Presented to:

_____

By: _____

On: _____

Old Testament Chronology

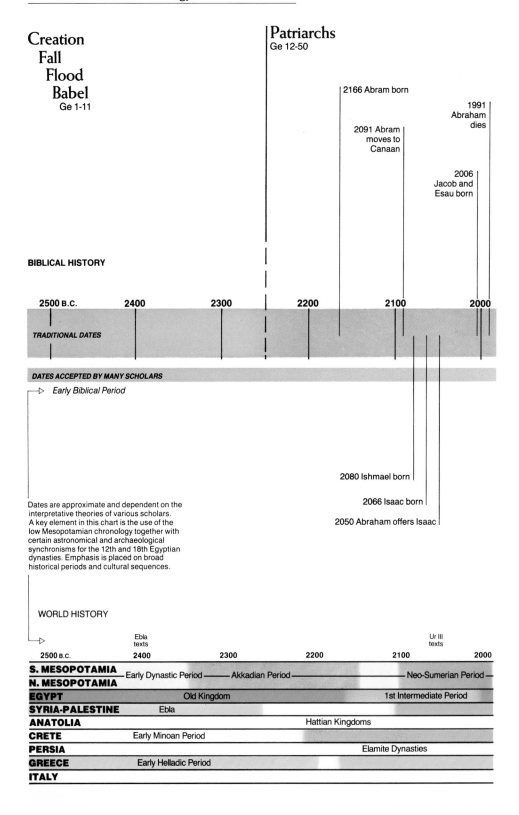

Creation
Fall
Flood
Babel
Ge 1-11

Patriarchs
Ge 12-50

2166 Abram born

1991 Abraham dies

2091 Abram moves to Canaan

2006 Jacob and Esau born

BIBLICAL HISTORY

2500 B.C.   2400   2300   2200   2100   2000

TRADITIONAL DATES

DATES ACCEPTED BY MANY SCHOLARS

▷ *Early Biblical Period*

2080 Ishmael born

2066 Isaac born

2050 Abraham offers Isaac

Dates are approximate and dependent on the interpretative theories of various scholars. A key element in this chart is the use of the low Mesopotamian chronology together with certain astronomical and archaeological synchronisms for the 12th and 18th Egyptian dynasties. Emphasis is placed on broad historical periods and cultural sequences.

WORLD HISTORY

▷

	Ebla texts			Ur III texts	
2500 B.C.	2400	2300	2200	2100	2000
S. MESOPOTAMIA	Early Dynastic Period —— Akkadian Period ——			—— Neo-Sumerian Period ——	
N. MESOPOTAMIA					
EGYPT	Old Kingdom		1st Intermediate Period		
SYRIA-PALESTINE	Ebla				
ANATOLIA			Hattian Kingdoms		
CRETE	Early Minoan Period				
PERSIA			Elamite Dynasties		
GREECE	Early Helladic Period				
ITALY					

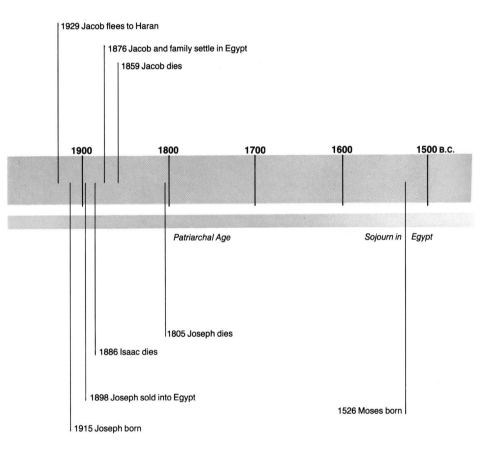

1929 Jacob flees to Haran

1876 Jacob and family settle in Egypt

1859 Jacob dies

1900 1800 1700 1600 1500 B.C.

Patriarchal Age *Sojourn in | Egypt*

1805 Joseph dies

1886 Isaac dies

1898 Joseph sold into Egypt

1526 Moses born

1915 Joseph born

	Cappadocian texts		Mari texts	Hammurapi texts		
	1900	1800		1700	1600	1500 B.C.
Isin-Larsa Period			Old Babylonian Period			
Middle Kingdom			2nd Intermediate (Hyksos) Period		New Kingdom	
Amorite Period				Hyksos Period	Late Canaanite Per.	
					Hittite Old Kingdom	
Middle Minoan Period						
Middle Helladic Period						

Ⓒ 1985 The Zondervan Corporation

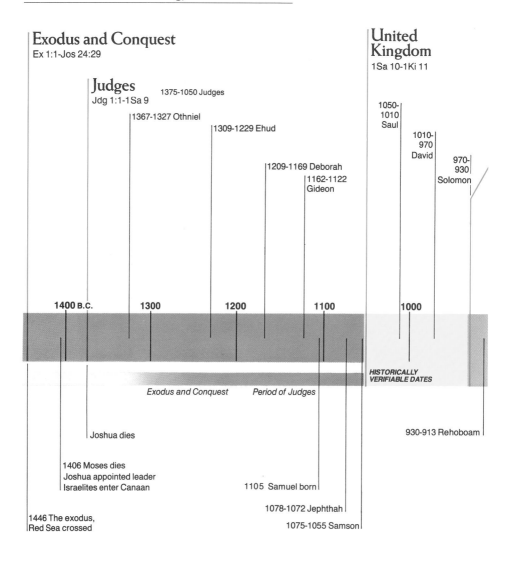

Exodus and Conquest
Ex 1:1-Jos 24:29

Judges
Jdg 1:1-1Sa 9

1375-1050 Judges

1367-1327 Othniel

1309-1229 Ehud

1209-1169 Deborah

1162-1122 Gideon

United Kingdom
1Sa 10-1Ki 11

1050-1010 Saul

1010-970 David

970-930 Solomon

| 1400 B.C. | 1300 | 1200 | 1100 | 1000 |

HISTORICALLY VERIFIABLE DATES

Exodus and Conquest   Period of Judges

Joshua dies

1406 Moses dies
Joshua appointed leader
Israelites enter Canaan

1105 Samuel born

930-913 Rehoboam

1078-1072 Jephthah

1446 The exodus,
Red Sea crossed

1075-1055 Samson

	Nuzi texts	Ugaritic texts		Merneptah inscription	Medinet Habu inscriptions			Shishak inscription
		Amarna texts						
1400 B.C.		**1300**		**1200**		**1100**	**1000**	
S. MESOPOTAMIA		Kassite Period						
N. MESOPOTAMIA	← Mitannian Kingdom			Middle Assyrian Period				
EGYPT		New Kingdom						
SYRIA-PALESTINE	Late Canaanite Period				Sea Peoples		Phoenician,	
ANATOLIA	Hittite Empire				Phrygian Period			
CRETE	Late Minoan Period						Dorian States	
PERSIA								
GREECE	Late Helladic (Mycenean) Period						Dorian States	
ITALY								

Divided Kingdom
1Ki 12-2Ki 17

Exile
Daniel

KINGS OF ISRAEL

930-909 Jeroboam I
908-886 Baasha
885-874 Omri
874-853 Ahab
852-841 Joram
841-814 Jehu
793-753 Jeroboam II
752-742 Menahem
752-732 Pekah
732-722 Hoshea
722 FALL of the NORTHERN KINGDOM

Restoration
Ezra-Esther

538 First
group returns
under
Zerubbabel

Between the Testaments
432-5 B.C.

432 Last
group returns
under Nehemiah

458 Second
group returns
under Ezra

586 Fall
of Jerusalem

Prophets
of Israel

Elijah 875-848
Elisha 848-797
Jonah 785-775
Amos 760-750
Hosea 750-715

900	800	700	600	500	400 B.C.

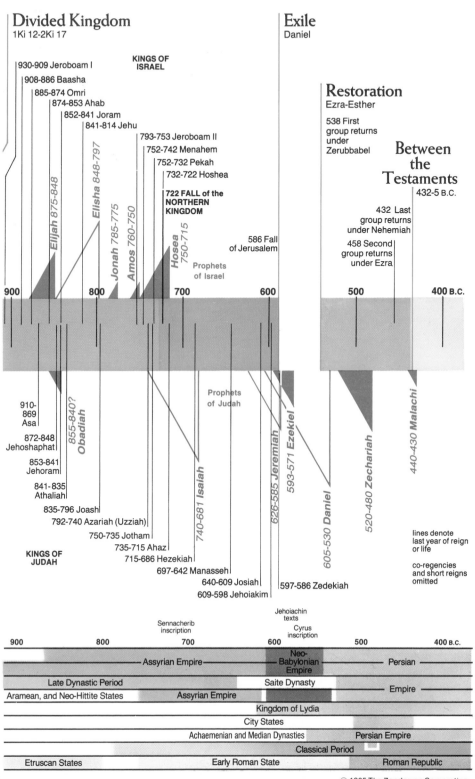

Prophets
of Judah

910-
869
Asa

855-840? Obadiah

872-848
Jehoshaphat

853-841
Jehoram

841-835
Athaliah

835-796 Joash

792-740 Azariah (Uzziah)

750-735 Jotham

KINGS OF JUDAH

735-715 Ahaz

715-686 Hezekiah

697-642 Manasseh

640-609 Josiah

609-598 Jehoiakim

597-586 Zedekiah

740-681 Isaiah
626-585 Jeremiah
593-571 Ezekiel
605-530 Daniel
520-480 Zechariah
440-430 Malachi

lines denote
last year of reign
or life

co-regencies
and short reigns
omitted

Sennacherib
inscription

Jehoiachin
texts

Cyrus
inscription

900	800	700	600	500	400 B.C.

			Neo-Babylonian Empire		
	Assyrian Empire			Persian	
Late Dynastic Period			Saite Dynasty	Empire	
Aramean, and Neo-Hittite States		Assyrian Empire			
			Kingdom of Lydia		
		City States			
		Achaemenian and Median Dynasties		Persian Empire	
			Classical Period		
Etruscan States		Early Roman State		Roman Republic	

© 1985 The Zondervan Corporation

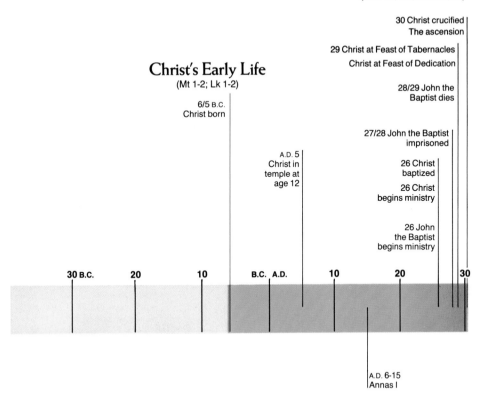

Christ's Ministry
(Mt 2-28; Mk; Lk 3-24; Jn)

30 Christ crucified |
The ascension

29 Christ at Feast of Tabernacles
Christ at Feast of Dedication

Christ's Early Life
(Mt 1-2; Lk 1-2)

28/29 John the
Baptist dies

6/5 B.C.
Christ born

27/28 John the Baptist |
imprisoned

A.D. 5
Christ in
temple at
age 12

26 Christ |
baptized
26 Christ |
begins ministry

26 John
the Baptist
begins ministry

30 B.C.   20   10   B.C. A.D.   10   20   30

A.D. 6-15
Annas I

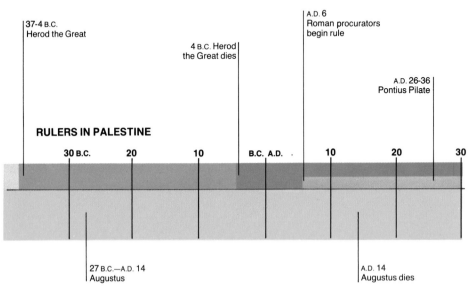

37-4 B.C.
Herod the Great

A.D. 6
Roman procurators
begin rule

4 B.C. Herod |
the Great dies

A.D. 26-36 |
Pontius Pilate

RULERS IN PALESTINE

30 B.C.   20   10   B.C. A.D. .   10   20   30

27 B.C.—A.D. 14
Augustus

A.D. 14
Augustus dies

ROMAN EMPERORS

The Early Church
(Acts-Revelation)

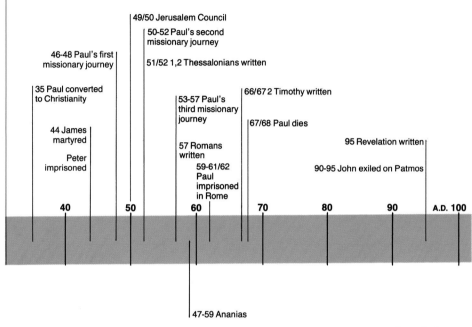

30 Pentecost

49/50 Jerusalem Council

50-52 Paul's second
missionary journey

46-48 Paul's first
missionary journey

51/52 1,2 Thessalonians written

35 Paul converted
to Christianity

66/67 2 Timothy written

53-57 Paul's
third missionary
journey

67/68 Paul dies

44 James
martyred

95 Revelation written

57 Romans
written

Peter
imprisoned

59-61/62
Paul
imprisoned
in Rome

90-95 John exiled on Patmos

40   50   60   70   80   90   A.D. 100

47-59 Ananias

Lines to timeline denote
end of journey or reign

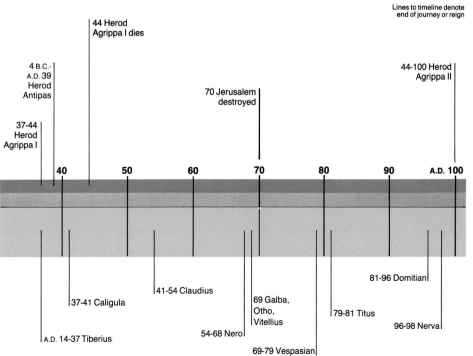

44 Herod
Agrippa I dies

4 B.C.-
A.D. 39
Herod
Antipas

44-100 Herod
Agrippa II

70 Jerusalem
destroyed

37-44
Herod
Agrippa I

40   50   60   70   80   90   A.D. 100

81-96 Domitian

41-54 Claudius

37-41 Caligula

69 Galba,
Otho,
Vitellius

79-81 Titus

96-98 Nerva

A.D. 14-37 Tiberius

54-68 Nero

69-79 Vespasian

© 1985 The Zondervan Corporation

Family Record

BIRTHS

NAME	DATE	NAME	DATE

DEATHS

NAME	DATE	NAME	DATE

MARRIAGES

NAME	PLACE	DATE

SPECIAL EVENTS

EVENT	PLACE	DATE

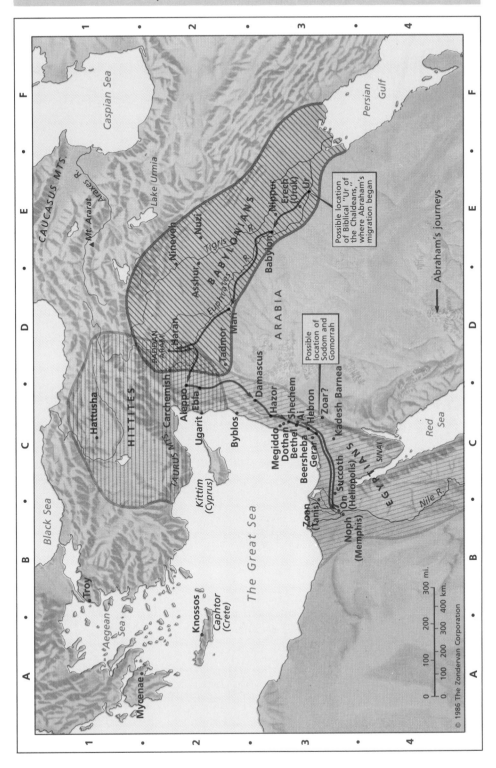

Map 1: WORLD OF THE PATRIARCHS

Caspian Sea

CAUCASUS MTS.

Mt. Ararat

Araxes R.

Lake Urmia

Nineveh

Nuzi

Asshur

BABYLONIANS

Tigris

Haran

Euphrates

PADDAN ARAM

Tadmor

Mari

Carchemish

TAURUS MTS.

HITTITES

Hattusha

Aleppo

Ebla

Ugarit

Byblos

Damascus

Nippur

Erech (Uruk)

Ur

Babylon

ARABIA

Possible location of Biblical "Ur of the Chaldeans," where Abraham's migration began

Persian Gulf

Abraham's journeys

Possible location of Sodom and Gomorrah

Hazor

Shechem

Ai

Megiddo

Dothan

Bethel

Gerar

Beersheba

Hebron

Zoar?

Kadesh Barnea

Succoth

Zoan (Tanis)

On (Heliopolis)

Noph (Memphis)

EGYPTIANS

SINAI

Nile R.

Red Sea

Kittim (Cyprus)

The Great Sea

Knossos

Caphtor (Crete)

Aegean Sea

Troy

Mycenae

Black Sea

0   100   200   300 mi.

0   100   200   300   400 km.

© 1986 The Zondervan Corporation

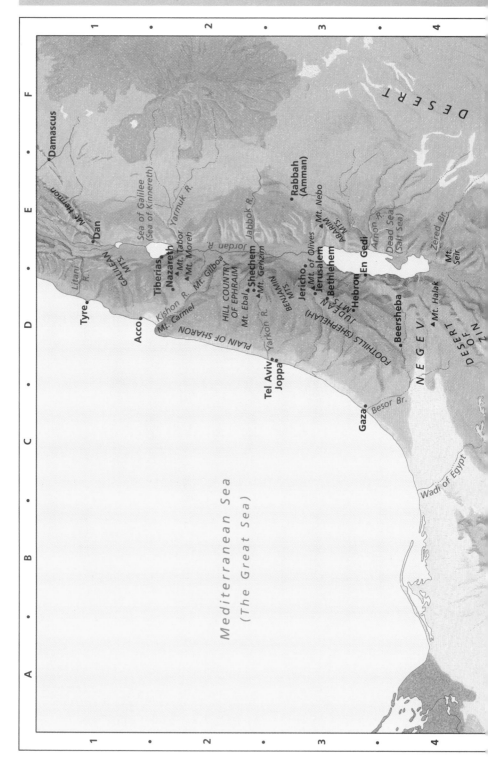

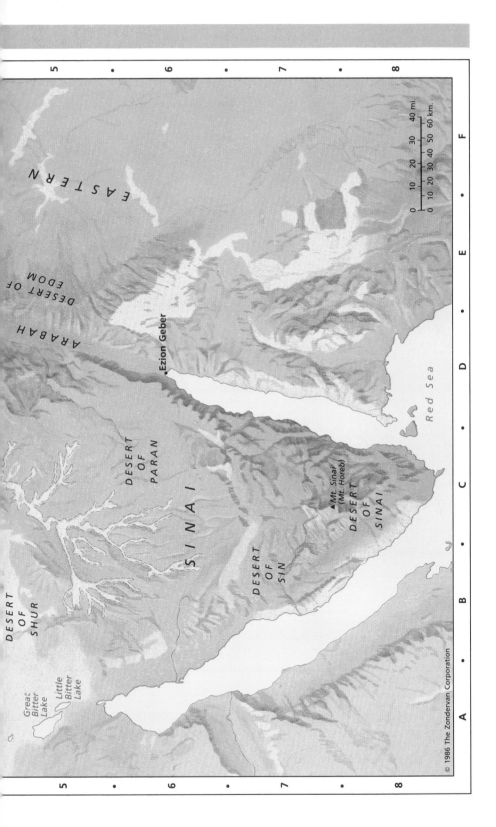

© 1986 The Zondervan Corporation

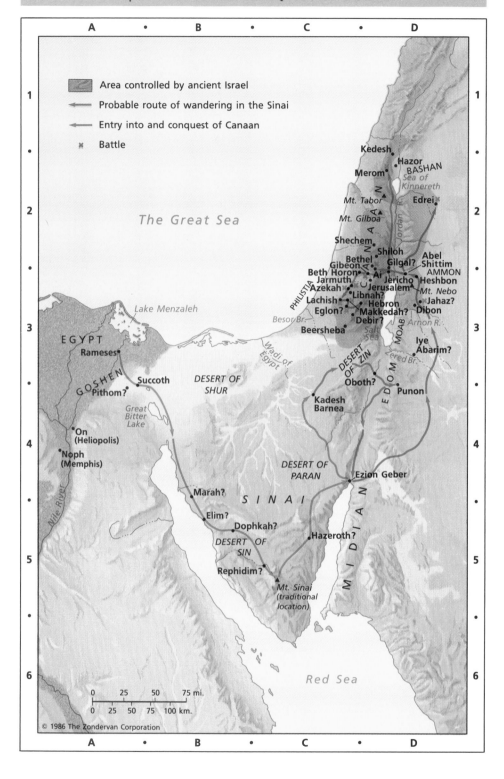

Map 3: **EXODUS AND CONQUEST OF CANAAN**

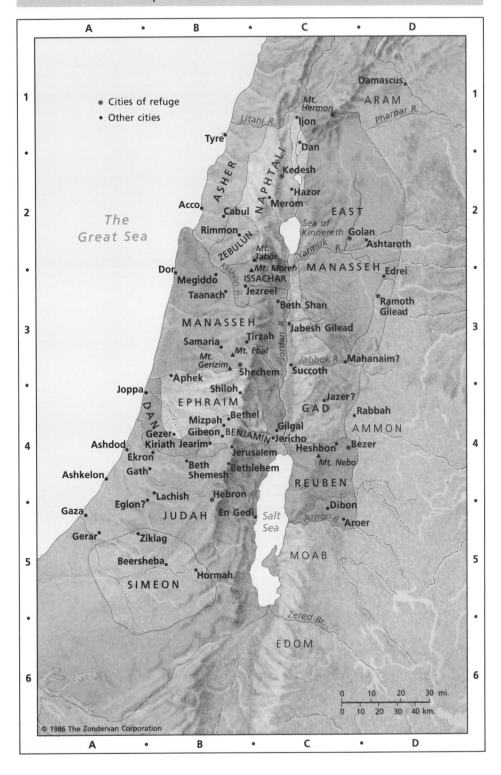

Map 4: LAND OF THE TWELVE TRIBES

Cities of refuge
Other cities

Damascus
ARAM
Pharpar R.
Mt. Hermon
Ijon
Litani R.
Tyre
Dan
Kedesh
Hazor
Merom
Acco
Cabul
EAST
Rimmon
Sea of Kinnereth
Golan
Ashtaroth
Yarmuk R.
Mt. Tabor
Mt. Moreh
MANASSEH
Edrei
Dor
Megiddo
ISSACHAR
Jezreel
Taanach
Beth Shan
Ramoth Gilead
MANASSEH
Jabesh Gilead
Jordan R.
Samaria
Tirzah
Mt. Ebal
Jabbok R.
Mahanaim?
Mt. Gerizim
Shechem
Succoth
Aphek
Shiloh
Jazer?
EPHRAIM
GAD
Rabbah
Joppa
Bethel
Mizpah
AMMON
Gezer
Gibeon
Gilgal
Kiriath Jearim
BENJAMIN
Jericho
Bezer
Ashdod
Jerusalem
Heshbon
Ekron
Mt. Nebo
Beth Shemesh
Bethlehem
Ashkelon
Gath
REUBEN
Lachish
Hebron
Dibon
Gaza
Eglon?
En Gedi
Salt Sea
Arnon R.
Aroer
Gerar
JUDAH
Ziklag
MOAB
Beersheba
Hormah
SIMEON
Zered Br.
EDOM

The Great Sea

ASHER
NAPHTALI
ZEBULUN
DAN

0   10   20   30 mi.
0 10 20 30 40 km.

© 1986 The Zondervan Corporation

Map 5: KINGDOM OF DAVID AND SOLOMON

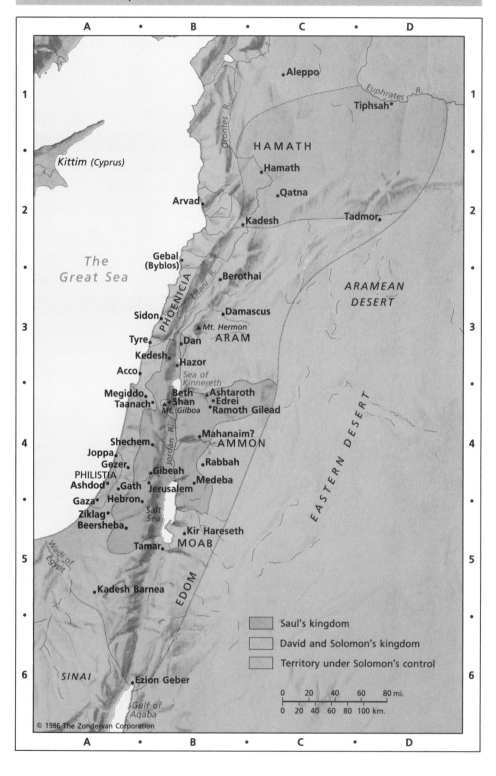

A • B • C • D

1
•Aleppo

Euphrates R.

Tiphsah•

HAMATH

Orontes R.

Kittim (Cyprus)

•Hamath

•Qatna

2
Arvad•

Tadmor•

•Kadesh

The
Great Sea

Gebal
(Byblos)•

•Berothai

ARAMEAN
DESERT

PHOENICIA

Litani R.

Sidon•

•Damascus

3
Tyre•

▲Mt. Hermon

•Dan

ARAM

Kedesh•

•Hazor

Acco•

Sea of
Kinnereth

Megiddo•

•Beth

•Ashtaroth

Taanach•

▲Shan

•Edrei

Mt. Gilboa

•Ramoth Gilead

EASTERN DESERT

Jordan R.

•Mahanaim?

Shechem•

AMMON

4
Joppa•

Gezer•

•Rabbah

PHILISTIA

•Gibeah

Ashdod•

•Gath

Medeba

Gaza•

•Hebron•

Jerusalem

Ziklag•

Salt
Sea

Beersheba•

•Kir Hareseth

Tamar•

MOAB

5

Wadi of
Egypt

EDOM

Kadesh Barnea•

Saul's kingdom

David and Solomon's kingdom

Territory under Solomon's control

6
SINAI

•Ezion Geber

| 0 | 20 | 40 | 60 | 80 mi. |

| 0 | 20 | 40 | 60 | 80 | 100 km. |

Gulf of
Aqaba

© 1986 The Zondervan Corporation

A • B • C • D

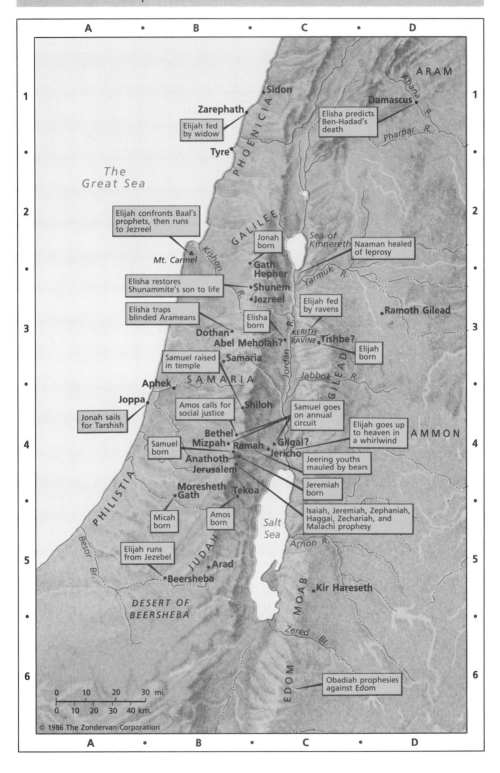

A • B • C • D

ARAM

Abana R.

•Sidon

Zarephath•
Elijah fed
by widow

Damascus•

Elisha predicts
Ben-Hadad's
death

Pharpar R.

Tyre•

P H O E N I C I A

*The
Great Sea*

Elijah confronts Baal's
prophets, then runs
to Jezreel

G A L I L E E

Jonah
born

*Sea of
Kinnereth*

Naaman healed
of leprosy

Kishon R.

Mt. Carmel

•Gath
Hepher

Yarmuk R.

Elisha restores
Shunammite's son to life

•Shunem

•Jezreel

Elijah fed
by ravens

•Ramoth Gilead

Elisha traps
blinded Arameans

Elisha
born

KERITH
RAVINE

Tishbe?•

Elijah
born

Dothan•

G I L E A D

Abel Meholah?

•Tishbe?

Samuel raised
in temple

•Samaria

Jordan R.

Jabbok R.

Aphek•

S A M A R I A

Joppa•

Amos calls for
social justice

•Shiloh

Samuel goes
on annual
circuit

Elijah goes up
to heaven in
a whirlwind

AMMON

Jonah sails
for Tarshish

Bethel•

Samuel
born

Mizpah•

Ramah•

Gilgal?•

•Jericho

Anathoth•

Jeering youths
mauled by bears

Jerusalem•

Jeremiah
born

Moresheth•
Gath

Tekoa•

Isaiah, Jeremiah, Zephaniah,
Haggai, Zechariah, and
Malachi prophesy

P H I L I S T I A

Micah
born

Amos
born

*Salt
Sea*

Arnon R.

Elijah runs
from Jezebel

J U D A H

•Arad

M O A B

•Kir Hareseth

•Beersheba

Besor Br.

*DESERT OF
BEERSHEBA*

Zered Br.

E D O M

Obadiah prophesies
against Edom

0   10   20   30 mi.

0 10 20 30 40 km.

© 1986 The Zondervan Corporation

A • B • C • D

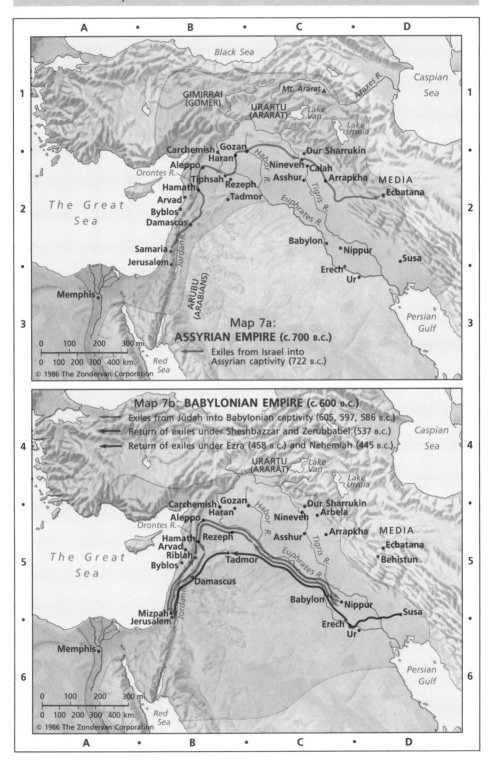

**Map 7a:
ASSYRIAN EMPIRE (c. 700 B.C.)**

→ Exiles from Israel into
Assyrian captivity (722 B.C.)

0 100 200 300 mi.
0 100 200 300 400 km.
© 1986 The Zondervan Corporation

Map 7b: BABYLONIAN EMPIRE (c. 600 B.C.)

→ Exiles from Judah into Babylonian captivity (605, 597, 586 B.C.)
→ Return of exiles under Sheshbazzar and Zerubbabel (537 B.C.)
→ Return of exiles under Ezra (458 B.C.) and Nehemiah (445 B.C.)

0 100 200 300 mi.
0 100 200 300 400 km.
© 1986 The Zondervan Corporation

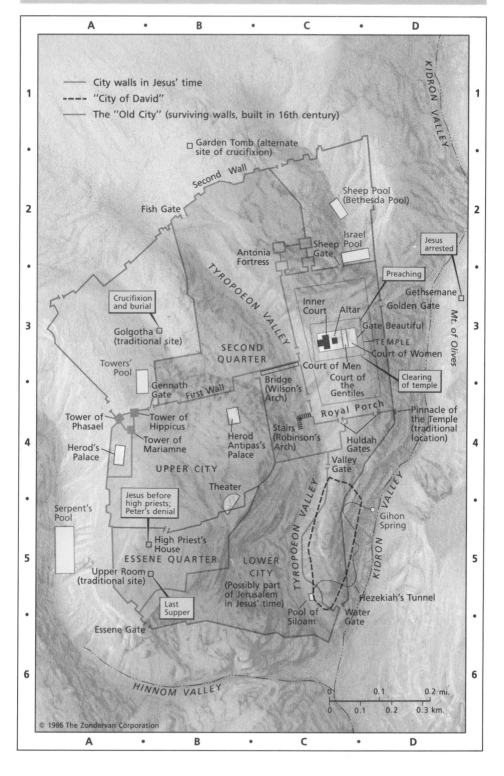

A • B • C • D

— City walls in Jesus' time

- - - "City of David"

— The "Old City" (surviving walls, built in 16th century)

KIDRON VALLEY

Garden Tomb (alternate site of crucifixion)

Second Wall

Sheep Pool (Bethesda Pool)

Fish Gate

Israel Pool

Jesus arrested

Antonia Fortress

Sheep Gate

Preaching

Golden Gate

Gethsemane

TYROPOEON VALLEY

Crucifixion and burial

Inner Court

Altar

Gate Beautiful

Mt of Olives

Golgotha (traditional site)

SECOND QUARTER

TEMPLE

Court of Women

Towers' Pool

Court of Men

Clearing of temple

Gennath Gate

First Wall

Bridge (Wilson's Arch)

Court of the Gentiles

Royal Porch

Pinnacle of the Temple (traditional location)

Tower of Phasael

Tower of Hippicus

Stairs (Robinson's Arch)

Huldah Gates

Tower of Mariamne

Herod Antipas's Palace

Herod's Palace

Valley Gate

UPPER CITY

Theater

TYROPOEON VALLEY

KIDRON VALLEY

Gihon Spring

Serpent's Pool

Jesus before high priests; Peter's denial

High Priest's House

ESSENE QUARTER

LOWER CITY (Possibly part of Jerusalem in Jesus' time)

Hezekiah's Tunnel

Upper Room (traditional site)

Last Supper

Pool of Siloam

Water Gate

Essene Gate

HINNOM VALLEY

0   0.1   0.2 mi.

0   0.1   0.2   0.3 km.

© 1986 The Zondervan Corporation

A • B • C • D

Map 9: JESUS' MINISTRY

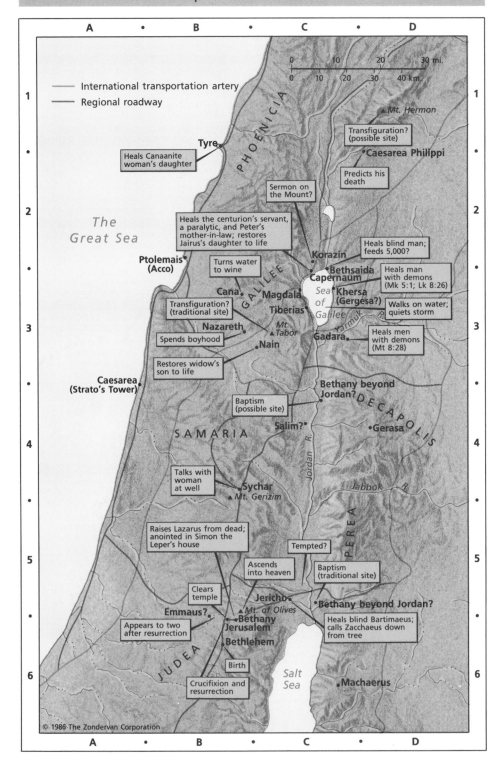

International transportation artery
Regional roadway

Mt. Hermon

Transfiguration?
(possible site)

Caesarea Philippi

Tyre

Heals Canaanite
woman's daughter

PHOENICIA

Predicts his
death

Sermon on
the Mount?

The
Great Sea

Heals the centurion's servant,
a paralytic, and Peter's
mother-in-law; restores
Jairus's daughter to life

Heals blind man;
feeds 5,000?

Ptolemais
(Acco)

Turns water
to wine

Korazin

Capernaum

Bethsaida

Heals man
with demons
(Mk 5:1; Lk 8:26)

Cana

GALILEE

Magdala

Sea
of
Galilee

Khersa
(Gergesa?)

Walks on water;
quiets storm

Transfiguration?
(traditional site)

Tiberias

Nazareth

Mt.
Tabor

Yarmuk

Heals men
with demons
(Mt 8:28)

Gadara

DECAPOLIS

Spends boyhood

Nain

Restores widow's
son to life

Caesarea
(Strato's Tower)

Bethany beyond
Jordan?

Baptism
(possible site)

Salim?

Gerasa

SAMARIA

Jordan R.

Jabbok R.

Talks with
woman
at well

Sychar

Mt. Gerizim

PEREA

Raises Lazarus from dead;
anointed in Simon the
Leper's house

Tempted?

Ascends
into heaven

Baptism
(traditional site)

Clears
temple

Jericho

Bethany beyond Jordan?

Emmaus?

Mt. of Olives

Bethany

Appears to two
after resurrection

Jerusalem

Heals blind Bartimaeus;
calls Zacchaeus down
from tree

Bethlehem

JUDEA

Birth

Salt
Sea

Crucifixion and
resurrection

Machaerus

© 1986 The Zondervan Corporation

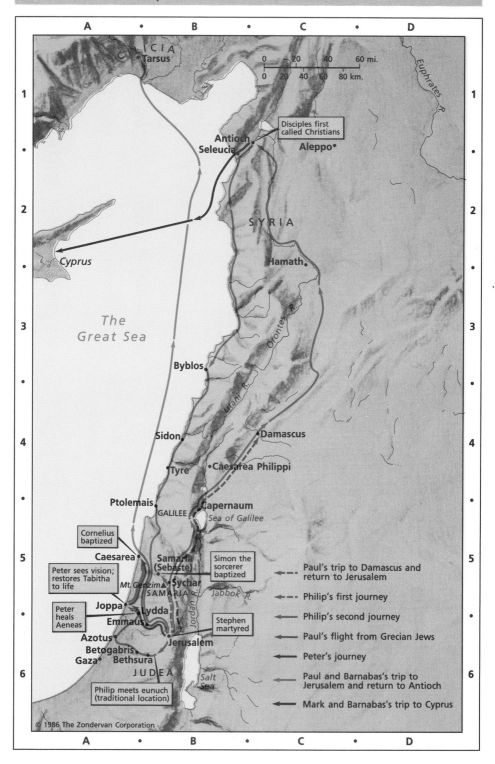

Map 10: APOSTLES' EARLY TRAVELS

CILICIA
Tarsus

Antioch
Seleucia

Disciples first
called Christians

Aleppo

SYRIA

Cyprus

Hamath

The
Great Sea

Byblos

Orontes R.

Litani R.

Sidon

Damascus

Tyre

Caesarea Philippi

Ptolemais

Capernaum

GALILEE

Sea of Galilee

Cornelius
baptized

Caesarea

Samaria
(Sebaste)

Simon the
sorcerer
baptized

Peter sees vision;
restores Tabitha
to life

Mt. Gerizim

Sychar
SAMARIA

Jabbok R.

Peter
heals
Aeneas

Joppa

Lydda

Emmaus

Stephen
martyred

Azotus

Jerusalem

Betogabris
Gaza   Bethsura

JUDEA

Salt
Sea

Philip meets eunuch
(traditional location)

© 1986 The Zondervan Corporation

0   20   40   60 mi.
0   20   40 60   80 km.

Euphrates R.

- - - Paul's trip to Damascus and
return to Jerusalem

- - - Philip's first journey

——— Philip's second journey

——— Paul's flight from Grecian Jews

——— Peter's journey

——— Paul and Barnabas's trip to
Jerusalem and return to Antioch

——— Mark and Barnabas's trip to Cyprus

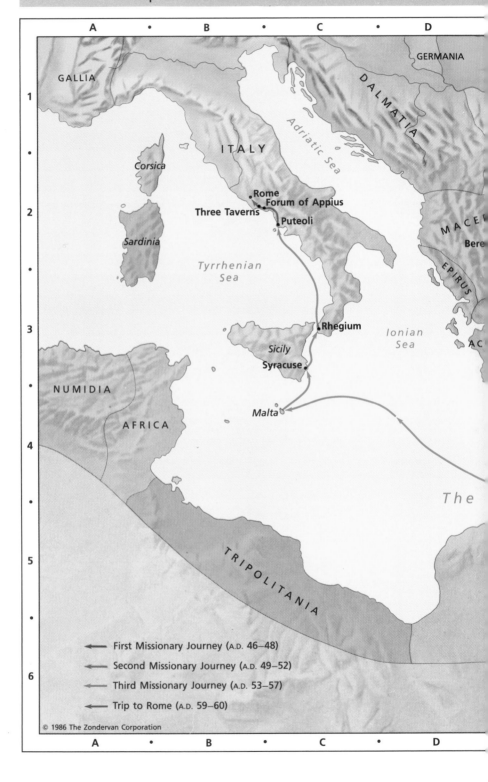

First Missionary Journey (A.D. 46–48)
Second Missionary Journey (A.D. 49–52)
Third Missionary Journey (A.D. 53–57)
Trip to Rome (A.D. 59–60)

© 1986 The Zondervan Corporation

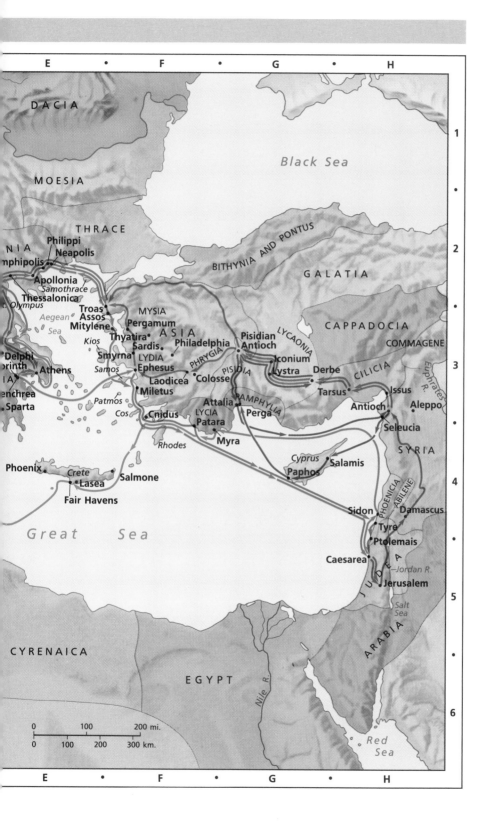

A • B • C • D

1

North
Atlantic
Ocean

GREENLAND
(DEN.)

ALASKA
(U.S.)

CANADA

ICELAND

NORW

North
Pacific
Ocean

UNITED STATES

MOROCCO

2

See inset below

MEXICO

WESTERN
SAHARA
(MOR.)

ALGER

MAURITANIA

MALI

HAWAII (U.S.)

CAPE VERDE

SENEGAL
GAMBIA
GUINEA-BISSAU
SIERRA LEONE
LIBERIA

BURKINA
GUINEA
IVORY
COAST
GHANA

BE
N
TO

VENEZUELA
COLOMBIA

GUYANA
SURINAME
FRENCH GUIANA
(FR.)

SAO TOME AND PRINCIPE
EQUATORIAL GUIN

ECUADOR

PERU

BRAZIL

South
Atlantic
Ocean

3

BOLIVIA

PARAGUAY

CHILE

South
Pacific
Ocean

URUGUAY

ARGENTINA

4

FALKLAND
IS. (U.K.)

a • b • c

U.S.

THE
BAHAMAS

TURKS & CAICOS IS. (U.K.)

5

CUBA

PUERTO
RICO
(U.S.)

VIRGIN IS. (U.K.–U.S.)
ANGUILLA (U.K.)
ANTIGUA AND
BARBUDA

5

CAYMAN IS.
(U.K.)

DOMINICAN
REPUBLIC

HAITI

MEXICO

BELIZE

JAMAICA

ST. KITTS
AND NEVIS
MONTSERRAT (U.K.)

GUADELOUPE (FR.)
DOMINICA
MARTINIQUE (FR.)
ST. LUCIA

GUATEMALA

HONDURAS

NETHERLANDS
ANTILLES (NETH.)

ARUBA (NETH.)

ST. VINCENT AND
THE GRENADINES

BARBADOS
GRENADA

EL SALVADOR

NICARAGUA

TRINIDAD AND
TOBAGO

6

COSTA RICA

PANAMA

VENEZUELA

GUYANA

6

COLOMBIA

a • b • c • D

E • F • G • H

SVALBARD
(NOR.)

FINLAND See inset below
SWEDEN

RUSSIA

1

KAZAKHSTAN

MONGOLIA

North
Pacific
Ocean

UZBEKISTAN KYRGYZSTAN
TURKMENISTAN TAJIKISTAN

NORTH
KOREA

TURKEY

NISIA

IRAQ

AFGHANISTAN

CHINA

SOUTH
KOREA

JAPAN

IRAN

PAKISTAN

NEPAL

LIBYA

EGYPT

SAUDI
ARABIA

QATAR

BHUTAN

TAIWAN

2

UNITED ARAB
EMIRATES

OMAN

BANGLADESH

BURMA
(MYANMAR)

LAOS

ER

CHAD

SUDAN

YEMEN

INDIA

THAILAND

PHILIPPINES

CENTRAL
AFRICAN
REPUBLIC

DJIBOUTI

ETHIOPIA

CAMBODIA

VIETNAM

MEROON

UGANDA

SOMALIA

SRI LANKA

BRUNEI

ON

RWANDA

KENYA

MALDIVES

MALAYSIA

CONGO

BURUNDI

SINGAPORE

ZAIRE

TANZANIA

SEYCHELLES

Indian Ocean

INDONESIA

PAPUA
NEW
GUINEA

3

ANGOLA

COMOROS

SOLOMON
ISLANDS

MALAWI

ZAMBIA

MOZAMBIQUE

VANUATU

NAMIBIA ZIMBABWE

BOTSWANA

MADAGASCAR

MAURITIUS
RÉUNION (FR.)

AUSTRALIA

NEW
CALEDONIA
(FR.)

SWAZILAND

SOUTH LESOTHO
AFRICA

NEW
ZEALAND

4

© 1992 The Zondervan Corporation

f • g • h

FAEROE IS.
(DEN.)

NORWAY

FINLAND

EST.

SWEDEN

LATVIA
LITH.

RUSSIA

UNITED
KINGDOM

DENMARK

BELARUS

5

IRELAND

NETHERLANDS

GERMANY

POLAND

BELGIUM

CZECHOSLOVAKIA

UKRAINE

KAZAKHSTAN

LUXEMBOURG

SWITZERLAND AUSTRIA HUNGARY

LIECH. SLOV.

MOLDOVA

FRANCE

CROATIA

BOS. &

ROMANIA

MONACO

SAN
MARINO

HERC.

YUGO.

GEORGIA

ANDORRA

ITALY

BULGARIA

MACED.

PORTUGAL

ALBANIA

ARMENIA

SPAIN

GREECE

TURKEY

AZERBAIJAN

GIBRALTAR (U.K.)

6

MALTA

CYPRUS

SYRIA

MOROCCO

TUNISIA

LEBANON
WEST BANK
ISRAEL

IRAQ

ALGERIA

LIBYA

JORDAN

KUWAIT

EGYPT

E • f • g • h

Map 13: ROMAN EMPIRE

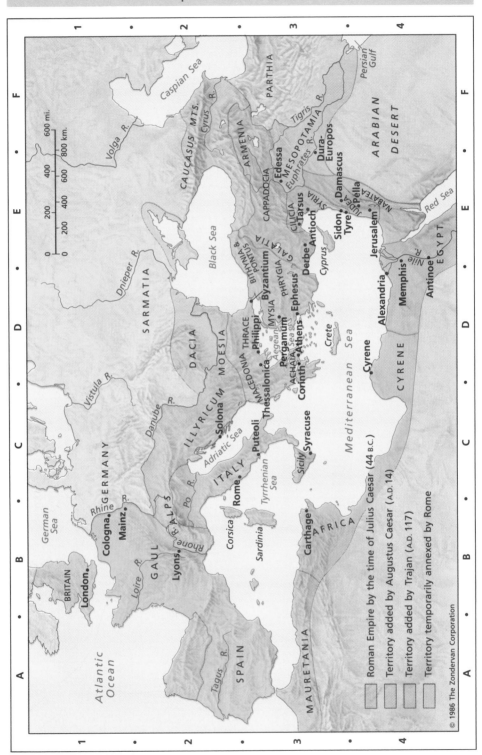

Roman Empire by the time of Julius Caesar (44 B.C.)

Territory added by Augustus Caesar (A.D. 14)

Territory added by Trajan (A.D. 117)

Territory temporarily annexed by Rome

© 1986 The Zondervan Corporation

The NIV
Study Bible
New International Version

General Editor
KENNETH BARKER

Associate Editors
DONALD BURDICK
JOHN STEK
WALTER WESSEL
RONALD YOUNGBLOOD

ZONDERVAN
BIBLE PUBLISHERS
GRAND RAPIDS, MICHIGAN 49506, U.S.A.

The NIV Study Bible
Copyright © 1985 by The Zondervan Corporation
All Rights Reserved

The Holy Bible, New International Version
Copyright © 1973, 1978, 1984 by International Bible Society

Notes, Book Introductions, Essays, Indexes, Maps, Charts, Diagrams, Color
Time Lines, copyright © 1985; The Center-Column Cross-Reference System,
copyright © 1984; The NIV Concordance, copyright © 1982, 1984 by the
Zondervan Corporation.

Artwork:
The Tabernacle, Solomon's Temple, Zerubbabel's Temple, Herod's Temple,
copyright © 1981; Solomon's Jerusalem, Jerusalem during the Time of the
Prophets, Jerusalem of the Returning Exiles, Jerusalem during the Ministry of
Jesus, Passion Week, The City of the Jebusites, David's Jerusalem, copyright
© 1982; by Hugh Claycombe; Color maps and index, copyright © 1986 by
The Zondervan Corporation; Ezekiel's Temple, plan adapted from the
design given in the Zondervan Pictorial Bible Dictionary. Copyright © 1975 by
The Zondervan Corporation. Used by permission.

*The NIV text may be quoted and/or reprinted up to and inclusive of one
thousand (1,000) verses without express written permission of the publisher,
providing the verses quoted do not amount to a complete book of the Bible
nor do the verses quoted account for 50% of the total work in which they are
quoted.*

*Notice of copyright must appear on the title or copyright page of the work as
follows:*

> *"Scripture taken from the HOLY BIBLE, NEW INTERNATIONAL VERSION.
> Copyright © 1973, 1978, 1984 International Bible Society. Used by
> permission of Zondervan Bible Publishers."*

*When quotations from the NIV text are used in non-saleable media, such as
church bulletins, orders of service, posters, transparencies or similar media,
the initials (NIV) may be used at the end of each quotation.*

*Quotations and/or reprints in excess of one thousand (1,000) verses, or other
permission requests, must be directed and approved in writing by Zondervan
Bible Publishers.*

Library of Congress Catalog Card Number 85-50591
Published by The Zondervan Corporation
Grand Rapids, Michigan 49506, U.S.A.
Printed in the United States of America

Twelfth printing—1,805,000 copies in print
RRD(C)—3/90

You will be pleased to know that a portion of the purchase price of your new NIV Bible
has been provided to the International Bible Society to help spread the Gospel of
Jesus Christ around the world!

Tribute to Edwin H. Palmer

Edwin H. Palmer, who had served so capably as Executive Secretary of the NIV Committee on Bible Translation and as coordinator of all translation work on the NIV, was appointed General Editor of *The NIV Study Bible* by Zondervan Bible Publishers in 1979. On September 16, 1980, he departed this life to "be with Christ, which is better by far" (Philippians 1:23). Before his death, however, he had laid most of the plans for the Study Bible, had recruited the majority of the contributors, and had done some editorial work on the first manuscripts submitted. We gratefully acknowledge his significant contributions to the earliest stages of this project.

Table of Contents

Tribute to Edwin H. Palmer	v
Contents: Maps	ix
Contents: Charts	x
Preface to the New International Version	xi
Introduction to the NIV Study Bible	xv
Acknowledgments	xviii
Contributors	xix
Abbreviations	xx
Transliterations	xxi

Introduction to Genesis	1
Genesis	**6**
Introduction to Exodus	84
Exodus	**88**
Introduction to Leviticus	145
Leviticus	**147**
Introduction to Numbers	185
Numbers	**189**
Introduction to Deuteronomy	243
Deuteronomy	**245**
Introduction to Joshua	288
Joshua	**292**
Introduction to Judges	325
Judges	**329**
Introduction to Ruth	363
Ruth	**365**
Introduction to 1 Samuel	371
1 Samuel	**375**
Introduction to 2 Samuel	421
2 Samuel	**423**
Introduction to 1 Kings	464
1 Kings	**470**
Introduction to 2 Kings	523
2 Kings	**524**
Introduction to 1 Chronicles	578
1 Chronicles	**583**
Introduction to 2 Chronicles	624
2 Chronicles	**625**
Introduction to Ezra	670
Ezra	**673**
Introduction to Nehemiah	692
Nehemiah	**694**
Introduction to Esther	718
Esther	**720**

Introduction to Job	731
Job	**735**
Introduction to Psalms	781
Psalms	**787**
Introduction to Proverbs	942
Proverbs	**946**
Introduction to Ecclesiastes	991
Ecclesiastes	**992**
Introduction to Song of Songs	1003
Song of Songs	**1005**
Introduction to Isaiah	1014
Isaiah	**1018**
Introduction to Jeremiah	1115
Jeremiah	**1119**
Introduction to Lamentations	1215
Lamentations	**1217**
Introduction to Ezekiel	1226
Ezekiel	**1231**
Introduction to Daniel	1298
Daniel	**1300**
The Book of the Twelve, or the Minor Prophets	1320
Introduction to Hosea	1321
Hosea	**1323**
Introduction to Joel	1338
Joel	**1339**
Introduction to Amos	1345
Amos	**1348**
Introduction to Obadiah	1360
Obadiah	**1361**
Introduction to Jonah	1363
Jonah	**1366**

TABLE OF CONTENTS

Introduction to Micah	1370
Micah	**1372**
Introduction to Nahum	1380
Nahum	**1382**
Introduction to Habakkuk	1386
Habakkuk	**1388**
Introduction to Zephaniah	1393
Zephaniah	**1395**
Introduction to Haggai	1400
Haggai	**1402**
Introduction to Zechariah	1405
Zechariah	**1408**
Introduction to Malachi	1423
Malachi	**1425**
The Time between the Testaments	1431
The Synoptic Gospels	1437
Introduction to Matthew	1439
Matthew	**1441**
Introduction to Mark	1490
Mark	**1493**
Introduction to Luke	1532
Luke	**1535**
Introduction to John	1591
John	**1593**
Introduction to Acts	1641
Acts	**1644**
Introduction to Romans	1703
Romans	**1706**
Introduction to 1 Corinthians	1732
1 Corinthians	**1735**
Introduction to 2 Corinthians	1761
2 Corinthians	**1763**
Introduction to Galatians	1779
Galatians	**1781**
Introduction to Ephesians	1789
Ephesians	**1791**

Introduction to Philippians	1801
Philippians	**1803**
Introduction to Colossians	1811
Colossians	**1813**
Introduction to 1 Thessalonians	1819
1 Thessalonians	**1821**
Introduction to 2 Thessalonians	1827
2 Thessalonians	**1828**
The Pastoral Letters	1832
Introduction to 1 Timothy	1833
1 Timothy	**1835**
Introduction to 2 Timothy	1843
2 Timothy	**1844**
Introduction to Titus	1849
Titus	**1851**
Introduction to Philemon	1855
Philemon	**1856**
Introduction to Hebrews	1857
Hebrews	**1859**
The General Letters	1878
Introduction to James	1879
James	**1881**
Introduction to 1 Peter	1886
1 Peter	**1888**
Introduction to 2 Peter	1897
2 Peter	**1899**
Introduction to 1 John	1905
1 John	**1908**
Introduction to 2 John	1914
2 John	**1915**
Introduction to 3 John	1916
3 John	**1917**
Introduction to Jude	1918
Jude	**1920**
Introduction to Revelation	1923
Revelation	**1926**

Table of Weights & Measures

Index to Subjects

Index to Maps

Concordance

Index to Color Maps

Contents: Maps

BOOK	TITLE	PAGE
Genesis	Table of Nations	21
	Jacob's Journeys	53
Exodus	The Exodus	106
Numbers	Cities of Refuge	241
Joshua	Conquest of Canaan	308
Judges	Five Cities of the Philistines	330
	Gideon's Battles	341
Ruth	The Book of Ruth	365
1 Samuel	David the Fugitive	405
	Exploits of David	415
2 Samuel	The City of the Jebusites/David's Jerusalem	430
	David's Conquests	442
1 Kings	Solomon's Jerusalem	473
	The Divided Kingdom	495
	Lives of Elijah and Elisha	513
2 Kings	Assyrian Campaigns against Israel and Judah	550
	Exile of Northern Kingdom	556
	Nebuchadnezzar's Campaigns against Judah	572
	Exile of Southern Kingdom	576
Ezra	Return from Exile	671
Nehemiah	Jerusalem of the Returning Exiles	696
Daniel	The Neo-Babylonian Empire	1305
Hosea	Jerusalem during the Time of the Prophets	1320
Jonah	The Book of Jonah	1366
Matthew	Journey to Bethlehem: Flight to and Return from Egypt	1445
	Jesus' Baptism and Temptation	1447
Mark	Jerusalem during the Ministry of Jesus	1499
	The Decapolis and the Lands beyond the Jordan	1502
	The Territories of Tyre and Sidon	1508
Luke	Palestine under Herod the Great	1542
John	Jesus in Judea and Samaria	1601
	Jesus in Galilee	1606
Acts	Countries of People Mentioned at Pentecost	1646
	Philip's and Peter's Missionary Journeys	1658
	Roman Damascus	1661
	The Spread of the Gospel	1668
	Paul's First Missionary Journey	1672
	Paul's Second Missionary Journey	1677
	Paul's Third Missionary Journey	1682
	Paul's Journey to Rome	1697
Romans	Rome	1702
1 Corinthians	Corinth	1733
Ephesians	Ephesus	1789

CONTENTS: MAPS AND CHARTS

Philippians	Philippi	1801
1 Timothy	Paul's Fourth Missionary Journey	1836
Revelation	The Seven Churches of Revelation	1928

Contents: Charts

BOOK	TITLE	PAGE
	Old & New Testament Chronology	
Genesis	Ancient Texts Relating to the Old Testament	5
	Major Covenants in the Old Testament	19
	The Tribes of Israel	81
Exodus	Hebrew Calendar	102
	The Tabernacle	124
	Tabernacle Furnishings	126
Leviticus	Old Testament Sacrifices	150
	Old Testament Feasts and Other Sacred Days	176
Numbers	Encampment of the Tribes of Israel/Marching Orders of the Tribes	192
Deuteronomy	Major Social Concerns in the Covenant	271
1 Samuel	David's Family Tree	399
1 Kings	Solomon's Temple	481
	Temple Furnishings	484
	Rulers of Israel and Judah	502
Ezra	Chronology: Ezra-Nehemiah	674
	Zerubbabel's Temple	678
Ezekiel	Dates in Ezekiel	1227
	Ezekiel's Temple	1284
Daniel	Identification of the Four Kingdoms	1311
	Ptolemies and Seleucids	1318
Malachi	From Malachi to Christ	1430
Matthew	Dating the Synoptic Gospels	1437
	House of Herod	1443
	Herod's Temple	1448
	Jewish Sects	1476
	The Life of Christ	1480
Mark	Passion Week	1524
Luke	Capernaum Synagogue	1546
	Parables of Jesus	1570
	Resurrection Appearances	1588
John	Miracles of Jesus	1596
Acts	Major Archaeological Finds Relating to the New Testament	1640
	Timeline of Paul's Life	1664
1 Timothy	Qualifications for Elders/Overseers and Deacons	1839

Preface

The New International Version is a completely new translation of the Holy Bible made by over a hundred scholars working directly from the best available Hebrew, Aramaic and Greek texts. It had its beginning in 1965 when, after several years of exploratory study by committees from the Christian Reformed Church and the National Association of Evangelicals, a group of scholars met at Palos Heights, Illinois, and concurred in the need for a new translation of the Bible in contemporary English. This group, though not made up of official church representatives, was transdenominational. Its conclusion was endorsed by a large number of leaders from many denominations who met in Chicago in 1966.

Responsibility for the new version was delegated by the Palos Heights group to a self-governing body of fifteen, the Committee on Bible Translation, composed for the most part of biblical scholars from colleges, universities and seminaries. In 1967 the New York Bible Society (now the International Bible Society) generously undertook the financial sponsorship of the project—a sponsorship that made it possible to enlist the help of many distinguished scholars. The fact that participants from the United States, Great Britain, Canada, Australia and New Zealand worked together gave the project its international scope. That they were from many denominations—including Anglican, Assemblies of God, Baptist, Brethren, Christian Reformed, Church of Christ, Evangelical Free, Lutheran, Mennonite, Methodist, Nazarene, Presbyterian, Wesleyan and other churches—helped to safeguard the translation from sectarian bias.

How it was made helps to give the New International Version its distinctiveness. The translation of each book was assigned to a team of scholars. Next, one of the Intermediate Editorial Committees revised the initial translation, with constant reference to the Hebrew, Aramaic or Greek. Their work then went to one of the General Editorial Committees, which checked it in detail and made another thorough revision. This revision in turn was carefully reviewed by the Committee on Bible Translation, which made further changes and then released the final version for publication. In this way the entire Bible underwent three revisions, during each of which the translation was examined for its faithfulness to the original languages and for its English style.

All this involved many thousands of hours of research and discussion regarding the meaning of the texts and the precise way of putting them into English. It may well be that no other translation has been made by a more thorough process of review and revision from committee to committee than this one.

From the beginning of the project, the Committee on Bible Translation held to certain goals for the New International Version: that it would be an accurate translation and one that would have clarity and literary quality and so prove suitable for public and private reading, teaching, preaching, memorizing and liturgical use. The Committee also sought to preserve some measure of continuity with the long tradition of translating the Scriptures into English.

In working toward these goals, the translators were united in their commitment to the authority and infallibility of the Bible as God's Word in written form. They believe that it contains the divine answer to the deepest needs of humanity, that it sheds unique light on our path in a dark world, and that it sets forth the way to our eternal well-being.

The first concern of the translators has been the accuracy of the translation and its fidelity to the thought of the biblical writers. They have weighed the significance of the lexical and grammatical details of the Hebrew, Aramaic and Greek texts. At the same time, they have striven for more than a word-for-word translation. Because thought patterns and syntax differ from language to language, faithful communication of the meaning of the writers of the Bible demands frequent modifications in sentence structure and constant regard for the contextual meanings of words.

A sensitive feeling for style does not always accompany scholarship. Accordingly the Committee on Bible Translation submitted the developing version to a number of stylistic consultants. Two of them read every book of both Old and New Testaments twice—once before and once after the last major revision—and made invaluable suggestions. Samples of the translation were tested for clarity and ease of reading by various kinds of people—young and old, highly educated and less well educated, ministers and laymen.

Concern for clear and natural English—that the New International Version should be idiomatic but

not idiosyncratic, contemporary but not dated—motivated the translators and consultants. At the same time, they tried to reflect the differing styles of the biblical writers. In view of the international use of English, the translators sought to avoid obvious Americanisms on the one hand and obvious Anglicisms on the other. A British edition reflects the comparatively few differences of significant idiom and of spelling.

As for the traditional pronouns "thou," "thee" and "thine" in reference to the Deity, the translators judged that to use these archaisms (along with the old verb forms such as "doest," "wouldest" and "hadst") would violate accuracy in translation. Neither Hebrew, Aramaic nor Greek uses special pronouns for the persons of the Godhead. A present-day translation is not enhanced by forms that in the time of the King James Version were used in everyday speech, whether referring to God or man.

For the Old Testament the standard Hebrew text, the Masoretic Text as published in the latest editions of *Biblia Hebraica,* was used throughout. The Dead Sea Scrolls contain material bearing on an earlier stage of the Hebrew text. They were consulted, as were the Samaritan Pentateuch and the ancient scribal traditions relating to textual changes. Sometimes a variant Hebrew reading in the margin of the Masoretic Text was followed instead of the text itself. Such instances, being variants within the Masoretic tradition, are not specified by footnotes. In rare cases, words in the consonantal text were divided differently from the way they appear in the Masoretic Text. Footnotes indicate this. The translators also consulted the more important early versions—the Septuagint; Aquila, Symmachus and Theodotion; the Vulgate; the Syriac Peshitta; the Targums; and for the Psalms the *Juxta Hebraica* of Jerome. Readings from these versions were occasionally followed where the Masoretic Text seemed doubtful and where accepted principles of textual criticism showed that one or more of these textual witnesses appeared to provide the correct reading. Such instances are footnoted. Sometimes vowel letters and vowel signs did not, in the judgment of the translators, represent the correct vowels for the original consonantal text. Accordingly some words were read with a different set of vowels. These instances are usually not indicated by footnotes.

The Greek text used in translating the New Testament was an eclectic one. No other piece of ancient literature has such an abundance of manuscript witnesses as does the New Testament. Where existing manuscripts differ, the translators made their choice of readings according to accepted principles of New Testament textual criticism. Footnotes call attention to places where there was uncertainty about what the original text was. The best current printed texts of the Greek New Testament were used.

There is a sense in which the work of translation is never wholly finished. This applies to all great literature and uniquely so to the Bible. In 1973 the New Testament in the New International Version was published. Since then, suggestions for corrections and revisions have been received from various sources. The Committee on Bible Translation carefully considered the suggestions and adopted a number of them. These were incorporated in the first printing of the entire Bible in 1978. Additional revisions were made by the Committee on Bible Translation in 1983 and appear in printings after that date.

As in other ancient documents, the precise meaning of the biblical texts is sometimes uncertain. This is more often the case with the Hebrew and Aramaic texts than with the Greek text. Although archaeological and linguistic discoveries in this century aid in understanding difficult passages, some uncertainties remain. The more significant of these have been called to the reader's attention in the footnotes.

In regard to the divine name YHWH, commonly referred to as the *Tetragrammaton,* the translators adopted the device used in most English versions of rendering that name as "Lord" in capital letters to distinguish it from *Adonai,* another Hebrew word rendered "Lord," for which small letters are used. Wherever the two names stand together in the Old Testament as a compound name of God, they are rendered "Sovereign Lord."

Because for most readers today the phrases "the Lord of hosts" and "God of hosts" have little meaning, this version renders them "the Lord Almighty" and "God Almighty." These renderings convey the sense of the Hebrew, namely, "he who is sovereign over all the 'hosts' (powers) in heaven and on earth, especially over the 'hosts' (armies) of Israel." For readers unacquainted with Hebrew this does not make clear the distinction between *Sabaoth* ("hosts" or "Almighty") and *Shaddai* (which can also be translated "Almighty"), but the latter occurs infrequently and is always footnoted. When *Adonai* and *YHWH Sabaoth* occur together, they are rendered "the Lord, the Lord Almighty."

As for other proper nouns, the familiar spellings of the King James Version are generally retained.

Names traditionally spelled with "ch," except where it is final, are usually spelled in this translation with "k" or "c," since the biblical languages do not have the sound that "ch" frequently indicates in English—for example, in *chant*. For well-known names such as Zechariah, however, the traditional spelling has been retained. Variation in the spelling of names in the original languages has usually not been indicated. Where a person or place has two or more different names in the Hebrew, Aramaic or Greek texts, the more familiar one has generally been used, with footnotes where needed.

To achieve clarity the translators sometimes supplied words not in the original texts but required by the context. If there was uncertainty about such material, it is enclosed in brackets. Also for the sake of clarity or style, nouns, including some proper nouns, are sometimes substituted for pronouns, and vice versa. And though the Hebrew writers often shifted back and forth between first, second and third personal pronouns without change of antecedent, this translation often makes them uniform, in accordance with English style and without the use of footnotes.

Poetical passages are printed as poetry, that is, with indentation of lines and with separate stanzas. These are generally designed to reflect the structure of Hebrew poetry. This poetry is normally characterized by parallelism in balanced lines. Most of the poetry in the Bible is in the Old Testament, and scholars differ regarding the scansion of Hebrew lines. The translators determined the stanza divisions for the most part by analysis of the subject matter. The stanzas therefore serve as poetic paragraphs.

As an aid to the reader, italicized sectional headings are inserted in most of the books. They are not to be regarded as part of the NIV text, are not for oral reading, and are not intended to dictate the interpretation of the sections they head.

The footnotes in this version are of several kinds, most of which need no explanation. Those giving alternative translations begin with "Or" and generally introduce the alternative with the last word preceding it in the text, except when it is a single-word alternative; in poetry quoted in a footnote a slant mark indicates a line division. Footnotes introduced by "Or" do not have uniform significance. In some cases two possible translations were considered to have about equal validity. In other cases, though the translators were convinced that the translation in the text was correct, they judged that another interpretation was possible and of sufficient importance to be represented in a footnote.

In the New Testament, footnotes that refer to uncertainty regarding the original text are introduced by "Some manuscripts" or similar expressions. In the Old Testament, evidence for the reading chosen is given first and evidence for the alternative is added after a semicolon (for example: Septuagint; Hebrew *father*). In such notes the term "Hebrew" refers to the Masoretic Text.

It should be noted that minerals, flora and fauna, architectural details, articles of clothing and jewelry, musical instruments and other articles cannot always be identified with precision. Also measures of capacity in the biblical period are particularly uncertain (see the table of weights and measures following the text).

Like all translations of the Bible, made as they are by imperfect man, this one undoubtedly falls short of its goals. Yet we are grateful to God for the extent to which he has enabled us to realize these goals and for the strength he has given us and our colleagues to complete our task. We offer this version of the Bible to him in whose name and for whose glory it has been made. We pray that it will lead many into a better understanding of the Holy Scriptures and a fuller knowledge of Jesus Christ the incarnate Word, of whom the Scriptures so faithfully testify.

The Committee on Bible Translation

June 1978
(Revised August 1983)

Names of the translators and editors may be secured
from the International Bible Society,
translation sponsors of the New International Version,
P.O. Box 62970, Colorado Springs, Colorado 80962-2970 U.S.A.

Introduction

About the Study Bible

The New International Version of the Bible is unsurpassed in accuracy, clarity and literary grace. The commitments that led to the completion of this version later guided several of its translators to spearhead publication of *The NIV Study Bible.* Their purpose was unchanged: to communicate the word of God to the hearts of people.

Like the NIV itself, *The NIV Study Bible* is the work of a transdenominational team of Biblical scholars. All confess the authority of the Bible as God's infallible word to humanity. They have sought to clarify understanding of, develop appreciation for, and provide insight into that word.

But why a study Bible when the NIV text itself is so clearly written? Surely there is no substitute for the reading of the text itself; nothing people write *about* God's word can be on a level with the word itself. Further, it is the Holy Spirit alone—not fallible human beings—who can open the human mind to the divine message.

However, the Spirit also uses people to explain God's word to others. It was the Spirit who led Philip to the Ethiopian eunuch's chariot, where he asked, "Do you understand what you are reading?" (Ac 8:31). "How can I," the Ethiopian replied, "unless someone explains it to me?" Philip then showed him how an Old Testament passage in Isaiah related to the good news of Jesus.

This interrelationship of the Scriptures—so essential to understanding the complete Biblical message —is a major theme of the Study Bible notes.

Doctrinally, the Study Bible reflects traditional evangelical theology. Where editors were aware of significant differences of opinion on key passages or doctrines, they tried to follow an evenhanded approach by indicating those differences (e.g., see note on Rev 20:2). In finding solutions to problems mentioned in the book introductions, they went only as far as evidence (Biblical and non-Biblical) could carry them.

The result is a study Bible that can be used profitably by all Christians who want to be serious Bible students.

Features of the NIV Study Bible

The NIV Study Bible features the text of the New International Version, study notes keyed to and listed with Bible verses, introductions and outlines to books of the Bible, text notes, a cross-reference system (100,000 entries), parallel passages, a concordance (over 35,000 references), charts, maps, essays and comprehensive indexes.

The text of the NIV, which is divided into paragraphs as well as verses, is organized into sections with headings.

Study Notes

The outstanding feature of this Study Bible is its nearly 20,000 study notes located on the same pages as the verses and passages they explain.

The study notes provide new information to supplement that found in the NIV text notes. Among other things, they

1. explain important words and concepts (see note on Lev 11:44 about "holiness");
2. interpret "difficult verses" (see notes on Mal 1:3 and Lk 14:26 for the concept of "hating" your parents);
3. draw parallels between specific people and events (see note on Ex 32:30 for the parallels between Moses and Christ as mediators);
4. describe historical and textual contexts of passages (see note on 1Co 8:1 for the practice of eating meat sacrificed to idols); and
5. demonstrate how one passage sheds light on another (see note on Ps 26:8 for how the presence of God's glory marked his presence in the tabernacle, in the temple, and finally in Jesus Christ himself).

Some elements of style should be noted:

1. Study notes on a *passage* precede notes on individual verses within that passage.
2. When a book of the Bible is referred to within a note on that book, the book name is not repeated. For example, a reference to 2 Timothy 2:18 within the notes on 2 Timothy is written 2:18, not 2Ti 2:18.

3. In lists of references within a note, references from the book under discussion are placed first. The rest appear in Biblical order.

Introductions to Books

Each introduction to each book of the Bible is different. Introductions vary in length and reflect both the nature of the material itself and the strengths and interests of contributing editors.

An introduction frequently reports on a book's title, author, and date of writing. It details the book's background and purpose, explores themes and theological significance, and points out special problems and distinctive literary features. Where appropriate, such as in Paul's letters to the churches, it describes the original recipients of a book and the city in which they lived.

A complete outline of the book's content is provided in each introduction (except for the introduction to Psalms). For Genesis, two outlines—a literary and a thematic—are given. Pairs of books that were originally one literary work, such as 1 and 2 Samuel, 1 and 2 Kings, and 1 and 2 Chronicles, are outlined together.

Text Notes

NIV text notes are indicated by raised, bold-faced letters following the words or phrases they explain. They examine such things as alternate translations, meanings of Hebrew and Greek terms, Old Testament quotations, and variant readings in ancient Biblical manuscripts. Text notes appear at the bottom of the right-hand column, preceded by their bold letters and verse numbers.

Cross-Reference System

The cross-reference system, developed over many years by June Gunden, John R. Kohlenberger III (OT) and Donald H. Madvig (NT), can be used to explore concepts, as well as specific words. For example, one can either study "angels as protectors" (see Mt 18:10) or focus on the word "angel" (see Jn 20:12).

The NIV cross-reference system resembles a series of interlocking chains with many links. The head, or organizing, link in each concept chain is indicated by the letter "S" (short for "See"). The appearance of a head link in a list of references usually signals another list of references that will cover a slightly different aspect of the concept or word being studied. The various chains in the cross-reference system—which is virtually inexhaustible—continually intersect and diverge.

Cross references are indicated by raised light-italic letters. When a single word is addressed by both text notes and cross references, the bold NIV text-note letter comes first. The cross references normally appear in the center column and, when necessary, continue at the bottom of the right-hand column preceding the NIV text notes.

The lists of references are in Biblical order with one exception: If reference is made to a verse within the same chapter, that verse (indicated by "ver") is listed first. If an Old Testament verse is quoted in the New Testament, the New Testament reference is marked with an asterisk (*).

Genesis 1:1 provides a good example of the resources of the cross-reference system.

The Beginning

1 In the beginning God created the heavens and the earth. 2Now the earth was formless and empty, darkness was over the surface of the deep, and the Spirit of God was hovering over the waters.

3And God said, "Let there be light," and there was light. 4God saw that the light was good, and he separated the light from the darkness. 5God called the light "day," and the darkness he called "night." And there was evening, and there was morning—the first day.

```
1:1 a Ps 102:25;
Pr 8:23;
Isa 40:21; 41:4,
26; Jn 1:1-2 b ver
21,27; Ge 2:3
c ver 6; Ne 9:6;
Job 9:8; 37:18;
Ps 96:5; 104:2;
115:15; 121:2;
136:5; Isa 40:22;
42:5; 51:13;
Jer 10:12; 51:15
d Ge 14:19;
2Ki 19:15;
Ne 9:6; Job 38:4;
Ps 90:2; 136:6;
146:6; Isa 37:16;
40:28; 42:5;
44:24; 45:12,18;
Jer 27:5; 32:17;
Ac 14:15; 17:24;
Eph 3:9;
Col 1:16;
Heb 3:4; 11:3;
Rev 4:11; 10:6
1:2 e Isa 23:1;
```

The four lists of references all relate to creation, but each takes a different perspective. Note *a* takes up the time of creation: "in the beginning." Note *b* lists three other occurrences of the word "created" in Genesis 1-2. Note *c* focuses on "the heavens" as God's creation. Because note *d* is attached to the end of the verse as well as to the word "earth," it deals with the word "earth," with the phrase "the heavens and the earth" and with creation itself (the whole verse).

Parallel Passages

When two or more passages of Scripture are nearly identical or deal with the same event, this

"parallel" is noted at the sectional headings for those passages. Such passages are especially common in Matthew, Mark, Luke and John, and in Samuel, Kings and Chronicles.

Identical or nearly identical passages are noted with *"pp."* Similar passages—those not dealing with the same event—are noted with *"Ref."*

To conserve space and avoid repetition, when a parallel passage is noted at a sectional heading, no further parallels are listed in the cross-reference system. It was compiled and edited by John R. Kohlenberger III and Edward W. Goodrick.

Concordance

The concordance is the largest ever bound together with an English Bible. By looking up key words, you can find verses for which you remember a word or two but not their location. For example, to find the verse that states that the word of God is "sharper than any double-edged sword," you could look in the concordance under either "sharper," "double-edged," or "sword."

Maps

The Study Bible includes 57 maps: 13 full color and 44 black and white. The 13 full-color maps at the end of this Bible cover nearly 4,000 years of history, from the patriarchs to Christianity in the world today.

Strategically placed throughout the text are almost four dozen black-and-white maps specially designed for the Study Bible. The Contents contains a complete list of the topics covered.

The cities of Damascus, Rome, Corinth, Ephesus and Philippi have been reconstructed as they might have been in New Testament times. These recreations allow Bible students to visualize the places through which Paul traveled on his missionary journeys.

Charts

Complementing the study notes are 35 charts, diagrams and drawings designed specifically for the Study Bible. Two full-color time lines, located in the front of this Bible, pinpoint significant dates in the Old and New Testaments. Other charts, carefully placed within the text, give detailed information about ancient non-Biblical texts, about Old Testament covenants, sacrifices, and feast days, about Jewish sects, and about major archaeological finds relating to the New Testament.

Essays

Four brief essays give additional information on specific sections of the Bible: the Minor Prophets, the Synoptic Gospels, the Pastoral Letters, and the General Letters.

A fifth essay details the history, literature and social developments of the 400 years between the Old and New Testaments.

Subject and Map Indexes

The subject index pinpoints other references to persons, places, events and topics mentioned in the Study Bible notes.

Two map indexes help in locating place-names on a map.

Acknowledgments

My greatest debt of gratitude is owed to God for giving me the privilege of serving as General Editor of *The NIV Study Bible*. Special thanks go to the four Associate Editors: Donald W. Burdick, John H. Stek, Walter W. Wessel, and Ronald Youngblood. Without their help, it would have been impossible to complete this project in a little over five years.

In addition, grateful acknowledgment is given to all those listed on the Contributors page. Obviously the editors and contributors have profited immensely from the labors of others. We feel deeply indebted to all the commentaries and other sources we have used in our work.

I should also thank the following individuals for rendering help in various ways (though I fear that I have inadvertently omitted a few names): Caroline Blauwkamp, David R. Douglass, Stanley N. Gundry, N. David Hill, Betty Hockenberry, Charles E. Hummel, Alan F. Johnson, Janet Johnston Murphy, Donald H. Madvig, Frances Steenwyk, and Edward Viening.

Nehemiah 8:7-8, 12 says:

> The Levites . . . instructed the people in the Law while the people were standing there. They read from the Book of the Law of God, making it clear and giving the meaning so that the people could understand what was being read. . . . Then all the people went away . . . to celebrate with great joy, because they now understood the words that had been made known to them.

My associates and I will feel amply rewarded if those who use this Study Bible have an experience similar to that of God's people in Nehemiah's time.

Kenneth L. Barker
General Editor

Contributors

General Editor:	Kenneth L. Barker
Associate Editors:	Donald W. Burdick
	John H. Stek
	Walter W. Wessel
	Ronald Youngblood

The individuals named below contributed and/or reviewed material for *The NIV Study Bible*. However, since the General Editor and the Associate Editors extensively edited the notes on most books, they alone are responsible for their final form and content.

The chief contributors of original material to the Study Bible are listed first. Where the Associate Editors and General Editor contributed an unusually large number of notes on certain books, their names are also listed.

Genesis	Ronald Youngblood	Micah	Allan A. MacRae;
Exodus	Ronald Youngblood;		Thomas E. McComiskey
	Walter C. Kaiser, Jr.	Nahum	G. Herbert Livingston;
Leviticus	R. Laird Harris;		Kenneth L. Barker
	Ronald Youngblood	Habakkuk	Roland K. Harrison;
Numbers	Ronald B. Allen;		William C. Williams
	Kenneth L. Barker	Zephaniah	Roland K. Harrison
Deuteronomy	Earl S. Kalland;	Haggai	Herbert Wolf
	Kenneth L. Barker	Zechariah	Kenneth L. Barker;
Joshua	Arthur Lewis		Larry L. Walker
Judges	John J. Davis;	Malachi	Herbert Wolf;
	Herbert Wolf		John H. Stek
Ruth	Marvin R. Wilson;	Matthew	Ralph Earle
	John H. Stek	Mark	Walter W. Wessel;
1,2 Samuel	J. Robert Vannoy		William L. Lane
1,2 Kings	J. Robert Vannoy	Luke	Lewis Foster
1,2 Chronicles	Raymond Dillard	John	Leon Morris
Ezra	Edwin Yamauchi;	Acts	Lewis Foster
	Ronald Youngblood	Romans	Walter W. Wessel
Nehemiah	Edwin Yamauchi;	1 Corinthians	W. Harold Mare
	Ronald Youngblood	2 Corinthians	Philip E. Hughes
Esther	Raymond Dillard;	Galatians	Robert Mounce
	Edwin Yamauchi	Ephesians	Walter L. Liefeld
Job	Elmer B. Smick;	Philippians	Richard B. Gaffin, Jr.
	Ronald Youngblood	Colossians	Gerald F. Hawthorne;
Psalms	John H. Stek		Wilber B. Wallis
Proverbs	Herbert Wolf	1,2 Thessalonians	Leon Morris
Ecclesiastes	Derek Kidner	1,2 Timothy	Walter W. Wessel;
Song of Songs	John H. Stek		George W. Knight, III
Isaiah	Herbert Wolf;	Titus	D. Edmond Hiebert
	John H. Stek	Philemon	John Werner
Jeremiah	Ronald Youngblood	Hebrews	Philip E. Hughes;
Lamentations	Ronald Youngblood		Donald W. Burdick
Ezekiel	Mark Hillmer	James	Donald W. Burdick
Daniel	Gleason L. Archer, Jr.;	1,2 Peter	Donald W. Burdick;
	Ronald Youngblood		John H. Skilton
Hosea	Jack P. Lewis	1,2,3 John	Donald W. Burdick
Joel	Jack P. Lewis	Jude	Donald W. Burdick;
Amos	Alan R. Millard;		John H. Skilton
	John H. Stek	Revelation	Robert Mounce
Obadiah	John M. Zinkand	"The Time between	David O'Brien
Jonah	Marvin R. Wilson;	the Testaments"	
	John H. Stek	(essay)	

Managing Editor:	Doris Wynbeek Rikkers
Copy Editor and Stylist:	June Gunden
Artist:	Hugh O. Claycombe
Art Consultant:	James E. Jennings

Abbreviations

General

c.	about, approximately
cf.	compare, confer
ch., chs.	chapter, chapters
e.g.	for example
etc.	and so on
i.e.	that is
lit.	literally
NT	New Testament
OT	Old Testament
v., vv.	verse, verses (in the chapter being commented on)

Standard abbreviations of month names are also sometimes used, as well as a few other common abbreviations.

Books of the Bible

Genesis	Ge	Nahum	Na
Exodus	Ex	Habakkuk	Hab
Leviticus	Lev	Zephaniah	Zep
Numbers	Nu	Haggai	Hag
Deuteronomy	Dt	Zechariah	Zec
Joshua	Jos	Malachi	Mal
Judges	Jdg	Matthew	Mt
Ruth	Ru	Mark	Mk
1 Samuel	1Sa	Luke	Lk
2 Samuel	2Sa	John	Jn
1 Kings	1Ki	Acts	Ac
2 Kings	2Ki	Romans	Ro
1 Chronicles	1Ch	1 Corinthians	1Co
2 Chronicles	2Ch	2 Corinthians	2Co
Ezra	Ezr	Galatians	Gal
Nehemiah	Ne	Ephesians	Eph
Esther	Est	Philippians	Php
Job	Job	Colossians	Col
Psalms	Ps	1 Thessalonians	1Th
Proverbs	Pr	2 Thessalonians	2Th
Ecclesiastes	Ecc	1 Timothy	1Ti
Song of Songs	SS	2 Timothy	2Ti
Isaiah	Isa	Titus	Tit
Jeremiah	Jer	Philemon	Phm
Lamentations	La	Hebrews	Heb
Ezekiel	Eze	James	Jas
Daniel	Da	1 Peter	1Pe
Hosea	Hos	2 Peter	2Pe
Joel	Joel	1 John	1Jn
Amos	Am	2 John	2Jn
Obadiah	Ob	3 John	3Jn
Jonah	Jnh	Jude	Jude
Micah	Mic	Revelation	Rev

Transliterations

A simplified system has been used for transliterating words from ancient Biblical languages into English. The only transliterations calling for comment are these:

Transliteration	Pronunciation
'	Glottal stop
ḥ	Similar to the "ch" in the German word *Buch*
ṭ	Similar to the "t" in the verb "tear"
'	Similar to the glottal stop
ṣ	Similar to the "ts" in "hits"
ś	Similar to the "s" in "sing"

THE OLD
TESTAMENT

GENESIS

Title

The first phrase in the Hebrew text of 1:1 is *bereshith* ("in [the] beginning"), which is also the Hebrew title of the book (books in ancient times customarily were named after their first word or two). The English title, Genesis, is Greek in origin and comes from the word *geneseos,* which appears in the Greek translation (Septuagint) of 2:4; 5:1. Depending on its context, the word can mean "birth," "genealogy," or "history of origin." In both its Hebrew and Greek forms, then, the title of Genesis appropriately describes its contents, since it is primarily a book of beginnings.

Background

Chs. 1-38 reflect a great deal of what we know from other sources about ancient Mesopotamian life and culture. Creation, genealogies, destructive floods, geography and mapmaking, construction techniques, migrations of peoples, sale and purchase of land, legal customs and procedures, sheep-herding and cattle-raising—all these subjects and many others were matters of vital concern to the peoples of Mesopotamia during this time. They were also of interest to the individuals, families and tribes of whom we read in the first 38 chapters of Genesis. The author appears to locate Eden, man's first home, in or near Mesopotamia; the tower of Babel was built there; Abram was born there; Isaac took a wife from there; and Jacob lived there for 20 years. Although these patriarchs settled in Palestine, their original homeland was Mesopotamia.

The closest ancient literary parallels to Ge 1-38 also come from Mesopotamia. *Enuma elish,* the story of the god Marduk's rise to supremacy in the Babylonian pantheon, is similar in some respects (though thoroughly mythical and polytheistic) to the Ge 1 creation account. Some of the features of certain king lists from Sumer bear striking resemblance to the genealogy in Ge 5. The 11th tablet of the *Gilgamesh* epic is quite similar in outline to the flood narrative in Ge 6-8. Several of the major events of Ge 1-8 are narrated in the same order as similar events in the *Atrahasis* epic. In fact, the latter features the same basic motif of creation-rebellion-flood as the Biblical account. Clay tablets found recently at the ancient (c. 2500-2300 B.C.) site of Ebla (modern Tell Mardikh) in northern Syria may also contain some intriguing parallels (see chart on "Ancient Texts Relating to the OT," p. 5).

Two other important sets of documents demonstrate the reflection of Mesopotamia in the first 38 chapters of Genesis. From the Mari letters (see chart on p. 5), dating from the patriarchal period, we learn that the names of the patriarchs (including especially Abram, Jacob and Job) were typical of that time. The letters also clearly illustrate the freedom of travel that was possible between various parts of the Amorite world in which the patriarchs lived. The Nuzi tablets (see chart on p. 5), though a few centuries later than the patriarchal period, shed light on patriarchal customs, which tended to survive virtually intact for many centuries. The inheritance right of an adopted household member or slave (see 15:1-4), the obligation of a barren wife to furnish her husband with sons through a servant girl (see 16:2-4), strictures against expelling such a servant girl and her son (see 21:10-11), the authority of oral statements in ancient Near Eastern law, such as the deathbed bequest (see 27:1-4,22-23,33)—these and other legal customs, social contracts and provisions are graphically illustrated in Mesopotamian documents.

As Ge 1-38 is Mesopotamian in character and background, so chs. 39-50 reflect Egyptian influence—though in not quite so direct a way. Examples of such influence are: Egyptian grape cultivation (40:9-11), the riverside scene (ch. 41), Egypt as Canaan's breadbasket (ch. 42), Canaan as the source of numerous products for Egyptian consumption (ch. 43), Egyptian religious and social customs (the end of chs. 43; 46), Egyptian administrative procedures (ch. 47), Egyptian funerary practices (ch. 50) and several Egyptian words and names used throughout these chapters. The closest specific literary parallel from Egypt is the *Tale of Two Brothers,* which bears some resemblance to the story of Joseph

and Potiphar's wife (ch. 39). Egyptian autobiographical narratives (such as the *Story of Sinuhe* and the *Report of Wenamun*) and certain historical legends offer more general literary parallels.

Author and Date of Writing

Historically, Jews and Christians alike have held that Moses was the author/compiler of the first five books of the OT. These books, known also as the Pentateuch (meaning "five-volumed book"), were referred to in Jewish tradition as the five fifths of the law (of Moses). The Bible itself suggests Mosaic authorship of Genesis, since Ac 15:1 refers to circumcision as "the custom taught by Moses," an allusion to Ge 17. However, a certain amount of later editorial updating does appear to be indicated (see, e.g., notes on 14:14; 36:31; 47:11).

The historical period during which Moses lived seems to be fixed with a fair degree of accuracy by 1 Kings. We are told that "the fourth year of Solomon's reign over Israel" was the same as "the four hundred and eightieth year after the Israelites had come out of Egypt" (1Ki 6:1). Since the former was c. 966 B.C., the latter—and thus the date of the exodus—was c. 1446 (assuming that the 480 in 1Ki 6:1 is to be taken literally; see Introduction to Judges: Background). The 40-year period of Israel's wanderings in the desert, which lasted from c. 1446 to c. 1406, would have been the most likely time for Moses to write the bulk of what is today known as the Pentateuch.

During the last two centuries some scholars have claimed to find in the Pentateuch four underlying sources. The presumed documents, allegedly dating from the tenth to the fifth centuries B.C., are called J (for Jahweh/Yahweh, the personal OT name for God), E (for Elohim, a generic name for God), D (for Deuteronomic) and P (for Priestly). Each of these documents is claimed to have its own characteristics and its own theology, which often contradicts that of the other documents. The Pentateuch is thus depicted as a patchwork of stories, poems and laws. However, this view is not supported by conclusive evidence, and intensive archaeological and literary research has undercut many of the arguments used to challenge Mosaic authorship.

Theme and Message

Genesis speaks of beginnings—of the heavens and the earth, of light and darkness, of seas and skies, of land and vegetation, of sun and moon and stars, of sea and air and land animals, of human beings (made in God's own image, the climax of his creative activity), of sin and redemption, of blessing and cursing, of society and civilization, of marriage and family, of art and craft and industry. The list could go on and on. A key word in Genesis is "account," which also serves to divide the book into its ten major parts (see Literary Features and Literary Outline) and which includes such concepts as birth, genealogy and history.

The book of Genesis is foundational to the understanding of the rest of the Bible. Its message is rich and complex, and listing its main elements gives a succinct outline of the Biblical message as a whole. It is supremely a book of relationships, highlighting those between God and nature, God and man, and man and man. It is thoroughly monotheistic, taking for granted that there is only one God worthy of the name and opposing the ideas that there are many gods (polytheism), that there is no god at all (atheism) or that everything is divine (pantheism). It clearly teaches that the one true God is sovereign over all that exists (i.e., his entire creation), and that by divine election he often exercises his unlimited freedom to overturn human customs, traditions and plans. It introduces us to the way in which God initiates and makes covenants with his chosen people, pledging his love and faithfulness to them and calling them to promise theirs to him. It establishes sacrifice as the substitution of life for life (ch. 22). It gives us the first hint of God's provision for redemption from the forces of evil (compare 3:15 with Ro 16:17-20) and contains the oldest and most profound definition of faith (15:6). More than half of Heb 11—the NT roll of the faithful—refers to characters in Genesis.

Literary Features

The message of a book is often enhanced by its literary structure and characteristics. Genesis is divided into ten main sections, each beginning with the word "account" (see 2:4; 5:1; 6:9; 10:1; 11:10; 11:27; 25:12; 25:19; 36:1—repeated for emphasis at 36:9—and 37:2). The first five sections can be grouped together and, along with the introduction to the book as a whole (1:1-2:3), can be appropriately called "primeval history" (1:1-11:26), sketching the period from Adam to Abraham. The last five sections constitute a much longer (but equally unified) account, and relate the story of God's dealings with Abraham, Isaac, Jacob and Joseph and their families—a section often called "patriarchal history" (11:27-50:26). This section is in turn composed of three narrative cycles (Abraham-Isaac,

11:27-25:11; Isaac-Jacob, 25:19-35:29; 37:1; Jacob-Joseph, 37:2-50:26), interspersed by the genealogies of Ishmael (25:12-18) and Esau (ch. 36).

The narrative frequently concentrates on the life of a later son in preference to the firstborn: Seth over Cain, Shem over Japheth (but see NIV text note on 10:21), Isaac over Ishmael, Jacob over Esau, Judah and Joseph over their brothers, and Ephraim over Manasseh. Such emphasis on divinely chosen men and their families is perhaps the most obvious literary and theological characteristic of the book of Genesis as a whole. It strikingly underscores the fact that the people of God are not the product of natural human developments, but are the result of God's sovereign and gracious intrusion into human history. He brings out of the fallen human race a new humanity consecrated to himself, called and destined to be the people of his kingdom and the channel of his blessing to the whole earth.

Numbers with symbolic significance figure prominently in Genesis. The number ten, in addition to being the number of sections into which Genesis is divided, is also the number of names appearing in the genealogies of chs. 5 and 11 (see note on 5:5). The number seven also occurs frequently. The Hebrew text of 1:1 consists of exactly seven words and that of 1:2 of exactly 14 (twice seven). There are seven days of creation, seven names in the genealogy of ch. 4 (see note on 4:17-18; see also 4:15,24; 5:31), various sevens in the flood story, 70 descendants of Noah's sons (ch. 10), a sevenfold promise to Abram (12:2-3), seven years of abundance and then seven of famine in Egypt (ch. 41), and 70 descendants of Jacob (ch. 46). Other significant numbers, such as 12 and 40, are used with similar frequency.

The book of Genesis is basically prose narrative, punctuated here and there by brief poems (the longest is the so-called Blessing of Jacob in 49:2-27). Much of the prose has a lyrical quality and uses the full range of figures of speech and other devices that characterize the world's finest epic literature. Vertical and horizontal parallelism between the two sets of three days in the creation account (see note on 1:11); the ebb and flow of sin and judgment in ch. 3 (the serpent and woman and man sin successively; then God questions them in reverse order; then he judges them in the original order); the powerful monotony of "and then he died" at the end of paragraphs in ch. 5; the climactic hinge effect of the phrase "But God remembered Noah" (8:1) at the midpoint of the flood story; the hourglass structure of the account of the tower of Babel in 11:1-9 (narrative in vv. 1-2,8-9; discourse in vv. 3-4,6-7; v. 5 acting as transition); the macabre pun in 40:19 (see 40:13); the alternation between brief accounts about firstborn sons and lengthy accounts about younger sons—these and numerous other literary devices add interest to the narrative and provide interpretive signals to which the reader should pay close attention.

It is no coincidence that many of the subjects and themes of the first three chapters of Genesis are reflected in the last three chapters of Revelation. We can only marvel at the superintending influence of the Lord himself, who assures us that "all Scripture is God-breathed" (2Ti 3:16) and that the people who wrote it "spoke from God as they were carried along by the Holy Spirit" (2Pe 1:21).

Outlines

Literary Outline:

I. Introduction (1:1-2:3)
II. Body (2:4-50:26)
    A. "The account of the heavens and the earth" (2:4-4:26)
    B. "The written account of Adam's line" (5:1-6:8)
    C. "The account of Noah" (6:9-9:29)
    D. "The account of Shem, Ham and Japheth" (10:1-11:9)
    E. "The account of Shem" (11:10-26)
    F. "The account of Terah" (11:27-25:11)
    G. "The account of Abraham's son Ishmael" (25:12-18)
    H. "The account of Abraham's son Isaac" (25:19-35:29)
    I. "The account of Esau" (36:1-37:1)
    J. "The account of Jacob" (37:2-50:26)

Thematic Outline:

I. Primeval History (1:1-11:26)
    A. Creation (1:1-2:3)
        1. Introduction (1:1-2)

      2. Body (1:3-31)
      3. Conclusion (2:1-3)
  B. Adam and Eve in Eden (2:4-25)
  C. The Fall and Its Consequences (ch. 3)
  D. The Rapid "Progress" of Sin (4:1-16)
  E. Two Genealogies (4:17-5:32)
      1. The genealogy of pride (4:17-24)
      2. The genealogy of death (4:25-5:32)
  F. The Extent of Sin before the Flood (6:1-8)
  G. The Great Flood (6:9-9:29)
      1. Preparing for the flood (6:9-7:10)
      2. Judgment and redemption (7:11-8:19)
         a. The rising of the waters (7:11-24)
         b. The receding of the waters (8:1-19)
      3. The flood's aftermath (8:20-9:29)
         a. A new promise (8:20-22)
         b. New ordinances (9:1-7)
         c. A new relationship (9:8-17)
         d. A new temptation (9:18-23)
         e. A final word (9:24-29)
  H. The Spread of the Nations (10:1-11:26)
      1. The diffusion of nations (ch. 10)
      2. The confusion of tongues (11:1-9)
      3. The first Semitic genealogy (11:10-26)
II. Patriarchal History (11:27-50:26)
  A. The Life of Abraham (11:27-25:11)
      1. Abraham's background (11:27-32)
      2. Abraham's land (chs. 12-14)
      3. Abraham's people (chs. 15-24)
      4. Abraham's last days (25:1-11)
  B. The Descendants of Ishmael (25:12-18)
  C. The Life of Jacob (25:19-35:29)
      1. Jacob at home (25:19-27:46)
      2. Jacob abroad (chs. 28-30)
      3. Jacob at home again (chs. 31-35)
  D. The Descendants of Esau (36:1-37:1)
  E. The Life of Joseph (37:2-50:26)
      1. Joseph's career (37:2-41:57)
      2. Jacob's migration (chs. 42-47)
      3. Jacob's last days (48:1-50:14)
      4. Joseph's last days (50:15-26)

Ancient Texts Relating to the Old Testament

Major representative examples of ancient Near Eastern non-Biblical documents that provide parallels to or shed light on various OT passages.

AMARNA LETTERS
Canaanite Akkadian—*14th century B.C.*
Hundreds of letters, written primarily by Canaanite scribes, illuminate social, political and religious relationships between Canaan and Egypt during the reigns of Amunhotep III and Akhenaten.

AMENEMOPE'S WISDOM
Egyptian—*early 1st millennium B.C.*
Thirty chapters of wisdom instruction are similar to Pr 22:17-24:22 and provide the closest external parallels to OT wisdom literature.

ATRAHASIS EPIC
Akkadian—*early 2nd millennium B.C.*
A cosmological epic depicts creation and early human history, including the flood (cf. Ge 1-9).

BABYLONIAN THEODICY
Akkadian—*early 1st millennium B.C.*
A sufferer and his friend dialogue with each other (cf. Job).

CYRUS CYLINDER
Akkadian—*6th century B.C.*
King Cyrus of Persia records the conquest of Babylon (cf. Da 5:30; 6:28) and boasts of his generous policies toward his new subjects and their gods.

DEAD SEA SCROLLS
Hebrew, Aramaic, Greek—*3rd century B.C. to 1st century A.D.*
Several hundred scrolls and fragments include the oldest copies of OT books and passages.

EBLA TABLETS
Sumerian, Eblaite—*mid-3rd millennium B.C.*
Thousands of commercial, legal, literary and epistolary texts describe the cultural vitality and political power of a pre-patriarchal civilization in northern Syria.

ELEPHANTINE PAPYRI
Aramaic—*late 5th century B.C.*
Contracts and letters document life among Jews who fled to southern Egypt after Jerusalem was destroyed in 586 B.C.

ENUMA ELISH
Akkadian—*early 2nd millennium B.C.*
Marduk, the Babylonian god of cosmic order, is elevated to the supreme position in the pantheon. The 7-tablet epic contains an account of creation (cf. Ge 1-2).

GEZER CALENDAR
Hebrew—*10th century B.C.*
A schoolboy from west-central Israel describes the seasons, crops and farming activity of the agricultural year.

GILGAMESH EPIC
Akkadian—*early 2nd millennium B.C.*
Gilgamesh, ruler of Uruk, experiences numerous adventures, including a meeting with Utnapishtim, the only survivor of a great deluge (cf. Ge 6-9).

HAMMURAPI'S CODE
Akkadian—*18th century B.C.*
Together with similar law codes that preceded and followed it, the Code of Hammurapi exhibits close parallels to numerous passages in the Mosaic legislation of the OT.

HYMN TO THE ATEN
Egyptian—*14th century B.C.*
The poem praises the beneficence and universality of the sun in language somewhat similar to that used in Ps 104.

ISHTAR'S DESCENT
Akkadian—*1st millennium B.C.*
The goddess Ishtar temporarily descends to the netherworld, which is pictured in terms reminiscent of OT descriptions of Sheol.

JEHOIACHIN'S RATION DOCKETS
Akkadian—*early 6th century B.C.*
Brief texts from the reign of Nebuchadnezzar II refer to rations allotted to Judah's exiled king Jehoiachin and his sons (cf. 2Ki 25:27-30).

KING LISTS
Sumerian—*late 3rd millennium B.C.*
The reigns of Sumerian kings before the flood are described as lasting for thousands of years, reminding us of the longevity of the pre-flood patriarchs in Ge 5.

LACHISH LETTERS
Hebrew—*early 6th century B.C.*
Inscriptions on pottery fragments vividly portray the desperate days preceding the Babylonian siege of Jerusalem in 588-586 B.C. (cf. Jer 34:7).

LAMENTATION OVER THE DESTRUCTION OF UR
Sumerian—*early 2nd millennium B.C.*
The poem mourns the destruction of the city of Ur at the hands of the Elamites (cf. the OT book of Lamentations).

LUDLUL BEL NEMEQI
Akkadian—*late 2nd millennium B.C.*
A suffering Babylonian nobleman describes his distress in terms faintly reminiscent of the experiences of Job.

MARI TABLETS
Akkadian—*18th century B.C.*
Letters and administrative texts provide detailed information regarding customs, language and personal names that reflect the culture of the OT patriarchs.

MERNEPTAH STELE
Egyptian—*13th century B.C.*
Pharaoh Merneptah figuratively describes his victory over various peoples in western Asia, including "Israel."

MESHA STELE (MOABITE STONE)
Moabite—*9th century B.C.*
Mesha, king of Moab (see 2Ki 3:4), rebels against a successor of Israel's king Omri.

MURASHU TABLETS
Akkadian—*5th century B.C.*
Commercial documents describe financial transactions engaged in by Murashu and Sons, a Babylonian firm that did business with Jews and other exiles.

MURSILIS'S TREATY WITH DUPPI-TESSUB
Hittite—*mid-2nd millennium B.C.*
King Mursilis imposes a suzerainty treaty on King Duppi-Tessub. The literary outline of this and other Hittite treaties is strikingly paralleled in OT covenants established by God with his people.

NABONIDUS CHRONICLE
Akkadian—*mid-6th century B.C.*
The account describes the absence of King Nabonidus from Babylon. His son Belshazzar is therefore the regent in charge of the kingdom (cf. Da 5:29-30).

NEBUCHADNEZZAR CHRONICLE
Akkadian—*early 6th century B.C.*
A chronicle from the reign of Nebuchadnezzar II includes the Babylonian account of the siege of Jerusalem in 597 B.C. (see 2Ki 24:10-17).

NUZI TABLETS
Akkadian—*mid-2nd millennium B.C.*
Adoption, birthright-sale and other legal documents graphically illustrate OT patriarchal customs current centuries earlier.

PESSIMISTIC DIALOGUE
Akkadian—*early 1st millennium B.C.*
A master and his servant discuss the pros and cons of various activities (cf. Ecc 1-2).

RAS SHAMRA TABLETS
Ugaritic—*15th century B.C.*
Canaanite deities and rulers experience adventures in epics that enrich our understanding of Canaanite mythology and religion and of OT poetry.

SARGON LEGEND
Akkadian—*1st millennium B.C.*
Sargon I (the Great), ruler of Akkad in the late 3rd millennium B.C., claims to have been rescued as an infant from a reed basket found floating in a river (cf. Ex 2).

SARGON'S DISPLAY INSCRIPTION
Akkadian—*8th century B.C.*
Sargon II takes credit for the conquest of Samaria in 722/721 B.C. and states that he captured and exiled 27,290 Israelites.

SENNACHERIB'S PRISM
Akkadian—*early 7th century B.C.*
Sennacherib vividly describes his siege of Jerusalem in 701 B.C., making Hezekiah a prisoner in his own royal city (but cf. 2Ki 19:35-37).

SEVEN LEAN YEARS TRADITION
Egyptian—*2nd century B.C.*
Egypt experiences 7 years of low Niles and famine, which, by a contractual agreement between Pharaoh Djoser (28th century B.C.) and a god, will be followed by prosperity (cf. Ge 41).

SHALMANESER'S BLACK OBELISK
Akkadian—*9th century B.C.*
Israel's king Jehu (or his servant) presents tribute to Assyria's king Shalmaneser III. Additional Assyrian and Babylonian texts refer to other kings of Israel and Judah.

SHISHAK'S GEOGRAPHICAL LIST
Egyptian—*10th century B.C.*
Pharaoh Shishak lists the cities that he captured or made tributary during his campaign in Judah and Israel (cf. 1Ki 14:25-26).

SILOAM INSCRIPTION
Hebrew—*late 8th century B.C.*
A Judahite workman describes the construction of an underground conduit to guarantee Jerusalem's water supply during Hezekiah's reign (cf. 2Ki 20:20; 2Ch 32:30).

SINUHE'S STORY
Egyptian—*20th-19th centuries B.C.*
An Egyptian official of the 12th dynasty goes into voluntary exile in Syria and Canaan during the OT patriarchal period.

TALE OF TWO BROTHERS
Egyptian—*13th century B.C.*
A young man rejects the amorous advances of his older brother's wife (cf. Ge 39).

WENAMUN'S JOURNEY
Egyptian—*11th century B.C.*
An official of the Temple of Amun at Thebes in Egypt is sent to Byblos in Canaan to buy lumber for the ceremonial barge of his god.

The Beginning

1 In the beginning[a] God created[b] the heavens[c] and the earth. [d] 2Now the earth was[a] formless[e] and empty,[f] darkness was over the surface of the deep,[g] and the Spirit of God[h] was hovering[i] over the waters.

3And God said,[j] "Let there be light," and there was light.[k] 4God saw that the light was good,[l] and he separated the light from the darkness. [m] 5God called[n] the light "day," and the darkness he called "night."[o] And there was evening, and there was morning[p]—the first day.

6And God said,[q] "Let there be an expanse[r] between the waters[s] to separate water from water." 7So God made the expanse and separated the water under the expanse from the water above it. [t] And it was so. [u]

8God called[v] the expanse "sky." [w] And there was evening, and there was morning[x]—the second day.

9And God said, "Let the water under the sky be gathered to one place,[y] and let dry ground[z] appear." And it was so. [a] 10God called[b] the dry ground "land," and the gathered waters[c] he called "seas." [d] And God saw that it was good. [e]

11Then God said, "Let the land

1:1 aPs 102:25; Pr 8:23; Isa 40:21; 41:4, 26; Jn 1:1-2 bver 21,27; Ge 2:3 cver 6; Ne 9:6; Job 9:8; 37:18; Ps 96:5; 104:2; 115:15; 121:2; 136:5; Isa 40:22; 42:5; 51:13; Jer 10:12; 51:15 dGe 14:19; 2Ki 19:15; Ne 9:6; Job 38:4; Ps 90:2; 136:6; 146:6; Isa 37:16; 40:28; 42:5; 44:24; 45:12,18; Jer 27:5; 32:17; Ac 14:15; 17:24; Eph 3:9; Col 1:16; Heb 3:4; 11:3; Rev 4:11; 10:6 1:2 eIsa 23:1; 24:10; 27:10; 32:14; 34:11 fIsa 45:18; Jer 4:23 gGe 8:2; Job 7:12; 26:8; 38:9; Ps 36:6; 42:7; 104:6; 107:24; Pr 30:4 hGe 2:7;

Job 33:4; Ps 104:30; Isa 32:15 iDt 32:11; Isa 31:5 1:3 jver 6; Ps 33:6,9; 148:5; Heb 11:3 k2Co 4:6*; 1Jn 1:5-7 1:4 lver 10,12,18,21,25,31; Ps 104:31; 119:68; Jer 31:35 mver 14; Ex 10:21-23; Job 26:10; 38:19; Ps 18:28; 104:20; 105:28; Isa 42:16; 45:7 1:5 nver 8,10; Ge 2:19,23 oPs 74:16 pver 8, 13,19,23,31 1:6 qS ver 3 rS ver 1; Isa 44:24; 2Pe 3:5 sver 9; Ps 24:2; 136:6 1:7 tGe 7:11; Job 26:10; 38:8-11,16; Ps 68:33; 148:4; Pr 8:28 uver 9,11,15,24 1:8 vS ver 5 wJob 9:8; 37:18; Ps 19:1; 104:2; Isa 40:22; 44:24; 45:12; Jer 10:12; Zec 12:1 xS ver 5 1:9 yJob 38:8-11; Ps 33:7; 104:6-9; Pr 8:29; Jer 5:22; 2Pe 3:5 zPs 95:5; Jnh 1:9; Hag 2:6 aS ver 7 1:10 bS ver 5 cPs 33:7 dJob 38:8; Ps 90:2; 95:5 eS ver 4

a2 Or possibly became

1:1 A summary statement introducing the six days of creative activity. The truth of this majestic verse was joyfully affirmed by poet (Ps 102:25) and prophet (Isa 40:21). *In the beginning God.* The Bible always assumes, and never argues, God's existence. Although everything else had a beginning, God has always been (Ps 90:2). *In the beginning.* Jn 1:1–10, which stresses the work of Christ in creation, opens with the same phrase. *God created.* The Hebrew noun *Elohim* is plural but the verb is singular, a normal usage in the OT when reference is to the one true God. This use of the plural expresses intensification rather than number and has been called the plural of majesty, or of potentiality. In the OT the Hebrew verb for "create" is used only of divine, never of human, activity. *the heavens and the earth.* "All things" (Isa 44:24). That God created everything is also taught in Ecc 1:5; Jer 10:16; Jn 1:3; Col 1:16; Heb 1:2. The positive, life-oriented teaching of v. 1 is beautifully summarized in Isa 45:18.
1:2 *earth.* The focus of this account. *formless and empty.* The phrase, which appears elsewhere only in Jer 4:23, gives structure to the rest of the chapter (see note on v. 11). God's "separating" and "gathering" on days 1–3 gave form, and his "making" and "filling" on days 4–6 removed the emptiness. *darkness ... the waters.* Completes the picture of a world awaiting God's light-giving, order-making and life-creating word. *and.* Or "but." The awesome (and, for ancient man, fearful) picture of the original state of the visible creation is relieved by the majestic announcement that the mighty Spirit of God hovers over creation. The announcement anticipates God's creative words that follow. *Spirit of God.* He was active in creation, and his creative power continues today (see Job 33:4; Ps 104:30). *hovering over.* Like a bird that provides for and protects its young (see Dt 32:11; Isa 31:5). The imagery may also suggest the winged sun disk, which throughout the ancient Near East was a symbol of divine majesty.
1:3 *God said.* Merely by speaking, God brought all things into being (Ps 33:6,9; 148:5; Heb 11:3). *Let there be light.* God's first creative word called forth light in the midst of the primeval darkness. Light is necessary for making God's creative works visible and life possible. In the OT it is also symbolic of life and blessing (see 2Sa 22:29; Job 3:20; 30:26; 33:30; Ps 49:19; 56:13; 97:11; 112:4; Isa 53:11; 58:8,10; 59:9; 60:1,3). Paul uses this word to illustrate

God's re-creating work in sin-darkened hearts (2Co 4:6).
1:4 Everything God created is good (see vv. 10,12,18,21, 25); in fact, the conclusion declares it to be "very good" (v. 31). The creation, as fashioned and ordered by God, had no lingering traces of disorder and no dark and threatening forces arrayed against God or man. Even darkness and the deep were given benevolent functions in a world fashioned to bless and sustain life (see Ps 104:19–26; 127:2).
1:5 *called.* See vv. 8,10. In ancient times, to name something or someone implied having dominion or ownership (see 17:5,15; 41:45; 2Ki 23:34; 24:17; Da 1:7). Both day and night belong to the Lord (Ps 74:16). *first day.* Some say that the creation days were 24-hour days, others that they were indefinite periods.
1:6 *expanse.* The atmosphere, or "sky" (v. 8), as seen from the earth. "Hard as a mirror" (Job 37:18) and "like a canopy" (Isa 40:22) are among the many pictorial phrases used to describe it.
1:7 *And it was so.* The only possible outcome, whether stated (vv. 9,11,15,24,30) or implied, to God's "Let there be."
1:9 *one place.* A picturesque way of referring to the "seas" (v. 10) that surround the dry ground on all sides and into which the waters of the lakes and rivers flow. The earth was "formed out of water" (2Pe 3:5) and "founded ... upon the seas" (Ps 24:2), and the waters are not to cross the boundaries set for them (Ps 104:7–9; Jer 5:22).
1:11 *God said.* This phrase is used twice on the third day (vv. 9,11) and three times (vv. 24,26,29) on the sixth day. These two days are climactic, as the following structure of ch. 1 reveals (see note on v. 2 regarding "formless and empty"):

Days of forming	Days of filling
1. "light" (v. 3)	4. "lights" (v. 14)
2. "water under the expanse ... water above it" (v. 7)	5. "every living and moving thing with which the water teems ... every winged bird" (v. 21)
3a. "dry ground" (v. 9)	6a[1]. "livestock, creatures that move along the ground, and wild animals" (v. 24)
	a[2]. "man" (v. 26)
b. "vegetation" (v. 11)	b. "every green plant for food" (v. 30)

produce vegetation:/ seed-bearing plants and trees on the land that bear fruit with seed in it, according to their various kinds.*g* " And it was so.*h* ¹²The land produced vegetation: plants bearing seed according to their kinds*i* and trees bearing fruit with seed in it according to their kinds. And God saw that it was good.*j* ¹³And there was evening, and there was morning*k*—the third day.

¹⁴And God said, "Let there be lights*l* in the expanse of the sky to separate the day from the night,*m* and let them serve as signs*n* to mark seasons*o* and days and years,*p* ¹⁵and let them be lights in the expanse of the sky to give light on the earth." And it was so.*q* ¹⁶God made two great lights—the greater light*r* to govern*s* the day and the lesser light to govern*t* the night.*u* He also made the stars.*v* ¹⁷God set them in the expanse of the sky to give light on the earth, ¹⁸to govern the day and the night,*w* and to separate light from darkness. And God saw that it was good.*x* ¹⁹And there was evening, and there was morning*y*—the fourth day.

²⁰And God said, "Let the water teem with living creatures,*z* and let birds fly above the earth across the expanse of the sky."*a* ²¹So God created*b* the great creatures of the sea*c* and every

living and moving thing with which the water teems,*d* according to their kinds, and every winged bird according to its kind.*e* And God saw that it was good.*f* ²²God blessed them and said, "Be fruitful and increase in number and fill the water in the seas, and let the birds increase on the earth."*g* ²³And there was evening, and there was morning*h*—the fifth day.

²⁴And God said, "Let the land produce living creatures*i* according to their kinds:*j* livestock, creatures that move along the ground, and wild animals, each according to its kind." And it was so.*k* ²⁵God made the wild animals*l* according to their kinds, the livestock according to their kinds, and all the creatures that move along the ground according to their kinds.*m* And God saw that it was good.*n*

²⁶Then God said, "Let us*o* make man*p* in our image,*q* in our likeness,*r* and let them rule*s* over the fish of the sea and the birds of the air,*t* over the livestock, over all the earth,*b* and over all the creatures that move along the ground."

1:11 /Ps 65:9-13; 104:14 *g*ver 12, 21,24,25; Ge 2:5; 6:20; 7:14; Lev 11:14,19,22; Dt 14:13,18; 1Co 15:38 *h*S ver 7
1:12 /S ver 11 /S ver 4
1:13 *k*S ver 5
1:14 /Ps 74:16; 136:7 *m*S ver 4 *n*Jer 10:2 *o*Ps 104:19 *p*Ge 8:22; Jer 31:35-36; 33:20,25
1:15 *q*S ver 7
1:16 *r*Dt 17:3; Job 31:26; Jer 43:13; Eze 8:16 *s*Ps 136:8 *t*Ps 136:9 *u*Job 38:33; Ps 74:16; 104:19; Jer 31:35; Jas 1:17 *v*Dt 4:19; Job 9:9; 38:7, 31-32; Ps 8:3; 33:6; Ecc 12:2; Isa 40:26; Jer 8:2; Am 5:8
1:18 *w*Jer 33:20, 25 *x*S ver 4
1:19 *y*S ver 5
1:20 *z*Ps 146:6 *a*Ge 2:19
1:21 *b*S ver 1 *c*Job 3:8; 7:12; Ps 74:13; 148:7; Isa 27:1; Eze 32:2
1:22 *d*Ps 104:25-26 *e*S ver 11 /S ver 4
1:22 *g*ver 28; Ge 8:17; 9:1,7, 19; 47:27; Lev 26:9; Eze 36:11
1:23 *h*S ver 5
1:24 *i*Ge 2:19 /S ver 11 *k*S ver 7
1:25 /Ge 7:21-22; Jer 27:5 *m*S ver

11 *n*S ver 4 **1:26** *o*Ge 3:5,22; 11:7; Ps 100:3; Isa 6:8 *p*Isa 45:18 *q*ver 27; Ge 5:3; 9:6; Ps 8:5; 82:6; 89:6; 1Co 11:7; 2Co 4:4; Col 1:15; 3:10; Jas 3:9 *r*Ac 17:28-29 *s*Ge 9:2; Ps 8:6-8 *t*Ps 8:8

*b*26 Hebrew; Syriac *all the wild animals*

Both the horizontal and vertical relationships between the days demonstrate the literary beauty of the chapter and stress the orderliness and symmetry of God's creative activity. *kinds.* See vv. 12,21,24–25. Both creation and reproduction are orderly.

1:14 *serve as signs.* In the ways mentioned here, not in any astrological or other such sense.

1:16 *two great lights.* The words "sun" and "moon" seem to be avoided deliberately here, since both were used as proper names for the pagan deities associated with these heavenly bodies. They are light-givers to be appreciated, not powers to be feared, because the one true God made them (see Isa 40:26). Perhaps because of the emphasis on the greater light and lesser light, the stars seem to be mentioned almost as an afterthought. But Ps 136:9 indicates that the stars help the moon "govern the night." *to govern.* The great Creator-King assigns subordinate regulating roles to certain of his creatures (see vv. 26,28).

1:17–18 The three main functions of the heavenly bodies.

1:21 *creatures of the sea.* The Hebrew word underlying this phrase was used in Canaanite mythology to name a dreaded sea monster. He is often referred to figuratively in OT poetry as one of God's most powerful opponents. He is pictured as national (Babylon, Jer 51:34; Egypt, Isa 51:9; Eze 29:3; 32:2) or cosmic (Job 7:12; Ps 74:13; Isa 27:1, though some take the latter as a reference to Egypt). In Genesis, however, the creatures of the sea are portrayed not

as enemies to be feared but as part of God's good creation to be appreciated. *winged bird.* The term denotes anything that flies, including insects (see Dt 14:19–20).

1:22 *Be fruitful and increase in number.* God's benediction on living things that inhabit the water and that fly in the air. By his blessing they flourish and fill both realms with life (see note on v. 28). God's rule over his created realm promotes and blesses life.

1:26 *us . . . our . . . our.* God speaks as the Creator-King, announcing his crowning work to the members of his heavenly court (see 3:22; 11:7; Isa 6:8; see also 1Ki 22:19–23; Job 15:8; Jer 23:18). *image . . . likeness.* No distinction should be made between "image" and "likeness," which are synonyms in both the OT (5:1; 9:6) and the NT (1Co 11:7; Col 3:10; Jas 3:9). Since man is made in God's image, every human being is worthy of honor and respect; he is neither to be murdered (9:6) nor cursed (Jas 3:9). "Image" includes such characteristics as "righteousness and holiness" (Eph 4:24) and "knowledge" (Col 3:10). Believers are to be "conformed to the likeness" of Christ (Ro 8:29) and will someday be "like him" (1Jn 3:2). *rule.* Man is the climax of God's creative activity, and God has "crowned him with glory and honor" and "made him ruler" over the rest of his creation (Ps 8:5–8). Since man was created in the image of the divine King, delegated sovereignty (kingship) was bestowed on him. (For redeemed man's ultimate kingship see notes on Heb 2:5–9.)

27So God created^u man^v in his own
   image,^{w}
in the image of God^x he created
   him;
male and female^y he created them.^{z}

28God blessed them and said to them,^{a} "Be fruitful and increase in number;^{b} fill the earth^c and subdue it. Rule over^d the fish of the sea and the birds of the air and over every living creature that moves on the ground.^{e}"

29Then God said, "I give you every seed-bearing plant on the face of the whole earth and every tree that has fruit with seed in it. They will be yours for food.^{f} 30And to all the beasts of the earth and all the birds of the air and all the creatures that move on the ground—everything that has the breath of life^g in it—I give every green plant for food.^{h}" And it was so.

31God saw all that he had made,^{i} and it was very good.^{j} And there was evening, and there was morning^k—the sixth day.

2

Thus the heavens and the earth were completed in all their vast array.^{l}

2By the seventh day^m God had finished the work he had been doing; so on the seventh day he rested^c from all his work.^{n} 3And God blessed the seventh day and made it holy,^{o} because on it he rested^p from all the work of creating^q that he had done.

Adam and Eve

4This is the account^r of the heavens and the earth when they were created.^{s}

When the LORD God made the earth and the heavens— 5and no shrub of the field had yet appeared on the earth^d and no plant of the field had yet sprung up,^{t} for the LORD God had not sent rain on the earth^{du} and there was no man to work the ground, 6but streams^e came up from the earth and watered the whole surface of the ground— 7the LORD God formed^v the

---

1:27 ^{u}S ver 1; ^{v}Ge 2:7; Ps 103:14; 119:73 ^{w}S ver 26 ^{x}Ge 5:1 ^{y}Ge 5:2; Mt 19:4*; Mk 10:6*; Gal 3:28 ^{z}Dt 4:32
1:28 ^{a}Ge 33:5; Jos 24:3; Ps 113:9; 127:3,5 ^{b}S Ge 17:6 ^{c}S ver 22; Ge 6:1; Ac 17:26 ^{d}ver 26; Ps 115:16 ^{e}Ps 8:6-8
1:29 ^{f}Ge 9:3; Dt 12:15; Ps 104:14; 1Ti 4:3
1:30 ^{g}Ge 2:7; 7:22 ^{h}Job 38:41; Ps 78:25; 104:14, 27; 111:5; 136:25; 145:15; 147:9
1:31 ^{i}Ps 104:24; 136:5; Pr 3:19; Jer 10:12 ^{j}S ver 4; 1Ti 4:4 ^{k}S ver 5

2:1 ^{l}Dt 4:19; 17:3; 2Ki 17:16; 21:3; Ps 104:2; Isa 44:24; 45:12; 48:13; 51:13
2:2 ^{m}Dt 5:14 ^{n}ver 2-3; Ex 20:11; 31:17; 34:21; Jn 5:17; Heb 4:4*
2:3 ^{o}Ex 16:23; 20:10; 23:12; 31:15; 35:2; Lev 23:3; Ne 9:14; Isa 58:13;

Jer 17:22 ^{p}Ps 95:11; Heb 4:1-11 ^{q}S Ge 1:1 2:4 ^{r}Ge 5:1; 6:9; 10:1; 11:10,27; 25:12,19; 36:1,9; 37:2 ^{s}Ge 1:1; Job 38:8-11 2:5 ^{t}S Ge 1:11 ^{u}Job 38:28; Ps 65:9-10; Jer 10:13 2:7 ^{v}Isa 29:16; 43:1,21; 44:2

^{c}2 Or ceased; also in verse 3 ^{d}5 Or land; also in verse 6 ^{e}6 Or mist

---

1:27 This highly significant verse is the first occurrence of poetry in the OT (which is about 40 percent poetry). created. The word is used here three times to describe the central divine act of the sixth day (see note on v. 1). male and female. Alike they bear the image of God, and together they share in the divine benediction that follows.
1:28 God blessed them . . . fill . . . subdue . . . Rule. Man goes forth under this divine benediction—flourishing, filling the earth with his kind, and exercising dominion over the other earthly creatures (see v. 26; 2:15; Ps 8:6-8). Human culture, accordingly, is not anti-God (though fallen man often has turned his efforts into proud rebellion against God). Rather, it is the expression of man's bearing the image of his Creator and sharing, as God's servant, in God's kingly rule. As God's representative in the creaturely realm, he is steward of God's creatures. He is not to exploit, waste or despoil them, but to care for them and use them in the service of God and man.
1:29-30 People and animals seem to be portrayed as originally vegetarian (see 9:3).
1:31 very good. See note on v. 4. the sixth day. Perhaps to stress the finality and importance of this day, in the Hebrew text the definite article is first used here in regard to the creation days.
2:2 finished . . . rested. God rested on the seventh day, not because he was weary, but because nothing formless or empty remained (see NIV text note). His creative work was completed—and it was totally effective, absolutely perfect, "very good" (1:31). It did not have to be repeated, repaired or revised, and the Creator rested to commemorate it.
2:3 God blessed the seventh day and made it holy . . . rested. Although the word "Sabbath" is not used here, the Hebrew verb translated "rested" (see v. 2) is the origin of the noun "Sabbath." Ex 20:11 quotes the first half of v. 3, but substitutes "Sabbath" for "seventh," clearly equating the

two. The first record of obligatory Sabbath observance is of Israel on her way from Egypt to Sinai (Ex 16), and according to Ne 9:13-14 the Sabbath was not an official covenant obligation until the giving of the law at Mount Sinai.
2:4 account. The word occurs ten times in Genesis—at the beginning of each main section (see Introduction: Literary Features). the heavens and the earth. See note on 1:1. The phrase "the account of the heavens and the earth" introduces the record of what happened to God's creation. The blight of sin and rebellion brought a threefold curse that darkens the story of Adam and Eve in God's good and beautiful garden: (1) on Satan (3:14); (2) on the ground, because of man (3:17); and (3) on Cain (4:11). 1:1-2:3 is a general account of creation, while 2:4-4:26 focuses on the beginning of human history. LORD God. "LORD" (Hebrew YHWH, "Yahweh") is the personal and covenant name of God (see note on Ex 3:15), emphasizing his role as Israel's Redeemer and covenant Lord (see note on Ex 6:6), while "God" (Hebrew Elohim) is a general term. Both names occur thousands of times in the OT, and often, as here, they appear together—clearly indicating that they refer to the same one and only God.
2:7 formed. The Hebrew for this verb commonly referred to the work of a potter (see Isa 45:9; Jer 18:6), who fashions vessels from clay (see Job 33:6). "Make" (1:26), "create" (1:27) and "form" are used to describe God's creation of both man and animals (v. 19; 1:21,25). breath of life. Humans and animals alike have the breath of life in them (see 1:30; Job 33:4). man became a living being. The Hebrew phrase here translated "living being" is translated "living creatures" in 1:20,24. The words of 2:7 therefore imply that people, at least physically, have affinity with the animals. The great difference is that man is made "in the image of God" (1:27) and has an absolutely unique relation both to God as his servant and to the other creatures as their divinely ap-

man[f][w] from the dust[x] of the ground[y] and breathed into his nostrils the breath[z] of life,[a] and the man became a living being.[b]

[8]Now the LORD God had planted a garden in the east, in Eden;[c] and there he put the man he had formed. [9]And the LORD God made all kinds of trees grow out of the ground—trees[d] that were pleasing to the eye and good for food. In the middle of the garden were the tree of life[e] and the tree of the knowledge of good and evil.[f]

[10]A river[g] watering the garden flowed from Eden;[h] from there it was separated into four headwaters. [11]The name of the first is the Pishon; it winds through the entire land of Havilah,[i] where there is gold. [12](The gold of that land is good; aromatic resin[g][j] and onyx are also there.) [13]The name of the second river is the Gihon; it winds through the entire land of Cush.[h] [14]The name of the third river is the Tigris;[k] it runs along the east side of Asshur. And the fourth river is the Euphrates.[l]

[15]The LORD God took the man and put him in the Garden of Eden[m] to work it and take care of it. [16]And the LORD God commanded the man, "You are free to eat from any tree in the garden;[n] [17]but you must not eat from the tree of the knowledge of good and evil,[o] for when you eat of it you will surely die."[p]

[18]The LORD God said, "It is not good for the man to be alone. I will make a helper suitable for him."[q]

[19]Now the LORD God had formed out of the ground all the beasts of the field[r] and all the birds of the air.[s] He brought them to the man to see what he would name them; and whatever the man called[t] each living creature,[u] that was its name. [20]So the man gave names to all the livestock, the birds of the air and all the beasts of the field.

But for Adam[i] no suitable helper[v] was found. [21]So the LORD God caused the man to fall into a deep sleep;[w] and while he was sleeping, he took one of the man's ribs[j] and closed up the place with flesh. [22]Then the LORD God made a woman from the rib[k][x] he had taken out of the man, and he brought her to the man.

[23]The man said,

"This is now bone of my bones
    and flesh of my flesh;[y]
she shall be called[z] 'woman,[l]'
    for she was taken out of man.[a]"

[24]For this reason a man will leave his fa-

Cross-references (center column)

2:7 [w]S Ge 1:27; [x]Ge 3:19; 18:27; Job 4:19; 10:9; 17:16; 34:15; Ps 90:3; Ecc 3:20; 12:7 [y]Ge 3:23; 4:2; Ps 103:14; Jer 18:6; 1Co 15:47 [z]S Ge 1:2; Job 27:3; Isa 2:22 [a]S Ge 1:30; Isa 42:5; Ac 17:25 [b]Job 12:10; 32:8; 33:4; 34:14; Ps 104:29; Isa 57:16; Eze 37:5; 1Co 15:45*
2:8 [c]ver 10,15; Ge 3:23,24; 4:16; 13:10; Isa 51:3; Eze 28:13; 31:9, 16; 36:35; Joel 2:3
2:9 [d]Eze 31:8 [e]Ge 3:22,24; Pr 3:18; 11:30; S Rev 2:7 [f]Eze 47:12
2:10 [g]Nu 24:6; Ps 46:4; Eze 47:5 [h]S ver 8
2:11 [i]Ge 10:7; 25:18
2:12 [j]Nu 11:7
2:14 [k]Ge 41:1; Da 10:4 [l]Ge 15:18; 31:21; Ex 23:31; Nu 22:5; Dt 1:7; 11:24; Jos 1:4; 2Sa 8:3; 1Ki 4:21; 2Ki 23:29; 24:7; 1Ch 5:9; 18:3; 2Ch 35:20; Jer 13:4; 46:2; 51:63; S Rev 9:14
2:15 [m]S ver 8
2:16 [n]Ge 3:1-2
2:17 [o]Ge 3:11,17 [p]Ge 3:1,3; 5:5; 9:29; Dt 30:15, 19; Jer 42:16; Eze 3:18;

[S column] S Ro 5:12; S 6:23 **2:18** [q]Pr 31:11; 1Co 11:9; 1Ti 2:13 **2:19** [r]Ps 8:7 [s]S Ge 1:20 [t]S Ge 1:5 [u]Ge 1:24 **2:20** [v]Ge 3:20; 4:1 **2:21** [w]Ge 15:12; 1Sa 26:12; Job 33:15 **2:22** [x]1Co 11:8,9,12; 1Ti 2:13 **2:23** [y]Ge 29:14; Eph 5:28-30 [z]S Ge 1:5 [a]1Co 11:8

[f]7 The Hebrew for *man (adam)* sounds like and may be related to the Hebrew for *ground (adamah)*; it is also the name *Adam* (see Gen. 2:20).   [g]12 Or *good; pearls*   [h]13 Possibly southeast Mesopotamia   [i]20 Or *the man*   [j]21 Or *took part of the man's side*   [k]22 Or *part*   [l]23 The Hebrew for *woman* sounds like the Hebrew for *man.*

Study notes (bottom)

pointed steward (Ps 8:5–8).

2:8 *in the east.* From the standpoint of the author of Genesis. The garden was perhaps near where the Tigris and Euphrates rivers (see v. 14) meet, in what is today southern Iraq. *Eden.* A name synonymous with "paradise" and related to either (1) a Hebrew word meaning "bliss" or "delight" or (2) a Mesopotamian word meaning "a plain." Perhaps the author subtly suggests both.

2:9 *tree of life.* Signifying and giving life, without death, to those who eat its fruit (see 3:22; Rev 2:7; 22:2,14). *tree of the knowledge of good and evil.* Signifying and giving knowledge, leading ultimately to death, to those who eat its fruit (v. 17; 3:3). "Knowledge of good and evil" refers to moral knowledge or ethical discernment (see Dt 1:39; Isa 7:15–16). Adam and Eve possessed both life and moral discernment as they came from the hand of God. Their access to the fruit of the tree of life showed that God's will and intention for them was life. Ancient pagans believed that the gods intended for man always to be mortal. In eating the fruit of the tree of the knowledge of good and evil, Adam and Eve sought a creaturely source of discernment in order to be morally independent of God.

2:11 *Pishon.* Location unknown. The Hebrew word may be a common noun meaning "gusher." *Havilah.* Location unknown; perhaps mentioned again in 10:29. It is probably to be distinguished from the Havilah of 10:7, which was in Egypt.

2:13 *Gihon.* Location unknown. The Hebrew word may be

a common noun meaning "spurter." Both the Pishon and the Gihon may have been streams in Lower Mesopotamia near the Persian Gulf. The names were those current when Moses wrote.

2:14 *Asshur.* An ancient capital city of Assyria ("Assyria" and "Asshur" are related words). *Euphrates.* Often called simply "the River" (1Ki 4:21,24) because of its size and importance.

2:15 *work . . . take care.* See note on 1:28. Man is now charged to govern the earth responsibly under God's sovereignty.

2:16 *any tree.* Including the tree of life (v. 9).

2:17 *surely die.* Despite the serpent's denial (3:4), disobeying God ultimately results in death.

2:18–25 The only full account of the creation of woman in ancient Near Eastern literature.

2:18 *not good . . . to be alone.* Without female companionship and a partner in reproduction, the man could not fully realize his humanity.

2:19 *name them.* His first act of dominion over the creatures around him (see note on 1:5).

2:24 *leave his father and mother.* Instead of remaining under the protective custody of his parents a man leaves them and, with his wife, establishes a new family unit. *united . . . one flesh.* The divine intention for husband and wife was monogamy. Together they were to form an inseparable union, of which "one flesh" is both a sign and an expression.

ther and mother and be united[b] to his wife, and they will become one flesh.[c]

[25]The man and his wife were both naked,[d] and they felt no shame.

The Fall of Man

3 Now the serpent[e] was more crafty than any of the wild animals the LORD God had made. He said to the woman, "Did God really say, 'You must not eat from any tree in the garden'?[f]"

[2]The woman said to the serpent, "We may eat fruit from the trees in the garden,[g] [3]but God did say, 'You must not eat fruit from the tree that is in the middle of the garden, and you must not touch it, or you will die.'"[h]

[4]"You will not surely die," the serpent said to the woman.[i] [5]"For God knows that when you eat of it your eyes will be opened, and you will be like God,[j] knowing good and evil."

[6]When the woman saw that the fruit of the tree was good for food and pleasing to the eye, and also desirable[k] for gaining wisdom, she took some and ate it. She also gave some to her husband,[l] who was with her, and he ate it.[m] [7]Then the eyes of both of them were opened, and they realized they were naked;[n] so they sewed fig leaves together and made coverings for themselves.[o]

[8]Then the man and his wife heard the sound of the LORD God as he was walk-ing[p] in the garden in the cool of the day, and they hid[q] from the LORD God among the trees of the garden. [9]But the LORD God called to the man, "Where are you?"[r]

[10]He answered, "I heard you in the garden, and I was afraid[s] because I was naked;[t] so I hid."

[11]And he said, "Who told you that you were naked?[u] Have you eaten from the tree that I commanded you not to eat from?[v]"

[12]The man said, "The woman you put here with me[w]—she gave me some fruit from the tree, and I ate it."

[13]Then the LORD God said to the woman, "What is this you have done?" The woman said, "The serpent deceived me,[x] and I ate."

[14]So the LORD God said to the serpent, "Because you have done this,

"Cursed[y] are you above all the livestock
and all the wild animals!
You will crawl on your belly
and you will eat dust[z]
all the days of your life.
[15]And I will put enmity
between you and the woman,
and between your offspring[m][a] and hers;[b]

2:24 [b]Mal 2:15;
[c]Mt 19:5*;
Mk 10:7-8*;
1Co 6:16*;
Eph 5:31*
2:25 [d]Ge 3:7,
10-11; Isa 47:3;
La 1:8
3:1 [e]Job 1:7; 2:2;
2Co 11:3;
Rev 12:9; 20:2
[f]S Ge 2:17
3:2 [g]Ge 2:16
3:3 [h]S Ge 2:17
3:4 [i]S Jn 8:44;
2Co 11:3
3:5 [j]S Ge 1:26;
14:18,19; Ps 7:8;
Isa 14:14;
Eze 28:2
3:6 [k]Jas 1:14-15;
1Jn 2:16
[l]Nu 30:7-8;
Jer 44:15,19,24
[m]2Co 11:3;
1Ti 2:14
3:7 [n]Ge 2:25
[o]ver 21

3:8 [p]Lev 26:12;
Dt 23:14
[q]Job 13:16; 23:7;
31:33; 34:22,23;
Ps 5:5; 139:7-12;
Isa 29:15;
Jer 16:17; 23:24;
49:10;
Rev 6:15-16
3:9 [r]Ge 4:9;
16:8; 18:9;
1Ki 19:9,13
3:10 [s]Ex 19:16;
20:18; Dt 5:5;
1Sa 12:18
[t]Ge 2:25
3:11 [u]Ge 2:25
[v]S Ge 2:17
3:12 [w]Ge 2:22
3:13 [x]Ro 7:11;
2Co 11:3;
1Ti 2:14
3:14
[y]Dt 28:15-20
[z]Ps 72:9;
Isa 49:23; 65:25;

Mic 7:17 3:15 [a]Jn 8:44; Ac 13:10; 1Jn 3:8 [b]Ge 16:11;
Jdg 13:5; Isa 7:14; 8:3; 9:6; Mt 1:23; Lk 1:31; Gal 4:4;
Rev 12:17

[m]15 Or seed

2:25 *naked... no shame.* Freedom from shame, signifying moral innocence, would soon be lost as a result of sin (see 3:7).
3:1 *serpent.* The great deceiver clothed himself as a serpent, one of God's good creatures. He insinuated a falsehood and portrayed rebellion as clever, but essentially innocent, self-interest. Therefore "the devil, or Satan," is later referred to as "that ancient serpent" (Rev 12:9; 20:2). *crafty.* The Hebrew words for "crafty" and "naked" are almost identical. Though naked, the man and his wife felt no shame (2:25). The craftiness of the serpent led them to sin, and they then became ashamed of their nakedness (see v. 7). *Did God really say...?* The question and the response changed the course of human history. By causing the woman to doubt God's word, Satan brought evil into the world. Here the deceiver undertook to alienate man from God. In Job 1–2 he, as the accuser, acted to alienate God from man (see also Zec 3:1).
3:3 *and you must not touch it.* The woman adds to God's word, distorting his directive and demonstrating that the serpent's subtle challenge was working its poison.
3:4 *You will not surely die.* The blatant denial of a specific divine pronouncement (see 2:17).
3:5 *God knows.* Satan accuses God of having unworthy motives. In Job 1:9–11; 2:4–5 he accuses the righteous man of the same. *your eyes will be opened, and you will be like God.* The statement is only half true. Their eyes were opened, to be sure (see v. 7), but the result was quite different from what the serpent had promised. *knowing good*

and evil. See note on 2:9.
3:6 *good for food... pleasing to the eye... desirable for gaining wisdom.* Three aspects of temptation. Cf. 1Jn 2:16; Lk 4:3,5,9.
3:7 *they realized they were naked.* No longer innocent like children, they had a new awareness of themselves and of each other in their nakedness and shame. *they... made coverings.* Their own feeble and futile attempt to hide their shame, which only God could cover (see note on v. 21).
3:8 *the garden.* Once a place of joy and fellowship with God, it became a place of fear and of hiding from God.
3:9 *Where are you?* A rhetorical question (see 4:9).
3:12 *The woman you put here... gave me.* The man blames God and the woman—anyone but himself—for his sin.
3:13 *The serpent deceived me.* The woman blames the serpent rather than herself.
3:14 *Cursed.* The serpent, the woman and the man were all judged, but only the serpent and the ground were cursed—the latter because of Adam (v. 17). *dust.* The symbol of death itself (v. 19) would be the serpent's food.
3:15 *he will crush your head, and you will strike his heel.* The antagonism between people and snakes is used to symbolize the outcome of the titanic struggle between God and the evil one, a struggle played out in the hearts and history of mankind. The offspring of the woman would eventually crush the serpent's head, a promise fulfilled in Christ's victory over Satan—a victory in which all believers will share (see Ro 16:20).

he will crush[n] your head,[c]
  and you will strike his heel.''

16To the woman he said,

"I will greatly increase your pains in
    childbearing;
  with pain you will give birth to
    children.[d]
Your desire will be for your husband,
  and he will rule over you.[e]''

17To Adam he said, "Because you listened to your wife and ate from the tree
about which I commanded you, 'You must
not eat of it,'[f]

"Cursed[g] is the ground[h] because of
    you;
  through painful toil[i] you will eat of it
    all the days of your life.[j]
18It will produce thorns and thistles[k] for
    you,
  and you will eat the plants of the
    field.[l]
19By the sweat of your brow[m]
  you will eat your food[n]
until you return to the ground,
  since from it you were taken;
for dust you are
  and to dust you will return.''[o]

20Adam[o] named his wife Eve,[p][p] because she would become the mother of all
the living.
21The LORD God made garments of skin
for Adam and his wife and clothed them.[q]

Cross references (center column):

3:15 cRo 16:20;
Heb 2:14
3:16 dPs 48:5-6;
Isa 13:8; 21:3;
26:17; Jer 4:31;
6:24; Mic 4:9;
1Ti 2:15
eICo 11:3;
S Eph 5:22
3:17 fS Ge 2:17
gGe 5:29;
Nu 35:33;
Ps 106:39;
Isa 24:5; Jer 3:1;
Ro 8:20-22
hGe 6:13; 8:21;
Isa 54:9
iGe 29:32; 31:42;
Ex 3:7; Ps 66:11;
127:2; Ecc 1:13
jGe 47:9; Job 5:7;
7:1; 14:1;
Ecc 2:23;
Jer 20:18
3:18 kJob 31:40;
Isa 5:6; Heb 6:8
lPs 104:14
3:19 mPs 104:23
nGe 14:18;
Dt 8:3,9; 23:4;
Ru 1:6; 2:14;
2Th 3:10
oS Ge 2:7;
S Job 7:21;
S Ps 146:4;
1Co 15:47;
Heb 9:27
3:20 pS Ge 2:20;
2Co 11:3;
1Ti 2:13
3:21 qS ver 7
3:22 rS Ge 1:26
sS Ge 2:9;
S Rev 2:7
3:23 tS Ge 2:8
uS Ge 2:7
3:24 vS Ge 2:8
wEx 25:18-22;
1Sa 4:4; 2Sa 6:2;
22:11; 1Ki 6:27;
8:6; 2Ki 19:15;
2Ch 5:8;
Ps 18:10; 80:1;
99:1; Isa 37:16;

22And the LORD God said, "The man has
now become like one of us,[r] knowing
good and evil. He must not be allowed to
reach out his hand and take also from the
tree of life[s] and eat, and live forever.'' 23So
the LORD God banished him from the Garden of Eden[t] to work the ground[u] from
which he had been taken. 24After he drove
the man out, he placed on the east side[q] of
the Garden of Eden[v] cherubim[w] and a
flaming sword[x] flashing back and forth to
guard the way to the tree of life.[y]

Cain and Abel

4 Adam[o] lay with his wife[z] Eve,[a] and
  she became pregnant and gave birth to
Cain.[r][b] She said, "With the help of the
LORD I have brought forth[s] a man.'' 2Later
she gave birth to his brother Abel.[c]
  Now Abel kept flocks, and Cain worked
the soil.[d] 3In the course of time Cain
brought some of the fruits of the soil as an
offering[e] to the LORD.[f] 4But Abel brought
fat portions[g] from some of the firstborn of
his flock.[h] The LORD looked with favor on
Abel and his offering,[i] 5but on Cain and
his offering he did not look with favor. So

Eze 10:1; 28:16 xJob 40:19; Ps 104:4; Isa 27:1 yS Ge 2:9 4:1
zver 17,25 aS Ge 2:20 bHeb 11:4; 1Jn 3:12; Jude 1:11 4:2
cMt 23:35; Lk 11:51; Heb 11:4; 12:24 dS Ge 2:7 4:3
eLev 2:1-2; Isa 43:23; Jer 41:5 fNu 18:12 4:4 gLev 3:16;
2Ch 29:35 hHeb 13:2,12; Dt 15:19 iHeb 11:4

n15 Or strike   o20,1 Or The man   p20 Eve
probably means living.   q24 Or placed in front
r1 Cain sounds like the Hebrew for brought forth or
acquired.   s1 Or have acquired

3:16 pains in childbearing. Her judgment fell on what was
most uniquely hers as a woman and as a "suitable helper''
(2:20) for her husband. Similarly, the man's "painful toil'' (v.
17) was a judgment on him as worker of the soil. Some
believe that the Hebrew root underlying "pains,'' "pain'' and
"painful toil'' should here be understood in the sense of
burdensome labor (see Pr 5:10, "toil''; 14:23, "hard
work''). give birth to children. As a sign of grace in the midst
of judgment, the human race would continue. desire . . .
rule. Her sexual attraction for the man, and his headship over
her, will become intimate aspects of her life in which she
experiences trouble and anguish rather than unalloyed joy
and blessing.
3:17-19 you will eat. Though he would have to work hard
and long (judgment), the man would be able to produce food
that would sustain life (grace).
3:19 return to the ground . . . to dust you will return.
Man's labor would not be able to stave off death. The origin
of his body (see 2:7) and the source of his food (see v. 17)
became a symbol of his eventual death.
3:21 clothed them. God graciously provided Adam and
Eve with more effective clothing (cf. v. 7) to cover their
shame (cf. v. 10).
3:22 us. See note on 1:26. knowing good and evil. In a
terribly perverted way, Satan's prediction (v. 5) came true.
live forever. Sin, which always results in death (Ro 6:23; Jas
1:14-15), cuts the sinner off from God's gift of eternal
life.
3:23 banished him from the Garden . . . to work the

ground. Before he sinned, man had worked in a beautiful
and pleasant garden (2:15). Now he would have to work
hard ground cursed with thorns and thistles (v. 18).
3:24 cherubim. Similar to the statues of winged, human-
headed bulls or lions that stood guard at the entrances to
palaces and temples in ancient Mesopotamia (see note on Ex
25:18). to guard. The sword of God's judgment stood between fallen man and God's garden. The reason is given in v.
22. Only through God's redemption in Christ does man have
access again to the tree of life (see Rev 2:7; 22:2,14,19).
4:1 With the help of the LORD. Eve acknowledged that God
is the ultimate source of life (see Ac 17:25).
4:2 Abel. The name means "breath'' or "temporary'' or
"meaningless'' (the translation of the same basic Hebrew
word that is in Ecc 1:2; 12:8) and hints at the shortness of
Abel's life.
4:3-4 Cain brought some of the fruits . . . But Abel
brought fat portions from some of the firstborn of his flock.
The contrast is not between an offering of plant life and an
offering of animal life, but between a careless, thoughtless
offering and a choice, generous offering (cf. Lev 3:16). Motivation and heart attitude are all-important, and God looked
with favor on Abel and his offering because of Abel's faith
(Heb 11:4). firstborn. Indicative of the recognition that all
the productivity of the flock is from the Lord and all of it
belongs to him.
4:5 angry. God did not look with favor on Cain and his
offering, and Cain (whose motivation and attitude were bad
from the outset) reacted predictably.

Cain was very angry, and his face was
downcast.
6Then the LORD said to Cain, "Why are
you angry?[j] Why is your face downcast?
7If you do what is right, will you not be
accepted? But if you do not do what is
right, sin is crouching at your door;[k] it
desires to have you, but you must master
it.[l]"
8Now Cain said to his brother Abel,
"Let's go out to the field."[t] And while
they were in the field, Cain attacked his
brother Abel and killed him.[m]
9Then the LORD said to Cain, "Where is
your brother Abel?"[n]
"I don't know,[o]" he replied. "Am I my
brother's keeper?"
10The LORD said, "What have you done?
Listen! Your brother's blood cries out to
me from the ground.[p] 11Now you are under a curse[q] and driven from the ground,
which opened its mouth to receive your
brother's blood from your hand. 12When
you work the ground, it will no longer
yield its crops for you.[r] You will be a restless wanderer[s] on the earth.[t]"
13Cain said to the LORD, "My punishment is more than I can bear. 14Today you
are driving me from the land, and I will be
hidden from your presence;[u] I will be a
restless wanderer on the earth,[v] and whoever finds me will kill me."[w]
15But the LORD said to him, "Not so[u]; if
anyone kills Cain[x], he will suffer vengeance[y] seven times over.[z]" Then the
LORD put a mark on Cain so that no one
who found him would kill him. 16So Cain
went out from the LORD's presence[a] and
lived in the land of Nod,[v] east of Eden.[b]
17Cain lay with his wife,[c] and she
became pregnant and gave birth to Enoch.
Cain was then building a city,[d] and he
named it after his son[e] Enoch. 18To Enoch
was born Irad, and Irad was the father of
Mehujael, and Mehujael was the father of
Methushael, and Methushael was the father of Lamech.
19Lamech married[f] two women,[g] one
named Adah and the other Zillah. 20Adah

4:6 [j]Jnh 4:4
4:7 [k]Ge 44:16; Nu 32:23; Isa 59:12 [l]Job 11:15; 22:27; Ps 27:3; 46:2; S Ro 6:16
4:8 [m]Mt 23:35; Lk 11:51; 1Jn 3:12; Jude 1:11
4:9 [n]S Ge 3:9 [o]S Jn 8:44
4:10 [p]Ge 9:5; 37:20,26; Ex 21:12; Nu 35:33; Dt 21:7,9; 2Sa 4:11; Job 16:18; 24:2; 31:38; Ps 9:12; 106:38; Heb 12:24; Rev 6:9-10
4:11 [q]Dt 11:28; 2Ki 2:24
4:12 [r]Dt 28:15-24 [s]Ps 37:25; 59:15; 109:10 [t]ver 14
4:14 [u]2Ki 17:18; Ps 51:11; 139:7-12; Jer 7:15; 52:3 [v]ver 12; Dt 28:64-67 [w]Ge 9:6; Ex 21:12,14; Lev 24:17; Nu 35:19,21,27, 33; 1Ki 2:32; 2Ki 11:16
4:15 [x]Eze 9:4,6 [y]Ex 21:20 [z]ver 24; Lev 26:21; Ps 79:12
4:16 [a]Jude 1:11 [b]S Ge 2:8 **4:17** [c]S ver 1 [d]Ps 55:9 [e]Ps 49:11
4:19 [f]Ge 6:2 [g]Ge 29:28; Dt 21:15; Ru 4:11; 1Sa 1:2

[t]*8* Samaritan Pentateuch, Septuagint, Vulgate and Syriac; Masoretic Text does not have *"Let's go out to the field."*
[u]*15* Septuagint, Vulgate and Syriac; Hebrew *Very well*
[v]*16* *Nod* means *wandering* (see verses 12 and 14).

4:7 *sin is crouching at your door.* The Hebrew word for "crouching" is the same as an ancient Babylonian word referring to an evil demon crouching at the door of a building to threaten the people inside. Sin may thus be pictured here as just such a demon, waiting to pounce on Cain—it desires to have him. He may already have been plotting his brother's murder. *it desires to have you.* In Hebrew, the same expression as that for "Your desire will be for [your husband]" in 3:16 (see also SS 7:10).
4:8 *attacked his brother . . . and killed him.* The first murder was especially monstrous because it was committed with deliberate deceit ("Let's go out to the field"), against a brother (see vv. 9–11; 1Jn 3:12) and against a good man (Mt 23:35; Heb 11:4)—a striking illustration of the awful consequences of the fall.
4:9 *Where . . . ?* A rhetorical question (see 3:9). *I don't know.* An outright lie. *Am I my brother's keeper?* A statement of callous indifference—all too common through the whole course of human history.
4:10 *Your brother's blood cries out.* Abel, in one sense a prophet (Lk 11:50–51), "still speaks, even though he is dead" (Heb 11:4), for his spilled blood continues to cry out to God against all those who do violence to their human brothers. But the blood of Christ "speaks a better word" (Heb 12:24).
4:11 *curse.* The ground had been cursed because of human sin (3:17), and now Cain himself is cursed. Formerly he had worked the ground, and it had produced life for him (vv. 2–3). Now the ground, soaked with his brother's blood, would symbolize death and would no longer yield for him its produce (v. 12).
4:12 *wanderer.* Estranged from his fellowman and finding even the ground inhospitable, he became a wanderer in the land of wandering (see NIV text note on v. 16).
4:13 *My punishment is more than I can bear.* Confronted with his crime and its resulting curse, Cain responded not with remorse but with self-pity. His sin was virtually uninterrupted: impiety (v. 3), anger (v. 5), jealousy, deception and murder (v. 8), falsehood (v. 9) and self-seeking (v. 13). The final result was alienation from God himself (vv. 14,16).
4:14–15 *whoever . . . anyone . . . no one.* These words seem to imply the presence of substantial numbers of people outside Cain's immediate family, but perhaps they only anticipate the future rapid growth of the race.
4:15 *mark.* A warning sign to protect him from an avenger. For the time being, the life of the murderer is spared (but see 6:7; 9:6). For a possible parallel see Eze 9:4.
4:16 *Nod.* Location unknown. See NIV text note.
4:17–18 *Cain . . . Enoch . . . Irad . . . Mehujael . . . Methushael . . . Lamech.* Together with that of Adam, these names add up to a total of seven, a number often signifying completeness (see v. 15). Each of the six names listed here is paralleled by a similar or identical name in the genealogy of Seth in ch. 5 as follows: Kenan (5:12), Enoch (5:21), Jared (5:18), Mahalalel (5:15), Methuselah (5:25), Lamech (5:28). The similarity between the two sets of names is striking and may suggest the selective nature of such genealogies (see note on 5:5). See also Introduction to 1 Chronicles: Genealogies.
4:17 *city.* The Hebrew for this word can refer to any permanent settlement, however small. Cain tried to redeem himself from his wandering state by the activity of his own hands—in the land of wandering he builds a city.
4:19 *married two women.* Polygamy entered history. Haughty Lamech, the seventh from Adam in the line of Cain, perhaps sought to attain the benefits of God's primeval blessing (see 1:28 and note) by his own device—multiplying his wives. Monogamy, however, was the original divine intention (see 2:23–24).
4:20–22 *Jabal . . . Jubal . . . Tubal-Cain.* Lamech's three sons had similar names, each derived from a Hebrew verb meaning "to bring, carry, lead," and emphasizing activity. Tubal-Cain's name was especially appropriate, since "Cain" means "metalsmith."

gave birth to Jabal; he was the father of those who live in tents and raise livestock. 21His brother's name was Jubal; he was the father of all who play the harp ʰ and flute. ⁱ 22Zillah also had a son, Tubal-Cain, who forgedʲ all kinds of tools out ofʷ bronze and iron. Tubal-Cain's sister was Naamah.

23Lamech said to his wives,

"Adah and Zillah, listen to me;
    wives of Lamech, hear my words.
I have killedˣ ᵏ a man for wounding
    me,
    a young man for injuring me.
24If Cain is avengedˡ seven times, ᵐ
    then Lamech seventy-seven times. ⁿ"

25Adam lay with his wifeᵒ again, and she gave birth to a son and named him Seth,ʸ ᵖ saying, "God has granted me another child in place of Abel, since Cain killed him." q 26Seth also had a son, and he named him Enosh. ʳ

At that time men began to call onᶻ the name of the LORD.ˢ

From Adam to Noah

5 This is the written accountᵗ of Adam's line. ᵘ

When God created man, he made him in the likeness of God.ᵛ 2He created themʷ male and femaleˣ and blessed them. And when they were created, he called them "man. ᵃ"

3When Adam had lived 130 years, he had a son in his own likeness, in his own image;ʸ and he named him Seth. ᶻ 4After

Seth was born, Adam lived 800 years and had other sons and daughters. 5Altogether, Adam lived 930 years, and then he died. ᵃ

6When Seth had lived 105 years, he became the fatherᵇ of Enosh. ᵇ 7And after he became the father of Enosh, Seth lived 807 years and had other sons and daughters. 8Altogether, Seth lived 912 years, and then he died.

9When Enosh had lived 90 years, he became the father of Kenan. ᶜ 10And after he became the father of Kenan, Enosh lived 815 years and had other sons and daughters. 11Altogether, Enosh lived 905 years, and then he died.

12When Kenan had lived 70 years, he became the father of Mahalalel. ᵈ 13And after he became the father of Mahalalel, Kenan lived 840 years and had other sons and daughters. 14Altogether, Kenan lived 910 years, and then he died.

15When Mahalalel had lived 65 years, he became the father of Jared. ᵉ 16And after he became the father of Jared, Mahalalel lived 830 years and had other sons and daughters. 17Altogether, Mahalalel lived 895 years, and then he died.

18When Jared had lived 162 years, he became the father of Enoch.ᶠ 19And after he became the father of Enoch, Jared lived 800 years and had other sons and daugh-

---

4:21 ʰGe 31:27; Ex 15:20; 1Sa 16:16; 1Ch 25:3; Ps 33:2; 43:4; Isa 16:11; Da 3:5 ʲJob 21:12; 30:31; Ps 150:4
4:22 ʲEx 35:35; 1Sa 13:19; 2Ki 24:14
4:23 ᵏGe 9:5-6; Ex 20:13; 21:12; 23:7; Lev 19:18; 24:17; Dt 27:24; 32:35
4:24 ˡDt 32:35; 2Ki 9:7; Ps 18:47; 94:1; Isa 35:4; Jer 51:56; Na 1:2 ᵐS ver 15 ⁿMt 18:22
4:25 ᵒver 1 ᵖGe 5:3; 1Ch 1:1 qver 8
4:26 ʳGe 5:6; 1Ch 1:1; Lk 3:38 ˢGe 12:8; 13:4; 21:33; 22:9; 26:25; 33:20; 35:1; Ex 17:15; 1Ki 18:24; Ps 116:17; Joel 2:32; Zep 3:9; S Ac 2:21
5:1 ᵗS Ge 2:4 ᵘ1Ch 1:1 ᵛS Ge 1:27; Col 3:10
5:2 ʷGe 1:28 ˣS Ge 1:27; Mt 19:4; Mk 10:6; Gal 3:28
5:3 ʸS Ge 1:26; 1Co 15:49 ᶻS Ge 4:25; Lk 3:38
5:5 ᵃS Ge 2:17; Heb 9:27
5:6 ᵇS Ge 4:26; Lk 3:38
5:9 ᶜ1Ch 1:2; Lk 3:37
5:12 ᵈ1Ch 1:2; Lk 3:37

5:15 ᵉ1Ch 1:2; Lk 3:37 **5:18** ᶠ1Ch 1:3; Lk 3:37; Jude 1:14

ʷ22 Or *who instructed all who work in* ˣ23 Or *I will kill* ʸ25 *Seth* probably means *granted.* ᶻ26 Or *to proclaim* ᵃ2 Hebrew *adam* ᵇ6 *Father* may mean *ancestor,* also in verses 7-26.

4:22 *tools.* For agriculture and construction, but they were also weapons.

4:23 *killed a man for wounding me.* Violent and wanton destruction of human life by one who proclaimed his complete independence from God by taking vengeance with his own hands (see Dt 32:35). Lamech proudly claimed to be master of his own destiny, thinking that he and his sons, by their own achievements, would redeem themselves from the curse on the line of Cain. This titanic claim climaxes the catalog of sins that began with Cain's prideful selfishness at the beginning of the chapter.

4:24 *seventy-seven times.* Lamech's vicious announcement of personal revenge found its counterpoint in Jesus' response to Peter's question about forgiveness in Mt 18:21–22.

4:25 *again . . . another child.* Abel was dead, and Cain was alienated; so Adam and Eve were granted a third son to carry on the family line.

4:26 *Enosh.* The name, like "Adam" (see NIV text note on 2:7), means "man." *began to call on the name of the LORD.* Lamech's proud self-reliance, so characteristic of the line of Cain, is contrasted with dependence on God found in the line of Seth.

5:1 *account.* See note on 2:4. *likeness.* See note on 1:26.
5:2 *male and female.* See note on 1:27. *blessed them.* See

1:28 and note. *called them.* See note on 1:5. *man.* Often refers to both sexes (mankind) in the early chapters of Genesis (see, e.g., 3:22–24).

5:3 *his own likeness . . . his own image.* See note on 1:26. As God created man in his own perfect image, so now sinful Adam has a son in his own imperfect image.

5:5 *930 years.* See notes on v. 27; 6:3. Whether the large numbers describing human longevity in the early chapters of Genesis are literal or have a conventional literary function—or both—is uncertain. Some believe that several of the numbers have symbolic significance, such as Enoch's 365 (v. 23) years (365 being the number of days in a year, thus a full life) and Lamech's 777 (v. 31) years (777 being an expansion and multiple of seven, the number of completeness; cf. the "seventy-seven times" of Lamech's namesake in 4:24). The fact that there are exactly ten names in the Ge 5 list (as in the genealogy of 11:10–26) makes it likely that it includes gaps, the lengths of which may be summarized in the large numbers. Other ancient genealogies outside the Bible exhibit similarly large figures. For example, three kings in a Sumerian list (which also contains exactly ten names) are said to have reigned 72,000 years each—obviously exaggerated time spans. *and then he died.* Repeated as a sad refrain throughout the chapter, the only exception being Enoch (see note on v. 24). The phrase is a stark reminder of God's judgment on sin resulting from Adam's fall.

ters. 20Altogether, Jared lived 962 years, and then he died.

21When Enoch had lived 65 years, he became the father of Methuselah.g 22And after he became the father of Methuselah, Enoch walked with Godh 300 years and had other sons and daughters. 23Altogether, Enoch lived 365 years. 24Enoch walked with God;i then he was no more, because God took him away.j

25When Methuselah had lived 187 years, he became the father of Lamech.k 26And after he became the father of Lamech, Methuselah lived 782 years and had other sons and daughters. 27Altogether, Methuselah lived 969 years, and then he died.

28When Lamech had lived 182 years, he had a son. 29He named him Noahcl and said, "He will comfort us in the labor and painful toil of our hands caused by the ground, the LORD has cursed.m" 30After Noah was born, Lamech lived 595 years and had other sons and daughters. 31Altogether, Lamech lived 777 years, and then he died.

32After Noah was 500 years old,n he became the father of Shem,o Ham and Japheth.p

The Flood

6 When men began to increase in number on the earthq and daughters were born to them, 2the sons of Godr saw that the daughters of mens were beautiful,t and they marriedu any of them they chose. 3Then the LORD said, "My Spiritv will not contend withd man forever,w for he is mortale;x his days will be a hundred and twenty years."

4The Nephilimy were on the earth in those days—and also afterward—when the sons of God went to the daughters of menz and had children by them. They were the heroes of old, men of renown.a

5The LORD saw how great man's wickedness on the earth had become,b and that every inclination of the thoughts of his heart was only evil all the time.c 6The LORD was grievedd that he had made man on the earth, and his heart was filled with pain. 7So the LORD said, "I will wipe mankind, whom I have created, from the face of the earthe—men and animals, and creatures that move along the ground, and

---

Cross references (center column):

5:21 g1Ch 1:3; Lk 3:37
5:22 hver 24; Ge 6:9; 17:1; 24:40; 48:15; 2Ki 20:3; Ps 116:9; Mic 6:8; Mal 2:6
5:24 iS ver 22 /2Ki 2:1,11; Ps 49:15; 73:24; 89:48; Heb 11:5
5:25 k1Ch 1:3; Lk 3:36
5:29 l1Ch 1:3; Lk 3:36 mS Ge 3:17; Ro 8:20
5:32 nGe 7:6,11; 8:13 oLk 3:36 pGe 6:10; 9:18; 10:1; 1Ch 1:4; Isa 65:20

6:1 qS Ge 1:28
6:2 rJob 1:6 fn; 2:1 sver 4 tDt 21:11 uS Ge 4:19
6:3 vJob 34:14; Gal 5:16-17 wIsa 57:16; 1Pe 3:20 xJob 10:9; Ps 78:39; 103:14; Isa 40:6
6:4 yNu 13:33 zver 2 aGe 11:4
6:5 bGe 38:7; Job 34:26; Jer 1:16; 44:5; Eze 3:19 cGe 8:21; Ps 14:1-3
6:6 dEx 32:14; 1Sa 15:11,35; 2Sa 24:16;

1Ch 21:15; Isa 63:10; Jer 18:7-10; Eph 4:30 6:7 eEze 33:28; Zep 1:2,18

c29 Noah sounds like the Hebrew for comfort.   d3 Or My spirit will not remain in   e3 Or corrupt

---

5:22 walked with God. The phrase replaces the word "lived" in the other paragraphs of the chapter and reminds us that there is a difference between walking with God and merely living.

5:24 then he was no more, because God took him away. The phrase replaces "and then he died" in the other paragraphs of the chapter. Like Elijah, who was "taken" (2Ki 2:10) to heaven, Enoch was taken away (cf. Ps 49:15; 73:24) to the presence of God without experiencing death (Heb 11:5). Lamech, the seventh from Adam in the genealogy of Cain, was evil personified. But "Enoch, the seventh from Adam" (Jude 14) in the genealogy of Seth, "was commended as one who pleased God" (Heb 11:5).

5:27 969 years. Only Noah and his family survived the flood. If the figures concerning life spans are literal, Methuselah died in the year of the flood (the figures in vv. 25,28 and 7:6 add up to exactly 969).

6:1 increase in number. See note on 1:22.

6:2 sons of God saw . . . daughters of men . . . and they married. See v. 4. The phrase "sons of God" here has been interpreted to refer either to angels or to human beings. In such places as Job 1:6; 2:1 it refers to angels, and perhaps also in Ps 29:1 (where it is translated "mighty ones"). Some interpreters also appeal to Jude 6–7 (as well as to Jewish literature) in referring the phrase here to angels.

Others, however, maintain that intermarriage and cohabitation between angels and human beings, though commonly mentioned in ancient mythologies, are surely excluded by the very nature of the created order (ch. 1; Mk 12:25). Elsewhere, expressions equivalent to "sons of God" often refer to human beings, though in contexts quite different from the present one (see Dt 14:1; 32:5; Ps 73:15; Isa 43:6; Hos 1:10; 11:1; Lk 3:38; 1Jn 3:1–2,10). "Sons of God" (vv. 2,4) possibly refers to godly men, and "daughters of men" to sinful women (significantly, they are not called "daughters of

God"), probably from the wicked line of Cain. If so, the context suggests that vv. 1–2 describe the intermarriage of the Sethites ("sons of God") of ch. 5 with the Cainites ("daughters of men") of ch. 4, indicating a breakdown in the separation of the two groups.

Another plausible suggestion is that the "sons of God" refers to royal figures (kings were closely associated with gods in the ancient Near East) who proudly perpetuated and aggravated the corrupt life-style of Lamech son of Cain (virtually a royal figure) and established for themselves royal harems.

6:3 Two key phrases in the Hebrew of this verse are obscure: the one rendered "contend with" (see NIV text note) and the one rendered "for he is mortal." The verse seems to announce that the period of grace between God's declaration of judgment and its arrival would be 120 years (cf. 1Pe 3:20). But if the NIV text note reading is accepted, the verse announces that man's life span would henceforth be limited to 120 years (but see 11:10–26).

6:4 Nephilim. People of great size and strength (see Nu 13:31–33). The Hebrew word means "fallen ones." In men's eyes they were "the heroes of old, men of renown," but in God's eyes they were sinners ("fallen ones") ripe for judgment.

6:5 One of the Bible's most vivid descriptions of total depravity. And because man's nature remained unchanged, things were no better after the flood (8:21).

6:6 The LORD was grieved . . . his heart was filled with pain. Man's sin is God's sorrow (see Eph 4:30).

6:7 I will wipe mankind . . . from the face of the earth. The period of grace (see v. 3 and note) was coming to an end. animals . . . creatures . . . birds. Though morally innocent, the animal world, as creatures under man's corrupted rule, shared in his judgment.

birds of the air—for I am grieved that I have made them. *f* " [8] But Noah[g] found favor in the eyes of the Lord. [h]

[9] This is the account[i] of Noah.

Noah was a righteous man, blameless[j] among the people of his time,[k] and he walked with God. [l] [10] Noah had three sons: Shem, [m] Ham and Japheth. [n]

[11] Now the earth was corrupt[o] in God's sight and was full of violence. [p] [12] God saw how corrupt[q] the earth had become, for all the people on earth had corrupted their ways. [r] [13] So God said to Noah, "I am going to put an end to all people, for the earth is filled with violence because of them. I am surely going to destroy[s] both them and the earth. [t] [14] So make yourself an ark of cypress[f] wood;[u] make rooms in it and coat it with pitch[v] inside and out. [15] This is how you are to build it: The ark is to be 450 feet long, 75 feet wide and 45 feet high. [g] [16] Make a roof for it and finish[h] the ark to within 18 inches[i] of the top. Put a door in the side of the ark and make lower, middle and upper decks. [17] I am going to bring floodwaters[w] on the earth to destroy all life under the heavens, every creature that has the breath of life in it. Everything on earth will perish. [x] [18] But I

will establish my covenant with you, [y] and you will enter the ark[z]—you and your sons and your wife and your sons' wives with you. [19] You are to bring into the ark two of all living creatures, male and female, to keep them alive with you. [a] [20] Two[b] of every kind of bird, of every kind of animal and of every kind[c] of creature that moves along the ground will come to you to be kept alive. [d] [21] You are to take every kind of food that is to be eaten and store it away as food for you and for them."

[22] Noah did everything just as God commanded him. [e]

7 The Lord then said to Noah, "Go into the ark, you and your whole family,[f] because I have found you righteous[g] in this generation. [2] Take with you seven[j] of

Cross-reference column

6:7 *f* ver 17; Ge 7:4,21;
Dt 28:63; 29:20
6:8 *g* Eze 14:14
h Ge 19:19; 39:4;
Ex 33:12,13,17;
34:9; Nu 11:15;
Ru 2:2; Lk 1:30;
Ac 7:46
6:9 *i* S Ge 2:4
j Ge 7:1;
Dt 18:13;
2Sa 22:24;
Job 1:1; 4:6;
9:21; 12:4; 31:6;
Ps 15:2; 18:23;
19:13; 37:37;
Pr 2:7 *k* Ge 7:1;
Ps 37:39;
Jer 15:1;
Eze 14:14,20;
Da 10:11;
l S Lk 1:6;
Heb 11:7; 2Pe 2:5
6:10 *m* Lk 3:36
n S Ge 5:32
6:11 *o* Dt 31:29;
Jdg 2:19 *p* Ps 7:9;
73:6; Eze 7:23;
8:17; 28:16;
Mal 2:16
6:12 *q* Ex 32:7;
Dt 4:16; 9:12,24
r Ps 14:1-3
6:13 *s* Dt 28:63;
2Ki 8:19;
Ezr 9:14;
Jer 44:11 *t* ver 17;
Ge 7:4,21-23;
Job 34:15;
Isa 5:6; 24:1-3;
Jer 44:27;
Eze 7:2-3
6:14 *u* Heb 11:7;
1Pe 3:20 *v* Ex 2:3
6:17 *w* Ps 29:10
x S ver 7,S 13;

2Pe 2:5 6:18 *y* Ge 9:9-16; 17:7; 19:12; Ex 6:4; 34:10,27; Dt 29:13,14-15; Ps 25:10; 74:20; 106:45; Isa 55:3; Jer 32:40; Eze 16:60; Hag 2:5; 1Pe 3:20 *z* Ge 7:1,7,13 6:19 *a* Ge 7:15 6:20 *b* Ge 7:15 *c* S Ge 1:11 *d* Ge 7:3 6:22 *e* Ge 7:5, 9,16; Ex 7:6; 39:43; 40:16,19,21,23,25,27,29,32 7:1 *f* S Ge 6:18; Mt 24:38; Lk 17:26-27; Heb 11:7; 1Pe 3:20; 2Pe 2:5 *g* S Ge 6:9; Eze 14:14

t 14 The meaning of the Hebrew for this word is uncertain. *g* 15 Hebrew *300 cubits long, 50 cubits wide and 30 cubits high* (about 140 meters long, 23 meters wide and 13.5 meters high) *h* 16 Or *Make an opening for light by finishing* *i* 16 Hebrew *a cubit* (about 0.5 meter) *j* 2 Or *seven pairs;* also in verse 3

6:8–9 *found favor . . . righteous . . . blameless . . . walked with God.* See note on 5:22. Noah's godly life was a powerful contrast to the wicked lives of his contemporaries (see v. 5 and note; see also v. 12). This description of Noah does not imply sinless perfection.

6:9 *account.* See note on 2:4. *righteous.* See note on Ps 1:5.

6:14 *ark.* The Hebrew for this word is used elsewhere only in reference to the basket that saved the baby Moses (Ex 2:3,5). *coat it with pitch.* Moses' mother made his basket watertight in the same way (see Ex 2:3).

6:16 *roof.* Perhaps overhanging, to keep the rain from coming in. *within 18 inches of the top.* Noah's ark probably had a series of small windows (see 8:6) encircling the entire vessel 18 inches from the top to admit light and air.

6:17 *floodwaters on the earth to destroy all life under the heavens.* Some believe that the deluge was worldwide, partly because of the apparently universal terms of the text—both here and elsewhere (vv. 7,12–13; 7:4,19, 21–23; 8:21; 9:11,15). Others argue that nothing in the narrative of chs. 6–9 prevents the flood from being understood as regional—destroying everything in its wake, but of relatively limited scope and universal only from the standpoint of Moses' geographic knowledge. "Earth," e.g., may be defined in the more restricted sense of "land" (see 2:5). "All life under the heavens" may mean all life within the range of Noah's perception. (See the universal language used to describe the drought and famine in the time of Joseph—41:54,57; see also note on 41:57.) Since the purpose of the floodwaters was to destroy sinful mankind (see v. 13), and since the writer possibly had in mind only the inhabitants of the ancient Near East, this flood may not have had to be worldwide to destroy them. The apostle Peter, however, seems to assume that the flood and its devastation were

universal and total, except for Noah and his family (2Pe 3:6; but see note there).

6:18 *covenant.* See note on 9:9. Noah would understand the full implications of God's covenant with him only after the floodwaters had dried up (see 9:8–17). *enter the ark.* The story of Noah's salvation from the flood illustrates God's redemption of his children (see Heb 11:7; 2Pe 2:5) and typifies baptism (see 1Pe 3:20–21). *your sons and your wife and your sons' wives with you.* God extends his loving concern to the whole family of righteous Noah—a consistent pattern in God's dealings with his people, underscoring the moral and responsible relationship of parents to their children (see 17:7–27; 18:19; Dt 30:19; Ps 78:1–7; 102:28; 103:17–18; 112:1–2; Ac 2:38–39; 16:31; 1Co 7:14).

6:19 *two of all living creatures . . . to keep them alive.* Most animals were doomed to die in the flood (see note on v. 7), but at least one pair of each kind was preserved to restock the earth after the waters subsided.

6:20 *kind.* See note on 1:11.

6:22 *did everything just as God commanded.* The account stresses Noah's obedience (see 7:5,9,16).

7:1 *Go into the ark.* The beginning of God's final word to Noah before the flood. God's first word to Noah after the flood begins similarly: "Come out of the ark" (8:16). *righteous.* See note on 6:8–9. As a "preacher of righteousness" (2Pe 2:5), Noah warned his contemporaries of coming judgment and testified to the vitality of his own faith (see Heb 11:7).

7:2 *seven of every kind of clean animal . . . two of every kind of unclean animal.* The ceremonially unclean animals would only have to reproduce themselves after the flood, but ceremonially clean animals would be needed also for the burnt offerings that Noah would sacrifice (see 8:20) and for food (see 9:3).

every kind of clean[h] animal, a male and its mate, and two of every kind of unclean animal, a male and its mate, [3]and also seven of every kind of bird, male and female, to keep their various kinds alive[i] throughout the earth. [4]Seven days from now I will send rain[j] on the earth[k] for forty days[l] and forty nights,[m] and I will wipe from the face of the earth every living creature I have made.[n]"

[5]And Noah did all that the LORD commanded him.[o]

[6]Noah was six hundred years old[p] when the floodwaters came on the earth. [7]And Noah and his sons and his wife and his sons' wives entered the ark[q] to escape the waters of the flood. [8]Pairs of clean and unclean[r] animals, of birds and of all creatures that move along the ground, [9]male and female, came to Noah and entered the ark, as God had commanded Noah.[s] [10]And after the seven days[t] the floodwaters came on the earth.

[11]In the six hundredth year of Noah's life,[u] on the seventeenth day of the second month[v]—on that day all the springs of the great deep[w] burst forth, and the floodgates of the heavens[x] were opened. [12]And rain fell on the earth forty days and forty nights.[y]

[13]On that very day Noah and his sons,[z] Shem, Ham and Japheth, together with his wife and the wives of his three sons, entered the ark.[a] [14]They had with them every wild animal according to its kind, all livestock according to their kinds, every creature that moves along the ground according to its kind and every bird according to its kind,[b] everything with wings. [15]Pairs of all creatures that have the breath of life in them came to Noah and entered the ark.[c] [16]The animals going in were

male and female of every living thing, as God had commanded Noah.[d] Then the LORD shut him in.

[17]For forty days[e] the flood kept coming on the earth, and as the waters increased they lifted the ark high above the earth. [18]The waters rose and increased greatly on the earth, and the ark floated on the surface of the water. [19]They rose greatly on the earth, and all the high mountains under the entire heavens were covered.[f] [20]The waters rose and covered the mountains to a depth of more than twenty feet.[k],[l] [21]Every living thing that moved on the earth perished—birds, livestock, wild animals, all the creatures that swarm over the earth, and all mankind.[h] [22]Everything on dry land that had the breath of life[i] in its nostrils died. [23]Every living thing on the face of the earth was wiped out; men and animals and the creatures that move along the ground and the birds of the air were wiped from the earth.[j] Only Noah was left, and those with him in the ark.[k]

[24]The waters flooded the earth for a hundred and fifty days.[l]

8 But God remembered[m] Noah and all the wild animals and the livestock that were with him in the ark, and he sent a wind over the earth,[n] and the waters receded. [2]Now the springs of the deep and the floodgates of the heavens[o] had been closed, and the rain[p] had stopped falling from the sky. [3]The water receded steadily from the earth. At the end of the hundred

7:2 [h]ver 8; Ge 8:20; Lev 10:10; 11:1-47; Dt 14:3-20; Eze 44:23; Hag 2:12; Ac 10:14-15
7:3 [i]Ge 6:20
7:4 [j]Ge 8:2
[k]1Ki 13:34; Jer 28:16
[l]Nu 13:25; Dt 9:9; 1Sa 17:16; 1Ki 19:8
[m]ver 12, 17; Ex 24:18; 32:1; 34:28; Dt 9:9,11,18,25; 10:10; Job 37:6, 13; Mt 4:2
[n]S Ge 6:7,13
7:5 [o]S Ge 6:22
7:6 [p]S Ge 5:32
7:7 [q]S Ge 6:18
7:8 [r]S ver 2
7:9 [s]S Ge 6:22
7:10 [t]S ver 4
7:11 [u]S Ge 5:32
[v]Ge 8:4,14
[w]S Ge 1:7; Job 28:11; Ps 36:6; 42:7; Pr 8:24; Isa 51:10; Eze 26:19
[x]Ge 8:2; 2Ki 7:2; Ps 78:23; Isa 24:18; Mal 3:10
7:12 [y]S ver 4; S 1Sa 12:17; S Job 28:26
7:13 [z]Ge 8:16; 1Pe 3:20; 2Pe 2:5
[a]S Ge 6:18
7:14 [b]S Ge 1:11
7:15 [c]ver 8-9; Ge 6:19
7:16 [d]S Ge 6:22
7:17 [e]S ver 4
7:19 [f]S Ps 104:6
7:20 [g]Ge 8:4-5, 2Pe 3:6
7:21 [h]S Ge 6:7, 13; 2Pe 3:6
7:22 [i]S Ge 1:30
7:23 [j]Job 14:19; 21:18; 22:11,16; Ps 90:5; Isa 28:2; Mt 24:39; Lk 17:27; 1Pe 3:20; 2Pe 2:5
[k]Heb 11:7
7:24 [l]Ge 8:3; Job 12:15

8:1 [m]Ge 9:15; 19:29; 21:1; 30:22; Ex 2:24; Nu 10:9; Ru 4:13; 1Sa 1:11,19; 2Ki 20:3; 1Ch 16:15; Ne 1:8; 5:19; 12:22,23,31; Job 14:13; Ps 105:42; 106:4; Lk 1:54,72
[n]Ex 14:21; Jos 2:10; 3:16; Job 12:15; Ps 66:6; Isa 11:15; 44:27; Na 1:4 **8:2** [o]S Ge 7:11 [p]S Ge 7:4

[k]20 Hebrew *fifteen cubits* (about 6.9 meters)   [l]20 Or *rose more than twenty feet, and the mountains were covered*

7:4 *forty days and forty nights.* A length of time often characterizing a critical period in redemptive history (see v. 12; Dt 9:11; Mt 4:1-11).

7:7 *entered the ark to escape the waters.* Noah and his family were saved, but life as usual continued for everyone else until it was too late (see Mt 24:37-39).

7:13 *Noah and his sons . . . together with his wife and the wives of his three sons.* "Only a few people, eight in all" (1Pe 3:20; see 2Pe 2:5), survived the flood.

7:14 *every wild animal . . . all livestock . . . every creature that moves along the ground . . . every bird.* Four of the five categories of animate life mentioned in 1:21-25. The fifth category—sea creatures—could remain alive outside the ark.

7:16 *God had commanded Noah . . . the LORD shut him in.* "God" gave the command, but in his role as redeeming "LORD" (see notes on 2:4; Ex 6:6) he closed the door of the ark behind Noah and his family. Neither divine name is mentioned in the rest of ch. 7, as the full fury of the flood was unleashed on sinful mankind.

7:20 *covered the mountains to a depth of more than twenty feet.* The ark was 45 feet high (6:15), so the water was deep enough to keep it from running aground.

7:22 *breath of life.* God's gift at creation (see 1:30; 2:7) was taken away because of sin.

8:1 So far the flood narrative has been an account of judgment; from this point on it is a story of redemption. *God remembered Noah.* Though he had not been mentioned since 7:16 or heard from for 150 days (see 7:24), God had not forgotten Noah and his family. To "remember" in the Bible is not merely to recall to mind; it is to express concern for someone, to act with loving care for him. When God remembers his people, he does so "with favor" (Ne 5:19; 13:31). *wind.* The Hebrew word translated "Spirit" in 1:2 is here rendered "wind," and introduces a series of parallels between the events of chs. 8-9 and those of ch. 1 in their literary order: Compare 8:2 with 1:7; 8:5 with 1:9; 8:7 with 1:20; 8:17 with 1:25; 9:1 with 1:28a; 9:2 with 1:28b; 9:3 with 1:30. Ch. 1 describes the original beginning, while chs. 8-9 describe a new beginning after the flood.

and fifty days[q] the water had gone down, [4]and on the seventeenth day of the seventh month[r] the ark came to rest on the mountains[s] of Ararat.[t] [5]The waters continued to recede until the tenth month, and on the first day of the tenth month the tops of the mountains became visible.

[6]After forty days[u] Noah opened the window he had made in the ark [7]and sent out a raven,[v] and it kept flying back and forth until the water had dried up from the earth.[w] [8]Then he sent out a dove[x] to see if the water had receded from the surface of the ground. [9]But the dove could find no place to set its feet because there was water over all the surface of the earth; so it returned to Noah in the ark. He reached out his hand and took the dove and brought it back to himself in the ark. [10]He waited seven more days and again sent out the dove from the ark. [11]When the dove returned to him in the evening, there in its beak was a freshly plucked olive leaf! Then Noah knew that the water had receded from the earth.[y] [12]He waited seven more days and sent the dove out again, but this time it did not return to him.

[13]By the first day of the first month of Noah's six hundred and first year,[z] the water had dried up from the earth. Noah then removed the covering from the ark and saw that the surface of the ground was dry. [14]By the twenty-seventh day of the second month[a] the earth was completely dry.

[15]Then God said to Noah, [16]"Come out of the ark, you and your wife and your sons and their wives.[b] [17]Bring out every kind of living creature that is with you—the birds, the animals, and all the creatures that move along the ground—so they can multiply on the earth and be fruitful and increase in number upon it."[c]

[18]So Noah came out, together with his sons and his wife and his sons' wives.[d] [19]All the animals and all the creatures that move along the ground and all the birds—everything that moves on the earth—came out of the ark, one kind after another.

[20]Then Noah built an altar to the LORD[e] and, taking some of all the clean animals and clean[f] birds, he sacrificed burnt offerings[g] on it. [21]The LORD smelled the pleasing aroma[h] and said in his heart: "Never again will I curse the ground[i] because of man, even though[m] every inclination of his heart is evil from childhood.[j] And never again will I destroy[k] all living creatures,[l] as I have done.

[22]"As long as the earth endures,
    seedtime and harvest,[m]
    cold and heat,
    summer and winter,[n]
    day and night
    will never cease."[o]

God's Covenant With Noah

9 Then God blessed Noah and his sons, saying to them, "Be fruitful and in-

8:3 qS Ge 7:24
8:4 rS Ge 7:11
sGe 7:20
t2Ki 19:37; Jer 51:27
8:6 uGe 7:12
8:7 vLev 11:15; Dt 14:14; 1Ki 17:4,6; Job 38:41; Ps 147:9; Pr 30:17; Isa 34:11;
Lk 12:24 wver 11
8:8 xJob 30:31; Ps 55:6; 74:19; SS 2:12,14; Isa 38:14; 59:11; 60:8; Jer 48:28; Eze 7:16; Hos 7:11; 11:11; Na 2:7; Mt 3:16; 10:16; Jn 1:32
8:11 yver 7
8:13 zS Ge 5:32
8:14 aS Ge 7:11

8:16 bS Ge 7:13
8:17 cS Ge 1:22
8:18 d1Pe 3:20; 2Pe 2:5
8:20 eGe 12:7-8; 13:18; 22:9; 26:25; 33:20; 35:7; Ex 17:15; 24:4 fS Ge 7:8 gGe 22:2,13; Ex 10:25; 20:24; 40:29; Lev 1:3; 4:29; 6:8-13; Nu 6:11; Jdg 6:26; 11:31; 1Sa 20:29; Job 1:5; 42:8
8:21 hEx 29:18, 25; Lev 1:9,13; 2:9; 4:31; Nu 15:3,7; 2Co 2:15 iS Ge 3:17 jGe 6:5; Ps 51:5; Jer 17:9; Mt 15:19; Ro 1:21 kJer 44:11 lGe 9:11,15; Isa 54:9
8:22 mJos 3:15; Ps 67:6; Jer 5:24

nPs 74:17; Zec 14:8 oS Ge 1:14

m21 Or man, for

8:4 *mountains.* The word is plural and refers to a range of mountains. *Ararat.* The name is related to Assyrian Urartu, which became an extensive and mountainous kingdom (see Jer 51:27; see also Isa 37:38), including much of the territory north of Mesopotamia and east of modern Turkey. The ark's landfall was probably in southern Urartu.
8:6 *window.* See note on 6:16.
8:11 *the dove returned . . . in its beak was a freshly plucked olive leaf.* Olives do not grow at high elevations, and the fresh leaf was a sign to Noah that the water had receded from the earth. The modern symbol of peace represented by a dove carrying an olive branch in its beak has its origin in this story.
8:13 *first day of the first month of Noah's six hundred and first year.* The date formula signals mankind's new beginning after the flood.
8:14 *twenty-seventh day of the second month.* More than a year after the flood began (see 7:11).
8:16 *Come out of the ark.* See note on 7:1.
8:17 *multiply . . . be fruitful . . . increase in number.* See 1:22 and note. The animals and birds could now repopulate their former habitats.
8:20 *LORD.* Since worship is a very personal matter, it is to God as "the LORD" (see note on 2:4) that Noah brought his sacrifice (see 4:4). *burnt offerings.* See Lev 1:4.
8:21 *smelled the pleasing aroma.* A figurative way of

saying that the Lord takes delight in his children's worship of him (see Eph 5:2; Php 4:18). *curse the ground.* Although the Hebrew here has a different word for "curse," the reference appears to be to the curse of 3:17. It may be that the Lord here pledged never to add curse upon curse as he had in regard to Cain (4:12). *even though every inclination of his heart is evil.* For almost identical phraseology see 6:5. Because of man's extreme wickedness, God had destroyed him (6:7) by means of a flood (6:17). Although righteous Noah and his family had been saved, he and his offspring were descendants of Adam and carried in their hearts the inheritance of sin. God graciously promises never again to deal with sin by sending such a devastating deluge (see 9:11,15). Human history is held open for God's dealing with sin in a new and redemptive way—the way that was prepared for by God's action at Babel (see notes on 11:6,8) and that begins to unfold with the call of Abram (12:1). *from childhood.* The phrase replaces "all the time" in 6:5 and emphasizes the truth that sin infects a person's life from his conception and birth (Ps 51:5; 58:3).
8:22 Times and seasons, created by God in the beginning (see 1:14), will never cease till the end of history.
9:1-7 At this new beginning, God renewed his original benediction (1:28) and his provision for man's food (cf. v. 3; 1:29–30). But because sin had brought violence into man's world and because God now appointed meat as a part of

crease in number and fill the earth. *p* ²The fear and dread of you will fall upon all the beasts of the earth and all the birds of the air, upon every creature that moves along the ground, and upon all the fish of the sea; they are given into your hands. *q* ³Everything that lives and moves will be food for you. *r* Just as I gave you the green plants, I now give you everything. *s*

⁴"But you must not eat meat that has its lifeblood still in it. *t* ⁵And for your lifeblood I will surely demand an accounting. *u* I will demand an accounting from every animal. *v* And from each man, too, I will demand an accounting for the life of his fellow man. *w*

⁶"Whoever sheds the blood of man,
　by man shall his blood be shed; *x*
for in the image of God *y*
　has God made man.

⁷As for you, be fruitful and increase in number; multiply on the earth and increase upon it." *z*

⁸Then God said to Noah and to his sons with him: ⁹"I now establish my covenant with you *a* and with your descendants after you ¹⁰and with every living creature that was with you—the birds, the livestock and all the wild animals, all those that came out of the ark with you—every living creature on earth. ¹¹I establish my covenant *b* with you: *c* Never again will all life be cut

off by the waters of a flood; never again will there be a flood to destroy the earth. *d* "

¹²And God said, "This is the sign of the covenant *e* I am making between me and you and every living creature with you, a covenant for all generations to come: *f* ¹³I have set my rainbow *g* in the clouds, and it will be the sign of the covenant between me and the earth. ¹⁴Whenever I bring clouds over the earth and the rainbow *h* appears in the clouds, ¹⁵I will remember my covenant *i* between me and you and all living creatures of every kind. Never again will the waters become a flood to destroy all life. *j* ¹⁶Whenever the rainbow *k* appears in the clouds, I will see it and remember the everlasting covenant *l* between God and all living creatures of every kind on the earth."

¹⁷So God said to Noah, "This is the sign of the covenant *m* I have established between me and all life on the earth."

The Sons of Noah

¹⁸The sons of Noah who came out of the ark were Shem, Ham and Japheth. *n* (Ham was the father of Canaan.) *o* ¹⁹These were the three sons of Noah, *p* and from them came the people who were scattered over the earth. *q*

Cross references (center column)

9:1 *p*S Ge 1:22
9:2 *q*S Ge 1:26
9:3 *r*S Ge 1:29
*s*S Ac 10:15;
Col 2:16
9:4 *t*Lev 3:17;
7:26; 17:10-14;
19:26; Dt 12:16,
23-25; 15:23;
1Sa 14:33;
Eze 33:25;
Ac 15:20,29
9:5 *u*Ge 42:22;
50:15; 1Ki 2:32;
2Ch 24:22;
Ps 9:12
*v*Ex 21:28-32
*w*S Ge 4:10
9:6 *x*S Ge 4:14;
S Jdg 9:24;
S Mt 26:52
*y*S Ge 1:26
9:7 *z*S Ge 1:22
9:9 *a*ver 11;
S Ge 6:18
9:11 *b*ver 16;
Isa 24:5; 33:8;
Hos 6:7 *c*S ver 9
*d*S Ge 8:21
9:12 *e*ver 17;
Ge 17:11
*f*Ge 17:12;
Ex 12:14;
Lev 3:17; 6:18;
17:7; Nu 10:8
9:13 *g*ver 14;
Eze 1:28;
Rev 4:3; 10:1
9:14 *h*S ver 13
9:15 *i*S Ge 8:1;
Ex 2:24; 6:5;
34:10; Lev 26:42,
45; Dt 7:9;
Ps 89:34; 103:18;
105:8; 106:45;
Eze 16:60
*j*S Ge 8:21
9:16 *k*ver 13
*l*S ver 11;
Ge 17:7,13,19;
2Sa 7:13; 23:5;
Ps 105:9-10;
Isa 9:7; 54:10;
55:3; 59:21;
61:8;
Jer 31:31-34; 32:40; 33:21; Eze 16:60; 37:26; S Heb 13:20
9:17 *m*S ver 12 9:18 *n*S Ge 5:32; Lk 3:36 *o*ver 25-27;
Ge 10:6,15 9:19 *p*Ge 5:32 *q*S Ge 1:22; 10:32; 11:4,8,9

Study notes (bottom)

man's food (v. 3), further divine provisions and stipulations are added (vv. 4–6). Yet God's benediction dominates and encloses the whole (see v. 7).

9:2 *they are given into your hands.* God reaffirmed that mankind would rule over all creation, including the animals (see note on 1:26).

9:3 *Everything that lives and moves will be food.* Meat would now supplement mankind's diet.

9:4 *you must not eat meat that has its lifeblood.* Lev 17:14 stresses the intimate relationship between blood and life by twice declaring that "the life of every creature is its blood." Life is the precious and mysterious gift of God, and man is not to seek to preserve it or increase the life-force within him by eating "life" that is "in the blood" (Lev 17:11)—as many pagan peoples throughout history have thought they could do.

9:5 *for your lifeblood ... I will demand an accounting from every animal.* God himself is the great defender of human life (see 4:9–12), which is precious to him because man was created in his image (v. 6) and because man is the earthly representative and focal point of God's kingdom. In the theocracy (kingdom of God) established at Sinai, a domestic animal that had taken human life was to be stoned to death (Ex 21:28–32).

9:6 *Whoever sheds the blood of man, by man shall his blood be shed.* In the later theocracy, those guilty of premeditated murder were to be executed (see Ex 21:12–14; Nu 35:16–32; see also Ro 13:3–4; 1Pe 2:13–14). *for in the image of God has God made man.* See

1:26 and note. In killing a human being, a murderer demonstrates his contempt for God as well as for his fellowman.

9:9 *I now establish my covenant.* God sovereignly promised in this covenant to Noah, to Noah's descendants and to all other living things (as a kind of gracious reward to righteous Noah, the new father of the human race—see 6:18) never again to destroy man and the earth until his purposes for his creation are fully realized ("as long as the earth endures," 8:22). For similar commitments by God see his covenants with Abram (15:18–20), Phinehas (Nu 25:10–13) and David (2Sa 7). See chart on "Major Covenants in the OT," p. 19.

9:11 *Never again will all life be cut off by the waters of a flood.* A summary of the provisions of the Lord's covenant with Noah—an eternal covenant, as seen in such words and phrases as "never again" (vv. 11,15), "for all generations to come" (v. 12) and "everlasting" (v. 16).

9:12 *sign.* A covenant sign was a visible seal and reminder of covenant commitments. Circumcision would become the sign of the covenant with Abraham (see 17:11), and the Sabbath would be the sign of the covenant with Israel at Sinai (see Ex 31:16–17).

9:13 *rainbow.* Rain and the rainbow doubtless existed long before the time of Noah's flood, but after the flood the rainbow took on new meaning as the sign of the Noahic covenant.

9:19 *scattered.* Thus anticipating the table of nations (see note on 11:8).

Major Covenants in the Old Testament

COVENANTS	REFERENCE	TYPE	PARTICIPANT	DESCRIPTION
Noahic	Ge 9:8-17	Royal Grant	Made with "righteous" (6:9) Noah (and his descendants and every living thing on earth—all life that is subject to man's jurisdiction)	An unconditional divine promise never to destroy all earthly life with some natural catastrophe; the covenant "sign" being the rainbow in the storm cloud
Abrahamic A	Ge 15:9-21	Royal (land) Grant	Made with "righteous" (his faith was "credited to him as righteousness," v. 6) Abram (and his descendants, v. 16)	An unconditional divine promise to fulfill the grant of the land; a self-maledictory oath symbolically enacted it (v. 17)
Abrahamic B	Ge 17	Suzerain-vassal	Made with Abraham as patriarchal head of his household	A conditional divine pledge to be Abraham's God and the God of his descendants (cf. "As for me," v. 4; "As for you," v. 9); the condition: total consecration to the Lord as symbolized by circumcision
Sinaitic	Ex 19-24	Suzerain-vassal	Made with Israel as the descendants of Abraham, Isaac and Jacob and as the people the Lord has redeemed from bondage to an earthly power	A conditional divine pledge to be Israel's God (as her Protector and the Guarantor of her blessed destiny); the condition: Israel's total consecration to the Lord as his people (his kingdom) who live by his rule and serve his purposes in history
Phinehas	Nu 25:10-13	Royal Grant	Made with the zealous priest Phinehas	An unconditional divine promise to maintain the family of Phinehas in a "lasting priesthood" (implicitly a pledge to Israel to provide her forever with a faithful priesthood)
Davidic	2Sa 7:5-16	Royal Grant	Made with faithful King David after his devotion to God as Israel's king and the Lord's anointed vassal had come to special expression (v. 2)	An unconditional divine promise to establish and maintain the Davidic dynasty on the throne of Israel (implicitly a pledge to Israel) to provide her forever with a godly king like David and through that dynasty to do for her what he had done through David—bring her into rest in the promised land (1Ki 4:20-21; 5:3-4).
New	Jer 31:31-34	Royal Grant	Promised to rebellious Israel as she is about to be expelled from the promised land in actualization of the most severe covenant curse (Lev 26:27-39; Dt 28:36-37, 45-68)	An unconditional divine promise to unfaithful Israel to forgive her sins and establish his relationship with her on a new basis by writing his law "on their hearts"—a covenant of pure grace

Major Types of Royal Covenants/Treaties in the Ancient Near East

Royal Grant (unconditional)

A king's grant (of land or some other benefit) to a loyal servant for faithful or exceptional service. The grant was normally perpetual and unconditional, but the servant's heirs benefited from it only as they continued their father's loyalty and service. (Cf. 1Sa 8:14; 22:7; 27:6; Est 8:1.)

Parity

A covenant between equals, binding them to mutual friendship or at least to mutual respect for each other's spheres and interests. Participants called each other "brothers." (Cf. Ge 21:27; 26:31; 31:44-54; 1Ki 5:12; 15:19; 20:32-34; Am 1:9.)

Suzerain-vassal (conditional)

A covenant regulating the relationship between a great king and one of his subject kings. The great king claimed absolute right of sovereignty, demanded total loyalty and service (the vassal must "love" his suzerain) and pledged protection of the subject's realm and dynasty, conditional on the vassal's faithfulness and loyalty to him. The vassal pledged absolute loyalty to his suzerain—whatever service his suzerain demanded—and exclusive reliance on the suzerain's protection. Participants called each other "lord" and "servant" or "father" and "son." (Cf. Jos 9:6,8; Eze 17:13-18; Hos 12:1.)

Commitments made in these covenants were accompanied by self-maledictory oaths (made orally, ceremonially or both). The gods were called upon to witness the covenants and implement the curses of the oaths if the covenants were violated.

20Noah, a man of the soil, proceeded[n] to plant a vineyard. 21When he drank some of its wine,[r] he became drunk and lay uncovered inside his tent. 22Ham, the father of Canaan, saw his father's nakedness[s] and told his two brothers outside. 23But Shem and Japheth took a garment and laid it across their shoulders; then they walked in backward and covered their father's nakedness. Their faces were turned the other way so that they would not see their father's nakedness.

24When Noah awoke from his wine and found out what his youngest son had done to him, 25he said,

"Cursed[t] be Canaan![u]
    The lowest of slaves
    will he be to his brothers.[v] "

26He also said,

"Blessed be the LORD, the God of
        Shem![w]
    May Canaan be the slave[x] of Shem.[o]
27May God extend the territory of
        Japheth[p];[y]
    may Japheth live in the tents of
        Shem,[z]
    and may Canaan be his[q] slave."

28After the flood Noah lived 350 years. 29Altogether, Noah lived 950 years, and then he died.[a]

The Table of Nations

10 This is the account[b] of Shem, Ham and Japheth,[c] Noah's sons,[d] who themselves had sons after the flood.

The Japhethites

10:2-5pp — 1Ch 1:5-7

2The sons[r] of Japheth:
    Gomer,[e] Magog,[f] Madai, Javan,[g]
    Tubal,[h] Meshech[i] and Tiras.
3The sons of Gomer:
    Ashkenaz,[j] Riphath and Togarmah.[k]
4The sons of Javan:
    Elishah,[l] Tarshish,[m] the Kittim[n]
    and the Rodanim.[s] 5(From these
    the maritime peoples spread out
    into their territories by their clans

Cross references (center column):

9:21 [r]Ge 19:35
9:22 [s]Hab 2:15
9:25 [t]Ge 27:12
[u]ver 18; Ex 20:5;
Ps 79:8;
Isa 14:21;
Jer 31:29; 32:18
[v]Ge 25:23;
27:29,37,40;
37:10; 49:8;
Nu 24:18;
Jos 9:23
9:26 [w]Ge 14:20;
Ex 18:10; Ps 7:17
[x]1Ki 9:21
9:27 [y]Ge 10:2-5
[z]Eph 2:13-14;
3:6

9:29 [a]S Ge 2:17
10:1 [b]S Ge 2:4
[c]S Ge 5:32 [d]ver
32; 1Ch 1:4
10:2 [e]Eze 38:6
[f]Eze 38:2; 39:6;
Rev 20:8
[g]Eze 27:19
[h]Isa 66:19;
Eze 27:13; 32:26
[i]Eze 39:1
10:3 [j]Jer 51:27
[k]Eze 27:14; 38:6
10:4 [l]Eze 27:7
[m]Ps 48:7; 72:10;
Isa 2:16; 23:1,6,
10,14; 60:9;
66:19; Jer 10:9;
Eze 27:12,25;
38:13; Jnh 1:3
[n]Nu 24:24;
Isa 23:12;
Jer 2:10;
Eze 27:6;
Da 11:30

Footnotes (center column):

[n]20 Or *soil, was the first*   [o]26 Or *be his slave*
[p]27 *Japheth* sounds like the Hebrew for *extend.*
[q]27 Or *their*   [r]2 *Sons* may mean *descendants* or *successors* or *nations*; also in verses 3, 4, 6, 7, 20-23, 29 and 31.   [s]4 Some manuscripts of the Masoretic Text and Samaritan Pentateuch (see also Septuagint and 1 Chron. 1:7); most manuscripts of the Masoretic Text *Dodanim*

9:20 *man of the soil.* Noah, like his father Lamech (see 5:29), was a farmer.
9:21 *When he drank some of its wine, he became drunk.* The first reference to wine connects it with drunkenness. *uncovered inside his tent.* Excessive use of wine led, among other things, to immodest behavior (see 19:30-35).
9:22 *father of Canaan.* Mentioned here because Ham, in acting as he did, showed himself to be the true father of Canaan (i.e., of the Canaanites; see note on 15:16). *told his two brothers.* He broadcast, rather than covered, his father's immodesty.
9:23 *faces were turned . . . so that they would not see.* They wanted to avoid further disgrace to their father.
9:24 *from his wine.* From the drunkenness caused by the wine.
9:25 *Cursed be Canaan!* Some maintain that Ham's son (see vv. 18,22) was to be punished because of his father's sin (see Ex 20:5), but Ex 20 restricts such punishment to "those who hate me." It is probably better to hold that Canaan and his descendants were to be punished because they were going to be even worse than Ham (Lev 18:2-3,6-30). *lowest of slaves.* Joshua's subjection of the Gibeonites (Jos 9:27) is one of the fulfillments (see also Jos 16:10; Jdg 1:28,30, 33,35; 1Ki 9:20-21). Noah's prophecy cannot be used to justify the enslavement of blacks, since those cursed here were Canaanites, who were Caucasian.
9:26 *Blessed be the LORD.* The Lord (instead of Shem) is blessed (praised) because he is the source of Shem's blessing. He is also the "God of Shem" (and his descendants, the Semites—which included the Israelites) in a special sense.
9:27 *live in the tents of Shem.* Share in the blessings bestowed on Shem.
9:29 *and then he died.* See note on 5:5. As the tenth and last member of the genealogy of Seth (5:3-32), Noah had an obituary that ends like those of his worthy ancestors.
10:1 *account.* See note on 2:4. The links affirmed here

may not all be based on strictly physical descent, but may include geographical, historical and linguistic associations (see note on v. 5 and NIV text notes on vv. 2,8; 11:10). See also Introduction to 1 Chronicles: Genealogies.
10:2 *Japheth.* As the least involved in the Biblical narrative and perhaps also as the oldest of Noah's sons (see v. 21 and NIV text note), his descendants or successors are listed first. The genealogy of Shem, the chosen line, appears last in the chapter (see vv. 21-31; see also 11:10-26). The 14 nations that came from Japheth plus the 30 from Ham and the 26 from Shem add up to 70 (the multiple of 10 and 7, both numbers signifying completeness; see note on 5:5), perhaps in anticipation of the 70 members of Jacob's family in Egypt (see 46:27; Ex 1:5; cf. Dt 32:8). The Japhethites lived generally north and west of Palestine in Eurasia. *Gomer.* The people of Gomer (the later Cimmerians) and related nations (see v. 3) lived near the Black Sea. *Magog.* Possibly the father of a Scythian people who inhabited the Caucasus and adjacent regions southeast of the Black Sea. *Madai.* The later Medes. *Javan.* Ionia (southern Greece) and perhaps western Asia Minor. *Tubal, Meshech.* Not related to Tobolsk and Moscow in modern Russia. Together with Magog they are mentioned in later Assyrian inscriptions. See also Eze 38:2. Probably Tubal was in Pontus, and Meshech was in the Moschian Mountains. Their movement was from eastern Asia Minor north to the Black Sea. *Tiras.* Possibly the Thrace of later times.
10:3 *Ashkenaz.* The later Scythians. All three names in this verse refer to peoples located in the upper Euphrates region.
10:4 *Elishah.* Either Alashia (an ancient name for Cyprus) or a reference to Sicily and southern Italy. *Tarshish.* Probably southern Spain. *the Kittim.* A people living on Cyprus. *Rodanim.* A people whose name is perhaps reflected in Rhodes (a Greek isle).
10:5 See vv. 20,31. *territories . . . clans . . . nations . . . language.* Geographic, ethnic, political and linguistic terms,

within their nations, each with its own language.)*o*

The Hamites

10:6-20pp — 1Ch 1:8-16

⁶The sons of Ham:

Cush,*p* Mizraim,*t* Put*q* and Canaan.*r*

⁷The sons of Cush:

Seba,*s* Havilah,*t* Sabtah, Raamah*u* and Sabteca.

The sons of Raamah:

Sheba*v* and Dedan.*w*

⁸Cush was the father*u* of Nimrod,*x* who grew to be a mighty warrior on the earth. ⁹He was a mighty*y* hunter*z* before the Lord; that is why it is said, "Like Nimrod, a mighty hunter before the Lord." ¹⁰The first centers of his kingdom were Babylon,*a* Erech,*b* Akkad and Calneh,*c* in*v*

Shinar.*w d* ¹¹From that land he went to Assyria,*e* where he built Nineveh,*f* Rehoboth Ir,*x* Calah ¹²and Resen, which is between Nineveh and Calah; that is the great city.

¹³Mizraim was the father of
the Ludites, Anamites, Lehabites, Naphtuhites, ¹⁴Pathrusites, Casluhites (from whom the Philistines*g* came) and Caphtorites.*h*
¹⁵Canaan*i* was the father of

10:5 *o*Ge 9:27
10:6 *p*2Ki 19:9;
2Ch 12:3; 16:8;
Isa 11:11; 18:1;
20:3; 43:3;
Jer 46:9;
Eze 30:4,9; 38:5;
Na 3:9; Zep 2:12;
3:10 *q*Eze 27:10;
38:5 *r*S Ge 9:18
10:7 *s*Isa 43:3
*t*S Ge 2:11
*u*Eze 27:22
*v*Ge 25:3;
1Ki 10:1;
2Ch 9:1;
Job 1:15; 6:19;
16:11; Ps 72:10,
15; Isa 60:6;
Jer 6:20;
Eze 27:22; 38:13;
Joel 3:8
*w*1Ch 1:32;
Isa 21:13;
Jer 25:23-24;
49:8; Eze 27:15,
20; 38:13
10:8 *x*Mic 5:6
10:9 *y*2Ch 14:9;
16:8; Isa 18:2
*z*Ge 25:27; 27:3
10:10 *a*Ge 11:9;
2Ch 36:17;

Isa 13:1; 47:1; Jer 21:2; 25:12; 50:1 *b*Ezr 4:9 *c*Isa 10:9;
Am 6:2 *d*Ge 11:2; 14:1; Zec 5:11 **10:11** *e*Ps 83:8; Mic 5:6
*f*2Ki 19:36; Isa 37:37; Jnh 1:2; 3:2,3; 4:11; Na 1:1; Zep 2:13
10:14 *g*Ge 21:32,34; 26:1,8; Jos 13:2; Jdg 3:3; Isa 14:31;
Jer 47:1,4; Am 9:7 *h*Dt 2:23; 1Ch 1:12 **10:15** *i*S Ge 9:18

*t*6 That is, Egypt; also in verse 13   *u*8 *Father* may mean *ancestor* or *predecessor* or *founder;* also in verses 13, 15, 24 and 26.   *v*10 Or *Erech and Akkad—all of them in*   *w*10 That is, Babylonia   *x*11 Or *Nineveh with its city squares*

---

respectively. These several criteria were used to differentiate the various groups of people.

10:6 *Ham.* The Hamites were located in southwestern Asia and northeast Africa. *Cush.* The upper Nile region, south of Egypt. *Mizraim.* Means "two Egypts," a reference to Upper and Lower Egypt. *Put.* Either Libya (see note on v. 13) or the land the ancient Egyptians called Punt (modern Somalia). *Canaan.* The name means "land of purple" (as does Phoenicia, the Greek name for the same general region)—so called because Canaan was a major producer and exporter of purple dye, highly prized by royalty. The territory was much later called Palestine after the Philistines (see v. 14).

10:7 *sons of Cush.* The seven Cushite nations here mentioned were all in Arabia. Sheba and Dedan (or their namesakes) reappear as two of Abraham's grandsons (see 25:3). Together with Raamah they are mentioned in Eze 27:20–22.

10:8 *Cush.* Probably not the same as that in vv. 6–7.

Located in Mesopotamia, its name may be related to that of the later Kassites. *Nimrod.* Possibly the Hebrew name of Sargon I, an early ruler of Akkad (see v. 10).

10:10 *Erech.* The Hebrew name for Uruk (modern Warka), one of the important cities in ancient Mesopotamia.

10:12 *great city.* Possibly a reference to Calah (or even Resen), but most likely to Nineveh (see Jnh 1:2; 3:2; 4:11), either alone or including the surrounding urban areas.

10:13 *Ludites.* Perhaps the Lydians in Asia Minor (see note on v. 22). *Anamites.* Located in north Africa, west of Egypt, near Cyrene. *Lehabites.* Perhaps the Libyan desert tribes (see note on v. 6). *Naphtuhites.* People of Lower Egypt.

10:14 *Pathrusites.* The inhabitants of Upper Egypt (see note on v. 6). *Caphtorites.* Crete, known as Caphtor in ancient times, was for a while the homeland of various Philistine groups (see Jer 47:4; Am 9:7). The Philistines themselves were a vigorous Indo-European maritime people who invaded Egypt early in the 12th century B.C. After being

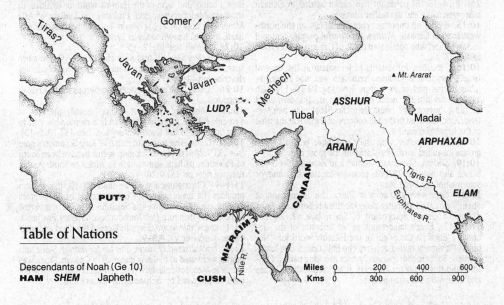

Table of Nations

Descendants of Noah (Ge 10)
HAM *SHEM* Japheth

Sidon,[j] his firstborn,[y][k] and of the Hittites,[l] [16]Jebusites,[m] Amorites,[n] Girgashites,[o] [17]Hivites,[p] Arkites, Sinites, [18]Arvadites,[q] Zemarites and Hamathites.[r]

Later the Canaanite[s] clans scattered [19]and the borders of Canaan[t] reached from Sidon[u] toward Gerar[v] as far as Gaza,[w] and then toward Sodom, Gomorrah, Admah and Zeboiim,[x] as far as Lasha.

[20]These are the sons of Ham by their clans and languages, in their territories and nations.

The Semites

10:21-31pp — Ge 11:10-27; 1Ch 1:17-27

[21]Sons were also born to Shem, whose older brother was[z] Japheth; Shem was the ancestor of all the sons of Eber.[y]

[22]The sons of Shem:

Elam,[z] Asshur,[a] Arphaxad,[b] Lud and Aram.[c]

[23]The sons of Aram:

Uz,[d] Hul, Gether and Meshech.[a]

[24]Arphaxad was the father of[b] Shelah, and Shelah the father of Eber.[e]

[25]Two sons were born to Eber:

One was named Peleg,[c] because in his time the earth was divided; his brother was named Joktan.

[26]Joktan was the father of

Almodad, Sheleph, Hazarmaveth, Jerah, [27]Hadoram, Uzal,[f] Diklah,

[28]Obal, Abimael, Sheba,[g] [29]Ophir,[h] Havilah and Jobab. All these were sons of Joktan.

[30]The region where they lived stretched from Mesha toward Sephar, in the eastern hill country.

[31]These are the sons of Shem by their clans and languages, in their territories and nations.

[32]These are the clans of Noah's sons,[i] according to their lines of descent, within their nations. From these the nations spread out over the earth[j] after the flood.

The Tower of Babel

11 Now the whole world had one language[k] and a common speech. [2]As men moved eastward,[d] they found a plain in Shinar[e][l] and settled there.

[3]They said to each other, "Come, let's

10:15 [j]ver 19; Jos 11:8; Jdg 10:6; Isa 23:2, 4; Jer 25:22; 27:3; 47:4; Eze 28:21; 32:30; Joel 3:4; Zec 9:2 [k]Ex 4:22; Nu 1:20; 3:2; 18:15; 26:5; 33:4 [l]Ge 15:20; 23:3, 20; 25:10; 26:34; 27:46; 49:32; Nu 13:29; Jos 1:4; 1Sa 26:6; Eze 16:3 **10:16** [m]Jdg 19:10; 1Ch 11:4; Ezr 9:1 [n]Ex 3:8; Nu 13:29; 21:13; 32:39; Dt 1:4; Jos 2:10; 2Ch 8:7 [o]Ge 15:18-21; Dt 7:1 **10:17** [p]Ge 34:2; 36:2; Ex 3:8; Dt 7:1; Jdg 3:3 **10:18** [q]Eze 27:8 [r]1Ch 18:3 [s]Ge 12:6; 13:7; 50:11; Ex 13:11; Nu 13:29; 14:25; 21:3; 33:40; Dt 1:7; Jdg 1:1 **10:19** [t]Ge 11:31; 12:1; 13:12; 17:8; 24:3; 26:34; 27:46; 28:1,6,8; 31:18; 35:6; 37:1; Lev 25:38 [u]S ver 15; Ge 49:13; Jos 19:28; Jdg 1:31; 18:28; 2Sa 24:6 [v]2Ch 14:13 [w]Dt 2:23; Jos 10:41; 11:22; 15:47; Jdg 1:18; 6:4; 16:1,21; 1Sa 6:17; Jer 25:20; 47:1; Am 1:6; Zep 2:4 [x]Ge 14:2; Dt 29:23 **10:21** [y]ver 24; Nu 24:24 **10:22** [z]Ge 14:1; Isa 11:11; 21:2; Jer 25:25; 49:34; Eze 32:24; Da 8:2 [a]Nu 24:22,24; Eze 27:23 [b]Lk 3:36 [c]Jdg 3:10; 1Ki 11:25; 19:15; 20:34; 22:31; 2Ki 5:1; 8:7 **10:23** [d]Ge 22:21; Job 1:1; Jer 25:20; La 4:21 **10:24** [e]S ver 21; Lk 3:35 **10:27** [f]Eze 27:19 **10:28** [g]1Ki 10:1; Job 6:19; Ps 72:10,15; Isa 60:6; Eze 27:22 **10:29** [h]1Ki 9:28; 10:11; 1Ch 29:4; Job 22:24; 28:16; Ps 45:9; Isa 13:12 **10:32** [i]S ver 1 [j]S Ge 9:19 **11:1** [k]ver 6 **11:2** [l]S Ge 10:10

[y]15 Or *of the Sidonians, the older brother of* [z]21 Or *Shem, the older brother of* [a]23 See Septuagint and 1 Chron. 1:17; Hebrew *Mash* [b]24 Hebrew; Septuagint *father of Cainan, and Cainan was the father of* [c]25 *Peleg* means *division.* [d]2 Or *from the east;* or *in the east* [e]2 That is, Babylonia

driven out, they migrated in large numbers to southwest Canaan, later extending their influence over most of the land. The Philistines of the patriarchal period (see 21:32,34; 26:1,8,14–15,18) no doubt had earlier settled in Canaan more peacefully and in smaller numbers.

10:15 *Sidon.* An important commercial city on the northwest coast of Canaan. *Hittites.* A powerful people, centered in Asia Minor, who dominated much of Canaan from c. 1800 to c. 1200 B.C.

10:16 *Jebusites.* Inhabitants of Jerusalem at the time of Israel's conquest of Canaan. Jerusalem was also known as Jebus during part of its history (see Jdg 19:10–11; 1Ch 11:4). *Amorites.* The name comes from an Akkadian word meaning "westerner" (west from the Babylonian perspective). Amorites lived in the hill country of Canaan at the time of the Israelite conquest.

10:17–18 Together with the Girgashites (v. 16), these groups inhabited small city-states for the most part.

10:19 *Sodom, Gomorrah, Admah and Zeboiim.* See 14:2, 8 (see also note on 13:10); probably located east and/or southeast of the Dead Sea.

10:21 *Sons were also born to Shem.* The descendants of Shem were called Shemites (later modified to Semites). *Eber.* Though a distant descendant of Shem (see vv. 24–25; 11:14–17), Eber's importance as the ancestor of the Hebrews ("Eber" is the origin of the Hebrew word for "Hebrew") is already hinted at here. The Ebla tablets (see Introduction: Background) frequently refer to a king named Ebrium, who ruled Ebla for 28 years. It is possible that Ebrium and Eber were the same person.

10:22 *Elam.* The Elamites lived east of Mesopotamia. *Asshur.* An early name for Assyria (see note on 2:14) in northern Mesopotamia. *Arphaxad.* See also 11:10–13; perhaps a compound form of the Hebrew word for Chaldea, in southern Mesopotamia. *Lud.* Probably the Lydians of Asia Minor (see note on v. 13). *Aram.* Located northeast of Canaan, the area known today as Syria.

10:24 *Shelah.* See 11:12–15.

10:25 *Peleg.* See NIV text note and 11:16–19. *the earth was divided.* Perhaps resulting from the dispersion of peoples described in 11:1–9.

10:26 *Joktan.* The predecessor of numerous south Arabian kingdoms.

10:28 *Sheba.* In southwest Arabia (roughly the area of Yemen). A later queen of Sheba made a memorable visit to King Solomon in the tenth century B.C. (see 1Ki 10:1–13).

10:29 *Ophir.* The source of much of King Solomon's gold (see 1Ki 9:28; 10:11). Its location seems to have been south of Palestine, perhaps somewhere in Africa or south Arabia (but see note on 1Ki 9:28).

11:1–9 Chronologically earlier than ch. 10, this section provides the main reason for the scattering of the peoples listed there. The narrative is a beautiful example of inverted or hourglass structure (see Introduction: Literary Features).

11:1 *the whole world.* The survivors of the flood and their descendants (see vv. 4,8–9).

11:3 *brick instead of stone, and tar for mortar.* Stone and mortar were used as building materials in Canaan. Stone was scarce in Mesopotamia, however, so mud brick and tar were used (as indicated by archaeological excavations).

make bricks ^m and bake them thoroughly." They used brick instead of stone, ⁿ and tar ^o for mortar. ⁴Then they said, "Come, let us build ourselves a city, with a tower that reaches to the heavens, ^p so that we may make a name ^q for ourselves and not be scattered ^r over the face of the whole earth." ^s

⁵But the LORD came down ^t to see the city and the tower that the men were building. ⁶The LORD said, "If as one people speaking the same language ^u they have begun to do this, then nothing they plan to do will be impossible for them. ⁷Come, let us ^v go down ^w and confuse their language so they will not understand each other." ^x

⁸So the LORD scattered them from there over all the earth, ^y and they stopped building the city. ⁹That is why it was called Babel ^{f z}—because there the LORD confused the language ^a of the whole world. ^b From there the LORD scattered ^c them over the face of the whole earth.

From Shem to Abram

11:10–27pp — Ge 10:21–31; 1Ch 1:17–27

¹⁰This is the account ^d of Shem.

Two years after the flood, when Shem was 100 years old, he became the father ^g of Arphaxad. ^e ¹¹And after he became the father of Arphaxad, Shem lived 500 years and had other sons and daughters.

¹²When Arphaxad had lived 35 years, he became the father of Shelah. ^f ¹³And after he became the father of Shelah, Arphaxad lived 403 years and had other sons and daughters. ^h

¹⁴When Shelah had lived 30 years, he became the father of Eber. ^g ¹⁵And after he became the father of Eber, Shelah lived 403 years and had other sons and daughters.

¹⁶When Eber had lived 34 years, he became the father of Peleg. ^h ¹⁷And after he became the father of Peleg, Eber lived 430 years and had other sons and daughters.

¹⁸When Peleg had lived 30 years, he became the father of Reu. ⁱ ¹⁹And after he became the father of Reu, Peleg lived 209 years and had other sons and daughters.

²⁰When Reu had lived 32 years, he became the father of Serug. ^j ²¹And after he became the father of Serug, Reu lived 207 years and had other sons and daughters.

²²When Serug had lived 30 years, he became the father of Nahor. ^k ²³And after he became the father of Nahor, Serug lived 200 years and had other sons and daughters.

²⁴When Nahor had lived 29 years, he became the father of Terah. ^l ²⁵And after he became the father of Terah, Nahor lived 119 years and had other sons and daughters.

²⁶After Terah had lived 70 years, he

Cross references (center column)

11:3 mEx 1:14; 5:7; Jer 43:9
nIsa 9:10; Am 5:11
oGe 14:10
11:4 pDt 1:28; 6:10; 9:1; Job 20:6; Jer 51:53 qGe 6:4 rDt 30:3; 1Ki 22:17; Est 3:8; Ps 44:11; Jer 31:10; 40:15; Eze 6:8; Joel 3:2 sS Ge 9:19; Dt 4:27
11:5 tver 7; Ge 18:21; Ex 3:8; 19:11,18,20; Ps 18:9; 144:5
11:6 uS ver 1
11:7 vS Ge 1:26 wS ver 5
xGe 42:23; Dt 28:49; Isa 28:11; 33:19; Jer 5:15; 1Co 14:2,11
11:8 yS Ge 9:19; Dt 32:8; S Lk 1:51
11:9 zS Ge 10:10 aPs 55:9 bAc 2:5-11 cIsa 2:10,21; 13:14; 24:1
11:10 dS Ge 2:4 eLk 3:36
11:12 fLk 3:35
11:14 gLk 3:35
11:16 hLk 3:35
11:18 iLk 3:35
11:20 jLk 3:35
11:22 kLk 3:34
11:24 lLk 3:34

Text notes

^f9 That is, Babylon; *Babel* sounds like the Hebrew for *confused.* ^g10 *Father* may mean *ancestor;* also in verses 11-25. ^h12,13 Hebrew; Septuagint (see also Luke 3:35, 36 and note at Gen. 10:24) 35 years, he became the father of Cainan. 13And after he became the father of Cainan, Arphaxad lived 430 years and had other sons and daughters, and then he died. When Cainan had lived 130 years, he became the father of Shelah. And after he became the father of Shelah, Cainan lived 330 years and had other sons and daughters

Study notes

11:4 *us . . . ourselves . . . we . . . ourselves.* The people's plans were egotistical and proud. *tower.* The typical Mesopotamian temple-tower, known as a ziggurat, was square at the base and had sloping, stepped sides that led upward to a small shrine at the top. *reaches to the heavens.* A similar ziggurat may be described in 28:12. Other Mesopotamian ziggurats were given names demonstrating that they, too, were meant to serve as staircases from earth to heaven: "The House of the Link between Heaven and Earth" (at Larsa), "The House of the Seven Guides of Heaven and Earth" (at Borsippa), "The House of the Foundation-Platform of Heaven and Earth" (at Babylon), "The House of the Mountain of the Universe" (at Asshur). *name.* In the OT, "name" also refers to reputation, fame or renown. (The Nephilim were "men of renown [lit. 'name']," 6:4.) At Babel (see note on v. 9) rebellious man undertook a united and godless effort to establish for himself, by a titanic human enterprise, a world renown by which he would dominate God's creation (cf. 10:8–12; 2Sa 18:18). *scattered.* See note on v. 8.
11:6 *If . . . then.* If the whole human race remained united in the proud attempt to take its destiny into its own hands and, by its man-centered efforts, to seize the reins of history, there would be no limit to its unrestrained rebellion against God. The kingdom of man would displace and exclude the kingdom of God.

11:7 *let us.* See notes on 1:1,26. God's "Come, let us" from above counters proud man's "Come, let us" (v. 4) from below. *not understand each other.* Without a common language, joint effort became impossible (see v. 8).
11:8 *scattered.* See v. 4; 9:19. God dispersed the people because of their rebellious pride. Even the greatest of human powers cannot defy God and long survive.
11:9 *Babel.* See NIV text note and 10:10. The word is of Akkadian origin and means "gateway to a god" (Jacob's stairway was similarly called "gate of heaven"; see 28:17). *confused.* The Hebrew word used here (*balal*) sounds like "Babel," the Hebrew word for Babylon and the origin of the English word "babel."
11:10–26 A ten-name genealogy, like that of Seth (see 5:3–31; see also note on 5:5). Unlike the Sethite genealogy, however, the genealogy of Shem does not give total figures for the ages of the men at death and does not end each paragraph with "and then he died." It covers the centuries between Shem and Abram as briefly as possible.
11:10 *account.* See note on 2:4.
11:26 *Terah . . . became the father of Abram, Nahor and Haran.* As in the case of Shem, Ham and Japheth, the names of the three sons may not be in chronological order by age (see 9:24; see also 10:21 and NIV text note). Haran died while his father was still alive (see v. 28).

became the father of Abram, *m* Nahor *n* and Haran. *o*

27This is the account *p* of Terah.

Terah became the father of Abram, Nahor *q* and Haran. And Haran became the father of Lot. *r* 28While his father Terah was still alive, Haran died in Ur of the Chaldeans, *s* in the land of his birth. 29Abram and Nahor *t* both married. The name of Abram's wife was Sarai, *u* and the name of Nahor's wife was Milcah; *v* she was the daughter of Haran, the father of both Milcah and Iscah. 30Now Sarai was barren; she had no children. *w*

31Terah took his son Abram, his grandson Lot *x* son of Haran, and his daughter-in-law *y* Sarai, the wife of his son Abram, and together they set out from Ur of the Chaldeans *z* to go to Canaan. *a* But when they came to Haran, *b* they settled there.

32Terah *c* lived 205 years, and he died in Haran.

The Call of Abram

12 The LORD had said to Abram, "Leave your country, your people and your father's household *d* and go to the land *e* I will show you. *f*

2"I will make you into a great nation *g* and I will bless you; *h*

I will make your name great,
    and you will be a blessing. *i*
3I will bless those who bless you,
    and whoever curses you I will
        curse; *j*
and all peoples on earth
    will be blessed through you. *k* "

4So Abram left, as the LORD had told him; and Lot *l* went with him. Abram was seventy-five years old *m* when he set out from Haran. *n* 5He took his wife Sarai, *o* his nephew Lot, all the possessions they had accumulated *p* and the people *q* they had acquired in Haran, and they set out for the land of Canaan, *r* and they arrived there.

6Abram traveled through the land *s* as far as the site of the great tree of Moreh *t* at Shechem. *u* At that time the Canaanites *v* were in the land. 7The LORD ap-

11:26 *m*Lk 3:34
*n*Jos 24:2
*o*2Ki 19:12;
Isa 37:12;
Eze 27:23
11:27 *p*S Ge 2:4
*q*ver 29;
Ge 31:53 *r*ver 31;
Ge 12:4; 13:1,5,
8,12; 14:12;
19:1; Lk 17:28;
2Pe 2:7
11:28 *s*ver 31;
Ge 15:7; Ne 9:7;
Job 1:17; 16:11;
Eze 23:23; Ac 7:4
11:29 *t*S ver 27,
31; Ge 22:20,23;
24:10,15,24;
29:5 *u*Ge 12:5,
11; 16:1; 17:15
*v*Ge 22:20
11:30 *w*Ge 16:1;
18:11; 25:21;
29:31; 30:1,22;
Jdg 13:2; 1Sa 1:5;
Ps 113:9; Lk 1:7,
36
11:31 *x*S ver 27
*y*Ge 38:11;
Lev 18:15; 20:12;
Ru 1:6,22; 2:20;
4:15; 1Sa 4:19;
1Ch 2:4;
Eze 22:11;
Mic 7:6 *z*S ver
28; Ac 7:4
*a*S Ge 10:19
*b*S ver 29;
Ge 12:4; 27:43;
28:5,10; 29:4;
2Ki 19:12;
Eze 27:23
11:32 *c*Jos 24:2
12:1 *d*Ge 20:13;
24:4,27,40
*e*S Ge 10:19
*f*Ge 15:7; 26:2;
Jos 24:3; Ac 7:3*;
Heb 11:8

12:2 *g*Ge 13:16; 15:5; 17:2,4; 18:18; 22:17; 26:4; 28:3,14;
32:12; 35:11; 41:49; 46:3; 47:27; 48:4,16,19; Ex 1:7; 5:5;
32:13; Dt 1:10; 10:22; 13:17; 26:5; Jos 11:4; 24:3;
2Sa 17:11; 1Ki 3:8; 4:20; 1Ch 27:23; 2Ch 1:9; Ne 9:23;
Ps 107:38; Isa 6:13; 10:22; 48:19; 51:2; 54:3; 60:22;
Jer 33:22; Mic 4:7 *h*Ge 24:1,35; 25:11; 26:3; 28:4;
Ex 20:24; Nu 22:12; 23:8,20; 24:9; Ps 67:6; 115:12;
Isa 44:3; 61:9; 65:23; Mal 3:12 *i*Ge 22:18; Isa 19:24;
Jer 4:2; Hag 2:19; Zec 8:13 **12:3** *j*Ge 27:29; Ex 23:22;
Nu 24:9; Dt 30:7 *k*Ge 15:5; 18:18; 22:18; 26:4; 28:4,14;
Dt 9:5; Ps 72:17; Isa 19:25; Ac 3:25; Gal 3:8* **12:4**
*l*S Ge 11:27 *m*Ge 16:3,16; 17:1,17,24; 21:5 *n*S Ge 11:31
12:5 *o*S Ge 11:29 *p*ver 16; Ge 13:2,6; 31:18; 46:6
*q*Ge 14:14; 15:3; 17:23; Ecc 2:7 *r*Ge 11:31; 16:3; Heb 11:8
12:6 *s*Heb 11:9 *t*Ge 35:4; Dt 11:30; Jos 24:26; Jdg 7:1; 9:6
*u*Ge 33:18; 37:12; Jos 17:7; 20:7; 24:1; Jdg 8:31; 21:19;
1Ki 12:1; Ps 60:6; 108:7 *v*S Ge 10:18

11:27 *account.* See note on 2:4.

11:28 *Ur of the Chaldeans.* Possibly in northern Mesopotamia, but more likely the site on the Euphrates in southern Iraq excavated by Leonard Woolley between 1922 and 1934. Ruins and artifacts from Ur reveal a civilization and culture that reached high levels before Abram's time. King Ur-Nammu, who may have been Abram's contemporary, is famous for his law code.

11:30 *Sarai was barren.* The sterility of Abram's wife (see 15:2–3; 17:17) emphasized the fact that God's people would not come by natural generation from the post-Babel peoples. God was bringing a new humanity into being, of whom Abram was father (17:5), just as Adam and Noah were fathers of the fallen human race.

11:31 *they came to Haran.* In Hebrew the name of the town is spelled differently from that of Abram's brother (v. 26). The moon-god was worshiped at both Ur and Haran, and since Terah was an idolater (see Jos 24:2) he probably felt at home in either place. Haran was a flourishing caravan city in the 19th century B.C. In the 18th century it was ruled by Amorites (see note on 10:16).

12:1 *had said.* God had spoken to Abram "while he was still in Mesopotamia, before he lived in Haran" (Ac 7:2). *Leave . . . show you.* Abram must leave the settled world of the post-Babel nations and begin a pilgrimage with God to a better world of God's making (see 24:7).

12:2–3 God's promise to Abram has a sevenfold structure: (1) "I will make you into a great nation," (2) "I will bless you," (3) "I will make your name great," (4) "you will be a blessing," (5) "I will bless those who bless you," (6) "whoever curses you I will curse," and (7) "all peoples on earth will be blessed through you." God's original blessing on all

mankind (1:28) would be restored and fulfilled through Abram and his offspring. In various ways and degrees, these promises were reaffirmed to Abram (v. 7; 15:5–21; 17:4–8; 18:18–19; 22:17–18), to Isaac (26:2–4), to Jacob (28:13–15; 35:11–12; 46:3) and to Moses (Ex 3:6–8; 6:2–8). The seventh promise is quoted in Ac 3:25 with reference to Peter's Jewish listeners (see Ac 3:12)—Abram's physical descendants—and in Gal 3:8 with reference to Paul's Gentile listeners—Abram's spiritual descendants.

12:4 *Abram left, as the LORD had told him.* See Heb 11:8. Prompt obedience grounded in faith characterized this patriarch throughout his life (see 17:23; 21:14; 22:3). *Lot went with him.* See 13:1,5. Lot at first was little more than Abram's ward. *seventy-five years old.* Although advanced in age at the time of his call, Abram would live for another full century (see 25:7; see also note on 5:5).

12:5 *people they had acquired.* Wealthy people in that ancient world always had servants to help them with their flocks and herds (see 15:3; 24:2). Not all servants were slaves; many were voluntarily employed.

12:6 *site of the great tree of Moreh.* See perhaps 35:4; Jdg 9:6,37. A famous sanctuary was located at Shechem in central Canaan, and a large tree was often a conspicuous feature at such holy places. But Abram worshiped the Lord there, not the local deity.

12:7 *The LORD appeared.* The Lord frequently appeared visibly to Abram and to others, but not in all his glory (see Ex 33:18–20; Jn 1:18). *an altar.* The first of several that Abram built at places where he had memorable spiritual experiences (see v. 8; 13:18; 22:9). He acknowledged that the land of Canaan belonged to the Lord in a special way (see Ex 20:24; Jos 22:19).

peared to Abram[w] and said, "To your off-spring[i] I will give this land.[x]"[y] So he built an altar there to the LORD,[z] who had appeared to him.

[8]From there he went on toward the hills east of Bethel[a] and pitched his tent,[b] with Bethel on the west and Ai[c] on the east. There he built an altar to the LORD and called on the name of the LORD.[d] [9]Then Abram set out and continued toward the Negev.[e]

Abram in Egypt

12:10–20Ref — Ge 20:1–18; 26:1–11

[10]Now there was a famine in the land,[f] and Abram went down to Egypt to live there for a while because the famine was severe.[g] [11]As he was about to enter Egypt, he said to his wife Sarai,[h] "I know what a beautiful woman[i] you are. [12]When the Egyptians see you, they will say, 'This is his wife.' Then they will kill me but will let you live. [13]Say you are my sister,[j] so that I will be treated well for your sake and my life will be spared because of you."

[14]When Abram came to Egypt, the Egyptians saw that she was a very beautiful woman.[k] [15]And when Pharaoh's officials saw her, they praised her to Pharaoh, and she was taken into his palace. [16]He treated Abram well for her sake, and Abram acquired sheep and cattle, male and female donkeys, menservants and maidservants, and camels.[l]

[17]But the LORD inflicted[m] serious diseases on Pharaoh and his household[n] because of Abram's wife Sarai. [18]So Pharaoh summoned Abram. "What have you done to me?"[o] he said. "Why didn't you tell me she was your wife?[p] [19]Why did you say,

'She is my sister,'[q] so that I took her to be my wife? Now then, here is your wife. Take her and go!" [20]Then Pharaoh gave orders about Abram to his men, and they sent him on his way, with his wife and everything he had.

Abram and Lot Separate

13 So Abram went up from Egypt[r] to the Negev,[s] with his wife and everything he had, and Lot[t] went with him. [2]Abram had become very wealthy[u] in livestock[v] and in silver and gold.

[3]From the Negev[w] he went from place to place until he came to Bethel,[x] to the place between Bethel and Ai[y] where his tent had been earlier [4]and where he had first built an altar.[z] There Abram called on the name of the LORD.[a]

[5]Now Lot,[b] who was moving about with Abram, also had flocks and herds and tents. [6]But the land could not support them while they stayed together, for their possessions were so great that they were not able to stay together.[c] [7]And quarreling[d] arose between Abram's herdsmen and the herdsmen of Lot. The Canaanites[e] and Perizzites[f] were also living in the land[g] at that time.

[8]So Abram said to Lot,[h] "Let's not have any quarreling between you and me,[i] or between your herdsmen and mine, for we

Cross references (center column)

12:7 wGe 17:1; 18:1; 26:2; 35:1; Ex 6:3; Ac 7:2
xEx 3:8; Nu 10:29; Dt 30:5; Heb 11:8
yGe 13:15,17; 15:18; 17:8; 23:18; 24:7; 26:3-4; 28:13; 35:12; 48:4; 50:24; Ex 6:4,8; 13:5,11; 32:13; 33:1; Nu 11:12; Dt 1:8; 2:31; 9:5; 11:9; 34:4; 2Ki 25:21; 1Ch 16:16; 2Ch 20:7; Ps 105:9-11; Jer 25:5; Eze 47:14; Ac 7:5; Ro 4:13; Gal 3:16*
zS Ge 8:20; 13:4
12:8 aGe 13:3; 28:11,19; 35:1,8, 15; Jos 7:2; 8:9; 1Sa 7:16; 1Ki 12:29; Hos 12:4; Am 3:14; 4:4
bGe 26:25; 33:19; Heb 11:9
cJos 7:2; 12:9; Ezr 2:28; Ne 7:32; Jer 49:3
dS Ge 4:26; S 8:20
12:9 eGe 13:1,3; 20:1; 24:62; Nu 13:17; 33:40; Dt 34:3; Jos 10:40
12:10 fGe 41:27, 57; 42:5; 43:1; 47:4,13; Ru 1:1; 2Sa 21:1; 2Ki 8:1; Ps 105:19
gGe 41:30,54,56; 47:20; Ps 105:16
12:11 hS Ge 11:29 iver 14; Ge 24:16; 26:7; 29:17; 39:6
12:13 jGe 20:2; 26:7
12:14 kS ver 11
12:16 lS ver 5; Ge 24:35; 26:14; 30:43; 32:5; 34:23; 47:17; Job 1:3; 31:25
12:17 m2Ki 15:5; Job 30:11; Isa 53:4,10 n1Ch 16:21; Ps 105:14 12:18 oGe 20:9; 26:10; 29:25; 31:26; 44:15 pIsa 43:27; 51:2; Eze 16:3 12:19 qGe 20:5; 26:9 13:1 rGe 45:25 sS Ge 12:9 tS Ge 11:27 13:2 uS Ge 12:5; 26:13; Pr 10:22 vGe 32:15; Job 1:3; 42:12 13:3 wS Ge 12:9 xS Ge 12:8 yJos 7:2 13:4 zS Ge 12:7 aS Ge 4:26 13:5 bS Ge 11:27 13:6 cS Ge 12:5; 33:9; 36:7 13:7 dGe 26:20, 21; Nu 20:3 eS Ge 10:18 fGe 15:20; 34:30; Ex 3:8; Jdg 1:4 gGe 12:6; 34:30 13:8 hS Ge 11:27 iPr 15:18; 20:3

i7 Or seed

12:8 *Bethel.* Just north of Jerusalem, it was an important town in the religious history of God's ancient people (see, e.g., 28:10–22; 35:1–8; 1Ki 12:26–29). Only Jerusalem is mentioned more often in the OT.

12:9 *Negev.* The dry wasteland stretching southward from Beersheba. The same Hebrew word is translated "south" in 13:14.

12:10 *went down to Egypt . . . because the famine was severe.* Egypt's food supply was usually plentiful because the Nile's water supply was normally dependable.

12:11 *beautiful.* See v. 14. She was 65 at the time (see v. 4; 17:17). The Genesis Apocryphon (one of the Dead Sea Scrolls) praises Sarai's beauty. Abram's experience in this episode foreshadows Israel's later experience in Egypt, as the author of Genesis, writing after the exodus, was very much aware. Abram was truly the "father" of Israel.

12:13 *Say you are my sister.* If Pharaoh were to add Sarai to his harem while knowing that she was Abram's wife, he would have to kill Abram first.

12:15 *Pharaoh.* See note on Ex 1:11.

12:16 Livestock was an important measure of wealth in ancient times (see 13:2). *menservants and maidservants.*

See note on v. 5. *camels.* Although camels were not widely used until much later (see, e.g., Jdg 6:5), archaeology has confirmed their occasional domestication as early as the patriarchal period.

12:19 *Why did you say, 'She is my sister' . . . ?* Egyptian ethics emphasized the importance of absolute truthfulness, and Abram was put in the uncomfortable position of being exposed as a liar.

12:20 *Pharaoh gave orders.* See Ex 12:31–32.

13:2 *had become very wealthy.* Abram left Egypt with greater wealth than he had before—even as Israel would later leave Egypt laden with wealth from the Egyptians (Ex 3:22; 12:36).

13:4 *Abram called on the name of the LORD.* As he had done earlier at the same place (see 12:8).

13:6 *the land could not support them.* Livestock made up the greater part of their possessions, and the region around Bethel and Ai did not have enough water or pasture for such large flocks and herds (see v. 10; 26:17–22,32; 36:7).

13:7 *Perizzites.* May refer to rural inhabitants in contrast to city dwellers.

13:8 *brothers.* Relatives (as often in the Bible).

are brothers.*j* ⁹Is not the whole land before you? Let's part company. If you go to the left, I'll go to the right; if you go to the right, I'll go to the left."*k*

¹⁰Lot looked up and saw that the whole plain*l* of the Jordan*m* was well watered, like the garden of the LORD,*n* like the land of Egypt,*o* toward Zoar.*p* (This was before the LORD destroyed Sodom*q* and Gomorrah.)*r* ¹¹So Lot chose for himself the whole plain of the Jordan and set out toward the east. The two men parted company: ¹²Abram lived in the land of Canaan,*s* while Lot*t* lived among the cities of the plain*u* and pitched his tents near Sodom.*v* ¹³Now the men of Sodom*w* were wicked and were sinning greatly against the LORD.*x*

¹⁴The LORD said to Abram after Lot had parted from him, "Lift up your eyes from where you are and look north and south, east and west.*y* ¹⁵All the land that you see I will give to you and your offspring*i* forever.*z* ¹⁶I will make your offspring like the dust of the earth, so that if anyone could count the dust, then your offspring could be counted.*a* ¹⁷Go, walk through the length and breadth of the land,*b* for I am giving it to you."*c*

¹⁸So Abram moved his tents and went to live near the great trees of Mamre*d* at Hebron,*e* where he built an altar to the LORD.*f*

Abram Rescues Lot

14 At this time Amraphel king of Shinar,*k g* Arioch king of Ellasar, Ked-

orlaomer*h* king of Elam*i* and Tidal king of Goiim ²went to war against Bera king of Sodom, Birsha king of Gomorrah, Shinab king of Admah, Shemeber king of Zeboiim,*j* and the king of Bela (that is, Zoar).*k* ³All these latter kings joined forces in the Valley of Siddim*l* (the Salt Sea*l m*). ⁴For twelve years they had been subject to Kedorlaomer,*n* but in the thirteenth year they rebelled.

⁵In the fourteenth year, Kedorlaomer*o* and the kings allied with him went out and defeated the Rephaites*p* in Ashteroth Karnaim, the Zuzites in Ham, the Emites*q* in Shaveh Kiriathaim ⁶and the Horites*r* in the hill country of Seir,*s* as far as El Paran*t* near the desert. ⁷Then they turned back and went to En Mishpat (that is, Kadesh),*u* and they conquered the whole territory of the Amalekites,*v* as well as the Amorites*w* who were living in Hazazon Tamar.*x*

⁸Then the king of Sodom, the king of Gomorrah,*y* the king of Admah, the king of Zeboiim*z* and the king of Bela (that is,

Cross references (center column)

13:8 /Ge 19:9; Ex 2:14;
Nu 16:13; Ps 133:1
13:9 *k*Ge 20:15; 34:10; 47:6; Jer 40:4
13:10 /1Ki 7:46; 2Ch 4:17 *m*Nu 13:29; 33:48 *n*Ge 2:8-10; Isa 51:3; Eze 31:8-9 *o*Ge 46:7 *p*Ge 14:2; 19:22, 30; Dt 34:3; Isa 15:5; Jer 48:34 *q*Dt 29:23; Job 39:6; Ps 107:34; Jer 4:26 *r*Ge 14:8; 19:17-29
13:12 *s*Ge 10:19 *t*Ge 11:27 *u*Ge ver 10; Ge 19:17,25,29 *v*Ge 14:12
13:13 *w*Ge 19:4; Isa 1:10; 3:9 *x*Ge 18:20; 19:5; 20:6; 39:9; Nu 32:23; 1Sa 12:23; 2Sa 12:13; Ps 51:4; Eze 16:49-50; 2Pe 2:8
13:14 *y*Ge 28:14; 32:12; 48:16; Dt 3:27; 13:17; Isa 54:3
13:15 *z*Ge 12:7; Gal 3:16*
13:16 *a*Ge 12:2; 16:10; 17:20; 21:13,18; 25:16; Nu 23:10
13:17 *b*ver 15; Nu 13:17-25 *c*Ge 12:7; 15:7
13:18 *d*Ge 14:13, 24; 18:1; 23:17, 19; 25:9; 49:30; 50:13 *e*Ge 23:2;

35:27; 37:14; Nu 13:22; Jos 10:3,36; Jdg 1:10; 1Sa 30:31; 2Sa 2:1,3,11; 1Ch 11:1 /S Ge 8:20 14:1 *g*S Ge 10:10 *h*ver 4, 9,17 /S Ge 10:22 14:2 /S Ge 10:19 *k*S Ge 13:10 14:3 /ver 8, 10 *m*Nu 34:3,12; Dt 3:17; Jos 3:16; 12:3; 15:2,5; 18:19 14:4 *n*S ver 1 14:5 *o*S ver 1 *p*Ge 15:20; Dt 2:11,20; 3:11, 13; Jos 12:4; 13:12; 17:15; 1Ch 20:4 *q*Dt 2:10 14:6 *r*Ge 36:20; Dt 2:12,22 *s*Ge 32:3; 33:14,16; 36:8; Dt 1:2; 2:1,5,22; Jos 11:17; 24:4; 1Ch 4:42; Isa 34:5; Eze 25:8; 35:2; Am 1:6 *t*Ge 21:21; Nu 10:12; 12:16; 13:3,26; Hab 3:3 14:7 *u*Ge 16:14; 20:1; Nu 13:26; 20:1; 32:8; Dt 1:2; Jos 10:41; Jdg 11:16; Ps 29:8 *v*Ex 17:8; Nu 13:29; 14:25; 24:20; Dt 25:17; Jdg 3:13; 6:3; 10:12; 12:15; 1Sa 14:48; 15:2; 28:18; 2Sa 1:1; 1Ch 4:43; Ps 83:7 *w*Nu 13:29; Dt 1:4; Jos 2:10; 13:4 *x*2Ch 20:2; Eze 48:28 14:8 *y*S Ge 13:10 *z*Dt 29:23; Hos 11:8

*i*15 Or *seed*; also in verse 16   *k l* That is, Babylonia; also in verse 9   *l*3 That is, the Dead Sea

---

13:9 Abram, always generous, gave his young nephew the opportunity to choose the land he wanted. He himself would not obtain wealth except by the Lord's blessing (see 14:22–24).
13:10 *plain.* The Hebrew for this word picturesquely describes this section of the Jordan Valley as oval in shape. *like the land of Egypt.* Because of its abundant and dependable water supply (see note on 12:10), Egypt came the closest to matching Eden's ideal conditions (see 2:10). *the LORD destroyed Sodom and Gomorrah.* See especially 18:16–19:29. The names of Sodom and Gomorrah became proverbial for vile wickedness and for divine judgment on sin. Archaeology has confirmed that, prior to this catastrophe, the now dry area east and southeast of the Dead Sea (see note on 10:19) had ample water and was well populated.
13:12 *Lot . . . pitched his tents near Sodom.* Since the men of Sodom were known to be wicked (see v. 13), Lot was flirting with temptation by choosing to live near them. Contrast the actions of Abram (v. 18).
13:14 *Lift up your eyes . . . and look.* See Dt 34:1–4. Lot and Abram are a study in contrasts. The former looked selfishly and coveted (v. 10); the latter looked as God commanded and was blessed.
13:16 *like the dust of the earth.* A simile (common in the ancient Near East) for the large number of Abram's offspring (see 28:14; 2Ch 1:9; see also Nu 23:10). Similar phrases

are: "as numerous as the stars in the sky" and "as the sand on the seashore" (22:17).
13:17 *walk through . . . the land.* Either to inspect it or to exercise authority over it, demonstrating the promised ownership.
13:18 *great trees.* See note on 12:6. *Mamre.* A town named after one of Abram's allies (see 14:13). *Hebron.* Kiriath Arba (see note on 23:2). *altar.* See note on 12:7.
14:1 *Amraphel king of Shinar.* Not the great Babylonian king Hammurapi, as once thought. *Elam.* See note on 10:22. *Goiim.* The Hebrew word means "Gentile nations" and may be a common noun here (as in Isa 9:1).
14:3 *Salt Sea.* The Dead Sea, whose water contains a 25 percent concentration of chloride and bromide salts, making it the densest large body of water on earth.
14:6 *Horites.* Formerly thought to be cave dwellers (the Hebrew word *hor* means "cave"), they are now known to have been the Hurrians, a non-Semitic people widely dispersed throughout the ancient Near East.
14:7 *En Mishpat.* Another name for Kadesh, it means "spring of judgment/justice." It is called Meribah Kadesh, "quarreling/litigation at Kadesh," in Dt 32:51 (see Nu 27:14). *Kadesh.* Located in the southwest Negev (see note on 12:9), it was later called Kadesh Barnea (see Nu 32:8). *Amalekites.* A tribal people living in the Negev and in the Sinai peninsula. *Amorites.* See note on 10:16.

Zoar)[a] marched out and drew up their battle lines in the Valley of Siddim[b] [9]against Kedorlaomer[c] king of Elam,[d] Tidal king of Goiim, Amraphel king of Shinar and Arioch king of Ellasar—four kings against five. [10]Now the Valley of Siddim[e] was full of tar[f] pits, and when the kings of Sodom and Gomorrah[g] fled, some of the men fell into them and the rest fled to the hills.[h] [11]The four kings seized all the goods[i] of Sodom and Gomorrah and all their food; then they went away. [12]They also carried off Abram's nephew Lot[j] and his possessions, since he was living in Sodom.

[13]One who had escaped came and reported this to Abram the Hebrew.[k] Now Abram was living near the great trees of Mamre[l] the Amorite, a brother[m] of Eshcol[m] and Aner, all of whom were allied with Abram. [14]When Abram heard that his relative[n] had been taken captive, he called out the 318 trained[o] men born in his household[p] and went in pursuit as far as Dan.[q] [15]During the night Abram divided his men[r] to attack them and he routed them, pursuing them as far as Hobah, north of Damascus.[s] [16]He recovered[t] all the goods[u] and brought back his relative Lot and his possessions, together with the women and the other people.

[17]After Abram returned from defeating

Kedorlaomer[v] and the kings allied with him, the king of Sodom[w] came out to meet him in the Valley of Shaveh (that is, the King's Valley).[x]

[18]Then Melchizedek[y] king of Salem[n] [z] brought out bread[a] and wine.[b] He was priest of God Most High,[c] [19]and he blessed Abram,[d] saying,

"Blessed be Abram by God Most High,[e]
    Creator[o] of heaven and earth.[f]
[20]And blessed be[p] God Most High,[g]
    who delivered your enemies into
        your hand."

Then Abram gave him a tenth of everything.[h]

[21]The king of Sodom[i] said to Abram, "Give me the people and keep the goods[j] for yourself."

[22]But Abram said to the king of Sodom,[k] "I have raised my hand[l] to the LORD, God Most High,[m] Creator of heaven and earth,[n] and have taken an oath [23]that I will accept nothing belonging to you,[o]

Cross references (center column):

14:8 [a]S Ge 13:10
[b]S ver 3
14:9 [c]S ver 1
[d]S Ge 10:22
14:10 [e]S ver 3
[f]Ge 11:3 [g]ver 17, 21 [h]Ge 19:17,30; Jos 2:16; Ps 11:1
14:11 [i]ver 16,21
14:12 [j]S Ge 11:27
14:13 [k]Ge 37:28; 39:14,17; 40:15; 41:12; 43:32; Ex 3:18; 1Sa 4:6; 14:11
[l]S Ge 13:18
[m]Nu 13:23; 32:9; Dt 1:24
14:14 [n]ver 12
[o]Dt 4:9; Pr 22:6
[p]S Ge 12:5
[q]Dt 34:1; Jdg 18:29; 1Ki 15:20
14:15 [r]Jdg 7:16
[s]Ge 15:2; 2Sa 8:5; 1Ki 20:34; 2Ki 16:9; Isa 7:8; 8:4; 10:9; 17:1; Jer 49:23,27; Eze 27:18; Am 1:3-5
14:16 [t]1Sa 30:8, 18 [u]S ver 11
14:17 [v]S ver 1
[w]S ver 10
[x]2Sa 18:18
14:18 [y]Ps 110:4; Heb 5:6; 7:17,21
[z]Ps 76:2; Heb 7:2
[a]S Ge 3:19
[b]Jdg 9:13; 19:19; Est 1:10; Ps 104:15; Pr 31:6; Ecc 10:19; SS 1:2
[c]ver 22; Ps 7:8, 17; Da 7:27
14:19 [d]Heb 7:6 [e]ver 18 [f]ver 22; S Ge 1:1; 24:3; Jos 2:11; Ps 148:5; Mt 11:25 **14:20** [g]S Ge 9:26; S 24:27 [h]Ge 28:22; Dt 14:22; 26:12; Lk 18:12; Heb 7:4 **14:21** [i]S ver 10 /S ver 11 **14:22** [k]S ver 10 [l]Ex 6:8; Nu 14:30; Dt 32:40; Ne 9:15; Eze 20:5; Da 12:7; Rev 10:5-6 [m]S ver 18 [n]S ver 19 **14:23** [o]1Sa 15:3,19; 2Ki 5:16; Est 8:11; 9:10,15

[m]*13* Or *a relative*; or *an ally*   [n]*18* That is, Jerusalem
[o]*19* Or *Possessor*, also in verse 22   [p]*20* Or *And praise be to*

14:10 *tar pits.* Lumps of asphalt are often seen even today floating in the southern end of the Dead Sea. *hills.* The Dead Sea, the lowest body of water on earth (about 1,300 feet below sea level), is flanked by hills on both sides.

14:12 *Lot . . . was living in Sodom.* He moved into the town and was living among its wicked people (see 2Pe 2:8). Though Lot was "righteous," he was now in danger of imitating the "filthy lives of lawless men" (2Pe 2:7).

14:13 *Hebrew.* Abram, the father of the Hebrew people, is the first Biblical character to be called a Hebrew (see "Eber" in note on 10:21). Usually an ethnic term in the Bible, it was normally used by non-Israelites in a disparaging sense (see, e.g., 39:17). Outside the Bible, people known as the Habiru/Apiru (a word probably related to Hebrew) are referred to as a propertyless, dependent, immigrant (foreign) social class rather than as a specific ethnic group. Negative descriptions of them are given in the Amarna letters (clay tablets found in Egypt). *Mamre.* A town was named after him (see 13:18 and note).

14:14 *318 trained men born in his household.* A clear indication of Abram's great wealth. The Hebrew for "trained men" is found only here in the Bible. A related word used elsewhere in very ancient texts means "armed retainers." *Dan.* This well-known city in the north was not given the name "Dan" until the days of the judges (see Jdg 18:29). The designation here is thus an editorial updating subsequent to Moses' time.

14:17 *King's Valley.* Near Jerusalem, probably to the east (see 2Sa 18:18).

14:18 *Melchizedek king of Salem . . . priest.* See Heb 7:1. In ancient times, particularly in non-Israelite circles, kingly and priestly duties were often performed by the same indi-

vidual. "Melchizedek" means "My king is righteousness" or "king of righteousness" (see Heb 7:2). "Salem" is a shortened form of "Jerusalem" (see Ps 76:2) and is related to the Hebrew word for "peace" (see Heb 7:2). The name of Adoni-Zedek, another king of Jerusalem (see Jos 10:1), is very similar to that of Melchizedek and means "My lord is righteousness" or "lord of righteousness." *bread and wine.* An ordinary meal (see Jdg 19:19), in no way related to the NT ordinance of communion. Melchizedek offered the food and drink as a show of friendship and hospitality.

14:19 *God Most High, Creator of heaven and earth.* The titles "most high," "lord of heaven" and "creator of earth" were frequently applied to the chief Canaanite deity in ancient times. Terminology and location (Jerusalem was in central Canaan) thus indicate that Melchizedek was probably a Canaanite king-priest. But Abram, by identifying Melchizedek's "God Most High" with "the LORD" (see v. 22), bore testimony to the one true God, whom Melchizedek had come to know.

14:20 *Abram gave him a tenth of everything.* Although Melchizedek's view of God was no doubt deficient, and perhaps even corrupted, Abram's response to his blessing seems to indicate that he recognized that Melchizedek served the same God as he (see v. 18). So Abram took the occasion to offer him a tithe of his spoils for God Most High. A tenth was the king's share (see 1Sa 8:15,17). Melchizedek is later spoken of as a type or prefiguration of Jesus, our "great high priest" (Heb 4:14), whose priesthood is therefore "in the order of Melchizedek, not in the order of Aaron" (Heb 7:11; see Ps 110:4).

14:22 *I have raised my hand.* A standard oath-taking practice in ancient times (see Dt 32:40; Rev 10:5–6).

not even a thread or the thong of a sandal, so that you will never be able to say, 'I made Abram rich.' [24]I will accept nothing but what my men have eaten and the share that belongs to the men who went with me—to Aner, Eshcol and Mamre.[p] Let them have their share."

God's Covenant With Abram

15 After this, the word of the LORD came to Abram[q] in a vision:[r]

"Do not be afraid,[s] Abram.
    I am your shield,[q][t]
    your very great reward.[r][u]"

[2]But Abram said, "O Sovereign LORD,[v] what can you give me since I remain childless[w] and the one who will inherit[s] my estate is Eliezer of Damascus?[x]" [3]And Abram said, "You have given me no children; so a servant[y] in my household[z] will be my heir."

[4]Then the word of the LORD came to him: "This man will not be your heir, but a son coming from your own body will be your heir.[a]" [5]He took him outside and said, "Look up at the heavens and count the stars[b]—if indeed you can count them." Then he said to him, "So shall your offspring be."[c]

[6]Abram believed the LORD, and he credited it to him as righteousness.[d]

[7]He also said to him, "I am the LORD, who brought you out[e] of Ur of the Chaldeans[f] to give you this land to take possession of it."[g]

[8]But Abram said, "O Sovereign LORD,[h] how can I know[i] that I will gain possession of it?"[j]

[9]So the LORD said to him, "Bring me a heifer,[k] a goat and a ram, each three years old,[l] along with a dove and a young pigeon.[m]"

[10]Abram brought all these to him, cut them in two and arranged the halves opposite each other;[n] the birds, however, he did not cut in half.[o] [11]Then birds of prey came down on the carcasses,[p] but Abram drove them away.

[12]As the sun was setting, Abram fell into a deep sleep,[q] and a thick and dreadful darkness came over him. [13]Then the LORD said to him, "Know for certain that your descendants will be strangers in a country not their own, and they will be enslaved[r] and mistreated four hundred years.[s] [14]But I will punish the nation they serve as slaves, and afterward they will come out[t] with great possessions.[u] [15]You, however, will go to your fathers[v] in peace and be buried at a good old age.[w] [16]In the fourth

---

14:24
pS Ge 13:18
15:1 q1Sa 15:10; 2Sa 7:4; 1Ki 6:11; 12:22; Jer 1:13; Eze 3:16; Da 10:1
rGe 46:2; Nu 12:6; 24:4; Ru 1:20; Job 33:15
sGe 21:17; 26:24; 46:3; Ex 14:13; 20:20; 2Ki 6:16; 2Ch 20:15,17; Ps 27:1; Isa 7:4; 41:10,13-14; 43:1,5; Jer 1:8; Hag 2:5
tDt 33:29; 2Sa 22:3,31; Ps 3:3; 5:12; 18:2; 28:7; 33:20; 84:11; 119:114; 144:2; Pr 2:7; 30:5
uPs 18:20; 37:25; 58:11; Isa 3:10
15:2 vver 8; Isa 49:22; Jer 44:26; Eze 5:11; 16:48
wAc 7:5
xS Ge 14:15
15:3 yGe 24:2,34
zS Ge 12:5
15:4 aGal 4:28
15:5 bJob 11:8; 35:5; Ps 8:3; 147:4; Jer 33:22
cS Ge 12:2; S Jer 30:19; Ro 4:18*; Heb 11:12
15:6 dPs 106:31; Ro 4:3*,20-24*; Gal 3:6*; Jas 2:23*
15:7 eGe 12:1; Ex 20:2; Ac 7:3; Heb 11:8
fS Ge 11:28; Ac 7:4
gS Ge 13:17; 17:8; 28:4; 35:12; 48:4; Ex 6:8; Dt 9:5
15:8 hS ver 2 iLk 1:18 jDt 12:20; 19:8 **15:9** kNu 19:2; Dt 21:3; Hos 4:16; Am 4:1 l1Sa 1:24 mLev 1:14; 5:7,11; 12:8 **15:10** nver 17; Jer 34:18 oLev 1:17; 5:8 **15:11** pDt 28:26; Jer 7:33 **15:12** qS Ge 2:21 rEx 1:11; 3:7; 5:6,10-14,18; 6:5; Dt 5:15; Job 3:18 sver 16; Ex 12:40; Nu 20:15; Ac 7:6,17; Gal 3:17 **15:14** tGe 50:24; Ex 3:8; 6:6-8; 12:25; Nu 10:29; Jos 1:2; Ac 7:7* uEx 12:32-38 **15:15** vGe 47:30; 49:29; Dt 31:16; 2Sa 7:12; 1Ki 1:21; Ps 49:19 wGe 25:8; 35:29; Ex 23:26; Dt 34:7; Jos 14:11; Jdg 8:32; 1Ch 29:28; Job 5:26; 21:23; 42:17; Ps 91:16; Pr 3:16; 9:11; Isa 65:20

q1 Or sovereign   r1 Or shield; / your reward will be very great   s2 The meaning of the Hebrew for this phrase is uncertain.

14:23 *I will accept nothing belonging to you.* Cf. 2Ki 5:16. Abram refused to let himself become obligated to anyone but the Lord. Had he done so, this Canaanite king might later have claimed the right of kingship over Abram.

15:1 *I am your shield.* Whether "shield" or "sovereign" is meant (see NIV text note), the reference is to the Lord as Abram's King. As elsewhere, "shield" stands for king (e.g., Dt 33:29; 2Sa 22:3; Ps 7:10; 84:9). *your very great reward.* Though Abram was quite rich (13:2), God himself was Abram's greatest treasure (cf. Dt 10:9).

15:2 *Eliezer of Damascus.* A servant probably acquired by Abram on his journey southward from Haran (see 12:5). He may also be the unnamed "chief servant" of 24:2.

15:3–4 Ancient documents uncovered at Nuzi (see chart on "Ancient Texts Relating to the OT," p. 5) near Kirkuk on a branch of the Tigris River, as well as at other places, demonstrate that a childless man could adopt one of his own male servants to be heir and guardian of his estate. Abram apparently contemplated doing this with Eliezer, or perhaps had already done so.

15:5 *count the stars—if indeed you can.* See 22:17. More than 8,000 stars are clearly visible in the darkness of a Near Eastern night. *So shall your offspring be.* The promise was initially fulfilled in Egypt (see Ex 1; see also Dt 1:10; Heb 11:12). Ultimately, all who belong to Christ are Abram's offspring (see Gal 3:29).

15:6 Abram is the "father of all who believe" (Ro 4:11),

and this verse is the first specific reference to faith in God's promises. It also teaches that God graciously responds to a man's faith by crediting righteousness to him (see Heb 11:7).

15:7 *I am the LORD, who brought you out.* Ancient royal covenants often began with (1) the self-identification of the king and (2) a brief historical prologue, as here (see Ex 20:2).

15:8 *how can I know . . . ?* Cf. Lk 1:18. Abram believed God's promise of a son, but he asked for a guarantee of the promise of the land.

15:9 *three years old.* The prime age for most sacrificial animals (see 1Sa 1:24).

15:10 *the birds . . . he did not cut in half.* Perhaps because they were too small (see Lev 1:17).

15:13 *a country not their own.* Egypt (see 46:3–4). *four hundred years.* A round number. According to Ex 12:40 Israel spent 430 years in Egypt.

15:15 The fulfillment is recorded in 25:8.

15:16 *In the fourth generation.* That is, after 400 years (see v. 13). A "generation" was the age of a man when his first son (from the legal standpoint) was born—in Abram's case, 100 years (see 21:5). *the sin of the Amorites has not yet reached its full measure.* Just how sinful many Canaanite religious practices are is now known from archaeological artifacts and from their own epic literature, discovered at Ras Shamra (ancient Ugarit) on the north Syrian coast beginning in 1929 (see chart on "Ancient Texts Relating to the OT," p. 5). Their "worship" was polytheistic and included child

generation,^x your descendants will come back here,^y for the sin of the Amorites^z has not yet reached its full measure."

¹⁷When the sun had set and darkness had fallen, a smoking firepot with a blazing torch^a appeared and passed between the pieces.^b ¹⁸On that day the LORD made a covenant with Abram^c and said, "To your descendants I give this land,^d from the river^t of Egypt^e to the great river, the Euphrates^f— ¹⁹the land of the Kenites,^g Kenizzites, Kadmonites, ²⁰Hittites,^h Perizzites,ⁱ Rephaites,^j ²¹Amorites, Canaanites, Girgashites and Jebusites."^k

Hagar and Ishmael

16 Now Sarai,^l Abram's wife, had borne him no children.^m But she had an Egyptian maidservantⁿ named Hagar;^o ²so she said to Abram, "The LORD has kept me from having children.^p Go, sleep with my maidservant; perhaps I can build a family through her."^q

Abram agreed to what Sarai said. ³So after Abram had been living in Canaan^r ten years,^s Sarai his wife took her Egyptian maidservant Hagar and gave her to her husband to be his wife. ⁴He slept with Hagar,^t and she conceived.

When she knew she was pregnant, she began to despise her mistress.^u ⁵Then Sarai said to Abram, "You are responsible

for the wrong I am suffering. I put my servant in your arms, and now that she knows she is pregnant, she despises me. May the LORD judge between you and me."^v

⁶"Your servant is in your hands,^w" Abram said. "Do with her whatever you think best." Then Sarai mistreated^x Hagar; so she fled from her.

⁷The angel of the LORD^y found Hagar near a spring^z in the desert; it was the spring that is beside the road to Shur.^a ⁸And he said, "Hagar,^b servant of Sarai, where have you come from, and where are you going?"^c

"I'm running away from my mistress Sarai," she answered.

⁹Then the angel of the LORD told her, "Go back to your mistress and submit to her." ¹⁰The angel added, "I will so increase your descendants that they will be too numerous to count."^d

15:16 ^xS ver 13; Ex 12:40 ^yGe 28:15; 46:4; 48:21; 50:24; Ex 3:8,17 ^zLev 18:28; Jos 13:4; Jdg 10:11; 1Ki 21:26; 2Ki 16:3; 21:11; Eze 16:3 **15:17** ^aJdg 7:16, 20; 15:4,5 ^bS ver 10 **15:18** ^cGe 17:2, 4,7; Ex 6:4; 34:10,27; 1Ch 16:16; Ps 105:9 ^dS Ge 12:7 ^eNu 34:5; Jos 15:4,47; 1Ki 8:65; 2Ki 24:7; 2Ch 7:8; Isa 27:12; Jer 37:5; 46:2; La 4:17; Eze 30:22; 47:19 ^fS Ge 2:14 **15:19** ^gNu 24:21; Jdg 1:16; 4:11, 17; 5:24; 1Sa 15:6; 27:10; 30:29; 1Ch 2:55 **15:20** ^hS Ge 10:15; S Dt 7:1 ⁱS Ge 13:7 **15:21** ^kS Ge 10:16; Jos 3:10; 24:11; Ne 9:8 **16:1** ^lS Ge 11:29 ^mS Ge 11:30; Lk 1:7,36; Gal 4:24-25 ⁿGe 24:61; 29:24,29; 31:33;

46:18 ^over 3-4,8,15; Ge 21:14; 25:12 **16:2** ^pGe 29:31; 30:2 ^qGe 19:32; 30:3-4,9-10 **16:3** ^rS Ge 12:5 ^sS Ge 12:4 **16:4** ^tS ver 1 ^uGe 30:1; 1Sa 1:6 **16:5** ^vGe 31:53; Ex 5:21; Jdg 11:27; 1Sa 24:12,15; 26:10,23; Ps 50:6; 75:7 **16:6** ^wJos 9:25 ^xGe 31:50 **16:7** ^yver 11; Ge 21:17; 22:11,15; 24:7,40; 31:11; 48:16; Ex 3:2; 14:19; 23:20,23; 32:34; 33:2; Nu 22:22; Jdg 2:1; 6:11; 13:3; 2Sa 24:16; 1Ki 19:5; 2Ki 1:3; 19:35; Ps 34:7; Zec 1:11; S Ac 5:19 ^zver 14; Ge 21:19 ^aGe 20:1; 25:18; Ex 15:22; 1Sa 15:7; 27:8 **16:8** ^bS ver 1 ^cS Ge 3:9 **16:10** ^dS Ge 13:16

^t18 Or Wadi

---

sacrifice, idolatry, religious prostitution and divination (cf. Dt 18:9–12). God was patient in judgment, even with the wicked Canaanites.

15:17 *a smoking firepot with a blazing torch.* Symbolizing the presence of God (see Ex 3:2; 14:24; 19:18; 1Ki 18:38; Ac 2:3–4). *passed between the pieces.* Of the slaughtered animals (v. 10). In ancient times the parties solemnized a covenant by walking down an aisle flanked by the pieces of slaughtered animals (see Jer 34:18–19). The practice signified a self-maledictory oath: "May it be so done to me if I do not keep my oath and pledge." Having credited Abram's faith as righteousness, God now graciously ministered to his need for assurance concerning the land. He granted Abram a promissory covenant, as he had to Noah (see 9:9 and note; see also chart on "Major Covenants in the OT," p. 19).

15:18 *made a covenant.* Lit. "cut a covenant," referring to the slaughtering of the animals (the same Hebrew verb is translated "made" and "cut" in Jer 34:18). *I give this land.* The Lord initially fulfilled this covenant through Joshua (see Jos 1:2–9; 21:43; see also 1Ki 4:20–21). *river of Egypt.* Probably the modern Wadi el-Arish in northeastern Sinai.

15:19–21 A similar list of ten peoples is found in 10:15–18 (see notes there). The number ten signifies completeness.

16:1 *no children.* See note on 11:30. *Egyptian.* Perhaps Hagar was acquired while Abram and Sarai were in Egypt (see 12:10–20).

16:2 *The LORD has kept me from having children.* Some time had passed since the revelation of 15:4 (see 16:3), and Sarai impatiently implied that God was not keeping his promise. *Go, sleep with my maidservant.* An ancient custom, illustrated in Old Assyrian marriage contracts, the Code

of Hammurapi and the Nuzi tablets (see note on 15:3–4), to ensure the birth of a male heir. Sarai would herself solve the problem of her barrenness.

16:3 *ten years.* Abram was now 85 years old (see 12:4; 16:16).

16:4 *despise her mistress.* Peninnah acted similarly toward Hannah (see 1Sa 1:6).

16:5 *May the LORD judge between you and me.* An expression of hostility or suspicion (see 31:53; see also 31:49).

16:7 *The angel of the LORD.* Since the angel of the Lord speaks for God in the first person (v. 10) and Hagar is said to name "the LORD who spoke to her: 'You are the God who sees me' " (v. 13), the angel appears to be both distinguished from the Lord (in that he is called "messenger"—the Hebrew for "angel" means "messenger") and identified with him. Similar distinction and identification can be found in 19:1,21; 31:11,13; Ex 3:2,4; Jdg 2:1–5; 6:11–12,14; 13:3,6,8–11,13,15–17,20–23; Zec 3:1–6; 12:8. Traditional Christian interpretation has held that this "angel" was a preincarnate manifestation of Christ as God's Messenger-Servant. It may be, however, that, as the Lord's personal messenger who represented him and bore his credentials, the angel could speak on behalf of (and so be identified with) the One who sent him (see especially 19:21; cf. 18:2,22; 19:2). Whether this "angel" was the second person of the Trinity remains therefore uncertain. *Shur.* Located east of Egypt (see 25:18; 1Sa 15:7).

16:8 *I'm running away from my mistress.* Not yet knowing exactly where she was going, Hagar answered only the first of the angel's questions.

16:10 A promise reaffirmed in 17:20 and fulfilled in 25:13–16.

11The angel of the LORD e also said to her:

"You are now with child
and you will have a son.f
You shall name himg Ishmael,u h
for the LORD has heard of your
misery. i
12He will be a wild donkeyj of a man;
his hand will be against everyone
and everyone's hand against him,
and he will live in hostility
towardv all his brothers. k"

13She gave this name to the LORD who spoke to her: "You are the God who sees me,l" for she said, "I have now seenw the One who sees me." m 14That is why the welln was called Beer Lahai Roix; o it is still there, between Kadeshp and Bered.

15So Hagarq bore Abram a son,r and Abram gave the name Ishmaels to the son she had borne. 16Abram was eighty-six years oldt when Hagar bore him Ishmael.

The Covenant of Circumcision

17 When Abram was ninety-nine years old,u the LORD appeared to himv and said, "I am God Almightyy; w walk before me and be blameless. x 2I will confirm my covenant between me and youy and will greatly increase your numbers."z

3Abram fell facedown, a and God said to him, 4"As for me, this is my covenant with you: b You will be the father of many nations. c 5No longer will you be called Abramz; your name will be Abraham, a d for I have made you a father of many nations. e 6I will make you very fruitful;f I will make nations of you, and kings will come from you.g 7I will establish my covenanthi as an everlasting covenanti k between me and you and your descendants after you for the generations to come, to be your God l and the God of your descendants after you. m 8The whole land of Canaan, n where you are now an alien,o I will give as an everlasting possession to

Cross references (center column)

16:11 eS ver 7; S Ac 5:19 /S Ge 3:15 gGe 12:2-3; 18:19; Ne 9:7; Isa 44:1; Am 3:2; Mt 1:21; Lk 1:13, 31 hGe 17:19; 21:3; 37:25,28; 39:1; Jdg 8:24 iGe 29:32; 31:42; Ex 2:24; 3:7,9; 4:31; Nu 20:16; Dt 26:7; 1Sa 9:16 16:12 jJob 6:5; 11:12; 24:5; 39:5; Ps 104:11; Jer 2:24; Hos 8:9 kGe 25:18 16:13 lPs 139:1-12 mGe 32:30; 33:10; Ex 24:10; 33:20,23; Nu 12:8; Jdg 6:22; 13:22; Isa 6:5 16:14 nS ver 7 oGe 24:62; 25:11 pS Ge 14:7 16:15 qS ver 1 rGe 21:9; Gal 4:22 sGe 17:18; 25:12; 28:9 16:16 tS Ge 12:4 17:1 uS Ge 12:4 vS Ge 12:7 wGe 28:3; 35:11; 43:14; 48:3; 49:25; Ex 6:3; Ru 1:20; Job 5:17; 6:4,14; 22:21; 33:19; 36:16; Isa 13:6; Joel 1:15; Mic 6:9 xS Ge 5:22; 20:5; Dt 18:13; 1Ki 3:6; 9:4; Job 1:1; Ps 15:2; 18:23; 78:72;

101:2 17:2 yS Ge 15:18; S 22:16-18 zS Ge 12:2 17:3 aver 17; Ge 18:2; 19:1; 33:3; Ex 18:7; Nu 14:5; Jos 5:14; 7:6; Jdg 13:20; Eze 1:28; 3:23 17:4 bS Ge 15:18 cver 16; S Ge 12:2; 25:23 17:5 dver 15; Ge 32:28; 35:10; 37:3,13; 43:6; 46:2; 1Ki 18:31; 2Ki 17:34; 1Ch 1:34; Ne 9:7; Isa 48:1; S Jn 1:42 eRo 4:17* 17:6 fGe 1:28; 22:17; 26:22; 28:3; 35:11; 41:52; 47:27; 48:4; 49:22; Lev 26:9; Dt 7:13 gver 16,19; Ge 18:10; 21:1; 36:31; Isa 51:2; Mt 1:6 17:7 hS Ge 15:18; Lev 26:9,15 iS Ge 6:18 /S Heb 13:20 kS Ge 9:16 lEx 6:7; 20:2; 29:45,46; Lev 11:44-45; 18:2; 22:33; 25:38; 26:12,45; Nu 15:41; Dt 4:20; 7:6,21; 29:13; 2Sa 7:24; Jer 14:9; Rev 21:7 mRo 9:8; Gal 3:16 17:8 nS Ge 10:19 oGe 23:4; 28:4; 35:27; 37:1; Ex 6:4; 1Ch 29:15

u11 Ishmael means God hears. v12 Or live to the east / of w13 Or seen the back of x14 Beer Lahai Roi means well of the Living One who sees me. y1 Hebrew El-Shaddai z5 Abram means exalted father. a5 Abraham means father of many.

Study notes (bottom)

16:11 Ishmael. See NIV text note and 17:20.
16:12 wild donkey. Away from human settlements, Ishmael would roam the desert like a wild donkey (see Job 24:5; Hos 8:9). hostility. The hostility between Sarai and Hagar (see vv. 4–6) was passed on to their descendants (see 25:18).
16:13 I have now seen the One who sees me. See NIV text note and cf. Ex 33:23. To see God's face was believed to bring death (see 32:30; Ex 33:20).
16:14 Beer Lahai Roi. See NIV text note. Another possible translation that fits the context equally well is: "well of the one who sees me and who lives." Kadesh. See note on 14:7.
17:1 ninety-nine years old. Thirteen years had passed since Ishmael's birth (see 16:16; 17:24–25). appeared. See note on 12:7. I am. See note on 15:7. God Almighty. The Hebrew (El-Shaddai) perhaps means "God, the Mountain One," either highlighting the invincible power of God or referring to the mountains as God's symbolic home (see Ps 121:1). It was the special name by which God revealed himself to the patriarchs (see Ex 6:3). Shaddai occurs 31 times in the book of Job and 17 times in the rest of the Bible. walk before me and be blameless. Perhaps equivalent to "walk with me and be blameless" (see notes on 5:22; 6:8–9). After Abram's and Sarai's attempt to obtain the promised offspring by using a surrogate mother, God appeared to Abram. The Lord made it clear that, if Abram was to receive God's promised and covenanted benefits, he must be God's faithful and obedient servant. His faith must be accompanied by the "obedience that comes from faith" (Ro 1:5; see ch. 22).
17:2 my covenant. See 12:2–3; 13:14–16; 15:4–5. The

covenant is God's. God calls it "my covenant" nine times in vv. 2–21, and he initiates (see 15:18), confirms (v. 2) and establishes (v. 7) it. numbers. See 13:16 and note. Earlier God had covenanted to keep his promise concerning the land (ch. 15); here he broadens his covenant to include the promised offspring. See chart on "Major Covenants in the OT," p. 19.
17:5 Abram . . . Abraham. See NIV text notes. The first name means "Exalted Father," probably in reference to God (i.e., "[God is] Exalted Father"); the second means "father of many," in reference to Abraham. your name will be. By giving Abram a new name (see Ne 9:7) God marked him in a special way as his servant (see notes on 1:5; 2:19).
17:6 nations . . . kings. This promise came also to Sarah (v. 16) and was renewed to Jacob (35:11; see 48:19). It referred to the proliferation of Abraham's offspring, who, like the descendants of Noah (see ch. 10), would someday become many nations and spread over the earth. Ultimately it finds fulfillment in such passages as Ro 4:16–18; 15:8–12; Gal 3:29; Rev 7:9; 21:24.
17:7 everlasting. From God's standpoint (see vv. 13,19), but capable of being broken from man's standpoint (see v. 14; cf. Isa 24:5; Jer 31:32). to be your God. The heart of God's covenant promise, repeated over and over in the OT (see, e.g., v. 8; Jer 24:7; 31:33; Eze 34:30–31; Hos 2:23; Zec 8:8). This is God's pledge to be the protector of his people and the One who provides for their well-being and guarantees their future blessing (see 15:1).
17:8 land. See 12:7; 15:18; Ac 7:5. everlasting possession. The land, though an everlasting possession given by God, could be temporarily lost because of disobedience (see Dt 28:62–63; 30:1–10).

you and your descendants after you; *p* and I will be their God. *q* "

9Then God said to Abraham, "As for you, you must keep my covenant, *r* you and your descendants after you for the generations to come. *s* 10This is my covenant with you and your descendants after you, the covenant you are to keep: Every male among you shall be circumcised. *t* 11You are to undergo circumcision, *u* and it will be the sign of the covenant *v* between me and you. 12For the generations to come *w* every male among you who is eight days old must be circumcised, *x* including those born in your household or bought with money from a foreigner—those who are not your offspring. 13Whether born in your household or bought with your money, they must be circumcised. *y* My covenant in your flesh is to be an everlasting covenant. *z* 14Any uncircumcised male, who has not been circumcised *a* in the flesh, will be cut off from his people; *b* he has broken my covenant. *c* "

15God also said to Abraham, "As for Sarai *d* your wife, you are no longer to call her Sarai; her name will be Sarah. *e* 16I will bless her and will surely give you a son by her. *f* I will bless her so that she will be the mother of nations; *g* kings of peoples will come from her."

17Abraham fell facedown; *h* he laughed *i* and said to himself, "Will a son be born to a man a hundred years old? *j* Will Sarah bear a child at the age of ninety?" *k* 18And Abraham said to God, "If only Ishmael *l* might live under your blessing!" *m*

19Then God said, "Yes, but your wife Sarah will bear you a son, *n* and you will call him Isaac. *b o* I will establish my covenant with him *p* as an everlasting covenant *q* for his descendants after him. 20And as for Ishmael, I have heard you: I will surely bless him; I will make him fruitful and will greatly increase his numbers. *r* He will be the father of twelve rulers, *s* and I will make him into a great nation. *t* 21But my covenant *u* I will establish with Isaac, whom Sarah will bear to you *v* by this time next year." *w* 22When he had finished speaking with Abraham, God went up from him. *x*

23On that very day Abraham took his son Ishmael and all those born in his household *y* or bought with his money, every male in his household, and circumcised them, as God told him. *z* 24Abraham was ninety-nine years old *a* when he was circumcised, *b* 25and his son Ishmael *c* was thirteen; 26Abraham and his son Ishmael

---

17:8 *p*S Ge 12:7; S 15:7 *q*S ver 7; Jer 31:1
17:9 *r*Ge 22:18; Ex 19:5; Dt 5:2 *s*Ge 18:19
17:10 *t*ver 23; Ge 21:4; Lev 12:3; Jos 5:2, 5,7; Jn 7:22; Ac 7:8; Ro 4:11
17:11 *u*Ex 12:48; Dt 10:16 *v*S Ge 9:12; Ro 4:11
17:12 *w*S Ge 9:12 *x*Ge 21:4; Lev 12:3; Jos 5:2; S Lk 1:59
17:13 *y*Ex 12:44, 48 *z*S Ge 9:16
17:14 *a*ver 23 *b*Ex 4:24-26; 12:15,19; 30:33; Lev 7:20,25; 17:4; 18:29; 19:8; 20:17; Nu 9:13; 15:30; 19:13; Dt 17:12; Jos 5:2-8; Job 38:15; Ps 37:28 *c*Eze 44:7
17:15 *d*S Ge 11:29 *e*S ver 5
17:16 *f*S ver 6; S Isa 29:22 *g*S ver 4; Ge 24:60; Gal 4:31
17:17 *h*S ver 3 *i*Ge 18:12; 21:6
17:18 *l*S Ge 16:15

*m*Ge 21:11 17:19 *n*S ver 6,21; Ge 18:14; 21:2; 1Sa 1:20 *o*S Ge 16:11; Mt 1:21; Lk 1:13,31 *p*Ge 26:3; 50:24; Ex 13:11; Dt 1:8 *q*S Ge 9:16; S Gal 3:16 *r*S Ge 13:16 *s*Ge 25:12-16 *t*Ge 25:18; 48:19 17:21 *u*Ex 34:10 *v*S ver 19 *w*Ge 18:10,14 17:22 *x*Ge 18:33; 35:13; Nu 12:9 17:23 *y*S Ge 12:5 *z*S ver 10,S 14 17:24 *a*S Ge 12:4 *b*Ro 4:11 17:25 *c*Ge 16:16

b *19* Isaac means *he laughs.*

17:9 *As for you.* Balances the "As for me" of v. 4. Having reviewed his covenanted commitment to Abraham (see 15:8–21), and having broadened it to include the promise of offspring, God now called upon Abraham to make a covenanted commitment to him—to "walk before me and be blameless" (v. 1). *keep my covenant.* Participation in the blessings of the Abrahamic covenant was conditioned on obedience (see 18:19; 22:18; 26:4–5).
17:10 *circumcised.* Circumcision was God's appointed "sign of the covenant" (v. 11), which signified Abraham's covenanted commitment to the Lord—that the Lord alone would be his God, whom he would trust and serve. It symbolized a self-maledictory oath (analogous to the oath to which God had submitted himself; see note on 15:17): "If I am not loyal in faith and obedience to the Lord, may the sword of the Lord cut off me and my offspring (see v. 14) as I have cut off my foreskin." Thus Abraham was to place himself under the rule of the Lord as his King, consecrating himself, his offspring and all he possessed to the service of the Lord. For circumcision as signifying consecration to the Lord see Ex 6:12 (NIV text note); Lev 19:23 (NIV text note); 26:41; Dt 10:16; 30:6; Jer 4:4; 6:10 (NIV text note); 9:25–26; Eze 44:7,9. Other nations also practiced circumcision (see Jer 9:25–26; Eze 32:18–19), but not for the covenant reasons that Israel did.
17:11 *sign of the covenant.* See notes on 9:12; 15:17. As the covenant sign, circumcision also (see note on v. 10) marked Abraham as the one to whom God had made covenant commitment (15:7–21) in response to Abraham's faith, which he "credited . . . to him as righteousness"

(15:6). Paul comments on this aspect of the covenant sign in Ro 4:11.
17:12 *eight days old.* See 21:4 and Ac 7:8 (Isaac); Lk 1:59 (John the Baptist); 2:21 (Jesus); Php 3:5 (Paul). Abraham was 99 years old when the newly initiated rite of circumcision was performed on him (see v. 24). The Arabs, who consider themselves descendants of Ishmael, are circumcised at the age of 13 (see v. 25). For them, as for other peoples, it serves as a rite of transition from childhood to manhood, thus into full participation in the community.
17:14 *cut off from his people.* Removed from the covenant people by divine judgment (see note on v. 10).
17:15 *Sarai . . . Sarah.* Both names evidently mean "princess." The renaming stressed that she was to be the mother of nations and kings (see v. 16) and thus to serve the Lord's purpose (see note on v. 5).
17:16 *son.* Fulfilled in Isaac (see 21:2–3).
17:17 *laughed.* In temporary disbelief (see 18:12; cf. Ro 4:19–21). The verb is a pun on the name "Isaac," which means "he laughs" (see NIV text notes on v. 19 and 21:3; see also 18:12–15; 21:6).
17:20 *numbers.* See note on 13:16. *father of twelve rulers.* Fulfilled in 25:16.
17:21 Paul cites the choice of Isaac (and not Ishmael) as one proof of God's sovereign right to choose to save by grace alone (see Ro 9:6–13). *by this time next year.* See 21:2.
17:22 *God went up from him.* A solemn conclusion to the conversation.
17:23 *On that very day.* Abraham was characterized by prompt obedience (see note on 12:4).

were both circumcised on that same day. [27]And every male in Abraham's household[d], including those born in his household or bought from a foreigner, was circumcised with him.

The Three Visitors

18 The LORD appeared to Abraham[e] near the great trees of Mamre[f] while he was sitting at the entrance to his tent[g] in the heat of the day. [2]Abraham looked up[h] and saw three men[i] standing nearby. When he saw them, he hurried from the entrance of his tent to meet them and bowed low to the ground.[j]

[3]He said, "If I have found favor in your eyes,[k] my lord,[c] do not pass your servant[l] by. [4]Let a little water be brought, and then you may all wash your feet[m] and rest under this tree. [5]Let me get you something to eat,[n] so you can be refreshed and then go on your way—now that you have come to your servant."

"Very well," they answered, "do as you say."

[6]So Abraham hurried into the tent to Sarah. "Quick," he said, "get three seahs[d] of fine flour and knead it and bake some bread."[o]

[7]Then he ran to the herd and selected a choice, tender calf[p] and gave it to a servant, who hurried to prepare it. [8]He then brought some curds[q] and milk[r] and the calf that had been prepared, and set these before them.[s] While they ate, he stood near them under a tree.

[9]"Where is your wife Sarah?"[t] they asked him.

"There, in the tent,[u]" he said.

[10]Then the LORD[e] said, "I will surely return to you about this time next year,[v] and Sarah your wife will have a son."[w] Now Sarah was listening at the entrance to the tent, which was behind him. [11]Abraham and Sarah were already old and well advanced in years,[x] and Sarah was past the age of childbearing.[y] [12]So Sarah laughed[z] to herself as she thought, "After I am worn out and my master[a] is old, will I now have this pleasure?"

[13]Then the LORD said to Abraham, "Why did Sarah laugh and say, 'Will I really have a child, now that I am old?'[b] [14]Is anything too hard for the LORD?[c] I will return to you at the appointed time next year[d] and Sarah will have a son."[e]

[15]Sarah was afraid, so she lied and said, "I did not laugh."

But he said, "Yes, you did laugh."

Abraham Pleads for Sodom

[16]When the men[f] got up to leave, they looked down toward Sodom, and Abraham walked along with them to see them on their way. [17]Then the LORD said, "Shall I hide from Abraham[g] what I am about to do?[h] [18]Abraham will surely become a great and powerful nation,[i] and all nations on earth will be blessed through him. [19]For I have chosen him[j], so that he will direct

Cross references

17:27 dGe 14:14
18:1 eS Ge 12:7;
Ac 7:2
fS Ge 13:18
gGe 19:1; 23:10,
18; 34:20,24;
Ru 4:1; Ps 69:12;
Heb 11:9
18:2 hGe 24:63
iver 16,22;
Ge 19:1,10;
32:24; Jos 5:13;
Jdg 13:6-11;
Hos 12:3-4;
Heb 13:2
jS Ge 17:3;
S 43:28
18:3 kGe 19:19;
39:4; Ru 2:2,10,
13; 1Sa 1:18;
Est 2:15 lGe 32:4,
18,20; 33:5
18:4 mGe 19:2;
24:32; 43:24;
Jdg 19:21;
2Sa 11:8;
S Lk 7:44
18:5 nJdg 13:15;
19:5
18:6 oGe 19:3;
2Sa 13:8
18:7 pIsa 28:24;
Lk 15:23
18:8 qIsa 7:15,22
rJdg 4:19; 5:25
sJdg 6:19
18:9 tS Ge 3:9

uGe 24:67;
Heb 11:9
18:10
vS Ge 17:21;
21:2; 2Ki 4:16
wS Ge 17:6;
Ro 9:9*
18:11
xS Ge 17:17;
Lk 1:18
yS Ge 11:30;
Ro 4:19;
Heb 11:11-12
18:12
zS Ge 17:17
a1Pe 3:6
18:13
bS Ge 17:17
18:14 cJob 42:2;
Isa 40:29; 50:2;
51:9; Jer 32:17,
27; S Mt 19:26;

Ro 4:21 dS ver 10 eS Ge 17:19; Ro 9:9*; Gal 4:23 18:16
fS ver 2 18:17 gAm 3:7 hGe 19:24; Job 1:16; Ps 107:34
18:18 iS Ge 12:2; Gal 3:8* 18:19 jGe 17:9

c3 Or O Lord   d6 That is, probably about 20 quarts
(about 22 liters)   e10 Hebrew Then he   f12 Or
husband

Footnotes

18:1 appeared. See note on 12:7. great trees. See note on 12:6. Mamre. See note on 13:18. the heat of the day. Early afternoon.

18:2 three men. At least two of the "men" were angels (see 19:1; see also note on 16:7). The third may have been the Lord himself (see vv. 1,13,17,20,26,33; see especially v. 22). hurried. The story in vv. 2–8 illustrates Near Eastern hospitality in several ways: 1. Abraham gave prompt attention to the needs of his guests (vv. 2,6–7). 2. He bowed low to the ground (v. 2). 3. He politely addressed one of his guests as "my lord" and called himself "your servant" (vv. 3,5), a common way of speaking when addressing a superior (see, e.g., 19:2,18–19). 4. He acted as if it would be a favor to him if they allowed him to serve them (vv. 3–5). 5. He asked that water be brought to wash their feet (see v. 4), an act of courtesy to refresh a traveler in a hot, dusty climate (see 19:2; 24:32; 43:24). 6. He prepared a lavish meal for them (vv. 5–8; a similar lavish offering was presented to a divine messenger in Jdg 6:18–19; 13:15–16). 7. He stood nearby (v. 8), assuming the posture of a servant (see v. 22), to meet their every wish. Heb 13:2 is probably a reference to vv. 2–8 and 19:1–3.

18:6 bread. A plural word referring to round, thin loaves.
18:10 See 17:21. Paul quotes this promise of Isaac's birth (see v. 14) in Ro 9:9 and relates it to Abraham's spiritual

offspring (see Ro 9:7–8).
18:12 laughed. In disbelief, as also Abraham had at first (see note on 17:17).
18:14 Is anything too hard for the LORD? The answer is no, for Sarah as well as for her descendants Mary and Elizabeth (see Lk 1:34–37). Nothing within God's will, including creation (see Jer 32:17) and redemption (see Mt 19:25–26), is impossible for him.
18:16 Sodom. See notes on 10:19; 13:10.
18:17 Abraham was God's friend (see v. 19; 2Ch 20:7; Jas 2:23; see also Isa 41:8, but see note there). And because he was now God's covenant friend (see Job 29:4), God convened his heavenly council (see note on 1:26) at Abraham's tent. There he announced his purpose for Abraham (v. 10) and for the wicked of the plain (vv. 20–21)—redemption and judgment. He thus even gave Abraham opportunity to speak in his court and to intercede for the righteous in Sodom and Gomorrah. Abraham was later called a prophet (20:7). Here, in Abraham, is exemplified the great privilege of God's covenant people throughout the ages: God has revealed his purposes to them and allows their voice to be heard (in intercession) in the court of heaven.
18:18 a great and powerful nation . . . blessed through him. See note on 12:2–3.
18:19 chosen. Lit. "known" (as in Am 3:2).

his children[k] and his household after him to keep the way of the LORD[l] by doing what is right and just,[m] so that the LORD will bring about for Abraham what he has promised him." [n]

20Then the LORD said, "The outcry against Sodom[o] and Gomorrah is so great[p] and their sin so grievous[q] 21that I will go down[r] and see if what they have done is as bad as the outcry that has reached me. If not, I will know."

22The men[s] turned away and went toward Sodom,[t] but Abraham remained standing before the LORD.[g][u] 23Then Abraham approached him and said: "Will you sweep away the righteous with the wicked?[v] 24What if there are fifty righteous people in the city? Will you really sweep it away and not spare[h] the place for the sake of the fifty righteous people in it?[w] 25Far be it from you to do such a thing[x]—to kill the righteous with the wicked, treating the righteous[y] and the wicked alike.[z] Far be it from you! Will not the Judge[ia] of all the earth do right?" [b]

26The LORD said, "If I find fifty righteous people in the city of Sodom, I will spare the whole place for their sake.[c]"

27Then Abraham spoke up again: "Now that I have been so bold as to speak to the Lord, though I am nothing but dust and ashes,[d] 28what if the number of the righteous is five less than fifty? Will you destroy the whole city because of five people?"

"If I find forty-five there," he said, "I will not destroy it."

29Once again he spoke to him, "What if only forty are found there?"

He said, "For the sake of forty, I will not do it."

30Then he said, "May the Lord not be angry,[e] but let me speak. What if only thirty can be found there?"

He answered, "I will not do it if I find thirty there."

31Abraham said, "Now that I have been so bold as to speak to the Lord, what if only twenty can be found there?"

He said, "For the sake of twenty, I will not destroy it."

32Then he said, "May the Lord not be angry, but let me speak just once more.[f] What if only ten can be found there?"

He answered, "For the sake of ten,[g] I will not destroy it."

33When the LORD had finished speaking[h] with Abraham, he left,[i] and Abraham returned home.[j]

Sodom and Gomorrah Destroyed

19 The two angels[k] arrived at Sodom[l] in the evening, and Lot[m] was sitting in the gateway of the city.[n] When he saw them, he got up to meet them and bowed down with his face to the ground.[o] 2"My lords," he said, "please turn aside to your servant's house. You can wash your feet[p] and spend the night and then go on your way early in the morning."

"No," they answered, "we will spend the night in the square." [q]

3But he insisted[r] so strongly that they did go with him and entered his house.[s]

18:19 [k]Dt 4:9-10; 6:7 [l]Jos 24:15; Eph 6:4 [m]Ge 22:12,18; 26:5; 2Sa 8:15; Ps 17:2; 99:4; Jer 23:5 [n]S Ge 16:11; S Isa 14:1
18:20 [o]Isa 1:10; Jer 23:14; Eze 16:46 [p]Ge 19:13 [q]S Ge 13:13
18:21 [r]S Ge 11:5
18:22 [s]S ver 2 [t]Ge 19:1 [u]Ge 19:27
18:23 [v]Ex 23:7; Lev 4:3,22,27; Nu 16:22; Dt 27:25; 2Sa 24:17; Ps 11:4-7; 94:21; Eze 18:4; 2Pe 2:9
18:24 [w]ver 26; Jer 5:1
18:25 [x]Ge 44:7, 17; Job 8:3-7; 34:10 [y]Isa 5:20; Am 5:15; Mal 2:17; 3:18 [z]Pr 1:16-17 [a]Jdg 11:27; Job 9:15; Ps 7:11; 94:2; Heb 12:23 [b]Ge 20:4; Dt 32:4; 2Ch 19:7; Ezr 9:15; Ne 9:33; Job 8:3, 20; 34:10; 36:23; Ps 58:11; 75:7; 94:2; 119:137; Isa 3:10-11; Eze 18:25; Da 4:37; 9:14; Mal 2:17; Ro 3:6
18:26 [c]S ver 24
18:27 [d]S Ge 2:7; S Job 2:8
18:30 [e]ver 32; Ge 44:18; Ex 32:22
18:32 [f]S ver 30; Jdg 6:39 [g]Jer 5:1
18:33 [h]Ex 31:18 [i]S Ge 17:22 [j]Ge 31:55
19:1 [k]S Ge 18:2; Heb 13:2

[l]Ge 18:22 [m]S Ge 11:27 [n]S Ge 18:1 [o]S Ge 17:3; 48:12; Ru 2:10; 1Sa 25:23; 2Sa 14:33; 2Ki 2:15 19:2 [p]S Ge 18:4; Lk 7:44 [q]Jdg 19:15,20 19:3 [r]Ge 33:11 [s]Job 31:32

[g]22 Masoretic Text; an ancient Hebrew scribal tradition *but the LORD remained standing before Abraham* [h]24 Or *forgive*; also in verse 26 [i]25 Or *Ruler*

18:20 *outcry.* A cry of righteous indignation (cf. the blood of Abel, 4:10) that became one of the reasons for the destruction of the cities (see 19:13). *Gomorrah.* See notes on 10:19; 13:10. *sin so grievous.* The sin of Sodom (and probably of Gomorrah as well) was already proverbial (see 13:13) and remained so for centuries (see Eze 16:49-50).
18:21 *I will go down.* The result would be judgment (as in 11:5-9), but God also comes down to redeem (as in Ex 3:8). *see.* Not a denial of God's infinite knowledge but a figurative way of stating that he does not act out of ignorance or on the basis of mere complaints.
18:22 *Abraham remained standing before the LORD.* The text and NIV text note both illustrate the mutual accessibility that existed between God and his servant.
18:23 The second time Abraham intervened for his relatives and for Sodom (see 14:14-16).
18:25 *Judge of all the earth.* Abraham based his plea on the justice and authority (see NIV text note) of God, confident that God would do what was right (see Dt 32:4).
18:27 *Lord.* Abraham used the title "Lord," not the intimate name "LORD," throughout his prayer. He was appealing to God as "Judge of all the earth." *dust and ashes.* In

contrast to God's exalted position, Abraham described himself as insignificant (see Job 30:19; 42:6).
18:32 *just once more.* Abraham's questioning in vv. 23-32 did not arise from a spirit of haggling but of compassion for his relatives and of wanting to know God's ways. *ten.* Perhaps Abraham stopped at ten because he had been counting while praying: Lot, his wife, possibly two sons (see 19:12), at least two married daughters and their husbands (see 19:14 and NIV text note), and two unmarried daughters (see 19:8).
18:33 *home.* To Mamre (see v. 1). The next morning Abraham went back to see what God had done (see 19:27).
19:1-3 See note on 18:2.
19:1 *The two angels.* See notes on 16:7; 18:2. *Lot was sitting in the gateway of the city.* Lot had probably become a member of Sodom's ruling council, since a city gateway served as the administrative and judicial center where legal matters were discussed and prosecuted (see Ru 4:1-12).
19:2 *square.* A large open space near the main city gateway (see 2Ch 32:6) where public gatherings were held. Important cities like Jerusalem could have two or more squares (see Ne 8:16).

He prepared a meal for them, baking bread without yeast,[t] and they ate.[u] [4]Before they had gone to bed, all the men from every part of the city of Sodom[v]—both young and old—surrounded the house. [5]They called to Lot, "Where are the men who came to you tonight? Bring them out to us so that we can have sex with them."[w]

[6]Lot went outside to meet them[x] and shut the door behind him [7]and said, "No, my friends. Don't do this wicked thing. [8]Look, I have two daughters who have never slept with a man. Let me bring them out to you, and you can do what you like with them. But don't do anything to these men, for they have come under the protection of my roof."[y]

[9]"Get out of our way," they replied. And they said, "This fellow came here as an alien,[z] and now he wants to play the judge![a] We'll treat you worse than them." They kept bringing pressure on Lot and moved forward to break down the door.

[10]But the men[b] inside reached out and pulled Lot back into the house and shut the door. [11]Then they struck the men who were at the door of the house, young and old, with blindness[c] so that they could not find the door.

[12]The two men said to Lot, "Do you have anyone else here—sons-in-law, sons or daughters, or anyone else in the city who belongs to you?[d] Get them out of here, [13]because we[e] are going to destroy this place. The outcry to the LORD against its people is so great[f] that he has sent us to destroy it."[g]

[14]So Lot went out and spoke to his sons-in-law, who were pledged to marry[i] his daughters. He said, "Hurry and get out of this place, because the LORD is about to destroy the city![h]" But his sons-in-law thought he was joking.[i]

[15]With the coming of dawn, the angels urged Lot, saying, "Hurry! Take your wife and your two daughters who are here, or you will be swept away[j] when the city is punished.[k]"

[16]When he hesitated, the men grasped his hand and the hands of his wife and of his two daughters[l] and led them safely out of the city, for the LORD was merciful to them.[m] [17]As soon as they had brought them out, one of them said, "Flee for your lives![n] Don't look back,[o] and don't stop anywhere in the plain![p] Flee to the mountains[q] or you will be swept away!"

[18]But Lot said to them, "No, my lords,[k] please! [19]Your[l] servant has found favor in your[l] eyes,[r] and you[l] have shown great kindness[s] to me in sparing my life. But I can't flee to the mountains;[t] this disaster will overtake me, and I'll die. [20]Look, here is a town near enough to run to, and it is small. Let me flee to it—it is very small, isn't it? Then my life will be spared."

[21]He said to him, "Very well, I will grant this request[u] too; I will not overthrow the town you speak of. [22]But flee there quickly, because I cannot do anything until you reach it." (That is why the town was called Zoar.[m][v])

[23]By the time Lot reached Zoar,[w] the sun had risen over the land. [24]Then the LORD rained down burning sulfur[x] on Sodom and Gomorrah[y]—from the LORD out of the heavens.[z] [25]Thus he overthrew those cities[a] and the entire plain,[b] including all those living in the cities—and also the vegetation in the land.[c] [26]But Lot's wife looked back,[d] and she became a pillar of salt.[e]

Cross references

19:3 [t]Ex 12:39
[u]S Ge 18:6
19:4 [v]S Ge 13:13
19:5
[w]S Ge 13:13;
Lev 18:22;
Dt 23:18;
Jdg 19:22;
Ro 1:24-27
19:6 [x]Jdg 19:23
19:8 [y]Jdg 19:24;
2Pe 2:7-8
19:9 [z]Ge 23:4
[a]S Ge 13:8;
Ac 7:27
19:10 [b]S Ge 18:2
19:11
[c]Dt 28:28-29;
2Ki 6:18;
Ac 13:11
19:12 [d]S Ge 6:18
19:13 [e]Ex 12:29;
2Sa 24:16;
2Ki 19:35;
1Ch 21:12;
2Ch 32:21
[f]Ge 18:20
[g]1Ch 21:15;
Ps 78:49;
Jer 21:12; 25:18;
44:22; 51:45
19:14
[h]Nu 16:21;
Rev 18:4
[i]Ex 9:21;
1Ki 13:18;
Jer 5:12; 43:2;
Lk 17:28

19:15 [i]Nu 16:26;
Job 21:18;
Ps 58:9; 73:19;
90:5 [k]Rev 18:4
19:16 [l]2Pe 2:7
[m]Ex 34:6;
Ps 33:18-19
19:17 [n]1Ki 19:3;
Jer 48:6 [o]ver 26
[p]S Ge 13:12
[q]S ver 19;
S Ge 14:10;
Mt 24:16
19:19 [r]S Ge 6:8;
S 18:3 [s]Ge 24:12;
39:21; 40:14;
47:29; Ru 1:8;
2:20; 3:10 [t]S ver 17,30
19:21
[u]1Sa 25:35;
2Sa 14:8;
Job 42:9
19:22
[v]S Ge 13:10
19:23
[w]S Ge 13:10
19:24
[x]Job 18:15;
Ps 11:6;
Isa 30:33; 34:9;
Eze 38:22
[y]Dt 29:23;

Isa 1:9; 13:19; Jer 49:18; 50:40; Am 4:11 [z]S Ge 18:17;
S Lev 10:2; S Mt 10:15; Lk 17:29 19:25 [a]S ver 24;
Eze 26:16; Zep 3:8; Hag 2:22 [b]S Ge 13:12 [c]Ps 107:34;
Isa 1:10; Jer 20:16; 23:14; La 4:6; Eze 16:48 19:26 [d]S ver
17 [e]Lk 17:32

[i]14 Or *were married to*   [k]18 Or *No, Lord*; or *No, my
lord*   [l]19 The Hebrew is singular.   [m]22 *Zoar* means
small.

19:3 *bread without yeast.* So that it could be baked quickly (see 18:6; Ex 12:39).

19:4–9 See Jdg 19:22–25.

19:5 *have sex with them.* Homosexuality was so characteristic of the men of Sodom (see Jude 7) that it is still often called sodomy.

19:8 *under the protection of my roof.* Ancient hospitality obliged a host to protect his guests in every situation.

19:9 *This fellow came here as an alien, and now he wants to play the judge.* Centuries later, Moses was also considered an outsider and accused of setting himself up as a judge (see Ex 2:14; Ac 7:27).

19:13 *we are going to destroy this place.* Sodom's wickedness had made it ripe for destruction (see Isa 3:9; Jer 23:14; La 4:6; Zep 2:8–9; 2Pe 2:6; Jude 7).

19:14 *his sons-in-law thought he was joking.* Lot appar-

ently had lost his power of moral persuasion even among his family members.

19:16 *hesitated.* Perhaps because of reluctance to leave his material possessions. *his hand and the hands of his wife and of his two daughters.* The ten righteous people required to save Sodom (see 18:32) had now been reduced to four. *the LORD was merciful to them.* Deliverance is due to divine mercy, not to human righteousness (cf. Tit 3:5).

19:24 *rained down burning sulfur.* Perhaps from a violent earthquake spewing up asphalt, such as is still found in this region.

19:26 *Lot's wife looked back, and she became a pillar of salt.* Her disobedient hesitation (see v. 17) became proverbial in later generations (see Lk 17:32). Even today, grotesque salt formations near the southern end of the Dead Sea are reminders of her folly.

²⁷Early the next morning Abraham got up and returned to the place where he had stood before the Lord.ᶠ ²⁸He looked down toward Sodom and Gomorrah, toward all the land of the plain, and he saw dense smoke rising from the land, like smoke from a furnace.ᵍ

²⁹So when God destroyed the cities of the plain,ʰ he remembered ⁱ Abraham, and he brought Lot out of the catastropheʲ that overthrew the cities where Lot had lived.ᵏ

Lot and His Daughters

³⁰Lot and his two daughters left Zoarˡ and settled in the mountains,ᵐ for he was afraid to stay in Zoar. He and his two daughters lived in a cave. ³¹One day the older daughter said to the younger, "Our father is old, and there is no man around here to lie with us, as is the custom all over the earth. ³²Let's get our father to drink wine and then lie with him and preserve our family lineⁿ through our father."ᵒ

³³That night they got their father to drink wine, and the older daughter went in and lay with him. He was not aware of it when she lay down or when she got up.ᵖ

³⁴The next day the older daughter said to the younger, "Last night I lay with my father. Let's get him to drink wine again tonight, and you go in and lie with him so we can preserve our family line through our father."ᑫ ³⁵So they got their father to drink wineʳ that night also, and the younger daughter went and lay with him. Again he was not aware of it when she lay down or when she got up.ˢ

³⁶So both of Lot's daughters became pregnant by their father.ᵗ ³⁷The older daughter had a son, and she named him Moabⁿ;ᵘ he is the father of the Moabitesᵛ of today. ³⁸The younger daughter also had a son, and she named him Ben-Ammiᵒ; he is the father of the Ammonitesʷ of today.

Abraham and Abimelech

20:1–18Ref — Ge 12:10–20; 26:1–11

20 Now Abraham moved on from thereˣ into the region of the Negevʸ and lived between Kadeshᶻ and Shur.ᵃ For a whileᵇ he stayed in Gerar,ᶜ ²and there Abraham said of his wife Sarah, "She is my sister.ᵈ" Then Abimelechᵉ king of Gerar sent for Sarah and took her.ᶠ

³But God came to Abimelechᵍ in a dreamʰ one night and said to him, "You are as good as deadⁱ because of the woman you have taken; she is a married woman."ʲ

⁴Now Abimelech had not gone near her, so he said, "Lord, will you destroy an innocent nation?ᵏ ⁵Did he not say to me, 'She is my sister,'ˡ and didn't she also say, 'He is my brother'? I have done this with a clear conscienceᵐ and clean hands.ⁿ"

⁶Then God said to him in the dream, "Yes, I know you did this with a clear conscience, and so I have keptᵒ you from sinning against me.ᵖ That is why I did not let you touch her. ⁷Now return the man's wife, for he is a prophet,ᑫ and he will pray for youʳ and you will live. But if you do not return her, you may be sure that you and all yours will die."ˢ

⁸Early the next morning Abimelech summoned all his officials, and when he told them all that had happened, they were very much afraid. ⁹Then Abimelech called Abraham in and said, "What have you done to us? How have I wronged you that you have brought such great guilt upon me and my kingdom? You have done things to me that should not be done.ᵗ" ¹⁰And Abimelech asked Abraham, "What was your reason for doing this?"

19:27 ᶠGe 18:22
19:28 ᵍGe 15:17; Ex 19:18; Rev 9:2; 18:9
19:29 ʰS Ge 13:12 ⁱS Ge 8:1 ʲ2Pe 2:7 ᵏGe 14:12; Eze 14:16
19:30 ˡver 22; S Ge 13:10 ᵐS ver 19; S Ge 14:10
19:32 ⁿS Ge 16:2 ᵒver 34,36; Ge 38:18
19:33 ᵖver 35
19:34 ᑫS ver 32
19:35 ʳGe 9:21 ˢver 33
19:36 ᵗS ver 32
19:37 ᵘGe 36:35; Ex 15:15; Nu 25:1; Isa 15:1; 25:10; Jer 25:21; 48:1; Eze 25:8; Zep 2:9 ᵛNu 22:4; 24:17; Dt 2:9; Jdg 3:28; Ru 1:4,22; 1Sa 14:47; 22:3-4; 2Sa 8:2; 2Ki 1:1; 3:4; Ezr 9:1; Ps 108:9; Jer 48:1
19:38 ʷNu 21:24; Dt 2:19; 23:3; Jos 12:2; Jdg 3:13; 10:6,7; 1Sa 11:1-11; 14:47; 1Ch 19:1; 2Ch 20:23; 26:8; 27:5; Ne 2:19; 4:3; Jer 25:21; 40:14; 49:1; Eze 21:28; 25:2; Am 1:13

20:1 ˣGe 18:1 ʸS Ge 12:9 ᶻS Ge 14:7 ᵃS Ge 16:7 ᵇGe 26:3 ᶜGe 26:1,6,17
20:2 ᵈS Ge 12:13 ᵉver 14; Ge 21:22; 26:1 ᶠS Ge 12:15
20:3 ᵍNu 22:9,20 ʰGe 28:12; 31:10,24; 37:5,9; 40:5; 41:1; Nu 12:6; Dt 13:1; Job 33:15; Da 2:1; 4:5 ⁱEx 10:7; 12:33; Ps 105:38 ʲver 7; Ge 26:11; 1Ch 16:21; Ps 105:14
20:4 ᵏS Ge 18:25
20:5 ˡS Ge 12:19 ᵐS Ge 17:1 ⁿPs 7:8; 25:21; 26:6; 41:12

20:6 ᵒ1Sa 25:26,34 ᵖS Ge 13:13; Ps 41:4; 51:4 20:7 ᑫDt 18:18; 34:10; 2Ki 3:11; 5:3; 1Ch 16:22; Ps 105:15 ʳver 17; Ex 8:8; Nu 11:2; 12:13; 1Sa 7:5; 1Ki 13:6; Job 42:8; Jer 18:20; 37:3; 42:2 ˢS ver 3; S Ps 9:5 20:9 ᵗS Ge 12:18; 34:7

ⁿ37 Moab sounds like the Hebrew for from father.
ᵒ38 Ben-Ammi means son of my people.

19:29 God . . . remembered Abraham. See note on 8:1. he brought Lot out of the catastrophe. Lot's deliverance was the main concern of Abraham's prayer (18:23–32), which God now answered.

19:33 they got their father to drink wine, and the older daughter went in and lay with him. Though Lot's role was somewhat passive, he bore the basic responsibility for the drunkenness and incest that eventually resulted in his two daughters' becoming pregnant by him (see v. 36).

19:36–38 The sons born to Lot's daughters were the ancestors of the Moabites and Ammonites (see Dt 2:9,19), two nations that were to become bitter enemies of Abraham's descendants (see, e.g., 1Sa 14:47; 2Ch 20:1).

20:1 between Kadesh and Shur. See notes on 14:7; 16:7. Gerar. Located at the edge of Philistine territory, about halfway between Gaza on the Mediterranean coast and Beersheba in the northern Negev.

20:2 Abimelech. Probably the father or grandfather of the later king who bore the same name (see 26:1).

20:3 dream. Once again God intervened to spare the mother of the promised offspring. Dreams were a frequent mode of revelation in the OT (see 28:12; 31:10–11; 37:5–9; 40:5; 41:1; Nu 12:6; Jdg 7:13; 1Ki 3:5; Da 2:3; 4:5; 7:1).

20:7 prophet. See note on 18:17. Abraham was the first man to bear this title (see Ps 105:15).

[11] Abraham replied, "I said to myself, 'There is surely no fear of God[u] in this place, and they will kill me because of my wife.'[v] [12] Besides, she really is my sister,[w] the daughter of my father though not of my mother; and she became my wife. [13] And when God had me wander[x] from my father's household,[y] I said to her, 'This is how you can show your love to me: Everywhere we go, say of me, "He is my brother."'"

[14] Then Abimelech[z] brought sheep and cattle and male and female slaves and gave them to Abraham,[a] and he returned Sarah his wife to him. [15] And Abimelech said, "My land is before you; live wherever you like."[b]

[16] To Sarah he said, "I am giving your brother a thousand shekels[p] of silver. This is to cover the offense against you before all who are with you; you are completely vindicated."

[17] Then Abraham prayed to God,[c] and God healed Abimelech, his wife and his slave girls so they could have children again, [18] for the LORD had closed up every womb in Abimelech's household because of Abraham's wife Sarah.[d]

The Birth of Isaac

21 Now the LORD was gracious to Sarah[e] as he had said, and the LORD did for Sarah what he had promised.[f] [2] Sarah became pregnant and bore a son[g] to Abraham in his old age,[h] at the very time God had promised him.[i] [3] Abraham gave the name Isaac[q][j] to the son Sarah bore him. [4] When his son Isaac was eight days old, Abraham circumcised him,[k] as God commanded him. [5] Abraham was a hundred years old[l] when his son Isaac was born to him.

[6] Sarah said, "God has brought me laughter,[m] and everyone who hears about this will laugh with me." [7] And she added, "Who would have said to Abraham that Sarah would nurse children? Yet I have borne him a son in his old age."[n]

Hagar and Ishmael Sent Away

[8] The child grew and was weaned,[o] and on the day Isaac was weaned Abraham held a great feast. [9] But Sarah saw that the son whom Hagar the Egyptian had borne to Abraham[p] was mocking,[q] [10] and she said to Abraham, "Get rid of that slave woman[r] and her son, for that slave woman's son will never share in the inheritance with my son Isaac."[s]

[11] The matter distressed Abraham greatly because it concerned his son.[t] [12] But God said to him, "Do not be so distressed about the boy and your maidservant. Listen to whatever Sarah tells you, because it is through Isaac that your offspring[r] will be reckoned.[u] [13] I will make the son of the maidservant into a nation[v] also, because he is your offspring."

[14] Early the next morning Abraham took some food and a skin of water and gave them to Hagar.[w] He set them on her shoulders and then sent her off with the

---

p[16] That is, about 25 pounds (about 11.5 kilograms)
q[3] *Isaac* means *he laughs.*
r[12] Or *seed*

Cross references (center column)

20:11
u Ge 42:18;
Ne 5:15;
Job 31:23;
Ps 36:1; Pr 16:6
v S Ge 12:12;
31:31
20:12
w S Ge 12:13
20:13 x Dt 26:5;
1Ch 16:20;
Isa 30:28; 63:17
y S Ge 12:1
20:14 z S ver 2
a S Ge 12:16
20:15
b S Ge 13:9;
S 45:18
20:17 c S ver 7;
Job 42:9
20:18 d Ge 12:17
21:1 e 1Sa 2:21
f S Ge 8:1; S 17:6,
21; 18:14;
Gal 4:23;
Heb 11:1
21:2
g S Ge 17:19;
S 30:6 h Gal 4:22;
Heb 11:11
i S Ge 18:10
21:3 j S Ge 16:11;
S 17:19; Jos 24:3
21:4
k S Ge 17:10,12;
Ac 7:8
21:5 l S Ge 12:4;
Heb 6:15
21:6 m Ge 17:17;
Job 8:21;
Ps 126:2;
Isa 12:6; 35:2;
44:23; 52:9; 54:1
21:7 n S Ge 17:17
21:8 o 1Sa 1:23
21:9 p S Ge 16:15
q Ge 39:14;
Gal 4:29
21:10 r Ge 39:17
s Ge 25:6;
Gal 4:30*
21:11 t Ge 17:18
21:12 u Mt 1:2;
Ro 9:7*;
Heb 11:18*
21:13
v S Ge 13:16
21:14
w S Ge 16:1

Notes (bottom)

20:11 *fear of God.* A conventional phrase equivalent to "true religion." "Fear" in this phrase has the sense of reverential trust in God that includes commitment to his revealed will (word).

20:12 *she really is my sister, the daughter of my father though not of my mother.* Abraham's half-truth was a sinful deception, not a legitimate explanation.

20:14–16 Abimelech's generosity was a strong contrast to Abraham's fearfulness and deception.

20:16 *shekels.* Though not in the Hebrew, the word is correctly supplied here as the most common unit of weight in ancient times. Originally the shekel was only a weight, not a coin, since coinage was not invented till the seventh century B.C.

21:1 *was gracious to Sarah as he had said.* See 17:16. *did for Sarah what he had promised.* See Gal 4:22–23,28.

21:3 *Isaac.* See note on 17:17.

21:4 See notes on 17:10,12.

21:5 Abraham, in fulfillment of the promise made to him (see 17:16), miraculously became a father at the age of 100 years (see 17:17).

21:6 *laughter . . . laugh.* See note on 17:17.

21:8 *weaned.* At age two or three, as was customary in the ancient Near East.

21:9 *the son whom Hagar the Egyptian had borne.* Ishmael, who was in his late teens at this time (see 16:15–16). *mocking.* Or "at play." In either case, Sarah saw Ishmael as a potential threat to Isaac's inheritance (v. 10).

21:10 *of that slave woman and her son.* See Gal 4:21–31. Driving them out would have had the effect of disinheriting Ishmael.

21:11 *The matter distressed Abraham.* Both love and legal custom played a part in Abraham's anguish. He knew that the customs of his day, illustrated later in the Nuzi tablets (see chart on "Ancient Texts Relating to the OT," p. 5), prohibited the arbitrary expulsion of a servant girl's son (whose legal status was relatively weak in any case).

21:12 *Listen to whatever Sarah tells you.* God overruled in this matter (as he had done earlier; see 15:4), promising Abraham that both Isaac and Ishmael would have numerous descendants. *it is through Isaac that your offspring will be reckoned.* See Ro 9:6–8 and Heb 11:17–19 for broader spiritual applications of this statement.

21:14 *Early the next morning.* Though Abraham would now be separated from Ishmael for the first time, he responded to God's command with prompt obedience (see note on 12:4). *Beersheba.* See note on v. 31.

boy. She went on her way and wandered in the desert of Beersheba. *x*

15When the water in the skin was gone, she put the boy under one of the bushes. 16Then she went off and sat down nearby, about a bowshot away, for she thought, "I cannot watch the boy die." And as she sat there nearby, she*s* began to sob. *y*

17God heard the boy crying, *z* and the angel of God*a* called to Hagar from heaven*b* and said to her, "What is the matter, Hagar? Do not be afraid; *c* God has heard the boy crying as he lies there. 18Lift the boy up and take him by the hand, for I will make him into a great nation. *d*"

19Then God opened her eyes*e* and she saw a well of water.*f* So she went and filled the skin with water and gave the boy a drink.

20God was with the boy*g* as he grew up. He lived in the desert and became an archer. 21While he was living in the Desert of Paran,*h* his mother got a wife for him*i* from Egypt.

The Treaty at Beersheba

22At that time Abimelech*j* and Phicol the commander of his forces*k* said to Abraham, "God is with you in everything you do. *l* 23Now swear*m* to me here before God that you will not deal falsely with me or my children or my descendants. *n* Show to me and the country where you are living as an alien the same kindness I have shown to you." *o*

24Abraham said, "I swear it."

25Then Abraham complained to Abimelech about a well of water that Abimelech's servants had seized. *p* 26But Abime-

lech said, "I don't know who has done this. You did not tell me, and I heard about it only today."

27So Abraham brought sheep and cattle and gave them to Abimelech, and the two men made a treaty. *q* 28Abraham set apart seven ewe lambs from the flock, 29and Abimelech asked Abraham, "What is the meaning of these seven ewe lambs you have set apart by themselves?"

30He replied, "Accept these seven lambs from my hand as a witness*r* that I dug this well. *s*"

31So that place was called Beersheba,*t* *t* because the two men swore an oath*u* there.

32After the treaty*v* had been made at Beersheba, *w* Abimelech and Phicol the commander of his forces*x* returned to the land of the Philistines.*y* 33Abraham planted a tamarisk tree*z* in Beersheba, and there he called upon the name of the LORD, *a* the Eternal God. *b* 34And Abraham stayed in the land of the Philistines*c* for a long time.

Abraham Tested

22 Some time later God tested*d* Abraham. He said to him, "Abraham!"

"Here I am," *e* he replied.

2Then God said, "Take your son*f*, your only son, Isaac, whom you love, and go to

---

21:14 *x*ver 31, 32; Ge 22:19; 26:33; 28:10; 46:1,5; Jos 15:28; 19:2; Jdg 20:1; 1Sa 3:20; 1Ch 4:28; Ne 11:27
21:16 *y*Jer 6:26; Am 8:10; Zec 12:10
21:17 *z*Ex 3:7; Nu 20:16; Dt 26:7; Ps 6:8
*a*S Ge 16:7
*b*Ge 22:11,15
*c*S Ge 15:1
21:18 *d*S Ge 17:20
21:19 *e*Nu 22:31
*f*S Ge 16:7
21:20 *g*Ge 26:3, 24; 28:15; 39:2, 21,23; Lk 1:66
21:21 *h*S Ge 14:6
*i*Ge 24:4,38; 28:2; 34:4,8; Jdg 14:2
21:22 *j*S Ge 20:2
*k*ver 32; Ge 26:26
*l*ver 23; Ge 26:28; 28:15; 31:3,5,42; 39:2, 3; 1Sa 3:19; 16:18; 2Ch 1:1; Ps 46:7; Isa 7:14; 8:8,10; 41:10; 43:5
21:23 *m*ver 31; Ge 25:33; 26:31; 31:53; Jos 2:12; Ki 2:8
*n*1Sa 24:21 *o*S ver 22; Jos 2:12
21:25 *p*Ge 26:15, 18,20-22
21:27 *q*ver 31, 32; Ge 26:28,31; 31:44,53
21:30 *r*Ge 31:44, 47,48,50,52; Jos 22:27,28,34; 24:27; Isa 19:20; Mal 2:14 *s*ver 25; Ge 26:25,32
21:31 *t*S ver 14
*u*S ver 23,S 27
21:32 *v*S ver 27
*w*S ver 14 *x*S ver 22 *y*S Ge 10:14
21:33 *z*1Sa 22:6; 31:13 *a*S Ge 4:26

*b*Ex 15:18; Dt 32:40; 33:27; Job 36:26; Ps 10:16; 45:6; 90:2; 93:2; 102:24; 103:19; 146:10; Isa 40:28; Jer 10:10; Hab 1:12; 3:6; Heb 13:8 **21:34** *c*S Ge 10:14 **22:1** *d*Ex 15:25; 16:4; 20:20; Dt 8:2,16; 13:3; Jdg 2:22; 3:1; 2Ch 32:31; Ps 66:10; Heb 11:17; Jas 1:12-13 *e*ver 11; Ge 31:11; 46:2; 1Sa 3:4,6,8; Isa 6:8 **22:2** *f*ver 12,16; Jn 3:16; Heb 11:17; 1Jn 4:9

s16 Hebrew; Septuagint *the child*   **t**31 *Beersheba* can mean *well of seven* or *well of the oath.*

21:15 *one of the bushes.* See note on v. 33.
21:17 *God heard . . . God has heard.* A pun on the name "Ishmael" (see NIV text note on 16:11; see also 17:20).
21:21 *Desert of Paran.* Located in north central Sinai. *his mother got a wife for him from Egypt.* Parents often arranged their children's marriages (see ch. 24).
21:22 *Abimelech.* See 20:2 and note. *Phicol.* Either a family name or an official title, since it reappears over 60 years later (25:26) in a similar context (26:26).
21:23 *swear to me . . . before God . . . Show to me . . . kindness.* Phrases commonly used when making covenants or treaties (see vv. 27,32). "Kindness" as used here refers to acts of friendship (cf. v. 27; 20:14). Such covenants always involved oaths.
21:27 *sheep and cattle.* Probably to be used in the treaty ceremony (see 15:10).
21:31 *Beersheba, because the two men swore an oath there.* See NIV text note. For a similar pun on the name see 26:33. Beersheba, an important town in the northern Negev, marked the southernmost boundary of the Israelite monarchy in later times (see, e.g., 2Sa 17:11). An ancient well there is still pointed out as "Abraham's well" (see v. 25), but its authenticity is not certain.

21:32 *Philistines.* See note on 10:14.
21:33 *tamarisk.* A shrub or small tree that thrives in arid regions. Its leafy branches provide welcome shade, and it is probably the unidentified bush under which Hagar put Ishmael in v. 15. *Eternal God.* The Hebrew is *El Olam,* a phrase unique to this passage. It is one of a series of names that include *El,* "God," as an element (see 14:19 and note; 17:1 and note; 33:20; 35:7).
22:1 *Some time later.* Isaac had grown into adolescence or young manhood, as implied also by 21:34 ("a long time"). *tested.* Not "tempted," for God does not tempt (Jas 1:13). Satan tempts us (see 1Co 7:5) in order to make us fall; God tests us in order to confirm our faith (Ex 20:20) or prove our commitment (Dt 8:2). See note on Mt 4:1. *Here I am.* Abraham answered with the response of a servant, as did Moses and Samuel when God called them by name (see Ex 3:4; 1Sa 3:4,6,8).
22:2 *your son, your only son, Isaac, whom you love.* In the Hebrew text "Isaac" follows the clause "whom you love," in order to heighten the effect: "your son, your only son, whom you love—Isaac." Isaac was the "only son" of the promise (21:12). *region of Moriah.* The author of Chronicles identifies the area as the temple mount in Jerusalem (2Ch 3:1).

the region of Moriah.*g* Sacrifice him there as a burnt offering*h* on one of the mountains I will tell you about.*i* "

³Early the next morning*j* Abraham got up and saddled his donkey. He took with him two of his servants and his son Isaac. When he had cut enough wood for the burnt offering, he set out for the place God had told him about. ⁴On the third day Abraham looked up and saw the place in the distance. ⁵He said to his servants, "Stay here with the donkey while I and the boy go over there. We will worship and then we will come back to you.*k* "

⁶Abraham took the wood for the burnt offering and placed it on his son Isaac,*l* and he himself carried the fire and the knife.*m* As the two of them went on together, ⁷Isaac spoke up and said to his father Abraham, "Father?"

"Yes, my son?" Abraham replied.

"The fire and wood are here," Isaac said, "but where is the lamb*n* for the burnt offering?"

⁸Abraham answered, "God himself will provide*o* the lamb*p* for the burnt offering, my son." And the two of them went on together.

⁹When they reached the place God had told him about,*q* Abraham built an altar*r* there and arranged the wood*s* on it. He bound his son Isaac and laid him on the altar,*t* on top of the wood. ¹⁰Then he reached out his hand and took the knife*u*

to slay his son.*v* ¹¹But the angel of the LORD*w* called out to him from heaven,*x* "Abraham! Abraham!"*y*

"Here I am,"*z* he replied.

¹²"Do not lay a hand on the boy," he said. "Do not do anything to him. Now I know that you fear God,*a* because you have not withheld from me your son, your only son.*b* "

¹³Abraham looked up and there in a thicket he saw a ram*u* caught by its horns.*c* He went over and took the ram and sacrificed it as a burnt offering instead of his son.*d* ¹⁴So Abraham called*e* that place The LORD*f* Will Provide. And to this day it is said, "On the mountain of the LORD it will be provided.*g* "

¹⁵The angel of the LORD*h* called to Abraham from heaven*i* a second time ¹⁶and said, "I swear by myself,*j* declares the LORD, that because you have done this and have not withheld your son, your only son,*k* ¹⁷I will surely bless you*l* and make your descendants*m* as numerous as the stars in the sky*n* and as the sand on the seashore.*o* Your descendants will take possession of the cities of their enemies,*p* ¹⁸and through your offspring*v* all nations

---

22:2 *g*2Ch 3:1
*h*S Ge 8:20 *i*ver 9
22:3 *j*Jos 8:10
22:5 *k*Ex 24:14
22:6 *l*Jn 19:17
*m*ver 10;
Jdg 19:29
22:7
*n*Ex 29:38-42;
Lev 1:10;
Rev 13:8
22:8 *o*ver 14
*p*ver 13; S Jn 1:29
22:9 *q*ver 2
*r*S Ge 4:26;
S 8:20 *s*Lev 1:7;
1Ki 18:33
*t*Heb 11:17-19;
Jas 2:21
22:10 *u*S ver 6

*v*ver 3;
S Ge 18:19
22:11
*w*S Ge 16:7
*x*S Ge 21:17
*y*Ge 46:2 *z*S ver 1
22:12
*a*S Ge 18:19;
42:18; Ex 18:21;
1Sa 15:22;
Job 1:1; 37:24;
Pr 8:13;
Jas 2:21-22 *b*S ver
2; Jn 3:16;
1Jn 4:9
22:13 *c*S ver 8
*d*S Ge 8:20;
Ro 8:32
22:14 *e*Ex 17:15;
Jdg 6:24
*f*Isa 30:29 *g*ver 8
22:15 *h*S Ge 16:7
*i*S Ge 21:17
22:16 *j*Ex 13:11;
32:13; 33:1;
Isa 45:23; 62:8;
Jer 22:5; 44:26;
49:13; 51:14;
Am 6:8; Lk 1:73;
Heb 6:13 *k*S ver 2
22:17 *l*S Ge 12:2
*m*Heb 6:14*
*n*S Ge 15:5;
Ex 32:13; Dt 7:7;

28:62 *o*S Ge 12:2; S 26:24; Hos 1:10; Ro 9:27; Heb 11:12
*p*Ge 24:60; Est 9:2

*u*13 Many manuscripts of the Masoretic Text, Samaritan Pentateuch, Septuagint and Syriac; most manuscripts of the Masoretic Text *a ram behind him*   *v*18 Or *seed*

Today "Mount Moriah" is occupied by the Dome of the Rock, an impressive Muslim structure erected in A.D. 691. A large outcropping of rock inside the building is still pointed to as the traditional site of the intended sacrifice of Isaac. *Sacrifice him.* Abraham had committed himself by covenant to be obedient to the Lord and had consecrated his son Isaac to the Lord by circumcision. The Lord put his servant's faith and loyalty to the supreme test, thereby instructing Abraham, Isaac and their descendants as to the kind of total consecration the Lord's covenant requires. The test also foreshadowed the perfect consecration in sacrifice that another offspring of Abraham would undergo (see note on v. 16) in order to wholly consecrate Abraham and his spiritual descendants to God and to fulfill the covenant promises.
22:3 *Early the next morning.* Prompt obedience, even under such trying circumstances, characterized Abraham's response to God (see note on 12:4).
22:4 *third day.* Three days would be necessary for the journey from Beersheba (see v. 19) to Jerusalem.
22:5 *boy.* See v. 12. The Hebrew for this word has a wide range of meaning, from an infant (see Ex 2:6) to a young man of military age (see 1Ch 12:28). *we will come back to you.* Abraham, the man of faith and "the father of all who believe" (Ro 4:11), "reasoned that God could raise the dead" (Heb 11:19) if that were necessary to fulfill his promise.
22:8 *God himself will provide the lamb.* The immediate fulfillment of Abraham's trusting response was the ram of v. 13, but its ultimate fulfillment is the Lamb of God (Jn 1:29, 36).

22:9 *laid him on the altar, on top of the wood.* Isaac is here a type (prefiguration) of Christ (see note on v. 16).
22:11 *angel of the LORD.* See note on 16:7. *Abraham! Abraham!* The repetition of the name indicates urgency (see 46:2; Ex 3:4; 1Sa 3:10; Ac 9:4). *Here I am.* See note on v. 1.
22:12 *fear God.* See note on 20:11. *you have not withheld from me your son, your only son.* See v. 16. Abraham's "faith was made complete by what he did" (Jas 2:21–22).
22:13 *instead of.* Substitutionary sacrifice of one life for another is mentioned here for the first time. As the ram died in Isaac's place, so also Jesus gave his life as a ransom "for" (lit. "instead of") many (Mk 10:45).
22:14 *mountain of the LORD.* During the Israelite monarchy the phrase referred to the temple mount in Jerusalem (see Ps 24:3; Isa 2:3; 30:29; Zec 8:3).
22:16 *I swear by myself.* There is no greater name in which the Lord can take an oath (see Heb 6:13). *you . . . have not withheld your son, your only son.* Abraham's devotion is paralleled by God's love to us in Christ as reflected in Jn 3:16 and Ro 8:32, which may allude to this verse.
22:17 *descendants as numerous as the stars in the sky.* See 13:16; 15:5 and notes. *sand on the seashore.* Fulfilled, at least in part, during Solomon's reign (see 1Ki 4:20). *cities.* Lit. "gates." Taking possession of the gate of a city was tantamount to occupying the city itself (see 24:60).
22:18 *all nations on earth will be blessed.* See note on 12:2–3. *because you have obeyed me.* See note on 17:9.

on earth will be blessed,^{q} because you have obeyed me."^{r}

[19] Then Abraham returned to his servants, and they set off together for Beersheba.^{s} And Abraham stayed in Beersheba.

Nahor's Sons

[20] Some time later Abraham was told, "Milcah is also a mother; she has borne sons to your brother Nahor:^{t} [21] Uz^u the firstborn, Buz^v his brother, Kemuel (the father of Aram), [22] Kesed, Hazo, Pildash, Jidlaph and Bethuel.^{w}" [23] Bethuel became the father of Rebekah.^{x} Milcah bore these eight sons to Abraham's brother Nahor.^{y} [24] His concubine,^{z} whose name was Reumah, also had sons: Tebah, Gaham, Tahash and Maacah.

The Death of Sarah

23 Sarah lived to be a hundred and twenty-seven years old. [2] She died at Kiriath Arba^a (that is, Hebron)^b in the land of Canaan, and Abraham went to mourn for Sarah and to weep over her.^{c}

[3] Then Abraham rose from beside his dead wife and spoke to the Hittites.^{wd} He said, [4] "I am an alien and a stranger^e among you. Sell me some property for a burial site here so I can bury my dead.^{f}"

[5] The Hittites replied to Abraham, [6] "Sir, listen to us. You are a mighty prince^g among us. Bury your dead in the choicest of our tombs. None of us will refuse you his tomb for burying your dead."

[7] Then Abraham rose and bowed down before the people of the land, the Hittites. [8] He said to them, "If you are willing to let me bury my dead, then listen to me and intercede with Ephron son of Zohar^h on my behalf [9] so he will sell me the cave of Machpelah,^{i} which belongs to him and is at the end of his field. Ask him to sell it to me for the full price as a burial site among you."

[10] Ephron the Hittite was sitting among his people and he replied to Abraham in the hearing of all the Hittites^j who had come to the gate^k of his city. [11] "No, my lord," he said. "Listen to me; I give^{xl} you the field, and I give^x you the cave that is in it. I give^x it to you in the presence of my people. Bury your dead."

[12] Again Abraham bowed down before the people of the land [13] and he said to Ephron in their hearing, "Listen to me, if you will. I will pay the price of the field. Accept it from me so I can bury my dead there."

[14] Ephron answered Abraham, [15] "Listen to me, my lord; the land is worth four hundred shekels^y of silver,^{m} but what is that between me and you? Bury your dead."

[16] Abraham agreed to Ephron's terms and weighed out for him the price he had named in the hearing of the Hittites: four

Cross references
22:18 ^{q}S Ge 12:2,3; Ac 3:25*; Gal 3:8* ^{r}S ver 10; Ge 17:2,9; Ps 105:9
22:19 ^{s}Ge 21:14; 26:23; 28:10
22:20 ^{t}S Ge 11:29
22:21 ^{u}S Ge 10:23 ^{v}Job 32:2; Jer 25:23
22:22 ^{w}Ge 24:15,47; 25:20
22:23 ^{x}Ge 24:15 ^{y}S Ge 11:29
22:24 ^{z}Ge 25:6; 35:22; 36:12; Jdg 8:31; 2Sa 3:7; 1Ki 2:22; 11:3; 1Ch 1:32; SS 6:8
23:2 ^{a}Jos 14:15; 15:13; 20:7; 21:11 ^{b}S Ge 13:18 ^{c}Ge 24:67
23:3 ^{d}S Ge 10:15
23:4 ^{e}S Ge 17:8; 19:9; Ex 2:22; Lev 25:23; Ps 39:12; 105:12; 119:19; Heb 11:9,13 ^{f}Ge 49:30; Ac 7:16
23:6 ^{g}Ge 14:14-16; 24:35
23:8 ^{h}Ge 25:9
23:9 ^{i}ver 17,19; Ge 25:9; 47:30; 49:30; 50:13
23:10 ^{j}ver 18 ^{k}S Ge 18:1; Dt 22:15; 25:7; Jos 20:4; Ru 4:11; 2Sa 15:2; 2Ki 15:35; Ps 127:5; Pr 31:23; Jer 26:10; 36:10
23:11 ^{l}2Sa 24:23
23:15 ^{m}Eze 45:12

^{w}3 Or *the sons of Heth*; also in verses 5, 7, 10, 16, 18 and 20 ^{x}11 Or *sell* ^{y}15 That is, about 10 pounds (about 4.5 kilograms)

22:23–24 Abraham's brother Nahor (see 11:26) became the father of eight sons by his wife and four by his concubine. They would later become the ancestors of 12 Aramean (see v. 21) tribes, just as Abraham's grandson Jacob would become the ancestor of the 12 tribes of Israel (see 49:28).
23:2 *Kiriath Arba.* Means "the town of Arba" (Arba was the most prominent member of a tribe living in the Hebron area [see Jos 14:15]). It can also mean "the town of four," referring to the place where Anak (see Jos 15:13–14; 21:11) and his three sons lived (see Jdg 1:10,20). *went.* Either from Beersheba to Hebron or into where Sarah's body was lying.
23:3 *Hittites.* See note on 10:15. They were apparently in control of the Hebron area at this time.
23:4 *an alien and a stranger.* The phrase was used often by the patriarchs and their descendants in reference to themselves (see 1Ch 29:15; Ps 39:12; see also Heb 11:13). On this earth Abraham "lived in tents" (Heb 11:9), the most temporary of dwellings. But he looked forward to the more permanent home promised him, which the author of Hebrews calls "the city with foundations, whose architect and builder is God" (Heb 11:10).
23:6 *You are a mighty prince.* Probably intended as words of flattery.
23:9 *cave of Machpelah.* Though inaccessible today, the tombs of several patriarchs and their wives—Abraham and Sarah, Isaac and Rebekah, Jacob and Leah (see v. 19; 25:8–10; 49:30–31; 50:12–13)—are, according to tradi-

tion, located in a large cave deep beneath the Mosque of Abraham, a Muslim shrine in Hebron. *end of his field.* Because buying the entire field would have made Abraham responsible for certain additional financial and social obligations, he wanted to buy only a small part of it. Hittite laws stipulated that when a landowner sold only part of his property to someone else, the original and principal landowner had to continue paying all dues on the land. But if the landowner disposed of an entire tract, the new owner had to pay the dues.
23:10 *in the hearing of all the Hittites who had come to the gate.* The main gateway of a city was usually the place where legal matters were transacted and attested (see v. 18; see also note on 19:1).
23:11 *my lord.* Perhaps intended to flatter Abraham (see v. 15). *give.* See NIV text note.
23:15 *four hundred shekels of silver, but what is that between me and you?* See note on 20:16. Despite Ephron's pretense of generosity, 400 shekels of silver was an exorbitant price for a field (see, e.g., Jer 32:9). Ephron was taking advantage of Abraham during a time of grief and bereavement. He knew that Abraham had to deal quickly in order to have a place to bury Sarah, so he insisted that Abraham buy the entire lot and assume responsibility for the dues as well.
23:16 *weight current among the merchants.* Subject to more variation and therefore greater dishonesty than the later royal standard (see 2Sa 14:26), which was carefully

hundred shekels of silver,[n] according to the weight current among the merchants.[o]

[17]So Ephron's field in Machpelah[p] near Mamre[q]—both the field and the cave in it, and all the trees within the borders of the field—was deeded [18]to Abraham as his property[r] in the presence of all the Hittites[s] who had come to the gate[t] of the city. [19]Afterward Abraham buried his wife Sarah in the cave in the field of Machpelah[u] near Mamre (which is at Hebron[v]) in the land of Canaan.[w] [20]So the field and the cave in it were deeded[x] to Abraham by the Hittites as a burial site.[y]

Isaac and Rebekah

24 Abraham was now old and well advanced in years,[z] and the LORD had blessed[a] him in every way.[b] [2]He said to the chief[z] servant[c] in his household, the one in charge of all that he had,[d] "Put your hand under my thigh.[e] [3]I want you to swear[f] by the LORD, the God of heaven[g] and the God of earth,[h] that you will not get a wife for my son[i] from the daughters of the Canaanites,[j] among whom I am living,[k] [4]but will go to my country and my own relatives[l] and get a wife for my son Isaac.[m]"

[5]The servant asked him, "What if the woman is unwilling to come back with me to this land?[n] Shall I then take your son back to the country you came from?[o]"

[6]"Make sure that you do not take my son back there,"[p] Abraham said. [7]"The LORD, the God of heaven,[q] who brought me out of my father's household and my native land[r] and who spoke to me and promised me on oath, saying, 'To your off-

spring[a s] I will give this land'[t]—he will send his angel before you[u] so that you can get a wife for my son from there. [8]If the woman is unwilling to come back with you, then you will be released from this oath[v] of mine. Only do not take my son back there." [w] [9]So the servant put his hand under the thigh[x] of his master[y] Abraham and swore an oath to him concerning this matter.

[10]Then the servant took ten of his master's camels[z] and left, taking with him all kinds of good things[a] from his master. He set out for Aram Naharaim[b b] and made his way to the town of Nahor.[c] [11]He had the camels kneel down near the well[d] outside the town; it was toward evening, the time the women go out to draw water.[e]

[12]Then he prayed, "O LORD, God of my master Abraham,[f] give me success[g] today, and show kindness[h] to my master Abraham. [13]See, I am standing beside this spring, and the daughters of the townspeople are coming out to draw water.[i] [14]May it be that when I say to a girl, 'Please let down your jar that I may have a drink,' and she says, 'Drink,[j] and I'll water your camels too'[k]—let her be the one you have chosen for your servant Isaac.[l] By this I will know[m] that you have shown kindness to my master."

[15]Before he had finished praying,[n] Re-

Cross references (center column)

23:16
[n]2Sa 24:24;
Jer 32:9;
Zec 11:12
[o]2Sa 14:26
23:17 [p]S ver 9
[q]S Ge 13:18
23:18 [r]S Ge 12:7
[s]ver 10
[t]S Ge 18:1
23:19 [u]S ver 9
[v]S Ge 13:18;
Jos 14:13;
1Ch 29:27
[w]Ge 49:31
23:20 [x]Jer 32:10
[y]S Ge 10:15;
35:29; 47:30;
49:30; 50:5,13
24:1
[z]S Ge 17:17;
Jos 23:1
[a]Ge 12:2; Gal 3:9
[b]ver 35
24:2 [c]S Ge 15:3
[d]Ge 39:4-6 [e]ver 9; Ge 47:29
24:3 [f]Ge 47:31;
50:25 [g]ver 7
[h]S Ge 14:19;
S Nu 20:14
[i]Dt 7:3;
2Co 6:14-17
[j]S Ge 10:15-19
[k]ver 37
24:4 [l]S Ge 12:1;
Jdg 14:3 [m]S ver
29; S Ge 21:21
24:5 [n]ver 39
[o]Heb 11:15
24:6 [p]ver 8
24:7 [q]ver 3
[r]Ge 12:1

[s]Ro 4:13;
Gal 3:16*
[t]S Ge 12:7
[u]S Ge 16:7
24:8 [v]ver 41;
Jos 2:12,17,20;
9:20 [w]S ver 6
24:9 [x]S ver 2
[y]Ge 32:4; 33:8
24:10 [z]ver 19;
1Ki 10:2;
1Ch 12:40;
Isa 30:6 [a]ver 22,
30,47,53;
Ge 43:11; 45:23
[b]Nu 23:7;
Dt 23:4; Jdg 3:8
[c]S Ge 11:29

24:11 [d]Ex 2:15 [e]ver 13; Ge 29:2,9-10; Ex 2:16; 1Sa 9:11; Jn 4:7 24:12 [f]ver 27,42,48; Ge 26:24; 28:13; 31:42,53; 32:9; 43:23; 46:3; Ex 3:6,15,16; 4:5; 1Ki 18:36; Ps 75:9; 94:7 [g]ver 21,40,51,56; Ge 27:20; Ne 1:11 [h]S Ge 19:19; Jos 2:12; Job 10:12 24:13 [i]S ver 11,43; Ge 29:8 24:14 [j]ver 18,46 [k]ver 19 [l]ver 44 [m]Jos 2:12; Jdg 6:17,37; 1Sa 14:10; 1Ki 13:3; Ps 86:17; Isa 38:7; Jer 44:29 24:15 [n]ver 45

[z]2 Or *oldest*   [a]7 Or *seed*   [b]10 That is, Northwest Mesopotamia

---

Study notes (bottom)

regulated and more precise.
23:17 *the field and the cave in it, and all the trees.* In order to be free of all obligations relating to the field in which the cave of Machpelah was located, Ephron had held out for the sale of the entire field and its contents (see note on v. 9).
23:19 *buried his wife . . . in the land of Canaan.* In that culture, people had a strong desire to be buried "with their fathers" (see note on 25:8) in their native land. By purchasing a burial place in Canaan, Abraham indicated his unswerving commitment to the Lord's promise. Canaan was his new homeland.
24:2 *chief servant in his household.* Probably Eliezer of Damascus (see note on 15:2). *Put your hand under my thigh.* Near the organ of procreation, probably because this oath was related to the continuation of Abraham's line through Isaac (see 47:29).
24:3 *the LORD, the God of heaven and the God of earth.* See v. 7. For a similar majestic title used by Abraham in an oath see 14:22.
24:4 *my country.* Mesopotamia (see note on v. 10). *get a wife for my son.* See note on 21:21.
24:7 *To your offspring I will give this land.* Repeats the

promise of 12:7. *his angel.* See note on 16:7.
24:10 *camels.* See note on 12:16. *Aram Naharaim.* See NIV text note; lit. "Aram of the two rivers"—the Euphrates and the Tigris. Aram (see note on 10:22) Naharaim was the northern part of the area called later by the Greeks "Mesopotamia"—lit. "between the rivers." *town of Nahor.* Perhaps named after Abraham's brother (see v. 15; 11:26). It is mentioned in clay tablets excavated by the French beginning in 1933 at the ancient city of Mari on the Euphrates (see chart on "Ancient Texts Relating to the OT," p. 5). Nahor was located in the Haran (see note on 11:31) district and was ruled by an Amorite prince in the 18th century B.C.
24:11 *toward evening, the time the women go out to draw water.* The coolest time of day.
24:14 *By this I will know.* Like his master Abraham, the servant asked God for a sign to validate his errand (see note on 15:8). *kindness.* See v. 27; probably a reference to God's covenant with Abraham, which had promised numerous descendants through Isaac (see 17:19; 21:12).
24:15 *Before he had finished praying.* God had already begun to answer. *Rebekah . . . was the daughter of Bethuel son of . . . the wife of Abraham's brother.* Isaac would thus be marrying his father's grandniece (see v. 48).

bekah[o] came out with her jar on her shoulder. She was the daughter of Bethuel[p] son of Milcah,[q] who was the wife of Abraham's brother Nahor.[r] 16The girl was very beautiful,[s] a virgin;[t] no man had ever lain with her. She went down to the spring, filled her jar and came up again.

17The servant hurried to meet her and said, "Please give me a little water from your jar."[u]

18"Drink,[v] my lord," she said, and quickly lowered the jar to her hands and gave him a drink.

19After she had given him a drink, she said, "I'll draw water for your camels[w] too,[x] until they have finished drinking." 20So she quickly emptied her jar into the trough, ran back to the well to draw more water, and drew enough for all his camels.[y] 21Without saying a word, the man watched her closely to learn whether or not the LORD had made his journey successful.[z]

22When the camels had finished drinking, the man took out a gold nose ring[a] weighing a beka[c] and two gold bracelets[b] weighing ten shekels.[d] 23Then he asked, "Whose daughter are you?[c] Please tell me, is there room in your father's house for us to spend the night?[d]"

24She answered him, "I am the daughter of Bethuel, the son that Milcah bore to Nahor.[e]" 25And she added, "We have plenty of straw and fodder,[f] as well as room for you to spend the night."

26Then the man bowed down and worshiped the LORD,[g] 27saying, "Praise be to the LORD,[h] the God of my master Abraham,[i] who has not abandoned his kindness and faithfulness[j] to my master. As for me, the LORD has led me on the journey[k] to the house of my master's relatives."[l]

28The girl ran and told her mother's household about these things. [m] 29Now Rebekah had a brother named Laban,[n] and he hurried out to the man at the spring. 30As soon as he had seen the nose ring, and the bracelets on his sister's arms,[o] and had heard Rebekah tell what the man said to her, he went out to the man and found him standing by the camels near the spring. 31"Come, you who are blessed by the LORD,"[p] he said. "Why are you stand-

ing out here? I have prepared the house and a place for the camels."

32So the man went to the house, and the camels were unloaded. Straw and fodder[q] were brought for the camels, and water for him and his men to wash their feet.[r] 33Then food was set before him, but he said, "I will not eat until I have told you what I have to say."

"Then tell us," Laban said.

34So he said, "I am Abraham's servant.[s] 35The LORD has blessed[t] my master abundantly,[u] and he has become wealthy.[v] He has given him sheep and cattle, silver and gold, menservants and maidservants, and camels and donkeys.[w] 36My master's wife Sarah has borne him a son in her[e] old age,[x] and he has given him everything he owns.[y] 37And my master made me swear an oath,[z] and said, 'You must not get a wife for my son from the daughters of the Canaanites, in whose land I live,[a] 38but go to my father's family and to my own clan, and get a wife for my son.'[b]

39"Then I asked my master, 'What if the woman will not come back with me?'[c]

40"He replied, 'The LORD, before whom I have walked,[d] will send his angel with you[e] and make your journey a success,[f] so that you can get a wife for my son from my own clan and from my father's family.[g] 41Then, when you go to my clan, you will be released from my oath even if they refuse to give her to you—you will be released from my oath.'[h]

42"When I came to the spring today, I said, 'O LORD, God of my master Abraham, if you will, please grant success[i] to the journey on which I have come. 43See, I am standing beside this spring;[j] if a maiden[k] comes out to draw water and I say to her, "Please let me drink a little water from your jar,"[l] 44and if she says to me, "Drink, and I'll draw water for your camels too," let her be the one the LORD has chosen for my master's son.'[m]

45"Before I finished praying in my heart,[n] Rebekah came out, with her jar on her shoulder.[o] She went down to the spring and drew water, and I said to her, 'Please give me a drink.'[p]

46"She quickly lowered her jar from her

24:15
oS Ge 22:23
pS Ge 22:22
qS Ge 11:29
rS Ge 11:29
24:16
sS Ge 12:11
tDt 22:15-21
24:17 uver 45;
1Ki 17:10; Jn 4:7
24:18 vS ver 14
24:19 wS ver 10
xver 14
24:20 yver 46
24:21 zS ver 12
24:22 aver 47;
Ge 41:42;
Isa 3:21;
Eze 16:11-12
bS ver 10
24:23 cver 47
dJdg 19:15; 20:4
24:24 ever 29,
47; S Ge 11:29
24:25 fver 32;
Jdg 19:19
24:26 gver 48,
52; Ex 4:31;
12:27;
1Ch 29:20;
2Ch 20:18
24:27
hGe 14:20;
Ex 18:10;
Ru 4:14;
1Sa 25:32;
2Sa 18:28;
1Ki 1:48; 8:56;
Ps 28:6; 41:13;
68:19; 106:48;
Lk 1:68 iS ver 12
jver 49;
Ge 32:10; 47:29;
Jos 2:14; Ps 98:3
kver 21 lS ver 12,
48; S Ge 12:1
24:28 mGe 29:12
24:29 nver 4;
Ge 25:20; 27:43;
28:2,5; 29:5,12,
13
24:30 oS ver 10;
Eze 23:42
24:31
pGe 26:29;
Ps 115:15

24:32 qS ver 25
rS Ge 18:4
24:34 sS Ge 15:3
24:35 tS Ge 12:2
uver 1 vS Ge 23:6
wS Ge 12:16
24:36
xS Ge 17:17
yGe 25:5; 26:14
24:37 zGe 50:5,
25 aver 3
24:38
bS Ge 21:21
24:39 cS ver 5
24:40 dS Ge 5:22
eS Ge 16:7 fS ver
12 gS Ge 12:1
24:41 hS ver 8
24:42 iS ver 12
24:43 jS ver 13
kPr 30:19;
Isa 7:14 lS ver 14
24:44 mver 14
24:45 niSa 1:13
over 15 pS ver
17; Jn 4:7

c22 That is, about 1/5 ounce (about 5.5 grams)
d22 That is, about 4 ounces (about 110 grams)
e36 Or his

24:22 *beka.* Half a shekel (see Ex 38:26); see note on 20:16.
24:32–33 See note on 18:2.
24:34–49 The servant explained his mission to Rebekah's family. His speech, which summarizes the narrative of the

earlier part of the chapter, is an excellent example of the ancient storyteller's art, which was designed to fix the details of a story in the hearer's memory.
24:40 *before whom I have walked.* See notes on 5:22; 6:8–9; 17:1.

shoulder and said, 'Drink, and I'll water your camels too.' *q* So I drank, and she watered the camels also. *r*

47"I asked her, 'Whose daughter are you?' *s*

"She said, 'The daughter of Bethuel *t* son of Nahor, whom Milcah bore to him.' *u*

"Then I put the ring in her nose *v* and the bracelets on her arms, *w* 48and I bowed down and worshiped the LORD. *x* I praised the LORD, the God of my master Abraham, *y* who had led me on the right road to get the granddaughter of my master's brother for his son. *z* 49Now if you will show kindness and faithfulness *a* to my master, tell me; and if not, tell me, so I may know which way to turn."

50Laban and Bethuel *b* answered, "This is from the LORD; *c* we can say nothing to you one way or the other. *d* 51Here is Rebekah; take her and go, and let her become the wife of your master's son, as the LORD has directed. *e* "

52When Abraham's servant heard what they said, he bowed down to the ground before the LORD. *f* 53Then the servant brought out gold and silver jewelry and articles of clothing *g* and gave them to Rebekah; he also gave costly gifts *h* to her brother and to her mother. 54Then he and the men who were with him ate and drank and spent the night there.

When they got up the next morning, he said, "Send me on my way *i* to my master."

55But her brother and her mother replied, "Let the girl remain with us ten days or so; *j* then you *f* may go."

56But he said to them, "Do not detain me, now that the LORD has granted success *k* to my journey. Send me on my way *l* so I may go to my master."

57Then they said, "Let's call the girl and ask her about it." *m* 58So they called Rebekah and asked her, "Will you go with this man?"

"I will go," *n* she said.

59So they sent their sister Rebekah on her way, *o* along with her nurse *p* and Abraham's servant and his men. 60And they blessed *q* Rebekah and said to her,

"Our sister, may you increase
    to thousands upon thousands; *r*
may your offspring possess
    the gates of their enemies." *s*

61Then Rebekah and her maids *t* got ready and mounted their camels and went back with the man. So the servant took Rebekah and left.

62Now Isaac had come from Beer Lahai Roi, *u* for he was living in the Negev. *v* 63He went out to the field one evening to meditate, *g w* and as he looked up, *x* he saw camels approaching. 64Rebekah also looked up and saw Isaac. She got down from her camel *y* 65and asked the servant, "Who is that man in the field coming to meet us?"

"He is my master," the servant answered. So she took her veil *z* and covered herself.

66Then the servant told Isaac all he had done. 67Isaac brought her into the tent *a* of his mother Sarah, *b* and he married Rebekah. *c* So she became his wife, and he loved her; *d* and Isaac was comforted after his mother's death. *e*

The Death of Abraham

25:1–4pp — 1Ch 1:32-33

25 Abraham took *h* another wife, whose name was Keturah. 2She bore him Zimran, *f* Jokshan, Medan, Midian, *g* Ishbak and Shuah. *h* 3Jokshan was the father of Sheba *i* and Dedan; *j* the descendants of Dedan were the Asshurites, the Letushites and the Leummites. 4The sons of Midian were Ephah, *k* Epher, Hanoch, Abida and Eldaah. All these were descendants of Keturah.

5Abraham left everything he owned to Isaac. *l* 6But while he was still living, he gave gifts to the sons of his concubines *m*

25:4 *k*Isa 60:6 **25:5** *l*S Ge 24:36 **25:6** *m*S Ge 22:24

*f*55 Or *she*   *g*63 The meaning of the Hebrew for this word is uncertain.   *h*1 Or *had taken*

Cross references (center column):

24:46 *q*ver 18-19 *r*ver 20
24:47 *s*ver 23 *t*S Ge 22:22 *u*S ver 24 *v*S ver 22 *w*S ver 10; Isa 3:19; Eze 16:11-12
24:48 *x*S ver 26 *y*S ver 12 *z*S ver 27
24:49 *a*S ver 27
24:50 *b*Ge 22:22 *c*Ps 118:23 *d*Ge 31:7,24,29, 42; 48:16
24:51 *e*S ver 12
24:52 *f*S ver 26
24:53 *g*Ge 45:22; Ex 3:22; 12:35; 2Ki 5:5 *h*S ver 10
24:54 *i*ver 56,59; Ge 30:25
24:55 *j*Jdg 19:4
24:56 *k*S ver 12 *l*S ver 54
24:57 *m*Jdg 19:3
24:58 *n*Ru 1:16

24:59 *o*S ver 54 *p*Ge 35:8
24:60 *q*Ge 27:4, 19; 28:1; 31:55; 48:9,15,20; Jos 22:6 *r*S Ge 17:16 *s*Ge 22:17; Ps 127:5; Pr 27:11
24:61 *t*S Ge 16:1; 30:3; 46:25
24:62 *u*S Ge 16:14 *v*S Ge 12:9
24:63 *w*Jos 1:8; Ps 1:2; 77:12; 119:15,27,48,97, 148; 143:5; 145:5 *x*Ge 18:2
24:64 *y*Ge 31:17, 34; 1Sa 30:17
24:65 *z*Ge 38:14; SS 1:7; 4:1,3; 6:7; Isa 47:2
24:67 *a*Ge 31:33 *b*S Ge 18:9 *c*Ge 25:20; 49:31 *d*Ge 29:18,20; 34:3; Jdg 16:4 *e*Ge 23:1-2
25:2 *f*Jer 25:25 *g*Ge 36:35; 37:28,36; Ex 2:15; Nu 22:4; 25:6,18; 31:2; Jos 13:21; Jdg 6:1,3; 7:1; 8:1,22,24; 9:17; 1Ki 11:18; Ps 83:9; Isa 9:4; 10:26; 60:6; Hab 3:7 *h*Job 2:11; 8:1
25:3 *i*S Ge 10:7 *j*S Ge 10:7

24:53 The rich gifts bestowed on Rebekah and her family indicated the wealth of the household into which she was being asked to marry—far from her loved ones and homeland.
24:60 See 22:17 and note.
24:62 *Beer Lahai Roi.* See note on 16:14.
24:65 *she took her veil and covered herself.* Apparently a sign that she was unmarried (cf. 38:14,19).
24:67 *tent.* Often used as a bridal chamber (see Ps 19:4–5).
25:1 *took another wife.* Or "married another woman"—his "concubine" (1Ch 1:32). *took.* Or "had tak-

en" (see NIV text note), since Abraham would have been 140 years old at this time if the order is chronological.
25:5 *left everything he owned to Isaac.* The law of primogeniture provided that at least a double share of the father's property be given to the firstborn son when the father died (Dt 21:15–17). Parallels to this practice come from Nuzi, from Larsa in the Old Babylonian period and from Assyria in the Middle Assyrian period. Isaac was Abraham's firstborn son according to law.
25:6 *gifts.* These doubtless represented the inheritance left to Abraham's other sons. *concubines.* Polygamy was practiced even by godly men in ancient times, though it was not

and sent them away from his son Isaac[n] to the land of the east.[o]

[7]Altogether, Abraham lived a hundred and seventy-five years.[p] [8]Then Abraham breathed his last and died at a good old age,[q] an old man and full of years; and he was gathered to his people.[r] [9]His sons Isaac and Ishmael buried him[s] in the cave of Machpelah[t] near Mamre,[u] in the field of Ephron[v] son of Zohar the Hittite,[w] [10]the field Abraham had bought from the Hittites.[i][x] There Abraham was buried with his wife Sarah. [11]After Abraham's death, God blessed his son Isaac,[y] who then lived near Beer Lahai Roi.[z]

Ishmael's Sons

25:12-16pp — 1Ch 1:29-31

[12]This is the account[a] of Abraham's son Ishmael, whom Sarah's maidservant, Hagar[b] the Egyptian, bore to Abraham.[c]

[13]These are the names of the sons of Ishmael, listed in the order of their birth: Nebaioth[d] the firstborn of Ishmael, Kedar,[e] Adbeel, Mibsam, [14]Mishma, Dumah,[f] Massa, [15]Hadad, Tema,[g] Jetur,[h] Naphish and Kedemah. [16]These were the sons of Ishmael, and these are the names of the twelve tribal rulers[i] according to their settlements and camps.[j] [17]Altogether, Ishmael lived a hundred and thirty-seven years. He breathed his last and died, and he was gathered to his people.[k] [18]His descendants[l] settled in the area from Havilah to Shur,[m] near the border of Egypt, as you go toward Asshur. And they lived in hostility toward[j] all their brothers.[n]

Jacob and Esau

[19]This is the account[o] of Abraham's son Isaac.

Abraham became the father of Isaac, [20]and Isaac was forty years old[p] when he married Rebekah[q] daughter of Bethuel[r] the Aramean from Paddan Aram[k][s] and sister of Laban[t] the Aramean.[u]

[21]Isaac prayed to the LORD on behalf of his wife, because she was barren.[v] The LORD answered his prayer,[w] and his wife Rebekah became pregnant. [22]The babies jostled each other within her, and she said, "Why is this happening to me?" So she went to inquire of the LORD.[x]

[23]The LORD said to her,

"Two nations[y] are in your womb,
    and two peoples from within you will
        be separated;
one people will be stronger than the
        other,
    and the older will serve the
        younger.[z]"

[24]When the time came for her to give birth,[a] there were twin boys in her womb.[b] [25]The first to come out was red,[c] and his whole body was like a hairy garment;[d] so they named him Esau.[l][e] [26]After this, his brother came out,[f] with his

Cross references

25:6 [n]S Ge 21:10; [o]Ge 29:1; Jdg 6:3,33; 1Ki 4:30; Job 1:3; Eze 25:4
25:7 [p]ver 26; Ge 12:4; 35:28; 47:9,28; 50:22,26; Job 42:16
25:8 [q]S Ge 15:15; [r]ver 17; Ge 35:29; 49:29,33; Nu 20:24; 31:2; Dt 31:14; 32:50; 34:5
25:9 [s]Ge 35:29; 47:30; 49:31; [t]S Ge 23:9; [u]S Ge 13:18; [v]Ge 23:8; [w]Ge 49:29; 50:13
25:10 [x]S Ge 10:15
25:11 [y]S Ge 12:2; [z]S Ge 16:14
25:12 [a]S Ge 2:4; [b]S Ge 16:1; [c]S Ge 17:20;
21:18
25:13 [d]Ge 28:9; 36:3 [e]Ps 120:5; SS 1:5; Isa 21:16; 42:11; 60:7; Jer 2:10; 49:28; Eze 27:21
25:14 [f]Jos 15:52; Isa 21:11; Ob 1:1
25:15 [g]Job 6:19; Isa 21:14; Jer 25:23
[h]1Ch 5:19
25:16 [i]Ge 17:20; [j]S Ge 13:16; Ps 83:6
25:17 [k]S ver 8
25:18 [l]S Ge 17:20; 21:18 [m]S Ge 16:7; [n]Ge 16:12
25:19 [o]S Ge 2:4
25:20 [p]ver 26; Ge 26:34; 35:28; [q]S Ge 24:67; [r]S Ge 22:22; [s]Ge 28:2,5,6; 30:20; 31:18; 33:18; 35:9,26; 46:15; 48:7; [t]S Ge 24:29; [u]Ge 31:20,24; Dt 26:5
25:21 [v]S Ge 11:30 [w]Ge 30:17,22; 1Sa 1:17,23; 1Ch 5:20; 2Ch 33:13; Ezr 8:23; Ps 127:3 25:22 [x]Ex 18:15; 28:30; 33:7; Lev 24:12; Nu 9:6-8; 27:5,21; Dt 17:9; Jdg 18:5; 1Sa 9:9; 10:22; 14:36; 22:10; 1Ki 22:8; 2Ki 3:11; 22:13; Isa 30:2; Jer 21:2; 37:7,17; Eze 14:7; 20:1,3 25:23 [y]S Ge 17:4 [z]S Ge 9:25; 48:14,19; Ro 9:11-12* 25:24 [a]Lk 1:57; 2:6 [b]Ge 38:27 25:25 [c]1Sa 16:12 [d]Ge 27:11 [e]Ge 27:1,15 25:26 [f]Ge 38:29

[i]10 Or the sons of Heth   [j]18 Or lived to the east of   [k]20 That is, Northwest Mesopotamia   [l]25 Esau may mean hairy; he was also called Edom, which means red.

Study notes

the original divine intention (see note on 4:19).
25:7 *a hundred and seventy-five years.* Abraham lived for a full century after "he set out from Haran" (12:4).
25:8 *died at a good old age.* As God had promised (see 15:15). *an old man and full of years.* A phrase used also of the patriarch Job (see Job 42:17). *was gathered to his people.* Joined his ancestors and/or deceased relatives in death (see 2Ki 22:20; 2Ch 34:28).
25:9 *Isaac and Ishmael.* Isaac, legally the firstborn (see note on v. 5), is listed first.
25:11 *Beer Lahai Roi.* See note on 16:14.
25:12 *account.* See note on 2:4.
25:13 *names of the sons of Ishmael.* Many are Arab names, giving credence to the Arab tradition that Ishmael is their ancestor.
25:16 *twelve tribal rulers.* Twelve major tribes descended from Abraham's son Ishmael (as predicted in 17:20)—as was also true of Abraham's brother Nahor (see note on 22:23-24).
25:18 *in hostility toward.* See note on 16:12; or possibly "to the east of" (see NIV text notes here and on 16:12; see also 25:6).
25:19 *account.* See note on 2:4.

25:20 *Paddan Aram.* See NIV text note; means "plain of Aram," another name for Aram Naharaim (see note on 24:10).
25:22 *jostled each other.* The struggle between Jacob and Esau began in the womb (see also v. 26). *went.* Perhaps to a nearby place of worship.
25:23 *the older will serve the younger.* The ancient law of primogeniture (see note on v. 5) provided that, under ordinary circumstances, the younger of two sons would be subservient to the older. God's election of the younger son highlights the fact that God's people are the product not of natural or worldly development but of his sovereign intervention in the affairs of men (see note on 11:30). Part of this verse is quoted in Ro 9:10-12 as an example of God's sovereign right to do "whatever pleases him" (Ps 115:3)—not in an arbitrary way (see Ro 9:14), but according to his own perfect will.
25:24-26 For another unusual birth of twin boys see 38:27-30.
25:25 *red.* A pun on Edom, one of Esau's other names (see v. 30 and NIV text note).
25:26 *his hand grasping Esau's heel.* Hostility between the Israelites (Jacob's descendants) and Edomites (Esau's de-

hand grasping Esau's heel;*g* so he was named Jacob.*m h* Isaac was sixty years old*i* when Rebekah gave birth to them.

27The boys grew up, and Esau became a skillful hunter,*j* a man of the open country,*k* while Jacob was a quiet man, staying among the tents. 28Isaac, who had a taste for wild game,*l* loved Esau, but Rebekah loved Jacob.*m*

29Once when Jacob was cooking some stew,*n* Esau came in from the open country,*o* famished. 30He said to Jacob, "Quick, let me have some of that red stew!*p* I'm famished!" (That is why he was also called Edom.*n*)*q*

31Jacob replied, "First sell me your birthright.*r* "

32"Look, I am about to die," Esau said. "What good is the birthright to me?"

33But Jacob said, "Swear*s* to me first." So he swore an oath to him, selling his birthright*t* to Jacob.

34Then Jacob gave Esau some bread and some lentil stew.*u* He ate and drank, and then got up and left.

So Esau despised his birthright.

Isaac and Abimelech

26:1–11Ref — Ge 12:10–20; 20:1–18

26 Now there was a famine in the land*v*—besides the earlier famine of Abraham's time—and Isaac went to Abimelech king of the Philistines*w* in Gerar.*x* 2The LORD appeared*y* to Isaac and said, "Do not go down to Egypt;*z* live in the land where I tell you to live.*a* 3Stay in this land for a while,*b* and I will be with you*c* and will bless you.*d* For to you and your descendants I will give all these lands*e* and will confirm the oath I swore to your father Abraham.*f* 4I will make your descendants*g* as numerous as the stars in the sky*h* and will give them all these lands,*i* and through your offspring*o* all nations on earth will be blessed,*j* 5because Abraham obeyed me*k* and kept my requirements, my commands, my decrees*l* and my laws.*m*" 6So Isaac stayed in Gerar.*n*

7When the men of that place asked him about his wife, he said, "She is my sister,*o*" because he was afraid to say, "She is my wife." He thought, "The men of this place might kill me on account of Rebekah, because she is beautiful."

8When Isaac had been there a long time, Abimelech king of the Philistines*p* looked down from a window and saw Isaac caressing his wife Rebekah. 9So Abimelech summoned Isaac and said, "She is really your wife! Why did you say, 'She is my sister'?*q*"

Isaac answered him, "Because I thought I might lose my life on account of her."

10Then Abimelech said, "What is this you have done to us?*r* One of the men

25:26 *g*Hos 12:3
*h*Ge 27:36;
32:27; Dt 23:7;
Jos 24:4; Ob 1:10,
12 *i*S ver 7,S 20
25:27 *j*S Ge 10:9
*k*ver 29; Ge 27:3,
5
25:28 *l*Ge 27:3,4,
9,14,19
*m*Ge 27:6; 37:3
25:29
*n*2Ki 4:38-40
*o*S ver 27
25:30 *p*ver 34
*q*Ge 32:3; 36:1,8,
8-9,19; Nu 20:14;
Dt 23:7;
Ps 137:7;
Jer 25:21; 40:11;
49:7
25:31
*r*Dt 21:16-17;
1Ch 5:1-2
25:33
*s*S Ge 21:23;
S 47:31
*t*Ge 27:36;
Heb 12:16
25:34 *u*ver 30
26:1
*v*S Ge 12:10;
S Dt 32:24
*w*S Ge 10:14;
Jdg 10:6
*x*S Ge 20:1
26:2 *y*S Ge 12:7
*z*Ge 46:3
*a*S Ge 12:1
26:3 *b*Ge 20:1
*c*S Ge 21:20;
27:45; 31:3,5;
32:9; 35:3;
48:21; Ex 3:12;
33:14-16;
Nu 23:21;
Dt 31:23; Jos 1:5;
Isa 43:2; Jer 1:8,
19; Hag 1:13 *d*ver
12; S Ge 12:2
*e*S Ge 12:7;
Ac 7:5
*f*S Ge 17:19
26:4 *g*ver 24;
Ge 48:4
*h*S Ge 12:2;

S Nu 10:36 *i*S Ge 12:7 *j*S Ge 12:3; Ac 3:25*; Gal 3:8 26:5
*k*S Ge 18:19 *l*Ps 119:80,112; Eze 18:21 *m*Lev 18:4,5,26;
19:19,37; 20:8,22; 25:18; 26:3; Nu 15:40; Dt 4:40; 6:2;
11:1; 1Ki 2:3 26:6 *n*S Ge 20:1 26:7 *o*S Ge 12:13 26:8
*p*S Ge 10:14 26:9 *q*S Ge 12:19 26:10 *r*S Ge 12:18

*m*26 Jacob means *he grasps the heel* (figuratively, *he deceives*). *n*30 Edom means *red*. *o*4 Or *seed*

scendants) became the rule rather than the exception (see, e.g., Nu 20:14–21; Ob 9–10). *Jacob.* See NIV text note. The name became proverbial for the unsavory quality of deceptiveness (see NIV text note on Jer 9:4).

25:31 *sell me your birthright.* In ancient times the birthright included the inheritance rights of the firstborn (see Heb 12:16; see also note on v. 5). Jacob was ever the schemer, seeking by any means to gain advantage over others. But it was by God's appointment and care, not Jacob's wits, that he came into the blessing.

25:33 *Swear to me first.* A verbal oath was all that was required to make the transaction legal.

25:34 *lentil.* A small pea-like annual plant, the pods of which turn reddish-brown when boiled. It grows well even in bad soil and has provided an important source of nourishment in the Near East since ancient times (see 2Sa 17:28; 23:11; Eze 4:9). *Esau despised his birthright.* In so doing, he proved himself to be "godless" (Heb 12:16), since at the heart of the birthright were the covenant promises that Isaac had inherited from Abraham.

26:1–33 The events of some of these verses (e.g. vv. 1–11) occurred before the birth of Esau and Jacob. Verses 1–33 are placed here to highlight the fact that the birthright and blessing Jacob struggled to obtain from his father (see 25:22, 31–33; 27:5–29) involved the covenant inheritance of Abraham that Isaac had received.

26:1 *the earlier famine of Abraham's time.* See 12:10.

Abimelech. Probably the son or grandson of the earlier king who bore the same name (see 20:2). *Philistines.* See note on 10:14. *Gerar.* See note on 20:1.

26:2 *appeared.* See note on 12:7.

26:3 *I will be with you.* God's promise to be a sustainer and protector of his people is repeated often (see, e.g., v. 24; 28:15; 31:3; Jos 1:5; Isa 41:10; Jer 1:8,19; Mt 28:20; Ac 18:10; see also Ge 17:7 and note). *the oath I swore to your father Abraham.* See 22:16–18.

26:4 *descendants as numerous as the stars in the sky.* See 13:16; 15:5 and notes. *through your offspring all nations on earth will be blessed.* See note on 12:2–3.

26:5 *because Abraham obeyed me.* See note on 17:9. *requirements . . . commands . . . decrees . . . laws.* Legal language describing various aspects of the divine regulations that God's people were expected to keep (see Lev 26:14–15,46; Dt 11:1). Addressing Israel after the covenant at Sinai, the author of Genesis used language that strictly applied only to that covenant. But he emphasized to Israel that their father Abraham had been obedient to God's will in his time and that they must follow his example if they were to receive the covenant promises.

26:7 *because she is beautiful.* See 12:11,14.

26:8 *caressing.* The word in Hebrew (a form of the verb translated "laugh" in 17:17; 18:12–13,15; 21:6 and "mock" in 21:9) is yet another pun on Isaac's name.

might well have slept with your wife, and you would have brought guilt upon us."

[11]So Abimelech gave orders to all the people: "Anyone who molests[s] this man or his wife shall surely be put to death."[t]

[12]Isaac planted crops in that land and the same year reaped a hundredfold,[u] because the LORD blessed him.[v] [13]The man became rich, and his wealth continued to grow until he became very wealthy.[w] [14]He had so many flocks and herds and servants[x] that the Philistines envied him.[y] [15]So all the wells[z] that his father's servants had dug in the time of his father Abraham, the Philistines stopped up,[a] filling them with earth.

[16]Then Abimelech said to Isaac, "Move away from us;[b] you have become too powerful for us.[c]"

[17]So Isaac moved away from there and encamped in the Valley of Gerar[d] and settled there. [18]Isaac reopened the wells[e] that had been dug in the time of his father Abraham, which the Philistines had stopped up after Abraham died, and he gave them the same names his father had given them.

[19]Isaac's servants dug in the valley and discovered a well of fresh water there. [20]But the herdsmen of Gerar quarreled[f] with Isaac's herdsmen and said, "The water is ours!"[g] So he named the well Esek,[p] because they disputed with him. [21]Then they dug another well, but they quarreled[h] over that one also; so he named it Sitnah.[q] [22]He moved on from there and dug another well, and no one quarreled over it. He named it Rehoboth,[r][i] saying, "Now the LORD has given us room[j] and we will flourish[k] in the land."

[23]From there he went up to Beersheba.[l] [24]That night the LORD appeared to him and said, "I am the God of your father Abra-

ham.[m] Do not be afraid,[n] for I am with you;[o] I will bless you and will increase the number of your descendants[p] for the sake of my servant Abraham."[q]

[25]Isaac built an altar[r] there and called on the name of the LORD.[s] There he pitched his tent, and there his servants dug a well.[t]

[26]Meanwhile, Abimelech had come to him from Gerar, with Ahuzzath his personal adviser and Phicol the commander of his forces.[u] [27]Isaac asked them, "Why have you come to me, since you were hostile to me and sent me away?[v]"

[28]They answered, "We saw clearly that the LORD was with you;[w] so we said, 'There ought to be a sworn agreement between us'—between us and you. Let us make a treaty[x] with you [29]that you will do us no harm,[y] just as we did not molest you but always treated you well and sent you away in peace. And now you are blessed by the LORD."[z]

[30]Isaac then made a feast[a] for them, and they ate and drank. [31]Early the next morning the men swore an oath[b] to each other. Then Isaac sent them on their way, and they left him in peace.

[32]That day Isaac's servants came and told him about the well[c] they had dug. They said, "We've found water!" [33]He called it Shibah,[s] and to this day the name of the town has been Beersheba.[t][d]

[34]When Esau was forty years old,[e] he married Judith daughter of Beeri the Hittite, and also Basemath daughter of Elon the Hittite.[f] [35]They were a source of grief to Isaac and Rebekah.[g]

26:11 [s]1Sa 24:6; 26:9; Ps 105:15
[t]S Ge 20:3
26:12 [u]Mt 13:8
[v]ver 3
26:13 [w]S Ge 13:2; S Dt 8:18
26:14 [x]S Ge 12:16; S 24:36; 32:23
[y]Ge 37:11
26:15 [z]S Ge 21:30
[a]S Ge 21:25
26:16 [b]ver 27; Jdg 11:7 [c]Ex 1:9; Ps 105:24-25
26:17 [d]S Ge 20:1
26:18 [e]S Ge 21:30
26:20 [f]S Ge 13:7 [g]Ge 21:25
26:21 [h]S Ge 13:7
26:22 [i]Ge 36:37 [j]Ps 18:19; Isa 33:20; 54:2; Am 9:11 [k]S Ge 17:6
26:23 [l]S Ge 22:19

26:24 [m]S Ge 24:12 [n]S Ge 15:1; S Jos 8:1 [o]S Ge 21:20 [p]S ver 4 [q]ver 4; Ge 17:7; S 22:17; 28:14; 30:27; 39:5; Dt 13:17
26:25 [r]S Ge 8:20 [s]S Ge 4:26; S Ac 2:21 [t]S Ge 21:30
26:26 [u]S Ge 21:22
26:27 [v]S ver 16
26:28 [w]S Ge 21:22 [x]S Ge 21:27; Jos 9:6
26:29 [y]Ge 31:29, 52 [z]S Ge 24:31
26:30 [a]Ge 31:54; Ex 18:12; 24:11; 1Sa 20:27
26:31 [b]S Ge 21:23,27
26:32 [c]S Ge 21:30
26:33 [d]S Ge 21:14
26:34 [e]S Ge 25:20 [f]S Ge 10:15; 28:9; 36:2; Jos 3:10; 1Sa 26:6; 1Ki 10:29

26:35 [g]Ge 27:46; 28:8; Job 7:16

[p]20 Esek means dispute.   [q]21 Sitnah means opposition.   [r]22 Rehoboth means room.   [s]33 Shibah can mean oath or seven.   [t]33 Beersheba can mean well of the oath or well of seven.

26:16 you have become too powerful for us. An indication that the covenant promises were being fulfilled. Already in the days of the patriarchs, the presence of God's people in the land was seen as a threat by the peoples of the world. As the world's people pursued their own godless living, God's people aroused their hostility. A similar complaint was voiced by an Egyptian pharaoh hundreds of years later (Ex 1:9).
26:20 The water is ours! In those arid regions, disputes over water rights and pasturelands were common (see 13:6–11; 21:25; 36:7).
26:25 built an altar. See note on 12:7. called on the name of the LORD. See 4:26 and note.
26:26 Phicol. See note on 21:22.
26:30 made a feast. Covenants were often concluded with a shared meal, signifying the bond of friendship (see 31:54; Ex 24:11).

26:33 the name of the town has been Beersheba. See note on 21:31.
26:34 When Esau was forty years old, he married. As had his father Isaac (see 25:20). Forty years was roughly equivalent to a generation in later times (see Nu 32:13). Judith . . . Basemath. In addition to these two wives, Esau also married Mahalath, "sister of Nebaioth and daughter of Ishmael" (28:9). The Esau genealogy of ch. 36 also mentions three wives, but they are identified as "Adah daughter of Elon the Hittite," "Oholibamah daughter of Anah . . . the Hivite" and "Basemath daughter of Ishmael and sister of Nebaioth" (36:2–3). Possibly the lists have suffered in transmission, or perhaps alternate names or nicknames are used. It may also be that Esau married more than three wives.
26:35 They were a source of grief. Isaac and Rebekah were determined not to allow Jacob to make the same mistake of marrying Hittite or Canaanite women (see 27:46–28:2).

Jacob Gets Isaac's Blessing

27 When Isaac was old and his eyes were so weak that he could no longer see,[h] he called for Esau his older son[i] and said to him, "My son."

"Here I am," he answered.

[2]Isaac said, "I am now an old man and don't know the day of my death.[j] [3]Now then, get your weapons—your quiver and bow—and go out to the open country[k] to hunt some wild game for me. [4]Prepare me the kind of tasty food I like[l] and bring it to me to eat, so that I may give you my blessing[m] before I die." [n]

[5]Now Rebekah was listening as Isaac spoke to his son Esau. When Esau left for the open country[o] to hunt game and bring it back, [6]Rebekah said to her son Jacob,[p] "Look, I overheard your father say to your brother Esau, [7]'Bring me some game and prepare me some tasty food to eat, so that I may give you my blessing in the presence of the LORD before I die.'[q] [8]Now, my son, listen carefully and do what I tell you:[r] [9]Go out to the flock and bring me two choice young goats,[s] so I can prepare some tasty food for your father, just the way he likes it.[t] [10]Then take it to your father to eat, so that he may give you his blessing[u] before he dies."

[11]Jacob said to Rebekah his mother, "But my brother Esau is a hairy man,[v] and I'm a man with smooth skin. [12]What if my father touches me?[w] I would appear to be tricking him and would bring down a curse[x] on myself rather than a blessing."

[13]His mother said to him, "My son, let the curse fall on me.[y] Just do what I say;[z] go and get them for me."

[14]So he went and got them and brought them to his mother, and she prepared some tasty food, just the way his father liked it.[a] [15]Then Rebekah took the best clothes[b] of Esau her older son,[c] which she had in the house, and put them on her

younger son Jacob. [16]She also covered his hands and the smooth part of his neck with the goatskins. [d] [17]Then she handed to her son Jacob the tasty food and the bread she had made.

[18]He went to his father and said, "My father."

"Yes, my son," he answered. "Who is it?" [e]

[19]Jacob said to his father, "I am Esau your firstborn.[f] I have done as you told me. Please sit up and eat some of my game[g] so that you may give me your blessing." [h]

[20]Isaac asked his son, "How did you find it so quickly, my son?"

"The LORD your God gave me success,[i]" he replied.

[21]Then Isaac said to Jacob, "Come near so I can touch you,[j] my son, to know whether you really are my son Esau or not."

[22]Jacob went close to his father Isaac,[k] who touched[l] him and said, "The voice is the voice of Jacob, but the hands are the hands of Esau." [23]He did not recognize him, for his hands were hairy like those of his brother Esau;[m] so he blessed him. [24]"Are you really my son Esau?" he asked.

"I am," he replied.

[25]Then he said, "My son, bring me some of your game to eat, so that I may give you my blessing." [n]

Jacob brought it to him and he ate; and he brought some wine and he drank. [26]Then his father Isaac said to him, "Come here, my son, and kiss me."

[27]So he went to him and kissed[o] him.[p] When Isaac caught the smell of his clothes,[q] he blessed him and said,

"Ah, the smell of my son
　is like the smell of a field
　that the LORD has blessed.[r]
[28]May God give you of heaven's dew[s]
　and of earth's richness[t] —

27:1 *hGe 48:10;
Dt 34:7; 1Sa 3:2
iS Ge 25:25*
27:2 *jGe 47:29;
1Ki 2:1*
27:3 *kS Ge 25:27*
27:4 *lS Ge 25:28
mver 10,25,31;
S Ge 24:60;
49:28; Dt 33:1;
Heb 11:20 nver 7*
27:5 *oS Ge 25:27*
27:6 *pS Ge 25:28*
27:7 *qver 4*
27:8 *rver 13,43*
27:9 *s1Sa 16:20
tS Ge 25:28*
27:10 *uS ver 4*
27:11 *vGe 25:25
wver 22
xS Ge 9:25*
27:13 *yMt 27:25
zS ver 8*
27:14 *aS Ge 25:28*
27:15 *bver 27;
SS 4:11
cS Ge 25:25*

27:16 *dver 22-23*
27:18 *ever 32*
27:19 *fver 32
gS Ge 25:28
hS ver 4*
27:20 *iS Ge 24:12*
27:21 *jver 12*
27:22 *kGe 45:4
lver 12*
27:23 *mver 16*
27:25 *nS ver 4*
27:27 *oGe 31:28,
55; 33:4; 48:10;
Ex 4:27; 18:7;
Ru 1:9;
1Sa 20:41;
2Sa 14:33; 19:39
pHeb 11:20
qS ver 15
rPs 65:9-13*
27:28 *sDt 33:13;
2Sa 1:21;
Job 18:16; 29:19;
Pr 3:20;
Isa 26:19;
Hos 14:5;
Hag 1:10;
Zec 8:12 tver 39;
Ge 49:25;
Lev 26:20;
Dt 33:13*

27:1 *eyes were so weak that he could no longer see.* In ancient times, blindness and near blindness were common among elderly people (see 48:10; 1Sa 4:15). *Here I am.* See note on 22:1.

27:4 *the kind of tasty food I like.* Rebekah and Jacob took advantage of Isaac's love for a certain kind of food (see vv. 9,14). *give you my blessing before I die.* Oral statements, including deathbed bequests (see 49:28–33), had legal force in ancient Near Eastern law. *blessing.* See note on v. 36.

27:5 *listening.* Eavesdropping.

27:6 *Rebekah.* Throughout the Jacob story the author develops a wordplay on "birthright" (*bekorah*) and "blessing" (*berakah*), both of which Jacob seeks to obtain; and Rebekah (*ribqah*) does her best to further the cause of her favorite son. *said to her son Jacob.* The parental favoritism mentioned in 25:28 is about to bear its poisonous fruit.

27:8 *my son, . . . do what I tell you.* Rebekah proves to be just as deceitful as Jacob, whose very name signifies deceit (see NIV text notes on v. 36; 25:26).

27:13 *let the curse fall on me.* Cf. the similar self-imprecation in Mt 27:25.

27:20 *your God.* Consistent with Jacob's language elsewhere (31:5,42; 32:9). Not until his safe return from Haran did he speak of the Lord as his own God (cf. 28:20–22; 33:18–20).

27:24 *Are you really my son Esau?* To the very end of the charade, Isaac remained suspicious.

27:27 *kissed him.* In his attempt to obtain the covenant blessing, Jacob the father of Israel betrayed with a kiss. Jesus the great Son of Israel, who ultimately obtained the blessing for Israel, was betrayed with a kiss (Mt 26:48–49; Lk 22:48).

an abundance of grain[u] and new wine.[v]

[29]May nations serve you
and peoples bow down to you.[w]
Be lord over your brothers,
and may the sons of your mother
bow down to you.[x]
May those who curse you be cursed
and those who bless you be
blessed.[y]"

[30]After Isaac finished blessing him and Jacob had scarcely left his father's presence, his brother Esau came in from hunting. [31]He too prepared some tasty food and brought it to his father. Then he said to him, "My father, sit up and eat some of my game, so that you may give me your blessing."[z]

[32]His father Isaac asked him, "Who are you?"[a]

"I am your son," he answered, "your firstborn, Esau.[b]"

[33]Isaac trembled violently and said, "Who was it, then, that hunted game and brought it to me?[c] I ate it just before you came and I blessed him—and indeed he will be blessed![d]"

[34]When Esau heard his father's words, he burst out with a loud and bitter cry[e] and said to his father, "Bless[f] me—me too, my father!"

[35]But he said, "Your brother came deceitfully[g] and took your blessing."[h]

[36]Esau said, "Isn't he rightly named Jacob[u]?[i] He has deceived[j] me these two times: He took my birthright,[k] and now he's taken my blessing!"[l] Then he asked, "Haven't you reserved any blessing for me?"

[37]Isaac answered Esau, "I have made him lord over you and have made all his relatives his servants, and I have sustained him with grain and new wine.[m] So what can I possibly do for you, my son?"

[38]Esau said to his father, "Do you have only one blessing, my father? Bless me too, my father!" Then Esau wept aloud.[n]

[39]His father Isaac answered him,[o]

"Your dwelling will be
away from the earth's richness,
away from the dew[p] of heaven
above.[q]
[40]You will live by the sword
and you will serve[r] your brother.[s]
But when you grow restless,
you will throw his yoke
from off your neck.[t]"

Jacob Flees to Laban

[41]Esau held a grudge[u] against Jacob[v] because of the blessing his father had given him. He said to himself, "The days of mourning[w] for my father are near; then I will kill[x] my brother Jacob."[y]

[42]When Rebekah was told what her older son Esau[z] had said, she sent for her younger son Jacob and said to him, "Your brother Esau is consoling himself with the thought of killing you.[a] [43]Now then, my son, do what I say:[b] Flee at once to my brother Laban[c] in Haran.[d] [44]Stay with him for a while[e] until your brother's fury subsides. [45]When your brother is no longer angry with you and forgets what you did to him,[f] I'll send word for you to come back from there.[g] Why should I lose both of you in one day?"

[46]Then Rebekah said to Isaac, "I'm disgusted with living because of these Hittite[h] women. If Jacob takes a wife from among the women of this land,[i] from Hittite women like these, my life will not be worth living."[j]

28
So Isaac called for Jacob and blessed[v][k] him and commanded him: "Do not marry a Canaanite woman.[l]

27:28 uPs 65:9; 72:16 vver 37; Nu 18:12; Dt 7:13; 33:28; 2Ki 18:32; Ps 4:7; Isa 36:17; Jer 31:12; 40:10 27:29 wZSa 8:14; Ps 68:31; 72:11; Isa 19:21,23; 27:13; 45:14,23; 49:7,23; 60:12,14; 66:23; Jer 12:17; Da 2:44; Zec 14:17-18 xS Ge 9:25; S 25:23; S 37:7 yver 33; Ge 12:3 27:31 zS ver 4 27:32 aver 18 bver 19 27:33 cver 35 dS ver 29 27:34 eHeb 12:17 fEx 12:32 27:35 gJer 9:4; 12:6 hver 19,45 27:36 iS Ge 25:26 jGe 29:25; 31:20, 26; 34:13; 1Sa 28:12 kS Ge 25:33 lHeb 12:16-17 27:37 mS ver 28; Dt 16:13; Ezr 6:9; Isa 16:10; Jer 40:12

27:38 nGe 29:11; Nu 14:1; Jdg 2:4; 21:2; Ru 1:9; 1Sa 11:4; 30:4; Heb 12:17 27:39 oHeb 11:20 pver 28 qGe 36:6 27:40 r2Sa 8:14 sS Ge 9:25 t2Ki 8:20-22 27:41 uGe 37:4; 49:23; 50:15; 1Sa 17:28 vGe 31:17; 32:11; Hos 10:14 wGe 50:4,10; Nu 20:29 xver 42 yOb 1:10 27:42 zGe 32:3, 11; 33:4 aver 41 27:43 bS ver 8 cS Ge 24:29 dS Ge 11:31 27:44 eGe 31:38, 41 27:45 fS ver 35 gS Ge 26:3 27:46 hS Ge 10:15

iS Ge 10:15-19 jS Ge 26:35; S Job 7:7 28:1 kS Ge 24:60 lGe 24:3

u36 Jacob means he grasps the heel (figuratively, he deceives). v1 Or greeted

---

27:29 *Be lord over your brothers.* Isaac was unwittingly blessing Jacob and thus fulfilling God's promise to Rebekah in 25:23.
27:33 *indeed he will be blessed.* The ancient world believed that blessings and curses had a kind of magical power to accomplish what they pronounced. But Isaac, as heir and steward of God's covenant blessing, acknowledged that he had solemnly transmitted that heritage to Jacob by way of a legally binding bequest (see note on v. 4).
27:34 *loud and bitter cry.* Esau's tears "could bring about no change of mind" (Heb 12:17).
27:36 *Isn't he rightly named Jacob?* See NIV text notes here and on 25:26. *He took my birthright, and now he's taken my blessing!* The Hebrew for "birthright" is *bekorah*, and for "blessing" it is *berakah* (see note on v. 6). Though

Esau tried to separate birthright from blessing, the former led inevitably to the latter, since both involved the inheritance of the firstborn (see Heb 12:16–17).
27:39 *away from the earth's richness, away from the dew of heaven.* Cf. v. 28. Isaac's secondary blessing of Esau could be only a parody of his primary blessing of Jacob.
27:40 See 25:23 and notes on 25:22,26.
27:43 *do what I say.* Bad advice earlier (see vv. 8,13), but sensible counsel this time.
27:44 *for a while.* Twenty years, as it turned out (see 31:38,41).
27:45 *both of you.* Either Jacob and Isaac or Jacob and Esau, who would become a target for blood revenge if he killed Jacob (cf. 2Sa 14:6–7).
27:46 See note on 26:35.

2Go at once to Paddan Aram,w m to the house of your mother's father Bethuel. n Take a wife for yourself there, from among the daughters of Laban, your mother's brother.o 3May God Almightyx p blessq you and make you fruitfulr and increase your numberss until you become a community of peoples. 4May he give you and your descendants the blessing given to Abraham,t so that you may take possession of the landu where you now live as an alien,v the land God gave to Abraham." 5Then Isaac sent Jacob on his way,w and he went to Paddan Aram,x to Laban son of Bethuel the Aramean,y the brother of Rebekah,z who was the mother of Jacob and Esau.

6Now Esau learned that Isaac had blessed Jacob and had sent him to Paddan Aram to take a wife from there, and that when he blessed him he commanded him, "Do not marry a Canaanite woman,"a 7and that Jacob had obeyed his father and mother and had gone to Paddan Aram. 8Esau then realized how displeasing the Canaanite womenb were to his father Isaac;c 9so he went to Ishmaeld and married Mahalath, the sister of Nebaiothe and daughter of Ishmael son of Abraham, in addition to the wives he already had.f

Jacob's Dream at Bethel

10Jacob left Beershebag and set out for Haran.h 11When he reached a certain place,i he stopped for the night because the sun had set. Taking one of the stones there, he put it under his headj and lay down to sleep. 12He had a dreamk in which he saw a stairwayy resting on the earth, with its top reaching to heaven, and the angels of God were ascending and descending on it.l 13There above itz stood the Lord,m and he said: "I am the Lord, the God of your father Abraham and God of Isaac.n I will give you and your descendants the lando on which you are lying.p 14Your descendants will be like the dust of the earth, and youq will spread out to the west and to the east, to the north and to the south.r All peoples on earth will be blessed through you and your offspring.s 15I am with yout and will watch over youuv wherever you go,w and I will bring you back to this land.x I will not leave youy until I have done what I have promised you.z " a

16When Jacob awoke from his sleep,b he thought, "Surely the Lord is in this place, and I was not aware of it." 17He was afraid and said, "How awesome is this place!c This is none other than the house of God;d this is the gate of heaven."

18Early the next morning Jacob took the stone he had placed under his heade and set it up as a pillarf and poured oil on top of it.g 19He called that place Bethel,a h though the city used to be called Luz.i

20Then Jacob made a vow,j saying, "If God will be with me and will watch over mek on this journey I am taking and will give me food to eat and clothes to wearl 21so that I return safelym to my father's

Cross references (center column)

28:2 mS Ge 25:20
nS Ge 25:20
nS Ge 21:21;
S 24:29
28:3 pS Ge 17:1
qGe 48:16;
Nu 6:24; Ru 2:4;
Ps 129:8; 134:3;
Jer 31:23
rS Ge 17:6
sS Ge 12:2
28:4 tS Ge 12:2,3
uS Ge 15:7
vS Ge 17:8
28:5 wS Ge 11:31
xHos 12:12
yS Ge 25:20
zS Ge 24:29
28:6 aS ver 1
28:8
bS Ge 10:15-19
cS Ge 26:35
28:9 dS Ge 16:15
eS Ge 25:13
fS Ge 26:34
28:10
gS Ge 21:14
hS Ge 11:31
28:11 iS Ge 12:8
/ver 18
28:12
kS Ge 20:3; 37:19
lJn 1:51
28:13
mS Ge 12:7;
35:7,9; 48:3
nS Ge 24:12;
48:16; 49:25;
50:17 oS Ge 12:7
pGe 46:4; 48:21
28:14 qGe 26:4
rS Ge 12:2;
S 13:14; S 26:24
sS Ge 12:3;
Ac 3:25; Gal 3:8
28:15
tS Ge 21:20
uPs 121:5,7-8
vver 20 wver 22;
Ge 35:3 xver 21;
S Ge 15:16;
30:25; 31:30
yDt 31:6,8;
Jos 1:5; Ne 4:14;
Ps 9:10
zLev 26:42
aPs 105:10
28:16 b1Ki 3:15;
Jer 31:26
28:17 cEx 3:5;
19:21; Jos 5:15;
Ps 68:24,35 dver
22; Ge 32:2; 1Ch 22:1; 2Ch 3:1 28:18 ever 11 /ver 22;
Ge 31:13,45,51; 35:14; Ex 24:4; Jos 24:26,27; Isa 19:19
gLev 8:11; Jos 4:9 28:19 hS Ge 12:8 iGe 35:6; 48:3;
Jos 16:2; 18:13; Jdg 1:23,26 28:20 /Ge 31:13; Lev 7:16;
22:18; 23:38; 27:2,9; Nu 6:2; 15:3; Dt 12:6; Jdg 11:30;
1Sa 1:21; 2Sa 15:8 kS ver 15 /1Ti 6:8 28:21 mJdg 11:31

w2 That is, Northwest Mesopotamia; also in verses 5, 6 and 7   x3 Hebrew El-Shaddai   y12 Or ladder
z13 Or There beside him   a19 Bethel means house of God.

28:2 Paddan Aram. Means "plain of Aram," another name for Aram Naharaim (see note on 24:10). Take a wife for yourself there. See 24:3-4.
28:3 God Almighty. See note on 17:1.
28:4 the blessing given to Abraham. For Paul's application of this phrase to Christian believers see Gal 3:14.
28:5 See map of "Jacob's Journeys," p. 53.
28:9 in addition to the wives he already had. See 26:34 and note.
28:11 one of the stones . . . under his head. In ancient times headrests (e.g., in Egypt) were often quite hard, sometimes being made of metal. People were used to sleeping on the ground.
28:12 stairway. Not a ladder with rungs, it was more likely a stairway such as mounted the sloping side of a ziggurat (see note on 11:4). angels of God were ascending and descending on it. A sign that the Lord offered to be Jacob's God. Jesus told a disciple that he would "see heaven open, and the angels of God ascending and descending on the Son of Man" (Jn 1:51). Jesus himself is the bridge between heaven and earth (see Jn 14:6), the only "mediator between God and men" (1Ti 2:5).

28:13 above it stood the Lord. Mesopotamian ziggurats were topped with a small shrine where worshipers prayed to their gods.
28:14 like the dust of the earth. See note on 13:16. All peoples on earth will be blessed through you. Repeats the blessing of 12:3.
28:15 I am with you. See note on 26:3. I will not leave you. Unlike the gods of pagan religions, in which the gods were merely local deities who gave protection only within their own territories, the one true God assured Jacob that he would always be with him wherever he went.
28:17 house of God . . . gate of heaven. Phrases that related Jacob's stairway to the Mesopotamian ziggurats (see notes on 11:4,9).
28:18 pillar. A memorial of worship or of communion between man and God, common in ancient times. poured oil on top of it. To consecrate it (see Ex 30:25-29).
28:21 return safely. Partially fulfilled in 33:18. the Lord will be my God. For the first time Jacob considered (conditionally: "If . . .") acknowledging the God of Abraham and Isaac (see v. 13; 27:20) as his own. His full acknowledgment came only after his safe return from Haran (see 33:20 and

house,[n] then the Lord[b] will be my God[o] [22]and[c] this stone that I have set up as a pillar[p] will be God's house,[q] and of all that you give me I will give you a tenth.[r] "

Jacob Arrives in Paddan Aram

29 Then Jacob continued on his journey and came to the land of the eastern peoples.[s] [2]There he saw a well in the field, with three flocks of sheep lying near it because the flocks were watered from that well.[t] The stone[u] over the mouth of the well was large. [3]When all the flocks were gathered there, the shepherds would roll the stone[v] away from the well's mouth and water the sheep.[w] Then they would return the stone to its place over the mouth of the well.

[4]Jacob asked the shepherds, "My brothers, where are you from?"[x]

"We're from Haran,[y]" they replied.

[5]He said to them, "Do you know Laban, Nahor's grandson?"[z]

"Yes, we know him," they answered.

[6]Then Jacob asked them, "Is he well?"

"Yes, he is," they said, "and here comes his daughter Rachel[a] with the sheep.[b]"

[7]"Look," he said, "the sun is still high; it is not time for the flocks to be gathered. Water the sheep and take them back to pasture."

[8]"We can't," they replied, "until all the flocks are gathered and the stone[c] has been rolled away from the mouth of the well. Then we will water[d] the sheep."

[9]While he was still talking with them, Rachel came with her father's sheep,[e] for she was a shepherdess. [10]When Jacob saw Rachel[f] daughter of Laban, his mother's brother, and Laban's sheep, he went over and rolled the stone[g] away from the mouth of the well and watered[h] his uncle's sheep.[i] [11]Then Jacob kissed[j] Rachel and began to weep aloud.[k] [12]He had told Rachel that he was a relative[l] of her father

and a son of Rebekah.[m] So she ran and told her father.[n]

[13]As soon as Laban[o] heard the news about Jacob, his sister's son, he hurried to meet him. He embraced him[p] and kissed him and brought him to his home, and there Jacob told him all these things. [14]Then Laban said to him, "You are my own flesh and blood."[q]

Jacob Marries Leah and Rachel

After Jacob had stayed with him for a whole month, [15]Laban said to him, "Just because you are a relative[r] of mine, should you work for me for nothing? Tell me what your wages[s] should be."

[16]Now Laban had two daughters; the name of the older was Leah,[t] and the name of the younger was Rachel.[u] [17]Leah had weak[d] eyes, but Rachel[v] was lovely in form, and beautiful. [18]Jacob was in love with Rachel[x] and said, "I'll work for you seven years in return for your younger daughter Rachel."[y]

[19]Laban said, "It's better that I give her to you than to some other man. Stay here with me." [20]So Jacob served seven years to get Rachel,[z] but they seemed like only a few days to him because of his love for her.[a]

[21]Then Jacob said to Laban, "Give me my wife. My time is completed, and I want to lie with her.[b]"

[22]So Laban brought together all the people of the place and gave a feast.[c] [23]But when evening came, he took his daughter Leah[d] and gave her to Jacob, and Jacob lay with her. [24]And Laban gave his servant girl Zilpah[e] to his daughter as her maidservant.[f]

[25]When morning came, there was Leah!

28:21 [n]S ver 15 [o]Ex 15:2; Dt 26:17; Jos 24:18; Ps 48:14; 118:28 **28:22** [p]S ver 18; 1Sa 7:12 [q]S ver 17 [r]S Ge 14:20; S Nu 18:21; Lk 18:12 **29:1** [s]S Ge 25:6 **29:2** [t]S Ge 24:11 [u]ver 3,8,10 **29:3** [v]S ver 2 [w]ver 8 **29:4** [x]Ge 42:7; Jdg 19:17 [y]S Ge 11:31 **29:5** [z]S Ge 11:29 **29:6** [a]Ge 30:22-24; 35:16; 46:19,22 [b]Ex 2:16 **29:8** [c]S ver 2 [d]S Ge 24:13 **29:9** [e]Ex 2:16 **29:10** [f]ver 16 [g]S ver 2 [h]S Ge 24:11 [i]ver 3; Ex 2:17 **29:11** [j]ver 13 [k]Ge 33:4; 42:24; 43:30; 45:2, 14-15; 46:29; 50:1,17; Ru 1:9 **29:12** [l]ver 15

[m]S Ge 24:29 [n]Ge 24:28 **29:13** [o]S Ge 24:29 [p]Ge 33:4; 45:14-15,14; 48:10; Ex 4:27; 18:7; Lk 15:20 **29:14** [q]Ge 2:23; 37:27; Jdg 9:2; 2Sa 5:1; 19:12-13; 20:1; Ne 5:5; Isa 58:7 **29:15** [r]ver 12 [s]Ge 30:28,32; 31:7,41 **29:16** [t]ver 17,23, 28,30; Ge 30:9; 35:23; 47:30; 49:31; Ru 4:11 [u]ver 9-10 **29:17** [v]S ver 16 [w]S Ge 12:11 **29:18** [x]S Ge 24:67 [y]ver 20,27,30; Ge 30:26; Hos 12:12 **29:20** [z]S ver 18; Ge 31:15 [a]SS 8:7; Hos 12:12 **29:21** [b]Jdg 15:1 **29:22** [c]Jdg 14:10; Isa 25:6; Jn 2:1-2

29:23 [d]S ver 16 **29:24** [e]Ge 30:9 [f]S Ge 16:1

[b]20,21 Or Since God ... father's house, the Lord
[c]21,22 Or house, and the Lord will be my God, [22]then
[d]17 Or delicate

---

note).
28:22 this stone ... will be God's house. In the sense that it would memorialize Jacob's meeting with God at Bethel (see NIV text note on v. 19). of all that you give me I will give you a tenth. A way of acknowledging the Lord as his God and King (see note on 14:20).
29:5 Laban, Nahor's grandson. See 24:15,29. The Hebrew word here for "grandson" is lit. "son," which can refer to any male descendant (see NIV text note on 10:2).
29:9 shepherdess. The task of caring for sheep and goats in the Middle East was shared by men and women.
29:10 rolled the stone away. A feat of unusual strength for one man, because the stone was large (see v. 2).
29:11 weep aloud. For joy.
29:14 flesh and blood. The English equivalent of a Hebrew phrase that means lit. "bone and flesh" and that stresses

blood kinship (see, e.g., 2:23).
29:16 Leah ... Rachel. The names mean "cow" and "ewe" respectively, appropriate in a herdsman's family.
29:21 my wife. If Jacob had said "Rachel," Laban would have had no excuse for giving him Leah.
29:22 feast. A wedding feast was usually seven days long (see vv. 27-28; Jdg 14:10,12).
29:23 when evening came ... Jacob lay with her. The darkness, or perhaps a veil (see 24:65), may have concealed Leah's identity.
29:24 See v. 29; a wedding custom documented in Old Babylonian marriage contracts.
29:25 you deceived me. Jacob, the deceiver in name (see NIV text notes on 25:26; 27:36) as well as in behavior (see 27:36), had himself been deceived. The one who had tried everything to obtain the benefits of the firstborn had now,

So Jacob said to Laban, "What is this you
have done to me?[g] I served you for Rachel, didn't I? Why have you deceived
me?[h]"
26 Laban replied, "It is not our custom
here to give the younger daughter in marriage before the older one.[i] 27 Finish this
daughter's bridal week;[j] then we will give
you the younger one also, in return for another seven years of work.[k]"
28 And Jacob did so. He finished the
week with Leah, and then Laban gave him
his daughter Rachel to be his wife.[l] 29 Laban gave his servant girl Bilhah[m] to his
daughter Rachel as her maidservant.[n]
30 Jacob lay with Rachel also, and he loved
Rachel more than Leah.[o] And he worked
for Laban another seven years.[p]

Jacob's Children

31 When the LORD saw that Leah was not
loved,[q] he opened her womb,[r] but Rachel
was barren. 32 Leah became pregnant and
gave birth to a son.[s] She named him Reuben,[e t] for she said, "It is because the
LORD has seen my misery.[u] Surely my husband will love me now."
33 She conceived again, and when she
gave birth to a son she said, "Because the
LORD heard that I am not loved,[v] he gave
me this one too." So she named him Simeon.[f w]
34 Again she conceived, and when she
gave birth to a son she said, "Now at last
my husband will become attached to me,[x]
because I have borne him three sons." So
he was named Levi.[g y]
35 She conceived again, and when she
gave birth to a son she said, "This time I
will praise the LORD." So she named him
Judah.[h z] Then she stopped having children.[a]

30 When Rachel saw that she was not
bearing Jacob any children,[b] she
became jealous of her sister.[c] So she said
to Jacob, "Give me children, or I'll die!"
2 Jacob became angry with her and said,
"Am I in the place of God,[d] who has kept
you from having children?"[e]
3 Then she said, "Here is Bilhah,[f] my
maidservant.[g] Sleep with her so that she
can bear children for me and that through
her I too can build a family."[h]
4 So she gave him her servant Bilhah as a
wife.[i] Jacob slept with her,[j] 5 and she
became pregnant and bore him a son.
6 Then Rachel said, "God has vindicated
me;[k] he has listened to my plea and given
me a son."[l] Because of this she named
him Dan.[i m]
7 Rachel's servant Bilhah[n] conceived
again and bore Jacob a second son. 8 Then
Rachel said, "I have had a great struggle
with my sister, and I have won."[o] So she
named him Naphtali.[j p]
9 When Leah[q] saw that she had stopped
having children,[r] she took her maidservant Zilpah[s] and gave her to Jacob as a
wife.[t] 10 Leah's servant Zilpah[u] bore Jacob
a son. 11 Then Leah said, "What good fortune!"[k] So she named him Gad.[l v]
12 Leah's servant Zilpah bore Jacob a second son. 13 Then Leah said, "How happy I
am! The women will call me[w] happy."[x]
So she named him Asher.[m y]
14 During wheat harvest,[z] Reuben went
out into the fields and found some man-

29:25 [g]S Ge 12:18 [h]S Ge 27:36 **29:26** [i]Jdg 15:2; 1Sa 14:49; 18:17, 20; 2Sa 6:23 **29:27** [j]Jdg 14:12 [k]S ver 18; Ge 31:41 **29:28** [l]S ver 16; S Ge 4:19 **29:29** [m]Ge 30:3; 35:22; 49:4; Dt 22:30; 1Ch 5:1 [n]S Ge 16:1 **29:30** [o]S ver 16 [p]S ver 20 **29:31** [q]ver 33; Dt 21:15-17 [r]S Ge 11:30; S 16:2; Ru 4:13; 1Sa 1:19; Ps 127:3 **29:32** [s]Ge 30:23; Ru 4:13; 1Sa 1:20 [t]Ge 37:21; 46:8; 48:5,14; 49:3; Ex 6:14; Nu 1:5, 20; 26:5; Dt 33:6; Jos 4:12; 1Ch 5:1,3 [u]S Ge 16:11 **29:33** [v]S ver 31 [w]Ge 34:25; 46:10; 48:5; 49:5; Ex 6:15; Nu 1:6,22; 34:20; 1Ch 4:24; Eze 48:24 **29:34** [x]Ge 30:20; 1Sa 1:2-4 [y]Ge 34:25; 46:11; 49:5-7; Ex 2:1; 6:16,19; Nu 1:47; 3:17-20; 26:57; Dt 33:8; 1Ch 6:1, 16; 23:6-24, 13-14 **29:35** [z]Ge 35:23; 37:26; 38:1; 43:8; 44:14,18; 46:12; 49:8; 1Ch 2:3; 4:1; Isa 48:1; Mt 1:2-3 [a]Ge 30:9 **30:1** [b]S Ge 11:30; Isa 49:21; 54:1 [c]S Ge 16:4; Lev 18:18 **30:2** [d]Ge 50:19; Dt 32:35; 2Ki 5:7 [e]S Ge 16:2 **30:3** [f]ver 7; S Ge 29:29 [g]S Ge 24:61 [h]Ge 16:2 **30:4** [i]ver 9,18 [j]Ge 16:3-4

30:6 [k]Ps 35:24; 43:1 [l]ver 23; Ge 21:2; Ru 4:13; 1Sa 1:20 [m]Ge 46:23; 49:16-17; Nu 26:42-43; Jos 19:40-48; Jdg 1:34; 13:2; 18:2; Jer 4:15; 8:16; Eze 48:1 **30:7** [n]S ver 3 **30:8** [o]Ge 32:28; Hos 12:3-4 [p]Ge 35:25; 46:24; 49:21; Nu 1:42; 26:48; Dt 33:23; Jdg 4:6; 5:18; 1Ch 7:13 **30:9** [q]S Ge 29:16 [r]Ge 29:35 [s]Ge 29:24 [t]S ver 4 **30:10** [u]Ge 46:18 **30:11** [v]Ge 35:26; 46:16; 49:19; Ex 1:4; Nu 1:24; 26:18; Jos 4:12; 1Ch 5:11; 12:8; Jer 49:1 **30:13** [w]Ps 127:3 [x]Ru 4:14; Ps 127:4-5; Lk 1:48 [y]Ge 35:26; 46:17; 49:20; Nu 1:40; 26:47; Dt 33:24; Jos 19:24-31; 1Ch 7:30-31 **30:14** [z]Ex 34:22; Jdg 15:1; Ru 2:23; 1Sa 6:13; 12:17

[e]32 *Reuben* sounds like the Hebrew for *he has seen my misery*; the name means *see, a son.* [f]33 *Simeon* probably means *one who hears.* [g]34 *Levi* sounds like and may be derived from the Hebrew for *attached.* [h]35 *Judah* sounds like and may be derived from the Hebrew for *praise.* [i]6 *Dan* here means *he has vindicated.* [j]8 *Naphtali* means *my struggle.* [k]11 Or *"A troop is coming!"* [l]11 *Gad* can mean *good fortune* or *a troop.* [m]13 *Asher* means *happy.*

against his will, received the firstborn (vv. 16,26).

29:28 *then Laban gave him his daughter Rachel.* Before Jacob worked another seven years (see v. 30).

29:30 *Jacob . . . loved Rachel more than Leah.* Not only because Rachel had been his choice from the beginning but also, no doubt, because Laban had tricked Jacob into marrying Leah.

29:31–35 Leah, though unloved, nevertheless became the mother of Jacob's first four sons, including Levi (ancestor of the Aaronic priestly line) and Judah (ancestor of David and his royal line, and ultimately of Jesus).

29:32 *named him Reuben . . . because the LORD has seen my misery.* Ishmael had received his name in similar circumstances (see 16:11).

30:1 *she became jealous of her sister.* As Jacob was of his older brother. *Give me children, or I'll die!* Tragically prophetic words (see 35:16–19).

30:2 *Am I in the place of God . . . ?* Jacob was forever trying to secure the blessing by his own efforts. Here he has to acknowledge that the blessing of offspring could come only from God (see 31:7–13 for the blessing of flocks). Joseph later echoed these words (see 50:19).

30:3 *Sleep with her.* See v. 9; see also 16:2 and note. *for me.* Lit. "on my knees," apparently an expression symbolic of adoption (see 48:10–16) and meaning "as though my own" (see 50:23 and NIV text note).

30:4 *as a wife.* As a concubine (see 35:22).

30:5–12 Jacob's fifth, sixth, seventh and eighth sons were born to him through his maidservant concubines.

30:14 *give me some of your son's mandrakes.* The man-

drake plants, *a* which he brought to his mother Leah. Rachel said to Leah, "Please give me some of your son's mandrakes."

[15]But she said to her, "Wasn't it enough *b* that you took away my husband? Will you take my son's mandrakes too?"

"Very well," Rachel said, "he can sleep with you tonight in return for your son's mandrakes." *c*

[16]So when Jacob came in from the fields that evening, Leah went out to meet him. "You must sleep with me," she said. "I have hired you with my son's mandrakes." *d* So he slept with her that night.

[17]God listened to Leah, *e* and she became pregnant and bore Jacob a fifth son. [18]Then Leah said, "God has rewarded me for giving my maidservant to my husband." *f* So she named him Issachar. *n g*

[19]Leah conceived again and bore Jacob a sixth son. [20]Then Leah said, "God has presented me with a precious gift. This time my husband will treat me with honor, *h* because I have borne him six sons." So she named him Zebulun. *o i*

[21]Some time later she gave birth to a daughter and named her Dinah. *j*

[22]Then God remembered Rachel; *k* he listened to her *l* and opened her womb. *m* [23]She became pregnant and gave birth to a son *n* and said, "God has taken away my disgrace." *o* [24]She named him Joseph, *p p* and said, "May the LORD add to me another son." *q*

Jacob's Flocks Increase

[25]After Rachel gave birth to Joseph, Jacob said to Laban, "Send me on my way *r* so I can go back to my own homeland. *s* [26]Give me my wives and children, for whom I have served you, *t* and I will be on my way. You know how much work I've done for you."

[27]But Laban said to him, "If I have found favor in your eyes, *u* please stay. I

have learned by divination *v* that *q* the LORD has blessed me because of you." *w* [28]He added, "Name your wages, *x* and I will pay them."

[29]Jacob said to him, "You know how I have worked for you *y* and how your livestock has fared under my care. *z* [30]The little you had before I came has increased greatly, and the LORD has blessed you wherever I have been. *a* But now, when may I do something for my own household?" *b* "

[31]"What shall I give you?" he asked.

"Don't give me anything," Jacob replied. "But if you will do this one thing for me, I will go on tending your flocks and watching over them: [32]Let me go through all your flocks today and remove from them every speckled or spotted sheep, every dark-colored lamb and every spotted or speckled goat. *c* They will be my wages. *d* [33]And my honesty will testify for me in the future, whenever you check on the wages you have paid me. Any goat in my possession that is not speckled or spotted, or any lamb that is not dark-colored, *e* will be considered stolen. *f* "

[34]"Agreed," said Laban. "Let it be as you have said." [35]That same day he removed all the male goats that were streaked or spotted, and all the speckled or spotted female goats (all that had white on them) and all the dark-colored lambs, *g* and he placed them in the care of his sons. *h* [36]Then he put a three-day journey *i* between himself and Jacob, while Jacob continued to tend the rest of Laban's flocks.

[37]Jacob, however, took fresh-cut

30:14 *a*ver 15, 16; SS 7:13
30:15 *b*Nu 16:9, 13; Isa 7:13; Eze 34:18
*c*Ge 38:16; Eze 16:33; Hos 9:1
30:16 *d*S ver 14
30:17 *e*S Ge 25:21
30:18 *f*S ver 4 *g*Ge 46:13; 49:1; Nu 1:8,28, 29; 26:25; Dt 27:12; 33:18; Jos 17:10; 19:17; 21:6,28; Jdg 5:15; 10:1; 1Ch 7:1
30:20 *h*S Ge 29:34; 1Pe 3:7 *i*Ge 35:23; 46:14; 49:13; Nu 1:30; 26:27; 34:25; Dt 33:18; Jdg 5:18
30:21 *j*Ge 34:1; 46:15
30:22 *k*S Ge 8:1 *l*S Ge 25:21 *m*S Ge 11:30
30:23 *n*S ver 6; S Ge 29:32 *o*Isa 4:1; 25:8; 45:17; 54:4; Lk 1:25
30:24 *p*S Ge 29:6; 32:22; 33:2,7; 35:24; 37:2; 39:1; 49:22-26; Dt 33:13 *q*Ge 35:17; 1Sa 4:20
30:25 *r*S Ge 24:54 *s*S Ge 28:15
30:26 *t*S Ge 29:18
30:27 *u*Ge 33:10; 50:4; Est 2:15
*v*Ge 44:5,15; Lev 19:26; Nu 22:7; 23:23; 24:1; Jos 13:22; 2Ki 17:17; Jer 27:9 *w*ver 30; S Ge 26:24; 31:38; Dt 28:11; 2Sa 6:11
30:28 *x*S Ge 29:15
30:29 *y*Ge 31:6 *z*Ge 31:38-40
30:30 *a*S ver 27 *b*1Ti 5:8
30:32 *c*ver 33,35, 39,40; Ge 31:8,

12 *d*S Ge 29:15 **30:33** *e*S ver 32 *f*Ge 31:39 **30:35** *g*S ver 32 *h*Ge 31:1 **30:36** *i*Ge 31:22; Ex 3:18; 5:3; 8:27

n18 Issachar sounds like the Hebrew for *reward.* *o20 Zebulun* probably means *honor.* *p24 Joseph* means *may he add.* *q27* Or possibly *have become rich and*

---

drake has fleshy, forked roots that resemble the lower part of a human body and were therefore superstitiously thought to induce pregnancy when eaten (see SS 7:13). Rachel, like Jacob (vv. 37–43), tried to obtain what she wanted by magical means.
30:16 *hired.* The Hebrew for this word is a pun on the name Issachar (see NIV text note on v. 18).
30:17–20 Jacob's ninth and tenth sons were born through Leah, who was thus the mother of half of Jacob's 12 sons (see note on 29:31–35).
30:20 *presented . . . gift.* The Hebrew terms for these words are puns on the name Zebulun (see NIV text note).
30:21 *Dinah.* See ch. 34.
30:22 *God remembered Rachel.* See note on 8:1.
30:23 *disgrace.* Barrenness was considered to be shameful, a mark of divine disfavor (see 16:2; 30:2).

30:24 *May the LORD add to me another son.* The fulfillment of Rachel's wish would bring about her death (see 35:16–19).
30:27 *divination.* The attempt to discover hidden knowledge through mechanical means (see 44:5), the interpretation of omens (see Eze 21:21) or the aid of supernatural powers (see Ac 16:16). It was strictly forbidden to Israel (Lev 19:26; Dt 18:10,14) because it reflected a pagan concept of the world controlled by evil forces, and therefore obviously not under the sovereign rule of the Lord. *the LORD has blessed me because of you.* Cf. 21:22; 26:28–29. The offspring of Abraham were a source of blessing (see 12:2).
30:35 *he removed.* Secretly and without telling Jacob.
30:37 *poplar . . . white.* The Hebrew terms for these words are puns on the name Laban. As Jacob had gotten the best of Esau (whose other name, Edom, means "red"; see note on

branches from poplar, almond[j] and plane trees[k] and made white stripes on them by peeling the bark and exposing the white inner wood of the branches.[l] 38Then he placed the peeled branches[m] in all the watering troughs,[n] so that they would be directly in front of the flocks when they came to drink. When the flocks were in heat[o] and came to drink, 39they mated in front of the branches.[p] And they bore young that were streaked or speckled or spotted.[q] 40Jacob set apart the young of the flock by themselves, but made the rest face the streaked and dark-colored animals[r] that belonged to Laban. Thus he made separate flocks for himself and did not put them with Laban's animals. 41Whenever the stronger females were in heat,[s] Jacob would place the branches in the troughs in front of the animals so they would mate near the branches,[t] 42but if the animals were weak, he would not place them there. So the weak animals went to Laban and the strong ones to Jacob.[u] 43In this way the man grew exceedingly prosperous and came to own large flocks, and maidservants and menservants, and camels and donkeys.[v]

Jacob Flees From Laban

31 Jacob heard that Laban's sons[w] were saying, "Jacob has taken everything our father owned and has gained all this wealth from what belonged to our father."[x] 2And Jacob noticed that Laban's attitude toward him was not what it had been.[y]

3Then the LORD said to Jacob, "Go back[z] to the land of your fathers and to your relatives, and I will be with you."[a]

4So Jacob sent word to Rachel and Leah to come out to the fields where his flocks were. 5He said to them, "I see that your father[b]'s attitude toward me is not what it was before,[c] but the God of my father has

been with me.[d] 6You know that I've worked for your father with all my strength,[e] 7yet your father has cheated[f] me by changing my wages[g] ten times.[h] However, God has not allowed him to harm me.[i] 8If he said, 'The speckled ones will be your wages,' then all the flocks gave birth to speckled young; and if he said, 'The streaked ones will be your wages,'[j] then all the flocks bore streaked young. 9So God has taken away your father's livestock[k] and has given them to me.[l]

10"In breeding season I once had a dream[m] in which I looked up and saw that the male goats mating with the flock were streaked, speckled or spotted. 11The angel of God[n] said to me in the dream,[o] 'Jacob.' I answered, 'Here I am.'[p] 12And he said, 'Look up and see that all the male goats mating with the flock are streaked, speckled or spotted,[q] for I have seen all that Laban has been doing to you.[r] 13I am the God of Bethel,[s] where you anointed a pillar[t] and where you made a vow[u] to me. Now leave this land at once and go back to your native land.'[v]"

14Then Rachel and Leah replied, "Do we still have any share[w] in the inheritance of our father's estate? 15Does he not regard us as foreigners?[x] Not only has he sold us, but he has used up what was paid for us.[y] 16Surely all the wealth that God took away from our father belongs to us and our children.[z] So do whatever God has told you."

17Then Jacob put his children and his wives[a] on camels,[b] 18and he drove all his livestock ahead of him, along with all the goods he had accumulated[c] in Paddan Aram,[r][d] to go to his father Isaac[e] in the land of Canaan.[f]

19When Laban had gone to shear his sheep,[g] Rachel stole her father's house-

---

Cross references (center column):

30:37 /Jer 1:11; kEze 31:8; lver 38,41
30:38 mS ver 37; nEx 2:16 over 41; Jer 2:24
30:39 pver 41; qS ver 32
30:40 rS ver 32
30:41 sS ver 38; tS ver 37
30:42 uGe 31:1, 9,16,43
30:43 vS Ge 12:16
31:1 wGe 30:35; xS Ge 30:42
31:2 yver 5
31:3 zver 13; Ge 32:9; Dt 30:3; Isa 10:21; 35:10; Jer 30:3; 42:12 aS Ge 21:22; S 26:3
31:5 bver 29,42, 53; Ge 43:23; Da 2:23 cver 2

dS Ge 21:22; S 26:3
31:6 eGe 30:29
31:7 fLev 6:2; Am 8:5 gS Ge 29:15 hver 41; Nu 14:22; Job 19:3 iver 52; S Ge 24:50
31:8 jS Ge 30:32
31:9 kJob 39:2; Eze 31:6 lS Ge 30:42
31:10 mS Ge 20:3
31:11 nS Ge 16:7 oS Ge 20:3 pS Ge 22:1; S Ex 3:4
31:12 qS Ge 30:32 rEx 3:7
31:13 sGe 28:10-22 tS Ge 28:18 uS Ge 28:20 vS ver 3
31:14 w2Sa 20:1; 1Ki 12:16
31:15 xDt 15:3; 23:20; Ru 2:10; 2Sa 15:19; 1Ki 8:41; Ob 1:11 yS Ge 29:20
31:16 zS Ge 30:42
31:17 aS Ge 27:41 bS Ge 24:63-64
31:18 cS Ge 12:5 dS Ge 25:20 eGe 35:27 fS Ge 10:19

31:19 gGe 38:12,13; 1Sa 25:2,4,7; 2Sa 13:23

r18 That is, Northwest Mesopotamia

25:25) by means of red stew (25:30), so he now tries to get the best of Laban (whose name means "white") by means of white branches. In effect, Jacob was using Laban's own tactic (deception) against him.

30:39 The scheme worked—but only because of God's intervention (see Jacob's own admission in 31:9), not because of Jacob's superstition.

30:43 *the man grew exceedingly prosperous.* Over a period of six years (see 31:41). While in Haran Jacob obtained both family and wealth.

31:3 *Go back to the land of your fathers.* Every sign Jacob was getting—from his wives (see vv. 14–16), from Laban (see v. 2), from Laban's sons (see v. 1) and now from God himself—told him that it was time to return to Canaan. *I will be with you.* See note on 26:3.

31:4 *Rachel and Leah.* At long last (see v. 14) Rachel, the

younger, has been given precedence over Leah—but she will soon become a deceiver like her husband Jacob (see vv. 31,35).

31:7 *ten times.* See v. 41. "Ten" here probably signifies completeness. In effect, Jacob accused Laban of cheating him at every turn.

31:9 See note on 30:39.

31:11 *angel of God.* See note on 16:7. *Here I am.* See note on 22:1.

31:13 *Bethel, where you anointed a pillar.* See note on 28:18.

31:18 *Paddan Aram.* Means "plain of Aram," another name for Aram Naharaim (see note on 24:10). See map of "Jacob's Journeys," p. 53.

31:19 *household gods.* Small portable idols, which Rachel probably stole because she thought they would bring her

hold gods.[h] [20]Moreover, Jacob deceived[i] Laban the Aramean[j] by not telling him he was running away.[k] [21]So he fled[l] with all he had, and crossing the River,[s][m] he headed for the hill country of Gilead.[n]

Laban Pursues Jacob

[22]On the third day[o] Laban was told that Jacob had fled.[p] [23]Taking his relatives[q] with him,[r] he pursued Jacob for seven days and caught up with him in the hill country of Gilead.[s] [24]Then God came to Laban the Aramean[t] in a dream at night and said to him,[u] "Be careful not to say anything to Jacob, either good or bad."[v]

[25]Jacob had pitched his tent in the hill country of Gilead[w] when Laban overtook him, and Laban and his relatives camped there too. [26]Then Laban said to Jacob, "What have you done?[x] You've deceived

me,[y] and you've carried off my daughters like captives in war.[z] [27]Why did you run off secretly and deceive me? Why didn't you tell me,[a] so I could send you away with joy and singing to the music of tambourines[b] and harps?[c] [28]You didn't even let me kiss my grandchildren and my daughters good-by.[d] You have done a foolish thing. [29]I have the power to harm you;[e] but last night the God of your father[f] said to me, 'Be careful not to say anything to Jacob, either good or bad.'[g] [30]Now you have gone off because you

31:19 [h]ver 30, 32,34-35; Ge 35:2; Jos 24:14; Jdg 17:5; 18:14, 17,24,30; 1Sa 7:3; 19:13; 2Ki 23:24; Hos 3:4
31:20 [i]S Ge 27:36 [j]S Ge 25:20 [k]ver 27
31:21 [l]ver 22; Ex 2:15; 14:5; 1Ki 18:46; 19:3; Jer 26:21 [m]S Ge 2:14 [n]ver 23,25; Ge 37:25; Nu 26:30; 32:1; Dt 3:10; Jos 12:2; Jer 22:6
31:22 [o]S Ge 30:36 [p]S ver 21
31:23 [q]ver 37 [r]Ex 14:9 [s]S ver 21
31:24 [t]S Ge 25:20 [u]S Ge 20:3 [v]S Ge 24:50

31:25 [w]S ver 21 **31:26** [x]S Ge 12:18 [y]S Ge 27:36 [z]Ge 34:29; 1Sa 30:2-3 **31:27** [a]ver 20 [b]Ex 15:20; Jdg 11:34; 1Sa 10:5; 2Sa 6:5; Ps 68:25; Isa 24:8; Jer 31:4 [c]S Ge 4:21 **31:28** [d]S Ge 27:27; Ru 1:14; Ac 20:37 **31:29** [e]S ver 7; S Ge 26:29 [f]S ver 5 [g]S Ge 24:50

[s]21 That is, the Euphrates

---

protection and blessing. Or perhaps she wanted to have something tangible to worship on the long journey ahead, a practice referred to much later in the writings of Josephus, a first-century Jewish historian. In any case, Rachel was not yet free of her pagan background (see 35:2; Jos 24:2).
31:21 *So he fled.* As he had fled earlier from Esau,

(27:42–43). Jacob's devious dealings produced only hostility from which he had to flee. *Gilead.* A fertile region southeast of the Sea of Galilee.
31:26 *deceived.* Jacob's character, reflected in his name (see NIV text notes on 25:26; 27:36), is emphasized in the narrative again and again.

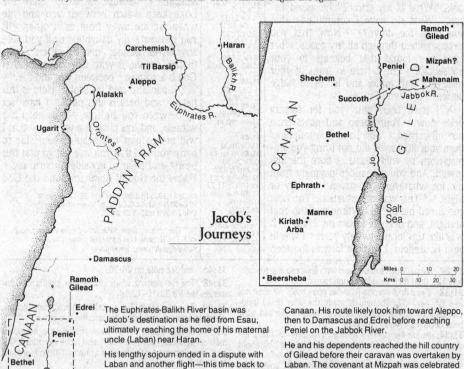

Jacob's Journeys

The Euphrates-Balikh River basin was Jacob's destination as he fled from Esau, ultimately reaching the home of his maternal uncle (Laban) near Haran.

His lengthy sojourn ended in a dispute with Laban and another flight—this time back to

Canaan. His route likely took him toward Aleppo, then to Damascus and Edrei before reaching Peniel on the Jabbok River.

He and his dependents reached the hill country of Gilead before their caravan was overtaken by Laban. The covenant at Mizpah was celebrated on one of the hills later used as a border station between Aramean and Israelite territories.

Jacob tarried at Succoth, entered Canaan and proceeded to Shechem, where he erected an altar to the Lord.

longed to return to your father's house. [h] But why did you steal [i] my gods? [j] "

[31] Jacob answered Laban, "I was afraid, because I thought you would take your daughters away from me by force. [k] [32] But if you find anyone who has your gods, he shall not live. [l] In the presence of our relatives, see for yourself whether there is anything of yours here with me; and if so, take it." Now Jacob did not know that Rachel had stolen the gods. [m]

[33] So Laban went into Jacob's tent and into Leah's tent [n] and into the tent of the two maidservants, [o] but he found nothing. [p] After he came out of Leah's tent, he entered Rachel's tent. [34] Now Rachel had taken the household gods [q] and put them inside her camel's saddle [r] and was sitting on them. Laban searched [s] through everything in the tent but found nothing.

[35] Rachel said to her father, "Don't be angry, my lord, that I cannot stand up in your presence; [t] I'm having my period. [u] " So he searched but could not find the household gods. [v]

[36] Jacob was angry and took Laban to task. "What is my crime?" he asked Laban. "What sin have I committed [w] that you hunt me down? [x] [37] Now that you have searched through all my goods, what have you found that belongs to your household? [y] Put it here in front of your relatives [z] and mine, and let them judge between the two of us. [a]

[38] "I have been with you for twenty years now. [b] Your sheep and goats have not miscarried, [c] nor have I eaten rams from your flocks. [39] I did not bring you animals torn by wild beasts; I bore the loss myself. And you demanded payment from me for whatever was stolen [d] by day or night. [e] [40] This was my situation: The heat consumed me in the daytime and the cold at night, and sleep fled from my eyes. [f] [41] It was like this for the twenty years [g] I was in your household. I worked for you fourteen years for your two daughters [h] and six years for your flocks, [i] and you changed my wages [j] ten times. [k] [42] If the God of my father, [l] the God of Abraham [m] and the Fear of Isaac, [n] had not been with me, [o] you would surely have sent me away empty-handed. But God has seen my hardship and the toil of my hands, [p] and last night he rebuked you. [q] "

[43] Laban answered Jacob, "The women are my daughters, the children are my children, and the flocks are my flocks. [r] All you see is mine. Yet what can I do today about these daughters of mine, or about the children they have borne? [44] Come now, let's make a covenant, [s] you and I, and let it serve as a witness between us." [t]

[45] So Jacob took a stone and set it up as a pillar. [u] [46] He said to his relatives, "Gather some stones." So they took stones and piled them in a heap, [v] and they ate there by the heap. [47] Laban called it Jegar Sahadutha, [t] and Jacob called it Galeed. [u] [w]

[48] Laban said, "This heap [x] is a witness between you and me today." [y] That is why it was called Galeed. [49] It was also called Mizpah, [v] [z] because he said, "May the LORD keep watch between you and me when we are away from each other. [50] If you mistreat [a] my daughters or if you take any wives besides my daughters, even though no one is with us, remember that God is a witness [b] between you and me." [c]

[51] Laban also said to Jacob, "Here is this heap, [d] and here is this pillar [e] I have set up between you and me. [52] This heap is a witness, and this pillar is a witness, [f] that I will not go past this heap to your side to harm you and that you will not go past this heap [g] and pillar to my side to harm me. [h] [53] May the God of Abraham [i] and the God

Cross references (center column)

31:30 [h]S Ge 28:15; [i]Job 29:2 [j]Ge 44:8 /S ver 19
31:31 [k]S Ge 20:11
31:32 [l]Ge 44:9 [m]S ver 19
31:33 [n]Ge 24:67 [o]S Ge 16:1 [p]ver 37
31:34 [q]S ver 19 [r]S Ge 24:63-64 [s]ver 37; Ge 44:12
31:35 [t]Ex 20:12; Lev 19:3,32; Dt 21:18; 27:16; Jer 35:18 [u]Lev 15:19-23 [v]ver 19
31:36 [w]1Sa 19:5; 20:32 [x]1Sa 23:23; 24:11
31:37 [y]ver 33 [z]ver 23 [a]Dt 1:16; 16:18
31:38 [b]S Ge 27:44 [c]S Ge 30:27
31:39 [d]Ge 30:33 [e]Ex 22:13
31:40 [f]Ps 132:4; 2Co 11:27
31:41 [g]S Ge 27:44
[h]Ge 29:30 [i]S Ge 30:32 [j]S Ge 29:15 [k]S ver 7
31:42 [l]S ver 5; S Ex 3:15 [m]S Ge 24:12 [n]ver 53; Ge 46:1 [o]S Ge 21:22; Ps 124:1-2 [p]S Ge 3:17 [q]S Ge 24:50
31:43 [r]Ge 30:32, 42
31:44 [s]S Ge 21:27 [t]S Ge 21:30
31:45 [u]S Ge 28:18
31:46 [v]ver 48,51, 52
31:47 [w]S Ge 21:30
31:48 [x]S ver 46 [y]S Ge 21:30; Jer 29:23; 42:5
31:49 [z]Jos 11:3; Jdg 10:17; 11:29
31:50 [a]Ge 16:6 [b]Dt 31:19; Jos 24:27; Jdg 11:10; 1Sa 12:5; 20:14, 23,42; Job 16:19; Jer 29:23; 42:5; Mic 1:2
[c]S Ge 21:30; S Dt 4:26; S Jer 7:11 **31:51** [d]S ver 46 [e]S Ge 28:18 **31:52** [f]S Ge 21:30 [g]S ver 46 [h]S ver 7; S Ge 26:29 **31:53** [i]S Ge 24:12

[t]47 The Aramaic *Jegar Sahadutha* means *witness heap.*
[u]47 The Hebrew *Galeed* means *witness heap.*
[v]49 *Mizpah* means *watchtower.*

31:27 *harps.* Much smaller, and with fewer strings (usually 6 to 12), than their modern counterparts.
31:32 *if you find anyone who has your gods, he shall not live.* Cf. 44:7–12. Though he made the offer in all innocence, Jacob almost lost his beloved Rachel. He had now been deceived even by his wife.
31:34 *inside her camel's saddle . . . sitting on them.* Indicating the small size and powerlessness of the household gods.
31:35 *I'm having my period.* In later times, anything a menstruating woman sat on was considered ritually unclean (Lev 15:20). Rachel, too, had become a deceiver.
31:42 *Fear.* Here a surrogate for God. Or perhaps the Hebrew for this word means "Kinsman," stressing the intimacy of God's relationship to the patriarch.

31:46 *ate.* See note on 26:30.
31:48 For the naming of an altar under similar circumstances see Jos 22:10–12,34.
31:49 *May . . . other.* The so-called Mizpah benediction, which in context is in fact a denunciation or curse.
31:51 *heap . . . pillar . . . between you and me.* Boundary markers between Laban's territory and Jacob's territory. Galeed, Jacob's name for the heap, is a pun on Gilead (see v. 47 and NIV text note).
31:53 *God of their father.* Or possibly "gods of their father [i.e., Terah]," reflecting Laban's polytheistic background (see Jos 24:2). *Fear of his father Isaac.* See note on v. 42. Jacob had met the "God of Isaac" (28:13) at Bethel 20 years earlier.

of Nahor,/ the God of their father, judge between us." k

So Jacob took an oath l in the name of the Fear of his father Isaac. m 54He offered a sacrifice n there in the hill country and invited his relatives to a meal. o After they had eaten, they spent the night there.

55Early the next morning Laban kissed his grandchildren and his daughters p and blessed q them. Then he left and returned home. r

Jacob Prepares to Meet Esau

32 Jacob also went on his way, and the angels of God s met him. 2When Jacob saw them, he said, "This is the camp of God!" t So he named that place Mahanaim. w u

3Jacob sent messengers v ahead of him to his brother Esau w in the land of Seir, x the country of Edom. y 4He instructed them: "This is what you are to say to my master z Esau: 'Your servant a Jacob says, I have been staying with Laban b and have remained there till now. 5I have cattle and donkeys, sheep and goats, menservants and maidservants. c Now I am sending this message to my lord, d that I may find favor in your eyes. e ' "

6When the messengers returned to Jacob, they said, "We went to your brother Esau, and now he is coming to meet you, and four hundred men are with him." f

7In great fear g and distress h Jacob divided the people who were with him into two groups, x i and the flocks and herds and camels as well. 8He thought, "If Esau comes and attacks one group, y the group y that is left may escape."

9Then Jacob prayed, "O God of my father Abraham, j God of my father Isaac, k

O LORD, who said to me, 'Go back to your country and your relatives, and I will make you prosper,' l 10I am unworthy of all the kindness and faithfulness m you have shown your servant. I had only my staff n when I crossed this Jordan, but now I have become two groups. o 11Save me, I pray, from the hand of my brother Esau, for I am afraid p he will come and attack me, q and also the mothers with their children. r 12But you have said, 'I will surely make you prosper and will make your descendants like the sand s of the sea, which cannot be counted. t ' "

13He spent the night there, and from what he had with him he selected a gift u for his brother Esau: 14two hundred female goats and twenty male goats, two hundred ewes and twenty rams, v 15thirty female camels with their young, forty cows and ten bulls, and twenty female donkeys and ten male donkeys. w 16He put them in the care of his servants, each herd by itself, and said to his servants, "Go ahead of me, and keep some space between the herds." x

17He instructed the one in the lead: "When my brother Esau meets you and asks, 'To whom do you belong, and where are you going, and who owns all these animals in front of you?' 18then you are to say, 'They belong to your servant y Jacob. They are a gift z sent to my lord Esau, and he is coming behind us.' "

19He also instructed the second, the third and all the others who followed the

---

Cross references:

31:53 /S Ge 11:27 kS Ge 16:5 /S Ge 21:23,27 mS ver 42
31:54 nGe 46:1; Ex 24:5; Lev 3:1 oS Ge 26:30
31:55 pS ver 28; Ru 1:9 qS Ge 24:60; S Ex 39:43 rGe 18:33
32:1 sS Ge 16:11; 2Ki 6:16-17; 1Ch 21:15; Ps 34:7; 35:5; 91:11; Da 6:22
32:2 tS Ge 28:17 uJos 13:26,30; 21:38; 2Sa 2:8; 29; 17:24; 19:32; 1Ki 2:8; 4:14; 1Ch 6:80
32:3 vNu 21:21; Jdg 11:17 wS Ge 27:41-42 xS Ge 14:6; S Nu 24:18 yS Ge 25:30;
32:4 zS Ge 24:9 aS Ge 18:3 bGe 31:41
32:5 cS Ge 12:16 dS Ge 24:9 eGe 33:8,10,15; 34:11; 47:25,29; 50:4; Ru 2:13
32:6 fGe 33:1
32:7 gver 11 hGe 35:3; Ps 4:1; 77:2; 107:6 iver 10; Ge 33:1
32:9 jS Ge 24:12 kS Ge 28:13

32:10 lS Ge 26:3; 31:13
32:10 mS Ge 24:27 nGe 38:18; 47:31; Nu 17:2 oS ver 7
32:11 pS ver 7 qGe 43:18; Ps 59:2 rS Ge 27:41
32:12 sS Ge 22:17; 1Ki 4:20,29 tS Ge 12:2; S 13:14; Hos 1:10; Ro 9:27

32:13 uver 13-15,18,20,21; Ge 33:10; 43:11,15,25,26; 1Sa 16:20; Pr 18:16; 21:14 32:14 vNu 7:88 32:15 wS Ge 13:2; 42:26; 45:23 32:16 xGe 33:8 32:18 yS Ge 18:3 zS ver 13

w2 Mahanaim means two camps.   x7 Or camps; also in verse 10   y8 Or camp

---

31:54 *sacrifice . . . meal.* Two important aspects of the covenant-making (see v. 44) process (see Ex 24:5–8,11). *relatives.* Those with whom he had now entered into a covenant. The common meal indicated mutual acceptance (see note on 26:30).

31:55 *blessed.* Or "said farewell to" (see NIV text note on 47:10; see also 31:28).

32:1 *angels of God met him.* Jacob had just left the region of the hostile Laban and is about to enter the region of the hostile Esau. He was met by the angels of God, whom he had seen at Bethel when he was fleeing from Esau to go to Laban (28:12). Thus God was with Jacob, as he had promised (see 28:15; 31:3; see also note on 26:3).

32:2 *Mahanaim.* Located in Gilead (see note on 31:21) east of the Jordan and north of the Jabbok (see note on v. 22). Two camps (see NIV text note) had just met in hostility and separated in peace. Two camps were again about to meet (in hostility, Jacob thought) and separate in peace. But Jacob called this crucial place "two camps" after seeing the angelic encampment, suggesting that he saw God's encampment as a divine assurance. God's host had come to escort him safely

to Canaan (see 33:12,15). Yet he also feared meeting with Esau, so he divided his household into two camps (see vv. 7,10 and NIV text note on v. 7), still trying to protect himself by his own devices.

32:3 *Seir . . . Edom.* Far to the south of Jacob's ultimate destination, but he assumed that Esau would come seeking revenge as soon as he heard that Jacob was on his way back.

32:4 *Your servant.* A phrase suggesting both courtesy and humility.

32:6 *four hundred.* A round number for a sizable unit of fighting men (see 1Sa 22:2; 25:13; 30:10).

32:9 *Jacob prayed.* His first recorded prayer since leaving Bethel.

32:11 *mothers with their children.* Jacob was afraid that Esau's wrath would extend to Jacob's family as well.

32:12 *your descendants like the sand of the sea.* A reference to God's promise in 28:14 (see 22:17 and note).

32:13 *gift.* Probably a wordplay: Out of his "two camps" (Hebrew *mahanayim,* v. 2; see vv. 7–8,10) Jacob selects a "gift" (*minhah*) for his brother.

herds: "You are to say the same thing to Esau when you meet him. 20And be sure to say, 'Your servant*a* Jacob is coming behind us.' " For he thought, "I will pacify him with these gifts*b* I am sending on ahead; *c* later, when I see him, perhaps he will receive me."*d* 21So Jacob's gifts*e* went on ahead of him, but he himself spent the night in the camp.

Jacob Wrestles With God

22That night Jacob got up and took his two wives, his two maidservants and his eleven sons*f* and crossed the ford of the Jabbok.*g* 23After he had sent them across the stream, he sent over all his possessions.*h* 24So Jacob was left alone,*i* and a man*j* wrestled with him till daybreak. 25When the man saw that he could not overpower him, he touched the socket of Jacob's hip*k* so that his hip was wrenched as he wrestled with the man. 26Then the man said, "Let me go, for it is daybreak."

But Jacob replied, "I will not let you go unless you bless me."*l*

27The man asked him, "What is your name?"

"Jacob," *m* he answered.

28Then the man said, "Your name*n* will no longer be Jacob, but Israel,*z o* because you have struggled with God and with men and have overcome."*p*

29Jacob said, "Please tell me your name."*q*

But he replied, "Why do you ask my name?"*r* Then he blessed*s* him there.

30So Jacob called the place Peniel,*a* say-

ing, "It is because I saw God face to face,*t* and yet my life was spared."

31The sun rose above him as he passed Peniel,*b u* and he was limping because of his hip. 32Therefore to this day the Israelites do not eat the tendon attached to the socket of the hip,*v* because the socket of Jacob's hip was touched near the tendon.

Jacob Meets Esau

33 Jacob looked up and there was Esau, coming with his four hundred men;*w* so he divided the children among Leah, Rachel and the two maidservants.*x* 2He put the maidservants and their children*y* in front, Leah and her children next, and Rachel and Joseph*z* in the rear. 3He himself went on ahead and bowed down to the ground*a* seven times*b* as he approached his brother.

4But Esau*c* ran to meet Jacob and embraced him; he threw his arms around his neck and kissed him.*d* And they wept.*e* 5Then Esau looked up and saw the women and children. "Who are these with you?" he asked.

Jacob answered, "They are the children God has graciously given your servant.*f* "

6Then the maidservants and their children*g* approached and bowed down.*h* 7Next, Leah and her children*i* came and bowed down.*j* Last of all came Joseph and Rachel,*k* and they too bowed down.

8Esau asked, "What do you mean by all these droves I met?"*l*

---

z28 Israel means he struggles with God. *a30 Peniel means face of God.* *b31 Hebrew Penuel, a variant of Peniel*

Cross references

32:20 *a*S Ge 18:3
*b*S ver 13;
1Sa 9:7; 2Ki 8:8;
Jer 40:5
*c*1Sa 25:19
*d*Ge 33:10;
Ex 28:38;
Lev 1:4; Mal 1:8
32:21 *e*S ver 13
32:22 */*S Ge 30:24
*g*Nu 21:24;
Dt 2:37; 3:16;
Jos 12:2
32:23 *h*S Ge 26:14
32:24 */*Da 10:8
*i*S Ge 18:2
32:25 *k*ver 32
32:26 */*Hos 12:4
32:27 *m*S Ge 25:26
32:28 *n*Isa 1:26;
56:5; 60:14;
62:2,4,12; 65:15
*o*S Ge 17:5
*p*S Ge 30:8
32:29 *q*Ex 3:13;
6:3; Jdg 13:17
*r*Jdg 13:18
*s*Ge 25:11; 35:9;
48:3
32:30 *t*S Ge 16:13;
1Co 13:12
32:31 *u*Jdg 8:9
32:32 *v*ver 25
33:1 *w*S Ge 32:6
*x*S Ge 32:7
33:2 *y*ver 6
*z*S Ge 30:24
33:3 *a*ver 6,7;
S Ge 17:3;
37:7-10; 42:6;
43:26; 44:14;
48:12; 1Sa 20:41
*b*2Ki 5:10,14
33:4 *c*S Ge 27:41-42
*d*S Ge 29:11;
Lk 15:20
*e*S Ge 27:27
33:5 */*S Ge 18:3;
Ge 48:9;
Ps 127:3; Isa 8:18
33:6 *g*ver 2
*h*S ver 3
33:7 *i*ver 2 /S ver
3 *k*S Ge 30:24
33:8 */*Ge 32:14-16

32:22 *Jabbok.* Today called the Wadi Zerqa, flowing westward into the Jordan about 20 miles north of the Dead Sea.
32:24 *left alone.* As he had been at Bethel (28:10–22). *a man.* God himself (as Jacob eventually realized; see v. 30) in the form of an angel (see Hos 12:3–4 and note on Ge 16:7). *wrestled.* God wrestled (*ye'abeq*) with Jacob (*ya'aqob*) by the Jabbok (*yabboq*)—the author delighted in wordplay. Jacob had struggled all his life to prevail, first with Esau, then with Laban. Now, as he was about to reenter Canaan, he was shown that it was with God that he must "wrestle." It was God who held his destiny in his hands.
32:25 *could not overpower him . . . touched the socket.* God came to him in such a form that Jacob could wrestle with him successfully, yet he showed Jacob that he could disable him at will.
32:26 *I will not let you go.* Jacob's persistence was soon rewarded (v. 29). *unless you bless me.* Jacob finally acknowledged that the blessing must come from God.
32:28 *Your name will no longer be Jacob.* Now that Jacob had acknowledged God as the source of blessing and was about to reenter the promised land, the Lord acknowledged Jacob as his servant by changing his name (see 17:5 and note). *Israel.* See NIV text note. Here in Father Jacob/Israel, the nation of Israel got her name and her characterization:

the people who struggle with God (memorialized in the name Israel) and with men (memorialized in the name Jacob) and overcome. God later confirmed Jacob's new name (35:10).
32:29 *Why do you ask my name?* Such a request of God is both unworthy and impossible to fulfill (see Jdg 13:17–18).
32:30 *I saw God face to face, and yet my life was spared.* See note on 16:13; see also Jdg 6:22–23; 13:22. Only God's "back" (see Ex 33:23) or "feet" (see Ex 24:10) or "form" (see Nu 12:8), in a symbolic sense, may be seen.
32:32 *do not eat the tendon.* Probably the sciatic muscle. Mentioned nowhere else in the Bible, this dietary prohibition is found in the later writings of Judaism. Jacob retained in his body, and Israel retained in her dietary practice, a perpetual reminder of this fateful encounter with God.
33:2 *Rachel and Joseph in the rear.* Jacob wanted to keep his favorite wife and child farthest away from potential harm.
33:3 *bowed down to the ground seven times.* A sign of total submission, documented also in texts found at Tell el-Amarna in Egypt and dating to the 14th century B.C. (see chart on "Ancient Texts Relating to the OT," p. 5).
33:4 All Jacob's fears proved unfounded. God had been at work and had so blessed Esau (v. 9) that he no longer held a grudge against Jacob.

"To find favor in your eyes, my lord," [m] he said.

[9]But Esau said, "I already have plenty, [n] my brother. Keep what you have for yourself."

[10]"No, please!" said Jacob. "If I have found favor in your eyes, [o] accept this gift [p] from me. For to see your face is like seeing the face of God, [q] now that you have received me favorably. [r] [11]Please accept the present [s] that was brought to you, for God has been gracious to me [t] and I have all I need." [u] And because Jacob insisted, [v] Esau accepted it.

[12]Then Esau said, "Let us be on our way; I'll accompany you."

[13]But Jacob said to him, "My lord [w] knows that the children are tender and that I must care for the ewes and cows that are nursing their young. [x] If they are driven hard just one day, all the animals will die. [14]So let my lord go on ahead of his servant, while I move along slowly at the pace of the droves [y] before me and that of the children, until I come to my lord in Seir. [z]"

[15]Esau said, "Then let me leave some of my men with you."

"But why do that?" Jacob asked. "Just let me find favor in the eyes of my lord." [a]

[16]So that day Esau started on his way back to Seir. [b] [17]Jacob, however, went to Succoth, [c] where he built a place for himself and made shelters for his livestock. That is why the place is called Succoth. [c]

[18]After Jacob came from Paddan Aram, [d] [d] he arrived safely at the [e] city of Shechem [e] in Canaan and camped within sight of the city. [19]For a hundred pieces of silver, [f] he bought from the sons of Hamor, [f] the father of Shechem, [g] the plot of

ground [h] where he pitched his tent. [i] [20]There he set up an altar [j] and called it El Elohe Israel. [g]

Dinah and the Shechemites

34 Now Dinah, [k] the daughter Leah had borne to Jacob, went out to visit the women of the land. [2]When Shechem [l] son of Hamor [m] the Hivite, [n] the ruler of that area, saw her, he took her and violated her. [o] [3]His heart was drawn to Dinah [p] daughter of Jacob, [q] and he loved [r] the girl and spoke tenderly [s] to her. [4]And Shechem said to his father Hamor, "Get me this girl as my wife." [t]

[5]When Jacob heard that his daughter Dinah had been defiled, [u] his sons were in the fields with his livestock; so he kept quiet about it until they came home.

[6]Then Shechem's father Hamor went out to talk with Jacob. [v] [7]Now Jacob's sons had come in from the fields as soon as they heard what had happened. They were filled with grief [w] and fury, [x] because Shechem had done a disgraceful thing in [h] Israel [y] by lying with Jacob's daughter—a thing that should not be done. [z]

[8]But Hamor said to them, "My son Shechem has his heart set on your daughter. Please give her to him as his wife. [a] [9]Intermarry with us; give us your daughters and take our daughters for yourselves. [b] [10]You

---

33:8
[m]S Ge 24:9; S 32:5
33:9 [n]ver 11; S Ge 13:6
33:10
[o]S Ge 30:27; S 32:5
[p]S Ge 32:13
[q]S Ge 16:13
[r]S Ge 32:20
33:11
[s]1Sa 25:27; 30:26 [t]Ge 30:43
[u]S ver 9 [v]Ge 19:3
33:13 [w]ver 8
[x]Isa 40:11; Jer 31:8
33:14 [y]Ex 12:38
[z]S Ge 14:6
33:15 [a]S Ge 32:5
33:16 [b]S Ge 14:6
33:17 [c]Jos 13:27; Jdg 8:5,6,8,14, 14-16,15,16; 1Ki 7:46; 2Ch 4:17; Ps 60:6; 108:7
33:18
[d]S Ge 25:20
[e]S Ge 12:6

33:19 [f]Ge 34:2; Jdg 9:28; Ac 7:16
[g]Ge 34:2; Jos 24:32
[h]Ge 34:10,16,21; 47:27; Jn 4:5
[i]S Ge 12:8
33:20 [j]S Ge 4:26; S 8:20
34:1 [k]S Ge 30:21
34:2 [l]S Ge 33:19
[m]S Ge 33:19
[n]S Ge 10:17
[o]Dt 21:14; 2Sa 13:14
34:3 [p]ver 26
[q]ver 19
[r]S Ge 24:67
[s]Ge 50:21; Isa 14:1; 40:2
34:4 [t]S Ge 21:21
34:5 [u]ver 2,13, 27; S 35:22; 49:4; Dt 27:20; 33:6; 1Ch 5:1
34:6 [v]Jdg 14:2-5
34:7 [w]1Co 5:2
[x]Ge 39:19; 49:6-7; 2Sa 12:5; 13:21; Est 7:7; Pr 6:34
[y]Dt 22:21;

Jdg 19:23; 20:6; 2Sa 13:12; Jer 29:23 [z]S Ge 20:9 **34:8**
[a]S Ge 21:21; Dt 21:11 **34:9** [b]ver 16,21; Dt 7:3; Jos 23:12

[c]17 *Succoth* means *shelters*.   [d]18 That is, Northwest Mesopotamia   [e]18 Or *arrived at Shalem, a*
[f]19 Hebrew *hundred kesitahs*; a kesitah was a unit of money of unknown weight and value.   [g]20 *El Elohe Israel* can mean *God, the God of Israel* or *mighty is the God of Israel.*   [h]7 Or *against*

33:9 *my brother.* Esau's generous and loving response was in contrast to Jacob's cautious and fearful "my lord" (v. 8).
33:11 *present.* The Hebrew for "present" is the same as that used for "blessing" in 27:35. The author of Genesis was conscious of the irony that Jacob now acknowledged that the blessing he had struggled for was from God. In his last attempt to express reconciliation with Esau, Jacob in a sense gave back the "blessing" he had stolen from his brother, doing so from the blessings the Lord had given him.
33:14 *until I come to my lord in Seir.* But Jacob, still the deceiver, had no intention of following Esau all the way to Seir.
33:18 *Paddan Aram.* Means "plain of Aram," another name for Aram Naharaim (see note on 24:10). *arrived safely.* The answer to Jacob's prayer of 20 years earlier (see 28:21). *Shechem.* An important city in central Canaan, first built and inhabited during the patriarchal period. Jacob followed in the footsteps of Father Abraham (see 12:6). Jacob dug a well there (see Jn 4:5–6) that can still be seen today.
33:19 *pieces of silver.* See NIV text note. The Hebrew word translated by this phrase is always found in patriarchal

contexts (see Jos 24:32; Job 42:11).
33:20 *set up an altar.* See note on 12:7. *called it El Elohe Israel.* See NIV text note. Jacob formally acknowledged the God of his fathers as his God also (see 28:21). But he lingered at Shechem and did not return to Bethel (see 35:1), and that meant trouble (see ch. 34).
34:1–31 The name of God ends ch. 33 and begins ch. 35, but it is completely absent from this sordid chapter (see note on 7:16).
34:2 *Shechem.* See 33:19. He was probably named after the city.
34:4 *Get me this girl as my wife.* See note on 21:21.
34:7 *Israel.* The clan of Israel. *a thing that should not be done.* Cf. Tamar's plea to Amnon in a similar situation (2Sa 13:12).
34:9 *Intermarry with us.* The Canaanites wanted to absorb Israel (see v. 16) in order to benefit from the blessings Jacob had received from the Lord (both his offspring and his possessions—vv. 21–23). This was a danger Israel constantly faced from other peoples and nations—either absorption or hostility, both of which are perpetual threats to the people of God.

can settle among us; *c* the land is open to you. *d* Live in it, trade[i] in it, *e* and acquire property in it. *f* "

[11]Then Shechem said to Dinah's father and brothers, "Let me find favor in your eyes, *g* and I will give you whatever you ask. [12]Make the price for the bride *h* and the gift I am to bring as great as you like, and I'll pay whatever you ask me. Only give me the girl as my wife."

[13]Because their sister Dinah had been defiled, *i* Jacob's sons replied deceitfully[j] as they spoke to Shechem and his father Hamor. [14]They said to them, "We can't do such a thing; we can't give our sister to a man who is not circumcised. *k* That would be a disgrace to us. [15]We will give our consent to you on one condition[l] only: that you become like us by circumcising all your males. *m* [16]Then we will give you our daughters and take your daughters for ourselves. *n* We'll settle among you and become one people with you. *o* [17]But if you will not agree to be circumcised, we'll take our sister[j] and go."

[18]Their proposal seemed good to Hamor and his son Shechem. [19]The young man, who was the most honored *p* of all his father's household, lost no time in doing what they said, because he was delighted with Jacob's daughter. *q* [20]So Hamor and his son Shechem went to the gate of their city *r* to speak to their fellow townsmen. [21]"These men are friendly toward us," they said. "Let them live in our land and trade in it; *s* the land has plenty of room for them. We can marry their daughters and they can marry ours. *t* [22]But the men will consent to live with us as one people only on the condition that our males be circumcised, *u* as they themselves are. [23]Won't their livestock, their property and all their other animals become ours? *v* So let us give our consent to them, and they will settle among us. *w* "

[24]All the men who went out of the city gate *x* agreed with Hamor and his son She-

chem, and every male in the city was circumcised.

[25]Three days later, while all of them were still in pain, *y* two of Jacob's sons, Simeon *z* and Levi, *a* Dinah's brothers, took their swords *b* and attacked the unsuspecting city, *c* killing every male. *d* [26]They put Hamor and his son Shechem to the sword *e* and took Dinah *f* from Shechem's house and left. [27]The sons of Jacob came upon the dead bodies and looted the city *g* where *k* their sister had been defiled. *h* [28]They seized their flocks and herds and donkeys *i* and everything else of theirs in the city and out in the fields. *j* [29]They carried off all their wealth and all their women and children, *k* taking as plunder *l* everything in the houses. *m*

[30]Then Jacob said to Simeon and Levi, "You have brought trouble *n* on me by making me a stench *o* to the Canaanites and Perizzites, the people living in this land. *p* We are few in number, *q* and if they join forces against me and attack me, I and my household will be destroyed."

[31]But they replied, "Should he have treated our sister like a prostitute? *r* "

Jacob Returns to Bethel

35 Then God said to Jacob, "Go up to Bethel *s* and settle there, and build an altar *t* there to God, *u* who appeared to you *v* when you were fleeing from your brother Esau." *w*

[2]So Jacob said to his household *x* and to all who were with him, "Get rid of the foreign gods *y* you have with you, and purify yourselves and change your clothes. *z* [3]Then come, let us go up to Bethel, where I will build an altar to God, *a* who answered me in the day of my distress *b* and who has been with me wherever I have gone. *c* " [4]So they gave

---

34:10 *c*ver 23; Ge 46:34; 47:6, 27 *d*S Ge 13:9 *e*Ge 42:34 *f*S Ge 33:19
34:11 *g*S Ge 32:5
34:12 *h*Ex 22:16; Dt 22:29; 1Sa 18:25
34:13 *j*S ver 5 *j*S Ge 27:36
34:14 *k*Ge 17:14; Jdg 14:3; 1Sa 31:4; Isa 52:1
34:15 *l*1Sa 11:2 *m*ver 22; Ex 12:48
34:16 *n*S ver 9 *o*S Ge 33:19
34:19 *p*Ge 49:3; 1Ch 11:21 *q*ver 3
34:20 *r*S Ge 18:1
34:21 *s*S Ge 33:19 *t*S ver 9
34:22 *u*S ver 15
34:23 *v*ver 28; S Ge 12:16 *w*S ver 10
34:24 *x*S Ge 18:1
34:25 *y*Jos 5:8 *z*S Ge 29:33 *a*S Ge 29:34 *b*Ge 49:5; Mal 2:16 *c*Jdg 18:7,10,27; Eze 38:11 *d*Ge 49:7
34:26 *e*S ver 7; Ge 48:22 *f*ver 3
34:27 *g*2Ki 21:14 *h*S ver 5
34:28 *i*Ge 43:18 *j*S ver 23
34:29 *k*S Ge 31:26 *l*Nu 14:3; 31:9, 53; Dt 2:35; Jos 7:21 *m*2Ki 8:12; Isa 13:16; La 5:11; Am 1:13; Zec 14:2
34:30 *n*Ge 43:6; Ex 5:23; Nu 11:11 *o*Ex 5:21; 6:9; 1Sa 13:4; 27:12; 2Sa 10:6; 1Ch 19:6 *p*S Ge 13:7 *q*Ge 35:26; 46:27; Ex 1:5; Dt 10:22; 26:5; 1Ch 16:19; Ps 105:12
34:31 *r*ver 2
35:1 *s*S Ge 12:8 *t*S Ge 4:26; 8:20 *u*ver 3 *v*S Ge 12:7 *w*ver 7; Ge 27:43
35:2 *x*Ge 18:19; Jos 24:15

*y*S Ge 31:19; S Jos 24:14 *z*Ex 19:10,14; Nu 8:7,21; 19:19
35:3 *a*ver 1 *b*S Ge 32:7; S Jdg 2:15 *c*S Ge 26:3

[i]10 Or *move about freely*; also in verse 21
[j]17 Hebrew *daughter*   [k]27 Or *because*

34:12 *the price for the bride and the gift I am to bring.* For a specific example of this marriage custom see 24:53.
34:13 *Jacob's sons replied deceitfully.* Like father, like son (see 27:24; see also note on 25:26).
34:15 Using a sacred ceremony for a sinful purpose (see vv. 24–25).
34:20 *gate of their city.* See notes on 19:1; 23:10.
34:23 The greed of the men of Shechem led to their destruction.
34:24 The Canaanites were even willing to submit to Israel's covenant rite in order to attain their purposes.
34:25 *Simeon and Levi.* Because they slaughtered the men of Shechem, their own descendants would be scattered far and wide (see note on 49:7). *Dinah's brothers.* All three

were children of Leah (29:33–34; 30:21). *killing every male.* Shechem's crime, serious as it was, hardly warranted such brutal and extensive retaliation (see vv. 27–29).
34:30 *Perizzites.* See note on 13:7.
35:1 *God . . . appeared to you when you were fleeing.* See v.7; 28:13.
35:2 *foreign gods you have with you.* See note on 31:19 (see also Jos 24:23).
35:3 *God . . . who has been with me.* See 28:15; see also note on 26:3.
35:4 *rings.* Worn as amulets or charms; a pagan religious custom (cf. Hos 2:13). *the oak at Shechem.* Obviously a well-known tree, perhaps the "great tree" mentioned in 12:6 (see Jos 24:26).

Jacob all the foreign gods they had and the rings in their ears, *d* and Jacob buried them under the oak *e* at Shechem. *f* 5Then they set out, and the terror of God *g* fell upon the towns all around them so that no one pursued them. *h*

6Jacob and all the people with him came to Luz *i* (that is, Bethel) in the land of Canaan. *j* 7There he built an altar, *k* and he called the place El Bethel, 1*l* because it was there that God revealed himself to him *m* when he was fleeing from his brother. *n*

8Now Deborah, Rebekah's nurse, *o* died and was buried under the oak *p* below Bethel. *q* So it was named Allon Bacuth. *m*

9After Jacob returned from Paddan Aram, *n r* God appeared to him again and blessed him. *s* 10God said to him, "Your name is Jacob, *o* but you will no longer be called Jacob; your name will be Israel. *p*" *t* So he named him Israel.

11And God said to him, "I am God Almighty *q*; *u* be fruitful and increase in number. *v* A nation *w* and a community of nations will come from you, and kings will come from your body. *x* 12The land I gave to Abraham and Isaac I also give to you, and I will give this land to your descendants after you.' "*z* 13Then God went up from him *a* at the place where he had talked with him.

14Jacob set up a stone pillar *b* at the place where God had talked with him, and he poured out a drink offering *c* on it; he also poured oil on it. *d* 15Jacob called the place where God had talked with him Bethel. *r e*

The Deaths of Rachel and Isaac

35:23–26pp — 1Ch 2:1–2

16Then they moved on from Bethel. While they were still some distance from Ephrath, *f* Rachel *g* began to give birth and had great difficulty. 17And as she was having great difficulty in childbirth, the midwife *h* said to her, "Don't be afraid, for you have another son." *i* 18As she breathed her last—for she was dying—she named her son Ben-Oni. *s j* But his father named him Benjamin. *t k*

19So Rachel died and was buried on the way to Ephrath *l* (that is, Bethlehem *m*). 20Over her tomb Jacob set up a pillar, and to this day *n* that pillar marks Rachel's tomb. *o*

21Israel moved on again and pitched his tent beyond Migdal Eder. *p* 22While Israel was living in that region, Reuben went in and slept with his father's concubine *q* Bilhah, *r* and Israel heard of it.

Jacob had twelve sons:

23The sons of Leah: *s*

　Reuben the firstborn *t* of Jacob,

Cross-references column

35:4
*d*S Ge 24:22;
Ex 32:3; 35:22;
Jdg 8:24; Pr 25:12
*e*ver 8 /S Ge 12:6
35:5 *g*Ex 15:16;
23:27; Dt 2:25;
Jos 2:9; 1Sa 7:10;
13:7; 14:15;
2Ch 14:14;
17:10; 20:29;
Ps 9:20;
Isa 19:17;
Zec 14:13
*h*Ps 105:14
35:6 /S Ge 28:19
/S Ge 10:19
35:7 *k*S Ge 8:20
*l*Ge 28:19
*m*S Ge 28:13
*n*S ver 1
35:8 *o*Ge 24:59
*p*ver 4
*q*S Ge 12:8;
1Sa 10:3
35:9 *r*S Ge 25:20
*s*S Ge 28:13;
S 32:29
35:10 *t*S Ge 17:5
35:11 *u*S Ge 17:1
*v*S Ge 12:2
*w*S Ge 12:2
*x*S Ge 17:6
35:12
*y*S Ge 28:13
*z*S Ge 12:7;
S 15:7
35:13
*a*S Ge 17:22
35:14
*b*S Ge 28:22
*c*Ex 29:40;
Lev 23:13;
Nu 6:15,17; 15:5;
28:7,14;
2Sa 23:16;
2Ch 29:35
*d*S Ge 28:18
35:15 *e*S Ge 12:8

35:16 /ver 19;
Ge 48:7; Ru 1:2;
4:11; 1Sa 17:12;
Mic 5:2
*g*S Ge 29:6
35:17
*h*Ge 38:28;
Ex 1:15
/S Ge 30:24
35:18 /1Sa 4:21;
14:3 *k*ver 24;

Ge 42:4; 43:16,29; 45:12,14; 49:27; Nu 1:36; Dt 33:12
35:19 /S ver 16 *m*Ge 48:7; Jos 19:15; Jdg 12:8; 17:7; 19:1, 18; Ru 1:1,19; 1Sa 17:12; Mic 5:2 35:20 *n*Jos 4:9; 7:26; 8:28; 10:27; 1Sa 6:18 *o*1Sa 10:2 35:21 *p*Jos 15:21 35:22 *q*S Ge 22:24 *r*S Ge 29:29; S 34:5; S Lev 18:8 35:23 *s*S Ge 29:16 *t*Ge 43:33; 46:8

1*7 El Bethel* means *God of Bethel.*　　*m8 Allon Bacuth* means *oak of weeping.*　*n9* That is, Northwest Mesopotamia; also in verse 26　*o10 Jacob* means *he grasps the heel* (figuratively, *he deceives*).　*p10 Israel* means *he struggles with God.*　*q11* Hebrew *El-Shaddai*　*r15 Bethel* means *house of God.*　*s18 Ben-Oni* means *son of my trouble.*　*t18 Benjamin* means *son of my right hand.*

35:5 *the terror of God.* God protected his servant.
35:7 *built an altar.* See note on 12:7.
35:8 *Deborah, Rebekah's nurse, died.* After long years of faithful service (see 24:59). *the oak.* Again probably a well-known tree (see note on v. 4), perhaps the "great tree" mentioned in 1Sa 10:3. *below.* Either "lower than" or "to the south of."
35:9 *Jacob returned.* See map of "Jacob's Journeys," p. 53. *Paddan Aram.* Means "plain of Aram," another name for Aram Naharaim (see note on 24:10).
35:10 *Jacob . . . Israel.* The previous assignment of an additional name (see 32:28) is here confirmed. For similar examples compare 21:31 with 26:33, and 28:19 with 35:15.
35:11–12 This event climaxes the Isaac-Jacob cycle (see Introduction: Literary Features). Now that Jacob at last back at Bethel, where God had begun his direct relationship with him, God confirmed to this chosen son of Isaac the covenant promises made to Abraham (17:1–8; see 28:3). His words echo his original benediction pronounced on man in the beginning (1:28) and renewed after the flood (9:1,7). God's blessing on mankind would be fulfilled in and through Jacob and his offspring. See also 47:27; Ex 1:7.
35:13 See note on 17:22.

35:14 See 28:18 and note. *drink offering.* A liquid poured out as a sacrifice to a deity.
35:15 See 28:19; see also note on v. 10.
35:16 *Ephrath.* The older name for Bethlehem (see v. 19) in Judah (see Ru 1:2; Mic 5:2).
35:17 *another son.* An echo of Rachel's own plea at the time of Joseph's birth (see 30:24).
35:18 *Benjamin.* See NIV text note. The name can also mean "son of the south"—in distinction from the other sons, who were born in the north. One set of Hebrew terms for indicating direction was based on facing east, so south was on the right.
35:19 *Rachel died.* In childbirth (see note on 30:1).
35:20 *Rachel's tomb.* See 1Sa 10:2. The traditional, though not authentic, site is near Bethlehem.
35:21 *Migdal Eder.* Means "tower of the flock," doubtless referring to a watchtower built to discourage thieves from stealing sheep and other animals (see, e.g., 2Ch 26:10). The same Hebrew phrase is used figuratively in Mic 4:8, where "flock" refers to the people of Judah (see Mic 4:6–7).
35:22 Reuben's act was an arrogant and premature claim to the rights of the firstborn—here the right to inherit his father's concubine. For this he would lose his legal status as firstborn (see 49:3–4; 1Ch 5:1; see also note on 37:21).

Simeon, Levi, Judah, [u] Issachar and Zebulun. [v]

24The sons of Rachel:

Joseph [w] and Benjamin. [x]

25The sons of Rachel's maidservant Bilhah: [y]

Dan and Naphtali. [z]

26The sons of Leah's maidservant Zilpah: [a]

Gad [b] and Asher. [c]

These were the sons of Jacob, [d] who were born to him in Paddan Aram. [e]

27Jacob came home to his father Isaac [f] in Mamre, [g] near Kiriath Arba [h] (that is, Hebron), [i] where Abraham and Isaac had stayed. [j] 28Isaac lived a hundred and eighty years. [k] 29Then he breathed his last and died and was gathered to his people, [l] old and full of years. [m] And his sons Esau and Jacob buried him. [n]

Esau's Descendants

36:10–14pp — 1Ch 1:35–37
36:20–28pp — 1Ch 1:38–42

36 This is the account [o] of Esau (that is, Edom). [p]

2Esau took his wives from the women of Canaan: [q] Adah daughter of Elon the Hittite, [r] and Oholibamah [s] daughter of Anah [t] and granddaughter of Zibeon the Hivite [u]— 3also Basemath [v] daughter of Ishmael and sister of Nebaioth. [w]

4Adah bore Eliphaz to Esau, Basemath bore Reuel, [x] 5and Oholibamah bore Jeush, Jalam and Korah. [y] These were the sons of Esau, who were born to him in Canaan.

6Esau took his wives and sons and daughters and all the members of his household, as well as his livestock and all his other animals and all the goods he had acquired in Canaan, [z] and moved to a land some distance from his brother Jacob. [a] 7Their possessions

were too great for them to remain together; the land where they were staying could not support them both because of their livestock. [b] 8So Esau [c] (that is, Edom) [d] settled in the hill country of Seir. [e]

9This is the account [f] of Esau the father of the Edomites [g] in the hill country of Seir.

10These are the names of Esau's sons:
Eliphaz, the son of Esau's wife Adah, and Reuel, the son of Esau's wife Basemath. [h]

11The sons of Eliphaz: [i]
Teman, [j] Omar, Zepho, Gatam and Kenaz. [k]

12Esau's son Eliphaz also had a concubine [l] named Timna, who bore him Amalek. [m] These were grandsons of Esau's wife Adah. [n]

13The sons of Reuel:
Nahath, Zerah, Shammah and Mizzah. These were grandsons of Esau's wife Basemath. [o]

14The sons of Esau's wife Oholibamah [p] daughter of Anah and granddaughter of Zibeon, whom she bore to Esau:
Jeush, Jalam and Korah. [q]

15These were the chiefs [r] among Esau's descendants:

The sons of Eliphaz the firstborn of Esau:
Chiefs Teman, [s] Omar, Zepho, Kenaz, [t] 16Korah, [u] Gatam and Amalek. These were the chiefs descended from Eliphaz [u] in Edom; [v] they were grandsons of Adah. [w]

17The sons of Esau's son Reuel: [x]
Chiefs Nahath, Zerah, Shammah and Mizzah. These were the chiefs

---

35:23 uS Ge 29:35 vS Ge 30:20 **35:24** wS Ge 30:24 xS ver 18 **35:25** yGe 37:2 zS Ge 30:8 **35:26** aGe 37:2 bS Ge 30:11 cS Ge 30:13 dS Ge 34:30; 46:8; Ex 1:1-4 eS Ge 25:20 **35:27** fGe 31:18 gS Ge 13:18 hGe 23:2; Jos 15:54; Jdg 1:10; Ne 11:25 iS Ge 13:18 jS Ge 17:8 **35:28** kS Ge 25:7,20 **35:29** lS Ge 25:8 mS Ge 15:15 nS Ge 23:20; S 25:9 **36:1** oS Ge 2:4 pS Ge 25:30 **36:2** qGe 28:8-9 rGe 26:34 sver 14,18 tver 25; 1Ch 1:40 uver 24; S Ge 10:17; 1Ch 1:40 **36:3** vver 4,10, 13,17 wS Ge 25:13 **36:4** xS ver 3; 1Ch 1:35 **36:5** yver 14,18; 1Ch 1:35 **36:6** zGe 12:5 aGe 27:39

36:7 bS Ge 13:6 **36:8** cDt 2:4 dS Ge 25:30 eS Ge 14:6 **36:9** fS Ge 2:4 gver 1,43 **36:10** hS ver 3 **36:11** iver 15-16; 1Ch 1:45; Job 2:11; 4:1 jJer 49:7,20; Eze 25:13; Am 1:12; Ob 1:9; Hab 3:3 kver 15 **36:12** lS Ge 22:24 mEx 17:8,16; Nu 24:20; Dt 25:17,19; 1Sa 15:2; 27:8 nver 16 **36:13** oS ver 3 **36:14** pS ver 2 qS ver 5 **36:15** rver 19,40; Ex 15:15 sJob 2:11;

Jer 49:7; Eze 25:13; Am 1:12; Hab 3:3 tS ver 11 **36:16** uS ver 11 vGe 32:3; Ex 15:15; Nu 20:14; 33:37 wver 12 **36:17** x1Ch 1:37

u 16 Masoretic Text; Samaritan Pentateuch (see also Gen. 36:11 and 1 Chron. 1:36) does not have Korah.

35:26 *sons of Jacob . . . born to him in Paddan Aram.* Obviously a summary statement since Benjamin was born in Canaan (see vv. 16–18).

35:27 *Mamre, near Kiriath Arba (that is, Hebron).* See notes on 13:18; 23:2.

35:29 See note on 25:8. *buried him.* In the family tomb, the cave of Machpelah (49:30–31).

36:1 *account.* See note on 2:4. Though repeated in v. 9, the word does not mark the start of a new main section there since the information in vv. 9–43 is merely an expansion of that in v. 1–8. *Esau (that is, Edom)* See 25:30 and NIV text note. Reddish rock formations, primarily sandstone, are conspicuous in the territory of the Edomites, located south and southeast of the Dead Sea.

36:2–3 See note on 26:34.

36:7 See 13:6; see also 26:20 and note.

36:8 *Seir.* Another name for Edom. The word itself is related to the Hebrew word meaning "hair," a possible meaning also for the name "Esau" (see NIV text note on 25:25). Esau's clan must have driven away the original Horite (see v. 20) inhabitants of Seir (see 14:6 and note). The descendants of Seir are listed in vv. 20–28.

36:10–14 The same list of Esau's descendants (see 1Ch 1:35–37) is repeated in vv. 15–19 as a list of tribal chieftains.

36:11 *Eliphaz: Teman.* One of Job's friends was named Eliphaz the Temanite (Job 2:11), and Job himself was from the land of Uz (Job 1:1). Thus Job probably lived in Edom (see vv. 28,34).

36:12 *Amalek.* See note on 14:7.

descended from Reuel in Edom; they were grandsons of Esau's wife Basemath.*y*

[18]The sons of Esau's wife Oholibamah:*z*

Chiefs Jeush, Jalam and Korah.*a* These were the chiefs descended from Esau's wife Oholibamah daughter of Anah.

[19]These were the sons of Esau*b* (that is, Edom),*c* and these were their chiefs.*d*

[20]These were the sons of Seir the Horite,*e* who were living in the region:

Lotan, Shobal, Zibeon, Anah,*f* [21]Dishon, Ezer and Dishan. These sons of Seir in Edom were Horite chiefs.*g*

[22]The sons of Lotan:

Hori and Homam.*v* Timna was Lotan's sister.

[23]The sons of Shobal:

Alvan, Manahath, Ebal, Shepho and Onam.

[24]The sons of Zibeon:*h*

Aiah and Anah. This is the Anah who discovered the hot springs*w i* in the desert while he was grazing the donkeys*j* of his father Zibeon.

[25]The children of Anah:*k*

Dishon and Oholibamah*l* daughter of Anah.

[26]The sons of Dishon*x*:

Hemdan, Eshban, Ithran and Keran.

[27]The sons of Ezer:

Bilhan, Zaavan and Akan.

[28]The sons of Dishan:

Uz and Aran.

[29]These were the Horite chiefs:

Lotan, Shobal, Zibeon, Anah,*m* [30]Dishon, Ezer and Dishan. These were the Horite chiefs,*n* according to their divisions, in the land of Seir.

The Rulers of Edom

36:31–43pp — 1Ch 1:43–54

[31]These were the kings who reigned in Edom before any Israelite king*o* reigned:*y* [32]Bela son of Beor became king of

Edom. His city was named Dinhabah.

[33]When Bela died, Jobab son of Zerah from Bozrah*p* succeeded him as king.

[34]When Jobab died, Husham from the land of the Temanites*q* succeeded him as king.

[35]When Husham died, Hadad son of Bedad, who defeated Midian*r* in the country of Moab,*s* succeeded him as king. His city was named Avith.

[36]When Hadad died, Samlah from Masrekah succeeded him as king.

[37]When Samlah died, Shaul from Rehoboth*t* on the river*z* succeeded him as king.

[38]When Shaul died, Baal-Hanan son of Acbor succeeded him as king.

[39]When Baal-Hanan son of Acbor died, Hadad*a* succeeded him as king. His city was named Pau, and his wife's name was Mehetabel daughter of Matred, the daughter of Me-Zahab.

[40]These were the chiefs*u* descended from Esau, by name, according to their clans and regions:

Timna, Alvah, Jetheth, [41]Oholibamah, Elah, Pinon, [42]Kenaz, Teman, Mibzar, [43]Magdiel and Iram. These were the chiefs of Edom, according to their settlements in the land they occupied.

This was Esau the father of the Edomites.*v*

Joseph's Dreams

37 Jacob lived in the land where his father had stayed,*w* the land of Canaan.*x*

[2]This is the account*y* of Jacob.

36:17 *y*S ver 3
36:18 *z*S ver 2
*a*S ver 5
36:19 *b*1Ch 1:35
*c*S Ge 25:30
*d*S ver 15
36:20 *e*S Ge 14:6
*f*ver 29
36:21 *g*ver 30
36:24 *h*S ver 2
*i*Jos 15:19
*j*Job 1:14
36:25 *k*S ver 2
*l*S ver 2
36:29 *m*ver 20
36:30 *n*ver 21
36:31 *o*S Ge 17:6

36:33 *p*Isa 34:6; 63:1; Jer 49:13, 22
36:34 *q*Jer 49:7; Eze 25:13; Ob 1:9
36:35 *r*S Ge 25:2
*s*S Ge 19:37; Nu 21:11; 22:1; Dt 1:5; Jdg 3:30; Ru 1:1,6
36:37 *t*Ge 26:22
36:40 *u*S ver 15
36:43 *v*S ver 9
37:1 *w*S Ge 17:8
*x*S Ge 10:19
37:2 *y*S Ge 2:4

*v*22 Hebrew *Hemam*, a variant of *Homam* (see 1 Chron. 1:39)   *w*24 Vulgate; Syriac *discovered water;* the meaning of the Hebrew for this word is uncertain.   *x*26 Hebrew *Dishan*, a variant of *Dishon*   *y*31 Or *before an Israelite king reigned over them*   *z*37 Possibly the Euphrates   *a*39 Many manuscripts of the Masoretic Text, Samaritan Pentateuch and Syriac (see also 1 Chron. 1:50); most manuscripts of the Masoretic Text *Hadar*

36:20—28 See note on v. 8. The same list of Seir's descendants (see 1Ch 1:38–42) is repeated in abbreviated form in vv. 29–30 as a list of tribal chieftains.

36:24 *This is the Anah who . . . Zibeon.* To distinguish him from the other Anah mentioned in vv. 2,14,18. The two Anahs appear together in v. 25.

36:31 *before any Israelite king reigned.* Presupposes the later Israelite monarchy and is therefore an editorial updating subsequent to Moses' time (see note on 14:14).

36:43 *This . . . Edomites.* A summary statement for the whole chapter (just as v. 1 is a title for the whole chapter).

37:1 *Canaan.* Jacob made the promised land his homeland and was later buried there (49:29–30; 50:13). His son Joseph also insisted on being buried in Canaan, which he recognized as the land the Lord had promised to Israel (50:24–25). The Jacob-Joseph cycle (see Introduction: Literary Features) begins and ends with references to the land of promise.

Joseph,[z] a young man of seventeen,[a] was tending the flocks[b] with his brothers, the sons of Bilhah[c] and the sons of Zilpah,[d] his father's wives, and he brought their father a bad report[e] about them.

[3]Now Israel[f] loved Joseph more than any of his other sons,[g] because he had been born to him in his old age;[h] and he made a richly ornamented[b] robe[i] for him.[j] [4]When his brothers saw that their father loved him more than any of them, they hated him[k] and could not speak a kind word to him.

[5]Joseph had a dream,[l] and when he told it to his brothers,[m] they hated him all the more.[n] [6]He said to them, "Listen to this dream I had: [7]We were binding sheaves[o] of grain out in the field when suddenly my sheaf rose and stood upright, while your sheaves gathered around mine and bowed down to it."[p]

[8]His brothers said to him, "Do you intend to reign over us? Will you actually rule us?"[q] And they hated him all the more[r] because of his dream and what he had said.

[9]Then he had another dream,[s] and he told it to his brothers. "Listen," he said, "I had another dream, and this time the sun and moon and eleven stars[t] were bowing down to me."[u]

[10]When he told his father as well as his brothers,[v] his father rebuked[w] him and said, "What is this dream you had? Will your mother and I and your brothers actually come and bow down to the ground before you?"[x] [11]His brothers were jealous of him,[y] but his father kept the matter in mind.[z]

Joseph Sold by His Brothers

[12]Now his brothers had gone to graze their father's flocks near Shechem,[a] [13]and Israel[b] said to Joseph, "As you know, your brothers are grazing the flocks near Shechem.[c] Come, I am going to send you to them."

"Very well," he replied.

[14]So he said to him, "Go and see if all is well with your brothers[d] and with the flocks, and bring word back to me." Then he sent him off from the Valley of Hebron.[e]

When Joseph arrived at Shechem, [15]a man found him wandering around in the fields and asked him, "What are you looking for?"

[16]He replied, "I'm looking for my brothers. Can you tell me where they are grazing their flocks?"

[17]"They have moved on from here," the man answered. "I heard them say, 'Let's go to Dothan.'[f]"

So Joseph went after his brothers and found them near Dothan. [18]But they saw him in the distance, and before he reached them, they plotted to kill him.[g]

[19]"Here comes that dreamer![h]" they said to each other. [20]"Come now, let's kill him and throw him into one of these cisterns[i] and say that a ferocious animal[j] devoured him.[k] Then we'll see what comes of his dreams."[l]

[21]When Reuben[m] heard this, he tried to

Cross references (center column)

37:2 [z]S Ge 30:24
[a]Ge 41:46;
2Sa 5:4
[b]Ge 46:32;
1Sa 16:11; 17:15;
Ps 78:71;
Am 7:15
[c]Ge 35:25
[d]Ge 35:26
[e]1Sa 2:24
37:3 [f]S Ge 17:5
[g]S Ge 25:28
[h]Ge 43:27; 44:20
[i]ver 23,31,32;
2Sa 13:18-19
[j]Ge 43:34; 45:22;
1Sa 1:4-5; Est 2:9
37:4 [k]S ver 24;
S Ge 27:41;
Ac 7:9
37:5 [l]S Ge 20:3;
S 28:12 [m]ver 10
[n]ver 8
37:7 [o]Ru 2:7,15
[p]ver 9,10;
Ge 27:29; 42:6,9;
43:26,28; 44:14;
50:18; 2Sa 1:2;
9:6
37:8 [q]Ge 41:44;
42:10; 44:16,18;
48:22; 49:26;
Dt 33:16 [r]ver 5
37:9 [s]S ver 7;
Ge 28:12
[t]Rev 12:1
[u]Dt 4:19; 17:3
37:10 [v]ver 5
[w]Ru 2:16; Ps 9:5;
68:30; 106:9;
119:21;
Isa 17:13; 54:9;
Zec 3:2 [x]S ver 7;
S Ge 9:25; S 33:3
37:11 [y]Ge 26:14;
Ac 7:9 [z]Lk 2:19,
51
37:12 [a]S Ge 12:6
37:13 [b]S Ge 17:5
[c]Ge 33:19
37:14 [d]1Sa 17:18
[e]S Ge 13:18
37:17 [f]2Ki 6:13
37:18 [g]1Sa 19:1;
2Ch 24:21;
Ps 31:13,20;
37:12,32;
S Mt 12:14;
Mk 14:1;
Ac 23:12
37:19
[h]S Ge 28:12

37:20 [i]ver 22; Jer 38:6,9 [j]ver 33; Lev 26:6,22; Dt 32:24; 2Ki 17:25; Eze 34:25 [k]ver 31-33; S Ge 4:10 [l]Ge 50:20 37:21 [m]S Ge 29:32

[b]3 The meaning of the Hebrew for *richly ornamented* is uncertain; also in verses 23 and 32.

37:2 *account.* See note on 2:4. The word here introduces the tenth and final main section of Genesis. *Joseph.* The author immediately introduces Joseph, on whom the last cycle of the patriarchal narrative centers. In his generation, he, more than any other, represented Israel—as a people who struggled with God and with men and overcame (see note on 32:28) and as a source of blessing to the nations (see 12:2–3). It is, moreover, through the life of Joseph that the covenant family in Canaan becomes an emerging nation in Egypt, thus setting the stage for the exodus. The story of God's dealings with the patriarchs foreshadows the subsequent Biblical account of God's purpose with Israel. It begins with the election and calling out of Abram from the post-Babel nations and ends with Israel in Egypt (in the person of Joseph) preserving the life of the nations (see 41:57; 50:20). So God would deliver Israel out of the nations (the exodus), eventually to send them on a mission of life to the nations (cf. Mt 28:18–20; Ac 1:8). *a bad report about them.* Doubtless about all his brothers (as the later context indicates), not just the sons of his father's concubines.

37:3 *richly ornamented robe.* A mark of Jacob's favoritism, "the kind of garment the virgin daughters of the king wore" (2Sa 13:18).

37:5 *dream.* See note on 20:3.

37:7 *bowed down.* Joseph's dream would later come true (42:6; 43:26; 44:14).

37:8 *Will you actually rule us?* Joseph would later become the "prince among his brothers" (Dt 33:16) and receive "the rights of the firstborn" (1Ch 5:2), at least the double portion of the inheritance (see note on 25:5), since his father adopted his two sons (48:5).

37:10 *your mother.* Jacob possibly refers to Leah, since Rachel has already died (see 35:19). *bow down ... before you.* An unsettling echo of a hope expressed earlier to Jacob by his father Isaac (see 27:29).

37:11 *kept the matter in mind.* A hint that Jacob later recalled Joseph's dreams when events brought about their fulfillment. Cf. Mary's equally sensitive response to events during Jesus' boyhood days (Lk 2:19,51).

37:12 *Shechem.* See note on 33:18.

37:17 *Dothan.* Located about 13 miles north of Shechem, Dothan was already an ancient city by this time.

37:19 *dreamer.* The Hebrew for this word means "master of dreams" or "dream expert" and is here used with obvious sarcasm.

37:21 *Reuben ... tried to rescue him.* As Jacob's firstborn,

rescue him from their hands. "Let's not take his life," he said. *n* 22"Don't shed any blood. Throw him into this cistern *o* here in the desert, but don't lay a hand on him." Reuben said this to rescue him from them and take him back to his father. *p*

23So when Joseph came to his brothers, they stripped him of his robe—the richly ornamented robe *q* he was wearing—24and they took him and threw him into the cistern. *r* Now the cistern was empty; there was no water in it.

25As they sat down to eat their meal, they looked up and saw a caravan of Ishmaelites *s* coming from Gilead. *t* Their camels were loaded with spices, balm *u* and myrrh, *v* and they were on their way to take them down to Egypt. *w*

26Judah *x* said to his brothers, "What will we gain if we kill our brother and cover up his blood? *y* 27Come, let's sell him to the Ishmaelites and not lay our hands on him; after all, he is our brother, *z* our own flesh and blood. *a*" His brothers agreed.

28So when the Midianite *b* merchants came by, his brothers pulled Joseph up out of the cistern *c* and sold *d* him for twenty shekels *e* of silver *e* to the Ishmaelites, *f* who took him to Egypt. *g*

29When Reuben returned to the cistern and saw that Joseph was not there, he tore his clothes. *h* 30He went back to his brothers and said, "The boy isn't there! Where can I turn now?" *i*

31Then they got Joseph's robe, *j* slaughtered a goat and dipped the robe in the blood. *k* 32They took the ornamented robe *l* back to their father and said, "We found this. Examine it to see whether it is your son's robe."

33He recognized it and said, "It is my son's robe! Some ferocious animal *m* has devoured him. Joseph has surely been torn to pieces." *n*

34Then Jacob tore his clothes, *o* put on sackcloth *p* and mourned for his son many days. *q* 35All his sons and daughters came to comfort him, *r* but he refused to be comforted. *s* "No," he said, "in mourning will I go down to the grave *d* *t* to my son. *u*" So his father wept for him.

36Meanwhile, the Midianites *e* *v* sold Joseph *w* in Egypt to Potiphar, one of Pharaoh's officials, the captain of the guard. *x*

Judah and Tamar

38 At that time, Judah *y* left his brothers and went down to stay with a man of Adullam *z* named Hirah. *a* 2There

37:21 *n*Ge 42:22
37:22 *o*S ver 20
*p*ver 29-30
37:23 *q*ver 3
37:24 *r*S ver 4;
Ge 49:23;
Jer 38:6; 41:7;
Eze 22:27
37:25 *s*S Ge 16:11
*t*S Ge 31:21;
S SS 4:1
*u*Jer 8:22; 22:6;
46:11 *v*Ge 43:11;
Ex 30:23;
Ps 45:8; Pr 7:17;
SS 1:13; Mt 2:11
*w*ver 28;
Ge 39:1;
Ps 105:17
37:26 *x*S Ge 29:35
*y*S Ge 4:10
37:27 *z*Ge 42:21
*a*S Ge 29:14
37:28 *b*S Ge 25:2
*c*Jer 38:13
*d*Ex 21:16
*e*Lev 27:5;
Mt 26:15
*f*S Ge 16:11 *g*ver
36; Ge 39:1;
45:4-5;
Ps 105:17;
Jer 12:6; Ac 7:9
37:29 *h*ver 34;
Ge 44:13;
Nu 14:6; Jos 7:6;
2Sa 1:11;
2Ki 2:12; 5:7;
11:14; 22:11;
Job 1:20; 2:12;
Isa 36:22; 37:1;
Jer 36:24; 41:5;
Joel 2:13
37:30 *i*ver 22

37:31 *j*S ver 3
*k*Rev 19:13
37:32 *l*S ver 3
37:33 *m*S ver 20
*n*Ge 42:13,38;
44:20,28
37:34 *o*S ver 29
*p*2Sa 3:31;

1Ki 20:31; 21:27; 2Ki 6:30; 19:1,2; Job 16:15; Ps 69:11; Isa 3:24; 15:3; 22:12; 32:11; 37:1; Jer 48:37; 49:3; Joel 1:13 *q*Ge 50:3,10,11; Nu 20:29; Dt 34:8 37:35 *r*Job 2:11; 15:11; 16:5; 42:11 *s*2Sa 12:17; Ps 77:2; Jer 31:15 *t*Ge 42:38; 44:22,29,31 *u*2Sa 12:23 37:36 *v*S Ge 25:2 *w*S ver 28 *x*Ge 39:1; 40:3; 41:10,12; 1Sa 22:14 38:1 *y*S Ge 29:35 *z*Jos 12:15; 15:35; 1Sa 22:1; 2Sa 23:13; 2Ch 11:7 *a*ver 12,20

*c*28 That is, about 8 ounces (about 0.2 kilogram)
*d*35 Hebrew *Sheol*   *e*36 Samaritan Pentateuch,
Septuagint, Vulgate and Syriac (see also verse 28);
Masoretic Text *Medanites*

he felt responsible for Joseph. He would later remind his brothers of this day (42:22). Initially Reuben's attempts to influence events seemed successful (30:14–17). But after his arrogant incest with Bilhah (see 35:22 and note) his efforts were always ineffective (see 42:37–38)—demonstrating his loss of the status of firstborn (see 49:3–4). Effective leadership passed to Judah (see vv. 26–27; 43:3–5,8–10; 44:14–34; 46:28; 49:8–12).

37:23–24 Similarly, in Egypt Joseph (though innocent of any wrongdoing) would be stripped of his position of privilege and thrown into prison—also as a result of domestic intrigue (ch. 39). His cloak also would be torn from him and shown to Potiphar, but he would be rescued (41:14).

37:25 *Ishmaelites.* Also called Midianites (v. 28; see Jdg 8:22,24,26) and Medanites (see NIV text note on v. 36). These various tribal groups were interrelated, since Midian and Medan, like Ishmael, were also sons of Abraham (25:2). *Gilead.* See note on 31:21. *balm.* An oil or gum, with healing properties (see Jer 51:8), exuded by the fruit or stems of one or more kinds of small trees. The balm of Gilead was especially effective (see Jer 8:22; 46:11). *myrrh.* Probably to be identified with labdanum, an aromatic gum (see Ps 45:8; Pr 7:17; SS 3:6; 5:13) exuded from the leaves of the cistus rose. Its oil was used in beauty treatments (see Est 2:12), and it was sometimes mixed with wine and drunk to relieve pain (see Mk 15:23). As a gift fit for a king, myrrh was brought to Jesus after his birth (Mt 2:11) and applied to his body after his death (Jn 19:39–40).

37:28 *twenty shekels of silver.* In later times, this amount was the value of a male of Joseph's age who had been dedicated to the Lord (see Lev 27:5).

37:31–33 Again a slaughtered goat figures prominently in an act of deception (see 27:5–13).

37:34 *tore his clothes.* See v. 29. *put on sackcloth.* Wearing coarse and uncomfortable sackcloth instead of ordinary clothes was a sign of mourning.

37:35 *daughters.* The term can include daughters-in-law (e.g., a daughter-in-law of Jacob is mentioned in 38:2). *grave.* According to some, the Hebrew word *Sheol* (see NIV text note) can also refer in a more general way to the realm of the dead, the netherworld, where, it was thought, departed spirits live (for a description of *Sheol* see, e.g., Job 3:13–19).

37:36 *sold.* "As a slave" (Ps 105:17). The peoples of the Arabian Desert were long involved in international slave trade (cf. Am 1:6,9). *guard.* The Hebrew for this word can mean "executioners" (the captain of whom was in charge of the royal prisoners; see 40:4), or it can mean "butchers" (the captain of whom was the chief cook in the royal court; cf. 1Sa 9:23–24).

38:1–30 The unsavory events of this chapter illustrate the danger that Israel as God's separated people faced if they remained among the Canaanites (see 15:16 and note). In Egypt the Israelites were kept separate because the Egyptians despised them (43:32; 46:34). While there, God's people were able to develop into a nation without losing their identity. Judah's actions contrasted with those of Joseph (ch. 39)—demonstrating the moral superiority of Joseph, to

Judah met the daughter of a Canaanite man named Shua.[b] He married her and lay with her; ³she became pregnant and gave birth to a son, who was named Er.[c] ⁴She conceived again and gave birth to a son and named him Onan.[d] ⁵She gave birth to still another son and named him Shelah.[e] It was at Kezib that she gave birth to him.

⁶Judah got a wife for Er, his firstborn, and her name was Tamar.[f] ⁷But Er, Judah's firstborn, was wicked in the LORD's sight;[g] so the LORD put him to death.[h]

⁸Then Judah said to Onan, "Lie with your brother's wife and fulfill your duty to her as a brother-in-law to produce offspring for your brother."[i] ⁹But Onan knew that the offspring would not be his; so whenever he lay with his brother's wife, he spilled his semen on the ground to keep from producing offspring for his brother. ¹⁰What he did was wicked in the LORD's sight; so he put him to death also.[j]

¹¹Judah then said to his daughter-in-law[k] Tamar,[l] "Live as a widow in your father's house[m] until my son Shelah[o] grows up." For he thought, "He may die too, just like his brothers." So Tamar went to live in her father's house.

¹²After a long time Judah's wife, the daughter of Shua,[p] died. When Judah had recovered from his grief, he went up to Timnah,[q] to the men who were shearing his sheep,[r] and his friend Hirah the Adullamite[s] went with him.

¹³When Tamar[t] was told, "Your father-in-law is on his way to Timnah to shear his sheep,"[u] ¹⁴she took off her widow's

clothes,[v] covered herself with a veil[w] to disguise herself, and then sat down[x] at the entrance to Enaim, which is on the road to Timnah.[y] For she saw that, though Shelah[z] had now grown up, she had not been given to him as his wife.

¹⁵When Judah saw her, he thought she was a prostitute,[a] for she had covered her face. ¹⁶Not realizing[b] that she was his daughter-in-law,[c] he went over to her by the roadside and said, "Come now, let me sleep with you."[d]

"And what will you give me to sleep with you?"[e] she asked.

¹⁷"I'll send you a young goat[f] from my flock," he said.

"Will you give me something as a pledge[g] until you send it?" she asked.

¹⁸He said, "What pledge should I give you?"

"Your seal[h] and its cord, and the staff[i] in your hand," she answered. So he gave them to her and slept with her, and she became pregnant by him.[j] ¹⁹After she left, she took off her veil and put on her widow's clothes[k] again.

²⁰Meanwhile Judah sent the young goat by his friend the Adullamite[l] in order to get his pledge[m] back from the woman, but he did not find her. ²¹He asked the men who lived there, "Where is the shrine prostitute[n] who was beside the road at Enaim?"

"There hasn't been any shrine prostitute here," they said.

²²So he went back to Judah and said, "I didn't find her. Besides, the men who lived

38:2 *b*ver 12; 1Ch 2:3
38:3 *c*ver 6; Ge 46:12; Nu 26:19
38:4 *d*ver 8,9; Ge 46:12; Nu 26:19
38:5 *e*Nu 26:20; 1Ch 2:3; 4:21
38:6 *f*ver 11,13
38:7 *g*S Ge 6:5 *h*ver 10; Ge 46:12; Lev 10:1-2; 1Ch 2:3
38:8 *i*Dt 25:5-6; Ru 4:5; Mt 22:24-28
38:10 *j*S ver 7; Dt 25:7-10
38:11 *k*S Ge 11:31 *l*S ver 6 *m*Ru 1:8 *n*ver 14,26 *o*Ru 1:13
38:12 *p*S ver 2 *q*ver 14; Jos 15:10,57; 19:43; Jdg 14:1,2; 2Ch 28:18 *r*S Ge 31:19 *s*S ver 1
38:13 *t*S ver 6 *u*S Ge 31:19
38:14 *v*ver 19 *w*S Ge 24:65 *x*Jer 3:2 *y*S ver 12 *z*S ver 11
38:15 *a*Jdg 11:1; 16:1
38:16 *b*Ge 42:23 *c*Lev 18:15; 20:12; Ru 1:6 *d*Ge 39:7,12; 2Sa 13:11 *e*S Ge 30:15
38:17 *f*Jdg 15:1 *g*ver 20
38:18 *h*ver 25; 1Ki 21:8; Est 3:12; 8:8; SS 8:6; Isa 49:16; Jer 22:24; Hag 2:23; 2Co 1:22; Eph 1:13 *i*S Ge 32:10; S Ex 4:2 *j*S Ge 19:32
38:19 *k*ver 14

38:20 *l*S ver 1 *m*ver 17 38:21 *n*S Ge 19:5; Lev 19:29; Dt 22:21; 23:17; 2Ki 23:7; Hos 4:14

whom leadership in Israel fell in his generation (see 37:5–9).
38:1 *left his brothers.* Joseph was separated from his brothers by force, but Judah voluntarily separated himself to seek his fortune among the Canaanites. *Adullam.* A town southwest of Jerusalem (see 2Ch 11:5,7).
38:3–4 *Er . . . Onan.* The names also appear as designations of tribes in Mesopotamian documents of this time.
38:5 *Kezib.* Probably the same as Aczib (Jos 15:44), three miles west of Adullam. The "men of Cozeba" (another form of the same word) were descendants of Shelah son of Judah (see 1Ch 4:21–22). The Hebrew root of the name means "deception" (see Mic 1:14 and NIV text note), a theme running throughout the story of Jacob and his sons.
38:6 *Judah got a wife for Er.* See note on 21:21.
38:8 A concise description of the custom known as "levirate marriage" (Latin *levir* means "brother-in-law"). Details of the practice are given in Dt 25:5–6, where it is laid down as a legal obligation within Israel (cf. Mt 22:24). The custom is illustrated in Ru 4:5, though there it is extended to the nearest living relative ("kinsman-redeemer," Ru 3:12), since neither Boaz nor the nearer kinsman was a brother-in-law.
38:9 *knew that the offspring would not be his.* Similarly, Ruth's nearest kinsman was fearful that if he married Ruth he

would endanger his own estate (Ru 4:5–6). *spilled his semen on the ground.* A means of birth control sometimes called "onanism" (after Onan).
38:10 *What he did.* His refusal to perform his levirate duty.
38:11 *he thought, "He may die too, just like his brothers."* Thus Judah had no intention of giving Shelah to Tamar (see v. 14).
38:12 *Timnah.* Exact location unknown, but somewhere in the hill country of Judah (see Jos 15:48,57).
38:14 *sat down . . . the road.* Prostitutes (see v. 15) customarily stationed themselves by the roadside (Jer 3:2). *Enaim.* Means "two springs"; probably the same as Enam in the western foothills of Judah (see Jos 15:33–34).
38:18 *seal and its cord.* Probably a small cylinder seal of the type used to sign clay documents by rolling them over the clay. The owner wore it around his neck on a cord threaded through a hole drilled lengthwise through it.
38:21 *shrine prostitute.* The Hebrew here differs from that used for "prostitute" in v. 15. Judah's friend perhaps deliberately used the more acceptable term, since ritual prostitutes enjoyed a higher social status in Canaan than did ordinary prostitutes.

there said, 'There hasn't been any shrine
prostitute here.' "
23Then Judah said, "Let her keep what
she has,[o] or we will become a laughing-
stock.[p] After all, I did send her this young
goat, but you didn't find her."
24About three months later Judah was
told, "Your daughter-in-law Tamar is
guilty of prostitution, and as a result she is
now pregnant."
Judah said, "Bring her out and have her
burned to death!"[q]
25As she was being brought out, she sent
a message to her father-in-law. "I am pregnant by the man who owns these," she
said. And she added, "See if you recognize
whose seal and cord and staff these are."[r]
26Judah recognized them and said, "She
is more righteous than I,[s] since I wouldn't
give her to my son Shelah.[t]" And he did
not sleep with her again.
27When the time came for her to give
birth, there were twin boys in her womb.[u]
28As she was giving birth, one of them put
out his hand; so the midwife[v] took a scarlet thread and tied it on his wrist[w] and
said, "This one came out first." 29But
when he drew back his hand, his brother
came out,[x] and she said, "So this is how
you have broken out!" And he was named
Perez.[f][y] 30Then his brother, who had the
scarlet thread on his wrist,[z] came out and
he was given the name Zerah.[g][a]

Joseph and Potiphar's Wife

39 Now Joseph[b] had been taken
down to Egypt. Potiphar, an Egyptian who was one of Pharaoh's officials, the
captain of the guard,[c] bought him from
the Ishmaelites who had taken him there.[d]
2The LORD was with Joseph[e] and he
prospered, and he lived in the house of his
Egyptian master. 3When his master saw
that the LORD was with him[f] and that the
LORD gave him success in everything he
did,[g] 4Joseph found favor in his eyes[h] and
became his attendant. Potiphar put him in
charge of his household,[i] and he entrusted to his care everything he owned.[j]
5From the time he put him in charge of his
household and of all that he owned, the
LORD blessed the household[k] of the Egyptian because of Joseph.[l] The blessing of
the LORD was on everything Potiphar had,
both in the house and in the field.[m] 6So he
left in Joseph's care everything he had;[n]
with Joseph in charge, he did not concern
himself with anything except the food he
ate.
Now Joseph was well-built and handsome,[o] 7and after a while his master's wife
took notice of Joseph and said, "Come to
bed with me!"[p]
8But he refused.[q] "With me in charge,"
he told her, "my master does not concern
himself with anything in the house; everything he owns he has entrusted to my
care.[r] 9No one is greater in this house
than I am.[s] My master has withheld nothing from me except you, because you are
his wife. How then could I do such a
wicked thing and sin against God?"[t]

38:23 [o]ver 18 [p]Ex 32:25; Job 12:4; Jer 20:7; La 3:14 **38:24** [q]Lev 20:10,14; 21:9; Dt 22:21, 22; Jos 7:25; Jdg 15:6; 1Sa 31:12; Job 31:11,28; Eze 16:38 **38:25** [r]S ver 18 **38:26** [s]1Sa 24:17 [t]S ver 11 **38:27** [u]Ge 25:24 **38:28** [v]S Ge 35:17 [w]ver 30 **38:29** [x]Ge 25:26 [y]Ge 46:12; Nu 26:20,21; Ru 4:12,18; 2Sa 5:20; 6:8; 1Ch 2:4; 9:4; Isa 28:21; Mt 1:3 **38:30** [z]ver 28 [a]Ge 46:12; 1Ch 2:4; Ne 11:24 **39:1** [b]S Ge 30:24 [c]S Ge 37:36 [d]S Ge 37:25 **39:2** [e]S Ge 21:20,22; Jos 1:5; 6:27; Jdg 1:19; 1Sa 18:14; Ac 7:9 **39:3** [f]S Ge 21:22 [g]ver 23; 1Sa 18:14; 2Ki 18:7; 2Ch 20:20; Ps 1:3; 128:2; Isa 33:6 **39:4** [h]S Ge 6:8; S 18:3 [i]Ge 47:6; 1Ki 11:28; Pr 22:29 [j]ver 8, 22; Ge 40:4; 42:37 **39:5** [k]2Sa 6:11 [l]S Ge 26:24 [m]Dt 28:3; Ps 128:4 **39:6** [n]Ge 24:2 [o]S Ge 12:11; Ex 2:2; 1Sa 9:2; 16:12; 17:42; Est 2:7; Da 1:4 **39:7** [p]S Ge 38:16; Pr 7:15-18 **39:8** [q]Pr 6:23-24 [r]S ver 4 **39:9** [s]Ge 41:33,40 [t]S Ge 13:13; S Nu 22:34

[f]29 *Perez* means *breaking out.* [g]30 *Zerah* can mean *scarlet* or *brightness.*

38:24 *have her burned to death.* In later times, burning was the legal penalty for prostitution (see Lev 21:9).

38:27–30 For a similarly unusual birth of twin boys see 25:24–26.

38:29 *Perez.* Became the head of the leading clan in Judah and the ancestor of David (see Ru 4:18–22) and ultimately of Christ (see Mt 1:1–6).

39:1 See 37:36. *taken down to Egypt.* Joseph's experiences in Egypt, as well as those of his youth in Canaan (see note on 37:23–24), are similar to Israel's national experiences in Egypt. Initially, because of God's blessing, Joseph attains a position of honor (in Potiphar's house); he is then unjustly thrown into prison, his only crime being his attractiveness and moral integrity; and finally he is raised up among the Egyptians as the one who, because God is with him, holds their lives in his hands. Similarly Israel was first received with honor in Egypt (because of Joseph); then she was subjected to cruel bondage, her only crime being God's evident blessings upon her; and finally God raised her up in the eyes of the Egyptians (through the ministry of Moses) as they came fearfully to recognize that these people and their God did indeed hold their lives in their hands. The author of Genesis knew the events of the exodus and shows how the history of God and the patriarchs moved forward to and foreshadowed that event (see also 15:13–16; 48:21–22; 50:24–25). *Ishmaelites.* See note on 37:25.

39:2–6 See vv. 20–23. Though Joseph's situation changed drastically, God's relationship to him remained the same.

39:2 *The LORD was with Joseph.* See note on 26:3. This fact, mentioned several times here (vv. 3,21,23), is stressed also by Stephen (Ac 7:9).

39:5 *the LORD blessed the household of the Egyptian because of Joseph.* The offspring of Abraham are becoming a blessing to the nations (see 12:2–3; 30:27).

39:6 *left in Joseph's care everything he had.* Joseph had full responsibility for the welfare of Potiphar's house, as later he would have full responsibility in prison (vv. 22–23) and later still in all Egypt (41:41). Always this Israelite came to hold the welfare of his "world" in his hands—but always by the blessing and overruling of God, never by his own wits, as his father Jacob had so long attempted. In the role that he played in Israel's history and in the manner in which he lived it, Joseph was a true representative of Israel.

39:7 *took notice of.* Looked with desire at. The phrase is used in the same sense in Akkadian in Section 25 of the Code of Hammurapi.

39:9 *sin against God.* All sin is against God, first and foremost (see Ps 51:4).

[10]And though she spoke to Joseph day after day, he refused[u] to go to bed with her or even be with her.

[11]One day he went into the house to attend to his duties,[v] and none of the household servants[w] was inside. [12]She caught him by his cloak[x] and said, "Come to bed with me!"[y] But he left his cloak in her hand and ran out of the house.[z]

[13]When she saw that he had left his cloak in her hand and had run out of the house, [14]she called her household servants.[a] "Look," she said to them, "this Hebrew[b] has been brought to us to make sport of us![c] He came in here to sleep with me, but I screamed.[d] [15]When he heard me scream for help, he left his cloak beside me and ran out of the house."[e]

[16]She kept his cloak beside her until his master came home. [17]Then she told him this story:[f] "That Hebrew[g] slave[h] you brought us came to me to make sport of me. [18]But as soon as I screamed for help, he left his cloak beside me and ran out of the house."

[19]When his master heard the story his wife told him, saying, "This is how your slave treated me," he burned with anger.[i] [20]Joseph's master took him and put him in prison,[j] the place where the king's prisoners were confined.

But while Joseph was there in the prison, [21]the LORD was with him;[k] he showed him kindness[l] and granted him favor in the eyes of the prison warden.[m] [22]So the warden put Joseph in charge of all those held in the prison, and he was made responsible for all that was done there.[n] [23]The warden paid no attention to anything under Joseph's[o] care, because the LORD was with Joseph and gave him success in whatever he did.[p]

The Cupbearer and the Baker

40 Some time later, the cupbearer[q] and the baker[r] of the king of Egypt offended their master, the king of Egypt. [2]Pharaoh was angry[s] with his two officials,[t] the chief cupbearer and the chief baker, [3]and put them in custody in the house of the captain of the guard,[u] in the same prison where Joseph was confined. [4]The captain of the guard[v] assigned them to Joseph,[w] and he attended them.

After they had been in custody[x] for some time, [5]each of the two men—the cupbearer and the baker of the king of Egypt, who were being held in prison—had a dream[y] the same night, and each dream had a meaning of its own.[z]

[6]When Joseph came to them the next morning, he saw that they were dejected. [7]So he asked Pharaoh's officials who were in custody[a] with him in his master's house, "Why are your faces so sad today?"[b]

[8]"We both had dreams," they answered, "but there is no one to interpret them."[c]

Then Joseph said to them, "Do not interpretations belong to God?[d] Tell me your dreams."

[9]So the chief cupbearer[e] told Joseph his dream. He said to him, "In my dream I saw a vine in front of me, [10]and on the vine were three branches. As soon as it budded, it blossomed,[f] and its clusters ripened into grapes. [11]Pharaoh's cup was in my hand, and I took the grapes, squeezed them into Pharaoh's cup and put the cup in his hand."

[12]"This is what it means,[g]" Joseph said to him. "The three branches are three days.[h] [13]Within three days[i] Pharaoh will lift up your head[j] and restore you to your position, and you will put Pharaoh's cup in his hand, just as you used to do when you were his cupbearer.[k] [14]But when all goes

---

Cross references (center column)

39:10 [u]Est 3:4
39:11 [v]Ex 18:20; Dt 1:18 [w]ver 14
39:12 [x]2Sa 13:11; Pr 7:13 [y]S Ge 38:16 [z]ver 15; Pr 5:8; 2Ti 2:22
39:14 [a]ver 11 [b]S Ge 14:13 [c]S Ge 21:9 [d]Dt 22:24,27
39:15 [e]S ver 12
39:17 [f]Ex 20:16; 23:1,7; Dt 5:20; Ps 101:5 [g]S Ge 14:13 [h]Ge 21:10
39:19 [i]S Ge 34:7; S Est 1:12
39:20 [j]Ge 40:3; 41:10; Ps 105:18
39:21 [k]S Ge 21:20 [l]S Ge 19:19 [m]Ex 3:21; 11:3; 12:36; Est 2:9; Ps 106:46; Pr 16:7; Da 1:9
39:22 [n]S ver 4
39:23 [o]S Ge 21:20; S Nu 14:43 [p]S ver 3

40:1 [q]ver 9,13, 21; Ne 1:11 [r]ver 16,20
40:2 [s]Pr 16:14, 15; 19:12 [t]Ge 41:10; Est 2:21
40:3 [u]S Ge 37:36; S 39:20
40:4 [v]S Ge 37:36 [w]S Ge 39:4 [x]ver 7; Ge 42:17
40:5 [y]S Ge 20:3 [z]Ge 41:11
40:7 [a]S ver 4 [b]Ne 2:2
40:8 [c]Ge 41:8,15 [d]Ge 41:16,25,28, 32; Dt 29:29; Da 2:22,28,47
40:9 [e]S ver 1
40:10 [f]Isa 27:6; 35:1-2; Hos 14:7
40:12 [g]ver 16; Ge 41:12,15,25; Da 2:36; 4:19 [h]ver 18
40:13 [i]ver 19,20; Jos 1:11; 3:2; Ezr 8:32; Ne 2:11 [j]ver 19 [k]S ver 1

39:10 *though she spoke to Joseph day after day, he refused.* Samson twice succumbed under similar pressure (Jdg 14:17; 16:16–17).

39:14 *this Hebrew.* See v. 17; see also note on 14:13.

39:20–23 See note on vv. 2–6.

39:20 *the place where the king's prisoners were confined.* Though understandably angry (see v. 19), Potiphar put Joseph in the "house of the captain of the guard" (40:3)—certainly not the worst prison available.

40:2 *chief cupbearer.* Would be the divinely appointed agent for introducing Joseph to Pharaoh (see 41:9–14).

40:5 *each dream had a meaning.* Throughout the ancient Near East it was believed that dreams had specific meanings and that proper interpretation of them could help the dreamer predict his future (see note on 20:3). God was beginning

to prepare the way for Joseph's rise in Egypt.

40:8 *interpretations belong to God.* Only God can interpret dreams properly and accurately (see 41:16,25,28; Da 2:28). *Tell me.* Joseph presents himself as God's agent through whom God will make known the revelation contained in their dreams—Israel is God's prophetic people through whom God's revelation comes to the nations (see 18:17 and note; 41:16,28,32).

40:13 *lift up your head and restore you to your position.* See Ps 3:3; 27:6. For this meaning of the idiom "lift up one's head" see 2Ki 25:27 and Jer 52:31, where the Hebrew for "released" in the context of freeing a prisoner means lit. "lifted up the head of."

40:14 *when all goes well with you, remember me.* Unfortunately, the cupbearer "forgot him" (v. 23) until two full years later (see 41:1,9–13).

well with you, remember me[l] and show me kindness;[m] mention me to Pharaoh[n] and get me out of this prison. [15]For I was forcibly carried off from the land of the Hebrews,[o] and even here I have done nothing to deserve being put in a dungeon."[p]

[16]When the chief baker[q] saw that Joseph had given a favorable interpretation,[r] he said to Joseph, "I too had a dream: On my head were three baskets[s] of bread.[h] [17]In the top basket were all kinds of baked goods for Pharaoh, but the birds were eating them out of the basket on my head."

[18]"This is what it means," Joseph said. "The three baskets are three days.[t] [19]Within three days[u] Pharaoh will lift off your head[v] and hang you on a tree.[i w] And the birds will eat away your flesh."[x]

[20]Now the third day[y] was Pharaoh's birthday,[z] and he gave a feast for all his officials.[a] He lifted up the heads of the chief cupbearer and the chief baker[b] in the presence of his officials: [21]He restored the chief cupbearer[c] to his position,[d] so that he once again put the cup into Pharaoh's hand,[e] [22]but he hanged[j] the chief baker,[f] just as Joseph had said to them in his interpretation.[g]

[23]The chief cupbearer, however, did not remember Joseph; he forgot him.[h]

Pharaoh's Dreams

41 When two full years had passed, Pharaoh had a dream:[i] He was standing by the Nile,[j] [2]when out of the river there came up seven cows, sleek and fat,[k] and they grazed among the reeds.[l] [3]After them, seven other cows, ugly and gaunt, came up out of the Nile and stood beside those on the riverbank. [4]And the cows that were ugly and gaunt ate up the seven sleek, fat cows. Then Pharaoh woke up.[m]

[5]He fell asleep again and had a second dream: Seven heads of grain,[n] healthy and good, were growing on a single stalk. [6]Af-

ter them, seven other heads of grain sprouted—thin and scorched by the east wind.[o] [7]The thin heads of grain swallowed up the seven healthy, full heads. Then Pharaoh woke up;[p] it had been a dream.

[8]In the morning his mind was troubled,[q] so he sent for all the magicians[r] and wise men of Egypt. Pharaoh told them his dreams, but no one could interpret them for him.[s]

[9]Then the chief cupbearer said to Pharaoh, "Today I am reminded of my shortcomings.[t] [10]Pharaoh was once angry with his servants,[u] and he imprisoned me and the chief baker in the house of the captain of the guard.[v] [11]Each of us had a dream the same night, and each dream had a meaning of its own.[w] [12]Now a young Hebrew[x] was there with us, a servant of the captain of the guard.[y] We told him our dreams, and he interpreted them for us, giving each man the interpretation of his dream.[z] [13]And things turned out exactly as he interpreted them to us: I was restored to my position, and the other man was hanged.[i a]"

[14]So Pharaoh sent for Joseph, and he was quickly brought from the dungeon.[b] When he had shaved[c] and changed his clothes,[d] he came before Pharaoh.

[15]Pharaoh said to Joseph, "I had a dream, and no one can interpret it.[e] But I have heard it said of you that when you hear a dream you can interpret it."[f]

[16]"I cannot do it," Joseph replied to Pharaoh, "but God will give Pharaoh the answer he desires."[g]

[17]Then Pharaoh said to Joseph, "In my dream I was standing on the bank of the Nile,[h] [18]when out of the river there came up seven cows, fat and sleek, and they

---

40:14
[l]1Sa 25:31;
Lk 23:42
[m]S Ge 19:19;
1Sa 20:14,42;
2Sa 9:1; 1Ki 2:7
[n]ver 23; Ge 41:9;
Ecc 9:15
40:15
[o]S Ge 14:13
[p]Ge 39:20;
Job 13:27
40:16 [q]S ver 1
[r]S ver 12
[s]Am 8:1-2
40:18 [t]ver 12
40:19 [u]ver 13
[v]S ver 13 [w]ver 22; Dt 21:22-23;
Est 2:23; 7:10
[x]Dt 28:26;
1Sa 17:44;
2Sa 21:10;
1Ki 14:11; 16:4;
21:24; Eze 39:4
40:20 [y]S ver 13
[z]Mt 14:6-10
[a]Est 2:18;
Mk 6:21 [b]S ver 1
40:21 [c]S ver 1
[d]2Ki 25:27;
Jer 52:31 [e]ver 13
40:22 [f]S ver 19
[g]Ge 41:13;
Ps 105:19
40:23 [h]S ver 14;
S Ecc 1:11
41:1 [i]S Ge 20:3
[j]ver 17;
S Ge 2:14;
Ex 1:22; 2:5;
7:15
41:2 [k]ver 26;
Jer 5:28 [l]ver 18;
Ex 2:3;
Job 40:21;
Isa 19:6
41:4 [m]ver 7
41:5 [n]Jos 13:3;
2Ki 4:42;
1Ch 13:5;
Isa 23:3; Jer 2:18

41:6 [o]Ex 10:13;
14:21; Job 6:26;
11:2; 15:2;
Ps 11:6; 48:7;
Isa 11:15; 27:8;
Jer 4:11; 18:17;
Eze 19:12; 27:26;
Hos 12:1; 13:15;
Jnh 4:8
41:7 [p]ver 4
41:8 [q]Job 7:14;
Da 2:1,3; 4:5,19
[r]Ex 7:11,22;
Da 1:20; 2:2,27;
4:7; 5:7 [s]ver 24;
S Ge 40:8;
Da 4:18
41:9 [t]S Ge 40:14
41:10 [u]S Ge 40:2
[v]S Ge 37:36;
S 39:20

41:11 [w]Ge 40:5 **41:12** [x]S Ge 14:13; 39:17 [y]S Ge 37:36;
40:4 [z]S Ge 40:12 **41:13** [a]S Ge 40:22 **41:14** [b]Ps 105:20
[c]Isa 18:2,7 [d]S Ge 35:2; 45:22; Ru 3:3; 2Sa 12:20 **41:15**
[e]S Ge 40:8 [f]S Ge 40:12; Da 4:18; 5:16 **41:16** [g]S Ge 40:8
41:17 [h]S ver 1

[h]16 Or three wicker baskets   [i]19 Or and impale you
on a pole   [j]22,13 Or impaled

40:15 *dungeon.* Probably hyperbole to reflect Joseph's despair (see note on 39:20). Since the same Hebrew word is translated "cistern" in 37:24, the author Genesis has established a link with Joseph's earlier experience at the hands of his brothers.
40:19 *lift off your head.* A grisly pun based on the same idiom used in v. 13.
40:20 *Pharaoh's birthday.* Centuries later, the birthday of Herod the tetrarch would become the occasion for another beheading (see Mt 14:6–10).
41:2 *out of the river there came up seven cows.* Cattle often submerged themselves up to their necks in the Nile to escape sun and insects.
41:6 *scorched by the east wind.* The Palestinian sirocco

(in Egypt the khamsin), which blows in from the desert (see Hos 13:15) in late spring and early fall, often withers vegetation (see Isa 40:7; Eze 17:10).
41:8 *his mind was troubled.* See 40:6–7. *magicians.* Probably priests who claimed to possess occult knowledge. *no one could interpret them.* See Da 2:10–11.
41:13 *things turned out exactly as he interpreted them.* Because his words were from the Lord (see Ps 105:19).
41:14 *Pharaoh sent for Joseph.* Effecting his permanent release from prison (see Ps 105:20). *shaved.* Egyptians were normally smooth-shaven, while Palestinians wore beards (see 2Sa 10:5; Jer 41:5).
41:16 *I cannot do it . . . but God will give Pharaoh the answer.* See 40:8; Da 2:27–28,30; 2Co 3:5.

grazed among the reeds. [i] 19After them, seven other cows came up—scrawny and very ugly and lean. I had never seen such ugly cows in all the land of Egypt. 20The lean, ugly cows ate up the seven fat cows that came up first. 21But even after they ate them, no one could tell that they had done so; they looked just as ugly as before. Then I woke up.

22"In my dreams I also saw seven heads of grain, full and good, growing on a single stalk. 23After them, seven other heads sprouted—withered and thin and scorched by the east wind. 24The thin heads of grain swallowed up the seven good heads. I told this to the magicians, but none could explain it to me. [j]"

25Then Joseph said to Pharaoh, "The dreams of Pharaoh are one and the same. [k] God has revealed to Pharaoh what he is about to do. [l] 26The seven good cows [m] are seven years, and the seven good heads of grain are seven years; it is one and the same dream. 27The seven lean, ugly cows that came up afterward are seven years, and so are the seven worthless heads of grain scorched by the east wind: They are seven years of famine. [n]

28"It is just as I said to Pharaoh: God has shown Pharaoh what he is about to do. [o] 29Seven years of great abundance [p] are coming throughout the land of Egypt, 30but seven years of famine [q] will follow them. Then all the abundance in Egypt will be forgotten, and the famine will ravage the land. [r] 31The abundance in the land will not be remembered, because the famine that follows it will be so severe. 32The reason the dream was given to Pharaoh in two forms is that the matter has been firmly decided [s] by God, and God will do it soon. [t]

33"And now let Pharaoh look for a discerning and wise man [u] and put him in charge of the land of Egypt. [v] 34Let Pharaoh appoint commissioners [w] over the land to take a fifth [x] of the harvest of Egypt during the seven years of abundance. [y] 35They should collect all the food of these good years that are coming and store up the grain under the authority of Pharaoh, to be kept in the cities for food. [z] 36This food should be held in reserve for the country, to be used during the seven years of famine that will come upon Egypt, [a] so that the country may not be ruined by the famine."

37The plan seemed good to Pharaoh and to all his officials. [b] 38So Pharaoh asked them, "Can we find anyone like this man, one in whom is the spirit of God [k]?" [c]

39Then Pharaoh said to Joseph, "Since God has made all this known to you, [d] there is no one so discerning and wise as you. [e] 40You shall be in charge of my palace, [f] and all my people are to submit to your orders. [g] Only with respect to the throne will I be greater than you. [h]"

Joseph in Charge of Egypt

41So Pharaoh said to Joseph, "I hereby put you in charge of the whole land of Egypt." [i] 42Then Pharaoh took his signet ring [j] from his finger and put it on Joseph's finger. He dressed him in robes [k] of fine linen [l] and put a gold chain around his neck. [m] 43He had him ride in a chariot [n] as his second-in-command, [l o] and men shouted before him, "Make way [m]!" [p] Thus he put him in charge of the whole land of Egypt. [q]

44Then Pharaoh said to Joseph, "I am Pharaoh, but without your word no one will lift hand or foot in all Egypt." [r] 45Phar-

Cross references

41:18 [i]S ver 2.
41:24 [j]S ver 8
41:25 [k]S Ge 40:12
[l]S Ge 40:8;
Isa 46:11;
Da 2:45
41:26 [m]S ver 2
41:27 [n]S Ge 12:10
41:28 [o]S Ge 40:8
41:29 [p]ver 47
41:30 [q]ver 54;
Ge 45:6,11;
47:13; Ps 105:16
[r]ver 56;
41:32 [s]Ge 12:10
[s]Ge 2:5
41:33 [t]S Ge 40:8
[u]ver 39

[v]S Ge 39:9
41:34 [w]Est 2:3
[x]Ge 47:24,26;
1Sa 8:15 [y]ver 48;
Ge 47:14
41:35 [z]ver 48
41:36 [a]ver 56;
Ge 42:6; 47:14
41:37 [b]Ge 45:16;
Est 2:4; Isa 19:11
41:38 [c]Nu 27:18;
Dt 34:9; Da 2:11;
4:8,8,9-18; 5:11,
14
41:39 [d]Da 2:11;
5:11 [e]ver 33
41:40 [f]1Ki 4:6;
2Ki 15:5;
Isa 22:15; 36:3
[g]S Ge 39:9;
Ps 105:21-22;
Ac 7:10 [h]Est 10:3
41:41 [i]ver 43,55;
Ge 42:6; 45:8,13,
26; Est 8:2;
Jer 40:7; Da 6:3
41:42 [j]S Ge 24:22;
Est 3:10; 8:2,8
[k]1Sa 17:38; 18:4;
1Ki 19:19;
Est 6:8,11;
Da 5:29; Zec 3:4
[l]Ex 25:4;
Est 8:15; Da 5:29
[m]Ps 73:6; SS 4:9;
Isa 3:18;
Eze 16:11;
Da 5:7,16,29
41:43 [n]Ge 46:29; 50:9;
Isa 2:7; 22:18
[o]Est 10:3
[p]Est 6:9 [q]S ver 41
41:44 [r]S Ge 37:8; Est
10:2; Ps 105:22

[k]38 Or *of the gods* [l]43 Or *in the chariot of his second-in-command*; or *in his second chariot* [m]43 Or *Bow down*

41:27 *seven years of famine.* See Ac 7:11. Long famines were rare in Egypt because of the regularity of the annual overflow of the Nile, but not uncommon elsewhere (see 2Ki 8:1). According to the NT, the great famine in the time of Elijah lasted three and a half years (Jas 5:17), thus half of seven years; it had been cut short by Elijah's intercession (1Ki 18:42; Jas 5:18).

41:32 Repetition of a divine revelation was often used for emphasis (see 37:5-9; Am 7:1-6,7-9; 8:1-3).

41:38 *in whom is the spirit of God.* See NIV text note. The word "spirit" should probably not be capitalized in such passages, since reference to the Holy Spirit would be out of character in statements by pagan rulers.

41:40 *You shall be in charge.* Pharaoh took Joseph's advice (see v. 33) and decided that Joseph himself should be "ruler over Egypt" (Ac 7:10; see also Ps 105:21). *all my people are to submit to your orders.* More lit. "at your command all my people are to kiss (you)"—i.e., kiss your hands or feet in an

act of homage and submission (see Ps 2:12 and note).

41:42 Three symbols of transfer and/or sharing of royal authority, referred to also in Est 3:10 (signet ring); Est 6:11 (robe); and Da 5:7,16,29 (gold chain).

41:43 *second-in-command.* The position was probably that of vizier, the highest executive office below that of the king himself. *Make way!* See NIV text note. The Hebrew here may be an Egyptian imperative of a Semitic loanword, meaning "Bow the knee!"

41:45 *gave Joseph the name Zaphenath-Paneah.* As a part of assigning Joseph an official position within his royal administration (see note on 1:5). Pharaoh presumed to use this marvelously endowed servant of the Lord for his own royal purposes—as a later Pharaoh would attempt to use divinely blessed Israel for the enrichment of Egypt (Ex 1). He did not recognize that Joseph served a Higher Power, whose kingdom and redemptive purposes were being advanced. (The meaning of Joseph's Egyptian name is uncertain.) *Asenath.*

aoh gave Joseph[s] the name Zaphenath-Paneah and gave him Asenath daughter of Potiphera, priest[t] of On,[n][u] to be his wife.[v] And Joseph went throughout the land of Egypt.

[46]Joseph was thirty years old[w] when he entered the service[x] of Pharaoh king of Egypt. And Joseph went out from Pharaoh's presence and traveled throughout Egypt. [47]During the seven years of abundance[y] the land produced plentifully. [48]Joseph collected all the food produced in those seven years of abundance in Egypt and stored it in the cities.[z] In each city he put the food grown in the fields surrounding it. [49]Joseph stored up huge quantities of grain, like the sand of the sea;[a] it was so much that he stopped keeping records because it was beyond measure.

[50]Before the years of famine came, two sons were born to Joseph by Asenath daughter of Potiphera, priest of On.[b] [51]Joseph named his firstborn[c] Manasseh[o][d] and said, "It is because God has made me forget all my trouble and all my father's household." [52]The second son he named Ephraim[p][e] and said, "It is because God has made me fruitful[f] in the land of my suffering."

[53]The seven years of abundance in Egypt came to an end, [54]and the seven years of famine[g] began,[h] just as Joseph had said. There was famine in all the other lands, but in the whole land of Egypt there was food. [55]When all Egypt began to feel the famine,[i] the people cried to Pharaoh for food. Then Pharaoh told all the Egyptians, "Go to Joseph and do what he tells you."[j]

[56]When the famine had spread over the whole country, Joseph opened the store-houses and sold grain to the Egyptians,[k] for the famine[l] was severe throughout Egypt.[m] [57]And all the countries came to Egypt to buy grain from Joseph,[n] because the famine was severe in all the world.[o]

Joseph's Brothers Go to Egypt

42 When Jacob learned that there was grain in Egypt,[p] he said to his sons, "Why do you just keep looking at each other?" [2]He continued, "I have heard that there is grain in Egypt. Go down there and buy some for us,[q] so that we may live and not die."[r]

[3]Then ten of Joseph's brothers went down to buy grain[s] from Egypt. [4]But Jacob did not send Benjamin,[t] Joseph's brother, with the others, because he was afraid that harm might come to him.[u] [5]So Israel's sons were among those who went to buy grain,[v] for the famine was in the land of Canaan[w] also.[x]

[6]Now Joseph was the governor of the land,[y] the one who sold grain to all its people.[z] So when Joseph's brothers arrived, they bowed down to him with their faces to the ground.[a] [7]As soon as Joseph saw his brothers, he recognized them, but he pretended to be a stranger and spoke harshly to them.[b] "Where do you come from?"[c] he asked.

"From the land of Canaan," they replied, "to buy food."

[8]Although Joseph recognized his brothers, they did not recognize him.[d] [9]Then he

---

41:45 [s]Est 2:7
[t]Ex 2:16
[u]Eze 30:17 [v]ver 50; Ge 46:20,27
41:46 [w]S Ge 37:2
[x]1Sa 8:11; 16:21; Pr 22:29; Da 1:19
41:47 [y]ver 29
41:48 [z]S ver 34
41:49 [a]S Ge 12:2
41:50 [b]S ver 45
41:51 [c]Ge 48:14, 18,20; 49:3
[d]Ge 46:20; 48:1; 50:23; Nu 1:34; Dt 33:17;
Jos 4:12; 17:1;
1Ch 7:14
41:52 [e]Ge 46:20; 48:1,5; 50:23;
Nu 1:32; 26:28;
Dt 33:17;
Jos 14:4;
Jdg 5:14;
1Ch 7:20;
2Ch 30:1;
Ps 60:7; Jer 7:15;
Ob 1:19
[f]S Ge 17:6
41:54 [g]S Ge 12:10
[h]Ac 7:11
41:55 [i]Dt 32:24; 2Ch 20:9;
Isa 51:19;
Jer 5:12; 27:8; 42:16; 44:27
[j]S ver 41; Jn 2:5
41:56 [k]S ver 36
[l]S Ge 12:10
[m]S ver 30
41:57 [n]Ge 42:5; 47:15
[o]S Ge 12:10
42:1 [p]Ac 7:12
42:2 [q]Ge 43:2,4; 44:25 [r]ver 19,33;
Ge 43:8; 47:19;
Ps 33:18-19
42:3 [s]ver 10;
Ge 43:20
42:4 [t]S Ge 35:18
[u]ver 38
42:5 [v]S Ge 41:57
[w]ver 13,29;
Ge 31:18; 45:17
[x]S Ge 12:10;
S Dt 32:24;
Ac 7:11
42:6 [y]S Ge 41:41;
S Ne 5:14

[z]S Ge 41:36 [a]S Ge 33:3 **42:7** [b]ver 30 [c]S Ge 29:4 **42:8** [d]Ge 37:2

[n]45 That is, Heliopolis; also in verse 50
[o]51 *Manasseh* sounds like and may be derived from the Hebrew for *forget.* [p]52 *Ephraim* sounds like the Hebrew for *twice fruitful.*

The name is Egyptian and probably means "She belongs to (the goddess) Neith." *Potiphera.* Not the same person as "Potiphar" (37:36; 39:1); the name (also Egyptian) means "he whom (the sun-god) Ra has given." *On.* Located ten miles northeast of modern Cairo, it was called Heliopolis ("city of the sun") by the Greeks and was an important center for the worship of Ra, who had a temple there. Potiphera therefore bore an appropriate name.
41:46 *thirty years old.* In just 13 years (see 37:2), Joseph had become second-in-command (v. 43) in Egypt.
41:49 *like the sand of the sea.* A simile also for the large number of offspring promised to Abraham and Jacob (see 22:17; 32:12).
41:52 *Ephraim.* The meaning of the name (see NIV text note) reflects the fact that God gave Joseph "two" (see v. 50) sons.
41:57 *all the world.* The known world from the writer's perspective (the Middle East). This description of the famine in the time of Joseph echoes the author's description of the flood in the time of Noah. God saved only Noah and his family from the flood, so that Noah became the new (after Adam) father of the race. With the call of Abram out of the

post-flood and post-Babel nations, God once more singled out one man, now to be the father of his special people. God promised that, through this man and his descendants, "all peoples on earth will be blessed" (12:3). The author highlights the fact that in this new crisis hope rested with one of these descendants.
42:2-3 Stephen refers to this incident (Ac 7:12).
42:4 *did not send Benjamin, Joseph's brother.* Their mother Rachel had died (35:19), and Jacob thought Joseph also was dead (37:33). Jacob did not want to lose Benjamin, the remaining son of his beloved Rachel.
42:5 *famine was in the land of Canaan also.* As in the time of Abram (see 12:10 and note).
42:6 *bowed down.* In fulfillment of Joseph's dreams (see 37:7,9).
42:8 *Joseph recognized his brothers.* Although at least 20 years had passed since he had last seen them (see 37:2; 41:46,53–54), they had been adults at the time and their appearance had not changed much. *they did not recognize him.* Joseph, a teenager at the time of his enslavement, was now an adult in an unexpected position of authority, wearing Egyptian clothes and speaking to his brothers through an

remembered his dreams[e] about them and said to them, "You are spies![f] You have come to see where our land is unprotected."[g]

10"No, my lord,[h]" they answered. "Your servants have come to buy food.[i] 11We are all the sons of one man. Your servants[j] are honest men,[k] not spies.[l]"

12"No!" he said to them. "You have come to see where our land is unprotected."[m]

13But they replied, "Your servants[n] were twelve brothers, the sons of one man, who lives in the land of Canaan.[o] The youngest is now with our father, and one is no more."[p]

14Joseph said to them, "It is just as I told you: You are spies![q] 15And this is how you will be tested: As surely as Pharaoh lives,[r] you will not leave this place unless your youngest brother comes here.[s] 16Send one of your number to get your brother;[t] the rest of you will be kept in prison,[u] so that your words may be tested to see if you are telling the truth.[v] If you are not, then as surely as Pharaoh lives, you are spies![w]" 17And he put them all in custody[x] for three days.

18On the third day, Joseph said to them, "Do this and you will live, for I fear God:[y] 19If you are honest men,[z] let one of your brothers stay here in prison,[a] while the rest of you go and take grain back for your starving households.[b] 20But you must bring your youngest brother to me,[c] so that your words may be verified and that you may not die." This they proceeded to do.

21They said to one another, "Surely we are being punished because of our brother.[d] We saw how distressed he was when he pleaded with us for his life, but we would not listen; that's why this distress[e] has come upon us."

22Reuben replied, "Didn't I tell you not to sin against the boy?[f] But you wouldn't listen! Now we must give an accounting[g] for his blood."[h] 23They did not realize[i] that Joseph could understand them,[j] since he was using an interpreter.

24He turned away from them and began

to weep,[k] but then turned back and spoke to them again. He had Simeon taken from them and bound before their eyes.[l]

25Joseph gave orders to fill their bags with grain,[m] to put each man's silver back in his sack,[n] and to give them provisions[o] for their journey.[p] After this was done for them, 26they loaded their grain on their donkeys[q] and left.

27At the place where they stopped for the night one of them opened his sack to get feed for his donkey,[r] and he saw his silver in the mouth of his sack.[s] 28"My silver has been returned," he said to his brothers. "Here it is in my sack."

Their hearts sank[t] and they turned to each other trembling[u] and said, "What is this that God has done to us?"[v]

29When they came to their father Jacob in the land of Canaan,[w] they told him all that had happened to them.[x] They said, 30"The man who is lord over the land spoke harshly to us[y] and treated us as though we were spying on the land.[z] 31But we said to him, 'We are honest men; we are not spies.[a] 32We were twelve brothers, sons of one father. One is no more, and the youngest is now with our father in Canaan.'[b]

33"Then the man who is lord over the land said to us, 'This is how I will know whether you are honest men: Leave one of your brothers here with me, and take food for your starving households and go.[c] 34But bring your youngest brother to me so I will know that you are not spies but honest men.[d] Then I will give your brother back to you,[e] and you can trade[q] in the land.[f]'"

35As they were emptying their sacks, there in each man's sack was his pouch of silver![g] When they and their father saw the money pouches, they were frightened.[h] 36Their father Jacob said to them, "You have deprived me of my children. Joseph is no more and Simeon is no more,[i] and now you want to take Benjamin.[j] Everything is against me![k]"

42:9 [e]S Ge 37:7
[f]ver 14,16,30;
Dt 1:22; Jos 2:1;
6:22 [g]ver 12
42:10 [h]S Ge 37:8
[i]S ver 3
42:11 [j]ver 13;
Ge 44:7,9,16,19,
21,31; 46:34;
47:3 [k]ver 15,16,
19,20,34 [l]ver 31
42:12 [m]ver 9
42:13 [n]S ver 11
[o]S ver 5;
Ge 46:31; 47:1
[p]ver 24,32,36;
S Ge 37:33; 43:7,
29,33; 44:8;
Jer 31:15
42:14 [q]S ver 9
42:15 [r]1Sa 17:55
[s]S ver 11;
Ge 43:3,5,7;
44:21,23
42:16 [t]ver 19
[u]ver 19 [v]S ver 11
[w]S ver 9
42:17 [x]S Ge 40:4
42:18
[y]S Ge 20:11;
S 22:12;
Lev 19:14; 25:43;
2Sa 23:3
42:19 [z]S ver 11
[a]ver 16 [b]S ver 2
42:20 [c]S ver 15
42:21
[d]Ge 37:26-28
[e]Ge 45:5
42:22
[f]Ge 37:21-22
[g]S Ge 9:5
[h]Ge 45:24
42:23 [i]Ge 38:16
[j]S Ge 11:7

42:24
[k]S Ge 29:11
[l]S ver 13;
Ge 43:14,23
42:25 [m]Ge 43:2
[n]ver 27,35;
Ge 43:12,18,21;
44:1,8 [o]Jer 40:5
[p]Ge 45:21,23
42:26
[q]S Ge 32:15;
44:13; 45:17;
1Sa 25:18;
Isa 30:6
42:27 [r]Jdg 19:19;
Job 39:9; Isa 1:3
[s]S ver 25
42:28 [t]Jos 2:11;
5:1; 7:5
[u]Mk 5:33
[v]Ge 43:23
42:29 [w]S ver 5
[x]Ge 44:24
42:30 [y]ver 7
[z]S ver 9
42:31 [a]ver 11
42:32 [b]S ver 13
42:33 [c]S ver 2
42:34 [d]S ver 11
[e]S ver 24
[f]Ge 34:10
42:35 [g]S ver 25
[h]Ge 43:18
42:36 [i]S ver 13
[j]S ver 24

[k]Job 3:25; Pr 10:24; Ro 8:31

[q]34 Or *move about freely*

---

interpreter (see v. 23). He was, moreover, shaven in the Egyptian manner (see note on 41:14).
42:10 *my lord . . . Your servants.* Unwittingly, Joseph's brothers again fulfilled his dreams and their own scornful fears (see 37:8).
42:15 *As surely as Pharaoh lives.* The most solemn oaths were pronounced in the name of the reigning monarch (as here) or of the speaker's deities (Ps 16:4; Am 8:14) or of the Lord himself (Jdg 8:19; 1Sa 14:39,45; 19:6).

42:21 *how distressed he was . . . distress has come upon us.* The brothers realized they were beginning to reap what they had sown (see Gal 6:7).
42:22 See 37:21–22 and note on 37:21.
42:24 *He had Simeon taken.* Jacob's second son (see 29:32–33) is imprisoned instead of the firstborn Reuben, perhaps because the latter had saved Joseph's life years earlier (37:21–22).

37Then Reuben said to his father, "You may put both of my sons to death if I do not bring him back to you. Entrust him to my care,[l] and I will bring him back."[m] 38But Jacob said, "My son will not go down there with you; his brother is dead[n] and he is the only one left. If harm comes to him[o] on the journey you are taking, you will bring my gray head down to the grave[r][p] in sorrow.[q]"

The Second Journey to Egypt

43 Now the famine was still severe in the land.[r] 2So when they had eaten all the grain they had brought from Egypt,[s] their father said to them, "Go back and buy us a little more food."[t]

3But Judah[u] said to him, "The man warned us solemnly, 'You will not see my face again unless your brother is with you.'[v] 4If you will send our brother along with us, we will go down and buy food for you.[w] 5But if you will not send him, we will not go down, because the man said to us, 'You will not see my face again unless your brother is with you.[x]'"

6Israel[y] asked, "Why did you bring this trouble[z] on me by telling the man you had another brother?"

7They replied, "The man questioned us closely about ourselves and our family. 'Is your father still living?'[a] he asked us. 'Do you have another brother?'[b] We simply answered his questions. How were we to know he would say, 'Bring your brother down here'?[c]"

8Then Judah[d] said to Israel[e] his father, "Send the boy along with me and we will go at once, so that we and you and our children may live and not die.[f] 9I myself will guarantee his safety; you can hold me personally responsible for him.[g] If I do not bring him back to you and set him here before you, I will bear the blame[h] before you all my life.[i] 10As it is, if we had not delayed,[j] we could have gone and returned twice."

11Then their father Israel[k] said to them, "If it must be, then do this: Put some of the best products[l] of the land in your bags and take them down to the man as a gift[m]—a little balm[n] and a little honey, some spices[o] and myrrh,[p] some pistachio nuts and almonds. 12Take double the amount[q] of silver with you, for you must return the silver that was put back into the mouths of your sacks.[r] Perhaps it was a mistake. 13Take your brother also and go back to the man at once.[s] 14And may God Almighty[s][t] grant you mercy[u] before the man so that he will let your other brother and Benjamin come back with you.[v] As for me, if I am bereaved, I am bereaved."[w]

15So the men took the gifts and double the amount of silver,[x] and Benjamin also. They hurried[y] down to Egypt and presented themselves[z] to Joseph. 16When Joseph saw Benjamin[a] with them, he said to the steward of his house,[b] "Take these men to my house, slaughter an animal and prepare dinner;[c] they are to eat with me at noon."

17The man did as Joseph told him and took the men to Joseph's house.[d] 18Now the men were frightened[e] when they were taken to his house.[f] They thought, "We were brought here because of the silver that was put back into our sacks[g] the first time. He wants to attack us[h] and overpower us and seize us as slaves[i] and take our donkeys.[j]"

19So they went up to Joseph's steward[k] and spoke to him at the entrance to the house. 20"Please, sir," they said, "we came down here the first time to buy food.[l] 21But at the place where we stopped for the night we opened our sacks and each of us found his silver—the exact weight—in the mouth of his sack. So we have brought it back with us.[m] 22We have also brought additional silver with us to buy food. We don't know who put our silver in our sacks."

23"It's all right," he said. "Don't be

42:37 [l]S Ge 39:4
[m]Ge 43:9; 44:32
42:38
[n]S Ge 37:33 [o]ver 4 [p]S Ge 37:35
[q]Ge 44:29,34; 48:7
43:1 [r]S Ge 12:10
43:2 [s]Ge 42:25
[t]S Ge 42:2
43:3 [u]ver 8;
Ge 44:14,18; 46:28
[v]S Ge 42:15
43:4 [w]S Ge 42:2
43:5
[x]S Ge 42:15;
44:26; 2Sa 3:13
43:6 [y]ver 8,11;
S Ge 17:5
[z]S Ge 34:30
43:7 [a]ver 27;
Ge 45:3
[b]S Ge 42:13;
44:19
[c]S Ge 42:15
43:8 [d]S ver 3;
S Ge 29:35 [e]S ver 6 [f]S Ge 42:2;
Ps 33:18-19
43:9 [g]1Sa 23:20
[h]Ge 44:10,17
[i]S Ge 42:37;
Phm 1:18-19
43:10 [j]Ge 45:9
43:11 [k]S ver 6

[l]S Ge 24:10
[m]S Ge 32:13
[n]S Ge 37:25;
Eze 27:17
[o]Ex 30:23;
1Ki 10:2;
Eze 27:22
[p]S Ge 37:25
43:12 [q]ver 15;
Ex 22:4,7;
Pr 6:31
[r]S Ge 42:25
43:13 [s]ver 3
43:14 [t]S Ge 17:1
[u]Dt 13:17;
Ps 25:6
[v]S Ge 42:24
[w]2Sa 18:33;
Est 4:16
43:15 [x]ver 12
[y]Ge 45:9,13
[z]Ge 47:2,7;
Mt 2:11
43:16
[a]S Ge 35:18 [b]ver 17,24,26;
Ge 44:1,4,12;
2Sa 19:17;
Isa 22:15 [c]ver 31;
Lk 15:23
43:17 [d]S ver 16
43:18 [e]Ge 42:35
[f]Ge 44:14
[g]S Ge 42:25
[h]S Ge 32:11
[i]Ge 44:9,16,33;
50:18 [j]Ge 34:28
43:19 [k]ver 16
43:20 [l]S Ge 42:3

43:21 [m]S ver 15; S Ge 42:25

[r]38 Hebrew Sheol   [s]14 Hebrew El-Shaddai

42:37 *both of my sons.* Reuben's generous offer as security for Benjamin's safety (see note on 37:21).

43:3 *Judah said.* From this point on, Judah became the spokesman for his brothers (see vv. 8–10; 44:14–34; 46:28). His tribe would become preeminent among the 12 (see 49:8–10), and he would be an ancestor of Jesus (see Mt 1:2,17; Lk 3:23,33).

43:9 Judah offered himself as security for Benjamin's safety—an even more generous gesture than that of Reuben (see 42:37 and note).

43:11 *take them . . . as a gift.* A customary practice when approaching one's superior, whether political (see 1Sa

16:20), military (see 1Sa 17:18) or religious (see 2Ki 5:15). *balm . . . myrrh.* See 37:25 and note. *honey.* Either that produced by bees, or an inferior substitute made by boiling grape or date juice down to a thick syrup. *pistachio nuts.* Mentioned only here in the Bible; the fruit of a small, broad-crowned tree that is native to Asia Minor, Syria and Palestine but not to Egypt.

43:14 *God Almighty.* See note on 17:1. *if I am bereaved, I am bereaved.* Cf. Esther's similar phrase of resignation in Est 4:16.

43:21 The brothers' statement to Joseph's steward compressed the details (see 42:27,35).

afraid. Your God, the God of your father, [n] has given you treasure in your sacks; [o] I received your silver." Then he brought Simeon out to them. [p]

[24] The steward took the men into Joseph's house, [q] gave them water to wash their feet [r] and provided fodder for their donkeys. [25] They prepared their gifts [s] for Joseph's arrival at noon, [t] because they had heard that they were to eat there.

[26] When Joseph came home, [u] they presented to him the gifts [v] they had brought into the house, and they bowed down before him to the ground. [w] [27] He asked them how they were, and then he said, "How is your aged father [x] you told me about? Is he still living?" [y]

[28] They replied, "Your servant our father [z] is still alive and well." And they bowed low [a] to pay him honor. [b]

[29] As he looked about and saw his brother Benjamin, his own mother's son, [c] he asked, "Is this your youngest brother, the one you told me about?" [d] And he said, "God be gracious to you, [e] my son." [30] Deeply moved [f] at the sight of his brother, Joseph hurried out and looked for a place to weep. He went into his private room and wept [g] there.

[31] After he had washed his face, he came out and, controlling himself, [h] said, "Serve the food." [i]

[32] They served him by himself, the brothers by themselves, and the Egyptians who ate with him by themselves, because Egyptians could not eat with Hebrews, [j] for that is detestable to Egyptians. [k] [33] The men had been seated before him in the order of their ages, from the firstborn [l] to the youngest; [m] and they looked at each other in astonishment. [34] When portions were served to them from Joseph's table, Benjamin's portion was five times as much as anyone else's. [n] So they feasted [o] and drank freely with him.

A Silver Cup in a Sack

44 Now Joseph gave these instructions to the steward of his house: [p] "Fill the men's sacks with as much food as they can carry, and put each man's silver in the mouth of his sack. [q] [2] Then put my cup, [r] the silver one, [s] in the mouth of the youngest one's sack, along with the silver for his grain." And he did as Joseph said.

[3] As morning dawned, the men were sent on their way with their donkeys. [t] [4] They had not gone far from the city when Joseph said to his steward, [u] "Go after those men at once, and when you catch up with them, say to them, 'Why have you repaid good with evil? [v] [5] Isn't this the cup [w] my master drinks from and also uses for divination? [x] This is a wicked thing you have done.'"

[6] When he caught up with them, he repeated these words to them. [7] But they said to him, "Why does my lord say such things? Far be it from your servants [y] to do anything like that! [z] [8] We even brought back to you from the land of Canaan [a] the silver [b] we found inside the mouths of our sacks. [c] So why would we steal [d] silver or gold from your master's house? [9] If any of your servants [e] is found to have it, he will die; [f] and the rest of us will become my lord's slaves. [g]"

[10] "Very well, then," he said, "let it be as you say. Whoever is found to have it [h] will become my slave; [i] the rest of you will be free from blame." [j]

[11] Each of them quickly lowered his sack to the ground and opened it. [12] Then the steward [k] proceeded to search, [l] beginning with the oldest and ending with the youngest. [m] And the cup was found in Benjamin's sack. [n] [13] At this, they tore their clothes. [o] Then they all loaded their donkeys [p] and returned to the city.

43:23
[n] S Ge 24:12; [l] S 31:5; Ex 3:6
[o] Ge 42:28
[p] S Ge 42:24
43:24 [q] S ver 16
[r] S Ge 18:4
43:25
[s] S Ge 32:13 [t] ver 16
43:26 [u] S ver 16
[v] S Ge 32:13; - [.] Mt 2:11
[w] S Ge 33:3
43:27 [x] S Ge 37:3
[y] S ver 7
43:28 [z] Ge 44:24, 27,30 [a] Ge 18:2; Ex 18:7
[b] S Ge 37:7
43:29
[c] S Ge 35:18
[d] S Ge 42:13
[e] Nu 6:25; Ps 67:1; 119:58; Isa 30:18-19; 33:2
43:30 [f] Jn 11:33, 38 [g] S Ge 29:11
43:31 [h] Ge 45:1; Isa 30:18; 42:14; 63:15; 64:12
[i] S ver 16
43:32
[j] S Ge 14:13; Gal 2:12
[k] Ge 46:34; Ex 8:26
43:33
[l] S Ge 35:23
[m] S Ge 42:13; 44:12
43:34
[n] S Ge 37:3; S 2Ki 25:30
[o] Lk 15:23

44:1 [p] S Ge 43:16
[q] S Ge 42:25
44:2 [r] ver 5,10, 12,16 [s] ver 8
44:3 [t] Jdg 19:9
44:4 [u] S Ge 43:16
[v] Ps 35:12; 38:20; 109:5; Pr 17:13; Jer 18:20
44:5 [w] S ver 2
[x] S Ge 30:27; Dt 18:10-14
44:7 [y] S Ge 42:11
[z] S Ge 18:25
44:8 [a] S Ge 42:13
[b] ver 2
[c] S Ge 42:25; S 43:15
[d] Ge 31:30
44:9 [e] S Ge 42:11
[f] Ge 31:32 [g] S ver 10; S Ge 43:18
44:10 [h] S ver 2
[i] ver 9,17,33
[j] S Ge 43:9

44:12 [k] S Ge 43:16 [l] S Ge 31:34 [m] S Ge 43:33 [n] ver 2 **44:13**
[o] S Ge 37:29 [p] S Ge 42:26

43:23 *Your God . . . has given you treasure.* The steward spoke better than he knew.
43:24 See note on 18:2.
43:26 *bowed down.* Additional fulfillment of Joseph's dreams (37:7,9; see also 42:6; 43:28).
43:29 *Benjamin, his own mother's son.* Joseph's special relationship to Benjamin is clear. *God be gracious to you.* Later blessings and benedictions would echo these words (see Nu 6:25; Ps 67:1).
43:30 *Joseph . . . wept.* Both emotional and sensitive, he wept often (see 42:24; 45:2,14–15; 46:29).
43:32 *Egyptians could not eat with Hebrews.* The taboo was probably based on ritual or religious reasons (see Ex 8:26), unlike the Egyptian refusal to associate with shepherds (see 46:34), which was probably based on social custom.

43:34 *Benjamin's portion was five times as much.* Again reflecting his special status with Joseph (see note on v. 29; see also 45:22).
44:4 *the city.* Identity unknown, though Memphis (about 13 miles south of modern Cairo) and Zoan (in the eastern delta region) have been suggested.
44:5 *divination.* See v. 15; see also note on 30:27.
44:9 *If any of your servants is found to have it, he will die.* Years earlier, Jacob had given Laban a similar rash response (see 31:32 and note).
44:10 The steward softened the penalty contained in the brothers' proposal.
44:12 *beginning with the oldest and ending with the youngest.* For a similar building up of suspense see 31:33.
44:13 *tore their clothes.* A sign of distress and grief (see 37:29).

[14]Joseph was still in the house[q] when Judah[r] and his brothers came in, and they threw themselves to the ground before him.[s] [15]Joseph said to them, "What is this you have done?[t] Don't you know that a man like me can find things out by divination?[u]"

[16]"What can we say to my lord?[v]" Judah[w] replied. "What can we say? How can we prove our innocence?[x] God has uncovered your servants'[y] guilt. We are now my lord's slaves[z]—we ourselves and the one who was found to have the cup.[a]"

[17]But Joseph said, "Far be it from me to do such a thing![b] Only the man who was found to have the cup will become my slave.[c] The rest of you, go back to your father in peace."[d]

[18]Then Judah[e] went up to him and said: "Please, my lord,[f] let your servant speak a word to my lord. Do not be angry[g] with your servant, though you are equal to Pharaoh himself. [19]My lord asked his servants,[h] 'Do you have a father or a brother?'[i] [20]And we answered, 'We have an aged father, and there is a young son born to him in his old age.[j] His brother is dead,[k] and he is the only one of his mother's sons left, and his father loves him.'[l]

[21]"Then you said to your servants,[m] 'Bring him down to me so I can see him for myself.'[n] [22]And we said to my lord,[o] 'The boy cannot leave his father; if he leaves him, his father will die.'[p] [23]But you told your servants, 'Unless your youngest brother comes down with you, you will not see my face again.'[q] [24]When we went back to your servant my father,[r] we told him what my lord[s] had said.[t]

[25]"Then our father said, 'Go back and buy a little more food.'[u] [26]But we said, 'We cannot go down. Only if our youngest brother is with us will we go. We cannot see the man's face unless our youngest brother is with us.'[v]

[27]"Your servant my father[w] said to us, 'You know that my wife bore me two sons.[x] [28]One of them went away from me, and I said, "He has surely been torn to pieces."[y] And I have not seen him since.[z] [29]If you take this one from me too and harm comes to him, you will bring my gray head down to the grave[a] in misery.'[b]

[30]"So now, if the boy is not with us when I go back to your servant my father[c] and if my father, whose life is closely bound up with the boy's life,[d] [31]sees that the boy isn't there, he will die.[e] Your servants[f] will bring the gray head of our father down to the grave[g] in sorrow. [32]Your servant guaranteed the boy's safety to my father. I said, 'If I do not bring him back to you, I will bear the blame before you, my father, all my life!'[h]

[33]"Now then, please let your servant remain here as my lord's slave[i] in place of the boy,[j] and let the boy return with his brothers. [34]How can I go back to my father if the boy is not with me? No! Do not let me see the misery[k] that would come upon my father."[l]

Joseph Makes Himself Known

45 Then Joseph could no longer control himself[m] before all his attendants, and he cried out, "Have everyone leave my presence!"[n] So there was no one with Joseph when he made himself known to his brothers. [2]And he wept[o] so loudly that the Egyptians heard him, and Pharaoh's household heard about it.[p]

[3]Joseph said to his brothers, "I am Joseph! Is my father still living?"[q] But his brothers were not able to answer him,[r] because they were terrified at his presence.[s]

[4]Then Joseph said to his brothers, "Come close to me."[t] When they had done so, he said, "I am your brother Joseph, the one you sold into Egypt![u] [5]And

---

44:14 [q]Ge 43:18 [r]ver 16; [s]Ge 29:35; [s]43:3 [s]S Ge 33:3
44:15 [t]S Ge 12:18 [u]S Ge 30:27
44:16 [v]ver 22, 24; S Ge 37:8 [w]S ver 14 [x]Ps 26:6; 73:13 [y]S Ge 42:11 [z]S Ge 43:18 [a]S ver 2
44:17 [b]S Ge 18:25 [c]S ver 10 [d]S Ge 43:9
44:18 [e]S Ge 29:35 [f]S ver 16 [g]S Ge 18:30
44:19 [h]S Ge 42:11 [i]S Ge 43:7
44:20 [j]S Ge 37:3 [k]S Ge 37:33 [l]S Ge 42:13
44:21 [m]S Ge 42:11 [n]S Ge 42:15
44:22 [o]S ver 16 [p]S Ge 37:35
44:23 [q]S Ge 42:15; [s]43:5
44:24 [r]S Ge 43:28 [s]S ver 16 [t]Ge 42:29
44:25 [u]S Ge 42:2
44:26 [v]S Ge 43:5
44:27 [w]S Ge 43:28
44:28 [x]Ge 46:19 [y]S Ge 37:33 [z]Ge 45:26,28; 46:30; 48:11
44:29 [a]S Ge 37:35 [b]S Ge 42:38
44:30 [c]S Ge 43:28 [d]1Sa 18:1; 2Sa 1:26
44:31 [e]S ver 22 [f]S Ge 42:11 [g]S Ge 37:35
44:32 [h]S Ge 42:37
44:33 [i]S ver 10; S Ge 43:18 [j]Jn 15:13
44:34 [k]S Ge 42:38 [l]Est 8:6
45:1 [m]S Ge 43:31 [n]2Sa 13:9
45:2 [o]S Ge 29:11 [p]ver 16; Ac 7:13
45:3 [q]S Ge 43:7 [r]ver 15

[s]Ge 44:20; Job 21:6; 23:15; Mt 17:6; Mk 6:49-50 **45:4** [t]Ge 27:21-22 [u]S 37:28

[t]29 Hebrew *Sheol*; also in verse 31

44:14 *threw themselves to the ground before him.* Further fulfillment of Joseph's dreams in 37:7,9 (see 42:6; 43:26, 28).
44:16 *God has uncovered your servants' guilt.* Like Joseph's steward (see note on 43:23), Judah spoke better than he knew—or perhaps his words had a double meaning (see 42:21).
44:18 *Judah . . . said.* See note on 43:3. *lord . . . servant.* See note on 42:10. *you are equal to Pharaoh.* Words more flattering than true (see 41:40,43).
44:30 *whose life is closely bound up with the boy's life.* The Hebrew underlying this clause is later used of Jonathan's becoming "one in spirit with David" (1Sa 18:1).
44:33 *in place of the boy.* Judah's willingness to be a

substitute for Benjamin helped make amends for his role in selling Joseph (see 37:26–27).
44:34 *Do not let me see the misery.* Judah remembers an earlier scene (37:34–35).
45:2 *wept.* See vv. 14–15; see also 43:30 and note.
45:3 *brothers . . . were terrified.* Either because they thought they were seeing a ghost or because they were afraid of what Joseph would do to them.
45:4 *I am your brother Joseph.* See v. 3; Ac 7:13. This time Joseph emphasized his relationship to them. *you sold.* See note on 37:28.
45:5 *God sent me.* See vv. 7–9; Ac 7:9. God had a purpose to work through the brothers' thoughtless and cruel act (see Ac 2:23; 4:28).

now, do not be distressed[v] and do not be angry with yourselves for selling me here,[w] because it was to save lives that God sent me ahead of you.[x] [6]For two years now there has been famine[y] in the land, and for the next five years there will not be plowing and reaping. [7]But God sent me ahead of you to preserve for you a remnant[z] on earth and to save your lives by a great deliverance.[u] [a]

[8]"So then, it was not you who sent me here, but God.[b] He made me father[c] to Pharaoh, lord of his entire household and ruler of all Egypt.[d] [9]Now hurry[e] back to my father and say to him, 'This is what your son Joseph says: God has made me lord of all Egypt. Come down to me; don't delay.[f] [10]You shall live in the region of Goshen[g] and be near me—you, your children and grandchildren, your flocks and herds, and all you have.[h] [11]I will provide for you there,[i] because five years of famine[j] are still to come. Otherwise you and your household and all who belong to you will become destitute.'[k]

[12]"You can see for yourselves, and so can my brother Benjamin,[l] that it is really I who am speaking to you.[m] [13]Tell my father about all the honor accorded me in Egypt[n] and about everything you have seen. And bring my father down here quickly.[o]"

[14]Then he threw his arms around his brother Benjamin and wept, and Benjamin[p] embraced him,[q] weeping. [15]And he kissed[r] all his brothers and wept over them.[s] Afterward his brothers talked with him.[t]

[16]When the news reached Pharaoh's palace that Joseph's brothers had come,[u] Pharaoh and all his officials[v] were pleased.[w] [17]Pharaoh said to Joseph, "Tell your brothers, 'Do this: Load your animals[x] and return to the land of Canaan,[y] [18]and bring your father and your families back to me. I will give you the best of the land of Egypt[z] and you can enjoy the fat of the land.' [a]

[19]"You are also directed to tell them, 'Do this: Take some carts[b] from Egypt for your children and your wives, and get your father and come. [20]Never mind about your belongings,[c] because the best of all Egypt[d] will be yours.' "

[21]So the sons of Israel did this. Joseph gave them carts,[e] as Pharaoh had commanded, and he also gave them provisions for their journey.[f] [22]To each of them he gave new clothing,[g] but to Benjamin he gave three hundred shekels[v] of silver and five sets of clothes.[h] [23]And this is what he sent to his father: ten donkeys[i] loaded with the best things[j] of Egypt, and ten female donkeys loaded with grain and bread and other provisions for his journey.[k] [24]Then he sent his brothers away, and as they were leaving he said to them, "Don't quarrel on the way!"[l]

[25]So they went up out of Egypt[m] and came to their father Jacob in the land of Canaan.[n] [26]They told him, "Joseph is still alive! In fact, he is ruler of all Egypt."[o] Jacob was stunned; he did not believe them.[p] [27]But when they told him everything Joseph had said to them, and when he saw the carts[q] Joseph had sent to carry him back, the spirit of their father Jacob revived. [28]And Israel said, "I'm convinced![r] My son Joseph is still alive. I will go and see him before I die."[s]

Jacob Goes to Egypt

46 So Israel[t] set out with all that was his, and when he reached Beer-

45:5 [v]Ge 42:21 [w]Ge 42:22 [x]ver 7-8; Ge 50:20; Job 10:12; Ps 105:17
45:6 [y]S Ge 41:30 45:7 [z]2Ki 19:4, 30,31; Ezr 9:8, 13; Isa 1:9; 10:20,21; 11:11, 16; 46:3; Jer 6:9; 42:2; 50:20; Mic 4:7; 5:7; Zep 2:7 [a]S ver 5; Ge 49:18; Ex 15:2; 1Sa 14:45; 2Ki 13:5; Est 4:14; Isa 25:9; Mic 7:7
45:8 [b]ver 5 [c]Jdg 17:10; 2Ki 6:21; 13:14 [d]S Ge 41:41
45:9 [e]S Ge 43:15 [f]Ge 43:10; Ac 7:14
45:10 [g]Ge 46:28, 34; 47:1,11,27; 50:8; Ex 8:22; 9:26; 10:24 [h]Ge 46:6-7
45:11 [i]Ge 47:12; 50:21 [j]S Ge 41:30 [k]Ps 102:17
45:12 [l]S Ge 35:18 [m]Mk 6:50
45:13 [n]S Ge 41:41 [o]S Ge 43:15; Ac 7:14
45:14 [p]S Ge 35:18 [q]S Ge 29:13
45:15 [r]S Ge 29:11; Lk 15:20 [s]S Ge 29:11,13; S 46:4 [t]ver 3
45:16 [u]S ver 2; Ac 7:13 [v]Ge 50:7 [w]S Ge 41:37
45:17 [x]S Ge 42:26 [y]S Ge 42:5
45:18 [z]ver 20; Ge 20:15; 46:34; 47:6,11,27; Jer 40:4 [a]Ezr 9:12; Ps 37:19; Isa 1:19
45:19 [b]ver 21, 27; Ge 46:5; Nu 7:3-8
45:20 [c]Ge 46:6, 32 [d]S ver 18
45:21 [e]S ver 19 [f]S Ge 42:25
45:22 [g]S Ge 24:53
45:23 [h]S Ge 37:3; S 41:14; Jdg 14:12,13; 2Ki 5:22 [i]S Ge 42:26 /S Ge 24:10 [k]S Ge 42:25 45:24 [l]Ge 42:21-22
45:25 [m]Ge 13:1 [n]Ge 42:29 45:26 [o]S Ge 41:41 [p]S Ge 44:28; 1Ki 10:7 45:27 [q]S ver 19 45:28 [r]Lk 16:31 [s]S Ge 44:28 46:1 [t]ver 5

[u]7 Or save you as a great band of survivors   [v]22 That is, about 7 1/2 pounds (about 3.5 kilograms)

45:6 Joseph was now 39 years old (see 41:46,53).
45:7 a remnant. Although none had been lost, they had escaped a great threat to them all; so Joseph called them a remnant in the confidence that they would live to produce a great people.
45:8 father. A title of honor given to viziers (see note on 41:43) and other high officials (in the Apocrypha see 1 Maccabees 11:32). All three titles of Joseph in this verse were originally Egyptian.
45:9 hurry back . . . don't delay. Joseph is anxious to see Jacob as soon as possible (see v. 13).
45:10 Goshen. A region in the eastern part of the Nile delta, it was very fertile (see v. 18) and remains so today.
45:12 I . . . am speaking. Not through an interpreter as before (see 42:23).

45:14 wept. See 43:30 and note.
45:15 his brothers talked with him. In intimate fellowship and friendship, rather than hostility or fear, for the first time in over 20 years (see 37:2 and note on 45:6).
45:18 you can enjoy the fat of the land. An echo of Isaac's blessing on Jacob (see 27:28).
45:22 to Benjamin he gave . . . five sets of clothes. See note on 43:34. shekels. See note on 20:16.
45:24 Don't quarrel. Joseph wanted nothing to delay their return (see note on v. 9), and he wanted them to avoid mutual accusation and recrimination concerning the past.
46:1 set out. Probably from the family estate at Hebron (see 35:27). when he reached Beersheba, he offered sacrifices. Abraham and Isaac had also worshiped the Lord there (see 21:33; 26:23-25).

sheba,[u] he offered sacrifices[v] to the God of his father Isaac.[w]

[2]And God spoke to Israel[x] in a vision at night[y] and said, "Jacob! Jacob!"

"Here I am,"[z] he replied.

[3]"I am God, the God of your father,"[a] he said. "Do not be afraid[b] to go down to Egypt,[c] for I will make you into a great nation[d] there.[e] [4]I will go down to Egypt with you, and I will surely bring you back again.[f] And Joseph's own hand will close your eyes.[g]"

[5]Then Jacob left Beersheba,[h] and Israel's[i] sons took their father Jacob and their children and their wives in the carts[j] that Pharaoh had sent to transport him. [6]They also took with them their livestock and the possessions[k] they had acquired in Canaan, and Jacob and all his offspring went to Egypt.[m] [7]He took with him to Egypt[n] his sons and grandsons and his daughters and granddaughters—all his offspring.[o]

[8]These are the names of the sons of Israel[p] (Jacob and his descendants) who went to Egypt:

Reuben the firstborn[q] of Jacob.

[9]The sons of Reuben:[r]
Hanoch, Pallu,[s] Hezron and Carmi.[t]

[10]The sons of Simeon:[u]
Jemuel,[v] Jamin, Ohad, Jakin, Zohar[w] and Shaul the son of a Canaanite woman.

[11]The sons of Levi:[x]
Gershon,[y] Kohath[z] and Merari.[a]

[12]The sons of Judah:[b]
Er,[c] Onan,[d] Shelah, Perez[e] and Zerah[f] (but Er and Onan had died in the land of Canaan).[g]
The sons of Perez:[h]
Hezron and Hamul.[i]

[13]The sons of Issachar:[j]
Tola, Puah,[w][k] Jashub[x][l] and Shimron.

[14]The sons of Zebulun:[m]

Sered, Elon and Jahleel.

[15]These were the sons Leah bore to Jacob in Paddan Aram,[y][n] besides his daughter Dinah.[o] These sons and daughters of his were thirty-three in all.

[16]The sons of Gad:[p]
Zephon,[z][q] Haggi, Shuni, Ezbon, Eri, Arodi and Areli.

[17]The sons of Asher:[r]
Imnah, Ishvah, Ishvi and Beriah.
Their sister was Serah.
The sons of Beriah:
Heber and Malkiel.

[18]These were the children born to Jacob by Zilpah,[s] whom Laban had given to his daughter Leah[t]—sixteen in all.

[19]The sons of Jacob's wife Rachel:[u]
Joseph and Benjamin.[v] [20]In Egypt, Manasseh[w] and Ephraim[x] were born to Joseph[y] by Asenath daughter of Potiphera, priest of On.[a][z]

[21]The sons of Benjamin:[a]
Bela, Beker, Ashbel, Gera, Naaman, Ehi, Rosh, Muppim, Huppim and Ard.[b]

[22]These were the sons of Rachel[c] who were born to Jacob—fourteen in all.

[23]The son of Dan:[d]
Hushim.[e]

[24]The sons of Naphtali:[f]
Jahziel, Guni, Jezer and Shillem.

[25]These were the sons born to Jacob by Bilhah,[g] whom Laban had given to his daughter Rachel[h]—seven in all.

46:1 [u]S Ge 21:14
[v]S Ge 31:54
[w]S Ge 31:42
46:2 [x]S Ge 17:5
[y]S Ge 15:1
[z]S Ge 22:1
46:3 [a]S Ge 28:13
[b]S Ge 15:1
[c]S Ge 26:2
[d]S Ge 12:2
[e]Ex 1:7
46:4 [f]S Ge 15:16; S 28:13 [g]ver 29; Ge 45:14-15; 50:1
46:5 [h]S Ge 21:14 [i]ver 1 /S Ge 45:19
46:6 [k]S Ge 45:20 [l]S Ge 12:5
[m]Nu 20:15; Dt 26:5; Jos 24:4; 1Sa 12:8; Ps 105:23; Isa 52:4; Ac 7:15
46:7 [n]Ge 13:10 [o]ver 6; Ge 45:10
46:8 [p]S Ge 35:26; Ex 1:1; Nu 26:4 [q]S Ge 29:32
46:9 [r]Ex 6:14; Nu 1:20; 26:7; 1Ch 5:3 [s]Nu 26:5; 1Ch 5:3 [t]Nu 26:6
46:10 [u]S Ge 29:33; Nu 26:14 [v]Ex 6:15; Nu 26:12 [w]Nu 26:13
46:11 [x]S Ge 29:34; S Nu 3:17 [y]Ex 6:16; Nu 3:21; 4:38 [z]Ex 6:16; Nu 3:27; 1Ch 23:12 [a]Ex 6:19; Nu 3:20,33; 4:29; 26:57; 1Ch 6:19
46:12 [b]S Ge 29:35 [c]S Ge 38:3 [d]S Ge 38:4 [e]S Ge 38:29 [f]S Ge 38:30 [g]S Ge 38:7; Nu 26:19 [h]1Ch 2:5; Mt 1:3 [i]Nu 26:21
46:13 [j]S Ge 30:18 [k]Nu 26:23; Jdg 10:1; 1Ch 7:1 [l]Nu 26:24
46:14 [m]S Ge 30:20
46:15 [n]S Ge 25:20; 29:31-35 [o]S Ge 30:21
46:16 [p]S Ge 30:11; S Nu 1:25 [q]Nu 26:15 46:17 [r]S Ge 30:13 46:18 [s]Ge 30:10 [t]S Ge 16:1 46:19 [u]S Ge 29:6 [v]Ge 44:27 46:20 [w]S Ge 41:51 [x]S Ge 41:52 [y]Nu 26:28-37 [z]S Ge 41:45 46:21 [a]Nu 26:38-41; 1Ch 7:6-12; 8:1 [b]Nu 26:40; 1Ch 8:3 46:22 [c]S Ge 29:6 46:23 [d]S Ge 30:6 [e]Nu 26:42 46:24 [f]S Ge 30:8 46:25 [g]Ge 30:8 [h]S Ge 24:61

[w]13 Samaritan Pentateuch and Syriac (see also 1 Chron. 7:1); Masoretic Text Puvah   [x]13 Samaritan Pentateuch and some Septuagint manuscripts (see also Num. 26:24 and 1 Chron. 7:1); Masoretic Text Iob   [y]15 That is, Northwest Mesopotamia   [z]16 Samaritan Pentateuch and Septuagint (see also Num. 26:15); Masoretic Text Ziphion   [a]20 That is, Heliopolis

---

46:2 *God spoke to Israel in a vision at night.* See 26:24. *Jacob! Jacob!* See note on 22:11. *Here I am.* See note on 22:1.

46:3–4 As Israel and his family were about to leave Canaan, God reaffirmed his covenant promises.

46:3 *I am . . . the God of your father . . . Do not be afraid.* A verbatim repetition of God's statement to Isaac in 26:24. *I will make you into a great nation.* The Lord reaffirmed one aspect of his promise to Abraham (see 12:2). *there.* See Ex 1:7.

46:4 *I will go down to Egypt with you.* God would be with Jacob as he went south to Egypt just as he was with him when he went north to Haran, and would again bring him

back as he had done before (see 28:15; see also 15:16; 48:21).

46:8 *These are the names of the sons of Israel . . . who went to Egypt.* Repeated verbatim in Ex 1:1 (see note there), where it introduces the background for the story of the exodus (predicted here in v. 4).

46:15 *Paddan Aram.* See note on 25:20. *thirty-three in all.* There are 34 names in vv. 8–15. To bring the number to 33 the name Ohad in v. 10 should probably be removed, since it does not appear in the parallel lists in Nu 26:12–13; 1Ch 4:24. The Hebrew form of "Ohad" looks very much like that of the nearby "Zohar" (see Ex 6:15), and a later scribe probably added Ohad to the text accidentally.

46:20 See note on 41:45.

26All those who went to Egypt with Jacob—those who were his direct descendants, not counting his sons' wives—numbered sixty-six persons. [i] 27With the two sons [b] who had been born to Joseph in Egypt, [j] the members of Jacob's family, which went to Egypt, were seventy [c] in all. [k]

28Now Jacob sent Judah [l] ahead of him to Joseph to get directions to Goshen. [m] When they arrived in the region of Goshen, 29Joseph had his chariot [n] made ready and went to Goshen to meet his father Israel. [o] As soon as Joseph appeared before him, he threw his arms around his father [d] and wept [p] for a long time. [q]

30Israel [r] said to Joseph, "Now I am ready to die, since I have seen for myself that you are still alive." [s]

31Then Joseph said to his brothers and to his father's household, "I will go up and speak to Pharaoh and will say to him, 'My brothers and my father's household, who were living in the land of Canaan, [t] have come to me. [u] 32The men are shepherds; [v] they tend livestock, [w] and they have brought along their flocks and herds and everything they own.' [x] 33When Pharaoh calls you in and asks, 'What is your occupation?' [y] 34you should answer, 'Your servants [z] have tended livestock from our boyhood on, just as our fathers did.' [a] Then you will be allowed to settle [b] in the region of Goshen, [c] for all shepherds are detestable to the Egyptians. [d]"

47 Joseph went and told Pharaoh, "My father and brothers, with their flocks and herds and everything they own, have come from the land of Canaan [e] and are now in Goshen." [f] 2He chose five of his brothers and presented them [g] before Pharaoh.

3Pharaoh asked the brothers, "What is your occupation?" [h]

"Your servants [i] are shepherds, [j]" they replied to Pharaoh, "just as our fathers were." 4They also said to him, "We have come to live here awhile, [k] because the famine is severe in Canaan [l] and your servants' flocks have no pasture. [m] So now, please let your servants settle in Goshen." [n]

5Pharaoh said to Joseph, "Your father and your brothers have come to you, 6and the land of Egypt is before you; settle [o] your father and your brothers in the best part of the land. [p] Let them live in Goshen. And if you know of any among them with special ability, [q] put them in charge of my own livestock. [r]"

7Then Joseph brought his father Jacob in and presented him [s] before Pharaoh. After Jacob blessed [e] Pharaoh, [t] 8Pharaoh asked him, "How old are you?"

9And Jacob said to Pharaoh, "The years of my pilgrimage are a hundred and thirty. [u] My years have been few and difficult, [v] and they do not equal the years of the pilgrimage of my fathers. [w]" 10Then Jacob blessed [f] Pharaoh [x] and went out from his presence.

11So Joseph settled his father and his brothers in Egypt and gave them property in the best part of the land, [y] the district of Rameses, [z] as Pharaoh directed. 12Joseph also provided his father and his brothers and all his father's household with food, according to the number of their children. [a]

Joseph and the Famine

13There was no food, however, in the whole region because the famine was

Cross references

46:26 [i] ver 5-7; Ex 1:5; Dt 10:22
46:27 [j] S Ge 41:45 [k] S Ge 34:30; Ac 7:14
46:28 [l] S Ge 43:3 [m] S Ge 45:10
46:29 [n] S Ge 41:43 [o] ver 1,30; S Ge 32:28; 47:29,31 [p] S Ge 29:11 [q] S ver 4; Lk 15:20
46:30 [r] S ver 29 [s] S Ge 44:28
46:31 [t] S Ge 42:13 [u] S Ge 45:10
46:32 [v] Ge 47:3 [w] S Ge 37:2 [x] S Ge 45:20
46:33 [y] Ge 47:3
46:34 [z] S Ge 42:11 [a] Ge 47:3 [b] S Ge 34:10 [c] S Ge 45:10 [d] S Ge 43:32
47:1 [e] S Ge 42:13 [f] S Ge 46:31
47:2 [g] S Ge 43:15
47:3 [h] Ge 46:33

[i] S Ge 42:11 [j] Ge 46:32
47:4 [k] Ru 1:1 [l] S Ge 12:10 [m] 1Ki 18:5; Jer 14:5-6; Joel 1:18 [n] Ge 46:34
47:6 [o] S Ge 34:10 [p] S Ge 13:9; S 45:18 [q] Ex 18:21,25; Dt 1:13,15; 2Ch 19:5; Ps 15:2 [r] S Ge 39:4
47:7 [s] S Ge 43:15 [t] ver 10;
2Sa 14:22; 19:39; 1Ki 8:66
47:9 [u] S Ge 25:7 [v] S Ge 3:17; Ps 39:4; 89:47 [w] Job 8:9; Ps 39:12
47:10 [x] S ver 7
47:11 [y] S Ge 45:10,18 [z] Ex 1:11; 12:37; Nu 33:3,5
47:12 [a] S Ge 45:11

[b] 27 Hebrew; Septuagint *the nine children*
[c] 27 Hebrew (see also Exodus 1:5 and footnote);
Septuagint (see also Acts 7:14) *seventy-five*
[d] 29 Hebrew *around him*   [e] 7 Or *greeted*   [f] 10 Or
said farewell to

46:26 *All those who went to Egypt with Jacob . . . numbered sixty-six persons.* The total of 33 (see v. 15 and note), 16 (v. 18), 14 (v. 22) and 7 (see v. 25) is 70 (v. 27). To arrive at 66 we must subtract Er and Onan, who "had died in the land of Canaan" (v. 12), and Manasseh and Ephraim (v. 20), who "had been born . . . in Egypt" (v. 27).
46:27 *seventy.* See NIV text note; see also Dt 10:22. Seventy is the ideal and complete number (see Introduction: Literary Features; see also notes on 5:5; 10:2) of Jacob's descendants who would have been in Egypt if Er and Onan had not died earlier (see 38:7-10). For the number 75 in Ac 7:14 see note there.
46:28 *Jacob sent Judah ahead.* See note on 43:3.
46:29 *wept.* See 43:30 and note.
46:34 *shepherds are detestable to the Egyptians.* See note on 43:32.
47:9 *pilgrimage.* Jacob referred to the itinerant nature of

patriarchal life in general and of his own in particular as he hopefully awaited the fulfillment of the promise of a land (see also Dt 26:5). *they do not equal the years of . . . my fathers.* Abraham lived to the age of 175 (25:7), Isaac to 180 (35:28).
47:11 *best part of the land.* See note on 45:10. *district of Rameses.* The city of Rameses is mentioned in Ex 1:11; 12:37; Nu 33:3,5. The name doubtless refers to the great Egyptian pharaoh Rameses II, who reigned centuries later (the designation here involves an editorial updating). In addition to being known as Goshen (see v. 27), the "district of Rameses" was called the "region of Zoan" in Ps 78:12,43 (see note on Ge 44:4).
47:13 *the famine was severe.* After the people used up all their money to buy grain (see vv. 14-15), they traded their livestock (vv. 16-17), then their land (v. 20), then themselves (v. 21).

severe; both Egypt and Canaan wasted away because of the famine. [b] [14]Joseph collected all the money that was to be found in Egypt and Canaan in payment for the grain they were buying, [c] and he brought it to Pharaoh's palace. [d] [15]When the money of the people of Egypt and Canaan was gone, [e] all Egypt came to Joseph [f] and said, "Give us food. Why should we die before your eyes? [g] Our money is used up."

[16]"Then bring your livestock, [h]" said Joseph. "I will sell you food in exchange for your livestock, since your money is gone. [i]" [17]So they brought their livestock to Joseph, and he gave them food in exchange for their horses, [j] their sheep and goats, their cattle and donkeys. [k] And he brought them through that year with food in exchange for all their livestock.

[18]When that year was over, they came to him the following year and said, "We cannot hide from our lord the fact that since our money is gone [l] and our livestock belongs to you, [m] there is nothing left for our lord except our bodies and our land. [19]Why should we perish before your eyes [n]—we and our land as well? Buy us and our land in exchange for food, [o] and we with our land will be in bondage to Pharaoh. [p] Give us seed so that we may live and not die, [q] and that the land may not become desolate."

[20]So Joseph bought all the land in Egypt for Pharaoh. The Egyptians, one and all, sold their fields, because the famine was too severe [r] for them. The land became Pharaoh's, [21]and Joseph reduced the people to servitude, [g] [s] from one end of Egypt to the other. [22]However, he did not buy the land of the priests, [t] because they received a regular allotment from Pharaoh and had food enough from the allotment [u] Pharaoh gave them. That is why they did not sell their land.

[23]Joseph said to the people, "Now that I have bought you and your land today for Pharaoh, here is seed [v] for you so you can plant the ground. [w] [24]But when the crop comes in, give a fifth [x] of it to Pharaoh. The other four-fifths you may keep as seed

for the fields and as food for yourselves and your households and your children."

[25]"You have saved our lives," they said. "May we find favor in the eyes of our lord; [y] we will be in bondage to Pharaoh." [z]

[26]So Joseph established it as a law concerning land in Egypt—still in force today—that a fifth [a] of the produce belongs to Pharaoh. It was only the land of the priests that did not become Pharaoh's. [b]

[27]Now the Israelites settled in Egypt in the region of Goshen. [c] They acquired property there [d] and were fruitful and increased greatly in number. [e]

[28]Jacob lived in Egypt [f] seventeen years, and the years of his life were a hundred and forty-seven. [g] [29]When the time drew near for Israel [h] to die, [i] he called for his son Joseph and said to him, "If I have found favor in your eyes, [j] put your hand under my thigh [k] and promise that you will show me kindness [l] and faithfulness. [m] Do not bury me in Egypt, [30]but when I rest with my fathers, [n] carry me out of Egypt and bury me where they are buried." [o]

"I will do as you say," he said.

[31]"Swear to me," [p] he said. Then Joseph swore to him, [q] and Israel [r] worshiped as he leaned on the top of his staff. [h] [s]

Manasseh and Ephraim

48 Some time later Joseph was told, "Your father is ill." So he took his two sons Manasseh and Ephraim [t] along with him. [2]When Jacob was told, "Your son Joseph has come to you," Israel [u] rallied his strength and sat up on the bed.

[3]Jacob said to Joseph, "God Almighty [i] [v] appeared to me at Luz [w] in the land of Canaan, and there he blessed me [x] [4]and said to me, 'I am going to make you fruitful and will increase your numbers. [y] I will make you a community of peoples, and I will give this land [z] as an everlasting possession to your descendants after you.' [a]

[5]"Now then, your two sons born to you

47:13
[b]S Ge 12:10;
S 41:30
47:14
[c]S Ge 41:36
[d]S Ge 41:34;
Ex 7:23; 8:24;
Jer 43:9
47:15 [e]ver 16,18
[f]S Ge 41:57 [g]ver
19; Ex 16:3
47:16 [h]ver 18,19
[i]ver 15
47:17 [j]Ex 14:9
[k]S Ge 12:16
47:18 [l]S ver 15
[m]S ver 16
47:19 [n]S ver 15
[o]S ver 16 [p]ver
21,25 [q]S Ge 42:2
47:20
[r]S Ge 12:10
47:21 [s]S ver 19
47:22 [t]ver 26
[u]Dt 14:28-29
47:23 [v]Isa 55:10;
61:11 [w]Ne 5:3
47:24
[x]S Ge 41:34

47:25 [y]S Ge 32:5
[z]S ver 19
47:26
[a]S Ge 41:34
[b]ver 22
47:27
[c]S Ge 45:10,18
[d]S Ge 33:19
[e]S Ge 1:22;
S 12:2; S 17:6
47:28 [f]Ps 105:23
[g]S Ge 25:7
47:29
[h]S Ge 46:29
[i]S Ge 27:2
[j]S Ge 32:5
[k]S Ge 24:2
[l]S Ge 19:19
[m]S Ge 24:27;
Jdg 1:24; 2Sa 2:6
47:30
[n]S Ge 15:15
[o]S Ge 23:20;
S 25:9; S 29:16;
50:25; Ex 13:19;
Jos 24:32;
Ac 7:15-16
47:31
[p]Ge 21:23;
Jos 2:20;
Jdg 15:12;
1Sa 24:21; 30:15
[q]S Ge 24:3
[r]S Ge 46:29
[s]S Ge 32:10;
Heb 11:21 [fn]
1Ki 1:47
48:1 [t]S Ge 41:52;
Heb 11:21
48:2 [u]ver 8,9,11,
14,20
48:3 [v]S Ge 17:1
[w]S Ge 28:19
[x]S Ge 28:13;
S 32:29
48:4 [y]S Ge 12:2;
S 17:6
[z]S Ge 12:7;
S 28:13
[a]S Ge 15:7

[g]21 Samaritan Pentateuch and Septuagint (see also Vulgate); Masoretic Text *and he moved the people into the cities*   [h]31 Or *Israel bowed down at the head of his bed*   [i]3 Hebrew *El-Shaddai*

47:21 The NIV text note reading would mean that the Egyptians were to move temporarily into the cities until seed could be distributed to them for planting (see v. 23).
47:26 *a fifth of the produce belongs to Pharaoh.* The same was true "during the seven years of abundance" (41:34)—but now all the land on which the produce grew belonged to Pharaoh as well.
47:27 *the Israelites . . . were fruitful and increased greatly in number.* See 35:11–12; 46:3 and notes.
47:29 *put your hand under my thigh.* See 24:2 and note.

In both cases, ties of family kinship are being stressed.
47:30 *rest with my fathers.* See note on 25:8. *bury me where they are buried.* In the cave of Machpelah (see 50:12–13).
47:31 *worshiped as he leaned on the top of his staff.* Quoted in Heb 11:21. Compare 48:2 with the NIV text note reading here.
48:3 *God Almighty.* See note on 17:1. *Luz.* The older name for Bethel (see 28:19).
48:5 *your two sons . . . will be reckoned as mine.* Jacob

in Egypt[b] before I came to you here will be reckoned as mine; Ephraim and Manasseh will be mine,[c] just as Reuben[d] and Simeon[e] are mine. [6]Any children born to you after them will be yours; in the territory they inherit they will be reckoned under the names of their brothers. [7]As I was returning from Paddan,[j][f] to my sorrow[g] Rachel died in the land of Canaan while we were still on the way, a little distance from Ephrath. So I buried her there beside the road to Ephrath" (that is, Bethlehem).[h]

[8]When Israel[i] saw the sons of Joseph,[j] he asked, "Who are these?"

[9]"They are the sons God has given me here,"[k] Joseph said to his father.

Then Israel said, "Bring them to me so I may bless[l] them."

[10]Now Israel's eyes were failing because of old age, and he could hardly see.[m] So Joseph brought his sons close to him, and his father kissed them[n] and embraced them.[o]

[11]Israel[p] said to Joseph, "I never expected to see your face again,[q] and now God has allowed me to see your children too."[r]

[12]Then Joseph removed them from Israel's knees[s] and bowed down with his face to the ground.[t] [13]And Joseph took both of them, Ephraim on his right toward Israel's left hand and Manasseh on his left toward Israel's right hand,[u] and brought them close to him. [14]But Israel[v] reached

out his right hand and put it on Ephraim's head,[w] though he was the younger,[x] and crossing his arms, he put his left hand on Manasseh's head, even though Manasseh was the firstborn.[y]

[15]Then he blessed[z] Joseph and said,

"May the God before whom my fathers
    Abraham and Isaac walked,[a]
the God who has been my shepherd[b]
    all my life to this day,
[16]the Angel[c] who has delivered me from
    all harm[d]
—may he bless[e] these boys.[f]
May they be called by my name
    and the names of my fathers
    Abraham and Isaac,[g]
and may they increase greatly
    upon the earth."[h]

[17]When Joseph saw his father placing his right hand[i] on Ephraim's head[j] he was displeased; so he took hold of his father's hand to move it from Ephraim's head to Manasseh's head. [18]Joseph said to him, "No, my father, this one is the firstborn; put your right hand on his head."[k]

[19]But his father refused and said, "I know, my son, I know. He too will become a people, and he too will become great.[l] Nevertheless, his younger brother will be greater than he,[m] and his descendants will become a group of nations.[n]"

Cross references:

48:5 [b]S Ge 41:50-52 [c]1Ch 5:1 [d]S Ge 29:32 [e]S Ge 29:33
48:7 [f]S Ge 25:20 [g]S Ge 42:38 [h]Ge 35:19; Ru 1:2; 1Sa 16:4
48:8 [i]S ver 2 [j]ver 10
48:9 [k]S Ge 33:5 [l]S Ge 24:60
48:10 [m]S Ge 27:1 [n]S Ge 27:27 [o]S Ge 29:13
48:11 [p]S ver 2 [q]S Ge 44:28 [r]Ge 50:23; Job 42:16; Ps 103:17; 128:6
48:12 [s]Ge 50:23; Job 3:12 [t]S Ge 19:1; S 33:3; 37:10
48:13 [u]Ps 16:8; 73:23; 110:1; Mt 25:33
48:14 [v]S ver 2

[w]ver 17,18 [x]S Ge 25:23 [y]S Ge 29:32; S 41:51
48:15 [z]S Ge 24:60 [a]S Ge 5:22; [b]Ge 49:24; 2Sa 5:2; Ps 23:1; 80:1; Isa 40:11; Jer 23:4
48:16 [c]S Ge 16:7 [d]S Ge 24:50; 2Sa 4:9; Ps 71:4; Jer 15:21; Da 3:17 [e]S Ge 28:3 [f]1Ch 5:1; Eze 47:13; Heb 11:21 [g]S Ge 28:13 [h]S Ge 12:2; S 13:14
48:17 [i]ver 13 [j]S ver 14

48:18 [k]S ver 14 48:19 [l]S Ge 17:20 [m]S Ge 25:23 [n]S Ge 12:2

17 That is, Northwest Mesopotamia

---

would adopt them as his own. *Ephraim and Manasseh.* See v. 1 for the expected order, since Manasseh was Joseph's firstborn (see 41:51). Jacob mentions Ephraim first because he intends to give him the primary blessing and thus "put Ephraim ahead of Manasseh" (v. 20). *mine, just as Reuben and Simeon are mine.* Joseph's first two sons would enjoy equal status with Jacob's first two sons (35:23) and in fact would eventually supersede them. Because of an earlier sinful act (see 35:22 and note), Reuben would lose his birthright to Jacob's favorite son, Joseph (see 49:3–4; 1Ch 5:2), and thus to Joseph's sons (see 1Ch 5:1).

48:6 *children born to you after them will be yours.* They would take the place of Ephraim and Manasseh, whom Jacob had adopted. *in the territory they inherit they will be reckoned under the names of their brothers.* They would perpetuate the names of Ephraim and Manasseh for purposes of inheritance (for a similar provision see 38:8 and note; Dt 25:5–6). Joseph's territory would thus be divided between Ephraim and Manasseh, but Levi (Jacob's third son; see 35:23) would receive "no share of the land" (Jos 14:4). The total number of tribal allotments would therefore remain the same.

48:7 *Paddan.* That is, Paddan Aram, meaning "plain of Aram," another name for Aram Naharaim (see note on 24:10). *Rachel died.* See 35:16–19. Adopted by Joseph's father, Ephraim and Manasseh in effect took the place of other sons whom Joseph's mother, Rachel, might have borne had she not died. *Ephrath.* See note on 35:16.

48:8 *Israel . . . asked, "Who are these?"* Either because he had never met them or because, being old, he could not see them clearly.

48:10 *because of old age . . . he could hardly see.* See note on 27:1. *kissed them and embraced them.* While they were on Jacob's knees (see v. 12), probably symbolizing adoption (see note on 30:3).

48:13–20 See note on Ac 6:6.

48:13 *Manasseh . . . toward Israel's right hand.* Joseph wanted Jacob to bless Manasseh, Joseph's firstborn, by placing his right hand on Manasseh's head.

48:15 *blessed.* As his father Isaac had blessed him (27:27–29). *Joseph.* Used here collectively for Ephraim and Manasseh (see NIV text note on v. 21). *before whom . . . Abraham and Isaac . . . walked.* See notes on 5:22; 17:1. *shepherd.* An intimate royal metaphor for God (see Ps 23:1), used in Genesis only here and in Jacob's later blessing of Joseph (49:24).

48:16 *Angel.* See note on 16:7. The angel—God himself—had earlier blessed Jacob (see 32:29; see also note on 32:24).

48:19 *his younger brother will be greater than he.* See note on 25:23. During the divided monarchy (930–722 B.C.), Ephraim's descendants were the most powerful tribe in the north. "Ephraim" was often used to refer to the northern kingdom as a whole (see, e.g., Isa 7:2,5,8–9; Hos 9:13; 12:1,8).

[20]He blessed[o] them that day[p] and said,

"In your[k] name will Israel[q] pronounce
    this blessing:[r]
'May God make you like Ephraim[s]
    and Manasseh.[t]'"

So he put Ephraim ahead of Manasseh.

[21]Then Israel said to Joseph, "I am about
to die, but God will be with you[1][u] and
take you[1] back to the land of your[1] fathers.[v] [22]And to you, as one who is over
your brothers,[w] I give the ridge of land[m][x] I
took from the Amorites with my sword[y]
and my bow."

Jacob Blesses His Sons

49:1–28Ref — Dt 33:1–29

49 Then Jacob called for his sons and
said: "Gather around so I can tell
you what will happen to you in days to
come.[z]

[2]"Assemble[a] and listen, sons of Jacob;
    listen to your father Israel.[b]

[3]"Reuben, you are my firstborn,[c]
    my might, the first sign of my
      strength,[d]
    excelling in honor,[e] excelling in
      power.
[4]Turbulent as the waters,[f] you will no
    longer excel,
    for you went up onto your father's
      bed,
    onto my couch and defiled it.[g]

[5]"Simeon[h] and Levi[i] are brothers—

    their swords[n] are weapons of
      violence.[j]
[6]Let me not enter their council,
    let me not join their assembly,[k]
    for they have killed men in their anger[l]
    and hamstrung[m] oxen as they
      pleased.
[7]Cursed be their anger, so fierce,
    and their fury,[n] so cruel![o]
I will scatter them in Jacob
    and disperse them in Israel.[p]

[8]"Judah,[o][q] your brothers will praise
    you;
    your hand will be on the neck[r] of
      your enemies;
    your father's sons will bow down to
      you.[s]
[9]You are a lion['s cub,[u] O Judah;[v]
    you return from the prey,[w] my son.
Like a lion he crouches and lies down,
    like a lioness—who dares to rouse
      him?
[10]The scepter will not depart from
    Judah,[x]
    nor the ruler's staff from between his
      feet,

48:20
oS Ge 24:60
pHeb 11:21
qS ver 2
rLev 9:22;
Nu 6:23; Dt 10:8;
21:5 sNu 2:18;
Jer 31:9
tS Ge 41:51;
Nu 2:20; 10:23;
Ru 4:11
48:21 uS Ge 26:3
vS Ge 15:16;
S 28:13; Dt 30:3;
Ps 126:1;
Jer 29:14;
Eze 34:13
48:22
wS Ge 37:8
xJos 24:32; Jn 4:5
yS Ge 34:26
49:1 zNu 24:14;
Dt 31:29;
Jer 23:20;
Da 2:28,45
49:2 aJos 24:1
bver 16,28;
Ps 34:11
49:3
cS Ge 29:32;
S 41:51
dDt 21:17;
Ps 78:51; 105:36
eS Ge 34:19
49:4 fIsa 57:20;
Jer 49:23
gS Ge 29:29;
S 34:5
49:5 hS Ge 29:33
iGe 29:34

jS Ge 34:25;
S Pr 4:17
49:6 kPs 1:1;
Pr 1:15; Eph 5:11
lS Ge 34:26
mJos 11:6,9;
2Sa 8:4; 1Ch 18:4
49:7 nGe 34:7
oGe 34:25
pJos 19:1,9;
21:1-42
49:8 qS Ge 29:35
rDt 28:48
sS Ge 9:25;
1Ch 5:2

49:9 tNu 24:9; Ps 7:2; 10:9; Eze 19:5; Mic 5:8 uEze 19:2
vRev 5:5 wver 27; Nu 23:24; Job 38:39; Ps 17:12; 22:13;
104:21 **49:10** xNu 24:17,19; Jdg 1:1-2; 20:18; 1Ch 5:2;
28:4; Ps 60:7; 108:8

k20 The Hebrew is singular.   l21 The Hebrew is
plural.   m22 Or *And to you I give one portion more
than to your brothers—the portion*   n5 The meaning
of the Hebrew for this word is uncertain.   o8 *Judah*
sounds like and may be derived from the Hebrew for
praise.

48:20 *he put Ephraim ahead of Manasseh.* Jacob, the
younger son who struggled with Esau for the birthright and
blessing and who preferred the younger sister (Rachel) above
the older (Leah), now advanced Joseph's younger son ahead
of the older.

48:21 *Joseph.* See note on v. 15. *I am about to die.* Years
later, Joseph spoke these words to his brothers (50:24).

48:22 *ridge of land.* The Hebrew for this phrase is identical
with the place-name Shechem, where Joseph was later buried in a plot of ground inherited by his descendants (see Jos
24:32; see also 33:19; Jn 4:5). *I took from the Amorites.*
Possibly referring to the event of 34:25–29.

49:2–27 Often called the "Blessing of Jacob," this is the
longest poem in Genesis. Its various blessings were intended
not only for Jacob's 12 sons but also for the tribes that
descended from them (see v. 28). For other poetic blessings
in Genesis see 9:26–27; 14:19–20; 27:27–29; 27:39–40;
48:15–16; 48:20.

49:4 *Turbulent.* Reuben's descendants were characterized
by indecision (see Jdg 5:15–16). *You will no longer excel, for
you went up onto your father's bed.* See 35:22 and note; see
also notes on 37:21; 48:5.

49:5 *Simeon and Levi are brothers.* They shared the traits
of violence, anger and cruelty (see vv. 6–7).

49:7 *I will scatter them.* Fulfilled when Simeon's descendants were absorbed into the territory of Judah (see Jos 19:1,
9) and when Levi's descendants were dispersed throughout

the land, living in 48 towns and the surrounding pasturelands (see note on 48:6; see also Nu 35:2,7; Jos 14:4;
21:41).

49:8 Cf. 27:29,40; 37:7,9. *Judah, your brothers ... will
bow down to you.* See note on 43:3. As those who would
become the leading tribes of southern and northern Israel
respectively, Judah and Joseph were given the longest (vv.
8–12 and vv. 22–26) of Jacob's blessings. Judah was the
fourth of Leah's sons and also the fourth son born to Jacob
(29:35), but Reuben, Simeon and Levi had forfeited their
right of leadership. So Jacob assigns leadership to Judah (a
son of Leah) but a double portion to Joseph (a son of Rachel).
See also 1Ch 5:2.

49:9 *You are a lion's cub.* A symbol of sovereignty, strength
and courage. Judah (or Israel) is often pictured as a lion in
later times (see Eze 19:1–7; Mic 5:8; and especially Nu
24:9). Judah's greatest descendant, Jesus Christ (see note on
43:3), is himself called "the Lion of the tribe of Judah" (Rev
5:5).

49:10 Though difficult to translate (see NIV text note), the
verse has been traditionally understood as Messianic. It was
initially fulfilled in David, and ultimately in Christ. *scepter.*
See Nu 24:17 and note. *until he comes to whom it belongs.*
Repeated almost verbatim in Eze 21:27 in a section where
Zedekiah, the last king of Judah, is told to "remove the
crown" (Eze 21:26) from his head because dominion over
Jerusalem will ultimately be given to the one "to whom it
rightfully belongs."

until he comes to whom it belongs[p] [y]
   and the obedience of the nations is
   his. [z]
[11]He will tether his donkey[a] to a vine,
   his colt to the choicest branch; [b]
he will wash his garments in wine,
   his robes in the blood of grapes. [c]
[12]His eyes will be darker than wine,
   his teeth whiter than milk. [q] [d]

[13]"Zebulun [e] will live by the seashore
   and become a haven for ships;
his border will extend toward
   Sidon. [f]

[14]"Issachar [g] is a rawboned[r] donkey
   lying down between two
   saddlebags. [s] [h]
[15]When he sees how good is his resting
   place
   and how pleasant is his land, [i]
he will bend his shoulder to the
   burden[j]
and submit to forced labor. [k]

[16]"Dan[t] [l] will provide justice for his
   people
   as one of the tribes of Israel. [m]
[17]Dan [n] will be a serpent by the roadside,
   a viper along the path, [o]
that bites the horse's heels[p]
   so that its rider tumbles backward.

[18]"I look for your deliverance, [q]
   O LORD. [r]

[19]"Gad[u] [s] will be attacked by a band of
   raiders,
   but he will attack them at their
   heels. [t]

[20]"Asher's [u] food will be rich; [v]

he will provide delicacies fit for a
   king. [w]
[21]"Naphtali [x] is a doe set free
   that bears beautiful fawns.[v] [y]

[22]"Joseph [z] is a fruitful vine, [a]
   a fruitful vine near a spring,
   whose branches[b] climb over a wall.[w]
[23]With bitterness archers attacked him; [c]
   they shot at him with hostility. [d]
[24]But his bow remained steady, [e]
   his strong arms[f] stayed[x] limber,
because of the hand of the Mighty One
   of Jacob, [g]
because of the Shepherd, [h] the Rock
   of Israel, [i]
[25]because of your father's God, [j] who
   helps[k] you,
because of the Almighty, [v][l] who
   blesses you
with blessings of the heavens above,
   blessings of the deep that lies
   below, [m]
   blessings of the breast[n] and womb. [o]
[26]Your father's blessings are greater
   than the blessings of the ancient
   mountains,

49:10 [y]Eze 21:27; [z]Ps 2:9; 72:8-11; 98:3; 110:2; Isa 2:4; 26:18; 42:1,4; 45:22; 48:20; 49:6; 51:5
49:11 [a]Jdg 5:10; 10:4; Zec 9:9 [b]Dt 8:8; 2Ki 18:32 [c]Dt 32:14; Isa 63:2
49:12 [d]SS 5:12
49:13 [e]S Ge 30:20 [f]S Ge 10:19
49:14 [g]S Ge 30:18 [h]Jdg 5:16; Ps 68:13
49:15 [i]Jos 19:17-23 /Eze 29:18 [k]1Ki 4:6; 5:13; 9:21; Isa 14:2; 31:8
49:16 [l]Ge 30:6 [m]S ver 2
49:17 [n]Jdg 18:27 [o]Jer 8:17; Am 9:3 [p]ver 19
49:18 [q]S Ge 45:7; Ps 40:1-3 [r]Ps 119:166,174
49:19 [s]S Ge 30:11 [t]ver 17
49:20 [u]S Ge 30:13 [v]Isa 25:6
[w]Job 29:6
49:21 [x]S Ge 30:8 [y]Job 39:1
49:22 [z]Ge 30:24 [a]S Ge 17:6; Ps 128:3; Eze 19:10 [b]Ps 80:10
49:23 [c]1Ch 10:3 [d]S Ge 27:41; S 37:24
49:24 [e]Job 29:20 [f]Ps 18:34; Isa 63:12 [g]Ps 132:2,5; Isa 1:24; 10:34; 49:26; 60:16 [h]S Ge 48:15 [i]Dt 32:4,15,18, 31; 1Sa 2:2; 2Sa 22:32;

Ps 18:2,31; 19:14; 78:35; 89:26; 144:1; Isa 17:10; 26:4; 30:29; 44:8; Hab 1:12 **49:25** [j]S Ge 28:13 [k]Ex 18:4; Ps 27:9 [l]S Ge 17:1 [m]S Ge 27:28 [n]Isa 66:11 [o]Dt 7:13; 28:4; Ps 107:38; Pr 10:22

P10 Or until Shiloh comes; or until he comes to whom tribute belongs   **q**12 Or will be dull from wine, / his teeth white from milk   **r**14 Or strong   **s**14 Or campfires   he provides justice.   **u**19 Gad can mean attack and band of raiders.   **v**21 Or free; / he utters beautiful words   **w**22 Or Joseph is a wild colt, / a wild colt near a spring, / a wild donkey on a terraced hill   **x**23,24 Or archers will attack . . . will shoot . . . will remain . . . will stay   **y**25 Hebrew Shaddai

---

49:11 Judah's descendants would someday enjoy a settled and prosperous life.
49:13 Though landlocked by the tribes of Asher and Manasseh, the descendants of Zebulun were close enough to the Mediterranean (within ten miles) to "feast on the abundance of the seas" (Dt 33:19).
49:17 *Dan will be a serpent.* The treachery of a group of Danites in later times is described in Jdg 18:27. *that bites the horse's heels.* Samson, from the tribe of Dan, would single-handedly hold the Philistines at bay (Jdg 14–16).
49:18 Jacob pauses midway through his series of blessings to utter a brief prayer for God's help.
49:19 *Gad will be attacked.* Located east of the Jordan (see Jos 13:24–27), the descendants of Gad were vulnerable to raids by the Moabites to the south, as the Mesha (see 2Ki 3:4) Stele (a Moabite inscription dating from the late ninth century B.C.) illustrates (see chart on "Ancient Texts Relating to the OT," p. 5).
49:20 *Asher's food will be rich.* Fertile farmlands near the Mediterranean (see Jos 19:24–30) would ensure the prosperity of Asher's descendants.
49:21 *Naphtali is a doe set free.* Perhaps a reference to an independent spirit fostered in the descendants of Naphtali by

their somewhat isolated location in the hill country north of the Sea of Galilee (see Jos 19:32–38).
49:22 *fruitful . . . fruitful.* A pun on the name Ephraim (see NIV text note on 41:52), who Jacob predicted would be greater than Joseph's firstborn son Manasseh (48:19–20). *branches climb over a wall.* Ephraim's descendants tended to expand their territory (see Jos 17:14–18).
49:24 *his bow remained steady.* The warlike Ephraimites (see Jdg 8:1; 12:1) would often prove victorious in battle (see Jos 17:18). *Mighty One of Jacob.* Stresses the activity of God in saving and redeeming his people (see Isa 49:26). *Shepherd.* See note on 48:15. *Rock of Israel.* Israel's sure defense (see Dt 32:4,15,18,30–31)—a figure often used also in Psalms and Isaiah.
49:25 *Almighty.* See note on 17:1. *blessings of the heavens . . . of the deep.* The fertility of the soil watered by rains from above and springs and streams from below. *of the breast and womb.* The fertility of man and animals. For the later prosperity of Ephraim's descendants see Hos 12:8.
49:26 *Joseph . . . the prince among his brothers.* See note on v. 8. Ephraim would gain supremacy, especially over the northern tribes (see Jos 16:9; Isa 7:1–2; Hos 13:1).

than[z] the bounty of the age-old
    hills.[p]
Let all these rest on the head of
    Joseph,[q]
on the brow of the prince among[a]
    his brothers.[r]

27"Benjamin[s] is a ravenous wolf;[t]
in the morning he devours the prey,[u]
in the evening he divides the
    plunder."[v]

28All these are the twelve tribes of Israel,[w] and this is what their father said to them when he blessed them, giving each the blessing[x] appropriate to him.

The Death of Jacob

29Then he gave them these instructions:[y] "I am about to be gathered to my people.[z] Bury me with my fathers[a] in the cave in the field of Ephron the Hittite,[b] 30the cave in the field of Machpelah,[c] near Mamre[d] in Canaan, which Abraham bought as a burial place[e] from Ephron the Hittite, along with the field.[f] 31There Abraham[g] and his wife Sarah[h] were buried, there Isaac and his wife Rebekah[i] were buried, and there I buried Leah.[j]

32The field and the cave in it were bought from the Hittites.[b][k]"

33When Jacob had finished giving instructions to his sons, he drew his feet up into the bed, breathed his last and was gathered to his people.[l]

50 Joseph threw himself upon his father and wept over him and kissed him.[m] 2Then Joseph directed the physicians in his service to embalm his father Israel. So the physicians embalmed him,[n] 3taking a full forty days, for that was the time required for embalming. And the Egyptians mourned for him seventy days.[o]

4When the days of mourning[p] had passed, Joseph said to Pharaoh's court,[q] "If I have found favor in your eyes,[r] speak to Pharaoh for me. Tell him, 5'My father made me swear an oath[s] and said, "I am about to die;[t] bury me in the tomb I dug for myself[u] in the land of Canaan." Now let me go up and bury my father;[w] then I will return.'"

49:26 [p]Hab 3:6
[q]1Ch 5:1;
Eze 47:13
[r]S Ge 37:8
49:27 [s]Ge 35:18;
Jdg 20:12-13
[t]Hab 1:8; Zep 3:3
[u]S ver 9
[v]Nu 31:11;
Dt 2:35; Jos 7:21;
8:2; 22:8;
Jdg 8:24
49:28 [w]S ver 2
[x]S Ge 27:4
49:29 [y]Ge 50:16
[z]S Ge 25:8
[a]S Ge 15:15;
50:25; 2Sa 2:32;
19:37 [b]S Ge 25:9
49:30 [c]S Ge 23:9
[d]S Ge 13:18
[e]S Ge 23:4
[f]S Ge 23:20
49:31 [g]Ge 25:9
[h]Ge 23:19
[i]S Ge 24:67
[j]S Ge 23:20;
S 29:16

49:32
[k]S Ge 10:15
49:33 [l]S Ge 25:8;
Ac 7:15
50:1
[m]S Ge 29:11;
S 46:4
50:2 [n]ver 26;
2Ch 16:14;
Mt 26:12;
Mk 16:1;
Jn 19:39-40
50:3
[o]S Ge 37:34;
S Dt 1:3

50:4 [p]S Ge 27:41 [q]ver 7 [r]S Ge 30:27; S 32:5 50:5
[s]S Ge 24:37 [t]ver 24 [u]2Sa 18:18; 2Ch 16:14; Isa 22:16;
Mt 27:60 [v]Ge 47:31 [w]Mt 8:21

[z]26 Or of my progenitors, / as great as   [a]26 Or the
one separated from   [b]32 Or the sons of Heth

49:27 *Benjamin is a ravenous wolf.* See the exploits of Ehud (Jdg 3:12–30) and Saul and Jonathan (1Sa 11–15). See Jdg 19–21 for examples of the savagery that characterized one group of Benjamin's descendants.
49:28 *twelve tribes of Israel.* See note on vv. 2–27.
49:29 *Bury me with my fathers.* See note on 25:8. Jacob does not forget that the land of his fathers is his God-appointed homeland (see note on 23:19).
49:33 *was gathered to his people.* See note on 25:8.
50:1 *wept.* See note on 43:30.

50:2 *physicians embalmed him.* Professional embalmers could have been hired for the purpose, but Joseph perhaps wanted to avoid involvement with the pagan religious ceremonies accompanying their services.
50:3 *forty days . . . seventy days.* The two periods probably overlapped.
50:5 *My father made me swear an oath.* See 47:29–31. *dug.* Or "bought," as the Hebrew for this verb is translated in Hos 3:2 (see also Dt 2:6). *go up.* To Hebron, which has a higher elevation than Goshen.

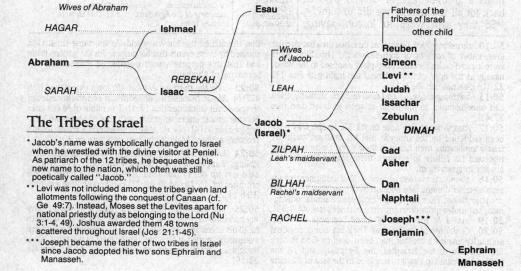

The Tribes of Israel

* Jacob's name was symbolically changed to Israel when he wrestled with the divine visitor at Peniel. As patriarch of the 12 tribes, he bequeathed his new name to the nation, which often was still poetically called "Jacob."

** Levi was not included among the tribes given land allotments following the conquest of Canaan (cf. Ge 49:7). Instead, Moses set the Levites apart for national priestly duty as belonging to the Lord (Nu 3:1-4, 49). Joshua awarded them 48 towns scattered throughout Israel (Jos 21:1-45).

*** Joseph became the father of two tribes in Israel since Jacob adopted his two sons Ephraim and Manasseh.

Wives of Abraham

HAGAR............ Ishmael

Abraham

    REBEKAH

SARAH............ Isaac

Esau

Wives of Jacob

LEAH............

Jacob (Israel)*

ZILPAH............ *Leah's maidservant*

BILHAH............ *Rachel's maidservant*

RACHEL............

Fathers of the tribes of Israel
    other child

Reuben
Simeon
Levi **
Judah
Issachar
Zebulun
    DINAH
Gad
Asher
Dan
Naphtali
Joseph***
Benjamin
    Ephraim
    Manasseh

6 Pharaoh said, "Go up and bury your
father, as he made you swear to do."
7 So Joseph went up to bury his father.
All Pharaoh's officials[x] accompanied
him—the dignitaries of his court[y] and all
the dignitaries of Egypt— 8 besides all the
members of Joseph's household and his
brothers and those belonging to his father's
household.[z] Only their children and their
flocks and herds were left in Goshen.[a]
9 Chariots[b] and horsemen[c] also went up
with him. It was a very large company.
10 When they reached the threshing
floor[c] of Atad, near the Jordan, they la-
mented loudly and bitterly;[d] and there Joseph observed a seven-day period[e] of
mourning[f] for his father.[g] 11 When the
Canaanites[h] who lived there saw the
mourning at the threshing floor of Atad,
they said, "The Egyptians are holding a
solemn ceremony of mourning."[i] That is
why that place near the Jordan is called
Abel Mizraim.[d]
12 So Jacob's sons did as he had commanded them:[j] 13 They carried him to the
land of Canaan and buried him in the cave
in the field of Machpelah,[k] near Mamre,[l]
which Abraham had bought as a burial
place from Ephron the Hittite,[m] along with
the field.[n] 14 After burying his father, Joseph returned to Egypt, together with his
brothers and all the others who had gone
with him to bury his father.[o]

Joseph Reassures His Brothers

15 When Joseph's brothers saw that their
father was dead, they said, "What if Joseph
holds a grudge[p] against us and pays us
back for all the wrongs we did to him?"[q]
16 So they sent word to Joseph, saying,
"Your father left these instructions[r] before
he died: 17 'This is what you are to say to
Joseph: I ask you to forgive your brothers
the sins[s] and the wrongs they committed
in treating you so badly.'[t] Now please forgive the sins of the servants of the God of
your father.[u]" When their message came
to him, Joseph wept.[v]
18 His brothers then came and threw
themselves down before him.[w] "We are
your slaves,"[x] they said.
19 But Joseph said to them, "Don't be
afraid. Am I in the place of God?[y] 20 You
intended to harm me,[z] but God intended[a]
it for good[b] to accomplish what is now
being done, the saving of many lives.[c] 21 So
then, don't be afraid. I will provide for you
and your children.[d]" And he reassured
them and spoke kindly[e] to them.

The Death of Joseph

22 Joseph stayed in Egypt, along with all
his father's family. He lived a hundred and
ten years[f] 23 and saw the third generation[g]
of Ephraim's[h] children.[i] Also the children
of Makir[j] son of Manasseh[k] were placed
at birth on Joseph's knees.[e][l]
24 Then Joseph said to his brothers, "I
am about to die.[m] But God will surely
come to your aid[n] and take you up out of
this land to the land[o] he promised on oath
to Abraham,[p] Isaac[q] and Jacob."[r] 25 And
Joseph made the sons of Israel swear an
oath[s] and said, "God will surely come to

50:7 [x]Ge 45:16 [y]ver 4 **50:8** [z]ver 14 [a]S Ge 45:10 **50:9** [b]S Ge 41:43 **50:10** [c]Nu 15:20; Ru 3:2; 2Sa 24:18; 1Ki 22:10 [d]2Sa 1:17; 3:33; 2Ch 35:25; Eze 32:16; Ac 8:2 [e]1Sa 31:13; Job 2:13; Eze 3:15 [f]S Ge 27:41; S Lev 10:6 [g]S Ge 37:34 **50:11** [h]S Ge 10:18 [i]S Ge 37:34 **50:12** [j]Ge 49:29 **50:13** [k]S Ge 23:9 [l]S Ge 13:18 [m]S Ge 25:9 [n]S Ge 23:20 **50:14** [o]ver 8 **50:15** [p]S Ge 27:41 [q]ver 17; S Ge 9:5; 37:28; Zep 3:11; 1Pe 3:9 **50:16** [r]Ge 49:29 **50:17** [s]S Mt 6:14 [t]S ver 15 [u]S Ge 28:13 [v]S Ge 29:11 **50:18** [w]S Ge 37:7 [x]S Ge 43:18 **50:19** [y]S Ge 30:2; S Ex 32:34; Ro 12:19; Heb 10:30 **50:20** [z]Ge 37:20 [a]Isa 10:7; Mic 4:11-12 [b]Ro 8:28 [c]S Ge 45:5; Est 4:14 **50:21** [d]S Ge 45:11 [e]S Ge 34:3; Eph 4:32 **50:22** [f]S Ge 25:7; Jos 24:29 **50:23** [g]Job 42:16 [h]S Ge 41:52 [i]S Ge 48:11 [j]Nu 26:29; 27:1; 32:39,40; 36:1; Dt 3:15; Jos 13:31; 17:1; Jdg 5:14 [k]S Ge 41:51 [l]S Ge 48:12 **50:24** [m]ver 5 [n]Ru 1:6; Ps 35:2; 106:4; Isa 38:14 [o]S Ge 15:14 [p]S Ge 13:17 [q]S Ge 17:19 [r]S Ge 12:7; S 15:16 **50:25** [s]S Ge 24:37

[c]9 Or *charioteers* [d]11 *Abel Mizraim* means *mourning of the Egyptians.* [e]23 That is, were counted as his

50:10 *threshing floor.* Grain was threshed on a flat circular area, either of rock or of pounded earth. Threshing floors were located on an elevated open place exposed to the wind, usually at the edge of town or near the main gate (see 1Ki 22:10). See note on Ru 1:22.

50:15 *holds a grudge . . . and pays us back.* Similarly, Esau had once planned to kill Jacob as soon as Isaac died (see 27:41).

50:17 *Joseph wept.* See note on 43:30. Joseph may have been saddened by the thought that his brothers might be falsely implicating their father in their story. Or he may have regretted his failure to reassure them sooner that he had already forgiven them.

50:18 *threw themselves down.* A final fulfillment of Joseph's earlier dreams (see note on 37:7; see also 37:9). *We are your slaves.* They had earlier expressed a similar willingness, but under quite different circumstances (see 44:9,33).

50:19 *Am I in the place of God?* See note on 30:2.

50:20 *God intended it for good.* Their act, out of personal animosity toward a brother, had been used by God to save life—the life of the Israelites, the Egyptians and all the nations that came to Egypt to buy food in the face of a famine that threatened the known world. At the same time, God showed by these events that his purpose for the nations is life and that this purpose would be effected through the descendants of Abraham.

50:23 *saw the third generation.* Cf. Job's experience (Job 42:16). *Makir.* Manasseh's firstborn son and the ancestor of the powerful Gileadites (Jos 17:1). The name of Makir later became almost interchangeable with that of Manasseh himself (see Jdg 5:14). *placed at birth on Joseph's knees.* Joseph probably adopted Makir's children (see note on 30:3).

50:24 *brothers.* Perhaps used here in a broader sense than siblings. *I am about to die.* See note on 48:21. *God will . . . take you up out of this land.* Joseph did not forget God's promises (cf. 15:16; 46:4; 48:21) concerning "the exodus" (Heb 11:22).

50:25 See 47:29–31 for a similar request by Jacob. *carry my bones up from this place.* Centuries later Moses did so to fulfill his ancestor's oath (see Ex 13:19). Joseph's bones were eventually "buried at Shechem in the tract of land that Jacob bought . . . from the sons of Hamor" (Jos 24:32; see Ge 33:19).

your aid, and then you must carry my bones[t] up from this place." [u]

²⁶So Joseph died[v] at the age of a hun-

dred and ten. [w] And after they embalmed him, [x] he was placed in a coffin in Egypt.

50:25
[t] S Ge 49:29
[u] S Ge 47:29-30; Heb 11:22

50:26 [v] Ex 1:6 [w] S Ge 25:7 [x] S ver 2

50:26 *Joseph died at the age of a hundred and ten.* See v. 22. Ancient Egyptian records indicate that 110 years was considered to be the ideal life span; to the Egyptians this would have signified divine blessing upon Joseph.

EXODUS

Title

"Exodus" is a Latin word derived from Greek *Exodos,* the name given to the book by those who translated it into Greek. The word means "exit," "departure" (see Lk 9:31; Heb 11:22). The name was retained by the Latin Vulgate, by the Jewish author Philo (a contemporary of Christ) and by the Syriac version. In Hebrew the book is named after its first two words, *we'elleh shemoth* ("These are the names of"). The same phrase occurs in Ge 46:8, where it likewise introduces a list of the names of those Israelites "who went to Egypt with Jacob" (1:1). Thus Exodus was not intended to exist separately, but was thought of as a continuation of a narrative that began in Genesis and was completed in Leviticus, Numbers and Deuteronomy. The first five books of the Bible are together known as the Pentateuch (see Introduction to Genesis: Author and Date of Writing).

Author and Date of Writing

Several statements in Exodus indicate that Moses wrote certain sections of the book (see 17:14; 24:4; 34:27). In addition, Jos 8:31 refers to the command of Ex 20:25 as having been "written in the Book of the Law of Moses." The NT also claims Mosaic authorship for various passages in Exodus (see, e.g., Mk 7:10; 12:26 and NIV text notes; see also Lk 2:22-23). Taken together, these references strongly suggest that Moses was largely responsible for writing the book of Exodus—a traditional view not convincingly challenged by the commonly held notion that the Pentateuch as a whole contains four underlying sources (see Introduction to Genesis: Author and Date of Writing).

Chronology

According to 1Ki 6:1, the exodus took place 480 years before "the fourth year of Solomon's reign over Israel." Since that year was c. 966 B.C., it has been traditionally held that the exodus occurred c. 1446. The "three hundred years" of Jdg 11:26 fits comfortably within this time span (see Introduction to Judges: Background). In addition, although Egyptian chronology relating to the 18th dynasty remains somewhat uncertain, recent research tends to support the traditional view that two of this dynasty's pharaohs, Thutmose III and his son Amunhotep II, were the pharaohs of the oppression and the exodus respectively (see notes on 2:15,23; 3:10).

On the other hand, the appearance of the name Rameses in 1:11 has led many to the conclusion that the 19th-dynasty pharaoh Seti I and his son Rameses II were the pharaohs of the oppression and the exodus respectively. Furthermore, archaeological evidence of the destruction of numerous Canaanite cities in the 13th century B.C. has been interpreted as proof that Joshua's troops invaded the promised land in that century. These and similar lines of argument lead to a date for the exodus of c. 1290 (see Introduction to Joshua: Historical Setting).

The identity of the cities' attackers, however, cannot be positively ascertained. The raids may have been initiated by later Israelite armies, or by Philistines or other outsiders. In addition, the archaeological evidence itself has become increasingly ambiguous, and recent evaluations have tended to redate some of it to the 18th dynasty. Also, the name Rameses in 1:11 could very well be the result of an editorial updating by someone who lived centuries after Moses—a procedure that probably accounts for the appearance of the same word in Ge 47:11 (see note there).

In short, there are no compelling reasons to modify in any substantial way the traditional 1446 B.C. date for the exodus of the Israelites from Egyptian bondage.

The Route of the Exodus

At least three routes of escape from Pithom and Rameses (1:11) have been proposed: (1) a northern route through the land of the Philistines (but see 13:17); (2) a middle route leading eastward across

Sinai to Beersheba; and (3) a southern route along the west coast of Sinai to the southeastern extremities of the peninsula. The southern route seems most likely, since several of the sites in Israel's desert itinerary have been tentatively identified along it. See map No. 3 at the end of the Study Bible. The exact place where Israel crossed the "Red Sea" is uncertain, however (see notes on 13:18; 14:2).

Themes and Theology

Exodus lays a foundational theology in which God reveals his name, his attributes, his redemption, his law and how he is to be worshiped. It also reports the appointment and work of the first covenant mediator (Moses), describes the beginnings of the priesthood, defines the role of the prophet and relates how the ancient covenant relationship between God and his people came under a new administration (the Sinai covenant).

Profound insights into the nature of God are found in chs. 3; 6; 33-34. The focus of these texts is on the fact and importance of his presence (as signified by his name Yahweh and by his glory). But emphasis is also placed on his attributes of justice, truthfulness, mercy, faithfulness and holiness. Thus to know God's "name" is to know him and to know his character (see 3:13-15; 6:3).

God is also the Lord of history, for there is no one like him: "majestic in holiness, awesome in glory, working wonders" (15:11). Neither the affliction of Israel nor the plagues in Egypt were outside his control. Pharaoh, the Egyptians and all Israel saw the power of God.

It is reassuring to know that God remembers and is concerned about his people (see 2:24). What he had promised centuries earlier to Abraham, Isaac and Jacob he now begins to bring to fruition as Israel is freed from Egyptian bondage and sets out for the land of promise. The covenant at Sinai is but another step in God's fulfillment of his promise to the patriarchs (3:15-17; 6:2-8; 19:3-8).

The theology of salvation is likewise one of the strong emphases of the book. The verb "redeem" is used, e.g., in 6:6; 15:13. But the heart of redemption theology is best seen in the Passover narrative of ch. 12 and the sealing of the covenant in ch. 24. The apostle Paul viewed the death of the Passover lamb as fulfilled in Christ (1Co 5:7). Indeed, John the Baptist called Jesus the "Lamb of God, who takes away the sin of the world" (Jn 1:29).

The foundation of Biblical ethics and morality is laid out first in the gracious character of God as revealed in the exodus itself and then in the Ten Commandments (20:1-17) and the ordinances of the Book of the Covenant (20:22-23:33), which taught Israel how to apply in a practical way the principles of the commandments.

The book concludes with an elaborate discussion of the theology of worship. Though costly in time, effort and monetary value, the tabernacle, in meaning and function, points to the chief end of man: "to glorify God and to enjoy him forever" (Westminster Shorter Catechism). By means of the tabernacle, the omnipotent, unchanging and transcendent God of the universe came to "dwell" or "tabernacle" with his people, thereby revealing his gracious nearness as well. God is not only mighty in Israel's behalf; he is also present in her midst.

However, these theological elements do not merely sit side by side in the Exodus narrative. They receive their fullest and richest significance from the fact that they are embedded in the account of God's raising up his servant Moses (1) to liberate his people from Egyptian bondage, (2) to inaugurate his earthly kingdom among them by bringing them into a special national covenant with him, and (3) to erect within Israel God's royal tent. And this account of redemption from bondage leading to consecration in covenant and the pitching of God's royal tent in the earth, all through the ministry of a chosen mediator, discloses God's purpose in history—the purpose he would fulfill through Israel, and ultimately through Jesus Christ the supreme Mediator.

Outline

I. Divine Redemption (chs. 1-18)
  A. Fulfilled Multiplication (ch. 1)
    1. The promised increase (1:1-7)
    2. The first pogrom (1:8-14)
    3. The second pogrom (1:15-21)
    4. The third pogrom (1:22)
  B. Preparations for Deliverance (2:1-4:26)
    1. Preparing a leader (2:1-10)
    2. Extending the time of preparation (2:11-22)
    3. Preparing the people (2:23-25)

    4. Calling a deliverer (3:1-10)
    5. Answering inadequate objections (3:11-4:17)
    6. Preparing a leader's family (4:18-26)
  C. First Steps in Leadership (4:27-7:5)
    1. Reinforced by brothers (4:27-31)
    2. Rebuffed by the enemy (5:1-14)
    3. Rebuffed by the enslaved (5:15-21)
    4. Revisited by old objections (5:22-23)
    5. Reinforced by the name of God (6:1-8)
    6. Reminded of one's lowly origins (6:9-7:5)
  D. Judgment and Salvation through the Plagues (7:6-11:10)
    1. Presenting the signs of divine authority (7:6-13)
    2. First plague: water turned to blood (7:14-24)
    3. Second plague: frogs (7:25-8:15)
    4. Third plague: gnats (8:16-19)
    5. Fourth plague: flies (8:20-32)
    6. Fifth plague: against livestock (9:1-7)
    7. Sixth plague: boils (9:8-12)
    8. Seventh plague: hail (9:13-35)
    9. Eighth plague: locusts (10:1-20)
    10. Ninth plague: darkness (10:21-29)
    11. Tenth plague announced: death of the firstborn (ch. 11)
  E. The Passover (12:1-28)
    1. Preparations for the Passover (12:1-13)
    2. Preparations for Unleavened Bread (12:14-20)
    3. Celebration of the Passover (12:21-28)
  F. The Exodus from Egypt (12:29-51)
    1. Death at midnight (12:29-32)
    2. Expulsion from Egypt (12:33-42)
    3. Regulations for the Passover (12:43-51)
  G. The Consecration of the Firstborn (13:1-16)
  H. Crossing the "Red Sea" (13:17-15:21)
    1. Into the wilderness (13:17-22)
    2. At the "Red Sea" (14:1-14)
    3. Across the "Red Sea" (14:15-31)
    4. Song at the sea (15:1-21)
  I. Journey to Sinai (15:22-18:27)
    1. The waters of Marah (15:22-27)
    2. The manna and the quail (ch. 16)
    3. The waters of Meribah (17:1-7)
    4. The war with Amalek (17:8-16)
    5. The wisdom of Jethro (ch. 18)
II. Covenant at Sinai (chs. 19-24)
  A. The Covenant Proposed (ch. 19)
  B. The Decalogue (20:1-17)
  C. The Reaction of the People to God's Fiery Presence (20:18-21)
  D. The Book of the Covenant (20:22-23:33)
    1. Prologue (20:22-26)
    2. Laws on slaves (21:1-11)
    3. Laws on homicide (21:12-17)
    4. Laws on bodily injuries (21:18-32)
    5. Laws on property damage (21:33-22:15)
    6. Laws on society (22:16-31)
    7. Laws on justice and neighborliness (23:1-9)
    8. Laws on sacred seasons (23:10-19)
    9. Epilogue (23:20-33)

    E. Ratification of the Covenant (ch. 24)
III. Divine Worship (chs. 25-40)
    A. Instructions concerning the Tabernacle (chs. 25-31)
        1. Collection of the materials (25:1-9)
        2. Ark and atonement cover (25:10-22)
        3. Table of the bread of the Presence (25:23-30)
        4. Gold lampstand (25:31-40)
        5. Curtains and frames (ch. 26)
        6. Altar of burnt offering (27:1-8)
        7. Courtyard (27:9-19)
        8. Priesthood (27:20-28:5)
        9. Garments of the priests (28:6-43)
     10. Ordination of the priests (ch. 29)
     11. Altar of incense (30:1-10)
     12. Census tax (30:11-16)
     13. Bronze basin (30:17-21)
     14. Anointing oil and incense (30:22-38)
     15. Appointment of craftsmen (31:1-11)
     16. Sabbath rest (31:12-18)
    B. False Worship (chs. 32-34)
        1. The golden calf (32:1-29)
        2. Moses' mediation (32:30-35)
        3. Threatened separation and Moses' prayer (ch. 33)
        4. Renewal of the covenant (ch. 34)
    C. The Building of the Tabernacle (chs. 35-40)
        1. Summons to build (35:1-19)
        2. Voluntary gifts (35:20-29)
        3. Bezalel and his craftsmen (35:30-36:7)
        4. Progress of the work (36:8-39:31)
        5. Moses' blessing (39:32-43)
        6. Erection of the tabernacle (40:1-33)
        7. Dedication of the tabernacle (40:34-38)

The Israelites Oppressed

1 These are the names of the sons of Israel[a] who went to Egypt with Jacob, each with his family: [2]Reuben, Simeon, Levi and Judah; [3]Issachar, Zebulun and Benjamin; [4]Dan and Naphtali; Gad and Asher.[b] [5]The descendants of Jacob numbered seventy[a] in all;[c] Joseph was already in Egypt.

[6]Now Joseph and all his brothers and all that generation died,[d] [7]but the Israelites were fruitful and multiplied greatly and became exceedingly numerous,[e] so that the land was filled with them.

[8]Then a new king, who did not know about Joseph, came to power in Egypt.[f] [9]"Look," he said to his people, "the Israelites have become much too numerous[g] for us.[h] [10]Come, we must deal shrewdly[i] with them or they will become even more numerous and, if war breaks out, will join our enemies, fight against us and leave the country."[j]

[11]So they put slave masters[k] over them to oppress them with forced labor,[l] and they built Pithom and Rameses[m] as store cities[n] for Pharaoh. [12]But the more they were oppressed, the more they multiplied and spread; so the Egyptians came to dread the Israelites [13]and worked them ruthlessly.[o] [14]They made their lives bitter with hard labor[p] in brick[q] and mortar and with all kinds of work in the fields; in all their hard labor the Egyptians used them ruthlessly.[r]

[15]The king of Egypt said to the Hebrew midwives,[s] whose names were Shiphrah and Puah, [16]"When you help the Hebrew women in childbirth and observe them on the delivery stool, if it is a boy, kill him; but if it is a girl, let her live."[t] [17]The midwives, however, feared[u] God and did not do what the king of Egypt had told them to do;[v] they let the boys live. [18]Then the king of Egypt summoned the midwives and asked them, "Why have you done this? Why have you let the boys live?"

[19]The midwives answered Pharaoh, "Hebrew women are not like Egyptian women; they are vigorous and give birth before the midwives arrive."[w]

[20]So God was kind to the midwives[x] and the people increased and became even more numerous. [21]And because the midwives feared[y] God, he gave them families[z] of their own.

[22]Then Pharaoh gave this order to all his people: "Every boy that is born[b] you must throw into the Nile,[a] but let every girl live."[b]

The Birth of Moses

2 Now a man of the house of Levi[c] married a Levite woman,[d] [2]and she

Cross references (center column)

1:1 aS Ge 46:8
1:4 bGe 35:22-26; Nu 1:20-43
1:5 cS Ge 46:26
1:6 dGe 50:26; Ac 7:15
1:7 ever 9; S Ge 12:2; Dt 7:13; Eze 16:7
1:8 fJer 43:11; 46:2
1:9 gS ver 7 hS Ge 26:16
1:10 iGe 15:13; Ex 3:7; 18:11; Ps 64:2; 71:10; 83:3; Isa 53:3 jPs 105:24-25; Ac 7:17-19
1:11 kEx 3:7; 5:10,13,14 lS Ge 15:13; Ex 2:11; 5:4; 6:6-7; Jos 9:27; 1Ki 9:21; 1Ch 22:2; Isa 60:10 mS Ge 47:11 n1Ki 9:19; 2Ch 8:4
1:13 over 14; Ge 15:13-14; Ex 5:21; 16:3; Lev 25:43,46,53; Dt 4:20; 26:6; 1Ki 8:51; Ps 129:1; Isa 30:6; 48:10; Jer 11:4
1:14 pDt 26:6; Ezr 9:9; Isa 14:3 qS Ge 11:3 rEx 2:23; 3:9; Nu 20:15; 1Sa 10:18; 2Ki 13:4; Ps 66:11; 81:6; Ac 7:19
1:15 sS Ge 35:17
1:16 tver 22
1:17 uver 21; Pr 16:6 vISa 22:17; Da 3:16-18; Ac 4:18-20; 5:29

1:19 wLev 19:11; Jos 2:4-6; 1Sa 19:14; 2Sa 17:20 1:20 xPr 11:18; 22:8; Ecc 8:12; Isa 3:10; Heb 6:10 1:21 yS ver 17 zISa 2:35; 2Sa 7:11,27-29; 1Ki 11:38; 14:10 1:22 aS Ge 41:1 bver 16; Ac 7:19 2:1 cS Ge 29:34 dver 2; Ex 6:20; Nu 26:59

a5 Masoretic Text (see also Gen. 46:27); Dead Sea Scrolls and Septuagint (see also Acts 7:14 and note at Gen. 46:27) seventy-five b22 Masoretic Text; Samaritan Pentateuch, Septuagint and Targums born to the Hebrews

---

1:1–5 These verses clearly indicate that Exodus was written as a continuation of Genesis. The Israelites lived in Egypt 430 years (see 12:40).
1:1 *These are the names of.* The same expression appears in Ge 46:8 at the head of a list of Jacob's descendants. *Israel . . . Jacob.* Jacob had earlier been given the additional name Israel (see Ge 32:28; 35:10 and notes).
1:2–4 The sons of Leah (Reuben through Zebulun) and Rachel (Benjamin; Joseph is not mentioned because the list includes only those "who entered Egypt with Jacob," v. 1) are listed in the order of their seniority and before the sons of Rachel's and Leah's maidservants: Bilhah had Dan and Naphtali, Zilpah had Gad and Asher (see Ge 35:23–26).
1:5 *seventy.* See note on Ge 46:27.
1:6–7 From the death of Joseph to the rise of a new king (v. 8) was more than 200 years.
1:7 See Ac 7:17. God's promised blessing of fruitfulness and increase had been given to Adam (Ge 1:28), Noah (Ge 8:17; 9:1,7), Abraham (Ge 17:2,6; 22:17), Isaac (Ge 26:4) and Jacob (Ge 28:14; 35:11; 48:4). God continued to fulfill his promise during the 430-year sojourn in Egypt. *the land was filled with them.* The Hebrew used here echoes the blessing of Adam (Ge 1:28)—God's initial blessing of mankind was being fulfilled in Israel. The Israelites who left Egypt are said to number about 600,000 men, "besides women and children" (12:37). *land.* Goshen (see note on Ge 45:10).

1:8 See Ac 7:18. *new king.* Probably Ahmose, the founder of the 18th dynasty, who expelled the Hyksos (foreign—predominantly Semitic—rulers of Egypt).
1:11 *slave masters.* The same official Egyptian designation appears on a wall painting in the Theban tomb of Rekhmire during the reign of the 18th-dynasty pharaoh Thutmose III (see Introduction: Chronology). *Rameses.* See note on Ge 47:11. *Pharaoh.* The word, which is Egyptian in origin and means "great house," is a royal title rather than a personal name.
1:14 *made their lives bitter.* A fact commemorated in the Passover meal, which was eaten "with bitter herbs" (12:8). *all kinds of work in the fields.* Including pumping the waters of the Nile into the fields to irrigate them (see Dt 11:10).
1:15 *Hebrew.* See note on Ge 14:13. *Shiphrah and Puah.* Semitic, not Egyptian, names. Since the Israelites were so numerous, there were probably other midwives under Shiphrah and Puah.
1:16 *delivery stool.* The Hebrew term means lit. "two stones"; a woman sat on them while giving birth.
1:17 See Ac 5:29 for a parallel in the early church. *feared God.* See note on Ge 20:11.
2:1 *a man . . . a Levite woman.* Perhaps Amram and Jochebed (but see note on 6:20).
2:2 *a fine child.* Moses was "no ordinary child" (Ac 7:20; Heb 11:23), "fair in the sight of God" (see NIV text note on Ac 7:20). The account of Moses' remarkable deliverance in

became pregnant and gave birth to a son. When she saw that he was a fine *e* child, she hid him for three months.*f* 3But when she could hide him no longer, she got a papyrus *g* basket for him and coated it with tar and pitch.*h* Then she placed the child in it and put it among the reeds *i* along the bank of the Nile. 4His sister *j* stood at a distance to see what would happen to him.

5Then Pharaoh's daughter went down to the Nile to bathe, and her attendants were walking along the river bank.*k* She saw the basket among the reeds and sent her slave girl to get it. 6She opened it and saw the baby. He was crying, and she felt sorry for him. "This is one of the Hebrew babies," she said.

7Then his sister asked Pharaoh's daughter, "Shall I go and get one of the Hebrew women to nurse the baby for you?"

8"Yes, go," she answered. And the girl went and got the baby's mother. 9Pharaoh's daughter said to her, "Take this baby and nurse him for me, and I will pay you." So the woman took the baby and nursed him. 10When the child grew older, she took him to Pharaoh's daughter and he became her son. She named *l* him Moses,*c* saying, "I drew *m* him out of the water."

Moses Flees to Midian

11One day, after Moses had grown up, he went out to where his own people *n* were and watched them at their hard labor.*o* He saw an Egyptian beating a Hebrew, one of his own people. 12Glancing this way and that and seeing no one, he killed the Egyptian and hid him in the sand. 13The next day he went out and saw two Hebrews fighting. He asked the one in the wrong, "Why are you hitting your fellow Hebrew?" *p*

14The man said, "Who made you ruler and judge over us? *q* Are you thinking of killing me as you killed the Egyptian?" Then Moses was afraid and thought, "What I did must have become known."

15When Pharaoh heard of this, he tried to kill *r* Moses, but Moses fled *s* from Pharaoh and went to live in Midian,*t* where he sat down by a well. 16Now a priest of Midian *u* had seven daughters, and they came to draw water *v* and fill the troughs *w* to water their father's flock. 17Some shepherds came along and drove them away, but Moses got up and came to their rescue *x* and watered their flock.*y*

18When the girls returned to Reuel *z* their father, he asked them, "Why have you returned so early today?"

19They answered, "An Egyptian rescued us from the shepherds. He even drew water for us and watered the flock."

20"And where is he?" he asked his daughters. "Why did you leave him? Invite him to have something to eat." *a*

21Moses agreed to stay with the man, who gave his daughter Zipporah *b* to Moses in marriage. 22Zipporah gave birth to a son, and Moses named him Gershom,*d c* saying, "I have become an alien *d* in a foreign land."

23During that long period, *e* the king of

Cross references (center column):

2:2 *e*S Ge 39:6
/Heb 11:23
2:3 *g*Isa 18:2
*h*Ge 6:14
*i*S Ge 41:2;
S Job 8:11;
Ac 7:21
2:4 /Ex 15:20
2:5 *k*Ex 7:15;
8:20
2:10 /1Sa 1:20
*m*2Sa 22:17
2:11 *n*Ac 7:23;
Heb 11:24-26
*o*S Ex 1:11

2:13 *p*Ac 7:26
2:14 *q*S Ge 13:8;
Ac 7:27*
2:15 *r*Ex 4:19
*s*S Ge 31:21
*t*Heb 11:27
2:16 *u*Ex 3:1;
18:1 *v*S Ge 24:11
*w*S Ge 30:38
2:17 *x*1Sa 30:8;
Ps 31:2
*y*S Ge 29:10
2:18 *z*Ex 3:1;
4:18; 18:1,5,12;
Nu 10:29
2:20 *a*Ge 18:2-5
2:21 *b*Ex 4:25;
18:2; Nu 12:1
2:22 *c*Jdg 18:30
*d*S Ge 23:4;
Heb 11:13
2:23 *e*Ac 7:30

c 10 Moses sounds like the Hebrew for *draw out.*
d 22 Gershom sounds like the Hebrew for *an alien there.*

---

infancy foreshadows the deliverance from Egypt that God would later effect through him.
2:3 *papyrus basket.* Each of the two Hebrew words lying behind this phrase is of Egyptian origin. The word for "basket" is used only here and of Noah's ark (see note on Ge 6:14). Moses' basket was a miniature version of the large, seaworthy "papyrus boats" mentioned in Isa 18:2. *reeds.* A word of Egyptian derivation, reflected in the proper name "Red Sea" (see NIV text note on 10:19).
2:4 *his sister.* Miriam (see 15:20).
2:5 *Pharaoh's daughter.* Perhaps the famous 18th-dynasty princess who later became Queen Hatshepsut. *attendants.* They stayed on the river bank to bathe the princess.
2:10 See Ac 7:21-22. *he became her son.* Throughout this early part of Exodus, all the pharaoh's efforts to suppress Israel were thwarted by women: the midwives (1:17), the Israelite mothers (1:19), Moses' mother and sister (vv. 3-4, 7-9), the pharaoh's daughter (here). The pharaoh's impotence to destroy the people of God is thus ironically exposed. *Moses.* The name, of Egyptian origin, means "is born" and forms the second element in such pharaonic names as Ahmose (see note on 1:8), Thutmose and Rameses (see note on 1:11). *drew him out.* A Hebrew wordplay on the name Moses (see NIV text note), emphasizing his providential rescue from the Nile. Thus Moses' name may also have

served as a reminder of the great act of deliverance God worked through him at the "Red Sea" (see 13:17-14:31).
2:11-15 See Ac 7:23-29; Heb 11:24-27.
2:11 *Moses had grown up.* He was now 40 years old (see Ac 7:23).
2:14 *Who made you ruler and judge . . . ?* Unwittingly, the speaker made a prediction that would be fulfilled 40 years later (see Ac 7:27,30,35). The Hebrew word for "judge" could also refer to a deliverer, as in the book of Judges (see Ac 7:35); it was often a synonym for "ruler" in the OT (see Ge 18:25 and note) as well as in ancient Canaanite usage. *Moses was afraid.* See note on Heb 11:27.
2:15 *Pharaoh.* Probably Thutmose III (see Introduction: Chronology). *Midian.* Named after one of Abraham's younger sons (see Ge 25:2; see also note on Ge 37:25). Midian was located in southeastern Sinai and west central Arabia, flanking the eastern arm of the Red Sea (Gulf of Aqaba) on either side. Dry and desolate, it formed a stark contrast to Moses' former home in the royal court. He lived in Midian 40 years (see Ac 7:29-30).
2:16 *priest of Midian.* Reuel (see v. 18), which means "friend of God." His other name, Jethro (see 3:1), may be a title meaning "his excellency."
2:23 *During that long period.* Thutmose III (see note on v. 15) enjoyed a long reign.

Egypt died.*f* The Israelites groaned in their slavery*g* and cried out, and their cry*h* for help because of their slavery went up to God. ²⁴God heard their groaning and he remembered*i* his covenant*j* with Abraham, with Isaac and with Jacob. ²⁵So God looked on the Israelites and was concerned*k* about them.

Moses and the Burning Bush

3 Now Moses was tending the flock of Jethro*l* his father-in-law, the priest of Midian,*m* and he led the flock to the far side of the desert and came to Horeb,*n* the mountain*o* of God. ²There the angel of the LORD*p* appeared to him in flames of fire*q* from within a bush.*r* Moses saw that though the bush was on fire it did not burn up. ³So Moses thought, "I will go over and see this strange sight—why the bush does not burn up."

⁴When the LORD saw that he had gone over to look, God called*s* to him from within the bush,*t* "Moses! Moses!"

And Moses said, "Here I am."*u*

⁵"Do not come any closer,"*v* God said. "Take off your sandals, for the place where you are standing is holy ground."*w* ⁶Then he said, "I am the God of your father, the God of Abraham, the God of Isaac and the God of Jacob."*x* At this, Moses hid*y* his face, because he was afraid to look at God.*z*

⁷The LORD said, "I have indeed seen*a* the misery*b* of my people in Egypt. I have heard them crying out because of their

slave drivers, and I am concerned*c* about their suffering.*d* ⁸So I have come down*e* to rescue them from the hand of the Egyptians and to bring them up out of that land into a good and spacious land,*f* a land flowing with milk and honey*g*—the home of the Canaanites, Hittites, Amorites, Perizzites, Hivites*h* and Jebusites.*i* ⁹And now the cry of the Israelites has reached me, and I have seen the way the Egyptians are oppressing*j* them. ¹⁰So now, go. I am sending*k* you to Pharaoh to bring my people the Israelites out of Egypt."*l*

¹¹But Moses said to God, "Who am I,*m* that I should go to Pharaoh and bring the Israelites out of Egypt?"

¹²And God said, "I will be with you.*n* And this will be the sign*o* to you that it is I who have sent you: When you have brought the people out of Egypt, you*e* will worship God on this mountain.*p*"

¹³Moses said to God, "Suppose I go to the Israelites and say to them, 'The God of your fathers has sent me to you,' and they

2:23 *f*Ex 4:19
*g*S Ex 1:14 *h*ver 24; Ex 3:7,9; 6:5; Nu 20:15-16; Dt 26:7; Jdg 2:18; 1Sa 12:8; Ps 5:2; 18:6; 39:12; 81:7; 102:1; Jas 5:4 **2:24** *i*S Ge 8:1 *j*S Ge 9:15; 15:15; 17:4; 22:16-18; 26:3; 28:13-15; Ex 32:13; 2Ki 13:23; Ps 105:10,42; Jer 14:21 **2:25** *k*Ex 3:7; 4:31; Lk 1:25 **3:1** *l*S Ex 2:18; Jdg 1:16 *m*S Ex 2:16 *n*ver 12; Ex 17:6; 19:1-11,5; 33:6; Dt 1:2,6; 4:10; 5:2; 29:1; 1Ki 19:8; Mal 4:4 *o*Ex 4:27; 18:5; 24:13; Dt 4:11,15 **3:2** *p*S Ge 16:7; S Ex 12:23; S Ac 5:19 *q*Ex 19:18; 1Ki 19:12 *r*ver 4; Ex 2:2-6; Dt 33:16; Mk 12:26; Lk 20:37; Ac 7:30 **3:4** *s*Ex 19:3; Lev 1:1 *t*Ex 4:5 *u*Ge 31:11; 1Sa 3:4; Isa 6:8 **3:5** *v*Jer 30:21 *w*S Ge 28:17; Ac 7:33* **3:6** *x*S Ge 24:12; S Ex 4:5; Mt 22:32*; Mk 12:26*; Lk 20:37*; Ac 3:13; 7:32* *y*1Ki 19:13 *z*Ex 24:11; 33:20; Jdg 13:22; Job 13:11; 23:16; 30:15; Isa 6:5

3:7 *a*1Sa 9:16 *b*ver 16; S Ge 16:11; 1Sa 1:11; Ne 9:9; Ps 106:44 *c*S Ex 2:25; Ac 7:34* *d*S Ex 1:10 **3:8** *e*S Ge 11:5; Ac 7:34* *f*S Ge 12:7; S 15:14 *g*ver 17; Ex 13:5; 33:3; Lev 20:24; Nu 13:27; Dt 1:25; 6:3; 8:7-9; 11:9; 26:9; 27:3; Jos 5:6; Jer 11:5; 32:22; Eze 20:6 *h*Jos 11:3; Jdg 3:3; 2Sa 24:7 *i*S Ge 15:18-21; Ezr 9:1 **3:9** *j*S Ex 1:14; S Nu 10:9 **3:10** *k*Ex 4:12; Jos 24:5; 1Sa 12:8; Ps 105:26; Ac 7:34* *l*Ex 6:13,26; 12:41,51; 20:2; Dt 4:20; 1Sa 12:6; 1Ki 8:16; Mic 6:4 **3:11** *m*Ex 4:10; 6:12,30; Jdg 6:15; 1Sa 9:21; 15:17; 18:18; 2Sa 7:18; 2Ch 2:6; Isa 6:5; Jer 1:6 **3:12** *n*S Ge 26:3; S Ex 14:22; Ro 8:31 *o*Nu 26:10; Jos 4:6; 1Sa 2:34; 10:7; Ps 86:17; Isa 7:14; 8:18; 20:3; Jer 44:29 *p*S ver 1; Ac 7:7

*e*12 The Hebrew is plural.

2:24 *covenant with Abraham.* See Ge 15:17–18; 17:7 and notes. *with Isaac.* See Ge 17:19; 26:24. *with Jacob.* See Ge 35:11–12.

3:1 Like David (2Sa 7:8), Moses was called from tending the flock to be the shepherd of God's people. *Jethro.* See note on 2:16. *Horeb.* Means "desert," "desolation"; either (1) an alternate name for Mount Sinai or (2) another high mountain in the same vicinity in the southeast region of the Sinai peninsula. Tradition identifies Mount Horeb with Ras es-Safsaf ("willow peak"), 6,500 feet high, and Mount Sinai with Jebel Musa ("mountain of Moses"), 7,400 feet high, but both identifications are uncertain.

3:2 *angel of the LORD.* Used interchangeably with "the LORD" and "God" in v. 4 (see note on Ge 16:7). *appeared to him in flames of fire.* God's revelation of himself and his will was often accompanied by fire (see 13:21; 19:18; 1Ki 18:24,38).

3:4 Every true prophet was called by God (see, e.g., 1Sa 3:4; Isa 6:8; Jer 1:4–5; Eze 2:1–8; Hos 1:2; Am 7:15; Jnh 1:1–2; see also note on 7:1–2). *Moses, Moses! . . . Here I am.* See notes on 22:1,11.

3:5 *Take off your sandals.* A practice still followed by Muslims before entering a mosque. *holy.* The ground was not holy by nature but was made so by the divine presence (see, e.g., Ge 2:3). Holiness involves being consecrated to the Lord's service and thus being separated from the commonplace.

3:6 See 2:24 and note. *afraid to look at God.* See notes on Ge 16:13; 32:30. Later, as the Lord's servant, Moses would meet with God on Mount Sinai (19:3) and even ask to see God's glory (33:18).

3:8 *I have come down to rescue.* God may also come down to judge (see Ge 11:5–9; 18:21). *land flowing with milk and honey.* The traditional and proverbial description of the hill country of Canaan—in its original pastoral state (see note on Isa 7:15). *Canaanites . . . Jebusites.* See notes on Ge 10:6, 15–16; 13:7. The list of the Canaanite nations ranges from two names (see Ge 13:7) to five (see Nu 13:29) to six (as here; see also Jdg 3:5) to ten (see Ge 15:19–21) to twelve (see Ge 10:15–18). The classic description includes seven names (see, e.g., Dt 7:1), seven being the number of completeness (see note on Ge 4:17–18).

3:10 *Pharaoh.* Probably Amunhotep II (see Introduction: Chronology).

3:11 Moses' first expression of reluctance (see v. 13; 4:1, 10,13).

3:12 *I will be with you.* See note on Ge 26:3. The Hebrew word translated "I will be" is the same as the one translated "I AM" in v. 14. *sign.* A visible proof or guarantee that what God had promised he would surely fulfill (see notes on 4:8; Ge 15:8).

3:13 Moses' second expression of reluctance. *What is his name?* God had not yet identified himself to Moses by name (see v. 6; cf. Ge 17:1).

ask me, 'What is his name?'[q] Then what shall I tell them?"

[14]God said to Moses, "I AM WHO I AM.[f] This is what you are to say to the Israelites: 'I AM[r] has sent me to you.' "

[15]God also said to Moses, "Say to the Israelites, 'The LORD,[g] the God of your fathers[s]—the God of Abraham, the God of Isaac and the God of Jacob[t]—has sent me to you.' This is my name[u] forever, the name by which I am to be remembered from generation to generation.[v]

[16]"Go, assemble the elders[w] of Israel and say to them, 'The LORD, the God of your fathers—the God of Abraham, Isaac and Jacob[x]— appeared to me and said: I have watched over you and have seen[y] what has been done to you in Egypt. [17]And I have promised to bring you up out of your misery in Egypt[z] into the land of the Canaanites, Hittites, Amorites, Perizzites, Hivites and Jebusites—a land flowing with milk and honey.'[a]

[18]"The elders of Israel will listen[b] to you. Then you and the elders are to go to the king of Egypt and say to him, 'The LORD, the God of the Hebrews,[c] has met[d] with us. Let us take a three-day journey[e] into the desert to offer sacrifices[f] to the LORD our God.' [19]But I know that the king of Egypt will not let you go unless a mighty hand[g] compels him. [20]So I will stretch out my hand[h] and strike the Egyptians with all the wonders[i] that I will perform among them. After that, he will let you go.[j]

[21]"And I will make the Egyptians favorably disposed[k] toward this people, so that when you leave you will not go empty-handed.[l] [22]Every woman is to ask her

neighbor and any woman living in her house for articles of silver[m] and gold[n] and for clothing, which you will put on your sons and daughters. And so you will plunder[o] the Egyptians."[p]

Signs for Moses

4 Moses answered, "What if they do not believe me or listen[q] to me and say, 'The LORD did not appear to you'?"

[2]Then the LORD said to him, "What is that in your hand?"

"A staff,"[r] he replied.

[3]The LORD said, "Throw it on the ground."

Moses threw it on the ground and it became a snake,[s] and he ran from it. [4]Then the LORD said to him, "Reach out your hand and take it by the tail." So Moses reached out and took hold of the snake and it turned back into a staff in his hand. [5]"This," said the LORD, "is so that they may believe[t] that the LORD, the God of their fathers—the God of Abraham, the God of Isaac and the God of Jacob—has appeared to you."

[6]Then the LORD said, "Put your hand inside your cloak." So Moses put his hand

---

3:13 [q]S Ge 32:29
3:14 [r]Ex 6:2-3; Jn 8:58; Heb 13:8; Rev 1:8; 4:8
3:15 [s]Ge 31:42; Da 2:23
[t]S Ge 24:12
[u]Ex 6:3,7; 15:3; 23:21; 34:5-7; Lev 24:11; Dt 28:58; Ps 30:4; 83:18; 96:2; 97:12; 135:13; 145:21; Isa 42:8; Jer 16:21; 33:2; Hos 12:5
[v]Ps 45:17; 72:17; 102:12
3:16 [w]Ex 4:29; 17:5; Lev 4:15; Nu 11:16; 16:25; Dt 5:23; 19:12; Jdg 8:14; Ru 4:2; Pr 31:23; Eze 8:11
[x]S Ge 24:12
[y]Ex 4:31; 2Ki 19:16; 2Ch 6:20; Ps 33:18; 66:7
3:17 [z]S Ge 15:16; 46:4; Ex 6:6
[a]S ver 8
3:18 [b]Ex 4:1,8, 31; 6:12,30
[c]S Ge 14:13
[d]Nu 23:4,16
[e]S Ge 30:36
[f]Ex 4:23; 5:1,3; 6:11; 7:16; 8:20, 27; 9:13; 10:9,26
3:19 [g]Ex 4:21; 6:6; 7:3; 10:1; 11:9; Dt 4:34; 2Ch 6:32
3:20 [h]Ex 6:1,6; 7:4-5; 9:15; 13:3,9,14,16; 15:6,12; Dt 4:34, 37; 5:15; 7:8; 26:8; 2Ki 17:36; 2Ch 6:32; Ps 118:15-16; 136:12; Isa 41:10; 63:12; Jer 21:5; 51:25; Da 9:15
[i]Ex 4:21; 7:3; 11:9,10; 15:11; 34:10; Nu 14:11; Dt 3:24; 4:34;

6:22; Ne 9:10; Ps 71:19; 72:18; 77:14; 78:43; 86:10; 105:27; 106:22; 135:9; 136:4; Jer 32:20; Mic 7:15; Ac 7:36
[j]Ex 11:1; 12:31-33 **3:21** [k]S Ge 39:21
[l]Ex 11:2; 2Ch 30:9; Ne 1:11; Ps 105:37; 106:46; Jer 42:12 **3:22** [m]Job 27:16-17
[n]Ex 11:2; 12:35; Ezr 1:4,6; 7:16; Ps 105:37
[o]S Ge 15:14; Eze 39:10
[p]Eze 29:10 **4:1** [q]S Ex 3:18 **4:2** [r]ver 17,20; Ge 38:18; Ex 7:19; 8:5,16; 14:16,21; 17:5-6,9; Nu 17:2; 20:8; Jos 8:18; Jdg 6:21; 1Sa 14:27; 2Ki 4:29 **4:3**
[s]Ex 7:8-12,15 **4:5** [t]ver 31; S Ex 3:6; 14:31; 19:9

[f]14 Or I WILL BE WHAT I WILL BE   [g]15 The Hebrew for LORD sounds like and may be derived from the Hebrew for I AM in verse 14.

3:14 I AM WHO I AM. The name by which God wished to be known and worshiped in Israel—the name that expressed his character as the dependable and faithful God who desires the full trust of his people (see v. 12, where "I will be" is completed by "with you"; see also 34:5-7). I AM. The shortened form of the name is perhaps found also in Ps 50:21 (see NIV text note there). Jesus applied the phrase to himself; in so doing he claimed to be God and risked being stoned for blasphemy (see Jn 8:58-59).
3:15 The LORD. The Hebrew for this name is Yahweh (often incorrectly spelled "Jehovah"; see note on Dt 28:58). It means "He is" or "He will be" and is the third-person form of the verb translated "I will be" in v. 12 and "I AM" in v. 14. When God speaks of himself he says, "I AM," and when we speak of him we say, "He is."
3:16 elders. The Hebrew for this word means lit. "bearded ones," perhaps reflecting the age, wisdom, experience and influence necessary for a man specially to function as an elder. As heads of local families and tribes, "elders" had a recognized position also among the Babylonians, Hittites, Egyptians (see Ge 50:7), Moabites and Midianites (see Nu 22:7). Their duties included judicial arbitration and sentenc-

ing (see Dt 22:13-19) as well as military leadership (see Jos 8:10) and counsel (see 1Sa 4:3).
3:18 Hebrews. See note on Ge 14:13. three-day journey. Probably a conventional expression for a short trip rather than a journey of exactly three days. desert. God had met with Moses there (see vv. 1-2) and would meet with him there again (see v. 12).
3:20 wonders. A prediction of the plagues that God would send against Egypt (see 7:14-12:30).
3:21-22 See 11:2-3; 12:35-36.
3:21 when you leave you will not go empty-handed. God had promised Abraham that after Israel had served for 400 years they would "come out with great possessions" (Ge 15:14; see Ps 105:37). Israel herself was to live by the same principle of providing gifts to a released slave (see Dt 15:12-15).
4:1 Moses' third expression of reluctance (in spite of God's assurance in 3:18).
4:2 staff. Probably a shepherd's crook.
4:3 snake. See 7:9-10 and note. Throughout much of Egypt's history the pharaoh wore a cobra made of metal on the front of his headdress as a symbol of his sovereignty.

into his cloak, and when he took it out, it was leprous,[h] like snow.[u]

[7]"Now put it back into your cloak," he said. So Moses put his hand back into his cloak, and when he took it out, it was restored,[v] like the rest of his flesh.

[8]Then the LORD said, "If they do not believe[w] you or pay attention to the first miraculous sign,[x] they may believe the second. [9]But if they do not believe these two signs or listen to you, take some water from the Nile and pour it on the dry ground. The water you take from the river will become blood[y] on the ground."

[10]Moses said to the LORD, "O Lord, I have never been eloquent, neither in the past nor since you have spoken to your servant. I am slow of speech and tongue."[z]

[11]The LORD said to him, "Who gave man his mouth? Who makes him deaf or mute?[a] Who gives him sight or makes him blind?[b] Is it not I, the LORD? [12]Now go;[c] I will help you speak and will teach you what to say."[d]

[13]But Moses said, "O Lord, please send someone else to do it."[e]

[14]Then the LORD's anger burned[f] against Moses and he said, "What about your brother, Aaron the Levite? I know he can speak well. He is already on his way to meet[g] you, and his heart will be glad when he sees you. [15]You shall speak to him and put words in his mouth;[h] I will help both of you speak and will teach you what to do. [16]He will speak to the people for you, and it will be as if he were your mouth[i] and as if you were God to him.[j]

[17]But take this staff[k] in your hand[l] so you can perform miraculous signs[m] with it."

Moses Returns to Egypt

[18]Then Moses went back to Jethro his father-in-law and said to him, "Let me go back to my own people in Egypt to see if any of them are still alive."

Jethro said, "Go, and I wish you well."

[19]Now the LORD had said to Moses in Midian, "Go back to Egypt, for all the men who wanted to kill[n] you are dead.[o]" [20]So Moses took his wife and sons,[p] put them on a donkey and started back to Egypt. And he took the staff[q] of God in his hand.

[21]The LORD said to Moses, "When you return to Egypt, see that you perform before Pharaoh all the wonders[r] I have given you the power to do. But I will harden his heart[s] so that he will not let the people go.[t] [22]Then say to Pharaoh, 'This is what the LORD says: Israel is my firstborn son,[u] [23]and I told you, "Let my son go,[v] so he may worship[w] me." But you refused to let him go; so I will kill your firstborn son.' "[x]

[24]At a lodging place on the way, the LORD met Moses,[i] and was about to kill[y] him. [25]But Zipporah[z] took a flint knife, cut off her son's foreskin[a] and touched

Cross references

4:6 [u]Lev 13:2,11; Nu 12:10; Dt 24:9; 2Ki 5:1,27; 2Ch 26:21
4:7 [v]2Ki 5:14; Mt 8:3; Lk 17:12-14
4:8 [w]S Ex 3:18 [x]ver 30; Jdg 6:17; 1Ki 13:3; Isa 7:14; Jer 44:29
4:9 [y]Ex 7:17-21
4:10 [z]S Ex 3:11
4:11 [a]Lk 1:20,64 [b]Ps 94:9; 146:8; Mt 11:5; Jn 10:21
4:12 [c]S Ex 3:10 [d]ver 15-16; Nu 23:5; Dt 18:15,18; Isa 50:4; 51:16; Jer 1:9; Mt 10:19-20; Mk 13:11; S Lk 12:12
4:13 [e]Jnh 1:1-3
4:14 [f]Nu 11:1, 10,33; 12:9; 16:15; 22:22; 24:10; 32:13; Dt 7:25; Jos 7:1; Job 17:8 [g]ver 27; 1Sa 10:2-5
4:15 [h]ver 30; Nu 23:5,12,16; Dt 18:18; Jos 1:8; Isa 51:16; 59:21; Jer 1:9; 31:33
4:16 [i]Ex 7:1-2; Jer 15:19; 36:6 [j]Nu 33:1; Ps 77:20; 105:26; Mic 6:4
4:17 [k]S ver 2 [l]ver 20; Ex 17:9 [m]Ex 7:9-21; 8:5, 16; 9:22; 10:12-15,21-23; 14:15-18,26; Nu 14:11; Dt 4:34; Ps 74:9; 78:43; 105:27
4:19 [n]Ex 2:15 [o]Ex 2:23; Mt 2:20
4:20 [p]Ex 2:22; 18:3; Ac 7:29 [q]S ver 2
4:21 [r]S Ex 3:19,20 [s]Ex 7:3,13; 8:15; 9:12,35; 10:1,20,27; 11:10; 14:4,8; Dt 2:30; Jos 11:20; 1Sa 6:6; Ps 105:25; Isa 6:10; 63:17; Jn 12:40; Ro 9:18 [t]Ex 8:32; 9:17
4:22 [u]S Ge 10:15; Dt 32:6; Isa 9:6; 63:16; 64:8; Jer 3:19; 31:9; Hos 11:1; Mal 2:10; Ro 9:4; 2Co 6:18 [v]Ex 5:1; 7:16
4:23 [w]S Ex 3:18 [x]Ge 49:3; Ex 11:5; 12:12,29; Nu 8:17; 33:4; Ps 78:51; 105:36; 135:8; 136:10
4:24 [y]Nu 22:22
4:25 [z]S Ex 2:21 [a]Ge 17:14; Jos 5:2,3

[h]6 The Hebrew word was used for various diseases affecting the skin—not necessarily leprosy.   [i]24 Or Moses' son; Hebrew him

---

4:8 *miraculous sign.* A supernatural event or phenomenon designed to demonstrate authority, provide assurance (see Jos 2:12-13), bear testimony (see Isa 19:19-20), give warning (see Nu 17:10) or encourage faith. See note on 3:12.
4:10 Moses' fourth expression of reluctance. *I am slow of speech and tongue.* Not in the sense of a speech impediment (see Ac 7:22). He complained, instead, of not being eloquent or quick-witted enough to respond to the pharaoh (see 6:12). Cf. the description of Paul in 2Co 10:10.
4:13 Moses' fifth and final expression of reluctance.
4:14 *the LORD's anger burned against Moses.* Although the Lord is "slow to anger" (34:6), he does not withhold his anger or punishment from his disobedient children forever (see 34:7). *Levite.* Under Aaron's leadership Israel's priesthood would come from the tribe of Levi.
4:15-16 See note on 7:1-2.
4:19 *all the men . . . are dead.* Including Thutmose III (see 2:15,23; see also Introduction: Chronology).
4:20 *sons.* Gershom (see 2:22) and Eliezer. The latter, though unmentioned by name until 18:4, had already been born.
4:21 *wonders.* See note on 3:20. *I will harden his heart.* Nine times in Exodus the hardening of the pharaoh's heart is ascribed to God (here; 7:3; 9:12; 10:1,20,27; 11:10; 14:4, 8; see Ro 9:17-18 and notes); another nine times the phar-

aoh is said to have hardened his own heart (7:13-14,22; 8:15,19,32; 9:7,34-35). The pharaoh alone was the agent of the hardening in each of the first five plagues. Not until the sixth plague did God confirm the pharaoh's willful action (see 9:12), as he had told Moses he would do (see similarly Ro 1:24-28).
4:22 *firstborn son.* A figure of speech indicating Israel's special relationship with God (see Jer 31:9; Hos 11:1). *son.* Used collectively of the Israelites also in Hos 11:1.
4:23 *kill your firstborn son.* Anticipates the tenth plague (see 11:5; 12:12).
4:24 *lodging place.* Perhaps near water, where travelers could spend the night. *The LORD . . . was about to kill him.* Evidently because Moses had failed to circumcise his son (see Ge 17:9-14).
4:25 *Zipporah . . . cut off her son's foreskin.* Sensing that divine displeasure had threatened Moses' life, she quickly performed the circumcision on their young son. *flint knife.* Continued to be used for circumcision long after metal was introduced, probably because flint knives were sharper than the metal instruments available and thus more efficient for the surgical procedure (see Jos 5:2 and note). *feet.* Probably a euphemism for "genitals," as in Dt 28:57 ("womb," lit. "feet").

⌊Moses'⌋ feet with it.[j] "Surely you are a
bridegroom of blood to me," she said. 26So
the LORD let him alone. (At that time she
said "bridegroom of blood," referring to
circumcision.)

27The LORD said to Aaron, "Go into the
desert to meet Moses." So he met Moses
at the mountain[b] of God and kissed[c] him.
28Then Moses told Aaron everything the
LORD had sent him to say,[d] and also about
all the miraculous signs he had commanded him to perform.

29Moses and Aaron brought together all
the elders[e] of the Israelites, 30and Aaron
told them everything the LORD had said to
Moses. He also performed the signs[f] before the people, 31and they believed.[g] And
when they heard that the LORD was concerned[h] about them and had seen their
misery,[i] they bowed down and worshiped.[j]

Bricks Without Straw

5 Afterward Moses and Aaron went to
Pharaoh and said, "This is what the
LORD, the God of Israel, says: 'Let my
people go,[k] so that they may hold a festival[l] to me in the desert.' "

2Pharaoh said, "Who is the LORD,[m] that
I should obey him and let Israel go? I do
not know the LORD and I will not let Israel
go."[n]

3Then they said, "The God of the Hebrews has met with us. Now let us take a
three-day journey[o] into the desert to offer
sacrifices to the LORD our God, or he may
strike us with plagues[p] or with the
sword."

4But the king of Egypt said, "Moses and
Aaron, why are you taking the people
away from their labor?[q] Get back to your
work!" 5Then Pharaoh said, "Look, the
people of the land are now numerous,[r]
and you are stopping them from working."

6That same day Pharaoh gave this order
to the slave drivers[s] and foremen in
charge of the people: 7"You are no longer
to supply the people with straw for making
bricks;[t] let them go and gather their own
straw. 8But require them to make the same
number of bricks as before; don't reduce
the quota.[u] They are lazy;[v] that is why
they are crying out, 'Let us go and sacrifice
to our God.'[w] 9Make the work harder for
the men so that they keep working and pay
no attention to lies."

10Then the slave drivers[x] and the foremen went out and said to the people,
"This is what Pharaoh says: 'I will not give
you any more straw. 11Go and get your
own straw wherever you can find it, but
your work will not be reduced[y] at all.' "
12So the people scattered all over Egypt to
gather stubble to use for straw. 13The slave
drivers kept pressing them, saying, "Complete the work required of you for each
day, just as when you had straw." 14The
Israelite foremen appointed by Pharaoh's
slave drivers were beaten[z] and were
asked, "Why didn't you meet your quota
of bricks yesterday or today, as before?"

15Then the Israelite foremen went and
appealed to Pharaoh: "Why have you
treated your servants this way? 16Your servants are given no straw, yet we are told,
'Make bricks!' Your servants are being
beaten, but the fault is with your own
people."

17Pharaoh said, "Lazy, that's what you
are—lazy![a] That is why you keep saying,
'Let us go and sacrifice to the LORD.'
18Now get to work.[b] You will not be given
any straw, yet you must produce your full
quota of bricks."

19The Israelite foremen realized they
were in trouble when they were told,
"You are not to reduce the number of
bricks required of you for each day."
20When they left Pharaoh, they found
Moses and Aaron waiting to meet them,
21and they said, "May the LORD look upon
you and judge[c] you! You have made us a
stench[d] to Pharaoh and his officials and
have put a sword[e] in their hand to kill
us."[f]

God Promises Deliverance

22Moses returned to the LORD and said,
"O Lord, why have you brought trouble

j25 Or *and drew near ⌊Moses'⌋ feet*

4:27 [b]S Ex 3:1 [c]S Ge 27:27; S 29:13 **4:28** [d]ver 16 **4:29** [e]S Ex 3:16 **4:30** [f]S ver 8 **4:31** [g]S Ex 3:18 [h]S Ex 2:25 [i]S Ge 16:11 [j]S Ge 24:26 **5:1** [k]S Ex 4:23 [l]S Ex 3:18 **5:2** [m]Jdg 2:10; Job 21:15; Mal 3:14 [n]Ex 3:19 **5:3** [o]S Ge 30:36 [p]Lev 26:25; Nu 14:12; Dt 28:21; 2Sa 24:13 **5:4** [q]S Ex 1:11; 6:6-7 **5:5** [r]S Ge 12:2 **5:6** [s]S Ge 15:13 **5:7** [t]S Ge 11:3
5:8 [u]ver 14,18 [v]ver 17 [w]Ex 10:11 **5:10** [x]ver 13; Ex 1:11 **5:11** [y]ver 19 **5:14** [z]ver 16; Isa 10:24 **5:17** [a]ver 8 **5:18** [b]S Ge 15:13 **5:21** [c]S Ge 16:5 [d]S Ge 34:30 [e]Ex 16:3; Nu 14:3; 20:3 [f]S Ex 1:13; S 14:11

4:26 *bridegroom of blood.* Circumcision may have been repulsive to Zipporah—though it was practiced for various reasons among many peoples of the ancient Near East.
4:30 *Aaron told them everything the LORD had said to Moses.* See note on 7:1–2.
5:1 *Pharaoh.* See note on 3:10.
5:3 See 3:18 and note. The reason for sacrificing where the Egyptians could not see them is given in 8:26 (see note on Ge 43:32).
5:6 *slave drivers.* Probably the same as the Egyptian "slave masters" in 1:11 (see note there). *foremen.* Israelite supervisors whose method of appointment and whose functions are indicated in vv. 14–16.
5:7 *straw.* Chopped and mixed with the clay as binder to make the bricks stronger.
5:9 *lies.* The pharaoh labels all hopes of a quick release for Israel as presumptuous and false.
5:21 *May the LORD look upon you and judge you!* See Ge 16:5; 31:49 and notes.

upon this people?g Is this why you sent me? 23Ever since I went to Pharaoh to speak in your name, he has brought trouble upon this people, and you have not rescuedh your people at all."

6 Then the LORD said to Moses, "Now you will see what I will do to Pharaoh: Because of my mighty handi he will let them go;j because of my mighty hand he will drive them out of his country."k

2God also said to Moses, "I am the LORD.l 3I appeared to Abraham, to Isaac and to Jacob as God Almighty,km but by my namen the LORDlo I did not make myself known to them.m 4I also established my covenantp with them to give them the landq of Canaan, where they lived as aliens.r 5Moreover, I have heard the groanings of the Israelites, whom the Egyptians are enslaving, and I have remembered my covenant.t

6"Therefore, say to the Israelites: 'I am the LORD, and I will bring you out from under the yoke of the Egyptians.u I will free you from being slaves to them, and I will redeemv you with an outstretched armw and with mighty acts of judgment.x 7I will take you as my own people, and I will be your God.y Then you will knowz that I am the LORD your God, who brought you out from under the yoke of the Egyptians. 8And I will bring you to the landa I sworeb with uplifted handc to give to Abraham, to Isaac and to Jacob.d I will give it to you as a possession. I am the LORD.'"e

9Moses reported this to the Israelites, but they did not listen to him because of their discouragement and cruel bondage.f

10Then the LORD said to Moses, 11"Go, tellg Pharaoh king of Egypt to let the Israelites go out of his country."h

12But Moses said to the LORD, "If the Israelites will not listeni to me, why would Pharaoh listen to me, since I speak with faltering lipsn?"j

Family Record of Moses and Aaron

13Now the LORD spoke to Moses and Aaron about the Israelites and Pharaoh king of Egypt, and he commanded them to bring the Israelites out of Egypt.k

14These were the heads of their families°:l

The sons of Reubenm the firstborn son of Israel were Hanoch and Pallu, Hezron and Carmi. These were the clans of Reuben.

15The sons of Simeonn were Jemuel, Jamin, Ohad, Jakin, Zohar and Shaul the son of a Canaanite woman. These were the clans of Simeon.

16These were the names of the sons of Levi° according to their records: Gershon,p Kohath and Merari.q Levi lived 137 years.

Cross references

5:22 gNu 11:11; Dt 1:12; Jos 7:7 5:23 hJer 4:10; 20:7; Eze 14:9 6:1 iS Ex 3:20; S Dt 5:15 jS Ex 3:20 kEx 11:1; 12:31, 33,39 6:2 lver 6,7,8,29; Ex 3:14,15; 7:5, 17; 8:22; 10:2; 12:12; 14:4,18; 16:12; Lev 11:44; 18:21; 20:7; Isa 25:3; 41:20; 43:11; 49:23; 60:16; Eze 13:9; 25:17; 36:38; 37:6,13; Joel 2:27 6:3 mS Ge 17:1 nS Ex 3:15; 2Sa 7:26; Ps 48:1; 61:5; 68:4; 83:18; 99:3; Isa 52:6 oEx 3:14; Jn 8:58 6:4 pS Ge 6:18; S 15:18 qS Ge 12:7; Ac 7:5; Ro 4:13; Gal 3:16; Heb 11:8-10 rS Ge 17:8 6:5 sS Ex 2:23; Ac 7:34 tS Ge 9:15 6:6 uver 7; Ex 3:8; 12:17,51; 16:1,6; 18:1; 19:1; 20:2; 29:46; Lev 22:33; 26:13; Dt 6:12; Ps 81:10; 136:11; Jer 2:6; Hos 13:4; Am 2:10; Mic 6:4 vEx 15:13; Dt 7:8; 9:26; 1Ch 17:21; Job 19:25; Ps 19:14; 34:22; 74:2; 77:15; 107:2; Isa 29:22; 35:9; 43:1; 44:23; 48:20; Jer 15:21; 31:11; 50:34 wS Ex 3:19,20; S Jer 32:21; Ac 13:17 xEx 3:20; Ps 9:16; 105:27 6:7 yS Ge 17:7; S Ex 34:9; Eze 11:19-20; Ro 9:4 zS ver 2; 1Ki 20:13,28; Isa 43:10; 48:7; Eze 39:6; Joel 3:17 6:8 aS Ge 12:7; Ex 3:8 bJer 11:5; Eze 20:6 cS Ge 14:22; Rev 10:5-6 dPs 136:21-22 eLev 18:21 6:9 fS Ge 34:30; Ex 2:23 6:11 gver 29 hS Ex 3:18 6:12 iS Ex 3:18 jEx 4:10. 6:13 kS Ex 3:10 6:14 lEx 13:3; Nu 1:1; 26:4 mS Ge 29:32 6:15 nS Ge 29:33 6:16 oS Ge 29:34 pS Ge 46:11 qNu 3:17; Jos 21:7; 1Ch 6:1,16

k3 Hebrew El-Shaddai l3 See note at Exodus 3:15. m3 Or Almighty, and by my name the LORD did I not let myself be known to them? n12 Hebrew I am uncircumcised of lips; also in verse 30 °14 The Hebrew for families here and in verse 25 refers to units larger than clans.

Footnotes

6:1 Now. Without further delay, God will act.
6:2 I am the LORD. Appears four times in this passage: (1) to introduce the message; (2) to confirm God's promise of redemption (v. 6) based on the evidence of vv. 2–5; (3) to underscore God's intention to adopt Israel (v. 7); (4) to confirm his promise of the land and to conclude the message (v. 8).
6:3 God Almighty. See note on Ge 17:1. by my name the LORD I did not make myself known to them. See notes on 3:14–15. This does not necessarily mean that the patriarchs were totally ignorant of the name Yahweh ("the LORD"), but it indicates that they did not understand its full implications as the name of the One who would redeem his people (see notes on v. 6; Ge 2:4). That fact could be comprehended only by the Israelites who were to experience the exodus, and by their descendants. make myself known. This experiential sense of the verb "to know" is intended also in its repeated use throughout the account of the plagues (see v. 7; 7:17; 8:10,22; 9:14,29; 10:2; 11:7) and in connection with the exodus itself (see 14:4,18; 16:6,8,12; 18:11).
6:5 remembered. See note on Ge 8:1.
6:6 I will bring you out . . . will free you . . . will redeem you. The verbs stress the true significance of the name Yah-

weh—"the LORD"—who is the Redeemer of his people (see note on v. 3). mighty acts of judgment. See 7:4. The Lord's acts include redemption (for Israel) and judgment (against Egypt).
6:7–8 brought you out from . . . will bring you to. Redemption means not only release from slavery and suffering but also deliverance to freedom and joy.
6:7 I will take you as my own people, and I will be your God. Words that anticipate the covenant at Mount Sinai (see 19:5–6; see also Jer 31:33).
6:8 See Ge 22:15–17. swore with uplifted hand. See note on Ge 14:22.
6:12 I speak with faltering lips. See note on 4:10.
6:13 Moses and Aaron. The genealogy contained in vv. 14–25 gives details concerning the background of Moses and Aaron. Only the first three of Jacob's 12 sons (Reuben, Simeon and Levi) are listed since Moses and Aaron were from the third tribe.
6:16 Merari. The name is of Egyptian origin, as are those of Putiel and Phinehas (see v. 25) and of Moses himself (see note on 2:10). Levi lived 137 years. See vv. 18,20. In the OT, attention is usually called to a person's life span only when it exceeds 100 years.

¹⁷The sons of Gershon, by clans, were Libni and Shimei. *r*

¹⁸The sons of Kohath *s* were Amram, Izhar, Hebron and Uzziel. *t* Kohath lived 133 years.

¹⁹The sons of Merari were Mahli and Mushi. *u*

These were the clans of Levi according to their records.

²⁰Amram *v* married his father's sister Jochebed, who bore him Aaron and Moses. *w* Amram lived 137 years.

²¹The sons of Izhar *x* were Korah, Nepheg and Zicri.

²²The sons of Uzziel were Mishael, Elzaphan *y* and Sithri.

²³Aaron married Elisheba, daughter of Amminadab *z* and sister of Nahshon, *a* and she bore him Nadab and Abihu, *b* Eleazar *c* and Ithamar. *d*

²⁴The sons of Korah *e* were Assir, Elkanah and Abiasaph. These were the Korahite clans.

²⁵Eleazar son of Aaron married one of the daughters of Putiel, and she bore him Phinehas. *f*

These were the heads of the Levite families, clan by clan.

²⁶It was this same Aaron and Moses to whom the LORD said, "Bring the Israelites out of Egypt *g* by their divisions." *h* ²⁷They were the ones who spoke to Pharaoh *i* king of Egypt about bringing the Israelites out of Egypt. It was the same Moses and Aaron. *j*

Aaron to Speak for Moses

²⁸Now when the LORD spoke to Moses in Egypt, ²⁹he said to him, "I am the LORD. *k* Tell Pharaoh king of Egypt everything I tell you."

³⁰But Moses said to the LORD, "Since I speak with faltering lips, *l* why would Pharaoh listen to me?"

7 Then the LORD said to Moses, "See, I have made you like God *m* to Pharaoh, and your brother Aaron will be your prophet. *n* ²You are to say everything I command you, and your brother Aaron is to tell Pharaoh to let the Israelites go out of his country. ³But I will harden Pharaoh's heart, *o* and though I multiply my miraculous signs and wonders *p* in Egypt, ⁴he will not listen *q* to you. Then I will lay my hand on Egypt and with mighty acts of judgment *r* I will bring out my divisions, *s* my people the Israelites. ⁵And the Egyptians will know that I am the LORD *t* when I stretch out my hand *u* against Egypt and bring the Israelites out of it."

⁶Moses and Aaron did just as the LORD commanded *v* them. ⁷Moses was eighty years old *w* and Aaron eighty-three when they spoke to Pharaoh.

Aaron's Staff Becomes a Snake

⁸The LORD said to Moses and Aaron, ⁹"When Pharaoh says to you, 'Perform a miracle, *x* then say to Aaron, 'Take your staff and throw it down before Pharaoh,' and it will become a snake." *y*

¹⁰So Moses and Aaron went to Pharaoh and did just as the LORD commanded. Aaron threw his staff down in front of Pharaoh and his officials, and it became a snake. ¹¹Pharaoh then summoned wise men and sorcerers, *z* and the Egyptian magicians *a* also did the same things by their secret arts: *b* ¹²Each one threw down

6:17 *r*Nu 3:18; 1Ch 6:17
6:18 *s*Nu 3:27; 1Ch 23:12
*t*Nu 3:19; 1Ch 6:2,18
6:19 *u*Nu 3:20, 33; 1Ch 6:19; 23:21
6:20 *v*1Ch 23:13 *w*Ex 2:1-2; Nu 26:59
6:21 *x*1Ch 6:38
6:22 *y*Lev 10:4; Nu 3:30; 1Ch 15:8; 2Ch 29:13
6:23 *z*Ru 4:19, 20; 1Ch 2:10 *a*Nu 1:7; 2:3; Mt 1:4 *b*Ex 24:1; 28:1; Lev 10:1; *c*Lev 10:6; Nu 3:2,32; 16:37, 39; Dt 10:6; Jos 14:1 *d*Ex 28:1; Lev 10:12,16; Nu 3:2; 4:28; 26:60; 1Ch 6:3; 24:1
6:24 *e*ver 21; Nu 16:1; 1Ch 6:22,37
6:25 *f*Nu 25:7, 11; 31:6; Jos 24:33; Ps 106:30
6:26 *g*S Ex 3:10 *h*Ex 7:4; 12:17, 41,51
6:27 *i*Ex 5:1 *j*Nu 3:1; Ps 77:20
6:29 *k*S ver 2

6:30 *l*S Ex 3:11
7:1 *m*S Ex 4:16 *n*Ex 4:15; Ac 14:12
7:3 *o*S Ex 4:21; Ro 9:18 *p*S Ex 3:20; S 10:1; Ac 7:36
7:4 *q*ver 13,16, 22; Ex 8:15,19; 9:12; 11:9 *r*S Ex 3:20; Ac 7:36 *s*S Ex 6:26
7:5 *t*S Ex 6:2 *u*Ex 3:20; Ps 138:7; Eze 6:14; 25:13
7:6 *v*ver 2,10,20; Ge 6:22
7:7 *w*Dt 31:2; 34:7; Ac 7:23,30

7:9 *x*Dt 6:22; 2Ki 19:29; Ps 78:43; 86:17; 105:27; 135:9; Isa 7:11; 37:30; 38:7-8; 55:13; S Jn 2:11 *y*Ex 4:2-5 **7:11** *z*Ex 22:18; Dt 18:10; 1Sa 6:2; 2Ki 21:6; Isa 2:6; 47:12; Jer 27:9; Mal 3:5 *a*S Ge 41:8; 2Ti 3:8 *b*ver 22; Ex 8:7,18; S Mt 24:24

6:20 *Amram . . . Aaron and Moses.* There is some reason to believe that Amram and Jochebed were not the immediate parents but the ancestors of Aaron and Moses. Kohath, Amram's father (see v. 18), was born before Jacob's (Israel's) descent into Egypt (see Ge 46:11), where the Israelites then stayed 430 years (see 12:40–41). Since Moses was 80 years old at the time of the exodus (see 7:7), he must have been born at least 350 years after Kohath, who consequently could not have been Moses' grandfather (see v. 18). Therefore Amram must not have been Moses' father, and the Hebrew verb for "bore" must have the same meaning it sometimes has in Ge 10 (see NIV text note on Ge 10:8, where it is translated "was the father of"). *Jochebed.* The name appears to mean "The LORD is glory." If so, it shows that the name Yahweh (here abbreviated as *Jo-*) was known before Moses was born (see note on v. 3). *Aaron and Moses.* Aaron, as the firstborn (see 7:7), is listed first in the official genealogy.

6:30 *faltering lips.* See v. 12 and note on 4:10.
7:1–2 As God transmits his word through his prophets to

his people, so Moses will transmit God's message through Aaron to the pharaoh. The prophet's task was to speak God's word on God's behalf. He was God's "mouth" (4:15–16).
7:3 *harden.* See note on 4:21. *miraculous signs.* See notes on 3:12; 4:8.
7:4 *mighty acts of judgment.* See note on 6:6.
7:7 *Moses was eighty years old.* See notes on 2:11,15.
7:9–10 *snake.* The Hebrew for this word is different from that used in 4:3 (see Ps 74:13, "monster"). A related word (also translated "monster") is used in Eze 29:3 as a designation for Egypt and her king.
7:11 *wise men and . . . magicians.* See note on Ge 41:8. According to tradition, two of the magicians who opposed Moses were named Jannes and Jambres (see 2Ti 3:8; the first is also mentioned in the pre-Christian Dead Sea Scrolls). *did the same things by their secret arts.* Either through sleight of hand or by means of demonic power.
7:12 *Aaron's staff swallowed up their staffs.* Demonstrating God's mastery over the pharaoh and the gods of Egypt.

his staff and it became a snake. But Aaron's staff swallowed up their staffs. 13Yet Pharaoh's heart[c] became hard and he would not listen[d] to them, just as the LORD had said.

The Plague of Blood

14Then the LORD said to Moses, "Pharaoh's heart is unyielding;[e] he refuses to let the people go. 15Go to Pharaoh in the morning as he goes out to the water.[f] Wait on the bank of the Nile[g] to meet him, and take in your hand the staff that was changed into a snake. 16Then say to him, 'The LORD, the God of the Hebrews, has sent me to say to you: Let my people go, so that they may worship[h] me in the desert. But until now you have not listened.[i] 17This is what the LORD says: By this you will know that I am the LORD:[j] With the staff that is in my hand I will strike the water of the Nile, and it will be changed into blood.[k] 18The fish in the Nile will die, and the river will stink;[l] the Egyptians will not be able to drink its water.' "[m]

19The LORD said to Moses, "Tell Aaron, 'Take your staff[n] and stretch out your hand[o] over the waters of Egypt—over the streams and canals, over the ponds and all the reservoirs'—and they will turn to blood. Blood will be everywhere in Egypt, even in the wooden buckets and stone jars."

20Moses and Aaron did just as the LORD had commanded.[p] He raised his staff in the presence of Pharaoh and his officials and struck the water of the Nile,[q] and all the water was changed into blood.[r] 21The fish in the Nile died, and the river smelled so bad that the Egyptians could not drink its water. Blood was everywhere in Egypt.

22But the Egyptian magicians[s] did the same things by their secret arts,[t] and Pharaoh's heart[u] became hard; he would not listen to Moses and Aaron, just as the LORD had said. 23Instead, he turned and went into his palace, and did not take even this to heart. 24And all the Egyptians dug along the Nile to get drinking water,[v] because they could not drink the water of the river.

The Plague of Frogs

25Seven days passed after the LORD struck the Nile. **8** 1Then the LORD said to Moses, "Go to Pharaoh and say to him, 'This is what the LORD says: Let my people go, so that they may worship[w] me. 2If you refuse to let them go, I will plague your whole country with frogs.[x] 3The Nile will teem with frogs. They will come up into your palace and your bedroom and onto your bed, into the houses of your officials and on your people,[y] and into your ovens and kneading troughs.[z] 4The frogs will go up on you and your people and all your officials.' "

5Then the LORD said to Moses, "Tell Aaron, 'Stretch out your hand with your staff[a] over the streams and canals and ponds, and make frogs[b] come up on the land of Egypt.' "

6So Aaron stretched out his hand over the waters of Egypt, and the frogs[c] came up and covered the land. 7But the magicians did the same things by their secret arts;[d] they also made frogs come up on the land of Egypt.

8Pharaoh summoned Moses and Aaron and said, "Pray[e] to the LORD to take the frogs away from me and my people, and I will let your people go to offer sacrifices[f] to the LORD."

Cross references (center column):

7:13 cS Ex 4:21
dS ver 4
7:14 ever 22;
Ex 8:15,32; 9:7;
10:1,20,27
7:15 fEx 8:20
gS Ge 41:1
7:16 hS Ex 3:18
iS ver 4
7:17 jS Ex 6:2;
14:25 kver 19-21;
Ex 4:9; Rev 11:6;
16:4
7:18 lIsa 19:6
mver 21,24;
Ps 78:44
7:19 nS Ex 4:2
oEx 14:21;
2Ki 5:11
7:20 pS ver 6
qEx 17:5
rPs 78:44;
105:29; 114:3;
Hab 3:8

7:22 sS Ge 41:8
tS ver 11;
S Mt 24:24 uver
13,S 14; Ex 8:19;
Ps 105:28
7:24 vS ver 18
8:1 wEx 3:12;
4:23; 5:1; 9:1
8:2 xPs 78:45;
105:30;
Rev 16:13
8:3 yEx 10:6
zEx 12:34
8:5 aS Ex 4:2;
7:9-20; 9:23;
10:13,21-22;
14:27 bS Ex 4:17
8:6 cPs 78:45;
105:30
8:7 dS Ex 7:11;
S Mt 24:24
8:8 ever 28;
Ex 9:28; 10:17;
Nu 21:7;
1Sa 12:19;
1Ki 13:6;
Jer 42:2; Ac 8:24
fver 25; Ex 10:8,
24; 12:31

7:13 heart became hard. See note on 4:21.

7:14–10:29 The first nine plagues can be divided into three groups of three plagues each—7:14–8:19; 8:20–9:12; 9:13–10:29—with the first plague in each group (the first, the fourth and the seventh) introduced by a warning delivered to the pharaoh in the morning as he went out to the Nile (see v. 15; 8:20; 9:13).

7:17 my. Moses'. the water of the Nile . . . will be changed into blood. See Ps 78:44; 105:29. The first nine plagues may have been a series of miraculous intensifications of natural events taking place in less than a year, and coming at God's bidding and timing. If so, the first plague resulted from the flooding of the Nile in late summer and early fall as large quantities of red sediment were washed down from Ethiopia, causing the water to become as red as blood (see the similar incident in 2Ki 3:22).

7:19 your staff. Aaron was acting on Moses' behalf (see v. 17). in the wooden buckets and stone jars. Lit. "in/on the wooden things and in/on the stone things." Some think that, since the Egyptians believed that their gods inhabited idols

and images made of wood, clay and stone (see Dt 29:16–17), the plague may have been intended as a rebuke to their religion (see 12:12).

7:20 Nile. Egypt's dependence on the life-sustaining waters of the Nile led to its deification as the god Hopi, for whom hymns of adoration were composed. See note on v. 19.

7:24 dug along the Nile to get drinking water. Filtered through sandy soil near the river bank, the polluted water would become safe for drinking.

7:25 Seven days passed. The plagues did not follow each other in rapid succession.

8:2 I will plague your whole country with frogs. The frog (or toad) was deified in the goddess Heqt, who assisted women in childbirth.

8:3 come up. The frogs abandoned the Nile and swarmed over the land, perhaps because the unusually high concentration of bacteria-laden algae had by now proved fatal to most of the fish, thus polluting the river.

9Moses said to Pharaoh, "I leave to you the honor of setting the time*g* for me to pray for you and your officials and your people that you and your houses may be rid of the frogs, except for those that remain in the Nile."

10"Tomorrow," Pharaoh said.

Moses replied, "It will be as you say, so that you may know there is no one like the LORD our God. *h* 11The frogs will leave you and your houses, your officials and your people; they will remain only in the Nile."

12After Moses and Aaron left Pharaoh, Moses cried out to the LORD about the frogs he had brought on Pharaoh. 13And the LORD did what Moses asked.*i* The frogs died in the houses, in the courtyards and in the fields. 14They were piled into heaps, and the land reeked of them. 15But when Pharaoh saw that there was relief,*j* he hardened his heart*k* and would not listen to Moses and Aaron, just as the LORD had said.

The Plague of Gnats

16Then the LORD said to Moses, "Tell Aaron, 'Stretch out your staff*l* and strike the dust of the ground,' and throughout the land of Egypt the dust will become gnats." 17They did this, and when Aaron stretched out his hand with the staff and struck the dust of the ground, gnats*m* came upon men and animals. All the dust throughout the land of Egypt became gnats. 18But when the magicians*n* tried to produce gnats by their secret arts,*o* they could not. And the gnats were on men and animals.

19The magicians said to Pharaoh, "This is the finger*p* of God." But Pharaoh's heart*q* was hard and he would not listen,*r* just as the LORD had said.

The Plague of Flies

20Then the LORD said to Moses, "Get up early in the morning*s* and confront Pharaoh as he goes to the water and say to him, 'This is what the LORD says: Let my people go, so that they may worship*t* me. 21If you do not let my people go, I will send swarms of flies on you and your officials, on your people and into your houses. The houses of the Egyptians will be full of flies, and even the ground where they are.

22"'But on that day I will deal differently with the land of Goshen,*u* where my people live;*v* no swarms of flies will be there, so that you will know*w* that I, the LORD, am in this land. 23I will make a distinction*p* between my people and your people.*x* This miraculous sign will occur tomorrow.'"

24And the LORD did this. Dense swarms of flies poured into Pharaoh's palace and into the houses of his officials, and throughout Egypt the land was ruined by the flies.*y*

25Then Pharaoh summoned*z* Moses and Aaron and said, "Go, sacrifice to your God here in the land."

26But Moses said, "That would not be right. The sacrifices we offer the LORD our God would be detestable to the Egyptians.*a* And if we offer sacrifices that are detestable in their eyes, will they not stone us? 27We must take a three-day journey*b* into the desert to offer sacrifices*c* to the LORD our God, as he commands us."

28Pharaoh said, "I will let you go to offer sacrifices to the LORD your God in the desert, but you must not go very far. Now pray*d* for me."

29Moses answered, "As soon as I leave you, I will pray to the LORD, and tomorrow the flies will leave Pharaoh and his officials and his people. Only be sure that Pharaoh does not act deceitfully*e* again by not letting the people go to offer sacrifices to the LORD."

30Then Moses left Pharaoh and prayed to the LORD,*f* 31and the LORD did what Moses asked: The flies left Pharaoh and his officials and his people; not a fly remained. 32But this time also Pharaoh hardened his

---

Cross references (center column):

8:9 *g*Ex 9:5
8:10 *h*Ex 9:14; 15:11; Dt 3:24; 4:35; 33:26; 2Sa 7:22; 1Ki 8:23; 1Ch 17:20; 2Ch 6:14; Ps 71:19; 86:8; 89:6; 113:5; Isa 40:18; 42:8; 46:9; Jer 10:6; 49:19; Mic 7:18
8:13 *i*Jas 5:16-18
8:15 *j*Ecc 8:11
*k*S Ex 7:14
8:16 *l*S Ex 4:2
8:17 *m*Ps 105:31
8:18 *n*Ex 9:11; *o*S Ex 7:11
8:19 *p*Ex 7:5; 10:7; 12:33; 31:18; 1Sa 6:9; Ne 9:6; Ps 8:3; 33:6; Lk 11:20
*q*S Ex 7:22
*r*S Ex 7:4
8:20 *s*Ex 7:15; 9:13

*t*S Ex 3:18
8:22 *u*S Ge 45:10
*v*Ex 9:4,6,26; 10:23; 11:7; 12:13; 19:5; Dt 4:20; 7:6; 14:2; 26:18; 1Ki 8:36; Job 36:11; Ps 33:12; 135:4; Mal 3:17
*w*Ex 7:5; 9:29
8:23 *x*Ex 9:4,6; 10:23; 11:7; 12:13,23,27
8:24 *y*Ps 78:45; 105:31
8:25 *z*ver 8; Ex 9:27; 10:16; 12:31
8:26 *a*S Ge 43:32
8:27 *b*S Ge 30:36
*c*S Ex 3:18
8:28 *d*S ver 8; S Jer 37:3; Ac 8:24
8:29 *e*ver 15; Ex 9:30; 10:11; Isa 26:10
8:30 *f*ver 12; Ex 9:33; 10:18

*p*23 Septuagint and Vulgate; Hebrew *will put a deliverance*

8:13 *the LORD did what Moses asked.* For similar occurrences see v. 31; 1Sa 12:18; 1Ki 18:42–45; Am 7:1–6. *The frogs died.* Probably because they had been infected by the bacteria (*Bacillus anthracis*) in the Nile algae (see note on v. 3).

8:16 *dust will become gnats.* The word "dust" is perhaps a reference to the enormous number (see, e.g., Ge 13:16) of the gnats, bred in the flooded fields of Egypt in late autumn.

8:19 *finger of God.* A concise and colorful figure of speech referring to God's miraculous power (see 31:18; Ps 8:3). Jesus drove out demons "by the finger of God" (Lk 11:20). Cf. the similar use of the phrase "hand of the LORD" in 9:3.

8:21 *I will send swarms of flies.* Probably *Stomoxys calci-*

trans, which would have multiplied rapidly as the receding Nile left breeding places in its wake. Full-grown, such flies infest houses and stables and bite men and animals.

8:22 *I will deal differently.* See 33:16. God makes a "distinction" (v. 23) between Moses' people and the pharaoh's people in this plague as well as in the fifth (see 9:4,6), the seventh (see 9:26), the ninth (see 10:23) and the tenth (see 11:7)—and probably also the sixth and eighth (see 9:11; 10:6)—demonstrating that the Lord can preserve his own people while judging Egypt. *Goshen.* See note on Ge 45:10.

8:26 *detestable to the Egyptians.* See Ge 46:34; see also Ge 43:32 and note.

8:31 *the LORD did what Moses asked.* See note on v. 13.

heart[g] and would not let the people go.

The Plague on Livestock

9 Then the LORD said to Moses, "Go to Pharaoh and say to him, 'This is what the LORD, the God of the Hebrews, says: "Let my people go, so that they may worship[h] me." [2]If you refuse to let them go and continue to hold them back, [3]the hand[i] of the LORD will bring a terrible plague[j] on your livestock in the field—on your horses and donkeys and camels and on your cattle and sheep and goats. [4]But the LORD will make a distinction between the livestock of Israel and that of Egypt,[k] so that no animal belonging to the Israelites will die.' "

[5]The LORD set a time and said, "Tomorrow the LORD will do this in the land." [6]And the next day the LORD did it: All the livestock[l] of the Egyptians died,[m] but not one animal belonging to the Israelites died. [7]Pharaoh sent men to investigate and found that not even one of the animals of the Israelites had died. Yet his heart[n] was unyielding and he would not let the people go.[o]

The Plague of Boils

[8]Then the LORD said to Moses and Aaron, "Take handfuls of soot from a furnace and have Moses toss it into the air in the presence of Pharaoh. [9]It will become fine dust over the whole land of Egypt, and festering boils[p] will break out on men and animals throughout the land."

[10]So they took soot from a furnace and stood before Pharaoh. Moses tossed it into the air, and festering boils broke out on men and animals. [11]The magicians[q] could not stand before Moses because of the boils that were on them and on all the

Egyptians. [12]But the LORD hardened Pharaoh's heart[r] and he would not listen[s] to Moses and Aaron, just as the LORD had said to Moses.

The Plague of Hail

[13]Then the LORD said to Moses, "Get up early in the morning, confront Pharaoh and say to him, 'This is what the LORD, the God of the Hebrews, says: Let my people go, so that they may worship[t] me, [14]or this time I will send the full force of my plagues against you and against your officials and your people, so you may know[u] that there is no one like[v] me in all the earth. [15]For by now I could have stretched out my hand and struck you and your people[w] with a plague that would have wiped you off the earth. [16]But I have raised you up[q] for this very purpose,[x] that I might show you my power[y] and that my name might be proclaimed in all the earth. [17]You still set yourself against my people and will not let them go. [18]Therefore, at this time tomorrow I will send the worst hailstorm[z] that has ever fallen on Egypt, from the day it was founded till now.[a] [19]Give an order now to bring your livestock and everything you have in the field to a place of shelter, because the hail will fall on every man and animal that has not been brought in and is still out in the field, and they will die.' "

[20]Those officials of Pharaoh who feared[b] the word of the LORD hurried to bring their slaves and their livestock inside. [21]But those who ignored[c] the word of the LORD left their slaves and livestock in the field.

[22]Then the LORD said to Moses, "Stretch

8:32 gS Ex 7:14
9:1 hS Ex 8:1
9:3 iEx 7:4; 1Sa 5:6; Job 13:21; Ps 32:4; 39:10; Ac 13:11
jLev 26:25; Ps 78:50; Am 4:10
9:4 kver 26; S Ex 8:23
9:6 lver 19-21; Ex 11:5; 12:29
mPs 78:48-50
9:7 nS Ex 7:22
oEx 7:14; 8:32
9:9 pLev 13:18, 19; Dt 28:27,35; 2Ki 20:7; Job 2:7; Isa 38:21; Rev 16:2
9:11 qS Ex 8:18

9:12 rS Ex 4:21
sS Ex 7:4
9:13 tS Ex 3:18
9:14 uS Ex 8:10
vEx 15:11; 1Sa 2:2; 2Sa 7:22; 1Ki 8:23; 1Ch 17:20; Ps 35:10; 71:19; 86:8; 89:6; Isa 46:9; Jer 10:6; Mic 7:18
9:15 wEx 3:20
9:16 xPr 16:4
yEx 14:4,17,31; Ps 20:6; 25:11; 68:28; 71:18; 106:8; 109:21; Ro 9:17*
9:18 zver 23; Jos 10:11; Ps 78:47-48; 105:32; 148:8; Isa 30:30; Eze 38:22; Hag 2:17 aver 24; Ex 10:6
9:20 bPr 13:13
9:21 cS Ge 19:14; Eze 33:4-5

q16 Or *have spared you*

9:3 *hand of the LORD.* See note on 8:19. *terrible plague on your livestock.* The flies of the fourth plague (see note on 8:21) probably carried the anthrax bacteria (see note on 8:13) that would now infect the animals, which had been brought into the fields again as the floodwaters subsided. The Egyptians worshiped many animals and animal-headed deities, including the bull-gods Apis and Mnevis, the cow-god Hathor and the ram-god Khnum. Thus Egyptian religion is again rebuked and ridiculed (see note on 7:19).
9:4 *distinction.* See note on 8:22.
9:5 *Tomorrow.* To give those Egyptians who feared God time to bring their livestock in from the fields and out of danger (see also v. 20).
9:6 *All the livestock of the Egyptians died.* That is, all that were left out in the fields. Protected livestock remained alive (see vv. 19-21).
9:8 *Take ... soot ... toss it into the air.* Perhaps symbolizing either the widespread extent of the plague of boils or their black coloration. *furnace.* Possibly a kiln for firing bricks, the symbol of Israel's bondage (see 1:14; 5:7-19).

The same word is used in Ge 19:28 as a simile for the destruction of Sodom and Gomorrah.
9:9 *boils.* Probably skin anthrax (a variety of the plague that struck the livestock in vv. 1-7), a black, burning abscess that develops into a pustule. *men and animals.* The plague on the livestock now extended to other animals as well as to the people of Egypt.
9:11 *magicians could not stand.* The "boils of Egypt" (Dt 28:27) seriously affected the knees and legs (see Dt 28:35).
9:12 *the LORD hardened Pharaoh's heart.* See note on 4:21.
9:16 Paul quotes this verse as an outstanding illustration of the sovereignty of God (see Ro 9:17).
9:18 *I will send ... hailstorm.* The flooding of the Nile (the probable occasion of the first six plagues) came to an end late in the fall. The hailstorm is thus in the proper chronological position, taking place in January or February when the flax and barley were in flower but the wheat and spelt had not yet germinated (see vv. 31-32).
9:19-21 See note on v. 6.

out your hand toward the sky so that hail will fall all over Egypt—on men and animals and on everything growing in the fields of Egypt." [23]When Moses stretched out his staff toward the sky, the LORD sent thunder[d] and hail,[e] and lightning flashed down to the ground. So the LORD rained hail on the land of Egypt; [24]hail fell and lightning flashed back and forth. It was the worst storm in all the land of Egypt since it had become a nation.[f] [25]Throughout Egypt hail struck everything in the fields—both men and animals; it beat down everything growing in the fields and stripped every tree.[g] [26]The only place it did not hail was the land of Goshen,[h] where the Israelites were.[i]

[27]Then Pharaoh summoned Moses and Aaron. "This time I have sinned,"[j] he said to them. "The LORD is in the right,[k] and I and my people are in the wrong. [28]Pray[l] to the LORD, for we have had enough thunder and hail. I will let you go;[m] you don't have to stay any longer."

[29]Moses replied, "When I have gone out of the city, I will spread out my hands[n] in prayer to the LORD. The thunder will stop and there will be no more hail, so you may know that the earth[o] is the LORD's. [30]But I know that you and your officials still do not fear[p] the LORD God."

[31](The flax and barley[q] were destroyed, since the barley had headed and the flax was in bloom. [32]The wheat and spelt,[r] however, were not destroyed, because they ripen later.)

[33]Then Moses left Pharaoh and went out of the city. He spread out his hands toward the LORD; the thunder and hail stopped, and the rain no longer poured down on the land. [34]When Pharaoh saw that the rain and hail and thunder had stopped, he sinned again: He and his officials hardened their hearts. [35]So Pharaoh's heart[s] was hard and he would not let the Israelites go, just as the LORD had said through Moses.

The Plague of Locusts

10 Then the LORD said to Moses, "Go to Pharaoh, for I have hardened his heart[t] and the hearts of his officials so that I may perform these miraculous signs[u] of mine among them [2]that you may tell your children[v] and grandchildren how I dealt harshly[w] with the Egyptians and how I performed my signs among them, and that you may know that I am the LORD."[x]

[3]So Moses and Aaron went to Pharaoh and said to him, "This is what the LORD, the God of the Hebrews, says: 'How long will you refuse to humble[y] yourself before me? Let my people go, so that they may worship me. [4]If you refuse[z] to let them go, I will bring locusts[a] into your country tomorrow. [5]They will cover the face of the ground so that it cannot be seen. They will devour what little you have left[b] after the hail, including every tree that is growing in your fields.[c] [6]They will fill your houses[d] and those of all your officials and all the Egyptians—something neither your fathers nor your forefathers have ever seen from the day they settled in this land till now.'"[e] Then Moses turned and left Pharaoh.

[7]Pharaoh's officials said to him, "How long will this man be a snare[f] to us? Let the people go, so that they may worship the LORD their God. Do you not yet realize that Egypt is ruined?"[g]

[8]Then Moses and Aaron were brought back to Pharaoh. "Go, worship[h] the LORD your God," he said. "But just who will be going?"

[9]Moses answered, "We will go with our young and old, with our sons and daughters, and with our flocks and herds, because we are to celebrate a festival[i] to the LORD."

9:23 [d]Ex 20:18; 1Sa 7:10; 12:17; Ps 18:13; 29:3; 68:33; 77:17; 104:7 [e]S ver 18; Rev 8:7; 16:21 9:24 [f]S ver 18 9:25 [g]Ps 105:32-33; Eze 13:13 9:26 [h]S ver 4; Isa 32:18-20 [i]Ex 10:23; 11:7; 12:13; Am 4:7 9:27 [j]ver 34; Ex 10:16; Nu 14:40; Dt 1:41; Jos 7:11; Jdg 10:10; 1Sa 15:24; 24:17; 26:21 [k]Ps 11:7; 116:5; 119:137; 129:4; 145:17; Jer 12:1; La 1:18 9:28 [l]S Ex 8:8; Ac 8:24 [m]S Ex 8:8 9:29 [n]ver 33; 1Ki 8:22,38; Job 11:13; Ps 77:2; 88:9; 143:6; Isa 1:15 [o]Ex 19:5; Job 41:11; Ps 24:1; 50:12; 1Co 10:26 9:30 [p]S Ex 8:29 9:31 [q]Dt 8:8; Ru 1:22; 2:23; 2Sa 14:30; 17:28; Isa 28:25; Eze 4:9; Joel 1:11 9:32 [r]Isa 28:25 9:35 [s]S Ex 4:21

10:1 [t]S Ex 4:21 [u]S Ex 3:19; S 7:3; Jos 24:17; Ne 9:10; Ps 74:9; 105:26-36 10:2 [v]Ex 12:26-27; 13:8,14; Dt 4:9; 6:20; 32:7; Jos 4:6; Ps 44:1; 71:18; 78:4,5; Joel 1:3 [w]1Sa 6:6 [x]S Ex 6:2 10:3 [y]1Ki 21:29; 2Ki 22:19; 2Ch 7:14; 12:7; 33:23; 34:27; Job 42:6; Isa 58:3; Da 5:22; Jas 4:10; 1Pe 5:6 10:4 [z]Ex 8:2; 9:2 [a]Dt 28:38; Ps 105:34; Pr 30:27; Joel 1:4; Rev 9:3 10:5 [b]Ex 9:32; Joel 1:4 [c]ver 15

10:6 [d]Joel 2:9 [e]S Ex 9:18 10:7 [f]Ex 23:33; 34:12; Dt 7:16; 12:30; 20:18; Jos 23:7-13,13; Jdg 2:3; 8:27; 16:5; 1Sa 18:21; Ps 106:36; Ecc 7:26 [g]S Ge 20:3; S Ex 8:19 10:8 [h]S Ex 8:8 10:9 [i]S Ex 3:18

9:27 *This time I have sinned.* For the first time the pharaoh acknowledges his sinfulness and perceives its devastating results.

9:29 *spread out my hands.* See 1Ki 8:22,38,54; 2Ch 6:12–13,29; Ezr 9:5; Ps 44:20; 88:9; 143:6; Isa 1:15; 1Ti 2:8. Statues of men praying with hands upraised have been found by archaeologists at several ancient sites in the Middle East.

9:30 LORD *God.* See note on Ge 2:4.

9:31–32 See note on v. 18.

9:32 *spelt.* Grains of spelt, a member of the grass family allied to wheat, have been found in ancient Egyptian tombs. Although inferior to wheat, it grows well in poorer and drier soil.

10:2 *tell your children.* The memory of God's redemptive acts is to be kept alive by reciting them to our descendants (see 12:26–27; 13:8,14–15; Dt 4:9; Ps 77:11–20; 78:4–6,43–53; 105:26–38; 106:7–12; 114:1–3; 135:8–9; 136:10–15).

10:4 *I will bring locusts.* In March or April the prevailing east winds (see v. 13) would bring in hordes of migratory locusts at their immature and most voracious stage. As also today, locust plagues were greatly feared in ancient times and became a powerful symbol of divine judgment (see Joel 1:4–7; 2:1–11; Am 7:1–3).

10:7 *How long . . . ?* The pharaoh's officials ironically echo the phrase used by Moses in v. 3. *Egypt is ruined.* Human rebellion and disobedience always bring death and destruction in their wake.

¹⁰Pharaoh said, "The LORD be with you—if I let you go, along with your women and children! Clearly you are bent on evil.ʳ ¹¹No! Have only the men go; and worship the LORD, since that's what you have been asking for." Then Moses and Aaron were driven out of Pharaoh's presence.

¹²And the LORD said to Moses, "Stretch out your handʲ over Egypt so that locusts will swarm over the land and devour everything growing in the fields, everything left by the hail."

¹³So Moses stretched out his staffᵏ over Egypt, and the LORD made an east wind blow across the land all that day and all that night. By morning the wind had brought the locusts;ˡ ¹⁴they invaded all Egypt and settled down in every area of the country in great numbers. Never before had there been such a plague of locusts,ᵐ nor will there ever be again. ¹⁵They covered all the ground until it was black. They devouredⁿ all that was left after the hail—everything growing in the fields and the fruit on the trees. Nothing green remained on tree or plant in all the land of Egypt.

¹⁶Pharaoh quickly summonedᵒ Moses and Aaron and said, "I have sinnedᵖ against the LORD your God and against you. ¹⁷Now forgiveᵠ my sin once more and prayʳ to the LORD your God to take this deadly plague away from me."

¹⁸Moses then left Pharaoh and prayed to the LORD.ˢ ¹⁹And the LORD changed the wind to a very strong west wind, which caught up the locusts and carried them into the Red Sea.ˢ Not a locust was left anywhere in Egypt. ²⁰But the LORD hardened Pharaoh's heart,ᵗ and he would not let the Israelites go.

The Plague of Darkness

²¹Then the LORD said to Moses, "Stretch out your hand toward the sky so that darknessᵘ will spread over Egypt—darkness that can be felt." ²²So Moses stretched out his hand toward the sky, and total darknessᵛ covered all Egypt for three days. ²³No one could see anyone else or leave his place for three days. Yet all the Israelites had light in the places where they lived.ʷ

²⁴Then Pharaoh summoned Moses and said, "Go,ˣ worship the LORD. Even your women and childrenʸ may go with you; only leave your flocks and herds behind."ᶻ

²⁵But Moses said, "You must allow us to have sacrifices and burnt offeringsᵃ to present to the LORD our God. ²⁶Our livestock too must go with us; not a hoof is to be left behind. We have to use some of them in worshiping the LORD our God, and until we get there we will not know what we are to use to worship the LORD."

²⁷But the LORD hardened Pharaoh's heart,ᵇ and he was not willing to let them go. ²⁸Pharaoh said to Moses, "Get out of my sight! Make sure you do not appear before me again! The day you see my face you will die."

²⁹"Just as you say," Moses replied, "I will never appearᶜ before you again."

The Plague on the Firstborn

11 Now the LORD had said to Moses, "I will bring one more plague on Pharaoh and on Egypt. After that, he will let you goᵈ from here, and when he does, he will drive you out completely.ᵉ ²Tell the people that men and women alike are to ask their neighbors for articles of silver and gold."ᶠ ³(The LORD made the Egyptians favorably disposedᵍ toward the people, and Moses himself was highly regardedʰ in Egypt by Pharaoh's officials and by the people.)

⁴So Moses said, "This is what the LORD says: 'About midnightⁱ I will go throughout Egypt.ʲ ⁵Every firstbornᵏ son in Egypt will die, from the firstborn son of Pharaoh,

---

Cross references (center column):

10:12 /Ex 7:19
10:13 ᵏver 21-22; Ex 4:17; 8:5,17; 9:23; 14:15-16,26-27; 17:5; Nu 20:8
ˡver 4; 1Ki 8:37; Ps 78:46; 105:34; Am 4:9; Na 3:16
10:14 ᵐDt 28:38; Ps 78:46; Isa 33:4; Joel 1:4; 2:1-11,25; Am 4:9
10:15 ⁿDt 28:38; Ps 105:34-35; Joel 1:4; Am 7:2; Mal 3:11
10:16 ᵒS Ex 8:25 ᵖS Ex 9:27
10:17 ᵠ1Sa 15:25 ʳS Ex 8:8
10:18 ˢS Ex 8:30
10:20 ᵗS Ex 4:21
10:21 ᵘDt 28:29

10:22 ᵛPs 105:28; Isa 13:10; 45:7; 50:3; Rev 16:10
10:23 ʷS Ex 8:22; Am 4:7
10:24 ˣS Ex 8:8 ʸver 8-10 ᶻS Ge 45:10
10:25 ᵃS Ge 8:20; S Ex 18:12
10:27 ᵇS Ex 4:21
10:29 ᶜEx 11:8; Heb 11:27
11:1 ᵈS Ex 3:20 ᵉS Ex 6:1
11:2 ᶠS Ex 3:21, 22
11:3 ᵍS Ge 39:21 ʰDt 34:11; 2Sa 7:9; 8:13; 22:44; 23:1; Est 9:4; Ps 89:27
11:4 ⁱEx 12:29; /Ex 12:23; Ps 81:5
11:5 ᵏS Ex 4:23

ʳ*10* Or *Be careful, trouble is in store for you!*
ˢ*19* Hebrew *Yam Suph*; that is, Sea of Reeds

10:11 *Have only the men go.* From the pharaoh's standpoint, (1) the women and children should remain behind as hostages, and (2) it was typically only the men who participated fully in worship.

10:13 *east wind.* See note on v. 4.

10:19 *the LORD changed the wind.* The forces of nature are compelled to obey his sovereign will (see 14:21; Mt 8:23-27). *Red Sea.* See NIV text note.

10:21 *darkness will spread over Egypt.* Like the third and sixth plagues, this ninth plague was unannounced to Pharaoh. It was possibly caused by the arrival of an unusually severe khamsin, the blinding sandstorm that blows in from the desert each year in the early spring. The darkness was an insult to the sun-god Ra (or Re), one of the chief deities of Egypt.

10:28 Pharaoh declares that he will never again grant Moses an audience. *The day you see my face.* During a plague of darkness, these words are somewhat ironic.

11:1 *and when he does.* The Hebrew for this phrase can also be read "as one sends away [a bride]"—i.e., laden with gifts (see Ge 24:53).

11:2–3 See 12:35–36.

11:4 *Moses said.* Continuing the speech of 10:29.

11:5 *Every firstborn son in Egypt will die.* See Ps 78:51; 105:36; 135:8; 136:10. This is the ultimate disaster, since all the plans and dreams of a father were bound up in his firstborn son, who received a double share of the family estate when the father died (see Dt 21:17 and note). More-

who sits on the throne, to the firstborn son of the slave girl, who is at her hand mill,*l* and all the firstborn of the cattle as well. [6]There will be loud wailing*m* throughout Egypt—worse than there has ever been or ever will be again. [7]But among the Israelites not a dog will bark at any man or animal.' Then you will know that the LORD makes a distinction*n* between Egypt and Israel. [8]All these officials of yours will come to me, bowing down before me and saying, 'Go,*o* you and all the people who follow you!' After that I will leave.'*p* Then Moses, hot with anger, left Pharaoh.

[9]The LORD had said to Moses, "Pharaoh will refuse to listen*q* to you—so that my wonders*r* may be multiplied in Egypt." [10]Moses and Aaron performed all these wonders before Pharaoh, but the LORD hardened Pharaoh's heart,*s* and he would not let the Israelites go out of his country.

The Passover

12:14–20pp — Lev 23:4–8; Nu 28:16–25; Dt 16:1–8

12 The LORD said to Moses and Aaron in Egypt, [2]"This month is to be for you the first month,*t* the first month of your year. [3]Tell the whole community of Israel that on the tenth day of this month each man is to take a lamb*t u* for his family, one for each household.*v* [4]If any household is too small for a whole lamb, they must share one with their nearest neighbor, having taken into account the number of people there are. You are to determine the amount of lamb needed in accordance with what each person will

eat. [5]The animals you choose must be year-old males without defect,*w* and you may take them from the sheep or the goats. [6]Take care of them until the fourteenth day of the month,*x* when all the people of the community of Israel must slaughter them at twilight.*y* [7]Then they are to take some of the blood*z* and put it on the sides and tops of the doorframes of the houses where they eat the lambs. [8]That same night*a* they are to eat the meat roasted*b* over the fire, along with bitter herbs,*c* and bread made without yeast.*d* [9]Do not eat the meat raw or cooked in water, but roast it over the fire—head, legs and inner parts.*e* [10]Do not leave any of it till morning;*f* if some is left till morning, you must burn it. [11]This is how you are to eat it: with your cloak tucked into your belt, your sandals on your feet and your staff in your hand. Eat it in haste;*g* it is the LORD's Passover. *h*

[12]"On that same night I will pass through*i* Egypt and strike down*j* every firstborn*k*—both men and animals—and I will bring judgment on all the gods*l* of Egypt. I am the LORD. *m* [13]The blood will be a sign for you on the houses where you are; and when I see the blood, I will pass over*n* you. No destructive plague will touch you when I strike Egypt.*o*

11:5 *l*Isa 47:2
11:6 *m*Ex 12:30;
Pr 21:13;
Am 5:17
11:7 *n*S Ex 8:22
11:8
*o*Ex 12:31-33
*p*Heb 11:27
11:9 *q*S Ex 7:4
*r*S Ex 3:20
11:10
*s*S Ex 4:21;
Ro 2:5
12:2 *t*ver 18;
Ex 13:4; 23:15;
34:18; 40:2;
Dt 16:1
12:3 *u*Mk 14:12;
1Co 5:7 *v*ver 21

12:5 *w*Ex 29:1;
Lev 1:3; 3:1; 4:3;
22:18-21; 23:12;
Nu 6:14; 15:8;
28:3; Dt 15:21;
17:1; Heb 9:14;
1Pe 1:19
12:6 *x*ver 19;
Lev 23:5;
Nu 9:1-3,5,11;
Jos 5:10;
2Ch 30:2
*y*Ex 16:12;
Dt 16:4,6
12:7 *z*ver 13,23;
Eze 9:6
12:8 *a*ver 10;
Ex 16:19; 23:18;
34:25; Lev 7:15;
Nu 9:12
*b*Dt 16:7;
2Ch 35:13
*c*Nu 9:11 *d*ver
19-20; Ex 13:3;
Dt 16:3-4;
1Co 5:8
12:9 *e*Ex 29:13,
17,22; Lev 3:3
12:10 *f*S ver 8;
Ex 13:7; 29:34;
Lev 22:30;
Dt 16:4
12:11 *g*ver 33;
Dt 16:3;
Isa 48:20; 52:12
*h*ver 13,21,27,43;
Lev 23:5; Nu 9:2,
4; 28:16;
Dt 16:1; Jos 5:10;

2Ki 23:21,23; 2Ch 30:1; Ezr 6:19; Isa 31:5; Eze 45:21 **12:12**
*i*Am 5:17 *j*Isa 10:33; 31:8; 37:36 *k*ver 29; S Ex 4:23; 13:15
*l*Ex 15:11; 18:11; Nu 33:4; 2Ch 2:5; Ps 95:3; 97:9; 135:5;
Isa 19:1; Jer 43:12; 44:8 *m*S Ex 6:2 **12:13** *n*S ver 11,23;
Heb 11:28 *o*S Ex 8:23

---

t3 The Hebrew word can mean *lamb* or *kid*; also in verse 4.

---

over, judgment on the firstborn represented judgment on the entire community. *slave girl, who is at her hand mill.* The lowliest of occupations (see Isa 47:2).
11:7 *distinction.* See note on 8:22.
12:2 *This month is . . . the first month.* The inauguration of the religious calendar in Israel (see chart on "Hebrew Calendar," p. 102). In the ancient Near East, new year festivals normally coincided with the new season of life in nature. The designation of this month as Israel's religious New Year reminded Israel that her life as the people of God was grounded in God's redemptive act in the exodus. The Canaanite name for this month was Abib (see 13:4; 23:15; 34:18; Dt 16:1), which means "young head of grain." Later the Babylonian name Nisan was used (see Ne 2:1; Est 3:7). Israel's agricultural calendar began in the fall (see note on 23:16), and during the monarchy it dominated the nation's civil calendar. Both calendars (civil and religious) existed side by side until after the exile. Judaism today uses only the calendar that begins in the fall.
12:3 *community of Israel.* The Israelites gathered in assembly.
12:5 *animals . . . without defect.* See Lev 22:18–25. Similarly, Jesus was like "a lamb without blemish or defect" (1Pe 1:19).
12:6 *at twilight.* Lit. "between the two evenings," an idiom meaning either (1) between the decline of the sun and

sunset, or (2) between sunset and nightfall—which has given rise to disputes about when the Sabbath and other holy days begin.
12:7 *blood.* Symbolizes a sacrifice offered as a substitute, one life laid down for another (see Lev 17:11). Thus Israel escapes the judgment about to fall on Egypt only through the mediation of a sacrifice (see Heb 9:22; 1Jn 1:7).
12:8 *bitter herbs.* Endive, chicory and other bitter-tasting plants are indigenous to Egypt. Eating them would recall the bitter years of servitude there (see 1:14). *bread made without yeast.* Reflecting the haste with which the people left Egypt (see vv. 11,39; Dt 16:3).
12:9 *roast it . . . head, legs and inner parts.* The method wandering shepherds used to cook meat.
12:11 *Passover.* Explained in vv. 13,23,27 to mean that the Lord would "pass over" and not destroy the occupants of houses that were under the sign of the blood.
12:12 *judgment on all the gods of Egypt.* Some had already been judged (see notes on 7:19; 8:2; 9:3; 10:21), and now all would be: (1) They would be shown to be powerless to deliver from the impending slaughter, and (2) many animals sacred to the gods would be killed.
12:13 *sign.* Just as the plagues were miraculous signs of judgment on Pharaoh and his people (see 8:23), so the Lord's "passing over" the Israelites who placed themselves under the sign of blood was a pledge of God's mercy.

14"This is a day you are to commemorate;[p] for the generations to come you shall celebrate it as a festival to the LORD—a lasting ordinance.[q] 15For seven days you are to eat bread made without yeast.[r] On the first day remove the yeast from your houses, for whoever eats anything with yeast in it from the first day through the seventh must be cut off[s] from Israel. 16On the first day hold a sacred assembly, and another one on the seventh day. Do no work[t] at all on these days, except to prepare food for everyone to eat—that is all you may do.

17"Celebrate the Feast of Unleavened Bread,[u] because it was on this very day that I brought your divisions out of Egypt.[v] Celebrate this day as a lasting ordinance for the generations to come.[w] 18In the first month[x] you are to eat bread made with-out yeast, from the evening of the four-teenth day until the evening of the twenty-first day. 19For seven days no yeast is to be found in your houses. And whoever eats anything with yeast in it must be cut off[y] from the community of Israel, whether he is an alien[z] or native-born. 20Eat nothing made with yeast. Wherever you live,[a] you must eat unleavened bread."[b]

21Then Moses summoned all the elders of Israel and said to them, "Go at once and select the animals for your families and slaughter the Passover[c] lamb. 22Take a bunch of hyssop,[d] dip it into the blood in the basin and put some of the blood[e] on the top and on both sides of the doorframe. Not one of you shall go out the door of his

12:14 [p]Ex 13:9; 23:14; 32:5 [q]ver 17,24; Ex 13:5, 10; 27:21; Lev 3:17; 10:9; 16:29; 17:7; 23:14; 24:3; Nu 18:23
12:15 [r]Ex 13:6-7; 23:15; 34:18; Lev 23:6; Nu 28:17; Dt 16:3; 1Co 5:7 [s]Ge 17:14
12:16 [t]Nu 29:35
12:17 [u]Ex 23:15; 34:18; Dt 16:16; 2Ch 8:13; 30:21; Ezr 6:22; Mt 26:17; Lk 22:1; Ac 12:3 [v]ver 41; S Ex 6:6, 26; 13:3; Lev 19:36 [w]Lev 3:17
12:18 [x]S ver 2
12:19 [y]S Ge 17:14 [z]Nu 9:14; 15:14; 35:15; Dt 1:16; Jos 8:33 **12:20** [a]Lev 3:17; Nu 35:29; Eze 6:6 [b]Ex 13:6 **12:21** [c]S ver 11; Mk 14:12-16 **12:22** [d]Lev 14:4,6; Nu 19:18; Ps 51:7 [e]Heb 11:28

12:14 *celebrate it as ... a lasting ordinance.* Frequent references to Passover observance occur in the rest of Scripture (see Nu 9:1–5; Jos 5:10; 2Ki 23:21–23; 2Ch 30:1–27; 35:1–19; Ezr 6:19–22; Lk 2:41–43; Jn 2:13,23; 6:4; 11:55–12:1). The ordinance is still kept by orthodox Jews today.

12:15 *remove the yeast from your houses.* Yeast later was often used as a symbol of sin, such as "hypocrisy" (Lk 12:1) or "malice and wickedness" (1Co 5:8). Before celebrating Passover, the observant Jew today conducts a systematic (often symbolic) search of his house to remove every crumb of leavened bread that might be there (see v. 19). *cut off from*

Hebrew calendar and selected events

NUMBER of MONTH			HEBREW NAME	MODERN EQUIVALENT
1	Sacred sequence begins	7	Abib; Nisan	MARCH—APRIL
2		8	Ziv (Iyyar)*	APRIL—MAY
3		9	Sivan	MAY—JUNE
4		10	(Tammuz)*	JUNE—JULY
5		11	(Ab)*	JULY—AUGUST
6		12	Elul	AUGUST—SEPTEMBER
7	Civil sequence	1	Ethanim (Tishri)*	SEPTEMBER—OCTOBER
8		2	Bul (Marcheshvan)*	OCTOBER—NOVEMBER
9		3	Kislev	NOVEMBER—DECEMBER
10		4	Tebeth	DECEMBER—JANUARY
11		5	Shebat	JANUARY—FEBRUARY
12		6	Adar	FEBRUARY—MARCH
			(Adar Sheni)* Second Adar	This intercalary month was added about every three years so the lunar calendar would correspond to the solar year.

* Names in parentheses are not in the Bible

house until morning. 23When the LORD goes through the land to strike*f* down the Egyptians, he will see the blood*g* on the top and sides of the doorframe and will pass over*h* that doorway, and he will not permit the destroyer*i* to enter your houses and strike you down.

24"Obey these instructions as a lasting ordinance*j* for you and your descendants. 25When you enter the land*k* that the LORD will give you as he promised, observe this ceremony. 26And when your children*l* ask you, 'What does this ceremony mean to you?' 27then tell them, 'It is the Passover*m* sacrifice to the LORD, who passed over the houses of the Israelites in Egypt and spared our homes when he struck down the Egyptians.' "*n* Then the people bowed down and worshiped.*o* 28The Israelites did

just what the LORD commanded*p* Moses and Aaron.

29At midnight*q* the LORD*r* struck down all the firstborn*s* in Egypt, from the firstborn of Pharaoh, who sat on the throne, to the firstborn of the prisoner, who was in the dungeon, and the firstborn of all the livestock*t* as well. 30Pharaoh and all his officials and all the Egyptians got up during the night, and there was loud wailing*u* in Egypt, for there was not a house without someone dead.

The Exodus

31During the night Pharaoh summoned Moses and Aaron and said, "Up! Leave my people, you and the Israelites! Go, worship*v* the LORD as you have requested. 32Take your flocks and herds,*w* as you have said, and go. And also bless*x* me."

12:23 *f*Isa 19:22
*g*S ver 7; Rev 7:3
*h*S ver 13
*i*S Ge 16:7;
Isa 37:36;
Jer 6:26; 48:8;
1Co 10:10;
Heb 11:28
12:24 *j*S ver 14
12:25
*k*S Ge 15:14;
Ex 3:17
12:26 *l*Ex 10:2
12:27 *m*S ver 11
*n*S Ex 8:23
*o*S Ge 24:26

12:28 *p*ver 50
12:29 *q*S Ex 11:4
*r*S Ge 19:13
*s*S Ex 4:23
*t*S Ex 9:6
12:30 *u*S Ex 11:6
12:31 *v*S Ex 8:8
12:32 *w*Ex 10:9,
26 *x*Ge 27:34

Israel. Removed from the covenant people by execution (see, e.g., 31:14; Lev 20:2–3) or banishment. See also Ge 17:14 and note.
12:17 *Feast of Unleavened Bread.* Began with the Passover meal and continued for seven days (see vv. 18–19; see also Mk 14:12).

12:21 *Passover lamb.* Jesus is "our Passover lamb" (1Co 5:7), sacrificed "once for all" (Heb 7:27) for us.
12:22 *hyssop.* Here probably refers to an aromatic plant *(Origanum maru)* of the mint family with a straight stalk (see Jn 19:29) and white flowers. The hairy surface of its leaves and branches held liquids well and made it suitable as a

---

BIBLICAL REFERENCES	AGRICULTURE	FEASTS
Ex 12:2; 13:4; 23:15; 34:18; Dt 16:1; Ne 2:1; Est 3:7	Spring (later) rains; barley and flax harvest begins	Passover; Unleavened Bread; Firstfruits
1 Ki 6:1, 37	Barley harvest; dry season begins	
Est 8:9	Wheat harvest	Pentecost (Weeks)
	Tending vines	
	Ripening of grapes, figs and olives	
Ne 6:15	Processing grapes, figs and olives	
1 Ki 8:2	Autumn (early) rains begin; plowing	Trumpets; Atonement; Tabernacles (Booths)
1 Ki 6:38	Sowing of wheat and barley	
Ne 1:1; Zec 7:1	Winter rains begin (snow in some areas)	Hanukkah ("Dedication")
Est 2:16		
Zec 1:7		
Ezr 6:15; Est 3:7,13; 8:12; 9:1,15,17,19,21	Almond trees bloom; citrus fruit harvest	Purim

33The Egyptians urged the people to hurry[y] and leave[z] the country. "For otherwise," they said, "we will all die!"[a] 34So the people took their dough before the yeast was added, and carried it on their shoulders in kneading troughs[b] wrapped in clothing. 35The Israelites did as Moses instructed and asked the Egyptians for articles of silver and gold[c] and for clothing.[d] 36The LORD had made the Egyptians favorably disposed[e] toward the people, and they gave them what they asked for; so they plundered[f] the Egyptians.

37The Israelites journeyed from Rameses[g] to Succoth.[h] There were about six hundred thousand men[i] on foot, besides women and children. 38Many other people[j] went up with them, as well as large droves of livestock, both flocks and herds. 39With the dough they had brought from Egypt, they baked cakes of unleavened bread. The dough was without yeast because they had been driven out[k] of Egypt and did not have time to prepare food for themselves.

40Now the length of time the Israelite people lived in Egypt[u] was 430 years.[l] 41At the end of the 430 years, to the very day, all the LORD's divisions[m] left Egypt. [n] 42Because the LORD kept vigil that night to bring them out of Egypt, on this night all the Israelites are to keep vigil to honor the LORD for the generations to come.[o]

Passover Restrictions

43The LORD said to Moses and Aaron, "These are the regulations for the Passover:[p]

"No foreigner[q] is to eat of it. 44Any slave you have bought may eat of it after you have circumcised[r] him, 45but a temporary resident and a hired worker[s] may not eat of it.

46"It must be eaten inside one house; take none of the meat outside the house. Do not break any of the bones.[t] 47The whole community of Israel must celebrate it.

48"An alien living among you who wants to celebrate the LORD's Passover must have all the males in his household circumcised; then he may take part like one born in the land.[u] No uncircumcised[v] male may eat of it. 49The same law applies to the native-born and to the alien[w] living among you."

50All the Israelites did just what the LORD had commanded[x] Moses and Aaron. 51And on that very day the LORD brought the Israelites out of Egypt[y] by their divisions.[z]

Consecration of the Firstborn

13 The LORD said to Moses, 2"Consecrate to me every firstborn male.[a] The first offspring of every womb among the Israelites belongs to me, whether man or animal."

3Then Moses said to the people, "Commemorate this day, the day you came out

12:33 [y]S ver 11
[z]S Ex 6:1; 1Sa 6:6
[a]S Ge 20:3;
S Ex 8:19
12:34 [b]Ex 8:3
12:35 [c]S Ex 3:22
[d]S Ge 24:53
12:36
[e]S Ge 39:21
[f]S Ex 3:22
12:37
[g]S Ge 47:11
[h]Ex 13:20;
Nu 33:3-5
[i]Ge 12:2;
Ex 38:26;
Nu 1:46; 2:32;
11:13,21; 26:51
12:38 [j]Nu 11:4;
Jos 8:35
12:39 [k]Ex 3:20;
11:1
12:40
[l]S Ge 15:13;
Ac 7:6; Gal 3:17
12:41 [m]S Ex 6:26
[n]S Ex 3:10
12:42 [o]Ex 13:10;
Lev 3:17; Nu 9:3;
Dt 16:1,6
12:43 [p]S ver 11

[q]ver 48; Nu 9:14;
15:14;
2Ch 6:32-33;
Isa 14:1; 56:3,6;
60:10
12:44
[r]S Ge 17:12-13
12:45 [s]Lev 22:10
12:46 [t]Nu 9:12;
Ps 34:20;
51:8; Pr 17:22;
Jn 19:36*
12:48 [u]ver 49;
Lev 19:18,34;
24:22; Nu 9:14;
10:32 [v]Eze 44:7
12:49
[w]Lev 24:22;
Nu 15:15-16,29;
Dt 1:16
12:50 [x]ver 28
12:51
[y]S Ex 3:10; S 6:6
[z]S Ex 6:26
13:2 [a]ver 12,13,
15; Ex 22:29;
34:20; Lev 27:26;
Nu 3:13; 8:17;

18:15; Dt 15:19; Ne 10:36; Lk 2:23*

[u]40 Masoretic Text; Samaritan Pentateuch and Septuagint Egypt and Canaan

sprinkling device for use in purification rituals (see Lev 14:4,6,49,51–52; Nu 19:6,18; Heb 9:19; see also Ps 51:7). *dip it into the blood.* Today at Passover meals a sprig of parsley or other plant is dipped in salt water to symbolize the lowly diet and tears of the Israelites during their time of slavery.
12:23 *pass over.* See note on v. 11. *the destroyer.* In Ps 78:49 the agent of God's wrath against the Egyptians is described as "a band of destroying angels." God often used angels to bring destructive plagues (see 2Sa 24:15–16; 2Ki 19:35; see also 1Co 10:10, a reference to Nu 16:41–49).
12:26 *your children ask you, 'What does this ceremony mean to you?'* See 13:14. The Passover was to be observed as a memorial feast commemorating Israel's redemption and appropriating it anew. As observed today, it includes the asking of similar questions by the youngest child present.
12:27 *Passover sacrifice.* See note on v. 21. *passed over.* See note on v. 11.
12:29 *prisoner, who was in the dungeon.* The lowliest of situations (see note on 11:5).
12:31 *Pharaoh summoned Moses.* Though he had sworn never again to grant Moses an audience (see 10:28 and note), Pharaoh now summons Moses (and Aaron) into his presence.
12:35–36 See 3:21–22; 11:2–3.

12:37 *journeyed from Rameses.* See 1:11; see also note on Ge 47:11. The Israelite departure took place "the day after the Passover" (Nu 33:3). *Succoth.* Probably modern Tell el-Maskhutah in the Wadi Tumeilat, west of the Bitter Lakes. *about six hundred thousand men.* A round number for 603,550 (see note on 38:26).

12:38 *many other people.* Possibly including such Egyptians as those mentioned in 9:20.

12:41 *430 years, to the very day.* See note on Ac 7:6.

12:46 *Do not break any of the bones.* See Nu 9:12; Ps 34:20; quoted in Jn 19:36 in reference to Jesus.

12:48 *No uncircumcised male may eat of it.* Only those consecrated to the Lord in covenant commitment could partake of Passover; only for them could it have its full meaning (see Ge 17:9–14). Concerning participants in the Lord's Supper see 1Co 11:28.

13:2 *Consecrate to me every firstborn male.* God had adopted Israel as his firstborn (see 4:22) and had delivered every firstborn among the Israelites, whether man or animal, from the tenth plague (see 12:12–13). All the firstborn in Israel were therefore his. Jesus, Mary's firstborn son (see Lk 2:7), was presented to the Lord in accordance with this law (see Lk 2:22–23).

of Egypt,[b] out of the land of slavery, because the LORD brought you out of it with a mighty hand.[c] Eat nothing containing yeast.[d] 4Today, in the month of Abib,[e] you are leaving. 5When the LORD brings you into the land of the Canaanites,[f] Hittites, Amorites, Hivites and Jebusites[g]—the land he swore to your forefathers to give you, a land flowing with milk and honey[h]—you are to observe this ceremony[i] in this month: 6For seven days eat bread made without yeast and on the seventh day hold a festival[j] to the LORD. 7Eat unleavened bread during those seven days; nothing with yeast in it is to be seen among you, nor shall any yeast be seen anywhere within your borders. 8On that day tell your son,[k] 'I do this because of what the LORD did for me when I came out of Egypt.' 9This observance will be for you like a sign on your hand[l] and a reminder on your forehead[m] that the law of the LORD is to be on your lips. For the LORD brought you out of Egypt with his mighty hand.[n] 10You must keep this ordinance[o] at the appointed time[p] year after year.

11"After the LORD brings you into the land of the Canaanites[q] and gives it to you, as he promised on oath[r] to you and your forefathers,[s] 12you are to give over to the LORD the first offspring of every womb. All the firstborn males of your livestock belong to the LORD.[t] 13Redeem with a lamb every firstborn donkey,[u] but if you do not redeem it, break its neck.[v] Redeem[w] every firstborn among your sons.[x]

14"In days to come, when your son[y] asks you, 'What does this mean?' say to him, 'With a mighty hand the LORD brought us out of Egypt, out of the land of slavery.[z] 15When Pharaoh stubbornly

refused to let us go, the LORD killed every firstborn in Egypt, both man and animal. This is why I sacrifice to the LORD the first male offspring of every womb and redeem each of my firstborn sons.'[a] 16And it will be like a sign on your hand and a symbol on your forehead[b] that the LORD brought us out of Egypt with his mighty hand."

Crossing the Sea

17When Pharaoh let the people go, God did not lead them on the road through the Philistine country, though that was shorter. For God said, "If they face war, they might change their minds and return to Egypt."[c] 18So God led[d] the people around by the desert road toward the Red Sea.[v] The Israelites went up out of Egypt armed for battle.[e]

19Moses took the bones of Joseph[f] with him because Joseph had made the sons of Israel swear an oath. He had said, "God will surely come to your aid, and then you must carry my bones up with you from this place."[w][g]

20After leaving Succoth[h] they camped at Etham on the edge of the desert.[i] 21By day the LORD went ahead[j] of them in a pillar of cloud[k] to guide them on their way and by night in a pillar of fire to give them light, so that they could travel by day or night. 22Neither the pillar of cloud by day nor the pillar of fire by night left[l] its place in front of the people.

14 Then the LORD said to Moses, 2"Tell the Israelites to turn back and encamp near Pi Hahiroth, between

Cross references (center column)

13:3 [b]ver 14; Ex 7:4; Lev 26:13; Nu 1:1; 9:1; 22:5; 26:4; Dt 4:45; 5:6; Ps 81:10; 114:1 [c]S Ex 3:20 [d]S Ex 12:8
13:4 [e]S Ex 12:2
13:5 [f]ver 11
[g]S Ex 3:8
[h]S Ex 3:8
[i]Ex 12:25-26
13:6 [j]S Ex 12:15-20
13:8 [k]S Ex 10:2; Ps 78:5-6
13:9 [l]Isa 44:5 [m]ver 16; Dt 6:8; 11:18; Pr 3:3; Mt 23:5 [n]S Ex 3:20
13:10 [o]S Ex 12:14 [p]Ps 75:2; 102:13
13:11 [q]S ver 5 [r]S Ge 22:16; Dt 1:8 [s]S Ge 12:7; S 17:19; Ps 105:42-45
13:12 [t]S Ge 4:4; Lev 27:26; Nu 3:13; 18:15, 17; Lk 2:23*
13:13 [u]ver 15; Lev 27:11 [v]Ex 34:20; Isa 66:3 [w]Nu 3:46-47 [x]Nu 18:15
13:14 [y]S Ex 10:2 [z]Ex 20:2; Dt 7:8; 28:68
13:15 [a]S ver 2
13:16 [b]S ver 9
13:17 [c]Ex 14:11; Nu 14:1-4; Dt 17:16; Hos 11:5
13:18 [d]Ex 15:22; Ps 136:16; Eze 20:10 [e]Jos 1:14; 4:13
13:19 [f]Jos 24:32; Ac 7:16; Heb 11:22 [g]S Ge 47:29-30
13:20 [h]S Ex 12:37 [i]Nu 33:6
13:21 [j]Ex 32:1; 33:14; Dt 2:7; 31:8; Jdg 4:14; 5:4; Ps 68:7;

13:3 [b]ver 14; 77:20; Jer 2:2; Hab 3:13 [k]Ex 14:19,24; 24:16; 33:9-10; 34:5; 40:38; Nu 9:16; 12:5; 14:14; Dt 1:33; Ne 9:12,19; Ps 78:14; 99:7; 105:39; Isa 4:5; 1Co 10:1 13:22 [l]Ne 9:19

[v]18 Hebrew *Yam Suph*; that is, Sea of Reeds   [w]19 See Gen. 50:25.

13:5 See note on 3:8.
13:9 *like a sign on your hand and a reminder on your forehead.* A figure of speech (see v. 16; Dt 6:8; 11:18; see also Pr 3:3; 6:21; 7:3; SS 8:6). A literal reading of this verse has led to the practice of writing the texts of vv. 1–10, vv. 11–16, Dt 6:4–9 and Dt 11:13–21 on separate strips of parchment and placing them in two small leather boxes, which the observant Jew straps on his forehead and left arm before his morning prayers. The boxes are called "phylacteries" (Mt 23:5). This practice seems to have originated after the exile to Babylon.
13:13 *Redeem.* See 6:6. The verb means "obtain release by means of payment." *every firstborn donkey.* The economic importance of pack animals allowed for their redemption through sacrificing a lamb. *every firstborn among your sons.* Humans were to be consecrated to the Lord by their life, not by their death (see Ge 22:12; Nu 3:39–51; cf. Ro 12:1).
13:14 See note on 12:26.
13:16 See note on v. 9.

13:17 *road through the Philistine country.* Although the most direct route from Goshen to Canaan, it was heavily guarded by a string of Egyptian fortresses.
13:18 *desert road.* Leading south along the west coast of the Sinai peninsula. *Red Sea.* See NIV text note. Various locations of the crossing have been proposed along the line of the modern Suez Canal and including the northern end of the Gulf of Suez (see map No. 2 at the end of the Study Bible; but see also note on 14:2). *armed for battle.* Probably only with spears, bows and slings.
13:19 See notes on Ge 50:24–25.
13:20 *Succoth.* See note on 12:37. *Etham.* Location unknown.
13:21 *pillar of cloud . . . pillar of fire.* The visible symbol of God's presence among his people (see 14:24; see also note on 3:2). The Lord often spoke to them from the pillar (see Nu 12:5–6; Dt 31:15–16; Ps 99:6–7).
14:2 *turn back.* Northward, in the general direction from which they had come. *Pi Hahiroth.* Located "east of Baal Zephon" (Nu 33:7). *Migdol.* Location unknown. The name

The Exodus

The exodus and conquest narratives form the classic historical and spiritual drama of OT times. Subsequent ages looked back to this period as one of obedient and victorious living under divine guidance. Close examination of the environment and circumstances also reveals the strenuous exertions, human sin and bloody conflicts of the era.

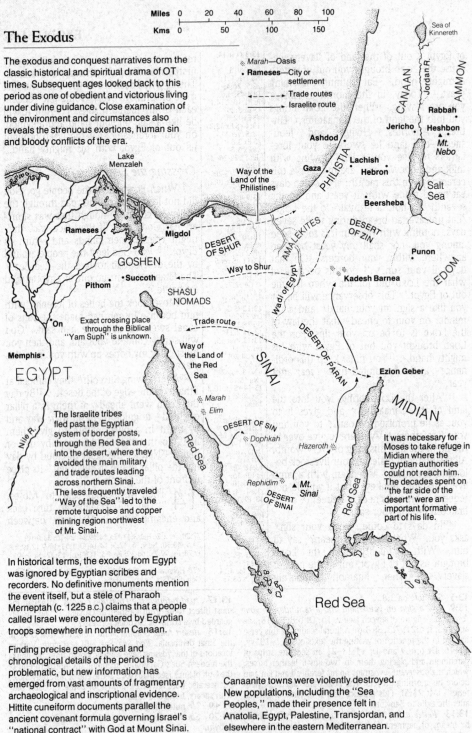

Miles 0 20 40 60 80 100
Kms 0 50 100 150

✳ *Marah*—Oasis
• **Rameses**—City or settlement
◄---► Trade routes
◄—— Israelite route

Lake Menzaleh

Rameses

Migdol

GOSHEN

Pithom

• Succoth

• On

Memphis •

EGYPT

Nile R.

SHASU NOMADS

Exact crossing place through the Biblical "Yam Suph" is unknown.

Way of the Land of the Red Sea

Trade route

✳ *Marah*
✳ *Elim*

DESERT OF SIN

✳ *Dophkah*

Rephidim ▲ Mt. Sinai

DESERT OF SINAI

Hazeroth ✳

Red Sea

SINAI

DESERT OF SHUR

Way to Shur

Way of the Land of the Philistines

Ashdod

Gaza

Lachish

Hebron

Beersheba

PHILISTIA

CANAAN

Jericho

Salt Sea

Jordan R.

Sea of Kinnereth

AMMON

Rabbah

Heshbon

Mt. Nebo

AMALEKITES

Wadi. of Egypt

DESERT OF ZIN

Kadesh Barnea

Punon

EDOM

DESERT OF PARAN

Ezion Geber

MIDIAN

Red Sea

Red Sea

The Israelite tribes fled past the Egyptian system of border posts, through the Red Sea and into the desert, where they avoided the main military and trade routes leading across northern Sinai. The less frequently traveled "Way of the Sea" led to the remote turquoise and copper mining region northwest of Mt. Sinai.

It was necessary for Moses to take refuge in Midian where the Egyptian authorities could not reach him. The decades spent on "the far side of the desert" were an important formative part of his life.

In historical terms, the exodus from Egypt was ignored by Egyptian scribes and recorders. No definitive monuments mention the event itself, but a stele of Pharaoh Merneptah (c. 1225 B.C.) claims that a people called Israel were encountered by Egyptian troops somewhere in northern Canaan.

Finding precise geographical and chronological details of the period is problematic, but new information has emerged from vast amounts of fragmentary archaeological and inscriptional evidence. Hittite cuneiform documents parallel the ancient covenant formula governing Israel's "national contract" with God at Mount Sinai.

The Late Bronze Age (c. 1550-1200 B.C.) was a time of major social migrations. Egyptian control over the Semites in the eastern Nile delta was harsh, with a system of brickmaking quotas imposed on the labor force, often the landless, low-class "Apiru." Numerous

Canaanite towns were violently destroyed. New populations, including the "Sea Peoples," made their presence felt in Anatolia, Egypt, Palestine, Transjordan, and elsewhere in the eastern Mediterranean.

Correspondence from Canaanite town rulers to the Egyptian court in the time of Akhenaten (c. 1375 B.C.) reveals a weak structure of alliances, with an intermittent Egyptian military presence and an ominous fear of people called "Habiru" ("Apiru").

Migdol[m] and the sea. They are to encamp by the sea, directly opposite Baal Zephon.[n] ³Pharaoh will think, 'The Israelites are wandering around the land in confusion, hemmed in by the desert.' ⁴And I will harden Pharaoh's heart,[o] and he will pursue them.[p] But I will gain glory[q] for myself through Pharaoh and all his army, and the Egyptians will know that I am the LORD."[r] So the Israelites did this.

⁵When the king of Egypt was told that the people had fled,[s] Pharaoh and his officials changed their minds[t] about them and said, "What have we done? We have let the Israelites go and have lost their services!" ⁶So he had his chariot made ready and took his army with him. ⁷He took six hundred of the best chariots,[u] along with all the other chariots of Egypt, with officers over all of them. ⁸The LORD hardened the heart[v] of Pharaoh king of Egypt, so that he pursued the Israelites, who were marching out boldly.[w] ⁹The Egyptians—all Pharaoh's horses[x] and chariots, horsemen[x] and troops[y]—pursued the Israelites and overtook[z] them as they camped by the sea near Pi Hahiroth, opposite Baal Zephon.[a]

¹⁰As Pharaoh approached, the Israelites looked up, and there were the Egyptians, marching after them. They were terrified and cried[b] out to the LORD. ¹¹They said to Moses, "Was it because there were no graves in Egypt that you brought us to the desert to die?[c] What have you done to us by bringing us out of Egypt? ¹²Didn't we say to you in Egypt, 'Leave us alone; let us serve the Egyptians'? It would have been better for us to serve the Egyptians than to die in the desert!"[d]

¹³Moses answered the people, "Do not be afraid.[e] Stand firm and you will see[f] the deliverance the LORD will bring you today. The Egyptians you see today you will never see[g] again. ¹⁴The LORD will

fight[h] for you; you need only to be still."[i]

¹⁵Then the LORD said to Moses, "Why are you crying out to me?[j] Tell the Israelites to move on. ¹⁶Raise your staff[k] and stretch out your hand over the sea to divide the water[l] so that the Israelites can go through the sea on dry ground. ¹⁷I will harden the hearts[m] of the Egyptians so that they will go in after them.[n] And I will gain glory through Pharaoh and all his army, through his chariots and his horsemen. ¹⁸The Egyptians will know that I am the LORD[o] when I gain glory through Pharaoh, his chariots and his horsemen."

¹⁹Then the angel of God,[p] who had been traveling in front of Israel's army, withdrew and went behind them. The pillar of cloud[q] also moved from in front and stood behind[r] them, ²⁰coming between the armies of Egypt and Israel. Throughout the night the cloud brought darkness[s] to the one side and light to the other side; so neither went near the other all night long.

²¹Then Moses stretched out his hand[t] over the sea,[u] and all that night the LORD drove the sea back with a strong east wind[v] and turned it into dry land.[w] The waters were divided,[x] ²²and the Israelites went through the sea[y] on dry ground,[z] with a wall[a] of water on their right and on their left.

²³The Egyptians pursued them, and all Pharaoh's horses and chariots and horsemen[b] followed them into the sea. ²⁴During the last watch of the night the LORD

14:2 mNu 33:7; Jer 44:1; Eze 29:10 nver 9
14:4 oS Ex 4:21 pver 8,17,23; Ps 71:11 qS Ex 9:16; Ro 9:17,22-23 rS Ex 6:2; Eze 32:15
14:5 sS Ge 31:21 tPs 105:25
14:7 uEx 15:4
14:8 vS Ex 11:10 wNu 33:3; Ac 13:17
14:9 xGe 47:17 yver 6-7,25; Jos 24:6; Isa 43:17 zEx 15:9 aver 2
14:10 bEx 15:25; Jos 24:7; Ne 9:9; Ps 5:2; 34:17; 50:15; 107:6,28
14:11 cS Ex 5:21; 16:3; 17:3; Nu 11:1; 14:22; 20:4; 21:5; Dt 9:7
14:12 dS Ex 5:21; 15:24; 17:2; Ps 106:7-8
14:13 eS Ge 15:1 fISa 12:16; 2Ch 20:17 gver 30
14:14 hver 25; Ex 15:3; Dt 1:30; 3:22; 20:4; Jos 10:14; 23:3, 10; 2Ch 20:29; Ne 4:20; Ps 24:8; 35:1; Isa 42:13; Jer 41:12
14:15 iISa 12:16; Ps 37:7; 46:10; 116:7; Isa 28:12; 30:15; Zec 2:13
14:15 jJos 7:10
14:16 kS Ex 4:2 lver 27; Isa 10:26
14:17 mEx 4:21 nS ver 4
14:18 oS Ex 6:2; Eze 32:15
14:19 pS Ge 16:7; 1Co 10:1 qS Ex 13:21; 1Co 10:1 rIsa 26:7; 42:16; 49:10; 52:12; 58:8
14:20 sJos 24:7

14:21 tS Ex 7:19 uS Ex 4:2; Job 26:12; Isa 14:27; 23:11; 51:15; Jer 31:35; Ac 7:36 vS Ge 41:6; Ex 15:8; 2Sa 22:16; 1Ki 19:11; Job 38:1; 40:6; Jer 23:19; Na 1:3 wS ver 22; S Ge 8:1 x2Ki 2:8; Ps 74:13; 78:13; 114:5; 136:13; Isa 63:12
14:22 yver 16; Nu 33:8; Jos 24:6; Isa 43:16; 63:11; 1Co 10:1 zver 21,29; S Ex 3:12; 15:19; Dt 31:6-8; Jos 3:16, 17; 4:22; Ne 9:11; Ps 66:6; 77:19; 106:9; Isa 11:15; 41:10; 43:5; 44:27; 50:2; 51:10; 63:13; Jer 46:28; Na 1:4; Heb 11:29 aEx 15:8; Jos 3:13; Ps 78:13 14:23 bver 7

x9 Or charioteers; also in verses 17, 18, 23, 26 and 28

---

means "watchtower." *sea.* The sea that the NIV, in accordance with established tradition, calls the Red Sea—in Hebrew *Yam Suph,* i.e., Sea of Reeds (see 13:18 and NIV text note). Reference can hardly be to the northern end of the Gulf of Suez since reeds do not grow in salt water. Moreover, an Egyptian papyrus locates Baal Zephon in the vicinity of Tahpanhes (see note on Jer 2:16), a site near Lake Menzaleh about 20 miles east of Rameses. The crossing of the "Red Sea" thus probably occurred at the southern end of Lake Menzaleh (see map of "The Exodus," p. 106; but see note on 13:18). *Baal Zephon.* Means "Baal of the north" or "Baal of North (Mountain)"—also the name of a Canaanite god.
14:4 *know that I am the LORD.* See note on 6:3.
14:7 *officers.* The Hebrew for the singular of this word means "third man," perhaps referring to his place in a chariot crew.
14:14 *The LORD will fight for you.* A necessary reminder that although Israel was "armed for battle" (13:18) and

"marching out boldly" (v. 8), the victory would be won by God alone.
14:19 *angel of God.* See note on Ge 16:7; here associated with the cloud (see 13:21).
14:20 *coming between the armies of Egypt and Israel.* The pillar of cloud (signifying the Lord's presence) protected Israel (see Ps 105:39).
14:21 *strong east wind.* See 10:13. In 15:8 the poet praises the Lord and calls the wind the "blast of your nostrils," affirming (as here) that the miracle occurred in accordance with God's timing and under his direction (see 15:10).
14:22 *through the sea on dry ground.* In later times, psalmists and prophets reminded Israel of what God had done for them (see Ps 66:6; 106:9; 136:13–14; Isa 51:10; 63:11–13). *wall of water.* See v. 29. The waters were "piled up" (15:8) on both sides.
14:24 *last watch of the night.* Often the time for surprise attack (see Jos 10:9; 1Sa 11:11). *the LORD looked down.* See

looked down from the pillar of fire and cloud*c* at the Egyptian army and threw it into confusion. *d* 25He made the wheels of their chariots come off*y* so that they had difficulty driving. And the Egyptians said, "Let's get away from the Israelites! The LORD is fighting*e* for them against Egypt."*f*

26Then the LORD said to Moses, "Stretch out your hand over the sea so that the waters may flow back over the Egyptians and their chariots and horsemen." 27Moses stretched out his hand over the sea, and at daybreak the sea went back to its place. *g* The Egyptians were fleeing toward*z* it, and the LORD swept them into the sea. *h* 28The water flowed back and covered the chariots and horsemen—the entire army of Pharaoh that had followed the Israelites into the sea. *i* Not one of them survived.*j*

29But the Israelites went through the sea on dry ground, *k* with a wall*l* of water on their right and on their left. 30That day the LORD saved *m* Israel from the hands of the Egyptians, and Israel saw the Egyptians lying dead on the shore. 31And when the Israelites saw the great power*n* the LORD displayed against the Egyptians, the people feared*o* the LORD and put their trust*p* in him and in Moses his servant.

The Song of Moses and Miriam

15 Then Moses and the Israelites sang this song*q* to the LORD:

"I will sing*r* to the LORD,
  for he is highly exalted.
The horse and its rider*s*
  he has hurled into the sea. *t*
2The LORD is my strength*u* and my song;
  he has become my salvation. *v*
He is my God, *w* and I will praise him,
  my father's God, and I will exalt*x*
  him.

3The LORD is a warrior;*y*
  the LORD is his name.*z*
4Pharaoh's chariots and his army*a*
  he has hurled into the sea.
The best of Pharaoh's officers
  are drowned in the Red Sea. *a*
5The deep waters*b* have covered them;
  they sank to the depths like a stone. *c*

6"Your right hand, *d* O LORD,
  was majestic in power.
Your right hand, *e* O LORD,
  shattered*f* the enemy.
7In the greatness of your majesty*g*
  you threw down those who opposed
    you.
You unleashed your burning anger; *h*
  it consumed*i* them like stubble.
8By the blast of your nostrils*j*
  the waters piled up. *k*
The surging waters stood firm like a
    wall; *l*
  the deep waters congealed in the
    heart of the sea. *m*

9"The enemy boasted,
  'I will pursue, *n* I will overtake them.
I will divide the spoils; *o*
  I will gorge myself on them.
I will draw my sword
  and my hand will destroy them.'
10But you blew with your breath, *p*

14:24
*c*S Ex 13:21;
1Co 10:1
*d*Ex 23:27;
Jos 10:10;
1Sa 5:9; 7:10;
14:15; 2Sa 5:24;
2Ki 7:6; 19:7
14:25 *e*S ver 14
*f*S ver 9;
Dt 32:31;
1Sa 2:2; 4:8
14:27 *g*Jos 4:18
*h*ver 28; Ex 15:1,
21; Dt 1:40; 2:1;
11:4; Ps 78:53;
106:11; 136:15;
Heb 11:29
14:28 *i*ver 23;
Ex 15:19;
Jos 24:7 /S ver 27;
Ex 15:5; Jdg 4:16;
Ne 9:11
14:29 *k*ver 21,
S 22; Jos 24:11;
2Ki 2:8; Ps 74:15
*l*Ps 78:13
14:30 *m*ver 29;
1Sa 14:23;
1Ch 11:14;
Ps 44:7; 106:8,
10,21; Isa 43:3;
50:2; 51:9-10;
60:16; 63:8,11
14:31
*n*S Ex 9:16;
Ps 147:5
*o*Ex 20:18;
Dt 31:13;
Jos 4:24;
1Sa 12:18;
Ps 76:7; 112:1
*p*S Ex 4:5;
Ps 22:4; 40:3;
106:12; Jn 2:11;
11:45
15:1 *q*Nu 21:17;
Jdg 5:1; 2Sa 22:1;
1Ch 16:9;
Job 36:24;
Ps 59:16; 105:2;
Rev 15:3 *r*Jdg 5:3;
Ps 13:6; 21:13;
27:6; 61:8;
104:33; 106:12;
Isa 12:5,6;
42:10;
44:23 *s*Dt 11:4;
Ps 76:6; Jer 51:21
*t*S Ex 14:27
15:2 *u*Ps 18:1;
59:17 *v*S Ge 45:7;
Ex 14:13;
Ps 18:2,46; 25:5;
27:1; 62:2;
118:14; Isa 12:2;
33:2; Jnh 2:9;
Hab 3:18
*w*S Ge 28:21

*x*Dt 10:21; 2Sa 22:47; Ps 22:3; 30:1; 34:3; 35:27; 99:5;
103:19; 107:32; 108:5; 109:1; 118:28; 145:11; 148:14;
Isa 24:15; 25:1; Jer 17:14; Da 4:37 **15:3** *y*S Ex 14:14;
Rev 19:11 *z*S Ex 3:15 **15:4** *a*Ex 14:6-7; Jer 51:21 **15:5**
*b*S Ex 14:28 *c*ver 10; Ne 9:11 **15:6** *d*Ps 16:11; 17:7; 21:8;
63:8; 74:11; 77:10; 89:13; 98:1; 118:15; 138:7 *e*S Ex 3:20;
S Job 40:14 *f*Nu 24:8; 1Sa 2:10; Ps 2:9 **15:7** *g*Dt 33:26;
Ps 150:2 *h*Ps 2:5; 78:49-50; Jer 12:13; 25:38 *i*Ex 24:17;
Dt 4:24; 9:3; Ps 18:8; 59:13; Heb 12:29 **15:8** *j*S Ex 14:21;
Ps 18:15 *k*Jos 3:13; Ps 78:13; Isa 43:16 *l*S Ex 14:22 *m*Ps 46:2
15:9 *n*Ex 14:5-9; Dt 28:45; Ps 7:5; La 1:3 *o*Jdg 5:30; Isa 9:3;
53:12; Lk 11:22 **15:10** *p*Job 4:9; 15:30; Isa 11:4; 30:33;
40:7

y25 Or *He jammed the wheels of their chariots* (see
Samaritan Pentateuch, Septuagint and Syriac)   *z27* Or
from   *a4* Hebrew *Yam Suph;* that is, Sea of Reeds; also
in verse 22

note on 13:21.
14:25 *The LORD is fighting for them.* See note on v. 14.
14:27 *The LORD swept them into the sea.* As he had done with the locusts of the eighth plague (see 10:19).
14:28 *Not one of them survived.* The Lord's victory over the pharaoh's army was complete.
14:31 *feared the LORD.* See note on Ge 20:11. *put their trust in him and in Moses.* Faith in God's mighty power and confidence in Moses' leadership. *his servant.* Here refers to one who has the status of a high official in the Lord's kingly administration (see Nu 12:8; Dt 34:5). See also the same title applied to Joshua (Jos 24:29), Samuel (1Sa 3:10), David (2Sa 3:18) and Elijah (2Ki 9:36).
15:1–18 A hymn celebrating God's spectacular victory over the pharaoh and his army. The focus of the song is God himself (see v. 11); the divine name Yahweh ("the LORD") appears ten times. Similes—"like a stone" (v. 5), "like a wall" (v. 8) and "like lead" (v. 10)—mark the conclusion of

three of the five stanzas. The first four stanzas (vv. 1–5, 6–8, 9–10, 11–12) retell the story of the "deliverance" (14:13) at the Red Sea, and the final stanza (vv. 13–18) anticipates the future approach to and conquest of Canaan.
15:1 *Moses and the Israelites sang.* As though one person, the whole community praises God. *I will sing.* A common way to begin a hymn of praise (see Jdg 5:3; Ps 89:1; 101:1; 108:1).
15:2 The first half of the verse is quoted verbatim in Ps 118:14 (see Isa 12:2).
15:3 *The LORD is a warrior.* See note on 14:14. God is often pictured as a king leading his people into battle (see, e.g., Dt 1:30; Jdg 4:14; 2Sa 5:24; 2Ch 20:17–18).
15:4 *officers.* See note on 14:7.
15:5 *sank . . . like a stone.* Babylon is similarly described in Jer 51:63–64.
15:8 See note on 14:22. *blast of your nostrils.* See note on 14:21; see also Ps 18:15.

and the sea covered them.
They sank like lead
in the mighty waters. *q*

11"Who among the gods is like you, *r*
O Lord?
Who is like you—
majestic in holiness, *s*
awesome in glory, *t*
working wonders? *u*
12You stretched out *v* your right hand
and the earth swallowed them. *w*

13"In your unfailing love you will lead *x*
the people you have redeemed. *y*
In your strength you will guide them
to your holy dwelling. *z*
14The nations will hear and tremble; *a*
anguish *b* will grip the people of
Philistia. *c*
15The chiefs *d* of Edom *e* will be terrified,
the leaders of Moab will be seized
with trembling, *f*
the people *b* of Canaan will melt *g* away;
16 terror *h* and dread will fall upon
them.
By the power of your arm
they will be as still as a stone *i* —
until your people pass by, O Lord,
until the people you bought *c j* pass
by. *k*
17You will bring *l* them in and plant *m*
them
on the mountain *n* of your
inheritance—
the place, O Lord, you made for your
dwelling, *o*
the sanctuary, *p* O Lord, your hands
established.

18The Lord will reign
for ever and ever." *q*

19When Pharaoh's horses, chariots and
horsemen *d* went into the sea, *r* the Lord
brought the waters of the sea back over
them, but the Israelites walked through
the sea on dry ground. *s* 20Then Miriam *t*
the prophetess, *u* Aaron's sister, took a
tambourine in her hand, and all the
women followed her, with tambourines *v*
and dancing. *w* 21Miriam sang *x* to them:

"Sing to the Lord,
for he is highly exalted.
The horse and its rider *y*
he has hurled into the sea." *z*

The Waters of Marah and Elim

22Then Moses led Israel from the Red
Sea and they went into the Desert *a* of
Shur. *b* For three days they traveled in the
desert without finding water. *c* 23When
they came to Marah, they could not drink
its water because it was bitter. (That is
why the place is called Marah. *e d*) 24So the
people grumbled *e* against Moses, saying,
"What are we to drink?" *f*

15:10 *you blew with your breath.* See note on 14:21.
15:11 *Who is like you . . . ?* See Ps 35:10; 71:19; 89:6; 113:5; Mic 7:18. The Lord, who tolerates no rivals, has defeated all the gods of Egypt and their worshipers.
15:12 *earth.* Perhaps refers to Sheol or the grave (see Ps 63:9; 71:20), the "realm of death below" (Dt 32:22), since it was the sea that swallowed the Egyptians.
15:13 *people you have redeemed.* See note on 6:6. *your holy dwelling.* Perhaps a reference to the house of worship at Shiloh (see Jer 7:12), and ultimately the temple on Mount Zion (see Ps 76:2), the "place" God would "choose" (Dt 12:14,18,26; 14:25; 16:7,15–16; 17:8,10; 31:11) to put "his Name" (Dt 12:5,11,21; 14:23–24; 16:2,6,11; 26:2). But the phrase may refer to the promised land, which is called "your dwelling" and "the sanctuary . . . your hands established" in v. 17.
15:14–15 *Philistia . . . Edom . . . Moab . . . Canaan.* The order is roughly that along the route Israel would follow from Mount Sinai to the promised land.
15:15 *chiefs.* The term used earlier of the Edomite rulers (see Ge 36:15–19,21,29–30,40,43).
15:16 *dread will fall upon them.* See note on 1Ch 14:17. *bought.* See NIV text note; see also Dt 32:6 and NIV text note. In Ps 74:2 the meaning "bought" or "purchased" is found in context with "redeemed" (see note on 13:13).

15:17 *inheritance.* The promised land (see 1Sa 26:19; Ps 79:1).
15:20 *prophetess.* See Nu 12:1–2 for a statement by Miriam concerning her prophetic gift (see note on 7:1–2). Other prophetesses in the Bible were Deborah (Jdg 4:4), Isaiah's wife (Isa 8:3, but see note there), Huldah (2Ki 22:14), Noadiah (Ne 6:14), Anna (Lk 2:36) and Philip's daughters (Ac 21:9). *women followed her, with tambourines and dancing.* Such celebration was common after victory in battle (see 1Sa 18:6; 2Sa 1:20).
15:21 Miriam repeats the first four lines of the victory hymn (see v. 1), changing only the form of the first verb.
15:22 *Desert of Shur.* Located east of Egypt (see Ge 25:18; 1Sa 15:7) in the northwestern part of the Sinai peninsula. In Nu 33:8 it is called the "Desert of Etham." Shur and Etham both mean "fortress wall" (Shur in Hebrew, Etham in Egyptian).
15:23 *Marah.* Probably modern Ain Hawarah, inland from the Gulf of Suez and 50 miles south of its northern end.
15:24 *grumbled.* During their desert wanderings, the Israelites grumbled against Moses and Aaron whenever they faced a crisis (see 16:2; 17:3; Nu 14:2; 16:11,41). In reality, however, they were grumbling "against the Lord" (16:8). Paul warns us not to follow their example (see 1Co 10:10).

15:10 *q*ver 5; Ne 9:11; Ps 29:3; 32:6; 77:19 15:11 *r*S Ex 8:10; Ps 77:13; S Isa 46:5 *s*Lev 19:2; 1Sa 2:2; 1Ch 16:29; Ps 99:3; 110:3; Isa 6:3; Rev 4:8 *t*S Ex 14:4; Ps 4:2; 8:1; 26:8; Isa 35:2; 40:5 *u*S Ex 3:20 15:12 *v*S Ex 7:5 *w*Nu 16:32; 26:10; Dt 11:6; Ps 106:17 15:13 *x*Ne 9:12; Ps 77:20 *y*S Ex 6:6; Job 33:28; Ps 71:23; 106:10; Isa 1:27; 41:14; 43:14; 44:22-24; 51:10; 63:9; Tit 2:14 *z*ver 17; Ps 68:16; 76:2; 78:54 15:14 *a*ver 16; Ex 23:27; Dt 2:25; Jos 2:9; 5:1; 9:24; 1Sa 4:7; Est 8:17; Ps 48:6; 96:9; 99:1; 114:7; Eze 38:20 *b*Isa 13:8 *c*Ps 83:7 15:15 *d*S Ge 36:15 *e*Dt 2:4 /Nu 22:3; Ps 114:7 *g*Jos 2:9, 24 15:16 *h*S ver 14; S Ge 35:5 *i*1Sa 25:37 *j*Ps 74:2; 2Pe 2:1 *k*Dt 2:4 15:17 *l*Ex 23:20; 32:34; 33:12 *m*2Sa 7:10; Ps 44:2; 80:8,15; Isa 5:2; 60:21; Jer 2:21; 11:17; 24:6; Am 9:15 *n*Dt 33:19; Ps 2:6; 3:4; 15:1; 78:54,68; 133:3; Da 9:16; Joel 2:1; Ob 1:16; Zep 3:11 *o*S ver 13; Ps 132:13-14 *p*Ps 78:69; 114:2 15:18 *q*S Ge 21:33; Ps 9:7; 29:10; 55:19; 66:7; 80:1; 102:12; 145:13; La 5:19 15:19 *r*S Ex 14:28 *s*S Ex 14:22 15:20 *t*ver 21; Ex 2:4; Nu 12:1; 20:1; 26:59; 1Ch 4:17; 6:3 *u*Jdg 4:4; 2Ki 22:14; 2Ch 34:22; Ne 6:14; Isa 8:3; Eze 13:17 *v*S Ge 31:27; 1Sa 18:6; Ps 81:2; Isa 30:32 *w*S Ge 4:21; Jdg 11:34; 21:21; 1Sa 18:6; 2Sa 6:5,14,16; Ps 30:11; 149:3; 150:4; SS 6:13; Jer 31:4,13 15:21 *x*1Sa 18:7 *y*Am 2:15; Hag 2:22 *z*S Ex 14:27 15:22 *a*Ps 78:52 *b*S Ge 16:7 *c*Ex 17:1,3; Nu 20:2,5; 33:14; Ps 107:5 15:23 *d*Nu 33:8; Ru 1:20 15:24 *e*S Ex 14:12; 16:2; 17:3; Nu 14:2; Jos 9:18; Ps 78:18,42; 106:13,25; Eze 16:43 /Mt 6:31

*b*15 Or *rulers*   *c*16 Or *created*   *d*19 Or *charioteers*
*e*23 *Marah* means *bitter.*

25Then Moses cried out[g] to the LORD,
and the LORD showed him a piece of
wood. He threw[h] it into the water, and
the water became sweet.

There the LORD made a decree and a
law for them, and there he tested[i] them.
26He said, "If you listen carefully to the
voice of the LORD your God and do what is
right in his eyes, if you pay attention to his
commands and keep[j] all his decrees,[k] I
will not bring on you any of the diseases[l] I
brought on the Egyptians, for I am the
LORD, who heals[m] you."

27Then they came to Elim, where there
were twelve springs and seventy palm
trees, and they camped[n] there near the
water.

Manna and Quail

16 The whole Israelite community set
out from Elim and came to the
Desert of Sin,[o] which is between Elim and
Sinai, on the fifteenth day of the second
month after they had come out of Egypt.[p]
2In the desert the whole community grumbled[q] against Moses and Aaron. 3The Israelites said to them, "If only we had died by
the LORD's hand in Egypt![r] There we sat
around pots of meat and ate all the food[s]
we wanted, but you have brought us out
into this desert to starve this entire assembly to death."[t]

4Then the LORD said to Moses, "I will
rain down bread from heaven[u] for you.
The people are to go out each day and
gather enough for that day. In this way I
will test[v] them and see whether they will
follow my instructions. 5On the sixth day
they are to prepare what they bring in, and
that is to be twice[w] as much as they gather
on the other days."

6So Moses and Aaron said to all the Israelites, "In the evening you will know that
it was the LORD who brought you out of
Egypt,[x] 7and in the morning you will see
the glory[y] of the LORD, because he has
heard your grumbling[z] against him. Who
are we, that you should grumble against
us?"[a] 8Moses also said, "You will know
that it was the LORD when he gives you
meat to eat in the evening and all the
bread you want in the morning, because
he has heard your grumbling[b] against him.
Who are we? You are not grumbling
against us, but against the LORD."[c]

9Then Moses told Aaron, "Say to the
entire Israelite community, 'Come before
the LORD, for he has heard your grumbling.' "

10While Aaron was speaking to the
whole Israelite community, they looked
toward the desert, and there was the
glory[d] of the LORD appearing in the
cloud.[e]

11The LORD said to Moses, 12"I have
heard the grumbling[f] of the Israelites. Tell
them, 'At twilight you will eat meat, and in
the morning you will be filled with bread.
Then you will know that I am the LORD
your God.' "[g]

13That evening quail[h] came and
covered the camp, and in the morning
there was a layer of dew[i] around the
camp. 14When the dew was gone, thin
flakes like frost[j] on the ground appeared
on the desert floor. 15When the Israelites
saw it, they said to each other, "What is
it?" For they did not know[k] what it was.

Moses said to them, "It is the bread[l]
the LORD has given you to eat. 16This is

15:25 [g]S Ex 14:10 [h]2Ki 2:21; 4:41; 6:6 [i]S Ge 22:1; Jdg 3:4; Job 23:10; Ps 81:7; Isa 48:10 **15:26** [j]Ex 23:22; Dt 11:13; 15:5; 28:1; Jer 11:6 [k]Ex 19:5-6; 20:2-17; Dt 7:12 [l]Dt 7:15; 28:27, 58-60; 32:39; 1Sa 5:6; Ps 30:2; 41:3-4; 103:3 [m]Ex 23:25-26; 2Ki 20:5; Ps 25:11; 103:3; 107:20; Jer 30:17; Hos 11:3 **15:27** [n]Nu 33:9 **16:1** [o]Ex 17:1; Nu 33:11,12 [p]S Ex 6:6; 12:1-2 **16:2** [q]S Ex 15:24; 1Co 10:10 **16:3** [r]Ex 17:3; Nu 14:2; 20:3 [s]Nu 11:4,34; Dt 12:20; Ps 78:18; 106:14; Jer 44:17 [t]S Ge 47:15; Dt 8:3 **16:4** [u]ver 14-15; Dt 8:3; Ne 9:15; Ps 78:24; 105:40; S Jn 6:31* [v]S Ge 22:1 **16:5** [w]ver 22; Lev 25:21 **16:6** [x]S Ex 6:6 **16:7** [y]ver 10; Ex 24:16; 29:43; 33:18,22; 40:34; Lev 9:6; Nu 16:19,42; Dt 5:24; 1Ki 8:11; Ps 63:2; Isa 6:3; 35:2; 40:5; 44:23; 60:1; 66:18; Eze 1:28; 10:4; 43:5; Hab 2:14; Hag 2:7; Jn 11:40 [z]ver 12; Nu 11:1, 18; 14:2,27,28; 17:5 [a]Nu 16:11 **16:8** [b]ver 7 [c]Nu 23:21; Dt 33:5; Jdg 8:23; 1Sa 8:7; 12:12; S Mt 10:40; Ro 13:2; 1Th 4:8 **16:10** [d]S ver 7; Jn 11:4 [e]Ex 13:21; 40:34-35; 1Ki 8:10; 2Ch 7:1; Eze 10:4 **16:12** [f]S ver 7 [g]S Ex 6:2; S 20:2 **16:13** [h]Nu 11:31; Ps 78:27-28; 105:40; 106:15 [i]Nu 11:9 **16:14** [j]ver 31; Nu 11:7-9; Dt 8:3,16; Ps 105:40 **16:15** [k]Dt 8:16 [l]S ver 4; Ne 9:20; S Jn 6:31

15:25 *He threw it into the water, and the water became sweet.* For a similar occurrence see 2Ki 2:19–22. *a decree and a law.* Technical terms presumably referring to what follows in v. 26. *tested.* See note on Ge 22:1. God tested Israel also in connection with his provision of manna (see 16:4; Dt 8:2–3) and the giving of the Ten Commandments (see 20:20).
15:27 *Elim.* Seven miles south of Ain Hawarah (see note on v. 23) in the well-watered valley of Gharandel. *palm trees.* Elim means "large trees."
16:1 *from Elim . . . to the Desert of Sin.* See Nu 33:10–11. The Desert of Sin was in southwestern Sinai ("Sin" is probably derived from "Sinai") in the region today called Debbet er-Ramleh. *fifteenth day of the second month.* Exactly one month had passed since Israel's exodus from Egypt (see 12:2,6,29,31).
16:2 *grumbled.* See note on 15:24.
16:3 *meat.* Nu 11:5 lists additional items of food from Egypt that the Israelites craved.
16:4 *bread from heaven.* Jesus called himself "the true bread from heaven" (Jn 6:32), "the bread of God" (Jn 6:33), "the bread of life" (Jn 6:35,48), "the living bread that came down from heaven" (Jn 6:51)—all in the spiritual sense (Jn 6:63). For a similar application see Dt 8:3 and Jesus' quotation of it in Mt 4:4. *go out each day and gather enough for that day.* Probably the background for Jesus' model petition in Mt 6:11; Lk 11:3. *test.* See notes on 15:25; Ge 22:1.
16:5 *sixth day . . . twice as much as they gather on the other days.* To provide for "the seventh day, the Sabbath" (v. 26), "a day of rest" (v. 23). See v. 29.
16:6 *know.* See note on 6:3.
16:8 *meat . . . in the evening and bread . . . in the morning.* See vv. 13–14.
16:10 *glory of the LORD appearing in the cloud.* See 24:15–17; see also note on 13:21.
16:12 *twilight.* See note on 12:6.
16:13 *quail came.* For a similar incident see Nu 11:31–33.
16:14 *thin flakes like frost.* See note on Nu 11:7.
16:15 *What is it?* See v. 31 and NIV text note.

what the Lord has commanded: 'Each one is to gather as much as he needs. Take an omer[f][m] for each person you have in your tent.' "

[17]The Israelites did as they were told; some gathered much, some little. [18]And when they measured it by the omer, he who gathered much did not have too much, and he who gathered little did not have too little.[n] Each one gathered as much as he needed.

[19]Then Moses said to them, "No one is to keep any of it until morning."[o]

[20]However, some of them paid no attention to Moses; they kept part of it until morning, but it was full of maggots and began to smell.[p] So Moses was angry[q] with them.

[21]Each morning everyone gathered as much as he needed, and when the sun grew hot, it melted away. [22]On the sixth day, they gathered twice[r] as much—two omers[g] for each person—and the leaders of the community[s] came and reported this to Moses. [23]He said to them, "This is what the Lord commanded: 'Tomorrow is to be a day of rest, a holy Sabbath[t] to the Lord. So bake what you want to bake and boil what you want to boil. Save whatever is left and keep it until morning.' "

[24]So they saved it until morning, as Moses commanded, and it did not stink or get maggots in it. [25]"Eat it today," Moses said, "because today is a Sabbath to the Lord. You will not find any of it on the ground today. [26]Six days you are to gather it, but on the seventh day, the Sabbath,[u] there will not be any."

[27]Nevertheless, some of the people went out on the seventh day to gather it, but they found none. [28]Then the Lord said to Moses, "How long will you[h] refuse to keep my commands[v] and my instructions? [29]Bear in mind that the Lord has given you the Sabbath; that is why on the sixth day he gives you bread for two days.

Everyone is to stay where he is on the seventh day; no one is to go out." [30]So the people rested on the seventh day.

[31]The people of Israel called the bread manna.[i][w] It was white like coriander seed and tasted like wafers made with honey. [32]Moses said, "This is what the Lord has commanded: 'Take an omer of manna and keep it for the generations to come, so they can see the bread I gave you to eat in the desert when I brought you out of Egypt.' "

[33]So Moses said to Aaron, "Take a jar and put an omer of manna[x] in it. Then place it before the Lord to be kept for the generations to come."

[34]As the Lord commanded Moses, Aaron put the manna in front of the Testimony,[y] that it might be kept. [35]The Israelites ate manna[z] forty years,[a] until they came to a land that was settled; they ate manna until they reached the border of Canaan.[b]

[36](An omer[c] is one tenth of an ephah.)[d]

Water From the Rock

17 The whole Israelite community set out from the Desert of Sin,[e] traveling from place to place as the Lord commanded. They camped at Rephidim,[f] but there was no water[g] for the people to drink. [2]So they quarreled with Moses and said, "Give us water[h] to drink."[i]

Moses replied, "Why do you quarrel with me? Why do you put the Lord to the test?"[j]

[3]But the people were thirsty[k] for water there, and they grumbled[l] against Moses. They said, "Why did you bring us up out of Egypt to make us and our children and livestock die[m] of thirst?"

[4]Then Moses cried out to the Lord,

16:16 [m]ver 32,36
16:18 [n]2Co 8:15*
16:19 [o]ver 23; Ex 12:10
16:20 [p]ver 24 [q]Ex 32:19
16:22 [r]S ver 5 [s]Ex 34:31
16:23 [t]S Ge 2:3; S Ex 20:8; Dt 5:13-14
16:26 [u]ver 23
16:28 [v]Jos 9:14; Ps 78:10; 106:13; 107:11; 119:1; Jer 32:23

16:31 [w]S ver 14
16:33 [x]Heb 9:4; Rev 2:17
16:34 [y]Ex 25:16, 21,22; 27:21; 31:18; 40:20; Lev 16:13; Nu 1:50; 7:89; 10:11; 17:4,10; Dt 10:2; 1Ki 8:9; 2Ch 5:10
16:35 [z]Jn 6:31, 49 [a]Nu 14:33; 33:38; Dt 1:3; 2:7; 8:2-4; Jos 5:6; Jdg 3:11; Ne 9:21; Ps 95:10; Am 5:25 [b]Jos 5:12
16:36 [c]S ver 16 [d]Lev 5:11; 6:20; Nu 5:15; 15:4; 28:5
17:1 [e]S Ex 16:1 [f]ver 8; Ex 19:2; Nu 33:15 [g]Nu 20:5; 21:5; 33:14
17:2 [h]Nu 20:2; 33:14; Ps 107:5 [i]S Ex 14:12 [j]Dt 6:16; Ps 78:18,41; 106:14; Mt 4:7; 1Co 10:9
17:3 [k]S Ex 15:22 [l]S Ex 15:24 [m]S Ex 14:11

[f]16 That is, probably about 2 quarts (about 2 liters); also in verses 18, 32, 33 and 36   [g]22 That is, probably about 4 quarts (about 4.5 liters)   [h]28 The Hebrew is plural.   [i]31 Manna means What is it? (see verse 15).

16:18 See 2Co 8:15, where Paul quotes the heart of the verse as an illustration of Christians who share with each other what they possess.
16:23 Sabbath. The first occurrence of the word itself, though the principle of the seventh day as a day of rest and holiness is set forth in the account of creation (see note on Ge 2:3).
16:29 See note on v. 5.
16:31 manna. See note on Nu 11:7.
16:33 jar. Said in Heb 9:4 to be made of gold.
16:34 Testimony. Anticipates the later description of the tablets containing the Ten Commandments as the "two tablets of the Testimony" (31:18; 32:15; 34:29), which gave their name to the "ark of the Testimony" (25:22; 26:33) in which they were placed (see 25:16,21) along with

the jar of manna (see Heb 9:4; see also Rev 2:17 and note).
16:35 ate manna forty years . . . until they reached . . . Canaan. The manna stopped at the time the Israelites celebrated their first Passover in Canaan (see Jos 5:10–12).
17:1 traveling from place to place. For a list of specific sites see Nu 33:12–14. Rephidim. Probably either the Wadi Refayid or the Wadi Feiran, both near Jebel Musa (see note on 3:1) in southern Sinai.
17:2 put the Lord to the test. Israel fails the Lord's testing of her (see 16:4) by putting the Lord to the test.
17:3 grumbled. See note on 15:24.
17:4 these people. The same note of distance and alienation ("these people" instead of "my people") in such situations is found often in the prophets (see, e.g., Isa 6:9; Hag 1:2).

"What am I to do with these people? They are almost ready to stone[n] me."

[5]The LORD answered Moses, "Walk on ahead of the people. Take with you some of the elders of Israel and take in your hand the staff[o] with which you struck the Nile,[p] and go. [6]I will stand there before you by the rock at Horeb.[q] Strike[r] the rock, and water[s] will come out of it for the people to drink." So Moses did this in the sight of the elders of Israel. [7]And he called the place Massah[j t] and Meribah[k u] because the Israelites quarreled and because they tested the LORD saying, "Is the LORD among us or not?"

The Amalekites Defeated

[8]The Amalekites[v] came and attacked the Israelites at Rephidim.[w] [9]Moses said to Joshua,[x] "Choose some of our men and go out to fight the Amalekites. Tomorrow I will stand on top of the hill with the staff[y] of God in my hands."

[10]So Joshua fought the Amalekites as Moses had ordered, and Moses, Aaron and Hur[z] went to the top of the hill. [11]As long as Moses held up his hands, the Israelites were winning,[a] but whenever he lowered his hands, the Amalekites were winning. [12]When Moses' hands grew tired, they took a stone and put it under him and he sat on it. Aaron and Hur held his hands up—one on one side, one on the other—so that his hands remained steady

till sunset.[b] [13]So Joshua overcame the Amalekite[c] army with the sword.

[14]Then the LORD said to Moses, "Write[d] this on a scroll as something to be remembered and make sure that Joshua hears it, because I will completely blot out[e] the memory of Amalek[f] from under heaven."

[15]Moses built an altar[g] and called[h] it The LORD is my Banner. [16]He said, "For hands were lifted up to the throne of the LORD. The[l] LORD will be at war against the Amalekites[i] from generation to generation."[j]

Jethro Visits Moses

18 Now Jethro,[k] the priest of Midian[l] and father-in-law of Moses, heard of everything God had done for Moses and for his people Israel, and how the LORD had brought Israel out of Egypt.[m]

[2]After Moses had sent away his wife Zipporah,[n] his father-in-law Jethro received her [3]and her two sons.[o] One son was named Gershom,[m] for Moses said, "I have become an alien in a foreign land";[p] [4]and the other was named Eliezer,[n q] for

Cross references (center column)

17:4 [n]Nu 14:10; 1Sa 30:6; SJn 8:59
17:5 [o]S Ex 4:2; S 10:12-13 [p]Ex 7:20
17:6 [q]S Ex 3:1 [r]Nu 20:8 [s]Nu 20:11; Dt 8:15; Jdg 15:19; 2Ki 3:20; Ne 9:15; Ps 74:15; 78:15-16; 105:41; 107:35; 114:8; Isa 30:25; 35:6; 43:19; 48:21; 1Co 10:4
17:7 [t]Dt 6:16; 9:22; 33:8; Ps 95:8 [u]Nu 20:13,24; 27:14; Ps 81:7; 106:32
17:8 [v]S Ge 36:12 [w]S ver 1
17:9 [x]Ex 24:13; 32:17; 33:11; Nu 11:28; 27:22; Dt 1:38; Jos 1:1; Ac 7:45 [y]S Ex 4:17
17:10 [z]ver 10-12; Ex 24:14; 31:2
17:11 [a]Jas 5:16
17:12 [b]Jos 8:26
17:13 [c]ver 8
17:14 [d]Ex 24:4; 34:27; Nu 33:2; Dt 31:9; Job 19:23; Isa 30:8; Jer 36:2; 45:1; 51:60 [e]Ex 32:33; Dt 29:20; Job 18:17; Ps 9:5; 34:16; 109:15; Eze 18:4 [f]ver 13; S Ge 36:12; Nu 24:7; Jdg 3:13; 1Sa 30:17-18; Ps 83:7
17:15 [g]S Ge 8:20 [h]S Ge 22:14 17:16 [i]Nu 24:7; 1Sa 15:8,32; 1Ch 4:43; Est 3:1; 8:3; 9:24 /Est 9:5 18:1 [k]S Ex 2:18 [l]S Ex 2:16 [m]S Ex 6:6 18:2 [n]S Ex 2:21 18:3 [o]S Ex 4:20; Ac 7:29 [p]Ex 2:22 18:4 [q]1Ch 23:15

[j]7 Massah means testing.   [k]7 Meribah means quarreling.   [l]16 Or "Because a hand was against the throne of the LORD, the   [m]3 Gershom sounds like the Hebrew for an alien there.   [n]4 Eliezer means my God is helper.

17:6 I will stand there . . . by the rock. Paul may have had this incident in mind when he spoke of Christ as "the spiritual rock that accompanied" Israel (see 1Co 10:4; see also Heb 11:24–26). Horeb. See note on 3:1. Strike the rock, and water will come out. The event was later celebrated by Israel's hymn writers and prophets (see Ps 78:15–16,20; 105:41; 114:8; Isa 48:21).

17:7 Massah and Meribah. Heb 3:7–8,15 (quoting Ps 95:7–8) gives the meaning "testing" for Massah and "rebellion" for Meribah. Another Meribah, where a similar incident occurred near Kadesh Barnea (see note on Ge 14:7), is referred to in Nu 20:13,24; 27:14; Dt 32:51; 33:8; Ps 81:7; 106:32; Eze 47:19; 48:28.

17:8 Amalekites. See note on Ge 14:7.

17:9 Joshua. The name given by Moses to Hoshea son of Nun (see Nu 13:16). "Hoshea" means "salvation," while "Joshua" means "The LORD saves." The Greek form of the name Joshua is the same as that of the name Jesus, for the meaning of which see NIV text note on Mt 1:21. Joshua was from the tribe of Ephraim (Nu 13:8), one of the most powerful of the 12 tribes (see notes on Ge 48:6,19). fight the Amalekites. Joshua's military prowess uniquely suited him to be the conqueror of Canaan 40 years later, while his faith in God and loyalty to Moses suited him to be Moses' "aide" (24:13; 33:11) and successor (see Dt 1:38; 3:28; 31:14; 34:9; Jos 1:5).

17:10 Hur. Perhaps the same Hur who was the son of Caleb and the grandfather of Bezalel (see 1Ch 2:19–20), one

of the builders of the tabernacle (see 31:2–5).

17:11 held up his hands. A symbol of appeal to God for help and enablement (see note on 9:29; see also 9:22; 10:12; 14:16).

17:14 Write. See 24:4; 34:27–28; Nu 33:2; Dt 28:58; 29:20,21,27; 30:10; 31:9,19,22,24; see also Introduction: Author and Date of Writing. scroll. A long strip of leather or papyrus on which scribes wrote in columns (see Jer 36:23) with pen (see Isa 8:1) and ink (see Jer 36:18), sometimes on both sides (see Eze 2:10; Rev 5:1). After being rolled up, a scroll was often sealed (see Isa 29:11; Da 12:4; Rev 5:1–2, 5,9) to protect its contents. Scrolls were of various sizes (see Isa 8:1; Rev 10:2,9–10). Certain Egyptian examples reached lengths of over 100 feet; Biblical scrolls, however, rarely exceeded 30 feet in length, as in the case of a book like Isaiah (see Lk 4:17). Reading the contents of a scroll involved the awkward procedure of unrolling it with one hand while rolling it up with the other (see Isa 34:4; Eze 2:10; Lk 4:17,20; Rev 6:14). Shortly after the time of Christ the scroll gave way to the book form still used today.

17:15 my Banner. Recalling Moses' petition with upraised hands (see vv. 11–12,16) and testifying to the power of God displayed in defense of his people.

18:1 Jethro the priest of Midian. See note on 2:16.

18:2 sent away his wife. Apparently Moses sent Zipporah to her father with the news that the Lord had blessed his mission (see v. 1) and that he was in the vicinity of Mount Sinai with Israel.

he said, "My father's God was my helper;[r] he saved me from the sword of Pharaoh."

[5]Jethro, Moses' father-in-law, together with Moses' sons and wife, came to him in the desert, where he was camped near the mountain[s] of God. [6]Jethro had sent word to him, "I, your father-in-law Jethro, am coming to you with your wife and her two sons."

[7]So Moses went out to meet his father-in-law and bowed down[t] and kissed[u] him. They greeted each other and then went into the tent. [8]Moses told his father-in-law about everything the LORD had done to Pharaoh and the Egyptians for Israel's sake and about all the hardships[v] they had met along the way and how the LORD had saved[w] them.

[9]Jethro was delighted to hear about all the good things[x] the LORD had done for Israel in rescuing them from the hand of the Egyptians. [10]He said, "Praise be to the LORD,[y] who rescued you from the hand of the Egyptians and of Pharaoh, and who rescued the people from the hand of the Egyptians. [11]Now I know that the LORD is greater than all other gods,[z] for he did this to those who had treated Israel arrogantly."[a] [12]Then Jethro, Moses' father-in-law,[b] brought a burnt offering[c] and other sacrifices[d] to God, and Aaron came with all the elders of Israel to eat bread[e] with Moses' father-in-law in the presence[f] of God.

[13]The next day Moses took his seat to serve as judge for the people, and they stood around him from morning till evening. [14]When his father-in-law saw all that Moses was doing for the people, he said, "What is this you are doing for the people? Why do you alone sit as judge, while all these people stand around you from morning till evening?"

[15]Moses answered him, "Because the people come to me to seek God's will.[g] [16]Whenever they have a dispute,[h] it is brought to me, and I decide between the parties and inform them of God's decrees and laws."[i]

[17]Moses' father-in-law replied, "What you are doing is not good. [18]You and these people who come to you will only wear yourselves out. The work is too heavy for you; you cannot handle it alone.[j] [19]Listen now to me and I will give you some advice, and may God be with you.[k] You must be the people's representative before God and bring their disputes[l] to him. [20]Teach them the decrees and laws,[m] and show them the way to live[n] and the duties they are to perform.[o] [21]But select capable men[p] from all the people—men who fear[q] God, trustworthy men who hate dishonest gain[r]—and appoint them as officials[s] over thousands, hundreds, fifties and tens. [22]Have them serve as judges for the people at all times, but have them bring every difficult case[t] to you; the simple cases they can decide themselves. That will make your load lighter, because they will share[u] it with you. [23]If you do this and God so commands, you will be able to stand the strain, and all these people will go home satisfied."

[24]Moses listened to his father-in-law and did everything he said. [25]He chose capable men from all Israel and made them leaders[v] of the people, officials over thousands, hundreds, fifties and tens.[w] [26]They served as judges[x] for the people at all times. The difficult cases[y] they brought to Moses, but the simple ones they decided themselves.[z]

[27]Then Moses sent his father-in-law on his way, and Jethro returned to his own country.[a]

At Mount Sinai

19 In the third month after the Israelites left Egypt[b]—on the very day—they came to the Desert of Sinai.[c] [2]After they set out from Rephidim,[d] they entered the Desert of Sinai, and Israel camped there in the desert in front of the mountain.[e]

19:2 [d]S Ex 17:1 [e]S ver 17; S Ex 3:1; Dt 5:2-4

Cross references (center column)

18:4 [r]S Ge 49:25; S Dt 33:29
18:5 [s]S Ex 3:1
18:7 [t]S Ge 17:3; S 43:28 [u]S Ge 29:13
18:8 [v]Nu 20:14; Ne 9:32 [w]Ex 15:6,16; Ps 81:7
18:9 [x]Jos 21:45; 1Ki 8:66; Ne 9:25; Ps 145:7; Isa 63:7
18:10 [y]S Ge 9:26; S 24:27
18:11 [z]S Ex 12:12; S 1Ch 16:25 [a]S Ex 1:10; S Lk 1:51
18:12 [b]S Ex 3:1 [c]Ex 10:25; 20:24; Lev 1:2-9 [d]Ge 31:54; Ex 24:5 [e]S Ge 26:30 [f]Dt 12:7
18:15 [g]S ver 19; S Ge 25:22
18:16 [h]Ex 24:14
[i]ver 15; Lev 24:12; Nu 15:34; Dt 1:17; 2Ch 19:7; Pr 24:23; Mal 2:9
18:18 [j]Nu 11:11,14,17; Dt 1:9,12
18:19 [k]Ex 3:12
[l]ver 15; Nu 27:5
18:20 [m]Dt 4:1,5; 5:1; Ps 119:12, 26,68 [n]Ps 143:8 [o]S Ge 39:11
18:21 [p]S Ge 47:6; Ac 6:3 [q]S Ge 22:12 [r]Ex 23:8; Dt 16:19; 1Sa 12:3; Ps 15:5; Pr 17:23; 28:8; Ecc 7:7; Eze 18:8; 22:12 [s]Nu 1:16; 7:2; 10:4; Dt 16:18; Ezr 7:25
18:22 [t]Lev 24:11; Dt 1:17-18 [u]Nu 11:17; Dt 1:9
18:25 [v]Nu 1:16; 7:2; 11:16; Dt 16:18 [w]Dt 1:13-15
18:26 [x]Dt 16:18; 2Ch 19:5; Ezr 7:25 [y]Dt 1:17 [z]ver 22
18:27 [a]Nu 10:29-30
19:1 [b]S Ex 6:6 [c]Nu 1:1; 3:14; 33:15

Bottom notes

18:5 *mountain of God.* See 3:1 and note.
18:11 *Now I know that the LORD is greater than all other gods.* See the similar confession of Naaman in 2Ki 5:15.
18:12 *brought.* The verb means "provided" an animal for sacrifice (see, e.g., 25:2; Lev 12:8), not "officiated at" a sacrifice. *eat bread with.* A token of friendship (contrast the battle with the Amalekites, 17:8–16). Such a meal often climaxed the establishment of a treaty (see Ge 31:54; Ex 24:11).
18:15 *seek God's will.* Inquire of God, usually by going to a place of worship (see Ge 25:22 and note; Nu 27:21) or to a prophet (see 1Sa 9:9; 1Ki 22:8).

18:16 *God's decrees and laws.* The process of compiling and systematizing the body of divine law that would govern the newly formed nation of Israel may have already begun (see 15:25–26 and note on Ge 26:5).

18:21 *men who fear God.* See note on Ge 20:11.

19:2 *Desert of Sinai.* Located in the southeast region of the peninsula (see note on 3:1). The narrator locates there the events recorded in the rest of Exodus, all of Leviticus, and Nu 1:1–10:10.

³Then Moses went up to God,ᶠ and the LORD calledᵍ to him from the mountain and said, "This is what you are to say to the house of Jacob and what you are to tell the people of Israel: ⁴'You yourselves have seen what I did to Egypt,ʰ and how I carried you on eagles' wingsⁱ and brought you to myself.ʲ ⁵Now if you obey me fullyᵏ and keep my covenant,ˡ then out of all nations you will be my treasured possession.ᵐ Although the whole earthⁿ is mine, ⁶youᵒ will be for me a kingdom of priestsᵒ and a holy nation.'ᵖ These are the words you are to speak to the Israelites."

⁷So Moses went back and summoned the eldersᑫ of the people and set before them all the words the LORD had commanded him to speak.ʳ ⁸The people all responded together, "We will do everything the LORD has said."ˢ So Moses brought their answer back to the LORD.

⁹The LORD said to Moses, "I am going to come to you in a dense cloud,ᵗ so that the people will hear me speakingᵘ with you and will always put their trustᵛ in you." Then Moses told the LORD what the people had said.

¹⁰And the LORD said to Moses, "Go to the people and consecrateʷ them today and tomorrow. Have them wash their clothesˣ ¹¹and be ready by the third day,ʸ because on that day the LORD will come downᶻ on Mount Sinaiᵃ in the sight of all the people. ¹²Put limitsᵇ for the people around the mountain and tell them, 'Be careful that you do not go up the mountain or touch the foot of it. Whoever touches the mountain shall surely be put to death. ¹³He shall surely be stonedᶜ or shot with arrows; not a hand is to be laid on him.

Whether man or animal, he shall not be permitted to live.' Only when the ram's hornᵈ sounds a long blast may they go up to the mountain."ᵉ

¹⁴After Moses had gone down the mountain to the people, he consecrated them, and they washed their clothes.ᶠ ¹⁵Then he said to the people, "Prepare yourselves for the third day. Abstainᵍ from sexual relations."

¹⁶On the morning of the third day there was thunderʰ and lightning, with a thick cloudⁱ over the mountain, and a very loud trumpet blast.ʲ Everyone in the camp trembled.ᵏ ¹⁷Then Moses led the people out of the camp to meet with God, and they stood at the foot of the mountain.ˡ ¹⁸Mount Sinai was covered with smoke,ᵐ because the LORD descended on it in fire.ⁿ The smoke billowed up from it like smoke from a furnace,ᵒ and the whole mountainᵖ trembledᵖ violently, ¹⁹and the sound of the trumpet grew louder and louder. Then Moses spoke and the voiceᑫ of God answeredʳ him.ᑫ

²⁰The LORD descended to the top of Mount Sinaiˢ and called Moses to the top of the mountain. So Moses went up ²¹and

Cross references

19:3 ᶠEx 20:21 ᵍS Ex 3:4; S 25:22; Ac 7:38 19:4 ʰDt 29:2; Jos 24:7 ⁱDt 32:11; Ps 103:5; Isa 40:31; Jer 4:13; 48:40; Rev 12:14 ʲDt 33:12; Isa 31:5; Eze 16:6 19:5 ᵏEx 15:26; Dt 6:3; Ps 78:10; Jer 7:23 ˡS Ge 17:9; S Ex 3:1 ᵐS Ex 8:22; S 34:9; S Dt 8:1; S Tit 2:14 ⁿS Ex 9:29; 1Co 10:26 19:6 ᵒIsa 61:6; 66:21; S 1Pe 2:5 ᵖGe 18:19; Lev 11:44-45; Dt 4:37; 7:6; 26:19; 28:9; 29:13; 33:3; Isa 4:3; 62:12; Jer 2:3; Am 3:2 19:7 ᑫEx 18:12; Lev 4:15; 9:1; Nu 16:25 ʳEx 4:30; 1Sa 8:10 19:8 ˢEx 24:3,7; Dt 5:27; 26:17 19:9 ᵗver 16; Ex 20:21; 24:15-16; 33:9; 34:5; Dt 4:11; 2Sa 22:10,12; 2Ch 6:1; Ps 18:11; 97:2; 99:7; Mt 17:5 ᵘDt 4:12,36; Jn 12:29-30 ᵛS Ex 4:5 19:10 ʷver 14, 22; Lev 11:44; Nu 11:18; 1Sa 16:5; Joel 2:16; Heb 10:22 ˣS Ge 35:2; Rev 22:14 19:11 ʸver 16 ᶻS Ge 11:5 ᵃver 3,20; S Ex 3:1; 24:16; 31:18; 34:2,4,29,32; Lev 7:38; 26:46; 27:34; Nu 3:1;

Dt 10:5; Ne 9:13; Gal 4:24-25 19:12 ᵇver 23 19:13 ᶜHeb 12:20* ᵈJos 6:4; 1Ch 15:28; Ps 81:3; 98:6 ᵉver 21; Ex 34:3 19:14 ᶠS Ge 35:2 19:15 ᵍ1Sa 21:4; 1Co 7:5 19:16 ʰ1Sa 2:10; Isa 29:6 ⁱS ver 9 ʲHeb 12:18-19; Rev 4:1 ᵏS Ge 3:10; 1Sa 13:7; 14:15; 28:5; Ps 99:1; Heb 12:21 19:17 ˡS ver 2; Dt 4:11 19:18 ᵐEx 20:18; Ps 104:32; Isa 6:4; Rev 15:8 ⁿS Ex 3:2; 24:17; Lev 9:24; Dt 4:11,24,33, 36; 5:4; 9:3; 1Ki 18:24,38; 1Ch 21:26; 2Ch 7:1; Ps 18:8; Heb 12:18 ᵒS Ge 19:28; Rev 9:2 ᵖJdg 5:5; 2Sa 22:8; Ps 18:7; 68:8; Isa 2:19; 5:25; 41:5; Jer 4:24; 10:10; Mic 1:4; Na 1:5; Hab 3:6,10; Hag 2:6 19:19 ᑫS ver 9; Dt 4:33; Ne 9:13 ʳPs 81:7 19:20 ˢS ver 11

ᵒ5,6 Or possession, for the whole earth is mine. ᵖYou ᵖ18 Most Hebrew manuscripts; a few Hebrew manuscripts and Septuagint all the people ᑫ19 Or and God answered him with thunder

---

19:3 Jacob . . . Israel. See note on 1:1.
19:4 I carried you on eagles' wings. The description best fits the female golden eagle.
19:5 if . . . then. The covenant between God and Israel at Mount Sinai is the outgrowth and extension of the Lord's covenant with Abraham and his descendants 600 years earlier (see chart on "Major Covenants in the OT," p. 19). Participation in the divine blessings is conditioned on obedience added to faith (see note on Ge 17:9). my covenant. See note on Ge 9:9. out of all nations . . . my treasured possession. The equivalent phrases used of Christians in 1Pe 2:9 are "chosen people" and "people belonging to God" (see Dt 7:6; 14:2; 26:18; Ps 135:4; Mal 3:17). the whole earth is mine. God is the Creator and Possessor of the earth and everything in it (see Ge 14:19,22; Ps 24:1–2).
19:6 kingdom of priests. Israel was to constitute the Lord's kingdom (the people who acknowledged him as their King) and, like priests, was to be wholly consecrated to his service (see Isa 61:6; cf. 1Pe 2:5; Rev 1:6; 5:10; 20:6). holy nation. See 1Pe 2:9. God's people, both individually and collectively, are to be "set apart" (see note on 3:5) to do his will (see Dt 7:6; 14:2,21; 26:19; Isa 62:12).

19:8 We will do everything the LORD has said. The people promised to obey the terms of the covenant (see 24:3,7; Dt 5:27).
19:9 dense cloud. See 13:21 and note. the people will hear me speaking. See Dt 4:33. put their trust in you. See 14:31 and note.
19:10–11 Outward preparation to meet God symbolizes the inward consecration God requires of his people.
19:12–13 The whole mountain becomes holy because of God's presence (see 3:5 and note). Israel must keep herself from the mountain even as she is to keep herself from the tabernacle (see Nu 3:10).
19:15 Abstain from sexual relations. Not because sex is sinful but because it may leave the participants ceremonially unclean (see Lev 15:18; see also 1Sa 21:4–5).
19:16 thunder . . . lightning . . . trumpet blast. God's appearance is often accompanied by an impressive display of meteorological sights and sounds (see, e.g., 1Sa 7:10; 12:18; Job 38:1; 40:6; Ps 18:13–14). thick cloud. See 13:21 and note.
19:18 fire . . . smoke from a furnace. See Ge 15:17 and note.

the LORD said to him, "Go down and warn the people so they do not force their way through to see[t] the LORD and many of them perish.[u] 22Even the priests, who approach[v] the LORD, must consecrate[w] themselves, or the LORD will break out against them."[x]

23Moses said to the LORD, "The people cannot come up Mount Sinai,[y] because you yourself warned us, 'Put limits[z] around the mountain and set it apart as holy.'"

24The LORD replied, "Go down and bring Aaron[a] up with you. But the priests and the people must not force their way through to come up to the LORD, or he will break out against them."[b]

25So Moses went down to the people and told them.

The Ten Commandments

20:1–17pp — Dt 5:6–21

20 And God spoke[c] all these words:[d] 2"I am the LORD your God,[e] who

brought you out[f] of Egypt,[g] out of the land of slavery.[h]

3"You shall have no other gods before[r] me.[i]

4"You shall not make for yourself an idol[j] in the form of anything in heaven above or on the earth beneath or in the waters below. 5You shall not bow down to them or worship[k] them; for I, the LORD your God, am a jealous God,[l] punishing the children for the sin of the fathers[m] to the third and fourth generation[n] of those who hate me, 6but showing love to a thousand[o] generations, of those who love me and keep my commandments.

7"You shall not misuse the name of the LORD your God, for the LORD

Cross references (center column)

19:21 [t]Ex 24:10-11; Nu 4:20; 1Sa 6:19 [u]S ver 13
19:22 [v]Lev 10:3 [w]1Sa 16:5; 2Ch 29:5; Joel 2:16 [x]ver 24; 2Sa 6:7
19:23 [y]ver 11 [z]ver 12
19:24 [a]Ex 24:1,9 [b]ver 22
20:1 [c]Dt 10:4 [d]Ne 9:13; Ps 119:9; 147:19; Mal 4:4
20:2 [e]S Ge 17:7; Ex 16:12; Lev 19:2; 20:7; Isa 43:3; Eze 20:19

[f]S Ge 15:7 [g]S Ex 6:6 [h]Ex 13:3; Eze 20:6
20:3 [i]ver 23; Ex 34:14; Dt 6:14; 13:10; 2Ki 17:35; Ps 44:20; 81:9; Jer 1:16; 7:6,9; 11:13; 19:4; 25:6; 35:15
20:4 [j]ver 5,23; Ex 32:8; 34:17; Lev 19:4; 26:1; Dt 4:15-19,23; 27:15; 2Sa 7:22;

1Ki 14:9; 2Ki 17:12; Isa 40:19; 42:8; 44:9 20:5 [k]Ex 23:13, 24; Jos 23:7; Jdg 6:10; 2Ki 17:35; Isa 44:15,17,19; 46:6 [l]Ex 34:14; Dt 4:24; Jos 24:19; Na 1:2 [m]S Ge 9:25; S Lev 26:39 [n]Ex 34:7; Nu 14:18; Jer 32:18 20:6 [o]Ex 34:7; Nu 14:18; Dt 7:9; Jer 32:18; Lk 1:50; Ro 11:28

[r]3 Or *besides*

Study notes

19:22 *priests.* See also v. 24. Before the Aaronic priesthood was established (see 28:1), priestly functions were performed either by the elders (see note on 3:16; see also 3:18; 12:21; 18:12) or by designated younger men (see 24:5). But perhaps the verse anticipates the regulations for the Aaronic priests who will be appointed. *who approach the LORD.* To officiate at sacrifices (see 40:32; Lev 21:23).

20:1–17 See Dt 5:6–21; see also Mt 5:21,27; 19:17–19; Mk 10:19; Lk 18:20; Ro 13:9; Eph 6:2–3.

20:1 *words.* A technical term for "(covenant) stipulations" in the ancient Near East (e.g., among the Hittites; see also 24:3,8; 34:28). The basic code in Israel's divine law is found in vv. 2–17, elsewhere called the "Ten Commandments" (34:28; Dt 4:13; 10:4), the Hebrew words for which mean lit. "Ten Words." "Decalogue," a term of Greek origin often used as a synonym for the Ten Commandments, also means lit. "Ten Words."

20:2 *I am the LORD your God, who brought you out.* The Decalogue reflects the structure of the contemporary royal treaties (see note on Ge 15:7). On the basis of (1) a preamble, in which the great king identified himself ("I am the LORD your God"), and (2) a historical prologue, in which he sketched his previous gracious acts toward the subject king or people ("who brought you out . . ."), he then set forth (3) the treaty (covenant) stipulations (see Dt 5:1–3,7–21) to be obeyed (in this case, ten in number: vv. 3–17). Use of this ancient royal treaty pattern shows that the Lord is here formally acknowledged as Israel's King and that Israel is his subject people. As his subjects, his covenant people are to render complete submission, allegiance and obedience to him out of gratitude for his mercies, reverence for his sovereignty, and trust in his continuing care. See chart on "Major Covenants in the OT," p. 19.

20:3 *before.* The Hebrew for this word is translated "in hostility toward" in Ge 16:12; 25:18. Something of that sense may be intended here. In any event, no deity, real or imagined, is to rival the one true God in Israel's heart and life.

20:4 *idol in the form of anything.* Because God has no visible form, any idol intended to resemble him would be a sinful misrepresentation of him (see Dt 4:12,15–18). Since other gods are not to be worshiped (see v. 5), making idols of them would be equally sinful (see Dt 4:19,23–28).

20:5 *jealous God.* God will not put up with rivalry or unfaithfulness. Usually his "jealousy" concerns Israel and assumes the covenant relationship (analogous to marriage) and the Lord's exclusive right to possess Israel and to claim her love and allegiance. Actually, jealousy is part of the vocabulary of love. The "jealousy" of God (1) demands exclusive devotion to himself (see 34:14; Dt 4:24; 32:16, 21; Jos 24:19; Ps 78:58; 1Co 10:22; Jas 4:5 and NIV text note), (2) delivers to judgment all who oppose him (see Dt 29:20; 1Ki 14:22; Ps 79:5; Isa 42:13; 59:17; Eze 5:13; 16:38; 23:25; 36:5; Na 1:2; Zep 1:18; 3:8) and (3) vindicates his people (see 2Ki 19:31; Isa 9:7; 26:11; Eze 39:25; Joel 2:18; Zec 1:14; 8:2). In some of these passages the meaning is closer to "zeal" (the same Hebrew word may be translated either way, depending on context). *to the third and fourth generation of those who hate me.* Those Israelites who blatantly violate God's covenant and thus show that they reject the Lord as their King will bring down judgment on themselves and their households (see, e.g., Nu 16:31–34; Jos 7:24 and note)—households were usually extended to "three or four" generations. See note on Ps 109:12. *hate.* In covenant contexts the terms "hate" and "love" (v. 6) were conventionally used to indicate rejection of or loyalty to the covenant Lord.

20:6 *a thousand generations of those.* See 1Ch 16:15; Ps 105:8. *love me and keep my commandments.* See Jn 14:15; 1Jn 5:3. In the treaty language of the ancient Near East the "love" owed to the great king was a conventional term for total allegiance and implicit trust expressing itself in obedient service.

20:7 *misuse the name of the LORD.* By profaning God's name—e.g., by swearing falsely by it (see Lev 19:12; see also Jer 7:9 and NIV text note), as on the witness stand in court. Jesus elaborates on oath-taking in Mt 5:33–37.

will not hold anyone guiltless who misuses his name.[p]

8"Remember the Sabbath[q] day by keeping it holy. [9]Six days you shall labor and do all your work,[r] [10]but the seventh day is a Sabbath[s] to the LORD your God. On it you shall not do any work, neither you, nor your son or daughter, nor your manservant or maidservant, nor your animals, nor the alien within your gates. [11]For in six days the LORD made the heavens and the earth,[t] the sea, and all that is in them, but he rested[u] on the seventh day.[v] Therefore the LORD blessed the Sabbath day and made it holy.

12"Honor your father and your mother,[w] so that you may live long[x] in the land[y] the LORD your God is giving you.

13"You shall not murder.[z]

14"You shall not commit adultery.[a]

15"You shall not steal.[b]

16"You shall not give false testimony[c] against your neighbor.[d]

17"You shall not covet[e] your neighbor's house. You shall not covet your neighbor's wife, or his manservant or maidservant, his ox or donkey, or anything that belongs to your neighbor."

[18]When the people saw the thunder and lightning and heard the trumpet[f] and saw the mountain in smoke,[g] they trembled with fear.[h] They stayed at a distance [19]and said to Moses, "Speak to us yourself and we will listen. But do not have God speak[i] to us or we will die."[j]

[20]Moses said to the people, "Do not be afraid.[k] God has come to test[l] you, so that the fear[m] of God will be with you to keep you from sinning."[n]

[21]The people remained at a distance, while Moses approached the thick darkness[o] where God was.

Idols and Altars

[22]Then the LORD said to Moses, "Tell the Israelites this: 'You have seen for yourselves that I have spoken to you from heaven:[p] [23]Do not make any gods to be

20:7 pEx 22:28; Lev 18:21; 19:12; 22:2; 24:11,16; Dt 6:13; 10:20; Job 2:5,9; Ps 63:11; Isa 8:21; Eze 20:39; 39:7; S Mt 5:33 **20:8** qS Ex 16:23; 31:13-16; 35:3; Lev 19:3,30; 26:2; Isa 56:2; Jer 17:21-27; Eze 22:8 **20:9** rEx 23:12; 31:13-17; 34:21; 35:2-3; Lev 23:3; Lk 13:14 **20:10** sS Ge 2:3; Ex 31:14; Lev 23:38; Nu 28:9; Isa 56:2; Eze 20:12,20 **20:11** tGe 1:3-2:1 uS Ge 2:2 vEx 31:17; Heb 4:4 **20:12** wS Ge 31:35; S Dt 5:16; Mt 15:4*; 19:19*; Mk 7:10*; 10:19*; Lk 18:20*; Eph 6:2 xDt 6:2; Eph 6:3 yDt 11:9; 25:15; Jer 35:7 **20:13** zS Ge 4:23; Mt 5:21*; 19:18*; Mk 10:19*; Lk 18:20*; Ro 13:9*; Jas 2:11* **20:14** aLev 18:20; 20:10; Nu 5:12,

13,29; Pr 6:29,32; Mt 5:27*; 19:18*; Mk 10:19*; Lk 18:20*; Ro 13:9*; Jas 2:11* **20:15** bLev 9:11,13; Eze 18:7; Mt 19:18*; Mk 10:19*; Lk 18:20*; Ro 13:9* **20:16** cLev 19:11; Jer 9:3,5 dEx 23:1,7; Lev 19:18; Ps 50:20; 101:5; 119:29; Mt 19:18*; Mk 10:19; Lk 3:14*; 18:20* **20:17** eLk 12:15; Ro 7:7*; 13:9*; Eph 5:3; Heb 13:5 **20:18** fEx 19:16-19; Dt 4:36; Isa 58:1; Jer 6:17; Eze 33:3; Heb 12:18-19; Rev 1:10 gS Ex 19:18 hS Ge 3:10; S Ex 14:31; S 19:16 **20:19** iJob 37:4,5; 40:9; Ps 29:3-4 /Dt 5:5,23-27; 18:16; Gal 3:19 **20:20** kS Ge 15:1 lS Ge 22:1 mDt 4:10; 6:2, 24; 10:12; Ps 111:10; 128:1; Pr 1:7; Ecc 12:13; Isa 8:13 nJob 1:8; 2:3; 28:28; Pr 3:7; 8:13; 14:16; 16:6 **20:21** oS Ex 19:9; Dt 5:22; Ps 18:9; 68:4; 97:2; Isa 19:1 **20:22** pDt 5:24,26; Ne 9:13

20:8 See Ge 2:3. *Sabbath.* See note on 16:23. *holy.* See note on 3:5.

20:9 *Six days.* The question of a shorter "work week" in a modern industrialized culture is not in view.

20:10 *On it you shall not do any work.* Two reasons (one here and one in Deuteronomy) are given: (1) Having completed his work of creation God "rested on the seventh day" (v. 11), and the Israelites are to observe the same pattern in their service of God in the creation; (2) the Israelites must cease all labor so that their servants can also participate in the Sabbath-rest—just as God had delivered his people from the burden of slavery in Egypt (see Dt 5:14-15). The Sabbath thus became a "sign" of the covenant between God and Israel at Mount Sinai (see 31:12-17; see also note on Ge 9:12).

20:12 *Honor.* (1) Prize highly (see Pr 4:8), (2) care for (see Ps 91:15), (3) show respect for (see Lev 19:3; 20:9), and (4) obey (see Dt 21:18-21; cf. Eph 6:1). *so that you may live long.* "The first commandment with a promise" (Eph 6:2). See also note on Dt 6:2.

20:13 See Mt 5:21-26. *murder.* The Hebrew for this verb usually refers to a premeditated and deliberate act.

20:14 See Mt 5:27-30. *adultery.* A sin "against God" (Ge 39:9) as well as against the marriage partner.

20:17 *covet.* Desire something with evil motivation (see Mt 15:19). To break God's commandments inwardly is equivalent to breaking them outwardly (see Mt 5:21-30).

20:18-21 Concludes the account of the giving of the Decalogue. The order of the narrative appears to be different from the order of events, since v. 18 is most likely a continua-

tion of 19:25. On this reading, the proclamation of the Decalogue took place after Moses approached God (v. 21). Biblical writers often did not follow chronological sequence in their narratives for various literary reasons. The purpose of chronological displacement here may have been either (1) to keep the Decalogue distinct from the "Book of the Covenant" (24:7) that follows (20:22-23:19), or (2) to conclude the account with the formal institution of Moses' office as covenant mediator—or both.

20:19 See Heb 12:19-20. Israel requests a mediator to stand between them and God, a role fulfilled by Moses and subsequently by priests, prophets and kings—and ultimately by Jesus Christ.

20:20 *Do not be afraid.* Do not think that God's display of his majesty is intended simply to fill you with abject fear. He has come to enter into covenant with you as your heavenly King. *test.* See note on Ge 22:1. *fear of God.* See note on Ge 20:11.

20:22-23:19 The stipulations of the "Book of the Covenant" (24:7), consisting largely of expansions on and expositions of the Ten Commandments. See chart on "Major Social Concerns in the Covenant," p. 271.

20:22-26 Initial stipulations governing Israel's basic relationship with God (cf. v. 3).

20:22 *heaven.* God's dwelling place. Even on "top of Mount Sinai" (19:20) God spoke from heaven.

20:23 See vv. 3-4. The contrast between the one true God "in heaven," who "does whatever pleases him" (Ps 115:3), and idols of silver or gold, who can do nothing at all (see Ps 115:4-7; see also Ps 135:5-6,15-17), is striking indeed.

alongside me; q do not make for yourselves gods of silver or gods of gold. r

24" 'Make an altar s of earth for me and sacrifice on it your burnt offerings t and fellowship offerings, s your sheep and goats and your cattle. Wherever I cause my name u to be honored, I will come to you and bless v you. 25If you make an altar of stones for me, do not build it with dressed stones, for you will defile it if you use a tool w on it. 26And do not go up to my altar on steps, lest your nakedness x be exposed on it.'

21

"These are the laws y you are to set before them:

Hebrew Servants

21:2–6pp — Dt 15:12–18
21:2–11Ref — Lev 25:39–55

2"If you buy a Hebrew servant, z he is to serve you for six years. But in the seventh year, he shall go free, a without paying anything. 3If he comes alone, he is to go free alone; but if he has a wife when he comes, she is to go with him. 4If his master gives him a wife and she bears him sons or daughters, the woman and her children shall belong to her master, and only the man shall go free.

5"But if the servant declares, 'I love my master and my wife and children and do not want to go free,' b 6then his master must take him before the judges. t c He shall take him to the door or the doorpost and pierce d his ear with an awl. Then he will be his servant for life. e

7"If a man sells his daughter as a ser-

vant, she is not to go free as menservants do. 8If she does not please the master who has selected her for himself, u he must let her be redeemed. He has no right to sell her to foreigners, because he has broken faith with her. 9If he selects her for his son, he must grant her the rights of a daughter. 10If he marries another woman, he must not deprive the first one of her food, clothing and marital rights. f 11If he does not provide her with these three things, she is to go free, without any payment of money.

Personal Injuries

12"Anyone who strikes a man and kills him shall surely be put to death. g 13However, if he does not do it intentionally, but God lets it happen, he is to flee to a place h I will designate. 14But if a man schemes and kills another man deliberately, i take him away from my altar and put him to death. j

15"Anyone who attacks v his father or his mother must be put to death.

16"Anyone who kidnaps another and either sells k him or still has him when he is caught must be put to death. l

17"Anyone who curses his father or mother must be put to death. m

18"If men quarrel and one hits the other with a stone or with his fist w and he does not die but is confined to bed, 19the one who struck the blow will not be held re-

Cross references (center column)

20:23 qS ver 3
rEx 22:20; 32:4,
8,31; 34:17;
Dt 29:17–18;
Ne 9:18
20:24 sEx 27:1;
40:29; Nu 16:38;
Dt 27:5; Jos 8:30;
2Ki 16:14;
2Ch 4:1; Ezr 3:2;
Eze 43:13
tS Ge 8:20;
S Ex 18:12
uDt 12:5; 16:6,
11; 26:2; 1Ki 9:3;
2Ki 21:4,7;
2Ch 6:6; 12:13;
Ezr 6:12
vS Ge 12:2; 22:17
20:25 wJos 8:31;
1Ki 6:7
20:26 xEze 43:17
21:1 yEx 24:3;
34:32; Dt 4:14;
6:1
21:2 zEx 22:3
aver 7; Jer 34:8,
14
21:5 bDt 15:16
21:6 cEx 22:8–9;
Dt 17:9; 19:17;
25:1 dPs 40:6
eJob 39:9; 41:4

21:10 f1Co 7:3–5
21:12 gver 15,
17; S Ge 4:14,23;
Ex 31:15;
Lev 20:9,10;
24:16; 27:29;
Nu 1:51; 35:16,
30–31; Dt 13:5;
19:11; 22:22;
27:16; Job 31:11;
Pr 20:20;
S Mt 26:52
21:13
hNu 35:10–34;
Dt 4:42; 19:2–13;
Jos 20:9
21:14 iGe 4:8;
Nu 35:20;
2Sa 3:27; 20:10;
Heb 10:26
jDt 19:11–12;
1Ki 2:28–34
21:16 kGe 37:28
lEx 22:4; Dt 24:7
21:17 mS ver 12;
S Dt 5:16;

Footnotes (center column, bottom)

s24 Traditionally peace offerings   t6 Or before God
u8 Or master so that he does not choose her   v15 Or
kills   w18 Or with a tool

Mt 15:4*; Mk 7:10*

20:24 altar of earth. Such an altar, with dimensions the same as those of the altar in the tabernacle (see 27:1), has been found in the excavated ruins of a small Iron Age (10th, or possibly 11th, century b.c.) Israelite temple at Arad in southern Palestine. burnt offerings. See note on Lev 1:3. fellowship offerings. See note on Lev 3:1. Wherever. Not the later central sanctuary at Jerusalem, but numerous temporary places of worship (see, e.g., Jos 8:30–31; Jdg 6:24; 21:4; 1Sa 7:17; 14:35; 2Sa 24:25; 1Ki 18:30).
20:25 do not build it with dressed stones. Many ancient altars of undressed stones (from various periods) have been found in Palestine. defile it if you use a tool on it. For reasons not now clear, but perhaps related to pagan practices.
20:26 steps. The oldest stepped altar known in Palestine is at Megiddo and dates between 3000 and 2500 b.c. nakedness be exposed. Men who ascended to such altars would expose their nakedness in the presence of God. Although Aaron and his descendants served at stepped altars (see Lev 9:22; Eze 43:17), they were instructed to wear linen undergarments (see 28:42–43; Lev 6:10; 16:3–4; Eze 44:17–18).
21:2–11 See Jer 34:8–22.
21:2 Hebrew. See note on Ge 14:13. in the seventh year, he shall go free. The Lord's servants are not to be anyone's perpetual slaves (see 20:10 and note).

21:6 the judges. See 22:8–9,28 and NIV text notes. pierce his ear with an awl. See Dt 15:17. Submission to this rite symbolized willing service (see Ps 40:6–8 and note on Ps 40:6).
21:12–15 See 20:13 and note; see also Nu 35:16–34; Dt 19:1–13; 21:1–9; 24:7; 27:24–25; Jos 20:1–9.
21:12 See Ge 9:6 and note.
21:13 does not do it intentionally. Related terms and expressions are "accidentally" (Nu 35:11), "without hostility" (Nu 35:22), "was not his enemy" (Nu 35:23), "did not intend to harm him" (Nu 35:23) and "without malice aforethought" (Dt 19:4). Premeditated murder is thus distinguished from accidental manslaughter. God lets it happen. The event is beyond human control—in modern legal terminology, an "act of God." place. A city of refuge (see Nu 35:6–32; Dt 19:1–13; Jos 20:1–9; 21:13,21,27,32, 38).
21:14 away from my altar. Or "even from my altar." The horns of the altar were a final refuge for those subject to judicial action (see 1Ki 1:50–51; 2:28; Am 3:14 and notes).
21:15 See 20:12.
21:16 See 20:15.
21:19 walks around outside with his staff. Is convalescing in a satisfactory way. the loss of his time. Lit. "his sitting," i.e., his enforced idleness.

sponsible if the other gets up and walks around outside with his staff; however, he must pay the injured man for the loss of his time and see that he is completely healed.

20"If a man beats his male or female slave with a rod and the slave dies as a direct result, he must be punished, 21but he is not to be punished if the slave gets up after a day or two, since the slave is his property. n

22"If men who are fighting hit a pregnant woman and she gives birth prematurelyx but there is no serious injury, the offender must be fined whatever the woman's husband demandso and the court allows. 23But if there is serious injury, you are to take life for life, p 24eye for eye, tooth for tooth, q hand for hand, foot for foot, 25burn for burn, wound for wound, bruise for bruise.

26"If a man hits a manservant or maidservant in the eye and destroys it, he must let the servant go free to compensate for the eye. 27And if he knocks out the tooth of a manservant or maidservant, he must let the servant go free to compensate for the tooth.

28"If a bull gores a man or a woman to death, the bull must be stoned to death, r and its meat must not be eaten. But the owner of the bull will not be held responsible. 29If, however, the bull has had the habit of goring and the owner has been warned but has not kept it penned ups and it kills a man or woman, the bull must be stoned and the owner also must be put to death. 30However, if payment is demanded of him, he may redeem his life by paying whatever is demanded. t 31This law also applies if the bull gores a son or daughter. 32If the bull gores a male or female slave, the owner must pay thirty shekelsy u of silver to the master of the slave, and the bull must be stoned.

33"If a man uncovers a pitv or digs one

and fails to cover it and an ox or a donkey falls into it, 34the owner of the pit must pay for the loss; he must pay its owner, and the dead animal will be his.

35"If a man's bull injures the bull of another and it dies, they are to sell the live one and divide both the money and the dead animal equally. 36However, if it was known that the bull had the habit of goring, yet the owner did not keep it penned up, w the owner must pay, animal for animal, and the dead animal will be his.

Protection of Property

22 "If a man steals an ox or a sheep and slaughters it or sells it, he must pay backx five head of cattle for the ox and four sheep for the sheep.

2"If a thief is caught breaking iny and is struck so that he dies, the defender is not guilty of bloodshed; z 3but if it happensz after sunrise, he is guilty of bloodshed.

"A thief must certainly make restitution, a but if he has nothing, he must be soldb to pay for his theft.

4"If the stolen animal is found alive in his possessionc—whether ox or donkey or sheep—he must pay back double. d

5"If a man grazes his livestock in a field or vineyard and lets them stray and they graze in another man's field, he must make restitutione from the best of his own field or vineyard.

6"If a fire breaks out and spreads into thornbushes so that it burns shocksf of grain or standing grain or the whole field, the one who started the fire must make restitution. g

7"If a man gives his neighbor silver or goods for safekeepingh and they are stolen from the neighbor's house, the thief, if he is caught, must pay back double. i 8But if the thief is not found, the owner of the

---

Cross references (center column):

21:21 nLev 25:44-46
21:22 over 30
21:23 pLev 24:19; Dt 19:21
21:24 qS ver 23; Mt 5:38*
21:28 rver 32; Ge 9:5
21:29 sver 36
21:30 tver 22
21:32 uGe 37:28; Zec 11:12-13; Mt 26:15; 27:3,9
21:33 vLk 14:5
21:36 wver 29
22:1 xLev 6:1-7; 2Sa 12:6; Pr 6:31; S Lk 19:8
22:2 yJob 24:16; Jer 2:34; Hos 7:1; Mt 6:19-20; 24:43 zNu 35:27
22:3 aver 1 bS Ex 21:2; S Mt 18:25
22:4 c1Sa 12:5 dS Ge 43:12
22:5 ever 1
22:6 fJdg 15:5 gver 1
22:7 hver 10; Lev 6:2 iS Ge 43:12

---

x22 Or *she has a miscarriage*   y32 That is, about 12 ounces (about 0.3 kilogram)   z3 Or *if he strikes him*

21:20–21 Benefit of doubt was granted to the slaveholder where no homicidal intentions could be proved.
21:23–25 See Dt 19:21. The so-called law of retaliation, as its contexts show, was meant to limit the punishment to fit the crime. By invoking the law of love, Jesus corrected the popular misunderstanding of the law of retaliation (see Mt 5:38–42).
21:23 *serious injury.* Either to mother or to child.
21:26–27 Humane applications of the law of retaliation.
21:28–32 The law of the goring bull.
21:28 *the bull must be stoned to death.* By killing someone, the bull becomes accountable for that person's life (see Ge 9:5).
21:30 *if payment is demanded.* If the victim's family is willing to accept a ransom payment instead of demanding the death penalty. *he may redeem his life by paying.* The pay-

ment (lit. "ransom," as in Nu 35:31) is not to compensate the victim's family but to save the negligent man's life.
21:32 *thirty shekels of silver.* Apparently the standard price for a slave. It was also the amount Judas was willing to accept as his price for betraying Jesus (see Mt 26:14–15; see also Zec 11:12–13). *shekels.* See note on Ge 20:16.
21:33–36 Laws concerning injuries to animals.
22:1–15 Laws concerning property rights (see 20:15).
22:2 An act of self-defense in darkness does not produce bloodguilt.
22:3 Killing an intruder in broad daylight is not justifiable.
22:5 *from the best.* Restitution should always err on the side of quality and generosity.
22:6 *thornbushes.* Often used as hedges (see Mic 7:4) bordering cultivated areas.

house must appear before the judges[a][i] to determine whether he has laid his hands on the other man's property. 9In all cases of illegal possession of an ox, a donkey, a sheep, a garment, or any other lost property about which somebody says, 'This is mine,' both parties are to bring their cases before the judges.[k] The one whom the judges declare[b] guilty must pay back double to his neighbor.

10"If a man gives a donkey, an ox, a sheep or any other animal to his neighbor for safekeeping[l] and it dies or is injured or is taken away while no one is looking, 11the issue between them will be settled by the taking of an oath[m] before the LORD that the neighbor did not lay hands on the other person's property. The owner is to accept this, and no restitution is required. 12But if the animal was stolen from the neighbor, he must make restitution[n] to the owner. 13If it was torn to pieces by a wild animal, he shall bring in the remains as evidence and he will not be required to pay for the torn animal.[o]

14"If a man borrows an animal from his neighbor and it is injured or dies while the owner is not present, he must make restitution.[p] 15But if the owner is with the animal, the borrower will not have to pay. If the animal was hired, the money paid for the hire covers the loss.[q]

Social Responsibility

16"If a man seduces a virgin[r] who is not pledged to be married and sleeps with her, he must pay the bride-price,[s] and she shall be his wife. 17If her father absolutely refuses to give her to him, he must still pay the bride-price for virgins.

18"Do not allow a sorceress[t] to live.

19"Anyone who has sexual relations with an animal[u] must be put to death.

20"Whoever sacrifices to any god[v] other than the LORD must be destroyed.[c][w]

21"Do not mistreat an alien[x] or oppress him, for you were aliens[y] in Egypt.

22"Do not take advantage of a widow or an orphan.[z] 23If you do and they cry out[a] to me, I will certainly hear their cry.[b] 24My anger will be aroused, and I will kill you with the sword; your wives will become widows and your children fatherless.[c]

25"If you lend money to one of my people among you who is needy, do not be like a moneylender; charge him no interest.[d][d] 26If you take your neighbor's cloak as a pledge,[e] return it to him by sunset, 27because his cloak is the only covering he has for his body. What else will he sleep in?[f] When he cries out to me, I will hear, for I am compassionate.[g]

28"Do not blaspheme God[e][h] or curse[i] the ruler of your people.[j]

29"Do not hold back offerings[k] from your granaries or your vats.[f]

"You must give me the firstborn of your sons.[l] 30Do the same with your cattle and

---

22:8 /S Ex 21:6
22:9 *ver 8;
Dt 25:1
22:10 /S ver 7
22:11 *mLev 6:3;
1Ki 8:31;
2Ch 6:22;
Heb 6:16
22:12 *nver 1
22:13 *oGe 31:39
22:14 *pver 1
22:15
*qLev 19:13;
Job 17:5
22:16 *rDt 22:28
*sGe 34:12
22:18 /S Ex 7:11;
Lev 19:26,31;
20:27; Dt 18:11;
1Sa 28:3;
2Ch 33:6;
Isa 57:3

22:19
*uLev 18:23;
20:15; Dt 27:21
22:20
*vS Ex 20:23;
34:15; Lev 17:7;
Nu 25:2;
Dt 32:17;
Ps 106:37
*wLev 27:29;
Dt 13:5; 17:2-5;
18:20; 1Ki 18:40;
19:1; 2Ki 10:25;
23:20; 2Ch 15:13
22:21 *xEx 23:9;
Lev 19:33; 24:22;
Nu 15:14;
Dt 1:16; 24:17;
Eze 22:29
*yDt 10:19; 27:19;
Zec 7:10; Mal 3:5
22:22 *zver 26;
Dt 10:18; 24:6,
10,12,17;
Job 22:6,9; 24:3,
21; Ps 68:5;
146:9; Pr 23:10;
Isa 1:17; Jer 7:5,
6; 21:12; 22:3;
Eze 18:5-9,12;
Zec 7:9-10;
Mal 3:5; Jas 1:27
22:23 *aLk 18:7
*bDt 10:18; 15:9;
24:15; Job 34:28;
35:9; Ps 10:14,
17; 12:5; 18:6;
34:15; Jas 5:4
22:24 *cPs 109:9;
La 5:3
22:25
*dLev 25:35-37;

Dt 15:7-11; 23:20; Ne 5:7,10; Ps 15:5; Eze 18:8 **22:26** *eS ver 22; Pr 20:16; Eze 33:15; Am 2:8 **22:27** /Dt 24:13,17; Job 22:6; 24:7; 29:11; 31:19-20; Eze 18:12,16 *gEx 34:6; Dt 4:31; 2Ch 30:9; Ne 9:17; Ps 99:8; 103:8; 116:5; 145:8; Joel 2:13; Jnh 4:2 **22:28** *hS Ex 20:7 /2Sa 16:5,9; 19:21; 1Ki 21:10; 2Ki 2:23; Ps 102:8 /Ecc 10:20; Ac 23:5* **22:29** *kEx 23:15,16,19; 34:20,26; Lev 19:24; 23:10; Nu 18:13; 28:26; Dt 18:4; 26:2,10; 1Sa 6:3; Ne 10:35; Pr 3:9; Mal 3:10 /S Ex 13:2; Nu 8:16-17; Lk 2:23

---

a8 Or *before God*; also in verse 9   **b**9 Or *whom God declares*   **c**20 The Hebrew term refers to the irrevocable giving over of things or persons to the LORD, often by totally destroying them.   **d**25 Or *excessive interest*   **e**28 Or *Do not revile the judges*   **f**29 The meaning of the Hebrew for this phrase is uncertain.

22:11 See 20:7 and note. *an oath before the LORD.* The judges were God's representatives in court cases (see 21:6; 22:8-9,28 and NIV text notes).
22:12-13 Similar laws apparently existed as early as the patriarchal period (see Ge 31:39).
22:16-31 General laws related to social obligations.
22:16 *bride-price.* A gift, usually substantial, given by the prospective groom to the bride's family as payment for her (see Ge 24:53). The custom is still followed today in parts of the Middle East.
22:18 See Dt 18:10,14; 1Sa 28:9; Isa 47:12-14.
22:19 Ancient myths and epics describe acts of bestiality performed by pagan gods and demigods in Babylon and Canaan.
22:20 See 20:3-5. The total destruction (see NIV text note) of the idolatrous Canaanites was later commanded by the Lord (see Nu 21:2; Dt 2:34; 3:6; 7:2; 13:15; 20:17; Jos 2:10; 6:17,21; 8:25; 10:1,28,35,37,39-40; 11:11-12, 20-21; Jdg 1:17).
22:21-27 That the poor, the widow, the orphan, the alien—in fact, all defenseless people—are objects of God's

special concern and providential care is clear from the writings of Moses (see 21:26-27; 23:6-12; Lev 19:9-10; Dt 14:29; 16:11,14; 24:19-21; 26:12-13), the psalmists (see Ps 10:14,17-18; 68:5; 82:3; 146:9) and the prophets (see Isa 1:23; 10:2; Jer 7:6; 22:3; Zec 7:10; Mal 3:5) as well as from the teachings of Jesus (see, e.g., Mt 25:34-45).
22:25-27 Laws dealing with interest on loans (see Lev 25:35-37; Dt 15:7-11; 23:19-20; see also Ne 5:7-12; Job 24:9; Pr 28:8; Eze 18:13; 22:12). Interest for profit was not to be charged at the expense of the poor. Generosity in such matters was extended even further by Jesus (see Lk 6:34-35).
22:26-27 If all that a man had to offer as his pledge for a loan was his cloak, he was among the poorest of the poor (see Am 2:8 and note).
22:28 *Do not . . . curse the ruler of your people.* A ruler was God's representative; quoted by a penitent Paul after he had unwittingly insulted the high priest (see Ac 23:4-5).
22:29 *give me the firstborn.* See notes on 4:22; 13:2,13; see also 13:15.
22:30 *Do the same with your cattle and your sheep.* See

your sheep. *m* Let them stay with their mothers for seven days, but give them to me on the eighth day. *n*

31"You are to be my holy people. *o* So do not eat the meat of an animal torn by wild beasts; *p* throw it to the dogs.

Laws of Justice and Mercy

23 "Do not spread false reports. *q* Do not help a wicked man by being a malicious witness. *r*

2"Do not follow the crowd in doing wrong. When you give testimony in a lawsuit, do not pervert justice *s* by siding with the crowd, *t* 3and do not show favoritism *u* to a poor man in his lawsuit.

4"If you come across your enemy's *v* ox or donkey wandering off, be sure to take it back to him. *w* 5If you see the donkey *x* of someone who hates you fallen down under its load, do not leave it there; be sure you help him with it.

6"Do not deny justice *y* to your poor people in their lawsuits. 7Have nothing to do with a false charge *z* and do not put an innocent *a* or honest person to death, *b* for I will not acquit the guilty. *c*

8"Do not accept a bribe, *d* for a bribe blinds those who see and twists the words of the righteous.

9"Do not oppress an alien; *e* you yourselves know how it feels to be aliens, because you were aliens in Egypt.

Sabbath Laws

10"For six years you are to sow your fields and harvest the crops, 11but during the seventh year let the land lie unplowed and unused. *f* Then the poor among your

people may get food from it, and the wild animals may eat what they leave. Do the same with your vineyard and your olive grove.

12"Six days do your work, *g* but on the seventh day do not work, so that your ox and your donkey may rest and the slave born in your household, and the alien as well, may be refreshed. *h*

13"Be careful *i* to do everything I have said to you. Do not invoke the names of other gods; *j* do not let them be heard on your lips. *k*

The Three Annual Festivals

14"Three times *l* a year you are to celebrate a festival to me.

15"Celebrate the Feast of Unleavened Bread; *m* for seven days eat bread made without yeast, as I commanded you. Do this at the appointed time in the month of Abib, *n* for in that month you came out of Egypt.

"No one is to appear before me empty-handed. *o*

16"Celebrate the Feast of Harvest *p* with the firstfruits *q* of the crops you sow in your field.

"Celebrate the Feast of Ingathering *r* at the end of the year, when you gather in your crops from the field. *s*

17"Three times *t* a year all the men are to appear before the Sovereign LORD.

Cross references (center column)

22:30
m Ex 34:19;
Dt 15:19
n Ge 17:12;
Lev 12:3; 22:27
22:31 *o* Ex 19:6;
Lev 19:2; 22:31;
Ezr 9:2
p Lev 7:24; 17:15;
22:8; Dt 14:21;
Eze 4:14; 44:31
23:1
q S Ge 39:17;
Mt 19:18;
Lk 3:14
r S Ex 20:16;
Dt 5:20;
19:16-21;
Ps 27:12; 35:11;
Pr 19:5; Ac 6:11
23:2 *s* ver 3,6,9;
Lev 19:15,33;
Dt 1:17; 16:19;
24:17; 27:19;
1Sa 8:3
23:3 *u* Dt 1:17
23:4 *v* Ro 12:20
w Lev 6:3; 19:11;
Dt 22:1-3
23:5 *x* Dt 22:4
23:6 *y* S ver 2;
Dt 23:16;
Pr 22:22
23:7
z S Ex 20:16;
S Eph 4:25
a Mt 27:4
b S Ge 18:23
c Ex 34:7;
Dt 19:18; 25:1
23:8
d S Ex 18:21;
Lev 19:15;
Dt 10:17; 27:25;
Job 15:34; 36:18;
Ps 26:10; Pr 6:35;
15:27; 17:8;
Isa 1:23; 5:23;
Mic 3:11; 7:3
23:9 *e* S ver 2;
S Ex 22:21;
Lev 19:33-34;
Eze 22:7
23:11
f Lev 25:1-7;
Ne 10:31
23:12
g S Ex 20:9;
Lk 13:14
h Ge 2:2-3

23:13 *i* Dt 4:9,23; 1Ti 4:16 *j* ver 32; Dt 12:3; Jos 23:7; Ps 16:4; Zec 13:2 *k* Dt 18:20; Jos 23:7; Ps 16:4; Hos 2:17 23:14 *l* ver 17; S Ex 12:14; 34:23,24; Dt 16:16; 1Ki 9:25; 2Ch 8:13; Eze 46:9 23:15 *m* S Ex 12:17; Mt 26:17; Lk 22:1; Ac 12:3 *n* S Ex 12:2 *o* S Ex 22:29 23:16 *p* Lev 23:15-21; Nu 28:26; Dt 16:9; 2Ch 8:13 *q* S Ex 22:29; S 34:22 *r* Ex 34:22; Lev 23:34,42; Dt 16:16; 31:10; Ezr 3:4; Ne 8:14; Zec 14:16 *s* Lev 23:39; Dt 16:13; Jer 40:10 23:17 *t* S ver 14

---

notes on 13:2; 13:13; see also 13:12,15. *give them to me on the eighth day.* The same principle applied in a different way to firstborn sons as well (see note on Ge 17:12).
22:31 Since God's people were "a kingdom of priests" (see 19:6 and note), they were to obey a law later specified for members of the Aaronic priesthood (see Lev 22:8) as well.
23:1–9 Most of the regulations in this section pertain to 20:16.
23:1 See Lev 19:16; Dt 22:13–19; 1Ki 21:10–13.
23:4–5 Those hostile to you are to be shown the same consideration as others (see Dt 22:1–4; Pr 25:21). Jesus teaches that this means "Love your enemies" (Mt 5:44).
23:7 1Ki 21:10–13 is a vivid illustration of violation of this law.
23:8 See Dt 16:19. Samuel exemplifies faithful stewardship in this regard (see 1Sa 12:3), while his sons do not (see 1Sa 8:3).
23:10–13 Extensions of the principles taught in 20:8–11; Dt 5:12–15.
23:14–19 See 34:18–26; Lev 23:4–44; Nu 28:16–29:40; Dt 16:1–17.
23:15 *Feast of Unleavened Bread.* Celebrated from the

15th through the 21st days of the first month (usually about mid-March to mid-April; see note on 12:2) at the beginning of the barley harvest; it commemorated the exodus.
23:16 *Feast of Harvest.* Also called the "Feast of Weeks" (34:22) because it was held seven weeks after the Feast of Unleavened Bread. It was celebrated on the sixth day of the third month (usually about mid-May to mid-June) during the wheat harvest. In later Judaism it came to commemorate the giving of the law on Mount Sinai, though there is no evidence of this significance in the OT. In NT times it was called "(the day of) Pentecost" (Ac 2:1; 20:16; 1Co 16:8), which means "50" (see Lev 23:16). *Feast of Ingathering.* Also called the "Feast of Tabernacles" (Lev 23:34) or "Booths" because the Israelites lived in temporary shelters when God brought them out of Egypt (see Lev 23:43). It was celebrated from the 15th through the 22nd days of the seventh month (usually about mid-September to mid-October) when the produce of the orchards and vines had been harvested; it commemorated the desert wanderings after the exodus. *end of the year.* End of the agricultural year, which began in the fall (see note on 12:2).
23:17 *all the men.* Normally accompanied by their families (see, e.g., 1Sa 1).

18"Do not offer the blood of a sacrifice to me along with anything containing yeast. *u*

"The fat of my festival offerings must not be kept until morning. *v*

19"Bring the best of the firstfruits *w* of your soil to the house of the LORD your God.

"Do not cook a young goat in its mother's milk. *x*

God's Angel to Prepare the Way

20"See, I am sending an angel *y* ahead of you to guard you along the way and to bring you to the place I have prepared. *z* 21Pay attention to him and listen *a* to what he says. Do not rebel against him; he will not forgive *b* your rebellion, *c* since my Name *d* is in him. 22If you listen carefully to what he says and do *e* all that I say, I will be an enemy *f* to your enemies and will oppose those who oppose you. 23My angel will go ahead of you and bring you into the land of the Amorites, Hittites, Perizzites, Canaanites, Hivites and Jebusites, *g* and I will wipe them out. 24Do not bow down before their gods or worship *h* them or follow their practices. *i* You must demolish *j* them and break their sacred stones *k* to pieces. 25Worship the LORD your God, *l* and his blessing *m* will be on your food and water. I will take away sickness *n* from among you, 26and none will miscarry or be barren *o* in your land. I will give you a full life span. *p*

27"I will send my terror *q* ahead of you and throw into confusion *r* every nation you encounter. I will make all your enemies turn their backs and run. *s* 28I will send the hornet *t* ahead of you to drive the Hivites, Canaanites and Hittites *u* out of your way. 29But I will not drive them out in a single year, because the land would become desolate and the wild animals *v* too numerous for you. 30Little by little I will drive them out before you, until you have increased enough to take possession *w* of the land.

31"I will establish your borders from the Red Sea *g* to the Sea of the Philistines, *h* and from the desert to the River. *i x* I will hand over to you the people who live in the land and you will drive them out *y* before you. 32Do not make a covenant *z* with them or with their gods. 33Do not let them live in your land, or they will cause you to sin against me, because the worship of their gods will certainly be a snare *a* to you."

The Covenant Confirmed

24 Then he said to Moses, "Come up to the LORD, you and Aaron, *b* Nadab and Abihu, *c* and seventy of the elders *d* of Israel. You are to worship at a distance, 2but Moses alone is to approach *e* the LORD; the others must not come near. And the people may not come up with him."

Cross references (center column)

23:18 *u*Ex 34:25; Lev 2:11 *v*S Ex 12:8
23:19 *w*S Ex 22:29; S 34:22; S Nu 18:12 *x*Ex 34:26; Dt 14:21
23:20 *y*S Ge 16:7 *z*Ex 15:17
23:21 *a*Dt 18:19; Jer 13:15 *b*Dt 29:20; 2Ki 24:4; La 1:17 *c*Nu 17:10; Dt 9:7; 31:27; Jos 24:19; Ps 25:7; 78:8,40, 56; 106:33; 107:11; 1Jn 5:16 *d*S Ex 3:15
23:22 *e*S Ex 15:26 *f*S Ge 12:3; Isa 41:11; Jer 30:20
23:23 *g*Nu 13:29; 21:21; Jos 3:10; 24:8,11; Ezr 9:1; Ps 135:11
23:24 *h*S Ex 20:5 *i*Lev 18:3; 20:23; Dt 9:4; 12:30-31; Jer 10:2 *j*Ex 34:13; Nu 33:52; Dt 7:5; 12:3; Jdg 2:2; 2Ki 18:4; 23:14 *k*Lev 26:1; Dt 16:22; 1Ki 14:23; 2Ki 3:2; 10:26; 17:10; 2Ch 14:3; Isa 27:9
23:25 *l*Mt 4:10 *m*Lev 26:3-13; Dt 7:12-15; 28:1-14 *n*S Ex 15:26
23:26 *o*Lev 26:3-4; Dt 7:14; 28:4; Mal 3:11 *p*S Ge 15:15; Dt 4:1,40; 32:47; Ps 90:10
23:27 *q*S Ge 35:5; S Ex 15:14 *r*S Ex 14:24; Dt 7:23

*s*2Sa 22:41; Ps 18:40; 21:12 **23:28** *t*Dt 7:20; Jos 24:12 *u*Ex 33:2; 34:11,24; Nu 13:29; Dt 4:38; 11:23; 18:12; Jos 3:10; 24:11; Ps 78:55 **23:29** *v*Dt 7:22 **23:30** *w*Jos 23:5 **23:31** *x*S Ge 2:14; Dt 34:2; Ezr 4:20 *y*Dt 7:24; 9:3; Jos 21:44; 24:12,18; Ps 80:8 **23:32** *z*S Ge 26:28; Ex 34:12; Dt 7:2; Jos 9:7; Jdg 2:2; 1Sa 11:1; 1Ki 15:19; 20:34; Eze 17:13 **23:33** *a*S Ex 10:7 *b*S Ex 19:24 *c*S Ex 6:23 *d*ver 9; Nu 11:16 **24:2** *e*Nu 12:6-8

g31 Hebrew *Yam Suph*; that is, Sea of Reeds *h31* That is, the Mediterranean *i31* That is, the Euphrates

---

23:18 *not . . . with anything containing yeast.* See note on 12:15. *not be kept until morning.* See 12:9–10.

23:19 *firstfruits.* Representative of the whole harvest. The offering of firstfruits was an acknowledgment that the harvest was from the Lord and belonged wholly to him. *Do not cook a young goat in its mother's milk.* Perhaps a protest against a Canaanite pagan ritual (see v. 33; 34:15).

23:20 *angel.* See 14:19; see also note on Ge 16:7. *place I have prepared.* Canaan (cf. the similar statement of Jesus in Jn 14:2–3).

23:21 *Name.* Representing God's presence.

23:22 *If.* See note on 19:5.

23:23 See 3:8 and note.

23:28 *hornet.* The meaning of the Hebrew for this word is uncertain. The Septuagint (the Greek translation of the OT) renders it "wasp," but the translators may have been guessing. In any event, the Lord promises to send some agent to disable or frighten the peoples of Canaan so that they will not be able to resist Israel's invasion. But probably the word involves concrete imagery and the focus of the statement is on the effects—therefore we are not to look for some historical agent to which the word metaphorically refers (cf. Isa

7:18).

23:30 *Little by little.* See Jdg 1.

23:31 See Ge 15:18; 1Ki 4:21. *Red Sea.* The (south)eastern border (here the modern Gulf of Aqaba; see note on 1Ki 9:26). *Sea of the Philistines.* The western border (see NIV text note). *the desert.* The southern border (northeastern Sinai; see note on Ge 15:18). *the River.* The northern border (see NIV text note).

23:33 *snare.* A symbol of destruction (see 10:7; Job 18:9; Ps 18:5; Pr 13:14; 21:6; Isa 24:17–18).

24:1 *Come up.* The action, temporarily interrupted for the Book of the Covenant (20:22–23:33), is resumed from 20:21. Moses and his associates would ascend the mountain after the events of vv. 3–8. *Nadab and Abihu.* Aaron's two oldest sons. Nadab would have succeeded Aaron as high priest, but he and his brother died because they offered unauthorized fire before the Lord (see Lev 10:1–2; Nu 3:4). *seventy . . . elders.* Cf. Nu 11:16; perhaps representing Jacob's 70 descendants (see 1:5; Ge 46:27 and note). *elders.* See note on 3:16. *at a distance.* See 20:21.

24:2 *Moses alone.* The mediator between God and the people of Israel. Jesus, the second Moses (see Heb 3:1–6), is the "mediator of a new covenant" (Heb 12:24).

3When Moses went and told the people all the LORD's words and laws,[f] they responded with one voice, "Everything the LORD has said we will do."[g] 4Moses then wrote[h] down everything the LORD had said.

He got up early the next morning and built an altar[i] at the foot of the mountain and set up twelve stone pillars[j] representing the twelve tribes of Israel. 5Then he sent young Israelite men, and they offered burnt offerings[k] and sacrificed young bulls as fellowship offerings[l] to the LORD. 6Moses[m] took half of the blood[n] and put it in bowls, and the other half he sprinkled[o] on the altar. 7Then he took the Book of the Covenant[p] and read it to the people. They responded, "We will do everything the LORD has said; we will obey."[q]

8Moses then took the blood, sprinkled it on the people[r] and said, "This is the blood of the covenant[s] that the LORD has made with you in accordance with all these words."

9Moses and Aaron, Nadab and Abihu, and the seventy elders[t] of Israel went up 10and saw[u] the God of Israel. Under his feet was something like a pavement made of sapphire,[k][v] clear as the sky[w] itself. 11But God did not raise his hand against these leaders of the Israelites; they saw[x] God, and they ate and drank.[y]

12The LORD said to Moses, "Come up to me on the mountain and stay here, and I will give you the tablets of stone,[z] with the law and commands I have written for their instruction."

13Then Moses set out with Joshua[a] his aide, and Moses went up on the mountain[b] of God. 14He said to the elders, "Wait here for us until we come back to you. Aaron and Hur[c] are with you, and anyone involved in a dispute[d] can go to them."

15When Moses went up on the mountain, the cloud[e] covered it, 16and the glory[f] of the LORD settled on Mount Sinai.[g] For six days the cloud covered the mountain, and on the seventh day the LORD called to Moses from within the cloud.[h] 17To the Israelites the glory of the LORD looked like a consuming fire[i] on top of the mountain. 18Then Moses entered the cloud as he went on up the mountain. And he stayed on the mountain forty[j] days and forty nights.[k]

Offerings for the Tabernacle

25:1–7pp — Ex 35:4–9

25 The LORD said to Moses, 2"Tell the Israelites to bring me an offering. You are to receive the offering for me from each man whose heart prompts[l] him to give. 3These are the offerings you are to receive from them: gold, silver and bronze; 4blue, purple and scarlet yarn[m] and fine linen; goat hair; 5ram skins dyed

Cross references (center column)

24:3 /S Ex 21:1; Gal 3:19
gS Ex 19:8; Jos 24:24
24:4 hS Ex 17:14
iS Ge 8:20
jS Ge 28:18; S Dt 27:2
24:5 kLev 1:3
lS Ge 31:54
24:6 mEx 14:15; 32:31; Ps 99:6
nHeb 9:18
oLev 1:11; 3:2,8, 13; 5:9; Mt 26:28
24:7 p2Ki 23:2, 21; Heb 9:19
qEx 19:8; Jer 40:3; 42:6,21; 43:2
24:8 rHeb 9:19; 1Pe 1:2
sLev 26:3; Dt 5:2-3; Jos 24:25; 2Ki 11:17; Jer 11:4,8; 31:32; 34:13; Zec 9:11; S Mt 26:28; S Lk 22:20; Heb 9:20*
24:9 tS ver 1
24:10 uS Ge 16:13; Nu 12:6; Isa 6:1; Eze 1:1; 8:3; 40:2; S Jn 1:18
vJob 28:16; Isa 54:11; Eze 1:26; 10:1
wRev 4:3
24:11 xS ver 10; S Ex 3:6; S 19:21
yEze 44:3; Mt 26:29
24:12 zEx 31:18; 32:15-16; 34:1, 28,29; Dt 4:13; 5:22; 8:3; 9:9,10, 11; 10:4; 2Co 3:3
24:13 aS Ex 17:9
bS Ex 3:1
24:14 cS Ex 17:10
dEx 18:16
24:15 eS Ex 19:9; Mt 17:5
24:16 /S Ex 16:7; Lev 9:23; Nu 14:10; 1Sa 4:21,22; Eze 8:4; 11:22 gS Ex 19:11 hPs 99:7 24:17 /S Ex 15:7; S 19:18; Heb 12:18,29 24:18 /1Ki 19:8 kS Ge 7:4; Mt 4:2 25:2 /Ex 35:21,22,26,27,29; 36:2; 2Ki 12:4; 1Ch 29:5,7,9; 2Ch 24:10; 29:31; Ezr 2:68; Ne 7:70-72; 2Co 8:11-12; 9:7 25:4 mEx 28:4-8

i5 Traditionally *peace offerings*   k10 Or *lapis lazuli*

Study notes (bottom)

24:3 *words.* Probably refers to the Ten Commandments (see 20:1 and note). *laws.* Probably refers to the stipulations of the Book of the Covenant (21:1–23:19). *we will do.* See v. 7; see also 19:8 and note.
24:4 *Moses . . . wrote.* See note on 17:14; see also Introduction: Author and Date of Writing. *twelve stone pillars representing.* See Jos 4:5,20; 1Ki 18:31.
24:5 *young Israelite men . . . offered.* See note on 19:22.
24:6 *half of the blood . . . the other half.* The division of the blood points to the twofold aspect of the "blood of the covenant" (v. 8): The blood on the altar symbolizes God's forgiveness and his acceptance of the offering; the blood on the people points to an oath that binds them in obedience (see vv. 3,7).
24:7 *Book of the Covenant.* Strictly speaking, 20:22–23:19 (see note there)—but here implying also the stipulations of 20:2–17; 23:20–33. *We will do . . . we will obey.* See v. 3; see also 19:8 and note.
24:8 *then.* Only after the people agreed to obey the Lord could they participate in his covenant with them. *blood of the covenant.* See Mk 14:24 and note.
24:9 *went up.* See v. 1 and note.
24:10 *saw . . . God.* But not in the fullness of his glory (see 33:20; see also notes on 3:6; Ge 16:13; Nu 12:8; Eze 1:28). *sapphire.* See NIV text note. *sky.* Symbolized by the blue color of the "sapphire" (see Eze 1:26).

24:11 *raise his hand against.* See 9:15. *leaders.* Lit. "corners," "corner supports"; used in the sense of "leaders" only here. Cf. Gal 2:9. *ate and drank.* A covenant meal (cf. Ge 26:30; 31:54), celebrating the sealing of the covenant described in vv. 3–8. It foreshadows the Lord's Supper, which celebrates the new covenant sealed by Christ's death (see 1Co 11:25–26).
24:12 *Come up.* See note on v. 1. *tablets of stone.* See note on 31:18. *their.* The people's. *instruction.* As instruction from the covenant Lord, the laws were divine directives.
24:13 *Joshua his aide.* See note on 17:9.
24:14 *Hur.* See note on 17:10.
24:17 *glory of the LORD.* See 16:10.
24:18 *stayed on the mountain.* Moses did not come down until he had received instructions concerning the tabernacle and its furnishings (see 32:15). *forty days and forty nights.* Jesus, the second Moses (see note on v. 2), fasted for the same length of time (see Mt 4:2).
25:2 *offering.* Here refers to a voluntary contribution.
25:4 *blue, purple and scarlet.* Royal colors. *blue, purple.* Dyes derived from various shellfish (primarily the *murex*) that swarm in the waters of the northeast Mediterranean. So important for the local economy was the dyeing industry that the promised land was known as Canaan (which means "land of purple"), later called Phoenicia (also meaning "land of purple") by the Greeks. *scarlet.* Derived from the eggs and

red and hides of sea cows[1];[n] acacia wood;[o] [6]olive oil[p] for the light; spices for the anointing oil and for the fragrant incense;[q] [7]and onyx stones and other gems to be mounted on the ephod[r] and breastpiece.[s]

[8]"Then have them make a sanctuary[t] for me, and I will dwell[u] among them. [9]Make this tabernacle and all its furnishings exactly like the pattern[v] I will show you.

The Ark

25:10–20pp — Ex 37:1–9

[10]"Have them make a chest[w] of acacia wood—two and a half cubits long, a cubit and a half wide, and a cubit and a half high.[m] [11]Overlay[x] it with pure gold, both inside and out, and make a gold molding around it. [12]Cast four gold rings for it and fasten them to its four feet, with two rings[y] on one side and two rings on the other. [13]Then make poles of acacia wood and overlay them with gold.[z] [14]Insert the poles[a] into the rings on the sides of the chest to carry it. [15]The poles are to remain in the rings of this ark; they are not to be

removed.[b] [16]Then put in the ark the Testimony,[c] which I will give you.

[17]"Make an atonement cover[n][d] of pure gold—two and a half cubits long and a cubit and a half wide.[o] [18]And make two cherubim[e] out of hammered gold at the ends of the cover. [19]Make one cherub on one end and the second cherub on the other; make the cherubim of one piece with the cover, at the two ends. [20]The cherubim[f] are to have their wings spread upward, overshadowing[g] the cover with them. The cherubim are to face each other, looking toward the cover. [21]Place the cover on top of the ark[h] and put in the ark the Testimony,[i] which I will give you. [22]There, above the cover between the two

Reference column

25:5 [n]Nu 4:6,10; [o]Dt 10:3
25:6 [p]Ex 27:20; 30:22-32; 35:28; 39:37; Nu 4:16
[q]Ex 30:1,7,35; 31:11; 35:28; Lev 16:12; Nu 4:16; 7:14; 2Ch 13:11
25:7 [r]Ex 28:4, 6-14; 29:5; Jdg 8:27; Hos 3:4
[s]Lev 8:8
25:8 [t]Ex 36:1-5; Lev 4:6; 10:4,7; 21:12,23; Nu 3:28; Heb 9:1-2
[u]Ex 29:45; Lev 26:11-12; Nu 5:3; Dt 12:11; 1Ki 6:13; Zec 2:10; 2Co 6:16
25:9 [v]ver 40; Ex 26:30; 27:8; 31:11; 39:32,42, 43; Nu 8:4; 1Ch 28:11,19; Ac 7:44; Heb 8:5
25:10 [w]Dt 10:1-5; 1Ki 6:19; Heb 9:4
25:11 [x]ver 24; Ex 30:3
25:12 [y]ver 26; Ex 30:4
25:13 [z]ver 28; Ex 27:6; 30:5; 37:28
25:14 [a]Ex 27:7; 40:20; 1Ch 15:15

25:15 [b]1Ki 8:8 25:16 [c]S Ex 16:34; Heb 9:4 25:17 [d]ver 21; Lev 16:13; Ro 3:25 25:18 [e]Ex 26:1,31; 36:35; 1Ki 6:23,27; 8:6; 2Ch 3:10-13; Heb 9:5 25:20 [f]S Ge 3:24 [g]Ex 37:9; 1Ki 8:7; 1Ch 28:18; Heb 9:5 25:21 [h]ver 10-15; Ex 26:34; 40:20; Dt 10:5 [i]S Ex 16:34; Heb 9:4

[1] 5 That is, dugongs   [m]10 That is, about 3 3/4 feet (about 1.1 meters) long and 2 1/4 feet (about 0.7 meter) wide and high   [n]17 Traditionally a mercy seat
[o]17 That is, about 3 3/4 feet (about 1.1 meters) long and 2 1/4 feet (about 0.7 meter) wide

---

carcasses of the worm *Coccus ilicis,* which attaches itself to the leaves of the holly plant. *fine linen.* A very high quality cloth (often used by Egyptian royalty) made from thread spun from the fibers of flax straw. The Hebrew for this term derives ultimately from Egyptian. Excellent examples of unusually white, tightly woven linen have been found in ancient Egyptian tombs. Some are so finely woven that they cannot be distinguished from silk without the use of a magnifying glass. *goat hair.* From long-haired goats. A coarse, black (cf. SS 1:5; 6:5) material, it was often used to weave cloth for tents.
25:5 *ram skins dyed red.* After all the wool had been removed from the skins. The final product was similar to present-day morocco leather. *sea cows.* Native to the Red Sea. *acacia.* The wood is darker and harder than oak and is avoided by wood-eating insects. It is common in the Sinai peninsula.
25:6 *spices.* Those used in the anointing oil are identified in 30:23–24 as myrrh (balsam sap), cinnamon (bark of the cinnamon tree, a species of laurel), cane (pith from the root of a reed plant) and cassia (made from dried flowers of the cinnamon tree). Those used in the fragrant incense are identified in 30:34 as gum resin (a powder taken from the middle of hardened drops of myrrh—rare and very valuable), onycha (made from mollusk shells) and galbanum (a rubbery resin taken from the roots of a flowering plant that thrives in Syria and Persia).
25:7 *other gems.* See 28:17–20.
25:8 *sanctuary.* Lit. "holy place," "place set apart." See note on 3:5.
25:9 *tabernacle.* Lit. "dwelling place." The word is rarely used of human dwellings; it almost always signifies the place where God dwells among his people (see v. 8; 29:45–46; Lev 26:11; Eze 37:27; cf. Jn 1:14; Rev 21:3). *pattern.* See note on v. 40.
25:10 *chest.* See v. 14. Such was its form and function. The Hebrew for this word is translated by the more traditional term "ark" throughout the rest of Exodus (see note on Dt

10:1–3); it is different from that used to refer to Noah's ark and to the reed basket in which the infant Moses was placed (see note on 2:3). Of all the tabernacle furnishings, the ark is mentioned first probably because it symbolized the throne of the Lord (see 1Sa 4:4; 2Sa 6:2), the great King, who chose to dwell among his people (see note on v. 9).
25:11 *pure gold.* Uncontaminated by silver or other impurities.
25:12 *rings.* Lit. "houses," "housings," into which poles were inserted to carry the ark (see v. 14).
25:16 *Testimony.* The two tablets on which were inscribed the Ten Commandments as the basic stipulations of the Sinai covenant (see 20:1–17; 31:18). The Hebrew word for "Testimony" is related to a Babylonian word meaning "covenant stipulations." See also notes on v. 22; 16:34.
25:17 *atonement.* Reconciliation, the divine act of grace whereby God draws to himself and makes "at one" with him those who were once alienated from him. In the OT, the shed blood of sacrificial offerings effected atonement (see Lev 17:11 and note); in the NT, the blood of Jesus, shed once for all time, does the same (see Ro 3:25; 1Jn 2:2). *atonement cover.* See NIV text note; see also Lev 16:2 and note. That God's symbolic throne was capped with an atonement cover signified his great mercy toward his people—only such a God can be revered (see Ps 130:3–4).
25:18 *cherubim.* Probably similar to the carvings of winged sphinxes that adorned the armrests of royal thrones (see note on v. 10) in many parts of the ancient Near East (see also note on Ge 3:24). In the OT the cherubim were symbolic attendants that marked the place of the Lord's "enthronement" in his earthly kingdom (see 1Sa 4:4; 2Sa 6:2; 2Ki 19:15; Ps 99:1). From the cover of the ark (God's symbolic throne) the Lord gave directions to Moses (see v. 22; Nu 7:89). Later the ark's presence in the temple at Jerusalem would designate it as God's earthly royal city (see Ps 9:11; 18:10 and notes).
25:22 *ark of the Testimony.* Called this because it contained the Testimony (see note on v. 16). The phrase "ark of the Testimony" is a synonym of the more familiar phrase

cherubim[j] that are over the ark of the Testimony, I will meet[k] with you and give you all my commands for the Israelites.[l]

The Table

25:23–29pp — Ex 37:10–16

23"Make a table[m] of acacia wood—two cubits long, a cubit wide and a cubit and a half high.[p] 24Overlay it with pure gold and make a gold molding around it. 25Also make around it a rim a handbreadth[q] wide and put a gold molding on the rim. 26Make four gold rings for the table and fasten them to the four corners, where the four legs are. 27The rings are to be close to the rim to hold the poles used in carrying the table. 28Make the poles of acacia wood, overlay them with gold[n] and carry the table with them. 29And make its plates and dishes of pure gold, as well as its pitchers

25:22 /Nu 7:89;
1Sa 4:4; 2Sa 6:2;
22:11; 2Ki 19:15;
1Ch 13:6; 28:18;
Ps 18:10; 80:1;
99:1; Isa 37:16
[k]Ex 19:3;
29:42; 30:6,36;
Lev 1:1; 16:2;
Nu 17:4 /Jer 3:16
25:23 mver 30;
Ex 26:35; 40:4,
22; Lev 24:6;
Nu 3:31;
1Ki 7:48;
1Ch 28:16;
2Ch 4:8,19;
Eze 41:22; 44:16;
Heb 9:2
25:28 [n]S ver 13

25:29 [o]Nu 4:7
25:30 [p]Ex 35:13;
39:36; 40:4,23;
Lev 24:5-9;
Nu 4:7;
1Sa 21:4-6;
1Ki 7:48;
1Ch 23:29
25:31 [q]Ex 26:35;
31:8; 35:14;
39:37; 40:4,24;

and bowls for the pouring out of offerings.[o] 30Put the bread of the Presence[p] on this table to be before me at all times.

The Lampstand

25:31–39pp — Ex 37:17–24

31"Make a lampstand[q] of pure gold and hammer it out, base and shaft; its flower-like cups, buds and blossoms shall be of one piece with it. 32Six branches are to extend from the sides of the lampstand—three on one side and three on the other. 33Three cups shaped like almond flowers with buds and blossoms are to be on one branch, three on the next branch,

Lev 24:4; Nu 3:31; 1Ki 7:49; 2Ch 4:7; Zec 4:2; Heb 9:2; Rev 1:12

[p]*23* That is, about 3 feet (about 0.9 meter) long and 1 1/2 feet (about 0.5 meter) wide and 2 1/4 feet (about 0.7 meter) high   [q]*25* That is, about 3 inches (about 8 centimeters)

"ark of the covenant" (see, e.g., Nu 10:33). *I will meet with you.* See note on 27:21.
25:23 *table.* The table taken from the second (Zerubbabel's) temple by Antiochus Epiphanes is depicted on the Arch of Titus among the items the Romans took back to Rome after conquering Jerusalem in A.D. 70.

25:26 *rings.* See note on v. 12.
25:30 *bread of the Presence.* Traditionally "showbread." In this phrase, "Presence" refers to the presence of God himself (as in 33:14–15; Isa 63:9). The bread (twelve loaves, one for each tribe) represented a perpetual bread offering to the Lord by which Israel declared that she conse-

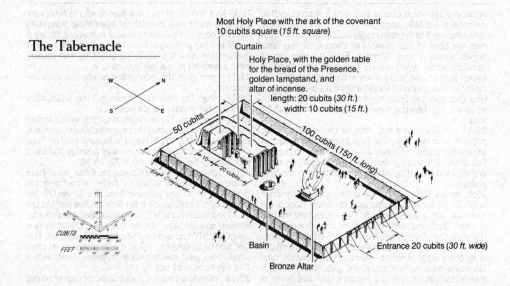

The Tabernacle

Most Holy Place with the ark of the covenant
10 cubits square (*15 ft. square*)

Curtain

Holy Place, with the golden table
for the bread of the Presence,
golden lampstand, and
altar of incense.
length: 20 cubits (*30 ft.*)
width: 10 cubits (*15 ft.*)

W   N
S   E

50 cubits

100 cubits (*150 ft. long*)

10   20 cubits

CUBITS
0   5   10   15   20

FEET
0   10   30

Basin

Entrance 20 cubits (*30 ft. wide*)

Bronze Altar

The new religious observances taught by Moses in the desert centered on rituals connected with the tabernacle, and amplified Israel's sense of separateness, purity and oneness under the Lordship of Yahweh.

A few desert shrines have been found in Sinai, notably at Serabit el-Khadem and at Timnah in the Negev, and show marked Egyptian influence.

Specific cultural antecedents to portable shrines carried on poles and covered with thin sheets of gold can be found in

ancient Egypt as early as the Old Kingdom (2800-2250 B.C.), but were especially prominent in the 18th and 19th dynasties (1570-1180). The best examples come from the fabulous tomb of Tutankhamun, c. 1350.

Comparisons of construction details in the text of Ex 25-40 with the frames, shrines, poles, sheathing, draped fabric covers, gilt rosettes, and winged protective figures from the shrine of Tutankhamun are instructive. The period, the Late Bronze Age, is equivalent in all dating systems to the era of Moses and the exodus.   © Hugh Claycombe 1981

and the same for all six branches extending from the lampstand. 34And on the lampstand there are to be four cups shaped like almond flowers with buds and blossoms. 35One bud shall be under the first pair of branches extending from the lampstand, a second bud under the second pair, and a third bud under the third pair—six branches in all. 36The buds and branches shall all be of one piece with the lampstand, hammered out of pure gold. r

37"Then make its seven lamps s and set them up on it so that they light the space in front of it. 38Its wick trimmers and trays t are to be of pure gold. 39A talent r of pure gold is to be used for the lampstand and all these accessories. 40See that you make them according to the pattern u shown you on the mountain.

The Tabernacle

26:1–37pp — Ex 36:8–38

26 "Make the tabernacle v with ten curtains of finely twisted linen and blue, purple and scarlet yarn, with cherubim w worked into them by a skilled craftsman. 2All the curtains are to be the same size x—twenty-eight cubits long and four cubits wide. s 3Join five of the curtains together, and do the same with the other five. 4Make loops of blue material along the edge of the end curtain in one set, and do the same with the end curtain in the other set. 5Make fifty loops on one curtain and fifty loops on the end curtain of the other set, with the loops opposite each other. 6Then make fifty gold clasps and use

them to fasten the curtains together so that the tabernacle is a unit. y

7"Make curtains of goat hair for the tent over the tabernacle—eleven altogether. 8All eleven curtains are to be the same size z—thirty cubits long and four cubits wide. t 9Join five of the curtains together into one set and the other six into another set. Fold the sixth curtain double at the front of the tent. 10Make fifty loops along the edge of the end curtain in one set and also along the edge of the end curtain in the other set. 11Then make fifty bronze clasps and put them in the loops to fasten the tent together as a unit. a 12As for the additional length of the tent curtains, the half curtain that is left over is to hang down at the rear of the tabernacle. 13The tent curtains will be a cubit u longer on both sides; what is left will hang over the sides of the tabernacle so as to cover it. 14Make for the tent a covering b of ram skins dyed red, and over that a covering of hides of sea cows. v c

15"Make upright frames of acacia wood for the tabernacle. 16Each frame is to be ten cubits long and a cubit and a half wide, w 17with two projections set parallel to each other. Make all the frames of the tabernacle in this way. 18Make twenty frames for the south side of the tabernacle 19and make forty silver bases d to go under

Cross-references (center column)

25:36 rver 18; Nu 8:4
25:37 sEx 27:21; 30:8; Lev 24:3-4; Nu 8:2; 1Sa 3:3; 2Ch 13:11
25:38 tS ver 37; Nu 4:9
25:40 uS ver 9; Ac 7:44; Heb 8:5*
26:1 vEx 29:42; 40:2; Lev 8:10; Nu 1:50; Jos 22:19,29; 2Sa 7:2; 1Ki 1:39; Ac 7:44; Heb 8:2, 5; 13:10; S Rev 21:3 wS Ex 25:18
26:2 xver 8

26:6 yver 11
26:8 zver 2
26:11 aver 6
26:14 bNu 3:25 cNu 4:25
26:19 dver 21, 25,32; Ex 38:27

Footnotes (center column)

r39 That is, about 75 pounds (about 34 kilograms)
s2 That is, about 42 feet (about 12.5 meters) long and 6 feet (about 1.8 meters) wide   t8 That is, about 45 feet (about 13.5 meters) long and 6 feet (about 1.8 meters) wide   u13 That is, about 1 1/2 feet (about 0.5 meter)
v14 That is, dugongs   w16 That is, about 15 feet (about 4.5 meters) long and 2 1/4 feet (about 0.7 meter) wide

---

crated to God the fruits of her labors, and by which she at the same time acknowledged that all such fruit had been hers only by God's blessing. See Lev 24:5–9.
25:31 *flowerlike cups, buds and blossoms.* The design is patterned after an almond tree (see v. 33), the first of the trees in the Near East to blossom in spring. The cups of the lampstand resemble either the calyx (outer covering of the flower) or the almond nut.
25:37 *seven.* Signifying completeness. *lamps.* The ancient lamp was a small clay saucer with part of its rim pinched together to form a spout from which protruded the top of a wick fed by oil contained in the saucer. (Examples of seven-spouted lamps come from the time of Moses.) The ruins of Beth Shan and Megiddo have yielded examples of a metal pedestal topped by a ledge designed to carry a lamp. The classic representation of the shape of the tabernacle lampstand comes from the time of Herod the Great and may be seen on the Arch of Titus in Rome. The lamps were to burn all night in the tabernacle, tended by the priests. Oil for the lamps was to be supplied by the people; the light from the lamps represented the glory of the Lord reflected in the consecrated lives of the Israelites—Israel's glory answering to God's glory in the tabernacle (29:43). See 27:20–21.
25:40 Quoted in Heb 8:5 in order to contrast the "shad-

ow" (the trappings of the old covenant) with the reality (the Christ of the new covenant). See also Heb 10:1.
26:1 *tabernacle.* See note on 25:9. Its basic structure was to be 15 feet wide by 45 feet long by 15 feet high. Over an inner lining of embroidered linen (vv. 1–6), it was to have a covering woven of goat hair (vv. 7–13) and two additional coverings of leather, one made from ram skins dyed red and one from the hides of sea cows (v. 14). Internally, the ceiling was probably flat, but whether the leather coverings had a ridge line with sloping sides (like a tent) is not known. Symbolically the tabernacle represented God's royal tent. *finely twisted linen and blue, purple and scarlet yarn.* See note on 25:4. *cherubim.* Signifying a royal chamber (see 25:18 and note).
26:7 *goat hair.* See note on 25:4.
26:14 *ram skins dyed red . . . sea cows.* See note on 25:5.
26:17 *projections.* Lit. "hands"; probably the two tenons at the bottom of each frame that were inserted into its two bases (see v. 19).
26:19 *forty silver bases.* These plus the 40 in v. 21, the 16 in v. 25 and the 4 in v. 32 make up a grand total of 100, the number of talents of silver obtained from the Israelite community to be used to cast the bases (see 38:27).

them—two bases for each frame, one under each projection. [20]For the other side, the north side of the tabernacle, make twenty frames [21]and forty silver bases e—two under each frame. [22]Make six frames for the far end, that is, the west end of the tabernacle, [23]and make two frames for the corners at the far end. [24]At these two corners they must be double from the bottom all the way to the top, and fitted into a single ring; both shall be like that. [25]So there will be eight frames and sixteen silver bases—two under each frame.

[26]"Also make crossbars of acacia wood: five for the frames on one side of the tabernacle, [27]five for those on the other side, and five for the frames on the west, at the far end of the tabernacle. [28]The center crossbar is to extend from end to end at the middle of the frames. [29]Overlay the frames with gold and make gold rings to hold the crossbars. Also overlay the crossbars with gold.

[30]"Set up the tabernacle f according to the plan g shown you on the mountain.

[31]"Make a curtain h of blue, purple and scarlet yarn and finely twisted linen, with cherubim i worked into it by a skilled craftsman. [32]Hang it with gold hooks on four posts of acacia wood overlaid with gold and standing on four silver bases. j [33]Hang the curtain from the clasps and place the ark of the Testimony behind the curtain. k The curtain will separate the Holy Place from the Most Holy Place. l [34]Put the atonement cover m on the ark of the Testimony in the Most Holy Place. [35]Place the table n outside the curtain on the north side of the tabernacle and put

26:21 e S ver 19

26:30 f Ex 40:2; Nu 9:15
g S Ex 25:9
26:31 h Nu 4:5; 2Ch 3:14; Mt 27:51; Lk 23:45; Heb 9:3
i S Ex 25:18
26:32 j S ver 19
26:33 k Ex 27:21; 35:12; 40:3,21; Lev 16:2; Nu 3:31; 4:5; 2Ch 3:14
l Lev 16:2,16; 1Ki 6:16; 7:50; 8:6; 2Ch 3:8; 5:7; Eze 41:4; Heb 9:2-3
26:34 m Ex 25:21; 30:6; 37:6; Lev 16:2; Heb 9:5
26:35 n S Ex 25:23; Heb 9:2

26:23 *corners.* Or "angles," perhaps referring to mitered joints at the corners.
26:26 *crossbars.* To strengthen the frames on the north, south and west sides of the courtyard.
26:29 *rings.* Lit. "houses," "housings" (see note on 25:12).

26:30 *plan.* See note on 25:40.
26:31–35 A curtain was to divide the tabernacle into two rooms, the Holy Place and the Most Holy Place, with the former twice as large as the latter. The Most Holy Place probably formed a perfect cube, 15 feet by 15 feet by 15 feet. Enclosed with linen curtains embroidered with cherubim

Tabernacle Furnishings

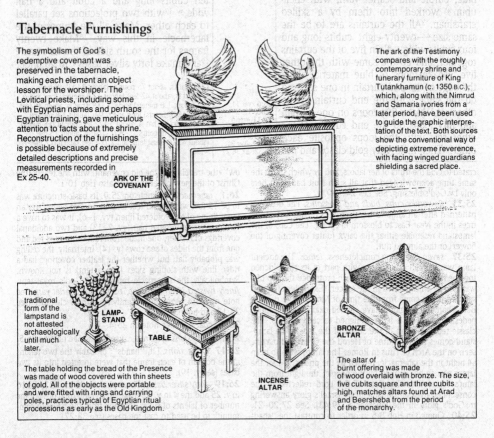

The symbolism of God's redemptive covenant was preserved in the tabernacle, making each element an object lesson for the worshiper. The Levitical priests, including some with Egyptian names and perhaps Egyptian training, gave meticulous attention to facts about the shrine. Reconstruction of the furnishings is possible because of extremely detailed descriptions and precise measurements recorded in Ex 25-40.

ARK OF THE COVENANT

The ark of the Testimony compares with the roughly contemporary shrine and funerary furniture of King Tutankhamun (c. 1350 B.C.), which, along with the Nimrud and Samaria ivories from a later period, have been used to guide the graphic interpretation of the text. Both sources show the conventional way of depicting extreme reverence, with facing winged guardians shielding a sacred place.

The traditional form of the lampstand is not attested archaeologically until much later.

LAMP-STAND

TABLE

The table holding the bread of the Presence was made of wood covered with thin sheets of gold. All of the objects were portable and were fitted with rings and carrying poles, practices typical of Egyptian ritual processions as early as the Old Kingdom.

INCENSE ALTAR

BRONZE ALTAR

The altar of burnt offering was made of wood overlaid with bronze. The size, five cubits square and three cubits high, matches altars found at Arad and Beersheba from the period of the monarchy.

the lampstand[o] opposite it on the south side.

36"For the entrance to the tent make a curtain[p] of blue, purple and scarlet yarn and finely twisted linen—the work of an embroiderer.[q] 37Make gold hooks for this curtain and five posts of acacia wood overlaid with gold. And cast five bronze bases for them.

The Altar of Burnt Offering

27:1–8pp — Ex 38:1–7

27 "Build an altar[r] of acacia wood, three cubits[x] high; it is to be square, five cubits long and five cubits wide.[y] 2Make a horn[s] at each of the four corners, so that the horns and the altar are of one piece, and overlay the altar with bronze. 3Make all its utensils of bronze—its pots to remove the ashes, and its shovels, sprinkling bowls,[t] meat forks and firepans.[u] 4Make a grating for it, a bronze network, and make a bronze ring at each of the four corners of the network. 5Put it under the ledge of the altar so that it is halfway up the altar. 6Make poles of acacia wood for the altar and overlay them with bronze.[v] 7The poles are to be inserted into the rings so they will be on two sides of the altar when it is carried.[w] 8Make the altar hollow, out of boards. It is to be made just as you were shown[x] on the mountain.

The Courtyard

27:9–19pp — Ex 38:9–20

9"Make a courtyard[y] for the tabernacle. The south side shall be a hundred cubits[z] long and is to have curtains of finely twisted linen, 10with twenty posts and twenty bronze bases and with silver hooks and bands on the posts. 11The north side shall also be a hundred cubits long and is to have curtains, with twenty posts and twenty bronze bases and with silver hooks and bands on the posts.

12"The west end of the courtyard shall be fifty cubits[a] wide and have curtains, with ten posts and ten bases. 13On the east end, toward the sunrise, the courtyard shall also be fifty cubits wide. 14Curtains fifteen cubits[b] long are to be on one side of the entrance, with three posts and three bases, 15and curtains fifteen cubits long are to be on the other side, with three posts and three bases.

16"For the entrance to the courtyard, provide a curtain[z] twenty cubits[c] long, of blue, purple and scarlet yarn and finely twisted linen—the work of an embroiderer[a]—with four posts and four bases. 17All the posts around the courtyard are to have silver bands and hooks, and bronze

Cross references (center column)

26:35 *o* Ex 25:31
26:36 *p* Ex 35:15; 40:5,28
q Ps 45:14; Eze 16:10; 26:16; 27:7
27:1 *r* S Ex 20:24; S 40:6; S 1Ki 8:64
27:2 *s* Ex 29:12; 30:2; 37:25; Lev 4:7; 1Ki 1:50; 2:28; Ps 118:27; Jer 17:1; Eze 43:15; Am 3:14; Zec 9:15
27:3 *t* Nu 7:13; 1Ki 7:40,45; 2Ki 12:13
u Nu 4:14; 1Ch 28:17; Jer 52:18
27:6 *v* S Ex 25:13
27:7 *w* Ex 25:14, 28
27:8 *x* S Ex 25:9

27:9 *y* Ex 35:17; 40:8,33; Lev 6:16,26; Eze 40:14; 42:1
27:16 *z* Ex 40:33
a Ex 36:37

Footnotes

x 1 That is, about 4 1/2 feet (about 1.3 meters)
y 1 That is, about 7 1/2 feet (about 2.3 meters) long and wide   *z 9* That is, about 150 feet (about 46 meters); also in verse 11   *a 12* That is, about 75 feet (about 23 meters); also in verse 13   *b 14* That is, about 22 1/2 feet (about 6.9 meters); also in verse 15   *c 16* That is, about 30 feet (about 9 meters)

---

and containing only the ark of the Testimony, it represented God's throne room. The Holy Place represented his royal guest chamber where his people symbolically came before him in the bread of the Presence (see note on 25:30), the light from the lampstand (see note on 25:37) and the incense from the altar of incense (see note on 30:1).
26:31 *curtain.* To separate the Holy Place from the Most Holy Place (see v. 33). It was called the "shielding curtain" (39:34; 40:21; Nu 4:5) because it shielded the ark (see 27:21; see also notes on 16:34; 25:22). At the moment when Christ died, the curtain of Herod's temple was torn, thereby giving the believer direct access to the presence of God (see Mk 15:38; Heb 6:19–20; 10:19–22). *cherubim.* See v. 1 and note. The curtain at the entrance to the Holy Place did not have cherubim (see v. 36).
26:37 *bronze.* Inside the tabernacle, gold was the metal of choice; outside—beginning with the bases of the outer curtain (see v. 36)—the metal of choice was bronze. The furnishings close to the place of God's dwelling were made of, or overlaid with, gold; those farther away (see 27:2–6; 30:18) were made of, or overlaid with, bronze. The bases that supported the frames of the tabernacle and the four posts holding the dividing curtain were of silver (see vv. 19,21, 25,32).
27:1 *altar.* The altar of burnt offering (see Lev 4:7,10,18). *acacia wood.* See note on 25:5.
27:2 *horns.* Projections of the four corner posts. They were symbols of help and refuge (see 1Ki 1:50; 2:28; Ps 18:2). They

also symbolized the atoning power of the altar: Some of the blood was put on the horns of the altar before the rest was poured out at the base (see 29:12; Lev 4:7,18,25,30, 34; 8:15; 9:9; 16:18).

27:3 *pots to remove the ashes.* From the grating (see v. 4). *shovels.* To haul the ashes away. *sprinkling bowls.* To catch the blood of the animals slain beside the altar and to sprinkle it at the base. *meat forks.* Three-pronged forks for arranging the sacrifice or removing the priests' portion from the container in which it was being boiled (see 1Sa 2:13–14). *firepans.* Probably for carrying fire from the altar of burnt offering to the altar of incense inside the Holy Place (see Lev 10:1; 16:12–13).

27:4 *grating.* Placed midway between the top and bottom of the boxlike structure. Since the intense heat of the fire built inside the upper half of the altar would have eventually destroyed it, perhaps the hollow altar (see v. 8) was designed to be filled with earth when it was in use. *ring.* See note on 25:12.

27:12–13 *west end . . . east end.* The courtyard is described as having two equal parts. The Most Holy Place probably occupied the central position in the western half, the altar of burnt offering the central position in the eastern half.

27:13–14 *toward the sunrise . . . the entrance.* The entrance to the tabernacle courtyard faced east, as did that of Solomon's temple (see Eze 8:16) and of Herod's temple.

bases. [18]The courtyard shall be a hundred cubits long and fifty cubits wide,[d] with curtains of finely twisted linen five cubits[e] high, and with bronze bases. [19]All the other articles used in the service of the tabernacle, whatever their function, including all the tent pegs for it and those for the courtyard, are to be of bronze.

Oil for the Lampstand

27:20–21pp — Lev 24:1–3

[20]"Command the Israelites to bring you clear oil[b] of pressed olives for the light so that the lamps may be kept burning. [21]In the Tent of Meeting,[c] outside the curtain that is in front of the Testimony,[d] Aaron and his sons are to keep the lamps[e] burning before the LORD from evening till morning. This is to be a lasting ordinance[f] among the Israelites for the generations to come.

The Priestly Garments

28 "Have Aaron[g] your brother brought to you from among the Israelites, along with his sons Nadab and Abihu,[h] Eleazar and Ithamar,[i] so they may serve me as priests.[j] [2]Make sacred garments[k] for your brother Aaron, to give him dignity and honor.[l] [3]Tell all the skilled men[m] to whom I have given wisdom[n] in such matters that they are to make garments for Aaron, for his consecration, so he may serve me as priest. [4]These are the garments they are to make: a breastpiece,[o] an ephod,[p] a robe,[q] a woven tunic,[r] a turban[s] and a sash. They are to make these sacred garments for your brother Aaron and his sons, so they may serve me as priests. [5]Have them use gold, and blue, purple and scarlet yarn, and fine linen.[t]

(center reference column)

27:20 [b]S Ex 25:6
27:21 [c]Ex 28:43;
29:42; 30:36;
33:7; Lev 1:1;
6:26; 8:3,31;
Nu 1:1; 31:54;
Jos 18:1; 1Ki 1:39
[d]S Ex 16:34
[e]S Ex 25:37
[f]Ex 29:9; 30:21;
Lev 3:17; 16:34;
17:7; Nu 18:23;
19:21; 1Sa 30:25
28:1 [g]Lev 8:30;
Ps 99:6; Heb 5:4
[h]S Ex 6:23; 24:9
[i]S Ex 6:23
[j]Lev 8:2; 21:1;
Nu 18:1-7;
Dt 18:5;
1Sa 2:28; Heb 5:1
28:2 [k]Ex 29:5,
29; 31:10; 35:19;
39:1; Lev 8:7-9,
30; 16:32;
Nu 20:26-28 [l]ver
40
28:3 [m]Ex 31:6;
35:10,25,35;
36:1 [n]Ex 31:3;
Dt 34:9; Isa 11:2;
1Co 12:8;
S Eph 1:17
28:4 [o]ver 15-30
[p]S Ex 25:7 [q]ver
31-35 [r]ver 39;
Lev 10:5 [s]ver 37
28:5 [t]Ex 25:4

28:6 [u]S Ex 25:7
28:8 [v]Ex 29:5
28:9 [w]SS 8:6;
Isa 49:16;
Hag 2:23
28:12 [x]Dt 33:12;
Job 31:36 [y]ver
29; Ex 30:16;
Nu 10:10; 31:54;
Jos 4:7; Zec 6:14
28:15 [z]S Ex 25:7
28:17
[a]Eze 28:13;
Rev 21:19-20

The Ephod

28:6–14pp — Ex 39:2–7

[6]"Make the ephod[u] of gold, and of blue, purple and scarlet yarn, and of finely twisted linen—the work of a skilled craftsman. [7]It is to have two shoulder pieces attached to two of its corners, so it can be fastened. [8]Its skillfully woven waistband[v] is to be like it—of one piece with the ephod and made with gold, and with blue, purple and scarlet yarn, and with finely twisted linen.

[9]"Take two onyx stones and engrave[w] on them the names of the sons of Israel [10]in the order of their birth—six names on one stone and the remaining six on the other. [11]Engrave the names of the sons of Israel on the two stones the way a gem cutter engraves a seal. Then mount the stones in gold filigree settings [12]and fasten them on the shoulder pieces of the ephod as memorial stones for the sons of Israel. Aaron is to bear the names on his shoulders[x] as a memorial[y] before the LORD. [13]Make gold filigree settings [14]and two braided chains of pure gold, like a rope, and attach the chains to the settings.

The Breastpiece

28:15–28pp — Ex 39:8–21

[15]"Fashion a breastpiece[z] for making decisions—the work of a skilled craftsman. Make it like the ephod: of gold, and of blue, purple and scarlet yarn, and of finely twisted linen. [16]It is to be square—a span[f] long and a span wide—and folded double. [17]Then mount four rows of precious stones[a] on it. In the first row there shall be a ruby, a topaz and a beryl; [18]in the second row a turquoise, a sapphire[g] and an em-

[d]18 That is, about 150 feet (about 46 meters) long and 75 feet (about 23 meters) wide   [e]18 That is, about 7 1/2 feet (about 2.3 meters)   [f]16 That is, about 9 inches (about 22 centimeters)   [g]18 Or *lapis lazuli*

27:18 *five cubits.* See NIV text note; high enough to block the view of people standing outside the courtyard, thus protecting the sanctity and privacy of the worship taking place inside.
27:20 *clear oil of pressed olives.* Unripe olives were crushed in a mortar. The pulpy mass was then placed in a cloth basket through the bottom of which the oil dripped, producing a clear fuel that burned with little or no smoke.
27:21 *Tent of Meeting.* The tabernacle; it was not a place where God's people met for collective worship but one where God himself met—by appointment, not by accident—with his people (see 29:42–43). *curtain that is in front of the Testimony.* See note on 26:31. *lamps burning . . . from evening till morning.* The lamps were lit in the evening (see 30:8) and apparently extinguished in the morning (1Sa 3:3).
28:1 *Nadab and Abihu.* See note on 24:1. *serve me as priests.* In order "to offer gifts and sacrifices for sins" and "to

deal gently with those who are ignorant and are going astray" (Heb 5:1–2). Another important function of the priests was to read the law of Moses to the people and remind them of their covenant obligations (see Dt 31:9–13; Ne 8:2–3).
28:2 *to give him dignity and honor.* The garments were to exalt the office and functions of lesser priests (see v. 40) as well as of the high priest.
28:6 *ephod.* A sleeveless vestment worn by the high priest. Sometimes the word refers to an otherwise unidentified object of worship (see, e.g., Jdg 8:27; 18:17; Hos 3:4).
28:8 *waistband.* Apparently to hold the front and the back of the ephod to the priest's body.
28:12 *Aaron is to bear the names on his shoulders.* To symbolize the fact that the high priest represents all Israel when he ministers in the tabernacle.
28:15 *for making decisions.* By means of the Urim and Thummim (see note on v. 30).

erald; [19]in the third row a jacinth, an agate and an amethyst; [20]in the fourth row a chrysolite,[b] an onyx and a jasper.[h] Mount them in gold filigree settings. [21]There are to be twelve stones, one for each of the names of the sons of Israel,[c] each engraved like a seal with the name of one of the twelve tribes. [d]

[22]"For the breastpiece make braided chains of pure gold, like a rope. [23]Make two gold rings for it and fasten them to two corners of the breastpiece. [24]Fasten the two gold chains to the rings at the corners of the breastpiece, [25]and the other ends of the chains to the two settings, attaching them to the shoulder pieces of the ephod at the front. [26]Make two gold rings and attach them to the other two corners of the breastpiece on the inside edge next to the ephod. [27]Make two more gold rings and attach them to the bottom of the shoulder pieces on the front of the ephod, close to the seam just above the waistband of the ephod. [28]The rings of the breastpiece are to be tied to the rings of the ephod with blue cord, connecting it to the waistband, so that the breastpiece will not swing out from the ephod.

[29]"Whenever Aaron enters the Holy Place,[e] he will bear the names of the sons of Israel over his heart on the breastpiece of decision as a continuing memorial before the LORD. [30]Also put the Urim and the Thummim[f] in the breastpiece, so they may be over Aaron's heart whenever he enters the presence of the LORD. Thus Aaron will always bear the means of making decisions for the Israelites over his heart before the LORD.

Other Priestly Garments

28:31–43pp — Ex 39:22–31

[31]"Make the robe of the ephod entirely of blue cloth, [32]with an opening for the head in its center. There shall be a woven edge like a collar[i] around this opening, so that it will not tear. [33]Make pomegran-

ates[g] of blue, purple and scarlet yarn around the hem of the robe, with gold bells between them. [34]The gold bells and the pomegranates are to alternate around the hem of the robe. [35]Aaron must wear it when he ministers. The sound of the bells will be heard when he enters the Holy Place before the LORD and when he comes out, so that he will not die.

[36]"Make a plate[h] of pure gold and engrave on it as on a seal: HOLY TO THE LORD.[i] [37]Fasten a blue cord to it to attach it to the turban; it is to be on the front of the turban. [38]It will be on Aaron's forehead, and he will bear the guilt[j] involved in the sacred gifts the Israelites consecrate, whatever their gifts may be. It will be on Aaron's forehead continually so that they will be acceptable[k] to the LORD.

[39]"Weave the tunic[l] of fine linen and make the turban[m] of fine linen. The sash is to be the work of an embroiderer. [40]Make tunics, sashes and headbands for Aaron's sons,[n] to give them dignity and honor. [o] [41]After you put these clothes[p] on your brother Aaron and his sons, anoint[q] and ordain them. Consecrate them so they may serve me as priests.[r]

[42]"Make linen undergarments[s] as a covering for the body, reaching from the waist to the thigh. [43]Aaron and his sons must wear them whenever they enter the Tent of Meeting[t] or approach the altar to minister in the Holy Place,[u] so that they will not incur guilt and die.[v]

"This is to be a lasting ordinance[w] for Aaron and his descendants.

Consecration of the Priests

29:1–37pp — Lev 8:1–36

29 "This is what you are to do to consecrate[x] them, so they may serve me as priests: Take a young bull and two rams without defect.[y] [2]And from fine

Cross references (center column)

28:20 [b]Eze 1:16; 10:9; Da 10:6
28:21 [c]Jos 4:8 [d]Rev 21:12
28:29 [e]ver 43
28:30 [f]Lev 8:8; Nu 27:21; Dt 33:8; 1Sa 28:6; Ezr 2:63; Ne 7:65

28:33 [g]Nu 13:23; 1Sa 14:2; 1Ki 7:18; SS 4:3; Jer 52:22; Joel 1:12; Hag 2:19
28:36 [h]ver 37; Ex 29:6; Lev 8:9 [i]Zec 14:20
28:38 [j]Lev 5:1; 10:17; 16:22; 22:9,16; Nu 18:1; Isa 53:5,6,11; Eze 4:4-6; Heb 9:28; 1Pe 2:24 [k]S Ge 32:20; Lev 22:20,27; 23:11; Isa 56:7
28:39 [l]ver 4 [m]Ex 29:6; Lev 16:4; Eze 24:17,23; 44:18
28:40 [n]ver 4; Ex 29:8-9; 39:41; 40:14; Lev 8:13 [o]ver 2
28:41 [p]Ex 40:13 [q]Ex 29:7; Lev 6:20; 10:7; 21:12; Nu 35:25 [r]Ex 29:7-9; 30:30; 40:15; Lev 4:3; 6:22; 8:1-36; Nu 3:3; Heb 7:28
28:42 [s]Lev 6:10; 16:4,23; Eze 44:18
28:43 [t]S Ex 27:21 [u]ver 29 [v]Ex 30:20,21; Lev 16:13; 22:9; Nu 1:51; 4:15,20; 18:22 [w]S Ex 27:21
29:1 [x]ver 21,44; Lev 20:7; Jos 3:5; 1Ch 15:12 [y]Eze 43:23

[h]20 The precise identification of some of these precious stones is uncertain.   [i]32 The meaning of the Hebrew for this word is uncertain.

Footnotes (bottom)

28:29 Aaron . . . will bear the names . . . over his heart. Thus the nation was doubly represented before the Lord (see v. 12 and note).

28:30 the Urim and the Thummim. The Hebrew for this phrase probably means "the curses and the perfections." The Hebrew word Urim begins with the first letter of the Hebrew alphabet (aleph) and Thummim begins with the last letter (taw). They were sacred lots and were often used in times of crisis to determine the will of God (see Nu 27:21). It has been suggested that if Urim ("curses") dominated when the lots were cast the answer was "no," but if Thummim ("perfections") dominated it was "yes." In any event, their "every decision" was "from the LORD" (Pr 16:33).
28:31 robe. Worn under the ephod.

28:35 According to Jewish tradition, one end of a length of rope was tied to the high priest's ankle and the other end remained outside the tabernacle. If the bells on his robe stopped tinkling while he was in the Holy Place, the assumption that he had died could be tested by pulling gently on the rope.
28:38 bear the guilt. Symbolically.
28:39 tunic. Worn under the robe.
28:40 to give them dignity and honor. See note on v. 2.
28:42–43 See note on 20:26.
28:43 Tent of Meeting. See note on 27:21.
29:1 consecrate them. See note on 19:10–11. without defect. See note on 12:5.

wheat flour, without yeast, make bread, and cakes mixed with oil, and wafers spread with oil.z 3Put them in a basket and present them in it—along with the bull and the two rams.a 4Then bring Aaron and his sons to the entrance to the Tent of Meeting and wash them with water.b 5Take the garmentsc and dress Aaron with the tunic, the robe of the ephod, the ephod itself and the breastpiece. Fasten the ephod on him by its skillfully woven waistband.d 6Put the turbane on his head and attach the sacred diademf to the turban. 7Take the anointing oilg and anoint him by pouring it on his head. 8Bring his sons and dress them in tunicsh 9and put headbands on them. Then tie sashes on Aaron and his sons.i The priesthood is theirs by a lasting ordinance.j In this way you shall ordain Aaron and his sons.

10"Bring the bull to the front of the Tent of Meeting, and Aaron and his sons shall lay their hands on its head.k 11Slaughter it in the LORD's presencel at the entrance to the Tent of Meeting. 12Take some of the bull's blood and put it on the hornsm of the altar with your finger, and pour out the rest of it at the base of the altar.n 13Then take all the fato around the inner parts,p the covering of the liver, and both kidneys with the fat around them, and burn them on the altar. 14But burn the bull's flesh and its hide and its offalq outside the camp.r It is a sin offering.

15"Take one of the rams,s and Aaron and his sons shall lay their hands on its head.t 16Slaughter it and take the blood and sprinkle it against the altar on all sides. 17Cut the ram into pieces and washu the inner parts and the legs, putting them with the head and the other pieces. 18Then burn the entire ram on the altar. It is a burnt offering to the LORD, a pleasing aroma,v an offering made to the LORD by fire.

19"Take the other ram,w and Aaron and his sons shall lay their hands on its head.x 20Slaughter it, take some of its blood and put it on the lobes of the right ears of

Aaron and his sons, on the thumbs of their right hands, and on the big toes of their right feet.y Then sprinkle blood against the altar on all sides.z 21And take some of the blooda on the altar and some of the anointing oilb and sprinkle it on Aaron and his garments and on his sons and their garments. Then he and his sons and their garments will be consecrated.c

22"Take from this ram the fat,d the fat tail, the fat around the inner parts, the covering of the liver, both kidneys with the fat around them, and the right thigh. (This is the ram for the ordination.) 23From the basket of bread made without yeast, which is before the LORD, take a loaf, and a cake made with oil, and a wafer. 24Put all these in the hands of Aaron and his sons and wave them before the LORD as a wave offering.e 25Then take them from their hands and burn them on the altar along with the burnt offering for a pleasing aroma to the LORD, an offering made to the LORD by fire.f 26After you take the breast of the ram for Aaron's ordination, wave it before the LORD as a wave offering, and it will be your share.g

27"Consecrate those parts of the ordination ram that belong to Aaron and his sons:h the breast that was waved and the thigh that was presented. 28This is always to be the regular share from the Israelites for Aaron and his sons. It is the contribution the Israelites are to make to the LORD from their fellowship offerings.k i

29"Aaron's sacred garmentsj will belong to his descendants so that they can be anointed and ordained in them.k 30The sonl who succeeds him as priest and comes to the Tent of Meeting to minister in the Holy Place is to wear them seven days.

31"Take the ramm for the ordination and

29:2 zver 23; Lev 2:1,4; 6:19-23; Nu 6:15
29:3 aver 15,19
29:4 bEx 40:12; Lev 14:8; 16:4; Heb 10:22
29:5 cS Ex 28:2
dEx 28:8
29:6 eEx 28:39; Isa 3:23; Zec 3:5 fS Ex 28:36
29:7 gver 21; S Ex 28:41; 30:25,30,31; 37:29; 40:9; Lev 21:10; 1Sa 10:1; 1Ki 1:39; Ps 89:20; 133:2; 141:5
29:8 hS Ex 28:4; Lev 16:4
29:9 iEx 28:40 jS Ex 27:21; 40:15; Nu 3:10; 18:7; 25:13; Dt 18:5; Jdg 17:5; 1Sa 2:30; 1Ki 12:31
29:10 kver 19; Lev 1:4; 4:15; 16:21; Nu 8:12
29:11 lLev 1:5, 11; 4:24; 6:16, 25; 14:13
29:12 mS Ex 27:2 nLev 4:7; 9:9
29:13 over 22; Lev 1:8; 3:3,5,9; 4:10; 6:12; 7:3,5, 31; 9:10; Nu 18:17; 1Sa 2:15; 1Ki 8:64; 2Ch 7:7; 29:35; 35:14; Isa 43:24; Eze 44:15 pS Ex 12:9
29:14 qNa 3:6; Mal 2:3 rLev 4:12,21; 16:27; Nu 19:3-5; Heb 13:11
29:15 sS ver 3 tver 10; Lev 3:2; 2Ch 29:23
29:17 uLev 1:9, 13
29:18 vS Ge 8:21; 2Co 2:15
29:19 wS ver 3 xS ver 10

29:20 yLev 14:14,25 zver 16; Lev 1:5, 11; 3:2
29:21 aHeb 9:22 bS ver 5 cS ver 1
29:22 dS ver 13
29:24 eLev 7:30; 9:21; 10:15; 14:12; 23:11,20; Nu 6:20; 8:11,13,

15 29:25 fver 18 29:26 gLev 7:31-34 29:27 hEx 22:29; Lev 7:31,34; Nu 18:11,12; Dt 18:3 29:28 iver 22-27; Lev 7:30,34; 10:15 29:29 jS Ex 28:2; S Lev 16:4 kNu 20:28 29:30 lLev 6:22; Nu 3:3; 20:28 29:31 mLev 7:37; 2Ch 13:9

19 Hebrew; Septuagint on them   k28 Traditionally peace offerings

---

29:4 Tent of Meeting. See note on 27:21. wash them with water. Symbolizing the removal of ceremonial uncleanness (cf. Heb 10:22) and thus signifying the purity that must characterize them.
29:7 anoint him. Symbolizing spiritual enduement for serving God (see Isa 61:1).
29:10 Bring the bull. As a sin offering (see v. 14) to atone for the past sins of Aaron and his sons (see Lev 4:3). lay their hands on its head. As a symbol of (1) the animal's becoming their substitute and (2) transferring their sins to the sin-bearer (see Lev 16:20-22 and note).
29:12 horns of the altar. See note on 27:2.

29:13 fat. The most select parts of the bull (see Lev 3:3-5, 16) were burned on the altar as a sacrifice to the Lord.
29:14 flesh . . . hide . . . offal. Thought of as bearing sin, and thus burned outside the camp (see Heb 13:11-13).
29:18 burn the entire ram. Symbolizing total dedication.
29:20 right ears. Symbolizing sensitivity to God and his word. right hands . . . right feet. Symbolizing a life of service to others on God's behalf.
29:24 wave offering. See note on Lev 7:30-32.
29:28 regular share . . . for Aaron and his sons. Parts of certain sacrificial animals were set aside as food for the priests and their families (see Lev 10:14).

cook the meat in a sacred place.[n] [32]At the entrance to the Tent of Meeting, Aaron and his sons are to eat the meat of the ram and the bread[o] that is in the basket. [33]They are to eat these offerings by which atonement was made for their ordination and consecration. But no one else may eat[p] them, because they are sacred. [34]And if any of the meat of the ordination ram or any bread is left over till morning,[q] burn it up. It must not be eaten, because it is sacred.

[35]"Do for Aaron and his sons everything I have commanded you, taking seven days to ordain them. [36]Sacrifice a bull each day[r] as a sin offering to make atonement[s]. Purify the altar by making atonement for it, and anoint it to consecrate[t] it. [37]For seven days make atonement for the altar and consecrate it. Then the altar will be most holy, and whatever touches it will be holy.[u]

[38]"This is what you are to offer on the altar regularly each day: [v] two lambs a year old. [39]Offer one in the morning and the other at twilight.[w] [40]With the first lamb offer a tenth of an ephah[1] of fine flour mixed with a quarter of a hin[m] of oil[x] from pressed olives, and a quarter of a hin of wine as a drink offering.[y] [41]Sacrifice the other lamb at twilight[z] with the same grain offering[a] and its drink offering as in the morning—a pleasing aroma, an offering made to the LORD by fire.

[42]"For the generations to come[b] this burnt offering is to be made regularly[c] at the entrance to the Tent of Meeting[d] before the LORD. There I will meet you and speak to you;[e] [43]there also I will meet with the Israelites, and the place will be consecrated by my glory.[f]

[44]"So I will consecrate the Tent of Meeting and the altar and will consecrate Aaron and his sons to serve me as priests.[g] [45]Then I will dwell[h] among the Israelites and be their God.[i] [46]They will know that I am the LORD their God, who brought them out of Egypt[j] so that I might dwell among them. I am the LORD their God.[k]

The Altar of Incense

30:1–5pp — Ex 37:25–28

30 "Make an altar[l] of acacia wood for burning incense.[m] [2]It is to be square, a cubit long and a cubit wide, and two cubits high[n]—its horns[n] of one piece with it. [3]Overlay the top and all the sides and the horns with pure gold, and make a gold molding around it.[o] [4]Make two gold rings[p] for the altar below the molding—two on opposite sides—to hold the poles used to carry it. [5]Make the poles of acacia wood and overlay them with gold.[q] [6]Put the altar in front of the curtain that is before the ark of the Testimony—before the atonement cover[r] that is over the Testimony—where I will meet with you.

[7]"Aaron must burn fragrant incense[s] on the altar every morning when he tends the lamps. [8]He must burn incense again when he lights the lamps at twilight so incense will burn regularly before the LORD for the generations to come.[t] [9]Do not offer on this altar any other incense[u] or any burnt offering or grain offering, and do not pour a drink offering on it. [10]Once a year[v] Aaron shall make atonement[w] on its horns. This annual atonement must be made with the blood of the atoning sin offering[x] for the generations to come.[y] It is most holy to the LORD."

Atonement Money

[11]Then the LORD said to Moses, [12]"When you take a census[z] of the Israelites to count them, each one must pay the LORD a ransom[a] for his life at the time he

29:31 [n]Lev 10:14; Nu 19:9; Eze 42:13 **29:32** [o]Mt 12:4 **29:33** [p]Lev 22:10,13 **29:34** [q]S Ex 12:10 **29:36** [r]Heb 10:11 [s]ver 33,37; Ex 30:10; Lev 1:4; 4:20; 16:16; Nu 6:11; 8:12,19; 16:46; 25:13; 2Ch 29:24 [t]Ex 40:10; Nu 7:10 **29:37** [u]S Ex 30:28-29; 40:10; Eze 43:25; Mt 23:19 **29:38** [v]Lev 23:2; Nu 28:3-8; 1Ch 16:40; 2Ch 8:13; Eze 46:13-15; Da 12:11 **29:39** [w]Nu 28:4, 8; 1Ki 18:36; 2Ch 13:11; Ezr 3:3; Ps 141:2; Da 9:21 **29:40** [x]Ex 30:24; Nu 15:4; 28:5 [y]S Ge 35:14; Lev 23:37; 2Ki 16:13 **29:41** [z]1Ki 18:29,36; 2Ki 3:20; 16:15; Ezr 9:4,5; Ps 141:2; Da 9:21 [a]Lev 2:1; 5:13; 10:12; Nu 4:16; 6:17; 1Ki 8:64; Isa 43:23 **29:42** [b]Ex 30:8, 10,21,31; 31:13 [c]Eze 46:15 [d]S Ex 26:1; S 27:21 [e]ver 43; Ex 25:22; 33:9, 11; Nu 7:89 **29:43** [f]Ex 33:18; 40:34; Lev 9:6; 1Ki 8:11; 2Ch 5:14; 7:2; Ps 26:8; 85:9; Eze 1:28; 43:5; Hag 1:8; 2:7 **29:44** [g]S ver 1 **29:45** [h]S Ex 25:8; Nu 35:34; Jn 14:17; S Ro 8:10 [i]S Ge 17:7; 2Co 6:16 **29:46** [j]S Ex 6:6; 19:4-6; Dt 5:6; Ps 114:1; Hag 2:5 [k]S Ge 17:7

Eze 41:22 [m]S Ex 25:6; 37:29; Lk 1:11; Heb 9:4; Rev 8:3 **30:2** [n]S Ex 27:2; Rev 9:13 **30:3** [o]S Ex 25:11 **30:4** [p]S Ex 25:12 **30:5** [q]S Ex 25:13 **30:6** [r]Ex 25:22; S 26:34 **30:7** [s]S Ex 25:6; 40:27; Nu 3:10; Dt 33:10; 1Sa 2:28; 1Ch 6:49; 2Ch 2:4; 26:18; 29:7 **30:8** [t]S Ex 25:37; S 29:42 **30:9** [u]Lev 10:1; Nu 16:7,40 **30:10** [v]Lev 16:2 [w]Lev 9:7; 16:18-19, 30; 23:27,28; 25:9 [x]Ex 29:14; Lev 4:3; 6:25; 7:7; 8:2,14; Nu 6:11 [y]S Ex 29:42 **30:12** [z]Ex 38:25; Nu 1:2,49; 4:2,29; 14:29; 26:2; 31:26; 2Sa 24:1; 2Ki 12:4 [a]Ex 38:26; Nu 31:50; S Mt 20:28

[1]40 That is, probably about 2 quarts (about 2 liters) [m]40 That is, probably about 1 quart (about 1 liter) [n]2 That is, about 1 1/2 feet (about 0.5 meter) long and wide and about 3 feet (about 0.9 meter) high

---

29:31 *sacred place.* Probably the tabernacle courtyard.
29:38–39 Institution of the daily morning and evening offerings—sometimes observed even during days of apostasy (see 2Ki 16:15).
29:42–43 *I will meet.* See note on 27:21.
29:43 *my glory.* Symbolic of God's presence over the ark of the covenant (see note on 25:10; see also 40:34–35; 1Ki 8:10–13).
29:45–46 *dwell among.* See note on 25:9.
29:45 *I will . . . be their God.* Commonly denotes the essence of the divine promise pledged in his covenant with his people (see note on 6:7).

29:46 *I am the LORD . . . who brought them out.* See note on 20:2.
30:1 *incense.* Its fragrant smoke symbolized the prayers of God's people (see Ps 141:2; Lk 1:10; Rev 5:8; 8:3–4).
30:3 *gold.* See note on 26:37.
30:4 *rings.* See note on 25:12.
30:6 *curtain that is before the ark of the Testimony.* See notes on 25:16,22; 26:31.
30:10 *annual atonement.* See Lev 16:34.
30:12 *take a census.* Perhaps such censuses were taken on various occasions (and at stated intervals) to enter the Israelites into an official roll for public duties in the Lord's service

is counted. Then no plague[b] will come on them when you number them. [13]Each one who crosses over to those already counted is to give a half shekel,[o] according to the sanctuary shekel,[c] which weighs twenty gerahs. This half shekel is an offering to the LORD. [14]All who cross over, those twenty years old or more,[d] are to give an offering to the LORD. [15]The rich are not to give more than a half shekel and the poor are not to give less[e] when you make the offering to the LORD to atone for your lives. [16]Receive the atonement[f] money from the Israelites and use it for the service of the Tent of Meeting.[g] It will be a memorial[h] for the Israelites before the LORD, making atonement for your lives."

Basin for Washing

[17]Then the LORD said to Moses, [18]"Make a bronze basin,[i] with its bronze stand, for washing. Place it between the Tent of Meeting and the altar, and put water in it. [19]Aaron and his sons are to wash their hands and feet[j] with water[k] from it. [20]Whenever they enter the Tent of Meeting, they shall wash with water so that they will not die.[l] Also, when they approach the altar to minister by presenting an offering made to the LORD by fire, [21]they shall wash their hands and feet so that they will not die. This is to be a lasting ordinance[m] for Aaron and his descendants for the generations to come."[n]

Anointing Oil

[22]Then the LORD said to Moses, [23]"Take the following fine spices:[o] 500 shekels[p] of liquid myrrh,[p] half as much (that is, 250 shekels) of fragrant cinnamon,[q] 250 shekels of fragrant cane,[r] [24]500 shekels[s] of cassia[t]—all according to the sanctuary shekel—and a hin[q] of olive oil. [25]Make these into a sacred anointing oil, a fragrant blend, the work of a perfumer.[u] It will be the sacred anointing oil.[v] [26]Then use it to anoint[w] the Tent of Meeting, the ark of the Testimony, [27]the table and all its articles, the lampstand and its accessories, the altar of incense, [28]the altar of burnt offering and all its utensils, and the basin with its stand.

[29]You shall consecrate them[x] so they will be most holy, and whatever touches them will be holy.[y]

[30]"Anoint Aaron and his sons and consecrate[z] them so they may serve me as priests.[a] [31]Say to the Israelites, 'This is to be my sacred anointing oil[b] for the generations to come.[c] [32]Do not pour it on men's bodies and do not make any oil with the same formula. It is sacred, and you are to consider it sacred.[d] [33]Whoever makes perfume like it and whoever puts it on anyone other than a priest must be cut off[e] from his people.'"

Incense

[34]Then the LORD said to Moses, "Take fragrant spices[f]—gum resin, onycha and galbanum—and pure frankincense, all in equal amounts, [35]and make a fragrant blend of incense,[g] the work of a perfumer.[h] It is to be salted and pure and sacred. [36]Grind some of it to powder and place it in front of the Testimony in the Tent of Meeting, where I will meet[i] with you. It shall be most holy[j] to you. [37]Do not make any incense with this formula for yourselves; consider it holy[k] to the LORD. [38]Whoever makes any like it to enjoy its fragrance must be cut off[l] from his people."

Bezalel and Oholiab

31:2–6pp — Ex 35:30–35

31 Then the LORD said to Moses, [2]"See, I have chosen Bezalel[m] son of Uri, the son of Hur,[n] of the tribe of Judah, [3]and I have filled him with the Spirit of God, with skill, ability and knowledge[o] in all kinds of crafts[p]— [4]to make artistic designs for work in gold, silver and bronze, [5]to cut and set stones, to work in wood, and to engage in all kinds of craftsmanship. [6]Moreover, I have appointed Oholiab[q] son of Ahisamach, of the tribe of

30:12
[b]Nu 14:12;
Dt 28:58-61;
2Sa 24:13;
1Ki 8:37
30:13 [c]ver 24;
Ex 38:24,26;
Lev 5:15; 27:3,
25; Nu 3:47;
7:13; 18:16;
Eze 4:10; 45:12;
Mt 17:24
30:14 [d]Ex 38:26;
Nu 1:3,18; 14:29;
26:2; 32:11;
2Ch 25:5
30:15 [e]Pr 22:2;
Eph 6:9
30:16 [f]ver 12
[g]Ex 38:25-28;
2Ch 24:5
[h]Nu 31:54
30:18 [i]Ex 31:9;
35:16; 38:8;
39:39; 40:7,30;
1Ki 7:38; 2Ch 4:6
30:19
[j]Ex 40:31-32;
Jn 13:10
[k]Ex 29:4; 40:12;
Lev 8:6; Ps 26:6;
Heb 10:22
30:20
[l]S Ex 28:43
30:21
[m]S Ex 27:21
[n]Ex 29:42
30:23
[o]S Ge 43:11
[p]S Ge 37:25
[q]Pr 7:17; SS 4:14
[r]SS 4:14;
Isa 43:24;
Jer 6:20
30:24 [s]S ver 13
[t]Ps 45:8;
Eze 27:19
30:25 [u]ver 35;
Ex 37:29;
1Ch 9:30
[v]S Ex 29:7;
S 1Sa 9:16
30:26 [w]Ex 40:9;
Lev 8:10; Nu 7:1

30:29
[x]Lev 8:10-11
[y]Ex 29:37;
Lev 6:18,27;
Mt 23:17
30:30 [z]Ex 29:7;
Lev 8:2,12,30;
10:7; 16:32;
21:10,12;
1Ch 15:12;
Ps 133:2
[a]S Ex 28:41
30:31 [b]S Ex 29:7
[c]S Ex 29:42
30:32 [d]ver 25,37
30:33 [e]ver 38;
S Ge 17:14
30:34 [f]SS 3:6
30:35 [g]S Ex 25:6
[h]S ver 25
30:36
[i]S Ex 25:22 [j]ver
32; S Ex 29:37;
Lev 2:3
30:37 [k]S ver 32

30:38 [l]S ver 33 **31:2** [m]Ex 36:1,2; 37:1; 38:22; 1Ch 2:20; 2Ch 1:5 [n]S Ex 17:10 **31:3** [o]S Ex 28:3 [p]1Ki 7:14; 1Co 12:4 **31:6** [q]Ex 36:1,2; 38:23

[o]13 That is, about 1/5 ounce (about 6 grams); also in verse 15 [p]23 That is, about 12 1/2 pounds (about 6 kilograms) [q]24 That is, probably about 4 quarts (about 4 liters)

(see Nu 1:2; 26:2). *pay . . . a ransom for his life.* An extension of the principle stated in 13:13,15 (see note on 13:13).
30:14 *twenty years old or more.* Of military age (see Nu 1:3).
30:16 *Tent of Meeting.* See note on 27:21.
30:18 *basin.* Made from bronze mirrors contributed by Israelite women (see 38:8). *washing.* See note on 29:4.
30:23–24 *myrrh . . . cinnamon . . . cane . . . cassia.* See note on 25:6.

30:33 *cut off from his people.* See note on 12:15.
30:34 *gum resin, onycha and galbanum.* See note on 25:6. *frankincense.* A resin from the bark of *Boswellia carteri,* which grows in southern Arabia.
31:2 *Bezalel.* Means "in the shadow/protection of God." *Hur.* See note on 17:10.
31:3 *filled him with the Spirit of God.* Ability to work as a skilled craftsman was a spiritual gift, equipping a person for special service to God.

Dan,[r] to help him. Also I have given skill to all the craftsmen[s] to make everything I have commanded you: [7]the Tent of Meeting,[t] the ark of the Testimony[u] with the atonement cover[v] on it, and all the other furnishings of the tent— [8]the table[w] and its articles, the pure gold lampstand[x] and all its accessories, the altar of incense,[y] [9]the altar of burnt offering[z] and all its utensils, the basin[a] with its stand— [10]and also the woven garments[b], both the sacred garments for Aaron the priest and the garments for his sons when they serve as priests, [11]and the anointing oil[c] and fragrant incense[d] for the Holy Place. They are to make them just as I commanded[e] you."

The Sabbath

[12]Then the LORD said to Moses, [13]"Say to the Israelites, 'You must observe my Sabbaths.[f] This will be a sign[g] between me and you for the generations to come,[h] so you may know that I am the LORD, who makes you holy.[r] [i]

[14]" 'Observe the Sabbath, because it is holy to you. Anyone who desecrates it must be put to death;[j] whoever does any work on that day must be cut off from his people. [15]For six days, work[k] is to be done, but the seventh day is a Sabbath of rest,[l] holy to the LORD. Whoever does any work on the Sabbath day must be put to death. [16]The Israelites are to observe the Sabbath,[m] celebrating it for the generations to come as a lasting covenant. [17]It will be a sign[n] between me and the Israelites for-

ever, for in six days the LORD made the heavens and the earth, and on the seventh day he abstained from work and rested.[o]' "[p]

[18]When the LORD finished speaking to Moses on Mount Sinai,[q] he gave him the two tablets of the Testimony, the tablets of stone[r] inscribed by the finger of God.[s]

The Golden Calf

32 When the people saw that Moses was so long in coming down from the mountain,[t] they gathered around Aaron and said, "Come, make us gods[s] who will go before[u] us. As for this fellow Moses who brought us up out of Egypt, we don't know what has happened to him."[v]

[2]Aaron answered them, "Take off the gold earrings[w] that your wives, your sons and your daughters are wearing, and bring them to me." [3]So all the people took off their earrings and brought them to Aaron. [4]He took what they handed him and made it into an idol[x] cast in the shape of a calf,[y] fashioning it with a tool. Then they said, "These are your gods,[t][z] O Israel, who brought you up out of Egypt."[a]

[5]When Aaron saw this, he built an altar in front of the calf and announced, "Tomorrow there will be a festival[b] to the LORD." [6]So the next day the people rose

---

Cross references (center column):

31:6 [r]1Ki 7:14; 2Ch 2:14
[s]S Ex 28:3
31:7 [t]Ex 36:8-38
[u]Ex 37:1-5
[v]Ex 37:6; 40:20
31:8
[w]Ex 37:10-16
[x]Ex 37:17-24; Lev 24:4
[y]Ex 37:25-28
31:9 [z]Ex 38:3; Nu 4:14
[a]S Ex 30:18
31:10 [b]S Ex 28:2
31:11
[c]Ex 30:22-32; 37:29 [d]S Ex 25:6
[e]S Ex 25:9
31:13 [f]S Ex 20:8
[g]ver 17; Isa 56:4; Eze 20:12,20
[h]S Ex 29:42
[i]Lev 11:44; 20:8; 21:8; Eze 37:28
31:14 [j]Ex 35:2; Nu 15:32-36
31:15 [k]S Ex 20:8, 9-11; 35:2;
Lev 16:29; 23:3;
Nu 29:7 [l]S Ge 2:3
31:16 [m]S Ex 20:8
31:17 [n]S ver 13

[o]S Ge 2:2-3
[p]S Ge 2:2;
S Ex 20:9;
Isa 56:2; 58:13; 66:23;
Jer 17:21-22;
Eze 20:12,20
31:18
[q]S Ex 19:11
[r]S Ex 24:12;
2Co 3:3; Heb 9:4
[s]Ex 32:15-16; 34:1,28; Dt 4:13; 9:10
32:1 [t]S Ge 7:4; Dt 9:9-12
[u]S Ex 13:21 [v]ver 23; Ac 7:40*
32:2
[w]Jdg 8:24-27
32:4
[x]S Ex 20:23;
Jdg 17:3-4;
Isa 30:22 [y]ver 8, 24,35; Dt 9:16;

Ne 9:18; Ps 106:19; Ac 7:41 [z]Ex 20:23; Isa 42:17
[a]1Ki 12:28; 14:9; 2Ki 10:29; 17:16; 2Ch 13:8; Hos 8:6; 10:5 32:5 [b]Lev 23:2,37; 2Ki 10:20; Joel 2:15

[r]13 Or who sanctifies you; or who sets you apart as holy
[s]1 Or a god; also in verses 23 and 31   [t]4 Or This is your god; also in verse 8

Study notes (bottom):

31:6 *Oholiab.* Means "The (divine) father is my tent/tabernacle." The names of Bezalel (see note on v. 2) and Oholiab were appropriate for the chief craftsmen working on the tabernacle.

31:7 *Tent of Meeting.* See note on 27:21.

31:13 *observe my Sabbaths.* Instructions for building the tabernacle and making the priestly garments are concluded by impressing on the Israelites the importance and necessity of keeping the Sabbath even while carrying out this special task.

31:14 *cut off from his people.* See note on 12:15.

31:16-17 *covenant . . . sign.* In her rhythm of work and rest in the service of God, Israel is to emulate God's pattern in creation as an ever-renewed sign of her covenant with God (see note on Ge 9:12).

31:18 *two tablets.* In keeping with ancient Near Eastern practice, these were duplicates of the covenant document, not two sections of the Ten Commandments. One copy belonged to each party of the covenant. Since Israel's copy was to be laid up in the presence of her God (according to custom), both covenant tablets (God's and Israel's) were placed in the ark (see 25:21). *Testimony.* See notes on 16:34; 25:16. *inscribed by the finger of God.* Because it was God's covenant (see 19:5-6), and the stipulations of the covenant (20:1-17) were his.

32:1 *so long.* Forty days and forty nights (see 24:18 and

note). *they.* Probably the tribe and clan leaders. *gods.* See NIV text note. *Moses who brought us up out of Egypt.* A rebellious contrast to the gracious statement of Israel's covenant Lord (see 20:2 and note; 29:46).

32:2 *gold earrings.* Probably part of the plunder brought from Egypt (see 3:21–22; 11:2–3; 12:35–36).

32:4 *cast in the shape of a calf.* Either gold plating over a carved wooden calf (it was later burned, v. 20) or crudely cast in solid gold and then further shaped with a tool, later to be melted down in the fire. The calf was probably similar to representations of the Egyptian bull-god Apis (see note on Jer 46:15). Its manufacture was a flagrant violation of the second commandment (20:4–5). *they.* The leaders among the people (see note on v. 1). *These are your gods . . . up out of Egypt.* A parody of 20:2 (see note on v. 1). Centuries later, King Jeroboam would quote these words when he set up two golden calves in the northern kingdom of Israel (see 1Ki 12:28–29).

32:5 *altar in front of the calf . . . festival to the LORD.* Apparently Aaron recognized the idolatrous consequences of his deed and acted quickly to keep the people from turning completely away from the Lord.

32:6 *they sat down . . . indulge in revelry.* A pagan symbol evoked pagan religious practices. Paul quotes this sentence as a vivid example of Israel's tendency toward idolatry (see 1Co 10:7). The Hebrew verb translated "indulge in revelry"

early and sacrificed burnt offerings and presented fellowship offerings.[u][c] Afterward they sat down to eat and drink[d] and got up to indulge in revelry.[e]

[7]Then the LORD said to Moses, "Go down, because your people, whom you brought up out of Egypt,[f] have become corrupt.[g] [8]They have been quick to turn away[h] from what I commanded them and have made themselves an idol[i] cast in the shape of a calf.[j] They have bowed down to it and sacrificed[k] to it and have said, 'These are your gods, O Israel, who brought you up out of Egypt.'[l]

[9]"I have seen these people," the LORD said to Moses, "and they are a stiff-necked[m] people. [10]Now leave me alone[n] so that my anger may burn against them and that I may destroy[o] them. Then I will make you into a great nation."[p]

[11]But Moses sought the favor[q] of the LORD his God. "O LORD," he said, "why should your anger burn against your people, whom you brought out of Egypt with great power and a mighty hand?[r] [12]Why should the Egyptians say, 'It was with evil intent that he brought them out, to kill them in the mountains and to wipe them off the face of the earth'?[s] Turn from your fierce anger; relent and do not bring disaster[t] on your people. [13]Remember[u] your servants Abraham, Isaac and Israel, to whom you swore by your own self:[v] 'I will make your descendants as numerous as the stars[w] in the sky and I will give your descendants all this land[x] I promised them, and it will be their inheritance forever.'" [14]Then the LORD relented[y] and did not bring on his people the disaster he had threatened.

[15]Moses turned and went down the mountain with the two tablets of the Testimony[z] in his hands.[a] They were in-

scribed[b] on both sides, front and back. [16]The tablets were the work of God; the writing was the writing of God, engraved on the tablets.[c]

[17]When Joshua[d] heard the noise of the people shouting, he said to Moses, "There is the sound of war in the camp."

[18]Moses replied:

"It is not the sound of victory,
　it is not the sound of defeat;
　it is the sound of singing that I hear."

[19]When Moses approached the camp and saw the calf[e] and the dancing,[f] his anger burned[g] and he threw the tablets out of his hands, breaking them to pieces[h] at the foot of the mountain. [20]And he took the calf they had made and burned[i] it in the fire; then he ground it to powder,[j] scattered it on the water[k] and made the Israelites drink it.

[21]He said to Aaron, "What did these people do to you, that you led them into such great sin?"

[22]"Do not be angry,[l] my lord," Aaron answered. "You know how prone these people are to evil.[m] [23]They said to me, 'Make us gods who will go before us. As for this fellow Moses who brought us up out of Egypt, we don't know what has happened to him.'[n] [24]So I told them, 'Whoever has any gold jewelry, take it off.' Then they gave me the gold, and I threw it into the fire, and out came this calf!"[o]

[25]Moses saw that the people were run-

32:6 [c]Ex 20:24; 34:15; Lev 3:1; 4:10; 6:12; 9:4; 22:21; Nu 6:14; 25:2; Dt 27:7; Jdg 20:26; Eze 43:27; Ac 7:41 [d]Jdg 19:4; Ru 3:3; 1Sa 1:9; 2Sa 11:11; 1Ki 13:23; 18:42; Ne 8:12; Job 1:4; Ecc 5:18; 8:15; Jer 16:8 [e]ver 17-19; 1Co 10:7*
32:7 [f]ver 4,11; Ex 33:1 [g]S Ge 6:11-12; Eze 20:8
32:8 [h]Jer 7:26; 16:12; Mal 2:8; 3:7 [i]S Ex 20:4 [j]S ver 4
[k]Ex 22:20 [l]1Ki 12:28; Eze 23:8
32:9 [m]Ex 33:3,5; 34:9; Dt 9:6,13; 10:16; 31:27; Jdg 2:19; 2Ki 17:14; 2Ch 30:8; 36:13; Ne 9:16; Ps 78:8; Pr 29:1; Isa 46:12; 48:4; Jer 7:26; Eze 2:4; Hos 4:16; Ac 7:51
32:10 [n]1Sa 2:25; Jer 7:16; 11:14; 14:11 [o]Ex 22:24; 33:3,5; Nu 16:21, 45; Dt 9:14,19; Ps 106:23; Jer 14:12; Eze 20:13 [p]Nu 14:12; Dt 9:14
32:11 [q]Dt 9:18; 2Sa 21:1; 2Ch 15:2; Ps 9:10; 34:4; 106:23; Isa 9:13; Jer 15:1 [r]ver 13; Dt 9:26; 1Sa 7:9; Ne 1:10; Ps 136:12
32:12 [s]Nu 14:13-16; Dt 9:28 [t]ver 14; Ex 33:13
32:13 [u]S Ex 2:24; 33:13 [v]S Ge 22:16; Heb 6:13 [w]Ge 15:5; 22:17 [x]S Ge 12:7

32:14 [y]Dt 9:19; 1Sa 15:11; 2Sa 24:16; 1Ki 21:29; 1Ch 21:15; Ps 106:45; Jer 18:8; 26:3,19; Am 7:3,6; Jnh 3:10 **32:15** [z]Ex 31:18; Heb 9:4 [a]S Ex 19:18; 34:4,29; Dt 9:15 [b]2Co 3:3 **32:16** [c]S Ex 24:12 **32:17** [d]S Ex 17:9 **32:19** [e]Dt 9:16 [f]ver 6; 1Co 10:7 [g]Ezr 9:3; Ps 119:53,158 [h]Ex 34:1; Dt 9:17 **32:20** [i]Dt 7:25; 12:3; Jos 7:1; 2Ki 23:6; 1Ch 14:12 [j]2Ch 34:7; Mic 1:7 [k]Dt 9:21 **32:22** [l]S Ge 18:30 [m]Dt 9:24; 28:20; 2Ki 21:15; Ezr 9:13; Ne 9:28; Jer 4:4; 44:3; Eze 6:9 **32:23** [n]S ver 1; Ac 7:40 **32:24** [o]S ver 4

[u]6 Traditionally *peace offerings*

---

often has sexual connotations (see, e.g., "caressing," Ge 26:8). Immoral orgies frequently accompanied pagan worship in ancient times.
32:7,9 *your people . . . these people.* By not calling Israel "my people" (as, e.g., in 3:10), God indicates that he is disowning them for breaking his covenant with them.
32:7 *corrupt.* And, therefore, ripe for destruction (see v. 10; Ge 6:11-13).
32:9 *stiff-necked.* Like unresponsive oxen or horses (see Jer 27:11-12; see also note on Ne 3:5).
32:10 *I will make you into a great nation.* After Israel—Abraham's descendants—has been destroyed, God will transfer to Moses the pledge originally given to Abraham (see Ge 12:2).
32:11 *your people.* Using God's own words (see v. 7 and note), Moses appeals to God's special relationship to Israel, then to God's need to vindicate his name in the eyes of the Egyptians (see v. 12), and finally to the great patriarchal promises (see v. 13).

32:13 *Israel.* Jacob (see 33:1; see also Ge 32:28).
32:14 *the LORD relented.* See note on Jer 18:7-10; see also 2Sa 24:16; Ps 106:45; Am 7:1-6; Jas 5:16.
32:15 *went down the mountain.* See note on 24:18. *two tablets.* See note on 31:18. *Testimony.* See notes on 16:34; 25:16. *inscribed on both sides.* Tablets were often thus inscribed in ancient times.
32:16 *work of God . . . writing of God.* See 31:18.
32:17 *Joshua.* Perhaps he had accompanied Moses part of the way up the mountain (see 24:13).
32:19 *breaking them to pieces.* Thus testifying against Israel that they had broken the covenant.
32:20 *burned it . . . ground it to powder.* King Jeroboam's altar (see note on v. 4) at Bethel received the same treatment (see 2Ki 23:15).
32:22-24 In his desperation, Aaron blamed the people (see notes on Ge 3:12-13).
32:24 *out came this calf.* Aaron could hardly have thought that Moses would believe such an incredible story.

ning wild and that Aaron had let them get out of control and so become a laughing-stock[p] to their enemies. [26]So he stood at the entrance to the camp and said, "Whoever is for the LORD, come to me." And all the Levites rallied to him.

[27]Then he said to them, "This is what the LORD, the God of Israel, says: 'Each man strap a sword to his side. Go back and forth through the camp from one end to the other, each killing his brother and friend and neighbor.' "[q] [28]The Levites did as Moses commanded, and that day about three thousand of the people died. [29]Then Moses said, "You have been set apart to the LORD today, for you were against your own sons and brothers, and he has blessed you this day."

[30]The next day Moses said to the people, "You have committed a great sin.[r] But now I will go up to the LORD; perhaps I can make atonement[s] for your sin."

[31]So Moses went back to the LORD and said, "Oh, what a great sin these people have committed![t] They have made themselves gods of gold.[u] [32]But now, please forgive their sin[v]—but if not, then blot me[w] out of the book[x] you have written."

[33]The LORD replied to Moses, "Whoever has sinned against me I will blot out[y] of my book. [34]Now go, lead[z] the people to the place[a] I spoke of, and my angel[b] will go before you. However, when the time comes for me to punish,[c] I will punish them for their sin."

[35]And the LORD struck the people with a plague because of what they did with the calf[d] Aaron had made.

33

Then the LORD said to Moses, "Leave this place, you and the people you brought up out of Egypt, and go up to the land I promised on oath[e] to Abraham, Isaac and Jacob, saying, 'I will give it to your descendants.'[f] [2]I will send an angel[g] before you and drive out the Canaanites, Amorites, Hittites, Perizzites, Hivites and Jebusites.[h] [3]Go up to the land flowing with milk and honey.[i] But I will not go with you, because you are a stiff-necked[j] people and I might destroy[k] you on the way."

[4]When the people heard these distressing words, they began to mourn[l] and no one put on any ornaments. [5]For the LORD had said to Moses, "Tell the Israelites, 'You are a stiff-necked people.[m] If I were to go with you even for a moment, I might destroy[n] you. Now take off your ornaments and I will decide what to do with you.' " [6]So the Israelites stripped off their ornaments at Mount Horeb.[o]

The Tent of Meeting

[7]Now Moses used to take a tent and pitch it outside the camp some distance away, calling it the "tent of meeting."[p] Anyone inquiring[q] of the LORD would go to the tent of meeting outside the camp. [8]And whenever Moses went out to the tent, all the people rose and stood at the entrances to their tents,[r] watching Moses

32:25 *p* S Ge 38:23
32:27 *q* Nu 25:3, 5; Dt 33:9; Eze 9:5
32:30 *r* 1Sa 12:20; Ps 25:11; 85:2 *s* Lev 1:4; 4:20, 26; 5:6,10,13; 6:7
32:31 *t* Ex 34:9; Dt 9:18 *u* S Ex 20:23
32:32 *v* Nu 14:19 *w* Ro 9:3 *x* Ps 69:28; Eze 13:9; Da 7:10; 12:1; Mal 3:16; S Lk 10:20
32:33 *y* S Ex 17:14; S Job 21:20; Rev 3:5
32:34 *z* S Ex 15:17 *a* Ex 3:17 *b* S Ex 14:19 *c* S Ge 50:19; Dt 32:35; Ps 89:32; 94:23; 99:8; 109:20; Isa 27:1; Jer 5:9; 11:22; 23:2; 44:13,29; Hos 12:2; Ro 2:5-6
32:35 *d* S ver 4
33:1 *e* S Ex 13:11; S Nu 14:23; Heb 6:13 *f* S Ge 12:7
33:2 *g* S Ex 14:19 *h* S Ex 23:28
33:3 *i* S Ex 3:8 *j* Ex 32:9; Ac 7:51 *k* S Ex 32:10
33:4 *l* Nu 14:39; Ezr 9:3; Est 4:1; Ps 119:53
33:5 *m* S Ex 32:9 *n* S Ex 32:10
33:6 *o* S Ex 3:1
33:7 *p* S Ex 27:21 *q* S Ge 25:22; S 1Ki 22:5
33:8 *r* ver 10; Nu 16:27

32:25 *were running wild . . . get out of control.* The same Hebrew root underlies both phrases and is found also in Pr 29:18 ("cast off restraint"). Anarchy reigns among people who refuse to obey and worship the Lord.
32:26 *Whoever is for the LORD, come to me.* See Jos 24:15; 1Ki 18:21; Mt 6:24. *all.* A generalization since Dt 33:9 implies that some of the Levites were also slain. *Levites.* The descendants of Levi (Ge 29:34) may have originally been regarded as priests (Dt 18:6–8). But at some stage they became subordinate to the priests who were descendants of Aaron, the brother of Moses (38:21; Nu 3:9–10; 1 Ch 16:4–6,37–42).
32:27 *killing his brother and friend and neighbor.* See Mt 10:37; Lk 14:26.
32:28 *The Levites did as Moses commanded.* Their zeal for the Lord is later matched by Aaron's grandson Phinehas, resulting in a perpetual covenant of the priesthood (see Nu 25:7–13).
32:29 *You have been set apart to the LORD today.* Because of their zeal for the Lord the Levites were set apart to be caretakers of the tabernacle and aides to the priests (see Nu 1:47–53; 3:5–9,12,41,45; 4:2–3).
32:30 *make atonement for your sin.* By making urgent intercession before God, as the mediator God had appointed between himself and Israel. No sacrifice that Israel or Moses might bring could atone for this sin. But Moses so identified

himself with Israel that he made his own death the condition for God's destruction of the nation (see v. 32). Jesus Christ, the great Mediator, offered himself on the cross to make atonement for his people.
32:32 *book you have written.* See notes on Ps 9:5; 51:1; 69:28.
32:33 *Whoever has sinned . . . I will blot out.* Moses' gracious offer is refused, because the person who sins is responsible for his own sin (see Dt 24:16; Eze 18:4 and note).
32:34 *Now go, lead the people.* Thus Moses received assurance that the Lord will continue his covenant with wayward Israel and fulfill his promise concerning the land. *the place I spoke of.* Canaan (see 33:1).
33:2 *Canaanites . . . Jebusites.* See note on 3:8.
33:3 *land flowing with milk and honey.* See note on 3:8. *I will not go with you.* The Lord's presence, earlier assured to his people (see 23:21 and note), is now temporarily withdrawn because of sin. *stiff-necked.* See note on 32:9.
33:6 *stripped off their ornaments.* As a sign of mourning (see Eze 26:16–17).
33:7 *tent of meeting outside the camp.* Not the tabernacle (contrast 27:21), which occupied a central location within the Israelite camp, but a temporary structure where the people could inquire of the Lord until the more durable tabernacle was completed.

until he entered the tent. [9]As Moses went into the tent, the pillar of cloud[s] would come down and stay at the entrance, while the LORD spoke[t] with Moses. [10]Whenever the people saw the pillar of cloud standing at the entrance to the tent, they all stood and worshiped, each at the entrance to his tent. [u] [11]The LORD would speak to Moses face to face,[v] as a man speaks with his friend. Then Moses would return to the camp, but his young aide Joshua[w] son of Nun did not leave the tent.

Moses and the Glory of the LORD

[12]Moses said to the LORD, "You have been telling me, 'Lead these people,'[x] but you have not let me know whom you will send with me. You have said, 'I know you by name[y] and you have found favor[z] with me.' [13]If you are pleased with me, teach me your ways[a] so I may know you and continue to find favor with you. Remember that this nation is your people." [b]

[14]The LORD replied, "My Presence[c] will go with you, and I will give you rest." [d]

[15]Then Moses said to him, "If your Presence[e] does not go with us, do not send us up from here. [16]How will anyone know that you are pleased with me and with your people unless you go with us?[f] What else will distinguish me and your people from all the other people on the face of the earth?" [g]

[17]And the LORD said to Moses, "I will do the very thing you have asked,[h] because I am pleased with you and I know you by name." [i]

[18]Then Moses said, "Now show me your glory." [j]

[19]And the LORD said, "I will cause all my goodness to pass[k] in front of you, and I

will proclaim my name,[l] the LORD, in your presence. I will have mercy on whom I will have mercy, and I will have compassion on whom I will have compassion. [m] [20]But," he said, "you cannot see my face, for no one may see[n] me and live."

[21]Then the LORD said, "There is a place near me where you may stand on a rock. [22]When my glory passes by, I will put you in a cleft in the rock[o] and cover you with my hand[p] until I have passed by. [23]Then I will remove my hand and you will see my back; but my face must not be seen."

The New Stone Tablets

34 The LORD said to Moses, "Chisel out two stone tablets like the first ones,[q] and I will write on them the words that were on the first tablets,[r] which you broke.[s] [2]Be ready in the morning, and then come up on Mount Sinai.[t] Present yourself to me there on top of the mountain. [3]No one is to come with you or be seen anywhere on the mountain;[u] not even the flocks and herds may graze in front of the mountain."

[4]So Moses chiseled[v] out two stone tablets like the first ones and went up Mount Sinai early in the morning, as the LORD had commanded him; and he carried the two stone tablets in his hands. [w] [5]Then the LORD came down in the cloud[x] and stood there with him and proclaimed his name, the LORD. [y] [6]And he passed in front of Moses, proclaiming, "The LORD, the LORD, the compassionate[z] and gracious God,

---

33:9 [s]Ex 13:21; S 19:9; Dt 31:15; 1Co 10:1
[t]S Ex 29:42; 31:18; Ps 99:7
33:10 [u]S ver 8
33:11 [v]Nu 12:8; Dt 5:4; 34:10
[w]S Ex 17:9
33:12 [x]Ex 3:10; S 15:17 [y]ver 17; 49:1;
Jn 10:14-15; 2Ti 2:19
[z]S Ge 6:8
33:13 [a]Ps 25:4; 27:11; 51:13; 86:11; 103:7; 143:8 [b]Ex 3:7; Dt 9:26,29; Ps 77:15
33:14 [c]S Ex 13:21; Dt 4:37; Isa 63:9; Hag 1:13; 2:4
[d]Dt 12:9,10; 25:19; Jos 1:13; 11:23; 21:44; 22:4; 23:1; 1Ki 8:56; Isa 63:14; Jer 31:2; Mt 11:28; Heb 4:1-11
33:15 [e]ver 3; Ex 34:9; 2Ki 13:23; 17:18; 23:27; 24:20; Ps 51:11; 80:3,7, 19; Jer 7:15; 52:3
33:16 [f]Ex 34:5; 40:34,35;
Nu 9:15; 14:14
[g]Ex 34:10; Lev 20:24,26; Nu 23:9; Dt 4:7, 32,34; 32:9; 33:28
33:17 [h]Ex 34:28; Dt 9:18,25; 10:10; Jas 5:16
[i]S Ge 6:8
33:18 [j]S Ex 16:7; Jn 1:14; 12:41; 1Ti 6:16; Rev 15:8
33:19 [k]1Ki 19:11
[l]Ex 6:3; 34:5-7
[m]Ro 9:15*
33:20 [n]S Ge 16:13; S Ex 3:6; S Dt 5:26;

[l]S Jn 1:18 **33:22** [o]Ge 49:24; 1Ki 19:9; Ps 27:5; 31:20; 62:7; 91:1; Isa 2:21; Jer 4:29 [p]Ps 91:4; Isa 49:2; 51:16 **34:1** [q]S Ex 24:12 [r]Dt 10:2,4 [s]S Ex 32:19 **34:2** [t]S Ex 19:11 **34:3** [u]S Ex 19:13 **34:4** [v]Dt 10:3 [w]S Ex 32:15 **34:5** [x]S Ex 13:21; S 19:9 [y]Ex 6:3; 33:19 **34:6** [z]S Ex 22:27; S Nu 14:20; S Ps 86:15

33:9 *pillar of cloud would come down.* Symbolizing God's communication with Moses "as a man speaks with his friend" (v. 11). Later, a similar descent crowned the completion of the tabernacle (see 40:33–34; see also note on 13:21).
33:11 *The LORD would speak to Moses face to face.* As the OT mediator, Moses was unique among the prophets. *Joshua . . . did not leave the tent.* Probably his task was to guard the tent against intrusion by others.
33:12 *you have not let me know whom you will send with me.* See note on v. 3. Moses objects that a mere angel is no substitute for God's own presence. *I know you by name.* I have chosen you for my special purpose.
33:13 *teach me your ways.* A prayer that is answered in 34:6–7.
33:14 *My Presence will go with you.* The Lord's gracious response to Moses' concern (see note on v. 3).
33:17 *because I am pleased with you.* How much more does God hear the prayers of his Son Jesus Christ (see Mt 17:5; Heb 3:1–6)!
33:18 See v. 22. In a sense, Moses' prayer was finally

answered on the Mount of Transfiguration (Lk 9:30–32), where he shared a vision—however brief—of the Lord's glory with Elijah and three of Jesus' disciples.
33:19 *goodness.* God's nature and character. *name.* A further symbol of God's nature, character and person (see Ps 20:1; Jn 1:12; 17:6 and NIV text note). Here his name implies his mercy (grace) and his compassion (as it does also in 34:6).
33:20 See note on Ge 16:13; see also Jn 1:18; 6:46; 1Ti 1:17; 1Jn 4:12.
33:21–23 God speaks of himself in human language. See 34:5–7 for the fulfillment of his promise.
34:1 *two stone tablets . . . I will write on them.* See note on 31:18. *words.* See note on 20:1.
34:5 *name.* See note on 33:19.
34:6–7 See 33:19 and note. The Lord's proclamation of the meaning and implications of his name in these verses became a classic exposition that was frequently recalled elsewhere in the OT (see Nu 14:18; Ne 9:17; Ps 86:15; 103:8; 145:8; Joel 2:13; Jnh 4:2). See also notes on 3:14–15; 6:2–3.

slow to anger,[a] abounding in love[b] and faithfulness,[c] [7]maintaining love to thousands,[d] and forgiving wickedness, rebellion and sin.[e] Yet he does not leave the guilty unpunished;[f] he punishes the children and their children for the sin of the fathers to the third and fourth generation."[g]

[8]Moses bowed to the ground at once and worshiped. [9]"O Lord, if I have found favor[h] in your eyes," he said, "then let the Lord go with us.[i] Although this is a stiffnecked[j] people, forgive our wickedness and our sin,[k] and take us as your inheritance."[l]

[10]Then the LORD said: "I am making a covenant[m] with you. Before all your people I will do wonders[n] never before done in any nation in all the world.[o] The people you live among will see how awesome is the work that I, the LORD, will do for you. [11]Obey what I command[p] you today. I will drive out before you the Amorites, Canaanites, Hittites, Perizzites, Hivites and Jebusites.[q] [12]Be careful not to make a treaty[r] with those who live in the land where you are going, or they will be a snare[s] among you. [13]Break down their altars, smash their sacred stones and cut down their Asherah poles.[v t] [14]Do not worship any other god,[u] for the LORD, whose name[v] is Jealous, is a jealous God.[w]

[15]"Be careful not to make a treaty[x] with those who live in the land; for when they prostitute[y] themselves to their gods and sacrifice to them, they will invite you and you will eat their sacrifices.[z] [16]And when you choose some of their daughters as wives[a] for your sons and those daughters prostitute themselves to their gods,[b] they will lead your sons to do the same.

[17]"Do not make cast idols.[c]

[18]"Celebrate the Feast of Unleavened Bread.[d] For seven days eat bread made without yeast,[e] as I commanded you. Do this at the appointed time in the month of Abib,[f] for in that month you came out of Egypt.

[19]"The first offspring[g] of every womb belongs to me, including all the firstborn males of your livestock, whether from herd or flock. [20]Redeem the firstborn donkey with a lamb, but if you do not redeem it, break its neck.[h] Redeem all your firstborn sons.[i]

"No one is to appear before me empty-handed.[j]

[21]"Six days you shall labor, but on the seventh day you shall rest;[k] even during the plowing season and harvest[l] you must rest.

[22]"Celebrate the Feast of Weeks with the firstfruits[m] of the wheat harvest, and the Feast of Ingathering[n] at the turn of the year.[w] [23]Three times[o] a year all your men are to appear before the Sovereign LORD, the God of Israel. [24]I will drive out nations[p] before you and enlarge your territory,[q] and no one will covet your land when you go up three times each year to appear before the LORD your God.

[25]"Do not offer the blood of a sacrifice to me along with anything containing yeast,[r] and do not let any of the sacrifice from the Passover Feast remain until morning.[s]

[26]"Bring the best of the firstfruits[t] of your soil to the house of the LORD your God.

"Do not cook a young goat in its mother's milk."[u]

34:6 [a]Nu 14:18; Ps 78:38; Jer 15:15; Ro 2:4 [b]S Ge 19:16 [c]Ps 61:7; 108:4; 115:1; 138:2; 143:1; La 3:23; Jas 5:11 **34:7** [d]S Ex 20:6; Dt 5:10 [e]1Ki 8:30; Ps 86:5; 103:3; 130:4,8; Isa 43:25; Da 9:9; 1Jn 1:9 [f]Ex 23:7; Jos 24:19; Job 7:20-21; 9:28; 10:14; Mic 6:1-16; Na 1:3 [g]S Ex 20:5 **34:9** [h]Ex 33:13; Nu 11:15 [i]S Ex 33:15 [j]Ex 32:9 [k]Nu 14:19; 1Ki 8:30; 2Ch 6:21; Ps 19:12; 25:11; Jer 33:8; Hos 14:2 [l]S Ex 6:7; 19:5; Dt 4:20; 7:6; 9:26,29; 14:2; 26:18; 32:9; 1Sa 10:1; 2Sa 14:16; 1Ki 8:51,53; Ps 28:9; 33:12; 74:2; 79:1; 94:14; 106:5,40; Isa 19:25; 63:17; Jer 10:16; 51:19; Mic 7:18; Zec 2:12 **34:10** [m]S Ge 6:18; S 9:15; S 15:18; Dt 5:2-3 [n]S Ex 3:20 [o]S Ex 33:16 **34:11** [p]Dt 6:25; Jos 11:15 [q]S Ex 23:28 **34:12** [r]Jdg 2:2 [s]S Ex 10:7 **34:13** [t]S Ex 23:24; Nu 33:52; Dt 7:5; 12:3; Jdg 6:26; 1Ki 15:13; 2Ch 15:10; 17:6; 34:3-4; Mic 5:14 **34:14** [u]S Ex 20:3 [v]Isa 9:6 [w]S Ex 20:5 **34:15** [x]ver 12; Dt 23:6; Ezr 9:12 [y]Ex 22:20; 32:8; Dt 31:16; Jdg 2:17; 2Ki 17:8; 1Ch 5:25; 2Ch 11:15; Am 2:4 [z]Ex 32:6; 1Co 8:4 **34:16** [a]Dt 7:3; 17:17; Jos 23:12; Jdg 3:6; 14:3; 1Ki 11:1,2; 16:31; Ezr 9:2; 10:3; Ne 10:30; 13:25,26 [b]Dt 7:4; 12:31; 20:18; 1Ki 11:4; 2Ki 21:3-15; Ps 106:34-41; Mal 2:11 **34:17** [c]S Ex 20:4 **34:18** [d]S Ex 12:17; Mt 26:17; Lk 22:1; Ac 12:3 [e]S Ex 12:15 [f]S Ex 12:2 **34:19** [g]S Ex 13:2 **34:20** [h]S Ex 13:13 [i]S Ex 13:2 [j]S Ex 22:29; Dt 16:16; Eze 46:9 **34:21** [k]Ge 2:2-3 [l]Ne 13:15; Isa 56:2; 58:13 **34:22** [m]ver 26; Ex 23:19; Lev 2:12,14; 7:13; 23:10,17; Nu 28:26 [n]S Ex 23:16 **34:23** [o]S Ex 23:14 **34:24** [p]S Ex 23:28 [q]Dt 12:20; 19:8; Job 12:23 **34:25** [r]S Ex 23:18 [s]S Ex 12:8 **34:26** [t]S Ex 22:29; S Nu 18:12 [u]S Ex 23:19

[v]13 That is, symbols of the goddess Asherah
[w]22 That is, in the fall

34:7 *thousands.* Or "a thousand generations" (see 20:6). *wickedness, rebellion and sin.* See Isa 59:12 and note. **34:10** *making a covenant.* Renewing the covenant he had earlier made (chs. 19–24). Verses 10–26, many of which are quoted almost verbatim from previous sections of Exodus (compare especially vv. 18–26 with 23:14–19), are sometimes referred to as the Ritual Decalogue since they can be convincingly divided into ten sections (see, e.g., the NIV paragraphing of vv. 15–26). **34:12** *not to make a treaty with those who live in the land.* Israel is not to make a treaty of peace with any of the people of Canaan to let them live in the land. *treaty.* The Hebrew for this word is the same as that for "covenant" in v. 10 (see also v. 15). **34:13** *Asherah poles.* Asherah was the name of the consort (wife) of El, the chief Canaanite god. Wooden poles, perhaps carved in her image, were often set up in her honor and placed near other pagan objects of worship (see, e.g., Jdg 6:25).

34:14 *whose name is Jealous.* See note on 20:5. **34:15** *prostitute themselves.* See Jdg 2:17 and note. *eat their sacrifices.* Partaking of food sacrificed to a pagan deity invites compromise (cf. 1Co 8; 10:18–21).

34:17 *Do not make cast idols.* As Aaron had done when he made the golden calf (see 32:4).

34:18–26 See notes on 23:14–19.

34:21 *even during the plowing season and harvest you must rest.* Just as they were also to rest while building the tabernacle (see notes on 31:13,16–17).

27Then the LORD said to Moses, "Write[v] down these words, for in accordance with these words I have made a covenant[w] with you and with Israel." 28Moses was there with the LORD forty days and forty nights[x] without eating bread or drinking water.[y] And he wrote on the tablets[z] the words of the covenant—the Ten Commandments. [a]

The Radiant Face of Moses

29When Moses came down from Mount Sinai[b] with the two tablets of the Testimony in his hands,[c] he was not aware that his face was radiant[d] because he had spoken with the LORD. 30When Aaron and all the Israelites saw Moses, his face was radiant, and they were afraid to come near him. 31But Moses called to them; so Aaron and all the leaders of the community[e] came back to him, and he spoke to them. 32Afterward all the Israelites came near him, and he gave them all the commands[f] the LORD had given him on Mount Sinai.

33When Moses finished speaking to them, he put a veil[g] over his face. 34But whenever he entered the LORD's presence to speak with him, he removed the veil until he came out. And when he came out and told the Israelites what he had been commanded, 35they saw that his face was radiant.[h] Then Moses would put the veil back over his face until he went in to speak with the LORD.

Sabbath Regulations

35 Moses assembled the whole Israelite community and said to them, "These are the things the LORD has commanded[i] you to do: 2For six days, work is to be done, but the seventh day shall be your holy day, a Sabbath[j] of rest to the LORD. Whoever does any work on it must be put to death. [k] 3Do not light a fire in any

of your dwellings on the Sabbath day. [l] "

Materials for the Tabernacle

35:4–9pp — Ex 25:1–7
35:10–19pp — Ex 39:32–41

4Moses said to the whole Israelite community, "This is what the LORD has commanded: 5From what you have, take an offering for the LORD. Everyone who is willing is to bring to the LORD an offering of gold, silver and bronze; 6blue, purple and scarlet yarn and fine linen; goat hair; 7ram skins dyed red and hides of sea cows[x]; acacia wood; 8olive oil[m] for the light; spices for the anointing oil and for the fragrant incense; 9and onyx stones and other gems to be mounted on the ephod and breastpiece.

10"All who are skilled among you are to come and make everything the LORD has commanded: [n] 11the tabernacle[o] with its tent and its covering, clasps, frames, crossbars, posts and bases; 12the ark[p] with its poles and the atonement cover and the curtain[q] that shields it; 13the table[r] with its poles and all its articles and the bread of the Presence; 14the lampstand[s] that is for light with its accessories, lamps and oil for the light; 15the altar[t] of incense with its poles, the anointing oil[u] and the fragrant incense;[v] the curtain for the doorway at the entrance to the tabernacle;[w] 16the altar[x] of burnt offering with its bronze grating, its poles and all its utensils; the bronze basin[y] with its stand; 17the curtains of the courtyard with its posts and bases, and the curtain for the entrance to the courtyard;[z] 18the tent pegs[a] for the tabernacle and for the courtyard, and their ropes; 19the woven garments worn for ministering in the sanctuary—both the sacred garments[b] for Aaron the priest and the garments for his sons when they serve as priests."

[x]7 That is, dugongs; also in verse 23

Cross references (center column):

34:27
[v]S Ex 17:14
[w]S Ge 6:18;
S 15:18
34:28 [x]S Ge 7:4;
Mt 4:2; Lk 4:2
[y]Dt 9:9,18;
Ezr 10:6 [z]ver 1;
Ex 31:18
[a]Dt 4:13; 10:4
34:29
[b]S Ex 19:11
[c]S Ex 32:15 [d]ver
35; Ps 34:5;
Isa 60:5; Mt 17:2;
2Co 3:7,13
34:31 [e]Ex 16:22
34:32 [f]S Ex 21:1;
35:1,4
34:33 [g]2Co 3:13
34:35 [h]S ver 29
35:1 [i]S Ex 34:32
35:2 [j]S Ge 2:3;
Ex 34:21;
Dt 5:13-14
[k]S Ex 31:14

35:3 [l]Ex 16:23
35:8 [m]S Ex 25:6
35:10 [n]Ex 31:6;
39:43
35:11
[o]Ex 26:1-37;
36:8-38
35:12
[p]Ex 25:10-22;
37:1-9
[q]S Ex 26:33
35:13
[r]Ex 25:23-30;
37:10-16
35:14
[s]S Ex 25:31
35:15
[t]Ex 30:1-6;
37:25-28
[u]Ex 30:25
[v]Ex 30:34-38
[w]S Ex 26:36
35:16
[x]Ex 27:1-8;
38:1-7
[y]S Ex 30:18
35:17
[z]S Ex 27:9;
38:9-20
35:18 [a]Ex 27:19;
38:20
35:19 [b]S Ex 28:2

34:27 *Write down these words.* As he had earlier written down similar words (see 24:4).
34:28 *he wrote.* Here the Lord, rather than Moses, is probably the subject (see v. 1). *the words of the covenant—the Ten Commandments.* The two phrases are synonymous (see note on 20:1).
34:29 *Testimony.* See notes on 16:34; 25:16. *was radiant.* He who had asked to see God's glory (33:18) now, quite unawares, reflects the divine glory. The Hebrew for "was radiant" is related to the Hebrew noun for "horn." The meaning of the phrase was therefore misunderstood by the Vulgate (the Latin translation), and thus European medieval art often showed horns sprouting from Moses' head.
34:33 *he put a veil over his face.* So that the Israelites would not see the fading away of the radiance but would continue to honor Moses as the one who represented God. For a NT reflection on Moses' action see 2Co 3:7–18 and

notes.
35:1–3 Just as the Israelites had been reminded of the importance of Sabbath observance immediately after the instructions for building the tabernacle and making the priestly garments (see note on 31:13), so now—just before the fulfilling of those instructions—the people are given the same reminder.
35:4–39:43 For the most part repeated from chs. 25–28; 30:1–5; 31:1–11 (see notes on those passages), sometimes verbatim, but with the verbs primarily in the past rather than the future tense and with the topics arranged in a different order. Such repetition was a common feature of ancient Near Eastern literature and was intended to fix the details of a narrative in the reader's mind (see note on Ge 24:34–49).
35:5 *Everyone who is willing.* The voluntary motivation behind the offering of materials and services for the tabernacle is stressed (see vv. 21–22,26,29; 36:2–3).

²⁰Then the whole Israelite community withdrew from Moses' presence, ²¹and everyone who was willing and whose heart moved him came and brought an offering to the Lord for the work on the Tent of Meeting, for all its service, and for the sacred garments. ²²All who were willing, men and women alike, came and brought gold jewelry of all kinds: brooches, earrings, rings and ornaments. They all presented their gold as a wave offering to the Lord. ²³Everyone who had blue, purple or scarlet yarn *c* or fine linen, or goat hair, ram skins dyed red or hides of sea cows brought them. ²⁴Those presenting an offering of silver or bronze brought it as an offering to the Lord, and everyone who had acacia wood for any part of the work brought it. ²⁵Every skilled woman *d* spun with her hands and brought what she had spun—blue, purple or scarlet yarn or fine linen. ²⁶And all the women who were willing and had the skill spun the goat hair. ²⁷The leaders *e* brought onyx stones and other gems *f* to be mounted on the ephod and breastpiece. ²⁸They also brought spices and olive oil for the light and for the anointing oil and for the fragrant incense. *g* ²⁹All the Israelite men and women who were willing *h* brought to the Lord freewill offerings *i* for all the work the Lord through Moses had commanded them to do.

Bezalel and Oholiab

35:30-35pp — Ex 31:2-6

³⁰Then Moses said to the Israelites, "See, the Lord has chosen Bezalel son of Uri, the son of Hur, of the tribe of Judah, ³¹and he has filled him with the Spirit of God, with skill, ability and knowledge in all kinds of crafts *j*— ³²to make artistic designs for work in gold, silver and bronze, ³³to cut and set stones, to work in wood and to engage in all kinds of artistic craftsmanship. ³⁴And he has given both him and Oholiab *k* son of Ahisamach, of the tribe of Dan, the ability to teach *l* others. ³⁵He has filled them with skill to do all kinds of work *m* as craftsmen, designers, embroiderers in blue, purple and scarlet yarn and fine linen, and weavers—all of them master craftsmen and designers. ¹So **36** Bezalel, Oholiab and every skilled person *n* to whom the Lord has given skill and ability to know how to carry out all the work of constructing the sanctuary *o*

are to do the work just as the Lord has commanded."

²Then Moses summoned Bezalel *p* and Oholiab *q* and every skilled person to whom the Lord had given ability and who was willing *r* to come and do the work. ³They received from Moses all the offerings *s* the Israelites had brought to carry out the work of constructing the sanctuary. And the people continued to bring freewill offerings morning after morning. ⁴So all the skilled craftsmen who were doing all the work on the sanctuary left their work ⁵and said to Moses, "The people are bringing more than enough *t* for doing the work the Lord commanded to be done."

⁶Then Moses gave an order and they sent this word throughout the camp: "No man or woman is to make anything else as an offering for the sanctuary." And so the people were restrained from bringing more, ⁷because what they already had was more *u* than enough to do all the work.

The Tabernacle

36:8-38pp — Ex 26:1-37

⁸All the skilled men among the workmen made the tabernacle with ten curtains of finely twisted linen and blue, purple and scarlet yarn, with cherubim worked into them by a skilled craftsman. ⁹All the curtains were the same size—twenty-eight cubits long and four cubits wide. *y* ¹⁰They joined five of the curtains together and did the same with the other five. ¹¹Then they made loops of blue material along the edge of the end curtain in one set, and the same was done with the end curtain in the other set. ¹²They also made fifty loops on one curtain and fifty loops on the end curtain of the other set, with the loops opposite each other. ¹³Then they made fifty gold clasps and used them to fasten the two sets of curtains together so that the tabernacle was a unit. *v*

¹⁴They made curtains of goat hair for the tent over the tabernacle—eleven altogether. ¹⁵All eleven curtains were the same size—thirty cubits long and four cubits wide. *z* ¹⁶They joined five of the curtains into one set and the other six into another

---

35:23 *c*Ex 39:1
35:25 *d*S Ex 28:3
35:27 *e*S Ex 25:2; 1Ch 29:6
*f*1Ch 29:8
35:28 *g*S Ex 25:6
35:29 *h*S Ex 25:2
*i*ver 4-9; Ex 25:1-7; 36:3; 2Ki 12:4
35:31 *j*ver 35; 2Ch 2:7,14
35:34 *k*S Ex 31:6
*l*2Ch 2:14
35:35 *m*ver 31
36:1 *n*S Ex 28:3
*o*Ex 25:8

36:2 *p*S Ex 31:2
*q*S Ex 31:6
*r*S Ex 25:2
36:3 *s*S Ex 35:29
36:5 *t*2Ch 24:14; 31:10; 2Co 8:2-3
36:7 *u*1Ki 7:47
36:13 *v*ver 18

*y*9 That is, about 42 feet (about 12.5 meters) long and 6 feet (about 1.8 meters) wide   *z*15 That is, about 45 feet (about 13.5 meters) long and 6 feet (about 1.8 meters) wide

---

35:21 *Tent of Meeting.* See note on 27:21.   **36:1-38** See note on 35:4-39:43.

set. [17]Then they made fifty loops along the edge of the end curtain in one set and also along the edge of the end curtain in the other set. [18]They made fifty bronze clasps to fasten the tent together as a unit.[w] [19]Then they made for the tent a covering of ram skins dyed red, and over that a covering of hides of sea cows.[a]

[20]They made upright frames of acacia wood for the tabernacle. [21]Each frame was ten cubits long and a cubit and a half wide,[b] [22]with two projections set parallel to each other. They made all the frames of the tabernacle in this way. [23]They made twenty frames for the south side of the tabernacle [24]and made forty silver bases to go under them—two bases for each frame, one under each projection. [25]For the other side, the north side of the tabernacle, they made twenty frames [26]and forty silver bases—two under each frame. [27]They made six frames for the far end, that is, the west end of the tabernacle, [28]and two frames were made for the corners of the tabernacle at the far end. [29]At these two corners the frames were double from the bottom all the way to the top and fitted into a single ring; both were made alike. [30]So there were eight frames and sixteen silver bases—two under each frame.

[31]They also made crossbars of acacia wood: five for the frames on one side of the tabernacle, [32]five for those on the other side, and five for the frames on the west, at the far end of the tabernacle. [33]They made the center crossbar so that it extended from end to end at the middle of the frames. [34]They overlaid the frames with gold and made gold rings to hold the crossbars. They also overlaid the crossbars with gold.

[35]They made the curtain[x] of blue, purple and scarlet yarn and finely twisted linen, with cherubim worked into it by a skilled craftsman. [36]They made four posts of acacia wood for it and overlaid them with gold. They made gold hooks for them and cast their four silver bases. [37]For the entrance to the tent they made a curtain of blue, purple and scarlet yarn and finely twisted linen—the work of an embroiderer;[y] [38]and they made five posts with hooks for them. They overlaid the tops of the posts and their bands with gold and made their five bases of bronze.

The Ark

37:1–9pp — Ex 25:10–20

37 Bezalel[z] made the ark[a] of acacia wood—two and a half cubits long, a cubit and a half wide, and a cubit and a half high.[c] [2]He overlaid it with pure gold,[b] both inside and out, and made a gold molding around it. [3]He cast four gold rings for it and fastened them to its four feet, with two rings on one side and two rings on the other. [4]Then he made poles of acacia wood and overlaid them with gold. [5]And he inserted the poles into the rings on the sides of the ark to carry it.

[6]He made the atonement cover[c] of pure gold—two and a half cubits long and a cubit and a half wide.[d] [7]Then he made two cherubim[d] out of hammered gold at the ends of the cover. [8]He made one cherub on one end and the second cherub on the other; at the two ends he made them of one piece with the cover. [9]The cherubim had their wings spread upward, overshadowing[e] the cover with them. The cherubim faced each other, looking toward the cover.[f]

The Table

37:10–16pp — Ex 25:23–29

[10]They[e] made the table[g] of acacia wood—two cubits long, a cubit wide, and a cubit and a half high.[f] [11]Then they overlaid it with pure gold[h] and made a gold molding around it. [12]They also made around it a rim a handbreadth[g] wide and put a gold molding on the rim. [13]They cast four gold rings for the table and fastened them to the four corners, where the four legs were. [14]The rings[i] were put close to the rim to hold the poles used in carrying the table. [15]The poles for carrying the table were made of acacia wood and were overlaid with gold. [16]And they made from pure gold the articles for the table—its plates and dishes and bowls and its pitchers for the pouring out of drink offerings.

[a] 19 That is, dugongs   [b] 21 That is, about 15 feet (about 4.5 meters) long and 2 1/4 feet (about 0.7 meter) wide   [c] 1 That is, about 3 3/4 feet (about 1.1 meters) long and 2 1/4 feet (about 0.7 meter) wide and high   [d] 6 That is, about 3 3/4 feet (about 1.1 meters) long and 2 1/4 feet (about 0.7 meter) wide   [e] 10 Or He; also in verses 11-29   [f] 10 That is, about 3 feet (about 0.9 meter) long, 1 1/2 feet (about 0.5 meter) wide, and 2 1/4 feet (about 0.7 meter) high   [g] 12 That is, about 3 inches (about 8 centimeters)

Cross references (center column)

36:18 [w] ver 13
36:35 [x] Ex 39:38; Mt 27:51; Lk 23:45; Heb 9:3
36:37 [y] Ex 27:16

37:1 [z] S Ex 31:2
[a] Ex 30:6; 39:35; Dt 10:3
37:2 [b] ver 11,26
37:6 [c] S Ex 26:34; S 31:7; Heb 9:5
37:7 [d] Eze 41:18
37:9 [e] Heb 9:5 /Dt 10:3
37:10 [g] Heb 9:2
37:11 [h] S ver 2
37:14 [i] ver 27

37:1–29 See note on 35:4–39:43.
37:1 *Bezalel made the ark.* The chief craftsman (see 31:2–3) was given the honor of making the most sacred object (see 25:10 and note) among the furnishings for the tabernacle.

The Lampstand

37:17–24pp — Ex 25:31–39

[17]They made the lampstand[j] of pure gold and hammered it out, base and shaft; its flowerlike cups, buds and blossoms were of one piece with it. [18]Six branches extended from the sides of the lampstand—three on one side and three on the other. [19]Three cups shaped like almond flowers with buds and blossoms were on one branch, three on the next branch and the same for all six branches extending from the lampstand. [20]And on the lampstand were four cups shaped like almond flowers with buds and blossoms. [21]One bud was under the first pair of branches extending from the lampstand, a second bud under the second pair, and a third bud under the third pair—six branches in all. [22]The buds and the branches were all of one piece with the lampstand, hammered out of pure gold.[k]

[23]They made its seven lamps,[l] as well as its wick trimmers and trays, of pure gold. [24]They made the lampstand and all its accessories from one talent[h] of pure gold.

The Altar of Incense

37:25–28pp — Ex 30:1–5

[25]They made the altar of incense[m] out of acacia wood. It was square, a cubit long and a cubit wide, and two cubits high[i]—its horns[n] of one piece with it. [26]They overlaid the top and all the sides and the horns with pure gold, and made a gold molding around it. [27]They made two gold rings[o] below the molding—two on opposite sides—to hold the poles used to carry it. [28]They made the poles of acacia wood and overlaid them with gold. [p]

[29]They also made the sacred anointing oil[q] and the pure, fragrant incense[r]—the work of a perfumer.

The Altar of Burnt Offering

38:1–7pp — Ex 27:1–8

38 They[j] built the altar of burnt offering of acacia wood, three cubits[k] high; it was square, five cubits long and five cubits wide.[l] [2]They made a horn at each of the four corners, so that the horns and the altar were of one piece, and they overlaid the altar with bronze.[s] [3]They made all its utensils[t] of bronze—its pots, shovels, sprinkling bowls, meat forks and

firepans. [4]They made a grating for the altar, a bronze network, to be under its ledge, halfway up the altar. [5]They cast bronze rings to hold the poles for the four corners of the bronze grating. [6]They made the poles of acacia wood and overlaid them with bronze. [7]They inserted the poles into the rings so they would be on the sides of the altar for carrying it. They made it hollow, out of boards.

Basin for Washing

[8]They made the bronze basin[u] and its bronze stand from the mirrors of the women[v] who served at the entrance to the Tent of Meeting.

The Courtyard

38:9–20pp — Ex 27:9–19

[9]Next they made the courtyard. The south side was a hundred cubits[m] long and had curtains of finely twisted linen, [10]with twenty posts and twenty bronze bases, and with silver hooks and bands on the posts. [11]The north side was also a hundred cubits long and had twenty posts and twenty bronze bases, with silver hooks and bands on the posts. [12]The west end was fifty cubits[n] wide and had curtains, with ten posts and ten bases, with silver hooks and bands on the posts. [13]The east end, toward the sunrise, was also fifty cubits wide. [14]Curtains fifteen cubits[o] long were on one side of the entrance, with three posts and three bases, [15]and curtains fifteen cubits long were on the other side of the entrance to the courtyard, with three posts and three bases. [16]All the curtains around the courtyard were of finely twisted linen. [17]The bases for the posts were bronze. The hooks and bands on the posts were silver, and their tops were overlaid with silver; so all the posts of the courtyard had silver bands.

[18]The curtain for the entrance to the courtyard was of blue, purple and scarlet yarn and finely twisted linen—the work of an embroiderer. It was twenty cubits[p] long and, like the curtains of the courtyard,

37:17 /Heb 9:2; Rev 1:12
37:22 kver 17; Nu 8:4
37:23 /Ex 40:4, 25
37:25 mEx 30:34-36; Lk 1:11; Heb 9:4; Rev 8:3 nS Ex 27:2; Rev 9:13
37:27 over 14
37:28 pS Ex 25:13
37:29 qS Ex 31:11 rEx 30:1,25; 39:38
38:2 sS2Ch 1:5
38:3 tS Ex 31:9

38:8 uS Ex 30:18; S 40:7 vDt 23:17; 1Sa 2:22; 1Ki 14:24

h[24] That is, about 75 pounds (about 34 kilograms)
i[25] That is, about 1 1/2 feet (about 0.5 meter) long and wide, and about 3 feet (about 0.9 meter) high   j[1] Or *He;* also in verses 2-9   k[1] That is, about 4 1/2 feet (about 1.3 meters)   l[1] That is, about 7 1/2 feet (about 2.3 meters) long and wide   m[9] That is, about 150 feet (about 46 meters)   n[12] That is, about 75 feet (about 23 meters)   o[14] That is, about 22 1/2 feet (about 6.9 meters)   p[18] That is, about 30 feet (about 9 meters)

38:1–31 See note on 35:4–39:43.
38:8 *bronze . . . mirrors.* Mirrored glass was unknown in ancient times, but highly polished bronze gave adequate reflection. *Tent of Meeting.* See note on 27:21.

five cubits^q high, ¹⁹with four posts and four bronze bases. Their hooks and bands were silver, and their tops were overlaid with silver. ²⁰All the tent pegs^w of the tabernacle and of the surrounding courtyard were bronze.

The Materials Used

²¹These are the amounts of the materials used for the tabernacle, the tabernacle of the Testimony,^x which were recorded at Moses' command by the Levites under the direction of Ithamar^y son of Aaron, the priest. ²²(Bezalel^z son of Uri, the son of Hur, of the tribe of Judah, made everything the LORD commanded Moses; ²³with him was Oholiab^a son of Ahisamach, of the tribe of Dan—a craftsman and designer, and an embroiderer in blue, purple and scarlet yarn and fine linen.) ²⁴The total amount of the gold from the wave offering used for all the work on the sanctuary^b was 29 talents and 730 shekels,^r according to the sanctuary shekel.^c

²⁵The silver obtained from those of the community who were counted in the census^d was 100 talents and 1,775 shekels,^s according to the sanctuary shekel— ²⁶one beka per person,^e that is, half a shekel,^t according to the sanctuary shekel,^f from everyone who had crossed over to those counted, twenty years old or more,^g a total of 603,550 men.^h ²⁷The 100 talents^u of silver were used to cast the basesⁱ for the sanctuary and for the curtain—100 bases from the 100 talents, one talent for each base. ²⁸They used the 1,775 shekels^v to make the hooks for the posts, to overlay the tops of the posts, and to make their bands.

²⁹The bronze from the wave offering was 70 talents and 2,400 shekels. ^w ³⁰They used it to make the bases for the entrance to the Tent of Meeting, the bronze altar with its bronze grating and all its utensils, ³¹the bases for the surrounding courtyard and those for its entrance and all the tent pegs for the tabernacle and those for the surrounding courtyard.

The Priestly Garments

39 From the blue, purple and scarlet yarn^j they made woven garments for ministering in the sanctuary.^k They

also made sacred garments^l for Aaron, as the LORD commanded Moses.

The Ephod

39:2–7pp — Ex 28:6–14

²They^x made the ephod of gold, and of blue, purple and scarlet yarn, and of finely twisted linen. ³They hammered out thin sheets of gold and cut strands to be worked into the blue, purple and scarlet yarn and fine linen—the work of a skilled craftsman. ⁴They made shoulder pieces for the ephod, which were attached to two of its corners, so it could be fastened. ⁵Its skillfully woven waistband was like it—of one piece with the ephod and made with gold, and with blue, purple and scarlet yarn, and with finely twisted linen, as the LORD commanded Moses.

⁶They mounted the onyx stones in gold filigree settings and engraved them like a seal with the names of the sons of Israel. ⁷Then they fastened them on the shoulder pieces of the ephod as memorial^m stones for the sons of Israel, as the LORD commanded Moses.

The Breastpiece

39:8–21pp — Ex 28:15–28

⁸They fashioned the breastpieceⁿ—the work of a skilled craftsman. They made it like the ephod: of gold, and of blue, purple and scarlet yarn, and of finely twisted linen. ⁹It was square—a span^y long and a span wide—and folded double. ¹⁰Then they mounted four rows of precious stones on it. In the first row there was a ruby, a topaz and a beryl; ¹¹in the second row a turquoise, a sapphire^z and an emerald; ¹²in the third row a jacinth, an agate and an amethyst; ¹³in the fourth row a chrysolite, an onyx and a jasper.^a They were mounted in gold filigree settings. ¹⁴There

38:20
wS Ex 35:18
38:21 xNu 1:50,
53; 8:24; 9:15;
10:11; 17:7;
1Ch 23:32;
2Ch 24:6;
Ac 7:44; Rev 15:5
yNu 4:28,33
38:22 zS Ex 31:2
38:23 aS Ex 31:6
38:24
bS Ex 30:16
cS Ex 30:13
38:25
dS Ex 30:12
38:26
eS Ex 30:12
gS Ex 30:14
fS Ex 30:13
hS Ex 12:37
38:27
iS Ex 26:19
39:1 jEx 35:23
kEx 35:19

lver 41; Ex 28:2
39:7 mLev 24:7;
Jos 4:7
39:8 nLev 8:8

q*18* That is, about 7 1/2 feet (about 2.3 meters)
r*24* The weight of the gold was a little over one ton (about 1 metric ton).   s*25* The weight of the silver was a little over 3 3/4 tons (about 3.4 metric tons).
t*26* That is, about 1/5 ounce (about 5.5 grams)
u*27* That is, about 3 3/4 tons (about 3.4 metric tons)
v*28* That is, about 45 pounds (about 20 kilograms)
w*29* The weight of the bronze was about 2 1/2 tons (about 2.4 metric tons).   x*2* Or *He*; also in verses 7, 8 and 22   y*9* That is, about 9 inches (about 22 centimeters)   z*11* Or *lapis lazuli*   a*13* The precise identification of some of these precious stones is uncertain.

38:25 *100 talents and 1,775 shekels.* Since there are 3,000 shekels in a talent, 100 talents equals 300,000 shekels, which, when added to the 1,775 shekels, gives a grand total of 301,775—half a shekel for each of the 603,-550 men of military age (v. 26).
38:26 *603,550 men.* The number is doubtless to be understood literally, since the figures in the tribal census (see Nu 1:21–43; 2:4–31) total 603,550 (see Nu 1:46 and note). See Introduction to Numbers: Special Problem.
38:27 *one talent for each base.* See note on 26:19.
39:1–43 See note on 35:4–39:43.

were twelve stones, one for each of the names of the sons of Israel, each engraved like a seal with the name of one of the twelve tribes. *o*

15For the breastpiece they made braided chains of pure gold, like a rope. 16They made two gold filigree settings and two gold rings, and fastened the rings to two of the corners of the breastpiece. 17They fastened the two gold chains to the rings at the corners of the breastpiece, 18and the other ends of the chains to the two settings, attaching them to the shoulder pieces of the ephod at the front. 19They made two gold rings and attached them to the other two corners of the breastpiece on the inside edge next to the ephod. 20Then they made two more gold rings and attached them to the bottom of the shoulder pieces on the front of the ephod, close to the seam just above the waistband of the ephod. 21They tied the rings of the breastpiece to the rings of the ephod with blue cord, connecting it to the waistband so that the breastpiece would not swing out from the ephod—as the LORD commanded Moses.

Other Priestly Garments

39:22–31pp — Ex 28:31–43

22They made the robe of the ephod entirely of blue cloth—the work of a weaver— 23with an opening in the center of the robe like the opening of a collar, *b* and a band around this opening, so that it would not tear. 24They made pomegranates of blue, purple and scarlet yarn and finely twisted linen around the hem of the robe. 25And they made bells of pure gold and attached them around the hem between the pomegranates. 26The bells and pomegranates alternated around the hem of the robe to be worn for ministering, as the LORD commanded Moses.

27For Aaron and his sons, they made tunics of fine linen *p*—the work of a weaver— 28and the turban *q* of fine linen, the linen headbands and the undergarments of finely twisted linen. 29The sash was of finely twisted linen and blue, purple and scarlet yarn—the work of an embroiderer—as the LORD commanded Moses.

30They made the plate, the sacred diadem, out of pure gold and engraved on it,

like an inscription on a seal: HOLY TO THE LORD. *r* 31Then they fastened a blue cord to it to attach it to the turban, *s* as the LORD commanded Moses.

Moses Inspects the Tabernacle

39:32–41pp — Ex 35:10–19

32So all the work on the tabernacle, the Tent of Meeting, was completed. The Israelites did everything just as the LORD commanded Moses. *t* 33Then they brought the tabernacle *u* to Moses: the tent and all its furnishings, its clasps, frames, crossbars, posts and bases; 34the covering of ram skins dyed red, the covering of hides of sea cows *c* and the shielding curtain; 35the ark of the Testimony *v* with its poles and the atonement cover; 36the table *w* with all its articles and the bread of the Presence; *x* 37the pure gold lampstand *y* with its row of lamps and all its accessories, *z* and the oil *a* for the light; 38the gold altar, *b* the anointing oil, *c* the fragrant incense, *d* and the curtain *e* for the entrance to the tent; 39the bronze altar *f* with its bronze grating, its poles and all its utensils; the basin *g* with its stand; 40the curtains of the courtyard with its posts and bases, and the curtain for the entrance to the courtyard; *h* the ropes and tent pegs for the courtyard; all the furnishings for the tabernacle, the Tent of Meeting; 41and the woven garments *i* worn for ministering in the sanctuary, both the sacred garments for Aaron the priest and the garments for his sons when serving as priests.

42The Israelites had done all the work just as the LORD had commanded Moses. *j* 43Moses inspected the work and saw that they had done it just as the LORD had commanded. *k* So Moses blessed *l* them.

Setting Up the Tabernacle

40 Then the LORD said to Moses: 2"Set up *m* the tabernacle, the Tent of Meeting, *n* on the first day of the first month. *o* 3Place the ark *p* of the Testimony in it and shield the ark with the curtain. 4Bring in the table *q* and set out what belongs on it. *r* Then bring in the lampstand *s* and set up its lamps. 5Place the gold altar *t*

Cross references (center column)

39:14
*o*Rev 21:12
39:27 *p*Lev 6:10;
8:2
39:28 *q*ver 31;
S Ex 28:4;
Lev 8:9; Isa 61:10

39:30 *r*Isa 23:18;
Zec 14:20
39:31 *s*S ver 28
39:32 *t*S Ex 25:9
39:33
*u*Ex 25:8-40;
36:8-38
39:35 *v*S Ex 37:1
39:36
*w*Ex 25:23-30;
37:10-16
*x*S Ex 25:30
39:37
*y*S Ex 25:31
*z*Ex 25:31-39
*a*S Ex 25:6
39:38
*b*Ex 30:1-10;
37:25-28
*c*Ex 30:22-32;
37:29
*d*Ex 30:34-38;
S 37:29
*e*S Ex 36:35
39:39
*f*Ex 27:1-8;
38:1-7
*g*S Ex 30:18
39:40
*h*Ex 27:9-19;
38:9-20
39:41 *i*S ver 1
39:42 *j*S Ex 25:9
39:43
*k*S Ex 25:9;
S 35:10
*l*Ge 31:55;
Lev 9:22,23;
Nu 6:23-27;
Dt 21:5; 26:15;
2Sa 6:18;
1Ki 8:14,55;
1Ch 16:2;
2Ch 30:27
40:2 *m*S Ex 26:30
*n*ver 34,35;
Lev 1:1; 3:2;
6:26; 9:23;
16:16; Nu 1:1;
7:89; 11:16;
17:4; 20:6;
Jos 18:1; 19:51;
Jer 7:12 *o*ver 17;
S Ex 12:2; Nu 9:1
40:3 *p*S Ex 26:33
40:4 *q*S Ex 25:23
*r*S Ex 25:30
*s*S Ex 25:31
40:5 *t*S Ex 30:1

b23 The meaning of the Hebrew for this word is uncertain.   c34 That is, dugongs

---

39:30 *sacred diadem.* An official designation (not found in 28:36–37) for the plate of the turban.
39:32 *all the work . . . was completed.* Reminiscent of the concluding words of the creation narrative (see Ge 2:1–3).
39:43 *Moses blessed them.* For the faithfulness with which the Israelites had donated their gifts, time and talents

in building the tabernacle and all its furnishings —faithfulness in service brings divine benediction.
40:2 *first day of the first month.* The tabernacle was set up almost a year after the institution of the Passover (see v. 17; 12:2,6).

of incense in front of the ark of the Testimony and put the curtain at the entrance to the tabernacle.

⁶"Place the altar *u* of burnt offering in front of the entrance to the tabernacle, the Tent of Meeting; ⁷place the basin *v* between the Tent of Meeting and the altar and put water in it. ⁸Set up the courtyard *w* around it and put the curtain at the entrance to the courtyard.

⁹"Take the anointing oil and anoint *x* the tabernacle and everything in it; consecrate it and all its furnishings, *y* and it will be holy. ¹⁰Then anoint the altar of burnt offering and all its utensils; consecrate *z* the altar, and it will be most holy. ¹¹Anoint the basin and its stand and consecrate them.

¹²"Bring Aaron and his sons to the entrance to the Tent of Meeting *a* and wash them with water. *b* ¹³Then dress Aaron in the sacred garments, *c* anoint him and consecrate *d* him so he may serve me as priest. ¹⁴Bring his sons and dress them in tunics. *e* ¹⁵Anoint them just as you anointed their father, so they may serve me as priests. Their anointing will be to a priesthood that will continue for all generations to come. *f* " ¹⁶Moses did everything just as the LORD commanded *g* him.

¹⁷So the tabernacle *h* was set up on the first day of the first month *i* in the second year. ¹⁸When Moses *j* set up the tabernacle, he put the bases in place, erected the frames, *k* inserted the crossbars and set up the posts. ¹⁹Then he spread the tent over the tabernacle and put the covering *l* over the tent, as the LORD commanded *m* him.

²⁰He took the Testimony *n* and placed it in the ark, *o* attached the poles to the ark and put the atonement cover *p* over it. ²¹Then he brought the ark into the tabernacle and hung the shielding curtain *q* and shielded the ark of the Testimony, as the LORD commanded *r* him.

²²Moses placed the table *s* in the Tent of Meeting on the north side of the tabernacle outside the curtain ²³and set out the

bread *t* on it before the LORD, as the LORD commanded *u* him.

²⁴He placed the lampstand *v* in the Tent of Meeting opposite the table on the south side of the tabernacle ²⁵and set up the lamps *w* before the LORD, as the LORD commanded *x* him.

²⁶Moses placed the gold altar *y* in the Tent of Meeting in front of the curtain ²⁷and burned fragrant incense on it, as the LORD commanded *z* him. ²⁸Then he put up the curtain *a* at the entrance to the tabernacle.

²⁹He set the altar *b* of burnt offering near the entrance to the tabernacle, the Tent of Meeting, and offered on it burnt offerings and grain offerings, *c* as the LORD commanded *d* him.

³⁰He placed the basin *e* between the Tent of Meeting and the altar and put water in it for washing, ³¹and Moses and Aaron and his sons used it to wash *f* their hands and feet. ³²They washed whenever they entered the Tent of Meeting or approached the altar, *g* as the LORD commanded *h* Moses.

³³Then Moses set up the courtyard *i* around the tabernacle and altar and put up the curtain *j* at the entrance to the courtyard. And so Moses finished the work.

The Glory of the LORD

³⁴Then the cloud *k* covered the Tent of Meeting, and the glory *l* of the LORD filled the tabernacle. ³⁵Moses could not enter the Tent of Meeting because the cloud had settled upon it, and the glory *m* of the LORD filled the tabernacle. *n*

³⁶In all the travels of the Israelites, whenever the cloud lifted from above the tabernacle, they would set out; *o* ³⁷but if the cloud did not lift, they did not set out—until the day it lifted. ³⁸So the cloud *p* of the LORD was over the tabernacle by day, and fire was in the cloud by night, in the sight of all the house of Israel during all their travels.

40:6 *u*S Ex 27:1; 2Ki 16:14; 2Ch 4:1
40:7 *v*Ex 30:18
40:8 *w*S Ex 27:9
40:9 *x*S Ex 30:26 *y*Nu 7:1
40:10 *z*S Ex 29:36
40:12 *a*Nu 8:9 *b*S Ex 29:4; S 30:19
40:13 *c*S Ex 28:41 *d*Lev 8:12
40:14 *e*S Ex 28:40; Lev 10:5
40:15 *f*S Ex 29:9
40:16 *g*S Ge 6:22
40:17 *h*Nu 7:1 *i*S ver 2
40:18 *j*2Ch 1:3 *k*Ex 36:20-34
40:19 *l*Ex 36:19 *m*S Ge 6:22
40:20 *n*S Ex 16:34; Heb 9:4 *o*S Ex 25:21 *p*Ex 25:17-22; S 26:34; S 31:7
40:21 *q*S Ex 26:33 *r*S Ge 6:22
40:22 *s*S Ex 25:23
40:23 *t*S Ex 25:30; Lev 24:5-8 *u*S Ge 6:22
40:24 *v*S Ex 25:31
40:25 *w*S Ex 37:23 *x*S Ge 6:22
40:26 *y*S Ex 30:1
40:27 *z*S Ge 6:22
40:28 *a*S Ex 26:36
40:29 *b*S Ex 20:24 *c*Ex 29:38-42 *d*S Ge 6:22
40:30 *e*S ver 7; S Ex 30:18
40:31 *f*Ex 30:19-21
40:32 *g*Ex 30:20 *h*S Ge 6:22
40:33 *i*S Ex 27:9; 38:9-20 *j*Ex 27:16
40:34 *k*Ex 19:16; Lev 16:2; Nu 9:15-23; 1Ki 8:12; 2Ch 5:13; Isa 6:4; Eze 10:4 *l*S Ex 16:7; Jn 1:14; 12:41; Rev 15:8
40:35 *m*S Ex 16:10 *n*1Ki 8:11; 2Ch 5:13-14; 7:2
40:36 *o*Nu 9:17-23; 10:13 **40:38** *p*S Ex 13:21; 1Co 10:1

40:16 *Moses did . . . just as the LORD commanded.* Moses' obedience to God's command is a key theme of the final chapter of Exodus (see vv. 19,21,23,25,27,29,32). It was the people who provided all the resources and made all the components, but it was the Lord's servant Moses who was authorized to erect the tabernacle and prepare it for the Lord's entry.

40:33 *Moses finished the work.* See note on 39:32.

40:34 With the glory of the Lord entering the tabernacle,

the great series of events that began with the birth of Moses and his rescue from the Nile, foreshadowing the deliverance of Israel from Egypt, comes to a grand climax. From now on, the Israelites march through the desert, and through history, with the Lord tenting among them and leading them to the land of fulfilled promises.

40:38 See note on 13:21. *house of Israel.* The nation, viewed as an extended family household.

LEVITICUS

Author and Date

See note on 1:1 and Introduction to Genesis: Author and Date of Writing.

Title

Leviticus receives its name from the Septuagint (the Greek translation of the OT) and means "relating to the Levites." Its Hebrew title, *wayyiqra'*, is the first word in the Hebrew text of the book and means "And he [i.e., the Lord] called." Although Leviticus does not deal only with the special duties of the Levites, it is so named because it concerns mainly the service of worship at the tabernacle, which was conducted by the priests who were the sons of Aaron, assisted by many from the rest of the tribe of Levi. Exodus gave the directions for building the tabernacle, and now Leviticus gives the laws and regulations for worship there including instructions on ceremonial cleanness, moral laws, holy days, the sabbath year and the Year of Jubilee. These laws were given, at least for the most part, during the year that Israel camped at Mount Sinai, when God directed Moses in organizing Israel's worship, government and military forces. The book of Numbers continues the history with preparations for moving on from Sinai to Canaan.

Themes

The key thought of Leviticus is holiness (see note on 11:44)—the holiness of God and man (man must revere God in "holiness"). In Leviticus spiritual holiness is symbolized by physical perfection. Therefore the book demands perfect animals for its many sacrifices (chs. 1-7) and requires priests without deformity (chs. 8-10). A woman's hemorrhaging after giving birth (ch. 12); sores, burns or baldness (chs. 13-14); a man's bodily discharge (15:1-18); specific activities during a woman's monthly period (15:19-33)—all may be signs of blemish (a lack of perfection) and may symbolize man's spiritual defects, which break his spiritual wholeness. The person with visible skin disease must be banished from the camp, the place of God's special presence, just as Adam and Eve were banished from the Garden of Eden. Such a person can return to the camp (and therefore to God's presence) when he is pronounced whole again by the examining priests. Before he can reenter the camp, however, he has to offer the prescribed, perfect sacrifices (symbolizing the perfect, whole sacrifice of Christ).

After the covenant at Sinai, Israel was the earthly representation of God's kingdom (the theocracy), and, as her King, the Lord established his administration over all of Israel's life. Her religious, communal and personal life was so regulated as to establish her as God's holy people and to instruct her in holiness. Special attention was given to Israel's religious ritual. The sacrifices were to be offered at an approved sanctuary, which would symbolize both God's holiness and his compassion. They were to be controlled by the priests, who by care and instruction would preserve them in purity and carefully teach their meaning to the people. Each particular sacrifice was to have meaning for the people of Israel but would also have spiritual and symbolic import.

For more information on the meaning of sacrifice in general see the solemn ritual of the Day of Atonement (ch. 16). For the meaning of the blood of the offering see 17:11; Ge 9:4. For the emphasis on substitution see 16:21.

Some suppose that the OT sacrifices were remains of old agricultural offerings—a human desire to offer part of one's possessions as a love gift to the deity. But the OT sacrifices were specifically prescribed by God and received their meaning from the Lord's covenant relationship with Israel—whatever their superficial resemblances to pagan sacrifices. They indeed include the idea of a gift, but this is accompanied by such other values as dedication, communion, propitiation (appeasing God's judicial wrath against sin) and restitution. The various offerings have differing functions, the primary ones being atonement (see note on Ex 25:17) and worship.

Outline

The subjects treated in Leviticus, as in any book of laws and regulations, cover several categories:

I. The Five Main Offerings (chs. 1-7)
   A. Their Content, Purpose and Manner of Offering (1:1-6:7)
   B. Additional Regulations (6:8-7:38)
II. The Ordination, Installation and Work of Aaron and His Sons (chs. 8-10)
III. Laws of Cleanness—Food, Childbirth, Infections, etc. (chs. 11-15)
IV. The Day of Atonement and the Centrality of Worship at the Tabernacle (chs. 16-17)
V. Moral Laws Covering Incest, Honesty, Thievery, Idolatry, etc. (chs. 18-20)
VI. Regulations for the Priests, the Offerings and the Annual Feasts (21:1-24:9)
VII. Punishment for Blasphemy, Murder, etc. (24:10-23)
VIII. The Sabbath Year, Jubilee, Land Tenure and Reform of Slavery (ch. 25)
IX. Blessings and Curses for Covenant Obedience and Disobedience (ch. 26)
X. Regulations for Offerings Vowed to the Lord (ch. 27)

The Burnt Offering

1 The LORD called to Moses[a] and spoke to him from the Tent of Meeting.[b] He said, 2"Speak to the Israelites and say to them: 'When any of you brings an offering to the LORD,[c] bring as your offering an animal from either the herd or the flock.[d]

3" 'If the offering is a burnt offering[e] from the herd,[f] he is to offer a male without defect.[g] He must present it at the entrance to the Tent[h] of Meeting so that it[a] will be acceptable[i] to the LORD. 4He is to lay his hand on the head[j] of the burnt offering,[k] and it will be accepted[l] on his behalf to make atonement[m] for him. 5He is to slaughter[n] the young bull[o] before the LORD, and then Aaron's sons[p] the priests shall bring the blood and sprinkle it against the altar on all sides[q] at the entrance to the Tent of Meeting. 6He is to skin[r] the burnt offering and cut it into pieces.[s] 7The sons of Aaron the priest are to put fire on the altar and arrange wood[t] on the fire. 8Then Aaron's sons the priests shall arrange the pieces, including the head and the fat,[u] on the burning wood[v] that is on the altar. 9He is to wash the inner parts and the legs with water,[w] and the priest is to burn all of it[x] on the altar.[y] It is a burnt offering,[z] an offering made by fire,[a] an aroma pleasing to the LORD.[b]

10" 'If the offering is a burnt offering from the flock, from either the sheep[c] or the goats,[d] he is to offer a male without defect. 11He is to slaughter it at the north side of the altar[e] before the LORD, and Aaron's sons the priests shall sprinkle its blood against the altar on all sides.[f] 12He is to cut it into pieces, and the priest shall arrange them, including the head and the fat,[g] on the burning wood that is on the altar. 13He is to wash the inner parts and the legs with water,[h] and the priest is to bring all of it and burn it[i] on the altar.[j] It is a burnt offering,[k] an offering made by fire, an aroma pleasing to the LORD.

14" 'If the offering to the LORD is a burnt offering of birds, he is to offer a dove or a young pigeon.[l] 15The priest shall bring it to the altar, wring off the head[m] and burn

---

1:1 aS Ex 3:4; S 25:22
bS Ex 27:21; S 40:2
1:2 cLev 7:16,38; 22:21; 23:38; 27:9
dLev 22:18-19; Nu 15:3
1:3 eS Ge 8:20 /ver 10; Lev 22:27; Ezr 8:35; Mal 1:8 gS ver 5; S Ex 12:5; S Lev 22:19,20; Heb 9:14; 1Pe 1:19 hLev 6:25; 17:9; Nu 6:16; Dt 12:5-6,11 /Isa 58:5
1:4 /S Ex 29:10, 15 kver 3; Lev 4:29; 6:25; Eze 45:15 /S Ge 32:20 mS Ex 29:36; S 32:30
1:5 nEx 29:11; Lev 3:2,8 oS ver 3; Ex 29:1; Nu 15:8; Dt 18:3; Ps 50:9; 69:31 pLev 8:2; 10:6; 21:1 qS Ex 29:20; Heb 12:24; 1Pe 1:2
1:6 rLev 7:8 sEx 29:17
1:7 tver 17; S Ge 22:9; Lev 3:5; 6:12
1:8 uver 12; S Ex 29:13;

Lev 8:20 vLev 9:13 1:9 wS Ex 29:17 xLev 6:22 yver 13; Ex 29:18; Lev 9:14 zver 3 aLev 23:8,25,36; Nu 28:6,19 bver 13; Ge 8:21; Lev 2:2; 3:5,16; 17:6; Nu 18:17; 28:11-13; Eph 5:2 1:10 cS Ge 22:7 dS ver 3; Ex 12:5; Lev 3:12; 4:23, 28; 5:6; Nu 15:11 1:11 eS Ex 29:11 /S Ex 29:20 1:12 gS ver 8 1:13 hS Ex 29:17 iLev 6:22 /S ver 9 kDt 12:27 1:14 /S Ge 15:9; Lk 2:24 1:15 mLev 5:8

a3 Or he

1:1 Emphasizes that the contents of Leviticus were given to Moses by God at Mount Sinai. Cf. also the concluding verse (27:34). In more than 50 places it is said that the Lord spoke to Moses. Modern criticism has attributed practically the whole book to priestly legislation written during or after the exile. But this is without objective evidence, is against the repeated claim of the book to be Mosaic, is against the traditional Jewish view, and runs counter to other OT and NT witness (Ro 10:5). Many items in Leviticus are now seen to be best explained in terms of a second-millennium B.C. date, which is also the most likely time for Moses to have written the Pentateuch (see Introduction to Genesis: Author and Date of Writing). There is no convincing reason not to take at face value the many references to Moses and his work. *Tent of Meeting.* The tabernacle, where God met with Israel (see note on Ex 27:21).
1:2 *brings an offering.* The Hebrew word for "offering" used here comes from the word translated "brings." An "offering" is something that someone "brings" to God as a gift (most offerings were voluntary, such as the burnt offering). *Corban* is the word for "offering" and is used in Mk 7:11, where Mark also translates it "gift" (see note there).
1:3 *burnt offering.* See further priestly regulations in 6:8–13 (see also chart on "OT Sacrifices," p. 150). A burnt offering was offered every morning and evening for all Israel (Ex 29:39–42). Double burnt offerings were brought on the Sabbath (Nu 28:9–10) and extra ones on feast days (Nu 28–29). In addition, anyone could offer special burnt offerings to express devotion to the Lord. *male.* The burnt offering had to be a male animal because of its greater value, and also perhaps because it was thought to better represent vigor and fertility. It was usually a young sheep or goat (for the average individual), but bulls (for the wealthy) and doves or pigeons (for the poor) were also specified. *without defect.* The animal had to be unblemished (cf. Mal 1:8). As in all offerings, the offerer was to lay his hand on the head of the animal to

express identification between himself and the animal (16:21), whose death would then be accepted in "atonement" (v. 4). The blood was sprinkled on the sides of the great altar (located outside the tabernacle—later the temple—in the eastern half of the courtyard), where the fire of sacrifice was never to go out (6:13). The whole sacrifice was to be burned up (v. 9), including the head, legs, fat and inner organs. It is therefore sometimes called a holocaust offering *(holo* means "whole," and *caust* means "burnt"). When a bull was offered, however, the officiating priest could keep its hide (7:8). The burnt offering may have been the usual sacrifice offered by the patriarchs. It was the most comprehensive in its meaning. Its Hebrew name means "going up," perhaps symbolizing worship and prayer as its aroma ascended to the Lord (v. 17). The completeness of its burning also speaks of dedication on the part of the worshiper. *entrance to the Tent of Meeting.* Where the altar of burnt offering was (see Ex 40:29). *acceptable to the LORD.* See Ro 12:1; Php 4:18.
1:4 *lay his hand on.* See notes on v. 3; Ex 29:10. *atonement.* See notes on 16:20–22; 17:11.
1:5 Only after the offerer killed the animal (symbolizing substitution of a perfect animal sacrifice for a sinful human life) did the priestly work begin. *blood.* See notes on 17:11; Heb 9:18. *sprinkle it against the altar.* See Ex 24:6; Heb 9:19–21.
1:6 *skin.* The whole animal was burned except the hide, which was given to the priest (7:8).
1:9,13,17 *aroma pleasing to the LORD.* The OT sacrifices foreshadowed Christ, who was a "fragrant offering" (Eph 5:2; cf. Php 4:18).
1:11 *north side.* See diagram of "The Tabernacle," p. 124.
1:14 *birds.* Three categories of sacrifices are mentioned: (1) herds (vv. 3–9), (2) flocks (vv. 10–13) and (3) birds (vv. 14–17). Sacrifices of birds were allowed for the poor (see 5:7; 12:8; Lk 2:24).

it on the altar; its blood shall be drained out on the side of the altar.[n] [16]He is to remove the crop with its contents[b] and throw it to the east side of the altar, where the ashes[o] are. [17]He shall tear it open by the wings, not severing it completely,[p] and then the priest shall burn it on the wood[q] that is on the fire on the altar. It is a burnt offering, an offering made by fire, an aroma pleasing to the LORD.

The Grain Offering

2 " 'When someone brings a grain offering[r] to the LORD, his offering is to be of fine flour.[s] He is to pour oil[t] on it,[u] put incense on it[v] [2]and take it to Aaron's sons the priests. The priest shall take a handful of the fine flour[w] and oil, together with all the incense,[x] and burn this as a memorial portion[y] on the altar, an offering made by fire,[z] an aroma pleasing to the LORD.[a] [3]The rest of the grain offering belongs to Aaron and his sons;[b] it is a most holy[c] part of the offerings made to the LORD by fire.

[4]" 'If you bring a grain offering baked in an oven,[d] it is to consist of fine flour: cakes made without yeast and mixed with oil, or[c] wafers[e] made without yeast and spread with oil.[f] [5]If your grain offering is prepared on a griddle,[g] it is to be made of fine flour mixed with oil, and without yeast. [6]Crumble it and pour oil on it; it is a grain offering. [7]If your grain offering is cooked in a pan,[h] it is to be made of fine flour and oil. [8]Bring the grain offering

made of these things to the LORD; present it to the priest, who shall take it to the altar. [9]He shall take out the memorial portion[i] from the grain offering and burn it on the altar as an offering made by fire, an aroma pleasing to the LORD.[j] [10]The rest of the grain offering belongs to Aaron and his sons;[k] it is a most holy part of the offerings made to the LORD by fire.[l]

[11]" 'Every grain offering you bring to the LORD must be made without yeast,[m] for you are not to burn any yeast or honey in an offering made to the LORD by fire. [12]You may bring them to the LORD as an offering of the firstfruits,[n] but they are not to be offered on the altar as a pleasing aroma. [13]Season all your grain offerings with salt.[o] Do not leave the salt of the covenant[p] of your God out of your grain offerings; add salt to all your offerings.

[14]" 'If you bring a grain offering of firstfruits[q] to the LORD, offer crushed heads of new grain roasted in the fire. [15]Put oil and incense[r] on it; it is a grain offering. [16]The priest shall burn the memorial portion[s] of the crushed grain and the oil, together with all the incense,[t] as an offering made to the LORD by fire.[u]

The Fellowship Offering

3 " 'If someone's offering is a fellowship offering,[d][v] and he offers an animal

Cross references (center column)

1:15 [n]Lev 5:9
1:16 [o]Lev 4:12; 6:10; Nu 4:13
1:17 [p]S Ge 15:10
[q]S ver 7
2:1 [r]S Ex 29:41; Lev 6:14-18
[s]Ex 29:2,40; Lev 5:11
[t]Nu 15:4; 28:5
[u]S Ex 29:2; Lev 7:12 [v]ver 2, 15,16; Lev 24:7; Ne 13:9; Isa 43:23
2:2 [w]Lev 5:11
[x]Lev 6:15; Isa 1:13; 65:3; 66:3 [y]ver 9,16; Lev 5:12; 6:15; 24:7; Nu 5:26; 18:8; Ps 16:5; 73:26; Isa 53:12 [z]ver 16
[a]S Lev 1:9
2:3 [b]ver 10; Lev 6:16; 10:12, 13 [c]S Ex 30:36
2:4 [d]Lev 7:9; 26:26 [e]Lev 7:12; 8:26 [f]S Ex 29:2
2:5 [g]Lev 6:21; 7:9; Eze 4:3
2:7 [h]Lev 7:9

2:9 [i]S ver 2 [j]S Ge 8:21
2:10 [k]ver 3 [l]Ezr 2:63
2:11 [m]S Ex 23:18; Lev 6:16
2:12 [n]S Ex 34:22
2:13 [o]Mk 9:49 [p]Nu 18:19; 2Ch 13:5; Eze 43:24
2:14 [q]S Ex 34:22; Nu 15:20; Dt 16:13; 26:2; Ru 3:2
2:15 [r]S ver 1
2:16 [s]S ver 2 [t]S ver 1 [u]Nu 4:16; Jer 14:12

3:1 [v]S ver 6; S Ex 32:6; Lev 7:11-34; S 17:5

[b]16 Or crop and the feathers; the meaning of the Hebrew for this word is uncertain.   [c]4 Or and
[d]1 Traditionally peace offering; also in verses 3, 6 and 9

Study notes (bottom)

1:17 not severing it completely. See note on Ge 15:10.
2:1 grain offering. See further priestly regulations in 6:14–23; 7:9–10. It was made of grain or fine flour. If baked or cooked, it consisted of cakes or wafers made in a pan or oven or on a griddle. It was the only bloodless offering, but it was to accompany the burnt offering (see Nu 28:3–6), sin offering (see Nu 6:14–15) and fellowship offering (see 9:4; Nu 6:17). The amounts of grain offering ingredients specified to accompany a bull, ram or lamb sacrificed as a burnt offering are given in Nu 28:12–13. A representative handful of flour was to be burned on the altar with the accompanying offerings, and the balance was to be baked without yeast and eaten by the priests in their holy meals (6:14–17). The flour that was burned on the altar was mixed with olive oil for shortening, salted for taste and accompanied by incense, but it was to have no yeast or honey—neither of which was allowed on the altar (vv. 11–13). The cooked product was similar to pie crust. The worshiper was not to eat any of the grain offering, and the priests were not to eat any of their own grain offerings, which were to be totally burned (6:22–23). The Hebrew word for grain offering can mean "present" or "gift" and is often used in that way (see Ge 43:11). The sacred gifts expressed devotion to God (see v. 2). fine flour. Grain that was milled and sifted. oil. Olive oil is often mentioned in connection with grain and new wine as fresh products of the harvest (see Dt 7:13). Used extensively in cooking, it was a suitable part of the worshiper's gift.

incense. Frankincense was the chief ingredient (see Ex 30:34–35).
2:3 most holy part. For this reason, the priests were to eat it in the sanctuary area proper and not feed their families with it (6:16–18).
2:4 without yeast. See notes on Ex 12:8,15.
2:5 griddle. A clay pan that rested on a stone heated by a fire. Later, iron pans were sometimes used.
2:11 honey. It was forbidden on the altar perhaps because of its use in brewing beer (as an aid to fermentation), though some suggest that it was because of its use in Canaanite cultic practice.
2:12 firstfruits. See 23:10–11; Ex 23:16,19; Nu 15:18–20; Dt 18:4–5; 26:1–11.
2:13 salt of the covenant. In ancient times salt was often costly and a valuable part of the diet. Perhaps this is why it was used as a covenant sign and was required for sacrifices.
3:1 fellowship offering. See further priestly regulations in 7:11–21,28–34. Two basic ideas are included in this offering: peace and fellowship. The traditional translation is "peace offering," a name that comes from the Hebrew word for the offering, which in turn is related to the Hebrew word shalom, meaning "peace" or "wholeness." Thus the offering perhaps symbolized peace between God and man as well as the inward peace that resulted. The fellowship offering was the only sacrifice of which the offerer might eat a part. Fellowship was involved because the offerer, on the basis of

from the herd, whether male or female, he
is to present before the LORD an animal
without defect.[w] 2He is to lay his hand on
the head[x] of his offering and slaughter it[y]
at the entrance to the Tent of Meeting.[z]
Then Aaron's sons the priests shall sprinkle[a] the blood against the altar[b] on all
sides.[c] 3From the fellowship offering he is
to bring a sacrifice made to the LORD by
fire: all the fat[d] that covers the inner
parts[e] or is connected to them, 4both
kidneys[f] with the fat on them near the
loins, and the covering of the liver, which
he will remove with the kidneys. 5Then
Aaron's sons[g] are to burn it on the altar[h]
on top of the burnt offering[i] that is on the
burning wood,[j] as an offering made by
fire, an aroma pleasing to the LORD.[k]

6" 'If he offers an animal from the flock
as a fellowship offering[l] to the LORD, he is
to offer a male or female without defect. 7If
he offers a lamb,[m] he is to present it before
the LORD.[n] 8He is to lay his hand on the
head of his offering and slaughter it[o] in
front of the Tent of Meeting. Then Aaron's
sons shall sprinkle its blood against the altar on all sides. 9From the fellowship offering he is to bring a sacrifice[p] made to the
LORD by fire: its fat, the entire fat tail cut
off close to the backbone, all the fat that
covers the inner parts or is connected to
them, 10both kidneys with the fat on them
near the loins, and the covering of the liver, which he will remove with the kidneys.
11The priest shall burn them on the altar[q]
as food,[r] an offering made to the LORD by
fire.[s]

12" 'If his offering is a goat,[t] he is to
present it before the LORD. 13He is to lay
his hand on its head and slaughter it in
front of the Tent of Meeting. Then Aaron's
sons shall sprinkle[u] its blood against the
altar on all sides.[v] 14From what he offers
he is to make this offering to the LORD by
fire: all the fat that covers the inner parts
or is connected to them, 15both kidneys
with the fat on them near the loins, and
the covering of the liver, which he will
remove with the kidneys.[w] 16The priest
shall burn them on the altar[x] as food,[y] an
offering made by fire, a pleasing aroma.[z]
All the fat[a] is the LORD's.[b]

17" 'This is a lasting ordinance[c] for the
generations to come,[d] wherever you
live:[e] You must not eat any fat or any
blood.[f] ' "

The Sin Offering

4 The LORD said to Moses, 2"Say to the
Israelites: 'When anyone sins unintentionally[g] and does what is forbidden in any
of the LORD's commands[h]—

3" 'If the anointed priest[i] sins,[j] bringing guilt on the people, he must bring to
the LORD a young bull[k] without defect[l] as
a sin offering[m] for the sin he has committed.[n] 4He is to present the bull at the entrance to the Tent of Meeting before the
LORD.[o] He is to lay his hand on its head

3:1 [w]S Ex 12:5 **3:2** [x]S Ex 29:15; Nu 8:10 [y]S Lev 1:5 [z]S Ex 40:2 [a]S Ex 24:6 [b]Lev 17:6; Nu 18:17 [c]S Ex 29:20 **3:3** [d]S Ex 29:13 [e]S Ex 12:9 **3:4** [f]ver 10; Ex 29:13; Lev 4:9 **3:5** [g]Lev 7:29-34 [h]ver 11,16 [i]Ex 29:13,38-42; Nu 28:3-10 [j]S Lev 1:7 [k]S Lev 1:9 **3:6** [l]S ver 1; Lev 22:21; Nu 15:3,8 **3:7** [m]Lev 17:3; Nu 15:5; 28:5,7,8 [n]Lev 17:8-9; 1Ki 8:62 **3:8** [o]S Lev 1:5 **3:9** [p]Isa 34:6; Jer 46:10; Eze 39:19; Zep 1:7 **3:11** [q]S ver 5 [r]ver 16; Lev 21:6, 17; Nu 28:2 [s]Lev 9:18 **3:12** [t]S Lev 1:10; S 4:3 **3:13** [u]S Ex 24:6 [v]Lev 1:5 **3:15** [w]Lev 7:4 **3:16** [x]S ver 5; Lev 7:31 [y]S ver 11 [z]S Lev 1:9 [a]S Ge 4:4 [b]1Sa 2:16 **3:17** [c]S Ex 12:14; S 27:21 [d]S Ge 9:12 [e]S Ex 12:20 [f]Ge 9:4; Lev 7:25-26; 17:10-16; Dt 12:16; Ac 15:20 **4:2** [g]ver 13,27; Lev 5:15-18; 22:14; Nu 15:24-29; 35:11-15; Jos 20:3,9; Heb 9:7 [h]ver 22; Nu 15:22 **4:3** [i]S Ex 28:41 [j]S Ge 18:23 [k]ver 14; Lev 3:12; 8:14; 10:16; 16:3,5; Nu 15:27; Ps 66:15; Eze 43:19,23 [l]S Ex 12:5 [m]S ver 24; S Ex 30:10; Lev 5:6-13; 9:2-22; Heb 9:13-14 [n]ver 32 **4:4** [o]ver 15,24; Lev 1:3; Nu 8:12

---

the sacrifice, had fellowship with God and with the priest, who also ate part of the offering (7:14–15,31–34). This sacrifice—along with others—was offered by the thousands during the three annual festivals in Israel (see Ex 23:14–17; Nu 29:39) because multitudes of people came to the temple to worship and share in a communal meal. During the monarchy, the animals offered by the people were usually supplemented by large numbers given by the king. At the dedication of the temple, Solomon offered 20,000 cattle and 120,000 sheep and goats as fellowship offerings over a period of 14 days (1Ki 8:63–65).

3:2 *lay his hand on.* See notes on 1:3; Ex 29:10.

3:5 *on top of the burnt offering.* The burnt offerings for the nation as a whole were offered every morning and evening, and the fellowship offerings were offered on top of them.

3:9 *fat tail.* A breed of sheep still much used in the Middle East has a tail heavy with fat.

3:11,16 *on the altar as food.* Israelite sacrifices were not "food for the gods" (as in other ancient cultures; see Eze 16:20; cf. Ps 50:9–13) but were sometimes called "food" metaphorically (21:6,8,17,21; 22:25) in the sense that they were gifts to God and that he received them with delight.

3:17 *not eat any fat or any blood.* See note on 17:11.

4:2 *unintentionally.* See 5:15; contrast Nu 15:30–31. Four classes of people involved in committing unintentional sins are listed: (1) "the anointed priest" (vv. 3–12), (2) the "whole Israelite community" (vv. 13–21), (3) a "leader" (vv. 22–26) and (4) a "member of the community" (vv. 27–35). Heb 9:7 speaks of sins "committed in ignorance" in referring to the Day of Atonement.

4:3 *anointed priest.* The high priest (see 6:20,22). *sins.* All high priests sinned except the high priest Jesus Christ (Heb 5:1–3; 7:26–28). *on the people.* The relationship of the priests to the people was so intimate in Israel (as a nation consecrated to God) that the people became guilty when the priest sinned. *must.* Although the burnt, grain and fellowship offerings (chs. 1–3) were voluntary, the sin offering was compulsory (see vv. 14,23,28). *without defect.* A defective sacrifice could not be a substitute for a defective people. The final perfect sacrifice for the sins of God's people was the crucified Christ, who was without any moral defect (Heb 9:13–14; 1Pe 1:19). *sin offering.* See further priestly regulations in 6:24–30; Nu 15:22–29. As soon as an "anointed priest" (or a person from one of the other classes of people) became aware of unintentional sin, he was to bring his sin offering to the Lord. On the other hand, should the priest (or others) remain unaware of unintentional sin, this lack was atoned for on the Day of Atonement.

4:4 Three principles of atonement are found in this verse: (1) substitution ("present the bull"), (2) identification ("lay his hand on its head") and (3) the death of the substitute ("slaughter it").

NAME	OT REFERENCES	ELEMENTS	PURPOSE
BURNT OFFERING	Lev 1; 6:8-13; 8:18-21; 16:24	Bull, ram or male bird (dove or young pigeon for poor); wholly consumed; no defect	Voluntary act of worship; atonement for unintentional sin in general; expression of devotion, commitment and complete surrender to God
GRAIN OFFERING	Lev 2; 6:14-23	Grain, fine flour, olive oil, incense, baked bread (cakes or wafers), salt; no yeast or honey; accompanied burnt offering and fellowship offering (along with drink offering)	Voluntary act of worship; recognition of God's goodness and provisions; devotion to God
FELLOWSHIP OFFERING	Lev 3; 7:11-34	Any animal without defect from herd or flock; variety of breads	Voluntary act of worship; thanksgiving and fellowship (it included a communal meal)
SIN OFFERING	Lev 4:1-5:13; 6:24-30; 8:14-17; 16:3-22	1. Young bull: for high priest and congregation 2. Male goat: for leader 3. Female goat or lamb: for common person 4. Dove or pigeon: for the poor 5. Tenth of an ephah of fine flour: for the very poor	Mandatory atonement for specific unintentional sin; confession of sin; forgiveness of sin; cleansing from defilement
GUILT OFFERING	Lev 5:14-6:7; 7:1-6	Ram or lamb	Mandatory atonement for unintentional sin requiring restitution; cleansing from defilement; make restitution; pay 20% fine

When more than one kind of offering was presented (as in Nu 6:16, 17), the procedure was usually as follows: (1) sin offering or guilt offering, (2) burnt offering, (3) fellowship offering and grain offering (along with a drink offering). This sequence furnishes part of the spiritual significance of the sacrificial system. First, sin had to be dealt with (sin offering or guilt offering). Second, the worshiper committed himself completely to God (burnt offering and grain offering). Third, fellowship or communion between the Lord, the priest and the worshiper (fellowship offering) was established. To state it another way, there were sacrifices of expiation (sin offerings and guilt offerings), consecration (burnt offerings and grain offerings) and communion (fellowship offerings—these included vow offerings, thank offerings and freewill offerings).

and slaughter it before the LORD. [5]Then the anointed priest shall take some of the bull's blood[p] and carry it into the Tent of Meeting. [6]He is to dip his finger into the blood and sprinkle[q] some of it seven times before the LORD,[r] in front of the curtain of the sanctuary.[s] [7]The priest shall then put some of the blood on the horns[t] of the altar of fragrant incense that is before LORD in the Tent of Meeting. The rest of the bull's blood he shall pour out at the base of the altar[u] of burnt offering[v] at the entrance to the Tent of Meeting. [8]He shall remove all the fat[w] from the bull of the sin offering—the fat that covers the inner parts or is connected to them, [9]both kidneys with the fat on them near the loins, and the covering of the liver, which he will remove with the kidneys[x]— [10]just as the fat is removed from the ox[e][y] sacrificed as a fellowship offering.[f][z] Then the priest shall burn them on the altar of burnt offering.[a] [11]But the hide of the bull and all its flesh, as well as the head and legs, the inner parts and offal[b]— [12]that is, all the rest of the bull—he must take outside the camp[c] to a place ceremonially clean,[d] where the ashes[e] are thrown, and burn it[f] in a wood fire on the ash heap.[g]

[13]" 'If the whole Israelite community sins unintentionally[h] and does what is forbidden in any of the LORD's commands, even though the community is unaware of the matter, they are guilty. [14]When they become aware of the sin they committed,

the assembly must bring a young bull[i] as a sin offering[j] and present it before the Tent of Meeting. [15]The elders[k] of the community are to lay their hands[l] on the bull's head[m] before the LORD, and the bull shall be slaughtered before the LORD.[n] [16]Then the anointed priest is to take some of the bull's blood[o] into the Tent of Meeting. [17]He shall dip his finger into the blood and sprinkle[p] it before the LORD[q] seven times in front of the curtain. [18]He is to put some of the blood[r] on the horns of the altar that is before the LORD[s] in the Tent of Meeting. The rest of the blood he shall pour out at the base of the altar[t] of burnt offering at the entrance to the Tent of Meeting. [19]He shall remove all the fat[u] from it and burn it on the altar,[v] [20]and do with this bull just as he did with the bull for the sin offering. In this way the priest will make atonement[w] for them, and they will be forgiven.[x] [21]Then he shall take the bull outside the camp[y] and burn it as he burned the first bull. This is the sin offering for the community.[z]

[22]" 'When a leader[a] sins unintentionally[b] and does what is forbidden in any of the commands of the LORD his God, he is guilty. [23]When he is made aware of the sin he committed, he must bring as his offering a male goat[c] without defect. [24]He is to

---

4:5 *p*ver 16; Lev 16:14
4:6 *q*Ex 24:8 *r*ver 17; Lev 16:14,19 *s*S Ex 25:8
4:7 *t*S Ex 27:2 *u*ver 34; S Ex 29:12; Lev 8:15 *v*ver 18, 30; Lev 5:9; 9:9; 16:18
4:8 *w*ver 19
4:9 *x*S Lev 3:4
4:10 *y*Lev 9:4 *z*S Ex 32:6 *a*S Ex 29:13
4:11 *b*Ex 29:14; Lev 8:17; 9:11; Nu 19:5
4:12 *c*S Ex 29:14; Lev 8:17; 9:11; Heb 13:11 *d*Lev 6:11; 10:14; Nu 19:9 *e*S Lev 1:16 *f*Lev 6:30 *g*Lev 16:3
4:13 *h*S ver 2
4:14 *i*S ver 3 /Nu 15:24
4:15 *k*S Ex 3:16; S 19:7 /2Ch 29:23 *m*S Ex 29:10; Lev 8:14,22; Nu 8:10 *n*S ver 4
4:16 *o*S ver 5
4:17 *p*Nu 19:4, 18 *q*S ver 6
4:18 *r*Lev 8:15; 17:6; 2Ch 29:22 *s*ver 7; Lev 6:30; 10:18 *t*Lev 5:9
4:19 *u*ver 8 *v*ver 26
4:20 *w*S Ex 29:36; S 32:30; S Ro 3:25; Heb 10:10-12 *x*ver 26,31,35; Nu 15:25
4:21 *y*S ver 12 *z*Lev 16:5,15;

2Ch 29:21 **4:22** *a*Nu 31:13 *b*ver 2 **4:23** *c*S ver 3; S Lev 1:10

e10 The Hebrew word can include both male and female.
f10 Traditionally *peace offering;* also in verses 26, 31 and 35

4:5 *blood.* See note on 17:11. There were two types of sin offerings. The first (vv. 3–21) and more important involved sprinkling the blood in the tabernacle in front of the inner curtain or, in the case of the solemn Day of Atonement (ch. 16), on and in front of the atonement cover (traditionally "mercy seat") itself. This type of sin offering was not eaten. The fat, kidneys and covering of the liver were burned on the great altar, but all the rest was burned outside the camp (v. 12). Heb 13:11–13 clearly draws the parallel to our sin offering, Jesus, who suffered outside the city gate. This type of sin offering was offered by and for a priest or by the elders for the whole community. In general, the animal to be sacrificed was a young bull, but on the Day of Atonement the sin offering was to be a goat (16:9).

The second type of sin offering (4:22–5:13) was for a leader of the nation or a private individual. Some of the blood was applied to the horns of the great altar, the rest poured out at its base. The fat, etc., was burned on the altar, but the rest of the offering was given to the priest and his male relatives as food to be eaten in a holy place (6:29–30; see 10:16–20). The sin offering brought by a private person was to be a female goat or lamb. If the person was poor, he could bring a dove or young pigeon (5:7–8; 12:6,8; cf. Lk 2:24), or even about two quarts of flour (5:11). The offering included confession (5:5) and the symbolic transfer of guilt by laying hands on the sacrifice (v. 29; 16:21). Then the priest who offered the sacrifice made atonement for the sin, and the Lord promised forgiveness (5:13). By bringing such a sin

offering, a faithful Israelite under conviction of sin sought restoration of fellowship with God.
4:6 *finger.* The right forefinger (see 14:16). *seven.* The number was symbolic of perfection and completeness (see note on Ge 5:5). *curtain.* The great curtain that separated the Holy Place from the Most Holy Place (Ex 26:33).
4:7 *horns.* The four horns of the altar (see Ex 30:1–3) were symbols of the atoning power of the sin offering (Ex 30:10).
4:8–10 See 3:3–5.
4:12 *outside the camp.* See note on 13:45–46. So also Jesus was crucified outside Jerusalem (Heb 13:11–13; see 9:11; 16:26–28; Nu 19:3; Eze 43:21). *ceremonially clean.* The distinction between clean and unclean was a matter of ritual or religious purity, not a concern for physical cleanliness (see chs. 11–15 for examples; see also Mk 7:1–4). *burn.* Since the sins of the offerer were symbolically transferred to the sacrificial bull, the bull had to be entirely destroyed and not thrown on the ash pile of 1:16.
4:15 *elders.* See note on Ex 3:16.
4:18 *altar.* Of incense (see v. 7).
4:20 *sin offering.* The offering of the priest who had sinned (v. 3). *will be forgiven.* In 4:20–6:7 this is a key phrase, occurring nine times and referring to forgiveness by God.
4:23 *male goat.* Less valuable animals were sacrificed for those with lesser standing in the community or of lesser economic means. Thus a bull was required for the high priest (v. 3) and the whole community (v. 14), but a male goat for a civic leader (v. 23) and a female goat (v. 28) or lamb (v. 32)

lay his hand on the goat's head and slaughter it at the place where the burnt offering is slaughtered before the LORD. *d* It is a sin offering. *e* 25Then the priest shall take some of the blood of the sin offering with his finger and put it on the horns of the altar *f* of burnt offering and pour out the rest of the blood at the base of the altar. *g* 26He shall burn all the fat on the altar as he burned the fat of the fellowship offering. In this way the priest will make atonement *h* for the man's sin, and he will be forgiven. *i*

27" 'If a member of the community sins unintentionally *j* and does what is forbidden in any of the LORD's commands, he is guilty. 28When he is made aware of the sin he committed, he must bring as his offering *k* for the sin he committed a female goat *l* without defect. 29He is to lay his hand on the head *m* of the sin offering *n* and slaughter it at the place of the burnt offering. *o* 30Then the priest is to take some of the blood with his finger and put it on the horns of the altar of burnt offering *p* and pour out the rest of the blood at the base of the altar. 31He shall remove all the fat, just as the fat is removed from the fellowship offering, and the priest shall burn it on the altar *q* as an aroma pleasing to the LORD. *r* In this way the priest will make atonement *s* for him, and he will be forgiven. *t*

32" 'If he brings a lamb *u* as his sin offering, he is to bring a female without defect. *v* 33He is to lay his hand on its head and slaughter it *w* for a sin offering *x* at the place where the burnt offering is slaughtered. *y* 34Then the priest shall take some of the blood of the sin offering with his finger and put it on the horns of the altar of burnt offering and pour out the rest of the blood at the base of the altar. *z* 35He shall remove all the fat, just as the fat is removed from the lamb of the fellowship offering, and the priest shall burn it on the altar *a* on top of the offerings made to the LORD by fire. In this way the priest will make atonement for him for the sin he has committed, and he will be forgiven.

5 " 'If a person sins because he does not speak up when he hears a public charge to testify *b* regarding something he has seen or learned about, he will be held responsible. *c*

2 " 'Or if a person touches anything ceremonially unclean—whether the carcasses of unclean wild animals or of unclean livestock or of unclean creatures that move along the ground *d*—even though he is unaware of it, he has become unclean *e* and is guilty.

3 " 'Or if he touches human uncleanness *f*—anything that would make him unclean *g*—even though he is unaware of it, when he learns of it he will be guilty.

4 " 'Or if a person thoughtlessly takes an oath *h* to do anything, whether good or evil *i*—in any matter one might carelessly swear about—even though he is unaware of it, in any case when he learns of it he will be guilty.

5 " 'When anyone is guilty in any of these ways, he must confess *j* in what way he has sinned 6and, as a penalty for the sin he has committed, he must bring to the LORD a female lamb or goat *k* from the flock as a sin offering; *l* and the priest shall make atonement *m* for him for his sin.

7 " 'If he cannot afford *n* a lamb, *o* he is to bring two doves or two young pigeons *p* to the LORD as a penalty for his sin—one for a sin offering and the other for a burnt offering. 8He is to bring them to the priest, who shall first offer the one for the sin offering. He is to wring its head from its neck, *q* not severing it completely, *r* 9and is to sprinkle *s* some of the blood of the sin offering against the side of the altar; *t* the rest of the blood must be drained out at the base of the altar. *u* It is a sin offering. 10The priest shall then offer the other as a burnt offering in the prescribed way *v* and make atonement *w* for him for the sin he has committed, and he will be forgiven. *x*

11" 'If, however, he cannot afford *y* two doves or two young pigeons, *z* he is to bring as an offering for his sin a tenth of an

---

4:24 *d* S ver 4
e S ver 3; Lev 6:25
4:25 *f* Lev 16:18;
Eze 43:20,22
g Lev 9:9
4:26 *h* S Ex 32:30
i Lev 5:10; 12:8
4:27 *j* S ver 2
4:28 *k* Lev 5:6;
Eze 40:39; 44:27
l S ver 3;
S Lev 1:10
4:29 *m* ver 4,24
n S Lev 1:4
o S Ge 8:20
4:30 *p* S ver 7
4:31 *q* ver 35
r S Ge 8:21
s Lev 1:4 *t* S ver 20
4:32 *u* Ex 29:38;
Lev 9:3; 14:10
v Lev 1:3
4:33 *w* Lev 1:5
x Lev 1:4 *y* ver 29
4:34 *z* S ver 7
4:35 *a* ver 31

5:1 *b* Pr 29:24;
Mt 26:63 *c* ver
17; S Ex 28:38;
Lev 7:18; 17:16;
19:8; 20:17;
24:15; Nu 5:31;
9:13; 15:31;
19:20; 30:15
5:2 *d* Lev 11:11,
24-14,30; Nu
Isa 52:11 *e* ver 3;
Lev 7:21; 11:8,
24; 13:45;
Nu 19:22;
Job 15:16;
Ps 51:5; Isa 6:5;
64:6; Eze 36:17;
Hag 2:13
5:3 *f* Nu 19:11-16
g Lev 7:20; 11:25;
14:19; 21:1;
Nu 5:2; 9:6;
19:7; Eze 44:25
5:4 *h* Nu 30:6,8
i Isa 41:23
5:5 *j* Lev 16:21;
26:40; Nu 5:7;
Jos 7:19;
1Ki 8:47;
Pr 28:13
5:6 *k* S Lev 1:10;
S 4:3 *l* S Lev 4:28
m S Ex 32:30
5:7 *n* ver 11;
Lev 12:8; 14:21;
27:8 *o* Lev 12:8;
14:22,30
p S Ge 15:9;
Nu 6:10
5:8 *q* Lev 1:15
r Lev 1:17
5:9 *s* S Ex 24:6
t Lev 1:15
u S Lev 4:7
5:10
v Lev 1:14-17;
1Ch 15:13
w S Ex 32:30
x S Lev 4:26
5:11 *y* S ver 7
z S Ge 15:9

---

for an ordinary Israelite. If an offerer was too poor, then doves and pigeons were sufficient (5:7) or even a handful of fine flour (5:11–12).

4:25 *priest.* The priest who officiated for the civil authority or the lay person (see vv. 30,34).

4:28 *female goat.* See note on v. 23.

4:29 *lay his hand on.* See notes on 1:3; Ex 29:10.

4:30 *horns.* See note on v. 7.

4:32 *lamb . . . female.* See note on v. 23.

4:35 *fat . . . of the fellowship offering.* See 3:3–5.

5:1–4 Four examples of the unintentional sins (see 4:2–3,

13,22,27) the sin offering covers.

5:2 *ceremonially unclean.* See note on 4:12.

5:3 *human uncleanness.* See chs. 11–15.

5:5 *confess.* The offerer had to acknowledge his sin to God in order to receive forgiveness.

5:7 *two doves . . . pigeons.* See note on 4:23.

5:11 *fine flour.* See note on 4:23. Although no blood was used with a flour offering, it was offered "on top of the offerings made to the LORD by fire" (v. 12). Heb 9:22 may refer to such a situation.

ephah[g][a] of fine flour[b] for a sin offering. He must not put oil or incense on it, because it is a sin offering. [12]He is to bring it to the priest, who shall take a handful of it as a memorial portion[c] and burn it on the altar[d] on top of the offerings made to the LORD by fire. It is a sin offering. [13]In this way the priest will make atonement[e] for him for any of these sins he has committed, and he will be forgiven. The rest of the offering will belong to the priest,[f] as in the case of the grain offering.[g]' "

The Guilt Offering

[14]The LORD said to Moses: [15]"When a person commits a violation and sins unintentionally[h] in regard to any of the LORD's holy things, he is to bring to the LORD as a penalty[i] a ram[j] from the flock, one without defect and of the proper value in silver, according to the sanctuary shekel.[h][k] It is a guilt offering.[l] [16]He must make restitution[m] for what he has failed to do in regard to the holy things, add a fifth of the value[n] to that and give it all to the priest, who will make atonement for him with the ram as a guilt offering, and he will be forgiven.

[17]"If a person sins and does what is forbidden in any of the LORD's commands, even though he does not know it,[o] he is guilty and will be held responsible.[p] [18]He is to bring to the priest as a guilt offering[q] a ram from the flock, one without defect and of the proper value. In this way the priest will make atonement for him for the wrong he has committed unintentionally, and he will be forgiven.[r] [19]It is a guilt offering; he has been guilty of[i] wrongdoing against the LORD."[s]

6 The LORD said to Moses: [2]"If anyone sins and is unfaithful to the LORD[t] by deceiving his neighbor[u] about something entrusted to him or left in his care[v] or stolen, or if he cheats[w] him, [3]or if he finds lost property and lies about it,[x] or if he swears falsely,[y] or if he commits any such sin that people may do— [4]when he thus sins and becomes guilty, he must return[z] what he has stolen or taken by extortion,

or what was entrusted to him, or the lost property he found, [5]or whatever it was he swore falsely about. He must make restitution[a] in full, add a fifth of the value to it and give it all to the owner on the day he presents his guilt offering.[b] [6]And as a penalty he must bring to the priest, that is, to the LORD, his guilt offering,[c] a ram from the flock, one without defect and of the proper value.[d] [7]In this way the priest will make atonement[e] for him before the LORD, and he will be forgiven for any of these things he did that made him guilty."

The Burnt Offering

[8]The LORD said to Moses: [9]"Give Aaron and his sons this command: 'These are the regulations for the burnt offering[f]: The burnt offering is to remain on the altar hearth throughout the night, till morning, and the fire must be kept burning on the altar.[g] [10]The priest shall then put on his linen clothes,[h] with linen undergarments next to his body,[i] and shall remove the ashes[j] of the burnt offering that the fire has consumed on the altar and place them beside the altar. [11]Then he is to take off these clothes and put on others, and carry the ashes outside the camp to a place that is ceremonially clean.[k] [12]The fire on the altar must be kept burning; it must not go out. Every morning the priest is to add firewood[l] and arrange the burnt offering on the fire and burn the fat[m] of the fellowship offerings[i][n] on it. [13]The fire must be kept burning on the altar continuously; it must not go out.

The Grain Offering

[14]" 'These are the regulations for the grain offering:[o] Aaron's sons are to bring it before the LORD, in front of the altar. [15]The priest is to take a handful of fine flour and oil, together with all the incense[p] on the grain offering,[q] and burn the memorial

Cross references (center column)

5:11 [a]S Ex 16:36
[b]S Lev 2:1
5:12 [c]S Lev 2:2
[d]Lev 2:9
5:13 [e]S Ex 32:30
[f]Lev 2:3
[g]S Ex 29:41
5:15 [h]S Lev 4:2
[i]Lev 22:14
[j]S Ex 29:3;
Lev 6:6; Nu 5:8;
6:14; 15:6; 28:11
[k]S Ex 30:13 [l]ver
16,18; Lev 6:5,6;
7:1,7;
14:12-17; 19:21,
22; Nu 6:12;
18:9; 1Sa 6:3;
Ezr 10:19;
Isa 53:10
5:16 [m]Lev 6:4
[n]ver 15;
Lev 27:13;
Nu 5:7
5:17 [o]ver 15
[p]S ver 1
5:18 [q]Lev 6:6;
14:12 [r]S ver 15
5:19 [s]2Ki 12:16
6:2 [t]Nu 5:6;
Ps 73:27; Ac 5:4;
Col 3:9
[u]Lev 19:11;
Jer 9:4,5
[v]S Ex 22:7
[w]S Ge 31:7
6:3 [x]S Ex 23:4
[y]S Ex 22:11
6:4 [z]Lev 5:16;
Eze 33:15;
S Lk 19:8

6:5 [a]Nu 5:7
[b]S Lev 5:15
6:6 [c]S Lev 5:15
[d]Nu 5:8
6:7 [e]S Ex 32:30
6:9 [f]Lev 7:37
[g]ver 12
6:10 [h]S Ex 39:27
[i]Ex 28:39-42,43;
39:28 [j]S Lev 1:16
6:11 [k]S Lev 4:12
6:12 [l]S Lev 1:7
[m]S Ex 29:13
[n]S Ex 32:6
6:14 [o]S Lev 2:1;
Nu 6:15; 15:4;
28:13
6:15 [p]S Lev 2:1
[q]Lev 2:9

Footnotes

[g]11 That is, probably about 2 quarts (about 2 liters)
[h]15 That is, about 2/5 ounce (about 11.5 grams)
[i]19 Or has made full expiation for his
[i]12 Traditionally peace offerings

5:15 *guilt offering.* See further priestly regulations in 7:1–6 (see also Isa 53:10). Traditionally called the "trespass offering," it was very similar to the sin offering (cf. 7:7), and the Hebrew words for the two were apparently sometimes interchanged. The major difference between the guilt and sin offerings was that the guilt offering was brought in cases where restitution for the sin was possible and therefore required (v. 16). Thus in cases of theft and cheating (6:2–5) the stolen property had to be returned along with 20 percent indemnity. By contrast, the sin offering was prescribed in cases of sin where no restitution was possible. The animal sacrificed as a guilt offering was always a ram.

6:3 *lost property.* See Dt 22:1–3.
6:6 *to the priest, that is, to the LORD.* Sacrifices were brought to the Lord, but priests were his authorized representatives.
6:8–7:36 Further regulations concerning the sacrifices, dealing mainly with the portions to be eaten by the priests or, in the case of the fellowship offering, by the one offering the sacrifice.
6:9 *burnt offering.* See ch. 1; Nu 15:1–16 and notes.
6:13 The perpetual fire on the altar represented uninterrupted offering to and appeal to God on behalf of Israel.
6:14 *grain offering.* See ch. 2 and notes.

portion[r] on the altar as an aroma pleasing to the LORD. [16]Aaron and his sons[s] shall eat the rest[t] of it, but it is to be eaten without yeast[u] in a holy place;[v] they are to eat it in the courtyard[w] of the Tent of Meeting.[x] [17]It must not be baked with yeast; I have given it as their share[y] of the offerings made to me by fire.[z] Like the sin offering and the guilt offering, it is most holy.[a] [18]Any male descendant of Aaron may eat it.[b] It is his regular share[c] of the offerings made to the LORD by fire for the generations to come.[d] Whatever touches them will become holy.[k] [e'] "

[19]The LORD also said to Moses, [20]"This is the offering Aaron and his sons are to bring to the LORD on the day he[1] is anointed:[f] a tenth of an ephah[m][g] of fine flour[h] as a regular grain offering,[i] half of it in the morning and half in the evening. [21]Prepare it with oil on a griddle;[j] bring it well-mixed and present the grain offering broken[n] in pieces as an aroma pleasing to the LORD. [22]The son who is to succeed him as anointed priest[k] shall prepare it. It is the LORD's regular share and is to be burned completely.[l] [23]Every grain offering of a priest shall be burned completely; it must not be eaten."

The Sin Offering

[24]The LORD said to Moses, [25]"Say to Aaron and his sons: 'These are the regulations for the sin offering:[m] The sin offering is to be slaughtered before the LORD[n] in the place[o] the burnt offering is slaughtered; it is most holy. [26]The priest who offers it shall eat it; it is to be eaten in a holy place,[p] in the courtyard[q] of the Tent of Meeting.[r] [27]Whatever touches any of the flesh will become holy,[s] and if any of the blood is spattered on a garment, you must wash it in a holy place. [28]The clay pot[t] the meat is cooked in must be broken; but if it is cooked in a bronze pot, the pot is to be scoured and rinsed with water. [29]Any male in a priest's family may eat it;[u] it is most holy.[v] [30]But any sin offering whose blood is brought into the Tent of Meeting to make atonement[w] in the Holy

Place[x] must not be eaten; it must be burned.[y]

The Guilt Offering

7 " 'These are the regulations for the guilt offering,[z] which is most holy: [2]The guilt offering is to be slaughtered in the place where the burnt offering is slaughtered, and its blood is to be sprinkled against the altar on all sides. [3]All its fat[a] shall be offered: the fat tail and the fat that covers the inner parts, [4]both kidneys with the fat on them near the loins, and the covering of the liver, which is to be removed with the kidneys.[b] [5]The priest shall burn them on the altar[c] as an offering made to the LORD by fire. It is a guilt offering. [6]Any male in a priest's family may eat it,[d] but it must be eaten in a holy place; it is most holy.[e]

[7] " 'The same law applies to both the sin offering[f] and the guilt offering:[g] They belong to the priest[h] who makes atonement with them.[i] [8]The priest who offers a burnt offering for anyone may keep its hide[j] for himself. [9]Every grain offering baked in an oven[k] or cooked in a pan[l] or on a griddle[m] belongs to the priest who offers it, [10]and every grain offering, whether mixed with oil or dry, belongs equally to all the sons of Aaron.

The Fellowship Offering

[11]" 'These are the regulations for the fellowship offering[o] a person may present to the LORD:

[12]" 'If he offers it as an expression of thankfulness, then along with this thank offering[n] he is to offer cakes[o] of bread made without yeast[p] and mixed with oil, wafers[q] made without yeast and spread with oil,[r] and cakes of fine flour well-kneaded and mixed with oil. [13]Along with his fellowship offering of thanksgiving[s] he is to present an offering with cakes of

---

Cross-references (center column):

6:15 [r]S Lev 2:2
6:16 [s]S Lev 2:3
[t]Eze 44:29
[u]S Lev 2:11 [v]ver 26; S Ex 29:11; Lev 10:13; 16:24; 24:9; Nu 18:10
[w]S Ex 27:9
[x]Ex 29:31; Lev 8:31
6:17 [y]Nu 5:9
[z]Ex 29:28; Lev 7:7; 10:16-18
[a]ver 29; Ex 40:10; Lev 10:12; 21:22; 24:9; Nu 18:9,10
6:18 [b]ver 29; Lev 2:3; 7:6; Nu 18:9-10
[c]Nu 5:9
[d]S Ge 9:12
[e]S Ex 30:29
6:20 [f]S Ex 28:41
[g]S Ex 16:36
[h]Nu 5:15; 28:5
[i]Ex 29:2; Lev 23:13; Nu 4:16
6:21 [j]Lev 2:5
6:22
[k]S Ex 28:41; S 29:30 [l]S Lev 1:9
6:25
[m]S Ex 30:10; S Lev 4:24
[n]S Lev 1:3
[o]S Lev 29:11
6:26 [p]S ver 16
[q]S Ex 27:9
[r]S Ex 27:21; S 40:2
6:27 [s]S Ex 29:37; Lev 10:10; Eze 44:19; 46:20; Hag 2:12
6:28 [t]Lev 11:33; 15:12; Nu 19:15
6:29 [u]S ver 18
[v]S ver 17; Eze 42:13
6:30 [w]Eze 45:15

[x]S Lev 4:18
[y]Lev 4:12
7:1 [z]S Lev 5:15; Eze 40:39
7:3 [a]S Ex 29:13
7:4 [b]Lev 3:15
7:5 [c]S Ex 29:13
7:6 [d]S Lev 6:18
[e]Eze 42:13
7:7 [f]S Ex 30:10
[g]S Lev 5:15 [h]ver 6; Lev 2:3; 6:17, 26; 14:13; 2Ki 12:16; 1Co 9:13; 10:18
[i]Nu 5:8
7:8 [j]Lev 1:6
7:9 [k]S Lev 2:4
[l]Lev 2:7
[m]S Lev 2:5
7:12 [n]ver 13,15; Lev 22:29; Ps 50:14; 54:6; 107:22; 116:17; Jer 33:11
[o]Jer 44:19
[p]Nu 6:19

[q]S Lev 2:4 [r]S Lev 2:1 **7:13** [s]S ver 12; S Ex 34:22

[k]18 Or Whoever touches them must be holy; similarly in verse 27 [l]20 Or each [m]20 That is, probably about 2 quarts (about 2 liters) [n]21 The meaning of the Hebrew for this word is uncertain. [o]11 Traditionally peace offering; also in verses 13-37

6:25 *sin offering.* See 4:1–5:13 and notes.
6:28 *clay.* Ordinary kitchen utensils and domestic ware were made of clay, usually fired in a kiln and often painted or burnished.
7:2 *guilt offering.* See 5:14–6:7 and notes. *place.* On the north side of the altar of burnt offering in front of the tabernacle (1:11).
7:3 *fat tail.* See note on 3:9.
7:7–10 See Nu 18:8–20; 1Co 9:13.
7:11–36 This section supplements ch. 3, adding regula-

tions about (1) three types of fellowship offerings (thank, vv. 12–15; vow, v. 16; freewill, v. 16), (2) prohibition of eating fat and blood (vv. 22–27) and (3) the priests' share (vv. 28–36).
7:12–15 Thank offerings were given in gratitude for deliverance from sickness (Ps 116:17), trouble (Ps 107:22) or death (Ps 56:12), or for a blessing received.
7:13 *with yeast.* This regulation was not against the prohibition of 2:11 or Ex 23:18 since the offering here was not burned on the altar.

bread made with yeast.[t] [14]He is to bring one of each kind as an offering, a contribution to the LORD; it belongs to the priest who sprinkles the blood of the fellowship offerings. [15]The meat of his fellowship offering of thanksgiving must be eaten on the day it is offered; he must leave none of it till morning.[u]

[16]" 'If, however, his offering is the result of a vow[v] or is a freewill offering,[w] the sacrifice shall be eaten on the day he offers it, but anything left over may be eaten on the next day.[x] [17]Any meat of the sacrifice left over till the third day must be burned up.[y] [18]If any meat of the fellowship offering[z] is eaten on the third day, it will not be accepted.[a] It will not be credited[b] to the one who offered it, for it is impure; the person who eats any of it will be held responsible.[c]

[19]" 'Meat that touches anything ceremonially unclean must not be eaten; it must be burned up. As for other meat, anyone ceremonially clean may eat it. [20]But if anyone who is unclean[d] eats any meat of the fellowship offering belonging to the LORD, that person must be cut off from his people.[e] [21]If anyone touches something unclean[f]—whether human uncleanness or an unclean animal or any unclean, detestable thing—and then eats any of the meat of the fellowship offering belonging to the LORD, that person must be cut off from his people.' "

Eating Fat and Blood Forbidden

[22]The LORD said to Moses, [23]"Say to the Israelites: 'Do not eat any of the fat of cattle, sheep or goats.[g] [24]The fat of an animal found dead or torn by wild animals[h] may be used for any other purpose, but you must not eat it. [25]Anyone who eats the fat

of an animal from which an offering by fire may be[p] made to the LORD must be cut off from his people. [26]And wherever you live, you must not eat the blood[i] of any bird or animal. [27]If anyone eats blood,[j] that person must be cut off from his people.' "

The Priests' Share

[28]The LORD said to Moses, [29]"Say to the Israelites: 'Anyone who brings a fellowship offering to the LORD is to bring part of it as his sacrifice to the LORD. [30]With his own hands he is to bring the offering made to the LORD by fire; he is to bring the fat, together with the breast, and wave the breast before the LORD as a wave offering.[k] [31]The priest shall burn the fat on the altar,[l] but the breast belongs to Aaron and his sons.[m] [32]You are to give the right thigh of your fellowship offerings to the priest as a contribution.[n] [33]The son of Aaron who offers the blood and the fat of the fellowship offering shall have the right thigh as his share. [34]From the fellowship offerings of the Israelites, I have taken the breast that is waved and the thigh[o] that is presented and have given them to Aaron the priest and his sons[p] as their regular share from the Israelites.' "

[35]This is the portion of the offerings made to the LORD by fire that were allotted to Aaron and his sons on the day they were presented to serve the LORD as priests. [36]On the day they were anointed,[q] the LORD commanded that the Israelites give this to them as their regular share for the generations to come.

[37]These, then, are the regulations for the burnt offering,[r] the grain offering,[s] the sin offering, the guilt offering, the ordination

Cross references (center column)

7:13 [r]Lev 23:17; Am 4:5
7:15 [u]S Ex 12:10
7:16 [v]S Ge 28:20; S Lev 1:2; Dt 23:21-23
[w]Ex 35:29; Lev 22:18,21; 23:38; Nu 15:3; 29:39; Dt 12:6; Ps 54:6; Eze 46:12
[x]Lev 19:5-8
7:17 [y]Ex 12:10; Lev 19:6
7:18 [z]2Ch 33:16
[a]Lev 19:7
[b]Nu 18:27
[c]S Lev 5:1
7:20 [d]S Lev 5:3
[e]S Ge 17:14; Lev 22:3-7
7:21 [f]S Lev 5:2
7:23 [g]Lev 17:3; Dt 14:4
7:24 [h]S Ex 22:31

7:26 [i]S Ge 9:4
7:27 [j]S Ge 9:4
7:30 [k]S Ex 29:24
7:31 [l]S Ex 29:13
[m]S Ex 29:27
7:32 [n]Ex 29:27; Lev 10:14,15; Nu 5:9; 6:20; 18:18
7:34 [o]Ex 29:22; Lev 10:15; Nu 6:20; 1Sa 9:24
[p]S Ex 29:27
7:36 [q]Lev 8:12, 30
7:37 [r]Lev 6:9
[s]Lev 6:14

[p]25 Or fire is

7:15–18 See 19:5–8. All meat had to be eaten promptly (in the case of the thank offering on the same day, and in the case of the vow and freewill offerings within two days). One reason may have been that in Canaan meat spoiled quickly and thus became ceremonially impure (v. 18) because it was not then perfect (1:3; see 21:16–23). The prohibition applied also to the Passover (Ex 12:10).

7:16 vow. See 22:18–23. A vow was a solemn promise to offer a gift to God in response to a divine deliverance or blessing. Such vows often accompanied prayers for deliverance or blessing (see note on Ps 7:17). freewill offering. See 22:18–23.

7:19 ceremonially unclean. See note on 4:12.

7:20 cut off from his people. Removed from the covenant people through direct divine judgment (Ge 17:14), or (as here and in vv. 21,25,27; 17:4,9–10,14; 18:29; 19:8; 20:3,5–6,17–18; 23:29) through execution (see, e.g., 20:2–3; Ex 31:14), or possibly sometimes through banishment.

7:21 detestable. The penalty for doing things that were

abominable in the Lord's eyes was severe (see note on v. 20; see also 18:29; 20:13).

7:22–27 See note on 17:11.

7:23 fat. The prohibition of fat for food was as strict as that of blood, but the reason was different. The fat of the fellowship offerings was the Lord's and was to be burned on the altar. There was no explicit prohibition of eating the fat of hunted animals like the gazelle or deer, but probably that was included (see 3:17; Dt 12:15–22).

7:26 not eat the blood. See note on 17:11; see also 3:17; 19:26; Ge 9:4–6; Dt 12:16,23–25; 15:23; 1Sa 14:32–34; Eze 33:25.

7:28–36 See 10:12–15; Nu 18:8–20; Dt 18:1–5.

7:30–32 breast . . . right thigh. The breast and right thigh given to the priest were first presented to the Lord with gestures described as waving the breast and presenting the thigh (v. 34). See 8:25–29; 9:21; 10:14–15; Ex 29:26–27; Nu 6:20; 18:11,18.

7:37–38 A summary of chs. 1–7.

7:37 ordination offering. See 8:14–36; Ex 29:1–35.

offering[t] and the fellowship offering, [38]which the LORD gave Moses[u] on Mount Sinai[v] on the day he commanded the Israelites to bring their offerings to the LORD,[w] in the Desert of Sinai.

The Ordination of Aaron and His Sons

8:1–36pp — Ex 29:1–37

8 The LORD said to Moses, [2]"Bring Aaron and his sons,[x] their garments,[y] the anointing oil,[z] the bull for the sin offering,[a] the two rams[b] and the basket containing bread made without yeast,[c] [3]and gather the entire assembly[d] at the entrance to the Tent of Meeting." [4]Moses did as the LORD commanded him, and the assembly gathered at the entrance to the Tent of Meeting.

[5]Moses said to the assembly, "This is what the LORD has commanded to be done.[e]" [6]Then Moses brought Aaron and his sons forward and washed them with water.[f] [7]He put the tunic on Aaron, tied the sash around him, clothed him with the robe and put the ephod on him. He also tied the ephod to him by its skillfully woven waistband; so it was fastened on him.[g] [8]He placed the breastpiece[h] on him and put the Urim and Thummim[i] in the breastpiece. [9]Then he placed the turban[j] on Aaron's head and set the gold plate, the sacred diadem,[k] on the front of it, as the LORD commanded Moses.[l]

[10]Then Moses took the anointing oil[m] and anointed[n] the tabernacle[o] and everything in it, and so consecrated them. [11]He sprinkled some of the oil on the altar seven times, anointing the altar and all its utensils and the basin with its stand, to consecrate them.[p] [12]He poured some of the anointing oil on Aaron's head and anointed[q] him to consecrate him.[r] [13]Then he brought Aaron's sons[s] forward, put tunics[t] on them, tied sashes around them and put headbands on them, as the LORD commanded Moses.[u]

[14]He then presented the bull[v] for the sin offering,[w] and Aaron and his sons laid their hands on its head.[x] [15]Moses slaughtered the bull and took some of the blood,[y] and with his finger he put it on all the horns of the altar[z] to purify the altar. [a] He poured out the rest of the blood at the base of the altar. So he consecrated it to make atonement for it.[b] [16]Moses also took all the fat around the inner parts, the covering of the liver, and both kidneys and their fat, and burned it on the altar. [17]But the bull with its hide and its flesh and its offal[c] he burned up outside the camp,[d] as the LORD commanded Moses.

[18]He then presented the ram[e] for the burnt offering, and Aaron and his sons laid their hands on its head. [19]Then Moses slaughtered the ram and sprinkled the blood against the altar on all sides. [20]He cut the ram into pieces and burned the head, the pieces and the fat.[f] [21]He washed the inner parts and the legs with water and burned the whole ram on the altar as a burnt offering, a pleasing aroma, an offering made to the LORD by fire, as the LORD commanded Moses.

[22]He then presented the other ram, the ram for the ordination,[g] and Aaron and his sons laid their hands on its head.[h] [23]Moses slaughtered the ram and took some of its blood and put it on the lobe of Aaron's right ear, on the thumb of his right hand and on the big toe of his right foot.[i] [24]Moses also brought Aaron's sons forward and put some of the blood on the lobes of their right ears, on the thumbs of their right hands and on the big toes of their right feet. Then he sprinkled blood against the altar on all sides.[j] [25]He took the fat[k], the fat tail, all the fat around the inner parts, the covering of the liver, both kidneys and their fat and the right thigh. [26]Then from the basket of bread made without yeast, which was before the LORD, he took a cake of bread, and one made with oil, and a wafer;[l] he put these on the fat portions and on the right thigh. [27]He put all these in the hands of Aaron and his sons and waved them before the LORD [m] as

7:37 [t]S Ex 29:31
7:38 [u]Lev 26:46; Nu 36:13; Dt 4:5; 29:1 [v]S Ex 19:11 [w]S Lev 1:2
8:2 [x]S Ex 28:1; S Lev 1:5 [y]Ex 28:2,4,43; S 39:27 [z]Ex 30:23-25,30 [a]S Ex 30:10 [b]ver 18,22 [c]Ex 29:2-3
8:3 [d]Nu 8:9
8:5 [e]Ex 29:1
8:6 [f]S Ex 29:4; S 30:19;
S Ac 22:16
8:7 [g]Ex 28:4
8:8 [h]S Ex 25:7 [i]S Ex 28:30
8:9 [j]S Ex 39:28 [k]S Ex 28:36 [l]S Ex 28:2; Lev 21:10
8:10 [m]ver 2 [n]S Ex 30:26 [o]S Ex 26:1
8:11 [p]S Ex 30:29
8:12 [q]S Lev 7:36 [r]S Ex 30:30
8:13 [s]S Ex 28:40 [t]S Ex 28:4,39; 39:27 [u]Lev 21:10
8:14 [v]S Lev 4:3

[w]S Ex 30:10 [x]S Lev 4:15
8:15 [y]S Lev 4:18 [z]S Lev 4:7 [a]Heb 9:22 [b]Eze 43:20
8:17 [c]S Lev 4:11 [d]S Lev 4:12
8:18 [e]S ver 2
8:20 [f]S Lev 1:8
8:22 [g]S ver 2 [h]S Lev 4:15
8:23 [i]Lev 14:14, 25
8:24 [j]Heb 9:18-22
8:25 [k]Lev 3:3-5
8:26 [l]S Lev 2:4
8:27 [m]Nu 5:25

8:2 *their garments.* See Ex 39:1–31; 40:12–16. The garments that the high priest was to wear when he ministered are detailed in Ex 28:4–43 (see notes there). *anointing oil.* See note on Ex 25:6. The oil was used to anoint the tabernacle, sacred objects and consecrated priests (vv. 10–12,30). It was later used to anoint leaders and kings (1Sa 10:1; 16:13). See also note on Ex 29:7.
8:6 *washed them with water.* In the bronze basin (see v. 11) in the courtyard of the tabernacle (see Ex 30:17–21).
8:7 *ephod.* See note on Ex 28:6.
8:8 *Urim and Thummim.* See notes on Ex 28:30; 1Sa 2:28.

8:9 *sacred diadem.* See note on Ex 39:30.
8:11 *seven times.* See note on 4:6.
8:12 *oil on Aaron's head.* See Ps 133.
8:14 *sin offering.* See 4:3–11 and notes. The consecration service included a sin offering for atonement, a burnt offering for worship (v. 18) and a "ram for ordination" (v. 22), whose blood was applied to the high priest on his right ear, thumb and toe (v. 23). After this was done, Aaron offered sacrifices for the people (9:15–21). Then he blessed the people in his capacity as priest, and the Lord accepted his ministry with the sign of miraculous fire (9:23–24). *laid their hands on.* See notes on 1:3; Ex 29:15.

a wave offering. [28]Then Moses took them from their hands and burned them on the altar on top of the burnt offering as an ordination offering, a pleasing aroma, an offering made to the LORD by fire. [29]He also took the breast—Moses' share of the ordination ram[n]—and waved it before the LORD as a wave offering, as the LORD commanded Moses.

[30]Then Moses[o] took some of the anointing oil and some of the blood from the altar and sprinkled them on Aaron and his garments[p] and on his sons and their garments. So he consecrated[q] Aaron and his garments and his sons and their garments.

[31]Moses then said to Aaron and his sons, "Cook the meat at the entrance to the Tent of Meeting[r] and eat it there with the bread from the basket of ordination offerings, as I commanded, saying,[q] 'Aaron and his sons are to eat it.' [32]Then burn up the rest of the meat and the bread. [33]Do not leave the entrance to the Tent of Meeting for seven days, until the days of your ordination are completed, for your ordination will last seven days.[s] [34]What has been done today was commanded by the LORD[t] to make atonement for you. [35]You must stay at the entrance to the Tent of Meeting day and night for seven days and do what the LORD requires,[u] so you will not die; for that is what I have been commanded." [36]So Aaron and his sons did everything the LORD commanded through Moses.

The Priests Begin Their Ministry

9 On the eighth day[v] Moses summoned Aaron and his sons and the elders[w] of Israel. [2]He said to Aaron, "Take a bull calf for your sin offering and a ram for your burnt offering, both without defect, and present them before the LORD. [3]Then say to the Israelites: 'Take a male goat[x] for a sin offering,[y] a calf[z] and a lamb[a]—both a year old and without defect—for a burnt offering, [4]and an ox[r][b] and a ram for a fellowship offering[s][c] to sacrifice before the LORD, together with a grain offering mixed with oil. For today the LORD will appear to you.[d] '"

[5]They took the things Moses commanded to the front of the Tent of Meeting, and the entire assembly came near and

stood before the LORD. [6]Then Moses said, "This is what the LORD has commanded you to do, so that the glory of the LORD[e] may appear to you."

[7]Moses said to Aaron, "Come to the altar and sacrifice your sin offering and your burnt offering and make atonement for yourself and the people;[f] sacrifice the offering that is for the people and make atonement for them, as the LORD has commanded.[g]"

[8]So Aaron came to the altar and slaughtered the calf as a sin offering[h] for himself. [9]His sons brought the blood to him,[i] and he dipped his finger into the blood and put it on the horns of the altar; the rest of the blood he poured out at the base of the altar.[j][k] [10]On the altar he burned the fat, the kidneys and the covering of the liver from the sin offering, as the LORD commanded Moses; [11]the flesh and the hide[l] he burned up outside the camp.[m]

[12]Then he slaughtered the burnt offering.[n] His sons handed him the blood,[o] and he sprinkled it against the altar on all sides. [13]They handed him the burnt offering piece by piece, including the head, and he burned them on the altar.[p] [14]He washed the inner parts and the legs and burned them on top of the burnt offering on the altar.[q]

[15]Aaron then brought the offering that was for the people.[r] He took the goat for the people's sin offering and slaughtered it and offered it for a sin offering as he did with the first one.

[16]He brought the burnt offering and offered it in the prescribed way.[s] [17]He also brought the grain offering, took a handful of it and burned it on the altar in addition to the morning's burnt offering.[t]

[18]He slaughtered the ox and the ram as the fellowship offering for the people.[u] His sons handed him the blood, and he sprinkled it against the altar on all sides. [19]But the fat portions of the ox and the ram—the fat tail, the layer of fat, the kidneys and the covering of the liver— [20]these they laid on the breasts, and then Aaron burned the fat on the altar. [21]Aaron waved the breasts

8:29 nLev 7:31-34
8:30 oS Ex 28:1
pS Ex 28:2
qS Lev 7:36
8:31 rS Lev 6:16
8:33 sLev 14:8;
15:13,28;
Nu 19:11;
Eze 43:25
8:34 tHeb 7:16
8:35 uLev 18:30;
22:9; Nu 3:7;
9:19; Dt 11:1;
1Ki 2:3;
Eze 48:11;
Zec 3:7
9:1 vEze 43:27
wS Lev 4:15
9:3 xS Lev 4:3
yver 15;
Lev 10:16 zver 8
aS Lev 4:32
9:4 bLev 4:10
cS Ex 32:6
dEx 29:43

9:6 eS Ex 16:7
9:7 fLev 16:6
gS Ex 30:10;
Heb 5:1,3; 7:27
9:8 hLev 4:1-12;
10:19
9:9 iver 12,18
jS Ex 29:12
kEze 43:20
9:11 lS Lev 4:11
mS Lev 4:12
9:12 nLev 10:19
oS ver 9
9:13 pS Lev 1:8
9:14 qS Lev 1:9
9:15
rLev 4:27-31
9:16 sLev 1:1-13
9:17 tLev 3:5
9:18 uLev 3:1-11

q31 Or I was commanded;   r4 The Hebrew word can
include both male and female; also in verses 18 and 19.
s4 Traditionally peace offering; also in verses 18 and 22

8:28 on top of the burnt offering. See note on 3:5.
8:31 saying, 'Aaron and his sons are to eat it.' Quoted
from Ex 29:32.
9:1 eighth day. After the seven days of ordination (8:33).
9:2 sin offering. See notes on 4:3,5. burnt offering. See
note on 1:3.

9:4 fellowship offering. See note on 3:1. grain offering. See
note on 2:1. LORD will appear. See vv. 6,23; see also note on
Ge 12:7.
9:17 morning's burnt offering. See Ex 29:38-42.
9:21 wave offering. See note on 7:30-32.

and the right thigh before the LORD as a wave offering,[v] as Moses commanded.

22Then Aaron lifted his hands toward the people and blessed them.[w] And having sacrificed the sin offering, the burnt offering and the fellowship offering, he stepped down.

23Moses and Aaron then went into the Tent of Meeting.[x] When they came out, they blessed the people; and the glory of the LORD[y] appeared to all the people. 24Fire[z] came out from the presence of the LORD and consumed the burnt offering and the fat portions on the altar. And when all the people saw it, they shouted for joy and fell facedown.[a]

The Death of Nadab and Abihu

10 Aaron's sons Nadab and Abihu[b] took their censers,[c] put fire in them[d] and added incense;[e] and they offered unauthorized fire before the LORD,[f] contrary to his command.[g] 2So fire came out[h] from the presence of the LORD and consumed them,[i] and they died before the LORD.[j] 3Moses then said to Aaron, "This is what the LORD spoke of when he said:

"'Among those who approach me[k]
I will show myself holy;[l]
in the sight of all the people
I will be honored.[m]'"

Aaron remained silent.

4Moses summoned Mishael and Elzaphan,[n] sons of Aaron's uncle Uzziel,[o] and said to them, "Come here; carry your cousins outside the camp,[p] away from the front of the sanctuary.[q]" 5So they came and carried them, still in their tunics,[r] outside the camp, as Moses ordered.

6Then Moses said to Aaron and his sons Eleazar and Ithamar,[s] "Do not let your hair become unkempt,[t] and do not tear your clothes,[u] or you will die and the LORD will be angry with the whole com-

munity.[v] But your relatives, all the house of Israel, may mourn[w] for those the LORD has destroyed by fire. 7Do not leave the entrance to the Tent of Meeting[x] or you will die, because the LORD's anointing oil[y] is on you." So they did as Moses said.

8Then the LORD said to Aaron, 9"You and your sons are not to drink wine[z] or other fermented drink[a] whenever you go into the Tent of Meeting, or you will die. This is a lasting ordinance[b] for the generations to come. 10You must distinguish between the holy and the common, between the unclean and the clean,[c] 11and you must teach[d] the Israelites all the decrees the LORD has given them through Moses.[e]"

12Moses said to Aaron and his remaining sons, Eleazar and Ithamar, "Take the grain offering[f] left over from the offerings made to the LORD by fire and eat it prepared without yeast beside the altar,[g] for it is most holy. 13Eat it in a holy place,[h] because it is your share and your sons' share of the offerings made to the LORD by fire; for so I have been commanded.[i] 14But you and your sons and your daughters may eat the breast[j] that was waved and the thigh that was presented. Eat them in a ceremonially clean place;[k] they have been given to you and your children as your share of the Israelites' fellowship offerings.[u] 15The thigh[l] that was presented and the breast that was waved must be brought with the fat portions of the offerings made by fire, to be waved before the LORD as a wave offering.[m] This will be the regular share for you

---

9:21 [v]S Ex 29:24, 26
9:22 [w]S Ge 48:20; S Ex 39:43; Lk 24:50
9:23 [x]S Ex 40:2 [y]S Ex 24:16
9:24 [z]S Ex 19:18; Jdg 6:21; 13:20 [a]1Ki 18:39
10:1 [b]Ex 6:23; 24:1; 28:1; Nu 3:2-4; 26:61; 1Ch 6:3 [c]Nu 16:46; 1Ki 7:50; 2Ki 25:15; 2Ch 4:22; Jer 52:19; Eze 8:11 [d]Lev 16:12; Nu 16:7,18; Isa 6:6 [e]S Ex 30:9 [f]ver 2; Lev 16:1 [g]Ex 30:9
10:2 [h]Ps 106:18 [i]Nu 11:1; 16:35; Ps 2:12; 50:3; Isa 29:6 [j]S Ge 19:24; S 38:7; Nu 16:35; 1Ch 24:2; Job 1:16
10:3 [k]Ex 19:22 [l]Ex 30:29; Lev 21:6; 22:32; Nu 16:5; 20:13; Isa 5:16; Eze 28:22; 38:16 [m]Ex 14:4; Isa 44:23; 49:3; 55:5; 60:21
10:4 [n]S Ex 6:22 [o]Ex 6:18 [p]Ac 5:6, 9,10 [q]S Ex 25:8
10:5 [r]S Lev 8:13
10:6 [s]S Ex 6:23 [t]Lev 13:45; 21:10; Nu 5:18 [u]Jer 41:5; S Mk 14:63

[v]Nu 1:53; 16:22; Jos 7:1; 22:18 [w]Ge 50:3,10; Nu 20:29; 1Sa 25:1
10:7 [x]S Ex 25:8 [y]S Ex 28:41
10:9 [z]Ge 9:21; Ex 29:40; Lev 23:13; Nu 15:5; Dt 28:39; Isa 5:22; 22:13; 28:1; 29:9; 56:12; Jer 35:6; Hos 4:11; Hab 2:15-16 [a]Nu 6:3; 28:7; Dt 14:26; 29:6;

Jdg 13:4; Pr 20:1; 23:29-35; 31:4-7; Isa 28:7; Eze 44:21; Mic 2:11; Lk 1:15; S Eph 5:18; 1Ti 3:3; Tit 1:7 [b]S Ex 12:14
10:10 [c]S Ge 7:2; S Lev 6:27; 14:57; 20:25; Eze 22:26 10:11 [d]2Ch 15:3; 17:7; Ezr 7:25; Ne 8:7; Mal 2:7 [e]Dt 17:10,11; 24:8; 25:1; 33:10; Pr 4:27; Hag 2:11; Mal 2:7 10:12 [f]S Ex 29:41 [g]Lev 6:14-18 10:13 [h]S Lev 6:16 [i]Eze 42:13 10:14 [j]Nu 5:9 [k]S Ex 29:31; S Lev 4:12 10:15 [l]S Lev 7:34 [m]S Ex 29:28

[t]6 Or *Do not uncover your heads*   [u]14 Traditionally *peace offerings*

9:22 *blessed.* The Aaronic benediction, a threefold blessing, is given in Nu 6:23–26. Cf. the threefold apostolic benediction in 2Co 13:14.

9:23 *glory of the LORD.* See v. 6; cf. the display of the Lord's glory at the erection of the tabernacle (Ex 40:34–35); cf. also God's acceptance of sacrifices at the dedication of Solomon's temple (2Ch 7:1).

9:24 *Fire came out from the presence of the LORD.* See 10:2; 1Ki 18:38.

10:1 *censers.* Ceremonial vessels containing hot coals and used for burning incense (see 16:12–13; 2Ch 26:19; Rev 8:3–4).

10:2 *died before the LORD.* Aaron's older sons are mentioned also in Ex 6:23; 24:1,9; 28:1; Nu 3:2–4; 26:60–61; 1Ch 6:3; 24:1–2. They are regularly remembered as having

died before the Lord and as having had no sons. Their death was tragic and at first seems harsh, but more so than that of Ananias and Sapphira (Ac 5:1–11). In both cases a new era was being inaugurated (cf. also the judgment on Achan, Jos 7, and on Uzzah, 2Sa 6:1–7). The new community had to be made aware that it existed for God, not vice versa.

10:6 *tear your clothes.* See 21:10; see also note on Ge 44:13.

10:7 *Do not leave.* To join the mourners (see 21:11–12).

10:10 *between the holy and the common.* The distinction between what was holy (sacred) and what was common (profane) was carefully maintained (see Eze 22:26; 42:20; 44:23; 48:14–15).

10:12–15 See 7:28–36; Nu 18:8–20; Dt 18:1–5.

and your children, as the LORD has commanded."

[16]When Moses inquired about the goat of the sin offering[n] and found that it had been burned up, he was angry with Eleazar and Ithamar, Aaron's remaining sons, and asked, [17]"Why didn't you eat the sin offering[o] in the sanctuary area? It is most holy; it was given to you to take away the guilt[p] of the community by making atonement for them before the LORD. [18]Since its blood was not taken into the Holy Place,[q] you should have eaten the goat in the sanctuary area, as I commanded.[r]"

[19]Aaron replied to Moses, "Today they sacrificed their sin offering and their burnt offering[s] before the LORD, but such things as this have happened to me. Would the LORD have been pleased if I had eaten the sin offering today?" [20]When Moses heard this, he was satisfied.

Clean and Unclean Food

11:1–23pp — Dt 14:3–20

11 The LORD said to Moses and Aaron, [2]"Say to the Israelites: 'Of all the animals that live on land, these are the ones you may eat:[t] [3]You may eat any animal that has a split hoof completely divided and that chews the cud.

[4]"'There are some that only chew the cud or only have a split hoof, but you must not eat them.[u] The camel, though it chews the cud, does not have a split hoof; it is ceremonially unclean for you. [5]The coney,[v] though it chews the cud, does not have a split hoof; it is unclean for you. [6]The rabbit, though it chews the cud, does not have a split hoof; it is unclean for you. [7]And the pig,[v] though it has a split hoof completely divided, does not chew the cud; it is unclean for you. [8]You must not eat their meat or touch their carcasses; they are unclean for you.[w]

[9]"'Of all the creatures living in the water of the seas and the streams, you may eat any that have fins and scales. [10]But all creatures in the seas or streams that do not have fins and scales—whether among all the swarming things or among all the other living creatures in the water—you are to detest.[x] [11]And since you are to detest them, you must not eat their meat and you must detest their carcasses.[y] [12]Anything living in the water that does not have fins and scales is to be detestable to you.[z]

[13]"'These are the birds you are to detest and not eat because they are detestable: the eagle, the vulture, the black vulture, [14]the red kite, any kind[a] of black kite, [15]any kind of raven,[b] [16]the horned owl, the screech owl, the gull, any kind of hawk, [17]the little owl, the cormorant, the great owl, [18]the white owl,[c] the desert owl, the osprey, [19]the stork,[d] any kind[e] of heron, the hoopoe and the bat.[w][f]

[20]"'All flying insects that walk on all fours are to be detestable to you.[g] [21]There are, however, some winged creatures that walk on all fours that you may eat: those that have jointed legs for hopping on the ground. [22]Of these you may eat any kind of locust,[h] katydid, cricket or grasshopper. [23]But all other winged creatures that have four legs you are to detest.

[24]"'You will make yourselves unclean by these;[i] whoever touches their carcasses will be unclean till evening.[i] [25]Whoever picks up one of their carcasses must wash his clothes,[k] and he will be unclean till evening.[l]

[26]"'Every animal that has a split hoof not completely divided or that does not chew the cud is unclean for you; whoever touches the carcass of any of them will be unclean. [27]Of all the animals that walk on

Cross-references (center column)

10:16 [n]S Lev 9:3
10:17
[o]Lev 6:24-30; Eze 42:13
[p]S Ex 28:38
10:18
[q]S Lev 4:18; 6:26
[r]S Lev 6:17
10:19 [s]Lev 9:12
11:2
[t]Ac 10:12-14
11:4 [u]Ac 10:14
11:7 [v]Isa 65:4; 66:3,17
11:8 [w]S Lev 5:2; Heb 9:10

11:10 [x]ver 12
11:11 [y]S Lev 5:2
11:12 [z]ver 10
11:14 [a]S Ge 1:11
11:15 [b]S Ge 8:7
11:18 [c]Isa 13:21; 14:23; 34:11,13; Zep 2:14
11:19 [d]Zec 5:9
[e]S Ge 1:11
[f]Isa 2:20
11:20 [g]Ac 10:14
11:22 [h]Mt 3:4; Mk 1:6
11:24 [i]S Lev 5:2
[j]ver 27-40; Lev 13:3; 14:46; 15:5; 22:6; Nu 19:7,19
11:25 [k]ver 28; S Ex 19:10; Lev 13:6; 14:8, 47; 15:5; 16:26; Nu 8:7; 19:7
[l]Lev 13:34; Nu 19:8; 31:24

[v]*5* That is, the hyrax or rock badger   [w]*19* The precise identification of some of the birds, insects and animals in this chapter is uncertain.

10:18 *Since its blood was not taken into the Holy Place, you should have eaten.* There were two types of sin offerings: (1) those in which the blood was sprinkled within the tabernacle, and (2) those in which it was sprinkled only on the great altar. Portions of the second type normally should have been eaten (see note on 4:5). But Moses was satisfied when he learned that Aaron had acted sincerely and not in negligence or rebellion (vv. 19–20).

10:19 *such things as this have happened to me.* Perhaps referring to the death of his two oldest sons (v. 2), for which he mourned by fasting. Or possibly something had occurred that made him ceremonially unclean.

11:2 *the ones you may eat.* Ch. 11 is closely paralleled in Dt 14:3–21 but is more extensive. The animals acceptable for human consumption were those that chewed the cud and had a split hoof (v. 3). Of marine life, only creatures with fins and scales were permissible (v. 9). Birds and insects are also

covered in the instructions (vv. 13–23). The distinction between clean and unclean food was as old as the time of Noah (Ge 7:2). The main reason for the laws concerning clean and unclean food is the same as for other laws concerning the clean and unclean—to preserve the sanctity of Israel as God's holy people (see v. 44). Some hold that certain animal life was considered unclean for health considerations, but it is difficult to substantiate this idea. Uncleanness typified sin and defilement. For the uncleanness of disease and bodily discharges see chs. 13–15.

11:6 *rabbit.* Does not technically chew the cud with regurgitation. The apparent chewing movements of the rabbit caused it to be classified popularly with cud chewers.

11:20 *all fours.* Although insects have six legs, perhaps people in ancient times did not count as ordinary legs the two large hind legs used for jumping.

all fours, those that walk on their paws are unclean for you; whoever touches their carcasses will be unclean till evening. 28Anyone who picks up their carcasses must wash his clothes, and he will be unclean till evening. *m* They are unclean for you.

29" 'Of the animals that move about on the ground, these are unclean for you: *n* the weasel, the rat, *o* any kind of great lizard, 30the gecko, the monitor lizard, the wall lizard, the skink and the chameleon. 31Of all those that move along the ground, these are unclean for you. Whoever touches them when they are dead will be unclean till evening. 32When one of them dies and falls on something, that article, whatever its use, will be unclean, whether it is made of wood, cloth, hide or sackcloth. *p* Put it in water; it will be unclean till evening, and then it will be clean. 33If one of them falls into a clay pot, everything in it will be unclean, and you must break the pot. *q* 34Any food that could be eaten but has water on it from such a pot is unclean, and any liquid that could be drunk from it is unclean. 35Anything that one of their carcasses falls on becomes unclean; an oven or cooking pot must be broken up. They are unclean, and you are to regard them as unclean. 36A spring, however, or a cistern for collecting water remains clean, but anyone who touches one of these carcasses is unclean. 37If a carcass falls on any seeds that are to be planted, they remain clean. 38But if water has been put on the seed and a carcass falls on it, it is unclean for you.

39" 'If an animal that you are allowed to eat dies, *r* anyone who touches the carcass *s* will be unclean till evening. 40Anyone who eats some of the carcass *t* must wash his clothes, and he will be unclean till evening. *u* Anyone who picks up the carcass must wash his clothes, and he will be unclean till evening.

41" 'Every creature that moves about on the ground is detestable; it is not to be eaten. 42You are not to eat any creature that moves about on the ground, whether it moves on its belly or walks on all fours or on many feet; it is detestable. 43Do not defile yourselves by any of these creatures. *v* Do not make yourselves unclean by means of them or be made unclean by them. 44I am the LORD your God; *w* consecrate yourselves *x* and be holy, *y* because I am holy. *z* Do not make yourselves unclean by any creature that moves about on the ground. *a* 45I am the LORD who brought you up out of Egypt *b* to be your God; *c* therefore be holy, because I am holy. *d*

46" 'These are the regulations concerning animals, birds, every living thing that moves in the water and every creature that moves about on the ground. 47You must distinguish between the unclean and the clean, between living creatures that may be eaten and those that may not be eaten.' "

Purification After Childbirth

12 The LORD said to Moses, 2"Say to the Israelites: 'A woman who becomes pregnant and gives birth to a son will be ceremonially unclean for seven days, just as she is unclean during her monthly period. *f* 3On the eighth day *g* the boy is to be circumcised. *h* 4Then the woman must wait thirty-three days to be purified from her bleeding. She must not touch anything sacred or go to the sanctuary until the days of her purification are over. 5If she gives birth to a daughter, for two weeks the woman will be unclean, as during her period. Then she must wait sixty-six days to be purified from her bleeding.

6" 'When the days of her purification for a son or daughter are over, *i* she is to bring to the priest at the entrance to the Tent of Meeting a year-old lamb *j* for a burnt offering and a young pigeon or a dove for a sin

Cross references

11:28 *m*Heb 9:10
11:29 *n*ver 41
*o*Isa 66:17
11:32 *p*Lev 15:12; Nu 19:18; 31:20
11:33 *q*S Lev 6:28
11:39 *r*Lev 17:15; 22:8; Dt 14:21; Eze 4:14; 44:31
*s*ver 40; Lev 22:4; Nu 19:11
11:40 *t*S ver 39
*u*ver 25; Lev 14:8; 17:15; 22:8; Eze 44:31; Heb 9:10
11:43 *v*ver 44; Lev 20:25; 22:5
11:44 *w*S Ex 6:2, 7; 20:2; Isa 43:3; 51:15; Eze 20:5
*x*S Ex 19:10; Lev 20:7; Nu 15:40; Jos 3:5; 7:13; 1Ch 15:12; 2Ch 29:5; 35:6
*y*S Ex 22:31; S Dt 14:2
*z*S Ex 31:13; Lev 19:2; 20:7; Jos 24:19; 1Sa 2:2; Job 6:10; Ps 99:3; Eph 1:4; 1Th 4:7; 1Pe 1:15,16*
*a*S ver 43
11:45 *b*Lev 25:38,55
*c*S Ge 17:7
*d*S Ex 19:6; 1Pe 1:16*
11:47 *e*Lev 10:10
12:2 *f*Lev 15:19; 18:19; Isa 64:6; Eze 18:6; 22:10; 36:17
12:3 *g*S Ex 22:30
*h*S Ge 17:10; S Lk 1:59
12:6 *i*Lk 2:22
*j*Ex 29:38; Lev 23:12; Nu 6:12,14; 7:15

11:36 *cistern for collecting water.* The use of waterproof plaster for lining cisterns dug in the ground was an important factor in helping the Israelites to settle the dry areas of Canaan after the conquest (cf. 2Ch 26:10).

11:41 *ground.* Verses 29–30 identify the animals that move about (or swarm) on the ground.

11:44 *be holy, because I am holy.* Holiness is the key theme of Leviticus, ringing like a refrain in various forms throughout the book (e.g., v. 45; 19:2; 20:7,26; 21:8,15; 22:9,16,32). The word "holy" appears more often in Leviticus than in any other book of the Bible. Israel was to be totally consecrated to God. Her holiness was to be expressed in every aspect of her life, to the extent that all of life had a certain ceremonial quality. Because of who God is and what

he has done (v. 45), his people must dedicate themselves fully to him (cf. Mt 5:48). See Ro 12:1.

11:45 *brought . . . out of Egypt.* A refrain found 8 more times in Leviticus (19:36; 22:33; 23:43; 25:38,42,55; 26:13,45) and nearly 60 times in 18 other books of the OT.

11:46–47 A summary of ch. 11.

12:2 *unclean.* The uncleanness came from the bleeding (vv. 4–5,7), not from the birth. It is not clear why the period of uncleanness after the birth of a baby boy (40 days) was half the period for a girl (80 days). *monthly period.* See 15:19–24.

12:3 See notes on Ge 17:10,12.

12:6 *burnt offering.* See note on 1:3. *sin offering.* See notes on 4:3,5.

offering.[k] [7]He shall offer them before the LORD to make atonement for her, and then she will be ceremonially clean from her flow of blood.

" 'These are the regulations for the woman who gives birth to a boy or a girl. [8]If she cannot afford a lamb, she is to bring two doves or two young pigeons,[l] one for a burnt offering and the other for a sin offering.[m] In this way the priest will make atonement for her, and she will be clean.[n] "

Regulations About Infectious Skin Diseases

13 The LORD said to Moses and Aaron, [2]"When anyone has a swelling[o] or a rash or a bright spot[p] on his skin that may become an infectious skin disease,[x] [q] he must be brought to Aaron the priest[r] or to one of his sons[y] who is a priest. [3]The priest is to examine the sore on his skin, and if the hair in the sore has turned white and the sore appears to be more than skin deep,[z] it is an infectious skin disease. When the priest examines him, he shall pronounce him ceremonially unclean.[s] [4]If the spot[t] on his skin is white but does not appear to be more than skin deep and the hair in it has not turned white, the priest is to put the infected person in isolation for seven days.[u] [5]On the seventh day[v] the priest is to examine him,[w] and if he sees that the sore is unchanged and has not spread in the skin, he is to keep him in isolation another seven days. [6]On the seventh day the priest is to examine him again, and if the sore has faded and has not spread in the skin, the priest shall pronounce him clean;[x] it is only a rash. The man must wash his clothes,[y] and he will be clean.[z] [7]But if the rash does spread in his skin after he has shown himself to the priest to be pronounced clean, he must appear before the priest again.[a] [8]The priest is to examine him, and if the rash has spread in the skin, he shall pronounce him unclean; it is an infectious disease.

[9]"When anyone has an infectious skin disease, he must be brought to the priest. [10]The priest is to examine him, and if there is a white swelling in the skin that has turned the hair white and if there is raw flesh in the swelling, [11]it is a chronic skin disease[b] and the priest shall pronounce him unclean. He is not to put him in isolation, because he is already unclean.

[12]"If the disease breaks out all over his skin and, so far as the priest can see, it covers all the skin of the infected person from head to foot, [13]the priest is to examine him, and if the disease has covered his whole body, he shall pronounce that person clean. Since it has all turned white, he is clean. [14]But whenever raw flesh appears on him, he will be unclean. [15]When the priest sees the raw flesh, he shall pronounce him unclean. The raw flesh is unclean; he has an infectious disease.[c] [16]Should the raw flesh change and turn white, he must go to the priest. [17]The priest is to examine him, and if the sores have turned white, the priest shall pronounce the infected person clean;[d] then he will be clean.

[18]"When someone has a boil[e] on his skin and it heals, [19]and in the place where the boil was, a white swelling or reddish-white[f] spot[g] appears, he must present himself to the priest. [20]The priest is to examine it, and if it appears to be more than skin deep and the hair in it has turned white, the priest shall pronounce him unclean. It is an infectious skin disease[h] that has broken out where the boil was. [21]But if, when the priest examines it, there is no white hair in it and it is not more than skin deep and has faded, then the priest is to put him in isolation for seven days. [22]If it is spreading in the skin, the priest shall pronounce him unclean; it is infectious. [23]But if the spot is unchanged and has not spread, it is only a scar from the boil, and the priest shall pronounce him clean.[i]

Cross references (center column)

12:6 [k]Lev 5:7
12:8 [l]S Ge 15:9; Lev 14:22
[m]Lev 5:7; Lk 2:22-24*
[n]S Lev 4:26
13:2 [o]ver 10,19, 28,43 [p]ver 4,38, 39; Lev 14:56 [q]ver 3,9,15; S Ex 4:6; Lev 14:3,32; Nu 5:2; Dt 24:8
[r]Dt 24:8
13:3 [s]ver 8,11, 20,30; Lev 21:1; Nu 9:6
13:4 [t]S ver 2
[u]ver 5,21,26,33, 46; Lev 14:38; Nu 12:14,15; Dt 24:9
13:5 [v]Lev 14:9
[w]ver 27,32,34,51
13:6 [x]ver 13,17, 23,28,34; Mt 8:3; Lk 5:12-14
[y]S Lev 11:25
[z]Lev 11:25; 14:8, 9,20,48; 15:8; Nu 8:7
13:7 [a]Lk 5:14

13:11 [b]S Ex 4:6; S Lev 14:8; S Nu 12:10; Mt 8:2
13:15 [c]S ver 2
13:17 [d]S ver 6
13:18 [e]S Ex 9:9
13:19 [f]ver 24,42; Lev 14:37 [g]S ver 2
13:20 [h]ver 2
13:23 [i]S ver 6

[x]2 Traditionally *leprosy*; the Hebrew word was used for various diseases affecting the skin—not necessarily leprosy; also elsewhere in this chapter.   [y]2 Or *descendants*   [z]3 Or *be lower than the rest of the skin*; also elsewhere in this chapter

---

12:8 See 1:14-17 and note on 1:14; see also 5:7-10; 14:21-22; and especially Lk 2:24 (Mary's offering for Jesus). **13:1-46** This section deals with preliminary symptoms of skin diseases (vv. 1-8) and then with the symptoms of (1) raw flesh (vv. 9-17), (2) boils (vv. 18-23), (3) burns (vv. 24-28), (4) sores on the head or chin (vv. 29-37), (5) white spots (vv. 38-39) and (6) skin diseases on the head that cause baldness (vv. 40-44). **13:2** *infectious skin disease.* Occurs often in chs. 13-14; see also 22:4; Nu 5:2. Since it is unlikely that ancient people would have understood the concept of infectiousness, this rendering is questionable; the Hebrew should perhaps be translated simply "skin disease." Such diseases show visible defects that could function aptly as a symbol for defilement—as could mildew (cf. vv. 47-59). *disease.* See NIV text note; see also 22:4-8; Nu 5:2-4; Dt 24:8-9. The symptoms described, and the fact that they may rapidly change (vv. 6,26-27,32-37), show that the disease was not true leprosy (Hansen's disease). They apply also to a number of other diseases, as well as to rather harmless skin eruptions. The Hebrew word translated "infectious skin disease" can also mean "mildew" (v. 47; 14:34; and especially 14:57).

[24] "When someone has a burn on his skin and a reddish-white or white spot appears in the raw flesh of the burn, [25]the priest is to examine the spot, and if the hair in it has turned white, and it appears to be more than skin deep, it is an infectious disease that has broken out in the burn. The priest shall pronounce him unclean; it is an infectious skin disease.[j] [26]But if the priest examines it and there is no white hair in the spot and if it is not more than skin deep and has faded, then the priest is to put him in isolation for seven days.[k] [27]On the seventh day the priest is to examine him,[l] and if it is spreading in the skin, the priest shall pronounce him unclean; it is an infectious skin disease. [28]If, however, the spot is unchanged and has not spread in the skin but has faded, it is a swelling from the burn, and the priest shall pronounce him clean; it is only a scar from the burn.[m]

[29] "If a man or woman has a sore on the head[n] or on the chin, [30]the priest is to examine the sore, and if it appears to be more than skin deep and the hair in it is yellow and thin, the priest shall pronounce that person unclean; it is an itch, an infectious disease of the head or chin. [31]But if, when the priest examines this kind of sore, it does not seem to be more than skin deep and there is no black hair in it, then the priest is to put the infected person in isolation for seven days.[o] [32]On the seventh day the priest is to examine the sore,[p] and if the itch has not spread and there is no yellow hair in it and it does not appear to be more than skin deep, [33]he must be shaved except for the diseased area, and the priest is to keep him in isolation another seven days. [34]On the seventh day the priest is to examine the itch,[q] and if it has not spread in the skin and appears to be no more than skin deep, the priest shall pronounce him clean. He must wash his clothes, and he will be clean.[r] [35]But if the itch does spread in the skin after he is pronounced clean, [36]the priest is to examine him, and if the itch has spread in the skin, the priest does not need to look for yellow hair; the person is unclean.[s] [37]If, however, in his judgment it is unchanged and black hair has grown in it, the itch is

healed. He is clean, and the priest shall pronounce him clean.

[38] "When a man or woman has white spots on the skin, [39]the priest is to examine them, and if the spots are dull white, it is a harmless rash that has broken out on the skin; that person is clean.

[40] "When a man has lost his hair and is bald,[t] he is clean. [41]If he has lost his hair from the front of his scalp and has a bald forehead, he is clean. [42]But if he has a reddish-white sore on his bald head or forehead, it is an infectious disease breaking out on his head or forehead. [43]The priest is to examine him, and if the swollen sore on his head or forehead is reddish-white like an infectious skin disease, [44]the man is diseased and is unclean. The priest shall pronounce him unclean because of the sore on his head.

[45] "The person with such an infectious disease must wear torn clothes,[u] let his hair be unkempt,[a] cover the lower part of his face[v] and cry out, 'Unclean! Unclean!'[w] [46]As long as he has the infection he remains unclean. He must live alone; he must live outside the camp.[x]

Regulations About Mildew

[47] "If any clothing is contaminated with mildew—any woolen or linen clothing, [48]any woven or knitted material of linen or wool, any leather or anything made of leather— [49]and if the contamination in the clothing, or leather, or woven or knitted material, or any leather article, is greenish or reddish, it is a spreading mildew and must be shown to the priest.[y] [50]The priest is to examine the mildew[z] and isolate the affected article for seven days. [51]On the seventh day he is to examine it,[a] and if the mildew has spread in the clothing, or the woven or knitted material, or the leather, whatever its use, it is a destructive mildew; the article is unclean.[b] [52]He must burn up the clothing, or the woven or knitted material of wool or linen, or any leather article that has the contamination in it, because the mildew is destructive; the article must be burned up.[c]

[53] "But if, when the priest examines it,

13:25 /ver 11
13:26 kS ver 4
13:27 /S ver 5
13:28 mS ver 2
13:29 nver 43,44
13:31 over 4
13:32 pS ver 5
13:34 qS ver 5
rS Lev 11:25
13:36 sver 30

13:40 tLev 21:5; 2Ki 2:23; Isa 3:24; 15:2; 22:12; Eze 27:31; 29:18; Am 8:10; Mic 1:16
13:45 uS Lev 10:6
vEze 24:17,22; Mic 3:7
wS Lev 5:2; La 4:15; Lk 17:12
13:46 xNu 5:1-4; 12:14; 2Ki 7:3; 15:5
13:49 yMk 1:44
13:50 zEze 44:23
13:51 aS ver 5
bLev 14:44
13:52 cver 55,57

[a]45 Or *clothes, uncover his head*

13:45–46 The ceremonially unclean were excluded from the camp (the area around the tabernacle and courtyard), where the Israelites lived in tents. Later, no unclean person was allowed in the temple area, where he could mingle with others. Not only was God present in the tabernacle in a special way, but also in the camp (Nu 5:3; Dt 23:14). Therefore unclean people were not to be in the camp (see Nu 5:1–4; 12:14–15, Miriam; 31:19–24; see also Lev 10:4–5;

Nu 15:35–36; 2Ki 7:3–4; 2Ch 26:21, Uzziah). As a result of their separation from God, the unclean were to exhibit their grief by tearing their clothes, by having unkempt hair and by partially covering their faces (v. 45).

13:47 *mildew.* During Israel's rainy season (October through March), this is a problem along the coast and by the Sea of Galilee, where it is very humid.

the mildew has not spread in the clothing, or the woven or knitted material, or the leather article, 54he shall order that the contaminated article be washed. Then he is to isolate it for another seven days. 55After the affected article has been washed, the priest is to examine it, and if the mildew has not changed its appearance, even though it has not spread, it is unclean. Burn it with fire, whether the mildew has affected one side or the other. 56If, when the priest examines it, the mildew has faded after the article has been washed, he is to tear the contaminated part out of the clothing, or the leather, or the woven or knitted material. 57But if it reappears in the clothing, or in the woven or knitted material, or in the leather article, it is spreading, and whatever has the mildew must be burned with fire. 58The clothing, or the woven or knitted material, or any leather article that has been washed and is rid of the mildew, must be washed again, and it will be clean."

59These are the regulations concerning contamination by mildew in woolen or linen clothing, woven or knitted material, or any leather article, for pronouncing them clean or unclean.

Cleansing From Infectious Skin Diseases

14 The LORD said to Moses, 2"These are the regulations for the diseased person at the time of his ceremonial cleansing, when he is brought to the priest: d 3The priest is to go outside the camp and examine him. e If the person has been healed of his infectious skin disease, bf 4the priest shall order that two live clean birds and some cedar wood, scarlet yarn and hyssop g be brought for the one to be cleansed. h 5Then the priest shall order that one of the birds be killed over fresh water in a clay pot. i 6He is then to take the live bird and dip it, together with the cedar wood, the scarlet yarn and the hyssop, into the blood of the bird that was

killed over the fresh water.j 7Seven times k he shall sprinkle l the one to be cleansed of the infectious disease and pronounce him clean. Then he is to release the live bird in the open fields. m

8"The person to be cleansed must wash his clothes, n shave off all his hair and bathe with water; o then he will be ceremonially clean. p After this he may come into the camp, q but he must stay outside his tent for seven days. 9On the seventh day r he must shave off all his hair; s he must shave his head, his beard, his eyebrows and the rest of his hair. He must wash his clothes and bathe himself with water, and he will be clean. t

10"On the eighth day u he must bring two male lambs and one ewe lamb v a year old, each without defect, along with three-tenths of an ephah c w of fine flour mixed with oil for a grain offering, x and one log d of oil. y 11The priest who pronounces him clean shall present z both the one to be cleansed and his offerings before the LORD at the entrance to the Tent of Meeting. a

12"Then the priest is to take one of the male lambs and offer it as a guilt offering, b along with the log of oil; he shall wave them before the LORD as a wave offering. c 13He is to slaughter the lamb in the holy place d where the sin offering and the burnt offering are slaughtered. Like the sin offering, the guilt offering belongs to the priest; e it is most holy. 14The priest is to take some of the blood of the guilt offering and put it on the lobe of the right ear of the one to be cleansed, on the thumb of his right hand and on the big toe of his right foot.f 15The priest shall then take some of the log of oil, pour it in the palm of his own left hand, g 16dip his right forefinger into the oil in his palm, and with his finger sprinkle some of it before the LORD seven

14:2 dLev 13:57; Dt 24:8; Mt 8:2-4; Mk 1:40-44; Lk 5:12-14; 17:14
14:3 eLev 13:46 /S Lev 13:2
14:4 gS Ex 12:22 hver 6,49,51,52; Nu 19:6; Ps 51:7
14:5 iver 50

14:6 /S ver 4
14:7 kver 51 l2Ki 5:10,14; Isa 52:15; Eze 36:25 mver 53
14:8 nS Lev 11:25 over 9; S Ex 29:4; Lev 15:5; 17:15; 22:6; Nu 19:7,8 pver 20
14:9 qS Lev 13:11; Nu 5:2,3; 12:14, 15; 19:20; 31:24; 2Ch 26:21 rS Lev 13:5 sNu 6:9; Dt 21:12 tS Lev 13:6
14:10 uNu 6:10; Mt 8:4; Mk 1:44; Lk 5:14 vS Lev 4:32 wNu 15:9; 28:20 xLev 2:1 yver 12, 15,21,24
14:11 zNu 6:16 aNu 6:10
14:12 bS Lev 5:18 cS Ex 29:24
14:13 dS Ex 29:11 eLev 6:24-30; S 7:7
14:14 fS Ex 29:20
14:15 gver 26

b3 Traditionally leprosy; the Hebrew word was used for various diseases affecting the skin—not necessarily leprosy; also elsewhere in this chapter.   c10 That is, probably about 6 quarts (about 6.5 liters)   d10 That is, probably about 2/3 pint (about 0.3 liter); also in verses 12, 15, 21 and 24

13:54 washed. See vv. 34,55–56,58. The treatment of disorders commonly included washing.
13:59 A summary of ch. 13.
14:1–32 The ritual after the skin disease had been cured had three parts: (1) ritual for the first week (outside the camp, vv. 1–7), (2) ritual for the second week (inside the camp, vv. 8–20) and (3) special permission for the poor (vv. 21–32).
14:4 hyssop. A plant used in ceremonial cleansing (see note on Ex 12:22).
14:5 killed. Diseases and disorders were a symbol of sin and rendered a person or object ceremonially unclean. The prescribed cleansing included sacrifice as well as washing

(see note on 13:54).
14:6 cedar . . . yarn . . . hyssop. Also used for cleansing in vv. 51–52; Nu 19:6.
14:7,16,51 seven times. See note on 4:6.
14:7 clean. Perhaps the yarn and cedar stick were used as well as the hyssop plant to sprinkle the blood for cleansing (see Ps 51:7). Further sacrifices are specified in vv. 10–31. release the live bird. Cf. 16:22; see note on 16:5.
14:8 The Levites were similarly cleansed (see Nu 8:7).
14:10 grain offering. See note on 2:1.
14:12 guilt offering. See 5:14–6:7 and note on 5:15. wave offering. See note on 7:30–32.
14:14 See note on 8:14.

times. [h] [17]The priest is to put some of the oil remaining in his palm on the lobe of the right ear of the one to be cleansed, on the thumb of his right hand and on the big toe of his right foot, on top of the blood of the guilt offering. [i] [18]The rest of the oil in his palm the priest shall put on the head of the one to be cleansed [j] and make atonement for him before the LORD.

[19]"Then the priest is to sacrifice the sin offering and make atonement for the one to be cleansed from his uncleanness. [k] After that, the priest shall slaughter the burnt offering [20]and offer it on the altar, together with the grain offering, and make atonement for him, [l] and he will be clean. [m]

[21]"If, however, he is poor [n] and cannot afford these, [o] he must take one male lamb as a guilt offering to be waved to make atonement for him, together with a tenth of an ephah [e] of fine flour mixed with oil for a grain offering, a log of oil, [22]and two doves or two young pigeons, [p] which he can afford, one for a sin offering and the other for a burnt offering. [q]

[23]"On the eighth day he must bring them for his cleansing to the priest at the entrance to the Tent of Meeting, [r] before the LORD. [s] [24]The priest is to take the lamb for the guilt offering, [t] together with the log of oil, [u] and wave them before the LORD as a wave offering. [v] [25]He shall slaughter the lamb for the guilt offering and take some of its blood and put it on the lobe of the right ear of the one to be cleansed, on the thumb of his right hand and on the big toe of his right foot. [w] [26]The priest is to pour some of the oil into the palm of his own left hand, [x] [27]and with his right forefinger sprinkle some of the oil from his palm seven times before the LORD. [28]Some of the oil in his palm he is to put on the same places he put the blood of the guilt offering—on the lobe of the right ear of the one to be cleansed, on the thumb of his right hand and on the big toe of his right foot. [29]The rest of the oil in his palm the priest shall put on the head of the one to be cleansed, to make atonement for him before the LORD. [y] [30]Then he shall sacrifice the doves or the young pigeons, which the person can afford, [z] [31]one [f] as a sin offering and the other as a burnt offering, [a] together with the grain offering. In

this way the priest will make atonement before the LORD on behalf of the one to be cleansed. [b]"

[32]These are the regulations for anyone who has an infectious skin disease [c] and who cannot afford the regular offerings [d] for his cleansing.

Cleansing From Mildew

[33]The LORD said to Moses and Aaron, [34]"When you enter the land of Canaan, [e] which I am giving you as your possession, [f] and I put a spreading mildew in a house in that land, [35]the owner of the house must go and tell the priest, 'I have seen something that looks like mildew in my house.' [36]The priest is to order the house to be emptied before he goes in to examine the mildew, so that nothing in the house will be pronounced unclean. After this the priest is to go in and inspect the house. [37]He is to examine the mildew on the walls, and if it has greenish or reddish [g] depressions that appear to be deeper than the surface of the wall, [38]the priest shall go out the doorway of the house and close it up for seven days. [h] [39]On the seventh day [i] the priest shall return to inspect the house. If the mildew has spread on the walls, [40]he is to order that the contaminated stones be torn out and thrown into an unclean place outside the town. [j] [41]He must have all the inside walls of the house scraped and the material that is scraped off dumped into an unclean place outside the town. [42]Then they are to take other stones to replace these and take new clay and plaster the house.

[43]"If the mildew reappears in the house after the stones have been torn out and the house scraped and plastered, [44]the priest is to go and examine it and, if the mildew has spread in the house, it is a destructive mildew; the house is unclean. [k] [45]It must be torn down—its stones, timbers and all the plaster—and taken out of the town to an unclean place.

[46]"Anyone who goes into the house while it is closed up will be unclean till evening. [l] [47]Anyone who sleeps or eats in the house must wash his clothes. [m]

[48]"But if the priest comes to examine it

Cross references (center column)

14:16 [h]ver 27
14:17 [i]ver 28
14:18 [j]ver 31; Lev 15:15
14:19 [k]ver 31; S Lev 5:3; 15:15
14:20 [l]Lev 15:30 [m]ver 8
14:21 [n]S Lev 5:7 [o]ver 22,32
14:22 [p]S Lev 5:7 [q]Lev 15:30
14:23 [r]Lev 15:14,29 [s]ver 10,11
14:24 [t]Nu 6:14 [u]S ver 10 [v]ver 12
14:25 [w]S Ex 29:20
14:26 [x]ver 15
14:29 [y]ver 18
14:30 [z]S Lev 5:7
14:31 [a]ver 22; Lev 5:7; 15:15,30

[b]S ver 18,S 19
14:32 [c]S Lev 13:2 [d]S ver 21
14:34 [e]Ge 12:5; Ex 6:4; Nu 13:2 [f]Ge 17:8; 48:4; Nu 27:12; 32:22; Dt 3:27; 7:1; 32:49
14:37 [g]S Lev 13:19
14:38 [h]S Lev 13:4
14:39 [i]Lev 13:5
14:40 [j]ver 45
14:44 [k]Lev 13:51
14:46 [l]S Lev 11:24
14:47 [m]S Lev 11:25

---

[e]21 That is, probably about 2 quarts (about 2 liters)
[f]31 Septuagint and Syriac; Hebrew 31such as the person can afford, one

---

14:19 sin offering. See 4:1–5:13 and notes on 4:3,5. burnt offering. See note on 1:3.

14:20 grain offering. See note on 2:1.

14:33–53 There are many similarities between this section

and the previous one, particularly in the manner of restoration.

14:45 torn down. A house desecrated by mildew, mold or fungus would be a defiled place to live in, so drastic measures had to be taken.

and the mildew has not spread after the house has been plastered, he shall pronounce the house clean, [n] because the mildew is gone. [49]To purify the house he is to take two birds and some cedar wood, scarlet yarn and hyssop. [o] [50]He shall kill one of the birds over fresh water in a clay pot. [p] [51]Then he is to take the cedar wood, the hyssop, [q] the scarlet yarn and the live bird, dip them into the blood of the dead bird and the fresh water, and sprinkle the house seven times. [r] [52]He shall purify the house with the bird's blood, the fresh water, the live bird, the cedar wood, the hyssop and the scarlet yarn. [53]Then he is to release the live bird in the open fields [s] outside the town. In this way he will make atonement for the house, and it will be clean. [t] "

[54]These are the regulations for any infectious skin disease, [u] for an itch, [55]for mildew [v] in clothing or in a house, [56]and for a swelling, a rash or a bright spot, [w] [57]to determine when something is clean or unclean.

These are the regulations for infectious skin diseases and mildew. [x]

Discharges Causing Uncleanness

15 The LORD said to Moses and Aaron, [2]"Speak to the Israelites and say to them: 'When any man has a bodily discharge, [y] the discharge is unclean. [3]Whether it continues flowing from his body or is blocked, it will make him unclean. This is how his discharge will bring about uncleanness:

[4]" 'Any bed the man with a discharge lies on will be unclean, and anything he sits on will be unclean. [5]Anyone who touches his bed must wash his clothes [z] and bathe with water, [a] and he will be unclean till evening. [b] [6]Whoever sits on anything that the man with a discharge sat on must wash his clothes and bathe with water, and he will be unclean till evening.

[7]" 'Whoever touches the man [c] who has a discharge [d] must wash his clothes and bathe with water, and he will be unclean till evening.

[8]" 'If the man with the discharge spits [e] on someone who is clean, that person must wash his clothes and bathe with water, and he will be unclean till evening.

[9]" 'Everything the man sits on when riding will be unclean, [10]and whoever touches any of the things that were under him will be unclean till evening; whoever picks up those things [f] must wash his clothes and bathe with water, and he will be unclean till evening.

[11]" 'Anyone the man with a discharge touches without rinsing his hands with water must wash his clothes and bathe with water, and he will be unclean till evening.

[12]" 'A clay pot [g] that the man touches must be broken, and any wooden article [h] is to be rinsed with water.

[13]" 'When a man is cleansed from his discharge, he is to count off seven days [i] for his ceremonial cleansing; he must wash his clothes and bathe himself with fresh water, and he will be clean. [j] [14]On the eighth day he must take two doves or two young pigeons [k] and come before the LORD to the entrance to the Tent of Meeting and give them to the priest. [15]The priest is to sacrifice them, the one for a sin offering [l] and the other for a burnt offering. [m] In this way he will make atonement before the LORD for the man because of his discharge. [n]

[16]" 'When a man has an emission of semen, [o] he must bathe his whole body with water, and he will be unclean till evening. [p] [17]Any clothing or leather that has semen on it must be washed with water, and it will be unclean till evening. [18]When a man lies with a woman and there is an emission of semen, [q] both must bathe with water, and they will be unclean till evening.

[19]" 'When a woman has her regular flow of blood, the impurity of her monthly period [r] will last seven days, and anyone who touches her will be unclean till evening.

[20]" 'Anything she lies on during her period will be unclean, and anything she sits

Cross-references (center column)

14:48 [n]S Lev 13:6
14:49 [o]1Ki 4:33
14:50 [p]ver 5
14:51 [q]ver 6;
Ps 51:7 [r]S ver 4,7
14:53 [s]S ver 7
[t]ver 20
14:54 [u]Lev 13:2
14:55
[v]Lev 13:47-52
14:56 [w]Lev 13:2
14:57
[x]S Lev 10:10
15:2 [y]ver 16,32;
Lev 22:4; Nu 5:2;
2Sa 3:29; Mt 9:20
15:5
[z]S Lev 11:25
[a]Lev 14:8
[b]S Lev 11:24
15:7 [c]ver 19;
Lev 22:5 [d]ver 16;
Lev 22:4

15:8 [e]Nu 12:14
15:10 [f]Nu 19:10
15:12
[g]S Lev 6:28
[h]S Lev 11:32
15:13 [i]S Lev 8:33
[j]ver 5
15:14 [k]Lev 14:22
15:15 [l]Lev 5:7
[m]Lev 14:31
15:16 [n]S Lev 14:18,19
[o]S ver 2;
Dt 23:10 [p]ver 5;
Dt 23:11
15:18 [q]1Sa 21:4
15:19 [r]S ver 24

15:1–33 The chapter deals with (1) male uncleanness caused by bodily discharge (vv. 2–15) or emission of semen (vv. 16–18); (2) female uncleanness caused by her monthly period (vv. 19–24) or lengthy hemorrhaging (vv. 25–30); (3) summary (vv. 31–33).

15:2 *bodily discharge.* Probably either diarrhea or urethral discharge (various kinds of infections). The contamination of anything under the man (v. 10), whether he sat (vv. 4,6,9) or lay (v. 4) on it, indicates that the bodily discharge had to do with the buttocks or genitals.

15:4 *bed.* Something like a mat (cf. 2Sa 11:13).

15:13 *cleansed.* God brought about the healing; the priest could only ascertain that a person was already healed.

15:16 *semen.* Normal sexual activity and a woman's menstruation required no sacrifices but only washing and a minimal period of uncleanness.

15:19 *seven days.* See 12:2. This regulation is the background of 2Sa 11:4 (Bathsheba).

15:20 See note on Ge 31:35.

on will be unclean. 21Whoever touches her bed must wash his clothes and bathe with water, and he will be unclean till evening. s 22Whoever touches anything she sits on must wash his clothes and bathe with water, and he will be unclean till evening. 23Whether it is the bed or anything she was sitting on, when anyone touches it, he will be unclean till evening.

24" 'If a man lies with her and her monthly flow t touches him, he will be unclean for seven days; any bed he lies on will be unclean.

25" 'When a woman has a discharge of blood for many days at a time other than her monthly period u or has a discharge that continues beyond her period, she will be unclean as long as she has the discharge, just as in the days of her period. 26Any bed she lies on while her discharge continues will be unclean, as is her bed during her monthly period, and anything she sits on will be unclean, as during her period. 27Whoever touches them will be unclean; he must wash his clothes and bathe with water, and he will be unclean till evening.

28" 'When she is cleansed from her discharge, she must count off seven days, and after that she will be ceremonially clean. 29On the eighth day she must take two doves or two young pigeons v and bring them to the priest at the entrance to the Tent of Meeting. 30The priest is to sacrifice one for a sin offering and the other for a burnt offering. In this way he will make atonement for her before the LORD for the uncleanness of her discharge. w

31" 'You must keep the Israelites separate from things that make them unclean, so they will not die in their uncleanness for defiling my dwelling place, g x which is among them.' "

32These are the regulations for a man with a discharge, for anyone made unclean by an emission of semen, y 33for a woman in her monthly period, for a man or a woman with a discharge, and for a man who lies with a woman who is ceremonially unclean. z

The Day of Atonement

16:2–34pp — Lev 23:26–32; Nu 29:7–11

16 The LORD spoke to Moses after the death of the two sons of Aaron who died when they approached the LORD. a 2The LORD said to Moses: "Tell your brother Aaron not to come whenever he chooses b into the Most Holy Place c behind the curtain d in front of the atonement cover e on the ark, or else he will die, because I appear f in the cloud g over the atonement cover.

3"This is how Aaron is to enter the sanc-

15:21 s ver 27
15:24 t ver 19; Lev 12:2; 18:19; 20:18; Eze 18:6
15:25 u Mt 9:20; Mk 5:25; Lk 8:43
15:29 v Lev 14:22

15:30 w Lev 5:10; 14:20,31; 18:19; 2Sa 11:4; Mk 5:25; Lk 8:43
15:31 x Lev 20:3; Nu 5:3; 19:13,20; 2Sa 15:25; 2Ki 21:7; Ps 33:14; 74:7; 76:2; Eze 5:11; 23:38
15:32 y S ver 2
15:33 z ver 19,24, 25
16:1 a S Lev 10:1
16:2 b Ex 30:10; Heb 9:7
c S Ex 26:33; Heb 9:25; 10:19
d S Ex 26:33; Heb 6:19
e S Ex 26:34
f S Ex 25:22
g S Ex 40:34; S 2Sa 22:10

g 31 Or my tabernacle

15:24 A case of the woman's period beginning during intercourse. This is different from 18:19 and 20:18. *flow.* During her period a woman was protected from sexual activity. No offering was required for uncleanness contracted by a man in this way, but the uncleanness lasted seven days. **15:25** *discharge of blood for many days.* As, e.g., the woman in Mt 9:20. *beyond her period.* An unnatural discharge, possibly caused by disease, was treated like a sickness and required an offering upon recovery (vv. 28–30; see vv. 14–15). **15:31** Addressed to the priests, thus emphasizing the importance of the regulations. Since God dwelt in the tabernacle, any unholiness, symbolized by the discharges of ch. 15, could result in death if the people came into his presence. Sin separates all people from a holy God and results in their death, unless atonement is made (see the next chapter). **16:1–34** See 23:26–32; 25:9; Ex 30:10; Nu 29:7–11; Heb 9:7. The order of ritual for the Day of Atonement was as follows: 1. The high priest went to the basin in the courtyard, removed his regular garments, washed himself (v. 4) and went into the Holy Place to put on the special garments for the Day of Atonement (v. 4). 2. He went out to sacrifice a bull at the altar of burnt offering as a sin offering for himself and the other priests (v. 11). 3. He went into the Most Holy Place with some of the bull's blood, with incense and with coals from the altar of burnt offering (vv. 12–13). The incense was placed on the burning coals, and the smoke of the incense hid the ark from view. 4. He sprinkled some of the bull's blood on and in front of the cover of the ark (v. 14). 5. He went outside the tabernacle and cast lots for two goats to see which was to be sacrificed and which was to be the scapegoat (vv. 7–8). 6. At the altar of burnt offering the high priest killed the goat for the sin offering for the people, and for a second time he went into the Most Holy Place, this time to sprinkle the goat's blood in front of and on the atonement cover (vv. 5,9,15–16a). 7. He returned to the Holy Place (called "Tent of Meeting" in v. 16) and sprinkled the goat's blood there (v. 16b). 8. He went outside to the altar of burnt offering and sprinkled it (v. 18) with the blood of the bull (for himself, v. 11) and of the goat (for the people, v. 15). 9. While in the courtyard, he laid both hands on the second goat, thus symbolizing the transfer of Israel's sin, and sent it out into the desert (vv. 20–22). 10. The man who took the goat away, after he accomplished his task, washed himself and his clothes outside the camp (v. 26) before rejoining the people. 11. The high priest entered the Holy Place to remove his special garments (v. 23). 12. He went out to the basin to wash and put on his regular priestly clothes (v. 24). 13. As a final sacrifice he went out to the great altar and offered a ram (v. 3) as a burnt offering for himself, and another ram (v. 5) for the people (v. 24). 14. The conclusion of the entire day was the removal of the sacrifices for the sin offerings to a place outside the camp, where they were burned, and there the man who performed this ritual bathed and washed his clothes (vv. 27–28) before rejoining the people. **16:1** *sons of Aaron who died.* See 10:1–3. **16:2** *atonement cover.* See Ex 25:17 and note. Blood sprinkled on the lid of the ark made atonement for Israel on the Day of Atonement (vv. 15–17). In the Septuagint (the Greek translation of the OT) the word for "atonement cover" is the same one used of Christ and translated "sacrifice of atonement" in Ro 3:25 (see NIV text note there).

tuary area:*h* with a young bull*i* for a sin offering and a ram for a burnt offering.*j* 4He is to put on the sacred linen tunic,*k* with linen undergarments next to his body; he is to tie the linen sash around him and put on the linen turban.*l* These are sacred garments;*m* so he must bathe himself with water*n* before he puts them on.*o* 5From the Israelite community*p* he is to take two male goats*q* for a sin offering and a ram for a burnt offering.

6"Aaron is to offer the bull for his own sin offering to make atonement for himself and his household.*r* 7Then he is to take the two goats and present them before the LORD at the entrance to the Tent of Meeting. 8He is to cast lots*s* for the two goats—one lot for the LORD and the other for the scapegoat.*h t* 9Aaron shall bring the goat whose lot falls to the LORD and sacrifice it for a sin offering. 10But the goat chosen by lot as the scapegoat shall be presented alive before the LORD to be used for making atonement*u* by sending it into the desert as a scapegoat.

11"Aaron shall bring the bull for his own sin offering to make atonement for himself and his household,*v* and he is to slaughter the bull for his own sin offering. 12He is to take a censer full of burning coals*w* from the altar before the LORD and two handfuls of finely ground fragrant incense*x* and take them behind the curtain. 13He is to put the incense on the fire before the LORD, and the smoke of the incense will conceal the atonement cover*y* above the Testimony, so that he will not die.*z* 14He is to take some of the bull's blood*a* and with his finger sprinkle it on the front of the atonement cover; then he shall sprinkle some of it with his finger seven times before the atonement cover.*b*

15"He shall then slaughter the goat for the sin offering for the people*c* and take its blood behind the curtain*d* and do with it

as he did with the bull's blood: He shall sprinkle*e* it on the atonement cover and in front of it. 16In this way he will make atonement*f* for the Most Holy Place*g* because of the uncleanness and rebellion of the Israelites, whatever their sins have been. He is to do the same for the Tent of Meeting,*h* which is among them in the midst of their uncleanness. 17No one is to be in the Tent of Meeting from the time Aaron goes in to make atonement in the Most Holy Place until he comes out, having made atonement for himself, his household and the whole community of Israel.

18"Then he shall come out to the altar*i* that is before the LORD and make atonement for it. He shall take some of the bull's blood and some of the goat's blood and put it on all the horns of the altar.*j* 19He shall sprinkle some of the blood on it with his finger seven times to cleanse it and to consecrate it from the uncleanness of the Israelites.*k*

20"When Aaron has finished making atonement for the Most Holy Place, the Tent of Meeting and the altar, he shall bring forward the live goat.*l* 21He is to lay both hands on the head of the live goat*m* and confess*n* over it all the wickedness and rebellion of the Israelites—all their sins—and put them on the goat's head. He shall send the goat away into the desert in the care of a man appointed for the task. 22The goat will carry on itself all their sins*o* to a solitary place; and the man shall release it in the desert.

23"Then Aaron is to go into the Tent of Meeting and take off the linen garments*p* he put on before he entered the Most Holy Place, and he is to leave them there.*q* 24He shall bathe himself with water in a holy

---

16:3 *h*ver 6; Lev 4:1-12; Heb 9:24,25
*i*S Lev 4:3 /ver 5
16:4 *k*S Lev 8:13
*l*S Ex 28:39 *m*ver 32; S Ex 28:42; 29:29,30; Lev 21:10; Nu 20:26,28
*n*S Ex 29:4; Heb 10:22
*o*Eze 9:2; 44:17-18
16:5 *p*S Lev 4:13-21
*q*ver 20; S Lev 4:3; 2Ch 29:23; Ps 50:9
16:6 *r*Lev 9:7; Heb 7:27; 9:7,12
16:8 *s*Nu 26:55, 56; 33:54; 34:13; Jos 14:2; 18:6; Jdg 20:9; Ne 10:34; Est 3:7; 9:24; Ps 22:18; Pr 16:33 *t*ver 10, 26
16:10 *u*Isa 53:4-10; S Ro 3:25
16:11 *v*S ver 6, 24,33
16:12 *w*S Lev 10:1; Rev 8:5
*x*S Ex 25:6; 30:34-38
16:13 *y*S Ex 25:17
*z*S Ex 28:43
16:14 *a*S Lev 4:5; Heb 9:7,13,25
*b*S Lev 4:6
16:15 *c*S Lev 4:13-21; Heb 7:27; 9:7,12; 13:11 *d*Heb 9:3
*e*S Lev 4:17; Nu 19:19; Isa 52:15; Eze 36:25
16:16 *f*S Ex 29:36; S Ro 3:25
*g*S Ex 26:33; Heb 9:25
*h*Ex 29:4; S 40:2
16:18 *i*S Lev 4:7
/S Lev 4:18
16:19 *k*Eze 43:20
16:20 *l*S ver 5
16:21 *m*S Ex 29:10
*n*S Lev 5:5
16:22 *o*S Ex 28:38; Isa 53:12

16:23 *p*S Ex 28:42 *q*Eze 42:14

*h*8 That is, the goat of removal; Hebrew *azazel*; also in verses 10 and 26

16:3 *sanctuary area.* The Most Holy Place (see v. 2). *bull.* For Aaron's cleansing (vv. 6,11). Before Aaron could minister in the Most Holy Place for the nation, he himself had to be cleansed (Heb 5:1–3); not so Christ, who is our high priest and Aaron's antitype (Heb 7:26–28).
16:5 *two male goats for a sin offering.* One was the usual sin offering (see notes on 4:3,5) and the other a scapegoat. No single offering could fully typify the atonement of Christ. The one goat was killed, its blood sprinkled in the Most Holy Place and its body burned outside the camp (vv. 15,27), symbolizing the payment of the price of Christ's atonement. The other goat, sent away alive and bearing the sins of the nation (v. 21), symbolized the removal of sin and its guilt. *ram.* For the sins of the people; the one in v. 3 was for the sins of the high priest. Both were sacrificed at the end of the ceremony (v. 24).

16:6–10 An outline of vv. 11–22.
16:11 *make atonement for himself.* See note on v. 3.
16:13 The smoke of the incense covered the ark so that the high priest would not see the glorious presence of God (v. 2) and thus die.
16:14 See Ro 3:25. *seven times.* See note on 4:6.
16:16 *Tent of Meeting.* Here and in vv. 17,20,33 the term means the Holy Place.
16:20–22 A summary description of substitutionary atonement. The sin of the worshipers was confessed and symbolically transferred to the sacrificial animal, on which hands were laid (see notes on 1:3; Ex 29:10; see also Lev 1:4; 3:8; 4:4).
16:24 *holy place.* Cf. 6:26. *burnt offering . . . burnt offering.* The two rams mentioned in vv. 3,5.

place[r] and put on his regular garments.[s] Then he shall come out and sacrifice the burnt offering for himself and the burnt offering for the people,[t] to make atonement for himself and for the people.[u] 25He shall also burn the fat of the sin offering on the altar.

26"The man who releases the goat as a scapegoat[v] must wash his clothes[w] and bathe himself with water;[x] afterward he may come into the camp. 27The bull and the goat for the sin offerings, whose blood was brought into the Most Holy Place to make atonement, must be taken outside the camp;[y] their hides, flesh and offal are to be burned up. 28The man who burns them must wash his clothes and bathe himself with water; afterward he may come into the camp.[z]

29"This is to be a lasting ordinance[a] for you: On the tenth day of the seventh month[b] you must deny yourselves[i][c] and not do any work[d]—whether native-born[e] or an alien living among you— 30because on this day atonement will be made[f] for you, to cleanse you. Then, before the LORD, you will be clean from all your sins.[g] 31It is a sabbath of rest, and you must deny yourselves;[h] it is a lasting ordinance.[i] 32The priest who is anointed and ordained[j] to succeed his father as high priest is to make atonement. He is to put on the sacred linen garments[k] 33and make atonement for the Most Holy Place, for the Tent of Meeting and the altar, and for the priests and all the people of the community.[l]

34"This is to be a lasting ordinance[m] for you: Atonement is to be made once a year[n] for all the sins of the Israelites."

And it was done, as the LORD commanded Moses.

Eating Blood Forbidden

17 The LORD said to Moses, 2"Speak to Aaron and his sons[o] and to all the Israelites and say to them: 'This is what the LORD has commanded: 3Any Israelite who sacrifices an ox,[j] a lamb[p] or a goat[q] in the camp or outside of it 4instead of bringing it to the entrance to the Tent of Meeting[r] to present it as an offering to the LORD in front of the tabernacle of the LORD[s]—that man shall be considered guilty of bloodshed; he has shed blood and must be cut off from his people.[t] 5This is so the Israelites will bring to the LORD the sacrifices they are now making in the open fields. They must bring them to the priest, that is, to the LORD, at the entrance to the Tent of Meeting and sacrifice them as fellowship offerings.[k][u] 6The priest is to sprinkle the blood against the altar[v] of the LORD[w] at the entrance to the Tent of Meeting and burn the fat as an aroma pleasing to the LORD.[x] 7They must no longer offer any of their sacrifices to the goat idols[l][y] to whom they prostitute themselves.[z] This is to be a lasting ordinance[a] for them and for the generations to come.'[b]

8"Say to them: 'Any Israelite or any alien living among them who offers a burnt offering or sacrifice 9and does not bring it to the entrance to the Tent[c] of Meeting[d] to sacrifice it to the LORD[e]—that man must be cut off from his people.

10" 'Any Israelite or any alien living among them who eats any blood—I will set my face against that person who eats blood[f] and will cut him off from his people. 11For the life of a creature is in the

Cross references

16:24 [r]S Lev 6:16
[s]ver 3-5 [t]Lev 1:3
[u]S ver 11
16:26 [v]S ver 8
[w]S Lev 11:25
[x]Lev 14:8
16:27
[y]S Ex 29:14
16:28 [z]Nu 19:8, 10
16:29
[a]S Ex 12:14
[b]Lev 25:9 [c]ver 31; Lev 23:27,32; Nu 29:7; Isa 58:3
[d]S Ex 31:15; S Lev 23:28
[e]Ex 12:19
16:30
[f]S Ex 30:10
[g]Ps 51:2; Jer 33:8; Eze 36:33; Zec 13:1; Eph 5:26
16:31 [h]Ezr 8:21; Isa 58:3,5; Da 10:12
[i]Ac 27:9
16:32
[j]S Ex 30:30 [k]S ver 4; S Ex 28:2
16:33 [l]S ver 11, 16-18; Eze 45:18
16:34
[m]S Ex 27:21
[n]Heb 9:7,25

17:2 [o]Lev 10:6, 12
17:3 [p]S Lev 3:7
[q]S Lev 7:23
17:4 [r]ver 9; 1Ki 8:4; 2Ch 1:3
[s]Dt 12:5-21
[t]S Ge 17:14
17:5 [u]S Lev 3:1; Eze 43:27
17:6 [v]S Lev 4:18
[w]S Lev 3:2
[x]S Lev 1:9
17:7 [y]S Ex 22:20
[z]S Ex 34:15; Jer 3:6,9; Eze 23:3; 1Co 10:20
[a]S Ex 12:14
[b]S Ge 9:12
17:9 [c]S Lev 1:3
[d]S ver 4
[e]S Lev 3:7
17:10 [f]S Ge 9:4

[i]29 Or must fast; also in verse 31   [j]3 The Hebrew word can include both male and female.   [k]5 Traditionally peace offerings   [l]7 Or demons

---

16:25 fat of the sin offering. See 4:8–10.
16:27 outside the camp. See note on 4:12.
16:29,31 deny yourselves. See NIV text note; more lit. "humble (or afflict) yourselves." The expression came to be used of fasting (Ps 35:13). The Day of Atonement was the only regular fast day stipulated in the OT (see 23:27,29,32 and NIV text note), though tradition later added other fast days to the Jewish calendar (see Zec 7:5; 8:19).
16:29 seventh month. Tishri, the seventh month, begins with the Feast of Trumpets (see note on 23:24). The Day of Atonement follows on the 10th day, and on the 15th day the Feast of Tabernacles begins (see 23:23–36).
16:30 clean from all your sins. On the Day of Atonement the repentant Israelite was assured of sins forgiven.
16:34 once a year. Heb 9:11–10:14 repeatedly points out this contrast with Christ's "once for all" sacrifice.
17:4 tabernacle of the LORD. The people, with few exceptions (e.g., Dt 12:15,20–21), were directed to sacrifice only at the central sanctuary (Dt 12:5–6). Sennacherib's representative referred to Hezekiah's requiring worship only in

Jerusalem (2Ki 18:22). One reason for such a regulation was to keep the Israelites from becoming corrupted by the Canaanites' pagan worship. cut off from his people. See note on 7:20.

17:5 to the priest, that is, to the LORD. See note on 6:6.
17:7 prostitute themselves. See 20:5–6; see also Jdg 2:17 and note.
17:11 the life of a creature is in the blood. See note on Ge 9:4. The blood shed in the sacrifices was sacred. It epitomized the life of the sacrificial victim. Since life was sacred, blood (a symbol of life) had to be treated with respect (Ge 9:5–6). Eating blood was therefore strictly forbidden (see 7:26–27; Dt 12:16,23–25; 15:23; 1Sa 14:32–34). blood . . . makes atonement. Practically every sacrifice included the sprinkling or smearing of blood on the altar or within the tabernacle (v. 6; 1:5; 3:2; 4:6,25; 7:2), thus teaching that atonement involves the substitution of life for life. The blood of the OT sacrifice pointed forward to the blood of the Lamb of God, who obtained for his people "eternal redemption" (Heb 9:12). "Without the shedding of blood there is no

blood,[g] and I have given it to you to make atonement for yourselves on the altar; it is the blood that makes atonement for one's life.[h] [12]Therefore I say to the Israelites, "None of you may eat blood, nor may an alien living among you eat blood."

[13]" 'Any Israelite or any alien living among you who hunts any animal or bird that may be eaten must drain out the blood and cover it with earth,[i] [14]because the life of every creature is its blood. That is why I have said to the Israelites, "You must not eat the blood of any creature, because the life of every creature is its blood; anyone who eats it must be cut off."[j]

[15]" 'Anyone, whether native-born or alien, who eats anything[k] found dead or torn by wild animals[l] must wash his clothes and bathe with water,[m] and he will be ceremonially unclean till evening;[n] then he will be clean. [16]But if he does not wash his clothes and bathe himself, he will be held responsible.[o] '"

Unlawful Sexual Relations

18 The LORD said to Moses, [2]"Speak to the Israelites and say to them: 'I am the LORD your God.[p] [3]You must not do as they do in Egypt, where you used to live, and you must not do as they do in the land of Canaan, where I am bringing you. Do not follow their practices.[q] [4]You must obey my laws[r] and be careful to follow my decrees.[s] I am the LORD your God.[t] [5]Keep my decrees and laws,[u] for the man who obeys them will live by them.[v] I am the LORD.

[6]" 'No one is to approach any close rela-

tive to have sexual relations. I am the LORD.

[7]" 'Do not dishonor your father[w] by having sexual relations with your mother.[x] She is your mother; do not have relations with her.

[8]" 'Do not have sexual relations with your father's wife;[y] that would dishonor your father.[z]

[9]" 'Do not have sexual relations with your sister,[a] either your father's daughter or your mother's daughter, whether she was born in the same home or elsewhere.[b]

[10]" 'Do not have sexual relations with your son's daughter or your daughter's daughter; that would dishonor you.

[11]" 'Do not have sexual relations with the daughter of your father's wife, born to your father; she is your sister.

[12]" 'Do not have sexual relations with your father's sister;[c] she is your father's close relative.

[13]" 'Do not have sexual relations with your mother's sister,[d] because she is your mother's close relative.

[14]" 'Do not dishonor your father's brother by approaching his wife to have sexual relations; she is your aunt.[e]

[15]" 'Do not have sexual relations with your daughter-in-law.[f] She is your son's wife; do not have relations with her.[g]

[16]" 'Do not have sexual relations with your brother's wife;[h] that would dishonor your brother.

[17]" 'Do not have sexual relations with both a woman and her daughter.[i] Do not

Cross references (center column)

17:11 gver 14; hHeb 9:22
17:13 iLev 7:26; Eze 24:7; 33:25; Ac 15:20
17:14 jS Ge 9:4
17:15 kS Lev 7:24; lS Ex 22:31; mS Lev 14:8; nS Lev 11:40
17:16 oS Lev 5:1
18:2 pS Ge 17:7
18:3 qver 24-30; S Eze 23:24; Dt 18:9; 2Ki 16:3; 17:8; 1Ch 5:25
18:4 rS Ge 26:5; sDt 4:1; 1Ki 11:11; Jer 44:10,23; Eze 11:12
18:5 tver 2; uS Ge 26:5; vDt 4:1; Ne 9:29; Isa 55:3; Eze 18:9; 20:11; Am 5:4-6; Mt 19:17; S Ro 10:5*; Gal 3:12*
18:7 wver 8; Lev 20:11; Dt 27:20; xEze 22:10
18:8 yiCo 5:1; zGe 35:22; Lev 20:11; Dt 22:30; 27:20
18:9 aver 11; Lev 20:17; Dt 27:22; bLev 20:17; Dt 27:22; 2Sa 13:13; Eze 22:11
18:12 cver 13; Lev 20:19
18:13 dS ver 12, 14; Lev 20:20
18:14 eS ver 13
18:15 fS Ge 11:31; S 38:16; gEze 22:11
18:16 hLev 20:21; Mt 14:4; Mk 6:18
18:17 iLev 20:14; Dt 27:23

---

forgiveness" (Heb 9:22).

17:15 *found dead or torn.* Such animals would not have had the blood drained from them and therefore would be forbidden.

18:1—20:27 Here God's people are given instructions concerning interpersonal relations and a morality reflecting God's holiness. Israel was thereby prepared for a life different from the Canaanites, whose life-style was deplorably immoral. Ch. 18 contains prohibitions in the moral sphere, ch. 19 expands the Ten Commandments to detail correct morality, and ch. 20 assesses the penalties for violating God's standard of morality. See chart on "Major Social Concerns in the Covenant," p. 271.

18:2 In chs. 18–26 The phrase "I am the LORD" occurs 42 times. The Lord's name (i.e., his revealed character as Yahweh, "the LORD") is the authority that stands behind his instructions. See note on Ex 3:15.

18:3 Six times in this chapter Israel is warned not to follow the example of pagans (here, two times; see also vv. 24, 26–27,30).

18:5 *live.* With God's full blessing. The law was the way of life for the redeemed (see Eze 20:11,13,21), not a way of salvation for the lost (see Ro 10:5; Gal 3:12).

18:6 A summary of the laws against incest (vv. 7–18).

Penalties for incestuous relations are given in ch. 20.

18:7 This prohibition probably applied even after the father's death. If the father was still living, the act was adulterous and therefore forbidden.

18:8 *your father's wife.* Other than your mother—assuming there is more than one wife.

18:11 *sister.* There would be many half-sisters in a polygamous society. Tamar claimed that an exception to this prohibition could be made (2Sa 13:12–13; but see note there).

18:14 *your aunt.* See 20:20. If the father's brother was alive, the act would be adulterous. If he was dead, one could rationalize such a marriage because the aunt was not a blood relative—but it was forbidden.

18:15 Cf. the account of Judah and Tamar (Ge 38:18).

18:16 *your brother's wife.* The law also applied to a time after divorce or the brother's death. To marry one's brother's widow was not immoral but might damage the brother's inheritance. The levirate law of Dt 25:5–6 offered an exception that preserved the dead brother's inheritance and continued his line.

18:17 *daughter.* Stepdaughter (granddaughter-in-law is also covered in the verse). The law applied even after the mother's death.

have sexual relations with either her son's daughter or her daughter's daughter; they are her close relatives. That is wickedness.

[18] " 'Do not take your wife's sister[j] as a rival wife and have sexual relations with her while your wife is living.

[19] " 'Do not approach a woman to have sexual relations during the uncleanness[k] of her monthly period.[l]

[20] " 'Do not have sexual relations with your neighbor's wife[m] and defile yourself with her.

[21] " 'Do not give any of your children[n] to be sacrificed[m] to Molech,[o] for you must not profane the name of your God.[p] I am the LORD.[q]

[22] " 'Do not lie with a man as one lies with a woman;[r] that is detestable.[s]

[23] " 'Do not have sexual relations with an animal and defile yourself with it. A woman must not present herself to an animal to have sexual relations with it; that is a perversion.[t]

[24] " 'Do not defile yourselves in any of these ways, because this is how the nations that I am going to drive out before you[u] became defiled.[v] [25]Even the land was defiled;[w] so I punished it for its sin,[x] and the land vomited out its inhabitants.[y] [26]But you must keep my decrees and my laws.[z] The native-born and the aliens living among you must not do any of these detestable things, [27]for all these things were done by the people who lived in the land before you, and the land became defiled. [28]And if you defile the land,[a] it will vomit you out[b] as it vomited out the nations that were before you.

[29] " 'Everyone who does any of these detestable things—such persons must be cut off from their people. [30]Keep my requirements[c] and do not follow any of the detestable customs that were practiced before you came and do not defile yourselves with them. I am the LORD your God.[d] ' "

Various Laws

19 The LORD said to Moses, [2]"Speak to the entire assembly of Israel[e]

and say to them: 'Be holy because I, the LORD your God,[f] am holy.[g]

[3] " 'Each of you must respect his mother and father,[h] and you must observe my Sabbaths.[i] I am the LORD your God.[j]

[4] " 'Do not turn to idols or make gods of cast metal for yourselves.[k] I am the LORD your God.[l]

[5] " 'When you sacrifice a fellowship offering[n] to the LORD, sacrifice it in such a way that it will be accepted on your behalf. [6]It shall be eaten on the day you sacrifice it or on the next day; anything left over until the third day must be burned up.[m] [7]If any of it is eaten on the third day, it is impure and will not be accepted.[n] [8]Whoever eats it will be held responsible[o] because he has desecrated what is holy[p] to the LORD; that person must be cut off from his people.[q]

[9] " 'When you reap the harvest of your land, do not reap to the very edges[r] of your field or gather the gleanings of your harvest.[s] [10]Do not go over your vineyard a second time[t] or pick up the grapes that have fallen.[u] Leave them for the poor and the alien.[v] I am the LORD your God.

[11] " 'Do not steal.[w]

" 'Do not lie.[x]

" 'Do not deceive one another.[y]

[12] " 'Do not swear falsely[z] by my name[a] and so profane[b] the name of your God. I am the LORD.

[13] " 'Do not defraud your neighbor[c] or rob[d] him.[e]

" 'Do not hold back the wages of a hired man[f] overnight.[g]

[14] " 'Do not curse the deaf or put a stumbling block in front of the blind,[h] but fear your God.[i] I am the LORD.

Cross references (center column)

18:18 /S Ge 30:1
18:19 kS Lev 15:25-30; lS Lev 15:24
18:20 mS Ex 20:14; Mt 5:27,28; 1Co 6:9; Heb 13:4
18:21 nDt 12:31; 18:10; 2Ki 16:3; 17:17; 21:6; 23:10; 2Ch 28:1-4; 33:6; Ps 106:37,38; Isa 57:5; Jer 7:30,31; 19:5; 32:35; Eze 16:20; Mic 6:7; oLev 20:2-5; Dt 9:4; 1Ki 11:5, 7,33; Isa 57:9; Jer 32:35; 49:1; Zep 1:5; pLev 19:12; 21:6; Isa 48:11; Eze 22:26; 36:20; Am 2:7; Mal 1:12; qS Ex 6:2
18:22 rLev 20:13; Dt 23:18; Ro 1:27; 1Co 6:9; sS Ge 19:5
18:23 tEx 22:19; Lev 20:15; Dt 27:21
18:24 uver 3,27, 30; Lev 20:23; vDt 9:4; 18:12
18:25 wNu 35:34; Dt 21:23; xLev 20:23; Dt 9:5; 12:31; 18:12 yver 28; Lev 20:22; Job 20:15; Jer 51:34
18:26 zS Ge 26:5
18:28 aLev 20:22; Ezr 9:11; La 1:17; bS ver 25
18:30 cS Lev 8:35 dver 2
19:2 eNu 14:5; Ps 68:26

/S Ex 20:2
gS Ex 15:11; 1Pe 1:16*;
S Lev 11:44; S 20:26
19:3 hEx 20:12; iS Ex 20:8; jLev 11:44
19:4 kS Ex 20:4; Jdg 17:3; Ps 96:5; 115:4-7; 135:15; lLev 11:44
19:6 mLev 7:16-17
19:7 nLev 7:18
19:8 oS Lev 5:1; pLev 22:2,15,16;

Nu 18:32 qS Ge 17:14 19:9 rRu 2:2,3,7,16,17 sLev 23:10, 22; Dt 24:19-22; Job 24:10 19:10 tDt 24:20 uver 9 vDt 24:19,21 19:11 wEx 20:15; S 23:4; Lk 3:14 xS Ex 20:16; S Eph 4:25 yS Lev 6:2 19:12 zJer 5:2; 7:9; Mal 3:5 aEx 3:13; 20:7; Dt 18:19; Pr 18:10; Isa 42:8; Jer 44:16,26; S Mt 5:33 bJer 34:16 19:13 cLev 25:14,17 dS Ex 20:15 eS Ex 22:15,25-27 fJob 7:2; 24:12; 31:39; Isa 16:14; Mal 3:5 gDt 24:15; Jer 22:13; Mt 20:8; 1Ti 5:18; Jas 5:4 19:14 hS Ex 4:11; Lev 21:18; Dt 27:18 iver 32; Lev 25:17,36

m21 Or to be passed through the fire
n5 Traditionally peace offering

Footnotes (bottom)

18:18 Cf. the account of Jacob with Leah and Rachel (Ge 29:23-30).
18:19 See Eze 18:6; 22:10.
18:21 *Molech.* The god of the Ammonites (see 20:2–5; 1Ki 11:5 and note). The detestable practice of sacrificing children to Molech was common in Phoenicia and other surrounding countries. Cf. 1Ki 3:26–27. King Manasseh evidently sacrificed his sons to Molech (2Ch 33:6; see 2Ki 23:10). Jer 32:35 protests the practice.
18:22 *lie with a man.* See 20:13, where the penalty for homosexual acts is death.
18:29 *detestable.* See note on 7:21. *cut off from their*

people. See note on 7:20.
19:1 See note on 18:1–20:27.
19:2 *Be holy.* See note on 11:44.
19:3–4 See v. 30; Ex 20:4–6,8–11. See also chart on "Major Social Concerns in the Covenant," p. 271.
19:5 *fellowship offering.* See note on 3:1.
19:6 *third day.* See note on 7:15–18.
19:8 *cut off from his people.* See note on 7:20.
19:9–10 See 23:22; see also Dt 24:19–21. Ru 2 gives an example of the application of the law of gleaning.
19:11–12 See Ex 20:7,15–16.
19:13 *wages of a hired man.* See Dt 24:14–15; Mt 20:8.

said to you, "You will possess their land; I will give it to you as an inheritance, a land flowing with milk and honey." [u] I am the LORD your God, who has set you apart from the nations. [v]

25" 'You must therefore make a distinction between clean and unclean animals and between unclean and clean birds. [w] Do not defile yourselves by any animal or bird or anything that moves along the ground—those which I have set apart as unclean for you. 26You are to be holy to me [t][x] because I, the LORD, am holy, [y] and I have set you apart from the nations [z] to be my own.

27" 'A man or woman who is a medium [a] or spiritist among you must be put to death. [b] You are to stone them; [c] their blood will be on their own heads.' "

Rules for Priests

21 The LORD said to Moses, "Speak to the priests, the sons of Aaron, [d] and say to them: 'A priest must not make himself ceremonially unclean [e] for any of his people who die, [f] 2except for a close relative, such as his mother or father, [g] his son or daughter, his brother, 3or an unmarried sister who is dependent on him since she has no husband—for her he may make himself unclean. [h] 4He must not make himself unclean for people related to him by marriage, [u] and so defile himself.

5" 'Priests must not shave [i] their heads or shave off the edges of their beards [j] or cut their bodies. [k] 6They must be holy to their God [l] and must not profane the name of their God. [m] Because they present the offerings made to the LORD by fire, [n] the food of their God, [o] they are to be holy. [p]

7" 'They must not marry women defiled by prostitution or divorced from their husbands, [q] because priests are holy to their God. [r] 8Regard them as holy, [s] because they offer up the food of your God. [t] Consider them holy, because I the LORD am holy—I who make you holy. [v] [u]

9" 'If a priest's daughter defiles herself by becoming a prostitute, she disgraces her father; she must be burned in the fire. [v]

10" 'The high priest, the one among his brothers who has had the anointing oil poured on his head [w] and who has been ordained to wear the priestly garments, [x] must not let his hair become unkempt [w] or tear his clothes. [y] 11He must not enter a place where there is a dead body. [z] He must not make himself unclean, [a] even for his father or mother, [b] 12nor leave the sanctuary [c] of his God or desecrate it, because he has been dedicated by the anointing oil [d] of his God. I am the LORD.

13" 'The woman he marries must be a virgin. [e] 14He must not marry a widow, a divorced woman, or a woman defiled by prostitution, but only a virgin from his own people, 15so he will not defile his offspring among his people. I am the LORD, who makes him holy. [x] ' "

16The LORD said to Moses, 17"Say to Aaron: 'For the generations to come none of your descendants who has a defect [f] may come near to offer the food of his God. [g] 18No man who has any defect [h] may come near: no man who is blind [i] or lame, [j] disfigured or deformed; 19no man with a crippled foot or hand, 20or who is hunchbacked or dwarfed, or who has any eye defect, or who has festering or running sores or damaged testicles. [k] 21No descendant of Aaron the priest who has any defect [l] is to come near to present the offerings made to the LORD by fire. [m] He has a defect; he must not come near to offer the food of his God. [n] 22He may eat the most holy food of his God, [o] as well as the holy food; 23yet because of his defect, [p] he must not go near the curtain or approach the altar, and so desecrate my sanctuary. [q] I am the LORD, who makes them holy. [y] [r] ' "

24So Moses told this to Aaron and his sons and to all the Israelites.

20:24 [u]S Ex 3:8; Nu 14:8; 16:14
[v]S Ex 33:16
20:25 [w]Lev 10:10; Dt 14:3-21; Ac 10:14
20:26 [x]Dt 14:2
[y]ver 8; Lev 19:2; Jos 24:19; 2Ki 19:22; Ps 99:3
[z]S Ex 33:16
20:27 [a]S Ex 22:18
[b]S Lev 19:31
[c]S ver 2; S Lev 24:14
21:1 [d]S Ex 28:1; S Lev 1:5
[e]S Lev 5:3; S 13:3
[f]ver 11; Nu 5:2; 6:6; 19:11; 31:19
21:2 [g]ver 11
21:3 [h]Nu 6:6
21:5 [i]S Lev 13:40; Jer 7:29; 10:6
[j]Eze 5:1; 44:20
[k]S Lev 19:28
21:6 [l]ver 8; Ezr 8:28
[m]Lev 18:21
[n]S Lev 3:11
[o]ver 17,22; Lev 22:25
[p]S Ex 19:22; S Lev 10:3
21:7 [q]ver 13,14
[r]Eze 44:22
21:8 [s]ver 6
[t]Lev 3:11
[u]S Ex 31:13

21:9
[v]S Ge 38:24; S Lev 19:29
21:10 [w]S Ex 29:7
[x]S Lev 8:7-9,13; S 16:4
[y]S Lev 10:6
21:11 [z]Nu 5:2; 6:6; 9:6; 19:11, 13,14; 31:19
[a]Lev 19:28 [b]ver 2
21:12 [c]S Ex 25:8
[d]S Ex 28:41
21:13 [e]Eze 44:22
21:17 [f]ver 18,21, 23 [g]S ver 6
21:18
[h]Lev 22:19-25
[i]S Lev 19:14
[j]2Sa 4:4; 9:3; 19:26
21:20
[k]Lev 22:24; Dt 23:1; Isa 56:3
21:21 [l]S ver 17
[m]S Lev 3:11
[n]Lev 22:19
21:22 [o]1Co 9:13
21:23 [p]S ver 17
[q]S Ex 25:8
[r]Lev 20:8

[t]26 Or be my holy ones   [u]4 Or unclean as a leader among his people   [v]8 Or who sanctify you; or who set you apart as holy   [w]10 Or not uncover his head   [x]15 Or who sanctifies him; or who sets him apart as holy   [y]23 Or who sanctifies them; or who sets them apart as holy

---

20:25 See ch. 11 and notes.
20:27 See note on v. 6.
21:1—22:33 Directions for the priests' conduct, especially about separation from ceremonial uncleanness.
21:1 for any . . . who die. Touching a corpse (Nu 19:11) or entering the home of a person who had died (Nu 19:14) made one unclean. A priest was only to contract such uncleanness at the death of a close relative (vv. 2–3), and the regulations for the high priest denied him even this (vv. 11–12).
21:5 cut their bodies. See 19:27–28. Such lacerations and disfigurement were common among pagans as signs of

mourning and to secure the attention of their deity (see 1Ki 18:28). Israelite faith had a much less grotesque view of death (see, e.g., vv. 1–4; Ge 5:24; 2Sa 12:23; Heb 11:19).
21:8 I . . . am holy. See note on 11:44.
21:9 See Ge 38:24 and note.
21:11—12 See note on v. 1.
21:17 defect. Like the sacrifices that had to be without defect, the priests were to typify Christ's perfection (Heb 9:13–14).
21:23 curtain. Between the Holy Place and the Most Holy Place (see Ex 26:33).

22 The LORD said to Moses, [2]"Tell Aaron and his sons to treat with respect the sacred offerings[s] the Israelites consecrate to me, so they will not profane my holy name.[t] I am the LORD.[u]

[3]"Say to them: 'For the generations to come, if any of your descendants is ceremonially unclean and yet comes near the sacred offerings that the Israelites consecrate to the LORD,[v] that person must be cut off from my presence.[w] I am the LORD.

[4]"'If a descendant of Aaron has an infectious skin disease[z] or a bodily discharge,[x] he may not eat the sacred offerings until he is cleansed. He will also be unclean if he touches something defiled by a corpse[y] or by anyone who has an emission of semen, [5]or if he touches any crawling thing[z] that makes him unclean, or any person[a] who makes him unclean, whatever the uncleanness may be. [6]The one who touches any such thing will be unclean[b] till evening.[c] He must not eat any of the sacred offerings unless he has bathed himself with water.[d] [7]When the sun goes down, he will be clean, and after that he may eat the sacred offerings, for they are his food.[e] [8]He must not eat anything found dead[f] or torn by wild animals,[g] and so become unclean[h] through it. I am the LORD.[i]

[9]"'The priests are to keep my requirements[j] so that they do not become guilty[k] and die[l] for treating them with contempt. I am the LORD, who makes them holy.[a] [m]

[10]"'No one outside a priest's family may eat the sacred offering, nor may the guest of a priest or his hired worker eat it.[n] [11]But if a priest buys a slave with money, or if a slave is born in his household, that slave may eat his food.[o] [12]If a priest's daughter marries anyone other than a priest, she may not eat any of the sacred contributions. [13]But if a priest's daughter becomes a widow or is divorced, yet has no children, and she returns to live in her father's house as in her youth, she may eat of her father's food. No unauthorized person, however, may eat any of it.

[14]"'If anyone eats a sacred offering by mistake,[p] he must make restitution to the priest for the offering and add a fifth of the value[q] to it. [15]The priests must not desecrate the sacred offerings[r] the Israelites present to the LORD[s] [16]by allowing them to eat[t] the sacred offerings and so bring upon them guilt[u] requiring payment.[v] I am the LORD, who makes them holy.[w]'"

Unacceptable Sacrifices

[17]The LORD said to Moses, [18]"Speak to Aaron and his sons and to all the Israelites and say to them: 'If any of you—either an Israelite or an alien living in Israel[x]—presents a gift[y] for a burnt offering to the LORD, either to fulfill a vow[z] or as a freewill offering,[a] [19]you must present a male without defect[b] from the cattle, sheep or goats in order that it may be accepted on your behalf.[c] [20]Do not bring anything with a defect,[d] because it will not be accepted on your behalf.[e] [21]When anyone brings from the herd or flock[f] a fellowship offering[b][g] to the LORD to fulfill a special vow or as a freewill offering,[h] it must be without defect or blemish[i] to be acceptable.[j] [22]Do not offer to the LORD the blind, the injured or the maimed, or anything with warts or festering or running sores. Do not place any of these on the altar as an offering made to the LORD by fire. [23]You may, however, present as a freewill offering an ox[c] or a sheep that is deformed or stunted, but it will not be accepted in fulfillment of a vow. [24]You must not offer to the LORD an animal whose testicles are bruised, crushed, torn or cut.[k] You must not do this in your own land, [25]and you must not accept such animals from the hand of a foreigner and offer them as the food of your God.[l] They will not be accepted on your behalf, because they are deformed and have defects.[m]'"

[26]The LORD said to Moses, [27]"When a

---

[z]4 Traditionally *leprosy*; the Hebrew word was used for various diseases affecting the skin—not necessarily leprosy.   [a]9 Or *who sanctifies them*; or *who sets them apart as holy*; also in verse 16   [b]21 Traditionally *peace offering*   [c]23 The Hebrew word can include both male and female.

Cross references:

22:2 [s]S Lev 19:8; [t]S Ex 20:7; S Mt 5:33; [u]Eze 44:8
22:3 [v]Ezr 8:28; [w]Lev 7:20,21; Nu 19:13
22:4 [x]Lev 15:2-15; [y]Lev 11:24-28,39
22:5 [z]Lev 11:24-28,43; [a]S Lev 15:7
22:6 [b]Hag 2:13; [c]S Lev 11:24; [d]S Lev 14:8
22:7 [e]Nu 18:11; [f]S Lev 11:39; [g]S Ex 22:31; [h]S Lev 11:40; [i]Lev 11:44
22:9 [j]S Lev 8:35; [k]S Ex 28:38 /ver 16; S Ex 28:43; [m]Lev 20:8
22:10 [n]ver 13; Ex 12:45; 29:33
22:11 [o]Ge 17:13; Ex 12:44

22:14 [p]S Lev 4:2; [q]Lev 5:15
22:15 [r]S Lev 19:8; [s]Nu 18:32
22:16 [t]Nu 18:11; [u]S Ex 28:38; [v]S ver 9; [w]Lev 20:8
22:18 [x]Nu 15:16; 19:10; Jos 8:33; [y]S Lev 1:2 [z]ver 21; S Ge 28:20; Nu 15:8; Ps 22:25; 76:11; 116:18; [a]S Lev 7:16
22:19 [b]S Lev 1:3; 21:18-21; Nu 28:11; Dt 15:21; [c]S Lev 1:2
22:20 [d]S Lev 1:3; Dt 15:21; 17:1; Eze 43:23; 45:18; 46:6; Mal 1:8; Heb 9:14; 1Pe 1:19; [e]S Ex 28:38
22:21 [f]S Lev 1:2; [g]S Ex 32:6; S Lev 3:6; [h]S Lev 7:16; [i]S Ex 12:5; Mal 1:14 /Am 4:5
22:24 [k]S Lev 21:20
22:25 [l]S Lev 21:6; [m]S Lev 1:3; S 3:1; Nu 19:2

Study notes:

22:3 *cut off from my presence.* Excluded from the worshiping community.
22:4 See 13:1–46 and note on 13:45–46; 15:1–18 and notes; 21:11.
22:5 See 11:29–31.
22:8 See 17:15 and note.
22:9 *die for treating them with contempt.* The laws of cleanness were the same for priests and people, but the penalties were far more severe for the priests, who had greater responsibility. Cf. Nadab and Abihu (10:1–3) and the faithless priests of Malachi's day (Mal 1:6–2:9). *holy.* See note on 11:44.

22:14 *make restitution . . . add a fifth.* Cf. 5:16.
22:16 *holy.* See note on 11:44.
22:18 *burnt offering.* See note on 1:3.
22:20–22 See Mal 1:8.
22:21 *fellowship offering.* See note on 3:1.
22:24 *bruised, crushed, torn or cut.* Castrated animals were not acceptable offerings.

calf, a lamb or a goat[n] is born, it is to remain with its mother for seven days.[o] From the eighth day[p] on, it will be acceptable[q] as an offering made to the LORD by fire. 28Do not slaughter a cow or a sheep and its young on the same day.[r]

29"When you sacrifice a thank offering[s] to the LORD, sacrifice it in such a way that it will be accepted on your behalf. 30It must be eaten that same day; leave none of it till morning.[t] I am the LORD.[u]

31"Keep[v] my commands and follow them.[w] I am the LORD. 32Do not profane my holy name.[x] I must be acknowledged as holy by the Israelites.[y] I am the LORD, who makes[d] you holy[ez] 33and who brought you out of Egypt[a] to be your God.[b] I am the LORD."

23 The LORD said to Moses, 2"Speak to the Israelites and say to them: 'These are my appointed feasts,[c] the appointed feasts of the LORD, which you are to proclaim as sacred assemblies.[d]

The Sabbath

3"'There are six days when you may work,[e] but the seventh day is a Sabbath of rest,[f] a day of sacred assembly. You are not to do any work;[g] wherever you live, it is a Sabbath to the LORD.

The Passover and Unleavened Bread

23:4–8pp — Ex 12:14–20; Nu 28:16–25; Dt 16:1–8

4"'These are the LORD's appointed feasts, the sacred assemblies you are to proclaim at their appointed times:[h] 5The LORD's Passover[i] begins at twilight on the fourteenth day of the first month.[j] 6On the fifteenth day of that month the LORD's Feast of Unleavened Bread[k] begins; for seven days[l] you must eat bread made without yeast. 7On the first day hold a sacred assembly[m] and do no regular work. 8For seven days present an offering made

to the LORD by fire.[n] And on the seventh day hold a sacred assembly and do no regular work.' "

Firstfruits

9The LORD said to Moses, 10"Speak to the Israelites and say to them: 'When you enter the land I am going to give you[o] and you reap its harvest,[p] bring to the priest a sheaf[q] of the first grain you harvest.[r] 11He is to wave the sheaf before the LORD[s] so it will be accepted[t] on your behalf; the priest is to wave it on the day after the Sabbath. 12On the day you wave the sheaf, you must sacrifice as a burnt offering to the LORD a lamb a year old[u] without defect,[v] 13together with its grain offering[w] of two-tenths of an ephah[fx] of fine flour mixed with oil—an offering made to the LORD by fire, a pleasing aroma—and its drink offering[y] of a quarter of a hin[g] of wine.[z] 14You must not eat any bread, or roasted or new grain,[a] until the very day you bring this offering to your God.[b] This is to be a lasting ordinance for the generations to come,[c] wherever you live.[d]

Feast of Weeks

23:15–22pp — Nu 28:26–31; Dt 16:9–12

15"'From the day after the Sabbath, the day you brought the sheaf of the wave offering, count off seven full weeks. 16Count off fifty days up to the day after the seventh Sabbath,[e] and then present an offering of new grain to the LORD. 17From wherever you live, bring two loaves made of two-tenths of an ephah[f] of fine flour, baked with yeast, as a wave offering of firstfruits[g] to the LORD. 18Present with this bread seven male lambs, each a year old and without defect, one young bull and two rams. They will be a burnt offering to the

22:27 nS Lev 1:3
oS Ex 22:30
pS Ex 22:30
qS Ex 28:38
22:28 rDt 22:6,7
22:29
sS Lev 7:12
22:30 tLev 7:15
uLev 11:44
22:31 vDt 4:2,
40; Ps 105:45
wS Ex 22:31
22:32 xLev 18:21
yS Lev 10:3
zLev 20:8
22:33 aS Ex 6:6
bS Ge 17:7
23:2 cver 4,37,
44; Nu 29:39;
Eze 44:24;
Col 2:16 dver 21,
27
23:3 eEx 20:9
fS Ex 20:10;
Heb 4:9,10 gver
7,21,35;
Nu 28:26
23:4 hNa 1:15
23:5 iS Ex 12:11
fS Ex 12:6
23:6 kEx 12:17
fS Ex 12:19
23:7 mver 3,8

23:8 nS Lev 1:9
23:10 oNu 15:2,
18 pS Lev 19:9
qS Lev 19:9
rS Ex 22:29;
S 34:22; Ro 11:16
23:11
sS Ex 29:24
tS Ex 28:38
23:12
uS Lev 12:6
vS Lev 12:5
23:13
wLev 2:14–16;
S 6:20 xver 17;
Lev 24:5;
Nu 15:6; 28:9
yS Ge 35:14
zS Lev 10:9
23:14 aJos 5:11;
Ru 2:14;
1Sa 17:17; 25:18;
2Sa 17:28
bEx 34:26
cLev 3:17;
Nu 10:8; 15:21
dJer 2:3
23:16 eAc 2:1;
20:16
23:17 fS ver 13
gS Ex 34:22

d32 Or made   e32 Or who sanctifies you; or who sets you apart as holy   f13 That is, probably about 4 quarts (about 4.5 liters); also in verse 17   g13 That is, probably about 1 quart (about 1 liter)

22:28 Perhaps the prohibition was humanitarian (see v. 27), or possibly it was practical: The mother was to be saved to build up the flock (see Dt 22:6–7). Or it may have been a law to avoid an otherwise unknown pagan custom (see note on Ex 23:19).

22:30 that same day. The rule applied also to the Passover (Ex 34:25); however, the fellowship offering could be saved and eaten on the following day (7:16).

23:2 appointed feasts. See Ex 23:14–17 and notes; 34:18–25; Nu 28–29; Dt 16:1–17. The parallel in Numbers (the fullest and closest to Leviticus) specifies in great detail the offerings to be made at each feast. See chart on "OT Feasts and Other Sacred Days," p. 176.

23:3 Sabbath. See notes on Ex 16:23; 20:9–10. The Sabbath is associated with the annual feasts also in Ex 23:12. Two additional lambs were to be sacrificed as a burnt offering

every weekly Sabbath (Nu 28:9–10).

23:5 Passover. See notes on Ex 12:11,14,21. first month. See note on Ex 12:2. The Israelites had three systems of referring to months. In one, the months were simply numbered (as here and in v. 24). In another, the Canaanite names were used (Abib, Bul, etc.), of which only four are known. In the third system, the Babylonian names (Nisan, Adar, Tishri, Kislev, etc.) were used—in the exilic and postexilic books only—and are still used today. See chart on "Hebrew Calendar," p. 102.

23:6 Feast of Unleavened Bread. See note on Ex 23:15. During the Feast the first sheaf of the barley harvest was brought (see vv. 10–11).

23:15 seven full weeks. See note on Ex 23:16.

23:16 fifty days. The NT name for the Feast of Weeks was Pentecost (see Ac 2:1; 20:16; 1Co 16:8), meaning "fifty."

LORD, together with their grain offerings and drink offerings h—an offering made by fire, an aroma pleasing to the LORD. 19Then sacrifice one male goat for a sin offering and two lambs, each a year old, for a fellowship offering. h 20The priest is to wave the two lambs before the LORD as a wave offering, i together with the bread of the firstfruits. They are a sacred offering to the LORD for the priest. 21On that same day you are to proclaim a sacred assembly j and do no regular work. k This is to be a lasting ordinance for the generations to come, wherever you live.

22"'When you reap the harvest l of your land, do not reap to the very edges of your field or gather the gleanings of your harvest. m Leave them for the poor and the alien. n I am the LORD your God.'"

23:18 hver 13;
Ex 29:41; 30:9;
37:16; Jer 19:13;
44:18
23:20
iS Ex 29:24
23:21 jS ver 2;
Ex 32:5 kS ver 3
23:22 lS Lev 19:9
mS Lev 19:10;
Dt 24:19-21;
Ru 2:15 nRu 2:2

23:24 over 27,
36; Ezr 3:1
pLev 25:9;
Nu 10:9,10; 29:1;
31:6; 2Ki 11:14;
2Ch 13:12;
Ps 98:6
23:25 qver 21
rS Lev 1:9
23:27
sS Lev 16:29
tS Ex 30:10
uS ver 2,S 24
23:28 vver 31

Feast of Trumpets

23:23–25pp — Nu 29:1–6

23The LORD said to Moses, 24"Say to the Israelites: 'On the first day of the seventh month you are to have a day of rest, a sacred assembly o commemorated with trumpet blasts. p 25Do no regular work, q but present an offering made to the LORD by fire. r'"

Day of Atonement

23:26–32pp — Lev 16:2–34; Nu 29:7–11

26The LORD said to Moses, 27"The tenth day of this seventh month s is the Day of Atonement. t Hold a sacred assembly u and deny yourselves, i and present an offering made to the LORD by fire. 28Do no work v on that day, because it is the Day of Atone-

h 19 Traditionally peace offering   i 27 Or and fast; also in verses 29 and 32

23:22 See note on 19:9–10.
23:24 first day of the seventh month. Today known as the Jewish New Year (Rosh Hashanah, "the beginning of the year"), but not so called in the Bible (the Hebrew expression is only used in Eze 40:1 in a date formula). trumpet blasts. Trumpets were blown on the first of every month (Ps 81:3).

With no calendars available, the trumpets sounding across the land were an important signal of the beginning of the new season, the end of the agricultural year. See note on 16:29; see also chart on "Hebrew Calendar," p. 102.
23:27 Day of Atonement. For details see notes on 16:1–34. Aaron was to enter the Most Holy Place only once

---

Old Testament Feasts AND OTHER SACRED DAYS

NAME	OT REFERENCES	OT TIME	MODERN EQUIVALENT
Sabbath	Ex 20:8–11; 31:12–17; Lev 23:3; Dt 5:12–15	7th day	Same
Sabbath Year	Ex 23:10–11; Lev 25:1–7	7th year	Same
Year of Jubilee	Lev 25:8–55; 27:17–24; Nu 36:4	50th year	Same
Passover	Ex 12:1–14; Lev 23:5; Nu 9:1–14; 28:16; Dt 16:1–3a, 4b–7	1st month (Abib) 14	Mar.-Apr.
Unleavened Bread	Ex 12:15–20; 13:3–10; 23:15; 34:18; Lev 23:6–8; Nu 28:17–25; Dt 16:3b, 4a, 8	1st month (Abib) 15-21	Mar.-Apr.
Firstfruits	Lev 23:9–14	1st month (Abib) 16	Mar.-Apr.
Weeks (Pentecost) (Harvest)	Ex 23:16a; 34:22a; Lev 23:15–21; Nu 28:26–31; Dt 16:9–12	3rd month (Sivan) 6	May-June
Trumpets (Later: Rosh Hashanah—New Year's Day)	Lev 23:23–25; Nu 29:1–6	7th month (Tishri) 1	Sept.-Oct.
Day of Atonement (Yom Kippur)	Lev 16; 23:26–32 Nu 29:7–11	7th month (Tishri) 10	Sept.-Oct.
Tabernacles (Booths) (Ingathering)	Ex 23:16b; 34:22b; Lev 23:33–36a, 39–43; Nu 29:12–34; Dt 16:13–15; Zec 14:16–19	7th month (Tishri) 15-21	Sept.-Oct.
Sacred Assembly	Lev 23:36b; Nu 29:35–38	7th month (Tishri) 22	Sept.-Oct.
Purim	Est 9:18–32	12th month (Adar) 14,15	Feb.-Mar.

On Kislev 25 (mid-December) Hanukkah, the feast of dedication or festival of lights, commemorated the purification of the temple and altar in the Maccabean period (165/4 B.C.). This feast is mentioned in Jn 10:22.

ment, when atonement is made for you before the LORD your God. 29Anyone who does not deny himself on that day must be cut off from his people.w 30I will destroy from among his peoplex anyone who does any work on that day. 31You shall do no work at all. This is to be a lasting ordinancey for the generations to come, wherever you live. 32It is a sabbath of restz for you, and you must deny yourselves. From the evening of the ninth day of the month until the following evening you are to observe your sabbath."a

Feast of Tabernacles

23:33–43pp — Nu 29:12–39; Dt 16:13–17

33The LORD said to Moses, 34"Say to the Israelites: 'On the fifteenth day of the seventhb month the LORD's Feast of Tabernaclesc begins, and it lasts for seven days.

35The first day is a sacred assembly;d do no regular work.e 36For seven days present offerings made to the LORD by fire, and on the eighth day hold a sacred assemblyf and present an offering made to the LORD by fire.g It is the closing assembly; do no regular work.

37(" 'These are the LORD's appointed feasts, which you are to proclaim as sacred assemblies for bringing offerings made to the LORD by fire—the burnt offerings and grain offerings, sacrifices and drink offeringsh required for each day. 38These offeringsi are in addition to those for the LORD's Sabbathsj andj in addition to your gifts and whatever you have vowed and all the freewill offeringsk you give to the LORD.)

Cross references:

23:29 wGe 17:14; Lev 7:20; Nu 5:2
23:30 xS Lev 20:3
23:31 yLev 3:17
23:32 zS Lev 16:31
aNe 13:19
23:34 biKi 8:2; Hag 2:1
cS Ex 23:16; Jn 7:2
23:35 dver 2
ever 3
23:36 fS ver 24; 1Ki 8:2; 2Ch 7:9; Ne 8:18; Jn 7:37
gS Lev 1:9
23:37 hver 13
iS Lev 1:2
23:38 iS Lev 1:2
jS Ex 20:10; 2Ch 2:4; Eze 45:17
kS Lev 7:16

j38 Or These feasts are in addition to the LORD's Sabbaths, and these offerings are

---

Notes:

a year (16:29–34) on the day called by modern Jews *Yom Kippur*. The Biblical name, however, is the plural *Yom Hakkippurim* (as in this verse), derived from the Hebrew words *yom* ("day") and *kipper* ("to atone"). The day was typological, foreshadowing the work of Christ, our high priest (see Heb 9:7; 13:11–12). *deny yourselves.* See note on 16:29,

31.
23:29 *cut off from his people.* See note on 7:20.
23:34 *Feast of Tabernacles.* See notes on Ex 23:16; Jn 7:37–39. Tabernacles was the last of the three annual pilgrimage festivals (Ex 23:14–17; Dt 16:16).

DESCRIPTION	PURPOSE	NT REFERENCES
		Mt 12:1–14; 28:1; Lk 4:16; Jn 5:9; Ac 13:42; Col 2:16; Heb 4:1–11
Day of rest; no work	Rest for people and animals	
Year of rest; fallow fields	Rest for land	
Canceled debts; liberation of slaves and indentured servants; land returned to original family owners	Help for poor; stabilize society	
Slaying and eating a lamb, together with bitter herbs and bread made without yeast, in every household	Remember Israel's deliverance from Egypt	Mt 26:17; Mk 14:12–26; Jn 2:13; 11:55; 1Co 5:7; Heb 11:28
Eating bread made without yeast; holding several assemblies; making designated offerings	Remember how the Lord brought the Israelites out of Egypt in haste	Mk 14:1,12; Ac 12:3; 1Co 5:6–8
Presenting a sheaf of the first of the barley harvest as a wave offering; making a burnt offering and a grain offering	Recognize the Lord's bounty in the land	Ro 8:23; 1Co 15:20–23
A festival of joy; mandatory and voluntary offerings, including the firstfruits of the wheat harvest	Show joy and thankfulness for the Lord's blessing of harvest	Ac 2:1–4; 20:16; 1Co 16:8
An assembly on a day of rest commemorated with trumpet blasts and sacrifices	Present Israel before the Lord for his favor	
A day of rest, fasting and sacrifices of atonement for priests and people and atonement for the tabernacle and altar	Cleanse priests and people from their sins and purify the Holy Place	Ro 3:24–26; Heb 9:7; 10:3, 19–22
A week of celebration for the harvest; living in booths and offering sacrifices	Memorialize the journey from Egypt to Canaan; give thanks for the productivity of Canaan	Jn 7:2,37
A day of convocation, rest and offering sacrifices	Commemorate the closing of the cycle of feasts	
A day of joy and feasting and giving presents	Remind the Israelites of their national deliverance in the time of Esther	

In addition, new moons were often special feast days (Nu 10:10; 1 Ch 23:31; Ezr 3:5; Ne 10:33; Ps 81:3; Isa 1:13–14; 66:23; Hos 5:7; Am 8:5; Col 2:16).

39" 'So beginning with the fifteenth day of the seventh month, after you have gathered the crops of the land, celebrate the festival ^{l} to the LORD for seven days; ^{m} the first day is a day of rest, and the eighth day also is a day of rest. 40On the first day you are to take choice fruit from the trees, and palm fronds, leafy branches ^{n} and poplars, ^{o} and rejoice ^{p} before the LORD your God for seven days. 41Celebrate this as a festival to the LORD for seven days each year. This is to be a lasting ordinance for the generations to come; celebrate it in the seventh month. 42Live in booths ^{q} for seven days: All native-born Israelites are to live in booths 43so your descendants will know ^{r} that I had the Israelites live in booths when I brought them out of Egypt. I am the LORD your God.' "

44So Moses announced to the Israelites the appointed feasts of the LORD.

Oil and Bread Set Before the LORD

24:1–3pp — Ex 27:20–21

24 The LORD said to Moses, 2"Command the Israelites to bring you clear oil of pressed olives for the light so that the lamps may be kept burning continually. 3Outside the curtain of the Testimony in the Tent of Meeting, Aaron is to tend the lamps before the LORD from evening till morning, continually. This is to be a lasting ordinance ^{s} for the generations to come. 4The lamps on the pure gold lampstand ^{t} before the LORD must be tended continually.

5"Take fine flour and bake twelve loaves of bread, ^{u} using two-tenths of an ephah $^{k\,v}$ for each loaf. 6Set them in two rows, six in each row, on the table of pure gold ^{w} before the LORD. 7Along each row put some pure incense ^{x} as a memorial portion ^{y} to represent the bread and to be an offering made to the LORD by fire. 8This bread is to be set out before the LORD regularly, ^{z} Sabbath after Sabbath, ^{a} on behalf of the Israelites, as a lasting covenant. 9It belongs to Aaron and his sons, ^{b} who are to eat it in a holy place, ^{c} because it is a most holy ^{d} part of their regular share of the offerings made to the LORD by fire."

A Blasphemer Stoned

10Now the son of an Israelite mother and an Egyptian father went out among the Israelites, and a fight broke out in the camp between him and an Israelite. 11The son of the Israelite woman blasphemed the Name ^{e} with a curse; ^{f} so they brought him to Moses. ^{g} (His mother's name was Shelomith, the daughter of Dibri the Danite.) ^{h} 12They put him in custody until the will of the LORD should be made clear to them. ^{i}

13Then the LORD said to Moses: 14"Take the blasphemer outside the camp. All those who heard him are to lay their hands on his head, and the entire assembly is to stone him. ^{j} 15Say to the Israelites: 'If anyone curses his God, ^{k} he will be held responsible; ^{l} 16anyone who blasphemes ^{m} the name of the LORD must be put to death. ^{n} The entire assembly must stone him. Whether an alien or native-born, when he blasphemes the Name, he must be put to death.

17" 'If anyone takes the life of a human being, he must be put to death. ^{o} 18Anyone who takes the life of someone's animal must make restitution ^{p}—life for life. 19If anyone injures his neighbor, whatever he has done must be done to him: 20fracture for fracture, eye for eye, tooth for tooth. ^{q} As he has injured the other, so he is to be

Cross references

23:39 ^{l}Isa 62:9
^{m}S Ex 23:16
23:40 ^{n}Ps 118:27
^{o}Ne 8:14-17;
Ps 137:2; Isa 44:4
^{p}Dt 12:7; 14:26;
28:47; Ne 8:10;
Ps 9:2; 66:6;
105:43; Joel 2:26
23:42
^{q}S Ex 23:16
23:43 ^{r}Ps 78:5
24:3 ^{s}S Ex 12:14
24:4 ^{t}S Ex 25:31
24:5
^{u}S Ex 25:30;
Heb 9:2
^{v}S Lev 23:13
24:6
^{w}Ex 25:23-30;
Nu 4:7
24:7 ^{x}S Lev 2:1
^{y}S Lev 2:2

24:8 ^{z}Ex 25:30;
Nu 4:7;
1Ch 9:32;
2Ch 2:4 ^{a}Mt 12:5
24:9 ^{b}Mt 12:4;
Mk 2:26; Lk 6:4
^{c}S Lev 6:16
^{d}S Lev 6:17
24:11 ^{e}S Ex 3:15
^{f}S Ex 20:7;
S 2Ki 6:33;
S Job 1:11
^{g}S Ex 18:22
^{h}Ex 31:2;
Nu 1:4; 7:2;
10:15; 13:2;
17:2; Jos 7:18;
1Ki 7:14
24:12
^{i}S Ex 18:16
24:14 ^{j}ver 23;
S Lev 20:2;
Dt 13:9; 17:5,7;
Ac 7:58
24:15
^{k}S Ex 22:28
^{l}S Lev 5:1
24:16
^{m}S Ex 22:28
^{n}S Ex 21:12;
1Ki 21:10,13;
Mt 26:66;
Mk 14:64;
Jn 10:33; 19:7;
Ac 7:58
24:17 ^{o}ver 21;
Ge 9:6;
S Ex 21:12;
Dt 27:24
24:18 ^{p}ver 21
24:20
^{q}S Ex 21:24;
Mt 5:38*

^{k}5 That is, probably about 4 quarts (about 4.5 liters)

23:42 *booths.* The Hebrew for this word is *Sukkot* and is also translated "Tabernacles" (as in v. 34), giving the feast its name. Even today, orthodox Jews construct small booths (see Ne 8:13–17) to remind them of the booths they lived in when God brought them out of Egypt at the time of the exodus (v. 43).

24:2–4 See Ex 27:20–21.

24:3 *Testimony.* See note on Ex 16:34. *tend the lamps.* So that they would burn all night. *continually.* Every night without interruption, but not throughout the day. See 1Sa 3:3 and note.

24:5 *two-tenths of an ephah.* See NIV text note. Either the loaves were quite large or a smaller unit of measurement is intended (the Hebrew word *ephah* is not expressed).

24:7 *pure incense.* Not used as a condiment for the bread, but burned either in piles on the table or in small receptacles alongside the rows of bread.

24:8 *This bread.* Often called the "bread of the Presence" (see Ex 25:30 and note). It represented a gift from the 12 tribes and signified the fact that God sustained his people. It was eaten by the priests (24:9).

24:9 See 1Sa 21:4–6.

24:10 *Egyptian father.* An alien. The laws, at least in the judicial sphere, applied equally to both the alien and the native-born Israelite (v. 22; see Ex 12:49).

24:11 *blasphemed.* See Ex 20:7 and note.

24:17,21 See Ge 9:6 and note.

24:20 *eye for eye, tooth for tooth.* See note on Ex 21:23–25. This represents a statement of principle: The penalty is to fit the crime, not exceed it. An actual eye or tooth was not to be required, nor is there evidence that such a penalty was ever exacted. A similar law of retaliation is found in the Code of Hammurapi, which also seems not to have been literally applied. Christ, like the middle-of-the-road Pharisees (school of Hillel), objected to an extremist use of this judicial principle to excuse private vengeance, such as by the strict Pharisees (school of Shammai); see Mt 5:38–42.

injured. [21]Whoever kills an animal must make restitution,[r] but whoever kills a man must be put to death.[s] [22]You are to have the same law for the alien[t] and the native-born.[u] I am the LORD your God.' "

[23]Then Moses spoke to the Israelites, and they took the blasphemer outside the camp and stoned him.[v] The Israelites did as the LORD commanded Moses.

The Sabbath Year

25 The LORD said to Moses on Mount Sinai,[w] [2]"Speak to the Israelites and say to them: 'When you enter the land I am going to give you, the land itself must observe a sabbath to the LORD. [3]For six years sow your fields, and for six years prune your vineyards and gather their crops.[x] [4]But in the seventh year the land is to have a sabbath of rest,[y] a sabbath to the LORD. Do not sow your fields or prune your vineyards.[z] [5]Do not reap what grows of itself[a] or harvest the grapes[b] of your untended vines.[c] The land is to have a year of rest. [6]Whatever the land yields during the sabbath year[d] will be food for you—for yourself, your manservant and maidservant, and the hired worker and temporary resident who live among you, [7]as well as for your livestock and the wild animals[e] in your land. Whatever the land produces may be eaten.

The Year of Jubilee

25:8–38Ref — Dt 15:1–11
25:39–55Ref — Ex 21:2–11; Dt 15:12–18

[8]" 'Count off seven sabbaths of years—seven times seven years—so that the seven sabbaths of years amount to a period of forty-nine years. [9]Then have the trumpet[f] sounded everywhere on the tenth day of the seventh month;[g] on the Day of Atonement[h] sound the trumpet throughout your land. [10]Consecrate the fiftieth year and proclaim liberty[i] through-

out the land to all its inhabitants. It shall be a jubilee[j] for you; each one of you is to return to his family property[k] and each to his own clan. [11]The fiftieth year shall be a jubilee[l] for you; do not sow and do not reap what grows of itself or harvest the untended vines.[m] [12]For it is a jubilee and is to be holy for you; eat only what is taken directly from the fields.

[13]" 'In this Year of Jubilee[n] everyone is to return to his own property.

[14]" 'If you sell land to one of your countrymen or buy any from him, do not take advantage of each other.[o] [15]You are to buy from your countryman on the basis of the number of years[p] since the Jubilee. And he is to sell to you on the basis of the number of years left for harvesting crops. [16]When the years are many, you are to increase the price, and when the years are few, you are to decrease the price,[q] because what he is really selling you is the number of crops. [17]Do not take advantage of each other,[r] but fear your God.[s] I am the LORD your God.[t]

[18]" 'Follow my decrees and be careful to obey my laws,[u] and you will live safely in the land.[v] [19]Then the land will yield its fruit,[w] and you will eat your fill and live there in safety.[x] [20]You may ask, "What will we eat in the seventh year[y] if we do not plant or harvest our crops?" [21]I will send you such a blessing[z] in the sixth year that the land will yield enough for three years.[a] [22]While you plant during the eighth year, you will eat from the old crop and will continue to eat from it until the harvest of the ninth year comes in.[b]

[23]" 'The land[c] must not be sold permanently, because the land is mine[d] and you are but aliens[e] and my tenants.

24:21 [r]S ver 18
[s]S ver 17
24:22
[t]S Ex 12:49;
S 22:21;
Eze 47:22
[u]Nu 9:14
24:23 [v]S ver 14
25:1 [w]Ex 19:11
25:3 [x]Ex 23:10
25:4 [y]ver 5,6,20;
Lev 26:35;
2Ch 36:21
[z]Isa 36:16; 37:30
25:5 [a]2Ki 19:29
[b]Ge 40:10;
Nu 6:3; 13:20;
Dt 23:24;
Ne 13:15; Isa 5:2
[c]ver 4,11
25:6 [d]S ver 4
25:7 [e]Ex 23:11
25:9 [f]Lev 23:24;
Nu 10:8; Jos 6:4;
Jdg 3:27; 7:16;
1Sa 13:3;
Isa 27:13;
Zec 9:14
[g]S Lev 16:29
[h]S Ex 30:10
25:10 [i]Isa 61:1;
Jer 34:8,15,17;
S Lk 4:19

[j]ver 11,28,50;
Lev 27:17,21;
Nu 36:4;
Eze 46:17 [k]ver 27
25:11 [l]S ver 10
[m]S ver 5
25:13 [n]ver 10
25:14
[o]S Lev 19:13;
1Sa 12:3,4;
1Co 6:8
25:15 [p]ver 27;
Lev 27:18,23
25:16 [q]ver 27,
51,52
25:17
[r]S Lev 19:13;
Job 31:16;
Pr 22:22; Jer 7:5,
6; 21:12; 22:3,
15; Zec 7:9-10;
1Th 4:6
[s]S Lev 19:14
[t]S Lev 19:32
25:18 [u]S Ge 26:5
[v]ver 19; Lev 26:4,
5; Dt 12:10;
33:28; Job 5:22;
Ps 4:8; Jer 23:6;
30:10; 32:37;
33:16; Eze 28:26;
34:25; 38:14
25:19 [w]Lev 26:4;
Dt 11:14; 28:12;
Isa 55:10 [x]S ver
18

25:20 [y]S ver 4 **25:21** [z]Dt 28:8,12; Ps 133:3; 134:3; 147:13;
Eze 44:30; Hag 2:19; Mal 3:10 [a]S Ex 16:5 **25:22** [b]Lev 26:10
25:23 [c]Nu 36:7; 1Ki 21:3; Eze 46:18 [d]Ex 19:5 [e]S Ge 23:4;
S Heb 11:13

24:22 See note on v. 10.
25:4 *land is to have a sabbath.* See Ex 23:10–11. The Israelites did not practice crop rotation, but the fallow year (when the crops were not planted) served somewhat the same purpose. And just as the land was to have a sabbath year, so the servitude of a Hebrew slave was limited to six years, apparently whether or not the year he was freed was a sabbath year (see Ex 21:2 and note). Dt 15:1–11 specifies that debts were also to be canceled in the sabbath year. The care for the poor in the laws of Israel (see Ex 23:11) is noteworthy. See 23:7,35; Dt 31:10; Ne 10:31.
25:9 *Day of Atonement.* See notes on 16:1–34; see also 23:27.
25:10 *fiftieth year.* Possibly a fallow year in addition to the seventh sabbath year, or perhaps the same as the 49th year (counting the first and last years). Jewish sources from the period between the Testaments favor the latter interpreta-

tion. *proclaim liberty . . . inhabitants.* See vv. 39–43,47–55. The Liberty Bell in Philadelphia is so named because this statement was written on it. Cf. Isa 61:1–2; Lk 4:16–21. *jubilee.* The Hebrew for this word is the same as and may be related to one of the Hebrew words for "[ram's] horn," "trumpet" (see, e.g., Ex 19:13), though in v. 9 a different Hebrew word for "trumpet" is used. Trumpets were blown at the close of the Day of Atonement to inaugurate the Year of Jubilee. Cf. 23:24.

25:13 *return to his own property.* See v. 10. The Lord prohibited the accumulation of property to the detriment of the poor. "The land is mine," said the Lord (v. 23). God's people are only tenants (see 1Ch 29:15; Heb 11:13).

25:15 *number of years left for harvesting.* In a way, the sale of land in Israel was a lease until the Year of Jubilee (see 27:18,23).

24Throughout the country that you hold as a possession, you must provide for the redemption f of the land.

25" 'If one of your countrymen becomes poor and sells some of his property, his nearest relative g is to come and redeem h what his countryman has sold. 26If, however, a man has no one to redeem it for him but he himself prospers i and acquires sufficient means to redeem it, 27he is to determine the value for the years j since he sold it and refund the balance to the man to whom he sold it; he can then go back to his own property. k 28But if he does not acquire the means to repay him, what he sold will remain in the possession of the buyer until the Year of Jubilee. It will be returned l in the Jubilee, and he can then go back to his property. m

29" 'If a man sells a house in a walled city, he retains the right of redemption a full year after its sale. During that time he may redeem it. 30If it is not redeemed before a full year has passed, the house in the walled city shall belong permanently to the buyer and his descendants. It is not to be returned in the Jubilee. 31But houses in villages without walls around them are to be considered as open country. They can be redeemed, and they are to be returned in the Jubilee.

32" 'The Levites always have the right to redeem their houses in the Levitical towns, n which they possess. 33So the property of the Levites is redeemable—that is, a house sold in any town they hold—and is to be returned in the Jubilee, because the houses in the towns of the Levites are their property among the Israelites. 34But the pastureland belonging to their towns must not be sold; it is their permanent possession. o

35" 'If one of your countrymen becomes poor p and is unable to support himself among you, help him q as you would an alien or a temporary resident, so he can continue to live among you. 36Do not take interest r of any kind1 from him, but fear your God, s so that your countryman may continue to live among you. 37You must not lend him money at interest t or sell him food at a profit. 38I am the LORD your God, who brought you out of Egypt to give

you the land of Canaan u and to be your God. v

39" 'If one of your countrymen becomes poor among you and sells himself to you, do not make him work as a slave. w 40He is to be treated as a hired worker x or a temporary resident among you; he is to work for you until the Year of Jubilee. 41Then he and his children are to be released, and he will go back to his own clan and to the property y of his forefathers. z 42Because the Israelites are my servants, whom I brought out of Egypt, a they must not be sold as slaves. 43Do not rule over them ruthlessly, b but fear your God. c

44" 'Your male and female slaves are to come from the nations around you; from them you may buy slaves. 45You may also buy some of the temporary residents living among you and members of their clans born in your country, and they will become your property. 46You can will them to your children as inherited property and can make them slaves for life, but you must not rule over your fellow Israelites ruthlessly.

47" 'If an alien or a temporary resident among you becomes rich and one of your countrymen becomes poor and sells himself d to the alien living among you or to a member of the alien's clan, 48he retains the right of redemption e after he has sold himself. One of his relatives f may redeem him: 49An uncle or a cousin or any blood relative in his clan may redeem him. Or if he prospers, g he may redeem himself. 50He and his buyer are to count the time from the year he sold himself up to the Year of Jubilee. h The price for his release is to be based on the rate paid to a hired man i for that number of years. 51If many years remain, he must pay for his redemption a larger share of the price paid for him. 52If only a few years remain until the Year of Jubilee, he is to compute that and pay for his redemption accordingly. j 53He is to be treated as a man hired from year to year; you must see to it that his owner does not rule over him ruthlessly. k

54" 'Even if he is not redeemed in any of these ways, he and his children are to be released in the Year of Jubilee, 55for the

1 36 Or take excessive interest; similarly in verse 37

25:24 f ver 29,48; Ru 4:7; Jer 32:8
25:25 g ver 48; Ru 2:20; Jer 32:7
h Lev 27:13,19, 31; Ru 4:4
25:26 i ver 49
25:27 j S ver 15
k ver 10
25:28 l Lev 27:24
m S ver 10
25:32 n Nu 35:1-8; Jos 21:2
25:34 o Nu 35:2-5; Eze 48:14
25:35 p Dt 24:14, 15 q Dt 15:8; Ps 37:21,26; Pr 21:26; Lk 6:35
25:36 r S Ex 22:25; Jer 15:10
s S Lev 19:32
25:37 t Ex 22:25

25:38 u S Ge 10:19
v S Ge 17:7
25:39 w I Ki 5:13; 9:22; Jer 34:14
25:40 x ver 53
25:41 y ver 28
25:42 a ver 38
25:43 b S Ex 1:13; Eze 34:4; Col 4:1
c S Ge 42:18
25:47 d Ne 5:5; Job 24:9
25:48 e S ver 24
f S ver 25
25:49 g ver 26
25:50 h S ver 10
i Job 7:1; 14:6; Isa 16:14; 21:16
25:52 j S ver 16
25:53 k Col 4:1

25:24 redemption of the land. That is, the right to repurchase the land by (or for) the original family.
25:25 nearest relative is to come and redeem. See Jer 32:6–15. This is apparently what the nearest relative was to do for Naomi and Ruth (Ru 4:1–4), but he was also obligated to marry the widow and support the family (see Dt

25:5–10). Only Boaz was willing to do both (Ru 4:9–10).
25:33 towns of the Levites. See Nu 35:1–8; Jos 21:1–42.
25:36 interest. The main idea (see NIV text note) was not necessarily to forbid all interest, but to assist the poor. The law did not forbid lending so much as it encouraged giving.
25:55 servants. Covenant terminology, similar to "vas-

Israelites belong to me as servants. They are my servants, whom I brought out of Egypt. [l] I am the LORD your God. [m]

Reward for Obedience

26 " 'Do not make idols [n] or set up an image [o] or a sacred stone [p] for yourselves, and do not place a carved stone [q] in your land to bow down before it. I am the LORD your God.

[2] " 'Observe my Sabbaths [r] and have reverence for my sanctuary. [s] I am the LORD.

[3] " 'If you follow my decrees and are careful to obey [t] my commands, [4]I will send you rain [u] in its season, [v] and the ground will yield its crops and the trees of the field their fruit. [w] [5]Your threshing will continue until grape harvest and the grape harvest will continue until planting, and you will eat all the food you want [x] and live in safety in your land. [y]

[6] " 'I will grant peace in the land, [z] and you will lie down [a] and no one will make you afraid. [b] I will remove savage beasts [c] from the land, and the sword will not pass through your country. [7]You will pursue your enemies, [d] and they will fall by the sword before you. [8]Five [e] of you will chase a hundred, and a hundred of you will chase ten thousand, and your enemies will fall by the sword before you. [f]

[9] " 'I will look on you with favor and make you fruitful and increase your numbers, [g] and I will keep my covenant [h] with you. [10]You will still be eating last year's harvest when you will have to move it out to make room for the new. [i] [11]I will put my dwelling place [m][j] among you, and I will not abhor you. [k] [12]I will walk [l] among you and be your God, [m] and you will be my people. [n] [13]I am the LORD your God, [o] who brought you out of Egypt [p] so that you would no longer be slaves to the Egyptians; I broke the bars of your yoke [q] and enabled you to walk with heads held high.

Punishment for Disobedience

[14] " 'But if you will not listen to me and

carry out all these commands, [r] [15]and if you reject my decrees and abhor my laws [s] and fail to carry out all my commands and so violate my covenant, [t] [16]then I will do this to you: I will bring upon you sudden terror, wasting diseases and fever [u] that will destroy your sight and drain away your life. [v] You will plant seed in vain, because your enemies will eat it. [w] [17]I will set my face [x] against you so that you will be defeated [y] by your enemies; [z] those who hate you will rule over you, [a] and you will flee even when no one is pursuing you. [b]

[18] " 'If after all this you will not listen to me, [c] I will punish [d] you for your sins seven times over. [e] [19]I will break down your stubborn pride [f] and make the sky above you like iron and the ground beneath you like bronze. [g] [20]Your strength will be spent in vain, [h] because your soil will not yield its crops, nor will the trees of the land yield their fruit. [i]

[21] " 'If you remain hostile [j] toward me and refuse to listen to me, I will multiply your afflictions seven times over, [k] as your sins deserve. [22]I will send wild animals [l] against you, and they will rob you of your children, destroy your cattle and make you so few [m] in number that your roads will be deserted. [n]

[23] " 'If in spite of these things you do not accept my correction [o] but continue to be hostile toward me, [24]I myself will be hostile [p] toward you and will afflict you for your sins seven times over. [25]And I will bring the sword [q] upon you to avenge [r] the breaking of the covenant. When you with-

---

25:55
[l] S Lev 11:45
[m] Lev 11:44
26:1 [n] S Ex 20:4
[o] Ps 97:7;
Isa 48:5;
Jer 44:19;
Hab 2:18
[p] S Ex 23:24
[q] Nu 33:52
26:2 [r] S Ex 20:8
[s] Lev 19:30
26:3 [t] S Ge 26:5;
S Ex 24:8;
Dt 6:17; 7:12;
11:13,22; 28:1,9
26:4 [u] Dt 11:14;
28:12; Ps 68:9;
Jer 5:24; Hos 6:3;
Joel 2:23;
Zec 10:1
[v] Job 5:10;
Ps 65:9; 104:13;
147:8; Jer 5:24
[w] S Ex 23:26;
S Lev 25:19;
S Job 14:9;
Ps 67:6
26:5 [x] Dt 6:11;
11:15;
Eze 36:29-30;
Joel 2:19,26
[y] S Lev 25:18
26:6 [z] Ps 29:11;
37:11; 85:8;
147:14; Isa 26:3;
54:13; 60:18;
Hag 2:9 [a] Ps 3:5;
4:8; Pr 3:24
[b] Job 11:18,19;
Isa 17:2;
Jer 30:10;
Mic 4:4; Zep 3:13
[c] S ver 22;
S Ge 37:20
26:7 [d] Ps 18:37;
44:5
26:8 [e] Isa 30:17
[f] Dt 28:7; 32:30;
Jos 23:10;
Jdg 15:15;
1Ch 12:14
26:9 [g] S Ge 1:22;
S 17:6; Ne 9:23
[h] S Ge 17:7
26:10 [i] Lev 25:22
26:11 [j] Ex 25:8;
Ps 74:7; 76:2;
Eze 37:27 [k] ver
15,43,44;
Dt 31:6;
1Sa 12:22;
1Ki 6:13;
2Ki 17:15
26:12 [l] S Ge 3:8
[m] S Ge 17:7
[n] Ex 6:7; Jer 7:23;
11:4; 24:7;
30:22; 31:1;
Zec 13:9;
2Co 6:16*
26:13 [o] Lev 11:44
[p] S Ex 6:6; S 13:3
[q] Isa 10:27;
Jer 2:20; 27:2;
28:10; 30:8;
Eze 30:18; 34:27;
Hos 11:4

26:14 [r] Dt 28:15-68; Mal 2:2 **26:15** [s] S ver 11 [t] S Ge 17:7
26:16 [u] Dt 28:22,35; Ps 78:33 [v] ver 39; 1Sa 2:33; Ps 107:17;
Eze 4:17; 24:23; 33:10 [w] Jdg 6:3-6; Job 31:8 **26:17**
[x] Lev 17:10; Eze 15:7 [y] Dt 28:48; Jos 7:12; Jdg 2:15;
1Ki 8:33; 2Ch 6:24 [z] Jos 7:4; Jer 19:7; 21:7 [a] Ps 106:41 [b] ver
36,37; Dt 28:7,25; Ps 53:5; Pr 28:1; Isa 30:17 **26:18** [c] ver 14
[d] Ps 99:8; Jer 21:14; Am 3:14 [e] ver 21 **26:19** [f] Ps 10:4; 73:6;
Isa 16:6; 25:11; 28:1-3; Jer 13:9; 48:29; Eze 24:21; Am 6:8;
Zep 3:11 [g] Dt 28:23; Job 38:38 **26:20** [h] Dt 28:38; Ps 127:1;
Isa 17:11; 49:4; Jer 12:13; Mic 6:15; Hag 1:6 [i] Dt 11:17;
28:24 **26:21** [j] ver 41 [k] ver 18; S Ge 4:15 **26:22** [l] S Ge 37:20
[m] Dt 28:62; Jer 42:2 [n] Jer 5:6; 14:16; 15:3; 16:4; Eze 14:15
26:23 [o] Jer 2:30; 5:3; 7:28; 17:23; 32:33; Zep 3:2 **26:24**
[p] 2Sa 22:27 **26:25** [q] ver 5:17; 15:3; 47:6; Eze 11:8; 14:17;
21:4; 33:2 [r] Jer 50:28; 51:6,11

[m] 11 Or *my tabernacle*

---

sals." Slavery, however demeaning, is not brutal where the masters truly recognize themselves as God's servants. Cf. Paul's exhortation to both slaves and masters (Eph 6:5–9; Col 3:22–4:1).

26:1 *Do not make idols.* This verse probably does not forbid making statues, but it does forbid worshiping God in any material form (see Ex 20:4 and note). "God is spirit" (Jn 4:24; see Dt 4:15–19).

26:3 *obey my commands.* Obedience is the key to blessing (see Gal 6:7–10; Jas 1:22–25). Compare the blessings promised in vv. 3–13 with those in Dt 28:1–14.

26:9 *fruitful and increase.* See note on Ge 1:22; contrast Lev 26:22.

26:12 *your God . . . my people.* Covenantal terms later made famous by Hosea (1:9–10; 2:23). See Jer 31:33; Eze 36:28; Heb 8:10.

26:14 *if you will not listen.* The list of curses for covenant disobedience (see vv. 14–39) is usually much longer than that of blessings for obedience (as in vv. 3–13; see Dt 28:15–29:28; cf. Dt 28:1–14).

26:17 See v. 36 and the allusion to this statement in Pr 28:1.

draw into your cities, I will send a plague[s] among you, and you will be given into enemy hands. [26]When I cut off your supply of bread,[t] ten women will be able to bake your bread in one oven, and they will dole out the bread by weight. You will eat, but you will not be satisfied.

[27] "If in spite of this you still do not listen to me[u] but continue to be hostile toward me, [28]then in my anger[v] I will be hostile[w] toward you, and I myself will punish you for your sins seven times over.[x] [29]You will eat[y] the flesh of your sons and the flesh of your daughters.[z] [30]I will destroy your high places,[a] cut down your incense altars[b] and pile your dead bodies on the lifeless forms of your idols,[c] and I will abhor[d] you. [31]I will turn your cities into ruins[e] and lay waste[f] your sanctuaries,[g] and I will take no delight in the pleasing aroma of your offerings.[h] [32]I will lay waste the land,[i] so that your enemies who live there will be appalled.[j] [33]I will scatter[k] you among the nations[l] and will draw out my sword[m] and pursue you. Your land will be laid waste,[n] and your cities will lie in ruins.[o] [34]Then the land will enjoy its sabbath years all the time that it lies desolate[p] and you are in the country of your enemies;[q] then the land will rest and enjoy its sabbaths. [35]All the time that it lies desolate, the land will have the rest[r] it did not have during the sabbaths you lived in it.

[36] "As for those of you who are left, I will make their hearts so fearful in the lands of their enemies that the sound of a windblown leaf[s] will put them to flight.[t] They will run as though fleeing from the sword, and they will fall, even though no one is pursuing them.[u] [37]They will stumble over one another[v] as though fleeing from the sword, even though no one is pursuing you. So you will not be able to stand before your enemies.[w] [38]You will perish[x] among the nations; the land of your enemies will devour you.[y] [39]Those of you who are left will waste away in the lands of their enemies because of their sins; also because of their fathers'[z] sins they will waste away.[a]

[40] "But if they will confess[b] their sins[c]

and the sins of their fathers[d]—their treachery against me and their hostility toward me, [41]which made me hostile[e] toward them so that I sent them into the land of their enemies—then when their uncircumcised hearts[f] are humbled[g] and they pay[h] for their sin, [42]I will remember my covenant with Jacob[i] and my covenant with Isaac[j] and my covenant with Abraham,[k] and I will remember the land. [43]For the land will be deserted[l] by them and will enjoy its sabbaths while it lies desolate without them. They will pay for their sins because they rejected[m] my laws and abhorred my decrees.[n] [44]Yet in spite of this, when they are in the land of their enemies,[o] I will not reject them or abhor[p] them so as to destroy them completely,[q] breaking my covenant[r] with them. I am the LORD their God. [45]But for their sake I will remember[s] the covenant with their ancestors whom I brought out of Egypt[t] in the sight of the nations to be their God. I am the LORD.' "

[46]These are the decrees, the laws and the regulations that the LORD established on Mount Sinai[u] between himself and the Israelites through Moses.[v]

Redeeming What Is the LORD's

27 The LORD said to Moses, [2]"Speak to the Israelites and say to them: 'If anyone makes a special vow[w] to dedicate persons to the LORD by giving equivalent values, [3]set the value of a male between the ages of twenty and sixty at fifty shekels[n] of silver, according to the sanctu-

---

26:25 [s]S Ex 5:3; S 9:3; Nu 16:46; 1Ki 8:37; Hab 3:5
26:26 [t]1Ki 8:37; 18:2; 2Ki 4:38; 6:25; 8:1; 25:3; Ps 105:16; Isa 3:1; 9:20; Jer 37:21; 52:6; Eze 4:16,17; 5:16; 14:13; Hos 4:10; Mic 6:14
26:27 [u]ver 14
26:28 [v]Dt 32:19; Jdg 2:14; Ps 78:59; 106:40
[w]Dt 7:10; Job 34:11; Isa 59:18; 65:6-7; 66:6; Jer 17:10; 25:29; Joel 3:4
[x]ver 18
26:29 [y]2Ki 6:29; Jer 19:9; La 4:10; Eze 5:10
[z]Dt 28:53
26:30 [a]Dt 12:2; 1Sa 9:12; 10:5; 1Ki 3:2,4; 12:31; 13:2,32; 2Ki 17:29; 23:20; 2Ch 34:3; Ps 78:58; Eze 6:3; 16:16; Am 7:9
[b]2Ch 34:4; Isa 17:8; 27:9; Eze 6:6 [c]Isa 21:9; Jer 50:2; Eze 6:13
[d]Ps 106:40; Am 6:8
26:31 [e]Ne 1:3; Isa 1:7; 3:8,26; 6:11; 24:12; 61:4; Jer 4:7; 9:11; 25:11; 34:22; 44:2,6,22; Eze 36:33; Mic 2:4; 3:12; Zep 2:5; 3:6 [f]2Ki 22:19 [g]Ps 74:3-7; Isa 63:18; 64:11; La 2:7; Eze 24:21; Am 7:9 [h]Am 5:21,22; 8:10
26:32 [i]Isa 5:6; Jer 9:11; 12:11; 25:11; 26:9; 33:10; 34:22; 44:22 / 1Ki 9:8; 2Ch 29:8; Isa 52:14; Jer 18:16; 19:8; 48:39; Eze 5:14; 26:16; 27:35; 28:19
26:33 [k]Jer 40:15; 50:17; Eze 34:4; Joel 3:2 [l]Dt 4:27; 28:64; Ne 1:8; Ps 44:11; 106:27; Jer 4:11; 9:16; 13:24; 31:10; Eze 5:10; 12:15; 17:21; 20:23; 22:15; Zec 7:14
[m]Jer 42:16; Am 9:4
[n]Isa 49:19;

Jer 7:34 [o]ver 31; 1Sa 15:22; Job 36:11; Jer 40:3 **26:34** [p]Isa 1:7; Jer 7:34; 25:11; 44:6; Eze 33:29 [q]ver 43; 2Ch 36:21 **26:35** [r]S Lev 25:4 **26:36** [s]Job 13:25 [t]2Ki 25:5; Ps 58:7; La 1:3,6; 4:19; Eze 21:7 [u]S ver 17 **26:37** [v]Jer 6:21; 13:16; 46:16; Eze 3:20; Na 3:3 [w]Jos 7:12 **26:38** [x]Job 4:9; 36:12; Ps 1:6; Isa 1:28; Jer 16:4; 44:27 [y]Dt 4:26 **26:39** [z]Ex 20:5; Isa 14:21 [a]S ver 16; Isa 24:16 **26:40** [b]S Lev 5:5 [c]Ps 32:5; 38:18 [d]Ne 9:2; Ps 106:6; Jer 3:12-15; 14:20; Hos 5:15; Lk 15:18; 1Jn 1:9 **26:41** [e]S ver 21./Dt 10:16; 30:6; Jer 4:4; 9:25,26; Eze 44:7,9; Ac 7:51 [g]2Ch 7:14; 12:6; Eze 20:43 [h]Isa 6:7; 33:24; 40:2; 53:5,6,11 **26:42** [i]Ge 28:15; 35:11-12 /S Ge 26:5 [k]S Ex 2:24 **26:43** [l]Ps 69:25; Isa 6:11; 32:14; 62:4; Jer 2:15; 44:2; La 1:1; Eze 36:4 [m]Nu 11:20; 14:31; 1Sa 8:7; Ps 106:24 [n]S ver 11; Eze 20:13 **26:44** [o]S ver 33; 2Ki 17:20; 25:11; 2Ch 6:36; 36:20.[p]S ver 11; Ro 11:2 [q]Dt 4:31; Jer 4:27; 5:10; 30:11 [r]Jdg 2:1; Jer 31:37; 33:26; 51:5 **26:45** [s]Dt 4:31 [t]Ex 6:8; Lev 25:38 **26:46** [u]S Ex 19:11 [v]S Lev 7:38; 27:34 **27:2** [w]S Ge 28:20

[n]3 That is, about 1 1/4 pounds (about 0.6 kilogram); also in verse 16

26:41 *uncircumcised hearts.* See note on Ge 17:10.
26:44 *not reject them.* See Jer 31:37; 33:25–26; Ro 11:1–29.
26:46 A summary statement concerning chs. 1–26.
27:1–34 This final chapter concerns things promised to the Lord in kind—servants, animals, houses or lands. But provisions were made to give money instead of the item, in which case usually the adding of a fifth of its value was

required. Such vows were expressions of special thanksgiving (cf. Hannah, 1Sa 1:28) and were given over and above the expected sacrifices.
27:2 *to dedicate persons.* Possibly to give slaves to the service of the temple, but more likely to offer oneself or a member of one's family. Since only Levites were acceptable for most work of this kind, other people gave the monetary equivalent—but see 1Sa 1:11.

ary shekel[o];[x] 4and if it is a female, set her
value at thirty shekels.[p] 5If it is a person
between the ages of five and twenty, set
the value of a male at twenty shekels[q][y]
and of a female at ten shekels.[r] 6If it is a
person between one month and five years,
set the value of a male at five shekels[s][z] of
silver and that of a female at three
shekels[t] of silver. 7If it is a person sixty
years old or more, set the value of a male
at fifteen shekels[u] and of a female at ten
shekels. 8If anyone making the vow is too
poor to pay[a] the specified amount, he is to
present the person to the priest, who will
set the value[b] for him according to what
the man making the vow can afford.

9" 'If what he vowed is an animal that is
acceptable as an offering to the LORD,[c]
such an animal given to the LORD becomes
holy.[d] 10He must not exchange it or substitute a good one for a bad one, or a bad
one for a good one;[e] if he should substitute one animal for another, both it and
the substitute become holy. 11If what he
vowed is a ceremonially unclean animal[f]—one that is not acceptable as an offering to the LORD—the animal must be
presented to the priest, 12who will judge its
quality as good or bad. Whatever value the
priest then sets, that is what it will be. 13If
the owner wishes to redeem[g] the animal,
he must add a fifth to its value.[h]

14" 'If a man dedicates his house as
something holy to the LORD, the priest will
judge its quality as good or bad. Whatever
value the priest then sets, so it will remain.
15If the man who dedicates his house redeems it,[i] he must add a fifth to its value,
and the house will again become his.

16" 'If a man dedicates to the LORD part
of his family land, its value is to be set
according to the amount of seed required
for it—fifty shekels of silver to a homer[v] of
barley seed. 17If he dedicates his field during the Year of Jubilee, the value that has
been set remains. 18But if he dedicates his
field after the Jubilee,[j] the priest will determine the value according to the number
of years that remain[k] until the next Year of
Jubilee, and its set value will be reduced.
19If the man who dedicates the field wishes
to redeem it,[l] he must add a fifth to its
value, and the field will again become his.
20If, however, he does not redeem the
field, or if he has sold it to someone else, it
can never be redeemed. 21When the field
is released in the Jubilee,[m] it will become
holy,[n] like a field devoted to the LORD;[o] it
will become the property of the priests.[w]

22" 'If a man dedicates to the LORD a
field he has bought, which is not part of his
family land, 23the priest will determine its
value up to the Year of Jubilee,[p] and the
man must pay its value on that day as
something holy to the LORD. 24In the Year
of Jubilee the field will revert to the person
from whom he bought it,[q] the one whose
land it was. 25Every value is to be set according to the sanctuary shekel,[r] twenty
gerahs[s] to the shekel.

26" 'No one, however, may dedicate the
firstborn of an animal, since the firstborn
already belongs to the LORD;[t] whether an
ox[x] or a sheep, it is the LORD's. 27If it is
one of the unclean animals,[u] he may buy
it back at its set value, adding a fifth of the
value to it. If he does not redeem it, it is to
be sold at its set value.

28" 'But nothing that a man owns and
devotes[y][v] to the LORD—whether man or
animal or family land—may be sold or redeemed; everything so devoted is most
holy[w] to the LORD.

29" 'No person devoted to destruction[z]
may be ransomed; he must be put to
death.[x]

27:3 [x]S Ex 30:13 **27:5** [y]S Ge 37:28 **27:6** [z]Nu 3:47; 18:16 **27:8** [a]S Lev 5:11 [b]ver 12,14 **27:9** [c]S Ge 28:20; S Lev 1:2 [d]ver 21, 26,28; Ex 40:9; Nu 6:20; 18:17; Dt 15:19 **27:10** [e]ver 33 **27:11** [f]ver 27; S Ex 13:13; Nu 18:15 **27:13** [g]S Lev 25:25 [h]S Lev 5:16 **27:15** [i]ver 13,20 **27:18** [j]Lev 25:10 [k]Lev 25:15 **27:19** [l]S Lev 25:25 **27:21** [m]S Lev 25:10 [n]S ver 9 [o]ver 28; Nu 18:14; Eze 44:29 **27:23** [p]S Lev 25:15 **27:24** [q]Lev 25:28 **27:25** [r]S Ex 30:13 [s]Nu 3:47; Eze 45:12 **27:26** [t]S Ex 13:12 **27:27** [u]S ver 11 **27:28** [v]Nu 18:14; Jos 6:17-19 [w]S ver 9 **27:29** [x]Dt 7:26

[o]*3* That is, about 2/5 ounce (about 11.5 grams); also in verse 25 [p]*4* That is, about 12 ounces (about 0.3 kilogram) [q]*5* That is, about 8 ounces (about 0.2 kilogram) [r]*5* That is, about 4 ounces (about 110 grams); also in verse 7 [s]*6* That is, about 2 ounces (about 55 grams) [t]*6* That is, about 1 1/4 ounces (about 35 grams) [u]*7* That is, about 6 ounces (about 170 grams) [v]*16* That is, probably about 6 bushels (about 220 liters) [w]*21* Or *priest* [x]*26* The Hebrew word can include both male and female. [y]*28* The Hebrew term refers to the irrevocable giving over of things or persons to the LORD. [z]*29* The Hebrew term refers to the irrevocable giving over of things or persons to the LORD, often by totally destroying them.

27:9 *becomes holy.* An animal given for a sacrifice could not be exchanged for another (v. 10). The people of Malachi's day chose the poorest animals after having vowed to offer good ones (Mal 1:13–14). If an unclean animal was given, it could be redeemed with the 20 percent penalty (vv. 11–13).

27:28 *devotes to the LORD.* See NIV text note. Devoting something was far more serious than dedicating it to sacred use. The devoted thing became totally the Lord's. Achan's sin was the greater because he stole what had been devoted to the Lord (Jos 7:11). Persons devoted to destruction were usually the captives in the wars of Canaan (cf. 1Sa 15:3,18).

27:29 Saul sinned in this regard when he did not totally destroy the Amalekites (1Sa 15).

27:30 *tithe.* A tenth (see Nu 18:21–29; Dt 12:6–18; 14:22–29; 26:12). From these passages it appears that Israel actually had three tithes: (1) the general tithe (here), paid to the Levites (Nu 18:21), who in turn had to give a tenth of that to the priests (Nu 18:26); (2) the tithe associated with the sacred meal involving offerer and Levite (Dt 14:22–27); (3) the tithe paid every three years to the poor (Dt 14:28–29).

30 " 'A tithe[y] of everything from the land, whether grain from the soil or fruit from the trees, belongs to the LORD; it is holy[z] to the LORD. 31 If a man redeems[a] any of his tithe, he must add a fifth of the value[b] to it. 32 The entire tithe of the herd and flock—every tenth animal that passes under the shepherd's rod[c]—will be holy to the LORD. 33 He must not pick out the good from the bad or make any substitution. [d] If he does make a substitution, both the animal and its substitute become holy and cannot be redeemed.[e] ' "

34 These are the commands the LORD gave Moses on Mount Sinai[f] for the Israelites.[g]

27:30
yNu 18:26;
Dt 12:6,17;
14:22,28;
2Ch 31:6;
Ne 10:37; 12:44;
13:5; Mal 3:8;
zDt 7:6; Ezr 9:2;
Isa 6:13
27:31
aS Lev 25:25
bLev 5:16
27:32 cPs 89:32;
Jer 33:13;
Eze 20:37

27:33 dver 10 eNu 18:21 27:34 fS Ex 19:11 gS Lev 7:38;
Ac 7:38

27:34 *the LORD gave Moses.* See 1:1; 7:37–38; 25:1; 26:46. This is strong testimony for the Mosaic authorship and divine origin of the book.

NUMBERS

Title

The English name of the book comes from the Septuagint (the Greek translation of the OT) and is based on the census lists found in chs. 1; 26. The Hebrew title of the book (*bemidbar,* "in the desert") is more descriptive of its contents. Numbers presents an account of the 38-year period of Israel's wandering in the desert following the establishment of the covenant of Sinai (compare 1:1 with Dt 1:1).

Author and Date

The book has traditionally been ascribed to Moses. This conclusion is based on (1) statements concerning Moses' writing activity (e.g., 33:1-2; Ex 17:14; 24:4; 34:27) and (2) the assumption that the first five books of the Bible, the Pentateuch, are a unit and come from one author. See Introduction to Genesis: Author and Date of Writing.

It is not necessary, however, to claim that Numbers came from Moses' hand complete and in final form. Portions of the book were probably added by scribes or editors from later periods of Israel's history. For example, the protestation of the humility of Moses (12:3) would hardly be convincing if it came from his own mouth. But it seems reasonable to assume that Moses wrote the essential content of the book.

Contents

Numbers relates the story of Israel's journey from Mount Sinai to the plains of Moab on the border of Canaan. Much of its legislation for people and priests is similar to that in Exodus, Leviticus and Deuteronomy. The book tells of the murmuring and rebellion of God's people and of their subsequent judgment. Those whom God had redeemed from slavery in Egypt and with whom he had made a covenant at Mount Sinai responded not with faith, gratitude and obedience but with unbelief, ingratitude and repeated acts of rebellion, which came to extreme expression in their refusal to undertake the conquest of Canaan (ch. 14). The community of the redeemed forfeited their part in the promised land. They were condemned to live out their lives in the desert; only their children would enjoy the fulfillment of the promise that had originally been theirs (cf. Heb 3:7-4:11).

Theological Teaching

In telling the story of Israel's desert wanderings, Numbers offers much that is theologically significant. During the first year after Israel's deliverance from Egypt, she entered into covenant with the Lord at Sinai to be the people of his kingdom, among whom he pitched his royal tent (the tabernacle)—this is the story of Exodus. As the account of Numbers begins, the Lord organizes Israel into a military camp. Leaving Sinai, she marches forth as his conquering army, with the Lord at her head, to establish his kingdom in the promised land in the midst of the nations. The book graphically portrays Israel's identity as the Lord's redeemed covenant people and her vocation as the servant people of God, charged with establishing his kingdom on earth. God's purpose in history is implicitly disclosed: to invade the arena of fallen humanity and effect the redemption of his creation—the mission in which his people are also to be totally engaged.

Numbers also presents the chastening wrath of God against his disobedient people. Because of her rebellion (and especially her refusal to undertake the conquest of Canaan), Israel was in breach of covenant. The fourth book of the Pentateuch presents a sobering reality: The God who had entered into covenant with Abraham (Ge 15; 17), who had delivered his people from bondage in the exodus (Ex 14-15), who had brought Israel into covenant with himself as his "treasured possession" (Ex 19; see especially Ex 19:5) and who had revealed his holiness and the gracious means of approaching him

(Lev 1-7) was also a God of wrath. His wrath extended to his errant children as well as to the enemy nations of Egypt and Canaan.

Even Moses, the great prophet and servant of the Lord, was not exempt from God's wrath when he disobeyed God. Ch. 20, which records his error, begins with the notice of Miriam's death (20:1) and concludes with the record of Aaron's death (20:22-29). Here is the passing of the old guard. Those whom God has used to establish the nation are dying before the nation has come into its own.

The questions arise: Is God finished with the nation as a whole (cf. Ro 11:1)? Are his promises a thing of the past? In one of the most remarkable sections of the Bible—the account of Balaam, the pagan diviner (chs. 22-24)—the reply is given. The Lord, working in a providential and direct way, proclaims his continued faithfulness to his purpose for his people despite their unfaithfulness to him.

Balaam is Moab's answer to Moses, the man of God. He is an internationally known prophet who shares the pagan belief that the God of Israel is like any other deity who might be manipulated by acts of magic or sorcery. But from the early part of the narrative, when Balaam first encounters the one true God in visions, and in the narrative of the journey on the donkey (ch. 22), he begins to learn that dealing with the true God is fundamentally different from anything he has ever known. When he attempts to curse Israel at the instigation of Balak king of Moab, Balaam finds his mouth unable to express the curse he desires to pronounce. Instead, from his lips come blessings on Israel and curses on her enemies (chs. 23-24).

In his seven prophetic oracles, Balaam proclaims God's great blessing for his people (see 23:20). Though the immediate enjoyment of this blessing will always depend on the faithfulness of his people, the ultimate realization of God's blessing is sure—because of the character of God (see 23:19). Thus Numbers reaffirms the ongoing purposes of God. Despite his judgment on his rebellious people, God is still determined to bring Israel into the land of promise. His blessing to her rests in his sovereign will.

The teaching of the book has lasting significance for Israel and for the church (cf. Ro 15:4; 1Co 10:6,11). God does display his wrath even against his errant people, but his grace is renewed as surely as is the dawn and his redemptive purpose will not be thwarted.

Special Problem

The large numbers of men conscripted into Israel's army puzzle modern scholars (see, e.g., the figures in 1:46; 26:51). These numbers of men mustered for warfare demand a total population in excess of 2,000,000. Such numbers seem to be exceedingly large for the times, for the locale, for the desert wanderings, and in comparison with the inhabitants of Canaan. See note on 3:43.

Various possibilities have been suggested to solve this problem. Some have thought that the numbers may have been corrupted in transmission. The present text, however, does not betray textual difficulties with the numbers.

Others have felt that the Hebrew word for "thousand" might have a different meaning here from its usual numerical connotation. In some passages, for example, the word is a technical term for a company of men that may or may not equal 1,000 (e.g., Jos 22:14, "family division"; 1Sa 23:23, "clans"). Further, some have postulated that this Hebrew word means "chief" (as in Ge 36:15). In this way the figure 53,400 (26:47) would mean "53 chiefs plus 400 men." Such a procedure would yield a greatly reduced total, but it would also be at variance with the fact that the Hebrew text adds the "thousands" in the same way it adds the "hundreds" for a large total. Also, this would make the proportion of chiefs to fighting men top-heavy (59 chiefs for 300 men in Simeon).

Another option is to read the Hebrew word for "thousand" with a dual meaning of "chief" and "1,000," with the chiefs numbering one less than the stated figure. For example, the 46,500 of Reuben (1:20) is read as 45 chiefs and 1,500 fighting men, the 59,300 of Simeon (1:23) is read as 58 chiefs and 1,300 fighting men, etc. But in this case, as in the former, the totals of 1:46 and 2:32 must then be regarded as errors of understanding (perhaps by later scribes).

Still another approach is to regard the numbers as symbolic figures rather than as strictly mathematical. The numerical value of the Hebrew letters in the expression *bene yisra'el* ("the Israelite community," 1:2) equals 603 (the number of the thousands of the fighting men, 1:46); the remaining 550 (plus 1 for Moses) might come from the numerical equivalent of the Hebrew letters in the expression "all the men ... who are able to serve in the army" (1:3). This symbolic use of numbers (called "gematria") is not unknown in the Bible (see Rev 13:18), but it is not likely in Numbers, where there are no literary clues pointing in that direction.

While the problem of the large numbers has not been satisfactorily solved, the Bible does point to

a remarkable increase of Jacob's descendants during the four centuries of their sojourn in Egypt (see Ex 1:7-12). With all their difficulties, these numbers also point to the great role of providence and miracles in God's dealings with his people during their life in the desert (see note on 1:46).

Structure and Outline

The book has three major divisions, based on Israel's geographical locations. Each of the three divisions has two parts, as the following breakdown demonstrates: (1) Israel at Sinai, preparing to depart for the land of promise (1:1-10:10), followed by the journey from Sinai to Kadesh (10:11-12:16); (2) Israel at Kadesh, delayed as a result of rebellion (13:1-20:13), followed by the journey from Kadesh to the plains of Moab (20:14-22:1); (3) Israel on the plains of Moab, anticipating the conquest of the land of promise (22:2-32:42), followed by appendixes dealing with various matters (chs. 33-36).

I. Israel at Sinai, Preparing to Depart for the Promised Land (1:1-10:10)
    A. The Commands for the Census of the People (chs. 1-4)
        1. The numbers of men from each tribe mustered for war (ch. 1)
        2. The placement of the tribes around the tabernacle and their order for march (ch. 2)
        3. The placement of the Levites around the tabernacle, and the numbers of the Levites and the firstborn of Israel (ch. 3)
        4. The numbers of the Levites in their tabernacle service for the Lord (ch. 4)
    B. The Commands for Purity of the People (5:1-10:10)
        1. The test for purity in the law of jealousy (ch. 5)
        2. The Nazirite vow and the Aaronic benediction (ch. 6)
        3. The offerings of the 12 leaders at the dedication of the tabernacle (ch. 7)
        4. The setting up of the lamps and the separation of the Levites (ch. 8)
        5. The observance of the Passover (9:1-14)
        6. The covering cloud and the silver trumpets (9:15-10:10)
II. The Journey from Sinai to Kadesh (10:11-12:16)
    A. The Beginning of the Journey (10:11-36)
    B. The Beginning of the Sorrows: Fire and Quail (ch. 11)
    C. The Opposition of Miriam and Aaron (ch. 12)
III. Israel at Kadesh, the Delay Resulting from Rebellion (13:1-20:13)
    A. The 12 Spies and Their Mixed Report of the Good Land (ch. 13)
    B. The People's Rebellion against God's Commission, and Their Defeat (ch. 14)
    C. A Collection of Laws on Offerings, the Sabbath and Tassels on Garments (ch. 15)
    D. The Rebellion of Korah and His Allies (ch. 16)
    E. The Budding of Aaron's Staff: A Sign for Rebels (ch. 17)
    F. Concerning Priests, Their Duties and Their Support (ch. 18)
    G. The Red Heifer and the Cleansing Water (ch. 19)
    H. The Sin of Moses (20:1-13)
IV. The Journey from Kadesh to the Plains of Moab (20:14-22:1)
    A. The Resistance of Edom (20:14-21)
    B. The Death of Aaron (20:22-29)
    C. The Destruction of Arad (21:1-3)
    D. The Bronze Snake (21:4-9)
    E. The Song of the Well (21:10-20)
    F. The Defeat of Sihon and Og (21:21-30)
    G. Israel Enters Moab (21:31-22:1)
V. Israel on the Plains of Moab, in Anticipation of Taking the Promised Land (22:2-32:42)
    A. Balak of Moab Hires Balaam to Curse Israel (22:2-41)
    B. Balaam Blesses Israel in Seven Oracles (chs. 23-24)
    C. The Baal of Peor and Israel's Apostasy (ch. 25)
    D. The Second Census (ch. 26)
    E. Instructions for the New Generation (chs. 27-30)
        1. The inheritance for women (27:1-11)
        2. The successor to Moses (27:12-23)
        3. Commands regarding offerings (28:1-15)
        4. Commands regarding festivals (28:16-29:40)

        5. Commands regarding vows (ch. 30)
    F. The War against Midian (ch. 31)
    G. The Settlement of the Transjordan Tribes (ch. 32)
VI. Appendixes Dealing with Various Matters (chs. 33-36)
    A. The Stages of the Journey (ch. 33)
    B. The Land of Inheritance (chs. 34-35)
    C. The Inheritance for Women (ch. 36)

The Census

1 The LORD spoke to Moses in the Tent of Meeting[a] in the Desert of Sinai[b] on the first day of the second month[c] of the second year after the Israelites came out of Egypt.[d] He said: [2]"Take a census[e] of the whole Israelite community by their clans and families,[f] listing every man by name,[g] one by one. [3]You and Aaron[h] are to number by their divisions all the men in Israel twenty years old or more[i] who are able to serve in the army.[j] [4]One man from each tribe,[k] each the head of his family,[l] is to help you.[m] [5]These are the names[n] of the men who are to assist you:

from Reuben,[o] Elizur son of Shedeur;[p]
[6]from Simeon,[q] Shelumiel son of Zurishaddai;[r]
[7]from Judah,[s] Nahshon son of Amminadab;[t]
[8]from Issachar,[u] Nethanel son of Zuar;[v]
[9]from Zebulun,[w] Eliab son of Helon;[x]
[10]from the sons of Joseph:
from Ephraim,[y] Elishama son of Ammihud;[z]
from Manasseh,[a] Gamaliel son of Pedahzur;[b]
[11]from Benjamin,[c] Abidan son of Gideoni;[d]
[12]from Dan,[e] Ahiezer son of Ammishaddai;[f]
[13]from Asher,[g] Pagiel son of Ocran;[h]
[14]from Gad,[i] Eliasaph son of Deuel;[j]
[15]from Naphtali,[k] Ahira son of Enan.[l]"

[16]These were the men appointed from the community, the leaders[m] of their ancestral tribes.[n] They were the heads of the clans of Israel.[o]

[17]Moses and Aaron took these men whose names had been given, [18]and they called the whole community together on the first day of the second month.[p] The people indicated their ancestry[q] by their clans and families,[r] and the men twenty years old or more[s] were listed by name, one by one, [19]as the LORD commanded Moses. And so he counted[t] them in the Desert of Sinai:

[20]From the descendants of Reuben[u] the firstborn son[v] of Israel:

All the men twenty years old or more who were able to serve in the army were listed by name, one by one, according to the records of their clans and families. [21]The number from the tribe of Reuben[w] was 46,500.

[22]From the descendants of Simeon:[x]

All the men twenty years old or more who were able to serve in the army were counted and listed by name, one by one, according to the records of their clans and families. [23]The number from the tribe of Simeon was 59,300.[y]

1:1 aS Ex 27:21; S 40:2 bS Ex 19:1 cver 18 dS Ex 6:14 1:2 eEx 30:11-16 fver 18 gNu 3:40 1:3 hEx 4:14; Nu 17:3 iS Ex 30:14 jver 20; Nu 26:2; Jos 5:4; 1Ch 5:18 1:4 kS Lev 24:11; S Jos 7:1 lver 16; Nu 7:2; 30:1; 31:26 mEx 18:21; Nu 34:18; Dt 1:15; Jos 22:14 1:5 nNu 17:2 oS Ge 29:32; Rev 7:5 pNu 2:10; 7:30; 10:18 1:6 qver 22; Nu 25:14 rNu 2:12; 7:36, 41; 10:19 1:7 sver 26; S Ge 29:35; Ps 78:68 tEx 6:23; Nu 7:12; Ru 4:20; 1Ch 2:10; Mt 1:4; Lk 3:32 1:8 uS Ge 30:18; Nu 10:15 vNu 2:5; 7:18 1:9 wver 30; Nu 10:16 xNu 2:7; 7:24 1:10 yver 32 zNu 2:18; 7:48, 53; 10:22 aver 34; Nu 10:23 bNu 2:20; 7:54 1:11 cNu 10:24 dNu 2:22; 7:60; Ps 68:27 1:12 ever 38 fNu 2:25; 7:66; 10:25 1:13 gver 40; Nu 10:26 hNu 2:27; 7:72 1:14 iver 24; Nu 10:20 jNu 2:14; 7:42 1:15 kver 42; Nu 10:27 lNu 2:29; 7:78 1:16 mS Ex 18:25 nNu 32:28 oS ver 4 1:18 pver 1 qEzr 2:59; Heb 7:3 rver 2 sS Ex 30:14 tEx 30:12; Nu 26:63; 31:49 1:20 uS Ge 29:32; S 46:9; Rev 7:5 vS Ge 10:15 1:21 wNu 26:7 1:22 xS Ge 29:33; Rev 7:7 1:23 yNu 26:14

1:1 *The LORD spoke to Moses.* One of the most pervasive emphases in Numbers is the fact that the Lord spoke to Moses and through Moses to Israel. From the opening words to the closing words (36:13), this is stated over 150 times and in more than 20 ways. The Lord's use of Moses as his prophet is described in 12:6–8. One of the Hebrew names for the book is *wayedabber* ("And he [the LORD] spoke"), from the first word in the Hebrew text. *Tent of Meeting.* See tabernacle. *Desert of Sinai.* The more common Hebrew name for Numbers is *bemidbar* ("in the desert"), the fifth word in the Hebrew text. The events of Numbers cover a period of 38 years and nine or ten months, i.e., the period of Israel's desert wanderings. *first day . . . second month . . . second year.* Thirteen months after the exodus, Numbers begins. Israel had spent the previous year in the region of Mount Sinai receiving the law and erecting the tabernacle. Now she was to be mustered as a military force for an orderly march. Dating events from the exodus (for another example see 1Ki 6:1) is similar to the Christian practice of dating years in reference to the incarnation of Christ (B.C. and A.D.). The exodus was God's great act of deliverance of his people from bondage.
1:2 *Take.* The Hebrew for this word is plural, indicating that Moses and Aaron were to complete this task together (see v. 3, "You and Aaron"), but the primary responsibility lay with Moses. *census.* Its main purpose was to form a

military roster, not a social, political or taxing document.
1:3 *able to serve in the army.* Refers to the principal military purpose of the census. The phrase occurs 14 times in ch. 1 and again in 26:2.
1:4 *One man from each tribe.* By having a representative from each tribe assist Moses and Aaron, the count would be regarded as legitimate by all.
1:5–16 The names of these men occur again in chs. 2; 7; 10. Most contain within them a reference to the name of God. Levi is not represented in the list (see vv. 47–53).
1:19 *And so he counted them in the Desert of Sinai.* A summary statement; vv. 20–43 provide the details.
1:20–43 For each tribe there are two verses in repetitive formulaic structure, giving: (1) the name of the tribe, (2) the specifics of those numbered, (3) the name of the tribe again and (4) the total count for that tribe. The numbers for each tribe are rounded off to the hundred (but Gad to the 50, v. 25). The same numbers are given for each tribe in ch. 2, where there are four triads of tribes. A peculiarity in the numbers that leads some to believe that they are symbolic is that the hundreds are grouped between 200 and 700. Also, various speculations have arisen regarding the meaning of the Hebrew word for "thousand" (see Introduction: Special Problem). In this chapter, the word has been used to mean 1,000 in order for the totals to be achieved.

24From the descendants of Gad: z

All the men twenty years old or more who were able to serve in the army were listed by name, according to the records of their clans and families. 25The number from the tribe of Gad a was 45,650.

26From the descendants of Judah: b

All the men twenty years old or more who were able to serve in the army were listed by name, according to the records of their clans and families. 27The number from the tribe of Judah c was 74,600.

28From the descendants of Issachar: d

All the men twenty years old or more who were able to serve in the army were listed by name, according to the records of their clans and families. 29The number from the tribe of Issachar e was 54,400.f

30From the descendants of Zebulun: g

All the men twenty years old or more who were able to serve in the army were listed by name, according to the records of their clans and families. 31The number from the tribe of Zebulun was 57,400.h

32From the sons of Joseph: i

From the descendants of Ephraim: j

All the men twenty years old or more who were able to serve in the army were listed by name, according to the records of their clans and families. 33The number from the tribe of Ephraim k was 40,500.

34From the descendants of Manasseh: l

All the men twenty years old or more who were able to serve in the army were listed by name, ac-

cording to the records of their clans and families. 35The number from the tribe of Manasseh was 32,200.

36From the descendants of Benjamin: m

All the men twenty years old or more who were able to serve in the army were listed by name, according to the records of their clans and families. 37The number from the tribe of Benjamin n was 35,400.

38From the descendants of Dan: o

All the men twenty years old or more who were able to serve in the army were listed by name, according to the records of their clans and families. 39The number from the tribe of Dan was 62,700.p

40From the descendants of Asher: q

All the men twenty years old or more who were able to serve in the army were listed by name, according to the records of their clans and families. 41The number from the tribe of Asher r was 41,500.

42From the descendants of Naphtali: s

All the men twenty years old or more who were able to serve in the army were listed by name, according to the records of their clans and families. 43The number from the tribe of Naphtali t was 53,400.u

44These were the men counted by Moses and Aaron v and the twelve leaders of Israel, each one representing his family. 45All the Israelites twenty years old or more w who were able to serve in Israel's army were counted according to their families.x 46The total number was 603,550.y

47The families of the tribe of Levi, z

1:24
zS Ge 30:11;
S Jos 13:24-28;
Rev 7:5
1:25 aGe 46:16;
Nu 26:18;
1Ch 5:11
1:26 bS ver 7;
Mt 1:2; Rev 7:5
1:27 cNu 26:22
1:28
dS Ge 30:18;
Rev 7:7
1:29 eS Ge 30:18
fNu 26:25
1:30
gS Ge 30:20;
Rev 7:8
1:31 hNu 26:27
1:32 iGe 49:26
jS Ge 41:52
1:33 kNu 26:37;
1Ch 7:20
1:34 lS Ge 41:51;
Rev 7:6

1:36
mS Ge 35:18;
2Ch 17:17;
Jer 32:44;
Ob 1:19; Rev 7:8
1:37 nNu 26:41
1:38 oGe 30:6;
Dt 33:22
1:39 pNu 26:43
1:40
qS Ge 30:13;
Nu 26:44;
Rev 7:6
1:41 rNu 26:47
1:42 sS Ge 30:8;
Rev 7:6
1:43 tNu 26:50
uS Ex 1:1-4
1:44 vNu 26:64
1:45 wver 3;
Nu 14:29
xNu 2:32
1:46 yS Ex 12:37;
2Sa 24:9
1:47
zS Nu 3:17-20

1:32–35 Because the descendants of Levi were excluded from the census (see note on v. 47), the descendants of Joseph are listed according to the families of his two sons, Ephraim (vv. 32–33) and Manasseh (vv. 34–35). In this way the traditional tribal number of 12 is maintained, and Joseph is given the "double portion" of the ranking heir (cf. Ge 49:22-26; Dt 33:13–17; 2Ki 2:9).
1:46 *603,550.* Except for Joshua and Caleb, all these died in the desert. The mathematics of these numbers is accurate and complex. It is complex in that the totals are reached in two ways: (1) a linear listing of 12 units (vv. 20–43), with the total given (v. 46); (2) four sets of triads, each with a subtotal, and then the grand total (2:3–32). These figures are also consistent with those in Ex 12:37; 38:26. This large

number of men conscripted for the army suggests a population for the entire community in excess of 2,000,000 (see Introduction: Special Problem). Ex 1:7 describes the remarkable growth of the Hebrew people in Egypt during the 400-year sojourn. They had become so numerous that they were regarded as a grave threat to the security of Egypt (Ex 1:9–10,20). Israel's amazing growth from the 70 who entered Egypt (Ge 1:5) was an evidence of God's great blessing and his faithfulness to his covenant with Abraham (Ge 12:2; 15:5; 17:4–6; 22:17).
1:47 Because of their special tasks, the Levites were excluded from this military count. They too had to perform service to the Lord, but they were to be engaged in the ceremonies and maintenance of the tabernacle (see note on

however, were not counted[a] along with the others. [48]The LORD had said to Moses: [49]"You must not count the tribe of Levi or include them in the census of the other Israelites. [50]Instead, appoint the Levites to be in charge of the tabernacle[b] of the Testimony[c]—over all its furnishings[d] and everything belonging to it. They are to carry the tabernacle and all its furnishings; they are to take care of it and encamp around it. [51]Whenever the tabernacle[e] is to move,[f] the Levites are to take it down, and whenever the tabernacle is to be set up, the Levites shall do it.[g] Anyone else who goes near it shall be put to death.[h] [52]The Israelites are to set up their tents by divisions, each man in his own camp under his own standard.[i] [53]The Levites, however, are to set up their tents around the tabernacle[j] of the Testimony so that wrath will not fall[k] on the Israelite community. The Levites are to be responsible for the care of the tabernacle of the Testimony.[l] "

[54]The Israelites did all this just as the LORD commanded Moses.

The Arrangement of the Tribal Camps

2 The LORD said to Moses and Aaron: [2]"The Israelites are to camp around the Tent of Meeting some distance from it,

1:47 aNu 4:3,49
1:50 bEx 25:9;
S 26:1
cS Ex 16:34;
Ac 7:44; Rev 15:5
dNu 3:31
1:51 eS Ex 26:1
fNu 4:5
gNu 3:38; 4:15
hS Ex 21:12
1:52 iNu 10:14;
Ps 20:5; SS 2:4;
6:4
1:53 jNu 2:10;
3:23,29,38
kLev 10:6;
Nu 16:46; 18:5;
Dt 9:22
lS Ex 38:21;
Nu 18:2-4

2:2 mPs 74:4;
Isa 31:9; Jer 4:21
2:3 nS Ex 6:23
2:5 oNu 10:15
pS Nu 1:8
2:7 qNu 1:9;
10:16
2:9 rNu 10:14;
Jdg 1:1
2:10 sS Nu 1:53
tNu 1:5
2:12 uNu 10:19
vS Nu 1:6
2:14 wNu 10:20

each man under his standard[m] with the banners of his family."

[3]On the east, toward the sunrise, the divisions of the camp of Judah are to encamp under their standard. The leader of the people of Judah is Nahshon son of Amminadab.[n] [4]His division numbers 74,600.

[5]The tribe of Issachar[o] will camp next to them. The leader of the people of Issachar is Nethanel son of Zuar.[p] [6]His division numbers 54,400.

[7]The tribe of Zebulun will be next. The leader of the people of Zebulun is Eliab son of Helon.[q] [8]His division numbers 57,400.

[9]All the men assigned to the camp of Judah, according to their divisions, number 186,400. They will set out first.[r]

[10]On the south[s] will be the divisions of the camp of Reuben under their standard. The leader of the people of Reuben is Elizur son of Shedeur.[t] [11]His division numbers 46,500.

[12]The tribe of Simeon[u] will camp next to them. The leader of the people of Simeon is Shelumiel son of Zurishaddai.[v] [13]His division numbers 59,300.

[14]The tribe of Gad[w] will be next.

---

vv. 32–35).
1:50 *Testimony.* The Ten Commandments written on stone tablets (see Ex 31:18; 32:15; 34:29), which were placed in the ark (Ex 25:16,21; 40:20), leading to the phrase the "ark of the Testimony" (Ex 25:22; 26:33,34).
1:51 *Anyone else.* The Hebrew for this phrase is often translated "stranger," "alien" or "foreigner" (e.g., Isa 1:7; Hos 7:9). Thus a non-Levite Israelite was considered an alien to the religious duties of the tabernacle (see Ex 29:33; 30:33; Lev 22:12). *death.* See 3:10,38; 18:7; cf. 16:31–33; 1Sa 6:19.
1:53 *their tents around the tabernacle.* See 3:21–38. *wrath.* The Levites formed a protective hedge against trespassing by the non-Levites to keep them from experiencing divine wrath.
1:54 *as the LORD commanded Moses.* In view of Israel's great disobedience in the later chapters of Numbers, these words of initial compliance have a special poignancy.
2:1–34 This chapter is symmetrically structured:
    Summary command (vv. 1-2)
    Details of execution (vv. 3-33):
        Eastern camp (vv. 3-9)
        Southern camp (vv. 10-16)
            Tent and Levites (v. 17)
        Western camp (vv. 18-24)
        Northern camp (vv. 25-31)
            Summary totals (vv. 32-33)
    Summary conclusion (v. 34)
In ch. 1 the nation is mustered, and the genealogical relationships are clarified. In ch. 2 the nation is put in structural order, and the line of march and place of

encampment are established. The numbers of ch. 1 are given in a new pattern, and the same leaders are named here again.
2:2 *some distance from it.* See 1:52–53. *each man.* Each was to know his exact position within the camp. *standard . . . banners.* Each tribe had its banner, and each triad of tribes had its standard. Jewish tradition suggests that the tribal banners corresponded in color to the 12 stones in the breastpiece of the high priest (Ex 28:15–21). Tradition also holds that the standard of the triad led by Judah had the figure of a lion, that of Reuben the figure of a man, that of Ephraim the figure of an ox and that of Dan the figure of an eagle (see the four living creatures described by Eze 1:10; cf. Rev 4:7). But these traditions are not otherwise substantiated. See diagram of "Encampment of the Tribes of Israel," p. 192.
2:3–7 *Judah . . . Issachar . . . Zebulun.* The fourth, fifth and sixth sons of Jacob and Leah. It is somewhat surprising to have these three tribes first in the order of march, since Reuben is regularly noted as Jacob's firstborn son (1:20). However, because of the failure of the older brothers (Reuben, Simeon and Levi; see Ge 49:3–7), Judah is granted pride of place among his brothers (Ge 49:8). Judah produced the royal line from which the Messiah came (Ge 49:10; Ru 4:18–21; Mt 1:1–16).
2:10–12 *Reuben . . . Simeon.* The first and second sons of Jacob and Leah.
2:14 *Gad.* The first son of Jacob and Zilpah (Leah's maidservant). Levi, Leah's third son, is not included with the divisions of the congregation. *Deuel.* See NIV text note. The Hebrew letters for *d* and *r* were easily confused by scribes (copyists) because of their similarity in form (see note on Ge

The leader of the people of Gad is Eliasaph son of Deuel.[a][x] 15His division numbers 45,650.

16All the men assigned to the camp of Reuben,[y] according to their divisions, number 151,450. They will set out second.

17Then the Tent of Meeting and the camp of the Levites[z] will set out in the middle of the camps. They will set out in the same order as they encamp, each in his own place under his standard.

18On the west[a] will be the divisions of the camp of Ephraim[b] under their standard. The leader of the people of Ephraim is Elishama son of Ammihud.[c] 19His division numbers 40,-500.

20The tribe of Manasseh[d] will be next to them. The leader of the people of Manasseh is Gamaliel son of Pedahzur.[e] 21His division numbers 32,200.

22The tribe of Benjamin[f] will be next. The leader of the people of Benjamin is Abidan son of Gideoni.[g] 23His division numbers 35,400.

24All the men assigned to the camp of Ephraim,[h] according to their divisions, number 108,100. They will set out third.[i]

25On the north[j] will be the divisions of the camp of Dan, under their standard.[k] The leader of the people of Dan is Ahiezer son of Ammishaddai.[l] 26His division numbers 62,700.

27The tribe of Asher will camp next to them. The leader of the people of Asher is Pagiel son of Ocran.[m] 28His division numbers 41,500.

29The tribe of Naphtali[n] will be next. The leader of the people of Naphtali is Ahira son of Enan.[o] 30His division numbers 53,400.

31All the men assigned to the camp of Dan number 157,600. They will set out last,[p] under their standards.

32These are the Israelites, counted according to their families.[q] All those in the camps, by their divisions, number 603,550.[r] 33The Levites, however, were not counted[s] along with

2:14 xNu 1:14; 10:20
2:16 yNu 10:18
2:17 zNu 1:50; 10:21
2:18 aS Nu 1:53
bS Ge 48:20; Jer 31:18-20
cNu 1:10
2:20 dS Ge 48:20
eS Nu 1:10
2:22 fNu 10:24
gS Nu 1:11

2:24 hNu 10:22
iPs 80:2
2:25 jS Nu 1:53
kNu 10:25
lS Nu 1:12
2:27 mNu 1:13; 10:26
2:29 nNu 10:27
oNu 1:15; 10:27
2:31 pNu 10:25; Jos 6:9
2:32 qNu 1:45
rS Ex 12:37
2:33 sNu 1:47; 26:57-62

a/4 Many manuscripts of the Masoretic Text, Samaritan Pentateuch and Vulgate (see also Num. 1:14); most manuscripts of the Masoretic Text Reuel

---

10:4).
2:17 *Tent of Meeting.* Representing God's presence in the heart of the camp (see 1:1 and note). *Levites.* In the line of march, the Judah and Reuben triads would lead the community, then would come the tabernacle with the attendant protective hedge of Levites (see note on 1:53), and last would come the Ephraim and Dan triads.
2:18–22 The Rachel tribes (Joseph and Benjamin) were on the west. Joseph's two sons Manasseh and Ephraim received

a special blessing from their grandfather Jacob, but the younger son, Ephraim, was given precedence over Manasseh (Ge 48:5–20). Here, true to Jacob's words, Ephraim is ahead of Manasseh. Last comes Benjamin, the last son born to Jacob.
2:25 *Dan.* The first son of Bilhah, Rachel's maidservant.
2:27 *Asher.* The second son of Zilpah, Leah's maidservant.
2:29 *Naphtali.* The second son of Bilhah.
2:32 *603,550.* See 1:46 and note.
2:33 *Levites.* See notes on 1:47,53.

Encampment of the Tribes of Israel   NU 2:1-31   NU 10:11-33

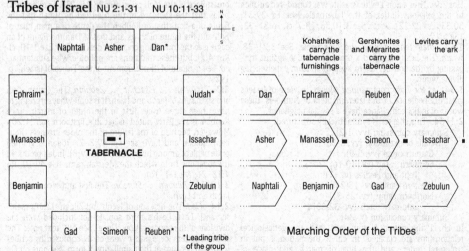

Marching Order of the Tribes

*Leading tribe of the group

the other Israelites, as the Lord commanded Moses.

34So the Israelites did everything the Lord commanded Moses; that is the way they encamped under their standards, and that is the way they set out, each with his clan and family.

The Levites

3 This is the account of the family of Aaron and Moses[t] at the time the Lord talked with Moses on Mount Sinai.[u]

2The names of the sons of Aaron were Nadab the firstborn[v] and Abihu, Eleazar and Ithamar.[w] 3Those were the names of Aaron's sons, the anointed priests,[x] who were ordained to serve as priests. 4Nadab and Abihu, however, fell dead before the Lord[y] when they made an offering with unauthorized fire before him in the Desert of Sinai.[z] They had no sons; so only Eleazar and Ithamar[a] served as priests during the lifetime of their father Aaron.[b]

5The Lord said to Moses, 6"Bring the tribe of Levi[c] and present them to Aaron the priest to assist him.[d] 7They are to perform duties for him and for the whole community[e] at the Tent of Meeting by doing the work[f] of the tabernacle. 8They are to take care of all the furnishings of the Tent of Meeting, fulfilling the obligations

of the Israelites by doing the work of the tabernacle. 9Give the Levites to Aaron and his sons;[g] they are the Israelites who are to be given wholly to him.[b] 10Appoint Aaron[h] and his sons to serve as priests;[i] anyone else who approaches the sanctuary must be put to death."[j]

11The Lord also said to Moses, 12"I have taken the Levites[k] from among the Israelites in place of the first male offspring[l] of every Israelite woman. The Levites are mine,[m] 13for all the firstborn are mine.[n] When I struck down all the firstborn in Egypt, I set apart for myself every firstborn in Israel, whether man or animal. They are to be mine. I am the Lord."[o]

14The Lord said to Moses in the Desert of Sinai,[p] 15"Count[q] the Levites by their families and clans. Count every male a month old or more."[r] 16So Moses counted them, as he was commanded by the word of the Lord.

17These were the names of the sons of Levi:[s]

Gershon,[t] Kohath[u] and Merari.[v]
18These were the names of the Gershonite clans:

Libni and Shimei.[w]
19The Kohathite clans:

[cross references column: 3:1 tS Ex 6:27; uS Ex 19:11; 3:2 vNu 1:20; wS Ex 6:23; 3:3 xS Ex 28:41; S 29:30; 3:4 yS Lev 10:2; zS Lev 10:1; aLev 10:6,12; Nu 4:28; b1Ch 24:1; 3:6 cDt 10:8; 31:9; 1Ch 15:2; dNu 8:6-22; 18:1-7; 2Ch 29:11; 3:7 eNu 1:53; 8:19 fS Lev 8:35; 3:9 gver 12,45; Nu 8:19; 18:6; 3:10 hS Ex 30:7; iS Ex 29:9; jNu 1:51; 3:12 kNe 13:29; Mal 2:4 lver 41; Nu 8:16,18 mS ver 9; Ex 13:2; Nu 8:14; 16:9 3:13 nS Ex 13:12 oLev 11:44 3:14 pS Ex 19:1 3:15 qver 39; S Nu 1:19 rver 22; Nu 18:16; 26:62 3:17 sS Ge 29:34; S 46:11; Nu 1:47; 1Ch 15:4; 23:6; 2Ch 29:12 tJos 21:6 uJos 21:4 vS Ex 6:16 3:18 wEx 6:17]

b9 Most manuscripts of the Masoretic Text; some manuscripts of the Masoretic Text, Samaritan Pentateuch and Septuagint (see also Num. 8:16) to me

---

2:34 *did everything the Lord commanded Moses.* As in 1:54, these words of absolute compliance contrast with Israel's later folly. *under their standards . . . each with his clan and family.* A major accomplishment for a people so numerous, so recently enslaved and more recently a mob in disarray. It may have been the orderliness of this encampment that led Balaam to say: "How beautiful are your tents, O Jacob, your dwelling places, O Israel!" (24:5).
3:1 *Aaron and Moses.* At first glance, the names seem out of order, but the emphasis is correct: It is the family of Aaron that is about to be described (see v. 2).
3:3 *anointed priests.* Ex 28:41 records God's command to Moses to anoint his brother Aaron and his sons as priests of the Lord (see Ex 30:30; Lev 8:30). By this solemn act they were consecrated in a special way to the Lord. Kings (1Sa 16:13) were also anointed with oil for special service to God. Physical objects could be anointed as well (see Ge 28:18; Ex 29:36). The Hebrew term for "anointed" (*mashiah*) later became the specific term for the Messiah (Christ); see NIV text note on Mt 1:17. *ordained.* The Hebrew for this word means lit. "fill the hand of" (see Ex 32:29). By this act there was an investing of authority, a consecration and a setting apart.
3:4 *Nadab and Abihu.* See Lev 10:1-3 and notes. *unauthorized fire.* Or "strange fire." This seems to be a deliberately obscure expression, as though the narrator finds the very concept distasteful. They were using fire that the Lord had not commanded (see Lev 10:1). Proximity to God's holiness requires righteousness and obedience from his priests. For all time, the deaths of Aaron's newly consecrated sons serve to warn God's ministers of the awesome seriousness of their tasks (cf. 1Sa 2:12-17,22-25,27-36; 3:11-14; 4:1-11).

For similar divine judgments at the beginning of new stages in salvation history see Jos 7; 2Sa 6:7; Ac 5:1-11.
3:5-10 These commands are not followed by a report of obedience as were the commands in chs. 1-2, but further details are given in ch. 8. Clear distinctions are made here between the priestly house (the sons of Aaron) and the Levites. The latter were to be aides to the priests, and they served not only Aaron but the whole nation in the process (see vv. 7-8).
3:9 *to him.* See NIV text note. It appears that the issue here is service to Aaron (and through him to the Lord); in 8:16 service is to the Lord.
3:10 *anyone else.* Lit. "stranger"—anyone lacking authorization. Service at the tabernacle may be performed only at the express appointment of the Lord. The words of v. 10 follow the paragraph telling of the death of Aaron's sons. They were authorized persons, but used unauthorized means. If the sons of Aaron were put to death at the commencement of their duties, how dare an unauthorized person even think to trespass? See v. 38; 18:7.
3:12-13 See note on Ex 13:2. *mine.* Repeated for emphasis.
3:12 *in place of.* An example of the practice of substitution (see Ge 22:13 and note; Mt 20:28).
3:15 *a month old or more.* The counting of the Levites corresponds to that of the other tribes in chs. 1-2, except that all males from the age of one month, rather than from 20 years, were to be counted. The Levites were not being mustered for war, but for special service in the sacred precincts of the Lord.
3:16 *as he was commanded.* The obedience of Moses to the Lord's command is explicit and total.

Amram, Izhar, Hebron and Uzziel.[x]

²⁰The Merarite clans:[y]

Mahli and Mushi.[z]

These were the Levite clans, according to their families.

²¹To Gershon[a] belonged the clans of the Libnites and Shimeites;[b] these were the Gershonite clans. ²²The number of all the males a month old or more who were counted was 7,500. ²³The Gershonite clans were to camp on the west, behind the tabernacle.[c] ²⁴The leader of the families of the Gershonites was Eliasaph son of Lael. ²⁵At the Tent of Meeting the Gershonites were responsible for the care of the tabernacle[d] and tent, its coverings,[e] the curtain at the entrance[f] to the Tent of Meeting,[g] ²⁶the curtains of the courtyard[h], the curtain at the entrance to the courtyard surrounding the tabernacle and altar,[i] and the ropes[j]—and everything[k] related to their use.

²⁷To Kohath[l] belonged the clans of the Amramites, Izharites, Hebronites and Uzzielites;[m] these were the Kohathite[n] clans. ²⁸The number of all the males a month old or more[o] was 8,600.[c] The Kohathites were responsible[p] for the care of the sanctuary.[q] ²⁹The Kohathite clans were to camp on the south side[r] of the tabernacle. ³⁰The leader of the families of the Kohathite clans was Elizaphan[s] son of Uzziel. ³¹They were responsible for the care of the ark,[t] the table,[u] the lampstand,[v] the altars,[w] the articles[x] of the sanctuary used in ministering, the curtain,[y] and everything related to their use.[z] ³²The chief leader of the Levites was Eleazar[a] son of

Aaron, the priest. He was appointed over those who were responsible[b] for the care of the sanctuary.[c]

³³To Merari belonged the clans of the Mahlites and the Mushites;[d] these were the Merarite clans.[e] ³⁴The number of all the males a month old or more[f] who were counted was 6,200. ³⁵The leader of the families of the Merarite clans was Zuriel son of Abihail; they were to camp on the north side of the tabernacle.[g] ³⁶The Merarites were appointed[h] to take care of the frames of the tabernacle,[i] its crossbars,[j] posts,[k] bases, all its equipment, and everything related to their use,[l] ³⁷as well as the posts of the surrounding courtyard[m] with their bases, tent pegs[n] and ropes.

³⁸Moses and Aaron and his sons were to camp to the east[o] of the tabernacle, toward the sunrise, in front of the Tent of Meeting.[p] They were responsible for the care of the sanctuary[q] on behalf of the Israelites. Anyone else who approached the sanctuary was to be put to death.[r]

³⁹The total number of Levites counted[s] at the LORD's command by Moses and Aaron according to their clans, including every male a month old or more, was 22,000.[t]

⁴⁰The LORD said to Moses, "Count all the firstborn Israelite males who are a month old or more[u] and make a list of their names.[v] ⁴¹Take the Levites for me in place of all the firstborn of the Israelites,[w] and the livestock of the Levites in place of

---

Cross-references (center column):

3:19 xS Ex 6:18
3:20 yS Ge 46:11; zS Ex 6:19
3:21 aS Ge 46:11; bEx 6:17
3:23 cS Nu 2:18
3:25 dEx 25:9; Nu 7:1 eEx 26:14 fEx 26:36; Nu 4:25 gEx 40:2
3:26 hEx 27:9 iver 31 jEx 35:18 kNu 4:26
3:27 lS Ge 46:11; S Ex 6:18
mEx 6:18; 1Ch 26:23 nNu 4:15,37
3:28 over 15 pNu 4:4,15 qS Ex 25:8; 30:13; 2Ch 30:19; Ps 15:1; 20:2; Eze 44:27
3:29 rS Nu 1:53
3:30 sS Ex 6:22
3:31 tS Ex 25:10-22; Dt 10:1-8; 2Ch 5:2; Jer 3:16 uS Ex 25:23 vS Ex 25:31; 1Ch 28:15; Jer 52:19 wver 26 xNu 1:50 yS Ex 26:33; Nu 4:5 zNu 4:15; 18:3
3:32 aS Ex 6:23

bver 28
cNu 4:19; 18:3 eS Ge 46:11
3:33 dS Ex 6:19 eS Ge 46:11
3:34 fver 15
3:35 gS Nu 2:25
3:36 hNu 4:32 iEx 26:15-25; 35:20-29 jEx 26:26-29 kEx 36:36 lNu 18:3
3:37 mEx 27:10-17 nEx 27:19
3:38 oNu 2:3 pS Nu 1:53; 1Ch 9:27; 23:32 qver 7; Nu 18:5 rver 10; Nu 1:51
3:39 sS ver 15 tNu 26:62
3:40 uver 15 vNu 1:2

3:41 wver 12

c28 Hebrew; some Septuagint manuscripts 8,300

3:21–38 The words of 1:53, "their tents around the tabernacle of the Testimony," are detailed by the four paragraphs in this section: (1) Gershon to the west (vv. 21–26); (2) Kohath to the south (vv. 27–32); (3) Merari to the north (vv. 33–37); (4) Moses and Aaron and sons to the east (v. 38). The other tribes began with the most favored: (1) Judah on the east (2:3); (2) Reuben on the south (2:10); (3) Ephraim on the west (2:18); (4) Dan on the north (2:25). The Levitical clans lead up to the most favored. The leaders of the Levitical houses correspond to the leaders of the other tribes (see note on 1:5–16). As do the names of the other tribal leaders, these names include a form of God's name.
3:24 *Eliasaph.* Means "(My) God has added." *Lael.* Means "belonging to God."
3:25–26 There were three curtains or covering screens for the tabernacle: (1) at the gate of the courtyard (v. 26; 4:26); (2) at the entrance to the Tent (vv. 25,31; 4:25); (3) between the Most Holy Place and the Holy Place (4:5).
3:27 *Amramites.* Aaron was an Amramite (see Ex 6:20); thus he and Moses were from the family of Kohath. To the Kohathites was given the care of the most holy things (see

4:4–18).
3:28 *8,600.* The total number of Levites given in v. 39 is 22,000—300 less than the totals of 7,500 Gershonites (v. 22), 8,600 Kohathites (here) and 6,200 Merarites (v. 34). Many believe that a copyist may have made a mistake here, and that the correct number is 8,300 (see NIV text note).
3:30 *Elizaphan.* Means "(My) God has protected." *Uzziel.* Means "My strength is God."
3:35 *Zuriel.* Means "My Rock is God." *Abihail.* Means "My (divine) Father is power."
3:38 *toward the sunrise.* The most honored location, but Moses and Aaron were placed there for a representative ministry (on behalf of the Israelites). *Anyone else . . . was to be put to death.* Service in the tabernacle was an act of mercy, a means for the people to come before God. Yet it was marked by strict discipline—it had to be done in God's way. The sovereignty of God was evident in his limitations on the means to approach him (see v. 10; 1:51; 18:7).
3:41 *I am the LORD.* What is being commanded conforms to God's character as Yahweh ("the LORD"; see note on Ex 3:14).

all the firstborn of the livestock of the Israelites. I am the LORD." [x]

[42]So Moses counted all the firstborn of
the Israelites, as the LORD commanded
him. [43]The total number of firstborn males
a month old or more,[y] listed by name, was
22,273.[z]

[44]The LORD also said to Moses, [45]"Take
the Levites in place of all the firstborn of
Israel, and the livestock of the Levites in
place of their livestock. The Levites are to
be mine.[a] I am the LORD.[b] [46]To redeem[c]
the 273 firstborn Israelites who exceed the
number of the Levites, [47]collect five
shekels[d][d] for each one, according to the
sanctuary shekel,[e] which weighs twenty
gerahs.[f] [48]Give the money for the redemption[g] of the additional Israelites to
Aaron and his sons."[h]

[49]So Moses collected the redemption
money[i] from those who exceeded the
number redeemed by the Levites. [50]From
the firstborn of the Israelites[j] he collected
silver weighing 1,365 shekels,[e][k] according to the sanctuary shekel. [51]Moses gave
the redemption money to Aaron and his
sons, as he was commanded by the word
of the LORD.

The Kohathites

4 The LORD said to Moses and Aaron:
[2]"Take a census[l] of the Kohathite
branch of the Levites by their clans and
families. [3]Count[m] all the men from thirty
to fifty years of age[n] who come to serve in
the work in the Tent of Meeting.

[4]"This is the work[o] of the Kohathites[p]
in the Tent of Meeting: the care of the
most holy things.[q] [5]When the camp is to
move,[r] Aaron and his sons are to go in
and take down the shielding curtain[s] and
cover the ark of the Testimony with it.[t]
[6]Then they are to cover this with hides of
sea cows,[t][u] spread a cloth of solid blue
over that and put the poles[v] in place.

[7]"Over the table of the Presence[w] they

are to spread a blue cloth and put on it the
plates, dishes and bowls, and the jars for
drink offerings;[x] the bread that is continually there[y] is to remain on it. [8]Over these
they are to spread a scarlet cloth, cover
that with hides of sea cows and put its
poles[z] in place.

[9]"They are to take a blue cloth and
cover the lampstand that is for light, together with its lamps, its wick trimmers
and trays,[a] and all its jars for the oil used
to supply it. [10]Then they are to wrap it and
all its accessories in a covering of hides of
sea cows and put it on a carrying frame.[b]

[11]"Over the gold altar[c] they are to
spread a blue cloth and cover that with
hides of sea cows and put its poles[d] in
place.

[12]"They are to take all the articles[e] used
for ministering in the sanctuary, wrap
them in a blue cloth, cover that with hides
of sea cows and put them on a carrying
frame.[f]

[13]"They are to remove the ashes[g] from
the bronze altar[h] and spread a purple cloth
over it. [14]Then they are to place on it all
the utensils[i] used for ministering at the
altar, including the firepans,[j] meat forks,[k]
shovels[l] and sprinkling bowls.[m] Over it
they are to spread a covering of hides of
sea cows and put its poles[n] in place.

[15]"After Aaron and his sons have finished covering the holy furnishings and all
the holy articles, and when the camp is
ready to move,[o] the Kohathites[p] are to
come to do the carrying.[q] But they must
not touch the holy things[r] or they will
die.[s][t] The Kohathites are to carry those
things that are in the Tent of Meeting.

[16]"Eleazar[u] son of Aaron, the priest, is
to have charge of the oil for the light,[v] the
fragrant incense,[w] the regular grain offer-

3:41 [x]Lev 11:44
3:43 [y]ver 15 [z]ver 39
3:45 [a]S ver 9 [b]Lev 11:44
3:46 [c]Ex 13:13; Nu 18:15
3:47 [d]S Lev 27:6 [e]S Ex 30:13 [f]S Lev 27:25
3:48 [g]ver 51 [h]ver 50
3:49 [i]ver 48
3:50 [j]ver 41,45 [k]S ver 46-48
4:2 [l]S Ex 30:12
4:3 [m]S Nu 1:47 [n]ver 23; Nu 8:25; 1Ch 23:3,24,27; Ezr 3:8
4:4 [o]S Nu 3:28 [p]Nu 7:9 [q]ver 19
4:5 [r]Nu 1:51 [s]S Ex 26:31,33 [t]1Ch 23:26
4:6 [u]S Ex 25:5 [v]S Ex 25:13-15; 1Ki 8:7; 2Ch 5:8
4:7 [w]S Lev 24:6

4:8 [z]Ex 26:26-28
4:9 [a]S Ex 25:38
4:10 [b]ver 12
4:11 [c]S Ex 30:1 [d]Ex 30:4
4:12 [e]Nu 3:31 [f]ver 10
4:13 [g]S Lev 1:16 [h]Ex 27:1-8; Nu 3:31
4:14 [i]S Ex 31:9 [j]S Ex 27:3 [k]1Ch 28:17; 2Ch 4:16 [l]2Ch 4:11 [m]Ex 27:3; Nu 7:84; 2Ch 4:8; Jer 52:18 [n]Ex 27:6
4:15 [o]ver 5 [p]S Nu 3:27 [q]Nu 7:9 [r]ver 4 [s]S Ex 28:43 [t]Nu 1:51; 2Sa 6:6,7
4:16 [u]Lev 10:6; Nu 3:32 [v]S Ex 25:6 [w]S Ex 25:6

[x]Ex 39:36; Jer 52:19
[y]S Ex 25:30

---

[d]47 That is, about 2 ounces (about 55 grams)
[e]50 That is, about 35 pounds (about 15.5 kilograms)
[f]6 That is, dugongs; also in verses 8, 10, 11, 12, 14 and 25

3:43 *22,273.* Seems too small for a population in excess of
2,000,000, and is used as an argument for attempting to give
a means of reducing the total number of the people (calculations based on this number suggest a total population of
about 250,000). Some suggest that the 22,273 firstborn of
Israel were those born since the exodus, all the firstborn at
the time of the exodus having already been set apart for the
Lord at the first Passover (see Ex 12:22–23). This, however,
creates a new problem since nowhere is that allegedly distinct group assigned any special service of the Lord. See
Introduction: Special Problem.
4:3 *thirty to fifty years.* Ch. 3 listed all males over the age of
one month (3:15). Ch. 4 lists those Levites who were of age
to serve in the tabernacle. Of the 22,000 Levite males (3:39),
8,580 were of age for service (v. 48). From 8:24 we learn

that the beginning age for service was 25; perhaps the first
5 years were something of an apprenticeship.

4:4 *most holy things.* Despite the fact that the primary care
of these holy things was given to the Kohathites, they were
forbidden to touch them (v. 15) or even to look at them (v.
20), on pain of death. All the work of the Kohathites was to
be strictly supervised by Aaron and his sons, and only the
priests were able to touch and look at the unveiled holy
things.

4:6 *sea cows.* See NIV text note.

4:16 *Eleazar ... the priest, is to have charge.* The high
priest could draw near to the most holy things on behalf of
the people. If he had not been able to do so, there could have
been no worship by the community.

ing[x] and the anointing oil. He is to be in charge of the entire tabernacle and everything in it, including its holy furnishings and articles."

[17]The LORD said to Moses and Aaron, [18]"See that the Kohathite tribal clans are not cut off from the Levites. [19]So that they may live and not die when they come near the most holy things,[y] do this for them: Aaron and his sons[z] are to go into the sanctuary and assign to each man his work and what he is to carry.[a] [20]But the Kohathites must not go in to look[b] at the holy things, even for a moment, or they will die."

The Gershonites

[21]The LORD said to Moses, [22]"Take a census also of the Gershonites by their families and clans. [23]Count all the men from thirty to fifty years of age[c] who come to serve in the work at the Tent of Meeting.

[24]"This is the service of the Gershonite clans as they work and carry burdens: [25]They are to carry the curtains of the tabernacle,[d] the Tent of Meeting,[e] its covering[f] and the outer covering of hides of sea cows, the curtains for the entrance to the Tent of Meeting, [26]the curtains of the courtyard surrounding the tabernacle and altar,[g] the curtain for the entrance,[h] the ropes and all the equipment[i] used in its service. The Gershonites are to do all that needs to be done with these things. [27]All their service, whether carrying or doing other work, is to be done under the direction of Aaron and his sons.[j] You shall assign to them as their responsibility[k] all they are to carry. [28]This is the service of the Gershonite clans[l] at the Tent of Meeting. Their duties are to be under the direction of Ithamar[m] son of Aaron, the priest.

The Merarites

[29]"Count[n] the Merarites by their clans and families.[o] [30]Count all the men from thirty to fifty years of age who come to serve in the work at the Tent of Meeting. [31]This is their duty as they perform service at the Tent of Meeting: to carry the frames of the tabernacle, its crossbars, posts and bases,[p] [32]as well as the posts of the sur-

4:16
x S Ex 29:41;
Lev 6:14-23
4:19 y S ver 15
z ver 27
a S Nu 3:32
4:20 b S Ex 19:21
4:23 c S ver 3
4:25
d Ex 27:10-18
e Nu 3:25
f Ex 26:14
4:26 g Ex 27:9
h Ex 27:16
i Nu 3:26
4:27 j ver 19
k Nu 3:25,26
4:28 l Nu 7:7
m S Ex 6:23
4:29 n S Ex 30:12
o S Ge 46:11
4:31 p Nu 3:36

4:32 q Nu 3:37
4:33 r S Ex 38:21
4:34 s ver 2
4:35 t ver 3
4:37 u S Nu 3:27
4:38 v S Ge 46:11
4:43 w ver 3
4:45 x ver 29
4:46 y Nu 1:19
4:47 z ver 3
4:48 a Nu 3:39
4:49 b S Nu 1:47

rounding courtyard with their bases, tent pegs, ropes,[q] all their equipment and everything related to their use. Assign to each man the specific things he is to carry. [33]This is the service of the Merarite clans as they work at the Tent of Meeting under the direction of Ithamar[r] son of Aaron, the priest."

The Numbering of the Levite Clans

[34]Moses, Aaron and the leaders of the community counted the Kohathites[s] by their clans and families. [35]All the men from thirty to fifty years of age[t] who came to serve in the work in the Tent of Meeting, [36]counted by clans, were 2,750. [37]This was the total of all those in the Kohathite clans[u] who served in the Tent of Meeting. Moses and Aaron counted them according to the LORD's command through Moses.

[38]The Gershonites[v] were counted by their clans and families. [39]All the men from thirty to fifty years of age who came to serve in the work at the Tent of Meeting, [40]counted by their clans and families, were 2,630. [41]This was the total of those in the Gershonite clans who served at the Tent of Meeting. Moses and Aaron counted them according to the LORD's command.

[42]The Merarites were counted by their clans and families. [43]All the men from thirty to fifty years of age[w] who came to serve in the work at the Tent of Meeting, [44]counted by their clans, were 3,200. [45]This was the total of those in the Merarite clans.[x] Moses and Aaron counted them according to the LORD's command through Moses.

[46]So Moses, Aaron and the leaders of Israel counted[y] all the Levites by their clans and families. [47]All the men from thirty to fifty years of age[z] who came to do the work of serving and carrying the Tent of Meeting [48]numbered 8,580.[a] [49]At the LORD's command through Moses, each was assigned his work and told what to carry.

Thus they were counted,[b] as the LORD commanded Moses.

The Purity of the Camp

5 The LORD said to Moses, [2]"Command the Israelites to send away from the

---

5:2 *infectious skin disease.* See NIV text note; see also note on Lev 13:2; cf. Lk 5:12–16; 17:11–19. *discharge of any kind.* See note on Lev 15:2. Such discharges were primarily from the sexual organs and were chronic in nature (cf. Lk 8:43–48). The people who suffered from them became living object lessons to the whole camp on the necessity for all people to be "clean" in their approach to

God. *unclean.* Ceremonially unfit to be with the community, and a possible contaminant to the tabernacle and the pure worship of the Lord. Aspects of uncleanness were not left in the abstract or theoretical; the focus was on tangible issues, such as clearly evident skin diseases and discharges. *dead body.* The ultimate tangible sign of uncleanness. Processes of decay and disease in dead flesh were evident to all. Physical

camp anyone who has an infectious skin disease[g][c] or a discharge[d] of any kind, or who is ceremonially unclean[e] because of a dead body.[f] [3]Send away male and female alike; send them outside the camp so they will not defile their camp, where I dwell among them.[g]" [4]The Israelites did this; they sent them outside the camp. They did just as the LORD had instructed Moses.

Restitution for Wrongs

[5]The LORD said to Moses, [6]"Say to the Israelites: 'When a man or woman wrongs another in any way[h] and so is unfaithful[h] to the LORD, that person is guilty[i] [7]and must confess[j] the sin he has committed. He must make full restitution[k] for his wrong, add one fifth to it and give it all to the person he has wronged. [8]But if that person has no close relative to whom restitution can be made for the wrong, the restitution belongs to the LORD and must be given to the priest, along with the ram[l] with which atonement is made for him.[m] [9]All the sacred contributions the Israelites bring to a priest will belong to him.[n] [10]Each man's sacred gifts are his own, but what he gives to the priest will belong to the priest.[o]' "

The Test for an Unfaithful Wife

[11]Then the LORD said to Moses, [12]"Speak to the Israelites and say to them:

'If a man's wife goes astray[p] and is unfaithful to him [13]by sleeping with another man,[q] and this is hidden from her husband and her impurity is undetected (since there is no witness against her and she has not been caught in the act), [14]and if feelings of jealousy[r] come over her husband and he suspects his wife and she is impure—or if he is jealous and suspects her even though she is not impure— [15]then he is to take his wife to the priest. He must also take an offering of a tenth of an ephah[i][s] of barley flour[t] on her behalf. He must not pour oil on it or put incense on it, because it is a grain offering for jealousy,[u] a reminder[v] offering to draw attention to guilt.

[16]"'The priest shall bring her and have her stand before the LORD. [17]Then he shall take some holy water in a clay jar and put some dust from the tabernacle floor into the water. [18]After the priest has had the woman stand before the LORD, he shall loosen her hair[w] and place in her hands the reminder offering, the grain offering for jealousy,[x] while he himself holds the bitter water that brings a curse.[y] [19]Then the priest shall put the woman under oath and

Cross references (center column)

5:2 [c]S Lev 13:2
[d]S Lev 15:2;
Mt 9:20
[e]Lev 13:3;
Nu 9:6-10
[f]S Lev 21:11
5:3 [g]S Ex 29:45;
Lev 26:12;
2Co 6:16
5:6 [h]S Lev 6:2
[i]Lev 5:14-6:7
5:7 [j]S Lev 5:5;
S Lk 19:8
[k]S Lev 5:16
5:8 [l]S Lev 5:15
[m]Lev 6:6,7
5:9 [n]Lev 6:17
5:10
[o]Lev 7:29-34

5:12 [p]ver 19-21;
S Ex 20:14
5:13 [q]S Ex 20:14
5:14 [r]ver 30;
Pr 6:34; 27:4;
SS 8:6
5:15 [s]S Ex 16:36
[t]S Lev 6:20 [u]ver 18,25
[v]Eze 21:23;
29:16
5:18
[w]S Lev 10:6;
1Co 11:6 [x]ver 15
[y]ver 19

[g]2 Traditionally *leprosy*; the Hebrew word was used for various diseases affecting the skin—not necessarily leprosy.   [h]6 Or *woman commits any wrong common to mankind*   [i]15 That is, probably about 2 quarts (about 2 liters)

---

contact with a corpse was a sure mark of uncleanness; normal contacts with the living would have to be curtailed until proper cleansing had been made. See note on 6:6 for application to the Nazirite vow. Jesus reached out to the dead as well as to the living; his raising of Jairus's daughter began with holding her limp hand (Lk 8:54).
5:3 *male and female alike.* The concept of clean versus unclean cuts across sexual lines. The essential issue was the presence of the Lord in the camp; there can be no uncleanness where he dwells. In the new Jerusalem (Rev 21:2–3) the dwelling of God with man will be uncompromised by any form of uncleanness (Rev 21:27).
5:5–10 The connection of these verses (on personal wrongs) with the first paragraph (on ritual uncleanness) may be that of moving from the outward, visible defects to the inward, more secret faults that mar the purity of the community. Those with evident marks of uncleanness are to be expelled for the duration of their malady. But more insidious are those people who have overtly sinned against others in the community, and who think that they may continue to function as though there was no wrong.
5:11–31 Again, the connection with the preceding four paragraphs seems to be a movement from the more open, obvious sins to the more personal, hidden ones. Issues of purity begin with physical marks (vv. 1–4), are expanded to interpersonal relationships (vv. 5–10), and then intrude into the most intimate of relationships—the purity of a man and woman in their marriage bed. A test for marital fidelity is far more difficult to prove than a test for a skin disorder; hence, the larger part of the chapter is given to this most sensitive of issues.

5:14 *feelings of jealousy.* These may have been provoked on the basis of good cause, and the issue must be faced. The concern is not just for the bruised feelings of the husband but is ultimately based on the reality of God's dwelling among his people (v. 3). Yet the chapter is designed to prevent unfounded charges of unfaithfulness. This text was not to be used by a capricious, petty or malevolent husband to badger an innocent woman. *impure.* The subject of the chapter is consistent; the purity of the camp where God dwells (v. 3) is the burden of the passage.
5:15–28 The actions presented here seem severe and harsh. But the consequences would have been worse for a woman charged with adultery by an angry husband if there was no provision for her guilt or innocence to be demonstrated. That she was taken to the priest (v. 15) is finally an act of mercy. The gravity of the ritual for a suspected unfaithful wife shows that the law regards marital infidelity most seriously. This was not just a concern of a jealous husband. The entire community was affected by this breach of faith; hence, the judgment was in the context of the community.
5:18 *loosen her hair.* A sign of openness; for the guilty, an expectation of judgment and mourning. *bitter water that brings a curse.* Or "curse-bringing water of bitterness." It is not just that the water was bitter tasting but that the water had the potential of bringing with it a bitter curse. The Lord's role in the proceedings (vv. 16,21,25) is emphasized repeatedly to show that this potion was neither simply a tool of magic nor merely a psychological device to determine stress. The verdict with respect to the woman was precipitated by her physiological and psychological responses to the bitter water, but the judgment was from the Lord.

say to her, "If no other man has slept with you and you have not gone astray[z] and become impure while married to your husband, may this bitter water that brings a curse[a] not harm you. [20]But if you have gone astray[b] while married to your husband and you have defiled yourself by sleeping with a man other than your husband"— [21]here the priest is to put the woman under this curse of the oath[c]—"may the LORD cause your people to curse and denounce you when he causes your thigh to waste away and your abdomen to swell.[j] [22]May this water[d] that brings a curse[e] enter your body so that your abdomen swells and your thigh wastes away.[k]"

" 'Then the woman is to say, "Amen. So be it.[f]"

[23]" 'The priest is to write these curses on a scroll[g] and then wash them off into the bitter water. [24]He shall have the woman drink the bitter water that brings a curse, and this water will enter her and cause bitter suffering. [25]The priest is to take from her hands the grain offering for jealousy, wave it before the LORD[h] and bring it to the altar. [26]The priest is then to take a handful of the grain offering as a memorial offering[i] and burn it on the altar; after that, he is to have the woman drink the water. [27]If she has defiled herself and been unfaithful to her husband, then when she is made to drink the water that brings a curse, it will go into her and cause bitter suffering; her abdomen will swell and her thigh waste away,[l] and she will become accursed[j] among her people. [28]If, however, the woman has not defiled herself and is free from impurity, she will be cleared of guilt and will be able to have children.

[29]" 'This, then, is the law of jealousy

when a woman goes astray[k] and defiles herself while married to her husband, [30]or when feelings of jealousy[l] come over a man because he suspects his wife. The priest is to have her stand before the LORD and is to apply this entire law to her. [31]The husband will be innocent of any wrongdoing, but the woman will bear the consequences[m] of her sin.' "

The Nazirite

6 The LORD said to Moses, [2]"Speak to the Israelites and say to them: 'If a man or woman wants to make a special vow[n], a vow of separation[o] to the LORD as a Nazirite,[p] [3]he must abstain from wine[q] and other fermented drink and must not drink vinegar[r] made from wine or from other fermented drink. He must not drink grape juice or eat grapes[s] or raisins. [4]As long as he is a Nazirite, he must not eat anything that comes from the grapevine, not even the seeds or skins.

[5]" 'During the entire period of his vow of separation no razor[t] may be used on his head.[u] He must be holy until the period of his separation to the LORD is over; he must let the hair of his head grow long. [6]Throughout the period of his separation to the LORD he must not go near a dead body.[v] [7]Even if his own father or mother or brother or sister dies, he must not make himself ceremonially unclean[w] on account of them, because the symbol of his separation to God is on his head. [8]Throughout the period of his separation he is consecrated to the LORD.

[9]" 'If someone dies suddenly in his presence, thus defiling the hair he has dedicat-

Cross references (center column)

5:19 zver 12,29
aver 18
5:20 bver 12
5:21 cJos 6:26;
1Sa 14:24;
Ne 10:29
5:22 dPs 109:18
ever 18 /Dt 27:15
5:23 gJer 45:1
5:25 hLev 8:27
5:26 iS Lev 2:2
5:27 /Isa 43:28;
65:15; Jer 26:6;
29:18; 42:18;
44:12,22;
Zec 8:13

5:29 kS ver 19
5:30 lS ver 14
5:31 mS Lev 5:1
6:2 nver 5;
S Ge 28:20;
Ac 21:23 over 6
pJdg 13:5; 16:17
S Lk 1:15
6:3 qS Lev 10:9;
rRu 2:14;
Ps 69:21;
Pr 10:26
sS Lev 25:5
6:5 tPs 52:2;
57:4; 59:7;
Isa 7:20; Eze 5:1
uS 1Sa 1:11
6:6
vS Lev 21:1-3;
Nu 19:11-22
6:7 wNu 9:6

j21 Or causes you to have a miscarrying womb and barrenness k22 Or body and cause you to be barren and have a miscarrying womb l27 Or suffering; she will have barrenness and a miscarrying womb

---

5:21 *your thigh to waste away and your abdomen to swell.* See NIV text note. The figurative language here (and in vv. 22,27) speaks of the loss of the capacity for childbearing (and, if pregnant, the miscarriage of the child). This is demonstrated by the determination of the fate of a woman wrongly charged (v. 28). For a woman in the ancient Near East to be denied the ability to bear children was a personal loss of inestimable proportions. Since it was in the bearing of children that a woman's worth was realized in the ancient world, this was a grievous punishment indeed.

6:2 *man or woman.* See ch. 30 for the differences between the vows of men and women. *vow ... Nazirite.* Involved separation or consecration for a specific period of special devotion to God—on occasion even for life. Attention is usually given to the prohibitions for the Nazirite; more important to the Lord is the positive separation (see v. 8). This was not just a vow of personal self-discipline; it was an act of total devotion to the Lord.

6:4 *anything that comes from the grapevine.* Not only was

the fermented beverage forbidden, but even the seed and skin of the grape. During the period of a Nazirite's vow, three areas of his (or her) life were governed: (1) diet, (2) appearance and (3) associations. Every Israelite was regulated in these areas, but for the Nazirite each regulation was heightened. An analogy may be the practice of some Christians to forgo certain (good) foods during the period of Lent to enhance spiritual devotion to Christ in the special period of remembering his sufferings.

6:5 *no razor.* See Jdg 13:5. The unusually long hair of a Nazirite would become a physical mark of his (or her) vow of special devotion to the Lord. Cf. Lev 21:5.

6:6 *dead body.* See note on 5:2. For the Nazirite, the prohibition of contact with dead bodies extended even to the deceased within his (or her) own family (v. 7; contrast Lev 21:1-3).

6:9–12 The provisions of the Nazirite vow concerned areas where he (or she) was able to make conscious decisions. This section deals with the unexpected and the un-

ed,[x] he must shave his head on the day of
his cleansing[y]—the seventh day. 10Then
on the eighth day[z] he must bring two
doves or two young pigeons[a] to the priest
at the entrance to the Tent of Meeting.[b]
11The priest is to offer one as a sin offering[c] and the other as a burnt offering[d] to
make atonement[e] for him because he
sinned by being in the presence of the dead
body. That same day he is to consecrate his
head. 12He must dedicate himself to the
LORD for the period of his separation and
must bring a year-old male lamb[f] as a guilt
offering.[g] The previous days do not count,
because he became defiled during his separation.

13" 'Now this is the law for the Nazirite
when the period of his separation is over.[h]
He is to be brought to the entrance to the
Tent of Meeting.[i] 14There he is to present
his offerings to the LORD: a year-old male
lamb without defect[j] for a burnt offering,
a year-old ewe lamb without defect for a
sin offering,[k] a ram[l] without defect for a
fellowship offering,[m][m] 15together with
their grain offerings[n] and drink offerings,[o]
and a basket of bread made without
yeast—cakes made of fine flour mixed
with oil, and wafers spread with oil.[p]

16" 'The priest is to present them[q] before the LORD[r] and make the sin offering
and the burnt offering.[s] 17He is to present
the basket of unleavened bread and is to
sacrifice the ram as a fellowship offering[t]
to the LORD, together with its grain offering[u] and drink offering.[v]

18" 'Then at the entrance to the Tent of
Meeting, the Nazirite must shave off the
hair that he dedicated.[w] He is to take the
hair and put it in the fire that is under the
sacrifice of the fellowship offering.

19" 'After the Nazirite has shaved off the
hair of his dedication, the priest is to place
in his hands a boiled shoulder of the ram,
and a cake and a wafer from the basket,
both made without yeast.[x] 20The priest
shall then wave them before the LORD as a
wave offering;[y] they are holy[z] and belong
to the priest, together with the breast that
was waved and the thigh that was
presented.[a] After that, the Nazirite may
drink wine.[b]

21" 'This is the law of the Nazirite[c] who
vows his offering to the LORD in accordance with his separation, in addition to
whatever else he can afford. He must fulfill
the vow[d] he has made, according to the
law of the Nazirite.' "

The Priestly Blessing

22The LORD said to Moses, 23"Tell Aaron
and his sons, 'This is how you are to bless[e]
the Israelites. Say to them:

24" ' "The LORD bless you[f]
and keep you;[g]
25the LORD make his face shine upon
you[h]
and be gracious to you;[i]
26the LORD turn his face[j] toward you
and give you peace.[k]" '

27"So they will put my name[l] on the
Israelites, and I will bless them."

Offerings at the Dedication of the Tabernacle

7 When Moses finished setting up the
tabernacle,[m] he anointed[n] it and consecrated it and all its furnishings.[o] He also
anointed and consecrated the altar and all
its utensils.[p] 2Then the leaders of Israel,[q]
the heads of families who were the tribal
leaders in charge of those who were counted,[r] made offerings. 3They brought as
their gifts before the LORD six covered
carts[s] and twelve oxen—an ox from each
leader and a cart from every two. These
they presented before the tabernacle.

m *14* Traditionally *peace offering*; also in verses 17 and 18

6:9 [x]ver 18 [y]S Lev 14:9 **6:10** [z]S Lev 14:10 [a]S Lev 5:7 [b]Lev 14:11 **6:11** [c]S Ex 30:10 [d]S Ge 8:20 [e]S Ex 29:36 **6:12** [f]S Lev 12:6 [g]S Lev 5:15 **6:13** [h]Ac 21:26 [i]Lev 14:11 **6:14** [j]S Ex 12:5 [k]ver 11; Lev 4:3; 14:10 [l]S Lev 5:15 [m]Lev 3:1 **6:15** [n]Lev 2:1; S 6:14 [o]S Ge 35:14 [p]S Ex 29:2 **6:16** [q]Lev 1:3 [r]ver 10 [s]ver 11 **6:17** [t]Lev 3:1 [u]S Ex 29:41 [v]Lev 23:13 **6:18** [w]ver 9; Ac 21:24
6:19 [x]Lev 7:12 **6:20** [y]Lev 7:30 [z]S Lev 27:9 [a]S Lev 7:34 [b]Ecc 9:7 **6:21** [c]ver 13 [d]ver 2 **6:23** [e]Dt 21:5; 1Ch 23:13 **6:24** [f]S Ge 28:3; Dt 28:3-6; Ps 28:9; 128:5 [g]1Sa 2:9; Ps 17:8 **6:25** [h]Job 29:24; Ps 4:6; 31:16; 80:3; 119:135 [i]Ge 43:29; Ps 25:16; 86:16; 119:29 **6:26** [j]Ps 4:6; 44:3 [k]Ps 4:8; 29:11; 37:11,37; 127:2; Isa 14:7; Jer 33:6; Jn 14:27 **6:27** [l]Dt 28:10; 2Sa 7:23; 2Ch 7:14; Ne 9:10; Jer 25:29; Eze 36:23 **7:1** [m]Ex 40:17 [n]S Ex 30:26 [o]S Ex 40:9 [p]ver 84,88; Ex 40:10; 2Ch 7:9 **7:2** [q]Nu 1:5-16 [r]Nu 1:19 **7:3** [s]Ge 45:19; 1Sa 6:7-14; 1Ch 13:7

planned events of daily living.

6:13–20 The offerings of the Nazirite at the completion of the period of the vow were extensive, expensive and expressive of the spirit of total commitment to the Lord during this time of special devotion. In addition to these several offerings the Nazirite burned his (or her) hair (the sign of the vow).

6:21 *This is the law of the Nazirite.* Summary statements such as this not only end a section, but also solemnize its contents.

6:24–26 The Aaronic benediction. The threefold repetition of the divine name Yahweh ("the LORD") is for emphasis and gives force to the expression in v. 27: "So they will put my name on the Israelites." Each verse conveys two elements of benediction, and the verses are progressively longer (in the Hebrew text, the first verse has three words, the second has five and the third has seven).

6:25 *make his face shine upon you.* In acceptance and favor.

6:26 *peace.* The Hebrew for this word is *shalom,* here seen in its most expressive fullness—not the absence of war, but a positive state of rightness and well-being. Such peace comes only from the Lord.

7:1–89 See Ex 40, which describes the setting up of the tabernacle and ends with the report of the cloud covering and the presence of the Lord filling the tabernacle. With much repetition of language, this chapter (the longest in the Pentateuch) records the magnificent (and identical) gifts to the Lord for tabernacle service from the leaders of the 12 tribes. The fact that the record of these gifts follows the text of the Aaronic benediction (6:24–26) seems fitting: In response to God's promise to bless his people, they bring gifts to him in 12 sequential days of celebrative pageantry.

4The LORD said to Moses, 5"Accept
these from them, that they may be used in
the work at the Tent of Meeting. Give
them to the Levites as each man's work
requires."
6So Moses took the carts and oxen and
gave them to the Levites. 7He gave two
carts and four oxen to the Gershonites,[t] as
their work required, 8and he gave four
carts and eight oxen to the Merarites,[u] as
their work required. They were all under
the direction of Ithamar son of Aaron, the
priest. 9But Moses did not give any to the
Kohathites,[v] because they were to carry
on their shoulders[w] the holy things, for
which they were responsible.
10When the altar was anointed,[x] the
leaders brought their offerings for its dedication[y] and presented them before the altar. 11For the LORD had said to Moses,
"Each day one leader is to bring his offering for the dedication of the altar."

12The one who brought his offering on the
first day was Nahshon[z] son of Amminadab
of the tribe of Judah.
13His offering was one silver plate
weighing a hundred and thirty
shekels,[n] and one silver sprinkling
bowl[a] weighing seventy shekels,[o][b]
both according to the sanctuary
shekel,[c] each filled with fine flour
mixed with oil as a grain offering;[d]
14one gold dish[e] weighing ten
shekels,[p][f] filled with incense;[g] 15one
young bull,[h] one ram and one male
lamb a year old, for a burnt offering;[i]
16one male goat for a sin offering;[j]
17and two oxen, five rams, five male
goats and five male lambs a year old,
to be sacrificed as a fellowship offering.[q][k] This was the offering of Nahshon son of Amminadab.[l]

18On the second day Nethanel son of
Zuar,[m] the leader of Issachar, brought his
offering.
19The offering he brought was one silver plate weighing a hundred and
thirty shekels, and one silver sprinkling bowl weighing seventy shekels,
both according to the sanctuary
shekel, each filled with fine flour
mixed with oil as a grain offering;
20one gold dish[n] weighing ten
shekels, filled with incense; 21one
young bull, one ram and one male
lamb a year old, for a burnt offering;
22one male goat for a sin offering;
23and two oxen, five rams, five male
goats and five male lambs a year old,
to be sacrificed as a fellowship offering. This was the offering of Nethanel
son of Zuar.

24On the third day, Eliab son of Helon,[o]
the leader of the people of Zebulun,
brought his offering.
25His offering was one silver plate
weighing a hundred and thirty
shekels, and one silver sprinkling bowl
weighing seventy shekels, both according to the sanctuary shekel, each
filled with fine flour mixed with oil as
a grain offering; 26one gold dish
weighing ten shekels, filled with incense; 27one young bull, one ram and
one male lamb a year old, for a burnt
offering; 28one male goat for a sin offering; 29and two oxen, five rams, five
male goats and five male lambs a year
old, to be sacrificed as a fellowship offering. This was the offering of Eliab
son of Helon.

30On the fourth day Elizur son of Shedeur,[p] the leader of the people of Reuben,
brought his offering.
31His offering was one silver plate
weighing a hundred and thirty
shekels, and one silver sprinkling bowl
weighing seventy shekels, both according to the sanctuary shekel, each
filled with fine flour mixed with oil as
a grain offering; 32one gold dish
weighing ten shekels, filled with incense; 33one young bull, one ram and
one male lamb a year old, for a burnt
offering; 34one male goat for a sin offering; 35and two oxen, five rams, five
male goats and five male lambs a year
old, to be sacrificed as a fellowship offering. This was the offering of Elizur
son of Shedeur.

36On the fifth day Shelumiel son of Zuri-

7:7 [t]Nu 4:24-26, 28 **7:8** [u]Nu 4:31-33 **7:9** [v]Nu 4:4 [w]Nu 4:15 **7:10** [x]ver 1; S Ex 29:36 [y]2Ch 7:9 **7:12** [z]S Nu 1:7 **7:13** [a]S Ex 27:3 [b]ver 85 [c]S Ex 30:13; Lev 27:3-7 [d]Lev 2:1; Nu 6:15; 15:4 **7:14** [e]ver 20; 1Ki 7:50; 2Ki 25:14; 2Ch 4:22; 24:14 [f]ver 86 [g]S Ex 25:6 **7:15** [h]Ex 24:5; 29:3; Nu 28:11 [i]Lev 1:3 **7:16** [j]Lev 4:3 **7:17** [k]Lev 3:1 [l]Nu 1:7 **7:18** [m]S Nu 1:8 **7:20** [n]S ver 14 **7:24** [o]S Nu 1:9 **7:30** [p]S Nu 1:5

[n] *13* That is, about 3 1/4 pounds (about 1.5 kilograms); also elsewhere in this chapter [o] *13* That is, about 1 3/4 pounds (about 0.8 kilogram); also elsewhere in this chapter [p] *14* That is, about 4 ounces (about 110 grams); also elsewhere in this chapter [q] *17* Traditionally *peace offering*; also elsewhere in this chapter

7:12–78 The leaders of the 12 tribes have already been named in 1:5–15; 2:3–32. The order of the presentation of their offerings to the Lord is the same as the order of march: first, the triad of tribes camped east of the tabernacle (Judah, Issachar and Zebulun: 2:3–9; 7:12,18,24); second, the triad camped to the south (Reuben, Simeon and Gad: 2:10–16; 7:30,36,42); third, the triad to the west (Ephraim, Manasseh and Benjamin: 2:18–24; 7:48,54,60); finally, those to the north (Dan, Asher and Naphtali: 2:25–31; 7:66,72,78). See diagram of "Encampment of the Tribes of Israel," p. 192.

shaddai,^{q} the leader of the people of Simeon, brought his offering.

^{37}His offering was one silver plate weighing a hundred and thirty shekels, and one silver sprinkling bowl weighing seventy shekels, both according to the sanctuary shekel, each filled with fine flour mixed with oil as a grain offering; ^{38}one gold dish weighing ten shekels, filled with incense; ^{39}one young bull, one ram and one male lamb a year old, for a burnt offering; ^{40}one male goat for a sin offering; ^{41}and two oxen, five rams, five male goats and five male lambs a year old, to be sacrificed as a fellowship offering. This was the offering of Shelumiel son of Zurishaddai.

^{42}On the sixth day Eliasaph son of Deuel,^{r} the leader of the people of Gad, brought his offering.

^{43}His offering was one silver plate weighing a hundred and thirty shekels, and one silver sprinkling bowl weighing seventy shekels, both according to the sanctuary shekel, each filled with fine flour mixed with oil as a grain offering; ^{44}one gold dish weighing ten shekels, filled with incense; ^{45}one young bull, one ram and one male lamb a year old, for a burnt offering; ^{46}one male goat for a sin offering; ^{47}and two oxen, five rams, five male goats and five male lambs a year old, to be sacrificed as a fellowship offering. This was the offering of Eliasaph son of Deuel.

^{48}On the seventh day Elishama son of Ammihud,^{s} the leader of the people of Ephraim, brought his offering.

^{49}His offering was one silver plate weighing a hundred and thirty shekels, and one silver sprinkling bowl weighing seventy shekels, both according to the sanctuary shekel, each filled with fine flour mixed with oil as a grain offering; ^{50}one gold dish weighing ten shekels, filled with incense; ^{51}one young bull, one ram and one male lamb a year old, for a burnt offering; ^{52}one male goat for a sin offering; ^{53}and two oxen, five rams, five male goats and five male lambs a year old, to be sacrificed as a fellowship offering. This was the offering of Elishama son of Ammihud.^{t}

^{54}On the eighth day Gamaliel son of

7:36 ^{q}S Nu 1:6
7:42 ^{r}S Nu 1:14
7:48 ^{s}S Nu 1:10
7:53 ^{t}S Nu 1:10

7:54 ^{u}S Nu 1:10
7:60 ^{v}S Nu 1:11
7:66 ^{w}S Nu 1:12

Pedahzur,^{u} the leader of the people of Manasseh, brought his offering.

^{55}His offering was one silver plate weighing a hundred and thirty shekels, and one silver sprinkling bowl weighing seventy shekels, both according to the sanctuary shekel, each filled with fine flour mixed with oil as a grain offering; ^{56}one gold dish weighing ten shekels, filled with incense; ^{57}one young bull, one ram and one male lamb a year old, for a burnt offering; ^{58}one male goat for a sin offering; ^{59}and two oxen, five rams, five male goats and five male lambs a year old, to be sacrificed as a fellowship offering. This was the offering of Gamaliel son of Pedahzur.

^{60}On the ninth day Abidan son of Gideoni,^{v} the leader of the people of Benjamin, brought his offering.

^{61}His offering was one silver plate weighing a hundred and thirty shekels, and one silver sprinkling bowl weighing seventy shekels, both according to the sanctuary shekel, each filled with fine flour mixed with oil as a grain offering; ^{62}one gold dish weighing ten shekels, filled with incense; ^{63}one young bull, one ram and one male lamb a year old, for a burnt offering; ^{64}one male goat for a sin offering; ^{65}and two oxen, five rams, five male goats and five male lambs a year old, to be sacrificed as a fellowship offering. This was the offering of Abidan son of Gideoni.

^{66}On the tenth day Ahiezer son of Ammishaddai,^{w} the leader of the people of Dan, brought his offering.

^{67}His offering was one silver plate weighing a hundred and thirty shekels, and one silver sprinkling bowl weighing seventy shekels, both according to the sanctuary shekel, each filled with fine flour mixed with oil as a grain offering; ^{68}one gold dish weighing ten shekels, filled with incense; ^{69}one young bull, one ram and one male lamb a year old, for a burnt offering; ^{70}one male goat for a sin offering; ^{71}and two oxen, five rams, five male goats and five male lambs a year old, to be sacrificed as a fellowship offering. This was the offering of Ahiezer son of Ammishaddai.

^{72}On the eleventh day Pagiel son of

Ocran,[x] the leader of the people of Asher, brought his offering.

[73]His offering was one silver plate weighing a hundred and thirty shekels, and one silver sprinkling bowl weighing seventy shekels, both according to the sanctuary shekel, each filled with fine flour mixed with oil as a grain offering; [74]one gold dish weighing ten shekels, filled with incense; [75]one young bull, one ram and one male lamb a year old, for a burnt offering; [76]one male goat for a sin offering; [77]and two oxen, five rams, five male goats and five male lambs a year old, to be sacrificed as a fellowship offering. This was the offering of Pagiel son of Ocran.

[78]On the twelfth day Ahira son of Enan,[y] the leader of the people of Naphtali, brought his offering.

[79]His offering was one silver plate weighing a hundred and thirty shekels, and one silver sprinkling bowl weighing seventy shekels, both according to the sanctuary shekel, each filled with fine flour mixed with oil as a grain offering; [80]one gold dish weighing ten shekels, filled with incense; [81]one young bull, one ram and one male lamb a year old, for a burnt offering; [82]one male goat for a sin offering; [83]and two oxen, five rams, five male goats and five male lambs a year old, to be sacrificed as a fellowship offering. This was the offering of Ahira son of Enan.

[84]These were the offerings of the Israelite leaders for the dedication of the altar when it was anointed:[z] twelve silver plates, twelve silver sprinkling bowls[a] and twelve gold dishes.[b] [85]Each silver plate weighed a hundred and thirty shekels, and each sprinkling bowl seventy shekels. Altogether, the silver dishes weighed two thousand four hundred shekels,[r] according to the sanctuary shekel.[c] [86]The twelve gold dishes filled with incense weighed ten shekels each, according to the sanctuary shekel.[d] Altogether, the gold dishes

weighed a hundred and twenty shekels.[s] [87]The total number of animals for the burnt offering[e] came to twelve young bulls, twelve rams and twelve male lambs a year old, together with their grain offering.[f] Twelve male goats were used for the sin offering.[g] [88]The total number of animals for the sacrifice of the fellowship offering[h] came to twenty-four oxen, sixty rams, sixty male goats and sixty male lambs[i] a year old. These were the offerings for the dedication of the altar after it was anointed.[j]

[89]When Moses entered the Tent of Meeting[k] to speak with the LORD,[l] he heard the voice speaking to him from between the two cherubim above the atonement cover[m] on the ark of the Testimony.[n] And he spoke with him.

Setting Up the Lamps

8 The LORD said to Moses, [2]"Speak to Aaron and say to him, 'When you set up the seven lamps, they are to light the area in front of the lampstand.[o]'"

[3]Aaron did so; he set up the lamps so that they faced forward on the lampstand, just as the LORD commanded Moses. [4]This is how the lampstand was made: It was made of hammered gold[p]—from its base to its blossoms. The lampstand was made exactly like the pattern[q] the LORD had shown Moses.

The Setting Apart of the Levites

[5]The LORD said to Moses: [6]"Take the Levites from among the other Israelites and make them ceremonially clean.[r] [7]To purify them, do this: Sprinkle the water of cleansing[s] on them; then have them shave their whole bodies[t] and wash their clothes,[u] and so purify themselves.[v] [8]Have them take a young bull with its grain offering of fine flour mixed with oil;[w] then you are to take a second young bull for a sin offering.[x] [9]Bring the Levites to the front of the Tent of Meeting[y] and assemble the whole Israelite community.[z] [10]You are to bring the Levites before the LORD,

---

Cross-references:

7:72 [x]S Nu 1:13
7:78 [y]S Nu 1:15
7:84 [z]ver 1,10
[a]S Nu 4:14 [b]ver 14
7:85 [c]ver 13
7:86 [d]ver 13

7:87 [e]ver 15 [f]ver 16 [g]ver 13
7:88 [h]ver 17
[i]Ge 32:14 [j]S ver 1,10
7:89 [k]S Ex 40:2 [l]S Ex 29:42
[m]S Ex 16:34; Ps 80:1; 99:1
[n]Nu 3:31
8:2 [o]Ex 25:37
8:4 [p]S Ex 25:36 [q]S Ex 25:9
8:6 [r]Lev 22:2; Isa 1:16; 52:11; 31:23
[s]Lev 14:9; Nu 6:9; Dt 21:12
[u]S Ge 35:2; Lev 14:8
[v]S Ge 35:2
8:8 [w]Lev 2:1; Nu 15:8-10
[x]Lev 4:3
8:9 [y]Ex 40:12
[z]Lev 8:3

---

[r]85 That is, about 60 pounds (about 28 kilograms)
[s]86 That is, about 3 pounds (about 1.4 kilograms)

7:84–88 The totals of the 12 sets of gifts.
7:89 The climax: Communion is established between the Lord and his prophet. The people have an advocate with God.
8:2 *area in front of the lampstand.* The Holy Place in the tabernacle (see Ex 25:37; 26:33; 27:21).
8:5–26 Describes the cleansing of the Levites and may be compared with the account of the ordination of Aaron and his sons to the priesthood (Lev 8). The Levites are helpers to

the priests, and the language describing their consecration is somewhat different from that of the priests. The priests were made holy, the Levites clean; the priests were anointed and washed, the Levites sprinkled; the priests were given new garments, the Levites washed theirs; blood was applied to the priests, it was waved over the Levites.
8:7 *shave their whole bodies.* Symbolic of the completeness of their cleansing, as in the case of the ritual cleansing of one cured of skin disease (Lev 14:8).

sounded, the tribes camping on the east are to set out. [n] [6]At the sounding of a second blast, the camps on the south are to set out. [o] The blast will be the signal for setting out. [7]To gather the assembly, blow the trumpets, [p] but not with the same signal. [q]

[8]"The sons of Aaron, the priests, are to blow the trumpets. This is to be a lasting ordinance for you and the generations to come. [r] [9]When you go into battle in your own land against an enemy who is oppressing you, [s] sound a blast on the trumpets. [t] Then you will be remembered [u] by the LORD your God and rescued from your enemies. [v] [10]Also at your times of rejoicing—your appointed feasts and New Moon festivals [w]—you are to sound the trumpets [x] over your burnt offerings [y] and fellowship offerings, [t][z] and they will be a memorial for you before your God. I am the LORD your God. [a]"

The Israelites Leave Sinai

[11]On the twentieth day of the second month of the second year, [b] the cloud lifted [c] from above the tabernacle of the Testimony. [d] [12]Then the Israelites set out from the Desert of Sinai and traveled from place to place until the cloud came to rest in the Desert of Paran. [e] [13]They set out, this first time, at the LORD's command through Moses. [f]

[14]The divisions of the camp of Judah went first, under their standard. [g] Nahshon son of Amminadab [h] was in command. [15]Nethanel son of Zuar was over the division of the tribe [i] of Issachar, [j] [16]and Eliab son of Helon [k] was over the division of the tribe of Zebulun. [l] [17]Then the tabernacle was taken down, and the Gershonites and Merarites, who carried it, set out. [m]

[18]The divisions of the camp of Reuben [n] went next, under their standard. [o] Elizur

son of Shedeur [p] was in command. [19]Shelumiel son of Zurishaddai was over the division of the tribe of Simeon, [q] [20]and Eliasaph son of Deuel was over the division of the tribe of Gad. [r] [21]Then the Kohathites [s] set out, carrying the holy things. [t] The tabernacle was to be set up before they arrived. [u]

[22]The divisions of the camp of Ephraim [v] went next, under their standard. Elishama son of Ammihud [w] was over the division of the tribe of Manasseh, [x] [24]and Abidan son of Gideoni was over the division of the tribe of Benjamin. [y]

[25]Finally, as the rear guard [z] for all the units, the divisions of the camp of Dan set out, under their standard. Ahiezer son of Ammishaddai [a] was in command. [26]Pagiel son of Ocran was over the division of the tribe of Asher, [b] [27]and Ahira son of Enan was over the division of the tribe of Naphtali. [c] [28]This was the order of march for the Israelite divisions as they set out.

[29]Now Moses said to Hobab [d] son of Reuel [e] the Midianite, Moses' father-in-law, [f] "We are setting out for the place about which the LORD said, 'I will give it to you.' [g] Come with us and we will treat you well, for the LORD has promised good things to Israel."

[30]He answered, "No, I will not go; [h] I am going back to my own land and my own people. [i] "

[31]But Moses said, "Please do not leave us. You know where we should camp in the desert, and you can be our eyes. [j] [32]If you come with us, we will share with you [k] whatever good things the LORD gives us. [l] "

10:5 [n]ver 14
10:6 [o]ver 18
10:7 [p]Jer 4:5; 6:1; Eze 33:3; Joel 2:1 [q]1Co 14:8
10:8 [r]S Ge 9:12; Nu 15:14; 35:29
10:9 [s]Ex 3:9; Jdg 2:18; 6:9; 1Sa 10:18; 2Ki 13:4; Ps 106:42 [t]S Lev 23:24 [u]S Ge 8:1 [v]2Ch 13:12; Ps 106:4
10:10 [w]Nu 28:11; 1Sa 20:5,24; 2Ki 4:23; 2Ch 8:13; Ps 81:3; Isa 1:13; Eze 45:17; 46:6; Am 8:5 [y]Lev 1:3 [z]Lev 3:1; Nu 6:14 [a]Lev 11:44
10:11 [b]Ex 40:17 [c]Nu 9:17 [d]S Ex 38:21
10:12 [e]S Ge 14:6; Dt 1:1; 33:2
10:13 [f]Dt 1:6
10:14 [g]S Nu 1:52; S 2:3-9 [h]Nu 1:7
10:15 [i]S Lev 24:11 [j]S Nu 1:8
10:16 [k]S Nu 2:7 [l]S Nu 1:9
10:17 [m]ver 21; Nu 4:21-32
10:18 [n]Nu 2:16 [o]Nu 2:10-16

[p]S Nu 1:5
10:19 [q]Nu 1:6
10:20 [r]S Nu 1:14
10:21 [s]S Nu 2:17 [t]Nu 4:20 [u]S ver 17
10:22 [v]Nu 2:24 [w]S Nu 1:10
10:23 [x]S Nu 1:10 [y]Nu 1:11
10:24 [y]Nu 1:11
10:25 [z]S Nu 2:31 [a]S Nu 1:12
10:26 [b]S Nu 1:13
10:27 [c]S Nu 1:15
10:29 [d]Jdg 4:11 [e]S Ex 2:18 [f]S Ex 3:1 [g]S Ge 12:7; S 15:14

10:30 [h]Mt 21:29 [i]S Ex 18:27 **10:31** [j]Job 29:15 **10:32** [k]S Ex 12:48; Dt 10:18 [l]Ps 22:27-31; 67:5-7

[t]10 Traditionally peace offerings

10:10 at your . . . appointed feasts . . . sound the trumpets. As an introit to prepare the people for communion with God. Later, David expanded the instruments to include the full orchestra in the worship of the Lord (see, e.g., 1Ch 25), but he maintained the playing of the silver trumpets regularly before the ark of the covenant (1Ch 16:6).
10:11–28 The structure of this section is: (1) v. 11, time frame; (2) vv. 12–13, introductory summary of setting out; (3) vv. 14–17, setting out of the tribes led by Judah (see 2:3–9); (4) vv. 18–21, setting out of the tribes led by Reuben (see 2:10–16); (5) vv. 22–24, setting out of the tribes led by Ephraim (see 2:18–24); (6) vv. 25–27, setting out of the tribes led by Dan (see 2:25–31); (7) v. 28, concluding summary of the line of march.
10:11 twentieth day of the second month. After 11 months in the region of Mount Sinai, the people set out for the promised land, led by the cloud. This verse begins the second great section of the book of Numbers (10:11–22:1).

Israel leaves on a journey that in a few months should have led to the conquest of Canaan.
10:14–27 The names of the leaders of the 12 tribes are given for the fourth time in the book (see 1:5–15; 2:3–31; 7:12–83). The order of the line of march is essentially the same as that in ch. 2. The new details are that the Gershonites and Merarites, who carry the tabernacle, follow the triad of the Judah tribes (v. 17), and the Kohathites, who carry the holy things, follow the triad of the Reuben tribes (v. 21) (see diagram of "Encampment of the Tribes of Israel," p. 192).
10:14 standard. As in 2:3,10,18,25, each of the four triads of tribes had a standard or banner for rallying and organization.
10:29 Hobab son of Reuel. Thus Hobab was Moses' brother-in-law. Reuel. Jethro (see Ex 2:18; 3:1).
10:31 be our eyes. Jdg 1:16 indicates that Hobab acceded to Moses' request.

LORD, "Why have you brought this trouble[o] on your servant? What have I done to displease you that you put the burden of all these people on me?[p] 12Did I conceive all these people? Did I give them birth? Why do you tell me to carry them in my arms, as a nurse carries an infant,[q] to the land you promised on oath[r] to their forefathers?[s] 13Where can I get meat for all these people?[t] They keep wailing to me, 'Give us meat to eat!' 14I cannot carry all these people by myself; the burden is too heavy for me.[u] 15If this is how you are going to treat me, put me to death[v] right now[w]—if I have found favor in your eyes—and do not let me face my own ruin."

16The LORD said to Moses: "Bring me seventy of Israel's elders[x] who are known to you as leaders and officials among the people.[y] Have them come to the Tent of Meeting,[z] that they may stand there with you. 17I will come down and speak with you[a] there, and I will take of the Spirit that is on you and put the Spirit on them.[b] They will help you carry the burden of the people so that you will not have to carry it alone.[c]

18"Tell the people: 'Consecrate yourselves[d] in preparation for tomorrow, when you will eat meat. The LORD heard you when you wailed,[e] "If only we had meat to eat! We were better off in Egypt!"[f] Now the LORD will give you meat,[g] and you will eat it. 19You will not eat it for just one day, or two days, or five, ten or twenty days, 20but for a whole month—until it comes out of your nostrils and you loathe it[h]—because you have rejected the LORD,[i] who is among you, and have

wailed before him, saying, "Why did we ever leave Egypt?" ' "[j]

21But Moses said, "Here I am among six hundred thousand men[k] on foot, and you say, 'I will give them meat to eat for a whole month!' 22Would they have enough if flocks and herds were slaughtered for them? Would they have enough if all the fish in the sea were caught for them?"[l]

23The LORD answered Moses, "Is the LORD's arm too short?[m] You will now see whether or not what I say will come true for you.[n]"

24So Moses went out and told the people what the LORD had said. He brought together seventy of their elders and had them stand around the Tent. 25Then the LORD came down in the cloud[o] and spoke with him,[p] and he took of the Spirit[q] that was on him and put the Spirit on the seventy elders.[r] When the Spirit rested on them, they prophesied,[s] but they did not do so again.[v]

26However, two men, whose names were Eldad and Medad, had remained in the camp. They were listed among the elders, but did not go out to the Tent. Yet the Spirit also rested on them,[t] and they prophesied in the camp. 27A young man ran and told Moses, "Eldad and Medad are prophesying in the camp."

28Joshua son of Nun,[u] who had been Moses' aide[v] since youth, spoke up and said, "Moses, my lord, stop them!"[w]

29But Moses replied, "Are you jealous for my sake? I wish that all the LORD's

11:11 oS Ge 34:30 pS Ex 5:22; S 18:18
11:12 qIsa 40:11; 49:23; 66:11,12 rNu 14:16 sS Ge 12:7; Ex 13:5
11:13 tS Ex 12:37; Jn 6:5-9
11:14 uS Ex 18:18
11:15 vEx 32:32 w1Ki 19:4; Job 6:9; 7:15-16; 9:21; 10:1; Isa 38:12; Jnh 4:3
11:16 xS Ex 3:16 yS Ex 18:25 zS Ex 40:2
11:17 aEx 19:20 bver 25,29; 1Sa 10:6; 2Ki 2:9, 15; 3:12; Isa 32:15; 40:5; 63:11; Joel 2:28; Hag 2:5 cS Ex 18:18; Jer 19:1
11:18 dS Ex 19:10 eS Ex 16:7 fver 5; Ac 7:39 gPs 78:20
11:20 hPs 78:29; 106:14,15 iS Lev 26:43; Jos 24:27; Jdg 8:23; 1Sa 10:19; Job 31:28; Isa 59:13; Hos 13:11
jver 33; Job 20:13,23
11:21 kS Ex 12:37
11:22 lMt 15:33
11:23 mIsa 50:2; 59:1 nNu 23:19; 1Sa 15:29; Eze 12:25; 24:14
11:25 oS Ex 19:9; Nu 12:5 pver 17 qver 29; 1Sa 10:6; 19:23 rS Ac 2:17 sver 26; Nu 24:2; Jdg 3:10; 1Sa 10:10; 19:20; 2Ch 15:1

11:26 tS ver 25; 1Ch 12:18; Rev 1:10 11:28 uEx 17:9; Nu 13:8; 26:65; Jos 14:10 vEx 33:11; Jos 1:1 wMk 9:38-40

v25 Or prophesied and continued to do so

11:12 Did I conceive all these people? The implication is that the Lord conceived the people of Israel, that he was their nurse and that their promises were his. Moses asks that he be relieved of his mediatorial office, for "the burden is too heavy for me" (v. 14; cf. Elijah, 1Ki 19). Even death, Moses asserts (v. 15), would be preferable to facing the continuing complaints of the people.

11:16–34 The Lord's response to the great distress of his prophet was twofold—mercy and curse: 1. There was mercy to Moses in that his responsibility was now to be shared by 70 leaders (vv. 16–17). 2. There was a curse on the people that was analogous to their complaint: They asked for meat and would now become sick with meat (vv. 18–34).

11:18 you will eat meat. Their distress at the lack of variety in the daily manna had led the people to challenge the Lord's goodness. They had wailed for meat. Now they were going to get their fill of meat, so much that it would make them physically ill (v. 20).

11:20 you have rejected the LORD. The principal issue was not meat at all, but a failure to demonstrate proper gratitude to the Lord, who was in their midst and who was their

constant source of good.

11:21 six hundred thousand men on foot. The numbers are consistent: A marching force of this size suggests a total population of over 2,000,000 (see note on 1:46). Moses' distress at providing meat for this immense number of people (v. 22) is nearly comical—the task is impossible.

11:23 Is the LORD's arm too short? The human impossibility is an occasion for demonstrating the Lord's power.

11:25 they prophesied. Probably means that they gave ecstatic expression to an intense religious experience (see 1Sa 10:5–6; 18:10; 19:20–24; 1Ki 18:29). but they did not do so again. It seems that the temporary gift of prophecy to the elders was primarily to establish their credentials as Spirit-empowered leaders.

11:29 Are you jealous for my sake? Here the true spirit of Moses is demonstrated. Rather than being threatened by the public demonstration of the gifts of the Spirit by Eldad and Medad, Moses desired that all God's people might have the full gifts of the Spirit (cf. Php 1:15–18). This verse is a fitting introduction to the inexcusable challenge to Moses' leadership in ch. 12.

people were prophets [x] and that the LORD would put his Spirit [y] on them!" [z] 30Then Moses and the elders of Israel returned to the camp.

31Now a wind went out from the LORD and drove quail [a] in from the sea. It brought them [w] down all around the camp to about three feet [x] above the ground, as far as a day's walk in any direction. 32All that day and night and all the next day the people went out and gathered quail. No one gathered less than ten homers. [y] Then they spread them out all around the camp. 33But while the meat was still between their teeth [b] and before it could be consumed, the anger [c] of the LORD burned against the people, and he struck them with a severe plague. [d] 34Therefore the place was named Kibroth Hattaavah, [z] [e] because there they buried the people who had craved other food.

35From Kibroth Hattaavah the people traveled to Hazeroth [f] and stayed there.

Miriam and Aaron Oppose Moses

12 Miriam [g] and Aaron began to talk against Moses because of his Cushite wife, [h] for he had married a Cushite. 2"Has the LORD spoken only through Moses?" they asked. "Hasn't he also spoken through us?" [i] And the LORD heard this. [j]

3(Now Moses was a very humble man, [k] more humble than anyone else on the face of the earth.)

4At once the LORD said to Moses, Aaron and Miriam, "Come out to the Tent of Meeting, all three of you." So the three of them came out. 5Then the LORD came down in a pillar of cloud; [l] he stood at the entrance to the Tent and summoned Aaron and Miriam. When both of them stepped forward, 6he said, "Listen to my words:

"When a prophet of the LORD is among you,
   I reveal [m] myself to him in visions, [n]
   I speak to him in dreams. [o]
7But this is not true of my servant Moses; [p]
   he is faithful in all my house. [q]
8With him I speak face to face,
   clearly and not in riddles; [r]
   he sees the form of the LORD. [s]
Why then were you not afraid
   to speak against my servant Moses?" [t]

9The anger of the LORD burned against them, [u] and he left them. [v]

10When the cloud lifted from above the Tent, [w] there stood Miriam—leprous, [a] like snow. [x] Aaron turned toward her and saw that she had leprosy; [y] 11and he said to Moses, "Please, my lord, do not hold against us the sin we have so foolishly committed. [z] 12Do not let her be like a

11:29 xISa 10:5; 19:20; 2Ch 24:19; Jer 7:25; 44:4; 1Co 14:5 ySer 17 zNu 27:18
11:31 aSEx 16:13; Ps 78:26-28
11:33 bPs 78:30 cNu 14:18; Dt 9:7; Jdg 2:12; 2Ki 22:17; Ps 106:29; Jer 44:3; Eze 8:17 dSver 18-20; Ps 106:15; Isa 10:16
11:34 eNu 33:16; Dt 9:22
11:35 fNu 33:17
12:1 gSEx 15:20 hSEx 2:21
12:2 iNu 16:3 /SNu 11:1
12:3 kMt 11:29
12:5 ISEx 13:21; S Nu 11:25
12:6 mISa 3:7,21 nSGe 15:1 oSGe 20:3; SMt 27:19; Heb 1:1
12:7 pDt 34:5; Jos 1:1-2,1; Ps 105:26 qHeb 3:2,5
12:8 rJdg 14:12; 1Ki 10:1; Ps 49:4; Pr 1:6; Da 5:12 sEx 20:4; Job 19:26; Ps 17:15; 140:13; Isa 6:1 tEx 24:2
12:9 uSEx 4:14 vSGe 17:22
12:10 wEx 40:2 xSEx 4:6; Dt 24:9 ySLev 13:11; 2Ki 5:1,27; 2Ch 16:12; 21:12-15; 26:19
12:11 z2Sa 19:19; 24:10

24:10

w31 Or *They flew*   x31 Hebrew *two cubits* (about 1 meter)   y32 That is, probably about 60 bushels (about 2.2 kiloliters)   z34 *Kibroth Hattaavah* means *graves of craving.*   a10 The Hebrew word was used for various diseases affecting the skin—not necessarily leprosy.

11:31–32 Cf. the great provision of Jesus in the feeding of the 5,000 (Jn 6:5–13) and the 4,000 (Mt 15:29–39). In those cases the feeding was a demonstration of God's grace; in this instance it was of God's wrath.

11:34 *Kibroth Hattaavah.* See NIV text note. These graves marked the death camp of those who had turned against the food of the Lord's mercy.

12:1 *his Cushite wife.* Cush was the first son of Ham, the father of the southernmost peoples known to the Hebrews (Ge 10:6–7), living in the southern Nile valley. Moses' wife Zipporah may be referred to here (see Ex 2:15–22); if so, the term "Cushite" is used in contempt of her Midianite ancestry. It is more likely, however, that the reference is to a new wife taken by Moses, perhaps after the death of his first wife. The attack on the woman was a pretext; its focus was the prophetic gift of Moses and his special relationship with the Lord (v. 2).

12:2 *Hasn't he also spoken through us?* Of course he had. Mic 6:4 speaks of Moses, Aaron and Miriam as God's gracious provision for Israel. The prophetic gifting of the 70 elders (11:24–30) seems to have been the immediate provocation for the attack of Miriam and Aaron on their brother.

12:3 Perhaps a later addition to the text, alerting the reader to the great unfairness of the charge of arrogance against Moses.

12:4 *At once.* The abruptness of the Lord's response instilled terror (see Job 22:10; Isa 47:11; Jer 4:20).

12:5 *came down.* Often used of divine manifestations. In 11:25 the Lord came down in grace; here and in Ge 11:5 he came down in judgment. In a sense every theophany (appearance of God) is a picture and promise of the grand theophany, the incarnation of Jesus, both in grace and in judgment.

12:6–8 The poetic cast of these words adds a sense of solemnity to them. The point of the poem is clear: All true prophetic vision is from the Lord, but in the case of Moses his position and faithfulness enhance his special relationship with the Lord.

12:7 *my servant.* See notes on Ex 14:31; Ps 18 title; Isa 41:8–9; 42:1. *my house.* The household of God's people Israel.

12:8 *clearly and not in riddles.* God's revelation does not come with equal clarity to his servants. There may be oracles of the Lord that a prophet might not fully understand at the time; to him they may be riddles and mysteries (cf. 1Pe 1:10–11). But to Moses, God spoke with special clarity, as though face to face (see also Dt 34:10).

12:10 *leprous.* See NIV text note. Miriam, the principal offender against her brother Moses, has become an outcast, as she now suffers from a skin disease that would exclude her from the community of Israel (see 5:1–4).

12:11 *Please, my lord.* Aaron's repentance for the sin of presumption is touching, both in its intensity and in his concern for his (and Moses') sister.

stillborn infant coming from its mother's womb with its flesh half eaten away."

13So Moses cried out to the LORD, "O God, please heal her! *a* "

14The LORD replied to Moses, "If her father had spit in her face, *b* would she not have been in disgrace for seven days? Confine her outside the camp *c* for seven days; after that she can be brought back." 15So Miriam was confined outside the camp *d* for seven days, *e* and the people did not move on till she was brought back.

16After that, the people left Hazeroth *f* and encamped in the Desert of Paran. *g*

Exploring Canaan

13 The LORD said to Moses, 2"Send some men to explore *h* the land of Canaan, *i* which I am giving to the Israelites. *j* From each ancestral tribe *k* send one of its leaders."

3So at the LORD's command Moses sent them out from the Desert of Paran. All of them were leaders of the Israelites. *l* 4These are their names:

from the tribe of Reuben, Shammua son of Zaccur;

5from the tribe of Simeon, Shaphat son of Hori;

6from the tribe of Judah, Caleb son of Jephunneh; *m*

7from the tribe of Issachar, Igal son of Joseph;

8from the tribe of Ephraim, Hoshea son of Nun; *n*

9from the tribe of Benjamin, Palti son of Raphu;

10from the tribe of Zebulun, Gaddiel son of Sodi;

11from the tribe of Manasseh (a tribe of Joseph), Gaddi son of Susi;

12from the tribe of Dan, Ammiel son of Gemalli;

13from the tribe of Asher, Sethur son of Michael;

14from the tribe of Naphtali, Nahbi son of Vophsi;

15from the tribe of Gad, Geuel son of Maki.

16These are the names of the men Moses sent to explore *o* the land. (Moses gave Hoshea son of Nun *p* the name Joshua.) *q*

17When Moses sent them to explore Canaan, *r* he said, "Go up through the Negev *s* and on into the hill country. *t* 18See what the land is like and whether the people who live there are strong or weak, few or many. 19What kind of land do they live in? Is it good or bad? What kind of towns do they live in? Are they unwalled or fortified? 20How is the soil? Is it fertile or poor? Are there trees on it or not? Do your best to bring back some of the fruit of the land. *u*" (It was the season for the first ripe grapes.) *v*

21So they went up and explored the land from the Desert of Zin *w* as far as Rehob, *x* toward Lebo *b* Hamath. *y* 22They went up through the Negev and came to Hebron, *z* where Ahiman, Sheshai and Talmai, *a* the descendants of Anak, *b* lived. (Hebron had been built seven years before Zoan in

---

Cross references (center column):

12:13 *a*Ex 15:26; Ps 6:2; 147:3; Isa 1:6; 30:26; 53:5; Jer 17:14; Hos 6:1
12:14 *b*Dt 25:9; Job 17:6; 30:9-10; Isa 50:6 *c*S Lev 13:46
12:15 *d*S Lev 14:8 *e*S Lev 13:4 *f*Nu 11:35 *g*Ge 21:21; Nu 10:12; 15:32
13:2 *h*ver 16; Dt 1:22 *i*S Lev 14:34 *j*Jos 1:3 *k*S Lev 24:11
13:3 *l*Nu 1:16
13:6 *m*ver 30; Nu 14:6,24; 34:19; Dt 1:36; Jdg 1:12-15
13:8 *n*S Nu 11:28
13:16 *o*S ver 2 *p*ver 8 *q*Dt 32:44
13:17 *r*ver 2; Jos 14:7 *s*S Ge 12:9 *t*Dt 1:7; Jos 9:1; Jdg 1:9
13:20 *u*Dt 1:25. *v*S Lev 25:5
13:21 *w*Nu 20:1; 27:14; 33:36; Dt 32:51; Jos 15:1 *x*Jos 19:28; Jdg 1:31; 18:28; 2Sa 10:6; 1Ch 6:75 *y*Nu 34:8; Jos 13:5; Jdg 3:3; 1Ki 8:65; 2Ki 14:25; 1Ch 13:5; 2Ch 7:8; Jer 52:9; Eze 47:16,20; Am 6:14
13:22 *z*S Ge 13:18; S 23:19 *a*Jos 15:14; Jdg 1:10 *b*ver 28; Dt 2:10; 9:2; Jos 11:21; 15:13; Jdg 1:20

*b*21 Or *toward the entrance to*

12:14 *disgrace for seven days.* An act of public rebuke (see Dt 25:9) demands a period of public shame. A period of seven days was a standard time for uncleanness occasioned by being in contact with a dead body (see 19:11,14,16).
12:16 *Desert of Paran.* The southernmost region of the promised land. The people's opportunity to conquer the land was soon to come.
13:2 *Send some men to explore the land of Canaan.* The use of spies was a common practice in the ancient Near East (see note on Jos 2:1–24). From Dt 1:22–23 it appears that this directive of the Lord was in response to the people's request. Thus the very sending of the spies was an expression of God's grace.
13:4–15 The names listed here are different from those in chs. 1–2; 7; 10. Presumably the tribal leaders in the four earlier lists were older men. The task for the spies called for men who were younger and more robust, but no less respected by their peers.
13:16 *Moses gave Hoshea son of Nun the name Joshua.* A parenthetical statement anticipating the later prominence of Joshua. The reader is alerted to the significance of this name in the list of the spies; here is a man of destiny. Hoshea means "salvation"; Joshua means "The LORD saves" (see NIV text note on Mt 1:21).

13:17–20 Moses' instruction to the 12 spies was comprehensive; a thorough report of the land and its produce and the peoples and their towns was required in their reconnaissance mission.
13:21 *explored the land.* The journey of the spies began in the southernmost extremity of the land (the Desert of Zin) and took them to the northernmost point (Rehob, near Lebo Hamath; see 34:8). This journey of about 250 miles each way took them 40 days (v. 25), perhaps a round number.
13:22 *Hebron.* The first city the spies came to in Canaan. The parenthetical comment about the city's being built seven years before Zoan in Egypt may have been prompted by their amazement at the size and fortifications of the city that was so closely associated with the lives of their ancestors four centuries before this time (see Ge 13:14–18; 14:13; 23:2; 25:9; 35:27–29; 50:13). In the stories of the ancestors of their people, Hebron had not been a great city, but a dwelling and trading place for shepherds and herdsmen. *descendants of Anak.* Three notable Anak descendants are mentioned as living at Hebron. The Anakites were men of great stature; their physical size brought fear to the people (see vv. 32–33). In a later day of faith, Caleb was to drive them from their city (Jos 15:14; Jdg 1:10).

Egypt.)*c* ²³When they reached the Valley of Eshcol,*c d* they cut off a branch bearing a single cluster of grapes. Two of them carried it on a pole between them, along with some pomegranates*e* and figs.*f* ²⁴That place was called the Valley of Eshcol because of the cluster of grapes the Israelites cut off there. ²⁵At the end of forty days*g* they returned from exploring the land.*h*

Report on the Exploration

²⁶They came back to Moses and Aaron and the whole Israelite community at Kadesh*i* in the Desert of Paran.*j* There they reported to them*k* and to the whole assembly and showed them the fruit of the land.*l* ²⁷They gave Moses this account: "We went into the land to which you sent us, and it does flow with milk and honey!*m* Here is its fruit.*n* ²⁸But the people who live there are powerful, and the cities are fortified and very large.*o* We even saw descendants of Anak*p* there.*q* ²⁹The Amalekites*r* live in the Negev; the Hittites,*s* Jebusites*t* and Amorites*u* live in the hill country;*v* and the Canaanites*w* live near the sea and along the Jordan.*x*"

³⁰Then Caleb*y* silenced the people before Moses and said, "We should go up and take possession of the land, for we can certainly do it."

³¹But the men who had gone up with him said, "We can't attack those people; they are stronger than we are."*z* ³²And they spread among the Israelites a bad report*a* about the land they had explored. They said, "The land we explored devours*b* those living in it. All the people we saw there are of great size.*c* ³³We saw the Nephilim*d* there (the descendants of Anak*e* come from the Nephilim). We seemed like grasshoppers*f* in our own eyes, and we looked the same to them."

The People Rebel

14 That night all the people of the community raised their voices and wept aloud.*g* ²All the Israelites grumbled*h* against Moses and Aaron, and the whole assembly said to them, "If only we had died in Egypt!*i* Or in this desert!*j* ³Why is the LORD bringing us to this land only to let us fall by the sword?*k* Our wives and children*l* will be taken as plunder.*m* Wouldn't it be better for us to go back to Egypt?*n*" ⁴And they said to each other, "We should choose a leader and go back to Egypt.*o*"

⁵Then Moses and Aaron fell facedown*p* in front of the whole Israelite assembly*q* gathered there. ⁶Joshua son of Nun*r* and Caleb son of Jephunneh, who were among those who had explored the land, tore their clothes*s* ⁷and said to the entire Israelite assembly, "The land we passed through and explored is exceedingly good.*t* ⁸If the LORD is pleased with us,*u* he will lead us into that land, a land flowing with milk and honey,*v* and will give it to us.*w* ⁹Only do not rebel*x* against the LORD. And do not be afraid*y* of the people of the land,*z* because we will swallow them up. Their protection is gone, but the LORD is with*a* us.*b* Do not be afraid of them."*c*

¹⁰But the whole assembly talked about stoning*d* them. Then the glory of the LORD*e* appeared at the Tent of Meeting to all the Israelites. ¹¹The LORD said to Moses,

13:22 *c*Ps 78:12, 43; Isa 19:11,13; 30:4; Eze 30:14
13:23 *d*S Ge 14:13 *e*S Ex 28:33 *f*Ge 3:7; Nu 20:5; Dt 8:8; 2Ki 18:31; Ne 13:15
13:25 *g*S Ge 7:4 *h*Nu 14:34
13:26 *i*S Ge 14:7 *j*S Ge 14:6 *k*Nu 32:8 *l*Dt 1:25
13:27 *m*S Ex 3:8 *n*Dt 1:25; Jer 2:7
13:28 *o*Dt 1:28; 9:1,2 *p*S ver 22 *q*Jos 14:12
13:29 *r*S Ge 14:7 *s*S Ge 10:15; Dt 7:1; 20:17; 1Ki 9:20; 10:29; 2Ki 7:6 *t*S Ex 3:8 *u*S Ge 10:16 *v*ver 17 *w*S Ge 10:18 *x*S Ge 13:10; Nu 22:1; 32:5; Dt 1:1; Jos 1:2; Jdg 3:28; Ps 42:6
13:30 *y*S ver 6
13:31 *z*Dt 9:1; Jos 14:8
13:32 *a*Nu 14:36, 37 *b*Eze 36:13,14 *c*Dt 1:28; Am 2:9
13:33 *d*Ge 6:4 *e*ver 28; Dt 1:28; Jos 11:22; 14:12 *f*Ecc 12:5; Isa 40:22

14:1 *g*S Ge 27:38; Ex 33:4; Nu 25:6; Dt 1:45; Jdg 20:23,26; 2Sa 3:32; Job 31:29
14:2 *h*S Ex 15:24; Heb 3:16 *i*S Ex 16:3 *j*S Nu 11:1; 16:13; 20:4; 21:5
14:3 *k*S Ex 5:21 *l*ver 31 *m*S Ge 34:29; Dt 1:39; Ps 109:11; Isa 33:4; Eze 7:21; 25:7; 26:5 *n*Ac 7:39
14:4 *o*Ne 9:17
14:5 *p*S Lev 9:24; Nu 16:4,22,45; 20:6; Jos 5:14;

2Sa 14:4; 1Ch 21:16; Eze 1:28 *q*S Lev 19:2 **14:6** *r*Nu 11:28 *s*S Ge 37:29,34; Jdg 11:35; 2Sa 13:31; 2Ki 19:1; Ezr 9:3; Est 4:1; S Mk 14:63 **14:7** *t*Nu 13:27; Dt 1:25 **14:8** *u*Dt 7:8; 10:15; Ps 18:19; 22:8; 37:23; 41:11; 56:9; 147:11; Pr 11:20; Isa 62:4; Mal 2:17 *v*Nu 13:27 *w*Dt 1:21 **14:9** *x*Dt 1:26; 9:7,23,24 *y*Ge 26:24; 2Ch 32:7; Ps 118:6; Jer 41:18; 42:11 *z*Dt 1:21; 7:18; 20:1 *a*Hag 2:4 *b*S Ge 21:22; Dt 1:30; 2Ch 13:12; Jer 15:20; 46:28; Hag 1:13 *c*ver 24
14:10 *d*S Ex 17:4 *e*S Ex 24:16

c23 Eshcol means *cluster;* also in verse 24.

13:23 *Valley of Eshcol.* See NIV text note. This valley is near Hebron; presumably the spies cut the cluster of grapes on their return journey. The size of the grape cluster should have indicated the goodness of the land God was giving them.

13:26–29 The first part of the spies' report was truthful, but the goodness of the land was offset in their fearful eyes by the powerful peoples who lived there.

13:30 *Caleb silenced the people.* Only Caleb and Hoshea (Joshua) gave a report prompted by faith in God.

13:32 *bad report about the land.* The promised land was a good land, a gracious gift from God. By speaking bad things about it, the faithless spies were speaking evil of the Lord (cf. 10:29).

13:33 Their words became exaggerations and distortions. The Anakites were now said to be Nephilim (see note on Ge 6:4). The reference to the Nephilim seems deliberately intended to evoke fear. The exaggeration of the faithless led to

their final folly: "We seemed like grasshoppers."

14:1 *all the people . . . wept.* The frightening words of the faithless spies led to mourning by the entire community and to their great rebellion against the Lord. They forgot all the miracles the Lord had done for them, they despised his mercies, and they spurned his might. In their ingratitude they preferred death (v. 2).

14:3 *children.* The most reprehensible charge against God's grace was that concerning their children. Only their children would survive (see vv. 31–33).

14:9 *the LORD is with us.* There are no walls, no fortifications, no factors of size or bearing, and certainly no gods that can withstand the onslaught of God's people when the Lord is with them.

14:10 *the glory of the LORD appeared.* The theophany (manifestation of God) must have been staggering in its sudden and intense display of his majesty and wrath.

14:11 *treat me with contempt.* By refusing to believe in

"How long will these people treat me with contempt?[f] How long will they refuse to believe in me,[g] in spite of all the miraculous signs[h] I have performed among them? [12]I will strike them down with a plague[i] and destroy them, but I will make you into a nation[j] greater and stronger than they."[k]

[13]Moses said to the LORD, "Then the Egyptians will hear about it! By your power you brought these people up from among them.[l] [14]And they will tell the inhabitants of this land about it. They have already heard[m] that you, O LORD, are with these people[n] and that you, O LORD, have been seen face to face,[o] that your cloud stays over them,[p] and that you go before them in a pillar of cloud by day and a pillar of fire by night.[q] [15]If you put these people to death all at one time, the nations who have heard this report about you will say, [16]'The LORD was not able to bring these people into the land he promised them on oath;[r] so he slaughtered them in the desert.'[s]

[17]"Now may the Lord's strength be displayed, just as you have declared: [18]'The LORD is slow to anger, abounding in love and forgiving sin and rebellion.[t] Yet he does not leave the guilty unpunished; he punishes the children for the sin of the fathers to the third and fourth generation.'[u] [19]In accordance with your great love, forgive[v] the sin of these people,[w] just as you have pardoned them from the time they left Egypt until now."[x]

[20]The LORD replied, "I have forgiven them,[y] as you asked. [21]Nevertheless, as surely as I live[z] and as surely as the glory of the LORD[a] fills the whole earth,[b] [22]not one of the men who saw my glory and the miraculous signs[c] I performed in Egypt and in the desert but who disobeyed me

and tested me ten times[d]— [23]not one of them will ever see the land I promised on oath[e] to their forefathers. No one who has treated me with contempt[f] will ever see it.[g] [24]But because my servant Caleb[h] has a different spirit and follows me wholeheartedly,[i] I will bring him into the land he went to, and his descendants will inherit it.[j] [25]Since the Amalekites[k] and Canaanites[l] are living in the valleys, turn[m] back tomorrow and set out toward the desert along the route to the Red Sea.[d] [n]"

[26]The LORD said to Moses and Aaron: [27]"How long will this wicked community grumble against me? I have heard the complaints of these grumbling Israelites.[o] [28]So tell them, 'As surely as I live,[p] declares the LORD, I will do to you[q] the very things I heard you say: [29]In this desert your bodies will fall[r]—every one of you twenty years old or more[s] who was counted in the census[t] and who has grumbled against me. [30]Not one of you will enter the land[u] I swore with uplifted hand[v] to make your home, except Caleb son of Jephunneh[w] and Joshua son of Nun.[x] [31]As for your children that you said would be taken as plunder, I will bring them in to enjoy the land you have rejected.[y] [32]But you—your bodies will fall[z] in this desert. [33]Your children will be shepherds here for forty years,[a] suffering for your unfaithfulness, until the last of your bodies lies in the desert. [34]For forty years[b]—one year for each of the forty days you explored the

---

14:11 [f]Ex 23:21; Nu 15:31; 16:30; 1Sa 2:17; Eze 31:14; Mal 1:13
[g]Dt 1:32; Ps 78:22; 106:24; Jn 3:15
[h]S Ex 3:20; S 4:17; S 10:1
14:12 [i]S Ex 5:3; S 30:12
[j]S Ex 32:10
[k]Dt 9:14; 29:20; 32:26; Ps 109:13
14:13 [l]Ex 32:11-14; Ps 106:23
14:14 [m]Ex 15:14
[n]Nu 5:3; 16:3; Jos 2:9 [o]Dt 5:4; 34:10
[p]S Ex 33:16
[q]S Ex 13:21
14:16 [r]Nu 11:12
[s]Ex 32:12; Jos 7:7
14:18 [t]S Ex 20:6; 34:6; Ps 145:8; Jnh 4:2; Jas 5:11
[u]Ex 20:5
14:19
[v]S Ex 34:9; 1Ki 8:34; Ps 85:2; 103:3 [w]Ps 106:45
[x]Ps 78:38
14:20 [y]Ex 34:6; Ps 99:8; 106:23; Mic 7:18-20
14:21 [z]ver 28; Dt 32:40; Jdg 8:19; Ru 3:13; 1Sa 14:39; 19:6; Isa 49:18; Jer 4:2; Eze 5:11; Zep 2:9
[a]Lev 9:6
[b]Ps 72:19; Isa 6:3; 40:5; Hab 2:14
14:22 [c]ver 11

[d]S Ex 14:11; 17:7; 32:1; Ps 81:7; 1Co 10:5
14:23 [e]ver 16; S Ex 33:1; Nu 32:11; Dt 1:34; Ps 95:11; 106:26 [f]ver 11 [g]Heb 3:18
14:24 [h]Nu 13:6 [i]ver 6-9; Dt 1:36; Jos 14:8,14
[j]Nu 26:65; 32:12; Ps 25:13; 37:9,11

14:25 [k]S Ge 14:7 [l]S Ge 10:18 [m]Dt 1:40 [n]Ex 23:31; Nu 21:4; 1Ki 9:26 14:27 [o]Ex 16:12; Dt 1:34,35 14:28 [p]S ver 21 [q]Nu 33:56 14:29 [r]ver 23,30,32; Nu 26:65; 32:13; 1Co 10:5; Heb 3:17; Jude 1:5 [s]S Nu 1:45 [t]S Ex 30:12 14:30 [u]S ver 29 [v]Ex 6:8; Dt 32:40; Ne 9:15; Ps 106:26; Eze 20:5; 36:7 [w]Nu 13:6 [x]Nu 11:28 14:31 [y]S Lev 26:43 14:32 [z]S ver 29,35 14:33 [a]ver 34; S Ex 16:35; Ac 13:18; Heb 3:9 14:34 [b]S ver 33

[d]25 Hebrew Yam Suph; that is, Sea of Reeds

---

the Lord's power, especially in view of all the wonders they had experienced, the people of Israel were holding him in contempt.

14:12 *I will make you into a nation.* For the second time since the exodus, God speaks of starting over with Moses in creating a people faithful to himself (see Ex 32:10).

14:13 *the Egyptians will hear about it!* Moses desires to protect the Lord's reputation. The enemies of God's people will charge the Lord with inability to complete his deliverance and will be contemptuous of his power.

14:17–19 Moses now moves from the Lord's reputation to his character, presenting a composite quotation of his own words of loyal love for and faithful discipline of his people (see Ex 20:6; 34:6–7).

14:22 *ten times.* Perhaps to be enumerated as follows: (1) Ex 14:10–12; (2) Ex 15:22–24; (3) Ex 16:1–3; (4) Ex 16:19–20; (5) Ex 16:27–30; (6) Ex 17:1–4; (7) Ex 32:1–35; (8) Nu 11:1–3; (9) 11:4–34; (10) 14:3. But "ten times" may also be a way of saying "many times."

14:24 *my servant Caleb has a different spirit.* Caleb seems to be singled out; perhaps the words of vv. 7–9 were his, and he was joined in them by Joshua. Caleb's ultimate vindication came 45 years later (see note on 13:22; see also Jos 14:10).

14:28 *I will do to you the very things I heard you say.* The people of Israel brought upon themselves their punishment. They had said that they would rather die in the desert (v. 2) than be led into Canaan to die by the sword. All those 20 years old or more, who were counted in the census, were to die in the desert (v. 29). The only exceptions would be Joshua and Caleb (v. 30). Only their children would survive (v. 31)—the children that the people said God would allow to die in the desert (v. 3).

14:34 The 40 days of the travels of the spies became the numerical pattern for their suffering: one year for one day—for 40 years they would recount their misjudgment, and for 40 years the people 20 years old or more would be dying, so that only the young generation might enter the

land c—you will suffer for your sins and know what it is like to have me against you.' 35I, the LORD, have spoken, and I will surely do these things d to this whole wicked community, which has banded together against me. They will meet their end in this desert; here they will die. e"

36So the men Moses had sent f to explore the land, who returned and made the whole community grumble g against him by spreading a bad report h about it— 37these men responsible for spreading the bad report i about the land were struck down and died of a plague j before the LORD. 38Of the men who went to explore the land, k only Joshua son of Nun and Caleb son of Jephunneh survived. l

39When Moses reported this m to all the Israelites, they mourned n bitterly. 40Early the next morning they went up toward the high hill country. o "We have sinned p," they said. "We will go up to the place the LORD promised."

41But Moses said, "Why are you disobeying the LORD's command? This will not succeed! q 42Do not go up, because the LORD is not with you. You will be defeated by your enemies, r 43for the Amalekites s and Canaanites t will face you there. Because you have turned away from the LORD, he will not be with you u and you will fall by the sword."

44Nevertheless, in their presumption they went up v toward the high hill country, though neither Moses nor the ark of the LORD's covenant moved from the camp. w 45Then the Amalekites and Canaanites x who lived in that hill country y came down and attacked them and beat them down all the way to Hormah. z

Supplementary Offerings

15 The LORD said to Moses, 2"Speak to the Israelites and say to them:

'After you enter the land I am giving you a as a home 3and you present to the LORD offerings made by fire, from the herd or the flock, b as an aroma pleasing to the LORD c—whether burnt offerings d or sacrifices, for special vows or freewill offerings e or festival offerings f— 4then the one who brings his offering shall present to the LORD a grain offering g of a tenth of an ephah e of fine flour h mixed with a quarter of a hin f of oil. 5With each lamb i for the burnt offering or the sacrifice, prepare a quarter of a hin of wine j as a drink offering. k

6" 'With a ram l prepare a grain offering m of two-tenths of an ephah g n of fine flour mixed with a third of a hin h of oil, o 7and a third of a hin of wine p as a drink offering. q Offer it as an aroma pleasing to the LORD. r

8" 'When you prepare a young bull s as a burnt offering or sacrifice, for a special vow t or a fellowship offering i u to the LORD, 9bring with the bull a grain offering v of three-tenths of an ephah j w of fine flour mixed with half a hin k of oil. 10Also bring half a hin of wine x as a drink offering. y It will be an offering made by fire, an aroma pleasing to the LORD. z 11Each bull or ram, each lamb or young goat, is to be prepared in this manner. 12Do this for each one, for as many as you prepare. a

13" 'Everyone who is native-born b must do these things in this way when he brings an offering made by fire as an aroma pleasing to the LORD. c 14For the generations to

Cross references (center column)

14:34 cNu 13:25
14:35 dNu 23:19
eS ver 32
14:36
fNu 13:4-16 gver 2 hS Nu 13:32
14:37
iS Nu 13:32; 1Co 10:10; Heb 3:17
jNu 16:49; 25:9; 26:1; 31:16; Dt 4:3
14:38 kver 30; Nu 13:4-16 lver 24; Jos 14:6
14:39 mver 28-35 nS Ex 33:4
14:40 over 45; Nu 13:17 pS Ex 9:27
14:41 q2Ch 24:20
14:42 rDt 1:42
14:43 sJdg 3:13 tver 45; Nu 13:29 uS Ge 39:23; Dt 31:8; Jos 6:27; Jdg 1:19; 6:16; 1Sa 3:19; 18:14; 2Ch 1:1
14:44 vDt 1:43 wNu 31:6
14:45 xS ver 43 yS ver 40 zNu 21:3; Dt 1:44; Jos 12:14; 15:30; 19:4; Jdg 1:17; 1Sa 30:30; 1Ch 4:30

15:2 aS Lev 23:10
15:3 bS Lev 1:2 cver 24; S Lev 1:9 dLev 1:3; Nu 28:13 eS Lev 7:16; S Ezr 1:4 fLev 23:1-44
15:4 gS Lev 6:14 hS Ex 16:36
15:5 iS Lev 3:7 jS Lev 10:9 kS Ge 35:14
15:6 lS Lev 5:15 mNu 28:12; 29:14 nS Lev 23:13 oEze 46:14
15:7 pver 5 qLev 23:13; Nu 28:14; 29:18 rS Lev 1:9
15:8 sS Ex 12:5; S Lev 1:5 tS Lev 22:18 uS Lev 3:6
15:9 vLev 2:1 wS Lev 14:10

15:10 xNu 28:14 yLev 23:13 zLev 1:9 15:12 aEzr 7:17
15:13 bS Lev 16:29 cLev 1:9

e4 That is, probably about 2 quarts (about 2 liters)
f4 That is, probably about 1 quart (about 1 liter); also in verse 5   g6 That is, probably about 4 quarts (about 4.5 liters)   h6 That is, probably about 1 1/4 quarts (about 1.2 liters); also in verse 7   i8 Traditionally peace offering   j9 That is, probably about 6 quarts (about 6.5 liters)   k9 That is, probably about 2 quarts (about 2 liters); also in verse 10

---

land. Significantly, Israel's refusal to carry out the Lord's commission to conquer his land is the climactic act of rebellion for which God condemns Israel to die in the desert. **14:37** these men responsible for spreading the bad report . . . were struck down. The judgment on the ten evil spies was immediate; the generation that they influenced would live out their lives in the desert.

14:40 We will go up. Now, too late, the people determine to go up to the land they had refused. Such a course of action was doomed to failure. Not only was the Lord not with them; he was against them (v. 41). Their subsequent defeat (v. 45) was another judgment the rebellious people brought down upon their own heads.

15:1–41 This chapter is divided into three units, each introduced by the phrase, "The LORD said to Moses" (vv. 1,17,37). The people were under terrible judgment because they had disobeyed the specific commands of the Lord and

had despised his character.

15:2 After you enter the land. The juxtaposition of this clause with the sad ending of ch. 14 is dramatic. The sins of the people were manifold; they would be judged. The grace and mercy of the Lord are magnified as he points to the ultimate realization of his ancient promise to Abraham (Ge 12:7), as well as to his continuing promise to the nation that they would indeed enter the land.

15:3–12 Grain and wine offerings were to accompany the offerings by fire; the grain was to be mixed with oil. The offerings increased in amounts with the increase of size of the sacrificial animal (vv. 6–12). These passages are the first to indicate that wine offerings must accompany all burnt and fellowship offerings.

15:14 alien. As in the case of the celebration of the Passover (see note on 9:14), the alien had the same regulations as the native-born Israelite. The commonwealth of Israel would

come,[d] whenever an alien[e] or anyone else living among you presents an offering[f] made by fire[g] as an aroma pleasing to the LORD, he must do exactly as you do. [15]The community is to have the same rules for you and for the alien living among you; this is a lasting ordinance for the generations to come.[h] You and the alien shall be the same before the LORD: [16]The same laws and regulations will apply both to you and to the alien living among you.[i] ' "

[17]The LORD said to Moses, [18]"Speak to the Israelites and say to them: 'When you enter the land to which I am taking you[j] [19]and you eat the food of the land,[k] present a portion as an offering to the LORD.[l] [20]Present a cake from the first of your ground meal[m] and present it as an offering from the threshing floor.[n o] [21]Throughout the generations to come[p] you are to give this offering to the LORD from the first of your ground meal.[q]

Offerings for Unintentional Sins

[22]" 'Now if you unintentionally fail to keep any of these commands the LORD gave Moses[r]— [23]any of the LORD's commands to you through him, from the day the LORD gave them and ·continuing through the generations to come[s]— [24]and if this is done unintentionally[t] without the community being aware of it,[u] then the whole community is to offer a young bull for a burnt offering[v] as an aroma pleasing to the LORD,[w] along with its prescribed grain offering[x] and drink offering,[y] and a male goat for a sin offering.[z] [25]The priest is to make atonement for the whole Israelite community, and they will be forgiven,[a] for it was not intentional[b] and they have brought to the LORD for their wrong an offering made by fire[c] and a sin offering.[d] [26]The whole Israelite community and the aliens living among them will be forgiven,

because all the people were involved in the unintentional wrong.[e]

[27]" 'But if just one person sins unintentionally,[f] he must bring a year-old female goat for a sin offering.[g] [28]The priest is to make atonement[h] before the LORD for the one who erred by sinning unintentionally, and when atonement has been made for him, he will be forgiven.[i] [29]One and the same law applies to everyone who sins unintentionally, whether he is a native-born Israelite or an alien.[j]

[30]" 'But anyone who sins defiantly,[k] whether native-born or alien,[l] blasphemes the LORD,[m] and that person must be cut off from his people.[n] [31]Because he has despised[o] the LORD's word and broken his commands,[p] that person must surely be cut off; his guilt remains on him.[q]' "

The Sabbath-Breaker Put to Death

[32]While the Israelites were in the desert,[r] a man was found gathering wood on the Sabbath day.[s] [33]Those who found him gathering wood brought him to Moses and Aaron and the whole assembly, [34]and they kept him in custody, because it was not clear what should be done to him.[t] [35]Then the LORD said to Moses, "The man must die.[u] The whole assembly must stone him outside the camp.[v]" [36]So the assembly took him outside the camp and stoned him[w] to death,[x] as the LORD commanded Moses.[y]

Tassels on Garments

[37]The LORD said to Moses, [38]"Speak to the Israelites and say to them: 'Throughout the generations to come[z] you are to make tassels on the corners of your garments,[a] with a blue cord on each tassel. [39]You will have these tassels to look at and so you

15:14 [d]Lev 3:17; Nu 10:8
[e]S Ex 12:19,43; S 22:21
[f]S Lev 22:18 [g]ver 25
15:15 [h]ver 14,21
15:16 [i]Ex 12:49; S Lev 22:18; Nu 9:14
15:18 [j]S Lev 23:10
15:19 [k]Jos 5:11, 12 [l]Nu 18:8
15:20 [m]S Lev 23:14 [n]S Lev 2:14; S Nu 18:27 [o]S Ge 50:10
15:21 [p]S Lev 23:14 [q]Eze 44:30; Ro 11:16
15:22 [r]S Lev 4:2
15:23 [s]ver 21
15:24 [t]ver 25,26 [u]S Lev 5:15 [v]Lev 4:14 [w]S ver 3 [x]Lev 2:1 [y]Lev 23:13; Nu 6:15 [z]Lev 4:3
15:25 [a]Lev 4:20; S Ro 3:25 [b]ver 22,S 24 [c]ver 14 [d]Lev 4:3
15:26 [e]S ver 24
15:27 [f]Lev 4:27 [g]Lev 4:3; Nu 6:14
15:28 [h]Nu 8:12; 28:22 [i]Lev 4:20
15:29 [j]S Ex 12:49
15:30 [k]Nu 14:40-44; Dt 1:43; 17:13; Ps 19:13 [l]ver 14 [m]2Ki 19:6,20; Isa 37:6,23; Eze 20:27 [n]S Ge 17:14; S Job 31:22
15:31 [o]S Nu 14:11 [p]1Sa 15:23,26; 2Sa 11:27; 12:9; Ps 119:126; Pr 13:13 [q]S Lev 5:1; Eze 18:20
15:32 [r]S Nu 12:16 [s]Ex 31:14,15; 35:2,3
15:34 [t]Nu 9:8
15:35 [u]Ex 31:14, 15 [v]S Lev 20:2; Lk 4:29; Ac 7:58
15:36 [w]S Lev 20:2

[x]S Ex 31:14 [y]Jer 17:21 15:38 [z]Lev 3:17; Nu 10:8 [a]Dt 22:12; Mt 23:5

---

always be open to proselytes. Indeed, the charter of Israel's faith embraces all peoples of the earth (Ge 12:3).

15:20 *Present a cake from the first.* This law also looks forward to the time when the Israelites would be in the land. The first of the threshed grain was to be made into a cake and presented to the Lord. This concept of the firstfruits is a symbol that all blessing is from the Lord and all produce belongs to him.

15:22 *unintentionally fail.* Sins may be unintentional, but they still need to be dealt with (see note on Lev 4:2). Such unintentional sins may be committed by the people as a whole (vv. 22–26) or by an individual (vv. 27–29).

15:30 *defiantly.* Lit. "with a high hand." Unlike unintentional sins, for which there are provisions of God's mercy, one who sets his hand defiantly to despise the word of God and to blaspheme his name must be punished. This was the experience of the nation in ch. 14, and it is described in the

case of an individual here in vv. 32–36. *cut off from his people.* See note on Ex 12:15.

15:32 *gathering wood on the Sabbath day.* The penalty for breaking the Sabbath was death (v. 36; Ex 31:15; 35:2). As in the case of the willful blasphemer (Lev 24:10–16), the Sabbath-breaker was guilty of high-handed rebellion (see note on v. 30) and was judged with death. By the time of Christ, Sabbath-keeping had become distorted to the point that its regulations were regarded as more important than the needs of people. Jesus confronted the Pharisees on this issue on several occasions (see, e.g., Mt 12:1–14). From their point of view, these regulations (vv. 32–36) gave them reasons to seek his death (Mt 12:14).

15:38 *tassels on the corners of your garments.* As one would walk along, the tassels would swirl about at the edge of his garment (cf. v. 39), serving as excellent memory prods to obey God's commands (cf. Dt 6:4–9).

will remember[b] all the commands of the
Lord, that you may obey them and not
prostitute yourselves[c] by going after the
lusts of your own hearts[d] and eyes. 40Then
you will remember to obey all my commands[e] and will be consecrated to your
God.[f] 41I am the Lord your God, who
brought you out of Egypt to be your God.[g]
I am the Lord your God.[h]' "

Korah, Dathan and Abiram

16 Korah[i] son of Izhar, the son of
Kohath, the son of Levi, and certain Reubenites—Dathan and Abiram[j],
sons of Eliab,[k] and On son of
Peleth—became insolent[l] 2and rose up
against Moses.[l] With them were 250 Israelite men, well-known community leaders
who had been appointed members of the
council.[m] 3They came as a group to oppose
Moses and Aaron[n] and said to them, "You
have gone too far! The whole community
is holy,[o] every one of them, and the Lord
is with them.[p] Why then do you set yourselves above the Lord's assembly?"[q]

4When Moses heard this, he fell facedown.[r] 5Then he said to Korah and all his
followers: "In the morning the Lord will
show who belongs to him and who is
holy,[s] and he will have that person come
near him.[t] The man he chooses[u] he will
cause to come near him. 6You, Korah, and
all your followers[v] are to do this: Take
censers[w] 7and tomorrow put fire[x] and incense[y] in them before the Lord. The man
the Lord chooses[z] will be the one who is
holy.[a] You Levites have gone too far!"

8Moses also said to Korah, "Now listen,
you Levites! 9Isn't it enough[b] for you that
the God of Israel has separated you from
the rest of the Israelite community and
brought you near himself to do the work at
the Lord's tabernacle and to stand before
the community and minister to them?[c]

10He has brought you and all your fellow
Levites near himself, but now you are trying to get the priesthood too.[d] 11It is
against the Lord that you and all your followers have banded together. Who is
Aaron that you should grumble[e] against
him?[f] "

12Then Moses summoned Dathan and
Abiram,[g] the sons of Eliab. But they said,
"We will not come![h] 13Isn't it enough that
you have brought us up out of a land flowing with milk and honey[i] to kill us in the
desert?[j] And now you also want to lord it
over us?[k] 14Moreover, you haven't
brought us into a land flowing with milk
and honey[l] or given us an inheritance of
fields and vineyards.[m] Will you gouge out
the eyes of[m] these men?[n] No, we will not
come![o] "

15Then Moses became very angry[p] and
said to the Lord, "Do not accept their offering. I have not taken so much as a donkey[q] from them, nor have I wronged any
of them."

16Moses said to Korah, "You and all
your followers are to appear before the
Lord tomorrow—you and they and
Aaron.[r] 17Each man is to take his censer
and put incense in it—250 censers in
all—and present it before the Lord. You
and Aaron are to present your censers
also.[s]" 18So each man took his censer,[t]
put fire and incense in it, and stood with
Moses and Aaron at the entrance to the
Tent of Meeting. 19When Korah had gathered all his followers in opposition to
them[u] at the entrance to the Tent of
Meeting, the glory of the Lord[v] appeared

15:39 bDt 4:23;
6:12; Ps 73:27
cS Lev 17:7;
Jdg 2:17;
Ps 106:39;
Jer 3:2; Hos 4:12
dPs 78:37;
Jer 7:24;
Eze 20:16
15:40
eS Ge 26:5;
Dt 11:13;
Ps 103:18;
119:56
fS Lev 11:44;
Ro 12:1;
Col 1:22;
1Pe 1:15
15:41 gS Ge 17:7
hS Ex 20:2
16:1 iS Ex 6:24;
Jude 1:11 jver 24;
Ps 106:17
kNu 26:8;
Dt 11:6
16:2 lNu 27:3
mNu 1:16; 26:9
16:3 nver 7;
Ps 106:16
oEx 19:6
pS Nu 14:14
qNu 12:2
16:4 rNu 14:5
16:5 sS Lev 10:3;
2Ti 2:19*
tJer 30:21
uNu 17:5;
Ps 65:4; 105:26;
Jer 50:44
16:6 vver 7,16
wS Lev 10:1;
Rev 8:3
16:7 xS Lev 10:1
yS Ex 30:9 zS ver
6 aver 5
16:9 bS Ge 30:15
cNu 3:6; Dt 10:8;
17:12; 21:5;
1Sa 2:11;
Ps 134:1;
Eze 44:11

16:10 dNu 3:10;
18:7; Jdg 17:5,12
1Co 10:10
16:11 ever 41;
fS Ex 16:7
16:12 gS ver 1,27
hver 14
16:13 iNu 13:27
jNu 14:2
kS Ge 13:8;
Ac 7:27,35
16:14
lS ver 6
mEx 22:5; 23:11;
Nu 20:5;
1Ki 4:25;
Ne 13:15;

Ps 105:33; Jer 5:17; Hos 2:12; Joel 2:22; Hag 2:19; Zec 3:10
nJdg 16:21; 1Sa 11:2; Jer 39:7 over 12 16:15 pS Ex 4:14
q1Sa 12:3 16:16 rS ver 6 16:17 sEze 8:11 16:18 tLev 10:1
16:19 uver 42; Nu 20:2 vS Ex 16:7; Nu 14:10; 20:6

1 l Or Peleth—took men   m 14 Or you make slaves
of; or you deceive

15:41 I am the Lord your God, who brought you out. The
demands that God made upon his people were grounded in
his act of redemption (see Ex 20:2 and note).
16:1–7 Earlier, Miriam and Aaron had led a rebellion
against the leadership of Moses (ch. 12). Now Korah and his
allies attack the leadership of Moses and Aaron. Korah was
descended from Levi through Kohath. As a Kohathite, he had
high duties in the service of the Lord at the tabernacle (see
4:1–20), but he desired more. His passion was to assume the
role of priest, and he used deception to advance his claim.
Korah was joined by the Reubenites, Dathan, Abiram and
On, and about 250 other leaders of Israel who had their own
complaints. Their charge was that Moses had "gone too far"
(v. 3) in taking the role of spiritual leadership of the people;
"the whole community is holy" (v. 3). To this abusive charge
Moses retorts, "You Levites have gone too far!" (v. 7), and
sets up a trial by fire.
16:12 Dathan and Abiram. Their charge against Moses

was that he had not led them into the land of promise. They
claimed that Moses had in fact led the people "out of a land
flowing with milk and honey" (v. 13). By this strange alche-
my, in their minds the land of Egypt has been transformed
from prison to paradise.

16:15 nor have I wronged any of them. Moses' humanity
is seen in his plea of innocence.

16:18–21 The trial was to be by fire: Which men would
the Lord accept as his priests in the holy tabernacle? The 250
men allied with Korah came with arrogance to withstand
Moses and Aaron at the entrance to the Tent of Meeting. The
revelation of the Lord's glory was sure and sudden (v. 19),
with words of impending doom for the rebellious people (v.
21). The punishment was fittingly ironic. Those 250 men
who dared to present themselves as priests before the Lord
with fire in their censers were themselves put to death by fire
(perhaps lightning) from the Lord (see v. 35).

to the entire assembly. [20]The LORD said to Moses and Aaron, [21]"Separate yourselves[w] from this assembly so I can put an end to them at once."[x]

[22]But Moses and Aaron fell facedown[y] and cried out, "O God, God of the spirits of all mankind,[z] will you be angry with the entire assembly[a] when only one man sins?"[b]

[23]Then the LORD said to Moses, [24]"Say to the assembly, 'Move away from the tents of Korah, Dathan and Abiram.'"

[25]Moses got up and went to Dathan and Abiram, and the elders of Israel[c] followed him. [26]He warned the assembly, "Move back from the tents of these wicked men![d] Do not touch anything belonging to them, or you will be swept away[e] because of all their sins.[f]" [27]So they moved away from the tents of Korah, Dathan and Abiram.[g] Dathan and Abiram had come out and were standing with their wives, children[h] and little ones at the entrances to their tents.[i]

[28]Then Moses said, "This is how you will know[j] that the LORD has sent me[k] to do all these things and that it was not my idea: [29]If these men die a natural death and experience only what usually happens to men, then the LORD has not sent me.[l] [30]But if the LORD brings about something totally new, and the earth opens its mouth[m] and swallows them, with everything that belongs to them, and they go down alive into the grave,[n][n] then you will know that these men have treated the LORD with contempt.[o]"

[31]As soon as he finished saying all this, the ground under them split apart[p] [32]and the earth opened its mouth and swallowed them,[q] with their households and all Korah's men and all their possessions. [33]They went down alive into the grave,[r] with everything they owned; the earth closed over them, and they perished and were gone from the community. [34]At their cries, all the Israelites around them fled,

shouting, "The earth is going to swallow us too!"

[35]And fire came out from the LORD[s] and consumed[t] the 250 men who were offering the incense.

[36]The LORD said to Moses, [37]"Tell Eleazar[u] son of Aaron, the priest, to take the censers[v] out of the smoldering remains and scatter the coals some distance away, for the censers are holy— [38]the censers of the men who sinned at the cost of their lives.[w] Hammer the censers into sheets to overlay the altar,[x] for they were presented before the LORD and have become holy. Let them be a sign[y] to the Israelites."

[39]So Eleazar the priest[z] collected the bronze censers brought by those who had been burned up,[a] and he had them hammered out to overlay the altar, [40]as the LORD directed him through Moses. This was to remind the Israelites that no one except a descendant of Aaron should come to burn incense[b] before the LORD,[c] or he would become like Korah and his followers.[d]

[41]The next day the whole Israelite community grumbled against Moses and Aaron. "You have killed the LORD's people," they said.

[42]But when the assembly gathered in opposition[e] to Moses and Aaron and turned toward the Tent of Meeting, suddenly the cloud covered it and the glory of the LORD[f] appeared. [43]Then Moses and Aaron went to the front of the Tent of Meeting, [44]and the LORD said to Moses, [45]"Get away from this assembly so I can put an end[g] to them at once." And they fell facedown.

[46]Then Moses said to Aaron, "Take your censer[h] and put incense in it, along with fire from the altar, and hurry to the assembly[i] to make atonement[j] for them. Wrath has come out from the LORD;[k] the

---

16:21 [w]ver 24; [x]S Ge 19:14; S Ex 32:10
16:22 [y]S Nu 14:5; [z]Nu 27:16; Job 12:10; 27:8; 33:4; 34:14; Jer 32:27; Eze 18:4; Heb 12:9; [a]S Lev 10:6; [b]S Ge 18:23; S Job 21:20
16:25 [c]S Ex 19:7
16:26 [d]Isa 52:11; [e]S Ge 19:15; [f]Jer 51:6
16:27 [g]S ver 12; [h]ver 32; Jos 7:24; Isa 13:16; 14:21; [i]S Ex 33:8
16:28 [j]1Ki 18:36; [k]Ex 3:12; Jn 5:36; 6:38
16:29 [l]Nu 24:13; Job 31:2; Ecc 3:19
16:30 [m]Ps 141:7; Isa 5:14 [n]ver 33; S Ge 37:35; 1Sa 2:6; Job 5:26; 21:13; Ps 9:17; 16:10; 55:15; Isa 14:11; 38:18; [o]S Nu 14:11; S Eze 26:20
16:31 [p]Isa 64:1-2; Eze 47:1-12; Mic 1:3-4; Zec 14:4
16:32 [q]S Ex 15:12
16:33 [r]S ver 30; S Ecc 9:10
16:35 [s]S Nu 11:1-3; 26:10; Rev 11:5 [t]S Lev 10:2
16:37 [u]S Ex 6:23 [v]ver 6
16:38 [w]Lev 10:1; Pr 20:2 [x]S Ex 20:24; 38:1-7 [y]Nu 26:10; Dt 28:46; Jer 44:29; Eze 14:8; 2Pe 2:6
16:39 [z]2Ch 26:18 [a]S Lev 20:14
16:40 [b]S Ex 30:1; 2Ki 12:3; Isa 1:13; 66:3; Jer 41:5; 44:3 [c]S Ex 30:9; 2Ch 26:18 [d]S Nu 3:10
16:42 [e]S ver 19 [f]Ex 16:7; Nu 14:10
16:45 [g]S Ex 32:10

16:46 [h]S Lev 10:1 [i]Lev 10:6 [j]S Ex 29:36 [k]S Nu 1:53

[n]30 Hebrew Sheol; also in verse 33

16:22 Here the magnanimity of Moses and Aaron is seen.
16:24 Move away. God's judgment was going to be severe, but he did not want to lash out against bystanders. It appears that Korah had left the 250 false priests and was standing with Dathan and Abiram to continue their opposition to Moses.
16:30 something totally new. Moses wished to assure the people that the imminent judgment was the direct work of the Lord and not a chance event that might be interpreted differently. The opening of the earth to swallow the rebels was a sure sign of the wrath of God and the vindication of Moses and Aaron.
16:32 swallowed them, with their households. The sons of

Korah did not die (26:11); apparently they did not join their father in his rash plan. The households of the other rebels died with them.
16:37 take the censers. The true priests took the censers of the 250 deceased impostors from their charred remains and hammered them into bronze sheets for the altar as a memorial of the folly of a self-proclaimed priest (v. 40).
16:41 the whole Israelite community grumbled. Again the community attacked Moses, unfairly charging him with the death of the Lord's people. Except for the intervention of Moses and Aaron (see vv. 4,22), the entire nation might have been destroyed because of their continued rebellion (see v. 45).

plague[l] has started." [47]So Aaron did as Moses said, and ran into the midst of the assembly. The plague had already started among the people,[m] but Aaron offered the incense and made atonement for them. [48]He stood between the living and the dead, and the plague stopped.[n] [49]But 14,-700 people died from the plague, in addition to those who had died because of Korah.[o] [50]Then Aaron returned to Moses at the entrance to the Tent of Meeting, for the plague had stopped.

The Budding of Aaron's Staff

17 The LORD said to Moses, [2]"Speak to the Israelites and get twelve staffs[p] from them, one from the leader of each of their ancestral tribes.[q] Write the name of each man on his staff. [3]On the staff of Levi write Aaron's name,[r] for there must be one staff for the head of each ancestral tribe. [4]Place them in the Tent of Meeting[s] in front of the Testimony,[t] where I meet with you.[u] [5]The staff belonging to the man I choose[v] will sprout,[w] and I will rid myself of this constant grumbling[x] against you by the Israelites."

[6]So Moses spoke to the Israelites, and their leaders gave him twelve staffs, one for the leader of each of their ancestral tribes, and Aaron's staff was among them. [7]Moses placed the staffs before the LORD in the Tent of the Testimony.[y]

[8]The next day Moses entered the Tent of the Testimony[z] and saw that Aaron's staff,[a] which represented the house of Levi, had not only sprouted but had budded, blossomed and produced almonds.[b]

[9]Then Moses brought out all the staffs[c] from the LORD's presence to all the Israelites. They looked at them, and each man took his own staff.

[10]The LORD said to Moses, "Put back Aaron's staff[d] in front of the Testimony, to be kept as a sign to the rebellious.[e] This will put an end to their grumbling against me, so that they will not die." [11]Moses did just as the LORD commanded him.

[12]The Israelites said to Moses, "We will die! We are lost, we are all lost![f] [13]Anyone who even comes near the tabernacle of the LORD will die.[g] Are we all going to die?"

Duties of Priests and Levites

18 The LORD said to Aaron, "You, your sons and your father's family are to bear the responsibility for offenses against the sanctuary,[h] and you and your sons alone are to bear the responsibility for offenses against the priesthood. [2]Bring your fellow Levites from your ancestral tribe to join you and assist you when you and your sons minister[i] before the Tent of the Testimony. [3]They are to be responsible to you[j] and are to perform all the duties of the Tent,[k] but they must not go near the furnishings of the sanctuary or the altar, or both they and you will die.[l] [4]They are to join you and be responsible for the care of the Tent of Meeting—all the work at the Tent—and no one else may come near where you are.[m]

[5]"You are to be responsible for the care of the sanctuary and the altar,[n] so that wrath will not fall on the Israelites again. [6]I myself have selected your fellow Levites

Cross references (center column)

16:46 /S Lev 26:25; Nu 8:19; Ps 106:29
16:47 mNu 25:6-8
16:48 nNu 25:8; Ps 106:30
16:49 over 32
17:2 pS Ge 32:10; S Ex 4:2 qNu 1:4
17:3 rS Nu 1:3
17:4 sS Ex 40:2 tver 7; S Ex 16:34 uEx 25:22
17:5 vS Nu 16:5 wver 8 xS Ex 16:7
17:7 yS Ex 38:21
17:8 zver 7; Nu 1:50 aver 2,10 bEze 17:24; Heb 9:4

17:9 cver 2
17:10 dS ver 8 eS Ex 23:21; Dt 9:24; Ps 66:7; 68:18; Pr 24:21
17:12 fJdg 13:22; Isa 6:5; 15:1
17:13 gNu 1:51
18:1 hS Ex 28:38
18:2 iNu 3:10
18:3 jS Nu 3:32 kNu 1:51 lver 7
18:4 mS Nu 3:38
18:5 nver 3; Lev 6:12

16:49 *14,700 people died.* The number makes sense only if the community is as large as the census lists of ch. 2 suggest.

17:1–13 This story follows the account of the divine judgment of Korah (16:1–35) and the narrative of the symbolic use given to the censers of the rebels and its aftermath (16:36–50). Ch. 17 is thus the third in a series of accounts vindicating the Aaronic priesthood against all opposition. The selection of 12 staffs, one from each tribe, was a symbolic act whereby the divine choice of Aaron would be indicated again.

17:3 *On the staff of Levi write Aaron's name.* The test needed to be unequivocal because of the wide support given to Korah's rebellion. The 250 who had joined with Korah were from many, perhaps all, of the tribes.

17:4 *in front of the Testimony.* In front of the ark, with the Ten Commandments, thus probably in the Holy Place, near the altar of incense.

17:8 *had not only sprouted but had budded, blossomed and produced almonds.* God exceeded the demands of the test so that there might be no uncertainty as to who had acted or what he intended by his action.

17:10 *in front of the Testimony.* Aaron's rod joined the stone tablets of the law of Moses (see note on Ex 25:16) and the jar of manna (Ex 16:33–34) within or near the ark of the

covenant (see Heb 9:4). These holy symbols were ever before the Lord as memorials of his special deeds in behalf of his people. Moreover, should anyone of a later age dare to question the unique and holy place of the Aaronic priests in the Lord's service, this symbolic memorial of God's choice of Aaron would stand in opposition to his audacity. It is difficult to overestimate the importance of the role of Aaron and his sons in the worship of Israel (see note on 18:1–7).

17:12 *We will die!* At last the people realized the sin of their arrogance in challenging Aaron's role. The appropriate ways of approaching the Lord are detailed in chs. 18–19.

18:1–7 Aaron and his family, chosen by the Lord to be the true priests of holy worship, faced a burdensome task. The lament of the people in 17:12–13 was real; grievous sins against the holy meeting place of the Lord and his people would be judged by death. The Lord's mercy in providing a legitimate priesthood was actually an aspect of his grace (cf. Ps 99:6–8), because it was the people's only hope for deliverance from judgment.

18:2 *Bring your fellow Levites.* The Aaronic priests were to be assisted by the others in the tribe of Levi, but the assistants were not to go beyond their serving role. If they did so, not only would they die, but so would the priests who were responsible (v. 3).

from among the Israelites as a gift to you,[o] dedicated to the LORD to do the work at the Tent of Meeting.[p] [7]But only you and your sons may serve as priests in connection with everything at the altar and inside the curtain.[q] I am giving you the service of the priesthood as a gift.[r] Anyone else who comes near the sanctuary must be put to death.[s]"

Offerings for Priests and Levites

[8]Then the LORD said to Aaron, "I myself have put you in charge of the offerings presented to me; all the holy offerings the Israelites give me I give to you and your sons as your portion[t] and regular share.[u] [9]You are to have the part of the most holy offerings[v] that is kept from the fire. From all the gifts they bring me as most holy offerings, whether grain[w] or sin[x] or guilt offerings,[y] that part belongs to you and your sons. [10]Eat it as something most holy; every male shall eat it.[z] You must regard it as holy.[a]

[11]"This also is yours: whatever is set aside from the gifts of all the wave offerings[b] of the Israelites. I give this to you and your sons and daughters as your regular share.[c] Everyone in your household who is ceremonially clean[d] may eat it.

[12]"I give you all the finest olive oil and all the finest new wine and grain[e] they give the LORD[g] as the firstfruits of their harvest.[g] [13]All the land's firstfruits that they bring to the LORD will be yours.[h] Everyone in your household who is ceremonially clean may eat it.[i]

[14]"Everything in Israel that is devoted[o] to the LORD[j] is yours. [15]The first offspring of every womb, both man and animal, that is offered to the LORD is yours.[k] But you must redeem[l] every firstborn[m] son and every firstborn male of unclean animals.[n] [16]When they are a month old,[o] you must redeem them at the redemption price set

at five shekels[p] of silver, according to the sanctuary shekel,[q] which weighs twenty gerahs.[r]

[17]"But you must not redeem the firstborn of an ox, a sheep or a goat; they are holy.[s] Sprinkle their blood[t] on the altar and burn their fat[u] as an offering made by fire, an aroma pleasing to the LORD.[v] [18]Their meat is to be yours, just as the breast of the wave offering[w] and the right thigh are yours.[x] [19]Whatever is set aside from the holy[y] offerings the Israelites present to the LORD I give to you and your sons and daughters as your regular share. It is an everlasting covenant of salt[z] before the LORD for both you and your offspring."

[20]The LORD said to Aaron, "You will have no inheritance in their land, nor will you have any share among them;[a] I am your share and your inheritance[b] among the Israelites.

[21]"I give to the Levites all the tithes[c] in Israel as their inheritance[d] in return for the work they do while serving at the Tent of Meeting.[e] [22]From now on the Israelites must not go near the Tent of Meeting, or they will bear the consequences of their sin and will die.[f] [23]It is the Levites who are to do the work at the Tent of Meeting and bear the responsibility for offenses against it. This is a lasting ordinance[g] for the generations to come.[h] They will receive no inheritance[i] among the Israelites.[j] [24]Instead, I give to the Levites as their inheritance the tithes that the Israelites present as an offering to the LORD.[k] That is why I said concerning them: 'They will have no inheritance among the Israelites.'"

[25]The LORD said to Moses, [26]"Speak to

18:6 [o]S Nu 3:9 [p]Nu 3:8
18:7 [q]Heb 9:3,6 [r]ver 20; Ex 29:9; 40:13; Heb 5:4 [s]ver 3; Nu 3:10
18:8 [t]S Lev 2:2 [u]Lev 6:16; 7:6, 31-34,36; Dt 18:1; 2Ch 31:4
18:9 [v]S Lev 6:17 [w]Lev 2:1 [x]Lev 6:25 [y]S Lev 5:15
18:10 [z]S Lev 6:16 [a]Lev 6:17,18
18:11 [b]Ex 29:26; Lev 7:30; Nu 6:20 [c]Lev 7:31-34 [d]Lev 13:3; 22:1-16
18:12 [e]Dt 7:13; 11:14; 12:17; 28:51; 2Ki 18:32; 2Ch 31:5; Ne 10:37; Jer 31:12; Eze 23:41; Hos 2:8; Joel 1:10; Hag 1:11 [f]S Ge 4:3 [g]Ex 23:19; 34:26; Ne 10:35
18:13 [h]S Ex 29:27 [i]ver 11
18:14 [j]S Lev 27:21; Jos 6:17-19
18:15 [k]Ex 13:2 [l]S Nu 3:46 [m]S Ge 10:15 [n]S Ex 13:13
18:16 [o]S Nu 3:15

[p]S Lev 27:6 [q]S Ex 30:13 [r]Nu 3:47
18:17 [s]S Lev 27:9 [t]S Lev 3:2 [u]S Ex 29:13 [v]S Lev 1:9
18:18 [w]Lev 7:30 [x]ver 11
18:19 [y]2Ki 12:4 [z]S Lev 2:13
18:20 [a]Nu 26:62; Dt 12:12 [b]ver 24; Dt 10:9; 14:27; 18:1-2; Jos 13:33; Eze 44:28
18:21 [c]ver 24; S Ge 28:22; Nu 31:28; Dt 14:22; Ne 10:37; 13:5;

Mal 3:8 [d]Lev 27:30-33; Heb 7:5 [e]Nu 1:53 **18:22** [f]S Ex 28:43
18:23 [g]S Ex 12:14; S 27:21 [h]Nu 10:8 [i]ver 20; Nu 26:62; Dt 10:9 [j]Eze 44:10 **18:24** [k]Lev 27:30; Dt 26:12

[o]*14* The Hebrew term refers to the irrevocable giving over of things or persons to the LORD. [p]*16* That is, about 2 ounces (about 55 grams)

18:7 *the service of the priesthood as a gift.* Of all men, the priests were privileged to approach the Holy Place and minister before the Lord. The priesthood was a gift of God's grace to both priests and people.
18:8 *your portion and regular share.* The priests were to be supported in their work of ministry (see Lev 6:14–7:36). Since the Levites as a whole and the priests in particular had no part in the land that God was going to give them, it was necessary that the means for their provision be spelled out fully. They were not to have a part in the land; their share was the Lord himself (v. 20).
18:11 *your sons and daughters.* Provision was made not only for the priests, but for their families as well. Only family members who were ceremonially unclean were forbidden to eat the gifts and offerings of the people (see v. 13). Provisions for cleansing were stated in Lev 22:4–8.

18:12 *finest olive oil . . . finest new wine and grain.* Since the best items of produce were to be given to the Lord, these became the special foods of the priests and their families. The NT writers similarly argue that those who minister the word of God in the present period should also be paid suitably for their work (see, e.g., 1Co 9:3–10 and notes).
18:19 *everlasting covenant of salt.* A permanent provision for the priests. The phrase "covenant of salt" (see 2Ch 13:5) remains obscure. In Lev 2:13 the salt that must accompany grain offerings is called the "salt of the covenant." According to Eze 43:24, salt is also to be sprinkled on burnt offerings, and Ex 30:35 specifies salt as one of the ingredients in the special incense compounded for the sanctuary. A "covenant of salt" is perhaps an allusion to the salt used in the sacrificial meal that commonly accompanied the making of a covenant (see Ge 31:54; Ex 24:5–11; Ps 50:5).

the Levites and say to them: 'When you receive from the Israelites the tithe I give you[l] as your inheritance, you must present a tenth of that tithe as the LORD's offering.[m] 27Your offering will be reckoned[n] to you as grain from the threshing floor[o] or juice from the winepress.[p] 28In this way you also will present an offering to the LORD from all the tithes[q] you receive from the Israelites. From these tithes you must give the LORD's portion to Aaron the priest. 29You must present as the LORD's portion the best and holiest part of everything given to you.'

30"Say to the Levites: 'When you present the best part, it will be reckoned to you as the product of the threshing floor or the winepress.[r] 31You and your households may eat the rest of it anywhere, for it is your wages for your work at the Tent of Meeting.[s] 32By presenting the best part[t] of it you will not be guilty in this matter;[u] then you will not defile the holy offerings[v] of the Israelites, and you will not die.' "

The Water of Cleansing

19 The LORD said to Moses and Aaron: 2"This is a requirement of the law that the LORD has commanded: Tell the Israelites to bring you a red heifer[w] without defect or blemish[x] and that has never been under a yoke.[y] 3Give it to Eleazar[z] the priest; it is to be taken outside the camp[a] and slaughtered in his presence. 4Then Eleazar the priest is to take some of its blood on his finger and sprinkle[b] it seven times toward the front of the Tent of Meeting. 5While he watches, the heifer is to be burned—its hide, flesh, blood and offal.[c] 6The priest is to take some cedar wood, hyssop[d] and scarlet wool[e] and throw them onto the burning

heifer. 7After that, the priest must wash his clothes and bathe himself with water.[f] He may then come into the camp, but he will be ceremonially unclean till evening. 8The man who burns it must also wash his clothes and bathe with water, and he too will be unclean till evening.

9"A man who is clean shall gather up the ashes of the heifer[g] and put them in a ceremonially clean place[h] outside the camp. They shall be kept by the Israelite community for use in the water of cleansing;[i] it is for purification from sin.[j] 10The man who gathers up[k] the ashes of the heifer must also wash his clothes, and he too will be unclean till evening.[l] This will be a lasting ordinance[m] both for the Israelites and for the aliens living among them.[n]

11"Whoever touches the dead body[o] of anyone will be unclean for seven days.[p] 12He must purify himself with the water on the third day and on the seventh day;[q] then he will be clean. But if he does not purify himself on the third and seventh days, he will not be clean.[r] 13Whoever touches the dead body[s] of anyone and fails to purify himself defiles the LORD's tabernacle.[t] That person must be cut off from Israel.[u] Because the water of cleansing has not been sprinkled on him, he is unclean;[v] his uncleanness remains on him.

14"This is the law that applies when a person dies in a tent: Anyone who enters the tent and anyone who is in it will be unclean for seven days, 15and every open container[w] without a lid fastened on it will be unclean.

16"Anyone out in the open who touches someone who has been killed with a sword or someone who has died a natural death,[x] or anyone who touches a human

---

Cross references (center column):

18:26 [l]ver 21
[m]ver 28;
Ne 10:38
18:27 [n]Lev 7:18
[o]Ge 50:10;
Dt 15:14;
Jdg 6:37; Ru 3:3,
6,14; 1Sa 23:1
[p]ver 12,30
18:28 [q]Mal 3:8
18:30 [r]S ver 27
18:31 [s]ver 23
18:32 [t]Lev 22:15
[u]ver 29
[v]S Lev 19:8
19:2 [w]S Ge 15:9;
Heb 9:13
[x]S Lev 22:19-25
[y]Dt 21:3; 1Sa 6:7
19:3 [z]Nu 3:4
[a]S Ex 29:14
19:4 [b]S Lev 4:17
19:5 [c]S Ex 29:14
19:6 [d]ver 18;
Ps 51:7
[e]S Lev 14:4

19:7
[f]S Lev 11:25;
S 14:8
19:9 [g]Heb 9:13
[h]S Ex 29:31;
S Lev 4:12 [i]ver
13; Nu 8:7
[j]S Ge 35:2
19:10 [k]Lev 15:10
[l]Lev 14:46
[m]Lev 3:17
[n]S Lev 22:18
19:11
[o]S Lev 21:1
[p]S Lev 8:33;
Nu 31:19
19:12 [q]ver 19;
Nu 31:19 [r]ver 20;
2Ch 26:21
19:13
[s]S Lev 21:11
[t]S Lev 15:31;
2Ch 36:14;
Ps 79:1
[u]Lev 7:20; 22:3
[v]ver 22; Hag 2:13
19:15
[w]S Lev 6:28
19:16 [x]Nu 31:19

18:26–32 Although the Levites were the recipients of the tithe given to the Lord, they were not themselves exempt from worshiping God by tithing. They in turn were to give a tenth of their income to Aaron (v. 28) and were to be sure that the best part was given as the Lord's portion (v. 29). By obedient compliance the Levites would escape judicial death (v. 32).

19:2 *red heifer.* The qualifying words, "without defect or blemish," are familiar in contexts of sacrificial worship in the OT. But this is not a sacrificial animal. It is a cow, not an ox; it is to be slaughtered, not sacrificed; and it is to be killed outside the camp, not at the holy altar. The ashes of the red heifer (v. 9) are the primary focus of this act, for they will be used in the ritual of the water of cleansing. The burning of the animal with its blood and offal (v. 5) is unprecedented in the OT. The normal pattern for the sacrifice of the burnt offering is given in Lev 1:3–9. In every respect the killing of the red heifer is distinct: A female animal was taken outside the camp to be killed; the priest had to be present, but he did

not identify himself with it; and a bit of the heifer's blood was sprinkled from the priest's finger toward the tabernacle seven times, but the rest of the animal was to be burned in its entirety, without the draining of its blood or the cleansing of its offal.

19:6 *cedar wood, hyssop and scarlet wool.* Associated with the cleansing properties of the ashes of the red heifer.

19:12 *purify himself with the water.* The ashes from the red heifer were kept outside the camp and would be mixed as needed with water to provide a means of cleansing after contact with dead bodies.

19:13 *defiles the LORD's tabernacle.* Willful neglect of the provision for cleansing brought not only judgment on the person, but also a pollution of the tabernacle itself. *cut off from Israel.* See note on Ex 12:15.

19:14 *anyone who is in it.* There would be many occasions in which a person would become unclean, not because of deliberate contact with a dead body, but just by being in the proximity of one who died.

bone[y] or a grave,[z] will be unclean for seven days.[a]

[17]"For the unclean person, put some ashes[b] from the burned purification offering into a jar and pour fresh water[c] over them. [18]Then a man who is ceremonially clean is to take some hyssop,[d] dip it in the water and sprinkle[e] the tent and all the furnishings and the people who were there. He must also sprinkle anyone who has touched a human bone or a grave[f] or someone who has been killed or someone who has died a natural death. [19]The man who is clean is to sprinkle[g] the unclean person on the third and seventh days, and on the seventh day he is to purify him.[h] The person being cleansed must wash his clothes[i] and bathe with water, and that evening he will be clean. [20]But if a person who is unclean does not purify himself, he must be cut off from the community, because he has defiled[j] the sanctuary of the LORD.[k] The water of cleansing has not been sprinkled on him, and he is unclean.[l] [21]This is a lasting ordinance[m] for them.

"The man who sprinkles the water of cleansing must also wash his clothes, and anyone who touches the water of cleansing will be unclean till evening. [22]Anything that an unclean[n] person touches becomes unclean, and anyone who touches it becomes unclean till evening."

Water From the Rock

20 In the first month the whole Israelite community arrived at the Desert of Zin,[o] and they stayed at Ka-

desh.[p] There Miriam[q] died and was buried.

[2]Now there was no water[r] for the community,[s] and the people gathered in opposition[t] to Moses and Aaron. [3]They quarreled[u] with Moses and said, "If only we had died when our brothers fell dead[v] before the LORD![w] [4]Why did you bring the LORD's community into this desert,[x] that we and our livestock should die here?[y] [5]Why did you bring us up out of Egypt to this terrible place? It has no grain or figs, grapevines or pomegranates.[z] And there is no water to drink![a]"

[6]Moses and Aaron went from the assembly to the entrance to the Tent of Meeting[b] and fell facedown,[c] and the glory of the LORD[d] appeared to them. [7]The LORD said to Moses, [8]"Take the staff,[e] and you and your brother Aaron gather the assembly together. Speak to that rock before their eyes and it will pour out its water.[f] You will bring water out of the rock for the community so they and their livestock can drink."

[9]So Moses took the staff[g] from the LORD's presence,[h] just as he commanded him. [10]He and Aaron gathered the assembly together[i] in front of the rock and Moses said to them, "Listen, you rebels, must we bring you water out of this rock?"[j] [11]Then Moses raised his arm and struck the rock twice with his staff. Water[k] gushed out, and the community and their livestock drank.

[12]But the LORD said to Moses and

Cross references (center column)

19:16 [y]1Ki 13:2; 2Ki 23:14; Eze 6:5
19:17 [z]2Ki 23:6; Mt 23:27; [a]S Lev 5:3; [b]ver 9; [c]S Nu 8:7
19:18 [d]S ver 6; S Ex 12:22; [e]S Lev 4:17 /ver 16
19:19 [g]S Lev 16:14-15; [h]Nu 31:19; Eze 36:25; Heb 10:22; [i]S Ge 35:2
19:20 /Ps 74:7; [k]S Lev 15:31; /S ver 12; S Lev 14:8
19:21 [m]S Ex 27:21
19:22 [n]S Lev 5:2; 15:4-12
20:1 [o]Nu 13:21
[p]ver 14; Nu 13:26; 33:36; Dt 1:46; Jdg 11:17; Ps 29:8
20:2 [q]S Ex 15:20; [r]S Ex 15:22
20:3 [s]Ex 17:1; [t]S Nu 16:19; [u]ver 13; S Ge 13:7; Ex 17:2; 21:18
20:4 [v]S Ex 5:21; [w]S Nu 14:2; 16:31-35; [x]S Nu 14:2; [y]S Ex 14:11; Nu 14:3; 16:13
20:5 [z]Nu 13:23; 16:14; [a]S Ex 17:1
20:6 [b]S Ex 40:2; [c]Nu 14:5; [d]S Nu 16:19
20:8 [e]S Ex 4:2; S 10:12-13; /Ex 17:6; Isa 41:18; 43:20; Jer 31:9
20:9 [g]Nu 17:2; [h]Nu 17:10
20:10 /ver 8; /Ps 106:32,33
20:11 [k]S Ex 17:6; S Isa 33:21

19:18 *hyssop, dip it in the water and sprinkle.* Here the method of the cleansing ritual is explained. A ceremonially clean person had to sprinkle the ceremonially unclean person or thing. The cleansing power of the blood of Christ is specifically contrasted ("much more"; Heb 9:13–14) with the cleansing effectiveness of the water of the ashes of the red heifer. *cut off from his people.* See note on Lev 7:20.
20:1–29 This chapter begins with the death of Miriam (v. 1), concludes with the death of Aaron (v. 28), includes the record of the conflict with Edom (vv. 14–21) and centers on the tragic sin of Moses (vv. 11–12). Such was the sad beginning of Israel's last year in the desert.
20:1 *first month.* The year is not given, but a comparison of vv. 22–29 with 33:38 leads to the conclusion that this chapter begins in the 40th year after the exodus (see notes on 1:1; 9:1). Most of the people 20 years old or more at the time of the rebellion at Kadesh (chs. 13–14) would already have died. *at Kadesh.* The larger part of the desert wandering is left without record. The people may have gone through a cycle of roving travels, seeking the water sources and the sparse vegetation, supported primarily by manna. But their circuits would bring them back to the central camp at Kadesh, the scene of their great rebellion (chs. 13–14). They have now come full circle; the land of promise lies before them again.

20:2 *no water.* Forty years earlier, the Lord had instructed Moses to take the staff he had used to strike the Nile (Ex 7:17) and to strike the rock at Horeb to initiate a flow of water (Ex 17:1–7). Now, 40 years later, at the place of Israel's worst acts of rebellion, the scene was recurring. The children of the rebellious nation now desire to die with their parents; the complaints about the bread from heaven are repeated by the sons.
20:8 *Speak to that rock.* Moses was told to take his staff, through which God had performed wonders in Egypt and in the desert all these years, but this time he was merely to speak to the rock and it would pour out its water for the people. Cf. Ps 114:8.
20:10 *Listen, you rebels.* At once the accumulated anger, exasperation and frustration of 40 years came to expression (see Ps 106:33).
20:11 *struck the rock twice with his staff.* In his rage Moses disobeyed the Lord's instruction to speak to the rock (v. 8). Moses' rash action brought a stern rebuke from the Lord (v. 12). The nature of Moses' offense is not clearly stated in this text, but these factors appear to be involved: 1. Moses' action was a lack of trust in God (v. 12), as though he believed that a word alone would not suffice. 2. God's holiness was offended by Moses' rash action (v. 12), for he had not shown proper deference to God's presence.

Aaron, "Because you did not trust in me enough to honor me as holy[l] in the sight of the Israelites, you will not bring this community into the land I give them."[m]

13These were the waters of Meribah,[q n] where the Israelites quarreled[o] with the LORD and where he showed himself holy among them.[p]

Edom Denies Israel Passage

14Moses sent messengers from Kadesh[q] to the king of Edom,[r] saying:

"This is what your brother Israel says: You know[s] about all the hardships[t] that have come upon us. 15Our forefathers went down into Egypt,[u] and we lived there many years.[v] The Egyptians mistreated[w] us and our fathers, 16but when we cried out to the LORD, he heard our cry[x] and sent an angel[y] and brought us out of Egypt.[z]

"Now we are here at Kadesh, a town on the edge of your territory.[a] 17Please let us pass through your country. We will not go through any field or vineyard, or drink water from any well. We will travel along the king's highway and not turn to the right or to the left until we have passed through your territory.[b]"

18But Edom[c] answered:

"You may not pass through here; if you try, we will march out and attack you with the sword.[d]"

19The Israelites replied:

"We will go along the main road, and if we or our livestock[e] drink any of your water, we will pay for it.[f] We only want to pass through on foot—nothing else."

20Again they answered:

"You may not pass through.[g]"

Then Edom[h] came out against them with a large and powerful army. 21Since Edom refused to let them go through their territory,[i] Israel turned away from them.[j]

The Death of Aaron

22The whole Israelite community set out from Kadesh[k] and came to Mount Hor.[l] 23At Mount Hor, near the border of Edom,[m] the LORD said to Moses and Aaron, 24"Aaron will be gathered to his people.[n] He will not enter the land I give the Israelites, because both of you rebelled against my command[o] at the waters of Meribah.[p] 25Get Aaron and his son Eleazar and take them up Mount Hor.[q] 26Remove Aaron's garments[r] and put them on his son Eleazar, for Aaron will be gathered to his people;[s] he will die there."

27Moses did as the LORD commanded: They went up Mount Hor[t] in the sight of the whole community. 28Moses removed Aaron's garments and put them on his son Eleazar.[u] And Aaron died there[v] on top of the mountain. Then Moses and Eleazar came down from the mountain, 29and when the whole community learned that Aaron had died,[w] the entire house of Israel mourned for him[x] thirty days.

Arad Destroyed

21 When the Canaanite king of Arad,[y] who lived in the Negev,[z]

20:12 [l]Nu 27:14; Dt 32:51; Isa 5:16; 8:13
[m]ver 24; Dt 1:37; 3:27
20:13 [n]S Ex 17:7
[o]S ver 3
[p]S Lev 10:3
20:14 [q]S ver 1
[r]S ver 16;
S Ge 25:30;
S 36:16 [s]Ge 24:3;
Dt 4:39; Jos 2:11;
9:9 [t]S Ex 18:8
20:15 [u]S Ge 46:6
[v]S Ge 15:13
[w]S Ex 1:14
20:16
[x]S Ge 16:11;
S 21:17;
S Ex 2:23
[y]Ex 14:19
[z]Ex 12:42;
Dt 26:8 [a]ver 14, 23; Nu 33:37
20:17 [b]ver 20; Nu 21:22;
Dt 2:27;
Jdg 11:17
20:18 [c]ver 14
[d]Nu 21:23
20:19 [e]Ex 12:38
[f]Dt 2:6,28

20:20 [g]S ver 17, 18 [h]ver 14
20:21 [i]Nu 21:23
[j]Nu 21:4; Dt 2:8;
Jdg 11:18
20:22 [k]Dt 1:46
[l]Nu 33:37; 34:7;
Dt 32:50
20:23 [m]S ver 16
20:24 [n]S Ge 25:8
[o]S ver 10
[p]S Ex 17:7
20:25 [q]Nu 33:38
20:26
[r]Ex 28:1-4;
40:13; S Lev 16:4
[s]ver 24;
Nu 27:13; 31:2
20:27 [t]Nu 33:38
20:28
[u]S Ex 29:29 [v]ver 26; Nu 33:38;
Dt 10:6; 32:50
20:29 [w]Dt 32:50
[x]S Ge 27:41;
S Lev 10:6;
S Dt 34:8
21:1 [y]Nu 33:40;
Jos 12:14
[z]S Ge 12:9;

Nu 13:17; Dt 1:7; Jdg 1:9,16

[q]13 Meribah means quarreling.

20:12 *you will not bring this community into the land.* The end result of Moses' action is sure: Neither Aaron nor Moses would enter the land of promise. Of their contemporaries only Joshua and Caleb would survive to enter the land. The inclusion of Aaron demonstrates his partnership with his brother in the breach against God's holiness.
20:13 *Meribah.* See NIV text note. The same name was used 40 years earlier at the first occasion of bringing water from the rock (Ex 17:7, where it is also called Massah, "testing"). Ps 95:8 laments the rebellion at Meribah and Massah.
20:14–21 Moses' attempt to pass through the territory of Edom by peaceful negotiation and payment for services rendered is met by arrogant rebuff.
20:14 *your brother Israel.* The people of Edom were descended from Esau, the brother of Jacob (see Ge 36:1).
20:17 *king's highway.* The major north-south trade route in Transjordan, extending from Arabia to Damascus.
20:20 *large and powerful army.* The show of force by Edom caused Israel to turn away so as not to risk conflict with this brother nation. Israel was forbidden by the Lord to

take even a foothold in Edom (see Dt 2:4–6).
20:22 *Mount Hor.* Other than its proximity to the border of Edom (v. 23), nothing is known for certain about its location.
20:24 *gathered to his people.* A euphemism for death (see, e.g., Ge 25:8,17; 35:29). *both of you.* Aaron had joined Moses in rebellion against God (v. 12); his impending death was a precursor of Moses' death as well (see Dt 34).
20:25 *Aaron and his son Eleazar.* There was no doubt about Aaron's successor, just as there was no doubt about Moses' successor (see Dt 34).
20:26–28 While Aaron was still alive, his garments were to be placed on his son; only then did he die.
20:29 *mourned for him.* His death (and that of Moses) marked the passing of a generation. The old generation was now nearly gone; in 40 years there had been almost a complete turnover of the people 20 years old or more.
21:1–3 The first battle of the new community against the Canaanites was provoked by the king of Arad, perhaps as he was raiding them. The result was a complete victory for the Israelites—a new day for them, since they had been defeated by the Amalekites and Canaanites a generation before

heard that Israel was coming along the road to Atharim, he attacked the Israelites and captured some of them. [2]Then Israel made this vow[a] to the LORD: "If you will deliver these people into our hands, we will totally destroy[r][b] their cities." [3]The LORD listened to Israel's plea and gave the Canaanites[c] over to them. They completely destroyed them[d] and their towns; so the place was named Hormah.[s] [e]

The Bronze Snake

[4]They traveled from Mount Hor[f] along the route to the Red Sea,[t][g] to go around Edom.[h] But the people grew impatient on the way;[i] [5]they spoke against God[j] and against Moses, and said, "Why have you brought us up out of Egypt[k] to die in the desert?[l] There is no bread! There is no water![m] And we detest this miserable food!"[n]

[6]Then the LORD sent venomous snakes[o] among them; they bit the people and many Israelites died.[p] [7]The people came to Moses[q] and said, "We sinned[r] when we spoke against the LORD and against you. Pray that the LORD[s] will take the snakes away from us." So Moses prayed[t] for the people.

[8]The LORD said to Moses, "Make a snake and put it up on a pole;[u] anyone who is bitten can look at it and live." [9]So Moses made a bronze snake[v] and put it up on a pole. Then when anyone was bitten by a snake and looked at the bronze snake, he lived.[w]

The Journey to Moab

[10]The Israelites moved on and camped at Oboth.[x] [11]Then they set out from

21:2 *a*Lev 7:16
*b*ver 3; Ex 22:20;
Dt 2:34; Jos 2:10;
8:26; Jer 25:9;
50:21
21:3 *c*S Ge 10:18
*d*S ver 2
*e*S Nu 14:45
21:4 *f*Nu 20:22
*g*Nu 14:25;
Dt 2:1; 11:4
*h*S Nu 20:21
*i*Dt 2:8; Jdg 11:18
21:5 *j*Ps 78:19
*k*Nu 11:20
*l*S Ex 14:11;
Nu 14:2,3
*m*Nu 20:5
*n*S Nu 11:5
21:6 *o*ver 7;
Dt 8:15; 32:33;
Job 20:14;
Ps 58:4; 140:3;
Jer 8:17
*p*1Co 10:9
21:7 *q*Ps 78:34;
Hos 5:15
*r*Nu 14:40
*s*Ex 8:8; 1Sa 7:8;
Jer 27:18; 37:3;
Ac 8:24
*t*S Nu 11:2
21:8 *u*Jn 3:14
21:9 *v*2Ki 18:4
*w*Jn 3:14-15
21:10 *x*Nu 33:43
21:11
*y*S Ge 36:35;
Nu 33:44;
Dt 34:8; Jer 40:11

21:12 *z*Dt 2:13,
14
21:13
*a*Nu 22:36;
Dt 2:24; Jos 12:1;
Jdg 11:13,18;
2Ki 10:33;
Isa 16:2;
Jer 48:20
*b*S Ge 10:16
21:14
*c*1Sa 17:47;
18:17; 25:28
21:15 *d*ver 28;
Dt 2:9,18;
Isa 15:1
21:16 *e*Nu 25:1;
33:49; Jdg 9:21;
Isa 15:8
21:17 *f*S Ex 15:1
21:20
*g*Nu 23:14;
Dt 3:17,27; 34:1;
Jos 12:3; 13:20

Oboth and camped in Iye Abarim, in the desert that faces Moab[y] toward the sunrise. [12]From there they moved on and camped in the Zered Valley.[z] [13]They set out from there and camped alongside the Arnon[a], which is in the desert extending into Amorite territory. The Arnon is the border of Moab, between Moab and the Amorites.[b] [14]That is why the Book of the Wars[c] of the LORD says:

> ". . . Waheb in Suphah[u] and the
>   ravines,
>   the Arnon [15]and[v] the slopes of the
>   ravines
> that lead to the site of Ar[d]
>   and lie along the border of Moab."

[16]From there they continued on to Beer,[e] the well where the LORD said to Moses, "Gather the people together and I will give them water."

[17]Then Israel sang this song:[f]

> "Spring up, O well!
>   Sing about it,
> [18]about the well that the princes dug,
>   that the nobles of the people sank—
>   the nobles with scepters and staffs."

Then they went from the desert to Mattanah, [19]from Mattanah to Nahaliel, from Nahaliel to Bamoth, [20]and from Bamoth to the valley in Moab where the top of Pisgah[g] overlooks the wasteland.

(14:41–45).
21:2 *totally destroy.* See NIV text note.
21:3 *Hormah.* See NIV text note; the association with Israel's earlier defeat is made certain by the use of this place-name (see 14:45).
21:4 With Moses' determination not to engage Edom in battle (see note on 20:20), the people became impatient with him and with the direction the Lord was taking them. Flushed with victory, they were confident in themselves. They forgot that their victory over Arad was granted by the Lord in response to their solemn pledge (v. 2); now they were ready to rebel again.
21:5 *we detest this miserable food!* The people's impatience (v. 4) led them to blaspheme God, to reject his servant Moses and to despise the bread from heaven. This is the most bitter of their several attacks on the manna (see note on 11:7). Just as Moses' attack on the rock was more than it appeared to be (see note on 20:11), so the people's contempt for the heavenly bread was more serious than one might think. Rejecting the heavenly manna was tantamount to

spurning God's grace (cf. Jn 6:32–35,48–51,58).
21:8–9 In response to the people's confession of sin (v. 7), God directed Moses to make an image of a snake and put it on a pole, so that anyone who had been bitten could look at it and live. See the typological use of this incident in Jn 3:14–15.
21:10–13 The people skirt Edom and make their way to the Arnon, the wadi that serves as the border between Moab and the region of the Amorites and that flows west into the midpoint of the Dead Sea.
21:14 *Book of the Wars of the LORD.* Mentioned only here in the OT. This is not in existence today; it was presumably an ancient collection of songs of war in praise of God (see note on 10:3 for music in war). Cf. the "Book of Jashar" (Jos 10:13; 2Sa 1:18).
21:16 *I will give them water.* The quest for water had been a constant problem during the desert experience (see ch. 20; Ex 17).
21:17–18 The "song of the well" may also come from the Book of the Wars of the Lord (v. 14).

Defeat of Sihon and Og

21Israel sent messengers[h] to say to Sihon[i] king of the Amorites:[j]

22"Let us pass through your country. We will not turn aside into any field or vineyard, or drink water from any well. We will travel along the king's highway until we have passed through your territory.[k]"

23But Sihon would not let Israel pass through his territory.[l] He mustered his entire army and marched out into the desert against Israel. When he reached Jahaz,[m] he fought with Israel.[n] 24Israel, however, put him to the sword[o] and took over his land[p] from the Arnon to the Jabbok,[q] but only as far as the Ammonites,[r] because their border was fortified. 25Israel captured all the cities of the Amorites[s] and occupied them,[t] including Heshbon[u] and all its surrounding settlements. 26Heshbon was the city of Sihon[v] king of the Amorites,[w] who had fought against the former king of Moab[x] and had taken from him all his land as far as the Arnon.[y]

27That is why the poets say:

"Come to Heshbon and let it be rebuilt;
   let Sihon's city be restored.

28"Fire went out from Heshbon,
   a blaze from the city of Sihon.[z]
It consumed[a] Ar[b] of Moab,
   the citizens of Arnon's heights.[c]
29Woe to you, O Moab![d]
   You are destroyed, O people of
      Chemosh![e]
He has given up his sons as fugitives[f]
   and his daughters as captives[g]
to Sihon king of the Amorites.

30"But we have overthrown them;
   Heshbon is destroyed all the way to
      Dibon.[h]
We have demolished them as far as
   Nophah,

which extends to Medeba.[i]"

31So Israel settled in the land of the Amorites.[j]

32After Moses had sent spies[k] to Jazer,[l] the Israelites captured its surrounding settlements and drove out the Amorites who were there. 33Then they turned and went up along the road toward Bashan[m,n] and Og king of Bashan and his whole army marched out to meet them in battle at Edrei.[o]

34The LORD said to Moses, "Do not be afraid of him, for I have handed him over to you, with his whole army and his land. Do to him what you did to Sihon king of the Amorites, who reigned in Heshbon.[p]"

35So they struck him down, together with his sons and his whole army, leaving them no survivors.[q] And they took possession of his land.[r]

Balak Summons Balaam

22 Then the Israelites traveled to the plains of Moab[s] and camped along the Jordan[t] across from Jericho.[w][u]

2Now Balak son of Zippor[v] saw all that Israel had done to the Amorites, 3and Moab was terrified because there were so many people. Indeed, Moab was filled with dread[w] because of the Israelites.

4The Moabites[x] said to the elders of Midian,[y] "This horde is going to lick up everything[z] around us, as an ox licks up the grass of the field.[a]"

21:21 [h]S Ge 32:3 [i]Nu 32:33; Dt 1:4; Jos 2:10; 12:2,4; 13:10; Jdg 11:19-21; 1Ki 4:19; Ne 9:22; Ps 135:11; 136:19; Jer 48:45 [j]S Ex 23:23 21:22 [k]S Nu 20:17 21:23 [l]Nu 20:21 [m]Dt 2:32; Jos 13:18; 21:36; Jdg 11:20; Isa 15:4; Jer 48:21,34 [n]Nu 20:18 21:24 [o]Dt 2:33; 3:3; 29:7; Ps 135:10-11; Am 2:9 [p]ver 35; Dt 3:4 [q]S Ge 32:22; Nu 32:33; Jdg 11:13,22 [r]S Ge 19:38; Dt 2:37; Jos 13:10 21:25 [s]Nu 13:29; Jdg 10:11; Am 2:10 [t]Jdg 11:26 [u]ver 30; Nu 32:3; Dt 1:4; 29:7; Jos 9:10; 12:2; Isa 15:4; 16:8; Jer 48:2,34 21:26 [v]ver 21; Dt 29:7; Ps 135:11 [w]Nu 13:29 [x]Nu 21:11 [y]ver 13 21:28 [z]Jer 48:45 [a]S Nu 11:1 [b]S ver 15 [c]Nu 22:41; Dt 12:2; Jos 13:17; Isa 15:2; Jer 19:5 21:29 [d]Nu 24:17; 2Sa 8:2; 1Ch 18:2; Ps 60:8; Isa 25:10; Jer 48:46 [e]Jdg 10:6; 11:24; Ru 1:15; 1Ki 11:7,33; 2Ki 23:13; Jer 48:7,46 [f]Isa 15:5 [g]Isa 16:2 21:30 [h]Nu 32:3; Jos 13:9,17; Ne 11:25; Isa 15:2; Jer 48:18,22 [i]Jos 13:16;

1Ch 19:7 21:31 [j]Nu 13:29 21:32 [k]Jos 2:1; 6:22; 7:2; Jdg 18:2; 2Sa 10:3; 1Ch 19:3 [l]Nu 32:1,3,35; Jos 13:25; 2Sa 24:5; 1Ch 6:81; Isa 16:8; Jer 48:32 21:33 [m]Nu 32:33; Dt 3:3; 31:4; Jos 2:10; 12:4; 13:30; 1Ki 4:19; Ne 9:22; Ps 135:11; 136:20 [n]Dt 3:4; 32:14; Jos 9:10; 1Ki 4:13 [o]Dt 1:4; 3:1,10; Jos 12:4; 13:12,31; 19:37 21:34 [p]Dt 3:2 21:35 [q]Jos 9:10 [r]S ver 24 22:1 [s]S Nu 21:11 [t]S Nu 13:29; S Jos 2:7 [u]Nu 31:12; 33:48; Dt 32:49; Jos 2:1 22:2 [v]Nu 23:1-3; Jos 24:9; Jdg 11:25; Mic 6:5; Rev 2:14 22:3 [w]S Ex 15:15 22:4 [x]S Ge 19:37 [y]S Ge 25:2 [z]Nu 32:17,18,29 [a]Job 5:25; Ps 72:16

[w] 1 Hebrew *Jordan of Jericho*; possibly an ancient name for the Jordan River

---

21:21–26 As with Edom (20:14–19), Israel requested freedom to pass through the land of the Amorites. When Sihon, their king, tried to meet Israel with a show of force, he suffered an overwhelming defeat. The land of the Amorites was in Transjordan, extending from the Arnon River (at the midpoint of the Dead Sea) to the Jabbok River (v. 24), which flows into the Jordan some 24 miles north of the Dead Sea.
21:27–30 This third ancient poem in ch. 21 was an Amorite taunt song about their earlier victory over Moab (v. 29). Perhaps the "song of Heshbon" was also preserved in the Book of the Wars of the Lord (v. 14).
21:33 *Bashan.* The region northeast of the Sea of Galilee.
21:35 *struck him down.* By defeating Og, Israel now controlled Transjordan from Moab to the heights of Bashan in the vicinity of Mount Hermon. The victory over Sihon and Og became a subject of song (Ps 135:11; 136:19–20), and is

a regular part of the commemoration of the works of the Lord in the Passover celebration.

22:1 *plains of Moab.* Israel now marched back to their staging area east of the Jordan and just north of the Dead Sea. From this point they would launch their attack on Canaan, beginning with the ancient city of Jericho. Moab did not trust Israel's intentions, however. Moab's fear leads to a remarkable interval in the story of Israel: the account of Balak and Balaam (chs. 22–24).

22:3 *Moab was terrified.* Balak king of Moab did not know that Israel had no plans against him.

22:4 *said to the elders of Midian.* Balak made an alliance with the Midianites to oppose Israel (see v. 7). *as an ox licks up the grass of the field.* A proverbial simile particularly fitting for a pastoral people.

So Balak son of Zippor, who was king of Moab at that time, [5]sent messengers to summon Balaam son of Beor,[b] who was at Pethor, near the River,[xc] in his native land. Balak said:

"A people has come out of Egypt;[d] they cover the face of the land and have settled next to me. [6]Now come and put a curse[e] on these people, because they are too powerful for me. Perhaps then I will be able to defeat them and drive them out of the country.[f] For I know that those you bless are blessed, and those you curse are cursed."

[7]The elders of Moab and Midian left, taking with them the fee for divination.[g] When they came to Balaam, they told him what Balak had said.

[8]"Spend the night here," Balaam said to them, "and I will bring you back the answer the LORD gives me.[h]" So the Moabite princes stayed with him.

[9]God came to Balaam[i] and asked,[j] "Who are these men with you?"

[10]Balaam said to God, "Balak son of Zippor, king of Moab, sent me this message: [11]'A people that has come out of Egypt covers the face of the land. Now come and put a curse on them for me. Perhaps then I will be able to fight them and drive them away.' "

[12]But God said to Balaam, "Do not go with them. You must not put a curse on those people, because they are blessed.[k] "

[13]The next morning Balaam got up and said to Balak's princes, "Go back to your own country, for the LORD has refused to let me go with you."

[14]So the Moabite princes returned to Balak and said, "Balaam refused to come with us."

[15]Then Balak sent other princes, more numerous and more distinguished than the first. [16]They came to Balaam and said:

"This is what Balak son of Zippor says: Do not let anything keep you from coming to me, [17]because I will reward you handsomely[l] and do whatever you say. Come and put a curse[m] on these people for me."

[18]But Balaam answered them, "Even if Balak gave me his palace filled with silver and gold, I could not do anything great or small to go beyond the command of the LORD my God.[n] [19]Now stay here tonight as the others did, and I will find out what else the LORD will tell me.[o]"

[20]That night God came to Balaam[p] and said, "Since these men have come to summon you, go with them, but do only what I tell you."[q]

Balaam's Donkey

[21]Balaam got up in the morning, saddled his donkey and went with the princes of Moab. [22]But God was very angry[r] when he went, and the angel of the LORD[s] stood in the road to oppose him. Balaam was riding on his donkey, and his two servants were with him. [23]When the donkey saw the angel of the LORD standing in the road with a drawn sword[t] in his hand, she turned off the road into a field. Balaam beat her[u] to get her back on the road. [24]Then the angel of the LORD stood in a narrow path between two vineyards, with walls on both sides. [25]When the donkey saw the angel of the LORD, she pressed

22:5 *b*ver 7; Nu 24:25; 31:8, 16; Dt 23:4; Jos 13:22; Ne 13:2; Mic 6:5; S 2Pe 2:15 *c*S Ge 2:14 *d*S Ex 13:3
22:6 *e*ver 12,17; Nu 23:7,11,13; 24:9,10 *f*ver 11
22:7 *g*S Ge 30:27
22:8 *h*ver 19
22:9 *i*S Ge 20:3 *j*ver 20; Nu 23:5; 24:4,16
22:12 *k*S Ge 12:2
22:17 *l*ver 37; Nu 24:11 *m*S ver 6
22:18 *n*ver 38; Nu 23:12,26; 24:13; 1Ki 22:14; 2Ch 18:13; Jer 42:4
22:19 *o*ver 8
22:20 *p*S Ge 20:3 *q*ver 35,38;
Nu 23:5,12,16, 26; 24:13; 2Ch 18:13
22:22 *r*S Ex 4:14 *s*S Ge 16:7; Jdg 13:3,6,13
22:23 *t*Jos 5:13 *u*ver 25,27

[x]5 That is, the Euphrates

22:5 *summon Balaam son of Beor.* Since Balak believed that there was no military way to withstand Israel, he sought to oppose them through pagan divination (vv. 6–7), sending for a diviner with an international reputation. (One of Balaam's non-Biblical prophecies is preserved in an Aramaic text from Deir Alla in the Jordan Valley dating to c. 700 B.C.)
22:8 *the answer the LORD gives me.* The language here and in v. 18 ("the LORD my God") has led some to believe that Balaam was a believer in Yahweh ("the LORD"), God of Israel. Based on the subsequent narrative, however, it seems best to take Balaam's words as claiming to be the spokesman for any god. Balaam is universally condemned in Scripture for moral, ethical and religious faults (see 31:7–8,15–16; Dt 23:3–6; Jos 13:22; 24:9–10; Ne 13:1–3; Mic 6:5; 2Pe 2:15–16; Jude 11; Rev 2:14).
22:9 *God came to Balaam.* The author shows his aversion to the pagan prophet Balaam by using "God" instead of "the LORD" (Yahweh), as Balaam does (e.g., in v. 8). By this subtle device, the narrator distances himself from Balaam's outrageous claims. That God spoke to Balaam is not to be denied,

but Balaam did not yet realize that the God of Israel was unlike the supposed deities that he usually schemed against.
22:12 *they are blessed.* Israel was under the Lord's blessing promised to Abraham (see note on Ge 12:2–3).
22:20 *go with them.* There appears to be a contradiction between the permission God grants Balaam here and the prohibition he had given earlier (v. 12), and then the anger the Lord displayed against Balaam on his journey (v. 22). The difficulty is best understood as lying in the contrary character of Balaam. God had forbidden him to go to curse Israel. He then allowed Balaam to go, but only if he would follow the Lord's direction. But Balaam's real intentions were known to the Lord, and so with severe displeasure he confronted the pagan prophet.
22:23 *the donkey saw the angel of the LORD.* The internationally known seer is blind to spiritual reality, but his proverbially dumb beast is able to see the angel of the Lord on the path. As a pagan prophet, Balaam was a specialist in animal divination, but his animal saw what he was blind to observe.

close to the wall, crushing Balaam's foot against it. So he beat her again.

26Then the angel of the LORD moved on ahead and stood in a narrow place where there was no room to turn, either to the right or to the left. 27When the donkey saw the angel of the LORD, she lay down under Balaam, and he was angry[v] and beat her with his staff. 28Then the LORD opened the donkey's mouth,[w] and she said to Balaam, "What have I done to you to make you beat me these three times?[x]"

29Balaam answered the donkey, "You have made a fool of me! If I had a sword in my hand, I would kill you right now.[y]"

30The donkey said to Balaam, "Am I not your own donkey, which you have always ridden, to this day? Have I been in the habit of doing this to you?"

"No," he said.

31Then the LORD opened Balaam's eyes,[z] and he saw the angel of the LORD standing in the road with his sword drawn. So he bowed low and fell facedown.

32The angel of the LORD asked him, "Why have you beaten your donkey these three times? I have come here to oppose you because your path is a reckless one before me.[y] 33The donkey saw me and turned away from me these three times. If she had not turned away, I would certainly have killed you by now,[a] but I would have spared her."

34Balaam said to the angel of the LORD, "I have sinned.[b] I did not realize you were standing in the road to oppose me. Now if you are displeased, I will go back."

35The angel of the LORD said to Balaam, "Go with the men, but speak only what I tell you." So Balaam went with the princes of Balak.

36When Balak[c] heard that Balaam was coming, he went out to meet him at the

Moabite town on the Arnon[d] border, at the edge of his territory. 37Balak said to Balaam, "Did I not send you an urgent summons? Why didn't you come to me? Am I really not able to reward you?"

38"Well, I have come to you now," Balaam replied. "But can I say just anything? I must speak only what God puts in my mouth."[e]

39Then Balaam went with Balak to Kiriath Huzoth. 40Balak sacrificed cattle and sheep,[f] and gave some to Balaam and the princes who were with him. 41The next morning Balak took Balaam up to Bamoth Baal,[g] and from there he saw part of the people.[h]

Balaam's First Oracle

23 Balaam said, "Build me seven altars here, and prepare seven bulls and seven rams[i] for me." 2Balak did as Balaam said, and the two of them offered a bull and a ram on each altar.[j]

3Then Balaam said to Balak, "Stay here beside your offering while I go aside. Perhaps the LORD will come to meet with me.[k] Whatever he reveals to me I will tell you." Then he went off to a barren height.

4God met with him,[l] and Balaam said, "I have prepared seven altars, and on each altar I have offered a bull and a ram."

5The LORD put a message in Balaam's mouth[m][n] and said, "Go back to Balak and give him this message."[o]

6So he went back to him and found him standing beside his offering, with all the princes of Moab.[p] 7Then Balaam[q] uttered his oracle:[r]

"Balak brought me from Aram,[s]

Cross references (center column)

22:27 vNu 11:1; Jas 1:19
22:28 w2Pe 2:16
xver 32
22:29 yver 33; Dt 25:4; Pr 12:10; 27:23-27; Mt 15:19
22:31 zGe 21:19
22:33 aS ver 29
22:34 bGe 39:9; Nu 14:40; 1Sa 15:24,30; 2Sa 12:13; 24:10; Job 33:27; Ps 51:4
22:36 cver 2

dS Nu 21:13
22:38 eNu 23:5, 16,26
22:40 fNu 23:1, 14,29; Eze 45:23
22:41 gS Nu 21:28
hNu 23:13
23:1 iS Nu 22:40
23:2 jver 14,30
23:3 kver 15
23:4 lver 16
23:5 mS Ex 4:12; Isa 59:21
nS Ex 4:15
oS Nu 22:20
23:6 pver 17
23:7 qNu 22:5; Jos 24:9 rver 18; Nu 24:3,21; 2Sa 23:1 s2Ki 5:1

y32 The meaning of the Hebrew for this clause is uncertain.

22:29 *If I had a sword.* A ridiculous picture of the hapless Balaam. A sword was nearby (see vv. 23,31–33), but its victim was not going to be the donkey.

22:31 *Then the LORD opened Balaam's eyes.* The language follows the same structure as the opening words of v. 28. In some ways, the opening of the eyes of the pagan prophet to see the reality of the angel was the greater miracle.

22:35 *speak only what I tell you.* The one great gain was that Balaam was now more aware of the seriousness of the task before him; he would not be able to change the word the Lord would give him (see 23:12,20,26).

22:37 *Did I not send you an urgent summons?* The comic element of the story is seen not only in the hapless Balaam but also in the frustrated Balak (see 23:11,25; 24:10).

22:40 *Balak sacrificed cattle and sheep.* Not sacrifices to the Lord. The pieces given to Balaam would have included the livers, for, as a pagan diviner, Balaam was a specialist in liver divination. Balaam subsequently gave up his acts of sorcery as the power of the Lord's word came upon him

(24:1).

23:1 *seven altars . . . seven bulls and seven rams.* These sacrifices were prepared as a part of Balaam's pagan actions. The number seven (signifying completeness) was held in high regard among Semitic peoples in general; the many animals would provide abundant liver and organ materials for the diviner from the east.

23:2 *Balak did as Balaam said.* Balaam is in charge; Balak is now his subordinate.

23:7–24:24 There are seven poetic oracles here: The first four are longer, have introductory narrative bridges and are written in exquisite poetry (23:7–10; 23:18–24; 24:3–9; 24:15–19). The last three are brief, are much more difficult to understand, and follow one another in a staccato pattern (24:20,21–22,23–24).

23:7 *oracle.* Hebrew *mashal,* usually translated "proverb," but here "oracle" is appropriate. By this word the distinctive nature of Balaam's prophecies is established; none of the prophecies of Israel's true prophets is described by this term.

the king of Moab from the eastern
    mountains. [t]
'Come,' he said, 'curse Jacob for me;
    come, denounce Israel.' [u]
[8]How can I curse
    those whom God has not cursed? [v]
How can I denounce
    those whom the LORD has not
    denounced? [w]
[9]From the rocky peaks I see them,
    from the heights I view them. [x]
I see a people who live apart
    and do not consider themselves one
    of the nations. [y]
[10]Who can count the dust of Jacob [z]
    or number the fourth part of Israel?
Let me die the death of the righteous, [a]
    and may my end be like theirs! [b]"

[11]Balak said to Balaam, "What have you
done to me? I brought you to curse my
enemies, [c] but you have done nothing but
bless them!" [d]

[12]He answered, "Must I not speak what
the LORD puts in my mouth?" [e]

Balaam's Second Oracle

[13]Then Balak said to him, "Come with
me to another place [f] where you can see
them; you will see only a part but not all of
them. [g] And from there, curse them for
me. [h]" [14]So he took him to the field of
Zophim on the top of Pisgah, [i] and there
he built seven altars and offered a bull and
a ram on each altar. [j]

[15]Balaam said to Balak, "Stay here beside your offering while I meet with him
over there."

[16]The LORD met with Balaam and put a
message in his mouth [k] and said, "Go back
to Balak and give him this message."

[17]So he went to him and found him
standing beside his offering, with the
princes of Moab. [l] Balak asked him,
"What did the LORD say?"

[18]Then he uttered his oracle: [m]

"Arise, Balak, and listen;
    hear me, son of Zippor. [n]
[19]God is not a man, [o] that he should lie, [p]
    nor a son of man, that he should
    change his mind. [q]
Does he speak and then not act?
    Does he promise [r] and not fulfill?
[20]I have received a command to bless; [s]
    he has blessed, [t] and I cannot change
    it. [u]

[21]"No misfortune is seen in Jacob, [v]
    no misery observed in Israel. [z] [w]
The LORD their God is with them; [x]
    the shout of the King [y] is among
    them.
[22]God brought them out of Egypt; [z]
    they have the strength of a wild ox. [a]
[23]There is no sorcery against Jacob,
    no divination [b] against Israel.
It will now be said of Jacob
    and of Israel, 'See what God has
    done!'
[24]The people rise like a lioness; [c]
    they rouse themselves like a lion [d]
that does not rest till he devours his
    prey
    and drinks the blood [e] of his
    victims."

[25]Then Balak said to Balaam, "Neither
curse them at all nor bless them at all!"
[26]Balaam answered, "Did I not tell you I
must do whatever the LORD says?" [f]

Balaam's Third Oracle

[27]Then Balak said to Balaam, "Come, let
me take you to another place. [g] Perhaps it
will please God to let you curse them for
me [h] from there." [28]And Balak took Balaam to the top of Peor, [i] overlooking the
wasteland.

23:7 [t]S Ge 24:10
[u]S Nu 22:6;
Ne 13:2
23:8 [v]Nu 22:12
[w]ver 20;
Isa 43:13
23:9 [x]Nu 22:41
[y]S Ex 33:16;
S Dt 32:8
23:10
[z]S Ge 13:16
[a]Ps 16:3; 116:15;
Isa 57:1
[b]Ps 37:37
23:11 [c]S Nu 22:6
[d]Nu 24:10;
Jos 24:10;
Ne 13:2
23:12
[e]S Nu 22:18,20
23:13 [f]ver 27
[g]Nu 22:41
[h]S Nu 22:6
23:14
[i]S Nu 21:20;
27:12 [j]S ver 2
23:16
[k]S Ex 4:15;
S Nu 22:38
23:17 [l]ver 6
23:18 [m]S ver 7

[n]Nu 22:2
23:19 [o]Job 9:32;
Isa 55:9; Hos 11:9
[p]S Nu 11:23
[q]1Sa 15:29;
Job 12:13; 36:5;
Ps 33:11; 89:34;
102:27; 110:4;
Jer 4:28; 7:16;
Mal 3:6; Tit 1:2;
Heb 6:18; 7:21;
Jas 1:17
[r]2Sa 7:25;
Ps 119:38
23:20 [s]ver 5,16;
Nu 24:1
[t]Ge 22:17;
Nu 22:12 [u]S ver
8; S Job 9:12
23:21 [v]Ps 32:2,5;
85:2; Ro 4:7-8
[w]Isa 33:24; 40:2;
Jer 50:20
[x]S Ge 26:3;
Ex 29:45,46;
Dt 4:7;
Ps 34:17-18;
145:18; Zec 2:10
[y]Dt 32:15; 33:5;
Ps 89:15-18;
Isa 44:2
23:22 [z]Nu 24:8;
Jos 2:10; 9:9
[a]Dt 33:17;
Job 39:9;
Ps 22:21; 29:6;
92:10; Isa 34:7
23:23 [b]ver 3;
S Ge 30:27;
Nu 24:1

23:24 [c]Nu 24:9; Eze 19:2; Na 2:11 [d]S Ge 49:9 [e]Isa 49:26
23:26 [f]S Nu 22:18,20 **23:27** [g]ver 13 [h]Nu 24:10 **23:28**
[i]Nu 25:3,18; 31:16; Dt 3:29; 4:3; Jos 22:17; Ps 106:28;
Hos 9:10

[z]21 Or *He has not looked on Jacob's offenses / or on
the wrongs found in Israel.*

23:8 *How can I curse those whom God has not cursed?*
That which Balaam had been hired to do he was unable to
do. God kept him from pronouncing a curse on his people,
who were unlike the nations of the world (v. 9).

23:10 *Let me die the death of the righteous.* A wish not
granted (see 31:8,16). *may my end be like theirs!* He who
had come to curse desired to share in Israel's blessing.

23:13 *a part but not all.* Balak attempted to reduce Israel's
power by selecting a point where their immense numbers
would be obscured. Unfortunately for Balak, the oracle that
followed (vv. 18–24) exceeded the first in its blessing on
Israel.

23:19 *God is not a man, that he should lie.* These sublime
words describe the immutability of the Lord and the integrity
of his word. Balaam is a foil for God—constantly shifting,

prevaricating, equivocating, changing—a prime example of
the distinction between God and man.

23:21 *the shout of the King is among them.* That the first
explicit declaration of the Lord's kingship in the Pentateuch
was made by Balaam is a suitable improbability. Because God
is King (Sovereign), he was able to use Balaam for his own
ends—to bless his people in a new and wonderful manner.

23:22 *wild ox.* Or "aurochs" or "oryx," a traditional image
of power in the ancient Near East (see also 24:8).

23:23 *no sorcery against Jacob.* Balaam speaks from his
frightful experience. He had no means in his bag of tricks to
withstand God's blessing of Israel.

23:24 *like a lioness.* Israel was about to arise and devour its
foes, like a lioness on the hunt (see 24:9; Ge 49:9).

²⁹Balaam said, "Build me seven altars here, and prepare seven bulls and seven rams for me." ³⁰Balak did as Balaam had said, and offered a bull and a ram on each altar.ʲ

24 Now when Balaam saw that it pleased the LORD to bless Israel,ᵏ he did not resort to sorceryˡ as at other times, but turned his face toward the desert.ᵐ ²When Balaam looked out and saw Israel encamped tribe by tribe, the Spirit of God came upon himⁿ ³and he uttered his oracle:

"The oracle of Balaam son of Beor,
  the oracle of one whose eye sees
    clearly,ᵒ
⁴the oracle of one who hears the words
    of God,ᵖ
  who sees a vision from the
    Almighty,ᵃ ᑫ
  who falls prostrate, and whose eyes
    are opened:

⁵"How beautiful are your tents,ʳ
    O Jacob,
  your dwelling places, O Israel!

⁶"Like valleys they spread out,
  like gardens beside a river,ˢ
like aloesᵗ planted by the LORD,
  like cedars beside the waters.ᵘ
⁷Water will flow from their buckets;
  their seed will have abundant water.

"Their king will be greater than Agag;ᵛ
  their kingdom will be exalted.ʷ

⁸"God brought them out of Egypt;
  they have the strength of a wild ox.
They devour hostile nations
  and break their bones in pieces;ˣ
  with their arrows they pierce them.ʸ
⁹Like a lion they crouch and lie down,

like a lionessᶻ—who dares to rouse
    them?

"May those who bless you be blessedᵃ
  and those who curse you be
    cursed!"ᵇ

¹⁰Then Balak's anger burnedᶜ against Balaam. He struck his hands togetherᵈ and said to him, "I summoned you to curse my enemies,ᵉ but you have blessed themᶠ these three times.ᵍ ¹¹Now leave at once and go home!ʰ I said I would reward you handsomely,ⁱ but the LORD has kept you from being rewarded."

¹²Balaam answered Balak, "Did I not tell the messengers you sent me,ʲ ¹³'Even if Balak gave me his palace filled with silver and gold, I could not do anything of my own accord, good or bad, to go beyond the command of the LORDᵏ—and I must say only what the LORD says'?ˡ ¹⁴Now I am going back to my people, but come, let me warn you of what this people will do to your people in days to come."ᵐ

Balaam's Fourth Oracle

¹⁵Then he uttered his oracle:

"The oracle of Balaam son of Beor,
  the oracle of one whose eye sees
    clearly,
¹⁶the oracle of one who hears the wordsⁿ
    of God,
  who has knowledge from the Most
    High,ᵒ
  who sees a vision from the Almighty,
  who falls prostrate, and whose eyes
    are opened:

¹⁷"I see him, but not now;
  I behold him, but not near.ᵖ

Cross references (center column):

23:30 ʲS ver 2
24:1 ᵏS Nu 23:20
  ˡS Nu 23:23
  ᵐNu 23:28
24:2
  ⁿS Nu 11:25,26
24:3 ᵒver 15
24:4 ᵖS Nu 22:9
  ᑫS Ge 15:1
24:5 ʳJer 4:20; 30:18; Mal 2:12
24:6 ˢS Ge 2:10
  ᵗPs 45:8; SS 4:14
  ᵘJob 29:19; Ps 1:3; 104:16; Eze 31:5
24:7 ᵛS Ex 17:8-16,14
  ʷDt 28:1; 2Sa 5:12; 1Ch 14:2; Ps 89:27; 145:11-13
24:8 ˣS Ex 15:6; Jer 50:17
  ʸ2Sa 18:14; Ps 45:5
24:9 ᶻS Nu 23:24
  ᵃS Ge 12:2
  ᵇS Ge 12:3
24:10 ᶜS Ex 4:14
  ᵈJob 27:23; 34:37; La 2:15; Eze 21:14; 22:13; 25:6 ᵉS Nu 22:6
  ᶠS Nu 23:11; S Dt 23:5 ᵍver 3-9; Nu 23:7-10, 18-24
24:11 ʰver 14,25
  ⁱS Nu 22:17
24:12 ʲNu 22:18
24:13 ᵏS Nu 22:18
  ˡS Nu 22:20
24:14 ᵐS Ge 49:1; Nu 31:8,16; Mic 6:5
24:16 ⁿS Nu 22:9
  ᵒGe 14:18; Isa 14:14
24:17 ᵖRev 1:7

ᵃ4 Hebrew *Shaddai;* also in verse 16

24:1 *sorcery as at other times.* Balaam's magic and sorcery are identified here (see notes on 22:40; 23:1).

24:2 *the Spirit of God came upon him.* Not to be confused with the filling of the Spirit (Ac 2:1–4), or with the anointing of the Spirit (Isa 61:1). This unexpected language prepares the reader for the heightened revelation that is about to come from the unwitting messenger.

24:3–4 The extensive introduction of this oracle describes Balaam's experience in the Lord's presence. Now Balaam's eyes were opened (see note on 22:31).

24:6–7 Balaam speaks here in general, but luxuriant, terms of the blessings that will come to the Israelites as they settle in their new land. The lushness of their blessing from the Lord is reminiscent of Eden.

24:7 *greater than Agag.* Possibly a specific future prophecy concerning the opponent of King Saul (1Sa 15:32–33)—setting the stage for the even more remarkable words of the fourth oracle (vv. 15–19). But it may be that Agag was a common name among Amalekite kings and that the allusion here is to the Amalekites who attacked Israel when she came out of Egypt (see Ex 17:8–13) and again when she first

approached Canaan (see 14:45).

24:8 *God brought them out of Egypt.* These central words about Israel's salvation are recited by one who was a hostile outsider (see note on 25:1).

24:9 *May those who bless you be blessed . . . cursed!* The theology of blessing and cursing in the promises made to Abraham (Ge 12:2–3) is now a part of this oracle of blessing. Perhaps here Balaam was reasserting his desire to be a part of Israel's blessing (see note on 23:10).

24:11 *the LORD has kept you from being rewarded.* In his disgust with Balaam's failure to curse Israel, Balak now dismisses him without pay—the ultimate insult to his greed (see 2Pe 2:15).

24:14 *in days to come.* The distant (Messianic) future is usually indicated by this expression (see, e.g., Jer 48:47 and note).

24:15–16 As in the third oracle (see vv. 3–4), the introduction to the fourth oracle is lengthy, helping to prepare the reader for the startling words of the prophecy.

24:17 *star . . . scepter.* Perhaps fulfilled initially in David, but ultimately in the coming Messianic ruler. Israel's future

A star will come out of Jacob; [q]
    a scepter will rise out of Israel. [r]
He will crush the foreheads of Moab, [s]
    the skulls [b] [t] of [c] all the sons of
        Sheth. [d]
[18]Edom [u] will be conquered;
    Seir, [v] his enemy, will be
        conquered, [w]
    but Israel [x] will grow strong.
[19]A ruler will come out of Jacob [y]
    and destroy the survivors of the city."

Balaam's Final Oracles

[20]Then Balaam saw Amalek [z] and uttered his oracle:

"Amalek was first among the nations,
    but he will come to ruin at last." [a]

[21]Then he saw the Kenites [b] and uttered
his oracle:

"Your dwelling place is secure, [c]
    your nest is set in a rock;
[22]yet you Kenites will be destroyed
    when Asshur [d] takes you captive."

[23]Then he uttered his oracle:

"Ah, who can live when God does
    this? [e]
[24] Ships will come from the shores of
        Kittim; [e]
    they will subdue Asshur [f] and Eber, [g]
    but they too will come to ruin. [h]"

[25]Then Balaam [i] got up and returned
home and Balak went his own way.

Moab Seduces Israel

25 While Israel was staying in Shittim, [j] the men began to indulge in
sexual immorality [k] with Moabite [l]
women, [m] [2]who invited them to the sacrifices [n] to their gods. [o] The people ate and
bowed down before these gods. [3]So Israel
joined in worshiping [p] the Baal of Peor. [q]
And the LORD's anger burned against
them.

[4]The LORD said to Moses, "Take all the
leaders [r] of these people, kill them and expose [s] them in broad daylight before the
LORD, [t] so that the LORD's fierce anger [u]
may turn away from Israel."

[5]So Moses said to Israel's judges, "Each
of you must put to death [v] those of your
men who have joined in worshiping the
Baal of Peor." [w]

[6]Then an Israelite man brought to his
family a Midianite [x] woman right before
the eyes of Moses and the whole assembly
of Israel while they were weeping [y] at the
entrance to the Tent of Meeting. [7]When
Phinehas [z] son of Eleazar, the son of
Aaron, the priest, saw this, he left the assembly, took a spear [a] in his hand [8]and
followed the Israelite into the tent. He
drove the spear through both of
them—through the Israelite and into the
woman's body. Then the plague against
the Israelites was stopped; [b] [9]but those

24:17 [q]Mt 2:2
[r]S Ge 49:10
[s]S Ge 19:37;
S Nu 21:29;
S Dt 23:6;
Isa 15:1-16:14
[t]Jer 48:45
24:18 [u]2Sa 8:12;
1Ch 18:11;
Ps 60:8;
Isa 11:14;
Am 9:12
[v]S Ge 14:6;
Dt 1:44; Jos 12:7;
15:10, Jdg 5:4
[w]Ob 1:2
[x]S Ge 9:25
24:19
[y]S Ge 49:10;
Mic 5:2
24:20
[z]S Ge 14:7;
S Ex 17:14
[a]Dt 25:19;
1Sa 15:20;
30:17-20;
2Sa 8:12;
1Ch 18:11
24:21
[b]S Ge 15:19
[c]Ps 37:27;
Pr 1:33;
Isa 32:18;
Eze 34:27
24:22
[d]S Ge 10:22
24:24 [e]S Ge 10:4
[f]ver 22
[g]S Ge 10:21 [h]ver
20
24:25 [i]S Nu 22:5
25:1
[j]S Nu 21:16;
Jos 2:1; Isa 66:11;
Joel 3:18; Mic 6:5

[k]Jer 5:7; 7:9;
9:2; 1Co 10:8;
Rev 2:14
[l]S Ge 19:37
[m]Nu 31:16
25:2 [n]S Ex 32:6
[o]Ex 20:5;
Dt 32:38;
1Co 10:20
25:3 [p]Dt 4:19;
Jdg 2:19; 1Ki 9:9;
Jer 1:16; 44:3
[q]S Nu 23:28
25:4 [r]Nu 7:2;
13:3 [s]2Sa 21:6
[t]Dt 4:3
[u]Ex 32:12;

Dt 13:17; Jos 7:26; 2Ki 23:26; 2Ch 28:11; 29:10; 30:8;
Ezr 10:14; Jer 44:3 **25:5** [v]S Ex 32:27 [w]Hos 9:10 **25:6**
[x]S Ge 25:2 [y]S Nu 14:1; Jdg 2:4; Ru 1:9; 1Sa 11:4; 2Sa 15:30;
Ezr 10:1; Ps 126:6; Jer 41:6 **25:7** [z]S Ex 6:25; Jos 22:13;
Jdg 20:28 [a]Jdg 5:8; 1Sa 13:19,22; 1Ki 18:28; Ps 35:3; 46:9;
Joel 3:10; Mic 4:3 **25:8** [b]Ps 106:30

[b]17 Samaritan Pentateuch (see also Jer. 48:45); the
meaning of the word in the Masoretic Text is uncertain.
[c]17 Or possibly Moab, / batter   [d]17 Or all the noisy
boasters   [e]23 Masoretic Text; with a different word
division of the Hebrew A people will gather from the
north.

Deliverer will be like a star (cf. Rev 22:16) and scepter in his
royalty and will bring victory over the enemies of his people
(see v. 19). *Sheth.* Possibly the early inhabitants of Moab
known as the Shutu people in ancient Egyptian documents.
24:20 *Amalek was first.* The first to attack Israel and
oppose the Lord's purpose with his people (see Ex 17:8–13).
24:21 *Kenites.* The name suggests a tribe of metal workers.
In other passages the Kenites are allied with Israel (see, e.g.,
Jdg 1:16; 4:11; 1Sa 15:6). Since Moses' father-in-law was a
Kenite but also associated with Midian (see Ex 2:16), it may
be that Balaam's reference is to Midianites (see 22:4,7). *nest.*
Hebrew *qen,* a wordplay on the word for Kenites (Hebrew
qeni).
24:22 *Asshur.* Assyria.
24:24 *Kittim.* Probably ancient Kition in Cyprus. *they will
subdue Asshur and Eber, but . . . ruin.* One nation will rise
and supplant another, only to face its own doom. By contrast,
there is the implied ongoing blessing on Israel, and their sure
promise of a future deliverer who will have the final victory
(vv. 17–19).
25:1–18 It is not until 31:8,16 that we learn that the
principal instigator of Israel's apostasy was Balaam (see notes
on 22:5,8). Failing to destroy Israel by pronouncing curses

on her, Balaam seduced Israel by the Canaanite fertility rites
of Baal.
25:1 *Shittim.* Another name for the region of Israel's staging for the conquest of Canaan; it was across the Jordan River
opposite the ancient city of Jericho (see Jos 2:1). *indulge in
sexual immorality.* Israel's engagement in the fertility rites of
Baal involved not only the evil of sexual immorality; it was
also a breach of covenant with the Lord, a worship of the
gods of the land (vv. 2–3) and a foretaste of the people's ruin
in the unfolding of their history.
25:4 *kill them and expose them in broad daylight.* The
special display of the corpses would warn survivors of the
consequences of sin.
25:6 *brought to his family a Midianite woman.* The contempt for the holy things and the word of the Lord shown by
Zimri (v. 14) and his lover Cozbi (v. 15) is unimagin-
able.
25:9 *24,000.* The number of those who died because of the
flagrant actions of the people in their worship of Baal exceeded even those who died in the rebellion of Korah and his
allies (14,700; see 16:49). Again, the large number of those
who died fits well with the immense number of the people
stated in the first census (1:46) and the second (26:51).

who died in the plague[c] numbered 24,-000.[d]

[10]The LORD said to Moses, [11]"Phinehas son of Eleazar, the son of Aaron, the priest, has turned my anger away from the Israelites; [e] for he was as zealous as I am for my honor[f] among them, so that in my zeal I did not put an end to them. [12]Therefore tell him I am making my covenant of peace[g] with him. [13]He and his descendants will have a covenant of a lasting priesthood, [h] because he was zealous[i] for the honor[j] of his God and made atonement[k] for the Israelites." [l]

[14]The name of the Israelite who was killed with the Midianite woman[m] was Zimri son of Salu, the leader of a Simeonite family. [n] [15]And the name of the Midianite woman who was put to death was Cozbi[o] daughter of Zur, a tribal chief of a Midianite family.[p]

[16]The LORD said to Moses, [q] [17]"Treat the Midianites[r] as enemies[s] and kill them, [t] [18]because they treated you as enemies when they deceived you in the affair of Peor[u] and their sister Cozbi, the daughter of a Midianite leader, the woman who was killed when the plague came as a result of Peor."

The Second Census

26 After the plague[v] the LORD said to Moses and Eleazar son of Aaron, the priest, [2]"Take a census[w] of the whole Israelite community by families—all those twenty years old or more who are able to serve in the army[x] of Israel." [3]So on the plains of Moab[y] by the Jordan across from Jericho,[t z] Moses and Eleazar the priest

spoke with them and said, [4]"Take a census of the men twenty years old or more, as the LORD commanded Moses."

These were the Israelites who came out of Egypt: [a]

[5]The descendants of Reuben,[b] the firstborn son of Israel, were:

through Hanoch,[c] the Hanochite clan;

through Pallu, [d] the Palluite clan;

[6]through Hezron,[e] the Hezronite clan;

through Carmi,[f] the Carmite clan.

[7]These were the clans of Reuben; those numbered were 43,730.

[8]The son of Pallu was Eliab, [9]and the sons of Eliab[g] were Nemuel, Dathan and Abiram. The same Dathan and Abiram were the community[h] officials who rebelled against Moses and Aaron and were among Korah's followers when they rebelled against the LORD. [i] [10]The earth opened its mouth and swallowed them[j] along with Korah, whose followers died when the fire devoured the 250 men. [k] And they served as a warning sign. [l] [11]The line of Korah, [m] however, did not die out. [n]

[12]The descendants of Simeon by their clans were:

through Nemuel,[o] the Nemuelite clan;

through Jamin, [p] the Jaminite clan;

through Jakin, the Jakinite clan;

[13]through Zerah, [q] the Zerahite clan;

25:9
cS Nu 14:37;
1Co 10:8
dNu 31:16
25:11 ePs 106:30
fEx 20:5;
Dt 32:16,21;
Ps 78:58
25:12 gIsa 11:9;
54:10; Eze 34:25;
37:26; Mal 2:4,5
25:13 hS Ex 29:9
iKi 19:10;
2Ki 10:16 jver 11
kS Ex 29:36;
S Ro 3:25
lPs 106:31;
Jer 33:18
25:14 mver 6
nS Nu 1:6
25:15 over 18
pNu 31:8;
Jos 13:21;
Hab 3:7
25:16 qNu 31:7
25:17 rNu 31:1-3
sEx 23:22;
Jdg 2:16-18;
Ne 9:27; Ps 8:2;
21:8; 74:23
tDt 21:1;
1Sa 17:9,35;
2Ki 9:27; 10:25
25:18
uS Nu 23:28
26:1
vS Nu 14:37;
25:8
26:2
wEx 30:11-16
xS Nu 1:3
26:3 yver 63;
Nu 33:48;
Jos 13:32
zNu 22:1

26:4 aS Ex 6:14;
S 13:3
26:5 bNu 1:20
cS Ge 46:9
d1Ch 5:3
26:6 e1Ch 5:3
fGe 46:9
26:9 gNu 16:1
hNu 1:16
iS Nu 16:2
26:10
jS Ex 15:12
kS Nu 16:35
lS Ex 3:12;
S Nu 16:38
26:11 mEx 6:24
nNu 16:33;

Dt 5:9; 24:16; 2Ki 14:6; 2Ch 25:4; Eze 18:20 26:12 oS Ge 46:10 p1Ch 4:24 26:13 qS Ge 46:10

t3 Hebrew Jordan of Jericho; possibly an ancient name for the Jordan River; also in verse 63

25:11 *He was as zealous as I am for my honor.* Cf. Ex 20:4–6. The zeal of Phinehas for the Lord's honor became the occasion for the Lord's covenanting with him and his descendants as God's true priests (see note on Ge 9:9). This son of Eleazar contrasts with the casual wickedness of his uncles, Nadab and Abihu (see Lev 10:1–3 and notes).
25:17 *Treat the Midianites as enemies.* Because of their active participation in the seduction of the Israelites. Midianites had been in league with Balak from the beginning of the confrontation (see 22:4,7) and became the objects of a holy war (31:1–24).
26:1–51 The first census of those who were mustered for the war of conquest had been taken over 38 years earlier. That first generation of men 20 years or more had nearly all died. It was now time for the new generation to be numbered and mustered for the campaign that awaited them. The aged Moses was joined in the task this time by his nephew Eleazar; Aaron was dead (see 20:28). In this second census the prominent clans of each tribe are listed. The numbers of most of the tribes increase. Reuben is one of the tribes that shows a decline. It is possible that the slight reduction of the families of Reuben was brought about by the judgment on their members during the rebellion of Korah

and his Reubenite allies (see note on v. 9). In the intervening years the family of Reuben had nearly caught up with its former numbers (see note on v. 14). Note the comparison of the numbers of each tribe from the first census to the second:

Tribe	First Census	Second Census
Reuben	46,500	43,730
Simeon	59,300	22,200
Gad	45,650	40,500
Judah	74,600	76,500
Issachar	54,400	64,300
Zebulun	57,400	60,500
Ephraim	40,500	32,500
Manasseh	32,200	52,700
Benjamin	35,400	45,600
Dan	62,700	64,400
Asher	41,500	53,400
Naphtali	53,400	45,400
Total	603,550	601,730

26:9 *Dathan and Abiram.* The listing of Reuben's families becomes an occasion to remind the reader of the part that certain of their number had in Korah's rebellion (see 16:1; cf. Jude 11).

through Shaul, the Shaulite clan.

[14]These were the clans of Simeon;[r] there were 22,200 men.[s]

[15]The descendants of Gad by their clans were:

through Zephon,[t] the Zephonite clan;

through Haggi, the Haggite clan;

through Shuni, the Shunite clan;

[16]through Ozni, the Oznite clan;

through Eri, the Erite clan;

[17]through Arodi,[g] the Arodite clan;

through Areli, the Arelite clan.

[18]These were the clans of Gad;[u] those numbered were 40,500.

[19]Er[v] and Onan[w] were sons of Judah, but they died[x] in Canaan.

[20]The descendants of Judah by their clans were:

through Shelah,[y] the Shelanite clan;

through Perez,[z] the Perezite clan;

through Zerah, the Zerahite clan.[a]

[21]The descendants of Perez[b] were:

through Hezron,[c] the Hezronite clan;

through Hamul, the Hamulite clan.

[22]These were the clans of Judah;[d] those numbered were 76,500.

[23]The descendants of Issachar by their clans were:

through Tola,[e] the Tolaite clan;

through Puah, the Puite[h] clan;

[24]through Jashub,[f] the Jashubite clan;

through Shimron, the Shimronite clan.

[25]These were the clans of Issachar;[g] those numbered were 64,300.

[26]The descendants of Zebulun[h] by their clans were:

through Sered, the Seredite clan;

through Elon, the Elonite clan;

through Jahleel, the Jahleelite clan.

[27]These were the clans of Zebulun;[i] those numbered were 60,500.

[28]The descendants of Joseph[j] by their clans through Manasseh and Ephraim[k] were:

[29]The descendants of Manasseh:[l]

through Makir,[m] the Makirite clan

(Makir was the father of Gilead[n]);

through Gilead, the Gileadite clan.

[30]These were the descendants of Gilead:[o]

through Iezer,[p] the Iezerite clan;

through Helek, the Helekite clan;

[31]through Asriel, the Asrielite clan;

through Shechem, the Shechemite clan;

[32]through Shemida, the Shemidaite clan;

through Hepher, the Hepherite clan.

[33](Zelophehad[q] son of Hepher had no sons;[r] he had only daughters, whose names were Mahlah, Noah, Hoglah, Milcah and Tirzah.)[s]

[34]These were the clans of Manasseh; those numbered were 52,700.[t]

[35]These were the descendants of Ephraim[u] by their clans:

through Shuthelah, the Shuthelahite clan;

through Beker, the Bekerite clan;

through Tahan, the Tahanite clan.

[36]These were the descendants of Shuthelah:

through Eran, the Eranite clan.

[37]These were the clans of Ephraim;[v] those numbered were 32,500.

These were the descendants of Joseph by their clans.

[38]The descendants of Benjamin[w] by their clans were:

through Bela, the Belaite clan;

through Ashbel, the Ashbelite clan;

through Ahiram, the Ahiramite clan;

[39]through Shupham,[i] the Shuphamite clan;

through Hupham, the Huphamite clan.

[40]The descendants of Bela through Ard[x] and Naaman were:

26:14 [r]S Ge 46:10 [s]Nu 1:23
26:15 [t]Ge 46:16
26:18 [u]S Ge 30:11; S Nu 1:25; S Jos 13:24-28
26:19 [v]S Ge 38:3 [w]S Ge 38:4 [x]Ge 38:7
26:20 [y]S Ge 38:5 [z]S Ge 38:29 [a]Jos 7:17
26:21 [b]S Ge 38:29 [c]Ru 4:19; 1Ch 2:9
26:22 [d]Nu 1:27
26:23 [e]S Ge 46:13
26:24 [f]Ge 46:13
26:25 [g]S Ge 30:18
26:26 [h]Nu 1:30
26:27 [i]S Ge 30:20
26:28 [j]Nu 1:32; 36:1 [k]S Ge 41:52
26:29 [l]Nu 1:34 [m]S Ge 50:23
26:30 [o]Nu 27:1; 36:1; 1Ch 7:14, 17 [p]Jos 17:2; Jdg 6:11; 8:2
26:33 [q]Nu 27:1; 36:2; Jos 17:3; 1Ch 7:15 [r]Nu 27:3 [s]Nu 36:11
26:34 [t]Nu 1:35
26:35 [u]Nu 1:32
26:37 [v]S Nu 1:33
26:38 [w]Ge 46:21; Nu 1:36; 1Ch 8:40
26:40 [x]S Ge 46:21
[n]Jdg 11:1

[g]17 Samaritan Pentateuch and Syriac (see also Gen. 46:16); Masoretic Text *Arod*   [h]23 Samaritan Pentateuch, Septuagint, Vulgate and Syriac (see also 1 Chron. 7:1); Masoretic Text *through Puvah, the Punite*   [i]39 A few manuscripts of the Masoretic Text, Samaritan Pentateuch, Vulgate and Syriac (see also Septuagint); most manuscripts of the Masoretic Text *Shephupham*

26:14 *22,200.* The greatest loss was in the tribe of Simeon (down from 59,300). Zimri was from the house of Simeon (25:14). Perhaps most of the 24,000 who died in the plague of that time were from Simeon. The judgment was so recent that the tribe had not had time to recover, as had the tribe of Reuben (see note on vv. 1–51).

26:19 *Er and Onan.* The names of the evil sons of Judah had not been forgotten, but they had no heritage (see Ge 38:1–10).

26:20 *Perez.* The line of David and Jesus would be traced through him (Ru 4:18–22; Mt 1:1–3).

26:29,35 *Manasseh . . . Ephraim.* The order of the tribes is the same as in ch. 1, except for the inversion of Ephraim and Manasseh.

26:33 *Zelophehad . . . daughters.* See 27:1–11; 36.

26:34 *52,700.* The greatest gain was in the tribe of Manasseh (up from 32,200). The reason for this increase is not known.

through Ard, i the Ardite clan;
through Naaman, the Naamite clan.
⁴¹These were the clans of Benjamin; ʸ those numbered were 45,600.

⁴²These were the descendants of Dan ᶻ by their clans: ᵃ
through Shuham, ᵇ the Shuhamite clan.
These were the clans of Dan: ⁴³All of them were Shuhamite clans; and those numbered were 64,400. ʲ

⁴⁴The descendants of Asher ᶜ by their clans were:
through Imnah, the Imnite clan;
through Ishvi, the Ishvite clan;
through Beriah, the Beriite clan;
⁴⁵and through the descendants of Beriah:
through Heber, the Heberite clan;
through Malkiel, the Malkielite clan.
⁴⁶(Asher had a daughter named Serah.)
⁴⁷These were the clans of Asher; ᵈ those numbered were 53,400.

⁴⁸The descendants of Naphtali ᵉ by their clans were:
through Jahzeel, the Jahzeelite clan;
through Guni, the Gunite clan;
⁴⁹through Jezer, the Jezerite clan;
through Shillem, the Shillemite clan.
⁵⁰These were the clans of Naphtali; ᶠ those numbered were 45,400. ᵍ

⁵¹The total number of the men of Israel was 601,730. ʰ

⁵²The LORD said to Moses, ⁵³"The land is to be allotted to them as an inheritance based on the number of names. i ⁵⁴To a larger group give a larger inheritance, and to a smaller group a smaller one; each is to receive its inheritance according to the number ʲ of those listed. ᵏ ⁵⁵Be sure that the land is distributed by lot. ˡ What each group inherits will be according to the names for its ancestral tribe. ⁵⁶Each inheritance is to be distributed by lot among the larger and smaller groups."

⁵⁷These were the Levites ᵐ who were counted by their clans:
through Gershon, the Gershonite clan;
through Kohath, the Kohathite clan;
through Merari, the Merarite clan.
⁵⁸These also were Levite clans:
the Libnite clan,
the Hebronite clan,
the Mahlite clan,
the Mushite clan,
the Korahite clan.
(Kohath was the forefather of Amram; ⁿ ⁵⁹the name of Amram's wife was Jochebed, ᵒ a descendant of Levi, who was born to the Levites ᵏ in Egypt. To Amram she bore Aaron, Moses ᵖ and their sister ᵠ Miriam. ʳ ⁶⁰Aaron was the father of Nadab and Abihu, Eleazar and Ithamar. ˢ ⁶¹But Nadab and Abihu ᵗ died when they made an offering before the LORD with unauthorized fire.) ᵘ

⁶²All the male Levites a month old or more numbered 23,000. ᵛ They were not counted ʷ along with the other Israelites because they received no inheritance ˣ among them. ʸ

⁶³These are the ones counted ᶻ by Moses and Eleazar the priest when they counted the Israelites on the plains of Moab ᵃ by the Jordan across from Jericho. ᵇ ⁶⁴Not one of them was among those counted ᶜ by Moses and Aaron ᵈ the priest when they counted the Israelites in the Desert of Sinai. ⁶⁵For the LORD had told those Israelites they would surely die in the desert, ᵉ and not one of them was left except Caleb ᶠ son of Jephunneh and Joshua son of Nun. ᵍ

Zelophehad's Daughters

27:1–11pp — Nu 36:1–12

27 The daughters of Zelophehad ʰ son of Hepher, i the son of Gilead, ʲ the son of Makir, ᵏ the son of Manasseh,

26:41 ʸNu 1:37
26:42 ᶻNu 1:38
ᵃJdg 18:19
ᵇGe 46:23
26:44 ᶜS Nu 1:40
26:47 ᵈNu 1:41
26:48 ᵉS Ge 30:8
26:50 ᶠNu 1:43
ᵍNu 1:42
26:51
ʰS Ex 12:37
26:53 ʲver 55;
Jos 11:23; 14:1;
Eze 45:8
26:54 ʲNu 33:54
ᵏNu 35:8
26:55 ˡS Lev 16:8

26:57
ᵐS Ge 46:11
26:58 ⁿEx 6:20
26:59 ᵒS Ex 2:1
ᵖEx 6:20
ᵠEx 2:4
ʳEx 15:20
26:60 ˢEx 6:23
26:61
ᵗS Lev 10:1-2
ᵘNu 3:4
26:62 ᵛNu 3:39
ʷNu 1:47
ˣS Nu 18:23
ʸS Nu 2:33
26:63 ᶻS Nu 1:19
ᵃS ver 3 ᵇNu 22:1
26:64
ᶜS Nu 14:29
ᵈNu 1:44
26:65
ᵉNu 14:28;
1Co 10:5
ᶠNu 13:6
ᵍS Nu 11:28
27:1 ʰS Nu 26:33
iJos 17:2,3
ʲS Nu 26:30
ᵏS Ge 50:23;
1Ch 2:21

i40 Samaritan Pentateuch and Vulgate (see also Septuagint); Masoretic Text does not have *through Ard.*
ᵏ59 Or *Jochebed, a daughter of Levi, who was born to Levi*

26:46 *daughter named Serah.* The listing of this solitary daughter is striking.
26:51 *601,730.* Despite all that the people had been through during the years of desert experience, their total number was nearly the same as that of those who were first numbered. This remarkable fact is to be regarded as the blessing of the Lord, in fulfillment of his many promises to give numerical strength to the people descended from Abraham through Jacob (see note on Ge 12:2–3). This grand total and its parts are in accord with the general pattern of the

numbers in the book (see note on 1:46).
26:53 *allotted ... based on the number.* Larger tribes would receive larger shares, but decisions of place would be made by lot (v. 65).
26:57 *Levites.* As in the first census (ch. 3), the Levites were counted separately.
27:1–11 The daughters of a man who had no son (see 26:33) were concerned about their rights of inheritance and the preservation of their father's name in the land (v. 4). Their action in approaching Moses, Eleazar and the leaders

belonged to the clans of Manasseh son of Joseph. The names of the daughters were Mahlah, Noah, Hoglah, Milcah and Tirzah. They approached [2]the entrance to the Tent of Meeting[l] and stood before Moses,[m] Eleazar the priest, the leaders[n] and the whole assembly, and said, [3]"Our father died in the desert.[o] He was not among Korah's followers, who banded together against the LORD,[p] but he died for his own sin and left no sons.[q] [4]Why should our father's name disappear from his clan because he had no son? Give us property among our father's relatives."

[5]So Moses brought their case[r] before the LORD[s] [6]and the LORD said to him, [7]"What Zelophehad's daughters are saying is right. You must certainly give them property as an inheritance[t] among their father's relatives and turn their father's inheritance over to them.[u]

[8]"Say to the Israelites, 'If a man dies and leaves no son, turn his inheritance over to his daughter. [9]If he has no daughter, give his inheritance to his brothers. [10]If he has no brothers, give his inheritance to his father's brothers. [11]If his father had no brothers, give his inheritance to the nearest relative in his clan, that he may possess it. This is to be a legal requirement[v] for the Israelites, as the LORD commanded Moses.'"

Joshua to Succeed Moses

[12]Then the LORD said to Moses, "Go up this mountain[w] in the Abarim range[x] and see the land[y] I have given the Israelites.[z] [13]After you have seen it, you too will be gathered to your people,[a] as your brother Aaron[b] was, [14]for when the community rebelled at the waters in the Desert of Zin,[c] both of you disobeyed my command

to honor me as holy[d] before their eyes." (These were the waters of Meribah[e] Kadesh, in the Desert of Zin.)

[15]Moses said to the LORD, [16]"May the LORD, the God of the spirits of all mankind,[f] appoint a man over this community [17]to go out and come in before them, one who will lead them out and bring them in, so the LORD's people will not be like sheep without a shepherd."[g]

[18]So the LORD said to Moses, "Take Joshua son of Nun, a man in whom is the spirit,[1][h] and lay your hand on him.[i] [19]Have him stand before Eleazar the priest and the entire assembly and commission him[j] in their presence.[k] [20]Give him some of your authority so the whole Israelite community will obey him.[l] [21]He is to stand before Eleazar the priest, who will obtain decisions for him by inquiring[m] of the Urim[n] before the LORD. At his command he and the entire community of the Israelites will go out, and at his command they will come in."

[22]Moses did as the LORD commanded him. He took Joshua and had him stand before Eleazar the priest and the whole assembly. [23]Then he laid his hands on him and commissioned him,[o] as the LORD instructed through Moses.

Daily Offerings

28 The LORD said to Moses, [2]"Give this command to the Israelites and say to them: 'See that you present to me at the appointed time[p] the food[q] for my offerings made by fire, as an aroma pleasing to me.'[r] [3]Say to them: 'This is the offering made by fire that you are to present to the LORD: two lambs a year old without de-

Cross references (center column)

27:2 [l]Ex 40:2,17
[m]S Nu 9:6
[n]Nu 1:16; 31:13; 32:2; 36:1
27:3 [o]Nu 26:65
[p]Nu 16:2
[q]Nu 26:33
27:5 [r]S Ge 25:22; S Ex 18:19
[s]S Nu 9:8
27:7 [t]Job 42:15
[u]ver 8; Jos 17:4
27:11 [v]Nu 35:29
27:12 [w]Nu 23:14
[x]Nu 33:47; Jer 22:20
[y]Dt 3:23-27; 32:48-52
[z]S Lev 14:34
27:13 [a]Nu 20:12; 31:2; Dt 4:22; 31:14; 32:50; 1Ki 2:1
[b]Nu 20:28
27:14 [c]S Nu 20:1,2-5
[d]S Nu 20:12
[e]S Ex 17:7
27:16 [f]S Nu 16:22; S Job 21:20
27:17 [g]1Ki 22:17; 2Ch 18:16; Eze 34:5; Zec 10:2; S Mt 9:36
27:18 [h]S Ge 41:38; Nu 11:25-29
[i]ver 23; Dt 34:9; Ac 6:6
27:19 [j]ver 23; Dt 3:28; 31:14,23
[k]Dt 31:7
27:20 [l]Jos 1:16,17
27:21 [m]S Ge 25:22; Jos 9:14; Ps 106:13; Isa 8:19; Hag 1:13; Mal 2:7; 3:1
[n]S Ex 28:30
27:23 [o]S ver 19
28:2 [p]Lev 23:1-44
[q]S Lev 3:11
[r]Lev 1:9

[1]18 Or Spirit

---

of the nation was unprecedented, an act of courage and conviction.

27:3 *he died for his own sin.* A particular case from among those who died in the desert (see 26:64–65). These pious women had a sound understanding of the nature of the desert experience and a just claim for their family.

27:5 *Moses brought their case before the LORD.* This verse indicates how case law might have operated in Israel. The general laws would be proclaimed. Then legitimate exceptions or special considerations would come to the elders, and perhaps to Moses himself. He then would await a decision from the Lord. In this case, the Lord gave a favorable decision for these women. Ch. 36 provides an appendix to this account.

27:12–23 The juxtaposition of the story of Zelophehad's daughters' request for an inheritance in the land (vv. 1–11) and the Lord's words to Moses about his own exclusion from the land (vv. 12–14) is touching. Provisions are made for exceptions and irregularities in the inheritance laws, but there is no provision for Moses. His sin at the waters of

Meribah at Kadesh (20:1–13) was always before him.

27:16 *appoint a man.* Moses' reaction to this reassertion of his restriction is a prayer for his successor.

27:18 *Take Joshua.* As Moses and Aaron needed to determine the true successor of Aaron before his death (20:22–29), so the true successor of Moses also needed to be established. Joshua and Caleb were the two heroes in the darkest hour of Israel's apostasy (chs. 13–14). It was fitting that the Lord selected one of them (cf. Ex 17:9–14; 24:13; 32:17; 33:11).

27:20 *Give him some of your authority.* The transition from Moses' leadership to that of any successor would be difficult. The change would be smoother by a gradual shift of power while Moses was still alive.

28:1–29:40 These chapters attest to the all-pervasiveness of sacrifice in the life of the people and to the enormity of the work of the priests. Perhaps the reason for these passages at this time is to give continuity to the impending transition from the leadership of Moses to that of Joshua (27:12–23).

28:1–8 See Ex 29:38–41; Lev 1–7 and notes.

fect,[s] as a regular burnt offering each day.[t] [4]Prepare one lamb in the morning and the other at twilight,[u] [5]together with a grain offering[v] of a tenth of an ephah[m] of fine flour[w] mixed with a quarter of a hin[n] of oil[x] from pressed olives. [6]This is the regular burnt offering[y] instituted at Mount Sinai[z] as a pleasing aroma, an offering made to the LORD by fire.[a] [7]The accompanying drink offering[b] is to be a quarter of a hin of fermented drink[c] with each lamb. Pour out the drink offering to the LORD at the sanctuary.[d] [8]Prepare the second lamb at twilight,[e] along with the same kind of grain offering and drink offering that you prepare in the morning.[f] This is an offering made by fire, an aroma pleasing to the LORD.[g]

Sabbath Offerings

[9]" 'On the Sabbath[h] day, make an offering of two lambs a year old without defect,[i] together with its drink offering and a grain offering of two-tenths of an ephah[o] of fine flour mixed with oil.[k] [10]This is the burnt offering for every Sabbath,[l] in addition to the regular burnt offering[m] and its drink offering.

Monthly Offerings

[11]" 'On the first of every month,[n] present to the LORD a burnt offering of two young bulls,[o] one ram[p] and seven male lambs a year old, all without defect.[q] [12]With each bull there is to be a grain offering[r] of three-tenths of an ephah[p][s] of fine flour mixed with oil; with the ram, a grain offering of two-tenths[t] of an ephah of fine flour mixed with oil; [13]and with each lamb, a grain offering[u] of a tenth[v] of an ephah of fine flour mixed with oil. This is for a burnt offering,[w] a pleasing aroma, an offering made to the LORD[x] by fire. [14]With each bull there is to be a drink offering[y] of half a hin[q] of wine; with the ram, a third of a hin[r]; and with each lamb, a quarter of a hin. This is the monthly burnt offering to be made at each new moon[z] during the year. [15]Besides the regular burnt offering[a] with its drink offering, one male goat[b] is to be presented to the LORD as a sin offering.[c]

28:3 sS Ex 12:5
tEx 29:38;
Am 4:4
28:4 uS Ex 29:39
28:5 vNu 29:6
wLev 6:20
xS Lev 2:1
28:6 yLev 1:3
zEx 19:3
aS Lev 1:9
28:7 bNu 6:15
cS Lev 10:9;
S 23:13
dS Lev 3:7;
Nu 3:28
28:8 eS Ex 29:39
fS Lev 3:7 gver 2;
Lev 1:9
28:9
hS Ex 20:10;
Mt 12:5 iver 3
jS Lev 23:13 kver 5
28:10
lS Lev 23:38 mver 3
28:11
nNu 10:10
oNu 7:15
pS Lev 5:15
qLev 1:3
28:12
rS Nu 15:6;
S 29:3 sNu 15:9
tver 20
28:13
uS Lev 6:14 vver 21 wS Nu 15:3
xLev 1:9
28:14 yS Nu 15:7
zver 11; 2Ch 2:4;
Ezr 3:5
28:15 aver 3,23, 24 bver 30
cLev 4:3;
Nu 29:16,19

28:16
dS Ex 12:11;
2Ch 30:13; 35:1
28:17
eS Ex 12:19
fS Ex 12:15
28:18
gS Ex 12:16
28:19 hS Lev 1:9
iver 11
28:20
jS Lev 14:10 kver 12
28:21 lver 13
28:22 mLev 4:3;
Ro 8:3
nS Nu 15:28
28:24 oLev 1:9
28:26
pS Ex 34:22
qS Ex 23:16 rver 18
28:27 sver 19
28:28 tver 12
28:29 uver 13
28:30 vver 15

The Passover

28:16–25pp — Ex 12:14–20; Lev 23:4–8; Dt 16:1–8

[16]" 'On the fourteenth day of the first month the LORD's Passover[d] is to be held. [17]On the fifteenth day of this month there is to be a festival; for seven days[e] eat bread made without yeast.[f] [18]On the first day hold a sacred assembly and do no regular work.[g] [19]Present to the LORD an offering made by fire,[h] a burnt offering of two young bulls, one ram and seven male lambs a year old, all without defect.[i] [20]With each bull prepare a grain offering of three-tenths of an ephah[j] of fine flour mixed with oil; with the ram, two-tenths;[k] [21]and with each of the seven lambs, one-tenth.[l] [22]Include one male goat as a sin offering[m] to make atonement for you.[n] [23]Prepare these in addition to the regular morning burnt offering. [24]In this way prepare the food for the offering made by fire every day for seven days as an aroma pleasing to the LORD;[o] it is to be prepared in addition to the regular burnt offering and its drink offering. [25]On the seventh day hold a sacred assembly and do no regular work.

Feast of Weeks

28:26–31pp — Lev 23:15–22; Dt 16:9–12

[26]" 'On the day of firstfruits,[p] when you present to the LORD an offering of new grain during the Feast of Weeks,[q] hold a sacred assembly and do no regular work.[r] [27]Present a burnt offering of two young bulls, one ram and seven male lambs a year old as an aroma pleasing to the LORD.[s] [28]With each bull there is to be a grain offering of three-tenths of an ephah of fine flour mixed with oil; with the ram, two-tenths;[t] [29]and with each of the seven lambs, one-tenth.[u] [30]Include one male goat[v] to make atonement for you. [31]Prepare these together with their drink offerings, in addition to the regular burnt offer-

m5 That is, probably about 2 quarts (about 2 liters); also in verses 13, 21 and 29   n5 That is, probably about 1 quart (about 1 liter); also in verses 7 and 14   o9 That is, probably about 4 quarts (about 4.5 liters); also in verses 12, 20 and 28   p12 That is, probably about 6 quarts (about 6.5 liters); also in verses 20 and 28   q14 That is, probably about 2 quarts (about 2 liters)   r14 That is, probably about 1 1/4 quarts (about 1.2 liters)

28:9–10 The Sabbath offerings were in addition to the daily offerings.
28:11–15 The sacrifices at the beginning of the month were of great significance. These were times for celebration and blowing of trumpets in worship (see 10:10).
28:16–25 The priests are instructed as to the proper preparation for the Passover in the first month of the year. Passover is also associated with the Feast of Unleavened Bread (see Ex 12:15; Lev 23:4–8). The number 7 (and 14, its multiple) reappears frequently in the paragraph.
28:26–31 The Feast of Weeks came 50 days after the Feast of Unleavened Bread (see Lev 23:9–22); from this number the term "Pentecost" (meaning "fifty") was used in the NT (Ac 2:1).

ing[w] and its grain offering. Be sure the animals are without defect.

Feast of Trumpets
29:1–6pp — Lev 23:23–25

29 " 'On the first day of the seventh month hold a sacred assembly and do no regular work.[x] It is a day for you to sound the trumpets. [2]As an aroma pleasing to the LORD,[y] prepare a burnt offering[z] of one young bull, one ram and seven male lambs a year old,[a] all without defect.[b] [3]With the bull prepare a grain offering[c] of three-tenths of an ephah[s] of fine flour mixed with oil; with the ram, two-tenths[t]; [4]and with each of the seven lambs, one-tenth.[u][d] [5]Include one male goat[e] as a sin offering to make atonement for you. [6]These are in addition to the monthly[f] and daily burnt offerings[g] with their grain offerings[h] and drink offerings[i] as specified. They are offerings made to the LORD by fire—a pleasing aroma.[i]

Day of Atonement
29:7–11pp — Lev 16:2–34; 23:26–32

[7]" 'On the tenth day of this seventh month hold a sacred assembly. You must deny yourselves[v][k] and do no work.[l] [8]Present as an aroma pleasing to the LORD a burnt offering of one young bull, one ram and seven male lambs a year old, all without defect.[m] [9]With the bull prepare a grain offering[n] of three-tenths of an ephah of fine flour mixed with oil; with the ram, two-tenths;[o] [10]and with each of the seven lambs, one-tenth.[p] [11]Include one male goat[q] as a sin offering, in addition to the sin offering for atonement and the regular burnt offering[r] with its grain offering, and their drink offerings.[s]

Feast of Tabernacles
29:12–39pp — Lev 23:33–43; Dt 16:13–17

[12]" 'On the fifteenth day of the seventh[t] month,[u] hold a sacred assembly and do no regular work. Celebrate a festival to the LORD for seven days. [13]Present an offering made by fire as an aroma pleasing to the LORD,[v] a burnt offering of thirteen young bulls, two rams and fourteen male lambs a year old, all without defect.[w] [14]With each of the thirteen bulls prepare a

grain offering[x] of three-tenths of an ephah of fine flour mixed with oil; with each of the two rams, two-tenths; [15]and with each of the fourteen lambs, one-tenth.[y] [16]Include one male goat as a sin offering,[z] in addition to the regular burnt offering with its grain offering and drink offering. [a]

[17]" 'On the second day[b] prepare twelve young bulls, two rams and fourteen male lambs a year old, all without defect.[c] [18]With the bulls, rams and lambs, prepare their grain offerings[d] and drink offerings[e] according to the number specified.[f] [19]Include one male goat as a sin offering,[g] in addition to the regular burnt offering[h] with its grain offering, and their drink offerings.[i]

[20]" 'On the third day prepare eleven bulls, two rams and fourteen male lambs a year old, all without defect.[j] [21]With the bulls, rams and lambs, prepare their grain offerings and drink offerings according to the number specified.[k] [22]Include one male goat as a sin offering, in addition to the regular burnt offering with its grain offering and drink offering.

[23]" 'On the fourth day prepare ten bulls, two rams and fourteen male lambs a year old, all without defect. [24]With the bulls, rams and lambs, prepare their grain offerings and drink offerings according to the number specified. [25]Include one male goat as a sin offering, in addition to the regular burnt offering with its grain offering and drink offering.

[26]" 'On the fifth day prepare nine bulls, two rams and fourteen male lambs a year old, all without defect. [27]With the bulls, rams and lambs, prepare their grain offerings and drink offerings according to the number specified. [28]Include one male goat as a sin offering, in addition to the regular burnt offering with its grain offering and drink offering.

[29]" 'On the sixth day prepare eight bulls, two rams and fourteen male lambs a year old, all without defect. [30]With the bulls, rams and lambs, prepare their grain

28:31 [w]ver 3,19
29:1 [x]Nu 28:18
29:2 [y]Nu 28:2
[z]Lev 1:9;
Nu 28:11 [a]ver 36
[b]Lev 1:3;
Nu 28:3
29:3 [c]ver 14;
Nu 28:12
29:4 [d]Nu 28:13
29:5 [e]Nu 28:15
29:6 [f]Nu 28:11
[g]Nu 28:3
[h]Nu 28:5
[i]Nu 28:7
[j]Lev 1:9; Nu 28:2
29:7 [k]Ac 27:9
[l]S Ex 31:15
29:8 [m]ver 2
29:9 [n]S ver 3,18
[o]Nu 28:12
29:10 [p]Nu 28:13
29:11 [q]ver 5;
Nu 28:15
[r]S Lev 16:3 [s]S ver 6
29:12 [t]1Ki 8:2; 12:32
[u]S Lev 23:24
29:13 [v]ver 2;
Nu 28:2
[w]Nu 28:3

29:14 [x]S ver 3;
S Nu 15:6
29:15 [y]ver 4;
Nu 28:13
29:16 [z]ver 5;
S Nu 28:15 [a]ver 6
29:17 [b]Lev 23:36
[c]ver 2; Nu 28:3
29:18 [d]S ver 9
[e]Nu 28:7
[f]Nu 15:4-12
29:19
[g]S Nu 28:15
[h]Nu 28:3 [i]ver 6
29:20 [j]S ver 17
29:21 [k]S ver 18

[s]3 That is, probably about 6 quarts (about 6.5 liters); also in verses 9 and 14   [t]3 That is, probably about 4 quarts (about 4.5 liters); also in verses 9 and 14   [u]4 That is, probably about 2 quarts (about 2 liters); also in verses 10 and 15   [v]7 Or *must fast*

29:1–6 The Feast of Trumpets came at the beginning of the seventh month, a busy month for the worship of the Lord in holy festivals (see Lev 23:23–25; see also chart on "OT Feasts and Other Sacred Days," p. 176). Later in Jewish tradition this feast commemorated the New Year, *Rosh Hashanah*. The trumpet used was the *shophar*, the ram's horn. **29:7–11** The Feast of Trumpets leads into the Day of

Atonement, a time of confession, contrition and celebration (see Lev 16; 23:26–32).
29:12–34 In the seventh month the Feast of Trumpets took place on the first day, the Day of Atonement occurred on the tenth day, and the Feast of Tabernacles began on the 15th day and lasted for seven days (see Lev 23:33–44). Each day of the Feast of Tabernacles had its own order for sacrifice.

offerings and drink offerings according to the number specified. ³¹Include one male goat as a sin offering, in addition to the regular burnt offering with its grain offering and drink offering.

³²"'On the seventh day prepare seven bulls, two rams and fourteen male lambs a year old, all without defect. ³³With the bulls, rams and lambs, prepare their grain offerings and drink offerings according to the number specified. ³⁴Include one male goat as a sin offering, in addition to the regular burnt offering with its grain offering and drink offering.

³⁵"'On the eighth day hold an assembly[l] and do no regular work. ³⁶Present an offering made by fire as an aroma pleasing to the LORD,[m] a burnt offering of one bull, one ram and seven male lambs a year old,[n] all without defect. ³⁷With the bull, the ram and the lambs, prepare their grain offerings and drink offerings according to the number specified. ³⁸Include one male goat as a sin offering, in addition to the regular burnt offering with its grain offering and drink offering.

³⁹"'In addition to what you vow[o] and your freewill offerings,[p] prepare these for the LORD at your appointed feasts:[q] your burnt offerings,[r] grain offerings, drink offerings and fellowship offerings.[w][s]'"

⁴⁰Moses told the Israelites all that the LORD commanded him.

Vows

30 Moses said to the heads of the tribes of Israel:[t] "This is what the LORD commands: ²When a man makes a vow to the LORD or takes an oath to obligate himself by a pledge, he must not break his word but must do everything he said.[u]

³"When a young woman still living in her father's house makes a vow to the LORD or obligates herself by a pledge ⁴and her father hears about her vow or pledge but says nothing to her, then all her vows and every pledge by which she obligated

herself will stand.[v] ⁵But if her father forbids her[w] when he hears about it, none of her vows or the pledges by which she obligated herself will stand; the LORD will release her because her father has forbidden her.

⁶"If she marries after she makes a vow[x] or after her lips utter a rash promise by which she obligates herself ⁷and her husband hears about it but says nothing to her, then her vows or the pledges by which she obligated herself will stand. ⁸But if her husband[y] forbids her when he hears about it, he nullifies the vow that obligates her or the rash promise by which she obligates herself, and the LORD will release her.[z]

⁹"Any vow or obligation taken by a widow or divorced woman will be binding on her.

¹⁰"If a woman living with her husband makes a vow or obligates herself by a pledge under oath ¹¹and her husband hears about it but says nothing to her and does not forbid her, then all her vows or the pledges by which she obligated herself will stand. ¹²But if her husband nullifies them when he hears about them, then none of the vows or pledges that came from her lips will stand.[a] Her husband has nullified them, and the LORD will release her. ¹³Her husband may confirm or nullify any vow she makes or any sworn pledge to deny herself. ¹⁴But if her husband says nothing to her about it from day to day, then he confirms all her vows or the pledges binding on her. He confirms them by saying nothing to her when he hears about them. ¹⁵If, however, he nullifies them[b] some time after he hears about them, then he is responsible for her guilt."

¹⁶These are the regulations the LORD gave Moses concerning relationships between a man and his wife, and between a father and his young daughter still living in his house.

Cross references (center column)

29:35
[l] S Lev 23:36
29:36 [m] Lev 1:9
[n] ver 2
29:39 [o] Nu 6:2
[p] S Lev 7:16
[q] S Lev 23:2
[r] Lev 1:3;
1Ch 23:31;
2Ch 31:3
[s] Lev 3:1
30:1 [t] S Nu 1:4
30:2
[u] Dt 23:21-23;
Jdg 11:35;
Job 22:27;
Ps 22:25; 50:14;
61:5,8; 76:11;
116:14; Pr 20:25;
Ecc 5:4,5;
Isa 19:21;
Jnh 1:16; 2:9

30:4 [v] ver 7
30:5 [w] ver 8,12, 15
30:6 [x] S Lev 5:4
30:8 [y] S Ge 3:6
[z] ver 5
30:12 [a] Eph 5:22; Col 3:18
30:15 [b] S ver 5

[w] 39 Traditionally *peace offerings*

29:40 *Moses told the Israelites.* The recapitulation of these festivals was a necessary part of the transfer of power from Moses to Joshua.

30:1–16 The principal OT passage on vows (see Dt 23:21–23). A vow is not to be made rashly (cf. Ecc 5:1–7), and a vow to the Lord must be kept.

30:3–5 The vow of an unmarried woman still under her father's protection might be nullified by her father. This and the following law were probably designed for the protection of the woman, who in ancient Near Eastern society was subject to strong societal pressures, some of which would leave her without defense.

30:6–8 The vow of a married woman might be nullified by her husband.

30:9 *widow or divorced woman.* She is her own agent in the taking of vows.

30:10–15 Further examples of the complications that come in the taking of vows within the husband-wife relationship. Such complications may have come up much as in the case of Zelophehad's daughters (27:1–11). One case after another presented itself, resulting in this final codification. Presumably, in the centuries leading up to the NT, the legal decisions on vows became even more complex. The words of Jesus that one is to avoid complications connected with oaths (Mt 5:33–37) are liberating.

Vengeance on the Midianites

31 The LORD said to Moses, [2]"Take vengeance on the Midianites[c] for the Israelites. After that, you will be gathered to your people.[d]"

[3]So Moses said to the people, "Arm some of your men to go to war against the Midianites and to carry out the LORD's vengeance[e] on them. [4]Send into battle a thousand men from each of the tribes of Israel." [5]So twelve thousand men armed for battle,[f] a thousand from each tribe, were supplied from the clans of Israel. [6]Moses sent them into battle,[g] a thousand from each tribe, along with Phinehas[h] son of Eleazar, the priest, who took with him articles from the sanctuary[i] and the trumpets[j] for signaling.

[7]They fought against Midian, as the LORD commanded Moses,[k] and killed every man.[l] [8]Among their victims were Evi, Rekem, Zur, Hur and Reba[m]—the five kings of Midian.[n] They also killed Balaam son of Beor[o] with the sword.[p] [9]The Israelites captured the Midianite women[q] and children and took all the Midianite herds, flocks and goods as plunder.[r] [10]They burned[s] all the towns where the Midianites had settled, as well as all their camps.[t] [11]They took all the plunder and spoils, including the people and animals,[u] [12]and brought the captives, spoils[v] and plunder to Moses and Eleazar the priest and the Israelite assembly[w] at their camp on the plains of Moab, by the Jordan across from Jericho.[x x]

[13]Moses, Eleazar the priest and all the leaders of the community went to meet them outside the camp. [14]Moses was angry with the officers of the army[y]—the commanders of thousands and commanders of hundreds—who returned from the battle.

[15]"Have you allowed all the women to live?" he asked them. [16]"They were the ones who followed Balaam's advice[z] and were the means of turning the Israelites away from the LORD in what happened at Peor,[a] so that a plague[b] struck the LORD's people. [17]Now kill all the boys. And kill every woman who has slept with a man,[c] [18]but save for yourselves every girl who has never slept with a man.

[19]"All of you who have killed anyone or touched anyone who was killed[d] must stay outside the camp seven days.[e] On the third and seventh days you must purify yourselves[f] and your captives. [20]Purify every garment[g] as well as everything made of leather, goat hair or wood.[h]"

[21]Then Eleazar the priest said to the soldiers who had gone into battle,[i] "This is the requirement of the law that the LORD gave Moses: [22]Gold, silver, bronze, iron,[j] tin, lead [23]and anything else that can withstand fire must be put through the fire,[k] and then it will be clean. But it must also be purified with the water of cleansing.[l] And whatever cannot withstand fire must be put through that water. [24]On the seventh day wash your clothes and you will be clean.[m] Then you may come into the camp.[n]"

Dividing the Spoils

[25]The LORD said to Moses, [26]"You and Eleazar the priest and the family heads[o] of the community are to count all the people[p] and animals that were captured.[q] [27]Divide[r] the spoils between the soldiers

---

31:2 [c]S Ge 25:2
[d]S Nu 20:26
31:3 [e]Jdg 11:36;
1Sa 24:12;
2Sa 4:8; 22:48;
Ps 94:1; 149:7;
Isa 34:8;
Jer 11:20; 46:10;
Eze 25:17
31:5 [f]ver 6,21
31:6 [g]S ver 5
[h]S Ex 6:25
[i]Nu 14:44
[j]S Nu 10:2
31:7 [k]Nu 25:16
[l]Dt 20:13;
Jdg 21:11;
1Ki 11:15,16
31:8 [m]Jos 13:21
[n]S Nu 25:15
[o]S Nu 22:5;
S 24:14
[p]Jos 13:22
31:9 [q]ver 15
[r]S Ge 34:29
31:10 [s]Jos 6:24;
8:28; 11:11;
Jdg 18:27
[t]Ge 25:16;
1Ch 6:54;
Ps 69:25;
Eze 25:4
31:11 [u]ver 26;
Dt 20:14;
2Ch 28:8
31:12 [v]ver 32,
53; Ge 49:27;
Ex 15:9
[w]S Nu 27:2
[x]Nu 22:1
31:14 [y]ver 48;
Ex 18:21;
Dt 1:15; 2Sa 18:1
31:16
[z]S Nu 22:5;
S 24:14;
S 2Pe 2:15
[a]S Nu 23:28;
25:1-9
[b]S Nu 14:37
31:17 [c]Dt 7:2;
20:16-18;
Jdg 21:11
31:19 [d]Nu 19:16
[e]S Lev 21:1
[f]Nu 19:12
31:20 [g]Nu 19:19
[h]S Lev 11:32
31:21 [i]S ver 5
31:22 [j]Jos 6:19;
22:8
31:23
[k]S 1Co 3:13
[l]S Nu 8:7
31:24
[m]S Lev 11:25

[n]S Lev 14:8 **31:26** [o]S Nu 1:4 [p]S Nu 1:19 [q]S ver 11,12 **31:27**
[r]Jos 22:8; 1Sa 25:13; 30:24

[x]12 Hebrew *Jordan of Jericho*; possibly an ancient name for the Jordan River

---

31:1–24 The Lord declares a holy war (see Introduction to Joshua: The Conquest and the Ethical Question of War) against the Midianites as one of Moses' last actions before the end of his life. Moses was not motivated by petty jealousy; rather, the war was "the LORD's vengeance" (v. 3) for the Midianites' part in seducing the Israelites to engage in sexual immorality and to worship the Baal of Peor. (See 25:16–18, where the specific mention of Cozbi, a Midianite woman, heightens the anger expressed in ch. 31.)
31:1 *gathered to your people*. A euphemism for death (see, e.g., Ge 25:8,17; 35:29).
31:4 *a thousand men from each of the tribes of Israel*. The burden of the holy war had to be shared equally among the tribes.
31:6 *Phinehas*. His zeal for the Lord's honor led him to execute Zimri and Cozbi (25:8). Now he leads in the sacred aspects of the battle to demonstrate that this is a holy war. *trumpets*. See note on 10:3.
31:7 *as the LORD commanded Moses*. The battle was the Lord's.

31:8 *They also killed Balaam*. Ch. 25 lacks the name of the principal instigator of the seduction of the Israelite men to the depraved worship of Baal. But here he is found among the dead. What Balaam had been unable to accomplish through acts of magic or sorcery (chs. 22–24) he was almost able to achieve by his advice to the Midianites (v. 16).
31:9–18 While the troops killed the men of Midian, they spared the women and children as plunder. Moses commanded that only the virgin women (who were thus innocent of the indecencies at Peor) could be spared; the guilty women and the boys (who might endanger the inheritance rights of Israelite men) were to be put to death (vv. 15–17).
31:19–24 Since this was holy war, both people (vv. 19–20) and things (vv. 21–24) had to be cleansed (cf. 19:11–13).
31:26–35 Another aspect of holy war was the fair distribution of the spoils of war, both among those who fought in the battle and among those who stayed with the community, with appropriate shares to be given to the Lord, whose battle it was (v. 28).

who took part in the battle and the rest of the community. 28From the soldiers who fought in the battle, set apart as tribute for the LORD[s] one out of every five hundred, whether persons, cattle, donkeys, sheep or goats. 29Take this tribute from their half share and give it to Eleazar the priest as the LORD's part. 30From the Israelites' half, select one out of every fifty, whether persons, cattle, donkeys, sheep, goats or other animals. Give them to the Levites, who are responsible for the care of the LORD's tabernacle.[t]" 31So Moses and Eleazar the priest did as the LORD commanded Moses.

32The plunder remaining from the spoils[u] that the soldiers took was 675,000 sheep, 33372,000 cattle, 3461,000 donkeys 35and 32,000 women who had never slept with a man.

36The half share of those who fought in the battle was:

337,500 sheep, 37of which the tribute for the LORD[v] was 675;

3836,000 cattle, of which the tribute for the LORD was 72;

3930,500 donkeys, of which the tribute for the LORD was 61;

4016,000 people, of which the tribute for the LORD was 32.

41Moses gave the tribute to Eleazar the priest as the LORD's part,[w] as the LORD commanded Moses.[x]

42The half belonging to the Israelites, which Moses set apart from that of the fighting men— 43the community's half—was 337,500 sheep, 4436,000 cattle, 4530,500 donkeys 46and 16,000 people. 47From the Israelites' half, Moses selected one out of every fifty persons and animals, as the LORD commanded him, and gave them to the Levites, who were responsible for the care of the LORD's tabernacle.

48Then the officers[y] who were over the units of the army—the commanders of thousands and commanders of hundreds—went to Moses 49and said to him, "Your servants have counted[z] the soldiers under our command, and not one is missing.[a] 50So we have brought as an offering to the LORD the gold articles each of us acquired—armlets, bracelets, signet rings, earrings and necklaces—to make atonement for ourselves[b] before the LORD."

51Moses and Eleazar the priest accepted from them the gold—all the crafted articles. 52All the gold from the commanders of thousands and commanders of hundreds that Moses and Eleazar presented as a gift to the LORD weighed 16,750 shekels.[y] 53Each soldier had taken plunder[c] for himself. 54Moses and Eleazar the priest accepted the gold from the commanders of thousands and commanders of hundreds and brought it into the Tent of Meeting[d] as a memorial[e] for the Israelites before the LORD.

The Transjordan Tribes

32 The Reubenites and Gadites, who had very large herds and flocks,[f] saw that the lands of Jazer[g] and Gilead[h] were suitable for livestock.[i] 2So they came to Moses and Eleazar the priest and to the leaders of the community,[j] and said, 3"Ataroth,[k] Dibon,[l] Jazer,[m] Nimrah,[n] Heshbon,[o] Elealeh,[p] Sebam,[q] Nebo[r] and Beon[s]— 4the land the LORD subdued[t] before the people of Israel—are suitable for livestock,[u] and your servants have livestock. 5If we have found favor in your eyes," they said, "let this land be given to your servants as our possession. Do not make us cross the Jordan.[v]"

6Moses said to the Gadites and Reubenites, "Shall your countrymen go to war while you sit here? 7Why do you discourage the Israelites from going over into the land the LORD has given them?[w] 8This is what your fathers did when I sent them from Kadesh Barnea to look over the land.[x] 9After they went up to the Valley of Eshcol[y] and viewed the land, they discouraged the Israelites from entering the land the LORD had given them. 10The LORD's anger was aroused[z] that day and he swore this oath: a 11'Because they have not followed me wholeheartedly, not one of the men twenty years old or more[b] who came up out of Egypt[c] will see the land I promised on oath[d] to Abraham, Isaac and Jacob[e]— 12not one except Caleb son of Jephunneh the Kenizzite and Joshua son of Nun, for they followed the LORD wholeheartedly.'[f] 13The LORD's anger burned against Israel[g] and he made them wander

31:28 sver 37-41;
S Nu 18:21
31:30 tNu 3:7; 18:3
31:32 uS ver 12
31:37 vver 38-41
31:41 wNu 5:9; 18:8 xver 21,28
31:48 yS ver 14
31:49 zS Nu 1:19 aJer 23:4
31:50 bS Ex 30:16

31:53 cS Ge 34:29; Dt 20:14
31:54 dS Ex 27:21; 40:2 eS Ex 28:12
32:1 fver 24,36; Jdg 5:16 gS Nu 21:32 hS Ge 31:21 iEx 12:38
32:2 jLev 4:22; Nu 27:2
32:3 kver 34; Jos 16:2,7; 18:13 lver 34; S Nu 21:30 mver 36; nver 36; Jos 13:27 oNu 21:25 pver 37; Isa 15:4; 16:9; Jer 48:34 qJos 13:19; Isa 16:8,9; Jer 48:32 rNu 33:47; Dt 32:49; 34:1; 1Ch 5:8 sver 38; Jos 13:17; Eze 25:9
32:4 tNu 21:34 uEx 12:38
32:5 vS Nu 13:29
32:7 wNu 13:27-14:4 26; Dt 1:19-25
32:8 xNu 13:3, 26; Dt 1:24
32:9 yNu 13:23; Dt 1:24
32:10 zNu 11:1 aS Nu 14:20-23
32:11 bS Ex 30:14 cNu 1:1 dS Nu 14:23 eNu 14:28-30
32:12 fNu 14:24, 30; Ps 63:8
32:13 gS Ex 4:14

y52 That is, about 420 pounds (about 190 kilograms)

32:1 *Reubenites and Gadites.* The abundance of fertile grazing land in Transjordan prompted the leaders of these two tribes to request that they be allowed to settle there and not cross the Jordan. This area too was a gift of God won by conquest.

32:8 *This is what your fathers did.* Moses' fear was that the failure of these two tribes to stay with the whole community in conquering Canaan would be the beginning of a general revolt against entering the land. It would be the failure of Kadesh (chs. 13–14) all over again. Moreover, the conquest of Canaan was a commission to all Israel.

in the desert forty years, until the whole generation of those who had done evil in his sight was gone.[h]

14"And here you are, a brood of sinners, standing in the place of your fathers and making the LORD even more angry with Israel.[i] 15If you turn away from following him, he will again leave all this people in the desert, and you will be the cause of their destruction.[j]"

16Then they came up to him and said, "We would like to build pens[k] here for our livestock[l] and cities for our women and children. 17But we are ready to arm ourselves and go ahead of the Israelites[m] until we have brought them to their place.[n] Meanwhile our women and children will live in fortified cities, for protection from the inhabitants of the land. 18We will not return to our homes until every Israelite has received his inheritance.[o] 19We will not receive any inheritance with them on the other side of the Jordan, because our inheritance[p] has come to us on the east side of the Jordan."[q]

20Then Moses said to them, "If you will do this—if you will arm yourselves before the LORD for battle,[r] 21and if all of you will go armed over the Jordan before the LORD until he has driven his enemies out before him[s]— 22then when the land is subdued before the LORD, you may return[t] and be free from your obligation to the LORD and to Israel. And this land will be your possession[u] before the LORD.[v]

23"But if you fail to do this, you will be sinning against the LORD; and you may be sure that your sin will find you out.[w] 24Build cities for your women and children, and pens for your flocks,[x] but do what you have promised.[y]"

25The Gadites and Reubenites said to Moses, "We your servants will do as our lord commands.[z] 26Our children and wives, our flocks and herds will remain here in the cities of Gilead.[a] 27But your servants, every man armed for battle, will cross over to fight[b] before the LORD, just as our lord says."

28Then Moses gave orders about them[c] to Eleazar the priest and Joshua son of Nun[d] and to the family heads of the Israel-

ite tribes.[e] 29He said to them, "If the Gadites and Reubenites, every man armed for battle, cross over the Jordan with you before the LORD, then when the land is subdued before you,[f] give them the land of Gilead as their possession.[g] 30But if they do not cross over[h] with you armed, they must accept their possession with you in Canaan.[i]"

31The Gadites and Reubenites answered, "Your servants will do what the LORD has said.[j] 32We will cross over before the LORD into Canaan armed,[k] but the property we inherit will be on this side of the Jordan.[l]"

33Then Moses gave to the Gadites,[m] the Reubenites and the half-tribe of Manasseh[n] son of Joseph the kingdom of Sihon king of the Amorites[o] and the kingdom of Og king of Bashan[p]—the whole land with its cities and the territory around them.[q]

34The Gadites built up Dibon, Ataroth, Aroer,[r] 35Atroth Shophan, Jazer,[s] Jogbehah,[t] 36Beth Nimrah[u] and Beth Haran as fortified cities, and built pens for their flocks.[v] 37And the Reubenites rebuilt Heshbon,[w] Elealeh[x] and Kiriathaim,[y] 38as well as Nebo[z] and Baal Meon (these names were changed) and Sibmah.[a] They gave names to the cities they rebuilt.

39The descendants of Makir[b] son of Manasseh went to Gilead,[c] captured it and drove out the Amorites[d] who were there. 40So Moses gave Gilead to the Makirites,[e] the descendants of Manasseh, and they settled there. 41Jair,[f] a descendant of Manasseh, captured their settlements and called them Havvoth Jair.[z g] 42And Nobah captured Kenath[h] and its surrounding settlements and called it Nobah[i] after himself.[j]

Stages in Israel's Journey

33 Here are the stages in the journey[k] of the Israelites when they came out of Egypt[l] by divisions under the lead-

32:13
[h]Nu 14:28-35; 26:64,65
32:14 [i]S ver 10; Dt 1:34; Ps 78:59
32:15 [j]Dt 30:17-18; 2Ch 7:20
32:16 [k]ver 24, 36; 1Sa 24:3; Ps 50:9; 78:70
[l]Ex 12:38; Dt 3:19
32:17 [m]Dt 3:18; Jos 4:12,13
[n]S Nu 22:4; Dt 3:20
32:18
[o]Jos 22:1-4
32:19 [p]ver 22,29
[q]Nu 21:33; Jos 12:1; 22:7
32:20 [r]ver 17
32:21 [s]ver 17
32:22 [t]Jos 22:4
[u]S Lev 14:34
[v]Dt 3:18-20
32:23 [w]S Ge 4:7; S Isa 3:9
32:24 [x]S ver 1,16
[y]Nu 30:2
32:25 [z]ver 29; Jos 1:16,18; 22:2
32:26 [a]ver 16, 24; Jos 1:14; 12:2; 22:9; 2Sa 2:9; 1Ch 5:9
32:27 [b]ver 17,21
32:28 [c]ver 29; Dt 3:18-20; Jos 1:13
[d]Nu 11:28

[e]Nu 1:16
32:29 [f]S Nu 22:4
[g]S ver 19
32:30 [h]ver 23
[i]ver 29,32
32:31 [j]ver 29
32:32 [k]ver 17
[l]S ver 30; Jos 12:6
32:33
[m]Jos 13:24-28; 1Sa 13:7
[n]Jos 1:12
[o]Nu 21:21;
Dt 2:26 [p]S ver 19; S Jos 12:5
[q]S Nu 21:24; 34:14; Dt 2:36; Jos 12:6
32:34 [r]Dt 2:36; 3:12; 4:48; Jos 12:2; 13:9; Jdg 11:26; 1Sa 30:28; 1Ch 5:8; Jer 48:19
32:35 [s]ver 3
[t]Jdg 8:11
32:36 [u]S ver 3
[v]S ver 1
32:37 [w]Nu 21:25
[x]S ver 3
[y]Jos 13:19; 1Ch 6:76; Jer 48:1,23; Eze 25:9
32:38 [z]S ver 3; Isa 15:2; Jer 48:1, 22 [a]S ver 3
32:39
[b]S Ge 50:23

[c]Nu 26:29; Dt 2:36 [d]S Ge 10:16 **32:40** [e]S Ge 50:23; Dt 3:15
32:41 [f]1Ki 4:13 [g]Dt 3:14; Jos 13:30; Jdg 10:4; 1Ch 2:23
32:42 [h]1Ch 2:23 [i]Jdg 8:11 [j]1Sa 15:12; 2Sa 18:18; Ps 49:11; Isa 22:16; 56:5 **33:1** [k]Ex 17:1; 40:36 [l]Nu 1:1

[z]41 Or them the settlements of Jair

32:17 *we are ready to arm ourselves.* The leaders of Reuben and Gad sought to assure Moses that they did not wish to shirk their duty in helping to conquer the land. They would join their brothers in battle but wished to leave their families and livestock behind in the territory of their choosing.

32:23 *your sin will find you out.* The bargain was struck, but not without strong warnings if they failed to live up to

their word.

32:33 *and the half-tribe of Manasseh.* It appears that after the requirements for Transjordan settlement were established with the tribes of Reuben and Gad, half the tribe of Manasseh joined with them.

33:1—49 The numerous places (significantly 40 in number between Rameses and the plains of Moab) in Israel's desert experience are listed. Unfortunately, most of the sites were

ership of Moses and Aaron.[m] 2At the LORD's command Moses recorded[n] the stages in their journey[o]. This is their journey by stages:

3The Israelites set out[p] from Rameses[q] on the fifteenth day of the first month, the day after the Passover.[r] They marched out boldly[s] in full view of all the Egyptians, 4who were burying all their firstborn,[t] whom the LORD had struck down among them; for the LORD had brought judgment[u] on their gods.[v]

5The Israelites left Rameses and camped at Succoth.[w]

6They left Succoth and camped at Etham, on the edge of the desert.[x]

7They left Etham, turned back to Pi Hahiroth, to the east of Baal Zephon,[y] and camped near Migdol.[z]

8They left Pi Hahiroth[aa] and passed through the sea[b] into the desert, and when they had traveled for three days in the Desert of Etham, they camped at Marah.[c]

9They left Marah and went to Elim, where there were twelve springs and seventy palm trees, and they camped[d] there.

10They left Elim[e] and camped by the Red Sea.[b]

11They left the Red Sea and camped in the Desert of Sin.[f]

12They left the Desert of Sin and camped at Dophkah.

13They left Dophkah and camped at Alush.

14They left Alush and camped at Rephidim, where there was no water for the people to drink.[g]

15They left Rephidim[h] and camped in the Desert of Sinai.[i]

16They left the Desert of Sinai and camped at Kibroth Hattaavah.[j]

17They left Kibroth Hattaavah and camped at Hazeroth.[k]

18They left Hazeroth and camped at Rithmah.

19They left Rithmah and camped at Rimmon Perez.

20They left Rimmon Perez and camped at Libnah.[l]

21They left Libnah and camped at Rissah.

22They left Rissah and camped at Kehelathah.

23They left Kehelathah and camped at Mount Shepher.

24They left Mount Shepher and camped at Haradah.

25They left Haradah and camped at Makheloth.

26They left Makheloth and camped at Tahath.

27They left Tahath and camped at Terah.

28They left Terah and camped at Mithcah.

29They left Mithcah and camped at Hashmonah.

30They left Hashmonah and camped at Moseroth.[m]

31They left Moseroth and camped at Bene Jaakan.[n]

32They left Bene Jaakan and camped at Hor Haggidgad.

33They left Hor Haggidgad and camped at Jotbathah.[o]

34They left Jotbathah and camped at Abronah.

35They left Abronah and camped at Ezion Geber.[p]

36They left Ezion Geber and camped at Kadesh, in the Desert of Zin.[q]

37They left Kadesh and camped at Mount Hor,[r] on the border of Edom.[s] 38At the LORD's command Aaron the priest went up Mount Hor, where he died[t] on the first day of the fifth month of the fortieth year[u] after the Israelites came out of Egypt.[v] 39Aaron was a hundred and twenty-three years old when he died on Mount Hor.

40The Canaanite king[w] of Arad,[x] who lived in the Negev[y] of Canaan,

33:1 mS Ex 4:16; 6:26
33:2 nS Ex 17:14 oS ver 1
33:3 pNu 10:2 qS Ge 47:11 rJos 5:10 sS Ex 14:8
33:4 tS Ex 4:23 u2Ch 24:24; Jer 15:3; Eze 14:21 vS Ex 12:12
33:5 wEx 12:37
33:6 xEx 13:20
33:7 yEx 14:9 zS Ex 14:2
33:8 aEx 14:2 bS Ex 14:22 cS Ex 15:23
33:9 dEx 15:27
33:10 eEx 16:1
33:11 fS Ex 16:1
33:14 gS Ex 15:22; S 17:2
33:15 hS Ex 17:1 iS Ex 19:1
33:16 jS Nu 11:34
33:17 kNu 11:35

33:20 lJos 10:29; 12:15; 15:42; 21:13; 2Ki 8:22; 19:8; 23:31; 1Ch 6:57; 2Ch 21:10; Isa 37:8; Jer 52:1
33:30 mDt 10:6
33:31 nDt 10:6
33:33 oDt 10:7
33:35 pDt 2:8; 1Ki 9:26; 22:48
33:36 qS Nu 13:21
33:37 rS Nu 20:22 sS Ge 36:16; S Nu 20:16
33:38 tS Nu 27:13 uS Ex 16:35 vNu 20:25-28
33:40 wS Ge 10:18 xS Nu 21:1 yS Ge 12:9

a8 Many manuscripts of the Masoretic Text, Samaritan Pentateuch and Vulgate; most manuscripts of the Masoretic Text *left from before Hahiroth*   b10 Hebrew *Yam Suph*; that is, Sea of Reeds; also in verse 11

desert encampments, not cities with lasting archaeological records; so they are difficult to locate. Many of the places (e.g., in vv. 19–29) are not recorded elsewhere in Exodus and Numbers. Some of the places mentioned elsewhere (e.g., Taberah, 11:2; see 21:19) are missing here. The data warrant these conclusions: 1. Moses recorded the list at the Lord's command (v. 2). 2. The list should be taken seriously, as an accurate recapitulation of the stages of the journey, despite difficulty in locating many of the sites. 3. The numerical factor of 40 sites between Rameses and the plains of Moab suggests some styling of the list, which helps to account for the sites not included. 4. As in the case of genealogies in the Pentateuch, some factors of ancient significance may not be clear to us today. 5. Ultimately the record is a recital of the Lord's blessing on his people for the extended period of their desert experience. Although certainly not without geographical importance, the listing of the stages of Israel's experience in the desert is fundamentally a religious document, a litany of the Lord's deliverance of his people.

heard that the Israelites were coming.

41They left Mount Hor and camped at Zalmonah.

42They left Zalmonah and camped at Punon.

43They left Punon and camped at Oboth. z

44They left Oboth and camped at Iye Abarim, on the border of Moab. a

45They left Iyimc and camped at Dibon Gad.

46They left Dibon Gad and camped at Almon Diblathaim.

47They left Almon Diblathaim and camped in the mountains of Abarim, b near Nebo. c

48They left the mountains of Abarimd and camped on the plains of Moabe by the Jordanf across from Jericho.dg 49There on the plains of Moab they camped along the Jordan from Beth Jeshimothh to Abel Shittim. i

50On the plains of Moab by the Jordan across from Jerichoj the LORD said to Moses, 51"Speak to the Israelites and say to them: 'When you cross the Jordan into Canaan,k 52drive out all the inhabitants of the land before you. Destroy all their carved images and their cast idols, and demolish all their high places.l 53Take possession of the land and settle in it, for I have given you the land to possess. m 54Distribute the land by lot, n according to your clans. o To a larger group give a larger inheritance, and to a smaller group a smaller one. p Whatever falls to them by lot will be theirs. Distribute it according to your ancestral tribes. q

55" 'But if you do not drive out the inhabitants of the land, those you allow to remain will become barbs in your eyes and thornsr in your sides. They will give you trouble in the land where you will live. 56And then I will do to you what I plan to do to them. s ' "

Boundaries of Canaan

34 The LORD said to Moses, 2"Command the Israelites and say to them: 'When you enter Canaan,t the land

that will be allotted to you as an inheritanceu will have these boundaries: v

3" 'Your southern side will include some of the Desert of Zinw along the border of Edom. On the east, your southern boundary will start from the end of the Salt Sea,ex 4cross south of Scorpionf Pass,y continue on to Zin and go south of Kadesh Barnea. z Then it will go to Hazar Addar and over to Azmon, a 5where it will turn, join the Wadi of Egyptb and end at the Sea.g

6" 'Your western boundary will be the coast of the Great Sea. c This will be your boundary on the west. d

7" 'For your northern boundary, e run a line from the Great Sea to Mount Horf 8and from Mount Hor to Leboh Hamath.g Then the boundary will go to Zedad, 9continue to Ziphron and end at Hazar Enan. This will be your boundary on the north.

10" 'For your eastern boundary,h run a line from Hazar Enan to Shepham. 11The boundary will go down from Shepham to Riblahi on the east side of Ainj and continue along the slopes east of the Sea of Kinnereth.ik 12Then the boundary will go down along the Jordan and end at the Salt Sea.

" 'This will be your land, with its boundaries on every side.' "

13Moses commanded the Israelites: "Assign this land by lotl as an inheritance. m The LORD has ordered that it be given to the nine and a half tribes, 14because the families of the tribe of Reuben, the tribe of Gad and the half-tribe of Manasseh have received their inheritance. n 15These two and a half tribes have received their inheritance on the east side of the Jordan of Jericho,j toward the sunrise."

16The LORD said to Moses, 17"These are the names of the men who are to assign the land for you as an inheritance: Eleazar

---

33:43 zNu 21:10
33:44
aS Nu 21:11
33:47 bNu 27:12
cNu 32:3
33:48 dNu 27:12
eS Nu 26:3
fS Ge 13:10
gNu 22:1;
Jos 12:9
33:49 hJos 12:3;
13:20; Eze 25:9
iS Nu 21:16
33:50 /ver 48
33:51 kNu 34:2;
Jos 3:17
33:52
lS Lev 26:1;
Ps 106:34-36
33:53
mDt 11:31;
17:14; Jos 1:11;
21:43
33:54
nS Lev 16:8;
Nu 36:2
oNu 26:54
pNu 35:8
qJos 18:10
33:55 rJos 23:13;
Jdg 2:3;
Ps 106:36;
Isa 55:13;
Eze 2:6; 28:24;
Mic 7:4;
2Co 12:7
33:56 sNu 14:28
34:2 tS Nu 33:51

uGe 17:8;
Dt 1:7-8;
Jos 23:4;
Ps 78:54-55;
105:11
vEze 47:15
34:3 wNu 13:21;
Jos 15:1-3
xS Ge 14:3
34:4 yJos 15:3;
Jdg 1:36
zNu 32:8
aJos 15:4
34:5 bGe 15:18
34:6 cJos 1:4;
9:1; 15:12,47;
23:4; Eze 47:10,
15; 48:28
dEze 47:19-20
34:7
eEze 47:15-17
fS Nu 20:22
34:8 gNu 13:21;
Jos 13:5
34:10 hJos 15:5
34:11
i2Ki 23:33; 25:6,
21; Jer 39:5;
52:9,27
jJos 15:32; 21:16;
1Ch 4:32
kDt 3:17;
Jos 11:2; 13:27
34:13
lS Lev 16:8;
Jos 18:10;
Mic 2:5
mJos 13:6;
14:1-5; Isa 49:8;
65:9; Eze 45:1
34:14
nNu 32:19;
Dt 33:21;
Jos 14:3

---

c45 That is, Iye Abarim   d48 Hebrew Jordan of Jericho; possibly an ancient name for the Jordan River; also in verse 50   e3 That is, the Dead Sea; also in verse 12   f4 Hebrew Akrabbim   g5 That is, the Mediterranean; also in verses 6 and 7   h8 Or to the entrance to   i11 That is, Galilee   j15 Jordan of Jericho was possibly an ancient name for the Jordan River.

33:52 drive out all the inhabitants of the land . . . Destroy all their . . . idols. What Israel had accomplished in the war against the Midianites (ch. 31) was now to be extended to all the inhabitants of Canaan. Particularly important was the command to destroy all symbols of the pagan religious system of the Canaanites.
34:3–12 The listing of the four boundaries is not only for information, but also to display again the dimensions of

God's great gift to his people.
34:13–15 The new realities that the settlement of Reuben, Gad and the half-tribe of Manasseh in Transjordan brought about (see ch. 32).
34:16–29 The listing of the new tribal leaders recalls the listing of the leaders of the first generation (1:5–16). This time the promise will be realized; these new leaders will assist Eleazar and Joshua in actually allotting the land.

the priest and Joshua[o] son of Nun. [18]And appoint one leader from each tribe to help[p] assign the land.[q] [19]These are their names:[r]

Caleb[s] son of Jephunneh,
from the tribe of Judah;[t]
[20]Shemuel son of Ammihud,
from the tribe of Simeon;[u]
[21]Elidad son of Kislon,
from the tribe of Benjamin;[v]
[22]Bukki son of Jogli,
the leader from the tribe of Dan;
[23]Hanniel son of Ephod,
the leader from the tribe of Manasseh[w] son of Joseph;
[24]Kemuel son of Shiphtan,
the leader from the tribe of Ephraim[x] son of Joseph;
[25]Elizaphan son of Parnach,
the leader from the tribe of Zebulun;[y]
[26]Paltiel son of Azzan,
the leader from the tribe of Issachar;
[27]Ahihud son of Shelomi,
the leader from the tribe of Asher;[z]
[28]Pedahel son of Ammihud,
the leader from the tribe of Naphtali."

[29]These are the men the LORD commanded to assign the inheritance to the Israelites in the land of Canaan.[a]

Towns for the Levites

35 On the plains of Moab by the Jordan across from Jericho,[k][b] the LORD said to Moses, [2]"Command the Israelites to give the Levites towns to live in[c] from the inheritance the Israelites will possess. And give them pasturelands[d] around the towns. [3]Then they will have towns to live in and pasturelands for their cattle, flocks and all their other livestock.[e]

[4]"The pasturelands around the towns that you give the Levites will extend out fifteen hundred feet[l] from the town wall. [5]Outside the town, measure three thousand feet[m][f] on the east side, three thousand on the south side, three thousand on the west and three thousand on the north,

Cross references
34:17
[o]Nu 11:28;
Dt 1:38
34:18 [p]S Nu 1:4
[q]Jos 14:1
34:19 [r]ver 29
[s]S Nu 26:65
[t]Ge 29:35;
Dt 33:7; Ps 60:7
34:20
[u]S Ge 29:33
34:21 [v]Ge 49:27;
Jdg 5:14;
Ps 68:27
34:23 [w]Nu 1:34
34:24 [x]Nu 1:32
34:25
[y]S Ge 30:20
34:27 [z]Nu 1:40
34:29 [a]ver 19
35:1 [b]Nu 22:1
35:2
[c]Lev 25:32-34;
Jos 14:3,4
[d]Jos 21:1-42
35:3 [e]Dt 18:6;
Jos 14:4; 21:2
35:5 [f]Jos 3:4

with the town in the center. They will have this area as pastureland for the towns.[g]

Cities of Refuge

35:6–34Ref – Dt 4:41–43; 19:1–14; Jos 20:1–9

[6]"Six of the towns you give the Levites will be cities of refuge, to which a person who has killed someone may flee.[h] In addition, give them forty-two other towns. [7]In all you must give the Levites forty-eight towns, together with their pasturelands. [8]The towns you give the Levites from the land the Israelites possess are to be given in proportion to the inheritance of each tribe: Take many towns from a tribe that has many, but few from one that has few."[i]

[9]Then the LORD said to Moses: [10]"Speak to the Israelites and say to them: 'When you cross the Jordan into Canaan,[j] [11]select some towns to be your cities of refuge, to which a person who has killed someone[k] accidentally[l] may flee. [12]They will be places of refuge from the avenger,[m] so that a person accused of murder[n] may not die before he stands trial before the assembly.[o] [13]These six towns you give will be your cities of refuge.[p] [14]Give three on this side of the Jordan and three in Canaan as cities of refuge. [15]These six towns will be a place of refuge for Israelites, aliens and any other people living among them, so that anyone who has killed another accidentally can flee there.

[16] 'If a man strikes someone with an iron object so that he dies, he is a murderer; the murderer shall be put to death.[q] [17]Or if anyone has a stone in his hand that could kill, and he strikes someone so that he dies, he is a murderer; the murderer shall be put to death. [18]Or if anyone has a wooden object in his hand that could kill, and he hits someone so that he dies, he is a murderer; the murderer shall be put to death. [19]The avenger of blood[r] shall put the murderer to death; when he meets him, he shall put him to death.[s] [20]If any-

Cross references (column 2)
[g]Lev 25:34;
2Ch 11:14; 13:9;
23:2; 31:19
35:6 [h]ver 11;
Jos 21:13
35:8 [i]Nu 26:54;
33:54
35:10 [j]Nu 33:51;
Dt 9:1; Jos 1:2,11
35:11 [k]ver 22-25
[l]S Ex 21:13
35:12 [m]ver 19;
Dt 19:6; Jos 20:3;
2Sa 14:11 [n]ver
26,27,28 [o]ver 24,
25
35:13 [p]ver 6,14
35:16
[q]S Ex 21:12
35:19 [r]S ver 12
[s]ver 21

[k]1 Hebrew *Jordan of Jericho*; possibly an ancient name for the Jordan River   [l]4 Hebrew *a thousand cubits* (about 450 meters)   [m]5 Hebrew *two thousand cubits* (about 900 meters)

35:1–5 Since the Levites would not receive an allotment with the other tribes in the land (1:47–53), they would need towns in which to live and to raise their families and care for their livestock. The Levites were to be spread throughout the land, not in an isolated encampment. Jos 21 presents the fulfillment of this command.
35:6–15 Six Levitical cities were to be stationed strategi-

cally in the land—three in Transjordan and three in Canaan proper—as cities of refuge, where a person guilty of unintentional manslaughter might escape blood revenge. Jos 20 describes the sites that were chosen.
35:16–21 Various descriptions of the taking of life are presented that would indicate willful murder.

one with malice aforethought shoves another or throws something at him intentionally[t] so that he dies [21]or if in hostility he hits him with his fist so that he dies, that person shall be put to death;[u] he is a murderer. The avenger of blood[v] shall put the murderer to death when he meets him.

[22]" 'But if without hostility someone suddenly shoves another or throws something at him unintentionally[w] [23]or, without seeing him, drops a stone on him that could kill him, and he dies, then since he was not his enemy and he did not intend to harm him, [24]the assembly[x] must judge between him and the avenger of blood according to these regulations. [25]The assembly must protect the one accused of murder from the avenger of blood and send him back to the city of refuge to which he fled. He must stay there until the death of the high priest,[y] who was anointed[z] with the holy oil.[a]

[26]" 'But if the accused ever goes outside the limits of the city of refuge to which he has fled [27]and the avenger of blood finds him outside the city, the avenger of blood may kill the accused without being guilty

of murder. [28]The accused must stay in his city of refuge until the death of the high priest; only after the death of the high priest may he return to his own property.

[29]" 'These are to be legal requirements[b] for you throughout the generations to come,[c] wherever you live.[d]

[30]" 'Anyone who kills a person is to be put to death as a murderer only on the testimony of witnesses. But no one is to be put to death on the testimony of only one witness.[e]

[31]" 'Do not accept a ransom[f] for the life of a murderer, who deserves to die. He must surely be put to death.

[32]" 'Do not accept a ransom for anyone who has fled to a city of refuge and so allow him to go back and live on his own land before the death of the high priest.

[33]" 'Do not pollute the land where you are. Bloodshed pollutes the land,[g] and atonement cannot be made for the land on which blood has been shed, except by the blood of the one who shed it. [34]Do not defile the land[h] where you live and where I dwell,[i] for I, the LORD, dwell among the Israelites.' "

35:20
[t]S Ex 21:14
35:21 [u]Ex 21:14
[v]ver 19
35:22
[w]S Ex 21:13
35:24 [x]S ver 12
35:25 [y]ver 32
[z]S Ex 28:41
[a]S Ex 29:7

35:29 [b]Nu 27:11
[c]Nu 10:8
[d]S Ex 12:20
35:30 [e]Dt 17:6; 19:15;
S Mt 18:16; Jn 7:51
35:31 [f]Ex 21:30; Job 6:22; Ps 49:8; Pr 13:8
35:33 [g]S Ge 4:10
35:34
[h]Lev 18:24,25
[i]S Ex 29:45

35:22 *without hostility.* The cities of refuge were to be established for the person who had committed an act of involuntary manslaughter.
35:24 *according to these regulations.* Any gracious provision is subject to abuse. For this reason the case of the involuntary slayer had to be determined by the judges. Further, the accused man had to stay in the city of refuge until the death of the high priest (when there would be a general amnesty). If the accused left the city of refuge, he would become fair game again for the avenger of blood.

35:25–28 See note on Jos 20:6.
35:30 *witnesses.* To avoid the possibility of an innocent party being accused and sentenced to death on insufficient evidence.
35:32 Not even an involuntary slayer could leave the city of refuge on the payment of a ransom.
35:33 *Bloodshed pollutes the land.* The crime of murder is not only an offense against the sanctity of life; it is in fact a pollutant to the Lord's sacred land.

Cities of Refuge

The idea of providing cities of refuge (Jos 20:1-9) for capital offenses is rooted in the tension between customary tribal law (retaliation or revenge, in which the blood relative is obligated to execute vengeance) and civil law (carried out less personally by an assembly according to a standard code of justice).

Blood feuds are usually associated with nomadic groups; legal procedures, with villages and towns. Israel, a society in the process of sedentarization, found it necessary to adopt an intermediate step regulating manslaughter, so that an innocent person would not be killed before standing trial. Absolution was possible only by being cleared by his hometown assembly, and by the eventual death of the high priest, which freed the offender from ritual pollution.

Kedesh
Acco
Golan
Dor
Beth Shan
Ramoth
Shechem
Peniel
Gezer
Gibeon
Bezer
Heshbon
Hebron

The six cities of refuge are shown in bold type.

Miles 10 5 0   10   20
Kms 10 5 0 10 20 30

Beersheba

Inheritance of Zelophehad's Daughters

36:1–12pp — Nu 27:1–11

36 The family heads of the clan of Gilead/ son of Makir,^{k} the son of Manasseh, who were from the clans of the descendants of Joseph,^{l} came and spoke before Moses and the leaders,^{m} the heads of the Israelite families. ²They said, "When the LORD commanded my lord to give the land as an inheritance to the Israelites by lot,^{n} he ordered you to give the inheritance of our brother Zelophehad^o to his daughters. ³Now suppose they marry men from other Israelite tribes; then their inheritance will be taken from our ancestral inheritance and added to that of the tribe they marry into. And so part of the inheritance allotted to us will be taken away. ⁴When the Year of Jubilee^p for the Israelites comes, their inheritance will be added to that of the tribe into which they marry, and their property will be taken from the tribal inheritance of our forefathers."

⁵Then at the LORD's command Moses gave this order to the Israelites: "What the tribe of the descendants of Joseph is saying is right. ⁶This is what the LORD commands for Zelophehad's daughters: They may marry anyone they please as long as they marry within the tribal clan of their father. ⁷No inheritance^q in Israel is to pass from tribe to tribe, for every Israelite shall keep the tribal land inherited from his forefathers. ⁸Every daughter who inherits land in any Israelite tribe must marry someone in her father's tribal clan,^{r} so that every Israelite will possess the inheritance of his fathers. ⁹No inheritance may pass from tribe to tribe, for each Israelite tribe is to keep the land it inherits."

¹⁰So Zelophehad's daughters did as the LORD commanded Moses. ¹¹Zelophehad's daughters—Mahlah, Tirzah, Hoglah, Milcah and Noah^s—married their cousins on their father's side. ¹²They married within the clans of the descendants of Manasseh son of Joseph, and their inheritance remained in their father's clan and tribe.^{t}

¹³These are the commands and regulations the LORD gave through Moses^u to the Israelites on the plains of Moab by the Jordan across from Jericho.^{n} ^{v}

^{n}13 Hebrew *Jordan of Jericho*; possibly an ancient name for the Jordan River

---

Cross references:

36:1 /S Nu 26:30
kS Ge 50:23
lS Nu 26:28
mS Nu 27:2
36:2 nS Nu 33:54
oS Nu 26:33
36:4 pS Lev 25:10
36:7 qS Lev 25:23
36:8 rI Ch 23:22
36:11 sNu 26:33
36:12 tI Ch 7:15
36:13 uS Lev 7:38; S 27:34 vNu 22:1

36:1–13 Presents an interesting further development of the account of Zelophehad's daughters (see 27:1–11). Since the Lord had instructed Moses that the women might inherit their father's land, new questions arose: What will happen to the family lands if these daughters marry among other tribes? Will not the original intention of the first provision be frustrated? Such questions led to the decision that marriage is to be kept within one's own tribe, so that the family allotments will not "pass from tribe to tribe" (v. 9). **36:10** *Zelophehad's daughters did as the LORD commanded.* The book of Numbers, which so often presents the rebellion of God's people against his grace and in defiance of his will, ends on a happy note. These noble women, who were concerned for their father's name and their own place in the land, obeyed the Lord.

DEUTERONOMY

Title

The word "Deuteronomy" (meaning "repetition of the law"), as the name of the last book of the Pentateuch, arose from a mistranslation in the Greek Septuagint and the Latin Vulgate of a phrase in Dt 17:18, which in Hebrew means "copy of this law." The error is not serious, however, since Deuteronomy is, in a certain sense, a "repetition of the law" (see Structure and Outline). The Hebrew name of the book is *'elleh haddebarim* ("These are the words") or, more simply, *debarim* ("words"; see 1:1).

Author

The book itself testifies that, for the most part, Moses wrote it (1:5; 31:9,22,24), and other OT books agree (1Ki 2:3; 8:53; 2Ki 14:6; 18:12)—though, of course, the preamble (1:1-5) and the report of Moses' death (ch. 34) were written by someone else. Jesus also bears testimony to Mosaic authorship (Mt 19:7-8; Mk 10:3-5; Jn 5:46-47), and so do other NT writers (Ac 3:22-23; 7:37-38; Ro 10:19). Moreover, Jesus quotes Deuteronomy as authoritative (Mt 4:4,7,10). In the NT there are almost 100 quotations of and allusions to Deuteronomy. Tradition uniformly testifies to the Mosaic authorship of the book (see, e.g., Mk 12:19). See Introduction to Genesis: Author and Date of Writing.

Date

The book is probably to be dated c. 1406 B.C. (see Introduction to Genesis: Author and Date of Writing).

Historical Setting

Deuteronomy locates Moses and the Israelites in the territory of Moab in the area where the Jordan flows into the Dead Sea (1:5). As his final act at this important time of transferring leadership to Joshua, Moses delivered his farewell addresses to prepare the people for their entrance into Canaan. These addresses were actually a covenant renewal (see Structure and Outline). In them, Moses emphasized the laws that were especially needed at such a time, and he presented them in a way appropriate to the situation. In contrast to the matter-of-fact narratives of Leviticus and Numbers, the book of Deuteronomy comes to us from Moses' heart in a warm, personal, sermonic form of expression.

Theological Teaching

The love relationship of the Lord to his people and that of the people to the Lord as their sovereign God pervade the whole book. Deuteronomy's spiritual emphasis and its call to total commitment to the Lord in worship and obedience inspired references to its message throughout the rest of Scripture.

Structure and Outline

Deuteronomy's literary structure supports its historical setting. By its interpretive, repetitious, reminiscent and somewhat irregular style it shows that it is a series of more or less extemporaneous addresses, sometimes describing events in nonchronological order (see, e.g., 10:3). But it also bears in its structure clear reflections of the suzerain-vassal treaties (see chart on "Major Covenants in the OT," p. 19) of the preceding and then-current Near Eastern states, a structure that lends itself to the Biblical emphasis on the covenant between the Lord and his people. In this sense Deuteronomy is a covenant renewal document, as the following outline shows:

I. The Preamble (1:1-5)
II. The Historical Prologue (1:6-4:43)
III. The Stipulations of the Covenant (4:44-26:19)

    A. The Great Commandment: The Demand for Absolute Allegiance (4:44-11:32)
    B. Supplementary Requirements (chs. 12-26)
       1. Ceremonial consecration (12:1-16:17)
       2. Governmental leaders and a righteous nation (16:18-21:21)
       3. Sanctity of God's kingdom (21:22-25:19)
       4. Confession of God as Redeemer-King (ch. 26)
 IV. Ratification; Curses and Blessings (chs. 27-30)
  V. Leadership Succession under the Covenant (chs. 31-34)
    A. Change of Leadership (31:1-29)
    B. Song of Moses (31:30-32:47)
    C. Moses' Testamental Blessing on the Tribes (32:48-33:29)
    D. Death of Moses and Succession of Joshua (ch. 34)
The book is sometimes divided into three addresses:
  I. First Address (1:1-4:43)
 II. Second Address (4:44-28:68)
III. Third Address (chs. 29-33)
IV. Moses' Death (ch. 34)

The Command to Leave Horeb

1 These are the words Moses spoke to all Israel in the desert east of the Jordan[a]—that is, in the Arabah[b]—opposite Suph, between Paran[c] and Tophel, Laban, Hazeroth and Dizahab. [2](It takes eleven days to go from Horeb[d] to Kadesh Barnea[e] by the Mount Seir[f] road.)[g]

[3]In the fortieth year,[h] on the first day of the eleventh month,[i] Moses proclaimed[j] to the Israelites all that the LORD had commanded him concerning them. [4]This was after he had defeated Sihon[k] king of the Amorites,[l] who reigned in Heshbon,[m] and at Edrei had defeated Og[n] king of Bashan, who reigned in Ashtaroth.[o]

[5]East of the Jordan in the territory of Moab,[p] Moses began to expound this law, saying:

[6]The LORD our God said to us[q] at Horeb,[r] "You have stayed long enough[s] at this mountain. [7]Break camp and advance into the hill country of the Amorites;[t] go to all the neighboring peoples in the Arabah,[u] in the mountains, in the western foothills, in the Negev[v] and along the coast, to the land of the Canaanites[w] and to Lebanon,[x] as far as the great river, the Euphrates.[y] [8]See, I have given you this land.[z],[a] Go in and take possession of the land that the LORD swore[b] he would give to your fathers—to Abraham, Isaac and Jacob—and to their descendants after them."

The Appointment of Leaders

[9]At that time I said to you, "You are too heavy a burden[c] for me to carry alone.[d]

[10]The LORD your God has increased[e] your numbers[f] so that today you are as many[g] as the stars in the sky.[h] [11]May the LORD, the God of your fathers, increase[i] you a thousand times and bless you as he has promised![j] [12]But how can I bear your problems and your burdens and your disputes all by myself?[k] [13]Choose some wise, understanding and respected men[l] from each of your tribes, and I will set them over you."

[14]You answered me, "What you propose to do is good."

[15]So I took[m] the leading men of your tribes,[n] wise and respected men,[o] and appointed them to have authority over you—as commanders[p] of thousands, of hundreds, of fifties and of tens and as tribal officials.[q] [16]And I charged your judges at that time: Hear the disputes between your brothers and judge[r] fairly,[s] whether the case is between brother Israelites or between one of them and an alien.[t] [17]Do not show partiality[u] in judging; hear both small and great alike. Do not be afraid of any man,[v] for judgment belongs to God. Bring me any case too hard for you, and I will hear it.[w] [18]And at that time I told you everything you were to do.[x]

Spies Sent Out

[19]Then, as the LORD our God commanded us, we set out from Horeb and went toward the hill country of the Amo-

---

1:1 [a]S Nu 13:29; Dt 4:46 [b]ver 7; Dt 2:8; 3:17; Jos 3:16; 8:14; 11:2; Eze 47:8 [c]S Nu 10:12
1:2 [d]S Ex 3:1 [e]S Ge 14:7; Dt 2:14; 9:23; Jos 15:3 [f]S Nu 24:18 [g]ver 19
1:3 [h]Nu 14:33; 32:13; Dt 8:2; Heb 3:7-9 [i]Ge 50:3; Dt 34:8; Jos 4:19 [j]Dt 4:1-2
1:4 [k]Nu 21:21-26 [l]S Ge 10:16; S 14:7 [m]S Nu 21:25 [n]Nu 21:33-35; Dt 3:10 [o]Jos 9:10; 12:4; 1Ch 11:44
1:5 [p]S Nu 21:11
1:6 [q]Nu 10:13 [r]S Ex 3:1 [s]Dt 2:3
1:7 [t]ver 19; Dt 2:24; 7:1; Jos 10:5 [u]S ver 1 [v]S Nu 21:1; Jos 11:16; 12:8; 2Sa 24:7 [w]S Ge 10:18 [x]Dt 11:24 [y]S Ge 2:14
1:8 [z]S Jos 23:13 [a]S Nu 34:2 [b]S Ex 13:11; S Nu 14:23; Heb 6:13-14
1:9 [c]S Nu 11:14; Ps 38:4 [d]S Ex 18:18

1:10 [e]ver 11; Eze 16:7 [f]S Dt 7:13 [g]S Ge 15:5; Isa 51:2; 60:22; Eze 33:24 [h]S Ge 22:17; S Nu 10:36
1:11 [i]S ver 10 [j]ver 8; Ex 32:13; 2Sa 24:3; 1Ch 21:3
1:12 [k]S Ge 5:22; S 18:18

1:13 [l]S Ge 47:6 **1:15** [m]Ex 18:25 [n]Ex 5:14; Nu 11:16; Jos 1:10; 3:2 [o]S Ge 47:6 [p]Nu 31:14; 1Sa 8:12; 22:7; 1Ki 1:9; 4 [q]S Nu 1:4 **1:16** [r]1Ki 3:9; Ps 72:1; Pr 2:9 [s]S Ge 31:37; Jn 7:24 [t]S Ex 12:19,49; S 22:21 **1:17** [u]S Ex 18:16; S Lev 19:15; Ac 10:34; Jas 2:1 [v]Pr 29:25 [w]Ex 18:26 **1:18** [x]S Ge 39:11

1:1–5 The preamble gives the historical setting for the entire book.

1:1 *Moses spoke.* Almost all of Deuteronomy is made up of speeches by Moses during the final months of his life, just before the Israelites crossed the Jordan to enter Canaan. *Arabah.* Includes the valley of the Jordan (from the Sea of Galilee to the southern end of the Dead Sea) and the valley extending down to the Gulf of Aqaba. *Suph . . . Paran . . . Tophel, Laban, Hazeroth and Dizahab.* Places along the route from Sinai to the territory of Moab.

1:2 *Horeb.* The usual name for Mount Sinai in Deuteronomy (the only exception is in 33:2). *Kadesh Barnea.* See note on Ge 14:7. *Seir.* See note on Ge 36:8.

1:3 *fortieth year.* After leaving Egypt. The Lord had condemned Israel to 40 years of wandering in Sinai as punishment for not entering Canaan as he had commanded them to do at Kadesh (Nu 14:33–34). The 40 years included the time spent at Sinai and on the journey to Kadesh as well as the next 38 years (see 2:14). See 8:2–5; 29:5–6; Nu 14:29–35; 32:13; Heb 3:7–19. *eleventh month.* January-February.

1:5 *this law.* The Ten Commandments and other laws given at Mount Sinai and recorded in Ex 20–24, Leviticus and Numbers. In Deuteronomy the laws are summarized and interpreted, and adjusted to the new, specific situation

Israel would face in Canaan. Thus Deuteronomy is, in essence, a covenant renewal (and updating) document.

1:7 See Jos 1:4. The land is described by its various geographical areas (see map No. 2 at the end of the Study Bible). *Arabah.* See note on v. 1; here the Jordan Valley and the Dead Sea area. *mountains.* The midsection running north and south. *western foothills.* Sloping toward the Mediterranean. *Negev.* See note on Ge 12:9. *coast.* The Mediterranean coastal strip. The "land of the Canaanites" and "Lebanon, as far as . . . the Euphrates" make up the northern sector. The "hill country of the Amorites" is, in general, the central and southern mountains. This description of the land agrees with that in the promise (see v. 8) to Abraham in Ge 15:18–21, a promise later limited to Isaac's descendants (Ge 26:2–4) and still later to the descendants of Jacob (Ge 35:11–12).

1:9–18 Cf. 16:18–20; Ex 18:13–26.

1:10 *The LORD your God.* This title occurs almost 300 times in Deuteronomy in addition to the many times that "LORD" is used alone or in other combinations. *as the stars in the sky.* See 10:22; 28:62; Ge 13:16 and note; 15:5 and note; 22:17; 26:4; Ex 32:13.

1:19–46 See Nu 13–14.

rites^y through all that vast and dreadful desert^z that you have seen, and so we reached Kadesh Barnea.^{a} ^{20}Then I said to you, "You have reached the hill country of the Amorites, which the LORD our God is giving us. ^{21}See, the LORD your God has given you the land. Go up and take possession^b of it as the LORD, the God of your fathers, told you. Do not be afraid;^{c} do not be discouraged." ^{d}

^{22}Then all of you came to me and said, "Let us send men ahead to spy^e out the land^f for us and bring back a report about the route we are to take and the towns we will come to."

^{23}The idea seemed good to me; so I selected^g twelve of you, one man from each tribe. ^{24}They left and went up into the hill country, and came to the Valley of Eshcol^h and explored it. ^{25}Taking with them some of the fruit of the land, they brought it down to us and reported,^{i} "It is a good land^j that the LORD our God is giving us." ^{k}

Rebellion Against the LORD

^{26}But you were unwilling to go up;^{l} you rebelled^m against the command of the LORD your God. ^{27}You grumbled^n in your tents and said, "The LORD hates us; so he brought us out of Egypt to deliver us into the hands of the Amorites to destroy us. ^{28}Where can we go? Our brothers have made us lose heart. They say, 'The people are stronger and taller^o than we are; the cities are large, with walls up to the sky. We even saw the Anakites^p there.' "

^{29}Then I said to you, "Do not be terrified; do not be afraid^q of them.^{r} ^{30}The LORD your God, who is going before you, will fight^s for you, as he did for you in Egypt, before your very eyes, ^{31}and in the desert. There you saw how the LORD your God carried^t you, as a father carries his

son, all the way you went until you reached this place." ^{u}

^{32}In spite of this,^{v} you did not trust^w in the LORD your God, ^{33}who went ahead of you on your journey, in fire by night and in a cloud by day,^{x} to search^y out places for you to camp and to show you the way you should go.

^{34}When the LORD heard^z what you said, he was angry^a and solemnly swore: ^{b} ^{35}"Not a man of this evil generation shall see the good land^c I swore to give your forefathers, ^{36}except Caleb^d son of Jephunneh. He will see it, and I will give him and his descendants the land he set his feet on, because he followed the LORD wholeheartedly. ^{e} "

^{37}Because of you the LORD became angry^f with me also and said, "You shall not enter^g it, either. ^{38}But your assistant, Joshua^h son of Nun, will enter it. Encourage^i him, because he will lead^j Israel to inherit^k it. ^{39}And the little ones that you said would be taken captive,^{l} your children who do not yet know^m good from bad—they will enter the land. I will give it to them and they will take possession of it. ^{40}But as for you, turn around and set out toward the desert along the route to the Red Sea.^{a} ^{n} "

^{41}Then you replied, "We have sinned against the LORD. We will go up and fight, as the LORD our God commanded us." So every one of you put on his weapons, thinking it easy to go up into the hill country.

^{42}But the LORD said to me, "Tell them, 'Do not go up and fight, because I will not be with you. You will be defeated by your enemies.' " ^{o}

^{43}So I told you, but you would not lis-

1:19 ^{y}S ver 7
^{z}Dt 2:7; 8:15;
32:10; Ps 136:16;
Jer 2:2,6;
Hos 13:5 ^{a}ver 2;
Nu 13:26
1:21 ^{b}Dt 9:23
^{c}S Nu 14:9;
Jos 1:6,9,18;
2Sa 10:12;
Ps 27:14
^{d}Dt 7:18; Jos 8:1;
10:8
1:22 ^{e}Nu 13:1-3
/S Ge 42:9
1:23 ^{g}Nu 13:1-3
1:24
^{h}Nu 13:21-25;
S 32:9
1:25 ^{i}S Nu 13:27
/S Nu 14:7
^{k}Jos 1:2
1:26 ^{l}Nu 14:1-4
^{m}S Nu 14:9
1:27 ^{n}Dt 9:28;
Ps 106:25
1:28 ^{o}S Nu 13:32
^{p}S Nu 13:33;
Dt 9:1-3
1:29 ^{q}Dt 3:22;
20:3; Ne 4:14
^{r}Dt 7:18; 20:1;
31:6
1:30 ^{s}S Ex 14:14
1:31 ^{t}Ex 19:4;
Dt 32:10-12;
Ps 28:9;
Isa 46:3-4; 63:9;
Hos 11:3;
Ac 13:18

^{u}Jer 31:32
1:32 ^{v}S Nu 14:11
^{w}Dt 9:23;
Ps 78:22; 106:24;
Zep 3:2;
Heb 3:19;
Jude 1:5
1:33 ^{x}Ex 13:21;
Nu 9:15-23;
Ne 9:12; Ps 78:14
^{y}S Nu 10:33
1:34 ^{z}S Nu 11:1
^{a}S Nu 32:14
^{b}S Nu 14:23,
28-30; Eze 20:15;
Heb 3:11
1:35 ^{c}S Nu 14:29
1:36 ^{d}S Nu 13:6
^{e}S Nu 14:24
1:37 ^{f}Ps 106:32
^{g}S Nu 27:13
1:38 ^{h}S Nu 11:28
^{i}Dt 31:7 /Dt 3:28
^{k}Jos 11:23;
Ps 78:55; 136:21
1:39 ^{l}S Nu 14:3
^{m}Isa 7:15-16

1:40 ^{n}S Ex 14:27; Jdg 11:16 1:42 ^{o}S Nu 14:41-43

^{a}40 Hebrew *Yam Suph*; that is, Sea of Reeds

1:21 *as the LORD . . . told you.* The promise of the land (see note on v. 7) was reaffirmed to Moses at the burning bush (v. 8; Ex 3:8,17). Now the Israelites are told to enter the land and conquer it. *Do not be afraid . . . discouraged.* See 31:8; Jos 1:9; 8:1; 10:25.
1:23 *twelve.* They are named in Nu 13:4–15.
1:24 *Eshcol.* See NIV text note on Nu 13:23.
1:26 *you rebelled.* Although they themselves had not rebelled, the people were being addressed as a nation united with the earlier rebellious generation (see 5:2; cf. 29:1).
1:27 *grumbled.* See note on Ex 15:24. *The LORD hates us.* The people's statement is ironic indeed in the light of Deuteronomy's major theme (see Introduction: Theological Teaching).
1:28 *Anakites.* Earlier inhabitants of Canaan, described as giants (see 2:10,21; 9:2; Nu 13:32).
1:30 *as he did for you in Egypt.* See Ex 14:1–15:19.
1:31 *God carried you.* See notes on Isa 41:10,13; 43:1–2;

cf. Isa 40:11; Jer 31:10; Eze 34:11–16.
1:33 *in fire by night and in a cloud by day.* The presence of the Lord was in the cloud over the tabernacle to guide the Israelites through their desert journeys (see Ex 13:21 and note; 40:34–38).
1:36 *Caleb.* See Nu 13:30–14:38; Jos 14:6–15.
1:37 *Because of you.* See 3:26; 4:21. God was angry with Moses when in a wrong spirit he struck the rock at Meribah to get water (Nu 20:9–13; 27:12–14). And since it was the Israelites who had incited him to sin, God was angry with them too. This event (v. 37) occurred almost 40 years after that of the preceding verses (vv. 34–36), but Moses, interested in telling of the Israelites' sin and his own, brings the two events together.
1:39 *do not yet know good from bad.* See notes on Ge 2:9; Isa 7:15.
1:41 *you.* See note on v. 26.
1:43 *You rebelled against the LORD's command.* The same

ten. You rebelled against the LORD's command and in your arrogance you marched up into the hill country. ⁴⁴The Amorites who lived in those hills came out against you; they chased you like a swarm of bees^p and beat you down from Seir^q all the way to Hormah.^r ⁴⁵You came back and wept before the LORD,^s but he paid no attention^t to your weeping and turned a deaf ear^u to you. ⁴⁶And so you stayed in Kadesh^v many days—all the time you spent there.

Wanderings in the Desert

2 Then we turned back and set out toward the desert along the route to the Red Sea,^b^w as the LORD had directed me. For a long time we made our way around the hill country of Seir.^x

²Then the LORD said to me, ³"You have made your way around this hill country long enough;^y now turn north. ⁴Give the people these orders:^z 'You are about to pass through the territory of your brothers the descendants of Esau,^a who live in Seir.^b They will be afraid^c of you, but be very careful. ⁵Do not provoke them to war, for I will not give you any of their land, not even enough to put your foot on. I have given Esau the hill country of Seir as his own.^d ⁶You are to pay them in silver for the food you eat and the water you drink.' "

⁷The LORD your God has blessed you in all the work of your hands. He has watched^e over your journey through this vast desert.^f These forty years^g the LORD your God has been with you, and you have not lacked anything.^h

⁸So we went on past our brothers the descendants of Esau, who live in Seir. We turned fromⁱ the Arabah^j road, which comes up from Elath and Ezion Geber,^k

and traveled along the desert road of Moab.^l

⁹Then the LORD said to me, "Do not harass the Moabites or provoke them to war, for I will not give you any part of their land. I have given Ar^m to the descendants of Lotⁿ as a possession."

¹⁰(The Emites^o used to live there—a people strong and numerous, and as tall as the Anakites.^p ¹¹Like the Anakites, they too were considered Rephaites,^q but the Moabites called them Emites. ¹²Horites^r used to live in Seir, but the descendants of Esau drove them out. They destroyed the Horites from before them and settled in their place, just as Israel did^s in the land the LORD gave them as their possession.)

¹³And the LORD said, "Now get up and cross the Zered Valley.^t" So we crossed the valley.

¹⁴Thirty-eight years^u passed from the time we left Kadesh Barnea^v until we crossed the Zered Valley. By then, that entire generation^w of fighting men had perished from the camp, as the LORD had sworn to them.^x ¹⁵The LORD's hand was against them until he had completely eliminated^y them from the camp.

¹⁶Now when the last of these fighting men among the people had died, ¹⁷the LORD said to me, ¹⁸"Today you are to pass by the region of Moab at Ar.^z ¹⁹When you come to the Ammonites,^a do not harass them or provoke them to war,^b for I will not give you possession of any land belonging to the Ammonites. I have given it as a possession to the descendants of Lot.^c"

²⁰(That too was considered a land of the Rephaites,^d who used to live there; but the Ammonites called them Zamzummites. ²¹They were a people strong and numer-

Cross references (center column)

1:44 ^pPs 118:12
^qS Nu 24:18
^rS Nu 14:45
1:45 ^sS Nu 14:1
^tJob 27:9; 35:13;
Ps 18:41; 66:18;
Pr 1:28; Isa 1:15;
Jer 14:12; La 3:8;
Mic 3:4; S Jn 9:31
^uPs 28:1; 39:12;
Pr 28:9
1:46 ^vS Nu 20:1
2:1 ^wS Ex 14:27;
S Nu 21:4
^xS Nu 24:18
2:3 ^yDt 1:6
2:4 ^zNu 20:14-21
^aGe 36:8 ^bver 1
^cEx 15:16
2:5 ^dJos 24:4
2:7 ^eDt 8:2-4
^fS Ex 13:21;
S Dt 1:19 ^gver
14; S Nu 14:33;
32:13; Jos 5:6
^hNe 9:21;
Am 2:10
2:8 ⁱS Nu 20:21
^jS Dt 1:1
^kNu 33:35;
1Ki 9:26

^lS Nu 21:4
2:9 ^mS Nu 21:15
ⁿGe 19:38;
Ps 83:8
2:10 ^oGe 14:5
^pS Nu 13:22,33
2:11 ^qS Ge 14:5
2:12 ^rS Ge 14:6
^sNu 21:25,35
2:13 ^tS Nu 21:12
2:14 ^uS ver 7
^vS Dt 1:2
^wNu 14:29-35
^xDt 1:34-35;
Jos 5:6
2:15 ^yPs 106:26;
Jude 1:5
2:18 ^zS Nu 21:15
2:19 ^aS Ge 19:38
^b2Ch 20:10
^cS ver 9
2:20 ^dS Ge 14:5

^b1 Hebrew *Yam Suph*; that is, Sea of Reeds

---

charge as in v. 26. First the people rebelled against the Lord's command to go into the land, then against his command not to enter the land. After their first rebellion the Lord would not go with them. His presence was essential, and Israel needed to learn that lesson.
1:44 *bees.* See note on Ex 23:28.
1:45 *before the LORD.* At the tabernacle.
2:1–3:11 See Nu 20:14–21:35.
2:1 *Red Sea.* Here probably the Gulf of Aqaba (see note on 1Ki 9:26). *hill country of Seir.* The mountainous area south of the Dead Sea.
2:5 *I will not give you any of their land.* See vv. 9,19. The Lord told Moses to bypass Edom, Moab and Ammon because of their blood relationship to Israel. The Israelites were to take over only those lands east of the Jordan that were in the hands of the Amorites (see v. 24; 3:2). *I have given.* See vv. 9,19. The Lord had given the descendants of Esau (Edomites) and Lot (Moabites and Ammonites) their lands, just as he was giving the Israelites the territories of Transjordan and

Canaan.
2:8 *Elath and Ezion Geber.* At the head of the Gulf of Aqaba. The "Arabah road" ran from the head of the gulf northward and to the east of Moab.
2:9 *Ar.* Location unknown.
2:10 *Emites.* Possibly meaning "terrors." *Anakites.* See note on 1:28.
2:11 *Rephaites.* Ancient people of large stature.
2:12 *Horites.* See note on Ge 14:6. *the land the LORD gave them.* Either (1) the Transjordan regions (see 2:24–3:20), (2) Canaan itself or (3) Transjordan and Canaan. If either (2) or (3) is intended, editorial updating is involved (see note on Ge 14:14).
2:13 *Zered.* The main stream (intermittent) that flows into the southern end of the Dead Sea from the east (see map No. 4 at the end of the Study Bible).
2:14 *Thirty-eight years.* See note on 1:3.
2:20 *Zamzummites.* Possibly meaning "murmurers," and perhaps to be identified with the Zuzites of Ge 14:5.

ous, and as tall as the Anakites. *e* The LORD destroyed them from before the Ammonites, who drove them out and settled in their place. 22The LORD had done the same for the descendants of Esau, who lived in Seir, *f* when he destroyed the Horites from before them. They drove them out and have lived in their place to this day. 23And as for the Avvites *g* who lived in villages as far as Gaza, *h* the Caphtorites *i* coming out from Caphtor *cj* destroyed them and settled in their place.)

Defeat of Sihon King of Heshbon

24"Set out now and cross the Arnon Gorge. *k* See, I have given into your hand Sihon the Amorite, *l* king of Heshbon, and his country. Begin to take possession of it and engage *m* him in battle. 25This very day I will begin to put the terror *n* and fear *o* of you on all the nations under heaven. They will hear reports of you and will tremble *p* and be in anguish because of you."

26From the desert of Kedemoth *q* I sent messengers to Sihon *r* king of Heshbon offering peace *s* and saying, 27"Let us pass through your country. We will stay on the main road; we will not turn aside to the right or to the left. *t* 28Sell us food to eat *u* and water to drink for their price in silver. Only let us pass through on foot *v* — 29as the descendants of Esau, who live in Seir, and the Moabites, who live in Ar, did for us—until we cross the Jordan into the land the LORD our God is giving us." 30But Sihon king of Heshbon refused to let us pass through. For the LORD *w* your God had made his spirit stubborn *x* and his heart obstinate *y* in order to give him into your hands, *z* as he has now done.

31The LORD said to me, "See, I have begun to deliver Sihon and his country over to you. Now begin to conquer and possess his land." *a*

32When Sihon and all his army came out to meet us in battle *b* at Jahaz, 33the LORD our God delivered *c* him over to us and we struck him down, *d* together with his sons and his whole army. 34At that time we took all his towns and completely destroyed *d e* them—men, women and children. We left no survivors. 35But the livestock *f* and the plunder *g* from the towns we had captured we carried off for ourselves. 36From Aroer *h* on the rim of the Arnon Gorge, and from the town in the gorge, even as far as Gilead, *i* not one town was too strong for us. The LORD our God gave *j* us all of them. 37But in accordance with the command of the LORD our God, *k* you did not encroach on any of the land of the Ammonites, *l* neither the land along the course of the Jabbok *m* nor that around the towns in the hills.

Defeat of Og King of Bashan

3 Next we turned and went up along the road toward Bashan, and Og king of Bashan *n* with his whole army marched out to meet us in battle at Edrei. *o* 2The LORD said to me, "Do not be afraid *p* of him, for I have handed him over to you with his whole army and his land. Do to him what you did to Sihon king of the Amorites, who reigned in Heshbon."

3So the LORD our God also gave into our hands Og king of Bashan and all his army. We struck them down, *q* leaving no survivors. *r* 4At that time we took all his cities. *s* There was not one of the sixty cities that we did not take from them—the whole region of Argob, Og's kingdom *t* in Bashan. *u* 5All these cities were fortified with high walls and with gates and bars, and there were also a great many unwalled villages. 6We completely destroyed *d* them, as we had done with Sihon king of Heshbon,

Cross references

2:21 *e* ver 10
2:22 *f* S Ge 14:6
2:23 *g* Jos 13:3; 18:23; 2Ki 17:31
h S Ge 10:19
i S Ge 10:14
j Jer 47:4; Am 9:7
2:24 *k* Nu 21:13-14; Jdg 11:13,18
l S Dt 1:7 *m* Dt 3:6
2:25 *n* S Ge 35:5; Dt 11:25 *o* Jos 2:9,11; 1Ch 14:17; 2Ch 14:14; 17:10; 20:29; Isa 2:19; 13:13; 19:16
p Ex 15:14-16
2:26 *q* Jos 13:18; 1Ch 6:79 *r* Dt 1:4; Jdg 11:21-22
s Dt 20:10;
Jdg 21:13;
2Sa 20:19
2:27 *t* Nu 21:21-22
2:28 *u* Dt 23:4
v S Nu 20:19
2:30 *w* Jdg 14:4; 1Ki 12:15
x S Ex 4:21; Ro 9:18
y S Ex 14:17
z La 3:65
2:31 *a* S Ge 12:7

2:32 *b* S Nu 21:23
2:33 *c* Ex 23:31; Dt 7:2; 31:5
d S Nu 21:24
2:34 *e* S Nu 21:2; Dt 3:6; 7:2; Ps 106:34
2:35 *f* Dt 3:7
g S Ge 34:29; S 49:27
2:36 *h* S Nu 32:34
i S Nu 32:39
j Ps 44:3
2:37 *k* ver 18-19
l S Nu 21:24
m S Ge 32:22
3:1 *n* S Nu 32:19
o S Nu 21:33
3:2 *p* Jos 10:8; 2Ki 19:6; Isa 7:4
3:3 *q* S Nu 21:24
r Nu 21:35
3:4 *s* S Nu 21:24
t ver 13
u S Nu 21:33

c 23 That is, Crete   *d* 34,6 The Hebrew term refers to the irrevocable giving over of things or persons to the LORD, often by totally destroying them.

2:23 *Avvites.* Pre-Philistine people otherwise unknown (Jos 13:3). *Caphtorites.* See note on Ge 10:14.
2:24 *Arnon.* See note on Nu 21:10–13.
2:26 *Kedemoth.* Means "eastern regions."
2:30 *his spirit stubborn and his heart obstinate.* In the OT, actions are often attributed to God without the mention of mediate or contributing situations or persons. Sihon by his own conscious will refused Israel passage, but it was God who would give Sihon's land to Israel (see note on Ex 4:21).
2:32 *Jahaz.* See note on Isa 15:4.
2:34 *completely destroyed.* See NIV text note. The Hebrew for this expression usually denotes the destruction of everyone and everything that could be destroyed. Objects like gold, silver and bronze, not subject to destruction, were put in a secure place as God's possession. Destruction of people and things made them useless to the conquerors but

put them in the hands of God. So the word is sometimes translated "destroyed" and sometimes "devoted" (see, e.g., Jos 6:17). The practice was sometimes limited, as when God assigned captured livestock and other plunder to his people as recompense for service in his army (see v. 35; 3:7; Jos 8:2).
2:36 *Aroer.* See note on Isa 17:2. *Gilead.* See note on Ge 31:21.
2:37 *Jabbok.* See note on Ge 32:22.
3:3 *gave into our hands Og.* As in 2:26–37.
3:4 *sixty cities.* The cities were large and walled (1Ki 4:13), implying a heavily populated territory (see v. 5). *region of Argob.* An otherwise unidentified area in Bashan (see vv. 13–14; 1Ki 4:13).
3:6–7 See note on 2:34.

destroying[ev] every city—men, women and children. [7]But all the livestock[w] and the plunder from their cities we carried off for ourselves.

[8]So at that time we took from these two kings of the Amorites[x] the territory east of the Jordan, from the Arnon Gorge as far as Mount Hermon.[y] [9](Hermon is called Sirion[z] by the Sidonians; the Amorites call it Senir.)[a] [10]We took all the towns on the plateau, and all Gilead, and all Bashan as far as Salecah[b] and Edrei, towns of Og's kingdom in Bashan. [11](Only Og king of Bashan was left of the remnant of the Rephaites.[c] His bed[f] was made of iron and was more than thirteen feet long and six feet wide.[g] It is still in Rabbah[d] of the Ammonites.)

Division of the Land

[12]Of the land that we took over at that time, I gave the Reubenites and the Gadites the territory north of Aroer[e] by the Arnon Gorge, including half the hill country of Gilead, together with its towns. [13]The rest of Gilead and also all of Bashan, the kingdom of Og, I gave to the half tribe of Manasseh.[f] (The whole region of Argob in Bashan used to be known as a land of the Rephaites.[g] [14]Jair,[h] a descendant of Manasseh, took the whole region of Argob as far as the border of the Geshurites and the Maacathites;[i] it was named[j] after him, so that to this day Bashan is called Havvoth Jair.[h]) [15]And I gave Gilead to Makir.[k] [16]But to the Reubenites and the Gadites I gave the territory extending from Gilead down to the Arnon Gorge (the middle of the gorge being the border) and out to the Jabbok River,[l] which is the border of the Ammonites. [17]Its western border was the Jordan in the Arabah,[m] from Kin-

nereth[n] to the Sea of the Arabah[o] (the Salt Sea[i][p]), below the slopes of Pisgah.

[18]I commanded you at that time: "The LORD your God has given[q] you this land to take possession of it. But all your able-bodied men, armed for battle, must cross over ahead of your brother Israelites.[r] [19]However, your wives,[s] your children and your livestock[t] (I know you have much livestock) may stay in the towns I have given you, [20]until the LORD gives rest to your brothers as he has to you, and they too have taken over the land that the LORD your God is giving them, across the Jordan. After that, each of you may go back to the possession I have given you."

Moses Forbidden to Cross the Jordan

[21]At that time I commanded Joshua: "You have seen with your own eyes all that the LORD your God has done to these two kings. The LORD will do the same to all the kingdoms over there where you are going. [22]Do not be afraid[u] of them;[v] the LORD your God himself will fight[w] for you."

[23]At that time I pleaded[x] with the LORD: [24]"O Sovereign LORD, you have begun to show to your servant your greatness[y] and your strong hand. For what god[z] is there in heaven or on earth who can do the deeds and mighty works[a] you do?[b] [25]Let me go over and see the good land[c] beyond the Jordan—that fine hill country and Lebanon.[d]"

[26]But because of you the LORD was angry[e] with me and would not listen to me. "That is enough," the LORD said. "Do not

Cross references (center column)

3:6 [v]Dt 2:24
3:7 [w]Dt 2:35
3:8 [x]Nu 32:33; Jos 13:8-12
[y]Dt 4:48; Jos 11:3,17; 12:1; 13:5; Jdg 3:3; 1Ch 5:23; Ps 42:6; 89:12; 133:3; SS 4:8
3:9 [z]Ps 29:6
[a]1Ch 5:23; SS 4:8; Eze 27:5
3:10 [b]Jos 12:5; 1Ch 5:11
3:11 [c]Ge 14:5
[d]Jos 13:25; 15:60; 2Sa 11:1; 12:26; 17:27; 1Ch 20:1; Jer 49:2; Eze 21:20; 25:5; Am 1:14
3:12 [e]Dt 2:36
3:13 [f]Dt 29:8
[g]Ge 14:5
3:14 [h]S Nu 32:41
[i]Jos 12:5; 13:11, 13; 2Sa 10:6; 23:34; 2Ki 25:23; 1Ch 4:19; Jer 40:8
[j]Jos 19:47; Ps 49:11
3:15 [k]S Ge 50:23; Nu 32:39-40
3:16 [l]S Nu 21:24
3:17 [m]2Sa 2:29; 4:7; Eze 47:8
[n]S Nu 34:11
[o]S Dt 1:1
[p]S Ge 14:3
3:18 [q]Jos 1:13
[r]S Nu 32:17
3:19 [s]S Nu 1:14
[t]S Nu 32:16
3:22 [u]S Dt 1:29
[v]Dt 7:18; 20:1; 31:6; 2Ch 32:8; Ps 23:4; Isa 41:10
[w]S Ex 14:14
3:23 [x]Dt 1:37; 31:2; 32:52; 34:4
3:24 [y]Dt 5:24; 11:2; 32:3
[z]S Ex 8:10
[a]Ps 71:16; 106:2; 145:12; 150:2
[b]2Sa 7:22
3:25 [c]Dt 4:22
[d]Dt 1:7; Jos 1:4; 9:1; 11:17; 12:7; 13:5; Jdg 3:3; 9:15; 1Ki 4:33
3:26 [e]ver 27; Dt 1:37; 31:2

Footnotes (center column bottom)

[e]6 The Hebrew term refers to the irrevocable giving over of things or persons to the LORD, often by totally destroying them. [f]11 Or sarcophagus [g]11 Hebrew nine cubits long and four cubits wide (about 4 meters long and 1.8 meters wide) [h]14 Or called the settlements of Jair [i]17 That is, the Dead Sea

---

3:8 *Mount Hermon.* Snowcapped throughout the year and rising to a height of over 9,200 feet, it is one of the most prominent and beautiful mountains in Lebanon.
3:9 *Sirion.* This name for Mount Hermon is found also in a Canaanite document contemporary with Moses. *Senir.* This name for Mount Hermon is also found in Assyrian sources.
3:10 *Salecah.* A city marking the eastern boundary of Bashan (see Jos 13:11).
3:11 *bed . . . of iron.* Sarcophagi (stone coffins) of basalt have been found in Bashan, and the Hebrew for "bed" (see NIV text note) and "iron" may reflect this. If an actual bed, it was probably made of wood but with certain iron fixtures, as were the "iron chariots" (see note on Jos 17:16). *Rabbah of the Ammonites.* Called Philadelphia in NT times, Rabbah was the capital of ancient Ammon (Am 1:13–14). Today its name is Amman, the capital of the kingdom of Jordan.
3:12–20 See Nu 32; 34:13–15.
3:14 *Jair . . . Havvoth Jair.* See NIV text note; see also note on Jdg 10:3. *the Geshurites and the Maacathites.* Two

comparatively small kingdoms, Geshur was east of the Sea of Galilee and Maacah was east of the Waters of Merom (see note on Jos 11:5) and north of Geshur.
3:15 *Makir.* See note on Ge 50:23.
3:17 *Kinnereth.* See note on Mk 1:16. *Pisgah.* On the edge of the high plateau overlooking the Dead Sea from the east.
3:20 *rest.* A peaceful situation—free from external threat and oppression, and untroubled within by conflict, famine or plague (see 12:9–10; 25:19; see also notes on Jos 1:13; 1Ki 5:4; Heb 4:1–11).
3:22 *God himself.* The conquest narratives emphasize the truth that without the Lord's help Israel's victory would be impossible. The Lord's power, not Israel's unaided strength, achieved victory. Moses bolstered Israel's resolve and faith by this assurance (see 1:30; 2:21–22,31; 20:4).
3:23–25 Moses' final plea to be allowed to enter the land (see 1:37 and note; 31:2).
3:26 *because of you.* See note on 1:37.

speak to me anymore about this matter. [27]Go up to the top of Pisgah[f] and look west and north and south and east.[g] Look at the land with your own eyes, since you are not going to cross[h] this Jordan. [i] [28]But commission[j] Joshua, and encourage[k] and strengthen him, for he will lead this people across[l] and will cause them to inherit the land that you will see." [29]So we stayed in the valley near Beth Peor. [m]

Obedience Commanded

4 Hear now, O Israel, the decrees[n] and laws I am about to teach[o] you. Follow them so that you may live[p] and may go in and take possession of the land that the LORD, the God of your fathers, is giving you. [2]Do not add[q] to what I command you and do not subtract[r] from it, but keep[s] the commands[t] of the LORD your God that I give you.

[3]You saw with your own eyes what the LORD did at Baal Peor. [u] The LORD your God destroyed from among you everyone who followed the Baal of Peor, [4]but all of you who held fast to the LORD your God are still alive today.

[5]See, I have taught[v] you decrees and laws[w] as the LORD my God commanded[x] me, so that you may follow them in the land you are entering[y] to take possession of it. [6]Observe[z] them carefully, for this will show your wisdom[a] and understanding to the nations, who will hear about all these decrees and say, "Surely this great nation is a wise and understanding people."[b] [7]What other nation is so great[c] as to have their gods near[d] them the way the LORD our God is near us whenever we pray to him? [8]And what other nation is so great as to have such righteous decrees and laws[e] as this body of laws I am setting before you today?

[9]Only be careful,[f] and watch yourselves closely so that you do not forget the things your eyes have seen or let them slip from your heart as long as you live. Teach[g] them to your children[h] and to their children after them. [10]Remember the day you stood before the LORD your God at Horeb,[i] when he said to me, "Assemble the people before me to hear my words so that they may learn[j] to revere[k] me as long as they live in the land[l] and may teach[m] them to their children." [11]You came near and stood at the foot of the mountain[n] while it blazed with fire[o] to the very heavens, with black clouds and deep darkness.[p] [12]Then the LORD spoke[q] to you out of the fire. You heard the sound of words but saw no form;[r] there was only a voice.[s] [13]He declared to you his covenant,[t] the Ten Commandments,[u] which he commanded you to follow and then wrote them on two stone tablets. [14]And the LORD directed me at that time to teach you the decrees and laws[v] you are to follow in the land that you are crossing the Jordan to possess.

Idolatry Forbidden

[15]You saw no form[w] of any kind the day the LORD spoke to you at Horeb[x] out of the fire. Therefore watch yourselves very carefully,[y] [16]so that you do not become corrupt[z] and make for yourselves an idol,[a] an image of any shape, whether formed like a man or a woman, [17]or like any animal on earth or any bird that flies in the air,[b] [18]or like any creature that moves

3:27 [f]S Nu 21:20
[g]S Ge 13:14
[h]S ver 26;
S Nu 20:12;
Dt 32:52
[i]S Nu 27:12
3:28
[j]Nu 27:18-23
[k]Dt 31:7
[l]Dt 1:38; 31:3,23
3:29
[m]S Nu 23:28;
Dt 4:46; 34:6;
Jos 13:20
4:1 [n]S Lev 18:4
[o]Dt 1:3
[p]S Lev 18:5;
Dt 30:15-20;
S Ro 10:5
4:2 [q]Dt 12:32;
Jos 1:7; Pr 30:6;
Rev 22:18-19
[r]Jer 26:2
[s]S Lev 22:31
[t]Dt 10:12-13;
Ecc 12:13
4:3 [u]Nu 25:1-9;
Ps 106:28
4:5 [v]Ps 71:17;
119:102;
Jer 32:33
[w]S Ex 18:20
[x]S Lev 27:34
[y]Ezr 9:11
4:6 [z]Dt 29:9;
1Ki 2:3
[a]Dt 30:19-20;
32:46-47;
Ps 19:7; 119:98;
Pr 1:7; 2Ti 3:15
[b]Job 1:1; 28:28;
Ps 111:10; Pr 2:5;
3:7; 9:10;
Ecc 12:13;
Eze 5:5
4:7 [c]ver 32-34;
2Sa 7:23
[d]S Nu 23:21;
S Ps 46:1;
Ac 17:27
4:8 [e]Ps 89:14;
97:2; 119:7,62,
144,160,172;
Ro 3:2
4:9 [f]S Ex 23:13
[g]S Ge 14:14;
18:19;
Dt 6:20-25;
Eph 6:4
[h]S Ex 10:2
4:10 [i]S Ex 3:1
[j]Dt 14:23; 17:19;
31:12-13;
Ps 2:11; 111:10;
147:11; Isa 8:13;
Jer 32:40
[k]S Ex 20:20

[l]Dt 12:1 [m]ver 9 **4:11** [n]S Ex 3:1; S 19:17 [o]S Ex 19:18 [p]S Ex 19:9; Ps 18:11; 97:2 **4:12** [q]Ex 20:22; Dt 5:4,22; S Mt 3:17; Heb 12:19 [r]Jn 5:37 [s]S Ex 19:9 **4:13** [t]Dt 9:9; Ro 9:4 [u]S Ex 24:12 **4:14** [v]S Ex 21:1 **4:15** [w]Isa 40:18; 41:22-24 [x]S Ex 3:1 [y]Jos 23:11; Mal 2:15 **4:16** [z]S Ge 6:11-12; Dt 9:12; 31:29; 32:5; Jdg 2:19 [a]Ex 20:4-5; Ro 1:23 **4:17** [b]Ro 1:23

3:27 *Go up to the top of Pisgah.* Moses did so after he had expounded the law to the Israelites to prepare them for life in the promised land (see 32:48–52; 34:1–6). *Pisgah.* See note on v. 17. *look west and north and south and east.* Like Abraham (see Ge 13:14), Moses would inherit the promised land only through his descendants (see 34:1–4).
3:28 *commission Joshua.* See 31:7–8.
3:29 *Beth Peor.* Means "house/sanctuary of Peor." Very likely, reference is to the cult place where the Baal of Peor was worshiped (see Nu 23:28; 25:3,5).
4:1 *Hear . . . O Israel.* God's call to his people to hear and obey is a frequent theme in Deuteronomy (see, e.g., 5:1; 6:3–4; 9:1; 20:3) and elsewhere in the OT. See also note on 6:4–9.
4:2 *Do not add . . . do not subtract.* The revelation the Lord gives is sufficient. All of it must be obeyed, and anything that adulterates or contradicts it cannot be tolerated (see 12:32; Pr 30:6; Gal 3:15; Rev 22:18–19).
4:4 *held fast.* See note on 10:20.

4:7 *near us whenever we pray.* The Israelites always had access to the Lord in prayer. His presence was symbolized by the tabernacle in the center of the camp, and by the pillar of cloud over the tabernacle (see Ex 40:34–38; Nu 23:21).
4:9 *Teach them to your children.* See v. 10; 11:19; cf. Ex 12:26–27.
4:10–14 See Ex 19–24.
4:10 *Remember.* The divine call to Israel to remember the Lord's past redemptive acts—especially how he delivered them from slavery in Egypt—is a common theme in Deuteronomy (5:15; 7:18; 8:2,18; 9:7,27; 11:2; 15:15; 16:3,12; 24:9,18,22; 25:17) and is summarized in 32:7: "Remember the days of old."
4:12 *no form.* See v. 15; see also note on Ex 20:4. "God is spirit" (Jn 4:24; cf. Isa 31:3).
4:13 *his covenant, the Ten Commandments.* See notes on Ex 20:1; 34:28. *two stone tablets.* See note on Ex 31:18.
4:15–18 See note on Ex 20:4.

along the ground or any fish in the waters below. [19]And when you look up to the sky and see the sun,[c] the moon and the stars[d]—all the heavenly array[e]—do not be enticed[f] into bowing down to them and worshiping[g] things the LORD your God has apportioned to all the nations under heaven. [20]But as for you, the LORD took you and brought you out of the iron-smelting furnace,[h] out of Egypt,[i] to be the people of his inheritance,[j] as you now are.

[21]The LORD was angry with me[k] because of you, and he solemnly swore that I would not cross the Jordan and enter the good land the LORD your God is giving you as your inheritance. [22]I will die in this land;[l] I will not cross the Jordan; but you are about to cross over and take possession of that good land. [m] [23]Be careful not to forget the covenant[n] of the LORD your God that he made with you; do not make for yourselves an idol[o] in the form of anything the LORD your God has forbidden. [24]For the LORD your God is a consuming fire,[p] a jealous God. [q]

[25]After you have had children and grandchildren and have lived in the land a long time—if you then become corrupt[r] and make any kind of idol,[s] doing evil[t] in the eyes of the LORD your God and provoking him to anger, [26]I call heaven and earth as witnesses[u] against you[v] this day that you will quickly perish[w] from the land that you are crossing the Jordan to possess. You will not live there long but will certainly be destroyed. [27]The LORD will scatter[x] you among the peoples, and only a few of you will survive[y] among the nations to which the LORD will drive you. [28]There you will worship man-made gods[z] of wood and stone,[a] which cannot see or hear or eat or smell. [b] [29]But if from there you seek[c] the LORD your God, you will find him if you look for him with all your heart[d] and with all your soul. [e] [30]When you are in distress[f]

and all these things have happened to you, then in later days[g] you will return[h] to the LORD your God and obey him. [31]For the LORD your God is a merciful[i] God; he will not abandon[j] or destroy[k] you or forget[l] the covenant with your forefathers, which he confirmed to them by oath.

The LORD Is God

[32]Ask[m] now about the former days, long before your time, from the day God created man on the earth;[n] ask from one end of the heavens to the other. [o] Has anything so great[p] as this ever happened, or has anything like it ever been heard of? [33]Has any other people heard the voice of God[j] speaking out of fire, as you have, and lived?[q] [34]Has any god ever tried to take for himself one nation out of another nation,[r] by testings,[s] by miraculous signs[t] and wonders,[u] by war, by a mighty hand and an outstretched arm,[v] or by great and awesome deeds,[w] like all the things the LORD your God did for you in Egypt before your very eyes?

[35]You were shown these things so that you might know that the LORD is God; besides him there is no other.[x] [36]From heaven he made you hear his voice[y] to discipline[z] you. On earth he showed you his great fire, and you heard his words from out of the fire. [37]Because he loved[a] your forefathers and chose their descendants after them, he brought you out of

---

4:19 [c]Dt 17:3; 2Ki 23:11; Job 31:26; Jer 8:2; 43:13; Eze 8:16 [d]S Ge 1:16 [e]S Ge 2:1; S 37:9; Ro 1:25 [f]Dt 13:5 [g]S Nu 25:3 **4:20** [h]S Ex 1:13 [i]S Ex 3:10 [j]S Ge 17:7; S Ex 8:22; S 34:9; Tit 2:14 **4:21** [k]Nu 20:12; Dt 1:37 **4:22** [l]Nu 27:13-14 [m]Dt 3:25 **4:23** [n]ver 9 [o]S Ex 20:4 **4:24** [p]S Ex 15:7; S 19:18; Heb 12:29 [q]S Ex 20:5 **4:25** [r]ver 16 [s]ver 23 [t]1Ki 11:6; 15:26; 16:25,30; 2Ki 17:2,17; 21:2 **4:26** [u]Ge 31:50; Pr 14:5 [v]Dt 30:18-19; 31:28; 32:1; Ps 50:4; Isa 1:2; 34:1; Jer 6:19; Mic 6:2 [w]Dt 6:15; 7:4 **4:27** [x]S Lev 26:33; Dt 28:36,64; 29:28; 1Ki 8:46; 2Ki 17:6; Ps 44:11; 106:27; Jer 3:8; Mic 1:16; Ob 1:5 **4:28** [z]Dt 13:2; 28:36,64; 1Sa 26:19; Jer 5:19; 16:13; Ac 19:26 [a]Dt 29:17 [b]Ps 115:4-8; 135:15-18; Isa 8:19; 26:14; 44:17-20; Rev 9:20 **4:29** [c]1Sa 13:12; 2Ki 13:4; 2Ch 7:14; 15:4; 33:12; Ps 78:34; 119:58; Isa 45:19,22; 55:6; Jer 26:19; Da 9:13; Hos 3:5; Am 5:4 [d]1Sa 7:3; 1Ki 8:48; Jer 29:13 [e]Dt 6:5; 30:1-3,10 **4:30** [f]Lev 26:41; Dt 31:17,21;

[g]Ps 4:1; 18:6; 46:1; 59:16; 107:6 [g]Dt 31:29; Jer 23:20; Hos 3:5; Heb 1:2 [h]Dt 30:2; 1Ki 8:48; Ne 1:9; Jer 3:1,12,22; 4:1; 18:11; Joel 2:12 **4:31** [i]Ex 34:6; Ne 9:31; Ps 111:4 [j]Dt 31:6,8; Jos 1:5; 1Ki 8:57; 1Ch 28:9,20; Ps 9:10; 27:9; 71:9; Isa 42:16; Heb 13:5 [k]S Lev 26:44 [l]Heb 26:45 **4:32** [m]Dt 32:7 [n]S Ge 1:27; Isa 45:12 [o]Dt 28:64; 30:1; Jer 9:16; Mt 24:31 [p]ver 7; 2Sa 7:23 **4:33** [q]Ex 20:22; Dt 5:24-26 **4:34** [r]Ex 14:30 [s]Isa 7:12 [t]S Ex 4:17 [u]Dt 7:19; 26:8; 29:3; 1Ch 16:12; Ps 9:1; 40:5; Jer 32:20 [v]S Ex 3:20; Dt 5:15; 6:21; 15:15 [w]Ex 15:11; Dt 34:12; Ps 45:4; 65:5 **4:35** [x]ver 39; Ex 8:10; Dt 7:9; 32:4,12; 1Sa 2:2; 1Ki 8:60; 2Ki 19:19; Isa 43:10; Mk 12:32 **4:36** [y]S Ex 19:19; Heb 12:25 [z]Dt 8:5 **4:37** [a]Dt 7:8; 10:15; 23:5; 33:3; Ps 44:3; Jer 31:3; Hos 11:1; Mal 1:2; 2:11

[j]33 Or *of a god*

4:19 *do not be enticed.* As kings of Judah would be later (2Ki 23:5).
4:20 *iron-smelting furnace.* Suggests that the period in Egypt was a time of affliction, testing and refinement for the Israelites (see 1Ki 8:51; Jer 11:4; see also Isa 48:10).
4:21 *because of you.* See note on 1:37.
4:24 *consuming fire.* See 9:3; see also note on Ex 24:17. *jealous God.* See 5:9; 6:15; see also note on Ex 20:5.
4:25 *After you ... have lived in the land.* The pattern of Israel's rebellion, resulting in expulsion from the land, and then their repentance, leading to restoration to the land, is prominent in Deuteronomy (see, e.g., the blessing and curse formulas in chs. 27–28).
4:26 *heaven and earth as witnesses.* See notes on 30:19; Ps 50:1; Isa 1:2.
4:27 *will scatter you.* See note on 28:64.

4:29 *with all your heart and ... soul.* Indicates total involvement and commitment. The phrase is applied not only to how the Lord's people should seek him, but also to how they should fear (revere) him, live in obedience to him, love and serve him (6:5; 10:12; 11:13; 13:3; 30:6), and, after forsaking him, renew their allegiance and commitment (26:16; 30:2,10).
4:31 *covenant ... confirmed ... by oath.* See notes on Ge 21:23; 22:16; Heb 6:13,18. In ancient times, parties to a covenant were expected to confirm their intentions by means of a self-maledictory oath (see note on Ge 15:17).
4:35 *so that you might know.* See v. 10. *besides him there is no other.* See v. 39; 5:7; 6:4 and note; 32:39. Moses' belief in one God was total and uncompromising (see note on Ge 1:1).
4:37 *he loved.* The first reference in Deuteronomy to God's

Egypt by his Presence and his great strength,[b] [38]to drive out before you nations greater and stronger than you and to bring you into their land to give it to you for your inheritance,[c] as it is today.

[39]Acknowledge[d] and take to heart this day that the LORD is God in heaven above and on the earth below. There is no other.[e] [40]Keep[f] his decrees and commands,[g] which I am giving you today, so that it may go well[h] with you and your children after you and that you may live long[i] in the land the LORD your God gives you for all time.

Cities of Refuge

4:41–43Ref — Nu 35:6–34; Dt 19:1–14; Jos 20:1–9

[41]Then Moses set aside three cities east of the Jordan, [42]to which anyone who had killed a person could flee if he had unintentionally[j] killed his neighbor without malice aforethought. He could flee into one of these cities and save his life. [43]The cities were these: Bezer in the desert plateau, for the Reubenites; Ramoth[k] in Gilead, for the Gadites; and Golan in Bashan, for the Manassites.

Introduction to the Law

[44]This is the law Moses set before the Israelites. [45]These are the stipulations, decrees and laws Moses gave them when they came out of Egypt [46]and were in the valley near Beth Peor east of the Jordan, in the land of Sihon[l] king of the Amorites, who reigned in Heshbon and was defeated by Moses and the Israelites as they came out of Egypt. [47]They took possession of his land and the land of Og king of Bashan, the two Amorite kings east of the Jordan. [48]This land extended from Aroer[m] on the rim of the Arnon Gorge to Mount Siyon[k] [n] (that is, Hermon[o]), [49]and included all the Arabah east of the Jordan, as far as the Sea of the Arabah,[l] below the slopes of Pisgah.

4:37 [b]S Ex 3:20; S 33:14
4:38 [c]Nu 34:14-15; Dt 7:1; 9:5
4:39 [d]Ex 8:10 [e]S ver 35; Ex 15:11
4:40 [f]S Lev 22:31 [g]ver 1; S Ge 26:5; Dt 5:29; 11:1; Ps 105:45; Isa 48:18 [h]Dt 5:16; 12:25; Isa 3:10 [i]S Ex 23:26; Eph 6:2-3
4:42 [j]S Ex 21:13
4:43 [k]Jos 21:38; 1Ki 22:3; 2Ki 8:28; 9:14
4:46 [l]Nu 21:26
4:48 [m]Dt 2:36 [n]Dt 3:9 [o]S Dt 3:8

5:1 [p]S Ex 18:20
5:2 [q]Ex 19:5; Jer 11:2; Heb 9:15; 10:15-17 [r]S Ge 17:9; S Ex 3:1
5:3 [s]Dt 11:2-7 [t]Nu 26:63-65; Heb 8:9
5:4 [u]S Dt 4:12 [v]S Nu 14:14 [w]S Ex 19:18
5:5 [x]Gal 3:19 [y]S Ge 3:10; Heb 12:18-21
5:6 [z]S Ex 13:3; S 29:46 [a]Lev 26:1; Dt 6:4; Ps 81:10
5:8 [b]Lev 26:1; Dt 4:15-18; Ps 78:58; 97:7
5:9 [c]S Nu 26:11 [d]Ex 34:7; S Nu 10:35; 14:18
5:10 [e]S Ex 34:7 [f]Nu 14:18; Dt 7:9; Ne 1:5; Jer 32:18; Da 9:4
5:11 [g]Ps 139:20 [h]Lev 19:12; Dt 10:20; Mt 5:33-37

The Ten Commandments

5:6–21pp — Ex 20:1–17

5 Moses summoned all Israel and said: Hear, O Israel, the decrees and laws[p] I declare in your hearing today. Learn them and be sure to follow them. [2]The LORD our God made a covenant[q] with us at Horeb.[r] [3]It was not with our fathers that the LORD made this covenant, but with us,[s] with all of us who are alive here today.[t] [4]The LORD spoke[u] to you face to face[v] out of the fire[w] on the mountain. [5](At that time I stood between[x] the LORD and you to declare to you the word of the LORD, because you were afraid[y] of the fire and did not go up the mountain.) And he said:

[6]"I am the LORD your God, who brought you out of Egypt,[z] out of the land of slavery.[a]

[7]"You shall have no other gods before[m] me.

[8]"You shall not make for yourself an idol in the form of anything in heaven above or on the earth beneath or in the waters below.[b] [9]You shall not bow down to them or worship them; for I, the LORD your God, am a jealous God, punishing the children for the sin of the fathers[c] to the third and fourth generation of those who hate me,[d] [10]but showing love to a thousand[e] generations, of those who love me and keep my commandments.[f]

[11]"You shall not misuse the name[g] of the LORD your God, for the LORD will not hold anyone guiltless who misuses his name.[h]

[12]"Observe the Sabbath day by keeping

[k]48 Hebrew; Syriac (see also Deut. 3:9) *Sirion*
[l]49 That is, the Dead Sea   [m]7 Or *besides*

love for his people (see Introduction: Theological Teaching). See note on 7:8; see also 5:10; 7:9,13; 10:15; 23:5. The corollary truth is that his people should love him (see note on 6:5).
4:39 See v. 35 and note.
4:41–43 See 19:1–13; Nu 35:9–28; Jos 20.
4:43 *Bezer.* About 20 miles east of the northeast corner of the Dead Sea.
5:1 *Hear, O Israel.* See note on 4:1.
5:2 *covenant with us at Horeb.* See note on Ex 19:5. God's covenant with Israel, given at Mount Horeb (Sinai) and now being confirmed, bound Israel to the Lord as their absolute Sovereign, and to his laws and regulations as their way of life. Adherence to the covenant would bring to Israel the blessings of the Lord, while breaking the covenant would bring against them the punishments described as "curses" (see,

e.g., 28:15–20). Jer 31:31–34 predicted the establishing of a new covenant, which made the Sinaitic covenant obsolete (see Heb 7:22; see also Heb 8:6–13; 10:15–18 and notes). See chart on "Major Covenants in the OT," p. 19.
5:3 *not with our fathers . . . but with us.* The covenant was made with those who were present at Sinai, but since they were representatives of the nation, it was made with all succeeding generations as well.
5:5 See vv. 23–26; Ex 20:18–21.
5:6–21 The Ten Commandments are both the basis and the heart of Israel's relationship with the Lord. It is almost impossible to exaggerate their effect on subsequent history. They constitute the basis of moral principles throughout the Western world, and they summarize what the one true God expects of his people in terms of faith, worship and conduct (see notes on Ex 20:3–17).

it holy,[i] as the LORD your God has commanded you. [13]Six days you shall labor and do all your work, [14]but the seventh day[j] is a Sabbath to the LORD your God. On it you shall not do any work, neither you, nor your son or daughter, nor your manservant or maidservant,[k] nor your ox, your donkey or any of your animals, nor the alien within your gates, so that your manservant and maidservant may rest, as you do.[l] [15]Remember that you were slaves[m] in Egypt and that the LORD your God brought you out of there with a mighty hand[n] and an outstretched arm.[o] Therefore the LORD your God has commanded you to observe the Sabbath day.

[16]"Honor your father[p] and your mother,[q] as the LORD your God has commanded you, so that you may live long[r] and that it may go well with you in the land the LORD your God is giving you.

[17]"You shall not murder.[s]

[18]"You shall not commit adultery.[t]

[19]"You shall not steal.[u]

[20]"You shall not give false testimony against your neighbor.[v]

[21]"You shall not covet your neighbor's wife. You shall not set your desire on your neighbor's house or land, his manservant or maidservant, his ox or donkey, or anything that belongs to your neighbor."[w]

[22]These are the commandments the LORD proclaimed in a loud voice to your whole assembly there on the mountain from out of the fire, the cloud and the deep darkness;[x] and he added nothing more. Then he wrote them on two stone tablets[y] and gave them to me.

[23]When you heard the voice out of the darkness, while the mountain was ablaze with fire, all the leading men of your tribes

and your elders[z] came to me. [24]And you said, "The LORD our God has shown us[a] his glory and his majesty,[b] and we have heard his voice from the fire. Today we have seen that a man can live even if God speaks with him.[c] [25]But now, why should we die? This great fire will consume us, and we will die if we hear the voice of the LORD our God any longer.[d] [26]For what mortal man has ever heard the voice of the living God speaking out of fire, as we have, and survived?[e] [27]Go near and listen to all that the LORD our God says.[f] Then tell us whatever the LORD our God tells you. We will listen and obey."[g]

[28]The LORD heard you when you spoke to me and the LORD said to me, "I have heard what this people said to you. Everything they said was good.[h] [29]Oh, that their hearts would be inclined to fear me[i] and keep all my commands[j] always, so that it might go well with them and their children forever![k]

[30]"Go, tell them to return to their tents. [31]But you stay here[l] with me so that I may give you all the commands, decrees and laws you are to teach them to follow in the land I am giving them to possess."

[32]So be careful to do what the LORD your God has commanded you; [m] do not turn aside to the right or to the left.[n] [33]Walk in all the way that the LORD your God has commanded you,[o] so that you may live and prosper and prolong your days[p] in the land that you will possess.

Love the LORD Your God

6 These are the commands, decrees and laws the LORD your God directed me to teach you to observe in the land that you are crossing the Jordan to possess, [2]so that you, your children and their children after them may fear[q] the LORD your God as long as you live[r] by keeping all his decrees and commands[s] that I give you, and so that you may enjoy long life.[t] [3]Hear, O

Cross references

5:12 [i]Ex 16:23-30; 31:13-17; Mk 2:27-28
5:14 [j]S Ge 2:2; Mt 12:2; Mk 2:27; Heb 4:4 [k]Job 31:13; Jer 34:9-11 [l]Jer 17:21,24
5:15 [m]S Ge 15:13 [n]Ex 6:1; Ps 108:6; Jer 32:21 [o]S Dt 4:34
5:16 [p]Mal 1:6 [q]Ex 21:17; Lev 19:3; Eze 22:7; Mt 15:4*; 19:19*; Mk 7:10*; 10:9*; Lk 18:20*; Eph 6:2-3* [r]S Dt 4:40; 11:9; Pr 3:1-2
5:17 [s]Ge 9:6; Lev 24:17; Ecc 3:3; Jer 40:15; 41:3; Mt 5:21-22*; 19:19*; Mk 10:19*; Lk 18:20*; Ro 13:9*; Jas 2:11*
5:18 [t]Lev 20:10; Mt 5:27-30; 19:18*; Mk 10:19*; Lk 18:20*; Ro 13:9*; Jas 2:11*
5:19 [u]Lev 19:11; Mt 19:19*; Mk 10:19*; Lk 18:20*; Ro 13:9*
5:20 [v]S Ex 23:1; Mt 19:18*; Mk 10:19*; Lk 18:20*
5:21 [w]Ro 7:7*; 13:9*
5:22 [x]S Ex 20:21 [y]S Ex 24:12
5:23 [z]S Ex 3:16
5:24 [a]Dt 4:34; 8:5; 11:2; Isa 53:4 [b]S Dt 3:24 [c]Ex 19:19
5:25 [d]Ex 20:18-19; Dt 18:16; Heb 12:19
5:26 [e]S Ex 33:20; Dt 4:33; Jdg 6:22-23; 13:22; Isa 6:5
5:27 [f]S Ex 19:8 [g]S Ex 24:7
5:28 [h]Dt 18:17
5:29 [i]Ps 81:8,13 [j]Jos 22:5; Ps 78:7 [k]ver 33; S Dt 4:1, 40; 12:25; 22:7 5:31 [l]Ex 24:12 5:32 [m]S Dt 4:29; 10:12 [n]Dt 17:11,20; 28:14; Jos 1:7; 1Ki 15:5; 2Ki 22:2; Pr 4:27 5:33 [o]Isa 3:10; Jer 7:23; 38:20; S Lk 1:6 [p]S ver 29 6:2 [q]S Ex 20:20; S 1Sa 12:24 [r]Dt 4:9 [s]S Ge 26:5 [t]S Ex 20:12

5:12 *as the LORD your God has commanded you.* Missing from the parallel verse in Exodus (20:8), this clause reminds the people of the divine origin of the Ten Commandments 40 years earlier (see vv. 15–16).
5:14 *so that your manservant and maidservant may rest.* See note on Ex 20:10; see also v. 15.
5:15 *Remember.* See note on 4:10.
5:16–21 The NT quotes often from this section of the Ten Commandments.
5:20 See 19:18–19.
5:22 *commandments.* Lit. "words" (see note on Ex 20:1).

two stone tablets. See note on Ex 31:18.
5:25 *we will die.* See notes on Ge 16:13; 32:30.
5:27 *We will listen and obey.* See note on Ex 19:8.
6:2 *fear the LORD.* See note on Ge 20:11. *enjoy long life.* See 4:40; 5:16,33. By obeying the Lord and keeping his decrees, individual Israelites would enjoy long life in the land, and the people as a whole would enjoy a long national existence in the land.
6:3–4 *Hear, O Israel.* See note on 4:1.
6:3 *land flowing with milk and honey.* See note on Ex 3:8. The phrase is used 14 times from Exodus through

Israel, and be careful to obey[u] so that it may go well with you and that you may increase greatly[v] in a land flowing with milk and honey,[w] just as the LORD, the God of your fathers, promised[x] you.

[4]Hear, O Israel: The LORD our God, the LORD is one.[n][y] [5]Love[z] the LORD your God with all your heart[a] and with all your soul and with all your strength.[b] [6]These commandments that I give you today are to be upon your hearts.[c] [7]Impress them on your children. Talk about them when you sit at home and when you walk along the road, when you lie down and when you get up.[d] [8]Tie them as symbols on your hands and bind them on your foreheads.[e] [9]Write them on the doorframes of your houses and on your gates.[f]

[10]When the LORD your God brings you into the land he swore to your fathers, to Abraham, Isaac and Jacob, to give you—a land with large, flourishing cities you did not build,[g] [11]houses filled with all kinds of good things you did not provide, wells you did not dig,[h] and vineyards and olive groves you did not plant—then when you eat and are satisfied,[i] [12]be careful that you do not forget[j] the LORD, who brought you out of Egypt, out of the land of slavery.

[13]Fear the LORD[k] your God, serve him only[l] and take your oaths[m] in his name.[n] [14]Do not follow other gods, the gods of the peoples around you; [15]for the LORD your God[o], who is among you, is a jealous God and his anger will burn against you, and he will destroy you from the face of the land. [16]Do not test the LORD your God[p] as you did at Massah. [17]Be sure to keep[q] the commands of the LORD your God and the stipulations and decrees he has given you.[r] [18]Do what is right and good in the

LORD's sight,[s] so that it may go well[t] with you and you may go in and take over the good land that the LORD promised on oath to your forefathers, [19]thrusting out all your enemies[u] before you, as the LORD said.

[20]In the future, when your son asks you,[v] "What is the meaning of the stipulations, decrees and laws the LORD our God has commanded you?" [21]tell him: "We were slaves of Pharaoh in Egypt, but the LORD brought us out of Egypt with a mighty hand.[w] [22]Before our eyes the LORD sent miraculous signs and wonders—great and terrible—upon Egypt and Pharaoh and his whole household. [23]But he brought us out from there to bring us in and give us the land that he promised on oath to our forefathers. [24]The LORD commanded us to obey all these decrees and to fear the LORD our God,[x] so that we might always prosper and be kept alive, as is the case today.[y] [25]And if we are careful to obey all this law[z] before the LORD our God, as he has commanded us, that will be our righteousness.[a]"

Driving Out the Nations

7 When the LORD your God brings you into the land you are entering to possess[b] and drives out before you many nations[c]—the Hittites,[d] Girgashites,[e] Amorites,[f] Canaanites, Perizzites,[g] Hivites[h] and Jebusites,[i] seven nations larger and

6:3 [u]S Ex 19:5
[v]Ge 15:5; Dt 5:33
[w]S Ex 3:8;
Dt 32:13-14
[x]Ex 13:5
6:4 [y]Dt 4:35,39;
Ne 9:6; Ps 86:10;
Isa 44:6;
Zec 14:9;
Mk 12:29*;
Jn 10:30;
1Co 8:4; Eph 4:6;
Jas 2:19
6:5 [z]Dt 11:1,22;
Mt 22:37*;
Mk 12:30*;
Lk 10:27*
[a]1Sa 12:24
[b]Dt 4:29; 10:12;
Jos 22:5
6:6 [c]ver 8;
Dt 11:18; 30:14;
32:46; Ps 26:2;
37:31; 40:8;
119:11; Pr 3:3;
Isa 51:7; Jer 17:1;
31:33; Eze 40:4
6:7 [d]Dt 4:9;
11:19; Pr 22:6;
Eph 6:4
6:8 [e]S ver 6;
S Ex 13:9;
Mt 23:5
6:9 [f]Dt 11:20
6:10 [g]S Ge 11:4;
Dt 12:29; 19:1;
Jos 24:13;
Ps 105:44
6:11 [h]Jer 2:13
[i]S Lev 26:5;
Dt 8:10; 14:29;
31:20
6:12 [j]Dt 4:9,23;
2Ki 17:38;
Ps 44:17; 78:7;
103:2
6:13 [k]Ps 33:8;
34:9 [l]Dt 13:4;
1Sa 7:3;
Jer 44:10;
Mt 4:10*;
Lk 4:4*; 4:8
[m]1Sa 20:3
[n]S Ex 20:7;
S Mt 5:33
6:15 [o]Dt 4:24;
5:9
6:16 [p]S Ex 17:2;
Mt 4:7*;
Lk 4:12*
6:17 [q]S Lev 26:3
[r]Dt 11:22;
Ps 119:4,56,100,
134,168

6:18 [s]2Ki 18:6; Isa 36:7; 38:3 [t]Dt 4:40 **6:19** [u]Ex 23:27;
Jos 21:44; Ps 78:53; 107:2; 136:24 **6:20** [v]S Ex 10:2 **6:21**
[w]S Dt 4:34 **6:24** [x]Dt 10:12; 30:6; Ps 86:11; Jer 32:39
[y]Ps 27:12; 41:2; S Ro 10:5 **6:25** [z]Ps 103:18; 119:34,55
[a]Dt 24:13; S Ro 9:31 **7:1** [b]S Lev 14:34; S Dt 4:38
[c]Dt 20:16-18; 31:3 [d]Ge 15:20 [e]S Ge 10:16 [f]S Dt 1:7
[g]Ge 13:7 [h]S Ge 10:17 [i]Jos 3:10

n4 Or *The LORD our God is one LORD*; or *The LORD is our God, the LORD is one*; or *The LORD is our God, the LORD alone*

6:4–9 Known as the *Shema*, Hebrew for "Hear." It has become the Jewish confession of faith, recited daily by the pious (see Mt 22:37–38; Mk 12:29–30; Lk 10:27).

6:4 *the LORD is one.* A divinely revealed insight, especially important in view of the multiplicity of Baals and other gods of Canaan and elsewhere (see, e.g., Jdg 2:11–13).

6:5 *Love the LORD.* Love for God and neighbor (see Lev 19:18) is built on the love that the Lord has for his people (1Jn 4:19–21) and on his identification with them. Such love is to be total, involving one's whole being (see notes on 4:29; Jos 22:5).

6:6 *commandments . . . upon your hearts.* A feature that would especially characterize the "new covenant" (see Jer 31:33).

6:8–9 Many Jews take these verses literally and tie phylacteries (see note on Mt 23:5) to their foreheads and left arms. They also attach mezuzot (small wooden or metal containers in which passages of Scripture are placed) to the doorframes of their houses. But a figurative interpretation is

supported by 11:18–20; Ex 13:9,16. See note on Ex 13:9.

6:10–12 Because the emphasis in Scripture is always on what God does and not on what his people achieve, they are never to forget what he has done for them.

6:13 Quoted in part by Jesus in response to Satan's temptation (Mt 4:10; Lk 4:8). Jesus quoted from Deuteronomy in response to the devil's other two temptations as well (see notes on v. 16; 8:3).

6:15 *jealous God.* See note on Ex 20:5.

6:16 Quoted in part by Jesus in Mt 4:7; Lk 4:12 (see also note on v. 13). *as you did at Massah.* See 9:22; 33:8; see also note on Ex 17:7.

6:20 See Ex 12:26 and note.

6:23 *brought us out . . . to bring us in.* See note on Ex 6:7–8.

6:25 *righteousness.* Probably here refers to a true, personal relationship with the covenant Lord that manifests itself in the daily lives of God's people (see 24:13).

7:1 *Hittites . . . Jebusites.* See 20:17; see also notes on Ge 10:6,15–18; 13:7. *seven nations.* See note on Ex 3:8.

stronger than you— [2]and when the LORD your God has delivered[j] them over to you and you have defeated them, then you must destroy[k] them totally.[o][l] Make no treaty[m] with them, and show them no mercy.[n] [3]Do not intermarry with them.[o] Do not give your daughters to their sons or take their daughters for your sons, [4]for they will turn your sons away from following me to serve other gods,[p] and the LORD's anger will burn against you and will quickly destroy[q] you. [5]This is what you are to do to them: Break down their altars, smash their sacred stones, cut down their Asherah poles[p][r] and burn their idols in the fire.[s] [6]For you are a people holy[t] to the LORD your God.[u] The LORD your God has chosen[v] you out of all the peoples on the face of the earth to be his people, his treasured possession.[w]

[7]The LORD did not set his affection on you and choose you because you were more numerous[x] than other peoples, for you were the fewest[y] of all peoples.[z] [8]But it was because the LORD loved[a] you and kept the oath he swore[b] to your forefathers that he brought you out with a mighty hand[c] and redeemed[d] you from the land of slavery,[e] from the power of Pharaoh king of Egypt. [9]Know therefore that the LORD your God is God;[f] he is the faithful God,[g] keeping his covenant of love[h] to a thousand generations[i] of those who love him and keep his commands.[j] [10]But

> those who hate him he will repay to
>   their face by destruction;
> he will not be slow to repay to their
>   face those who hate him.[k]

[11]Therefore, take care to follow the commands, decrees and laws I give you today.

[12]If you pay attention to these laws and are careful to follow them, then the LORD

your God will keep his covenant of love with you, as he swore to your forefathers.[l] [13]He will love you and bless you[m] and increase your numbers.[n] He will bless the fruit of your womb,[o] the crops of your land—your grain, new wine[p] and oil[q]—the calves of your herds and the lambs of your flocks in the land that he swore to your forefathers to give you.[r] [14]You will be blessed more than any other people; none of your men or women will be childless, nor any of your livestock without young.[s] [15]The LORD will keep you free from every disease.[t] He will not inflict on you the horrible diseases you knew in Egypt,[u] but he will inflict them on all who hate you.[v] [16]You must destroy all the peoples the LORD your God gives over to you.[w] Do not look on them with pity[x] and do not serve their gods,[y] for that will be a snare[z] to you.

[17]You may say to yourselves, "These nations are stronger than we are. How can we drive them out?[a]" [18]But do not be afraid[b] of them; remember well what the LORD your God did to Pharaoh and to all Egypt.[c] [19]You saw with your own eyes the great trials, the miraculous signs and wonders, the mighty hand[d] and outstretched arm, with which the LORD your God brought you out. The LORD your God will do the same to all the peoples you now fear.[e] [20]Moreover, the LORD your God will send the hornet[f] among them until even

---

7:2 /S Dt 2:33
kS Dt 2:34
/Nu 31:17;
Dt 33:27;
Jos 11:11
mS Ex 23:32 nver 16; Dt 13:8;
19:13; 25:12
7:3
oEx 34:15-16;
Jos 22:16; Da 9:7
7:4 pJdg 3:6
qS Dt 4:26
7:5 rS Ex 34:13;
Dt 16:21
sS Ex 23:24
7:6 tEx 19:6;
S Lev 27:30
uDt 26:19;
Ps 30:4; 37:28;
50:5; 52:9
vDt 14:2;
1Ki 3:8; Isa 41:9;
Eze 20:5
wS Ge 17:7;
S Ex 8:22; S 34:9;
Isa 43:1; Ro 9:4;
Tit 2:14
7:7 xS Ge 22:17
yGe 34:30
zDt 4:37; 10:22
7:8 aS Dt 4:37;
1Ki 10:9;
2Ch 2:11; Ps 44:3
bEx 32:13;
S Nu 14:8;
Ro 11:28
cS Ex 3:20
dS Ex 6:6
eS Ex 13:14
7:9 /S Dt 4:35
gPs 18:25; 33:4;
108:4; 145:13;
146:6; Isa 49:7;
Jer 42:5;
Hos 11:12;
S 1Co 1:9 hver 12; 1Ki 8:23;
2Ch 6:14;
Ne 1:5; 9:32
iS Ex 20:6
/S Dt 5:10
7:10
kS Lev 26:28;
S Nu 10:35;
Na 1:2

7:12
lLev 26:3-13;
Dt 28:1-14;
Ps 105:8-9;
Mic 7:20
7:13 mPs 11:5;
146:8; Pr 15:9;
Isa 51:1; Jn 14:21
nS Ge 17:6;
Ex 1:7; Dt 1:10;
13:17; 30:5;
Ps 107:38

oS Ge 49:25 pS Ge 27:28 qS Nu 18:12 rDt 28:4 **7:14**
sEx 23:26 **7:15** tS Ex 15:26 uS Ex 9:9 vS Ex 23:25;
Dt 30:8-10 **7:16** wver 24; Jos 6:2; 10:26 xS ver 2 yJdg 3:6;
Ezr 9:1; Ps 106:36 zver 25; S Ex 10:7 **7:17** aNu 33:53 **7:18**
bS Nu 14:9; S Dt 1:21,29 cPs 105:5; 119:52 **7:19**
dPs 136:12 eDt 4:34 **7:20** /S Ex 23:28

o2 The Hebrew term refers to the irrevocable giving over of things or persons to the LORD, often by totally destroying them; also in verse 26.   p5 That is, symbols of the goddess Asherah; here and elsewhere in Deuteronomy

---

7:2–5 *Make no treaty . . . Do not intermarry . . . Break down their altars.* Israel was to have no association—political, social or religious—with the idol worshipers of Canaan (see v. 16; see also note on 2:34).

7:2 *destroy them totally.* See note on 2:34.

7:4 *turn your sons . . . to serve other gods.* The Lord's command against intermarriage with foreigners was not racially motivated but was intended to prevent spiritual contamination and apostasy (see, e.g., 1Ki 11:1–11; Ne 13:25–27).

7:5 *altars . . . sacred stones . . . Asherah poles.* Cult objects of Canaanite idolatrous worship (see 12:3; 16:21–22). See also NIV text note; Ex 34:13 and note.

7:6 *holy.* Separated from all corrupting people or things and consecrated totally to the Lord (see note on Ex 3:5). *treasured possession.* See note on Ex 19:5.

7:8 *because the LORD loved you.* The "covenant of love" (vv. 9,12) stems from God's love for his people, based on his

character and embodied in his covenant; it does not stem from the numerical greatness of the people or any virtue of theirs. His love must be reciprocated by his people (see vv. 9–10; 9:4–6; see also note on 6:5).

7:9 *Know . . . that the LORD . . . is God.* See Ps 100:3. *thousand generations of those who love him.* See note on Ex 20:6.

7:12–15 The blessings are elaborated in 28:1–14; 30:1–10.

7:13 *grain, new wine and oil.* A common OT summary of the produce of field, vineyard and olive grove (see, e.g., 11:14; 14:23; 18:4; 28:51).

7:15 *not inflict . . . diseases.* See note on 28:60.

7:16 See Introduction to Joshua: The Conquest and the Ethical Question of War.

7:18 *remember.* See note on 4:10.

7:20 *hornet.* See note on Ex 23:28.

the survivors who hide from you have perished. 21Do not be terrified by them, for the LORD your God, who is among you,*g* is a great and awesome God.*h* 22The LORD your God will drive out those nations before you, little by little.*i* You will not be allowed to eliminate them all at once, or the wild animals will multiply around you. 23But the LORD your God will deliver them over to you, throwing them into great confusion until they are destroyed.*j* 24He will give their kings*k* into your hand,*l* and you will wipe out their names from under heaven. No one will be able to stand up against you;*m* you will destroy them.*n* 25The images of their gods you are to burn*o* in the fire. Do not covet*p* the silver and gold on them, and do not take it for yourselves, or you will be ensnared*q* by it, for it is detestable*r* to the LORD your God. 26Do not bring a detestable thing into your house or you, like it, will be set apart for destruction.*s* Utterly abhor and detest it, for it is set apart for destruction.

Do Not Forget the LORD

8 Be careful to follow every command I am giving you today, so that you may live*t* and increase and may enter and possess the land that the LORD promised on oath to your forefathers.*u* 2Remember how the LORD your God led*v* you all the way in the desert these forty years, to humble you and to test*w* you in order to know what was in your heart, whether or not you would keep his commands. 3He humbled*x* you, causing you to hunger and then feeding you with manna,*y* which neither you nor your fathers had known, to teach*z* you that man does not live on bread*a* alone but on every word that comes from the mouth*b* of the LORD.*c* 4Your clothes did not wear out and your feet did not swell during these forty years.*d* 5Know then in your heart that as a man disciplines his

son, so the LORD your God disciplines you.*e*

6Observe the commands of the LORD your God, walking in his ways*f* and revering him.*g* 7For the LORD your God is bringing you into a good land*h*—a land with streams and pools of water, with springs flowing in the valleys and hills;*i* 8a land with wheat and barley,*j* vines*k* and fig trees,*l* pomegranates, olive oil and honey;*m* 9a land where bread*n* will not be scarce and you will lack nothing;*o* a land where the rocks are iron and you can dig copper out of the hills.*p*

10When you have eaten and are satisfied,*q* praise the LORD your God for the good land he has given you. 11Be careful that you do not forget*r* the LORD your God, failing to observe his commands, his laws and his decrees that I am giving you this day. 12Otherwise, when you eat and are satisfied, when you build fine houses and settle down,*s* 13and when your herds and flocks grow large and your silver and gold increase and all you have is multiplied, 14then your heart will become proud and you will forget*t* the LORD your God, who brought you out of Egypt, out of the land of slavery. 15He led you through the vast and dreadful desert,*u* that thirsty and waterless land, with its venomous snakes*v* and scorpions. He brought you water out of hard rock.*w* 16He gave you manna*x* to eat in the desert, something your fathers had never known,*y* to humble and to test*z* you so that in the end it might go well with you. 17You may say to yourself,*a* "My power and the strength of my hands*b* have produced this wealth for me." 18But remember the LORD your God, for it is he

Cross references (center column)

7:21 *g*S Ge 17:7; Jos 3:10
*h*Dt 10:17; Ne 1:5; 9:32; Ps 47:2; 66:3; 68:35; Isa 9:6; Da 9:4
7:22 *i*Ex 23:28-30
7:23 *j*Ex 23:27; Jos 10:10
7:24 *k*Jos 10:24; Ps 110:5 *l*S ver 16
*m*S Ex 23:31; Dt 11:25; Jos 1:5; 10:8; 23:9
*n*Jos 21:44
7:25 *o*S Ex 4:14; S 32:20
*p*Ex 20:17; Jos 7:21 *q*S ver 16
*r*Dt 17:1
7:26 *s*Lev 27:28-29
8:1 *t*Dt 4:1
*u*S Ex 19:5; Job 36:11; Ps 16:11; Eze 20:19
8:2 *v*Dt 29:5; Ps 136:16; Am 2:10
*w*S Ge 22:1
8:3 *x*2Ch 36:12; Ps 44:9; Pr 18:12; Isa 2:11; Jer 44:10
*y*S Ex 16:4
*z*1Ki 8:36; Ps 25:5; 94:12; 119:171 *a*ver 9; S Ge 3:19; Job 23:12; Ps 104:15; Pr 28:21; Isa 51:14; Jer 42:14
*b*Job 22:22; Ps 119:13; 138:4
*c*S Ex 16:2-3; Mt 4:4*; Lk 4:4*
8:4 *d*Dt 29:5; Ne 9:21
8:5 *e*Dt 4:36; 2Sa 7:14; Job 5:17; 33:19; Pr 3:11-12; Heb 12:5-11; Rev 3:19
8:6 *f*S Ex 33:13; 1Ki 3:14; Ps 81:13; 95:10
*g*Dt 5:33
8:7 *h*Ps 106:24; Jer 3:19; Eze 20:6
*i*Dt 11:9-12; Jer 2:7
8:8 *j*S Ex 9:31
*k*S Ge 49:11
*l*S Nu 13:23; S 1Ki 4:25

*m*Dt 32:13; Ps 81:16 8:9 *n*S ver 3 *o*Jdg 18:10 *p*Job 28:2 8:10 *q*Dt 6:10-12 8:11 *r*Dt 4:9 8:12 *s*Pr 30:9; Hos 13:6 8:14 *t*ver 11; Ps 78:7; 106:21 8:15 *u*S Dt 1:19; S 32:10 *v*Nu 21:6; Isa 14:29; 30:6 *w*Ex 17:6; Dt 32:13; Job 28:9; Ps 78:15; 114:8 8:16 *x*S Ex 16:14 *y*Ex 16:15 *z*S Ge 22:1 8:17 *a*Dt 9:4, 7,24; 31:27 *b*Jdg 7:2; Ps 44:3; Isa 10:13

Footnotes (bottom)

7:22 *God will drive out.* See note on 3:22.
7:25–26 Cf. the story of Achan (Jos 6:17–19; 7:1,20–25).
7:26 *set apart for destruction.* See note on 2:34.
8:2 *Remember.* See note on 4:10. *test.* See v. 16; see also note on Ge 22:1.
8:3 *manna.* See v. 16; see also note on Nu 11:7. *man does not live on bread alone.* See note on 6:13; quoted by Jesus in response to the devil's temptation (see Mt 4:4; Lk 4:4). Bread sustains but does not guarantee life, which is God's gift to those who trust in and live by his word: his commands and promises (see vv. 1,18). God's "discipline" (v. 5) of his people by bringing them through the desert taught them this fundamental truth. There they were humbled (cf. v. 14) by being cast in total dependence on the Lord.
8:7–9 A concise description of the rich and fertile land of promise that the Israelites were about to enter and possess

(see 11:8–12). See map No. 2 at the end of the Study Bible.
8:9 *iron . . . copper.* The mountains of southern Lebanon and the regions east of the Sea of Galilee and south of the Dead Sea contain iron. Both copper and iron were plentiful in the part of the Arabah south of the Dead Sea. Some of the copper mines date to the time of Solomon and earlier. Zarethan was a center for bronze works in Solomon's time (1Ki 7:45–46). Some bronze objects from this site precede the Solomonic period, and today there are copper works at Timnah in the Negev.
8:11,14,19 *forget.* See note on 4:10.
8:15 *water out of hard rock.* See Ex 17:6 and note.
8:16 *test.* See v. 2; see also note on Ge 22:1.
8:17–18 See Zec 4:6 and note.
8:18 *remember.* See note on 4:10.

who gives you the ability to produce wealth,*c* and so confirms his covenant, which he swore to your forefathers, as it is today.

19If you ever forget the LORD your God and follow other gods*d* and worship and bow down to them, I testify against you today that you will surely be destroyed.*e* 20Like the nations*f* the LORD destroyed before you, so you will be destroyed for not obeying the LORD your God.*g*

Not Because of Israel's Righteousness

9 Hear, O Israel. You are now about to cross the Jordan*h* to go in and dispossess nations greater and stronger than you,*i* with large cities*j* that have walls up to the sky.*k* 2The people are strong and tall—Anakites! You know about them and have heard it said: "Who can stand up against the Anakites?"*l* 3But be assured today that the LORD your God is the one who goes across ahead of you*m* like a devouring fire.*n* He will destroy them; he will subdue them before you. And you will drive them out and annihilate them quickly,*o* as the LORD has promised you.

4After the LORD your God has driven them out before you, do not say to yourself,*p* "The LORD has brought me here to take possession of this land because of my righteousness." No, it is on account of the wickedness*q* of these nations*r* that the LORD is going to drive them out before you. 5It is not because of your righteousness or your integrity*s* that you are going in to take possession of their land; but on account of the wickedness*t* of these nations,*u* the LORD your God will drive them out*v* before you, to accomplish what he swore*w* to your fathers, to Abraham, Isaac and Jacob.*x* 6Understand, then, that it is not because of your righteousness that the LORD your God is giving you this good land to possess, for you are a stiff-necked people.*y*

The Golden Calf

7Remember this and never forget how you provoked*z* the LORD your God to an-

ger in the desert. From the day you left Egypt until you arrived here, you have been rebellious*a* against the LORD.*b* 8At Horeb you aroused the LORD's wrath*c* so that he was angry enough to destroy you.*d* 9When I went up on the mountain to receive the tablets of stone, the tablets of the covenant*e* that the LORD had made with you, I stayed on the mountain forty days*f* and forty nights; I ate no bread and drank no water.*g* 10The LORD gave me two stone tablets inscribed by the finger of God.*h* On them were all the commandments the LORD proclaimed to you on the mountain out of the fire, on the day of the assembly.*i*

11At the end of the forty days and forty nights,*j* the LORD gave me the two stone tablets,*k* the tablets of the covenant. 12Then the LORD told me, "Go down from here at once, because your people whom you brought out of Egypt have become corrupt.*l* They have turned away quickly*m* from what I commanded them and have made a cast idol for themselves."

13And the LORD said to me, "I have seen this people*n*, and they are a stiff-necked people indeed! 14Let me alone,*o* so that I may destroy them and blot out*p* their name from under heaven.*q* And I will make you into a nation stronger and more numerous than they."

15So I turned and went down from the mountain while it was ablaze with fire. And the two tablets of the covenant were in my hands.*q r* 16When I looked, I saw that you had sinned against the LORD your God; you had made for yourselves an idol cast in the shape of a calf.*s* You had turned aside quickly from the way that the LORD had commanded you. 17So I took the two tablets and threw them out of my hands, breaking them to pieces before your eyes.

18Then once again I fell*t* prostrate before the LORD for forty days and forty nights; I ate no bread and drank no water,*u* because of all the sin you had committed,*v* doing what was evil in the

Cross references (center column)

8:18 *c*Ge 26:13; Dt 26:10; 28:4; 1Sa 2:7; Ps 25:13; 112:3; Pr 8:18; 10:22; Ecc 9:11; Hos 2:8
8:19 *d*Dt 6:14; Ps 16:4; Jer 7:6; 13:10; 25:6
*e*Dt 4:26; 30:18
8:20 *f*2Ki 21:2; Ps 10:16
*g*Eze 5:5-17
9:1 *h*S Nu 35:10
*i*Dt 4:38
*j*S Nu 13:28
*k*S Ge 11:4
9:2 *l*Nu 13:22; Jos 11:22
9:3 *m*Dt 31:3; Jos 3:11
*n*S Ex 15:7; S 19:18; Heb 12:29
*o*S Ex 23:31
9:4 *p*S Dt 8:17
*q*2Ki 16:3; 17:8; 21:2; Ezr 9:11
*r*S Ex 23:24; S Lev 18:21, 24-30; Dt 18:9-14
9:5 *s*S Eph 2:9
*t*Dt 18:9
*u*S Lev 18:25
*v*Dt 4:38; 11:23
*w*S Ge 12:7
*x*Eze 36:32
9:6 *y*S Ex 32:9; Ac 7:51
9:7 *z*S Nu 11:33

*a*S Ex 23:21
*b*S Ex 14:11
9:8 *c*Nu 16:46; 1Sa 28:18; Job 20:28; Ps 2:12; 7:11; 69:24; 110:5; Isa 9:19; Eze 20:13
*d*Ex 32:7-10; Ezr 9:14; Ps 106:19
9:9 *e*S Dt 4:13
*f*S Ge 7:4
*g*S Ex 24:12
9:10 *h*S Ex 31:18
*i*Dt 10:4; 18:16
9:11 *j*S Ge 7:4
*k*S Ex 24:12
9:12 *l*S Dt 4:16
*m*Jdg 2:17
9:13 *n*ver 6; Dt 10:16
9:14 *o*Ex 32:10
*p*S Nu 14:12
*q*Jer 7:16
9:15 *r*S Ex 32:15
9:16 *s*S Ex 32:4
9:18 *t*S Ex 34:28
*u*ver 9
*v*S Ex 32:31

*q*15 Or *And I had the two tablets of the covenant with me, one in each hand*

9:1 *Hear, O Israel.* See note on 4:1.
9:2 *Anakites.* See note on 1:28.
9:3 *devouring fire.* See 4:24; see also note on Ex 24:17. *he will subdue them before you . . . you will drive them out.* The Lord not only went ahead of the Israelites, but he also exerted his power alongside them and through them to assure victory. The Lord's involvement, together with that of the Israelite armies, continues throughout Deuteronomy and the conquest narratives.
9:4 *because of my righteousness.* See note on 7:8. *wicked-*

ness of these nations. See note on Ge 15:16.
9:6,13 *stiff-necked.* See 10:16; 31:27; see also note on Ex 32:9.
9:7,27 *Remember.* See note on 4:10.
9:9 *tablets of stone . . . of the covenant.* See notes on Ex 20:1; 34:28.
9:10 *two stone tablets.* See note on Ex 31:18. *finger of God.* See note on Ex 8:19.
9:11–21 See Ex 31:18–32:20.

LORD's sight and so provoking him to anger. [19]I feared the anger and wrath of the LORD, for he was angry enough with you to destroy you.[w] But again the LORD listened to me.[x] [20]And the LORD was angry enough with Aaron to destroy him, but at that time I prayed for Aaron too. [21]Also I took that sinful thing of yours, the calf you had made, and burned it in the fire. Then I crushed it and ground it to powder as fine as dust[y] and threw the dust into a stream that flowed down the mountain.[z]

[22]You also made the LORD angry[a] at Taberah,[b] at Massah[c] and at Kibroth Hattaavah.[d]

[23]And when the LORD sent you out from Kadesh Barnea,[e] he said, "Go up and take possession[f] of the land I have given you." But you rebelled[g] against the command of the LORD your God. You did not trust[h] him or obey him. [24]You have been rebellious against the LORD ever since I have known you.[i]

[25]I lay prostrate before the LORD those forty days and forty nights[j] because the LORD had said he would destroy you.[k] [26]I prayed to the LORD and said, "O Sovereign LORD, do not destroy your people,[l] your own inheritance[m] that you redeemed[n] by your great power and brought out of Egypt with a mighty hand.[o] [27]Remember your servants Abraham, Isaac and Jacob. Overlook the stubbornness[p] of this people, their wickedness and their sin. [28]Otherwise, the country[q] from which you brought us will say, 'Because the LORD was not able to take them into the land he had promised them, and because he hated them,[r] he brought them out to put them to death in the desert.'[s] [29]But they are your people,[t] your inheritance[u] that you brought out by your great power and your outstretched arm.[v]"

Tablets Like the First Ones

10 At that time the LORD said to me, "Chisel out two stone tablets[w] like the first ones and come up to me on the mountain. Also make a wooden chest.[r] [2]I will write on the tablets the words that were on the first tablets, which you broke. Then you are to put them in the chest."[x]

[3]So I made the ark out of acacia wood[y] and chiseled[z] out two stone tablets like the first ones, and I went up on the mountain with the two tablets in my hands. [4]The LORD wrote on these tablets what he had written before, the Ten Commandments[a] he had proclaimed[b] to you on the mountain, out of the fire, on the day of the assembly.[c] And the LORD gave them to me. [5]Then I came back down the mountain[d] and put the tablets in the ark[e] I had made,[f] as the LORD commanded me, and they are there now.[g]

[6](The Israelites traveled from the wells of the Jaakanites to Moserah.[h] There Aaron died[i] and was buried, and Eleazar[j] his son succeeded him as priest.[k] [7]From there they traveled to Gudgodah and on to Jotbathah, a land with streams of water.[l] [8]At that time the LORD set apart the tribe of Levi[m] to carry the ark of the covenant[n] of the LORD, to stand before the LORD to minister[o] and to pronounce blessings[p] in his name, as they still do today.[q] [9]That is why the Levites have no share or inheritance among their brothers; the LORD is their inheritance,[r] as the LORD your God told them.)

[10]Now I had stayed on the mountain forty days and nights, as I did the first time, and the LORD listened to me at this time also. It was not his will to destroy you.[s] [11]"Go," the LORD said to me, "and lead the people on their way, so that they may enter and possess the land that I swore to their fathers to give them."

Fear the LORD

[12]And now, O Israel, what does the LORD your God ask of you[t] but to fear[u] the LORD your God, to walk[v] in all his

9:19
[w]S Ex 32:14;
Heb 12:21* [x]ver
26; Ex 34:10;
S Nu 11:2;
1Sa 7:9; Jer 15:1
9:21 [y]Ps 18:42;
Isa 29:5; 40:15
[z]Ex 32:20;
Isa 2:18; Mic 1:7
9:22 [a]S Nu 1:53
[b]Nu 11:3
[c]S Ex 17:7
[d]Nu 11:34
9:23 [e]S Dt 1:2
[f]Dt 1:21
[g]S Nu 14:9
[h]S Dt 1:32;
Ps 106:24
9:24 [i]S Dt 8:17
9:25 [j]S Ge 7:4
[k]ver 18;
S Ex 33:17
9:26 [l]S Ex 33:13
[m]S Ex 34:9
[n]S Ex 6:6;
Dt 15:15;
2Sa 7:23;
Ps 78:35 [o]S ver
19; S Ex 32:11
9:27 [p]ver 6;
S Ex 33:17
9:28 [q]Dt 32:27
[r]S Dt 1:27
[s]S Ex 32:12;
Jos 7:9
9:29 [t]S Ex 33:13
[u]S Ex 34:9;
Dt 32:9 [v]Dt 4:34;
Ne 1:10; Jer 27:5;
32:17
10:1 [w]Ex 34:1-2

10:2 [x]Ex 25:16,
21; 2Ch 5:10;
6:11
10:3 [y]Ex 37:1-9
[z]Ex 34:4
10:4
[a]S Ex 24:12;
S 34:28 [b]Ex 20:1
[c]S Dt 9:10
10:5 [d]S Ex 19:11
[e]S Ex 25:10;
S 1Sa 3:3
[f]S Ex 25:21
[g]1Ki 8:9
10:6 [h]Nu 33:30
[i]S Nu 27:13
[j]S Ex 6:23
[k]S Nu 20:25-28
10:7
[l]Nu 33:32-34;
Ps 42:1; SS 5:12;
Isa 32:2
10:8 [m]S Nu 3:6
[n]S Nu 10:33
[o]S Nu 16:9
[p]S Ge 48:20
[q]1Ch 23:26
10:9 [r]S Nu 18:20
10:10
[s]S Ex 33:17
10:12 [t]Mic 6:8
[u]S Ex 20:20
[v]1Ki 2:3; 3:3; 9:4

[r]l That is, an ark

9:19 *But again the LORD listened to me.* Moses' intercessory prayer on this occasion (vv. 26–29) ranks among the great prayers for Israel's national survival (see 1Sa 7:5,8–9; Jer 15:1).
9:22 *Taberah.* See Nu 11:3 and NIV text note. *Massah.* See 6:16; 33:8; see also note on Ex 17:7. *Kibroth Hattaavah.* See Nu 11:34 and NIV text note.
9:23 *Kadesh Barnea.* See note on Ge 14:7.
9:27 *Overlook.* See note on Ac 17:30.
10:1–3 *chest . . . ark.* Both words translate the same Hebrew word, which means "chest" or "box." After initially translating "chest" for clarity, the NIV reverts to the more traditional and familiar rendering "ark."

10:1 *two stone tablets.* See note on Ex 31:18.
10:2 *put them in the chest.* See notes on Ex 16:34; 25:16.
10:3 Ex 34–37 shows that the order of events here is different from that in Exodus (see Introduction: Structure and Outline).
10:6–9 A historical parenthesis, apparently stemming from Moses' prayer for Aaron and the Israelites (9:26–29) and the reference to the ark (vv. 1–5).
10:8 *carry the ark.* See note on Nu 1:50. *to minister.* See note on 21:5.
10:9 See Nu 18:20,24.
10:12 *fear the LORD.* See note on Ge 20:11. *love him.* See notes on 4:29,37; 6:5.

ways, to love him,[w] to serve the LORD[x] your God with all your heart[y] and with all your soul,[z] [13]and to observe the LORD's commands[a] and decrees that I am giving you today for your own good?[b]

[14]To the LORD your God belong the heavens,[cde] even the highest heavens,[f g] the earth and everything in it.[h] [15]Yet the LORD set his affection on your forefathers and loved[i] them, and he chose you,[j] their descendants, above all the nations, as it is today.[k] [16]Circumcise[l] your hearts,[m] therefore, and do not be stiff-necked[n] any longer. [17]For the LORD your God is God of gods[o] and Lord of lords,[p] the great God, mighty and awesome,[q] who shows no partiality[r] and accepts no bribes.[s] [18]He defends the cause of the fatherless and the widow,[t] and loves the alien, giving him food and clothing.[u] [19]And you are to love[v] those who are aliens,[w] for you yourselves were aliens in Egypt.[x] [20]Fear the LORD your God and serve him.[y] Hold fast[z] to him and take your oaths in his name.[a] [21]He is your praise;[b] he is your God, who performed for you those great[c] and awesome wonders[d] you saw with your own eyes. [22]Your forefathers who went down into Egypt were seventy in all,[e] and now the LORD your God has made you as numerous as the stars in the sky.[f]

Love and Obey the LORD

11 Love[g] the LORD your God and keep his requirements, his decrees, his laws and his commands always.[h] [2]Remember today that your children[i] were not the ones who saw and experienced the discipline of the LORD your God:[j] his majesty,[k] his mighty hand, his outstretched arm;[l] [3]the signs he performed and the things he did in the heart of Egypt, both to Pharaoh king of Egypt and to his whole country;[m] [4]what he did to the Egyptian army, to its horses and chariots,[n] how he overwhelmed them with the waters of the Red Sea[s o] as they were pursuing you, and how the LORD brought lasting ruin on them. [5]It was not

your children who saw what he did for you in the desert until you arrived at this place, [6]and what he did[p] to Dathan and Abiram, sons of Eliab the Reubenite, when the earth opened[q] its mouth right in the middle of all Israel and swallowed them up with their households, their tents and every living thing that belonged to them. [7]But it was your own eyes that saw all these great things the LORD has done.[r]

[8]Observe therefore all the commands[s] I am giving you today, so that you may have the strength to go in and take over the land that you are crossing the Jordan to possess,[t] [9]and so that you may live long[u] in the land that the LORD swore[v] to your forefathers to give to them and their descendants, a land flowing with milk and honey.[w] [10]The land you are entering to take over is not like the land of Egypt,[x] from which you have come, where you planted your seed and irrigated it by foot as in a vegetable garden. [11]But the land you are crossing the Jordan to take possession of is a land of mountains and valleys[y] that drinks rain from heaven.[z] [12]It is a land the LORD your God cares for; the eyes[a] of the LORD your God are continually on it from the beginning of the year to its end.

[13]So if you faithfully obey[b] the commands I am giving you today—to love[c] the LORD your God and to serve him with all your heart and with all your soul[d]— [14]then I will send rain[e] on your land in its season, both autumn and spring rains,[f] so that you may gather in your grain, new wine and oil. [15]I will provide grass[g] in the fields for your cattle, and you will eat and be satisfied.[h]

[16]Be careful, or you will be enticed to turn away and worship other gods and

Cross references (center column)

10:12 wDt 5:33; 6:13; Mt 22:37; 1Ti 1:5
xDt 11:13; 28:47; Ps 100:2
yS Dt 6:5; Ps 119:2
zS Dt 5:32
10:13 aS Dt 4:2
bDt 5:33; 6:24
10:14 cPs 148:4; Isa 19:1; Hab 3:8
dNe 9:6; Job 35:5; Ps 8:3; 89:11; 104:3
eDt 33:26
fPs 115:16
g1Ki 8:27
hEx 19:5; Ps 24:1; Ac 17:24
10:15 iS Dt 4:37
jPs 105:6; 135:4
kS Nu 14:8; Ro 11:28; 1Pe 2:9
10:16
lS Ge 17:11
mS Lev 26:41; Dt 30:6; Jer 32:39
nS Ex 32:9; S Dt 9:13
10:17
oJos 22:22; Ps 135:5; 136:2; Da 2:47; 11:36
pPs 136:3; S 1Ti 6:15
qS Dt 7:21
rDt 1:17; Mal 2:9
sS Ex 23:8; S Lev 19:16
10:18 tEx 22:21, 22-24; 23:9; Lev 19:33; Dt 27:19; Job 29:13; Ps 94:6; Isa 10:2; Jer 49:11
uS Nu 10:32
10:19 vDt 7:12
wS Ex 22:21; S Dt 24:19
xS Lev 19:34; Eze 47:22-23
10:20 yMt 4:10
zDt 11:22; 13:4; 30:20; Jos 23:8; Ru 1:14; 2Ki 18:6; Ps 119:31; Isa 38:3
aS Ex 20:7
10:21 bS Ex 15:2
c1Sa 12:24; Ps 126:2
d2Sa 7:23
10:22
eS Ge 34:30; S 46:26; Ac 7:14
fS Ge 12:2; S Nu 10:36
11:1 gS Dt 6:5; hS Lev 8:35
11:2 iDt 31:13; Ps 78:6 jS Dt 5:24
kS Dt 3:24
lPs 136:12

11:3 mEx 7:8-21 11:4 nS Ex 15:1 oS Ex 14:27; S Nu 21:4
11:6 pNu 16:1-35; Ps 106:16-18 qIsa 24:19 11:7 rDt 5:3
11:8 sEzr 9:10 tDt 31:6-7,23; Jos 1:7 11:9 uS Dt 5:16
vDt 9:5 wS Ex 3:8 11:10 xIsa 11:15; 37:25 11:11 yEze 36:4
zDt 8:7; Ne 9:25 11:12 a1Ki 8:29; 9:3 11:13 bS Dt 6:17
cS Dt 10:12 dDt 4:29; Jer 17:24 11:14 eS Lev 26:4;
Ac 14:17 fPs 147:8; Jer 3:3; 5:24; Joel 2:23; Jas 5:7 11:15
gPs 104:14 hS Lev 26:5

s4 Hebrew *Yam Suph*; that is, Sea of Reeds

10:13 *for your own good.* See 6:24; see also note on 6:2.
10:16 *Circumcise your hearts.* See note on Ge 17:10. *stiff-necked.* See 9:6,13; 31:27; see also note on Ex 32:9.
10:20 *Hold fast.* As a man is "united" to his wife (Ge 2:24), and as Ruth "clung" to Naomi (Ru 1:14). See 4:4; 11:22; 13:4; 30:20.
10:22 *seventy.* See notes on Ge 46:26–27; see also Ex 1:5. *as the stars in the sky.* See note on 1:10.
11:2–7 Moses continually emphasizes the involvement of his listeners in the Lord's works of providence and deliverance. In 5:3 it was not the fathers but they themselves with whom the covenant was made. Here it is not their children

but they themselves who saw God's great deeds.
11:2 *Remember.* See note on 4:10.
11:8–12 See note on 8:7–9.
11:9 *live long.* See note on 6:2.
11:10 *irrigated it by foot.* Irrigation channels dug by foot and/or fed by devices powered by foot brought the water of the Nile to the gardens in Egypt, in contrast to the rains that watered Canaan (v. 11).
11:13 See note on 4:29.
11:14 *autumn and spring rains.* The rainy season in Palestine begins in October and ends in April.

bow down to them.[l] [17]Then the LORD's anger[j] will burn against you, and he will shut[k] the heavens so that it will not rain and the ground will yield no produce,[l] and you will soon perish[m] from the good land the LORD is giving you. [18]Fix these words of mine in your hearts and minds; tie them as symbols on your hands and bind them on your foreheads.[n] [19]Teach them to your children,[o] talking about them when you sit at home and when you walk along the road, when you lie down and when you get up.[p] [20]Write them on the doorframes of your houses and on your gates,[q] [21]so that your days and the days of your children may be many[r] in the land that the LORD swore to give your forefathers, as many as the days that the heavens are above the earth.[s]

[22]If you carefully observe[t] all these commands I am giving you to follow—to love[u] the LORD your God, to walk in all his ways and to hold fast[v] to him— [23]then the LORD will drive out[w] all these nations[x] before you, and you will dispossess nations larger and stronger than you.[y] [24]Every place where you set your foot will be yours:[z] Your territory will extend from the desert to Lebanon, and from the Euphrates River[a] to the western sea.[t] [25]No man will be able to stand against you. The LORD your God, as he promised you, will put the terror[b] and fear of you on the whole land, wherever you go.[c]

[26]See, I am setting before you today a blessing[d] and a curse[e]— [27]the blessing[f] if you obey the commands of the LORD your God that I am giving you today; [28]the curse if you disobey[g] the commands of the LORD your God and turn from the way that I command you today by following other gods,[h] which you have not known. [29]When the LORD your God has brought you into the land you are entering to possess, you are to proclaim on Mount Gerizim[i] the blessings, and on Mount Ebal[j]

the curses.[k] [30]As you know, these mountains are across the Jordan, west of the road,[u] toward the setting sun, near the great trees of Moreh,[l] in the territory of those Canaanites living in the Arabah in the vicinity of Gilgal.[m] [31]You are about to cross the Jordan to enter and take possession[n] of the land the LORD your God is giving[o] you. When you have taken it over and are living there, [32]be sure that you obey all the decrees and laws I am setting before you today.

The One Place of Worship

12 These are the decrees[p] and laws you must be careful to follow in the land that the LORD, the God of your fathers, has given you to possess—as long as you live in the land.[q] [2]Destroy completely all the places on the high mountains[r] and on the hills and under every spreading tree[s] where the nations you are dispossessing worship their gods. [3]Break down their altars, smash[t] their sacred stones and burn[u] their Asherah[v] poles in the fire; cut down the idols of their gods and wipe out their names[w] from those places.

[4]You must not worship the LORD your God in their way.[x] [5]But you are to seek the place the LORD your God will choose from among all your tribes to put his Name[y] there for his dwelling.[z] To that place you must go; [6]there bring your burnt offerings and sacrifices, your tithes[a] and special gifts, what you have vowed[b] to give and your freewill offerings, and the firstborn of your herds and flocks.[c] [7]There, in the presence[d] of the LORD your God,

---

11:16 /Dt 4:19; 8:19; 29:18; Job 31:9,27
11:17 /Dt 6:15; 9:19 k1Ki 17:1; 2Ch 6:26; 7:13 /S Lev 26:20 mDt 4:26; 28:12, 24
11:18 nS Ex 13:9; Dt 6:6-8
11:19 oS Ex 12:26; Dt 6:7; Ps 145:4; Isa 38:19; Jer 32:39 pDt 4:9-10
11:20 qDt 6:9
11:21 rJob 5:26; Pr 3:2; 4:10; 9:11 sPs 72:5
11:22 tS Dt 6:17 uS Dt 6:5 vS Dt 10:20
11:23 wS Dt 9:5 xS Ex 23:28 yDt 9:1
11:24 zGe 15:18; Dt 1:36; 12:20; 19:8; Jos 1:3; 14:9 aS Ge 2:14
11:25 bS Dt 2:25 cEx 23:27; Dt 7:24
11:26 dPs 24:5 eLev 26:14-17; Dt 27:13-26; 30:1,15,19; La 2:17; Da 9:11; Hag 1:11; Mal 2:2; 3:9; 4:6
11:27 /Dt 28:1-14; Ps 24:5
11:28 g2Ch 24:20; Jer 42:13; 44:16 hS Dt 4:28; 13:6, 13; 29:26; 1Sa 26:19
11:29 iJdg 9:7 /Dt 27:4; Jos 8:30

kDt 27:12-13; Jos 8:33; Jn 4:20
11:30 lS Ge 12:6 mJos 4:19; 5:9; 9:6; 10:6; 14:6; 15:7; Jdg 2:1; 2Ki 2:1; Mic 6:5
11:31 nS Nu 33:53 oDt 12:10; Jos 11:23
12:1 pPs 119:5 qDt 4:9-10; 6:15; 1Ki 8:40; Eze 20:19
12:2 rS Nu 21:28 s1Ki 14:23; 2Ki 17:10; Isa 57:5; Jer 2:20;

3:6,13 12:3 t2Ki 11:18 uS Ex 32:20 vEx 34:13; 1Ki 14:15,23 wS Ex 23:13 12:4 xver 30; 2Ki 17:15; Jer 10:2 12:5 yS Ex 20:24; S 2Sa 7:13 zver 11,13; Dt 14:23; 15:20; 16:2, 11; 18:6; 26:2; 1Sa 2:29; 1Ki 5:5; 8:16; 9:3; 2Ch 2:4; 6:6; 7:12,16; Ezr 6:12; 7:15; Ps 26:8; 78:68; Zec 2:12 12:6 aS Lev 27:30 bS Ge 28:20 cJos 22:27; Isa 66:20 12:7 dS Ex 18:12

t24 That is, the Mediterranean   u30 Or Jordan, westward

11:17 *shut the heavens.* The all-important seasonal rains (see v. 14) were controlled by the LORD—not by Baal, as the inhabitants of Canaan thought (cf. Hos 2:8,17).
11:18–20 See note on 6:8–9.
11:22 *hold fast.* See note on 10:20.
11:24 *Every place where you set your foot.* See note on 1:7.
11:26–30 The blessings and curses proclaimed on Mount Gerizim and Mount Ebal are detailed in chs. 27–28.
11:28 *known.* Experienced or acknowledged (see 13:2,6, 13; 28:64; 29:26; 32:17; see also note on Ex 6:3).
11:30 *road.* Probably the north-south road that ran parallel to the Jordan between the Sea of Galilee and the Dead Sea. *great trees of Moreh.* See note on Ge 12:6. *Arabah.* See note on 1:1. The Canaanites who lived there controlled the terri-

tory around Gerizim and Ebal.
12:3 *altars . . . sacred stones . . . Asherah poles.* See note on 7:5.
12:4 *in their way.* The rituals and accessories of idolatrous worship were not to be used to worship the Lord, the one true God (cf. vv. 29–31).
12:5 *the place the LORD . . . will choose . . . to put his Name.* The tabernacle, the Lord's dwelling place during the desert journey, will be located in the city in Canaan where the Lord would choose to dwell. Moses stresses the importance of centralizing the place of worship as he prepares the people for settlement in the promised land, where the Canaanites had established many places of worship. See vv. 11,14,18,21,26; 14:23–24; 16:2,6,11; 26:2.
12:6 See v. 11 and chart on "OT Sacrifices," p. 150.

you and your families shall eat and shall rejoice[e] in everything you have put your hand to, because the LORD your God has blessed you.

[8]You are not to do as we do here today, everyone as he sees fit,[f] [9]since you have not yet reached the resting place[g] and the inheritance[h] the LORD your God is giving you. [10]But you will cross the Jordan and settle in the land the LORD your God is giving[i] you as an inheritance, and he will give you rest[j] from all your enemies around you so that you will live in safety. [11]Then to the place the LORD your God will choose as a dwelling for his Name[k]—there you are to bring everything I command you: your burnt offerings and sacrifices, your tithes and special gifts, and all the choice possessions you have vowed to the LORD.[l] [12]And there rejoice[m] before the LORD your God, you, your sons and daughters, your menservants and maidservants, and the Levites[n] from your towns, who have no allotment or inheritance[o] of their own. [13]Be careful not to sacrifice your burnt offerings anywhere you please.[p] [14]Offer them only at the place the LORD will choose[q] in one of your tribes, and there observe everything I command you.

[15]Nevertheless, you may slaughter your animals in any of your towns and eat as much of the meat as you want, as if it were gazelle or deer,[r] according to the blessing the LORD your God gives you. Both the ceremonially unclean and the clean may eat it. [16]But you must not eat the blood;[s] pour[t] it out on the ground like water.[u] [17]You must not eat in your own towns the tithe[v] of your grain and new wine and oil,[w] or the firstborn of your herds and flocks, or whatever you have vowed to give,[x] or your freewill offerings or special gifts.[y] [18]Instead, you are to eat[z] them in the presence of the LORD your God at the place the LORD your God will choose[a]—you, your sons and daughters, your menservants and maidservants, and the Levites from your towns—and you are to rejoice[b] before the LORD your God in

everything you put your hand to. [19]Be careful not to neglect the Levites[c] as long as you live in your land.[d]

[20]When the LORD your God has enlarged your territory[e] as he promised[f] you, and you crave meat[g] and say, "I would like some meat," then you may eat as much of it as you want. [21]If the place where the LORD your God chooses to put his Name[h] is too far away from you, you may slaughter animals from the herds and flocks the LORD has given you, as I have commanded you, and in your own towns you may eat as much of them as you want.[i] [22]Eat them as you would gazelle or deer.[j] Both the ceremonially unclean and the clean may eat. [23]But be sure you do not eat the blood,[k] because the blood is the life, and you must not eat the life with the meat.[l] [24]You must not eat the blood; pour it out on the ground like water.[m] [25]Do not eat it, so that it may go well[n] with you and your children after you, because you will be doing what is right[o] in the eyes of the LORD.

[26]But take your consecrated things and whatever you have vowed to give,[p] and go to the place the LORD will choose. [27]Present your burnt offerings[q] on the altar of the LORD your God, both the meat and the blood. The blood of your sacrifices must be poured beside the altar of the LORD your God, but you may eat[r] the meat. [28]Be careful to obey all these regulations I am giving you, so that it may always go well[s] with you and your children after you, because you will be doing what is good and right in the eyes of the LORD your God.

[29]The LORD your God will cut off[t] before you the nations you are about to invade and dispossess. But when you have driven them out and settled in their land,[u] [30]and after they have been destroyed before you, be careful not to be ensnared[v] by inquiring about their gods, saying, "How do these nations serve their gods? We will do the same."[w] [31]You must not worship the LORD your God in their way, because in worshiping their gods, they do all kinds

12:7 eS Lev 23:40; Ecc 3:12-13; 5:18-20; S Isa 62:9
12:8 fJdg 17:6; 21:25
12:9 gS Ex 33:14; Dt 3:20; Ps 95:11; Mic 2:10; hDt 4:21
12:10 iS Dt 11:31; jS Ex 33:14
12:11 kS ver 5; lS Lev 1:3; Jos 22:23
12:12 mver 7; nDt 26:11-13; oS Nu 18:20
12:13 pS ver 5
12:14 qver 11
12:15 rver 22; Dt 14:5; 15:22
12:16 sS Ge 9:4; Ac 15:20 tver 23-24; S Ge 35:14; 1Ch 11:18; Jer 7:18; uS Lev 17:13; S Dt 15:23; Jn 19:34
12:17 vS Lev 27:30; wS Nu 18:12 xver 26; Nu 18:19; yDt 14:23; 15:20
12:18 zDt 14:23; 15:20 aver 5 bver 7,12; Dt 14:26; Ne 8:10; Ecc 3:12-13; 5:18-20
12:19 cver 12; Dt 14:27; Ne 13:10; dMal 3:8
12:20 eS Ex 34:24 fS Ge 15:8; S Dt 11:24 gS Ex 16:3
12:21 hDt 14:24 iLev 17:4
12:22 jS ver 15
12:23 kS Lev 7:26 lEze 33:25
12:24 mver 16
12:25 nS Dt 4:40 over 28; Ex 15:26; Dt 13:18; 1Ki 11:38; 2Ki 12:2
12:26 pS ver 17; Nu 5:9-10
12:27 qS Lev 1:13 rLev 3:1-17
12:28 sDt 4:40; Ecc 8:12
12:29 tJos 23:4 uS Dt 6:10
12:30 vS Ex 10:7 wS ver 4

12:8 *as we do here today.* Israel was not able to follow all the procedures of the sacrificial system during the desert wandering and conquest periods. Moses was giving directives for their worship and way of life when settled in the land (vv. 10–14). *as he sees fit.* See note on Jdg 17:6. **12:9** *resting place.* See note on 3:20. **12:11** *dwelling for his Name.* Equivalent to "dwelling for himself." See notes on Ex 3:13–14. **12:12** *rejoice before the LORD.* Joy, based on the Lord's blessings, was to be a major feature of Hebrew life and

worship in the promised land (vv. 7,18). *Levites . . . have no . . . inheritance.* See 10:9; Nu 18:20,24.

12:13 *not . . . anywhere you please.* Sacrifices and offerings to the Lord were to be brought only to the central sanctuary, not to the various Canaanite worship sites.

12:16,24 *you must not eat the blood.* See notes on Ge 9:4; Lev 17:11.

12:31 *burn . . . sons and daughters . . . as sacrifices.* See 18:10; see also note on Lev 18:21.

of detestable things the LORD hates.[x] They even burn their sons[y] and daughters in the fire as sacrifices to their gods.[z]

³²See that you do all I command you; do not add[a] to it or take away from it.

Worshiping Other Gods

13 If a prophet,[b] or one who foretells by dreams,[c] appears among you and announces to you a miraculous sign or wonder, ²and if the sign[d] or wonder of which he has spoken takes place, and he says, "Let us follow other gods"[e] (gods you have not known) "and let us worship them," ³you must not listen to the words of that prophet[f] or dreamer.[g] The LORD your God is testing[h] you to find out whether you love[i] him with all your heart and with all your soul. ⁴It is the LORD your God you must follow,[j] and him you must revere.[k] Keep his commands and obey him; serve him and hold fast[l] to him. ⁵That prophet or dreamer must be put to death,[m] because he preached rebellion against the LORD your God, who brought you out of Egypt and redeemed you from the land of slavery; he has tried to turn[n] you from the way the LORD your God commanded you to follow. You must purge the evil[o] from among you.

⁶If your very own brother, or your son or daughter, or the wife you love, or your closest friend secretly entices[p] you, saying, "Let us go and worship other gods"[q] (gods that neither you nor your fathers have known, ⁷gods of the peoples around you, whether near or far, from one end of the land to the other), ⁸do not yield[r] to him or listen to him. Show him no pity.[s] Do not spare him or shield him. ⁹You must certainly put him to death.[t] Your hand[u] must be the first in putting him to death, and then the hands of all the people. ¹⁰Stone him to death, because he tried to turn you away[v] from the LORD your God, who brought you out of Egypt, out of the land of slavery. ¹¹Then all Israel will hear and be afraid,[w] and no one among you will do such an evil thing again.

¹²If you hear it said about one of the towns the LORD your God is giving you to live in ¹³that wicked men[x] have arisen among you and have led the people of their town astray, saying, "Let us go and worship other gods" (gods you have not known), ¹⁴then you must inquire, probe and investigate it thoroughly.[y] And if it is true and it has been proved that this detestable thing has been done among you,[z] ¹⁵you must certainly put to the sword all who live in that town. Destroy it completely,[v][a] both its people and its livestock.[b] ¹⁶Gather all the plunder of the town into the middle of the public square and completely burn the town[c] and all its plunder as a whole burnt offering to the LORD your God.[d] It is to remain a ruin[e] forever, never to be rebuilt. ¹⁷None of those condemned things[v] shall be found in your hands, so that the LORD will turn from his fierce anger;[f] he will show you mercy,[g] have compassion[h] on you, and increase your numbers,[i] as he promised[j] on oath to your forefathers, ¹⁸because you obey the LORD your God, keeping all his commands that I am giving you today and doing what is right[k] in his eyes.

Clean and Unclean Food

14:3–20pp — Lev 11:1–23

14 You are the children[l] of the LORD your God. Do not cut yourselves or shave the front of your heads for the dead, ²for you are a people holy[m] to the LORD your God.[n] Out of all the peoples on the

12:31
xS Lev 18:25
yS Lev 18:21
zS 2Ki 3:27
12:32 aS Dt 4:2;
Rev 22:18-19
13:1 bMt 24:24;
Mk 13:22;
2Th 2:9
cS Ge 20:3;
Jer 23:25; 27:9;
29:8
13:2 dDt 18:22;
1Sa 2:34; 10:9;
2Ki 19:29; 20:9;
Isa 7:11
eS Dt 11:28
13:3 f2Pe 2:1
g1Sa 28:6,15
hS Ge 22:1;
1Ki 13:18;
22:22-23;
Jer 29:31; 43:2;
Eze 13:9;
1Co 11:19
iDt 6:5
13:4 j2Ki 23:3;
2Ch 34:31;
2Jn 1:6
kS Dt 6:13;
S Ps 5:7
lS Dt 10:20
13:5
mS Ex 21:12;
S 22:20 nver 10;
Dt 4:19 oDt 17:7,
12; 19:19; 24:7;
Jdg 20:13;
S 1Co 5:13
13:6 pDt 17:2-7;
29:18
qS Dt 11:28
13:8 rPr 1:10
sS Dt 7:2
13:9 tver 5
uS Lev 24:14
13:10 vS Ex 20:3
13:11
wDt 17:13;
19:20; 21:21;
1Ti 5:20
13:13
xJdg 19:22;
20:13; 1Sa 2:12;
10:27; 11:12;
25:17; 1Ki 21:10
13:14 yJdg 20:12
zDt 17:4
13:15 aIsa 24:6;
34:5; 43:28;
47:6; La 2:6;
Da 9:11;
Zec 8:13; Mal 4:6
bEx 22:20
13:16 c2Ki 25:9;
Jer 39:8; 52:13;
Eze 16:41
dDt 7:25,26;
Jos 6:24
eJos 8:28;
Isa 7:16; 17:1;
24:10; 25:2;

27:10; 32:14,19; 37:26; Jer 49:2; Mic 1:6 **13:17** fEx 32:12;
Nu 25:4 gS Ge 43:14 hDt 30:3 iS Dt 7:13 jS Ge 12:2;
S 13:14; S 26:24 **13:18** kS Dt 12:25 **14:1** lS Jn 1:12;
S Ro 8:14; 9:8 **14:2** mS Ge 28:14; Ex 22:31; Isa 6:13;
Mal 2:15 nS Lev 20:26; Ro 12:1

v 15,17 The Hebrew term refers to the irrevocable giving over of things or persons to the LORD, often by totally destroying them.

12:32 do not add . . . or take away. See note on 4:2.
13:1–5 Eventual fulfillment is one test of true prophecy (18:21–22), but the more stringent rule given here guards against intelligent foresight masquerading as prophecy and against coincidental fulfillment of the predictions of false prophets.
13:3 testing. See note on Ge 22:1. all your heart. See note on 4:29.
13:4 hold fast. See note on 10:20.
13:5 prophet . . . must be put to death. See 18:20; Jer 28:15–17. You must purge the evil from among you. Repeated in 17:7; 19:19; 21:21; 22:21,24; 24:7, and quoted in 1Co 5:13. The purpose was to eliminate the evildoers as well as the evil itself.
13:13 wicked. See 1Sa 1:16; 2:12; 25:17. The same

Hebrew word is also used, e.g., in 1Sa 10:27; 30:22 ("troublemakers"); 1Ki 21:10,13 ("scoundrels"); Pr 6:12 ("scoundrel"). Later, this word (Belial in Hebrew) was used as a name for Satan (2Co 6:15), who is the personification of wickedness and lawlessness.

13:15 Destroy it completely. See note on 2:34.

14:1 cut yourselves. A pagan religious custom (see 1Ki 18:28). shave the front of your heads. Shaving the forehead was a practice of mourners in Canaan.

14:2,21 holy to the LORD. See note on Lev 11:44. The regulations regarding clean and unclean foods were intended to separate Israel from things the Lord had identified as detestable and ceremonially unclean.

14:2 treasured possession. See note on Ex 19:5.

face of the earth, the LORD has chosen you to be his treasured possession. [o]

3Do not eat any detestable thing. [p] 4These are the animals you may eat: [q] the ox, the sheep, the goat, [r] 5the deer, [s] the gazelle, the roe deer, the wild goat, [t] the ibex, the antelope and the mountain sheep. [w] 6You may eat any animal that has a split hoof divided in two and that chews the cud. 7However, of those that chew the cud or that have a split hoof completely divided you may not eat the camel, the rabbit or the coney. [x] Although they chew the cud, they do not have a split hoof; they are ceremonially unclean for you. 8The pig is also unclean; although it has a split hoof, it does not chew the cud. You are not to eat their meat or touch their carcasses. [u]

9Of all the creatures living in the water, you may eat any that has fins and scales. 10But anything that does not have fins and scales you may not eat; for you it is unclean.

11You may eat any clean bird. 12But these you may not eat: the eagle, the vulture, the black vulture, 13the red kite, the black kite, any kind [v] of falcon, [w] 14any kind of raven, [x] 15the horned owl, the screech owl, the gull, any kind of hawk, 16the little owl, the great owl, the white owl, 17the desert owl, [y] the osprey, the cormorant, 18the stork, any kind of heron, the hoopoe and the bat.

19All flying insects that swarm are unclean to you; do not eat them. 20But any winged creature that is clean you may eat. [z]

21Do not eat anything you find already dead. [a] You may give it to an alien living in any of your towns, and he may eat it, or you may sell it to a foreigner. But you are a people holy to the LORD your God. [b]

Do not cook a young goat in its mother's milk. [c]

Tithes

22Be sure to set aside a tenth [d] of all that

your fields produce each year. 23Eat [e] the tithe of your grain, new wine [f] and oil, and the firstborn of your herds and flocks in the presence of the LORD your God at the place he will choose as a dwelling for his Name, [g] so that you may learn [h] to revere [i] the LORD your God always. 24But if that place is too distant and you have been blessed by the LORD your God and cannot carry your tithe (because the place where the LORD will choose to put his Name is so far away), 25then exchange [j] your tithe for silver, and take the silver with you and go to the place the LORD your God will choose. 26Use the silver to buy whatever you like: cattle, sheep, wine or other fermented drink, [k] or anything you wish. Then you and your household shall eat there in the presence of the LORD your God and rejoice. [l] 27And do not neglect the Levites [m] living in your towns, for they have no allotment or inheritance of their own. [n]

28At the end of every three years, bring all the tithes [o] of that year's produce and store it in your towns, [p] 29so that the Levites (who have no allotment [q] or inheritance [r] of their own) and the aliens, [s] the fatherless and the widows who live in your towns may come and eat and be satisfied, [t] and so that the LORD your God may bless [u] you in all the work of your hands.

The Year for Canceling Debts

15:1–11Ref — Lev 25:8–38

15 At the end of every seven years you must cancel debts. [v] 2This is how it is to be done: Every creditor shall cancel the loan he has made to his fellow Israelite. He shall not require payment from his fellow Israelite or brother, because the LORD's time for canceling debts has been proclaimed. 3You may require payment from a foreigner, [w] but you must cancel any

---

14:2 [o]S Ex 8:22; S Dt 7:6
14:3 [p]Eze 4:14
14:4 [q]Ac 10:14 [r]S Lev 7:23
14:5 [s]S Dt 12:15 [t]Job 39:1; Ps 104:18
14:8 [u]S Lev 5:2
14:13 [v]S Ge 1:11 [w]Isa 34:15
14:14 [x]S Ge 8:7
14:17 [y]Ps 102:6; Isa 13:21; 14:23; 34:11; Zep 2:14
14:20 [z]S Lev 20:25
14:21 [a]S Lev 11:39 [b]ver 2 [c]S Ex 23:19
14:22 [d]S Ge 14:20; S Lev 27:30; S Nu 18:21
14:23 [e]S Dt 12:17,18 [f]Ps 4:7 [g]S Dt 12:5; 1Ki 3:2 [h]S Dt 4:10 [i]Ps 22:23; 33:8; Mal 2:5
14:25 [j]Mt 21:12; Jn 2:14
14:26 [k]S Lev 10:9; Ecc 10:16-17 [l]S Lev 23:40; S Dt 12:18
14:27 [m]S Dt 12:19 [n]S Nu 18:20; 26:62; Dt 18:1-2
14:28 [o]S Lev 27:30 [p]Dt 26:12
14:29 [q]Ge 47:22 [r]Nu 26:62 [s]Dt 16:11; 24:19-21; Ps 94:6; Isa 1:17; 58:6 [t]S Dt 6:11 [u]Dt 15:10; Ps 41:1; Pr 22:9; Mal 3:10
15:1 [v]Dt 31:10; Ne 10:31
15:3 [w]S Ge 31:15; Dt 23:20; 28:12; Ru 2:10

[w]5 The precise identification of some of the birds and animals in this chapter is uncertain.   [x]7 That is, the hyrax or rock badger

---

14:3–21 The subject of clean and unclean food is discussed in greater detail in Lev 11 (see notes there).
14:21 Do not eat . . . already dead. Because of the prohibition against eating blood, since the dead animal's blood would not be properly drained (see 12:16,24; see also notes on Ge 9:4; Lev 17:11). Do not cook a young goat in its mother's milk. See note on Ex 23:19.
14:22–29 See Nu 18:21–29. Taken together, the two passages suggest the following: 1. Annually, a tenth of all Israelite produce was to be taken to the city of the central sanctuary for distribution to the Levites. 2. At that time, at an initial festival, all Israelites ate part of the tithe. 3. The rest, which would be by far the major part of it, belonged to the Levites. 4. Every third year the tithe was gathered in the

towns and stored for distribution to the Levites and the less fortunate: aliens, fatherless and widows (see 26:12). 5. The Levites were to present to the Lord a tenth of their tithe. See note on Lev 27:30.
14:22 set aside a tenth. See notes on Ge 14:20; 28:22.
14:23 dwelling for his Name. See note on 12:5.
14:25 silver. Pieces of silver of various weights were a common medium of exchange, but not in the form of coins (see note on Ge 20:16).
15:1 every seven years. See Ex 23:10–11; Lev 25:1–7.
15:3 require payment from a foreigner. Since he was not subject to the command to allow his fields to lie fallow during the seventh year, a foreigner would probably be financially able to pay his debts if asked to do so.

debt your brother owes you. [4]However, there should be no poor among you, for in the land the LORD your God is giving you to possess as your inheritance, he will richly bless[x] you, [5]if only you fully obey the LORD your God and are careful to follow[y] all these commands I am giving you today. [6]For the LORD your God will bless you as he has promised, and you will lend to many nations but will borrow from none. You will rule over many nations but none will rule over you.[z]

[7]If there is a poor man[a] among your brothers in any of the towns of the land that the LORD your God is giving you, do not be hardhearted or tightfisted[b] toward your poor brother. [8]Rather be openhanded[c] and freely lend him whatever he needs. [9]Be careful not to harbor this wicked thought: "The seventh year, the year for canceling debts,[d] is near," so that you do not show ill will[e] toward your needy brother and give him nothing. He may then appeal to the LORD against you, and you will be found guilty of sin.[f] [10]Give generously to him and do so without a grudging heart;[g] then because of this the LORD your God will bless[h] you in all your work and in everything you put your hand to. [11]There will always be poor people[i] in the land. Therefore I command you to be openhanded toward your brothers and toward the poor and needy in your land.[j]

Freeing Servants

15:12–18pp — Ex 21:2–6
15:12–18Ref — Lev 25:38–55

[12]If a fellow Hebrew, a man or a woman, sells himself to you and serves you six years, in the seventh year you must let him go free.[k] [13]And when you release him, do not send him away empty-handed.

[14]Supply him liberally from your flock, your threshing floor[l] and your winepress. Give to him as the LORD your God has blessed you. [15]Remember that you were slaves[m] in Egypt and the LORD your God redeemed you.[n] That is why I give you this command today.

[16]But if your servant says to you, "I do not want to leave you," because he loves you and your family and is well off with you, [17]then take an awl and push it through his ear lobe into the door, and he will become your servant for life. Do the same for your maidservant.

[18]Do not consider it a hardship to set your servant free, because his service to you these six years has been worth twice as much as that of a hired hand. And the LORD your God will bless you in everything you do.

The Firstborn Animals

[19]Set apart for the LORD[o] your God every firstborn male[p] of your herds and flocks.[q] Do not put the firstborn of your oxen to work, and do not shear the firstborn of your sheep.[r] [20]Each year you and your family are to eat them in the presence of the LORD your God at the place he will choose.[s] [21]If an animal has a defect,[t] is lame or blind, or has any serious flaw, you must not sacrifice it to the LORD your God.[u] [22]You are to eat it in your own towns. Both the ceremonially unclean and the clean may eat it, as if it were gazelle or deer.[v] [23]But you must not eat the blood; pour it out on the ground like water.[w]

Passover

16:1–8pp — Ex 12:14–20; Lev 23:4–8; Nu 28:16–25

16 Observe the month of Abib[x] and celebrate the Passover[y] of the LORD your God, because in the month of

Cross references (center column)

15:4 [x]Dt 28:8
15:5 [y]S Ex 15:26; Dt 7:12; 28:1
15:6 [z]Dt 28:12-13,44
15:7 [a]ver 11; Mt 26:11
[b]1Jn 3:17
15:8 [c]Mt 5:42; Lk 6:34; S Ac 24:17
15:9 [d]ver 1 [e]Mt 20:15 [f]S Ex 22:23; S Job 5:15; Jas 5:4
15:10 [g]2Co 9:5 [h]S Dt 14:29
15:11 [i]S ver 7 [j]Mt 26:11; Mk 14:7; Jn 12:8
15:12 [k]Jer 34:14

15:14 [l]S Nu 18:27
15:15 [m]Ex 13:3; Jer 34:13 [n]Ex 20:2; S Dt 4:34; S 9:26; 16:12; 24:18; Jer 16:14; 23:7
15:19 [o]S Lev 27:9 [p]S Ex 13:2 [q]S Ge 4:4 [r]S Ex 22:30
15:20 [s]S Lev 7:15-18; Dt 12:5-7,17,18
15:21 [t]S Ex 12:5 [u]S Lev 22:19-25; Dt 17:1; Mal 1:8, 13
15:22 [v]S Dt 12:15
15:23 [w]S Ge 9:4; Dt 12:16; Eze 33:25
16:1 [x]S Ex 12:2 [y]S Ex 12:11; 2Ki 23:21; Mt 26:17-29

Study notes (bottom)

15:4 *there should be no poor among you.* Because of the Lord's reward for obedience (vv. 4–6), and because of the sabbath-year arrangement (vv. 7–11). This "year for canceling debts" (v. 9) gave Israelites who had experienced economic reverses a way to gain release from indebtedness and so, in a measure, a way to equalize wealth. Cf. the provisions of the Year of Jubilee (Lev 25:8–38).

15:6 *you will lend.* If Israel failed to follow the Lord's commands, the reverse would be true (see 28:43–44).

15:11 *There will always be poor people.* See also Jesus' statement in Mt 26:11. Even in the best of societies under the most enlightened laws, the uncertainties of life and the variations among citizens result in some people becoming poor. In such cases the Lord commands that generosity and kindness be extended to them.

15:15 *Remember.* See note on 4:10.

15:16 *because he loves you.* In Ex 21:5–6 an additional reason is given: The servant may want to stay with his family.

15:17 *take an awl and push it through his ear lobe.* See

note on Ex 21:6.

15:18 *worth twice as much as.* A Hebrew servant worked twice as many years as the Code of Hammurapi, e.g., required for release from debt (see chart on "Ancient Texts Relating to the OT," p. 5). Other ancient legal texts, however, support "equivalent to" as a possible translation of the phrase.

15:19 *Set apart . . . every firstborn male.* Because the Lord saved his people from the plague of death on the firstborn in Egypt (see Ex 12:12,29; 13:2 and note; 13:15).

15:21 *If an animal has a defect . . . you must not sacrifice it.* See note on Lev 1:3.

15:23 See 12:16,24; see also notes on Ge 9:4; Lev 17:11.

16:1–17 See chart on "OT Feasts and Other Sacred Days," p. 176; see also Ex 23:14–19 and notes; 34:18–26; Lev 23:4–44 and notes; Nu 28:16–29:40.

16:1–8 See Ex 12:1–28; 13:1–16 and notes.

16:1 *Abib.* See chart on "Hebrew Calendar," p. 102.

Abib he brought you out of Egypt by night. [2]Sacrifice as the Passover to the LORD your God an animal from your flock or herd at the place the LORD will choose as a dwelling for his Name.[z] [3]Do not eat it with bread made with yeast, but for seven days eat unleavened bread, the bread of affliction,[a] because you left Egypt in haste[b]—so that all the days of your life you may remember the time of your departure from Egypt.[c] [4]Let no yeast be found in your possession in all your land for seven days. Do not let any of the meat you sacrifice on the evening[d] of the first day remain until morning.[e]

[5]You must not sacrifice the Passover in any town the LORD your God gives you [6]except in the place he will choose as a dwelling for his Name. There you must sacrifice the Passover in the evening, when the sun goes down, on the anniversary[v][f] of your departure from Egypt. [7]Roast[g] it and eat it at the place the LORD your God will choose. Then in the morning return to your tents. [8]For six days eat unleavened bread and on the seventh day hold an assembly[h] to the LORD your God and do no work.[i]

Feast of Weeks
16:9–12pp — Lev 23:15–22; Nu 28:26–31

[9]Count off seven weeks[j] from the time you begin to put the sickle to the standing grain.[k] [10]Then celebrate the Feast of Weeks to the LORD your God by giving a freewill offering in proportion to the blessings the LORD your God has given you. [11]And rejoice[l] before the LORD your God at the place he will choose as a dwelling for his Name[m]—you, your sons and daughters, your menservants and maidservants, the Levites[n] in your towns, and the aliens,[o] the fatherless and the widows living among you.[p] [12]Remember that you were slaves in Egypt,[q] and follow carefully these decrees.

Feast of Tabernacles
16:13–17pp — Lev 23:33–43; Nu 29:12–39

[13]Celebrate the Feast of Tabernacles for seven days after you have gathered the produce of your threshing floor[r] and your winepress.[s] [14]Be joyful[t] at your Feast—you, your sons and daughters, your menservants and maidservants, and the Levites, the aliens, the fatherless and the widows who live in your towns. [15]For seven days celebrate the Feast to the LORD your God at the place the LORD will choose. For the LORD your God will bless you in all your harvest and in all the work of your hands, and your joy[u] will be complete.

[16]Three times a year all your men must appear[v] before the LORD your God at the place he will choose: at the Feast of Unleavened Bread,[w] the Feast of Weeks and the Feast of Tabernacles.[x] No man should appear before the LORD empty-handed:[y] [17]Each of you must bring a gift in proportion to the way the LORD your God has blessed you.

Judges

[18]Appoint judges[z] and officials for each of your tribes in every town the LORD your God is giving you, and they shall judge the people fairly.[a] [19]Do not pervert justice[b] or show partiality.[c] Do not accept a bribe,[d] for a bribe blinds the eyes of the wise and twists the words of the righteous. [20]Follow justice and justice alone, so that you may live and possess the land the LORD your God is giving you.

Worshiping Other Gods

[21]Do not set up any wooden Asherah pole[z][e] beside the altar you build to the LORD your God,[f] [22]and do not erect a sacred stone,[g] for these the LORD your God hates.

17 Do not sacrifice to the LORD your God an ox or a sheep that has any

y6 Or down, at the time of day   z21 Or Do not plant any tree dedicated to Asherah

Cross references (center column)
16:2 zDt 12:5,26
16:3 aEx 12:8,39; 34:18; 1Co 5:8
bEx 12:11
cDt 4:9
16:4 dS Ex 12:6
eS Ex 12:8; Mk 14:12
16:6 fS Ex 12:42
16:7 gS Ex 12:8
16:8 hS Lev 23:8
iMt 26:17; Lk 2:41; 22:7; Jn 2:13
16:9 jAc 2:1
kS Ex 23:16
16:11 lDt 12:7
mS Ex 20:24; S 2Sa 7:13
nDt 12:12
oS Dt 14:29
pNe 8:10
16:12 qS Dt 15:15
16:13 rS Lev 2:14
sS Ge 27:37; S Ex 23:16
16:14 tver 11
16:15 uJob 38:7; Ps 4:7; 28:7; 30:11
16:16 vDt 31:11; Ps 84:7
wS Ex 12:17
xS Ex 23:14,16; Ezr 3:4
yS Ex 34:20
16:18 zS Ex 18:21,26
aS Ge 31:37
16:19 bS Ex 23:2
cS Lev 19:15
dS Ex 18:21; S 1Sa 8:3
16:21 eS Dt 7:5
fEx 34:13; 1Ki 14:15; 2Ki 17:16; 21:3; 2Ch 33:3
16:22 gS Ex 23:24

16:3,12 *remember.* See note on 4:10.
16:6 *on the anniversary.* Referring either to the time of day (see NIV text note), as the preceding phrases do, or to the anniversary of the day it first occurred, as the NIV has translated.
16:7 *to your tents.* To wherever they were staying while at the festival, whether in permanent or temporary quarters.
16:8 *assembly.* The Hebrew for this word probably means "closing assembly," as the NIV translates it in Lev 23:36.
16:9 *the time you begin to put the sickle to the standing grain.* Abib 16, the second day of the Passover Feast.

16:15 *your joy will be complete.* As a result of God's blessing (cf. Jn 3:29; 15:11; 16:24; Php 2:2; 1Jn 1:4; 2Jn 12).
16:16 *Three times a year.* The three annual pilgrimage festivals (see Ex 23:14,17; 34:23).
16:17 *bring a gift in proportion.* See v. 10; cf. 2Co 8:12.
16:18–20 Cf. 1:9–18; Ex 18:13–26.
16:19 See Ex 23:8 and note.
16:21–22 *Asherah pole . . . sacred stone.* See note on 7:5.
17:1 *defect or flaw.* See note on Lev 1:3.

defect[h] or flaw in it, for that would be detestable[i] to him.[j]

[2]If a man or woman living among you in one of the towns the LORD gives you is found doing evil in the eyes of the LORD your God in violation of his covenant,[k] [3]and contrary to my command[l] has worshiped other gods,[m] bowing down to them or to the sun[n] or the moon or the stars of the sky,[o] [4]and this has been brought to your attention, then you must investigate it thoroughly. If it is true[p] and it has been proved that this detestable thing has been done in Israel,[q] [5]take the man or woman who has done this evil deed to your city gate and stone that person to death.[r] [6]On the testimony of two or three witnesses a man shall be put to death, but no one shall be put to death on the testimony of only one witness.[s] [7]The hands of the witnesses must be the first in putting him to death,[t] and then the hands of all the people.[u] You must purge the evil[v] from among you.

Law Courts

[8]If cases come before your courts that are too difficult for you to judge[w] —whether bloodshed, lawsuits or assaults[x]—take them to the place the LORD your God will choose.[y] [9]Go to the priests, who are Levites,[z] and to the judge[a] who is in office at that time. Inquire of them and they will give you the verdict.[b] [10]You must act according to the decisions they give you at the place the LORD will choose. Be careful to do everything they direct you to do. [11]Act according to the law they teach you and the decisions they give you. Do not turn aside from what they tell you, to the right or to the left.[c] [12]The man who shows contempt[d] for the judge or for the priest who stands ministering[e] there to the LORD your God must be put to death.[f] You must purge the

evil from Israel.[g] [13]All the people will hear and be afraid, and will not be contemptuous again.[h]

The King

[14]When you enter the land the LORD your God is giving you and have taken possession[i] of it and settled in it,[j] and you say, "Let us set a king over us like all the nations around us,"[k] [15]be sure to appoint[l] over you the king the LORD your God chooses. He must be from among your own brothers.[m] Do not place a foreigner over you, one who is not a brother Israelite. [16]The king, moreover, must not acquire great numbers of horses[n] for himself[o] or make the people return to Egypt[p] to get more of them,[q] for the LORD has told you, "You are not to go back that way again."[r] [17]He must not take many wives,[s] or his heart will be led astray.[t] He must not accumulate[u] large amounts of silver and gold.[v]

[18]When he takes the throne[w] of his kingdom, he is to write[x] for himself on a scroll a copy[y] of this law, taken from that of the priests, who are Levites. [19]It is to be with him, and he is to read it all the days of his life[z] so that he may learn to revere the LORD his God and follow carefully all the words of this law and these decrees[a] [20]and not consider himself better than his brothers and turn from the law[b] to the right or to the left.[c] Then he and his descendants will reign a long time over his kingdom in Israel.[d]

Offerings for Priests and Levites

18 The priests, who are Levites[e]—indeed the whole tribe of

17:1 [h]S Ex 12:5; S Lev 22:20
[i]Dt 7:25
[j]S Dt 15:21
17:2 [k]Dt 13:6-11
17:3 [l]Jer 7:31
[m]Ex 22:20
[n]S Ge 1:16
[o]S Ge 2:1; S 37:9
17:4 [p]Dt 22:20
[q]Dt 13:12-14
17:5 [r]S Lev 24:14
17:6 [s]Nu 35:30; Dt 19:15; S Mt 18:16
17:7 [t]Nu 8:7
[u]S Lev 24:14; Ac 7:58
[v]S Dt 13:5; 1Co 5:13*
17:8 [w]Ex 21:6
[x]2Ch 19:10
[y]Dt 12:5; Ps 122:3-5
17:9 [z]Dt 24:8; 27:9 [a]S Ex 21:6
[b]S Ge 25:22; Dt 19:17; Eze 44:24; Hag 2:11
17:11 [c]S Lev 10:11; S Dt 5:32
17:12 [d]Nu 15:30 [e]S Nu 16:9 [f]ver 13; S Ge 17:14; Dt 13:11; 18:20; 19:20; 1Ki 18:40; Jer 14:14; Hos 4:4; Zec 13:3
[g]S Dt 13:5
17:13 [h]S ver 12
17:14 [i]S Nu 33:53 [j]Jos 21:43 [k]1Sa 8:5,19-20; 10:19
17:15 [l]1Sa 16:3; 2Sa 5:3 [m]Jer 30:21
17:16 [n]Isa 2:7; 30:16 [o]1Sa 8:11; 1Ki 4:26; 9:19; 10:26; 2Ch 1:14; Ps 20:7 [p]1Ki 10:29; Isa 31:1; Jer 42:14 [q]1Ki 10:28; Isa 31:1; Eze 17:15 [r]S Ex 13:17
17:17 [s]S Ex 34:16; 2Sa 5:13; 12:11; 1Ki 11:3; 2Ch 11:21 [t]1Ki 11:2; Pr 31:3 [u]1Ki 10:27 [v]2Ch 1:11;

Isa 2:7 17:18 [w]1Ki 1:46; 1Ch 29:23 [x]Dt 31:22,24; Jos 24:26; 1Sa 10:25 [y]2Ch 23:11 17:19 [z]Dt 4:9-10; Jos 1:8 [a]Dt 11:13; 1Ki 3:3; 11:38; 2Ki 22:2 17:20 [b]Jos 23:6; Job 23:12; Ps 119:102 [c]S Dt 5:32; S 1Ki 9:4 [d]1Sa 8:5; 10:25; 1Ki 2:3; 1Ch 28:8 18:1 [e]Jer 33:18,21

17:3 *bowing down to . . . the sun or the moon or the stars.* See 2Ki 17:16; 21:3,5; 23:4–5.

17:6 *two or three witnesses.* A further specification of the law set forth in Nu 35:30. See 19:15; cf. Mt 18:16; 2Co 13:1; 1Ti 5:19; Heb 10:28.

17:7 *You must purge the evil from among you.* See v. 12; see also note on 13:5.

17:14 *a king . . . like all the nations around us.* Moses, Joshua and a succession of judges were chosen directly by the Lord to govern Israel on his behalf. As Gideon later said, "The LORD will rule over you" (Jdg 8:23; see note there). Moses here, however, anticipates a time when the people would ask for a king (see 1Sa 8:4–9) contrary to the Lord's ideal for them (see notes on 7:2–5; 1Sa 8:1–12:25; see also Lev 20:23). So Moses gives guidance concerning the eventual selection of a king.

17:16–17a The very things that later kings were guilty of,

beginning especially with Solomon (1Ki 4:26; 11:1–4)—except that they did not make Israel return to Egypt (but see Jer 42:13–43:7).

17:18 *write for himself . . . a copy of this law.* As a sign of submission to the Lord as his King, and as a guide for his rule in obedience to his heavenly Suzerain. This was required procedure for vassal kings under the suzerainty treaties among the Hittites and others before and during this period (see note on 31:9). See chart on "Major Covenants in the OT," p. 19.

17:20 *not consider himself better.* The king was not above God's law, any more than were the humblest of his subjects.

18:1 *no allotment or inheritance.* No private ownership of land. Towns and surrounding pasturelands were set aside for the use of the Levites (Jos 21:41–42), as were the tithes and parts of sacrifices (see 14:22–29 and note; Lev 27:30 and note; Nu 18:21–29).

Levi—are to have no allotment or inheritance with Israel. They shall live on the offerings[f] made to the LORD by fire, for that is their inheritance.[g] [2]They shall have no inheritance among their brothers; the LORD is their inheritance,[h] as he promised them.[i]

[3]This is the share due the priests[j] from the people who sacrifice a bull[k] or a sheep: the shoulder, the jowls and the inner parts.[l] [4]You are to give them the firstfruits of your grain, new wine and oil, and the first wool from the shearing of your sheep,[m] [5]for the LORD your God has chosen them[n] and their descendants out of all your tribes to stand and minister[o] in the LORD's name always.[p]

[6]If a Levite moves from one of your towns anywhere in Israel where he is living, and comes in all earnestness to the place the LORD will choose,[q] [7]he may minister in the name[r] of the LORD his God like all his fellow Levites who serve there in the presence of the LORD. [8]He is to share equally in their benefits, even though he has received money from the sale of family possessions.[s]

Detestable Practices

[9]When you enter the land the LORD your God is giving you, do not learn to imitate[t] the detestable ways[u] of the nations there. [10]Let no one be found among you who sacrifices his son or daughter in[a] the fire,[v] who practices divination[w] or sorcery,[x] interprets omens, engages in witchcraft,[y] [11]or casts spells,[z] or who is a medium or spiritist[a] or who consults the dead. [12]Anyone who does these things is detestable to the LORD, and because of these detestable practices the LORD your God will drive out those nations before you.[b] [13]You must be blameless[c] before the LORD your God.[d]

The Prophet

[14]The nations you will dispossess listen to those who practice sorcery or divination.[e] But as for you, the LORD your God has not permitted you to do so. [15]The LORD your God will raise up for you a prophet like me from among your own brothers.[f] You must listen to him. [16]For this is what you asked of the LORD your God at Horeb on the day of the assembly when you said, "Let us not hear the voice of the LORD our God nor see this great fire anymore, or we will die."[g]

[17]The LORD said to me: "What they say is good. [18]I will raise up for them a prophet[h] like you from among their brothers; I will put my words[i] in his mouth,[j] and he will tell them everything I command him.[k] [19]If anyone does not listen[l] to my words that the prophet speaks in my name,[m] I myself will call him to account.[n] [20]But a prophet who presumes to speak in my name anything I have not commanded him to say, or a prophet who speaks in the name of other gods,[o] must be put to death."[p]

[21]You may say to yourselves, "How can we know when a message has not been spoken by the LORD?" [22]If what a prophet proclaims in the name of the LORD does not take place or come true,[q] that is a message the LORD has not spoken.[r] That prophet has spoken presumptuously.[s] Do not be afraid of him.

Cities of Refuge

19:1–14Ref — Nu 35:6–34; Dt 4:41–43; Jos 20:1–9

19 When the LORD your God has destroyed the nations whose land he is giving you, and when you have driven

Cross references (center column)

18:1 /S Nu 18:8
gS Nu 18:20;
1Co 9:13
18:2 hNu 18:20
iJos 13:14
18:3 /S Ex 29:27
kS Lev 1:5
lLev 7:28-34;
Nu 18:12
18:4 mEx 22:29;
Nu 18:12
18:5 nS Ex 28:1
oDt 10:8
pS Ex 29:9
18:6
qS Nu 35:2-3;
S Dt 12:5
18:7 rver 19;
1Ki 18:32; 22:16;
Ps 118:26
18:8 sNu 18:24;
2Ch 31:4;
Ne 12:44,47;
13:12
18:9 tDt 9:5;
12:29-31
uS Lev 18:3;
2Ki 21:2;
2Ch 28:3; 33:2;
34:33; Ezr 6:21;
9:11; Jer 44:4
18:10
vS Lev 18:21
w1Sa 15:23
xS Ex 7:11
yS Lev 19:31
18:11 zIsa 47:9
aS Ex 22:18;
S 1Sa 28:13
18:12
bS Lev 18:24
18:13 cS Ge 6:9;
Ps 119:1
dMt 5:48

18:14 eS 2Ki 21:6
18:15
/S Mt 21:11;
Lk 2:25-35;
Jn 1:21;
Ac 3:22*; 7:37*
18:16
gS Ex 20:19;
Dt 5:23-27
18:18 hS Ge 20:7
iIsa 2:3; 26:8;
51:4; Mic 4:2
/S Ex 4:12
kJn 4:25-26;
S 14:24; Ac 3:22*
18:19
/S Ex 23:21
mS ver 7;
S Lev 19:12;
2Ki 2:24
nJos 22:23;
Ac 3:23*;
Heb 12:25
18:20
oS Ex 23:13
pDt 13:1-5;
S 17:12

18:22 qS Dt 13:2; 1Sa 3:20 rKi 22:28; Jer 28:9 sver 20

a 10 Or who makes his son or daughter pass through

18:4 *firstfruits.* See Ex 23:19 and note; 34:26; Lev 23:10–11; Nu 15:18–20; 18:12–13.
18:5 See note on 21:5.
18:9 *detestable ways of the nations.* What follows is the most complete list of magical or spiritistic arts in the OT. All were practiced in Canaan, and all are condemned and prohibited. The people are not to resort to such sources for their information, guidance or revelation. Rather, they are to listen to the Lord's true prophets (see vv. 14–22).
18:10 *sacrifices his son or daughter.* See 12:31; see also note on Lev 18:21.
18:15 *prophet like me.* Verse 16, as well as the general context (see especially vv. 20–22), indicates that a series of prophets is meant. At Mount Horeb the people requested that Moses take the message from God and deliver it to them (see Ex 20:19 and note). But now that Moses is to leave

them, he says that another spokesman will take his place, and then another will be necessary for the next generation. This is therefore a collective reference to the prophets who will follow. As such, it is also the basis for Messianic expectation and receives a unique fulfillment in Jesus (see Jn 1:21, 25,45; 5:46; 6:14; 7:40; Ac 3:22–26; 7:37).
18:16 See Ex 20:18–19; Heb 12:18–21.
18:18 *my words in his mouth.* See Ex 4:15–16; see also note on Ex 7:1–2.
18:20 *prophet who presumes to speak.* See note on 13:1–5. *must be put to death.* See 13:5; Jer 28:15–17.
18:21–22 This negative form of statement is always true. But the positive statement, "If the prophecy comes true, it is from the Lord," may not always be true (see note on 13:1–5).
19:1–13 See 4:41–43; Nu 35:9–28; Jos 20.

them out and settled in their towns and houses,[t] [2]then set aside for yourselves three cities centrally located in the land the LORD your God is giving you to possess. [3]Build roads to them and divide into three parts the land the LORD your God is giving you as an inheritance, so that anyone who kills a man may flee there.

[4]This is the rule concerning the man who kills another and flees there to save his life—one who kills his neighbor unintentionally, without malice aforethought. [5]For instance, a man may go into the forest with his neighbor to cut wood, and as he swings his ax to fell a tree, the head may fly off and hit his neighbor and kill him. That man may flee to one of these cities and save his life. [6]Otherwise, the avenger of blood[u] might pursue him in a rage, overtake him if the distance is too great, and kill him even though he is not deserving of death, since he did it to his neighbor without malice aforethought. [7]This is why I command you to set aside for yourselves three cities.

[8]If the LORD your God enlarges your territory,[v] as he promised[w] on oath to your forefathers, and gives you the whole land he promised them, [9]because you carefully follow all these laws I command you today—to love the LORD your God and to walk always in his ways[x]—then you are to set aside three more cities. [10]Do this so that innocent blood[y] will not be shed in your land, which the LORD your God is giving you as your inheritance, and so that you will not be guilty of bloodshed.[z]

[11]But if a man hates his neighbor and lies in wait for him, assaults and kills him,[a] and then flees to one of these cities, [12]the elders of his town shall send for him, bring him back from the city, and hand him over to the avenger of blood to die. [13]Show him no pity.[b] You must purge from Israel the guilt of shedding innocent blood,[c] so that it may go well with you.

[14]Do not move your neighbor's boundary stone set up by your predecessors in the inheritance you receive in the land the LORD your God is giving you to possess.[d]

Witnesses

[15]One witness is not enough to convict a man accused of any crime or offense he may have committed. A matter must be established by the testimony of two or three witnesses.[e]

[16]If a malicious witness[f] takes the stand to accuse a man of a crime, [17]the two men involved in the dispute must stand in the presence of the LORD before the priests and the judges[g] who are in office at the time. [18]The judges must make a thorough investigation,[h] and if the witness proves to be a liar, giving false testimony against his brother, [19]then do to him as he intended to do to his brother.[i] You must purge the evil from among you. [20]The rest of the people will hear of this and be afraid,[j] and never again will such an evil thing be done among you. [21]Show no pity:[k] life for life, eye for eye, tooth for tooth, hand for hand, foot for foot.[l]

Going to War

20 When you go to war against your enemies and see horses and chariots and an army greater than yours,[m] do not be afraid[n] of them,[o] because the LORD your God, who brought you up out of Egypt, will be with[p] you. [2]When you are about to go into battle, the priest shall come forward and address the army. [3]He shall say: "Hear, O Israel, today you are going into battle against your enemies. Do not be fainthearted[q] or afraid; do not be terrified or give way to panic before them. [4]For the LORD your God is the one who goes with you[r] to fight[s] for you against your enemies to give you victory.[t]"

[5]The officers shall say to the army: "Has anyone built a new house and not dedicated[u] it? Let him go home, or he may die in battle and someone else may dedicate it. [6]Has anyone planted[v] a vineyard and not begun to enjoy it?[w] Let him go home, or he may die in battle and someone else enjoy it. [7]Has anyone become pledged to a woman and not married her? Let him go home, or he may die in battle and someone else marry her.[x]" [8]Then the officers

Cross references

19:1 [t]Dt 6:10-11
19:6 [u]S Nu 35:12
19:8 [v]S Ex 34:24
  [w]S Ge 15:8;
  S Dt 11:24
19:9 [x]Dt 6:5
19:10 [y]Pr 6:17;
  Jer 7:6; 26:15
  [z]Dt 21:1-9
19:11
  [a]S Ex 21:12;
  1Jn 3:15
19:13 [b]Dt 7:2
  [c]Dt 21:9;
  1Ki 2:31
19:14 [d]Dt 27:17;
  Job 24:2; Ps 16:6;
  Pr 15:25; 22:28;
  23:10; Isa 1:23;
  Hos 5:10

19:15
  [e]S Dt 17:6;
  S Mt 18:16*;
  26:60; 2Co 13:1*
19:16 [f]Ex 23:1;
  Pr 6:19
19:17 [g]S Ex 21:6
19:18 [h]S Ex 23:7
19:19 [i]Pr 19:5,9;
  1Co 5:13*
19:20
  [j]S Dt 13:11
19:21 [k]ver 13
  [l]S Ex 21:24;
  Mt 5:38*
20:1 [m]Ps 20:7;
  Isa 31:1
  [n]S Nu 14:9
  [o]S Dt 3:22;
  S 1Sa 17:45
  [p]Isa 41:10
20:3 [q]1Sa 17:32;
  Job 23:16;
  Ps 22:14; Isa 7:4;
  35:4; Jer 51:46
20:4
  [r]2Ch 20:14-22
  [s]S Ex 14:14;
  1Ch 5:22;
  Ne 4:20
  [t]Jdg 12:3; 15:18;
  Ps 44:7; 144:10
20:5 [u]Ne 12:27
20:6 [v]Jer 31:5;
  Eze 28:26;
  Mic 1:6 [w]1Co 9:7
20:7 [x]Dt 24:5;
  Pr 5:18

19:14 *boundary stone.* Such stones were set up to indicate the perimeters of fields and landed estates. Moving them illegally to increase one's own holdings was considered a serious crime.
19:15 See note on 17:6.
19:18 *giving false testimony.* See 5:20; Lev 19:11–13; 1Ki 21:10,13.
19:19 *You must purge the evil from among you.* See note on 13:5.
19:21 *life for life.* See notes on Ex 21:24–25; Lev 24:20;

see also Mt 5:38–42.
20:2 *priest shall . . . address.* Not merely a recitation of ritual. Priests sometimes accompanied the army when it went into battle (see, e.g., Jos 6:4–21; 2Ch 20:14–22).
20:3 *Hear, O Israel.* See note on 4:1.
20:4 See note on 3:22.
20:5–8 *Let him go home.* See the curses in 28:30. Israel was not to trust in the size of its army but in the Lord. Exemptions from military duty were sometimes extensive (see, e.g., Jdg 7:2–8).

shall add, "Is any man afraid or fainthearted? Let him go home so that his brothers will not become disheartened too."[y] [9]When the officers have finished speaking to the army, they shall appoint commanders over it.

[10]When you march up to attack a city, make its people an offer of peace.[z] [11]If they accept and open their gates, all the people in it shall be subject[a] to forced labor[b] and shall work for you. [12]If they refuse to make peace and they engage you in battle, lay siege to that city. [13]When the LORD your God delivers it into your hand, put to the sword all the men in it.[c] [14]As for the women, the children, the livestock[d] and everything else in the city,[e] you may take these as plunder[f] for yourselves. And you may use the plunder the LORD your God gives you from your enemies. [15]This is how you are to treat all the cities that are at a distance[g] from you and do not belong to the nations nearby.

[16]However, in the cities of the nations the LORD your God is giving you as an inheritance, do not leave alive anything that breathes.[h] [17]Completely destroy[b] them—the Hittites, Amorites, Canaanites, Perizzites, Hivites and Jebusites—as the LORD your God has commanded you. [18]Otherwise, they will teach you to follow all the detestable things they do in worshiping their gods,[i] and you will sin[j] against the LORD your God.

[19]When you lay siege to a city for a long time, fighting against it to capture it, do not destroy its trees by putting an ax to them, because you can eat their fruit. Do not cut them down. Are the trees of the field people, that you should besiege them?[c] [20]However, you may cut down trees that you know are not fruit trees[k] and use them to build siege works until the city at war with you falls.

Atonement for an Unsolved Murder

21 If a man is found slain, lying in a field in the land the LORD your God is giving you to possess, and it is not known who killed him,[l] [2]your elders and judges shall go out and measure the distance from the body to the neighboring towns. [3]Then the elders of the town nearest the body shall take a heifer that has never been worked and has never worn a yoke[m] [4]and lead her down to a valley that has not been plowed or planted and where there is a flowing stream. There in the valley they are to break the heifer's neck. [5]The priests, the sons of Levi, shall step forward, for the LORD your God has chosen them to minister and to pronounce blessings[n] in the name of the LORD and to decide all cases of dispute and assault.[o] [6]Then all the elders of the town nearest the body shall wash their hands[p] over the heifer whose neck was broken in the valley, [7]and they shall declare: "Our hands did not shed this blood, nor did our eyes see it done. [8]Accept this atonement for your people Israel, whom you have redeemed, O LORD, and do not hold your people guilty of the blood of an innocent man." And the bloodshed will be atoned for.[q] [9]So you will purge[r] from yourselves the guilt of shedding innocent blood, since you have done what is right in the eyes of the LORD.

Marrying a Captive Woman

[10]When you go to war against your enemies and the LORD your God delivers them into your hands[s] and you take captives,[t] [11]if you notice among the captives a beautiful[u] woman and are attracted to her,[v] you may take her as your wife. [12]Bring her into your home and have her shave her head,[w] trim her nails [13]and put aside the clothes she was wearing when captured. After she has lived in your house and mourned her father and mother for a full month,[x] then you may go to her and be her husband and she shall be your wife. [14]If you are not pleased with her, let her go

Cross references (center column)

20:8 [y]Jdg 7:3
20:10 [z]S Dt 2:26; Lk 14:31-32
20:11 [a]ver 15; 2Ki 6:22
[b]1Ki 9:21; 1Ch 22:2; Isa 31:8
20:13 [c]Nu 31:7
20:14 [d]Jos 8:2; 22:8 [e]S Nu 31:11
[f]S Nu 31:53
20:15 [g]S ver 11; Jos 9:9
20:16 [h]Ex 23:31-33; Nu 21:2-3; S Dt 7:2; Jos 6:21; 10:1; 11:14
20:18 [i]S Ex 34:16 [j]S Ex 10:7
20:20 [k]Jer 6:6

21:1 [l]S Nu 25:17
21:3 [m]S Nu 19:2
21:5 [n]S Ge 48:20; S Ex 39:43 [o]Dt 17:8-11
21:6 [p]Mt 27:24
21:8 [q]Nu 35:33-34
21:9 [r]Dt 19:13
21:10 [s]Jos 21:44 1Ki 8:46; 1Ch 9:1; Ezr 5:12; Jer 40:1; Eze 1:1; 17:12; Da 2:25; Mic 4:10
21:11 [u]Ge 6:2 [v]S Ge 34:8
21:12 [w]S Lev 14:9; S Nu 8:7; 1Co 11:5
21:13 [x]Ps 45:10

Footnotes

[b]17 The Hebrew term refers to the irrevocable giving over of things or persons to the LORD, often by totally destroying them.   [c]19 Or down to use in the siege, for the fruit trees are for the benefit of man.

20:10–15 Rules regarding warfare against nations outside the promised land.

20:11 *subject to forced labor.* A fulfillment of Noah's curse on Canaan (see Ge 9:25 and note).

20:17 *Hittites . . . Jebusites.* See 7:1; see also notes on Ge 10:6,15–18; 13:7.

20:19 *do not destroy its trees.* The failure of later armies to follow this wise rule stripped bare much of Palestine (though the absence of woodlands there today is of relatively recent origin).

21:5 *to minister.* To officiate at the place of worship before the Lord on behalf of the people (see 10:8; 18:5). *to pro-*

nounce blessings. See Nu 6:22–27.

21:6 *wash their hands.* Symbolic of a declaration of innocence (v. 7; see Mt 27:24).

21:10 *against your enemies.* The enemies here are those outside Canaan (see 20:14–15); so the woman (v. 11) could be taken captive and would not be subject to total destruction.

21:12 *shave her head.* Indicative of leaving her former life and beginning a new life, or perhaps symbolic of mourning (v. 13; see, e.g., Jer 47:5; Mic 1:16) or of humiliation (see note on Isa 7:20). For cleansing rites see Lev 14:8; Nu 8:7; cf. 2Sa 19:24.

wherever she wishes. You must not sell her or treat her as a slave, since you have dishonored her.[y]

The Right of the Firstborn

[15]If a man has two wives,[z] and he loves one but not the other, and both bear him sons but the firstborn is the son of the wife he does not love,[a] [16]when he wills his property to his sons, he must not give the rights of the firstborn to the son of the wife he loves in preference to his actual firstborn, the son of the wife he does not love.[b] [17]He must acknowledge the son of his unloved wife as the firstborn by giving him a double[c] share of all he has. That son is the first sign of his father's strength.[d] The right of the firstborn belongs to him.[e]

A Rebellious Son

[18]If a man has a stubborn and rebellious[f] son[g] who does not obey his father and mother[h] and will not listen to them when they discipline him, [19]his father and mother shall take hold of him and bring him to the elders at the gate of his town. [20]They shall say to the elders, "This son of ours is stubborn and rebellious. He will not obey us. He is a profligate and a drunkard." [21]Then all the men of his town shall stone him to death.[i] You must purge the evil[j] from among you. All Israel will hear of it and be afraid.[k]

Various Laws

[22]If a man guilty of a capital offense[l] is put to death and his body is hung on a tree, [23]you must not leave his body on the tree overnight.[m] Be sure to bury[n] him that same day, because anyone who is hung on a tree is under God's curse.[o] You must not

Center reference column

21:14 [y]S Ge 34:2
21:15 [z]S Ge 4:19
[a]Ge 29:33
21:16
[b]1Ch 26:10
21:17 [c]2Ki 2:9;
Isa 40:2; 61:7;
Zec 9:12
[d]S Ge 49:3
[e]Ge 25:31;
Lk 15:12
21:18 [f]Ps 78:8;
Jer 5:23; Zep 3:1
[g]Pr 30:17
[h]S Ge 31:35;
Pr 1:8; Isa 30:1;
Eph 6:1-3
21:21 [i]S Lev 20:9
/Dt 19:19
[k]S Dt 13:11
21:22 [l]Dt 22:26;
Mt 26:66;
Mk 14:64;
Ac 23:29
21:23 [m]Jos 8:29;
10:27; Jn 19:31
[n]Eze 39:12
[o]Ezr 6:11;
Est 2:23; 7:9;
8:7; 9:13,25;
Isa 50:11;
Gal 3:13*

[p]S Lev 18:25
22:1 [q]Ex 23:4-5;
Pr 27:10; Zec 7:9
22:4 [r]Ex 23:5
[s]1Co 9:9
22:6 [t]Lev 22:28
22:7
[u]S Lev 22:28
[v]S Dt 5:29
22:8 [w]Jos 2:8;
1Sa 9:25;
2Sa 11:2
22:9 [x]Lev 19:19
22:10 [y]2Co 6:14
22:11 [z]Lev 19:19
22:12
[a]Nu 15:37-41;
Mt 23:5

desecrate[p] the land the LORD your God is giving you as an inheritance.

22

If you see your brother's ox or sheep straying, do not ignore it but be sure to take it back to him.[q] [2]If the brother does not live near you or if you do not know who he is, take it home with you and keep it until he comes looking for it. Then give it back to him. [3]Do the same if you find your brother's donkey or his cloak or anything he loses. Do not ignore it.

[4]If you see your brother's donkey[r] or his ox fallen on the road, do not ignore it. Help him get it to its feet.[s]

[5]A woman must not wear men's clothing, nor a man wear women's clothing, for the LORD your God detests anyone who does this.

[6]If you come across a bird's nest beside the road, either in a tree or on the ground, and the mother is sitting on the young or on the eggs, do not take the mother with the young.[t] [7]You may take the young, but be sure to let the mother go,[u] so that it may go well with you and you may have a long life.[v]

[8]When you build a new house, make a parapet around your roof so that you may not bring the guilt of bloodshed on your house if someone falls from the roof.[w]

[9]Do not plant two kinds of seed in your vineyard;[x] if you do, not only the crops you plant but also the fruit of the vineyard will be defiled.[d]

[10]Do not plow with an ox and a donkey yoked together.[y]

[11]Do not wear clothes of wool and linen woven together.[z]

[12]Make tassels on the four corners of the cloak you wear.[a]

[d]9 Or be forfeited to the sanctuary

21:14 *dishonored.* Twelve other times the Hebrew for this word is used of men forcing women to have sexual intercourse with them (22:24,29; Ge 34:2; Jdg 19:24; 20:5; 2Sa 13:12,14,22,32; La 5:11; Eze 22:10–11).
21:15 *two wives.* See notes on Ge 4:19; 25:6.
21:16 *in preference to.* The order of birth rather than parental favoritism governed succession, though the rule was sometimes set aside with divine approval (cf., e.g., Jacob or Solomon).
21:17 *double share.* In Israel the oldest son enjoyed a double share of the inheritance. Parallels to this practice come from Nuzi, Larsa in the Old Babylonian period, and Assyria in the Middle Assyrian period (see chart on "Ancient Texts Relating to the OT," p. 5). Receiving a double portion of an estate was also tantamount to succession. Thus Elisha succeeded Elijah (2Ki 2:9). *first sign of his father's strength.* The first result of a man's procreative ability.
21:18 *stubborn and rebellious . . . does not obey.* In wicked defiance of the fifth commandment (see 5:16; Ex 20:12 and note).

21:21 *stone him to death.* See 5:16; 27:16; Ex 21:15,17. *You must purge the evil from among you.* See note on 13:5.
21:22 *put to death and . . . hung on a tree.* The offender was first executed, then "hung on a tree" (see Ge 40:19), or, as the Hebrew for this phrase doubtless intends, "impaled on a pole" (see NIV text notes on Ge 40:19; Est 2:23).
21:23 *not leave his body on the tree overnight.* Prolonged exposure gives undue attention to the crime and the criminal. *under God's curse.* God had condemned murder, and hanging on a tree symbolized divine judgment and rejection. Christ accepted the full punishment of our sins, thus becoming "a curse for us" (Gal 3:13).
22:1 *do not ignore it.* See vv. 3–4. The Biblical legislation was intended not only to punish criminal behavior but also to express concern for people and their possessions. See chart on "Major Social Concerns in the Covenant," p. 271.
22:5 Probably intended to prohibit such perversions as transvestism and homosexuality, especially under religious auspices. The God-created differences between men and women are not to be disregarded (see Lev 18:22; 20:13).

Marriage Violations

13If a man takes a wife and, after lying with her*b*, dislikes her 14and slanders her and gives her a bad name, saying, "I married this woman, but when I approached her, I did not find proof of her virginity," 15then the girl's father and mother shall bring proof that she was a virgin to the town elders at the gate.*c* 16The girl's father will say to the elders, "I gave my daughter in marriage to this man, but he dislikes her. 17Now he has slandered her and said, 'I did not find your daughter to be a virgin.' But here is the proof of my daughter's virginity." Then her parents shall display the cloth before the elders of the town, 18and the elders*d* shall take the man and punish him. 19They shall fine him a hundred shekels of silver*e* and give them to the girl's father, because this man has giv-

en an Israelite virgin a bad name. She shall continue to be his wife; he must not divorce her as long as he lives.

20If, however, the charge is true*e* and no proof of the girl's virginity can be found, 21she shall be brought to the door of her father's house and there the men of her town shall stone her to death. She has done a disgraceful thing*f* in Israel by being promiscuous while still in her father's house. You must purge the evil from among you.

22If a man is found sleeping with another man's wife, both the man who slept*g* with her and the woman must die.*h* You must purge the evil from Israel.

23If a man happens to meet in a town a virgin pledged to be married and he sleeps with her, 24you shall take both of them to

22:13 *b*Dt 24:1
22:15
*c*S Ge 23:10
22:18 *d*Ex 18:21;
Dt 1:9-18

22:20 *e*Dt 17:4
22:21 *f*S Ge 34:7;
S 38:24;
S Lev 19:29;
Dt 23:17-18;
1Co 5:13*
22:22 *g*2Sa 11:4
*h*S Ge 38:24;
S Ex 21:12;
Mt 5:27-28;
Jn 8:5; 1Co 6:9;
Heb 13:4

e19 That is, about 2 1/2 pounds (about 1 kilogram)

22:14 *proof of her virginity.* A blood-stained cloth or garment (see vv. 15,17,20).
22:15 *elders at the gate.* See 25:7; see also notes on Ge 19:1; Ru 4:1.
22:19 *hundred shekels of silver.* A heavy fine—several times what Hosea paid to buy Gomer back (Hos 3:2) or

what Jeremiah paid for the field at Anathoth (Jer 32:9). It may have been about twice the average bride-price (see note on v. 29). The high fine, in addition to the no-divorce rule, was intended to restrain not only a husband's charges against his wife but also easy divorce.
22:21,24 *You must purge the evil from among you.* See v.

Major Social Concerns in the Covenant

1. Personhood
Everyone's person is to be secure (Ex 20:13; Dt 5:17; Ex 21:16-21,26-31; Lev 19:14; Dt 24:7; 27:18).

2. False Accusation
Everyone is to be secure against slander and false accusation (Ex 20:16; Dt 5:20; Ex 23:1-3; Lev 19:16; Dt 19:15-21).

3. Woman
No woman is to be taken advantage of within her subordinate status in society (Ex 21:7-11,20, 26-32; 22:16-17; Dt 21:10-14; 22:13-30; 24:1-5).

4. Punishment
Punishment for wrongdoing shall not be excessive so that the culprit is dehumanized (Dt 25:1-5).

5. Dignity
Every Israelite's dignity and right to be God's freedman and servant are to be honored and safeguarded (Ex 21:2,5-6; Lev 25; Dt 15:12-18).

6. Inheritance
Every Israelite's inheritance in the promised land is to be secure (Lev 25; Nu 27:5-7; 36:1-9; Dt 25:5-10).

7. Property
Everyone's property is to be secure (Ex 20:15; Dt 5:19; Ex 21:33-36; 22:1-15; 23:4-5; Lev 19:35-36; Dt 22:1-4; 25:13-15).

8. Fruit of Labor
Everyone is to receive the fruit of his labors (Lev 19:13; Dt 24:14; 25:4).

9. Fruit of the Ground
Everyone is to share the fruit of the ground (Ex 23:10-11; Lev 19:9-10; 23:22; 25:3-55; Dt 14:28-29; 24:19-21).

10. Rest on Sabbath
Everyone, down to the humblest servant and the resident alien, is to share in the weekly rest of God's Sabbath (Ex 20:8-11; Dt 5:12-15; Ex 23:12).

11. Marriage
The marriage relationship is to be kept inviolate (Ex 20:14; Dt 5:18; see also Lev 18:6-23; 20:10-21; Dt 22:13-30).

12. Exploitation
No one, however disabled, impoverished or powerless, is to be oppressed or exploited (Ex 22:21-27; Lev 19:14,33-34; 25:35-36; Dt 23:19; 24:6,12-15,17; 27:18).

13. Fair Trial
Everyone is to have free access to the courts and is to be afforded a fair trial (Ex 23:6,8; Lev 19:15; Dt 1:17; 10:17-18; 16:18-20; 17:8-13; 19:15-21).

14. Social Order
Every person's God-given place in the social order is to be honored (Ex 20:12; Dt 5:16; Ex 21:15,17; 22:28; Lev 19:3,32; 20:9; Dt 17:8-13; 21:15-21; 27:16).

15. Law
No one shall be above the law, not even the king (Dt 17:18-20).

16. Animals
Concern for the welfare of other creatures is to be extended to the animal world (Ex 23:5,11; Lev 25:7; Dt 22:4,6-7; 25:4).

the gate of that town and stone them to death—the girl because she was in a town and did not scream for help, and the man because he violated another man's wife. You must purge the evil from among you. [i]

25But if out in the country a man happens to meet a girl pledged to be married and rapes her, only the man who has done this shall die. 26Do nothing to the girl; she has committed no sin deserving death. This case is like that of someone who attacks and murders his neighbor, 27for the man found the girl out in the country, and though the betrothed girl screamed, [j] there was no one to rescue her.

28If a man happens to meet a virgin who is not pledged to be married and rapes her and they are discovered, [k] 29he shall pay the girl's father fifty shekels of silver. [f] He must marry the girl, for he has violated her. He can never divorce her as long as he lives.

30A man is not to marry his father's wife; he must not dishonor his father's bed. [l]

Exclusion From the Assembly

23 No one who has been emasculated [m] by crushing or cutting may enter the assembly of the LORD.

2No one born of a forbidden marriage [g] nor any of his descendants may enter the assembly of the LORD, even down to the tenth generation.

3No Ammonite [n] or Moabite or any of his descendants may enter the assembly of the LORD, even down to the tenth generation. [o] 4For they did not come to meet you with bread and water [p] on your way when you came out of Egypt, and they hired Balaam [q] son of Beor from Pethor in Aram Naharaim [h] [r] to pronounce a curse on you. [s] 5However, the LORD your God would not listen to Balaam but turned the

curse [t] into a blessing for you, because the LORD your God loves [u] you. 6Do not seek a treaty [v] of friendship with them as long as you live. [w]

7Do not abhor an Edomite, [x] for he is your brother. [y] Do not abhor an Egyptian, because you lived as an alien in his country. [z] 8The third generation of children born to them may enter the assembly of the LORD.

Uncleanness in the Camp

9When you are encamped against your enemies, keep away from everything impure. [a] 10If one of your men is unclean because of a nocturnal emission, he is to go outside the camp and stay there. [b] 11But as evening approaches he is to wash himself, and at sunset [c] he may return to the camp. [d]

12Designate a place outside the camp where you can go to relieve yourself. 13As part of your equipment have something to dig with, and when you relieve yourself, dig a hole and cover up your excrement. 14For the LORD your God moves [e] about in your camp to protect you and to deliver your enemies to you. Your camp must be holy, [f] so that he will not see among you anything indecent and turn away from you.

Miscellaneous Laws

15If a slave has taken refuge [g] with you, do not hand him over to his master. [h] 16Let him live among you wherever he likes and in whatever town he chooses. Do not oppress [i] him.

17No Israelite man [j] or woman is to become a shrine prostitute. [k] 18You must not bring the earnings of a female prostitute or of a male prostitute [l] into the house

---

Cross references (center column):

22:24 [i] 1Co 5:13*
22:27 /S Ge 39:14
22:28 [k] Ex 22:16
22:30 /S Ge 29:29; S Lev 18:8; S 20:9; 1Co 5:1
23:1 [m] S Lev 21:20
23:3 [n] S Ge 19:38 over 4; Ne 13:2
23:4 [p] Dt 2:28 [q] S Nu 23:7; S 2Pe 2:15 [r] S Ge 24:10 [s] S ver 3
23:5 [t] Nu 24:10; Jos 24:10; Pr 26:2 [u] S Dt 4:37
23:6 [v] S Nu 24:17; Isa 15:1; 25:10; Jer 25:21; 27:3; 48:1; Eze 25:8; Zep 2:9 [w] Ezr 9:12; Mt 5:43
23:7 [x] S Ge 25:30 [y] S Ge 25:26 [z] S Lev 19:34
23:9 [a] Lev 15:1-33
23:10 [b] Lev 15:16
23:11 [c] S Lev 15:16 [d] 1Sa 21:5
23:14 [e] S Ge 3:8 [Ex 3:5
23:15 [g] 2Sa 23:3; Ps 2:12; 71:1 [h] 1Sa 30:15
23:16 [i] Ex 22:21; S 23:6
23:17 /1Ki 14:24; 15:12; 22:46; 2Ki 23:7; Job 36:14 [k] S Ge 38:21

Footnotes:

[f] 29 That is, about 1 1/4 pounds (about 0.6 kilogram)   [g] 2 Or one of illegitimate birth   [h] 4 That is, Northwest Mesopotamia   [i] 18 Hebrew of a dog

---

Study notes (bottom):

22; see also note on 13:5.
22:22 See Lev 20:10.
22:29 fifty shekels of silver. Probably equaled the average bride-price, which must have varied with the economic status of the participants (see note on Ex 22:16).
22:30 his father's wife. Refers to a wife other than his mother (see 27:20). dishonor his father's bed. Lit. "uncover the corner of his father's garment" (see notes on Ru 3:9; Eze 16:8).
23:1 For blessings on eunuchs in later times see Isa 56:4-5; Ac 8:26-39.
23:2-3 down to the tenth generation. Perhaps forever, since ten is symbolic of completeness or finality. In v. 6 the equivalent expression is "as long as you live" (lit. "all your days forever").
23:3 Ruth is an outstanding exception to Moabite exclusion from Israel (see Introduction to Ruth: Theme and

Theology).
23:4 Balaam son of Beor. See Nu 22:4-24:25.
23:6 Do not seek a treaty of friendship with them. See the prophets' denunciation of Moab, Ammon and Edom (Isa 15-16; Jer 48:1-49:6; Eze 25:1-11; Am 1:13-2:3; Zep 2:8-11).
23:7 Edomite . . . your brother. Edom (Esau) is often condemned for his hostility against his brother Jacob (Israel; see Am 1:11; Ob 10; see also notes on Ge 25:22,26).
23:9-14 Sanitary rules for Israel's military camps. For similar rules for the people in general see Lev 15.
23:15 If a slave has taken refuge. A foreign slave seeking freedom in Israel (see v. 16). Cf. 24:7.
23:17-18 See notes on Ex 34:15-16.
23:18 male prostitute. Lit. "dog" (see NIV text note), a word often associated with moral or spiritual impurity (cf. Mt 7:6; 15:26; Php 3:2).

of the LORD your God to pay any vow, because the LORD your God detests them both.[l]

19Do not charge your brother interest, whether on money or food or anything else that may earn interest.[m] 20You may charge a foreigner[n] interest, but not a brother Israelite, so that the LORD your God may bless[o] you in everything you put your hand to in the land you are entering to possess.

21If you make a vow to the LORD your God, do not be slow to pay it,[p] for the LORD your God will certainly demand it of you and you will be guilty of sin.[q] 22But if you refrain from making a vow, you will not be guilty.[r] 23Whatever your lips utter you must be sure to do, because you made your vow freely to the LORD your God with your own mouth.

24If you enter your neighbor's vineyard, you may eat all the grapes you want, but do not put any in your basket. 25If you enter your neighbor's grainfield, you may pick kernels with your hands, but you must not put a sickle to his standing grain.[s]

24 If a man marries a woman who becomes displeasing to him[t] because he finds something indecent about her, and he writes her a certificate of divorce,[u] gives it to her and sends her from his house, 2and if after she leaves his house she becomes the wife of another man, 3and her second husband dislikes her and writes her a certificate of divorce, gives it to her and sends her from his house, or if he dies, 4then her first husband, who divorced her, is not allowed to marry her again after she has been defiled. That would be detestable in the eyes of the LORD. Do not bring sin upon the land the LORD[v] your God is giving you as an inheritance.

5If a man has recently married, he must not be sent to war or have any other duty laid on him. For one year he is to be free to stay at home and bring happiness to the wife he has married.[w]

6Do not take a pair of millstones—not even the upper one—as security for a debt, because that would be taking a man's livelihood as security.[x]

7If a man is caught kidnapping one of his brother Israelites and treats him as a slave or sells him, the kidnapper must die.[y] You must purge the evil from among you.[z]

8In cases of leprous[j] diseases be very careful to do exactly as the priests, who are Levites,[a] instruct you. You must follow carefully what I have commanded them.[b] 9Remember what the LORD your God did to Miriam along the way after you came out of Egypt.[c]

10When you make a loan of any kind to your neighbor, do not go into his house to get what he is offering as a pledge.[d] 11Stay outside and let the man to whom you are making the loan bring the pledge out to you. 12If the man is poor, do not go to sleep with his pledge[e] in your possession. 13Return his cloak to him by sunset[f] so that he may sleep in it.[g] Then he will thank you, and it will be regarded as a righteous act in the sight of the LORD your God.[h]

14Do not take advantage of a hired man who is poor and needy, whether he is a brother Israelite or an alien living in one of your towns.[i] 15Pay him his wages each day before sunset, because he is poor[j] and is counting on it.[k] Otherwise he may cry to the LORD against you, and you will be guilty of sin.[l]

16Fathers shall not be put to death for their children, nor children put to death for their fathers; each is to die for his own sin.[m]

17Do not deprive the alien or the fatherless[n] of justice,[o] or take the cloak of the widow as a pledge. 18Remember that you were slaves in Egypt[p] and the LORD your God redeemed you from there. That is why I command you to do this.

19When you are harvesting in your field and you overlook a sheaf, do not go back

23:18 lS Ge 19:5; S Lev 20:13; Rev 22:15
23:19 mS Lev 25:35-37, 36; Ne 5:2-7
23:20 nS Ge 31:15; S Dt 15:3 oDt 15:10
23:21 pS Nu 6:21; Jdg 11:35; Ps 15:4 qNu 30:1-2; Job 22:27; Ps 61:8; 65:1; 76:11; Ecc 5:4-5; Isa 19:21; S Mt 5:33; Ac 5:3
23:22 rAc 5:4
23:25 sMt 12:1; Mk 2:23; Lk 6:1
24:1 tDt 22:13 uver 3; 2Ki 17:6; Isa 50:1; Jer 3:8; Mal 2:16; Mt 1:19; 5:31*; 19:7-9; Mk 10:4-5
24:4 vJer 3:1
24:5 wS Dt 20:7
24:6 xS Ex 22:22
24:7 yS Ex 21:16 z1Co 5:13*
24:8 aS Dt 17:9 bLev 13:1-46; S 14:2
24:9 cS Nu 12:10
24:10 dEx 22:25-27
24:12 eS Ex 22:26
24:13 fEx 22:26 gS Ex 22:27 hDt 6:25; Ps 106:31; Da 4:27
24:14 iLev 19:13; 25:35-43; Dt 15:12-18; Job 24:4; Pr 14:31; 19:17; Am 4:1; 1Ti 5:18
24:15 jS Lev 25:35 kS Lev 19:13; Mt 20:8 lS Ex 22:23; S Job 12:19; Jas 5:4
24:16 mS Nu 26:11; Jer 31:29-30
24:17 nEx 22:22; Job 6:27; 24:9; 29:12; Ps 10:18; 82:3; Pr 23:10; Eze 22:7 oS Ex 22:21; S 23:2; S Dt 10:18
24:18 pS Dt 15:15

18 The Hebrew word was used for various diseases affecting the skin—not necessarily leprosy.

23:19 interest. See notes on Ex 22:25-27; Lev 25:36.
23:20 charge a foreigner. A foreign businessman would come into Israel for financial advantage and so would be subject to paying interest.
23:21-23 See notes on Nu 30; see also Ecc 5:4-6.
24:1-4 In the books of Moses divorce was permitted and regulated (see Lev 21:7,14; 22:13; Nu 30:9). Jesus conditioned the law of 24:1 in the Sermon on the Mount (Mt 5:31-32) and cited the higher law of creation (Mt 19:3-9).
24:5 happiness. Marital bliss was held in high regard.
24:6 millstones. Used for grinding grain for flour and daily food (see note on Jdg 9:53).
24:7 as a slave. Cf. 23:15. You must purge the evil from among you. See note on 13:5.
24:8 leprous diseases. See NIV text note; see also note on Lev 13:2.
24:9,18,22 Remember. See note on 4:10.
24:10-13 See note on Ex 22:26-27.
24:16 each is to die for his own sin. See Eze 18:4 and note.
24:17-18 When the Israelites were in trouble, the Lord helped them. Therefore they were not to take advantage of others in difficulty.
24:19-21 See note on Lev 19:9-10.

to get it. *q* Leave it for the alien, *r* the fatherless and the widow, *s* so that the LORD your God may bless *t* you in all the work of your hands. ²⁰When you beat the olives from your trees, do not go over the branches a second time. *u* Leave what remains for the alien, the fatherless and the widow. ²¹When you harvest the grapes in your vineyard, do not go over the vines again. Leave what remains for the alien, the fatherless and the widow. ²²Remember that you were slaves in Egypt. That is why I command you to do this. *v*

25 When men have a dispute, they are to take it to court and the judges *w* will decide the case, *x* acquitting *y* the innocent and condemning the guilty. *z* ²If the guilty man deserves to be beaten, *a* the judge shall make him lie down and have him flogged in his presence with the number of lashes his crime deserves, ³but he must not give him more than forty lashes. *b* If he is flogged more than that, your brother will be degraded in your eyes. *c*

⁴Do not muzzle an ox while it is treading out the grain. *d*

⁵If brothers are living together and one of them dies without a son, his widow must not marry outside the family. Her husband's brother shall take her and marry her and fulfill the duty of a brother-in-law to her. *e* ⁶The first son she bears shall carry on the name of the dead brother so that his name will not be blotted out from Israel. *f*

⁷However, if a man does not want to marry his brother's wife, *g* she shall go to the elders at the town gate *h* and say, "My husband's brother refuses to carry on his brother's name in Israel. He will not fulfill the duty of a brother-in-law to me." *i* ⁸Then the elders of his town shall summon him and talk to him. If he persists in saying, "I do not want to marry her," ⁹his brother's widow shall go up to him in the presence of the elders, take off one of his sandals, *j* spit in his face *k* and say, "This is what is done to the man who will not

build up his brother's family line." ¹⁰That man's line shall be known in Israel as The Family of the Unsandaled.

¹¹If two men are fighting and the wife of one of them comes to rescue her husband from his assailant, and she reaches out and seizes him by his private parts, ¹²you shall cut off her hand. Show her no pity. *l*

¹³Do not have two differing weights in your bag—one heavy, one light. *m* ¹⁴Do not have two differing measures in your house—one large, one small. ¹⁵You must have accurate and honest weights and measures, so that you may live long *n* in the land the LORD your God is giving you. ¹⁶For the LORD your God detests anyone who does these things, anyone who deals dishonestly. *o*

¹⁷Remember what the Amalekites *p* did to you along the way when you came out of Egypt. ¹⁸When you were weary and worn out, they met you on your journey and cut off all who were lagging behind; they had no fear of God. *q* ¹⁹When the LORD your God gives you rest *r* from all the enemies *s* around you in the land he is giving you to possess as an inheritance, you shall blot out the memory of Amalek *t* from under heaven. Do not forget!

Firstfruits and Tithes

26 When you have entered the land the LORD your God is giving you as an inheritance and have taken possession of it and settled in it, ²take some of the firstfruits *u* of all that you produce from the soil of the land the LORD your God is giving you and put them in a basket. Then go to the place the LORD your God will choose as a dwelling for his Name *v* ³and say to the priest in office at the time, "I declare today to the LORD your God that I have come to the land the LORD swore to our forefathers to give us." ⁴The priest shall take the basket from your hands and set it down in front of the altar of the LORD your God. ⁵Then you shall declare before the

Cross references (center column):

24:19
q S Lev 19:9
r Dt 10:19; 27:19;
Eze 47:22;
Zec 7:10; Mal 3:5
s ver 20; Dt 14:29
t S Dt 14:29;
Pr 19:17; 28:27;
Ecc 11:1
24:20 *u* Lev 19:10
24:22 *v* ver 18
25:1 *w* S Ex 21:6
x Dt 17:8-13;
19:17; Ac 23:3
y 1Ki 8:32
z S Ex 23:7;
Dt 1:16-17
25:2 *a* Pr 10:13;
19:29;
Lk 12:47-48
25:3 *b* Mt 27:26;
Jn 19:1;
2Co 11:24
c Jer 20:2
25:4
d S Nu 22:29;
1Co 9:9*;
1Ti 5:18*
25:5 *e* Ru 4:10,
13; Mt 22:24;
Mk 12:19;
Lk 20:28
25:6 *f* Ge 38:9;
Ru 4:5,10
25:7 *g* Ru 1:15
h S Ge 23:10
i Ru 4:1-2,5-6
25:9 *j* Jos 24:22;
Ru 4:7-8,11
k Nu 12:14;
Job 17:6; 30:10;
Isa 50:6

25:12 *l* S Dt 7:2
25:13 *m* Pr 11:1;
20:23; Mic 6:11
25:15
n S Ex 20:12
25:16 *o* Pr 11:1
25:17
p S Ge 36:12
25:18 *q* Ps 36:1;
Ro 3:18
25:19
r S Ex 33:14;
Heb 3:18-19
s Est 9:16
t S Ge 36:12
26:2 *u* S Ex 22:29
v S Ex 20:24;
S Dt 12:5

25:3 *not . . . more than forty lashes.* Beating could subject the culprit to abuse, so the law kept the punishment from becoming inhumane. Cf. Paul's experience (2Co 11:24).
25:4 Applied to ministers of Christ in 1Co 9:9–10; 1Ti 5:17–18. *treading out the grain.* See notes on Ge 50:10; Ru 1:22.
25:5–6 The continuity of each family and the decentralized control of land through family ownership were basic to the Mosaic economy (see note on Ge 38:8).
25:7 *if a man does not want to marry his brother's wife.* See vv. 8–10; note the experiences, with some variations, described in Ge 38:8–10; Ru 4:1–12. *elders at the town gate.* See 22:15; see also notes on Ge 19:1; Ru 4:1.
25:11–12 Cf. Ex 21:22–25.

25:13–16 See note on Lev 19:35.
25:14 *measures.* Of quantity.
25:17 *Remember.* See note on 4:10. *Amalekites.* See Ex 17:8–16; Nu 14:45.
25:18 *fear of God.* See note on Ge 20:11.
25:19 *rest.* See note on 3:20.
26:1 *inheritance.* See note on Ex 32:13.
26:2 *firstfruits.* The offering described here occurred only once and must not be confused with the annual offerings of firstfruits (see 18:4 and note). *the place the LORD . . . will choose as a dwelling for his Name.* See note on 12:5.
26:5 *wandering Aramean.* A reference to Jacob, who had wandered from southern Canaan to Haran and back (Ge 27–35) and who later migrated to Egypt (see Ge 46:3–7).

LORD your God: "My father was a wandering[w] Aramean,[x] and he went down into Egypt with a few people[y] and lived there and became a great nation,[z] powerful and numerous. 6But the Egyptians mistreated us and made us suffer,[a] putting us to hard labor.[b] 7Then we cried out to the LORD, the God of our fathers, and the LORD heard our voice[c] and saw[d] our misery,[e] toil and oppression.[f] 8So the LORD brought us out of Egypt[g] with a mighty hand and an outstretched arm,[h] with great terror and with miraculous signs and wonders.[i] 9He brought us to this place and gave us this land, a land flowing with milk and honey;[j] 10and now I bring the firstfruits of the soil that you, O LORD, have given me.[k]" Place the basket before the LORD your God and bow down before him. 11And you and the Levites[l] and the aliens among you shall rejoice[m] in all the good things the LORD your God has given to you and your household.

12When you have finished setting aside a tenth[n] of all your produce in the third year, the year of the tithe,[o] you shall give it to the Levite, the alien, the fatherless and the widow, so that they may eat in your towns and be satisfied. 13Then say to the LORD your God: "I have removed from my house the sacred portion and have given it to the Levite, the alien, the fatherless and the widow, according to all you commanded. I have not turned aside from your commands nor have I forgotten any of them.[p] 14I have not eaten any of the sacred portion while I was in mourning, nor have I removed any of it while I was unclean,[q] nor have I offered any of it to the dead. I have obeyed the LORD my God; I have done everything you commanded me. 15Look down from heaven,[r] your holy dwelling place, and bless[s] your people Israel and the land you have given us as you promised on oath to our forefathers, a land flowing with milk and honey."

Follow the LORD's Commands

16The LORD your God commands you

this day to follow these decrees and laws; carefully observe them with all your heart and with all your soul.[t] 17You have declared this day that the LORD is your God and that you will walk in his ways, that you will keep his decrees, commands and laws, and that you will obey him.[u] 18And the LORD has declared this day that you are his people, his treasured possession[v] as he promised, and that you are to keep all his commands. 19He has declared that he will set you in praise,[w] fame and honor high above all the nations[x] he has made and that you will be a people holy[y] to the LORD your God, as he promised.

The Altar on Mount Ebal

27 Moses and the elders of Israel commanded the people: "Keep all these commands[z] that I give you today. 2When you have crossed the Jordan[a] into the land the LORD your God is giving you, set up some large stones[b] and coat them with plaster.[c] 3Write on them all the words of this law when you have crossed over to enter the land the LORD your God is giving you, a land flowing with milk and honey,[d] just as the LORD, the God of your fathers, promised you. 4And when you have crossed the Jordan, set up these stones on Mount Ebal,[e] as I command you today, and coat them with plaster. 5Build there an altar[f] to the LORD your God, an altar of stones. Do not use any iron tool[g] upon them. 6Build the altar of the LORD your God with fieldstones and offer burnt offerings on it to the LORD your God. 7Sacrifice fellowship offerings[k][h] there, eating them and rejoicing[i] in the presence of the LORD your God.[j] 8And you shall write very clearly all the words of this law on these stones[k] you have set up."[l]

Curses From Mount Ebal

9Then Moses and the priests, who are Levites,[m] said to all Israel, "Be silent, O Israel, and listen! You have now become

Cross references (center column)

26:5 [w]S Ge 20:13
[x]S Ge 25:20
[y]S Ge 34:30;
43:14 [z]S Ge 12:2
26:6 [a]S Nu 20:15
[b]S Ex 1:13
26:7 [c]S Ge 21:17
[d]Ex 3:9;
2Ki 13:4; 14:26
[e]S Ge 16:11
[f]Ps 42:9; 44:24;
72:14
26:8 [g]S Nu 20:16
[h]S Ex 3:20
[i]S Dt 4:34;
34:11-12
26:9 [j]S Ex 3:8
26:10 [k]S Dt 8:18
26:11 [l]Dt 12:12
[m]S Dt 16:11
26:12
[n]S Ge 14:20
[o]S Nu 18:24;
Dt 14:28-29;
Heb 7:5,9
26:13
[p]Ps 119:141,153,
176
26:14 [q]Lev 7:20;
Hos 9:4
26:15 [r]Ps 68:5;
80:14; 102:19;
Isa 63:15;
Zec 2:13
[s]S Ex 39:43

26:16 [t]Dt 4:29
26:17 [u]Ex 19:8;
Ps 48:14
26:18 [v]Ex 6:7;
Dt 7:6
26:19 [w]Isa 62:7;
Zep 3:20
[x]Dt 4:7-8; 28:1,
13,44; 1Ch 14:2;
Ps 148:14;
Isa 40:11
[y]S Dt 7:6
27:1 [z]Ps 78:7
27:2 [a]Jos 4:1
[b]Ex 24:4;
Jos 24:26;
1Sa 7:12
[c]Jos 8:31
27:3 [d]S Ex 3:8
27:4 [e]S Dt 11:29
27:5 [f]S Ex 20:24
[g]Ex 20:25
27:7 [h]S Ex 32:6
[i]S Dt 16:11
[j]Jos 8:31
27:8 [k]Isa 8:1;
30:8; Hab 2:2
[l]Jos 8:32
27:9 [m]S Dt 17:9

[k]7 Traditionally *peace offerings*

He also married two Aramean women (see Ge 28:5; 29:16, 28). *with a few people . . . became a great nation.* See Ex 1:5; 1:7 and note.
26:11 *rejoice.* See note on 12:12.
26:12 See note on 14:22–29.
26:16 *with all your heart . . . soul.* See note on 4:29.
26:17 The terminology is that of a covenant or treaty, involving a renewal of Israel's vow that the Lord was God and that they would obey him (see note on Ex 19:8).
26:18 *treasured possession.* See note on Ex 19:5.
27:2–8 Setting up stones inscribed with messages to be remembered was a common practice in the ancient Near

East.
27:2,4 *coat them with plaster.* So that the writing inscribed on them would stand out clearly (see v. 8).
27:3,8 *all the words of this law.* The stipulations (see note on Ex 20:1) of the covenant that Moses' reaffirmation contained.
27:5 *Build . . . an altar of stones.* Different from the altars of the tabernacle, both in form and in use (see note on Ex 20:25).
27:9 *You have now become the people of the LORD.* The language of covenant renewal.

the people of the LORD your God.[n] 10Obey the LORD your God and follow his commands and decrees that I give you today."

11On the same day Moses commanded the people:

12When you have crossed the Jordan, these tribes shall stand on Mount Gerizim[o] to bless the people: Simeon, Levi, Judah, Issachar,[p] Joseph and Benjamin.[q] 13And these tribes shall stand on Mount Ebal[r] to pronounce curses: Reuben, Gad, Asher, Zebulun, Dan and Naphtali.

14The Levites shall recite to all the people of Israel in a loud voice:

15"Cursed is the man who carves an image or casts an idol[s]—a thing detestable[t] to the LORD, the work of the craftsman's hands—and sets it up in secret."

Then all the people shall say, "Amen!"[u]

16"Cursed is the man who dishonors his father or his mother."[v]

Then all the people shall say, "Amen!"

17"Cursed is the man who moves his neighbor's boundary stone."[w]

Then all the people shall say, "Amen!"

18"Cursed is the man who leads the blind astray on the road."[x]

Then all the people shall say, "Amen!"

19"Cursed is the man who withholds justice from the alien,[y] the fatherless or the widow."[z]

Then all the people shall say, "Amen!"

20"Cursed is the man who sleeps with his father's wife, for he dishonors his father's bed."[a]

Then all the people shall say, "Amen!"

21"Cursed is the man who has sexual relations with any animal."[b]

Then all the people shall say, "Amen!"

22"Cursed is the man who sleeps with his sister, the daughter of his father or the daughter of his mother."[c]

Then all the people shall say, "Amen!"

23"Cursed is the man who sleeps with his mother-in-law."[d]

Then all the people shall say, "Amen!"

24"Cursed is the man who kills[e] his neighbor secretly."[f]

Then all the people shall say, "Amen!"

25"Cursed is the man who accepts a bribe to kill an innocent person."[g]

Then all the people shall say, "Amen!"

26"Cursed is the man who does not uphold the words of this law by carrying them out."[h]

Then all the people shall say, "Amen!"[i]

Blessings for Obedience

28 If you fully obey the LORD your God and carefully follow[j] all his commands[k] I give you today, the LORD your God will set you high above all the nations on earth.[l] 2All these blessings will come upon you[m] and accompany you if you obey the LORD your God:

3You will be blessed[n] in the city and blessed in the country.[o]

4The fruit of your womb will be blessed, and the crops of your land and the young of your livestock—the calves of your herds and the lambs of your flocks.[p]

5Your basket and your kneading trough will be blessed.

27:9 [n]Dt 26:18
27:12
27:12 [o]S Dt 11:29
[p]S Ge 30:18
[q]Jos 8:35
27:13
[r]S Dt 11:29
27:15 [s]S Ex 20:4
[t]1Ki 11:5,7;
2Ki 23:13;
Isa 44:19; 66:3
[u]Nu 5:22;
S 1Co 14:16
27:16
[v]S Ge 31:35;
S Ex 21:12;
S Dt 5:16
27:17
[w]S Dt 19:14
27:18
[x]S Lev 19:14
27:19
[y]S Ex 22:21;
S Dt 24:19
[z]S Ex 23:2;
S Dt 10:18
27:20
[a]S Ge 34:5;
S Lev 18:7

27:21
[b]S Ex 22:19
27:22
[c]S Lev 18:9
27:23
[d]S Lev 20:14
27:24 [e]S Ge 4:23
[f]Ex 21:12
27:25
[g]Ex 23:7-8;
S Lev 19:16
27:26
[h]S Lev 26:14;
Dt 28:15;
Ps 119:21;
Jer 11:3;
Gal 3:10*
[i]Jer 11:5
28:1 [j]S Dt 15:5
[k]S Lev 26:3
[l]S Nu 24:7;
S Dt 26:19
28:2 [m]Jer 32:24;
Zec 1:6
28:3 [n]Ps 144:15
[o]S Ge 39:5
28:4
[p]S Ge 49:25;
S Dt 8:18

27:12 *these tribes shall stand on Mount Gerizim.* All six were descendants of Jacob by Leah and Rachel (see Ge 35:23–24). See 11:30 and note. *to bless.* No blessings appear in vv. 15–26, which consist entirely of 12 curses (see 28:15–68). Blessings, however, are listed and described in 28:1–14.

27:13 *these tribes shall stand on Mount Ebal.* Reuben and Zebulun were descendants of Jacob by Leah; the rest were his descendants by the maidservants Zilpah and Bilhah (see Ge 35:23,25–26).

27:15 *carves an image . . . casts an idol.* In violation of the first and second commandments of the Decalogue (see note on Ex 20:1). See 4:28; 5:6–10; 31:29; Isa 40:19–20; 41:7; 44:9–20; 45:16; Jer 10:3–9; Hos 8:4–6; 13:2. *Amen!* Not simply approval but a solemn, formal assertion that the people accept and agree to the covenant and its curses and blessings (see vv. 16–26).

27:16 See 5:16; Ex 20:12 and note.
27:17 See note on 19:14.
27:19 See 24:17–18 and note.
27:20 Cf. 22:30; see Lev 18:8.
27:21 See Ex 22:19 and note; Lev 18:23; 20:15–16.
27:22 See Lev 18:9.
27:23 See Lev 18:8.
27:24–25 See 5:17; Ex 20:13; 21:12; Lev 24:17,21.
27:26 Quoted in Gal 3:10 to prove that mankind is under a curse because no one follows the law of God fully. *by carrying them out.* It is not enough to assert allegiance to the law; one must live according to its stipulations.
28:1–14 These blessings are the opposites of the curses in vv. 15–44 (compare especially vv. 3–6 with vv. 16–19).
28:5,17 *basket . . . kneading trough.* Used at home for storage and for the preparation of foods, particularly bread.

⁶You will be blessed when you come in and blessed when you go out. q

⁷The LORD will grant that the enemies r who rise up against you will be defeated before you. They will come at you from one direction but flee from you in seven. s

⁸The LORD will send a blessing on your barns and on everything you put your hand to. The LORD your God will bless t you in the land he is giving you.

⁹The LORD will establish you as his holy people, u as he promised you on oath, if you keep the commands v of the LORD your God and walk in his ways. ¹⁰Then all the peoples on earth will see that you are called by the name w of the LORD, and they will fear you. ¹¹The LORD will grant you abundant prosperity—in the fruit of your womb, the young of your livestock x and the crops of your ground—in the land he swore to your forefathers to give you. y

¹²The LORD will open the heavens, the storehouse z of his bounty, a to send rain b on your land in season and to bless c all the work of your hands. You will lend to many nations but will borrow from none. d ¹³The LORD will make you the head, not the tail. If you pay attention to the commands of the LORD your God that I give you this day and carefully follow e them, you will always be at the top, never at the bottom. f ¹⁴Do not turn aside from any of the commands I give you today, to the right or to the left, g following other gods and serving them.

Curses for Disobedience

¹⁵However, if you do not obey h the LORD your God and do not carefully follow all his commands and decrees I am giving you today, i all these curses will come upon you and overtake you: j

¹⁶You will be cursed in the city and cursed in the country. k

¹⁷Your basket and your kneading trough will be cursed. l

¹⁸The fruit of your womb will be cursed, and the crops of your land, and the calves of your herds and the lambs of your flocks. m

¹⁹You will be cursed when you

come in and cursed when you go out. n

²⁰The LORD will send on you curses, o confusion and rebuke p in everything you put your hand to, until you are destroyed and come to sudden ruin q because of the evil r you have done in forsaking him. ¹ ²¹The LORD will plague you with diseases until he has destroyed you from the land you are entering to possess. s ²²The LORD will strike you with wasting disease, t with fever and inflammation, with scorching heat and drought, u with blight v and mildew, which will plague w you until you perish. x ²³The sky over your head will be bronze, the ground beneath you iron. y ²⁴The LORD will turn the rain z of your country into dust and powder; it will come down from the skies until you are destroyed.

²⁵The LORD will cause you to be defeated a before your enemies. You will come at them from one direction but flee from them in seven, b and you will become a thing of horror c to all the kingdoms on earth. d ²⁶Your carcasses will be food for all the birds of the air e and the beasts of the earth, and there will be no one to frighten them away. f ²⁷The LORD will afflict you with the boils of Egypt g and with tumors, festering sores and the itch, from which you cannot be cured. ²⁸The LORD will afflict you with madness, blindness and confusion of mind. ²⁹At midday you will grope h about like a blind man in the dark. You will be unsuccessful in everything you do; day after day you will be oppressed and robbed, with no one to rescue i you.

³⁰You will be pledged to be married to a woman, but another will take her and ravish her. j You will build a house, but you will not live in it. k You will plant a vineyard, but you will not even begin to enjoy its fruit. l ³¹Your ox will be slaughtered before your eyes, but you will eat none of it. Your donkey will be forcibly taken from

---

28:6 qPs 121:8
28:7 rAch 6:34
sS Lev 26:8,17
28:8 tDt 15:4
28:9 uS Ex 19:6
vS Lev 26:3
28:10
wS Nu 6:27;
1Ki 8:43;
Jer 25:29;
Da 9:18
28:11
xS Ge 30:27 yver
4; Dt 30:9
28:12
zJob 38:22;
Ps 135:7;
Jer 10:13; 51:16
aPs 65:11; 68:10;
Jer 31:12
bS Lev 26:4;
1Ki 8:35-36;
18:1; Ps 104:13;
Isa 5:6; 30:23;
32:20 cIsa 61:9;
65:23;
Jer 32:38-41;
Mal 3:12 dver 44;
S Lev 25:19;
S Dt 15:3,6;
Eze 34:26
28:13 eJer 11:6
fS Dt 26:19
28:14
gS Dt 5:32;
Jos 1:7
28:15 h1Ki 9:6;
2Ch 7:19
iS Dt 27:26
jDt 29:27;
Jos 23:15;
2Ch 12:5;
Da 9:11; Mal 2:2
28:16 kver 3
28:17 lver 5
28:18 mver 4

28:19 nver 6
28:20 over 8,15;
Lev 26:16;
Jer 42:18;
Mal 2:2; 3:9; 4:6
pPs 39:11; 76:6;
80:16; Isa 17:13;
51:20; 54:9;
66:15; Eze 5:15
qDt 4:26
rS Ex 32:22
28:21
sLev 26:25;
Nu 14:12;
Jer 24:10;
Am 4:10
28:22 tver 48;
Dt 32:24
uLev 26:16;
2Ki 8:1;
Job 12:15;
Ps 105:16;
Jer 14:1;
Hag 1:11; Mal 3:9
vHag 2:17
wS Lev 26:25
xDt 4:26; Am 4:9
28:23
yS Lev 26:19
28:24
zLev 26:19;
Dt 11:17;
1Ki 8:35; 17:1;
Isa 5:6; Jer 14:1;
Hag 1:10
28:25 a1Sa 4:10;
Ps 78:62
bS Lev 26:17 cver

37 dAch 29:8; 30:7; Jer 15:4; 24:9; 26:6; 29:18; 44:12;
Eze 23:46 28:26 eS Ge 40:19 fPs 79:2; Isa 18:6; Jer 7:33;
12:9; 15:2; 16:4; 19:7; 34:20 28:27 gDt 7:15 28:29
hGe 19:11; Ex 10:21; Job 5:14; 12:25; 24:13; 38:15;
Isa 59:10 iJdg 3:9; 2Ki 13:5; Est 4:14; Isa 19:20; 43:11;
Hos 13:4; Ob 1:21 28:30 jJob 31:10 kIsa 65:22; Am 5:11
lJer 12:13

l 20 Hebrew me

28:7 For the reverse see v. 25.
28:12 the heavens, the storehouse. For the heavens as the storehouse of rain, snow, hail and wind see Job 38:22; Ps 135:7; Jer 10:13; 51:16. You will lend. For the opposite see v. 44; see also note on 15:6.
28:13 the head, not the tail. For the reverse see v. 44.

28:23 sky . . . bronze . . . ground . . . iron. No rain would pierce the sky or penetrate the ground.
28:25 For the reverse see v. 7.
28:27 boils of Egypt. See note on Ex 9:9.
28:30 See 20:5-7.

you and will not be returned. Your sheep will be given to your enemies, and no one will rescue them. ³²Your sons and daughters will be given to another nation,^m and you will wear out your eyes watching for them day after day, powerless to lift a hand. ³³A people that you do not know will eat what your land and labor produce, and you will have nothing but cruel oppressionⁿ all your days.^o ³⁴The sights you see will drive you mad.^p ³⁵The LORD will afflict your knees and legs with painful boils^q that cannot be cured, spreading from the soles of your feet to the top of your head.^r

³⁶The LORD will drive you and the king^s you set over you to a nation unknown to you or your fathers.^t There you will worship other gods, gods of wood and stone.^u ³⁷You will become a thing of horror^v and an object of scorn^w and ridicule^x to all the nations where the LORD will drive you.^y

³⁸You will sow much seed in the field but you will harvest little,^z because locusts^a will devour^b it. ³⁹You will plant vineyards and cultivate them but you will not drink the wine^c or gather the grapes, because worms will eat^d them.^e ⁴⁰You will have olive trees throughout your country but you will not use the oil, because the olives will drop off.^f ⁴¹You will have sons and daughters but you will not keep them, because they will go into captivity.^g ⁴²Swarms of locusts^h will take over all your trees and the crops of your land.

⁴³The alien who lives among you will rise above you higher and higher, but you will sink lower and lower.ⁱ ⁴⁴He will lend to you, but you will not lend to him.^j He will be the head, but you will be the tail.^k

⁴⁵All these curses will come upon you. They will pursue you and overtake you^l until you are destroyed,^m because you did not obey the LORD your God and observe the commands and decrees he gave you. ⁴⁶They will be a sign and a wonder to you and your descendants forever.ⁿ ⁴⁷Because you did not serve^o the LORD your God joyfully and gladly^p in the time of prosperity, ⁴⁸therefore in hunger and thirst,^q in

nakedness and dire poverty, you will serve the enemies the LORD sends against you. He will put an iron yoke^r on your neck^s until he has destroyed you.

⁴⁹The LORD will bring a nation against you^t from far away, from the ends of the earth,^u like an eagle^v swooping down, a nation whose language you will not understand,^w ⁵⁰a fierce-looking nation without respect for the old^x or pity for the young. ⁵¹They will devour the young of your livestock and the crops of your land until you are destroyed. They will leave you no grain, new wine^y or oil,^z nor any calves of your herds or lambs of your flocks until you are ruined.^a ⁵²They will lay siege^b to all the cities throughout your land until the high fortified walls in which you trust fall down. They will besiege all the cities throughout the land the LORD your God is giving you.^c

⁵³Because of the suffering that your enemy will inflict on you during the siege, you will eat the fruit of the womb, the flesh of the sons and daughters the LORD your God has given you.^d ⁵⁴Even the most gentle and sensitive man among you will have no compassion on his own brother or the wife he loves or his surviving children, ⁵⁵and he will not give to one of them any of the flesh of his children that he is eating. It will be all he has left because of the suffering your enemy will inflict on you during the siege of all your cities.^e ⁵⁶The most gentle and sensitive^f woman among you—so sensitive and gentle that she would not venture to touch the ground with the sole of her foot—will begrudge the husband she loves and her own son or daughter^g ⁵⁷the afterbirth from her womb and the children she bears. For she intends to eat them^h secretly during the siege and in the distress that your enemy will inflict on you in your cities.

⁵⁸If you do not carefully follow all the words of this law,ⁱ which are written in

28:32 ^mver 41
28:33 ⁿJer 6:6;
22:17
^oJer 5:15-17;
Eze 25:4
28:34 ^pver 67
28:35 ^qDt 7:15;
Rev 16:2 ^rJob 2:7;
7:5; 13:28;
30:17,30; Isa 1:6
28:36 ^s1Sa 12:25
^tS Dt 4:27;
2Ki 24:14; 25:7,
11; 2Ch 33:11;
36:21; Ezr 5:12;
Jer 15:14; 16:13;
27:20; 39:1-9;
52:28; La 1:3
^uS Dt 4:28
28:37 ^vver 25;
Jer 42:18;
Eze 5:15
^wPs 22:7; 39:8;
44:13; 64:8;
Jer 18:16; 48:27;
Mic 6:16
^x2Ch 7:20;
Ezr 9:7; Jer 44:8
^y1Ki 9:7;
Ps 44:14;
Jer 19:8; 24:9;
25:9,18; 29:18;
La 2:15
28:38
^zLev 26:20;
Ps 129:7;
Isa 5:10;
Jer 12:13;
Hos 8:7;
Mic 6:15;
Hag 1:6,9; 2:16
^aS Ex 10:4
^bS Ex 10:15
28:39
^cS Lev 10:9
^dJoel 1:4; 2:25;
Mal 3:11
^eIsa 5:10;
17:10-11;
Zep 1:13
28:40 ^fJer 11:16;
Mic 6:15
28:41 ^gver 32
28:42 ^hver 38;
Jdg 6:5; 7:12;
Jer 46:23
28:43 ⁱver 13
28:44 ^jS ver 12
^kS Dt 26:19
28:45 ^lS Ex 15:9
^mver 15;
Dt 4:25-26
28:46
ⁿS Nu 16:38;
Ps 71:7; Isa 8:18;
20:3; Eze 5:15;
Zec 3:8
28:47
^oS Dt 10:12
^pS Lev 23:40;
Ne 9:35
28:48 ^qJer 14:3;
La 4:4

^rJer 28:13-14;
La 1:14 ^sGe 49:8
28:49
^tS Lev 26:44
^uIsa 5:26-30,26;
7:18-20; 39:3;
Jer 4:16; 5:15;
6:22; 25:32; 31:8; Hab 1:6 ^v2Sa 1:23; Jer 4:13; 48:40;
49:22; La 4:19; Eze 17:3; Hos 8:1 ^wS Ge 11:7; 1Co 14:21*
28:50 ^xIsa 47:6 **28:51** ^yPs 4:7; Isa 36:17; Hag 1:11
^zS Nu 18:12 ^aver 33; Jdg 6:4 **28:52** ^b2Ki 6:24 ^cJer 10:18;
Eze 6:10; Zep 1:14-16,17 **28:53** ^dver 57; Lev 26:29;
2Ki 6:28-29; La 2:20 **28:55** ^e2Ki 6:29 **28:56** ^fIsa 47:1
^gLa 4:10 **28:57** ^hS ver 53 **28:58** ⁱDt 31:24

28:35 See note on Ex 9:11.
28:44 See notes on vv. 12–13.
28:49 *ends of the earth.* An indefinite figurative expression meaning "far away"—anywhere from the horizon to the perimeter of the then-known world. *eagle swooping down.* Symbolic of the speed and power of the Assyrians (see Hos 8:1) and Babylonians (see Jer 48:40; 49:22). *whose language you will not understand.* Though related to Hebrew, the languages of Assyria and Babylonia were not understood

by the average Israelite (see Isa 28:11; 33:19 and note; 1Co 14:21).
28:53 *suffering that your enemy will inflict on you during the siege.* See vv. 55, 57. The repetition of the clause emphasizes the distress that the Israelites would suffer if they refused to obey the Lord. *you will eat . . . sons and daughters.* For the actualizing of this curse see 2Ki 6:24–29; La 2:20; 4:10.
28:58 *words of this law.* See note on 31:24. *this glorious*

this book, and do not revere[j] this glorious and awesome name[k]—the LORD your God— [59]the LORD will send fearful plagues on you and your descendants, harsh and prolonged disasters, and severe and lingering illnesses. [60]He will bring upon you all the diseases of Egypt[l] that you dreaded, and they will cling to you. [61]The LORD will also bring on you every kind of sickness and disaster not recorded in this Book of the Law,[m] until you are destroyed.[n] [62]You who were as numerous as the stars in the sky[o] will be left but few[p] in number, because you did not obey the LORD your God. [63]Just as it pleased[q] the LORD to make you prosper and increase in number, so it will please[r] him to ruin and destroy you.[s] You will be uprooted[t] from the land you are entering to possess.

[64]Then the LORD will scatter[u] you among all nations,[v] from one end of the earth to the other.[w] There you will worship other gods—gods of wood and stone, which neither you nor your fathers have known.[x] [65]Among those nations you will find no repose, no resting place[y] for the sole of your foot. There the LORD will give you an anxious mind, eyes[z] weary with longing, and a despairing heart.[a] [66]You will live in a constant suspense, filled with dread both night and day, never sure of your life. [67]In the morning you will say, "If only it were evening!" and in the evening, "If only it were morning!"—because of the terror that will fill your hearts and the sights that your eyes will see.[b] [68]The LORD will send you back in ships to Egypt on a journey I said you should never make again.[c] There you will offer yourselves for sale to your enemies as male and female slaves, but no one will buy you.

Renewal of the Covenant

29 These are the terms of the covenant the LORD commanded Moses to make with the Israelites in Moab,[d] in addition to the covenant he had made with them at Horeb.[e]

[2]Moses summoned all the Israelites and said to them:

Your eyes have seen all that the LORD did in Egypt to Pharaoh, to all his officials and to all his land.[f] [3]With your own eyes you saw those great trials, those miraculous signs and great wonders.[g] [4]But to this day the LORD has not given you a mind that understands or eyes that see or ears that hear.[h] [5]During the forty years that I led[i] you through the desert, your clothes did not wear out, nor did the sandals on your feet.[j] [6]You ate no bread and drank no wine or other fermented drink.[k] I did this so that you might know that I am the LORD your God.[l]

[7]When you reached this place, Sihon[m] king of Heshbon[n] and Og king of Bashan came out to fight against us, but we defeated them.[o] [8]We took their land and gave it as an inheritance[p] to the Reubenites, the Gadites and the half-tribe of Manasseh.[q]

[9]Carefully follow[r] the terms of this covenant,[s] so that you may prosper in everything you do.[t] [10]All of you are standing today in the presence of the LORD your God—your leaders and chief men, your elders and officials, and all the other men of Israel, [11]together with your children and your wives, and the aliens living in your camps who chop your wood and carry your water.[u] [12]You are standing here in order to enter into a covenant with the LORD your God, a covenant the LORD is making with you this day and sealing with an oath, [13]to confirm you this day as his people,[v] that he may be your God[w] as he promised you and as he swore to your fa-

---

28:58 /Ps 96:4; Jer 5:22; Mal 1:14; 2:5; 3:5,16; 4:2 *kS Ex 3:15; S Jos 7:9
28:60 /Ex 15:26
28:61 *mDt 29:21; 30:10; 31:26; Jos 1:8; 8:34; 23:6; 24:26; 2Ki 14:6; 22:8; 2Ch 17:9; 25:4; Ne 8:1,18; Mal 4:4 *nDt 4:25-26
28:62 *oS Ge 22:17; Dt 4:27; 10:22 *pS Lev 26:22
28:63 *qDt 30:9; Isa 62:5; 65:19; Jer 32:41; Zep 3:17 *rPr 1:26 *sS Ge 6:7 *tPs 52:5; Jer 12:14; 31:28; 45:4
28:64 *uS Dt 4:27; Ezr 9:7; Isa 6:12; Jer 32:23; 43:11; 52:27 *vNe 1:8; Ps 44:11; Jer 13:24; 18:17; 22:22 *wS Dt 4:32; S Jer 8:19 *xDt 11:28; 32:17
28:65 *yLa 1:3 *zJob 11:20 *aLev 26:16,36; Hos 9:17
28:67 *bver 34
28:68 *cS Ex 13:14
29:1 *dS Lev 7:38 *eS Ex 3:1
29:2 /Ex 19:4
29:3 *gS Dt 4:34
29:4 *hIsa 6:10; 32:3; 48:8; Jer 5:21; Eze 12:2; S Mt 13:15; Ro 11:8*; Eph 4:18
29:5 /S Dt 8:2 /S Dt 8:4
29:6 *kS Lev 10:9 /Dt 8:3
29:7 *mS Nu 21:26 *nS Nu 21:25 *oNu 21:21-24, 33-35; Dt 2:26-3:11
29:8 *pPs 78:55; 135:12; 136:22 *qNu 32:33;
Dt 3:12-13 **29:9** *rS Dt 4:6; S Jos 1:7 *sEx 19:5; Ps 25:10; 103:18 *tJos 1:8; 2Ch 31:21 **29:11** *uJos 9:21,23,27; 1Ch 20:3 **29:13** *vS Ge 6:18; S Ex 19:6 *wS Ge 17:7

---

and awesome name—the LORD. See note and NIV text note on Ex 3:15. One of the oddities of history and revelation is the loss of the proper pronunciation of the Hebrew word *YHWH,* the most intimate and personal name of God in the OT (see note on Ge 2:4). "Jehovah" is a spelling that developed from combining the consonants of the name with the vowels of a word for "Lord" (*Adonai*). "Yahweh" is probably the original pronunciation. The name eventually ceased to be pronounced because later Jews thought it too holy to be uttered and feared violating Ex 20:7 and Lev 24:16. It is translated "LORD" in this version (see Preface to the NIV).
28:60 *diseases of Egypt.* Those brought on the Egyptians during the plagues (see 7:15; Ex 15:26).
28:61 *Book of the Law.* See note on 31:24.
28:62 *as the stars in the sky.* See 1:10; see also notes on Ge 13:16; 15:5.

28:64 *will scatter you.* Experienced by Israel in the Assyrian (722-721 B.C.) and Babylonian (586 B.C.) exiles (see 2Ki 17:6; 25:21).
28:68 *a journey I said you should never make again.* See 17:16; Ex 13:17; Nu 14:3-4.
29:1 See notes on 5:2-3.
29:2 *Your eyes have seen.* Only those who were less than 20 years old (Nu 14:29) when Israel followed the majority spy report at Kadesh Barnea and refused to enter Canaan would have actually experienced life in Egypt before the exodus. But Moses is speaking to the people as a nation and referring to the national experience (see note on 5:3).
29:4 Quoted in Ro 11:8 and applied to hardened Israel.
29:8 *gave it as an inheritance.* See 3:12-17.
29:9-15 A clear summary of the nature of covenant reaffirmation.

thers, Abraham, Isaac and Jacob. [14]I am making this covenant,[x] with its oath, not only with you [15]who are standing here with us today in the presence of the LORD our God but also with those who are not here today.[y]

[16]You yourselves know how we lived in Egypt and how we passed through the countries on the way here. [17]You saw among them their detestable images and idols of wood and stone, of silver and gold.[z] [18]Make sure there is no man or woman, clan or tribe among you today whose heart turns[a] away from the LORD our God to go and worship the gods of those nations; make sure there is no root among you that produces such bitter poison.[b]

[19]When such a person hears the words of this oath, he invokes a blessing[c] on himself and therefore thinks, "I will be safe, even though I persist in going my own way.' [d] This will bring disaster on the watered land as well as the dry.[m] [20]The LORD will never be willing to forgive[e] him; his wrath and zeal[f] will burn[g] against that man. All the curses written in this book will fall upon him, and the LORD will blot[h] out his name from under heaven. [21]The LORD will single him out from all the tribes of Israel for disaster,[i] according to all the curses of the covenant written in this Book of the Law.[j]

[22]Your children who follow you in later generations and foreigners who come from distant lands will see the calamities that have fallen on the land and the diseases with which the LORD has afflicted it.[k] [23]The whole land will be a burning waste[l] of salt[m] and sulfur—nothing planted, nothing sprouting, no vegetation growing on it. It will be like the destruction of Sodom and Gomorrah,[n] Admah and Zeboiim, which the LORD overthrew in fierce anger.[o] [24]All the nations will ask: "Why has the LORD done this to this land?[p] Why this fierce, burning anger?"

[25]And the answer will be: "It is because this people abandoned the covenant of the

LORD, the God of their fathers, the covenant he made with them when he brought them out of Egypt.[q] [26]They went off and worshiped other gods and bowed down to them, gods they did not know, gods he had not given them. [27]Therefore the LORD's anger burned against this land, so that he brought on it all the curses written in this book.[r] [28]In furious anger and in great wrath[s] the LORD uprooted[t] them from their land and thrust them into another land, as it is now."

[29]The secret things belong to the LORD our God,[u] but the things revealed belong to us and to our children forever, that we may follow all the words of this law.[v]

Prosperity After Turning to the LORD

30 When all these blessings and curses[w] I have set before you come upon you and you take them to heart wherever the LORD your God disperses you among the nations,[x] [2]and when you and your children return[y] to the LORD your God and obey him with all your heart[z] and with all your soul according to everything I command you today, [3]then the LORD your God will restore your fortunes[n][a] and have compassion[b] on you and gather[c] you again from all the nations where he scattered[d] you.[e] [4]Even if you have been banished to the most distant land under the heavens,[f] from there the LORD your God will gather[g] you and bring you back. [5]He will bring[i] you to the land that belonged to your fathers, and you will take possession of it. He will make you more prosperous and numerous[j] than your fathers. [6]The LORD your God will circumcise your hearts and the hearts of your descendants,[k] so that you may love[l] him with all your heart and with all your soul, and live. [7]The LORD your God will put all these curses[m] on your enemies who hate

---

29:14 [x]Ex 19:5; Isa 59:21; Jer 31:31; 32:40; 50:5; Eze 16:62; 37:26; Heb 8:7-8
29:15 [y]S Ge 6:18; Ac 2:39
29:17 [z]Ex 20:23; Dt 4:28
29:18 [a]S Dt 13:6 [b]S Dt 11:16; Heb 12:15
29:19 [c]Ps 72:17; Isa 65:16 [d]Ps 36:2
29:20 [e]S Ex 23:21 [f]Ex 34:14; Eze 23:25; Zep 1:18 [g]Ps 74:1; 79:5; 80:4; Eze 36:5 [h]2Ki 13:23; 14:27; Rev 3:5
29:21 [i]Dt 32:23; Eze 7:26 [j]S Dt 28:61
29:22 [k]Jer 19:8; 49:17; 50:13
29:23 [l]Isa 1:7; 6:11; 9:18; 64:10; Jer 12:11; 44:2,6; Mic 5:11 [m]S Ge 13:10; Eze 47:11 [n]S Ge 19:24,25; Zep 2:9; S Mt 10:15; Ro 9:29 [o]S Ge 14:8
29:24 [p]1Ki 9:8; 2Ch 36:19; Jer 16:10; 22:8-9; 52:13
29:25 [q]2Ki 17:23; 2Ch 36:21
29:27 [r]S Dt 28:15
29:28 [s]Ps 7:11 [t]1Ki 14:15; 2Ch 7:20; Ps 9:6; 52:5; Pr 2:22; Jer 12:14; 31:28; 42:10; Eze 19:12
29:29 [u]Ac 1:7 [v]Jn 5:39; Ac 17:11; 2Ti 3:16
30:1 [w]S Dt 11:26 [x]Lev 26:40-45; S Dt 4:32; 29:28
30:2 [y]S Dt 4:30 [z]Dt 4:29; Ps 119:2
30:3 [a]Ps 14:7; 53:6; 85:1; 126:4; Jer 30:18; 33:11; Eze 16:53; Joel 3:1; Zep 2:7 [b]Dt 13:17 [c]S Ge 48:21 [d]S Ge 11:4; Dt 4:27 [e]Isa 11:11; Jer 12:15; 16:15; 24:6; 29:14;
30:4 [f]Ps 19:6 [g]Isa 17:6; 24:13; 27:12; 40:11; 49:5; 56:8; Eze 20:34,41; 34:13 [h]Ne 1:8-9; Isa 11:12; 41:5; 42:10; 43:6; 48:20; 62:11; Jer 31:8,10; 50:2 30:5 [i]Jer 29:14 [j]S Dt 7:13 30:6 [k]S Dt 6:24; S 10:16 [l]Dt 6:5 30:7 [m]S Ge 12:3

[m]19 Or way, in order to add drunkenness to thirst."
[n]3 Or will bring you back from captivity

29:18 *root . . . that produces such bitter poison.* The poison of idolatry, involving the rejection of the Lord.
29:20 *The LORD will never be willing to forgive him.* Not to be taken as contradictory to 2Pe 3:9 ("not wanting anyone to perish"). Peter, too, says that those who deny the "sovereign Lord" bring "swift destruction on themselves" (2Pe 2:1). *this book.* See note on 31:24. *blot out his name.* See 9:14; Ex 32:32–33; Rev 3:5.
29:21 *Book of the Law.* See note on 31:24.
29:23 *destruction of Sodom.* See Ge 19:24–25; see also notes on Ge 10:19; 13:10.

29:27 *this book.* See note on 31:24.
29:28 *as it is now.* This would be said when Israel was in exile (see v. 25).
29:29 *secret things.* The hidden events of Israel's future relative to the blessings and curses; but the phrase can also have wider application. *things revealed.* Primarily the "words of this law."
30:2,6,10 *with all your heart . . . soul.* See note on 4:29.
30:3 *restore your fortunes.* See NIV text note.
30:6 *circumcise your hearts.* See note on Ge 17:10.
30:7 *curses on your enemies.* Fulfilling Ge 12:3.

and persecute you.[n] 8You will again obey the LORD and follow all his commands I am giving you today. 9Then the LORD your God will make you most prosperous in all the work of your hands and in the fruit of your womb, the young of your livestock and the crops of your land.[o] The LORD will again delight[p] in you and make you prosperous, just as he delighted in your fathers, 10if you obey the LORD your God and keep his commands and decrees that are written in this Book of the Law[q] and turn to the LORD your God with all your heart and with all your soul.[r]

The Offer of Life or Death

11Now what I am commanding you today is not too difficult for you or beyond your reach.[s] 12It is not up in heaven, so that you have to ask, "Who will ascend into heaven[t] to get it and proclaim it to us so we may obey it?"[u] 13Nor is it beyond the sea,[v] so that you have to ask, "Who will cross the sea to get it and proclaim it to us so we may obey it?"[w] 14No, the word is very near you; it is in your mouth and in your heart so you may obey it.[x]

15See, I set before you today life[y] and prosperity,[z] death[a] and destruction.[b] 16For I command you today to love[c] the LORD your God, to walk in his ways, and to keep his commands, decrees and laws; then you will live[d] and increase, and the LORD your God will bless you in the land you are entering to possess.

17But if your heart turns away and you are not obedient, and if you are drawn away to bow down to other gods and worship them, 18I declare to you this day that you will certainly be destroyed.[e] You will not live long in the land you are crossing the Jordan to enter and possess.

19This day I call heaven and earth as witnesses against you[f] that I have set be-

fore you life and death, blessings and curses.[g] Now choose life, so that you and your children may live 20and that you may love[h] the LORD your God, listen to his voice, and hold fast to him. For the LORD is your life,[i] and he will give[j] you many years in the land[k] he swore to give to your fathers, Abraham, Isaac and Jacob.

Joshua to Succeed Moses

31 Then Moses went out and spoke these words to all Israel: 2"I am now a hundred and twenty years old[l] and I am no longer able to lead you.[m] The LORD has said to me, 'You shall not cross the Jordan.'[n] 3The LORD your God himself will cross[o] over ahead of you.[p] He will destroy these nations[q] before you, and you will take possession of their land. Joshua also will cross[r] over ahead of you, as the LORD said. 4And the LORD will do to them what he did to Sihon and Og,[s] the kings of the Amorites, whom he destroyed along with their land. 5The LORD will deliver[t] them to you, and you must do to them all that I have commanded you. 6Be strong and courageous.[u] Do not be afraid or terrified[v] because of them, for the LORD your God goes with you;[w] he will never leave you[x] nor forsake[y] you."

7Then Moses summoned Joshua and said[z] to him in the presence of all Israel, "Be strong and courageous, for you must go with this people into the land that the LORD swore to their forefathers to give them,[a] and you must divide it among them as their inheritance. 8The LORD himself goes before you and will be with you;[b] he will never leave you nor forsake you.[c] Do not be afraid; do not be discouraged."

The Reading of the Law

9So Moses wrote[d] down this law and

Cross references (center column)

30:7 [n]Dt 7:15
30:9 [o]Jer 1:10; 24:6; 31:28; 32:41; 42:10; 45:4 [p]S Dt 28:63
30:10 [q]S Dt 28:61 [r]S Dt 4:29
30:11 [s]Ps 19:8; Isa 45:19,23; 63:1
30:12 [t]Pr 30:4 [u]Ro 10:6*
30:13 [v]Job 28:14 [w]Ro 10:7*
30:14 [x]S Dt 6:6; Ro 10:8*
30:15 [y]Pr 10:16; 11:19; 12:28; Jer 21:8 [z]Dt 28:11; Job 36:11; Ps 25:13; 106:5; Pr 3:1-2 [a]S Ge 2:17 [b]S Dt 11:26
30:16 [c]Dt 6:5 [d]ver 19; Dt 4:1; 32:47; Ne 9:29
30:18 [e]S Dt 8:19
30:19 [f]Dt 4:26
[g]S Dt 11:26
30:20 [h]Dt 6:5 [i]Dt 4:1; S 8:3; 32:47; Ps 27:1; Pr 3:22; S Jn 5:26; Ac 17:28 [j]Ge 12:7 [k]Ps 37:3
31:2 [l]S Ex 7:7 [m]Nu 27:17; 1Ki 3:7
31:3 [n]S Dt 3:23,26 [o]Nu 27:18 [p]S Dt 9:3 [q]S Dt 7:1 [r]S Dt 3:28
31:4 [s]S Nu 21:33
31:5 [t]S Dt 2:33
31:6 [u]ver 7,23; Jos 1:6,9,18; 10:25; 1Ch 22:13; 28:20; 2Ch 32:7 [v]Jer 1:8,17; Eze 2:6 [w]S Ge 28:15; S Dt 1:29; 20:4; S Mt 28:20 [x]Ps 56:9; 118:6 [y]S Dt 4:31; 1Sa 12:22; 1Ki 6:13; Ps 94:14; Isa 41:17; Heb 13:5*
31:7 [z]ver 23; Nu 27:23 [a]Jos 1:6
31:8 [b]S Ex 13:21 [c]S Ge 28:15;
S Dt 4:31 31:9 [d]S Ex 17:14

30:9 *your fathers.* The patriarchs (see v. 20).
30:10 *Book of the Law.* See note on 31:24.
30:12,14 *It is not up in heaven . . . the word is very near you.* Moses declares that understanding, believing and obeying the covenant were not beyond them. Paul applies this passage to the availability of the "word of faith" (Ro 10:6–10).
30:19 *I call heaven and earth as witnesses.* The typical ancient treaty outside the OT contained a list of gods who served as "witnesses" to its provisions. The covenant in Deuteronomy was "witnessed" by heaven and earth (see 31:28; 32:1; see also notes on Ps 50:1; Isa 1:2).
30:20 *hold fast.* See note on 10:20. *the LORD is your life.* When they chose the Lord, they chose life (v. 19). In 32:46–47 "all the words of this law" are said to be their life. The law, the Lord and life are bound together. "Life" in this context refers to all that makes life rich, full and produc-

tive—as God created it to be.
31:2 *no longer able to lead.* Not a reference to physical disability (see 34:7). The Lord did not allow Moses to lead the people into Canaan because of his sin (see 1:37; 3:23–27; 4:21–22; 32:48–52; Nu 20:2–13).
31:4 *what he did to Sihon and Og.* See 2:26–3:11.
31:6 *Be strong and courageous.* The Lord's exhortation, often through his servants, to the people of Israel (Jos 10:25), to Joshua (vv. 7,23; Jos 1:6–7,9,18), to Solomon (1Ch 22:13; 28:20) and to Hezekiah's military officers (2Ch 32:7). By trusting in the Lord and obeying him, his followers would be victorious in spite of great obstacles. *he will never leave you nor forsake you.* See v. 8; Jos 1:5; 1Ki 8:57; see also note on Ge 28:15.
31:9 *wrote down this law and gave it to the priests.* Ancient treaties specified that a copy of the treaty was to be placed before the gods at the religious centers of the nations

gave it to the priests, the sons of Levi, who carried[e] the ark of the covenant of the LORD, and to all the elders of Israel. [10]Then Moses commanded them: "At the end of every seven years, in the year for canceling debts,[f] during the Feast of Tabernacles,[g] [11]when all Israel comes to appear[h] before the LORD your God at the place he will choose,[i] you shall read this law[j] before them in their hearing. [12]Assemble the people—men, women and children, and the aliens living in your towns—so they can listen and learn[k] to fear[l] the LORD your God and follow carefully all the words of this law. [13]Their children,[m] who do not know this law, must hear it and learn to fear the LORD your God as long as you live in the land you are crossing the Jordan to possess."

Israel's Rebellion Predicted

[14]The LORD said to Moses, "Now the day of your death[n] is near. Call Joshua[o] and present yourselves at the Tent of Meeting, where I will commission him.[p]" So Moses and Joshua came and presented themselves at the Tent of Meeting. [q]

[15]Then the LORD appeared at the Tent in a pillar of cloud, and the cloud stood over the entrance to the Tent.[r] [16]And the LORD said to Moses: "You are going to rest with your fathers,[s] and these people will soon prostitute[t] themselves to the foreign gods of the land they are entering. They will forsake[u] me and break the covenant I made with them. [17]On that day I will become angry[v] with them and forsake[w] them; I will hide[x] my face[y] from them, and they will be destroyed. Many disasters[z] and difficulties will come upon them, and on that day they will ask, 'Have not these disasters come upon us because our God is not with us?'[a] [18]And I will certainly hide my face on that day because of all their wickedness in turning to other gods.

[19]"Now write[b] down for yourselves this song and teach it to the Israelites and have them sing it, so that it may be a witness[c] for me against them. [20]When I have

brought them into the land flowing with milk and honey, the land I promised on oath to their forefathers, [d] and when they eat their fill and thrive, they will turn to other gods[e] and worship them,[f] rejecting me and breaking my covenant.[g] [21]And when many disasters and difficulties come upon them,[h] this song will testify against them, because it will not be forgotten by their descendants. I know what they are disposed to do,[i] even before I bring them into the land I promised them on oath." [22]So Moses wrote[j] down this song that day and taught it to the Israelites.

[23]The LORD gave this command[k] to Joshua son of Nun: "Be strong and courageous,[l] for you will bring the Israelites into the land I promised them on oath, and I myself will be with you."

[24]After Moses finished writing[m] in a book the words of this law[n] from beginning to end, [25]he gave this command to the Levites who carried[o] the ark of the covenant of the LORD: [26]"Take this Book of the Law and place it beside the ark of the covenant of the LORD your God. There it will remain as a witness against you.[p] [27]For I know how rebellious[q] and stiff-necked[r] you are. If you have been rebellious against the LORD while I am still alive and with you, how much more will you rebel after I die! [28]Assemble before me all the elders of your tribes and all your officials, so that I can speak these words in their hearing and call heaven and earth to testify against them.[s] [29]For I know that after my death you are sure to become utterly corrupt[t] and to turn from the way I have commanded you. In days to come, disaster[u] will fall upon you because you will do evil in the sight of the LORD and provoke him to anger by what your hands have made."

The Song of Moses

[30]And Moses recited the words of this

Cross references (center column)

31:9 *e*ver 25; 1Ch 15:2
31:10 /S Dt 15:1 *g*S Ex 23:16; Dt 16:13
31:11 *h*S Dt 16:16 *i*Dt 12:5 /Jos 8:34-35; 2Ki 23:2; Ne 8:2
31:12 *k*Dt 4:10 *l*Hag 1:12; Mal 1:6; 3:5,16
31:13 *m*S Dt 11:2
31:14 *n*S Ge 25:8; S Nu 27:13 *o*Nu 27:23; Dt 34:9; Jos 1:1-9 *p*S Nu 27:19 *q*Ex 33:9-11
31:15 *r*S Ex 33:9
31:16 *s*S Ge 15:15 *t*S Ex 34:15; Dt 4:25-28; Jdg 2:12 *u*Jdg 10:6,13; 1Ki 9:9; 18:18; 19:10; Jer 2:13; 5:19; 19:4
31:17 *v*Dt 32:16; Jdg 2:14,20; 10:7; 2Ki 13:3; 22:13; Ps 106:29, 40; Jer 7:18; 21:5; 36:7 *w*Jdg 6:13; 2Ch 15:2; 24:20; Ezr 8:22; Ps 44:9; Isa 2:6 *x*Dt 32:20; Isa 1:15; 45:15; 53:3; 54:8 *y*Job 13:24; Ps 13:1; 27:9; 30:7; 104:29; Isa 50:6; Jer 33:5; Eze 39:29; Mic 3:4 *z*Jer 4:20; Eze 7:26 *a*Nu 14:42; Hos 9:12
31:19 *b*ver 22 *c*S Ge 31:50
31:20 *d*Dt 6:10-12 *e*Ps 4:2; 16:4; 40:4; Jer 13:25; Da 3:28; Am 2:4 /Dt 8:19; 11:16-17 *g*ver 16
31:21 *h*S Dt 4:30 *i*1Ch 28:9; Hos 5:3; Jn 2:24-25
31:22 /ver 19
31:23 *k*S ver 7 /Jos 1:6
31:24 *m*Dt 17:18; 2Ki 22:8 *n*Dt 28:58
31:25 *o*S ver 9
31:26 *p*ver 19
31:27 *q*S Ex 23:21
*r*S Dt 9:27 31:28 *s*Dt 4:26; 30:19; 32:1; Job 20:27; Isa 26:21 31:29 *t*S Dt 4:16; Rev 9:20 *u*1Ki 9:9; 22:23; 2Ki 22:16

---

involved. For Israel, that meant to place it in the ark of the covenant (see 33:9; see also notes on Ex 16:34; 31:18).
31:10 *every seven years.* See 15:4 and note; Ex 23:10-11; Lev 25:17; see also chart on "OT Feasts and Other Sacred Days," p. 176.
31:11 *place he will choose.* See note on 12:5. *read this law before them.* Reading the law to the Israelites (and teaching it to them) was one of the main duties of the priests (see 33:10; Mal 2:4-9).
31:14 *I will commission him.* See v. 23; cf. Nu 27:18-23.
31:19 *write down . . . this song and teach it.* See v. 22; 31:30-32:43.

31:23 *Be strong and courageous.* See note on v. 6.
31:24 *words of this law from beginning to end.* The book of Deuteronomy up to this place (see note on v. 9).
31:26 *place it beside the ark.* See note on v. 9.
31:27 *stiff-necked.* See 9:6,13; 10:16; see also note on Ex 32:9.
31:28 *heaven and earth to testify.* See note on 30:19.
31:29 *what your hands have made.* A reference to idols (see 4:28; 27:15 and note).
31:30—32:43 The song of Moses (see notes on Ex 15:1-18; Rev 15:3).

song from beginning to end in the hearing
of the whole assembly of Israel:

32 Listen,[v] O heavens,[w] and I will
speak;
  hear, O earth, the words of my
    mouth.[x]

[2]Let my teaching fall like rain[y]
  and my words descend like dew,[z][a]
like showers[b] on new grass,
  like abundant rain on tender plants.

[3]I will proclaim[c] the name of the
  LORD.[d]
  Oh, praise the greatness[e] of our God!
[4]He is the Rock,[f] his works are
  perfect,[g]
  and all his ways are just.
A faithful God[h] who does no wrong,
  upright[i] and just is he.[j]

[5]They have acted corruptly toward him;
  to their shame they are no longer his
    children,
  but a warped and crooked
    generation.[o][k]
[6]Is this the way you repay[l] the LORD,
  O foolish[m] and unwise people?[n]
Is he not your Father,[o] your Creator,[p]
  who made you and formed you?[p]

[7]Remember the days of old;[q]
  consider the generations long past.[r]
Ask your father and he will tell you,
  your elders, and they will explain to
    you.[s]

[8]When the Most High[t] gave the nations
  their inheritance,
  when he divided all mankind,[u]
he set up boundaries[v] for the peoples
  according to the number of the sons
    of Israel.[q][w]

[9]For the LORD's portion[x] is his people,
  Jacob his allotted inheritance.[y]

[10]In a desert[z] land he found him,
  in a barren and howling waste.[a]
He shielded[b] him and cared for him;
  he guarded him as the apple of his
    eye,[c]
[11]like an eagle that stirs up its nest

and hovers over its young,[d]
  that spreads its wings to catch them
  and carries them on its pinions.[e]
[12]The LORD alone led[f] him;[g]
  no foreign god was with him.[h]

[13]He made him ride on the heights[i] of
  the land
  and fed him with the fruit of the
    fields.
He nourished him with honey from the
  rock,[j]
  and with oil[k] from the flinty crag,
[14]with curds and milk from herd and
  flock
  and with fattened lambs and goats,
with choice rams of Bashan[l]
  and the finest kernels of wheat.[m]
You drank the foaming blood of the
  grape.[n]

[15]Jeshurun[r][o] grew fat[p] and kicked;
  filled with food, he became heavy
    and sleek.
He abandoned[q] the God who made
  him
  and rejected the Rock[r] his Savior.
[16]They made him jealous[s] with their
  foreign gods
  and angered[t] him with their
    detestable idols.
[17]They sacrificed[u] to demons,[v] which are
  not God—
  gods they had not known,[w]
  gods that recently appeared,[x]
  gods your fathers did not fear.
[18]You deserted the Rock, who fathered
  you;
  you forgot[y] the God who gave you
    birth.

32:1 [v]Ps 49:1;
Mic 1:2 [w]Jer 2:12
[x]S Dt 4:26
32:2 [y]2Sa 23:4
[z]Ps 107:20;
Isa 9:8; 55:11
[a]Mic 5:7
[b]Ps 65:10; 68:9;
72:6; 147:8
32:3 [c]Ps 118:17;
145:6 [d]Ex 33:19;
34:5-6 [e]S Dt 3:24
32:4 [f]S Ge 49:24
[g]2Sa 22:31;
Ps 18:30; 19:7
[h]S Dt 4:35
[i]Ps 92:15
[j]S Ge 18:25
32:5 [k]ver 20;
Mt 17:17;
Lk 9:41; Ac 2:40
32:6 [l]Ps 116:12
[m]Ps 94:8;
Jer 5:21 [n]ver 28
[o]S Ex 4:22;
2Sa 7:24 [p]ver 15
32:7 [q]Ps 44:1;
74:2; 77:5;
Isa 51:9; 63:9
[r]Dt 4:32; Job 8:8;
20:4; Ps 78:4;
Isa 46:9
[s]S Ex 10:2;
Job 15:18
32:8 [t]Ps 7:8
[u]S Ge 11:8;
Ac 8:1 [v]Ps 74:17
[w]Nu 23:9;
Dt 33:12,28;
Jer 23:6
32:9 [x]Ps 16:5;
73:26; 119:57;
142:5; Jer 10:16
[y]S Dt 9:29;
S 1Sa 26:19
32:10 [z]S Dt 1:19
[a]Dt 8:15;
Job 12:24;
Ps 107:40
[b]Ps 32:10;
Jer 31:22
[c]Ps 17:8; Pr 7:2;
Hos 13:5; Zec 2:8

32:11 [d]S Ex 19:4
[e]Ps 17:8;
18:10-19; 61:4
32:12 [f]Ps 106:9;
Isa 63:13;
Jer 31:32
[g]Dt 4:35 [h]ver 39;
Jdg 2:12;
Ps 18:31; 81:9;
Isa 43:12; 45:5
32:13 [i]Dt 33:29;
2Sa 22:34;
Ps 18:33;
Isa 33:16; 58:14;
Eze 36:2;
Hab 3:19
[j]S Dt 8:8
[k]Dt 33:24;
Job 29:6
32:14
[l]S Nu 21:33
[m]Ps 65:9; 81:16;

147:14 [n]S Ge 49:11 **32:15** [o]Dt 33:5,26; Isa 44:2 [p]Dt 31:20;
Jer 5:28 [q]Dt 31:16; Isa 1:4,28; 58:2; 65:11; Jer 15:6;
Eze 14:5 [r]S Ge 49:24 **32:16** [s]S Nu 25:11; S 1Co 10:22
[t]S Dt 31:17; S 1Ki 14:9 **32:17** [u]S Ex 32:8 [v]S Ex 22:20;
1Co 10:20 [w]S Dt 28:64 [x]Jdg 5:8 [y]Jdg 3:7; 1Sa 12:9;
Ps 44:17,20; 106:21; Jer 2:32; Eze 23:35; Hos 8:14; 13:6

[o]5 Or *Corrupt are they and not his children, / a
generation warped and twisted to their shame*   [p]6 Or
Father, who bought you   [q]8 Masoretic Text; Dead Sea
Scrolls (see also Septuagint) *sons of God*   [r]15 *Jeshurun*
means *the upright one,* that is, Israel.

32:1 *Listen, O heavens.* For similar introductions see Isa
1:2 and note; 34:1; Mic 1:2; 6:1–2.
32:4 *He is the Rock.* A major theme of the song of Moses
(see vv. 4,15,18,30–31; see also note on Ge 49:24).
32:5 *warped and crooked generation.* See Php 2:15.
32:6 *Father.* See Isa 63:16; 64:8.
32:7 *Remember the days of old.* See note on 4:10.
32:8 *Most High.* The only occurrence in Deuteronomy of
this name for God (see note on Ge 14:19). It emphasizes the
Lord's sovereignty over all creation. *gave the nations their
inheritance.* See Ge 10. *according to the number of the sons
of Israel.* Perhaps referring to the Lord's grant of Canaan to
Israel as sufficient to sustain their expected population (see

note on Ge 10:2).
32:10 *apple of his eye.* Lit. "little man of his eye," referring
to the pupil, a delicate part of the eye that is essential for
vision and that therefore must be protected at all costs.
32:11 *hovers over.* See note on Ge 1:2.
32:13 *honey from the rock.* See Ps 81:16. In Canaan, bees
sometimes built their hives in clefts of rocks (cf. Isa
7:18–19). *oil from the flinty crag.* Olive trees often grew on
rocky hillsides, as on the Mount of Olives east of Jerusalem.
32:14 *Bashan.* See note on Eze 39:18. *foaming blood of
the grape.* Wine (see Ge 49:11).
32:15 *Jeshurun.* See NIV text note; see also Isa 44:2 and
note. *Rock.* See v. 18 and note on v. 4.

¹⁹The LORD saw this and rejected them[z]
  because he was angered by his sons
    and daughters. [a]
²⁰"I will hide my face[b] from them," he
    said,
  "and see what their end will be;
for they are a perverse generation,[c]
  children who are unfaithful. [d]
²¹They made me jealous[e] by what is no
    god
  and angered me with their worthless
    idols.[f]
I will make them envious by those who
    are not a people;
  I will make them angry by a nation
    that has no understanding.[g]
²²For a fire has been kindled by my
    wrath,[h]
  one that burns to the realm of death[s]
    below.[i]
It will devour[j] the earth and its
    harvests[k]
  and set afire the foundations of the
    mountains.[l]

²³"I will heap calamities[m] upon them
  and spend my arrows[n] against them.
²⁴I will send wasting famine[o] against
    them,
  consuming pestilence[p] and deadly
    plague;[q]
I will send against them the fangs of
    wild beasts,[r]
  the venom of vipers[s] that glide in the
    dust.[t]
²⁵In the street the sword will make them
    childless;
  in their homes terror[u] will reign. [v]
Young men and young women will
    perish,
  infants and gray-haired men. [w]
²⁶I said I would scatter[x] them
  and blot out their memory from
    mankind,[y]
²⁷but I dreaded the taunt of the enemy,
  lest the adversary misunderstand[z]
and say, 'Our hand has triumphed;
  the LORD has not done all this.' " [a]

²⁸They are a nation without sense,
  there is no discernment[b] in them.
²⁹If only they were wise and would
    understand this[c]
  and discern what their end will be! [d]

³⁰How could one man chase a thousand,
  or two put ten thousand to flight,[e]
unless their Rock had sold them,[f]
  unless the LORD had given them
    up?[g]
³¹For their rock is not like our Rock,[h]
  as even our enemies concede. [i]
³²Their vine comes from the vine of
    Sodom[j]
  and from the fields of Gomorrah.
Their grapes are filled with poison,[k]
  and their clusters with bitterness. [l]
³³Their wine is the venom of serpents,
  the deadly poison of cobras. [m]

³⁴"Have I not kept this in reserve
  and sealed it in my vaults?[n]
³⁵It is mine to avenge;[o] I will repay.[p]
  In due time their foot will slip;[q]
their day of disaster is near
  and their doom rushes upon them.[r] "

³⁶The LORD will judge his people[s]
  and have compassion[t] on his
    servants[u]
when he sees their strength is gone
  and no one is left, slave[v] or free.
³⁷He will say: "Now where are their
    gods,
  the rock they took refuge in,[w]
³⁸the gods who ate the fat of their
    sacrifices
  and drank the wine of their drink
    offerings?[x]
Let them rise up to help you!
  Let them give you shelter!

³⁹"See now that I myself am He![y]
  There is no god besides me. [z]
I put to death[a] and I bring to life,[b]
  I have wounded and I will heal,[c]
  and no one can deliver out of my
    hand. [d]

32:19 [z]Lev 26:30;
Ps 78:59 [a]Am 6:8
32:20 [b]Dt 31:17,
29; Ps 4:6; 44:24
[c]S ver 5 [d]Dt 9:23
32:21
[e]S Nu 25:11;
S 1Co 10:22 [f]ver
17; 1Ki 16:13,26;
2Ki 17:15;
Ps 31:6; Jer 2:5;
8:19; 10:8;
16:19; Jnh 2:8
[g]Ro 10:9*
32:22 [h]Ps 7:11
[i]Nu 16:31-35;
Ps 18:7-8;
Jer 15:14; La 4:11
[j]Am 7:4
[k]Lev 26:20
[l]Ps 83:14
32:23
[m]S Dt 29:21 [n]ver
42; 2Sa 22:15;
Job 6:4; Ps 7:13;
18:14; 45:5;
77:17; 120:4;
Isa 5:28; 49:2;
Eze 5:16;
Hab 3:9,11
32:24 [o]Ge 26:1;
S 41:55; 42:5;
2Sa 24:13;
1Ch 21:12
[p]S Dt 28:22
[q]Ps 91:6
[r]S Ge 37:20 [s]ver
33; Job 20:16;
Ps 58:4; Jer 8:17;
Am 5:18-19;
Mic 7:17
[t]Job 20:16
32:25 [u]Isa 24:17
[v]Jer 14:18;
La 1:20;
Eze 7:15; 2Co 7:5
[w]2Ch 36:17;
Isa 13:18;
Jer 4:31; La 2:21
32:26 [x]Dt 4:27
[y]S Nu 14:12;
Job 18:17;
Ps 34:16; 37:28;
109:15; Isa 14:20
32:27
[z]Dt 9:26-28
[a]Ps 140:8;
Isa 10:13;
Jer 40:2-3
32:28 [b]Isa 1:3;
5:13; 27:11;
Jer 8:7
32:29 [c]Dt 5:29;
Ps 81:13
[d]Isa 47:7; La 1:9

32:30
[e]S Lev 26:8
[f]Jdg 2:14; 3:8;
4:2; 10:7;
1Sa 12:9
[g]Nu 21:34;
1Sa 23:7; Ps 31:8;
44:12; 106:41;
Isa 50:1; 54:6
32:31
[h]S Ge 49:24
[i]S Ex 14:25
32:32 [j]Jer 23:14
[k]Job 6:4; 20:16
[l]Dt 29:18
32:33 [m]S ver 24

32:34 [n]Job 14:17; Jer 2:22; Hos 13:12 **32:35** [o]S ver 41;
S Ge 4:24; S Jer 51:6 [p]S Ge 30:2; S Ex 32:34; S Ps 54:5;
S Ro 12:19*; Heb 10:30* [q]Ps 17:5; 35:6; 37:31; 38:16;
66:9; 73:2,18; 94:18; 121:3; Pr 4:19; Jer 23:12 [r]Eze 7:8-9
32:36 [s]Heb 10:30* [t]Am 7:3 [u]Lev 26:43-45; Dt 30:1-3;
Jdg 2:18; Ps 90:13; 102:13; 103:13; 106:45; 135:14;
Joel 2:14 [v]1Ki 14:10; 21:21; 2Ki 9:8 **32:37** [w]Jdg 10:14;
Jer 2:28; 11:12 **32:38** [x]Nu 25:1-2; Jer 11:12; 44:8,25 **32:39**
[y]Isa 41:4; 43:10; 44:7; 46:4; 48:12 [z]S ver 12 [a]1Sa 2:6
[b]1Sa 2:6; 2Ki 5:7; Ps 68:20; Jn 11:25-26 [c]Ex 15:26;
Job 5:18; 15:11; Ps 147:3; Isa 6:10; 19:22; 30:26; 53:5;
57:18; Jer 33:6; Hos 6:1; Mal 4:2; 1Pe 2:24 [d]Job 9:12; 10:7;
Ps 7:2; 50:22; Isa 43:13; Da 4:35; Hos 5:14

[s]22 Hebrew *to Sheol*

32:21 Quoted in part in Ro 10:19 to illustrate Israel's
failure to understand the good news about Christ.
32:22 *realm of death below.* See note on Ge 37:35.
32:30 *their Rock.* Israel's God.
32:31 *their rock.* The god of Israel's enemy.
32:34 *sealed it in my vaults.* The Lord's plans for the future
are fixed and certain. Sin will be punished in due time.

32:35–36 Quoted in part in Heb 10:30 as a warning
against rejecting the Son of God.

32:35 *It is mine to avenge; I will repay.* Quoted in Ro
12:19 to affirm that avenging is God's prerogative.

32:39 *no god besides me.* See note on 4:35. *I put to death
and I bring to life.* See Isa 45:7 and note.

⁴⁰I lift my hand^e to heaven and declare:
　As surely as I live forever,^f
⁴¹when I sharpen my flashing sword^g
　and my hand grasps it in judgment,
I will take vengeance^h on my
　adversaries
　and repay those who hate me.ⁱ
⁴²I will make my arrows drunk with
　blood,^j
　while my sword devours flesh:^k
the blood of the slain and the captives,
　the heads of the enemy leaders.''

⁴³Rejoice,^l O nations, with his people,^{t,u}
　for he will avenge the blood of his
　　servants;^m
he will take vengeance on his enemiesⁿ
　and make atonement for his land and
　　people.^o

⁴⁴Moses came with Joshua^{v,p} son of Nun and spoke all the words of this song in the hearing of the people. ⁴⁵When Moses finished reciting all these words to all Israel, ⁴⁶he said to them, ''Take to heart all the words I have solemnly declared to you this day,^q so that you may command^r your children to obey carefully all the words of this law. ⁴⁷They are not just idle words for you—they are your life.^s By them you will live long^t in the land you are crossing the Jordan to possess.''

Moses to Die on Mount Nebo

⁴⁸On that same day the LORD told Moses,^u ⁴⁹''Go up into the Abarim^v Range to Mount Nebo^w in Moab, across from Jericho,^x and view Canaan,^y the land I am giving the Israelites as their own possession. ⁵⁰There on the mountain that you have climbed you will die^z and be gathered to your people, just as your brother Aaron died^a on Mount Hor^b and was gathered to his people. ⁵¹This is because both of you broke faith with me in the presence of the Israelites at the waters of Meribah Kadesh^c in the Desert of Zin^d and because you did not uphold my holiness among the Israelites.^e ⁵²Therefore,

you will see the land only from a distance;^f you will not enter^g the land I am giving to the people of Israel.''

Moses Blesses the Tribes
33:1–29Ref — Ge 49:1–28

33 This is the blessing^h that Moses the man of Godⁱ pronounced on the Israelites before his death. ²He said:

''The LORD came from Sinai^j
　and dawned over them from Seir;^k
he shone forth^l from Mount Paran.^m
He came with^w myriads of holy onesⁿ
　from the south, from his mountain
　　slopes.^x
³Surely it is you who love^o the people;
　all the holy ones are in your hand.^p
At your feet they all bow down,^q
　and from you receive instruction,
⁴the law that Moses gave us,^r
　the possession of the assembly of
　　Jacob.^s
⁵He was king^t over Jeshurun^{y,u}
　when the leaders of the people
　　assembled,
　along with the tribes of Israel.

⁶''Let Reuben live and not die,
　nor^z his men be few.''^v

⁷And this he said about Judah:^w

''Hear, O LORD, the cry of Judah;
　bring him to his people.
With his own hands he defends his
　　cause.
　Oh, be his help against his foes!''

⁸About Levi^x he said:

''Your Thummim and Urim^y belong

Cross references (center column)

32:40 ^eS Ge 14:22; ^fS Ge 21:33; Rev 1:18
32:41 ^gJdg 7:20; Ps 7:12; 45:3; Isa 27:1; 34:6; 66:16; Jer 12:12; Eze 21:9-10 ^hver 35; Ps 149:7; Jer 46:10; Na 1:2 ⁱPs 137:8; Jer 25:14; 50:29; 51:24,56
32:42 ^jS ver 23 ^k2Sa 2:26; Jer 12:12; 44:1; 46:10,14
32:43 ^lPs 137:6; Isa 25:9; 65:18; 66:10; Ro 15:10* ^m2Ki 9:7; S Rev 6:10 ⁿIsa 1:24; Jer 9:9 ^oPs 65:3; 79:9
32:44 ^pNu 13:8, 16
32:46 ^qS Dt 6:6; Jn 1:17; 7:19 ^rDt 6:7
32:47 ^sS Dt 30:20 ^tS Ex 23:26; Dt 33:25; Isa 65:22
32:48 ^uNu 27:12
32:49 ^vNu 27:12 ^wS Nu 32:3 ^xS Nu 22:1 ^yS Lev 14:34
32:50 ^zS Ge 25:8; S Nu 27:13 ^aNu 20:29 ^bS Nu 20:22
32:51 ^cEze 47:19 ^dS Nu 13:21; 20:11-13 ^eNu 27:14
32:52 ^fDt 34:1-3 ^gS Dt 3:27
33:1 ^hS Ge 27:4 ⁱJos 14:6; 1Sa 2:27; 9:6; 1Ki 12:22; 13:1; 2Ki 1:9-13; 5:8; Jer 35:4
33:2 ^jEx 19:18; Ps 68:8 ^kJos 11:17; Jdg 5:4 ^lPs 50:2; 80:1; 94:1 ^mS Nu 10:12 ⁿPs 89:7; Da 4:13; 7:10; 8:13; Zec 14:5; Ac 7:53; Gal 3:19; Heb 2:2; Rev 5:11
33:3 ^oS Dt 4:37 ^pDt 7:6 ^qLk 10:39; Rev 4:10
33:4 ^rDt 4:2; Jn 1:17; 7:19

^sPs 119:111 **33:5** ^tS Ex 16:8; 1Sa 10:19; Ps 10:16; 149:2 ^uS Nu 23:21; S Dt 32:15 **33:6** ^vS Ge 34:5 **33:7** ^wS Ge 49:10 **33:8** ^xS Ge 29:34 ^yEx 28:30

^t43 Or *Make his people rejoice, O nations*
^u43 Masoretic Text; Dead Sea Scrolls (see also Septuagint) *people, / and let all the angels worship him /*
^v44 Hebrew *Hoshea*, a variant of *Joshua* ^w2 Or *from*
^x2 The meaning of the Hebrew for this phrase is uncertain. ^y5 *Jeshurun* means *the upright one*, that is, Israel; also in verse 26. ^z6 Or *but let*

Study notes (bottom)

32:43 *Rejoice, O nations, with his people.* One of the Dead Sea Scrolls adds a clause in Deuteronomy (see NIV text note), and the clause is quoted in Heb 1:6.
32:47 *they are your life.* See note on 30:20.
32:50 *gathered to your people.* See note on Ge 25:8. *Aaron died on Mount Hor.* See 10:6; Nu 20:22–29.
32:51 *you broke faith with me.* See 1:37; 3:23–26; 4:21–22; 31:2; Nu 20:12. *Meribah Kadesh in the Desert of Zin.* See 33:8; see also notes on Ex 17:7; Nu 20:13.
33:1 *blessing.* See Ge 12:1–3; 22:15–18; 27:27–29; 28:10–15; 49:1–28. Moses' blessings on the tribes (vv. 6–25) should be compared particularly with Jacob's blessings on his sons in Ge 49. *man of God.* The first occurrence of this

title. It appears next in Jos 14:6 (also of Moses; see Ps 90 title). Later it designates other messengers of God (see note on 1Sa 2:27).
33:2 *Sinai . . . Seir . . . Paran.* Mountains associated with the giving of the law (see Ge 21:21 and note; Jdg 5:4–5; Hab 3:3). *holy ones.* Angels.
33:3 *holy ones.* Israelites (see 7:6; 14:2; 26:19; 28:9).
33:5 *king.* The Lord, not an earthly monarch, was to be king over Israel (see Jdg 8:23 and note). *Jeshurun.* See NIV text note; see also Isa 44:2 and note.
33:8 *Thummim and Urim.* See note on Ex 28:30. *Massah.* See 6:16; 9:22; see also note on Ex 17:7. *Meribah.* See 32:51; see also note on Ex 17:7.

to the man you favored. *z*
You tested *a* him at Massah;
    you contended with him at the
      waters of Meribah. *b*
⁹He said of his father and mother, *c*
    'I have no regard for them.'
He did not recognize his brothers
    or acknowledge his own children,
but he watched over your word
    and guarded your covenant. *d*
¹⁰He teaches *e* your precepts to Jacob
    and your law to Israel. *f*
He offers incense before you *g*
    and whole burnt offerings on your
      altar. *h*
¹¹Bless all his skills, O LORD,
    and be pleased with the work of his
      hands. *i*
Smite the loins of those who rise up
    against him;
    strike his foes till they rise no more."

¹²About Benjamin *j* he said:

"Let the beloved of the LORD rest
    secure in him, *k*
for he shields him all day long, *l*
and the one the LORD loves *m* rests
    between his shoulders. *n* "

¹³About Joseph *o* he said:

"May the LORD bless his land
    with the precious dew from heaven
      above
and with the deep waters that lie
    below; *p*
¹⁴with the best the sun brings forth
    and the finest the moon can yield;
¹⁵with the choicest gifts of the ancient
    mountains *q*
and the fruitfulness of the everlasting
    hills;
¹⁶with the best gifts of the earth and its
    fullness
and the favor of him who dwelt in
    the burning bush. *r*
Let all these rest on the head of Joseph,
    on the brow of the prince among *a*
    his brothers. *s*

¹⁷In majesty he is like a firstborn bull;
    his horns *t* are the horns of a wild
      ox. *u*
With them he will gore *v* the nations,
    even those at the ends of the earth.
Such are the ten thousands of
    Ephraim; *w*
such are the thousands of
    Manasseh. *x* "

¹⁸About Zebulun *y* he said:

"Rejoice, Zebulun, in your going out,
    and you, Issachar, *z* in your tents.
¹⁹They will summon peoples to the
    mountain *a*
    and there offer sacrifices of
      righteousness; *b*
they will feast on the abundance of the
    seas, *c*
    on the treasures hidden in the sand."

²⁰About Gad *d* he said:

"Blessed is he who enlarges Gad's
    domain! *e*
Gad lives there like a lion,
    tearing at arm or head.
²¹He chose the best land for himself; *f*
    the leader's portion was kept for
      him. *g*
When the heads of the people
    assembled,
he carried out the LORD's righteous
    will, *h*
    and his judgments concerning Israel."

²²About Dan *i* he said:

"Dan is a lion's cub,
    springing out of Bashan."

²³About Naphtali *j* he said:

"Naphtali is abounding with the favor of
    the LORD
    and is full of his blessing;
he will inherit southward to the
    lake."

²⁴About Asher *k* he said:

33:8 *z* Ps 106:16
a S Nu 14:22
b S Ex 17:7
33:9
c Ex 32:26-29
d Ps 61:5; Mal 2:5
33:10 *e* Ezr 7:10;
Ne 8:18;
Ps 119:151;
Jer 23:22; Mal 2:6
f S Lev 10:11;
Dt 17:8-11;
31:9-13
g S Ex 30:7;
Lev 16:12-13
h Ps 51:19
33:11
i 2Sa 24:23;
Ps 20:3; 51:19
33:12
j S Ge 35:18
k Dt 4:37-38;
12:10; S 32:8
l S Ex 19:4
m Ps 60:5; 127:2;
Isa 5:1
n S Ex 28:12
33:13
o S Ge 30:24
p Ge 27:28;
Ps 148:7
33:15 *q* Hab 3:6
33:16 *r* S Ex 3:2
s S Ge 37:8

33:17 *t* 1Sa 2:10;
2Sa 22:3;
Eze 34:21
u S Nu 23:22
v 1Ki 22:11;
Ps 44:5
w S Ge 41:52
x S Ge 41:51
33:18
y S Ge 30:20
z S Ge 30:18
33:19
a S Ex 15:17;
Ps 48:1; Isa 2:3;
65:11; 66:20;
Jer 31:6 *b* Ps 4:5;
51:19 *c* Isa 18:7;
23:18; 45:14;
60:5,11; 61:6;
Hag 2:7;
Zec 14:14
33:20 *d* Ge 30:11
e Dt 3:12-17
33:21
f Nu 32:1-5,31-32
g S Nu 34:14
h Jos 22:1-3
33:22 *i* Ge 49:16;
S Nu 1:38
33:23 *j* S Ge 30:8
33:24
k S Ge 30:13

a 16 Or *of the one separated from*

33:9 *he watched over your word.* The Levites had charge of the tabernacle with its ark, in which the Book of the Law was placed (see note on 31:9).

33:10 *teaches your precepts to Jacob.* See note on 31:11.

33:13 *About Joseph.* Moses included the blessing on the two tribes of Ephraim and Manasseh (v. 17), Joseph's sons, with that of Joseph himself. *dew from heaven . . . deep waters.* See note on Ge 49:25.

33:15-16 See Ge 49:26 and note.

33:16 *best gifts of the earth.* Under the Lord's blessing, Joseph's land in the central part of Canaan was to be unusually fertile and productive. *who dwelt in the burning bush.* See Ex 3:1-6.

33:19 *abundance of the seas . . . treasures hidden in the sand.* References to maritime wealth (see note on Ge 49:13).

33:21 *He chose the best land.* For his livestock (see 3:12-20).

33:22 *springing out of Bashan.* The lion's cub, not Dan, is the subject. Another possible translation is "keeping away from the viper." Although someday he would be like a viper himself (see Ge 49:17), the early history of Dan pictured him as being somewhat more timid.

33:23 *lake.* The Sea of Galilee. Naphtali's area extended from north of the Waters of Merom to south of the Sea of Galilee.

"Most blessed of sons is Asher;
  let him be favored by his brothers,
  and let him bathe his feet in oil. *l*
25The bolts of your gates will be iron and
    bronze, *m*
  and your strength will equal your
    days. *n*

26"There is no one like the God of
    Jeshurun, *o*
  who rides *p* on the heavens to help
    you *q*
  and on the clouds *r* in his majesty. *s*
27The eternal *t* God is your refuge, *u*
  and underneath are the everlasting *v*
    arms.
He will drive out your enemy before
    you, *w*
  saying, 'Destroy him!' *x*
28So Israel will live in safety alone; *y*
  Jacob's spring is secure
  in a land of grain and new wine,
  where the heavens drop dew. *z*
29Blessed are you, O Israel! *a*
  Who is like you, *b*
  a people saved by the LORD? *c*
He is your shield and helper *d*
  and your glorious sword.
Your enemies will cower before you,
  and you will trample down their high
    places. *b e* "

The Death of Moses

34 Then Moses climbed Mount
    Nebo *f* from the plains of Moab to
the top of Pisgah, *g* across from Jericho. *h*
There the LORD showed *i* him the whole
land—from Gilead to Dan, *j* 2all of Naphtali, the territory of Ephraim and Manasseh, all the land of Judah as far as the
western sea, *c k* 3the Negev *l* and the

whole region from the Valley of Jericho,
the City of Palms, *m* as far as Zoar. *n* 4Then
the LORD said to him, "This is the land I
promised on oath *o* to Abraham, Isaac and
Jacob *p* when I said, 'I will give it *q* to your
descendants.' I have let you see it with
your eyes, but you will not cross *r* over
into it."

5And Moses the servant of the LORD *s*
died *t* there in Moab, as the LORD had said.
6He buried him *d* in Moab, in the valley
opposite Beth Peor, *u* but to this day no
one knows where his grave is. *v* 7Moses
was a hundred and twenty years old *w*
when he died, yet his eyes were not
weak *x* nor his strength gone. *y* 8The Israelites grieved for Moses in the plains of
Moab *z* thirty days, *a* until the time of
weeping and mourning *b* was over.

9Now Joshua son of Nun was filled with
the spirit *e* of wisdom *c* because Moses had
laid his hands on him. *d* So the Israelites
listened to him and did what the LORD had
commanded Moses.

10Since then, no prophet *e* has risen in
Israel like Moses, *f* whom the LORD knew
face to face, *g* 11who did all those miraculous signs and wonders *h* the LORD sent
him to do in Egypt—to Pharaoh and to all
his officials *i* and to his whole land. 12For
no one has *j* ever shown the mighty power
or performed the awesome deeds *k* that
Moses did in the sight of all Israel.

33:24
*l*S Ge 49:20;
S Dt 32:13
33:25 *m*Ne 3:3;
7:3; Ps 147:13
*n*S Dt 32:47
33:26
*o*S Dt 32:15
*p*Ps 18:10; 68:33
*q*S Dt 10:14;
S Ps 104:3
*r*2Sa 22:10;
Ps 18:9; 68:4;
Da 7:13
*s*S Ex 15:7
33:27 *t*Ex 15:18;
Isa 40:28; 57:15
*u*Ps 9:9; 84:1;
90:1; 91:9
*v*S Ge 21:33
*w*Ex 34:11;
Jos 24:18
*x*S Dt 7:2
33:28
*y*S Ex 33:16;
S Lev 25:18;
S Dt 32:8;
Ps 16:9; Pr 1:33;
Isa 14:30 *z*ver 13;
Ge 27:28
33:29 *a*Ps 1:1;
32:1-2; 144:15
*b*2Sa 22:45;
Ps 18:44; 66:3;
81:15 *c*Dt 4:7
*d*Ge 15:1;
Ex 18:4;
Ps 10:14; 18:1;
27:1,9; 30:10;
54:4; 70:5;
115:9-11; 118:7;
Isa 45:24;
Hos 13:9;
Hab 3:19
*e*S Nu 33:52;
S Dt 32:13
34:1 *f*S Nu 32:3
*g*S Nu 21:20
*h*Dt 32:49
*i*Dt 32:52
*j*S Ge 14:14
34:2 *k*S Ex 23:31
34:3 *l*S Ge 12:9

*m*Jdg 1:16; 3:13;
2Ch 28:15
*n*S Ge 13:10
34:4 *o*Ge 28:13
*p*Jos 21:43
*q*Ge 12:7
*r*S Dt 3:23
34:5 *s*S Nu 12:7
*t*S Ge 25:8
34:6 *u*S Dt 3:29
*v*Jude 1:9

34:7 *w*S Ex 7:7 *x*S Ge 27:1 *y*S Ge 15:15 **34:8** *z*S Nu 21:11
*a*S Ge 37:34; S Dt 1:3 *b*2Sa 11:27 **34:9** *c*S Ge 41:38;
S Ex 28:3; Isa 11:2 *d*S Dt 31:14; Ac 6:6 **34:10** *e*S Ge 20:7
*f*Dt 18:15,18 *g*S Ge 33:11 **34:11** *h*Dt 4:34 *i*S Ex 11:3 **34:12**
*j*Heb 3:1-6 *k*S Dt 4:34

*b*29 Or *will tread upon their bodies*   *c*2 That is, the
Mediterranean   *d*6 Or *He was buried*   *e*9 Or *Spirit*

33:26 *Jeshurun.* See note on 32:15. *rides . . . on the
clouds.* See note on Ps 68:4.
33:29 *shield.* See note on Ge 15:1. *high places.* See note
on 1Ki 3:2.
34:1 *Moses climbed Mount Nebo.* In obedience to the
Lord's command in 32:48–52.
34:4 *land I promised.* See 1:8; Ge 12:1; 15:18 and note;
Ex 33:1.
34:5 *servant of the LORD.* A special title used to refer to
those whom the Lord, as the Great King, has taken into his
service; they serve as members of God's royal administration. For example, it was used especially of Abraham (Ge
26:24), Moses (Ex 14:31), Joshua (Jos 24:29), David (2Sa
7:5), the prophets (2Ki 9:7), Israel collectively (Isa 41:8),

and even a foreign king the Lord used to carry out his
purposes (Jer 25:9). See notes on Ex 14:31; Isa 42:1–4.
34:6 *Beth Peor.* See note on 3:29.
34:7 *a hundred and twenty years old.* See 31:2; perhaps a
round number, indicating three generations of about 40
years each.
34:8 *grieved . . . thirty days.* See Ge 50:3 and note.
34:10 *no prophet has risen in Israel like Moses.* See note
on 18:15. *face to face.* See Nu 12:8 and note.
34:12 *no one has ever.* Until Jesus came, no one was
superior to Moses. See Heb 3:1–6, where Moses the "servant" (Heb 3:5) is contrasted with Christ the "son" (Heb
3:6).

JOSHUA

Title and Theme

Joshua is a story of conquest and fulfillment for the people of God. After many years of slavery in Egypt and 40 years in the desert, the Israelites were finally allowed to enter the land promised to their fathers. Abraham, always a migrant, never possessed the country to which he was sent, but he left to his children the legacy of God's covenant that made them the eventual heirs of all of Canaan (see Ge 15:13,16,18; 17:8). Joshua was destined to turn that promise into reality.

Where Deuteronomy ends, the book of Joshua begins: The tribes of Israel are still camped on the east side of the Jordan River. The narrative opens with God's command to move forward and pass through the river on dry land. Then it relates the series of victories in central, southern and northern Canaan that gave the Israelites control of all the hill country and the Negev. It continues with a description of the tribal allotments and ends with Joshua's final addresses to the people. The theme of the book, therefore, is the establishment of Israel in the promised land.

Earlier in his life Joshua was called simply Hoshea (Nu 13:8,16), meaning "salvation." But later Moses changed his name to Joshua, meaning "The LORD saves" (or "The LORD gives victory"). When this same name (the Greek form of which is Jesus; see NIV text note on Mt 1:21) was given to Mary's firstborn son, it became the most loved of names.

In the Hebrew Bible the book of Joshua initiates a division called the Former Prophets, including also Judges, Samuel and Kings—all historical in content but written from a prophetic standpoint. They do more than merely record the nation's development from Moses to the fall of Judah in 586 B.C. They prophetically interpret God's covenant ways with Israel in history—how he fulfills and remains true to his promises (especially through his servants such as Joshua, the judges, Samuel and David) and how he deals with the waywardness of the Israelites. In Joshua it was the Lord who won the victories and "gave Israel all the land he had sworn to give their forefathers" (21:43).

Author and Date

In the judgment of many scholars Joshua was not written until the end of the period of the kings, some 800 years after the actual events. But there are significant reasons to question this conclusion and to place the time of composition much earlier. The earliest Jewish traditions (Talmud) claim that Joshua wrote his own book except for the final section about his funeral, which is attributed to Eleazar son of Aaron (the last verse must have been added by a later editor).

On at least two occasions the text reports writing at Joshua's command or by Joshua himself. When the tribes received their territories, Joshua instructed his men "to make a survey of the land and write a description of it" (18:8). Then in the last scene of the book, when Joshua led Israel in a renewal of the covenant with the Lord, "he drew up decrees and laws" (24:25). On yet another occasion the one telling the story appears also to have been a participant in the event; he uses the pronouns "we" and "us" (5:1,6).

Moreover, the author's observations are accurate and precise. He is thoroughly at ease with the antiquated names of cities, such as "the Jebusite city" (15:8; 18:16,28) for Jerusalem, Kiriath Arba (14:15; 15:54; 20:7; 21:11) for Hebron, and Greater Sidon (11:8; 19:28) for what later became simply Sidon. Tyre is never mentioned because in the days of Joshua it had not yet developed into a port of major importance.

But if some features suggest Joshua's own lifetime, others point to a time somewhat later. The account of the long day when the sun stood still at Aijalon is substantiated by a quotation from another source, the Book of Jashar (10:13). This would hardly be natural for an eyewitness of the miracle, writing shortly after it happened. Also, there are 12 instances where the phrase "until this day" is employed by the author.

It seems safe to conclude that the book, at least in its early form, dates from the beginning of the monarchy. Some think that Samuel may have had a hand in shaping or compiling the materials of the book, but in fact we are unsure who the final author or editor was.

The Life of Joshua

Joshua's remarkable life was filled with excitement, variety, success and honor. He was known for nis deep trust in God and as "a man in whom is the spirit" (Nu 27:18). As a youth he lived through the bitter realities of slavery in Egypt, but he also witnessed the supernatural plagues and the miracle of Israel's escape from the army of the Egyptians when the waters of the sea opened before them. In the Sinai peninsula it was Joshua who led the troops of Israel to victory over the Amalekites (Ex 17:8-13). He alone was allowed to accompany Moses up the holy mountain where the tablets of the law were received (Ex 24:13-14). And it was he who stood watch at the temporary tent of meeting Moses set up before the tabernacle was erected (Ex 33:11).

Joshua was elected to represent his own tribe of Ephraim when the 12 spies were sent into Canaan to look over the land. Only Joshua and his friend Caleb were ready to follow God's will and take immediate possession of the land (see Nu 14:26-34). The rest were condemned to die in the desert. Even Moses died short of the goal and was told to turn everything over to Joshua. God promised to guide and strengthen Joshua, just as he had Moses (Dt 31:23).

Joshua proved to be not only a military strategist in the battles that followed, but also a statesman in the way he governed the tribes. Above all, he was God's chosen servant (see 24:29 and note on Dt 34:5) to bring Moses' work to completion and establish Israel in the promised land. In that role he was a striking OT type (foreshadowing) of Christ (see notes on Heb 4:1,6-8).

Historical Setting

At the time of the Israelite migration into Canaan the superpowers of the ancient Near East were relatively weak. The Hittites had faded from the scene. Neither Babylon nor Egypt could maintain a military presence in Canaan, and the Assyrians would not send in their armies until centuries later.

As the tribes circled east of the Dead Sea, only the stronghold of Edom offered any resistance. Moab was forced to let Israel pass through her territory and camp in her plains. When Og and Sihon, two regional Amorite kings of Transjordan, tried to stop the Israelites, they were easily defeated and their lands occupied.

Biblical archaeologists call this period the Late Bronze Age (1550-1200 B.C.). Today thousands of artifacts give testimony to the richness of the Canaanite material culture, which was in many ways superior to that of the Israelites. When the ruins of the ancient kingdom of Ugarit were discovered at modern Ras Shamra on the northern coast of Syria (see chart on "Ancient Texts Relating to the OT," p. 5), a wealth of new information came to light concerning the domestic, commercial and religious life of the Canaanites. From a language close to Hebrew came stories of ancient kings and gods that revealed their immoral behavior and cruelty. In addition, pagan temples, altars, tombs and ritual vessels have been uncovered, throwing more light on the culture and customs of the peoples surrounding Israel.

Excavations at the ancient sites of Megiddo, Beth Shan and Gezer show how powerfully fortified these cities were and why they were not captured and occupied by Israel in Joshua's day. Many other fortified towns were taken, however, so that Israel became firmly established in the land as the dominant power. Apart from Jericho and Ai, Joshua is reported to have burned only Hazor (11:13), so attempts to date these events by destruction levels in the mounds of Canaan's ancient cities are questionable undertakings. It must also be remembered that other groups were involved in campaigns in the region about this time, among whom were Egyptian rulers and the Sea Peoples (including the Philistines). There had also been much intercity warfare among the Canaanites, and afterward the period of the judges was marked by general turbulence.

Much of the data from archaeology appears to support a date for Joshua's invasion c. 1250 B.C. This fits well with an exodus that would then have taken place 40 years earlier under the famous Rameses II, who ruled from the Nile delta at a city with the same name (Ex 1:11). It also places Joseph in Egypt in a favorable situation. Four hundred years before Rameses II the pharaohs were the Semitic Hyksos, who also ruled from the delta near the land of Goshen.

On the other hand, a good case can be made for the traditional viewpoint that the invasion occurred c. 1406 B.C. The oppression would have taken place under Amunhotep II after the death of his father Thutmose III, who is known to have used slave labor in his building projects. The earlier date also fits

better with the two numbers found in Jdg 11:26 and 1Ki 6:1, since it allows for an additional 150 years between Moses and the monarchy. See also the Introductions to Genesis: Author and Date of Writing; Exodus: Chronology; and Judges: Background.

The Conquest and the Ethical Question of War

Many readers of Joshua (and other OT books) are deeply troubled by the role that warfare plays in this account of God's dealings with his people. Not a few relieve their ethical scruples by ascribing the author's perspective to a pre-Christian (and sub-Christian) stage of moral development that the Christian, in the light of Christ's teaching, must repudiate and transcend. Hence the main thread of the narrative line of Joshua is an offense to them.

It must be remembered, however, that the book of Joshua does not address itself to the abstract ethical question of war as a means for gaining human ends. It can only be understood in the context of the history of redemption unfolding in the Pentateuch, with its interplay of divine grace and judgment. Of that story it is the direct continuation.

Joshua is not an epic account of Israel's heroic generation or the story of Israel's conquest of Canaan with the aid of her national deity. It is rather the story of how God, to whom the whole world belongs, at one stage in the history of redemption reconquered a portion of the earth from the powers of this world that had claimed it for themselves, defending their claims by force of arms and reliance on their false gods. It tells how God commissioned his people, under his servant Joshua, to take Canaan in his name out of the hands of the idolatrous and dissolute Canaanites (whose measure of sin was now full; see Ge 15:16). It tells how he aided them in that enterprise and gave them conditional tenancy in his land in fulfillment of the ancient pledge.

Joshua is the story of the kingdom of God breaking into the world of nations at a time when national and political entities were viewed as the creation of the gods and living proofs of their power. Thus the Lord's triumph over the Canaanites testified to the world that the God of Israel is the one true and living God, whose claim on the world is absolute. It was also a warning to the nations that the irresistible advance of the kingdom of God would ultimately disinherit all those who opposed it, giving place in the earth only to those who acknowledge and serve the Lord. At once an act of redemption and of judgment, it gave notice of the outcome of history and anticipated the eschatological destiny of mankind and the creation.

The battles for Canaan were therefore the Lord's holy war, undertaken at a particular time in the program of redemption. God gave his people under Joshua no commission or license to conquer the world with the sword but a particular, limited mission. The conquered land itself would not become Israel's national possession by right of conquest, but it belonged to the Lord. So the land had to be cleansed of all remnants of paganism. Its people and their wealth were not for Israel to seize as the booty of war from which to enrich themselves (as Achan tried to do, ch. 7) but were placed under God's ban (were to be devoted to God to dispense with as he pleased). On that land Israel was to establish a commonwealth faithful to the righteous rule of God and thus be a witness (and a blessing) to the nations. If she herself became unfaithful and conformed to Canaanite culture and practice, she would in turn lose her place in the Lord's land—as she almost did in the days of the judges, and as she did eventually in the exile.

War is a terrible curse that the human race brings on itself as it seeks to possess the earth by its own unrighteous ways. But it pales before the curse that awaits all those who do not heed God's testimony to himself or his warnings—those who oppose the rule of God and reject his offer of grace. The God of the second Joshua (Jesus) is the God of the first Joshua also. Although now for a time he reaches out to the whole world with the gospel (and commissions his people urgently to carry his offer of peace to all nations), the sword of his judgment waits in the wings—and his second Joshua will wield it (Rev 19:11-16).

Outline

I. The Entrance into the Land (1:1-5:12)
    A. The Exhortations to Conquer (ch. 1)
    B. The Reconnaissance of Jericho (ch. 2)
    C. The Crossing of the Jordan (chs. 3-4)
    D. The Consecration at Gilgal (5:1-12)
II. The Conquest of the Land (5:13-12:24)
    A. The Initial Battles (5:13-8:35)

      1. The victory at Jericho (5:13-6:27)
      2. The failure at Ai because of Achan's sin (ch. 7)
      3. The victory at Ai (8:1-29)
      4. The covenant renewed at Shechem (8:30-35)
  B. The Campaign in the South (chs. 9-10)
      1. The treaty with the Gibeonites (ch. 9)
      2. The long day of Joshua (10:1-15)
      3. The southern cities conquered (10:16-43)
  C. The Campaign in the North (ch. 11)
  D. The Defeated Kings of Canaan (ch. 12)
III. The Distribution of the Land (chs. 13-21)
  A. Areas Yet to Be Conquered (13:1-7)
  B. The Land East of the Jordan for Reuben, Gad and Half of Manasseh (13:8-33)
  C. The Lands Given to Judah and "Joseph" at Gilgal (chs. 14-17)
  D. The Lands Given to the Remaining Tribes at Shiloh (chs. 18-19)
      1. The tabernacle at Shiloh (18:1-10)
      2. The allotments for Benjamin, Simeon, Zebulun, Issachar, Asher, Naphtali and Dan (18:11-19:48)
      3. The town given to Joshua (19:49-51)
  E. The Cities Assigned to the Levites (chs. 20-21)
      1. The 6 cities of refuge (ch. 20)
      2. The 48 cities of the priests (ch. 21)
IV. Epilogue: Tribal Unity and Loyalty to the Lord (chs. 22-24)
  A. The Altar of Witness by the Jordan (ch. 22)
  B. Joshua's Farewell Exhortation (ch. 23)
  C. The Renewal of the Covenant at Shechem (24:1-28)
  D. The Death and Burial of Joshua and Eleazar (24:29-33)

The LORD Commands Joshua

1 After the death of Moses the servant of the LORD,[a] the LORD said to Joshua[b] son of Nun, Moses' aide: 2"Moses my servant is dead. Now then, you and all these people, get ready to cross the Jordan River[c][d] into the land[e] I am about to give to them[f]—to the Israelites. 3I will give you every place where you set your foot,[g] as I promised Moses.[h] 4Your territory will extend from the desert to Lebanon,[i] and from the great river, the Euphrates[j]—all the Hittite[k] country—to the Great Sea[a] on the west.[l] 5No one will be able to stand up against you[m] all the days of your life. As I was with[n] Moses, so I will be with you; I will never leave you nor forsake[o] you.

6"Be strong[p] and courageous,[q] because you will lead these people to inherit the land I swore to their forefathers[r] to give them. 7Be strong and very courageous. Be careful to obey[s] all the law[t] my servant Moses[u] gave you; do not turn from it to the right or to the left,[v] that you may be successful wherever you go.[w] 8Do not let this Book of the Law[x] depart from your mouth;[y] meditate[z] on it day and night, so that you may be careful to do everything written in it. Then you will be prosperous

and successful.[a] 9Have I not commanded you? Be strong and courageous. Do not be terrified;[b] do not be discouraged,[c] for the LORD your God will be with you wherever you go."[d]

10So Joshua ordered the officers of the people:[e] 11"Go through the camp[f] and tell the people, 'Get your supplies[g] ready. Three days[h] from now you will cross the Jordan[i] here to go in and take possession[j] of the land the LORD your God is giving you for your own.'"

12But to the Reubenites, the Gadites and the half-tribe of Manasseh,[k] Joshua said, 13"Remember the command that Moses the servant of the LORD gave you: 'The LORD your God is giving you rest[l] and has granted you this land.' 14Your wives,[m] your children and your livestock may stay in the land[n] that Moses gave you east of the Jordan, but all your fighting men, fully armed,[o] must cross over ahead of your brothers.[p] You are to help your brothers

---

1:1 [a]Ex 14:31; Dt 34:5; Rev 15:3
[b]S Ex 17:9
1:2 [c]S Nu 13:29
[d]S Nu 35:10
[e]S Ge 15:14
[f]Ge 12:7; Dt 1:25
1:3 [g]S Dt 11:24
[h]Ge 50:24;
Nu 13:2; Dt 1:8
1:4 [i]S Dt 3:25
[j]S Ge 2:14
[k]S Ge 10:15;
23:10; Ex 3:8
[l]Nu 34:2-12;
Ezr 4:20
1:5 [m]S Dt 7:24
[n]ver 17;
S Ge 26:3;
S 39:2; Jdg 6:12;
1Sa 10:7; Jer 1:8;
30:11
[o]S Ge 28:15;
S Dt 4:31
1:6 [p]2Sa 2:7;
1Ki 2:2; Isa 41:6;
Joel 3:9-10
[q]S Dt 1:21;
S 31:6; S Jdg 5:21
[r]Jer 3:18; 7:7
1:7 [s]Dt 29:9;
1Ki 2:3; 3:3
[t]Ezr 7:26;
Ps 78:10;
119:136;
Isa 42:24;
Jer 26:4-6; 32:23;
44:10 [u]ver 2,15;
S Nu 12:7;
Job 1:8; 42:7
[v]S Dt 5:32;
Jos 23:6 [w]ver 9;
S Dt 4:2; 5:33;
S 11:8; Jos 11:15
1:8 [x]S Dt 28:61;
S Ps 147:19
[y]S Ex 4:15;
Isa 59:21

[z]S Ge 24:63 [a]Dt 29:9; 1Sa 18:14; Ps 1:1-3; Isa 52:13; 53:10;
Jer 23:5 1:9 [b]S Dt 31:6; Jos 10:8; 2Ki 19:6; Isa 35:4; 37:6
[c]S Dt 1:21; Job 4:5 [d]S ver 7; Dt 31:8; Jer 1:8 1:10
[e]S Dt 1:15 1:11 [f]Jos 3:2 [g]1Sa 17:22; Isa 10:28 [h]S Ge 40:13
[i]S Nu 35:10 [j]S Nu 33:53 1:12 [k]Nu 32:33 1:13 [l]S Ex 33:14;
Ps 55:6; Isa 11:10; 28:12; 30:15; 32:18; 40:31; Jer 6:16;
45:3; La 5:5 1:14 [m]Dt 3:19 [n]S Nu 32:26 [o]S Ex 13:18
[p]Jos 4:12

[a]4 That is, the Mediterranean

1:1–18 The Lord initiates the action by charging Joshua, his chosen replacement for Moses (see Dt 31:1–8), to lead Israel across the Jordan and take possession of the promised land. He urges courage and promises success—but only if Israel obeys the law of God that Moses has given them. The chapter consists of speeches significant in their content and order: The Lord commands Joshua as his appointed leader over his people (vv. 1–9); Joshua, as the Lord's representative, addresses Israel (vv. 10–15); Israel responds to Joshua as the Lord's representative and successor to Moses (vv. 16–18). Thus the events of the book are set in motion and the roles of the main actors indicated.

1:1 *After the death of Moses.* Immediately the time and occasion of the action are set forth, showing that the story will continue where Deuteronomy ended, with the death of Moses. Cf. "After the death of Joshua" (Jdg 1:1). *servant of the LORD.* See notes on Ex 14:31; Dt 34:5; Ps 18 title; Isa 41:8–9; 42:1. *Moses' aide.* The title by which Joshua served for many years as second in command (see Nu 11:28; see also Ex 24:13; 33:11; Dt 1:38).

1:2 *Jordan River.* The flow of the Jordan near Jericho was not large during most of the year (only 80–100 feet wide), but at flood stage in the spring it filled its wider bed, which at places was a mile wide and far more treacherous to cross. *land I am about to give to them.* A central theme of the Pentateuch (see Ge 12:1; 50:24; Ex 3:8; 23:31; Dt 1:8). Joshua records the fulfillment of this promise of God.
1:3–5 See Dt 11:24–25.
1:4 The dimensions of the land promised to Israel vary (compare this text and Ge 15:18 with Dt 34:1–4), but these are the farthest limits—conquered and held only by David and Solomon. Canaan was still called "Hatti-land" centuries after the Hittites had withdrawn to the north. But Joshua was to take all he set out to conquer; wherever he set his foot was

his. His victories gave to the 12 tribes most of the central hill country and much of the Negev.
1:5 *I will be with you.* To direct, sustain and assure success.
1:6 *land I swore to their forefathers.* The long-awaited inheritance pledged to the descendants of Abraham (Ge 15:7,8–21) and of Jacob (Ge 28:13).
1:7 *Be careful to obey.* Success was not guaranteed unconditionally (see Dt 8:1; 11:8,22–25).
1:8 *Book of the Law.* A documentary form of the laws from Sinai was already extant. *mouth.* See Dt 4:9–10; 6:6–7; 11:19. The law was usually read orally (cf. Dt 30:9–14; Ac 8:30). *meditate.* See Ps 1:2.
1:9 *Have I not commanded you?* A rhetorical question that emphasizes the authority of the speaker.
1:10 *Joshua ordered.* At this point Joshua assumes full command. *officers.* May refer to those whom Moses had appointed over the divisions within the tribes (Ex 18:21; Dt 1:15).
1:11 *supplies.* Foodstuffs needed for the next several days of march.
1:12–15 The threat from the two kings of Transjordan was overcome by military victory and the occupation of the lands north of Moab and east of the Jordan River. The two and a half tribes who asked to remain had been charged by Moses to send their fighting men across with the rest to conquer Canaan (Nu 21:21–35; 32:1–27). The conquest of the promised land must be an undertaking by all Israel.
1:13 *rest.* An important OT concept (see notes on Dt 3:20; 2Sa 7:1,11), implying secure borders, peace with neighboring countries and absence of threat to life and well-being within the land (see note on 1Ki 5:4).
1:14 *your fighting men, fully armed.* Those over 20 (see, e.g., Ex 38:26), known for their valor and able to equip themselves with the weapons of war.

15until the LORD gives them rest, as he has done for you, and until they too have taken possession of the land that the LORD your God is giving them. After that, you may go back and occupy your own land, which Moses the servant of the LORD gave you east of the Jordan toward the sunrise." q

16Then they answered Joshua, "Whatever you have commanded us we will do, and wherever you send us we will go. r 17Just as we fully obeyed Moses, so we will obey you. s Only may the LORD your God be with you as he was with Moses. 18Whoever rebels against your word and does not obey t your words, whatever you may command them, will be put to death. Only be strong and courageous! u "

Rahab and the Spies

2 Then Joshua son of Nun secretly sent two spies v from Shittim. w "Go, look over x the land," he said, "especially Jericho. y " So they went and entered the house of a prostitute b named Rahab z and stayed there.

2The king of Jericho was told, "Look! Some of the Israelites have come here tonight to spy out the land." 3So the king of Jericho sent this message to Rahab: a "Bring out the men who came to you and entered your house, because they have come to spy out the whole land."

4But the woman had taken the two men b and hidden them. c She said, "Yes,

the men came to me, but I did not know where they had come from. 5At dusk, when it was time to close the city gate, d the men left. I don't know which way they went. Go after them quickly. You may catch up with them." e 6(But she had taken them up to the roof and hidden them under the stalks of flax f she had laid out on the roof.) g 7So the men set out in pursuit of the spies on the road that leads to the fords of the Jordan, h and as soon as the pursuers i had gone out, the gate was shut.

8Before the spies lay down for the night, she went up on the roof j 9and said to them, "I know that the LORD has given this land to you and that a great fear k of you has fallen on us, so that all who live in this country are melting in fear because of you. 10We have heard how the LORD dried up l the water of the Red Sea c for you when you came out of Egypt, m and what you did to Sihon and Og, n the two kings of the Amorites o east of the Jordan, p whom you completely destroyed. d q 11When we heard of it, our hearts melted r and everyone's courage failed s because of you, t for the LORD your God u is God in heaven above and on the earth v below. 12Now

1:15
qNu 32:20-22;
Jos 22:1-4
1:16
rS Nu 27:20;
S 32:25
1:17 sS Nu 27:20
1:18 tS Nu 32:25
uS Dt 1:21;
S 31:6
2:1 vS ver 4;
S Ge 42:9
wS Nu 25:1;
Jos 3:1; Joel 3:18
xS Nu 21:32;
Jdg 18:2
yS Nu 33:48
zJos 6:17,25;
S Heb 11:31
2:3 aJos 6:23
2:4 bver 1;
Jos 6:22 cJos 6:17
2:5 dJdg 5:8;
9:35; 16:2
eS Heb 11:31
2:6 fJdg 15:14;
Pr 31:13; Isa 19:9
gS Ex 1:19;
Jos 6:25;
2Sa 17:19
2:7 hNu 22:1;
Jdg 3:28; 7:24;
12:5,6; Isa 16:2
iver 16,22
2:8 jS Dt 22:8;
Jdg 16:27;
2Sa 16:22;
Ne 8:16; Isa 15:3;
22:1; Jer 32:29
2:9 kS Ge 35:5;
S Ex 15:14
2:10 lS Ge 8:1;
Ex 14:21;
Jos 3:17; Ps 74:15
mS Nu 23:22
nS Nu 21:21
oS Ge 10:16;
S 14:7 pJos 9:10
qS Nu 21:2
2:11 rS Ge 42:28
sS Dt 2:25;
Ps 107:26;
Jnh 1:5
tEx 15:14;

Jos 5:1; 7:5; 2Sa 4:1; Ps 22:14; Isa 13:7; 19:1; Jer 51:30;
Na 2:10 u2Ki 5:15; 19:15; Da 6:26 vS Ge 14:19; S Nu 20:14

b1 Or possibly an innkeeper   c10 Hebrew Yam Suph;
that is, Sea of Reeds   d10 The Hebrew term refers to
the irrevocable giving over of things or persons to the
LORD, often by totally destroying them.

1:18 *Whoever rebels.* Having just taken the oath of allegiance to Joshua, they now agree to the death penalty for any act of treason (e.g., the sin of Achan, 7:15). *be strong and courageous.* The people's words of encouragement to Joshua echo and reinforce those from the Lord (vv. 6–7,9).

2:1–24 The mission of the two spies and the account of Rahab. The practice of reconnaissance and espionage is as old as war itself (cf. Jdg 7:10–11; 1Sa 26:16). Rahab became a convert to the God of Israel and a famous woman among the Hebrews. She is honored in the NT for her faith (Heb 11:31) and for her good works (Jas 2:25).

2:1 *sent . . . from Shittim.* The invasion point was in the plains of Moab facing the Jordan and Jericho (Nu 33:48–49). The Hebrew word *Shittim* means "acacia trees," which grow in the semi-arid conditions of the desert. *especially Jericho.* The primary focus of the spies. It was a fortified city, was well supplied by strong springs, which helped to make it an oasis, and was located just five miles west of the Jordan. Its name probably means "moon city," and archaeological excavations there reveal continuous occupation back to at least 7000 B.C. *prostitute.* Josephus and other early sources refer to Rahab as an "innkeeper" (see NIV text note), but see Heb 11:31; Jas 2:25.

2:2 *king of Jericho.* The major cities of Canaan were in reality small kingdoms, each ruled by a local king (attested also in the Amarna letters of the 14th century B.C.; see chart on "Ancient Texts Relating to the OT," p. 5).

2:6 *hidden . . . under the stalks of flax.* Rooftops in the Near East are still used for drying grain or stalks. Rahab's

cunning saved the lives of the two Israelites but put her own life in jeopardy.

2:7 *fords of the Jordan.* Shallow crossings of the Jordan, where the depth of normal flow averages only three feet.

2:8–11 Rahab's confession has a significant concentric structure:

a. "I know";
b. "a great fear . . . has fallen on us . . . all who live in this country";
c. "We have heard";
bb. "our hearts melted and everyone's courage failed";
aa. "the LORD your God is God".

Rahab's personal confession forms the outer frame (a.-aa.); the inner frame (b.-bb.) offers the military intelligence that the spies report back to Joshua. the center (c., v. 10) sums up the news about the Lord that occasioned both the Canaanite fear and also Rahab's abandonment of Canaan and its gods for the Lord and Israel. Her confession of faith in the Lord and her accurate information about the Lord's triumphs over powerful enemies are founding. That the hearts of the Canaanites were "melting in fear" (v. 9) was vital information to the spies.

2:10 *completely destroyed.* See NIV text note.

2:12 *show kindness to my family.* The Hebrew for "kindness" is frequently translated "love" or "unfailing love" and often summarizes God's covenant favor toward his people or the love that people are to show to others. Rahab had acted toward the spies as though she was an Israelite, and now she asks that Israel treat her similarly. *sure sign.* Their oath to

then, please swear to me[w] by the LORD that you will show kindness[x] to my family, because I have shown kindness to you. Give me a sure sign[y] ¹³that you will spare the lives of my father and mother, my brothers and sisters, and all who belong to them,[z] and that you will save us from death."

¹⁴"Our lives for your lives!"[a] the men assured her. "If you don't tell what we are doing, we will treat you kindly and faithfully[b] when the LORD gives us the land."

¹⁵So she let them down by a rope[c] through the window,[d] for the house she lived in was part of the city wall. ¹⁶Now she had said to them, "Go to the hills[e] so the pursuers[f] will not find you. Hide yourselves there three days[g] until they return, and then go on your way."[h]

¹⁷The men said to her, "This oath[i] you made us swear will not be binding on us ¹⁸unless, when we enter the land, you have tied this scarlet cord[j] in the window[k] through which you let us down, and unless you have brought your father and mother, your brothers and all your family[l] into your house. ¹⁹If anyone goes outside your house into the street, his blood will be on his own head;[m] we will not be responsible. As for anyone who is in the house with you, his blood will be on our head[n] if a hand is laid on him. ²⁰But if you tell what we are doing, we will be released from the oath you made us swear."[o]

²¹"Agreed," she replied. "Let it be as you say." So she sent them away and they departed. And she tied the scarlet cord[p] in the window.[q]

²²When they left, they went into the hills and stayed there three days,[r] until the pursuers[s] had searched all along the road and returned without finding them. ²³Then the two men started back. They went down out of the hills, forded the river and came to Joshua son of Nun and told him everything that had happened to them. ²⁴They said to Joshua, "The LORD has surely given the whole land into our hands;[t] all the people are melting in fear[u] because of us."

Crossing the Jordan

3 Early in the morning Joshua and all the Israelites set out from Shittim[v] and went to the Jordan,[w] where they camped before crossing over. ²After three days[x] the officers[y] went throughout the camp,[z] ³giving orders to the people: "When you see the ark of the covenant[a] of the LORD your God, and the priests,[b] who are Levites,[c] carrying it, you are to move out from your positions and follow it. ⁴Then you will know which way to go, since you have never been this way before. But keep a distance of about a thousand yards[e][d] between you and the ark; do not go near it."

⁵Joshua told the people, "Consecrate

[e4] Hebrew *about two thousand cubits* (about 900 meters)

Cross references

2:12 wS Ge 24:8; S 47:31
xS Ge 24:12; Ru 3:10
yS Ge 24:14; S Ex 3:12; Jos 4:6; 1Sa 2:34; 2Ki 19:29
2:13 zver 18; Jos 6:23
2:14 a1Ki 20:39, 42; 2Ki 10:24
bS Ge 47:29
2:15 cJer 38:6,11
dver 18,21; Ge 26:8; Jdg 5:28; 1Sa 19:12
2:16 eS Ge 14:10
fS ver 7 gver 22
hS Heb 11:31
2:17 iS Ge 24:8
2:18 jver 21
kS ver 15 lS ver 13
2:19 mS Lev 20:9
nMt 27:25
2:20 oS Ge 24:8; S 47:31

2:21 Pver 18
qS ver 15
2:22 rver 16
sS ver 7
2:24 tJos 10:8; 11:6; Jdg 3:28; 7:9,14; 20:28; 1Sa 14:10
uS Ex 15:15
3:1 vS Jos 2:1
wS Ge 13:10; Job 40:23
3:2 xS Ge 40:13; Jos 2:16
yS Dt 1:15
zJos 1:11
3:3 aS Nu 10:33
bver 8,17; Nu 4:15; Dt 31:9; 1Ki 8:3 c1Sa 6:15
3:4 dNu 35:5

Commentary

spare the whole family (v. 14).

2:14 *kindly and faithfully.* The terms of the pledge made by the spies echo Rahab's request (v. 12). *when the LORD gives us the land.* All were convinced of the inevitable victory of the Israelites over the city of Jericho.

2:15 *the house . . . was part of the city wall.* There is archaeological evidence that the people of Jericho would occasionally build their houses onto the city wall. Although this evidence predates the time of Joshua, it may still serve to illumine this verse. Alternatively, the Late Bronze fortifications at Jericho may have included a casemate wall (a hollow wall with partitions), and Rahab may have occupied one or more rooms inside it.

2:18 *scarlet cord in the window.* The function of the red marker was similar to that of the blood of the Passover lamb when the Lord struck down the firstborn of Egypt (see Ex 12:13,22–23). The early church viewed the blood-colored cord as a type (symbol) of Christ's atonement.

2:19 *his blood will be on our head.* A vow that accepted responsibility for the death of another, with its related guilt and the retribution meted out by either relatives or the state.

2:22 *into the hills.* Directly west of ancient Jericho were the high, rugged hills of the central mountain ridge in Palestine. They are honeycombed with caves, making the concealment and escape of the two spies relatively easy.

3:1–4:24 Details of the river crossing and the memorial of 12 stones set up in the camp at Gilgal. The great significance of this account can hardly be overemphasized, since it marks

the crossing of the boundary into the promised land and parallels the miracle of the "Red Sea" crossing in the exodus (Ex 14–15). The Israelites' faith in the God of their fathers was renewed and strengthened when it was about to be most severely challenged, while at the same time the Canaanites' fear was greatly increased (5:1). In this account the author uses an "overlay" technique in which, having narrated the crossing to its conclusion (ch. 3), he returns to various points in the event to enlarge on several details: the stones for a memorial (4:1–9); the successful crossing by all Israel (4:10–14); the renewed flow of the river after the crossing was completed (4:15–18). The final paragraph of ch. 4 (vv. 19–24) picks up the story again from 3:17 and completes the account by noting Israel's encampment at Gilgal and the erecting of the stone memorial.

3:3 *ark of the covenant.* The most sacred of the tabernacle furnishings (see Ex 25:10–22). Since it signified the Lord's throne, the Lord himself went into the Jordan ahead of his people as he led them into the land of rest (see Nu 10:33–36).

3:4 *distance of about a thousand yards.* There was evidently a line of march, with the priests and ark leading the way. Respect for the sacred symbol of the Lord's holy presence accounts for this gap between the people and the priests bearing the ark.

3:5 *Consecrate yourselves.* Before their meeting with God at Sinai this had involved washing all their garments as well as their bodies, and also abstinence from sexual intercourse

yourselves,[e] for tomorrow the LORD will do amazing things[f] among you."

[6]Joshua said to the priests, "Take up the ark of the covenant and pass on ahead of the people." So they took it up and went ahead of them.

[7]And the LORD said to Joshua, "Today I will begin to exalt you[g] in the eyes of all Israel, so they may know that I am with you as I was with Moses.[h] [8]Tell the priests[i] who carry the ark of the covenant: 'When you reach the edge of the Jordan's waters, go and stand in the river.' "

[9]Joshua said to the Israelites, "Come here and listen to the words of the LORD your God. [10]This is how you will know that the living God[j] is among you[k] and that he will certainly drive out before you the Canaanites, Hittites,[l] Hivites, Perizzites,[m] Girgashites, Amorites and Jebusites.[n] [11]See, the ark of the covenant of the Lord of all the earth[o] will go into the Jordan ahead of you.[p] [12]Now then, choose twelve men[q] from the tribes of Israel, one from each tribe. [13]And as soon as the priests who carry the ark of the LORD—the Lord of all the earth[r]—set foot in the Jordan, its waters flowing downstream[s] will be cut off[t] and stand up in a heap.[u] "

[14]So when the people broke camp to cross the Jordan, the priests carrying the ark of the covenant[v] went ahead[w] of

them. [15]Now the Jordan[x] is at flood stage[y] all during harvest.[z] Yet as soon as the priests who carried the ark reached the Jordan and their feet touched the water's edge, [16]the water from upstream stopped flowing.[a] It piled up in a heap[b] a great distance away, at a town called Adam in the vicinity of Zarethan,[c] while the water flowing down[d] to the Sea of the Arabah[e] (the Salt Sea[f]) was completely cut off.[g] So the people crossed over opposite Jericho.[h] [17]The priests[i] who carried the ark of the covenant of the LORD stood firm on dry ground in the middle of the Jordan,[j] while all Israel passed by until the whole nation had completed the crossing on dry ground.[k]

4 When the whole nation had finished crossing the Jordan,[l] the LORD said to Joshua, [2]"Choose twelve men[m] from among the people, one from each tribe, [3]and tell them to take up twelve stones[n] from the middle of the Jordan[o] from right where the priests stood and to carry them over with you and put them down at the place where you stay tonight.[p] "

[4]So Joshua called together the twelve men[q] he had appointed from the Israelites, one from each tribe, [5]and said to them,

---

Cross references (center column):

3:5 [e]S Ex 29:1; S Lev 11:44
[f]Jdg 6:13; 1Ch 16:9,24; Ps 26:7; 75:1
3:7 [g]Jos 4:14; 1Ch 29:25
[h]Jos 1:5
3:8 [i]S ver 3
3:10 [j]Dt 5:26; 1Sa 17:26,36; 2Ki 19:4,16; Ps 18:46; 42:2; 84:2; Isa 37:4,17; Jer 10:10; 23:36; Da 6:26; Hos 1:10; S Mt 16:16
[k]S Dt 7:21
[l]S Ge 26:34
[m]Jos 17:15; 24:11; Jdg 1:4; 3:5 [n]S Ex 3:8; S 23:23; S Dt 7:1; Jos 9:1; 11:3; 12:8; Jdg 19:11; 1Ch 11:4
3:11 [o]ver 13; Ex 19:5; Dt 10:14; Job 9:10; 28:24; 41:11; Ps 50:12; 97:5; Zec 6:5
[p]S Dt 9:3
3:12 [q]Jos 4:2,4
3:13 [r]S ver 11
[s]ver 16 [t]Jos 4:7
[u]S Ex 14:22; S Isa 11:15
3:14 [v]Ps 132:8
[w]Ac 7:44-45

3:15 [x]2Ki 2:6
[y]Jos 4:18; 1Ch 12:15; Isa 8:7 [z]S Ge 8:22
3:16 [a]Ps 66:6; 74:15; 114:3
[b]Job 38:37; Ps 33:7
[c]1Ki 4:12; 7:46
[d]ver 13 [e]S Dt 1:1
[f]S Ge 14:3

[g]S Ge 8:1; S Ex 14:22 [h]2Ki 2:4 3:17 [i]S ver 3 [j]Jos 4:3,5,8,9, 10 [k]S Ex 14:22; S Jos 2:10 4:1 [l]Dt 27:2 4:2 [m]S Jos 3:12 4:3 [n]ver 20 [o]S Jos 3:17 [p]ver 19 4:4 [q]S Jos 3:12

[f]16 That is, the Dead Sea

(see Ex 19:10,14–15).
3:7 *I will begin to exalt you.* A prime objective for the divine intervention at the Jordan was to validate the leadership of Joshua. With a miraculous event so much like that of the "Red Sea" crossing, Joshua's position as the Lord's servant would be shown to be comparable to that of Moses.
3:10 *This is how you will know.* The manner by which God is about to bring Israel across the Jordan River, the watery boundary of the promised land, will bring assurance that the one true God is with them and that he will surely dislodge the present inhabitants of Canaan. Two fundamental issues are at stake: 1. Who is the true and mighty God—the God of Israel or the god on whom the Canaanites depend (Baal, who was believed to reign as king among the gods because he had triumphed over the sea-god)? By opening the way through the flooded Jordan the Lord would show both Israel and the Canaanites that he is Lord over the waters (as he was at the "Red Sea," at the flood and at creation) and that he is able to establish his own order in the world. See 1Ki 20:23; 2Ki 18:32–35. 2. Who has the rightful claim to the land—the Lord or the Canaanites? (For the juridical aspect of such wars see Jdg 11:27.) By passing safely through the Jordan at the head of his army the Lord showed the rightness of his claim on the land. In the ancient Near East a common way for obtaining the judicial verdict of the gods was by compelling the accused to submit to trial by water ordeal. Usually this involved casting him into a river (if the accused drowned, the gods had found him guilty; if not, the gods had declared him innocent). In Israel, however, another form of water ordeal was practiced (see Nu 5:16–28). Significantly, the Lord

would enter the Jordan first and then remain there until his whole army had crossed safely over. Thus his claim to the land was vindicated before the eyes of all who heard about it. And it was his claim, not Israel's; she came through the Jordan only with him and as his army, "baptized" to his service. *Canaanites . . . Jebusites.* See notes on Ge 9:25; 10:6,15–16; 13:7; 15:16; 23:3; Ex 3:8; Jdg 3:3; 6:10.
3:12 *choose twelve men.* Joshua seems to anticipate the Lord's instructions concerning a stone monument of the event (see 4:2–3).
3:13 *cut off.* Blocked, stopped in its flow. *stand up in a heap.* The Hebrew for "heap" is found here, in v. 16 and also in the poetic accounts of the "Red Sea" crossing (Ex 15:8; Ps 78:13). It is possible that God used a physical means (such as a landslide) to dam up the Jordan at the place called Adam (v. 16), near the entrance of the Jabbok. (As recently as 1927 a blockage of the water in this area was recorded that lasted over 20 hours.) But if so, the miraculous element is not diminished (see Ex 14:21).
3:15 *at flood stage.* Because of the spring rains and the melting of snow on Mount Hermon. *harvest.* Grain harvest took place in April and May. *as soon as.* The stoppage nearly 20 miles upstream (v. 16) would have happened several hours earlier to make the events coincide.
3:17 *The priests who carried the ark . . . stood firm on dry ground in the middle of the Jordan.* Signifying that the Lord himself remained in the place of danger until all Israel had crossed the Jordan.
4:3 *at the place where you stay tonight.* Indicating that the entire nation made the crossing in one day.

"Go over before the ark of the LORD your God into the middle of the Jordan.[r] Each of you is to take up a stone on his shoulder, according to the number of the tribes of the Israelites, [6]to serve as a sign[s] among you. In the future, when your children[t] ask you, 'What do these stones mean?'[u] [7]tell them that the flow of the Jordan was cut off[v] before the ark of the covenant of the LORD. When it crossed the Jordan, the waters of the Jordan were cut off. These stones are to be a memorial[w] to the people of Israel forever."

[8]So the Israelites did as Joshua commanded them. They took twelve stones[x] from the middle of the Jordan,[y] according to the number of the tribes of the Israelites, as the LORD had told Joshua;[z] and they carried them over with them to their camp, where they put them down. [9]Joshua set up the twelve stones[a] that had been[g] in the middle of the Jordan at the spot where the priests who carried the ark of the covenant had stood. And they are there to this day.[b]

[10]Now the priests who carried the ark remained standing in the middle of the Jordan until everything the LORD had commanded Joshua was done by the people, just as Moses had directed Joshua. The people hurried over, [11]and as soon as all of them had crossed, the ark of the LORD and the priests came to the other side while the people watched. [12]The men of Reuben,[c] Gad[d] and the half-tribe of Manasseh[e] crossed over, armed, in front of the Israelites,[f] as Moses had directed them.[g] [13]About forty thousand armed for battle[h] crossed over[i] before the LORD to the plains of Jericho for war.

[14]That day the LORD exalted[j] Joshua in the sight of all Israel; and they revered him

all the days of his life, just as they had revered Moses.

[15]Then the LORD said to Joshua, [16]"Command the priests carrying the ark of the Testimony[k] to come up out of the Jordan."

[17]So Joshua commanded the priests, "Come up out of the Jordan."

[18]And the priests came up out of the river carrying the ark of the covenant of the LORD. No sooner had they set their feet on the dry ground than the waters of the Jordan returned to their place[l] and ran at flood stage[m] as before.

[19]On the tenth day of the first month the people went up from the Jordan and camped at Gilgal[n] on the eastern border of Jericho. [20]And Joshua set up at Gilgal the twelve stones[o] they had taken out of the Jordan. [21]He said to the Israelites, "In the future when your descendants ask their fathers, 'What do these stones mean?'[p] [22]tell them, 'Israel crossed the Jordan on dry ground.'[q] [23]For the LORD your God dried up the Jordan before you until you had crossed over. The LORD your God did to the Jordan just what he had done to the Red Sea[h] when he dried it up before us until we had crossed over.[r] [24]He did this so that all the peoples of the earth might know[s] that the hand of the LORD is powerful[t] and so that you might always fear the LORD your God.[u]"

Circumcision at Gilgal

5 Now when all the Amorite kings west of the Jordan and all the Canaanite kings along the coast[v] heard how the LORD had dried up the Jordan before the Israelites until we had crossed over, their

---

4:5 [r]S Jos 3:17
4:6 [s]S Jos 2:12
[t]S Ex 10:2 [u]ver 21; Ex 12:26; S 13:14
4:7 [v]Jos 3:13 [w]S Ex 28:12
4:8 [x]Ex 28:21 [y]S Jos 3:17 [z]ver 20
4:9 [a]S Ge 28:18; Jos 24:26; 1Sa 7:12
[b]S Ge 35:20
4:12 [c]S Ge 29:32 [d]S Ge 30:11 [e]S Ge 41:51 [f]S Nu 32:27 [g]Nu 32:29
4:13 [h]S Ex 13:18 [i]S Nu 32:17
4:14 [j]S Jos 3:7

4:16 [k]Ex 25:22
4:18 [l]Ex 14:27 [m]S Jos 3:15
4:19 [n]S Dt 11:30
4:20 [o]ver 3,8
4:21 [p]S ver 6
4:22 [q]S Ex 14:22
4:23
[r]Ex 14:19-22
4:24 [s]1Ki 8:60; 18:36; 2Ki 5:15; Ps 67:2; 83:18; 106:8; Isa 37:20; 52:10 [t]Ex 15:16; 1Ch 29:12; Ps 44:3; 89:13; 98:1; 118:15-16 [u]S Ex 14:31
5:1 [v]S Nu 13:29

[g]9 Or *Joshua also set up twelve stones*   [h]23 Hebrew *Yam Suph;* that is, Sea of Reeds

---

4:6 *What do these stones mean?* A stone monument was commonly used as a memorial to remind future generations of what had happened at that place (24:26; 1Sa 7:12).

4:9 *Joshua set up the twelve stones.* Each tribe brought a stone for the monument from the riverbed to the new campsite at Gilgal, and Joshua constructed the monument there. An alternative translation suggests that Joshua set up a second pile in the middle of the river (see NIV text note).

4:13 *About forty thousand.* Seems too few for the number of men listed in Nu 26 for Reuben, Gad and half of Manasseh; the contingents were very likely representative since it would have been imprudent to leave the people undefended who settled in Transjordan (cf. 22:8, "brothers"; Nu 32:17).

4:19 *tenth day of the first month.* The day the Passover lamb was to be selected (Ex 12:3). *Gilgal.* Usually identified with the ruins at Khirbet el-Mafjer, two miles northeast of Jericho.

4:23 *God dried up the Jordan.* Still another descriptive phrase for the miracle, along with "the water . . . cut off,"

"piled up in a heap" and "stopped flowing" (3:16).

4:24 *so that all . . . might know.* The Lord's revelation of his power to the Israelites was a public event that all the Canaanites heard about (see 5:1), just as they had heard of the crossing of the "Red Sea" and defeat of Sihon and Og (2:10). *you.* The Hebrew can also be read as "they." *fear the LORD.* Worship and serve him according to his commandments.

5:1—12 Two covenantal ceremonies were resumed at Gilgal in accordance with the laws from Sinai: the rite of circumcision and the Feast of the Passover. Both were significant preparations for the conquest of the promised land.

5:1 *Amorite . . . Canaanite.* Usually interchangeable, these general names included the many smaller nations in the land. Amorite meant "westerner," and Canaanite referred to the people living along the Mediterranean coast. This verse perhaps concludes the account of the crossing since it notes the effect of that event on the peoples of Canaan (see note on 3:10).

hearts melted[w] and they no longer had the courage to face the Israelites.

[2]At that time the LORD said to Joshua, "Make flint knives[x] and circumcise[y] the Israelites again." [3]So Joshua made flint knives and circumcised the Israelites at Gibeath Haaraloth.[i]

[4]Now this is why he did so: All those who came out of Egypt—all the men of military age[z]—died in the desert on the way after leaving Egypt.[a] [5]All the people that came out had been circumcised, but all the people born in the desert during the journey from Egypt had not. [6]The Israelites had moved about in the desert[b] forty years[c] until all the men who were of military age when they left Egypt had died, since they had not obeyed the LORD. For the LORD had sworn to them that they would not see the land that he had solemnly promised their fathers to give us,[d] a land flowing with milk and honey.[e] [7]So he raised up their sons in their place, and these were the ones Joshua circumcised. They were still uncircumcised because they had not been circumcised on the way. [8]And after the whole nation had been circumcised, they remained where they were in camp until they were healed.[f]

[9]Then the LORD said to Joshua, "Today I have rolled away the reproach of Egypt from you." So the place has been called Gilgal[g] to this day.

[10]On the evening of the fourteenth day of the month,[h] while camped at Gilgal on the plains of Jericho, the Israelites celebrated the Passover.[i] [11]The day after the Passover, that very day, they ate some of the produce of the land:[j] unleavened bread[k] and roasted grain.[l] [12]The manna stopped the day after[k] they ate this food from the land; there was no longer any manna for the Israelites, but that year they ate of the produce of Canaan.[m]

The Fall of Jericho

[13]Now when Joshua was near Jericho, he looked up and saw a man[n] standing in front of him with a drawn sword[o] in his hand. Joshua went up to him and asked, "Are you for us or for our enemies?"

[14]"Neither," he replied, "but as commander of the army of the LORD I have now come." Then Joshua fell facedown[p] to the ground[q] in reverence, and asked him, "What message does my Lord[1] have for his servant?"

[15]The commander of the LORD's army replied, "Take off your sandals, for the place where you are standing is holy."[r] And Joshua did so.

5:1 [w]S Ge 42:28
5:2 [x]S Ex 4:25
         [y]S Ge 17:10,12, 14
5:4 [z]S Nu 1:3
         [a]Dt 2:14
5:6 [b]Nu 32:13;
         Jos 14:10;
         Ps 107:4
         [c]S Ex 16:35
         [d]Nu 14:23,29-35;
         Dt 2:14 [e]S Ex 3:8
5:8 [f]Ge 34:25
5:9 [g]S Dt 11:30

5:10 [h]S Ex 12:6
          [i]S Ex 12:11
5:11 [j]S Nu 15:19
          [k]Ex 12:15
          [l]S Lev 23:14
5:12 [m]Ex 16:35
5:13 [n]S Ge 18:2
          [o]Nu 22:23
5:14 [p]S Ge 17:3
          [q]S Ge 19:1
5:15
          [r]S Ge 28:17;
          Ex 3:5; Ac 7:33

13 Gibeath Haaraloth means hill of foreskins. *19 Gilgal sounds like the Hebrew for roll.* **k**12 Or the day **l**14 Or lord

---

5:2 *flint knives.* Metal knives were available, but flint made a more efficient surgical tool, as modern demonstrations have shown. Israel had to be consecrated to the Lord's service before she could undertake the Lord's warfare and take possession of the land (cf. Ex 4:24–26). *circumcise.* Circumcision marked every male as a son of Abraham (Ge 17:10–11) bound to the service of the Lord, and it was a prerequisite for the Passover (Ex 12:48).
5:3 *Gibeath Haaraloth.* See NIV text note.
5:6 *forty years.* The time between their departure from Egypt and the crossing of the Jordan. Only 38 years had passed since they turned back at Kadesh Barnea (Nu 14:20–22; Dt 2:14).
5:9 *reproach of Egypt.* Although the reference may be to Egypt's enslavement of Israel, it is much more likely that the author had in mind the reproach the Egyptians would have cast upon her and her God if Israel had perished in the desert (see Ex 32:12; Nu 14:13; Dt 9:28). Now that the desert journey is over and Israel is safely in the promised land as his special people consecrated to him by circumcision, the reproach of Egypt is rolled away.
5:10 *Passover.* The ceremonies took place in the month of Abib, the first month of the year (Ex 12:2). At twilight on the 14th day of the month the Passover lamb was to be slaughtered, then roasted and eaten that same night (Ex 12:5–8). Israel had not celebrated Passover since Sinai, one year after her release from Egypt (Nu 9:1–5). Before the next season she had rebelled at the border of Canaan, and the generation of the exodus had been condemned to die in the desert (Nu 14:21–23,29–35). For that generation the celebration of Passover (deliverance from judgment) could have had little meaning.
5:11 *unleavened bread.* Bread baked without yeast. It was to be eaten during the seven feast days that followed (Ex 12:15; Lev 23:6).
5:12 *manna stopped.* This transition from eating manna to eating the "produce of the land" (v. 11) ended 40 years of dependence on God's special provision. Manna was God's gift for the desert journey; from now on he provided Israel with food from the promised land.
5:13—6:5 The narration of the conquest is introduced by the sudden appearance of a heavenly figure who calls himself the "commander of the army of the LORD" (5:14).
5:13 *Joshua was near Jericho.* The leader of God's army went to scout the nearest Canaanite stronghold, but another warrior was already on the scene. *a man standing.* The experience is taken by many to be an encounter with God in human form (theophany), or with Christ (Christophany). But angels also were sent on missions of this kind (Jdg 6:11; 13:3), and some were identified as captains over the heavenly armies (Da 10:5,20; 12:1).
5:14 *Neither.* Joshua and Israel must know their place—it is not that God is on their side; rather, they must fight God's battles. *commander of the army of the LORD.* God has sent the commander of his heavenly armies to take charge of the battle on earth. Joshua must take orders from him (6:2–5), and he can also lead the armies of heaven are committed to this war—as later events confirm. *my Lord.* A term of respect for a superior.
5:15 Joshua is commissioned to undertake the Lord's battles for Canaan, just as Moses had been commissioned to confront Pharaoh (Ex 3:5).

6 Now Jericho[s] was tightly shut up because of the Israelites. No one went out and no one came in.

[2]Then the LORD said to Joshua, "See, I have delivered[t] Jericho into your hands, along with its king and its fighting men. [3]March around the city once with all the armed men. Do this for six days. [4]Have seven priests carry trumpets of rams' horns[u] in front of the ark. On the seventh day, march around the city seven times, with the priests blowing the trumpets.[v] [5]When you hear them sound a long blast[w] on the trumpets, have all the people give a loud shout;[x] then the wall of the city will collapse and the people will go up, every man straight in."

[6]So Joshua son of Nun called the priests and said to them, "Take up the ark of the covenant of the LORD and have seven priests carry trumpets in front of it."[y] [7]And he ordered the people, "Advance[z]! March around the city, with the armed guard going ahead of the ark[a] of the LORD."

[8]When Joshua had spoken to the people, the seven priests carrying the seven trumpets before the LORD went forward, blowing their trumpets, and the ark of the LORD's covenant followed them. [9]The armed guard marched ahead of the priests who blew the trumpets, and the rear guard[b] followed the ark. All this time the trumpets were sounding. [10]But Joshua had commanded the people, "Do not give a war cry, do not raise your voices, do not say a word until the day I tell you to shout. Then shout![c]" [11]So he had the ark of the LORD carried around the city, circling it once. Then the people returned to camp and spent the night there.

[12]Joshua got up early the next morning and the priests took up the ark of the LORD. [13]The seven priests carrying the seven trumpets went forward, marching before the ark of the LORD and blowing the trumpets. The armed men went ahead of them and the rear guard followed the ark of the LORD, while the trumpets kept sounding. [14]So on the second day they marched around the city once and returned to the camp. They did this for six days.

[15]On the seventh day, they got up at daybreak and marched around the city seven times in the same manner, except that on that day they circled the city seven times.[d] [16]The seventh time around, when the priests sounded the trumpet blast, Joshua commanded the people, "Shout! For the LORD has given you the city![e] [17]The city and all that is in it are to be

Cross references (center column):
6:1 [s]Jos 24:11
6:2 [t]ver 16; Dt 7:24; Jos 8:1
6:4 [u]S Ex 19:13 [v]S Lev 25:9
6:5 [w]Ex 19:13 [x]ver 20; 1Sa 4:5; 2Sa 6:15; Ezr 3:11; 10:12; Ps 42:4; 95:1; Isa 8:9; 42:13
6:6 [y]ver 4
6:7 [z]Ex 14:15 [a]Nu 10:35; 1Sa 4:3; 7:1
6:9 [b]ver 13; S Nu 2:31; Isa 52:12
6:10 [c]ver 20; 1Sa 4:5; Ezr 3:11
6:15 [d]1Ki 18:44; 2Ki 4:35; 5:14
6:16 [e]S ver 2

6:1 *Jericho.* Modern Tell es-Sultan, site of more than two dozen ancient cities, built and destroyed, one above the other. Many had powerful, double walls, but none of the levels has been positively identified as the one that fell under Joshua. The tell (mound) is roughly 400 by 200 yards in size. Since Jericho may have been a center for the worship of the moon-god (Jericho probably means "moon city"), God was destroying not only Canaanite cities, but also Canaanite religion. See map No. 3 at the end of the Study Bible.

6:2 *the LORD.* The Lord's command no doubt comes to Joshua through the "commander of the army of the LORD" (5:14), who orders the first conquest of a Canaanite city.

6:3 *March around the city.* A ritual act, signifying a siege of the city, that was to be repeated for six days.

6:4 *trumpets of rams' horns.* Instruments not of music but of signaling, in both religious and military contexts (which appear to come together here). The trumpets were to be sounded (v. 8), as on the seventh day, announcing the presence of the Lord (see 2Sa 6:15; 1Ch 15:28; Zec 9:14). *ark.* Signified that the Lord was laying siege to the city. *seventh day.* No note is taken of the Sabbath during this seven-day siege, but perhaps that was the day the Lord gave the city to Israel as the first pledge of the land of rest. To arrive at the goal of a long march on the seventh day is a motif found also in other ancient Near Eastern literature. In any event, the remarkable constellation of sevens (seven priests with trumpets, seven days, seven encirclements on the seventh day) underscores the sacred significance of the event (see Introduction to Revelation: Distinctive Feature) and is, perhaps, a deliberate evoking of the seven days of creation to signal the beginning of God's new order in the world.

6:5 *long blast . . . loud shout.* Signaling the onset of the attack—psychological warfare, intended to create panic and confusion (see Jdg 7). In the Dead Sea Scroll of "The War of the Sons of Light against the Sons of Darkness," the Levites are instructed to blow in unison a great battle fanfare to melt the heart of the enemy. (For Dead Sea Scrolls see "The Time between the Testaments," p. 1431.) *every man straight in.* Not a breach here and there but a general collapse of the walls, giving access to the city from all sides.

6:7 *armed guard.* The Hebrew for this term differs from that in v. 3 but may be synonymous with it. It is to be expected that the ark led the procession. If so, the present reference may be to a kind of royal guard (but see v. 9 and note).

6:8–14 Throughout these verses the ark of the Lord is made the center of focus, highlighting the fact that it was the Lord himself who besieged the city.

6:9 *rear guard.* If the rear guard was made up of the final contingents of the army (see Nu 10:25), the armed guard of vv. 7,9 constituted the main body of troops.

6:12–14 Literary repetition reflects repetition in action, a common feature in ancient Near Eastern literature.

6:17 *devoted.* See NIV text note. The ban placed all of Jericho's inhabitants under the curse of death and all of the city's treasures that could not be destroyed under consignment to the Lord's house (v. 19). According to the law of Moses this ban could be applied to animals for sacrifice, to property given to God, or to any person found worthy of death (Lev 27:28–29). It was Moses himself who ruled that all the inhabitants of Canaan be "devoted" by execution for their idolatry and all its accompanying moral corruption (Dt 20:16–18). See note on Dt 2:34. *Rahab . . . and . . . her house shall be spared.* Honoring the pledge made by the two spies (2:14).

devoted[m][f] to the Lord. Only Rahab the prostitute[n][g] and all who are with her in her house shall be spared, because she hid[h] the spies we sent. [18]But keep away from the devoted things,[i] so that you will not bring about your own destruction by taking any of them. Otherwise you will make the camp of Israel liable to destruction[j] and bring trouble[k] on it. [19]All the silver and gold and the articles of bronze and iron[l] are sacred to the Lord and must go into his treasury."

[20]When the trumpets sounded,[m] people shouted, and at the sound of the trumpet, when the people gave a loud shout,[n] the wall collapsed; so every man charged straight in, and they took the city.[o] [21]They devoted[p] the city to the Lord and destroyed[q] with the sword every living thing in it—men and women, young and old, cattle, sheep and donkeys.

[22]Joshua said to the two men[r] who had spied out[s] the land, "Go into the prostitute's house and bring her out and all who belong to her, in accordance with your oath to her.[t]" [23]So the young men who had done the spying went in and brought out Rahab, her father and mother and brothers and all who belonged to her.[u] They brought out her entire family and put them in a place outside the camp of Israel.

[24]Then they burned the whole city[v] and everything in it, but they put the silver and gold and the articles of bronze and iron[w] into the treasury of the Lord's house.[x] [25]But Joshua spared[y] Rahab the prostitute,[z] with her family and all who belonged to her, because she hid the men Joshua had sent as spies to Jericho[a]—and she lives among the Israelites to this day. [26]At that time Joshua pronounced this

solemn oath:[b] "Cursed[c] before the Lord is the man who undertakes to rebuild this city, Jericho:

"At the cost of his firstborn son
    will he lay its foundations;
at the cost of his youngest
    will he set up its gates."[d]

[27]So the Lord was with Joshua,[e] and his fame spread[f] throughout the land.

Achan's Sin

7 But the Israelites acted unfaithfully in regard to the devoted things[o];[g] Achan[h] son of Carmi, the son of Zimri,[p] the son of Zerah,[i] of the tribe of Judah,[j] took some of them. So the Lord's anger burned[k] against Israel.[l]

[2]Now Joshua sent men from Jericho to Ai,[m] which is near Beth Aven[n] to the east of Bethel,[o] and told them, "Go up and spy out[p] the region." So the men went up and spied out Ai.

[3]When they returned to Joshua, they said, "Not all the people will have to go up against Ai. Send two or three thousand men to take it and do not weary all the people, for only a few men are there." [4]So about three thousand men went up; but they were routed by the men of Ai,[q] [5]who killed about thirty-six[r] of them. They chased the Israelites from the city gate as

---

6:17 [f]ver 21; Lev 27:28; Dt 20:17; Isa 13:5; 24:1; 34:2,5; Mal 4:6
[g]S Jos 2:1 [h]ver 25; Jos 2:4
6:18 [i]Jos 7:1; 1Ch 2:7 [j]Jos 7:12 [k]Jos 7:25,26
6:19 [l]ver 24; Nu 31:22
6:20 [m]Lev 25:9; Jdg 6:34; 7:22; 1Ki 1:41; Isa 18:3; 27:13; Jer 4:21; 42:14; Am 2:2 [n]S ver 5, S 10 [o]Heb 11:30
6:21 [p]S ver 17 [q]S Dt 20:16
6:22 [r]S Ge 42:9; S Jos 2:4 [s]S Nu 21:32 [t]Jos 2:14; Heb 11:31
6:23 [u]S Jos 2:13
6:24 [v]S Nu 31:10 [w]S ver 19 [x]S Dt 13:16
6:25 [y]Jdg 1:25 [z]S Jos 2:1 [a]S ver 17; S Jos 2:6

6:26 [b]1Sa 14:24 [c]S Nu 5:21 [d]1Ki 16:34
6:27 [e]S Ge 39:2; S Nu 14:43 [f]Jos 9:1; 1Ch 14:17
7:1 [g]S Jos 6:18 [h]ver 26; 1Ch 2:7 [i]Jos 22:20 [j]ver 18; Nu 1:4 [k]S Ex 4:14; S 32:20 [l]S Lev 10:6
7:2 [m]S Ge 12:8; S Jos 8:1,28 [n]Jos 18:12; 1Sa 13:5; 14:23; Hos 4:15; 5:8; 10:5 [o]Ge 12:8; Jos 12:16; 16:1; Jdg 1:22; 1Sa 30:27; 2Ki 23:15; Jer 48:13; Am 3:14; 4:4; 5:5-6; 7:10,13 [p]S Nu 21:32
7:4 [q]S Lev 26:17; S Dt 28:25

7:5 [r]Jos 22:20

[m]17 The Hebrew term refers to the irrevocable giving over of things or persons to the Lord, often by totally destroying them; also in verses 18 and 21. [n]17 Or possibly *innkeeper*; also in verses 22 and 25 [o]1 The Hebrew term refers to the irrevocable giving over of things or persons to the Lord, often by totally destroying them; also in verses 11, 12, 13 and 15. [p]1 See Septuagint and 1 Chron. 2:6; Hebrew *Zabdi*; also in verses 17 and 18.

6:18 *your own destruction.* See NIV text note on v. 17. If Israel took for herself anything that was under God's ban, she herself would fall under the ban.

6:25 *she lives among the Israelites.* The faith of Rahab is noted twice in the NT (Heb 11:31; Jas 2:25).

6:26 *Cursed . . . is the man.* Jericho itself was to be devoted to the Lord as a perpetual sign of God's judgment on the wicked Canaanites and as a firstfruits offering of the land. This was a way of signifying that the conquered land belonged to the Lord. The curse was fulfilled in the rebellious days of King Ahab (1Ki 16:34).

7:1-26 The tragic story of Achan, which stands in sharp contrast to the story of Rahab. In the earlier event a Canaanite prostitute, because of her courageous allegiance to Israel and her acknowledgment of the Lord, was spared and received into Israel. She abandoned Canaan and its gods on account of the Lord and Israel, and so received Canaan back. In the present event an Israelite (of the tribe of Judah, no less), because of his disloyalty to the Lord and Israel, is executed as the Canaanites were. He stole the riches of

Canaan from the Lord, and so lost his inheritance in the promised land. This is also a story of how one man's sin adversely affected the entire nation. Throughout this account (as often in the OT) Israel is considered a corporate unity in covenant with and in the service of the Lord. Thus even in the acts of one (Achan) or a few (the 3,000 defeated at Ai) all Israel is involved (see vv. 1,11; 22:20).

7:2 *from Jericho to Ai.* An uphill march of some 15 miles through a ravine to the top of the central Palestinian ridge. Strategically, an advance from Gilgal to Ai would bring Israel beyond the Jordan Valley and provide them a foothold in the central highlands. Ai in Hebrew means "the ruin." It is usually identified with et-Tell (meaning "the ruin" in Arabic), just two miles east of Bethel, but some dispute this precise identification. *Beth Aven.* Means "house of wickedness," a derogatory designation of either Bethel itself or a pagan shrine nearby (see 1Sa 13:5; Hos 4:15; Am 5:5). *spy out the region.* See note on 2:1-24.

7:5 *stone quarries.* Or a place called Shebarim (see NIV text note), meaning "breaks," a fitting term for the rocky bluffs overlooking the Jordan Valley.

far as the stone quarries[q] and struck them down on the slopes. At this the hearts of the people melted[s] and became like water.

[6]Then Joshua tore his clothes[t] and fell facedown[u] to the ground before the ark of the LORD, remaining there till evening.[v] The elders of Israel[w] did the same, and sprinkled dust[x] on their heads. [7]And Joshua said, "Ah, Sovereign LORD, why[y] did you ever bring this people across the Jordan to deliver us into the hands of the Amorites to destroy us?[z] If only we had been content to stay on the other side of the Jordan! [8]O Lord, what can I say, now that Israel has been routed by its enemies? [9]The Canaanites and the other people of the country will hear about this and they will surround us and wipe out our name from the earth.[a] What then will you do for your own great name?[b] "

[10]The LORD said to Joshua, "Stand up! What are you doing down on your face? [11]Israel has sinned;[c] they have violated my covenant,[d] which I commanded them to keep. They have taken some of the devoted things; they have stolen, they have lied,[e] they have put them with their own possessions.[f] [12]That is why the Israelites cannot stand against their enemies;[g] they turn their backs[h] and run[i] because they have been made liable to destruction.[j] I will not be with you anymore[k] unless you destroy whatever among you is devoted to destruction.

[13]"Go, consecrate the people. Tell them, 'Consecrate yourselves[l] in preparation for tomorrow; for this is what the LORD, the God of Israel, says: That which is devoted is among you, O Israel. You cannot stand against your enemies until you remove it.

[14]" 'In the morning, present[m] yourselves tribe by tribe. The tribe that the LORD

takes[n] shall come forward clan by clan; the clan that the LORD takes shall come forward family by family; and the family that the LORD takes shall come forward man by man. [15]He who is caught with the devoted things[o] shall be destroyed by fire,[p] along with all that belongs to him.[q] He has violated the covenant[r] of the LORD and has done a disgraceful thing in Israel!' "[s]

[16]Early the next morning Joshua had Israel come forward by tribes, and Judah was taken. [17]The clans of Judah came forward, and he took the Zerahites.[t] He had the clan of the Zerahites come forward by families, and Zimri was taken. [18]Joshua had his family come forward man by man, and Achan son of Carmi, the son of Zimri, the son of Zerah, of the tribe of Judah,[u] was taken.[v]

[19]Then Joshua said to Achan, "My son, give glory[w] to the LORD,[r] the God of Israel, and give him the praise.[s] Tell[x] me what you have done; do not hide it from me."

[20]Achan replied, "It is true! I have sinned against the LORD, the God of Israel. This is what I have done: [21]When I saw in the plunder[y] a beautiful robe from Babylonia,[t] two hundred shekels[u] of silver and a wedge of gold weighing fifty shekels,[v] I coveted[z] them and took them. They are hidden in the ground inside my tent, with the silver underneath."

[22]So Joshua sent messengers, and they ran to the tent, and there it was, hidden in his tent, with the silver underneath.

Cross-reference column:

7:5 sS Ge 42:28; Ps 22:14; Isa 13:7; Eze 21:7; Na 2:10
7:6 tS Ge 37:29 uS Ge 17:3; 1Ch 21:16; Eze 9:8 vJdg 20:23 wJos 8:10; 9:11; 20:4; 23:2 x1Sa 4:12; 2Sa 13:19; 15:32; Ne 9:1; Job 2:12; La 2:10; Eze 27:30; Rev 18:19
7:7 y1Sa 4:3 zS Ex 5:22; S Nu 14:16
7:9 aEx 32:12; S Dt 9:28 bDt 28:58; 1Sa 12:22; Ps 48:10; 106:8; Jer 14:21
7:11 cS Ex 9:27; Dt 29:27; Jos 24:16-27; 2Ki 17:7; Hos 10:9 dver 15; Jos 6:17-19; 23:16; Jdg 2:20; 1Sa 15:24; Ps 78:10 eAc 5:1-2 fver 21
7:12 gLev 26:37 hPs 18:40; 21:12 iS Lev 26:17 jJos 6:18 kPs 44:9; 60:10
7:13 lS Lev 11:44
7:14 m1Sa 10:19
nPr 16:33
7:15 oJos 6:18 pDt 7:25; 2Ki 25:9; 1Ch 14:12; Isa 37:19; Jer 43:12; Eze 30:16 q1Sa 14:39 rS ver 11 sGe 34:7
7:17 tNu 26:20
7:18 uS ver 1; S Lev 24:11 vJnh 1:7
7:19 wEx 14:17; 1Sa 6:5; Ps 96:8; Isa 42:12; Jer 13:16; Jn 9:24* xS Lev 5:5; 1Sa 14:43
7:21 yS Ge 34:29; S 49:27

zS Dt 7:25; Eph 5:5; 1Ti 6:10

q5 Or as far as Shebarim   r19 A solemn charge to tell the truth   s19 Or and confess to him   t21 Hebrew Shinar   u21 That is, about 5 pounds (about 2.3 kilograms)   v21 That is, about 1 1/4 pounds (about 0.6 kilogram)

7:6 *Joshua tore his clothes.* A sign of great distress (see Ge 37:29,34; 44:13; Jdg 11:35). Joshua's dismay (and that of the people), as indicated by his prayer, arose from his recognition that the Lord had not been with Israel's troops in the battle. And without the Lord the whole venture for which Israel had crossed the Jordan would be impossible. Moreover, the Canaanites would now judge that neither Israel nor her God was invincible. They would pour out of their fortified cities, combine forces and descend on Israel in the Jordan Valley, from which Israel could not escape across the flooding Jordan.

7:9 *your own great name.* Joshua pleads, as Moses had (Nu 14:13-16; Dt 9:28-29), that God's honor in the eyes of all the world was at stake in the fortunes of his people.

7:11 *Israel has sinned.* One soldier's theft of the devoted goods brought collective guilt on the entire nation (see 22:20). *violated my covenant.* See v. 15. This is the main indictment; what follows is further specification.

7:12 *devoted to destruction.* See note on 6:18.

7:13 *Consecrate yourselves.* A series of purifications to be undertaken by every Israelite in preparation for meeting with God, as before a solemn religious feast or a special assembly called by the Lord (see note on 3:5). Here God summons his people before him for his judgment.

7:14 *tribe that the LORD takes.* When the lots are cast, one of the tribes is "taken by the LORD" so that the search is narrowed until the Lord exposes the guilty persons. The lots may have been the Urim and Thummim from the ephod of the high priest (see notes on Ex 28:30; 1Sa 2:28; see also NIV text note on 1Sa 14:41).

7:15 *disgraceful thing in Israel.* An act that within Israel, as the covenant people of the Lord, is an outrage of utter folly (see Dt 22:21; Jdg 19:23-24; 20:6,10; 2Sa 13:12).

7:19 *My son.* Joshua took a fatherly attitude toward Achan. *give glory to the LORD.* See NIV text note. *give him the praise.* See NIV text note.

7:21 *robe from Babylonia.* A valuable import. *two hundred shekels . . . fifty shekels.* See NIV text notes.

23They took the things from the tent, brought them to Joshua and all the Israelites and spread them out before the LORD.

24Then Joshua, together with all Israel, took Achan son of Zerah, the silver, the robe, the gold wedge, his sons[a] and daughters, his cattle, donkeys and sheep, his tent and all that he had, to the Valley of Achor.[b] 25Joshua said, "Why have you brought this trouble[c] on us? The LORD will bring trouble on you today."

Then all Israel stoned him,[d] and after they had stoned the rest, they burned them.[e] 26Over Achan they heaped[f] up a large pile of rocks, which remains to this day.[g] Then the LORD turned from his fierce anger.[h] Therefore that place has been called the Valley of Achor[w][i] ever since.

Ai Destroyed

8 Then the LORD said to Joshua, "Do not be afraid;[j] do not be discouraged.[k] Take the whole army[l] with you, and go up and attack Ai.[m] For I have delivered[n] into your hands the king of Ai, his people, his city and his land. 2You shall do to Ai and its king as you did to Jericho and its king, except that you may carry off their plunder[o] and livestock for yourselves.[p] Set an ambush[q] behind the city."

3So Joshua and the whole army moved out to attack Ai. He chose thirty thousand of his best fighting men and sent them out at night 4with these orders: "Listen carefully. You are to set an ambush behind the city. Don't go very far from it. All of you be on the alert. 5I and all those with me will advance on the city, and when the men come out against us, as they did before, we will flee from them. 6They will pursue us until we have lured them away from the city, for they will say, 'They are running away from us as they did before.' So when

we flee from them, 7you are to rise up from ambush and take the city. The LORD your God will give it into your hand.[r] 8When you have taken the city, set it on fire.[s] Do what the LORD has commanded.[t] See to it; you have my orders."

9Then Joshua sent them off, and they went to the place of ambush[u] and lay in wait between Bethel and Ai, to the west of Ai—but Joshua spent that night with the people.

10Early the next morning[v] Joshua mustered his men, and he and the leaders of Israel[w] marched before them to Ai. 11The entire force that was with him marched up and approached the city and arrived in front of it. They set up camp north of Ai, with the valley between them and the city. 12Joshua had taken about five thousand men and set them in ambush between Bethel and Ai, to the west of the city. 13They had the soldiers take up their positions—all those in the camp to the north of the city and the ambush to the west of it. That night Joshua went into the valley.

14When the king of Ai saw this, he and all the men of the city hurried out early in the morning to meet Israel in battle at a certain place overlooking the Arabah.[x] But he did not know[y] that an ambush had been set against him behind the city. 15Joshua and all Israel let themselves be driven back[z] before them, and they fled toward the desert.[a] 16All the men of Ai were called to pursue them, and they pursued Joshua and were lured away[b] from the city. 17Not a man remained in Ai or Bethel who did not go after Israel. They left the city open and went in pursuit of Israel.

18Then the LORD said to Joshua, "Hold out toward Ai the javelin[c] that is in your

7:24 aS Nu 16:27
bver 26; Jos 15:7;
Isa 65:10;
Hos 2:15
7:25 cS Jos 6:18
dS Lev 20:2;
Dt 17:5;
1Ki 12:18;
2Ch 10:18;
24:21; Ne 9:26
eS Ge 38:24
7:26 f2Sa 18:17
gS Ge 35:20
hS Nu 25:4 iS ver
24
8:1 jGe 26:24;
Dt 31:6
kS Nu 14:9;
S Dt 1:21
lJos 10:7
mJos 7:2; 9:3;
10:1; 12:9
nS Jos 6:2
8:2 oS Ge 49:27
pver 27; Dt 20:14
qver 4,12;
Jdg 9:43; 20:29

8:7 rJdg 7:7;
1Sa 23:4
8:8 sJdg 20:29-38
tver 19
8:9 u2Ch 13:13
8:10 vGe 22:3
wS Jos 7:6
8:14 xS Dt 1:1
yJdg 20:34
8:15 zJdg 20:36
aJos 15:61; 16:1;
18:12
8:16 bJdg 20:31
8:18 cJob 41:26;
Ps 35:3

w26 Achor means trouble.

7:23 before the LORD. Who is here the Judge.
7:24 Joshua . . . all Israel. Joshua and all Israel were God's agents for executing his judgment on both the Canaanites and this violator of the covenant. all that he had. As the head of (and example for) his family, Achan involved his whole household in his guilt and punishment. This is in accordance with the principle of corporate solidarity—the whole community is represented in one member (especially the head of that community).
7:25 stoned him. Because he had been found guilty of violating the covenant of the holy Lord (see Ex 19:13; Lev 24:23; Nu 15:36). Afterward the bodies were burned to purge the land of the evil.
7:26 large pile of rocks. A second monument in the land to the events of the conquest—alongside the memorial at Gilgal (4:20). Achor. See NIV text note. Achor was also another form of Achan's name (see 1Ch 2:7, "Achar," and NIV text note there).

8:1—29 Renewal of the conquest and the taking of Ai.
8:1 Do not be afraid. Now that Israel is purged, the Lord reassures Joshua once more (see 1:3–5; 3:11–13; 6:2–5).
8:2 you may carry off their plunder. The Lord now assigns the wealth of Canaan to his troops who fight his battles. Set an ambush. Still in command, the Lord directs the attack.
8:12 five thousand. Verse 3 speaks of a contingent of 30,000 assigned to the ambush. Perhaps Joshua assigned two different units to the task to assure success. Or from the original 30,000 a unit of 5,000 may have been designated to attack Ai itself while the remaining 25,000 served as a covering force to block the threat from Bethel (see v. 17).
8:13 the camp to the north. In full visibility Joshua's main force moved north of the city, then pretended to flee to the east, drawing out the entire army of defenders.
8:17 Ai or Bethel. Their joint action indicates that the two cities were closely allied, though each is said to have had a king (12:9,16).

hand,[d] for into your hand I will deliver the city." So Joshua held out his javelin[e] toward Ai. [19]As soon as he did this, the men in the ambush rose quickly[f] from their position and rushed forward. They entered the city and captured it and quickly set it on fire.[g]

[20]The men of Ai looked back and saw the smoke of the city rising against the sky,[h] but they had no chance to escape in any direction, for the Israelites who had been fleeing toward the desert had turned back against their pursuers. [21]For when Joshua and all Israel saw that the ambush had taken the city and that smoke was going up from the city, they turned around[i] and attacked the men of Ai. [22]The men of the ambush also came out of the city against them, so that they were caught in the middle, with Israelites on both sides. Israel cut them down, leaving them neither survivors nor fugitives.[j] [23]But they took the king of Ai alive[k] and brought him to Joshua.

[24]When Israel had finished killing all the men of Ai in the fields and in the desert where they had chased them, and when every one of them had been put to the sword, all the Israelites returned to Ai and killed those who were in it. [25]Twelve thousand men and women fell that day—all the people of Ai.[l] [26]For Joshua did not draw back the hand that held out

his javelin[m] until he had destroyed[x][n] all who lived in Ai.[o] [27]But Israel did carry off for themselves the livestock and plunder of this city, as the LORD had instructed Joshua.[p]

[28]So Joshua burned[q] Ai[r] and made it a permanent heap of ruins,[s] a desolate place to this day.[t] [29]He hung the king of Ai on a tree and left him there until evening. At sunset,[u] Joshua ordered them to take his body from the tree and throw it down at the entrance of the city gate. And they raised a large pile of rocks[v] over it, which remains to this day.

The Covenant Renewed at Mount Ebal

[30]Then Joshua built on Mount Ebal[w] an altar[x] to the LORD, the God of Israel, [31]as Moses the servant of the LORD had commanded the Israelites. He built it according to what is written in the Book of the Law of Moses—an altar of uncut stones, on which no iron tool[y] had been used. On it they offered to the LORD burnt offerings and sacrificed fellowship offerings.[y][z] [32]There, in the presence of the Israelites, Joshua copied on stones the law of Moses, which he had written.[a] [33]All Israel, aliens and citizens[b] alike, with their elders, offi-

Cross references (center column)

8:18 [d]S Ex 4:2; 17:9-12 [e]ver 26
8:19 [f]Jdg 20:33
[g]S ver 8
8:20 [h]Jdg 20:40
8:21 [i]Jdg 20:41
8:22 [j]Dt 7:2; Jos 10:1
8:23 [k]1Sa 15:8
8:25
[l]Dt 20:16-18

8:26 [m]ver 18
[n]S Nu 21:2
[o]Ex 17:12
8:27 [p]S ver 2
8:28 [q]S Nu 31:10
[r]Jos 7:2; Jer 49:3
[s]S Dt 13:16;
Jos 10:1
[t]S Ge 35:20
8:29
[u]S Dt 21:23;
Jn 19:31
[v]2Sa 18:17
8:30 [w]ver 33;
S Dt 11:29
[x]S Ex 20:24
8:31 [y]S Ex 20:25
[z]Dt 27:6-7
8:32 [a]Dt 27:8
8:33
[b]S Lev 16:29

[x]26 The Hebrew term refers to the irrevocable giving over of things or persons to the LORD, often by totally destroying them. [y]31 Traditionally *peace offerings*

8:26 *he had destroyed.* For the second time Joshua ordered the holy ban on the inhabitants of a Canaanite city (see NIV text note).

8:28 *burned Ai.* As he had Jericho (6:24) and would later do to Hazor (11:11). *desolate place to this day.* If the ruins of Ai have been correctly identified (see note on 7:2), the site shows signs of later occupation only from c. 1200 to 1100 B.C.

8:29 *hung the king of Ai on a tree.* The Israelites did not execute by hanging. "Tree" may refer to a pole on which the king's body was impaled after execution (see note on Dt 21:22). *until evening.* According to Mosaic instructions (see Dt 21:22–23). *large pile of rocks.* A third monument in the land (see note on 7:26).

8:30–35 The renewal of the covenant with the Lord as Moses had ordered (Dt 11:26–30; 27:1–8) concludes the account of the initial battles (see Introduction: Outline). The conquest of Canaan has already been put into rich theological perspective. This final event (see also Joshua's final official act, ch. 24) underscores Israel's servant relationship to the Lord. In conquest and occupation she must faithfully acknowledge her one identity as the people of the kingdom of God, subject to his commission and rule (see note on 5:14).

How Israel could assemble peacefully between Mount Ebal and Mount Gerizim without further conquest is a worrisome question—and has led to some radical reconstructions of Israel's history. It must be noted, however, that Biblical narrators at times followed a thematic rather than a strictly chronological order of events. That may be the case here, since it is clear that the story of the Gibeonite deception

and submission (ch. 9) is included in the thematic development of how Israel came into possession of the rest of Canaan (see the author's introduction in 9:1–2). The Shechemites (Shechem was a major city lying between the two mountains mentioned) were Hivites (or were under Hivite domination; see Ge 34:2) and thus were related to the people of the Gibeonite cities (9:7; 11:19). Also, there was no important town between Gibeon and Shechem (Bethel and Ai had been subdued). Perhaps the treaty of submission established between Israel and the Gibeonites (ch. 9) applied also to the Hivites of Shechem, and the covenant renewal ceremony that concludes ch. 8 (and the previous narrative section) actually took place chronologically after the events narrated in ch. 9. If this suggestion is correct, the Gibeonites or their representatives would have been among the "aliens" who participated with Israel in the covenant event (vv. 33, 35).

8:30 *Mount Ebal.* At the foot of this peak was the fortress city of Shechem, where Abraham had built an altar (Ge 12:6–7).

8:31 *burnt offerings.* See Lev 1:1–17. *fellowship offerings.* See Lev 3:1–17; 7:11–18.

8:32 *copied on stones.* Moses had ordered the people first to plaster the stones, then to inscribe on them the words of the law (Dt 27:2–4). These stones are the fourth monument in the land (see note on v. 29).

8:33 *aliens and citizens alike.* Israel now included the "other people" (Ex 12:38) who had come out of Egypt, plus others who had associated with them during the desert wanderings (see note on vv. 30–35).

cials and judges, were standing on both sides of the ark of the covenant of the LORD, facing those who carried it—the priests, who were Levites.*c* Half of the people stood in front of Mount Gerizim and half of them in front of Mount Ebal,*d* as Moses the servant of the LORD had formerly commanded when he gave instructions to bless the people of Israel.

34Afterward, Joshua read all the words of the law—the blessings and the curses—just as it is written in the Book of the Law.*e* 35There was not a word of all that Moses had commanded that Joshua did not read to the whole assembly of Israel, including the women and children, and the aliens who lived among them.*f*

The Gibeonite Deception

9 Now when all the kings west of the Jordan heard about these things —those in the hill country,*g* in the western foothills, and along the entire coast of the Great Sea*z h* as far as Lebanon*i* (the kings of the Hittites, Amorites, Canaanites, Perizzites,*j* Hivites*k* and Jebusites)*l*— 2they came together to make war against Joshua and Israel.

3However, when the people of Gibeon*m* heard what Joshua had done to Jericho and Ai,*n* 4they resorted to a ruse: They went as a delegation whose donkeys were loaded*a* with worn-out sacks and old wineskins, cracked and mended. 5The men put worn and patched sandals on their feet and wore old clothes. All the bread of their food supply was dry and moldy. 6Then they went to Joshua in the camp at Gilgal*o* and said to him and the men of Israel, "We have come from a distant country;*p* make a treaty*q* with us."

7The men of Israel said to the Hivites,*r*

"But perhaps you live near us. How then can we make a treaty*s* with you?"

8"We are your servants,*t*" they said to Joshua.

But Joshua asked, "Who are you and where do you come from?"

9They answered: "Your servants have come from a very distant country*u* because of the fame of the LORD your God. For we have heard reports*v* of him: all that he did in Egypt,*w* 10and all that he did to the two kings of the Amorites east of the Jordan—Sihon king of Heshbon,*x* and Og king of Bashan,*y* who reigned in Ashtaroth.*z* 11And our elders and all those living in our country said to us, 'Take provisions for your journey; go and meet them and say to them, "We are your servants; make a treaty with us." ' 12This bread of ours was warm when we packed it at home on the day we left to come to you. But now see how dry and moldy it is. 13And these wineskins that we filled were new, but see how cracked they are. And our clothes and sandals are worn out by the very long journey."

14The men of Israel sampled their provisions but did not inquire*a* of the LORD. 15Then Joshua made a treaty of peace*b* with them to let them live,*c* and the leaders of the assembly ratified it by oath.

16Three days after they made the treaty with the Gibeonites, the Israelites heard that they were neighbors, living near*d* them. 17So the Israelites set out and on the third day came to their cities: Gibeon, Kephirah, Beeroth*e* and Kiriath Jearim.*f* 18But the Israelites did not attack them,

---

8:33 cDt 31:12
dDt 11:29;
Jn 4:20
8:34 eS Dt 28:61;
31:11
8:35 fS Ex 12:38;
Dt 31:12
9:1 gS Nu 13:17
hS Nu 34:6
iS Dt 3:25
jGe 13:7;
S Jos 3:10 kver 7;
Jos 11:19
lS Jos 3:10
9:3 mver 17;
Jos 10:10; 11:19;
18:25; 21:17;
2Sa 2:12; 5:25;
20:8; 1Ki 3:4;
9:2; 1Ch 8:29;
14:16; 16:39;
21:29; 2Ch 1:3;
Ne 3:7; Isa 28:21;
Jer 28:1; 41:12
nGe 12:8;
S Jos 8:1
9:6 oS Dt 11:30
pver 22
qS Ge 26:28
9:7 rS ver 1

5S Ex 23:32;
S 1Ki 5:12
9:8 t2Ki 10:5
9:9 uS Dt 20:15
vver 24
wS Nu 23:22
9:10 xS Nu 21:25
yS Nu 21:33
zS Nu 21:24,35;
Jos 2:10
9:14
aS Ex 16:28;
S Nu 27:21
9:15 bS ver 3,7;
Jos 10:1,4; 11:19;
2Sa 21:2; 24:1
cver 21; Jdg 1:21;
Ps 106:34
9:16 dver 22
9:17 eJos 18:25;
2Sa 4:2; 23:37
fJos 15:9,60;
18:14,15;
Jdg 18:12;
1Sa 6:21; 7:2;
Ps 132:6;
Jer 26:20

z1 That is, the Mediterranean   a4 Most Hebrew manuscripts; some Hebrew manuscripts, Vulgate and Syriac (see also Septuagint) *They prepared provisions and loaded their donkeys*

8:34 *the blessings and the curses.* See Dt 27–28 and notes.

9:1–27 The account of how the Gibeonites deceived the leaders of the tribes and obtained a treaty of submission to Israel. It is the first of three sections telling how Israel came into possession of the bulk of the land. Verses 1–2 introduce the three units.

9:1 *kings west of the Jordan.* Small, independent city-kingdoms were scattered over Canaan, inhabited by a variety of peoples who had come earlier from outside the land (compare vv. 1–2 with Ge 15:19).

9:3 *Gibeon.* A site just north of Jerusalem called el-Jib, showing the remains of a Late Bronze Age city with an excellent water supply. The Gibeonites were in league with a number of neighboring towns (v. 17) but seem to have been dominant in the confederation.

9:4 *they resorted to a ruse.* Motivated by their fear of Israel's God, the Gibeonites used pretense to trick Joshua into a treaty that would allow them to live.

9:6 *make a treaty with us.* In this request they were offering

to submit themselves by treaty to be subjects of the Israelites (see v. 11, where they call themselves "your servants"—unmistakable language in the international diplomacy of that day). They chose submission rather than certain death (v. 24).

9:7 *Hivites.* Possibly Horites, an ethnic group living in Canaan related to the Hurrians of northern Mesopotamia (11:19; Ge 10:17; Ex 23:23; Jdg 3:3).

9:9 *heard reports of him.* The same reports that had been heard in Jericho (see 2:10).

9:14 *did not inquire of the LORD.* Did not consult their King, whose mission they were on.

9:15 *treaty of peace.* A covenant to let them live was sworn by the heads of the tribes—i.e., an oath was taken in the holy name of God. All such oaths were binding in Israel (see Ex 20:7; Lev 19:12; 1Sa 14:24).

9:18 *The whole assembly grumbled.* Perhaps the people feared the consequences of not following through on the earlier divine order to destroy all the Canaanites, but more likely they grumbled because they could not take over the

because the leaders of the assembly had sworn an oath[g] to them by the Lord, the God of Israel.

The whole assembly grumbled[h] against the leaders, [19]but all the leaders answered, "We have given them our oath by the Lord, the God of Israel, and we cannot touch them now. [20]This is what we will do to them: We will let them live, so that wrath will not fall on us for breaking the oath[i] we swore to them." [21]They continued, "Let them live,[j] but let them be woodcutters and water carriers[k] for the entire community." So the leaders' promise to them was kept.

[22]Then Joshua summoned the Gibeonites and said, "Why did you deceive us by saying, 'We live a long way[l] from you,' while actually you live near[m] us? [23]You are now under a curse:[n] You will never cease to serve as woodcutters and water carriers for the house of my God."

[24]They answered Joshua, "Your servants were clearly told[o] how the Lord your God had commanded his servant Moses to give you the whole land and to wipe out all its inhabitants from before you. So we feared for our lives because of you, and that is why we did this. [25]We are now in your hands.[p] Do to us whatever seems good and right[q] to you."

[26]So Joshua saved them from the Israelites, and they did not kill them. [27]That day he made the Gibeonites[r] woodcutters and water carriers[s] for the community and for the altar of the Lord at the place the Lord would choose.[t] And that is what they are to this day.

The Sun Stands Still

10 Now Adoni-Zedek[u] king of Jerusalem[v] heard that Joshua had taken Ai[w] and totally destroyed[b][x] it, doing to Ai and its king as he had done to Jericho and its king, and that the people of Gibeon[y] had made a treaty of peace[z] with Israel and were living near them. [2]He and his people were very much alarmed at this, because Gibeon was an important city, like one of the royal cities; it was larger than Ai, and all its men were good fighters. [3]So Adoni-Zedek king of Jerusalem appealed to Hoham king of Hebron,[a] Piram king of Jarmuth,[b] Japhia king of Lachish[c] and Debir[d] king of Eglon.[e] [4]"Come up and help me attack Gibeon," he said, "because it has made peace[f] with Joshua and the Israelites."

[5]Then the five kings[g] of the Amorites[h]—the kings of Jerusalem, Hebron, Jarmuth, Lachish and Eglon—joined forces. They moved up with all their troops and took up positions against Gibeon and attacked it.

[6]The Gibeonites then sent word to Joshua in the camp at Gilgal:[i] "Do not abandon your servants. Come up to us quickly and save us! Help us, because all the Amorite kings from the hill country have joined forces against us."

[7]So Joshua marched up from Gilgal with his entire army,[j] including all the best fighting men. [8]The Lord said to Joshua, "Do not be afraid[k] of them; I have given

Cross references column:

9:18 [g]ver 15; Jdg 21:1,7,18; 1Sa 20:17; Ps 15:4; [h]S Ex 15:24
9:20 [i]S Ge 24:8
9:21 [j]S ver 15; [k]S Dt 29:11
9:22 [l]ver 6; [m]ver 16
9:23 [n]S Ge 9:25
9:24 [o]ver 9
9:25 [p]Ge 16:6; [q]Jer 26:14
9:27 [r]S Ex 1:11; [s]S Dt 29:11; [t]Dt 12:5

10:1 [u]ver 3; [v]Jos 12:10; 15:8, 63; 18:28; Jdg 1:7 [w]S Jos 8:1; [x]S Dt 20:16; S Jos 8:22 [y]Jos 9:3; [z]S Jos 9:15
10:3 [a]S Ge 13:18; [b]ver 5; Jos 12:11; 15:35; 21:29; Ne 11:29 [c]ver 5, 31; Jos 12:11; 15:39; 2Ki 14:19; 2Ch 11:9; 25:27; 32:9; Ne 11:30; Isa 36:2; 37:8; Jer 34:7; Mic 1:13 [d]ver 38; Jos 11:21; 12:13; 13:26; 15:7,49; 21:15; Jdg 1:11; 1Ch 6:58 [e]ver 23, 34,36; Jos 12:12; 15:39
10:4 [f]S Jos 9:15
10:5 [g]ver 16; [h]Nu 13:29; S Dt 1:7
10:6 [i]S Dt 11:30
10:7 [j]Jos 8:1
10:8 [k]S Dt 3:2; S Jos 1:9

[b][l] The Hebrew term refers to the irrevocable giving over of things or persons to the Lord, often by totally destroying them; also in verses 28, 35, 37, 39 and 40.

Gibeonite cities and possessions.
9:21 *woodcutters and water carriers.* A conventional phrase for household servants.
9:23 *under a curse.* Noah's prediction that Canaan would someday "be the slave of Shem" (Ge 9:25–26) has part of its fulfillment in this event. *for the house of my God.* Probably specifies how the Gibeonites were to serve "the entire community" (v. 21). Worship at the tabernacle (and later at the temple) required much wood and water (for sacrifices and washing) and consequently a great deal of menial labor. From now on, that labor was to be supplied by the Gibeonites, perhaps on a rotating basis. In this way they entered the Lord's service. When Solomon became king, the tabernacle and altar were at Gibeon (2Ch 1:3,5).
9:27 *the place the Lord would choose.* Joshua moved the tabernacle (and its altar) to Shiloh, and there it would reside at least until the days of Samuel (1Sa 4:3). Later, the Lord chose Jerusalem (1Ki 9:3).
10:1–43 The army under Joshua comes to the defense of Gibeon and defeats the coalition of southern kings at Aijalon, then subdues all the southern cities of Judah and the Negev.
10:1 *Adoni-Zedek.* Means "lord of righteousness" or "My (divine) lord is righteous." An earlier king of Jerusalem had a

similar name (Melchizedek; see Ge 14:18 and note). *Jerusalem.* City of the Jebusites.
10:2 *important city.* Gibeon was not only larger in size than Bethel or Ai, but also closer to Jerusalem. With Bethel and Ai conquered and the Gibeonite league in submission, the Israelites were well established in the central highlands, virtually cutting the land in two. Naturally the king of Jerusalem felt threatened, and he wanted to reunite all the Canaanites against Israel. Perhaps he also held (or claimed) some political dominion over the Gibeonite cities and viewed their submission to Israel as rebellion. *good fighters.* Men famous for their courage in battle, yet wise enough to have made peace with the Israelites.
10:5 *five kings of the Amorites.* Rulers over five of the major cities in the southern mountains. The Amorites of the hills are here distinguished from the Canaanites along the coast.
10:6 *Come . . . and save us!* An urgent appeal for deliverance to a man whose name means "The Lord saves." A treaty such as Joshua had made with the Gibeonites usually obliged the ruling nation to come to the aid of the subject peoples if they were attacked.

them into your hand.[l] Not one of them will be able to withstand you."[m]

[9]After an all-night march from Gilgal, Joshua took them by surprise. [10]The LORD threw them into confusion[n] before Israel,[o] who defeated them in a great victory at Gibeon.[p] Israel pursued them along the road going up to Beth Horon[q] and cut them down all the way to Azekah[r] and Makkedah.[s] [11]As they fled before Israel on the road down from Beth Horon to Azekah, the LORD hurled large hailstones[t] down on them from the sky,[u] and more of them died from the hailstones than were killed by the swords of the Israelites.

[12]On the day the LORD gave the Amorites[v] over to Israel, Joshua said to the LORD in the presence of Israel:

"O sun, stand still over Gibeon,
    O moon, over the Valley of
        Aijalon.[w]"
[13]So the sun stood still,[x]
    and the moon stopped,
    till the nation avenged itself on[c] its
        enemies,

as it is written in the Book of Jashar.[y]
The sun stopped[z] in the middle of the sky and delayed going down about a full day. [14]There has never been a day like it before or since, a day when the LORD listened to a man. Surely the LORD was fighting[a] for Israel!

[15]Then Joshua returned with all Israel to the camp at Gilgal.[b]

Five Amorite Kings Killed

[16]Now the five kings had fled[c] and hidden in the cave at Makkedah. [17]When Joshua was told that the five kings had been found hiding in the cave at Makkedah, [18]he said, "Roll large rocks up to the mouth of the cave, and post some men there to guard it. [19]But don't stop! Pursue your enemies, attack them from the rear and don't let them reach their cities, for the LORD your God has given them into your hand."

[20]So Joshua and the Israelites destroyed them completely[d]—almost to a man—but the few who were left reached their fortified cities.[e] [21]The whole army then returned safely to Joshua in the camp at Makkedah, and no one uttered a word against the Israelites.

[22]Joshua said, "Open the mouth of the cave and bring those five kings out to me." [23]So they brought the five kings out of the cave—the kings of Jerusalem, Hebron, Jarmuth, Lachish and Eglon. [24]When they had brought these kings[f] to Joshua, he summoned all the men of Israel and said to the army commanders who had come with him, "Come here and put your feet[g] on the necks of these kings." So they came forward and placed their feet[h] on their necks.

[25]Joshua said to them, "Do not be afraid; do not be discouraged. Be strong and courageous.[i] This is what the LORD will do to all the enemies you are going to fight." [26]Then Joshua struck and killed the kings and hung them on five trees, and they were left hanging on the trees until evening.

[27]At sunset[j] Joshua gave the order and they took them down from the trees and threw them into the cave where they had been hiding. At the mouth of the cave they placed large rocks, which are there to this day.[k]

[28]That day Joshua took Makkedah. He

10:8 [l]S Jos 2:24
[m]S Dt 7:24
10:10 [n]S Ex 14:24
[o]S Dt 7:23
[p]S Jos 9:3
[q]Jos 16:3,5;
18:13,14; 21:22;
1Sa 13:18;
1Ki 9:17;
1Ch 6:68; 7:24;
2Ch 8:5; 25:13
[r]Jos 15:35;
1Sa 17:1;
2Ch 11:9;
Ne 11:30;
Jer 34:7 [s]ver 16,
17,21; Jos 12:16;
15:41
10:11 [t]S Ex 9:18;
Ps 18:12;
Isa 28:2,17;
32:19; Eze 13:11,
13 [u]Jdg 5:20
10:12 [v]Am 2:9
[w]Jos 19:42;
21:24; Jdg 1:35;
12:12; 1Sa 14:31;
1Ch 6:69; 8:13;
2Ch 11:10; 28:18
10:13 [x]Hab 3:11
[y]2Sa 1:18
[z]Isa 38:8
10:14 [a]ver 42;
S Ex 14:14;
Ps 106:43;
136:24;
Isa 63:10;
Jer 21:5
10:15 [b]ver 43
10:16 [c]Ps 68:12

10:20 [d]Dt 20:16
[e]2Ch 11:10;
Jer 4:5; 5:17;
8:14; 35:11
10:24 [f]S Dt 7:24
[g]Mal 4:3
[h]2Sa 22:40;
Ps 110:1;
Isa 51:23
10:25 [i]S Dt 31:6
10:27
[j]S Dt 21:23
[k]S Ge 35:20

[c]13 Or nation triumphed over

10:9 *all-night march.* Gilgal was about 20 miles east of Gibeon, a steep uphill climb for Joshua's men. *by surprise.* Joshua attacked early in the morning, perhaps while the moon was still up (v. 12).
10:10 *confusion.* The Hebrew for this word implies terror or panic.
10:11 *down from Beth Horon.* A long descent to the plain of Aijalon below, following the main east-west crossroad just north of Jerusalem. *large hailstones.* For the Lord's use of the elements of nature as his armaments see Jdg 5:20; 1Sa 7:10; Job 38:22.
10:13 *Book of Jashar.* An early account of Israel's wars (perhaps all in poetic form; see 2Sa 1:18; see also note on Jdg 5:1–31), but never a part of canonical Scripture. *delayed going down.* Some believe that God extended the hours of daylight for the Israelites to defeat their enemies. Others suggest that the sun remained cool (perhaps as the result of an overcast sky) for an entire day, allowing the fighting to continue through the afternoon. The fact is we do not know what happened, except that it involved divine intervention.

10:16 *Makkedah.* A town near Azekah (v. 10) in the western foothills where Joshua's troops made their camp.
10:19 *Pursue your enemies.* Most of the fighting men defending the southern cities were caught and killed before they could reach the safety of their fortresses.
10:21 *no one uttered a word.* The thought here appears to be that no one dared even to raise his voice against the Israelites anymore.
10:24 *put your feet on the necks.* Public humiliation of defeated enemy chieftains was the usual climax of warfare in the ancient Near East.
10:26 *hung them on five trees.* See note on Dt 21:22.
10:27 *they placed large rocks.* A fifth monument in the land to the events of the conquest (see note on 8:32).
10:28 *totally destroyed everyone.* The holy ban was placed on the people of Makkedah, meaning they were "devoted to death" for their wicked deeds (see NIV text note on v. 1). The same fate came to the other major cities of the south (vv. 29–42).

put the city and its king to the sword and totally destroyed everyone in it. He left no survivors. [l] And he did to the king of Makkedah as he had done to the king of Jericho. [m]

Southern Cities Conquered

29Then Joshua and all Israel with him moved on from Makkedah to Libnah [n] and attacked it. 30The LORD also gave that city and its king into Israel's hand. The city and everyone in it Joshua put to the sword. He left no survivors there. And he did to its king as he had done to the king of Jericho.

31Then Joshua and all Israel with him moved on from Libnah to Lachish; [o] he took up positions against it and attacked it. 32The LORD handed Lachish over to Israel, and Joshua took it on the second day. The city and everyone in it he put to the sword, just as he had done to Libnah. 33Meanwhile, Horam king of Gezer [p] had come up to help Lachish, but Joshua defeated him and his army—until no survivors were left.

34Then Joshua and all Israel with him moved on from Lachish to Eglon; [q] they took up positions against it and attacked it. 35They captured it that same day and put it to the sword and totally destroyed everyone in it, just as they had done to Lachish.

36Then Joshua and all Israel with him went up from Eglon to Hebron [r] and attacked it. 37They took the city and put it to the sword, together with its king, its villages and everyone [s] in it. They left no survivors. Just as at Eglon, they totally destroyed it and everyone in it.

38Then Joshua and all Israel with him turned around and attacked Debir. [t] 39They took the city, its king and its villages, and put them to the sword. Everyone in it they totally destroyed. They left no survivors. They did to Debir and its

king as they had done to Libnah and its king and to Hebron. [u]

40So Joshua subdued the whole region, including the hill country, the Negev, [v] the western foothills and the mountain slopes, [w] together with all their kings. [x] He left no survivors. He totally destroyed all who breathed, just as the LORD, the God of Israel, had commanded. [y] 41Joshua subdued them from Kadesh Barnea [z] to Gaza [a] and from the whole region of Goshen [b] to Gibeon. 42All these kings and their lands Joshua conquered in one campaign, because the LORD, the God of Israel, fought [c] for Israel.

43Then Joshua returned with all Israel to the camp at Gilgal. [d]

Northern Kings Defeated

11 When Jabin [e] king of Hazor [f] heard of this, he sent word to Jobab king of Madon, to the kings of Shimron [g] and Acshaph, [h] 2and to the northern kings who were in the mountains, in the Arabah [i] south of Kinnereth, [j] in the western foothills and in Naphoth Dor [d] [k] on the west; 3to the Canaanites in the east and west; to the Amorites, Hittites, Perizzites [l] and Jebusites in the hill country; [m] and to the Hivites [n] below Hermon [o] in the region of Mizpah. [p] 4They came out with all their troops and a large number of horses and chariots—a huge army, as numerous as the sand on the seashore. [q] 5All these kings joined forces [r] and made camp together at the Waters of Merom, [s] to fight against Israel.

6The LORD said to Joshua, "Do not be afraid of them, because by this time tomor-

Cross references (center column)

10:28 [l]Dt 20:16
[m]ver 30,32,35, 39; Jos 6:21
10:29 [n]S Nu 33:20
10:31 [o]S ver 3
10:33 [p]Jos 12:12; 16:3, 10; 21:21; Jdg 1:29; 2Sa 5:25; 1Ki 9:15; 1Ch 6:67
10:34 [q]S ver 3
10:36 [r]S Ge 13:18; Jos 14:13; 15:13; 20:7; 21:11; Jdg 16:3
10:37 [s]S ver 28
10:38 [t]S ver 3
10:39 [u]S ver 28
10:40 [v]S Ge 12:9; Jos 12:8; 15:19, 21; 18:25; 19:8; 1Sa 30:27
[w]S Dt 1:7
[x]Dt 7:24
[y]Dt 20:16-17
10:41 [z]S Ge 14:7
[a]S Ge 10:19
[b]Jos 11:16; 15:51
10:42 [c]S ver 14
10:43 [d]ver 15; Jos 5:9; 1Sa 7:16; 10:8; 11:14; 13:12
11:1 [e]Jdg 4:2,7, 23; Ps 83:9 [f]ver 10; Jos 12:19; 15:23,25; 19:36; Jdg 4:2,17; 1Sa 12:9; 1Ki 9:15; 2Ki 15:29; Ne 11:33; Jer 49:28,33
[g]Jos 19:15
[h]Jos 12:20; 19:25
11:2 [i]ver 16; S Dt 1:1; Dt 2:1; 18:18 [j]S Nu 34:11; Dt 3:17; Jos 19:35; 1Ki 15:20
[k]Jos 12:23; 17:11; Jdg 1:27; 1Ki 4:11; 1Ch 7:29
11:3 [l]S Jos 3:10
[m]Nu 13:17
[n]S Ex 3:8; Dt 7:1; Jdg 3:3,5; 1Ki 9:20
[o]S Dt 3:8 [p]ver 8;

S Ge 31:49; Jos 15:38; 18:26; Jdg 1:11; 20:1; 21:1; 1Sa 7:5,6; 1Ki 15:22; 2Ki 25:23 11:4 [q]S Ge 12:2; Jdg 7:12; 1Sa 13:5 11:5 [r]Jdg 5:19 [s]ver 7

[d]2 Or in the heights of Dor

10:33 *Horam king of Gezer.* An important detail: the defeat of the king of the most powerful city in the area. Gezer was eventually taken over by the Egyptians and given to King Solomon as a wedding gift (see 1Ki 9:16).

10:38 *Debir.* In the past, Debir (also known as Kiriath Sepher, 15:15) was identified with Tell Beit Mirsim. More recently, however, it has been equated with Khirbet Rabud, about five miles southwest of Hebron.

10:41 *Kadesh Barnea to Gaza.* The south-to-north limits in the western part of the region. *Goshen.* A seldom-used name for the eastern Negev, not to be confused with the Goshen in the delta of Egypt; it is also the name of a town (15:51). Goshen and Gibeon mark the south-to-north limits in the eastern part of the region.

11:1–23 Only the northern cities remained to be conquered. The major battle for the hills of Galilee is fought and won against Hazor and the coalition of other northern city-states. A summary follows of all Joshua's victories in the southern and central regions as well.

11:1 *Jabin king of Hazor.* Jabin is perhaps a dynastic name, used again in the days of Deborah (Jdg 4:2). The archaeological excavation of Hazor shows that it was the largest and best fortified of all the Canaanite cities. Its lower city measured 175 acres.

11:2 *Kinnereth.* Means "harp"; the Sea of Galilee.

11:4 *as numerous as the sand.* A widely used figure of speech for indicating large numbers (see note on Ge 22:17).

11:5 *All these kings.* Jabin's muster extended as far as the Arabah (v. 2) in the Jordan Valley and as far as Dor on the Mediterranean, south of Mount Carmel. *Merom.* Probably modern Meirun, just northwest of Safed near the source of the Wadi Ammud (Marun)—some eight miles northwest of the Sea of Galilee.

11:6 *hamstring their horses.* Done by cutting the tendon above the hock or ankle, crippling the horse so that it cannot walk again. *burn their chariots.* These advanced implements of war were not used by the armies of Israel until the time of Solomon (see 1Ki 9:22; 10:26–29).

row I will hand all of them over[t] to Israel, slain. You are to hamstring[u] their horses and burn their chariots."[v]

7So Joshua and his whole army came against them suddenly at the Waters of Merom and attacked them, 8and the LORD gave them into the hand of Israel. They defeated them and pursued them all the way to Greater Sidon,[w] to Misrephoth Maim,[x] and to the Valley of Mizpah on the east, until no survivors were left. 9Joshua did to them as the LORD had directed: He hamstrung their horses and burned their chariots.

10At that time Joshua turned back and captured Hazor and put its king to the sword.[y] (Hazor had been the head of all these kingdoms.) 11Everyone in it they put to the sword. They totally destroyed[e] them,[z] not sparing anything that breathed,[a] and he burned up[b] Hazor itself.

12Joshua took all these royal cities and their kings and put them to the sword. He totally destroyed them, as Moses the servant of the LORD had commanded.[c] 13Yet Israel did not burn any of the cities built on their mounds—except Hazor, which Joshua burned. 14The Israelites carried off for themselves all the plunder and livestock of these cities, but all the people they put to the sword until they completely destroyed them, not sparing anyone that breathed.[d] 15As the LORD commanded his servant Moses, so Moses commanded Joshua, and Joshua did it; he left nothing undone of all that the LORD commanded Moses.[e]

16So Joshua took this entire land: the hill country,[f] all the Negev,[g] the whole region of Goshen, the western foothills,[h] the Arabah and the mountains of Israel with their foothills, 17from Mount Halak, which rises toward Seir,[i] to Baal Gad[j] in the Valley of Lebanon[k] below Mount Hermon.[l] He captured all their kings and struck them down, putting them to death.[m] 18Joshua waged war against all these kings for a long time. 19Except for the Hivites[n] living in Gibeon,[o] not one city made a treaty of peace[p] with the Israelites, who took them all in battle. 20For it was the LORD himself who hardened their hearts[q] to wage war against Israel, so that he might destroy them totally, exterminating them without mercy, as the LORD had commanded Moses.[r]

21At that time Joshua went and destroyed the Anakites[s] from the hill country: from Hebron, Debir[t] and Anab,[u] from all the hill country of Judah, and from all the hill country of Israel. Joshua totally destroyed them and their towns. 22No Anakites were left in Israelite territory; only in Gaza,[v] Gath[w] and Ashdod[x] did any survive. 23So Joshua took the entire land,[y] just as the LORD had directed Moses, and he gave it as an inheritance[z] to Israel according to their tribal divisions.[a] [b]

Then the land had rest[c] from war.[d]

List of Defeated Kings

12 These are the kings of the land whom the Israelites had defeated

[column of cross-references:]
11:6 tS Jos 2:24; uS Ge 49:6 vver 9
11:8 wS Ge 10:15; S Jdg 18:7 xJos 13:6
11:10 yIsa 3:25; Jer 41:2; 44:18
11:11 zS Dt 7:2 aDt 20:16-17 bS Nu 31:10
11:12 cNu 33:50-52; Dt 7:2
11:14 dS Dt 20:16
11:15 eEx 34:11; Dt 7:2; S Jos 1:7
11:16 fNu 13:17 gS Dt 1:7 hS Jos 10:41
11:17 iS Ge 14:6; S Nu 24:18; S Dt 33:2 jJos 13:5 kS Dt 3:25; Jos 12:7 lDt 3:9; Jos 12:8 mDt 7:24
11:19 nS Jos 9:1 oS Jos 9:3 pS Jos 9:15
11:20 qS Ex 4:21; S 14:17; Ro 9:18 rDt 7:16; Jdg 14:4
11:21 sS Nu 13:22,33 tS Jos 10:3 uJos 15:50
11:22 vS Ge 10:19 wJos 12:17; 19:13; 1Sa 5:8; 17:4; 1Ki 2:39; 2Ki 14:25; 1Ch 8:13; Am 6:2 xJos 15:47; 1Sa 5:1; Isa 20:1
11:23 yJos 21:43-45; Ne 9:24 zS Dt 1:38; 12:9-10; S 25:19; S Jos 13:7 aNu 26:53 bPs 105:44 cS Ex 33:14 dJos 14:15

e11 The Hebrew term refers to the irrevocable giving over of things or persons to the LORD, often by totally destroying them; also in verses 12, 20 and 21.

11:10 *Joshua . . . captured Hazor.* Perhaps his greatest victory. Hazor's armed forces, however, had been defeated earlier at Merom. The archaeological site reveals extensive damage and the burning of the Canaanite city c. 1400 B.C., c. 1300 and again c. 1230. Since the destruction level at c. 1300 probably indicates the burning of the city by Pharaoh Seti I, this leaves the destruction levels at c. 1400 and c. 1230 for Joshua's conquest. Those who hold to the late date of the conquest opt for the 1230 level; those who hold to the early date opt for 1400 (see Introduction: Historical Setting). Once again the ban of total destruction was applied (v. 11).
11:13 *mounds.* The Hebrew word is *tel* (Arabic *tell*), a hill formed by the accumulated debris of many ancient settlements one above the other (see note on 7:2).
11:15 *he left nothing undone.* Joshua's success should be measured in the light of the specific orders given by God, which he carried out fully, rather than by the total area that eventually would have to be occupied by Israel.
11:16 *this entire land.* A lesson in the geography of Canaan follows.
11:17 *Mount Halak.* A desert peak to the east of Kadesh Barnea marking Israel's southern extremity. *Baal Gad.* The first valley west of Mount Hermon.

11:18 *for a long time.* An estimation of the duration of Joshua's conquests can be made from the life-span of Caleb: Seven years had elapsed from the beginning of the conquest (age 78; compare 14:7 with Dt 2:14) until he took Hebron (age 85; see 14:10).
11:20 *the LORD . . . hardened their hearts.* God has sovereign control of history, yet his will never denies our personal and moral freedom (cf. the case of Pharaoh, Ex 8:32; 9:12).
11:21 *Anakites.* Had been reported by the 12 spies to be a people "of great size" (Nu 13:32), whom the Israelites had feared so much that they had refused to undertake the conquest. They were related to the Nephilim (see note on Ge 6:4) and were named after their forefather, Anak. Joshua shared with Caleb his victory over the Anakites (14:12–15).
12:1–24 A conclusion to the first section of Joshua, and a summary of the victories of the Israelites and the cities whose kings had been defeated (see map No. 3 at the end of the Study Bible).
12:1 *territory . . . east of the Jordan.* The unity of the nation is reaffirmed by the inclusion of these lands in Transjordan. *Arnon Gorge.* Marked the border with Moab to the south. *Mount Hermon.* The upper limits of Israel's land to the north.

and whose territory they took[e] over east of the Jordan,[f] from the Arnon[g] Gorge to Mount Hermon,[h] including all the eastern side of the Arabah:[i]

[2]Sihon king of the Amorites, who reigned in Heshbon.[j] He ruled from Aroer[k] on the rim of the Arnon Gorge—from the middle of the gorge—to the Jabbok River,[l] which is the border of the Ammonites.[m] This included half of Gilead.[n] [3]He also ruled over the eastern Arabah from the Sea of Kinnereth[f][o] to the Sea of the Arabah (the Salt Sea[g][p]), to Beth Jeshimoth,[q] and then southward below the slopes of Pisgah.[r]

[4]And the territory of Og king of Bashan,[s] one of the last of the Rephaites,[t] who reigned in Ashtaroth[u] and Edrei. [5]He ruled over Mount Hermon, Salecah,[v] all of Bashan[w] to the border of the people of Geshur[x] and Maacah,[y] and

half of Gilead[z] to the border of Sihon king of Heshbon.

[6]Moses, the servant of the LORD, and the Israelites conquered them.[a] And Moses the servant of the LORD gave their land to the Reubenites, the Gadites and the half-tribe of Manasseh to be their possession.[b]

[7]These are the kings of the land that Joshua and the Israelites conquered on the west side of the Jordan, from Baal Gad in the Valley of Lebanon[c] to Mount Halak, which rises toward Seir (their lands Joshua gave as an inheritance to the tribes of Israel according to their tribal divisions— [8]the hill country, the western foothills, the Arabah, the mountain slopes, the desert and the Negev[d]—the lands of the Hittites,

12:1 ePs 136:21
fS Nu 32:19
gS Nu 21:13
hS Dt 3:8
iS Jos 11:2
12:2 jver 5;
S Nu 21:21,25;
Jos 13:10;
Jdg 11:19
kS Nu 32:34;
S Jos 13:16
lS Ge 32:22
mS Ge 19:38
nS Ge 31:21;
S Nu 32:26;
Dt 2:36; S 3:15;
Jos 13:11,25;
17:1; 20:8;
21:38; Jdg 5:17;
7:3; 10:8
12:3 oJos 11:2
pS Ge 14:3
qS Nu 33:49;
Jos 13:20
rS Nu 21:20
12:4
sS Nu 21:21,33;
Jos 13:30
tS Ge 14:5
uS Dt 1:4
12:5 vS Dt 3:10
wNu 32:33;
Jos 17:1; 20:8;
21:27; 22:7
xJos 13:2,13;
1Sa 27:8

yS Dt 3:14 zver 2 **12:6** aS Dt 3:8 bNu 32:29,33; Jos 13:8
12:7 cS Jos 11:17 **12:8** dS Dt 1:7

f3 That is, Galilee   g3 That is, the Dead Sea

12:4 *Og king of Bashan.* Og and Sihon (v. 2) met defeat under the command of Moses, a long-remembered tribute to God's mighty power (see Ne 9:22; Ps 135:11).

12:7 *the land . . . on the west side.* Canaan proper (9:1; 11:16–17; 24:11; Ge 15:18–19).

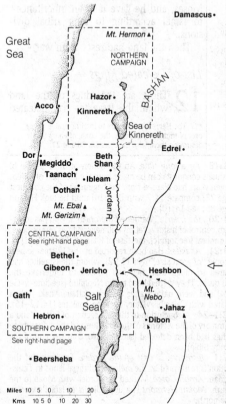

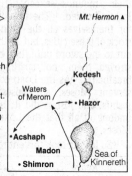

4. THE NORTHERN CAMPAIGN

Late Bronze Age Hazor was burned by Joshua (Jos 11:13). Excavations have revealed three clearly datable destruction layers, one of which may provide the strongest evidence yet for a historically verifiable date for the conquest.

The excavator thought Joshua burned the latest level (c. 1230 B.C.), but others argue that it must actually have been the earliest of the three levels, c. 1400 B.C.

Conquest of Canaan

⟵ 1. ENTRY INTO CANAAN

When the Israelite tribes approached Canaan after four decades of desert existence, they had to overcome the two Amorite kingdoms on the Medeba plateau and in Bashan. Under Moses' leadership, they also subdued the Midianites in order to consolidate their control over the Transjordanian region.

The conquest of Canaan followed a course that in retrospect appears as though it had been planned by a brilliant strategist. Taking Jericho gave Israel control of its strategic plains, fords and roads as a base of operations. When Israel next gained control of the Bethel, Gibeon and the Upper Beth Horon region, she dominated the center of the north-south Palestinian ridge. Subsequently, she was able to break the power of the allied urban centers in separate campaigns south and north.

Amorites, Canaanites, Perizzites, Hivites and Jebusites): *e*

[9]the king of Jericho *f*	one
the king of Ai *g* (near Bethel *h*)	one
[10]the king of Jerusalem *i*	one
the king of Hebron	one
[11]the king of Jarmuth	one
the king of Lachish *j*	one
[12]the king of Eglon *k*	one
the king of Gezer *l*	one
[13]the king of Debir *m*	one
the king of Geder	one
[14]the king of Hormah *n*	one
the king of Arad *o*	one
[15]the king of Libnah *p*	one
the king of Adullam *q*	one
[16]the king of Makkedah *r*	one
the king of Bethel *s*	one
[17]the king of Tappuah *t*	one
the king of Hepher *u*	one
[18]the king of Aphek *v*	one
the king of Lasharon	one
[19]the king of Madon	one
the king of Hazor *w*	one
[20]the king of Shimron Meron	one
the king of Acshaph *x*	one
[21]the king of Taanach *y*	one
the king of Megiddo *z*	one
[22]the king of Kedesh *a*	one
the king of Jokneam *b* in Carmel *c*	one
[23]the king of Dor (in Naphoth Dor *h d*)	one
the king of Goyim in Gilgal	one
[24]the king of Tirzah *e*	one

thirty-one kings in all. *f*

Land Still to Be Taken

13 When Joshua was old and well advanced in years, *g* the LORD said to him, "You are very old, and there are still

12:8 *e*S Jos 3:10; S 11:17; Ezr 9:1
12:9 *f*S Nu 33:48
*g*S Ge 12:8; S Jos 8:1
*h*S Jos 7:2; 8:9; 18:13; Jdg 1:23; 4:5; 20:18; 21:2; Ne 11:31
12:10 *i*S Jos 10:1
12:11 *j*S Jos 10:3
12:12 *k*S Jos 10:3
*l*S Jos 10:33
12:13
*m*S Jos 10:3
12:14
*n*S Nu 14:45
*o*S Nu 21:1
12:15
*p*S Nu 33:20
*q*S Ge 38:1; Jos 15:35; Mic 1:15
12:16
*r*S Jos 10:10
*s*S Jos 7:2
12:17 *t*Jos 15:34; 16:8; 17:8
*u*S Jos 11:22; 1Ki 4:10
12:18 *v*Jos 13:4; 19:30; Jdg 1:31; 1Sa 4:1; 29:1
12:19
*w*S Jos 11:1
12:20 *x*S Jos 11:1

12:21 *y*Jos 17:11; 21:25 *z*Jdg 1:27; 5:19; 1Ki 4:12 **12:22** *a*Jos 15:23; 19:37; 20:7; 21:32; Jdg 4:6,9 *b*Jos 19:11; 21:34 *c*Jos 15:55; 19:26; 1Sa 15:12; 2Sa 23:35 **12:23** *d*S Jos 11:2 **12:24** *e*1Ki 14:17; 15:33; 16:8,23; SS 6:4 *f*Ps 135:11; 136:18 **13:1** *g*Ge 24:1; Jos 14:10; 23:1,2; 1Ki 1:1

*h*23 Or *in the heights of Dor*

12:12 *king of Gezer.* Had been defeated in the siege of Lachish (10:33), but the city itself was not captured by Joshua, nor were the cities of Aphek, Taanach, Megiddo or Dor (vv. 18–23; see Jdg 1:27–31).

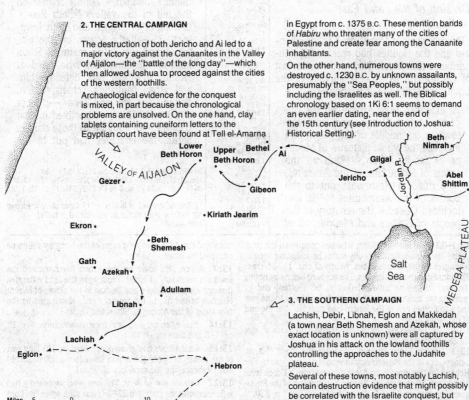

2. THE CENTRAL CAMPAIGN

The destruction of both Jericho and Ai led to a major victory against the Canaanites in the Valley of Aijalon—the "battle of the long day"—which then allowed Joshua to proceed against the cities of the western foothills.

Archaeological evidence for the conquest is mixed, in part because the chronological problems are unsolved. On the one hand, clay tablets containing cuneiform letters to the Egyptian court have been found at Tell el-Amarna

in Egypt from c. 1375 B.C. These mention bands of *Habiru* who threaten many of the cities of Palestine and create fear among the Canaanite inhabitants.

On the other hand, numerous towns were destroyed c. 1230 B.C. by unknown assailants, presumably the "Sea Peoples," but possibly including the Israelites as well. The Biblical chronology based on 1Ki 6:1 seems to demand an even earlier dating, near the end of the 15th century (see Introduction to Joshua: Historical Setting).

3. THE SOUTHERN CAMPAIGN

Lachish, Debir, Libnah, Eglon and Makkedah (a town near Beth Shemesh and Azekah, whose exact location is unknown) were all captured by Joshua in his attack on the lowland foothills controlling the approaches to the Judahite plateau.

Several of these towns, most notably Lachish, contain destruction evidence that might possibly be correlated with the Israelite conquest, but with Jericho and Ai, the historical implications are not clear.

very large areas of land to be taken over.

2"This is the land that remains: all the regions of the Philistines[h] and Geshurites:[i] 3from the Shihor River[j] on the east of Egypt to the territory of Ekron[k] on the north, all of it counted as Canaanite (the territory of the five Philistine rulers[l] in Gaza, Ashdod,[m] Ashkelon,[n] Gath and Ekron—that of the Avvites);[o] 4from the south, all the land of the Canaanites, from Arah of the Sidonians as far as Aphek,[p] the region of the Amorites,[q] 5the area of the Gebalites[i];[r] and all Lebanon[s] to the east, from Baal Gad below Mount Hermon[t] to Lebo[j] Hamath.[u]

6"As for all the inhabitants of the mountain regions from Lebanon to Misrephoth Maim,[v] that is, all the Sidonians, I myself will drive them out[w] before the Israelites. Be sure to allocate this land to Israel for an inheritance, as I have instructed you,[x] 7and divide it as an inheritance[y] among the nine tribes and half of the tribe of Manasseh."

Division of the Land East of the Jordan

8The other half of Manasseh,[k] the Reubenites and the Gadites had received the inheritance that Moses had given them east of the Jordan, as he, the servant of the LORD, had assigned[z] it to them.[a]

9It extended from Aroer[b] on the rim of the Arnon Gorge, and from the town in the middle of the gorge, and included the whole plateau[c] of Medeba as far as Dibon,[d] 10and all the towns of Sihon king of the Amorites, who ruled in Heshbon,[e] out to the border of the Ammonites.[f] 11It also included Gilead,[g] the territory of the people of Geshur and Maacah, all of

Mount Hermon and all Bashan as far as Salecah[h]— 12that is, the whole kingdom of Og in Bashan,[i] who had reigned in Ashtaroth[j] and Edrei[k] and had survived as one of the last of the Rephaites.[l] Moses had defeated them and taken over their land.[m] 13But the Israelites did not drive out the people of Geshur[n] and Maacah,[o] so they continue to live among the Israelites to this day.[p]

14But to the tribe of Levi he gave no inheritance, since the offerings made by fire to the LORD, the God of Israel, are their inheritance, as he promised them.[q]

15This is what Moses had given to the tribe of Reuben, clan by clan:

16The territory from Aroer[r] on the rim of the Arnon Gorge, and from the town in the middle of the gorge, and the whole plateau past Medeba[s] 17to Heshbon and all its towns on the plateau,[t] including Dibon,[u] Bamoth Baal,[v] Beth Baal Meon,[w] 18Jahaz,[x] Kedemoth,[y] Mephaath,[z] 19Kiriathaim,[a] Sibmah,[b] Zereth Shahar on the hill in the valley, 20Beth Peor,[c] the slopes of Pisgah, and Beth Jeshimoth 21—all the towns on the plateau[d] and the entire realm of Sihon king of the Amorites, who ruled at Heshbon. Moses had defeated him and the Midianite chiefs,[e] Evi, Rekem, Zur, Hur and Reba[f]—princes allied with Sihon—who lived in that country. 22In addition to those slain in battle, the Israelites had put to the

13:2
hS Ge 10:14;
S Jdg 3:31
iS Jos 12:5
13:3 iI Ch 13:5;
Isa 23:3; Jer 2:18
kJos 15:11,45;
19:43; Jdg 1:18;
1Sa 5:10; 7:14
lJdg 3:3; 16:5,18;
1Sa 6:4,17;
Isa 14:29;
Jer 25:20;
Eze 25:15
mS Jos 11:22;
Am 3:9
nJdg 1:18; 14:19;
2Sa 1:20
oS Dt 2:23
13:4 pS Jos 12:18
qS Ge 14:7;
S 15:16; Am 2:10
13:5 rI Ki 5:18;
Ps 83:7; Eze 27:9
sS Jos 11:17
tS Dt 3:8
uS Nu 13:21;
34:8; Jdg 3:3
13:6 vJos 11:8
wPs 80:8
xNu 33:54;
S 34:13
13:7
yS Jos 11:23;
Ps 78:55
13:8 zS Jos 12:6
aJos 18:7
13:9 bver 16;
S Nu 32:34;
Dt 2:36;
Jdg 11:26;
2Sa 24:5 cver 17,
21; Jer 48:8,21
dS Nu 21:30;
S 32:3; Isa 15:2;
Jer 48:18,22
13:10 eS Jos 12:2
fS Nu 21:24
13:11 gS Jos 12:2

hJos 12:5
13:12 iS Dt 1:4
jJos 12:4
kS Nu 21:33
lS Ge 14:5
mS Dt 3:8
13:13 nS Jos 12:5
oS Dt 3:14
pDt 3:12
13:14 qver 33;
Dt 18:1-2;
Jos 14:3
13:16 rS ver 9;
Jos 12:2;
1Sa 30:28
sS Nu 21:30;
Isa 15:2
13:17 tS ver 9
uS Nu 32:3
vNu 22:41
wI Ch 5:8;

Jer 48:23; Eze 25:9 **13:18** xS Nu 21:23 yS Dt 2:26
zJos 21:37; Jer 48:21 **13:19** aS Nu 32:37 bS Nu 32:3 **13:20**
cS Dt 3:29 **13:21** dS ver 9 eS Ge 25:2; S Nu 25:15 fNu 31:8

i5 That is, the area of Byblos   i5 Or to the entrance to
k8 Hebrew With it (that is, with the other half of
Manasseh)

13:1–32 The heavenly King, who has conquered the land, begins the administration of his realm by assigning specific territories to the several tribes. Much of chs. 13–21 reads like administrative documents. The account begins by noting the land still to be subdued (but to be allotted) and by recalling the assignments already made by Moses to the two and a half tribes east of the Jordan (see map No. 4 at the end of the Study Bible).
13:1 *Joshua was old.* Between 90 and 100 years of age; Caleb was 85 (14:10).
13:3 *Shihor River.* Another name for the Wadi el-Arish below Gaza at the eastern entrance to the Sinai. *rulers.* The Hebrew for this word is probably derived from a Greek term for "tyrant," indicating the Aegean background of the Philistines. See map on "Five Cities of the Philistines," p. 330.
13:5 *Gebalites.* Inhabitants of the ancient city of Byblos (see NIV text note) just north of modern Beirut. The Phoeni-

cians and the Philistines held most of the territory still to be occupied by Israel.
13:9 *Aroer.* This town on the Arnon River marked the southern boundary of Israel. From here the land extended through Ammon, Gilead and Bashan to the slopes of Mount Hermon in the north, the territory once dominated by the two kings of the Amorites, Sihon and Og.
13:14 *the offerings . . . are their inheritance.* See Dt 18:1–8 and note on Dt 18:1.
13:15 *what Moses had given to . . . Reuben.* The land east of the Jordan between the Arnon River (boundary of Moab) and Heshbon (the old royal city of Sihon).
13:22 *Balaam son of Beor.* The one who supposedly had influence with the gods (Nu 22–24) was slain when the Lord punished the Midianites for trying to seduce Israel into idolatry and sexual immorality (see Nu 25; 31:8).

sword Balaam son of Beor,[g] who practiced divination.[h] 23The boundary of the Reubenites was the bank of the Jordan. These towns and their villages were the inheritance of the Reubenites, clan by clan.[i]

24This is what Moses had given to the tribe of Gad, clan by clan:

25The territory of Jazer,[j] all the towns of Gilead[k] and half the Ammonite country as far as Aroer, near Rabbah;[l] 26and from Heshbon[m] to Ramath Mizpah and Betonim, and from Mahanaim[n] to the territory of Debir;[o] 27and in the valley, Beth Haram, Beth Nimrah,[p] Succoth[q] and Zaphon[r] with the rest of the realm of Sihon king of Heshbon (the east side of the Jordan, the territory up to the end of the Sea of Kinnereth[1s]). 28These towns and their villages were the inheritance of the Gadites,[t] clan by clan.

29This is what Moses had given to the half-tribe of Manasseh, that is, to half the family of the descendants of Manasseh, clan by clan:

30The territory extending from Mahanaim[u] and including all of Bashan,[v] the entire realm of Og king of Bashan[w]—all the settlements of Jair[x] in Bashan, sixty towns, 31half of Gilead, and Ashtaroth and Edrei (the royal cities of Og in Bashan).[y] This was for the descendants of Makir[z] son of Manasseh—for half of the sons of Makir, clan by clan.[a]

32This is the inheritance Moses had given when he was in the plains of Moab[b] across the Jordan east of Jericho.[c] 33But to the tribe of Levi, Moses had given no inheritance;[d] the LORD, the God of Israel, is their inheritance,[e] as he promised them.[f]

Division of the Land West of the Jordan

14 Now these are the areas the Israelites received as an inheritance[g] in the land of Canaan, which Eleazar[h] the priest, Joshua son of Nun and the heads of the tribal clans of Israel[i] allotted[j] to them.[k] 2Their inheritances were assigned by lot[l] to the nine-and-a-half tribes,[m] as the LORD had commanded through Moses. 3Moses had granted the two-and-a-half tribes their inheritance east of the Jordan[n] but had not granted the Levites an inheritance among the rest,[o] 4for the sons of Joseph had become two tribes—Manasseh and Ephraim.[p] The Levites received no share of the land but only towns to live in, with pasturelands for their flocks and herds.[q] 5So the Israelites divided the land, just as the LORD had commanded Moses.[r]

Hebron Given to Caleb

6Now the men of Judah approached Joshua at Gilgal,[s] and Caleb son of Jephunneh[t] the Kenizzite said to him, "You know what the LORD said to Moses the man of God[u] at Kadesh Barnea[v] about you and me.[w] 7I was forty years old when Moses the servant of the LORD sent me from Kadesh Barnea[x] to explore the land.[y] And I brought him back a report according to my convictions,[z] 8but my brothers who went up with me made the hearts of the people melt with fear.[a] I, however, followed the LORD my God wholeheartedly.[b] 9So on that day Moses swore to me, 'The land on which your feet have walked will be your inheritance[c] and that of your children[d] forever, because you have followed the LORD my God wholeheartedly.'[m]

10"Now then, just as the LORD promised,[e] he has kept me alive for forty-five years since the time he said this to Moses, while Israel moved[f] about in the desert.

127 That is, Galilee   m9 Deut. 1:36

Cross references (center column):

13:22 gS Nu 22:5
hS Ge 30:27;
S Nu 23:23
13:23 i1Ch 5:7
13:25 jS Nu 21:32;
Jos 21:39
kS Jos 12:2
lS Dt 3:11
13:26 mS Nu 21:25;
Jer 49:3
nS Ge 32:2
oS Ge 10:3
13:27 pS Nu 32:3
qS Ge 33:17
rJdg 12:1; Ps 48:2
sS Nu 34:11
13:28 tGe 46:16;
S Nu 32:33;
Eze 48:27
13:30 uS Ge 32:2
vS Nu 21:33
wS Jos 12:4
xS Nu 32:41
13:31 yNu 21:33
zS Ge 50:23
aJos 17:5
13:32 bS Nu 26:3
cS Nu 22:1
13:33 dNu 26:62
eS Nu 18:20
fS ver 14;
Jos 18:7;
Eze 44:28

14:1 gS Jos 11:23;
Ps 16:6; 136:21
hS Ex 6:23
iJos 21:1
jS Nu 26:53
kNu 34:17-18;
Jos 19:51
14:2 lS Lev 16:8
mNu 34:13
14:3 nS Nu 32:33;
S 34:14
oS Nu 35:2;
S Jos 13:14
14:4 pS Ge 41:52;
S Jdg 1:29
qS Nu 35:2-3;
Jos 21:2
14:5 rS Nu 34:13
14:6 sS Dt 11:30
tNu 13:6; 14:30
uS Dt 33:1
vNu 13:26
wS Nu 14:38
14:7 xJos 15:3
yS Nu 13:17
zNu 13:30;
S 14:6-9
14:8 aS Nu 13:31
bS Nu 14:24;
S 32:12
14:9 cS Dt 11:24
dS Nu 14:24
14:10 eS Nu 11:28;
14:30 fS Jos 5:6

13:24 *what Moses had given to . . . Gad.* The central area, beginning near Heshbon on the south and reaching, along the Jordan, to the southern end of the Sea of Galilee. It included most of Gilead, but the exact boundary between Gad and the half-tribe of Manasseh remains somewhat uncertain since not all the places named can now be located.

13:29 *what Moses had given to the half-tribe of Manasseh.* The lands east and north of the Sea of Galilee, but also including the upper part of Gilead. Makir led in the occupation of these lands (see Nu 32:32,39–42).

13:33 *the LORD . . . is their inheritance.* See v.14; see also Dt 18:1–8 and note on Dt 18:1.

14:1–15 A short introductory chapter for the following

section (chs. 15–19), with a special note on the Lord's faithfulness to Caleb.

14:1 *Eleazar the priest.* Son of Aaron, Eleazar as high priest was the highest official over the casting of the lots. The Urim and Thummim (see notes on Ex 28:30; 1Sa 2:28) may have been used.

14:4 *Manasseh and Ephraim.* Sons of Joseph. Since Jacob had adopted them as his own sons (Ge 48:5), they constituted two separate tribes. This made possible the 12-part nation, with the Levites serving as a nonpolitical tribe.

14:6 *what the LORD said.* Caleb now recalls the promise from the Lord 38 years earlier at Kadesh Barnea when he brought back a good report of the land (Nu 13:30; 14:6–9; Dt 1:34–36).

So here I am today, eighty-five years old![g] [11]I am still as strong[h] today as the day Moses sent me out; I'm just as vigorous[i] to go out to battle now as I was then. [12]Now give me this hill country that the LORD promised me that day.[j] You yourself heard then that the Anakites[k] were there and their cities were large and fortified,[l] but, the LORD helping me, I will drive them out just as he said."

[13]Then Joshua blessed[m] Caleb son of Jephunneh[n] and gave him Hebron[o] as his inheritance.[p] [14]So Hebron has belonged to Caleb son of Jephunneh the Kenizzite ever since, because he followed the LORD, the God of Israel, wholeheartedly.[q] [15](Hebron used to be called Kiriath Arba[r] after Arba,[s] who was the greatest man among the Anakites.)

Then the land had rest[t] from war.

Allotment for Judah

15:15-19pp — Jdg 1:11-15

15 The allotment for the tribe of Judah, clan by clan, extended down to the territory of Edom,[u] to the Desert of Zin[v] in the extreme south.[w]

[2]Their southern boundary started from the bay at the southern end of the Salt Sea,[n][x] [3]crossed south of Scorpion[o] Pass,[y] continued on to Zin and went over to the south of Kadesh Barnea.[z] Then it ran past Hezron up to Addar and curved around to Karka. [4]It then passed along to Azmon[a] and joined the Wadi of Egypt,[b] ending at the sea. This is their[p] southern boundary.

[5]The eastern boundary[c] is the Salt Sea[d] as far as the mouth of the Jordan.

The northern boundary[e] started from the bay of the sea at the mouth of the Jordan, [6]went up to Beth Hoglah[f] and continued north of Beth Arabah[g] to the Stone of Bohan[h] son of Reuben. [7]The boundary then went up

to Debir[i] from the Valley of Achor[j] and turned north to Gilgal,[k] which faces the Pass of Adummim south of the gorge. It continued along to the waters of En Shemesh[l] and came out at En Rogel.[m] [8]Then it ran up the Valley of Ben Hinnom[n] along the southern slope of the Jebusite[o] city (that is, Jerusalem[p]). From there it climbed to the top of the hill west of the Hinnom Valley[q] at the northern end of the Valley of Rephaim.[r] [9]From the hilltop the boundary headed toward the spring of the waters of Nephtoah,[s] came out at the towns of Mount Ephron and went down toward Baalah[t] (that is, Kiriath Jearim).[u] [10]Then it curved westward from Baalah[v] to Mount Seir,[w] ran along the northern slope of Mount Jearim (that is, Kesalon), continued down to Beth Shemesh[x] and crossed to Timnah.[y] [11]It went to the northern slope of Ekron,[z] turned toward Shikkeron, passed along to Mount Baalah[a] and reached Jabneel.[b] The boundary ended at the sea.

[12]The western boundary is the coastline of the Great Sea.[q][c]

These are the boundaries around the people of Judah by their clans.

[13]In accordance with the LORD's command to him, Joshua gave to Caleb[d] son of Jephunneh a portion in Judah—Kiriath Arba[e], that is, Hebron.[f] (Arba was the forefather of Anak.)[g] [14]From Hebron Caleb drove out the three Anakites[h]—Sheshai, Ahiman and Talmai[i]—descendants of Anak.[j] [15]From there he marched against the people living

Cross references (center column)

14:10 gS Jos 13:1
14:11 hS Dt 34:7
iS Ge 15:15
14:12 jS Nu 14:24
kS Nu 13:33
lNu 13:28
14:13 mJos 22:6, 7 nISa 25:3; 30:14
oS Ge 23:19; S Jos 10:36
pJdg 1:20; 1Ch 6:56
14:14 qS Nu 14:24
14:15 rS Ge 23:2
sJos 15:13
tJos 11:23; Jdg 3:11; 1Ki 4:24; 5:4; 1Ch 22:9
15:1 uNu 34:3
vS Nu 13:21
wJos 18:5
15:2 xS Ge 14:3
15:3 yS Nu 34:4
zS Dt 1:2
15:4 aNu 34:4
bS Ge 15:18
15:5 cNu 34:10
dS Ge 14:3
eJos 18:15-19
15:6 fJos 18:19, 21 gver 61; Jos 18:18
hJos 18:17
15:7 iS Jos 10:3
jS Jos 7:24
kS Dt 11:30
lJos 18:17
mJos 18:16; 2Sa 17:17; 1Ki 1:9
15:8 n2Ch 28:3; Jer 19:6 over 63; Jos 18:16,28; Jdg 1:21; 19:10; 2Sa 5:6; 1Ch 11:4; Ezr 9:1 pS Jos 10:1 q2Ki 23:10; Jer 7:31; 19:2 r2Sa 5:18,22; 1Ch 14:9; Isa 17:5
15:9 sJos 18:15 tver 10,11,29; 2Sa 6:2; 1Ch 13:6 uS Jos 9:17
15:10 vS ver 9 wS Nu 24:18 xJos 19:22,38; 21:16; Jdg 1:33; 1Sa 6:9; 1Ki 4:9; 2Ki 14:11 yS Ge 38:12
15:11 zS Jos 13:3 aS ver 9 bJos 19:33
15:12 cS Nu 34:6

15:13 dISa 25:3; 30:14 eS Ge 23:2 fS Jos 10:36; 21:12; 1Ch 6:56 gS Nu 13:22 15:14 hS Nu 13:33 iS Nu 13:22 jJdg 1:10,20

n2 That is, the Dead Sea; also in verse 5   o3 Hebrew Akrabbim   p4 Hebrew your   q12 That is, the Mediterranean; also in verse 47

Study notes (bottom)

14:12 *this hill country.* Hebron is situated high in the Judahite hill country, about 25 miles south of Jerusalem. *Anakites.* See note on 11:21.

14:15 *Kiriath Arba.* Means "the town of Arba" and was named for Arba, the father of the Anakites (15:13; 21:11). It can also mean "the town of four." Hebron means "union." *Then the land had rest from war.* Since the Judahites and Caleb approached Joshua concerning their territory while he was still headquartered at Gilgal, it may be that they did so shortly before the wars fought under Joshua were ended (see 11:23).

15:1-63 Judah is the first of the west bank tribes to have its territory delineated. First the outer limits are listed, then the area apportioned to Caleb and Othniel; finally the Canaanite cities allotted to the clans of Judah are named region by

region.

15:1 *tribe of Judah.* Judah's priority is anchored in the oracle of Jacob (Ge 49:8–12) and upheld in the history of the nation (2Ki 17:18).

15:4 *southern boundary.* The points listed formed a curved line beginning at the lower tip of the Dead Sea and moving under Kadesh Barnea to join the Mediterranean coast at the mouth of the Wadi el-Arish (see note on 13:3).

15:5 *northern boundary.* Judah's border with Benjamin ran in a westerly line from the mouth of the Jordan through the Hinnom Valley, just south of Jerusalem, over to Timnah, then northwest to the coastal city of Jabneel (later called Jamnia), about ten miles south of Joppa.

15:15 *he marched against . . . Debir.* See note on 10:38.

in Debir (formerly called Kiriath Sepher). [16]And Caleb said, "I will give my daughter Acsah[k] in marriage to the man who attacks and captures Kiriath Sepher." [17]Othniel[l] son of Kenaz, Caleb's brother, took it; so Caleb gave his daughter Acsah to him in marriage.

[18]One day when she came to Othniel, she urged him[r] to ask her father for a field. When she got off her donkey, Caleb asked her, "What can I do for you?"

[19]She replied, "Do me a special favor. Since you have given me land in the Negev,[m] give me also springs of water." So Caleb gave her the upper and lower springs.[n]

[20]This is the inheritance of the tribe of Judah, clan by clan:

[21]The southernmost towns of the tribe of Judah in the Negev[o] toward the boundary of Edom were:

Kabzeel,[p] Eder,[q] Jagur, [22]Kinah, Dimonah, Adadah, [23]Kedesh,[r] Hazor,[s] Ithnan, [24]Ziph,[t] Telem, Bealoth, [25]Hazor Hadattah, Kerioth Hezron (that is, Hazor),[u] [26]Amam, Shema, Moladah,[v] [27]Hazar Gaddah, Heshmon, Beth Pelet, [28]Hazar Shual,[w] Beersheba,[x] Biziothiah, [29]Baalah,[y] Iim, Ezem,[z] [30]Eltolad,[a] Kesil, Hormah,[b] [31]Ziklag,[c] Madmannah,[d] Sansannah, [32]Lebaoth, Shilhim, Ain[e] and Rimmon[f]—a total of twenty-nine towns and their villages.

[33]In the western foothills:

Eshtaol,[g] Zorah,[h] Ashnah,[i] [34]Zanoah,[j] En Gannim,[k] Tappuah,[l] Enam, [35]Jarmuth,[m] Adullam,[n] Socoh,[o] Azekah,[p] [36]Shaaraim,[q] Adithaim and Gederah[r] (or Gederothaim)[s]—fourteen towns and their villages.

[37]Zenan, Hadashah, Migdal Gad, [38]Dilean, Mizpah,[s] Joktheel,[t] [39]Lachish,[u] Bozkath,[v] Eglon,[w] [40]Cabbon, Lahmas, Kitlish, [41]Gederoth,[x] Beth Dagon,[y] Naamah and Makkedah[z]—sixteen towns and their villages.

[42]Libnah,[a] Ether, Ashan,[b] [43]Iphtah, Ashnah,[c] Nezib, [44]Keilah,[d] Aczib[e] and Mareshah[f]—nine towns and their villages.

[45]Ekron,[g] with its surrounding settlements and villages; [46]west of Ekron, all that were in the vicinity of Ashdod,[h] together with their villages; [47]Ashdod,[i] its surrounding settlements and villages; and Gaza, its settlements and villages, as far as the Wadi of Egypt[j] and the coastline of the Great Sea.[k]

[48]In the hill country:

Shamir,[l] Jattir,[m] Socoh,[n] [49]Dannah, Kiriath Sannah (that is, Debir[o]), [50]Anab,[p] Eshtemoh,[q] Anim, [51]Goshen,[r] Holon[s] and Giloh[t]—eleven towns and their villages.

[52]Arab, Dumah,[u] Eshan, [53]Janim, Beth Tappuah, Aphekah, [54]Humtah, Kiriath Arba[v] (that is, Hebron) and Zior—nine towns and their villages.

[55]Maon,[w] Carmel,[x] Ziph,[y] Juttah,[z] [56]Jezreel,[a] Jokdeam, Zanoah,[b] [57]Kain, Gibeah[c] and Timnah[d]—ten towns and their villages.

[58]Halhul, Beth Zur,[e] Gedor,[f] [59]Maarath, Beth Anoth and Eltekon—six towns and their villages.

[60]Kiriath Baal[g] (that is, Kiriath Jearim[h]) and Rabbah[i]—two towns and their villages.

[61]In the desert:[j]

Beth Arabah,[k] Middin, Secacah, [62]Nibshan, the City of Salt and En

Cross references (center column)

15:16 [k]1Ch 2:49
15:17 [l]Jdg 3:9, 11; 1Ch 4:13; 27:15
15:19 [m]S Jos 10:40 [n]Ge 36:24
15:21 [o]S Jos 10:40 [p]2Sa 23:20; 1Ch 11:22 [q]Ge 35:21
15:23 [r]S Jos 12:22 [s]S Jos 11:1
15:24 [t]ver 55; 1Sa 23:14; 2Ch 11:8
15:25 [u]S Jos 11:1
15:26 [v]Jos 19:2; 1Ch 4:28; Ne 11:26
15:28 [w]Jos 19:3; 1Ch 4:28 [x]S Ge 21:14
15:29 [y]S ver 9 [z]Jos 19:3; 1Ch 4:29
15:30 [a]Jos 19:4 [b]S Nu 14:45
15:31 [c]Jos 19:5; 1Sa 27:6; 1Ch 4:30; 12:1; Ne 11:28 [d]1Ch 2:49
15:32 [e]S Nu 34:11 [f]Jos 19:7; Jdg 20:45; 21:13; Zec 14:10
15:33 [g]Jos 19:41; Jdg 13:25; 16:31; 18:2 [h]Jdg 13:2; 18:11; 2Ch 11:10; Ne 11:29 [i]ver 43
15:34 [j]ver 56; 1Ch 4:18; Ne 3:13; 11:30 [k]Jos 19:21; 21:29 [l]S Jos 12:17
15:35 [m]S Jos 10:3 [n]S Ge 38:1 [o]ver 48; 1Ki 4:10 [p]S Jos 10:10
15:36 [q]1Sa 17:52; 1Ch 4:31 [r]1Ch 12:4
15:38 [s]S Jos 11:3 [t]2Ki 14:7
15:39 [u]S Jos 10:3 [v]2Ki 22:1 [w]S Jos 10:3
15:41 [x]2Ch 28:18 [y]Jos 19:27 [z]S Jos 10:10
15:42 [a]S Nu 33:20 [b]Jos 19:7; 1Sa 30:30; 1Ch 4:32; 6:59
15:43 [c]ver 33
15:44 [d]1Sa 23:1-2,1; 1Ch 4:19; Ne 3:17,18

[e]Jos 19:29; Jdg 1:31; Mic 1:14 [f]Mic 1:15 15:45 [g]S Jos 13:3
15:46 [h]Jos 11:22 15:47 [i]S Jos 11:22 [j]S Ge 15:18 [k]S Nu 34:6
15:48 [l]Jos 10:1 [m]Jos 21:14; 1Sa 30:27; 1Ch 6:57 [n]S ver 35
15:49 [o]S Jos 10:3 15:50 [p]Jos 11:21 [q]Jos 21:14; 1Sa 30:28
15:51 [r]S Jos 10:41 [s]Jos 21:15; Jer 48:21 [t]2Sa 15:12 15:52 [u]S Ge 25:14 15:54 [v]S Ge 35:27 15:55 [w]Jdg 10:12; 1Sa 23:24,25; 25:1,2; 1Ch 2:45 [x]S Jos 12:22 [y]S ver 24 [z]Jos 21:16 15:56 [a]Jos 17:16; 19:18; Jdg 6:33; 1Sa 25:43; 1Ki 18:45; 1Ch 3:1; Hos 1:5 [b]S ver 34 15:57 [c]Jos 18:28; 24:33; Jdg 19:12; 20:4; 2Sa 23:29; 1Ch 11:31 [d]S Ge 38:12
15:58 [e]1Ch 2:45; 2Ch 11:7; Ne 3:16 [f]1Ch 4:39; 12:7
15:60 [g]ver 9 [h]S Jos 9:17 [i]S Dt 3:11 15:61 [j]S Jos 8:15
[k]S ver 6

[r]18 Hebrew and some Septuagint manuscripts; other Septuagint manuscripts (see also note at Judges 1:14) *Othniel, he urged her* [s]36 Or *Gederah and Gederothaim*

15:17 *Othniel.* See Jdg 3:7–11 for his service as judge in Israel.

15:19 *upper and lower springs.* They still water the local farms in Hebron.

15:21 *southernmost towns.* Most of the first 29 villages were assigned to the tribe of Simeon (cf. 19:1–9).

15:33 *western foothills.* The Hebrew for this term is *Shephelah,* meaning "lowland." This area between the highlands of central Judah and the Philistine coast was for the most part not occupied by Israel until the victories of King

David. Some of the places on this list were reassigned to the tribe of Dan (cf. 19:41–43).

15:48 *hill country.* The high region south of Jerusalem. The Septuagint adds 11 names, including Tekoa and Bethlehem, to this list.

15:61 *desert.* The chalky, dry region east and south of Jerusalem that borders the Dead Sea.

15:62 Only En Gedi can be positively located, though the "City of Salt" is believed by many to be Qumran, where, centuries later, the scribes who produced the Dead Sea

Gedi *l*—six towns and their villages.
63Judah could not *m* dislodge the Jebusites *n*, who were living in Jerusalem; *o* to this day the Jebusites live there with the people of Judah. *p*

Allotment for Ephraim and Manasseh

16 The allotment for Joseph began at the Jordan of Jericho, *t* east of the waters of Jericho, and went up from there through the desert *q* into the hill country of Bethel. *r* 2It went on from Bethel (that is, Luz *s*), *u* crossed over to the territory of the Arkites *t* in Ataroth, *u* 3descended westward to the territory of the Japhletites as far as the region of Lower Beth Horon *v* and on to Gezer, *w* ending at the sea.

4So Manasseh and Ephraim, the descendants of Joseph, received their inheritance. *x*

5This was the territory of Ephraim, clan by clan:

The boundary of their inheritance went from Ataroth Addar *y* in the east to Upper Beth Horon *z* 6and continued to the sea. From Micmethath *a* on the north it curved eastward to Taanath Shiloh, passing by it to Janoah *b* on the east. 7Then it went down from Janoah *c* to Ataroth *d* and Naarah, touched Jericho and came out at the Jordan. 8From Tappuah *e* the border went west to the Kanah Ravine *f* and ended at the sea. This was the inheritance of the tribe of the Ephraimites, clan by clan. 9It also included all the towns and their villages that were set aside for the Ephraimites within the inheritance of the Manassites. *g*

10They did not dislodge the Canaanites living in Gezer; to this day the Canaanites live among the people of Ephraim but are required to do forced labor. *h*

17 This was the allotment for the tribe of Manasseh *i* as Joseph's first-born, *j* that is, for Makir, *k* Manasseh's firstborn. Makir was the ancestor of the Gileadites, who had received Gilead *l* and Bashan *m* because the Makirites were great soldiers. 2So this allotment was for the rest of the people of Manasseh *n*—the clans of Abiezer, *o* Helek, Asriel, *p* Shechem, Hepher *q* and Shemida. *r* These are the other male descendants of Manasseh son of Joseph by their clans.

3Now Zelophehad son of Hepher, *s* the son of Gilead, the son of Makir, the son of Manasseh, had no sons but only daughters, *t* whose names were Mahlah, Noah, Hoglah, Milcah and Tirzah. 4They went to Eleazar the priest, Joshua son of Nun, and the leaders and said, "The LORD commanded Moses to give us an inheritance among our brothers." So Joshua gave them an inheritance along with the brothers of their father, according to the LORD's command. *u* 5Manasseh's share consisted of ten tracts of land besides Gilead and Bashan east of the Jordan, *v* 6because the daughters of the tribe of Manasseh received an inheritance among the sons. The land of Gilead belonged to the rest of the descendants of Manasseh.

7The territory of Manasseh extended from Asher *w* to Micmethath *x* east of Shechem. *y* The boundary ran southward from there to include the people living at En Tappuah. 8(Manasseh had the land of Tappuah, but Tappuah *z* itself, on the boundary of Manasseh, belonged to the Ephraimites.) 9Then the boundary continued south to the Kanah Ravine. *a* There were towns belonging to Ephraim lying among the towns of Manasseh,

Cross references (center column)

15:62
l Isa 23:29; 24:1;
Eze 47:10
15:63
m Jos 16:10;
17:12; Jdg 1:21;
1Ki 9:21 *n* S ver 8
o S Jos 10:1
p Eze 48:7
16:1 *q* S Jos 8:15
r S Jos 12:9
16:2 *s* S Ge 28:19
t 2Sa 15:32 *u* S ver
5; S Nu 32:3
16:3 *v* S Jos 10:10
w S Jos 10:33
16:4 *x* Jos 18:5
16:5 *y* ver 2;
Jos 18:13
z S Jos 10:10
16:6 *a* Jos 17:7
b ver 7; 2Ki 15:29
16:7 *c* S ver 6
d S Nu 32:3
16:8 *e* S Jos 12:17
f Jos 17:9; 19:28
16:9 *g* Eze 48:5
16:10
h S Jos 15:63;
17:13;
Jdg 1:28-29;
1Ki 9:16

17:1 *i* S Nu 1:34;
1Ch 7:14
j S Ge 41:51
k S Ge 50:23
l S Jos 12:2
m S Jos 13:11
17:2 *n* Jos 22:7
o S Nu 26:30;
Jdg 6:11,34; 8:2;
1Ch 7:18
p 1Ch 7:14
q S Nu 27:1
r 1Ch 7:19
17:3 *s* S Nu 27:1
t S Nu 26:33
17:4 *u* Nu 27:5-7
17:5
v Jos 13:30-31
17:7 *w* ver 10;
Jos 19:24,31;
21:6,30;
Jdg 1:31; 5:17;
6:35; 7:23
x Jos 16:6
y S Ge 12:6;
Jos 21:21; 24:25;
Jdg 9:1
17:8 *z* S Jos 12:17
17:9 *a* S Jos 16:8

t 1 Jordan of Jericho was possibly an ancient name for the Jordan River.   *u 2* Septuagint; Hebrew *Bethel to Luz*

Scrolls lived.

15:63 *Jebusites.* A victory over the city of the Jebusites by the men of Judah is recorded in Jdg 1:8, but evidently this did not result in its permanent occupation. Both Benjamin and Judah failed to take the Jebusite fortress of Jerusalem (Jdg 1:21).

16:1—17:18 Two chapters are devoted to the lands given to the "house of Joseph" (Ephraim and the half-tribe of Manasseh that settled west of the Jordan). Following Judah, the Joseph tribes were given priority.

16:1 *allotment for Joseph.* Ephraim's southern border moved west from Jericho past Bethel and down to Gezer and the Mediterranean coast.

16:5 *boundary.* Ephraim's northern border began down by the Jordan and ran west near Shiloh, but south of Shechem, then followed the Wadi Kanah down to the Mediterranean Sea.

16:10 *Gezer.* See note on 10:33. *but are required to do forced labor.* Since Gezer does not appear to have come under Israelite control until the days of Solomon (1Ki 9:15-16), this may be a note added after that event (but see 2Sa 5:25).

17:1 *Manasseh as Joseph's firstborn.* A reminder to the proud Ephraimites that Manasseh had been the firstborn, though Jacob gave priority to Ephraim when he adopted Joseph's two sons (Ge 48:14,19).

17:3 *Zelophehad . . . had . . . only daughters.* Before Moses died, he promised the daughters an allotment along with their relatives (see Nu 26:33; 27:1-7).

17:5 *ten tracts of land.* Manasseh's territory was second only to Judah's in size. Then ten portions went to the five brothers (minus Hepher) and to the five daughters of Hepher. For the law protecting the inheritance rights of a daughter without brothers see Nu 27:8-11.

but the boundary of Manasseh was the northern side of the ravine and ended at the sea. ¹⁰On the south the land belonged to Ephraim, on the north to Manasseh. The territory of Manasseh reached the sea and bordered Asher*b* on the north and Issachar*c* on the east.*d*

¹¹Within Issachar*e* and Asher, Manasseh also had Beth Shan,*f* Ibleam*g* and the people of Dor,*h* Endor,*i* Taanach*j* and Megiddo,*k* together with their surrounding settlements (the third in the list is Naphoth*v*).*l*

¹²Yet the Manassites were not able*m* to occupy these towns, for the Canaanites were determined to live in that region. ¹³However, when the Israelites grew stronger, they subjected the Canaanites to forced labor but did not drive them out completely.*n*

¹⁴The people of Joseph said to Joshua, "Why have you given us only one allotment and one portion for an inheritance? We are a numerous people and the LORD has blessed us abundantly."*o*

¹⁵"If you are so numerous," Joshua answered, "and if the hill country of Ephraim is too small for you, go up into the forest*p* and clear land for yourselves there in the land of the Perizzites*q* and Rephaites.*r*"

¹⁶The people of Joseph replied, "The hill country is not enough for us, and all the Canaanites who live in the plain have iron chariots,*s* both those in Beth Shan*t* and its settlements and those in the Valley of Jezreel."*u*

¹⁷But Joshua said to the house of Joseph—to Ephraim and Manasseh—"You are numerous and very powerful. You will have not only one allotment*v* ¹⁸but the forested hill country*w* as well. Clear it, and its farthest limits will be yours; though the Canaanites have iron chariots*x* and though they are strong, you can drive them out."

Division of the Rest of the Land

18 The whole assembly of the Israelites gathered at Shiloh*y* and set up the Tent of Meeting*z* there. The country was brought under their control, ²but there were still seven Israelite tribes who had not yet received their inheritance.

³So Joshua said to the Israelites: "How long will you wait before you begin to take possession of the land that the LORD, the God of your fathers, has given you? ⁴Appoint three men from each tribe. I will send them out to make a survey of the land and to write a description of it,*a* according to the inheritance of each.*b* Then they will return to me. ⁵You are to divide the land into seven parts. Judah is to remain in its territory on the south*c* and the house of Joseph in its territory on the north.*d* ⁶After you have written descriptions of the seven parts of the land, bring them here to me and I will cast lots*e* for you in the presence of the LORD our God. ⁷The Levites, however, do not get a portion among you, because the priestly service of the LORD is their inheritance.*f* And Gad, Reuben and the half-tribe of Manasseh have already received their inheritance on the east side of

---

Cross references (center column):

17:10 *b*S ver 7
*c*S Ge 30:18
*d*Eze 48:5
17:11 *e*ver 10
*f*ver 16; Jdg 1:27;
1Sa 31:10;
2Sa 21:12;
1Ki 4:12;
1Ch 7:29
*g*2Ki 9:27
*h*S Jos 11:2
*i*1Sa 28:7;
Ps 83:10
*j*S Jos 12:21
*k*1Ki 9:15
*l*Eze 48:4
17:12
*m*S Jos 15:63
17:13
*n*Jdg 1:27-28
17:14
*o*Nu 26:28-37
17:15 *p*2Sa 18:6
*q*S Jos 3:10
*r*S Ge 14:5;
Jos 15:8; 18:16;
2Sa 5:18; 23:13;
Isa 17:5
17:16 *s*ver 18;
Jdg 1:19; 4:3,13
*t*S ver 11
*u*S Jos 15:56;
S 1Sa 29:1

17:17 *v*Eze 48:5
17:18 *w*1Sa 1:1
*x*S ver 16
18:1 *y*ver 8;
Jos 19:51; 21:2;
Jdg 18:31; 21:12,
19; 1Sa 1:3;
3:21; 4:3;
1Ki 14:2;
Ps 78:60;
Jer 7:12; 26:6;
41:5 *z*S ver 10;
S Ex 27:21;
S 40:2; Ac 7:45
18:4 *a*ver 8
*b*Mic 2:5
18:5 *c*Jos 15:1
*d*Jos 16:1-4
18:6 *e*S Lev 16:8
18:7 *f*S Jos 13:33

v 11 That is, Naphoth Dor

17:11 *Beth Shan . . . Megiddo.* These powerfully fortified cities, and others along Manasseh's common border with Issachar and Asher, were not conquered until later. When King Saul died in battle, the victorious Philistines fastened his body to the wall of Beth Shan (see 1Sa 31:10), which suggests that that city was in league with the Philistines.

17:13 *when the Israelites grew stronger.* Possibly referring to the days of David and Solomon (see note on 16:10).

17:14 *people of Joseph . . . numerous.* The reference is to both Ephraim and Manasseh (see v. 17). The allotment to the Joseph tribes is here handled as one (see 16:1,4)—though the two subdivisions are then described separately (16:5–17:11).

17:15 *hill country of Ephraim.* The territory of the Joseph tribes—under the name of the legal firstborn (see note on v. 1). *clear land for yourselves.* This region of Canaan was still heavily forested. It seems that the Israelites viewed their assigned territories primarily in terms of the number of cities that had their land cleared for farming and pasturage, not in terms of the size of the region in which these cities were located. The region assigned to the Joseph tribes was at the time not as heavily populated as others. *Perizzites and Rephaites.* Here listed as neighboring peoples, though elsewhere the Perizzites are said to have lived on the west bank in Canaan (3:10; 12:8) and the Rephaites in the Transjordan

kingdom of Og (12:4; 13:12). See notes on Ge 13:7; Dt 2:11.

17:16 *in the plain.* Only in the plains were chariots effective. *iron chariots.* Chariots with certain parts made of iron (see note on 2Sa 8:7), perhaps the axles—the use of iron was a new development (see note on 11:6).

18:1–19:51 Seven tribes remained to be assigned land: Benjamin, Simeon, Zebulun, Issachar, Asher, Naphtali and Dan. Their lots were cast at Shiloh, after which a special portion was awarded to Joshua.

18:1 *Shiloh.* About ten miles northeast of Bethel, a little east of the main road from Bethel to Shechem. *Tent of Meeting.* The tabernacle (see note on Ex 27:21) with its sacred ark of the covenant. It would remain at Shiloh until the time of Samuel (1Sa 4:3).

18:3 *take possession.* Conquest had to be followed by settlement, which required a survey, then a fair distribution, and then a full occupation of the land. A distinction must therefore be made between the national wars of conquest (Joshua) and the tribal wars of occupation (Jdg 1–2).

18:5 *north.* Relative to the territory of Judah.

18:6 *I will cast lots for you.* See note on 14:1.

18:7 *priestly service of the LORD is their inheritance.* See 13:14; see also Dt 18:1–8 and note on Dt 18:1.

the Jordan. Moses the servant of the LORD gave it to them. g"

8As the men started on their way to map out the land, Joshua instructed them, "Go and make a survey of the land and write a description of it. h Then return to me, and I will cast lots for you here at Shiloh i in the presence of the LORD." 9So the men left and went through the land. They wrote its description on a scroll, town by town, in seven parts, and returned to Joshua in the camp at Shiloh. 10Joshua then cast lots j for them in Shiloh in the presence k of the LORD, and there he distributed the land to the Israelites according to their tribal divisions. l

Allotment for Benjamin

11The lot came up for the tribe of Benjamin, clan by clan. Their allotted territory lay between the tribes of Judah and Joseph:

12On the north side their boundary began at the Jordan, passed the northern slope of Jericho and headed west into the hill country, coming out at the desert m of Beth Aven. n 13From there it crossed to the south slope of Luz o (that is, Bethel p) and went down to Ataroth Addar q on the hill south of Lower Beth Horon.

14From the hill facing Beth Horon r on the south the boundary turned south along the western side and came out at Kiriath Baal (that is, Kiriath Jearim), s a town of the people of Judah. This was the western side.

15The southern side began at the outskirts of Kiriath Jearim on the west, and the boundary came out at the spring of the waters of Nephtoah. t 16The boundary went down to the foot of the hill facing the Valley of Ben Hinnom, north of the Valley of Rephaim. u It continued down the Hinnom Valley v along the southern slope of the Jebusite city and so to En Rogel. w 17It then curved north, went to En Shemesh, continued to Geliloth, x which faces the Pass of Adummim, y and ran down to the Stone of Bohan z son of Reuben. 18It continued to the northern slope of Beth Arabah w a and on down into the Arabah. b 19It then

went to the northern slope of Beth Hoglah c and came out at the northern bay of the Salt Sea, x d at the mouth of the Jordan in the south. This was the southern boundary.

20The Jordan formed the boundary on the eastern side.

These were the boundaries that marked out the inheritance of the clans of Benjamin on all sides. e

21The tribe of Benjamin, clan by clan, had the following cities:

Jericho, Beth Hoglah, f Emek Keziz, 22Beth Arabah, g Zemaraim, h Bethel, i 23Avvim, j Parah, Ophrah, k 24Kephar Ammoni, Ophni and Geba l —twelve towns and their villages.

25Gibeon, m Ramah, n Beeroth, o 26Mizpah, p Kephirah, q Mozah, 27Rekem, Irpeel, Taralah, 28Zelah, Haeleph, the Jebusite city s (that is, Jerusalem t), Gibeah u and Kiriath —fourteen towns and their villages. v

This was the inheritance of Benjamin for its clans. w

Allotment for Simeon

19:2–10pp — 1Ch 4:28–33

19 The second lot came out for the tribe of Simeon, clan by clan. Their inheritance lay within the territory of Judah. x 2It included:

Beersheba y (or Sheba), v Moladah, z 3Hazar Shual, a Balah, Ezem, b 4Eltolad, c Bethul, Hormah, d 5Ziklag, e Beth Marcaboth, Hazar Susah, 6Beth Lebaoth and Sharuhen —thirteen towns and their villages;

7Ain, Rimmon, f Ether and Ashan g—four towns and their villages— 8and all the villages around these towns as far as Baalath Beer (Ramah in the Negev). h

This was the inheritance of the tribe of Simeonites, clan by clan. 9The inheritance of the Simeonites was taken from the share of Judah, i because Judah's portion was more than they needed. So the Simeonites

Cross references (center column)

18:7 *g*Jos 13:8
18:8 *h*ver 4 *i*S ver 1
18:10 *j*S Nu 34:13 *k*S ver 1; Jer 7:12 *l*Nu 33:54; Jos 19:51
18:12 *m*S Jos 8:15 *n*S Jos 7:2
18:13 *o*S Ge 28:19 *p*S Jos 12:9 *q*S Nu 32:3; S Jos 16:5
18:14 *r*Jos 10:10 *s*S Jos 9:17
18:15 *t*Jos 15:9
18:16 *u*S Jos 17:15 *v*Jos 15:8 *w*S Jos 15:7
18:17 *x*Jos 22:10 *y*Jos 15:7 *z*Jos 15:6
18:18 *a*S Jos 15:6 *b*S Jos 11:2
18:19 *c*S Jos 15:6 *d*S Ge 14:3
18:20 *e*1Sa 9:1
18:21 *f*S Jos 15:6
18:22 *g*Jos 15:6 *h*2Ch 13:4 *i*Jos 16:1
18:23 *j*S Dt 2:23 *k*Jdg 6:11,24; 8:27,32; 9:5; 1Sa 13:17
18:24 *l*Jos 21:17; 1Sa 13:3,16; 14:5; 19:13; 2Ki 23:8; Isa 10:29
18:25 *m*Jos 9:3 *n*S Jos 10:40; Jdg 4:5; 19:13; 1Sa 1:1,19; 2:11; 7:17; 25:1; 1Ki 15:17,21; Ezr 2:26; Ne 11:33; Isa 10:29; Jer 31:15; 40:1 *o*S Jos 9:17; Ezr 2:25; Ne 7:29
18:26 *p*S Jos 11:3 *q*Jos 9:17; Ezr 2:25; Ne 7:29
18:28 *r*2Sa 21:14 *s*S Jos 15:8 *t*S Jos 10:1 *u*S Jos 15:57 *v*S Jos 9:17 *w*Eze 48:23
19:1 *x*S Ge 49:7
19:2 *y*S Ge 21:14; 1Ki 19:3 *z*S Jos 15:26
19:3 *a*S Jos 15:28 *b*S Jos 15:29
19:4 *c*Jos 15:30 *d*S Nu 14:45
19:5 *e*S Jos 15:31
19:7 *f*S Jos 15:32 *g*S Jos 15:42
19:8 *h*S Jos 10:40
19:9 *i*S Ge 49:7

Text notes

w 18 Septuagint; Hebrew *slope facing the Arabah*
x 19 That is, the Dead Sea   y 2 Or *Beersheba, Sheba;* 1 Chron. 4:28 does not have *Sheba.*

18:9 *scroll.* Presumed form of the document; the Hebrew for this word is not specific.
18:11 *lot ... for ... Benjamin.* A buffer zone between Judah and Ephraim, the two dominant tribes. Its northern line was the same as Ephraim's southern border (see note on 16:1), and its southern line was the same as Judah's northern-

most boundary (see note on 15:5).

18:23 *Avvim.* The people of Ai.

19:1 *second lot ... for ... Simeon.* Cities within the borders of Judah (15:21) in the Negev along Judah's southern border (1Ch 4:24–42).

received their inheritance within the territory of Judah.[j]

Allotment for Zebulun

[10]The third lot came up for Zebulun,[k] clan by clan:

The boundary of their inheritance went as far as Sarid.[l] [11]Going west it ran to Maralah, touched Dabbesheth, and extended to the ravine near Jokneam.[m] [12]It turned east from Sarid[n] toward the sunrise to the territory of Kisloth Tabor and went on to Daberath[o] and up to Japhia. [13]Then it continued eastward to Gath Hepher[p] and Eth Kazin; it came out at Rimmon[q] and turned toward Neah. [14]There the boundary went around on the north to Hannathon and ended at the Valley of Iphtah El.[r] [15]Included were Kattath, Nahalal,[s] Shimron,[t] Idalah and Bethlehem.[u] There were twelve towns and their villages.

[16]These towns and their villages were the inheritance of Zebulun,[v] clan by clan.[w]

Allotment for Issachar

[17]The fourth lot came out for Issachar,[x] clan by clan. [18]Their territory included:

Jezreel,[y] Kesulloth, Shunem,[z] [19]Hapharaim, Shion, Anaharath, [20]Rabbith, Kishion,[a] Ebez, [21]Remeth, En Gannim,[b] En Haddah and Beth Pazzez. [22]The boundary touched Tabor,[c] Shahazumah and Beth Shemesh,[d] and ended at the Jordan. There were sixteen towns and their villages.

[23]These towns and their villages were the inheritance of the tribe of Issachar,[e] clan by clan.[f]

Allotment for Asher

[24]The fifth lot came out for the tribe of Asher,[g] clan by clan. [25]Their territory included:

Helkath, Hali, Beten, Acshaph,[h] [26]Allammelech, Amad and Mishal.[i] On the west the boundary touched Carmel[j] and Shihor Libnath. [27]It then turned east toward Beth Dagon,[k]

touched Zebulun[l] and the Valley of Iphtah El,[m] and went north to Beth Emek and Neiel, passing Cabul[n] on the left. [28]It went to Abdon,[z o] Rehob,[p] Hammon[q] and Kanah,[r] as far as Greater Sidon.[s] [29]The boundary then turned back toward Ramah[t] and went to the fortified city of Tyre,[u] turned toward Hosah and came out at the sea[v] in the region of Aczib,[w] [30]Ummah, Aphek[x] and Rehob.[y] There were twenty-two towns and their villages.

[31]These towns and their villages were the inheritance of the tribe of Asher,[z] clan by clan.

Allotment for Naphtali

[32]The sixth lot came out for Naphtali, clan by clan:

[33]Their boundary went from Heleph and the large tree in Zaanannim,[a] passing Adami Nekeb and Jabneel[b] to Lakkum and ending at the Jordan. [34]The boundary ran west through Aznoth Tabor and came out at Hukkok.[c] It touched Zebulun[d] on the south, Asher on the west and the Jordan[a] on the east. [35]The fortified cities were Ziddim, Zer, Hammath,[e] Rakkath, Kinnereth,[f] [36]Adamah, Ramah,[g] Hazor,[h] [37]Kedesh,[i] Edrei,[j] En Hazor, [38]Iron, Migdal El, Horem, Beth Anath[k] and Beth Shemesh.[l] There were nineteen towns and their villages.

[39]These towns and their villages were the inheritance of the tribe of Naphtali, clan by clan.[m]

Allotment for Dan

[40]The seventh lot came out for the tribe of Dan, clan by clan. [41]The territory of their inheritance included:

Zorah, Eshtaol,[n] Ir Shemesh, [42]Shaalabbin, Aijalon,[o] Ithlah, [43]Elon,

---

19:9 [j]Eze 48:24
19:10 [k]ver 16,27, 34; Jos 21:7,34
[l]ver 12
19:11 [m]S Jos 12:22
19:12 [n]ver 10
[o]Jos 21:28; 1Ch 6:72
19:13 [p]S Jos 11:22
[q]Jos 15:32
19:14 [r]ver 27
19:15 [s]Jos 21:35
[t]Jos 11:1
[u]S Ge 35:19
19:16 [v]S ver 10
[w]Eze 48:26
19:17 [x]S Ge 30:18
19:18 [y]S Jos 15:56
[z]1Sa 28:4;
1Ki 1:3; 2Ki 4:8
19:20 [a]Jos 21:28
19:21 [b]S Jos 15:34
19:22 [c]Jdg 4:6, 12; 8:18;
Ps 89:12;
Jer 46:18
[d]S Jos 15:10
19:23 [e]Jos 17:10
[f]Ge 49:15;
Eze 48:25
19:24 [g]S Jos 17:7
19:25 [h]S Jos 11:1
19:26 [i]Jos 21:30
[j]S Jos 12:22;
1Ki 18:19;
2Ki 2:25
19:27 [k]Jos 15:41

[l]S ver 10 [m]ver 14
[n]1Ki 9:13
19:28
[o]Jos 21:30;
1Ch 6:74 [p]ver 30; Nu 13:21;
Jos 21:31;
Jdg 1:31
[q]1Ch 6:76
[r]S Jos 16:8
[s]S Ge 10:19
19:29 [t]Jos 18:25
[u]2Sa 5:11; 24:7;
Ezr 3:7; Ps 45:12;
Isa 23:1;
Jer 25:22;
Eze 26:2
[v]Jdg 5:17
[w]S Jos 15:44
19:30
[x]S Jos 12:18
[y]S ver 28
19:31
[z]S Ge 30:13;
S Jos 17:7;
Eze 48:2
19:33 [a]Jdg 4:11
[b]Jos 15:11
19:34 [c]1Ch 6:75
[d]S ver 10
19:35 [e]1Ch 2:55
[f]S Jos 11:2
19:36 [g]Jos 18:25
[h]S Jos 11:1
19:37
[i]S Jos 12:22
[j]S Nu 21:33

19:38 [k]Jdg 1:33 [l]S Jos 15:10 19:39 [m]Eze 48:3 19:41
[n]S Jos 15:33 19:42 [o]S Jos 10:12

[z]28 Some Hebrew manuscripts (see also Joshua 21:30); most Hebrew manuscripts *Ebron* [a]34 Septuagint; Hebrew *west, and Judah, the Jordan,*

19:10 *third lot . . . for Zebulun.* To this tribe went a portion of lower Galilee west of the Sea of Galilee and in the vicinity of NT Nazareth.
19:17 *fourth lot . . . for Issachar.* Southwest of the Sea of Galilee reaching down to Beth Shan and west to the Jezreel Valley. Mount Tabor marked its northern border.
19:24 *fifth lot . . . for . . . Asher.* Asher was given the coastal area as far north as Sidon in Phoenicia and as far south as Mount Carmel.

19:32 *sixth lot . . . for Naphtali.* An area mostly to the north of the Sea of Galilee, taking in the modern Huleh Valley and the mountains bordering on Asher to the west. Its southernmost point was at the lower edge of the Sea of Galilee.
19:40 *seventh lot . . . for . . . Dan.* An elbow of land squeezed between Ephraim and Judah and west of Benjamin. The port of Joppa marked the northwestern corner of Dan.

Timnah,[p] Ekron,[q] 44Eltekeh, Gibbethon,[r] Baalath,[s] 45Jehud, Bene Berak, Gath Rimmon,[t] 46Me Jarkon and Rakkon, with the area facing Joppa.[u]

47(But the Danites had difficulty taking possession of their territory,[v] so they went up and attacked Leshem[w], took it, put it to the sword and occupied it. They settled in Leshem and named[x] it Dan after their forefather.)[y]

48These towns and their villages were the inheritance of the tribe of Dan,[z] clan by clan.

Allotment for Joshua

49When they had finished dividing the land into its allotted portions, the Israelites gave Joshua son of Nun an inheritance among them, 50as the LORD had commanded. They gave him the town he asked for—Timnath Serah[b][a] in the hill country of Ephraim. And he built up the town and settled there.

51These are the territories that Eleazar the priest, Joshua son of Nun and the heads of the tribal clans of Israel assigned by lot at Shiloh in the presence of the LORD at the entrance to the Tent of Meeting. And so they finished dividing[b] the land.[c]

Cities of Refuge

20:1-9Ref — Nu 35:9-34; Dt 4:41-43; 19:1-14

20 Then the LORD said to Joshua: 2"Tell the Israelites to designate the cities of refuge, as I instructed you through Moses, 3so that anyone who kills a person accidentally and unintentionally[d] may flee there and find protection from the avenger of blood.[e]

4"When he flees to one of these cities, he is to stand in the entrance of the city gate[f] and state his case before the elders[g] of that city. Then they are to admit him into their city and give him a place to live with them. 5If the avenger of blood pursues him, they must not surrender the one accused, because he killed his neighbor unintentionally and without malice aforethought. 6He is to stay in that city until he has stood trial before the assembly[h] and until the death of the high priest who is serving at that time. Then he may go back to his own home in the town from which he fled."

7So they set apart Kedesh[i] in Galilee in the hill country of Naphtali, Shechem[j] in the hill country of Ephraim, and Kiriath Arba[k] (that is, Hebron[l]) in the hill country of Judah.[m] 8On the east side of the Jordan of Jericho[c] they designated Bezer[n] in the desert on the plateau in the tribe of Reuben, Ramoth in Gilead[o][p] in the tribe of Gad, and Golan in Bashan[q] in the tribe of Manasseh. 9Any of the Israelites or any alien living among them who killed some-

Cross references (center column)

19:43
pS Ge 38:12
qS Jos 13:3
19:44 rJos 21:23;
1Ki 15:27; 16:15
s1Ki 9:18;
2Ch 8:6
19:45 tJos 21:24;
1Ch 6:69
19:46
u2Ch 2:16;
Ezr 3:7; Jnh 1:3;
Ac 9:36
19:47 vJdg 18:1
wJdg 18:7,14
xS Dt 3:14
yJdg 18:27,29
19:48 zS Ge 30:6
19:50 aJos 24:30;
Jdg 2:9
19:51 bJos 23:4
cS Jos 14:1;
S 18:10; Ac 13:19

20:3 dS Lev 4:2
eS Nu 35:12
20:4 fS Ge 23:10;
Jer 38:7 gS Jos 7:6
20:6 hS Nu 35:12
20:7 iS Jos 12:22
jS Ge 12:6
kS Ge 35:27
lS Jos 10:36
mLk 1:39
20:8 nJos 21:36;
1Ch 6:78
oS 1Ch 6:80
pS Jos 12:2
qS Jos 12:5;
1Ch 6:71

b 50 Also known as Timnath Heres (see Judges 2:9)
c 8 Jordan of Jericho was possibly an ancient name for the Jordan River.

19:47 *Danites had difficulty.* The Amorites of this area "confined the Danites to the hill country" (Jdg 1:34), so most of the tribe migrated to the upper Jordan Valley, where they seized the town of Leshem (or Laish, Jdg 18:2-10, 27-29) and renamed it Dan.

19:49 *gave Joshua ... an inheritance.* In the account of the distribution of the promised land (the territory west of the Jordan), the assignment to Caleb is treated first (14:6-15), the assignment to Joshua last. Thus the allotting of inheritance to these two dauntless servants of the Lord from the desert generation (see Nu 13:30; 14:6,24,30) frames the whole account—and both received the territory they asked for. Appropriately, Joshua's allotment came last; he was not a king or a warlord but the servant of God commissioned to bring the Lord's people into the promised land.

19:50 *Timnath Serah.* Located in the southwestern corner of Ephraim, facing out to the sea. Here Joshua was also buried (24:30).

20:1-9 Having distributed the land to the tribes, the Lord's next administrative regulation (see note on 13:1-32) provided an elementary system of government, specifically a system of regional courts to deal with capital offenses having to do with manslaughter. Thus this most inflammatory of cases was removed from local jurisdiction, and a safeguard was created against the easy miscarriage of justice (with its potential for endless blood feuds) when retribution for manslaughter was left in the hands of family members. The cities chosen were among those also assigned to the Levites, where ideally the law of Moses would especially be known and honored.

20:2 *as I instructed you through Moses.* See Nu 35:6-34.

20:3 *avenger of blood.* Also translated "kinsman-redeemer" (Ru 3:9), or "Redeemer" (Ps 19:14). The avenger was a near relative with the obligation of exacting retribution (see Lev 24:17; Nu 35:16-28).

20:4 *city gate.* Traditional place for trials, where the elders sat to hold court (see Ru 4:1 and note; see also Job 29:7).

20:6 *assembly.* Made up of the adult males of the city. Their function in the trial before the elders (v. 4) is not clear, but perhaps they witnessed the trial to see that it was fair (closed courts are notoriously corruptible). *and.* Or "or." *death of the high priest.* See Nu 35:25-28. Either an atoning effect or a kind of amnesty was achieved by the high priest's death.

20:7 *they set apart Kedesh.* A wordplay in the Hebrew: "they consecrated (the town of) consecration." The other two cities west of the Jordan already had sacred associations: For Shechem see 8:30-35 and note; Ge 12:6-7; for Hebron see Ge 23:2; 49:29-32. The geographical distribution of the cities was important: one in the north, one in the midlands and one in the south. (See v. 8, where the order of the three cities of refuge that served in Transjordan is reversed: Bezer in the south, Ramoth in the midlands and Golan in the north.) See "Cities of Refuge," p. 241.

20:9 *or any alien.* Evidence of the equal protection granted to the foreigners living in Israel (cf. Lev 19:33-34; Dt 10:18-19).

one accidentally[r] could flee to these designated cities and not be killed by the avenger of blood prior to standing trial before the assembly.[s]

Towns for the Levites

21:4–39pp — 1Ch 6:54–80

21 Now the family heads of the Levites approached Eleazar the priest, Joshua son of Nun, and the heads of the other tribal families of Israel[t] 2at Shiloh[u] in Canaan and said to them, "The LORD commanded through Moses that you give us towns[v] to live in, with pasturelands for our livestock."[w] 3So, as the LORD had commanded, the Israelites gave the Levites the following towns and pasturelands out of their own inheritance:

4The first lot came out for the Kohathites,[x] clan by clan. The Levites who were descendants of Aaron the priest were allotted thirteen towns from the tribes of Judah, Simeon and Benjamin.[y] 5The rest of Kohath's descendants were allotted ten towns from the clans of the tribes of Ephraim, Dan and half of Manasseh.[z]

6The descendants of Gershon[a] were allotted thirteen towns from the clans of the tribes of Issachar,[b] Asher,[c] Naphtali and the half-tribe of Manasseh in Bashan.

7The descendants of Merari,[d] clan by clan, received twelve[e] towns from the tribes of Reuben, Gad and Zebulun.[f]

8So the Israelites allotted to the Levites these towns and their pasturelands, as the LORD had commanded through Moses.

9From the tribes of Judah and Simeon they allotted the following towns by name 10(these towns were assigned to the descendants of Aaron who were from the Kohathite clans of the Levites, because the first lot fell to them):

11They gave them Kiriath Arba[g] (that is, Hebron[h]), with its surrounding pastureland, in the hill country of Judah. (Arba was the forefather of Anak.) 12But the fields and villages around the city they had given to Caleb son of Jephunneh as his possession.[i]

13So to the descendants of Aaron the priest they gave Hebron (a city of refuge[j] for one accused of murder), Libnah,[k] 14Jattir,[l] Eshtemoa,[m] 15Holon,[n] Debir,[o] 16Ain,[p] Juttah[q] and Beth Shemesh,[r] together with their pasturelands—nine towns from these two tribes.

17And from the tribe of Benjamin they gave them Gibeon,[s] Geba,[t] 18Anathoth[u] and Almon, together with their pasturelands—four towns.

19All the towns[v] for the priests, the descendants of Aaron, were thirteen, together with their pasturelands.[w]

20The rest of the Kohathite clans of the Levites were allotted towns from the tribe of Ephraim:

21In the hill country of Ephraim they were given Shechem[x] (a city of refuge for one accused of murder) and Gezer,[y] 22Kibzaim and Beth Horon,[z] together with their pasturelands—four towns.[a]

23Also from the tribe of Dan they received Eltekeh, Gibbethon,[b] 24Aijalon[c] and Gath Rimmon,[d] together with their pasturelands—four towns.

25From half the tribe of Manasseh they received Taanach[e] and Gath Rimmon, together with their pasturelands—two towns.

26All these ten towns and their pasturelands were given to the rest of the Kohathite clans.[f]

27The Levite clans of the Gershonites were given:

from the half-tribe of Manasseh, Golan in Bashan[g] (a city of refuge for one accused of murder[h]) and Be Eshtarah, together with their pasturelands—two towns;

28from the tribe of Issachar,[i] Kishion,[j] Daberath,[k] 29Jarmuth[l] and En Gannim,[m] together with their pasturelands—four towns;

30from the tribe of Asher,[n] Mishal,[o] Abdon,[p] 31Helkath and Rehob,[q] together with their pasturelands—four towns;

32from the tribe of Naphtali, Kedesh[r] in Galilee (a city of refuge for one accused of murder[s]), Hammoth

Cross references

20:9 [r]S Lev 4:2; [s]S Ex 21:13
21:1 [t]Jos 14:1
21:2 [u]S Jos 18:1; [v]S Lev 25:32; [w]S Nu 35:2-3; S Jos 14:4
21:4 [x]Nu 3:17; [y]ver 19
21:5 [z]ver 26
21:6 [a]Nu 3:17; [b]S Ge 30:18; [c]S Jos 17:7
21:7 [d]S Ex 6:16; [e]ver 40; [f]S Jos 19:10
21:11 [g]S Ge 23:2; [h]S Jos 10:36
21:12 [i]S Jos 15:13
21:13 [j]Nu 35:6; [k]S Nu 33:20
21:14 [l]S Jos 15:48; [m]S Jos 15:50
21:15 [n]S Jos 15:51; [o]S Jos 10:3
21:16 [p]S Nu 34:11; [q]Jos 15:55; [r]S Jos 15:10
21:17 [s]S Jos 9:3; [t]S Jos 18:24; S Ne 11:31
21:18 [u]2Sa 23:27; 1Ki 2:26; Ezr 2:23; Ne 7:27; 11:32; Isa 10:30; Jer 1:1; 11:21; 32:7
21:19 [v]2Ch 31:15; [w]ver 4
21:21 [x]S Jos 17:7; [y]S Jos 10:33
21:22 [z]S Jos 10:10; [a]1Sa 1:1
21:23 [b]S Jos 19:44
21:24 [c]S Jos 10:12; [d]S Jos 19:45
21:25 [e]S Jos 12:21
21:26 [f]ver 5
21:27 [g]S Jos 12:5; [h]Nu 35:6
21:28 [i]S Ge 30:18; [j]Jos 19:20; [k]S Jos 19:12
21:29 [l]S Jos 10:3; [m]S Jos 15:34
21:30 [n]S Jos 17:7; [o]Jos 19:26; [p]S Jos 19:28
21:31 [q]S Jos 19:28
21:32 [r]S Jos 12:22; [s]Nu 35:6

21:1–45 Finally the Levites are allotted their towns and adjoining pasturelands—with the priestly families being given precedence (see v. 10).

21:4 *Kohathites.* The three sons of Levi were Kohath, Gershon and Merari (Ex 6:16; Nu 3:17). *Judah, Simeon and Benjamin.* Tribal areas close to Jerusalem, which would later be the site of the temple. The remaining Kohathites received cities in adjoining tribes.

21:11 *Hebron.* Caleb's city (14:13–15). The priests and Levites were to be given space in their assigned cities along with the other inhabitants.

21:27 *Gershonites.* Received cities in the northern tribes of Asher, Naphtali and Issachar.

Dor and Kartan, together with their pasturelands—three towns.

33All the towns of the Gershonite[t] clans were thirteen, together with their pasturelands.

34The Merarite clans (the rest of the Levites) were given:

from the tribe of Zebulun,[u]
Jokneam,[v] Kartah, 35Dimnah and Nahalal,[w] together with their pasturelands—four towns;

36from the tribe of Reuben,
Bezer,[x] Jahaz,[y] 37Kedemoth and Mephaath,[z] together with their pasturelands—four towns;

38from the tribe of Gad,
Ramoth[a] in Gilead[b] (a city of refuge for one accused of murder), Mahanaim,[c] 39Heshbon and Jazer,[d] together with their pasturelands—four towns in all.

40All the towns allotted to the Merarite clans, who were the rest of the Levites, were twelve.[e]

41The towns of the Levites in the territory held by the Israelites were forty-eight in all, together with their pasturelands.[f] 42Each of these towns had pasturelands surrounding it; this was true for all these towns.

43So the LORD gave Israel all the land he had sworn to give their forefathers,[g] and they took possession[h] of it and settled there.[i] 44The LORD gave them rest[j] on every side, just as he had sworn to their forefathers. Not one of their enemies[k] withstood them; the LORD handed all their enemies[l] over to them.[m] 45Not one of all the LORD's good promises[n] to the house of Israel failed; every one was fulfilled.

Eastern Tribes Return Home

22 Then Joshua summoned the Reubenites, the Gadites and the half-

tribe of Manasseh 2and said to them, "You have done all that Moses the servant of the LORD commanded,[o] and you have obeyed me in everything I commanded. 3For a long time now—to this very day—you have not deserted your brothers but have carried out the mission the LORD your God gave you. 4Now that the LORD your God has given your brothers rest[p] as he promised, return to your homes[q] in the land that Moses the servant of the LORD gave you on the other side of the Jordan.[r] 5But be very careful to keep the commandment[s] and the law that Moses the servant of the LORD gave you: to love the LORD[t] your God, to walk in all his ways, to obey his commands,[u] to hold fast to him and to serve him with all your heart and all your soul.[v]"

6Then Joshua blessed[w] them and sent them away, and they went to their homes. 7(To the half-tribe of Manasseh Moses had given land in Bashan,[x] and to the other half of the tribe Joshua gave land on the west side[y] of the Jordan with their brothers.) When Joshua sent them home, he blessed them,[z] 8saying, "Return to your homes with your great wealth—with large herds of livestock,[a] with silver, gold, bronze and iron,[b] and a great quantity of clothing—and divide[c] with your brothers the plunder[d] from your enemies."

9So the Reubenites, the Gadites and the half-tribe of Manasseh left the Israelites at Shiloh[e] in Canaan to return to Gilead,[f] their own land, which they had acquired in accordance with the command of the LORD through Moses.

10When they came to Geliloth[g] near the Jordan in the land of Canaan, the Reubenites, the Gadites and the half-tribe of Manasseh built an imposing altar[h] there by the Jordan. 11And when the Israelites heard that they had built the altar on the border of Canaan at Geliloth near the Jor-

Cross references

21:33 [t]ver 6
21:34 [u]S Jos 19:10
  [v]S Jos 12:22
21:35 [w]Jos 19:15
21:36 [x]S Jos 20:8
  [y]S Nu 21:23;
  Dt 2:32;
  Jdg 11:20
21:37 [z]S Jos 13:18
21:38 [a]S Dt 4:43
  [b]S Jos 12:2
  [c]S Ge 32:2
21:39 [d]S Jos 13:25
21:40 [e]ver 7
21:41 [f]Nu 35:7
21:43 [g]Dt 34:4
  [h]Dt 11:31
  [i]S Dt 17:14
21:44 [j]S Ex 33:14
  [k]S Dt 6:19
  [l]S Ex 23:31
  [m]Dt 21:10
21:45 [n]Jos 23:14;
  Ne 9:8

22:2 [o]S Nu 32:25
22:4 [p]S Ex 33:14
  [q]Nu 32:22;
  Dt 3:20
  [r]Nu 32:18;
  S Jos 1:13-15
22:5 [s]Isa 43:22;
  Mal 3:14
  [t]Jos 23:11
  [u]S Dt 5:29
  [v]S Dt 6:5
22:6 [w]S Ge 24:60;
  S Ex 39:43
22:7 [x]S Nu 32:19;
  S Jos 12:5
  [y]Jos 17:2
  [z]S Jos 14:13;
  Lk 24:50
22:8 [a]S Dt 20:14
  [b]S Nu 31:22
  [c]S Nu 31:27
  [d]S Ge 49:27;
  1Sa 30:16;
  2Sa 1:1; Isa 9:3
22:9 [e]Jos 18:1
  [f]S Nu 32:26
22:10 [g]Jos 18:17
  [h]ver 19,26-27;
  Isa 19:19; 56:7

21:34 *Merarite clans.* Their 12 cities were scattered over Reuben, Gad and Zebulun.
21:43–45 A concluding summary statement of how the Lord had fulfilled his sworn promise to give Israel this land (see Ge 15:18–21). The occupation of the land was not yet complete (see 23:4–5; Jdg 1–2), but the national campaign was over and Israel was finally established in the promised land. No power was left in Canaan that could threaten to dislodge her.
21:44 *rest on every side.* See note on 1:13.
22:1–34 The two and a half tribes from east of the Jordan, faithful in battle, are now commended by Joshua and sent to their homes. But their "altar of witness" (see vv. 26–27,34) was misunderstood, and disciplinary action against them was narrowly averted.
22:2 *all that Moses . . . commanded.* Moses had ordered

them to join the other tribes in the conquest of Canaan (Nu 32:16–27; Dt 3:18).
22:5 *love the LORD . . . serve him with all your heart.* Both Moses and Joshua saw that obedience to the laws of God would require love and service from the heart. In the ancient Near East, "love" was also a political term, indicating true-hearted loyalty to one's king.
22:8 *divide with your brothers.* Moses also had seen the need for a fair sharing of the spoils of war (Nu 31:25–27).
22:10 *Geliloth.* Understood in the Septuagint to be Gilgal, next to Jericho; more likely it was a site east of Shiloh along the Jordan River (18:17).
22:11 *when the Israelites heard.* Anxiety about apostasy led to hasty conclusions. They thought the altar had been set up as a rival to the true altar at Shiloh.

dan on the Israelite side, [12]the whole assembly of Israel gathered at Shiloh[i] to go to war against them.

[13]So the Israelites sent Phinehas[j] son of Eleazar,[k] the priest, to the land of Gilead—to Reuben, Gad and the half-tribe of Manasseh. [14]With him they sent ten of the chief men, one for each of the tribes of Israel, each the head of a family division among the Israelite clans.[l]

[15]When they went to Gilead—to Reuben, Gad and the half-tribe of Manasseh—they said to them: [16]"The whole assembly of the LORD says: 'How could you break faith[m] with the God of Israel like this? How could you turn away from the LORD and build yourselves an altar in rebellion[n] against him now? [17]Was not the sin of Peor[o] enough for us? Up to this very day we have not cleansed ourselves from that sin, even though a plague fell on the community of the LORD! [18]And are you now turning away from the LORD?

" 'If you rebel against the LORD today, tomorrow he will be angry with the whole community[p] of Israel. [19]If the land you possess is defiled, come over to the LORD's land, where the LORD's tabernacle[q] stands, and share the land with us. But do not rebel against the LORD or against us by building an altar[r] for yourselves, other than the altar of the LORD our God. [20]When Achan son of Zerah acted unfaithfully regarding the devoted things,[d][s] did not wrath[t] come upon the whole community[u] of Israel? He was not the only one who died for his sin.' "[v]

[21]Then Reuben, Gad and the half-tribe of Manasseh replied to the heads of the clans of Israel: [22]"The Mighty One, God, the LORD! The Mighty One, God,[w] the LORD![x] He knows![y] And let Israel know! If this has been in rebellion or disobedience to the LORD, do not spare us this day. [23]If we have built our own altar to turn away from the LORD and to offer burnt offerings and grain offerings,[z] or to sacrifice fellowship offerings[e] on it, may the LORD himself call us to account.[a]

[24]"No! We did it for fear that some day your descendants might say to ours, 'What do you have to do with the LORD, the God of Israel? [25]The LORD has made the Jordan a boundary between us and you—you Reubenites and Gadites! You have no share in the LORD.' So your descendants might cause ours to stop fearing the LORD.

[26]"That is why we said, 'Let us get ready and build an altar—but not for burnt offerings or sacrifices.' [27]On the contrary, it is to be a witness[b] between us and you and the generations that follow, that we will worship the LORD at his sanctuary with our burnt offerings, sacrifices and fellowship offerings.[c] Then in the future your descendants will not be able to say to ours, 'You have no share in the LORD.'

[28]"And we said, 'If they ever say this to us, or to our descendants, we will answer: Look at the replica of the LORD's altar, which our fathers built, not for burnt offerings and sacrifices, but as a witness[d] between us and you.'

[29]"Far be it from us to rebel[e] against the LORD and turn away from him today by building an altar for burnt offerings, grain offerings and sacrifices, other than the altar of the LORD our God that stands before his tabernacle.[f] "

[30]When Phinehas the priest and the leaders of the community—the heads of the clans of the Israelites—heard what Reuben, Gad and Manasseh had to say, they were pleased. [31]And Phinehas son of Eleazar, the priest, said to Reuben, Gad and Manasseh, "Today we know that the LORD is with us,[g] because you have not

22:12 [i]Jos 18:1
22:13 [j]S Nu 25:7
[k]Nu 3:32;
Jos 24:33
22:14 [l]ver 32;
S Nu 1:4
22:16 [m]S Dt 7:3;
1Sa 13:13; 15:11
[n]Dt 12:13-14
22:17
[o]S Nu 23:28;
25:1-9
22:18
[p]S Lev 10:6
22:19 [q]S Ex 26:1
[r]S ver 10
22:20 [s]Jos 7:1
[t]Ps 7:11
[u]Lev 10:6
[v]Jos 7:5
22:22
[w]S Dt 10:17
[x]Ps 50:1
[y]1Sa 2:3; 16:7;
1Ki 8:39;
1Ch 28:9;
Ps 11:4; 40:9;
44:21; 139:4;
Jer 17:10

22:23 [z]Jer 41:5
[a]S Dt 12:11;
S 18:19;
1Sa 20:16
22:27
[b]S Ge 21:30;
Jos 24:27;
Isa 19:20
[c]S Dt 12:6
22:28
[d]S Ge 21:30
22:29 [e]Jos 24:16
[f]S Ex 26:1
22:31 [g]2Ch 15:2

[d]20 The Hebrew term refers to the irrevocable giving over of things or persons to the LORD, often by totally destroying them.   [e]23 Traditionally *peace offerings*; also in verse 27

22:12 *gathered at Shiloh.* In the presence of God at the tabernacle. *to go to war against them.* To take disciplinary action (cf. Dt 13:12–18; Jdg 20).
22:13–14 A prestigious delegation is sent to try to turn the Transjordan tribes from their (supposed) act of rebellion against the Lord.
22:16 *How could you . . . ?* The accusations were very grave: You have committed apostasy and rebellion.
22:17 *Peor.* Where some of the Israelites became involved in the Moabite worship of Baal of Peor (Nu 25:1–5).
22:19 *is defiled.* By pagan worship, corrupting its inhabitants. *the LORD's land.* The promised land proper had never included Transjordan territory. Canaan was the land the Lord especially claimed as his own and promised to the descendants of Abraham, Isaac and Jacob.
22:20 *Achan . . . the whole community of Israel.* See note

on 7:1–26.
22:22 *The Mighty One, God, the LORD!* See note on Ps 50:1. The repetition of the sacred names gives an oath-like quality to this strong denial of any wrongdoing.
22:27 *witness.* The altar, presumably of uncut stone (see 8:31; Ex 20:25), was to serve as a testimony to the commitment of the Transjordan tribes to remain loyal to the Lord, and to their continued right to worship the Lord at the tabernacle—even though they lived outside the land of promise. It constitutes the sixth memorial monument in the land noted by the author of Joshua (see note on 10: 27).
22:31 *you have rescued the Israelites.* Their words prevented a terrible punishment that the other tribes were about to inflict as a divine act of judgment (consider the implications of v. 20).

acted unfaithfully toward the LORD in this matter. Now you have rescued the Israelites from the LORD's hand."

32Then Phinehas son of Eleazar, the priest, and the leaders returned to Canaan from their meeting with the Reubenites and Gadites in Gilead and reported to the Israelites.[h] 33They were glad to hear the report and praised God.[i] And they talked no more about going to war against them to devastate the country where the Reubenites and the Gadites lived.

34And the Reubenites and the Gadites gave the altar this name: A Witness[j] Between Us that the LORD is God.

Joshua's Farewell to the Leaders

23 After a long time had passed and the LORD had given Israel rest[k] from all their enemies around them, Joshua, by then old and well advanced in years,[l] 2summoned all Israel—their elders,[m] leaders, judges and officials[n]—and said to them: "I am old and well advanced in years.[o] 3You yourselves have seen everything the LORD your God has done to all these nations for your sake; it was the LORD your God who fought for you.[p] 4Remember how I have allotted[q] as an inheritance[r] for your tribes all the land of the nations that remain—the nations I conquered—between the Jordan and the Great Sea[f s] in the west. 5The LORD your God himself will drive them out[t] of your way. He will push them out[u] before you, and you will take possession of their land, as the LORD your God promised you.[v]

6"Be very strong; be careful to obey all that is written in the Book of the Law[w] of Moses, without turning aside[x] to the right or to the left.[y] 7Do not associate with these nations that remain among you; do not invoke the names of their gods or swear[z] by them. You must not serve them

or bow down[a] to them. 8But you are to hold fast to the LORD[b] your God, as you have until now.

9"The LORD has driven out before you great and powerful nations;[c] to this day no one has been able to withstand you.[d] 10One of you routs a thousand,[e] because the LORD your God fights for you,[f] just as he promised. 11So be very careful[g] to love the LORD[h] your God.

12"But if you turn away and ally yourselves with the survivors of these nations that remain among you and if you intermarry with them[i] and associate with them,[j] 13then you may be sure that the LORD your God will no longer drive out[k] these nations before you. Instead, they will become snares[l] and traps for you, whips on your backs and thorns in your eyes,[m] until you perish from this good land,[n] which the LORD your God has given you.

14"Now I am about to go the way of all the earth.[o] You know with all your heart and soul that not one of all the good promises the LORD your God gave you has failed. Every promise[p] has been fulfilled; not one has failed.[q] 15But just as every good promise[r] of the LORD your God has come true, so the LORD will bring on you all the evil[s] he has threatened, until he has destroyed you[t] from this good land he has given you.[u] 16If you violate the covenant of the LORD your God, which he commanded you, and go and serve other gods and bow down to them, the LORD's anger will burn against you, and you will quickly perish from the good land he has given you.[v]"

The Covenant Renewed at Shechem

24 Then Joshua assembled[w] all the tribes of Israel at Shechem.[x] He summoned[y] the elders,[z] leaders, judges

22:32 [h]S ver 14
22:33 [i]1Ch 29:20; Da 2:19; Lk 2:28
22:34 [j]S Ge 21:30
23:1 [k]S Dt 12:9; Jos 21:44 [l]S Jos 13:1
23:2 [m]S Jos 7:6 [n]Jos 24:1 [o]S Jos 13:1
23:3 [p]S Ex 14:14; S Dt 20:4
23:4 [q]Jos 19:51 [r]S Nu 34:2; Ps 78:55 [s]S Nu 34:6
23:5 [t]ver 13; Jdg 2:21 [u]Ps 44:5; Jer 46:15 [v]Ex 23:30
23:6 [w]S Dt 28:61 [x]S Dt 17:20 [y]Jos 1:7
23:7 [z]Ex 23:13; Jer 5:7; 12:16

[a]S Ex 20:5
23:8 [b]S Dt 10:20
23:9 [c]Dt 11:23 [d]Dt 7:24
23:10 [e]Lev 26:8; Jdg 3:31 [f]S Ex 14:14
23:11 [g]S Dt 4:15 [h]Jos 22:5
23:12 [i]S Ge 34:9 [j]S Ex 34:16; Ps 106:34-35
23:13 [k]S ver 5 [l]S Ex 10:7 [m]S Nu 33:55 [n]Dt 1:8; 1Ki 9:7; 2Ki 25:21
23:14 [o]1Ki 2:2 [p]Ps 119:140; 145:13 [q]S Jos 21:45
23:15 [r]1Ki 8:56; Jer 33:14 [s]1Ki 14:10; 2Ki 22:16; Isa 24:6; 34:5; 43:28; Jer 6:19; 11:8; 35:17; 39:16; Mal 4:6 [t]Jos 24:20 [u]Lev 26:17; Dt 28:15; Jer 40:2
23:16 [v]Dt 4:25-26
24:1 [w]Ge 49:2 [x]S Ge 12:6 [y]1Sa 12:7; 1Ki 8:14 [z]Jos 7:6

[f]4 That is, the Mediterranean

22:34 *name.* Such extended names were common in the ancient Near East.

23:1–16 Joshua, the Lord's servant, delivers a farewell address recalling the victories the Lord has given, but also reminding the people of areas yet to be possessed and of the need to be loyal to God's covenant laws. Their mission remains—to be the people of God's kingdom in the world.

23:1 *rest.* See note on 1:13. *well advanced in years.* Joshua was approaching the age of 110 (24:29).

23:6 *be careful to obey.* Echoing the Lord's instructions at the beginning (1:7–8; see 22:5). *Book of the Law.* A reference to canonical written materials from the time of Moses (cf. Dt 30:10,19; 31:9,24,26).

23:11 *love the LORD your God.* A concluding summation (see note on 22:5).

23:12 *But if you turn away.* Remaining in the promised land was conditioned on faithfulness to the Lord and separation from the idolaters still around them. Failure to meet these conditions would bring Israel's banishment from the land (cf. vv. 13,15–16; 2Ki 17:7–8; 2Ch 7:14–20). *ally yourselves . . . intermarry.* The Lord prohibited alliances, either national or domestic, with the peoples of Canaan because such alliances would tend to compromise Israel's loyalty to the Lord (see Ex 34:15–16; Dt 7:2–4).

23:13 *snares and traps.* Joshua's warning echoes Ex 23:33; 34:12; Dt 7:16.

24:1–33 Once more Joshua assembled the tribes at Shechem to call Israel to a renewal of the covenant (see 8:30–35). It was his final official act as the Lord's servant, mediator of the Lord's rule over his people. In this he followed the example of Moses, whose final official act was also a call to covenant renewal—of which Deuteronomy is the preserved document.

and officials of Israel,[a] and they presented themselves before God.

[2]Joshua said to all the people, "This is what the LORD, the God of Israel, says: 'Long ago your forefathers, including Terah the father of Abraham and Nahor,[b] lived beyond the River[g] and worshiped other gods.[c] [3]But I took your father Abraham from the land beyond the River and led him throughout Canaan[d] and gave him many descendants.[e] I gave him Isaac,[f] [4]and to Isaac I gave Jacob and Esau.[g] I assigned the hill country of Seir[h] to Esau, but Jacob and his sons went down to Egypt.[i]

[5]" 'Then I sent Moses and Aaron,[j] and I afflicted the Egyptians by what I did there, and I brought you out.[k] [6]When I brought your fathers out of Egypt, you came to the sea,[l] and the Egyptians pursued them with chariots and horsemen[h][m] as far as the Red Sea.[i][n] [7]But they cried[o] to the LORD for help, and he put darkness[p] between you and the Egyptians; he brought the sea over them and covered them.[q] You saw with your own eyes what I did to the Egyptians.[r] Then you lived in the desert for a long time.[s]

[8]" 'I brought you to the land of the Amorites[t] who lived east of the Jordan. They fought against you, but I gave them into your hands. I destroyed them from before you, and you took possession of their land.[u] [9]When Balak son of Zippor,[v] the king of Moab, prepared to fight against Israel, he sent for Balaam son of Beor[w] to put a curse on you.[x] [10]But I would not listen to Balaam, so he blessed you[y] again and again, and I delivered you out of his hand.

[11]" 'Then you crossed the Jordan[z] and came to Jericho.[a] The citizens of Jericho fought against you, as did also the Amorites, Perizzites,[b] Canaanites, Hittites, Girgashites, Hivites and Jebusites,[c] but I gave them into your hands.[d] [12]I sent the hornet[e] ahead of you, which drove them out[f] before you—also the two Amorite kings. You did not do it with your own sword and bow.[g] [13]So I gave you a land[h] on which you did not toil and cities you did not build; and you live in them and eat from vineyards and olive groves that you did not plant.'[i]

[14]"Now fear the LORD[j] and serve him with all faithfulness.[k] Throw away the gods[l] your forefathers worshiped beyond the River and in Egypt,[m] and serve the LORD. [15]But if serving the LORD seems undesirable to you, then choose for yourselves this day whom you will serve, whether the gods your forefathers served beyond the River, or the gods of the Amorites,[n] in whose land you are living. But as for me and my household,[o] we will serve the LORD."[p]

[16]Then the people answered, "Far be it from us to forsake[q] the LORD to serve other gods! [17]It was the LORD our God himself who brought us and our fathers up out of Egypt, from that land of slavery,[r] and performed those great signs[s] before our eyes. He protected us on our entire journey and among all the nations through which we traveled. [18]And the LORD drove out[t] before us all the nations,[u] including the Amorites, who lived in the land.[v] We too will serve the LORD, because he is our God.[w]"

[19]Joshua said to the people, "You are not able to serve the LORD. He is a holy

---

24:1 [a]Jos 23:2
24:2 [b]Ge 11:26
[c]Ge 11:32
24:3 [d]S Ge 12:1
[e]S Ge 1:28;
S 12:2 /S Ge 21:3
24:4 [g]S Ge 25:26
[h]S Ge 14:6;
S Nu 24:18
[i]Ge 46:5-6
24:5 /S Ex 3:10
[k]Ex 12:51
24:6 /S Ex 14:22
[m]S Ex 14:9
[n]Ex 14:23
24:7 [o]S Ex 14:10
[p]Ex 14:20
[q]S Ex 14:28
[r]S Ex 19:4
[s]Dt 1:46
24:8 /S Ex 23:23
[u]S Nu 21:31
24:9 [v]Nu 22:2
[w]S Nu 23:7
[x]S Nu 22:6
24:10
[y]S Nu 23:11;
S Dt 23:5
24:11
[z]S Ex 14:29
[a]Jos 6:1

[b]S Jos 3:10
[c]S Ge 15:18-21
[d]Ex 23:23; Dt 7:1
24:12
[e]S Ex 23:28;
Ps 44:3,6-7
/S Ex 23:31
[g]Ps 135:11
24:13 [h]Ex 6:8
[i]Dt 6:10-11
24:14
/1Sa 12:14;
Job 23:15;
Ps 19:9; 119:120
[k]Dt 10:12; 18:13;
1Sa 12:24;
2Co 1:12 /ver 23;
S Ge 31:19;
Ex 12:12; 18:11;
20:3; Nu 25:2;
Dt 11:28;
Jdg 10:16;
Ru 1:15; Isa 55:7
[m]Eze 23:3
24:15 [n]Jdg 6:10;
Ru 1:15
[o]S Ge 35:2
[p]Ru 1:16; 2:12;
1Ki 18:21;
Da 3:18
24:16 [q]Jos 22:29
24:17 [r]Jdg 6:8
[s]S Ex 10:1
24:18
[t]S Ex 23:31
[u]S Dt 33:27

[v]Ac 7:45 [w]S Ge 28:21

[g]2 That is, the Euphrates; also in verses 3, 14 and 15 [h]6 Or *charioteers* [i]6 Hebrew *Yam Suph*; that is, Sea of Reeds

---

24:2 *This is what the LORD . . . says.* Only a divinely appointed mediator would dare to speak for God with direct discourse, as in vv. 2–13. *Long ago.* In accordance with the common ancient Near Eastern practice of making treaties (covenants), a brief recital of the past history of the relationship precedes the making of covenant commitments. Joshua here focuses on the separation of Abraham from his polytheistic family, the deliverance of Israel from Egypt and the Lord's establishment of his people in Canaan. *the River.* See NIV text note.
24:6 *Red Sea.* See NIV text note.
24:10 *I would not listen to Balaam.* Not only did the Lord reject Balaam's prayers; he also turned his curse into a blessing (see Nu 23–24).
24:12 *the hornet.* Lower (northern) Egypt had long used the hornet as a national symbol, so Egypt's military campaigns in Canaan may have been in mind. But "the hornet" may also refer to the reports about Israel that spread panic among the Canaanites (2:11; 5:1; 9:24). See note on Ex

23:28.
24:14 *fear the LORD.* Trust, serve and worship him. *gods your forefathers worshiped beyond the River and in Egypt.* See v. 2. Joshua appealed to the Israelites to put away the gods their forefathers had worshiped in Mesopotamia and Egypt. In Ur and Haran, Terah's family would have been exposed to the worship of the moon-god, Nanna(r) or Sin. The golden calf of Ex 32:4 may be an example of their worship of the gods of Egypt. It was probably patterned after Apis, the sacred bull of Egypt; see note on Ex 32:4. (Jeroboam's golden calves at Bethel and Dan, on the other hand, probably represented mounts or pedestals for a riding or standing deity; see 1Ki 12:28–29.)
24:15 *as for me.* Joshua publicly makes his commitment, hoping to elicit the same from Israel.
24:17–18 A creedal statement based on the miraculous events of the exodus and ending with "he is our God."
24:19 *You are not able.* Strong words to emphasize the danger of overconfidence.

God;[x] he is a jealous God.[y] He will not forgive[z] your rebellion[a] and your sins. 20If you forsake the LORD[b] and serve foreign gods, he will turn[c] and bring disaster[d] on you and make an end of you,[e] after he has been good to you."

21But the people said to Joshua, "No! We will serve the LORD."

22Then Joshua said, "You are witnesses[f] against yourselves that you have chosen[g] to serve the LORD."

"Yes, we are witnesses,[h]" they replied.

23"Now then," said Joshua, "throw away the foreign gods[i] that are among you and yield your hearts[j] to the LORD, the God of Israel."

24And the people said to Joshua, "We will serve the LORD our God and obey him."[k]

25On that day Joshua made a covenant[l] for the people, and there at Shechem[m] he drew up for them decrees and laws.[n] 26And Joshua recorded[o] these things in the Book of the Law of God.[p] Then he took a large stone[q] and set it up there under the oak[r] near the holy place of the LORD.

27"See!" he said to all the people. "This stone[s] will be a witness[t] against us. It has heard all the words the LORD has said to us. It will be a witness against you if you are untrue[u] to your God."[v]

Buried in the Promised Land
24:29–31pp — Jdg 2:6–9

28Then Joshua sent the people away, each to his own inheritance.[w]

29After these things, Joshua son of Nun, the servant of the LORD, died[x] at the age of a hundred and ten.[y] 30And they buried him in the land of his inheritance, at Timnath Serah[i][z] in the hill country of Ephraim, north of Mount Gaash.[a]

31Israel served the LORD throughout the lifetime of Joshua and of the elders[b] who outlived him and who had experienced everything the LORD had done for Israel.

32And Joseph's bones,[c] which the Israelites had brought up from Egypt,[d] were buried at Shechem in the tract of land[e] that Jacob bought for a hundred pieces of silver[k] from the sons of Hamor, the father of Shechem. This became the inheritance of Joseph's descendants.

33And Eleazar son of Aaron[f] died and was buried at Gibeah,[g] which had been allotted to his son Phinehas[h] in the hill country[i] of Ephraim.

Cross references
24:19 xS Lev 11:44; S 20:26
yS Ex 20:5
zS Ex 34:7
aS Ex 23:21
24:20 b1Ch 28:9; 20; 2Ch 24:18
cAc 7:42
d1Sa 12:25; Hos 13:11
eJos 23:15
24:22 fver 27; Ru 4:10; Isa 8:2; 43:10; 44:8; Jer 42:5; Mal 2:14
gPs 119:30,173
hS Dt 25:9
24:23 iS ver 14
j1Ki 8:58; Ps 119:36; 141:4; Jer 31:33
24:24 kEx 19:8; Jer 42:6
24:25 lS Ex 24:8
mS Jos 17:7
nEx 15:25
24:26 oS Dt 17:18
pS Dt 28:61; S 31:24
qS Ge 28:18; S Dt 27:2
rS Ge 12:6; S Jdg 4:11
24:27 sS Ge 28:18; Hab 2:11 tS ver 22; S Jos 21:30; S Jos 22:27
uS Jos 7:11
vS Nu 11:20; S Pr 30:9
24:28 wJdg 21:23,24
24:29 xJdg 1:1
yS Ge 50:22
24:30 zS Jos 19:50

a2Sa 23:30 24:31 bJos 7:6 24:32 cHeb 11:22 dS Ge 47:29-30 eGe 33:19; Jn 4:5; Ac 7:16 24:33 fS Jos 22:13 gS Jos 15:57 hS Ex 6:25 i1Sa 9:4; 1Ki 4:8

i30 Also known as Timnath Heres (see Judges 2:9)
k32 Hebrew hundred kesitahs; a kesitah was a unit of money of unknown weight and value.

24:22 witnesses. See v. 27; a normal part of treaty/covenant-making (see Dt 30:19).

24:23 foreign gods. The other gods were represented by idols of wood and metal, which could be thrown away and destroyed.

24:25 covenant for the people. Consisting of the pledges they had agreed to and the decrees and laws from God.

24:26 large stone. Set up as a witness to the covenant renewal that closed Joshua's ministry, this is the seventh memorial in the land reminding Israel of what the Lord had done for them through his servant (see note on 22:27). To these memorials were added the perpetual ruins of Jericho (6:26). Thus the promised land itself bore full testimony to Israel (seven being the number of completeness)—how she had come into possession of the land and how she would remain in the land only by fulfilling the covenant conditions. The land shouted its own story. oak. See note on Ge 12:6.

24:29–33 Three burials. Since it was a deep desire of the ancients to be buried in their homeland, these notices not only mark the conclusion of the story and the close of an era

but also underscore the fact that Israel had indeed been established in the promised homeland—the Lord had kept his covenant.

24:29 a hundred and ten. For the significance of this number see note on Ge 50:26.

24:30 buried him . . . at Timnath Serah. See 19:50 and note.

24:31 The story told in Joshua is a testimony to Israel's faithfulness in that generation. The author anticipates the quite different story that would follow.

24:32 Joseph's bones. Returning his bones to Shechem was significant not only because of the ancient plot of land Jacob bought from Hamor (Ge 33:19), but also because Shechem was to be the center of the tribes of Ephraim and Manasseh, the two sons of Joseph. Also, the return fulfilled an oath sworn to Joseph on his deathbed (Ge 50:25; Ex 13:19).

24:33 Eleazar. The high priest who served Joshua, as Aaron had served Moses. Gibeah. Not the Benjamite city, but a place in Ephraim near Shiloh.

JUDGES

Title

The title describes the leaders Israel had from the time of the elders who outlived Joshua until the time of the monarchy. Their principal purpose is best expressed in 2:16: "Then the LORD raised up judges, who saved them out of the hands of . . . raiders." Since it was God who permitted the oppressions and raised up deliverers, he himself was Israel's ultimate Judge and Deliverer (11:27; see 8:23, where Gideon, a judge, insists that the Lord is Israel's true ruler).

Author and Date

Although, according to tradition, Samuel wrote the book, authorship is actually uncertain. It is possible that Samuel assembled some of the accounts from the period of the judges and that such prophets as Nathan and Gad, both of whom were associated with David's court, had a hand in shaping and editing the material (see 1Ch 29:29).

The date of composition is also unknown, but it was undoubtedly during the monarchy. The frequent expression "In those days Israel had no king" (17:6; 18:1; 19:1; 21:25) suggests a date after the establishment of the monarchy. The observation that the Jebusites still controlled Jerusalem (1:21) has been taken to indicate a time before David's capture of the city c. 1000 B.C. (see 2Sa 5:6-10). But the new conditions in Israel alluded to in chs. 17-21 suggest a time after the Davidic dynasty had been effectively established (tenth century B.C.).

Theme and Theology

The book of Judges characterizes the life of Israel in the promised land from the death of Joshua to the rise of the monarchy. On the one hand, it is an account of frequent apostasy, provoking divine chastening. On the other hand, it tells of urgent appeals to God in times of crisis, moving the Lord to raise up leaders (judges) through whom he throws off foreign oppressors and restores the land to peace.

After Israel was established in the promised land through the ministry of Joshua, her pilgrimage ended. Many of the covenant promises God had given to the patriarchs in Canaan and to the fathers in the desert had now been fulfilled. The Lord's land, where Israel was to enter into rest, lay under her feet; it remained only for her to occupy it, to displace the Canaanites and to cleanse it of paganism. The time had come for Israel to be the kingdom of God in the form of an established commonwealth on earth.

But in Canaan Israel quickly forgot the acts of God that had given her birth and had established her in the land. Consequently she lost sight of her unique identity as God's people, chosen and called to be his army and the loyal citizens of his emerging kingdom. She settled down and attached herself to Canaan's peoples, morals, gods, and religious beliefs and practices as readily as to Canaan's agriculture and social life.

Throughout Judges the fundamental issue is the lordship of God in Israel—i.e., Israel's acknowledgment of and loyalty to his rule. His kingship over Israel had been uniquely established by the covenant at Sinai (Ex 19-24), which was later renewed by Moses on the plains of Moab (Dt 29) and by Joshua at Shechem (Jos 24). The author accuses Israel of having rejected the kingship of the Lord again and again. She stopped fighting the Lord's battles, turned to the gods of Canaan to secure the blessings of family, flocks and fields, and abandoned God's laws for daily living. In the very center of the cycle of the judges (see Outline), Gideon had to remind Israel that the Lord was her King (see note on 8:23). The recurring lament, and indictment, of chs. 17-21 (see Outline) is: "In those days Israel had no king; everyone did as he saw fit" (see note on 17:6). The primary reference here is doubtless to the earthly mediators of the Lord's rule (i.e., human kings), but the implicit charge is that Israel did not truly acknowledge or obey her heavenly King either.

Only by the Lord's sovereign use of foreign oppression to chasten his people—thereby implementing the covenant curses (see Lev 26:14-45; Dt 28:15-68)—and by his raising up deliverers when his people cried out to him did he maintain his kingship in Israel and preserve the embryonic kingdom from extinction. Israel's flawed condition was graphically exposed; she continued to need new saving acts by God in order to enter into the promised rest (see note on Jos 1:13).

Out of the recurring cycles of disobedience, foreign oppression, cries of distress, and deliverance (see 2:11-19; Ne 9:26-31) emerges another important theme—the covenant faithfulness of the Lord. The amazing patience and long-suffering of God are no better demonstrated than during this unsettled period.

Remarkably, this age of Israel's failure, following directly on the redemptive events that came through Moses and Joshua, is in a special way the OT age of the Spirit. God's Spirit enabled men to accomplish feats of victory in the Lord's holy war against the powers that threatened his kingdom (see 3:10; 6:34; 11:29; 13:25; 14:6,19; 15:14; see also 1Sa 10:6,10; 11:6; 16:13). This same Spirit, poured out on the church following the redemptive work of the second Joshua (Jesus), empowered the people of the Lord to begin the task of preaching the gospel to all nations and of advancing the kingdom of God (see notes on Ac 1:2,8).

Background

Fixing precise dates for the judges is difficult and complex. The dating system followed here is based primarily on 1Ki 6:1, which speaks of an interval of 480 years between the exodus and the fourth year of Solomon's reign. This would place the exodus c. 1446 B.C. and the period of the judges between c. 1380 and the rise of Saul, c. 1050. Jephthah's statement that Israel had occupied Heshbon for 300 years (11:26) generally agrees with these dates.

Some maintain, however, that the number 480 in 1Ki 6:1 is somewhat artificial, arrived at by multiplying 12 (perhaps in reference to the 12 judges) by 40 (a conventional number of years for a generation). They point out the frequent use of the round numbers 10, 20, 40 and 80 in the book of Judges itself. A later date for the exodus would of course require a much shorter period of time for the judges (see Introduction to Exodus: Chronology).

Literary Features

Even a quick reading of Judges discloses its basic threefold division: (1) a prologue (1:1-3:6), (2) a main body (3:7-16:31) and (3) an epilogue (chs. 17-21). Closer study brings to light a more complex structure, with interwoven themes that bind the whole into an intricately designed portrayal of the character of an age.

The prologue (1:1-3:6) has two parts, and each serves a different purpose. They are not chronologically related, nor does either offer a strict chronological scheme of the time as a whole. The first part (1:1-2:5) sets the stage historically for the narratives that follow. It describes Israel's occupation of the promised land—from her initial success to her large-scale failure and divine rebuke.

The second part (2:6-3:6) indicates a basic perspective on the period from the time of Joshua to the rise of the monarchy, a time characterized by recurring cycles of apostasy, oppression, cries of distress and gracious divine deliverance. The author summarizes and explains the Lord's dealings with his rebellious people and introduces some of the basic vocabulary and formulas he will use in the later narratives: "did evil in the eyes of the LORD," 2:11 (see 3:7,12; 4:1; 6:1; 10:6); "handed them over to," 2:14 (see 6:1; 13:1); and "sold them," 2:14 (see 3:8; 4:2; 10:7).

The main body of the book (3:7-16:31), which gives the actual accounts of the recurring cycles (apostasy, oppression, distress, deliverance), has its own unique design. Each cycle has a similar beginning ("the Israelites did evil in the eyes of the LORD"; see note on 3:7) and a recognizable conclusion ("the land had peace . . . years" or "led Israel . . . years"; see note on 3:11). The first of these cycles (Othniel; see 3:7-11 and note) provides the "report form" used for each successive story of oppression and deliverance.

The remaining five cycles form the following narrative units, built around the rest of the major judges:

1. Ehud (3:12-30), a lone hero from the tribe of Benjamin who delivers Israel from oppression from the east.
2. Deborah (chs. 4-5), a woman from one of the Joseph tribes (Ephraim, west of the Jordan) who judges at a time when Israel is being overrun by a coalition of Canaanites under Sisera.
3. Gideon and his son Abimelech (chs. 6-9), who form the central account. In many ways Gideon

is the ideal judge, evoking memory of Moses, while his son is the very antithesis of a responsible and faithful judge.

4. Jephthah (10:6-12:7), a social outcast from the other Joseph tribe (Manasseh, east of the Jordan) who judges at a time when Israel is being threatened by a coalition of powers under the king of Ammon.

5. Samson (chs. 13-16), a lone hero from the tribe of Dan who delivers Israel from oppression from the west.

The arrangement of these narrative units is significant. The central accounts of Gideon (the Lord's ideal judge) and Abimelech (the anti-judge) are bracketed by the parallel narratives of the woman Deborah and the social outcast Jephthah—which in turn are framed by the stories of the lone heroes Ehud and Samson. In this way even the structure focuses attention on the crucial issue of the period of the judges: Israel's attraction to the Baals of Canaan (shown by Abimelech; see note on 9:1-57) versus the Lord's kingship over his people (encouraged by Gideon; see note on 8:23).

The epilogue (chs. 17-21) characterizes the era in yet another way, depicting religious and moral corruption on the part of individuals, cities and tribes. Like the introduction, it has two divisions that are neither chronologically related nor expressly dated to the careers of specific judges. The events must have taken place, however, rather early in the period of the judges (see notes on 18:30; 20:1,28).

By dating the events of the epilogue only in relationship to the monarchy (see the recurring refrain in 17:6; 18:1; 19:1; 21:25), the author contrasts the age of the judges with the better time that the monarchy inaugurated, undoubtedly having in view the rule of David and his dynasty (see note on 17:1-21:25). The book mentions two instances of the Lord's assigning leadership to the tribe of Judah: (1) in driving out the Canaanites (1:1-2), and (2) in disciplining a tribe in Israel (20:18). The author views the ruler from the tribe of Judah as the savior of the nation.

The first division of the epilogue (chs. 17-18) relates the story of Micah's development of a paganized place of worship and tells of the tribe of Dan abandoning their allotted territory while adopting Micah's corrupted religion. The second division (chs. 19-21) tells the story of a Levite's sad experience at Gibeah in Benjamin and records the disciplinary removal of the tribe of Benjamin because it had defended the degenerate town of Gibeah.

The two divisions have several interesting parallels:

1. Both involve a Levite's passing between Bethlehem (in Judah) and Ephraim across the Benjamin-Dan corridor.

2. Both mention 600 warriors—those who led the tribe of Dan and those who survived from the tribe of Benjamin.

3. Both conclude with the emptying of a tribal area in that corridor (Dan and Benjamin).

Not only are these Benjamin-Dan parallels significant within the epilogue, but they also form a notable link to the main body of the book. The tribe of Benjamin, which in the epilogue undertook to defend gross immorality, setting ties of blood above loyalty to the Lord, was the tribe from which the Lord raised the deliverer Ehud (3:15). The tribe of Dan, which in the epilogue retreated from its assigned inheritance and adopted pagan religious practices, was the tribe from which the Lord raised the deliverer Samson (13:2,5). Thus the tribes that in the epilogue depict the religious and moral corruption of Israel are the very tribes from which the deliverers were chosen whose stories frame the central account of the book (Gideon-Abimelech).

The whole design of the book from prologue to epilogue, the unique manner in which each section deals with the age as a whole, and the way the three major divisions are interrelated clearly portray an age gone awry—an age when "Israel had no king" and "everyone did as he saw fit" (see note on 17:6). Of no small significance is the fact that the story is in episodes and cycles. It is given as the story of all Israel, though usually only certain areas are directly involved. The book portrays the centuries after Joshua as a time of Israelite unfaithfulness to the Lord and of her surrender to the allurements of Canaan. Only by the mercies of God was Israel not overwhelmed and absorbed by the pagan nations around her. Meanwhile, however, the history of redemption virtually stood still—awaiting the forward thrust of the Lord's servant David and the establishment of his dynasty.

Outline

I. Prologue: Incomplete Conquest and Apostasy (1:1-3:6)
  A. First Episode: Israel's Failure to Purge the Land (1:1-2:5)
  B. Second Episode: God's Dealings with Israel's Rebellion (2:6-3:6)
II. Oppression and Deliverance (3:7-16:31)

Major Judges   *Minor Judges*

  A. Othniel Defeats Aram Naharaim (3:7-11)
  B. Ehud Defeats Moab (3:12-30)

                                   1. Shamgar (3:31)

  C. Deborah Defeats Canaan (chs. 4-5)
  D. Gideon Defeats Midian (chs. 6-8)
               (Abimelech, the anti-judge, ch. 9)

                                   2. Tola (10:1-2)
                                   3. Jair (10:3-5)
  E. Jephthah Defeats Ammon (10:6-12:7)
                                   4. Ibzan (12:8-10)
                                   5. Elon (12:11-12)
                                   6. Abdon (12:13-15)
  F. Samson Checks Philistia (chs. 13-16)
III. Epilogue: Religious and Moral Disorder (chs. 17-21)
  A. First Episode (chs. 17-18; see 17:6; 18:1)
    1. Micah's corruption of religion (ch. 17)
    2. The Danites' departure from their tribal territory (ch. 18)
  B. Second Episode (chs. 19-21; see 19:1; 21:25)
    1. Gibeah's corruption of morals (ch. 19)
    2. The Benjamites' removal from their tribal territory (chs. 20-21)

Israel Fights the Remaining Canaanites

1:11–15pp — Jos 15:15–19

1 After the death[a] of Joshua, the Israelites asked the LORD, "Who will be the first[b] to go up and fight for us against the Canaanites?[c]"

²The LORD answered, "Judah[d] is to go; I have given the land into their hands.[e]"

³Then the men of Judah said to the Simeonites their brothers, "Come up with us into the territory allotted to us, to fight against the Canaanites. We in turn will go with you into yours." So the Simeonites[f] went with them.

⁴When Judah attacked, the LORD gave the Canaanites and Perizzites[g] into their hands and they struck down ten thousand men at Bezek.[h] ⁵It was there that they found Adoni-Bezek[i] and fought against him, putting to rout the Canaanites and Perizzites. ⁶Adoni-Bezek fled, but they chased him and caught him, and cut off his thumbs and big toes.

⁷Then Adoni-Bezek said, "Seventy kings with their thumbs and big toes cut off have picked up scraps under my table. Now God has paid me back[j] for what I did to them." They brought him to Jerusalem,[k] and he died there.

⁸The men of Judah attacked Jerusalem[l]

also and took it. They put the city to the sword and set it on fire.

⁹After that, the men of Judah went down to fight against the Canaanites living in the hill country,[m] the Negev[n] and the western foothills. ¹⁰They advanced against the Canaanites living in Hebron[o] (formerly called Kiriath Arba[p]) and defeated Sheshai, Ahiman and Talmai.[q]

¹¹From there they advanced against the people living in Debir[r] (formerly called Kiriath Sepher). ¹²And Caleb said, "I will give my daughter Acsah in marriage to the man who attacks and captures Kiriath Sepher." ¹³Othniel son of Kenaz, Caleb's younger brother, took it; so Caleb gave his daughter Acsah to him in marriage.

¹⁴One day when she came to Othniel, she urged him[a] to ask her father for a field. When she got off her donkey, Caleb asked her, "What can I do for you?"

¹⁵She replied, "Do me a special favor. Since you have given me land in the Negev, give me also springs of water." Then Caleb gave her the upper and lower springs.[s]

¹⁶The descendants of Moses' father-in-law,[t] the Kenite,[u] went up from the City of Palms[b][v] with the men of Judah to live

1:1 [a]Jos 24:29
[b]S Nu 2:3-9;
Jdg 20:18;
1Ki 20:14 [c]ver
27; S Ge 10:18;
Jdg 3:1-6
1:2 [d]S Ge 49:10
[e]ver 4; Jdg 3:28;
4:7,14; 7:9
1:3 [f]ver 17
1:4 [g]S Ge 13:7;
S Jos 3:10
[h]1Sa 11:8
1:5 [i]ver 6,7
1:7 [j]Lev 24:19;
Jer 25:12
[k]S Jos 10:1
1:8 [l]ver 21;
Jos 15:63; 2Sa 5:6

1:9 [m]S Nu 13:17
[n]S Ge 12:9;
S Nu 21:1;
Isa 30:6
1:10 [o]S Ge 13:18
[p]S Ge 35:27 [q]ver
20; S Nu 13:22;
Jos 15:14
1:11 [r]Jos 10:38
1:15 [s]S Nu 13:6
1:16 [t]Nu 10:29
[u]S Ge 15:19
[v]Dt 34:3;
Jdg 3:13;
2Ch 28:15

[a]*14* Hebrew; Septuagint and Vulgate *Othniel, he urged her*　[b]*16* That is, Jericho

---

1:1–3:6 An introduction in two parts: (1) an account of Israel's failure to lay claim completely to the promised land as the Lord had directed (1:1–36) and of his rebuke for their disloyalty (2:1–5); (2) an overview of the main body of the book (3:7–16:31), portraying Israel's rebellious ways in the centuries after Joshua's death and showing how the Lord dealt with her in that period (2:6–3:6). See Introduction: Literary Features.

1:1–36 Judah is assigned leadership in occupying the land (v. 2; see 20:18). Her vigorous efforts (together with those of Simeon) highlight by contrast the sad story of failure that follows. Only Ephraim's success at Bethel (vv. 22–26) breaks the monotony of that story.

1:1 *After the death of Joshua.* The book of Judges, like that of Joshua, tells of an era following the death of a leading figure in the history of redemption (see Jos 1:1). Joshua probably died c. 1390 B.C. The battles under his leadership broke the power of the Canaanites to drive the Israelites out of the land. The task that now confronted Israel was the actual occupation of Canaanite territory (see notes on Jos 18:3; 21:43–45). *asked the LORD.* Probably by the priestly use of Urim and Thummim (see notes on Ex 28:30; 1Sa 2:28). *go up.* The main Israelite encampment was at Gilgal, near Jericho in the Jordan Valley (about 800 feet below sea level), while the Canaanite cities were mainly located in the central hill country (about 2,500–3,500 feet above sea level).

1:2 *Judah is to go.* See 20:18. Judah was also the first to be assigned territory west of the Jordan (Jos 15). The leadership role of the tribe of Judah had been anticipated in the blessing of Jacob (Ge 49:8–12).

1:3 *Simeonites.* Joshua assigned to Simeon cities within the territory of Judah (Jos 19:1,9; see Ge 49:5–7).

1:4 *Canaanites.* See note on Ge 10:6. *Perizzites.* See note on Ge 13:7. *Bezek.* Location unknown. Saul marshaled his army there before going to Jabesh Gilead (1Sa 11:8).

1:5 *Adoni-Bezek.* Means "lord of Bezek."

1:6 *cut off his thumbs and big toes.* Physically mutilating prisoners of war was a common practice in the ancient Near East (see note on 16:21). It rendered them unfit for military service.

1:7 *Seventy kings.* Canaan was made up of many small city-states, each of which was ruled by a king. "Seventy" may be a round number, or it may be symbolic of a large number. *under my table.* Humiliating treatment, like that given to a dog (see Mt 15:27; Lk 16:21). *God has paid me back.* See note on Ex 21:23–25.

1:8 *attacked Jerusalem.* Although the city was defeated, it was not occupied by the Israelites at this time (see v. 21). Israel did not permanently control the city until David captured it c. 1000 B.C. (2Sa 5:6–10).

1:10 *Kiriath Arba.* See note on Jos 14:15.

1:11 *Debir.* See note on Jos 10:38.

1:12 *Caleb.* He and Joshua had brought back an optimistic report about the prospects of conquering Canaan (Nu 14:6–9). *daughter . . . in marriage.* Victory in battle was one way to pay the bride-price for a girl (see 1Sa 18:25).

1:13 *Othniel.* First major judge (see 3:7–11).

1:15 *upper and lower springs.* They still water the local farms in Hebron.

1:16 *Moses' father-in-law.* See note on Ex 2:16.

among the people of the Desert of Judah in the Negev near Arad. *w*

[17]Then the men of Judah went with the Simeonites[x] their brothers and attacked the Canaanites living in Zephath, and they totally destroyed[c] the city. Therefore it was called Hormah. [d][y] [18]The men of Judah also took[e] Gaza,[z] Ashkelon[a] and Ekron—each city with its territory.

[19]The LORD was with[b] the men of Judah. They took possession of the hill country,[c] but they were unable to drive the people from the plains, because they had iron chariots. [d] [20]As Moses had promised, Hebron[e] was given to Caleb, who drove from it the three sons of Anak.[f] [21]The Benjamites, however, failed[g] to dislodge the Jebusites, who were living in Jerusalem;[h] to this day the Jebusites live there with the Benjamites.

[22]Now the house of Joseph[i] attacked Bethel,[j] and the LORD was with them. [23]When they sent men to spy out Bethel (formerly called Luz),[k] [24]the spies saw a man coming out of the city and they said to him, "Show us how to get into the city and we will see that you are treated well." [25]So he showed them, and they put the city to the sword but spared[m] the man and his whole family. [26]He then went to the land of the Hittites,[n] where he built a city and called it Luz,[o] which is its name to this day.

[27]But Manasseh did not[p] drive out the people of Beth Shan or Taanach or Dor[q] or Ibleam[r] or Megiddo[s] and their surrounding settlements, for the Canaanites[t] were

1:16 *w*Nu 21:1; Jos 12:14
1:17 *x*ver 3 *y*S Nu 14:45
1:18 *z*Jos 11:22 *a*S Jos 13:3
1:19 *b*S Nu 14:43 *c*Nu 13:17 *d*S Jos 17:16
1:20 *e*Jos 10:36 *f*S ver 10; S Jos 14:13
1:21 *g*S Jos 9:15; S 15:63 *h*S ver 8

1:22 *i*Jdg 10:9 *j*S Jos 7:2
1:23 *k*S Ge 28:19
1:24 *l*S Ge 47:29
1:25 *m*Jos 6:25
1:26 *n*S Dt 7:1; Eze 16:3 *o*S Ge 28:19
1:27 *p*1Ki 9:21 *q*S Jos 11:2 *r*S Jos 17:11 *s*S Jos 12:21 *t*S ver 1

c 17 The Hebrew term refers to the irrevocable giving over of things or persons to the LORD, often by totally destroying them.   d 17 *Hormah* means *destruction.*
e 18 Hebrew; Septuagint *Judah did not take*

1:17 *men of Judah . . . Simeonites.* Judah was fulfilling her commitment (v. 3).
1:18 *Gaza, Ashkelon and Ekron.* Three of the five main cities inhabited by the Philistines (see map below).
1:19 *unable to drive the people from.* Israel failed to comply with God's commands (Dt 7:1–5; 20:16–18) to drive the Canaanites out of the land. Five factors were involved in that failure: (1) The Canaanites possessed superior weapons (v. 19); (2) Israel disobeyed God by making treaties with the Canaanites (2:1–3); (3) Israel violated the covenant the Lord had made with their forefathers (2:20–21); (4) God was testing Israel's faithfulness to obey his commands

Five Cities of the Philistines

Like a string of opulent pearls along the Mediterranean coast, the five cities of the Philistines comprise a litany of familiar Biblical names: Gaza, Ashkelon, Ashdod, Ekron and Gath.

Each was a commercial emporium with important connections reaching as far as Egypt along the coastal route, the "interstate highway" of the ancient world. The ships of Phoenicia, Cyprus, Crete and the Aegean called at Philistia's seaports, which included a site today called Tell Qasile, where a Philistine temple has been found, on the Yarkon River just north of modern Tel Aviv.

The Philistine plain itself was an arid, loess-covered lowland bordering on the desert to the south—a stretch of undulating sand dunes adjacent to the sea—and the foothills of the Judahite plateau on the east. No area in Biblical history was more frequently contested than the western foothills (the Shephelah region), lying on the border between Judea and Philistia. Beth Shemesh, Timnah, Azekah and Ziklag were among the towns coveted by both Israelites and Philistines, and they figure in the stories of Samson, Goliath and David.

The area to the north of Philistia, the plain of Sharon, was also contested at various periods: During Saul's reign the Philistines even held Beth Shan and the Esdraelon valley. Later, from about the time of Baasha on, a long border war was conducted by the Israelites at Gibbethon. Originally a part of Judah's tribal allotment, the coastal area was never totally wrested away from the Philistines who may have begun their occupation as early as the time of Abraham.

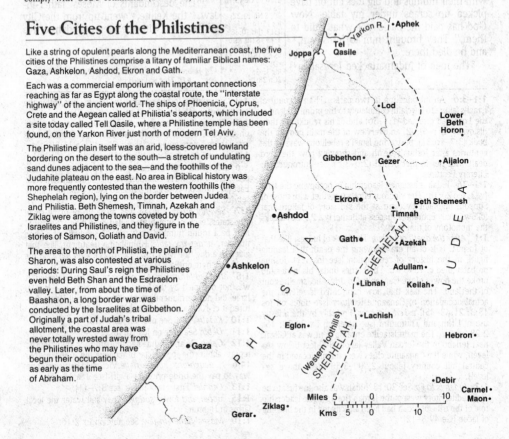

determined to live in that land. 28When Israel became strong, they pressed the Canaanites into forced labor but never drove them out completely.u 29Nor did Ephraimv drive out the Canaanites living in Gezer,w but the Canaanites continued to live there among them.x 30Neither did Zebulun drive out the Canaanites living in Kitron or Nahalol, who remained among them; but they did subject them to forced labor. 31Nor did Ashery drive out those living in Acco or Sidonz or Ahlab or Acziba or Helbah or Aphekb or Rehob,c 32and because of this the people of Asher lived among the Canaanite inhabitants of the land. 33Neither did Naphtali drive out those living in Beth Shemeshd or Beth Anathe; but the Naphtalites too lived among the Canaanite inhabitants of the land, and those living in Beth Shemesh and Beth Anath became forced laborers for them. 34The Amoritesf confined the Danitesg to the hill country, not allowing them to come down into the plain.h 35And the Amorites were determined also to hold out in Mount Heres,i Aijalonj and Shaalbim,k but when the power of the house of Joseph increased, they too were pressed into forced labor. 36The boundary of the Amorites was from Scorpionf Passl to Selam and beyond.n

The Angel of the LORD at Bokim

2 The angel of the LORDo went up from Gilgalp to Bokimq and said, "I brought you up out of Egyptr and led you into the land that I swore to give to your forefathers.s I said, 'I will never break my covenant with you,t 2and you shall not make a covenant with the people of this land,u but you shall break down their altars.v Yet you have disobeyedw me. Why have you done this? 3Now therefore I tell you that I will not drive them out before you;x they will be thorns,y in your sides and their gods will be a snarez to you."

4When the angel of the LORD had spoken these things to all the Israelites, the people wept aloud,a 5and they called that place Bokim.gb There they offered sacrifices to the LORD.

Disobedience and Defeat

2:6–9pp — Jos 24:29–31

6After Joshua had dismissed the Israelites, they went to take possession of the land, each to his own inheritance. 7The people served the LORD throughout the lifetime of Joshua and of the elders who outlived him and who had seen all the great things the LORD had done for Israel.c

8Joshua son of Nun,d the servant of the

f36 Hebrew Akrabbim   g5 Bokim means weepers.

Cross references (center column):

1:28 uJos 17:12-13
1:29 vJos 14:4; Jdg 5:14 wS Jos 10:33 xJos 16:10
1:31 yS Jos 17:7 zS Ge 49:13 aS Jos 15:44 bS Jos 12:18 cS Nu 13:21
1:33 dS Jos 15:10 eJos 19:38
1:34 fNu 13:29; Jdg 10:11; 1Sa 7:14 gS Ge 30:6 hJdg 18:1
1:35 iJdg 8:13 jJos 19:42 k1Ki 4:9
1:36 lJos 15:3 m2Ki 14:7; Isa 16:1; 42:11 nPs 106:34

2:1 oS Ge 16:7 pS Dt 11:30 qver 5 rEx 20:2; Jdg 6:8 sGe 17:8 tS Lev 26:42-44; Dt 7:9
2:2 uS Ex 23:32; S 34:12; Dt 7:2 vS Ex 23:24; 34:13; Dt 7:5; 2Ch 14:3 wJer 7:28
2:3 xJos 23:13 yS Nu 33:55 zS Ex 10:7
2:4 aS Ge 27:38; S Nu 25:6; 2Ki 17:13
2:5 bver 1
2:7 cver 7
2:8 dJos 1:1

(2:22–23; 3:4); (5) God was giving Israel, as his army, the opportunity to develop her skills in warfare (3:1–2). iron chariots. Wooden vehicles with certain iron fittings, perhaps axles.
1:20 *As Moses had promised.* See Nu 14:24; Dt 1:36; Jos 14:9–14. *Anak.* See note on Nu 13:22.
1:21 *Benjamites . . . failed to dislodge.* See note on v. 8. Jerusalem lay on the border between Benjamin and Judah but was allotted to Benjamin (Jos 18:28). *Jebusites.* See note on Ge 10:16.
1:22 *house of Joseph.* Ephraim and West Manasseh. *Bethel.* See note on Ge 12:8. There is archaeological evidence of a destruction in the 13th century B.C. that may reflect the battle mentioned in this verse.
1:23 *spy out.* See note on Nu 13:2.
1:25 *spared the man.* Cf. the treatment of Rahab (Jos 6:25).
1:26 *land of the Hittites.* A name for Aram (Syria) at the time of the conquest (see note on Ge 10:15).
1:27–29 See Jos 17:16–18.
1:28 *forced labor.* See note on 1Ki 5:13.
1:33 *Beth Shemesh.* Location unknown. The name means "house of the sun(-god)." There was also a Beth Shemesh in Judah (see note on v. 35). *Beth Anath.* Means "house of (the goddess) Anath" (see note on 3:31).
1:34 *Amorites.* See note on Ge 10:16. *confined the Danites.* Joshua had defeated the Amorites earlier (Jos 10:5–11), but they were still strong enough to withstand the Danites. For this reason a large number of Danites migrated northward a short time later (see ch. 18).
1:35 *Mount Heres.* Means "mountain of the sun(-god)"; probably the Beth Shemesh in Judah, which is also called Ir

Shemesh, "city of the sun(-god)" (Jos 19:41).
1:36 *boundary of the Amorites.* Their southern boundary (see Jos 15:2–3).
2:1–5 Because Israel had not zealously laid claim to the land as the Lord had directed (see 1:27–36), he withdrew his helping hand. On this note the first half of the introduction ends. Although the actual time of the Lord's rebuke is not indicated, it was probably early in the period of the judges and may even have been connected with the event in Jos 9 (or possibly Jos 18:1–3).
2:1 *angel of the LORD.* See note on Ge 16:7. The role of the angel of the Lord in this passage parallels that of the unnamed prophet in 6:8–10 and the word of the Lord in 10:11–14, calling his people to account. *Gilgal.* The place where Israel first became established in the land under Joshua (see Jos 4:19–5:12). *out of Egypt.* The theme of Exodus, frequently referred to as the supreme evidence of God's redemptive love for his people (see Ex 20:2). *swore to give.* See Ge 15:18; see also note on Heb 6:13.
2:2 *not make a covenant.* To have done so would have broken their covenant with the Lord (see Ex 23:32).
2:6–3:6 The second half of the introduction continues the narrative of Jos 24:28–31. It is a preliminary survey of the accounts narrated in Jdg 3:7–16:31, showing that Israel's first centuries in the promised land are a recurring cycle of apostasy, oppression, cries of distress and gracious deliverance (see Introduction: Literary Features). The author reminds Israel that she will enjoy God's promised rest in the promised land only when she is loyal to him and to his covenant.
2:6 *take possession of the land.* See note on 1:1.
2:8 *servant of the LORD.* Joshua is identified as the Lord's

LORD, died at the age of a hundred and ten. [9]And they buried him in the land of his inheritance, at Timnath Heres[h][e] in the hill country of Ephraim, north of Mount Gaash.

[10]After that whole generation had been gathered to their fathers, another generation grew up, who knew neither the LORD nor what he had done for Israel.[f] [11]Then the Israelites did evil[g] in the eyes of the LORD[h] and served the Baals.[i] [12]They forsook the LORD, the God of their fathers, who had brought them out of Egypt. They followed and worshiped various gods[j] of the peoples around them.[k] They provoked[l] the LORD to anger[m] [13]because they forsook[n] him and served Baal and the Ashtoreths.[o] [14]In his anger[p] against Israel the LORD handed them over[q] to raiders who plundered[r] them. He sold them[s] to their enemies all around, whom they were no longer able to resist.[t] [15]Whenever Israel went out to fight, the hand of the LORD was against them[u] to defeat them, just as he had sworn to them. They were in great distress.[v]

[16]Then the LORD raised up judges,[i][w] who saved[x] them out of the hands of these raiders. [17]Yet they would not listen to their judges but prostituted[y] themselves to other gods[z] and worshiped them.[a] Unlike their fathers, they quickly turned[b] from the way in which their fathers had walked, the way of obedience to the LORD's commands.[c] [18]Whenever the LORD

raised up a judge for them, he was with the judge and saved[d] them out of the hands of their enemies as long as the judge lived; for the LORD had compassion[e] on them as they groaned[f] under those who oppressed and afflicted[g] them. [19]But when the judge died, the people returned to ways even more corrupt[h] than those of their fathers,[i] following other gods and serving and worshiping them.[j] They refused to give up their evil practices and stubborn[k] ways.

[20]Therefore the LORD was very angry[l] with Israel and said, "Because this nation has violated the covenant[m] that I laid down for their forefathers and has not listened to me, [21]I will no longer drive out[n] before them any of the nations Joshua left when he died. [22]I will use them to test[o] Israel and see whether they will keep the way of the LORD and walk in it as their forefathers did." [23]The LORD had allowed those nations to remain; he did not drive them out at once by giving them into the hands of Joshua.[p]

3 These are the nations the LORD left to test[q] all those Israelites who had not experienced any of the wars in Canaan

2:9 [e]S Jos 19:50
2:10 [f]S Ex 5:2;
Gal 4:8
2:11 [g]1Ki 15:26
[h]Jdg 3:12; 4:1;
6:1; 10:6
[i]Jdg 3:7; 8:33;
1Ki 16:31; 22:53;
2Ki 10:18; 17:16
2:12 [j]S Dt 32:12;
Ps 106:36
[k]S Dt 31:16;
Jdg 10:6
[l]S Nu 11:33
[m]Dt 4:25;
Ps 78:58; 106:40
2:13 [n]1Sa 7:3;
1Ki 11:5,33;
2Ki 23:13
[o]Jdg 3:7; 5:8;
6:25; 8:33; 10:6;
1Sa 31:10;
Ne 9:26;
Ps 78:56;
Jer 11:10
2:14 [p]S Dt 31:17
[q]Ne 9:27;
Ps 106:41
[r]Ps 44:10; 89:41;
Eze 34:8
[s]S Dt 32:30;
S Jdg 3:8
[t]S Dt 28:25
2:15 [u]Ru 1:13;
Job 19:21;
Ps 32:4 [v]Ge 35:3;
2Sa 22:7;
2Ch 15:4;
Job 5:5; 20:22;
Ps 4:1; 18:6
2:16 [w]Ru 1:1;
1Sa 4:18; 7:6,15;
2Sa 7:11;
1Ch 17:10;
Ac 13:20
[x]1Sa 11:3;
Ps 106:43
2:17 [y]S Ex 34:15;
S Nu 15:39
[z]S Ps 4:2
[a]Ne 9:28;
Ps 106:36
[b]Dt 9:12 [c]ver 7
2:18 [d]1Sa 7:3;
2Ki 13:5;

Isa 19:20; 43:3,11; 45:15,21; 49:26; 60:16; 63:8
[e]S Dt 32:36 [f]S Ex 2:23 [g]S Nu 10:9 2:19 [h]S Ge 6:11;
S Dt 4:16 [i]Dt 32:17; Ne 9:2; Ps 78:57; Jer 44:3,9 [j]Jdg 4:1;
8:33 [k]S Ex 32:9 2:20 [l]S Dt 31:17; Jos 23:16 [m]S Jos 7:11;
S 2Ki 17:15 2:21 [n]S Jos 23:5 2:22 [o]S Ge 22:1; S Ex 15:25
2:23 [p]Jdg 1:1 3:1 [q]S Ex 15:25

official representative (see notes on Ex 14:31; Ps 18 title; Isa 41:8–9; 42:1). *a hundred and ten.* For the significance of this number see note on Ge 50:26.

2:10–15 The Lord withdraws his help because of Israel's apostasy. He "sells" the people he had "bought" (Ex 15:16) and redeemed (Ex 15:13; cf. Ps 74:2).

2:10 *gathered to their fathers.* See Ge 15:15; see also note on Ge 25:8. *who knew neither the LORD . . . Israel.* They had no direct experience of the Lord's acts (see Ex 1:8).

2:11 *did evil in the eyes of the LORD.* The same expression is used in 3:7,12; 4:1; 6:1; 10:6. *Baals.* The many local forms of this Canaanite deity (see note on v. 13).

2:12 *provoked the LORD to anger.* See Dt 4:25; see also note on Zec 1:2.

2:13 *Baal.* Means "lord," the god worshiped by the Canaanites and Phoenicians, was variously known to them as the son of Dagon and the son of El. In Aram (Syria) he was called Hadad and in Babylonia Adad. Believed to give fertility to the womb and life-giving rain to the soil, he is pictured as standing on a bull, a popular symbol of fertility and strength (see 1Ki 12:28). The storm cloud was his chariot, thunder his voice, and lightning his spear and arrows. The worship of Baal involved sacred prostitution and sometimes even child sacrifice (see Jer 19:5). The stories of Elijah and Elisha (1Ki 17–2Ki 13), as well as many other OT passages, directly or indirectly protest Baalism (e.g., Ps 29:3–9; 68:1–4,32–34; 93:1–5; 97:1–5; Jer 10:12–16; 14:22; Hos 2:8,16–17; Am 5:8). *Ashtoreths.* Female deities such as Ashtoreth (con-

sort of Baal) and Asherah (consort of El, the chief god of the Canaanite pantheon). Ashtoreth was associated with the evening star and was the beautiful goddess of war and fertility. She was worshiped as Ishtar in Babylonia and as Athtart in Aram. To the Greeks she was Astarte or Aphrodite, and to the Romans, Venus. Worship of the Ashtoreths involved extremely lascivious practices (1Ki 14:24; 2Ki 23:7).

2:14 *handed them over to.* The same expression is used in 6:1; 13:1. *sold them.* The same expression is used in 3:8; 4:2; 10:7.

2:16–19 The Lord was merciful to his people in times of distress, sending deliverers to save them from oppression. But Israel continually forgot these saving acts, just as she had those he had performed through Moses and Joshua.

2:16 *judges.* See Introduction: Title. There were six major judges (Othniel, Ehud, Deborah, Gideon, Jephthah and Samson) and six minor ones (Shamgar, Tola, Jair, Ibzan, Elon and Abdon).

2:17 *prostituted themselves.* Since the Hebrew for Baal (meaning "lord") was also used by women to refer to their husbands, it is understandable that the metaphor of adultery was commonly used in connection with Israelite worship of Baal (see Hos 2:2–3,16–17).

2:18 *groaned . . . oppressed.* The language of the Egyptian bondage (see Ex 2:24; 3:9; 6:5).

2:20–23 The Lord decided to leave the remaining nations to test Israel's loyalty.

3:1–6 The list of nations the Lord left roughly describes an

2(he did this only to teach warfare to the descendants of the Israelites who had not had previous battle experience): 3the five *r* rulers of the Philistines, *s* all the Canaanites, the Sidonians, and the Hivites *t* living in the Lebanon mountains from Mount Baal Hermon *u* to Lebo Hamath. *v* 4They were left to test *w* the Israelites to see whether they would obey the LORD's commands, which he had given their forefathers through Moses.

5The Israelites lived *x* among the Canaanites, Hittites, Amorites, Perizzites, *y* Hivites and Jebusites. *z* 6They took their daughters *a* in marriage and gave their own daughters to their sons, and served their gods. *b c*

Othniel

7The Israelites did evil in the eyes of the LORD; they forgot the LORD *d* their God and served the Baals and the Asherahs. *e* 8The anger of the LORD burned against Israel so that he sold *f* them into the hands of Cushan-Rishathaim *g* king of Aram Naharaim, *k h* to whom the Israelites were subject for eight years. 9But when they cried out *i* to the LORD, he raised up for them a deliverer, *j* Othniel *k* son of Kenaz, Caleb's younger brother, who saved them.

10The Spirit of the LORD came upon him, *l* so that he became Israel's judge1 and went to war. The LORD gave Cushan-Rishathaim *m* king of Aram *n* into the hands of Othniel, who overpowered him. 11So the land had peace *o* for forty years, *p* until Othniel son of Kenaz *q* died.

Ehud

12Once again the Israelites did evil in the eyes of the LORD, *r* and because they did this evil the LORD gave Eglon king of Moab *s* power over Israel. 13Getting the Ammonites *t* and Amalekites *u* to join him, Eglon came and attacked Israel, and they took possession of the City of Palms. *m v* 14The Israelites were subject to Eglon king of Moab *w* for eighteen years.

15Again the Israelites cried out to the LORD, and he gave them a deliverer *x*—Ehud *y*, a left-handed *z* man, the son of Gera the Benjamite. The Israelites sent him with tribute *a* to Eglon king of Moab.

3:3 *r*S Jos 13:3
*s*S Ge 10:14
*t*S Ge 10:17;
S Ex 3:8 *u*S Dt 3:8
*v*S Nu 13:21
3:4 *w*S Ex 15:25
3:5 *x*Ps 106:35
*y*S Jos 3:10
*z*S Jos 11:3;
Ezr 9:1
3:6 *a*Ezr 10:18;
Ne 13:23;
Mal 2:11
*b*S Ex 34:16;
Dt 7:3-4
*c*S Dt 7:16
3:7 *d*Dt 4:9;
S 32:18; Jdg 8:34;
Ps 78:11,42;
106:7; Jer 23:27
*e*S Ex 34:13;
S Jdg 2:11,13;
1Ki 16:33;
2Ch 34:7;
Isa 17:8
3:8 *f*Jdg 2:14;
Ps 44:12;
Isa 50:1; 52:3
*g*ver 10
*h*S Ge 24:10
3:9 *i*ver 15;
Jdg 6:6,7; 10:10;
1Sa 12:10;
Ps 106:44;
107:13
*j*S Dt 28:29;
Ne 9:27
*k*S Jos 15:17

3:10
*l*S Nu 11:25;
Jdg 6:34; 11:29;
13:25; 14:6,19;
15:14; 1Sa 11:6;
16:13; 1Ki 18:46;
1Ch 12:18;
2Ch 24:20;
Isa 11:2 *m*ver 8

*n*S Ge 10:22 3:11 *o*ver 30; S Jos 14:15; Jdg 5:31; 8:28
*p*S Ex 16:35 *q*S Jos 15:17 3:12 *r*S Jdg 2:11 *s*1Sa 12:9 3:13
*t*S Ge 19:38; Jdg 10:11 *u*S Ge 14:7 *v*S Jdg 1:16 3:14
*w*Jer 48:1 3:15 *x*S ver 9 *y*ver 16; Jdg 4:1 *z*Jdg 20:16;
1Ch 12:2 *a*ver 17,18; 2Sa 8:2,6; 1Ki 4:21; 2Ki 17:3;
Est 10:1; Ps 68:29; 72:10; 89:22; Ecc 2:8; Isa 60:5; Hos 10:6

j3 Or *to the entrance to*   k8 That is, Northwest
Mesopotamia   l10 Or *leader*   m13 That is, Jericho

arc along the western and northern boundaries of the area actually occupied by Israel at the death of Joshua (vv. 1–4). Within Israelite-occupied territory there were large groups of native peoples (v. 5; see 1:27–36) with whom the Israelites intermingled, often adopting their religions (v. 6).
3:2 *only to teach warfare.* As his covenant servant, Israel was the Lord's army for fighting against the powers of the world that were settled in his land. In view of the incomplete conquest, succeeding generations in Israel needed to become capable warriors. "Only" probably here means "especially."
3:3 *five rulers.* The Hebrew for "rulers" is related to the word "tyrant" (see note on Jos 13:3) and is used only of Philistine rulers. These rulers had control of a five-city confederacy. At one point Judah defeated three of these cities (1:18) but was unable to hold them. *Sidonians.* Here used collectively of the Phoenicians. *Hivites.* Here identified with a region in northern Canaan reaching all the way to Hamath (see also Jos 11:3). *Mount Baal Hermon.* Probably Mount Hermon (see 1Ch 5:23).
3:6 *took their daughters . . . and served their gods.* See note on Jos 23:12. The degenerating effect of such intermarriage is well illustrated in Solomon's experience (1Ki 11:1–8).
3:7–11 In the account of Othniel's judgeship the author provides the basic literary form he uses in his accounts of the major judges (i.e., beginning statement; cycle of apostasy, oppression, distress, deliverance; recognizable conclusion), adding only the brief details necessary to complete the report (see Introduction: Literary Features).
3:7 *did evil in the eyes of the LORD.* A recurring expression (see v. 12; 4:1; 6:1; 10:6; 13:1) used to introduce the cycles of the judges (see Introduction: Literary Features). *Baals.* See note on 2:13. *Asherahs.* See notes on 2:13; Ex 34:13.
3:8 *Cushan-Rishathaim.* Probably means "doubly wicked

Cushan," perhaps a caricature of his actual name (see note on 10:6 regarding Baal-Zebub). *Aram Naharaim.* See note on Ge 24:10.
3:9 *they cried out to the LORD.* The Israelites' cries of distress occurred in each recurring cycle of the judges (see Introduction: Literary Features). *Othniel.* See 1:13.
3:10 *Spirit of the LORD came upon him.* The Spirit empowered Othniel to deliver his people, as he did Gideon (6:34), Jephthah (11:29), Samson (14:6,19) and also David (1Sa 16:13). Cf. Nu 11:25–29.
3:11 *the land had peace . . . years.* A recognizable conclusion to the cycle of a judge (noted only here and in v. 30; 5:31; 8:28). After the judgeship of Gideon this formula is replaced by "led Israel . . . years" (12:7; 15:20; 16:31). See Introduction: Literary Features. *forty years.* A conventional number of years for a generation (see Introduction: Background).
3:12–30 Ehud's triumph over Eglon king of Moab. The left-handed Benjamite was an authentic hero. All alone, and purely by his wits, he cut down the king of Moab, who had established himself in Canaan near Jericho. This account balances that of Samson in the five narrative units central to the book of Judges (see Introduction: Literary Features).
3:12 *Moab.* See note on Ge 19:33.
3:13 *Ammonites.* See note on Ge 19:33. *Amalekites.* These descendants of Esau (Ge 36:12,16) lived in the Negev (Nu 13:29). See note on Ge 14:7.
3:14 *Israelites.* Here mainly Benjamin and Ephraim.
3:15 *left-handed man.* Left-handedness was noteworthy among Benjamites (see 20:15–16)—which is ironic since Benjamin means "son of (my) right hand." Being left-handed, Ehud could conceal his dagger on the side where it was not expected (see v. 21). *tribute.* An annual payment, perhaps of agricultural products (cf. 2Ki 3:4).

16Now Ehud[b] had made a double-edged sword about a foot and a half[n] long, which he strapped to his right thigh under his clothing. 17He presented the tribute[c] to Eglon king of Moab, who was a very fat man.[d] 18After Ehud had presented the tribute, he sent on their way the men who had carried it. 19At the idols[o] near Gilgal he himself turned back and said, "I have a secret message for you, O king."

The king said, "Quiet!" And all his attendants left him.

20Ehud then approached him while he was sitting alone in the upper room of his summer palace[p] [e] and said, "I have a message from God for you." As the king rose[f] from his seat, 21Ehud reached with his left hand, drew the sword[g] from his right thigh and plunged it into the king's belly. 22Even the handle sank in after the blade, which came out his back. Ehud did not pull the sword out, and the fat closed in over it. 23Then Ehud went out to the porch[q]; he shut the doors of the upper room behind him and locked them.

24After he had gone, the servants came and found the doors of the upper room locked. They said, "He must be relieving himself[h] in the inner room of the house." 25They waited to the point of embarrassment,[i] but when he did not open the doors of the room, they took a key and unlocked them. There they saw their lord fallen to the floor, dead.

26While they waited, Ehud got away. He passed by the idols and escaped to Seirah. 27When he arrived there, he blew a trumpet[j] in the hill country of Ephraim, and the Israelites went down with him from the hills, with him leading them.

28"Follow me," he ordered, "for the LORD has given Moab,[k] your enemy, into your hands.[l]" So they followed him down and, taking possession of the fords of the Jordan[m] that led to Moab, they allowed no one to cross over. 29At that time they struck down about ten thousand Moabites, all vigorous and strong; not a man escaped. 30That day Moab[n] was made subject to Israel, and the land had peace[o] for eighty years.

Shamgar

31After Ehud came Shamgar son of Anath,[p] who struck down six hundred[q] Philistines[r] with an oxgoad. He too saved Israel.

Deborah

4 After Ehud[s] died, the Israelites once again did evil[t] in the eyes of the LORD.[u] 2So the LORD sold them[v] into the hands of Jabin, a king of Canaan, who reigned in Hazor.[w] The commander of his army was Sisera,[x] who lived in Harosheth Haggoyim. 3Because he had nine hundred iron chariots[y] and had cruelly oppressed[z]

[n]16 Hebrew *a cubit* (about 0.5 meter)   [o]19 Or *the stone quarries*; also in verse 26   [p]20 The meaning of the Hebrew for this phrase is uncertain.   [q]23 The meaning of the Hebrew for this word is uncertain.

3:16 [b]S ver 15
3:17 [c]S ver 15
[d]Job 15:27;
Ps 73:4
3:20 [e]Am 3:15
/Ne 8:5
3:21 [g]2Sa 2:16;
3:27; 20:10
3:24 [h]1Sa 24:3
3:25 [i]2Ki 2:17;
8:11

3:27 [j]S Lev 25:9;
Jdg 6:34; 7:18;
2Sa 2:28;
Isa 18:3;
Jer 42:14
3:28 [k]S Ge 19:37
[l]S Jos 2:24;
S Jdg 1:2
[m]S Nu 13:29;
S Jos 2:7
3:30 [n]S Ge 36:35
[o]S ver 11
3:31 [p]Jdg 5:6
[q]S Jos 23:10
[r]Jos 13:2;
Jdg 10:11; 13:1;
1Sa 5:1; 31:1;
2Sa 8:1;
Jer 25:20; 47:1
4:1 [s]S Jdg 3:15
[t]S Jdg 2:19
[u]S Jdg 2:11
4:2 [v]S Dt 32:30
[w]S Jos 11:1
[x]1Sa 12:9;
Ps 83:9
4:3 [y]S Jos 17:16
[z]Jdg 10:12;
Ps 106:42

3:16 *made a double-edged sword.* During the period of the judges, Israelite weapons were often fashioned or improvised for the occasion: Shamgar's oxgoad (v. 31), Jael's tent peg (4:22), Gideon's jars and torches (7:20), the woman's millstone (9:53) and Samson's donkey jawbone (15:15). See 1Sa 13:19.

3:19 *idols.* Lit. "carved (stone) things," a frequent Hebrew word for stone idols (see NIV text note). But here the reference may be to carved stone statues of Eglon, marking the boundary of the territory he now claims as part of his expanded realm—a common practice in the ancient Near East.

3:20 *upper room.* Rooms were built on the flat roofs of houses (2Ki 4:10–11) and palaces (Jer 22:13–14), and had latticed windows (2Ki 1:2) that provided comfort in the heat of summer.

3:22 *which came out his back.* Or "and the offal in his belly came out."

3:28 *taking possession of the fords.* This move prevented the Moabites from sending reinforcements and also enabled the Israelites to cut off the Moabites fleeing Jericho.

3:30 *eighty years.* Round numbers are frequently used in Judges (see Introduction: Background).

3:31 *Shamgar.* The first of six minor judges and a contemporary of Deborah (see 5:6–7). His name is foreign, so he was probably not an Israelite. *son of Anath.* Indicates either that Shamgar came from the town of Beth Anath (see 1:33) or that his family worshiped the goddess Anath. Since Anath, Baal's sister, was a goddess of war who fought for Baal, the

expression "son of Anath" may have been a military title, meaning "a warrior." *oxgoad.* A long, wooden rod, sometimes having a metal tip, used for driving draft animals (see 1Sa 13:21).

4:1–5:31 Deborah's triumph over Sisera (commander of a Canaanite army)—first narrated in prose (ch. 4), then celebrated in song (ch. 5). At the time of the Canaanite threat from the north, Israel remained incapable of united action until a woman (Deborah) summoned them to the Lord's battle. Because the warriors of Israel lacked the courage to rise up and face the enemy, the glory of victory went to a woman (Jael)—and she may not have been an Israelite.

4:1–2 Except for the Canaanites, Israel's enemies came from outside the territory she occupied. Nations like Aram Naharaim, Moab, Midian and Ammon were mainly interested in plunder, but the Canaanite uprising of chs. 4–5 was an attempt to restore Canaanite power in the north. The Philistines engaged in continual struggle with Israel for permanent control of the land in the southern and central regions.

4:2 *Jabin.* See Ps 83:9–10. The name was possibly royal rather than personal. Joshua is credited with having earlier slain a king by the same name (Jos 11:1,10). *Hazor.* The original royal city of the Jabin dynasty; it may still have been in ruins (see note on Jos 11:10). Sisera sought to recover the territory once ruled by the kings of Hazor. *Sisera.* His name suggests he was not a Canaanite.

4:3 *nine hundred.* The number probably represents a coali-

the Israelites for twenty years, they cried to the LORD for help.

[4]Deborah,[a] a prophetess,[b] the wife of Lappidoth, was leading[r] Israel at that time. [5]She held court[c] under the Palm of Deborah between Ramah[d] and Bethel[e] in the hill country of Ephraim, and the Israelites came to her to have their disputes decided. [6]She sent for Barak son of Abinoam[f] from Kedesh[g] in Naphtali and said to him, "The LORD, the God of Israel, commands you: 'Go, take with you ten thousand men of Naphtali[h] and Zebulun[i] and lead the way to Mount Tabor.[j] [7]I will lure Sisera, the commander of Jabin's[k] army, with his chariots and his troops to the Kishon River[l] and give him into your hands.[m] '"

[8]Barak said to her, "If you go with me, I will go; but if you don't go with me, I won't go."

[9]"Very well," Deborah said, "I will go with you. But because of the way you are going about this,[s] the honor will not be yours, for the LORD will hand Sisera over to a woman." So Deborah went with Barak to Kedesh,[n] [10]where he summoned[o] Zebulun and Naphtali. Ten thousand men followed him, and Deborah also went with him.

[11]Now Heber the Kenite had left the other Kenites,[p] the descendants of Hobab,[q] Moses' brother-in-law,[t] and

pitched his tent by the great tree[r] in Zaanannim[s] near Kedesh.

[12]When they told Sisera that Barak son of Abinoam had gone up to Mount Tabor,[t] [13]Sisera gathered together his nine hundred iron chariots[u] and all the men with him, from Harosheth Haggoyim to the Kishon River.[v]

[14]Then Deborah said to Barak, "Go! This is the day the LORD has given Sisera into your hands.[w] Has not the LORD gone ahead[x] of you?" So Barak went down Mount Tabor, followed by ten thousand men. [15]At Barak's advance, the LORD routed[y] Sisera and all his chariots and army by the sword, and Sisera abandoned his chariot and fled on foot. [16]But Barak pursued the chariots and army as far as Harosheth Haggoyim. All the troops of Sisera fell by the sword; not a man was left.[z]

[17]Sisera, however, fled on foot to the tent of Jael,[a] the wife of Heber the Kenite,[b] because there were friendly relations between Jabin king of Hazor[c] and the clan of Heber the Kenite.

[18]Jael[d] went out to meet Sisera and said to him, "Come, my lord, come right in. Don't be afraid." So he entered her tent, and she put a covering over him.

[19]"I'm thirsty," he said. "Please give me

Cross references (center column)

4:4 [a]Jdg 5:1,7,12, 15 [b]S Ex 15:20
4:5 [c]1Sa 14:2; 22:6 [d]S Jos 18:25 [e]S Jos 12:9
4:6 [f]Jdg 5:1,12, 15; 1Sa 12:11; Heb 11:32 [g]S Jos 12:22 [h]S Ge 30:8 [i]Jdg 5:18; 6:35 [j]S Jos 19:22
4:7 [k]S Jos 11:1 [l]ver 13; Jdg 5:21; 1Ki 18:40; Ps 83:9 [m]S Jdg 1:2
4:9 [n]S Jos 12:22
4:10 [o]2Ch 36:23; Ezr 1:2; Isa 41:2; 42:6; 45:3; 46:11; 48:15
4:11 [p]S Ge 15:19 [q]Nu 10:29
[r]Jos 24:26; Jdg 9:6 [s]Jos 19:33
4:12 [t]S Jos 19:22
4:13 [u]S Jos 17:16 [v]S ver 7; Jdg 5:19
4:14 [w]S Jdg 1:2 [x]Dt 9:3; 1Sa 8:20; 2Sa 5:24; Ps 68:7 [y]S Ex 14:24; Ps 18:14
4:16 [z]S Ex 14:28; Ps 83:9
4:17 [a]ver 18,21, 22; Jdg 5:6,24 [b]S Ge 15:19 [c]S Jos 11:1
4:18 [d]S ver 17

[r]4 Traditionally judging   [s]9 Or But on the expedition you are undertaking   [t]11 Or father-in-law

---

tion rather than the chariot force of one city. In the 15th century B.C., Pharaoh Thutmose III boasted of having captured 924 chariots at the battle of Megiddo. *Israelites.* Mainly Zebulun and Naphtali, but West Manasseh, Issachar and Asher were also affected.
4:4 *Deborah.* Means "bee"; cf. Dt 1:44. She is the only judge said to have been a prophet(ess). Other women spoken of as prophetesses are Miriam (Ex 15:20), Huldah (2Ki 22:14), Noadiah (Ne 6:14) and Anna (Lk 2:36), but see also Ac 21:9.
4:6 *Barak.* Means "thunderbolt"—which suggests that he is summoned to be the Lord's "flashing sword" (Dt 32:41). He is named among the heroes of faith in Heb 11:32. *Kedesh in Naphtali.* A town affected by the Canaanite oppression. *Naphtali and Zebulun.* Issachar, a near neighbor of these tribes, is not mentioned here but is included in the poetic description of the battle in 5:15. In all, six tribes are mentioned as having participated in the battle. *Mount Tabor.* A mountain about 1,300 feet high, northeast of the battle site.
4:7 With the Israelites encamped on the slopes of Mount Tabor, safe from chariot attack, the Lord's strategy was to draw Sisera into a trap. For the battle site, Sisera cleverly chose the Valley of Jezreel along the Kishon River, where his chariot forces would have ample maneuvering space to range the battlefield and attack in numbers from any quarter. But that was his undoing, for he did not know the power of the Lord, who would fight from heaven for Israel with storm and flood (see 5:20–21), as he had done in the days of Joshua (10:11–14). Even in modern times storms have rendered the plain along the Kishon virtually impassable. In April of 1799 the flooded Kishon River aided Napoleon's victory over a

Turkish army.
4:9 *a woman.* Barak's timidity (and that of Israel's other warriors, whom he exemplified) was due to lack of trust in the Lord and was thus rebuked (see note on 9:54).
4:11 *Heber the Kenite.* Since one meaning of Heber's name is "ally," and since "Kenite" identifies him as belonging to a clan of metalworkers, the author hints at the truth that this member of a people allied with Israel since the days of Moses has moved from south to north to ally himself (see v. 17) with the Canaanite king who is assembling a large force of "iron chariots." It is no doubt he who informs Sisera of Barak's military preparations. *other Kenites.* Settled in the south not far from Kadesh Barnea in the Negev (see 1:16). *Hobab.* See Nu 10:29.
4:14 *gone ahead of you.* As a king at the head of his army (see 1Sa 8:20). See also Ex 15:3 ("the LORD is a warrior"); Jos 10:10–11; 2Sa 5:24; 2Ch 20:15–17,22–24. *Barak went down Mount Tabor.* The Lord's "thunderbolt" (see note on v. 6) descends the mountain to attack the Canaanite army.
4:15 *routed.* See note on v. 7. The Hebrew for this word is also used of the panic that overcame the Egyptians at the "Red Sea" (Ex 14:24) and the Philistines at Mizpah (1Sa 7:10).
4:18 *he entered her tent.* Since ancient Near Eastern custom prohibited any man other than a woman's husband or father from entering her tent, Jael seemed to offer Sisera an ideal hiding place.
4:19 *skin.* Containers for liquids were normally made from the skins of goats or lambs. *milk.* See note on 5:25. Jael, whose name means "mountain goat," gave him milk to drink—and it was most likely goat's milk (see Ex 23:19; Pr

some water." She opened a skin of milk, *e*
gave him a drink, and covered him up.

20"Stand in the doorway of the tent," he
told her. "If someone comes by and asks
you, 'Is anyone here?' say 'No.' "

21But Jael, *f* Heber's wife, picked up a
tent peg and a hammer and went quietly to
him while he lay fast asleep, *g* exhausted.
She drove the peg through his temple into
the ground, and he died. *h*

22Barak came by in pursuit of Sisera, and
Jael *i* went out to meet him. "Come," she
said, "I will show you the man you're
looking for." So he went in with her, and
there lay Sisera with the tent peg through
his temple—dead. *j*

23On that day God subdued *k* Jabin, *l*
the Canaanite king, before the Israelites.
24And the hand of the Israelites grew
stronger and stronger against Jabin, the Canaanite king, until they destroyed him. *m*

The Song of Deborah

5 On that day Deborah *n* and Barak son
of Abinoam *o* sang this song: *p*

2"When the princes in Israel take the
　　lead,
　when the people willingly offer *q*
　　themselves—
　praise the LORD! *r*

3"Hear this, you kings! Listen, you
　　rulers!
　I will sing to *u* the LORD, I will sing; *s*

I will make music to *v* the LORD, the
　　God of Israel. *t*

4"O LORD, when you went out *u* from
　　Seir, *v*
　when you marched from the land of
　　Edom,
　the earth shook, *w* the heavens poured,
　　the clouds poured down water. *x*
5The mountains quaked *y* before the
　　LORD, the One of Sinai,
　before the LORD, the God of Israel.

6"In the days of Shamgar son of Anath, *z*
　　in the days of Jael, *a* the roads *b* were
　　abandoned;
　travelers took to winding paths. *c*
7Village life *w* in Israel ceased,
　　ceased until I, *x* Deborah, *d* arose,
　　arose a mother in Israel.
8When they chose new gods, *e*
　　war came to the city gates, *f*
　and not a shield or spear *g* was seen
　　among forty thousand in Israel.
9My heart is with Israel's princes,
　　with the willing volunteers *h* among
　　the people.
　Praise the LORD!

10"You who ride on white donkeys, *i*
　　sitting on your saddle blankets,
　and you who walk along the road,
　consider 11the voice of the singers *y* at
　　the watering places.

Cross-reference column:

4:19 *e*S Ge 18:8
4:21 *f*S ver 17
*g*Ge 2:21; 15:12;
1Sa 26:12;
Isa 29:10; Jnh 1:5
*h*Jdg 5:26
4:22 *i*S ver 17
*j*Jdg 5:27
4:23 *k*Ne 9:24;
Ps 18:47; 44:2;
47:3; 144:2
*l*S Jos 11:1
4:24 *m*Ps 83:9;
106:43
5:1 *n*S Jdg 4:4
*o*S Jdg 4:6
*p*S Ex 15:1;
Ps 32:7
5:2 *q*2Ch 17:16;
Ps 110:3 *r*ver 9
5:3 *s*S Ex 15:1
*t*Ps 27:6
5:4 *u*S Ex 13:21
*v*S Nu 24:18;
S Dt 33:2
*w*2Sa 22:8;
Ps 18:7; 77:18;
82:5; Isa 2:19,21;
13:13; 24:18;
64:3; Jer 10:10;
50:46; 51:29;
Joel 3:16; Na 1:5;
Hab 3:6 *x*Ps 68:8;
77:17
5:5 *y*S Ex 19:18;
Ps 29:6; 46:3;
77:18; 114:4;
Isa 64:3
5:6 *z*Jdg 3:31
*a*S Jdg 4:17
*b*Lev 26:22;
Isa 33:8
*c*Ps 125:5;
Isa 59:8
5:7 *d*S Jdg 4:4
5:8 *e*Dt 32:17;
S Jdg 2:13 *f*ver
11; S Jos 2:5
*g*S Nu 25:7
5:9 *h*S ver 2
5:10 *i*S Ge 49:11;
Jdg 12:14

*u*3 Or *of*　*v*3 Or / *with song I will praise*　*w*7 Or
Warriors　*x*7 Or *you*　*y*11 Or *archers*; the meaning
of the Hebrew for this word is uncertain.

27:27).

4:21 *drove the peg through his temple.* The laws of hospitality normally meant that one tried to protect a guest from
any harm (see 19:23; Ge 18:8). Jael remained true to her
family's previous alliance with Israel (she may have been an
Israelite) and so undid her husband's deliberate breach of
faith. Armed only with domestic implements, this dauntless
woman destroyed the great warrior whom Barak had earlier
feared.

4:22 *there lay Sisera . . . dead.* With Sisera dead the kingdom of Jabin was no longer a threat. The land "flowing with
milk and honey" had been saved by the courage and faithfulness of "Bee" (see note on v. 4) and "Mountain Goat" (see
note on v. 19).

5:1–31 To commemorate a national victory with songs
was a common practice (see Ex 15:1–18; Nu 21:27–30; Dt
32:1–43; 1Sa 18:7). The "Book of the Wars of the LORD"
(see note on Nu 21:14) and the "Book of Jashar" (see note
on Jos 10:13) were probably collections of such songs.

The song was probably written by Deborah or a contemporary (see v. 7 and NIV text note) and is thus one of the oldest
poems in the Bible. It highlights some of the central themes
of the narrative (cf. Ex 15:1–18; 1Sa 2:1–10; 2Sa 22;
23:1–7; Lk 1:46–55,68–79). In particular, it celebrates before the nations (v. 3) the righteous acts of the Lord and of his
warriors (v. 11). The song may be divided into the following
sections: (1) the purpose of the song (praise) and the occasion for the deeds it celebrates (vv. 2–9); (2) the exhortation

to Israel to act in accordance with her heroic past (vv.
10–11a); (3) the people's appeal to Deborah (vv. 11b–12);
(4) the gathering of warriors (vv. 13–18); (5) the battle (vv.
19–23); (6) the crafty triumph of Jael over Sisera (vv.
24–27); (7) the anxious waiting of Sisera's mother (vv.
28–30); and (8) the conclusion (v. 31).

5:4–5 Poetic recalling of the Lord's terrifying appearance in
a storm cloud many years before, when he had brought Israel
through the desert into Canaan (see Dt 33:2; Ps 68:7–8;
Mic 1:3–4; see also Ps 18:7–15).

5:4 *Seir.* Edom. For a similar association of Seir (and Mount
Paran) with Sinai see Dt 33:2. *the heavens poured.* See Ps
68:7–10.

5:5 *the One of Sinai.* See Ps 68:8. An earthquake and
thunderstorm occurred when God appeared at Mount Sinai
(Ex 19:16–18).

5:6 *Shamgar.* See note on 3:31. *roads were abandoned.*
Because of enemy garrisons and marauding bands (see note
on 4:1–2) the roads were unsafe.

5:7 *Village life . . . ceased.* The inhabitants of villages fled
to walled towns for protection.

5:8 *not a shield or spear was seen.* Either because Israel
had made peace with the native Canaanites (see 3:5–6) or
because she had been disarmed (see 1Sa 13:19–22).

5:10 *who ride on white donkeys.* An allusion to the nobles
and the wealthy (see 10:4; 12:14).

5:11 *voice of the singers.* The leaders are encouraged by
the songs of the minstrels at the watering places—songs that

They recite the righteous acts[j] of the
  LORD,
  the righteous acts of his warriors[z] in
    Israel.

"Then the people of the LORD
  went down to the city gates.[k]
12'Wake up,[l] wake up, Deborah![m]
  Wake up, wake up, break out in
    song!
  Arise, O Barak![n]
  Take captive your captives,[o] O son of
    Abinoam.'

13"Then the men who were left
  came down to the nobles;
  the people of the LORD
  came to me with the mighty.
14Some came from Ephraim,[p] whose
    roots were in Amalek;[q]
  Benjamin[r] was with the people who
    followed you.
  From Makir[s] captains came down,
  from Zebulun those who bear a
    commander's staff.
15The princes of Issachar[t] were with
    Deborah;[u]
  yes, Issachar was with Barak,[v]
  rushing after him into the valley.
  In the districts of Reuben
  there was much searching of heart.
16Why did you stay among the
    campfires[a] [w]
  to hear the whistling for the flocks?[x]
  In the districts of Reuben
  there was much searching of heart.
17Gilead[y] stayed beyond the Jordan.

And Dan, why did he linger by the
    ships?
  Asher[z] remained on the coast[a]
  and stayed in his coves.
18The people of Zebulun[b] risked their
    very lives;
  so did Naphtali[c] on the heights of
    the field.[d]

19"Kings came[e], they fought;
  the kings of Canaan fought
  at Taanach by the waters of Megiddo,[f]
  but they carried off no silver, no
    plunder.[g]
20From the heavens[h] the stars fought,
  from their courses they fought against
    Sisera.
21The river Kishon[i] swept them away,
  the age-old river, the river Kishon.
  March on, my soul; be strong![j]
22Then thundered the horses' hoofs—
  galloping, galloping go his mighty
    steeds.[k]
23'Curse Meroz,' said the angel of the
    LORD.
  'Curse its people bitterly,
  because they did not come to help the
    LORD,
  to help the LORD against the mighty.'

24"Most blessed of women[l] be Jael,[m]
  the wife of Heber the Kenite,[n]
  most blessed of tent-dwelling
    women.
25He asked for water, and she gave him
    milk;[o]

5:11 /1Sa 12:7;
Da 9:16; Mic 6:5
kS ver 8
5:12 /Ps 44:23;
57:8; Isa 51:9,17
mS Jdg 4:4
nS Jdg 4:6
oPs 68:18;
Eph 4:8
5:14
pS Ge 41:52;
S Jdg 1:29
qJdg 3:13
rS Nu 34:21
sS Ge 50:23
5:15 tS Ge 30:18
uS Jdg 4:4
vS Jdg 4:6
5:16 wS Ge 49:14
xS Nu 32:1
5:17 yS Jos 12:2

zS Jos 17:7
aJos 19:29
5:18 bS Ge 30:20
cS Ge 30:8;
Ps 68:27
dS Jdg 4:6
5:19 eJos 11:5;
S Jdg 4:13;
Rev 16:16
fS Jos 12:21 gver
30
5:20 hS Jos 10:11
5:21 iS Jdg 4:7
jJos 1:6
5:22 kJer 8:16
5:24 lLk 1:42
mS Jdg 4:17
nS Ge 15:19
5:25 oS Ge 18:8   z11 Or villagers   a16 Or saddlebags

---

rehearse the past heroic achievements of the Lord and his
warriors.
5:12 *Wake up.* A plea to take action (see Ps 44:23; Isa
51:9). *Take captive your captives.* The same action is applied
to God in Ps 68:18 and to Christ in Eph 4:8.
5:13–18 The warriors of the Lord who gathered for the
battle. The tribes who came were Ephraim, Benjamin, Manasseh ("Makir" is possibly both East and West Manasseh;
see Dt 3:15; Jos 13:29–31; 17:1), Zebulun (vv. 14,18),
Issachar (v. 15) and Naphtali (v. 18). Especially involved
were Zebulun and Naphtali (v. 18; see 4:10), the tribes most
immediately affected by Sisera's tyranny. Reuben (vv.
15–16) and Gad (here referred to as Gilead, v. 17), from east
of the Jordan, and Dan and Asher, from along the coast (v.
17), are rebuked for not responding. Judah and Simeon are
not even mentioned, perhaps because they were already
engaged with the Philistines. Levi is not mentioned because
it did not have military responsibilities in the theocracy
(kingdom of God).
5:14 *roots . . . in Amalek.* Some Amalekites apparently
once lived in the hill country of Ephraim (see 12:15). *Makir.*
The firstborn son of Manasseh (Jos 17:1). Although the
descendants of Makir settled on both sides of the Jordan (see
Dt 3:15; Jos 13:29–31; 17:1; 1Ch 7:14–19), reference
here is to those west of the Jordan (see v. 17; Jos 17:5).
5:18 *on the heights of the field.* Perhaps connected to Ge

49:21, where Naphtali is described as a "doe set free."
5:19 *Megiddo.* Megiddo and Taanach dominated the main
pass that runs northeast through the hill country from the
plain of Sharon to the Valley of Jezreel. Because of its strategic location, the "plain of Megiddo" (2Ch 35:22) has been a
frequent battleground from the earliest times. There Pharaoh
Thutmose III defeated a Canaanite coalition in 1468 B.C.,
and there in A.D. 1917 the British under General Allenby
ended the rule of the Turks in Palestine by vanquishing them
in the Valley of Jezreel opposite Megiddo. In Biblical history
the forces of Israel under Deborah and Barak crushed the
Canaanites "by the waters of Megiddo" (v. 19), and there
Judah's good king Josiah died in battle against Pharaoh Neco
II in 609 B.C. (2Ki 23:29). See also the reference in Rev
16:16 to "the place that in Hebrew is called Armageddon"
(i.e., "Mount Megiddo") as the site of the "battle on the
great day of God Almighty" (Rev 16:14).
5:20 *stars fought.* A poetic way of saying that the powers of
heaven fought in Israel's behalf (see note on 4:7).
5:21 *swept them away.* See note on 4:7.
5:23 *Meroz.* Because of its refusal to help the army of the
Lord, this Israelite town in Naphtali was cursed. Other cities
were also punished severely for refusing to participate in the
wars of the Lord (see 8:15–17; 21:5–10).
5:25 *curdled milk.* Artificially soured milk made by shaking
milk in a skin-bottle and then allowing it to ferment (due to

in a bowl fit for nobles she brought
  him curdled milk.
26Her hand reached for the tent peg,
  her right hand for the workman's
  hammer.
She struck Sisera, she crushed his head,
  she shattered and pierced his
  temple.*p*
27At her feet he sank,
  he fell; there he lay.
At her feet he sank, he fell;
  where he sank, there he fell—dead*q*.

28"Through the window*r* peered Sisera's
  mother;
  behind the lattice she cried out,*s*
  'Why is his chariot so long in coming?
  Why is the clatter of his chariots
  delayed?'
29The wisest of her ladies answer her;
  indeed, she keeps saying to herself,
30'Are they not finding and dividing the
  spoils:*t*
  a girl or two for each man,
  colorful garments as plunder for
  Sisera,
  colorful garments embroidered,
  highly embroidered garments*u* for my
  neck—
  all this as plunder?*v*'

31"So may all your enemies perish,*w*
  O LORD!
But may they who love you be like
  the sun*x*
  when it rises in its strength."*y*

Then the land had peace*z* forty years.

5:26 *p* Jdg 4:21
5:27 *q* Jdg 4:22
5:28 *r* S Jos 2:15
  s Pr 7:6
5:30 *t* Ex 15:9;
1Sa 30:24;
Ps 68:12
u Ps 45:14;
Eze 16:10 *v* ver
19; 2Sa 1:24
5:31
w S Nu 10:35
x 2Sa 23:4;
Job 37:21;
Ps 19:4; 89:36;
Isa 18:4
y 2Sa 18:32
z S Jdg 3:11

6:1 *a* S Jdg 2:11
b S Ge 25:2
6:2 *c* 1Sa 13:6;
26:16; 37:3
d Isa 2:19;
Jer 48:28; 49:8,
30 *e* Job 24:8;
Jer 41:9;
Heb 11:38
6:3 *f* Nu 13:29
g S Ge 25:6;
Isa 11:14;
Jer 49:28
6:4 *h* Lev 26:16;
Dt 28:30,51;
Isa 10:6; 39:6;
42:22
i S Ge 10:19
6:5 *j* S Dt 28:42
k Jdg 8:10;
Isa 21:7; 60:6;
Jer 49:32
6:6 *l* S Jdg 3:9
6:7 *m* S Jdg 3:9
6:8 *n* Dt 18:15;
1Ki 20:13,22;
2Ki 17:13,23;
Ne 9:29;
Job 36:10;
Jer 25:5;
Eze 18:30-31
o S Jdg 2:1
p Jos 24:17
6:9 *q* S Nu 10:9;
Ps 136:24
r Ps 44:2
6:10 *s* S Ex 20:5
t S Jos 24:15
6:11 *u* S Ge 16:7

Gideon

6 Again the Israelites did evil in the eyes of the LORD,*a* and for seven years he gave them into the hands of the Midianites.*b* 2Because the power of Midian was so oppressive,*c* the Israelites prepared shelters for themselves in mountain clefts, caves*d* and strongholds.*e* 3Whenever the Israelites planted their crops, the Midianites, Amalekites*f* and other eastern peoples*g* invaded the country. 4They camped on the land and ruined the crops*h* all the way to Gaza*i* and did not spare a living thing for Israel, neither sheep nor cattle nor donkeys. 5They came up with their livestock and their tents like swarms of locusts.*j* It was impossible to count the men and their camels;*k* they invaded the land to ravage it. 6Midian so impoverished the Israelites that they cried out*l* to the LORD for help.

7When the Israelites cried*m* to the LORD because of Midian, 8he sent them a prophet,*n* who said, "This is what the LORD, the God of Israel, says: I brought you up out of Egypt,*o* out of the land of slavery.*p* 9I snatched you from the power of Egypt and from the hand of all your oppressors.*q* I drove them from before you and gave you their land.*r* 10I said to you, 'I am the LORD your God; do not worship*s* the gods of the Amorites,*t* in whose land you live.' But you have not listened to me."

11The angel of the LORD*u* came and sat

---

bacteria that remained in the skin from previous use).
5:28 This graphic picture of the anxious waiting of Sisera's mother heightens the triumph of Jael over the powerful Canaanite general and presents a contrast between this mother in Canaan and the triumphant Deborah, "a mother in Israel" (v. 7).
5:31 The song ends with a prayer that the present victory would be the pattern for all future battles against the Lord's enemies (see Nu 10:35; Ps 68:1–2). *your enemies . . . they who love you.* The two basic attitudes of people toward the Lord. As Lord of the covenant and royal Head of his people Israel, he demanded their love (see Ex 20:6), just as kings in the ancient Near East demanded the love of their subjects. *forty years.* A conventional number of years for a generation (see Introduction: Background).
6:1–9:57 The Gideon and Abimelech narratives are a literary unit and constitute the center account of the judges. They are bracketed by the stories of Deborah (from Ephraim, a son of Joseph; west of the Jordan) and Jephthah (from Manasseh, the other son of Joseph; east of the Jordan)—which in turn are bracketed by the stories of the heroes Ehud (from Benjamin) and Samson (from Dan). In this center narrative, the crucial issues of the period of the judges are emphasized: the worship of Baal, and the Lord's kingship over his covenant people Israel.
6:1 *Midianites.* See notes on Ge 37:25; Ex 2:15. Since

they were apparently not numerous enough to wage war against the Israelites alone, they often formed coalitions with surrounding peoples—as with the Moabites (Nu 22:4–6; 25:6–18), the Amalekites and other tribes from the east (v. 3). Their defeat was an event long remembered in Hebrew history (see Ps 83:9; Isa 9:4; 10:26; Hab 3:7).
6:3 *Amalekites.* See note on Ge 14:7. Normally they were a people of the Negev, but they are in coalition here with the Midianites and other eastern peoples, who were nomads from the desert east of Moab and Ammon.
6:5 *swarms of locusts.* A vivid picture of the marauders who swarmed across the land, leaving it stripped bare (see 7:12; Ex 10:13–15; Joel 1:4). *camels.* The earliest OT reference to the use of mounted camels in warfare.
6:7 *cried to the LORD.* The Israelites' cries of distress occurred in each recurring cycle of the judges (see Introduction: Literary Features).
6:8 *prophet.* See notes on 2:1; 10:11. The unnamed prophet rebuked Israel for forgetting that the Lord had saved them from Egyptian bondage and had given them the land (vv. 9–10).
6:10 *Amorites.* Probably here includes all the inhabitants of Canaan (see note on Ge 10:16).
6:11 *angel of the LORD.* See note on Ge 16:7. *Ophrah.* To be distinguished from the Benjamite Ophrah (Jos 18:23). *Abiezrite.* The Abiezrites (v. 24) were from the tribe of

down under the oak in Ophrah ^{v} that belonged to Joash ^{w} the Abiezrite, ^{x} where his son Gideon ^{y} was threshing ^{z} wheat in a winepress ^{a} to keep it from the Midianites. ^{12}When the angel of the LORD appeared to Gideon, he said, "The LORD is with you, ^{b} mighty warrior. ^{c}"

^{13}"But sir," Gideon replied, "if the LORD is with us, why has all this happened to us? Where are all his wonders ^{d} that our fathers told ^{e} us about when they said, 'Did not the LORD bring us up out of Egypt?' But now the LORD has abandoned ^{f} us and put us into the hand of Midian."

^{14}The LORD turned to him and said, "Go in the strength you have ^{g} and save ^{h} Israel out of Midian's hand. Am I not sending you?"

^{15}"But Lord, ^{b}" Gideon asked, "how can I save Israel? My clan ^{i} is the weakest in Manasseh, and I am the least in my family. ^{j}"

^{16}The LORD answered, "I will be with you ^{k}, and you will strike down all the Midianites together."

^{17}Gideon replied, "If now I have found favor in your eyes, give me a sign ^{l} that it is really you talking to me. ^{18}Please do not go away until I come back and bring my offering and set it before you."

And the LORD said, "I will wait until you return."

^{19}Gideon went in, prepared a young goat, ^{m} and from an ephah ^{cn} of flour he made bread without yeast. Putting the meat in a basket and its broth in a pot, he brought them out and offered them to him under the oak. ^{o}

^{20}The angel of God said to him, "Take the meat and the unleavened bread, place them on this rock, ^{p} and pour out the broth." And Gideon did so. ^{21}With the tip of the staff ^{q} that was in his hand, the angel of the LORD touched the meat and the un-

leavened bread. ^{r} Fire flared from the rock, consuming the meat and the bread. And the angel of the LORD disappeared. ^{22}When Gideon realized ^{s} that it was the angel of the LORD, he exclaimed, "Ah, Sovereign LORD! I have seen the angel of the LORD face to face!" ^{t}

^{23}But the LORD said to him, "Peace! Do not be afraid. ^{u} You are not going to die." ^{v}

^{24}So Gideon built an altar to the LORD there and called ^{w} it The LORD is Peace. To this day it stands in Ophrah ^{x} of the Abiezrites.

^{25}That same night the LORD said to him, "Take the second bull from your father's herd, the one seven years old. ^{d} Tear down your father's altar to Baal and cut down the Asherah pole ^{ey} beside it. ^{26}Then build a proper kind of ^{f} altar to the LORD your God on the top of this height. Using the wood of the Asherah pole that you cut down, offer the second ^{g} bull as a burnt offering. ^{z}"

^{27}So Gideon took ten of his servants and did as the LORD told him. But because he was afraid of his family and the men of the town, he did it at night rather than in the daytime.

^{28}In the morning when the men of the town got up, there was Baal's altar, ^{a} demolished, with the Asherah pole beside it cut down and the second bull sacrificed on the newly built altar!

^{29}They asked each other, "Who did this?"

When they carefully investigated, they were told, "Gideon son of Joash ^{b} did it."

^{30}The men of the town demanded of Joash, "Bring out your son. He must die, because he has broken down Baal's altar ^{c}

Cross references (center column):

6:11 ^{v}S Jos 18:23
^{w}ver 29;
Jdg 7:14; 8:13,29
^{x}S Nu 26:30
^{y}Jdg 7:1; 8:1;
Heb 11:32
^{z}Ru 2:17; 3:2;
1Sa 23:1;
1Ch 21:20
^{a}Ne 13:15;
Isa 16:10; 63:3;
La 1:15; Joel 3:13
6:12 ^{b}S Jos 1:5;
Ru 2:4; 1Sa 10:7;
Ps 129:8
^{c}Jdg 11:1
6:13 ^{d}S Jos 3:5
^{e}2Sa 7:22;
Ps 44:1; 78:3
^{f}S Dt 31:17
6:14 ^{g}Heb 11:34
^{h}ver 36; Jdg 10:1;
2Ki 14:27
6:15 ^{i}Isa 60:22
/1Sa 9:21
6:16 ^{k}Ex 3:12;
S Nu 14:43;
Jos 1:5
6:17 ^{l}ver 36-37;
S Ge 24:14;
S Ex 3:12; S 4:8
6:19 ^{m}Jdg 13:15
^{n}S Lev 19:36
^{o}Ge 18:7-8
6:20 ^{p}Jdg 13:19
6:21 ^{q}S Ex 4:2

^{r}S Lev 9:24
6:22 ^{s}Jdg 13:16,
21 ^{t}Ge 32:30;
Jdg 13:22
6:23 ^{u}Da 10:19
^{v}S Ge 16:13;
S Dt 5:26
6:24 ^{w}S Ge 22:14
^{x}S Jos 18:23
6:25 ^{y}ver 26,28,
30; Ex 34:13;
S Jdg 2:13
6:26 ^{z}S Ge 8:20
6:28 ^{a}ver 30;
1Ki 16:32;
2Ki 21:3
6:29 ^{b}S ver 11
6:30 ^{c}S ver 28

---

^{b}15 Or sir ^{c}19 That is, probably about 3/5 bushel (about 22 liters) ^{d}25 Or Take a full-grown, mature bull from your father's herd ^{e}25 That is, a symbol of the goddess Asherah; here and elsewhere in Judges ^{f}26 Or build with layers of stone an ^{g}26 Or full-grown; also in verse 28

Manasseh (Jos 17:2). *threshing wheat in a winepress.* Rather than in the usual, exposed area (see note on Ru 1:22). Gideon felt more secure threshing in this better protected but very confined space.

6:12 *mighty warrior.* Apparently Gideon belonged to the upper class, perhaps a kind of aristocracy (see v. 27), in spite of his disclaimer in v. 15.

6:14 *LORD turned.* See vv. 22–23. Apparently this appearance of the "angel of the LORD" (v. 11) was a theophany (a manifestation of God). *Go . . . Am I not sending you?* Gideon was commissioned to deliver Israel as Moses had been (see Ex 3:7–10).

6:15 *how can I . . . ?* The Lord usually calls the lowly rather than the mighty to act for him (see notes on Ge 25:23; 1Sa 9:21).

6:17 *give me a sign.* See vv. 36–40; cf. the signs the Lord

gave Moses as assurance that he would be with him in his undertaking (see Ex 3:12; 4:1–17).

6:21 *consuming the meat.* Indicating that Gideon's offering was accepted (see Lev 9:24).

6:23 *not going to die.* See 13:22 and notes on Ge 16:13; 32:30.

6:25 *Tear down . . . altar.* Gideon's first task as the Lord's warrior was to tear down an altar to Baal, as Israel had been commanded to do (see 2:2; Ex 34:13; Dt 7:5). *Baal.* See note on 2:13. *Asherah pole.* See NIV text note; see also notes on 2:13; Ex 34:13.

6:26 *proper kind of altar.* See Ex 20:25.

6:30 *He must die.* The Israelites were so apostate that they were willing to kill one of their own people for the cause of Baal (contrast Dt 13:6–10, where God told Moses that idolaters must be stoned).

and cut down the Asherah pole beside it.''

31But Joash replied to the hostile crowd around him, ''Are you going to plead Baal's cause?*d* Are you trying to save him? Whoever fights for him shall be put to death by morning! If Baal really is a god, he can defend himself when someone breaks down his altar.'' 32So that day they called Gideon ''Jerub-Baal,*h e*'' saying, ''Let Baal contend with him,'' because he broke down Baal's altar.

33Now all the Midianites, Amalekites*f* and other eastern peoples*g* joined forces and crossed over the Jordan and camped in the Valley of Jezreel.*h* 34Then the Spirit of the LORD came upon*i* Gideon, and he blew a trumpet,*j* to follow him. 35He sent messengers throughout Manasseh, calling them to arms, and also into Asher,*l* Zebulun and Naphtali,*m* so that they too went up to meet them.*n*

36Gideon said to God, ''If you will save*o* Israel by my hand as you have promised— 37look, I will place a wool fleece*p* on the threshing floor.*q* If there is dew only on the fleece and all the ground is dry, then I will know*r* that you will save Israel by my hand, as you said.'' 38And that is what happened. Gideon rose early the next day; he squeezed the fleece and wrung out the dew—a bowlful of water.

39Then Gideon said to God, ''Do not be angry with me. Let me make just one more request.*s* Allow me one more test with the fleece. This time make the fleece dry and the ground covered with dew.'' 40That night God did so. Only the fleece was dry; all the ground was covered with dew.*t*

Gideon Defeats the Midianites

7 Early in the morning, Jerub-Baal*u* (that is, Gideon*v*) and all his men camped at the spring of Harod.*w* The camp

of Midian*x* was north of them in the valley near the hill of Moreh.*y* 2The LORD said to Gideon, ''You have too many men for me to deliver Midian into their hands. In order that Israel may not boast against me that her own strength*z* has saved her, 3announce now to the people, 'Anyone who trembles with fear may turn back and leave Mount Gilead.*a*' '' So twenty-two thousand men left, while ten thousand remained.

4But the LORD said to Gideon, ''There are still too many*b* men. Take them down to the water, and I will sift them for you there. If I say, 'This one shall go with you,' he shall go; but if I say, 'This one shall not go with you,' he shall not go.''

5So Gideon took the men down to the water. There the LORD told him, ''Separate those who lap the water with their tongues like a dog from those who kneel down to drink.'' 6Three hundred men*c* lapped with their hands to their mouths. All the rest got down on their knees to drink.

7The LORD said to Gideon, ''With the three hundred men that lapped I will save you and give the Midianites into your hands.*d* Let all the other men go, each to his own place.''*e* 8So Gideon sent the rest of the Israelites to their tents but kept the three hundred, who took over the provisions and trumpets of the others.

Now the camp of Midian lay below him in the valley. 9During that night the LORD said to Gideon, ''Get up, go down against the camp, because I am going to give it into your hands.*f* 10If you are afraid to attack, go down to the camp with your servant Purah 11and listen to what they are saying. Afterward, you will be encouraged to attack the camp.'' So he and Purah his servant went down to the outposts of the camp. 12The Midianites, the Amalekites*g*

Cross references

6:31 *d*1Sa 24:15; Ps 43:1; Jer 30:13
6:32 *e*Jdg 7:1; 8:29,35; 9:1; 1Sa 12:11
6:33 *f*Nu 13:29 *g*S Ge 25:6 *h*S Jos 15:56; Eze 25:4; Hos 1:5
6:34 *i*S Jdg 3:10 *j*S Jos 6:20; S Jdg 3:27 *k*S Jos 17:2
6:35 *l*S Jos 17:7 *m*S Jdg 4:6 *n*Jdg 7:23
6:36 *o*S ver 14
6:37 *p*Job 31:20 *q*S Nu 18:27; 2Sa 6:6; 24:16 *r*S Ge 24:14
6:39 *s*Ge 18:32
6:40 *t*Ex 4:3-7; Isa 38:7
7:1 *u*S Jdg 6:32 *v*S Jdg 6:11 *w*2Sa 23:25
*x*S Ge 25:2 *y*S Ge 12:6
7:2 *z*S Dt 8:17; 2Co 4:7
7:3 *a*Dt 20:8; S Jos 12:2
7:4 *b*1Sa 14:6
7:6 *c*Ge 14:14
7:7 *d*S Jos 8:7 *e*1Sa 14:6
7:9 *f*ver 13-15; S Jos 2:24; S Jdg 1:2
7:12 *g*Nu 13:29

*h*32 *Jerub-Baal* means *let Baal contend.*

6:32 *Jerub-Baal.* See NIV text note. This name later occurs as Jerub-Besheth (2Sa 11:21) by substituting a degrading term (Hebrew *bosheth,* ''shameful thing'') for the name of Baal, as in the change of the names Esh-Baal and Merib-Baal (1Ch 8:33–34) to Ish-Bosheth and Mephibosheth (see notes on 2Sa 2:8; 4:4). *Let Baal contend with him.* Let Baal defend himself against Gideon.

6:33 *Valley of Jezreel.* See note on 5:19.

6:34 *Spirit . . . came upon.* Lit. ''Spirit . . . clothed himself with.'' This vivid figure, used only three times (here; 1Ch 12:18; 2Ch 24:20), emphasizes that the Spirit of the Lord empowered the human agent and acted through him (see note on 3:10).

6:35 *Manasseh.* West Manasseh. *Asher.* This tribe earlier had failed to answer the call to arms (5:17).

6:39 *just one more request.* Cf. Abraham's words in Ge 18:32.

7:1–8 As supreme commander of Israel, the Lord reduced the army so that Israel would know that the victory was by his power, not theirs.

7:1 *Harod.* Means ''trembling'' and may refer to either the timidity of the Israelites (v. 3) or the great panic of the Midianites when Gideon attacked (v. 21). The Hebrew verb form is translated ''routing'' in 8:12. *hill of Moreh.* Located across the Valley of Jezreel, approximately four miles from the Israelite army.

7:3 *may turn back.* Those who were afraid to fight the Lord's battle were not to go out with his army so that they would not demoralize the others (Dt 20:8). *Mount Gilead.* Perhaps used here as another name for Mount Gilboa.

7:6 *lapped.* The 300 remained on their feet, prepared for any emergency.

7:8–14 The Lord provided Gideon with encouraging intelligence information for the battle.

and all the other eastern peoples had settled in the valley, thick as locusts.[h] Their camels[i] could no more be counted than the sand on the seashore.[j]

¹³Gideon arrived just as a man was telling a friend his dream. "I had a dream," he was saying. "A round loaf of barley bread came tumbling into the Midianite camp. It struck the tent with such force that the tent overturned and collapsed."

¹⁴His friend responded, "This can be nothing other than the sword of Gideon son of Joash,[k] the Israelite. God has given the Midianites and the whole camp into his hands."

¹⁵When Gideon heard the dream and its interpretation, he worshiped God.[l] He returned to the camp of Israel and called out, "Get up! The LORD has given the Midianite camp into your hands."[m] ¹⁶Dividing the three hundred men[n] into three companies,[o] he placed trumpets[p] and empty jars[q] in the hands of all of them, with torches[r] inside.

¹⁷"Watch me," he told them. "Follow my lead. When I get to the edge of the camp, do exactly as I do. ¹⁸When I and all who are with me blow our trumpets,[s] then from all around the camp blow yours and shout, 'For the LORD and for Gideon.'"

¹⁹Gideon and the hundred men with him reached the edge of the camp at the beginning of the middle watch, just after they had changed the guard. They blew their trumpets and broke the jars[t] that were in their hands. ²⁰The three companies blew the trumpets and smashed the jars. Grasping the torches[u] in their left hands and holding in their right hands the

7:12 [h]S Dt 28:42; Jer 46:23   [i]Jer 49:29   [j]S Jos 11:4   **7:14** [k]S Jdg 6:11   **7:15** [l]1Sa 15:31   [m]S ver 9

7:16 [n]Ge 14:15   [o]Jdg 9:43; 1Sa 11:11; 2Sa 18:2   [p]S Lev 25:9   [q]ver 19; Ge 24:14   [r]S Ge 15:17   **7:18** [s]S Jdg 3:27   **7:19** [t]S ver 16   **7:20** [u]S Ge 15:17

7:13–14 Although revelations by dreams are frequently mentioned in the OT, here both dreamer and interpreter are non-Israelite. Contrast Joseph, who interpreted dreams in Egypt (Ge 40:1–22; 41:1–32), and Daniel, who interpreted dreams in Babylon (Da 2:1–45; 4:4–27).
7:13 *round loaf of barley bread.* Since barley was considered an inferior grain and only one-half the value of wheat (see 2Ki 7:1), it is a fitting symbol for Israel, which was inferior in numbers.
7:16 *three companies.* A strategy adopted by Israel on several occasions (9:43; 1Sa 11:11; 2Sa 18:2). *trumpets.* Rams' horns (see Ex 19:13).

Gideon's Battles

The story of Gideon begins with a graphic portrayal of one of the most striking facts of life in the Fertile Crescent: the periodic migration of nomadic people from the Aramean desert into the settled areas of Palestine. Each spring the tents of the *bedouin* herdsmen appear overnight almost as if by magic, scattered on the hills and fields of the farming districts. Conflict between these two ways of life (herdsmen and farmers) was inevitable.

In the Biblical period, the vast numbers and warlike practice of the herdsmen reduced the village people to near vassalage. Gideon's answer was twofold: (1) religious reform, starting with his own family; and (2) military action, based on a coalition of northern Israelite tribes. The location of Gideon's hometown, "Ophrah of the Abiezrites," is not known with certainty, but probably was ancient Aper (modern Afula) in the Valley of Jezreel.

The battle at the spring of Harod is justly celebrated for its strategic brilliance. Denied the use of the only local water source, the Midianites camped in the valley and fell victim to the small band of Israelites, who attacked them from the heights of the hill of Moreh.

The main battle took place north of the hill near the village of Endor at the foot of Mount Tabor. Fleeing by way of the Jordan Valley, the Midianites were trapped when the Ephraimites seized the fords of the Jordan from below Beth Shan to Beth Barah near Adam.

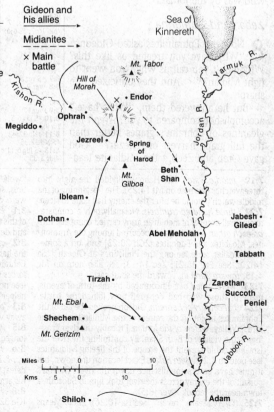

Gideon and his allies →
Midianites →
× Main battle

Sea of Kinnereth

Mt. Tabor
Hill of Moreh
Endor
Kishon R.
Ophrah
Megiddo
Jezreel
Spring of Harod
Mt. Gilboa
Beth Shan
Ibleam
Dothan
Abel Meholah
Jabesh Gilead
Tabbath
Tirzah
Zarethan
Succoth
Peniel
Mt. Ebal
Shechem
Mt. Gerizim
Jordan R.
Yarmuk R.
Jabbok R.
Shiloh
Adam

Miles 5   0   10
Kms 5   0   10

trumpets they were to blow, they shouted, "A sword[v] for the LORD and for Gideon!" [21]While each man held his position around the camp, all the Midianites ran, crying out as they fled.[w]

[22]When the three hundred trumpets sounded,[x] the LORD caused the men throughout the camp to turn on each other[y] with their swords.[z] The army fled to Beth Shittah toward Zererah as far as the border of Abel Meholah[a] near Tabbath. [23]Israelites from Naphtali, Asher[b] and all Manasseh were called out,[c] and they pursued the Midianites.[d] [24]Gideon sent messengers throughout the hill country of Ephraim, saying, "Come down against the Midianites and seize the waters of the Jordan[e] ahead of them as far as Beth Barah."

So all the men of Ephraim were called out and they took the waters of the Jordan as far as Beth Barah. [25]They also captured two of the Midianite leaders, Oreb and Zeeb.[f] They killed Oreb at the rock of Oreb,[g] and Zeeb at the winepress of Zeeb. They pursued the Midianites[h] and brought the heads of Oreb and Zeeb to Gideon, who was by the Jordan.[i]

Zebah and Zalmunna

8 Now the Ephraimites asked Gideon,[j] "Why have you treated us like this? Why didn't you call us when you went to fight Midian?"[k] [l] And they criticized him sharply.[m]

[2]But he answered them, "What have I accomplished compared to you? Aren't the gleanings of Ephraim's grapes better than the full grape harvest of Abiezer?[n] [3]God gave Oreb and Zeeb,[o] the Midianite lead-

ers, into your hands. What was I able to do compared to you?" At this, their resentment against him subsided.

[4]Gideon and his three hundred men, exhausted yet keeping up the pursuit, came to the Jordan[p] and crossed it. [5]He said to the men of Succoth,[q] "Give my troops some bread; they are worn out,[r] and I am still pursuing Zebah and Zalmunna,[s] the kings of Midian."

[6]But the officials of Succoth[t] said, "Do you already have the hands of Zebah and Zalmunna in your possession? Why should we give bread[u] to your troops?"[v]

[7]Then Gideon replied, "Just for that, when the LORD has given Zebah and Zalmunna[w] into my hand, I will tear your flesh with desert thorns and briers."

[8]From there he went up to Peniel[i] [x] and made the same request of them, but they answered as the men of Succoth had. [9]So he said to the men of Peniel, "When I return in triumph, I will tear down this tower."[y]

[10]Now Zebah and Zalmunna were in Karkor with a force of about fifteen thousand men, all that were left of the armies of the eastern peoples; a hundred and twenty thousand swordsmen had fallen.[z] [11]Gideon went up by the route of the nomads east of Nobah[a] and Jogbehah[b] and fell upon the unsuspecting army. [12]Zebah and Zalmunna, the two kings of Midian, fled, but he pursued them and captured them, routing their entire army.

[13]Gideon son of Joash[c] then returned from the battle by the Pass of Heres.[d] [14]He caught a young man of Succoth and ques-

[i] 8 Hebrew *Penuel*, a variant of *Peniel*; also in verses 9 and 17

Cross references (center column)

7:20 [v]S Dt 32:41
7:21 [w]2Ki 7:7
7:22 [x]S Jos 6:20
[y]1Sa 14:20;
2Ch 20:23;
Isa 9:21; 19:2;
Eze 38:21;
Hag 2:22;
Zec 14:13
[z]Hab 3:14
[a]1Sa 18:19;
1Ki 4:12; 19:16
7:23 [b]S Jos 17:7
[c]Jdg 6:35
[d]Ps 83:9
7:24 [e]S Jos 2:7
7:25 [f]Jdg 8:3;
Ps 83:11
[g]Isa 10:26
[h]Isa 9:4 [i]Jdg 8:4;
Ps 106:43
8:1 [j]S Jdg 6:11
[k]S Ge 25:2
[l]Jdg 12:1
[m]2Sa 19:41
8:2 [n]S Nu 26:30
8:3 [o]S Jdg 7:25

8:4 [p]Jdg 7:25
8:5 [q]S Ge 33:17
[r]Job 16:7; Ps 6:6;
Jer 45:3 [s]ver 7,
12; Ps 83:11
8:6 [t]ver 14
[u]1Sa 25:11
[v]ver 15
8:7 [w]S ver 5
8:8 [x]ver 9,17;
Ge 32:30;
1Ki 12:25
8:9 [y]ver 17
8:10 [z]S Jdg 6:5;
Isa 9:4
8:11 [a]Nu 32:42
[b]S Nu 32:35
8:13 [c]S Jdg 6:11
[d]Jdg 1:35

Study notes (bottom section)

7:19 *middle watch.* The Hebrews divided the night into three watches (see note on Mt 14:25). The "beginning of the middle watch" would be after the enemy had gone to sleep.
7:22 *three hundred trumpets.* Normally only a comparatively small number of men in an army carried trumpets. *turn on each other.* A similar panic occurred among the Ammonites, Moabites and Edomites (2Ch 20:23) and, on a somewhat smaller scale, among the Philistines at Gibeah (1Sa 14:20). See Eze 38:21; Zec 14:13; see also note on Jdg 4:15. *toward Zererah.* Toward the southeast.
7:23 *were called out.* Encouraged by the turn of events, many of those who had departed now joined the battle.
7:24 *hill country of Ephraim.* Gideon needed the aid of the Ephraimites to cut off the retreat of the Midianites into the Jordan Valley. *waters of the Jordan.* Probably the river crossings in the vicinity of Beth Shan. By controlling the river the Israelites could prevent the escape of the fleeing Midianites (see note on 3:28). *Beth Barah.* Exact location unknown, but it must have been some distance down the river. Gideon's pursuit of the enemy across the river took him to Succoth, a town near the Jabbok River (8:5).
7:25 *Oreb.* Means "raven" (see Isa 10:26). *Zeeb.* Means

"wolf." *heads.* Frequently parts of the bodies of dead victims, such as heads, hands (8:6) and foreskins (1Sa 18:25), were cut off and brought back as a kind of body count.
8:1 *Ephraimites.* Contrast Gideon, who placates the wrath of this tribe (vv. 2–3), with Jephthah, who brings humiliation and defeat to it (12:1–6).
8:2 *gleanings.* Leftover grain after the main gathering of the harvest (see note on Ru 1:22). Here Gideon implies that Ephraim has accomplished more than he and all the other forces involved in the initial attack. *Abiezer.* Gideon's clan (see note on 6:11). The name means "My (divine) Father is helper" or "My (divine) Father is strong."
8:3 *their resentment . . . subsided.* "A gentle answer turns away wrath" (Pr 15:1).
8:5 *kings of Midian.* Zebah and Zalmunna may have belonged to different Midianite tribes (see Nu 31:8).
8:6 *hands.* See note on 7:25. *Why should we give bread . . . ?* The officials of Succoth doubted Gideon's ability to defeat the Midianite coalition and feared reprisal if they gave his army food.
8:8 *Peniel.* The place where Jacob had wrestled with God (Ge 32:30–31).

tioned him, and the young man wrote down for him the names of the seventy-seven officials of Succoth, [e] the elders [f] of the town. [15]Then Gideon came and said to the men of Succoth, "Here are Zebah and Zalmunna, about whom you taunted me by saying, 'Do you already have the hands of Zebah and Zalmunna in your possession? Why should we give bread to your exhausted men?[g] '" [16]He took the elders of the town and taught the men of Succoth a lesson [h] by punishing them with desert thorns and briers. [17]He also pulled down the tower of Peniel [i] and killed the men of the town. [j]

[18]Then he asked Zebah and Zalmunna, "What kind of men did you kill at Tabor? [k] "

"Men like you," they answered, "each one with the bearing of a prince."

[19]Gideon replied, "Those were my brothers, the sons of my own mother. As surely as the LORD lives, [l] if you had spared their lives, I would not kill you." [20]Turning to Jether, his oldest son, he said, "Kill them!" But Jether did not draw his sword, because he was only a boy and was afraid.

[21]Zebah and Zalmunna said, "Come, do it yourself. 'As is the man, so is his strength.'" So Gideon stepped forward and killed them, and took the ornaments [m] off their camels' necks.

Gideon's Ephod

[22]The Israelites said to Gideon, "Rule over us—you, your son and your grandson—because you have saved us out of the hand of Midian."

[23]But Gideon told them, "I will not rule over you, nor will my son rule over you. The LORD will rule [n] over you." [24]And he said, "I do have one request, that each of you give me an earring [o] from your share of the plunder. [p] " (It was the custom of the Ishmaelites [q] to wear gold earrings.)

[25]They answered, "We'll be glad to give them." So they spread out a garment, and each man threw a ring from his plunder onto it. [26]The weight of the gold rings he asked for came to seventeen hundred shekels, [i] not counting the ornaments, the pendants and the purple garments worn by the kings of Midian or the chains [r] that were on their camels' necks. [27]Gideon made the gold into an ephod, [s] which he placed in Ophrah, [t] his town. All Israel prostituted themselves by worshiping it there, and it became a snare [u] to Gideon and his family. [v]

Gideon's Death

[28]Thus Midian was subdued before the Israelites and did not raise its head [w] again. During Gideon's lifetime, the land enjoyed peace [x] forty years.

[29]Jerub-Baal [y] son of Joash [z] went back home to live. [30]He had seventy sons [a] of his own, for he had many wives. [31]His concubine, [b] who lived in Shechem, also bore him a son, whom he named Abimelech. [c] [32]Gideon son of Joash died at a good old age [d] and was buried in the tomb of his father Joash in Ophrah of the Abiezrites.

[33]No sooner had Gideon died than the Israelites again prostituted themselves to the Baals. [e] They set up Baal-Berith [f] as their god [g] and [34]did not remember [h] the LORD their God, who had rescued them from the hands of all their enemies on every side. [35]They also failed to show kind-

i26 That is, about 43 pounds (about 19.5 kilograms)

8:14 *e*ver 6
/S Ex 3:16
8:15 *g*ver 6
8:16 *h*1Sa 14:12
8:17 *i*S ver 8 /ver 9
8:18 *k*S Jos 19:22
8:19 *l*S Nu 14:21
8:21 *m*ver 26;
Isa 3:18
8:23 *n*S Ex 16:8;
S Nu 11:20;
1Sa 12:12

8:24 *o*S Ge 35:4
*p*S Ge 49:27
*q*S Ge 16:11
8:26 *r*S ver 21
8:27 *s*S Ex 25:7;
Jdg 17:5; 18:14
*t*S Jos 18:23
*u*S Ex 10:7
*v*S Ex 32:2
8:28 *w*Ps 83:2
*x*S Jdg 3:11
8:29 *y*S Jdg 6:32
*z*S Jdg 6:11
8:30 *a*Jdg 9:2,5,
18,24; 12:14;
2Ki 10:1
8:31 *b*S Ge 22:24
*c*Jdg 9:1; 10:1;
2Sa 11:21
8:32 *d*S Ge 15:15
8:33 *e*S Jdg 2:11,
13,19 /Jdg 9:4
*g*Jdg 9:27,46
8:34 *h*S Jdg 3:7;
S Ne 9:17

8:19 *sons of my own mother.* In an age when men often had several wives it was necessary to distinguish between full brothers and half brothers.

8:21 *do it yourself.* Dying at the hands of a boy may have been considered a disgrace (see 1Sa 17:42). *ornaments.* Crescent necklaces, as in Isa 3:18.

8:23 *I will not rule . . . The LORD will rule.* Gideon, like Samuel (1Sa 8:4–20), rejected the establishment of a monarchy because he regarded it as a replacement of the Lord's rule. God's rule over Israel (theocracy) is a central issue in Judges.

8:24 *earring.* Or possibly "nose ring" (see Ge 24:47; Eze 16:12). *Ishmaelites.* Related to the Midianites (Ge 25:1–2) and sometimes identified with them (vv. 22,24; Ge 37:25–28; 39:1). See note on Ge 37:25.

8:27 *ephod.* Sometimes a holy garment associated with the priesthood (Ex 28:6–30; 39:2–26; Lev 8:7), at other times a pagan object associated with idols (17:5; 18:14,17).

8:28 *forty years.* A conventional number of years for a generation (see Introduction: Background).

8:29 *Jerub-Baal.* See note on 6:32.

8:30 *seventy sons.* A sign of power and prosperity (see 12:14; 2Ki 10:1).

8:31 *concubine.* She was originally a slave in his household (9:18; see note on Ge 16:2). *Abimelech.* Appears elsewhere as a royal title (Ge 20:2; 26:1; Ps 34 title) and means "My (divine) Father is King." Gideon, in naming his son, acknowledges that the Lord (here called "Father") is King.

8:32 *at a good old age.* A phrase used elsewhere only of Abraham (Ge 15:15; 25:8) and David (1Ch 29:28).

8:33 *Baals.* See notes on 2:11,13. *Baal-Berith.* Means "lord of the covenant"; the same deity is called El-Berith ("god of the covenant") in 9:46. There was a temple dedicated to him (see 9:4) in Shechem. The word "covenant" in his name probably refers to a solemn treaty that bound together a league of Canaanite cities whose people worshiped him as their god. Ironically, Shechem (v. 31), near Mount Ebal, was the site at which Joshua had twice renewed the Lord's covenant with Israel after they had entered Canaan (Jos 8:30–35; 24:25–27). See also note on 2:11.

ness to the family of Jerub-Baal[i] (that is, Gideon) for all the good things he had done for them.[j]

Abimelech

9 Abimelech[k] son of Jerub-Baal[l] went to his mother's brothers in Shechem and said to them and to all his mother's clan, [2]"Ask all the citizens of Shechem, 'Which is better for you: to have all seventy of Jerub-Baal's sons rule over you, or just one man?' Remember, I am your flesh and blood.[m]"

[3]When the brothers repeated all this to the citizens of Shechem, they were inclined to follow Abimelech, for they said, "He is our brother." [4]They gave him seventy shekels[k] of silver from the temple of Baal-Berith,[n] and Abimelech used it to hire reckless adventurers,[o] who became his followers. [5]He went to his father's home in Ophrah and on one stone murdered his seventy brothers,[p] the sons of Jerub-Baal. But Jotham,[q] the youngest son of Jerub-Baal, escaped by hiding.[r] [6]Then all the citizens of Shechem and Beth Millo[s] gathered beside the great tree[t] at the pillar in Shechem to crown Abimelech king.

[7]When Jotham[u] was told about this, he climbed up on the top of Mount Gerizim[v] and shouted to them, "Listen to me, citizens of Shechem, so that God may listen to you. [8]One day the trees went out to anoint a king for themselves. They said to the olive tree, 'Be our king.'

[9]"But the olive tree answered, 'Should I give up my oil, by which both gods and men are honored, to hold sway over the trees?'

[10]"Next, the trees said to the fig tree, 'Come and be our king.'

[11]"But the fig tree replied, 'Should I give up my fruit, so good and sweet, to hold sway over the trees?'

[12]"Then the trees said to the vine, 'Come and be our king.'

[13]"But the vine answered, 'Should I give up my wine,[w] which cheers both gods and men, to hold sway over the trees?'

[14]"Finally all the trees said to the thornbush, 'Come and be our king.'

[15]"The thornbush said to the trees, 'If you really want to anoint me king over you, come and take refuge in my shade;[x] but if not, then let fire come out[y] of the thornbush and consume the cedars of Lebanon!'[z]

[16]"Now if you have acted honorably and in good faith when you made Abimelech king, and if you have been fair to Jerub-Baal and his family, and if you have treated

Cross references

8:35 [i]S Jdg 6:32 / [j]Jdg 9:16
9:1 [k]S Jdg 8:31 / [l]S Jdg 6:32
9:2 [m]S Ge 29:14
9:4 [n]S Jdg 8:33 / [o]Jdg 11:3; 1Sa 25:25; 2Ch 13:7; Job 30:8
9:5 [p]S Jdg 8:30 qver 7,21,57 / [r]2Ki 11:2; 2Ch 22:9
9:6 [s]ver 20; 2Ki 12:20 / [t]S Ge 12:6; S Jdg 4:11
9:7 [u]S ver 5 / [v]S Dt 11:29; Jn 4:20
9:13 [w]S Ge 14:18; Ecc 2:3; SS 4:10
9:15 [x]Isa 30:2 / [y]ver 20 / [z]S Dt 3:25; 1Ki 5:6; Ps 29:5; 92:12; Isa 2:13

[k]4 That is, about 1 3/4 pounds (about 0.8 kilogram)

9:1–57 The stories of Gideon and Abimelech form the literary center of Judges (see Introduction: Literary Features). Abimelech, who tried to set himself up like a Canaanite city king with the help of Baal (v. 4), stands in sharp contrast to his father Gideon (Jerub-Baal), who had attacked Baal worship and insisted that the Lord ruled over Israel. Abimelech attempted this Canaanite revival in the very place where Joshua had earlier reaffirmed Israel's allegiance to the Lord (Jos 24:14–27). In every respect Abimelech was the antithesis of the Lord's appointed judges.
9:1 *Shechem.* See note on Ge 33:18. Ruins dating from the Canaanite era give evidence of a sacred area, probably to be associated with the temple of Baal-Berith or El-Berith (vv. 4,46). Archaeological evidence, which is compatible with the destruction of Shechem by Abimelech, indicates that its sacred area was never rebuilt after this time.
9:2 *citizens.* The singular form of the Hebrew for this word is *ba'al.* It means "lord" or "owner" and probably refers here to the aristocracy or landowners of the city. *flesh and blood.* Being half-Canaanite, Abimelech intimated that it was in their best interest to make him king rather than be under the rule of Gideon's 70 sons. The following he gathered was based on this relationship and became a threat to the people of Israel.
9:4 *from the temple.* Ancient temples served as depositories for personal and civic funds. The payments of vows and penalties, as well as gifts, were also part of the temple treasury. The temple of Baal-Berith is probably to be identified with a large building found at Shechem by archaeologists. *reckless adventurers.* Use of mercenaries to accomplish political or military goals was common in ancient times. Others who used them are Jephthah (11:3), David (1Sa

22:1–2), Absalom (2Sa 15:1), Adonijah (1Ki 1:5), Rezon (1Ki 11:23–24) and Jeroboam (2Ch 13:6–7).
9:5 *on one stone.* Abimelech's 70 brothers were slaughtered like sacrificial animals (see 13:19–20; 1Sa 14:33–34). In effect he inaugurated his kingship by using his Israelite half brothers as his coronation sacrifices (see 2Sa 15:10,12; 1Ki 1:5,9; 3:4).
9:6 *Beth Millo.* "Millo" is derived from a Hebrew verb meaning "to fill" and probably refers to the earthen fill used to erect a platform on which walls and other large structures were built. Beth Millo may be identical to the "stronghold" of v. 46. *great tree.* See Jos 24:25–26; see also note on Ge 12:6.
9:7 *top.* Probably a ledge that overlooked the city.
9:8 *trees went out.* Fables of this type, in which inanimate objects speak and act, were popular among Eastern peoples of that time (see 2Ki 14:9).
9:9–13 The olive tree, the fig tree and the vine were all plants that produced fruit of great importance to the people of the Near East.
9:13 *gods.* It was commonly believed that the gods participated in such human experiences as drinking wine.
9:14 *thornbush.* Probably the well-known buckthorn, a scraggly bush common in the hills of Palestine and a constant menace to farming. It produced nothing of value and was an apt figure for Abimelech.
9:15 *shade.* Ironically, in offering shade to the trees, the thornbush symbolized the traditional role of kings as protectors of their subjects (see Isa 30:2–3; 32:1–2; La 4:20; Da 4:12). *cedars of Lebanon.* The most valuable of Near Eastern trees, here symbolic of the leading men of Shechem (see v. 20).

him as he deserves— [17]and to think that my father fought for you, risked[a] his life to rescue you from the hand of Midian [18](but today you have revolted against my father's family, murdered his seventy sons[b] on a single stone, and made Abimelech, the son of his slave girl, king over the citizens of Shechem because he is your brother)— [19]if then you have acted honorably and in good faith toward Jerub-Baal and his family today,[c] may Abimelech be your joy, and may you be his, too! [20]But if you have not, let fire come out[d] from Abimelech and consume you, citizens of Shechem[e] and Beth Millo,[f] and let fire come out from you, citizens of Shechem and Beth Millo, and consume Abimelech!"

[21]Then Jotham[g] fled, escaping to Beer,[h] and he lived there because he was afraid of his brother Abimelech.

[22]After Abimelech had governed Israel three years, [23]God sent an evil spirit[i] between Abimelech and the citizens of Shechem, who acted treacherously against Abimelech. [24]God did this in order that the crime against Jerub-Baal's seventy sons,[j] the shedding[k] of their blood, might be avenged[l] on their brother Abimelech and on the citizens of Shechem, who had helped him[m] murder his brothers. [25]In opposition to him these citizens of Shechem set men on the hilltops to ambush and rob everyone who passed by, and this was reported to Abimelech.

[26]Now Gaal son of Ebed[n] moved with his brothers into Shechem, and its citizens put their confidence in him. [27]After they had gone out into the fields and gathered the grapes and trodden[o] them, they held a festival in the temple of their god.[p] While they were eating and drinking, they cursed Abimelech. [28]Then Gaal son of Ebed[q] said, "Who[r] is Abimelech, and who is Shechem, that we should be subject to him? Isn't he Jerub-Baal's son, and isn't Zebul his deputy? Serve the men of Hamor,[s] Shechem's father! Why should we serve

Abimelech? [29]If only this people were under my command![t] Then I would get rid of him. I would say to Abimelech, 'Call out your whole army!' "[1] [u]

[30]When Zebul the governor of the city heard what Gaal son of Ebed said, he was very angry. [31]Under cover he sent messengers to Abimelech, saying, "Gaal son of Ebed and his brothers have come to Shechem and are stirring up the city against you. [32]Now then, during the night you and your men should come and lie in wait[v] in the fields. [33]In the morning at sunrise, advance against the city. When Gaal and his men come out against you, do whatever your hand finds to do.[w]"

[34]So Abimelech and all his troops set out by night and took up concealed positions near Shechem in four companies. [35]Now Gaal son of Ebed had gone out and was standing at the entrance to the city gate[x] just as Abimelech and his soldiers came out from their hiding place.[y]

[36]When Gaal saw them, he said to Zebul, "Look, people are coming down from the tops of the mountains!"

Zebul replied, "You mistake the shadows of the mountains for men."

[37]But Gaal spoke up again: "Look, people are coming down from the center of the land, and a company is coming from the direction of the soothsayers' tree."

[38]Then Zebul said to him, "Where is your big talk now, you who said, 'Who is Abimelech that we should be subject to him?' Aren't these the men you ridiculed?[z] Go out and fight them!"

[39]So Gaal led out[m] the citizens of Shechem and fought Abimelech. [40]Abimelech chased him, and many fell wounded in the flight—all the way to the entrance to the gate. [41]Abimelech stayed in Arumah, and Zebul drove Gaal and his brothers out of Shechem.

Cross references (center column):

9:17 [a]Jdg 12:3; 1Sa 19:5; 28:21; Job 13:14; Ps 119:109
9:18 [b]S Jdg 8:30
9:19 [c]ver 16
9:20 [d]ver 15 [e]ver 45 [f]S ver 6
9:21 [g]S ver 5 [h]Nu 21:16
9:23 [i]1Sa 16:14, 23; 18:10; 19:9; 1Ki 22:22
9:24 [j]S Jdg 8:30 [k]S Ge 9:6; Nu 35:33; 1Ki 2:32 [l]ver 56-57 [m]Dt 27:25
9:26 [n]ver 28,31, 41
9:27 [o]Isa 16:10; Am 5:11; 9:13 [p]S Jdg 8:33
9:28 [q]S ver 26 [r]1Sa 25:10 [s]S Ge 33:19

9:29 [t]2Sa 15:4 [u]ver 38
9:32 [v]Jos 8:2
9:33 [w]1Sa 10:7
9:35 [x]S Jos 2:5 [y]Ps 32:7; Isa 28:15,17; Jer 49:10
9:38 [z]ver 28-29

---

[1]29 Septuagint; Hebrew *him.*" Then he said to Abimelech, "Call out your whole army!"   [m]39 Or Gaal went out in the sight of

---

9:20 *fire come out ... and consume.* A grim prediction that Abimelech and the people of Shechem would destroy each other. Fire spreads rapidly through bramble bushes and brings about swift destruction (see Ex 22:6; Isa 9:18).
9:21 *Beer.* A very common name, meaning "a well."
9:22 *Israel.* Those Israelites who recognized Abimelech's authority, mainly in the vicinity of Shechem.
9:23 *evil spirit.* Perhaps a spirit of distrust and bitterness. The Hebrew for "spirit" is often used to describe an attitude or disposition. *acted treacherously.* The one who founded his kingdom by treachery is himself undone by treachery.
9:26 *put their confidence in him.* Just as the fickle population had followed Abimelech, so they are now swayed by the deceptive proposals of Gaal.

9:27 *held a festival.* The vintage harvest was one of the most joyous times of the year (see Isa 16:9–10; Jer 25:30), but festivals and celebrations held at pagan temples often degenerated into debauched drinking affairs.
9:28 *Hamor.* The Hivite ruler who had founded the city of Shechem (34:2; Jos 24:32).
9:32 *lie in wait.* Ambush succeeded against Gibeah in Benjamin (20:37) and against Ai (Jos 8:2).
9:34 *four companies.* Smaller segments meant less chance of detection. Also, attack from several directions was good strategy.
9:37 *center of the land.* See note on Eze 38:12. *soothsayers' tree.* Probably a sacred tree in some way related to the temple of Baal-Berith (see note on Ge 12:6).

⁴²The next day the people of Shechem went out to the fields, and this was reported to Abimelech. ⁴³So he took his men, divided them into three companies[a] and set an ambush[b] in the fields. When he saw the people coming out of the city, he rose to attack them. ⁴⁴Abimelech and the companies with him rushed forward to a position at the entrance to the city gate. Then two companies rushed upon those in the fields and struck them down. ⁴⁵All that day Abimelech pressed his attack against the city until he had captured it and killed its people. Then he destroyed the city[c] and scattered salt[d] over it.

⁴⁶On hearing this, the citizens in the tower of Shechem went into the stronghold of the temple[e] of El-Berith. ⁴⁷When Abimelech heard that they had assembled there, ⁴⁸he and all his men went up Mount Zalmon.[f] He took an ax and cut off some branches, which he lifted to his shoulders. He ordered the men with him, "Quick! Do what you have seen me do!" ⁴⁹So all the men cut branches and followed Abimelech. They piled them against the stronghold and set it on fire over the people inside. So all the people in the tower of Shechem, about a thousand men and women, also died.

⁵⁰Next Abimelech went to Thebez[g] and besieged it and captured it. ⁵¹Inside the city, however, was a strong tower, to which all the men and women—all the people of the city—fled. They locked themselves in and climbed up on the tower roof. ⁵²Abimelech went to the tower and stormed it. But as he approached the en-

trance to the tower to set it on fire, ⁵³a woman dropped an upper millstone on his head and cracked his skull.[h]

⁵⁴Hurriedly he called to his armor-bearer, "Draw your sword and kill me,[i] so that they can't say, 'A woman killed him.'" So his servant ran him through, and he died. ⁵⁵When the Israelites saw that Abimelech was dead, they went home.

⁵⁶Thus God repaid the wickedness that Abimelech had done to his father by murdering his seventy brothers. ⁵⁷God also made the men of Shechem pay for all their wickedness.[j] The curse of Jotham[k] son of Jerub-Baal came on them.

Tola

10 After the time of Abimelech[l] a man of Issachar,[m] Tola son of Puah,[n] the son of Dodo, rose to save[o] Israel. He lived in Shamir,[p] in the hill country of Ephraim. ²He led[n] Israel twenty-three years; then he died, and was buried in Shamir.

Jair

³He was followed by Jair[q] of Gilead, who led Israel twenty-two years. ⁴He had thirty sons, who rode thirty donkeys.[r] They controlled thirty towns in Gilead, which to this day are called Havvoth Jair.[o][s] ⁵When Jair[t] died, he was buried in Kamon.

Jephthah

⁶Again the Israelites did evil in the eyes

Cross references (center column):
9:43 aS Jdg 7:16
bJos 8:2
9:45 cver 20
dJer 48:9
9:46 eS Jdg 8:33
9:48 fPs 68:14
9:50 g2Sa 11:21
9:53 h2Sa 11:21
9:54 i1Sa 31:4; 2Sa 1:9
9:57 jver 24; Ps 94:23 kS ver 5
10:1 lS Jdg 8:31 mS Ge 30:18
nS Ge 46:13 oS Jdg 6:14 pJos 15:48
10:3 qS Nu 32:41
10:4 rS Ge 49:11; S 1Ki 1:33 sS Nu 32:41
10:5 tS Nu 32:41

n2 Traditionally *judged*; also in verse 3   o4 Or *called the settlements of Jair*

9:43 *three companies.* See note on 7:16.

9:45 *scattered salt over it.* To condemn it to perpetual barrenness and desolation (see Dt 29:23; Ps 107:33–34; Jer 17:6; Zep 2:9).

9:46 *stronghold.* Probably the Beth Millo of v. 6. *El-Berith.* Baal-Berith (v. 4).

9:49 *set it on fire.* In fulfillment of Jotham's curse (v. 20).

9:53 *woman.* While the men used bows, arrows and spears, women helped to defend the tower by dropping heavy stones on those who came near it. *upper millstone.* See note on 3:16. The upper, revolving stone of a mill was circular, with a hole in the center. Grinding grain was women's work (see Ex 11:5), usually considered too lowly for men to perform (see 16:21). Abimelech was killed by a woman using a domestic implement (see also 4:21).

9:54 *armor-bearer.* A military leader usually had a young man carry his shield and spear (see 1Sa 14:6; 31:4). *A woman killed him.* It was considered a disgrace for a soldier to die at the hands of a woman. Abimelech's shameful death was long remembered (2Sa 11:21).

9:56 *God repaid.* God was in control of the events. As Israel's true King, he brought Abimelech's wickedness to a quick and shameful end.

9:57 *curse of Jotham.* See v. 20.

10:1 *a man of Issachar, Tola son of Puah.* Tola and Puah

bear names of two of the sons of Issachar (Ge 46:13; Nu 26:23; 1Ch 7:1).

10:3 *Jair.* Since Jair came from Gilead (the territory assigned to Manasseh) and since a descendant of Manasseh bore the same name (Nu 32:41; Dt 3:14; 1Ki 4:13), it appears that Jair was a Manassite.

10:4 *thirty sons . . . thirty donkeys . . . thirty towns.* Evidence of wealth and position. *Havvoth Jair.* See NIV text note.

10:6—12:7 Israel now turned to Jephthah, a social outcast whom they had driven from the land and caused to become an outlaw without an inheritance in Israel. The author notes this to Israel's shame. The account of Jephthah's judgeship balances that of Deborah in the story of the judges (see note on 4:1–5:31; see also Introduction: Literary Features).

10:6 *gods of Aram.* The chief gods were Hadad (Baal), Mot, Anath and Rimmon. *gods of Sidon.* The Sidonians worshiped essentially the same gods as the Canaanites (see notes on 2:11,13). *gods of Moab.* The chief deity of Moab was Chemosh. *gods of the Ammonites.* Molech was the chief Ammonite deity (see 1Ki 11:7) and was sometimes worshiped by the offering of human sacrifice (Lev 18:21; 20:2–5; 2Ki 23:10). This god is also called Milcom (see NIV text notes on 1Ki 11:5; 2Ki 23:13). Both Molech and Milcom are forms of a Semitic word for "king." *gods of the*

of the LORD.[u] They served the Baals and the Ashtoreths,[v] and the gods of Aram,[w] the gods of Sidon,[x] the gods of Moab, the gods of the Ammonites[y][z] and the gods of the Philistines.[a] And because the Israelites forsook the LORD[b] and no longer served him, [7]he became angry[c] with them. He sold them[d] into the hands of the Philistines and the Ammonites, [8]who that year shattered and crushed them. For eighteen years they oppressed all the Israelites on the east side of the Jordan in Gilead,[e] the land of the Amorites. [9]The Ammonites also crossed the Jordan to fight against Judah,[f] Benjamin and the house of Ephraim;[g] and Israel was in great distress. [10]Then the Israelites cried[h] out to the LORD, "We have sinned[i] against you, forsaking our God and serving the Baals."[j]

[11]The LORD replied, "When the Egyptians,[k] the Amorites,[l] the Ammonites,[m] the Philistines,[n] [12]the Sidonians, the Amalekites[o] and the Maonites[p][p] oppressed you[q] and you cried to me for help, did I not save you from their hands? [13]But you have forsaken[r] me and served other gods,[s] so I will no longer save you. [14]Go and cry out to the gods you have chosen. Let them save[t] you when you are in trouble![u]"

[15]But the Israelites said to the LORD, "We have sinned. Do with us whatever you think best,[v] but please rescue us now." [16]Then they got rid of the foreign gods among them and served the LORD.[w] And he could bear Israel's misery[x] no longer.[y]

[17]When the Ammonites were called to arms and camped in Gilead, the Israelites assembled and camped at Mizpah.[z] [18]The leaders of the people of Gilead said to each other, "Whoever will launch the attack against the Ammonites will be the head[a] of all those living in Gilead."

11 Jephthah[b] the Gileadite was a mighty warrior.[c] His father was Gilead;[d] his mother was a prostitute.[e] [2]Gilead's wife also bore him sons, and when they were grown up, they drove Jephthah away. "You are not going to get any inheritance in our family," they said, "because you are the son of another woman." [3]So Jephthah fled from his brothers and settled in the land of Tob,[f] where a group of adventurers[g] gathered around him and followed him.

[4]Some time later, when the Ammonites[h] made war on Israel, [5]the elders of Gilead went to get Jephthah from the land of Tob. [6]"Come," they said, "be our commander, so we can fight the Ammonites."

[7]Jephthah said to them, "Didn't you hate me and drive me from my father's house?[i] Why do you come to me now, when you're in trouble?"

[8]The elders of Gilead said to him, "Nevertheless, we are turning to you now; come with us to fight the Ammonites, and you will be our head[j] over all who live in Gilead."

[9]Jephthah answered, "Suppose you take me back to fight the Ammonites and the LORD gives them to me—will I really be your head?"

[10]The elders of Gilead replied, "The LORD is our witness;[k] we will certainly do as you say." [11]So Jephthah went with the elders[l] of Gilead, and the people made him head and commander over them. And he repeated[m] all his words before the LORD in Mizpah.[n]

[12]Then Jephthah sent messengers to the

Cross references (center column):

10:6 [u]S Jdg 2:11
[v]S Jdg 2:13
[w]Eze 27:16
[x]S Ge 10:15
[y]S Ge 19:38
[z]S Nu 21:29
[a]S Ge 26:1;
S Jdg 2:12
10:7 [b]S Dt 32:15
[c]S Dt 31:17
[d]S Dt 32:30
10:8 [e]S Jos 12:2
10:9 [f]ver 17;
Jdg 11:4
[g]Jdg 1:22
10:10 [h]S Jdg 3:9
[i]S Ex 9:27;
Ps 32:5; Jer 3:25;
8:14; 14:20
[j]Jer 2:27
10:11 [k]Ex 14:30
[l]S Ge 14:7
[m]S Jdg 3:13
[n]S Jdg 3:31
10:12 [o]S Ge 14:7
[p]S Jos 15:55
[q]S Jdg 4:3
10:13
[r]S Dt 32:15
[s]Jer 11:10; 13:10
10:14 [t]Isa 44:17;
57:13 [u]Dt 32:37;
Jer 2:28; 11:12;
Hab 2:18
10:15 [v]1Sa 3:18;
2Sa 10:12; 15:26;
Job 1:21; Isa 39:8
10:16
[w]Jos 24:23;
Jer 18:8 [x]Isa 63:9
[y]S Dt 32:36
10:17
[z]S Ge 31:49;
Jdg 11:29
10:18 [a]Jdg 11:8,9
11:1 [b]Jdg 12:1;
1Sa 12:11;
Heb 11:32
[c]Jdg 6:12
[d]Nu 26:29
[e]S Ge 38:15
11:3 [f]ver 5;
2Sa 10:6,8
[g]S Jdg 9:4
11:4 [h]S Jdg 10:9
11:7 [i]S Ge 26:16
11:8 [j]S Jdg 10:18
11:10
[k]S Ge 31:50;
S Isa 1:2
11:11 [l]1Sa 8:4;
2Sa 3:17
[m]Ex 19:9;
1Sa 8:21
[n]S Jos 11:3

---

[p]*12* Hebrew; some Septuagint manuscripts *Midianites*

Philistines. While the Philistines worshiped most of the Canaanite gods, their most popular deities appear to have been Dagon and Baal-Zebub. The name Dagon is the same as a Hebrew word for "grain," suggesting that he was a vegetation deity. He was worshiped in Babylonia as early as the second millennium B.C. Baal-Zebub was worshiped in Ekron (2Ki 1:2–3,6,16). The name means "lord of the flies," a deliberate change by followers of Baal (Yahweh) to ridicule and protest the worship of Baal-Zebul ("Baal the prince"), a name known from ancient Canaanite texts (see Mt 10:25; 12:24 and NIV text notes).

10:7 *Philistines.* The account of Philistine oppression is resumed in 13:1.

10:11 *The LORD replied.* See note on 2:1. The Lord rebuked Israel for forgetting that he had delivered them from their oppressors in Canaan (see notes on 2:16–19; 6:8).

10:12 *Maonites.* See NIV text note; or perhaps the same as the Meunites, who along with the Philistines and Arabs opposed Israel (2Ch 26:7).

10:17 *Mizpah.* Means "watchtower." Several places bore this name. Jephthah's headquarters was a town or fortress in Gilead (11:11) called "Mizpah of Gilead" (11:29). It may have been the same as Ramath Mizpah (Jos 13:26), located about 30 miles east of Beth Shan.

10:18 The Gileadites wanted to resist the Ammonite incursion but lacked the courageous military leadership to press their cause. *people.* Fighting men.

11:1 *his mother was a prostitute.* Therefore Jephthah was a social outcast.

11:3 *Tob.* The men of Tob were later allied with the Ammonites against David (2Sa 10:6–8). *adventurers.* See note on 9:4.

11:8 *be our head.* In addition to their initial offer of military command during the war with Ammon (v. 6), the Gileadites now also offer to make Jephthah regional head after the fighting is over.

11:11 The proposal of the elders was ratified by the people, a process followed in the election of Saul (1Sa 11:15), Rehoboam (1Ki 12:1) and Jeroboam (1Ki 12:20).

Ammonite king with the question: "What do you have against us that you have attacked our country?"

13The king of the Ammonites answered Jephthah's messengers, "When Israel came up out of Egypt, they took away my land from the Arnon o to the Jabbok, p all the way to the Jordan. Now give it back peaceably."

14Jephthah sent back messengers to the Ammonite king, 15saying:

"This is what Jephthah says: Israel did not take the land of Moab q or the land of the Ammonites. r 16But when they came up out of Egypt, Israel went through the desert to the Red Sea q s and on to Kadesh. t 17Then Israel sent messengers u to the king of Edom, saying, 'Give us permission to go through your country,' v but the king of Edom would not listen. They sent also to the king of Moab, w and he refused. x So Israel stayed at Kadesh.

18"Next they traveled through the desert, skirted the lands of Edom y and Moab, passed along the eastern side z of the country of Moab, and camped on the other side of the Arnon. a They did not enter the territory of Moab, for the Arnon was its border.

19"Then Israel sent messengers b to Sihon king of the Amorites, who ruled in Heshbon, c and said to him, 'Let us pass through your country to our own place.' d 20Sihon, however, did not trust Israel r to pass through his territory. He mustered all his men and encamped at Jahaz and fought with Israel. e

21"Then the LORD, the God of Israel, gave Sihon and all his men into Israel's hands, and they defeated them. Israel took over all the land of the Amorites who lived in that country, 22capturing all of it from the Arnon to the Jabbok and from the desert to the Jordan. f

23"Now since the LORD, the God of Israel, has driven the Amorites out before his people Israel, what right have you to take it over? 24Will you not take what your god Chemosh g gives you? Likewise, whatever the LORD our God has given us, h we will possess. 25Are you better than Balak son of Zippor, i king of Moab? Did he ever quarrel with Israel or fight with them? j 26For three hundred years Israel occupied k Heshbon, Aroer, l the surrounding settlements and all the towns along the Arnon. Why didn't you retake them during that time? 27I have not wronged you, but you are doing me wrong by waging war against me. Let the LORD, the Judge, s m decide n the dispute this day between the Israelites and the Ammonites. o "

28The king of Ammon, however, paid no attention to the message Jephthah sent him.

29Then the Spirit p of the LORD came upon Jephthah. He crossed Gilead and Manasseh, passed through Mizpah q of Gilead, and from there he advanced against the Ammonites. r 30And Jephthah made a vow s to the LORD: "If you give the Ammonites into my hands, 31whatever comes out of the door of my house to meet me

Cross references (center column)

11:13
oS Nu 21:13
pS Nu 21:24
11:15 qDt 2:9
rDt 2:19
11:16
sNu 14:25;
S Dt 1:40
tS Ge 14:7
11:17 uver 19;
S Ge 32:3;
Nu 20:14
vS Nu 20:17
wJer 48:1
xS Jos 24:9
11:18
yS Nu 20:21
zDt 2:8
aS Nu 21:13
11:19 bS ver 17
cS Jos 12:2
dNu 21:21-22
11:20 eNu 21:23

11:22
fNu 21:21-26;
S Dt 2:26
11:24
gS Nu 21:29;
S Jos 3:10
hDt 2:36
11:25 iNu 22:2
jS Jos 24:9
11:26 kNu 21:25
lS Nu 32:34;
S Jos 13:9
11:27
mS Ge 18:25
nS Ge 16:5
oS 2Ch 20:12
11:29 pS Jdg 3:10
qS Ge 31:49
rS Jdg 10:17
11:30
sS Ge 28:20;
Nu 30:10;
1Sa 1:11; Pr 31:2

q16 Hebrew Yam Suph; that is, Sea of Reeds   r20 Or however, would not make an agreement for Israel   s27 Or Ruler

---

11:13 *my land.* When the Israelites had first approached Canaan, this area was ruled by the Amorite king Sihon, who had taken it from the Moabites (Nu 21:29). The Ammonites had since become dominant over Moab and now claimed all previous Moabite territory.

11:14–27 Jephthah responded in accordance with international policies of the time; his letter is a classic example of contemporary international correspondence. It also reflects— and appeals to—the common recognition that the god(s) of a people established and protected their political boundaries and decided all boundary disputes. Jephthah's defense of Israel's claim to the land is threefold: (1) Israel took it from Sihon king of the Amorites, not from the Ammonites (vv. 15–22); (2) the Lord gave the land to Israel (vv. 23–25); (3) Israel had long possessed it (vv. 26–27).

11:16 *Kadesh.* Kadesh Barnea; see note on Nu 20:1.

11:21 *LORD, the God of Israel.* War was viewed not only in military terms but also as a contest between deities (see v. 24; Ex 12:12; Nu 33:4).

11:24 *Chemosh.* Reference to Chemosh, the chief deity of the Moabites, indicates either that at this time the king of

Ammon also ruled Moab or that there was a military confederacy of the two peoples.

11:25 *Balak.* See Nu 22–24.

11:26 *three hundred years.* For the relevance of this phrase in establishing the time span for Judges see Introduction: Background.

11:27 *Judge.* See 1Sa 24:15. As the divine Judge, the Lord is the final court of appeal. It is significant that in the book of Judges the singular noun "judge" is found only here, where it is used of the Lord, Israel's true Judge.

11:29 *Spirit of the LORD.* See note on 3:10. In the OT the unique empowering of the Spirit was given to an individual primarily to enable him to carry out the special responsibilities God had given him.

11:30 *made a vow.* A common practice among the Israelites (see Ge 28:20; 1Sa 1:11; 2Sa 15:8). The precise nature of this vow has been the subject of wide speculation, but v. 31 indicates the promise of a burnt offering and leads to the conclusion that Jephthah probably offered his daughter as a human sacrifice (v. 39). A vow was not to be broken (see Nu 30:2; Dt 23:21–23; see also Ecc 5:4–5).

when I return in triumph[t] from the Ammonites will be the LORD's, and I will sacrifice it as a burnt offering.[u]"

[32]Then Jephthah went over to fight the Ammonites, and the LORD gave them into his hands. [33]He devastated twenty towns from Aroer to the vicinity of Minnith,[v] as far as Abel Keramim. Thus Israel subdued Ammon.

[34]When Jephthah returned to his home in Mizpah, who should come out to meet him but his daughter, dancing[w] to the sound of tambourines![x] She was an only child.[y] Except for her he had neither son nor daughter. [35]When he saw her, he tore his clothes[z] and cried, "Oh! My daughter! You have made me miserable and wretched, because I have made a vow to the LORD that I cannot break.[a]"

[36]"My father," she replied, "you have given your word to the LORD. Do to me just as you promised,[b] now that the LORD has avenged you[c] of your enemies,[d] the Ammonites. [37]But grant me this one request," she said. "Give me two months to roam the hills and weep with my friends, because I will never marry."

[38]"You may go," he said. And he let her go for two months. She and the girls went into the hills and wept because she would never marry. [39]After the two months, she returned to her father and he did to her as he had vowed. And she was a virgin.

From this comes the Israelite custom [40]that each year the young women of Israel go out for four days to commemorate the daughter of Jephthah the Gileadite.

Jephthah and Ephraim

12 The men of Ephraim called out their forces, crossed over to Zaphon[e] and said to Jephthah,[f] "Why did you go to fight the Ammonites without calling us to go with you?[g] We're going to burn down your house over your head."

[2]Jephthah answered, "I and my people

were engaged in a great struggle with the Ammonites, and although I called, you didn't save me out of their hands. [3]When I saw that you wouldn't help, I took my life in my hands[h] and crossed over to fight the Ammonites, and the LORD gave me the victory[i] over them. Now why have you come up today to fight me?"

[4]Jephthah then called together the men of Gilead[j] and fought against Ephraim. The Gileadites struck them down because the Ephraimites had said, "You Gileadites are renegades from Ephraim and Manasseh.[k]" [5]The Gileadites captured the fords of the Jordan[l] leading to Ephraim, and whenever a survivor of Ephraim said, "Let me cross over," the men of Gilead asked him, "Are you an Ephraimite?" If he replied, "No," [6]they said, "All right, say 'Shibboleth.'" If he said, "Sibboleth," because he could not pronounce the word correctly, they seized him and killed him at the fords of the Jordan. Forty-two thousand Ephraimites were killed at that time.

[7]Jephthah led[t] Israel six years. Then Jephthah the Gileadite died, and was buried in a town in Gilead.

Ibzan, Elon and Abdon

[8]After him, Ibzan of Bethlehem[m] led Israel. [9]He had thirty sons and thirty daughters. He gave his daughters away in marriage to those outside his clan, and for his sons he brought in thirty young women as wives from outside his clan. Ibzan led Israel seven years. [10]Then Ibzan died, and was buried in Bethlehem.

[11]After him, Elon the Zebulunite led Israel ten years. [12]Then Elon died, and was buried in Aijalon[n] in the land of Zebulun. [13]After him, Abdon son of Hillel, from Pirathon,[o] led Israel. [14]He had forty sons and thirty grandsons,[p] who rode on seventy donkeys.[q] He led Israel eight years. [15]Then Abdon son of Hillel died, and was

---

11:31 [t]Ge 28:21
[u]S Ge 8:20;
Lev 1:3;
Jdg 13:16
11:33 [v]Eze 27:17
11:34
[w]S Ex 15:20
[x]S Ge 31:27;
S Ex 15:20
[y]Zec 12:10
11:35 [z]S Nu 14:6
[a]Nu 30:2;
S Dt 23:21;
Ecc 5:2,4,5
11:36 [b]Lk 1:38
[c]S Nu 31:3
[d]2Sa 18:19
12:1 [e]S Jos 13:27
[f]S Jdg 11:1
[g]Jdg 8:1

12:3 [h]S Jdg 9:17
[i]S Dt 20:4
12:4 [j]1Ki 17:1
[k]S Ge 46:20;
Isa 9:21; 19:2
12:5 [l]S Jos 2:7
12:8
[m]S Ge 35:19
12:12
[n]S Jos 10:12
12:13 [o]ver 15;
2Sa 23:30;
1Ch 11:31; 27:14
12:14 [p]S Jdg 8:30
[q]S Jdg 5:10

[t]7 Traditionally *judged*; also in verses 8-14

11:34 *dancing.* It was customary for women to greet armies returning victoriously from battle in this way (see Ex 15:20; 1Sa 18:6).
11:35 *tore his clothes.* A common practice for expressing extreme grief (see Ge 37:34 and note).
11:37 *I will never marry.* To be kept from marrying and rearing children was a bitter prospect for an Israelite girl.
11:39 *Israelite custom.* Probably a local custom, since no other mention of it is found in the OT.
12:1 *burn down your house.* The Philistines issued a similar threat to Samson's wife (14:15). See also 20:48.
12:2 *answered.* Again Jephthah tried diplomacy first (see 11:12,14; see also note on 8:1). *I called.* New information on the sequence of events.
12:6 *Shibboleth.* Ironically, the word meant "floods" (see,

e.g., Ps 69:2,15). Apparently the Israelites east of the Jordan pronounced its initial letter with a strong "sh" sound, while those in Canaan gave it a softer "s" sound. (Peter was similarly betrayed by his accent; see Mt 26:73.)
12:7 *led Israel . . . years.* A new formula for closing out the account of a judge (see note on 3:11; see also Introduction: Literary Features).
12:8 *Bethlehem.* Probably the Bethlehem in western Zebulun.
12:9 *thirty sons and thirty daughters.* See note on 10:4.
12:11 *Elon.* Also the name of a clan in the tribe of Zebulun (Ge 46:14; Nu 26:26).
12:14 *forty sons and thirty grandsons.* A total of 70 (see notes on 8:30; 10:4).
12:15 *hill country of the Amalekites.* See note on 5:14.

buried at Pirathon in Ephraim, in the hill country of the Amalekites. [r]

The Birth of Samson

13 Again the Israelites did evil in the eyes of the LORD, so the LORD delivered them into the hands of the Philistines [s] for forty years. [t]

[2] A certain man of Zorah, [u] named Manoah, [v] from the clan of the Danites, [w] had a wife who was sterile and remained childless. [x] [3] The angel of the LORD [y] appeared to her [z] and said, "You are sterile and childless, but you are going to conceive and have a son. [a] [4] Now see to it that you drink no wine or other fermented drink [b] and that you do not eat anything unclean, [c] [5] because you will conceive and give birth to a son. [d] No razor [e] may be used on his head, because the boy is to be a Nazirite, [f] set apart to God from birth, and he will begin [g] the deliverance of Israel from the hands of the Philistines."

[6] Then the woman went to her husband and told him, "A man of God [h] came to me. He looked like an angel of God, [i] very awesome. [j] I didn't ask him where he came from, and he didn't tell me his name. [7] But he said to me, 'You will conceive and give birth to a son. Now then, drink no wine [k] or other fermented drink [l] and do not eat anything unclean, because the boy will be a Nazirite of God from birth until the day of his death.' [m] "

[8] Then Manoah [n] prayed to the LORD: "O Lord, I beg you, let the man of God [o]

you sent to us come again to teach us how to bring up the boy who is to be born."

[9] God heard Manoah, and the angel of God came again to the woman while she was out in the field; but her husband Manoah was not with her. [10] The woman hurried to tell her husband, "He's here! The man who appeared to me [p] the other day!"

[11] Manoah got up and followed his wife. When he came to the man, he said, "Are you the one who talked to my wife?"

"I am," he said.

[12] So Manoah asked him, "When your words are fulfilled, what is to be the rule for the boy's life and work?"

[13] The angel of the LORD answered, "Your wife must do all that I have told her. [14] She must not eat anything that comes from the grapevine, nor drink any wine or other fermented drink [q] nor eat anything unclean. [r] She must do everything I have commanded her."

[15] Manoah said to the angel of the LORD, "We would like you to stay until we prepare a young goat [s] for you."

[16] The angel of the LORD replied, "Even though you detain me, I will not eat any of your food. But if you prepare a burnt offering, [t] offer it to the LORD." (Manoah did not realize [u] that it was the angel of the LORD.)

[17] Then Manoah inquired of the angel of the LORD, "What is your name, [v] so that we may honor you when your word comes true?"

[18] He replied, "Why do you ask my

Cross references (margin)

12:15 [r]Jdg 5:14
13:1 [s]S Jdg 3:31
[t]Jdg 14:4
13:2 [u]S Jos 15:33
[v]ver 8; Jdg 16:31
[w]S Ge 30:6
[x]S Ge 11:30
13:3 [y]S Ge 16:7
[z]ver 10 [a]Isa 7:14;
Lk 1:13
13:4 [b]S Lev 10:9
[c]ver 14;
Nu 6:2-4;
S Lk 1:15
13:5 [d]S Ge 3:15
[e]1Sa 1:11
[f]S Nu 6:2,13;
Am 2:11,12
[g]1Sa 7:13
13:6 [h]ver 8;
1Sa 2:27; 9:6;
1Ki 13:1; 17:18
[i]S Nu 22:22
[j]Ps 66:5
13:7 [k]Jer 35:6
[l]Lev 10:9
[m]1Sa 1:11,28
13:8 [n]S ver 2
[o]S ver 6

13:10 [p]ver 3
13:14 [q]Lev 10:9
[r]S ver 4
13:15 [s]Jdg 6:19
13:16
[t]S Jdg 11:31
[u]S Jdg 6:22
13:17
[v]S Ge 32:29

The background of this reference is unknown; the Amalekites are otherwise associated with the Negev (Nu 13:29). **13:1—16:31** Samson (from the tribe of Dan), like Ehud (from the tribe of Benjamin), was a loner, whose heroic exploits involved single-handed triumphs over powerful enemies. His story therefore balances that of Ehud (3:12–30). He typifies the nation of Israel—born by special divine provision, consecrated to the Lord from birth and endowed with unique power among his fellowmen. The likeness is even more remarkable in light of his foolish chasing of foreign women, some of ill repute, until he was cleverly subdued by one of them. In this he exemplified Israel, who during the period of the judges constantly prostituted herself to Canaanite gods to her own destruction. **13:1** *did evil in the eyes of the LORD.* See note on 3:7. **13:2** *Zorah.* A town first assigned to Judah (Jos 15:33), but later given to Dan (Jos 19:41). It became the point of departure for the Danite migration northward (18:2,8,11). *Danites.* See 1:34 and note. *sterile ... childless.* The same condition, before divine intervention, as that of Sarah, the mother of Isaac (Ge 11:30; 16:1); Rebekah, the mother of Jacob (Ge 25:21); Hannah, the mother of Samuel (1Sa 1:2); and Elizabeth, the mother of John the Baptist (Lk 1:7). **13:3** *angel of the LORD.* See note on Ge 16:7. *you are going to ... have a son.* Cf. the announcements of the births of Ishmael (Ge 16:11), Isaac (Ge 18:10), Immanuel (Isa 7:14), John the Baptist (Lk 1:13) and Jesus (Lk 1:31).

13:5 *Nazirite.* From the Hebrew word meaning "separated" or "dedicated." For the stipulations of this vow see Nu 6:1–21 and notes. Samson's vow was not voluntary, as it applied to his whole lifetime (v. 7). The same was true of Samuel (1Sa 1:11) and John the Baptist (Lk 1:15). *begin the deliverance ... from ... the Philistines.* The deliverance was continued in the time of Samuel (1Sa 7:10–14) and completed under David (2Sa 5:17–25; 8:1). **13:6** *man of God.* An expression often used of prophets (see Dt 33:1; 1Sa 2:27; 9:6–10; 1Ki 12:22), though it is clear from vv. 3,21 that this messenger was not a prophet but the angel of the Lord. **13:8** *teach us.* Not the usual parental concern, but a special concern based on the boy's special calling. **13:12** *When your words are fulfilled.* A declaration of faith. To Manoah it was not a matter of whether these events would occur, but of when (v. 17). **13:15** *stay until we prepare a young goat.* Such food was considered a special delicacy. Hospitality of this kind was common in the ancient Near East (see 6:18–19; Ge 18:1–8). **13:17** *What is your name ... ?* A messenger's identity was considered very important. *when your word comes true.* Fulfilled prophecy was a sign of the authenticity of a prophet (Dt 18:21–22; 1Sa 9:6). **13:18** *beyond understanding.* See NIV text note. In Isa 9:6 the Hebrew for this phrase (translated "Wonderful") applies

name?w It is beyond understanding.u" 19Then Manoah took a young goat, together with the grain offering, and sacrificed it on a rockx to the Lord. And the Lord did an amazing thing while Manoah and his wife watched: 20As the flamey blazed up from the altar toward heaven, the angel of the Lord ascended in the flame. Seeing this, Manoah and his wife fell with their faces to the ground.z 21When the angel of the Lord did not show himself again to Manoah and his wife, Manoah realizeda that it was the angel of the Lord.

22"We are doomedb to die!" he said to his wife. "We have seenc God!"

23But his wife answered, "If the Lord had meant to kill us, he would not have accepted a burnt offering and grain offering from our hands, nor shown us all these things or now told us this."d

24The woman gave birth to a boy and named him Samson.e He grewf and the Lord blessed him,g 25and the Spirit of the Lord began to stirh him while he was in Mahaneh Dan,i between Zorah and Eshtaol.

Samson's Marriage

14 Samsonj went down to Timnahk and saw there a young Philistine woman. 2When he returned, he said to his father and mother, "I have seen a Philistine woman in Timnah; now get her for me as my wife."l

3His father and mother replied, "Isn't there an acceptable woman among your relatives or among all our people?m Must you go to the uncircumcisedn Philistines to get a wife?o"

But Samson said to his father, "Get her for me. She's the right one for me." 4(His parents did not know that this was from the Lord,p who was seeking an occasion to confront the Philistines;q for at that time they were ruling over Israel.)r 5Samson went down to Timnah together with his father and mother. As they approached the vineyards of Timnah, suddenly a young lion came roaring toward him. 6The Spirit of the Lord came upon him in powers so that he tore the lion apartt with his bare hands as he might have torn a young goat. But he told neither his father nor his mother what he had done. 7Then he went down and talked with the woman, and he liked her.

8Some time later, when he went back to marry her, he turned aside to look at the lion's carcass. In it was a swarm of bees and some honey, 9which he scooped out with his hands and ate as he went along. When he rejoined his parents, he gave them some, and they too ate it. But he did not tell them that he had taken the honey from the lion's carcass.

10Now his father went down to see the woman. And Samson made a feastu there, as was customary for bridegrooms. 11When he appeared, he was given thirty companions.

12"Let me tell you a riddle,v" Samson

Cross references (center column)
13:18
wS Ge 32:29
13:19 xJdg 6:20
13:20
yS Lev 9:24
zS Ge 17:3
13:21 aS Jdg 6:22
13:22
bS Nu 17:12;
S Dt 5:26
cS Ge 16:13;
S Ex 3:6; S 24:10;
S Jdg 6:22
13:23 dPs 25:14
13:24 eJdg 14:1;
15:1; 16:1;
Heb 11:32
fISa 2:21,26;
3:19 gLk 1:80
13:25 hS Jdg 3:10
iJdg 18:12
14:1 jS Jdg 13:24
kS Ge 38:12
14:2 lS Ge 21:21

14:3 mS Ge 24:4
nS Ge 34:14;
S 1Sa 14:6
oS Ex 34:16
14:4 pS Dt 2:30
qS Jos 11:20
rJdg 13:1; 15:11
14:6 sS Jdg 3:10
tISa 17:35
14:10
uS Ge 29:22
14:12
vS Nu 12:8;
Eze 17:2; 20:49;
24:3; Hos 12:10

u18 Or is wonderful

---

to One who would come as "Mighty God."

13:22 *doomed to die.* See 6:23 and notes on Ge 16:13; 32:30.

13:24 *Samson.* The name is derived from a Hebrew word meaning "sun" or "brightness," and is used here either as an expression of joy over the birth of the child or as a reference to the nearby town of Beth Shemesh, "house of the sun(-god)." *He grew and the Lord blessed him.* Cf. 1Sa 2:26 (Samuel) and Lk 2:52 (Jesus).

13:25 *began to stir him.* See notes on 3:10; 11:29. *Mahaneh Dan.* Means "Dan's camp" (see NIV text note on 18:12).

14:1 *Timnah.* Identified as Tell Batash in the Sorek Valley, west of Beth Shemesh. Archaeologists have uncovered the Philistine layer of the town. *young Philistine woman.* The disappointment of Samson's parents (v. 3; cf. Esau, Ge 26:35; 27:46; 28:1) is understandable in light of the prohibition against marriage with the peoples of Canaan (Ex 34:11,16; Dt 7:1,3; see also Jdg 3:5–6).

14:2 *get her for me.* See Ge 34:4. As the head of the family, the father exercised authority in all matters, often including the choice of wives for his sons (see 12:9; Ge 24:3–9; Ne 10:30).

14:3 *uncircumcised.* A term of scorn, referring to those not bound by covenant to the Lord, used especially of the Philistines (see note on 1Sa 14:6). *right one for me.* The Hebrew

for this expression is similar to that translated "did as he saw fit" in 17:6; 21:25. The author anticipates this theme, which recurs in chs. 17–21.

14:4 *this was from the Lord.* See Jos 11:20; 1Ki 12:15. The Lord uses even the sinful weaknesses of men to accomplish his purposes and bring praise to his name (see Ge 45:8; 50:20; 2Ch 25:20; Ac 2:23; 4:28; Ro 8:28–29).

14:5 *vineyards of Timnah.* The Sorek Valley (in which Timnah was located) and its surrounding areas were noted for their luxurious vineyards. *young lion.* Lions were once common in southern Canaan (see 1Sa 17:34; 2Sa 23:20; 1Ki 13:24; 20:36).

14:6 *Spirit . . . came upon him.* See 13:25; 14:19; 15:14; see also notes on 3:10; 11:29. *tore the lion apart.* David (1Sa 17:34–37) and Benaiah (2Sa 23:20) later performed similar feats.

14:10 *feast.* Such a special feast was common in the ancient Near East (see Ge 29:22) and here lasted seven days (v. 12; see Ge 29:27). Since it would have included drinking wine, Samson may have violated his Nazirite vow (see 13:4, 7).

14:11 *companions.* These are the "guests of the bridegroom" (cf. Mt 9:15). They were probably charged with protecting the wedding party against marauders.

14:12 *riddle.* The use of riddles at feasts and special occasions was popular in the ancient world. *sets of clothes.*

said to them. "If you can give me the answer within the seven days of the feast,[w] I will give you thirty linen garments and thirty sets of clothes.[x] [13]If you can't tell me the answer, you must give me thirty linen garments and thirty sets of clothes."

"Tell us your riddle," they said. "Let's hear it."

[14]He replied,

"Out of the eater, something to eat;
  out of the strong, something
    sweet."[y]

For three days they could not give the answer.

[15]On the fourth[v] day, they said to Samson's wife, "Coax[z] your husband into explaining the riddle for us, or we will burn you and your father's household to death.[a] Did you invite us here to rob us?"

[16]Then Samson's wife threw herself on him, sobbing, "You hate me! You don't really love me.[b] You've given my people a riddle, but you haven't told me the answer."

"I haven't even explained it to my father or mother," he replied, "so why should I explain it to you?" [17]She cried the whole seven days[c] of the feast. So on the seventh day he finally told her, because she continued to press him. She in turn explained the riddle to her people.

[18]Before sunset on the seventh day the men of the town said to him,

"What is sweeter than honey?
  What is stronger than a lion?"[d]

Samson said to them,

"If you had not plowed with my heifer,
  you would not have solved my
    riddle."

[19]Then the Spirit of the LORD came upon him in power.[e] He went down to Ashke-

lon,[f] struck down thirty of their men, stripped them of their belongings and gave their clothes to those who had explained the riddle. Burning with anger,[g] he went up to his father's house. [20]And Samson's wife was given to the friend[h] who had attended him at his wedding.

Samson's Vengeance on the Philistines

15 Later on, at the time of wheat harvest,[i] Samson[j] took a young goat[k] and went to visit his wife. He said, "I'm going to my wife's room."[l] But her father would not let him go in.

[2]"I was so sure you thoroughly hated her," he said, "that I gave her to your friend.[m] Isn't her younger sister more attractive? Take her instead."

[3]Samson said to them, "This time I have a right to get even with the Philistines; I will really harm them." [4]So he went out and caught three hundred foxes[n] and tied them tail to tail in pairs. He then fastened a torch[o] to every pair of tails, [5]lit the torches[p] and let the foxes loose in the standing grain of the Philistines. He burned up the shocks[q] and standing grain, together with the vineyards and olive groves.

[6]When the Philistines asked, "Who did this?" they were told, "Samson, the Timnite's son-in-law, because his wife was given to his friend.[r]"

So the Philistines went up and burned her[s] and her father to death.[t] [7]Samson said to them, "Since you've acted like this, I won't stop until I get my revenge on you." [8]He attacked them viciously and slaughtered many of them. Then he went down and stayed in a cave in the rock[u] of Etam.[v]

[9]The Philistines went up and camped in

Cross references (center column)

14:12 [w]Ge 29:27
[x]S Ge 45:22;
S 2Ki 5:5
14:14 [y]ver 18
14:15 [z]Jdg 16:5;
Ecc 7:26
[a]S Lev 20:14;
Jdg 15:6
14:16 [b]Jdg 16:15
14:17 [c]Est 1:5
14:18 [d]ver 14
14:19 [e]S Jdg 3:10

[f]S Jos 13:3
[g]1Sa 11:6
14:20 [h]Jdg 15:2,
6; Jn 3:29
15:1 [i]S Ge 30:14
[j]S Jdg 13:24
[k]S Ge 38:17
[l]Ge 29:21
15:2
[m]S Jdg 14:20
15:4 [n]SS 2:15
[o]S Ge 15:17
15:5 [p]S Ge 15:17
[q]Ex 22:6;
2Sa 14:30-31
15:6 [r]S Jdg 14:20
[s]S Ge 38:24
[t]S Jdg 14:15
15:8 [u]Isa 2:21
[v]ver 11

[v]15 Some Septuagint manuscripts and Syriac; Hebrew *seventh*

Mentioned, together with silver, as gifts of great value in Ge 45:22; 2Ki 5:22 (see also Zec 14:14).

14:16 *don't really love me.* Delilah used the same tactics (16:15).

14:18 *my heifer.* Samson's wife (see v. 15). Since heifers were not used for plowing, Samson is accusing them of unfairness.

14:19 *Spirit . . . came upon him.* God's purposes for Samson included humbling the Philistines. *Ashkelon.* One of the five principal cities of the Philistines (see map, p. 330).

14:20 *friend.* See 15:2; probably the young man who had attended Samson (cf. Jn 3:29), in all likelihood one of his 30 companions (v. 11).

15:1 *time of wheat harvest.* Near the end of May or the beginning of June (see note on Ru 1:22). *young goat.* Such a gift was customary, as with Judah and Tamar (Ge 38:17).

15:2 *younger sister.* Samson's father-in-law felt he had to

make a counterproposal because he had received the bride-price from Samson. Similar marital transactions were made by Laban and Jacob (Ge 29:16–28) and Saul and David (1Sa 18:19–21).

15:4 *foxes.* The Hebrew word may refer to foxes or jackals, both of which are still found in modern Israel.

15:5 *burned up.* The wheat harvest (v. 1) comes at the end of a long dry season, thus making the fields extremely vulnerable to fire.

15:7 *revenge.* A common feature of life in the ancient Near East. Six cities of refuge were designated by the Lord to prevent endless killings (Jos 20:1–9).

15:9 *Lehi.* Means "jawbone." This locality probably did not receive the name until after the events described here; the author uses the name in anticipation of those events—a common device in Hebrew narrative. The exact site of Lehi is not known.

Judah, spreading out near Lehi.ʷ ¹⁰The men of Judah asked, "Why have you come to fight us?"

"We have come to take Samson prisoner," they answered, "to do to him as he did to us."

¹¹Then three thousand men from Judah went down to the cave in the rock of Etam and said to Samson, "Don't you realize that the Philistines are rulers over us?ˣ What have you done to us?"

He answered, "I merely did to them what they did to me."

¹²They said to him, "We've come to tie you up and hand you over to the Philistines."

Samson said, "Swear to meʸ that you won't kill me yourselves."

¹³"Agreed," they answered. "We will only tie you up and hand you over to them. We will not kill you." So they bound him with two new ropesᶻ and led him up from the rock. ¹⁴As he approached Lehi,ᵃ the Philistines came toward him shouting. The Spirit of the LORD came upon him in power.ᵇ The ropes on his arms became like charred flax,ᶜ and the bindings dropped from his hands. ¹⁵Finding a fresh jawbone of a donkey, he grabbed it and struck down a thousand men.ᵈ

¹⁶Then Samson said,

"With a donkey's jawbone
   I have made donkeys of them.ʷᵉ
With a donkey's jawbone
   I have killed a thousand men."

¹⁷When he finished speaking, he threw away the jawbone; and the place was called Ramath Lehi.ˣ ᶠ

¹⁸Because he was very thirsty, he cried out to the LORD,ᵍ "You have given your servant this great victory.ʰ Must I now die of thirst and fall into the hands of the uncircumcised?" ¹⁹Then God opened up the hollow place in Lehi, and water came out of it. When Samson drank, his strength returned and he revived.ⁱ So the springʲ was called En Hakkore,ʸ and it is still there in Lehi.

²⁰Samson ledᶻ Israel for twenty yearsᵏ in the days of the Philistines.

Samson and Delilah

16 One day Samsonˡ went to Gaza,ᵐ where he saw a prostitute.ⁿ He went in to spend the night with her. ²The people of Gaza were told, "Samson is here!" So they surrounded the place and lay in wait for him all night at the city gate.ᵒ They made no move during the night, saying, "At dawnᵖ we'll kill him."

³But Samson lay there only until the middle of the night. Then he got up and took hold of the doors of the city gate, together with the two posts, and tore them loose, bar and all. He lifted them to his shoulders and carried them to the top of the hill that faces Hebron.�q

⁴Some time later, he fell in loveʳ with a woman in the Valley of Sorek whose name was Delilah.ˢ ⁵The rulers of the Philistinesᵗ went to her and said, "See if you can lureᵘ him into showing you the secret

---

15:9 ʷver 14,17, 19
15:11 ˣS Jdg 14:4; Ps 106:40-42
15:12 ʸS Ge 47:31
15:13 ᶻJdg 16:11, 12
15:14 ᵃS ver 9
ᵇS Jdg 3:10
ᶜS Jos 2:6
15:15 ᵈS Lev 26:8
15:16 ᵉJer 22:19

15:17 ᶠS ver 9
15:18 ᵍJdg 16:28
ʰS Dt 20:4
15:19 ⁱGe 45:27; 1Sa 30:12; Isa 40:29
ʲS Ex 17:6
15:20 ᵏJdg 16:31
16:1 ˡS Jdg 13:24
ᵐS Ge 10:19
ⁿS Ge 38:15
16:2 ᵒS Jos 2:5
ᵖ1Sa 19:11
16:3 qS Jos 10:36
16:4 ʳS Ge 24:67; S 34:3 ˢver 6
16:5 ᵗS Jos 13:3
ᵘS Ex 10:7; S Jdg 14:15

ʷ16 Or *made a heap or two*; the Hebrew for *donkey* sounds like the Hebrew for *heap.* ˣ17 *Ramath Lehi* means *jawbone hill.* ʸ19 *En Hakkore* means *caller's spring.* ᶻ20 Traditionally *judged*

15:11 *three thousand men from Judah.* The only time a force from Judah is explicitly mentioned in connection with any of the judges (but see note on 1:2). The men of Judah were well aware of Samson's capabilities, and even with a large force they did not attempt to tie him up without his consent (vv. 12–13). *Philistines are rulers over us.* Much of Judah was under Philistine rule, and the tribe was apparently content to accept it. They mustered a force, not to support Samson, but to capture him for the Philistines.

15:14 *shouting.* A battle cry (see 1Sa 17:52). They came shouting against Samson as the lion had come roaring against him (14:5). *Spirit of the LORD.* See notes on 3:10; 11:29; 14:19.

15:15 *struck down a thousand men.* Cf. the exploits of Shamgar, who struck down 600 Philistines with an oxgoad (3:31).

15:18 *Must I now die of thirst . . . ?* Mighty Samson was, after all, only a mortal man.

15:19 *water came out of it.* God provided for Samson as he had for Israel in the desert. See Ex 17:1–7 (Massah and Meribah); Nu 20:2–13 (Meribah).

15:20 *led Israel . . . years.* See note on 12:7. *twenty years.* Round numbers are frequently used in Judges (see Introduction: Background).

16:1 *Gaza.* An important Philistine seaport on the Mediterranean coast of southwest Palestine. *prostitute.* While Samson certainly possessed physical strength, he lacked moral strength, which ultimately led to his ruin.

16:2 *dawn.* By that time they expected Samson to be exhausted and sleeping soundly.

16:3 *bar.* Probably made of bronze (1Ki 4:13) or iron (Ps 107:16; Isa 45:2). *faces Hebron.* That is, in the direction of Hebron, which was 38 miles away in the hill country. Since Hebron was the chief city of Judah, this must be seen as Samson's response to what the men of Judah had done to him (see 15:11–13).

16:5 *rulers of the Philistines.* See note on 3:3. *subdue him.* The Philistines were not interested in killing him quickly; they sought revenge by a prolonged period of torture. *eleven hundred shekels.* An extraordinarily generous payment in light of 17:10 (see note there). (The total amount paid by the five Philistines would have been equivalent to the price of 275 slaves, at the rate offered for Joseph centuries earlier; see Ge 37:28.) Micah stole a similar amount of silver from his mother (17:2).

of his great strength[v] and how we can overpower him so we may tie him up and subdue him. Each one of us will give you eleven hundred shekels[a] of silver." [w]

[6]So Delilah[x] said to Samson, "Tell me the secret of your great strength and how you can be tied up and subdued."

[7]Samson answered her, "If anyone ties me with seven fresh thongs[b] that have not been dried, I'll become as weak as any other man."

[8]Then the rulers of the Philistines brought her seven fresh thongs that had not been dried, and she tied him with them. [9]With men hidden in the room,[y] she called to him, "Samson, the Philistines are upon you!"[z] But he snapped the thongs as easily as a piece of string snaps when it comes close to a flame. So the secret of his strength was not discovered.

[10]Then Delilah said to Samson, "You have made a fool of me;[a] you lied to me. Come now, tell me how you can be tied."

[11]He said, "If anyone ties me securely with new ropes[b] that have never been used, I'll become as weak as any other man."

[12]So Delilah took new ropes and tied him with them. Then, with men hidden in the room, she called to him, "Samson, the Philistines are upon you!"[c] But he snapped the ropes off his arms as if they were threads.

[13]Delilah then said to Samson, "Until now, you have been making a fool of me and lying to me. Tell me how you can be tied."

He replied, "If you weave the seven braids of my head into the fabric on the loom, and tighten it with the pin, I'll become as weak as any other man." So while he was sleeping, Delilah took the seven braids of his head, wove them into the fabric [14]and[c] tightened it with the pin.

Again she called to him, "Samson, the Philistines are upon you!"[d] He awoke

from his sleep and pulled up the pin and the loom, with the fabric.

[15]Then she said to him, "How can you say, 'I love you,'[e] when you won't confide in me? This is the third time[f] you have made a fool of me and haven't told me the secret of your great strength.[g]" [16]With such nagging she prodded him day after day until he was tired to death.

[17]So he told her everything.[h] "No razor has ever been used on my head," he said, "because I have been a Nazirite[i] set apart to God since birth. If my head were shaved, my strength would leave me, and I would become as weak as any other man."

[18]When Delilah saw that he had told her everything, she sent word to the rulers of the Philistines,[j] "Come back once more; he has told me everything." So the rulers of the Philistines returned with the silver in their hands.[k] [19]Having put him to sleep on her lap, she called a man to shave off the seven braids of his hair, and so began to subdue him.[d] And his strength left him.[l]

[20]Then she called, "Samson, the Philistines are upon you!"[m]

He awoke from his sleep and thought, "I'll go out as before and shake myself free." But he did not know that the LORD had left him.[n]

[21]Then the Philistines[o] seized him, gouged out his eyes[p] and took him down to Gaza.[q] Binding him with bronze shackles, they set him to grinding[r] in the prison. [22]But the hair on his head began to grow again after it had been shaved.

The Death of Samson

[23]Now the rulers of the Philistines assembled to offer a great sacrifice to Da-

Cross references (center column)

16:5 [v]ver 6,15
[w]ver 18
16:6 [x]ver 4
16:9 [y]ver 12 [z]ver 14
16:10 [a]ver 13
16:11
[b]S Jdg 15:13
16:12 [c]ver 14
16:14 [d]ver 9,20

16:15 [e]Jdg 14:16
[f]Nu 24:10
[g]S ver 5
16:17 [h]ver 18;
Mic 7:5 [i]S Nu 6:2
16:18 [j]S Jos 13:3;
1Sa 5:8 [k]ver 5
16:19
[l]Pr 7:26-27
16:20 [m]S ver 14
[n]Nu 14:42;
Jos 7:12;
1Sa 16:14; 18:12;
28:15
16:21 [o]Jer 47:1
[p]S Nu 16:14
[q]S Ge 10:19
[r]Job 31:10;
Isa 47:2

Text notes

[a]5 That is, about 28 pounds (about 13 kilograms)
[b]7 Or bowstrings; also in verses 8 and 9
[c]13,14 Some Septuagint manuscripts; Hebrew "I can, if you weave the seven braids of my head into the fabric on the loom." [c]14So she   [d]19 Hebrew; some Septuagint manuscripts and he began to weaken

---

16:7 *seven fresh thongs.* The number seven had special significance to the ancients, symbolizing completeness or fullness. Note that Samson's hair was divided into seven braids (v. 13).

16:11 *new ropes.* The Philistines apparently did not know that this method had already been tried and had failed (15:13–14).

16:13 Out of disdain, Samson arrogantly played with his Philistine adversaries. *tighten it with the pin.* Probably from a weaver's shuttle. The details of the account suggest that the loom in question was the vertical type with a crossbeam from which warp threads were suspended. Samson's long hair was woven into the warp and beaten up into the web with the pin, thus forming a tight fabric.

16:19–20 *his strength left him . . . the LORD had left him.*

The source of Samson's strength was ultimately God himself. **16:20** *he did not know.* One of the most tragic statements in the OT. Samson was unaware that he had betrayed his calling. He had permitted a Philistine woman to rob him of the sign of his special consecration to the Lord. The Lord's champion lay asleep and helpless in the arms of his paramour.

16:21 *gouged out his eyes.* Brutal treatment of prisoners of war to humiliate and incapacitate them was common (see 1Sa 11:2; 2Ki 25:7; see also note on Jdg 1:6). *to Gaza.* In shame and weakness, Samson was led to Gaza, the place where he had displayed great strength (vv. 1–3). *set him to grinding.* See note on 9:53.

16:23 *Dagon.* See note on 10:6. *Our god has delivered.* It was common to attribute a victory to the national deities.

gon[s] their god and to celebrate, saying, "Our god has delivered Samson, our enemy, into our hands."

24When the people saw him, they praised their god,[t] saying,

"Our god has delivered our enemy
    into our hands,[u]
the one who laid waste our land
    and multiplied our slain."

25While they were in high spirits,[v] they shouted, "Bring out Samson to entertain us." So they called Samson out of the prison, and he performed for them.

When they stood him among the pillars, 26Samson said to the servant who held his hand, "Put me where I can feel the pillars that support the temple, so that I may lean against them." 27Now the temple was crowded with men and women; all the rulers of the Philistines were there, and on the roof[w] were about three thousand men and women watching Samson perform. 28Then Samson prayed to the LORD,[x] "O Sovereign LORD, remember me. O God, please strengthen me just once more, and let me with one blow get revenge[y] on the Philistines for my two eyes." 29Then Samson reached toward the two central pillars on which the temple stood. Bracing himself against them, his right hand on the one and his left hand on the other, 30Samson said, "Let me die with the Philistines!" Then he pushed with all his might, and down came the temple on the rulers and all the people in it. Thus he killed many

more when he died than while he lived. 31Then his brothers and his father's whole family went down to get him. They brought him back and buried him between Zorah and Eshtaol in the tomb of Manoah[z] his father. He had led[e][a] Israel twenty years.[b]

Micah's Idols

17 Now a man named Micah[c] from the hill country of Ephraim 2said to his mother, "The eleven hundred shekels[f] of silver that were taken from you and about which I heard you utter a curse—I have that silver with me; I took it."

Then his mother said, "The LORD bless you,[d] my son!"

3When he returned the eleven hundred shekels of silver to his mother, she said, "I solemnly consecrate my silver to the LORD for my son to make a carved image and a cast idol.[e] I will give it back to you."

4So he returned the silver to his mother, and she took two hundred shekels[g] of silver and gave them to a silversmith, who made them into the image and the idol.[f] And they were put in Micah's house.

5Now this man Micah had a shrine,[g] and he made an ephod[h] and some idols[i] and installed[j] one of his sons as his priest.[k] 6In those days Israel had no king;[l] everyone did as he saw fit.[m]

7A young Levite[n] from Bethlehem in

Cross references
16:23 sISa 5:2; 1Ch 10:10
16:24 tDa 5:4; uISa 31:9; 1Ch 10:9
16:25 vJdg 9:27; 19:6,9,22; Ru 3:7; Est 1:10
16:27 wS Jos 2:8
16:28 xJdg 15:18; yJer 15:15
16:31 zS Jdg 13:2; aRu 1:1; 1Sa 4:18; 7:6; bJdg 15:20
17:1 cJdg 18:2,13
17:2 dRu 2:20; 3:10; 1Sa 15:13; 23:21; 2Sa 2:5
17:3 eS Ex 20:4
17:4 fS Ex 32:4; S Isa 17:8
17:5 gIsa 44:13; Eze 8:10; hS Jdg 8:27; iS Ge 31:19; jS Nu 16:10; kS Ex 29:9
17:6 lJdg 18:1; 19:1; 21:25; mS Dt 12:8
17:7 nJdg 18:3

e31 Traditionally judged   f2 That is, about 28 pounds (about 13 kilograms)   g4 That is, about 5 pounds (about 2.3 kilograms)

16:27 on the roof. The temple complex probably surrounded an open court and had a flat roof where a large number of people had gathered to get a glimpse of the fallen champion.
16:30 pushed. Samson pushed the wooden pillars from their stone bases. Archaeologists have discovered a Philistine temple with a pair of closely spaced pillar bases. killed many more. Samson previously had slain well over 1,000 people (see 15:15; see also 14:19; 15:8).
16:31 went down to get him. The freedom of his family to secure his body and give it a burial indicates that the Philistines had no intention of further dishonoring him (contrast Saul's death, 1Sa 31:9–10). led Israel . . . years. See note on 12:7. twenty years. Round numbers are frequently used in Judges (see Introduction: Background).
17:1–21:25 Two episodes forming an epilogue to the story of the judges (see Introduction: Literary Features). The events narrated evidently took place fairly early in the period of the judges (see notes on 18:30; 20:1,28). They illustrate the religious and moral degeneracy that characterized the age—when "Israel had no king" and "everyone did as he saw fit" (17:6; 21:25). Writing at a time when the monarchy under the Davidic dynasty had brought cohesion and order to the land and had reestablished a center for the worship of the Lord, the author portrays this earlier era of the judges as a dismal period of national decay, from which it was to be rescued by the house of David.

17:1–18:31 The first episode illustrates corruption in Israelite worship by telling of Micah's establishment of a local place of worship in Ephraim, aided by a Levite claiming descent from Moses. This paganized worship of the Lord is taken over by the tribe of Dan when that tribe abandons its appointed inheritance and migrates to Israel's northern frontier.
17:2 eleven hundred shekels. See note on 16:5. I heard you utter a curse. Fear of the curse seems to have motivated his returning the stolen money. The LORD bless you. A blessing to counteract the curse.
17:3 mother . . . son. With their paganized view of the God of Israel, both were idolaters in disobedience to the law (Ex 20:4,23; Dt 4:16). a carved image and a cast idol. The image was probably made of wood overlaid with silver; the idol was made of solid silver or of cheaper metal overlaid with silver.
17:4 silversmith. A maker of idols, as in Ac 19:24 (cf. Isa 40:19 and Jer 10:9, where the Hebrew for this word is translated "goldsmith").
17:5 ephod. See 8:27 and note on Ex 28:6. idols. Household gods, used in this case for divining (cf. Eze 21:21; Zec 10:2). Some of them were in human form (1Sa 19:13).
17:6 had no king. See 18:1; 19:1; 21:25; suggests that Judges was written after the establishment of the monarchy (see Introduction: Author and Date). did as he saw fit. The expression implies that Israel had departed from the cov-

Judah,[o] who had been living within the clan of Judah, [8]left that town in search of some other place to stay. On his way[h] he came to Micah's house in the hill country of Ephraim.

[9]Micah asked him, "Where are you from?"

"I'm a Levite from Bethlehem in Judah,[p]" he said, "and I'm looking for a place to stay."

[10]Then Micah said to him, "Live with me and be my father[q] and priest,[r] and I'll give you ten shekels[i] of silver a year, your clothes and your food." [11]So the Levite agreed to live with him, and the young man was to him like one of his sons. [12]Then Micah installed[s] the Levite, and the young man became his priest[t] and lived in his house. [13]And Micah said, "Now I know that the LORD will be good to me, since this Levite has become my priest."[u]

Danites Settle in Laish

18 In those days Israel had no king.[v] And in those days the tribe of the Danites was seeking a place of their own where they might settle, because they had not yet come into an inheritance among the tribes of Israel.[w] [2]So the Danites[x] sent five warriors[y] from Zorah and Eshtaol to spy out[z] the land and explore it. These men represented all their clans. They told them, "Go, explore the land."[a]

The men entered the hill country of Ephraim and came to the house of Micah,[b] where they spent the night. [3]When they were near Micah's house,

they recognized the voice[o] of the young Levite;[c] so they turned in there and asked him, "Who brought you here? What are you doing in this place? Why are you here?"

[4]He told them what Micah had done for him, and said, "He has hired me and I am his priest.[d]"

[5]Then they said to him, "Please inquire of God[e] to learn whether our journey will be successful."

[6]The priest answered them, "Go in peace[f]. Your journey has the LORD's approval."

[7]So the five men[g] left and came to Laish,[h] where they saw that the people were living in safety, like the Sidonians, unsuspecting and secure.[i] And since their land lacked nothing, they were prosperous.[j] Also, they lived a long way from the Sidonians[j] and had no relationship with anyone else.[k]

[8]When they returned to Zorah and Eshtaol, their brothers asked them, "How did you find things?"

[9]They answered, "Come on, let's attack them! We have seen that the land is very good. Aren't you going to do something? Don't hesitate to go there and take it over.[k] [10]When you get there, you will find an unsuspecting people and a spacious land that God has put into your hands, a land that lacks nothing[l] whatever.[m]"

[11]Then six hundred men[n] from the clan

Cross references (center column):

17:7
oS Ge 35:19;
Mt 2:1
17:9 pRu 1:1
17:10 qS Ge 45:8
rJdg 18:19
17:12
sS Nu 16:10
tJdg 18:4
17:13 uNu 18:7
18:1 vS Jdg 17:6
wJos 19:47;
Jdg 1:34
18:2 xS Ge 30:6
yver 17
zS Nu 21:32
aS Jos 2:1
bS Jdg 17:1

18:3 cJdg 17:7
18:4 dJdg 17:12
18:5
eS Ge 25:22;
Jdg 20:18,23,27;
1Sa 14:18;
2Sa 5:19; 2Ki 1:2;
8:8
18:6 f1Ki 22:6
18:7 gver 17
hS Jos 19:47
iS Ge 34:25 /ver
28; Jos 11:8
18:9 kNu 13:30;
1Ki 22:3
18:10 /Dt 8:9
m1Ch 4:40
18:11 nver 16,17

[h]8 Or To carry on his profession   [i]10 That is, about 4 ounces (about 110 grams)   [j]7 The meaning of the Hebrew for this clause is uncertain.   [k]7 Hebrew; some Septuagint manuscripts with the Arameans

---

enant standards of conduct found in the law (see Dt 12:8).
17:7 *Bethlehem in Judah.* Not among the 48 designated Levitical cities (Jos 21).
17:8 *left that town.* The failure of the Israelites to obey the law probably resulted in a lack of support for the Levites, which explains the man's wandering in search of his fortune.
17:10 *father.* A term of respect used also for Elijah (2Ki 2:12) and Elisha (2Ki 6:21; 13:14). See Ge 45:8; Mt 23:9.
ten shekels. See NIV text note. In the light of this remuneration for a year's service, the stated amounts in 16:5 and 17:2 take on special significance. The offer of wages, clothing and food was more than this Levite could resist (v. 11). Clearly material concerns were at the root of his decision, because later he accepts an even more attractive offer (18:19–20).
17:12 *installed the Levite.* An attempt to make his shrine legitimate and give it prestige. Micah probably removed his son (see v. 5).
18:1 *seeking a place.* The Danite allotment was at the west end of the strip of land between Judah and Ephraim (Jos 19:41–46), but, due to the opposition of the Amorites (Jdg 1:34) and the Philistines, they were unable to occupy that territory (see note on 13:2).
18:2 *spy out.* See 1:23 and note on Nu 13:2.
18:3 *recognized the voice.* Perhaps they recognized him by his dialect or accent.

18:5 *inquire of God.* The request is for an oracle, probably by using the ephod and household gods (see note on 17:5). God had already revealed his will by the allotments given to the various tribes (Jos 14–20). They were searching for an oracle that would guarantee the success of their journey.
18:6 *Go in peace.* The Levite gave them the message they wanted to hear. He was even careful to use the name of the Lord to give the message credibility and authority.
18:7 *Laish.* The journey northward was about 100 miles from Zorah and Eshtaol (v. 2). This town is called Leshem in Jos 19:47. After its capture by the Danites, Laish was renamed Dan (v. 29), and it was Israel's northernmost settlement (see 20:1; 1Sa 3:20; 2Sa 3:10). Excavations there have disclosed that the earliest Israelite occupation of Dan was in the 12th century B.C. and that the first Israelite inhabitants apparently lived in tents or temporary huts. Occupation of the site continued into the Assyrian period, but the town was destroyed and rebuilt many times. A large high place attached to the city was often extensively rebuilt and refurbished and was in use into the Hellenistic period. *Sidonians.* A peaceful Phoenician people who engaged in commerce throughout the Mediterranean world. *had no relationship.* They did not feel threatened by other powers and therefore sought no treaties for mutual defense.
18:11 *six hundred men.* As leaders of the tribe of Dan, they

of the Danites,[o] armed for battle, set out from Zorah and Eshtaol. [12]On their way they set up camp near Kiriath Jearim[p] in Judah. This is why the place west of Kiriath Jearim is called Mahaneh Dan[1][q] to this day. [13]From there they went on to the hill country of Ephraim and came to Micah's house.[r]

[14]Then the five men who had spied out the land of Laish[s] said to their brothers, "Do you know that one of these houses has an ephod,[t] other household gods, a carved image and a cast idol?[u] Now you know what to do." [15]So they turned in there and went to the house of the young Levite at Micah's place and greeted him. [16]The six hundred Danites,[v] armed for battle, stood at the entrance to the gate. [17]The five men who had spied out the land went inside and took the carved image, the ephod, the other household gods[w] and the cast idol while the priest and the six hundred armed men[x] stood at the entrance to the gate.

[18]When these men went into Micah's house and took[y] the carved image, the ephod, the other household gods[z] and the cast idol, the priest said to them, "What are you doing?"

[19]They answered him, "Be quiet![a] Don't say a word. Come with us, and be our father and priest.[b] Isn't it better that you serve a tribe and clan[c] in Israel as priest rather than just one man's household?" [20]Then the priest was glad. He took the ephod, the other household gods and the carved image and went along with the people. [21]Putting their little children, their livestock and their possessions in front of them, they turned away and left.

[22]When they had gone some distance from Micah's house, the men who lived near Micah were called together and over-

took the Danites. [23]As they shouted after them, the Danites turned and said to Micah, "What's the matter with you that you called out your men to fight?"

[24]He replied, "You took[d] the gods I made, and my priest, and went away. What else do I have? How can you ask, 'What's the matter with you?' "

[25]The Danites answered, "Don't argue with us, or some hot-tempered men will attack you, and you and your family will lose your lives." [26]So the Danites went their way, and Micah, seeing that they were too strong for him,[e] turned around and went back home.

[27]Then they took what Micah had made, and his priest, and went on to Laish, against a peaceful and unsuspecting people.[f] They attacked them with the sword and burned[g] down their city.[h] [28]There was no one to rescue them because they lived a long way from Sidon[i] and had no relationship with anyone else. The city was in a valley near Beth Rehob.[j]

The Danites rebuilt the city and settled there. [29]They named it Dan[k] after their forefather Dan, who was born to Israel—though the city used to be called Laish.[l] [30]There the Danites set up for themselves the idols, and Jonathan son of Gershom,[m] the son of Moses,[m] and his sons were priests for the tribe of Dan until the time of the captivity of the land. [31]They continued to use the idols Micah had made,[n] all the time the house of God[o] was in Shiloh.[p]

A Levite and His Concubine

19 In those days Israel had no king. Now a Levite who lived in a

Cross references (center column)

18:11 [o]Jdg 13:2
18:12 [p]S Jos 9:17
[q]Jdg 13:25
18:13 [r]S Jdg 17:1
18:14
[s]S Jos 19:47
[t]S Jdg 8:27
[u]S Ge 31:19
18:16 [v]S ver 11
18:17
[w]S Ge 31:19;
Mic 5:13 [x]ver 11
18:18 [y]ver 24;
Isa 46:2;
Jer 43:11; 48:7;
49:3; Hos 10:5
[z]S Ge 31:19
18:19 [a]Job 13:5;
21:5; 29:9; 40:4;
Isa 52:15;
Mic 7:16
[b]Jdg 17:10
[c]Nu 26:42

18:24 [d]S ver 17-18
18:26 [e]2Sa 3:39;
Ps 18:17; 35:10
18:27
[f]S Ge 34:25
[g]S Nu 31:10
[h]Ge 49:17;
S Jos 19:47
18:28 [i]S ver 7;
S Ge 10:19
[j]S Nu 13:21
18:29
[k]S Ge 14:14
[l]S Jos 19:47;
1Ki 15:20
18:30 [m]Ex 2:22
18:31 [n]ver 17
[o]Jdg 19:18; 20:18
[p]S Jos 18:1;
Jer 7:14

[1]*12 Mahaneh Dan* means *Dan's camp.*   [m]*30* An ancient Hebrew scribal tradition, some Septuagint manuscripts and Vulgate; Masoretic Text *Manasseh*

---

represented the entire tribe's migration to its new location in the north. Cf. the 600 men who constituted the remnant of the tribe of Benjamin (20:47).

18:19 *father.* See note on 17:10. *a tribe and clan.* Only one clan from the tribe of Dan is ever mentioned—Shuham (Nu 26:42; called Hushim in Ge 46:23). The Danites appealed to the Levite's vanity and materialism.

18:21 *in front of them.* For protection in case of attack; see Ge 33:2–3 (Jacob and Esau).

18:24 *You took the gods.* Micah was concerned about the loss of gods that could not protect themselves. *What else do I have?* The agonizing cry of one whose faith is centered in helpless gods.

18:28 *Beth Rehob.* Probably the same as Rehob in Nu 13:21.

18:30 *Jonathan.* The Levite is here identified as Jonathan son of Gershom, the son of Moses (Ex 2:22; 18:3; 1Ch 23:14–15). In an effort to prevent desecration of the name of Moses, later scribes modified the name slightly, making it

read "Manasseh" (see NIV text note). If Jonathan was the grandson of Moses, the events in this chapter must have occurred early in the period of the judges (see notes on 20:1,28). *captivity of the land.* The date of this captivity has not been determined (see note on v. 7 regarding Laish).

18:31 *all the time the house of God was in Shiloh.* See Jos 18:1. For Shiloh's destruction see Ps 78:60; Jer 7:12,14; 26:6. Archaeological work at Shiloh indicates that the site was destroyed c. 1050 B.C. and was left uninhabited for many centuries.

19:1–21:25 The second episode of the epilogue (see note on 17:1–18:31). It illustrates Israel's moral corruption by telling of the degenerate act of the men of Gibeah—an act remembered centuries later (Hos 9:9; 10:9). Although that town showed itself to be as wicked as any Canaanite town, it was defended by the rest of the tribe of Benjamin against the Lord's discipline through the Israelites, until nearly the whole tribe was destroyed.

19:1–30 An account of an Israelite town that revived the

remote area in the hill country of Ephraim[q] took a concubine from Bethlehem in Judah.[r] [2]But she was unfaithful to him. She left him and went back to her father's house in Bethlehem, Judah. After she had been there four months, [3]her husband went to her to persuade her to return. He had with him his servant and two donkeys. She took him into her father's house, and when her father saw him, he gladly welcomed him. [4]His father-in-law, the girl's father, prevailed upon him to stay; so he remained with him three days, eating and drinking,[s] and sleeping there.

[5]On the fourth day they got up early and he prepared to leave, but the girl's father said to his son-in-law, "Refresh yourself[t] with something to eat; then you can go." [6]So the two of them sat down to eat and drink together. Afterward the girl's father said, "Please stay tonight and enjoy yourself.[u]" [7]And when the man got up to go, his father-in-law persuaded him, so he stayed there that night. [8]On the morning of the fifth day, when he rose to go, the girl's father said, "Refresh yourself. Wait till afternoon!" So the two of them ate together.

[9]Then when the man, with his concubine and his servant, got up to leave, his father-in-law, the girl's father, said, "Now look, it's almost evening. Spend the night here; the day is nearly over. Stay and enjoy yourself. Early tomorrow morning you can get up and be on your way home." [10]But, unwilling to stay another night, the man left and went toward Jebus[v] (that is, Jerusalem), with his two saddled donkeys and his concubine.

[11]When they were near Jebus and the day was almost gone, the servant said to his master, "Come, let's stop at this city of the Jebusites[w] and spend the night."

[12]His master replied, "No. We won't go into an alien city, whose people are not Israelites. We will go on to Gibeah." [13]He added, "Come, let's try to reach Gibeah or Ramah[x] and spend the night in one of those places." [14]So they went on, and the sun set as they neared Gibeah in Benjamin.[y] [15]There they stopped to spend the night.[z] They went and sat in the city square,[a] but no one took them into his home for the night.

[16]That evening[b] an old man from the hill country of Ephraim,[c] who was living in Gibeah (the men of the place were Benjamites), came in from his work in the fields. [17]When he looked and saw the traveler in the city square, the old man asked, "Where are you going? Where did you come from?"[d]

[18]He answered, "We are on our way from Bethlehem in Judah to a remote area in the hill country of Ephraim where I live. I have been to Bethlehem in Judah and now I am going to the house of the LORD.[e] No one has taken me into his house. [19]We have both straw and fodder[f] for our donkeys[g] and bread and wine[h] for ourselves your servants—me, your maidservant, and the young man with us. We don't need anything."

[20]"You are welcome at my house," the old man said. "Let me supply whatever you need. Only don't spend the night in the square." [21]So he took him into his house and fed his donkeys. After they had washed their feet, they had something to eat and drink.[i]

[22]While they were enjoying themselves,[j] some of the wicked men[k] of the city surrounded the house. Pounding on the door, they shouted to the old man who owned the house, "Bring out the man who came to your house so we can have sex with him.[l]"

[23]The owner of the house went outside[m] and said to them, "No, my friends,

19:1 [q]ver 16,18
[r]Ru 1:1
19:4 [s]ver 6,8;
S Ex 32:6
19:5 [t]ver 8;
19:6 [u]S Jdg 16:25
Ge 18:5
19:10
[v]S Ge 10:16;
S Jos 15:8
19:11
[w]S Ge 10:16;
S Jos 3:10

19:13
[x]S Jos 18:25
19:14 [y]Jos 15:57;
1Sa 10:26; 11:4;
13:2; 15:34;
Isa 10:29
19:15
[z]S Ge 24:23
[a]S Ge 19:2
19:16 [b]Ps 104:23
[c]S ver 1
19:17 [d]S Ge 29:4
19:18
[e]S Jdg 18:31
19:19 [f]Ge 24:25
[g]S Ge 42:27
[h]S Ge 14:18
19:21
[i]Ge 24:32-33;
Lk 7:44
19:22
[j]S Jdg 16:25
[k]S Dt 13:13
[l]Ge 19:4-5;
Jdg 20:5;
Ro 1:26-27
19:23 [m]Ge 19:6

ways of Sodom (see Ge 19).
19:1 *Levite.* Unlike the Levite of chs. 17–18, this man is not named. *concubine.* See note on Ge 25:6.
19:3 *gladly welcomed him.* The separation of the concubine from the Levite was probably a matter of family disgrace, and so his father-in-law was glad for the prospect of the two being reunited.
19:10 *Jebus.* See 1:21; see also note on Ge 10:16.
19:12 *alien city.* With the city under the control of the Jebusites, the Levite was afraid that he would receive no hospitality and might be in mortal danger.
19:14 *Gibeah in Benjamin.* Distinguished from the Gibeah in Judah (Jos 15:20,57) and the Gibeah in the hill country of Ephraim (Jos 24:33). As the political capital of Saul's kingdom, it is called Gibeah of Saul in 1Sa 11:4; see also 1Sa 13:15.
19:15 *took them into his home.* See notes on 13:15; Ge 18:2.

19:18 *house of the LORD.* Apparently the Levite was planning to go to Shiloh (see 18:31; Jos 18:1) to present a thank offering to the Lord or a sin offering for himself and his concubine.
19:21 *washed their feet.* An evidence of hospitality in the ancient Near East, where travelers commonly wore sandals as they walked the dusty roads (see Ge 18:4; 24:32; 43:24; Lk 7:44; Jn 13:5–14).
19:22 *wicked men.* The Hebrew for this expression refers to the morally depraved (see note on Dt 13:13). Elsewhere the expression is associated with idolatry (Dt 13:13), drunkenness (1Sa 1:16) and rebellion (1Sa 2:12). Here the reference is to homosexuality. *Bring out the man.* The sexual perversion of these wicked men is yet another example of the decadence of an age when "everyone did as he saw fit" (17:6; 21:25). A similar request was made by the men of Sodom (Ge 19:5). Homosexuality was common among the Canaanites.

don't be so vile. Since this man is my guest, don't do this disgraceful thing. *n* ²⁴Look, here is my virgin daughter, *o* and his concubine. I will bring them out to you now, and you can use them and do to them whatever you wish. But to this man, don't do such a disgraceful thing."

²⁵But the men would not listen to him. So the man took his concubine and sent her outside to them, and they raped her *p* and abused her *q* throughout the night, and at dawn they let her go. ²⁶At daybreak the woman went back to the house where her master was staying, fell down at the door and lay there until daylight.

²⁷When her master got up in the morning and opened the door of the house and stepped out to continue on his way, there lay his concubine, fallen in the doorway of the house, with her hands on the threshold. ²⁸He said to her, "Get up; let's go." But there was no answer. Then the man put her on his donkey and set out for home.

²⁹When he reached home, he took a knife *r* and cut up his concubine, limb by limb, into twelve parts and sent them into all the areas of Israel. *s* ³⁰Everyone who saw it said, "Such a thing has never been seen or done, not since the day the Israelites came up out of Egypt. *t* Think about it! Consider it! Tell us what to do! *u* "

Israelites Fight the Benjamites

20 Then all the Israelites *v* from Dan to Beersheba *w* and from the land of Gilead came out as one man *x* and assembled *y* before the Lord in Mizpah. *z* ²The leaders of all the people of the tribes of

Israel took their places in the assembly of the people of God, four hundred thousand soldiers *a* armed with swords. ³(The Benjamites heard that the Israelites had gone up to Mizpah.) Then the Israelites said, "Tell us how this awful thing happened."

⁴So the Levite, the husband of the murdered woman, said, "I and my concubine came to Gibeah *b* in Benjamin to spend the night. *c* ⁵During the night the men of Gibeah came after me and surrounded the house, intending to kill me. *d* They raped my concubine, and she died. *e* ⁶I took my concubine, cut her into pieces and sent one piece to each region of Israel's inheritance, *f* because they committed this lewd and disgraceful act *g* in Israel. ⁷Now, all you Israelites, speak up and give your verdict. *h* "

⁸All the people rose as one man, saying, "None of us will go home. No, not one of us will return to his house. ⁹But now this is what we'll do to Gibeah: We'll go up against it as the lot directs. *i* ¹⁰We'll take ten men out of every hundred from all the tribes of Israel, and a hundred from a thousand, and a thousand from ten thousand, to get provisions for the army. Then, when the army arrives at Gibeah *n* in Benjamin, it can give them what they deserve for all this vileness done in Israel." ¹¹So all the men of Israel got together and united as one man *j* against the city.

¹²The tribes of Israel sent men throughout the tribe of Benjamin, saying, "What about this awful crime that was committed among you? *k* ¹³Now surrender those

Cross references (center column)

19:23
n S Ge 34:7;
S Lev 19:29;
S Jos 7:15;
S Jdg 20:6;
Ro 1:27
19:24 *o* Ge 19:8
19:25 *p* Jdg 20:5
q 1Sa 31:4
19:29 *r* S Ge 22:6
s Jdg 20:6;
1Sa 11:7
19:30 *t* Hos 9:9
u Jdg 20:7;
Pr 13:10
20:1 *v* Jdg 21:5
w S Ge 21:14;
1Sa 3:20;
2Sa 3:10; 17:11;
24:15; 1Ki 4:25;
2Ch 30:5 *x* ver
11; 1Sa 11:7
y 1Sa 7:5
z S Jos 11:3

20:2 *a* 1Sa 11:8
20:4 *b* S Jos 15:57
c S Ge 24:23
20:5 *d* S Jdg 19:22
e Jdg 19:25-26
20:6 *f* S Jdg 19:29
g S Jdg 19:23;
2Sa 13:12
20:7 *h* S Jdg 19:30
20:9 *i* S Lev 16:8
20:11 *j* S ver 1
20:12 *k* Dt 13:14

n *10* One Hebrew manuscript; most Hebrew manuscripts *Geba,* a variant of *Gibeah*

19:23 *don't be so vile.* An expression of outrage at the willful perversion of what is right and natural (see Ge 19:7; 2Sa 13:12; see also Ro 1:27).
19:24 *my virgin daughter, and his concubine.* The tragedy of this story lies not only in the decadence of Gibeah, but also in the callous selfishness of men who would betray defenseless women to be brutally violated for a whole night. Cf. Ge 19:8, where Lot offered his two daughters to the men of Sodom.
19:25 *took.* Here the Hebrew for this verb suggests taking by force.
19:29 *cut up his concubine.* Dismembering the concubine's body and sending parts to each of the 12 tribes was intended to awaken Israel from its moral lethargy and to marshal the tribes to face up to their responsibility. It is ironic that the one who issued such a call was himself so selfish and insensitive. See also Saul's similar action in 1Sa 11:7.
20:1–48 All Israel (except Jabesh Gilead; see 21:8–9) assembled before the Lord to deal with the moral outrage committed by the men of Gibeah. Having first inquired of God for divine direction, they marched against Gibeah and the Benjamites as the disciplinary arm of the Lord (see Jos 22:11–34), following him as their King.

20:1 *Dan to Beersheba.* A conventional way of speaking of all Israel from north (Dan) to south (Beersheba); see 1Sa 3:20; 2Sa 3:10; 24:2; 1Ch 21:2; 2Ch 30:5. The use of this expression, however, does not mean that the events of this chapter occurred after Dan's move to the north (18:27–29); rather, it indicates the author's perspective at the time of writing (Judges was probably written after the Davidic dynasty was fully established; see Introduction: Author and Date). Here the expression refers to the disciplinary action of all Israel (except Jabesh Gilead; see 21:8–9) against Gibeah and the rest of the Benjamites. Such a united response must have occurred early in the time of the judges, before the period of foreign domination of various parts of the land. *as one man.* Cf. vv. 8,11; 1Sa 11:7. *assembled . . . in Mizpah.* A gathering place of the tribes during the days of Saul (1Sa 7:5–17; 10:17).
20:9 *lot.* Casting lots was a common method of determining the will of God (see notes on Ex 28:30; Jnh 1:7; Ac 1:26).
20:10 *ten men.* Support for the large army had to be well organized and efficient. One man was responsible for providing food for nine men fighting at the front.
20:13 *surrender those wicked men.* The demand of Israel

wicked men[l] of Gibeah so that we may put them to death and purge the evil from Israel.[m]"

But the Benjamites would not listen to their fellow Israelites. [14]From their towns they came together at Gibeah to fight against the Israelites. [15]At once the Benjamites mobilized twenty-six thousand swordsmen from their towns, in addition to seven hundred chosen men from those living in Gibeah. [16]Among all these soldiers there were seven hundred chosen men who were left-handed,[n] each of whom could sling a stone at a hair and not miss.

[17]Israel, apart from Benjamin, mustered four hundred thousand swordsmen, all of them fighting men.

[18]The Israelites went up to Bethel[o] [o] and inquired of God.[p] They said, "Who of us shall go first[q] to fight[r] against the Benjamites?"

The LORD replied, "Judah[s] shall go first."

[19]The next morning the Israelites got up and pitched camp near Gibeah. [20]The men of Israel went out to fight the Benjamites and took up battle positions against them at Gibeah. [21]The Benjamites came out of Gibeah and cut down twenty-two thousand Israelites[t] on the battlefield that day. [22]But the men of Israel encouraged one another and again took up their positions where they had stationed themselves the first day. [23]The Israelites went up and wept before the LORD[u] until evening,[v] and they inquired of the LORD.[w] They said, "Shall we go up again to battle[x] against the Benjamites, our brothers?"

The LORD answered, "Go up against them."

[24]Then the Israelites drew near to Benjamin the second day. [25]This time, when the Benjamites came out from Gibeah to oppose them, they cut down another eighteen thousand Israelites,[y] all of them armed with swords.

[26]Then the Israelites, all the people, went up to Bethel, and there they sat weeping before the LORD.[z] They fasted[a] that day until evening and presented burnt offerings[b] and fellowship offerings[p] [c] to the LORD.[d] [27]And the Israelites inquired of the LORD.[e] (In those days the ark of the covenant of God[f] was there, [28]with Phinehas son of Eleazar,[g] the son of Aaron, ministering before it.)[h] They asked, "Shall we go up again to battle with Benjamin our brother, or not?"

The LORD responded, "Go, for tomorrow I will give them into your hands.[i]"

[29]Then Israel set an ambush[j] around Gibeah. [30]They went up against the Benjamites on the third day and took up positions against Gibeah as they had done before. [31]The Benjamites came out to meet them and were drawn away[k] from the city. They began to inflict casualties on the Israelites as before, so that about thirty men fell in the open field and on the roads—the one leading to Bethel[l] and the other to Gibeah.

[32]While the Benjamites were saying, "We are defeating them as before,"[m] the Israelites were saying, "Let's retreat and draw them away from the city to the roads."

[33]All the men of Israel moved from their places and took up positions at Baal Tamar, and the Israelite ambush charged out of its place[n] on the west[q] of Gibeah.[r] [34]Then ten thousand of Israel's finest men made a frontal attack on Gibeah. The fighting was so heavy that the Benjamites did not realize[o] how near disaster was.[p] [35]The LORD defeated Benjamin[q] before Israel, and on that day the Israelites struck down 25,100 Benjamites, all armed with swords. [36]Then the Benjamites saw that they were beaten.

20:13 /S Dt 13:13
mS Dt 13:5;
S 1Co 5:13
20:16 nS Jdg 3:15
20:18 oS Jos 12:9;
S Jdg 18:31
pS Jdg 18:5
qS Jdg 1:1 rver 23,28
sS Ge 49:10
20:21 tver 25
20:23 uS Nu 14:1
vJos 7:6
wS Jdg 18:5
xS ver 18
20:25 yver 21

20:26 zS Nu 14:1
a2Sa 12:21
bLev 1:3
cS Ex 32:6
dJdg 21:4
20:27 eS Jdg 18:5
fS Nu 10:33
20:28 gNu 25:7
hDt 18:5
iS Jos 2:24
20:29 jS Jos 8:2
20:31 kJos 8:16
lJos 16:1
20:32 mver 39
20:33 nJos 8:19
20:34 oJos 8:14
pver 41
20:35 qISa 9:21

o[18] Or to the house of God; also in verse 26   p[26] Traditionally peace offerings   q[33] Some Septuagint manuscripts and Vulgate; the meaning of the Hebrew for this word is uncertain.   r[33] Hebrew Geba, a variant of Gibeah

---

was not unreasonable. They wanted to punish only those directly involved in the crime. wicked men. See note on Dt 13:13. put them to death. The sin of the men of Gibeah called for the death penalty, and Israel had to punish the sin if she was to avoid guilt herself (see Dt 13:5; 17:7; 19:19–20).

20:16 left-handed. The Benjamite Ehud was also left-handed (3:15). sling a stone. Cf. Zec 9:15. The sling was a very effective weapon, as David later demonstrated in his encounter with Goliath (1Sa 17:49). A slingstone, weighing one pound or more, could be hurled at 90–100 miles an hour. miss. In other contexts the Hebrew for this verb is translated "to sin."

20:18 Bethel. At this time the ark of the covenant and the high priest Phinehas were at Bethel (see vv. 26–28). in-

quired of God. Probably by priestly use of Urim and Thummim (see notes on Ex 28:30; 1Sa 2:28). Who of us shall go first . . . ? See 1:1–36. Judah. See note on 1:2.

20:21 twenty-two thousand Israelites. A rousing victory for the Benjamites, who numbered 25,700 and therefore had slain nearly one man apiece.

20:27 ark. The only mention of the ark in Judges.

20:28 Phinehas. Phinehas was the priest in the tabernacle in the days of Joshua (Jos 22:13), and the fact that he was still serving is further evidence that these events took place early in the days of the judges (see notes on v. 1; 18:30).

20:29 set an ambush. See 9:32; Jos 8:2.

20:33 Baal Tamar. Location unknown.

20:36b–45 Details of the account in vv. 29–36a.

Now the men of Israel had given way[r] before Benjamin, because they relied on the ambush[s] they had set near Gibeah. [37]The men who had been in ambush made a sudden dash into Gibeah, spread out and put the whole city to the sword.[t] [38]The men of Israel had arranged with the ambush that they should send up a great cloud of smoke[u] from the city,[v] [39]and then the men of Israel would turn in the battle.

The Benjamites had begun to inflict casualties on the men of Israel (about thirty), and they said, "We are defeating them as in the first battle."[w] [40]But when the column of smoke began to rise from the city, the Benjamites turned and saw the smoke of the whole city going up into the sky.[x] [41]Then the men of Israel turned on them,[y] and the men of Benjamin were terrified, because they realized that disaster had come[z] upon them. [42]So they fled before the Israelites in the direction of the desert, but they could not escape the battle. And the men of Israel who came out of the towns cut them down there. [43]They surrounded the Benjamites, chased them and easily[s] overran them in the vicinity of Gibeah on the east. [44]Eighteen thousand Benjamites fell, all of them valiant fighters.[a] [45]As they turned and fled toward the desert to the rock of Rimmon,[b] the Israelites cut down five thousand men along the roads. They kept pressing after the Benjamites as far as Gidom and struck down two thousand more.

[46]On that day twenty-five thousand Benjamite[c] swordsmen fell, all of them valiant fighters. [47]But six hundred men turned and fled into the desert to the rock of Rimmon, where they stayed four months. [48]The men of Israel went back to Benjamin and put all the towns to the sword, including the animals and every-

thing else they found. All the towns they came across they set on fire.[d]

Wives for the Benjamites

21 The men of Israel had taken an oath[e] at Mizpah:[f] "Not one of us will give[g] his daughter in marriage to a Benjamite."

[2]The people went to Bethel,[t] where they sat before God until evening, raising their voices and weeping bitterly. [3]"O LORD, the God of Israel," they cried, "why has this happened to Israel? Why should one tribe be missing[h] from Israel today?"

[4]Early the next day the people built an altar and presented burnt offerings and fellowship offerings.[u][i]

[5]Then the Israelites asked, "Who from all the tribes of Israel[j] has failed to assemble before the LORD?" For they had taken a solemn oath that anyone who failed to assemble before the LORD at Mizpah should certainly be put to death.

[6]Now the Israelites grieved for their brothers, the Benjamites. "Today one tribe is cut off from Israel," they said. [7]"How can we provide wives for those who are left, since we have taken an oath[k] by the LORD not to give them any of our daughters in marriage?" [8]Then they asked, "Which one of the tribes of Israel failed to assemble before the LORD at Mizpah?" They discovered that no one from Jabesh Gilead[l] had come to the camp for the assembly. [9]For when they counted the people, they found that none of the people of Jabesh Gilead were there.

[10]So the assembly sent twelve thousand fighting men with instructions to go to Jabesh Gilead and put to the sword those living there, including the women and children. [11]"This is what you are to do,"

Cross references
20:36 [r]Jos 8:15; [s]Jos 8:2
20:37 [t]Jos 8:19
20:38 [u]Jos 8:20
[v]Jos 8:4-8
20:39 [w]ver 32; Ps 78:9
20:40 [x]Jos 8:20
20:41 [y]Jos 8:21
[z]ver 34
20:44 [a]1Sa 10:26; Ps 76:5
20:45 [b]S Jos 15:32
20:46 [c]1Sa 9:21
20:48 [d]Jdg 21:23
21:1 [e]S Jos 9:18
[f]S Jos 11:3 [g]ver 18,22
21:3 [h]ver 6,17
21:4 [i]Jdg 20:26
21:5 [j]Jdg 20:1
21:7 [k]S Jos 9:18
21:8 [l]1Sa 11:1; 31:11; 2Sa 2:4; 21:12; 1Ch 10:11

[s]43 The meaning of the Hebrew for this word is uncertain.   [t]2 Or to the house of God   [u]4 Traditionally peace offerings

---

20:46 *twenty-five thousand.* A round number for 25,100 (v. 35).

20:47 *six hundred men.* If these had not escaped, the tribe of Benjamin would have been annihilated. The same number of Danites went to Laish (18:11).

21:1-25 Second thoughts about the slaughter of their Benjamite brothers caused the Israelites to grieve over the loss. Only 600 Benjamites were left alive, and the men of Israel decided to provide wives for them in order to keep the tribe from disappearing. After slaughtering most of the people of Jabesh Gilead, the Israelites took 400 girls from the survivors and gave them to 400 Benjamites. Shortly afterward, each of the remaining Benjamites seized a wife from the girls of Shiloh, and Benjamin began to be restored.

21:1 *taken an oath.* This vow, probably taken in the name of the Lord, was not an ordinary vow but invoked a curse on oneself if the vow was broken (v. 18; see also Ac 23:12-15).

21:2 *Bethel.* See 20:18,26-27. *weeping bitterly.* Earlier the Israelites wept because they were defeated by the Benjamites (20:23,26). Now they weep because the disciplinary action against the Benjamites has nearly annihilated one of the tribes (see v. 3).

21:5 *failed to assemble.* The tribes had a mutual responsibility in times of military action (see note on 5:13-18). Those who failed to participate were often singled out and sometimes punished (5:15-17,23). *solemn oath.* Complicating the situation for Israel was the fact that they had taken a second oath, calling for the death of those who did not participate in the battle.

21:10 *twelve thousand.* A thousand from each tribe (see Nu 31:6), with 1,000 supplied to represent the tribe of Benjamin.

21:11 *Kill every male.* The punishment of Jabesh Gilead seems brutal, but the covenant bond between the tribes was

they said. "Kill every male[m] and every woman who is not a virgin.[n]" [12]They found among the people living in Jabesh Gilead four hundred young women who had never slept with a man, and they took them to the camp at Shiloh[o] in Canaan.

[13]Then the whole assembly sent an offer of peace[p] to the Benjamites at the rock of Rimmon.[q] [14]So the Benjamites returned at that time and were given the women of Jabesh Gilead who had been spared. But there were not enough for all of them.

[15]The people grieved for Benjamin,[r] because the LORD had made a gap in the tribes of Israel. [16]And the elders of the assembly said, "With the women of Benjamin destroyed, how shall we provide wives for the men who are left? [17]The Benjamite survivors must have heirs," they said, "so that a tribe of Israel will not be wiped out.[s] [18]We can't give them our daughters as wives, since we Israelites have taken this oath:[t] 'Cursed be anyone who gives[u] a wife to a Benjamite.' [19]But look, there is the annual festival of the LORD in Shiloh,[v] to the north of Bethel[w], and east of the road that goes from Bethel

to Shechem,[x] and to the south of Lebonah."

[20]So they instructed the Benjamites, saying, "Go and hide in the vineyards [21]and watch. When the girls of Shiloh come out to join in the dancing,[y] then rush from the vineyards and each of you seize a wife from the girls of Shiloh and go to the land of Benjamin. [22]When their fathers or brothers complain to us, we will say to them, 'Do us a kindness by helping them, because we did not get wives for them during the war, and you are innocent, since you did not give[z] your daughters to them.' "

[23]So that is what the Benjamites did. While the girls were dancing,[a] each man caught one and carried her off to be his wife. Then they returned to their inheritance[b] and rebuilt the towns and settled in them.[c]

[24]At that time the Israelites left that place and went home to their tribes and clans, each to his own inheritance.

[25]In those days Israel had no king; everyone did as he saw fit.[d]

Cross-references (center column):

21:11
[m]S Nu 31:7
[n]Nu 31:17-18
21:12 [o]S Jos 18:1
21:13 [p]S Dt 2:26
[q]S Jos 15:32
21:15 [r]ver 6
21:17 [s]S ver 3
21:18 [t]S Jos 9:18
[u]S ver 1
21:19 [v]S Jos 18:1
[w]Jos 16:1

[x]S Jos 17:7
21:21
[y]S Ex 15:20
21:22 [z]S ver 1
21:23 [a]ver 21
[b]S Jos 24:28
[c]Jdg 20:48
21:25 [d]S Dt 12:8

---

extremely important. Even though delinquency on some occasions was not punished (5:15–17), the nature of the crime in this case, coupled with Benjamin's refusal to turn over the criminals, caused Israel to take this oath (v. 5).
21:12 *in Canaan.* Emphasizes the fact that the women were brought across the Jordan from the east.
21:19 *festival of the LORD.* In light of the mention of vineyards (v. 20), it is likely that this reference is to the Feast of Tabernacles (see note on 1Sa 1:3), though it may have been a local festival. *north of Bethel . . . south of Lebonah.* This detailed description of Shiloh's location may indicate that this material was written at a time when Shiloh was in ruins, perhaps after its destruction during the battle of Aphek

(1Sa 4:1–11).
21:21 *seize a wife.* With the Benjamites securing wives in this manner, the other tribes were not actually "giving" their daughters to them (see note on v. 22).
21:22 *When their fathers or brothers complain.* It was customary for the brothers of a girl who had been abducted to demand satisfaction (see Ge 34:7–31; 2Sa 13:20–38). It was therefore important that the elders anticipate this response and be prepared to get cooperation from the girls' families.
21:24 *went home.* These soldiers had probably been away from home at least five months (see 20:47).
21:25 *Israel had no king.* See note on 17:6.

RUTH

Title

The book is named after one of its main characters, a young woman of Moab, the great-grandmother of David and an ancestress of Jesus (Mt 1:1,5). The only other Biblical book bearing the name of a woman is Esther.

Background

The story is set in the time of the judges, a time characterized in the book of Judges as a period of religious and moral degeneracy, national disunity and general foreign oppression. The book of Ruth reflects a temporary time of peace between Israel and Moab (contrast Jdg 3:12-30). Like 1Sa 1-2, it gives a series of intimate glimpses into the private lives of the members of an Israelite family. It also presents a delightful account of the remnant of true faith and piety in the period of the judges, relieving an otherwise wholly dark picture of that era.

Author and Date of Writing

The author is unknown. Jewish tradition points to Samuel, but it is unlikely that he is the author because the mention of David (4:17,22) implies a later date. Further, the literary style of Hebrew used in Ruth suggests that it was written during the period of the monarchy.

Theme and Theology

The author focuses on Ruth's unswerving and selfless devotion to desolate Naomi (1:16-17; 2:11-12; 3:10; 4:15) and on Boaz's kindness to these two widows (chs. 2-4). He presents striking examples of lives that embody in their daily affairs the self-giving love that fulfills God's law (Lev 19:18; cf. Ro 13:10). Such love also reflects God's love, in a marvelous joining of man's actions with God's (compare 2:12 with 3:9). In God's benevolence such lives are blessed and are made a blessing.

It may seem surprising that one who reflects God's love so clearly is a Moabitess (see map on "The Book of Ruth," p. 365). Yet her complete loyalty to the Israelite family into which she has been received by marriage and her total devotion to her desolate mother-in-law mark her as a true daughter of Israel and a worthy ancestress of David. She strikingly exemplifies the truth that participation in the coming kingdom of God is decided, not by blood and birth, but by the conformity of one's life to the will of God through the "obedience that comes from faith" (Ro 1:5). Her place in the ancestry of David signifies that all nations will be represented in the kingdom of David's greater Son.

As an episode in the ancestry of David, the book of Ruth sheds light on his role in the history of redemption. Redemption is a key concept throughout the account; the Hebrew word in its various forms occurs 23 times. The book is primarily a story of Naomi's transformation from despair to happiness through the selfless, God-blessed acts of Ruth and Boaz. She moves from emptiness to fullness (1:21; 3:17; see notes on 1:1,3,5-6,12,21-22; 3:17; 4:15), from destitution (1:1-5) to security and hope (4:13-17). Similarly, Israel was transformed from national desperation at the death of Eli (1Sa 4:18) to peace and prosperity in the early days of Solomon (1Ki 4:20-34; 5:4) through the selfless devotion of David, a true descendant of Ruth and Boaz. The author thus reminded Israel that the reign of the house of David, as the means of God's benevolent rule in Israel, held the prospect of God's promised peace and rest. But this rest would continue only so long as those who participated in the kingdom— prince and people alike—reflected in their daily lives the selfless love exemplified by Ruth and Boaz. In Jesus, the great "son of David" (Mt 1:1), and his redemptive work, the promised blessings of the kingdom of God find their fulfillment.

Literary Features

The book of Ruth is a Hebrew short story, told with consummate skill. Among historical narratives in Scripture it is unexcelled in its compactness, vividness, warmth, beauty and dramatic effectiveness— an exquisitely wrought jewel of Hebrew narrative art.

Marvelously symmetrical throughout (see Outline), the action moves from a briefly sketched account of distress (1:1-5; 71 words in Hebrew) through four episodes to a concluding account of relief and hope that is drawn with equal brevity (4:13-17; 71 words in Hebrew). The crucial turning point occurs exactly midway (see note on 2:20). The opening line of each of the four episodes signals its main development (1:6, the return; 2:1, the meeting with Boaz; 3:1, finding a home for Ruth; 4:1, the decisive event at the gate), while the closing line of each episode facilitates transition to what follows (see notes on 1:22; 2:23; 3:18; 4:12). Contrast is also used to good effect: pleasant (the meaning of "Naomi") and bitter (1:20), full and empty (1:21), and the living and the dead (2:20). Most striking is the contrast between two of the main characters, Ruth and Boaz: The one is a young, alien, destitute widow, while the other is a middle-aged, well-to-do Israelite securely established in his home community. For each there is a corresponding character whose actions highlight, by contrast, his or her selfless acts: Ruth—Orpah, Boaz—the unnamed kinsman.

When movements in space, time and circumstance all correspond in some way, a harmony results that both satisfies the reader's artistic sense and helps open doors to understanding. The author of Ruth keeps his readers from being distracted from the central story—Naomi's passage from emptiness to fullness through the selfless acts of Ruth and Boaz (see Theme and Theology). That passage, or restoration, first takes place in connection with her return from Moab to the promised land and to Bethlehem ("house of food"; see note on 1:1). It then progresses with the harvest season, when the fullness of the land is gathered in. All aspects of the story keep the reader's attention focused on the central issue. Consideration of these and other literary devices (mentioned throughout the notes) will aid understanding of the book of Ruth.

Outline

I. Introduction: Naomi Emptied (1:1-5)
II. Naomi Returns from Moab (1:6-22)
   A. Ruth Clings to Naomi (1:6-18)
   B. Ruth and Naomi Return to Bethlehem (1:19-22)
III. Ruth and Boaz Meet in the Harvest Fields (ch. 2)
   A. Ruth Begins Work (2:1-7)
   B. Boaz Shows Kindness to Ruth (2:8-16)
   C. Ruth Returns to Naomi (2:17-23)
IV. Ruth Goes to Boaz at the Threshing Floor (ch. 3)
   A. Naomi Instructs Ruth (3:1-5)
   B. Boaz Pledges to Secure Redemption (3:6-15)
   C. Ruth Returns to Naomi (3:16-18)
V. Boaz Arranges to Marry Ruth (4:1-12)
   A. Boaz Confronts the Unnamed Kinsman (4:1-8)
   B. Boaz Buys Naomi's Property and Announces His Marriage to Ruth (4:9-12)
VI. Conclusion: Naomi Filled (4:13-17)
VII. Epilogue: Genealogy of David (4:18-22)

Naomi and Ruth

1 In the days when the judges ruled,[a] [a] there was a famine in the land,[b] and a man from Bethlehem in Judah,[c] together with his wife and two sons, went to live for a while[d] in the country of Moab.[e] [2]The man's name was Elimelech,[f] his wife's name Naomi, and the names of his two sons were Mahlon and Kilion.[g] They were Ephrathites[h] from Bethlehem,[i] Judah. And they went to Moab and lived there.

[3]Now Elimelech, Naomi's husband, died, and she was left with her two sons. [4]They married Moabite women,[j] one named Orpah and the other Ruth.[k] After they had lived there about ten years, [5]both Mahlon and Kilion[l] also died,[m] and Naomi was left without her two sons and her husband.

[6]When she heard in Moab[n] that the LORD had come to the aid of his people[o] by providing food[p] for them, Naomi and her daughters-in-law[q] prepared to return home from there. [7]With her two daughters-in-law she left the place where she had been living and set out on the road that would take them back to the land of Judah.

[8]Then Naomi said to her two daughters-in-law, "Go back, each of you, to your mother's home.[r] May the LORD show kindness[s] to you, as you have shown to your dead[t] and to me. [9]May the LORD grant that each of you will find rest[u] in the home of another husband."

Then she kissed[v] them and they wept aloud[w] [10]and said to her, "We will go back with you to your people."

1:1 [a]Jdg 2:16-18
[b]S Ge 12:10;
2Ki 6:25;
Ps 105:16;
Hag 1:11
[c]S Ge 35:19
[d]Ge 47:4
[e]S Ge 36:35
1:2 [f]ver 3;
Ru 2:1; 4:3 [g]ver 5; Ru 4:9
[h]S Ge 35:16
[i]Ge 35:19;
1Sa 16:18
1:4 [j]1Ki 11:1;
2Ch 24:26;
Ezr 9:2; Ne 13:23
[k]ver 14; Ru 4:13;
Mt 1:5
1:5 [l]S ver 2 [m]ver 8; Ru 2:11

1:6 [n]S Ge 36:35
[o]S Ge 50:24;
Ex 4:31;
Jer 29:10; Zep 2:7
[p]Ps 132:15;
Mt 6:11
[q]S Ge 11:31;
S 38:16
1:8 [r]Ge 38:11
[s]S Ge 19:19;
2Ti 1:16 [t]S ver 5

1:9 [u]Ru 3:1 [v]S Ge 27:27; S 29:11 [w]S Ge 27:38; S Nu 25:6

[a] [j] Traditionally *judged*

1:1 *when the judges ruled.* Probably from c. 1380 to c. 1050 B.C. (see Introduction to Judges: Background). By mentioning the judges, the author calls to mind that period of Israel's apostasy, moral degradation and oppression. *famine.* Not mentioned in Judges. *Bethlehem in Judah.* David's hometown (1Sa 16:18). Bethlehem (the name suggests "house of food") is empty.
1:2 *Elimelech.* Means "(My) God is King" (see note on Jdg 8:23). *Naomi.* See NIV text note on v. 20. *Ephrathites.* Ephrathah was a name for the area around Bethlehem (see 4:11; Ge 35:19; 1Sa 17:12; Mic 5:2).
1:3 *Elimelech, Naomi's husband, died.* Naomi's emptying begins (see v. 21).
1:4 *They married.* Prospect of continuing the family line remained. *Moabite women.* See Ge 19:36–37. Marriage with Moabite women was not forbidden, though no Moabite—or his sons to the tenth generation—was allowed to "enter the assembly of the LORD" (Dt 23:3). *Ruth.* The name

sounds like the Hebrew for "friendship." Ruth is one of four women in Matthew's genealogy of Jesus. The others are Tamar, Rahab and Bathsheba (Mt 1:3,5–6).
1:5 *Mahlon.* Ruth's husband (4:10), whose name probably means "weakling." *Naomi was left.* Naomi's emptiness is complete: She has neither husband nor sons. She has only two young daughters-in-law, both of them foreigners and childless.
1:6 *the LORD had come to the aid of his people.* At several points in the account, God's sovereign control of events is acknowledged (here; vv. 13,21; 2:20; 4:12–15). *food.* Bethlehem ("house of food") again has food. *prepared to return home.* Empty Naomi returns to the newly filled land of promise.
1:8 *Go back.* Desolate Naomi repeatedly urges her daughters-in-law to return to their original homes in Moab (here; vv. 11–12,15); she has nothing to offer them. *show kindness.* See 2:20; 3:10.

The Book of Ruth

Set in the dark and bloody days of the judges, the story of Ruth is silent about the underlying hostility and suspicion the two peoples—Judahites and Moabites—felt for each other. The original onslaught of the invading Israelite tribes against towns that were once Moabite had never been forgotten or forgiven, while the Hebrew prophets denounced Moab's pride and arrogance for trying to bewitch, seduce and oppress Israel from the time of Balaam on. The Mesha stele (c. 830 B.C.) boasts of the massacre of entire Israelite towns.

Moab encompassed the expansive, grain-filled plateau between the Dead Sea and the eastern desert on both sides of the enormous rift of the Arnon River gorge. Much of eastern Moab was steppeland—semi-arid wastes not profitable for cultivation, but excellent for grazing flocks of sheep and goats. The tribute Moab paid to Israel in the days of Ahab was 100,000 lambs and the wool of 100,000 rams.

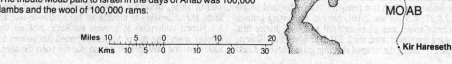

to Jericho ↑

ISRAEL

Jordan R.   Heshbon •

▲ Mt. Nebo

• Bethlehem

The main route through Moab was the King's Highway, a track connecting the cities of Heshbon, Dibon and Kir Hareseth with points north and south.

Dead Sea

• Dibon

• Aroer

Arnon R.

— King's Highway

MOAB

Miles 10 5 0   10   20
Kms 10 5 0   10   20   30

• Kir Hareseth

[11]But Naomi said, "Return home, my daughters. Why would you come with me? Am I going to have any more sons, who could become your husbands?[x] [12]Return home, my daughters; I am too old to have another husband. Even if I thought there was still hope for me—even if I had a husband tonight and then gave birth to sons— [13]would you wait until they grew up?[y] Would you remain unmarried for them? No, my daughters. It is more bitter[z] for me than for you, because the LORD's hand has gone out against me![a]"

[14]At this they wept[b] again. Then Orpah kissed her mother-in-law[c] good-by,[d] but Ruth clung to her.[e]

[15]"Look," said Naomi, "your sister-in-law[f] is going back to her people and her gods.[g] Go back with her."

[16]But Ruth replied, "Don't urge me to leave you[h] or to turn back from you. Where you go I will go,[i] and where you stay I will stay. Your people will be my people[j] and your God my God.[k] [17]Where you die I will die, and there I will be buried. May the LORD deal with me, be it ever so severely,[l] if anything but death separates you and me."[m] [18]When Naomi realized that Ruth was determined to go with her, she stopped urging her.[n]

[19]So the two women went on until they came to Bethlehem.[o] When they arrived in Bethlehem, the whole town was stirred[p] because of them, and the women exclaimed, "Can this be Naomi?"

[20]"Don't call me Naomi,[b]" she told them. "Call me Mara,[c] because the Almighty[d][q] has made my life very bitter.[r] [21]I went away full, but the LORD has brought me back empty.[s] Why call me Naomi? The LORD has afflicted[e] me;[t] the Almighty has brought misfortune upon me."

[22]So Naomi returned from Moab accompanied by Ruth the Moabitess,[u] her daughter-in-law,[v] arriving in Bethlehem as the barley harvest[w] was beginning.[x]

Ruth Meets Boaz

2 Now Naomi had a relative[y] on her husband's side, from the clan of Elimelech,[z] a man of standing,[a] whose name was Boaz.[b]

[2]And Ruth the Moabitess[c] said to Naomi, "Let me go to the fields and pick

---

1:11 xGe 38:11; Dt 25:5
1:13 yGe 38:11 zver 20; Ex 1:14; 15:23; 1Sa 30:6 aS Jdg 2:15; S Job 4:5
1:14 bver 9 cRu 2:11; 3:1; Mic 7:6 dS Ge 31:28 eS Dt 10:20
1:15 fDt 25:7 gJos 24:14 hGe 24:58
1:16 h2Ki 2:2 iGe 24:58 jPs 45:10 kS Jos 24:15
1:17 lS Sa 3:17; 14:44; 20:13; 25:22; 2Sa 3:9, 35; 19:13; 1Ki 2:23; 19:2; 20:10; 2Ki 6:31 m2Sa 15:21
1:18 nAc 21:14
1:19 oS Jdg 17:7 pMt 21:10
1:20 qS Ge 15:1; S 17:1; Ps 91:1 rS ver 13
1:21 sJob 1:21 tJob 30:11; Ps 88:7; Isa 53:4
1:22 uRu 2:2,6, 21; 4:5,10 vS Ge 11:31 wS Ex 9:31; S Lev 19:9 xS Sa 21:9
2:1 yRu 3:2; Pr 7:4 zS Ru 1:2 a1Sa 9:1; 1Ki 11:28 bRu 4:21; 1Ch 2:12; Mt 1:5; Lk 3:32
2:2 cS Ru 1:22

b*20 Naomi* means *pleasant;* also in verse 21.
c*20 Mara* means *bitter.* d*20* Hebrew *Shaddai;* also in verse 21 e*21* Or *has testified against*

1:11 *sons, who could become your husbands.* Naomi alludes to the Israelite law (Dt 25:5–6) regarding levirate marriage (see notes on Ge 38:8; Dt 25:5–10; see also Mk 12:18–23), which was given to protect the widow and guarantee continuance of the family line.

1:12 *I am too old.* Naomi can have no more sons; even her womb is empty.

1:13 *the LORD's hand . . . against me.* See notes on vv. 5–6; see also vv. 20–21.

1:14 Orpah's departure highlights the loyalty and selfless devotion of Ruth to her desolate mother-in-law.

1:15 *her gods.* The chief god of the Moabites was Chemosh.

1:16 This classic expression of loyalty and love discloses the true character of Ruth. Her commitment to Naomi is complete, even though it holds no prospect for her but to share in Naomi's desolation. For a similar declaration of devotion see 2Sa 15:21.

1:17 *May the LORD deal with me, be it ever so severely.* See note on 1Sa 3:17. Ruth, a Gentile, swears her commitment to Naomi in the name of Israel's God, thus acknowledging him as her God (see v. 16).

1:20 *Naomi . . . Mara.* See NIV text notes. In the ancient Near East a person's name was often descriptive. *Almighty.* See note on Ge 17:1.

1:21 *full . . . empty.* These words highlight the central theme of the story—how the empty Naomi becomes full again.

1:22 *Ruth the Moabitess.* Several times the author reminds the reader that Ruth is a foreigner from a despised people (2:2,6,21; 4:5,10; see 2:10). *harvest.* Harvesting grain in ancient Canaan took place in April and May (barley first, wheat a few weeks later; see 2:23). It involved the following steps: (1) cutting the ripened standing grain with hand sick-

les (Dt 16:9; 23:25; Jer 50:16; Joel 3:13)—usually done by men; (2) binding the grain into sheaves—usually done by women; (3) gleaning, i.e., gathering stalks of grain left behind (2:7); (4) transporting the sheaves to the threshing floor—often by donkey, sometimes by cart (Am 2:13); (5) threshing, i.e., loosening the grain from the straw—usually done by the treading of cattle (Dt 25:4; Hos 10:11), but sometimes by toothed threshing sledges (Isa 41:15; Am 1:3) or the wheels of carts (Isa 28:28); (6) winnowing—done by tossing the grain into the air with winnowing forks (Jer 15:7) so that the wind, which usually came up for a few hours in the afternoon, blew away the straw and chaff (Ps 1:4), leaving the grain at the winnower's feet; (7) sifting the grain (Am 9:9) to remove any residual foreign matter; (8) bagging for transportation and storage (Ge 42–44). Threshing floors, where both threshing and winnowing occurred, were hard, smooth, open places, prepared on either rock or clay and carefully chosen for favorable exposure to the prevailing winds. They were usually on the east side—i.e., downwind—of the village. *was beginning.* Naomi and Ruth arrive in Bethlehem just as the renewed fullness of the land is beginning to be harvested—an early hint that Naomi will be full again. Reference to the barley harvest also prepares the reader for the next major scene in the harvest fields (see Introduction: Literary Features).

2:1 *relative.* A sign of hope (see note on v. 20). *Boaz.* Probably means "In him is strength." Boaz is included in both genealogies of Jesus (Mt 1:5; Lk 3:32).

2:2 *Let me go.* Although Ruth is an alien and, as a young woman alone, obviously quite vulnerable in the harvest fields, she undertakes to provide for her mother-in-law. In 3:1 Naomi undertakes to provide for Ruth. *pick up the leftover grain.* The law of Moses instructed landowners to leave what the harvesters missed so that the poor, the alien,

up the leftover grain[d] behind anyone in whose eyes I find favor.[e] ''

Naomi said to her, "Go ahead, my daughter." [3]So she went out and began to glean in the fields behind the harvesters.[f] As it turned out, she found herself working in a field belonging to Boaz, who was from the clan of Elimelech.[g]

[4]Just then Boaz arrived from Bethlehem and greeted the harvesters, "The LORD be with you![h]"

"The LORD bless you![i]" they called back.

[5]Boaz asked the foreman of his harvesters, "Whose young woman is that?"

[6]The foreman replied, "She is the Moabitess[j] who came back from Moab with Naomi. [7]She said, 'Please let me glean and gather among the sheaves[k] behind the harvesters.' She went into the field and has worked steadily from morning till now, except for a short rest[l] in the shelter."

[8]So Boaz said to Ruth, "My daughter, listen to me. Don't go and glean in another field and don't go away from here. Stay here with my servant girls. [9]Watch the field where the men are harvesting, and follow along after the girls. I have told the men not to touch you. And whenever you are thirsty, go and get a drink from the water jars the men have filled."

[10]At this, she bowed down with her face to the ground.[m] She exclaimed, "Why have I found such favor in your eyes that you notice me[n]—a foreigner?[o]"

[11]Boaz replied, "I've been told all about what you have done for your mother-in-law[p] since the death of your husband[q]—how you left your father and mother and your homeland and came to live with a people you did not know[r] before.[s] [12]May the LORD repay you for what

you have done. May you be richly rewarded by the LORD,[t] the God of Israel,[u] under whose wings[v] you have come to take refuge.[w]"

[13]"May I continue to find favor in your eyes,[x] my lord," she said. "You have given me comfort and have spoken kindly to your servant—though I do not have the standing of one of your servant girls."

[14]At mealtime Boaz said to her, "Come over here. Have some bread[y] and dip it in the wine vinegar."

When she sat down with the harvesters,[z] he offered her some roasted grain.[a] She ate all she wanted and had some left over.[b] [15]As she got up to glean, Boaz gave orders to his men, "Even if she gathers among the sheaves,[c] don't embarrass her. [16]Rather, pull out some stalks for her from the bundles and leave them for her to pick up, and don't rebuke[d] her."

[17]So Ruth gleaned in the field until evening. Then she threshed[e] the barley she had gathered, and it amounted to about an ephah.[f][f] [18]She carried it back to town, and her mother-in-law saw how much she had gathered. Ruth also brought out and gave her what she had left over[g] after she had eaten enough.

[19]Her mother-in-law asked her, "Where did you glean today? Where did you work? Blessed be the man who took notice of you![h]"

Then Ruth told her mother-in-law about the one at whose place she had been working. "The name of the man I worked with today is Boaz," she said.

[20]"The LORD bless him![i]" Naomi said to her daughter-in-law.[j] "He has not stopped showing his kindness[k] to the liv-

Cross references (center column)

2:2 [d]S Lev 19:9; S 23:22
[e]S Ge 6:8; S 18:3
2:3 [f]ver 14; 2Ki 4:18; Jer 9:22; Am 9:13
[g]ver 1
2:4 [h]S Jdg 6:12; Lk 1:28; 2Th 3:16
[i]S Ge 28:3; S Nu 6:24
2:6 [j]S Ru 1:22
2:7 [k]S Ge 37:7; S Lev 19:9
[l]2Sa 4:5
2:10 [m]S Ge 19:1; S 1Sa 20:41 [n]ver 19; Ps 41:1
[o]S Ge 31:15; S Dt 15:3
2:11 [p]S Ru 1:14
[q]S Ru 1:5
[r]Isa 55:5
[s]Ru 1:16-17

2:12 [t]1Sa 24:19; 26:23,25; Ps 18:20; Pr 25:22; Jer 31:16
[u]S Jos 24:15
[v]Ps 17:8; 36:7; 57:1; 61:4; 63:7; 91:4 [w]Ps 71:1
2:13 [x]S Ge 18:3
2:14 [y]S Ge 3:19
[z]S ver 3
[a]S Lev 23:14 [b]ver 18
2:15 [c]S Ge 37:7; S Lev 19:9
2:16 [d]S Ge 37:10
2:17 [e]S Jdg 6:11
[f]S Lev 19:36
2:18 [g]ver 14
2:19 [h]S ver 10
2:20 [i]S Jdg 17:2; S 1Sa 23:21
[j]S Ge 11:31
[k]S Ge 19:19

[f]17 That is, probably about 3/5 bushel (about 22 liters)

---

the widow and the fatherless could glean for their needs (Lev 19:9; 23:22; Dt 24:19).

2:3 *As it turned out.* Divine providence is at work (vv. 19–20).

2:4 The exchange of greetings between Boaz and his laborers characterizes Boaz as a godly man with a kind spirit.

2:9 *follow along after the girls.* It was customary for the men to cut the grain and for the servant girls to go behind them to bind the grain into sheaves. Then Ruth could glean what they had left behind (see note on 1:22).

2:11 Ruth's commitment to care for her desolate mother-in-law remains the center of attention throughout the book.

2:12 *under whose wings.* A figure of a bird protecting her young under her wings (see Mt 23:37; see also note on 3:9).

2:13 *your servant.* A polite reference to herself.

2:15 *gave orders to his men.* Boaz goes beyond the requirement of the law in making sure that Ruth's labors are abundantly productive (see 3:15).

2:17 *threshed.* See note on 1:22. In Ruth's case, as in that

of Gideon (Jdg 6:11), the amount was small and could be threshed by hand simply by beating it with a club or stick. *ephah.* See NIV text note; an unusually large amount for one day's gleaning.

2:20 *The LORD . . . has not stopped showing his kindness.* See 1:8. In 3:10 Boaz credits Ruth with demonstrating this same virtue. *kinsman-redeemers.* Redemption is a key concept in Ruth (see Introduction: Theme and Theology). The kinsman-redeemer was responsible for protecting the interests of needy members of the extended family—e.g., to provide an heir for a brother who had died (Dt 25:5–10), to redeem land that a poor relative had sold outside the family (Lev 25:25–28), to redeem a relative who had been sold into slavery (Lev 25:47–49) and to avenge the killing of a relative (Nu 35:19–21; "avenger" and "kinsman-redeemer" are translations of the same Hebrew word). Naomi is encouraged when she hears that the Lord has led Ruth to the fields of a relative who might serve as their kinsman-redeemer. This moment of Naomi's awakened hope is the crucial turning point of the story.

ing and the dead." She added, "That man is our close relative; [he is one of our kinsman-redeemers. [m]"

[21]Then Ruth the Moabitess [n] said, "He even said to me, 'Stay with my workers until they finish harvesting all my grain.' "

[22]Naomi said to Ruth her daughter-in-law, "It will be good for you, my daughter, to go with his girls, because in someone else's field you might be harmed."

[23]So Ruth stayed close to the servant girls of Boaz to glean until the barley [o] and wheat harvests [p] were finished. And she lived with her mother-in-law.

Ruth and Boaz at the Threshing Floor

3 One day Naomi her mother-in-law [q] said to her, "My daughter, should I not try to find a home [g][r] for you, where you will be well provided for? [2]Is not Boaz, with whose servant girls you have been, a kinsman [s] of ours? Tonight he will be winnowing barley on the threshing floor. [t] [3]Wash [u] and perfume yourself, [v] and put on your best clothes. [w] Then go down to the threshing floor, but don't let him know you are there until he has finished eating and drinking. [x] [4]When he lies down, note the place where he is lying. Then go and uncover his feet and lie down. He will tell you what to do."

[5]"I will do whatever you say," [y] Ruth answered. [6]So she went down to the threshing floor [z] and did everything her mother-in-law told her to do.

[7]When Boaz had finished eating and drinking and was in good spirits, [a] he went over to lie down at the far end of the grain pile. [b] Ruth approached quietly, uncovered his feet and lay down. [8]In the middle of the night something startled the man, and he turned and discovered a woman lying at his feet.

[9]"Who are you?" he asked.

"I am your servant Ruth," she said. "Spread the corner of your garment [c] over me, since you are a kinsman-redeemer. [d]"

[10]"The LORD bless you, [e] my daughter," he replied. "This kindness is greater than that which you showed earlier: [f] You have not run after the younger men, whether rich or poor. [11]And now, my daughter, don't be afraid. I will do for you all you ask. All my fellow townsmen know that you are a woman of noble character. [g] [12]Although it is true that I am near of kin, there is a kinsman-redeemer [h] nearer than [i] I. [13]Stay here for the night, and in the morning if he wants to redeem, [j] good; let him redeem. But if he is not willing, as surely as the LORD lives [k] I will do it. [l] Lie here until morning."

[14]So she lay at his feet until morning, but got up before anyone could be recognized; and he said, "Don't let it be known that a woman came to the threshing floor. [m]" [n]

[15]He also said, "Bring me the shawl [o] you are wearing and hold it out." When she did so, he poured into it six measures of barley and put it on her. Then he [h] went back to town.

[16]When Ruth came to her mother-in-

2:20 [l]S Lev 25:25
[m]Ru 3:9,12; 4:1,14
2:21 [n]S Ru 1:22
2:23 [o]S Ex 9:31
[p]S Ge 30:14;
S 1Sa 6:13
3:1 [q]S Ru 1:14
[r]Ru 1:9
3:2 [s]S Ru 2:1
[t]S Lev 2:14;
S Nu 18:27;
S Jdg 6:11
3:3 [u]2Sa 12:20;
2Ki 5:10; Ps 26:6;
51:2; Isa 1:16;
Jer 4:14; Eze 16:9
[v]2Sa 14:2;
Isa 61:3
[w]S Ge 41:14
[x]S Ex 32:6;
S Ecc 2:3;
S Jer 15:17
3:5 [y]Eph 6:1;
Col 3:20
3:6 [z]S Nu 18:27
3:7 [a]Jdg 19:6,22;
1Sa 25:36;
2Sa 13:28;
1Ki 21:7; Est 1:10

[b]2Ch 31:6;
SS 7:2; Jer 50:26;
Hag 2:16
3:9 [c]Eze 16:8
[d]S Ru 2:20
3:10 [e]S Jdg 17:2
[f]S Jos 2:12
3:11 [g]Pr 12:4;
14:1; 31:10
3:12 [h]S Ru 2:20
[i]Ru 4:1
3:13 [j]Dt 25:5;
Ru 4:5; Mt 22:24
[k]S Nu 14:21;
Hos 4:15 [l]Ru 4:6
3:14 [m]S Nu 18:27
[n]Ro 14:16;
2Co 8:21
3:15 [o]Isa 3:22

[g][1] Hebrew *find rest* (see Ruth 1:9)   [h][15] Most Hebrew manuscripts; many Hebrew manuscripts, Vulgate and Syriac *she*

2:23 *until the barley and wheat harvests were finished.* This phrase rounds out the harvest episode and prepares for the next major scene on the threshing floor (see Introduction: Literary Features).

3:1 Naomi's awakened hope (cf. 1:8–13) now moves her to undertake provision for Ruth's future (see note on 2:2).

3:2 *Tonight he will be winnowing.* See note on 1:22. In the threshing season it was customary for the landowner to spend the night near the threshing floor to protect his grain from theft.

3:3 Ruth is instructed to prepare herself like a bride (see Eze 16:9–12). *go down to the threshing floor.* Women were not normally present at the evening reveleries of the threshers (v. 14). *eating and drinking.* Harvest was a time of festivity (Isa 9:3; 16:9–10; Jer 48:33).

3:4 *uncover his feet and lie down.* Although Naomi's instructions may appear forward, the moral integrity of Naomi and Ruth is never in doubt (see v. 11). Naomi's advice to Ruth is clearly for the purpose of appealing to Boaz's kinsman obligation. Ruth's actions were a request for marriage. Tamar, the mother of Perez (4:12), had also laid claim to the provision of the levirate (or kinsman-redeemer) law (Ge 38:13–30).

3:9 *Spread the corner of your garment over me.* A request

for marriage (see Eze 16:8); a similar custom is still practiced in some parts of the Middle East today. There is a play on the words "wings" of the Lord (2:12) and "corners" (lit. "wings") of the garment (here), both signifying protection. Boaz is vividly reminded that he must serve as the Lord's protective wing to watch over Ruth.

3:10 *kindness . . . you showed earlier.* See 2:11–12.

3:11 *woman of noble character.* See Pr 31:10. The Hebrew for this expression is similar to that used of Boaz in 2:1; thus the author maintains a balance between his descriptions of Ruth and Boaz.

3:12 *a kinsman-redeemer nearer than I.* How Boaz was related to Ruth's former husband (Mahlon) is unknown, but the closest male relative had the primary responsibility to marry a widow. Naomi instructed Ruth to approach Boaz because he had already shown himself willing to be Ruth's protector. Boaz, however, would not bypass the directives of the law, which clearly gave priority to the nearest relative.

3:13 *as surely as the LORD lives.* Boaz commits himself by oath (cf. 1:17) to redeem the family property and to arrange Ruth's honorable marriage.

3:15 Boaz goes beyond the requirement of the law in supplying Ruth with grain from the threshing floor (see 2:15).

law, Naomi asked, "How did it go, my daughter?"

Then she told her everything Boaz had done for her [17]and added, "He gave me these six measures of barley, saying, 'Don't go back to your mother-in-law empty-handed.' "

[18]Then Naomi said, "Wait, my daughter, until you find out what happens. For the man will not rest until the matter is settled today."[p]

Boaz Marries Ruth

4 Meanwhile Boaz went up to the town gate[q] and sat there. When the kinsman-redeemer[r] he had mentioned[s] came along, Boaz said, "Come over here, my friend, and sit down." So he went over and sat down.

[2]Boaz took ten of the elders[t] of the town and said, "Sit here," and they did so.[u] [3]Then he said to the kinsman-redeemer, "Naomi, who has come back from Moab, is selling the piece of land that belonged to our brother Elimelech.[v] [4]I thought I should bring the matter to your attention and suggest that you buy it in the presence of these seated here and in the presence of the elders of my people. If you will redeem it, do so. But if you[i] will not, tell me, so I will know. For no one has the right to do it except you,[w] and I am next in line."

"I will redeem it," he said.

[5]Then Boaz said, "On the day you buy the land from Naomi and from Ruth the Moabitess,[x] you acquire[j] the dead man's widow, in order to maintain the name of the dead with his property."[y]

[6]At this, the kinsman-redeemer said, "Then I cannot redeem[z] it because I might endanger my own estate. You redeem it yourself. I cannot do it."[a]

[7](Now in earlier times in Israel, for the redemption[b] and transfer of property to become final, one party took off his sandal[c] and gave it to the other. This was the method of legalizing transactions[d] in Israel.)[e]

[8]So the kinsman-redeemer said to Boaz, "Buy it yourself." And he removed his sandal.[f]

[9]Then Boaz announced to the elders and all the people, "Today you are witnesses[g] that I have bought from Naomi all the property of Elimelech, Kilion and Mahlon. [10]I have also acquired Ruth the Moabitess,[h] Mahlon's widow, as my wife,[i] in order to maintain the name of the dead with his property, so that his name will not disappear from among his family or from the town records.[j] Today you are witnesses![k]"

[11]Then the elders and all those at the gate[l] said, "We are witnesses.[m] May the LORD make the woman who is coming into your home like Rachel and Leah,[n] who together built up the house of Israel. May

Cross references (center column)

3:18 [p]Ps 37:3-5
4:1 [q]S Ge 18:1; S 23:10
[r]S Ru 2:20
[s]Ru 3:12
4:2 [t]S Ex 3:16
[u]S Dt 25:7
4:3 [v]S Lev 25:25; S Ru 1:2
4:4 [w]S Lev 25:25; Jer 32:7-8
4:5 [x]S Ru 1:22
[y]S Ge 38:8; S Ru 3:13
4:6 [z]Lev 25:25; Ru 3:13
[a]S Dt 25:7
4:7 [b]S Lev 25:24
[c]ver 8 [d]Isa 8:1-2, 16,20 [e]Dt 25:7-9
4:8 [f]Dt 25:9
4:9 [g]Isa 8:2; Jer 32:10,44
4:10 [h]S Ru 1:22
[i]S Dt 25:5
[j]S Dt 25:6
[k]S Jos 24:22
4:11 [l]S Ge 23:10
[m]S Dt 25:9
[n]S Ge 4:19; S 29:16

[i]4 Many Hebrew manuscripts, Septuagint, Vulgate and Syriac; most Hebrew manuscripts he   [i]5 Hebrew; Vulgate and Syriac Naomi, you acquire Ruth the Moabitess,

---

3:17 empty-handed. Again the empty-full motif (see note on 1:21).

3:18 Wait. The Hebrew underlying this word is translated "sat" in 4:1. Thus the author prepares the reader for the next major scene, in which Boaz sits at the town gate to see the matter through.

4:1 town gate. The "town hall" of ancient Israel, the normal place for business and legal transactions, where witnesses were readily available (vv. 9–12; see note on Ge 19:1). my friend. The other kinsman remains unnamed.

4:2 ten of the elders. A full court for legal proceedings.

4:3 selling the piece of land. See note on 2:20. Two interpretations are possible: 1. Naomi owns the land but is so destitute that she is forced to sell. It was the duty of the kinsman-redeemer to buy any land in danger of being sold outside the family. 2. Naomi does not own the land—it had been sold by Elimelech before the family left for Moab—but by law she retains the right of redemption to buy the land back. Lacking funds to do so herself, she is dependent on a kinsman-redeemer to do it for her. It is the right of redemption that Naomi is "selling." brother. Used in the broader sense of "relative."

4:5 you acquire the dead man's widow. Now Boaz reveals the other half of the obligation—the acquisition of Ruth. Levirate law (Dt 25:5–6) provided that Ruth's firstborn son would keep Mahlon's name alive and would possess the right of ownership of the family inheritance.

4:6 I cannot redeem it. Possibly he fears that, if he has a son by her and if that son is his only surviving heir, his own property will transfer to the family of Elimelech (see note on Ge 38:9). In that case his risk was no greater than that assumed by Boaz. This kinsman's refusal to assume the kinsman-redeemer's role highlights the kindness and generosity of Boaz toward the two widows—just as Orpah's return to her family highlights Ruth's selfless devotion and loyalty to Naomi.

4:7 one party took off his sandal. The process of renouncing one's property rights and passing them to another was publicly attested by taking off a sandal and transferring it to the new owner (cf. Am 2:6; 8:6). The Nuzi documents (see chart on "Ancient Texts Relating to the OT," p. 5) refer to a similar custom.

4:9 witnesses. The role of public witnesses was to attest to all legal transactions and other binding agreements.

4:10 name of the dead. See Dt 25:6.

4:11 Rachel and Leah . . . built up the house of Israel. Cf. Dt 25:9. The Israelite readers of Ruth would have associated the house of Jacob (Israel), built up by Rachel and Leah, with the house of Israel, rebuilt by David, the descendant of Ruth and Boaz, after it had been threatened with extinction (1Sa 4). They also knew that the Lord had covenanted to "build" the house of David as an enduring dynasty, through which Israel's blessed destiny would be assured (see 2Sa 7:27–29). Ephrathah. See note on 1:2.

you have standing in Ephrathah[o] and be famous in Bethlehem. [p] [12]Through the offspring the LORD gives you by this young woman, may your family be like that of Perez,[q] whom Tamar[r] bore to Judah."

The Genealogy of David

4:18–22pp — 1Ch 2:5–15; Mt 1:3–6; Lk 3:31–33

[13]So Boaz took Ruth and she became his wife. Then he went to her, and the LORD enabled her to conceive,[s] and she gave birth to a son.[t] [14]The women[u] said to Naomi: "Praise be to the LORD,[v] who this day has not left you without a kinsman-redeemer.[w] May he become famous throughout Israel! [15]He will renew your life and sustain you in your old age. For your daughter-in-law,[x] who loves you and who is better to you than seven sons,[y] has given him birth."

[16]Then Naomi took the child, laid him in her lap and cared for him. [17]The women living there said, "Naomi has a son." And they named him Obed. He was the father of Jesse,[z] the father of David.[a]

[18]This, then, is the family line of Perez[b]:

Perez was the father of Hezron,[c]
[19]Hezron the father of Ram,
Ram the father of Amminadab,[d]
[20]Amminadab the father of Nahshon,[e]
Nahshon the father of Salmon,[k]
[21]Salmon the father of Boaz,[f]
Boaz the father of Obed,
[22]Obed the father of Jesse,
and Jesse the father of David.

Cross references

4:11 *o*S Ge 35:16
*p*Ru 1:19
4:12 *q*S Ge 38:29
*r*Ge 38:6,24
4:13 *s*S Ge 8:1;
S 29:31
*t*S Ge 29:32;
S 30:6; Lk 1:57
4:14 *u*Lk 1:58
*v*S Ge 24:27
*w*S Ru 2:20
4:15 *x*S Ge 11:31
*y*1Sa 1:8; 2:5;
Job 1:2
4:17 *z*ver 22;
1Sa 16:1,18;
17:12,17,58;
1Ch 2:12,13;
Ps 72:20
*a*1Sa 16:13;
1Ch 2:15
4:18 *b*S Ge 38:29
*c*Nu 26:21
4:19 *d*S Ex 6:23
4:20 *e*S Nu 7:12
4:21 *f*S Ru 2:1

[k]20 A few Hebrew manuscripts, some Septuagint manuscripts and Vulgate (see also verse 21 and Septuagint of 1 Chron. 2:11); most Hebrew manuscripts *Salma*

4:12 *Perez, whom Tamar bore to Judah.* Perez was Boaz's ancestor (vv. 18–21; Mt 1:3; Lk 3:33). His birth to Judah was from a union based on the levirate practice (Ge 38:27–30; see note on 1:11). Perez was therefore an appropriate model within Boaz's ancestry for the blessing the elders gave to Boaz. Moreover, the descendants of Perez had raised the tribe of Judah to a prominent place in Israel. So the blessing of the elders—that, through the offspring Ruth would bear to Boaz, his family would be like that of Perez—was fully realized in David and his dynasty. Thus also v. 12 prepares the reader for the events briefly narrated in the conclusion.

4:13–17 The conclusion of the story balances the introduction (1:1–5): (1) In the Hebrew both have the same number of words; (2) both compress much into a short space; (3) both focus on Naomi; (4) the introduction emphasizes Naomi's emptiness, and the conclusion portrays her fullness.

4:13 *the LORD enabled her to conceive.* See note on 1:6.

4:14 *kinsman-redeemer.* The child Obed, as v. 15 makes clear. *May he become famous.* This same wish is expressed concerning Boaz in v. 11.

4:15 *better to you than seven sons.* See 1Sa 1:8. Since

seven was considered a number of completeness, to have seven sons was the epitome of all family blessings in Israel (see 1Sa 2:5; Job 1:2; 42:13). Ruth's selfless devotion to Naomi receives its climactic acknowledgment.

4:16 *laid him in her lap.* Possibly symbolizing adoption (see note on Ge 30:3).

4:17 *Naomi has a son.* Through Ruth, aged Naomi, who can no longer bear children, obtains an heir in place of Mahlon. *Obed.* The name means "servant," in its full form possibly "servant of the LORD."

4:18–22 See 1Ch 2:5–15; Mt 1:3–6; Lk 3:31–33. Like the genealogies of Ge 5:3–32; 11:10–26, this genealogy has ten names (see note on Ge 5:5). It brings to mind the reign of David, during which, in contrast to the turbulent period of the judges recalled in 1:1, Israel finally entered into rest in the promised land (see 1Ki 5:4). It signifies that, just as Naomi was brought from emptiness to fullness through the selfless love of Ruth and Boaz, so the Lord brought Israel from unrest to rest through their descendant David, who selflessly gave himself to fight Israel's battles on the Lord's behalf. The ultimate end of this genealogy is Jesus Christ, the great "son of David" (Mt 1:1), who fulfills prophecy and will bring the Lord's people into final rest.

1 SAMUEL

Title

1 and 2 Samuel are named after the person God used to establish kingship in Israel. Samuel not only anointed both Saul and David, Israel's first two kings, but he also gave definition to the new order of God's rule over Israel that began with the incorporation of kingship into its structure. Samuel's importance as God's representative in this period of Israel's history is close to that of Moses (see Ps 99:6; Jer 15:1) since he, more than any other person, provided for covenant continuity in the transition from the rule of the judges to that of the monarchy.

1 and 2 Samuel were originally one book. It was divided into two parts by the translators of the Septuagint (the Greek translation of the OT)—a division subsequently followed by Jerome (the Latin Vulgate) and by modern versions. The title of the book has varied from time to time, having been designated "The First and Second Books of Kingdoms" (Septuagint), "First and Second Kings" (Vulgate) and "First and Second Samuel" (Hebrew tradition and most modern versions).

Literary Features, Authorship and Date

Many questions have arisen pertaining to the literary character, authorship and date of 1,2 Samuel. Certain literary characteristics of the book suggest that it was compiled with the use of a number of originally independent sources, which the author may have incorporated into his own composition as much as possible in their original, unedited form.

Who the author was cannot be known with certainty since the book itself gives no indication of his identity. Some have suggested Zabud, son of Nathan the prophet, who is referred to in 1 Ki 4:5 as the "personal adviser" to King Solomon. He would have had access to information about David's reign from his father Nathan, as well as from court records. Whoever the author was, he must have lived shortly after Solomon's death (930 B.C.) and the division of the kingdom (see references to "Israel and Judah" in 11:8; 17:52; 18:16; 2Sa 5:5; 24:1-9 and the expression "kings of Judah" in 1Sa 27:6). Also, he doubtless had access to records of the life and times of Samuel, Saul and David. Explicit reference in the book itself is made to only one such source (the Book of Jashar, 2Sa 1:18), but the writer of Chronicles refers to four others that pertain to this period (the book of the annals of King David, 1Ch 27:24; the records of Samuel the seer; the records of Nathan the prophet; the records of Gad the seer, 1Ch 29:29).

Contents and Theme: Kingship and Covenant

1 Samuel portrays the establishment of kingship in Israel. Before the author describes this momentous change in the structure of the theocracy (God's rule), he effectively depicts the complexity of its context. The following events provide both historical and theological context for the birth of the monarchy:

1. *The birth, youth and calling of Samuel (chs. 1-3)*. In a book dealing for the most part with the reigns of Israel's first two kings, Saul and David, it is significant that the author chose not to include a birth narrative of either of these men, but to describe the birth of their forerunner and anointer, the prophet Samuel. This in itself accentuates the importance the author attached to Samuel's role in the events that follow. He seems to be saying in a subtle way that flesh and blood are to be subordinated to word and Spirit in the process of the establishment of kingship. For this reason chs. 1-3 should be viewed as integrally related to what follows, not as a more likely component of the book of Judges or as a loosely attached prefix to the rest of 1,2 Samuel. Kingship is given its birth and then nurtured by the prophetic word and work of the prophet Samuel. Moreover, the events of Samuel's nativity thematically anticipate the story of God's working that is narrated in the rest of the book.

2. *The "ark narratives" (chs. 4-6)*. This section describes how the ark of God was captured by the Philistines and then, after God wreaked havoc on several Philistine cities, how it was returned to Israel. These narratives reveal the folly of Israel's notion that possession of the ark automatically guaranteed

victory over her enemies. They also display the awesome power of the Lord (Yahweh, the God of Israel) and his superiority over the Philistine god Dagon. The Philistines were forced to confess openly their helplessness against God's power by their return of the ark to Israel. The entire ark episode performs a vital function in placing Israel's subsequent sinful desire for a human king in proper perspective.

3. *Samuel as a judge and deliverer (ch. 7)*. When Samuel called Israel to repentance and renewed dedication to the Lord, the Lord intervened mightily in Israel's behalf and gave victory over the Philistines. This narrative reaffirms the authority of Samuel as a divinely ordained leader; at the same time it provides evidence of divine protection and blessing for God's people when they place their confidence in the Lord and live in obedience to their covenant obligations.

All the material in chs. 1-7 serves as a necessary preface for the narratives of chs. 8-12, which describe the rise and establishment of kingship in Israel. The author has masterfully arranged the stories in chs. 8-12 in order to accentuate the serious theological conflict surrounding the historical events. In the study of these chapters, scholars have often noted the presence of a tension or ambivalence in the attitude toward the monarchy: On the one hand, Samuel is commanded by the Lord to give the people a king (8:7,9,22; 9:16-17; 10:24; 12:13); on the other hand, their request for a king is considered a sinful rejection of the Lord (8:7; 10:19; 12:12,17,19-20). These seemingly conflicting attitudes toward the monarchy must be understood in the context of Israel's covenant relationship with the Lord.

Moses had anticipated Israel's desire for a human king (Dt 17:18-20), but Israelite kingship was to be compatible with the continued rule of the Lord over his people as their Great King. Instead, when the elders asked Samuel to give them a king (8:5,19-20), they rejected the Lord's kingship over them (8:7; 10:19; 12:17,19). Their desire was for a king such as the nations around them had—to lead them in battle and give them a sense of national security and unity. The request for a king constituted a denial of their covenant relationship to the Lord, who was their King. Moreover, the Lord not only had promised to be their protector but had also repeatedly demonstrated his power in their behalf, most recently in the ark narratives (chs. 4-6), as well as in the great victory won over the Philistines under the leadership of Samuel (ch. 7).

Nevertheless the Lord instructed Samuel to give the people a king (8:7,9,22). By divine appointment Saul was brought into contact with Samuel, and Samuel was directed to anoint him privately as king (9:1-10:16). Subsequently, Samuel gathered the people at Mizpah, where, after again admonishing them concerning their sin in desiring a king (10:18-19), he presided over the selection of a king by lot. The lot fell on Saul and publicly designated him as the one whom God had chosen (10:24). Saul did not immediately assume his royal office, but returned home to work his fields (11:5,7). When the inhabitants of Jabesh Gilead were threatened by Nahash the Ammonite, Saul rose to the challenge, gathered an army and led Israel to victory in battle. His success placed a final seal of divine approval on Saul's selection to be king (cf. 10:24; 11:12-13) and occasioned the inauguration of his reign at Gilgal (11:14-12:25).

The question that still needed resolution, then, was not so much whether Israel should have a king (it was clearly the Lord's will to give them a king), but rather how they could maintain their covenant with God (i.e., preserve the theocracy) now that they had a human king. The problem was resolved when Samuel called the people to repentance and renewal of their allegiance to the Lord on the very occasion of the inauguration of Saul as king (11:14-12:25; see note on 10:25). By establishing kingship in the context of covenant renewal, Samuel placed the monarchy in Israel on a radically different footing from that in surrounding nations. The king in Israel was not to be autonomous in his authority and power; rather, he was to be subject to the law of the Lord and the word of the prophet (10:25; 12:23). This was to be true not only for Saul but also for all the kings who would occupy the throne in Israel in the future. The king was to be an instrument of the Lord's rule over his people, and the people as well as the king were to continue to recognize the Lord as their ultimate Sovereign (12:14-15).

Saul very quickly demonstrated that he was unwilling to submit to the requirements of his theocratic office (chs. 13-15). When he disobeyed the instructions of the prophet Samuel in preparation for battle against the Philistines (13:13), and when he refused to totally destroy the Amalekites as he had been commanded to do by the word of the Lord through Samuel (ch. 15), he ceased to be an instrument of the Lord's rule over his people. These abrogations of the requirements of his theocratic office led to his rejection as king (15:23).

The remainder of 1 Samuel (chs. 16-31) depicts the Lord's choice of David to be Saul's successor, and then describes the long road by which David is prepared for accession to the throne. Although Saul's rule became increasingly anti-theocratic in nature, David refused to usurp the throne by forceful means but left his accession to office in the Lord's hands. Eventually Saul was wounded in a battle

with the Philistines and, fearing capture, took his own life. Three of Saul's sons, including David's loyal friend Jonathan, were killed in the same battle (ch. 31).

Chronology

Even though the narratives of 1,2 Samuel contain some statements of chronological import (see, e.g., 1Sa 6:1; 7:2; 8:1,5; 13:1; 25:1; 2Sa 2:10-11; 5:4-5; 14:28; 15:7), the data are insufficient to establish a precise chronology for the major events of this period of Israel's history. Except for the dates of David's birth and the duration of his reign, which are quite firm (see 2Sa 5:4-5), most other dates can only be approximated. The textual problem with the chronological data on the age of Saul when he became king and the length of his reign (see NIV text notes on 1Sa 13:1) contributes to uncertainty concerning the precise time of his birth and the beginning of his reign. No information is given concerning the time of Samuel's birth (1Sa 1:1) or death (25:1). His lifetime must have spanned, at least in part, that of Samson and that of Obed, son of Ruth and Boaz and grandfather of David. It is indicated that he was well along in years when the elders of Israel asked him to give them a king (see 8:1,5). One other factor contributing to chronological uncertainty is that the author has not always arranged his material in strict chronological sequence. It seems clear, for example, that 2Sa 7 is to be placed chronologically after David's conquests described in 2Sa 8:1-14 (see notes on 2Sa 7:1; 8:1). The story of the famine sent by God on Israel during the reign of David because of Saul's violation of a treaty with the Gibeonites is found in 2Sa 21:1-4, though chronologically it occurred prior to the time of Absalom's rebellion recorded in 2Sa 15-18 (see further the notes on 2Sa 21:1-2). The following dates, however, provide an approximate chronological framework for the times of Samuel, Saul and David.

1105 B.C.	Birth of Samuel (1Sa 1:20)
1080	Birth of Saul
1050	Saul anointed to be king (1Sa 10:1)
1040	Birth of David
1025	David anointed to be Saul's successor (1Sa 16:1-13)
1010	Death of Saul and beginning of David's reign over Judah in Hebron (2Sa 1:1; 2:1,4,11)
1003	Beginning of David's reign over all Israel and capture of Jerusalem (2Sa 5)
997-992	David's wars (2Sa 8:1-14)
991	Birth of Solomon (2Sa 12:24; 1Ki 3:7; 11:42)
980	David's census (2Sa 24:1)
970	End of David's reign (2Sa 5:4-5; 1Ki 2:10-11)

Outline

I. Historical Setting for the Establishment of Kingship in Israel (1Sa 1-7)
   A. Samuel's Birth, Youth and Calling to Be a Prophet; Judgment on the House of Eli (1Sa 1-3)
   B. Israel Defeated by the Philistines, the Ark of God Taken and the Ark Restored; Samuel's Role as Judge and Deliverer (1Sa 4-7)
II. The Establishment of Kingship in Israel under the Guidance of Samuel the Prophet (1Sa 8-12)
   A. The People's Sinful Request for a King and God's Intent to Give Them a King (1Sa 8)
   B. Samuel Anoints Saul Privately to Be King (1Sa 9:1-10:16)
   C. Saul Chosen to Be King Publicly by Lot at Mizpah (1Sa 10:17-27)
   D. The Choice of Saul as King Confirmed by Victory over the Ammonites (1Sa 11:1-13)
   E. Saul's Reign Inaugurated at a Covenant Renewal Ceremony Convened by Samuel at Gilgal (1Sa 11:14-12:25)
III. Saul's Kingship a Failure (1Sa 13-15)
IV. David's Rise to the Throne; Progressive Deterioration and End of Saul's Reign (1Sa 16:1-2Sa 5:5)
   A. David Is Anointed Privately, Enters the Service of King Saul and Flees for His Life (1Sa 16-26)
   B. David Seeks Refuge in Philistia, and Saul and His Sons Are Killed in Battle (1Sa 27-31)
   C. David Becomes King over Judah (2Sa 1-4)
   D. David Becomes King over All Israel (2Sa 5:1-5)
V. David's Kingship in Its Accomplishments and Glory (2Sa 5:6-9:12)
   A. David Conquers Jerusalem and Defeats the Philistines (2Sa 5:6-25)
   B. David Brings the Ark to Jerusalem (2Sa 6)
   C. God Promises David an Everlasting Dynasty (2Sa 7)

    D. The Extension of David's Kingdom Externally and the Justice of His Rule Internally (2Sa 8)

    E. David's Faithfulness to His Covenant with Jonathan (2Sa 9)

  VI. David's Kingship in Its Weaknesses and Failures (2Sa 10-20)

    A. David Commits Adultery and Murder (2Sa 10-12)

    B. David Loses His Sons Amnon and Absalom (2Sa 13-20)

 VII. Final Reflections on David's Reign (2Sa 21-24)

The Birth of Samuel

1 There was a certain man from Rama-thaim,[a] a Zuphite[a b] from the hill country[c] of Ephraim,[d] whose name was Elkanah[e] son of Jeroham, the son of Elihu, the son of Tohu, the son of Zuph, an Ephraimite. [2]He had two wives;[f] one was called Hannah and the other Peninnah. Peninnah had children, but Hannah had none.

[3]Year after year[g] this man went up from his town to worship[h] and sacrifice to the LORD Almighty at Shiloh,[i] where Hophni and Phinehas, the two sons of Eli,[j] were priests of the LORD. [4]Whenever the day came for Elkanah to sacrifice,[k] he would give portions of the meat to his wife Peninnah and to all her sons and daughters.[l] [5]But to Hannah he gave a double portion[m] because he loved her, and the LORD had closed her womb.[n] [6]And because the LORD had closed her womb, her rival kept provoking her in order to irritate her.[o] [7]This went on year after year. Whenever Hannah went up to the house of the LORD, her rival provoked her till she wept and

would not eat.[p] [8]Elkanah her husband would say to her, "Hannah, why are you weeping? Why don't you eat? Why are you downhearted? Don't I mean more to you than ten sons?[q]"

[9]Once when they had finished eating and drinking in Shiloh, Hannah stood up. Now Eli the priest was sitting on a chair by the doorpost of the LORD's temple.[b r] [10]In bitterness of soul[s] Hannah wept much and prayed to the LORD. [11]And she made a vow,[t] saying, "O LORD Almighty[u], if you will only look upon your servant's misery and remember[v] me, and not forget your servant but give her a son, then I will give him to the LORD for all the days of his life,[w] and no razor[x] will ever be used on his head."

[12]As she kept on praying to the LORD, Eli observed her mouth. [13]Hannah was praying in her heart, and her lips were moving but her voice was not heard. Eli thought she was drunk [14]and said to her, "How long will you keep on getting drunk? Get rid of your wine."

Cross references (center column)

1:1 [a]S Jos 18:25
[b]1Sa 9:5
[c]Jos 17:17-18
[d]Jos 21:20-22
[e]1Ch 6:27,34
1:2 [f]S Ge 4:19
1:3 [g]ver 21;
Ex 23:14;
1Sa 2:19; 20:6,
29; Lk 2:41
[h]Dt 12:5-7
[i]S Jos 18:1
[j]1Sa 2:31; 14:3
1:4 [k]Lev 7:15-18;
Dt 12:17-18
[l]S Ge 29:34
1:5 [m]S Ge 37:3
[n]S Ge 11:30;
S 29:31
1:6 [o]S Ge 16:4

1:7 [p]2Sa 12:17;
Ps 102:4
1:8 [q]S Ru 4:15
1:9 [r]1Sa 3:3
1:10 [s]Job 3:20;
7:11; 10:1;
21:25; 23:2;
27:2; Isa 38:15;
Jer 20:18
1:11 [t]S Jdg 11:30
[u]S Ge 17:1;
Ps 24:10; 46:7;
Isa 1:9 [v]S Ge 8:1
[w]S Jdg 13:7
[x]Nu 6:1-21;
Jdg 13:5; Lk 1:15

[a] [1] Or *from Ramathaim Zuphim*   [b] [9] That is, tabernacle

---

1:1 *Ramathaim.* The name occurs only here in the OT and appears to be another name for Ramah (see 1:19; 2:11; 7:17; 19:18; 25:1). It is perhaps to be identified with the Ramah of Benjamin (see Jos 18:25) located in the hill country about five miles north of Jerusalem near the border of Ephraim and Benjamin. *Zuphite.* See NIV text note. It is not entirely clear whether this word refers to the man or the place. If it refers to the man, it indicates his descent from Zuph (see 1Ch 6:34-35). If it refers to the place, it designates the general area in which Ramathaim is located (see 9:5). *Ephraimite.* Although Elkanah is here called an Ephraimite, he was probably a Levite whose family belonged to the Kohathite clans that had been allotted towns in Ephraim (see Jos 21:20-21; 1Ch 6:22-26).
1:2 *two wives.* See notes on Ge 4:19; 16:2; 25:6.
1:3 *Year after year this man went up.* Three times a year every Israelite male was required to appear before the Lord at the central sanctuary (Ex 23:14-19; 34:23; Dt 16:16-17). The festival referred to here was probably the Feast of Tabernacles, which not only commemorated God's care for his people during the desert journey to Canaan (see Lev 23:43) but more especially celebrated, with joy and feasting, God's blessing on the year's crops (see Dt 16:13-15). On such festive occasions Hannah's deep sorrow because of her own barrenness was the more poignant. *the LORD Almighty.* Traditionally "the LORD of hosts." This is the first time in the Bible that God is designated by this title. The Hebrew for "host(s)" can refer to (1) human armies (Ex 7:4; Ps 44:9); (2) the celestial bodies such as the sun, moon and stars (Ge 2:1; Dt 4:19; Isa 40:26); or (3) the heavenly creatures such as angels (Jos 5:14; 1Ki 22:19; Ps 148:2). The title, "the LORD of hosts," is perhaps best understood as a general reference to the sovereignty of God over all powers in the universe (hence the NIV rendering, "the LORD Almighty"). In the account of the establishment of kingship in Israel it became particularly appropriate as a reference to God as the God of armies—both of the heavenly army (Dt 33:2; Jos 5:14; Ps 68:17; Hab 3:8) and of the army of Israel (1Sa 17:45). *Shiloh.* The town in

Ephraim between Bethel and Shechem where the central sanctuary and the ark of the covenant were located (see Jos 18:1; Jdg 21:19).
1:4 *sacrifice.* Here refers to a sacrifice that was combined with a festive meal signifying fellowship and communion with the Lord and grateful acknowledgment of his mercies (see Lev 7:11-18; Dt 12:7,17-18).
1:5 *the LORD had closed her womb.* The Lord gives and withholds children (see Ge 18:10; 29:31; 30:2,22).
1:6 *her rival.* See note on Ge 16:4.
1:9 *temple.* Here and in 3:3 the central sanctuary, the tabernacle (see NIV text note), is referred to as "the LORD's temple." It is also called "the house of the LORD" (v. 7; 3:15), "the Tent of Meeting" (2:22) and "my dwelling" (2:32). The references to the tabernacle as a "house" and a "temple," as well as those to sleeping quarters and doors (3:2,15), give the impression that at this time the tabernacle was part of a larger, more permanent building complex to which the term "temple" could legitimately be applied (cf. Jer 7:12,14; 26:6).
1:11 *vow.* See Ge 28:20-22; Nu 21:2; Ps 50:14; 76:11; 116:14,18; 132:2-5; Pr 20:25; 31:2. Regulations for the making of vows by women are found in Nu 30. *remember.* To remember is more than simply to recall that Hannah existed. It is to go into action in her behalf (see v. 19; see also note on Ge 8:1). *all the days of his life.* In contrast to the normal period of service for Levites, which was from age 25 to 50 (see Nu 8:23-26). *no razor.* Hannah voluntarily vows for her son that which God had required of Samson (Jdg 13:5). Long hair was a symbol of dedication to the service of the Lord and was one of the characteristics of the Nazirite vow (see Nu 6:1-21). The vow was normally taken for a limited time rather than for life.
1:13 *drunk.* Eli's mistake suggests that in those days it was not uncommon for drunken people to enter the sanctuary. Further evidence of the religious and moral deterioration of the time is found in the stories of Jdg 17-21.

¹⁵"Not so, my lord," Hannah replied, "I am a woman who is deeply troubled.ʸ I have not been drinking wine or beer; I was pouringᶻ out my soul to the LORD. ¹⁶Do not take your servant for a wicked woman; I have been praying here out of my great anguish and grief." ᵃ

¹⁷Eli answered, "Go in peace,ᵇ and may the God of Israel grant you what you have asked of him.ᶜ"

¹⁸She said, "May your servant find favor in your eyes.ᵈ" Then she went her way and ate something, and her face was no longer downcast.ᵉ

¹⁹Early the next morning they arose and worshiped before the LORD and then went back to their home at Ramah.ᶠ Elkanah lay with Hannah his wife, and the LORD remembered ᵍ her. ²⁰So in the course of time Hannah conceived and gave birth to a son.ʰ She named ⁱ him Samuel,ᶜʲ saying, "Because I asked the LORD for him."

Hannah Dedicates Samuel

²¹When the man Elkanah went up with all his family to offer the annual ᵏ sacrifice to the LORD and to fulfill his vow,ˡ ²²Hannah did not go. She said to her husband, "After the boy is weaned, I will take him and present ᵐ him before the LORD, and he will live there always."

²³"Do what seems best to you," Elkanah her husband told her. "Stay here until you have weaned him; only may the LORD make good ⁿ hisᵈ word." So the woman stayed at home and nursed her son until she had weaned ᵒ him.

²⁴After he was weaned, she took the boy with her, young as he was, along with a three-year-old bull,ᵉᵖ an ephahᶠ of flour and a skin of wine, and brought him to the house of the LORD at Shiloh. ²⁵When they had slaughtered the bull, they brought the boy to Eli, ²⁶and she said to him, "As surely as you live, my lord, I am the woman who stood here beside you praying to the LORD. ²⁷I prayed ᑫ for this child, and the LORD has granted me what I asked of him. ²⁸So now I give him to the LORD. For his whole life ʳ he will be given over to the LORD." And he worshiped the LORD there.

Hannah's Prayer

2 Then Hannah prayed and said: ˢ

"My heart rejoices ᵗ in the LORD;
in the LORD my horn ᵍᵘ is lifted high.
My mouth boasts ᵛ over my enemies,ʷ
for I delight in your deliverance.

²"There is no one holy ʰˣ like ʸ the
LORD;
there is no one besides you;
there is no Rock ᶻ like our God.

³"Do not keep talking so proudly
or let your mouth speak such
arrogance,ᵃ
for the LORD is a God who knows,ᵇ
and by him deeds ᶜ are weighed. ᵈ

Cross references (center column)

1:15 ʸ2Ki 4:27
ᶻPs 42:4; 62:8;
La 2:19
1:16 ᵃPs 55:2
1:17 ᵇNu 6:26;
1Sa 20:42;
2Ki 5:19;
S Ac 15:33
ᶜS Ge 25:21;
Ps 20:3-5
1:18 ᵈS Ge 18:3;
Ru 2:13
ᵉRo 15:13
1:19 ⁱS Jos 18:25
ᵍS Ge 8:1;
S 29:31
1:20
ʰS Ge 17:19;
S 29:32; S 30:6
ⁱEx 2:10; Mt 1:21
ʲ1Sa 7:5; 12:23;
1Ch 6:27;
Jer 15:1;
Heb 11:32
1:21 ᵏS ver 3
ˡS Ge 28:20;
Nu 30:2;
Dt 12:11
1:22 ᵐEx 13:2;
Lk 2:22
1:23 ⁿS Ge 25:21
ᵒGe 21:8
1:24
ᵖNu 15:8-10
1:27 ᑫ1Sa 2:20;
Ps 66:19-20
1:28 ʳS Jdg 13:7
2:1 ˢLk 1:46-55
ᵗPs 13:5; 33:21;
Zec 10:7
ᵘPs 18:2; 89:17,
24; 148:14
ᵛPs 6:8
ʷS Nu 10:35;
Ps 6:10
2:2 ˣS Ex 15:11;
S Lev 11:44
ʸS Ex 8:10;
Isa 40:25; 46:5
ᶻS Ge 49:24;
S Ex 33:22;
Dt 32:37;
2Sa 22:2,32;
23:3; Ps 31:3;
71:3
2:3 ᵃPs 17:10;
31:18; 73:8;
75:4; 94:4
ᵇS Jos 22:22
ᶜ1Sa 16:7;

1Ki 8:39; 1Ch 28:9; 2Ch 6:30; Pr 15:11; Jer 11:20; 17:10
ᵈPr 16:2; 24:11-12

ᶜ20 Samuel sounds like the Hebrew for heard of God.
ᵈ23 Masoretic Text; Dead Sea Scrolls, Septuagint and Syriac your   ᵉ24 Dead Sea Scrolls, Septuagint and Syriac; Masoretic Text with three bulls   ᶠ24 That is, probably about 3/5 bushel (about 22 liters)   ᵍ1 Horn here symbolizes strength; also in verse 10.   ʰ2 Or no Holy One

---

1:16 *wicked.* See note on Dt 13:13.
1:20 *Samuel.* See NIV text note.
1:21 *annual sacrifice.* See notes on vv. 3–4. *his vow.* Making vows to God was a common feature of OT piety, usually involving thank offerings and praise (see Lev 7:16; Ps 50:14; 56:12; 66:13–15; 116:17–18; Isa 19:21). Elkanah no doubt annually made vows to the Lord as he prayed for God's blessing on his crops and flocks, and fulfilled those vows at the Feast of Tabernacles (see note on v. 3).
1:22 *weaned.* It was customary in the East to nurse children for three years or longer (in the Apocrypha see 2 Maccabees 7:27) since there was no way to keep milk sweet.
1:23 *his word.* No previous word from God is mentioned, unless this refers to the pronouncement of Eli in v. 17. The Dead Sea Scrolls, Septuagint (the Greek translation of the OT) and Syriac version (see NIV text note) resolve this problem by reading "your word."
1:26 *As surely as you live.* A customary way of emphasizing the truthfulness of one's words.
2:1 *prayed.* Hannah's prayer is a song of praise and thanksgiving to God (see Ps 72:20, where the psalms of David are designated "prayers"). This song has sometimes been termed the "Magnificat of the OT" because it is so similar to the Magnificat of the NT (Mary's song, Lk 1:46–55). It also

has certain resemblances to the "Benedictus" (the song of Zechariah, Lk 1:67–79). Hannah's song of praise finds many echoes in David's song near the end of the book (2Sa 22). These two songs frame the main narrative, and their themes highlight the ways of God that the narrative relates—they contain the theology of the book in the form of praise. Hannah speaks prophetically at a time when Israel is about to enter an important new period of her history with the establishment of kingship through her son, Samuel. *rejoices in the LORD.* The supreme source of Hannah's joy is not in the child, but in the God who has answered her prayer. *my horn is lifted high.* See NIV text note; cf. Dt 33:17; Ps 75:5,10; 92:10; 112:9; Lk 1:69. To have one's horn lifted up by God is to be delivered from disgrace to a position of honor and strength.
2:2 *no one besides you.* See 2Sa 7:22; Dt 4:39; Isa 45:6. *Rock.* A metaphor to depict the strength and stability of the God of Israel as the unfailing source of security for his people (see 2Sa 22:32; Dt 32:4,31; Ps 18:31; Isa 30:29; 44:8).
2:3 *so proudly ... such arrogance.* After the manner of Peninnah (and others in the narratives of 1,2 Samuel—Eli's sons, the Philistines, Saul, Nabal, Goliath, Absalom, Shimei and Sheba). *the LORD is a God who knows.* See 16:7; 1Ki 8:39; Ps 139:1–6.

4"The bows of the warriors are broken,[e]
  but those who stumbled are armed
    with strength.[f]
5Those who were full hire themselves
    out for food,
  but those who were hungry[g] hunger
    no more.
She who was barren[h] has borne seven
    children,
  but she who has had many sons pines
    away.

6"The LORD brings death and makes
    alive;[i]
  he brings down to the grave[i] and
    raises up.[j]
7The LORD sends poverty and wealth;[k]
  he humbles and he exalts.[l]
8He raises[m] the poor[n] from the dust[o]
  and lifts the needy[p] from the ash
    heap;
he seats them with princes
  and has them inherit a throne of
    honor.[q]

"For the foundations[r] of the earth are
    the LORD's;
  upon them he has set the world.
9He will guard the feet[s] of his saints,[t]
  but the wicked will be silenced in
    darkness.[u]

"It is not by strength[v] that one prevails;

10 those who oppose the LORD will be
    shattered.[w]
He will thunder[x] against them from
    heaven;
  the LORD will judge[y] the ends of the
    earth.

"He will give strength[z] to his king
  and exalt the horn[a] of his anointed."

11Then Elkanah went home to Ramah,[b]
but the boy ministered[c] before the LORD
under Eli the priest.

Eli's Wicked Sons

12Eli's sons were wicked men; they had
no regard[d] for the LORD. 13Now it was the
practice[e] of the priests with the people
that whenever anyone offered a sacrifice
and while the meat[f] was being boiled, the
servant of the priest would come with a
three-pronged fork in his hand. 14He
would plunge it into the pan or kettle or
caldron or pot, and the priest would take
for himself whatever the fork brought up.
This is how they treated all the Israelites
who came to Shiloh. 15But even before the

2:4 [e]2Sa 1:27; Ps 37:15; 46:9; 76:3 [f]Job 17:9; Isa 40:31; 41:1; 52:1; 57:10
2:5 [g]Lk 1:53 [h]Ps 113:9; Isa 54:1; Jer 15:9
2:6 [i]Dt 32:39 [i]Isa 26:19; Eze 37:3,12
2:7 [k]S Dt 8:18 [l]Job 5:11; 40:12; Ps 75:7; Isa 2:12; 13:11; 22:19; Da 4:37
2:8 [m]Ps 113:7-8 [n]Jas 2:5 [o]1Ki 16:2 [p]Ps 72:12; 107:41; 145:14; 146:8; [s] Mt 23:12 [q]2Sa 7:8; Job 36:7; Isa 22:23; Eze 21:26 [r]Job 15:7; 38:4; Ps 104:5; Pr 8:29; Isa 40:12; Jer 10:12
2:9 [s]Ps 91:12; 121:3; Pr 3:26 [t]Pr 2:8 [u]Job 10:22; Isa 5:30; 8:22; 59:9; 60:2; Jer 13:16; Am 5:18,20; Zep 1:14-15; Mt 8:12 [v]1Sa 17:47; Ps 33:16-17; Zec 4:6

2:10 [w]S Ex 15:6 [x]S Ex 19:16; 1Sa 7:10; 12:17; 2Sa 22:14;

Job 37:4,5; 38:1; Ps 18:13; 29:3; Isa 66:6 [y]Ps 96:13; 98:9; Mt 25:31-32 [z]Ps 18:1; 21:1; 59:16 [a]S Dt 33:17; Ps 89:24; S Lk 1:69 2:11 [b]S Jos 18:25 [c]ver 18; S Nu 16:9; 1Sa 3:1 2:12 [d]Jer 2:8; 9:6 2:13 [e]Dt 18:3 [f]Lev 7:35-36

16 Hebrew Sheol

2:4–5 In a series of examples derived from everyday life Hannah shows that God often works contrary to natural expectations and brings about surprising reversals—seen frequently in the stories that follow.
2:5 *seven children.* See note on Ru 4:15.
2:6–8 Hannah declares that life and death, prosperity and adversity, are determined by the sovereign power of God—another theme richly illustrated in the following narrative (see Dt 32:39; 1Ki 17:20–24; 2Ki 4:32–35; Jn 5:21; 11:41–44).
2:6 *grave.* See NIV text note; see also note on Ge 37:35.
2:8 *foundations of the earth.* A common figure in the OT for the solid base on which the earth (the dry land on which man lives, not planet earth; Ge 1:10) is founded. The phrase does not teach a particular theory of the structure of the universe (see Job 9:6; 38:6; Ps 75:3; 104:5; Zec 12:1).
2:9 *guard the feet.* Travel in ancient Israel was for the most part by foot over trails that were often rocky and dangerous (see Ps 91:11–12; 121:3). *saints.* People who are faithful to the Lord. The Hebrew root underlying this word is used of both God and his people in 2Sa 22:26 (see also Ps 18:25) to characterize the nature of their mutual relationship. The word is also translated "godly" (Ps 12:1; 32:6) and "faithful ones" (Pr 2:8).
2:10 *judge.* Impose his righteous rule upon (see Ps 96:13; 98:9). *ends of the earth.* All nations and peoples (see Dt 33:17; Isa 45:22). *his king.* Hannah's prayer is here prophetic, anticipating the establishment of kingship in Israel and the initial realization of the Messianic ideal in David (Lk 1:69). Ultimately her expectation finds fulfillment in Christ and his complete triumph over the enemies of God. *horn.* See note on v. 1. *anointed.* The first reference in the Bible to the Lord's anointed—i.e., his anointed king. (Priests were also

anointed for God's service; see Ex 28:41; Lev 4:3.) The word is often synonymous with "king" (as here) and provides part of the vocabulary basis for the Messianic idea in the Bible. "Anointed" and "Messiah" are the translation and transliteration respectively of the same Hebrew word. The Greek translation of this Hebrew term is *Christos,* from which comes the English word "Christ" (see NIV text note on Mt 1:17). A king (coming from the tribe of Judah) is first prophesied by Jacob (Ge 49:10); kingship is further anticipated in the oracles of Balaam in Nu 24:7,17. Also Dt 17:14–20 looks forward to the time when the Lord will place a king of his choice over his people after they enter the promised land. 1,2 Samuel shows how this expectation of the theocratic king is realized in the person of David. Hannah's prophetic anticipation of a king at the time of the dedication of her son Samuel, who was to be God's agent for establishing kingship in Israel, is entirely appropriate.
2:11 *ministered.* Performed such services as a boy might render while assisting the high priest. *before the LORD.* At the "house of the LORD" (1:24).
2:12 *wicked.* See note on Dt 13:13. *had no regard for.* Lit. "did not know." In OT usage, to "know" the Lord is not just intellectual or theoretical recognition. To know the Lord is to enter into fellowship with him and acknowledge his claims on one's life. The term often has a covenantal connotation (see Jer 31:34; Hos 13:4, "acknowledge").
2:13–16 Apparently vv. 13–14 describe the practice that had come to be accepted for determining the priests' portion of the fellowship offerings (Lev 7:31–36; 10:14–15; Dt 18:1–5)—a tradition presumably based on the assumption that a random thrust of the fork would providentially determine a fair portion. Verses 15–16 then describe how Eli's sons arrogantly violated that custom and the law.

fat was burned, the servant of the priest would come and say to the man who was sacrificing, "Give the priest some meat to roast; he won't accept boiled meat from you, but only raw."

16If the man said to him, "Let the fat[g] be burned up first, and then take whatever you want," the servant would then answer, "No, hand it over now; if you don't, I'll take it by force."

17This sin of the young men was very great in the LORD's sight, for they[i] were treating the LORD's offering with contempt. h

18But Samuel was ministering[i] before the LORD—a boy wearing a linen ephod. j 19Each year his mother made him a little robe and took it to him when she went up with her husband to offer the annual[k] sacrifice. 20Eli would bless Elkanah and his wife, saying, "May the LORD give you children by this woman to take the place of the one she prayed[l] for and gave to the LORD." Then they would go home. 21And the LORD was gracious to Hannah; m she conceived and gave birth to three sons and two daughters. Meanwhile, the boy Samuel grew[n] up in the presence of the LORD.

22Now Eli, who was very old, heard about everything[o] his sons were doing to all Israel and how they slept with the women[p] who served at the entrance to the Tent of Meeting. 23So he said to them, "Why do you do such things? I hear from all the people about these wicked deeds of yours. 24No, my sons; it is not a good report that I hear spreading among the LORD's people. 25If a man sins against another man, God[k] may mediate for him; but if a man sins against the LORD, who will[q] intercede[r] for him?" His sons, however, did not listen to their father's rebuke, for it was the LORD's will to put them to death.

26And the boy Samuel continued to grow[s] in stature and in favor with the LORD and with men. t

Prophecy Against the House of Eli

27Now a man of God[u] came to Eli and said to him, "This is what the LORD says: 'Did I not clearly reveal myself to your father's house when they were in Egypt under Pharaoh? 28I chose[v] your father out of all the tribes of Israel to be my priest, to go up to my altar, to burn incense, w and to wear an ephod[x] in my presence. I also gave your father's house all the offerings[y] made with fire by the Israelites. 29Why do you[1] scorn my sacrifice and offering[z] that I prescribed for my dwelling?[a] Why do you honor your sons more than me by fat-

Cross references (center column):

2:16 gLev 3:3, 14-16; 7:29-34
2:17 hver 22,29; SNu 14:11; Jer 7:21; Eze 22:26; Mal 2:7-9
2:18 iS ver 11 jver 28; 1Sa 22:18; 23:9; 2Sa 6:14; 1Ch 15:27
2:19 kS 1Sa 1:3
2:20 lS 1Sa 1:27
2:21 mGe 21:1 nS Jdg 13:24; Lk 1:80; 2:40
2:22 oS ver 17 pS Ex 38:8

2:25 qEx 4:21; Jos 11:20 rS Ex 32:10; SNu 11:2; 1Sa 3:14; 1Ki 13:6; Job 9:33; Ps 106:30; Isa 1:18; 22:14; Jer 15:1; Heb 10:26
2:26 sS Jdg 13:24; Lk 2:52 tPr 3:4
2:27 uS Dt 33:1; S Jdg 13:6
2:28 vS Ex 28:1 wS Ex 30:7 x1Sa 22:18; 23:6, 9; 30:7 yLev 7:35-36
2:29 zver 12-17 aS Dt 12:5

Notes: i17 Or men k25 Or the judges l29 The Hebrew is plural.

2:15 *before the fat was burned.* On the altar as the Lord's portion, which he was to receive first (see Lev 3:16; 4:10, 26,31,35; 7:28,30–31; 17:6). *roast.* Boiling is the only form of cooking specified in the law for the priests' portion (Nu 6:19–20). Roasting this portion is nowhere expressly forbidden in the law, but it is specified only for the Passover lamb (Ex 12:8–9; Dt 16:7). The present passage seems to imply that for the priests to roast their portion of the sacrifices was unlawful.

2:16 *by force.* Presenting the priests' portion was to be a voluntary act on the part of the worshipers (see Lev 7:28–36; Dt 18:3).

2:18 *But Samuel.* Between 2:11 and 4:1 the author presents a series of sharp contrasts between Samuel and Eli's sons. *linen ephod.* A priestly garment worn by those who served before the Lord at his sanctuary (see 22:18; 2Sa 6:14). It was a close-fitting, sleeveless pullover, usually of hip length, and is to be distinguished from the special ephod worn by the high priest (see note on v. 28; cf. Ex 39:1–26).

2:19 *little robe.* A sleeveless garment reaching to the knees, worn over the undergarment and under the ephod (see 15:27; 18:4). *annual sacrifice.* See note on 1:3.

2:22 *slept with the women who served.* See Ex 38:8. There is no further reference to such women in the OT. Perhaps these women performed various menial tasks, but certainly their service is not to be confused with that of the Levites, which is prescribed in the Pentateuch (Nu 1:50; 3:6–8; 8:15; 16:9; 18:2–3). The immoral acts of Eli's sons are reminiscent of the religious prostitution (fertility rites) at the Canaanite sanctuaries (see 1Ki 14:24; 15:12; 22:46)—acts that were an abomination to the Lord and a desecration of his house (Dt 23:17–18).

2:23 *he said to them.* Eli rebuked his sons but did not remove them from office. God would do that.

2:25 *God.* See NIV text note. Eli's argument is that when someone commits an offense against another man, there is recourse to a third party to decide the issue (whether this be understood as God or as God's representatives, the judges; see NIV text notes on Ex 22:8–9); but when the offense is against the Lord, there is no recourse, for God is both the one wronged and the judge. *the LORD's will to put them to death.* This comment by the author of the narrative is not intended to excuse Eli's sons, but to indicate that Eli's warning was much too late. Eli's sons had persisted in their evil ways for so long that God's judgment on them was determined (v. 34; see Jos 11:20).

2:26 *grow in stature and in favor with the LORD and with men.* Cf. Luke's description of Jesus (Lk 2:52).

2:27 *man of God.* Often a designation for a prophet (see 9:6,10; Dt 33:1; Jos 14:6; 1Ki 13:1,6–8; 17:18,24; 2Ki 4:7). *father's house.* The descendants of Aaron.

2:28 *to be my priest.* Three tasks of the priests are mentioned: 1. *to go up to my altar.* To perform the sacrificial rites at the altar of burnt offering in the courtyard of the tabernacle. 2. *to burn incense.* At the altar of incense in the Holy Place (Ex 30:1–10). 3. *to wear an ephod.* See note on v. 18. It would appear that the reference here is to the special ephod of the high priest (see Ex 28:4–13). The breastplate containing the Urim and Thummim was attached to the ephod of the high priest. The Urim and Thummim were a divinely ordained means of communication with God, placed in the custody of the high priest (see Ex 28:30 and note; see also 1Sa 23:9–12; 30:7–8).

tening yourselves on the choice parts of every offering made by my people Israel?'

30"Therefore the LORD, the God of Israel, declares: 'I promised that your house and your father's house would minister before me forever.*b* But now the LORD declares: 'Far be it from me! Those who honor me I will honor,*c* but those who despise*d* me will be disdained.*e* 31The time is coming when I will cut short your strength and the strength of your father's house, so that there will not be an old man in your family line*f* 32and you will see distress*g* in my dwelling. Although good will be done to Israel, in your family line there will never be an old man.*h* 33Every one of you that I do not cut off from my altar will be spared only to blind your eyes with tears and to grieve your heart, and all your descendants*i* will die in the prime of life.

34"'And what happens to your two sons, Hophni and Phinehas, will be a sign*j* to you—they will both die*k* on the same day.*l* 35I will raise up for myself a faithful priest,*m* who will do according to what is in my heart and mind. I will firmly establish his house, and he will minister before my anointed*n* one always. 36Then everyone left in your family line will come and bow down before him for a piece of silver

and a crust of bread and plead,*o* "Appoint me to some priestly office so I can have food to eat.*p*" ' "

The LORD Calls Samuel

3 The boy Samuel ministered*q* before the LORD under Eli. In those days the word of the LORD was rare;*r* there were not many visions.*s*

2One night Eli, whose eyes*t* were becoming so weak that he could barely see,*u* was lying down in his usual place. 3The lamp*v* of God had not yet gone out, and Samuel was lying down in the temple*m w* of the LORD, where the ark*x* of God was. 4Then the LORD called Samuel.

Samuel answered, "Here I am.*y* 5And he ran to Eli and said, "Here I am; you called me."

But Eli said, "I did not call; go back and lie down." So he went and lay down.

6Again the LORD called, "Samuel!" And Samuel got up and went to Eli and said, "Here I am; you called me."

"My son," Eli said, "I did not call; go back and lie down."

7Now Samuel did not yet know*z* the

2:30 *b*S Ex 29:9;
*c*Ps 50:23; 91:15;
Pr 8:17 *d*Isa 53:3;
Na 3:6; Mal 2:9
*e*Jer 18:10
2:31
*f*1Sa 4:11-18;
22:16
2:32 *g*1Sa 4:3;
22:17-20;
Jer 7:12,14
*h*1Ki 2:26-27
2:33 *i*Jer 29:32;
Mal 2:12
2:34 *j*S Dt 13:2
*k*1Sa 4:11
*l*1Ki 13:3
2:35 *m*2Sa 8:17;
20:25; 1Ki 1:8,
32; 2:35; 4:4;
1Ch 16:39;
29:22;
Eze 44:15-16
*n*1Sa 9:16; 10:1;
16:13; 2Sa 2:4;
12:7; 23:1;
1Ki 1:34;
Ps 89:20

2:36
*o*Eze 44:10-14
*p*1Sa 3:12;
1Ki 2:27
3:1 *q*S 1Sa 2:11
*r*Ps 74:9; La 2:9;
Eze 7:26
*s*Am 8:11
3:2 *t*1Sa 4:15
*u*S Ge 27:1
3:3
*v*Ex 25:31-38;
Lev 24:1-4
*w*1Sa 1:9
*x*Dt 10:1-5;
1Ki 6:19; 8:1
3:4 *y*S Ge 22:1;
S Ex 3:4

3:7 *z*1Sa 2:12

*m*3 That is, tabernacle

2:30 *I promised.* See Ex 29:9; Lev 8–9; Nu 16–17; 25:13. *Far be it from me!* This is not to say that the promise of the priesthood to Aaron's house has been annulled, but rather that Eli and his house are to be excluded from participation in this privilege because of their sin. *Those who honor me I will honor.* See v. 29. Spiritual privileges bring responsibilities and obligations; they are not to be treated as irrevocable rights (see 2Sa 22:26–27).
2:31 *strength . . . strength.* Lit. "arm . . . arm," symbolic of strength. Eli's "arm" and that of his priestly family will be cut off (contrast David, 2Sa 22:35). *not be an old man in your family line.* A prediction of the decimation of Eli's priestly family in the death of his sons (4:11), in the massacre of his descendants by Saul at Nob (22:18–19) and in the removal of Abiathar from his priestly office (1Ki 2:26–27).
2:32 *distress in my dwelling.* Including the capture of the ark by the Philistines (4:1–10), the destruction of Shiloh (Jer 7:14) and the relocation of the tabernacle to Nob (21:1–6; see note on 21:1).
2:33 A reference apparently to Abiathar, who was expelled from office by Solomon (see 1Ki 2:26–27) after an unsuccessful attempt to make Adonijah king as the successor to David.
2:34 *a sign to you.* The death of Hophni and Phinehas (4:11) will confirm the longer-term predictions. Such confirmation of a prophetic word was not uncommon (see 10:7–9; 1Ki 13:3; Jer 28:15–17; Lk 1:18–20).
2:35 *I will raise up for myself a faithful priest.* Initially fulfilled in the person of Zadok, who served as a priest during the time of David (see 2Sa 8:17; 15:24,35; 20:25) and who eventually replaced Abiathar as high priest in the time of Solomon (see 1Ki 2:35; 1Ch 29:22). *firmly establish his house.* Lit. "build for him a faithful house"; the faithful priest will be given a "faithful" (i.e., enduring) priestly family. See

the similar word spoken concerning David (25:28, "lasting dynasty"; see also 2Sa 7:16; 1Ki 11:38). The line of Zadok was continued by his son Azariah (see 1Ki 4:1) and was still on the scene at the time of the return from the exile (see 1Ch 6:14–15; Ezr 3:2). It continued in intertestamental times until Antiochus IV Epiphanes (175–164 B.C.) sold the priesthood to Menelaus (in the Apocrypha see 2 Maccabees 4:23–50), who was not of the priestly line. *my anointed one.* David and his successors (see note on v. 10).

3:1 *boy Samuel.* See 2:11,18. Samuel is now no longer a little child (see 2:21,26). The Jewish historian Josephus places his age at 12 years; he may have been older. *the word of the LORD was rare.* See Pr 29:18; Am 8:11. During the entire period of the judges, apart from the prophet of 2:27–36, we are told of only two prophets (Jdg 4:4; 6:8) and of five revelations (Jdg 2:1–3; 6:11–23; 7:2–11; 10:11–14; 13:3–21). Possibly 2Ch 15:3 also refers to this period. *visions.* Cf. Ge 15:1.
3:3 *The lamp of God had not yet gone out.* The reference is to the golden lampstand, which stood opposite the table of the bread of the Presence (Ex 25:31–40) in the Holy Place. It was still night, but the early morning hours were approaching when the flame grew dim or went out (see Ex 27:20–21; 30:7–8; Lev 24:3–4; 2Ch 13:11; Pr 31:18). For the lamp to be permitted to go out before morning was a violation of the Pentateuchal regulations. *temple.* See NIV text note and note on 1:9.
3:5 *Eli said.* Eli's failure to recognize at once that the Lord had called Samuel may be indicative of his own unfamiliarity with the Lord.
3:7 *did not yet know the LORD.* In the sense of having a direct experience of him (see Ex 1:8), such as receiving a revelation from God (see the last half of the verse).

LORD: The word[a] of the LORD had not yet been revealed[b] to him.

[8]The LORD called Samuel a third time, and Samuel got up and went to Eli and said, "Here I am; you called me."

Then Eli realized that the LORD was calling the boy. [9]So Eli told Samuel, "Go and lie down, and if he calls you, say, 'Speak, LORD, for your servant is listening.' " So Samuel went and lay down in his place.

[10]The LORD came and stood there, calling as at the other times, "Samuel! Samuel!"[c]"

Then Samuel said, "Speak, for your servant is listening."

[11]And the LORD said to Samuel: "See, I am about to do something in Israel that will make the ears of everyone who hears of it tingle.[d] [12]At that time I will carry out against Eli everything[e] I spoke against his family—from beginning to end. [13]For I told him that I would judge his family forever because of the sin he knew about; his sons made themselves contemptible,[n] and he failed to restrain[f] them. [14]Therefore, I swore to the house of Eli, 'The guilt of Eli's house will never be atoned[g] for by sacrifice or offering.' "

[15]Samuel lay down until morning and then opened the doors of the house of the LORD. He was afraid to tell Eli the vision, [16]but Eli called him and said, "Samuel, my son."

Samuel answered, "Here I am."

[17]"What was it he said to you?" Eli asked. "Do not hide[h] it from me. May God deal with you, be it ever so severely,[i] if you hide from me anything he told you." [18]So Samuel told him everything, hiding nothing from him. Then Eli said, "He is the LORD; let him do what is good in his eyes."[j]

[19]The LORD was with[k] Samuel as he grew[l] up, and he let none[m] of his words fall to the ground. [20]And all Israel from Dan to Beersheba[n] recognized that Samuel was attested as a prophet of the LORD.[o] [21]The LORD continued to appear at Shiloh, and there he revealed[p] himself to Samuel through his word.

4

And Samuel's word came to all Israel.

The Philistines Capture the Ark

Now the Israelites went out to fight against the Philistines. The Israelites camped at Ebenezer,[q] and the Philistines at Aphek.[r] [2]The Philistines deployed their forces to meet Israel, and as the battle spread, Israel was defeated by the Philistines, who killed about four thousand of them on the battlefield. [3]When the soldiers returned to camp, the elders of Israel asked, "Why[s] did the LORD bring defeat upon us today before the Philistines? Let us bring the ark[t] of the LORD's covenant from Shiloh,[u] so that it[o] may go with us[v] and save us from the hand of our enemies."

[4]So the people sent men to Shiloh, and they brought back the ark of the covenant

3:7 [a]Jer 1:2
[b]S Nu 12:6;
Am 3:7
3:10 [c]Ex 3:4
3:11 [d]2Ki 21:12;
Job 15:21;
Jer 19:3
3:12
[e]S 1Sa 2:27-36
3:13 [f]1Ki 1:6
3:14 [g]S 1Sa 2:25
3:17 [h]1Ki 22:14;
Jer 23:28; 38:14;
42:4

[i]S Ru 1:17
3:18 [j]S Jdg 10:15
3:19
[k]S Ge 21:22;
S Nu 14:43
[l]S Jdg 13:24
[m]1Sa 9:6
3:20 [n]S Jdg 20:1
[o]S Dt 18:22;
Eze 33:33
3:21 [p]S Nu 12:6
4:1 [q]1Sa 5:1;
7:12 [r]Jos 12:18;
1Sa 29:1;
1Ki 20:26
4:3 [s]Jos 7:7
[t]S Jos 6:7
[u]S Jos 18:1;
S 2Ch 2:32
[v]2Ch 13:8

[n]*13* Masoretic Text; an ancient Hebrew scribal tradition and Septuagint *sons blasphemed God*   [o]*3* Or *he*

3:11–14 The Lord's first revelation to Samuel repeats the message Eli had already received from the "man of God" (2:27–36), thus confirming the fact that the youth had indeed received a revelation from God.
3:13 *contemptible.* See NIV text note and Lev 24:14.
3:15 *doors of the house of the LORD.* See note on 1:9. The tabernacle itself did not have doors. This may refer to an enclosure in which it stood. *vision.* See note on vv. 11–14.
3:17 *May God deal with you, be it ever so severely.* A curse formula (see 14:44; 20:13; 25:22; 2Sa 3:9,35; 19:13; Ru 1:17; 1Ki 2:23; 2Ki 6:31), usually directed against the speaker but here used by Eli against Samuel if he conceals anything the Lord said (see also note on 14:24).
3:18 *let him do what is good in his eyes.* Eli bows before God, accepting the judgment as righteous (see Ex 34:5–7).
3:19 *he let none of his words fall to the ground.* Because none of Samuel's words proved unreliable, he was recognized as a prophet who spoke the word of the Lord (see vv. 20–21).
3:20 *Dan to Beersheba.* A conventional expression often used in Samuel, Kings and Chronicles to denote the entire land (Dan was located in the far north and Beersheba in the far south).
3:21 *at Shiloh.* But not after the events narrated in chs. 4–6 (see Jer 7:12–14; 26:6).
4:1 *Samuel's word came to all Israel.* Contrast 3:1. *Ebenezer.* Means "stone of help." The precise location is unknown, but it was probably a short distance (see v. 6) to the east of Aphek—not to be confused with the location of the stone named Ebenezer that was later erected by Samuel between Mizpah and Shen (see 7:12) to commemorate a victory over the Philistines. *Aphek.* A town about 12 miles northeast of the coastal city of Joppa. Philistine presence this far north suggests an attempt to spread their control over the Israelite tribes of central Canaan (see v. 9; Jdg 15:11).
4:3 *Why did the LORD bring defeat . . . ?* The elders understood that their defeat was more an indication of God's displeasure than it was of Philistine military might. Israel's pagan neighbors also believed that the outcome of battle was decided by the gods. *so that it may go with us and save us.* See NIV text note. In an attempt to secure the Lord's presence with them in the struggle against the Philistines, the elders sent for the ark of the covenant. They were correct in thinking there was a connection between God's presence with his people and the ark (cf. v. 4), and no doubt they remembered the presence of the ark at notable victories in Israel's past history (see Nu 10:33–36; Jos 3:3,11,14–17; 6:6,12–20). But they incorrectly believed that the Lord's presence with the ark was guaranteed, rather than being subject to his free decision. They reflect the pagan notion that the deity is identified with the symbol of his presence, and that God's favor could automatically be gained by manipulating the symbol.
4:4 *enthroned between the cherubim.* On each end of the

of the LORD Almighty, who is enthroned between the cherubim.[w] And Eli's two sons, Hophni and Phinehas, were there with the ark of the covenant of God.

[5]When the ark of the LORD's covenant came into the camp, all Israel raised such a great shout[x] that the ground shook. [6]Hearing the uproar, the Philistines asked, "What's all this shouting in the Hebrew[y] camp?"

When they learned that the ark of the LORD had come into the camp, [7]the Philistines were afraid.[z] "A god has come into the camp," they said. "We're in trouble! Nothing like this has happened before. [8]Woe to us! Who will deliver us from the hand of these mighty gods? They are the gods who struck[a] the Egyptians with all kinds of plagues[b] in the desert. [9]Be strong, Philistines! Be men, or you will be subject to the Hebrews, as they[c] have been to you. Be men, and fight!"

[10]So the Philistines fought, and the Israelites were defeated[d] and every man fled to his tent. The slaughter was very great; Israel lost thirty thousand foot soldiers. [11]The ark of God was captured, and Eli's two sons, Hophni and Phinehas, died.[e]

Death of Eli

[12]That same day a Benjamite[f] ran from the battle line and went to Shiloh, his clothes torn and dust[g] on his head. [13]When he arrived, there was Eli[h] sitting on his chair by the side of the road, watching, because his heart feared for the ark of

God. When the man entered the town and told what had happened, the whole town sent up a cry.

[14]Eli heard the outcry and asked, "What is the meaning of this uproar?"

The man hurried over to Eli, [15]who was ninety-eight years old and whose eyes[i] were set so that he could not see. [16]He told Eli, "I have just come from the battle line; I fled from it this very day."

Eli asked, "What happened, my son?"

[17]The man who brought the news replied, "Israel fled before the Philistines, and the army has suffered heavy losses. Also your two sons, Hophni and Phinehas, are dead,[j] and the ark of God has been captured."[k]

[18]When he mentioned the ark of God, Eli fell backward off his chair by the side of the gate. His neck was broken and he died, for he was an old man and heavy. He had led[p][l] Israel forty years.[m]

[19]His daughter-in-law, the wife of Phinehas, was pregnant and near the time of delivery. When she heard the news that the ark of God had been captured and that her father-in-law and her husband were dead, she went into labor and gave birth, but was overcome by her labor pains. [20]As she was dying, the women attending her said, "Don't despair; you have given birth to a son." But she did not respond or pay any attention.

[21]She named the boy Ichabod,[q][n] say-

Cross-references (center column)

4:4 wS Ge 3:24; S Ex 25:22
4:5 xS Jos 6:5,10
4:6 yS Ge 14:13
4:7 zS Ex 15:14
4:8 aEx 12:30; 1Sa 5:12
bRev 11:6
4:9 cS Jdg 13:1
4:10 dS Dt 28:25
4:11 ePs 78:64; Jer 7:12
4:12 fEze 24:26; 33:21 gS Jos 7:6; S 2Sa 1:2
4:13 hver 18

4:15 iS 1Sa 3:2
4:17 jISa 22:18; Ps 78:64
kPs 78:61
4:18 lS Jdg 2:16; S 16:31
mISa 2:31
4:21 nS Ge 35:18

p18 Traditionally *judged*   q21 *Ichabod* means *no glory.*

---

atonement cover of the ark of the covenant were golden cherubim with their wings spread upward over the ark (see Ex 25:17–22). In the space between these cherubim God's presence with his people was localized in a special way, so that the atonement cover of the ark came to be viewed as the throne of Israel's divine King (see 2Sa 6:2; Ps 80:1; 99:1). *Hophni and Phinehas.* These wicked priests (see 2:12) did not restrain the army from its improper use of the ark but actually accompanied the ark to the battlefield.
4:6 *Hebrew.* See note on Ge 14:13.
4:7 *A god has come into the camp.* The Philistines also identified the God of Israel with the symbol of his presence (see note on v. 3).
4:8 *mighty gods.* The Philistines could think only in polytheistic terms. *Egyptians . . . plagues.* See note on 6:6.
4:11 *The ark of God was captured.* This phrase or a variation of it occurs five times in the chapter (here, vv. 17,19,21–22) and is the focal point of the narrative. In this disastrous event, God's word in 3:11 finds a swift fulfillment. *Hophni and Phinehas, died.* The fulfillment of 2:34; 3:12.
4:12 *his clothes torn and dust on his head.* A sign of grief and sorrow, here marking the messenger as a bearer of bad news (see 2Sa 1:2; 13:19; 15:32).
4:13 *his heart feared for the ark of God.* Eli had sufficient spiritual sensitivity to be aware of the danger inherent in the sinful and presumptuous act of taking the ark of God into the battle. And he seems to have been even more concerned for

the ark than for his sons (see v. 18).
4:18 *he died.* The death of Eli marked the end of an era that had begun with the death of Joshua and the elders who served with him (see Jos 24:29,31). Incapable of restraining Israel or his sons from their wicked ways, and weakened and blinded by age, the old priest is an apt epitome of the flawed age now coming to its tragic close. He is also a striking contrast to the reign of David, which is the main focus of this narrative. *heavy.* A bit of information that not only helps explain why Eli's fall was fatal but also links his death with the judgment announced earlier: "Why do you honor your sons more than me by fattening yourselves . . .?" (2:29). *He had led Israel forty years.* See NIV text note. Eli is here included among the judges (see 2Sa 7:11; Jdg 2:16–19; Ru 1:1), who served as leaders of Israel in the period between the deaths of Joshua and of the elders who outlived him and the establishment of kingship. It is likely that Eli's leadership of 40 years overlapped that of Jephthah, Ibzan, Elon and Abdon (Jdg 12:7–14), as well as that of Samson (Jdg 13–16).
4:21 *The glory has departed.* The glory of Israel was Israel's God, not the ark, and loss of the ark did not mean that God had abandoned his people—God was not inseparably bound to the ark (see Jer 3:16–17). Yet the removal of the ark from Israel did signal estrangement in the relationship between God and his people, and it demonstrated the gravity of their error in thinking that in spite of their wickedness they had the power to coerce God into doing their will simply

ing, "The glory° has departed from Israel"—because of the capture of the ark of God and the deaths of her father-in-law and her husband. 22She said, "The glory*p* has departed from Israel, for the ark of God has been captured."*q*

The Ark in Ashdod and Ekron

5 After the Philistines had captured the ark of God, they took it from Ebenezer*r* to Ashdod.*s* 2Then they carried the ark into Dagon's temple and set it beside Dagon.*t* 3When the people of Ashdod rose early the next day, there was Dagon, fallen*u* on his face on the ground before the ark of the Lord! They took Dagon and put him back in his place. 4But the following morning when they rose, there was Dagon, fallen on his face on the ground before the ark of the Lord! His head and hands had been broken*v* off and were lying on the threshold; only his body remained. 5That is why to this day neither the priests of Dagon nor any others who enter Dagon's temple at Ashdod step on the threshold.*w*

6The Lord's hand*x* was heavy upon the people of Ashdod and its vicinity; he brought devastation*y* upon them and afflicted them with tumors.*r z* 7When the men of Ashdod saw what was happening, they said, "The ark of the god of Israel must not stay here with us, because his hand is heavy upon us and upon Dagon

our god." 8So they called together all the rulers*a* of the Philistines and asked them, "What shall we do with the ark of the god of Israel?"

They answered, "Have the ark of the god of Israel moved to Gath.*b*" So they moved the ark of the God of Israel.

9But after they had moved it, the Lord's hand was against that city, throwing it into a great panic.*c* He afflicted the people of the city, both young and old, with an outbreak of tumors.*s* 10So they sent the ark of God to Ekron.*d*

As the ark of God was entering Ekron, the people of Ekron cried out, "They have brought the ark of the god of Israel around to us to kill us and our people." 11So they called together all the rulers*e* of the Philistines and said, "Send the ark of the god of Israel away; let it go back to its own place, or it*t* will kill us and our people." For death had filled the city with panic; God's hand was very heavy upon it. 12Those who did not die*f* were afflicted with tumors, and the outcry of the city went up to heaven.

The Ark Returned to Israel

6 When the ark of the Lord had been in Philistine territory seven months, 2the Philistines called for the priests and the di-

---

4:21 °S Ex 24:16; Ps 106:20; Jer 2:11; Eze 1:28; 9:3; 10:18
4:22 *p*S Ex 24:16; Ps 78:61 *q*Jer 7:12
5:1 *r*S 1Sa 4:1 *s*S Jos 11:22; S 13:3
5:2 *t*S Jdg 16:23; Isa 2:18; 19:1; 46:1
5:3 *u*Isa 40:20; 41:7; 46:7; Jer 10:4
5:4 *v*Eze 6:6; Mic 1:7
5:5 *w*Zep 1:9
5:6 *x*S Ex 9:3; Ac 13:11 *y*2Sa 6:7; Ps 78:66 *z*S Ex 15:26; 1Sa 6:5

5:8 *a*S Jdg 16:18 *b*S Jos 11:22
5:9 *c*S Ex 14:24
5:10 *d*S Jos 13:3
5:11 *e*ver 8
5:12 *f*S 1Sa 4:8

*r*6 Hebrew; Septuagint and Vulgate *tumors. And rats appeared in their land, and death and destruction were throughout the city*   *s*9 Or *with tumors in the groin* (see Septuagint)   *t*11 Or *he*

---

because they possessed the ark.

5:1 *Ashdod.* One of the five major cities of the Philistines (Jos 13:3), it was located near the Mediterranean coast about 35 miles west of Jerusalem. See map, p. 330.

5:2 *Dagon.* In Canaanite mythology the son (or brother) of El and the father of Baal. He was the principal god of the Philistines and was worshiped in temples at Gaza (Jdg 16:21,23,26), Ashdod (here) and Beth Shan (31:10–12; 1Ch 10:10). Veneration of this deity was widespread in the ancient world, extending from Mesopotamia to the Aramean and Canaanite area and attested in non-Biblical sources dating from the late third millennium B.C. until Maccabean times (second century B.C.; in the Apocrypha see 1 Maccabees 10:83–85). The precise nature of the worship of Dagon is obscure. Some have considered Dagon to be a fish god, but more recent evidence suggests either a storm or grain god. His name is related to a Hebrew word for "grain."

5:3 *Dagon, fallen on his face.* The ark was placed next to the image of Dagon by the Philistines in order to demonstrate Dagon's superiority over the God of Israel, but the symbolism was reversed when Dagon was toppled to a position of homage before the ark of the Lord.

5:5 *this day.* The time of the writing of 1,2 Samuel (see Introduction: Literary Features, Authorship and Date). *step on the threshold.* Apparently the threshold was considered to possess supernatural power because of its contact with parts of the fallen image of Dagon. Zep 1:9 appears to be a reference to a more general and rather widespread pagan idea that the threshold was the dwelling place of spirits.

5:6 *The Lord's hand was heavy.* Dagon's broken hand lay on the ground (v. 4), but the Lord shows the reality and strength of his own hand by bringing a plague (see note on 6:4) on the people of Ashdod and the surrounding area (see vv. 9,11). God would not be manipulated by his own people (see note on 4:3), nor would he permit the Philistines to think that their victory over the Israelites and the capture of the ark demonstrated the superiority of their god over the God of Israel.

5:8 *rulers.* Of the five major cities of the Philistines (see 6:16; Jos 13:3; Jdg 3:3). *Have the ark of the god of Israel moved to Gath.* Evidently the leaders of the Philistines did not share the opinion of the Ashdodites that there was a direct connection between what had happened in Ashdod and the presence of the ark; they seem to have suspected that the sequence of events was merely coincidental (see 6:9). The removal of the ark to Gath put the matter to a test.

5:10 *Ekron.* The northernmost of the five major Philistine cities, located 11 miles northeast of Ashdod and close to Israelite territory (see map, p. 330).

5:11 *Send the ark of the god of Israel away.* After three successive towns had been struck by disease upon the arrival of the ark, there was little doubt in the people's minds that the power of the God of Israel was the cause of their distress.

6:2 *priests and . . . diviners.* The experts on religious matters (priests) and the discerners of hidden knowledge by interpretation of omens (diviners) were consulted (see Dt 18:10; Isa 2:6; Eze 21:21).

viners*g* and said, "What shall we do with the ark of the LORD? Tell us how we should send it back to its place."

³They answered, "If you return the ark of the god of Israel, do not send it away empty,*h* but by all means send a guilt offering*i* to him. Then you will be healed, and you will know why his hand*j* has not been lifted from you."

⁴The Philistines asked, "What guilt offering should we send to him?"

They replied, "Five gold tumors and five gold rats, according to the number*k* of the Philistine rulers, because the same plague*l* has struck both you and your rulers. ⁵Make models of the tumors*m* and of the rats that are destroying the country, and pay honor*n* to Israel's god. Perhaps he will lift his hand from you and your gods and your land. ⁶Why do you harden*o* your hearts as the Egyptians and Pharaoh did? When he*u* treated them harshly,*p* did they*q* not send the Israelites out so they could go on their way?

⁷"Now then, get a new cart*r* ready, with two cows that have calved and have never been yoked.*s* Hitch the cows to the cart, but take their calves away and pen them up. ⁸Take the ark of the LORD and put it on the cart, and in a chest beside it put the gold objects you are sending back to him as a guilt offering. Send it on its way, ⁹but keep watching it. If it goes up to its own territory, toward Beth Shemesh,*t* then the LORD has brought this great disaster on us. But if it does not, then we will know that it was not his hand that struck us and that it happened to us by chance."

¹⁰So they did this. They took two such cows and hitched them to the cart and penned up their calves. ¹¹They placed the ark of the LORD on the cart and along with it the chest containing the gold rats and the models of the tumors. ¹²Then the cows went straight up toward Beth Shemesh, keeping on the road and lowing all the way; they did not turn to the right or to the left. The rulers of the Philistines followed them as far as the border of Beth Shemesh.

¹³Now the people of Beth Shemesh were harvesting their wheat*u* in the valley, and when they looked up and saw the ark, they rejoiced at the sight. ¹⁴The cart came to the field of Joshua of Beth Shemesh, and there it stopped beside a large rock. The people chopped up the wood of the cart and sacrificed the cows as a burnt offering*v* to the LORD. ¹⁵The Levites*w* took down the ark of the LORD, together with the chest containing the gold objects, and placed them on the large rock.*x* On that day the people of Beth Shemesh*y* offered burnt offerings and made sacrifices to the LORD. ¹⁶The five rulers of the Philistines saw all this and then returned that same day to Ekron.

¹⁷These are the gold tumors the Philistines sent as a guilt offering to the LORD—one each*z* for Ashdod, Gaza, Ashkelon, Gath and Ekron. ¹⁸And the number of the gold rats was according to the number of Philistine towns belonging to the five rulers—the fortified towns with their country villages. The large rock, on which*v* they set the ark of the LORD, is a witness to this day in the field of Joshua of Beth Shemesh.

¹⁹But God struck down*a* some of the

Cross references (center column):

6:2 *g*S Ex 7:11; S Isa 44:25
6:3 *h*S Ex 22:29; S 34:20
*i*S Lev 5:15 /ver 9
6:4 *k*S Jos 13:3
*l*2Sa 24:25
6:5 *m*S 1Sa 5:6
*n*S Jos 7:19; Rev 14:7
6:6 *o*S Ex 4:21
*p*Ex 10:2
*q*S Ex 12:33
6:7 *r*2Sa 6:3; 1Ch 13:7
*s*S Nu 19:2
6:9 *t*S Jos 15:10; 21:16

6:13
*u*S Ge 30:14; Ru 2:23; 1Sa 12:17
6:14 *v*1Sa 11:7; 2Sa 24:22; 1Ki 19:21
6:15 *w*Jos 3:3
*x*ver 18
*y*Jos 21:16
6:17 *z*S Jos 13:3
6:19 *a*2Sa 6:7

u6 That is, God   *v18* A few Hebrew manuscripts (see also Septuagint); most Hebrew manuscripts *villages as far as Greater Abel, where*

6:3 *guilt offering.* The priests and diviners suggest returning the ark with a gift, signifying recognition of guilt in taking the ark from Israel and compensation for this violation of the Lord's honor (see v. 5). For the guilt offering in Israel see Lev 5:14–6:7.

6:4 *Five gold tumors.* Corresponding to the symptoms of the plague (see 5:6). *five gold rats.* The disease was accompanied by a plague of rats (v. 5). The Greek translation of the OT (the Septuagint) includes this information earlier in the narrative (see NIV text note on 5:6). It is likely that the rats were carriers of the disease, which may have been a form of the plague.

6:5 *Make models . . . and pay honor to Israel's god.* The golden models were an acknowledgment that the disease and the rats were a judgment from the hand of the God of Israel (see note on v. 3).

6:6 *the Egyptians and Pharaoh.* The plagues that God inflicted on the Egyptians at the time of the exodus made a lasting impression on the surrounding nations (see 4:8; Jos 2:10).

6:7 *have never been yoked.* Have not been trained to pull a cart. *take their calves away.* Normally cows do not willingly leave their suckling calves.

6:9 *Beth Shemesh.* A town near the Philistine border, belonging to Judah (see Jos 15:10). Its name means "house (or sanctuary) of the sun(-god)."

6:13 *harvesting their wheat.* The time of wheat harvest is from mid-April until mid-June.

6:14–15 The termination of the trip at Beth Shemesh is just as much a revelation of the hand of God as the journey itself, because it was one of the towns of Judah assigned to the priests at the time of the conquest (see Jos 21:13–16).

6:17 *guilt offering.* See note on v. 3.

6:18 *witness.* A kind of monument to the event. *this day.* The time of the writing of 1,2 Samuel (see Introduction: Literary Features, Authorship and Date).

6:19 *seventy.* The additional 50,000 in most Hebrew manuscripts (see NIV text note) is apparently a copyist's mistake because it is added in an ungrammatical way (no conjunction). Furthermore, this small town could not have contained that many inhabitants. *looked into the ark.* The men of Beth Shemesh (Levites and priests among them) were

men of Beth Shemesh, putting seventy[w] of them to death because they had looked[b] into the ark of the LORD. The people mourned because of the heavy blow the LORD had dealt them, [20]and the men of Beth Shemesh asked, "Who can stand[c] in the presence of the LORD, this holy[d] God? To whom will the ark go up from here?"

[21]Then they sent messengers to the people of Kiriath Jearim,[e] saying, "The Philistines have returned the ark of the LORD. Come down and take it up to your place." [1]So the men of Kiriath Jearim came and took up the ark[f] of the LORD. They took it to Abinadab's[g] house on the hill and consecrated Eleazar his son to guard the ark of the LORD.

Samuel Subdues the Philistines at Mizpah

[2]It was a long time, twenty years in all, that the ark remained at Kiriath Jearim,[h] and all the people of Israel mourned and sought after the LORD.[i] [3]And Samuel said to the whole house of Israel, "If you are returning[j] to the LORD with all your hearts, then rid[k] yourselves of the foreign gods and the Ashtoreths[l] and commit[m] yourselves to the LORD and serve him only,[n] and he will deliver[o] you out of the hand of the Philistines." [4]So the Israelites put away their Baals and Ashtoreths, and served the LORD only.

[5]Then Samuel[p] said, "Assemble all Is-rael at Mizpah[q] and I will intercede[r] with the LORD for you." [6]When they had assembled at Mizpah,[s] they drew water and poured[t] it out before the LORD. On that day they fasted and there they confessed, "We have sinned against the LORD." And Samuel was leader[x][u] of Israel at Mizpah.

[7]When the Philistines heard that Israel had assembled at Mizpah, the rulers of the Philistines came up to attack them. And when the Israelites heard of it, they were afraid[v] because of the Philistines. [8]They said to Samuel, "Do not stop crying[w] out to the LORD our God for us, that he may rescue us from the hand of the Philistines." [9]Then Samuel[x] took a suckling lamb and offered it up as a whole burnt offering to the LORD. He cried out to the LORD on Israel's behalf, and the LORD answered him.[y]

[10]While Samuel was sacrificing the burnt offering, the Philistines drew near to engage Israel in battle. But that day the LORD thundered[z] with loud thunder against the Philistines and threw them into such a panic[a] that they were routed before the Israelites. [11]The men of Israel rushed out of Mizpah and pursued the Philistines, slaughtering them along the way to a point below Beth Car.

[12]Then Samuel took a stone[b] and set it

Cross references

6:19 [b]S Ex 19:21
6:20 [c]2Sa 6:9; Ps 130:3; [d]S Lev 11:45
6:21 [e]S Jos 9:17
7:1 [f]S Jos 6:7 [g]2Sa 6:3; 1Ch 13:7
7:2 [h]1Ch 13:5; Ps 132:6 [i]1Ch 13:3
7:3 [j]Dt 30:10; 2Ki 18:5; 23:25; Jer 24:7 [k]S Ge 31:19; S Jos 24:14 [l]S Jdg 2:12-13; 1Sa 12:10; 31:10 [m]Joel 2:12 [n]S Dt 6:13; Mt 4:10; Lk 4:8 [o]S Jdg 2:18
7:5 [p]S 1Sa 1:20; Ps 99:6; Jer 15:1 [q]S Jos 11:3; Jdg 21:5; 1Sa 10:17 [r]S ver 8; S Ge 20:7; S Dt 9:19
7:6 [s]S Jos 11:3 [t]La 2:19 [u]S Jdg 2:16; S 16:31
7:7 [v]1Sa 17:11
7:8 [w]ver 5; S Ex 32:30; S Nu 21:7; 1Sa 12:19,23; 1Ki 18:24; Isa 37:4; Jer 15:1; 27:18
7:9 [x]Ps 99:6 [y]S Ex 32:11; S Dt 9:19
7:10 [z]S Ex 9:23; S 1Sa 2:10 [a]S Ge 35:5; S Ex 14:24
7:12 [b]S Ge 28:22; S Dt 27:2; Jos 4:9

[w]19 A few Hebrew manuscripts; most Hebrew manuscripts and Septuagint 50,070 [x]6 Traditionally judge

Study notes

judged by God for their irreverent curiosity. Because God had so closely linked the manifestation of his own presence among his people with the ark, it was to be treated with great honor and respect (see 2Sa 6:7; Nu 4:17–20). This attitude of respect, however, is quite different from the superstitious attitude that led the elders to take the ark into battle against the Philistines, thus treating it as an object with magical power (see note on 4:3).

6:20 *To whom will the ark go up from here?* The inhabitants of Beth Shemesh respond to God's judgment in much the same way as the inhabitants of Ashdod, Gath and Ekron (see 5:8–10).

7:1 *Abinadab's house.* The ark remained in relative obscurity at Abinadab's house until David brought it to Jerusalem (2Sa 6:2–3). Somehow the Tent of Meeting (and the altar of burnt offering) escaped the destruction of Shiloh (Jer 7:12,14; 26:6). It apparently was first moved to Nob (21:1–9). In David's and Solomon's days it was located at Gibeon (1Ch 16:39; 21:29; 2Ch 1:3,13), the city whose people had been condemned to be menial laborers at the Lord's sanctuary (Jos 9:23,27). Later, we are told, Solomon brought the "Tent of Meeting" to the completed temple (see notes on 1Ki 3:4; 8:4).

7:2 *twenty years in all.* Probably the 20-year interval between the return of the ark to Israel and the assembly called by Samuel at Mizpah (see v. 5).

7:3 *Ashtoreths.* Ashtoreth was a goddess of love, fertility and war, worshiped in various forms by many peoples of the ancient Near East, including the Canaanites (see note on Jdg 2:13). The worship of Ashtoreth is frequently combined with the worship of Baal (see v. 4; 12:10; Jdg 2:13; 3:7; 10:6), in accordance with the common practice in fertility cults to associate male and female deities.

7:5 *Mizpah.* A town in the territory of Benjamin (Jos 18:26), located about seven and a half miles north of Jerusalem. It was here that the Israelites had previously gathered to undertake disciplinary action against Benjamin (Jdg 20:1; 21:1) after the abuse and murder of the concubine of a traveling Levite in Gibeah of Benjamin. Several other places bore the same name (see 2Sa 22:3; Ge 31:49; Jos 11:3,8; 15:38). *I will intercede.* See 7:8–9; 8:6; 12:17–19,23; 15:11. Samuel, like Moses, was later remembered as a great intercessor (see Ps 99:6; Jer 15:1). Both were appointed by God to mediate his rule over his people, representing God to Israel and speaking on Israel's behalf to God.

7:6 *they drew water and poured it out before the LORD.* There is no other reference to this type of ceremony in the OT. It appears to symbolize the pouring out of one's heart in repentance and humility before the Lord. For related expressions see 1:15; Ps 62:8; La 2:19. *Samuel was leader.* See NIV text note and v. 15; see also note on 4:18.

7:10 *the LORD thundered with loud thunder.* The Lord had promised to be the protector of his people when they were obedient to their covenant obligations (see Ex 23:22; Dt 20:1–4; see also 2Sa 5:19–25; Jos 10:11–14; Jdg 5:20–21; 2Ki 7:6; 19:35; 2Ch 20:17,22).

7:12 *Ebenezer.* See NIV text note and note on 4:1.

up between Mizpah and Shen. He named it Ebenezer,^{y}^{c} saying, "Thus far has the LORD helped us." [13]So the Philistines were subdued^d and did not invade Israelite territory again.

Throughout Samuel's lifetime, the hand of the LORD was against the Philistines. [14]The towns from Ekron^e to Gath that the Philistines had captured from Israel were restored to her, and Israel delivered the neighboring territory from the power of the Philistines. And there was peace between Israel and the Amorites.^{f}

[15]Samuel^g continued as judge^h over Israel all^i the days of his life. [16]From year to year he went on a circuit from Bethel^j to Gilgal^k to Mizpah, judging^l Israel in all those places. [17]But he always went back to Ramah,^{m} where his home was, and there he also judged^n Israel. And he built an altar^o there to the LORD.

Israel Asks for a King

8 When Samuel grew old, he appointed^p his sons as judges for Israel. [2]The name of his firstborn was Joel and the name of his second was Abijah,^{q} and they served at Beersheba.^{r} [3]But his sons^s did not walk in his ways. They turned aside^t after dishonest gain and accepted bribes^u and perverted^v justice.

[4]So all the elders^w of Israel gathered together and came to Samuel at Ramah.^{x} [5]They said to him, "You are old, and your sons do not walk in your ways; now appoint a king^y to lead^z^{z} us, such as all the other nations^a have."

[6]But when they said, "Give us a king^b to lead us," this displeased^c Samuel; so he prayed to the LORD. [7]And the LORD told him: "Listen^d to all that the people are saying to you; it is not you they have rejected,^{e} but they have rejected me as their king.^{f} [8]As they have done from the day I brought them up out of Egypt until this day, forsaking^g me and serving other gods, so they are doing to you. [9]Now listen to them; but warn them solemnly and let them know^h what the king who will reign over them will do."

[10]Samuel told^i all the words of the LORD to the people who were asking him for a king. [11]He said, "This is what the king who will reign over you will do: He will take^j your sons and make them serve^k with his chariots and horses, and they will run in front of his chariots.^{l} [12]Some he will assign to be commanders^m of thousands and commanders of fifties, and others to plow his ground and reap his harvest, and still others to make weapons of war and equipment for his chariots. [13]He will take your daughters to be perfumers and cooks and bakers. [14]He will take the best of your^n fields and vineyards^o and olive groves and give them to his attendants.^{p} [15]He will take a tenth^q of your grain and of your vintage and give it

Cross references (center column)

7:12 ^{c}S 1Sa 4:1
7:13 ^{d}Jdg 13:5
7:14 ^{e}S Jos 13:3
/S Jdg 1:34
7:15 ^{g}ver 6;
1Sa 12:11
^{h}S Jdg 2:16
/Jdg 2:18
7:16 /S Ge 12:8
^{k}S Jos 10:43;
S 1Sa 10:8;
Am 5:5 /ver 6;
Ac 13:20
7:17
^{m}S Jos 18:25;
1Sa 8:4; 15:34;
19:18; 25:1; 28:3
^{n}ver 6 ^{o}1Sa 9:12;
14:35; 20:6;
2Sa 24:25
8:1 ^{p}Dt 16:18-19
8:2 ^{q}1Ch 6:28
^{r}Ge 22:19;
1Ki 19:3;
Am 5:4-5
8:3 ^{s}1Sa 2:12
^{t}Ne 9:29;
Job 34:27;
Ps 14:3; 58:3;
Isa 53:6
^{u}Ex 23:8;
1Sa 12:3;
Job 8:22;
Pr 17:23
^{v}S Ex 23:2
8:4 ^{w}S Jdg 11:11;
1Sa 11:3
^{x}S 1Sa 7:17
8:5 ^{y}ver 19;
S Dt 17:14-20;
1Sa 10:19; 12:12,
13; Hos 13:11
^{z}1Sa 3:20; 12:2
^{a}ver 20

8:6 ^{b}Hos 13:10
^{c}1Sa 12:17;
15:11; 16:1
8:7 ^{d}ver 22;
1Sa 12:1
^{e}S Nu 11:20
/S Ex 16:8
8:8 ^{g}1Sa 12:10;
2Ki 21:22;
Jer 2:17
8:9 ^{h}ver 11-18;
S Dt 17:14-20;
1Sa 10:25

8:10 ^{i}S Ex 19:7 8:11 /1Sa 14:52 ^{k}S Ge 41:46 /S Dt 17:16;
2Sa 15:1; 1Ki 1:5; 2Ch 1:14; 9:25; SS 3:7 8:12 ^{m}S Dt 1:15
8:14 ^{n}Eze 46:18 ^{o}1Ki 21:7,15; Mic 2:2 ^{p}2Ki 22:12 8:15
^{q}S Ge 41:34; 1Sa 17:25

^{y}12 Ebenezer means stone of help. ^{z}5 Traditionally judge; also in verses 6 and 20

Study notes

7:13 *did not invade Israelite territory again.* Some interpreters see a contradiction between this statement and subsequent references to the Philistines in 9:16; 10:5; 13:3,5; 17:1; 23:27. This statement, however, only indicates that the Philistines did not immediately counterattack. See 2Ki 6:23–24 for a similar situation.
7:15 A summary statement marking the end of the author's account of Samuel's ministry as Israel's leader (see v. 6).
7:16 *judging Israel.* See note on 4:18.
7:17 *Ramah.* See note on 1:1.
8:1–12:25 See Introduction: Contents and Theme.
8:1 *When Samuel grew old.* Probably about 20 years after the victory at Mizpah, when Samuel was approximately 65 years old (see Introduction: Chronology).
8:3 *accepted bribes.* Perversion of justice through bribery was explicitly forbidden in Pentateuchal law (see Ex 23:8; Dt 16:19).
8:5 *appoint a king to lead us.* The elders cite Samuel's age and the misconduct of his sons as justifications for their request for a king. It soon becomes apparent, however, that the more basic reason for their request was a desire to be like the surrounding nations—to have a human king as a symbol of national power and unity who would lead them in battle and guarantee their security (see v. 20; 10:19; 12:12; see also Introduction: Contents and Theme).
8:7 *Listen to all that the people are saying to you.* Anticipa-

tions of kingship in Israel are present already in the Pentateuch (Ge 49:10; Nu 24:7,17; Dt 17:14–20); Samuel is therefore instructed to listen to the people's request (see vv. 9,22). *it is not you they have rejected, but they have rejected me as their king.* Cf. Jdg 8:23. The sin of Israel in requesting a king (see 10:19; 12:12,17,19–20) did not rest in any evil inherent in kingship itself, but rather in the kind of kingship the people envisioned and their reasons for requesting it (see Introduction: Contents and Theme). Their desire was for a form of kingship that denied their covenant relationship with the Lord, who himself was pledged to be their savior and deliverer. In requesting a king "like all the other nations" (v. 20) they broke the covenant, rejected the Lord who was their King (12:12; Nu 23:21; Dt 33:5) and forgot his constant provision for their protection in the past (10:18; 12:8–11).
8:11 *what the king . . . will do.* Using a description of the policies of contemporary Canaanite kings (vv. 11–17), Samuel warns the people of the burdens associated with the type of kingship they long for.
8:15 *tenth.* This king's portion would be over and above the tenth Israel was to devote to the Lord (Lev 27:30–32; Nu 18:26; Dt 14:22,28; 26:12). In fact, the demands of the king would parallel all that Israel was to consecrate to the Lord as her Great King (persons, lands, crops, livestock)—even the whole population (v. 17).

to his officials and attendants. [16]Your menservants and maidservants and the best of your cattle[a] and donkeys he will take for his own use. [17]He will take a tenth of your flocks, and you yourselves will become his slaves. [18]When that day comes, you will cry out for relief from the king you have chosen, and the LORD will not answer[r] you in that day.[s]"

[19]But the people refused[t] to listen to Samuel. "No!" they said. "We want[u] a king[v] over us. [20]Then we will be like all the other nations,[w] with a king to lead us and to go out before us and fight our battles."

[21]When Samuel heard all that the people said, he repeated[x] it before the LORD. [22]The LORD answered, "Listen[y] to them and give them a king."

Then Samuel said to the men of Israel, "Everyone go back to his town."

Samuel Anoints Saul

9 There was a Benjamite,[z] a man of standing,[a] whose name was Kish[b] son of Abiel, the son of Zeror, the son of Becorath, the son of Aphiah of Benjamin. [2]He had a son named Saul, an impressive[c] young man without equal[d] among the Israelites—a head taller[e] than any of the others.

[3]Now the donkeys[f] belonging to Saul's father Kish were lost, and Kish said to his son Saul, "Take one of the servants with you and go and look for the donkeys." [4]So he passed through the hill[g] country of Ephraim and through the area around Shalisha,[h] but they did not find them.

They went on into the district of Shaalim, but the donkeys[i] were not there. Then he passed through the territory of Benjamin, but they did not find them.

[5]When they reached the district of Zuph,[j] Saul said to the servant who was with him, "Come, let's go back, or my father will stop thinking about the donkeys and start worrying[k] about us."

[6]But the servant replied, "Look, in this town there is a man of God;[l] he is highly respected, and everything[m] he says comes true. Let's go there now. Perhaps he will tell us what way to take."

[7]Saul said to his servant, "If we go, what can we give the man? The food in our sacks is gone. We have no gift[n] to take to the man of God. What do we have?"

[8]The servant answered him again. "Look," he said, "I have a quarter of a shekel[b] of silver. I will give it to the man of God so that he will tell us what way to take." [9](Formerly in Israel, if a man went to inquire[o] of God, he would say, "Come, let us go to the seer," because the prophet of today used to be called a seer.)[p]

[10]"Good," Saul said to his servant. "Come, let's go." So they set out for the town where the man of God was.

[11]As they were going up the hill to the town, they met some girls coming out to draw[q] water, and they asked them, "Is the seer here?"

[12]"He is," they answered. "He's ahead of you. Hurry now; he has just come to our town today, for the people have a sacri-

Cross references (center column)

8:18 [r]1Sa 28:6; Job 27:9; 35:12, 13; Ps 18:41; 66:18; Pr 1:28; Isa 1:15; 58:4; 59:2; Jer 14:12; Eze 8:18; Mic 3:4
[s]1Sa 10:25; 1Ki 12:4
8:19 [t]Pr 1:24; Isa 50:2; 66:4; Jer 7:13; 8:12; 13:10; 44:16
[u]Ac 13:21
[v]S ver 5
8:20 [w]S ver 5
8:21 [x]S Jdg 11:11
8:22 [y]S ver 7
9:1 [z]Jos 18:11-20
[a]S Ru 2:1
[b]1Sa 14:51; 1Ch 8:33; 9:39; Est 2:5; Ac 13:21
9:2 [c]S Ge 39:6
[d]1Sa 10:24
[e]1Sa 10:23
9:3 [f]ver 20; 1Sa 10:14,16
9:4 [g]S Jos 24:33
[h]2Ki 4:42

[i]1Sa 10:2
9:5 [j]1Sa 1:1
[k]1Sa 10:2
9:6 [l]S Dt 33:1; S Jdg 13:6
[m]1Sa 3:19
9:7 [n]S Ge 32:20; 1Ki 13:7; 14:3; 2Ki 4:42; 5:5,15; Jer 40:5
9:9 [o]S Ge 25:22
[p]2Sa 15:27; 24:11; 2Ki 17:13; 1Ch 9:22; 21:9; 26:28; 29:29; 2Ch 19:2; Isa 29:10; 30:10; Am 7:12
9:11 [q]S Ge 24:11,13

[a]16 Septuagint; Hebrew *young men*　　[b]8 That is, about 1/10 ounce (about 3 grams)

Study notes (bottom)

8:18 *cry out for relief from the king.* See 1Ki 12:4; Jer 22:13–17.
8:20 *like all the other nations.* See notes on vv. 5,7.
9:2 *a head taller than any of the others.* Physically of kingly stature (see 10:23).
9:3 *donkeys . . . were lost.* Saul is introduced as a donkey wrangler sent in search of donkeys that had strayed from home—perhaps symbolizing Saul and the rebellious people who had asked for a king (cf. Isa 1:3). David would be introduced as a shepherd caring for his father's flock and later pictured as the shepherd over the Lord's flock (2Sa 5:2; 7:7–8; Ps 78:71–72).
9:6 *the servant replied.* Saul's ignorance of Samuel is indicative of his character. *this town.* Probably Ramah (see 7:17), the hometown of Samuel, to which he had just returned from a journey (see v. 12; 7:16). *man of God.* See note on 2:27; here a reference to Samuel. *everything he says comes true.* See 3:19 and note.
9:7 *what can we give the man?* Other examples of gifts offered to prophets are found in 1Ki 14:3; 2Ki 4:42; 5:15–16; 8:8–9. Whether Samuel accepted the gift and whether he was dependent on such gifts for a livelihood are not clear. Elisha refused the gift of Naaman (2Ki 5:16). In later times false prophets adjusted their message to the de-

sires of those who supported them (1Ki 22:6,8,18; Mic 3:5,11).
9:8 *a quarter of a shekel of silver.* See NIV text note. Before the use of coins, gold or silver was weighed out for each monetary transaction (see 13:21; Job 28:15). The value of that amount of silver in Saul's time is not known.
9:9 *the prophet of today used to be called a seer.* There was no essential difference between a seer and a prophet. The person popularly designated as a prophet at the time of the writing of 1,2 Samuel was termed a seer in the time of Saul. This need not mean that the term "prophet" was unknown in the time of Saul or that the term "seer" was unknown in later times (see Isa 30:10). The reference is to popular usage.
9:12 *high place.* See Lev 26:30. After entrance into the promised land, the Israelites often followed the custom of the Canaanites in building local altars on hills. (At this time the central sanctuary was not functioning because the ark of God was separated from the tabernacle; Shiloh had been destroyed, and the priestly family, after the death of Eli's sons, was apparently still inactive.) In later times, worship at the "high places" provided a means for the entrance of pagan practices into Israel's religious observances and, for this reason, it was condemned (see note on 1Ki 3:2).

fice[r] at the high place.[s] 13As soon as you enter the town, you will find him before he goes up to the high place to eat. The people will not begin eating until he comes, because he must bless[t] the sacrifice; afterward, those who are invited will eat. Go up now; you should find him about this time.''

14They went up to the town, and as they were entering it, there was Samuel, coming toward them on his way up to the high place.

15Now the day before Saul came, the LORD had revealed this to Samuel: 16''About this time tomorrow I will send you a man from the land of Benjamin. Anoint[u] him leader[v] over my people Israel; he will deliver[w] my people from the hand of the Philistines.[x] I have looked upon my people, for their cry[y] has reached me.''

17When Samuel caught sight of Saul, the LORD said to him, ''This[z] is the man I spoke to you about; he will govern my people.''

18Saul approached Samuel in the gateway and asked, ''Would you please tell me where the seer's house is?''

19''I am the seer,'' Samuel replied. ''Go up ahead of me to the high place, for today you are to eat with me, and in the morning I will let you go and will tell you all that is in your heart. 20As for the donkeys[a] you lost three days ago, do not worry about them; they have been found. And to whom is all the desire[b] of Israel turned, if not to you and all your father's family?''

21Saul answered, ''But am I not a Benjamite, from the smallest tribe[c] of Israel, and is not my clan the least[d] of all the clans of

the tribe of Benjamin?[e] Why do you say such a thing to me?''

22Then Samuel brought Saul and his servant into the hall and seated them at the head of those who were invited—about thirty in number. 23Samuel said to the cook, ''Bring the piece of meat I gave you, the one I told you to lay aside.''

24So the cook took up the leg[f] with what was on it and set it in front of Saul. Samuel said, ''Here is what has been kept for you. Eat, because it was set aside for you for this occasion, from the time I said, 'I have invited guests.' '' And Saul dined with Samuel that day.

25After they came down from the high place to the town, Samuel talked with Saul on the roof[g] of his house. 26They rose about daybreak and Samuel called to Saul on the roof, ''Get ready, and I will send you on your way.'' When Saul got ready, he and Samuel went outside together. 27As they were going down to the edge of the town, Samuel said to Saul, ''Tell the servant to go on ahead of us''—and the servant did so—''but you stay here awhile, so that I may give you a message from God.''

10 Then Samuel took a flask[h] of oil and poured it on Saul's head and kissed him, saying, ''Has not the LORD anointed[i] you leader over his inheritance?[c][j] 2When you leave me today, you will meet two men near Rachel's tomb,[k] at Zelzah on the border of Benjamin. They will say to you, 'The donkeys[l] you set out to look for have been found. And now your father has stopped thinking about them

c[j] Hebrew; Septuagint and Vulgate over his people Israel? You will reign over the LORD's people and save them from the power of their enemies round about. And this will be a sign to you that the LORD has anointed you leader over his inheritance:

Cross references (center column):
9:12 [r]Nu 28:11-15; S 1Sa 7:17 [s]S Lev 26:30
9:13 [t]S Mt 14:19; 1Co 10:16; 1Ti 4:3-5
9:16 [u]Ex 30:25; S 1Sa 2:35; 12:3; 15:1; 26:9; 2Ki 11:12; Ps 2:2 [v]2Sa 7:8; 1Ki 8:16; 1Ch 5:2 [w]Ex 3:8 [x]1Sa 23:4; 2Sa 3:18 [y]S Ge 16:11; Ps 102:1
9:17 [z]1Sa 16:12
9:20 [a]S ver 3 [b]1Sa 12:13; Ezr 6:8; Isa 60:4-9; Da 2:44; Hag 2:7; Mal 3:1
9:21 [c]Ps 68:27 [d]S Ex 3:11; Mt 2:6; 1Co 15:9
[e]Jdg 6:15; 20:35, 46; 1Sa 18:18
9:24 [f]S Lev 7:34
9:25 [g]S Dt 22:8; S Jos 2:8; S Mt 24:17; Lk 5:19
10:1 [h]1Sa 16:1; 2Ki 9:1 [i]S Ex 29:7; S 1Sa 9:16; S 1Ki 1:39; [j]S Ex 34:9; 2Sa 20:19; Ps 78:62,71
10:2 [k]Ge 35:20 [l]1Sa 9:4

9:13 *he must bless the sacrifice.* Samuel presided over the sacrificial meal (see 1:4; 2:13–16), at which he gave a prayer, probably similar to those referred to in the NT (see Mt 26:26–27; Jn 6:11, 23; 1Ti 4:3–5).

9:16 *Anoint him.* Priests were also anointed (see Ex 29:7; 40:12–15; Lev 4:3; 8:12), but from this point in the OT it is usually the king who is referred to as ''the anointed of the LORD'' (see note on 2:10; cf. 12:3; 24:6; 26:9,11,16; 2Sa 1:14,16; 19:21; 22:51; 23:1; Ps 2:2,6; but see also Zec 4:14). Anointing signifies separation to the Lord for a particular task and divine equipping for the task (see v. 6; 16:13; Isa 61:1). *leader.* The Hebrew for this word indicates one designated (here by the Lord) to be the chief in rank. It served as a useful term to ease the transition between the time of the judges and that of the kings. *Philistines.* See note on 7:13.

9:20 *all the desire of Israel.* A reference to Israel's desire for a king.

9:21 *smallest tribe . . . least of all the clans.* Saul's origins were among the humblest in Israel (Benjamin was the last of

Jacob's sons, and the tribe had been greatly reduced in the time of the judges; see Jdg 20:46–48). His elevation to king shows that God ''raises the poor'' (2:8), which is one of the central themes running throughout Samuel. God's use of the powerless to promote his kingdom in the world is a common feature in the Biblical testimony and underscores the truth that his kingdom is not of this world.

9:24 *leg.* The Hebrew for this word specifies the thigh, which was normally reserved for the Lord's consecrated priest (see Ex 29:22,27; Lev 7:32–33,35; Nu 6:20; 18:18). The presentation of this choice piece of the sacrificial animal to Saul was a distinct honor and anticipated his being designated the Lord's anointed.

10:1 *oil.* Perhaps spiced olive oil (see Ex 30:22–33). *Has not the LORD anointed you . . .?* See note on 9:16. *leader.* See 9:16 and note. *his inheritance.* ''My people Israel'' (9:16). The Lord's inheritance includes both the people (see Ex 34:9) and the land (see Ex 15:17). After departing from Samuel, Saul is to receive three signs (see vv. 2–7) to authenticate Samuel's words and to assure him that the Lord has indeed chosen him to be king.

and is worried _m_ about you. He is asking, "What shall I do about my son?"' _l_

³"Then you will go on from there until you reach the great tree of Tabor. Three men going up to God at Bethel _n_ will meet you there. One will be carrying three young goats, another three loaves of bread, and another a skin of wine. ⁴They will greet you and offer you two loaves of bread, _o_ which you will accept from them.

⁵"After that you will go to Gibeah _p_ of God, where there is a Philistine outpost. _q_ As you approach the town, you will meet a procession of prophets _r_ coming down from the high place _s_ with lyres, tambourines, _t_ flutes _u_ and harps _v_ being played before them, and they will be prophesying. _w_ ⁶The Spirit _x_ of the LORD will come upon you in power, and you will prophesy with them; and you will be changed _y_ into a different person. ⁷Once these signs are fulfilled, do whatever _z_ your hand _a_ finds to do, for God is with _b_ you.

⁸"Go down ahead of me to Gilgal. _c_ I will surely come down to you to sacrifice burnt offerings and fellowship offerings, _d_ but you must wait seven _d_ days until I come to you and tell you what you are to do."

Saul Made King

⁹As Saul turned to leave Samuel, God changed _e_ Saul's heart, and all these signs _f_ were fulfilled _g_ that day. ¹⁰When they arrived at Gibeah, a procession of prophets met him; the Spirit _h_ of God came upon him in power, and he joined in their prophesying. _i_ ¹¹When all those who had

formerly known him saw him prophesying with the prophets, they asked each other, "What is this _j_ that has happened to the son of Kish? Is Saul also among the prophets?" _k_

¹²A man who lived there answered, "And who is their father?" So it became a saying: "Is Saul also among the prophets?" _l_ ¹³After Saul stopped prophesying, _m_ he went to the high place.

¹⁴Now Saul's uncle _n_ asked him and his servant, "Where have you been?"

"Looking for the donkeys, _o_" he said. "But when we saw they were not to be found, we went to Samuel."

¹⁵Saul's uncle said, "Tell me what Samuel said to you."

¹⁶Saul replied, "He assured us that the donkeys _p_ had been found." But he did not tell his uncle what Samuel had said about the kingship.

¹⁷Samuel summoned the people of Israel to the LORD at Mizpah _q_ ¹⁸and said to them, "This is what the LORD, the God of Israel, says: 'I brought Israel up out of Egypt, and I delivered you from the power of Egypt and all the kingdoms that oppressed _r_ you.' ¹⁹But you have now rejected _s_ your God, who saves _t_ you out of all your calamities and distresses. And you have said, 'No, set a king _u_ over us.' _v_ So now present _w_ yourselves before the LORD by your tribes and clans."

²⁰When Samuel brought all the tribes of

Cross references (center column)

10:2 _m_ 1Sa 9:5
10:3 _n_ S Ge 35:8
10:4 _o_ ver 27;
1Sa 16:20;
Pr 18:16
10:5 _p_ ver 26;
1Sa 11:4; 15:34
_q_ 1Sa 13:3
_r_ S Nu 11:29;
1Ki 20:35;
2Ki 2:3,15; 4:1;
6:1; 9:1;
Am 7:14
_s_ S Lev 26:30
_t_ S Ge 31:27;
Jer 31:4
_u_ 1Ki 1:40;
Isa 30:29
_v_ 1Sa 16:16;
18:10; 19:9;
2Ki 3:15; Ps 92:3
_w_ ver 10;
1Sa 19:20;
1Ch 25:1;
1Co 14:1
10:6 _x_ S Nu 11:25
_y_ ver 9
10:7 _z_ 2Sa 7:3;
1Ki 8:17;
1Ch 22:7; 28:2;
2Ch 6:7; Ecc 9:10
_a_ Jdg 9:33
_b_ S Jos 1:5;
Lk 1:28; Heb 13:5
10:8 _c_ Jos 4:20;
S 10:43;
1Sa 7:16; 11:14
_d_ 1Sa 13:8
10:9 _e_ ver 6
_f_ S Dt 13:2 _g_ ver 7
10:10
_h_ S Nu 11:25;
1Sa 11:6 _i_ S ver 5

10:11 _j_ Mt 13:54;
Jn 7:15 _k_ ver 12;
1Sa 19:24;
2Ki 9:11;
Jer 29:26; Hos 9:7
10:12 _l_ S ver 11
10:13
_m_ 1Sa 19:23
10:14 _n_ 1Sa 14:50
_o_ S 1Sa 9:3
10:16 _p_ S 1Sa 9:3
10:17 _q_ S 1Sa 7:5
10:18 _r_ S Ex 1:14;
S Nu 10:9
10:19
_s_ S Nu 11:20;

_t_ Ps 7:10; 18:48; 68:20; 145:19 _u_ S 1Sa 8:5
_v_ S Dt 17:14 _w_ Jos 7:14

_d 8_ Traditionally _peace offerings_

10:5 _Gibeah of God._ Gibeah was Saul's hometown (see v. 26; 11:4), located in the tribal area of Benjamin (Jos 18:28; Jdg 19:12–14). It was usually called "Gibeah" or "Gibeah of Benjamin" (as in 13:2,15), but twice "Gibeah of Saul" (15:34; 2Sa 21:6). The present designation (used only here) may have been Samuel's way of reminding Saul that the land of Canaan belonged to God and not to the Philistines (see Dt 32:43; Isa 14:2; Hos 9:3). _prophets._ The bands of prophets with which Samuel was associated (as also the "sons of the prophets" with whom Elijah and Elisha were associated; see note on 1Ki 20:35) appear to have been small communities of men who banded together in spiritually decadent times for mutual cultivation of their religious zeal. _prophesying._ Here (and in vv. 6,10–11,13) appears to designate an enthusiastic praising of God inspired by the Holy Spirit (see Nu 11:24–30 for similar use of the term).
10:7 _do whatever your hand finds to do._ Saul is to take whatever action is appropriate when the situation presents itself to manifest publicly his royal leadership (see 11:4–11).
10:8 _Go down ahead of me to Gilgal._ At some unspecified future time, perhaps previously discussed (see 9:25), Saul is to go to Gilgal and wait seven days for Samuel's arrival (see 13:7–14).
10:11 _Is Saul also among the prophets?_ An expression of surprise at Saul's behavior (see note on v. 5) by those who

had known him previously—another subtle indication of his character (see notes on 9:3,6).
10:12 _who is their father?_ Some understand the question as an expression of contempt for prophets generally, others as implying the recognition that prophetic inspiration comes from God and therefore could be imparted to whomever God chose. However, since leading prophets were sometimes called "father" (2Ki 2:12; 6:21; 13:14), the speaker may have intended a disdainful reference to Samuel or an ironical gibe at Saul.
10:17 _Samuel summoned the people._ After the private designation and anointing of Saul to be king (9:1–10:16), an assembly is called by Samuel to make the Lord's choice known to the people (v. 21) and to define the king's task (v. 25). _Mizpah._ See note on 7:5.
10:18 _I delivered you._ Speaking through Samuel, the Lord emphasizes to the people that he has been their deliverer throughout their history. He brought them out of Egypt and delivered them from all their enemies during the time of the judges. Although the judges themselves are sometimes referred to as Israel's deliverers (see Jdg 3:9,15,31; 6:14; 10:1; 13:5), this was true only in a secondary sense, for they were instruments of the Lord's deliverance (see Jdg 2:18). It was the Lord who sent them (see 12:11; Jdg 6:14).
10:19 _rejected your God._ See note on 8:7.

Israel near, the tribe of Benjamin was chosen. [21]Then he brought forward the tribe of Benjamin, clan by clan, and Matri's clan was chosen.[x] Finally Saul son of Kish was chosen. But when they looked for him, he was not to be found. [22]So they inquired[y] further of the Lord, "Has the man come here yet?"

And the Lord said, "Yes, he has hidden himself among the baggage."

[23]They ran and brought him out, and as he stood among the people he was a head taller[z] than any of the others. [24]Samuel said to all the people, "Do you see the man the Lord has chosen?[a] There is no one like[b] him among all the people."

Then the people shouted, "Long live[c] the king!"

[25]Samuel explained[d] to the people the regulations[e] of the kingship.[f] He wrote them down on a scroll and deposited it before the Lord. Then Samuel dismissed the people, each to his own home.

[26]Saul also went to his home in Gibeah,[g] accompanied by valiant men[h] whose hearts God had touched. [27]But some troublemakers[i] said, "How can this fellow save us?" They despised him and brought him no gifts.[j] But Saul kept silent.

Saul Rescues the City of Jabesh

11 Nahash[k] the Ammonite went up and besieged Jabesh Gilead.[l] And all the men of Jabesh said to him, "Make a treaty[m] with us, and we will be subject to you."

[2]But Nahash the Ammonite replied, "I will make a treaty with you only on the condition[n] that I gouge[o] out the right eye of every one of you and so bring disgrace[p] on all Israel."

[3]The elders[q] of Jabesh said to him, "Give us seven days so we can send messengers throughout Israel; if no one comes to rescue[r] us, we will surrender[s] to you."

[4]When the messengers came to Gibeah[t] of Saul and reported these terms to the people, they all wept[u] aloud. [5]Just then Saul was returning from the fields, behind his oxen, and he asked, "What is wrong with the people? Why are they weeping?" Then they repeated to him what the men of Jabesh had said.

[6]When Saul heard their words, the Spirit[v] of God came upon him in power, and he burned with anger. [7]He took a pair of oxen,[w] cut them into pieces, and sent the pieces by messengers throughout Israel,[x] proclaiming, "This is what will be done to the oxen of anyone[y] who does not follow Saul and Samuel." Then the terror of the Lord fell on the people, and they turned out as one man.[z] [8]When Saul mustered[a] them at Bezek,[b] the men of Israel numbered three hundred thousand and the men of Judah thirty thousand.

[9]They told the messengers who had come, "Say to the men of Jabesh Gilead, 'By the time the sun is hot tomorrow, you will be delivered.'" When the messengers went and reported this to the men of Jabesh, they were elated. [10]They said to the

---

Cross references

10:21 [x]Est 3:7; Pr 16:33
10:22 [y]S Ge 25:22; S Jdg 18:5
10:23 [z]1Sa 9:2
10:24 [a]Dt 17:15; 2Sa 21:6 [b]1Sa 9:2 [c]1Ki 1:25,34,39; 2Ki 11:12
10:25 [d]S 1Sa 8:9 [e]S Dt 17:14-20; S 1Sa 8:11-18; 2Ki 11:12 [f]1Sa 11:14
10:26 [g]S ver 5; S Jdg 19:14 [h]S Jdg 20:44
10:27 [i]S Dt 13:13; S 1Sa 20:7 /S ver 4; 1Ki 10:25; 2Ch 17:5; 32:23; Ps 68:29
11:1 [k]S Ge 19:38; 1Sa 12:12; 2Sa 10:2; 17:27; 1Ch 19:1 [l]Jdg 21:8; 1Sa 31:11; 2Sa 2:4,5; 21:12 [m]S Ex 23:32; S Jer 37:1
11:2 [n]Ge 34:15 [o]S Nu 16:14 [p]1Sa 17:26
11:3 [q]S 1Sa 8:4 [r]S Jdg 2:16 [s]ver 10
11:4 [t]S 1Sa 10:5, 26 [u]S Ge 27:38; S Nu 25:6
11:6 [v]S Jdg 3:10
11:7 [w]S 1Sa 6:14 [x]S Jdg 19:29 [y]Jdg 21:5 [z]S Jdg 20:1
11:8 [a]Jdg 20:2 [b]Jdg 1:4

10:20 *tribe of Benjamin was chosen.* Probably by casting lots (see 14:41-42; Jos 7:15-18). The Urim and Thummim were used for this purpose (see notes on 2:28; Ex 28:30).
10:24 *Long live the king!* See 2Sa 16:16.
10:25 *regulations of the kingship.* Samuel here takes the first step toward resolving the tension that existed between Israel's misdirected desire for a king (and their misconceived notion of what the king's role and function should be) and the Lord's intent to give them one (see Introduction: Contents and Theme). This description of the duties and prerogatives of the Israelite king was given for the benefit of both the people and the king-designate. It was intended to clearly distinguish Israelite kingship from that of the surrounding nations and to ensure that the king's role in Israel was compatible with the continued rule of the Lord over Israel as her Great King (see Dt 17:14-20). *deposited it before the Lord.* The written constitutional-legal document defining the role of the king in governing God's covenant people was preserved at the sanctuary (the tabernacle, later the temple). Other written documents defining Israel's covenant relationship with the Lord are referred to in Ex 24:7; Dt 31:26; Jos 24:26.
10:27 *troublemakers.* See note on Dt 13:13. *How can this fellow save us?* Reflects the people's continued apostate idea that national security was to be sought in the person of the human king (see note on v. 18; cf. 8:20).
11:1 *Ammonite.* The Ammonites were descended from

Lot (see Ge 19:38; Dt 2:19) and lived east of the tribal territory of Gad near the upper regions of the Jabbok River (see Dt 2:37; Jos 12:2). Previous attempts by the Ammonites to occupy Israelite territory are referred to in Jdg 3:13; 11:4-32. The Philistine threat to Israel in the west presented the Ammonites with an opportunity to move against Israel from the east with supposed impunity. *Jabesh Gilead.* A town east of the Jordan in the tribal area of Manasseh.
11:2 *gouge out the right eye.* Besides causing humiliation (see note on Jdg 16:21), the loss of the right eye would destroy the military capability of the archers.
11:4 *Gibeah of Saul.* See 10:26 and note on 10:5. Close family ties undoubtedly prompted the inhabitants of Jabesh to seek help from the tribe of Benjamin (see Jdg 21:12-14).
11:5 *Saul was returning from the fields.* After Saul's public selection as the king-designate at Mizpah (10:17-27), he returned home (10:26) to resume his normal private activities and to wait for the Lord's leading for the next step in his elevation to the throne (see notes on v. 15; 10:7).
11:6 *the Spirit of God came upon him in power.* For similar endowment of Israel's deliverers with extraordinary vigor by God's Spirit see 10:6,10; Jdg 14:6,19; 15:14.
11:7 *sent the pieces by messengers throughout Israel.* For a similar case see Jdg 19:29.
11:8 *Bezek.* Located north of Shechem, west of the Jordan River but within striking distance of Jabesh Gilead.

Ammonites, "Tomorrow we will surrender[c] to you, and you can do to us whatever seems good to you."

[11]The next day Saul separated his men into three divisions;[d] during the last watch of the night they broke into the camp of the Ammonites[e] and slaughtered them until the heat of the day. Those who survived were scattered, so that no two of them were left together.

Saul Confirmed as King

[12]The people then said to Samuel, "Who[f] was it that asked, 'Shall Saul reign over us?' Bring these men to us and we will put them to death."

[13]But Saul said, "No one shall be put to death today,[g] for this day the LORD has rescued[h] Israel."

[14]Then Samuel said to the people, "Come, let us go to Gilgal[i] and there reaffirm the kingship.[j]" [15]So all the people went to Gilgal[k] and confirmed Saul as king[l] in the presence of the LORD. There they sacrificed fellowship offerings[e] before the LORD, and Saul and all the Israelites held a great celebration.

Samuel's Farewell Speech

12 Samuel said to all Israel, "I have listened[m] to everything you said to me and have set a king[n] over you. [2]Now

you have a king as your leader.[o] As for me, I am old and gray, and my sons[p] are here with you. I have been your leader from my youth until this day. [3]Here I stand. Testify against me in the presence of the LORD and his anointed.[q] Whose ox have I taken? Whose donkey[r] have I taken? Whom have I cheated? Whom have I oppressed? From whose hand have I accepted a bribe[s] to make me shut my eyes? If I have done[t] any of these, I will make it right."[u]

[4]"You have not cheated or oppressed us," they replied. "You have not taken anything from anyone's hand."

[5]Samuel said to them, "The LORD is witness[v] against you, and also his anointed is witness this day, that you have not found anything[w] in my hand.[x]"

"He is witness," they said.

[6]Then Samuel said to the people, "It is the LORD who appointed Moses and Aaron and brought[y] your forefathers up out of Egypt. [7]Now then, stand[z] here, because I am going to confront[a] you with evidence before the LORD as to all the righteous acts[b] performed by the LORD for you and your fathers.

[8]"After Jacob[c] entered Egypt, they cried[d] to the LORD for help, and the LORD sent[e] Moses and Aaron, who brought your

---

11:10 cver 3
11:11 dS Jdg 7:16; eS Ge 19:38
11:12 fS Dt 13:13; Lk 19:27
11:13 g2Sa 19:22; hSa 19:5; 1Ch 11:14
11:14 iS Jos 10:43; S 1Sa 10:8; jSa 10:25
11:15 kS Jos 5:9; 2Sa 19:15; lSa 12:1
12:1 mS 1Sa 8:7; nSa 11:15
12:2 oS 1Sa 8:5

p1Sa 8:3
12:3 qS 1Sa 9:16; 24:6; 26:9,11; 2Sa 1:14; 19:21; Ps 105:15; rNu 16:15; sS Ex 18:21; S 1Sa 8:3; tEx 20:17; Ac 20:33; uS Lev 25:14
12:5 vS Ge 31:50; wAc 23:9; 24:20; xEx 22:4
12:6 yS Ex 3:10; Mic 6:4
12:7 zS Jos 24:1; aIsa 1:18; 3:14; Jer 2:9; 25:31; Eze 17:20; 20:35; Mic 6:1-5; bS Jdg 5:11
12:8 cS Ge 46:6; dS Ex 2:23; eS Ex 3:10; 4:16

e15 Traditionally *peace offerings*

11:11 *last watch of the night.* The third watch, from about 2:00 A.M. until about 6:00 A.M. (see note on Mt 14:25).
11:13 *the LORD has rescued Israel.* Saul recognizes Israel's true deliverer (see note on 10:18). The victory, in combination with Saul's confession, places yet another seal of divine approval on Saul as the man the Lord has chosen to be king.
11:14 *let us go to Gilgal and there reaffirm the kingship.* Samuel perceives that it is now the appropriate time for the people to renew their allegiance to the Lord. The kingship of which he speaks is the Lord's, not Saul's. Samuel calls for an assembly to restore the covenant relationship between the Lord and his people. He wants to inaugurate Saul's rule in a manner demonstrating that the continued rule of the Lord as Israel's Great King is in no way diminished or violated in the new era of the monarchy (see Introduction: Contents and Theme). Verses 14–15 are a brief synopsis of the Gilgal assembly and are prefaced to the more detailed account of the same assembly in ch. 12. *Gilgal.* Located east of Jericho near the Jordan River. It was a particularly appropriate place for Israel to renew her allegiance to the Lord (see Jos 4:19–5:11; 10:8–15).
11:15 *confirmed Saul as king in the presence of the LORD.* Saul had previously been anointed in private by Samuel at Ramah (10:1) and publicly selected as the king-designate at Mizpah (10:17-27). In the subsequent Ammonite crisis (vv. 1–13) his leadership did not rest on public recognition of his royal authority, but on the military victory. Now at Gilgal Saul is inaugurated as God's chosen king and formally assumes the privileges and responsibilities of this office. *fellowship offerings.* This type of offering was an important element in the original ceremony of covenant ratification at

Sinai (Ex 24:5,11). It represented the communion or peace between the Lord and his people when the people lived in conformity with their covenant obligations (see Lev 7:11–17; 22:21–23). *held a great celebration.* Rejoicing is the expression of people who have renewed their commitment to the Lord, confessed their sin (see 12:19) and been given a king.
12:3 *Testify against me.* When Samuel presents the newly inaugurated king to the people, he seeks to establish publicly his own past faithfulness to the covenant as leader of the nation. His purpose is to exonerate himself and provide an example for Saul in his new responsibilities. *Whose ox have I taken? Whose donkey have I taken?* See Ex 20:17; 22:1,4, 9. Samuel has not used his position for personal gain (see Nu 16:15). *Whom have I cheated? Whom have I oppressed?* See Lev 19:13; Dt 24:14. *From whose hand have I accepted a bribe . . .?* See Ex 23:8; Dt 16:19.
12:6 *Samuel said to the people.* Samuel turns from consideration of his previous leadership to the matter of the people's request for a king, which he views as a covenant-breaking act and a serious apostasy. *It is the LORD.* Samuel emphasizes that in the past the Lord had provided the necessary leadership for the nation.
12:7 *confront you with evidence.* The terminology is that of a legal proceeding, as in vv. 2–5, but now the relationship of the parties is reversed. This time Samuel is the accuser, the people are the defendants, and the Lord is the Judge. *righteous acts performed by the LORD.* These righteous acts (see vv. 8–11) demonstrate the constancy of the Lord's covenant faithfulness toward his people in the past and, by way of contrast, serve as an indictment of their present apostasy.

Israel Without Weapons

15Then Samuel left Gilgal[n] and went up to Gibeah[f] in Benjamin, and Saul counted the men who were with him. They numbered about six hundred.[g]

16Saul and his son Jonathan and the men with them were staying in Gibeah[o][h] in Benjamin, while the Philistines camped at Micmash. 17Raiding[i] parties went out from the Philistine camp in three detachments. One turned toward Ophrah[j] in the vicinity of Shual, 18another toward Beth Horon,[k] and the third toward the borderland overlooking the Valley of Zeboim[l] facing the desert.

19Not a blacksmith[m] could be found in the whole land of Israel, because the Philistines had said, "Otherwise the Hebrews will make swords or spears![n]" 20So all Israel went down to the Philistines to have their plowshares, mattocks, axes and sickles[p] sharpened. 21The price was two thirds of a shekel[q] for sharpening plowshares and mattocks, and a third of a shekel[r] for sharpening forks and axes and for repointing goads.

22So on the day of the battle not a soldier with Saul and Jonathan[o] had a sword or spear[p] in his hand; only Saul and his son Jonathan had them.

Jonathan Attacks the Philistines

23Now a detachment of Philistines had gone out to the pass[q] at Micmash.[r] 14 1One day Jonathan son of Saul said to the young man bearing his armor, "Come, let's go over to the Philistine outpost on the other side." But he did not tell his father.

2Saul was staying[s] on the outskirts of Gibeah[t] under a pomegranate tree[u] in Migron.[v] With him were about six hundred men, 3among whom was Ahijah, who was wearing an ephod. He was a son of Ichabod's[w] brother Ahitub[x] son of Phinehas, the son of Eli,[y] the LORD's priest in Shiloh.[z] No one was aware that Jonathan had left.

4On each side of the pass[a] that Jonathan intended to cross to reach the Philistine outpost was a cliff; one was called Bozez, and the other Seneh. 5One cliff stood to the north toward Micmash, the other to the south toward Geba.[b]

6Jonathan said to his young armor-bearer, "Come, let's go over to the outpost of those uncircumcised[c] fellows. Perhaps the LORD will act in our behalf. Nothing[d] can hinder the LORD from saving, whether by many[e] or by few.[f] "

7"Do all that you have in mind," his armor-bearer said. "Go ahead; I am with you heart and soul."

8Jonathan said, "Come, then; we will cross over toward the men and let them see us. 9If they say to us, 'Wait there until we come to you,' we will stay where we are and not go up to them. 10But if they say, 'Come up to us,' we will climb up, because that will be our sign[g] that the LORD has given them into our hands.[h] "

11So both of them showed themselves to the Philistine outpost. "Look!" said the Philistines. "The Hebrews[i] are crawling out of the holes they were hiding[j] in." 12The men of the outpost shouted to Jonathan and his armor-bearer, "Come up to us and we'll teach you a lesson.[k] "

So Jonathan said to his armor-bearer, "Climb up after me; the LORD has given them into the hand[l] of Israel."

13Jonathan climbed up, using his hands

n15 Hebrew; Septuagint Gilgal and went his way; the rest of the people went after Saul to meet the army, and they went out of Gilgal   o16 Two Hebrew manuscripts; most Hebrew manuscripts Geba, a variant of Gibeah   p20 Septuagint; Hebrew plowshares   q21 Hebrew pim; that is, about 1/4 ounce (about 8 grams)   r21 That is, about 1/8 ounce (about 4 grams)

13:15 six hundred. The seven-day delay had greatly depleted Saul's forces (see vv. 2,4,6–8).
13:17 Raiding parties. The purpose of these Philistine contingents was not to engage the Israelites in battle, but to plunder the land and demoralize its inhabitants.
13:18 Valley of Zeboim. Located to the east toward the Jordan Valley.
13:19 Not a blacksmith. A Philistine monopoly on the technology of iron production placed the Israelites at a great disadvantage in the fashioning and maintenance of agricultural implements and military weapons.
13:22 not . . . a sword or spear. The Israelites fought with bow and arrow and slingshot.
14:1 on the other side. The Philistines were encamped to the north of the pass and the Israelites to the south.
14:2 Gibeah. Saul had retreated farther south from Geba (13:3) to Gibeah. under a pomegranate tree. It appears to

have been customary for leaders in early Israel to hold court under well-known trees (see 22:6; Jdg 4:5).
14:3 Ahijah. Either the brother and predecessor of Ahimelech son of Ahitub (referred to in 21:1; 22:9,11) or an alternate name for Ahimelech. wearing an ephod. See note on 2:28. Ichabod's brother. See 4:21.
14:6 uncircumcised fellows. A term of contempt (see 17:26,36; 31:4; 2Sa 1:20; Jdg 14:3; 15:18; 1Ch 10:4), which draws attention to Israel's covenant relationship to the Lord (see note on Ge 17:10) and, by implication, to the illegitimacy of the Philistine presence in the land. by many or by few. See note on 17:47. Jonathan's bold plan is undertaken as an act of faith (cf. Heb 11:33–34) founded on God's promise (9:16).
14:10 our sign. See Jdg 6:36–40; Isa 7:11.
14:11 Hebrews. See 4:6; 13:3,7 and note on Ge 14:13.

and feet, with his armor-bearer right behind him. The Philistines fell before Jonathan, and his armor-bearer followed and killed behind him. [14]In that first attack Jonathan and his armor-bearer killed some twenty men in an area of about half an acre.[s]

Israel Routs the Philistines

[15]Then panic[m] struck the whole army—those in the camp and field, and those in the outposts and raiding[n] parties—and the ground shook. It was a panic sent by God.[t]

[16]Saul's lookouts[o] at Gibeah in Benjamin saw the army melting away in all directions. [17]Then Saul said to the men who were with him, "Muster the forces and see who has left us." When they did, it was Jonathan and his armor-bearer who were not there.

[18]Saul said to Ahijah, "Bring[p] the ark[q] of God." (At that time it was with the Israelites.)[u] [19]While Saul was talking to the priest, the tumult in the Philistine camp increased more and more. So Saul said to the priest,[r] "Withdraw your hand."

[20]Then Saul and all his men assembled and went to the battle. They found the Philistines in total confusion, striking[s] each other with their swords. [21]Those Hebrews who had previously been with the Philistines and had gone up with them to their camp went[t] over to the Israelites who were with Saul and Jonathan. [22]When all the Israelites who had hidden[u] in the

hill country of Ephraim heard that the Philistines were on the run, they joined the battle in hot pursuit. [23]So the LORD rescued[v] Israel that day, and the battle moved on beyond Beth Aven.[w]

Jonathan Eats Honey

[24]Now the men of Israel were in distress that day, because Saul had bound the people under an oath,[x] saying, "Cursed be any man who eats food before evening comes, before I have avenged myself on my enemies!" So none of the troops tasted food.

[25]The entire army[v] entered the woods, and there was honey on the ground. [26]When they went into the woods, they saw the honey oozing out, yet no one put his hand to his mouth, because they feared the oath. [27]But Jonathan had not heard that his father had bound the people with the oath, so he reached out the end of the staff that was in his hand and dipped it into the honeycomb.[y] He raised his hand to his mouth, and his eyes brightened.[w] [28]Then one of the soldiers told him, "Your father bound the army under a strict oath, saying, 'Cursed be any man who eats food today!' That is why the men are faint."

[29]Jonathan said, "My father has made trouble[z] for the country. See how my eyes

---

Cross references (center column):

14:15
[m]S Ge 35:5;
[s]S Ex 14:24;
[s]S 19:16;
2Ki 7:5-7
[n]1Sa 13:17
14:16
[o]2Sa 18:24;
2Ki 9:17;
Isa 52:8; Eze 33:2
14:18 [p]1Sa 30:7
[q]S Jdg 18:5
14:19 [r]Nu 27:21
14:20
[s]S Jdg 7:22;
Eze 38:21;
Zec 14:13
14:21 [t]1Sa 29:4
14:22
[u]S 1Sa 13:6

14:23
[v]S Ex 14:30
[w]S Jos 7:2
14:24 [x]Jos 6:26
14:27 [y]ver 43;
Ps 19:10;
Pr 16:24; 24:13
14:29 [z]Jos 7:25;
1Ki 18:18

Text notes:

[s]14 Hebrew half a yoke; a "yoke" was the land plowed by a yoke of oxen in one day.   [t]15 Or a terrible panic   [u]18 Hebrew; Septuagint "Bring the ephod." (At that time he wore the ephod before the Israelites.)   [v]25 Or Now all the people of the land   [w]27 Or his strength was renewed

---

14:15 *ground shook.* See 7:10; Jos 10:11–14; Ps 77:18 for other instances of divine intervention in nature to bring deliverance to Israel.

14:18 *Bring the ark of God.* Saul decides to seek God's will before entering into battle with the Philistines (see Nu 27:21; Dt 20:2). Here the Septuagint (the Greek translation of the OT) may preserve the original text (see NIV text note) for the following reasons: 1. In 7:1 the ark was located at Kiriath Jearim, where it remained until David brought it to Jerusalem (2Sa 6), but the ephod was present in Saul's camp at Gibeah (see v. 3). 2. Nowhere else in the OT is the ark used to determine God's will, but the ephod (with the Urim and Thummim) was given for this purpose (see 23:9; 30:7 and notes on 2:18,28). 3. The command to the priest to withdraw his hand (v. 19) is more appropriate with the ephod than with the ark.

14:19 *Withdraw your hand.* Due to the urgency of the moment, Saul decides that to wait for the word of the Lord might jeopardize his military advantage. As in 13:8–12, his decision rests on his own insight rather than on dependence upon the Lord and a commitment to obey him.

14:23 *So the LORD rescued Israel that day.* The writer attributes the victory to the Lord, not to either Saul or Jonathan (see vv. 6,10,15; 11:13).

14:24–46 Following the account of the great victory the Lord had given, the author relates Saul's actions that strikingly illustrated his lack of fitness to be king. This foolish curse

before the battle (see note on v. 24) brought "distress" to the army and, as Jonathan tellingly observed, "made trouble for the country" (v. 29) rather than contributing to the victory. And later, when hindered from taking advantage of the battle's outcome by the Lord's refusal to answer (v. 37), Saul was ready to execute Jonathan as the cause, though Jonathan had contributed most to the victory, as everyone else recognized (v. 45). Saul's growing egocentrism was turning into an all-consuming passion that threatened the very welfare of the nation. Rather than serving the cause of the Lord and his people, he was in fact becoming a king "such as all the other nations have" (8:5).

14:24 *in distress.* Saul's rash action in requiring his troops to fast placed them at an unnecessary disadvantage in the battle (see vv. 29–30). *Cursed.* Thus Saul as king "bound the army under a strict oath" (v. 28), a most serious matter because an oath directly invoked God's involvement, whether it concerned giving testimony (Ex 20:7; Lev 19:12), making commitments (Ge 21:23–24; 24:3–4) or prohibiting action (here; Jos 6:24). It appealed to God as the supreme enforcement power and the all-knowing Judge of human actions. *I have avenged myself on my enemies.* Saul perceives the conflict with the Philistines more as a personal vendetta (see note on 15:12) than as a battle for the honor of the Lord and the security of the Lord's people (note the contrast between his attitude and that of Jonathan in vv. 6,10,12).

brightened[x] when I tasted a little of this honey. [30]How much better it would have been if the men had eaten today some of the plunder they took from their enemies. Would not the slaughter of the Philistines have been even greater?"

[31]That day, after the Israelites had struck down the Philistines from Micmash[a] to Aijalon,[b] they were exhausted. [32]They pounced on the plunder[c] and, taking sheep, cattle and calves, they butchered them on the ground and ate them, together with the blood.[d] [33]Then someone said to Saul, "Look, the men are sinning against the LORD by eating meat that has blood[e] in it."

"You have broken faith," he said. "Roll a large stone over here at once." [34]Then he said, "Go out among the men and tell them, 'Each of you bring me your cattle and sheep, and slaughter them here and eat them. Do not sin against the LORD by eating meat with blood still[f] in it.' "

So everyone brought his ox that night and slaughtered it there. [35]Then Saul built an altar[g] to the LORD; it was the first time he had done this.

[36]Saul said, "Let us go down after the Philistines by night and plunder them till dawn, and let us not leave one of them alive."

"Do whatever seems best to you," they replied.

But the priest said, "Let us inquire[h] of God here."

[37]So Saul asked God, "Shall I go down after the Philistines? Will you give them into Israel's hand?" But God did not answer[i] him that day.

[38]Saul therefore said, "Come here, all you who are leaders of the army, and let us find out what sin has been committed[j] today. [39]As surely as the LORD who rescues Israel lives,[k] even if it lies with my son Jonathan,[l] he must die." [m] But not one of the men said a word.

[40]Saul then said to all the Israelites, "You stand over there; I and Jonathan my son will stand over here."

"Do what seems best to you," the men replied.

[41]Then Saul prayed to the LORD, the God of Israel, "Give[n] me the right[o] answer."[y] And Jonathan and Saul were taken by lot, and the men were cleared. [42]Saul said, "Cast the lot[p] between me and Jonathan my son." And Jonathan was taken.

[43]Then Saul said to Jonathan, "Tell me what you have done." [q]

So Jonathan told him, "I merely tasted a little honey[r] with the end of my staff. And now must I die?"

[44]Saul said, "May God deal with me, be it ever so severely,[s] if you do not die, Jonathan.[t] "

[45]But the men said to Saul, "Should Jonathan die—he who has brought about this great deliverance in Israel? Never! As surely as the LORD lives, not a hair[u] of his head will fall to the ground, for he did this today with God's help." So the men rescued[v] Jonathan, and he was not put to death.

[46]Then Saul stopped pursuing the Philistines, and they withdrew to their own land.

[47]After Saul had assumed rule over Israel, he fought against their enemies on every side: Moab,[w] the Ammonites,[x] Edom,[y] the kings[z] of Zobah,[z] and the Philistines. Wherever he turned, he inflicted punishment on them.[a] [48]He fought valiantly and defeated the Amalekites,[a] delivering Israel from the hands of those who had plundered them.

Cross references (center column)

14:31 [a]ver 5
[b]S Jos 10:12
14:32 [c]1Sa 15:19; Est 9:10
[d]S Ge 9:4
14:33 [e]S Ge 9:4
14:34 [f]Lev 19:26
14:35 [g]S 1Sa 7:17
14:36 [h]S Ge 25:22; S Jdg 18:5
14:37 [i]1Sa 28:6, 15; 2Sa 22:42; Ps 18:41
14:38 [j]Jos 7:11
14:39 [k]S Nu 14:21; 2Sa 12:5; Job 19:25; Ps 18:46; 42:2
[l]ver 44 [m]Jos 7:15
14:41 [n]Ac 1:24
[o]Pr 16:33
14:42 [p]Jnh 1:7
14:43 [q]S Jos 7:19
[r]S ver 27
14:44 [s]S Ru 1:17
[t]ver 39
14:45 [u]1Ki 1:52; S Mt 10:30
[v]2Sa 14:11
14:47 [w]S Ge 19:37 [x]S Ge 19:38; 2Sa 12:31
[y]1Sa 21:7
[z]2Sa 8:3; 10:6; 23:36
14:48 [a]S Ge 36:12; Nu 13:29; Jdg 3:13; 1Sa 15:2,7; 27:8; 28:18; 30:13; 2Sa 1:13; 1Ch 4:43

Textual notes

[x]29 Or my strength was renewed   [y]41 Hebrew; Septuagint "Why have you not answered your servant today? If the fault is in me or my son Jonathan, respond with Urim, but if the men of Israel are at fault, respond with Thummim."   [z]47 Masoretic Text; Dead Sea Scrolls and Septuagint king   [a]47 Hebrew; Septuagint he was victorious

---

14:31 *Aijalon.* Located to the west near the Philistines' own territory (see Jos 10:12).

14:33 *eating meat that has blood in it.* The Israelites were not permitted to eat blood (see Ge 9:4; Lev 17:11; 19:26; Dt 12:16; Eze 33:25; Ac 15:20 and notes). *broken faith.* See Mal 2:10–11. The same Hebrew term is translated "faithless" (Ps 78:57; Jer 3:8–11) and "treacherous" (Isa 48:8).

14:35 *first time he had done this.* Another indication of Saul's personal lack of interest in religious matters (see notes on 9:6; 10:11).

14:36 *priest.* Ahijah (see v. 3).

14:37 *Saul asked God.* The means of ascertaining God's will appears to have been the ephod with its Urim and Thummim (see v. 3 and note on v. 18). *God did not answer.* Because an oath had been broken in the battle, God refused to answer Saul's inquiry concerning further military action.

14:39 *As surely as the LORD . . . lives.* An oath formula (see note on v. 24; see also 19:6; Jer 4:2; Hos 4:15).

14:41 *taken by lot.* See 10:20–21; Jos 7:14–18; Pr 16:33.

14:44 A curse formula (see note on v. 24; see also 3:17 and note).

14:45 *he did this today with God's help.* The men of Saul's army recognize the inappropriateness of taking the life of the one through whom God has delivered his people.

14:47–48 A summary of Saul's military victories to the east (Moab and the Ammonites), south (Edom) and north (Zobah).

14:47 *Ammonites.* See Dt 2:19–21,37.

14:48 *Amalekites.* See note on 15:2.

Saul's Family

49Saul's sons were Jonathan, Ishvi and Malki-Shua.[b] The name of his older daughter was Merab, and that of the younger was Michal.[c] 50His wife's name was Ahinoam daughter of Ahimaaz. The name of the commander of Saul's army was Abner[d] son of Ner, and Ner was Saul's uncle.[e] 51Saul's father Kish[f] and Abner's father Ner were sons of Abiel.

52All the days of Saul there was bitter war with the Philistines, and whenever Saul saw a mighty or brave man, he took[g] him into his service.

The LORD Rejects Saul as King

15 Samuel said to Saul, "I am the one the LORD sent to anoint[h] you king over his people Israel; so listen now to the message from the LORD. 2This is what the LORD Almighty says: 'I will punish the Amalekites[i] for what they did to Israel when they waylaid them as they came up from Egypt. 3Now go, attack the Amalekites and totally[j] destroy[b] everything that belongs to them. Do not spare them; put to death men and women, children and infants, cattle and sheep, camels and donkeys.'"

4So Saul summoned the men and mustered them at Telaim—two hundred thousand foot soldiers and ten thousand men

from Judah. 5Saul went to the city of Amalek and set an ambush in the ravine. 6Then he said to the Kenites,[k] "Go away, leave the Amalekites so that I do not destroy you along with them; for you showed kindness to all the Israelites when they came up out of Egypt." So the Kenites moved away from the Amalekites.

7Then Saul attacked the Amalekites[l] all the way from Havilah to Shur,[m] to the east of Egypt. 8He took Agag[n] king of the Amalekites alive,[o] and all his people he totally destroyed with the sword. 9But Saul and the army spared[p] Agag and the best of the sheep and cattle, the fat calves[c] and lambs—everything that was good. These they were unwilling to destroy completely, but everything that was despised and weak they totally destroyed.

10Then the word of the LORD came to Samuel: 11"I am grieved[q] that I have made Saul king, because he has turned[r] away from me and has not carried out my instructions."[s] Samuel was troubled,[t] and he cried out to the LORD all that night.

12Early in the morning Samuel got up and went to meet Saul, but he was told,

---

14:49 [b]1Sa 31:2; 1Ch 8:33 [c]Ge 29:26
14:50 [d]2Sa 2:8; 3:6; 1Ki 2:5 [e]1Sa 10:14
14:51 [f]S 1Sa 9:1
14:52 [g]1Sa 8:11
15:1 [h]S 1Sa 9:16
15:2 [i]S Ge 14:7; S 1Sa 14:48; S 2Sa 1:8
15:3 [j]ver 9,19; S Ge 14:23; Jos 6:17; 1Sa 22:19; 27:9; 28:18; Est 3:13; 9:5
15:6 [k]S Ge 15:19; Nu 24:22; Jdg 1:16; 1Sa 30:29
15:7 [l]S 1Sa 14:48 [m]S Ge 16:7
15:8 [n]Ex 17:8-16; S Nu 24:7 [o]S Jos 8:23
15:9 [p]S ver 3
15:11 [q]S Ge 6:6; S Ex 32:14 [r]S Jos 22:16 [s]Job 21:14; 34:27; Ps 28:5; Isa 5:12; 53:6; Jer 48:10; Eze 18:24 [t]S ver 35; S 1Sa 8:6

[b]3 The Hebrew term refers to the irrevocable giving over of things or persons to the LORD, often by totally destroying them; also in verses 8, 9, 15, 18, 20 and 21. [c]9 Or *the grown bulls*; the meaning of the Hebrew for this phrase is uncertain.

14:49 *Saul's sons.* See 2Sa 2:8,10; 1Ch 9:39; 10:2. *Merab . . . Michal.* See 18:17,20,27; 19:11–17; 25:44; 2Sa 6:16–23.
14:50 *Ahinoam.* The only reference to a wife of Saul. His concubine Rizpah is mentioned in 2Sa 3:7; 21:8–11.
14:52 *All the days of Saul.* Closes the main account of Saul's reign. *he took him into his service.* Saul developed a special cadre of professional soldiers bound to himself, much as David was to do later (see 22:2; 23:13; 25:13; 27:2–3; 29:2; 30:1,9; 2Sa 2:3; 5:6; 8:18; 15:18; 23:8–39).
15:1–35 The event that occasioned Saul's rejection. Although no time designation is given, it evidently occurred after the conflicts of 14:47, in a time of relative peace and security. It is likely that David was anointed (16:1–13) shortly after the rejection of Saul (vv. 22,26,28), thus c. 1025 B.C.
15:2 *Amalekites.* A Bedouin people descended from Esau (see Ge 36:12,16) usually located in the Negev and Sinai regions (see 27:8; 30:1; Ge 14:7; Ex 17:8; Nu 13:29). *what they did to Israel.* See Ex 17:8–13; Nu 14:43, 45; Dt 25:17–19; cf. Jdg 3:13; 6:3–5,33; 7:12; 10:12.
15:3 *totally destroy.* See NIV text note and Lev 27:28–29; Dt 13:12–18; see also notes on Jos 6:17–18. Saul is given an opportunity as king to demonstrate his allegiance to the Lord by obedience in this assigned task.
15:4 *Telaim.* Probably the same as Telem in Jos 15:24, located in the southern part of Judah.
15:5 *city of Amalek.* A settlement of Amalekites, most likely located between Telaim and Kadesh Barnea, possibly the residence of their king.
15:6 *Kenites.* A Bedouin people of the Sinai, closely related to the Midianites. Moses had married a Kenite woman (see

Ex 2:16,21–22; Nu 10:29; Jdg 1:16; 4:11), and some of the Kenites had accompanied the Israelites when they settled in the land of Canaan (see 27:10; Jdg 1:16; 4:17–23; 5:24; 1Ch 2:55).
15:7 *Havilah to Shur.* The location of Havilah is uncertain. Shur was on the eastern frontier of Egypt (see 27:8; Ge 16:7; 20:1). Ishmael's descendants occupied this area (see Ge 25:18).
15:8 *all his people.* All the Amalekites they encountered. Some Amalekites survived (see 27:8; 30:1,18; 2Sa 8:12; 1Ch 4:43).
15:9 When Israel refused to obey the Lord's command (v. 3), their holy war against the Amalekites degenerated into personal aggrandizement, much like that of Achan at the time of the conquest of Canaan (see Jos 7:1). Giving to the Lord by destruction only what was despised and weak was a contemptible act (see Mal 1:7–12), not to be excused (see v. 19) by the protestation that the best had been preserved for sacrifice to the Lord (vv. 15,21).
15:11 *grieved.* See note on v. 29. *he has turned away from me.* A violation of the fundamental requirement of his office as king (see notes on 12:14–15).
15:12 *Carmel.* Located about seven miles south of Hebron (see 25:2; Jos 15:55). *monument in his own honor.* Saul's self-glorification here contrasts sharply with his self-abasement after the victory over the Ammonites (see note on 11:13; cf. v. 17; 2Sa 18:18). *Gilgal.* Saul returns to the place where he was inaugurated and instructed in the responsibilities of his office (see 11:14–12:25). This was also the place where he had been told that he would not have a continuing dynasty because of his disobedience (see 13:13–14).

"Saul has gone to Carmel.[u] There he has set up a monument[v] in his own honor and has turned and gone on down to Gilgal."

[13]When Samuel reached him, Saul said, "The LORD bless you! I have carried out the LORD's instructions."

[14]But Samuel said, "What then is this bleating of sheep in my ears? What is this lowing of cattle that I hear?"

[15]Saul answered, "The soldiers brought them from the Amalekites; they spared the best of the sheep and cattle to sacrifice to the LORD your God, but we totally destroyed the rest."

[16]"Stop!" Samuel said to Saul. "Let me tell you what the LORD said to me last night."

"Tell me," Saul replied.

[17]Samuel said, "Although you were once small[w] in your own eyes, did you not become the head of the tribes of Israel? The LORD anointed you king over Israel. [18]And he sent you on a mission, saying, 'Go and completely destroy those wicked people, the Amalekites; make war on them until you have wiped them out.' [19]Why did you not obey the LORD? Why did you pounce on the plunder[x] and do evil in the eyes of the LORD?"

[20]"But I did obey[y] the LORD," Saul said. "I went on the mission the LORD assigned me. I completely destroyed the Amalekites and brought back Agag their king. [21]The soldiers took sheep and cattle from the plunder, the best of what was devoted to God, in order to sacrifice them to the LORD your God at Gilgal."

[22]But Samuel replied:

"Does the LORD delight in burnt
    offerings and sacrifices
    as much as in obeying the voice of
        the LORD?
To obey is better than sacrifice,[z]
    and to heed is better than the fat of
        rams.
[23]For rebellion is like the sin of
        divination,[a]
    and arrogance like the evil of idolatry.
Because you have rejected[b] the word of
        the LORD,
    he has rejected you as king."

[24]Then Saul said to Samuel, "I have sinned.[c] I violated[d] the LORD's command and your instructions. I was afraid[e] of the people and so I gave in to them. [25]Now I beg you, forgive[f] my sin and come back with me, so that I may worship the LORD."

[26]But Samuel said to him, "I will not go back with you. You have rejected[g] the word of the LORD, and the LORD has rejected you as king over Israel!"

[27]As Samuel turned to leave, Saul caught hold of the hem of his robe,[h] and it tore.[i] [28]Samuel said to him, "The LORD has torn[j] the kingdom[k] of Israel from you today and has given it to one of your neighbors—to one better than you.[l] [29]He who is the Glory of Israel does not lie[m] or change[n] his mind; for he is not a man, that he should change his mind."

Cross references (center column):

15:12 [u]Jos 15:55
[v]S Nu 32:42
15:17 [w]S Ex 3:11
15:19 [x]S Ge 14:23;
S 1Sa 14:32
15:20 [y]1Sa 28:18
15:22 [z]Ps 40:6-8;
51:16; Pr 21:3;
Isa 1:11-15;
Jer 7:22; Hos 6:6;
Am 5:25;
Mic 6:6-8;
S Mk 12:33
15:23 [a]Dt 18:10
[b]S 1Sa 13:13
15:24 [c]S Ex 9:27;
S Nu 22:34;
Ps 51:4
[d]S 1Sa 13:13
[e]Pr 29:25;
Isa 51:12-13;
Jer 42:11
15:25 [f]Ex 10:17
15:26 [g]S Nu 15:31;
S 1Sa 13:14;
S 1Ki 14:10
15:27 [h]1Sa 28:14
[i]1Ki 11:11,31;
14:8; 2Ki 17:21
15:28 [j]1Sa 28:17
[k]S 1Sa 13:14
[l]2Sa 6:21; 7:15
15:29 [m]Tit 1:2
[n]Nu 23:19;
Heb 7:21

15:13 *I have carried out the LORD's instructions.* Here and in v. 20 Saul is clearly less than honest in his statements to Samuel.

15:15 *The soldiers ... spared the best ... to sacrifice.* Saul attempts to shift responsibility from himself to the army and to excuse their action by claiming pious intentions. *the LORD your God.* Saul's use of the pronoun "your" instead of "my" here and in vv. 21,30 indicates an awareness of his own alienation from the Lord (see 12:19 for a similar case), even though he speaks of obedience and the intent to honor God by sacrifice.

15:17 *you were once small in your own eyes.* See 9:21; 10:22.

15:22 Samuel does not suggest that sacrifice is unimportant but that it is acceptable only when brought with an attitude of obedience and devotion to the Lord (see Ps 15; Isa 1:11-17; Hos 6:6; Am 5:21-27; Mic 6:6-8). *fat of rams.* The fat of sacrificed animals belonged to the Lord (see 2:15; Ex 23:18; Lev 3:14-16; 7:30).

15:23 *rebellion.* Samuel charges Saul with violating the central requirement of the covenant condition given to him when he became king (see 12:14-15). *sin of divination.* A serious offense against the Lord (see Lev 19:26; Dt 18:9-12), which Saul himself condemned (28:3,9). *you have rejected the word of the LORD.* A king who sets his own will above the command of the Lord ceases to be an instrument of the Lord's rule over his people, violating the very

nature of his theocratic office. *he has rejected you as king.* The judgment here goes beyond the one given earlier (see note on 13:14). Now Saul himself is to be set aside as king. Although this did not happen immediately, as chs. 16-31 show, the process began that led to his death. It included in its relentless course the removal of God's Spirit and favor from him (16:14), the defection of his son Jonathan and daughter Michal to David, and the insubordination of his own officials (22:17).

15:24 Saul's confession retains an element of self-justification and a shift of blame (contrast David's confession, 2Sa 12:13; Ps 51). Previously (vv. 15,21) he had attempted to justify his soldiers' actions.

15:25 *come back with me.* Saul's greatest concern was not to worship God but to avoid an open break with the prophet Samuel, a break that would undermine his authority as king (see v. 30).

15:28 *one of your neighbors.* David (see note on 13:14).

15:29 *Glory of Israel.* A title of God used elsewhere only in Mic 1:15, though in Ps 106:20; Jer 2:11; Hos 4:7 he is called "Glory" (see note on 4:21). Cf. 2Sa 1:19; Ps 89:17; Isa 13:19. *does not lie or change his mind.* See Nu 23:19; Ps 110:4; Jer 4:28; Mal 3:6 and notes. There is no conflict between this statement and vv. 11,35, where the Lord is said to "grieve" that he made made Saul king. God has real emotions (one of the marks of personality).

30Saul replied, "I have sinned.o But please honorp me before the elders of my people and before Israel; come back with me, so that I may worship the LORD your God." 31So Samuel went back with Saul, and Saul worshiped the LORD.

32Then Samuel said, "Bring me Agag king of the Amalekites."

Agag came to him confidently,d thinking, "Surely the bitterness of death is past."

33But Samuel said,

"As your sword has made women
       childless,
   so will your mother be childless
       among women."q

And Samuel put Agag to death before the LORD at Gilgal.

34Then Samuel left for Ramah,r but Saul went up to his home in Gibeahs of Saul. 35Until the day Samuelt died, he did not go to see Saul again, though Samuel mournedu for him. And the LORD was grievedv that he had made Saul king over Israel.

Samuel Anoints David

16 The LORD said to Samuel, "How long will you mournw for Saul, since I have rejectedx him as king over Israel? Fill your horn with oily and be on your way; I am sending you to Jessez of Bethlehem. I have chosena one of his sons to be king."

2But Samuel said, "How can I go? Saul will hear about it and kill me."

The LORD said, "Take a heifer with you and say, 'I have come to sacrifice to the LORD.' 3Invite Jesse to the sacrifice, and I will showb you what to do. You are to anointc for me the one I indicate."

4Samuel did what the LORD said. When he arrived at Bethlehem,d the elders of the town tremblede when they met him. They asked, "Do you come in peace?f "

5Samuel replied, "Yes, in peace; I have come to sacrifice to the LORD. Consecrateg yourselves and come to the sacrifice with me." Then he consecrated Jesse and his sons and invited them to the sacrifice.

6When they arrived, Samuel saw Eliabh and thought, "Surely the LORD's anointed stands here before the LORD."

7But the LORD said to Samuel, "Do not consider his appearance or his height, for I have rejected him. The LORD does not look at the things man looks at. Man looks at the outward appearance,i but the LORD looks at the heart."j

8Then Jesse called Abinadabk and had him pass in front of Samuel. But Samuel said, "The LORD has not chosen this one either." 9Jesse then had Shammahl pass by, but Samuel said, "Nor has the LORD chosen this one." 10Jesse had seven of his sons pass before Samuel, but Samuel said to him, "The LORD has not chosen these." 11So he asked Jesse, "Are these allm the sons you have?"

"There is still the youngest," Jesse answered, "but he is tending the sheep."n

Samuel said, "Send for him; we will not sit downe until he arrives."

12So heo sent and had him brought in. He was ruddy, with a fine appearance and handsomep features.

15:30
oS Nu 22:34
pIsa 29:13;
Jn 12:43
15:33
qEst 9:7-10;
Jer 18:21
15:34 rS 1Sa 7:17
sS Jdg 19:14;
S 1Sa 10:5
15:35 tisa 19:24
uver 11; 1Sa 16:1
vS Ge 6:6
16:1 wS 1Sa 8:6;
S 15:35
xS 1Sa 13:14
yS 1Sa 10:1
zS Ru 4:17
a2Sa 5:2; 7:8;
1Ki 8:16;
1Ch 12:23;
Ps 78:70;
Ac 13:22

16:3 bEx 4:15
cS Dt 17:15
16:4 dS Ge 48:7;
Lk 2:4; e1Sa 21:1
f1Ki 2:13;
2Ki 9:17
16:5 gS Ex 19:10,
22
16:6 h1Sa 17:13;
1Ch 2:13
16:7 iPs 147:10
/S 1Sa 2:3;
2Sa 7:20;
S Ps 44:21;
S 139:23;
S Rev 2:23
16:8 k1Sa 17:13
16:9 l1Sa 17:13;
2Sa 13:3; 21:21
16:11
m1Sa 17:12
nS Ge 37:2;
2Sa 7:8
16:12 o1Sa 9:17
pS Ge 39:6

d32 Or him trembling, yet   e11 Some Septuagint manuscripts; Hebrew not gather around

---

15:31 *So Samuel went back with Saul.* Samuel's purpose in agreeing to Saul's request is not to honor Saul, but to carry out the divine sentence on Agag and in so doing to reemphasize Saul's neglect of duty.

15:34 *Ramah.* Samuel's home (see 7:17). *Gibeah of Saul.* See note on 10:5.

15:35 *Samuel mourned.* Samuel regarded Saul as if dead (see the use of "mourned" in 6:19). Even though his love for him remained (see v. 11; 16:1), he sought no further contact with him because God had rejected him as king. Saul did come to Samuel on one other occasion (see 19:24).

16:1 *The LORD said to Samuel.* Probably c. 1025 B.C. (see note on 15:1–35). *Jesse.* For Jesse's genealogy see Ru 4:18–22; Mt 1:3–6. *Bethlehem.* A town five miles south of Jerusalem, formerly known as Ephrath (Ge 48:7). It was later to become renowned as the "town of David" (Lk 2:4) and the birthplace of Christ (Mic 5:2; Mt 2:1; Lk 2:4–7). *I have chosen one of his sons to be king.* See notes on 13:14; 15:28.

16:2 *Saul will . . . kill me.* The road from Ramah (where Samuel was, 15:34) to Bethlehem passed through Gibeah of Saul. Saul already knew that the Lord had chosen someone

to replace him as king (see 15:28). Samuel fears that jealousy will incite Saul to violence. Later incidents (18:10–11; 19:10; 20:33) demonstrate that Samuel's fears were well-founded. *say, 'I have come to sacrifice to the LORD.'* This response is true but incomplete, and it was intended to deceive Saul.

16:3 *anoint.* See note on 9:16.

16:5 *Consecrate yourselves.* Involves preparing oneself spiritually as well as making oneself ceremonially clean by washing and putting on clean clothes (see Ex 19:10,14; Lev 15; Nu 19:11–22).

16:6 *Eliab.* Jesse's oldest son (17:13).

16:7 *his appearance or his height.* Samuel is not to focus on these outward features, which had characterized Saul (see 9:2; 10:23–24). *heart.* The Lord is concerned with man's inner disposition and character (see 1Ki 8:39; 1Ch 28:9; Lk 16:15; Jn 2:25; Ac 1:24).

16:8 *Abinadab.* Jesse's second son.

16:9 *Shammah.* Jesse's third son.

16:11 *he is tending the sheep.* The Lord's chosen one is a shepherd (see note on 9:3; see also 2Sa 7:7–8; Ps 78:71–72).

Then the LORD said, "Rise and anoint him; he is the one."

¹³So Samuel took the horn of oil and anointed^q him in the presence of his brothers, and from that day on the Spirit of the LORD^r came upon David in power.^s Samuel then went to Ramah.

David in Saul's Service

¹⁴Now the Spirit of the LORD had departed^t from Saul, and an evil^f spirit^u from the LORD tormented him.^v

¹⁵Saul's attendants said to him, "See, an evil spirit from God is tormenting you. ¹⁶Let our lord command his servants here to search for someone who can play the harp.^w He will play when the evil spirit from God comes upon you, and you will feel better."

¹⁷So Saul said to his attendants, "Find someone who plays well and bring him to me."

¹⁸One of the servants answered, "I have seen a son of Jesse^x of Bethlehem who knows how to play the harp. He is a brave man and a warrior.^y He speaks well and is a fine-looking man. And the LORD is with^z him."

¹⁹Then Saul sent messengers to Jesse and said, "Send me your son David, who is with the sheep.^a" ²⁰So Jesse took a donkey loaded with bread,^b a skin of wine and a young goat and sent them with his son David to Saul.

²¹David came to Saul and entered his service.^c Saul liked him very much, and David became one of his armor-bearers. ²²Then Saul sent word to Jesse, saying,

---

16:13
^qS 1Sa 2:35;
S 2Sa 22:51
^r1Sa 18:12
^sS 1Sa 11:6
16:14
^tS Jdg 16:20 ^uver 23; S Jdg 9:23;
1Sa 18:10
^v2Sa 7:15
16:16 ^wver 23; S 1Sa 10:5,6;
2Ch 29:26-27;
Ps 49:4

16:18 ^xS Ru 4:17
^y2Sa 17:8
^zS Ge 39:2;
1Sa 17:37; 20:13;
1Ch 22:11;
Mt 1:23
16:19 ^a1Sa 17:15
16:20
^bS Ge 32:13;
S 1Sa 10:4
16:21
^cS Ge 41:46

^f14 Or *injurious*; also in verses 15, 16 and 23

16:13 *in the presence of his brothers.* The small circle of witnesses to David's anointing assured its confidentiality, but also provided ample testimony for the future that David had been anointed by Samuel and that he was not merely a usurper of Saul's office. *the Spirit of the LORD came upon David in power.* See 10:5–6,10; 11:6; Jdg 15:14.

16:14–17:58 In the next two episodes, David is introduced to Saul's court and to Israel as a gifted musician and warrior. With these two gifts he would become famous in Israel and would lead the nation to spiritual and political vigor (see 2Sa 22; 23:1–7). Also through these two gifts Saul would become dependent upon David.

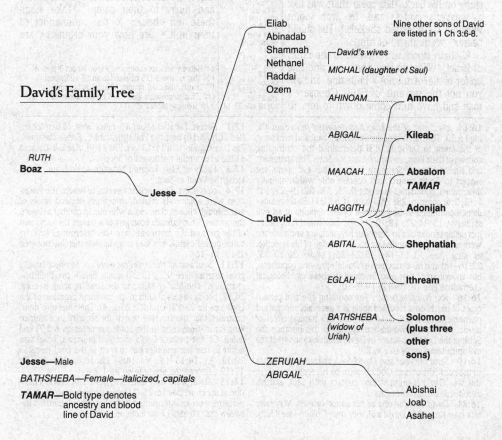

David's Family Tree

Eliab
Abinadab
Shammah
Nethanel
Raddai
Ozem

Nine other sons of David are listed in 1 Ch 3:6-8.

David's wives

MICHAL (daughter of Saul)

AHINOAM .... **Amnon**

ABIGAIL .... **Kileab**

MAACAH .... **Absalom**
                   TAMAR

HAGGITH .... **Adonijah**

ABITAL .... **Shephatiah**

EGLAH .... **Ithream**

BATHSHEBA .... **Solomon**
(widow of   **(plus three**
Uriah)   **other**
                      sons)

RUTH
Boaz

Jesse

David

ZERUIAH
ABIGAIL

Abishai
Joab
Asahel

Jesse—Male

BATHSHEBA—*Female—italicized, capitals*

TAMAR—**Bold type denotes**
            ancestry and blood
            line of David

"Allow David to remain in my service, for I am pleased with him."

[23]Whenever the spirit from God came upon Saul, David would take his harp and play. Then relief would come to Saul; he would feel better, and the evil spirit[d] would leave him.

David and Goliath

17 Now the Philistines gathered their forces for war and assembled[e] at Socoh in Judah. They pitched camp at Ephes Dammim, between Socoh[f] and Azekah.[g] [2]Saul and the Israelites assembled and camped in the Valley of Elah[h] and drew up their battle line to meet the Philistines. [3]The Philistines occupied one hill and the Israelites another, with the valley between them.

[4]A champion named Goliath,[i] who was from Gath, came out of the Philistine camp. He was over nine feet[g] tall. [5]He had a bronze helmet on his head and wore a coat of scale armor of bronze weighing five thousand shekels[h]; [6]on his legs he wore bronze greaves, and a bronze javelin[i] was slung on his back. [7]His spear shaft was like a weaver's rod,[k] and its iron point weighed six hundred shekels.[i] His shield bearer[l] went ahead of him.

[8]Goliath stood and shouted to the ranks of Israel, "Why do you come out and line up for battle? Am I not a Philistine, and are you not the servants of Saul? Choose[m] a man and have him come down to me. [9]If he is able to fight and kill me, we will become your subjects; but if I overcome him and kill you, you will become our subjects and serve us." [10]Then the Philistine said, "This day I defy[n] the ranks of Israel! Give me a man and let us fight each other.[o]" [11]On hearing the Philistine's words, Saul and all the Israelites were dismayed and terrified.

[12]Now David was the son of an Ephrathite[p] named Jesse,[q] who was from Bethlehem[r] in Judah. Jesse had eight[s] sons, and in Saul's time he was old and well advanced in years. [13]Jesse's three oldest sons had followed Saul to the war: The firstborn was Eliab;[t] the second, Abinadab;[u] and the third, Shammah.[v] [14]David was the youngest. The three oldest followed Saul, [15]but David went back and forth from Saul to tend[w] his father's sheep[x] at Bethlehem.

[16]For forty days the Philistine came forward every morning and evening and took his stand.

[17]Now Jesse said to his son David, "Take this ephah[i][y] of roasted grain[z] and these ten loaves of bread for your brothers and hurry to their camp. [18]Take along these ten cheeses to the commander of their unit.[k] See how your brothers[a] are

Cross references

16:23 [d]S ver 14; S Jdg 9:23
17:1 [e]1Sa 13:5 [f]Jos 15:35; 2Ch 28:18 [g]S Jos 10:10,11
17:2 [h]1Sa 21:9
17:4 [i]1Sa 21:9; 2Sa 21:19
17:6 [j]ver 45; 1Sa 18:10
17:7 [k]2Sa 21:19; 1Ch 11:23; 20:5 [l]ver 41
17:8 [m]2Sa 2:12-17
17:10 [n]ver 26, 45; 2Sa 21:21 [o]ver 23
17:12 [p]S Ge 35:16; S 48:7; Ps 132:6 [q]S Ru 4:17 [r]S Ge 35:19 [s]1Sa 16:11
17:13 [t]S 1Sa 16:6 [u]1Sa 16:8 [v]S 1Sa 16:9
17:15 [w]S Ge 37:2 [x]1Sa 16:19
17:17 [y]S Lev 19:36 [z]S Lev 23:14; 1Sa 25:18
17:18 [a]Ge 37:14

[g]4 Hebrew *was six cubits and a span* (about 3 meters) [h]5 That is, about 125 pounds (about 57 kilograms) [i]7 That is, about 15 pounds (about 7 kilograms) [j]17 That is, probably about 3/5 bushel (about 22 liters) [k]18 Hebrew *thousand*

16:14 *the Spirit of the LORD had departed from Saul.* Cf. Jdg 16:20. The removal of the Spirit from Saul and the giving of the Spirit to David (v. 13) determined the contrasting courses of their lives. *evil spirit from the LORD.* This statement and similar ones in Scripture indicate that evil spirits are subject to God's control and operate only within divinely determined boundaries (see Jdg 9:23; 1Ki 22:19-23; Job 1:12; 2:6; compare 2Sa 24:1 with 1Ch 21:1). Saul's disobedience continued to be punished by the assaults of an evil spirit (vv. 15-16,23; 18:10; 19:9). *tormented him.* Saul's increasing tendencies to despondency, jealousy and violence were no doubt occasioned by his knowledge of his rejection as king (see 13:13-14; 15:22-26; 18:9; 20:30-33; 22:16-18) and his awareness of David's growing popularity, but an evil spirit was also involved in these psychological aberrations (see 18:10-12; 19:9-10).

16:16 *you will feel better.* The soothing effect of certain types of music on a troubled spirit is a generally recognized phenomenon (see 2Ki 3:15). Beyond this natural effect of music, however, it would appear that in this instance the Spirit of the Lord was active in David's music to suppress the evil spirit temporarily (see v. 23).

16:19 *Send me your son David.* Saul unknowingly invites to the court the person God chose to be his replacement. In this way David is brought into contact with Saul, and his introduction to Israel begins.

16:21 *David became one of his armor-bearers.* May refer to a later time after David's victory over Goliath (see 18:2).

17:1 *Socoh.* Located about 15 miles west of Bethlehem (see 2Ch 28:18) near the Philistine border. *Ephes Dammim.* Pas Dammim in 1Ch 11:13 (see 2Sa 23:9). *Azekah.* Located a little over a mile northwest of Socoh.

17:2 *Valley of Elah.* Located between Azekah and Socoh along the Wadi es-Sant.

17:4 *champion.* The ancient Greeks, to whom the Philistines were apparently related, sometimes decided issues of war through chosen champions who met in combat between the armies. Through this economy of warriors the judgment of the gods on the matter at stake was determined (trial by battle ordeal). Israel too may have known this practice (see 2Sa 2:14-16).

17:11 *Saul and all the Israelites were . . . terrified.* Israel's giant warrior (see 9:2; 10:23) quails before the Philistine champion. The fear of Saul and the Israelite army (see vv. 24,32) betrays a loss of faith in the covenant promises of the Lord (see Ex 23:22; Dt 3:22; 20:1-4). Their fear also demonstrates that the Israelite search for security in a human king (apart from trust in the Lord; see notes on 8:5,7) had failed. On the basis of God's covenant promises, Israel was never to fear her enemies but to trust in the Lord (see 2Sa 10:12; Ex 14:13-14; Nu 14:9; Jos 10:8; 2Ch 20:17).

17:12 *Ephrathite.* See note on Ru 1:2.

17:15 *David went back and forth from Saul.* David's position at the court (see 16:21-23) was not permanent, but was performed on an intermittent basis. For the relationship between chs. 16 and 17 see note on v. 55.

and bring back some assurance[1] from them. [19]They are with Saul and all the men of Israel in the Valley of Elah, fighting against the Philistines."

[20]Early in the morning David left the flock with a shepherd, loaded up and set out, as Jesse had directed. He reached the camp as the army was going out to its battle positions, shouting the war cry. [21]Israel and the Philistines were drawing up their lines facing each other. [22]David left his things with the keeper of supplies,[b] ran to the battle lines and greeted his brothers. [23]As he was talking with them, Goliath, the Philistine champion from Gath, stepped out from his lines and shouted his usual[c] defiance, and David heard it. [24]When the Israelites saw the man, they all ran from him in great fear.

[25]Now the Israelites had been saying, "Do you see how this man keeps coming out? He comes out to defy Israel. The king will give great wealth to the man who kills him. He will also give him his daughter[d] in marriage and will exempt his father's family from taxes[e] in Israel."

[26]David asked the men standing near him, "What will be done for the man who kills this Philistine and removes this disgrace[f] from Israel? Who is this uncircumcised[g] Philistine that he should defy[h] the armies of the living[i] God?"

[27]They repeated to him what they had been saying and told him, "This is what will be done for the man who kills him."

[28]When Eliab, David's oldest brother, heard him speaking with the men, he burned with anger[j] at him and asked, "Why have you come down here? And with whom did you leave those few sheep in the desert? I know how conceited you are and how wicked your heart is; you came down only to watch the battle."

[29]"Now what have I done?" said David.

"Can't I even speak?" [30]He then turned away to someone else and brought up the same matter, and the men answered him as before. [31]What David said was overheard and reported to Saul, and Saul sent for him.

[32]David said to Saul, "Let no one lose heart[k] on account of this Philistine; your servant will go and fight him."

[33]Saul replied,[l] "You are not able to go out against this Philistine and fight him; you are only a boy, and he has been a fighting man from his youth."

[34]But David said to Saul, "Your servant has been keeping his father's sheep. When a lion[m] or a bear came and carried off a sheep from the flock, [35]I went after it, struck it and rescued the sheep from its mouth. When it turned on me, I seized[n] it by its hair, struck it and killed it. [36]Your servant has killed both the lion[o] and the bear; this uncircumcised Philistine will be like one of them, because he has defied the armies of the living God. [37]The LORD who delivered[p] me from the paw of the lion[q] and the paw of the bear will deliver me from the hand of this Philistine."

Saul said to David, "Go, and the LORD be with[r] you."

[38]Then Saul dressed David in his own[s] tunic. He put a coat of armor on him and a bronze helmet on his head. [39]David fastened on his sword over the tunic and tried walking around, because he was not used to them.

"I cannot go in these," he said to Saul, "because I am not used to them." So he took them off. [40]Then he took his staff in his hand, chose five smooth stones from the stream, put them in the pouch of his shepherd's bag and, with his sling in his hand, approached the Philistine.

17:22 [b]S Jos 1:11
17:23 [c]ver 8-10
17:25 [d]1Sa 18:17
[e]S 1Sa 8:15
[f]1Sa 11:2
[g]S 1Sa 14:6
[h]S ver 10
[i]Dt 5:26;
S Jos 3:10;
2Ki 18:35
17:28 [j]S Ge 27:41;
Pr 18:19

17:32 [k]S Dt 20:3;
Ps 18:45; Isa 7:4;
Jer 4:9; 38:4;
Da 11:30
17:33 [l]Nu 13:31
17:34
[m]Job 10:16;
Isa 31:4;
Jer 49:19;
Hos 13:8;
Am 3:12
17:35 [n]Jdg 14:6
17:36
[o]1Ch 11:22
17:37 [p]2Co 1:10
[q]Ti 4:17
[r]S 1Sa 16:18;
S 18:12
17:38
[s]S Ge 41:42

[1]18 Or *some token*; or *some pledge of spoils*

17:24 *great fear.* See note on v. 11.
17:25 *The king will give great wealth.* See 8:14; 22:7. *give him his daughter in marriage.* See 18:17–26; cf. Jos 15:16
17:26 *Who is this . . . ?* David sees the issues clearly—which sets him apart from Saul and all the other Israelites on that battlefield.
17:28 *he burned with anger.* Eliab's anger may arise from jealousy toward his brother and a sense of guilt for the defeatist attitude of the Israelites. He recognizes, but does not comprehend, David's indomitable spirit (see 16:13).
17:32 *Let no one lose heart on account of this Philistine.* David's confidence does not rest in his own prowess (see vv. 37,47) but in the power of the living God, whose honor has been violated by the Philistines and whose covenant promises have been scorned by the Israelites.
17:33 *You are not able.* Saul does not take into account the power of God (see vv. 37,47).
17:34 *lion.* For the presence of lions in Canaan at that time

see 2Sa 23:20; Jdg 14:5–18; 1Ki 13:24–26; Am 3:12. *bear.* See 2Sa 17:8; 2Ki 2:24; Am 5:19.

17:36 *this uncircumcised Philistine.* See note on 14:6.
17:37 *The LORD . . . will deliver me.* Reliance on the Lord was essential for the true theocratic king (see notes on 10:18; 11:13). Here David's faith contrasts sharply with Saul's loss of faith (see 11:6–7 for Saul's earlier fearlessness). *Saul said to David, "Go."* Saul is now dependent on David not only for his sanity (see note on 16:16) but also for the security of his realm.

17:40 *his staff.* God's newly appointed shepherd of his people (see 2Sa 5:2; 7:7; Ps 78:72) goes to defend the Lord's threatened and frightened flock. *stones.* Usually the stones chosen were round and smooth and somewhat larger than a baseball. When hurled by a master slinger, they probably traveled at close to 100 miles per hour. *his sling.* For the Benjamites' skill with a sling see Jdg 20:16.

41Meanwhile, the Philistine, with his
shield bearer[t] in front of him, kept coming
closer to David. 42He looked David over
and saw that he was only a boy, ruddy and
handsome,[u] and he despised[v] him. 43He
said to David, "Am I a dog,[w] that you
come at me with sticks?" And the Philistine cursed David by his gods. 44"Come
here," he said, "and I'll give your flesh to
the birds of the air[x] and the beasts of the
field![y]"

45David said to the Philistine, "You
come against me with sword and spear and
javelin,[z] but I come against you in the
name[a] of the LORD Almighty, the God of
the armies of Israel, whom you have defied.[b] 46This day the LORD will hand[c] you
over to me, and I'll strike you down and
cut off your head. Today I will give the
carcasses[d] of the Philistine army to the
birds of the air and the beasts of the earth,
and the whole world[e] will know that
there is a God in Israel.[f] 47All those gathered here will know that it is not by
sword[g] or spear that the LORD saves;[h] for
the battle[i] is the LORD's, and he will give
all of you into our hands."

48As the Philistine moved closer to attack him, David ran quickly toward the
battle line to meet him. 49Reaching into his
bag and taking out a stone, he slung it and
struck the Philistine on the forehead. The
stone sank into his forehead, and he fell
facedown on the ground.

50So David triumphed over the Philistine
with a sling[j] and a stone; without a sword
in his hand he struck down the Philistine
and killed him.

51David ran and stood over him. He
took hold of the Philistine's sword and
drew it from the scabbard. After he killed
him, he cut[k] off his head with the sword.[l]

When the Philistines saw that their hero
was dead, they turned and ran. 52Then the
men of Israel and Judah surged forward
with a shout and pursued the Philistines to
the entrance of Gath[m] and to the gates of
Ekron.[m] Their dead were strewn along the
Shaaraim[n] road to Gath and Ekron.
53When the Israelites returned from chasing the Philistines, they plundered their
camp. 54David took the Philistine's head
and brought it to Jerusalem, and he put the
Philistine's weapons in his own tent.

55As Saul watched David[o] going out to
meet the Philistine, he said to Abner, commander of the army, "Abner,[p] whose son
is that young man?"

Abner replied, "As surely as you live, O
king, I don't know."

56The king said, "Find out whose son
this young man is."

57As soon as David returned from killing
the Philistine, Abner took him and brought
him before Saul, with David still holding
the Philistine's head.

58"Whose son are you, young man?"
Saul asked him.

David said, "I am the son of your servant Jesse[q] of Bethlehem."

Saul's Jealousy of David

18 After David had finished talking
with Saul, Jonathan[r] became one
in spirit with David, and he loved[s] him as
himself.[t] 2From that day Saul kept David
with him and did not let him return to his

17:41 [t]ver 7 **17:42** [u]1Sa 16:12 [v]Ps 123:3-4; Pr 16:18 **17:43** [w]1Sa 24:14; 2Sa 3:8; 9:8; 2Ki 8:13 **17:44** [x]S Ge 40:19; Rev 19:17 [y]2Sa 21:10; Jer 34:20 **17:45** [z]S ver 6 [a]Dt 20:1; 2Ch 13:12; 14:11; 32:8; Ps 20:7-8; 124:8; Heb 11:32-34 [b]S ver 10 **17:46** [c]S 1Sa 14:12 [d]S Dt 28:26 [e]S Jos 4:24; S Isa 11:9 [f]1Ki 18:36; 2Ki 5:8; 19:19; Isa 37:20 **17:47** [g]Hos 1:7 [h]1Sa 14:6; 2Ch 14:11; Jer 39:18 [i]S Ex 14:14; S Nu 21:14; S 1Sa 2:9; 2Ch 20:15; Ps 44:6-7 **17:50** [j]1Sa 25:29 **17:51** [k]Heb 11:34 [l]1Sa 21:9; 22:10 **17:52** [m]Jos 15:11 [n]S Jos 15:36 **17:55** [o]1Sa 16:21 [p]1Sa 26:5 **17:58** [q]S Ru 4:17 **18:1** [r]1Sa 19:1; 20:16; 31:2; 2Sa 4:4 [s]2Sa 1:26 [t]S Ge 44:30

m52 Some Septuagint manuscripts; Hebrew *a valley*

17:43 *Am I a dog . . . ?* See note on 2Sa 9:8.
17:45 *in the name of the LORD Almighty.* David's strength was his reliance on the Lord (see Ps 9:10; Pr 18:10). For the expression "name of the LORD" see notes on Ex 3:13–14; Dt 12:11.
17:46 *the whole world will know.* The victory that David anticipates will demonstrate to all the world the existence and power of Israel's God (see Ex 7:17; 9:14,16,29; Dt 4:34–35; Jos 2:10–11; 4:23–24; 1Ki 8:59–60; 18:36–39; 2Ki 5:15; 19:19).
17:47 *the battle is the LORD's.* Both the Israelite and the Philistine armies will be shown the error of placing trust in human devices for personal or national security (see 2:10; 14:6; 2Ch 14:11; 20:15; Ps 33:16–17; 44:6–7; Ecc 9:11; Hos 1:7; Zec 4:6).
17:51 *they turned and ran.* Most likely the Philistines saw the fall of their champion as the judgment of the gods, but they did not honor Goliath's original proposal (see v. 9).
17:54 *brought it to Jerusalem.* Jerusalem had not at this time been conquered by the Israelites. David may have kept Goliath's head as a trophy of victory and brought the skull with him to Jerusalem when he took that city and made it his capital (see 2Sa 5:1–9). Or, having grown up almost under the shadow of the Jebusite city, he may have displayed Goliath's head to its defiant inhabitants as a warning of what the God of Israel was able to do and eventually would do. *put the Philistine's weapons in his own tent.* As his personal spoils of the battle. Since Goliath's sword is later in the custody of the priest at Nob (see 21:9), he must have dedicated it to the Lord, the true victor in the fight (cf. 31:10).
17:55 *whose son is that young man?* The seeming contradiction between vv. 55–58 and 16:14–23 may be resolved by noting that prior to this time David was not a permanent resident at Saul's court (see v. 15; 18:2; see also note on 16:21), so that Saul's knowledge of David and his family may have been minimal. Further, Saul may have been so incredulous at David's courage that he was wondering if his family background and social standing might explain his extraordinary conduct.
18:1 It appears that David spoke with Saul at length, and he may have explained his actions as an expression of his faith in the Lord, thus attracting the love and loyalty of Jonathan (see v. 3; 14:6; 19:5). Their friendship endured even when it became clear that David was to replace him as the successor to his father's throne.
18:2 *Saul kept David with him.* See note on 17:15.

father's house. ³And Jonathan made a covenant[u] with David because he loved him as himself. ⁴Jonathan took off the robe[v] he was wearing and gave it to David, along with his tunic, and even his sword, his bow and his belt.[w]

⁵Whatever Saul sent him to do, David did it so successfully[n][x] that Saul gave him a high rank in the army.[y] This pleased all the people, and Saul's officers as well.

⁶When the men were returning home after David had killed the Philistine, the women came out from all the towns of Israel to meet King Saul with singing and dancing,[z] with joyful songs and with tambourines[a] and lutes. ⁷As they danced, they sang:[b]

"Saul has slain his thousands,
    and David his tens[c] of thousands."

⁸Saul was very angry; this refrain galled him. "They have credited David with tens of thousands," he thought, "but me with only thousands. What more can he get but the kingdom?[d]" ⁹And from that time on Saul kept a jealous[e] eye on David.

¹⁰The next day an evil[o] spirit[f] from God came forcefully upon Saul. He was prophesying in his house, while David was playing the harp,[g] as he usually[h] did. Saul had a spear[i] in his hand ¹¹and he hurled it, saying to himself,[j] "I'll pin David to the wall." But David eluded[k] him twice.[l]

¹²Saul was afraid[m] of David, because the LORD[n] was with[o] David but had left[p] Saul. ¹³So he sent David away from him and gave him command over a thousand men, and David led[q] the troops in their campaigns.[r] ¹⁴In everything he did he had great success,[p][s] because the LORD was

with[t] him. ¹⁵When Saul saw how successful[q] he was, he was afraid of him. ¹⁶But all Israel and Judah loved David, because he led them in their campaigns.[u]

¹⁷Saul said to David, "Here is my older daughter[v] Merab. I will give her to you in marriage;[w] only serve me bravely and fight the battles[x] of the LORD." For Saul said to himself,[y] "I will not raise a hand against him. Let the Philistines do that!"

¹⁸But David said to Saul, "Who am I,[z] and what is my family or my father's clan in Israel, that I should become the king's son-in-law?[a]" ¹⁹So[r] when the time came for Merab,[b] Saul's daughter, to be given to David, she was given in marriage to Adriel of Meholah.[c]

²⁰Now Saul's daughter Michal[d] was in love with David, and when they told Saul about it, he was pleased.[e] ²¹"I will give her to him," he thought, "so that she may be a snare[f] to him and so that the hand of the Philistines may be against him." So Saul said to David, "Now you have a second opportunity to become my son-in-law."

²²Then Saul ordered his attendants: "Speak to David privately and say, 'Look, the king is pleased with you, and his attendants all like you; now become his son-in-law.'"

²³They repeated these words to David. But David said, "Do you think it is a small matter to become the king's son-in-law?[g] I'm only a poor man and little known."

²⁴When Saul's servants told him what David had said, ²⁵Saul replied, "Say to David, 'The king wants no other price[h] for

---

18:3 [u]1Sa 20:8, 16,17,42; 22:8; 23:18; 24:21; 2Sa 21:7
18:4 [v]S Ge 41:42 [w]2Sa 18:11
18:5 [x]ver 30 [y]2Sa 5:2
18:6 [z]S Ex 15:20; 2Sa 1:20 [a]Ps 68:25
18:7 [b]Ex 15:21 [c]1Sa 21:11; 29:5; 2Sa 18:3
18:8 [d]S 1Sa 13:14
18:9 [e]1Sa 19:1
18:10 [f]S Jdg 9:23; S 1Sa 16:14 [g]S 1Sa 10:5 [h]1Sa 16:21; 19:7 [i]S 1Sa 17:6
18:11 [j]ver 25; 1Sa 20:7,33 [k]1Sa 19:10 [l]Ps 132:1
18:12 [m]ver 29 [n]1Sa 16:13 [o]Jos 1:5; 1Sa 17:37; 20:13; 1Ch 22:11 [p]S Jdg 16:20
18:13 [q]Nu 27:17 [r]2Sa 5:2
18:14 [s]S Ge 39:3

[t]S Ge 39:2; S Nu 14:43; 2Sa 7:9
18:16 [u]2Sa 5:2
18:17 [v]1Sa 17:25 [w]S Ge 29:26 [x]S Nu 21:14 [y]ver 25; 1Sa 20:33
18:18 [z]S Ex 3:11; S 1Sa 9:21 [a]ver 23
18:19 [b]2Sa 21:8 [c]S Jdg 7:22
18:20 [d]ver 28; S Ge 29:26 [e]ver 29
18:21 [f]S Ge 10:7; S Dt 7:16
18:23 [g]ver 18
18:25 [h]S Ge 34:12

[n]5 Or wisely   [o]10 Or injurious   [p]14 Or he was very wise   [q]15 Or wise   [r]19 Or However,

---

18:3 *Jonathan made a covenant with David.* The initiative comes from Jonathan. The terms of the agreement are not here specified (see further 19:1; 20:8,13–16,41–42; 23:18) but would appear to involve a pledge of mutual loyalty and friendship. At the very least, Jonathan accepts David as his equal.
18:4 *took off the robe . . . and gave it to David.* Jonathan ratifies the covenant in an act that symbolizes giving himself to David. His act may even signify his recognition that David was to assume his place as successor to Saul (see 20:14–15, 31; 23:17)—a possibility that seems the more likely in that he also gave David "even his sword, his bow and his belt" (cf. 13:22).
18:5 *Whatever Saul sent him to do.* During the rest of the campaign.
18:7 *David his tens of thousands.* In accordance with the normal conventions of Hebrew poetry, this was the women's way of saying "Saul and David have slain thousands" (10,-000 was normally used as the parallel of 1,000—see Dt 32:30; Ps 91:7; Mic 6:7; also in Canaanite poetry found at Ugarit). It is a measure of Saul's insecurity and jealousy that he read their intentions incorrectly and took offense. His

resentment may have been initially triggered by the mention of David's name alongside his own. See note on 21:11 for how the Philistines interpreted the song.
18:10 *evil spirit from God.* See note on 16:14. *prophesying.* The Hebrew for this word is sometimes used to indicate uncontrolled ecstatic behavior (see note on 1Ki 18:29) and is best understood in that sense in this context (see also note on 10:5). *as he usually did.* See 16:14,23.
18:12 *the LORD was with David but had left Saul.* See 16:14 and note.
18:13 *he sent David away.* His apparent motive was the hope that David would be killed in battle (see vv. 17, 21, 25; 19:1), but the result was greater acclaim for David (see vv. 14,16,30).
18:17 *Here is my older daughter.* David was entitled to have Saul's daughter as his wife because of his victory over Goliath (see 17:25). This promise had not been kept and is now made conditional on further military service, in which Saul hoped David would be killed. *battles of the LORD.* See 25:28.
18:25 *no other price.* Normally a bride-price was paid by the bridegroom to the father of the bride (see Ge 34:12; Ex

the bride than a hundred Philistine fore-skins, to take revenge[i] on his enemies.'" Saul's plan[j] was to have David fall by the hands of the Philistines.

26When the attendants told David these things, he was pleased to become the king's son-in-law. So before the allotted time elapsed, 27David and his men went out and killed two hundred Philistines. He brought their foreskins and presented the full number to the king so that he might become the king's son-in-law. Then Saul gave him his daughter Michal[k] in marriage.

28When Saul realized that the LORD was with David and that his daughter Michal[l] loved David, 29Saul became still more afraid[m] of him, and he remained his enemy the rest of his days.

30The Philistine commanders continued to go out to battle, and as often as they did, David met with more success[s][n] than the rest of Saul's officers, and his name became well known.

Saul Tries to Kill David

19 Saul told his son Jonathan[o] and all the attendants to kill[p] David. But Jonathan was very fond of David, 2and warned him, "My father Saul is looking for a chance to kill you. Be on your guard to-morrow morning; go into hiding[q] and stay there. 3I will go out and stand with my father in the field where you are. I'll speak[r] to him about you and will tell you what I find out."

4Jonathan spoke[s] well of David to Saul his father and said to him, "Let not the king do wrong[t] to his servant David; he has not wronged you, and what he has done has benefited you greatly. 5He took his life[u] in his hands when he killed the Philistine. The LORD won a great victory[v] for all Israel, and you saw it and were glad. Why then would you do wrong to an inno-cent[w] man like David by killing him for no reason?"

6Saul listened to Jonathan and took this oath: "As surely as the LORD lives, David will not be put to death."

7So Jonathan called David and told him the whole conversation. He brought him to Saul, and David was with Saul as before.[x]

8Once more war broke out, and David went out and fought the Philistines. He struck them with such force that they fled before him.

9But an evil[t] spirit[y] from the LORD came upon Saul as he was sitting in his house with his spear in his hand. While David was playing the harp,[z] 10Saul tried to pin him to the wall with his spear, but David eluded[a] him as Saul drove the spear into the wall. That night David made good his escape.

11Saul sent men to David's house to watch[b] it and to kill him in the morning.[c] But Michal, David's wife, warned him, "If you don't run for your life tonight, tomor-row you'll be killed." 12So Michal let Da-vid down through a window,[d] and he fled and escaped. 13Then Michal took an idol[u][e] and laid it on the bed, covering it with a garment and putting some goats' hair at the head.

14When Saul sent the men to capture David, Michal said,[f] "He is ill."

15Then Saul sent the men back to see David and told them, "Bring him up to me in his bed so that I may kill him." 16But when the men entered, there was the idol in the bed, and at the head was some goats' hair.

17Saul said to Michal, "Why did you de-ceive me like this and send my enemy away so that he escaped?"

Michal told him, "He said to me, 'Let me get away. Why should I kill you?'"

Cross references

18:25 [i]Ps 8:2; 44:16; Jer 20:10 [j]S ver 11,S 17
18:27 [k]2Sa 3:14; 6:16
18:28 [l]S ver 20
18:29 [m]ver 12
18:30 [n]ver 5
19:1 [o]S 1Sa 18:1 [p]1Sa 18:9
19:2 [q]1Sa 20:5, 19
19:3 [r]1Sa 20:12
19:4 [s]1Sa 20:32; 22:14; Pr 31:8,9; Jer 18:20 [t]1Sa 25:21; Pr 17:13
19:5 [u]S Jdg 9:17; S 12:3 [v]S 1Sa 11:13

19:7 [w]S Ge 31:36; Dt 19:10-13
[x]S 1Sa 18:10
19:9 [y]S Jdg 9:23 [z]S 1Sa 10:5
19:10 [a]1Sa 18:11
19:11 [b]Ps 59 Title [c]Jdg 16:2
19:12 [d]S Jos 2:15; Ac 9:25; 2Co 11:33
19:13 [e]S Ge 31:19
19:14 [f]S Ex 1:19; Jos 2:4

[s]30 Or David acted more wisely   [t]9 Or injurious
[u]13 Hebrew teraphim; also in verse 16

22:16) as compensation for the loss of his daughter and insurance for her support if widowed. Saul requires David instead to pass a test appropriate for a great warrior, hoping that he will "fall" (see vv. 17,21).

18:28 *Michal loved David.* God's favor on David is re-vealed not only in his military accomplishments, but also in Michal's love for him—now added to that of Jonathan. Everything Saul seeks to use against David turns to David's advantage.

18:29 *Saul became still more afraid of him.* Saul's percep-tion that God's hand was on David did not lead him to repentance and acceptance of his own lot (see 15:26) but into greater fear and jealousy toward David.

19:1 *Saul told his son . . . to kill David.* Saul now abandons his indirect attempts on David's life (see 18:13,17,25) and adopts a more direct approach, leading to David's departure from the court and from service to Saul (see vv. 12,18; 20:42).

19:4 *Jonathan spoke well of David.* Jonathan does not let his own personal ambition distort his perception of David's true theocratic spirit (see v. 5 and notes on 14:6; 17:11; 18:1).

19:6 *Saul listened to Jonathan and took this oath.* See 14:24,44 for previous oaths that Saul did not keep (see note on 14:39).

19:9 *evil spirit from the LORD.* See note on 16:14; cf. 18:10-11.

19:10 *with his spear.* See 18:10-11; 20:33.

19:12 *through a window.* For similar escapes see Jos 2:15; Ac 9:25.

19:13 *idol.* See NIV text note and note on Ge 31:19.

[18]When David had fled and made his escape, he went to Samuel at Ramah[g] and told him all that Saul had done to him. Then he and Samuel went to Naioth and stayed there. [19]Word came to Saul: "David is in Naioth at Ramah"; [20]so he sent men to capture him. But when they saw a group of prophets[h] prophesying, with Samuel standing there as their leader, the Spirit of God came upon[i] Saul's men and they also prophesied.[j] [21]Saul was told about it, and he sent more men, and they prophesied too. Saul sent men a third time, and they also prophesied. [22]Finally, he himself left for Ramah and went to the great cistern at Secu. And he asked, "Where are Samuel and David?"

"Over in Naioth at Ramah," they said.

[23]So Saul went to Naioth at Ramah. But the Spirit of God came even upon him, and he walked along prophesying[k] until he came to Naioth. [24]He stripped[l] off his robes and also prophesied in Samuel's[m] presence. He lay that way all that day and night. This is why people say, "Is Saul also among the prophets?"[n]

David and Jonathan

20 Then David fled from Naioth at Ramah and went to Jonathan and asked, "What have I done? What is my crime? How have I wronged[o] your father, that he is trying to take my life?"[p]

[2]"Never!" Jonathan replied. "You are not going to die! Look, my father doesn't do anything, great or small, without confiding in me. Why would he hide this from me? It's not so!"

[3]But David took an oath[q] and said, "Your father knows very well that I have found favor in your eyes, and he has said to himself, 'Jonathan must not know this or he will be grieved.' Yet as surely as the LORD lives and as you live, there is only a step between me and death."

[4]Jonathan said to David, "Whatever you want me to do, I'll do for you."

[5]So David said, "Look, tomorrow is the New Moon festival,[r] and I am supposed to

Cross references (center column)
19:18
[g]S 1Sa 7:17
19:20
[h]S Nu 11:29
[i]S Nu 11:25
[j]S 1Sa 10:5
19:23 [k]1Sa 10:13
19:24 [l]2Sa 6:20; Isa 20:2
[m]1Sa 15:35
[n]S 1Sa 10:11
20:1 [o]1Sa 24:9
[p]1Sa 22:23;
23:15; 24:11;
25:29; Ps 40:14;
54:3; 63:9; 70:2
20:3 [q]Dt 6:13
20:5 [r]S Nu 10:10

19:18 *Ramah.* Samuel's home (see 7:17 and note on 1:1). *Naioth.* Means "habitations" or "dwellings." The term appears to designate a complex of houses in a certain section of Ramah where a company of prophets resided (see vv. 19–20,22–23).
19:20 *group of prophets.* See 10:5 and note. *prophesying.* See notes on 10:5; 18:10.
19:24 *He lay that way all that day and night.* Saul was so overwhelmed by the power of the Spirit of God that he was prevented from carrying out his intention to take David's life. His frustrated attempts to kill David—his own inability to harm David and the thwarting of his plans by Jonathan's loyalty, by Michal's deception and by David's own clever-

ness—all reach their climax here. *Is Saul also among the prophets?* This second occasion reinforced the first (see 10:11 and note). Its repetition underscores how alien Saul's spirit was from that of these zealous servants of the Lord.
20:1 *Naioth at Ramah.* See note on 19:18.
20:3 *as surely as the LORD lives.* See note on 14:39.
20:5 *New Moon festival.* Each month of the year was consecrated to the Lord by the bringing of special sacrifices (Nu 28:11–15) and the blowing of trumpets (Nu 10:10; Ps 81:3). This observance also involved cessation from normal work, especially at the beginning of the seventh month (Lev 23:24–25; Nu 29:1–6; 2Ki 4:23; Isa 1:13; Am 8:5).

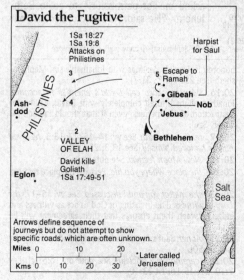

David the Fugitive

1Sa 18:27
1Sa 19:8
Attacks on Philistines

Harpist for Saul

3

5 Escape to Ramah

Ash-dod

4

1 • Gibeah

• Nob

• Jebus*

2
VALLEY OF ELAH

• Bethlehem

David kills Goliath
1Sa 17:49-51

Eglon

PHILISTINES

Salt Sea

Arrows define sequence of journeys but do not attempt to show specific roads, which are often unknown.

Miles 0   10   20
Kms 0 10 20 30

*Later called Jerusalem

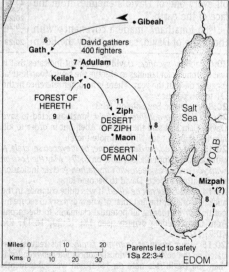

• Gibeah

6
Gath •

7 Adullam

Keilah •

10

FOREST OF HERETH

11 • Ziph

9

DESERT OF ZIPH

• Maon

DESERT OF MAON

8

Salt Sea

MOAB

Mizpah
• (?)

8

Miles 0   10   20
Kms 0 10 20 30

Parents led to safety
1Sa 22:3-4

EDOM

David gathers 400 fighters

dine with the king; but let me go and hide[s] in the field until the evening of the day after tomorrow. [6]If your father misses me at all, tell him, 'David earnestly asked my permission[t] to hurry to Bethlehem,[u] his hometown, because an annual[v] sacrifice is being made there for his whole clan.' [7]If he says, 'Very well,' then your servant is safe. But if he loses his temper,[w] you can be sure that he is determined[x] to harm me. [8]As for you, show kindness to your servant, for you have brought him into a covenant[y] with you before the LORD. If I am guilty, then kill[z] me yourself! Why hand me over to your father?"

[9]"Never!" Jonathan said. "If I had the least inkling that my father was determined to harm you, wouldn't I tell you?"

[10]David asked, "Who will tell me if your father answers you harshly?"

[11]"Come," Jonathan said, "let's go out into the field." So they went there together.

[12]Then Jonathan said to David: "By the LORD, the God of Israel, I will surely sound[a] out my father by this time the day after tomorrow! If he is favorably disposed toward you, will I not send you word and let you know? [13]But if my father is inclined to harm you, may the LORD deal with me, be it ever so severely,[b] if I do not let you know and send you away safely. May the LORD be with[c] you as he has been with my father. [14]But show me unfailing kindness[d] like that of the LORD as long as I live, so that I may not be killed, [15]and do not ever cut off your kindness from my family[e]—not even when the LORD has cut off every one of David's enemies from the face of the earth."

[16]So Jonathan[f] made a covenant[g] with the house of David, saying, "May the LORD

call David's enemies to account.[h]" [17]And Jonathan had David reaffirm his oath[i] out of love for him, because he loved him as he loved himself.

[18]Then Jonathan said to David: "Tomorrow is the New Moon festival. You will be missed, because your seat will be empty.[j] [19]The day after tomorrow, toward evening, go to the place where you hid[k] when this trouble began, and wait by the stone Ezel. [20]I will shoot three arrows[l] to the side of it, as though I were shooting at a target. [21]Then I will send a boy and say, 'Go, find the arrows.' If I say to him, 'Look, the arrows are on this side of you; bring them here,' then come, because, as surely as the LORD lives, you are safe; there is no danger. [22]But if I say to the boy, 'Look, the arrows are beyond[m] you,' then you must go, because the LORD has sent you away. [23]And about the matter you and I discussed—remember, the LORD is witness[n] between you and me forever."

[24]So David hid in the field, and when the New Moon festival[o] came, the king sat down to eat. [25]He sat in his customary place by the wall, opposite Jonathan,[v] and Abner sat next to Saul, but David's place was empty.[p] [26]Saul said nothing that day, for he thought, "Something must have happened to David to make him ceremonially unclean—surely he is unclean.[q]" [27]But the next day, the second day of the month, David's place was empty again. Then Saul said to his son Jonathan, "Why hasn't the son of Jesse come to the meal, either yesterday or today?"

[28]Jonathan answered, "David earnestly asked me for permission[r] to go to Bethlehem. [29]He said, 'Let me go, because our

20:5 [s]S 1Sa 19:2
20:6 [t]ver 28
[u]1Sa 17:58
[v]S 1Sa 1:3
20:7 [w]1Sa 10:27; 25:17
[x]S 1Sa 18:11
20:8 [y]S 1Sa 18:3
[z]2Sa 14:32
20:12 [a]1Sa 19:3
20:13 [b]S Ru 1:17
[c]S 1Sa 16:18; S 18:12
20:14 [d]S Ge 40:14
20:15 [e]1Sa 24:21; 2Sa 9:7
20:16 [f]S 1Sa 18:1
[g]S 1Sa 18:3

20:17 [h]S Jos 22:23
[i]S Jos 9:18; S 1Sa 18:3
20:18 [j]ver 25
20:19
20:20 [k]S 1Sa 19:2
20:22 [l]2Ki 13:15
[m]ver 37
20:23
20:24 [n]S Ge 31:50
20:25 [o]S Nu 10:10
20:26 [p]ver 18
20:28 [q]Lev 7:20-21
[r]ver 6

20:6 *annual sacrifice.* David's statement indicates that it was customary for families to observe the New Moon festival together once in the year. There is no other reference in the OT to this practice.

20:8 *covenant.* See note on 18:3.

20:11 *let's go out into the field.* Jonathan acted to save David. Cain had said the same to Abel, but in order to kill him (Ge 4:8; but see NIV text note there).

20:13 *may the LORD deal with me, be it ever so severely.* A common curse formula (see note on 3:17). *May the LORD be with you as he has been with my father.* A clear indication that Jonathan expects David to become king.

20:14 *that I may not be killed.* It was quite common in the ancient world for the first ruler of a new dynasty to secure his position by murdering all potential claimants to the throne from the preceding dynasty (see 1Ki 15:29; 16:11; 2Ki 10:7; 11:1).

20:15 *your kindness from my family.* This request was based on the covenant previously concluded between Jonathan and David (see note on 18:3) and was subsequently

honored in David's dealings with Jonathan's son Mephibosheth (see 2Sa 9:3,7; 21:7).

20:16 *May the LORD call David's enemies to account.* Jonathan aligns himself completely with David, calling for destruction of his enemies, even if that should include his father, Saul.

20:17 *reaffirm his oath.* See vv. 14–15, 42; 18:3. *he loved him as he loved himself.* See 18:3; 2Sa 1:26.

20:18 *New Moon festival.* See note on v. 5.

20:19 *the place where you hid.* Perhaps the place referred to in 19:2.

20:23 *the matter you and I discussed.* See vv. 15–17. *the LORD is witness.* The invoking of God to act as witness and judge between them ensures that their agreement will be kept.

20:25 *Abner.* Saul's cousin and the commander of his army (see 14:50).

20:26 *ceremonially unclean.* See note on 16:5; cf. Lev 7:19–21; 15:16; Dt 23:10.

family is observing a sacrifice *s* in the town and my brother has ordered me to be there. If I have found favor in your eyes, let me get away to see my brothers.' That is why he has not come to the king's table."

30Saul's anger flared up at Jonathan and he said to him, "You son of a perverse and rebellious woman! Don't I know that you have sided with the son of Jesse to your own shame and to the shame of the mother who bore you? 31As long as the son of Jesse lives on this earth, neither you nor your kingdom *t* will be established. Now send and bring him to me, for he must die!"

32"Why *u* should he be put to death? What *v* has he done?" Jonathan asked his father. 33But Saul hurled his spear at him to kill him. Then Jonathan knew that his father intended *w* to kill David.

34Jonathan got up from the table in fierce anger; on that second day of the month he did not eat, because he was grieved at his father's shameful treatment of David.

35In the morning Jonathan went out to the field for his meeting with David. He had a small boy with him, 36and he said to the boy, "Run and find the arrows I shoot." As the boy ran, he shot an arrow beyond him. 37When the boy came to the place where Jonathan's arrow had fallen, Jonathan called out after him, "Isn't the arrow beyond *x* you?" 38Then he shouted, "Hurry! Go quickly! Don't stop!" The boy picked up the arrow and returned to his master. 39(The boy knew nothing of all this; only Jonathan and David knew.) 40Then Jonathan gave his weapons to the boy and said, "Go, carry them back to town."

41After the boy had gone, David got up from the south side *of* the stone, and bowed down before Jonathan three times, with his face to the ground. *y* Then they kissed each other and wept together—but David wept the most.

42Jonathan said to David, "Go in peace, *z* for we have sworn friendship *a* with each other in the name of the LORD, *b* saying, 'The LORD is witness *c* between you and me, and between your descendants and my descendants forever. *d* '" Then David left, and Jonathan went back to the town.

David at Nob

21 David went to Nob, *e* to Ahimelech the priest. Ahimelech trembled *f* when he met him, and asked, "Why are you alone? Why is no one with you?"

2David answered Ahimelech the priest, "The king charged me with a certain matter and said to me, 'No one is to know anything about your mission and your instructions.' As for my men, I have told them to meet me at a certain place. 3Now then, what do you have on hand? Give me five loaves of bread, or whatever you can find."

4But the priest answered David, "I don't have any ordinary bread *g* on hand; however, there is some consecrated *h* bread here—provided the men have kept *i* themselves from women."

5David replied, "Indeed women have been kept from us, as usual *j* whenever *w* I set out. The men's things *x* are holy *k* even on missions that are not holy. How much more so today!" 6So the priest gave him

---

Cross references (center column)

20:29 *s* S Ge 8:20
20:31 *t* 1Sa 23:17; 24:20
20:32 *u* S 1Sa 19:4; Mt 27:23 *v* S Ge 31:36
20:33 *w* S 1Sa 18:11,17
20:37 *x* ver 22

20:41 *y* S Ge 33:3; Ru 2:10; 1Sa 24:8; 25:23; 2Sa 1:2
20:42 *z* S 1Sa 1:17; S Ac 15:33 *a* S Ge 40:14; 2Sa 1:26; Pr 18:24 *b* Isa 48:1 *c* S Ge 31:50; S 1Sa 18:3 *d* 2Sa 9:1
21:1 *e* 1Sa 22:9, 19; Ne 11:32; Isa 10:32 *f* 1Sa 16:4
21:4 *g* Lev 24:8-9 *h* Mt 12:4 *i* S Ex 19:15; S Lev 15:18
21:5 *j* Dt 23:9-11; Jos 3:5; 2Sa 11:11 *k* 1Th 4:4

w 5 Or *from us in the past few days since*   *x* 5 Or *bodies*

20:30 *son of a perverse and rebellious woman.* The Hebrew idiom intends to characterize Jonathan, not his mother.

20:31 *neither you nor your kingdom will be established.* Saul is now convinced that David will succeed him if David is not killed (see notes on 18:13,17,29; 19:1), and he is incapable of understanding Jonathan's lack of concern for his own succession to the throne.

20:33 *hurled his spear.* See 18:11; 19:10.

20:41 *bowed . . . three times.* A sign of submission and respect (see Ge 33:3; 42:6).

20:42 *sworn friendship.* See vv. 14–15,23; 18:3. *the town.* Gibeah (see 10:26).

21:1 *Nob.* A town northeast of Jerusalem and south of Gibeah where the tabernacle was relocated after the destruction of Shiloh (4:2–3; Jer 7:12). Although it appears that no attempt was made to bring the ark to this sanctuary (see note on 7:1), Ahimelech the high priest, 85 other priests (22:17–18), the ephod (v. 9) and the table of consecrated bread (v. 6) are mentioned in connection with it. *Ahimelech the priest.* See note on 14:3. It appears from 22:10,15 that

David's purpose in coming to Nob was to seek the Lord's guidance by means of the Urim and Thummim (see notes on 2:28; Ex 28:30).

21:2 It is not clear why David resorts to deception in his response to Ahimelech. Perhaps it was an attempt to protect Ahimelech from the charge of involvement in David's escape from Saul. If so, his strategy was not successful (see 22:13–18).

21:4 *consecrated bread.* The "bread of the Presence" (see v. 6; Ex 25:30), which was placed in the Holy Place in the tabernacle and later in the temple as a thank offering to the Lord, symbolizing his provision of daily bread. *provided the men have kept themselves from women.* Although the bread was to be eaten only by the priests (see Lev 24:9), Ahimelech agreed to give it to David and his men on the condition that they were ceremonially clean (see Ex 19:15; Lev 15:18). Jesus uses this incident to illustrate the principle that the ceremonial law was not to be viewed in a legalistic manner (see Mt 12:3–4). He also teaches that it is always lawful to do good and to save life (see Lk 6:9). Such compassionate acts are within the true spirit of the law.

the consecrated bread,[l] since there was no bread there except the bread of the Presence that had been removed from before the LORD and replaced by hot bread on the day it was taken away.

[7]Now one of Saul's servants was there that day, detained before the LORD; he was Doeg[m] the Edomite,[n] Saul's head shepherd.

[8]David asked Ahimelech, "Don't you have a spear or a sword here? I haven't brought my sword or any other weapon, because the king's business was urgent."

[9]The priest replied, "The sword[o] of Goliath[p] the Philistine, whom you killed in the Valley of Elah,[q] is here; it is wrapped in a cloth behind the ephod. If you want it, take it; there is no sword here but that one."

David said, "There is none like it; give it to me."

David at Gath

[10]That day David fled from Saul and went[r] to Achish king of Gath. [11]But the servants of Achish said to him, "Isn't this David, the king of the land? Isn't he the one they sing about in their dances:

" 'Saul has slain his thousands,
and David his tens of thousands'?"[s]

[12]David took these words to heart and was very much afraid of Achish king of Gath. [13]So he pretended to be insane[t] in their presence; and while he was in their hands he acted like a madman, making marks on the doors of the gate and letting saliva run down his beard.

[14]Achish said to his servants, "Look at the man! He is insane! Why bring him to me? [15]Am I so short of madmen that you have to bring this fellow here to carry on like this in front of me? Must this man come into my house?"

David at Adullam and Mizpah

22 David left Gath and escaped to the cave[u] of Adullam.[v] When his brothers and his father's household heard about it, they went down to him there. [2]All those who were in distress or in debt or discontented gathered[w] around him, and he became their leader. About four hundred men were with him.

[3]From there David went to Mizpah in Moab and said to the king of Moab, "Would you let my father and mother come and stay with you until I learn what God will do for me?" [4]So he left them with the king of Moab,[x] and they stayed with him as long as David was in the stronghold.

[5]But the prophet Gad[y] said to David, "Do not stay in the stronghold. Go into the land of Judah." So David left and went to the forest of Hereth.[z]

Saul Kills the Priests of Nob

[6]Now Saul heard that David and his men had been discovered. And Saul, spear in hand, was seated[a] under the tamarisk[b] tree on the hill at Gibeah, with all his officials standing around him. [7]Saul said to them, "Listen, men of Benjamin! Will the son of Jesse give all of you fields and vineyards? Will he make all of you commanders[c] of thousands and commanders of hundreds? [8]Is that why you have all conspired[d] against me? No one tells me when my son makes a covenant[e] with the son of

---

21:6 [l]S Ex 25:30; 1Sa 22:10; Mt 12:3-4; Mk 2:25-28; Lk 6:1-5
21:7 [m]1Sa 22:9, 22 [n]1Sa 14:47; Ps 52 Title
21:9 [o]S 1Sa 17:51 [p]S 1Sa 17:4 [q]1Sa 17:2
21:10 [r]1Sa 25:13; 27:2
21:11 [s]S 1Sa 18:7
21:13 [t]Ps 34 Title

22:1 [u]Ps 57 Title; 142 Title [v]S Ge 38:1
22:2 [w]1Sa 23:13; 25:13; 2Sa 15:20
22:4 [x]S Ge 19:37
22:5 [y]2Sa 24:11; 1Ch 21:9; 29:29; 2Ch 29:25 [z]2Sa 23:14
22:6 [a]S Jdg 4:5 [b]S Ge 21:33
22:7 [c]S Dt 1:15
22:8 [d]ver 13 [e]S 1Sa 18:3

21:9 *sword of Goliath.* See note on 17:54. *ephod.* See note on 2:28.

21:10 *Achish.* See note on Ps 34 title. *Gath.* One of the five major towns of the Philistines (Jos 13:3).

21:11 *king of the land.* The designation of David as "king" by the Philistines may be understood as a popular exaggeration expressing an awareness of the enormous success and popularity of David among the Israelite people.

22:1 *cave of Adullam.* See 2Sa 23:13; Ge 38:1; Jos 12:15; 15:35; 1Ch 11:15 and note on Ps 142 title.

22:2 *four hundred men were with him.* David, officially an outlaw, was joined by others in similar circumstances, so that he began to develop the power base that would sustain him throughout his later years as king.

22:3 *Mizpah in Moab.* Precise location unknown. *let my father and mother come and stay with you.* The king of Moab was a natural ally for David because Saul had warred against him (see 14:47) and David's own great-grandmother was a Moabitess (see Ru 4:13,22).

22:4 *stronghold.* Perhaps a specific fortress, but more likely a reference to a geographical area in which it was easy to hide (see 23:14; 2Sa 5:17; 23:14).

22:5 *prophet Gad.* The king-designate is now served also by a prophet. Later a priest would come to him (v. 20) and complete the basic elements of a royal entourage—and they were all refugees from Saul's administration. This is the first appearance of the prophet who later assisted David in musical arrangements for the temple services (see 2Ch 29:25), wrote a history of David's reign (see 1Ch 29:29) and confronted David with the Lord's rebuke for his sin of numbering the Israelites (see 2Sa 24:11–25). *forest of Hereth.* Located in the tribal area of Judah.

22:6 *tamarisk tree.* See note on 14:2. *Gibeah.* See note on 10:5.

22:7 *men of Benjamin.* Saul, a Benjamite (9:1–2; 10:21), seeks to strengthen his position with his own officials by emphasizing tribal loyalty. David was from the tribe of Judah (see note on 16:1; 2Sa 2:4). *give all of you fields and vineyards.* Saul does exactly what Samuel had warned him that he would do—become as the kings of other nations (see 8:14). His actions are contrary to the covenantal ideal for kingship (see notes on 8:7; 10:25). *commanders of thousands and of hundreds.* See 8:12.

Jesse.*f* None of you is concerned*g* about me or tells me that my son has incited my servant to lie in wait for me, as he does today."

9But Doeg*h* the Edomite, who was standing with Saul's officials, said, "I saw the son of Jesse come to Ahimelech son of Ahitub*i* at Nob.*j* 10Ahimelech inquired*k* of the LORD for him; he also gave him provisions*l* and the sword*m* of Goliath the Philistine."

11Then the king sent for the priest Ahimelech son of Ahitub and his father's whole family, who were the priests at Nob, and they all came to the king. 12Saul said, "Listen now, son of Ahitub."

"Yes, my lord," he answered.

13Saul said to him, "Why have you conspired*n* against me, you and the son of Jesse, giving him bread and a sword and inquiring of God for him, so that he has rebelled against me and lies in wait for me, as he does today?"

14Ahimelech answered the king, "Who*o* of all your servants is as loyal as David, the king's son-in-law, captain of your bodyguard and highly respected in your household? 15Was that day the first time I inquired of God for him? Of course not! Let not the king accuse your servant or any of his father's family, for your servant knows nothing at all about this whole affair."

16But the king said, "You will surely die, Ahimelech, you and your father's whole family.*p*"

17Then the king ordered the guards at his side: "Turn and kill the priests of the LORD, because they too have sided with David. They knew he was fleeing, yet they did not tell me."

But the king's officials were not willing*q* to raise a hand to strike the priests of the LORD.

18The king then ordered Doeg, "You turn and strike down the priests."*r* So Doeg the Edomite turned and struck them down. That day he killed eighty-five men who wore the linen ephod.*s* 19He also put to the sword*t* Nob,*u* the town of the priests, with its men and women, its chil-

dren and infants, and its cattle, donkeys and sheep.

20But Abiathar,*v* a son of Ahimelech son of Ahitub,*w* escaped and fled to join David.*x* 21He told David that Saul had killed the priests of the LORD. 22Then David said to Abiathar: "That day, when Doeg*y* the Edomite was there, I knew he would be sure to tell Saul. I am responsible for the death of your father's whole family. 23Stay with me; don't be afraid; the man who is seeking your life*z* is seeking mine also. You will be safe with me."

David Saves Keilah

23 When David was told, "Look, the Philistines are fighting against Keilah*a* and are looting the threshing floors,"*b* 2he inquired*c* of the LORD, saying, "Shall I go and attack these Philistines?"

The LORD answered him, "Go, attack the Philistines and save Keilah."

3But David's men said to him, "Here in Judah we are afraid. How much more, then, if we go to Keilah against the Philistine forces!"

4Once again David inquired*d* of the LORD, and the LORD answered him, "Go down to Keilah, for I am going to give the Philistines*e* into your hand.*f*" 5So David and his men went to Keilah, fought the Philistines and carried off their livestock. He inflicted heavy losses on the Philistines and saved the people of Keilah. 6(Now Abiathar*g* son of Ahimelech had brought the ephod*h* down with him when he fled to David at Keilah.)

Saul Pursues David

7Saul was told that David had gone to Keilah, and he said, "God has handed him over*i* to me, for David has imprisoned himself by entering a town with gates and bars."*j* 8And Saul called up all his forces for battle, to go down to Keilah to besiege David and his men.

9When David learned that Saul was plotting against him, he said to Abiathar*k* the priest, "Bring the ephod.*l*" 10David

22:8 *f*2Sa 20:1
*g*1Sa 23:21
22:9 *h*S 1Sa 21:7
*i*1Sa 14:3
/S 1Sa 21:1
22:10
*k*S Ge 25:22;
S 1Sa 23:2
/S 1Sa 21:6
*m*S 1Sa 17:51
22:13 *n*ver 8
22:14
*o*S 1Sa 19:4
22:16
*p*S 1Sa 2:31
22:17 *q*S Ex 1:17
22:18 *r*S 1Sa 4:17
*s*S 1Sa 2:18
22:19 *t*S 1Sa 15:3
*u*S 1Sa 21:1

22:20 *v*1Sa 23:6,
9; 30:7;
2Sa 15:24; 20:25;
1Ki 1:7; 2:22,26,
27; 4:4;
1Ch 15:11; 27:34
*w*S 1Sa 14:3
*x*S 1Sa 2:32
22:22
*y*S 1Sa 21:7
22:23
*z*S 1Sa 20:1
23:1 *a*S Jos 15:44
*b*S Nu 18:27;
S Jdg 6:11
23:2 *c*ver 4,12;
1Sa 22:10; 30:8;
2Sa 2:1; 5:19;
Ps 50:15
23:4 *d*S ver 2
*e*S 1Sa 9:16
/S Jos 8:7
23:6
*g*S 1Sa 22:20
*h*S 1Sa 2:28
23:7 *i*S Dt 32:30
/Ps 31:21
23:9
*k*S 1Sa 22:20
/S 1Sa 2:18

22:10 *Ahimelech inquired of the LORD for him.* See note on 21:1.

22:17 *They knew he was fleeing.* How much the priests really knew is not clear. David himself had not told them (see 21:2–3,8).

22:18 *linen ephod.* See note on 2:18.

22:19 *put to the sword Nob.* Thus the prophecy of judgment against the house of Eli is fulfilled (see 2:31).

22:20 *Abiathar ... escaped and fled to join David.* See

note on v. 5. Abiathar brought the high priestly ephod with him (see 23:6) and subsequently "inquired of the LORD" for David (see 23:2 and note; see also 23:4,9; 30:7–8; 2Sa 2:1; 5:19,23). He served as high priest until removed from office by Solomon for participating in the rebellion of Adonijah (see 1Ki 2:26–27).

23:2 *he inquired of the LORD.* By means of the Urim and Thummim through the high priest Abiathar (see vv. 6,9 and note on 2:28).

23:9 *Bring the ephod.* See note on v. 2.

said, "O LORD, God of Israel, your servant has heard definitely that Saul plans to come to Keilah and destroy the town on account of me. [11]Will the citizens of Keilah surrender to him? Will Saul come down, as your servant has heard? O LORD, God of Israel, tell your servant."

And the LORD said, "He will."

[12]Again David asked, "Will the citizens of Keilah surrender[m] me and my men to Saul?"

And the LORD said, "They will."

[13]So David and his men,[n] about six hundred in number, left Keilah and kept moving from place to place. When Saul was told that David had escaped from Keilah, he did not go there.

[14]David stayed in the desert[o] strongholds and in the hills of the Desert of Ziph.[p] Day after day Saul searched[q] for him, but God did not[r] give David into his hands.

[15]While David was at Horesh in the Desert of Ziph, he learned that Saul had come out to take his life.[s] [16]And Saul's son Jonathan went to David at Horesh and helped him find strength[t] in God. [17]"Don't be afraid," he said. "My father Saul will not lay a hand on you. You will be king[u] over Israel, and I will be second to you. Even my father Saul knows this." [18]The two of them made a covenant[v] before the LORD. Then Jonathan went home, but David remained at Horesh.

[19]The Ziphites[w] went up to Saul at Gibeah and said, "Is not David hiding among us[x] in the strongholds at Horesh, on the hill of Hakilah,[y] south of Jeshimon? [20]Now, O king, come down whenever it pleases you to do so, and we will be responsible for handing[z] him over to the king."

[21]Saul replied, "The LORD bless[a] you for your concern[b] for me. [22]Go and make further preparation. Find out where David usually goes and who has seen him there. They tell me he is very crafty. [23]Find out

about all the hiding places he uses and come back to me with definite information.[y] Then I will go with you; if he is in the area, I will track[c] him down among all the clans of Judah."

[24]So they set out and went to Ziph ahead of Saul. Now David and his men were in the Desert of Maon,[d] in the Arabah south of Jeshimon.[e] [25]Saul and his men began the search, and when David was told about it, he went down to the rock and stayed in the Desert of Maon. When Saul heard this, he went into the Desert of Maon in pursuit of David.

[26]Saul[f] was going along one side of the mountain, and David and his men were on the other side, hurrying to get away from Saul. As Saul and his forces were closing in on David and his men to capture them, [27]a messenger came to Saul, saying, "Come quickly! The Philistines are raiding the land." [28]Then Saul broke off his pursuit of David and went to meet the Philistines. That is why they call this place Sela Hammahlekoth.[z] [29]And David went up from there and lived in the strongholds[g] of En Gedi.[h]

David Spares Saul's Life

24 After Saul returned from pursuing the Philistines, he was told, "David is in the Desert of En Gedi.[i]" [2]So Saul took three thousand chosen men from all Israel and set out to look[j] for David and his men near the Crags of the Wild Goats.

[3]He came to the sheep pens along the way; a cave[k] was there, and Saul went in to relieve[l] himself. David and his men were far back in the cave. [4]The men said, "This is the day the LORD spoke[m] of when he said[a] to you, 'I will give your enemy into your hands for you to deal with as you wish.' "[n] Then David crept up unnoticed and cut[o] off a corner of Saul's robe.

[5]Afterward, David was conscience-

23:12 [m]ver 20
23:13
[n]S 1Sa 22:2
23:14 [o]Ps 55:7
[p]S Jos 15:24
[q]Ps 54:3-4
[r]Ps 32:7
23:15
[s]S 1Sa 20:1
23:16 [t]1Sa 30:6;
Ps 18:2; 27:14
23:17
[u]S 1Sa 20:31
23:18
[v]S 1Sa 18:3;
2Sa 9:1
23:19 [w]1Sa 26:1
[x]Ps 54 Title
[y]1Sa 26:3
23:20 [z]ver 12
23:21 [a]Ru 2:20;
2Sa 2:5 [b]1Sa 22:8

23:23
[c]S Ge 31:36
23:24
[d]S Jos 15:55
[e]1Sa 26:1
23:26 [f]Ps 17:9
23:29 [g]1Sa 24:22
[h]S Jos 15:62;
2Ch 20:2; SS 1:14
24:1 [i]S Jos 15:62
24:2 [j]1Sa 26:2
24:3 [k]Ps 57 Title;
142 Title
[l]Jdg 3:24
24:4
[m]1Sa 25:28-30
[n]2Sa 4:8 [o]ver 10,
11

[y]23 Or *me at Nacon*   [z]28 *Sela Hammahlekoth* means *rock of parting.*   [a]4 Or *"Today the LORD is saying*

23:13 *about six hundred.* The number of David's men has grown significantly (cf. 22:2).
23:14 *desert strongholds.* Inaccessible places (see note on 22:4). *Desert of Ziph.* Located south of Hebron. *God did not give David into his hands.* The reality of God's protection over David portrayed here contrasts sharply with the wishful thinking of Saul in v. 7.
23:17 *You will be king over Israel.* See notes on 18:4; 20:13,16,31. *I will be second to you.* Jonathan's love and respect for David enable him to accept a role subordinate to David without any sign of resentment or jealousy (see notes on 18:3; 19:4). This is the last recorded meeting between Jonathan and David. *Saul knows this.* See 18:8 and note on 20:31.

23:18 *covenant.* See notes on 18:3; 20:14–15.
23:19 *strongholds.* Inaccessible places (see note on 22:4).
24:4 *This is the day the LORD spoke of when he said.* There is no previous record of the divine revelation here alluded to by David's men. Perhaps this was their own interpretation of the anointing of David to replace Saul (see 16:13–14), or of assurances given to David that he would survive Saul's vendetta against him and ultimately become king (see 20:14–15; 23:17). If the alternative given in the NIV text note is taken, the reference would not be to a verbal communication from the Lord but to the providential nature of the incident itself, which David's men understood as a revelation from God that David should not ignore.

stricken [p] for having cut off a corner of his robe. [6]He said to his men, "The LORD forbid that I should do such a thing to my master, the LORD's anointed, [q] or lift my hand against him; for he is the anointed of the LORD." [7]With these words David rebuked his men and did not allow them to attack Saul. And Saul left the cave and went his way.

[8]Then David went out of the cave and called out to Saul, "My lord the king!" When Saul looked behind him, David bowed down and prostrated himself with his face to the ground. [r] [9]He said to Saul, "Why do you listen [s] when men say, 'David is bent on harming [t] you'? [10]This day you have seen with your own eyes how the LORD delivered you into my hands in the cave. Some urged me to kill you, but I spared [u] you; I said, 'I will not lift my hand against my master, because he is the LORD's anointed.' [11]See, my father, look at this piece of your robe in my hand! I cut [v] off the corner of your robe but did not kill you. Now understand and recognize that I am not guilty [w] of wrongdoing [x] or rebellion. I have not wronged [y] you, but you are hunting [z] me down to take my life. [a] [12]May the LORD judge [b] between you and me. And may the LORD avenge [c] the wrongs you have done to me, but my hand will not touch you. [13]As the old saying goes, 'From evildoers come evil deeds, [d]' so my hand will not touch you.

[14]"Against whom has the king of Israel come out? Whom are you pursuing? A dead dog? [e] A flea? [f] [15]May the LORD be our judge [g] and decide [h] between us. May

he consider my cause and uphold [i] it; may he vindicate [j] me by delivering [k] me from your hand."

[16]When David finished saying this, Saul asked, "Is that your voice, [l] David my son?" And he wept aloud. [17]"You are more righteous than I," [m] he said. "You have treated me well, [n] but I have treated you badly. [o] [18]You have just now told me of the good you did to me; the LORD delivered [p] me into your hands, but you did not kill me. [19]When a man finds his enemy, does he let him get away unharmed? May the LORD reward [q] you well for the way you treated me today. [20]I know that you will surely be king [r] and that the kingdom [s] of Israel will be established in your hands. [21]Now swear [t] to me by the LORD that you will not cut off my descendants or wipe out my name from my father's family. [u]"

[22]So David gave his oath to Saul. Then Saul returned home, but David and his men went up to the stronghold. [v]

David, Nabal and Abigail

25 Now Samuel died, [w] and all Israel assembled and mourned [x] for him; and they buried him at his home in Ramah. [y]

Then David moved down into the Desert of Maon. [b] [2]A certain man in Maon, [z] who had property there at Carmel, was very wealthy. [a] He had a thousand goats and three thousand sheep, which he was shearing [b] in Carmel. [3]His

---

24:5 [p]1Sa 26:9; 2Sa 24:10
24:6 [q]S Ge 26:11; S 1Sa 12:3
24:8 [r]S 1Sa 20:41
24:9 [s]1Sa 26:19 [t]1Sa 20:1
24:10 [u]S ver 4
24:11 [v]S ver 4 [w]Ps 7:3 [x]1Sa 25:28 [y]Ps 35:7 [z]S Ge 31:36; 1Sa 26:20 [a]S 1Sa 20:1
24:12 [b]S Ge 16:5; S 1Sa 25:38; S Job 9:15 [c]S Nu 31:3
24:13 [d]Mt 7:20
24:14 [e]S 1Sa 17:43 [f]1Sa 26:20
24:15 [g]ver 12 [h]S Ge 16:5
[i]Ps 35:1,23; Isa 49:25
[j]Ps 26:1; 35:24; 43:1; 50:4; 54:1; 135:14
[k]Ps 119:134,154
24:16 [l]1Sa 26:17
24:17 [m]Ge 38:26
[n]Mt 5:44 [o]S Ex 9:27
24:18 [p]1Sa 26:23
24:19 [q]S Ru 2:12; S 2Ch 15:7
24:20 [r]S 1Sa 20:31 [s]S 1Sa 13:14
24:21 [t]Ge 21:23; S 47:31; S 1Sa 18:3; 2Sa 21:1-9 [u]S 1Sa 20:14-15
24:22 [v]S 1Sa 23:29
25:1 [w]1Sa 28:3 [x]S Lev 10:6; Dt 34:8 [y]S 1Sa 7:17
25:2 [z]S Jos 15:55 [a]2Sa 19:32 [b]S Ge 31:19

[b] [j] Some Septuagint manuscripts; Hebrew Paran

24:6 *for he is the anointed of the LORD.* Because Saul's royal office carried divine sanction by virtue of his anointing (see note on 9:16), David is determined not to wrest the kingship from Saul but to leave its disposition to the Lord who gave it (see vv. 12,15; 26:10).

24:11 *my father.* Saul was David's father-in-law (see 18:27).

24:16 *he wept aloud.* Saul experiences temporary remorse (see 26:21) for his actions against David but quickly reverts to his former determination to kill him (see 26:2).

24:21 *not cut off my descendants.* See notes on 20:14–15.

24:22 *stronghold.* An inaccessible place (see note on 22:4). From previous experience David did not place any confidence in Saul's words of repentance.

25:1 *all Israel . . . mourned for him.* Samuel was recognized as a leader of national prominence who played a key role in the restructuring of the theocracy with the establishment of the monarchy (see chs. 8–12). The loss of his leadership was mourned much like that of other prominent figures in Israel's past history, including Jacob (Ge 50:10), Aaron (Nu 20:29) and Moses (Dt 34:8). *Ramah.* See 7:17 and note on 1:1.

25:2–44 Nabal, the "fool" (see v. 25), lived near Carmel, where Saul had erected a monument in his own honor (see 15:12) and had committed the act that led to his rejection

(see 15:26). The account of Nabal effectively serves the author's purpose in a number of ways: 1. Nabal's general character, his disdainful attitude toward David though David had guarded his flocks, and his sudden death at the Lord's hand all parallel Saul (whose "flock" David had also protected). This allows the author indirectly to characterize Saul as a fool (see 13:13; 26:21) and to foreshadow his end. 2. David's vengeful attitude toward Nabal displays his natural tendency and highlights his restraint toward Saul, the Lord's anointed (this event is sandwiched between the two instances in which David spared Saul in spite of the urging of his men). 3. Abigail's prudent action prevents David from using his power as leader for personal vengeance (the very thing Saul was doing). In this way the Lord (who avenged his servant) keeps David's sword clean, teaching him a lesson he does not forget. 4. Abigail's confident acknowledgment of David's future accession to the throne foreshadows that event and even anticipates the Lord's commitment to establish David's house as a "lasting dynasty" (v. 28; cf. 2Sa 7:11–16). 5. Abigail's marriage to David provides him with a wise and worthy wife, while Saul gives away David's wife Michal to another, illustrating how the Lord counters every move Saul makes against David.

25:3 *Calebite.* A descendant of Caleb (see Nu 14:24), who settled at Hebron (see Jos 14:13) after the conquest of Ca-

name was Nabal and his wife's name was
Abigail.[c] She was an intelligent and
beautiful woman, but her husband, a
Calebite,[d] was surly and mean in his dealings.
4While David was in the desert, he
heard that Nabal was shearing sheep. 5So
he sent ten young men and said to them,
"Go up to Nabal at Carmel and greet him
in my name. 6Say to him: 'Long life to you!
Good health[e] to you and your household!
And good health to all that is yours![f]
7" 'Now I hear that it is sheep-shearing
time. When your shepherds were with us,
we did not mistreat[g] them, and the whole
time they were at Carmel nothing of theirs
was missing. 8Ask your own servants and
they will tell you. Therefore be favorable
toward my young men, since we come at a
festive time. Please give your servants and
your son David whatever[h] you can find for
them.' "
9When David's men arrived, they gave
Nabal this message in David's name. Then
they waited.
10Nabal answered David's servants,
"Who[i] is this David? Who is this son of
Jesse? Many servants are breaking away
from their masters these days. 11Why
should I take my bread[j] and water, and
the meat I have slaughtered for my shearers, and give it to men coming from who
knows where?"
12David's men turned around and went
back. When they arrived, they reported
every word. 13David said to his men[k],
"Put on your swords!" So they put on
their swords, and David put on his. About
four hundred men went[l] up with David,
while two hundred stayed with the supplies.[m]
14One of the servants told Nabal's wife
Abigail: "David sent messengers from the
desert to give our master his greetings,[n]
but he hurled insults at them. 15Yet these
men were very good to us. They did not
mistreat[o] us, and the whole time we were
out in the fields near them nothing was
missing.[p] 16Night and day they were a
wall[q] around us all the time we were
herding our sheep near them. 17Now think
it over and see what you can do, because
disaster is hanging over our master and his
whole household. He is such a wicked[r]
man that no one can talk to him."
18Abigail lost no time. She took two
hundred loaves of bread, two skins of
wine, five dressed sheep, five seahs[c] of
roasted grain,[s] a hundred cakes of raisins[t]
and two hundred cakes of pressed figs, and
loaded them on donkeys.[u] 19Then she told
her servants, "Go on ahead;[v] I'll follow
you." But she did not tell[w] her husband
Nabal.
20As she came riding her donkey into a
mountain ravine, there were David and his
men descending toward her, and she met
them. 21David had just said, "It's been useless—all my watching over this fellow's
property in the desert so that nothing of his
was missing.[x] He has paid[y] me back evil[z]
for good. 22May God deal with David,[d] be
it ever so severely,[a] if by morning I leave
alive one male[b] of all who belong to him!"
23When Abigail saw David, she quickly
got off her donkey and bowed down before
David with her face to the ground.[c] 24She
fell at his feet and said: "My lord, let the
blame[d] be on me alone. Please let your
servant speak to you; hear what your servant has to say. 25May my lord pay no attention to that wicked man Nabal. He is
just like his name—his name is Fool[e],[f]
and folly goes with him. But as for me,
your servant, I did not see the men my
master sent.
26"Now since the LORD has kept you,
my master, from bloodshed[g] and from
avenging[h] yourself with your own hands,
as surely as the LORD lives and as you live,
may your enemies and all who intend to
harm my master be like Nabal.[i] 27And let
this gift,[j] which your servant has brought

25:3 [c]Pr 31:10 [d]S Jos 14:13; S 15:13 **25:6** [e]Ps 122:7; Mt 10:12 [f]1Ch 12:18 **25:7** [g]ver 15 **25:8** [h]Ne 8:10 **25:10** [i]Jdg 9:28 **25:11** [j]Jdg 8:6 **25:13** [k]S 1Sa 22:2 [l]S 1Sa 21:10 [m]S Nu 31:27 **25:14** [n]1Sa 13:10 **25:15** [o]ver 7 [p]ver 21 **25:16** [q]Ex 14:22; Job 1:10; Ps 139:5 **25:17** [r]S Dt 13:13; S 1Sa 20:7 **25:18** [s]S Lev 23:14; S 1Sa 17:17 [t]1Ch 12:40 [u]S Ge 42:26; 2Sa 16:1; Isa 30:6 **25:19** [v]Ge 32:20 [w]ver 36 **25:21** [x]ver 15 [y]Ps 109:5 [z]S 1Sa 19:4 **25:22** [a]S Ru 1:17 [b]1Ki 14:10; 21:21; 2Ki 9:8 **25:23** [c]S Ge 19:1; S 1Sa 20:41 **25:24** [d]2Sa 14:9 **25:25** [e]Pr 17:12 [f]Pr 12:16; 14:16; 20:3; Isa 32:5 **25:26** [g]ver 33 [h]Heb 10:30 [i]ver 34; 2Sa 18:32 **25:27** [j]S Ge 33:11

[c] *18* That is, probably about a bushel (about 37 liters)
[d] *22* Some Septuagint manuscripts; Hebrew *with David's enemies*

naan. Since Caleb's name can mean "dog," Nabal is subtly depicted as a dog as well as a fool. He would soon be a dead dog (see note on 2Sa 9:8), when the Lord would avenge his acts of contempt toward David. The hint is strong that, when the Lord avenges Saul's sins against David (see 24:12,15), the king will no longer pursue a dead dog (see 24:14) but will himself become one—a case of biting irony.

25:4 *shearing sheep.* A festive occasion (see v. 8; 2Sa 13:23–24).

25:8 *whatever you can find for them.* David and his men ask for some remuneration for their protection of Nabal's shepherds and flocks against pillage (see vv. 15–16,21).

25:17 *wicked man.* See note on Dt 13:13. *no one can talk to him.* In this way, too, Nabal is like Saul (cf., e.g., 20:27–33).

25:19 *did not tell her husband.* Cf. Michal's treatment of Saul (19:11–14).

25:22 *May God deal with David, be it ever so severely.* See note on 3:17. David invokes a curse on himself if he should fail to kill every male in Nabal's household and so obliterate Nabal's family.

25:25 *wicked man.* See note on Dt 13:13. *He is just like his name.* In ancient times a person's name was believed to reflect his nature and character. *his name is Fool.* In Hebrew the name Nabal means "fool."

25:26 *as surely as the LORD lives.* See note on 14:39.

to my master, be given to the men who follow you. [28]Please forgive[k] your servant's offense, for the LORD will certainly make a lasting[l] dynasty for my master, because he fights the LORD's battles.[m] Let no wrongdoing[n] be found in you as long as you live. [29]Even though someone is pursuing you to take your life,[o] the life of my master will be bound securely in the bundle of the living by the LORD your God. But the lives of your enemies he will hurl[p] away as from the pocket of a sling.[q] [30]When the LORD has done for my master every good thing he promised concerning him and has appointed him leader[r] over Israel, [31]my master will not have on his conscience the staggering burden of needless bloodshed or of having avenged himself. And when the LORD has brought my master success, remember[s] your servant."[t]

[32]David said to Abigail, "Praise[u] be to the LORD, the God of Israel, who has sent you today to meet me. [33]May you be blessed for your good judgment and for keeping me from bloodshed[v] this day and from avenging myself with my own hands. [34]Otherwise, as surely as the LORD, the God of Israel, lives, who has kept me from harming you, if you had not come quickly to meet me, not one male belonging to Nabal[w] would have been left alive by daybreak."

[35]Then David accepted from her hand what she had brought him and said, "Go home in peace. I have heard your words and granted[x] your request."

[36]When Abigail went to Nabal, he was in the house holding a banquet like that of a king. He was in high[y] spirits and very drunk.[z] So she told[a] him nothing until daybreak. [37]Then in the morning, when Nabal was sober, his wife told him all these things, and his heart failed him and he

became like a stone.[b] [38]About ten days later, the LORD struck[c] Nabal and he died.

[39]When David heard that Nabal was dead, he said, "Praise be to the LORD, who has upheld my cause against Nabal for treating me with contempt. He has kept his servant from doing wrong and has brought Nabal's wrongdoing down on his own head."

Then David sent word to Abigail, asking her to become his wife. [40]His servants went to Carmel and said to Abigail, "David has sent us to you to take you to become his wife."

[41]She bowed down with her face to the ground and said, "Here is your maidservant, ready to serve you and wash the feet of my master's servants." [42]Abigail[d] quickly got on a donkey and, attended by her five maids, went with David's messengers and became his wife. [43]David had also married Ahinoam[e] of Jezreel, and they both were his wives.[f] [44]But Saul had given his daughter Michal, David's wife, to Paltiel[eg] son of Laish, who was from Gallim.[h]

David Again Spares Saul's Life

26 The Ziphites[i] went to Saul at Gibeah and said, "Is not David hiding[j] on the hill of Hakilah, which faces Jeshimon?[k]"

[2]So Saul went down to the Desert of Ziph, with his three thousand chosen men of Israel, to search[l] there for David. [3]Saul made his camp beside the road on the hill of Hakilah[m] facing Jeshimon, but David stayed in the desert. When he saw that Saul had followed him there, [4]he sent out scouts and learned that Saul had definitely arrived.[f]

[5]Then David set out and went to the

25:28 *k*ver 24; 2Sa 14:9
*l*2Sa 7:11,26
*m*1Sa 18:17
*n*1Sa 24:11
25:29 *o*1Sa 20:1
*p*Jer 10:18; 22:26
*q*1Sa 17:50; 2Sa 4:8
25:30 *r*S 1Sa 12:12; S 13:14
25:31 *s*S Ge 40:14
*t*2Sa 3:10
25:32 *u*S Ge 24:27
25:33 *v*ver 26
25:34 *w*S ver 26
25:35 *x*S Ge 19:21
25:36 *y*S Ru 3:7
*z*Pr 20:1; Ecc 10:17;
Isa 5:11,22; 22:13; 28:7; 56:12; Hos 4:11
*a*ver 19

25:37 *b*Ex 15:16
25:38 *c*Dt 32:35; 1Sa 24:12; 26:10; 2Sa 6:7; 12:15
25:42 *d*2Sa 2:2; 3:3; 1Ch 3:1
25:43 *e*2Sa 3:2; 1Ch 3:1
*f*1Sa 27:3; 30:5; 2Sa 2:2
25:44 *g*2Sa 3:15
*h*Isa 10:30
26:1 *i*1Sa 23:19
*/Ps 54 Title
*k*1Sa 23:24
26:2 *l*1Sa 24:2
26:3 *m*1Sa 23:19

e44 Hebrew *Palti*, a variant of *Paltiel*   *f4* Or *had come to Nacon*

25:28 *the LORD will certainly make a lasting dynasty.* While the idea that David was destined to become king in place of Saul may have spread among the general populace, Abigail's assessment of David contrasts sharply with that of her husband (see v. 10). *he fights the LORD's battles.* Abigail is familiar with David's victories over the Philistines, in which he sought to glorify the Lord rather than advance his own honor (see 17:26,45–47; 18:16–17). *Let no wrongdoing be found in you.* Abigail shows concern for the preservation of David's integrity in view of the office he was later to assume (see vv. 30–31,39).
25:29 *bound securely in the bundle of the living.* Using the figure of placing a valuable possession in a carefully wrapped package for safekeeping, Abigail assures David that the Lord will preserve his life in the midst of danger.
25:30 *leader.* See note on 9:16.
25:31 *needless bloodshed.* See note on v. 28.
25:32 *who has sent you.* David recognizes the providential

leading of the Lord in his encounter with Abigail (see v. 39).
25:36 *holding a banquet.* See Pr 30:21–22. *like that of a king.* Another clue that the author is using Nabal as a subtle portrayal of Saul.
25:37 *became like a stone.* Perhaps he suffered a stroke—he who was without moral sensitivity (was a *nabal;* see v. 25 and note) became as senseless as a stone.
25:43 *Ahinoam.* David's first wife (see 27:3; 30:5; 2Sa 2:2) and mother of his first son, Amnon (see 2Sa 3:2). *Jezreel.* Located near Carmel (see v. 2; Jos 15:55) and not to be confused with the northern town of the same name, where Israel camped against the Philistines (see 29:1,11) and where Ahab resided in later times (see 1Ki 18:45–46).
25:44 *Michal, David's wife.* See 18:27.
26:1 *Ziphites.* See notes on 23:14,19. *Gibeah.* Saul's residence (see 10:26).
26:2 *three thousand.* Apparently Saul's standing army (see 24:2).

place where Saul had camped. He saw where Saul and Abner[n] son of Ner, the commander of the army, had lain down. Saul was lying inside the camp, with the army encamped around him.

[6]David then asked Ahimelech the Hittite[o] and Abishai[p] son of Zeruiah,[q] Joab's brother, "Who will go down into the camp with me to Saul?"

"I'll go with you," said Abishai.

[7]So David and Abishai went to the army by night, and there was Saul, lying asleep inside the camp with his spear stuck in the ground near his head. Abner and the soldiers were lying around him.

[8]Abishai said to David, "Today God has delivered your enemy into your hands. Now let me pin him to the ground with one thrust of my spear; I won't strike him twice."

[9]But David said to Abishai, "Don't destroy him! Who can lay a hand on the LORD's anointed[r] and be guiltless?[s] [10]As surely as the LORD lives," he said, "the LORD himself will strike[t] him; either his time[u] will come and he will die,[v] or he will go into battle and perish. [11]But the LORD forbid that I should lay a hand on the LORD's anointed. Now get the spear and water jug that are near his head, and let's go."

[12]So David took the spear and water jug near Saul's head, and they left. No one saw or knew about it, nor did anyone wake up. They were all sleeping, because the LORD had put them into a deep sleep.[w]

[13]Then David crossed over to the other side and stood on top of the hill some distance away; there was a wide space between them. [14]He called out to the army and to Abner son of Ner, "Aren't you going to answer me, Abner?"

Abner replied, "Who are you who calls to the king?"

[15]David said, "You're a man, aren't you? And who is like you in Israel? Why didn't you guard your lord the king? Someone came to destroy your lord the king. [16]What you have done is not good. As surely as the LORD lives, you and your men deserve to die, because you did not guard your master, the LORD's anointed. Look around you. Where are the king's spear and water jug that were near his head?"

[17]Saul recognized David's voice and said, "Is that your voice,[x] David my son?"

David replied, "Yes it is, my lord the king." [18]And he added, "Why is my lord pursuing his servant? What have I done, and what wrong[y] am I guilty of? [19]Now let my lord the king listen[z] to his servant's words. If the LORD has incited you against me, then may he accept an offering.[a] If, however, men have done it, may they be cursed before the LORD! They have now driven me from my share in the LORD's inheritance[b] and have said, 'Go, serve other gods.'[c] [20]Now do not let my blood[d] fall to the ground far from the presence of the LORD. The king of Israel has come out to look for a flea[e]—as one hunts a partridge in the mountains.[f]"

[21]Then Saul said, "I have sinned.[g] Come back, David my son. Because you considered my life precious[h] today, I will not try to harm you again. Surely I have acted like a fool and have erred greatly."

[22]"Here is the king's spear," David answered. "Let one of your young men come over and get it. [23]The LORD rewards[i] every man for his righteousness[j] and faithfulness. The LORD delivered[k] you into my hands today, but I would not lay a hand on the LORD's anointed. [24]As surely

Cross references column:

26:5 [n]1Sa 17:55
26:6 [o]S Ge 10:15
[p]2Sa 2:18; 10:10; 16:9; 18:2; 19:21; 23:18; 1Ch 11:20; 19:11
[q]1Ch 2:16
26:9 [r]ver 16; S Ge 26:11; S 1Sa 9:16; 2Sa 1:14; 19:21; La 4:20
[s]S 1Sa 24:5
26:10 [t]S Ge 16:5; S 1Sa 25:38; S Ro 12:19
[u]Dt 31:14; Ps 37:13
[v]1Sa 31:6; 2Sa 1:1
26:12 [w]S Jdg 4:21

26:17 [x]1Sa 24:16
26:18 [y]Job 13:23; Jer 37:18
26:19 [z]1Sa 24:9
[a]2Sa 16:11
[b]Dt 20:16; 32:9; 2Sa 14:16; 20:19; 21:3 [c]S Dt 4:28; S 11:28
26:20 [d]S 1Sa 24:11
[e]1Sa 24:14
[f]Jer 4:29; 16:16; Am 9:3
26:21 [g]S Ex 9:27
[h]Ps 72:14
26:23 [i]S Ge 16:5; S Ru 2:12; Ps 62:12
[j]2Sa 22:21,25; Ps 7:8; 18:20,24
[k]1Sa 24:18

26:5 *lain down.* David arrived at Saul's camp during the night when the men were sleeping. *Abner.* Saul's cousin (see 14:50).

26:6 *Ahimelech the Hittite.* Not referred to elsewhere. Hittites had long resided in Canaan (see note on Ge 10:15; see also Ge 15:20; 23:3–20; Dt 7:1; 20:17). Another Hittite in David's service was Uriah (see 2Sa 11:3; 23:39). *Abishai son of Zeruiah, Joab's brother.* Zeruiah was an older sister of David (1Ch 2:16), so Abishai and Joab (and their brother Asahel, 2Sa 2:18) were David's nephews as well as trusted military leaders. Joab would long serve as the commander of his army.

26:9 See note on 24:6.

26:10 *As surely as the LORD lives.* See note on 14:39.

26:12 *David took the spear and water jug.* In this way he sought to prove again to Saul that he did not seek his life.

26:19 *may he accept an offering.* David knows no reason why God should be angry with him; but if for some reason God is behind Saul's determined effort to kill him, David

appeals for God to accept an offering of appeasement (cf. 16:5)—in any event, to let the matter be settled between David and God, without Saul's involvement. *may they be cursed before the LORD!* David commits any such men to the judgment of God. *the LORD's inheritance.* See note on 10:1. David appeals to Saul's conscience by describing his present exclusion from the fellowship of God's people and from living at peace in the Lord's land. *Go, serve other gods.* In their view, to be expelled from the Lord's land was to be separated from the Lord's sanctuary (an OT form of excommunication) and left to serve the gods of whatever land one may settle in (see Jos 22:24–27).

26:20 *look for a flea.* See 24:14. David suggests that Saul is making a fool of himself in his fanatical pursuit of an innocent and undesigning man.

26:21 *I have sinned.* See 24:17. *I have acted like a fool.* Saul confesses that his behavior has been not only unwise but also ungodly (see notes on 13:13; 25:2–44).

26:23 *I would not lay a hand on the LORD's anointed.* See v. 9 and note on 24:6.

as I valued your life today, so may the LORD value my life and deliver[l] me from all trouble."

[25]Then Saul said to David, "May you be blessed,[m] my son David; you will do great things and surely triumph."

So David went on his way, and Saul returned home.

David Among the Philistines

27 But David thought to himself, "One of these days I will be destroyed by the hand of Saul. The best thing I can do is to escape to the land of the Philistines. Then Saul will give up searching for me anywhere in Israel, and I will slip out of his hand."

[2]So David and the six hundred men[n] with him left and went[o] over to Achish[p] son of Maoch king of Gath. [3]David and his men settled in Gath with Achish. Each

man had his family with him, and David had his two wives:[q] Ahinoam of Jezreel and Abigail of Carmel, the widow of Nabal. [4]When Saul was told that David had fled to Gath, he no longer searched for him.

[5]Then David said to Achish, "If I have found favor in your eyes, let a place be assigned to me in one of the country towns, that I may live there. Why should your servant live in the royal city with you?"

[6]So on that day Achish gave him Ziklag,[r] and it has belonged to the kings of Judah ever since. [7]David lived[s] in Philistine territory a year and four months.

[8]Now David and his men went up and raided the Geshurites,[t] the Girzites and the Amalekites.[u] (From ancient times these peoples had lived in the land extending to Shur[v] and Egypt.) [9]Whenever

26:24 [l]Ps 54:7
26:25
[m]S Ru 2:12
27:2 [n]1Sa 30:9;
2Sa 2:3
[o]S 1Sa 21:10
[p]1Ki 2:39

27:3
[q]S 1Sa 25:43
27:6 [r]Jos 15:31;
19:5; 1Sa 30:1;
1Ch 12:20;
Ne 11:28
27:7 [s]1Sa 29:3
27:8 [t]S Jos 12:5
[u]S Ex 17:14;
S 1Sa 14:48;
30:1; 2Sa 1:8;
8:12 [v]S Ge 16:7

26:25 *you will ... triumph.* Saul makes a veiled reference to his own conviction that David will replace him as king (see 24:20).
27:1 *I will be destroyed by the hand of Saul.* David falters in his faith (see 23:14; 25:29) and under pressure of Saul's superior forces feels compelled to seek security outside Israel's borders. *land of the Philistines.* For the second time David seeks refuge in the land of the Philistines (see 21:10–15).
27:2 *Achish ... king of Gath.* See 21:10. In contrast to David's previous excursion into Philistia, Achish is now ready to receive him because he has become known as a formidable adversary of Saul. Moreover, to offer sanctuary under the circumstances would obligate David and his men to serve at his call in any military venture (see 28:1).
27:3 *Ahinoam.* See note on 25:43. *Abigail.* See 25:39–42.
27:4 *he no longer searched for him.* Saul did not have sufficient military strength to make incursions into Philistine

territory, and with David out of the country he no longer faced an internal threat to his throne.
27:5 *in one of the country towns.* David desired more independence and freedom of movement than was possible while residing under the very eyes of the king of Gath. *Why should your servant live in the royal city with you?* David implies that he is not worthy of this honor.
27:6 *Ziklag.* Location unknown, but it is included in a list of towns in southern Judah (see Jos 15:31). It was given to the tribe of Simeon (see Jos 19:1–5) and was presumably occupied by them (cf. Jdg 1:17–18), only to be lost to the Philistines at a later, undisclosed time. *it has belonged to the kings of Judah ever since.* As royal property. This comment implies that the book of Samuel was written after the time of the division of Israel into the northern and southern kingdoms—an important consideration in determining the date of the writing of the book (see Introduction: Literary Features, Authorship and Date).

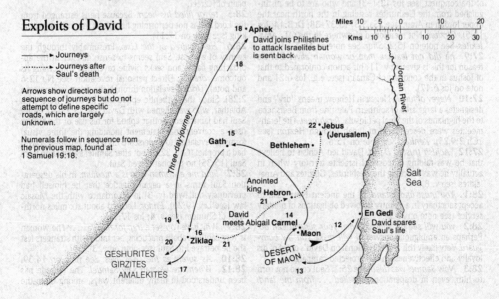

Exploits of David

──► Journeys

··········► Journeys after Saul's death

Arrows show directions and sequence of journeys but do not attempt to define specific roads, which are largely unknown.

Numerals follow in sequence from the previous map, found at 1 Samuel 19:18.

Miles 10　5　0　　10　　20
Kms 10 5 0　10　20　30

18 **Aphek**
David joins Philistines to attack Israelites but is sent back
18

Three-day journey

15 **Gath**

22 **Jebus (Jerusalem)**

Bethlehem •

Anointed king **Hebron**
21

19

David meets Abigail **Carmel**
14

16 **Ziklag**
20　　21

Maon •

DESERT OF MAON
13

En Gedi
David spares Saul's life
12

Salt Sea

Jordan River

GESHURITES
GIRZITES
AMALEKITES　17

David attacked an area, he did not leave a man or woman alive, w but took sheep and cattle, donkeys and camels, and clothes. Then he returned to Achish.

10When Achish asked, "Where did you go raiding today?" David would say, "Against the Negev of Judah" or "Against the Negev of Jerahmeel x" or "Against the Negev of the Kenites. y" 11He did not leave a man or woman alive to be brought to Gath, for he thought, "They might inform on us and say, 'This is what David did.'" And such was his practice as long as he lived in Philistine territory. 12Achish trusted David and said to himself, "He has become so odious z to his people, the Israelites, that he will be my servant forever. a"

Saul and the Witch of Endor

28 In those days the Philistines gathered b their forces to fight against Israel. Achish said to David, "You must understand that you and your men will accompany me in the army."

2David said, "Then you will see for yourself what your servant can do."

Achish replied, "Very well, I will make you my bodyguard c for life."

3Now Samuel was dead, d and all Israel had mourned for him and buried him in his own town of Ramah. e Saul had expelled f the mediums and spiritists g from the land.

4The Philistines assembled and came and set up camp at Shunem, h while Saul gathered all the Israelites and set up camp at Gilboa. i 5When Saul saw the Philistine army, he was afraid; terror j filled his heart. 6He inquired k of the LORD, but the LORD did not answer him by dreams l or Urim m or prophets. n 7Saul then said to his attendants, "Find me a woman who is a medium, o so I may go and inquire of her."

"There is one in Endor, p" they said.

8So Saul disguised q himself, putting on other clothes, and at night he and two men went to the woman. "Consult r a spirit for me," he said, "and bring up for me the one I name."

9But the woman said to him, "Surely you know what Saul has done. He has cut off s the mediums and spiritists from the land. Why have you set a trap t for my life to bring about my death?"

10Saul swore to her by the LORD, "As surely as the LORD lives, you will not be punished for this."

11Then the woman asked, "Whom shall I bring up for you?"

"Bring up Samuel," he said.

12When the woman saw Samuel, she

Cross references (center column)

27:9 wS 1Sa 15:3
27:10 x1Sa 30:29
y Jdg 1:16
27:12 zS Ge 34:30
28:1 a1Sa 29:6 b1Sa 29:1
28:2 c1Sa 29:2
28:3 d1Sa 25:1

eS 1Sa 7:17 fver 9
g S Ex 22:18
28:4 h S Jos 19:18
i1Sa 31:1,3; 2Sa 1:6,21; 21:12
28:5 j S Ex 19:16
28:6 k S 1Sa 8:18; 14:37 l S Dt 13:3
m S Ex 28:30; S Lev 8:8
n Eze 20:3; Am 8:11; Mic 3:7
28:7 o1Ch 10:13; Ac 16:16
p Jos 17:11; Ps 83:10
28:8 q1Ki 22:30; 2Ch 18:29; 35:22 r2Ki 1:3; Isa 8:19
28:9 s ver 3
t Job 18:10; Ps 31:4; 69:22; Isa 8:14

27:7 *David lived in Philistine territory a year and four months.* It was not until after the death of Saul that David moved his residence from Ziklag (see 2Sa 1:1; 2:1–3) to Hebron.

27:8 *Geshurites.* A people residing in the area south of Philistia who were not defeated by the Israelites at the time of the conquest (see Jos 13:1–3) and who are to be distinguished from the Geshurites residing in the north near the upper Jordan in Aram (see 2Sa 3:3; 13:37–38; Dt 3:14; Jos 12:5). *Girzites.* Not mentioned elsewhere in the OT. *Amalekites.* See note on 15:2. *Shur.* See note on 15:7.

27:9 *he did not leave a man or woman alive.* David's reason for this is given in v. 11; his action conformed to that of Joshua in the conquest of Canaan (see, e.g., Jos 6:21 and note on Jos 6:17).

27:10 *Negev of Judah.* Negev in Hebrew means "dry" and designates a large area of southern Palestine from Beersheba to the highlands of the Sinai peninsula. *Jerahmeel.* The Jerahmeelites were descendants of Judah through Hezron (see 1Ch 2:9,25). *Kenites.* See note on 15:6.

27:12 *Achish trusted David.* David led Achish to believe that he was raiding outposts of Israelite territory when in actuality he was attacking the Geshurites, Girzites and Amalekites (see v. 8).

28:1 *You must understand.* In the ancient Near East, to accept sanctuary in a country involved obligations of military service (see note on 27:2).

28:2 *you will see for yourself what your servant can do.* Perhaps an ambiguous answer. *I will make you my bodyguard.* Very likely this was conditional on David's proof of his loyalty and effectiveness in the projected campaign.

28:3 *Now Samuel was dead.* See 25:1. Saul could not turn to him, even in desperation. *expelled . . . from the land.*

Possibly a euphemism for "put to death," in agreement with Pentateuchal law (see vv. 9,21). *mediums and spiritists.* See Lev 19:31; 20:6,27; Dt 18:11.

28:4 *Shunem.* The Philistines assembled their forces far to the north, along the plain of Jezreel in the territory of Issachar (see Jos 19:18). *Gilboa.* A range of mountains east of the plain of Jezreel.

28:5 *terror filled his heart.* Because he is estranged from the Lord and is not performing his role as the true theocratic king (see note on 17:11).

28:6 *He inquired of the LORD.* Presumably through the agency of a priest. Saul seems to sense disaster in the approaching battle and seeks divine revelation concerning its outcome. *dreams.* Direct personal revelation (see Nu 12:6 and note). *Urim.* Revelation through the priest (see note on 2:28). Since the authentic ephod and its Urim were with Abiathar, who was aligned with David (see 23:2,6,9), either Saul had fabricated another ephod for his use or the author used a conventional statement including the three visual forms of revelation to underscore his point. *prophets.* David had a prophet (Gad, 22:5), but after Samuel's alienation from Saul (15:35) no prophet served Saul.

28:7 *Find me a woman who is a medium.* In his desperation Saul turns to a pagan practice that he himself had previously outlawed (v. 3) in accordance with the Mosaic law (see Lev 19:26). *Endor.* Located about six miles northwest of Shunem (see v. 4; Jos 17:11).

28:9 *Why have you set a trap for my life . . .?* The woman is very cautious about practicing her trade with strangers lest she be betrayed to Saul (see note on v. 3).

28:10 *As surely as the LORD lives.* See note on 14:39.

28:12 *When the woman saw Samuel.* The episode has been understood in many different ways, among them the

cried out at the top of her voice and said to
Saul, "Why have you deceived me?[u] You
are Saul!"
13The king said to her, "Don't be afraid.
What do you see?"
The woman said, "I see a spirit[g] coming
up out of the ground."[v]
14"What does he look like?" he asked.
"An old man wearing a robe[w] is coming
up," she said.
Then Saul knew it was Samuel, and he
bowed down and prostrated himself with
his face to the ground.
15Samuel said to Saul, "Why have you
disturbed me by bringing me up?"
"I am in great distress," Saul said. "The
Philistines are fighting against me, and God
has turned[x] away from me. He no longer
answers[y] me, either by prophets or by
dreams.[z] So I have called on you to tell
me what to do."
16Samuel said, "Why do you consult
me, now that the LORD has turned away
from you and become your enemy? 17The
LORD has done what he predicted through
me. The LORD has torn[a] the kingdom out
of your hands and given it to one of your
neighbors—to David. 18Because you did
not obey[b] the LORD or carry out his fierce
wrath[c] against the Amalekites,[d] the LORD
has done this to you today. 19The LORD
will hand over both Israel and you to the
Philistines, and tomorrow you and your
sons[e] will be with me. The LORD will also
hand over the army of Israel to the Philistines."
20Immediately Saul fell full length on the
ground, filled with fear because of Samuel's words. His strength was gone, for he
had eaten nothing all that day and night.
21When the woman came to Saul and
saw that he was greatly shaken, she said,
"Look, your maidservant has obeyed you. I
took my life[f] in my hands and did what
you told me to do. 22Now please listen to
your servant and let me give you some
food so you may eat and have the strength
to go on your way."
23He refused[g] and said, "I will not eat."
But his men joined the woman in urging
him, and he listened to them. He got up
from the ground and sat on the couch.
24The woman had a fattened calf[h] at the
house, which she butchered at once. She
took some flour, kneaded it and baked
bread without yeast. 25Then she set it before Saul and his men, and they ate. That
same night they got up and left.

Achish Sends David Back to Ziklag

29 The Philistines gathered[i] all their
forces at Aphek,[j] and Israel
camped by the spring in Jezreel.[k] 2As the
Philistine rulers marched with their units
of hundreds and thousands, David and his
men were marching at the rear[l] with
Achish. 3The commanders of the Philistines asked, "What about these Hebrews?"
Achish replied, "Is this not David,[m] who
was an officer of Saul king of Israel? He has
already been with me for over a year,[n] and
from the day he left Saul until now, I have
found no fault in him."
4But the Philistine commanders were
angry with him and said, "Send[o] the man
back, that he may return to the place you
assigned him. He must not go with us into
battle, or he will turn[p] against us during
the fighting. How better could he regain
his master's favor than by taking the heads
of our own men? 5Isn't this the David they
sang about in their dances:

"'Saul has slain his thousands,
and David his tens of thousands'?"[q]

6So Achish called David and said to him,

28:12 [u]S Ge 27:36; 1Ki 14:6 **28:13** [v]ver 15; S Lev 19:31; 2Ch 33:6 **28:14** [w]1Sa 15:27 **28:15** [x]S Jdg 16:20 [y]S 1Sa 14:37 [z]S Dt 13:3 **28:17** [a]1Sa 15:28 **28:18** [b]1Sa 15:20 [c]S Dt 9:8; S 1Sa 15:3 [d]S Ge 14:7; S 1Sa 14:48 **28:19** [e]1Sa 31:2; 1Ch 8:33 **28:21** [f]S Jdg 9:17; S 12:3 **28:23** [g]1Ki 21:4 **28:24** [h]S Ge 18:7 **29:1** [i]1Sa 28:1 [j]S 1Sa 4:1 [k]Jos 17:16; 1Ki 18:45; 21:1, 23; 2Ki 9:30; Jer 50:5; Hos 1:4, 5,11; 2:22 **29:2** [l]1Sa 28:2 **29:3** [m]1Ch 12:19 [n]1Sa 27:7 **29:4** [o]1Ch 12:19 [p]1Sa 14:21 **29:5** [q]S 1Sa 18:7

[g]*13* Or *see spirits*; or *see gods*

following: 1. God permitted the spirit of Samuel to appear to the woman. 2. The woman had contact with an evil or devilish spirit in the form of Samuel by whom she was deceived and controlled. 3. By using parapsychological powers such as telepathy or clairvoyance, the woman was able to discern Saul's thoughts and picture Samuel in her own mind. Whatever the explanation of this mysterious affair, the medium was used in some way to convey to Saul that the impending battle would bring death, would dash his hopes for a dynasty and would conclude his reign with a devastating defeat of Israel that would leave the nation at the mercy of the Philistines, the very people against whom he had struggled all his years as king. And this would come, as Samuel had previously announced (15:26,28), because of his unfaithfulness to the Lord. *she cried out . . . You are Saul!* By whatever means, the medium suddenly becomes aware that she is dealing with Saul.

28:14 *An old man wearing a robe.* Saul remembers Samuel as customarily dressed in this apparel (see 15:27).

28:21 *When the woman came to Saul.* This statement suggests that the woman removed herself from the direct view of Saul while she gave her oracles.

29:1 *The Philistines gathered all their forces.* The narrative flow broken at 28:2 is resumed. *Aphek.* A place in the vicinity of Shunem (28:4), to be distinguished from another place of the same name referred to in 4:1 (see 1Ki 20:26,30; 2Ki 13:17).

29:2 *Philistine rulers.* See note on 5:8.

29:3 *I have found no fault in him.* David's tactics described in 27:10–12 were highly successful.

29:4 *the place you assigned him.* See 27:6. *he will turn against us during the fighting.* The Philistines had experienced just such a reversal on a previous occasion (see 14:21).

29:6 *As surely as the LORD lives.* See note on 14:39. Achish swears by the God of Israel apparently as a means of proving his sincerity to David.

"As surely as the LORD lives, you have been reliable, and I would be pleased to have you serve with me in the army. From the day *r* you came to me until now, I have found no fault in you, but the rulers *s* don't approve of you. ⁷Turn back and go in peace; do nothing to displease the Philistine rulers."

⁸"But what have I done?" asked David. "What have you found against your servant from the day I came to you until now? Why can't I go and fight against the enemies of my lord the king?"

⁹Achish answered, "I know that you have been as pleasing in my eyes as an angel *t* of God; nevertheless, the Philistine commanders *u* have said, 'He must not go up with us into battle.' ¹⁰Now get up early, along with your master's servants who have come with you, and leave *v* in the morning as soon as it is light."

¹¹So David and his men got up early in the morning to go back to the land of the Philistines, and the Philistines went up to Jezreel.

David Destroys the Amalekites

30 David and his men reached Ziklag *w* on the third day. Now the Amalekites *x* had raided the Negev and Ziklag. They had attacked Ziklag and burned *y* it, ²and had taken captive the women and all who were in it, both young and old. They killed none of them, but carried them off as they went on their way.

³When David and his men came to Ziklag, they found it destroyed by fire and their wives and sons and daughters taken captive. *z* ⁴So David and his men wept *a* aloud until they had no strength left to weep. ⁵David's two wives *b* had been captured—Ahinoam of Jezreel and Abigail, the widow of Nabal of Carmel. ⁶David was greatly distressed because the men were talking of stoning *c* him; each one was bitter *d* in spirit because of his sons and daughters. But David found strength *e* in the LORD his God.

⁷Then David said to Abiathar *f* the priest, the son of Ahimelech, "Bring me the ephod. *g*" Abiathar brought it to him, ⁸and David inquired *h* of the LORD, "Shall I pursue this raiding party? Will I overtake them?"

"Pursue them," he answered. "You will certainly overtake them and succeed *i* in the rescue. *j* "

⁹David and the six hundred men *k* with him came to the Besor Ravine, where some stayed behind, ¹⁰for two hundred men were too exhausted *l* to cross the ravine. But David and four hundred men continued the pursuit.

¹¹They found an Egyptian in a field and brought him to David. They gave him water to drink and food to eat— ¹²part of a cake of pressed figs and two cakes of raisins. He ate and was revived, *m* for he had not eaten any food or drunk any water for three days and three nights.

¹³David asked him, "To whom do you belong, and where do you come from?"

He said, "I am an Egyptian, the slave of an Amalekite. *n* My master abandoned me when I became ill three days ago. ¹⁴We raided the Negev of the Kerethites *o* and the territory belonging to Judah and the Negev of Caleb. *p* And we burned *q* Ziklag."

¹⁵David asked him, "Can you lead me down to this raiding party?"

He answered, "Swear to me before God that you will not kill me or hand me over to my master, *r* and I will take you down to them."

¹⁶He led David down, and there they were, scattered over the countryside, eating, drinking and reveling *s* because of the great amount of plunder *t* they had taken from the land of the Philistines and from Judah. ¹⁷David fought *u* them from dusk until the evening of the next day, and none of them got away, except four hundred young men who rode off on camels and fled. *v* ¹⁸David recovered *w* everything the Amalekites had taken, including his two

Cross references (center column)

29:6
r 1Sa 27:8-12 *s* ver 3
29:9 *t* 2Sa 14:17, 20; 19:27 *u* ver 4
29:10
v 1Ch 12:19
30:1 *w* S 1Sa 27:6 *x* S 1Sa 27:8 *y* ver 14
30:3 *z* S Ge 31:26
30:4 *a* S Ge 27:38
30:5
b S 1Sa 25:43
30:6 *c* S Ex 17:4; Jn 8:59
d S Ru 1:13
e S 1Sa 23:16; Ro 4:20

30:7 *f* S 1Sa 22:20
g S 1Sa 2:28
30:8 *h* S 1Sa 23:2
i S Ge 14:16
j S Ex 2:17
30:9 *k* S 1Sa 27:2
30:10 *l* ver 21
30:12
m S Jdg 15:19
30:13
n S 1Sa 14:48
30:14 *o* 2Sa 8:18; 15:18; 20:7,23; 1Ki 1:38,44; 1Ch 18:17; Eze 25:16; Zep 2:5
p S Jos 14:13; S 15:13 *q* ver 1
30:15 *r* Dt 23:15
30:16 *s* Lk 12:19
t S ver 17; S Jos 22:8
30:17 *u* ver 16; 1Sa 11:11; 2Sa 1:1 *v* 2Sa 1:8
30:18
w S Ge 14:16

29:8 *But what have I done?* David pretends disappointment in order to keep intact his strategy of deception. In reality this turn of events rescued David from a serious dilemma. *Why can't I go and fight against the enemies of my lord the king?* David again uses an ambiguous statement (see 28:2). To whom was he referring as "my lord the king"—Achish or Saul or the Lord?
29:9 *as an angel of God.* A common simile.
29:11 *Jezreel.* The place of Israel's camp (see v. 1).
30:1–31:13 While Saul goes to his death at the hands of the Philistines, David is drawn into and pursues the Lord's continuing war with the Amalekites (see 15:2–3 and notes).
30:1 *Ziklag.* See note on 27:6. *Amalekites.* See 27:8 and

note on 15:2. The absence of David and his warriors gave the Amalekites opportunity for revenge. *Negev.* See note on 27:10.
30:5 *Ahinoam.* See note on 25:43. *Abigail.* See 25:42.
30:7 *Abiathar the priest.* See note on 22:20. *ephod.* See note on 2:28.
30:14 *Negev.* See note on 27:10. *Kerethites.* Along with the Pelethites, they later contributed contingents of professional warriors to David's private army (see 2Sa 15:18; 20:7; 1Ki 1:38). The name may indicate that they originally came from the island of Crete (see Am 9:7 and NIV text note there). *Negev of Caleb.* The area south of Hebron (see Jos 14:13).

wives. ¹⁹Nothing was missing: young or old, boy or girl, plunder or anything else they had taken. David brought everything back. ²⁰He took all the flocks and herds, and his men drove them ahead of the other livestock, saying, "This is David's plunder."

²¹Then David came to the two hundred men who had been too exhausted ˣ to follow him and who were left behind at the Besor Ravine. They came out to meet David and the people with him. As David and his men approached, he greeted them. ²²But all the evil men and troublemakers among David's followers said, "Because they did not go out with us, we will not share with them the plunder we recovered. However, each man may take his wife and children and go."

²³David replied, "No, my brothers, you must not do that with what the LORD has given us. He has protected us and handed over to us the forces that came against us. ²⁴Who will listen to what you say? The share of the man who stayed with the supplies is to be the same as that of him who went down to the battle. All will share alike. ʸ" ²⁵David made this a statute and ordinance for Israel from that day to this.

²⁶When David arrived in Ziklag, he sent some of the plunder to the elders of Judah, who were his friends, saying, "Here is a present ᶻ for you from the plunder of the LORD's enemies."

²⁷He sent it to those who were in Bethel, ᵃ Ramoth ᵇ Negev and Jattir; ᶜ ²⁸to those in Aroer, ᵈ Siphmoth, ᵉ Eshtemoa ᶠ ²⁹and Racal; to those in the towns of the Jerahmeelites ᵍ and the Kenites; ʰ ³⁰to those in Hormah, ⁱ Bor Ashan, ʲ Athach ³¹and Hebron; ᵏ and to those in all the other places where David and his men had roamed.

Saul Takes His Life

31:1–13pp — 2Sa 1:4–12; 1Ch 10:1–12

31 Now the Philistines fought against Israel; the Israelites fled before them, and many fell slain on Mount Gilboa. ˡ ²The Philistines pressed hard after Saul and his sons, ᵐ and they killed his sons Jonathan, ⁿ Abinadab and Malki-Shua. ᵒ ³The fighting grew fierce around Saul, and when the archers overtook him, they wounded ᵖ him critically.

⁴Saul said to his armor-bearer, "Draw your sword and run me through, ᑫ or these uncircumcised ʳ fellows will come and run me through and abuse me."

But his armor-bearer was terrified and would not do it; so Saul took his own sword and fell on it. ⁵When the armor-bearer saw that Saul was dead, he too fell on his sword and died with him. ⁶So Saul and his three sons and his armor-bearer and all his men died ˢ together that same day.

⁷When the Israelites along the valley and those across the Jordan saw that the Israelite army had fled and that Saul and his sons had died, they abandoned their towns and fled. And the Philistines came and occupied them.

⁸The next day, when the Philistines ᵗ came to strip the dead, they found Saul and his three sons fallen on Mount Gilboa. ⁹They cut off his head and stripped off his armor, and they sent messengers throughout the land of the Philistines to proclaim the news ᵘ in the temple of their idols and among their people. ᵛ ¹⁰They put his armor in the temple of the Ashtoreths ʷ and fastened his body to the wall of Beth Shan. ˣ

¹¹When the people of Jabesh Gilead ʸ heard of what the Philistines had done to Saul, ¹²all their valiant men ᶻ journeyed

Cross references (center column)

30:21 ˣver 10
30:24
ʸNu 31:27;
S Jdg 5:30
30:26
ᶻS Ge 33:11
30:27 ᵃS Jos 7:2
ᵇS Jos 10:40
ᶜS Jos 15:48
30:28
ᵈS Nu 32:34;
S Jos 13:16
ᵉ1Ch 27:27
ᶠS Jos 15:50
30:29 ᵍ1Sa 27:10
ʰS 1Sa 15:6
30:30
ⁱS Nu 14:45;
S 21:3
ʲS Jos 15:42
30:31
ᵏNu 13:22;
S Jos 10:36;
2Sa 2:1,4

31:1 ˡS 1Sa 28:4
31:2
ᵐS 1Sa 28:19
ⁿS 1Sa 18:1
ᵒS 1Sa 14:49
31:3 ᵖS 1Sa 28:4
31:4 ᑫS Jdg 9:54
ʳS Ge 34:14;
S 1Sa 14:6
31:6
ˢS 1Sa 26:10
31:8 ᵗ2Sa 1:20
31:9 ᵘ2Sa 1:20;
4:4 ᵛS Jdg 16:24
31:10
ʷS Jdg 2:12-13;
S 1Sa 7:3
ˣS Jos 17:11
31:11
ʸS Jdg 21:8;
S 1Sa 11:1
31:12 ᶻPs 76:5

30:22 *troublemakers.* See note on Dt 13:13.

30:23 *what the LORD has given us.* David gently but firmly rejects the idea that their victory is to be attributed to their own prowess. Because the Lord gave the victory, no segment of David's men could claim any greater right to the spoils than any other.

30:26 *elders of Judah, who were his friends.* David sent the plunder as an expression of gratitude to those who had assisted him during his flight from Saul (see v. 31), thus preparing the way for his later elevation to kingship in Judah (see 2Sa 2:1–4).

30:29 *Jerahmeelites.* See note on 27:10. *Kenites.* See note on 15:6.

30:31 *Hebron.* The most important city in the southern part of Judah. The other locations mentioned are to the southwest and southeast of Hebron.

31:2 *Jonathan, Abinadab and Malki-Shua.* See note on 14:49. The surviving son, Ish-Bosheth or Esh-Baal (1Ch 8:33; 9:39), was afterward promoted by Abner, who some-

how survived the battle, to succeed his father as king (2Sa 2:8–9).

31:4 *uncircumcised fellows.* See 14:6 and note. *abuse me.* A practice that was not uncommon; previously the Philistines had mutilated and humiliated Samson after his capture (see Jdg 16:23–25). *took his own sword and fell on it.* The culmination of a long process of self-destruction.

31:6 *all his men.* Those who had served around him in his administration (but see note on v. 2).

31:9 *They cut off his head.* David had done the same to Goliath (see 17:51). *sent messengers throughout the land.* Probably bearing Saul's head and armor as proof and trophies of their victory.

31:10 *They put his armor in the temple.* Symbolic of ascribing the victory to the Philistine gods.

31:11 *Jabesh Gilead.* See note on 11:1.

31:12 *They took down the bodies of Saul and his sons.* The men of Jabesh Gilead had not forgotten how Saul had come to their defense when they were threatened by the

through the night to Beth Shan. They took down the bodies of Saul and his sons from the wall of Beth Shan and went to Jabesh, where they burned[a] them. [13]Then they

31:12
[a]S Ge 38:24;
Am 6:10

31:13
[b]2Sa 21:12-14
[c]S Ge 21:33

took their bones[b] and buried them under a tamarisk[c] tree at Jabesh, and they fasted[d] seven days.[e]

[d]2Sa 3:35; 12:19-23 [e]S Ge 50:10

Ammonites (see ch. 11). *burned them.* Cremation was not customary in ancient Israel and here appears to have been done to prevent any further abuse of the bodies of Saul and his sons by the Philistines.

31:13 *took their bones and buried them.* David later had

their remains removed from Jabesh and placed in the family burial grounds of Zela in Benjamin (see 2Sa 21:12–14). *fasted seven days.* As an indication of their mourning for Saul (cf. 2Sa 1:12; 3:35; 12:16,21–23).

2 SAMUEL

Title

1 and 2 Samuel were originally one book (see Introduction to 1 Samuel: Title).

Literary Features, Authorship and Date

See Introduction to 1 Samuel: Literary Features, Authorship and Date.

Contents and Theme: Kingship and Covenant

2 Samuel depicts David as a true (though imperfect) representative of the ideal theocratic king. David was initially acclaimed king at Hebron by the tribe of Judah (chs. 1-4), and subsequently was accepted by the remaining tribes after the murder of Ish-Bosheth, one of Saul's surviving sons (5:1-5). David's leadership was decisive and effective. He captured Jerusalem from the Jebusites and made it his royal city and residence (5:6-14). Shortly afterward he brought the ark of the Lord from the house of Abinadab to Jerusalem, publicly acknowledging the Lord's kingship and rule over himself and the nation (ch. 6; Ps 132:3-5).

Under David's rule the Lord caused the nation to prosper, to defeat its enemies and, in fulfillment of his promise (see Ge 15:18), to extend its borders from Egypt to the Euphrates (ch. 8). David wanted to build a temple for the Lord—as his royal house, as a place for his throne (the ark) and as a place for Israel to worship him. But the prophet Nathan told David that he was not to build the Lord a house (temple); rather, the Lord would build David a house (dynasty). Ch. 7 announces the Lord's promise that this Davidic dynasty would endure forever. This climactic chapter also describes the establishment of the Davidic covenant (see Ps 89:34-37), a covenant that promises ultimate victory over the evil one through the offspring of Eve (see Ge 3:15 and note). This promise—which had come to be focused on Shem and his descendants (see Ge 9:26-27 and notes), then on Abraham and his descendants (see Ge 12:2-3; 13:16; 15:5 and notes) and then on Judah and his (royal) descendants (see Ge 49:8-11 and notes)—is now focused specifically on the royal family of David. Later the prophets make clear that a descendant of David who sits on David's throne will perfectly fulfill the role of the theocratic king. He will complete the redemption of God's people (see Isa 9:6-7; 11:1-16; Jer 23:5-6; 30:8-9; 33:14-16; Eze 34:23-24; 37:24-25), thus enabling them to achieve the promised victory with him (Ro 16:20).

After the description of David's rule in its glory and success, chs. 10-20 depict the darker side of his reign and describe David's weaknesses and failures. Even though David remained a king after God's own heart because he was willing to acknowledge his sin and repent (12:13), he nevertheless fell far short of the theocratic ideal and suffered the disciplinary results of his disobedience (12:10-12). His sin with Bathsheba (chs. 11-12) and his leniency both with the wickedness of his sons (13:21; 14:1,33; 19:4-6) and with the insubordination of Joab (3:29,39; 20:10,23) led to intrigue, violence and bloodshed within his own family and the nation. It eventually drove him from Jerusalem at the time of Absalom's rebellion. Nonetheless the Lord was gracious to David, and his reign became a standard by which the reigns of later kings were measured (see 2Ki 18:3; 22:2).

The book ends with David's own words of praise to God, who had delivered him from all his enemies (22:31-51), and with words of expectation for the fulfillment of God's promise that a king will come from the house of David and rule "over men in righteousness" (23:3-5). These songs echo many of the themes of Hannah's song (1Sa 2:1-10), and together they frame (and interpret) the basic narrative.

Chronology

See Introduction to 1 Samuel: Chronology.

Outline

Below is an abbreviated outline for 2 Samuel. For the complete outline see Introduction to 1 Samuel: Outline.

IV. David's Rise to the Throne; Progressive Deterioration and End of Saul's Reign (1Sa 16:1-2Sa 5:5)
   A. David Is Anointed Privately, Enters the Service of King Saul and Flees for His Life (1Sa 16-26)
   B. David Seeks Refuge in Philistia, and Saul and His Sons Are Killed in Battle (1Sa 27-31)
   C. David Becomes King over Judah (2Sa 1-4)
   D. David Becomes King over All Israel (2Sa 5:1-5)
V. David's Kingship in Its Accomplishments and Glory (2Sa 5:6-9:12)
   A. David Conquers Jerusalem and Defeats the Philistines (2Sa 5:6-25)
   B. David Brings the Ark to Jerusalem (2Sa 6)
   C. God Promises David an Everlasting Dynasty (2Sa 7)
   D. The Extension of David's Kingdom Externally and the Justice of His Rule Internally (2Sa 8)
   E. David's Faithfulness to His Covenant with Jonathan (2Sa 9)
VI. David's Kingship in Its Weaknesses and Failures (2Sa 10-20)
   A. David Commits Adultery and Murder (2Sa 10-12)
   B. David Loses His Sons Amnon and Absalom (2Sa 13-20)
VII. Final Reflections on David's Reign (2Sa 21-24)

David Hears of Saul's Death

1:4–12pp — 1Sa 31:1–13; 1Ch 10:1–12

1 After the death[a] of Saul, David returned from defeating[b] the Amalekites[c] and stayed in Ziklag two days. [2]On the third day a man[d] arrived from Saul's camp, with his clothes torn and with dust on his head. [e] When he came to David, he fell[f] to the ground to pay him honor.[g]

[3]"Where have you come from?" David asked him.

He answered, "I have escaped from the Israelite camp."

[4]"What happened?" David asked. "Tell me."

He said, "The men fled from the battle. Many of them fell and died. And Saul and his son Jonathan are dead."

[5]Then David said to the young man who brought him the report, "How do you know that Saul and his son Jonathan are dead?"

[6]"I happened to be on Mount Gilboa,[h]" the young man said, "and there was Saul, leaning on his spear, with the chariots and riders almost upon him. [7]When he turned around and saw me, he called out to me, and I said, 'What can I do?'

[8]"He asked me, 'Who are you?'

" 'An Amalekite,[i]' I answered.

[9]"Then he said to me, 'Stand over me and kill me![j] I am in the throes of death, but I'm still alive.'

[10]"So I stood over him and killed him, because I knew that after he had fallen he could not survive. And I took the crown[k]

that was on his head and the band on his arm and have brought them here to my lord."

[11]Then David and all the men with him took hold of their clothes and tore[l] them. [12]They mourned and wept and fasted till evening for Saul and his son Jonathan, and for the army of the LORD and the house of Israel, because they had fallen by the sword.

[13]David said to the young man who brought him the report, "Where are you from?"

"I am the son of an alien, an Amalekite,[m]" he answered.

[14]David asked him, "Why were you not afraid to lift your hand to destroy the LORD's anointed?[n]"

[15]Then David called one of his men and said, "Go, strike him down!"[o] So he struck him down, and he died. [p] [16]For David had said to him, "Your blood be on your own head. [q] Your own mouth testified against you when you said, 'I killed the LORD's anointed.' "

David's Lament for Saul and Jonathan

[17]David took up this lament[r] concerning Saul and his son Jonathan,[s] [18]and ordered that the men of Judah be taught this lament of the bow (it is written in the Book of Jashar):[t]

[19]"Your glory, O Israel, lies slain on your heights.

Cross references (center column)

1:1 [a]S 1Sa 26:10; 1Ch 10:13
[b]S Jos 22:8; S 1Sa 30:17
[c]S Ge 14:7; Nu 13:29
1:2 [d]2Sa 4:10
[e]S 1Sa 4:12; Job 2:12; Eze 27:30
[f]S 1Sa 20:41
[g]S Ge 37:7
1:6 [h]ver 21; S 1Sa 28:4
1:8 [i]ver 13; S 1Sa 15:2; S 27:8; 30:13,17
1:9 [j]S Jdg 9:54
1:10 [k]2Ki 11:12
1:11 [l]S Ge 37:29; S Nu 14:6
1:13 [m]S ver 8; S 1Sa 14:48
1:14 [n]S 1Sa 12:3; S 26:9
1:15 [o]2Sa 4:12
[p]2Sa 4:10
1:16 [q]S Lev 20:9; Mt 27:24-25; Ac 18:6
1:17 [r]S Ge 50:10; S Eze 32:2 [s]ver 26
1:18 [t]Jos 10:13

1:1 *After the death of.* See Jos 1:1; Jdg 1:1. The narrative thread of 1 Samuel is continued. 1 and 2 Samuel were originally one book (see Introduction to 1 Samuel: Title). *David returned from defeating the Amalekites.* See 1Sa 30:26. *Ziklag.* See note on 1Sa 27:6.
1:2 *his clothes torn . . . dust on his head.* See note on 1Sa 4:12; see also Jos 7:6; Ac 14:14.
1:8 *Amalekite.* It is not necessary to conclude from v. 3 that this Amalekite was a member of Saul's army. His statement that he "happened to be on Mount Gilboa" (v. 6) is probably not as innocent as it appears. He may have been there as a scavenger to rob the fallen soldiers of their valuables and weapons. It is ironic that Saul's death is reported by an Amalekite (see 1Sa 15).
1:10 *I stood over him and killed him.* The Amalekite's story conflicts with 1Sa 31:3–6, where David is depicted as taking his own life. It appears that the Amalekite fabricated this version of Saul's death, expecting David to reward him (see 4:10). His miscalculation of David's response cost him his life (see v. 15). *I took the crown.* Apparently he got to Saul before the Philistines did (see 1Sa 31:8–9).
1:11 *took hold of their clothes and tore them.* See note on 1Sa 4:12.
1:12 *mourned and wept.* David and his men expressed their grief in typical Near Eastern fashion (see Ge 23:2; 1Ki 13:30; Jer 22:18). *fasted.* See 3:35; 1Sa 31:13.
1:13 *Amalekite.* The man was probably unaware of David's

recent hostile encounters with the Amalekites (see v. 1; 1Sa 30; see also note on 1Sa 15:2).
1:14 The Amalekite understood nothing of the deep significance that David attached to the sanctity of the royal office in Israel (see note on 1Sa 24:6). *the LORD's anointed.* See note on 1Sa 9:16.
1:15 *strike him down!* David displays no personal satisfaction over Saul's death and condemns to death the one he believes to be his murderer (see note on v. 10; see also 4:10).
1:16 *Your blood be on your own head.* The Amalekite's own testimony brought about his execution (see Jos 2:19; 1Ki 2:37).
1:17 *lament.* It was a common practice in the ancient Near East to compose laments for fallen leaders and/or heroes.
1:18 *lament of the bow.* Perhaps David taught his men to sing this lament while they practiced the bow (Israel's most common weapon; see, e.g., 22:35) as a motivation to master the weapon thoroughly so they would not experience a similar defeat (see note on Eze 21:9). *Book of Jashar.* See note on Jos 10:13.
1:19 *Your glory.* A reference to Saul and Jonathan as divinely designated leaders of God's covenant people, who had achieved many significant victories over Israel's enemies (see 1Sa 14:47–48 and note). *heights.* Of Gilboa (see vv. 21,25; 1Sa 31:1). *How the mighty have fallen!* The theme of David's lament (see v. 27). David's words contain no suggestion of bitterness toward Saul but rather recall the good qualities

How the mighty[u] have fallen![v]

20"Tell it not in Gath,[w]
proclaim it not in the streets of
Ashkelon,[x]
lest the daughters of the Philistines[y] be
glad,
lest the daughters of the
uncircumcised rejoice.[z]

21"O mountains of Gilboa,[a]
may you have neither dew[b] nor
rain,[c]
nor fields that yield offerings[d] of
grain.
For there the shield of the mighty was
defiled,
the shield of Saul—no longer rubbed
with oil.[e]

22From the blood[f] of the slain,
from the flesh of the mighty,
the bow[g] of Jonathan did not turn
back,
the sword of Saul did not return
unsatisfied.

23"Saul and Jonathan—
in life they were loved and gracious,
and in death they were not parted.
They were swifter than eagles,[h]
they were stronger than lions.[i]

24"O daughters of Israel,
weep for Saul,
who clothed you in scarlet and finery,
who adorned your garments with
ornaments of gold.[j]

25"How the mighty have fallen in battle!

Jonathan lies slain on your heights.
26I grieve[k] for you, Jonathan[l] my
brother;[m]
you were very dear to me.
Your love for me was wonderful,[n]
more wonderful than that of women.

27"How the mighty have fallen!
The weapons of war have
perished!"[o]

David Anointed King Over Judah

2 In the course of time, David inquired[p]
of the LORD. "Shall I go up to one of
the towns of Judah?" he asked.
The LORD said, "Go up."
David asked, "Where shall I go?"
"To Hebron,"[q] the LORD answered.
2So David went up there with his two
wives,[r] Ahinoam of Jezreel and Abigail,[s]
the widow of Nabal of Carmel. 3David also
took the men who were with him,[t] each
with his family, and they settled in Hebron[u] and its towns. 4Then the men of
Judah came to Hebron[v] and there they
anointed[w] David king over the house of
Judah.
When David was told that it was the
men of Jabesh Gilead[x] who had buried
Saul, 5he sent messengers to the men of
Jabesh Gilead to say to them, "The LORD
bless[y] you for showing this kindness to
Saul your master by burying him. 6May the
LORD now show you kindness and faithfulness,[z] and I too will show you the same
favor because you have done this. 7Now
then, be strong[a] and brave, for Saul your

Cross references (center column):

1:19 [u]2Sa 23:8;
Ps 29:1; 45:3
[v]2Sa 3:38
1:20 [w]Mic 1:10
[x]Jos 13:3
[y]1Sa 31:8
[z]S 1Sa 18:6
1:21 [a]S ver 6
[b]S Ge 27:28;
S Isa 18:4
[c]Dt 11:17;
1Ki 8:35; 17:1;
18:1; 2Ch 6:26;
Job 36:27; 38:28;
Ps 65:10; 147:8;
Isa 5:6; Jer 5:24;
14:4; Am 1:2
[d]Jer 12:4;
Eze 31:15
[e]Isa 21:5
1:22 [f]Isa 34:3,7;
49:26 [g]Dt 32:42
1:23 [h]S Dt 28:49
[i]Jdg 14:18
1:24 [j]S Jdg 5:30

1:26 [k]Jer 22:18;
34:5 [l]ver 17
[m]S 1Sa 20:42
[n]S 1Sa 18:1
1:27 [o]S 1Sa 2:4
2:1 [p]S 1Sa 23:2,
11-12
[q]S Ge 13:18;
S 23:19
2:2 [r]S 1Sa 25:43
[s]S 1Sa 25:42
2:3 [t]S 1Sa 27:2;
1Ch 12:22
[u]S Ge 13:18;
23:2; 37:14
2:4 [v]S 1Sa 30:31
[w]S 1Sa 2:35;
2Sa 5:3-5;
1Ch 12:23-40
[x]S Jdg 21:8;
S 1Sa 11:1
2:5 [y]S Jdg 17:2;
S 1Sa 23:21;
2Ti 1:16
2:6 [z]Ex 34:6
2:7 [a]S Jos 1:6;
S Jdg 5:21

---

and accomplishments of Saul and Jonathan.
1:20 *Tell it not in Gath . . . Ashkelon.* As the major Philistine cities located the closest and farthest from Israel's borders, Gath and Ashkelon represent the entire Philistine nation. David does not want the enemies of God's covenant
people to take pleasure in Israel's defeat (as he knew they
would; see 1Sa 31:9–10) and thus bring reproach on the
name of the Lord (see Ex 32:12; Nu 14:13–19; Dt 9:28; Jos
7:9; Mic 1:10). *uncircumcised.* See note on 1Sa 14:6.
1:21 *O mountains of Gilboa.* As an expression of profound
grief, David rhetorically pronounces a curse on the place
where Israel was defeated and Saul and Jonathan were killed
(for other such rhetorical curses see Job 3:3–26; Jer
20:14–18). *no longer rubbed with oil.* Leather shields were
rubbed with oil to preserve them (but see note on Isa 21:5).
1:23 *in death they were not parted.* Even though Jonathan
opposed his father's treatment of David, he gave his life
beside his father in Israel's defense.
1:26 *more wonderful than that of women.* David is not
suggesting that marital love is inferior to that of friendship,
nor do his remarks have any sexual implications. He is simply
calling attention to Jonathan's nearly inexplicable self-de-
nying commitment to David, whom he had long recognized
as the Lord's choice to succeed his father rather than himself
(see notes on 1Sa 20:13–16).
1:27 *weapons of war.* Probably a metaphor for Saul and
Jonathan.

2:1 *David inquired of the LORD.* By means of the ephod
through the priest Abiathar (see notes on Ex 28:30; 1Sa
2:28; 23:2). *one of the towns of Judah.* Even though Saul
was dead and David had many friends and contacts among
the people of his own tribe (see 1Sa 30:26–31), David did
not presume to return from Philistine territory to assume the
kingship promised to him without first seeking the Lord's
guidance. *Hebron.* An old and important city (see Ge 13:18;
23:2; Jos 15:13–15; see also note on 1Sa 30:31) centrally
located in the tribe of Judah.
2:2 *Ahinoam of Jezreel.* See note on 1Sa 25:43. *Abigail.*
See 1Sa 25.
2:3 *men who were with him.* See 1Sa 22:2; 23:13; 30:3,9.
2:4 *anointed David king.* See notes on 1Sa 2:10; 9:16.
David had previously been anointed privately by Samuel in
the presence of his own family (see note on 1Sa 16:13). Here
the anointing ceremony is repeated as a public recognition by
his own tribe of his divine calling to be king. *over the house
of Judah.* Very likely the tribe of Simeon was also involved
(see Jos 19:1; Jdg 1:3), but the Judahites in every way
dominated the area. *men of Jabesh Gilead.* See notes on 1Sa
11:1; 31:12. *buried Saul.* See note on 1Sa 31:13.
2:7 *your master is dead, and the house of Judah has
anointed me king over them.* David's concluding statement
to the men of Jabesh Gilead is a veiled invitation to them to
recognize him as their king just as the tribe of Judah had
done. This appeal for their support, however, was ignored

master is dead, and the house of Judah has anointed me king over them."

War Between the Houses of David and Saul

3:2–5pp — 1Ch 3:1–4

8Meanwhile, Abner b son of Ner, the commander of Saul's army, had taken Ish-Bosheth c son of Saul and brought him over to Mahanaim. d 9He made him king over Gilead, e Ashuri a f and Jezreel, and also over Ephraim, Benjamin and all Israel. g

10Ish-Bosheth son of Saul was forty years old when he became king over Israel, and he reigned two years. The house of Judah, however, followed David. 11The length of time David was king in Hebron over the house of Judah was seven years and six months. h

12Abner son of Ner, together with the men of Ish-Bosheth son of Saul, left Mahanaim and went to Gibeon. i 13Joab j son of Zeruiah and David's men went out and met them at the pool of Gibeon. One group sat down on one side of the pool and one group on the other side.

14Then Abner said to Joab, "Let's have some of the young men get up and fight hand to hand in front of us."

"All right, let them do it," Joab said.

15So they stood up and were counted off—twelve men for Benjamin and Ish-Bosheth son of Saul, and twelve for David. 16Then each man grabbed his opponent by the head and thrust his dagger k into his opponent's side, and they fell down together. So that place in Gibeon was called Helkath Hazzurim. b

17The battle that day was very fierce, and Abner and the men of Israel were defeated l by David's men. m

18The three sons of Zeruiah n were there: Joab, o Abishai p and Asahel. q Now Asahel was as fleet-footed as a wild gazelle. r 19He chased Abner, turning neither to the right nor to the left as he pursued him. 20Abner looked behind him and asked, "Is that you, Asahel?"

"It is," he answered.

21Then Abner said to him, "Turn aside to the right or to the left; take on one of the young men and strip him of his weapons." But Asahel would not stop chasing him.

22Again Abner warned Asahel, "Stop chasing me! Why should I strike you down? How could I look your brother Joab in the face?" s

23But Asahel refused to give up the pur-

Cross references

2:8 b S 1Sa 14:50; S 2Sa 3:27
c 2Sa 4:5;
1Ch 8:33; 9:39
d S Ge 32:2
2:9 e S Nu 32:26
f S Jos 19:24-31
g 1Ch 12:29
2:11 h 2Sa 5:5
2:12 i S Jos 9:3
2:13 j 2Sa 8:16; 19:13; 1Ki 1:7; 1Ch 2:16; 11:6; 27:34
2:16 k S Jdg 3:21
2:17 l 2Sa 3:1
m S 1Sa 17:8
2:18 n 2Sa 3:39; 16:10; 19:22
o 2Sa 3:30; 10:7; 11:1; 14:1; 18:14; 20:8; 24:3; 1Ki 1:7; 2:5,34
p S 1Sa 26:6
q 2Sa 23:24; 1Ch 2:16; 11:26; 27:7 r 1Ch 12:8; Pr 6:5; SS 2:9
2:22 s 2Sa 3:27

a 9 Or Asher   b 16 Helkath Hazzurim means field of daggers or field of hostilities.

(see 1Sa 2:8–9).

2:8 *Abner son of Ner.* See note on 1Sa 14:50. *Saul's army.* His small standing army of professionals loyal to him and his family (see 1Sa 13:2,15; 14:2,52). *Ish-Bosheth.* The name was originally Ish-(or Esh-)Baal (1Ch 8:33) but was changed by the author of Samuel to Ish-Bosheth, meaning "man of the shameful thing" (see note on 4:4). Evidently Baal (meaning "lord" or "master") was at this time still used to refer to the Lord. Later this was discontinued because of confusion with the Canaanite god Baal, and the author of Samuel reflects the later sensitivity. *son of Saul.* See notes on 1Sa 14:49; 31:2. *brought him.* Abner takes the initiative in the power vacuum created by Saul's death, using the unassertive Ish-Bosheth as a pawn for his own ambitions (see 3:11; see also note on 4:1). There is no evidence that Ish-Bosheth had strong support among the Israelites generally. *Mahanaim.* A Gileadite town in Transjordan and thus beyond the sphere of Philistine domination—a kind of refugee capital.

2:9 *He made him king.* As a nephew of Saul (see note on 1Sa 14:50), Abner had both a family and a career interest in ensuring dynastic succession for Saul's house. *Gilead . . . all Israel.* This delineation of Ish-Bosheth's realm suggests that his actual rule, while involving territory both east and west of the Jordan, was quite limited and that the last entry ("all Israel") was more claim than reality. David ruled over Judah and Simeon, and the Philistines controlled large sections of the northern tribal regions.

2:11 *seven years and six months.* Cf. Ish-Bosheth's two-year reign in Mahanaim (v. 10). Because it appears that David was made king over all Israel shortly after Ish-Bosheth's death (5:1–5) and moved his capital to Jerusalem not long afterward (5:6–12), reconciling the lengths of David's and Ish-Bosheth's reigns is difficult. The difficulty is

best resolved by assuming that it took Ish-Bosheth a number of years to be recognized as his father's successor, and that the two years of his reign roughly correspond to the last two or three years of David's reign in Hebron.

2:12 Abner initiates an action to prevent David's sphere of influence from spreading northward out of Judah. Gibeon was located in the tribal area of Benjamin, to which Saul and his family belonged, and which the Philistines had not occupied.

2:13 *Joab son of Zeruiah.* See note on 1Sa 26:6. Joab became a figure of major importance during David's reign as a competent but ruthless military leader (see 10:7–14; 11:1; 12:26; 1Ki 11:15–16). At times David was unable to control him (3:39; 18:5,14; 1Ki 2:5–6), and he was eventually executed for his wanton assassinations and his part in the conspiracy to place Adonijah rather than Solomon on David's throne (1Ki 2:28–34). *David's men.* Some, at least, of David's small force of professionals that had gathered around him (see 1Sa 22:1–2; 23:13; 27:2; 30:9).

2:15 *Benjamin.* At this time Ish-Bosheth seems to have been supported mainly by his own tribesmen.

2:17 *The battle that day was very fierce.* Because the representative combat (see note on 1Sa 17:4) by 12 men from each side was indecisive, a full-scale battle ensued in which David's forces were victorious. The attempt to use representative combat to avoid the decimation of civil war failed (see 3:1).

2:21 *Turn aside.* Abner tried unsuccessfully to avoid the necessity of killing Asahel.

2:22 *How could I look your brother Joab in the face?* Abner did not want the hostility between himself and Joab to be intensified by the practice of blood revenge (see note on 3:27).

suit; so Abner thrust the butt of his spear into Asahel's stomach, [t] and the spear came out through his back. He fell there and died on the spot. And every man stopped when he came to the place where Asahel had fallen and died. [u]

24But Joab and Abishai pursued Abner, and as the sun was setting, they came to the hill of Ammah, near Giah on the way to the wasteland of Gibeon. 25Then the men of Benjamin rallied behind Abner. They formed themselves into a group and took their stand on top of a hill.

26Abner called out to Joab, "Must the sword devour[v] forever? Don't you realize that this will end in bitterness? How long before you order your men to stop pursuing their brothers?"

27Joab answered, "As surely as God lives, if you had not spoken, the men would have continued the pursuit of their brothers until morning.[c]"

28So Joab[w] blew the trumpet,[x] and all the men came to a halt; they no longer pursued Israel, nor did they fight anymore.

29All that night Abner and his men marched through the Arabah.[y] They crossed the Jordan, continued through the whole Bithron[d] and came to Mahanaim.[z]

30Then Joab returned from pursuing Abner and assembled all his men. Besides Asahel, nineteen of David's men were found missing. 31But David's men had killed three hundred and sixty Benjamites who were with Abner. 32They took Asahel and buried him in his father's tomb[a] at Bethlehem. Then Joab and his men marched all night and arrived at Hebron by daybreak.

3 The war between the house of Saul and the house of David lasted a long time.[b] David grew stronger and stronger,[c]

while the house of Saul grew weaker and weaker. [d]

2Sons were born to David in Hebron:
His firstborn was Amnon[e] the son of Ahinoam[f] of Jezreel;
3his second, Kileab the son of Abigail[g] the widow of Nabal of Carmel;
the third, Absalom[h] the son of Maacah daughter of Talmai king of Geshur;[i]
4the fourth, Adonijah[j] the son of Haggith;
the fifth, Shephatiah the son of Abital;
5and the sixth, Ithream the son of David's wife Eglah.
These were born to David in Hebron.

Abner Goes Over to David

6During the war between the house of Saul and the house of David, Abner[k] had been strengthening his own position in the house of Saul. 7Now Saul had had a concubine[l] named Rizpah[m] daughter of Aiah. And Ish-Bosheth said to Abner, "Why did you sleep with my father's concubine?"

8Abner was very angry because of what Ish-Bosheth said and he answered, "Am I a dog's head[n]—on Judah's side? This very day I am loyal to the house of your father Saul and to his family and friends. I haven't handed you over to David. Yet now you accuse me of an offense involving this woman! 9May God deal with Abner, be it ever so severely, if I do not do for David

Cross references

2:23 [t]2Sa 3:27; 4:6 [u]2Sa 20:12
2:26 [v]S Dt 32:42; Jer 46:10,14; Na 2:13; 3:15
2:28 [w]2Sa 18:16; 20:23 [x]S Jdg 3:27
2:29 [y]S Dt 3:17 [z]S Ge 32:2
2:32 [a]S Ge 49:29
3:1 [b]1Ki 14:30 [c]2Sa 5:10

[d]2Sa 2:17; 22:44; Est 9:4
3:2 [e]2Sa 13:1 [f]S 1Sa 25:43
3:3 [g]S 1Sa 25:42 [h]2Sa 13:1,28 [i]2Sa 13:37; 14:32; 15:8
3:4 [j]1Ki 1:5,11; 2:13,22
3:6 [k]S 1Sa 14:50
3:7 [l]S Ge 22:24; 2Sa 16:21-22; S 1Ki 1:3 [m]2Sa 21:8-11
3:8 [n]S 1Sa 17:43; 2Sa 9:8; 16:9; 2Ki 8:13

c27 Or *spoken this morning, the men would not have taken up the pursuit of their brothers*; or *spoken, the men would have given up the pursuit of their brothers by morning*   d29 Or *morning*; or *ravine*; the meaning of the Hebrew for this word is uncertain.

2:26 *Must the sword devour forever?* Abner proposes an armistice as a means of avoiding the awful consequences of civil war.
2:27 *As surely as God lives.* An oath formula (see note on 1Sa 14:39).
2:28 *nor did they fight anymore.* For the present the open conflict ceased, but the hostility remained (see 3:1).
2:29 *Arabah.* See note on Dt 1:1.
3:2–5 The list of six sons born to David in Hebron is given as an evidence of the strengthening of David's house in contrast to that of Saul (v. 1). That these six sons were each born of a different mother tells us that David married four additional wives (see 2:2) during his time in Hebron. The writer does not offer any direct criticism of this polygamous practice (see 5:13), which conflicts with Dt 17:17, but he lets the disastrous results in David's family life speak for themselves (see chs. 13–19; 1Ki 1–2). *Amnon.* Later raped his sister Tamar and was killed by his brother Absalom (see ch. 13). *Ahinoam of Jezreel.* See note on 1Sa 25:43.
3:3 *Kileab.* Called Daniel in 1Ch 3:1. *Abigail.* See 1Sa 25.

Absalom. Later avenged the rape of Tamar by killing Amnon, and conspired against his father David in an attempt to make himself king (see chs. 13–18). *Maacah daughter of Talmai.* David's marriage to Maacah undoubtedly had political implications. With Talmai as an ally on Ish-Bosheth's northern border, David flanked the northern kingdom both south and north. *Geshur.* A small Aramean city kingdom (see 15:8) located northeast of the Sea of Galilee (see Jos 12:5; 13:11–13).
3:4 *Adonijah.* Was put to death for attempting to take over the throne before Solomon could be crowned (see 1Ki 1–2).
3:7 *Rizpah.* See 21:8–11. *Why did you sleep with my father's concubine?* Ish-Bosheth suspects that Abner's act was part of a conspiracy to seize the kingship (cf. v. 6). Great significance was attached to taking the concubine of a former king (see note on 12:8; see also 16:21; 1Ki 2:22).
3:9 *May God deal with Abner, be it ever so severely.* A curse formula (see note on 1Sa 3:17). *what the LORD promised him on oath.* The knowledge of David's divine designation as successor to Saul had spread widely (see notes on 2:4; 1Sa 16:13; 25:28).

what the LORD promised[o] him on oath [10]and transfer the kingdom from the house of Saul and establish David's throne over Israel and Judah from Dan to Beersheba."[p] [11]Ish-Bosheth did not dare to say another word to Abner, because he was afraid of him.

[12]Then Abner sent messengers on his behalf to say to David, "Whose land is it? Make an agreement with me, and I will help you bring all Israel over to you."

[13]"Good," said David. "I will make an agreement with you. But I demand one thing of you: Do not come into my presence unless you bring Michal daughter of Saul when you come to see me."[q] [14]Then David sent messengers to Ish-Bosheth son of Saul, demanding, "Give me my wife Michal,[r] whom I betrothed to myself for the price of a hundred Philistine foreskins."

[15]So Ish-Bosheth gave orders and had her taken away from her husband[s] Paltiel[t] son of Laish. [16]Her husband, however, went with her, weeping behind her all the way to Bahurim.[u] Then Abner said to him, "Go back home!" So he went back.

[17]Abner conferred with the elders[v] of Israel and said, "For some time you have wanted to make David your king. [18]Now do it! For the LORD promised David, 'By my servant David I will rescue my people Israel from the hand of the Philistines[w] and from the hand of all their enemies.[x]' "

[19]Abner also spoke to the Benjamites in person. Then he went to Hebron to tell David everything that Israel and the whole

house of Benjamin[y] wanted to do. [20]When Abner, who had twenty men with him, came to David at Hebron, David prepared a feast[z] for him and his men. [21]Then Abner said to David, "Let me go at once and assemble all Israel for my lord the king, so that they may make a compact[a] with you, and that you may rule over all that your heart desires."[b] So David sent Abner away, and he went in peace.

Joab Murders Abner

[22]Just then David's men and Joab returned from a raid and brought with them a great deal of plunder. But Abner was no longer with David in Hebron, because David had sent him away, and he had gone in peace. [23]When Joab and all the soldiers with him arrived, he was told that Abner son of Ner had come to the king and that the king had sent him away and that he had gone in peace.

[24]So Joab went to the king and said, "What have you done? Look, Abner came to you. Why did you let him go? Now he is gone! [25]You know Abner son of Ner; he came to deceive you and observe your movements and find out everything you are doing."

[26]Joab then left David and sent messengers after Abner, and they brought him back from the well of Sirah. But David did not know it. [27]Now when Abner[c] returned to Hebron, Joab took him aside into the gateway, as though to speak with him privately. And there, to avenge the blood

3:9 [o]S 1Sa 15:28
3:10 [p]S Jdg 20:1; 1Sa 25:28–31; 2Sa 24:2
3:13 [q]S Ge 43:5
3:14 [r]S 1Sa 18:27
3:15 [s]Dt 24:1–4
[t]1Sa 25:44
3:16 [u]2Sa 16:5; 17:18
3:17 [v]S Jdg 11:11
3:18 [w]S 1Sa 9:16
[x]2Sa 8:6
3:19 [y]1Ch 12:2, 16,29
3:20 [z]1Ch 12:39
3:21 [a]2Sa 5:3
[b]1Ki 11:37
3:27 [c]2Sa 2:8; 4:1; 1Ki 2:5,32

3:10 *transfer the kingdom.* Abner was the real power behind the throne. *Dan to Beersheba.* See note on 1Sa 3:20.
3:12 *Whose land is it?* Possibly a rhetorical question that presumed that the land belonged either to Abner or to David. The former seems more likely from the following sentence. *Make an agreement with me.* Abner wants assurance that he will face no reprisals for his past loyalty to the house of Saul.
3:13 *Michal daughter of Saul.* Although Saul had given Michal to David (1Sa 18:27), he later gave her to another man after David fled from his court (1Sa 25:44). In the minds of the northern elders, the reunion of David and Michal would strengthen David's claim to the throne as a legitimate son-in-law of Saul.
3:14 *David sent messengers to Ish-Bosheth.* David wanted Michal returned as an open and official act of Ish-Bosheth himself, rather than as part of a subterfuge planned by Abner. David knew that Ish-Bosheth would not dare to defy Abner's wishes (see v. 11). *a hundred Philistine foreskins.* See 1Sa 18:25. Saul had required 100 Philistine foreskins; David presented him with 200 (1Sa 18:27).
3:16 *Bahurim.* The last Benjamite city on the way to Hebron (see 16:5; 17:18).
3:17 *elders of Israel.* The collective leadership of the various tribes comprised an informal national ruling body (see notes on Ex 3:16; Joel 1:2; Mt 15:2; Ac 24:1; see also 1Sa 8:4; 2Sa 5:3; 1Ki 8:1,3; 20:7; 2Ki 10:1; 23:1). *you have*

wanted to make David your king. Apparently Ish-Bosheth's support came mainly from the tribe of Benjamin (see 2:15 and note) and from Gilead in Transjordan (see 2:8; 1Sa 11:9–11; 31:11–13).
3:18 *the LORD promised David.* By this time Samuel's anointing of David must have become common knowledge (see 5:2). Abner probably interpreted the anointing as a promise from the Lord, since Samuel was the Lord's much-revered prophet.
3:19 *Abner also spoke to the Benjamites in person.* Because Saul and his family were from the tribe of Benjamin, Abner was careful to consult the Benjamites concerning the transfer of kingship to the tribe of Judah. Apparently they consented, but Abner was not above representing matters in a way that was favorable to his purpose.
3:21 *make a compact with you.* See 5:3 and note.
3:25 *he came to deceive you.* Joab despised Abner for killing his brother (2:18,23; 3:27) and sought to discredit him in David's eyes as a mere opportunist. Perhaps he also sensed that his own position of leadership would be threatened if Abner joined forces with David, since Abner was obviously a power among the northern tribes.
3:27 *Joab stabbed him in the stomach, and he died.* Joab's murder of Abner is not to be excused either as an act of war or as justifiable blood revenge (cf. Nu 35:12; Dt 19:11–13). Asahel had been killed by Abner in the course of battle (see 2:23; see also note on 2:21).

of his brother Asahel, Joab stabbed him [d] in the stomach, and he died. [e]

[28]Later, when David heard about this, he said, "I and my kingdom are forever innocent[f] before the LORD concerning the blood of Abner son of Ner. [29]May his blood[g] fall upon the head of Joab and upon all his father's house! [h] May Joab's house never be without someone who has a running sore[i] or leprosy[e] or who leans on a crutch or who falls by the sword or who lacks food."

[30](Joab and his brother Abishai murdered Abner because he had killed their brother Asahel in the battle at Gibeon.)

[31]Then David said to Joab and all the people with him, "Tear your clothes and put on sackcloth[j] and walk in mourning[k] in front of Abner." King David himself walked behind the bier. [32]They buried Abner in Hebron, and the king wept[l] aloud at Abner's tomb. All the people wept also.

[33]The king sang this lament[m] for Abner:

"Should Abner have died as the lawless die?
[34] Your hands were not bound,
   your feet were not fettered. [n]
You fell as one falls before wicked
   men."

And all the people wept over him again. [35]Then they all came and urged David to eat something while it was still day; but David took an oath, saying, "May God deal with me, be it ever so severely, [o] if I taste bread[p] or anything else before the sun sets!"

[36]All the people took note and were pleased; indeed, everything the king did pleased them. [37]So on that day all the people and all Israel knew that the king

had no part[q] in the murder of Abner son of Ner.

[38]Then the king said to his men, "Do you not realize that a prince and a great man has fallen[r] in Israel this day? [39]And today, though I am the anointed king, I am weak, and these sons of Zeruiah[s] are too strong[t] for me. [u] May the LORD repay[v] the evildoer according to his evil deeds!"

Ish-Bosheth Murdered

4 When Ish-Bosheth son of Saul heard that Abner[w] had died in Hebron, he lost courage, and all Israel became alarmed. [2]Now Saul's son had two men who were leaders of raiding bands. One was named Baanah and the other Recab; they were sons of Rimmon the Beerothite from the tribe of Benjamin—Beeroth[x] is considered part of Benjamin, [3]because the people of Beeroth fled to Gittaim[y] and have lived there as aliens to this day.

[4](Jonathan[z] son of Saul had a son who was lame in both feet. He was five years old when the news[a] about Saul and Jonathan came from Jezreel. His nurse picked him up and fled, but as she hurried to leave, he fell and became crippled. [b] His name was Mephibosheth.)[c]

[5]Now Recab and Baanah, the sons of Rimmon the Beerothite, set out for the house of Ish-Bosheth, [d] and they arrived there in the heat of the day while he was taking his noonday rest. [e] [6]They went into the inner part of the house as if to get some wheat, and they stabbed[f] him in the stomach. Then Recab and his brother Baanah slipped away.

[7]They had gone into the house while he

Cross references (center column)

3:27 [d]S Ex 21:14; S Jdg 3:21; S 2Sa 2:23; [e]2Sa 2:22
3:28 [f]ver 37; Dt 21:9
3:29 [g]S Lev 20:9 [h]1Ki 2:31-33 [i]S Lev 15:2
3:31 [j]Ps 30:11; 35:13; 69:11; Isa 20:2 [k]S Ge 37:34
3:32 [l]S Nu 14:1; Pr 24:17
3:33 [m]S Ge 50:10
3:34 [n]Job 36:8; Ps 2:3; 149:8; Isa 45:14; Na 3:10
3:35 [o]S Ru 1:17 [p]S 1Sa 31:13; 2Sa 12:17; Jer 16:7

3:37 [q]S ver 28
3:38 [r]2Sa 1:19
3:39 [s]S 2Sa 2:18 [t]2Sa 16:9; 18:11 [u]S Jdg 18:26 [v]1Ki 2:32; Ps 41:10; 101:8
4:1 [w]S 2Sa 3:27
4:2 [x]Jos 9:17
4:3 [y]Ne 11:33
4:4 [z]S 1Sa 18:1 [a]S 1Sa 31:9 [b]S Lev 21:18 [c]2Sa 9:8,12; 16:1-4; 19:24; 21:7-8; 1Ch 8:34; 9:40
4:5 [d]S 2Sa 2:8 [e]Ru 2:7
4:6 [f]S 2Sa 2:23

[e]29 The Hebrew word was used for various diseases affecting the skin—not necessarily leprosy.

3:29 *May his blood fall upon the head of Joab and upon all his father's house!* After disclaiming any personal or official involvement in the plot to assassinate Abner (v. 28), David cursed Joab and thereby called on God to judge his wicked act. In this crucial hour when David's relationship to the northern tribes hung in the balance, he appears not to have felt sufficiently secure in his own position to bring Joab publicly to justice (see v. 39). The crime went unpunished until early in the reign of Solomon (1Ki 2:5–6,29–35).

3:31 *Joab.* He too was compelled to join the mourners. It may be that Joab's involvement was not widely known and that David hoped to keep the matter secret for the time being.

3:32 *Hebron.* David's royal city at the time. *the king wept aloud at Abner's tomb.* Because Abner's murder had the potential of destroying the union of the nation under David's rule, David did everything possible to demonstrate his innocence to the people. In this he was successful (see vv. 36–37).

3:35 *May God deal with me, be it ever so severely.* A curse formula (see note on 1Sa 3:17).

3:39 *May the LORD repay the evildoer.* See note on v. 29.

4:1 *he lost courage.* Ish-Bosheth was very much aware of his dependence on Abner (see note on 2:8). *all Israel became alarmed.* Civil strife threatened, and the northern tribes were now without a strong leader.

4:2 *Beeroth.* One of the Gibeonite cities (Jos 9:17) assigned to Benjamin (Jos 18:25).

4:3 *Gittaim.* Its location is not known (but see Ne 11:33), so it is possible that the "because" at the beginning of this verse is unwarranted.

4:4 *Jonathan son of Saul had a son who was lame in both feet.* The writer emphasizes that with the death of Ish-Bosheth (see v. 6) there was no other viable claimant to the throne from the house of Saul. *news about Saul and Jonathan.* See 1:4; 1Sa 31:2–4. *Mephibosheth.* See 9:1–13; 16:1–4; 19:24–30; 21:7–8. The name was originally Merib-Baal (apparently meaning "opponent of Baal"; see 1Ch 8:34), perhaps to be spelled "Meri-Baal" (meaning "loved by Baal"), but was changed by the author of Samuel to Mephibosheth (meaning "from the mouth of the shameful thing"). See note on 2:8.

was lying on the bed in his bedroom. After
they stabbed and killed him, they cut off
his head. Taking it with them, they traveled all night by way of the Arabah.[g]
8They brought the head[h] of Ish-Bosheth to
David at Hebron and said to the king,
"Here is the head of Ish-Bosheth son of
Saul,[i] your enemy, who tried to take your
life. This day the LORD has avenged[j] my
lord the king against Saul and his offspring."

9David answered Recab and his brother
Baanah, the sons of Rimmon the Beerothite, "As surely as the LORD lives, who
has delivered[k] me out of all trouble,
10when a man told me, 'Saul is dead,' and
thought he was bringing good news, I
seized him and put him to death in Ziklag.[l] That was the reward I gave him for
his news! 11How much more—when
wicked men have killed an innocent man
in his own house and on his own
bed—should I not now demand his
blood[m] from your hand and rid the earth of
you!"

12So David gave an order to his men,
and they killed them.[n] They cut off their
hands and feet and hung the bodies by the
pool in Hebron. But they took the head of
Ish-Bosheth and buried it in Abner's tomb
at Hebron.

David Becomes King Over Israel

5:1-3pp — 1Ch 11:1-3

5 All the tribes of Israel[o] came to David
at Hebron and said, "We are your own
flesh and blood.[p] 2In the past, while Saul
was king over us, you were the one who
led Israel on their military campaigns.[q]
And the LORD said[r] to you, 'You will shepherd[s] my people Israel, and you will
become their ruler.[t]' "

3When all the elders of Israel had come
to King David at Hebron, the king made a
compact[u] with them at Hebron before the
LORD, and they anointed[v] David king over
Israel.

4David was thirty years old[w] when he
became king, and he reigned[x] forty[y]
years. 5In Hebron he reigned over Judah
seven years and six months,[z] and in
Jerusalem he reigned over all Israel and
Judah thirty-three years.

David Conquers Jerusalem

5:6-10pp — 1Ch 11:4-9
5:11-16pp — 1Ch 3:5-9; 14:1-7

6The king and his men marched to

4:7 [g]S Dt 3:17
4:8 [h]2Sa 20:21; 2Ki 10:7 [i]1Sa 24:4; 25:29 [j]S Nu 31:3
4:9 [k]S Ge 48:16; 1Ki 1:29
4:10 [l]2Sa 1:2-16
4:11 [m]S Ge 4:10; 9:5; Ps 9:12; 72:14
4:12 [n]2Sa 1:15
5:1 [o]2Sa 19:43 [p]S Ge 29:14; 35:26
5:2 [q]1Sa 18:5,13, 16 [r]S 1Sa 11:6 [s]S Ge 48:15; S 1Sa 16:1; 2Sa 7:7; Mt 2:6; Jn 21:16 [t]S 1Sa 12:12; S 13:14; S 2Sa 6:21
5:3 [u]2Sa 3:21 [v]S Dt 17:15; 2Sa 2:4
5:4 [w]S Ge 37:2; Lk 3:23 [x]1Ki 2:11; 1Ch 3:4 [y]1Ch 26:31
5:5 [z]2Sa 2:11; 1Ki 2:11; 1Ch 3:4

4:7 *Arabah.* See note on Dt 1:1.
4:8 *This day the LORD has avenged my lord the king against Saul.* Recab and Baanah depict their assassination of Ish-Bosheth in pious terms, expecting David to commend them for their act—a serious miscalculation.
4:9 *As surely as the LORD lives.* An oath formula (see note on 1Sa 14:39).
4:11 *demand his blood from your hand.* An expression for the death penalty (see Ge 9:5–6). David here does what he was unable to do with Joab (see note on 3:29).
4:12 *their hands and feet.* The hands that had assassinated Ish-Bosheth and the feet that had run with the news.
5:1–24:25 Beginning with ch. 5 there are sections of 2 Samuel that have parallel passages in 1 Chronicles (they are listed at the sectional headings). In some instances these parallel accounts are nearly identical; in others there are variations.
5:1 *All the tribes of Israel.* Representatives of each tribe, including elders and armed soldiers (see 1Ch 12:23–40). *your own flesh and blood.* The representatives of the various tribes cite three reasons for recognizing David as their king. The first of these is the acknowledgment that David is an Israelite. Even though national unity had been destroyed in the civil strife following Saul's death (2:8–3:1), this blood relationship had not been forgotten.
5:2 *the one who led Israel on their military campaigns.* The second reason (see note on v. 1) for recognizing David as king (see 1Sa 18:5,13–14,16,30). *the LORD said to you.* The third and most important reason (see 1Sa 13:13–14; 16:1, 13; 23:17; 25:26–31).
5:3 *the king made a compact with them ... before the LORD.* David and Israel entered into a covenant in which both the king and the people obligated themselves before the Lord to carry out their mutual responsibilities (see 2Ki 11:17 and note). Thus, while David was king over Judah as the one elevated to that position by his tribe and later became king over Jerusalem by conquest (vv. 6–10), his rule over the northern tribes was by virtue of a treaty (covenant) of submission. That treaty was not renewed with David's grandson Rehoboam because he refused to negotiate its terms at the time of his accession to the throne (1Ki 12:1–16). *they anointed David king over Israel.* The third time David was anointed (see note on 2:4).
5:5 *In Hebron he reigned . . . seven years and six months.* See 2:11. *Israel and Judah.* The specific relationship of David to these two segments of his realm appears to have remained distinct (see note on v. 3).
5:6 *Jerusalem.* One of the most significant accomplishments of David's reign was the establishment of Jerusalem as his royal city and the nation's capital (see Introduction: Contents and Theme). The site was first occupied in the third millennium B.C. and was a royal city in the time of Abraham (see note on Ge 14:18). It was located on the border between Judah and Benjamin but was controlled by neither tribe. At the time of the conquest both Judah and Benjamin had attacked the city (see notes on Jdg 1:8,21), but it was quickly lost again to the Jebusites (Jos 15:63) and was sometimes referred to by the name Jebus (see Jdg 19:10; 1Ch 11:4). The city David conquered covered somewhat less than 11 acres and could have housed not many more than 3,500 inhabitants. By locating his royal city in a newly conquered town on the border between the two segments of his realm, David united the kingdom under his rule without seeming to subordinate one part to the other. *Jebusites.* A Canaanite people (Ge 10:15–16) inhabiting the area in (Jos 15:8; 18:16) and around (Nu 13:29; Jos 11:3) Jerusalem. *the blind and lame can ward you off.* Jerusalem was a natural fortress because of its location on a rise surrounded on three sides by deep valleys; so the Jebusites were confident that their walls could easily be defended.

Jerusalem[a] to attack the Jebusites,[b] who lived there. The Jebusites said to David, "You will not get in here; even the blind and the lame can ward you off." They thought, "David cannot get in here." [7]Nevertheless, David captured the fortress of Zion,[c] the City of David.[d][e]

[8]On that day, David said, "Anyone who conquers the Jebusites will have to use the water shaft[f] to reach those 'lame and blind'[g] who are David's enemies.[g]" That is why they say, "The 'blind and lame' will not enter the palace."

[9]David then took up residence in the fortress and called it the City of David. He built up the area around it, from the supporting terraces[h][h] inward. [10]And he became more and more powerful,[i] because the LORD God Almighty[j] was with him.[k]

[11]Now Hiram[l] king of Tyre sent mes-

sengers to David, along with cedar logs and carpenters and stonemasons, and they built a palace for David. [12]And David knew that the LORD had established him as king over Israel and had exalted his kingdom[m] for the sake of his people Israel.

[13]After he left Hebron, David took more concubines and wives[n] in Jerusalem, and more sons and daughters were born to him. [14]These are the names of the children born to him there:[o] Shammua, Shobab, Nathan,[p] Solomon, [15]Ibhar, Elishua, Nepheg, Japhia, [16]Elishama, Eliada and Eliphelet.

David Defeats the Philistines
5:17–25pp — 1Ch 14:8–17

[17]When the Philistines heard that David had been anointed king over Israel, they

5:6 aS Jdg 1:8
bS Jos 15:8
5:7 cPs 76:2
dJer 21:13
e2Sa 6:12,16;
1Ki 2:10; 8:1;
Isa 29:1;
Jer 25:29
5:8 f2Ki 20:20;
2Ch 32:30
gMt 21:14
5:9 h1Ki 9:15,24
5:10 i2Sa 3:1
/Ps 24:10
k2Sa 7:9
5:11 l1Ki 5:1,18;
2Ch 2:3

5:12 mS Nu 24:7
5:13 nS Dt 17:17
5:14 o1Ch 3:5
pLk 3:31

f8 Or use scaling hooks   g8 Or are hated by David
h9 Or the Millo

5:7 *fortress.* Probably the fortified city itself. *Zion.* The first occurrence of the name in the OT (its meaning is unknown). Originally the name appears to have been given to the southernmost hill of the city on which the Jebusite fortress was located. As the city expanded (from the days of Solomon onward), the name continued to be applied to the entire city (see Isa 1:8; 2:3).
5:8 *On that day, David said.* 1Ch 11:6 may be combined with this verse for a more complete account. Joab's part in the conquest of the city demonstrated again his military prowess and reconfirmed him in the position of commander of David's armies. *water shaft.* Although the Hebrew for this term is obscure (see NIV text note), it appears that David knew of a secret tunnel—perhaps running from the Gihon spring outside the city into the fortress—that gave access to water when the city was under siege (see 2Ch 32:30). *lame and blind.* An ironic reference to the Jebusites (cf. v. 6). *The 'blind and lame' will not enter the palace.* The proverb may

mean that the Jebusites did not have access to the royal palace, though they were allowed to remain in the city and its environs.
5:9 *supporting terraces.* Stone terraces on the steep slopes of the hill, creating additional space for buildings (but see NIV text note; see also note on Jdg 9:6).
5:11 *Hiram king of Tyre.* This Phoenician king was the first to accord the newly established King David international recognition. It was vital to him that he have good relations with the king of Israel since Israel dominated the inland trade routes to Tyre, and Tyre was dependent on Israelite agriculture for much of its food (also true in the first century A.D.; see Ac 12:20). A close relationship existed between these two realms until the Babylonian invasions. *Tyre.* An important Phoenician seaport on the Mediterranean coast north of Israel (see Eze 26–27).
5:12 *David knew that the LORD had established him as king.* In the ideology of the ancient Near East the king's

---

Substantial historical evidence, both Biblical and extra-Biblical, places the temple of Herod (and before it the temples of Zerubbabel and of Solomon) on the holy spot where King David built an altar to the Lord. David had purchased the land from Araunah the Jebusite, who was using the exposed

bedrock as a threshing floor (2Sa 24:18-25). Tradition claims a much older sanctity for the site, associating it with the altar of Abraham on Mount Moriah (Ge 22:1-19). The writer of Genesis equates Moriah with "the Mountain of the LORD," and other OT shrines originated in altars erected by Abraham.

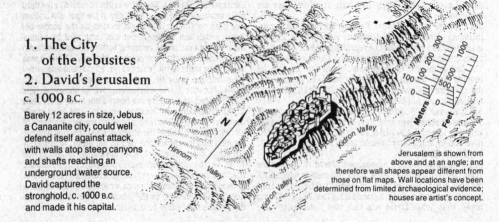

1. The City of the Jebusites
2. David's Jerusalem

c. 1000 B.C.

Barely 12 acres in size, Jebus, a Canaanite city, could well defend itself against attack, with walls atop steep canyons and shafts reaching an underground water source. David captured the stronghold, c. 1000 B.C. and made it his capital.

Jerusalem is shown from above and at an angle; and therefore wall shapes appear different from those on flat maps. Wall locations have been determined from limited archaeological evidence; houses are artist's concept.

went up in full force to search for him, but David heard about it and went down to the stronghold. *q* [18]Now the Philistines had come and spread out in the Valley of Rephaim; *r* [19]so David inquired *s* of the LORD, "Shall I go and attack the Philistines? Will you hand them over to me?"

The LORD answered him, "Go, for I will surely hand the Philistines over to you."

[20]So David went to Baal Perazim, and there he defeated them. He said, "As waters break out, the LORD has broken out against my enemies before me." So that place was called Baal Perazim.[i][t] [21]The Philistines abandoned their idols there, and David and his men carried them off. *u*

[22]Once more the Philistines came up and spread out in the Valley of Rephaim; [23]so David inquired of the LORD, and he answered, "Do not go straight up, but circle around behind them and attack them in front of the balsam trees. [24]As soon as you hear the sound *v* of marching in the tops of the balsam trees, move quickly, because that will mean the LORD has gone out in front *w* of you to strike the Philistine army." [25]So David did as the LORD commanded him, and he struck down the Philistines *x* all the way from Gibeon[j][y] to Gezer. *z*

The Ark Brought to Jerusalem

6:1–11pp — 1Ch 13:1–14
6:12–19pp — 1Ch 15:25–16:3

6 David again brought together out of Israel chosen men, thirty thousand in all. [2]He and all his men set out from Baalah *a* of Judah *k* to bring up from there the ark *b* of God, which is called by the Name,[l][c] the name of the LORD Almighty, who is enthroned *d* between the cherubim *e* that are on the ark. [3]They set the ark of God on a new cart *f* and brought it from the house of Abinadab, which was on the hill. *g* Uzzah and Ahio, sons of Abinadab, were guiding the new cart [4]with the ark of God on it, *m* and Ahio was walking in front of it. [5]David and the whole house of Israel were celebrating *h* with all their might before the LORD, with songs *n* and with harps, lyres, tambourines, sistrums and cymbals. *i*

[6]When they came to the threshing floor of Nacon, Uzzah reached out and took hold of *j* the ark of God, because the oxen

Cross references (center column)

5:17 *q*2Sa 23:14; 1Ch 11:16
5:18 *r*S Jos 15:8; S 17:15
5:19 *s*S Jdg 18:5; S 1Sa 23:2
5:20 *t*S Ge 38:29
5:21 *u*Dt 7:5; Isa 46:2
5:24 *v*S Ex 14:24 *w*Jdg 4:14
5:25 *x*2Sa 8:12; 21:15 *y*Isa 28:21 *z*S Jos 10:33

6:2 *a*S Jos 15:9 *b*1Sa 4:4; 7:1 *c*Lev 24:16; Dt 28:10; Isa 63:14 *d*Ps 99:1; 132:14 *e*S Ge 3:24; S Ex 25:22
6:3 *f*ver 7; Nu 7:4-9; S 1Sa 6:7 *g*2Sa 7:1
6:5 *h*S Ex 15:20 *i*Ezr 3:10; Ne 12:27; Ps 150:5
6:6 *j*S Nu 4:15, 19-20

Text notes (center column)

i20 Baal Perazim means *the lord who breaks out.* *j25* Septuagint (see also 1 Chron. 14:16); Hebrew *Geba* *k2* That is, Kiriath Jearim; Hebrew *Baale Judah,* a variant of *Baalah of Judah* *l2* Hebrew; Septuagint and Vulgate do not have *the Name.* *m3,4* Dead Sea Scrolls and some Septuagint manuscripts; Masoretic Text *cart* [4]*and they brought it with the ark of God from the house of Abinadab, which was on the hill* *n5* See Dead Sea Scrolls, Septuagint and 1 Chronicles 13:8; Masoretic Text *celebrating before the LORD with all kinds of instruments made of pine.*

Study notes (bottom)

possession of a palace was the chief symbolic indication of his status. *for the sake of his people Israel.* David acknowledged that his elevation to kingship over all Israel was the Lord's doing and that it was an integral part of his continuing redemptive program for Israel—just as the ministries of Moses, Joshua, the judges and Samuel had been.
5:13 *David took more concubines and wives.* See note on 3:2.
5:14 *Shammua, Shobab, Nathan, Solomon.* 1Ch 3:5 designates Bathsheba as their mother.
5:17 *When the Philistines heard that David had been anointed king.* Chronologically it is likely that the Philistine attack followed immediately after the events of v. 3 and before the capture of Jerusalem (vv. 6–14). (The author arranged his narrative by topics; see note on 7:1.) The Philistines had not been disturbed by David's reign over Judah, but now they acted to protect their interests in the north, much of which they dominated after the defeat of Saul (1Sa 31). *stronghold.* Probably a reference to the desert area in southern Judah where David had hidden from Saul (see notes on 1Sa 22:4; 23:14). This action of David suggests that he had not yet taken Jerusalem.
5:19 *David inquired of the LORD.* See notes on 2:1; 1Sa 2:28; 22:20; 23:2.
5:20 *the LORD has broken out . . . Baal Perazim.* See NIV text note. As a true theocratic king, David attributes the victory to the Lord and does not claim the glory for himself (see notes on 1Sa 10:18,27; 11:13; 12:11; 14:23; 17:11, 45–47).
5:21 *abandoned their idols there.* As the Israelites had taken the ark into battle (see note on 1Sa 4:3), so the

Philistines carried images of their deities into battle in the hope that this would ensure victory. *carried them off.* In compliance with the instruction of Dt 7:5, they also burned them (1Ch 14:12).
5:23 *he answered.* As had been true in the case of the conquest under Joshua, the Lord ordered the battle and he himself marched against the enemy with his heavenly host (see Jos 6:2–5; 8:1–2; 10:8,14; 11:6). David's wars were a continuation and completion of the wars fought by Joshua.
5:24 *sound of marching.* The heavenly host of the Lord going into battle.
6:2 *Baalah of Judah.* See NIV text note; see also Jos 15:60; 18:14; 1Sa 7:1. *ark of God.* See Ex 25:10–22; see also notes on 1Sa 4:3–4,21. The ark had remained at Kiriath Jearim during the reign of Saul. *called by the Name.* Used elsewhere to designate ownership (see 12:28; Dt 28:10; Isa 4:1; 63:19). *LORD Almighty.* See note on 1Sa 1:3. *enthroned between the cherubim.* See note on 1Sa 4:4; see also 1Ch 28:2 ("footstool of our God"). David recognized the great significance of the ark as the earthly throne of Israel's God. As a true theocratic king, he wished to acknowledge the Lord's kingship and rule over both himself and the people by restoring the ark to a place of prominence in the nation.
6:3 *new cart.* David follows the example of the Philistines (see 1Sa 6:7) rather than the instructions of Ex 25:12–14; Nu 4:5–6,15, which require that the ark be carried on the shoulders of the Levites (see 1Ch 15:13–15). *from the house of Abinadab.* See 1Sa 7:1. *Uzzah and Ahio, sons of Abinadab.* 1Sa 7:1 speaks of Eleazar as the son of Abinadab. The Hebrew word for "son" can have the broader meaning of "descendant."

stumbled. [7]The LORD's anger burned against Uzzah because of his irreverent act;[k] therefore God struck him down[l] and he died there beside the ark of God.

[8]Then David was angry because the LORD's wrath[m] had broken out against Uzzah, and to this day that place is called Perez Uzzah.[o] [n]

[9]David was afraid of the LORD that day and said, "How[o] can the ark of the LORD ever come to me?" [10]He was not willing to take the ark of the LORD to be with him in the City of David. Instead, he took it aside to the house of Obed-Edom[p] the Gittite. [11]The ark of the LORD remained in the house of Obed-Edom the Gittite for three months, and the LORD blessed him and his entire household.[q]

[12]Now King David[r] was told, "The LORD has blessed the household of Obed-Edom and everything he has, because of the ark of God." So David went down and brought up the ark of God from the house of Obed-Edom to the City of David with rejoicing. [13]When those who were carrying the ark of the LORD had taken six steps, he sacrificed[s] a bull and a fattened calf. [14]David, wearing a linen ephod,[t] danced[u] before the LORD with all his might, [15]while he and the entire house of Israel brought up the ark of the LORD with shouts[v] and the sound of trumpets.[w]

[16]As the ark of the LORD was entering the City of David,[x] Michal[y] daughter of Saul watched from a window. And when she saw King David leaping and dancing before the LORD, she despised him in her heart.

[17]They brought the ark of the LORD and set it in its place inside the tent that David had pitched for it,[z] and David sacrificed burnt offerings[a] and fellowship offerings[p] before the LORD. [18]After he had finished sacrificing[b] the burnt offerings and fellowship offerings, he blessed[c] the people in the name of the LORD Almighty. [19]Then he gave a loaf of bread, a cake of dates and a cake of raisins[d] to each person in the whole crowd of Israelites, both men and women.[e] And all the people went to their homes.

[20]When David returned home to bless his household, Michal daughter of Saul came out to meet him and said, "How the king of Israel has distinguished himself today, disrobing[f] in the sight of the slave girls of his servants as any vulgar fellow would!"

[21]David said to Michal, "It was before the LORD, who chose me rather than your father or anyone from his house when he appointed[g] me ruler[h] over the LORD's people Israel—I will celebrate before the LORD. [22]I will become even more undignified than this, and I will be humiliated in my own eyes. But by these slave girls you spoke of, I will be held in honor."

[23]And Michal daughter of Saul had no children to the day of her death.

God's Promise to David

7:1-17pp — 1Ch 17:1-15

7 After the king was settled in his palace[i] and the LORD had given him rest

Cross references column:

6:7
k 1Ch 15:13-15
l S 1Sa 5:6; 6:19;
S 25:38
6:8 m Ps 7:11
n S Ge 38:29
6:9 o S 1Sa 6:20
6:10
p 1Ch 15:18;
26:4-5
6:11
q S Ge 30:27;
39:5
6:12 r 1Ki 8:1
6:13 s 1Ki 8:5,62;
Ezr 6:17
6:14 t Ex 19:6;
S 1Sa 2:18
u S Ex 15:20
6:15 v S Jos 6:5
w Ps 47:5; 98:6
6:16 x S 2Sa 5:7
y S 1Sa 18:27

6:17 z 1Ki 8:6;
1Ch 15:1;
2Ch 1:4
a Lev 1:1-17;
1Ki 8:62-64
6:18 b 1Ki 8:22
c S Ex 39:43
6:19 d Hos 3:1
e Dt 26:13;
Ne 8:10
6:20 f S 1Sa 19:24
6:21 g 1Sa 13:14;
S 15:28 h 2Sa 5:2;
7:8; 1Ch 5:2;
17:7; Mic 5:2
7:1 i 2Sa 6:3

o 8 *Perez Uzzah* means *outbreak against Uzzah.*
p 17 Traditionally *peace offerings*; also in verse 18

6:7 *his irreverent act.* Although Uzzah's intent may have been good, he violated the clear instructions the Lord had given for handling the ark (see note on v. 3; cf. Ex 25:15; Nu 4:5-6,15; 1Ch 15:13-15; see also note on 1Sa 6:19). At this important new beginning in Israel's life with the Lord, the Lord gives a shocking and vivid reminder to David and Israel that those who claim to serve him must acknowledge his rule with absolute seriousness (see Lev 10:1-3; Jos 7:24-25; 24:19-20; Ac 5:1-11).
6:8 *David was angry.* David's initial reaction was resentment that his attempt to honor the Lord had resulted in a display of God's wrath. *to this day.* Until the time of the writing of 2 Samuel. *Perez Uzzah.* See NIV text note. The place-name memorialized a divine warning that was not soon forgotten (see Jos 7:26 and NIV text note).
6:9 *David was afraid of the LORD.* David's anger was accompanied by fear—not the wholesome fear of proper honor and respect for the Lord (1Sa 12:24; Jos 24:14) but an anxiety arising from an acute sense of his own guilt (Ge 3:10; Dt 5:5).
6:10 *Obed-Edom.* Perhaps means "servant of man." *Gittite.* He appears to have been a Levite (see note on 1Ch 13:13; cf. 1Ch 15:18,24; 16:5; 26:4-8,15; 2Ch 25:24), though many think the term "Gittite" fixes his place of birth

at the Philistine city of Gath (see 15:18). However, Gittite may be a reference to the Levitical city Gath Rimmon in Dan or Manasseh (Jos 21:20-25).
6:12 *David . . . brought up the ark.* God's blessing on the household of Obed-Edom showed David that God's anger had been appeased.
6:13 *those . . . carrying the ark.* David had become aware of his previous error (1Ch 15:13-15). *six steps.* Sufficient to show that now God's blessing was on the Levites (see 1Ch 15:26).
6:14 *linen ephod.* See note on 1Sa 2:18.
6:16 *she despised him.* Michal had no appreciation for the significance of the event and deeply resented David's public display as unworthy of the dignity of a king (see vv. 20-23).
6:17 *burnt offerings.* See Lev 1. *fellowship offerings.* See note on 1Sa 11:15.
6:18 *he blessed the people.* As Solomon would later do at the dedication of the temple (1Ki 8:55-61).
6:20 *disrobing.* An allusion to David's having worn only a linen ephod (v. 14) rather than his royal robe.
6:23 *Michal . . . had no children.* Probably a punishment for her pride and at the same time another manifestation of God's judgment on the house of Saul.
7:1-29 God's great promise to David (see Introduction:

from all his enemies*j* around him,*k* 2he said to Nathan*l* the prophet, "Here I am, living in a palace*m* of cedar, while the ark of God remains in a tent."*n*

3Nathan replied to the king, "Whatever you have in mind,*o* go ahead and do it, for the LORD is with you."

4That night the word of the LORD came to Nathan, saying:

5"Go and tell my servant David, 'This is what the LORD says: Are you*p* the one to build me a house to dwell in?*q* 6I have not dwelt in a house from the day I brought the Israelites up out of Egypt to this day.*r* I have been moving from place to place with a tent*s* as my dwelling.*t* 7Wherever I have moved with all the Israelites,*u* did I ever say to any of their rulers whom I commanded to shepherd*v* my people Israel, "Why have you not built me a house*w* of cedar?*x*" '

8"Now then, tell my servant David, 'This is what the LORD Almighty says: I took you from the pasture and from following the flock*y* to be ruler*z* over my people Israel.*a* 9I have been with you wherever you have gone,*b* and I have cut off all your enemies from be-fore you.*c* Now I will make your name great, like the names of the greatest men of the earth.*d* 10And I will provide a place for my people Israel and will plant*e* them so that they can have a home of their own and no longer be disturbed.*f* Wicked*g* people will not oppress them anymore,*h* as they did at the beginning 11and have done ever since the time I appointed leaders*q**i* over my people Israel. I will also give you rest from all your ene-mies.*j*

" 'The LORD declares*k* to you that the LORD himself will establish*l* a house*m* for you: 12When your days are over and you rest*n* with your fathers, I will raise up your offspring to succeed you, who will come from your own body,*o* and I will establish his king-dom.*p* 13He is the one who will build a house*q* for my Name,*r* and I will establish the throne of his kingdom

---

7:1 /ver 11
*k*1Ch 22:18
7:2 /2Sa 12:1;
1Ki 1:8,22;
1Ch 29:29;
2Ch 9:29
*m*2Sa 5:11;
1Ki 3:1; 7:1,2,7;
9:1; 2Ch 8:1;
Jer 22:14;
Hag 1:4
*n*S Ex 26:1;
Ps 132:3;
Ac 7:45-46
7:3 *o*S 1Sa 10:7;
Ps 132:1-5
7:5 *p*1Ki 8:19;
1Ch 22:8
*q*1Ki 5:3-5;
1Ch 28:3
7:6 *r*Ac 7:45
*s*Ex 40:18,34;
Jos 18:1 *t*1Ki 8:16
7:7 *u*Dt 23:14
*v*S 2Sa 5:2
*w*1Ki 8:27;
Isa 66:1
*x*Lev 26:11-12
7:8 *y*S 1Sa 16:11;
1Ch 21:17;
Ps 74:1; Am 7:15
*z*S 1Sa 2:7-8;
S 9:16; S 16:1;
S 2Sa 6:21
*a*Ps 78:70-72;
2Co 6:18*
7:9 *b*S 1Sa 18:14;
2Sa 5:10

*c*Ps 18:37-42
*d*S Ex 11:3
7:10
*e*S Ex 15:17;
Isa 5:1-7
*f*2Ki 21:8;
2Ch 33:8
*g*Ps 89:22-23

*h*Ps 147:14; Isa 54:14; 60:18 7:11 *i*S Jdg 2:16; 1Sa 12:9-11
/ver 1 *k*1Ki 2:24 *l*1Sa 25:28; Ps 89:35-37; S Mt 1:1;
Lk 1:32-33; Ac 13:22-23; 2Ti 2:8 *m*S Ex 1:21; Isa 7:2 7:12
*n*S Ge 15:15; 1Ki 2:1; Ac 13:36 *o*1Ki 8:20; Ps 132:11-12;
Jer 30:21; 33:15 *p*2Ch 23:3 7:13 *q*S Dt 12:5; 1Ki 6:12
*r*Dt 16:11; 1Ki 5:5; 8:19,29; 2Ki 21:4,7

*q*11 Traditionally *judges*

Contents and Theme). Although it is not expressly called a covenant here, it is elsewhere (23:5; Ps 89:3,28,34,39; cf. Ps 132:11), and David responds with language suggesting his recognition that a covenant had been made (see notes on vv. 20,28).

7:1 *After the king was settled in his palace.* See 5:11; see also note on 5:12. *and the LORD had given him rest from all his enemies.* Chronologically the victories noted in 8:1–14 probably preceded the events of this chapter. The arrangement of material is topical (see also note on 5:17)—ch. 6 records the bringing of the ark to Jerusalem; ch. 7 tells of David's desire to build a temple in Jerusalem in which to house the ark.

7:2 *Nathan.* The first reference to this prophet (see 12:1–14; 1Ki 1). *tent.* See v. 6; 6:17. Now that he himself had a royal palace (symbolic of his established kingship), a tent did not seem to David to be an appropriate place for the throne of Israel's divine King (see note on 6:2; see also Ps 132:2–5; Ac 7:46). He wanted to build Israel's heavenly King a royal house in the capital city of his kingdom.

7:3 *Nathan replied.* In consulting a prophet, David sought God's will, but Nathan boldly voiced approval of David's plans in the Lord's name before he had received a revelation from the Lord.

7:5 *Are you the one . . . ?* David's desire was commendable (1Ki 8:18–19), but his gift and mission were to fight the Lord's battles until Israel was securely at rest in the promised land (see v. 10; 1Ki 5:3).

7:7 *did I ever say . . . "Why have you not built me a house . . . ?"* David misunderstood the Lord's priorities. He reflected the pagan notion that the gods were interested in human beings only as builders and maintainers of their temples and as practitioners of their cult. Instead, the Lord had raised up rulers in Israel only to shepherd his people (that is also why he had brought David "from the pasture," v. 8).

7:9 *I have cut off all your enemies.* See note on v. 1.

7:10 *I will provide a place for my people Israel.* It is for this purpose that the Lord has made David king, and through David he will do it. *at the beginning.* In Egypt.

7:11 *leaders.* During the period of the judges (see NIV text note). *I will also give you rest from all your enemies.* See vv. 1,9. David's victories over threatening powers will be complete, so that the rest already enjoyed will be assured for the future. *the LORD himself will establish a house for you.* Compare this statement with the rhetorical question of v. 5. In a beautiful play on words God says that David is not to build him a house (temple); rather, God will build David a house (royal dynasty) that will last forever (v. 16). God has been building Israel ever since the days of Abraham, and now he commits himself to build David's royal house so that the promise to Israel may be fulfilled—rest in the promised land. It is God's building that effects his kingdom. This covenant with David is unconditional, like those with Noah, Abram and Phinehas (see note on Ge 9:9; see also chart on "Major Covenants in the OT," p. 19), grounded only in God's firm and gracious purpose. It finds its ultimate fulfillment in the kingship of Christ, who was born of the tribe of Judah and the house of David (see Ps 89:30–38; Isa 9:1–7; Mt 1:1; Lk 1:32–33,69; Ac 2:30; 13:23; Ro 1:2–3; 2Ti 2:8; Rev 3:7; 22:16).

7:12 *raise up your offspring to succeed you.* The royal line of David, in contrast to that of Saul, would continue after David's death by dynastic succession.

7:13 *He is the one who will build a house for my Name.* God's priorities are that his own royal house, where his throne (the ark) can finally come to rest (1Ch 6:31; 28:2), will wait until Israel is at rest and David's dynasty (in the person of his son) is secure. "Name" is equivalent to "me" in v. 5 (see note on 1Sa 25:25).

forever.[s] [14]I will be his father, and he will be my son.[t] When he does wrong, I will punish him[u] with the rod[v] of men, with floggings inflicted by men. [15]But my love will never be taken away from him,[w] as I took it away from Saul,[x] whom I removed from before you. [16]Your house and your kingdom will endure forever before me[r]; your throne[y] will be established[z] forever.[a]' "

[17]Nathan reported to David all the words of this entire revelation.

David's Prayer

7:18–29pp — 1Ch 17:16–27

[18]Then King David went in and sat before the LORD, and he said:

"Who am I,[b] O Sovereign LORD, and what is my family, that you have brought me this far? [19]And as if this were not enough in your sight, O Sovereign LORD, you have also spoken about the future of the house of your servant. Is this your usual way of dealing with man,[c] O Sovereign LORD?

[20]"What more can David say[d] to you? For you know[e] your servant,[f] O Sovereign LORD. [21]For the sake of your word and according to your will, you have done this great thing and made it known to your servant.

[22]"How great[g] you are,[h] O Sovereign LORD! There is no one like[i] you,

and there is no God[j] but you, as we have heard with our own ears.[k] [23]And who is like your people Israel—the one nation on earth that God went out to redeem as a people for himself, and to make a name[m] for himself, and to perform great and awesome wonders[n] by driving out nations and their gods from before your people, whom you redeemed[o] from Egypt?[s] [24]You have established your people Israel as your very own[p] forever, and you, O LORD, have become their God.[q]

[25]"And now, LORD God, keep forever the promise[r] you have made concerning your servant and his house. Do as you promised, [26]so that your name[s] will be great forever. Then men will say, 'The LORD Almighty is God over Israel!' And the house of your servant David will be established[t] before you.

[27]"O LORD Almighty, God of Israel, you have revealed this to your servant, saying, 'I will build a house for you.' So your servant has found courage to offer you this prayer. [28]O Sovereign

Cross references

7:13 [s] ver 16; S Ge 9:16; 2Sa 22:51; 1Ki 2:4,45; 1Ch 22:10; 28:6; 2Ch 6:16; 7:18; 13:5; 21:7; Ps 89:3-4,29, 35-37; Pr 25:5; Isa 9:7; 16:5; Jer 17:25; 33:17, 21; Da 7:27
7:14 [t] Ps 2:7; 89:26; Jer 3:19; [u] S Mt 3:17; Jn 1:49; 2Co 6:18*; Heb 1:5*; Rev 21:7 [v] S Dt 8:5; 1Ki 11:34; 1Ch 22:10; Heb 12:7 [w] Ps 89:30-33; Pr 13:24
7:15 [w] ver 25; 1Ki 2:4; 6:12; 8:25; 9:5; 11:13, 32; 2Ki 19:34; 2Ch 6:16; 7:18; 21:7; Ps 89:24, 33; Jer 33:17 [x] S 1Sa 13:13; S 15:28; 16:14
7:16 [y] Ps 89:36-37; S Lk 1:33 [z] Ps 9:7; 93:2; 103:19 [a] ver 13
7:18 [b] S Ex 3:11
7:19 [c] Isa 55:8-9
7:20 [d] Isa 38:15 [e] Jn 21:17 [f] S 1Sa 16:7
7:22 [g] Ps 48:1; 77:13; 86:10; Jer 10:6 [h] Dt 3:24 [i] S Ex 9:14

[j] S Ex 8:10; S 20:4 [k] Ex 10:2; S Jdg 6:13; Ps 44:1
7:23 [l] Dt 4:32-38; S 33:29; S 1Sa 12:22

[m] S Nu 6:27 [n] Dt 10:21 [o] Dt 7:7-8; S 9:26 7:24 [p] Dt 26:18 [q] Ex 6:6-7; Ps 48:14 7:25 [r] S ver 15; S Nu 23:19; 2Ch 1:9 7:26 [s] S Ex 6:3; Ne 9:5; Ps 72:19; 96:8; Mt 6:9 [t] S 1Sa 25:28

[r] 16 Some Hebrew manuscripts and Septuagint; most Hebrew manuscripts you   [s] 23 See Septuagint and 1 Chron. 17:21; Hebrew wonders for your land and before your people, whom you redeemed from Egypt, from the nations and their gods.

7:14 *his father . . . my son.* This familial language expresses the special relationship God promises to maintain with the descendant(s) of David whom he will establish on David's throne. It marks him as the one God has chosen and enthroned to rule in his name as the official representative of God's rule over his people (see notes on Ps 2:7; 45:6; 89:27). In Jesus Christ this promise comes to ultimate fulfillment (see Mt 1:1; Mk 1:11; Heb 1:5).
7:15 *my love.* God's special and unfailing favor (see note on Ps 6:4).
7:16 *your throne will be established forever.* See note on v. 11; see also Introduction: Contents and Theme. The promise of an everlasting kingdom for the house of David became the focal point for many later prophecies and powerfully influenced the development of the Messianic hope in Israel.
7:18–29 David's prayer expresses wonder that God would make such commitments to him and his descendants. But he also acknowledges that what God had pledged to him is for Israel's sake, that its purpose is the fulfillment of God's covenanted promises to his people—and that its ultimate effect will be the honor and praise of God throughout the world.
7:18 *went in.* Presumably into the tent (6:17) in which the ark was kept. *sat before the LORD.* The ark was the symbol of God's presence with his people (see Ex 25:22; see also notes on 1Sa 4:3–4,21).
7:19 *Is this your usual way of dealing with man, O Sovereign LORD?* The meaning of this clause is uncertain (cf. 1Ch

17:17). It has also been taken as an exclamation ("This is your law for man, O Sovereign LORD!") and understood as a summation of the divine decree concerning David and his house.
7:20 *know.* Or "especially acknowledge" or "choose" (see Ge 18:19, "chosen"; Am 3:2, "chosen"). David recognizes God's promise as a covenant (23:5).
7:21 *your word.* Probably God's covenant word of promise to his people.
7:22 *no God but you.* See 22:32; 1Sa 2:2.
7:23 *the one nation on earth that God went out to redeem as a people for himself.* Israel's uniqueness did not consist in her national achievements but in God's choice of her to be his own people (see Dt 7:6–8; 33:26–29). *to make a name for himself.* The basis for God's electing love, revealed in his dealings with Israel, did not lie in any meritorious characteristic of the Israelite people but in his own sovereign purposes (see Dt 7:6–8; 9:4–5; 1Sa 12:22; Ne 9:10; Isa 63:12; Jer 32:20–21; Eze 36:22–38).
7:24 *you, O LORD, have become their God.* What God has pledged to David, he has pledged as the God of Israel.
7:27 *your servant has found courage to offer you this prayer.* David's prayer lays claim on God's promise.
7:28 *good things.* A common summary expression for covenant benefits from God (see, e.g., 1Sa 2:32, "good"; Nu 10:29,32; Dt 26:11; Jos 21:45; 23:14, "good promises"; Isa 63:7; Jer 29:32; 32:40–41, "good"; 33:9).

LORD, you are God! Your words are trustworthy,[u] and you have promised these good things to your servant. [29]Now be pleased to bless the house of your servant, that it may continue forever in your sight; for you, O Sovereign LORD, have spoken, and with your blessing[v] the house of your servant will be blessed forever."

David's Victories

8:1–14pp — 1Ch 18:1–13

8 In the course of time, David defeated the Philistines[w] and subdued[x] them, and he took Metheg Ammah from the control of the Philistines.

[2]David also defeated the Moabites.[y] He made them lie down on the ground and measured them off with a length of cord. Every two lengths of them were put to death, and the third length was allowed to live. So the Moabites became subject to David and brought tribute.[z]

[3]Moreover, David fought Hadadezer[a] son of Rehob, king of Zobah,[b] when he went to restore his control along the Euphrates[c] River. [4]David captured a thousand of his chariots, seven thousand charioteers[t] and twenty thousand foot soldiers. He hamstrung[d] all but a hundred of the chariot horses.

[5]When the Arameans of Damascus[e] came to help Hadadezer king of Zobah, David struck down twenty-two thousand of them. [6]He put garrisons[f] in the Aramean kingdom of Damascus, and the Arameans became subject[g] to him and brought tribute. The LORD gave David victory wherever he went.[h]

[7]David took the gold shields[i] that belonged to the officers of Hadadezer and brought them to Jerusalem. [8]From Tebah[u] and Berothai,[j] towns that belonged to Hadadezer, King David took a great quantity of bronze.

[9]When Tou[v] king of Hamath[k] heard that David had defeated the entire army of Hadadezer,[l] [10]he sent his son Joram[w] to King David to greet him and congratulate him on his victory in battle over Hadadezer, who had been at war with Tou. Joram brought with him articles of silver and gold and bronze.

[11]King David dedicated[m] these articles to the LORD, as he had done with the silver and gold from all the nations he had subdued: [12]Edom[x][n] and Moab,[o] the Ammonites[p] and the Philistines,[q] and Amalek.[r] He also dedicated the plunder taken from Hadadezer son of Rehob, king of Zobah.

[13]And David became famous[s] after he returned from striking down eighteen thousand Edomites[y] in the Valley of Salt.[t]

[14]He put garrisons throughout Edom, and all the Edomites[u] became subject to David.[v] The LORD gave David victory[w] wherever he went.[x]

David's Officials

8:15–18pp — 1Ch 18:14–17

[15]David reigned over all Israel, doing what was just and right[y] for all his people. [16]Joab[z] son of Zeruiah was over the army;

Cross references

7:28 uEx 34:6; Jn 17:17
7:29 vNu 6:23-27
8:1 wPs 60:8; 87:4; 108:9 xHeb 11:32-33
8:2 yS Ge 19:37; S Nu 21:29 zS Jdg 3:15; S Isa 45:14
8:3 a2Sa 10:16, 19; 1Ki 11:23 bS 1Sa 14:47 cS Ge 2:14
8:4 dS Ge 49:6; Jos 11:9
8:5 eS Ge 14:15; 2Sa 10:6; 1Ki 11:24; 2Ki 8:7; 14:28
8:6 fIKi 20:34 g2Sa 10:19 h2Sa 3:18
8:7 iIKi 10:16; 14:26; 2Ki 11:10
8:8 jEze 47:16
8:9 kIKi 8:65; 2Ki 14:28; 2Ch 8:4 lLk 14:31-32
8:11 mver 12; 1Ki 7:51; 15:15; 1Ch 26:26; 2Ch 5:1
8:12 nS Nu 24:18 over 2 p2Sa 10:14 qS 2Sa 5:25 rS Nu 24:20; S 1Sa 27:8
8:13 s2Sa 7:9 t2Ki 14:7; 1Ch 18:12; Ps 60 Title
8:14 uNu 24:17-18; Ps 108:9; Isa 34:5; 63:1; Jer 49:7; Eze 25:12 vS Ge 27:29; 37-40 wPs 144:10 x2Sa 22:44; Ps 18:43
8:15 yS Ge 18:19; 1Ki 11:38; 14:8; 15:11; 22:43; 2Ki 12:2; Job 29:14; Ps 5:12; 119:121; Heb 11:33
8:16 zS 2Sa 2:13

Text notes

t4 Septuagint (see also Dead Sea Scrolls and 1 Chron. 18:4); Masoretic Text *captured seventeen hundred of his charioteers*   u8 See some Septuagint manuscripts (see also 1 Chron. 18:8); Hebrew *Betah.*   v9 Hebrew *Toi,* a variant of *Tou;* also in verse 10   w10 A variant of *Hadoram*   x12 Some Hebrew manuscripts, Septuagint and Syriac (see also 1 Chron. 18:11); most Hebrew manuscripts *Aram*   y13 A few Hebrew manuscripts, Septuagint and Syriac (see also 1 Chron. 18:12); most Hebrew manuscripts *Aram* (that is, Arameans)

8:1 *In the course of time.* Chronologically the events of this chapter, or many of them, are probably to be placed between chs. 5 and 6 (see 7:1 and note). *Metheg Ammah.* An unknown site, perhaps near Gath (see 1Ch 18:1).
8:2 *Moabites.* Descendants of Lot (Ge 19:37), occupying territory east of the Dead Sea. Saul fought with the Moabites (1Sa 14:47), and David sought refuge in Moab for his parents during his exile from Israel (1Sa 22:3–4). See note on Ru 1:22.
8:3 *Hadadezer.* Means "Hadad is (my) help." Hadad was an Aramean deity equivalent to the Canaanite Baal. *Zobah.* Saul had previously fought against the kings of Zobah (1Sa 14:47), whose territory was apparently located in the Beqaa Valley between the Lebanon and Anti-Lebanon mountains, thus on Israel's northern border. *restore.* Saul's earlier victories over the kings of Zobah had extended Israelite control, if only briefly, as far as the fringes of the Euphrates Valley. *Euphrates River.* The land promised to Abraham had included borders from Egypt to the Euphrates (Ge 15:18–21; Dt 1:7; 11:24; Jos 1:4). Here is at least another provisional fulfillment of this promise (see 1Ki 4:21–24; see also Ge

17:8; Jos 21:43–45). See map No. 5 at the end of the Study Bible.
8:4 See NIV text note. *hamstrung . . . the chariot horses.* See Jos 11:6 and note. David may not have understood the value of the chariot as a military weapon.
8:5 *came to help Hadadezer.* They feared Israelite expansion to the north.
8:7 *gold shields.* Shields adorned with gold—the phrase is similar to "iron chariots" (see Jos 17:16 and note).
8:8 *bronze.* Later used by Solomon in the construction of the temple (1Ch 18:8).
8:9 *Hamath.* A kingdom centered on the Orontes River, north of Zobah (see v. 3 and note).
8:13 *Valley of Salt.* See 2Ki 14:7; see also Ps 60 title.
8:15 *just and right.* As a true theocratic king, David's reign was characterized by adherence to God's standards of right rule (see notes on 1Sa 8:3; 12:3), as no doubt laid down in Samuel's "regulations of the kingship" (see 1Sa 10:25 and note; 1Ki 2:3–4).
8:16 *Joab son of Zeruiah was over the army.* See notes on 2:13; 5:8. *recorder.* The precise duties of this official are not

Jehoshaphat*a* son of Ahilud was recorder;*b* 17Zadok*c* son of Ahitub and Ahimelech son of Abiathar*d* were priests; Seraiah was secretary;*e* 18Benaiah*f* son of Jehoiada was over the Kerethites*g* and Pelethites; and David's sons were royal advisers.*z*

David and Mephibosheth

9 David asked, "Is there anyone still left of the house of Saul to whom I can show kindness for Jonathan's sake?"*h*

2Now there was a servant of Saul's household named Ziba.*i* They called him to appear before David, and the king said to him, "Are you Ziba?"

"Your servant," he replied.

3The king asked, "Is there no one still left of the house of Saul to whom I can show God's kindness?"

Ziba answered the king, "There is still a son of Jonathan;*j* he is crippled*k* in both feet."

4"Where is he?" the king asked.

Ziba answered, "He is at the house of Makir*l* son of Ammiel in Lo Debar."

5So King David had him brought from Lo Debar, from the house of Makir son of Ammiel.

6When Mephibosheth son of Jonathan, the son of Saul, came to David, he bowed down to pay him honor.*m*

David said, "Mephibosheth!"

"Your servant," he replied.

7"Don't be afraid," David said to him, "for I will surely show you kindness for the sake of your father Jonathan.*n* I will restore to you all the land that belonged to your grandfather Saul, and you will always eat at my table.*o*"

8Mephibosheth*p* bowed down and said, "What is your servant, that you should notice a dead dog*q* like me?"

9Then the king summoned Ziba, Saul's servant, and said to him, "I have given

---

8:16 *a*2Sa 20:24; 1Ki 4:3 *b*Isa 36:3, 22
8:17 *c*1Sa 2:35; 2Sa 15:24,29; 20:25; 1Ki 1:8; 4:4; 1Ch 6:8,53; 16:39; 24:3; 27:17; 2Ch 31:10; Eze 40:46; 43:19; 44:15; 48:11 *d*Mk 2:26 *e*1Ki 4:3; 2Ki 12:10; 19:2; 22:3; Isa 36:3; Jer 36:12
8:18 *f*2Sa 20:23; 23:20; 1Ki 1:8, 38; 2:25,35,46; 4:4 *g*S 1Sa 30:14
9:1 *h*S 1Sa 20:14-17, 42; S 23:18
9:2 *i*2Sa 16:1-4; 19:17,26,29
9:3 *j*1Ch 8:34 *k*S Lev 21:18
9:4 *l*2Sa 17:27-29
9:6 *m*S Ge 37:7
9:7 *n*S 1Sa 20:14-15 over 13; 2Sa 19:28; 21:7; 1Ki 2:7; 2Ki 25:29; Jer 52:33
9:8 *p*S 2Sa 4:4 *q*S 2Sa 3:8

z18 Or *were priests*

---

indicated, though the position was an important one in the court and was maintained throughout the period of the monarchy (see 2Ki 18:18,37; 2Ch 34:8; Isa 36:3,11,22). He may have been a kind of chancellor or chief administrator of royal affairs, responsible among other things for the royal chronicles and annals.
8:17 *Zadok son of Ahitub.* First mentioned here, Zadok was a descendant of Eleazar son of Aaron (see 1Ch 6:4–8, 50–52; 24:1–3). His father, Ahitub, is not to be identified with Ichabod's brother of the same name (1Sa 14:3). Zadok remained loyal to David throughout his reign (15:24–29; 17:15–16; 19:11) and eventually anointed Solomon as David's successor (1Ki 1:8,45; 2:35; 4:4). *Ahimelech son of Abiathar.* It appears that a copyist's error may have occurred here (repeated in 1Ch 24:3,6,31) in which these two names have been transposed. Abiathar is referred to as son of Ahimelech in 1Sa 22:20. While it is true that the Abiathar of 1Sa 22:20 could have had a son named Ahimelech (after his grandfather), such a person does not appear elsewhere in the narratives of Samuel and Kings as a colleague of Zadok, but Abiathar consistently does (15:29,35; 17:15; 19:11; 20:25; 1Ki 1:7–8,19; 2:27,35; 4:4). Abiathar was a descendant of Aaron through Ithamar (1Ch 24:3) in the line of Eli (see notes on 1Sa 2:31,33). *Seraiah.* Also called Sheva (20:25), Shisha (1Ki 4:3) and Shavsha (1Ch 18:16). *secretary.* His duties presumably included domestic and foreign correspondence, perhaps keeping records of important political events, and various administrative functions (2Ki 12:10–12).
8:18 *Kerethites and Pelethites.* See note on 1Sa 30:14. Under the leadership of Benaiah, they formed a sort of special royal guard for David (23:22–23). "Pelethite" is probably an alternate form of "Philistine." *royal advisers.* The Hebrew has the common word for "priests" (see NIV text note; see also 20:26), but the usage is obscure since that sense appears unlikely. Chronicles has "chief officials at the king's side" (see 1Ch 18:17 and note), which supports the meaning "royal advisers."
9:1–20:26 These chapters, together with 1Ki 1:1–2:46, are often referred to as the "Court History of David" and hailed as one of the finest examples of historical narrative to have been produced in the ancient world. Their intimate and

precise detail marks them as the work of an eyewitness.
9:1–13 The events of this chapter cannot be dated precisely, but they occurred a number of years after David's capture of Jerusalem. Mephibosheth was five years old at the time of his father's death (4:4); now he has a son of his own (v. 12).
9:1 *I can show kindness for Jonathan's sake.* David has not forgotten his promise to Jonathan (see 1Sa 20:15,42).
9:2 *Ziba.* The chief steward of Saul's estate, which had been inherited by Mephibosheth son of Jonathan, Saul's firstborn (see 1:1–4; 19:17).
9:3 *There is still a son of Jonathan.* Saul had other descendants (see 21:8), but Ziba mentions only the one in whom David would be chiefly interested.
9:4 *Makir.* Apparently a wealthy benefactor of Mephibosheth who later also came to David's aid (17:27). *Lo Debar.* A town deep in Gileadite territory in Transjordan (Jos 13:26, "Debir"), far from the family estate and from David's court (see note on 2:8).
9:7 *restore to you.* The property Saul had acquired as king had either been taken over by David, or Ziba as steward had virtually taken possession of it and was profiting from its income (see 16:1–4; 19:26–30). *you will always eat at my table.* More a matter of high honor than economic assistance. Mephibosheth's general financial needs were to be cared for by the produce of Saul's estate (v. 10).
9:8 *dead dog like me.* An expression of deep self-abasement. The author has used the "dead dog" motif with great effect. First Goliath, scornfully disdaining the young warrior David, asks, "Am I a dog . . . ?" (1Sa 17:43)—and unwittingly foreshadows his own end. Then David, in a self-deprecating manner, describes himself as a "dead dog" (1Sa 24:14) to suggest to Saul that the king of Israel should not consider him worth so much attention. In the Nabal episode, that "dog" (a Calebite) and his sudden death characterize Saul and foreshadow his unhappy end (see note on 1Sa 25:3). Here a grandson of Saul and in 16:9 a relative of the dead king who curses David are similarly described. For the author, "dead dog" fittingly characterizes those who foolishly scorn or oppose the Lord's anointed, while David's own self-depreciation (see 1Sa 18:18; 2Sa 7:18) is conducive to his exaltation.

your master's grandson everything that belonged to Saul and his family. [10]You and your sons and your servants are to farm the land for him and bring in the crops, so that your master's grandson[r] may be provided for. And Mephibosheth, grandson of your master, will always eat at my table." (Now Ziba had fifteen sons and twenty servants.)

[11]Then Ziba said to the king, "Your servant will do whatever my lord the king commands his servant to do." So Mephibosheth ate at David's[a] table like one of the king's sons.[s]

[12]Mephibosheth had a young son named Mica, and all the members of Ziba's household were servants of Mephibosheth.[t] [13]And Mephibosheth lived in Jerusalem, because he always ate at the king's table, and he was crippled in both feet.

David Defeats the Ammonites

10:1–19pp — 1Ch 19:1–19

10 In the course of time, the king of the Ammonites died, and his son Hanun succeeded him as king. [2]David thought, "I will show kindness to Hanun son of Nahash,[u] just as his father showed kindness to me." So David sent a delegation to express his sympathy to Hanun concerning his father.

When David's men came to the land of the Ammonites, [3]the Ammonite nobles said to Hanun their lord, "Do you think David is honoring your father by sending men to you to express sympathy? Hasn't David sent them to you to explore the city and spy it out[v] and overthrow it?" [4]So Hanun seized David's men, shaved off half of each man's beard,[w] cut off their garments in the middle at the buttocks,[x] and sent them away.

[5]When David was told about this, he sent messengers to meet the men, for they were greatly humiliated. The king said, "Stay at Jericho till your beards have grown, and then come back."

[6]When the Ammonites realized that they had become a stench[y] in David's nostrils, they hired twenty thousand Aramean[z] foot soldiers from Beth Rehob[a] and Zobah,[b] as well as the king of Maacah[c] with a thousand men, and also twelve thousand men from Tob.[d]

[7]On hearing this, David sent Joab[e] out with the entire army of fighting men. [8]The Ammonites came out and drew up in battle formation at the entrance to their city gate, while the Arameans of Zobah and Rehob and the men of Tob and Maacah were by themselves in the open country.

[9]Joab saw that there were battle lines in front of him and behind him; so he selected some of the best troops in Israel and deployed them against the Arameans. [10]He put the rest of the men under the command of Abishai[f] his brother and deployed them against the Ammonites. [11]Joab said, "If the Arameans are too strong for me, then you are to come to my rescue; but if the Ammonites are too strong for you, then I will come to rescue you. [12]Be strong[g] and let us fight bravely for our people and the cities of our God. The LORD will do what is good in his sight." [h]

[13]Then Joab and the troops with him advanced to fight the Arameans, and they fled before him. [14]When the Ammonites[i] saw that the Arameans were fleeing, they fled before Abishai and went inside the city. So Joab returned from fighting the Ammonites and came to Jerusalem.

[15]After the Arameans saw that they had been routed by Israel, they regrouped. [16]Hadadezer had Arameans brought from beyond the River[b]; they went to Helam, with Shobach the commander of Hadadezer's army leading them.

[17]When David was told of this, he gathered all Israel, crossed the Jordan and went to Helam. The Arameans formed their battle lines to meet David and fought against him. [18]But they fled before Israel, and Da-

Cross references (center column)

9:10 r2Sa 16:3
9:11 sJob 36:7; Ps 113:8
9:12 tS 2Sa 4:4
10:2 uS 1Sa 11:1
10:3 vS Nu 21:32
10:4 wS Lev 19:27; Isa 7:20; 15:2; 50:6; 52:14; Jer 48:37; Eze 5:1
xIsa 20:4

10:6 yS Ge 34:30
zS 2Sa 8:5
aS Nu 13:21
bS 1Sa 14:47
cS Dt 3:14
dJdg 11:3-5
10:7 eS 2Sa 2:18
10:10 fS 1Sa 26:6
10:12 gS Dt 1:21; 31:6; S Eph 6:10
hS Jdg 10:15; Ne 4:14
10:14 iS 2Sa 8:12

a11 Septuagint; Hebrew my   b16 That is, the Euphrates

9:12 *Mica.* See 1Ch 8:35–39 for his descendants.

10:1 *king.* Nahash (see v. 2; 1Sa 11). *Ammonites.* See note on 1Sa 11:1.

10:2 *show kindness.* The Hebrew for this expression suggests that a formal treaty existed between the Israelites and the Ammonites. Perhaps this explains why there is no account of a war against the Ammonites in ch. 8, and why the Ammonites did not come to the assistance of the Moabites (8:2).

10:3 *city.* Rabbah, the capital (11:1; 12:26).

10:4 *shaved off half of each man's beard.* In the Eastern world of that time this was considered an insult of the most serious kind. A beard was shaved only as a sign of deep mourning (see Isa 15:2; Jer 41:5; Eze 5:1). *cut off their*

garments in the middle at the buttocks. A customary way of degrading prisoners of war (see Isa 20:4).

10:5 *Jericho.* See notes on Jos 6:1,26; 1Ki 16:34. Jericho remained unrestored during the centuries between Joshua's conquest and the time of Ahab.

10:6 *Beth Rehob.* See Nu 13:21; Jdg 18:28. *Zobah.* See note on 8:3. *Maacah.* See Dt 3:14; Jos 12:5; 13:13. *Tob.* See Jdg 11:3,5.

10:10 *Abishai.* See note on 1Sa 26:6.

10:16 *Hadadezer.* See note on 8:3. *Helam.* A town close to the northern border of Gilead.

10:18 *seven hundred.* Evidently a copyist's mistake; in 1Ch 19:18 the figure is 7,000.

vid killed seven hundred of their charioteers and forty thousand of their foot sol-
diers.c He also struck down Shobach the
commander of their army, and he died
there. 19When all the kings who were vassals of Hadadezer saw that they had been
defeated by Israel, they made peace with
the Israelites and became subjectj to
them.

So the Arameansk were afraid to help
the Ammonites anymore.

David and Bathsheba

11 In the spring,l at the time when
kings go off to war, David sent
Joabm out with the king's men and the
whole Israelite army.n They destroyed the
Ammonites and besieged Rabbah.o But
David remained in Jerusalem.

2One evening David got up from his bed
and walked around on the roofp of the
palace. From the roof he sawq a woman
bathing. The woman was very beautiful,
3and David sent someone to find out about
her. The man said, "Isn't this Bathsheba,r
the daughter of Eliams and the wife of
Uriaht the Hittite?" 4Then David sent
messengers to get her.u She came to him,
and he sleptv with her. (She had purified
herself from her uncleanness.)w Thend she
went back home. 5The woman conceived
and sent word to David, saying, "I am
pregnant."

6So David sent this word to Joab: "Send
me Uriahx the Hittite." And Joab sent him
to David. 7When Uriah came to him, David asked him how Joab was, how the soldiers were and how the war was going.
8Then David said to Uriah, "Go down to
your house and wash your feet."y So
Uriah left the palace, and a gift from the
king was sent after him. 9But Uriah slept at
the entrance to the palace with all his master's servants and did not go down to his
house.

10When David was told, "Uriah did not
go home," he asked him, "Haven't you
just come from a distance? Why didn't you
go home?"

11Uriah said to David, "The arkz and
Israel and Judah are staying in tents, and
my master Joab and my lord's men are
camped in the open fields. How could I go
to my house to eat and drink and liea with
my wife? As surely as you live, I will not
do such a thing!"

12Then David said to him, "Stay here
one more day, and tomorrow I will send
you back." So Uriah remained in Jerusalem
that day and the next. 13At David's invitation, he ate and drank with him, and David made him drunk. But in the evening
Uriah went out to sleep on his mat among
his master's servants; he did not go home.

Cross references (center column):

10:19 j2Sa 8:6
k1Ki 11:25;
22:31; 2Ki 5:1
11:1 l1Ki 20:22,
26 m2Sa 2:18
n1Ch 20:1
oSt Dt 3:11
11:2 pS Dt 22:8;
S Jos 2:8
qMt 5:28
11:3 r1Ch 3:5
s2Sa 23:34
t2Sa 23:39
11:4
uS Lev 20:10;
Ps 51 Title;
Jas 1:14-15
vDt 22:22
wS Lev 15:25-30

11:6 x1Ch 11:41
11:8 yS Ge 18:4
11:11 z2Sa 7:2
aS 1Sa 21:5

c18 Some Septuagint manuscripts (see also 1 Chron.
19:18); Hebrew *horsemen*   d4 Or *with her. When she
purified herself from her uncleanness,*

10:19 *they made peace with the Israelites.* There is no
indication that Hadadezer himself made peace with Israel as
his vassals did in the aftermath of this defeat. These events
represent David's last major campaign against combined foreign powers.
11:1 *the spring.* Of the year following the events reported
in ch. 10. The time must have been about ten years after
David became established in Jerusalem. *the time when kings
go off to war.* Directly after the grain harvest in April and
May. *Rabbah.* See note on 10:3. Though now alone (see
10:19), the Ammonites had not yet been subjugated.
11:2 *walked around on the roof.* The roofs were flat (see
1Sa 9:25). David had probably gone there to enjoy the cool
evening air.
11:3 *Eliam.* Perhaps the same Eliam who was a member of
David's personal bodyguard (23:34) and a son of his counsel-
or Ahithophel. *Uriah.* Also listed among those comprising
David's royal guard (23:39). His name suggests that even
though he was a Hittite, he had adopted the Israelite faith
(Uriah means "My light is the LORD"). *Hittite.* See note on
1Sa 26:6.
11:4 *David sent messengers to get her.* Through this
action David eventually becomes guilty of breaking the sixth,
seventh, ninth and tenth commandments (Ex 20:13–17).
She came to him, and he slept with her. Bathsheba appears
to have been an unprotesting partner in this adulterous
relationship with David. (*She had purified herself from her
uncleanness.*) The purpose of this parenthetical statement is
to indicate Bathsheba's condition at the time of her sexual
relations with David. She had just become ceremonially

clean (Lev 15:28–30) after the seven-day period of monthly
impurity due to menstruation (Lev 15:19–30). The significance of this in the context is to make it clear that she was
not already pregnant by her own husband when David took
her.
11:5 *I am pregnant.* Bathsheba leaves the next step up to
David. The law prescribed the death penalty for both David
and Bathsheba (Lev 20:10; Dt 22:22), as they well knew.
11:6 *Send me Uriah.* Under the pretense of seeking information about the course of the war, David brings Uriah back
to Jerusalem.
11:8 *Go down to your house and wash your feet.* In
essence, David tells Uriah to go home and relax. What he
does not say specifically is what is most important, and well
understood by Uriah (v. 11). *a gift from the king was sent
after him.* The Hebrew word for "gift" has the meaning of
"food" in Ge 43:34 ("portions" from the king's table). David
wanted Uriah and Bathsheba to enjoy their evening together.
11:11 *ark.* Uriah's statement suggests that the ark was in
the field camp with the army rather than in the tent that
David had set up for it in Jerusalem (6:17). If so, it was
probably there for purposes of worship and to seek guidance
for the war. But then the circumstances are even more
damning for David—the Lord is in the field with his army
while David stays at home in leisure. *How could I go to my
house . . . ?* Uriah's devotion to duty exposes by sharp contrast David's dalliance at home while his men are in the field.
As surely as you live. See note on 1Sa 1:26.
11:13 *David made him drunk.* In the hope that in this
condition he would relent and go to Bathsheba.

¹⁴In the morning David wrote a letter^b to Joab and sent it with Uriah. ¹⁵In it he wrote, "Put Uriah in the front line where the fighting is fiercest. Then withdraw from him so he will be struck down^c and die.^d"

¹⁶So while Joab had the city under siege, he put Uriah at a place where he knew the strongest defenders were. ¹⁷When the men of the city came out and fought against Joab, some of the men in David's army fell; moreover, Uriah the Hittite died.

¹⁸Joab sent David a full account of the battle. ¹⁹He instructed the messenger: "When you have finished giving the king this account of the battle, ²⁰the king's anger may flare up, and he may ask you, 'Why did you get so close to the city to fight? Didn't you know they would shoot arrows from the wall? ²¹Who killed Abimelech^e son of Jerub-Besheth^e? Didn't a woman throw an upper millstone on him from the wall,^f so that he died in Thebez? Why did you get so close to the wall?' If he asks you this, then say to him, 'Also, your servant Uriah the Hittite is dead.' "

²²The messenger set out, and when he arrived he told David everything Joab had sent him to say. ²³The messenger said to David, "The men overpowered us and came out against us in the open, but we drove them back to the entrance to the city gate. ²⁴Then the archers shot arrows at your servants from the wall, and some of the king's men died. Moreover, your servant Uriah the Hittite is dead."

²⁵David told the messenger, "Say this to Joab: 'Don't let this upset you; the sword devours one as well as another. Press the attack against the city and destroy it.' Say this to encourage Joab."

²⁶When Uriah's wife heard that her husband was dead, she mourned for him.

²⁷After the time of mourning^g was over, David had her brought to his house, and she became his wife and bore him a son. But the thing David had done displeased^h the LORD.

Nathan Rebukes David

11:1; 12:29–31pp — 1Ch 20:1–3

12 The LORD sent Nathanⁱ to David.^j When he came to him,^k he said, "There were two men in a certain town, one rich and the other poor. ²The rich man had a very large number of sheep and cattle, ³but the poor man had nothing except one little ewe lamb he had bought. He raised it, and it grew up with him and his children. It shared his food, drank from his cup and even slept in his arms. It was like a daughter to him.

⁴"Now a traveler came to the rich man, but the rich man refrained from taking one of his own sheep or cattle to prepare a meal for the traveler who had come to him. Instead, he took the ewe lamb that belonged to the poor man and prepared it for the one who had come to him."

⁵David^l burned with anger^m against the manⁿ and said to Nathan, "As surely as the LORD lives,^o the man who did this deserves to die! ⁶He must pay for that lamb four times over,^p because he did such a thing and had no pity."

⁷Then Nathan said to David, "You are the man!^q This is what the LORD, the God of Israel, says: 'I anointed^r you^s king over Israel, and I delivered you from the hand of Saul. ⁸I gave your master's house to you,^t and your master's wives into your arms. I gave you the house of Israel and Judah. And if all this had been too little, I would have given you even more. ⁹Why did you

^e*21* Also known as *Jerub-Baal* (that is, Gideon)

Cross references (center column):

11:14 ^b1Ki 21:8
11:15 ^cver 14-17; 2Sa 12:9
^d2Sa 12:12
11:21 ^eS Jdg 8:31
^fJdg 9:50-54

11:27 ^gDt 34:8
^h2Sa 12:9; Ps 51:4-5
12:1 ⁱS 2Sa 7:2
^jPs 51 Title
^k2Sa 14:4
12:5 ^l1Ki 20:40
^mS Ge 34:7
ⁿRo 2:1
^oS 1Sa 14:39
12:6 ^pEx 22:1
12:7 ^q2Sa 14:13; Da 4:22
^rS 1Sa 2:35
^s1Ki 20:42
12:8 ^tS 2Sa 9:7

11:15 *so he will be struck down and die.* Unsuccessful in making it appear that Uriah was the father of Bathsheba's child, David plotted Uriah's death so he could marry Bathsheba himself as quickly as possible.

11:21 *Jerub-Besheth.* Another possible spelling is "Jerub-Bosheth." In Judges he is called Jerub-Baal (see note on Jdg 6:32; see also NIV text note here). For similar name changes by the author of Samuel see notes on 2:8; 4:4. *millstone.* See Jdg 9:52–53. *Uriah . . . is dead.* Joab knows that this news is of great importance to David, and he uses it to squelch any criticism David might otherwise have had of the battle tactics.

11:25 *David told the messenger.* David hid his satisfaction over the news with a hypocritical statement that war is war and the death of Uriah should not be a discouragement.

11:27 *time of mourning was over.* Presumably a period of seven days (Ge 50:10; 1Sa 31:13). *she became his wife.* See notes on 3:2–5; 5:14. *the thing David had done displeased the LORD.* Not only had David brazenly violated God's laws

(see note on v. 4) but, even worse, he had shamelessly abused his royal power, which the Lord had entrusted to him to shepherd the Lord's people (5:2; 7:7–8).

12:1 *The LORD sent.* Prophets were messengers from the Lord. Here the Great King sends his emissary to rebuke and announce judgment on the king he had enthroned over his people. *Nathan.* See note on 7:2. *There were two men.* Nathan begins one of the most striking parables in the OT.

12:5 *As surely as the LORD lives.* See note on 1Sa 14:39.

12:6 *four times over.* In agreement with the requirements of Ex 22:1.

12:8 *your master's wives.* Earlier narratives refer to only one wife of Saul (Ahinoam, 1Sa 14:50) and one concubine (Rizpah, 2Sa 3:7; 21:8). This statement suggests that there were others. But since it was customary for new kings to assume the harem of their predecessors (see note on 3:7), it may be that Nathan merely uses conventional language to emphasize that the Lord had placed David on Saul's throne. *I gave you the house of Israel and Judah.* See 2:4; 5:2–3.

despise[u] the word of the LORD by doing what is evil in his eyes? You struck down[v] Uriah[w] the Hittite with the sword and took his wife to be your own. You killed[x] him with the sword of the Ammonites. [10]Now, therefore, the sword[y] will never depart from your house, because you despised me and took the wife of Uriah the Hittite to be your own.'

[11]"This is what the LORD says: 'Out of your own household[z] I am going to bring calamity upon you. [a] Before your very eyes I will take your wives and give them to one who is close to you, and he will lie with your wives in broad daylight. [b] [12]You did it in secret, [c] but I will do this thing in broad daylight[d] before all Israel.' "

[13]Then David said to Nathan, "I have sinned[e] against the LORD."

Nathan replied, "The LORD has taken away[f] your sin. [g] You are not going to die. [h] [14]But because by doing this you have made the enemies of the LORD show utter contempt,[f][i] the son born to you will die."

[15]After Nathan had gone home, the LORD struck[j] the child that Uriah's wife had borne to David, and he became ill. [16]David pleaded with God for the child. He fasted and went into his house and spent the nights lying[k] on the ground. [17]The elders of his household stood beside him to get him up from the ground, but he refused, [l] and he would not eat any food with them. [m]

[18]On the seventh day the child died. David's servants were afraid to tell him that the child was dead, for they thought, "While the child was still living, we spoke to David but he would not listen to us.

How can we tell him the child is dead? He may do something desperate."

[19]David noticed that his servants were whispering among themselves and he realized the child was dead. "Is the child dead?" he asked.

"Yes," they replied, "he is dead."

[20]Then David got up from the ground. After he had washed, [n] put on lotions and changed his clothes, [o] he went into the house of the LORD and worshiped. Then he went to his own house, and at his request they served him food, and he ate.

[21]His servants asked him, "Why are you acting this way? While the child was alive, you fasted and wept, [p] but now that the child is dead, you get up and eat!"

[22]He answered, "While the child was still alive, I fasted and wept. I thought, 'Who knows? [q] The LORD may be gracious to me and let the child live.' [r] [23]But now that he is dead, why should I fast? Can I bring him back again? I will go to him, [s] but he will not return to me." [t]

[24]Then David comforted his wife Bathsheba, [u] and he went to her and lay with her. She gave birth to a son, and they named him Solomon. [v] The LORD loved him; [25]and because the LORD loved him, he sent word through Nathan the prophet to name him Jedidiah. [g] [w]

[26]Meanwhile Joab fought against Rabbah[x] of the Ammonites and captured the royal citadel. [27]Joab then sent messengers to David, saying, "I have fought against Rabbah and taken its water supply. [28]Now muster the rest of the troops and besiege

---

Cross references

12:9
[u]S Nu 15:31;
S 1Sa 13:14
[v]S 2Sa 11:15
[w]1Ki 15:5
[x]Ps 26:9; 51:14
12:10
[y]2Sa 13:28;
18:14-15;
1Ki 2:25
12:11 [z]2Sa 16:11
[a]Dt 28:30;
2Sa 16:21-22
[b]S Dt 17:17
12:12
[c]2Sa 11:4-15
[d]2Sa 16:22
12:13
[e]S Ge 13:13;
S 20:6;
S Nu 22:34
[f]Ps 32:1-5; 51:1,
9; 103:12;
Isa 43:25; 44:22;
Zec 3:4,9
[g]Pr 28:13;
Jer 2:35;
Mic 7:18-19
[h]Lev 20:10;
24:17
12:14 [i]Isa 52:5;
Ro 2:24
12:15
[j]S 1Sa 25:38
12:16 [k]Ps 5:7;
95:6
12:17
[l]S Ge 37:35;
S 1Sa 1:7
[m]S 2Sa 3:35;
Da 6:18

12:20 [n]Mt 6:17
[o]S Ge 41:14
12:21 [p]Jdg 20:26
12:22 [q]Jnh 3:9
[r]Isa 38:1-5
12:23 [s]Ge 37:35
[t]S 1Sa 31:13;
2Sa 13:39;
Job 7:10; 10:21
12:24 [u]1Ki 1:11
[v]1Ki 1:10;
1Ch 22:9; 28:5;
Mt 1:6
12:25 [w]Ne 13:26
12:26 [x]S Dt 3:11

[f]14 Masoretic Text; an ancient Hebrew scribal tradition this you have shown utter contempt for the LORD
[g]25 Jedidiah means loved by the LORD.

12:9 despise the word of the LORD. See notes on 11:4,27. You killed him. David is held directly responsible for Uriah's death even though he fell in battle (see 11:15).

12:10 the sword will never depart from your house. Three of David's sons came to violent deaths: Amnon (13:28–29), Absalom (18:14) and Adonijah (1Ki 2:25).

12:11 Out of your own household I am going to bring calamity upon you. David was driven from Jerusalem by Absalom's conspiracy to seize the kingship from his own father (15:1–15). he will lie with your wives in broad daylight. Fulfilled at the time of Absalom's rebellion (see note on 16:22).

12:13 I have sinned against the LORD. David recognizes his guilt and confesses his sin in response to Nathan's rebuke (see Ps 51). Notice the contrast between David's confession and Saul's (see note on 1Sa 15:24). The LORD has taken away your sin. David experienced the joy of knowing his sin was forgiven (see Ps 32:1,5; cf. Ps 51:8,12). You are not going to die. The Lord, in his grace, released David from the customary death penalty for adultery and murder (Lev 20:10; 24:17).

12:14 you have made the enemies of the LORD show utter contempt. David is required to suffer the disciplinary results of his sin in a manner open to public view. But see NIV text note.

12:20 he went into the house of the LORD and worshiped. In this way David clearly demonstrated his humble acceptance of the disciplinary results of his sin. Notice again (see note on v. 13) the contrast between David's attitude and Saul's (see note on 1Sa 15:25).

12:23 I will go to him. Like the child, David will die and join him in the grave (see note on Ge 37:35).

12:24 Solomon. See 1Ch 22:9 and NIV text note.

12:25 Jedidiah. See NIV text note. The giving of this name suggests that the Lord's special favor rested on Solomon from his birth. And since the name also contained an echo of David's name, it provided assurance to David that the Lord also loved him and would continue his dynasty.

12:26 Joab fought against Rabbah. The writer now returns to the outcome of the attack against the Ammonites (11:1, 25), which provided the background for the story of David and Bathsheba. Even while the Lord was displeased with David, he gave the Israelites victory over a people that had abused them.

the city and capture it. Otherwise I will take the city, and it will be named after me."

²⁹So David mustered the entire army and went to Rabbah, and attacked and captured it. ³⁰He took the crown^y from the head of their king^h—its weight was a talentⁱ of gold, and it was set with precious stones—and it was placed on David's head. He took a great quantity of plunder from the city ³¹and brought out the people who were there, consigning them to labor with saws and with iron picks and axes, and he made them work at brickmaking.^j He did this to all the Ammonite^z towns. Then David and his entire army returned to Jerusalem.

Amnon and Tamar

13 In the course of time, Amnon^a son of David fell in love with Tamar,^b the beautiful sister of Absalom^c son of David.

²Amnon became frustrated to the point of illness on account of his sister Tamar, for she was a virgin, and it seemed impossible for him to do anything to her.

³Now Amnon had a friend named Jonadab son of Shimeah,^d David's brother. Jonadab was a very shrewd man. ⁴He asked Amnon, "Why do you, the king's son, look so haggard morning after morning? Won't you tell me?"

Amnon said to him, "I'm in love with Tamar, my brother Absalom's sister."

⁵"Go to bed and pretend to be ill," Jonadab said. "When your father comes to see you, say to him, 'I would like my sister Tamar to come and give me something to eat. Let her prepare the food in my sight so I may watch her and then eat it from her hand.'"

⁶So Amnon lay down and pretended to be ill. When the king came to see him, Amnon said to him, "I would like my sister Tamar to come and make some special

bread in my sight, so I may eat from her hand."

⁷David sent word to Tamar at the palace: "Go to the house of your brother Amnon and prepare some food for him." ⁸So Tamar went to the house of her brother Amnon, who was lying down. She took some dough, kneaded it, made the bread in his sight and baked it. ⁹Then she took the pan and served him the bread, but he refused to eat.

"Send everyone out of here,"^e Amnon said. So everyone left him. ¹⁰Then Amnon said to Tamar, "Bring the food here into my bedroom so I may eat from your hand." And Tamar took the bread she had prepared and brought it to her brother Amnon in his bedroom. ¹¹But when she took it to him to eat, he grabbed^f her and said, "Come to bed with me, my sister."^g

¹²"Don't, my brother!" she said to him. "Don't force me. Such a thing should not be done in Israel!^h Don't do this wicked thing.ⁱ ¹³What about me?^j Where could I get rid of my disgrace? And what about you? You would be like one of the wicked fools in Israel. Please speak to the king; he will not keep me from being married to you." ¹⁴But he refused to listen to her, and since he was stronger than she, he raped her.^k

¹⁵Then Amnon hated her with intense hatred. In fact, he hated her more than he had loved her. Amnon said to her, "Get up and get out!"

¹⁶"No!" she said to him. "Sending me away would be a greater wrong than what you have already done to me."

But he refused to listen to her. ¹⁷He called his personal servant and said, "Get this woman out of here and bolt the door after her." ¹⁸So his servant put her out and bolted the door after her. She was wearing

---

12:30 ^yEst 8:15; Ps 21:3; 132:18
12:31 ^zS 1Sa 14:47
13:1 ^a2Sa 3:2
^b2Sa 14:27; 1Ch 3:9
^c2Sa 3:3
13:3 ^dS 1Sa 16:9

13:9 ^eGe 45:1
13:11 ^fS Ge 39:12
^gS Ge 38:16
13:12 ^hLev 20:17
ⁱS Ge 34:7
13:13 ^jS Lev 18:9;
S Dt 22:21,23-24
13:14 ^kS Ge 34:2;
Eze 22:11

^h30 Or of Milcom (that is, Molech)   ⁱ30 That is, about 75 pounds (about 34 kilograms)   ^j31 The meaning of the Hebrew for this clause is uncertain.

12:30 *the crown . . . was placed on David's head.* A crown of such weight (see NIV text note) would have been worn only briefly and on very special occasions. Perhaps it was worn only once in a symbolic act of transferring to David sovereignty over Ammon.

12:31 *consigning them to labor.* Victorious kings often used prisoners of war as menial laborers in royal building projects (see 1Ki 9:20–21; cf. also Ex 1:11).

13:1–39 The trouble within David's family begins (see note on 12:10).

13:1 *Amnon.* David's oldest son (3:2). *Tamar.* David's daughter by Maacah of Geshur (3:3), and Absalom's full sister.

13:3 *Shimeah.* Called Shammah in 1Sa 16:9.

13:13 *what about you?* This act would jeopardize Amnon's position as crown prince and heir to the throne. *he will not keep me from being married to you.* Possibly a futile attempt by Tamar to escape Amnon's immediate designs rather than a serious proposal, since such a marriage was prohibited in Israel (see Lev 18:9; 20:17; Dt 27:22).

13:15 *Amnon hated her.* The reversal in Amnon's feelings toward Tamar demonstrates that his former "love" (v. 1) was nothing but sensual desire.

13:16 *Sending me away would be a greater wrong.* No longer a virgin, she could not be offered by her father to any other potential husband (see v. 21 and note).

13:18 *richly ornamented robe.* See Ge 37:3 and note.

Great Sea

Orontes R.

Hamath

PHOENICIANS

ARAMEANS

Litani R.

• Damascus

Tyre

GESHUR

Kishon R.

Yarmuk R.

Dor •

Megiddo

Taanach

• Beth Shan

Jabbok R.

Jordan R.

• Rabbah

Jerusalem

AMMONITES

Hebron

Arnon R.

MOABITES

Zered R.

AMALEKITES

EDOMITES

Euphrates R.

Eastern arm of the
Red Sea

David's Conquests

Once he had become king over all Israel
(2Sa 5:1-5), David:

1. Conquered the Jebusite citadel of Zion/
   Jerusalem and made it his royal city
   (2Sa 5:6-10);

2. Received the recognition of and
   assurance of friendship from Hiram
   of Tyre, king of the Phoenicians
   (2Sa 5:11-12);

3. Decisively defeated the Philistines so that
   their hold on Israelite territory was broken
   and their threat to Israel eliminated
   (2Sa 5:17-25; 8:1);

4. Defeated the Moabites and imposed his
   authority over them (2Sa 8:2);

5. Crushed the Aramean kingdoms of
   Hadadezer (king of Zobah), Damascus
   and Maacah and put them under tribute
   (2Sa 8:3-8; 10:6-19). Talmai, the Aramean
   king of Geshur, apparently had made
   peace with David while he was still
   reigning in Hebron and sealed the alliance
   by giving his daughter in marriage to
   David (2Sa 3:3; see 1Ch 2:23);

6. Subdued Edom and incorporated it into
   his empire (2Sa 8:13-14);

7. Defeated the Ammonites and brought
   them into subjection (2Sa 12:19-31);

8. Subjugated the remaining Canaanite
   cities that had previously maintained their
   independence from and hostility toward
   Israel, such as Beth Shan, Megiddo,
   Taanach and Dor.

Since David had earlier crushed the
Amalekites (1Sa 30:17), his wars thus
completed the conquest begun by Joshua
and secured all the borders of Israel. His
empire (united Israel plus the subjugated
kingdoms) reached from Ezion Geber on
the eastern arm of the Red Sea to the
Euphrates River.

Miles	0		20		40		60		80		100
Kms	0	20	40	60	80	100	120	140			

a richly ornamented[k] robe,[l] for this was the kind of garment the virgin daughters of the king wore. [19]Tamar put ashes[m] on her head and tore the ornamented[l] robe she was wearing. She put her hand on her head and went away, weeping aloud as she went.

[20]Her brother Absalom said to her, "Has that Amnon, your brother, been with you? Be quiet now, my sister; he is your brother. Don't take this thing to heart." And Tamar lived in her brother Absalom's house, a desolate woman.

[21]When King David heard all this, he was furious.[n] [22]Absalom never said a word to Amnon, either good or bad;[o] he hated[p] Amnon because he had disgraced his sister Tamar.

Absalom Kills Amnon

[23]Two years later, when Absalom's sheepshearers[q] were at Baal Hazor near the border of Ephraim, he invited all the king's sons to come there. [24]Absalom went to the king and said, "Your servant has had shearers come. Will the king and his officials please join me?"

[25]"No, my son," the king replied. "All of us should not go; we would only be a burden to you." Although Absalom urged him, he still refused to go, but gave him his blessing.

[26]Then Absalom said, "If not, please let my brother Amnon come with us."

The king asked him, "Why should he go with you?" [27]But Absalom urged him, so he sent with him Amnon and the rest of the king's sons.

[28]Absalom[r] ordered his men, "Listen! When Amnon is in high[s] spirits from

drinking wine and I say to you, 'Strike Amnon down,' then kill him. Don't be afraid. Have not I given you this order? Be strong and brave.[t]" [29]So Absalom's men did to Amnon what Absalom had ordered. Then all the king's sons got up, mounted their mules and fled.

[30]While they were on their way, the report came to David: "Absalom has struck down all the king's sons; not one of them is left." [31]The king stood up, tore[u] his clothes and lay down on the ground; and all his servants stood by with their clothes torn.

[32]But Jonadab son of Shimeah, David's brother, said, "My lord should not think that they killed all the princes; only Amnon is dead. This has been Absalom's expressed intention ever since the day Amnon raped his sister Tamar. [33]My lord the king should not be concerned about the report that all the king's sons are dead. Only Amnon is dead."

[34]Meanwhile, Absalom had fled.

Now the man standing watch looked up and saw many people on the road west of him, coming down the side of the hill. The watchman went and told the king, "I see men in the direction of Horonaim, on the side of the hill."[m]

[35]Jonadab said to the king, "See, the king's sons are here; it has happened just as your servant said."

[36]As he finished speaking, the king's sons came in, wailing loudly. The king, too, and all his servants wept very bitterly.

[37]Absalom fled and went to Talmai[v] son

13:18
[l]S Ge 37:23
13:19 [m]S Jos 7:6;
Est 4:1; Da 9:3
13:21 [n]S Ge 34:7
13:22 [o]Ge 31:24
[p]Lev 19:17-18;
1Jn 2:9-11
13:23 [q]1Sa 25:7
13:28 [r]S 2Sa 3:3
[s]S Ru 3:7

[r]S 2Sa 12:10
13:31 [u]S Nu 14:6
13:37 [v]S 2Sa 3:3

[k]*18* The meaning of the Hebrew for this phrase is uncertain.   [l]*19* The meaning of the Hebrew for this word is uncertain.   [m]*34* Septuagint; Hebrew does not have this sentence.

13:19 *put ashes on her head.* A sign of great mourning. *tore the ornamented robe.* Thus expressing her anguish and announcing that her virginity had been violated. *put her hand on her head.* Also a sign of grief (see Jer 2:37).
13:20 *Be quiet now, my sister . . . Don't take this thing to heart.* Absalom urges his sister not to make the matter a public scandal, and attempts to quiet her by minimizing its significance. Meanwhile, he formulates his own secret plans for revenge (see vv. 22,28,32).
13:21 *he was furious.* Although David was incensed by Amnon's rape of Tamar, there is no record that he took any punitive action against him. Perhaps the memory of his own sin with Bathsheba adversely affected his judicious handling of the matter. Whatever the reason, David abdicated his responsibility both as king and as father. This disciplinary leniency toward his sons (see notes on 14:33; 1Ki 1:6) eventually led to the death of Amnon and the revolts of Absalom and Adonijah.
13:22 *Absalom never said a word to Amnon . . . he hated Amnon.* He quietly bided his time.
13:23 *he invited all the king's sons.* The time of sheepshearing was a festive occasion (see 1Sa 25:4,8).

13:26 *let my brother Amnon come.* Upon David's refusal of the invitation, Absalom diplomatically requested that Amnon, the crown prince and oldest son, be his representative. *Why should he go with you?* David's question suggests some misgivings because of the strained relationship between the two half brothers (see v. 22).
13:28 *kill him.* Absalom arranged for the murder of his half brother in violation of Eastern hospitality. In the wicked acts of Amnon and Absalom, David's oldest sons became guilty of sexual immorality and murder, as their father had before them. With the murder of Amnon, Absalom not only avenged the rape of his sister but also secured for himself the position of successor to the throne (see 3:3; 15:1–6). Kileab, David's second son (3:3), may have died in his youth since there is no reference to him beyond the announcement of his birth.
13:29 *mules.* Apparently the normal mount for royalty in David's kingdom (see 18:9; 1Ki 1:33,38,44; see also note on 1Ki 1:33).
13:31 *tore his clothes and lay down on the ground.* Common ways of expressing grief (see Jos 7:6; 1Ki 21:27; Est 4:1,3; Job 1:20; 2:8).

of Ammihud, the king of Geshur. But King David mourned for his son every day.

[38]After Absalom fled and went to Geshur, he stayed there three years. [39]And the spirit of the king[n] longed to go to Absalom,[w] for he was consoled[x] concerning Amnon's death.

Absalom Returns to Jerusalem

14 Joab[y] son of Zeruiah knew that the king's heart longed for Absalom. [2]So Joab sent someone to Tekoa[z] and had a wise woman[a] brought from there. He said to her, "Pretend you are in mourning. Dress in mourning clothes, and don't use any cosmetic lotions.[b] Act like a woman who has spent many days grieving for the dead. [3]Then go to the king and speak these words to him." And Joab[c] put the words in her mouth.

[4]When the woman from Tekoa went[o] to the king, she fell with her face to the ground to pay him honor, and she said, "Help me, O king!"

[5]The king asked her, "What is troubling you?"

She said, "I am indeed a widow; my husband is dead. [6]I your servant had two sons. They got into a fight with each other in the field, and no one was there to separate them. One struck the other and killed him. [7]Now the whole clan has risen up against your servant; they say, 'Hand over the one who struck his brother down, so that we may put him to death[d] for the life

of his brother whom he killed; then we will get rid of the heir[e] as well.' They would put out the only burning coal I have left,[f] leaving my husband neither name nor descendant on the face of the earth."

[8]The king said to the woman, "Go home,[g] and I will issue an order in your behalf."

[9]But the woman from Tekoa said to him, "My lord the king, let the blame[h] rest on me and on my father's family,[i] and let the king and his throne be without guilt.[j] "

[10]The king replied, "If anyone says anything to you, bring him to me, and he will not bother you again."

[11]She said, "Then let the king invoke the LORD his God to prevent the avenger[k] of blood from adding to the destruction, so that my son will not be destroyed."

"As surely as the LORD lives," he said, "not one hair[l] of your son's head will fall to the ground.[m] "

[12]Then the woman said, "Let your servant speak a word to my lord the king."

"Speak," he replied.

[13]The woman said, "Why then have you devised a thing like this against the people of God? When the king says this, does he not convict himself,[n] for the king has not brought back his banished son?[o] [14]Like water[p] spilled on the ground, which can-

Cross references (center column)

13:39
w2Sa 14:13
xS 2Sa 12:19-23
14:1 yS 2Sa 2:18
14:2 zNe 3:5;
Jer 6:1; Am 1:1
a2Sa 20:16
b S Ru 3:3;
S Isa 1:6
14:3 cver 19
14:7 dNu 35:19

eMt 21:38
fDt 19:10-13
14:8 g1Sa 25:35
14:9 h1Sa 25:24
iMt 27:25
j1Sa 25:28
14:11
kS Nu 35:12,21
lS Mt 10:30
mS 1Sa 14:45
14:13
nS 2Sa 12:7;
1Ki 20:40
o2Sa 13:38-39
14:14
pJob 14:11;
Ps 58:7; Isa 19:5

n39 Dead Sea Scrolls and some Septuagint manuscripts; Masoretic Text *But the spirit of David the king* o4 Many Hebrew manuscripts, Septuagint, Vulgate and Syriac; most Hebrew manuscripts *spoke*

13:37 *Talmai son of Ammihud, the king of Geshur.* Absalom's grandfather (see 3:3).
13:39 *longed to go to Absalom.* With Absalom a refugee, David had lost both of his oldest living sons.
14:1 *Joab son of Zeruiah.* See note on 2:13. *the king's heart longed for Absalom.* Torn between anger and love (and perhaps remorse), David again leaves the initiative to others.
14:2 *So Joab sent.* Joab appears to have been motivated by a concern for the political implications of the unresolved dispute between David and the son in line for the throne. He attempts to move David to action by means of a story designed to elicit a response clearly applicable, by analogy, to David's own predicament. A similar technique was used by Nathan the prophet (12:1–7; see 1Ki 20:38–43). *Tekoa.* A town a few miles south of Bethlehem, from which the prophet Amos also came (Am 1:1).
14:7 *the whole clan has risen up against your servant.* It was customary in Israel for a murder victim's next of kin to avenge the blood of his relative by putting the murderer to death (see note on 3:27; see also Nu 35:12; Dt 19:11–13). In the case presented, however, blood revenge would wipe out the family line, which was something Israelite law and custom tried to avoid if at all possible (see notes on Dt 25:5–6; Ru 2:20). *we will get rid of the heir as well.* The woman suggests that the motivation for blood revenge was more a selfish desire to acquire the family inheritance than a desire for justice (see Nu 27:11). *leaving my husband*

neither name nor descendant. The implication is that it would be a more serious offense to terminate the woman's family line than to permit a murder to go unpunished by blood revenge. Apparently Joab hoped subtly to suggest to David that if he did not restore Absalom, a struggle for the throne would eventually ensue.
14:8 *I will issue an order in your behalf.* David's judicial action may have rested on the legal ground that the murder was not premeditated (see Dt 19:4–6).
14:9 *blame.* For the unpunished crime.
14:11 *let the king invoke the LORD his God.* The woman wants David to confirm his promise by an oath in the Lord's name. *As surely as the LORD lives.* An oath formula (see notes on Ge 42:15; 1Sa 14:39) that solemnly binds David to his commitment.
14:13 *against the people of God.* The woman's suggestion is that David has done the same thing to Israel that her family members have done to her. The people of Israel want their crown prince returned safely to them. *does he not convict himself . . . ?* The argument is that when David exempted the fictitious murderer from blood revenge, he in effect rendered himself guilty for not doing the same in the case of Absalom. The analogy places David in the position of the blood avenger.
14:14 *Like water spilled on the ground.* Blood revenge will not return the victim of murder to life, just as water spilled on the ground cannot be recovered. *God does not take away life.* In the suggestion that the avenging of blood is contrary

some distance away. [18]All his men marched past him, along with all the Kerethites[x] and Pelethites; and all the six hundred Gittites who had accompanied him from Gath marched before the king.

[19]The king said to Ittai[y] the Gittite, "Why should you come along with us? Go back and stay with King Absalom. You are a foreigner,[z] an exile from your homeland. [20]You came only yesterday. And today shall I make you wander[a] about with us, when I do not know where I am going? Go back, and take your countrymen. May kindness and faithfulness[b] be with you."

[21]But Ittai replied to the king, "As surely as the LORD lives, and as my lord the king lives, wherever my lord the king may be, whether it means life or death, there will your servant be."[c]

[22]David said to Ittai, "Go ahead, march on." So Ittai the Gittite marched on with all his men and the families that were with him.

[23]The whole countryside wept aloud[d] as all the people passed by. The king also crossed the Kidron Valley,[ef] and all the people moved on toward the desert.

[24]Zadok[g] was there, too, and all the Levites who were with him were carrying the ark[h] of the covenant of God. They set down the ark of God, and Abiathar[i] offered sacrifices[s] until all the people had finished leaving the city.

[25]Then the king said to Zadok, "Take the ark of God back into the city. If I find favor in the LORD's eyes, he will bring me back and let me see it and his dwelling place[j] again. [26]But if he says, 'I am not

pleased with you,' then I am ready; let him do to me whatever seems good to him.[k]"

[27]The king also said to Zadok the priest, "Aren't you a seer?[l] Go back to the city in peace, with your son Ahimaaz and Jonathan[m] son of Abiathar. You and Abiathar take your two sons with you. [28]I will wait at the fords[n] in the desert until word comes from you to inform me." [29]So Zadok and Abiathar took the ark of God back to Jerusalem and stayed there.

[30]But David continued up the Mount of Olives, weeping[o] as he went; his head[p] was covered and he was barefoot. All the people with him covered their heads too and were weeping as they went up. [31]Now David had been told, "Ahithophel[q] is among the conspirators with Absalom." So David prayed, "O LORD, turn Ahithophel's counsel into foolishness."

[32]When David arrived at the summit, where people used to worship God, Hushai[r] the Arkite[s] was there to meet him, his robe torn and dust[t] on his head. [33]David said to him, "If you go with me, you will be a burden[u] to me. [34]But if you return to the city and say to Absalom, 'I will be your servant, O king; I was your father's servant in the past, but now I will be your servant,'[v] then you can help me by frustrating[w] Ahithophel's advice. [35]Won't the priests Zadok and Abiathar be there with you? Tell them anything you hear in the king's palace.[x] [36]Their two sons, Ahimaaz[y] son of Zadok and Jonathan[z] son of Abiathar, are there with them. Send them to me with anything you hear."

[37]So David's friend Hushai[a] arrived at Jerusalem as Absalom[b] was entering the city.

[s]24 Or *Abiathar went up*

Cross references (center column)

15:18 [x]S 1Sa 30:14; 2Sa 20:7,23; 1Ki 1:38,44; 1Ch 18:17
15:19 [y]2Sa 18:2 [z]S Ge 31:15
15:20 [a]S 1Sa 22:2 [b]2Sa 2:6
15:21 [c]Ru 1:16-17; Pr 17:17
15:23 [d]1Sa 11:4; Job 2:12 [e]1Ki 2:37; 2Ki 23:12; 2Ch 15:16; 29:16; 30:14; Jer 31:40 [f]Jn 18:1
15:24 [g]S 2Sa 8:17; 19:11 [h]Nu 4:15; S 10:33; 1Ki 2:26 [i]S 1Sa 22:20
15:25 [j]Ex 15:13; S Lev 15:31; Ps 43:3; 46:4; 84:1; 132:7
15:26 [k]S Jdg 10:15; 2Sa 22:20
15:27 [l]S 1Sa 9:9 [m]ver 36; 2Sa 17:17; 1Ki 1:42
15:28 [n]2Sa 17:16
15:30 [o]S Nu 25:6; S Ps 30:5 [p]Est 6:12
15:31 [q]S ver 12
15:32 [r]ver 37; 2Sa 16:16; 17:5; 1Ki 4:16 [s]Jos 16:2 [t]Jos 7:6
15:33 [u]2Sa 19:35
15:34 [v]2Sa 16:19 [w]2Sa 17:14; Pr 11:14
15:35 [x]2Sa 17:15-16
15:36 [y]2Sa 18:19 [z]S ver 27; 2Sa 17:17; 1Ki 1:42
15:37 [a]1Ch 27:33 [b]2Sa 16:15

15:18 *Kerethites and Pelethites.* See note on 8:18. *six hundred Gittites.* Philistine soldiers from Gath under the command of Ittai who for some unknown reason had joined David's personal military force (see 18:2).

15:19 *Go back and stay with King Absalom.* David releases the Philistine contingent from further obligations to him.

15:21 *As surely as the LORD lives.* An oath of loyalty and devotion taken in the name of Israel's God (see note on 1Sa 14:39). For a similar oath see Ru 1:16–17.

15:24 *Zadok.* See note on 8:17. *Abiathar.* See note on 8:17; see also 1Sa 22:20–23.

15:25 *Take the ark of God back into the city.* David reveals a true understanding of the connection between the ark and God's presence with his people. He knows that possession of the ark does not guarantee God's blessing (see notes on 1Sa 4:3,21). He also recognizes that the ark belongs in the capital city as a symbol of the Lord's rule over the nation (see note on 6:2), no matter who the king might be.

15:26 *let him do to me whatever seems good to him.* David confesses that he has no exclusive claim to the throne and that Israel's divine King is free to confer the kingship on

whomever he chooses.

15:27 *Aren't you a seer?* Perhaps an allusion to the high priest's custody of the Urim and Thummim as a means of divine revelation (see notes on Ex 28:30; 1Sa 2:28). See also note on 1Sa 9:9.

15:28 *fords in the desert.* Fords across the Jordan in the vicinity of Gilgal.

15:30 *his head was covered.* A sign of sorrow (see Est 6:12; Jer 14:3–4). *he was barefoot.* Another sign of sorrow (see Isa 20:2,4; Eze 24:17; Mic 1:8).

15:31 *Ahithophel.* See note on v. 12.

15:32 *Hushai the Arkite.* The Arkites were a clan (some think non-Israelite) that inhabited an area southwest of Bethel (Jos 16:2). Since Hushai was a trusted member of David's court (see note on v. 37), his appearance was the beginning of an answer to David's prayer (v. 31).

15:37 *David's friend Hushai.* 1Ch 27:33 calls him the "king's friend," which seems to be an official title for the king's most trusted adviser (see 1Ki 4:5, where the Hebrew for "king's friend" is translated "personal adviser to the king").

David and Ziba

16 When David had gone a short distance beyond the summit, there was Ziba,[c] the steward of Mephibosheth, waiting to meet him. He had a string of donkeys saddled and loaded with two hundred loaves of bread, a hundred cakes of raisins, a hundred cakes of figs and a skin of wine.[d]

[2]The king asked Ziba, "Why have you brought these?"

Ziba answered, "The donkeys are for the king's household to ride on, the bread and fruit are for the men to eat, and the wine is to refresh[e] those who become exhausted in the desert."

[3]The king then asked, "Where is your master's grandson?"[f]

Ziba[g] said to him, "He is staying in Jerusalem, because he thinks, 'Today the house of Israel will give me back my grandfather's kingdom.'"

[4]Then the king said to Ziba, "All that belonged to Mephibosheth[h] is now yours."

"I humbly bow," Ziba said. "May I find favor in your eyes, my lord the king."

Shimei Curses David

[5]As King David approached Bahurim,[i] a man from the same clan as Saul's family came out from there. His name was Shimei[j] son of Gera, and he cursed[k] as he came out. [6]He pelted David and all the king's officials with stones, though all the troops and the special guard were on David's right and left. [7]As he cursed, Shimei said, "Get out, get out, you man of blood, you scoundrel! [8]The LORD has repaid you for all the blood you shed in the household of Saul, in whose place you have reigned.[l] The LORD has handed the kingdom over to your son Absalom. You have come to ruin because you are a man of blood!"[m]

[9]Then Abishai[n] son of Zeruiah said to

16:1 c2Sa 9:1-13
d S 1Sa 25:18;
1Ch 12:40
16:2
e2Sa 17:27-29
16:3 f2Sa 9:9-10
g S 2Sa 9:2
16:4 h S 2Sa 4:4
16:5 i S 2Sa 3:16
j2Sa 19:16-23;
1Ki 2:8-9,36,44
k S Ex 22:28
16:8 l2Sa 19:28;
21:9 m2Sa 19:19;
Ps 55:3
16:9 n S 1Sa 26:6

o S 2Sa 3:8
p S 2Sa 3:39;
Lk 9:54
16:10
q S 2Sa 2:18;
19:22 r Ro 9:20
16:11 s2Sa 12:11
t S Ge 45:5;
1Sa 26:19
16:12 u Ps 4:1;
25:18 v Dt 23:5;
Ro 8:28
w Ps 109:28
16:14 x2Sa 17:2
16:15
y S 2Sa 15:37
z S 2Sa 15:12
16:16
a S 2Sa 15:32
16:17 b2Sa 19:25
16:19 c2Sa 15:34

the king, "Why should this dead dog[o] curse my lord the king? Let me go over and cut off his head."[p]

[10]But the king said, "What do you and I have in common, you sons of Zeruiah?[q] If he is cursing because the LORD said to him, 'Curse David,' who can ask, 'Why do you do this?'"[r]

[11]David then said to Abishai and all his officials, "My son,[s] who is of my own flesh, is trying to take my life. How much more, then, this Benjamite! Leave him alone; let him curse, for the LORD has told him to.[t] [12]It may be that the LORD will see my distress[u] and repay me with good[v] for the cursing I am receiving today."[w]

[13]So David and his men continued along the road while Shimei was going along the hillside opposite him, cursing as he went and throwing stones at him and showering him with dirt. [14]The king and all the people with him arrived at their destination exhausted.[x] And there he refreshed himself.

The Advice of Hushai and Ahithophel

[15]Meanwhile, Absalom[y] and all the men of Israel came to Jerusalem, and Ahithophel[z] was with him. [16]Then Hushai[a] the Arkite, David's friend, went to Absalom and said to him, "Long live the king! Long live the king!"

[17]Absalom asked Hushai, "Is this the love you show your friend? Why didn't you go with your friend?"[b]

[18]Hushai said to Absalom, "No, the one chosen by the LORD, by these people, and by all the men of Israel—his I will be, and I will remain with him. [19]Furthermore, whom should I serve? Should I not serve the son? Just as I served your father, so I will serve you."[c]

[20]Absalom said to Ahithophel, "Give us your advice. What should we do?"

[21]Ahithophel answered, "Lie with your

16:1 *Ziba.* See ch. 9. *Mephibosheth.* See note on 4:4.
16:2 *Ziba answered.* Since David assumed control of Saul's estate (9:7–10), Ziba, always the opportunist, seeks to profit from the political crisis.
16:3 *your master's grandson.* Mephibosheth (see 9:3,9).
16:4 *All that belonged to Mephibosheth is now yours.* Because the revolt was so widespread and loyalties so uncertain, David was quick to assume the worst.
16:5 *Bahurim.* On the eastern slope of the Mount of Olives (see note on 3:16). *same clan as Saul's family.* The clan of Matri (see 1Sa 10:21). *Gera.* His exact relation to Saul is unknown (see note on 1Ki 2:8).
16:6 *troops and special guard.* The Kerethites, Pelethites and 600 Gittites (see 15:18).
16:7 *scoundrel.* See note on Dt 13:13.
16:8 *blood you shed in the household of Saul.* Shimei may

be referring to the executions reported in 21:1–14, but the time of that event is uncertain (see note on 21:1).
16:9 *Abishai.* See note on 1Sa 26:6. *this dead dog.* An expression of absolute contempt (see note on 9:8).
16:10 *If . . . because the LORD said to him, 'Curse David.'* David leaves open the possibility that God has seen fit to terminate his rule—the verdict is not yet in (see 15:26). For David's later actions regarding Shimei see 19:18–23; 1Ki 2:8–9.
16:15 *Ahithophel.* See note on 15:12.
16:16 *Hushai the Arkite, David's friend.* See notes on 15:32,37.
16:21 *Lie with your father's concubines.* This would signify Absalom's assumption of royal power; it would also be a definitive and irreversible declaration of the break between father and son (see notes on 3:7; 12:8; 1Ki 2:22).

father's concubines whom he left to take care of the palace. Then all Israel will hear that you have made yourself a stench in your father's nostrils, and the hands of everyone with you will be strengthened." ²²So they pitched a tent for Absalom on the roof, and he lay with his father's concubines in the sight of all Israel. *d*

²³Now in those days the advice *e* Ahithophel gave was like that of one who inquires of God. That was how both David *f* and Absalom regarded all of Ahithophel's advice.

17 Ahithophel said to Absalom, "I would *t* choose twelve thousand men and set out tonight in pursuit of David. ²I would *u* attack him while he is weary and weak. *g* I would *u* strike him with terror, and then all the people with him will flee. I would *u* strike down only the king *h* ³and bring all the people back to you. The death of the man you seek will mean the return of all; all the people will be unharmed." ⁴This plan seemed good to Absalom and to all the elders of Israel.

⁵But Absalom said, "Summon also Hushai *i* the Arkite, so we can hear what he has to say." ⁶When Hushai came to him, Absalom said, "Ahithophel has given this advice. Should we do what he says? If not, give us your opinion."

⁷Hushai replied to Absalom, "The advice Ahithophel has given is not good this time. ⁸You know your father and his men; they are fighters, and as fierce as a wild bear robbed of her cubs. *j* Besides, your father is an experienced fighter; *k* he will not spend the night with the troops. ⁹Even now, he is hidden in a cave or some other place. *l* If he should attack your troops first, *v* whoever hears about it will say, 'There has been a slaughter among the troops who follow Absalom.' ¹⁰Then even the bravest soldier, whose heart is like the heart of a lion, *m* will melt *n* with fear, for all Israel knows that your father is a fighter and that those with him are brave. *o*

¹¹"So I advise you: Let all Israel, from Dan to Beersheba *p*—as numerous as the sand *q* on the seashore—be gathered to you, with you yourself leading them into battle. ¹²Then we will attack him wherever he may be found, and we will fall on him as dew settles on the ground. Neither he nor any of his men will be left alive. ¹³If he withdraws into a city, then all Israel will bring ropes to that city, and we will drag it down to the valley *r* until not even a piece of it can be found."

¹⁴Absalom and all the men of Israel said, "The advice *s* of Hushai the Arkite is better than that of Ahithophel." *t* For the Lord had determined to frustrate *u* the good advice of Ahithophel in order to bring disaster *v* on Absalom. *w*

¹⁵Hushai told Zadok and Abiathar, the priests, "Ahithophel has advised Absalom and the elders of Israel to do such and such, but I have advised them to do so and so. ¹⁶Now send a message immediately and tell David, 'Do not spend the night at the fords in the desert; *x* cross over without fail, or the king and all the people with him will be swallowed up.' "

¹⁷Jonathan *z* and Ahimaaz were staying at En Rogel. *a* A servant girl was to go and inform them, and they were to go and tell King David, for they could not risk being seen entering the city. ¹⁸But a young man saw them and told Absalom. So the two of them left quickly and went to the house of a man in Bahurim. *b* He had a well in his courtyard, and they climbed down into it. ¹⁹His wife took a covering and spread it out over the opening of the well and scattered grain over it. No one knew anything about it. *c*

²⁰When Absalom's men came to the woman *d* at the house, they asked, "Where are Ahimaaz and Jonathan?"

The woman answered them, "They

Cross references (center column):

16:22 *d*S 2Sa 3:7; 12:11-12; S 15:16
16:23 *e*2Sa 17:14,23 *f*S 2Sa 15:12
17:2 *g*2Sa 16:14 *h*1Ki 22:31; Zec 13:7
17:5 *i*S 2Sa 15:32
17:8 *j*Hos 13:8 *k*1Sa 16:18
17:9 *l*Jer 41:9
17:10 *m*1Ch 12:8 *n*Jos 2:9,11; Eze 21:15 *o*2Sa 23:8; 1Ch 11:11

17:11 *p*S Jdg 20:1 *q*S Ge 12:2; S Jos 11:4
17:13 *r*Mic 1:6
17:14 *s*S 2Sa 16:23 *t*S 2Sa 15:12 *u*S 2Sa 15:34; Ne 4:15 *v*Ps 9:16 *w*2Ch 10:8
17:16 *x*2Sa 15:28 *y*2Sa 15:35
17:17 *z*S 2Sa 15:27,36 *a*Jos 15:7; 18:16; 1Ki 1:9
17:18 *b*S 2Sa 3:16
17:19 *c*S Jos 2:6
17:20 *d*S Ex 1:19

*t*1 Or *Let me*   *u*2 Or *will*   *v*9 Or *When some of the men fall at the first attack*

16:22 *he lay with his father's concubines.* A fulfillment of Nathan's prophecy (12:11-12). For additional significance see note on v. 21.

17:1-3 Ahithophel's advice to Absalom envisioned a cheap and easy victory that would not leave the nation weakened.

17:4 *all the elders of Israel.* See note on 3:17. Absalom's rebellion appears to have gained extensive backing from prominent tribal leaders.

17:5 *Hushai the Arkite.* See 16:16-19; see also notes on 15:32,37.

17:7-13 Hushai's advice subtly capitalizes on Absalom's uncertainty, his fear and his egotism.

17:12 *we . . . we.* Hushai carefully links himself with the revolt.

17:14 *the Lord had determined to frustrate the good advice of Ahithophel.* An answer to David's prayer (see 15:31; cf. Ps 33:10; Pr 21:30).

17:15 *Zadok and Abiathar.* See 15:24-29,35-36.

17:16 *fords in the desert.* See 15:28 and note. *cross over.* Hushai advises David to cross the Jordan River, knowing that Absalom might change his mind and immediately set out after him.

17:17 *Jonathan and Ahimaaz.* See 15:36. *En Rogel.* A spring in the Kidron Valley just outside the walls of Jerusalem. *A servant girl.* A servant girl going to the spring for water would attract no attention.

17:18 *Bahurim.* See note on 16:5.

crossed over the brook." **w** The men searched but found no one, so they returned to Jerusalem.

21After the men had gone, the two climbed out of the well and went to inform King David. They said to him, "Set out and cross the river at once; Ahithophel has advised such and such against you." 22So David and all the people with him set out and crossed the Jordan. By daybreak, no one was left who had not crossed the Jordan.

23When Ahithophel saw that his advice *e* had not been followed, he saddled his donkey and set out for his house in his hometown. He put his house in order *f* and then hanged himself. So he died and was buried in his father's tomb.

24David went to Mahanaim, *g* and Absalom crossed the Jordan with all the men of Israel. 25Absalom had appointed Amasa *h* over the army in place of Joab. Amasa was the son of a man named Jether, *x* *i* an Israelite *y* who had married Abigail, *z* the daughter of Nahash and sister of Zeruiah the mother of Joab. 26The Israelites and Absalom camped in the land of Gilead.

27When David came to Mahanaim, Shobi son of Nahash *j* from Rabbah *k* of the Ammonites, and Makir *l* son of Ammiel from Lo Debar, and Barzillai *m* the Gileadite *n* from Rogelim 28brought bedding and bowls and articles of pottery. They also brought wheat and barley, flour and roasted grain, beans and lentils, *a* 29honey and curds, sheep, and cheese from cows' milk for David and his people to eat. *o* For they said, "The people have become hungry and tired and thirsty in the desert. *p* "

Absalom's Death

18 David mustered the men who were with him and appointed over them commanders of thousands and commanders of hundreds. 2David sent the troops out *q*—a third under the command of Joab, a third under Joab's brother Abishai *r* son of Zeruiah, and a third under Ittai *s* the Gittite. The king told the troops, "I myself will surely march out with you."

3But the men said, "You must not go out; if we are forced to flee, they won't care about us. Even if half of us die, they won't care; but you are worth ten *t* thousand of us. *b* It would be better now for you to give us support from the city." *u*

4The king answered, "I will do whatever seems best to you."

So the king stood beside the gate while all the men marched out in units of hundreds and of thousands. 5The king commanded Joab, Abishai and Ittai, "Be gentle with the young man Absalom for my sake." And all the troops heard the king giving orders concerning Absalom to each of the commanders.

6The army marched into the field to fight Israel, and the battle took place in the forest *v* of Ephraim. 7There the army of Israel was defeated by David's men, and the casualties that day were great—twenty thousand men. 8The battle spread out over the whole countryside, and the forest claimed more lives that day than the sword.

9Now Absalom happened to meet David's men. He was riding his mule, and as

Cross references:

17:23 *e* S 2Sa 16:23
f 2Ki 20:1
17:24 *g* S Ge 32:2
17:25 *h* 2Sa 19:13; 20:4, 9-12; 1Ki 2:5,32; 1Ch 12:18
i 1Ch 2:13-17
17:27 *j* S 1Sa 11:1
k S Dt 3:11
l 2Sa 9:4
m 2Sa 19:31-39; 1Ki 2:7
n 2Sa 19:31; Ezr 2:61
17:29 *o* 1Ch 12:40
p 2Sa 16:2; S Ro 12:13

18:2 *q* S Jdg 7:16; 1Sa 11:11
r S 1Sa 26:6
s 2Sa 15:19
18:3 *t* S 1Sa 18:7
u 2Sa 21:17
18:6 *v* S Jos 17:15

w20 Or *"They passed by the sheep pen toward the water."*   **x**25 Hebrew *Ithra*, a variant of *Jether*   **y**25 Hebrew and some Septuagint manuscripts; other Septuagint manuscripts (see also 1 Chron. 2:17) *Ishmaelite* or *Jezreelite*   **z**25 Hebrew *Abigal*, a variant of *Abigail*   **a**28 Most Septuagint manuscripts and Syriac; Hebrew *lentils, and roasted grain*   **b**3 Two Hebrew manuscripts, some Septuagint manuscripts and Vulgate; most Hebrew manuscripts *care; for now there are ten thousand like us*

17:23 *his hometown.* Giloh (see note on 15:12). *hanged himself.* Ahithophel was convinced that the rebellion would fail and that he would be found guilty of treason as a co-conspirator.

17:24 *Mahanaim.* Ironically the same place where Ish-Bosheth had sought refuge after Saul's death (2:8).

17:25 *Amasa.* Nephew of David and cousin of both Absalom and Joab son of Zeruiah. *Abigail, the daughter of Nahash and sister of Zeruiah.* Zeruiah was David's sister (1Ch 2:16). Since the father of Abigail and Zeruiah is Nahash rather than Jesse, it would appear that their unnamed mother married Jesse after the death of Nahash.

17:27 *Shobi son of Nahash.* Apparently the brother of Hanun (see 10:2–4), whom David had defeated earlier in his reign (12:26–31). *Rabbah of the Ammonites.* See note on 10:3. *Makir.* See note on 9:4. *Barzillai.* A wealthy benefactor of David during his flight to Mahanaim (see 19:32; 1Ki 2:7). After the Babylonian exile, there were claimants to the priesthood among his descendants (Ezr 2:61–63; Ne 7:63).

18:2 *Ittai the Gittite.* See 15:18–22.

18:3 *You must not go out.* In addition to the reason given, David was growing old and was no longer the warrior he had been (see note on 15:7). This is essentially the same idea that Ahithophel had expressed to Absalom (see 17:2).

18:5 *Be gentle with . . . Absalom for my sake.* David's love for his (now) oldest son was undying—and almost his undoing (see 19:5–7).

18:6 *Israel.* Absalom's army (see 15:13; 16:15; 17:4,11, 24–26). *forest of Ephraim.* The battle was apparently fought in Gilead, east of the Jordan (see 17:24,26). Why this area is termed the "forest of Ephraim" is not clear (perhaps it comes from an Ephraimite claim on the area; see Jdg 12:1–4).

18:8 *The battle spread out.* The armies apparently became dispersed, and many of the men got lost in the forest.

18:9 *his mule.* See note on 13:29. *Absalom's head got caught in the tree.* Whether by the entanglement of his abundant hair (14:26) or by some other means is not stated, but his handsome head (see 14:25) was in the end—ironically—his undoing.

the mule went under the thick branches of a large oak, Absalom's head[w] got caught in the tree. He was left hanging in midair, while the mule he was riding kept on going.

[10]When one of the men saw this, he told Joab, "I just saw Absalom hanging in an oak tree."

[11]Joab said to the man who had told him this, "What! You saw him? Why didn't you strike[x] him to the ground right there? Then I would have had to give you ten shekels[c] of silver and a warrior's belt.[y]"

[12]But the man replied, "Even if a thousand shekels[d] were weighed out into my hands, I would not lift my hand against the king's son. In our hearing the king commanded you and Abishai and Ittai, 'Protect the young man Absalom for my sake.[e]' [13]And if I had put my life in jeopardy[f]—and nothing is hidden from the king[z]—you would have kept your distance from me."

[14]Joab[a] said, "I'm not going to wait like this for you." So he took three javelins in his hand and plunged them into Absalom's heart while Absalom was still alive in the oak tree. [15]And ten of Joab's armor-bearers surrounded Absalom, struck him and killed him.[b]

[16]Then Joab[c] sounded the trumpet, and the troops stopped pursuing Israel, for Joab halted them. [17]They took Absalom, threw him into a big pit in the forest and piled up[d] a large heap of rocks[e] over him. Meanwhile, all the Israelites fled to their homes.

[18]During his lifetime Absalom had taken a pillar and erected it in the King's Valley[f] as a monument[g] to himself, for he thought, "I have no son[h] to carry on the memory of my name." He named the pillar after himself, and it is called Absalom's Monument to this day.

David Mourns

[19]Now Ahimaaz[i] son of Zadok said, "Let me run and take the news to the king

that the LORD has delivered him from the hand of his enemies.[j]"

[20]"You are not the one to take the news today," Joab told him. "You may take the news another time, but you must not do so today, because the king's son is dead."

[21]Then Joab said to a Cushite, "Go, tell the king what you have seen." The Cushite bowed down before Joab and ran off.

[22]Ahimaaz son of Zadok again said to Joab, "Come what may, please let me run behind the Cushite."

But Joab replied, "My son, why do you want to go? You don't have any news that will bring you a reward."

[23]He said, "Come what may, I want to run."

So Joab said, "Run!" Then Ahimaaz ran by way of the plain[g] and outran the Cushite.

[24]While David was sitting between the inner and outer gates, the watchman[k] went up to the roof of the gateway by the wall. As he looked out, he saw a man running alone. [25]The watchman called out to the king and reported it.

The king said, "If he is alone, he must have good news." And the man came closer and closer.

[26]Then the watchman saw another man running, and he called down to the gatekeeper, "Look, another man running alone!"

The king said, "He must be bringing good news,[l] too."

[27]The watchman said, "It seems to me that the first one runs like[m] Ahimaaz son of Zadok."

"He's a good man," the king said. "He comes with good news."

[28]Then Ahimaaz called out to the king, "All is well!" He bowed down before the

---

18:9 [w]2Sa 14:26
18:11 [x]2Sa 3:39
[y]1Sa 18:4
18:13 [z]2Sa 14:19-20
18:14 [a]2Sa 2:18
18:15 [b]2Sa 12:10
18:16 [c]2Sa 2:28
18:17 [d]Jos 7:26
[e]Jos 8:29
18:18 [f]Ge 14:17
[g]Ge 50:5; S Nu 32:42
[h]2Sa 14:27
18:19 [i]S 2Sa 15:36
[j]Jdg 11:36
18:24 [k]S 1Sa 14:16; S Jer 51:12
18:26 [l]1Ki 1:42; Isa 52:7; 61:1
18:27 [m]2Ki 9:20

[c]11 That is, about 4 ounces (about 115 grams)
[d]12 That is, about 25 pounds (about 11 kilograms)
[e]12 A few Hebrew manuscripts, Septuagint, Vulgate and Syriac; most Hebrew manuscripts may be translated Absalom, whoever you may be. [f]13 Or Otherwise, if I had acted treacherously toward him [g]23 That is, the plain of the Jordan

---

18:11 *I would have had to give you.* Joab must be referring to an announced intent on his part to reward anyone killing Absalom. His actions and interests did not always coincide with David's wishes (see note on 2:13).
18:15 *killed him.* The easiest and most certain way of ending the rebellion—but the brutal overkill is indicative of the deep animosity felt by David's men against Absalom.
18:17 *large heap of rocks.* A mound of rocks that mocked the monument Absalom himself had erected (v. 18). *all the Israelites.* See note on v. 6.
18:18 *erected it ... as a monument to himself.* As Saul had done (1Sa 15:12). *King's Valley.* Thought to be located near Jerusalem (see Ge 14:17; Josephus, *Antiquities,*

7.10.3). *I have no son.* See 14:27 and note. *Absalom's Monument.* Not to be confused with the much later monument of the same name that is still visible today in the valley east of Jerusalem.
18:19 *Ahimaaz son of Zadok.* See 15:27; 17:17–21.
18:20 *not the one to take the news.* The choice of a messenger depended on the content of the message (see v. 27 and note).
18:21 *Cushite.* An alien (see notes on Ge 10:6–8; Am 9:7).
18:27 *He comes with good news.* David presumed that Joab would not have sent someone like Ahimaaz to carry bad news (see v. 20 and note).

king with his face to the ground and said, "Praise be to the LORD your God! He has delivered up the men who lifted their hands against my lord the king."

29The king asked, "Is the young man Absalom safe?"

Ahimaaz answered, "I saw great confusion just as Joab was about to send the king's servant and me, your servant, but I don't know what it was."

30The king said, "Stand aside and wait here." So he stepped aside and stood there.

31Then the Cushite arrived and said, "My lord the king, hear the good news! The LORD has delivered you today from all who rose up against you."

32The king asked the Cushite, "Is the young man Absalom safe?"

The Cushite replied, "May the enemies of my lord the king and all who rise up to harm you be like that young man." n

33The king was shaken. He went up to the room over the gateway and wept. As he went, he said: "O my son Absalom! My son, my son Absalom! If only I had died o instead of you—O Absalom, my son, my son!" p

19 Joab was told, "The king is weeping and mourning for Absalom." 2And for the whole army the victory that day was turned into mourning, because on that day the troops heard it said, "The king is grieving for his son." 3The men stole into the city that day as men steal in who are ashamed when they flee from battle. 4The king covered his face and cried aloud, "O my son Absalom! O Absalom, my son, my son!"

5Then Joab went into the house to the king and said, "Today you have humiliated all your men, who have just saved your life and the lives of your sons and daughters and the lives of your wives and concubines. 6You love those who hate you and hate those who love you. You have made it

18:32 nJdg 5:31; S 1Sa 25:26
18:33 oEx 32:32
pGe 43:14; 2Sa 19:4

19:7 qPr 14:28
19:8 rS 2Sa 15:2
19:9 s2Sa 8:1-14
t2Sa 15:14
19:11
uS 2Sa 15:24
19:13
vS 2Sa 17:25
wS Ge 29:14
xS Ru 1:17
yS 2Sa 2:13

clear today that the commanders and their men mean nothing to you. I see that you would be pleased if Absalom were alive today and all of us were dead. 7Now go out and encourage your men. I swear by the LORD that if you don't go out, not a man will be left with you by nightfall. This will be worse for you than all the calamities that have come upon you from your youth till now." q

8So the king got up and took his seat in the gateway. When the men were told, "The king is sitting in the gateway," r they all came before him.

David Returns to Jerusalem

Meanwhile, the Israelites had fled to their homes. 9Throughout the tribes of Israel, the people were all arguing with each other, saying, "The king delivered us from the hand of our enemies; he is the one who rescued us from the hand of the Philistines. s But now he has fled the country because of Absalom; t 10and Absalom, whom we anointed to rule over us, has died in battle. So why do you say nothing about bringing the king back?"

11King David sent this message to Zadok u and Abiathar, the priests: "Ask the elders of Judah, 'Why should you be the last to bring the king back to his palace, since what is being said throughout Israel has reached the king at his quarters? 12You are my brothers, my own flesh and blood. So why should you be the last to bring back the king?' 13And say to Amasa, v 'Are you not my own flesh and blood? w May God deal with me, be it ever so severely, x if from now on you are not the commander of my army in place of Joab.' y "

14He won over the hearts of all the men of Judah as though they were one man. They sent word to the king, "Return, you and all your men." 15Then the king returned and went as far as the Jordan.

Now the men of Judah had come to Gil-

18:29 *I saw great confusion.* Ahimaaz avoids a direct answer to David's question, though he knew Absalom was dead.

18:33 *O my son Absalom!* One of the most moving expressions in all literature of a father's love for a son—in spite of all that Absalom had done.

19:5 *Joab went . . . to the king.* Apparently confident that the king was unaware of his part in Absalom's death. David never indicates that he learned of it (see 1Ki 2:5). *you have humiliated all your men.* Joab boldly rebukes David for allowing his personal grief to keep him from expressing his appreciation for the loyalty of those who risked their lives to preserve his throne. Joab warns David that his love for Absalom can still undo him.

19:9 *The king delivered us.* With Absalom dead, the north-

ern tribes remember what David had done for them (see 3:17–18; 5:2).

19:11 *Ask the elders of Judah.* Even though the rebellion had begun in Hebron in Judah (see 15:9–12), David appeals to the elders of his own tribe to take the initiative in restoring him to the throne in Jerusalem (see 2:4; 1Sa 30:26). This appeal produced the desired result, but it also led to the arousal of tribal jealousies (see vv. 41–42).

19:13 *Amasa.* See 17:25 and note. Although Amasa deserved death for treason, David appointed him commander of his army in place of Joab, hoping to secure the allegiance of those who had followed Amasa, especially the Judahites (see 20:5). *May God deal with me, be it ever so severely.* A curse formula (see note on 1Sa 3:17).

19:15 *Gilgal.* See note on Jos 4:19.

gal*z* to go out and meet the king and bring him across the Jordan. [16]Shimei*a* son of Gera, the Benjamite from Bahurim, hurried down with the men of Judah to meet King David. [17]With him were a thousand Benjamites, along with Ziba,*b* the steward of Saul's household,*c* and his fifteen sons and twenty servants. They rushed to the Jordan, where the king was. [18]They crossed at the ford to take the king's household over and to do whatever he wished.

When Shimei son of Gera crossed the Jordan, he fell prostrate before the king [19]and said to him, "May my lord not hold me guilty. Do not remember how your servant did wrong on the day my lord the king left Jerusalem.*d* May the king put it out of his mind. [20]For I your servant know that I have sinned, but today I have come here as the first of the whole house of Joseph to come down and meet my lord the king."

[21]Then Abishai*e* son of Zeruiah said, "Shouldn't Shimei be put to death for this? He cursed*f* the Lord's anointed."*g*

[22]David replied, "What do you and I have in common, you sons of Zeruiah?*h* This day you have become my adversaries! Should anyone be put to death in Israel today?*i* Do I not know that today I am king over Israel?" [23]So the king said to Shimei, "You shall not die." And the king promised him on oath.*j*

[24]Mephibosheth,*k* Saul's grandson, also went down to meet the king. He had not taken care of his feet or trimmed his mustache or washed his clothes from the day the king left until the day he returned safely. [25]When he came from Jerusalem to meet the king, the king asked him, "Why didn't you go with me,*l* Mephibosheth?" [26]He said, "My lord the king, since I your servant am lame,*m* I said, 'I will have my donkey saddled and will ride on it, so I can go with the king.' But Ziba*n* my servant betrayed me. [27]And he has slandered your servant to my lord the king. My lord the king is like an angel*o* of God; so do whatever pleases you. [28]All my grandfather's descendants deserved nothing but death*p* from my lord the king, but you gave your servant a place among those who sat at your table.*q* So what right do I have to make any more appeals to the king?"

[29]The king said to him, "Why say more? I order you and Ziba to divide the fields."

[30]Mephibosheth said to the king, "Let him take everything, now that my lord the king has arrived home safely."

[31]Barzillai*r* the Gileadite also came down from Rogelim to cross the Jordan with the king and to send him on his way from there. [32]Now Barzillai was a very old man, eighty years of age. He had provided for the king during his stay in Mahanaim, for he was a very wealthy*s* man. [33]The king said to Barzillai, "Cross over with me and stay with me in Jerusalem, and I will provide for you."

[34]But Barzillai answered the king, "How many more years will I live, that I should go up to Jerusalem with the king? [35]I am now eighty*t* years old. Can I tell the difference between what is good and what is not? Can your servant taste what he eats and drinks? Can I still hear the voices of men and women singers?*u* Why should your servant be an added*v* burden to my lord the king? [36]Your servant will cross over the Jordan with the king for a short distance, but why should the king reward me in this way? [37]Let your servant return, that I may die in my own town near the tomb of my father*w* and mother. But here is your servant Kimham.*x* Let him cross

19:15 *z*S 1Sa 11:15
19:16 *a*2Sa 16:5-13
19:17 *b*S 2Sa 9:2
*c*S Ge 43:16
19:19 *d*S 2Sa 16:6-8
19:21 *e*S 1Sa 26:6
*f*S Ex 22:28
*g*S 1Sa 12:3;
S 26:9
19:22 *h*S 2Sa 2:18;
S 16:10
*i*1Sa 11:13
19:23 *j*1Ki 2:8,42
19:24 *k*S 2Sa 4:4
19:25 *l*2Sa 16:17
19:26 *m*S Lev 21:18

*n*S 2Sa 9:2
19:27 *o*S 1Sa 29:9
19:28 *p*S 2Sa 16:8
*q*S 2Sa 9:7,13
19:31 *r*S 2Sa 17:27-29,
27; 1Ki 2:7
19:32 *s*1Sa 25:2
19:35 *t*Ps 90:10
*u*2Ch 35:25;
Ezr 2:65; Ecc 2:8;
12:1 *v*2Sa 15:33
19:37 *w*S Ge 49:29
*x*Jer 41:17

19:17 *a thousand Benjamites.* No doubt fearing they would be suspected by the king of being implicated in Shimei's deed.
19:20 *I your servant know that I have sinned.* Shimei's guilt was common knowledge; he could only seize the most appropriate time to plead for mercy. *house of Joseph.* A common way of referring to the northern tribes (see 1Ki 11:28; Eze 37:19; Am 5:6; Zec 10:6)—of which Ephraim and Manasseh (sons of Joseph) were the most prominent (see Nu 26:28; Jos 18:5; Jdg 1:22).
19:21 *Abishai.* See 16:9; see also note on 1Sa 26:6. *the Lord's anointed.* See note on 1Sa 9:16; see also 1Sa 24:6; 26:9-11; Ex 22:28; 1Ki 21:10.
19:22 *Should anyone be put to death in Israel today?* It was a day for general amnesty (see 1Sa 11:13).
19:23 *You shall not die.* David kept his pledge; he would not himself avenge the wrong committed against him (see note on 1Sa 25:2-44). But on his deathbed he instructed Solomon to take Shimei's case in hand (see 1Ki 2:8-9, 36-46).
19:24 *Mephibosheth.* See 9:6-13.
19:25 *Why didn't you go with me . . . ?* David remembers Ziba's previous allegations (see 16:3).
19:26 *lame.* See 4:4; 9:3.
19:27 *he has slandered your servant.* See 16:3. *like an angel of God.* See 14:17 and note. *do whatever pleases you.* Mephibosheth discreetly requests David to reconsider the grant of his property to Ziba (see 16:4).
19:29 *divide the fields.* Faced with conflicting testimony that could not be corroborated, David withholds judgment and orders the division of Saul's estate.
19:31 *Barzillai.* See note on 17:27.
19:35 *difference between what is good and what is not.* At his age, he would be indifferent to all the pleasures of the court.
19:37 *Kimham.* Likely a son of Barzillai (see 1Ki 2:7).

over with my lord the king. Do for him whatever pleases you."

38The king said, "Kimham shall cross over with me, and I will do for him whatever pleases you. And anything you desire from me I will do for you."

39So all the people crossed the Jordan, and then the king crossed over. The king kissed Barzillai and gave him his blessing,y and Barzillai returned to his home.

40When the king crossed over to Gilgal, Kimham crossed with him. All the troops of Judah and half the troops of Israel had taken the king over.

41Soon all the men of Israel were coming to the king and saying to him, "Why did our brothers, the men of Judah, steal the king away and bring him and his household across the Jordan, together with all his men?"z

42All the men of Judah answered the men of Israel, "We did this because the king is closely related to us. Why are you angry about it? Have we eaten any of the king's provisions? Have we taken anything for ourselves?"

43Then the men of Israela answered the men of Judah, "We have ten shares in the king; and besides, we have a greater claim on David than you have. So why do you treat us with contempt? Were we not the first to speak of bringing back our king?"

But the men of Judah responded even more harshly than the men of Israel.

Sheba Rebels Against David

20 Now a troublemaker named Sheba son of Bicri, a Benjamite, happened to be there. He sounded the trumpet and shouted,

"We have no shareb in David,c
  no part in Jesse's son!d
Every man to his tent, O Israel!"

2So all the men of Israel deserted David to follow Sheba son of Bicri. But the men of Judah stayed by their king all the way from the Jordan to Jerusalem.

3When David returned to his palace in Jerusalem, he took the ten concubinese he had left to take care of the palace and put them in a house under guard. He provided for them, but did not lie with them. They were kept in confinement till the day of their death, living as widows.

4Then the king said to Amasa,f "Summon the men of Judah to come to me within three days, and be here yourself." 5But when Amasa went to summon Judah, he took longer than the time the king had set for him.

6David said to Abishai,g "Now Sheba son of Bicri will do us more harm than Absalom did. Take your master's men and pursue him, or he will find fortified cities and escape from us." 7So Joab's men and the Kerethitesh and Pelethites and all the mighty warriors went out under the command of Abishai. They marched out from Jerusalem to pursue Sheba son of Bicri.

8While they were at the great rock in Gibeon,i Amasa came to meet them. Joabj was wearing his military tunic, and strapped over it at his waist was a belt with a dagger in its sheath. As he stepped forward, it dropped out of its sheath.

9Joab said to Amasa, "How are you, my brother?" Then Joab took Amasa by the beard with his right hand to kiss him. 10Amasa was not on his guard against the daggerk in Joabl's hand, and Joab plunged

Cross references (center column)

19:39 yS Ge 47:7
19:41 zJdg 8:1; 12:1
19:43 aS 2Sa 5:1

20:1 bS Ge 31:14
cS Ge 29:14;
1Ki 12:16
d1Sa 22:7-8
20:3
eS 2Sa 15:16
20:4 fS 2Sa 17:25
20:6 g2Sa 21:17
20:7
hS 1Sa 30:14;
S 2Sa 15:18
20:8 iS Jos 9:3
jS 2Sa 2:18
20:10 kS Jdg 3:21
l1Ki 2:5

Footnotes

19:41 Why did . . . the men of Judah, steal the king away and bring him . . . across the Jordan . . . ? It seems that the Jordan was a kind of psychological border to the land of Israel (see Jos 22:19,25; Jdg 12:4)—which may also explain why Ish-Bosheth (2:8), Mephibosheth (9:4) and even David himself (17:22) had sought refuge in Transjordan. That being the case, the protest of the Israelites may be that the Judahites had not waited for all Israel to assemble before bringing David across the Jordan, thus leaving the Israelites in a bad light—as though they were reluctant to receive the king back (see v. 43).
19:43 ten shares. The ten tribes, excluding Judah and Simeon (see note on 2:4). we have a greater claim on David. The grounds for this assertion may be that the Lord had chosen David to reign in the place of Saul (see 3:17–18; 5:2).
20:1 troublemaker. See note on Dt 13:13. Bicri. Benjamin's second son (Beker, Ge 46:21; 1Ch 7:6–9). Benjamite. Tribal jealousy still simmered over the transfer of the royal house from Benjamin (Saul's tribe) to Judah. there. In Gilgal (19:40–43). We have no share in David. Sheba appeals to the Israelite suspicion that David favored his own tribe Judah

over the other tribes (see 1Ki 12:16).
20:2 all the men of Israel. Those referred to in 19:41–43.
20:3 ten concubines. See notes on 15:16; 16:22.
20:4 Amasa. See notes on 17:25; 19:13. David bypasses Joab.
20:6 Abishai. David bypasses Joab a second time (see v. 7). your master's men. "Joab's men" (v. 7).
20:7 Joab's men. See 18:2. It becomes clear that Joab also accompanied the soldiers and, though not in command (by the king's order), he was obviously the leader recognized by the soldiers (see vv. 7,11,15). Kerethites and Pelethites. See note on 8:18. mighty warriors. See 23:8–39. Once more in a time of crisis David depended mainly on the small force of professionals (many of them non-Israelite) who made up his private army.
20:8 Gibeon. See note on 2:12. Amasa came. Apparently with some troops (see v. 11 and note).
20:10 into his belly. See 2:23; 3:27. For the second time Joab commits murder to secure his position as commander of David's army (see 1Ki 2:5–6). Joab and his brother Abishai. In defiance of David's order, Joab reassumes command on his own initiative (see v. 23).

it into his belly, and his intestines spilled out on the ground. Without being stabbed again, Amasa died. Then Joab and his brother Abishai pursued Sheba son of Bicri.

¹¹One of Joab's men stood beside Amasa and said, "Whoever favors Joab, and whoever is for David, let him follow Joab!" ¹²Amasa lay wallowing in his blood in the middle of the road, and the man saw that all the troops came to a halt ᵐ there. When he realized that everyone who came up to Amasa stopped, he dragged him from the road into a field and threw a garment over him. ¹³After Amasa had been removed from the road, all the men went on with Joab to pursue Sheba son of Bicri.

¹⁴Sheba passed through all the tribes of Israel to Abel Beth Maacah ʰ and through the entire region of the Berites, ⁿ who gathered together and followed him. ¹⁵All the troops with Joab came and besieged Sheba in Abel Beth Maacah. ᵒ They built a siege ramp ᵖ up to the city, and it stood against the outer fortifications. While they were battering the wall to bring it down, ¹⁶a wise woman ۹ called from the city, "Listen! Listen! Tell Joab to come here so I can speak to him." ¹⁷He went toward her, and she asked, "Are you Joab?"

"I am," he answered.

She said, "Listen to what your servant has to say."

"I'm listening," he said.

¹⁸She continued, "Long ago they used to say, 'Get your answer at Abel,' and that settled it. ¹⁹We are the peaceful ʳ and

faithful in Israel. You are trying to destroy a city that is a mother in Israel. Why do you want to swallow up the LORD's inheritance?" ˢ

²⁰"Far be it from me!" Joab replied, "Far be it from me to swallow up or destroy! ²¹That is not the case. A man named Sheba son of Bicri, from the hill country of Ephraim, has lifted up his hand against the king, against David. Hand over this one man, and I'll withdraw from the city."

The woman said to Joab, "His head ᵗ will be thrown to you from the wall."

²²Then the woman went to all the people with her wise advice, ᵘ and they cut off the head of Sheba son of Bicri and threw it to Joab. So he sounded the trumpet, and his men dispersed from the city, each returning to his home. And Joab went back to the king in Jerusalem.

²³Joab ᵛ was over Israel's entire army; Benaiah son of Jehoiada was over the Kerethites and Pelethites; ²⁴Adoniram ⁱ ʷ was in charge of forced labor; Jehoshaphat ˣ son of Ahilud was recorder; ²⁵Sheva was secretary; Zadok ʸ and Abiathar were priests; ²⁶and Ira the Jairite was David's priest.

The Gibeonites Avenged

21 During the reign of David, there was a famine ᶻ for three successive years; so David sought ᵃ the face of the

h *14* Or *Abel, even Beth Maacah*; also in verse 15
i *24* Some Septuagint manuscripts (see also 1 Kings 4:6 and 5:14); Hebrew *Adoram*

Cross references:
20:12 ᵐS 2Sa 2:23
20:14 ⁿNu 21:16
20:15 ᵒ1Ki 15:20; 2Ki 15:29 ᵖIsa 37:33; Jer 6:6; 32:24
20:16 ۹2Sa 14:2
20:19 ʳS Dt 2:26
ˢS 1Sa 26:19
20:21 ᵗS 2Sa 4:8
20:22 ᵘEcc 9:13
20:23 ᵛS 2Sa 2:28; 8:16-18; 24:2
20:24 ʷ1Ki 4:6; 5:14; 12:18; 2Ch 10:18; ˣ2Sa 8:16
20:25 ʸS 1Sa 2:35; S 2Sa 8:17
21:1 ᶻS Ge 12:10; S Dt 32:24 ᵃS Ex 32:11

20:11 *Whoever favors Joab, and whoever is for David.* To dispel any idea that Joab was aligned with Sheba's conspiracy, an appeal is made to Amasa's troops to support Joab if they are truly loyal to David.
20:14 *Abel Beth Maacah.* See NIV text note; located to the north of Dan (see 1Ki 15:20; 2Ch 16:4). Sheba's strategy was to gather as many volunteers for his revolt as possible, but he was obviously afraid to assemble his ragtag army anywhere within close reach of David's men. *Berites.* Otherwise unknown.
20:18 *Get your answer at Abel.* The city was famous for the wisdom of its inhabitants.
20:19 *a mother in Israel.* A town that produced faithful Israelites—cities were commonly personified as women (see Jer 50:12; Gal 4:26). *the LORD's inheritance.* See note on 1Sa 10:1.
20:21 *hill country of Ephraim.* Either Sheba, a Benjamite (see v. 1), lived in the tribal territory of Ephraim or this was the designation of a geographical, rather than a strictly tribal, region.
20:22 *Joab went back to the king in Jerusalem.* See notes on vv. 7,10.
20:23-26 These royal officials apparently served David during most of his reign (see 8:15-18).
20:23 *Joab was over Israel's entire army.* Though in some disfavor, he held this position until he participated in Adonijah's conspiracy (1Ki 1:7; 2:28-35). *Kerethites and Pele-*

thites. See note on 8:18.
20:24 *Adoniram was in charge of forced labor.* A position not established in the early years of David's reign (see 8:15-16). Adoniram must have been a late appointee of David since he continued to serve under Solomon (1Ki 4:6; 5:14) and was eventually killed in the early days of the reign of Rehoboam (1Ki 12:18; 2Ch 10:18). *forced labor.* Labor performed for the most part by prisioners of war from defeated nations (see 12:31; Jos 9:21; 1Ki 9:15,20-21). *recorder.* See note on 8:16.
20:25 *Sheva.* See note on 8:17 ("Seraiah"). *secretary.* See note on 8:17. *Zadok and Abiathar.* See note on 8:17.
20:26 *Jairite.* A reference either to Jair of the tribe of Manasseh (Nu 32:41) or to a judge from Gilead (Jdg 10:3,5). *priest.* See note on 8:18.
21:1-24:25 This concluding section forms an appendix to 1,2 Samuel and contains additional materials (without concern for chronology) relating to David's reign. While its topical arrangement is striking, it also employs a literary pattern, *a-b-c-c-b-a,* frequently found elsewhere in OT literature. The first and last units (21:1-14; 24:1-25) are narratives of two events in which David had to deal with God's wrath against Israel (the first occasioned by an act of Saul, the second by his own). The second and fifth units (21:15-22; 23:8-39) are accounts of David's warriors (the second much longer than the first). At the center (22:1-23:7) are two songs of David (the first much longer than the second), one of

LORD. The LORD said, "It is on account of Saul and his blood-stained house; it is because he put the Gibeonites to death."

2The king summoned the Gibeonites[b] and spoke to them. (Now the Gibeonites were not a part of Israel but were survivors of the Amorites; the Israelites had sworn to spare them, but Saul in his zeal for Israel and Judah had tried to annihilate them.) 3David asked the Gibeonites, "What shall I do for you? How shall I make amends so that you will bless the LORD's inheritance?"[c]

4The Gibeonites answered him, "We have no right to demand silver or gold from Saul or his family, nor do we have the right to put anyone in Israel to death."[d]

"What do you want me to do for you?" David asked.

5They answered the king, "As for the man who destroyed us and plotted against us so that we have been decimated and have no place anywhere in Israel, 6let seven of his male descendants be given to us to be killed and exposed[e] before the LORD at Gibeah of Saul—the Lord's chosen[f] one."

So the king said, "I will give them to you."

7The king spared Mephibosheth[g] son of Jonathan, the son of Saul, because of the oath[h] before the LORD between David and Jonathan son of Saul. 8But the king took Armoni and Mephibosheth, the two sons

of Aiah's daughter Rizpah,[i] whom she had borne to Saul, together with the five sons of Saul's daughter Merab,[j] whom she had borne to Adriel son of Barzillai the Meholathite.[j] 9He handed them over to the Gibeonites, who killed and exposed them on a hill before the LORD. All seven of them fell together; they were put to death[k] during the first days of the harvest, just as the barley harvest was beginning.[l]

10Rizpah daughter of Aiah took sackcloth and spread it out for herself on a rock. From the beginning of the harvest till the rain poured down from the heavens on the bodies, she did not let the birds of the air touch them by day or the wild animals by night.[m] 11When David was told what Aiah's daughter Rizpah, Saul's concubine, had done, 12he went and took the bones of Saul[n] and his son Jonathan from the citizens of Jabesh Gilead.[o] (They had taken them secretly from the public square at Beth Shan,[p] where the Philistines had hung[q] them after they struck Saul down on Gilboa.)[r] 13David brought the bones of Saul and his son Jonathan from there, and the bones of those who had been killed and exposed were gathered up.

14They buried the bones of Saul and his son Jonathan in the tomb of Saul's father Kish, at Zela[s] in Benjamin, and did every-

---

Cross references (center column):

21:2 [b]S Jos 9:15
21:3 [c]S 1Sa 26:19
21:4 [d]Nu 35:33-34
21:6 [e]Nu 25:4 [f]S 1Sa 10:24
21:7 [g]2Sa 4:4 [h]S 1Sa 18:3; S 2Sa 9:7
21:8 [i]2Sa 3:7 [j]1Sa 18:19
21:9 [k]S 2Sa 16:8 [l]S Ru 1:22
21:10 [m]S Ge 40:19; S 1Sa 17:44
21:12 [n]1Sa 31:11-13 [o]S Jdg 21:8; S 1Sa 11:1 [p]S Jos 17:11 [q]1Sa 31:10 [r]S 1Sa 28:4
21:14 [s]Jos 18:28

j8 Two Hebrew manuscripts, some Septuagint manuscripts and Syriac (see also 1 Samuel 18:19); most Hebrew and Septuagint manuscripts Michal

---

which celebrates David's victories as warrior-king while the other recalls his role as psalmist (see note on 1Sa 16:14–17:58). It is unknown if motivation for this arrangement went beyond aesthetic considerations. The triumph song of ch. 22 and the song of Hannah in 1Sa 2:1–10 clearly form a literary frame enclosing the main composition (see note on 1Sa 2:1).

21:1–14 This event appears to have occurred after David's kindness was extended to Mephibosheth (ch. 9) and before Absalom's rebellion (16:7–8; 18:28; see note on 16:8).
21:1 *he put the Gibeonites to death.* Saul's action against the Gibeonites is not related elsewhere but appears to have been instituted early in his reign, motivated by an excessive nationalism (if not tribalism—the Gibeonites occupied territory partly assigned to Benjamin, and Saul's great-grandfather was known as the "father of Gibeon," 1Ch 8:29; 9:35).
21:2 *Amorites.* A comprehensive name sometimes used to designate all the pre-Israelite inhabitants of Canaan (Ge 15:16; Jos 24:18; Jdg 6:10; Am 2:10). More precisely, the Gibeonites were called Hivites (Jos 9:7; 11:19). *the Israelites had sworn to spare them.* A pledge sworn in the name of the Lord (Jos 9:15,18–26). *tried to annihilate them.* The reason Saul was unsuccessful is not known.
21:3 *bless.* Since the oath sworn to them had been violated, they could rightly call down God's curse on the land. *the LORD's inheritance.* See note on 1Sa 10:1.
21:4 *nor do we have the right to put anyone in Israel to death.* Bloodguilt could only be redressed by the shedding of blood, but as subject aliens the Gibeonites had no right to

legal redress against an Israelite. This restriction must have been Saul's since it is contrary to the Mosaic law (see Ex 22:21; Lev 19:34; 24:22; Dt 1:16–17; 24:17; 27:19).
21:5 *the man.* Saul. *no place anywhere in Israel.* Those who escaped Saul's attack had been driven from their towns and lands (see 4:2–3 and notes).
21:6 *seven.* Because it would represent a full number (seven symbolized completeness)—though many more Gibeonites had been slain. *Gibeah.* The place of Saul's residence (see 1Sa 10:26).
21:7 *oath before the LORD between David and Jonathan.* See 4:4; 9:1–13; 1Sa 18:3; 20:15.
21:8 *Rizpah.* See 3:7. *Merab.* See 1Sa 18:19. *Barzillai the Meholathite.* Not to be confused with Barzillai the Gileadite (17:27; 19:31).
21:9 *All seven of them fell together.* This nearly extinguished the house of Saul, which God had rejected (see 1Sa 13:13–14; 15:23–26). In 1Ch 8:29–39; 9:35–44 no descendants of Saul are listed other than from the line of Jonathan. *barley harvest was beginning.* About the middle of April (see note on Ru 1:22).
21:10 *sackcloth.* See note on Ge 37:34. *rain poured down.* An indication that the famine was caused by drought and evidence that the judgment on Israel for breaking the oath sworn to the Gibeonites (see v. 1) was now over.
21:12 *bones of Saul and his son Jonathan.* See 1Sa 31:11–13. David's final act toward Saul and Jonathan was a deed of deep respect for the king he had honored and the friend he had loved.

thing the king commanded. After that,[t] God answered prayer[u] in behalf of the land.[v]

Wars Against the Philistines

21:15-22pp — 1Ch 20:4-8

15Once again there was a battle between the Philistines[w] and Israel. David went down with his men to fight against the Philistines, and he became exhausted. 16And Ishbi-Benob, one of the descendants of Rapha, whose bronze spearhead weighed three hundred shekels[k] and who was armed with a new sword, said he would kill David. 17But Abishai[x] son of Zeruiah came to David's rescue; he struck the Philistine down and killed him. Then David's men swore to him, saying, "Never again will you go out with us to battle, so that the lamp[y] of Israel will not be extinguished.[z]"

18In the course of time, there was another battle with the Philistines, at Gob. At that time Sibbecai[a] the Hushathite killed Saph, one of the descendants of Rapha.

19In another battle with the Philistines at Gob, Elhanan son of Jaare-Oregim[1] the Bethlehemite killed Goliath[m] the Gittite,[b] who had a spear with a shaft like a weaver's rod.[c]

20In still another battle, which took place at Gath, there was a huge man with six fingers on each hand and six toes on each foot—twenty-four in all. He also was descended from Rapha. 21When he taunt-

ed[d] Israel, Jonathan son of Shimeah,[e] David's brother, killed him.

22These four were descendants of Rapha in Gath, and they fell at the hands of David and his men.

David's Song of Praise

22:1-51pp — Ps 18:1-50

22 David sang[f] to the LORD the words of this song when the LORD delivered him from the hand of all his enemies and from the hand of Saul. 2He said:

"The LORD is my rock,[g] my fortress[h]
    and my deliverer;[i]
3 my God is my rock, in whom I take
        refuge,[j]
    my shield[k] and the horn[n][l] of my
        salvation.
He is my stronghold,[m] my refuge and
        my savior—
    from violent men you save me.
4I call to the LORD, who is worthy[n] of
        praise,
    and I am saved from my enemies.

5"The waves[o] of death swirled about
        me;
    the torrents of destruction
        overwhelmed me.
6The cords of the grave[o][p] coiled around
        me;
    the snares of death confronted me.

Cross references (center column):

21:14 [t]Jos 7:26; [u]2Sa 24:25; [v]1Ch 8:34
21:15 [w]S 2Sa 5:25
21:17 [x]2Sa 20:6; [y]1Ki 11:36; 15:4; 2Ki 8:19; 2Ch 21:7; Ps 132:17; [z]2Sa 18:3
21:18 [a]1Ch 11:29; 27:11
21:19 [b]S 1Sa 17:4; [c]S 1Sa 17:7
21:21 [d]S 1Sa 17:10; [e]S 1Sa 16:9
22:1 [f]S Ex 15:1
22:2 [g]S 1Sa 2:2; [h]Ps 31:3; 91:2; [i]Ps 144:2
22:3 [j]S Dt 23:15; S 32:37; Ps 14:6; 31:2; 59:16; 71:7; 91:2; 94:22; Pr 10:29; Isa 25:4; Jer 16:19; Joel 3:16; [k]S Ge 15:1; [l]S Dt 33:17; S Lk 1:69; [m]Ps 9:9; 52:7
22:4 [n]Ps 48:1; 96:4; 145:3
22:5 [o]Ps 69:14-15; Jnh 2:3
22:6 [p]Ps 116:3; Ac 2:24

---

k16 That is, about 7 1/2 pounds (about 3.5 kilograms) l19 Or *son of Jair the weaver* m19 Hebrew and Septuagint; 1 Chron. 20:5 *son of Jair killed Lahmi the brother of Goliath* n3 *Horn* here symbolizes strength. o6 Hebrew *Sheol*

21:15-22 These four Philistine episodes (vv. 15-17, 18, 19, 20-21) cannot be chronologically located with any certainty (see note on 21:1-24:25). Each involves a heroic accomplishment by one of David's mighty men, resulting in the death of a "descendant of Rapha" (see vv. 16,18,20,22).
21:16 *Rapha.* In calling the four formidable enemy warriors referred to in this series "descendants of Rapha" (v. 22), the writer most likely identifies them as giants, as suggested by Dt 2:10-11,20-21. In that case, they may have been related to the Anakites (see Jos 11:21-22). Cf. Ge 15:19-20, which in its list of ten peoples of Canaan mentions Rephaites but not Anakites, though the Anakites (but not Rephaites) figure significantly in the accounts of the conquest (Nu 13:22,28,33; Dt 1:28; 9:2; Jos 14:12,15; Jdg 1:20).
21:17 *Abishai.* See note on 1Sa 26:6. *so that the lamp of Israel will not be extinguished.* A striking metaphor depicting Israel's dependence on David for its security and continuing existence as a nation—its national hope (see 22:29; 23:3-4; 1Ki 11:36).
21:18 *Gob.* Probably in the near vicinity of Gezer, with 1Ch 20:4 locates this same battle. *Saph.* Called Sippai in 1Ch 20:4.
21:19 *Elhanan . . . killed Goliath.* See NIV text note. Since it is clear from 1Sa 17 that David killed Goliath, it is possible that an early copyist misread the Hebrew for "Lahmi the brother of" (see 1Ch 20:5) as "the Bethlehemite" (in He-

brew the word for "killed" stands first in the clause).
21:21 *taunted Israel.* As Goliath had done (see 1Sa 17:10, 25). *Shimeah.* Also called Shammah (1Sa 16:9; 17:13).
22:1 *this song.* Preserved also as Ps 18 (see notes on that psalm). Besides an introduction (vv. 2-4) and conclusion (vv. 47-51), the song consists of three major sections: The first describes David's deliverance from mortal danger at the hands of his enemies (vv. 5-20); the second sets forth the moral grounds for God's saving help (vv. 21-30); the third recounts the help that the Lord gave him (vv. 31-46). The song was probably composed shortly after David's victories over foreign enemies (8:1-14) and before his sin with Bathsheba (compare vv. 21-25 with 1Ki 15:5). *from . . . all his enemies.* See 8:1-14. *from . . . Saul.* See 1Sa 18-31.
22:2 *my rock.* A figure particularly appropriate to David's experience (see vv. 32,47; 23:3; Dt 32:4,15,18,31; Ps 28:1; 31:2; 61:2; 78:35; 89:36; 94:22; 95:1). He had often taken refuge among the rocks of the desert (1Sa 23:25; 24:2), but he realized that true security was found only in the Lord. *fortress.* The Hebrew for this word occurs in 5:17; 23:14; 1Sa 22:4-5; 24:22, referring to places where David sought refuge.
22:3 *my shield.* See vv. 31,36; Ge 15:1; Dt 33:29. *horn.* See NIV text note; Dt 33:17; Jer 48:25.
22:5 *waves of death.* In vv. 5-6 David depicts his experiences in poetic figures of mortal danger.
22:6 *grave.* See note on Jnh 2:2.

⁷In my distress*q* I called*r* to the LORD;
  I called out to my God.
From his temple he heard my voice;
  my cry came to his ears.

⁸"The earth*s* trembled and quaked,*t*
  the foundations*u* of the heavens*p*
    shook;
  they trembled because he was angry.
⁹Smoke rose from his nostrils;
  consuming fire*v* came from his
    mouth,
  burning coals*w* blazed out of it.
¹⁰He parted the heavens and came down;
  dark clouds*x* were under his feet.
¹¹He mounted the cherubim*y* and flew;
  he soared*q* on the wings of the
    wind.*z*
¹²He made darkness*a* his canopy around
    him—
  the dark*r* rain clouds of the sky.
¹³Out of the brightness of his presence
  bolts of lightning*b* blazed forth.
¹⁴The LORD thundered*c* from heaven;
  the voice of the Most High
    resounded.
¹⁵He shot arrows*d* and scattered the
    enemies,,
  bolts of lightning and routed them.
¹⁶The valleys of the sea were exposed
  and the foundations of the earth laid
    bare
at the rebuke*e* of the LORD,
  at the blast*f* of breath from his
    nostrils.

¹⁷"He reached down from on high*g* and
    took hold of me;
  he drew*h* me out of deep waters.
¹⁸He rescued*i* me from my powerful
    enemy,
  from my foes, who were too strong
    for me.
¹⁹They confronted me in the day of my
    disaster,

but the LORD was my support.*j*
²⁰He brought me out into a spacious*k*
    place;
  he rescued*l* me because he
    delighted*m* in me.*n*

²¹"The LORD has dealt with me according
    to my righteousness;*o*
  according to the cleanness*p* of my
    hands*q* he has rewarded me.
²²For I have kept*r* the ways of the LORD;
  I have not done evil by turning from
    my God.
²³All his laws are before me;*s*
  I have not turned*t* away from his
    decrees.
²⁴I have been blameless*u* before him
  and have kept myself from sin.
²⁵The LORD has rewarded me according
    to my righteousness,*v*
  according to my cleanness*s* in his
    sight.

²⁶"To the faithful you show yourself
    faithful,
  to the blameless you show yourself
    blameless,
²⁷to the pure*w* you show yourself pure,
  but to the crooked you show yourself
    shrewd.*x*
²⁸You save the humble,*y*
  but your eyes are on the haughty*z* to
    bring them low.*a*
²⁹You are my lamp,*b* O LORD;
  the LORD turns my darkness into
    light.

22:7 *q*Ge 35:3; S Jdg 2:15; 2Ch 15:4; Ps 4:1; 77:2; 120:1; Isa 26:16
*r*Ps 34:6,15; 116:4
22:8 *s*Jdg 5:4; Ps 97:4
*t*S Ex 19:18; S Jdg 5:4; Ps 68:8; 77:18; Jer 10:10
*u*Job 9:6; 26:11; Ps 75:3
22:9 *v*Ps 50:3; 97:3; Heb 12:29; S Rev 11:5
*w*Isa 6:6; Eze 1:13; 10:2
22:10 *x*S Ex 19:9; Lev 16:2; S Dt 33:26; 1Ki 8:12; Job 26:9; Ps 104:3; Isa 19:1; Jer 4:13; Na 1:3
22:11 *y*S Ge 3:24; S Ex 25:22
*z*Ps 104:3
22:12 *a*S Ex 19:9
22:13 *b*Job 37:3; Ps 77:18
22:14 *c*S 1Sa 2:10
22:15 *d*S Dt 32:23
22:16 *e*Ps 6:1; 50:8,21; 106:9; Na 1:4
*f*S Ex 14:21; Isa 30:33; 40:24
22:17 *g*Ps 144:7
*h*Ex 2:10
22:18 *i*Lk 1:71
22:19 *j*Ps 23:4
22:20 *k*Job 36:16; Ps 31:8 *l*Ps 118:5
*m*Ps 22:8; Isa 42:1; Mt 12:18
*n*S 2Sa 15:26
22:21 *o*S 1Sa 26:23
*p*Ps 26:6
*q*Job 17:9; 22:30; 42:7-8; Ps 24:4
22:22 *r*Ge 18:19; Ps 128:1; Pr 8:32
22:23 *s*Dt 6:4-9; Ps 119:30-32
*t*Ps 119:102
22:24 *u*S Ge 6:9; Eph 1:4

22:25 *v*S 1Sa 26:23 22:27 *w*Mt 5:8 *x*Lev 26:23-24 22:28 *y*S Ex 3:8; 1Sa 2:8-9; Ps 72:12-13 *z*Ps 131:1; Pr 30:13; Da 4:31; Zep 3:11 *a*Isa 2:12,17; 5:15; S Lk 1:51 22:29 *b*Ps 27:1; Isa 2:5; Mic 7:8; Rev 21:23; 22:5

p 8 Hebrew; Vulgate and Syriac (see also Psalm 18:7) *mountains* *q 11* Many Hebrew manuscripts (see also Psalm 18:10); most Hebrew manuscripts *appeared* *r 12* Septuagint and Vulgate (see also Psalm 18:11); Hebrew *massed* *s 25* Hebrew; Septuagint and Vulgate (see also Psalm 18:24) *to the cleanness of my hands*

22:7 *his temple.* Heaven, where the Lord is enthroned as King (see Ps 11:4; Isa 6:1; Jnh 2:7).
22:8–16 See note on Ps 18:7–15.
22:9 *Smoke rose from his nostrils.* God's power is portrayed in terms similar to those applied to the awesome beast, the leviathan (Job 41:19–21).
22:11 *cherubim.* See Eze 1 and 10, where cherubim are said to be the bearers of the throne of God; see also notes on Ge 3:24; 1Sa 4:4; Eze 1:5.
22:14 *The LORD thundered.* The reference to thunder as the voice of God is common in the OT (see Ps 29; Job 37:2–5). Thunder is particularly suited to expressing God's power and majesty.
22:17 *He reached down from on high.* In vv. 17–20 David describes his deliverance, initially in figurative terms (v. 17; cf. v. 5) and subsequently in more literal language (vv. 18–20).
22:20 *delighted in.* The Hebrew underlying this expres-

sion is used in 15:26 ("pleased"); Ps 22:8 (cf. Mt 3:17, "well pleased") and expresses the idea of the sovereign good pleasure and favor of God toward his anointed one (v. 51).
22:21 *according to my righteousness.* In vv. 21–25 David refers to the Lord's deliverances as a reward for his own righteousness. While these statements may give the impression of self-righteous boasting and a meritorious basis for divine favor, they should be understood in their context as: (1) David's desire to please the Lord in his service as the Lord's anointed (see note on v. 51); (2) his recognition that the Lord rewards those who faithfully seek to serve him.
22:26–30 Because God responds to man in kind (see Job 34:11; Pr 3:34), David has experienced the Lord's favor.
22:28 *the haughty to bring them low.* The words of this verse fit well with David's experience in his conflict with Saul (see Hannah's song, 1Sa 2:3–8).
22:29 *You are my lamp.* The Lord causes David's life and undertakings to flourish (see Job 18:5–6; 21:17; see also

30With your help I can advance against a
    troop[t];
  with my God I can scale a wall.

31"As for God, his way is perfect;[c]
  the word of the LORD is flawless.[d]
He is a shield[e]
  for all who take refuge in him.
32For who is God besides the LORD?
  And who is the Rock[f] except our
    God?[g]
33It is God who arms me with strength[u]
  and makes my way perfect.
34He makes my feet like the feet of a
    deer;[h]
  he enables me to stand on the
    heights.[i]
35He trains my hands[j] for battle;
  my arms can bend a bow[k] of bronze.
36You give me your shield[l] of victory;
  you stoop down to make me great.
37You broaden the path[m] beneath me,
  so that my ankles do not turn.

38"I pursued my enemies and crushed
    them;
  I did not turn back till they were
    destroyed.
39I crushed[n] them completely, and they
    could not rise;
  they fell beneath my feet.
40You armed me with strength for battle;
  you made my adversaries bow at my
    feet.[o]
41You made my enemies turn their
    backs[p] in flight,
  and I destroyed my foes.
42They cried for help,[q] but there was no
    one to save them—[r]
  to the LORD, but he did not answer.[s]
43I beat them as fine as the dust[t] of the
    earth;
  I pounded and trampled[u] them like
    mud[v] in the streets.

44"You have delivered[w] me from the
    attacks of my people;

you have preserved[x] me as the head
  of nations.
People[y] I did not know are subject to
  me,
45 and foreigners come cringing[z] to me;
  as soon as they hear me, they obey
    me.[a]
46They all lose heart;
  they come trembling[v][b] from their
    strongholds.

47"The LORD lives! Praise be to my Rock!
  Exalted[c] be God, the Rock, my
    Savior![d]
48He is the God who avenges[e] me,[f]
  who puts the nations under me,
49 who sets me free from my enemies.[g]
You exalted me[h] above my foes;
  from violent men you rescued me.
50Therefore I will praise you, O LORD,
  among the nations;
  I will sing praises[i] to your name.[j]
51He gives his king great victories;[k]
  he shows unfailing kindness to his
    anointed,[l]
  to David[m] and his descendants
    forever."[n]

The Last Words of David

23 These are the last words of David:

"The oracle of David son of Jesse,
  the oracle of the man exalted[o] by the
    Most High,
  the man anointed[p] by the God of Jacob,
  Israel's singer of songs[w]:

2"The Spirit[q] of the LORD spoke through
  me;
  his word was on my tongue.
3The God of Israel spoke,

Cross references (center column):

22:31 cS Dt 32:4; Mt 5:48 dPs 12:6; 119:140; Pr 30:5-6 eS Ge 15:1
22:32 fS 1Sa 2:2 gS 2Sa 7:22
22:34 hIsa 35:6; Hab 3:19 iS Dt 32:13
22:35 jPs 144:1 kPs 7:12; 11:2; Zec 9:13
22:36 lEph 6:16
22:37 mPr 4:11
22:39 nPs 44:5; 110:6; Mal 4:3
22:40 oS Jos 10:24; S 1Ki 5:3
22:41 pS Ex 23:27
22:42 qIsa 1:15 rPs 50:22 sS 1Sa 14:37
22:43 tIKi 20:10; 2Ki 13:7; Isa 41:2; Am 1:3 uPs 7:5; Isa 41:25; Mic 7:10; Zec 10:5 vIsa 5:25; 10:6; 22:5; Mic 7:10
22:44 wS Ex 11:3; S 2Sa 3:1
xDt 28:13 yS 2Sa 8:1-14; Isa 55:3-5
22:45 zPs 66:3; 81:15
aS Dt 33:29
22:46 bMic 7:17
22:47 cS Ex 15:2 dDt 32:15; Ps 18:31; 89:26; 95:1
22:48 eS Nu 31:3 fPs 144:2
22:49 gPs 140:1, 4 hPs 27:6
22:50 iPs 9:11; 47:6; 68:4 jRo 15:9*
22:51 kPs 21:1; 144:9-10 lSa 16:13; Ps 89:20; Ac 13:23 mS 2Sa 7:13 nPs 89:24,29
23:1 oS Ex 11:3; Ps 78:70-71; 89:27 pISa 2:10, 35; Ps 18:50; 20:6; 84:9; Isa 45:1; Hab 3:13
23:2 qMt 22:43; Mk 12:36; 2Pe 1:21

Footnotes (center column):

t30 Or *can run through a barricade*   *u33* Dead Sea Scrolls, some Septuagint manuscripts, Vulgate and Syriac (see also Psalm 18:32); Masoretic Text *who is my strong refuge*   *v46* Some Septuagint manuscripts and Vulgate (see also Psalm 18:45); Masoretic Text *they arm themselves.*   *w1* Or *Israel's beloved singer*

---

note on Ps 27:1).

22:31 *his way is perfect.* The remainder of the song (vv. 31–51) accentuates David's praise to God for his deliverances.

22:32 *Rock.* See note on v. 2.

22:47 *The LORD lives!* God's interventions and blessings in David's behalf have shown him to be the living God (see Dt 5:26).

22:50 *I will praise you, O LORD, among the nations.* For Paul's reference to this vow see Ro 15:9.

22:51 *his king . . . his anointed.* See notes on 1Sa 10:25; 12:14–15. David refers to himself in the third person in a way that acknowledges the covenantal character of his kingship. It is in the context of David's official capacity as the Lord's anointed that the entire song is to be read and understood (see note on v. 21). *his descendants forever.* David

speaks of God's promise through Nathan (see 7:12–16).

23:1 *last words of David.* Probably to be understood as David's last poetic testimony (in the manner of his psalms), perhaps composed at the time of his final instructions and warnings to his son Solomon (see 1Ki 2:1–10).

23:2 *The Spirit of the LORD spoke through me.* David was conscious of God's Spirit at work in him enabling him to speak under the Spirit's guidance (see notes on 2Ti 3:16; 2Pe 1:21).

23:3 *Rock.* See note on 22:2; see also 1Sa 2:2; Dt 32:4, 15,18,30–31. *When one rules over men in righteousness.* In brief and vivid strokes David portrays the ideal theocratic king—to be fully realized only in the rule of David's greater son, Jesus Christ. This prophetic utterance complements that of 7:12–16 and anticipates those of Isa 9:7; 11:1–5; Jer 23:5–6; 33:15–16; Zec 9:9.

the Rock[r] of Israel said to me:
'When one rules over men in
righteousness,[s]
when he rules in the fear[t] of God,[u]
4 he is like the light[v] of morning[w] at
sunrise[x]
on a cloudless morning,
like the brightness after rain[y]
that brings the grass from the earth.'

5 "Is not my house right with God?
Has he not made with me an
everlasting covenant,[z]
arranged and secured in every part?
Will he not bring to fruition my
salvation
and grant me my every desire?
6 But evil men are all to be cast aside like
thorns,[a]
which are not gathered with the
hand.
7 Whoever touches thorns
uses a tool of iron or the shaft of a
spear;
they are burned up where they lie."

David's Mighty Men

23:8–39pp — 1Ch 11:10–41

8 These are the names of David's mighty
men:[b]
Josheb-Basshebeth,[x][c] a Tahkemonite,[y]
was chief of the Three; he raised his spear
against eight hundred men, whom he
killed[z] in one encounter.
9 Next to him was Eleazar son of Dodai[d]
the Ahohite.[e] As one of the three mighty
men, he was with David when they taunted the Philistines gathered ⌞at Pas Dam-
mim⌟[a] for battle. Then the men of Israel
retreated, 10 but he stood his ground and
struck down the Philistines till his hand
grew tired and froze to the sword. The
LORD brought about a great victory that
day. The troops returned to Eleazar, but
only to strip the dead.
11 Next to him was Shammah son of
Agee the Hararite. When the Philistines
banded together at a place where there
was a field full of lentils, Israel's troops fled
from them. 12 But Shammah took his stand
in the middle of the field. He defended it
and struck the Philistines down, and the
LORD brought about a great victory.
13 During harvest time, three of the
thirty chief men came down to David at
the cave of Adullam,[f] while a band of
Philistines was encamped in the Valley of
Rephaim.[g] 14 At that time David was in the
stronghold,[h] and the Philistine garrison
was at Bethlehem.[i] 15 David longed for
water and said, "Oh, that someone would
get me a drink of water from the well near
the gate of Bethlehem!" 16 So the three
mighty men broke through the Philistine
lines, drew water from the well near the
gate of Bethlehem and carried it back to
David. But he refused to drink it; instead,
he poured[j] it out before the LORD. 17 "Far
be it from me, O LORD, to do this!" he
said. "Is it not the blood[k] of men who
went at the risk of their lives?" And David
would not drink it.
Such were the exploits of the three
mighty men.
18 Abishai[l] the brother of Joab son of
Zeruiah was chief of the Three.[b] He raised
his spear against three hundred men,
whom he killed, and so he became as famous as the Three. 19 Was he not held in
greater honor than the Three? He became

23:3 [r]Dt 32:4; S 1Sa 2:2; Ps 18:31 [s]Ps 72:3 [t]S Ge 42:18 [u]Isa 11:1-5 **23:4** [v]Jn 1:5 [w]Ps 119:147; 130:6; Pr 4:18 [x]S Jdg 5:31; Mt 13:43 [y]S Dt 32:2 **23:5** [z]S Ge 9:16; Ps 89:29 **23:6** [a]Isa 5:6; 9:18; 10:17; 27:4; 33:12; Mic 7:4; Na 1:10; Mt 13:40-41 **23:8** [b]S 2Sa 17:10 [c]1Ch 27:2 **23:9** [d]1Ch 27:4 [e]1Ch 8:4 **23:13** [f]S Ge 38:1; S Jos 12:15 [g]S Jos 17:15 **23:14** [h]1Sa 22:4-5; S 2Sa 5:17 [i]Ru 1:19 **23:16** [j]S Ge 35:14 **23:17** [k]Lev 17:10-12 **23:18** [l]S 1Sa 26:6

[x] *8* Hebrew; some Septuagint manuscripts suggest *Ish-Bosheth,* that is, *Esh-Baal* (see also 1 Chron. 11:11 *Jashobeam*). [y] *8* Probably a variant of *Hacmonite* (see 1 Chron. 11:11) [z] *8* Some Septuagint manuscripts (see also 1 Chron. 11:11); Hebrew and other Septuagint manuscripts *Three; it was Adino the Eznite who killed eight hundred men* [a] *9* See 1 Chron. 11:13; Hebrew *gathered there.* [b] *18* Most Hebrew manuscripts (see also 1 Chron. 11:20); two Hebrew manuscripts and Syriac *Thirty*

23:4 *like the light of morning.* See notes on Ps 27:1; 36:9.

23:5 *Is not my house right with God?* A rhetorical question recalling God's covenant with him and his dynasty (see 7:12–16). *everlasting covenant.* David expressly calls God's promise to him a covenant that will not be abrogated (see notes on 7:20,28; Isa 55:3; see also Ps 89:3,28,34,39; 132:11). *bring to fruition.* Through David's promised descendants.

23:6 *evil men . . . cast aside.* Godless people who have no interest in the righteous king will be destroyed (see Ps 2:9; 110:5–6).

23:8–39 See note on 21:1–24:25. This list of 37 (see v. 39) of David's most valiant warriors and the description of some of their exploits are paralleled in 1Ch 11:11–41. There the list is expanded by 16 names (1Ch 11:41–47).

23:8 *Tahkemonite.* 1Ch 11:11 reads "Hacmonite" (see NIV text note here), derived from an unknown place-name. *Three.* Two groups of three warriors (vv. 8–12 and 13–23) and one group of 30 warriors (vv. 23–39) are mentioned (see note on v. 39 for the total number of warriors).

23:9 *Ahohite.* A descendant of Ahoah from the tribe of Benjamin (1Ch 8:4).

23:13 *harvest time.* See 11:1 and note. The circumstances of this event suggest that it happened shortly after David had fled from Saul, when men first began to gather to his cause (see 1Sa 22:1–4), or shortly after his conquest of Jerusalem (see 2Sa 5:17–18). *three.* Not the same as the three mighty men of v. 9. *thirty chief men.* See vv. 23–24,39. *cave of Adullam.* See 1Sa 22:1. *Rephaim.* See 5:18.

23:14 *stronghold.* See note on 1Sa 22:4.

23:15–16 See note on 1Ch 11:15–19.

23:18 *Abishai.* See 10:10,14; 18:2; see also note on 1Sa 26:6. *Three.* Presumably those referred to in vv. 13–17.

their commander, even though he was not included among them.

20Benaiah m son of Jehoiada was a valiant fighter from Kabzeel, n who performed great exploits. He struck down two of Moab's best men. He also went down into a pit on a snowy day and killed a lion. 21And he struck down a huge Egyptian. Although the Egyptian had a spear in his hand, Benaiah went against him with a club. He snatched the spear from the Egyptian's hand and killed him with his own spear. 22Such were the exploits of Benaiah son of Jehoiada; he too was as famous as the three mighty men. 23He was held in greater honor than any of the Thirty, but he was not included among the Three. And David put him in charge of his bodyguard.

24Among the Thirty were:

Asahel o the brother of Joab,
Elhanan son of Dodo from Bethlehem,
25Shammah the Harodite, p
Elika the Harodite,
26Helez q the Paltite,
Ira r son of Ikkesh from Tekoa,
27Abiezer s from Anathoth, t
Mebunnai c the Hushathite,
28Zalmon the Ahohite,
Maharai u the Netophathite, v
29Heled d w son of Baanah the Netophathite,
Ithai son of Ribai from Gibeah x in Benjamin,
30Benaiah the Pirathonite, y

Hiddai e from the ravines of Gaash, z
31Abi-Albon the Arbathite,
Azmaveth the Barhumite, a
32Eliahba the Shaalbonite,
the sons of Jashen,
Jonathan 33son of f Shammah the Hararite,
Ahiam son of Sharar g the Hararite,
34Eliphelet son of Ahasbai the Maacathite, b
Eliam c son of Ahithophel d the Gilonite,
35Hezro the Carmelite, e
Paarai the Arbite,
36Igal son of Nathan from Zobah, f
the son of Hagri, h
37Zelek the Ammonite,
Naharai the Beerothite, g the armor-bearer of Joab son of Zeruiah,
38Ira the Ithrite, h
Gareb the Ithrite
39and Uriah i the Hittite.
There were thirty-seven in all.

David Counts the Fighting Men
24:1–17pp — 1Ch 21:1–17

24 Again j the anger of the LORD burned against Israel, k and he in-

Cross-references (center column)
23:20 mS 2Sa 8:18; 1Ch 27:5
nJos 15:21
23:24 oS 2Sa 2:18
23:25 pJdg 7:1
23:26 q1Ch 27:10 r1Ch 27:9
23:27 s1Ch 27:12 tS Jos 21:18
23:28 u1Ch 27:13 v2Ki 25:23; Ezr 2:22; Ne 7:26; Jer 40:8
23:29 w1Ch 27:15 xS Jos 15:57
23:30 yS Jdg 12:13
zJos 24:30
23:31 a2Sa 3:16
23:34 bS Dt 3:14 cS 2Sa 11:3 dS 2Sa 15:12
23:35 eS Jos 12:22
23:36 fS 1Sa 14:47
23:37 gS Jos 9:17
23:38 h1Ch 2:53
23:39 i2Sa 11:3
24:1 jS Jos 9:15
kJob 1:6; Zec 3:1

c27 Hebrew; some Septuagint manuscripts (see also 1 Chron. 11:29) Sibbecai d29 Some Hebrew manuscripts and Vulgate (see also 1 Chron. 11:30); most Hebrew manuscripts Heleb e30 Hebrew; some Septuagint manuscripts (see also 1 Chron. 11:32) Hurai f33 Some Septuagint manuscripts (see also 1 Chron. 11:34); Hebrew does not have son of. g33 Hebrew; some Septuagint manuscripts (see also 1 Chron. 11:35) Sacar h36 Some Septuagint manuscripts (see also 1 Chron. 11:38); Hebrew Haggadi

---

23:20 Benaiah son of Jehoiada. Commander of the Kerethites and Pelethites (8:18; 20:23; see v. 23 below) and of the division of troops for the third month of the year (1Ch 27:5). He supported Solomon's succession to the throne (1Ki 1–2) and eventually replaced Joab as commander of the army (1Ki 2:35).
23:24 Thirty. Twenty-nine names are listed in vv. 24–39. Since the three of vv. 13–17 are also included in the thirty (see v. 13), the total number of warriors mentioned is 32. 1Ch 11:26–47 lists 16 additional names for this group, so it appears that the list includes the names of replacements for vacancies when a warrior either dropped out or died. Asahel. See 2:18–23.
23:34 Eliam. Father of Bathsheba (see 11:3) and son of David's counselor Ahithophel, who joined in Absalom's conspiracy (see 15:12,31,34; 16:20–23; 17:1–23).
23:39 Uriah. Husband of Bathsheba (see 11:3–27). thirty-seven. The total number of warriors referred to in vv. 8–39, including the Three of vv. 8–12, the Three of vv. 13–17, Abishai (vv. 18–19), Benaiah (vv. 20–23) and the 29 whose names are recorded in vv. 24–39 (see note on v. 24).
24:1 Again. The previous occasion may have been the famine of 21:1. the anger of the LORD burned against Israel. The specific reason for the Lord's displeasure is not stated. Because the anger is said to be directed against Israel rather

than David, some have concluded that it was occasioned by the widespread support among the people for the rebellions of Absalom and Sheba against David (see 15:12; 17:11, 24–26; 18:7; 20:1–2), the divinely chosen and anointed theocratic king. This would mean that the events of this chapter are to be placed chronologically shortly after those of chs. 15–20 and so after 980 B.C. (see note on 15:7). the LORD ... incited David against them. 1Ch 21:1 says that Satan inspired David to take the census. Although Scripture is clear that God does not cause anyone to sin (Jas 1:13–15), it is also clear that man's—and Satan's—evil acts are under God's sovereign control (see Ex 4:21; 7:3; 9:12; 10:1,20,27; 11:10; 14:4; Jos 11:20; 1Ki 22:22–23; Job 1:12; 2:10; Eze 3:20; 14:9; Ac 4:28). take a census of Israel and Judah. David's military census (see vv. 2–3) does not appear to have been prompted by any immediate external threat. Since he wanted to "know how many there are" (v. 2), it is evident that his action was motivated either by pride in the size of the empire he had acquired or by reliance for his security on the size of the reserve of manpower he could muster in an emergency or, more likely, both. The mere taking of a census was hardly sinful (see Nu 1:2–3; 26:2–4), but in this instance it represented an unwarranted glorying in and dependence on human power rather than the Lord (not much different from Israel's initial desire to have a king for their

cited David against them, saying, "Go and take a census of[l] Israel and Judah."

²So the king said to Joab[m] and the army commanders[i] with him, "Go throughout the tribes of Israel from Dan to Beersheba[n] and enroll[o] the fighting men, so that I may know how many there are."

³But Joab[p] replied to the king, "May the LORD your God multiply the troops a hundred times over,[q] and may the eyes of my lord the king see it. But why does my lord the king want to do such a thing?"

⁴The king's word, however, overruled Joab and the army commanders; so they left the presence of the king to enroll the fighting men of Israel.

⁵After crossing the Jordan, they camped near Aroer,[r] south of the town in the gorge, and then went through Gad and on to Jazer.[s] ⁶They went to Gilead and the region of Tahtim Hodshi, and on to Dan Jaan and around toward Sidon.[t] ⁷Then they went toward the fortress of Tyre[u] and all the towns of the Hivites[v] and Canaanites. Finally, they went on to Beersheba[w] in the Negev[x] of Judah.

⁸After they had gone through the entire land, they came back to Jerusalem at the end of nine months and twenty days.

⁹Joab reported the number of the fighting men to the king: In Israel there were eight hundred thousand able-bodied men who could handle a sword, and in Judah five hundred thousand.[y]

¹⁰David was conscience-stricken[z] after he had counted the fighting men, and he said to the LORD, "I have sinned[a] greatly in what I have done. Now, O LORD, I beg you, take away the guilt of your servant. I have done a very foolish thing.[b]"

¹¹Before David got up the next morning, the word of the LORD had come to Gad[c] the prophet, David's seer:[d] ¹²"Go and tell

David, 'This is what the LORD says: I am giving you three options. Choose one of them for me to carry out against you.'"

¹³So Gad went to David and said to him, "Shall there come upon you three[j] years of famine[e] in your land? Or three months of fleeing from your enemies while they pursue you? Or three days of plague[f] in your land? Now then, think it over and decide how I should answer the one who sent me."

¹⁴David said to Gad, "I am in deep distress. Let us fall into the hands of the LORD, for his mercy[g] is great; but do not let me fall into the hands of men."

¹⁵So the LORD sent a plague on Israel from that morning until the end of the time designated, and seventy thousand of the people from Dan to Beersheba died.[h] ¹⁶When the angel stretched out his hand to destroy Jerusalem, the LORD was grieved[i] because of the calamity and said to the angel who was afflicting the people, "Enough! Withdraw your hand." The angel of the LORD[j] was then at the threshing floor of Araunah the Jebusite.

¹⁷When David saw the angel who was striking down the people, he said to the LORD, "I am the one who has sinned and done wrong. These are but sheep.[k] What have they done?[l] Let your hand fall upon me and my family."[m]

David Builds an Altar

24:18–25pp — 1Ch 21:18–26

¹⁸On that day Gad went to David and said to him, "Go up and build an altar to the LORD on the threshing floor of Araunah[n] the Jebusite." ¹⁹So David went up, as the LORD had commanded through Gad.

Cross references (center column):

24:1 /S Ex 30:12; 1Ch 27:23
24:2 mS 2Sa 20:23; nS 2Sa 3:10; o2Ch 2:17; 17:14; 25:5
24:3 pS 2Sa 2:18; qS Dt 1:11
24:5 rS Jos 13:9; sS Nu 21:32
24:6 tS Ge 10:19; Jdg 1:31
24:7 uS Jos 19:29; vS Ex 3:8; wGe 21:31; xS Dt 1:7
24:9 yS Nu 1:44-46
24:10 zS 1Sa 24:5; aS Nu 22:34; bS Nu 12:11
24:11 cS 1Sa 22:5; d1Sa 9:9
24:13 eDt 28:38-42,48; S 32:24; Eze 14:21; /S Ex 5:3; S 30:12; S Lev 26:25; Dt 28:21-22, 27-28,35
24:14 gNe 9:28; Ps 4:1; 51:1; 86:5; 103:8,13; 119:132; 130:4; Isa 54:7; 55:7; Jer 33:8; 42:12; Da 9:9
24:15 h1Ch 27:24
24:16 iS Ge 6:6; jS Ge 16:7; S 19:13; S Ex 12:23; Ac 12:23
24:17 kPs 74:1; 100:3; Jer 49:20; lS Ge 18:23; mJnh 1:12
24:18 nGe 22:2; 2Ch 3:1

---

l2 Septuagint (see also verse 4 and 1 Chron. 21:2); Hebrew Joab the army commander   i13 Septuagint (see also 1 Chron. 21:12); Hebrew seven

---

security; see 1Sa 8–12). The act was uncharacteristic of David (see 1Sa 17:26,37,45–47; 2Sa 22:2–4,47–51).

24:2 *Dan to Beersheba.* See note on 1Sa 3:20.

24:3 *But why . . . ?* David's directive does not go unchallenged. The fact that he does not answer suggests that he knew his reasons were highly questionable. In any event, Joab's challenge renders David the more guilty.

24:5–8 The military census was begun in southern Transjordan and moved northward, then back across the Jordan, moving from north to south.

24:9 *eight hundred thousand . . . five hundred thousand.* These figures differ from those of 1Ch 21:5 (see notes on 1Ch 21:5–6).

24:10 *I have sinned greatly.* See note on v. 1.

24:11 *Gad the prophet, David's seer.* See notes on 1Sa 9:9; 22:5.

24:12 *Go and tell David.* See 12:1 and note. *three options.* The three alternative judgments were all included in the curses that Moses said would come on God's people when

they failed to adhere to their covenant obligations (see Dt 28:15–25).

24:14 *not . . . into the hands of men.* David, who knew both God and war, knew that even in his anger God is more merciful than man let loose in the rampages of war (see Ps 30:5).

24:15 *Dan to Beersheba.* See note on 1Sa 3:20.

24:16 *angel.* Angels appear elsewhere in Scripture as instruments of God's judgment (see Ex 33:2; 2Ki 19:35; Ps 35:5–6; 78:49; Mt 13:41; Ac 12:23). *the LORD was grieved.* See note on 1Sa 15:29. *threshing floor of Araunah.* Located on Mount Moriah, immediately north of David's city and overlooking it. Later it would become the site of the temple (see 1Ch 22:1; 2Ch 3:1). *Jebusite.* See note on 5:6.

24:17 *Let your hand fall upon me and my family.* Although the people of Israel were not without guilt (see v. 1), David assumes full blame for his own act and acknowledges his responsibility as king for the well-being of the Lord's people (see 5:2; 7:7–8).

20When Araunah looked and saw the king and his men coming toward him, he went out and bowed down before the king with his face to the ground.

21Araunah said, "Why has my lord the king come to his servant?"

"To buy your threshing floor," David answered, "so I can build an altar to the LORD, that the plague on the people may be stopped." o

22Araunah said to David, "Let my lord the king take whatever pleases him and offer it up. Here are oxen p for the burnt offering, and here are threshing sledges and ox yokes for the wood. 23O king, Araunah gives q all this to the king." Arau-

nah also said to him, "May the LORD your God accept you."

24But the king replied to Araunah, "No, I insist on paying you for it. I will not sacrifice to the LORD my God burnt offerings that cost me nothing." r

So David bought the threshing floor and the oxen and paid fifty shekels k s of silver for them. 25David built an altar t to the LORD there and sacrificed burnt offerings and fellowship offerings.l Then the LORD answered prayer u in behalf of the land, and the plague on Israel was stopped.

24:21
oNu 16:44-50
24:22
pS 1Sa 6:14
24:23 qGe 23:11

24:24
rMal 1:13-14
sS Ge 23:16
24:25 tS 1Sa 7:17
u2Sa 21:14

k24 That is, about 1 1/4 pounds (about 0.6 kilogram)　l25 Traditionally *peace offerings*

24:19　*as the LORD had commanded.* The Lord himself appointed the atoning sacrifice in answer to David's prayer.
24:21　*To buy your threshing floor.* David does not simply expropriate the property for his royal purposes (see 1Sa 8:14).
24:24　*burnt offerings.* See Lev 1:1–17. *David bought the threshing floor.* Thus the later site of the temple (see note on

v. 16) became the royal property of the house of David. *and the oxen.* David's haste could not wait for oxen to be brought some distance from his own herds. *fifty shekels.* See note on 1Ch 21:25.
24:25　*fellowship offerings.* See note on 1Sa 11:15. Reconciliation and restoration of covenant fellowship were obtained by the king's repentance, intercessory prayer and the offering of sacrifices.

1 KINGS

Title

1 and 2 Kings (like 1 and 2 Samuel and 1 and 2 Chronicles) are actually one literary work, called in Hebrew tradition simply "Kings." The division of this work into two books was introduced by the translators of the Septuagint (the Greek translation of the OT) and subsequently followed in the Latin Vulgate and most modern versions. In 1448 the division into two sections also appeared in a Hebrew manuscript and was perpetuated in later printed editions of the Hebrew text. Both the Septuagint and the Latin Vulgate further designated Samuel and Kings in a way that emphasized the relationship of these two works (Septuagint: First, Second, Third and Fourth Book of Kingdoms; Latin Vulgate: First, Second, Third and Fourth Kings). Together Samuel and Kings relate the whole history of the monarchy, from its rise under the ministry of Samuel to its fall at the hands of the Babylonians.

The division between 1 and 2 Kings has been made at an appropriate but somewhat arbitrary place, shortly after the deaths of Ahab of the northern kingdom (22:37) and Jehoshaphat of the southern kingdom (22:50). Placing the division at this point causes the account of the reign of Ahaziah of Israel to overlap the end of 1 Kings (22:51-53) and the beginning of 2 Kings (ch. 1). The same is true of the narration of the ministry of Elijah, which for the most part appears in 1 Kings (chs. 17-19). However, his final act of judgment and the passing of his cloak to Elisha at the moment of his ascension to heaven in a whirlwind are contained in 2 Kings (1:1-2:17).

Author, Sources and Date

There is little conclusive evidence as to the identity of the author of 1,2 Kings. Although Jewish tradition credits Jeremiah, few today accept this as likely. Whoever the author was, it is clear that he was familiar with the book of Deuteronomy—as were many of Israel's prophets. It is also clear that he used a variety of sources in compiling his history of the monarchy. Three such sources are named: "the book of the annals of Solomon" (11:41), "the book of the annals of the kings of Israel" (14:19), "the book of the annals of the kings of Judah" (14:29). It is likely that other written sources were also employed (such as those mentioned in Chronicles; see below).

Although some scholars have concluded that the three sources specifically cited in 1,2 Kings are to be viewed as official court annals from the royal archives in Jerusalem and Samaria, this is by no means certain. It seems at least questionable whether official court annals would have included details of conspiracies such as those referred to in 16:20; 2Ki 15:15. It is also questionable whether official court annals would have been readily accessible for public scrutiny, as the author clearly implies in his references to them. Such considerations have led some scholars to conclude that these sources were records of the reigns of the kings of Israel and Judah compiled by the succession of Israel's prophets spanning the kingdom period. 1,2 Chronicles makes reference to a number of such writings: "the records of Samuel the seer, the records of Nathan the prophet and the records of Gad the seer" (1Ch 29:29), "the prophecy of Ahijah the Shilonite" and "the visions of Iddo the seer" (2Ch 9:29), "the records of Shemaiah the prophet" (2Ch 12:15), "the annals of Jehu son of Hanani," (2Ch 20:34), "the annotations on the book of the kings" (2Ch 24:27), the "events of Uzziah's reign . . . recorded by the prophet Isaiah son of Amoz" (2Ch 26:22; see also 2Ch 32:32)—and there may have been others. It is most likely, for example, that for the ministries of Elijah and Elisha the author depended on a prophetic source (perhaps from the eighth century) that had drawn up an account of those two prophets in which they were already compared with Moses and Joshua.

Some scholars place the date of composition of 1,2 Kings in the time subsequent to Jehoiachin's release from prison (562 B.C.; 2Ki 25:27-30) and prior to the end of the Babylonian exile in 538. This position is challenged by others on the basis of statements in 1,2 Kings that speak of certain things in the preexilic period that are said to have continued in existence "to this day" (see, e.g., 8:8, the poles

used to carry the ark; 9:20-21, conscripted labor; 12:19, Israel in rebellion against the house of David; 2Ki 8:22, Edom in rebellion against the kingdom of Judah). From such statements it is argued that the writer must have been a person living in Judah in the preexilic period rather than in Babylon in postexilic times. If this argument is accepted, one must conclude that the original book was composed about the time of the death of Josiah and that the material pertaining to the time subsequent to his reign was added during the exile c. 550. While this "two-edition" viewpoint is possible, it rests largely on the "to this day" statements.

An alternative is to understand these statements as those of the original source used by the author rather than statements of the author himself. A comparison of 2Ch 5:9 with 1Ki 8:8 suggests that this is a legitimate conclusion. Chronicles is clearly a postexilic writing, yet the wording of the statement concerning the poles used to carry the ark ("they are still there today") is the same in Chronicles as it is in Kings. Probably the Chronicler was simply quoting his source, namely, 1Ki 8:8. There is no reason that the author of 1,2 Kings could not have done the same thing in quoting from his earlier sources. This explanation allows for positing a single author living in exile and using the source materials at his disposal.

Theme: Kingship and Covenant

1,2 Kings contains no explicit statement of purpose or theme. Reflection on its content, however, reveals that the author has selected and arranged his material in a manner that provides a sequel to the history found in 1,2 Samuel—a history of kingship regulated by covenant. In general, 1,2 Kings describes the history of the kings of Israel and Judah in the light of God's covenants. The guiding thesis of the book is that the welfare of Israel and her kings depended on their obedience to their obligations as defined in the Mosaic covenant.

It is clearly not the author's intention to present a socio-politico-economic history of Israel's monarchy in accordance with the principles of modern historiography. The author repeatedly refers the reader to other sources for more detailed information about the reigns of the various kings (see, e.g., 11:41; 14:19,29; 15:7,31; 16:5,14,20,27), and he gives a covenantal rather than a social or political or economic assessment of their reigns. From the standpoint of a political historian, Omri would be considered one of the more important rulers in the northern kingdom. He established a powerful dynasty and made Samaria the capital city. According to the Moabite Stone (see chart on "Ancient Texts Relating to the OT," p. 5), Omri was the ruler who subjugated the Moabites to the northern kingdom. Long after Omri's death, Assyrian rulers referred to Jehu as the "son of Omri" (either mistakenly or merely in accordance with their literary conventions when speaking of a later king of a realm). Yet in spite of Omri's political importance, his reign is dismissed in six verses (16:23-28) with the statement that he "did evil in the eyes of the LORD and sinned more than all those before him" (16:25). Similarly, the reign of Jeroboam II, who presided over the northern kingdom during the time of its greatest political and economic power, is treated only briefly (2Ki 14:23-29).

Another example of the writer's covenantal rather than merely political or economic interest can be seen in the description of the reign of Josiah of Judah. Nothing is said about the early years of his reign, but a detailed description is given of the reformation and renewal of the covenant that he promoted in his 18th year as king (2Ki 22:3-23:28). Nor is anything said of the motives leading Josiah to oppose Pharaoh Neco of Egypt at Megiddo, or of the major shift in geopolitical power from Assyria to Babylon that was connected with this incident (see notes on 2Ki 23:29-30).

It becomes apparent, then, that the kings who receive the most attention in 1,2 Kings are those during whose reigns there was either notable deviation from or affirmation of the covenant (or significant interaction between a king and God's prophet; see below). Ahab son of Omri is an example of the former (17:1-22:39). His reign is given extensive treatment, not so much because of its extraordinary political importance, but because of the serious threat to covenant fidelity and continuity that arose in the northern kingdom during his reign. Ultimately the pagan influence of Ahab's wife Jezebel through Ahab's daughter Athaliah (whether she was Jezebel's daughter is unknown) nearly led to the extermination of the house of David in Judah (see 2Ki 11:1-3).

Manasseh (2Ki 21:1-18) is an example of a similar sort. Here again it is deviation from the covenant that is emphasized in the account of his reign rather than political features, such as involvement in the Assyrian-Egyptian conflict (mentioned in Assyrian records but not in 2 Kings). The extreme apostasy characterizing Manasseh's reign made exile for Judah inevitable (2Ki 21:10-15; 23:26-27).

On the positive side, Hezekiah (2Ki 18:1-20:21) and Josiah (2Ki 22:1-23:29) are given extensive treatment because of their involvement in covenant renewal. These are the only two kings given

unqualified approval by the writer for their loyalty to the Lord (2Ki 18:3; 22:2). It is noteworthy that all the kings of the northern kingdom are said to have done evil in the eyes of the Lord and walked in the ways of Jeroboam, who caused Israel to sin (see, e.g., 16:26,31; 22:52; 2Ki 3:3; 10:29). It was Jeroboam who established the golden calf worship at Bethel and Dan shortly after the division of the kingdom (see 12:26-33; 13:1-6).

While the writer depicts Israel's obedience or disobedience to the Sinai covenant as decisive for her historical destiny, he also recognizes the far-reaching historical significance of the Davidic covenant, which promised that David's dynasty would endure forever. This is particularly noticeable in references to the "lamp" that the Lord had promised David (see 11:36; 15:4; 2Ki 8:19; see also note on 2Sa 21:17). It also appears in more general references to the promise to David (8:20,25) and its consequences for specific historical developments in Judah's later history (11:12-13,32; 2Ki 19:34; 20:6). In addition, the writer uses the life and reign of David as a standard by which the lives of later kings are measured (see, e.g., 9:4; 11:4,6,33,38; 14:8; 15:3,5,11; 2Ki 16:2; 18:3; 22:2).

Another prominent feature of the narratives of 1,2 Kings is the emphasis on the relationship between prophecy and fulfillment in the historical developments of the monarchy. On at least 11 occasions a prophecy is recorded that is later said to have been fulfilled (see, e.g., 2Sa 7:13 and 1Ki 8:20; 1Ki 11:29-39 and 1Ki 12:15; 1Ki 13 and 2Ki 23:16-18). The result of this emphasis is that the history of the kingdom is not presented as a chain of chance occurrences or the mere interplay of human actions but as the unfolding of Israel's historical destiny under the guidance of an omniscient and omnipotent God—Israel's covenant Lord, who rules all history in accordance with his sovereign purposes (see 8:56; 2Ki 10:10).

The author also stresses the importance of the prophets themselves in their role as official emissaries from the court of Israel's covenant Lord, the Great King to whom Israel and her king were bound in service through the covenant. The Lord sent a long succession of such prophets to call king and people back to covenant loyalty (2Ki 17:13). For the most part their warnings and exhortations fell on deaf ears. Many of these prophets and prophetesses are mentioned in the narratives of 1,2 Kings (see, e.g., Ahijah, 11:29-40; 14:5-18; Shemaiah, 12:22-24; Micaiah, 22:8-28; Jonah, 2Ki 14:25; Isaiah, 2Ki 19:1-7,20-34; Huldah, 2Ki 22:14-20), but particular attention is given to the ministries of Elijah and Elisha (1Ki 17-19; 2Ki 1-13).

Reflection on these features of 1,2 Kings suggests that it was written to explain to a people in exile that the reason for their condition of humiliation was their stubborn persistence in breaking the covenant. In bringing the exile upon his people, God, after much patience, imposed the curses of the covenant, which had stood as a warning to them from the beginning (see Lev 26:27-45; Dt 28:64-68). This is made explicit with respect to the captivity of the northern kingdom in 2Ki 17:7-23; 18:10-12, and with respect to the southern kingdom in 2Ki 21. The reformation under Josiah in the southern kingdom is viewed as too little, too late (see 2Ki 23:26-27; 24:3).

The book, then, provides a retrospective analysis of Israel's history. It explains the reasons both for the destruction of Samaria and Jerusalem and their respective kingdoms and for the bitter experience of being forced into exile. This does not mean, however, that there is no hope for the future. The writer consistently keeps the promise to David in view as a basis on which Israel in exile may look to the future with hope rather than with despair. In this connection the final four verses of the book, reporting Jehoiachin's release from prison in Babylon and his elevation to a place of honor in the court there (2Ki 25:27-30), take on added significance. The future remains open for a new work of the Lord in faithfulness to his promise to the house of David.

It is important to note that, although the author was undoubtedly a Judahite exile, and although the northern kingdom had been dispersed for well over a century and a half at the time of his writing, the scope of his concern was all Israel—the whole covenant people. Neither he nor the prophets viewed the division of the kingdom as an excommunication of the ten tribes, nor did they see the earlier exile of the northern kingdom as a final exclusion of the northern tribes from Israel's future.

Chronology

1,2 Kings presents the reader with abundant chronological data. Not only is the length of the reign of each king given, but during the period of the divided kingdom the beginning of the reign of each king is synchronized with the regnal year of the ruling king in the opposite kingdom. Often additional data, such as the age of the ruler at the time of his accession, are also provided.

By integrating Biblical data with those derived from Assyrian chronological records, the year 853 B.C. can be fixed as the year of Ahab's death, and the year 841 as the year Jehu began to reign. The

years in which Ahab and Jehu had contacts with Shalmaneser III of Assyria can also be given definite dates (by means of astronomical calculations based on an Assyrian reference to a solar eclipse). With these fixed points, it is then possible to work both forward and backward in the lines of the kings of Israel and Judah to give dates for each king. By the same means it can be determined that the division of the kingdom occurred in 930, that Samaria fell to the Assyrians in 722-721 and that Jerusalem fell to the Babylonians in 586.

The synchronistic data correlating the reigns of the kings of Israel and Judah present some knotty problems, which have long been considered nearly insoluble. In more recent times, most of these problems have been resolved in a satisfactory way through recognizing such possibilities as overlapping reigns, co-regencies of sons with their fathers, differences in the time of the year in which the reign of a king officially began, and differences in the way a king's first year was reckoned (e.g., see notes on 15:33; 2Ki 8:25; see also chart on "Rulers of Israel and Judah," p. 502).

Content

1,2 Kings describes the history of Israel's monarchy from the closing days of the rule of David until the time of the Babylonian exile. After an extensive account of Solomon's reign, the narrative records the division of the kingdom and then, by means of its synchronistic accounts, presents an interrelated picture of developments within the two kingdoms.

Kingship in the northern kingdom was plagued with instability and violence. Twenty rulers represented nine different dynasties during the approximately 210 years from the division of the kingdom in 930 B.C. until the fall of Samaria in 722-721. In the southern kingdom there were also 20 rulers, but these were all descendants of David (except Athaliah, whose usurping of the throne interrupted the sequence for a few years) and spanned a period of about 345 years from the division of the kingdom until the fall of Jerusalem in 586.

Outline

1,2 Kings can be broadly outlined by relating its contents to the major historical periods it describes and to the ministries of Elijah and Elisha.

I. The Solomonic Era (1:1-12:24)
   A. Solomon's Succession to the Throne (1:1-2:12)
   B. Solomon's Throne Consolidated (2:13-46)
   C. Solomon's Wisdom (ch. 3)
   D. Solomon's Reign Characterized (ch. 4)
   E. Solomon's Building Projects (5:1-9:9)
      1. Preparation for building the temple (ch. 5)
      2. Building the temple (ch. 6)
      3. Building the palace (7:1-12)
      4. The temple furnishings (7:13-51)
      5. Dedication of the temple (ch. 8)
      6. The Lord's response and warning (9:1-9)
   F. Solomon's Reign Characterized (9:10-10:29)
   G. Solomon's Folly (11:1-13)
   H. Solomon's Throne Threatened (11:14-43)
   I. Rehoboam's Succession to the Throne (12:1-24)
II. Israel and Judah from Jeroboam I/Rehoboam to Ahab/Asa (12:25-16:34)
   A. Jeroboam I of Israel (12:25-14:20)
   B. Rehoboam of Judah (14:21-31)
   C. Abijah of Judah (15:1-8)
   D. Asa of Judah (15:9-24)
   E. Nadab of Israel (15:25-32)
   F. Baasha of Israel (15:33-16:7)
   G. Elah of Israel (16:8-14)
   H. Zimri of Israel (16:15-20)
   I. Omri of Israel (16:21-28)
   J. Ahab of Israel (16:29-34)

III. The Ministries of Elijah and Elisha and Other Prophets from Ahab/Asa to Joram/Jehoshaphat (17:1-2Ki 8:15)
   A. Elijah (and Other Prophets) in the Reign of Ahab (17:1-22:40)
      1. Elijah and the drought (ch. 17)
      2. Elijah on Mount Carmel (ch. 18)
      3. Elijah's flight to Horeb (ch. 19)
      4. A prophet condemns Ahab for sparing Ben-Hadad (ch. 20)
      5. Elijah condemns Ahab for seizing Naboth's vineyard (ch. 21)
      6. Micaiah prophesies Ahab's death; its fulfillment (22:1-40)
   B. Jehoshaphat of Judah (22:41-50)
   C. Ahaziah of Israel; Elijah's Last Prophecy (22:51-2Ki 1:18)
   D. Elijah's Translation; Elisha's Inauguration (2Ki 2:1-18)
   E. Elisha in the Reign of Joram (2:19-8:15)
      1. Elisha's initial miraculous signs (2:19-25)
      2. Elisha during the campaign against Moab (ch. 3)
      3. Elisha's ministry to needy ones in Israel (ch. 4)
      4. Elisha heals Naaman (ch. 5)
      5. Elisha's deliverance of one of the prophets (6:1-7)
      6. Elisha's deliverance of Joram from Aramean raiders (6:8-23)
      7. Aramean siege of Samaria lifted, as Elisha prophesied (6:24-7:20)
      8. The Shunammite's land restored (8:1-6)
      9. Elisha prophesies Hazael's oppression of Israel (8:7-15)
IV. Israel and Judah from Joram/Jehoram to the Exile of Israel (2Ki 8:16-17:41)
   A. Jehoram of Judah (8:16-24)
   B. Ahaziah of Judah (8:25-29)
   C. Jehu's Revolt and Reign (chs. 9-10)
      1. Elisha orders Jehu's anointing (9:1-13)
      2. Jehu's assassination of Joram and Ahaziah (9:14-29)
      3. Jehu's execution of Jezebel (9:30-37)
      4. Jehu's slaughter of Ahab's family (10:1-17)
      5. Jehu's eradication of Baal worship (10:18-36)
   D. Athaliah and Joash of Judah; Repair of the Temple (chs. 11-12)
   E. Jehoahaz of Israel (13:1-9)
   F. Jehoash of Israel; Elisha's Last Prophecy (13:10-25)
   G. Amaziah of Judah (14:1-22)
   H. Jeroboam II of Israel (14:23-29)
   I. Azariah of Judah (15:1-7)
   J. Zechariah of Israel (15:8-12)
   K. Shallum of Israel (15:13-16)
   L. Menahem of Israel (15:17-22)
   M. Pekahiah of Israel (15:23-26)
   N. Pekah of Israel (15:27-31)
   O. Jotham of Judah (15:32-38)
   P. Ahaz of Judah (ch. 16)
   Q. Hoshea of Israel (17:1-6)
   R. Exile of Israel; Resettlement of the Land (17:7-41)
V. Judah from Hezekiah to the Babylonian Exile (2Ki 18-25)
   A. Hezekiah (chs. 18-20)
      1. Hezekiah's good reign (18:1-8)
      2. The Assyrian threat and deliverance (18:9-19:37)
      3. Hezekiah's illness and alliance with Babylon (ch. 20)
   B. Manasseh (21:1-18)
   C. Amon (21:19-26)
   D. Josiah (22:1-23:30)
      1. Repair of the temple; discovery of the Book of the Law (ch. 22)
      2. Renewal of the covenant; end of Josiah's reign (23:1-30)
   E. Jehoahaz Exiled to Egypt (23:31-35)

F. Jehoiakim: First Babylonian Invasion (23:36-24:7)
G. Jehoiachin: Second Babylonian Invasion (24:8-17)
H. Zedekiah (24:18-20)
I. Babylonian Exile of Judah (25:1-21)
J. Removal of the Remnant to Egypt (25:22-26)
K. Elevation of Jehoiachin in Babylon (25:27-30)

Adonijah Sets Himself Up as King

1 When King David was old and well
advanced in years, he could not keep
warm even when they put covers over
him. [2]So his servants said to him, "Let us
look for a young virgin to attend the king
and take care of him. She can lie beside
him so that our lord the king may keep
warm."

[3]Then they searched throughout Israel
for a beautiful girl and found Abishag,[a] a
Shunammite,[b] and brought her to the
king. [4]The girl was very beautiful; she took
care of the king and waited on him, but
the king had no intimate relations with
her.

[5]Now Adonijah,[c] whose mother was
Haggith, put himself forward and said, "I
will be king." So he got chariots[d] and
horses[a] ready, with fifty men to run ahead
of him. [6](His father had never interfered[e]
with him by asking, "Why do you behave
as you do?" He was also very handsome
and was born next after Absalom.)

[7]Adonijah conferred with Joab[f] son of
Zeruiah and with Abiathar[g] the priest, and
they gave him their support. [8]But Zadok[h]
the priest, Benaiah[i] son of Jehoiada, Nathan[j] the prophet, Shimei[k] and Rei[b] and

David's special guard[l] did not join Adonijah.

[9]Adonijah then sacrificed sheep, cattle
and fattened calves at the Stone of
Zoheleth near En Rogel. [m] He invited all his
brothers, the king's sons, [n] and all the men
of Judah who were royal officials, [10]but he
did not invite[o] Nathan the prophet or Benaiah or the special guard or his brother
Solomon. [p]

[11]Then Nathan asked Bathsheba, [q] Solomon's mother, "Have you not heard that
Adonijah, [r] the son of Haggith, has become
king without our lord David's knowing it?
[12]Now then, let me advise[s] you how you
can save your own life and the life of your
son Solomon. [13]Go in to King David and
say to him, 'My lord the king, did you not
swear[t] to me your servant: "Surely Solomon your son shall be king after me, and
he will sit on my throne"? Why then has
Adonijah become king?' [14]While you are
still there talking to the king, I will come in
and confirm what you have said."

[15]So Bathsheba went to see the aged
king in his room, where Abishag[u] the Shunammite was attending him. [16]Bathsheba
bowed low and knelt before the king.

1:3 [a]ver 15;
S 2Sa 3:7;
1Ki 2:17,22
[b]S Jos 19:18
1:5 [c]S 2Sa 3:4
[d]S 1Sa 8:11
1:6 [e]1Sa 3:13
1:7 [f]S 2Sa 2:13,
18 [g]S 1Sa 22:20
1:8 [h]S 1Sa 2:35;
S 2Sa 8:17
[i]S 2Sa 8:18
[j]S 2Sa 7:2
[k]1Ki 4:18
[l]2Sa 23:8
1:9 [m]S 2Sa 17:17
[n]1Ch 29:24
1:10 [o]ver 26
[p]S 2Sa 12:24
1:11 [q]2Sa 12:24
[r]S 2Sa 3:4
1:12 [s]Pr 15:22
1:13 [t]ver 17,30
1:15 [u]S ver 3

[a]5 Or charioteers   [b]8 Or and his friends

1:1—12:24 The narrative of the Solomonic era is an exquisite example of literary inversion, in this case consisting of
nine sections. The first and last are parallel, as well as the
second and eighth, etc.—and the fifth section, which occupies the central position in the structure, is the longest of the
nine and describes Solomon's building projects (see Introduction: Outline).
1:1 *advanced in years.* 2Sa 5:4 indicates that David died at
about 70 years of age (cf. 1Ki 2:11).
1:3 *Shunammite.* Abishag came from Shunem (2Ki 4:8; Jos
19:18; 1Sa 28:4), located near the plain of Jezreel in the
tribal territory of Issachar.
1:4 *had no intimate relations with her.* Significant in connection with Adonijah's request to be given Abishag as his
wife after the death of David (see notes on 2:17,22).
1:5 *Adonijah.* The fourth son of David (see 2Sa 3:4), who
was at this time approximately 35 years of age. It is likely that
he was the oldest surviving son of David (see note on 2Sa
13:28; see also 2Sa 18:14). *put himself forward.* A unilateral
attempt to usurp the throne, bypassing King David's right to
designate his own successor (Adonijah must at least have
known that his father favored Solomon; see v. 10). If successful, it would have thwarted God's and David's choice of
Solomon (see vv. 13,17,30; 1Ch 22:9–10; see also note on
2Sa 12:25). *fifty men to run ahead of him.* Adonijah here
follows the example of Absalom before him (see note on 2Sa
15:1).
1:6 *never interfered.* David appears to have been consistently negligent in disciplining his sons (see notes on 2Sa
13:21; 14:33). *very handsome.* Attractive physical appearance was an important asset to an aspirant to the throne (see
1Sa 9:2; 16:12; 2Sa 14:25).
1:7 *Joab son of Zeruiah.* See notes on 1Sa 26:6; 2Sa 2:13;
19:13; 20:10,23. Joab's alignment with Adonijah may have

been motivated by a struggle for power with Benaiah (see v.
8; 2Sa 8:18; 20:23; 23:20–23). Joab held his position more
by his standing with the army than by the favor and confidence of David (see 2:5–6). *Abiathar the priest.* See note on
2Sa 8:17.
1:8 *Zadok the priest.* See note on 2Sa 8:17. *Benaiah son of
Jehoiada.* See note on 2Sa 23:20. *Nathan the prophet.* See
2Sa 12:1–25. *Shimei.* Not the Shimei of 2:8,46; 2Sa
16:5–8; perhaps the same as Shimei son of Ela (4:18). *Rei.*
See NIV text note. There is no other OT reference to Rei if
taken as a proper name. *David's special guard.* See 2Sa
23:8–39.
1:9 *Adonijah then sacrificed.* Here also (see note on v. 5)
Adonijah followed the example of Absalom (see 2Sa
15:7–12). *En Rogel.* Means "the spring of Rogel"; located
just south of Jerusalem in the Kidron Valley. Apparently the
site of a spring had some kind of symbolic significance for the
business at hand (see v. 33 and note).
1:11 *Bathsheba, Solomon's mother.* The queen mother
held an important and influential position in the royal court
(see 2:19; 15:13; 2Ki 10:13; 2Ch 15:16). *has become king.*
Although the preceding narrative does not relate the actual
proclamation of Adonijah's kingship, it can be assumed (see
v. 25; 2:15; cf. 2Sa 15:10).
1:12 *save your own life and the life of your son Solomon.*
It was common in the ancient Near East for a usurper to
liquidate all potential claimants to the throne in an attempt to
secure his own position (see 15:29; 2Ki 10:11; 11:1).
1:13 *did you not swear to me . . . ?* Although 2 Samuel
does not record David's oath concerning the succession of
Solomon, it does suggest that Solomon was the son through
whom the Lord's promise to David for an eternal dynasty
would be carried forward (see note on v. 5).

"What is it you want?" the king asked.
[17]She said to him, "My lord, you yourself swore[v] to me your servant by the LORD your God: 'Solomon your son shall be king after me, and he will sit on my throne.' [18]But now Adonijah has become king, and you, my lord the king, do not know about it. [19]He has sacrificed[w] great numbers of cattle, fattened calves, and sheep, and has invited all the king's sons, Abiathar the priest and Joab the commander of the army, but he has not invited Solomon your servant. [20]My lord the king, the eyes of all Israel are on you, to learn from you who will sit on the throne of my lord the king after him. [21]Otherwise, as soon as my lord the king is laid to rest[x] with his fathers, I and my son Solomon will be treated as criminals."

[22]While she was still speaking with the king, Nathan the prophet arrived. [23]And they told the king, "Nathan the prophet is here." So he went before the king and bowed with his face to the ground.

[24]Nathan said, "Have you, my lord the king, declared that Adonijah shall be king after you, and that he will sit on your throne? [25]Today he has gone down and sacrificed great numbers of cattle, fattened calves, and sheep. He has invited all the king's sons, the commanders of the army and Abiathar the priest. Right now they are eating and drinking with him and saying, 'Long live King Adonijah!' [26]But me your servant, and Zadok the priest, and Benaiah son of Jehoiada, and your servant Solomon he did not invite.[y] [27]Is this something my lord the king has done without letting his servants know who should sit on the throne of my lord the king after him?"

Cross references (center column)

1:17 [v]S ver 13
1:19 [w]ver 9
1:21
[x]S Ge 15:15;
1Ki 2:10
1:26 [y]ver 10

1:29 [z]S 2Sa 4:9
1:30 [a]S ver 13;
1Ch 23:1
1:32 [b]S 1Sa 2:35
1:33 [c]Jdg 10:4;
Zec 9:9 [d]ver 38;
2Ch 32:30; 33:14
1:34 [e]S 1Sa 2:35;
10:1 [f]S 2Sa 15:10
1:37 [g]Jos 1:5,17
[h]ver 47
1:38 [i]ver 8
/S 1Sa 30:14;
S 2Sa 15:18

David Makes Solomon King

1:28–53pp — 1Ch 29:21-25

[28]Then King David said, "Call in Bathsheba." So she came into the king's presence and stood before him.

[29]The king then took an oath: "As surely as the LORD lives, who has delivered me out of every trouble,[z] [30]I will surely carry out today what I swore[a] to you by the LORD, the God of Israel: Solomon your son shall be king after me, and he will sit on my throne in my place.'"

[31]Then Bathsheba bowed low with her face to the ground and, kneeling before the king, said, "May my lord King David live forever!"

[32]King David said, "Call in Zadok[b] the priest, Nathan the prophet and Benaiah son of Jehoiada." When they came before the king, [33]he said to them: "Take your lord's servants with you and set Solomon my son on my own mule[c] and take him down to Gihon.[d] [34]There have Zadok the priest and Nathan the prophet anoint[e] him king over Israel. Blow the trumpet[f] and shout, 'Long live King Solomon!' [35]Then you are to go up with him, and he is to come and sit on my throne and reign in my place. I have appointed him ruler over Israel and Judah."

[36]Benaiah son of Jehoiada answered the king, "Amen! May the LORD, the God of my lord the king, so declare it. [37]As the LORD was with my lord the king, so may he be with[g] Solomon to make his throne even greater[h] than the throne of my lord King David!"

[38]So Zadok[i] the priest, Nathan the prophet, Benaiah son of Jehoiada, the Kerethites[j] and the Pelethites went down and put Solomon on King David's mule

---

1:17 *you yourself swore to me . . . by the LORD your God.* An oath taken in the Lord's name was inviolable (see Ex 20:7; Lev 19:12; Jos 9:15,18,20; Jdg 11:30,35; Ecc 5:4–7). **1:21** *laid to rest with his fathers.* A conventional expression for death (see Ge 47:30; Dt 31:16). **1:24** Nathan approached David diplomatically by raising a question that revealed the dilemma. Either David had secretly encouraged Adonijah to claim the throne and thereby had broken his oath to Bathsheba and Solomon (see v. 27), or he had been betrayed by Adonijah. **1:25** *Long live King Adonijah!* An expression of recognition and acclamation of the new king (see 1Sa 10:24; 2Sa 16:16; 2Ki 11:12). **1:31** *May my lord King David live forever!* An expression of Bathsheba's thanks in the stereotyped hyperbolic language of the court (see Ne 2:3; Da 2:4; 3:9; 5:10; 6:21). **1:33** *your lord's servants.* Presumably including the Kerethites and Pelethites (see v. 38). *my own mule.* Although crossbreeding was forbidden in the Mosaic law (Lev 19:19), mules (perhaps imported; see Eze 27:14) were used in the time of David, at least as mounts for royalty (see 2Sa 13:29; 18:9). To ride on David's own mule was a public proclamation that Solomon's succession to the throne was sanctioned by David (see Ge 41:43 and first NIV text note; Est 6:7–8). *Gihon.* The site of a spring on the eastern slope of Mount Zion (see notes on v. 9; 2Sa 5:8). **1:34** *anoint him.* See notes on 1Sa 2:10; 9:16. *Blow the trumpet.* See 2Ki 9:13; 2Sa 15:10; 20:1. *Long live King Solomon!* See note on v. 25. **1:35** *Israel and Judah.* The distinction between Israel and Judah was rooted in the separate arrangements by which David became king over these two tribal units (see 2Sa 2:4; 5:3). **1:36** *Amen! May the LORD . . . so declare it.* See Jer 28:6. **1:37** *even greater.* Not a deprecation of David's accomplishments, but an expression of total loyalty to David and Solomon. Benaiah shared David's own desire for his chosen successor (see vv. 47–48). **1:38** *the Kerethites and the Pelethites.* See note on 2Sa 8:18.

and escorted him to Gihon.[k] [39]Zadok the priest took the horn of oil[l] from the sacred tent[m] and anointed Solomon. Then they sounded the trumpet[n] and all the people shouted,[o] "Long live King Solomon!" [40]And all the people went up after him, playing flutes[p] and rejoicing greatly, so that the ground shook with the sound.

[41]Adonijah and all the guests who were with him heard it as they were finishing their feast. On hearing the sound of the trumpet, Joab asked, "What's the meaning of all the noise in the city?"[q]

[42]Even as he was speaking, Jonathan[r] son of Abiathar the priest arrived. Adonijah said, "Come in. A worthy man like you must be bringing good news."[s]

[43]"Not at all!" Jonathan answered. "Our lord King David has made Solomon king. [44]The king has sent with him Zadok the priest, Nathan the prophet, Benaiah son of Jehoiada, the Kerethites and the Pelethites, and they have put him on the king's mule, [45]and Zadok the priest and Nathan the prophet have anointed him king at Gihon. From there they have gone up cheering, and the city resounds[t] with it. That's the noise you hear. [46]Moreover, Solomon has taken his seat[u] on the royal throne. [47]Also, the royal officials have come to congratulate our lord King David, saying, 'May your God make Solomon's name more famous than yours and his throne greater[v] than yours!' And the king bowed in worship on his bed [48]and said,

'Praise be to the LORD, the God of Israel, who has allowed my eyes to see a successor[w] on my throne today.' "

[49]At this, all Adonijah's guests rose in alarm and dispersed. [50]But Adonijah, in fear of Solomon, went and took hold of the horns[x] of the altar. [51]Then Solomon was told, "Adonijah is afraid of King Solomon and is clinging to the horns of the altar. He says, 'Let King Solomon swear to me today that he will not put his servant to death with the sword.' "

[52]Solomon replied, "If he shows himself to be a worthy man, not a hair[y] of his head will fall to the ground; but if evil is found in him, he will die." [53]Then King Solomon sent men, and they brought him down from the altar. And Adonijah came and bowed down to King Solomon, and Solomon said, "Go to your home."

David's Charge to Solomon

2:10–12pp — 1Ch 29:26–28

2 When the time drew near for David to die,[z] he gave a charge to Solomon his son.

[2]"I am about to go the way of all the earth,"[a] he said. "So be strong,[b] show yourself a man, [3]and observe[c] what the LORD your God requires: Walk in his ways, and keep his decrees and commands, his laws and requirements, as written in the Law of Moses, so that you may prosper[d] in all you do and wherever you go, [4]and that the LORD may keep his promise[e] to me: 'If

Cross references (center column)

1:38 *k*S ver 33
1:39 *l*S Ex 29:7; S 1Sa 10:1; 2Ki 11:12; Ps 89:20
*m*S Ex 26:1; S 27:21
*n*S 2Sa 15:10; 2Ki 11:14 *o*ver 34; Nu 23:21; Ps 47:5; Zec 9:9
1:40 *p*S 1Sa 10:5
1:41
*q*2Ch 23:12-13
1:42
*r*S 2Sa 15:27,36
*s*S 2Sa 18:26
1:45 *t*ver 40
1:46 *u*S Dt 17:18
1:47 *v*ver 37

1:48 *w*1Ki 3:6
1:50 *x*S Ex 27:2
1:52
*y*S 1Sa 14:45
2:1 *z*S Ge 27:2; S Nu 27:13
2:2 *a*Jos 23:14 *b*S Jos 1:6
2:3 *c*S Dt 4:6; S 10:12; S 17:14-20; S Jos 1:7
*d*1Ch 22:13
2:4 *e*S 2Sa 7:13, 15; 2Ch 23:3

1:39 *Zadok . . . anointed Solomon.* Kings chosen by God to rule over his people who were not in a line of dynastic succession were anointed by prophets (Saul, 1Sa 9:16; David, 1Sa 16:12; Jehu, 2Ki 9). Kings who assumed office in the line of dynastic succession were anointed by priests (Solomon, here; Joash, 2Ki 11:12). The distinction seems to be that the priest worked within the established order while the prophets introduced new divine initiatives. *horn of oil.* Perhaps containing the anointing oil described in Ex 30:22–33. *sacred tent.* The tent David had erected in Jerusalem to house the ark (see 2Sa 6:17) rather than the tabernacle at Gibeon (see 3:4 and note; 2Ch 1:3).

1:41 *heard it.* Although Gihon may not have been visible from En Rogel, the distance was not great and the sound would carry down the Kidron Valley.

1:42 *Jonathan son of Abiathar.* See 2Sa 17:17–21.

1:47 *more famous.* See note on v. 37.

1:48 *successor.* In Solomon's succession to the throne David sees a fulfillment of the promise in 2Sa 7:12,16.

1:49 *dispersed.* No one wanted to be identified with Adonijah's abortive coup now that it appeared certain to fail.

1:50 *took hold of the horns of the altar.* The horns of the altar were vertical projections at each corner. The idea of seeking asylum at the altar was rooted in the Pentateuch (see Ex 21:13–14). The priest smeared the blood of the sacrifice on the horns of the altar (see Ex 29:12; Lev 4:7,18,25,30, 34) during the sacrificial ritual. Adonijah thus seeks to place his own destiny under the protection of God.

1:52 *worthy man.* Who recognizes and submits to Solomon's office and authority. *if evil is found in him.* If he shows evidence of continuing opposition to Solomon's succession to the throne.

2:1 *he gave a charge.* Moses (Dt 31:1–8), Joshua (Jos 23:1–16) and Samuel (1Sa 12:1–25), as representatives of the Lord's rule, had all given final instructions and admonitions shortly before their deaths.

2:2 *the way of all the earth.* To the grave (see Jos 23:14). *be strong.* See Dt 31:7,23; Jos 1:6–7,9,18.

2:3 *observe what the LORD your God requires.* See Ge 26:5; Lev 18:30; Dt 11:1. *Walk in his ways.* A characteristic expression of Deuteronomy for obedience to covenant obligations (Dt 5:33; 8:6; 10:12; 11:22; 19:9; 26:17; 28:9; 30:16). *his decrees and commands, his laws and requirements.* Four generally synonymous terms for covenant obligations (see 6:12; 8:58; 2Ki 17:37; Dt 8:11; 11:1; 26:17; 28:15,45; 30:10,16). *that you may prosper.* See Dt 29:9.

2:4 *that the LORD may keep his promise to me.* David here alludes to the covenanted promise of an everlasting dynasty given to him by God through Nathan the prophet (see notes on 2Sa 7:11–16). Although the covenant promise to David was unconditional, individual participation in its blessing on the part of David's royal descendants was conditioned on obedience to the obligations of the Mosaic covenant (see 2Ch 7:17–22). *with all their heart and soul.* See Dt 4:29; 6:5; 10:12; 30:6. *you will never fail to have a man on the*

your descendants watch how they live, and if they walk faithfully[f] before me with all their heart and soul, you will never fail to have a man on the throne of Israel.'

[5]"Now you yourself know what Joab[g] son of Zeruiah did to me—what he did to the two commanders of Israel's armies, Abner[h] son of Ner and Amasa[i] son of Jether. He killed them, shedding their blood in peacetime as if in battle, and with that blood stained the belt around his waist and the sandals on his feet. [6]Deal with him according to your wisdom,[j] but do not let his gray head go down to the grave[c] in peace.

[7]"But show kindness[k] to the sons of Barzillai[l] of Gilead and let them be among those who eat at your table.[m] They stood by me when I fled from your brother Absalom.

[8]"And remember, you have with you Shimei[n] son of Gera, the Benjamite from

Bahurim, who called down bitter curses on me the day I went to Mahanaim.[o] When he came down to meet me at the Jordan, I swore[p] to him by the LORD: 'I will not put you to death by the sword.' [9]But now, do not consider him innocent. You are a man of wisdom;[q] you will know what to do to him. Bring his gray head down to the grave in blood."

[10]Then David rested with his fathers and was buried[r] in the City of David.[s] [11]He had reigned[t] forty years over Israel—seven years in Hebron and thirty-three in Jerusalem. [12]So Solomon sat on the throne[u] of his father David, and his rule was firmly established.[v]

Solomon's Throne Established

[13]Now Adonijah,[w] the son of Haggith, went to Bathsheba, Solomon's mother.

2:4 [f]2Ki 18:3-6; 20:3; Ps 26:1-3; 132:12
2:5 [g]S 2Sa 2:18 [h]S 1Sa 14:50; [i]S 2Sa 17:25
2:6 [j]ver 9
2:7 [k]S Ge 40:14 [l]S 2Sa 17:27; 19:31-39 [m]S 2Sa 9:7
2:8 [n]ver 36-46; 2Sa 16:5-13

[o]S Ge 32:2
[p]2Sa 19:18-23
2:9 [q]ver 6
2:10 [r]Ac 2:29 [s]S 2Sa 5:7
2:11 [t]S 2Sa 5:4,5
2:12
[u]1Ch 17:14; 29:23; 2Ch 9:8 [v]ver 46; 2Ch 1:1; 12:13; 17:1; 21:4
2:13 [w]S 2Sa 3:4

[c]6 Hebrew *Sheol*; also in verse 9

---

throne of Israel. Both Solomon and his descendants fell short of their covenant obligations. This led to the division of the kingdom and eventually to the exile of both the northern and southern kingdoms. It was only in the coming of Christ that the fallen tent of David would be restored (see notes on Am 9:11–15; Ac 15:16) and the promise of David's eternal dynasty ultimately fulfilled. When the nation and its king turned away from the requirements of the Sinai covenant, they experienced the covenant curses rather than blessings; but in all this God remained faithful to his covenant promises to Abraham and to David (see Lev 26:42–45; Isa 9:6–7; 11:1–16; 16:5; 55:3; Jer 23:5–6; 30:9; 33:17,20–22, 25–26; Eze 34:23–24; 37:24–28).

2:5 *Joab son of Zeruiah.* See note on 1:7. *Abner son of Ner.* See notes on 2Sa 3:25–32. *Amasa son of Jether.* See 2Sa 20:10. *shedding their blood in peacetime.* Joab's actions were unlawful assassinations (see Dt 19:1–13; 21:1–9) and

only served his own self-interest.
2:7 *sons of Barzillai.* See note on 2Sa 17:27. *eat at your table.* A position of honor that brought with it other benefits (see 18:19; 2Ki 25:29; 2Sa 9:7; 19:28; Ne 5:17).
2:8 See 2Sa 16:5–13. *Shimei son of Gera, the Benjamite.* Gera was probably the ancestor of Shimei's particular line of descent rather than his immediate father (see Ge 46:21; Jdg 3:15). See NIV text notes on Ge 10:2; Da 5:22.
2:9 *do not consider him innocent.* The Mosaic law prohibited cursing a ruler (21:10; Ex 22:28).
2:10 *rested with his fathers.* See note on 1:21. *City of David.* See 2Sa 5:7 and note. Peter implies that David's tomb is still known in his day (Ac 2:29).
2:11 *forty years.* See 2Sa 5:4–5. David ruled c. 1010–970 B.C. (see Introduction to 1 Samuel: Chronology).
2:13 *Adonijah, the son of Haggith.* See note on 1:5. *Do you come peacefully?* The question (see 1Sa 16:4; 2Ki 9:22)

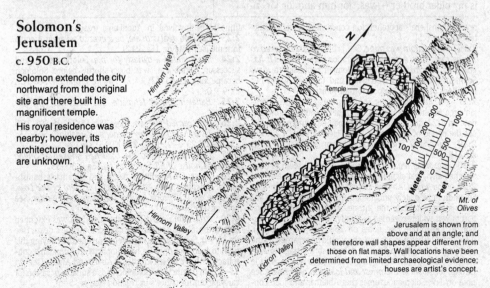

Solomon's Jerusalem

c. 950 B.C.

Solomon extended the city northward from the original site and there built his magnificent temple.

His royal residence was nearby; however, its architecture and location are unknown.

Hinnom Valley

Temple

Hinnom Valley

Kidron Valley

N

Meters

Feet

100 200 300
0 500 1000

Mt. of Olives

Jerusalem is shown from above and at an angle; and therefore wall shapes appear different from those on flat maps. Wall locations have been determined from limited archaeological evidence; houses are artist's concept.

Bathsheba asked him, "Do you come peacefully?" *x*

He answered, "Yes, peacefully." [14]Then he added, "I have something to say to you."

"You may say it," she replied.

[15]"As you know," he said, "the kingdom was mine. All Israel looked to me as their king. But things changed, and the kingdom has gone to my brother; for it has come to him from the LORD. [16]Now I have one request to make of you. Do not refuse me."

"You may make it," she said.

[17]So he continued, "Please ask King Solomon—he will not refuse you—to give me Abishag *y* the Shunammite as my wife."

[18]"Very well," Bathsheba replied, "I will speak to the king for you."

[19]When Bathsheba went to King Solomon to speak to him for Adonijah, the king stood up to meet her, bowed down to her and sat down on his throne. He had a throne brought for the king's mother, *z* and she sat down at his right hand. *a*

[20]"I have one small request to make of you," she said. "Do not refuse me."

The king replied, "Make it, my mother; I will not refuse you."

[21]So she said, "Let Abishag *b* the Shunammite be given in marriage to your brother Adonijah."

[22]King Solomon answered his mother, "Why do you request Abishag *c* the Shunammite for Adonijah? You might as well request the kingdom for him—after all, he is my older brother *d*—yes, for him and for

Abiathar *e* the priest and Joab son of Zeruiah!"

[23]Then King Solomon swore by the LORD: "May God deal with me, be it ever so severely, *f* if Adonijah does not pay with his life for this request! [24]And now, as surely as the LORD lives—he who has established me securely on the throne of my father David and has founded a dynasty for me as he promised *g*—Adonijah shall be put to death today!" [25]So King Solomon gave orders to Benaiah *h* son of Jehoiada, and he struck down Adonijah and he died. *i*

[26]To Abiathar *j* the priest the king said, "Go back to your fields in Anathoth. *k* You deserve to die, but I will not put you to death now, because you carried the ark *l* of the Sovereign LORD before my father David and shared all my father's hardships." *m* [27]So Solomon removed Abiathar from the priesthood of the LORD, fulfilling *n* the word the LORD had spoken at Shiloh about the house of Eli.

[28]When the news reached Joab, who had conspired with Adonijah though not with Absalom, he fled to the tent of the LORD and took hold of the horns *o* of the altar. [29]King Solomon was told that Joab had fled to the tent of the LORD and was beside the altar. *p* Then Solomon ordered Benaiah *q* son of Jehoiada, "Go, strike him down!"

[30]So Benaiah entered the tent *r* of the LORD and said to Joab, "The king says, 'Come out! *s* ' "

But he answered, "No, I will die here."

2:13 *x*S 1Sa 16:4
2:17 *y*S 1Ki 1:3
2:19 *z*1Ki 15:13; 2Ki 10:13; 24:15; 2Ch 15:16; Jer 13:18; 22:26; 29:2 *a*Ps 45:9
2:21 *b*1Ki 1:3
2:22 *c*S Ge 22:24; S 1Ki 1:3 *d*1Ch 3:2

2:23 *e*S 1Sa 22:20 *f*S Ru 1:17
2:24 *g*2Sa 7:11
2:25 *h*S 2Sa 8:18 *i*S 2Sa 12:10
2:26 *j*S 1Sa 22:20 *k*S Jos 21:18 *l*S 2Sa 15:24 *m*S 2Sa 15:14
2:27 *n*S 1Sa 2:27-36
2:28 *o*S Ex 27:2
2:29 *p*Ex 21:14 *q*ver 25
2:30 *r*2Ki 11:15 *s*Ex 21:14

reveals Bathsheba's apprehension concerning Adonijah's intention (see 1:5).

2:15 *the kingdom was mine.* See 1:11. *All Israel looked to me as their king.* A gross exaggeration (see 1:7–8). *it has come to him from the LORD.* Adonijah professes to view Solomon's kingship as God's will and to have no further intentions of seeking the position for himself.

2:17 *give me Abishag the Shunammite as my wife.* Adonijah's request has the appearance of being innocent (but see note on v. 22) since Abishag had remained a virgin throughout the period of her care for David (see 1:1–4; Dt 22:30).

2:19 *right hand.* The position of honor (see Ps 110:1; Mt 20:21).

2:20 *one small request.* Bathsheba does not seem to have attached any great significance to Adonijah's request.

2:22 *You might as well request the kingdom for him.* Solomon immediately understood Adonijah's request as another attempt to gain the throne. Possession of the royal harem was widely regarded as signifying the right of succession to the throne (see notes on 2Sa 3:7; 12:8; 16:21). Although Abishag was a virgin, she would be regarded by the people as belonging to David's harem; so marriage to Abishag would greatly strengthen Adonijah's claim to the throne. *for Abiathar the priest and Joab son of Zeruiah.* See note on 1:7. Solomon assumes that Abiathar and Joab con-

tinue to be involved in Adonijah's treacherous schemes.

2:23 *May God deal with me, be it ever so severely.* A curse formula (see note on 1Sa 3:17).

2:24 *has founded a dynasty for me.* Solomon's son and successor, Rehoboam, was born shortly before Solomon became king (cf. 11:42; 14:21). *as he promised.* See 1Ch 22:9–10.

2:25 *Benaiah son of Jehoiada.* See notes on 1:7; 2Sa 23:20.

2:26 *you carried the ark.* See 2Sa 15:24–25,29; 1Ch 15:11–12. *shared all my father's hardships.* See 1Sa 22:20–23; 23:6–9; 30:7; 2Sa 17:15; 19:11.

2:27 *fulfilling the word the LORD had spoken at Shiloh about the house of Eli.* See notes on 1Sa 2:30–35.

2:28 *news.* Of Adonijah's death and Abiathar's banishment. *conspired with Adonijah.* See 1:7. *tent of the LORD.* See note on 1:39. *took hold of the horns of the altar.* See note on 1:50.

2:29 *strike him down!* The right of asylum was extended only to those who accidentally caused someone's death (see Ex 21:14). Solomon was completely justified in denying this right to Joab, not only for his complicity in Adonijah's conspiracy, but also for his murder of Abner and Amasa (see vv. 31–33). In this incident Solomon finds a suitable occasion for carrying out his father's instruction (see vv. 5–6).

Benaiah reported to the king, "This is how Joab answered me."

³¹Then the king commanded Benaiah, "Do as he says. Strike him down and bury him, and so clear me and my father's house of the guilt of the innocent blood ᵗ that Joab shed. ³²The LORD will repay ᵘ him for the blood he shed, ᵛ because without the knowledge of my father David he attacked two men and killed them with the sword. Both of them—Abner son of Ner, commander of Israel's army, and Amasa ʷ son of Jether, commander of Judah's army—were better ˣ men and more upright than he. ³³May the guilt of their blood rest on the head of Joab and his descendants forever. But on David and his descendants, his house and his throne, may there be the LORD's peace forever."

³⁴So Benaiah ʸ son of Jehoiada went up and struck down Joab ᶻ and killed him, and he was buried on his own land ᵈ in the desert. ³⁵The king put Benaiah ᵃ son of Jehoiada over the army in Joab's position and replaced Abiathar with Zadok ᵇ the priest.

³⁶Then the king sent for Shimei ᶜ and said to him, "Build yourself a house in Jerusalem and live there, but do not go anywhere else. ³⁷The day you leave and cross the Kidron Valley, ᵈ you can be sure you will die; your blood will be on your own head." ᵉ

³⁸Shimei answered the king, "What you say is good. Your servant will do as my lord the king has said." And Shimei stayed in Jerusalem for a long time.

³⁹But three years later, two of Shimei's slaves ran off to Achish ᶠ son of Maacah,

king of Gath, and Shimei was told, "Your slaves are in Gath." ⁴⁰At this, he saddled his donkey and went to Achish at Gath in search of his slaves. So Shimei went away and brought the slaves back from Gath.

⁴¹When Solomon was told that Shimei had gone from Jerusalem to Gath and had returned, ⁴²the king summoned Shimei and said to him, "Did I not make you swear by the LORD and warn ᵍ you, 'On the day you leave to go anywhere else, you can be sure you will die'? At that time you said to me, 'What you say is good. I will obey.' ⁴³Why then did you not keep your oath to the LORD and obey the command I gave you?"

⁴⁴The king also said to Shimei, "You know in your heart all the wrong ʰ you did to my father David. Now the LORD will repay you for your wrongdoing. ⁴⁵But King Solomon will be blessed, and David's throne will remain secure ⁱ before the LORD forever."

⁴⁶Then the king gave the order to Benaiah ʲ son of Jehoiada, and he went out and struck Shimei ᵏ down and killed him.

The kingdom was now firmly established ˡ in Solomon's hands.

Solomon Asks for Wisdom

3:4–15pp — 2Ch 1:2–13

3 Solomon made an alliance with Pharaoh king of Egypt and married ᵐ his daughter. ⁿ He brought her to the City of David ᵒ until he finished building his palace ᵖ and the temple of the LORD, and the

---

Cross references (center column):

2:31 ᵗS Dt 19:13
2:32 ᵘJdg 9:57
ᵛS Ge 4:14; S Jdg 9:24
ʷS 2Sa 17:25
ˣ2Ch 21:13
2:34 ʸver 25
ᶻS 2Sa 2:18
2:35 ᵃS 2Sa 8:18
ᵇS 1Sa 2:35
2:36 ᶜS 2Sa 16:5
2:37
ᵈS 2Sa 15:23; Jn 18:1
ᵉS Lev 20:9
2:39 ᶠ1Sa 27:2

2:42
ᵍS 2Sa 19:23
2:44
ʰ2Sa 16:5-13
2:45 ⁱS 2Sa 7:13
2:46 ʲS 2Sa 8:18
ᵏS ver 8 ˡS ver 12
3:1 ᵐ1Ki 7:8; 11:1-13
ⁿ1Ki 9:24; 2Ch 8:11
ᵒ2Sa 5:7; 1Ki 2:10
ᵖS 2Sa 7:2; 1Ki 9:10

ᵈ34 Or *buried in his tomb*

2:32 *he attacked two men and killed them.* See 2Sa 3:27; 20:9-10. *Israel's army.* See 2Sa 2:8-9. *Judah's army.* See 2Sa 20:4.

2:34 *on his own land.* See NIV text note. The tomb of Joab's father was located near Bethlehem (see 2Sa 2:32). *desert.* Of Judah, east of Bethlehem.

2:35 *Benaiah son of Jehoiada.* See note on 2Sa 23:20. *Zadok the priest.* See notes on 1Sa 2:35; 2Sa 8:17.

2:36 *do not go anywhere else.* Confinement to Jerusalem would greatly reduce the possibility of Shimei's (see v. 8) conspiring with any remaining followers of Saul against Solomon's rule.

2:39 *Achish son of Maacah, king of Gath.* Gath was a major Philistine city (see Jos 13:3; 1Sa 6:16-17). It is likely that Gath was ruled successively by Maoch, Achish the elder (1Sa 27:2), Maacah and Achish the younger (here).

2:46 *struck Shimei down and killed him.* The third execution carried out by Benaiah (see vv. 25,34). It brought to completion the tasks assigned to Solomon by David just before his death (vv. 6,9).

3:1 *made an alliance with Pharaoh.* It appears likely that Solomon established his marriage alliance with either Siamun or Psusennes II, the last kings of the 21st Egyptian

dynasty (the first Egyptian pharaoh mentioned by name in the OT is Shishak—11:40; 14:25-26—who established the 22nd Egyptian dynasty c. 945 B.C.). Such an alliance attests Egyptian recognition of the growing importance and strength of the Israelite state. 1Ki 9:16 indicates that the pharaoh gave his daughter the Canaanite town of Gezer as a dowry at the time of her marriage to Solomon. Gezer was located near the crossing of two important trade routes. One, to the west of Gezer, went from Egypt to the north and was very important for Egypt's commercial interests. The other, to the north of Gezer, went from Jerusalem to the Mediterranean Sea and the port of Joppa and was important to Solomon as a supply line for his building projects. The marriage alliance enabled both Solomon and the pharaoh to accomplish important economic and political objectives. No precise date is given for the conclusion of the marriage alliance, though it appears to have occurred in the third or fourth year of Solomon's reign (see 2:39). Solomon began construction of the temple in his fourth year (6:1), and control of the Gezer area was important to him for the beginning of this project. *City of David.* The Egyptian princess was given a temporary residence in the old fortress (see 2Sa 5:7 and note) until a separate palace of her own could be constructed some 20 years later (7:8; 9:10; 2Ch 8:11).

wall around Jerusalem. ²The people, however, were still sacrificing at the high places,*q* because a temple had not yet been built for the Name*r* of the LORD. ³Solomon showed his love*s* for the LORD by walking*t* according to the statutes*u* of his father David, except that he offered sacrifices and burned incense on the high places.*v*

⁴The king went to Gibeon*w* to offer sacrifices, for that was the most important high place, and Solomon offered a thousand burnt offerings on that altar. ⁵At Gibeon the LORD appeared*x* to Solomon during the night in a dream,*y* and God said, "Ask*z* for whatever you want me to give you."

⁶Solomon answered, "You have shown great kindness to your servant, my father David, because he was faithful*a* to you and righteous and upright in heart. You have continued this great kindness to him and have given him a son*b* to sit on his throne this very day.

⁷"Now, O LORD my God, you have made your servant king in place of my father David. But I am only a little child*c* and do not know how to carry out my duties. ⁸Your servant is here among the people you have chosen,*d* a great people, too numerous to count or number.*e* ⁹So give your servant a discerning*f* heart to

govern your people and to distinguish*g* between right and wrong. For who is able*h* to govern this great people of yours?"

¹⁰The Lord was pleased that Solomon had asked for this. ¹¹So God said to him, "Since you have asked*i* for this and not for long life or wealth for yourself, nor have asked for the death of your enemies but for discernment*j* in administering justice, ¹²I will do what you have asked.*k* I will give you a wise*l* and discerning heart, so that there will never have been anyone like you, nor will there ever be. ¹³Moreover, I will give you what you have not*m* asked for—both riches and honor*n*—so that in your lifetime you will have no equal*o* among kings. ¹⁴And if you walk*p* in my ways and obey my statutes and commands as David your father did, I will give you a long life."*q* ¹⁵Then Solomon awoke*r*—and he realized it had been a dream.*s*

He returned to Jerusalem, stood before the ark of the Lord's covenant and sacrificed burnt offerings*t* and fellowship offerings.*e* *u* Then he gave a feast*v* for all his court.

3:2 *q*Lev 17:3-5; S 26:30; Dt 12:14; 1Ki 15:14; 22:43 *r*S Dt 14:23
3:3 *s*Dt 6:5; Ps 31:23; 145:20 *r*S Dt 10:12; S Jos 1:7 *u*S Dt 17:19; S 1Ki 14:8 *r*S ver 2; Lev 17:3-5; 2Ki 12:3; 15:4, 35; 16:4; 21:3
3:4 *w*S Jos 9:3
3:5 *x*1Ki 9:2; 11:9 *y*S Mt 27:19 *z*S Mt 7:7
3:6 *a*S Ge 17:1 *b*1Ki 1:48
3:7 *c*Nu 27:17; 1Ch 22:5; 29:1; Jer 1:6
3:8 *d*S Dt 7:6 *e*S Ge 12:2; S 1Ch 27:23
3:9 *f*S 2Sa 14:17; Jas 1:5

*g*S Dt 1:16; Heb 5:14 *h*2Co 2:16
3:11 *i*Jas 4:3 *j*1Ch 22:12
3:12 *k*1Jn 5:14-15 *l*S 2Sa 14:20; 1Ki 4:29,30,31; 5:12; 10:23; Ecc 1:16
3:13 *m*Mt 6:33; Eph 3:20 *n*Pr 3:1-2,16; 8:18 *o*1Ki 10:23; 2Ch 9:22; Ne 13:26
3:14 *p*1Ki 9:4; Ps 25:13; 101:2; 128:1; Pr 3:1-2, 16 *q*Ps 61:6

3:15 *r*S Ge 28:16 *s*ver 5 *t*Lev 6:8-13 *u*Lev 7:11-21 *v*Est 1:3, 9; 2:18; 5:8; 6:14; 9:17; Da 5:1

*e*15 Traditionally *peace offerings*

3:2 *high places.* Upon entering Canaan, the Israelites often followed the Canaanite custom of locating their altars on high hills, probably on the old Baal sites. The question of the legitimacy of Israelite worship at these high places has long been a matter of debate. It is clear that the Israelites were forbidden to take over pagan altars and high places and use them for the worship of the Lord (Nu 33:52; Dt 7:5; 12:3). It is also clear that altars were to be built only at divinely sanctioned sites (see Ex 20:24; Dt 12:5,8,13–14). It is not so clear whether multiplicity of altars was totally forbidden provided the above conditions were met (see 19:10,14; Lev 26:30–31; Dt 12; 1Sa 9:12). It seems, however, that these conditions were not followed even in the time of Solomon, and pagan high places were being used for the worship of the Lord. This would eventually lead to religious apostasy and syncretism and was strongly condemned (2Ki 17:7–18; 21:2–9; 23:4–25). *because a temple had not yet been built.* Worship at a variety of places was apparently considered normal prior to the building of the temple (see Jdg 6:24; 13:19; 1Sa 7:17; 9:12–13).
3:3 *except.* Solomon's one major fault early in his reign was inconsistency in meeting the Mosaic requirements concerning places of legitimate worship.
3:4 *Gibeon.* The Gibeonites tricked Joshua and Israel into a peace treaty at the time of the conquest of Canaan (see Jos 9:3–27). The city was subsequently given to the tribe of Benjamin and set apart for the Levites (Jos 18:25; 21:17). David avenged Saul's violation of the Gibeonite treaty by the execution of seven of Saul's descendants (see 2Sa 21:1–9). *most important high place.* The reason for Gibeon's importance was the presence there of the tabernacle and the ancient bronze altar (see 1Ch 21:29; 2Ch 1:2–6). These

must have been salvaged after the destruction of Shiloh by the Philistines (see note on 1Sa 7:1).
3:5 *dream.* Revelation through dreams is found elsewhere in the OT (see Ge 28:12; 31:11; 46:2; Nu 12:6; Jdg 7:13; Da 2:4; 7:1), as well as in the NT (see, e.g., Mt 1:20; 2:12,22).
3:6 *kindness.* The Hebrew for this word refers to God's covenant favors (see note on 2Sa 7:15). Solomon is praising the Lord for faithfulness to his promises to David (2Sa 7:8–16). *because.* See note on 2Sa 22:21.
3:7 *I am only a little child.* The birth of Solomon is generally placed in approximately the middle of David's 40-year reign, meaning that Solomon was about 20 years old at the beginning of his own reign (see 2:11–12) and lacked experience in assuming the responsibilities of his office (cf. Jer 1:6).
3:8 *great people, too numerous to count.* From the small beginnings of a single family living in Egypt (see Ge 46:26–27; Dt 7:7), the Israelites had increased to an extent approaching that anticipated in the promise given to Abraham (Ge 13:16; 22:17–18) and Jacob (Ge 32:12). See 4:20.
3:11 *long life ... wealth ... death of your enemies.* Typical desires of ancient Near Eastern monarchs.
3:12 *never ... anyone like you.* See 4:29–34; 10:1–13.
3:13 *I will give you what you have not asked for.* Cf. Jesus' promise in Lk 12:31.
3:14 *if you walk in my ways ... I will give you a long life.* Echoes Dt 6:2; 17:20; 22:7. Unfortunately Solomon did not remain obedient to the covenant as his father David had (11:6), and he did not live to be much more than 60 years of age (see note on v. 7; cf. 11:42).
3:15 *ark of the Lord's covenant.* See notes on 6:19; 2Sa 6:2. *fellowship offerings.* See note on 1Sa 11:15.

A Wise Ruling

[16]Now two prostitutes came to the king and stood before him. [17]One of them said, "My lord, this woman and I live in the same house. I had a baby while she was there with me. [18]The third day after my child was born, this woman also had a baby. We were alone; there was no one in the house but the two of us.

[19]"During the night this woman's son died because she lay on him. [20]So she got up in the middle of the night and took my son from my side while I your servant was asleep. She put him by her breast and put her dead son by my breast. [21]The next morning, I got up to nurse my son—and he was dead! But when I looked at him closely in the morning light, I saw that it wasn't the son I had borne."

[22]The other woman said, "No! The living one is my son; the dead one is yours."

But the first one insisted, "No! The dead one is yours; the living one is mine." And so they argued before the king.

[23]The king said, "This one says, 'My son is alive and your son is dead,' while that one says, 'No! Your son is dead and mine is alive.'"

[24]Then the king said, "Bring me a sword." So they brought a sword for the king. [25]He then gave an order: "Cut the living child in two and give half to one and half to the other."

[26]The woman whose son was alive was filled with compassion[w] for her son and said to the king, "Please, my lord, give her the living baby! Don't kill him!"

But the other said, "Neither I nor you shall have him. Cut him in two!"

[27]Then the king gave his ruling: "Give the living baby to the first woman. Do not kill him; she is his mother."

[28]When all Israel heard the verdict the king had given, they held the king in awe, because they saw that he had wisdom[x] from God to administer justice.

Solomon's Officials and Governors

4 So King Solomon ruled over all Israel. [2]And these were his chief officials:[y]

Azariah[z] son of Zadok—the priest;
[3]Elihoreph and Ahijah, sons of Shisha—secretaries;[a]
Jehoshaphat[b] son of Ahilud—recorder;
[4]Benaiah[c] son of Jehoiada—commander in chief;
Zadok[d] and Abiathar—priests;
[5]Azariah son of Nathan—in charge of the district officers;
Zabud son of Nathan—a priest and personal adviser to the king;
[6]Ahishar—in charge of the palace;[e]
Adoniram[f] son of Abda—in charge of forced labor.[g]

[7]Solomon also had twelve district governors[h] over all Israel, who supplied provisions for the king and the royal household. Each one had to provide supplies for one month in the year. [8]These are their names:

Ben-Hur—in the hill country[i] of Ephraim;
[9]Ben-Deker—in Makaz, Shaalbim,[j] Beth Shemesh[k] and Elon Bethhanan;
[10]Ben-Hesed—in Arubboth (Socoh[l] and all the land of Hepher[m] were his);

3:26 [w]Ps 102:13; Isa 49:15; 63:15; Jer 3:12; 31:20; Hos 11:8

3:28 [x]S 2Sa 14:20; Col 2:3
4:2 [y]1Ki 12:6; Job 12:12 [z]1Ch 6:10; 2Ch 26:17
4:3 [a]S 2Sa 8:17 [b]S 2Sa 8:16
4:4 [c]S 2Sa 8:18 [d]S 2Sa 8:17
4:6 [e]S Ge 41:40 [f]S 2Sa 20:24 [g]S Ge 49:15
4:7 [h]ver 27
4:8 [i]S Jos 24:33
4:9 [j]Jdg 1:35 [k]S Jos 15:10
4:10 [l]S Jos 15:35 [m]S Jos 12:17

3:16 *two prostitutes.* It is not known if these two were Israelites or Jebusites—possibly the latter. *came to the king.* It was possible for Israelites (and others within the realm) to bypass lower judicial officials (Dt 16:18) and appeal directly to the king (see 2Ki 8:3; 2Sa 15:2).
3:17 *live in the same house.* Brothels were common in ancient Near Eastern cities.
3:28 *they saw that he had wisdom from God.* This episode strikingly demonstrated that the Lord had answered Solomon's prayer for a discerning heart (vv. 9,12).
4:1 *ruled over all Israel.* Solomon ruled over an undivided kingdom, as his father had before him (see 2Sa 8:15).
4:2 *son.* According to 2Sa 15:27,36 and 1Ch 6:8–9, Azariah was the son of Ahimaaz and the grandson of Zadok (see note on 2:8). Apparently Zadok's son Ahimaaz had died, so that Zadok was succeeded by his grandson Azariah. *Zadok.* See 2:27,35.
4:3 *Shisha.* See note on 2Sa 8:17. *secretaries.* See note on 2Sa 8:17. *Jehoshaphat son of Ahilud.* The same person who served in David's court (see 2Sa 8:16). *recorder.* See note on 2Sa 8:16.
4:4 *Benaiah.* Replaced Joab as commander of the army (see

2:35; 2Sa 8:18). *Zadok and Abiathar.* Abiathar was banished at the beginning of Solomon's reign (2:27,35), and Zadok was succeeded by his grandson Azariah (v. 2).
4:5 *Nathan.* Either the prophet (1:11) or the son of David (2Sa 5:14). *district officers.* See vv. 7–19. *priest.* See note on 2Sa 8:18 ("royal advisers"). *personal adviser to the king.* See note on 2Sa 15:37.
4:6 *in charge of the palace.* The first OT reference to an office mentioned frequently in 1,2 Kings (1Ki 16:9; 18:3; 2Ki 18:18,37; 19:2). It is likely that this official was administrator of the palace and steward of the king's properties. *Adoniram.* Served not only under Solomon, but also under David before him (2Sa 20:24) and Rehoboam after him (1Ki 12:18). *forced labor.* See notes on 9:15; 2Sa 20:24.
4:7 *Solomon . . . had twelve district governors.* The 12 districts were not identical to tribal territories, possibly because the tribes varied greatly in agricultural productivity. But Solomon's administrative decision violated traditional tribal boundaries and probably stirred up ancient tribal loyalties, eventually contributing to the disruption of the united kingdom.
4:8 *Ben-Hur.* Hebrew *Ben* means "son of."

11Ben-Abinadab—in Naphoth Dor[f] [n] (he was married to Taphath daughter of Solomon);

12Baana son of Ahilud—in Taanach and Megiddo, and in all of Beth Shan[o] next to Zarethan[p] below Jezreel, from Beth Shan to Abel Meholah[q] across to Jokmeam;[r]

13Ben-Geber—in Ramoth Gilead (the settlements of Jair[s] son of Manasseh in Gilead[t] were his, as well as the district of Argob in Bashan and its sixty large walled cities[u] with bronze gate bars);

14Ahinadab son of Iddo—in Mahanaim;[v]

15Ahimaaz[w]—in Naphtali (he had married Basemath daughter of Solomon);

16Baana son of Hushai[x]—in Asher and in Aloth;

17Jehoshaphat son of Paruah—in Issachar;

18Shimei[y] son of Ela—in Benjamin;

19Geber son of Uri—in Gilead (the country of Sihon[z] king of the Amorites and the country of Og[a] king of Bashan). He was the only governor over the district.

Solomon's Daily Provisions

20The people of Judah and Israel were as numerous as the sand[b] on the seashore; they ate, they drank and they were happy.[c] 21And Solomon ruled[d] over all the kingdoms from the River[e] to the land of the Philistines, as far as the border of Egypt.[f] These countries brought tribute[g]

and were Solomon's subjects all his life.

22Solomon's daily provisions[h] were thirty cors[h] of fine flour and sixty cors[i] of meal, 23ten head of stall-fed cattle, twenty of pasture-fed cattle and a hundred sheep and goats, as well as deer, gazelles, roebucks and choice fowl.[i] 24For he ruled over all the kingdoms west of the River, from Tiphsah[j] to Gaza, and had peace[k] on all sides. 25During Solomon's lifetime Judah and Israel, from Dan to Beersheba,[l] lived in safety,[m] each man under his own vine and fig tree.[n]

26Solomon had four[j] thousand stalls for chariot horses,[o] and twelve thousand horses.[k]

27The district officers,[p] each in his month, supplied provisions for King Solomon and all who came to the king's table. They saw to it that nothing was lacking. 28They also brought to the proper place their quotas of barley and straw for the chariot horses and the other horses.

Solomon's Wisdom

29God gave Solomon wisdom[q] and very great insight, and a breadth of understanding as measureless as the sand[r] on the seashore. 30Solomon's wisdom was greater than the wisdom of all the men of the East,[s] and greater than all the wisdom of Egypt.[t] 31He was wiser[u] than any other man, including Ethan the Ezrahite—wiser

---

4:11 [n]S Jos 11:2
4:12 [o]S Jos 17:11
[p]S Jos 3:16
[q]S Jdg 7:22
[r]1Ch 6:68
4:13 [s]S Nu 32:41
[t]Nu 32:40
[u]Dt 3:4
4:14 [v]Jos 13:26
4:15 [w]2Sa 15:27
4:16
[x]S 2Sa 15:32
4:18 [y]1Ki 1:8
4:19 [z]S Jos 12:2
[a]Dt 3:8-10;
S Jos 12:4
4:20 [b]S Ge 12:2;
S 32:12
[c]1Ch 22:9
4:21 [d]2Ch 9:26;
Ezr 4:20;
Ps 72:11; La 1:1
[e]S Ge 2:14;
Ps 72:8
[f]S Ex 23:31
[g]S Jdg 3:15;
Eze 16:13

4:22 [h]1Ki 10:5
4:23 [i]Ne 5:18
4:24 [j]2Ki 15:16
[k]S Jos 14:15
4:25 [l]S Jdg 20:1
[m]1Ch 22:9;
Jer 23:6;
Eze 28:26; 39:26
[n]Dt 8:8;
2Ki 18:31;
Ps 105:33;
Isa 36:16;
Jer 5:17;
Joel 2:22;
Mic 4:4; Zec 3:10
4:26 [o]S Dt 17:16
4:27 [p]ver 7
4:29 [q]S 1Ki 3:12
[r]S Ge 32:12
4:30 [s]S Ge 25:6;
S Jdg 6:3;
Da 1:20; Mt 2:1
[t]Isa 19:11;
Ac 7:22
4:31 [u]S 1Ki 3:12

[f]11 Or in the heights of Dor   [g]21 That is, the Euphrates; also in verse 24   [h]22 That is, probably about 185 bushels (about 6.6 kiloliters)   [i]22 That is, probably about 375 bushels (about 13.2 kiloliters)   [j]26 Some Septuagint manuscripts (see also 2 Chron. 9:25); Hebrew forty   [k]26 Or charioteers

---

4:11 *Ben-Abinadab.* Most likely the "son of" David's brother Abinadab (see 1Sa 16:8; 17:13), making him Solomon's first cousin (he was also his son-in-law).
4:12 *Baana son of Ahilud.* Probably a brother of Jehoshaphat the recorder (v. 3).
4:16 *Baana son of Hushai.* Perhaps the son of David's trusted adviser (see notes on 2Sa 15:32,37).
4:18 *Shimei son of Ela.* Perhaps the same Shimei mentioned in 1:8.
4:20 *as numerous as the sand on the seashore.* See 3:8 and note; see also v. 29; Ge 22:17; 2Sa 17:11; Isa 10:22; Jer 33:22; Hos 1:10; cf. Ge 41:49; Jos 11:4; Jdg 7:12; Ps 78:27. *they ate, they drank and they were happy.* Judah and Israel prospered (see 5:4).
4:21 *from the River to the land of the Philistines, as far as the border of Egypt.* The borders of Solomon's empire extended to the limits originally promised to Abraham (see note on 2Sa 8:3). However, rebellion was brewing in Edom (11:14–21) and Damascus (11:23–25).
4:22 *Solomon's daily provisions.* For all his household, his palace servants and his court officials and their families.
4:24 *Tiphsah.* A city on the west bank of the Euphrates River. *Gaza.* The southernmost city of the Philistines on the Mediterranean coast.

4:26 *four thousand.* See NIV text note. 1Ki 10:26 and 2Ch 1:14 indicate that Solomon had 1,400 chariots, meaning he maintained stalls for two horses for each chariot, with places for about 1,200 reserve horses. By way of comparison, an Assyrian account of the battle of Qarqar in 853 B.C. (about a century after Solomon) speaks of 1,200 chariots from Damascus, 700 chariots from Hamath and 2,000 chariots from Israel (the northern kingdom).

4:29 *as measureless as the sand on the seashore.* See note on v. 20.

4:30 *men of the East.* The phrase is general and appears to refer to the peoples of Mesopotamia (see Ge 29:1) and Arabia (see Jer 49:28; Eze 25:4,10)—those associated with Israel's northeastern and eastern horizons, just as Egypt was the main region on her southwestern horizon. Many examples of Mesopotamian wisdom literature have been recovered. *wisdom of Egypt.* See Ge 41:8; Ex 7:11; Ac 7:22. Examples of Egyptian wisdom literature are to be found in the proverbs of Ptahhotep (c. 2450 B.C.) and Amenemope (see Introduction to Proverbs: Date).

4:31 *He was wiser than any other man.* Until Jesus came (see Lk 11:31). *Ethan the Ezrahite.* See Ps 89 title. *Heman, Calcol and Darda.* See note on 1Ch 2:6–7.

than Heman, Calcol and Darda, the sons of Mahol. And his fame spread to all the surrounding nations. [32]He spoke three thousand proverbs[v] and his songs[w] numbered a thousand and five. [33]He described plant life, from the cedar of Lebanon to the hyssop[x] that grows out of walls. He also taught about animals and birds, reptiles and fish. [34]Men of all nations came to listen to Solomon's wisdom, sent by all the kings[y] of the world, who had heard of his wisdom.

Preparations for Building the Temple

5:1–16pp — 2Ch 2:1–18

5 When Hiram[z] king of Tyre heard that Solomon had been anointed king to succeed his father David, he sent his envoys to Solomon, because he had always been on friendly terms with David. [2]Solomon sent back this message to Hiram:

[3]"You know that because of the wars[a] waged against my father David from all sides, he could not build[b] a temple for the Name of the LORD his God until the LORD put his enemies under his feet.[c] [4]But now the LORD my God has given me rest[d] on every side, and there is no adversary[e] or disaster. [5]I intend, therefore, to build a temple[f] for the Name of the LORD my God, as the LORD told my father David, when he said, 'Your son whom I will put on the throne in your place will build the temple for my Name.'[g]

[6]"So give orders that cedars[h] of Lebanon be cut for me. My men will work with yours, and I will pay you for your men whatever wages you set. You know that we have no one so skilled in felling timber as the Sidonians."

[7]When Hiram heard Solomon's message, he was greatly pleased and said, "Praise be to the LORD[i] today, for he has given David a wise son to rule over this great nation."

[8]So Hiram sent word to Solomon:

"I have received the message you sent me and will do all you want in providing the cedar and pine logs. [9]My men will haul them down from Lebanon to the sea[j], and I will float them in rafts by sea to the place you specify. There I will separate them and you can take them away. And you are to grant my wish by providing food[k] for my royal household."

[10]In this way Hiram kept Solomon supplied with all the cedar and pine logs he wanted, [11]and Solomon gave Hiram twenty thousand cors[1] of wheat as food[l] for his household, in addition to twenty thousand baths[m,n] of pressed olive oil. Solomon continued to do this for Hiram year after year. [12]The LORD gave Solomon wisdom,[m] just as he had promised him. There were peaceful relations between

Cross references (center column)

4:32 [v]Pr 1:1; 10:1; 25:1; Ecc 12:9
[w]Ps 78:63; SS 1:1; Eze 33:32
4:33 [x]S Lev 14:49
4:34 [y]2Ch 9:23
5:1 [z]S 2Sa 5:11
5:3 [a]1Ch 22:8; 28:3 [b]S 2Sa 7:5
[c]2Sa 22:40; Ps 8:6; 110:1; S Mt 22:44; 1Co 15:25
5:4 [d]S Jos 14:15; 1Ch 22:9; Lk 2:14
[e]1Ki 11:14,23
5:5 [f]S Dt 12:5; 1Ch 17:12; 1Co 3:16; Rev 21:22
[g]Dt 12:5; 2Sa 7:13
5:6 [h]1Ch 14:1; 22:4

5:7 [i]1Ki 10:9; Isa 60:6
5:9 [j]Ezr 3:7 [k]ver 11; Eze 27:17; Ac 12:20
5:11 [l]S ver 9
5:12 [m]S 1Ki 3:12

[1]11 That is, probably about 125,000 bushels (about 4,400 kiloliters)   [m]11 Septuagint (see also 2 Chron. 2:10); Hebrew *twenty cors*   [n]11 That is, about 115,000 gallons (about 440 kiloliters)

4:32 *three thousand proverbs.* Only some of these are preserved in the book of Proverbs.

4:33 *animals and birds, reptiles and fish.* Examples of Solomon's knowledge of these creatures are found in Pr 6:6–8; 26:2–3,11; 27:8; 28:1,15.

4:34 *all nations . . . all the kings of the world.* A general statement referring to the Near Eastern world (cf. Ge 41:57).

5:1 *Hiram king of Tyre.* Hiram ruled over Tyre c. 978–944 B.C. He may have also served as co-regent with his father Abibaal as early as 993. Before Solomon was born, Hiram provided timber and workmen for the building of David's palace (see 2Sa 5:11).

5:3 *he could not build a temple.* Although David was denied the privilege of building the temple, he did make plans and provisions for its construction (see 1Ch 22:2–5; 28:2; cf. also Ps 30 title).

5:4 *rest.* Described here as "no adversary or disaster." God's promises to his people (see Ex 33:14; Dt 25:19; Jos 1:13,15) and to David (2Sa 7:11) have now been fulfilled (see 8:56), so that the Israelites are free to concentrate their strength and resources on building their Great King's royal house (see note on 2Sa 7:11).

5:5 *Name.* Signifies God's revealed character or self-revelation as a person (see, e.g., 8:16; Ex 20:24; Dt 12:5; 2Sa 6:2; 7:13). *as the LORD told my father David.* See 2Sa 7:12–13; 1Ch 22:8–10.

5:6 *So give orders.* A more detailed account of Solomon's request is found in 2Ch 2:3–10. *cedars of Lebanon.* Widely used in the ancient Near East in the construction of royal houses and temples.

5:7 *Praise be to the LORD.* In polytheistic cultures it was common practice for the people of one nation to recognize the deities of another nation (see 10:9; 11:5) and even to ascribe certain powers to them (see 2Ki 18:25; see also 2Ch 2:12).

5:9 *place you specify.* Joppa (2Ch 2:16; see note on 1Ki 3:1). *providing food for my royal household.* Provision of food for Hiram's court personnel appears to cover only the cost of the wood itself. In addition, Solomon would have to provide for the wages of the Phoenician laborers (v. 6). Comparison of v. 11 with 2Ch 2:10 indicates that besides wheat and olive oil for Hiram's court, Solomon also sent barley and wine for labor costs. Hiram may have sold some of these provisions in order to pay the laborers.

5:11 *twenty thousand cors of wheat.* See NIV text note. By way of comparison, Solomon's court received 10,950 cors of flour and 21,900 cors of meal on an annual basis (see 4:22). Solomon's whole grain payment to Hiram of 20,000 cors of wheat and 20,000 cors of barley (2Ch 2:10) would probably yield about 26,666 cors of refined flour and meal, or about 20 percent less than the requirements of Solomon's own court.

Hiram and Solomon, and the two of them made a treaty.[n]

[13]King Solomon conscripted laborers[o] from all Israel—thirty thousand men. [14]He sent them off to Lebanon in shifts of ten thousand a month, so that they spent one month in Lebanon and two months at home. Adoniram[p] was in charge of the forced labor. [15]Solomon had seventy thousand carriers and eighty thousand stonecutters in the hills, [16]as well as thirty-three hundred[o] foremen[q] who supervised the project and directed the workmen. [17]At the king's command they removed from the quarry[r] large blocks of quality stone[s] to provide a foundation of dressed stone for the temple. [18]The craftsmen of Solomon and Hiram[t] and the men of Gebal[p] [u] cut and prepared the timber and stone for the building of the temple.

Solomon Builds the Temple

6:1–29pp — 2Ch 3:1–14

6 In the four hundred and eightieth[q] year after the Israelites had come out of Egypt, in the fourth year of Solomon's reign over Israel, in the month of Ziv, the second month,[v] he began to build the temple of the LORD.[w]

[2]The temple[x] that King Solomon built for the LORD was sixty cubits long, twenty wide and thirty high.[r] [3]The portico[y] at the front of the main hall of the temple extended the width of the temple, that is twenty cubits,[s] and projected ten cubits[t] from the front of the temple. [4]He made narrow clerestory windows[z] in the temple. [5]Against the walls of the main hall and inner sanctuary he built a structure around the building, in which there were side rooms.[a] [6]The lowest floor was five cubits[u] wide, the middle floor six cubits[v] and the third floor seven.[w] He made offset ledges around the outside of the temple so that nothing would be inserted into the temple walls.

[7]In building the temple, only blocks dressed[b] at the quarry were used, and no hammer, chisel or any other iron tool[c] was heard at the temple site while it was being built.

[8]The entrance to the lowest[x] floor was on the south side of the temple; a stairway led up to the middle level and from there to the third. [9]So he built the temple and completed it, roofing it with beams and cedar[d] planks. [10]And he built the side rooms all along the temple. The height of each was five cubits, and they were attached to the temple by beams of cedar.

[11]The word of the LORD came[e] to Solo-

Cross-references (center column):

5:12 [n]Jos 9:7; 1Ki 15:19; Am 1:9
5:13 [o]S Ge 49:15; S Lev 25:39; 1Ki 9:15
5:14 [p]S 2Sa 20:24; 1Ki 4:6; 2Ch 10:18
5:16 [q]1Ki 9:23
5:17 [r]1Ki 6:7 [s]1Ch 22:2
5:18 [t]S 2Sa 5:11 [u]S Jos 13:5
6:1 [v]Ezr 3:8 [w]Ezr 5:11
6:2 [x]Ex 26:1
6:3 [y]Eze 40:49

6:4 [z]Eze 41:16
6:5 [a]Jer 35:2; Eze 41:5-6
6:7 [b]S Ex 20:25 [c]S Dt 27:5
6:9 [d]SS 1:17
6:11 [e]1Ki 12:22; 13:20; 16:1,7; 17:2; 21:17; Jer 40:1

Text notes:

[o]16 Hebrew; some Septuagint manuscripts (see also 2 Chron. 2:2, 18) thirty-six hundred   [p]18 That is, Byblos   [q]1 Hebrew; Septuagint four hundred and fortieth   [r]2 That is, about 90 feet (about 27 meters) long and 30 feet (about 9 meters) wide and 45 feet (about 13.5 meters) high   [s]3 That is, about 30 feet (about 9 meters)   [t]3 That is, about 15 feet (about 4.5 meters)   [u]6 That is, about 7 1/2 feet (about 2.3 meters); also in verses 10 and 24   [v]6 That is, about 9 feet (about 2.7 meters)   [w]6 That is, about 10 1/2 feet (about 3.1 meters)   [x]8 Septuagint; Hebrew middle

---

5:13 *conscripted laborers.* See notes on 9:15; 2Sa 20:24. Resentment among the people toward this sort of forced labor eventually led to a civil uprising and the division of Solomon's kingdom immediately after his death (12:1–18).
5:15 *seventy thousand carriers and eighty thousand stonecutters.* Conscripted from the non-Israelite population that David had subdued and incorporated into his kingdom (see 2Ch 2:17–18). *hills.* The limestone hills of Palestine where the stone was quarried.
5:16 *thirty-three hundred foremen.* 1Ki 9:23 refers to 550 supervisors. If these are two different categories of supervisory personnel, the total is 3,850 men. 2Ch 2:2 refers to 3,600 foremen, and 2Ch 8:10 speaks of 250 supervisors, which again yields a total of 3,850 men in a supervisory capacity.
5:17 *large blocks of quality stone.* For the size of these stones see 7:10. Transportation of such stones to Jerusalem would require enormous manpower.
5:18 *men of Gebal.* See NIV text note; see also Eze 27:9.
6:1–38 See drawing of "Solomon's Temple," p. 481.
6:1 *four hundred and eightieth year . . . fourth year.* Synchronizations between certain events in the reigns of later Israelite kings and Assyrian chronological records fix the fourth year of Solomon's reign at c. 966 B.C. (see Introduction: Chronology). If Israel's exodus is placed 480 years prior to 966, it would have occurred c. 1446 (the chronology followed in this Study Bible) during the rule of the 18th-dynasty Egyptian pharaoh, Amunhotep II. On the basis of Ex 1:11 and certain other historical considerations, however,

some have concluded that the exodus could not have occurred prior to the rule of the 19th-dynasty pharaoh, Rameses II—thus not until c. 1290 (see note on Ge 47:11). This would mean that the 480 years of this verse would be understood as either a schematic (perhaps representative of 12 generations multiplied by the conventional, but not always actual, 40-year length of a generation) or aggregate figure (the combined total of a number of subsidiary time periods, which in reality were partly concurrent, examples of which are to be found in Egyptian and Mesopotamian records).
6:2 *temple that King Solomon built.* The temple was patterned after the tabernacle (and, in general, other temples of the time) and was divided into three major areas: the Most Holy Place, the Holy Place and the outer courtyard. The Most Holy Place in the temple was cubical, as it probably was in the tabernacle. The dimensions of the temple in most instances seem to be double those of the tabernacle (see Ex 26:15–30; 36:20–34).
6:6 *offset ledges.* To avoid making holes in the temple wall, it was built with a series of ledges on which the beams for the three floors of side chambers rested. This accounts for the different widths of the rooms on each floor.
6:8 *entrance to the lowest floor.* Of the side chambers.
6:11 *The word of the LORD came to Solomon.* As the temple neared completion the Lord spoke to Solomon, perhaps through an unnamed prophet (but see 3:5,11–14; 9:2–9).

mon: [12]"As for this temple you are building, if you follow my decrees, carry out my regulations and keep all my commands[f] and obey them, I will fulfill through you the promise[g] I gave to David your father. [13]And I will live among the Israelites and will not abandon[h] my people Israel."

[14]So Solomon[i] built the temple and completed[j] it. [15]He lined its interior walls with cedar boards, paneling them from the floor of the temple to the ceiling,[k] and covered the floor of the temple with planks of pine.[l] [16]He partitioned off twenty cubits[y] at the rear of the temple with cedar boards from floor to ceiling to form within the temple an inner sanctuary, the Most Holy Place.[m] [17]The main hall in front of this room was forty cubits[z] long. [18]The inside of the temple was cedar,[n] carved with

gourds and open flowers. Everything was cedar; no stone was to be seen.

[19]He prepared the inner sanctuary[o] within the temple to set the ark of the covenant[p] of the LORD there. [20]The inner sanctuary[q] was twenty cubits long, twenty wide and twenty high.[a] He overlaid the inside with pure gold, and he also overlaid the altar of cedar.[r] [21]Solomon covered the inside of the temple with pure gold, and he extended gold chains across the front of the inner sanctuary, which was overlaid with gold. [22]So he overlaid the whole interior with gold. He also overlaid with gold the altar that belonged to the inner sanctuary.

[23]In the inner sanctuary he made a pair

6:12 /1Ki 11:10
*g*2Sa 7:12-16;
1Ki 9:5
6:13
*h*S Lev 26:11;
S Dt 31:6;
Jn 14:18;
Heb 13:5
6:14 /Ac 7:47
/1Ch 28:20;
2Ch 5:1
6:15 *k*1Ki 7:7
/Eze 41:15-16
6:16 *m*S Ex 26:33
6:18 *n*ver 29;
Ps 74:6;
Eze 41:18

6:19 *o*1Ki 8:6
*p*S Ex 25:10;
S 1Sa 3:3
6:20 *q*Eze 41:3-4
*r*S Ex 30:1

y16 That is, about 30 feet (about 9 meters)   *z17* That is, about 60 feet (about 18 meters)   *a20* That is, about 30 feet (about 9 meters) long, wide and high

---

6:12 *if you follow my decrees . . . I will fulfill through you the promise.* In words similar to those spoken by David (see notes on 2:1–4), the Lord assures Solomon of a continuing dynasty (see 2Sa 7:12–16) if he is faithful to the covenant. **6:13** *I will live among the Israelites.* In the temple being built (see 9:3). To avoid any apprehension among the Israel-

ites concerning his presence with them (cf. Ps 78:60; Jer 26:6,9; see note on 1Sa 7:1), the Lord gives assurance that he will dwell in their midst (see 8:10–13; Lev 26:11). **6:16** *Most Holy Place.* The same terminology was used for the inner sanctuary housing the ark in the tabernacle (see Ex 26:33–34; Lev 16:2,16–17, 20, 23).

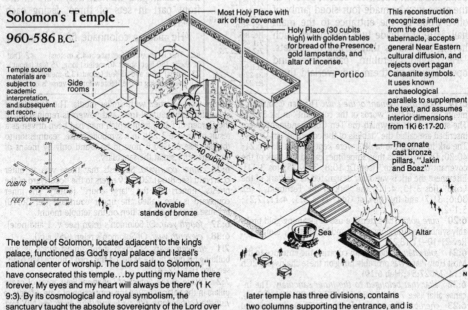

Solomon's Temple

960-586 B.C.

Temple source materials are subject to academic interpretation, and subsequent art reconstructions vary.

Side rooms

20

40 cubits

CUBITS

FEET

Movable stands of bronze

Most Holy Place with ark of the covenant

Holy Place (30 cubits high) with golden tables for bread of the Presence, gold lampstands, and altar of incense.

Portico

Sea

Altar

This reconstruction recognizes influence from the desert tabernacle, accepts general Near Eastern cultural diffusion, and rejects overt pagan Canaanite symbols. It uses known archaeological parallels to supplement the text, and assumes interior dimensions from 1Ki 6:17-20.

The ornate cast bronze pillars, "Jakin and Boaz"

N

The temple of Solomon, located adjacent to the king's palace, functioned as God's royal palace and Israel's national center of worship. The Lord said to Solomon, "I have consecrated this temple . . . by putting my Name there forever. My eyes and my heart will always be there" (1 K 9:3). By its cosmological and royal symbolism, the sanctuary taught the absolute sovereignty of the Lord over the whole creation and his special headship over Israel.

The floor plan is a type that has a long history in Semitic religion, particularly among the West Semites. An early example of the tripartite division into *'ulam, hekal,* and *debir* (portico, main hall, and inner sanctuary) has been found at Syrian Ebla (c. 2300 B.C.) and, much later but more contemporaneous with Solomon, at Tell Tainat in the Orontes basin (c. 900 B.C.). Like Solomon's, the

later temple has three divisions, contains two columns supporting the entrance, and is located adjacent to the royal palace.

Many archaeological parallels can be drawn to the methods of construction used in the temple, e.g., the "stone and cedar beam" technique described in 1Ki 6:36. Interestingly, evidence for the largest bronze-casting industry ever found in Palestine comes from the same locale and period as that indicated in Scripture: Zarethan in the Jordan Valley c. 1000 B.C.

© Hugh Claycombe 1986

of cherubim[s] of olive wood, each ten cubits[b] high. 24One wing of the first cherub was five cubits long, and the other wing five cubits—ten cubits from wing tip to wing tip. 25The second cherub also measured ten cubits, for the two cherubim were identical in size and shape. 26The height of each cherub was ten cubits. 27He placed the cherubim[t] inside the innermost room of the temple, with their wings spread out. The wing of one cherub touched one wall, while the wing of the other touched the other wall, and their wings touched each other in the middle of the room. 28He overlaid the cherubim with gold.

29On the walls[u] all around the temple, in both the inner and outer rooms, he carved cherubim,[v] palm trees and open flowers. 30He also covered the floors of both the inner and outer rooms of the temple with gold.

31For the entrance of the inner sanctuary he made doors of olive wood with five-sided jambs. 32And on the two olive wood doors[w] he carved cherubim, palm trees and open flowers, and overlaid the cherubim and palm trees with beaten gold. 33In the same way he made four-sided jambs of olive wood for the entrance to the main hall. 34He also made two pine doors, each having two leaves that turned in sockets. 35He carved cherubim, palm trees and open flowers on them and overlaid them

with gold hammered evenly over the carvings.

36And he built the inner courtyard[x] of three courses[y] of dressed stone and one course of trimmed cedar beams.

37The foundation of the temple of the LORD was laid in the fourth year, in the month of Ziv. 38In the eleventh year in the month of Bul, the eighth month, the temple was finished in all its details[z] according to its specifications.[a] He had spent seven years building it.

Solomon Builds His Palace

7 It took Solomon thirteen years, however, to complete the construction of his palace.[b] 2He built the Palace[c] of the Forest of Lebanon[d] a hundred cubits long, fifty wide and thirty high,[c] with four rows of cedar columns supporting trimmed cedar beams. 3It was roofed with cedar above the beams that rested on the columns—forty-five beams, fifteen to a row. 4Its windows were placed high in sets of three, facing each other. 5All the doorways had rectangular frames; they were in the front part in sets of three, facing each other.[d]

6He made a colonnade fifty cubits long

Cross references (center column):

6:23 ˢS Ex 37:7
6:27 ˡS Ge 3:24;
S Ex 25:18
6:29 ᵘS ver 18
ᵛver 32,35;
Eze 41:18,25
6:32 ʷEze 41:23

6:36 ˣ2Ch 4:9
ʸ1Ki 7:12;
Ezr 6:4
6:38 ᶻ1Ch 28:19
ᵃEx 25:9;
Heb 8:5
7:1 ᵇS 2Sa 7:2
7:2 ᶜS 2Sa 7:2
ᵈ1Ki 10:17;
2Ch 9:16;
Isa 22:8; 37:24;
Jer 22:6,23

b23 That is, about 15 feet (about 4.5 meters)   c2 That is, about 150 feet (about 46 meters) long, 75 feet (about 23 meters) wide and 45 feet (about 13.5 meters) high   d5 The meaning of the Hebrew for this verse is uncertain.

6:19 *ark of the covenant of the LORD.* The Ten Commandments are called the "words of the covenant" in Ex 34:28. The stone tablets on which the Ten Commandments were inscribed are called the "tablets of the covenant" in Dt 9:9. The ark in which the tablets were kept (see Ex 25:16,21; 40:20; Dt 10:1–5) is thus sometimes called the "ark of the covenant of the LORD" (see Dt 10:8; 31:9,25; Jos 3:11). Elsewhere the ark is variously designated as the "ark of the LORD" (Jos 3:13; 4:11), the "ark of the Testimony" (Ex 30:6; 31:7) and the "ark of God" (1Sa 3:3; 4:11,17,21; 5:1–2).
6:20 *pure gold.* The extensive use of gleaming gold probably symbolized the glory of God and his heavenly temple (cf. Rev 21:10–11,18,21).
6:21 *gold chains.* The curtain covering the entrance to the Most Holy Place was probably hung on these chains (see 2Ch 3:14; Mt 27:51; Heb 6:19).
6:22 *altar that belonged to the inner sanctuary.* The incense altar (see 7:48; Ex 30:1,6; 37:25–28; Heb 9:3–4).
6:23 *cherubim.* See note on Ex 25:18. They were to stand as sentries on either side of the ark (8:6–7; 2Ch 3:10–13). Two additional cherubim stood on the ark—one on each end of its atonement cover (Ex 25:17–22). *ten cubits high.* The Most Holy Place, where the cherubim stood, was 20 cubits high (v. 16).
6:29 *he carved cherubim.* Not a violation of the second commandment, which prohibited making anything to serve as a representation of God and worshiping it (see note on Ex 20:4). *palm trees and open flowers.* Early Jewish syna-

gogues were adorned with similar motifs. The depiction of cherubim and beautiful trees and flowers is reminiscent of the Garden of Eden, from which man had been driven as a result of sin (Ge 3:24). In a symbolic sense, readmission to the paradise of God is now to be found only by means of atonement for sin at the sanctuary.
6:36 *inner courtyard.* Suggests that there was an outer courtyard (see 8:64). 2Ch 4:9 refers to the "courtyard of the priests" (inner) and the "large court" (outer). The inner courtyard is also called the upper courtyard (Jer 36:10) because of its higher position on the temple mount.
6:37 *fourth year.* Of Solomon's reign (see v. 1 and note).
6:38 *eleventh year.* Of Solomon's reign (959 B.C.).
7:1 *thirteen years.* Solomon spent almost twice as long building his own house as he did the Lord's house (see 6:38; see also Hag 1:2–4).
7:2 *Palace of the Forest of Lebanon.* Four rows of cedar pillars in the palace created the impression of a great forest. *a hundred cubits long, fifty wide and thirty high.* See NIV text note. Compare these measurements with those of the temple in 6:2.
7:3 *forty-five beams, fifteen to a row.* Suggests that there were three floors in the building above the main hall on the ground level. The building included storage area for weaponry (see 10:16–17).
7:6 *colonnade.* Apparently an entrance hall to the Palace of the Forest of Lebanon. Its length (50 cubits) corresponds to the width of the palace.

and thirty wide.e In front of it was a portico, and in front of that were pillars and an overhanging roof.

7He built the throne hall, the Hall of Justice, where he was to judge,e and he covered it with cedar from floor to ceiling.ff 8And the palace in which he was to live, set farther back, was similar in design. Solomon also made a palace like this hall for Pharaoh's daughter, whom he had married.g

9All these structures, from the outside to the great courtyard and from foundation to eaves, were made of blocks of high-grade stone cut to size and trimmed with a saw on their inner and outer faces. 10The foundations were laid with large stones of good quality, some measuring ten cubitsg and some eight.h 11Above were high-grade stones, cut to size, and cedar beams. 12The great courtyard was surrounded by a wall of three coursesh of dressed stone and one course of trimmed cedar beams, as was the inner courtyard of the temple of the LORD with its portico.

The Temple's Furnishings

7:23–26pp — 2Ch 4:2–5
7:38–51pp — 2Ch 4:6,10–5:1

13King Solomon sent to Tyre and brought Huram,ii 14whose mother was a widow from the tribe of Naphtali and whose father was a man of Tyre and a craftsman in bronze. Huram was highly skilledj and experienced in all kinds of bronze work. He came to King Solomon and did allk the work assigned to him.

15He cast two bronze pillars,l each eighteen cubits high and twelve cubits around,i by line. 16He also made two capitalsm of cast bronze to set on the tops of the pillars; each capital was five cubitsk

high. 17A network of interwoven chains festooned the capitals on top of the pillars, seven for each capital. 18He made pomegranates in two rowsl encircling each network to decorate the capitals on top of the pillars.m He did the same for each capital. 19The capitals on top of the pillars in the portico were in the shape of lilies, four cubitsn high. 20On the capitals of both pillars, above the bowl-shaped part next to the network, were the two hundred pomegranatesn in rows all around. 21He erected the pillars at the portico of the temple. The pillar to the south he named Jakino and the one to the north Boaz.po 22The capitals on top were in the shape of lilies. And so the work on the pillarsp was completed.

23He made the Seaq of cast metal, circular in shape, measuring ten cubitsg from rim to rim and five cubits high. It took a liner of thirty cubitsq to measure around it. 24Below the rim, gourds encircled it—ten to a cubit. The gourds were cast in two rows in one piece with the Sea.

25The Sea stood on twelve bulls,s three facing north, three facing west, three facing south and three facing east. The Sea rested on top of them, and their hindquarters were toward the center. 26It was a

7:7 e1Sa 7:15; Ps 122:5; Pr 20:8 /1Ki 6:15
7:8 gS 1Ki 3:1
7:12 hS 1Ki 6:36
7:13 iver 45; 2Ch 2:13; 4:16
7:14 /Ex 31:2-5; S 35:31 k2Ch 4:11
7:15 l2Ki 11:14; 23:3; 25:17; 2Ch 3:15; 23:13; 34:31; Jer 27:19; 52:17,21; Eze 40:49
7:16 mver 20,42; 2Ki 25:17; Jer 52:22
7:20 nver 18; 2Ch 3:16; 4:13
7:21 o2Ch 3:17
7:22 p2Ki 25:17
7:23 qver 47; 2Ki 25:13; 1Ch 18:8; 2Ch 4:18; Jer 52:17; Rev 4:6 rJer 31:39; Zec 2:1
7:25 sJer 52:20

e6 That is, about 75 feet (about 23 meters) long and 45 feet (about 13.5 meters) wide f7 Vulgate and Syriac; Hebrew floor g10,23 That is, about 15 feet (about 4.5 meters) h10 That is, about 12 feet (about 3.6 meters) i13 Hebrew Hiram, a variant of Huram; also in verses 40 and 45 j15 That is, about 27 feet (about 8.1 meters) high and 18 feet (about 5.4 meters) around k16 That is, about 7 1/2 feet (about 2.3 meters); also in verse 23 l18 Two Hebrew manuscripts and Septuagint; most Hebrew manuscripts made the pillars, and there were two rows m18 Many Hebrew manuscripts and Syriac; most Hebrew manuscripts pomegranates n19 That is, about 6 feet (about 1.8 meters); also in verse 38 o21 Jakin probably means he establishes. p21 Boaz probably means in him is strength. q23 That is, about 45 feet (about 13.5 meters)

7:7 throne hall. It is not clear whether the throne hall, the Hall of Justice, Solomon's own living quarters (v. 8) and the palace for Pharaoh's daughter (v. 8) were separate buildings or locations within the Palace of the Forest of Lebanon.
7:9 trimmed with a saw. The pinkish white limestone of Palestine is easily cut when originally quarried, but gradually hardens with exposure.
7:12 great courtyard. Constructed in the same way as the inner courtyard of the temple (6:36).
7:13 King Solomon sent. Prior to the completion of the temple and the construction of Solomon's palace (see 2Ch 2:7,13–14). Huram. See NIV text note. His full name is Huram-Abi (2Ch 2:13).
7:14 widow from the tribe of Naphtali. 2Ch 2:14 indicates that Huram-Abi's mother was from Dan. Apparently she was born in the city of Dan in northern Israel close to the tribe of Naphtali, from which came her first husband. After he died, she married a man from Tyre. all kinds of bronze work. Huram-Abi had a much wider range of skills as well (see 2Ch 2:7,14).

7:15 two bronze pillars. One was placed on each side of the main entrance to the temple (v. 21). Surely decorative, they may also have embodied a symbolism not known to us. It has been suggested that they were not freestanding but supported a roof (forming a portico to the temple) and an architrave.
7:21 pillar to the south. The temple, like the tabernacle before it, faced east (see Eze 8:16).
7:23 Sea of cast metal. This enormous reservoir of water corresponded to the bronze basin made for the tabernacle (see Ex 30:17–21; 38:8). Its water was used by the priests for ritual cleansing (2Ch 4:6). thirty cubits. Technically speaking, this should be 31.416 cubits because of the ten-cubit diameter of the circular top. Thirty may be a round number here, or perhaps the measurement was taken a bit below the rim or on the inside circumference (see v. 26).
7:24 ten to a cubit. With ten gourds to a cubit it took 300 gourds to span the entire reservoir, or 600 gourds counting both rows.

handbreadth[r] in thickness, and its rim was like the rim of a cup, like a lily blossom. It held two thousand baths.[s]

27He also made ten movable stands[t] of bronze; each was four cubits long, four wide and three high.[t] 28This is how the stands were made: They had side panels attached to uprights. 29On the panels between the uprights were lions, bulls and cherubim—and on the uprights as well. Above and below the lions and bulls were wreaths of hammered work. 30Each stand[u] had four bronze wheels with bronze axles, and each had a basin resting on four supports, cast with wreaths on each side. 31On the inside of the stand there was an opening that had a circular frame one cubit[u] deep. This opening was round, and with its basework it measured a cubit and a half.[v] Around its opening there was engraving. The panels of the stands were square, not round. 32The four wheels were under the panels, and the axles of the wheels were attached to the stand. The diameter of each wheel was a cubit and a half. 33The wheels were made like chariot wheels; the axles, rims, spokes and hubs were all of cast metal.

34Each stand had four handles, one on each corner, projecting from the stand. 35At the top of the stand there was a circular band half a cubit[w] deep. The supports and panels were attached to the top of the stand. 36He engraved cherubim, lions and palm trees on the surfaces of the supports and on the panels, in every available space, with wreaths all around. 37This is the way

7:27 [2Ki 16:17]
7:30 [2Ki 16:17]

r26 That is, about 3 inches (about 8 centimeters)
s26 That is, probably about 11,500 gallons (about 44 kiloliters); the Septuagint does not have this sentence.
t27 That is, about 6 feet (about 1.8 meters) long and wide and about 4 1/2 feet (about 1.3 meters) high
u31 That is, about 1 1/2 feet (about 0.5 meter)
v31 That is, about 2 1/4 feet (about 0.7 meter); also in verse 32   w35 That is, about 3/4 foot (about 0.2 meter)

7:27 *ten movable stands.* These movable bronze stands were designed to hold water basins (see v. 38) of much smaller dimensions than the bronze Sea. The water from the basins was used to wash certain prescribed parts of the animals that were slaughtered for burnt offerings (see Lev 1:9,13; 2Ch 4:6).
7:36 *He engraved cherubim, lions and palm trees.* See note on 6:29.

Temple Furnishings

Glimpses of the rich ornamentation of Solomon's temple can be gained through recent discoveries that illumine the text of 1 Ki 6-7.

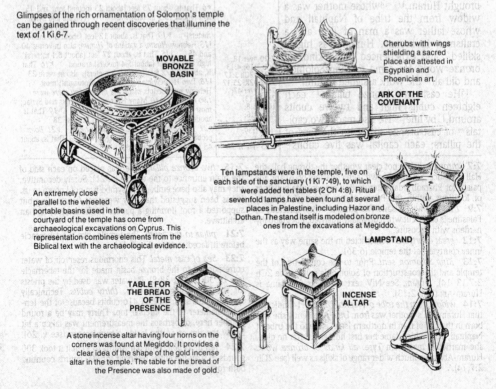

MOVABLE BRONZE BASIN

An extremely close parallel to the wheeled portable basins used in the courtyard of the temple has come from archaeological excavations on Cyprus. This representation combines elements from the Biblical text with the archaeological evidence.

Cherubs with wings shielding a sacred place are attested in Egyptian and Phoenician art.

ARK OF THE COVENANT

Ten lampstands were in the temple, five on each side of the sanctuary (1 Ki 7:49), to which were added ten tables (2 Ch 4:8). Ritual sevenfold lamps have been found at several places in Palestine, including Hazor and Dothan. The stand itself is modeled on bronze ones from the excavations at Megiddo.

LAMPSTAND

TABLE FOR THE BREAD OF THE PRESENCE

INCENSE ALTAR

A stone incense altar having four horns on the corners was found at Megiddo. It provides a clear idea of the shape of the gold incense altar in the temple. The table for the bread of the Presence was also made of gold.

he made the ten stands. They were all cast in the same molds and were identical in size and shape.

38He then made ten bronze basins,v each holding forty baths x and measuring four cubits across, one basin to go on each of the ten stands. 39He placed five of the stands on the south side of the temple and five on the north. He placed the Sea on the south side, at the southeast corner of the temple. 40He also made the basins and shovels and sprinkling bowls. w

So Huram finished all the work he had undertaken for King Solomon in the temple of the LORD:

41the two pillars;

the two bowl-shaped capitals on top of the pillars;

the two sets of network decorating the two bowl-shaped capitals on top of the pillars;

42the four hundred pomegranates for the two sets of network (two rows of pomegranates for each network, decorating the bowl-shaped capitals x on top of the pillars);

43the ten stands with their ten basins;

44the Sea and the twelve bulls under it;

45the pots, shovels and sprinkling bowls.y

All these objects that Huram z made for King Solomon for the temple of the LORD were of burnished bronze. 46The king had them cast in clay molds in the plain a of the Jordan between Succoth b and Zarethan. c 47Solomon left all these things unweighed, d because there were so many; e the weight of the bronze f was not determined.

48Solomon also made all g the furnishings that were in the LORD's temple:

the golden altar;

the golden table h on which was the bread of the Presence; i

49the lampstands j of pure gold (five on the right and five on the left, in front of the inner sanctuary);

the gold floral work and lamps and tongs;

50the pure gold basins, wick trimmers, sprinkling bowls, dishes k and censers; l

and the gold sockets for the doors of the innermost room, the Most Holy Place, and also for the doors of the main hall of the temple.

51When all the work King Solomon had done for the temple of the LORD was finished, he brought in the things his father David had dedicated m—the silver and gold and the furnishings n—and he placed them in the treasuries of the LORD's temple.

The Ark Brought to the Temple
8:1–21pp — 2Ch 5:2–6:11

8 Then King Solomon summoned into his presence at Jerusalem the elders of Israel, all the heads of the tribes and the chiefs o of the Israelite families, to bring up the ark p of the LORD's covenant from Zion, the City of David. q 2All the men of Israel came together to King Solomon at the time of the festival r in the month of Ethanim, the seventh month. s

3When all the elders of Israel had arrived, the priests t took up the ark, 4and they brought up the ark of the LORD and

x38 That is, about 230 gallons (about 880 liters)

Cross references
7:38 vS Ex 30:18
7:40 wS Ex 27:3; Jer 52:18
7:42 xS ver 16
7:45 yS Ex 27:3; Jer 52:18 zS ver 13
7:46 aS Ge 13:10 bS Ge 33:17 cJos 3:16
7:47 d1Ch 22:3; Jer 52:20 eEx 36:5-7 fS ver 23
7:48 gEx 39:32-43 hS Ex 25:23 iS Ex 25:30
7:49 jS Ex 25:31
7:50 kS Nu 7:14 l2Ki 25:13; Jer 52:19
7:51 mS 2Sa 8:11 n2Ki 12:13; 24:13; Jer 27:19
8:1 oNu 7:2 pS 1Sa 3:3; Rev 11:19 qS 2Sa 5:7
8:2 rver 65; S Lev 23:36; Ne 8:17 sS Lev 23:34; S Nu 29:12
8:3 tS Jos 3:3

7:40 basins. Perhaps used for cooking meat to be eaten in connection with the fellowship offerings (see Lev 7:11–17; 22:21–23). shovels. Used for removing ashes from the altar. sprinkling bowls. For use by the priests in various rites involving the sprinkling of blood or water (see Ex 27:3).
7:41 two sets of network. See v. 17.
7:42 four hundred pomegranates. See vv. 18,20.
7:43 ten stands with their ten basins. See vv. 27–37.
7:44 the Sea and the twelve bulls. See vv. 23–26.
7:45 pots, shovels and sprinkling bowls. See v. 40.
7:46 Succoth. Located on the east side of the Jordan (Ge 33:17; Jos 13:27; Jdg 8:4–5) just north of the Jabbok River. Excavations in this area have confirmed that Succoth was a center of metallurgy during the period of the monarchy. Zarethan. Located near Adamah (see Jos 3:16) and Abel Meholah (4:12).
7:48 golden altar. See 6:22. golden table. The bread of the Presence was placed on this table (see Ex 25:23–30; 1Ch 9:32; 2Ch 13:11; 29:18). Ten such golden tables are mentioned in 1Ch 28:16 and 2Ch 4:8,19, five placed on the north and five on the south side of the temple.
7:49 lampstands of pure gold. Only one lampstand with

seven arms had stood in the tabernacle, opposite the table for the bread of the Presence (Ex 25:31–40; 26:35). The ten lampstands in the temple, five on the north and five on the south side, created a lane of light in the Holy Place. gold floral work. See Ex 25:33. lamps. See Ex 25:37. tongs. See 2Ch 4:21; Isa 6:6.
7:50 censers. See 2Ki 25:15; 2Ch 4:22; Jer 52:18–19.
7:51 things his father David had dedicated. Valuable objects of silver and gold, either taken as booty in war or received as tribute from kings seeking David's favor (see 2Sa 8:9–12; 1Ch 18:7–11; 2Ch 5:1). treasuries of the Lord's temple. See 15:18; 2Ki 12:18; 1Ch 9:26; 26:20–26; 28:12.
8:1 bring up the ark of the Lord's covenant. David had previously brought the ark from the house of Obed-Edom to Jerusalem (see 2Sa 6). Zion, the City of David. See note on 2Sa 5:7.
8:2 festival. It is probable that Solomon waited 11 months (see 6:38) to dedicate the temple during the Feast of Tabernacles, which was observed in the seventh month of the year (Lev 23:34; Dt 16:13–15). seventh month. Presumably in the 12th year of Solomon's reign.

the Tent of Meeting[u] and all the sacred furnishings in it. The priests and Levites[v] carried them up, [5]and King Solomon and the entire assembly of Israel that had gathered about him were before the ark, sacrificing[w] so many sheep and cattle that they could not be recorded or counted.

[6]The priests then brought the ark of the LORD's covenant[x] to its place in the inner sanctuary of the temple, the Most Holy Place,[y] and put it beneath the wings of the cherubim.[z] [7]The cherubim spread their wings over the place of the ark and overshadowed[a] the ark and its carrying poles. [8]These poles were so long that their ends could be seen from the Holy Place in front of the inner sanctuary, but not from outside the Holy Place; and they are still there today.[b] [9]There was nothing in the ark except the two stone tablets[c] that Moses had placed in it at Horeb, where the LORD made a covenant with the Israelites after they came out of Egypt.

[10]When the priests withdrew from the Holy Place, the cloud[d] filled the temple of the LORD. [11]And the priests could not perform their service[e] because of the cloud, for the glory[f] of the LORD filled his temple.

[12]Then Solomon said, "The LORD has said that he would dwell in a dark cloud;[g] [13]I have indeed built a magnificent temple for you, a place for you to dwell[h] forever."

[14]While the whole assembly of Israel was standing there, the king turned around and blessed[i] them. [15]Then he said:

"Praise be to the LORD,[j] the God of Israel, who with his own hand has fulfilled what he promised with his own mouth to my father David. For he said, [16]'Since the day I brought my people Israel out of Egypt,[k] I have not chosen a city in any tribe of Israel to have a temple built for my Name[l] to be there, but I have chosen[m] David[n] to rule my people Israel.'

[17]"My father David had it in his heart[o] to build a temple[p] for the Name of the LORD, the God of Israel. [18]But the LORD said to my father David, 'Because it was in your heart to build a temple for my Name, you did well to have this in your heart. [19]Nevertheless, you[q] are not the one to build the temple, but your son, who is your own flesh and blood—he is the one who will build the temple for my Name.'[r]

[20]"The LORD has kept the promise he made: I have succeeded[s] David my father and now I sit on the throne of Israel, just as the LORD promised, and I have built[t] the temple for the Name of the LORD, the God of Israel. [21]I have provided a place there for the ark, in which is the covenant of the LORD that he made with our fathers when he brought them out of Egypt."

Solomon's Prayer of Dedication

8:22–53pp — 2Ch 6:12–40

[22]Then Solomon stood before the altar of the LORD in front of the whole assembly of Israel, spread out his hands[u] toward heaven [23]and said:

"O LORD, God of Israel, there is no God like[v] you in heaven above or on earth below—you who keep your covenant of love[w] with your servants who continue wholeheartedly in your way. [24]You have kept your promise to your servant David my father; with your mouth you have promised and with your hand you have fulfilled it—as it is today.

[25]"Now LORD, God of Israel, keep for your servant David my father the promises[x] you made to him when you said, 'You shall never fail to have a man to sit before me on the throne of Israel, if only your sons are careful in

---

8:4 uS Lev 17:4
v1Ch 15:13
8:5 wS 2Sa 6:13;
S 2Ch 30:24
8:6 xS Ex 26:33;
S 2Sa 6:17;
Rev 11:19
yS Ex 26:33
zS Ge 3:24;
S Ex 25:18
8:7 aS Ex 25:20
8:8 bEx 25:13-15
8:9 cS Ex 16:34;
S 25:16; Heb 9:4
8:10
dS Ex 16:10;
S Lev 16:2;
Rev 15:8
8:11 e2Ch 7:2;
Rev 15:8
fS Ex 16:7;
S 29:43
8:12
gS Ex 40:34;
S 2Sa 22:10
8:13 hEx 15:17;
Ps 132:13;
135:21; Mt 23:21
8:14 iS Ex 39:43
8:15 jS 1Ch 16:36;
Lk 1:68
8:16 kS Ex 3:10
lS Dt 12:5
mS 1Sa 9:16;
S 16:1 nPs 89:3-4

8:17 oS 1Sa 10:7;
Ac 7:46
p2Sa 7:27;
1Ch 22:7;
Ps 26:8; 132:5
8:19 qS 2Sa 7:5
rS 2Sa 7:13
8:20 sS 2Sa 7:12
t1Ch 28:6
8:22 uS Ex 9:29
8:23 vS Ex 9:14
wS Dt 7:9,12;
Ne 1:5; 9:32;
Da 9:4
8:25 xS 2Sa 7:15;
1Ch 17:23;
2Ch 1:9

8:4 *Tent of Meeting.* The tabernacle, which had been preserved at Gibeon (see notes on 3:4; 1Sa 7:1; see also 2Ch 5:4–5).

8:6 *put it beneath the wings of the cherubim.* See 6:23–28.

8:8 *their ends could be seen.* The carrying poles were always to remain in the gold rings of the ark (Ex 25:15). *they are still there today.* These words must be those of the original author of this description of the dedication of the temple rather than those of the final compiler of the books of Kings (see Introduction: Author, Sources and Date; see also 2Ch 5:9).

8:9 *two stone tablets.* See Ex 25:16; 40:20. *the Lord made a covenant.* See Ex 24.

8:10 *the cloud filled the temple.* Just as a visible manifestation of the presence of the Lord had descended on the tabernacle at Sinai, so now the Lord came to take up his abode in the temple (see Ex 40:33–35; Eze 10:3–5,18–19; 43:4–5).

8:12 *he would dwell in a dark cloud.* See Ex 19:9; 24:15, 18; 33:9–10; 34:5; Lev 16:2; Dt 4:11; 5:22; Ps 18:10–11.

8:15 *what he promised.* See 2Sa 7:5–16.

8:16 *my Name.* Equivalent to the Lord himself (see note on 5:5).

8:23 *no God like you.* No other god has acted in history as has the God of Israel, performing great miracles and directing the course of events so that his long-range covenant promises are fulfilled (see Ex 15:11; Dt 4:39; 7:9; Ps 86:8–10).

8:24 *your promise.* See v. 15; 2Sa 7:5–16.

8:25 *if only your sons . . . walk before me.* See 9:4–9; 2Ch 7:17–22; see also note on 1Ki 2:4.

all they do to walk before me as you have done.' [26]And now, O God of Israel, let your word that you promised[y] your servant David my father come true.

[27]"But will God really dwell[z] on earth? The heavens, even the highest heaven,[a] cannot contain[b] you. How much less this temple I have built! [28]Yet give attention to your servant's prayer and his plea for mercy, O LORD my God. Hear the cry and the prayer that your servant is praying in your presence this day. [29]May your eyes be open[c] toward[d] this temple night and day, this place of which you said, 'My Name[e] shall be there,' so that you will hear the prayer your servant prays toward this place. [30]Hear the supplication of your servant and of your people Israel when they pray[f] toward this place. Hear[g] from heaven, your dwelling place, and when you hear, forgive.[h]

[31]"When a man wrongs his neighbor and is required to take an oath and he comes and swears the oath[i] before your altar in this temple, [32]then hear from heaven and act. Judge between your servants, condemning the guilty and bringing down on his own head what he has done. Declare the innocent not guilty, and so establish his innocence.[j]

[33]"When your people Israel have been defeated[k] by an enemy because they have sinned[l] against you, and when they turn back to you and confess your name, praying and making supplication to you in this temple,[m] [34]then hear from heaven and forgive the sin of your people Israel and bring them back to the land you gave to their fathers.

[35]"When the heavens are shut up and there is no rain[n] because your people have sinned[o] against you, and when they pray toward this place and confess your name and turn from their sin because you have afflicted them, [36]then hear from heaven and forgive the sin of your servants, your people Israel. Teach[p] them the right way[q] to live, and send rain[r] on the land you gave your people for an inheritance.

[37]"When famine[s] or plague[t] comes to the land, or blight[u] or mildew, locusts or grasshoppers,[v] or when an enemy besieges them in any of their cities, whatever disaster or disease may come, [38]and when a prayer or plea is made by any of your people Israel—each one aware of the afflictions of his own heart, and spreading out his hands[w] toward this temple— [39]then hear[x] from heaven, your dwelling place. Forgive[y] and act;

8:26 yS 2Sa 7:25
8:27 zAc 7:48; 17:24
aS Dt 10:14
b2Ch 2:6;
Ps 139:7-16;
Isa 66:1;
Jer 23:24
8:29 cver 52;
2Ki 19:16;
2Ch 7:15;
Ne 1:6; Ps 5:1;
31:2; 102:17;
130:2; Isa 37:17
dPs 28:2; 138:2;
Da 6:10
eS Dt 11:12;
12:11; S 2Sa 7:13
8:30 fver 47;
Lev 26:40;
Ne 1:6; Jer 29:12;
Da 9:4 gver 39;
Ps 34:6
hS Ex 34:7,9;
Lev 26:40-42;
Ps 85:2
8:31 iS Ex 22:11
8:32 jDt 25:1;
Eze 18:20

8:33
kS Lev 26:17
lLev 26:39
mIsa 37:1,14,38
8:35
nS Dt 28:24;
S 2Sa 1:21
oJer 5:25
8:36 pS Dt 8:3;
S 1Sa 12:23
qPs 5:8; 27:11;
107:7; Pr 11:5;
Isa 45:13;
Jer 6:16; 7:23;
31:21 rver 35;
1Ki 17:1; 18:1,
45; Jer 5:24;
10:3; 14:22;
Zec 10:1
8:37
sS Lev 26:26
tS Ex 30:12;
S Lev 26:25
uS Dt 28:22
vS Ex 10:13;

Ps 105:34 **8:38** wS Ex 9:29 **8:39** xS ver 30 yPs 130:4

8:27 *How much less this temple I have built!* With the construction of the temple and the appearance of a visible manifestation of the presence of God within its courts, the erroneous notion that God was irreversibly and exclusively bound to the temple in a way that guaranteed his assistance to Israel no matter how the people lived could very easily arise (see Jer 7:4–14; Mic 3:11). Solomon confessed that even though God had chosen to dwell among his people in a special and localized way, he far transcended containment by anything in all creation.
8:29 *My Name.* I the Lord (see note on 5:5).
8:30 *pray toward this place.* When an Israelite was unable to pray in the temple itself, he was to direct his prayers toward the place where God had pledged to be present among his people (see Da 6:10). *heaven, your dwelling place.* See note on v. 27.
8:31 *required to take an oath.* In cases such as default in pledges (Ex 22:10–12) or alleged adultery (Nu 5:11–31), when there was insufficient evidence to establish the legitimacy of the charge, the supposed offender was required to take an oath of innocence at the sanctuary. Such an oath, with its attendant blessings and curses, was considered a divinely given means of determining innocence or guilt since the consequences of the oath became apparent in the life of the individual either by his experiencing the blessing or the curse or by direct divine revelation through the Urim and Thummim (see Ex 28:29–30; Lev 8:8; Nu 27:21).
8:32 *hear from heaven.* It is clear that Solomon viewed the oath as an appeal to God to act and not as an automatic

power that worked in a magical way.
8:33 *defeated by an enemy because they have sinned against you.* Defeat by enemies was listed in Dt 28:25 as one of the curses that would come on Israel if she disobeyed the covenant. Solomon's prayer reflects an awareness of the covenant obligations the Lord had placed on his people and a knowledge of the consequences that disobedience would entail.
8:34 *bring them back to the land.* A reference to prisoners taken in battle.
8:35 *no rain.* Drought was another of the covenant curses listed in Dt 28:22–24.
8:36 *right way to live.* In accordance with covenant obligations (see Dt 6:18; 12:25; 13:18; 1Sa 12:23).
8:37 *famine.* See Dt 32:24. *plague.* See Dt 28:21–22; 32:24. *locusts or grasshoppers.* See Dt 28:38,42. *an enemy besieges them in any of their cities.* See Dt 28:52. *disaster.* See Dt 28:61; 31:29; 32:23–25. *disease.* See Dt 28:22.
8:38 *aware of the afflictions of his own heart.* Conscious of one's guilt before God, with an attitude of repentance and the desire for God's forgiveness and grace (see 2Ch 6:29; Ps 38:17–18; Jer 17:9).
8:39 *deal with each man according to all he does.* Not to be viewed as a request for retribution for the wrong committed (forgiveness and retribution are mutually exclusive), but as a desire for whatever discipline God in his wisdom may use to correct his people and to instruct them in the way of the covenant (see v. 40; Pr 3:11; Heb 12:5–15).

deal with each man according to all he does, since you know[z] his heart (for you alone know the hearts of all men), [40]so that they will fear[a] you all the time they live in the land[b] you gave our fathers.

[41]"As for the foreigner[c] who does not belong to your people Israel but has come from a distant land because of your name— [42]for men will hear[d] of your great name and your mighty hand[e] and your outstretched arm—when he comes and prays toward this temple, [43]then hear from heaven, your dwelling place, and do whatever the foreigner asks of you, so that all the peoples of the earth may know[f] your name and fear[g] you, as do your own people Israel, and may know that this house I have built bears your Name.[h]

[44]"When your people go to war against their enemies, wherever you send them, and when they pray[i] to the LORD toward the city you have chosen and the temple I have built for your Name, [45]then hear from heaven their prayer and their plea, and uphold their cause.[j]

[46]"When they sin against you—for there is no one who does not sin[k]—and you become angry with them and give them over to the enemy, who takes them captive[l] to his own land, far away or near; [47]and if they have a change of heart in the land where they are held captive, and repent and plead[m] with you in the land of their conquerors and say, 'We have sinned, we have done wrong, we have acted wickedly';[n] [48]and if they turn back[o] to you with all their heart[p] and soul in the land of their

enemies who took them captive, and pray[q] to you toward the land you gave their fathers, toward the city you have chosen and the temple[r] I have built for your Name;[s] [49]then from heaven, your dwelling place, hear their prayer and their plea, and uphold their cause. [50]And forgive your people, who have sinned against you; forgive all the offenses they have committed against you, and cause their conquerors to show them mercy;[t] [51]for they are your people and your inheritance,[u] whom you brought out of Egypt, out of that iron-smelting furnace.[v]

[52]"May your eyes be open[w] to your servant's plea and to the plea of your people Israel, and may you listen to them whenever they cry out to you.[x] [53]For you singled them out from all the nations of the world to be your own inheritance,[y] just as you declared through your servant Moses when you, O Sovereign LORD, brought our fathers out of Egypt."

[54]When Solomon had finished all these prayers and supplications to the LORD, he rose from before the altar of the LORD, where he had been kneeling with his hands spread out toward heaven. [55]He stood and blessed[z] the whole assembly of Israel in a loud voice, saying:

[56]"Praise be to the LORD, who has given rest[a] to his people Israel just as he promised. Not one word has failed of all the good promises[b] he gave through his servant Moses. [57]May the LORD our God be with us as he was with our fathers; may he never leave us nor forsake[c] us. [58]May he turn our

Cross references (center column)

8:39
[z]S Jos 22:22;
S Ps 44:21;
Jn 2:24;
S Rev 2:23
8:40 [a]ver 39-40;
Dt 6:13;
Ps 103:11; 130:4
[b]S Dt 12:1
8:41
[c]S Ge 31:15;
Isa 56:3,6; 61:5
8:42 [d]1Ki 10:1;
Isa 60:3; Ac 8:27
[e]Dt 3:24
8:43 [f]S Jos 4:24;
S 1Sa 17:46
[g]Ps 102:15
[h]S Dt 28:10
8:44 [i]1Ch 5:20;
2Ch 14:11
8:45 [j]Ps 9:4;
140:12
8:46 [k]Ps 130:3;
143:2; Pr 20:9;
S Ro 3:9
[l]Lev 26:33-39;
S Dt 4:27;
S 21:10; S 28:64;
2Ki 25:21
8:47 [m]S ver 30;
S Lev 5:5;
Ezr 9:15; Ne 1:6;
Jer 14:20
[n]Ezr 9:7;
Ps 106:6; Jer 3:25
8:48 [o]S Dt 4:30
[p]S Dt 4:29

[q]1Jn 1:8-10
[r]Ps 5:7; 11:4;
Jnh 2:4
[s]Dt 12:11-14;
Ne 1:9; Jer 23:3;
31:8
8:50 [t]2Ki 25:28;
2Ch 30:9;
Ps 106:46; Da 1:9
8:51 [u]S Ex 34:9;
S Dt 9:29
[v]S Ex 1:13;
Isa 48:10;
Jer 11:4
8:52 [w]S ver 29
[x]Job 30:20;
Ps 3:4; 22:2;
77:1; 142:1
8:53 [y]Ex 19:5;
S 34:9
8:55
[z]S Ex 39:43;
Nu 6:23
8:56
[a]S Ex 33:14;
Dt 12:10; Heb 4:8
[b]S Jos 23:15;
S Jer 29:10

8:57 [c]S Dt 4:31; S 31:6; S Mt 28:20; Heb 13:5

8:40 *fear you.* Honor and obediently serve you (see Dt 5:29; 6:1-2; 8:6; 31:13; 2Ch 6:31; Ps 130:4).
8:41 *foreigner who does not belong to your people Israel.* One who comes from a foreign land to pray to Israel's God at the temple, as distinguished from a resident alien.
8:42 *men will hear.* See 9:9 (foreign nations generally); 10:1 (queen of Sheba); Jos 2:9-11 (Rahab); 1Sa 4:6-8 (Philistines). *your great name and your mighty hand and your outstretched arm.* God's great power, demonstrated by his interventions in the history of his people (see Dt 4:34; 5:15; 7:19; 11:2; 26:8).
8:44 *go to war . . . wherever you send them.* Military initiatives undertaken with divine sanction (see, e.g., Lev 26:7; Dt 20; 21:10; 1Sa 15:3; 23:2,4; 30:8; 2Sa 5:19,24). *toward the city you have chosen.* See note on v. 30.
8:46 *the enemy, who takes them captive.* On the basis of Lev 26:33-45; Dt 28:64-68; 30:1-5 Solomon knew that stubborn disobedience would lead to exile from the promised land.

8:51 *iron-smelting furnace.* See Dt 4:20 and note.
8:53 *you singled them out . . . to be your own inheritance.* Solomon began his prayer with an appeal to the Davidic covenant (vv. 23-30), and he closes with an appeal to the Sinaitic covenant (see Ex 19:5; Lev 20:24,26; Dt 7:6; 32:9).
8:54 *he had been kneeling.* Cf. v. 22; 2Sa 7:18; 2Ch 6:13; Lk 22:41; Eph 3:14.
8:56 *Praise be to the LORD.* Solomon understood this historic day to be a testimony to God's covenant faithfulness. *rest to his people.* After the conquest of Canaan under the leadership of Joshua, the Lord gave the Israelites a period of rest from their enemies (Jos 11:23; 21:44; 22:4), even though there remained much land to be possessed (Jos 13:1; Jdg 1). It was only with David's victories that the rest was made durable and complete (see 2Sa 7:1; see also note on 1Ki 5:4).
8:58 *turn our hearts to him.* Solomon asks for a divine work of grace within his people that will enable them to be faithful to the covenant (see Dt 30:6; Ps 51:10; Php 2:13).

hearts[d] to him, to walk in all his ways and to keep the commands, decrees and regulations he gave our fathers. [59]And may these words of mine, which I have prayed before the LORD, be near to the LORD our God day and night, that he may uphold the cause of his servant and the cause of his people Israel according to each day's need, [60]so that all the peoples[e] of the earth may know that the LORD is God and that there is no other.[f] [61]But your hearts[g] must be fully committed[h] to the LORD our God, to live by his decrees and obey his commands, as at this time."

The Dedication of the Temple

8:62–66pp — 2Ch 7:1–10

[62]Then the king and all Israel with him offered sacrifices[i] before the LORD. [63]Solomon offered a sacrifice of fellowship offerings[y] to the LORD: twenty-two thousand cattle and a hundred and twenty thousand sheep and goats. So the king and all the Israelites dedicated[j] the temple of the LORD.

[64]On that same day the king consecrated the middle part of the courtyard in front of the temple of the LORD, and there he offered burnt offerings, grain offerings and the fat[k] of the fellowship offerings, because the bronze altar[l] before the LORD was too small to hold the burnt offerings, the grain offerings and the fat of the fellowship offerings.[m]

[65]So Solomon observed the festival[n] at that time, and all Israel with him—a vast assembly, people from Lebo[z] Hamath[o] to the Wadi of Egypt.[p] They celebrated it before the LORD our God for seven days and seven days more, fourteen days in all. [66]On

8:58 [d]S Jos 24:23
8:60 [e]S Jos 4:24
/S Dt 4:35
8:61 [g]Dt 6:5
[h]1Ki 9:4; 11:4;
15:3,14; 22:43;
2Ki 20:3;
1Ch 28:9; 29:19;
2Ch 16:9; 17:6;
25:2; Ps 119:80;
Isa 38:3
8:62 [i]S 2Sa 6:13;
1Ch 29:21;
Eze 45:17
8:63 /Ezr 6:16
8:64 [k]S Ex 29:13
/S Ex 27:1;
2Ki 16:14;
2Ch 4:1; 8:12;
15:8;
Eze 43:13-17
[m]S 2Sa 6:17
8:65 [n]S ver 2
[o]S Nu 13:21
[p]S Ge 15:18

8:66 [q]S Ex 18:9
9:1 [r]S 2Sa 7:2
9:2 [s]S 1Ki 3:5
9:3 [t]S 1Sa 9:16;
2Ki 19:20; 20:5;
Ps 10:17; 34:17
[u]S Ex 20:24;
S Dt 12:5
[v]S Dt 11:12
9:4 [w]S Ge 17:1
[x]Dt 17:20;
1Ki 14:8; 15:5
[y]S 1Ki 3:14;
1Ch 28:9; Pr 4:4
9:5 [z]1Ch 22:10
[a]S 2Sa 7:15
9:6 [b]Dt 28:15;
2Sa 7:14;
2Ki 18:12;
Jer 17:27; 26:4;
32:23; 44:23
[c]1Ki 11:10
9:7
[d]Lev 18:24-28;
Dt 4:26;
S Jos 23:13;
2Ki 17:23;
Jer 24:10
[e]Dt 12:5; Jer 7:14
/Job 17:6;
Ps 44:14;
Jer 24:9; Joel 2:17
[g]S Dt 28:37;
Eze 5:15

the following day he sent the people away. They blessed the king and then went home, joyful and glad in heart for all the good[q] things the LORD had done for his servant David and his people Israel.

The LORD Appears to Solomon

9:1–9pp — 2Ch 7:11–22

9 When Solomon had finished[r] building the temple of the LORD and the royal palace, and had achieved all he had desired to do, [2]the LORD appeared[s] to him a second time, as he had appeared to him at Gibeon. [3]The LORD said to him:

"I have heard[t] the prayer and plea you have made before me; I have consecrated this temple, which you have built, by putting my Name[u] there forever. My eyes[v] and my heart will always be there.

[4]"As for you, if you walk before me in integrity of heart[w] and uprightness, as David[x] your father did, and do all I command and observe my decrees and laws,[y] [5]I will establish[z] your royal throne over Israel forever, as I promised David your father when I said, 'You shall never fail[a] to have a man on the throne of Israel.'

[6]"But if you[a] or your sons turn away[b] from me and do not observe the commands and decrees I have given you[a] and go off to serve other gods[c] and worship them, [7]then I will cut off Israel from the land[d] I have given them and will reject this temple I have consecrated for my Name.[e] Israel will then become a byword[f] and an object of ridicule[g] among all peo-

[y]63 Traditionally *peace offerings*; also in verse 64 [z]65 Or *from the entrance to* [a]6 The Hebrew is plural.

8:59 *his servant.* The king, who, as the Lord's anointed, serves as the earthly representative of God's rule over his people (see notes on Ps 2:2,7).

8:60 *so that all . . . may know.* See note on Ps 46:10.

8:63 *fellowship offerings.* Involved a communion meal (see note on 1Sa 11:15). *twenty-two thousand cattle and a hundred and twenty thousand sheep and goats.* Although these numbers may seem large, there were vast numbers of people who participated in the dedication ceremony, which lasted 14 days (see vv. 1–2; see also v. 65).

8:65 *Lebo Hamath.* See note on Eze 47:15. *Wadi of Egypt.* Probably Wadi el-Arish (see note on Ge 15:18). People came to Jerusalem for the dedication of the temple from nearly the entire area of Solomon's dominion (see note on 4:21). *seven days and seven days more, fourteen days in all.* It appears that the seven-day celebration for the dedication of the temple was followed by the seven-day Feast of Tabernacles (see note on v. 2), which was observed from the 15th to the 21st of the seventh month. According to Chronicles, this was followed by a final assembly on the next day, in accordance

with Lev 23:33–36; then on the 23rd of the month the people were sent to their homes (see 2Ch 7:8–10).

9:1 *When Solomon had finished.* At the earliest this would be in the 24th year (4+7+13=24) of Solomon's reign—946 B.C. (see 6:1,37–38; 7:1; 9:10).

9:2 *he had appeared to him at Gibeon.* See 3:4–15.

9:3 *putting my Name there forever.* See 8:10–13. *My eyes and my heart will always be there.* See 8:29.

9:4–5 *if you walk before me in integrity of heart . . . I will establish your royal throne over Israel forever.* See 8:25 and note on 2:4. The Lord reemphasizes to Solomon the importance of obedience to the covenant in order to experience its blessings rather than its curses. This was particularly necessary as Solomon's kingdom grew in influence and wealth, with all the potential for covenant-breaking that prosperity brought (see Dt 8:12–14,17; 31:20; 32:15).

9:6 *serve other gods and worship them.* See 11:4–8.

9:7 *a byword and an object of ridicule among all peoples.* See the covenant curse in Dt 28:37.

ples. [8]And though this temple is now imposing, all who pass by will be appalled[h] and will scoff and say, 'Why has the LORD done such a thing to this land and to this temple?'[i] [9]People will answer,[j] 'Because they have forsaken[k] the LORD their God, who brought their fathers out of Egypt, and have embraced other gods, worshiping and serving them—that is why the LORD brought all this disaster[l] on them.' "

Solomon's Other Activities

9:10–28pp — 2Ch 8:1–18

[10]At the end of twenty years, during which Solomon built these two buildings—the temple of the LORD and the royal palace— [11]King Solomon gave twenty towns in Galilee to Hiram king of Tyre, because Hiram had supplied him with all the cedar and pine and gold[m] he wanted. [12]But when Hiram went from Tyre to see the towns that Solomon had given him, he was not pleased with them. [13]"What kind of towns are these you have given me, my brother?" he asked. And he called them the Land of Cabul,[b][n] a name they have to this day. [14]Now Hiram had sent to the king 120 talents[c] of gold.[o]

[15]Here is the account of the forced labor King Solomon conscripted[p] to build the LORD's temple, his own palace, the supporting terraces,[d][q] the wall of Jerusalem, and Hazor,[r] Megiddo and Gezer.[s] [16](Pharaoh king of Egypt had attacked and captured Gezer. He had set it on fire. He

killed its Canaanite inhabitants and then gave it as a wedding gift to his daughter,[t] Solomon's wife. [17]And Solomon rebuilt Gezer.) He built up Lower Beth Horon,[u] [18]Baalath,[v] and Tadmor[e] in the desert, within his land, [19]as well as all his store cities[w] and the towns for his chariots[x] and for his horses[f]—whatever he desired to build in Jerusalem, in Lebanon and throughout all the territory he ruled.

[20]All the people left from the Amorites, Hittites,[y] Perizzites, Hivites and Jebusites[z] (these peoples were not Israelites), [21]that is, their descendants[a] remaining in the land, whom the Israelites could not exterminate[g][b]—these Solomon conscripted for his slave labor force,[c] as it is to this day. [22]But Solomon did not make slaves[d] of any of the Israelites; they were his fighting men, his government officials, his officers, his captains, and the commanders of his chariots and charioteers. [23]They were also the chief officials[e] in charge of Solomon's projects—550 officials supervising the men who did the work.

[24]After Pharaoh's daughter[f] had come up from the City of David to the palace Solomon had built for her, he constructed the supporting terraces.[g]

[25]Three[h] times a year Solomon sacrificed burnt offerings and fellowship offer-

Cross references (center column)

9:8 [h]S Lev 26:32
[i]S Dt 29:24;
Jer 7:4-15;
Mt 23:38
9:9 [j]Dt 29:25;
2Ki 22:17;
Jer 5:19; 13:22;
16:11,13; 22:9
[k]S Nu 25:3;
Jer 40:3; 44:23;
La 4:12
[l]S Dt 31:29
9:11 [m]ver 14
9:13 [n]Jos 19:27
9:14 [o]ver 11
9:15 [p]1Ki 5:13
[q]S 2Sa 5:9
[r]Jos 11:10-11
[s]S Jos 10:33

9:16 [t]1Ki 3:1;
Ps 45:12; 68:29;
72:10
9:17 [u]S Jos 10:10
9:18 [v]S Jos 19:44
9:19 [w]S Ex 1:11
[x]S Dt 17:16;
1Ki 4:26;
2Ch 1:14; 9:25
9:20 [y]S Nu 13:29
[z]S Jos 11:3
9:21
[a]S Ge 9:25-26
[b]S Jos 15:63
[c]S Ge 49:15;
S Ex 1:11;
S Dt 20:11
9:22
[d]S Lev 25:39
9:23 [e]1Ki 5:16
9:24 [f]S 1Ki 3:1
[g]2Sa 5:9;
1Ki 11:27
9:25 [h]S Ex 23:14

Text notes (center column footnotes)

[b]13 Cabul sounds like the Hebrew for good-for-nothing.
[c]14 That is, about 4 1/2 tons (about 4 metric tons)
[d]15 Or the Millo; also in verse 24   [e]18 The Hebrew may also be read Tamar.   [f]19 Or charioteers
[g]21 The Hebrew term refers to the irrevocable giving over of things or persons to the LORD, often by totally destroying them.

9:9 that is why the LORD brought all this disaster on them. See Dt 29:22–28; Jer 22:8–30.

9:10–28 See map No. 5 at the end of the Study Bible.

9:11 Solomon gave twenty towns in Galilee to Hiram king of Tyre. Comparison of vv. 10–14 with 5:1–12 suggests that during Solomon's 20 years of building activity he became more indebted to Hiram than anticipated in their original agreement (see note on 5:9), which had provided for payment for labor (5:6) and wood (5:10–11). From vv. 11,14 it is evident that in addition to wood and labor Solomon had also acquired great quantities of gold from Hiram. It appears that Solomon gave Hiram the 20 towns in the Phoenician-Galilee border area as a surety for repayment of the gold. 2Ch 8:1–2 indicates that at some later date when Solomon's gold reserves were increased, perhaps after the return of the expedition to Ophir (1Ki 9:26–28; 10:11) or the visit of the queen of Sheba (10:1–13), he settled his debt with Hiram and recovered the 20 towns held as collateral.

9:15 forced labor. Non-Israelite slave labor of a permanent nature (in contrast to the temporary conscription of Israelite workmen described in 5:13–16). supporting terraces. Probably for Solomon's expansion of Jerusalem on the ridge north from David's city (see note on 2Sa 5:9). Hazor. Solomon's building activity at Hazor, Megiddo and Gezer was intended to strengthen the fortifications of these ancient, strategically located towns (Solomonic gates, probably built by the same

masons, have been found at all three sites). Hazor was the most important fortress in the northern Galilee area, controlling the trade route running from the Euphrates River to Egypt. Megiddo. Another fortress along the great north-south trade route; it commanded the pass through the Carmel range from the plain of Jezreel to the coastal plain of Sharon. Gezer. See note on 3:1.

9:16 killed its Canaanite inhabitants. Although Joshua had killed the king of Gezer at the time of the conquest (Jos 10:33; 12:12), the tribe of Ephraim had been unable to drive out its inhabitants (Jos 16:10; Jdg 1:29).

9:17 Lower Beth Horon. Located about eight miles northwest of Jerusalem at a pass giving entrance to the Judahite highlands and Jerusalem from the coastal plain.

9:18 Baalath. To be identified with either the Bealoth of Jos 15:24 located to the south of Hebron in the tribe of Judah or the Baalath southwest of Beth Horon in the tribe of Dan (Jos 19:44). Tadmor. See NIV text note; see also 2Ch 8:4; Eze 47:19.

9:20 Amorites . . . Jebusites. See Dt 7:1; 20:17; see also notes on Ge 10:15–18; 13:7; 15:16; 23:9; Jos 5:1; Jdg 3:3; 6:10; 2Sa 21:2.

9:22 Solomon did not make slaves of any of the Israelites. See note on v. 15.

9:23 550 officials. See note on 5:16.

9:25 Three times a year. On the occasion of the three

ings[h] on the altar he had built for the LORD, burning incense before the LORD along with them, and so fulfilled the temple obligations.

26King Solomon also built ships[i] at Ezion Geber,[j] which is near Elath[k] in Edom, on the shore of the Red Sea.[i] 27And Hiram sent his men—sailors[l] who knew the sea—to serve in the fleet with Solomon's men. 28They sailed to Ophir[m] and brought back 420 talents[j] of gold,[n] which they delivered to King Solomon.

The Queen of Sheba Visits Solomon

10:1–13pp — 2Ch 9:1–12

10 When the queen of Sheba[o] heard about the fame[p] of Solomon and his relation to the name of the LORD, she came to test him with hard questions.[q] 2Arriving at Jerusalem with a very great caravan[r]—with camels carrying spices, large quantities of gold, and precious stones—she came to Solomon and talked with him about all that she had on her mind. 3Solomon answered all her questions; nothing was too hard for the king to explain to her. 4When the queen of Sheba saw all the wisdom of Solomon and the palace he had built, 5the food on his table,[s] the seating of his officials, the attending servants in their robes, his cupbearers, and the burnt offerings he made at[k] temple of the LORD, she was overwhelmed.

6She said to the king, "The report I

heard in my own country about your achievements and your wisdom is true. 7But I did not believe[t] these things until I came and saw with my own eyes. Indeed, not even half was told me; in wisdom and wealth[u] you have far exceeded the report I heard. 8How happy your men must be! How happy your officials, who continually stand before you and hear[v] your wisdom! 9Praise[w] be to the LORD your God, who has delighted in you and placed you on the throne of Israel. Because of the LORD's eternal love[x] for Israel, he has made you king, to maintain justice[y] and righteousness."

10And she gave the king 120 talents[l] of gold,[z] large quantities of spices, and precious stones. Never again were so many spices brought in as those the queen of Sheba gave to King Solomon.

11(Hiram's ships brought gold from Ophir;[a] and from there they brought great cargoes of almugwood[m] and precious stones. 12The king used the almugwood to make supports for the temple of the LORD and for the royal palace, and to make harps and lyres for the musicians. So much almugwood has never been imported or seen since that day.)

13King Solomon gave the queen of

Cross references (center column)

9:26 /1Ki 10:22; 22:48;
2Ch 20:37;
Isa 2:16
/S Nu 33:35
*k*2Ki 14:22; 16:6
9:27 /Eze 27:8
9:28
*m*S Ge 10:29 *n*ver 14; 1Ki 10:10,11, 14,21; 2Ch 1:15; Ecc 2:8
10:1 *o*S Ge 10:7, 28; S 25:3; Mt 12:42; Lk 11:31
*p*Eze 16:14
*q*S Nu 12:8; S Jdg 14:12
10:2 *r*S Ge 24:10
10:5 *s*1Ki 4:22

10:7 *t*S Ge 45:26
*u*1Ch 29:25
10:8 *v*Pr 8:34
10:9 *w*S 1Ki 5:7; S Isa 42:10
*x*S Dt 7:8
*y*Ps 11:7; 33:5; 72:2; 99:4; 103:6
10:10
*z*S 1Ki 9:28; Isa 60:6
10:11
*a*S Ge 10:29

Footnotes (center bottom)

h25 Traditionally *peace offerings*   i26 Hebrew *Yam Suph*; that is, Sea of Reeds   j28 That is, about 16 tons (about 14.5 metric tons)   k5 Or *the ascent by which he went up to*   l10 That is, about 4 1/2 tons (about 4 metric tons)   m11 Probably a variant of *algumwood*; also in verse 12

important annual festivals: the Feast of Unleavened Bread, the Feast of Weeks, and the Feast of Tabernacles (see Ex 23:14–17; 2Ch 8:13).

9:26 *ships.* Used in a large trading business that brought great wealth to Solomon's court (see v. 28; 10:11). *Ezion Geber.* Located at the northern tip of the Gulf of Aqaba (see 22:48; Nu 33:35; Dt 2:8). *Red Sea.* The Hebrew for this term, normally read as *Yam Suph* ("sea of reeds"; see NIV text note), refers to the body of water through which the Israelites passed at the time of the exodus (see notes on Ex 13:18; 14:2). It can also be read, however, as *Yam Soph* ("sea of land's end"), a more likely reading when referring to the Red Sea, and especially (as here) to its eastern arm (the Gulf of Aqaba).

9:28 *Ophir.* A source for gold (2Ch 8:18; Job 28:16; Ps 45:9; Isa 13:12), almugwood and precious stones (10:11), and silver, ivory, apes and baboons (10:22). Its location is disputed: Southeastern Arabia, southwestern Arabia, the northeastern African coast (in the area of Somalia), India and Zimbabwe have all been suggested. If Ophir was located in Arabia, it was probably a trading center for goods from farther east as well as from east Africa. But the three-year voyages of Solomon's merchant vessels (10:22) suggest a more distant location than the Arabian coast.

10:1 *Sheba.* Archaeological evidence suggests that Sheba is to be identified with a mercantile kingdom that flourished in southwest Arabia (see notes on Ge 10:28; Joel 3:8) c. 900–450 B.C. It profited from the sea trade of India and east

Africa by transporting luxury commodities north to Damascus and Gaza on caravan routes through the Arabian Desert. It is possible that Solomon's fleet of ships threatened Sheba's continued dominance of this trading business. *his relation to the name of the LORD.* The queen of Sheba recognized a connection between the wisdom of Solomon and the God he served. Jesus used her example to condemn the people of his own day who had not recognized that "one greater than Solomon" was in their midst (Mt 12:42; Lk 11:31).

10:9 *Praise be to the LORD your God.* The queen of Sheba's confession is beautifully worded and reflects a profound understanding of Israel's covenant relationship with the Lord. However, it does not necessarily imply anything more than her recognition of the Lord as Israel's national God in conformity with the ideas of polytheistic paganism (see note on 5:7; see also 2Ch 2:12; Da 3:28–29). There is no confession that Solomon's God has become her God to the exclusion of all others.

10:10 *120 talents of gold.* See notes on 9:11,28.

10:11 *Hiram's ships.* See 9:26–28. Hiram had supplied the wood, the sailors and the expertise in construction that Israel lacked. *almugwood.* See NIV text note and 2Ch 9:10–11. Its identity is unknown, though some suggest it is juniper. It was apparently available from Lebanon as well as Ophir (2Ch 2:8).

10:13 *all she desired and asked for.* The exchange of gifts between Solomon and the queen may have signified the effecting of a trade agreement (see note on v. 1). There is no

Sheba all she desired and asked for, besides what he had given her out of his royal bounty. Then she left and returned with her retinue to her own country.

Solomon's Splendor

10:14–29pp — 2Ch 1:14–17; 9:13–28

14The weight of the gold[b] that Solomon received yearly was 666 talents,[n] 15not including the revenues from merchants and traders and from all the Arabian kings and the governors of the land.

16King Solomon made two hundred large shields[c] of hammered gold; six hundred bekas[o] of gold went into each shield. 17He also made three hundred small shields of hammered gold, with three minas[p] of gold in each shield. The king put them in the Palace of the Forest of Lebanon.[d]

18Then the king made a great throne inlaid with ivory and overlaid with fine gold. 19The throne had six steps, and its back had a rounded top. On both sides of the seat were armrests, with a lion standing beside each of them. 20Twelve lions stood on the six steps, one at either end of each step. Nothing like it had ever been made for any other kingdom. 21All King Solomon's goblets were gold, and all the household articles in the Palace of the Forest of Lebanon were pure gold.[e] Nothing was made of silver, because silver was considered of little value in Solomon's days. 22The king had a fleet of trading ships[q][f] at sea along with the ships[g] of Hiram. Once every three years it returned, carrying gold, silver and ivory, and apes and baboons.

23King Solomon was greater in riches[h] and wisdom[i] than all the other kings of the earth. 24The whole world sought audience with Solomon to hear the wisdom[j] God had put in his heart. 25Year after year, everyone who came brought a gift[k]—articles of silver and gold, robes, weapons and spices, and horses and mules.

26Solomon accumulated chariots and horses;[l] he had fourteen hundred chariots and twelve thousand horses,[r] which he kept in the chariot cities and also with him in Jerusalem. 27The king made silver as common[m] in Jerusalem as stones,[n] and cedar as plentiful as sycamore-fig[o] trees in the foothills. 28Solomon's horses were imported from Egypt[s] and from Kue[t]—the royal merchants purchased them from Kue. 29They imported a chariot from Egypt for six hundred shekels[u] of silver, and a horse for a hundred and fifty.[v] They also exported them to all the kings of the Hittites[p] and of the Arameans.

Solomon's Wives

11 King Solomon, however, loved many foreign women[q] besides Pharaoh's daughter—Moabites, Ammonites,[r] Edomites, Sidonians and Hittites. 2They were from nations about which the Lord had told the Israelites, "You must not intermarry[s] with them, because they will surely turn your hearts after their gods." Nevertheless, Solomon held fast to them in love. 3He had seven hundred wives of royal birth and three hundred

Cross references

10:14
bS 1Ki 9:28
10:16 cS 2Sa 8:7
10:17 dS 1Ki 7:2
10:21 eIsa 60:17
10:22 fS 1Ki 9:26
gS 1Ki 9:27;
Ps 48:7; Isa 2:16;
23:1,14; 60:6,9
10:23 hS 1Ki 3:13;
Mt 6:29
iS 1Ki 3:12;
Mt 12:42

10:24
jS 2Sa 14:20
10:25
kS 1Sa 10:27
10:26
lS Dt 17:16
10:27 mDt 17:17
nJob 27:16;
Isa 60:17
oS 1Ch 27:28;
Am 7:14
10:29
pS Nu 13:29
11:1 qS ver 3;
S Ex 34:16
rS 1Ki 14:21,31
11:2 sS Ex 34:16;
1Ki 16:31

n14 That is, about 25 tons (about 23 metric tons)
o16 That is, about 7 1/2 pounds (about 3.5 kilograms)
p17 That is, about 3 3/4 pounds (about 1.7 kilograms)
q22 Hebrew *of ships of Tarshish*   r26 Or *charioteers*
s28 Or possibly *Muzur,* a region in Cilicia; also in verse 29   t28 Probably *Cilicia*   u29 That is, about 15 pounds (about 7 kilograms)   v29 That is, about 3 3/4 pounds (about 1.7 kilograms)

---

basis for the idea sometimes suggested that she desired offspring fathered by Solomon and left Jerusalem carrying his child.
10:15 *revenues from . . . Arabian kings.* Tribute from Bedouin sheiks for passage of their caravans into Israelite territory. *governors of the land.* See 4:7–19.
10:16 *large shields.* Rectangular shields that afforded maximum protection (in distinction from the smaller round shields). These gold shields were probably not intended for battle but for ceremonial use, symbolizing Israel's wealth and glory. They were probably made of wood overlaid with gold. Shishak of Egypt carried them off as plunder in the fifth regnal year of Solomon's son Rehoboam (see 14:25–26).
10:22 *fleet of trading ships.* See NIV text note; 2Ch 9:21. The same fleet is referred to in v. 11; 9:26–28. "Ships of Tarshish" are not necessarily ships that sail to Tarshish (see note on Jnh 1:3) but can designate large trading vessels.
10:26 *chariots and horses.* See note on 4:26. Accumulation of chariots and horses by the king was forbidden in the Mosaic law (Dt 17:16).
10:29 *exported them.* Through his agents Solomon was the middleman in a lucrative trading business. It appears that

he acquired horses from the north (Muzur and Kue in Asia Minor; see NIV text notes on v. 28) and sold them in the south, while at the same time acquiring chariots from the south (Egypt) and selling them in the north. See inset to map No. 4 at the end of the Study Bible.

11:1 *loved many foreign women.* Many of Solomon's marriages were no doubt for the purpose of sealing international relationships with various kingdoms, large and small—a common practice in the ancient Near East. But this violated not only Dt 17:17 with respect to the multiplicity of wives, but also the prohibition against taking wives from the pagan peoples among whom Israel settled (see Ex 34:16; Dt 7:1–3; Jos 23:12–13; Ezr 9:2; 10:2–3; Ne 13:23–27). *Moabites.* See note on Ge 19:36–38. *Ammonites.* See note on Ge 19:36–38; see also 14:21; Dt 23:3. *Edomites.* See notes on Ge 25:26; 36:1; Am 1:11; 9:12; see also Dt 23:7–8. *Sidonians.* See 16:31.

11:2 *they will surely turn your hearts after their gods.* An example in Israel's earlier history is found in Nu 25:1–15.

11:3 *seven hundred . . . three hundred.* Cf. SS 6:8, but see note there.

concubines, t and his wives led him astray. u 4As Solomon grew old, his wives turned his heart after other gods, v and his heart was not fully devoted w to the LORD his God, as the heart of David his father had been. 5He followed Ashtoreth x the goddess of the Sidonians, and Molech w y the detestable god of the Ammonites. 6So Solomon did evil z in the eyes of the LORD; he did not follow the LORD completely, as David his father had done.

7On a hill east a of Jerusalem, Solomon built a high place for Chemosh b the detestable god of Moab, and for Molech c the detestable god of the Ammonites. 8He did the same for all his foreign wives, who burned incense and offered sacrifices to their gods.

9The LORD became angry with Solomon because his heart had turned away from the LORD, the God of Israel, who had appeared d to him twice. 10Although he had forbidden Solomon to follow other gods, e Solomon did not keep the LORD's command. f 11So the LORD said to Solomon, "Since this is your attitude and you have not kept my covenant and my decrees, g which I commanded you, I will most certainly tear h the kingdom away from you and give it to one of your subordinates. 12Nevertheless, for the sake of David i your father, I will not do it during your lifetime. I will tear it out of the hand of your son. 13Yet I will not tear the whole kingdom from him, but will give him one tribe j for the sake k of David my servant and for the sake of Jerusalem, which I have chosen." l

Solomon's Adversaries

14Then the LORD raised up against Solomon an adversary, m Hadad the Edomite, from the royal line of Edom. 15Earlier when David was fighting with Edom, Joab the commander of the army, who had gone up to bury the dead, had struck down all the men in Edom. n 16Joab and all the Israelites stayed there for six months, until they had destroyed all the men in Edom. 17But Hadad, still only a boy, fled to Egypt with some Edomite officials who had served his father. 18They set out from Midian and went to Paran. o Then taking men from Paran with them, they went to Egypt, to Pharaoh king of Egypt, who gave Hadad a house and land and provided him with food.

19Pharaoh was so pleased with Hadad that he gave him a sister of his own wife, Queen Tahpenes, in marriage. 20The sister of Tahpenes bore him a son named Genubath, whom Tahpenes brought up in the royal palace. There Genubath lived with Pharaoh's own children.

21While he was in Egypt, Hadad heard that David rested with his fathers and that Joab the commander of the army was also dead. Then Hadad said to Pharaoh, "Let me go, that I may return to my own country."

22"What have you lacked here that you

11:3 t S Ge 22:24; S Est 2:14 u ver 1;
Dt 17:17;
Ne 13:26; Pr 31:3
11:4 v S Ex 34:16
w S 1Ki 8:61;
S 1Ch 29:19
11:5 x S Jdg 2:13
y ver 7;
S Lev 18:21;
Isa 57:9; Zep 1:5
11:6 z S Dt 4:25
11:7 a 2Ki 23:13
b S Nu 21:29
c S Lev 18:21;
20:2-5; Ac 7:43
11:9 d S 1Ki 3:5
11:10 e S 1Ki 9:6
f 1Ki 6:12
11:11
g S Lev 18:4 h ver
31; S 1Sa 15:27;
2Ki 17:21;
Mt 21:43
11:12 i Ps 89:33
11:13 j 1Ki 12:20
k S 2Sa 7:15
j Dt 12:11
11:14 m S 1Ki 5:4
11:15
n 1Ch 18:12
11:18 o Nu 10:12
w 5 Hebrew Milcom; also in verse 33

11:4 *his heart was not fully devoted to the LORD his God.* See 8:61. The atmosphere of paganism and idolatry introduced into Solomon's court by his foreign wives gradually led Solomon into syncretistic religious practices.
11:5 *Ashtoreth.* See v. 33; 14:15; 2Ki 23:13; see also note on Jdg 2:13. *Molech.* See 2Sa 12:30 and NIV text note. Molech and Milcom (see NIV text note) are alternate names for the same pagan deity. Worship of this god not only severely jeopardized the continued recognition of the absolute kingship of the Lord over his people, but also involved (on rare occasions) the abomination of child sacrifice (see 2Ki 16:3; 17:17; 21:6; Lev 18:21; 20:2-5; see also note on Jdg 10:6).
11:6 *as David his father had done.* Although David committed grievous sins, he was repentant, and he was never involved in idolatrous worship.
11:7 *high place.* See note on 3:2. *Chemosh.* See 2Ki 3:26-27.
11:9 *appeared to him twice.* See 3:4-5; 9:1-9.
11:11 *not kept my covenant.* Solomon had broken the most basic demands of the covenant (see Ex 20:2-5) and thereby severely undermined the entire covenant relationship between God and his people.
11:12 *for the sake of David your father.* Because of David's unwavering loyalty to the Lord and God's covenant with him (see 2Sa 7:11-16).
11:13 *one tribe.* Judah (see note on vv. 31-32; see also

12:20). *for the sake of Jerusalem, which I have chosen.* Now that Jerusalem contained the temple built by David's son in accordance with 2Sa 7:13, the destiny of Jerusalem and the Davidic dynasty were closely linked (see 2Ki 19:34; 21:7-8; Ps 132). The temple represented God's royal palace, where his earthly throne (the ark) was situated and where he had pledged to be present as Israel's Great King (9:3).
11:14 *Hadad.* A familiar name among Edomite kings (see Ge 36:35,39).
11:15 *David was fighting with Edom.* See 2Sa 8:13-14.
11:16 *all the Israelites . . . all the men in Edom.* All those, on both sides, who took part in the campaign.
11:17 *only a boy.* Probably in his early teens.
11:18 *Midian.* At this time Midianites inhabited a region on the eastern borders of Moab and Edom. *Paran.* A desert area southeast of Kadesh in the central area of the Sinai peninsula (see Nu 10:12; 12:16; 13:3). *Pharaoh king of Egypt.* See note on 3:1. *gave Hadad a house and land and . . . food.* In a time of Israel's growing strength it was in Egypt's interest to befriend those who would harass Israel and keep her power in check.
11:21 *Let me go.* It appears that Hadad returned to Edom during the early days of Solomon's reign.
11:22 *What have you lacked here . . . ?* Because Egypt had by this time established relatively good relations with Israel (see note on 3:1), the pharaoh was reluctant to see Hadad return to Edom and provoke trouble with Solomon.

want to go back to your own country?" Pharaoh asked.

"Nothing," Hadad replied, "but do let me go!"

23And God raised up against Solomon another adversary,*p* Rezon son of Eliada, who had fled from his master, Hadadezer*q* king of Zobah. 24He gathered men around him and became the leader of a band of rebels when David destroyed the forces*x* of Zobah₁; the rebels went to Damascus,*r* where they settled and took control. 25Rezon was Israel's adversary as long as Solomon lived, adding to the trouble caused by Hadad. So Rezon ruled in Aram*s* and was hostile toward Israel.

Jeroboam Rebels Against Solomon

26Also, Jeroboam son of Nebat rebelled*t* against the king. He was one of Solomon's officials, an Ephraimite from Zeredah, and his mother was a widow named Zeruah.

27Here is the account of how he rebelled against the king: Solomon had built the supporting terraces*v u* and had filled in the gap in the wall of the city of David his father. 28Now Jeroboam was a man of standing,*v* and when Solomon saw how well*w* the young man did his work, he put him in charge of the whole labor force of the house of Joseph.

29About that time Jeroboam was going out of Jerusalem, and Ahijah*x* the prophet of Shiloh met him on the way, wearing a new cloak. The two of them were alone out in the country, 30and Ahijah took hold of the new cloak he was wearing and tore*y* it into twelve pieces. 31Then he said to Jeroboam, "Take ten pieces for yourself, for this is what the LORD, the God of Israel, says: 'See, I am going to tear*z* the kingdom out of Solomon's hand and give you ten tribes. 32But for the sake*a* of my servant David and the city of Jerusalem, which I have chosen out of all the tribes of Israel, he will have one tribe. 33I will do this because they have*z* forsaken me and worshiped*b* Ashtoreth the goddess of the Sidonians, Chemosh the god of the Moabites, and Molech the god of the Ammonites, and have not walked*c* in my ways, nor done what is right in my eyes, nor kept my statutes*d* and laws as David, Solomon's father, did.

34"'But I will not take the whole kingdom out of Solomon's hand; I have made him ruler all the days of his life for the sake of David my servant, whom I chose and who observed my commands and statutes. 35I will take the kingdom from his son's hands and give you ten tribes. 36I will give one tribe*e* to his son so that David my servant may always have a lamp*f* before me in Jerusalem, the city where I chose to

11:23 *p* S 1Ki 5:4
q S 2Sa 8:3
11:24 *r* S 2Sa 8:5
11:25
s S Ge 10:22;
S 2Sa 10:19
11:26 *t* 2Ch 13:6
11:27
u S 1Ki 9:24
11:28 *v* S Ru 2:1
w S Ge 39:4;
Pr 22:29
11:29
x 1Ki 12:15; 14:2;
2Ch 9:29; 10:15

11:30 *y* 1Sa 15:27
11:31 *z* S ver 11;
S 1Sa 15:27
11:32
a S 2Sa 7:15
11:33 *b* S Jdg 2:13
c 2Ki 21:22
d 1Ki 3:3
11:36 *e* 1Ki 12:17
f S 2Sa 21:17

x 24 Hebrew *destroyed them*   *y 27* Or *the Millo*
z 33 Hebrew; Septuagint, Vulgate and Syriac *because he has*

11:24 *leader of a band of rebels.* As David had been (1Sa 22:1–2), and Jephthah before him (Jdg 11:3). *rebels went to Damascus, where they settled and took control.* Presumably this took place in the early part of Solomon's reign (see 2Sa 8:6 for the situation in Damascus during the time of David). It is likely that Solomon's expedition (2Ch 8:3) against Hamath Zobah (the kingdom formerly ruled by Hadadezer, 2Sa 8:3–6) was provoked by opposition led by Rezon. Even though Solomon was able to retain control of the territory north of Damascus to the Euphrates (4:21,24), he was not able to drive Rezon from Damascus itself.
11:26 *rebelled against the king.* See note on v. 40.
11:27 *supporting terraces.* See 9:15 and note.
11:28 *whole labor force of the house of Joseph.* See 5:13–18. Jeroboam's supervision of the conscripted laborers from the tribes of Ephraim and Manasseh made him aware of the smoldering discontent among the people over Solomon's policies (see 12:4).
11:31–32 *ten tribes . . . one tribe.* The tradition of considering the ten northern tribes as a unit distinct from the southern tribes (Judah and Simeon—Levi received no territorial inheritance; see Jos 21) goes back to the period of the judges (see Jdg 5:14–16). The reason, no doubt, was the continuing presence of a non-Israelite corridor (Jerusalem, Gibeonite league, Gezer) that separated the two Israelite regions (see map No. 3 at the end of the Study Bible). Political division along the same line during the early years of David's reign and the different arrangements that brought the southern and northern segments under David's rule (see 2Sa 2:4; 5:3) reinforced this sense of division. With the conquest of Jerusalem by David (2Sa 5:6–7) and the pharaoh's gift of Gezer to Solomon's wife (9:16–17), all Israel was for the first time territorially united. (Now that Jerusalem and Gezer were under Israelite control, the Gibeonite league, which had submitted already to Joshua—see Jos 9—could be effectively absorbed politically.) In the division here announced, the "one tribe" refers to the area dominated by Judah (but including Simeon; see Jos 19:1–9), and the "ten tribes" refers to the region that came under David's rule at the later date (Ephraim and Manasseh, Joseph's sons, being counted as two tribes; see Ge 48:5; see also note on Jos 14:4). For further refinement of the new boundaries that came about see note on 12:21.

11:33 *forsaken me.* See vv. 5–7. *have not walked in my ways.* See vv. 1–2; 3:14.
11:34 *I have made him ruler all the days of his life.* See vv. 12–13.
11:35 *from his son's hands.* From Rehoboam (see 12:1–24).
11:36 *a lamp before me in Jerusalem.* Symbolizes the continuance of the Davidic dynasty in the city where God had chosen to cause his Name to dwell (see v. 13 and note). In a number of passages, the burning or snuffing out of one's lamp signifies the flourishing or ceasing of one's life (Job 18:6; 21:17; Pr 13:9; 20:20; 24:20). Here (and in 15:4; 2Ki 8:19; 2Ch 21:7; Ps 132:17) the same figure is applied to David's dynasty (see especially Ps 132:17, where "set up a lamp for my anointed" is parallel to "make a horn grow for David"). In David's royal sons his "lamp" continues to burn before the Lord in Jerusalem.

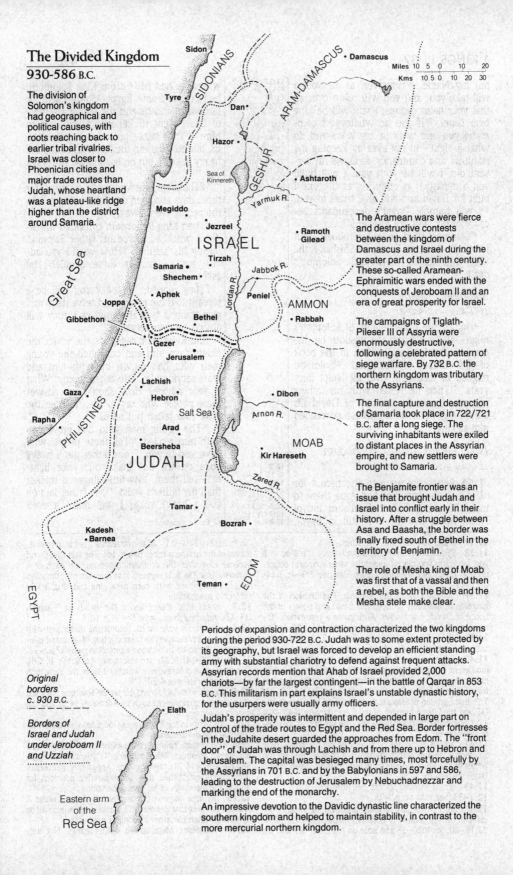

The Divided Kingdom
930-586 B.C.

The division of Solomon's kingdom had geographical and political causes, with roots reaching back to earlier tribal rivalries. Israel was closer to Phoenician cities and major trade routes than Judah, whose heartland was a plateau-like ridge higher than the district around Samaria.

Sidon

Damascus

Miles 10 5 0   10   20
Kms   10 5 0   10   20   30

Tyre

SIDONIANS

ARAM-DAMASCUS

Dan

Hazor

GESHUR

Sea of Kinnereth

Ashtaroth

Megiddo

Yarmuk R.

Jezreel

Ramoth Gilead

ISRAEL

Tirzah

Samaria

Shechem

Jabbok R.

Peniel

AMMON

Joppa

Aphek

Bethel

Rabbah

Gibbethon

Jordan R.

Gezer

Jerusalem

Lachish

Gaza

Hebron

Dibon

Salt Sea

Arnon R.

Rapha

Arad

PHILISTINES

Beersheba

MOAB

JUDAH

Kir Hareseth

Zered R.

Tamar

Bozrah

Kadesh Barnea

EDOM

Teman

EGYPT

Elath

Great Sea

Original borders c. 930 B.C.

Borders of Israel and Judah under Jeroboam II and Uzziah

Eastern arm of the Red Sea

The Aramean wars were fierce and destructive contests between the kingdom of Damascus and Israel during the greater part of the ninth century. These so-called Aramean-Ephraimitic wars ended with the conquests of Jeroboam II and an era of great prosperity for Israel.

The campaigns of Tiglath-Pileser III of Assyria were enormously destructive, following a celebrated pattern of siege warfare. By 732 B.C. the northern kingdom was tributary to the Assyrians.

The final capture and destruction of Samaria took place in 722/721 B.C. after a long siege. The surviving inhabitants were exiled to distant places in the Assyrian empire, and new settlers were brought to Samaria.

The Benjamite frontier was an issue that brought Judah and Israel into conflict early in their history. After a struggle between Asa and Baasha, the border was finally fixed south of Bethel in the territory of Benjamin.

The role of Mesha king of Moab was first that of a vassal and then a rebel, as both the Bible and the Mesha stele make clear.

Periods of expansion and contraction characterized the two kingdoms during the period 930-722 B.C. Judah was to some extent protected by its geography, but Israel was forced to develop an efficient standing army with substantial chariotry to defend against frequent attacks. Assyrian records mention that Ahab of Israel provided 2,000 chariots—by far the largest contingent—in the battle of Qarqar in 853 B.C. This militarism in part explains Israel's unstable dynastic history, for the usurpers were usually army officers.

Judah's prosperity was intermittent and depended in large part on control of the trade routes to Egypt and the Red Sea. Border fortresses in the Judahite desert guarded the approaches from Edom. The "front door" of Judah was through Lachish and from there up to Hebron and Jerusalem. The capital was besieged many times, most forcefully by the Assyrians in 701 B.C. and by the Babylonians in 597 and 586, leading to the destruction of Jerusalem by Nebuchadnezzar and marking the end of the monarchy.

An impressive devotion to the Davidic dynastic line characterized the southern kingdom and helped to maintain stability, in contrast to the more mercurial northern kingdom.

put my Name. 37However, as for you, I will take you, and you will rule^g over all that your heart desires;^h you will be king over Israel. 38If you do whatever I command you and walk in my ways and do what is rightⁱ in my eyes by keeping my statutes^j and commands, as David my servant did, I will be with you. I will build you a dynasty^k as enduring as the one I built for David and will give Israel to you. 39I will humble David's descendants because of this, but not forever.' "

40Solomon tried to kill Jeroboam, but Jeroboam fled^l to Egypt, to Shishak^m the king, and stayed there until Solomon's death.

Solomon's Death

11:41–43pp — 2Ch 9:29–31

41As for the other events of Solomon's reign—all he did and the wisdom he displayed—are they not written in the book of the annals of Solomon? 42Solomon reigned in Jerusalem over all Israel forty years. 43Then he rested with his fathers and was buried in the city of David his father. And Rehoboamⁿ his son succeeded him as king.

Israel Rebels Against Rehoboam

12:1–24pp — 2Ch 10:1–11:4

12 Rehoboam went to Shechem,^o for all the Israelites had gone there to make him king. 2When Jeroboam son of Nebat heard this (he was still in Egypt,

where he had fled^p from King Solomon), he returned from^a Egypt. 3So they sent for Jeroboam, and he and the whole assembly of Israel went to Rehoboam and said to him: 4"Your father put a heavy yoke^q on us, but now lighten the harsh labor and the heavy yoke he put on us, and we will serve you."

5Rehoboam answered, "Go away for three days and then come back to me." So the people went away.

6Then King Rehoboam consulted the elders^r who had served his father Solomon during his lifetime. "How would you advise me to answer these people?" he asked.

7They replied, "If today you will be a servant to these people and serve them and give them a favorable answer,^s they will always be your servants."

8But Rehoboam rejected^t the advice the elders gave him and consulted the young men who had grown up with him and were serving him. 9He asked them, "What is your advice? How should we answer these people who say to me, 'Lighten the yoke your father put on us'?"

10The young men who had grown up with him replied, "Tell these people who have said to you, 'Your father put a heavy yoke on us, but make our yoke lighter'—tell them, 'My little finger is thicker than my father's waist. 11My father laid on you a heavy yoke; I will make it even

Cross references (center column)

11:37 ^g1Ki 14:7
^h2Sa 3:21
11:38
ⁱS Dt 12:25;
S 2Sa 8:15
^jS Dt 17:19
^kS Ex 1:21
11:40 ^l1Ki 12:2;
2Ch 10:2
^m2Ch 12:2
11:43 ⁿMt 1:7
12:1 ^over 25;
S Ge 12:6;
Jos 24:32

12:2
^pS 1Ki 11:40
12:4
^qS 1Sa 8:11–18;
1Ki 4:20-28
12:6 ^rS 1Ki 4:2
12:7 ^sPr 15:1
12:8 ^tLev 19:32

^a2 Or *he remained in*

11:37 *Israel.* The northern ten tribes.

11:38 *If you do whatever I command you . . . I will be with you.* Jeroboam was placed under the same covenant obligations as David and Solomon before him (see 2:3–4; 3:14; 6:12–13).

11:39 *humble David's descendants.* The division of the kingdom considerably reduced the status and power of the house of David. *not forever.* Anticipates a restoration (announced also in the Messianic prophecies of Jer 30:9; Eze 34:23; 37:15–28; Hos 3:5; Am 9:11–12) in which the nation is reunited under the rule of the house of David.

11:40 *Solomon tried to kill Jeroboam.* Jeroboam, perhaps indifferent to the timing announced by Ahijah (vv. 34–35), may have made an abortive attempt to wrest the kingdom from Solomon (see v. 26). *Shishak the king.* See 14:25–26. This first Egyptian pharaoh to be mentioned by name in the OT was the Libyan founder of the 22nd dynasty (945–924 B.C.). Solomon's marriage ties were with the previous dynasty (see note on 3:1).

11:41 *annals of Solomon.* A written source concerning Solomon's life and administration, which was used by the writer of 1,2 Kings (see Introduction: Author, Sources and Date; see also 15:7,23).

11:43 *rested with his fathers.* See note on 1:21.

12:1–33 See map on p. 495.

12:1 *Shechem.* A city of great historical significance located in the hill country of northern Ephraim (see Ge 12:6; 33:18–20; Jos 8:30–35 and note on Jos 8:30; see also Jos

20:7; 21:21; 24:1–33). *all the Israelites.* That is, representatives of the northern tribes (see v. 16). The fact that David became king over the northern tribes on the basis of a covenant (see 2Sa 5:3) suggests that their act of submission was to be renewed with each new king and that it was subject to negotiation.

12:2 *heard this.* Heard about the death of Solomon (11:43). *returned from Egypt.* See 2Ch 10:2.

12:4 *put a heavy yoke on us.* Smoldering discontent with Solomon's heavy taxation and conscription of labor and military forces flared up into strong expression (see 4:7,22–23, 27–28; 5:13–14; 9:22; see also notes on 9:15; 11:28). Conditions had progressively worsened since the early days of Solomon's rule (see 4:20).

12:6 *elders who had served his father Solomon.* Officials of Solomon's government such as Adoniram (4:6) and the district governors (4:7–19).

12:7 Authority in the kingdom of God is for service, not for personal aggrandizement.

12:8 *young men.* Young in comparison to the officials who had served Solomon. Rehoboam was 41 years old when he became king (14:21). *serving him.* Apparently Rehoboam had quickly established new administrative positions for friends and associates of his own generation.

12:10 *My little finger is thicker than my father's waist.* A proverb claiming that Rehoboam's weakest measures will be far stronger than his father's strongest measures.

12:11 *scorpions.* Metal-spiked leather lashes. Not only

heavier. My father scourged you with whips; I will scourge you with scorpions.' "

12Three days later Jeroboam and all the people returned to Rehoboam, as the king had said, "Come back to me in three days." 13The king answered the people harshly. Rejecting the advice given him by the elders, 14he followed the advice of the young men and said, "My father made your yoke heavy; I will make it even heavier. My father scourged u you with whips; I will scourge you with scorpions." 15So the king did not listen to the people, for this turn of events was from the LORD, v to fulfill the word the LORD had spoken to Jeroboam son of Nebat through Ahijah w the Shilonite.

16When all Israel saw that the king refused to listen to them, they answered the king:

"What share x do we have in David,
    what part in Jesse's son?
To your tents, O Israel! y
    Look after your own house,
        O David!"

So the Israelites went home. z 17But as for the Israelites who were living in the towns of Judah, a Rehoboam still ruled over them.

18King Rehoboam sent out Adoniram, b b who was in charge of forced labor, but all

Israel stoned him to death. c King Rehoboam, however, managed to get into his chariot and escape to Jerusalem. 19So Israel has been in rebellion against the house of David d to this day.

20When all the Israelites heard that Jeroboam had returned, they sent and called him to the assembly and made him king over all Israel. Only the tribe of Judah remained loyal to the house of David. e

21When Rehoboam arrived in Jerusalem, he mustered the whole house of Judah and the tribe of Benjamin—a hundred and eighty thousand fighting men—to make war f against the house of Israel and to regain the kingdom for Rehoboam son of Solomon.

22But this word of God came to Shemaiah g the man of God: h 23"Say to Rehoboam son of Solomon king of Judah, to the whole house of Judah and Benjamin, and to the rest of the people, 24'This is what the LORD says: Do not go up to fight against your brothers, the Israelites. Go home, every one of you, for this is my doing.' " So they obeyed the word of the LORD and went home again, as the LORD had ordered.

Golden Calves at Bethel and Dan

25Then Jeroboam fortified Shechem i in

Cross references (center column)

12:14 uEx 1:14
12:15 vS Dt 2:30; 2Ch 25:20
wS 1Ki 11:29
12:16 xS Ge 31:14
yS 2Sa 20:1
zIsa 7:17
12:17 a1Ki 11:36
12:18 bS 2Sa 20:24
cS Jos 7:25
12:19 d2Ki 17:21
12:20 e1Ki 11:13; Eze 37:16
12:21 f1Ki 14:30; 15:6, 16; 2Ch 11:1
12:22 g2Ch 12:5-7
hS Dt 33:1; 2Ki 4:7
12:25 iS ver 1

b18 Some Septuagint manuscripts and Syriac (see also 1 Kings 4:6 and 5:14); Hebrew Adoram

Study notes (bottom)

will governmental burdens on the people be increased, but the punishment for not complying with the government's directives will also be intensified.

12:14 *followed the advice of the young men.* Rehoboam's answer reflects a despotic spirit completely contrary to the covenantal character of Israelite kingship (see Dt 17:14–20; see also note on 1Sa 10:25).

12:15 *this turn of events was from the LORD.* By this statement the writer of Kings does not condone either the foolish act of Rehoboam or the revolutionary spirit of the northern tribes, but he reminds the reader that all these things occurred to bring about the divinely announced punishment on the house of David for Solomon's idolatry and breach of the covenant (11:9–13). For the relationship between divine sovereignty over all things and human responsibility for evil acts see note on 2Sa 24:1. *the word the LORD had spoken to Jeroboam . . . through Ahijah.* See 11:29–39.

12:16 *all Israel.* The northern tribes (see note on v. 1). *David.* The Davidic dynasty (see 2Sa 20:1 for an earlier expression of the same sentiment).

12:17 *Israelites who were living in the towns of Judah.* People originally from the northern tribes who had settled in Judah. They were later to be joined by others from the north who desired to serve the Lord and worship at the temple (see 2Ch 11:16–17).

12:18 *Adoniram, who was in charge of forced labor.* He had served in the same capacity under both David (2Sa 20:24) and Solomon (1Ki 4:6; 5:14).

12:19 *this day.* The time of the writing of the source from which the author of 1 Kings derived this account (see Intro-

duction: Author, Sources and Date).

12:21 *tribe of Benjamin.* Although the bulk of Benjamin was aligned with the northern tribes (see note on 11:31–32), the area around Jerusalem remained under Rehoboam's control (as did the Gibeonite cities and Gezer). The northern boundary of Judah must have reached almost to Bethel (12 miles north of Jerusalem)—which Abijah, Rehoboam's son, even held for a short while (see 2Ch 13:19). *a hundred and eighty thousand fighting men.* Probably includes all support personnel together with those who would actually be committed to battle.

12:22 *Shemaiah.* Wrote a history of Rehoboam's reign (2Ch 12:15). Another of his prophecies is recorded in 2Ch 12:5–8. *man of God.* A common way of referring to a prophet (see, e.g., 13:1; Dt 18:18; 33:1; 1Sa 2:27; 9:9–10).

12:23 *rest of the people.* See note on v. 17.

12:24 *went home again.* Although full-scale civil war was averted, intermittent skirmishes and battles between Israel and Judah continued throughout the reigns of Rehoboam, Abijah and Asa, until political instability in Israel after the death of Baasha finally brought the conflict to a halt. Asa's son Jehoshaphat entered into an alliance with Ahab and sealed the relationship by the marriage of his son Jehoram to Ahab's daughter Athaliah (see 14:30; 15:6,16; 22:2,44; 2Ki 8:18).

12:25 *Peniel.* A town in Transjordan (see Ge 32:31; Jdg 8:9,17) of strategic importance for defense against the Arameans of Damascus (see 11:23–25) and the Ammonites.

the hill country of Ephraim and lived there. From there he went out and built up Peniel. c j

26Jeroboam thought to himself, "The kingdom will now likely revert to the house of David. 27If these people go up to offer sacrifices at the temple of the LORD in Jerusalem, k they will again give their allegiance to their lord, Rehoboam king of Judah. They will kill me and return to King Rehoboam."

28After seeking advice, the king made two golden calves. l He said to the people, "It is too much for you to go up to Jerusalem. Here are your gods, O Israel, who brought you up out of Egypt." m 29One he set up in Bethel, n and the other in Dan. o 30And this thing became a sin; p the people went even as far as Dan to worship the one there.

31Jeroboam built shrines q on high places and appointed priests r from all sorts of people, even though they were not Levites. 32He instituted a festival on the fifteenth day of the eighth s month, like the festival held in Judah, and offered sacrifices on the altar. This he did in Bethel, t sacrificing to the calves he had made. And at Bethel he also installed priests at the high places he had made. 33On the fifteenth day of the eighth month, a month of his own choosing, he offered sacrifices on the altar he

had built at Bethel. u So he instituted the festival for the Israelites and went up to the altar to make offerings.

The Man of God From Judah

13 By the word of the LORD a man of God v came from Judah to Bethel, w as Jeroboam was standing by the altar to make an offering. 2He cried out against the altar by the word of the LORD: "O altar, altar! This is what the LORD says: 'A son named Josiah x will be born to the house of David. On you he will sacrifice the priests of the high places y who now make offerings here, and human bones will be burned on you.'" 3That same day the man of God gave a sign: z "This is the sign the LORD has declared: The altar will be split apart and the ashes on it will be poured out."

4When King Jeroboam heard what the man of God cried out against the altar at Bethel, he stretched out his hand from the altar and said, "Seize him!" But the hand he stretched out toward the man shriveled up, so that he could not pull it back. 5Also, the altar was split apart and its ashes poured out according to the sign given by the man of God by the word of the LORD.

6Then the king said to the man of God,

c25 Hebrew Penuel, a variant of Peniel

Cross references

12:25 /S Jdg 8:8
12:27 kDt 12:5-6
12:28 /S Ex 32:4;
S 2Ch 11:15
mS Ex 32:8
12:29
nS Ge 12:8;
S Jos 7:2
oJdg 18:27-31;
Am 8:14
12:30
p1Ki 13:34;
14:16; 15:26,30;
16:2; 2Ki 3:3;
10:29; 13:2;
17:21
12:31
qS Lev 26:30;
1Ki 13:32;
2Ki 17:29
rS Ex 29:9;
1Ki 13:33;
2Ki 17:32;
2Ch 11:14-15;
13:9
12:32
sS Nu 29:12
t2Ki 10:29

12:33
u2Ki 23:15;
Am 7:13
13:1 vS Dt 33:1;
S Jdg 13:6
wAm 7:13
13:2
x2Ki 23:15-16,20;
2Ch 34:5
yS Lev 26:30
13:3
zS Ge 24:14;
S Ex 4:8;
S Jn 2:11

12:26 revert to the house of David. Jeroboam did not have confidence in the divine promise given to him through Ahijah (see 11:38) and thus took action that forfeited the theocratic basis for his kingship.

12:28 two golden calves. Pagan gods of the Arameans and Canaanites were often represented as standing on calves or bulls as symbols of their strength and fertility (see note on Jdg 2:13). Here are your gods, O Israel, who brought you up out of Egypt. Like Aaron (Ex 32:4-5), Jeroboam attempted to combine the pagan calf symbol with the worship of the Lord, though he attempted no physical representation of the Lord—no "god" stood on the backs of his bulls.

12:29 Bethel. Located about 12 miles north of Jerusalem close to the border of Ephraim but within the territory of Benjamin (Jos 18:11-13,22). Bethel held a prominent place in the history of Israel's worship of the Lord (see Ge 12:8; 28:11-19; 35:6-7; Jdg 20:26-28; 1Sa 7:16). Dan. Located in the far north of the land near Mount Hermon. A similarly paganized worship was practiced here during the period of the judges (Jdg 18:30-31).

12:30 this thing became a sin. Jeroboam's royal policy promoted violation of the second commandment (Ex 20:4-6). It inevitably led to Israel's violation of the first commandment also (Ex 20:3) and opened the door for the entrance of fully pagan practices into Israel's religious rites (especially in the time of Ahab). Jeroboam foolishly abandoned religious principle for political expediency and in so doing forfeited the promise given him by the prophet Ahijah (see 11:38).

12:31 Jeroboam built shrines on high places. See note on 3:2. not Levites. Many of the priests and Levites of the northern kingdom migrated to Judah because Jeroboam

bypassed them when appointing cult personnel in the north (see 2Ch 11:13-14).

12:32 festival held in Judah. Apparently the Feast of Tabernacles, observed in Judah on the 15th to the 21st of the seventh month (see 8:2; Lev 23:34). offered sacrifices on the altar. Jeroboam overstepped the limits of his prerogatives as king and assumed the role of a priest (see 2Ch 26:16-21).

13:1 man of God. See note on 12:22. from Judah to Bethel. God sent a prophet from the southern kingdom to Bethel in the northern kingdom. Possibly he did this to emphasize that the divinely appointed political division (11:11,29-39; 12:15,24) was not intended to establish rival religious systems in the two kingdoms. Two centuries later the prophet Amos from Tekoa in Judah also went to Bethel in the northern kingdom to pronounce God's judgment on Jeroboam II (Am 7:10-17).

13:2 Josiah. A prophetic announcement of the rule of King Josiah, who came to the throne in Judah nearly 300 years after the division of the kingdom. will sacrifice the priests of the high places. Fulfilled in 2Ki 23:15-20.

13:3 sign. The immediate fulfillment of a short-term prediction would serve to authenticate the reliability of the longer-term prediction (see Dt 18:21-22).

13:5 its ashes poured out. Visibly demonstrating God's power to fulfill the words of the prophet (see note on v. 3) and providing a clear sign that Jeroboam's offering was unacceptable to the Lord (see Lev 6:10-11).

13:6 your God. Should not be taken as implying that Jeroboam no longer considered the Lord as his own God (cf. 2:3; Ge 27:20), but as suggesting that he recognized the prophet as his superior in the theocratic order. king's hand

"Intercede[a] with the LORD your God and pray for me that my hand may be restored." So the man of God interceded with the LORD, and the king's hand was restored and became as it was before.

[7] The king said to the man of God, "Come home with me and have something to eat, and I will give you a gift."[b]

[8] But the man of God answered the king, "Even if you were to give me half your possessions,[c] I would not go with you, nor would I eat bread[d] or drink water here. [9] For I was commanded by the word of the LORD: 'You must not eat bread or drink water or return by the way you came.' " [10] So he took another road and did not return by the way he had come to Bethel.

[11] Now there was a certain old prophet living in Bethel, whose sons came and told him all that the man of God had done there that day. They also told their father what he had said to the king. [12] Their father asked them, "Which way did he go?" And his sons showed him which road the man of God from Judah had taken. [13] So he said to his sons, "Saddle the donkey for me." And when they had saddled the donkey for him, he mounted it [14] and rode after the man of God. He found him sitting under an oak tree and asked, "Are you the man of God who came from Judah?"

"I am," he replied.

[15] So the prophet said to him, "Come home with me and eat."

[16] The man of God said, "I cannot turn back and go with you, nor can I eat bread[e] or drink water with you in this place. [17] I have been told by the word of the LORD: 'You must not eat bread or drink water there or return by the way you came.' "

[18] The old prophet answered, "I too am a prophet, as you are. And an angel said to me by the word of the LORD:[f] 'Bring him back with you to your house so that he may eat bread and drink water.' " (But he was lying[g] to him.) [19] So the man of God returned with him and ate and drank in his house.

[20] While they were sitting at the table, the word of the LORD came to the old prophet who had brought him back. [21] He cried out to the man of God who had come from Judah, "This is what the LORD says: 'You have defied[h] the word of the LORD and have not kept the command the LORD your God gave you. [22] You came back and ate bread and drank water in the place where he told you not to eat or drink. Therefore your body will not be buried in the tomb of your fathers.' "

[23] When the man of God had finished eating and drinking, the prophet who had brought him back saddled his donkey for him. [24] As he went on his way, a lion[i] met him on the road and killed him, and his body was thrown down on the road, with both the donkey and the lion standing beside it. [25] Some people who passed by saw the body thrown down there, with the lion standing beside the body, and they went and reported it in the city where the old prophet lived.

[26] When the prophet who had brought him back from his journey heard of it, he said, "It is the man of God who defied[j] the word of the LORD. The LORD has given him over to the lion, which has mauled him and killed him, as the word of the LORD had warned him."

[27] The prophet said to his sons, "Saddle the donkey for me," and they did so. [28] Then he went out and found the body

---

Cross references:

13:6 [a] S Ge 20:7; S Nu 11:2; S Jer 37:3; Ac 8:24
13:7 [b] S 1Sa 9:7
13:8 [c] Nu 22:18
[d] ver 16
13:16 [e] ver 8

13:18 [f] 1Ki 22:6, 12; 2Ch 35:21; Isa 36:10
[g] S Ge 19:14; S Dt 13:3
13:21 [h] ver 26; S 1Sa 13:14; 1Ki 20:35
13:24 [i] 1Ki 20:36
13:26 [j] S ver 21

---

was restored. The Lord's gracious response to Jeroboam's request is to be seen as an additional sign (see v. 3) given to confirm the word of the prophet and to move Jeroboam to repentance.

13:7 *Come home with me.* Jeroboam attempted to renew his prestige in the eyes of the people by creating the impression that there was no fundamental break between himself and the prophetic order (see 1Sa 15:30 for a similar situation).

13:9 *You must not.* The prophet's refusal of Jeroboam's invitation rested on a previously given divine command. It underscored God's extreme displeasure with the apostate worship at Bethel.

13:18 *I too am a prophet, as you are.* A half-truth. It is likely that the old prophet in Bethel had faithfully proclaimed the word of the Lord in former days, but those days had long since passed.

13:19 *the man of God returned with him.* Neither the old prophet's lie nor his own need justified disobedience to the direct and explicit command of the Lord. His public action in this matter undermined respect for the divine authority of all

he had said at Bethel.

13:20 *the word of the LORD came to the old prophet.* The fundamental distinction between a true and a false prophecy here becomes apparent. The false prophecy arises from one's own imagination (Jer 23:16; Eze 13:2,7) while the true prophecy is from God (Ex 4:16; Dt 18:18; Jer 1:9; 2Pe 1:21).

13:22 *your body will not be buried in the tomb of your fathers.* The man of God from Judah will die far from his own home and family burial plot.

13:24 *killed him.* A stern warning to Jeroboam that God takes his word very seriously. *the donkey and the lion standing beside it.* The remarkable fact that the donkey did not run and the lion did not attack the donkey or disturb the man's body (v. 28) clearly stamped the incident as a divine judgment. This additional miracle was reported in Bethel (v. 25) and provided yet another sign authenticating the message that the man of God from Judah had delivered at Jeroboam's altar. But Jeroboam was still not moved to repentance (v. 33).

thrown down on the road, with the donkey and the lion standing beside it. The lion had neither eaten the body nor mauled the donkey. ²⁹So the prophet picked up the body of the man of God, laid it on the donkey, and brought it back to his own city to mourn for him and bury him. ³⁰Then he laid the body in his own tomb, ^k and they mourned over him and said, "Oh, my brother!" ^l

³¹After burying him, he said to his sons, "When I die, bury me in the grave where the man of God is buried; lay my bones ^m beside his bones. ³²For the message he declared by the word of the LORD against the altar in Bethel and against all the shrines on the high places ⁿ in the towns of Samaria ^o will certainly come true." ^p

³³Even after this, Jeroboam did not change his evil ways, ^q but once more appointed priests for the high places from all sorts ^r of people. Anyone who wanted to become a priest he consecrated for the high places. ³⁴This was the sin ^s of the house of Jeroboam that led to its downfall and to its destruction ^t from the face of the earth.

Ahijah's Prophecy Against Jeroboam

14 At that time Abijah son of Jeroboam became ill, ²and Jeroboam said to his wife, "Go, disguise yourself, so you won't be recognized as the wife of Jeroboam. Then go to Shiloh. Ahijah ^u the prophet is there—the one who told me I

would be king over this people. ³Take ten loaves of bread ^v with you, some cakes and a jar of honey, and go to him. He will tell you what will happen to the boy." ⁴So Jeroboam's wife did what he said and went to Ahijah's house in Shiloh.

Now Ahijah could not see; his sight was gone because of his age. ⁵But the LORD had told Ahijah, "Jeroboam's wife is coming to ask you about her son, for he is ill, and you are to give her such and such an answer. When she arrives, she will pretend to be someone else."

⁶So when Ahijah heard the sound of her footsteps at the door, he said, "Come in, wife of Jeroboam. Why this pretense? ^w I have been sent to you with bad news. ⁷Go, tell Jeroboam that this is what the LORD, the God of Israel, says: ^x 'I raised you up from among the people and made you a leader ^y over my people Israel. ⁸I tore ^z the kingdom away from the house of David and gave it to you, but you have not been like my servant David, who kept my commands and followed me with all his heart, doing only what was right ^a in my eyes. ⁹You have done more evil ^b than all who lived before you. ^c You have made for yourself other gods, idols ^d made of metal; you have provoked ^e me to anger and thrust me behind your back. ^f

¹⁰" 'Because of this, I am going to bring disaster ^g on the house of Jeroboam. I will cut off from Jeroboam every last male in Israel—slave or free. ^h I will burn up the

Cross references (center column)

13:30 ^k2Ki 23:17; ^lJer 22:18
13:31 ^m2Ki 23:18
13:32 ⁿS Lev 26:30; S 1Ki 12:31 ^o1Ki 16:24,28; 20:1; 2Ki 10:1; 15:13 ^p2Ki 23:16
13:33 ^q1Ki 15:26 ^rS 1Ki 12:31
13:34 ^sS 1Ki 12:30 ^t1Ki 14:10; 15:29; 2Ki 9:9; Jer 35:17; Am 7:9
14:2 ^uS 1Ki 11:29

14:3 ^vS 1Sa 9:7
14:6 ^wS 1Sa 28:12
14:7 ^x1Ki 15:29 ^y1Ki 11:37
14:8 ^zS 1Sa 15:27 ^aS 2Sa 8:15; 1Ki 3:3; 15:5; 2Ki 14:3; 15:3, 34; 16:2; 18:3; 20:3; 22:2
14:9 ^b1Ki 16:30, 33; 21:25; 2Ki 21:9,11; 24:3 ^c1Ki 16:2 ^dS Ex 20:4; S 32:4; 2Ch 11:15 ^eDt 32:16; 1Ki 16:2; Ps 78:58; Jer 7:18; 8:19; 32:32; 44:3; Eze 8:17; 16:26 ^fNe 9:26; Ps 50:17; Jer 2:27; 32:33; Eze 23:35
14:10 ^gS Jos 23:15; S 1Ki 13:34 ^hS Dt 32:36; 2Ki 9:8-9

13:30 *laid the body in his own tomb.* See v. 22. The old prophet did the only thing left for him to do in order to make amends for his deliberate and fatal deception.

13:31 *grave where the man of God is buried.* The old prophet chose in this way to identify himself with the message that the man of God from Judah had given at Bethel.

13:32 *Samaria.* As the capital of the northern kingdom, Samaria is used to designate the entire territory of the northern ten tribes (see note on 16:24). However, Samaria was not established until about 50 years after this (16:23–24). The use of the name here reflects the perspective of the author of Kings (see note on Ge 14:14 for a similar instance of the use of a place-name—Dan—of later origin than the historical incident with which it is connected).

13:33 *appointed priests . . . from all sorts of people.* See 12:31 and note.

13:34 *sin.* The sin in 12:30 was the establishment of a paganized worship; here it is persistence in this worship with all its attendant evils.

14:1 *At that time.* Probably indicating a time not far removed from the event narrated in ch. 13. *Abijah.* Means "My (divine) Father is the LORD," suggesting that Jeroboam, at least to some degree, desired to be regarded as a worshiper of the Lord.

14:2 *disguise yourself.* Jeroboam's attempt to mislead the prophet Ahijah into giving a favorable prophecy concerning the sick boy indicates (1) his consciousness of his own guilt, (2) his superstition that prophecy worked in a magical way

and (3) his confused but real respect for the power of the Lord's prophet. *who told me I would be king over this people.* See 11:29–39.

14:3 *ten loaves of bread.* The gift of an ordinary farmer (like Saul in 1Sa 9:7–8) rather than that of a king (see 2Ki 8:7–9).

14:5 *the LORD had told Ahijah.* See 1Sa 9:15–17; 2Ki 6:32 for other examples of divine revelation concerning an imminent visit.

14:6 *Come in, wife of Jeroboam.* Ahijah's recognition of the woman and his knowledge of the purpose of her visit served to authenticate his message as truly being the word of the Lord.

14:7–8 *raised you . . . made you a leader . . . tore the kingdom away.* Jeroboam is first reminded of the gracious acts of the Lord in his behalf (see 11:26,30–38).

14:8 *you have not been like my servant David.* Jeroboam had not responded to God's gracious acts and had ignored the requirements given when Ahijah told him he would become king (see 11:38).

14:9 *all who lived before you.* Jeroboam's wickedness surpassed that of Saul, David and Solomon in that he implemented a paganized system of worship for the entire populace of the northern kingdom. *other gods.* See notes on 12:28,30.

14:10 *slave or free.* Without exception (see 21:21; 2Ki 9:8; 14:26).

house of Jeroboam as one burns dung, until it is all gone.[i] [11]Dogs[j] will eat those belonging to Jeroboam who die in the city, and the birds of the air[k] will feed on those who die in the country. The LORD has spoken!'

[12]"As for you, go back home. When you set foot in your city, the boy will die. [13]All Israel will mourn for him and bury him. He is the only one belonging to Jeroboam who will be buried, because he is the only one in the house of Jeroboam in whom the LORD, the God of Israel, has found anything good.[l]

[14]"The LORD will raise up for himself a king over Israel who will cut off the family of Jeroboam. This is the day! What? Yes, even now.[d] [15]And the LORD will strike Israel, so that it will be like a reed swaying in the water. He will uproot[m] Israel from this good land that he gave to their forefathers and scatter them beyond the River,[e] because they provoked[n] the LORD to anger by making Asherah[o] poles.[f] [16]And he will give Israel up because of the sins[p] Jeroboam has committed and has caused Israel to commit."

[17]Then Jeroboam's wife got up and left and went to Tirzah.[q] As soon as she stepped over the threshold of the house, the boy died. [18]They buried him, and all Israel mourned for him, as the LORD had said through his servant the prophet Ahijah.

[19]The other events of Jeroboam's reign, his wars and how he ruled, are written in the book of the annals of the kings of Israel. [20]He reigned for twenty-two years and then rested with his fathers. And Nadab his son succeeded him as king.

Rehoboam King of Judah

14:21,25–31pp — 2Ch 12:9–16

[21]Rehoboam son of Solomon was king in Judah. He was forty-one years old when he became king, and he reigned seventeen years in Jerusalem, the city the LORD had chosen out of all the tribes of Israel in which to put his Name. His mother's name was Naamah; she was an Ammonite.[r]

[22]Judah[s] did evil in the eyes of the LORD. By the sins they committed they stirred up his jealous anger[t] more than their fathers had done. [23]They also set up for themselves high places, sacred stones[u] and Asherah poles[v] on every high hill and

---

Cross references (center column):

14:10 [i]1Sa 12:25; 15:26; 1Ki 15:29; Hos 13:11
14:11 [j]1Ki 16:4; 21:24 [k]S Ge 40:19; S Dt 28:26
14:13 [l]2Ch 12:12; 19:3
14:15 [m]S Dt 29:28; S 2Ch 7:20 [n]Jer 44:3 [o]S Dt 12:3
14:16 [p]S 1Ki 12:30; S 15:26
14:17 [q]S Jos 12:24; S 1Ki 15:33
14:21 [r]S 1Ki 11:1
14:22 [s]2Ki 17:19; 2Ch 12:1 [t]Dt 32:21; Ps 78:58; Jer 44:3; S 1Co 10:22
14:23 [u]S Ex 23:24; Dt 16:22; Hos 10:1 [v]S Dt 12:3

[d]*14* The meaning of the Hebrew for this sentence is uncertain. [e]*15* That is, the Euphrates [f]*15* That is, symbols of the goddess Asherah; here and elsewhere in 1 Kings

---

14:11 *birds of the air will feed on those who die in the country.* See note on 16:4. The covenant curse of Dt 28:26 is applied to Jeroboam's male descendants, none of whom will receive an honorable burial.

14:12 *boy.* The Hebrew for this word allows for wide latitude in age (the same term is used for the young advisers of Rehoboam; see 12:8 and note). *will die.* Although the death of Abijah was a severe disappointment to Jeroboam and his wife, it was an act of God's mercy to the prince, sparing him the disgrace and suffering that were to come on his father's house (see Isa 57:1–2).

14:13 *All Israel will mourn for him and bury him.* Perhaps an indication that Abijah was the crown prince, and was well known and loved by the people. *buried.* He alone of Jeroboam's descendants would receive an honorable burial.

14:14 *a king . . . who will cut off the family of Jeroboam.* Ahijah looked beyond the brief reign of Nadab, Jeroboam's son (15:25–26), to the revolt of Baasha (15:27–16:7).

14:15 *like a reed swaying in the water.* Descriptive of the instability of the royal house in the northern kingdom, which was to be characterized by assassinations and revolts (see 15:27–28; 16:16; 2Ki 9:24; 15:10,14,25,30). *He will uproot Israel.* The list of curses for covenant breaking found in Deuteronomy climaxes in forced exile for God's people from the land of promise (Dt 28:63–64; 29:25–28). *Asherah poles.* See NIV text note. Ahijah perceived that Jeroboam's use of golden bulls in worship would inevitably lead to the adoption of other elements of Canaanite nature religion. The goddess Asherah was the consort of Baal (cf. Jdg 3:7; 2Ki 23:4), and the Asherah poles were probably wooden representations of the goddess (see note on Ex 34:13).

14:16 *sins Jeroboam has committed.* See 12:26–33; 13:33–34. *caused Israel to commit.* A phrase repeated often in 1,2 Kings (e.g., 15:26; 16:2,13,19,26).

14:17 *Tirzah.* Used by the kings of Israel as the royal city until Omri purchased and built up Samaria to serve that purpose (16:24). It is probably modern Tell el-Far'ah, about seven miles north of Shechem (see note on SS 6:4).

14:19 *his wars.* See v. 30; 15:6; 2Ch 13:2–20. *annals of the kings of Israel.* A record of the reigns of the kings of the northern kingdom used by the author of 1,2 Kings and apparently accessible to those interested in further details of the history of the reigns of Israelite kings. It is not to be confused with the canonical book of 1,2 Chronicles, which was written later than 1,2 Kings and contains the history of the reigns of the kings of Judah only (see Introduction: Author, Sources and Date).

14:20 *twenty-two years.* 930–909 B.C. *rested with his fathers.* See note on 1:21. *Nadab.* See 15:25–32.

14:21 *forty-one years old.* Rehoboam was born shortly before David's death (see 11:42; see also note on 2:24). *seventeen years.* 930–913 B.C. *city the LORD had chosen . . . to put his Name.* See 9:3; Ps 132:13.

14:22 *Judah did evil in the eyes of the LORD.* The reign of Rehoboam is described in greater detail in 2Ch 11–12. The priests and Levites who immigrated to Judah from the north led the country to follow the way of David and Solomon for the first three years of Rehoboam's reign (see 12:24; 2Ch 11:17). In later years Rehoboam and the people of Judah turned away from the Lord (2Ch 12:1).

14:23 *high places.* See note on 3:2. *sacred stones.* Stone pillars, bearing a religious significance, that were placed next to the altars. The use of such pillars was common among the Canaanites and was explicitly forbidden to the Israelites in the Mosaic law (Ex 23:24; Lev 26:1; Dt 16:21–22). It is likely that the pillars were intended to be representations of the deity (2Ki 3:2). For legitimate uses of stone pillars see Ge 28:18; 31:45; Ex 24:4. *Asherah poles.* See note on v. 15.

Rulers of Israel and Judah

DATA AND DATES IN
ORDER OF SEQUENCE

Adapted from: *A Chronology of the Hebrew Kings* by Edwin R. Thiele.
© 1977 by The Zondervan Corporation. Used by permission.

1.	1Ki 12:1-24 14:21-31	**Rehoboam** (Judah)		17 years	930-913
2.	1Ki 12:25—14:20	**Jeroboam I** (Israel)		22 years	930-909
3.	1Ki 15:1-8	**Abijah** (Judah)	18th of Jeroboam	3 years	913-910
4.	1Ki 15:9-24	**Asa** (Judah)	20th of Jeroboam	41 years	910-869
5.	1Ki 15:25-31	**Nadab** (Israel)	2nd of Asa	2 years	909-908
6.	1Ki 15:32—16:7	**Baasha** (Israel)	3rd of Asa	24 years	908-886
7.	1Ki 16:8-14	**Elah** (Israel)	26th of Asa	2 years	886-885
8.	1Ki 16:15-20	**Zimri** (Israel)	27th of Asa	7 days	885
9.	1Ki 16:21-22	**Tibni** (Israel)		Overlap with Omri	885-880
10.	1Ki 16:23-28	**Omri** (Israel)	27th of Asa	Made king by the people	885
				Overlap with Tibni	885-880
			31st of Asa	12 years / Official reign = 11 actual years	885-874
				Beginning of sole reign	880
11.	1Ki 16:29—22:40	**Ahab** (Israel)	38th of Asa	22 years / Official reign = 21 actual years	874-853
12.	1Ki 22:41-50	**Jehoshaphat** (Judah)		Co-regency with Asa	872-869
				25 years / Official reign	872-848
			4th of Ahab	Beginning of sole reign	869
				Has Jehoram as regent	853-848
13.	1Ki 22:51—2Ki 1:18	**Ahaziah** (Israel)	17th of Jehoshaphat	2 years / Official reign = 1 yr. actual reign	853-852
14.	2Ki 1:17 2Ki 3:1—8:15	**Joram** (Israel)	2nd of Jehoram 18th of Jehoshaphat	852 12 years / Official reign = 11 actual years	852-841
15.	2Ki 8:16-24	**Jehoram** (Judah)	5th of Joram	Beginning of sole reign	848
				8 years / Official reign = 7 actual years	848-841
16.	2Ki 8:25-29 2Ki 9:29	**Ahaziah** (Judah)	12th of Joram 11th of Joram	1 year / Nonaccession-year reckoning Accession-year reckoning	841 841
17.	2Ki 9:30—10:36	**Jehu** (Israel)		28 years	841-814
18.	2Ki 11	**Athaliah** (Judah)		7 years	841-835
19.	2Ki 12	**Joash** (Judah)	7th of Jehu	40 years	835-796
20.	2Ki 13:1-9	**Jehoahaz** (Israel)	23rd of Joash	17 years	814-798
21.	2Ki 13:10-25	**Jehoash** (Israel)	37th of Joash	16 years	798-782

#	Reference	King	Synchronism	Length	Note	Dates
22.	2Ki 14:1-22	**Amaziah** (Judah)	2nd of Jehoash	29 years		**796-767**
					Overlap with Azariah	792-767
23.	2Ki 14:23-29	**Jeroboam II** (Israel)			Co-regency with Jehoash	793-782
				41 years	Total reign	**793-753**
			15th of Amaziah		Beginning of sole reign	782
24.	2Ki 15:1-7	**Azariah** (Judah)			Overlap with Amaziah	792-767
				52 years	Total reign	**792-740**
			27th of Jeroboam		Beginning of sole reign	767
25.	2Ki 15:8-12	**Zechariah** (Israel)	38th of Azariah	6 months		**753**
26.	2Ki 15:13-15	**Shallum** (Israel)	39th of Azariah	1 month		**752**
27.	2Ki 15:16-22	**Menahem** (Israel)	39th of Azariah	10 years	Ruled in Samaria	752-742
28.	2Ki 15:23-26	**Pekahiah** (Israel)	50th of Azariah	2 years		742-740
29.	2Ki 15:27-31	**Pekah** (Israel)			In Gilead; overlapping years	752-740
				20 years	Total reign	**752-732**
			52nd of Azariah		Beginning of sole reign	740
30.	2Ki 15:32-38	**Jotham** (Judah)			Co-regency with Azariah	750-740
	2Ki 15:30			16 years	Official reign	**750-735**
					Reign to his 20th year	750-732
			2nd of Pekah		Beginning of co-regency	750
31.	2Ki 16	**Ahaz** (Judah)			Total reign	735-715
			17th of Pekah			735
				16 years	From 20th of Jotham	**732-715**
32.	2Ki 15:30	**Hoshea** (Israel)			20th of Jotham	732
	2Ki 17		12th of Ahaz*	9 years		**732-722**
33.	2Ki 18:1—20:21	**Hezekiah** (Judah)	3rd of Hoshea*	29 years		**715-686**
34.	2Ki 21:1-18	**Manasseh** (Judah)			Co-regency with Hezekiah	697-686
				55 years	Total reign	**697-642**
35.	2Ki 21:19-26	**Amon** (Judah)		2 years		**642-640**
36.	2Ki 22:1—23:30	**Josiah** (Judah)		31 years		**640-609**
37.	2Ki 23:31-33	**Jehoahaz** (Judah)		3 months		**609**
38.	2Ki 23:34—24:7	**Jehoiakim** (Judah)		11 years		**609-598**
39.	2Ki 24:8-17	**Jehoiachin** (Judah)		3 months		**598-597**
40.	2Ki 24:18—25:26	**Zedekiah** (Judah)		11 years		**597-586**

*These data arise when the reign of Hoshea
is thrown 12 years in advance of its historical position.

*Italics denote kings of **Judah**.*
Non-italic type denotes kings of **Israel**.

under every spreading tree.ʷ ²⁴There were even male shrine prostitutesˣ in the land; the people engaged in all the detestableʸ practices of the nations the LORD had driven out before the Israelites.

²⁵In the fifth year of King Rehoboam, Shishak king of Egypt attackedᶻ Jerusalem. ²⁶He carried off the treasures of the templeᵃ of the LORD and the treasures of the royal palace. He took everything, including all the gold shieldsᵇ Solomon had made. ²⁷So King Rehoboam made bronze shields to replace them and assigned these to the commanders of the guard on duty at the entrance to the royal palace.ᶜ ²⁸Whenever the king went to the LORD's temple, the guards bore the shields, and afterward they returned them to the guardroom.

²⁹As for the other events of Rehoboam's reign, and all he did, are they not written in the book of the annals of the kings of Judah? ³⁰There was continual warfareᵈ between Rehoboam and Jeroboam. ³¹And Rehoboam rested with his fathers and was buried with them in the City of David. His mother's name was Naamah; she was an Ammonite.ᵉ And Abijahᵍ his son succeeded him as king.

Abijah King of Judah

15:1–2,6–8pp —2Ch 13:1–2,22–14:1

15 In the eighteenth year of the reign of Jeroboam son of Nebat, Abijahʰ became king of Judah, ²and he reigned in

Jerusalem three years. His mother's name was Maacahᶠ daughter of Abishalom.ⁱ

³He committed all the sins his father had done before him; his heart was not fully devotedᵍ to the LORD his God, as the heart of David his forefather had been. ⁴Nevertheless, for David's sake the LORD his God gave him a lampʰ in Jerusalem by raising up a son to succeed him and by making Jerusalem strong. ⁵For David had done what was right in the eyes of the LORD and had not failed to keepⁱ any of the LORD's commands all the days of his life—except in the case of Uriahʲ the Hittite.

⁶There was warᵏ between Rehoboamʲ and Jeroboam throughout Abijah's lifetime. ⁷As for the other events of Abijah's reign, and all he did, are they not written in the book of the annals of the kings of Judah? There was war between Abijah and Jeroboam. ⁸And Abijah rested with his fathers and was buried in the City of David. And Asa his son succeeded him as king.

Asa King of Judah

15:9–22pp — 2Ch 14:2–3; 15:16–16:6
15:23–24pp — 2Ch 16:11–17:1

⁹In the twentieth year of Jeroboam king of Israel, Asa became king of Judah, ¹⁰and he reigned in Jerusalem forty-one years.

Cross references (center column)

14:23
ʷS Dt 12:2;
Eze 6:13
14:24
ˣS Dt 23:17
ʸ1Ki 11:5-7;
2Ki 21:2;
Ezr 9:11;
Pr 21:27;
Isa 1:13;
Jer 16:18; 32:35;
44:4
14:25 ᶻ2Ch 12:2
14:26
ᵃ1Ki 15:15,18
ᵇS 2Sa 8:7
14:27 ᶜ2Ki 11:5
14:30 ᵈ2Sa 3:1;
S 1Ki 12:21
14:31
ᵉS 1Ki 11:1

15:2 ᶠver 10,13;
2Ch 11:20
15:3 ᵍS 1Ki 8:61
15:4
ʰS 2Sa 21:17
15:5 ⁱS Dt 5:32;
S 1Ki 9:4
ʲ2Sa 11:2-27;
12:9
15:6 ᵏver 16,32;
S 1Ki 12:21;
2Ch 16:9

ᵍ31 Some Hebrew manuscripts and Septuagint (see also 2 Chron. 12:16); most Hebrew manuscripts *Abijam* ʰ1 Some Hebrew manuscripts and Septuagint (see also 2 Chron. 12:16); most Hebrew manuscripts *Abijam*; also in verses 7 and 8 ʲ2 A variant of *Absalom*; also in verse 10 ʲ6 Most Hebrew manuscripts; some Hebrew manuscripts and Syriac *Abijam* (that is, Abijah)

14:24 *male shrine prostitutes.* Ritual prostitution was an important feature of Canaanite fertility religion. The Israelites had been warned by Moses not to engage in this abominable practice (see Dt 23:17–18; see also 1Ki 15:12; 2Ki 23:7; Hos 4:14).

14:25 *fifth year of King Rehoboam.* 926 B.C. *Shishak.* See notes on 3:1; 11:40. *attacked Jerusalem.* Shishak's invasion is described in more detail in 2Ch 12:2–4 and is also attested in a victory inscription found on the walls of the temple of Amun in Thebes, where numerous cities that Shishak plundered in both Judah and the northern kingdom are listed. 2Ch 12:5–8 indicates that fear of the impending invasion led to a temporary reformation in Judah.

14:26 *gold shields Solomon had made.* See 10:16–17.

14:27 *bronze shields.* The reduced realm could not match the great wealth Solomon had accumulated in Jerusalem (see 10:21,23,27).

14:29 *annals of the kings of Judah.* A record of the reigns of the kings of Judah similar to the one for the kings of the northern kingdom (see note on v. 19; see also Introduction: Author, Sources and Date).

14:30 *continual warfare.* See notes on v. 19; 12:24.

14:31 *rested with his fathers.* See note on 1:21.

15:1 *eighteenth year of the reign of Jeroboam.* The first of numerous synchronisms in 1,2 Kings between the reigns of the kings in the north and those in Judah (see, e.g., vv. 9,25, 33; 16:8,15,29; see also Introduction: Chronology). *Abijah.* See note on 14:1. Both Rehoboam and Jeroboam had sons by

this name.

15:2 *three years.* 913–910 B.C. *Maacah daughter of Abishalom.* See NIV text note. Abijah's mother is said to be a daughter of Uriel of Gibeah in 2Ch 13:2. It is likely that Maacah was the granddaughter of Absalom and the daughter of a marriage between Tamar (Absalom's daughter; see 2Sa 14:27) and Uriel. Absalom's mother was also named Maacah (2Sa 3:3).

15:3 *sins his father had done.* See 14:22–24. *not fully devoted to the LORD his God, as . . . David his forefather had been.* Although David fell into grievous sin, his heart was never divided between serving the Lord and serving the nature deities of the Canaanites.

15:4 *lamp in Jerusalem.* See note on 11:36.

15:5 *Uriah the Hittite.* See 2Sa 11.

15:6 *Rehoboam.* See NIV text note; see also note on 12:24.

15:7 *other events of Abijah's reign.* See 2Ch 13. *annals of the kings of Judah.* See note on 14:29. *war between Abijah and Jeroboam.* Cf. v. 6; 14:30. From 2Ch 13 it is clear that the chronic hostile relations of preceding years flared into serious combat in which Abijah defeated Jeroboam and took several towns from him, including Bethel (2Ch 13:19).

15:8 *rested with his fathers.* See note on 1:21.

15:9 *twentieth year of Jeroboam.* 910 B.C. (see note on 14:20).

15:10 *forty-one years.* 910–869 B.C. *Maacah daughter of Abishalom.* See note on v. 2.

His grandmother's name was Maacah[l] daughter of Abishalom.

[11]Asa did what was right in the eyes of the Lord, as his father David[m] had done. [12]He expelled the male shrine prostitutes[n] from the land and got rid of all the idols[o] his fathers had made. [13]He even deposed his grandmother Maacah[p] from her position as queen mother,[q] because she had made a repulsive Asherah pole. Asa cut the pole down[r] and burned it in the Kidron Valley. [14]Although he did not remove[s] the high places, Asa's heart was fully committed[t] to the Lord all his life. [15]He brought into the temple of the Lord the silver and gold and the articles that he and his father had dedicated.[u]

[16]There was war[v] between Asa and Baasha king of Israel throughout their reigns. [17]Baasha king of Israel went up against Judah and fortified Ramah[w] to prevent anyone from leaving or entering the territory of Asa king of Judah.

[18]Asa then took all the silver and gold that was left in the treasuries of the Lord's temple[x] and of his own palace. He entrusted it to his officials and sent[y] them to

Ben-Hadad[z] son of Tabrimmon, the son of Hezion, the king of Aram, who was ruling in Damascus. [19]"Let there be a treaty[a] between me and you," he said, "as there was between my father and your father. See, I am sending you a gift of silver and gold. Now break your treaty with Baasha king of Israel so he will withdraw from me."

[20]Ben-Hadad agreed with King Asa and sent the commanders of his forces against the towns of Israel. He conquered[b] Ijon, Dan, Abel Beth Maacah and all Kinnereth in addition to Naphtali. [21]When Baasha heard this, he stopped building Ramah[c] and withdrew to Tirzah.[d] [22]Then King Asa issued an order to all Judah—no one was exempt—and they carried away from Ramah[e] the stones and timber Baasha had been using there. With them King Asa[f] built up Geba[g] in Benjamin, and also Mizpah.[h]

[23]As for all the other events of Asa's reign, all his achievements, all he did and the cities he built, are they not written in the book of the annals of the kings of Judah? In his old age, however, his feet became diseased. [24]Then Asa rested with

---

Cross references (center column):

15:10 [l]S ver 2
15:11 [m]1Ki 9:4
15:12 [n]1Ki 14:24
[o]2Ch 15:8
15:13 [p]S ver 2
[q]S 1Ki 2:19
[r]S Ex 34:13
15:14 [s]2Ch 14:5;
17:6 [t]S 1Ki 8:61
15:15
[u]S 2Sa 8:11
15:16 [v]S ver 6;
S 1Ki 12:21
15:17
[w]S Jos 18:25
15:18
[x]S 1Ki 14:26
[y]2Ki 12:18; 16:8;
18:14-16,15;
Joel 3:5

[z]ver 18-20;
1Ki 20:1;
2Ki 6:24; 13:3;
Jer 49:27
15:19
[a]S Ex 23:32;
S 1Ki 5:12
15:20 [b]1Ki 20:34
15:21
[c]S Jos 18:25
[d]1Ki 16:15-17
15:22 [e]ver 17
[f]ver 9-24;
Jer 41:9
[g]S Jos 18:24;
2Ki 23:8
[h]S Jos 11:3

15:12 *male shrine prostitutes.* See note on 14:24. *got rid of all the idols his fathers had made.* See 14:23.

15:13 *deposed his grandmother Maacah.* 2Ch 14:1–15:16 indicates a progression in Asa's reform over a period of years. Although Asa had destroyed pagan idols and altars early in his reign (2Ch 14:2–3), it was not until after a victory over Zerah the Cushite (2Ch 14:8–15) that Asa responded to the message of the prophet Azariah son of Oded by calling for a covenant renewal assembly in Jerusalem in the 15th year of his reign (2Ch 15:10). After this assembly Asa deposed his grandmother Maacah because of her idolatry (2Ch 15:16). *made a repulsive Asherah pole.* See note on 14:15. It appears that Maacah's action was a deliberate attempt to counter Asa's reform.

15:14 *did not remove the high places.* The reference here and in 2Ch 15:17 is to those high places where the Lord was worshiped (for the question of legitimacy of worship of the Lord at high places see note on 3:2). When 2Ch 14:3 indicates that Asa removed the high places, it is to be taken as a reference to the high places that were centers of pagan Canaanite worship (see 2Ch 17:6; 20:33 for the same distinction). This same statement of qualified approval that is made of Asa is made of five other kings of Judah prior to the time of Hezekiah (Jehoshaphat, 22:43; Joash, 2Ki 12:3; Amaziah, 2Ki 14:4; Azariah, 2Ki 15:4; Jotham, 2Ki 15:35). *fully committed to the Lord.* See note on v. 3.

15:15 *silver and gold and the articles.* Most likely consisting of war booty that Abijah had taken from Jeroboam (2Ch 13) and that Asa acquired from Zerah the Cushite (2Ch 14:8–15).

15:16 *war between Asa and Baasha . . . throughout their reigns.* A reference to the chronic hostile relations that had existed ever since the division of the kingdom, rather than to full-scale combat (see notes on v. 7; 12:24; see also 2Ch 15:19).

15:17 *fortified Ramah.* Baasha had recaptured the territory previously taken from Jeroboam by Abijah (see note on v. 7; see also 2Ch 13:19) since Ramah was located south of Bethel

and only about five miles north of Jerusalem. *prevent anyone from leaving or entering the territory of Asa.* See 2Ch 15:9–10.

15:18 *silver and gold that was left.* That which remained after the plundering of Jerusalem by Shishak of Egypt (see 14:25). *Hezion.* It is not clear whether Hezion is to be identified with Rezon of Damascus (see 11:23–25) or regarded as the founder of a new dynasty.

15:19 *treaty . . . between my father and your father.* A reference to a previously unmentioned treaty between Abijah and Tabrimmon of Aram. When Tabrimmon died, Baasha succeeded in establishing a treaty with his successor Ben-Hadad. Asa saw no hope for success against Baasha without the assistance provided by a renewal of the old treaty with Aram. Although his plan seemed to be successful, it was condemned by Hanani the prophet as a foolish act and a denial of reliance on the Lord (see 2Ch 16:7–10). The true theocratic king was never to fear his enemies but to trust in the God of the covenant for security and protection (see note on 1Sa 17:11). Ahaz was later to follow Asa's bad example and seek Assyria's help when he was attacked by Israel and Aram (see 2Ki 16:5–9; Isa 7).

15:20 *Naphtali.* The cities that Ben-Hadad conquered in Naphtali were of particular importance because the major trade routes from Damascus going west to Tyre and southwest through the plain of Jezreel to the coastal plain and Egypt transversed this area. This same territory was later seized by the Assyrian ruler Tiglath-Pileser III (2Ki 15:29).

15:21 *Tirzah.* See note on 14:17.

15:22 *order to all Judah.* Asa's action is reminiscent of the labor force conscripted by Solomon (5:13–14; 11:28). *Geba . . . Mizpah.* Asa established two border fortresses to check Baasha's desire to expand his territory southward. Geba was east of Ramah, and Mizpah was southwest of Ramah.

15:23 *other events of Asa's reign.* See 2Ch 14:2–16:14. *annals of the kings of Judah.* See note on 14:29. *feet became diseased.* See 2Ch 16:12.

15:24 *rested with his fathers.* See note on 1:21. *Jehosha-*

his fathers and was buried with them in the city of his father David. And Jehoshaphat[i] his son succeeded him as king.

Nadab King of Israel

25Nadab son of Jeroboam became king of Israel in the second year of Asa king of Judah, and he reigned over Israel two years. 26He did evil[j] in the eyes of the LORD, walking in the ways of his father[k] and in his sin, which he had caused Israel to commit.

27Baasha son of Ahijah of the house of Issachar plotted against him, and he struck him down[l] at Gibbethon,[m] a Philistine town, while Nadab and all Israel were besieging it. 28Baasha killed Nadab in the third year of Asa king of Judah and succeeded him as king.

29As soon as he began to reign, he killed Jeroboam's whole family.[n] He did not leave Jeroboam anyone that breathed, but destroyed them all, according to the word of the LORD given through his servant Ahijah the Shilonite— 30because of the sins[o] Jeroboam had committed and had caused[p] Israel to commit, and because he provoked the LORD, the God of Israel, to anger.

31As for the other events of Nadab's reign, and all he did, are they not written in the book of the annals[q] of the kings of Israel? 32There was war[r] between Asa and

15:24 /Mt 1:8
15:26 /S Dt 4:25
   kS 1Ki 12:30
15:27 /1Ki 14:14
   mS Jos 19:44
15:29
   nS 1Ki 13:34
15:30
   oS 1Ki 12:30
   p1Ki 16:26;
   2Ki 3:3; 14:24;
   15:28; 21:16
15:31 q1Ki 11:41
15:32 rS ver 6

15:33
   s1Ki 14:17; 16:6,
   23; 2Ki 15:14;
   SS 6:4
15:34 tver 26
16:1 uver 7;
   2Ch 19:2; 20:34
   v2Ch 16:7
16:2 w1Sa 2:8
   xS 1Ki 14:7-9
   yS 1Ki 12:30
16:3 z2Ki 9:9
   aver 11;
   1Ki 21:22
16:4
   bS 1Ki 14:11
   cS Ge 40:19
16:5 d1Ki 15:31
16:6
   eS 1Ki 15:33
16:7 /S 1Ki 6:11
   gS ver 1

Baasha king of Israel throughout their reigns.

Baasha King of Israel

33In the third year of Asa king of Judah, Baasha son of Ahijah became king of all Israel in Tirzah,[s] and he reigned twenty-four years. 34He did evil[t] in the eyes of the LORD, walking in the ways of Jeroboam and in his sin, which he had caused Israel to commit.

16 Then the word of the LORD came to Jehu[u] son of Hanani[v] against Baasha: 2"I lifted you up from the dust[w] and made you leader[x] of my people Israel, but you walked in the ways of Jeroboam and caused[y] my people Israel to sin and to provoke me to anger by their sins. 3So I am about to consume Baasha[z] and his house,[a] and I will make your house like that of Jeroboam son of Nebat. 4Dogs[b] will eat those belonging to Baasha who die in the city, and the birds of the air[c] will feed on those who die in the country."

5As for the other events of Baasha's reign, what he did and his achievements, are they not written in the book of the annals[d] of the kings of Israel? 6Baasha rested with his fathers and was buried in Tirzah.[e] And Elah his son succeeded him as king.

7Moreover, the word of the LORD came[f] through the prophet Jehu[g] son of

---

phat his son succeeded him. For the reign of Jehoshaphat see 22:41–50; 2Ch 17:1–21:1.

15:25 second year of Asa. See note on v. 1. The second year of Asa of Judah corresponded to the 22nd and last year of Jeroboam of Israel (see v. 9; 14:20). two years. 909–908 B.C.

15:26 his sin, which he had caused Israel to commit. Jeroboam's sin (see note on 14:16). Although Abijah of Judah occupied Bethel during the reign of Jeroboam (see note on v. 7), it is probable that the paganized worship Jeroboam initiated was continued elsewhere until control of Bethel was regained by Baasha.

15:27 Gibbethon. A town located between Jerusalem and Joppa (probably a few miles west of Gezer) in the territory originally assigned to Dan (Jos 19:43–45). This Levitical city (Jos 21:23) probably fell into Philistine hands at the time of the Philistine expansion in the period of the judges.

15:28 third year of Asa. 908 B.C. (see note on v. 10). It is likely that Baasha was a commander in Nadab's army and was able to secure the support of the military for his revolt.

15:29 the word . . . given through . . . Ahijah. See 14:10–11.

15:30 sins Jeroboam had committed and had caused Israel to commit. See note on 14:16.

15:31 annals of the kings of Israel. See note on 14:19.

15:32 war . . . throughout their reigns. See note on v. 16. The demise of Jeroboam's dynasty did not improve relations between the two kingdoms.

15:33 third year of Asa. 908 B.C. (see note on v. 10). Tirzah. See note on 14:17. twenty-four years. 908–886 B.C.

His official years were counted as 24, though his actual years were 23 (see 16:8; see also Introduction: Chronology).

15:34 his sin, which he had caused Israel to commit. See note on 14:16. The assessment of Baasha's reign indicates no improvement over the reign of Nadab, whom he replaced (see v. 26).

16:1 Jehu. Like his father before him (see 2Ch 16:7–10), Jehu brought God's word of condemnation to a king. Much as the man of God from Judah (see note on 13:1) and later the prophet Amos, he was sent from the south to a northern king. His ministry continued for about 50 years until the reign of Jehoshaphat of Judah (2Ch 19:2; 20:34).

16:2 I lifted you up from the dust. Cf. 14:7. walked in the ways of Jeroboam. See note on 14:16.

16:3 consume Baasha and his house. Cf. 14:10 (the house of Jeroboam); 21:21 (the house of Omri and Ahab).

16:4 Identical to the prophecy against Jeroboam's dynasty in 14:11.

16:5 his achievements. For the purposes of the writer of Kings (see Introduction: Theme), it was not necessary to list any of Baasha's achievements. He may have been a very successful ruler from a military-political point of view. annals of the kings of Israel. See note on 14:19.

16:6 rested with his fathers. See note on 1:21.

16:7 evil he had done . . . like the house of Jeroboam. See v. 2; 15:34. he destroyed it. Although Baasha fulfilled God's purpose (14:10,14) in destroying the house of Jeroboam, he remained responsible for this violent and unlawful act (cf. Ge 50:20; Isa 10:5–7,12).

Hanani to Baasha and his house, because of all the evil he had done in the eyes of the LORD, provoking him to anger by the things he did, and becoming like the house of Jeroboam—and also because he destroyed it.

Elah King of Israel

8In the twenty-sixth year of Asa king of Judah, Elah son of Baasha became king of Israel, and he reigned in Tirzah two years.

9Zimri, one of his officials, who had command of half his chariots, plotted against him. Elah was in Tirzah at the time, getting drunk *h* in the home of Arza, the man in charge *i* of the palace at Tirzah. 10Zimri came in, struck him down and killed him in the twenty-seventh year of Asa king of Judah. Then he succeeded him as king. *j*

11As soon as he began to reign and was seated on the throne, he killed off Baasha's whole family. *k* He did not spare a single male, whether relative or friend. 12So Zimri destroyed the whole family of Baasha, in accordance with the word of the LORD spoken against Baasha through the prophet Jehu— 13because of all the sins Baasha and his son Elah had committed and had caused Israel to commit, so that they provoked the LORD, the God of Israel, to anger by their worthless idols. *l*

14As for the other events of Elah's reign, and all he did, are they not written in the book of the annals of the kings of Israel?

Zimri King of Israel

15In the twenty-seventh year of Asa king

of Judah, Zimri reigned in Tirzah seven days. The army was encamped near Gibbethon, *m* a Philistine town. 16When the Israelites in the camp heard that Zimri had plotted against the king and murdered him, they proclaimed Omri, the commander of the army, king over Israel that very day there in the camp. 17Then Omri and all the Israelites with him withdrew from Gibbethon and laid siege to Tirzah. 18When Zimri saw that the city was taken, he went into the citadel of the royal palace and set the palace on fire around him. So he died, 19because of the sins he had committed, doing evil in the eyes of the LORD and walking in the ways of Jeroboam and in the sin he had committed and had caused Israel to commit.

20As for the other events of Zimri's reign, and the rebellion he carried out, are they not written in the book of the annals of the kings of Israel?

Omri King of Israel

21Then the people of Israel were split into two factions; half supported Tibni son of Ginath for king, and the other half supported Omri. 22But Omri's followers proved stronger than those of Tibni son of Ginath. So Tibni died and Omri became king.

23In the thirty-first year of Asa king of Judah, Omri became king of Israel, and he reigned twelve years, six of them in Tirzah. *n* 24He bought the hill of Samaria from Shemer for two talents *k* of silver and built

---

Cross-references:
16:9 *h* 1Ki 20:12, 16; Pr 31:4-5
i 1Ki 18:3
16:10 *j* 2Ki 9:31
16:11 *k* S ver 3
16:13 *l* S Dt 32:21

16:15 *m* S Jos 19:44
16:23 *n* S Jos 12:24;
S 1Ki 15:33

k 24 That is, about 150 pounds (about 70 kilograms)

16:8 *twenty-sixth year of Asa.* 886 B.C. (see note on 15:10; see also Introduction: Chronology). *two years.* 886–885 B.C. **16:9** *getting drunk.* The fact that Elah was carousing at Tirzah while the army was laying siege to Gibbethon (v. 15) indicates he had little perception of his responsibilities as king. **16:10** *twenty-seventh year of Asa.* 885 B.C. **16:11** *killed off Baasha's whole family.* See 15:29; 2Ki 10:1–7; 11:1. *friend.* Probably the chief adviser to the king (see note on 2Sa 15:37). **16:12** *word of the LORD . . . through the prophet Jehu.* See vv. 1–4. Zimri did not consciously decide to fulfill Jehu's prophecy, but unwittingly he became the instrument by which Jehu's prediction was fulfilled (see note on v. 7) when he conspired against Elah and destroyed the dynasty of Baasha. **16:13** *sins Baasha and his son Elah had committed.* See 15:34. *worthless idols.* A reference to all the paganism in Israel's religious observances, including the use of the golden calves in worship (see 12:28; 14:9). **16:14** *annals of the kings of Israel.* See note on 14:19. **16:15** *twenty-seventh year of Asa.* 885 B.C. (see notes on 15:1,10). *Gibbethon.* See notes on v. 9; 15:27. **16:16** *plotted against the king and murdered him.* See vv. 9–12. *Omri, the commander of the army.* He held a higher

rank than Zimri did under Elah (v. 9). **16:17** *Tirzah.* The royal residence (see vv. 8–10; see also note on 14:17). **16:19** *ways of Jeroboam.* See note on 14:16. **16:20** *annals of the kings of Israel.* See note on 14:19. **16:22** *Tibni died.* It is not clear whether Tibni's death was due to natural causes or the result of the military struggle for control of the land. **16:23** *thirty-first year of Asa.* 880 B.C. (see note on 15:10; see also Introduction: Chronology). *became king.* Became sole king. The struggle for control of the northern kingdom between Omri and Tibni lasted four years (compare this verse with v. 15). *twelve years.* 885–874. The 12 years of Omri's reign include the four years of struggle between Omri and Tibni (cf. vv. 15,29). *Tirzah.* See note on 14:17. Omri had been able to capture Tirzah in a matter of days (vv. 15–19). **16:24** *Samaria.* Seven miles northwest of Shechem, Samaria rose about 300 feet above the surrounding fertile valleys (referred to as a "wreath" in Isa 28:1). The original owner may have been persuaded to sell his property (see 21:3) on the condition that the city be named after him (cf. Ru 4:5). The site provided an ideal location for a nearly impregnable capital city for the northern kingdom (see 20:1–21; 2Ki 6:25; 18:9–10). With the establishment of

a city on the hill, calling it Samaria,*o* after Shemer, the name of the former owner of the hill.

25But Omri did evil*p* in the eyes of the LORD and sinned more than all those before him. 26He walked in all the ways of Jeroboam son of Nebat and in his sin, which he had caused*q* Israel to commit, so that they provoked the LORD, the God of Israel, to anger by their worthless idols.*r*

27As for the other events of Omri's reign, what he did and the things he achieved, are they not written in the book of the annals of the kings of Israel? 28Omri rested with his fathers and was buried in Samaria.*s* And Ahab his son succeeded him as king.

Ahab Becomes King of Israel

29In the thirty-eighth year of Asa king of Judah, Ahab son of Omri became king of Israel, and he reigned in Samaria over Israel twenty-two years. 30Ahab son of Omri

did more*t* evil in the eyes of the LORD than any of those before him. 31He not only considered it trivial to commit the sins of Jeroboam son of Nebat, but he also married*u* Jezebel daughter*v* of Ethbaal king of the Sidonians, and began to serve Baal*w* and worship him. 32He set up an altar*x* for Baal in the temple*y* of Baal that he built in Samaria. 33Ahab also made an Asherah pole*z* and did more*a* to provoke the LORD, the God of Israel, to anger than did all the kings of Israel before him.

34In Ahab's time, Hiel of Bethel rebuilt Jericho. He laid its foundations at the cost of his firstborn son Abiram, and he set up its gates at the cost of his youngest son Segub, in accordance with the word of the LORD spoken by Joshua son of Nun.*b*

Elijah Fed by Ravens

17 Now Elijah*c* the Tishbite, from Tishbe1 in Gilead,*d* said to Ahab,

1 Or Tishbite, of the settlers

Cross references

16:24 *o*S 1Ki 13:32; S Mt 10:5
16:25 *p*ver 25-26; S Dt 4:25; Mic 6:16
16:26 *q*S 1Ki 15:30 *r*S Dt 32:21
16:28 *s*S 1Ki 13:32
16:30 *t*S 1Ki 14:9
16:31 *u*S 1Ki 11:2 *v*S Jdg 3:6; 2Ki 9:34 *w*S Jdg 2:11
16:32 *x*S Jdg 6:28 *y*2Ki 10:27; 11:18; Jer 43:12
16:33 *z*S Jdg 3:7; 2Ki 13:6 *a*S 1Ki 14:9; 21:25
16:34 *b*Jos 6:26
17:1 *c*Mal 4:5; Mt 11:14; 17:3 *d*Jdg 12:4

---

this royal city, the kings of the north came to possess a royal citadel-city like that of the Davidic dynasty (see 2Sa 5:6–12). Archaeologists have discovered that Omri and Ahab also adorned it with magnificent structures to rival those Solomon had erected in Jerusalem. From this time on, the northern kingdom could be designated by the name of the royal city, just as the southern kingdom could be designated by its capital, Jerusalem (see, e.g., 21:1; Isa 10:10; Am 6:1).

16:25 *sinned more than all.* Omri's alliance with Ethbaal of Tyre and Sidon (Omri's son Ahab married Ethbaal's daughter Jezebel to seal the alliance) led to widespread Baal worship in the northern kingdom (vv. 31–33) and eventually to the near extinction of the Davidic line in the southern kingdom (see 2Ki 11; see also note on 2Ki 8:18). This marriage alliance must have been established in the early years of Omri's reign (see note on v. 23), perhaps to strengthen his hand against Tibni (see vv. 21–22).

16:26 *sin, which he had caused Israel to commit.* See 12:26–33; see also note on 14:16. *worthless idols.* See note on v. 13.

16:27 *things he achieved.* Omri's military and political accomplishments were not of importance for the purposes of the writer of Kings (see Introduction: Theme). Apart from establishing Samaria as the capital of the northern kingdom, about all that is known of him is that he organized a governmental structure in the northern kingdom that was in place during the rule of his son, Ahab (see 20:14–15). Omri's dynasty, however, endured for over 40 years. A century and a half later (732 B.C.) Tiglath-Pileser III of Assyria referred to Israel as the "house of Omri" in his annals. *annals of the kings of Israel.* See note on 14:19.

16:28 *rested with his fathers.* See note on 1:21.

16:29 *thirty-eighth year of Asa.* 874 B.C. (see notes on 15:9–10). *twenty-two years.* 874–853 B.C.

16:30 *more evil . . . than any.* Omri sinned more than those before him (see v. 25), and Ahab sinned more than his father had. Evil became progressively worse in the royal house of the northern kingdom. Nearly a third of the narrative material in 1,2 Kings concerns the 34-year period of the reigns of Ahab and his two sons, Ahaziah and Joram. In this period the struggle between the kingdom of God (championed especially by Elijah and Elisha) and the kingdom of

Satan was especially intense.

16:31 *married Jezebel daughter of Ethbaal.* The Jewish historian Josephus refers to Ethbaal as a king-priest who ruled over Tyre and Sidon for 32 years. Ahab had already married Jezebel during the reign of his father (see note on v. 25). *Baal.* Perhaps Melqart, the local manifestation of Baal in Tyre, whose worship was brought to Israel by Jezebel. It is probable that Ahab participated in the worship of this deity at the time of his marriage. The names of Ahab's sons (Ahaziah, "The LORD grasps"; Joram, "The LORD is exalted") suggest that Ahab did not intend to replace the worship of the Lord with the worship of Baal but to worship both deities in a syncretistic way.

16:32 *temple of Baal that he built in Samaria.* Ahab imported the Phoenician Baal worship of his wife Jezebel into the northern kingdom by constructing a temple of Baal in Samaria, just as Solomon had erected the temple of the Lord in Jerusalem. This pagan temple and its sacred stone (see note on 14:23) were later destroyed by Jehu (2Ki 10:21–27).

16:33 *Asherah pole.* See note on 14:15. *than did all the kings of Israel.* See note on v. 30. Ahab elevated the worship of Baal to an official status in the northern kingdom at the beginning of his reign.

16:34 *rebuilt Jericho.* Does not mean that Jericho had remained uninhabited since its destruction by Joshua (see Jos 18:21; Jdg 1:16; 3:13; 2Sa 10:5), but that it had remained an unwalled town or village. During the rule of Ahab, Hiel fortified the city by reconstructing its walls and gates (see 9:17 for a similar use of "rebuild"). This violated God's intention that the ruins of Jericho (Jos 6:26) be a perpetual reminder that Israel had received the land of Canaan from God's hand as a gift of grace. Accordingly, Hiel suffered the curse Joshua had pronounced.

17:1 *Elijah.* Elijah's name (meaning "The LORD is my God") was the essence of his message (18:21,39). He was sent to oppose vigorously, by word and action, both Baal worship and those who engaged in it. *from Tishbe in Gilead.* See NIV text note. Gilead was in the northern Transjordan area. The precise location of Tishbe is unknown. *whom I serve.* Lit. "before whom I stand," a technical expression indicating one who stands in the service of a king. Kings and

"As the LORD, the God of Israel, lives, whom I serve, there will be neither dew nor rain[e] in the next few years except at my word."

[2]Then the word of the LORD came to Elijah: [3]"Leave here, turn eastward and hide[f] in the Kerith Ravine, east of the Jordan. [4]You will drink from the brook, and I have ordered the ravens[g] to feed you there."

[5]So he did what the LORD had told him. He went to the Kerith Ravine, east of the Jordan, and stayed there. [6]The ravens brought him bread and meat in the morning[h] and bread and meat in the evening, and he drank from the brook.

The Widow at Zarephath

[7]Some time later the brook dried up because there had been no rain in the land. [8]Then the word of the LORD came to him: [9]"Go at once to Zarephath[i] of Sidon and stay there. I have commanded a widow[j] in that place to supply you with food." [10]So he went to Zarephath. When he came to the town gate, a widow was there gathering sticks. He called to her and asked,

"Would you bring me a little water in a jar so I may have a drink?"[k] [11]As she was going to get it, he called, "And bring me, please, a piece of bread."

[12]"As surely as the LORD your God lives," she replied, "I don't have any bread—only a handful of flour in a jar and a little oil[l] in a jug. I am gathering a few sticks to take home and make a meal for myself and my son, that we may eat it—and die."

[13]Elijah said to her, "Don't be afraid. Go home and do as you have said. But first make a small cake of bread for me from what you have and bring it to me, and then make something for yourself and your son. [14]For this is what the LORD, the God of Israel, says: 'The jar of flour will not be used up and the jug of oil will not run dry until the day the LORD gives rain[m] on the land.' "

[15]She went away and did as Elijah had told her. So there was food every day for Elijah and for the woman and her family. [16]For the jar of flour was not used up and the jug of oil did not run dry, in keeping

17:1 [e]S Dt 11:17; S 28:24; S 2Sa 1:21; S 1Ki 8:36; Job 12:15; S Lk 4:25 **17:3** [f]1Ki 18:4, 10; Jer 36:19,26 **17:4** [g]S Ge 8:7 **17:6** [h]Ex 16:8 **17:9** [i]Ob 1:20 [j]Lk 4:26 **17:10** [k]S Ge 24:17; Jn 4:7 **17:12** [l]2Ki 4:2 **17:14** [m]ver 1

priests in Israel were supposed to be anointed to serve as official representatives of the Lord, Israel's Great King, leading Israel in the way of faithfulness to the Lord and channeling his covenantal care and blessings to them. Since the days of Jeroboam the northern kingdom had not had such a priest (12:31), and its kings had all been unfaithful. Now, in the great crisis brought on by Ahab's promotion of Baal worship, the Lord sent Elijah (and after him Elisha) to serve as his representative (instead of king and priest), much as Moses had done long ago. The author of Kings highlights many parallels between the ministries of Elijah and Moses. *neither dew nor rain.* The drought was not only a divine judgment on a nation that had turned to idolatry, but also a demonstration that even though Baal was considered the god of fertility and lord of the rain clouds, he was powerless to give rain (cf. Lev 26:3–4; Hos 2:5,8).

17:3 *Leave here.* With this command God withdrew his prophet from his land and people to leave them isolated from his word and blessings. The absence of the prophet confirmed and intensified the judgment. *Kerith Ravine, east of the Jordan.* The location of Kerith is uncertain. Perhaps it was a gorge formed by one of the northern tributaries to the Yarmuk River.

17:4 *ravens to feed you there.* The Lord's faithful servant Elijah was miraculously sustained beyond the Jordan (like Israel in the desert in the time of Moses) while Israel in the promised land was going hungry—a clear testimony against Israel's reliance on Baal. The fact that Elijah was sustained in a miraculous way apart from living among his own people demonstrated that the word of God was not dependent on the people, but the people were dependent on the word of God.

17:9 *Zarephath of Sidon.* A coastal town located between Tyre and Sidon in the territory ruled by Jezebel's father Ethbaal (16:31). Elijah is commanded to go and reside in the heart of the very land from which the Baal worship now being promoted in Israel had come. *I have commanded a widow in that place to supply you with food.* Elijah, as the

bearer of God's word, was now to be sustained by human hands, but they were the hands of a poor widow facing starvation (v. 12). She was, moreover, from outside the circle of God's own people (cf. Lk 4:25–26)—in fact, she was from the pagan nation that at that time (much like Egypt earlier and Babylon later) represented the forces arrayed against God's kingdom.

17:10 *So he went.* Elijah's reliance on the Lord demonstrated the faith in the Lord that Israel should have been living by.

17:12 *As surely as the LORD your God lives.* Her oath in the name of the Lord was either an accommodation to Elijah, whom she recognized as an Israelite (see notes on 5:7; 10:9), or a genuine expression of previous knowledge of and commitment to the God of Israel.

17:13 *first make a small cake of bread for me . . . then make something for yourself and your son.* As a prophet, Elijah's words are the command of the Lord. The widow is asked to give all she has to sustain the bearer of the word of God. The demand to give her all is in essence the demand of the covenant that Israel had broken.

17:14 *what the LORD, the God of Israel, says.* Elijah can tell the widow "Don't be afraid" (v. 13) because the demand of the covenant is not given without the promise of the covenant. The Lord does not ask more than he promises to give.

17:15 *did as Elijah had told her.* By an act of faith the woman received the promised blessing. Israel had forsaken the covenant and followed Baal and Asherah in search of prosperity. Now in the midst of a pagan kingdom a widow realized that trustful obedience to the word of God is the way that leads to life.

17:16 *jar of flour was not used up.* God miraculously provided for this non-Israelite who, in an act of faith in the Lord's word, had laid her life on the line. He gave her "manna" from heaven even while he was withholding food from his unfaithful people in the promised land. The warning of Dt 32:21 was being fulfilled (cf. Ro 10:19; 11:11,14).

with the word of the LORD spoken by Elijah.

¹⁷Some time later the son of the woman who owned the house became ill. He grew worse and worse, and finally stopped breathing. ¹⁸She said to Elijah, "What do you have against me, man of God? Did you come to remind me of my sinⁿ and kill my son?"

¹⁹"Give me your son," Elijah replied. He took him from her arms, carried him to the upper room where he was staying, and laid him on his bed. ²⁰Then he cried^o out to the LORD, "O LORD my God, have you brought tragedy also upon this widow I am staying with, by causing her son to die?" ²¹Then he stretched^p himself out on the boy three times and cried to the LORD, "O LORD my God, let this boy's life return to him!"

²²The LORD heard Elijah's cry, and the boy's life returned to him, and he lived. ²³Elijah picked up the child and carried him down from the room into the house. He gave him to his mother^q and said, "Look, your son is alive!"

²⁴Then the woman said to Elijah, "Now I know^r that you are a man of God^s and that the word of the LORD from your mouth is the truth."^t

Elijah and Obadiah

18 After a long time, in the third^u year, the word of the LORD came to Elijah: "Go and present^v yourself to Ahab,

and I will send rain^w on the land." ²So Elijah went to present himself to Ahab.

Now the famine was severe^x in Samaria, ³and Ahab had summoned Obadiah, who was in charge^y of his palace. (Obadiah was a devout believer^z in the LORD. ⁴While Jezebel^a was killing off the LORD's prophets, Obadiah had taken a hundred prophets and hidden^b them in two caves, fifty in each, and had supplied^c them with food and water.) ⁵Ahab had said to Obadiah, "Go through the land to all the springs^d and valleys. Maybe we can find some grass to keep the horses and mules alive so we will not have to kill any of our animals."^e ⁶So they divided the land they were to cover, Ahab going in one direction and Obadiah in another.

⁷As Obadiah was walking along, Elijah met him. Obadiah recognized^f him, bowed down to the ground, and said, "Is it really you, my lord Elijah?"

⁸"Yes," he replied. "Go tell your master, 'Elijah is here.'"

⁹"What have I done wrong," asked Obadiah, "that you are handing your servant over to Ahab to be put to death? ¹⁰As surely as the LORD your God lives, there is not a nation or kingdom where my master has not sent someone to look^g for you. And whenever a nation or kingdom claimed you were not there, he made them swear they could not find you. ¹¹But now you tell me to go to my master and say, 'Elijah is here.' ¹²I don't know where the

---

Cross references (center column)

17:18 ⁿLk 5:8
17:20 ^o2Ki 4:33
17:21 ^p2Ki 4:34; Ac 20:10
17:23 ^qHeb 11:35
17:24 ^rJn 16:30 ^sver 18 ^t1Ki 22:16; Ps 119:43; Jn 17:17
18:1 ^u1Ki 17:1; Lk 4:25 ^vver 15

^wS Dt 28:12
18:2 ^xS Lev 26:26
18:3 ^y1Ki 16:9 ^zNe 7:2
18:4 ^a1Ki 21:23; 2Ki 9:7 ^bS 1Ki 17:3; Isa 16:3; 25:4; 32:2; Ob 1:14 ^cJer 26:24
18:5 ^dJer 14:3 ^eS Ge 47:4
18:7 ^f2Ki 1:8; Zec 13:4
18:10 ^gS 1Ki 17:3

17:18 *Did you come to remind me of my sin and kill my son?* The widow concluded that Elijah's presence in her house had called God's attention to her sin, and that the death of her son was a divine punishment for this sin. Although her sense of guilt seems to have been influenced by pagan ideas, both she and Elijah are confronted with the question: Why did the God who promised life bring death instead?
17:21 *stretched himself out on the boy three times.* The apparent intent of this physical contact was to transfer the bodily warmth and stimulation of the prophet to the child. Elijah's prayer, however, makes it clear that he expected the life of the child to return as an answer to prayer, not as a result of bodily contact. *let this boy's life return to him.* Moved by a faith like that of Abraham (Ro 4:17; Heb 11:19), Elijah prayed for the child's return to life so that the veracity and trustworthiness of God's word might be demonstrated.
17:22 *the boy's life returned to him.* The first instance of raising the dead recorded in Scripture. This non-Israelite widow was granted the supreme covenant blessing, the gift of life rescued from the power of death. This blessing came in the person of her son, the only hope for a widow in ancient society (see 2Ki 4:14; Ru 1:11–12; 4:15–17; Lk 7:12).
17:24 *you are a man of God.* The widow had addressed Elijah as a man of God previously (v. 18), but now she knew in a much more experiential way that he truly was a prophet of the Lord (see note on 12:22). *the word of the LORD from your mouth is the truth.* God used this experience to con-

vince the Phoenician widow that his word was completely reliable. Her confession was one that the Lord's own people in Israel had failed to make.
18:1 *third year.* Apparently of the drought. Later Jewish tradition indicates that the drought lasted three and a half years (cf. Lk 4:25; Jas 5:17), but that probably represents a symbolic number for a drought cut short (half of seven years; see Ge 41:27; 2Ki 8:1). *present yourself to Ahab, and I will send rain on the land.* Elijah's return is not occasioned by repentance in Israel but by the command of the Lord, who in his sovereign grace determined to reveal himself anew to his people.
18:3 *Obadiah.* A common OT name, meaning "servant of the LORD." *in charge of his palace.* See note on 4:6.
18:5 The famine did not move Ahab to repentance (contrast Ahab's response to the famine with that of David years earlier, 2Sa 21:1). But when his military strength seemed to be jeopardized, he scoured the land for food and water (see 10:26; according to the annals of the Assyrian ruler Shalmaneser III, Ahab had a force of at least 2,000 chariots).
18:8 *tell your master, 'Elijah is here.'* This action would publicly identify Obadiah with Elijah in contrast to his previous clandestine support of the prophets sought by Jezebel (see vv. 4,13).
18:12 *I don't know where the Spirit of the LORD may carry you.* Elijah's disappearance earlier and now his sudden reappearance suggested to Obadiah that God's Spirit was miraculously transporting the prophet about (see 2Ki 2:16).

Spirit[h] of the LORD may carry you when I leave you. If I go and tell Ahab and he doesn't find you, he will kill me. Yet I your servant have worshiped the LORD since my youth. [13]Haven't you heard, my lord, what I did while Jezebel was killing the prophets of the LORD? I hid a hundred of the LORD's prophets in two caves, fifty in each, and supplied them with food and water. [14]And now you tell me to go to my master and say, 'Elijah is here.' He will kill me!"

[15]Elijah said, "As the LORD Almighty lives, whom I serve, I will surely present[i] myself to Ahab today."

Elijah on Mount Carmel

[16]So Obadiah went to meet Ahab and told him, and Ahab went to meet Elijah. [17]When he saw Elijah, he said to him, "Is that you, you troubler[j] of Israel?"

[18]"I have not made trouble for Israel," Elijah replied. "But you[k] and your father's family have. You have abandoned[l] the LORD's commands and have followed the Baals. [19]Now summon[m] the people from all over Israel to meet me on Mount Carmel.[n] And bring the four hundred and fifty prophets of Baal and the four hundred prophets of Asherah, who eat at Jezebel's table."[o]

[20]So Ahab sent word throughout all Israel and assembled the prophets on Mount Carmel.[p] [21]Elijah went before the people and said, "How long will you waver[q] between two opinions? If the LORD[r] is God, follow him; but if Baal is God, follow him."

But the people said nothing.

[22]Then Elijah said to them, "I am the only one of the LORD's prophets left,[s] but Baal has four hundred and fifty prophets.[t] [23]Get two bulls for us. Let them choose one for themselves, and let them cut it into pieces and put it on the wood but not set fire to it. I will prepare the other bull and put it on the wood but not set fire to it. [24]Then you call[u] on the name of your god, and I will call on the name of the LORD.[v] The god who answers by fire[w]—he is God."

Then all the people said, "What you say is good."

[25]Elijah said to the prophets of Baal, "Choose one of the bulls and prepare it first, since there are so many of you. Call on the name of your god, but do not light the fire." [26]So they took the bull given them and prepared it.

Then they called[x] on the name of Baal from morning till noon. "O Baal, answer us!" they shouted. But there was no response;[y] no one answered. And they danced around the altar they had made. [27]At noon Elijah began to taunt them. "Shout louder!" he said. "Surely he is a god! Perhaps he is deep in thought, or busy, or traveling. Maybe he is sleeping and must be awakened."[z] [28]So they shouted louder and slashed[a] themselves with swords and spears, as was their custom, until their blood flowed. [29]Midday passed, and they continued their frantic prophesying until the time for the evening

Cross references (center column)

18:12 [h]2Ki 2:16; Eze 3:14; Ac 8:39
18:15 [i]ver 1
18:17 [j]Jos 7:25; 1Sa 14:29; 1Ki 21:20; Jer 38:4
18:18 [k]1Ki 16:33; 21:25 [l]S Dt 31:16
18:19 [m]2Ki 10:19 [n]S Jos 19:26 [o]2Ki 9:22
18:20 [p]2Ki 2:25; 4:25
18:21 [q]Jos 24:15; 2Ki 17:41; Ps 119:113; Mt 6:24 [r]ver 39; Ps 100:3; 118:27
18:22 [s]1Ki 19:10 [t]Jer 2:8; 23:13
18:24 [u]S 1Sa 7:8 [v]S Ge 4:26 [w]S ver 38; S Ex 19:18; S Lev 9:24
18:26 [x]Isa 44:17; 45:20 [y]Ps 115:4-5; 135:16; Isa 41:26,28; 46:7; Jer 10:5; 1Co 8:4; 12:2
18:27 [z]Hab 2:19
18:28 [a]S Lev 19:28

18:13 *Jezebel was killing the prophets.* Possibly in an attempt to please Baal so he would send rain. *prophets of the LORD.* Probably members of the communities of "prophets" that had sprung up in Israel during this time of apostasy (see note on 20:35).

18:17 *you troubler of Israel.* Ahab holds Elijah to account for the drought and charges him with a crime against the state worthy of death (he calls him a "trouble bringer"; see Jos 7:25).

18:18 *You have abandoned the LORD's commands and have followed the Baals.* The source of Israel's trouble was not Elijah or even the drought, but the breach of covenantal loyalty.

18:19 *Mount Carmel.* A high ridge next to the Mediterranean Sea, where the effects of the drought would be least apparent (see Am 1:2) and the power of Baal to nurture life would seem to be strongest. *prophets of Baal ... prophets of Asherah.* See v. 29 and note. *Asherah.* See note on 14:15. *eat at Jezebel's table.* See note on 2:7.

18:21 *waver.* The Hebrew for this word is the same as that used for "danced" in v. 26 (see note there). Elijah speaks with biting irony: In her religious ambivalence Israel is but engaging in a wild and futile religious "dance." *If the LORD is God, follow him; but if Baal is God, follow him.* Elijah placed a clear choice before the people. He drew a sharp contrast between the worship of the Lord and that of Baal, to elimi-

nate the apostate idea that both deities could be worshiped in a syncretistic way.

18:22 *only one ... left.* At least the only one to stand boldly and publicly against the king and the prophets of Baal (but see v. 4; 19:10,14; 20:13,28,35; 22:6,8).

18:24 *The god who answers by fire—he is God.* Both the Lord and Baal were said to ride the thunderstorm as their divine chariot (see Ps 104:3 and note); thunder was their voice (see Ps 29:3–9 and note) and lightning their weapon (see Ps 18:14 and note). Elijah's challenge is direct. Cf. Lev 9:24.

18:26 *danced around the altar.* The ecstatic cultic dance was part of the pagan ritual intended to arouse the deity to perform some desired action.

18:27 *deep in thought ... sleeping.* Elijah ridicules, but as he does he shows knowledge of the Baal myths. *until their blood flowed.* Self-inflicted wounds (causing blood to flow) were symbolic of self-sacrifice as an extreme method of arousing the deity to action. Such mutilation of the body was strictly forbidden in the Mosaic law (Lev 19:28; Dt 14:1).

18:29 *frantic prophesying.* Indicative of ecstatic raving, in which the ritual reached its climax (see notes on 1Sa 10:5; 18:10). *time for the evening sacrifice.* See Ex 29:38–41; Nu 28:3–8. *no response.* Dramatic demonstration of Baal's impotence (see Ps 115:5–8; 135:15–18; Jer 10:5).

sacrifice.[b] But there was no response, no one answered, no one paid attention.[c]

[30]Then Elijah said to all the people, "Come here to me." They came to him, and he repaired the altar[d] of the LORD, which was in ruins. [31]Elijah took twelve stones, one for each of the tribes descended from Jacob, to whom the word of the LORD had come, saying, "Your name shall be Israel."[e] [32]With the stones he built an altar in the name[f] of the LORD, and he dug a trench around it large enough to hold two seahs[m] of seed. [33]He arranged[g] the wood, cut the bull into pieces and laid it on the wood. Then he said to them, "Fill four large jars with water and pour it on the offering and on the wood."

[34]"Do it again," he said, and they did it again.

"Do it a third time," he ordered, and they did it the third time. [35]The water ran down around the altar and even filled the trench.

[36]At the time[h] of sacrifice, the prophet Elijah stepped forward and prayed: "O LORD, God of Abraham,[i] Isaac and Israel, let it be known[j] today that you are God in Israel and that I am your servant and have done all these things at your command.[k] [37]Answer me, O LORD, answer me, so these people will know[l] that you, O LORD, are God, and that you are turning their hearts back again."

[38]Then the fire[m] of the LORD fell and burned up the sacrifice, the wood, the stones and the soil, and also licked up the water in the trench.

[39]When all the people saw this, they fell prostrate[n] and cried, "The LORD—he is God! The LORD—he is God!"[o]

[40]Then Elijah commanded them, "Seize the prophets of Baal. Don't let anyone get away!" They seized them, and Elijah had them brought down to the Kishon Valley[p] and slaughtered[q] there.

[41]And Elijah said to Ahab, "Go, eat and drink, for there is the sound of a heavy rain." [42]So Ahab went off to eat and drink, but Elijah climbed to the top of Carmel, bent down to the ground and put his face between his knees.[r]

[43]"Go and look toward the sea," he told his servant. And he went up and looked.

"There is nothing there," he said.

Seven times Elijah said, "Go back."

[44]The seventh time[s] the servant reported, "A cloud[t] as small as a man's hand is rising from the sea."

So Elijah said, "Go and tell Ahab, 'Hitch up your chariot and go down before the rain stops you.'"

[45]Meanwhile, the sky grew black with clouds, the wind rose, a heavy rain[u] came on and Ahab rode off to Jezreel.[v] [46]The power[w] of the LORD came upon Elijah and, tucking his cloak into his belt,[x] he ran ahead of Ahab all the way to Jezreel.

Elijah Flees to Horeb

19 Now Ahab told Jezebel[y] everything Elijah had done and how he had killed[z] all the prophets with the sword. [2]So Jezebel sent a messenger to Elijah to say, "May the gods deal with me, be it ever so severely,[a] if by this time tomor-

Cross references (center column):

18:29 [b]S Ex 29:41; [c]2Ki 19:12; Isa 16:12; Jer 10:5
18:30 [d]1Ki 19:10
18:31 [e]S Ge 17:5; 2Ki 17:34
18:32 [f]S Dt 18:7; Col 3:17
18:33 [g]S Ge 22:9
18:36 [h]S Ex 29:39,41; [i]S Ge 24:12; [j]S Ex 4:5; Mt 22:32; [j]S Jos 4:24; S 1Sa 17:46; S Ps 46:10; [k]Nu 16:28
18:37 [l]S Jos 4:24
18:38 [m]ver 24; S Ex 19:18; S Lev 9:24; 2Ki 1:10; 1Ch 21:26; 2Ch 7:1; Job 1:16
18:39 [n]S Lev 9:24; [o]S ver 21; S Ps 46:10
18:40 [p]S Jdg 4:7; [q]S Ex 22:20; S Dt 17:12; S 2Ki 11:18
18:42 [r]S 1Sa 12:17; Jas 5:18
18:44 [s]S Jos 6:15; [t]Lk 12:54
18:45 [u]S 1Ki 8:36; Job 37:13; [v]S 1Sa 29:1; S Hos 1:4
18:46 [w]S Jdg 3:10; S 1Sa 11:6; Lk 1:35; 4:14; [x]2Ki 4:29; 9:1
19:1 [y]1Ki 16:31; [z]S Ex 22:20
19:2 [a]S Ru 1:17

[m]32 That is, probably about 13 quarts (about 15 liters)

18:30 *altar of the LORD, which was in ruins.* It is possible that the altar had been built by people of the northern ten tribes after the division of the kingdom (see note on 3:2) and that it had been destroyed by the agents of Jezebel (vv. 4,13; 19:10,14).

18:31 *twelve stones, one for each of the tribes.* In this way Elijah called attention to the covenant unity of Israel as the people of God in spite of her political division. What was about to happen concerned the entire nation, not just the northern ten tribes.

18:33 *water.* By drenching the whole installation Elijah showed to all that he was using no tricks.

18:36 *prayed.* Elijah's simple but earnest prayer stands in sharp contrast to the frantic shouts and "dancing" and self-mutilation of the Baal prophets. *God of Abraham, Isaac and Israel.* An appeal to the Lord to remember his ancient covenant with the patriarchs, and to Israel to remember all that the Lord has done for her since the days of her forefathers.

18:38 *fire of the LORD fell.* See note on v. 24.

18:40 *slaughtered there.* Elijah, acting on the authority of the Lord, who sent him, carried out the sentence pronounced in the Mosaic law for prophets of pagan deities (Dt 13:13–18; 17:2–5).

18:41 *sound of a heavy rain.* Now that Baal worship has been struck a devastating blow, there is the promise of rain (see 17:1). Significantly, Ahab takes no action—either to carry out the Mosaic sentence or to halt Elijah.

18:42 *Elijah . . . bent down to the ground and put his face between his knees.* Now that the people had confessed that the Lord alone was God, Elijah prayed for the covenant curse to be lifted (see note on 17:1) by the coming of rain (see 8:35; 2Ch 7:13–14).

18:43 *Seven times.* The number symbolic of completeness.

18:44 *rising from the sea.* Appearing on the western horizon.

18:46 *ran ahead of Ahab all the way to Jezreel.* Divinely energized by extraordinary strength, Elijah ran before Ahab's chariot to Jezreel. This dramatic scene, with the Lord's prophet running before the king and the Lord himself racing behind him riding his mighty thundercloud chariot (see note on v. 24), served as a powerful appeal to Ahab to break once for all with Baal and henceforth to rule as the servant of the Lord.

19:2 *May the gods deal with me, be it ever so severely.* A curse formula (see note on 1Sa 3:17). *one of them.* The dead prophets of Baal (v. 1).

row I do not make your life like that of one of them." [b]

[3]Elijah was afraid [n] and ran [c] for his life. [d] When he came to Beersheba [e] in Judah, he left his servant there, [4]while he himself went a day's journey into the desert. He came to a broom tree, [f] sat down under it and prayed that he might die. "I have had enough, LORD," he said. "Take my life; [g] I am no better than my ancestors." [5]Then he lay down under the tree and fell asleep. [h]

All at once an angel [i] touched him and said, "Get up and eat." [6]He looked around, and there by his head was a cake of bread baked over hot coals, and a jar of water. He ate and drank and then lay down again.

[7]The angel of the LORD came back a second time and touched him and said, "Get

up and eat, for the journey is too much for you." [8]So he got up and ate and drank. Strengthened by that food, he traveled forty [j] days and forty nights until he reached Horeb, [k] the mountain of God. [9]There he went into a cave [l] and spent the night.

The LORD Appears to Elijah

And the word of the LORD came to him: "What are you doing here, Elijah?" [m]

[10]He replied, "I have been very zealous [n] for the LORD God Almighty. The Israelites have rejected your covenant, [o] broken down your altars, [p] and put your prophets to death with the sword. I am the only one left, [q] and now they are trying to kill me too."

[11]The LORD said, "Go out and stand on

19:2 [b]Ps 13:4; Jer 20:10; 26:21; 36:26
19:3 [c]S Ge 31:21 [d]S Ge 9:17 [e]S Jos 19:2
19:4 [f]Job 30:4 [g]S Nu 11:15; Job 6:9; 7:16; 10:1; Ps 69:19; Jer 20:18; Jnh 4:8
19:5 [h]Ge 28:11 [i]S Ge 16:7

19:8 [j]Ex 24:18; Mt 4:2 [k]S Ex 3:1
19:9 [l]S Ex 33:22 [m]S Ge 3:9
19:10 [n]S Nu 25:13; Ac 22:3; Gal 4:18 [o]S Dt 31:16 [p]1Ki 18:30 [q]1Ki 18:22; Jer 5:11; 9:2; Ro 11:3*

[n]3 Or *Elijah saw*

19:3 *Elijah was afraid and ran for his life.* In spite of Elijah's great triumph in the trial on Mount Carmel and the dramatic demonstration that Elijah's God is the Lord of heaven and earth and the source of Israel's blessings, Jezebel is undaunted. Hers is no empty threat, and Ahab has shown that he is either unwilling or unable to restrain her. So Elijah knows

that one of the main sources of Israel's present apostasy is still spewing out its poison and that his own life is in danger. *Beersheba.* The southernmost city in Judah (see notes on Ge 21:31; Am 5:5; see also Jdg 20:1).

19:4 *broom tree.* A desert shrub, sometimes large enough to offer some shade. *prayed that he might die.* Cf. Jnh 4:3,8.

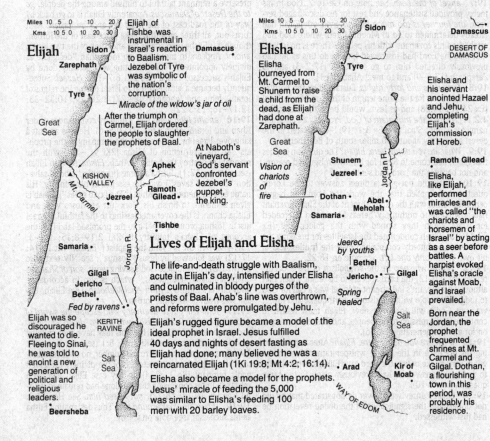

Elijah

Sidon · · Zarephath · Tyre · · Great Sea · Samaria · Gilgal · Jericho · Bethel · *Fed by ravens* · Mt. Carmel · KISHON VALLEY · Jezreel · Tishbe · Aphek · Ramoth Gilead · Jordan R. · KERITH RAVINE · Salt Sea · Beersheba

Miles 10 5 0 10 20 / Kms 10 5 0 10 20 30

Elijah of Tishbe was instrumental in Israel's reaction to Baalism. Jezebel of Tyre was symbolic of the nation's corruption.

— *Miracle of the widow's jar of oil*

After the triumph on Carmel, Elijah ordered the people to slaughter the prophets of Baal.

Damascus ·

At Naboth's vineyard, God's servant confronted Jezebel's puppet, the king.

Elijah was so discouraged he wanted to die. Fleeing to Sinai, he was told to anoint a new generation of political and religious leaders.

Elisha

Sidon · Tyre · Great Sea · Shunem · Jezreel · Dothan · Abel Meholah · Samaria · Jeered by youths · Bethel · Jericho · Gilgal · Spring healed · Salt Sea · Arad · Kir of Moab · Jordan R. · WAY OF EDOM

Miles 10 5 0 10 20 / Kms 10 5 0 10 20 30

Elisha journeyed from Mt. Carmel to Shunem to raise a child from the dead, as Elijah had done at Zarephath.

Vision of chariots of fire

DESERT OF DAMASCUS

Elisha and his servant anointed Hazael and Jehu, completing Elijah's commission at Horeb.

Ramoth Gilead

Elisha, like Elijah, performed miracles and was called "the chariots and horsemen of Israel" by acting as a seer before battles. A harpist evoked Elisha's oracle against Moab, and Israel prevailed.

Born near the Jordan, the prophet frequented shrines at Mt. Carmel and Gilgal. Dothan, a flourishing town in this period, was probably his residence.

Lives of Elijah and Elisha

The life-and-death struggle with Baalism, acute in Elijah's day, intensified under Elisha and culminated in bloody purges of the priests of Baal. Ahab's line was overthrown, and reforms were promulgated by Jehu.

Elijah's rugged figure became a model of the ideal prophet in Israel. Jesus fulfilled 40 days and nights of desert fasting as Elijah had done; many believed he was a reincarnated Elijah (1Ki 19:8; Mt 4:2; 16:14).

Elisha also became a model for the prophets. Jesus' miracle of feeding the 5,000 was similar to Elisha's feeding 100 men with 20 barley loaves.

the mountain[r] in the presence of the LORD, for the LORD is about to pass by."[s]

Then a great and powerful wind[t] tore the mountains apart and shattered[u] the rocks before the LORD, but the LORD was not in the wind. After the wind there was an earthquake, but the LORD was not in the earthquake. [12]After the earthquake came a fire,[v] but the LORD was not in the fire. And after the fire came a gentle whisper. [w] [13]When Elijah heard it, he pulled his cloak over his face[x] and went out and stood at the mouth of the cave.

Then a voice said to him, "What are you doing here, Elijah?"

[14]He replied, "I have been very zealous for the LORD God Almighty. The Israelites have rejected your covenant, broken down your altars, and put your prophets to death with the sword. I am the only one left,[y] and now they are trying to kill me too."

[15]The LORD said to him, "Go back the way you came, and go to the Desert of Damascus. When you get there, anoint Hazael[z] king over Aram. [16]Also, anoint[a] Jehu son of Nimshi king over Israel, and anoint Elisha[b] son of Shaphat from Abel Meholah[c] to succeed you as prophet. [17]Jehu will put to death any who escape the sword of Hazael,[d] and Elisha will put to death any who escape the sword of Jehu.[e] [18]Yet I reserve[f] seven thousand in Israel—all whose knees have not bowed down to Baal and all whose mouths have not kissed[g] him."

The Call of Elisha

[19]So Elijah went from there and found Elisha son of Shaphat. He was plowing with twelve yoke of oxen, and he himself was driving the twelfth pair. Elijah went up to him and threw his cloak[h] around him. [20]Elisha then left his oxen and ran after Elijah. "Let me kiss my father and

---

Cross references:

19:11 [r]Ex 34:2; Mt 17:1-3 [s]Ex 33:19 [t]S Ex 14:21; S 2Ki 2:1 [u]Na 1:6
19:12 [v]S Ex 3:2 [w]ver 11; S 1Sa 14:6; Job 4:16; Zec 4:6; 2Co 12:9
19:13 [x]Ex 3:6
19:14 [y]1Ki 18:22; Ro 11:3*
19:15 [z]2Ki 8:7-15
19:16 [a]2Ki 9:6 [b]ver 21; 2Ki 2:1; 3:11 [c]S Jdg 7:22
19:17 [d]2Ki 8:12, 29; 10:32; 12:17; 13:3,7,22; Am 1:4 [e]Jer 48:44
19:18 [f]Ro 11:4* [g]Hos 13:2
19:19 [h]S Ge 41:42; 2Ki 2:8,14

Elijah concluded that his work was fruitless and consequently that life was not worth living. He had lost his confidence in the triumph of the kingdom of God and was withdrawing from the arena of conflict.

19:7 *angel of the LORD.* See note on Ge 16:7. God in his mercy provided sustenance and rest for his discouraged servant. *the journey is too much for you.* Evidently Elijah had already determined to go to Mount Horeb, where God had established his covenant with his people. There is no indication that the Lord had instructed him to do this as he had previously directed him to go to Kerith (17:2–3) and to Zarephath (17:8–9) and to meet Ahab (18:1).

19:8 *forty days and forty nights.* Sustained by the Lord as Moses had been for the same length of time on Mount Sinai (Ex 24:18; 34:28) and as Jesus would be in the desert (Mt 4:2,11). *Horeb, the mountain of God.* Probably an alternate name for Mount Sinai (see Ex 3:1; 19:1–3), located in the desert apparently about 250 miles south of Beersheba.

19:9 *What are you doing here, Elijah?* The question implies that Elijah had come to Sinai for his own misguided reasons and not because the Lord had sent him.

19:10 Elijah did not give a direct answer to the Lord's question but implied that the work the Lord had begun centuries earlier with the establishment of the Sinai covenant had now come to nothing. Whereas Moses had interceded for Israel when they sinned with the golden calf (Ex 32:11–13), Elijah condemned the Israelites for breaking the covenant, and bitterly complained over the fruitlessness of his own work. *only one left.* See note on 18:22.

19:12 *gentle whisper.* In the symbolism of these occurrences (vv. 11–12) the Lord appears to be telling Elijah that although his servant's indictment of Israel was a call for God to judge his people with windstorm, earthquake and fire, it was not God's will to do so now. Elijah must return to continue God's mission to his people, and Elisha is to carry it on for another generation (v. 16).

19:13 *What are you doing here, Elijah?* After demonstrating his presence in the gentle whisper rather than in the wind, earthquake or fire, the Lord gave Elijah an opportunity to revise the answer he had previously given to the same question (vv. 9–10).

19:14 Elijah's unrevised answer demonstrated that he did not understand the significance of the divine revelation he had just witnessed.

19:15 *The LORD said to him.* Giving instructions to Elijah that revealed his sovereign power over people and nations. Even though Israel would experience divine judgment through Hazael, Jehu and Elisha, God would continue to preserve a remnant faithful to himself among the people. *go to the Desert of Damascus.* Apparently Elijah is to go back by way of the road east of the Dead Sea and the Jordan. As it turns out, all three anointings take place east of the Jordan, though it is Elisha who effects the anointing of the two kings. *anoint.* Appears to mean here no more than "designate as divinely appointed." This anointing was actually done by Elijah's successor Elisha (see 2Ki 8:7–15). *Hazael.* Subsequently became a serious threat to Israel during the reigns of Joram, Jehu and Jehoahaz (see 2Ki 8:28–29; 10:32–33; 12:17–18; 13:3,22).

19:16 *anoint Jehu.* Jehu was a military commander under Ahab and Joram, Ahab's son (2Ki 9:5–6). He was anointed king over Israel by a "man from the company of the prophets" at the instruction of Elisha (2Ki 9:1–16), with the mandate to destroy the house of Ahab. *Elisha.* As with Elijah (see note on 17:1), Elisha's name (meaning "God is salvation" or "God saves") was the essence of his ministry. His name evokes memory of Joshua ("The LORD saves"). Elijah is given someone to finish his work just as Moses was, and Elisha channels the covenant blessings to the faithful in Israel just as Joshua brought Israel into the promised land (see the account of Elisha's ministry in 2Ki 2:19–8:15; 9:1–3; 13:14–20). In the NT John the Baptist ("Elijah," Mt 11:14; 17:12) was followed by Jesus ("Joshua"; see NIV text note on Mt 1:21) to complete God's saving work. *son of Shaphat.* Shaphat means "He judges," which is also in accordance with Elisha's ministry. *from Abel Meholah.* Like Elijah, Elisha was from beyond the Jordan.

19:17 *Jehu will put to death any who escape the sword of Hazael.* See 2Ki 9:24. *Elisha will put to death any who escape the sword of Jehu.* How this may have been fulfilled we are not told, but see 2Ki 2:24; 8:1 (see also Hos 6:5).

19:18 *seven thousand.* A round number, no doubt symbolic of the fullness or completeness of the divinely preserved godly remnant (Ro 11:2–4). In any case Elijah had been mistaken in his conclusion that he alone had remained faithful (see vv. 10,14; 18:22). *not kissed him.* See Hos 13:2.

19:19 *threw his cloak around him.* Thus designating Elisha as his successor (see note on v. 16).

mother good-by," [i] he said, "and then I will come with you."

"Go back," Elijah replied. "What have I done to you?"

[21]So Elisha left him and went back. He took his yoke of oxen[j] and slaughtered them. He burned the plowing equipment to cook the meat and gave it to the people, and they ate. Then he set out to follow Elijah and became his attendant.[k]

Ben-Hadad Attacks Samaria

20 Now Ben-Hadad[l] king of Aram mustered his entire army. Accompanied by thirty-two kings with their horses and chariots, he went up and besieged Samaria[m] and attacked it. [2]He sent messengers into the city to Ahab king of Israel, saying, "This is what Ben-Hadad says: [3]'Your silver and gold are mine, and the best of your wives and children are mine.' "

[4]The king of Israel answered, "Just as you say, my lord the king. I and all I have are yours."

[5]The messengers came again and said, "This is what Ben-Hadad says: 'I sent to demand your silver and gold, your wives and your children. [6]But about this time tomorrow I am going to send my officials to search your palace and the houses of your officials. They will seize everything you value and carry it away.' "

[7]The king of Israel summoned all the elders[n] of the land and said to them, "See how this man is looking for trouble![o] When he sent for my wives and my children, my silver and my gold, I did not refuse him."

[8]The elders and the people all answered, "Don't listen to him or agree to his demands."

[9]So he replied to Ben-Hadad's messengers, "Tell my lord the king, 'Your servant will do all you demanded the first time, but this demand I cannot meet.' " They left and took the answer back to Ben-Hadad.

[10]Then Ben-Hadad sent another message to Ahab: "May the gods deal with me, be it ever so severely, if enough dust[p] remains in Samaria to give each of my men a handful."

[11]The king of Israel answered, "Tell him: 'One who puts on his armor should not boast[q] like one who takes it off.' "

[12]Ben-Hadad heard this message while he and the kings were drinking[r] in their tents,[o] and he ordered his men: "Prepare to attack." So they prepared to attack the city.

Ahab Defeats Ben-Hadad

[13]Meanwhile a prophet[s] came to Ahab king of Israel and announced, "This is what the LORD says: 'Do you see this vast army? I will give it into your hand today, and then you will know[t] that I am the LORD.' "

[14]"But who will do this?" asked Ahab.

The prophet replied, "This is what the LORD says: 'The young officers of the provincial commanders will do it.' "

"And who will start[u] the battle?" he asked.

The prophet answered, "You will."

[15]So Ahab summoned the young officers of the provincial commanders, 232 men.

Cross references (center column):

19:20 [i] Lk 9:61
19:21 [j] S 1Sa 6:14
[k] S ver 16
20:1 [l] S 1Ki 15:18
[m] S 1Ki 13:32
20:7 [n] 1Sa 11:3
[o] 2Ki 5:7
20:10 [p] S 2Sa 22:43
20:11 [q] Pr 27:1; Jer 9:23; Am 2:14
20:12 [r] S 1Ki 16:9
20:13 [s] S Jdg 6:8
[t] S Ex 6:7
20:14 [u] S Jdg 1:1

[o] 12 Or in Succoth; also in verse 16

19:21 *slaughtered them . . . burned the plowing equipment.* Elisha's break with his past vocation was complete, though he obviously came from a wealthy family. *attendant.* In Hebrew the same designation as used for Joshua's relationship to Moses ("aide," Ex 24:13; 33:11).

20:1 *Ben-Hadad king of Aram.* Chronological considerations suggest that this was Ben-Hadad II, either a son or a grandson of Ben-Hadad I, who had ruled Aram as early as 900–895 B.C. (see notes on 15:9–10,18–20,33). The events of this chapter span parts of two years (see vv. 22–26) followed by three years of peace between Israel and Aram (see 22:1). Ahab died at the conclusion of the three years of peace in a battle against the Arameans (22:37) in 853. This means that the events of this chapter are to be dated c. 857. *thirty-two kings.* Tribal chieftains or city-state kings who were vassals of Ben-Hadad II.

20:4 *I and all I have are yours.* Ahab's submission to Ben-Hadad's demand suggests that Israel saw little hope for the possibility of a military victory over the Aramean forces. The negotiated settlement would end the siege on Samaria, spare Ahab's life and avoid the plundering of the city.

20:6 *I am going to send my officials to search your palace and the houses of your officials.* Ben-Hadad's new demand required the surrender of the city to his forces.

20:9 *this demand I cannot meet.* Ahab replied in language conceding Ben-Hadad's superiority ("my lord the king, 'Your servant . . . ' ") but was adamant in refusing to surrender the city.

20:10 *May the gods deal with me, be it ever so severely.* A curse formula (see note on 1Sa 3:17).

20:11 *'One who puts on his armor should not boast like one who takes it off.'* A saying similar to the familiar "Don't count your chickens before they hatch."

20:13 *you will know that I am the LORD.* Although Ahab had not sought God's help in the crisis confronting the city, the Lord graciously chose to reveal himself yet another time (see 18:36–37) to the king and people, this time through a deliverance.

20:14 *young officers of the provincial commanders.* See note on 16:27. Organizational details of the provincial government of the northern kingdom are unknown.

20:15 *232 men . . . 7,000 in all.* Not a large military force (though a significant number for a city under siege) but one of fitting size for demonstrating that the imminent victory was from the Lord rather than from Israel's own military superiority (cf. Jdg 7:2).

Then he assembled the rest of the Israelites, 7,000 in all. 16They set out at noon
while Ben-Hadad and the 32 kings allied
with him were in their tents getting
drunk.[v] 17The young officers of the provincial commanders went out first.
Now Ben-Hadad had dispatched scouts,
who reported, "Men are advancing from
Samaria."
18He said, "If they have come out for
peace, take them alive; if they have come
out for war, take them alive."
19The young officers of the provincial
commanders marched out of the city with
the army behind them 20and each one
struck down his opponent. At that, the
Arameans fled, with the Israelites in pursuit. But Ben-Hadad king of Aram escaped
on horseback with some of his horsemen.
21The king of Israel advanced and overpowered the horses and chariots and inflicted heavy losses on the Arameans.
22Afterward, the prophet[w] came to the
king of Israel and said, "Strengthen your
position and see what must be done, because next spring[x] the king of Aram will
attack you again."
23Meanwhile, the officials of the king of
Aram advised him, "Their gods are gods[y]
of the hills. That is why they were too
strong for us. But if we fight them on the
plains, surely we will be stronger than
they. 24Do this: Remove all the kings from
their commands and replace them with
other officers. 25You must also raise an
army like the one you lost—horse for
horse and chariot for chariot—so we can
fight Israel on the plains. Then surely we
will be stronger than they." He agreed
with them and acted accordingly.
26The next spring[z] Ben-Hadad mustered the Arameans and went up to
Aphek[a] to fight against Israel. 27When the
Israelites were also mustered and given
provisions, they marched out to meet
them. The Israelites camped opposite them
like two small flocks of goats, while the
Arameans covered the countryside.[b]
28The man of God came up and told the
king of Israel, "This is what the LORD says:
'Because the Arameans think the LORD is a
god of the hills and not a god[c] of the valleys, I will deliver this vast army into your
hands, and you will know[d] that I am the
LORD.' "
29For seven days they camped opposite
each other, and on the seventh day the
battle was joined. The Israelites inflicted a
hundred thousand casualties on the Aramean foot soldiers in one day. 30The rest of
them escaped to the city of Aphek,[e] where
the wall collapsed[f] on twenty-seven thousand of them. And Ben-Hadad fled to the
city and hid[g] in an inner room.
31His officials said to him, "Look, we
have heard that the kings of the house of
Israel are merciful.[h] Let us go to the king
of Israel with sackcloth[i] around our waists
and ropes around our heads. Perhaps he
will spare your life."
32Wearing sackcloth around their waists
and ropes around their heads, they went to
the king of Israel and said, "Your servant
Ben-Hadad says: 'Please let me live.' "

20:16 [v]S 1Ki 16:9 **20:22** [w]S Jdg 6:8 [x]S 2Sa 11:1 **20:23** [y]ver 28; Isa 36:20; Ro 1:21-23

20:26 [z]S 2Sa 11:1 [a]ver 30; S 1Sa 4:1; 2Ki 13:17 **20:27** [b]Jdg 6:6; S 1Sa 13:6 **20:28** [c]S ver 23 [d]S Ex 6:7; Jer 16:19-21 **20:30** [e]S ver 26 [f]Ps 62:4; Isa 26:21; 30:13 [g]1Ki 22:25 **20:31** [h]Job 41:3 [i]S Ge 37:34

20:20 *each one struck down his opponent.* Apparently they were met by a small advance force like their own (see 2Sa 2:15–16). *escaped on horseback with some of his horsemen.* Since fighting on horseback did not come until later, reference must be to chariot horses and charioteers. After their defeat, the Arameans seem to have withdrawn to Damascus.

20:22 *the king of Aram will attack you again.* The anonymous prophet (see v. 13) warned Ahab against undue self-confidence. The prophet's announcement of an impending renewed attack by Ben-Hadad should have driven Ahab to more complete reliance on the God who had revealed himself on Mount Carmel and in the recent military victory.

20:23 *gods of the hills.* An expression of the pagan idea that a deity's power extended only over the limited area of his particular jurisdiction. *That is why they were too strong for us.* The Arameans believed that the outcome of military conflicts depended on the relative strength of the gods of the opposing forces rather than on the inherent strength of the two armies. For this reason, their strategy was to fight the next battle in a way that advantageously maximized the supposed strengths and weaknesses of the deities involved.

20:26 *Aphek.* Presumably the Aphek located a few miles east of the Sea of Galilee. The battle apparently took place in the Jordan Valley near the juncture of the Yarmuk and Jordan rivers.

20:28 *man of God.* Apparently the same prophet mentioned in vv. 13,22. *you will know that I am the LORD.* See note on v. 13. God will again demonstrate that he is the sovereign ruler over all nature and history and that the pagan nature deities are powerless before him.

20:29 *a hundred thousand casualties.* Probably includes all those who were driven from the field and the Aramean encampment, including support personnel.

20:30 *wall collapsed.* The God of Israel not only gave Israel's army a victory in battle but also caused an additional disaster to fall on the Aramean army. *twenty-seven thousand.* Aphek was certainly not so large a city that its wall could literally have collapsed on so many. Perhaps this is the number of troops that had taken refuge in Aphek and were left defenseless when the city walls gave way.

20:31 *kings of the house of Israel are merciful.* The Arameans recognized that Israel's kings were different from, e.g., the ruthless Assyrian kings. *sackcloth . . . ropes.* Perhaps here symbolic of humility and submission.

20:32 *Your servant.* In the diplomatic language of the time, Ben-Hadad acknowledged his inferiority and subordination to Ahab by designating himself Ahab's servant (see note on v. 9). *my brother.* Ahab disregarded Ben-Hadad's concession and responded in terminology used by rulers who considered themselves equals (see 9:13). In doing this, Ahab gave much more than Ben-Hadad had asked or expected.

The king answered, "Is he still alive? He is my brother."

[33] The men took this as a good sign and were quick to pick up his word. "Yes, your brother Ben-Hadad!" they said.

"Go and get him," the king said. When Ben-Hadad came out, Ahab had him come up into his chariot.

[34] "I will return the cities[j] my father took from your father," Ben-Hadad[k] offered. "You may set up your own market areas[l] in Damascus,[m] as my father did in Samaria."

Ahab said,[u] "On the basis of a treaty[n] I will set you free." So he made a treaty with him, and let him go.

A Prophet Condemns Ahab

[35] By the word of the LORD one of the sons of the prophets[o] said to his companion, "Strike me with your weapon," but the man refused.[p]

[36] So the prophet said, "Because you have not obeyed the LORD, as soon as you leave me a lion[q] will kill you." And after the man went away, a lion found him and killed him.

[37] The prophet found another man and said, "Strike me, please." So the man struck him and wounded him. [38] Then the prophet went and stood by the road waiting for the king. He disguised himself with his headband down over his eyes. [39] As the king passed by, the prophet called out to him, "Your servant went into the thick of the battle, and someone came to me with a captive and said, 'Guard this man. If he is missing, it will be your life for his life,[r] or you must pay a talent[p] of silver.' [40] While your servant was busy here and there, the man disappeared."

"That is your sentence,"[s] the king of Israel said. "You have pronounced it yourself."

[41] Then the prophet quickly removed the headband from his eyes, and the king of Israel recognized him as one of the prophets. [42] He said to the king, "This is what the LORD says: 'You[t] have set free a man I had determined should die.[q][u] Therefore it is your life for his life,[v] your people for his people.' " [43] Sullen and angry,[w] the king of Israel went to his palace in Samaria.

Naboth's Vineyard

21 Some time later there was an incident involving a vineyard belonging to Naboth[x] the Jezreelite. The vineyard was in Jezreel,[y] close to the palace of Ahab king of Samaria. [2] Ahab said to Naboth, "Let me have your vineyard to use for a vegetable garden, since it is close

20:34 /1Ki 15:20
*k*S Ge 10:22
/2Sa 8:6
*m*S Ge 14:15;
Jer 49:23-27
*n*S Ex 23:32
20:35
*o*S 1Sa 10:5;
Am 7:14
*p*S 1Ki 13:21
20:36 *q*1Ki 13:24

20:39 *r*S Jos 2:14
20:40 *s*2Sa 12:5;
S 14:13
20:42 *t*S 2Sa 12:7
*u*Jer 48:10
*v*S Jos 2:14
20:43 *w*1Ki 21:4
21:1 *x*2Ki 9:21
*y*S 1Sa 29:1;
2Ki 10:1

p39 That is, about 75 pounds (about 34 kilograms)
q42 The Hebrew term refers to the irrevocable giving over of things or persons to the LORD, often by totally destroying them.

20:33 *come up into his chariot.* Not the treatment normally accorded a defeated military opponent.
20:34 *cities my father took from your father.* Perhaps Ramoth Gilead (see 22:3) along with some of the cities Ben-Hadad I had taken from Baasha (15:20) at an even earlier time. *your own market areas.* Outlets for engaging in the lucrative international trade—a distinct economic advantage; usually such privileges were a jealously guarded local monopoly. *made a treaty with him, and let him go.* A parity treaty (a peace treaty between equals) that included among its provisions the political and trade agreements proposed by Ben-Hadad.
20:35 *sons of the prophets.* An expression designating members of prophetic companies (see 2Ki 2:3,5,7,15; 4:1, 38; 5:22; 6:1; 9:1). "Son" is not to be understood here as "male child" or "descendant" but as the member of a group. These companies of prophets were apparently religious communities that sprang up in the face of general indifference and apostasy for the purpose of mutual edification and the cultivation of the experience of God. It seems likely that they were known as prophets because their religious practices (sometimes ecstatic) were called prophesying (see 18:29; Nu 11:25–27; 1Sa 10:5–6,10–11; 18:10; 19:20–24)—to be distinguished from "prophet" in the sense of one bringing ("prophesying") a word from the Lord. The relationship of the Lord's great prophets (such as Samuel, Elijah and Elisha) to these communities probably being their spiritual mentors.
20:36 *as soon as you leave me a lion will kill you.* A penalty reminiscent of what happened to the man of God from Judah (13:23–24).

20:39 *talent.* See NIV text note. Because few soldiers could have paid such a large sum, it would appear to Ahab that the man's life was at stake.
20:40 *That is your sentence.* Ahab refused to grant clemency. Little did he know that he was pronouncing his own death sentence (cf. the similar technique used by Nathan the prophet, 2Sa 12:1–12).
20:42 *a man I had determined should die.* See NIV text note and notes on Lev 27:28; Jos 6:17. It is not clear whether Ahab violated a previous revelation or erred by simply neglecting to inquire of the Lord before releasing Ben-Hadad. In any case, the Lord had given Ben-Hadad into Ahab's hand (see v. 28), and Ahab was responsible to the Lord for his custody. *your life for his life, your people for his people.* Because Ahab sinned in his official capacity as king, the sentence fell not only on Ahab personally but also on the people of the northern kingdom. Ahab died in battle against the Arameans (22:29–39), and Israel was severely humiliated by them during the reigns of Jehu and Jehoahaz (2Ki 10:32; 13:3).
21:1 *close to the palace of Ahab.* Ahab maintained a residence in Jezreel in addition to his official palace in Samaria (see 18:45; 2Ki 9:30). *Samaria.* The entire northern kingdom is here represented by its capital city (see note on 16:24).
21:2 *Let me have your vineyard.* Because royal power in Israel was limited by covenantal law (see Dt 17:14–20; 1Sa 10:25), Ahab was unable simply to confiscate privately held land, as was customary with Canaanite kings (see note on v. 7; see also 1Sa 8:9–17).

to my palace. In exchange I will give you a better vineyard or, if you prefer, I will pay you whatever it is worth."

³But Naboth replied, "The LORD forbid that I should give you the inheritance*z* of my fathers."

⁴So Ahab went home, sullen and angry*a* because Naboth the Jezreelite had said, "I will not give you the inheritance of my fathers." He lay on his bed sulking and refused*b* to eat.

⁵His wife Jezebel came in and asked him, "Why are you so sullen? Why won't you eat?"

⁶He answered her, "Because I said to Naboth the Jezreelite, 'Sell me your vineyard; or if you prefer, I will give you another vineyard in its place.' But he said, 'I will not give you my vineyard.'"

⁷Jezebel his wife said, "Is this how you act as king over Israel? Get up and eat! Cheer up. I'll get you the vineyard*c* of Naboth the Jezreelite."

⁸So she wrote letters*d* in Ahab's name, placed his seal*e* on them, and sent them to the elders and nobles who lived in Naboth's city with him. ⁹In those letters she wrote:

"Proclaim a day of fasting and seat Naboth in a prominent place among the people. ¹⁰But seat two scoundrels*f* opposite him and have them testify that he has cursed*g* both God and the king. Then take him out and stone him to death."

¹¹So the elders and nobles who lived in Naboth's city did as Jezebel directed in the letters she had written to them. ¹²They proclaimed a fast*h* and seated Naboth in a

prominent place among the people. ¹³Then two scoundrels came and sat opposite him and brought charges against Naboth before the people, saying, "Naboth has cursed both God and the king." So they took him outside the city and stoned him to death. *i* ¹⁴Then they sent word to Jezebel: "Naboth has been stoned and is dead."

¹⁵As soon as Jezebel heard that Naboth had been stoned to death, she said to Ahab, "Get up and take possession of the vineyard*j* of Naboth the Jezreelite that he refused to sell you. He is no longer alive, but dead." ¹⁶When Ahab heard that Naboth was dead, he got up and went down to take possession of Naboth's vineyard.

¹⁷Then the word of the LORD came to Elijah the Tishbite: ¹⁸"Go down to meet Ahab king of Israel, who rules in Samaria. He is now in Naboth's vineyard, where he has gone to take possession of it. ¹⁹Say to him, 'This is what the LORD says: Have you not murdered a man and seized his property?'*k* Then say to him, 'This is what the LORD says: In the place where dogs licked up Naboth's blood,*l* dogs*m* will lick up your blood—yes, yours!'"

²⁰Ahab said to Elijah, "So you have found me, my enemy!"*n*

"I have found you," he answered, "because you have sold*o* yourself to do evil in the eyes of the LORD. ²¹I am going to bring disaster on you. I will consume your descendants and cut off from Ahab every last male*p* in Israel—slave or free.*q* ²²I will make your house*r* like that of Jeroboam son of Nebat and that of Baasha son of Ahijah, because you have provoked me to anger and have caused Israel to sin.'*s*

Cross references

21:3
*z*S Lev 25:23
21:4 *a*1Ki 20:43
*b*1Sa 28:23
21:7 *c*S 1Sa 8:14
21:8 *d*2Sa 11:14
*e*S Ge 38:18
21:10
*f*S Dt 13:13;
Ac 6:11
*g*S Ex 22:28;
Lev 24:15-16
21:12 *h*Isa 58:4

21:13
*i*S Lev 24:16
21:15 *j*S 1Sa 8:14
21:19 *k*Job 24:6;
31:39 *l*2Ki 9:26;
Ps 9:12; Isa 14:20
*m*1Ki 22:38;
Ps 68:23; Jer 15:3
21:20
*n*S 1Ki 18:17
*o*2Ki 17:17;
Ro 7:14
21:21 *p*Jdg 9:5;
2Ki 10:7
*q*S Dt 32:36
21:22 *r*1Ki 16:3
*s*S 1Ki 12:30

21:3 Naboth's refusal to dispose of his land was based on the conviction that the land was the Lord's, that he had granted a perpetual lease to each Israelite family and that this lease was to be jealously preserved as the family's permanent inheritance in the promised land.

21:7 *Is this how you act as king over Israel?* A sarcastic remark of incredulity spoken by one accustomed to the despotic practices of the Phoenician and Canaanite kings, who would not hesitate a moment to use their power to satisfy personal interests (contrast the attitude and practice of Samuel in the exercise of his civil power, 1Sa 12:3–4).

21:9 *Proclaim a day of fasting.* Jezebel attempted to create the impression that a disaster threatened the people that could be averted only if they would humble themselves before the Lord and remove any person whose sin had brought God's judgment on them (cf. Jdg 20:26; 1Sa 7:5–6; 2Ch 20:2–4).

21:10 *two.* Mosaic law required two witnesses for capital offenses (Nu 35:30; Dt 17:6; 19:15). *scoundrels.* See note on Dt 13:13. *have them testify.* The entire scenario was designed to give an appearance of legitimate judicial procedure (see Ex 20:16; 23:7; Lev 19:16). *he has cursed both*

God and the king. For this the Mosaic law prescribed death by stoning (Lev 24:15–16).

21:13 *outside the city.* In accordance with Mosaic law (Lev 24:14; Nu 15:35–36). Naboth was stoned on his own field (compare v. 19 with 2Ki 9:21,26), and his sons were stoned with him (see 2Ki 9:26; cf. the case of Achan, Jos 7: 24–25), thus also eliminating his heirs.

21:19 *Have you not murdered a man and seized his property?* Ahab's willing compliance with Jezebel's scheme made him guilty of murder and theft. *In the place where dogs licked up Naboth's blood, dogs will lick up your blood.* Ahab's subsequent repentance (v. 29) occasioned the postponement of certain aspects of this prophecy until the time of his son Joram, whose body was thrown on the field of Naboth (2Ki 9:25–26). Ahab himself was killed in battle at Ramoth Gilead (22:29–37) and his body brought to Samaria, where the dogs licked the blood being washed from his chariot (22:38).

21:21 *slave or free.* See note on 14:10.

21:22 *like that of Jeroboam.* See 14:10; 15:28–30. *that of Baasha.* See 16:3–4,11–13.

23"And also concerning Jezebel the Lord says: 'Dogs[t] will devour Jezebel by the wall of[r] Jezreel.'

24"Dogs[u] will eat those belonging to Ahab who die in the city, and the birds of the air[v] will feed on those who die in the country."

25(There was never[w] a man like Ahab, who sold himself to do evil in the eyes of the Lord, urged on by Jezebel his wife. 26He behaved in the vilest manner by going after idols, like the Amorites[x] the Lord drove out before Israel.)

27When Ahab heard these words, he tore his clothes, put on sackcloth[y] and fasted. He lay in sackcloth and went around meekly.[z]

28Then the word of the Lord came to Elijah the Tishbite: 29"Have you noticed how Ahab has humbled himself before me? Because he has humbled[a] himself, I will not bring this disaster in his day,[b] but I will bring it on his house in the days of his son."[c]

Micaiah Prophesies Against Ahab

22:1–28pp — 2Ch 18:1–27

22 For three years there was no war between Aram and Israel. 2But in the third year Jehoshaphat king of Judah went down to see the king of Israel. 3The king of Israel had said to his officials, "Don't you know that Ramoth Gilead[d] belongs to us and yet we are doing nothing to retake it from the king of Aram?"

4So he asked Jehoshaphat, "Will you go with me to fight[e] against Ramoth Gilead?"

Jehoshaphat replied to the king of Israel, "I am as you are, my people as your people, my horses as your horses." 5But Jehoshaphat also said to the king of Israel, "First seek the counsel[f] of the Lord."

6So the king of Israel brought together the prophets—about four hundred men—and asked them, "Shall I go to war against Ramoth Gilead, or shall I refrain?"

"Go,"[g] they answered, "for the Lord will give it into the king's hand."[h]

7But Jehoshaphat asked, "Is there not a prophet[i] of the Lord here whom we can inquire[j] of?"

8The king of Israel answered Jehoshaphat, "There is still one man through whom we can inquire of the Lord, but I hate[k] him because he never prophesies anything good[l] about me, but always bad. He is Micaiah son of Imlah."

"The king should not say that," Jehoshaphat replied.

9So the king of Israel called one of his officials and said, "Bring Micaiah son of Imlah at once."

10Dressed in their royal robes, the king of Israel and Jehoshaphat king of Judah were sitting on their thrones at the threshing floor[m] by the entrance of the gate of Samaria, with all the prophets prophesying before them. 11Now Zedekiah[n] son of Kenaanah had made iron horns[o] and he

Cross references

21:23 *t*2Ki 9:10, 34-36
21:24 *u*1Ki 14:11; *v*S Ge 40:19; S Dt 28:26
21:25 *w*S 1Ki 14:9; S 16:33
21:26 *x*S Ge 15:16
21:27 *y*S Ge 37:34; S Jer 4:8; *z*Isa 38:15
21:29 *a*S Ex 10:3; *b*S Ex 32:14; 2Ki 22:20; *c*Ex 20:5; 2Ki 9:26; 10:6-10
22:3 *d*S Dt 4:43
22:4 *e*2Ki 3:7
22:5 *f*Ex 33:7; 2Ki 3:11; Job 38:2; Ps 32:8; 73:24; 107:11
22:6 *g*S Jdg 18:6
*h*S 1Ki 13:18
22:7 *i*Dt 18:15; 2Ki 3:11; 5:8; *j*S Nu 27:21; 2Ki 3:11
22:8 *k*Am 5:10; *l*ver 13; Isa 5:20; 30:10; Jer 23:17
22:10 *m*S Jdg 6:37
22:11 *n*ver 24; *o*Dt 33:17; Jer 27:2; 28:10; Zec 1:18-21

r23 Most Hebrew manuscripts; a few Hebrew manuscripts, Vulgate and Syriac (see also 2 Kings 9:26) *the plot of ground at*

21:24 See notes on 14:11; 16:4.
21:25 *urged on by Jezebel.* See 16:31; 18:4; 19:1–2; 21:7.
21:26 *Amorites.* Here a designation for the entire pre-Israelite population of Canaan (see Ge 15:16; Dt 1:7).
21:27 *sackcloth.* See note on Ge 37:34.
21:29 *in the days of his son.* The judgment was postponed but not rescinded (see note on v. 19).
22:1 *three years.* See note on 20:1. *no war between Aram and Israel.* The annals of the Assyrian ruler Shalmaneser III (859–824 B.C.) record the participation of both "Ahab the Israelite" and Hadadezer (Ben-Hadad) of Damascus in a coalition of 12 rulers that fought against Assyrian forces at Qarqar on the Orontes River in 853. According to the Assyrian records, Ahab contributed 2,000 chariots and 10,000 foot soldiers to the allied forces. Assyrian claims of victory appear exaggerated since they withdrew and did not venture westward again for four or five years.
22:2 *Jehoshaphat king of Judah went down to see the king of Israel.* Perhaps to congratulate him on the success of the western alliance against the Assyrian threat (see notes on v. 1; 2Ch 18:2).
22:3 *Ramoth Gilead.* Located near the Yarmuk River in Transjordan; an Israelite city since the days of Moses (see 4:13; Dt 4:43; Jos 20:8). *belongs to us.* Israel could lay claim to Ramoth Gilead also by virtue of the treaty concluded with Ben-Hadad a few years earlier (see 20:34), the provi-

sions of which he had apparently failed to honor.
22:4 *Will you go with me . . . ?* Even though Ahab had just been allied with the Arameans against the Assyrians, now that the Assyrian threat was over he did not hesitate to seize an opportunity to free Ramoth Gilead from Aramean control. *I am as you are, my people as your people, my horses as your horses.* Jehoshaphat was later to be condemned by the prophet Jehu (2Ch 19:2) for violating the Lord's will by joining forces with Ahab. In this alliance, Jehoshaphat completely reversed the policy of his father Asa, who had entered into an alliance with the Arameans against Baasha of the northern kingdom (see 15:17–23).
22:5 *First seek the counsel of the Lord.* Jehoshaphat hesitated to proceed with the planned action without the assurance of the Lord's favor (see 1Sa 23:1–4; 2Sa 2:1).
22:6 *prophets.* No doubt associated with the paganized worship at Bethel (see notes on 12:28–29), they exercised their "office" by proclaiming messages designed to please the king (see Am 7:10–13).
22:7 *Is there not a prophet of the Lord here . . . ?* Jehoshaphat recognized that the 400 prophets were not to be relied on (see Eze 13:2–3) and asked for consultation with a true prophet of the Lord.
22:8 *never prophesies anything good.* Ahab's assessment of a prophet depended on whether his message was favorable to him (see 18:17; 21:20).
22:11 *Zedekiah.* Evidently the spokesman for the 400

declared, "This is what the LORD says: 'With these you will gore the Arameans until they are destroyed.'"

12All the other prophets were prophesying the same thing. "Attack Ramoth Gilead and be victorious," they said, "for the LORD will give it into the king's hand."

13The messenger who had gone to summon Micaiah said to him, "Look, as one man the other prophets are predicting success for the king. Let your word agree with theirs, and speak favorably."*p*

14But Micaiah said, "As surely as the LORD lives, I can tell him only what the LORD tells me."*q*

15When he arrived, the king asked him, "Micaiah, shall we go to war against Ramoth Gilead, or shall I refrain?"

"Attack and be victorious," he answered, "for the LORD will give it into the king's hand."

16The king said to him, "How many times must I make you swear to tell me nothing but the truth in the name of the LORD?"

17Then Micaiah answered, "I saw all Israel scattered*r* on the hills like sheep without a shepherd,*s* and the LORD said, 'These people have no master. Let each one go home in peace.'"

18The king of Israel said to Jehoshaphat, "Didn't I tell you that he never prophesies anything good about me, but only bad?"

19Micaiah continued, "Therefore hear the word of the LORD: I saw the LORD sitting on his throne*t* with all the host*u* of heaven standing around him on his right and on his left. 20And the LORD said, 'Who will entice Ahab into attacking Ramoth Gilead and going to his death there?'

"One suggested this, and another that.

21Finally, a spirit came forward, stood before the LORD and said, 'I will entice him.'

22"'By what means?' the LORD asked.

"'I will go out and be a lying*v* spirit in the mouths of all his prophets,' he said.

"'You will succeed in enticing him,' said the LORD. 'Go and do it.'

23"So now the LORD has put a lying*w* spirit in the mouths of all these prophets*x* of yours. The LORD has decreed disaster*y* for you."

24Then Zedekiah*z* son of Kenaanah went up and slapped*a* Micaiah in the face. "Which way did the spirit from*s* the LORD go when he went from me to speak*b* to you?" he asked.

25Micaiah replied, "You will find out on the day you go to hide*c* in an inner room."

26The king of Israel then ordered, "Take Micaiah and send him back to Amon the ruler of the city and to Joash the king's son 27and say, 'This is what the king says: Put this fellow in prison*d* and give him nothing but bread and water until I return safely.'"

28Micaiah declared, "If you ever return safely, the LORD has not spoken*e* through me." Then he added, "Mark my words, all you people!"

Ahab Killed at Ramoth Gilead
22:29–36pp — 2Ch 18:28–34

29So the king of Israel and Jehoshaphat king of Judah went up to Ramoth Gilead. 30The king of Israel said to Jehoshaphat, "I will enter the battle in disguise,*f* but you wear your royal robes." So the king of Israel disguised himself and went into battle.

31Now the king of Aram*g* had ordered his thirty-two chariot commanders, "Do not fight with anyone, small or great, ex-

Cross references (center column)
22:13 *p*S ver 8
22:14 *q*S Nu 22:18;
S 1Sa 3:17
22:17 *r*S Ge 11:4;
Na 3:18
*s*Nu 27:17;
Isa 13:14;
S Mt 9:36
22:19 *t*Ps 47:8;
Isa 6:1; 63:15;
Eze 1:26; Da 7:9
*u*Job 1:6; 15:8;
38:7;
Ps 103:20-21;
148:2; Jer 23:18,
22; Lk 2:13

22:22 *v*S Jdg 9:23;
2Th 2:11
22:23 *w*S Dt 13:3
*x*Eze 14:9
*y*S Dt 31:29
22:24 *z*ver 11
*a*Ac 23:2
*b*Job 26:4
22:25 *c*1Ki 20:30
22:27 *d*2Ch 16:10;
Jer 20:2; 26:21;
37:15; Heb 11:36
22:28 *e*S Dt 18:22
22:30 *f*S 1Sa 28:8
22:31 *g*S Ge 10:22;
S 2Sa 10:19

*s*24 Or *Spirit of*

---

prophets. *iron horns.* A symbol of power (see Dt 33:17).
22:13 *Let your word agree with theirs.* A bit of advice reflecting the view that all prophets were merely self-serving.
22:15 *we.* A subtle shift (see v. 6) that seeks a favorable response by including Jehoshaphat as a co-sponsor of the enterprise. *Attack . . . for the LORD will give it into the king's hand.* Micaiah sarcastically mimics the 400 false prophets (see v. 12).
22:16 *tell me nothing but the truth.* Micaiah apparently betrayed his lack of seriousness, and Ahab immediately recognizes this.
22:17 *like sheep without a shepherd . . . These people have no master.* Using the imagery of shepherd and sheep (see Nu 27:16–17; Zec 13:7; Mt 9:36; 26:31), Micaiah depicts Ahab's death in the upcoming battle.
22:19 *I saw the LORD sitting on his throne.* A true prophet was one who had, as it were, been made privy to what had transpired in God's heavenly throne room and so could truthfully declare what God intended to do (see Isa 6:1; Jer 23:16–22).
22:23 *the LORD has put a lying spirit in the mouths of all*

these prophets. Some view the lying spirit as Satan or one of his agents. Others have suggested a spirit of God who undertakes the task of a lying spirit (but see 1Sa 15:29). Still others understand the lying spirit as a symbolic picture of the power of the lie. The Lord had given the 400 prophets over to the power of the lie because they did not love the truth and had chosen to speak out of their own hearts (see Jer 14:14; 23:16,26; Eze 13:2–3,17; see also note on 2Sa 24:1).
22:24 *Which way did the spirit from the LORD go when he went from me to speak to you?* By this sarcastic question Zedekiah suggests that one prophet can be a liar just as well as another.
22:25 *hide in an inner room.* Where Zedekiah will seek refuge (cf. 20:30). This will vindicate Micaiah's prophetic authority.
22:30 *disguise.* By this strategy he thought he could direct attention away from himself and so minimize any chance for fulfillment of Micaiah's prediction.
22:31 *except the king of Israel.* If the leader was killed or captured, ancient armies usually fell apart (cf. vv. 35–36).

cept the king*h* of Israel." 32When the chariot commanders saw Jehoshaphat, they thought, "Surely this is the king of Israel." So they turned to attack him, but when Jehoshaphat cried out, 33the chariot commanders saw that he was not the king of Israel and stopped pursuing him.

34But someone drew his bow*i* at random and hit the king of Israel between the sections of his armor. The king told his chariot driver, "Wheel around and get me out of the fighting. I've been wounded." 35All day long the battle raged, and the king was propped up in his chariot facing the Arameans. The blood from his wound ran onto the floor of the chariot, and that evening he died. 36As the sun was setting, a cry spread through the army: "Every man to his town; everyone to his land!"*j*

37So the king died and was brought to Samaria, and they buried him there. 38They washed the chariot at a pool in Samaria (where the prostitutes bathed),*t* and the dogs*k* licked up his blood, as the word of the LORD had declared.

39As for the other events of Ahab's reign, including all he did, the palace he built and inlaid with ivory,*l* and the cities he fortified, are they not written in the book of the annals of the kings of Israel? 40Ahab rested with his fathers. And Ahaziah his son succeeded him as king.

Jehoshaphat King of Judah

22:41–50pp — 2Ch 20:31–21:1

41Jehoshaphat son of Asa became king of Judah in the fourth year of Ahab king of Israel. 42Jehoshaphat was thirty-five years old when he became king, and he reigned in Jerusalem twenty-five years. His mother's name was Azubah daughter of Shilhi. 43In everything he walked in the ways of his father Asa*m* and did not stray from them; he did what was right in the eyes of the LORD. The high places,*n* however, were not removed, and the people continued to offer sacrifices and burn incense there. 44Jehoshaphat was also at peace with the king of Israel.

45As for the other events of Jehoshaphat's reign, the things he achieved and his military exploits, are they not written in the book of the annals of the kings of Judah? 46He rid the land of the rest of the male shrine prostitutes*o* who remained there even after the reign of his father Asa. 47There was then no king*p* in Edom; a deputy ruled.

48Now Jehoshaphat built a fleet of trading ships*u* *q* to go to Ophir for gold, but they never set sail—they were wrecked at Ezion Geber.*r* 49At that time Ahaziah son of Ahab said to Jehoshaphat, "Let my men sail with your men," but Jehoshaphat refused.

50Then Jehoshaphat rested with his fathers and was buried with them in the city of David his father. And Jehoram his son succeeded him.

Ahaziah King of Israel

51Ahaziah son of Ahab became king of Israel in Samaria in the seventeenth year of Jehoshaphat king of Judah, and he reigned

---

22:31
*h*S 2Sa 17:2
22:34 *j*2Ki 9:24; 2Ch 35:23
22:36 *j*2Ki 14:12
22:38
*k*S 1Ki 21:19
22:39 *l*2Ch 9:17; Ps 45:8; Am 3:15

22:43
*m*S 1Ki 8:61; 2Ch 17:3
*n*S 1Ki 3:2
22:46
*o*S Dt 23:17
22:47
*p*1Ki 11:14-18; 2Ki 3:9; 8:20
22:48
*q*S 1Ki 9:26
*r*S Nu 33:35

t38 Or Samaria and cleaned the weapons
u48 Hebrew of ships of Tarshish

22:34 *chariot driver.* A war chariot normally carried two men—a fighter and a driver. Sometimes, it appears, there were three men, but the third seems to have been an officer who commanded a chariot unit (see 9:22; 2Ki 9:25; Ex 14:7; 15:4, where these officers are called lit. "the third"). **22:35** *that evening he died.* Fulfilling Micaiah's prophecy (vv. 17,28). **22:38** *as the word of the LORD had declared.* A partial fulfillment of Elijah's prophecy concerning Ahab's death (see note on 21:19). **22:39** *the palace he built and inlaid with ivory.* Excavators of Samaria have found ivory inlays in some of the buildings dating from this period of Israel's history. Ahab's use of ivory in this way is indicative of the realm's economic prosperity during his reign. *cities he fortified.* Excavators have found evidence that Ahab strengthened the fortifications of Megiddo and Hazor. *annals of the kings of Israel.* See note on 14:19. **22:40** *rested with his fathers.* See note on 1:21. *Ahaziah his son succeeded him.* For the reign of Ahaziah see vv. 51–53; 2Ki 1. **22:41** *Jehoshaphat . . . became king of Judah in the fourth year of Ahab.* Appears to refer to the beginning of Jehoshaphat's reign as sole king in 869 B.C. (see notes on v. 42; 16:29; see also Introduction: Chronology).

22:42 *twenty-five years.* 872–848 B.C. The full span of Jehoshaphat's reign dates from the 39th year of King Asa, when he became co-regent with his father (see note on 15:10; see also 2Ch 16:12). **22:43** *The high places, however, were not removed.* See notes on 3:2; 15:14. **22:44** *king.* Probably to be understood in the collective sense and as including Ahab, Ahaziah and Joram, all of whom ruled in the north during the reign of Jehoshaphat in the south (see note on v. 4). **22:45** *military exploits.* See 2Ki 3; 2Ch 17:11; 20. *annals of the kings of Judah.* See note on 14:29. **22:46** *male shrine prostitutes.* See note on 14:24. **22:47** *no king in Edom.* Suggests that Edom was subject to Judah (see 2Sa 8:14; 2Ki 8:20). **22:48** *Ophir.* See note on 9:28. *wrecked at Ezion Geber.* The destruction of the trading ships was a judgment of God on Jehoshaphat for entering into an alliance with Ahaziah of the northern kingdom (see 2Ch 20:35–37). **22:50** *rested with his fathers.* See note on 1:21. *Jehoram his son succeeded him.* For the reign of Jehoram see 2Ki 8:16–24; 2Ch 21. **22:51** *seventeenth year of Jehoshaphat.* 853 B.C. (see notes on vv. 41–42). *two years.* 853–852 (see note on 2Ki 1:17).

over Israel two years. [52]He did evil[s] in the eyes of the LORD, because he walked in the ways of his father and mother and in the ways of Jeroboam son of Nebat, who caused Israel to sin. [53]He served and worshiped Baal[t] and provoked the LORD, the God of Israel, to anger, just as his father[u] had done.

22:52 [s]1Ki 15:26

22:53 [t]S Jdg 2:11
[u]1Ki 21:25

22:52 *ways of his father and mother.* See 16:30–33.

ways of Jeroboam. See 12:28–33.

2 KINGS

See Introduction to 1 Kings.

Outline

Below is an abbreviated outline for 2 Kings. For the complete outline see Introduction to 1 Kings: Outline.

III. The Ministries of Elijah and Elisha and Other Prophets from Ahab/Asa to Joram/Jehoshaphat (1Ki 17:1-2Ki 8:15)
    A. Elijah (and Other Prophets) in the Reign of Ahab (1Ki 17:1-22:40)
    B. Jehoshaphat of Judah (1Ki 22:41-50)
    C. Ahaziah of Israel; Elijah's Last Prophecy (1Ki 22:51-2Ki 1:18)
    D. Elijah's Translation; Elisha's Inauguration (2Ki 2:1-18)
    E. Elisha in the Reign of Joram (2Ki 2:19-8:15)
IV. Israel and Judah from Joram/Jehoram to the Exile of Israel (2Ki 8:16-17:41)
    A. Jehoram of Judah (8:16-24)
    B. Ahaziah of Judah (8:25-29)
    C. Jehu's Revolt and Reign (chs. 9-10)
    D. Athaliah and Joash of Judah; Repair of the Temple (chs. 11-12)
    E. Jehoahaz of Israel (13:1-9)
    F. Jehoash of Israel; Elisha's Last Prophecy (13:10-25)
    G. Amaziah of Judah (14:1-22)
    H. Jeroboam II of Israel (14:23-29)
    I. Azariah of Judah (15:1-7)
    J. Zechariah of Israel (15:8-12)
    K. Shallum of Israel (15:13-16)
    L. Menahem of Israel (15:17-22)
    M. Pekahiah of Israel (15:23-26)
    N. Pekah of Israel (15:27-31)
    O. Jotham of Judah (15:32-38)
    P. Ahaz of Judah (ch. 16)
    Q. Hoshea of Israel (17:1-6)
    R. Exile of Israel; Resettlement of the Land (17:7-41)
V. Judah from Hezekiah to the Babylonian Exile (2Ki 18-25)
    A. Hezekiah (chs. 18-20)
    B. Manasseh (21:1-18)
    C. Amon (21:19-26)
    D. Josiah (22:1-23:30)
    E. Jehoahaz Exiled to Egypt (23:31-35)
    F. Jehoiakim: First Babylonian Invasion (23:36-24:7)
    G. Jehoiachin: Second Babylonian Invasion (24:8-17)
    H. Zedekiah (24:18-20)
    I. Babylonian Exile of Judah (25:1-21)
    J. Removal of the Remnant to Egypt (25:22-26)
    K. Elevation of Jehoiachin in Babylon (25:27-30)

The LORD's Judgment on Ahaziah

1 After Ahab's death, Moab[a] rebelled against Israel. [2]Now Ahaziah had fallen through the lattice of his upper room in Samaria and injured himself. So he sent messengers,[b] saying to them, "Go and consult Baal-Zebub,[c] the god of Ekron,[d] to see if I will recover[e] from this injury."

[3]But the angel[f] of the LORD said to Elijah[g] the Tishbite, "Go up and meet the messengers of the king of Samaria and ask them, 'Is it because there is no God in Israel[h] that you are going off to consult Baal-Zebub, the god of Ekron?' [4]Therefore this is what the LORD says: 'You will not leave[i] the bed you are lying on. You will certainly die!'" So Elijah went.

[5]When the messengers returned to the king, he asked them, "Why have you come back?"

[6]"A man came to meet us," they replied. "And he said to us, 'Go back to the king who sent you and tell him, "This is what the LORD says: Is it because there is no God in Israel that you are sending men to consult Baal-Zebub, the god of Ekron? Therefore you will not leave[j] the bed you

are lying on. You will certainly die!'"'"

[7]The king asked them, "What kind of man was it who came to meet you and told you this?"

[8]They replied, "He was a man with a garment of hair[k] and with a leather belt around his waist."

The king said, "That was Elijah the Tishbite."

[9]Then he sent[l] to Elijah a captain[m] with his company of fifty men. The captain went up to Elijah, who was sitting on the top of a hill, and said to him, "Man of God, the king says, 'Come down!'"

[10]Elijah answered the captain, "If I am a man of God, may fire come down from heaven and consume you and your fifty men!" Then fire[n] fell from heaven and consumed the captain and his men.

[11]At this the king sent to Elijah another captain with his fifty men. The captain said to him, "Man of God, this is what the king says, 'Come down at once!'"

[12]"If I am a man of God," Elijah replied, "may fire come down from heaven and consume you and your fifty men!" Then the fire of God fell from heaven and consumed him and his fifty men.

Cross references (center column):

1:1 [a]S Ge 19:37; 2Ki 3:5
1:2 [b]ver 16
[c]S Mk 3:22
[d]1Sa 6:2; Isa 2:6; 14:29 [e]S Jdg 18:5
1:3 [f]ver 15
[g]1Ki 17:1
[h]S 1Sa 28:8
1:4 [i]ver 6,16; Ps 41:8
1:6 [j]S ver 4
1:8 [k]S 1Ki 18:7; Mt 3:4; Mk 1:6
1:9 [l]2Ki 6:14
[m]Ex 18:25; Isa 3:3
1:10 [n]S 1Ki 18:38; S Rev 11:5; S 13:13

1:1 *After Ahab's death.* See 1Ki 22:37. *Moab rebelled.* Moab had been brought into subjection by David (see 2Sa 8:2), but when the northern and Transjordan tribes rebelled and made Jeroboam their king, political domination of Moab probably also shifted to the northern kingdom. An inscription of Mesha king of Moab (see chart on "Ancient Texts Relating to the OT," p. 5) indicates that during the reign of Omri's "son" (probably a reference to his grandson Joram, not to Ahab) the Moabites were able to free the area of Medeba from Israelite control (see map No. 5 at the end of the Study Bible).

1:2 *Baal-Zebub.* See note on Jdg 10:6. *Ekron.* The northernmost of the five major Philistine cities (see Jos 13:3; 1Sa 5:10 and notes). *if I will recover.* Ahaziah appears to have feared that his injury would be fatal. He turned to the pagan deity for a revelatory oracle, not for healing.

1:3 *angel of the LORD.* See 1Ki 19:7; see also note on Ge 16:7. The Lord usually spoke directly to the consciousness of the prophet (1Ki 17:2,8; 18:1; 19:9; 21:17). Perhaps the means of revelation was changed in this instance to heighten the contrast between the messengers of Ahaziah (vv. 2–3,5) and the angel (which means "messenger") of the Lord. *Elijah the Tishbite.* See note on 1Ki 17:1. *king of Samaria.* See note on 1Ki 21:1.

1:4 *You will certainly die!* Ahaziah will receive the oracle he sought, but it will come from the Lord through Elijah, not from Baal-Zebub.

1:5 *Why have you come back?* Ahaziah realized the messengers could not have traveled so quickly to Ekron and back.

1:8 *garment of hair.* See 1Ki 19:19. Elijah's cloak was probably of sheepskin or camel's hair, tied with a simple leather thong (cf. Mt 3:4). His dress contrasted sharply with the fine linen clothing (see Jer 13:1) of his wealthy contemporaries and constituted a protest against the materialistic attitudes of the king and the upper classes (cf. Mt 11:7–8; Lk 7:24–25). *That was Elijah the Tishbite.* Ahaziah was familiar

with Elijah's appearance because of the prophet's many encounters with Ahab, his father.

1:9 *he sent to Elijah a captain with his company of fifty men.* The pagan people of that time thought that the magical power of curses could be nullified either by forcing the pronouncer of the curse to retract his statement or by killing him so that his curse would go with him to the netherworld. It appears that Ahaziah shared this view and desired to take Elijah prisoner in order to counteract the pronouncement of his death. *Man of God, the king says, 'Come down!'* Ahaziah attempted to place the prophet under the authority of the king. This constituted a violation of the covenant nature of Israelite kingship, in which the king's actions were always to be placed under the scrutiny and authority of the word of the Lord spoken by his prophets (see notes on 1Sa 10:25; 12:23).

1:10 *fire fell from heaven and consumed the captain and his men.* See 1Ki 18:38. Another link between the ministries of Elijah and Moses (see Lev 10:2; Nu 16:35). At stake in this incident was the question of who was sovereign in Israel. Would Ahaziah recognize that the king in Israel was only a vice-regent under the authority and kingship of the Lord, or would he exercise despotic power, like pagan kings (see notes on 1Sa 12:14–15)? At Mount Carmel the Lord had revealed himself and authenticated his prophet by fire from heaven (see 1Ki 18:38–39). Now this previous revelation is confirmed to Ahaziah. Jesus' rebuke of his disciples for suggesting that fire be called down from heaven to destroy the Samaritans (Lk 9:51–56) is not to be understood as a disapproval of Elijah's action, but as an indication that the disciples failed to discern the difference between the issue at stake in Elijah's day and the unbelief of the Samaritans in their own day.

1:11 *the king sent to Elijah another captain.* Ahaziah refused to submit to the word of the Lord in spite of the dramatic revelation of God's power.

13So the king sent a third captain with
his fifty men. This third captain went up
and fell on his knees before Elijah. "Man of
God," he begged, "please have respect for
my life[o] and the lives of these fifty men,
your servants! 14See, fire has fallen from
heaven and consumed the first two captains and all their men. But now have respect for my life!"
15The angel[p] of the LORD said to Elijah,
"Go down with him; do not be afraid[q] of
him." So Elijah got up and went down
with him to the king.
16He told the king, "This is what the
LORD says: Is it because there is no God in
Israel for you to consult that you have sent
messengers[r] to consult Baal-Zebub, the
god of Ekron? Because you have done this,
you will never leave[s] the bed you are lying
on. You will certainly die!" 17So he died,[t]
according to the word of the LORD that
Elijah had spoken.
Because Ahaziah had no son, Joram[a] [u]
succeeded him as king in the second year
of Jehoram son of Jehoshaphat king of
Judah. 18As for all the other events of Ahaziah's reign, and what he did, are they not
written in the book of the annals of the
kings of Israel?

Elijah Taken Up to Heaven

2 When the LORD was about to take[v]
Elijah up to heaven in a whirlwind,[w]
Elijah and Elisha[x] were on their way from
Gilgal.[y] 2Elijah said to Elisha, "Stay here;[z]
the LORD has sent me to Bethel."
But Elisha said, "As surely as the LORD
lives and as you live, I will not leave
you."[a] So they went down to Bethel.
3The company[b] of the prophets at Bethel came out to Elisha and asked, "Do you
know that the LORD is going to take your
master from you today?"
"Yes, I know," Elisha replied, "but do
not speak of it."
4Then Elijah said to him, "Stay here, Elisha; the LORD has sent me to Jericho.[c]"
And he replied, "As surely as the LORD
lives and as you live, I will not leave you."
So they went to Jericho.
5The company[d] of the prophets at Jericho went up to Elisha and asked him, "Do
you know that the LORD is going to take
your master from you today?"
"Yes, I know," he replied, "but do not
speak of it."
6Then Elijah said to him, "Stay here;[e]
the LORD has sent me to the Jordan."[f]
And he replied, "As surely as the LORD
lives and as you live, I will not leave
you."[g] So the two of them walked on.
7Fifty men of the company of the prophets went and stood at a distance, facing the
place where Elijah and Elisha had stopped
at the Jordan. 8Elijah took his cloak,[h]
rolled it up and struck[i] the water with it.
The water divided[j] to the right and to the
left, and the two of them crossed over on
dry[k] ground.
9When they had crossed, Elijah said to
Elisha, "Tell me, what can I do for you
before I am taken from you?"
"Let me inherit a double[l] portion of
your spirit,"[m] Elisha replied.
10"You have asked a difficult thing," Elijah said, "yet if you see me when I am

1:13 [o]Ps 72:14 **1:15** [p]ver 3 [q]Isa 51:12; 57:11; Jer 1:17; Eze 2:6 **1:16** [r]S ver 2 [s]ver 4 **1:17** [t]2Ki 8:15; Jer 20:6; 28:17 [u]2Ki 3:1; 8:16 **2:1** [v]S Ge 5:24 [w]ver 11; 1Ki 19:11; Isa 5:28; 66:15; Jer 4:13; Na 1:3 [x]S 1Ki 19:16 [y]S Dt 11:30; 2Ki 4:38 **2:2** [z]ver 6 [a]Ru 1:16 **2:3** [b]S 1Sa 10:5 **2:4** [c]Jos 3:16 **2:5** [d]ver 3 **2:6** [e]ver 2 [f]Jos 3:15 [g]Ru 1:16 **2:8** [h]S 1Ki 19:19 [i]ver 14 [j]S Ex 14:21 [k]Ex 14:22,29 **2:9** [l]S Dt 21:17 [m]S Nu 11:17

[a]*17* Hebrew *Jehoram,* a variant of *Joram*

1:13 *fell on his knees before Elijah.* The third captain, recognizing that Elijah was the bearer of the word of the Lord, feared for his life and bowed before him with a humble request.
1:15 *The angel of the LORD said to Elijah.* See note on v. 3.
1:17 *died, according to the word of the LORD.* In the end Ahaziah was punished for turning away from the God of Israel to a pagan deity, and the word of the Lord was shown to be both reliable and beyond the power of the king to annul. *Joram.* Ahaziah's younger brother (see 3:1; 1Ki 22:51). *second year of Jehoram son of Jehoshaphat.* Jehoram's reign overlapped that of his father Jehoshaphat from 853 to 848 B.C. (see note on 8:16). The reference here is to the second year of that co-regency. The 18th year of Jehoshaphat (3:1) is therefore the same as the second year of Jehoram's co-regency (852).
1:18 *annals of the kings of Israel.* See note on 1Ki 14:19.
2:2 *I will not leave you.* Elisha was aware that Elijah's ministry was almost finished and that his departure was near (v. 5). He was determined to accompany him until the moment the Lord took him. His commitment to Elijah and to Elijah's ministry was unfailing (see v. 9; 1Ki 19:21).
2:3 *company of.* Lit. "sons of" (see note on 1Ki 20:35). During the days of Elijah and Elisha, companies of prophets were located at Bethel (here), Jericho (v. 5) and Gilgal (4:38). It appears that Elijah journeyed by divine instruction to Gilgal (v. 1), Bethel (v. 2) and Jericho (v. 4) for a last meeting with each of these companies.
2:7 *Fifty men.* These men were to witness the miracle by which Elijah and Elisha crossed the river.
2:8 *Elijah took his cloak . . . and struck the water with it.* Elijah used his cloak much as Moses had used his staff at the time of Israel's passage through the "Red Sea" (see Ex 14:16,21,26).
2:9 *Let me inherit a double portion.* Elisha was not expressing a desire for a ministry twice as great as Elijah's, but he was using terms derived from inheritance law to express his desire to carry on Elijah's ministry. Inheritance law assigned a double portion of a father's possessions to the firstborn son (see Dt 21:17 and note).
2:10 *difficult thing.* Although Elijah had previously been told to anoint Elisha as his successor (1Ki 19:16,19–21), Elijah's response clearly showed that the issue rested solely with the Lord's sovereign good pleasure. *If you see me . . . it will be yours—otherwise not.* Elijah left the answer to Elisha's request in the Lord's hands.

taken from you, it will be yours—otherwise not."

[11] As they were walking along and talking together, suddenly a chariot of fire[n] and horses of fire appeared and separated the two of them, and Elijah went up to heaven[o] in a whirlwind.[p] [12] Elisha saw this and cried out, "My father! My father! The chariots[q] and horsemen of Israel!" And Elisha saw him no more. Then he took hold of his own clothes and tore[r] them apart.

[13] He picked up the cloak that had fallen from Elijah and went back and stood on the bank of the Jordan. [14] Then he took the cloak[s] that had fallen from him and struck[t] the water with it. "Where now is the LORD, the God of Elijah?" he asked. When he struck the water, it divided to the right and to the left, and he crossed over.

[15] The company[u] of the prophets from Jericho, who were watching, said, "The spirit[v] of Elijah is resting on Elisha." And they went to meet him and bowed to the ground before him. [16] "Look," they said, "we your servants have fifty able men. Let them go and look for your master. Perhaps the Spirit[w] of the LORD has picked him

up[x] and set him down on some mountain or in some valley."

"No," Elisha replied, "do not send them."

[17] But they persisted until he was too ashamed[y] to refuse. So he said, "Send them." And they sent fifty men, who searched for three days but did not find him. [18] When they returned to Elisha, who was staying in Jericho, he said to them, "Didn't I tell you not to go?"

Healing of the Water

[19] The men of the city said to Elisha, "Look, our lord, this town is well situated, as you can see, but the water is bad and the land is unproductive."

[20] "Bring me a new bowl," he said, "and put salt in it." So they brought it to him. [21] Then he went out to the spring and threw[z] the salt into it, saying, "This is what the LORD says: 'I have healed this water. Never again will it cause death or make the land unproductive.'" [22] And the water has remained wholesome[a] to this day, according to the word Elisha had spoken.

Elisha Is Jeered

[23] From there Elisha went up to Bethel.

Cross references (center column):

2:11 *n*2Ki 6:17; Ps 68:17; 104:3, 4; Isa 66:15; Hab 3:8; Zec 6:1
*o*S Ge 5:24
*p*S ver 1
2:12 *q*2Ki 6:17; 13:14
*r*S Ge 37:29
2:14 *s*S 1Ki 19:19
*t*ver 8
2:15 *u*S 1Sa 10:5
*v*S Nu 11:17
2:16 *w*S 1Ki 18:12
*x*Ac 8:39
2:17 *y*S Jdg 3:25
2:21 *z*S Ex 15:25; 2Ki 4:41; 6:6
2:22 *a*Ex 15:25

2:11 *chariot of fire and horses of fire.* The Lord's heavenly host had accompanied and supported Elijah's ministry (as it had that of Moses; see Ex 15:1–10), and now at his departure Elisha is allowed to see it (cf. 6:17). *Elijah went up to heaven in a whirlwind.* Elijah, like Enoch before him (Ge 5:24), was taken up to heaven bodily without experiencing death; like Moses (Dt 34:4–6), he was taken away outside the promised land.

2:12 *chariots and horsemen of Israel!* Elisha depicted Elijah as embodying the true strength of the nation. He, rather than the apostate king, is the Lord's representative. The same description was later used of Elisha (13:14).

2:13 *He picked up the cloak.* See note on v. 8. Possession of Elijah's cloak symbolized Elisha's succession to Elijah's ministry (see 1Ki 19:19).

2:14 *When he struck the water, it divided.* See v. 8. The Lord authenticated Elisha's succession to Elijah's ministry and demonstrated that the same divine power that had accompanied Elijah's ministry was now operative in the ministry of Elisha. In crossing the Jordan as Joshua had before him, Elisha is shown to be Elijah's "Joshua" (Elisha and Joshua are very similar names, Elisha meaning "God saves" and Joshua "The LORD saves").

2:15 *bowed to the ground before him.* Indicated their recognition of Elisha's succession to Elijah's position. Elisha was now the Lord's official representative in this time of royal apostasy.

2:16 *Perhaps the Spirit of the LORD has picked him up and set him down.* Obadiah expressed the same idea years earlier (see 1Ki 18:12). *do not send them.* Elisha knew their search would be fruitless.

2:17 *Send them.* When the company of prophets refused to be satisfied with Elisha's answer, he permitted them to go so that the authority and truth of his words would be confirmed

to them.

2:19 *city.* Evidently Jericho (see v. 18). *the water is bad and the land is unproductive.* The inhabitants of Jericho were experiencing the effects of the covenant curse (contrast Dt 28:15–18 with Ex 23:25–26; Lev 26:9; Dt 28:1–4). See 1Ki 16:34; Jos 6:26.

2:20 *new bowl.* That which was to be used in the service of the Lord was to be undefiled by profane use (see Lev 1:3,10; Nu 19:2; Dt 21:3; 1Sa 6:7). *put salt in it.* Elisha may have used salt because of its known preservative qualities, but it is more likely that he used it to symbolize the covenant faithfulness of the Lord (see notes on Lev 2:13; Nu 18:19; see also 2Ch 13:5).

2:21 *I have healed this water.* Any idea of a magical effect of the salt in the purification of the water is excluded by the explicit statement that the Lord himself healed the water. In this symbolic way Elisha was able, as the first act of his ministry, to proclaim to the people that in spite of their disobedience the Lord was merciful and was still reaching out to them in his grace (see 13:23).

2:23 *Go on up.* Since Bethel was the royal cult center of the northern kings (1Ki 12:29; Am 7:13) and Elijah and Elisha were known to frequent Samaria (perhaps even as their main residence; see note on 5:3), the youths from Bethel no doubt assumed that Elisha was going up to Samaria to continue Elijah's struggle against royal apostasy. (Some believe that the youths, in their mocking, were telling Elisha to ascend to heaven as Elijah had done.) *you baldhead!* Baldness was uncommon among the ancient Jews, and luxuriant hair seems to have been viewed as a sign of strength and vigor (see note on 2Sa 14:26). By calling Elisha "baldhead," the youths from Bethel expressed that city's utter disdain for the Lord's representative, who, they felt, had no power.

As he was walking along the road, some youths came out of the town and jeered[b] at him. "Go on up, you baldhead!" they said. "Go on up, you baldhead!" [24]He turned around, looked at them and called down a curse[c] on them in the name[d] of the LORD. Then two bears came out of the woods and mauled forty-two of the youths. [25]And he went on to Mount Carmel[e] and from there returned to Samaria.

Moab Revolts

3 Joram[b][f] son of Ahab became king of Israel in Samaria in the eighteenth year of Jehoshaphat king of Judah, and he reigned twelve years. [2]He did evil[g] in the eyes of the LORD, but not as his father[h] and mother had done. He got rid of the sacred stone[i] of Baal that his father had made. [3]Nevertheless he clung to the sins[j] of Jeroboam son of Nebat, which he had caused Israel to commit; he did not turn away from them.

[4]Now Mesha king of Moab[k] raised sheep, and he had to supply the king of Israel with a hundred thousand lambs[l] and with the wool of a hundred thousand rams. [5]But after Ahab died, the king of Moab rebelled[m] against the king of Israel. [6]So at that time King Joram set out from Samaria and mobilized all Israel. [7]He also sent this message to Jehoshaphat king of Judah: "The king of Moab has rebelled against me. Will you go with me to fight[n] against Moab?"

"I will go with you," he replied. "I am as you are, my people as your people, my horses as your horses."

[8]"By what route shall we attack?" he asked.

"Through the Desert of Edom," he answered.

[9]So the king of Israel set out with the king of Judah and the king of Edom.[o] After a roundabout march of seven days, the army had no more water for themselves or for the animals with them.

[10]"What!" exclaimed the king of Israel. "Has the LORD called us three kings together only to hand us over to Moab?"

[11]But Jehoshaphat asked, "Is there no prophet of the LORD here, that we may inquire[p] of the LORD through him?"

An officer of the king of Israel answered, "Elisha[q] son of Shaphat is here. He used to pour water on the hands of Elijah.[c][r]"

[12]Jehoshaphat said, "The word[s] of the LORD is with him." So the king of Israel and Jehoshaphat and the king of Edom went down to him.

[13]Elisha said to the king of Israel, "What do we have to do with each other? Go to

---

2:23
b S Ex 22:28; 2Ch 30:10; 36:16; Job 19:18; Ps 31:18
2:24 c S Ge 4:11
d S Dt 18:19
2:25
e S 1Ki 18:20
3:1 f S 2Ki 1:17
3:2 g 1Ki 15:26
h 1Ki 16:30
i S Ex 23:24
3:3 j S 1Ki 12:30
3:4 k S Ge 19:37; 2Ki 1:1 l Ezr 7:17; Isa 16:1
3:5 m S 2Ki 1:1

3:7 n 1Ki 22:4
3:9 o S 1Ki 22:47
3:11
p S Ge 25:22; S 1Ki 22:5
q S Ge 20:7
r S 1Ki 19:16
3:12 s S Nu 11:17

---

b [7] Hebrew *Jehoram*, a variant of *Joram*; also in verse 6
c [11] That is, he was Elijah's personal servant.

2:24 *called down a curse on them in the name of the LORD.* Elisha pronounced a curse similar to the covenant curse of Lev 26:21–22. The result gave warning of the judgment that would come on the entire nation should it persist in disobedience and apostasy (see 2Ch 36:16). Thus Elisha's first acts were indicative of his ministry that would follow: God's covenant blessings would come to those who looked to him (vv. 19–22), but God's covenant curses would fall on those who turned away from him.

3:1 *Joram son of Ahab became king . . . in the eighteenth year of Jehoshaphat.* See note on 1:17. *twelve years.* 852–841 B.C.

3:2 *not as his father and mother had done.* Not as Ahab (see notes on 1Ki 16:30–34) and Jezebel (see 1Ki 18:4; 19:1–2; 21:7–15). *sacred stone of Baal that his father had made.* Apparently a reference to the stone representation of the male deity (see note on 1Ki 14:23) that Ahab placed in the temple he had constructed for Jezebel in Samaria (see 1Ki 16:32–33). From 10:27 it appears that this stone was later reinstated, perhaps by Jezebel.

3:3 *sins of Jeroboam . . . he had caused Israel to commit.* See note on 1Ki 14:16.

3:4 *Mesha king of Moab.* See note on 1:1. *a hundred thousand lambs and . . . the wool of a hundred thousand rams.* The heavy annual tribute (see Isa 16:1) that Israel required from the Moabites as a vassal state.

3:5 *king of Moab rebelled.* See note on 1:1.

3:7 *Will you go with me to fight against Moab?* Joram wished to attack Moab from the rear (v. 8), but to do that his army had to pass through Judah. *I am as you are, my people as your people, my horses as your horses.* See 1Ki 22:4. Jehoshaphat had already been condemned by prophets of the

Lord for his alliance with the northern kings Ahab (see 2Ch 18:1; 19:1–2) and Ahaziah (2Ch 20:35–37), yet he agreed to join with Joram against Moab. Perhaps he was disturbed by the potential danger to Judah posed by the growing strength of Moab (see 2Ch 20), and he may have considered Joram less evil than his predecessors (see v. 2).

3:8 *Through the Desert of Edom.* This route of attack took the armies of Israel and Judah south of the Dead Sea, enabling them to circumvent the fortifications of Moab's northern frontier and to avoid the possibility of a rearguard action against them by the Arameans of Damascus. The Edomites, who were subject to Judah, were in no position to resist the movement of Israel's army through their territory.

3:9 *king of Edom.* Although here designated a king, he was in reality a governor appointed by Jehoshaphat (see 8:20; 1Ki 22:47).

3:11 *Is there no prophet of the LORD here . . . ?* See 1Ki 22:7. Only after the apparent failure of their own strategies did the three rulers seek the word of the Lord (v. 12). *Elisha son of Shaphat is here.* Since Elijah is reported to have sent a letter to Jehoshaphat's son Jehoram after his father's death (2Ch 21:12–15), it seems that Elisha accompanied the armies on this campaign as the representative of the aged Elijah. The event is narrated here after the account of Elisha's initiation as Elijah's successor and the two events that foreshadowed the character of his ministry. Following this introduction to Elisha's ministry, the present episode is topically associated with the series of Elisha's acts that now occupies the narrative.

3:13 *Go to the prophets of your father and . . . mother.* See 1Ki 22:6.

the prophets of your father and the prophets of your mother."

"No," the king of Israel answered, "because it was the LORD who called us three kings together to hand us over to Moab."

[14]Elisha said, "As surely as the LORD Almighty lives, whom I serve, if I did not have respect for the presence of Jehoshaphat king of Judah, I would not look at you or even notice you. [15]But now bring me a harpist." [t]

While the harpist was playing, the hand[u] of the LORD came upon Elisha [16]and he said, "This is what the LORD says: Make this valley full of ditches. [17]For this is what the LORD says: You will see neither wind nor rain, yet this valley will be filled with water,[v] and you, your cattle and your other animals will drink. [18]This is an easy[w] thing in the eyes of the LORD; he will also hand Moab over to you. [19]You will overthrow every fortified city and every major town. You will cut down every good tree, stop up all the springs, and ruin every good field with stones."

[20]The next morning, about the time[x] for offering the sacrifice, there it was—water flowing from the direction of Edom! And the land was filled with water.[y]

[21]Now all the Moabites had heard that the kings had come to fight against them; so every man, young and old, who could bear arms was called up and stationed on the border. [22]When they got up early in the morning, the sun was shining on the water. To the Moabites across the way, the water looked red—like blood. [23]"That's blood!" they said. "Those kings must have fought and slaughtered each other. Now to the plunder, Moab!"

[24]But when the Moabites came to the camp of Israel, the Israelites rose up and fought them until they fled. And the Israelites invaded the land and slaughtered the Moabites. [25]They destroyed the towns, and each man threw a stone on every good field until it was covered. They stopped up all the springs and cut down every good tree. Only Kir Hareseth[z] was left with its stones in place, but men armed with slings surrounded it and attacked it as well.

[26]When the king of Moab saw that the battle had gone against him, he took with him seven hundred swordsmen to break through to the king of Edom, but they failed. [27]Then he took his firstborn[a] son, who was to succeed him as king, and offered him as a sacrifice on the city wall. The fury against Israel was great; they withdrew and returned to their own land.

The Widow's Oil

4 The wife of a man from the company[b] of the prophets cried out to Elisha, "Your servant my husband is dead, and you know that he revered the LORD. But now his creditor[c] is coming to take my two boys as his slaves."

[2]Elisha replied to her, "How can I help you? Tell me, what do you have in your house?"

"Your servant has nothing there at all," she said, "except a little oil." [d]

Cross references (center column):

3:15 [r]S 1Sa 10:5
[u]Jer 15:17;
Eze 1:3
3:17 [v]Ps 107:35;
Isa 12:3; 32:2;
35:6; 41:18;
65:13
3:18 [w]S Ge 18:14;
2Ki 20:10;
Isa 49:6;
Jer 32:17,27;
Mk 10:27
3:20 [x]S Ex 29:41
[y]S Ex 17:6

3:25 [z]Isa 15:1;
16:7; Jer 48:31,
36
3:27 [a]S Dt 12:31;
2Ki 16:3; 21:6;
2Ch 28:3;
Ps 106:38;
Jer 19:4-5;
Mic 6:7
4:1 [b]S 1Sa 10:5
[c]S Ex 22:26;
Lev 25:39-43;
Ne 5:3-5;
Job 22:6; 24:9
4:2 [d]S 1Ki 17:12

3:14 *if I did not have respect for . . . Jehoshaphat . . . I would not look at you.* Joram will share in the blessing of the word of God only because of his association with Jehoshaphat.
3:15 *bring me a harpist.* To create a disposition conducive to receiving the word of the Lord.
3:16 *this valley.* The Israelite armies were encamped in the broad valley (the Arabah) between the highlands of Moab on the east and those of Judah on the west, just south of the Dead Sea.
3:17 *will be filled with water.* The word of the Lord contained a promise and a directive. The Lord will graciously provide for his people, but they must respond to his word in faith and obedience (v. 16).
3:19 The two armies will devastate the rebellious country.
3:20 *time for offering.* See Ex 29:38–39; Nu 28:3–4.
water flowing from the direction of Edom. Flash floods in the distant mountains of Edom caused water to flow north through the broad, usually dry, valley that sloped toward the Dead Sea (see note on v. 16).
3:23 *Those kings must have . . . slaughtered each other.* The Moabites would have good reason to suspect that an internal conflict had arisen between the parties of an alliance whose members had previously been mutually hostile.
3:25 *Kir Hareseth.* The capital city of Moab (see Isa 16:7, 11; Jer 48:31,36), usually identified with present-day Kerak, located about 11 miles east of the Dead Sea and 15 miles south of the Arnon River.
3:26 *break through to the king of Edom.* A desperate attempt by the king of Moab to induce Edom to turn against Israel and Judah.
3:27 *offered him as a sacrifice on the city wall.* King Mesha offered his oldest son, the crown prince, as a burnt offering (see 16:3; Jer 7:31) to the Moabite god Chemosh (see 1Ki 11:7; Nu 21:29; Jer 48:46) in an attempt to induce the deity to come to his aid. *The fury against Israel was great.* The Hebrew underlying this clause would normally refer to a visitation of God's wrath. It may be that just when total victory appeared to be in Israel's grasp, God's displeasure with the Ahab dynasty showed itself in some way that caused the Israelite kings to give up the campaign. Comparing Aramaic and later Hebrew usage, a few scholars suggest that the Hebrew here can be translated, "There was great dismay upon/in Israel."
4:1 *company of the prophets.* See notes on 2:3; 1Ki 20:35. *to take my two boys as his slaves.* Servitude as a means of debt payment by labor was permitted in the Mosaic law (Ex 21:1–2; Lev 25:39–41; Dt 15:1–11). It appears that the practice was much abused (see Ne 5:5,8; Am 2:6; 8:6), even though the law limited the term of such bondage and required that those so held be treated as hired workers.

³Elisha said, "Go around and ask all your neighbors for empty jars. Don't ask for just a few. ⁴Then go inside and shut the door behind you and your sons. Pour oil into all the jars, and as each is filled, put it to one side."

⁵She left him and afterward shut the door behind her and her sons. They brought the jars to her and she kept pouring. ⁶When all the jars were full, she said to her son, "Bring me another one."

But he replied, "There is not a jar left." Then the oil stopped flowing.

⁷She went and told the man of God,ᵉ and he said, "Go, sell the oil and pay your debts. You and your sons can live on what is left."

The Shunammite's Son Restored to Life

⁸One day Elisha went to Shunem.ᶠ And a well-to-do woman was there, who urged him to stay for a meal. So whenever he came by, he stopped there to eat. ⁹She said to her husband, "I know that this man who often comes our way is a holy man of God. ¹⁰Let's make a small room on the roof and put in it a bed and a table, a chair and a lamp for him. Then he can stayᵍ there whenever he comes to us."

¹¹One day when Elisha came, he went up to his room and lay down there. ¹²He said to his servant Gehazi, "Call the Shunammite."ʰ So he called her, and she stood before him. ¹³Elisha said to him, "Tell her, 'You have gone to all this trou-

ble for us. Now what can be done for you? Can we speak on your behalf to the king or the commander of the army?'"

She replied, "I have a home among my own people."

¹⁴"What can be done for her?" Elisha asked.

Gehazi said, "Well, she has no son and her husband is old."

¹⁵Then Elisha said, "Call her." So he called her, and she stood in the doorway. ¹⁶"About this timeⁱ next year," Elisha said, "you will hold a son in your arms."

"No, my lord," she objected. "Don't mislead your servant, O man of God!"

¹⁷But the woman became pregnant, and the next year about that same time she gave birth to a son, just as Elisha had told her.

¹⁸The child grew, and one day he went out to his father, who was with the reapers.ʲ ¹⁹"My head! My head!" he said to his father.

His father told a servant, "Carry him to his mother." ²⁰After the servant had lifted him up and carried him to his mother, the boy sat on her lap until noon, and then he died. ²¹She went up and laid him on the bedᵏ of the man of God, then shut the door and went out.

²²She called her husband and said, "Please send me one of the servants and a donkey so I can go to the man of God quickly and return."

²³"Why go to him today?" he asked. "It's not the New Moonˡ or the Sabbath."

4:7 ᵉS 1Ki 12:22
4:8 ᶠS Jos 19:18
4:10 ᵍMt 10:41; S Ro 12:13
4:12 ʰ2Ki 8:1

4:16 ⁱS Ge 18:10
4:18 ʲS Ru 2:3
4:21 ᵏver 32
4:23 ˡS Nu 10:10; 1Ch 23:31; Ps 81:3

4:4 *shut the door behind you and your sons.* The impending miracle was not intended to be a public sensation but to demonstrate privately God's mercy and grace to this widow (cf. Ps 68:5). She did not hesitate to respond to the instructions of the Lord's prophet in faith and obedience.

4:8 *Shunem.* See note on 1Ki 1:3.

4:9 *holy man of God.* The woman recognized that Elisha was a person set apart to the Lord's work in a very special sense. Nowhere else in the OT is the term "holy" applied to a prophet.

4:10 *he can stay there whenever he comes to us.* By her hospitality the woman was able to assist in sustaining the proclamation of God's word through Elisha.

4:12 *Gehazi.* Referred to here for the first time; he appears to have served Elisha in some of the same ways as Elisha had served Elijah, though the two men were of drastically different character (see 5:19–27; 6:15).

4:13 *I have a home among my own people.* The Shunammite woman felt secure and content in the community of her own family and tribe, and she had no need or desire for favors from high government officials.

4:14 *she has no son and her husband is old.* A great disappointment because it meant that the family's name would cease and its land and possessions would pass on to others. It was also a great threat to this young wife's future in that she faced the likelihood of many years as a widow with no provider or protector—children were a widow's only

social security in old age (see 8:1–6; see also note on 1Ki 17:22).

4:16 *About this time next year.* See Ge 17:21; 18:14. *Don't mislead your servant, O man of God!* The woman's response revealed the depths of her desire for a son and her fear of disappointment more than it showed a lack of confidence in the word of Elisha.

4:17 *just as Elisha had told her.* The trustworthiness of Elisha's word was confirmed, and the birth of the son was shown to be the result of God's gracious intervention in her behalf.

4:20 *he died.* The child, given as an evidence of God's grace and the reliability of his word, was suddenly taken from the woman in a severe test of her faith. Her subsequent actions demonstrate the strength of her faith in the face of great calamity.

4:21 *laid him on the bed of the man of God.* In this way the woman concealed the child's death from the rest of the household while she went to seek the prophet at whose word the child had been born.

4:23 *Why go to him today?* The question suggests that it was not uncommon for the woman to go to Elisha, but that on this occasion the timing of her visit was unusual. *It's not the New Moon or the Sabbath.* The Sabbath and New Moon were observed by cessation from work (see notes on Ge 2:3; Ex 16:23; 20:9–10; 1Sa 20:5; see also Lev 23:3).

"It's all right," she said.

24She saddled the donkey and said to her servant, "Lead on; don't slow down for me unless I tell you." 25So she set out and came to the man of God at Mount Carmel. *m*

When he saw her in the distance, the man of God said to his servant Gehazi, "Look! There's the Shunammite! 26Run to meet her and ask her, 'Are you all right? Is your husband all right? Is your child all right?' "

"Everything is all right," she said.

27When she reached the man of God at the mountain, she took hold of his feet. Gehazi came over to push her away, but the man of God said, "Leave her alone! She is in bitter distress, *n* but the LORD has hidden it from me and has not told me why."

28"Did I ask you for a son, my lord?" she said. "Didn't I tell you, 'Don't raise my hopes'?"

29Elisha said to Gehazi, "Tuck your cloak into your belt, *o* take my staff *p* in your hand and run. If you meet anyone, do not greet him, and if anyone greets you, do not answer. Lay my staff on the boy's face."

30But the child's mother said, "As surely as the LORD lives and as you live, I will not leave you." So he got up and followed her.

31Gehazi went on ahead and laid the staff on the boy's face, but there was no sound or response. So Gehazi went back to meet Elisha and told him, "The boy has not awakened."

32When Elisha reached the house, there was the boy lying dead on his couch. *q* 33He went in, shut the door on the two of them and prayed *r* to the LORD. 34Then he

got on the bed and lay upon the boy, mouth to mouth, eyes to eyes, hands to hands. As he stretched *s* himself out upon him, the boy's body grew warm. 35Elisha turned away and walked back and forth in the room and then got on the bed and stretched out upon him once more. The boy sneezed seven times *t* and opened his eyes. *u*

36Elisha summoned Gehazi and said, "Call the Shunammite." And he did. When she came, he said, "Take your son." *v* 37She came in, fell at his feet and bowed to the ground. Then she took her son and went out.

Death in the Pot

38Elisha returned to Gilgal *w* and there was a famine *x* in that region. While the company of the prophets was meeting with him, he said to his servant, "Put on the large pot and cook some stew for these men."

39One of them went out into the fields to gather herbs and found a wild vine. He gathered some of its gourds and filled the fold of his cloak. When he returned, he cut them up into the pot of stew, though no one knew what they were. 40The stew was poured out for the men, but as they began to eat it, they cried out, "O man of God, there is death in the pot!" And they could not eat it.

41Elisha said, "Get some flour." He put it into the pot and said, "Serve it to the people to eat." And there was nothing harmful in the pot. *y*

Feeding of a Hundred

42A man came from Baal Shalishah, *z* bringing the man of God twenty loaves *a* of

---

Cross references (center column):

4:25 *m* S 1Ki 18:20
4:27 *n* 1Sa 1:15
4:29 *o* S 1Ki 18:46
p S Ex 4:2
4:32 *q* ver 21
4:33 *r* 1Ki 17:20; Mt 6:6

4:34 *s* 1Ki 17:21; Ac 20:10
4:35 *t* S Jos 6:15
u 2Ki 8:5
4:36 *v* Heb 11:35
4:38 *w* S 2Ki 2:1
x S Lev 26:26; 2Ki 8:1
4:41 *y* S Ex 15:25; S 2Ki 2:21
4:42 *z* 1Sa 9:4
a Mt 14:17; 15:36

4:26 *Everything is all right.* The woman was determined to share her distress with no one but the prophet from whom she had received the promise of the birth of her son.

4:28 *Didn't I tell you, 'Don't raise my hopes'?* The woman struggled with the question of why the Lord would take from her that which she had been given as a special demonstration of his grace and the trustworthiness of his word.

4:29 *Lay my staff on the boy's face.* It appears that Elisha expected the Lord to restore the boy's life when the staff was placed on him. This does not suggest that Elisha attributed magical power to the staff, but that he viewed it as a representation of his own presence and a symbol of divine power (see note on 2:8; cf. Ex 14:16; Ac 19:12).

4:30 *I will not leave you.* The woman was not convinced that Gehazi's mission would be successful and insisted that Elisha himself accompany her to Shunem.

4:33 *shut the door on the two of them and prayed.* Just as Elijah had done in a similar situation years before (see 1Ki 17:20–22), Elisha first turned to the Lord in earnest prayer for restoration of life to the dead child. His prayer is clear evidence that his subsequent actions were not intended as a

magical means of restoring life.

4:34 *lay upon the boy.* See note on 1Ki 17:21. Perhaps Elisha was familiar with the earlier similar action of Elijah.

4:37 *fell at his feet and bowed to the ground.* The woman gratefully acknowledged the special favor granted to her by the Lord through Elisha, and silently reaffirmed the verbal confession of the widow of Zarephath (see 1Ki 17:24).

4:38 *famine in that region.* Perhaps the same famine mentioned in 8:1. Famine was a covenant curse (see Lev 26:19–20,26; Dt 28:18,23–24; 1Ki 8:36–37) and evidence of God's anger with his people's disobedience to their covenant obligations. *company of the prophets.* See note on 2:3.

4:39 *wild vine . . . gourds.* The precise type of plant is not specified.

4:41 *flour.* The flour itself did not make the stew edible (see 2:21 and note). It was simply a means by which the Lord provided for those who were faithful to the covenant, at a time when others suffered under the covenant curse.

4:42 *first ripe grain.* Instead of bringing the firstfruits of the new harvest (see Lev 2:14; 23:15–17; Dt 18:3–5) to the

barley bread *b* baked from the first ripe grain, along with some heads of new grain. "Give it to the people to eat," Elisha said.

⁴³"How can I set this before a hundred men?" his servant asked.

But Elisha answered, "Give it to the people to eat. *c* For this is what the LORD says: 'They will eat and have some left over. *d* '" ⁴⁴Then he set it before them, and they ate and had some left over, according to the word of the LORD.

Naaman Healed of Leprosy

5 Now Naaman was commander of the army of the king of Aram. *e* He was a great man in the sight of his master and highly regarded, because through him the LORD had given victory to Aram. He was a valiant soldier, but he had leprosy. *d f*

²Now bands *g* from Aram had gone out and had taken captive a young girl from Israel, and she served Naaman's wife. ³She said to her mistress, "If only my master would see the prophet *h* who is in Samaria! He would cure him of his leprosy."

⁴Naaman went to his master and told him what the girl from Israel had said. ⁵"By all means, go," the king of Aram replied. "I will send a letter to the king of Israel." So Naaman left, taking with him

ten talents *e* of silver, six thousand shekels *f* of gold and ten sets of clothing. *i* ⁶The letter that he took to the king of Israel read: "With this letter I am sending my servant Naaman to you so that you may cure him of his leprosy."

⁷As soon as the king of Israel read the letter, *j* he tore his robes and said, "Am I God? *k* Can I kill and bring back to life? *l* Why does this fellow send someone to me to be cured of his leprosy? See how he is trying to pick a quarrel *m* with me!"

⁸When Elisha the man of God heard that the king of Israel had torn his robes, he sent him this message: "Why have you torn your robes? Have the man come to me and he will know that there is a prophet *n* in Israel." ⁹So Naaman went with his horses and chariots and stopped at the door of Elisha's house. ¹⁰Elisha sent a messenger to say to him, "Go, wash *o* yourself seven times *p* in the Jordan, and your flesh will be restored and you will be cleansed."

¹¹But Naaman went away angry and said, "I thought that he would surely come

Cross references (center column)

4:42 *b* S 1Sa 9:7
4:43 *c* Lk 9:13
d Mt 14:20; Jn 6:12
5:1 *e* S Ge 10:22; S 2Sa 10:19
f S Ex 4:6; S Nu 12:10; Lk 4:27
5:2 *g* 2Ki 6:23; 13:20; 24:2
5:3 *h* S Ge 20:7

5:5 *i* ver 22; S Ge 24:53; Jdg 14:12; S 1Sa 9:7
5:7 *j* 2Ki 19:14 *k* S Ge 30:2 *l* S Dt 32:39 *m* 1Ki 20:7
5:8 *n* S 1Ki 22:7
5:10 *o* Jn 9:7 *p* S Ge 33:3; S Lev 14:7

d 1 The Hebrew word was used for various diseases affecting the skin—not necessarily leprosy; also in verses 3, 6, 7, 11 and 27.   *e 5* That is, about 750 pounds (about 340 kilograms)   *f 5* That is, about 150 pounds (about 70 kilograms)

---

apostate priests at Bethel and Dan (see 1Ki 12:28–31), godly people in the northern kingdom may have contributed their offerings for the sustenance of Elisha and those associated with him (see note on v. 23). Thus they looked upon Elisha rather than the apostate king and priests as the true representative of their covenant Lord.

4:43 *the LORD says.* The bread was multiplied at the word of the Lord through Elisha apart from any intermediate means (contrast v. 41; 2:20; cf. Mk 6:35–43).

5:1 *king of Aram.* Probably Ben-Hadad II (see notes on 8:7; 13:3; 1Ki 20:1). *the LORD had given victory to Aram.* Probably a reference to an otherwise undocumented Aramean victory over the Assyrians in the aftermath of the battle of Qarqar in 853 B.C. (see note on 1Ki 22:1). In the narrator's theological perspective, this victory is attributable to the sovereignty of the God of Israel, who is seen as the ruler and controller of the destinies of all nations, not just that of Israel (see Eze 30:24; Am 2:1–3; 9:7).

5:2 *bands from Aram.* Although Israel had concluded a peace treaty with the Arameans during the reign of Ahab (see 1Ki 20:34), minor border skirmishes continued between the two states in the aftermath of the battle for control of Ramoth Gilead, in which Ahab had been killed (see note on 1Ki 22:4; see also 1Ki 22:35). *young girl from Israel.* In sharp contrast to the Israelite king in Samaria, this young girl held captive in Damascus was very much aware of God's saving presence with his people through his servant Elisha, and she selflessly shared that knowledge with her Aramean captors.

5:3 *prophet who is in Samaria.* Elisha, who maintained a residence in Samaria (see v. 9; 2:25; 6:19).

5:5 *I will send a letter to the king of Israel.* The border skirmishes had not nullified the official peace between the two nations as established by treaty. The king of Israel was Joram (see 1:17; 3:1; 9:24). *ten talents of silver.* See NIV

text note. An idea of the relative value of this amount of silver can be seen by comparing it with the price Omri paid for the hill of Samaria (see 1Ki 16:24).

5:6 *so that you may cure him of his leprosy.* Ben-Hadad assumed that the prophet described by the Israelite slave girl was subject to the authority of the king and that his services could be bought with a sufficiently large gift. He thought he could buy with worldly wealth one of the chief blessings of God's saving presence among his people.

5:7 *he is trying to pick a quarrel with me!* Joram concluded that the entire incident was an attempt by Ben-Hadad to create a pretext for a declaration of war. So blind was the king to God's saving presence through Elisha that he could think only of international intrigue.

5:8 *Why have you torn your robes?* Elisha chided Joram for his fear (see note on 1Sa 17:11) and for his failure to consult the Lord's prophet (see 3:13–14 for evidence of the tension that existed between Joram and Elisha).

5:9 *with his horses and chariots.* This proud pagan would command the healing by his lordly presence.

5:10 *wash yourself seven times in the Jordan.* The instruction is designed to demonstrate to Naaman that healing would come by the power of the God of Israel, but only if he obeyed the word of the Lord's prophet. The prophet himself was not a healer. Ritual washings were practiced among Eastern religions as a purification rite, and the number seven was generally known as a symbol of completeness. Naaman was to wash in the muddy waters of the Jordan River, demonstrating that there was no natural connection between the washing and the desired healing. Perhaps it also suggested that one needed to pass through the Jordan, as Israel had done (Jos 3–4), in order to obtain healing from the God of Israel.

5:11 *wave his hand over the spot and cure me of my*

out to me and stand and call on the name of the LORD his God, wave his hand ^q over the spot and cure me of my leprosy. ¹²Are not Abana and Pharpar, the rivers of Damascus, better than any of the waters^r of Israel? Couldn't I wash in them and be cleansed?" So he turned and went off in a rage.^s

¹³Naaman's servants went to him and said, "My father,^t if the prophet had told you to do some great thing, would you not have done it? How much more, then, when he tells you, 'Wash and be cleansed'!" ¹⁴So he went down and dipped himself in the Jordan seven times,^u as the man of God had told him, and his flesh was restored^v and became clean like that of a young boy.^w

¹⁵Then Naaman and all his attendants went back to the man of God^x. He stood before him and said, "Now I know^y that there is no God in all the world except in Israel. Please accept now a gift^z from your servant."

¹⁶The prophet answered, "As surely as the LORD lives, whom I serve, I will not accept a thing." And even though Naaman urged him, he refused.^a

¹⁷"If you will not," said Naaman, "please let me, your servant, be given as much earth^b as a pair of mules can carry, for your servant will never again make burnt offerings and sacrifices to any other god but the LORD. ¹⁸But may the LORD forgive your servant for this one thing: When my master enters the temple of Rimmon to

bow down and he is leaning^c on my arm and I bow there also—when I bow down in the temple of Rimmon, may the LORD forgive your servant for this."

¹⁹"Go in peace,"^d Elisha said.

After Naaman had traveled some distance, ²⁰Gehazi, the servant of Elisha the man of God, said to himself, "My master was too easy on Naaman, this Aramean, by not accepting from him what he brought. As surely as the LORD^e lives, I will run after him and get something from him."

²¹So Gehazi hurried after Naaman. When Naaman saw him running toward him, he got down from the chariot to meet him. "Is everything all right?" he asked.

²²"Everything is all right," Gehazi answered. "My master sent me to say, 'Two young men from the company of the prophets have just come to me from the hill country of Ephraim. Please give them a talent^g of silver and two sets of clothing.' "^f

²³"By all means, take two talents," said Naaman. He urged Gehazi to accept them, and then tied up the two talents of silver in two bags, with two sets of clothing. He gave them to two of his servants, and they carried them ahead of Gehazi. ²⁴When Gehazi came to the hill, he took the things from the servants and put them away in the house. He sent the men away and they left. ²⁵Then he went in and stood before his master Elisha.

5:11 ^qS Ex 7:19
5:12 ^rIsa 8:6
^sPr 14:17,29;
19:11; 29:11
5:13 ^t2Ki 6:21;
13:14
5:14 ^uS Ge 33:3;
S Lev 14:7;
S Jos 6:15
^vS Ex 4:7
^wJob 33:25
5:15 ^xS Jos 2:11
^yS Jos 4:24;
S 1Sa 17:46
^zS 1Sa 9:7
5:16 ^aver 20,26;
Ge 14:23;
Da 5:17
5:17 ^bEx 20:24

5:18 ^c2Ki 7:2
5:19 ^d1Sa 1:17;
S Ac 15:33
5:20 ^eEx 20:7
5:22 ^fS ver 5;
S Ge 45:22

^g*22 That is, about 75 pounds (about 34 kilograms)*

---

leprosy. Naaman expected to be healed by the magical technique of the prophet rather than by the power of God operative in connection with his own obedient response to God's word.

5:12 *Abana and Pharpar.* The Abana was termed the Golden River by the Greeks. It is usually identified with the Barada River of today, rising in the Anti-Lebanon mountains and flowing through the city of Damascus. The Pharpar River flows east from Mount Hermon just to the south of Damascus.

5:14 *his flesh was restored and became clean like that of a young boy.* Physically he was reborn (see also v. 15 and note). As he obeyed God's word, Naaman received the gift of God's grace. Naaman is here a sign to disobedient Israel that God's blessing is found only in the path of trustful obedience. When his own people turn away from covenant faithfulness, God will raise up those who will follow his word from outside the covenant nation (see notes on 1Ki 17:9–24; see also Mt 8:10–12; Lk 4:27).

5:15 *no God in all the world except in Israel.* Naaman's confession put to shame the Israelites who continued to waver in their opinion on whether Baal and the Lord (Yahweh) were both gods, or whether Yahweh alone was God (see note on 1Ki 18:21).

5:16 *I will not accept a thing.* Elisha did not seek monetary gain for proclaiming the word of the Lord (see Mt 10:8). Naaman was healed solely by divine grace, not by the power

of Elisha.

5:17 *let me . . . be given as much earth as a pair of mules can carry.* In the ancient world it was commonly thought that a deity could be worshiped only on the soil of the nation to which he was bound (see v. 15). For this reason Naaman wanted to take Israelite soil with him in order to have a place in Damascus for the worship of the Lord.

5:18 *my master.* Ben-Hadad, king of Aram. *Rimmon.* Also known as Hadad (and in Canaan and Phoenicia as Baal), this Aramean deity was the god of storm ("Rimmon" means "thunderer") and war. The two names were sometimes combined (see note on Zec 12:11).

5:19 *Go in peace.* Elisha did not directly address Naaman's problem of conscience (v. 18), but commended him to the leading and grace of God as he returned to his pagan environment and official responsibilities.

5:20 *As surely as the LORD lives.* An oath formula (see note on 1Sa 14:39).

5:22 *company of the prophets.* See note on 2:3. *Please give them a talent of silver and two sets of clothing.* Gehazi deceived Naaman in order to satisfy his desire for material gain. The evil of his lie was compounded in that it obscured the gracious character of the Lord's work in Naaman's healing and blurred the distinction between Elisha's function as a true prophet of the Lord and the self-serving actions of false prophets and pagan soothsayers.

5:24 *house.* Of Elisha (see v. 9).

"Where have you been, Gehazi?" Elisha asked.

"Your servant didn't go anywhere," Gehazi answered.

26But Elisha said to him, "Was not my spirit with you when the man got down from his chariot to meet you? Is this the time[g] to take money, or to accept clothes, olive groves, vineyards, flocks, herds, or menservants and maidservants?[h] 27Naaman's leprosy[i] will cling to you and to your descendants forever." Then Gehazi[j] went from Elisha's presence and he was leprous, as white as snow.[k]

An Axhead Floats

6 The company[l] of the prophets said to Elisha, "Look, the place where we meet with you is too small for us. 2Let us go to the Jordan, where each of us can get a pole; and let us build a place there for us to live."

And he said, "Go."

3Then one of them said, "Won't you please come with your servants?"

"I will," Elisha replied. 4And he went with them.

They went to the Jordan and began to cut down trees. 5As one of them was cutting down a tree, the iron axhead fell into the water. "Oh, my lord," he cried out, "it was borrowed!"

6The man of God asked, "Where did it fall?" When he showed him the place, Elisha cut a stick and threw[m] it there, and made the iron float. 7"Lift it out," he said. Then the man reached out his hand and took it.

5:26 gS ver 16
hJer 45:5
5:27 iS Nu 12:10
/Col 3:5 kS Ex 4:6
6:1 lS 1Sa 10:5
6:6 mS Ex 15:25;
S 2Ki 2:21

6:9 nver 12
6:10 oJer 11:18
6:12 pver 9
6:13 qGe 37:17
6:14 r2Ki 1:9
6:16 sS Ge 15:1
t2Ch 32:7;
Ps 55:18;
Ro 8:31; 1Jn 4:4

Elisha Traps Blinded Arameans

8Now the king of Aram was at war with Israel. After conferring with his officers, he said, "I will set up my camp in such and such a place."

9The man of God sent word to the king[n] of Israel: "Beware of passing that place, because the Arameans are going down there." 10So the king of Israel checked on the place indicated by the man of God. Time and again Elisha warned[o] the king, so that he was on his guard in such places.

11This enraged the king of Aram. He summoned his officers and demanded of them, "Will you not tell me which of us is on the side of the king of Israel?"

12"None of us, my lord the king[p]," said one of his officers, "but Elisha, the prophet who is in Israel, tells the king of Israel the very words you speak in your bedroom."

13"Go, find out where he is," the king ordered, "so I can send men and capture him." The report came back: "He is in Dothan."[q] 14Then he sent[r] horses and chariots and a strong force there. They went by night and surrounded the city.

15When the servant of the man of God got up and went out early the next morning, an army with horses and chariots had surrounded the city. "Oh, my lord, what shall we do?" the servant asked.

16"Don't be afraid,"[s] the prophet answered. "Those who are with us are more[t] than those who are with them."

17And Elisha prayed, "O LORD, open his

5:26 *Is this the time to take money . . . ?* Gehazi sought to use the grace of God granted to another individual for his own material advantage. This was equivalent to making merchandise of God's grace (see note on 2Co 2:17). "Money" here and elsewhere in 2 Kings refers to gold or silver in various weights, not to coins, which were a later invention. *clothes . . . maidservants.* Evidently what Gehazi secretly hoped to acquire with the two talents of silver (see note on v. 5).
5:27 *leprosy.* See NIV text note on v. 1. *to you and to your descendants forever.* For the extension of punishment to the children of an offender of God's law see Ex 20:5 and note; see also note on Jos 7:24. *white as snow.* See Ex 4:6.
6:1 *company of the prophets.* See note on 2:3.
6:2 *a place there for us to live.* Some have suggested that the company of prophets lived in a communal housing structure. The Hebrew for this phrase, however, could be translated "a place there for us to sit," referring to some type of assembly hall. It is implied in 4:1–7 that there were separate dwellings for the members of the prophetic companies (see note on 1Sa 19:18).
6:5 *it was borrowed.* At that time an iron axhead was a costly tool, too expensive for the members of the prophetic company to purchase. Having lost it, the borrower faced the prospect of having to work off the value as a bondservant.

6:6 *Elisha cut a stick and threw it there, and made the iron float.* The Lord demonstrated here his concern for the welfare of his faithful ones.
6:8 *king of Aram.* Probably Ben-Hadad II (see note on 5:1). *war with Israel.* A reference to border clashes rather than full-scale hostility (see v. 23; see also note on 5:2). Some indication of Israelite weakness and Aramean strength is seen in the ability of the Arameans to send forces to Dothan (only about 11 miles north of Samaria) without apparent difficulty (see vv. 13–14).
6:9 *man of God.* Elisha (see v. 10). *king of Israel.* Probably Joram (see 1:17; 3:1; 9:24).
6:11 *which of us is on the side of the king of Israel?* Repeated evidence that Israel possessed advance knowledge of Aramean military plans led the king of Aram to suspect that there was a traitor among his top officials.
6:13 *capture him.* The king of Aram thought he could eliminate Elisha's influence by denying him contact with Israel's king. *Dothan.* Located on a hill about halfway between Jezreel and Samaria, where the main royal residences were (see 1:2; 3:1; 8:29; 9:15; 10:1; 1Ki 21:1).
6:16 *Those who are with us are more than those who are with them.* Elisha knew that there was greater strength in the unseen reality of the hosts of heaven than in the visible reality of the Aramean forces (see 2Ch 32:7–8; 1Jn 4:4).

eyes so he may see." Then the LORD opened the servant's eyes, and he looked and saw the hills full of horses and chariots[u] of fire all around Elisha.

18As the enemy came down toward him, Elisha prayed to the LORD, "Strike these people with blindness."[v] So he struck them with blindness, as Elisha had asked.

19Elisha told them, "This is not the road and this is not the city. Follow me, and I will lead you to the man you are looking for." And he led them to Samaria.

20After they entered the city, Elisha said, "LORD, open the eyes of these men so they can see." Then the LORD opened their eyes and they looked, and there they were, inside Samaria.

21When the king of Israel saw them, he asked Elisha, "Shall I kill them, my father?[w] Shall I kill them?"

22"Do not kill them," he answered. "Would you kill men you have captured[x] with your own sword or bow? Set food and water before them so that they may eat and drink and then go back to their master." 23So he prepared a great feast for them, and after they had finished eating and drinking, he sent them away, and they returned to their master. So the bands[y] from Aram stopped raiding Israel's territory.

Famine in Besieged Samaria

24Some time later, Ben-Hadad[z] king of Aram mobilized his entire army and marched up and laid siege[a] to Samaria. 25There was a great famine[b] in the city; the siege lasted so long that a donkey's head sold for eighty shekels[h] of silver, and a quarter of a cab[i] of seed pods[j][c] for five shekels.[k]

26As the king of Israel was passing by on the wall, a woman cried to him, "Help me, my lord the king!"

27The king replied, "If the LORD does not help you, where can I get help for you? From the threshing floor? From the winepress?" 28Then he asked her, "What's the matter?"

She answered, "This woman said to me, 'Give up your son so we may eat him today, and tomorrow we'll eat my son.' 29So we cooked my son and ate[d] him. The next day I said to her, 'Give up your son so we may eat him,' but she had hidden him."

30When the king heard the woman's words, he tore[e] his robes. As he went along the wall, the people looked, and there, underneath, he had sackcloth[f] on his body. 31He said, "May God deal with

Cross references (center column):

6:17 [u]S 2Ki 2:11, 12
6:18 [v]Ge 19:11; Ac 13:11
6:21 [w]S 2Ki 5:13
6:22 [x]S Dt 20:11; 2Ch 28:8-15
6:23 [y]S 2Ki 5:2
6:24 [z]S 1Ki 15:18; 2Ki 8:7 [a]Dt 28:52
6:25 [b]S Lev 26:26; S Ru 1:1 [c]Isa 36:12
6:29 [d]S Lev 26:29; Dt 28:53-55
6:30 [e]2Ki 18:37; Isa 22:15
/S Ge 37:34

h25 That is, about 2 pounds (about 1 kilogram)   **i**25 That is, probably about 1/2 pint (about 0.3 liter)   **j**25 Or *of dove's dung*   **k**25 That is, about 2 ounces (about 55 grams)

6:17 *saw the hills full of horses and chariots.* In response to Elisha's prayer, his servant was able to see the protecting might of the heavenly hosts gathered about Elisha (see Ge 32:1–2; Ps 34:7; 91:11–12; Mt 18:10; 26:53; see also note on 2Ki 2:11).

6:18 *Strike these people with blindness.* Elisha had prayed for the eyes of his servant to be opened to the unseen reality of the heavenly hosts; now he prays for the eyes of the Aramean soldiers to be closed to earthly reality (see Ge 19:11).

6:19 *This is not the road and this is not the city.* Elisha's statement led the Aramean soldiers to believe that they were being directed to the city where Elisha could be found. Technically this statement was not an untruth, since Elisha accompanied them to Samaria, but it was a means of deceiving the Aramean soldiers into a trap inside Samaria, the fortress-like capital city of the northern kingdom (see Ex 1:19–20; Jos 2:6; 1Sa 16:1–2 for other instances of deception recorded in the OT).

6:20 *there they were, inside Samaria.* The power of the Lord operative through Elisha turned the intended captors into captives.

6:21 *king of Israel.* Joram (see note on v. 9).

6:22 *Do not kill them.* In reality the Aramean soldiers had been taken captive by the power of the Lord, not by Joram's military prowess. The Lord's purpose was to demonstrate to them and their king and to the Israelites and their king that Israel's national security ultimately was grounded in the Lord, not in military forces or strategies.

6:23 *bands from Aram stopped raiding Israel's territory.* See notes on v. 8; 5:2. Temporarily the Arameans recognized the futility of opposition to the power of the God of Israel.

6:24 *Ben-Hadad.* The same Ben-Hadad who had besieged Samaria on a previous occasion (see notes on 13:3; 1Ki 20:1). This siege is probably to be dated c. 850 B.C.

6:25 *donkey's head.* According to Pentateuchal law the donkey was unclean and not to be eaten (see Lev 11:2–7; Dt 14:4–8). The severity of the famine caused the inhabitants of Samaria not only to disregard the laws of uncleanness, but also to place a high value on the least edible part of the donkey. *eighty shekels of silver.* See NIV text note; see also note on 5:5.

6:27 *If the LORD does not help you, where can I get help for you?* Joram correctly recognized his own inability to assist the woman if the Lord himself did not act in Israel's behalf, but he wrongly implied that the Lord was to be blamed for a situation brought on by Israel's own disobedience and idolatry.

6:28 *tomorrow we'll eat my son.* The sins of the king and people were so great that the covenant curses of Lev 26:29 and Dt 28:53,57 were being inflicted (cf. La 4:10).

6:30 *tore his robes.* More an expression of anger toward Elisha and the Lord (see v. 31) than one of repentance and sorrow for the sins that had provoked the covenant curse. *sackcloth.* A coarse cloth usually worn as a sign of mourning (see note on Ge 37:34). It is not clear why Joram wore sackcloth hidden under his royal robe. Perhaps it was a testing of the Lord, a private ritual to attempt to gain divine favor.

6:31 *May God deal with me, be it ever so severely.* A curse formula (see note on 1Sa 3:17). *if the head of Elisha . . . remains on his shoulders today!* Joram considered Elisha in some way responsible for the conditions in the city. Cf.

me, be it ever so severely, if the head of Elisha son of Shaphat remains on his shoulders today!'"

[32]Now Elisha was sitting in his house, and the elders[g] were sitting with him. The king sent a messenger ahead, but before he arrived, Elisha said to the elders, "Don't you see how this murderer[h] is sending someone to cut off my head?[i] Look, when the messenger comes, shut the door and hold it shut against him. Is not the sound of his master's footsteps behind him?"

[33]While he was still talking to them, the messenger came down to him. And the king[j] said, "This disaster is from the LORD. Why should I wait[j] for the LORD any longer?"

7 Elisha said, "Hear the word of the LORD. This is what the LORD says: About this time tomorrow, a seah[1] of flour will sell for a shekel[m] and two seahs[n] of barley for a shekel[k] at the gate of Samaria."

[2]The officer on whose arm the king was leaning[l] said to the man of God, "Look, even if the LORD should open the floodgates[m] of the heavens, could this happen?"

"You will see it with your own eyes," answered Elisha, "but you will not eat[n] any of it!"

The Siege Lifted

[3]Now there were four men with leprosy[oo] at the entrance of the city gate. They said to each other, "Why stay here until we die? [4]If we say, 'We'll go into the city'—the famine is there, and we will die. And if we stay here, we will die. So let's go over to the camp of the Arameans and surrender. If they spare us, we live; if they kill us, then we die."

[5]At dusk they got up and went to the camp of the Arameans. When they reached the edge of the camp, not a man was there, [6]for the Lord had caused the Arameans to hear the sound[p] of chariots and horses and a great army, so that they said to one another, "Look, the king of Israel has hired[q] the Hittite[r] and Egyptian kings to attack

us!" [7]So they got up and fled[s] in the dusk and abandoned their tents and their horses and donkeys. They left the camp as it was and ran for their lives.

[8]The men who had leprosy[t] reached the edge of the camp and entered one of the tents. They ate and drank, and carried away silver, gold and clothes, and went off and hid them. They returned and entered another tent and took some things from it and hid them also.

[9]Then they said to each other, "We're not doing right. This is a day of good news and we are keeping it to ourselves. If we wait until daylight, punishment will overtake us. Let's go at once and report this to the royal palace."

[10]So they went and called out to the city gatekeepers and told them, "We went into the Aramean camp and not a man was there—not a sound of anyone—only tethered horses and donkeys, and the tents left just as they were." [11]The gatekeepers shouted the news, and it was reported within the palace.

[12]The king got up in the night and said to his officers, "I will tell you what the Arameans have done to us. They know we are starving; so they have left the camp to hide[u] in the countryside, thinking, 'They will surely come out, and then we will take them alive and get into the city.'"

[13]One of his officers answered, "Have some men take five of the horses that are left in the city. Their plight will be like that of all the Israelites left here—yes, they will only be like all these Israelites who are doomed. So let us send them to find out what happened."

[14]So they selected two chariots with their horses, and the king sent them after the Aramean army. He commanded the drivers, "Go and find out what has hap-

Cross references (center column)

6:32 [g]Eze 8:1; 14:1; 20:1
[h]1Ki 18:4 [i]ver 31
6:33 [j]Lev 24:11; Job 2:9; 14:14; Isa 40:31
7:1 [k]ver 16
7:2 [l]2Ki 5:18 [m]ver 19; Ge 7:11; Ps 78:23; Mal 3:10 [n]ver 17
7:3 [o]Lev 13:45-46; Nu 5:1-4
7:6 [p]S Ex 14:24; Eze 1:24 [q]2Sa 10:6; Jer 46:21 [r]S Nu 13:29

7:7 [s]Jdg 7:21; Ps 48:4-6; Pr 28:1; Isa 30:17
7:8 [t]Isa 33:23; 35:6
7:12 [u]Jos 8:4

1 [l] That is, probably about 7 quarts (about 7.3 liters); also in verses 16 and 18   [m] l That is, about 2/5 ounce (about 11 grams); also in verses 16 and 18   [n] l That is, probably about 13 quarts (about 15 liters); also in verses 16 and 18   [o]3 The Hebrew word is used for various diseases affecting the skin—not necessarily leprosy; also in verse 8.

Ahab's attitude toward Elijah (1Ki 18:10,16; 21:20).
6:32 *elders.* Leaders of the city (see notes on Ex 3:16; 2Sa 3:17). They sit with Elisha rather than with the king.
6:33 *Why should I wait for the LORD any longer?* Joram felt himself deceived by Elisha and abandoned by the Lord, whom he blamed for the disastrous conditions in the city.
7:1 *a seah of flour will sell for a shekel.* See NIV text notes. This was about double the normal cost of flour, but a phenomenal improvement.
7:2 *floodgates of the heavens.* See v. 19; Ge 8:2; Isa 24:18.
7:3 *entrance of the city gate.* Pentateuchal law excluded

persons with skin diseases from residence in the community (Lev 13:46; Nu 5:2–3).
7:6 *the LORD had caused the Arameans to hear the sound.* See 2Sa 5:24 and note. *Hittite . . . kings.* Kings of small city-states ruled by dynasties of Hittite origin, which had arisen in northern Aram after the fall of the Hittite empire c. 1200 B.C.
7:12 *what the Arameans have done to us.* Joram's unbelief caused him to conclude that the report of the four leprous men was part of an Aramean war strategy rather than an evidence of the fulfillment of Elisha's prophecy (see v. 1).

pened." [15]They followed them as far as the Jordan, and they found the whole road strewn with the clothing and equipment the Arameans had thrown away in their headlong flight.[v] So the messengers returned and reported to the king. [16]Then the people went out and plundered[w] the camp of the Arameans. So a seah of flour sold for a shekel, and two seahs of barley sold for a shekel,[x] as the LORD had said.

[17]Now the king had put the officer on whose arm he leaned in charge of the gate, and the people trampled him in the gateway, and he died,[y] just as the man of God had foretold when the king came down to his house. [18]It happened as the man of God had said to the king: "About this time tomorrow, a seah of flour will sell for a shekel and two seahs of barley for a shekel at the gate of Samaria."

[19]The officer had said to the man of God, "Look, even if the LORD should open the floodgates[z] of the heavens, could this happen?" The man of God had replied, "You will see it with your own eyes, but you will not eat any of it!" [20]And that is exactly what happened to him, for the people trampled him in the gateway, and he died.

The Shunammite's Land Restored

8 Now Elisha had said to the woman[a] whose son he had restored to life, "Go away with your family and stay for a while wherever you can, because the LORD has decreed a famine[b] in the land that will last

seven years."[c] [2]The woman proceeded to do as the man of God said. She and her family went away and stayed in the land of the Philistines seven years.

[3]At the end of the seven years she came back from the land of the Philistines and went to the king to beg for her house and land. [4]The king was talking to Gehazi, the servant of the man of God, and had said, "Tell me about all the great things Elisha has done." [5]Just as Gehazi was telling the king how Elisha had restored[d] the dead to life, the woman whose son Elisha had brought back to life came to beg the king for her house and land.

Gehazi said, "This is the woman, my lord the king, and this is her son whom Elisha restored to life." [6]The king asked the woman about it, and she told him.

Then he assigned an official to her case and said to him, "Give back everything that belonged to her, including all the income from her land from the day she left the country until now."

Hazael Murders Ben-Hadad

[7]Elisha went to Damascus,[e] and Ben-Hadad[f] king of Aram was ill. When the king was told, "The man of God has come all the way up here," [8]he said to Hazael,[g] "Take a gift[h] with you and go to meet the man of God. Consult[i] the LORD through him; ask him, 'Will I recover from this illness?'"

[9]Hazael went to meet Elisha, taking with him as a gift forty camel-loads of all

---

Cross references (center column):

7:15 [v]Job 27:22
7:16 [w]Isa 33:4, 23 [x]ver 1
7:17 [y]S ver 2
7:19 [z]S ver 2
8:1 [a]2Ki 4:8-37 [b]S Lev 26:26; S Dt 28:22; S Ru 1:1
[c]S Ge 12:10
8:5 [d]2Ki 4:35
8:7 [e]S 2Sa 8:5 [f]S 2Ki 6:24
8:8 [g]1Ki 19:15 [h]S Ge 32:20; S 1Sa 9:7 [i]S Jdg 18:5

7:16–20 *as the LORD had said . . . as the man of God had foretold . . . as the man of God had said . . . that is exactly what happened to him.* Emphasizing the trustworthiness of the prophetic word spoken by Elisha. In the fulfillment of Elisha's prophecy Israel was reminded that deliverance from her enemies was a gift of God's grace and that rejection of God's word provoked the wrath of divine judgment.

8:1 *the LORD has decreed a famine.* The famine should have been perceived by the people of the northern kingdom as a covenant curse sent on them because of their sin (see note on 4:38). *seven years.* It is not clear whether this famine began before or after the Aramean siege of Samaria (see 4:38; 6:24–7:20).

8:2 *She and her family went away.* Elisha's instruction enabled the woman and her family to escape the privations of the famine.

8:3 *went to the king.* See note on 1Ki 3:16. *beg for her house and land.* Either someone had illegally occupied the woman's property during her absence, or it had fallen to the domain of the king by virtue of its abandonment.

8:4 *Gehazi.* See 5:27. *Tell me about all the great things Elisha has done.* The king's lack of familiarity with Elisha's ministry is perhaps an indication that this incident occurred in the early days of the reign of Jehu rather than in the time of Joram, who had had numerous contacts with Elisha (see 3:13–14; 5:7–10; 6:10–23; 6:24–7:20). But see note on 5:7.

8:5 *as Gehazi was telling the king.* The woman's approach to the king providentially coincided with Gehazi's story of her son's miraculous restoration to life through the ministry of Elisha.

8:6 *Give back everything that belonged to her.* The widow and her son were living examples of the Lord's provision and blessing for those who were obedient to the word of the Lord through his prophets.

8:7 *Elisha went to Damascus.* The time had come for Elisha to carry out one of the three tasks originally given to Elijah at Mount Horeb (see notes on 1Ki 19:15–16). The annals of the Assyrian ruler Shalmaneser III record Assyrian victories over Ben-Hadad (Hadadezer) of Damascus in 846 B.C. and Hazael of Damascus in 842. Elisha's visit to Damascus is to be dated c. 843.

8:8 *Consult the LORD through him.* In a reversal of the situation described in 1:1–4, a pagan king seeks an oracle from Israel's God. *Will I recover . . . ?* The question is the same as that of Ahaziah in 1:2.

8:9 *forty camel-loads of all the finest wares of Damascus.* Damascus was the center for trade between Egypt, Asia Minor and Mesopotamia. Ben-Hadad evidently thought a generous gift would favorably influence Elisha's oracle. *Your son Ben-Hadad.* Use of father-son terminology is a tacit acknowledgment by Ben-Hadad of Elisha's superiority (see 6:21; 1Sa 25:8).

the finest wares of Damascus. He went in and stood before him, and said, "Your son Ben-Hadad king of Aram has sent me to ask, 'Will I recover from this illness?' "

[10]Elisha answered, "Go and say to him, 'You will certainly recover'; but[p] the LORD has revealed to me that he will in fact die." [11]He stared at him with a fixed gaze until Hazael felt ashamed.[k] Then the man of God began to weep.[l]

[12]"Why is my lord weeping?" asked Hazael.

"Because I know the harm[m] you will do to the Israelites," he answered. "You will set fire to their fortified places, kill their young men with the sword, dash[n] their little children[o] to the ground, and rip open[p] their pregnant women."

[13]Hazael said, "How could your servant, a mere dog,[q] accomplish such a feat?"

"The LORD has shown me that you will become king[r] of Aram," answered Elisha.

[14]Then Hazael left Elisha and returned to his master. When Ben-Hadad asked, "What did Elisha say to you?" Hazael replied, "He told me that you would certainly recover." [15]But the next day he took a thick cloth, soaked it in water and spread it over the king's face, so that he died.[s] Then Hazael succeeded him as king.

Jehoram King of Judah

8:16–24pp — 2Ch 21:5–10,20

[16]In the fifth year of Joram[t] son of Ahab king of Israel, when Jehoshaphat was king of Judah, Jehoram[u] son of Jehoshaphat began his reign as king of Judah. [17]He was thirty-two years old when he became king, and he reigned in Jerusalem eight years. [18]He walked in the ways of the kings of Israel, as the house of Ahab had done, for he married a daughter[v] of Ahab. He did evil in the eyes of the LORD. [19]Nevertheless, for the sake of his servant David, the LORD was not willing to destroy[w] Judah. He had promised to maintain a lamp[x] for David and his descendants forever.

[20]In the time of Jehoram, Edom rebelled against Judah and set up its own king.[y] [21]So Jehoram[q] went to Zair with all his chariots. The Edomites surrounded him and his chariot commanders, but he rose up and broke through by night; his army, however, fled back home. [22]To this day Edom has been in rebellion[z] against Judah. Libnah[a] revolted at the same time.

[23]As for the other events of Jehoram's reign, and all he did, are they not written

Cross references (center column)

8:10 /Isa 38:1
8:11 kS Jdg 3:25
/Lk 19:41
8:12
mS 1Ki 19:17
nPs 137:9;
Isa 13:16;
Hos 13:16;
Na 3:10;
Lk 19:44
oS Ge 34:29
p2Ki 15:16;
Am 1:13
8:13
qS 1Sa 17:43;
S 2Sa 3:8
r1Ki 19:15
8:15 sS 2Ki 1:17

8:16 tS 2Ki 1:17
u2Ch 21:1-4
8:18 vver 26;
2Ki 11:1
8:19 wS Ge 6:13
xS 2Sa 21:17;
Rev 21:23
8:20 yS 1Ki 22:47
8:22 zGe 27:40
aS Nu 33:20;
Jos 21:13;
2Ki 19:8

p10 The Hebrew may also be read *Go and say, 'You will certainly not recover,' for.*   q21 Hebrew *Joram*, a variant of *Jehoram*; also in verses 23 and 24

8:10 *You will certainly recover.* This reading of the Hebrew text (see NIV text note for an alternative reading) is to be preferred (see v. 14) and understood as an assertion that Ben-Hadad's illness was not terminal.

8:12 *harm you will do to the Israelites.* The Lord gave Elisha a clear picture of the severity of the judgment he was about to send on Israel by the hand of Hazael (see 9:14–16; 10:32; 12:17–18; 13:3,22). *set fire ... rip open their pregnant women.* These actions were characteristic of victorious armies in that time (see 15:16; Hos 10:14; 13:16; Am 1:13). Elisha's words do not sanction such acts but simply describe Hazael's future attacks on Israel.

8:13 *How could your servant, a mere dog, accomplish such a feat?* Hazael did not show repulsion at these violent acts but saw no possibility to gain the power necessary to accomplish them (for this metaphorical use of "dog" see note on 2Sa 9:8). *you will become king of Aram.* Elisha's prophecy suggests that Hazael was not a legitimate successor to Ben-Hadad. In an Assyrian inscription Hazael is designated "the son of a nobody" (i.e., a commoner) who usurped the throne.

8:15 *died.* Elisha's prophecy of Hazael's kingship did not legitimize the assassination. Hazael's murder of Ben-Hadad as well as his future acts of violence against Israel were wicked acts arising out of his own sinful heart (see Isa 10:5–19). His reign extended from c. 842 B.C. to c. 806 or 796, and he was followed by a son he named Ben-Hadad (13:24).

8:16 *fifth year of Joram.* 848 B.C. Jehoram had been co-regent with his father since 853 (see note on 1:17), but he now began his reign as sole king.

8:17 *reigned in Jerusalem eight years.* Jehoram's sole reign is to be dated 848–841 B.C.

8:18 *as the house of Ahab had done.* Jehoram introduced Baal worship in Judah, as Ahab had done in the northern kingdom (see 11:18). Baal worship now spread to the southern kingdom at the same time it was being restricted in the northern kingdom by Ahab's son Joram (see 3:1–2). *married a daughter of Ahab.* Jehoram's wife was Athaliah, a daughter of Ahab but probably not of Jezebel (see v. 26; 2Ch 18:1). Athaliah's influence on Jehoram paralleled that of Jezebel on Ahab (see 1Ki 16:31; 18:4; 19:1–2; 2Ch 21:6).

8:19 *lamp for David.* See note on 1Ki 11:36; see also Ps 132:17. The Lord spared Judah and its royal house the judgment he brought on the house of Ahab because of the covenant he had made with David (see 2Sa 7:16,29; 2Ch 21:7).

8:20 *set up its own king.* Previously Edom had been subject to Judah and had been ruled by a deputy (see note on 3:9; see also 1Ki 22:47).

8:21 *his army ... fled.* Although Jehoram and his army were able to break through an encirclement by Edomite forces, they were soundly defeated and forced to retreat to their own territory.

8:22 *To this day.* Until the time of the writing of the account of Jehoram's reign used by the author of 1,2 Kings (see Introduction to 1 Kings: Author, Sources and Date; see also note on 1Ki 8:8). Later, Amaziah of Judah was able to inflict a serious defeat on Edom (14:7), and his successor Azariah regained control of the trade route to Elath through Edomite territory (14:22; 2Ch 26:2). *Libnah revolted at the same time.* Libnah appears to have been located close to the Philistine border near Lachish (see 19:8). It is likely that the revolt of Libnah was connected with that of the Philistines and Arabs described in 2Ch 21:16–17.

8:23 *other events of Jehoram's reign.* See 2Ch 21:4–20. *annals of the kings of Judah.* See note on 1Ki 14:29.

in the book of the annals of the kings of Judah? [24]Jehoram rested with his fathers and was buried with them in the City of David. And Ahaziah his son succeeded him as king.

Ahaziah King of Judah

8:25–29pp — 2Ch 22:1–6

[25]In the twelfth [b] year of Joram son of Ahab king of Israel, Ahaziah son of Jehoram king of Judah began to reign. [26]Ahaziah was twenty-two years old when he became king, and he reigned in Jerusalem one year. His mother's name was Athaliah, [c] a granddaughter of Omri [d] king of Israel. [27]He walked in the ways of the house of Ahab [e] and did evil [f] in the eyes of the LORD, as the house of Ahab had done, for he was related by marriage to Ahab's family.

[28]Ahaziah went with Joram son of Ahab to war against Hazael king of Aram at Ramoth Gilead. [g] The Arameans wounded Joram; [29]so King Joram returned to Jezreel [h] to recover from the wounds the Arameans had inflicted on him at Ramoth [r] in his battle with Hazael [i] king of Aram.

Then Ahaziah [j] son of Jehoram king of Judah went down to Jezreel to see Joram son of Ahab, because he had been wounded.

Jehu Anointed King of Israel

9 The prophet Elisha summoned a man from the company [k] of the prophets and said to him, "Tuck your cloak into your belt, [l] take this flask of oil [m] with you and go to Ramoth Gilead. [n] [2]When you get there, look for Jehu son of Jehoshaphat, the son of Nimshi. Go to him, get him away from his companions and take him into an inner room. [3]Then take the flask and pour the oil [o] on his head and declare, 'This is

what the LORD says: I anoint you king over Israel.' Then open the door and run; don't delay!"

[4]So the young man, the prophet, went to Ramoth Gilead. [5]When he arrived, he found the army officers sitting together. "I have a message for you, commander," he said.

"For which of us?" asked Jehu.

"For you, commander," he replied.

[6]Jehu got up and went into the house. Then the prophet poured the oil [p] on Jehu's head and declared, "This is what the LORD, the God of Israel, says: 'I anoint you king over the LORD's people Israel. [7]You are to destroy the house of Ahab your master, and I will avenge [q] the blood of my servants [r] the prophets and the blood of all the LORD's servants shed by Jezebel. [s] [8]The whole house [t] of Ahab will perish. I will cut off from Ahab every last male [u] in Israel—slave or free. [9]I will make the house of Ahab like the house of Jeroboam [v] son of Nebat and like the house of Baasha [w] son of Ahijah. [10]As for Jezebel, dogs [x] will devour her on the plot of ground at Jezreel, and no one will bury her.' " Then he opened the door and ran.

[11]When Jehu went out to his fellow officers, one of them asked him, "Is everything all right? Why did this madman [y] come to you?"

"You know the man and the sort of things he says," Jehu replied.

[12]"That's not true!" they said. "Tell us."

Jehu said, "Here is what he told me: 'This is what the LORD says: I anoint you king over Israel.' "

[13]They hurried and took their cloaks and spread [z] them under him on the bare steps.

Cross reference column:

8:25 [b]2Ki 9:29
8:26 [c]S ver 18
[d]1Ki 16:23
8:27 [e]1Ki 16:30
[f]1Ki 15:26
8:28 [g]S Dt 4:43; 2Ki 9:1,14
8:29 [h]1Ki 21:29; 2Ki 9:21
[i]1Ki 19:15,17
[j]2Ki 10:13
9:1 [k]S 1Sa 10:5
[l]S 1Ki 18:46
[m]S 1Sa 10:1
[n]S 2Ki 8:28
9:3 [o]1Ki 19:16

9:6 [p]1Ki 19:16
9:7 [q]S Ge 4:24; S Rev 6:10
[r]S Dt 32:43
[s]S 1Ki 18:4
9:8 [t]2Ki 10:17
[u]S 1Sa 25:22
9:9 [v]S 1Ki 13:34; S 14:10
[w]1Ki 16:3
9:10 [x]S 1Ki 21:23
9:11 [y]S 1Sa 10:11; S Jn 10:20
9:13 [z]Mt 21:8; Lk 19:36

[r]29 Hebrew Ramah, a variant of Ramoth

8:24 *rested with his fathers.* See notes on 1Ki 1:21; 2Ch 21:20.

8:25 *twelfth year of Joram.* 841 B.C. In 9:29 the first year of Joram's reign was counted as his accession year and his second year as the first year of his reign, whereas here his accession year was counted as the first year of his reign (see Introduction to 1 Kings: Chronology).

8:26 *twenty-two years old when he became king.* See note on 2Ch 22:2. *Athaliah.* See note on v. 18.

8:27 *ways of the house of Ahab.* See 2Ch 22:3–5.

8:28 *Ahaziah went with Joram . . . to war against Hazael . . . at Ramoth Gilead.* As Jehoshaphat had joined Ahab in battle against the Arameans at Ramoth Gilead (1Ki 22), so now Ahaziah joined his uncle Joram in a similar venture. On the previous occasion Ahab met his death (1Ki 22:37). On this occasion Joram was wounded and, while recuperating in Jezreel (see note on 1Ki 21:1), both he and his nephew Ahaziah were assassinated by Jehu (see 9:14–28).

9:1 *company of the prophets.* See note on 2:3.

9:3 *I anoint you king.* See notes on 1Sa 2:10; 9:16; 1Ki 19:16.

9:7 *destroy the house of Ahab.* Jehu learned that he was the divinely appointed agent to inflict the judgment Elijah had pronounced many years earlier in his own hearing against the house of Ahab (see vv. 25–26; 1Ki 21:21–24). *blood of all the LORD's servants shed by Jezebel.* A reference to people such as Naboth and his family (1Ki 21:13), who were unjustly put to death through Jezebel's influence.

9:8 *slave or free.* See note on 1Ki 14:10.

9:9 *like the house of Jeroboam.* See 1Ki 14:7–11; 15:27–30. *like the house of Baasha.* See 1Ki 16:1–4,8–12. Elijah had spoken the same words to Ahab years before (see 1Ki 21:21–24).

9:11 *this madman.* The epithet betrays a scornful attitude on the part of the military officers of the northern kingdom toward members of the prophetic companies.

Then they blew the trumpet[a] and shouted, "Jehu is king!"

Jehu Kills Joram and Ahaziah

9:21–29pp — 2Ch 22:7–9

[14]So Jehu son of Jehoshaphat, the son of Nimshi, conspired against Joram. (Now Joram and all Israel had been defending Ramoth Gilead[b] against Hazael king of Aram, [15]but King Joram[s] had returned to Jezreel to recover[c] from the wounds the Arameans had inflicted on him in the battle with Hazael king of Aram.) Jehu said, "If this is the way you feel, don't let anyone slip out of the city to go and tell the news in Jezreel." [16]Then he got into his chariot and rode to Jezreel, because Joram was resting there and Ahaziah[d] king of Judah had gone down to see him.

[17]When the lookout[e] standing on the tower in Jezreel saw Jehu's troops approaching, he called out, "I see some troops coming."

"Get a horseman," Joram ordered. "Send him to meet them and ask, 'Do you come in peace?[f]'"

[18]The horseman rode off to meet Jehu and said, "This is what the king says: 'Do you come in peace?'"

"What do you have to do with peace?" Jehu replied. "Fall in behind me."

The lookout reported, "The messenger has reached them, but he isn't coming back."

[19]So the king sent out a second horseman. When he came to them he said, "This is what the king says: 'Do you come in peace?'"

Jehu replied, "What do you have to do with peace? Fall in behind me."

[20]The lookout reported, "He has reached them, but he isn't coming back either. The driving is like[g] that of Jehu son of Nimshi—he drives like a madman."

[21]"Hitch up my chariot," Joram ordered. And when it was hitched up, Joram king of Israel and Ahaziah king of Judah rode out, each in his own chariot, to meet Jehu. They met him at the plot of ground that had belonged to Naboth[h] the Jezreelite. [22]When Joram saw Jehu he asked, "Have you come in peace, Jehu?"

"How can there be peace," Jehu replied, "as long as all the idolatry and witchcraft of your mother Jezebel[i] abound?"

[23]Joram turned about and fled, calling out to Ahaziah, "Treachery,[j] Ahaziah!"

[24]Then Jehu drew his bow[k] and shot Joram between the shoulders. The arrow pierced his heart and he slumped down in his chariot. [25]Jehu said to Bidkar, his chariot officer, "Pick him up and throw him on the field that belonged to Naboth the Jezreelite. Remember how you and I were riding together in chariots behind Ahab his father when the LORD made this prophecy[l] about him: [26]'Yesterday I saw the blood of Naboth[m] and the blood of his sons, declares the LORD, and I will surely make you pay for it on this plot of ground, declares the LORD.'[t] Now then, pick him up and throw him on that plot, in accordance with the word of the LORD."[n]

[27]When Ahaziah king of Judah saw what had happened, he fled up the road to Beth Haggan.[u] Jehu chased him, shouting, "Kill him too!" They wounded him in his chariot on the way up to Gur near Ibleam,[o] but he escaped to Megiddo[p] and died there. [28]His servants took him by chariot[q] to Jerusalem and buried him with his fathers in his tomb in the City of David. [29](In the eleventh[r] year of Joram son of Ahab, Ahaziah had become king of Judah.)

Jezebel Killed

[30]Then Jehu went to Jezreel. When Jezebel heard about it, she painted[s] her eyes, arranged her hair and looked out of a window. [31]As Jehu entered the gate, she

---

Cross references

9:13 [a]S 2Sa 15:10
9:14 [b]S Dt 4:43; S 2Ki 8:28
9:15 [c]S 2Ki 8:29
9:16 [d]2Ch 22:7
9:17 [e]S 1Sa 14:16; Isa 21:6; [f]S 1Sa 16:4
9:20 [g]2Sa 18:27
9:21 [h]1Ki 21:1
9:22 [i]1Ki 18:19; Rev 2:20
9:23 [j]2Ki 11:14
9:24 [k]S 1Ki 22:34
9:25 [l]1Ki 21:19-22
9:26 [m]S 1Ki 21:19; [n]S 1Ki 21:29
9:27 [o]S Jdg 1:27; [p]2Ki 23:29
9:28 [q]2Ki 14:20; 23:30
9:29 [r]2Ki 8:25
9:30 [s]Jer 4:30; Eze 23:40

---

[s]15 Hebrew *Jehoram*, a variant of *Joram*; also in verses 17 and 21-24   [t]26 See 1 Kings 21:19.   [u]27 Or *fled by way of the garden house*

9:15 *don't let anyone . . . go and tell the news in Jezreel.* For the success of Jehu's revolt and to avoid a civil conflict it was important to take Joram totally by surprise.

9:16 *Jezreel.* About 45 miles from Ramoth Gilead. *Ahaziah . . . had gone down to see him.* See 8:29.

9:21 *plot of ground that had belonged to Naboth.* See notes on 1Ki 21:2–3,13,19.

9:22 *idolatry and witchcraft.* Both punishable by death (see Dt 13; 18:10–12). As long as these evils were promoted in the northern kingdom, there could be no peace.

9:26 *in accordance with the word of the LORD.* Jehu saw himself providentially placed in the position of fulfilling the prophecy of Elijah given years before (see 1Ki 21:18–24).

Even though Ahab's own blood was not shed on Naboth's field (see 1Ki 21:29 and note), Jehu saw in Joram's death the fulfillment of Elijah's prophecy (see note on 1Ki 21:19).

9:27 *escaped to Megiddo and died there.* It may be questioned whether Jehu was justified in extending the purge of Ahab's house (see Hos 1:4) to the descendants of the house of David through Ahab's daughter Athaliah (see 8:18,26).

9:31 *Zimri, you murderer of your master.* In bitter sarcasm Jezebel called Jehu by the name Zimri. About 45 years earlier Zimri had seized the throne from Elah by assassination and then had destroyed the whole house of Baasha. He ruled, however, for only seven days before Omri seized power (see 1Ki 16:8–20).

asked, "Have you come in peace, Zimri, *t* you murderer of your master?"*v*

³²He looked up at the window and called out, "Who is on my side? Who?" Two or three eunuchs looked down at him. ³³"Throw her down!" Jehu said. So they threw her down, and some of her blood spattered the wall and the horses as they trampled her underfoot. *u*

³⁴Jehu went in and ate and drank. "Take care of that cursed woman," he said, "and bury her, for she was a king's daughter." *v* ³⁵But when they went out to bury her, they found nothing except her skull, her feet and her hands. ³⁶They went back and told Jehu, who said, "This is the word of the LORD that he spoke through his servant Elijah the Tishbite: On the plot of ground at Jezreel dogs *w* will devour Jezebel's flesh. *wx* ³⁷Jezebel's body will be like refuse *y* on the ground in the plot at Jezreel, so that no one will be able to say, 'This is Jezebel.' "

Ahab's Family Killed

10 Now there were in Samaria *z* seventy sons *a* of the house of Ahab. So Jehu wrote letters and sent them to Samaria: to the officials of Jezreel, *xb* to the elders and to the guardians *c* of Ahab's children. He said, ²"As soon as this letter reaches you, since your master's sons are with you and you have chariots and horses, a fortified city and weapons, ³choose the best and most worthy of your master's sons and set him on his father's

throne. Then fight for your master's house."

⁴But they were terrified and said, "If two kings could not resist him, how can we?"

⁵So the palace administrator, the city governor, the elders and the guardians sent this message to Jehu: "We are your servants *d* and we will do anything you say. We will not appoint anyone as king; you do whatever you think best."

⁶Then Jehu wrote them a second letter, saying, "If you are on my side and will obey me, take the heads of your master's sons and come to me in Jezreel by this time tomorrow."

Now the royal princes, seventy of them, were with the leading men of the city, who were rearing them. ⁷When the letter arrived, these men took the princes and slaughtered all seventy *e* of them. They put their heads *f* in baskets and sent them to Jehu in Jezreel. ⁸When the messenger arrived, he told Jehu, "They have brought the heads of the princes."

Then Jehu ordered, "Put them in two piles at the entrance of the city gate until morning."

⁹The next morning Jehu went out. He stood before all the people and said, "You are innocent. It was I who conspired against my master and killed him, but who killed all these? ¹⁰Know then, that not a

---

9:31
*t*1Ki 16:9-10
9:33 *u*Ps 7:5
9:34 *v*S 1Ki 16:31
9:36 *w*Ps 68:23;
Jer 15:3
*x*S 1Ki 21:23
9:37 *y*Ps 83:10;
Isa 5:25; Jer 8:2;
9:22; 16:4;
25:33; Zep 1:17
10:1 *z*S 1Ki 13:32
*a*S Jdg 8:30
*b*S 1Ki 21:1
*c*ver 5

10:5 *d*Jos 9:8
10:7
*e*S 1Ki 21:21
*f*S 2Sa 4:8

v31 Or *"Did Zimri have peace, who murdered his master?"* *w36* See 1 Kings 21:23. *x1* Hebrew; some Septuagint manuscripts and Vulgate *of the city*

9:36 *the word of the LORD that he spoke through his servant Elijah.* In the manner of Jezebel's death the word of the Lord was confirmed—the word she had defied during her life (see 1Ki 21:23).

10:1 *Samaria.* In order to consolidate his coup and establish control of the northern kingdom, Jehu still faced the formidable problems of taking the nearly impregnable fortress of Samaria (see note on 1Ki 16:24) and then of completing the destruction of Ahab's house. *seventy sons of the house of Ahab.* The number of Ahab's wives is unknown (see 1Ki 20:5). The 70 presumably included both sons and grandsons. *officials.* Officers appointed by the king (see 1Ki 4:1–6). *elders.* Local leaders by virtue of their position in the tribal and family structure (see notes on Ex 3:16; 2Sa 3:17). *guardians of Ahab's children.* Those entrusted with the care and upbringing of the princes in the royal family.

10:3 *fight for your master's house.* Jehu's strategy was to induce the leaders of Samaria into submission to his rule by bluffing a military confrontation.

10:4 *terrified.* The leaders of Samaria were completely intimidated by Jehu's challenge.

10:5 *palace administrator.* See note on 1Ki 4:6. *city governor.* Probably an official appointed by the king who served as commander of the militia of the capital city. *the elders and the guardians.* See note on v. 1.

10:6 *take the heads of your master's sons and come to me.* The wording of Jehu's command contains what appears to be

a deliberate ambiguity. The "heads of your master's sons" could be understood as a reference to the leading figures among the 70 descendants of Ahab, such as the crown prince and several other sons of special ability and standing. On the other hand, the expression could be taken as a reference to the literal heads of all 70 princes.

10:7 *slaughtered all seventy.* The leaders of the city understood the communique in the literal sense, as Jehu most certainly had hoped they would. *put their heads in baskets and sent them to Jehu.* The leaders of Samaria did not carry the heads of the princes to Jezreel themselves as they had been ordered to do by Jehu (see v. 6). It is likely that they feared for their lives.

10:8 *Put them in two piles at the entrance of the city gate.* This gruesome procedure imitated the barbaric practice of the Assyrian rulers Ashurnasirpal and Shalmaneser III, whose reigns were characterized by acts of terror.

10:9 *It was I who . . . killed him.* Jehu openly confessed his own part in the overthrow of the government of Joram. *who killed all these?* Because of the ambiguous communique Jehu sent to the leaders of Samaria (see note on v. 6), he can now deny any personal responsibility for the slaughter of the 70 sons of Ahab and can lay the blame for it on the leaders of Samaria.

10:10 *what he promised through his servant Elijah.* See 1Ki 21:20–24,29. Jehu implies a divine sanction not only for what had already been done but also for his intent to con-

word the LORD has spoken against the house of Ahab will fail. The LORD has done what he promised[g] through his servant Elijah."[h] [11]So Jehu[i] killed everyone in Jezreel who remained of the house of Ahab, as well as all his chief men, his close friends and his priests, leaving him no survivor.[j]

[12]Jehu then set out and went toward Samaria. At Beth Eked of the Shepherds, [13]he met some relatives of Ahaziah king of Judah and asked, "Who are you?"

They said, "We are relatives of Ahaziah,[k] and we have come down to greet the families of the king and of the queen mother.[l]"

[14]"Take them alive!" he ordered. So they took them alive and slaughtered them by the well of Beth Eked—forty-two men. He left no survivor.[m]

[15]After he left there, he came upon Jehonadab[n] son of Recab,[o] who was on his way to meet him. Jehu greeted him and said, "Are you in accord with me, as I am with you?"

"I am," Jehonadab answered.

"If so," said Jehu, "give me your hand."[p] So he did, and Jehu helped him up into the chariot. [16]Jehu said, "Come with me and see my zeal[q] for the LORD." Then he had him ride along in his chariot.

[17]When Jehu came to Samaria, he killed all who were left there of Ahab's family;[r] he destroyed them, according to the word of the LORD spoken to Elijah.

Ministers of Baal Killed

[18]Then Jehu brought all the people together and said to them, "Ahab served[s] Baal a little; Jehu will serve him much. [19]Now summon[t] all the prophets of Baal, all his ministers and all his priests. See that no one is missing, because I am going to hold a great sacrifice for Baal. Anyone who

fails to come will no longer live." But Jehu was acting deceptively in order to destroy the ministers of Baal.

[20]Jehu said, "Call an assembly[u] in honor of Baal." So they proclaimed it. [21]Then he sent word throughout Israel, and all the ministers of Baal came; not one stayed away. They crowded into the temple of Baal until it was full from one end to the other. [22]And Jehu said to the keeper of the wardrobe, "Bring robes for all the ministers of Baal." So he brought out robes for them.

[23]Then Jehu and Jehonadab son of Recab went into the temple of Baal. Jehu said to the ministers of Baal, "Look around and see that no servants of the LORD are here with you—only ministers of Baal." [24]So they went in to make sacrifices and burnt offerings. Now Jehu had posted eighty men outside with this warning: "If one of you lets any of the men I am placing in your hands escape, it will be your life for his life."[v]

[25]As soon as Jehu had finished making the burnt offering, he ordered the guards and officers: "Go in and kill[w] them; let no one escape."[x] So they cut them down with the sword. The guards and officers threw the bodies out and then entered the inner shrine of the temple of Baal. [26]They brought the sacred stone[y] out of the temple of Baal and burned it. [27]They demolished the sacred stone of Baal and tore down the temple[z] of Baal, and people have used it for a latrine to this day.

[28]So Jehu[a] destroyed Baal worship in Israel. [29]However, he did not turn away from the sins[b] of Jeroboam son of Nebat, which he had caused Israel to commit—the worship of the golden calves[c] at Bethel[d] and Dan.

[30]The LORD said to Jehu, "Because you have done well in accomplishing what is

Cross references (center column)

10:10
g 2Ki 9:7-10
h S 1Ki 21:29
10:11 i Hos 1:4
j ver 14;
Job 18:19;
Mal 4:1
10:13 k 2Ki 8:29;
2Ch 22:8
l S 1Ki 2:19
10:14 m S ver 11
10:15 n Jer 35:6,
14-19 o 1Ch 2:55;
Jer 35:2
p Ezr 10:19;
Eze 17:18
10:16
q S Nu 25:13
10:17 r 2Ki 9:8
10:18 s S Jdg 2:11
10:19 t 1Ki 18:19

10:20 u S Ex 32:5
10:24 v S Jos 2:14
10:25
w S Ex 22:20;
S 2Ki 11:18
x S 1Ki 18:40
10:26
y S Ex 23:24
10:27
z S 1Ki 16:32
10:28 a 1Ki 19:17
10:29
b S 1Ki 12:30
c S Ex 32:4
d 1Ki 12:32

---

tinue the purge of Ahab's house and associates.
10:11 *all his chief men, his close friends and his priests.* Jehu went beyond the responsibility given to him (see 9:7; Hos 1:4) and acted solely on grounds of political self-interest. Jehu himself had been in the service of Ahab (see 9:25).
10:13 *relatives of Ahaziah.* See 2Ch 21:17. *families of the king and of the queen mother.* Members of the royal family from Judah who had not yet heard of the deaths of Joram and Jezebel.
10:15 *Jehonadab son of Recab.* Jehonadab was the leader of a conservative movement among the Israelites that was characterized by strong opposition to Baalism as well as to various practices of a settled agricultural society, including the building of houses, the sowing of crops and the use of wine. His followers still adhered to these principles over 200 years later and were known as Recabites (see Jer 35:6–10).
10:16 *had him ride along.* Public association with Jehonadab gave Jehu added credentials among the rural populace as

a follower of the Lord.
10:18 *Ahab served Baal a little; Jehu will serve him much.* After settling in Samaria, Jehu gave the appearance of having previously appealed to the word of the Lord as a mere political maneuver.
10:19 *will no longer live.* Jehu's reputation made this no idle threat.
10:26 *burned it.* May refer to the Asherah pole (see note on 1Ki 14:15) that usually accompanied a sacred stone (see 1Ki 16:32–33).
10:27 *sacred stone of Baal.* See note on 1Ki 14:23. *to this day.* See note on 8:22.
10:29 *sins of Jeroboam . . . he had caused Israel to commit.* See 1Ki 12:26–32; 13:33–34; 14:16.
10:30 *Because you have done . . . to the house of Ahab all I had in mind.* Jehu was the Lord's instrument to bring judgment on the house of Ahab, for which he was commended. But he was later condemned by the prophet Hosea for the

right in my eyes and have done to the house of Ahab all I had in mind to do, your descendants will sit on the throne of Israel to the fourth generation." *e* 31Yet Jehu was not careful*f* to keep the law of the LORD, the God of Israel, with all his heart. He did not turn away from the sins*g* of Jeroboam, which he had caused Israel to commit.

32In those days the LORD began to reduce*h* the size of Israel. Hazael*i* overpowered the Israelites throughout their territory 33east of the Jordan in all the land of Gilead (the region of Gad, Reuben and Manasseh), from Aroer*j* by the Arnon*k* Gorge through Gilead to Bashan.

34As for the other events of Jehu's reign, all he did, and all his achievements, are they not written in the book of the annals*l* of the kings of Israel?

35Jehu rested with his fathers and was buried in Samaria. And Jehoahaz his son succeeded him as king. 36The time that Jehu reigned over Israel in Samaria was twenty-eight years.

Athaliah and Joash
11:1–21pp — 2Ch 22:10–23:21

11 When Athaliah*m* the mother of Ahaziah saw that her son was dead, she proceeded to destroy the whole royal family. 2But Jehosheba, the daughter of King Jehoram*y* and sister of Ahaziah,

took Joash*n* son of Ahaziah and stole him away from among the royal princes, who were about to be murdered. She put him and his nurse in a bedroom to hide him from Athaliah; so he was not killed.*o* 3He remained hidden with his nurse at the temple of the LORD for six years while Athaliah ruled the land.

4In the seventh year Jehoiada sent for the commanders of units of a hundred, the Carites*p* and the guards and had them brought to him at the temple of the LORD. He made a covenant with them and put them under oath at the temple of the LORD. Then he showed them the king's son. 5He commanded them, saying, "This is what you are to do: You who are in the three companies that are going on duty on the Sabbath*q*—a third of you guarding the royal palace,*r* 6a third at the Sur Gate, and a third at the gate behind the guard, who take turns guarding the temple— 7and you who are in the other two companies that normally go off Sabbath duty are all to guard the temple for the king. 8Station yourselves around the king, each man with his weapon in his hand. Anyone who approaches your ranks*z* must be put to death. Stay close to the king wherever he goes."

y2 Hebrew Joram, a variant of Jehoram   z8 Or approaches the precincts

Cross references

10:30 *e*2Ki 15:12
10:31 *f*Dt 4:9; Pr 4:23
*g*1Ki 12:30
10:32 *h*2Ki 13:25; Ps 107:39
*i*S 1Ki 19:17
10:33 *j*S Nu 32:34; Dt 2:36; Jdg 11:26; Isa 17:2
*k*S Nu 21:13
10:34 *l*1Ki 15:31
11:1 *m*S 2Ki 8:18
11:2 *n*2Ki 12:1
*o*S Jdg 9:5
11:4 *p*ver 19
11:5 *q*1Ch 9:25
*r*1Ki 14:27

---

killing of all Ahab's associates, as well as Ahaziah of Judah and the 42 Judahite princes—the "massacre at Jezreel" (Hos 1:4). *fourth generation.* The restriction of this blessing to four generations is reflective of the qualified approval given to Jehu's reign. Nevertheless, his dynasty survived longer than any other dynasty of the northern kingdom, lasting nearly 100 years. It included the reigns of Jehoahaz, Jehoash, Jeroboam II and Zechariah (see note on 15:12).
10:31 *was not careful to keep the law of the LORD ... with all his heart.* Jehu seems to have been driven more by a political desire to secure his own position on the throne of the northern kingdom than by a desire to serve the Lord. In this he was guilty of using God's judgment on the house of Ahab to satisfy his self-interest.
10:32 *the LORD began to reduce the size of Israel.* The climax of the covenant curses enumerated in Lev 26 and Dt 28 was Israel's expulsion from Canaan. During the rule of Jehu the northern kingdom experienced the beginnings of this curse (see 17:7–18 for its full realization).
10:33 All of Transjordan was lost to Hazael and the Arameans of Damascus.
10:34 *other events of Jehu's reign.* The "Black Obelisk" of the Assyrian ruler Shalmaneser III informs us that Jehu paid tribute to the Assyrians shortly after coming to the throne of the northern kingdom in 841 B.C. In the Assyrian inscription Jehu is incorrectly called the "son of Omri," but this may simply be Shalmaneser's way of identifying Jehu with Samaria (or Israel). There is no reference to this payment of tribute in the Biblical narratives of Jehu's reign. *annals of the kings of Israel.* See note on 1Ki 14:19.
10:35 *rested with his fathers.* See note on 1Ki 1:21. *Jehoahaz his son succeeded him.* For the reign of Jehoahaz

see 13:1–9.
10:36 *twenty-eight years.* 841–814 B.C.
11:1 *Athaliah.* See note on 8:18. *her son was dead.* See 9:27. *destroy the whole royal family.* To secure the throne in Judah for herself. By this time the royal family in Judah had already been reduced to a mere remnant. Jehoram, the late husband of Athaliah and the father of Ahaziah, had killed all his brothers when he succeeded his father Jehoshaphat on the throne (see 2Ch 21:4). Jehu had slain another 42 members of the royal house of Judah, perhaps including many of the sons of Jehoram's brothers (10:12–14; 2Ch 22:8–9), and the brothers of Ahaziah had been killed by marauding Arabs (2Ch 22:1). It is likely that Athaliah's purge focused primarily on the children of Ahaziah, i.e., her own grandchildren. Ahaziah had died at the young age of 22 (see 8:26). This attempt to completely destroy the house of David was an attack on God's redemptive plan—a plan that centered in the Messiah, which the Davidic covenant promised (see notes on 2Sa 7:11,16; 1Ki 8:25).
11:2 *daughter of King Jehoram and sister of Ahaziah.* It is likely that Jehosheba was the daughter of Jehoram by a wife other than Athaliah, and thus she was a half sister of Ahaziah. She was married to the high priest Jehoiada (see 2Ch 22:11). *him and his nurse.* The child was not more than a year old and had not yet been weaned (see vv. 3,21).
11:4 *seventh year.* Of Athaliah's rule. *commanders of units of a hundred.* 2Ch 23:1 lists the names of five commanders, all native Israelites. *Carites.* Mercenary soldiers from Caria in southwest Asia Minor who served as royal bodyguards. *had them brought to him at the temple.* 2Ch 23:2 includes the Levites and family leaders of Judah in the conspiracy.

9The commanders of units of a hundred did just as Jehoiada the priest ordered. Each one took his men—those who were going on duty on the Sabbath and those who were going off duty—and came to Jehoiada the priest. 10Then he gave the commanders the spears and shields[s] that had belonged to King David and that were in the temple of the LORD. 11The guards, each with his weapon in his hand, stationed themselves around the king—near the altar and the temple, from the south side to the north side of the temple.

12Jehoiada brought out the king's son and put the crown on him; he presented him with a copy of the covenant[t] and proclaimed him king. They anointed[u] him, and the people clapped their hands[v] and shouted, "Long live the king!"[w]

13When Athaliah heard the noise made by the guards and the people, she went to the people at the temple of the LORD. 14She looked and there was the king, standing by the pillar,[x] as the custom was. The officers and the trumpeters were beside the king, and all the people of the land were rejoicing and blowing trumpets.[y] Then Athaliah tore[z] her robes and called out, "Treason! Treason!"[a]

15Jehoiada the priest ordered the commanders of units of a hundred, who were in charge of the troops: "Bring her out between the ranks[a] and put to the sword anyone who follows her." For the priest had said, "She must not be put to death in the temple[b] of the LORD." 16So they seized her as she reached the place where the horses enter[c] the palace grounds, and there she was put to death.[d]

17Jehoiada then made a covenant[e] be-

tween the LORD and the king and people that they would be the LORD's people. He also made a covenant between the king and the people.[f] 18All the people of the land went to the temple[g] of Baal and tore it down. They smashed[h] the altars and idols to pieces and killed Mattan the priest[i] of Baal in front of the altars.

Then Jehoiada the priest posted guards at the temple of the LORD. 19He took with him the commanders of hundreds, the Carites,[j] the guards and all the people of the land, and together they brought the king down from the temple of the LORD and went into the palace, entering by way of the gate of the guards. The king then took his place on the royal throne, 20and all the people of the land rejoiced.[k] And the city was quiet, because Athaliah had been slain with the sword at the palace.

21Joash[b] was seven years old when he began to reign.

Joash Repairs the Temple

12:1–21pp — 2Ch 24:1–14; 24:23–27

12 In the seventh year of Jehu, Joash[c1] became king, and he reigned in Jerusalem forty years. His mother's name was Zibiah; she was from Beersheba. 2Joash did what was right[m] in the eyes of the LORD all the years Jehoiada the priest instructed him. 3The high places,[n] however, were not removed; the people continued to offer sacrifices and burn incense there.

4Joash said to the priests, "Collect[o] all the money that is brought as sacred offer-

Cross references (center column)

11:10 sS 2Sa 8:7
11:12 tEx 25:16;
2Ki 23:3
uS 1Sa 9:16;
S 1Ki 1:39
vPs 47:1; 98:8;
Isa 55:12
wS 1Sa 10:24
11:14
xS 1Ki 7:15
yS 1Ki 1:39
zS Ge 37:29
a2Ki 9:23
11:15 b1Ki 2:30
11:16 cNe 3:28;
Jer 31:40
dS Ge 4:14
11:17
eS Ex 24:8;
2Sa 5:3;
2Ch 15:12; 23:3;
29:10; 34:31;
Ezr 10:3

f2Ki 23:3;
Jer 34:8
11:18
gS 1Ki 16:32
hS Dt 12:3
i1Ki 18:40;
2Ki 10:25; 23:20
11:19 jver 4
11:20 kPr 11:10;
28:12; 29:2
12:1 l2Ki 11:2
12:2
mS Dt 12:25;
S 2Sa 8:15
12:3 nS 1Ki 3:3;
S 2Ki 18:4
12:4 o2Ki 22:4

a15 Or *out from the precincts*   b21 Hebrew *Jehoash*, a variant of *Joash*   c1 Hebrew *Jehoash*, a variant of *Joash*; also in verses 2, 4, 6, 7 and 18

11:10 *spears and shields that had belonged to King David and that were in the temple.* David had probably taken the spears and gold shields as plunder in his battle with Hadadezer and then dedicated them to the Lord (see 2Sa 8:7–11). **11:12** *covenant.* Either (1) the Ten Commandments, (2) the entire Mosaic covenant or (3) a document dealing more specifically with the covenant responsibilities of the king (see Dt 17:14–20; see also note on 1Sa 10:25). The third option is most likely. *anointed him.* See notes on 1Sa 2:10; 9:16; 1Ki 1:39. *Long live the king!* See 1Sa 10:24; 1Ki 1:34,39. **11:14** *pillar.* Apparently one of the two bronze pillars of the portico of the temple, named Jakin and Boaz (see 23:3; 1Ki 7:15–22; 2Ch 23:13). *all the people of the land.* It is likely that Jehoiada had chosen to stage his coup on a Sabbath during one of the major religious festivals, when many from the realm who were loyal to the Lord would be in Jerusalem. **11:17** *covenant between the LORD and the king and people that they would be the LORD's people.* A renewal of the Mosaic covenant, by which Israel had been constituted as the Lord's people (see Ex 19:5–6; Dt 4:20). The years of apostasy, involving both the royal house and the people of Judah, necessitated a renewal of allegiance to the Lord at the

time of an important new beginning for the southern kingdom (see notes on 1Sa 11:14–15; 12:14–15,24–25). *covenant between the king and the people.* Defined responsibilities and mutual obligations of king and people that were compatible with Israel's covenant relationship with the Lord (see notes on 1Sa 10:25; 2Sa 5:3). **11:18** *idols.* Stone pillars (see note on 1Ki 14:23) and Asherah poles (see note on 1Ki 14:15). **11:19** *commanders of hundreds, the Carites, the guards.* See note on v. 4. **11:21** See v. 3. The Lord had preserved a lamp for David in Jerusalem (see 1Ki 11:36). **12:1** *seventh year of Jehu.* 835 B.C. (see note on 10:36). *forty years.* 835–796. **12:2** *all the years Jehoiada the priest instructed him.* After Jehoiada died, Joash turned away from the Lord (see 2Ch 24:17–27). **12:3** *high places . . . were not removed.* These were high places where the Lord was worshiped rather than pagan deities (see note on 1Ki 15:14). They were nevertheless potential sources for the entrance of pagan practices into Israel's worship (see note on 1Ki 3:2).

ings[p] to the temple of the LORD—the money collected in the census,[q] the money received from personal vows and the money brought voluntarily[r] to the temple. [5]Let every priest receive the money from one of the treasurers, and let it be used to repair[s] whatever damage is found in the temple."

[6]But by the twenty-third year of King Joash the priests still had not repaired the temple. [7]Therefore King Joash summoned Jehoiada the priest and the other priests and asked them, "Why aren't you repairing the damage done to the temple? Take no more money from your treasurers, but hand it over for repairing the temple." [8]The priests agreed that they would not collect any more money from the people and that they would not repair the temple themselves.

[9]Jehoiada the priest took a chest and bored a hole in its lid. He placed it beside the altar, on the right side as one enters the temple of the LORD. The priests who guarded the entrance[t] put into the chest all the money[u] that was brought to the temple of the LORD. [10]Whenever they saw that there was a large amount of money in the chest, the royal secretary[v] and the

high priest came, counted the money that had been brought into the temple of the LORD and put it into bags. [11]When the amount had been determined, they gave the money to the men appointed to supervise the work on the temple. With it they paid those who worked on the temple of the LORD—the carpenters and builders, [12]the masons and stonecutters. [w] They purchased timber and dressed stone for the repair of the temple of the LORD, and met all the other expenses of restoring the temple.

[13]The money brought into the temple was not spent for making silver basins, wick trimmers, sprinkling bowls, trumpets or any other articles of gold[x] or silver for the temple of the LORD; [14]it was paid to the workmen, who used it to repair the temple. [15]They did not require an accounting from those to whom they gave the money to pay the workers, because they acted with complete honesty.[y] [16]The money from the guilt offerings[z] and sin offerings[a] was not brought into the temple of the LORD; it belonged[b] to the priests.

[17]About this time Hazael[c] king of Aram went up and attacked Gath and captured it. Then he turned to attack Jerusalem.

Cross references (center column):

12:4 [p]Nu 18:19
[q]S Ex 30:12
[r]S Ex 25:2; S 35:29
12:5 [s]2Ki 22:5
12:9 [t]2Ki 25:18; Jer 35:4; 52:24
[u]Mk 12:41; Lk 21:1
12:10 [v]S 2Sa 8:17
12:12 [w]2Ki 22:5-6
12:13 [x]S 1Ki 7:51
12:15 [y]2Ki 22:7; 1Co 4:2
12:16 [z]Lev 5:14-19
[a]Lev 4:1-35
[b]S Lev 7:7
12:17 [c]2Ki 8:12

12:4 *money . . . brought as sacred offerings to the temple.* The money was derived from three different sources: 1. *money collected in the census.* At the age of 20, Israelite youths were required to register for military service and to make an offering of half a shekel (see note on 5:26) for use in the service of the central sanctuary (see Ex 30:11–16; 38:25–26; Nu 2:32). 2. *money received from personal vows.* Various types of vows and their equivalence in monetary assessments are described in Lev 27:1–25. 3. *money brought voluntarily to the temple.* For voluntary offerings see Lev 22:18–23; Dt 16:10.
12:5 *treasurers.* Temple functionaries who handled financial matters for the priests relative to the people's sacrifices and offerings. *whatever damage is found in the temple.* Construction of the temple had been completed 124 years before the beginning of the reign of Joash (see notes on v. 1; 1Ki 6:38). In addition to deterioration due to age, it had fallen into disrepair and abuse during the rule of Athaliah (see 2Ch 24:7).
12:6 *twenty-third year of King Joash.* Joash may have instituted his plan for restoration of the temple a few years before the 23rd year of his reign. Now at age 30 he asserts his royal authority and takes charge of the temple repairs.
12:7 *Take no more money from your treasurers.* The proceeds from the sources of revenue mentioned in v. 4 were no longer to be given to the priests.
12:8 *priests agreed.* Apparently a compromise was reached: The priests would no longer take the money received from the people, but neither would they pay for the temple repairs from the money they had already received.
12:9 *priests who guarded the entrance.* Three high-ranking priests charged with protecting the temple from unlawful (profane) entry (see 25:18; Jer 52:24). *put into the chest all the money.* When the people were assured that all their offerings would be used for the temple restoration, they

responded with greater generosity. See 22:3–7 for continuation (or renewal) of this practice in the reign of Josiah.
12:10 *royal secretary.* See note on 2Sa 8:17. Joash arranges for direct royal supervision of the temple's monetary affairs.
12:11 *men appointed.* The whole matter is taken out of the hands of the priests.
12:13 *articles of gold or silver for the temple.* All the money was initially designated for the restoration of the temple. When the restoration was completed, additional funds were used for the acquisition of silver and gold articles for use in the temple service (see 2Ch 24:14).
12:16 *money from the guilt offerings and sin offerings.* See Lev 5:16; 6:5; Nu 5:7–10 for references to priestly income in connection with the bringing of a guilt offering. There is no Pentateuchal reference to priestly income in connection with the bringing of a sin offering (but see Lev 7:7).
12:17 *About this time.* These events must have taken place toward the end of Joash's reign. From 2Ch 24:17–24 it is clear that the Aramean attack was occasioned by Joash's turning away from the Lord after Jehoiada's death. Joash's apostasy reached its climax in the stoning of Jehoiada's son Zechariah (2Ch 24:22). Probably because of Joash's earlier zeal for the temple, the author of Kings did not choose to relate these matters. *Hazael.* See 8:7–15; 10:32–33; 13:3, 22. *Gath.* One of the major Philistine cities (see Jos 13:3) that David had conquered (1Ch 18:1) and that continued to be subject to Judah during the reign of Rehoboam (2Ch 11:8). In the latter years of the reign of Joash of Judah (835–796 B.C.) and during the reign of Jehoahaz of Israel (814–798; see 13:3,7), the Arameans had virtually overrun the northern kingdom, enabling them to advance against the Philistines and the kingdom of Judah with little resistance. *he turned to attack Jerusalem.* See 2Ch 24:23–24.

18But Joash king of Judah took all the sacred objects dedicated by his fathers—Jehoshaphat, Jehoram and Ahaziah,
the kings of Judah—and the gifts he himself had dedicated and all the gold found in
the treasuries of the temple of the LORD
and of the royal palace, and he sent[d] them
to Hazael king of Aram, who then withdrew[e] from Jerusalem.
19As for the other events of the reign of
Joash, and all he did, are they not written
in the book of the annals of the kings of
Judah? 20His officials[f] conspired against
him and assassinated[g] him at Beth Millo,[h]
on the road down to Silla. 21The officials
who murdered him were Jozabad son of
Shimeath and Jehozabad son of Shomer.
He died and was buried with his fathers in
the City of David. And Amaziah his son
succeeded him as king.

Jehoahaz King of Israel

13 In the twenty-third year of Joash
son of Ahaziah king of Judah,
Jehoahaz son of Jehu became king of Israel
in Samaria, and he reigned seventeen
years. 2He did evil[i] in the eyes of the
LORD by following the sins of Jeroboam son
of Nebat, which he had caused Israel to
commit, and he did not turn away from
them. 3So the LORD's anger[j] burned
against Israel, and for a long time he kept
them under the power[k] of Hazael king of
Aram and Ben-Hadad[l] his son.
4Then Jehoahaz sought[m] the LORD's favor, and the LORD listened to him, for he
saw[n] how severely the king of Aram was
oppressing[o] Israel. 5The LORD provided a
deliverer[p] for Israel, and they escaped
from the power of Aram. So the Israelites
lived in their own homes as they had before. 6But they did not turn away from the
sins[q] of the house of Jeroboam, which he
had caused Israel to commit; they continued in them. Also, the Asherah pole[d][r]
remained standing in Samaria.
7Nothing had been left[s] of the army of
Jehoahaz except fifty horsemen, ten chariots and ten thousand foot soldiers, for the
king of Aram had destroyed the rest and
made them like the dust[t] at threshing
time.
8As for the other events of the reign of
Jehoahaz, all he did and his achievements,
are they not written in the book of the
annals of the kings of Israel? 9Jehoahaz
rested with his fathers and was buried in
Samaria. And Jehoash[e] his son succeeded
him as king.

Jehoash King of Israel

10In the thirty-seventh year of Joash king

12:18 [d]S 1Ki 15:18; S 2Ch 21:16-17 [e]1Ki 15:21; 2Ki 15:20; 19:36 **12:20** [f]2Ki 14:5 [g]2Ki 14:19; 15:10,14,25,30; 21:23; 25:25 [h]Jdg 9:6 **13:2** [i]1Ki 12:26-33 **13:3** [j]S Dt 31:17 [k]S 1Ki 19:17 [l]ver 24 **13:4** [m]S Dt 4:29 [n]S Dt 26:7 [o]S Nu 10:9; 2Sa 7:10 **13:5** [p]S Ge 45:7; S Dt 28:29; S Jdg 2:18 **13:6** [q]1Ki 12:30 [r]S 1Ki 16:33 **13:7** [s]2Ki 10:32-33 [t]S 2Sa 22:43

[d]6 That is, a symbol of the goddess Asherah; here and elsewhere in 2 Kings [e]9 Hebrew *Joash,* a variant of *Jehoash*; also in verses 12-14 and 25

12:18 *sacred objects . . . gold . . . he sent them to Hazael.* Years earlier, Asa had sought to secure assistance from the Arameans with a similar gift (see 1Ki 15:18).
12:19 *annals of the kings of Judah.* See note on 1Ki 14:29. A fuller account of the reign of Joash is also found in 2Ch 22:10–24:27.
12:20 *conspired against him.* The conspiracy was aroused in response to Joash's murder of Zechariah son of Jehoiada (see 2Ch 24:25). *Beth Millo.* Beth means "house"; for the meaning of Millo see note on Jdg 9:6. Here the reference may be to a building (perhaps a kind of barracks) built on the "Millo" in the old City of David (see 2Sa 5:9 and note; 1Ki 11:27). Perhaps the king was staying there temporarily with his troops at the time of his assassination; Chronicles says he was killed "in his bed" (2Ch 24:25). *Silla.* Perhaps refers to a steep descent from the City of David down into the Kidron Valley.
12:21 *officials.* Sons of Ammonite and Moabite mothers (2Ch 24:26), suggesting that they may have been mercenary military officers whose services could have been bought by others. *buried with his fathers.* But see 2Ch 24:25. *Amaziah his son succeeded him.* For the reign of Amaziah see 14:1–22.
13:1 *twenty-third year of Joash.* 814 B.C. (see note on 12:1; see also Introduction to 1 Kings: Chronology). *seventeen years.* 814–798.
13:2 *sins of Jeroboam.* See 1Ki 12:26–32; 13:33–34; 14:16.
13:3 *Hazael.* See notes on 8:12,13,15; 10:33. *Ben-Hadad.* See v. 24. His reign began in either 806 or 796 B.C.
13:4 *the LORD listened to him.* Although deliverance did not come during the lifetime of Jehoahaz (see v. 22), the Lord was merciful to his people in spite of their sin, because of his covenant with Abraham, Isaac and Jacob (v. 23).
13:5 *deliverer for Israel.* Probably either (1) the Assyrian ruler Adadnirari III (810–783 B.C.), whose attacks on the Arameans of Damascus in 806 and 804 enabled the Israelites to break Aramean control over Israelite territory (see v. 25; 14:25), or (2) Jehoash son of Jehoahaz (vv. 17,19,25), or (3) Jeroboam II, who was able to extend Israel's boundaries far to the north (see 14:25,27) after the Assyrians had broken the military power of the Arameans.
13:6 *Asherah pole remained standing.* This idol had been set up by Ahab (see 1Ki 16:33) and had either escaped destruction by Jehu when he purged Baal worship from Samaria (see 10:27–28) or had been reintroduced during the reign of Jehoahaz.
13:7 *ten chariots.* In effect, a small police force. According to the Assyrian annals of Shalmaneser III, Ahab had contributed 2,000 chariots to the coalition of forces that opposed the Assyrians at the battle of Qarqar in 853 B.C. (see note on 1Ki 22:1). *ten thousand foot soldiers.* At the battle of Qarqar Ahab had supplied 10,000 foot soldiers to the coalition of forces opposing the Assyrians. At that time this would have represented only a contingent of Israel's army, while now it represented the entire Israelite infantry. In 857 Ahab had inflicted 100,000 casualties on the Aramean foot soldiers in one day (see 1Ki 20:29).
13:8 *annals of the kings of Israel.* See note on 1Ki 14:19.
13:9 *rested with his fathers.* See note on 1Ki 1:21.
13:10 *thirty-seventh year of Joash.* 798 B.C. (see note on

of Judah, Jehoash son of Jehoahaz became king of Israel in Samaria, and he reigned sixteen years. [11]He did evil in the eyes of the LORD and did not turn away from any of the sins of Jeroboam son of Nebat, which he had caused Israel to commit; he continued in them.

[12]As for the other events of the reign of Jehoash, all he did and his achievements, including his war against Amaziah[u] king of Judah, are they not written in the book of the annals[v] of the kings of Israel? [13]Jehoash rested with his fathers, and Jeroboam[w] succeeded him on the throne. Jehoash was buried in Samaria with the kings of Israel.

[14]Now Elisha was suffering from the illness from which he died. Jehoash king of Israel went down to see him and wept over him. "My father! My father!" he cried. "The chariots[x] and horsemen of Israel!"

[15]Elisha said, "Get a bow and some arrows,"[y] and he did so. [16]"Take the bow in your hands," he said to the king of Israel. When he had taken it, Elisha put his hands on the king's hands.

[17]"Open the east window," he said, and he opened it. "Shoot!"[z] Elisha said, and he shot. "The LORD's arrow of victory, the arrow of victory over Aram!" Elisha declared. "You will completely destroy the Arameans at Aphek."[a]

[18]Then he said, "Take the arrows," and the king took them. Elisha told him, "Strike the ground." He struck it three times and stopped. [19]The man of God was angry with him and said, "You should have struck the ground five or six times; then you would have defeated Aram and completely destroyed it. But now you will defeat it only three times."[b]

[20]Elisha died and was buried.

Now Moabite raiders[c] used to enter the country every spring. [21]Once while some Israelites were burying a man, suddenly they saw a band of raiders; so they threw the man's body into Elisha's tomb. When the body touched Elisha's bones, the man came to life[d] and stood up on his feet.

[22]Hazael king of Aram oppressed[e] Israel throughout the reign of Jehoahaz. [23]But the LORD was gracious to them and had compassion and showed concern for them because of his covenant[f] with Abraham, Isaac and Jacob. To this day he has been unwilling to destroy[g] them or banish them from his presence.[h]

[24]Hazael king of Aram died, and Ben-Hadad[i] his son succeeded him as king. [25]Then Jehoash son of Jehoahaz recaptured from Ben-Hadad son of Hazael the towns he had taken in battle from his father Jehoahaz. Three times[j] Jehoash defeated him, and so he recovered[k] the Israelite towns.

Cross references (center column):

13:12 [u]2Ki 14:15; [v]1Ki 15:31
13:13 [w]2Ki 14:23; Hos 1:1
13:14 [x]S 2Ki 2:12
13:15 [y]1Sa 20:20
13:17 [z]Jos 8:18; [a]S 1Ki 20:26
13:19 [b]ver 25
13:20 [c]S 2Ki 5:2
13:21 [d]Mt 27:52
13:22 [e]S 1Ki 19:17
13:23 [f]S Ex 2:24; [g]S Dt 29:20; [h]S Ex 33:15; 2Ki 17:18; 24:3, 20
13:24 [i]ver 3
13:25 [j]ver 19; [k]S 2Ki 10:32

12:1). *sixteen years.* 798–782.
13:11 *sins of Jeroboam.* See 1Ki 12:26–32; 13:33–34; 14:16.
13:12 *war against Amaziah.* See 14:8–14; 2Ch 25:17–24. *annals of the kings of Israel.* See note on 1Ki 14:19.
13:13 *rested with his fathers.* See note on 1Ki 1:21. *Jeroboam succeeded him.* For the reign of Jeroboam II see 14:23–29.
13:14 *Elisha was suffering.* Ch. 9 contains the last previous reference to Elisha. Since Jehu had been anointed in 841 B.C. (see note on 10:36) and Jehoash began to reign in 798 (see note on v. 10), there is at least a 43-year period in which we are told nothing of Elisha's activities. Based on Elisha's relationship with Elijah, he must have been born prior to 880 and he must have lived to be more than 80 years of age. *The chariots and horsemen of Israel!* An expression of recognition by Jehoash that Elisha was of greater significance for Israel's military success than Israel's military forces were (see notes on 2:12; 6:13,16–23).
13:16 *put his hands on the king's hands.* By this symbolic act Elisha indicated that Jehoash was to engage the Arameans in battle with the Lord's blessing on him.
13:17 *east window.* Faced Transjordan, which was controlled by the Arameans (see 10:32–33). *Aphek.* About 60 years earlier Ahab had won a decisive victory at Aphek over the Arameans and Ben-Hadad II (see 1Ki 20:26–30 and note on 1Ki 20:26).
13:18 *struck it three times and stopped.* The moderately

enthusiastic response to Elisha's directive reflected insufficient zeal for accomplishing the announced task.
13:19 *defeat it only three times.* Jehoash's moderate enthusiasm in striking the ground with arrows symbolized the moderate success he would have against the Arameans. It would be left for Jeroboam II son of Jehoash to gain complete victory over them (see 14:25,28).
13:21 *When the body touched Elisha's bones, the man came to life.* The life-giving power of the God Elisha represented is demonstrated once again in this last OT reference to Elisha (for previous demonstrations of this power see 4:32–37 and 1Ki 17:17–24; for Elijah's translation to heaven without dying see 2:11–12).
13:23 *To this day.* Until the time of the writing of the source from which the author derived this account (see note on 1Ki 8:8; see also Introduction to 1 Kings: Author, Sources and Date). *unwilling to destroy them or banish them.* In his mercy and grace the Lord was long-suffering toward his people and refrained from full implementation of the covenant curse of exile from Canaan (see note on 10:32). This postponement of judgment provided Israel with the opportunity to repent and return to covenant faithfulness.
13:24 *Ben-Hadad.* See note on v. 3.
13:25 *towns he had taken . . . from . . . Jehoahaz.* Probably towns west of the Jordan, since the area east of the Jordan had been lost already in the time of Jehu (see 10:32–33). It was not until the time of Jeroboam II that the area east of the Jordan was fully recovered for Israel (see 14:25). *Three times.* In fulfillment of Elisha's prophecy (v. 19).

Amaziah King of Judah

14:1–7pp — 2Ch 25:1–4,11–12
14:8–22pp — 2Ch 25:17–26:2

14 In the second year of Jehoash[f] son of Jehoahaz king of Israel, Amaziah son of Joash king of Judah began to reign. ²He was twenty-five years old when he became king, and he reigned in Jerusalem twenty-nine years. His mother's name was Jehoaddin; she was from Jerusalem. ³He did what was right in the eyes of the LORD, but not as his father David had done. In everything he followed the example of his father Joash. ⁴The high places,[l] however, were not removed; the people continued to offer sacrifices and burn incense there.

⁵After the kingdom was firmly in his grasp, he executed[m] the officials[n] who had murdered his father the king. ⁶Yet he did not put the sons of the assassins to death, in accordance with what is written in the Book of the Law[o] of Moses where the LORD commanded: "Fathers shall not be put to death for their children, nor children put to death for their fathers; each is to die for his own sins."[g][p]

⁷He was the one who defeated ten thousand Edomites in the Valley of Salt[q] and captured Sela[r] in battle, calling it Joktheel, the name it has to this day.

⁸Then Amaziah sent messengers to Jehoash son of Jehoahaz, the son of Jehu, king of Israel, with the challenge: "Come, meet me face to face."

⁹But Jehoash king of Israel replied to Amaziah king of Judah: "A thistle[s] in Lebanon sent a message to a cedar in Lebanon, 'Give your daughter to my son in marriage.' Then a wild beast in Lebanon came along and trampled the thistle underfoot. ¹⁰You have indeed defeated Edom and now you are arrogant.[t] Glory in your victory, but stay at home! Why ask for trouble and cause your own downfall and that of Judah also?"

¹¹Amaziah, however, would not listen, so Jehoash king of Israel attacked. He and Amaziah king of Judah faced each other at Beth Shemesh[u] in Judah. ¹²Judah was routed by Israel, and every man fled to his home.[v] ¹³Jehoash king of Israel captured Amaziah king of Judah, the son of Joash, the son of Ahaziah, at Beth Shemesh. Then Jehoash went to Jerusalem and broke down the wall[w] of Jerusalem from the Ephraim Gate[x] to the Corner Gate[y]—a section about six hundred feet long.[h] ¹⁴He took all the gold and silver and all the articles found in the temple of the LORD and in the treasuries of the royal palace. He also took hostages and returned to Samaria.

¹⁵As for the other events of the reign of Jehoash, what he did and his achievements, including his war[z] against Amaziah king of Judah, are they not written in the book of the annals of the kings of Israel? ¹⁶Jehoash rested with his fathers and was

Cross references

14:4 [l]2Ki 12:3
14:5 [m]2Ki 21:24
[n]2Ki 12:20
14:6 [o]S Dt 28:61
[p]S Nu 26:11;
Job 21:20;
Jer 31:30; 44:3;
Eze 18:4,20
14:7 [q]S 2Sa 8:13
[r]S Jdg 1:36
14:9 [s]Jdg 9:8-15
14:10
[t]2Ch 26:16;
32:25
14:11
[u]S Jos 15:10
14:12 [v]1Ki 22:36
14:13 [w]1Ki 3:1;
2Ch 33:14;
36:19; Jer 39:2
[x]Ne 8:16; 12:39
[y]2Ch 26:9;
Jer 31:38;
Zec 14:10
14:15 [z]2Ki 13:12

---

f *1* Hebrew *Joash,* a variant of *Jehoash;* also in verses 13, 23 and 27   **g** *6* Deut. 24:16   **h** *13* Hebrew *four hundred cubits* (about 180 meters)

14:1 *second year of Jehoash.* 796 B.C. (see note on 13:10).

14:2 *twenty-nine years.* 796–767. Amaziah's 29-year reign included a 24-year co-regency with his son Azariah (see notes on v. 21; 15:1–2).

14:3 *not as his father David.* Amaziah did not remain completely free from involvement with the worship of pagan deities (see 2Ch 25:14–16). His loyalty to the Lord fell short of that of Asa and Jehoshaphat before him (see 1Ki 15:11,14; 22:43; see also 1Ki 9:4; 11:4).

14:4 *high places, however, were not removed.* See note on 1Ki 15:14.

14:7 *defeated ten thousand Edomites.* Amaziah was able to regain temporarily (see 2Ch 28:17) some of Judah's control over the Edomites, which had been lost during the reign of Jehoram (see 8:20–22). *Valley of Salt.* The same battlefield on which David had defeated the Edomites (see 2Sa 8:13; 1Ch 18:12; Ps 60 title), generally identified with the Arabah directly south of the Dead Sea. *Sela.* Means "rock"; often regarded as the Edomite stronghold presently known as Petra (a Greek word meaning "rock"; see Jdg 1:36; Isa 16:1; 42:11; Ob 3). *to this day.* Until the time of the writing of the account of Amaziah's reign used by the author (see note on 1Ki 8:8; see also Introduction to 1 Kings: Author, Sources and Date).

14:8 *meet me face to face.* A challenge amounting to a declaration of war. Perhaps it was provoked by the hostile actions of mercenary troops from the northern kingdom after their dismissal from the Judahite army (see 2Ch 25:10,13)

and by the refusal of Jehoash to establish a marriage alliance with Amaziah (see v. 9).

14:9 *Jehoash . . . replied.* For his reply Jehoash used a fable (see Jdg 9:8–15) in which he represented himself as a strong cedar and Amaziah as an insignificant thistle that could easily be trampled underfoot.

14:11 *would not listen.* See 2Ch 25:20. *Beth Shemesh.* A town about 15 miles west of Jerusalem near the border between Judah and Dan (see Jos 15:10; 1Sa 6:9).

14:13 *Jehoash . . . captured Amaziah.* It is likely that Amaziah was taken back to the northern kingdom as a prisoner, where he remained until being released to return to Judah after the death of Jehoash (see vv. 15–16; see also note on v. 21). *Ephraim Gate to the Corner Gate.* The Corner Gate (see Jer 31:38; Zec 14:10) was at the northwest corner of the wall around Jerusalem. The Ephraim Gate was on the north side of Jerusalem (see Ne 12:39), 600 feet east of the Corner Gate. This northwestern section of the wall of Jerusalem was the point at which the city was most vulnerable to attack.

14:14 *gold and silver and all the articles found in the temple . . . and . . . the royal palace.* The value of the plundered articles was probably not great, because Joash had previously stripped the temple and palace to pay tribute to Hazael of Damascus (see 12:17–18). *took hostages.* The hostages were probably intended to secure additional payments of tribute in view of the meager war booty.

14:15 *annals of the kings of Israel.* See note on 1Ki 14:19.

buried in Samaria with the kings of Israel. And Jeroboam his son succeeded him as king.

[17]Amaziah son of Joash king of Judah lived for fifteen years after the death of Jehoash son of Jehoahaz king of Israel. [18]As for the other events of Amaziah's reign, are they not written in the book of the annals of the kings of Judah?

[19]They conspired[a] against him in Jerusalem, and he fled to Lachish,[b] but they sent men after him to Lachish and killed him there. [20]He was brought back by horse[c] and was buried in Jerusalem with his fathers, in the City of David.

[21]Then all the people of Judah took Azariah,[i][d] who was sixteen years old, and made him king in place of his father Amaziah. [22]He was the one who rebuilt Elath[e] and restored it to Judah after Amaziah rested with his fathers.

Jeroboam II King of Israel

[23]In the fifteenth year of Amaziah son of Joash king of Judah, Jeroboam[f] son of Jehoash king of Israel became king in Samaria, and he reigned forty-one years. [24]He did evil in the eyes of the LORD and did not turn away from any of the sins of Jeroboam son of Nebat, which he had caused Israel to commit.[g] [25]He was the one who restored the boundaries of Israel from Lebo[j] Hamath[h] to the Sea of the Arabah,[k][i] in accordance with the word of the LORD, the God of Israel, spoken through his servant Jonah[j] son of Amittai, the prophet from Gath Hepher.

[26]The LORD had seen how bitterly everyone in Israel, whether slave or free,[k] was suffering;[l] there was no one to help them.[m] [27]And since the LORD had not said he would blot out[n] the name of Israel from under heaven, he saved[o] them by the hand of Jeroboam son of Jehoash.

[28]As for the other events of Jeroboam's reign, all he did, and his military achievements, including how he recovered for Israel both Damascus[p] and Hamath,[q] which had belonged to Yaudi,[l] are they not written in the book of the annals[r] of the kings of Israel? [29]Jeroboam rested with his fathers, the kings of Israel. And Zechariah his son succeeded him as king.

14:19
a S 2Ki 12:20
b S Jos 10:3
14:20
c S 2Ki 9:28
14:21 *d* 2Ki 15:1; 2Ch 26:23; Isa 1:1; Hos 1:1; Am 1:1
14:22
e S 1Ki 9:26
14:23
f S 2Ki 13:13; 1Ch 5:17; Am 1:1; 7:10
14:24
g S 1Ki 15:30
14:25
h S Nu 13:21
i Dt 3:17 /Jnh 1:1; Mt 12:39
14:26 *k* Dt 32:36
l 2Ki 13:4
m Ps 18:41; 22:11; 72:12; 107:12; Isa 63:5; La 1:7
14:27
n S Dt 29:20
o S Jdg 6:14
14:28 *p* S 2Sa 8:5
q S 2Sa 8:9
r 1Ki 15:31

i 21 Also called *Uzziah*   *j 25* Or *from the entrance to*   *k 25* That is, the Dead Sea   *l 28* Or *Judah*

14:16 *rested with his fathers.* See 13:12–13; see also note on 1Ki 1:21.

14:17 *lived for fifteen years after the death of Jehoash.* Jehoash died in 782 B.C. and Amaziah in 767.

14:18 *annals of the kings of Judah.* See note on 1Ki 14:29.

14:19 *conspired against him.* 2Ch 25:27 connects the conspiracy against Amaziah with his turning away from the Lord, but it did not serve the purpose of the author of Kings to note this. *Lachish.* A fortress city in southern Judah 15 miles west of Hebron, presently known as Tell ed-Duweir (see 18:14; 2Ch 11:9).

14:21 *Then all the people of Judah took Azariah, who was.* Or "Now all the people of Judah had taken Azariah, when he was." See NIV text note. *made him king in place of his father Amaziah.* It is likely that this occurred after Amaziah had been taken prisoner by Jehoash (see v. 13). Thus Azariah's reign substantially overlapped that of his father Amaziah (see notes on v. 2; 15:2).

14:22 *rebuilt Elath and restored it to Judah.* Azariah extended the subjection of the Edomites begun by his father (see v. 7) and reestablished Israelite control over the important port city on the Gulf of Aqaba (see 1Ki 9:26).

14:23 *fifteenth year of Amaziah.* 782 B.C. (see note on v. 2). This was the beginning of Jeroboam's sole reign. He had previously served as co-regent with his father Jehoash. *forty-one years.* 793–753 (including the co-regency with his father).

14:24 *sins of Jeroboam.* See 1Ki 12:26–32; 13:33–34; 14:16; Am 3:13–14; 4:4–5; 7:10–17.

14:25 *from Lebo Hamath.* Jeroboam II was able to free the northern kingdom from the oppression it had suffered at the hands of Hazael and Ben-Hadad (see 10:32; 12:17; 13:3, 22,25). He also extended Israelite political control over the Arameans of Damascus, an undertaking that had been begun by his father Jehoash (see 13:25). Assyrian pressure on the Arameans, including attacks on Damascus by Shalmaneser IV in 773 B.C. and Ashur-Dan III in 772, had weakened the Arameans enough to enable Jeroboam II to gain the upper hand over them. Meanwhile, Assyria also became too weak to suppress Jeroboam's expansion. *Sea of the Arabah.* See NIV text note. According to Am 6:14 the southern limit of Jeroboam's kingdom in Transjordan was the "valley of the Arabah"—probably to be connected with the Valley of Salt (see note on v. 7). If so, Jeroboam had also subdued Moab and the Ammonites. *Jonah . . . the prophet from Gath Hepher.* See Jnh 1:1. Gath Hepher was located in the tribe of Zebulun, northeast of Nazareth (see Jos 19:13). This reference to Jonah is of help in dating the ministry of the prophet.

14:26 *slave or free.* See note on 1Ki 14:10. *suffering.* At the hands of the Arameans (see 10:32–33; 13:3–7), the Moabites (13:20) and the Ammonites (Am 1:13).

14:27 *had not said.* The sin of the Israelites had not yet reached its full measure, and the Lord mercifully extended to the nation an additional period of grace in which there was opportunity to repent (see note on 13:23). Persistence in apostasy, however, would bring certain judgment (see Am 4:2–3; 6:14). *saved them by the hand of Jeroboam.* See note on 13:5.

14:28 *all he did.* During Jeroboam's reign the northern kingdom enjoyed greater material prosperity than it had at any time since the rule of David and Solomon. Unfortunately, it was also a time of religious formalism and apostasy as well as social injustice (see the books of Amos and Hosea, who prophesied during Jeroboam's reign). *Damascus and Hamath.* See note on v. 25. *Yaudi.* Thought by some to be a place in northern Aram referred to in a few Assyrian inscriptions. Others understand the word as a reference to Judah (see NIV text note) in the sense that Damascus and Hamath were once included in territory ruled by David and Solomon (see 2Sa 8:6; 2Ch 8:3). *annals of the kings of Israel.* See note on 1Ki 14:19.

14:29 *rested with his fathers.* See note on 1Ki 1:21. *Zechariah his son succeeded him.* For the reign of Zechariah see 15:8–12.

Azariah King of Judah

15:1–7pp — 2Ch 26:3–4,21–23

15 In the twenty-seventh year of Jeroboam king of Israel, Azariah[s] son of Amaziah king of Judah began to reign. [2]He was sixteen years old when he became king, and he reigned in Jerusalem fifty-two years. His mother's name was Jecoliah; she was from Jerusalem. [3]He did what was right[t] in the eyes of the LORD, just as his father Amaziah had done. [4]The high places, however, were not removed; the people continued to offer sacrifices and burn incense there.

[5]The LORD afflicted[u] the king with leprosy[m] until the day he died, and he lived in a separate house.[n][v] Jotham[w] the king's son had charge of the palace[x] and governed the people of the land.

[6]As for the other events of Azariah's reign, and all he did, are they not written in the book of the annals of the kings of Judah? [7]Azariah rested[y] with his fathers and was buried near them in the City of David. And Jotham[z] his son succeeded him as king.

Zechariah King of Israel

[8]In the thirty-eighth year of Azariah king of Judah, Zechariah son of Jeroboam became king of Israel in Samaria, and he reigned six months. [9]He did evil[a] in the eyes of the LORD, as his fathers had done. He did not turn away from the sins of Jeroboam son of Nebat, which he had caused Israel to commit.

[10]Shallum son of Jabesh conspired against Zechariah. He attacked him in front of the people,[o] assassinated[b] him and succeeded him as king. [11]The other events of Zechariah's reign are written in the book of the annals[c] of the kings of Israel. [12]So the word of the LORD spoken to Jehu was fulfilled:[d] "Your descendants will sit on the throne of Israel to the fourth generation."[p]

Shallum King of Israel

[13]Shallum son of Jabesh became king in the thirty-ninth year of Uzziah king of Judah, and he reigned in Samaria[e] one month. [14]Then Menahem son of Gadi went from Tirzah[f] up to Samaria. He attacked Shallum son of Jabesh in Samaria, assassinated[g] him and succeeded him as king.

[15]The other events of Shallum's reign, and the conspiracy he led, are written in the book of the annals[h] of the kings of Israel.

[16]At that time Menahem, starting out from Tirzah, attacked Tiphsah[i] and everyone in the city and its vicinity, because they refused to open[j] their gates. He sacked Tiphsah and ripped open all the pregnant women.

Menahem King of Israel

[17]In the thirty-ninth year of Azariah king

15:1 [s]S ver 32; S 2Ki 14:21
15:3 [t]S 1Ki 14:8
15:5 [u]S Ge 12:17 [v]Lev 13:46 [w]ver 7,32; 2Ch 27:1; Mic 1:1 [x]S Ge 41:40
15:7 [y]Isa 6:1; 14:28 [z]S ver 5
15:9 [a]1Ki 15:26
15:10 [b]S 2Ki 12:20
15:11 [c]1Ki 15:31
15:12 [d]2Ki 10:30
15:13 [e]S 1Ki 13:32
15:14 [f]S 1Ki 15:33 [g]S 2Ki 12:20
15:15 [h]1Ki 15:31
15:16 [i]1Ki 4:24 [j]S 2Ki 8:12; S Hos 13:16

[m]5 The Hebrew word was used for various diseases affecting the skin—not necessarily leprosy.   [n]5 Or *in a house where he was relieved of responsibility*   [o]10 Hebrew; some Septuagint manuscripts *in Ibleam*   [p]12 2 Kings 10:30

15:1 *twenty-seventh year of Jeroboam.* 767 B.C., based on dating the beginning of Jeroboam's co-regency with Jehoash in 793 (see note on 14:23). *Azariah . . . began to reign.* He began his sole reign, after a 24-year co-regency with his father Amaziah (see notes on v. 2; 14:2,21). (His actual years were one less than his official years.)
15:2 *fifty-two years.* 792–740 B.C. (but he was co-regent with his father Amaziah 792–767). See note on v. 1.
15:3 *as his father Amaziah had done.* See note on 14:3.
15:4 *high places, however, were not removed.* See 14:4; see also note on 1Ki 15:14.
15:5 *afflicted the king with leprosy.* A punishment for usurping the priestly function of burning incense on the altar in the temple (see 2Ch 26:16–21; cf. Lev 13:46). *had charge of the palace and governed the people of the land.* Jotham ruled for his father for the remainder of Azariah's life (750–740 B.C.; see note on v. 33).
15:6 *all he did.* A more detailed account of Azariah's accomplishments is found in 2Ch 26:1–15. *annals of the kings of Judah.* See note on 1Ki 14:29.
15:7 *rested with his fathers.* See note on 1Ki 1:21. *Jotham his son succeeded him.* For the reign of Jotham see vv. 32–38.
15:8 *thirty-eighth year of Azariah.* 753 B.C. (see note on v. 2).
15:9 *sins of Jeroboam.* See 1Ki 12:26–32; 13:33–34; 14:16.

15:11 *annals of the kings of Israel.* See note on 1Ki 14:19.
15:12 *word of the LORD . . . was fulfilled.* See NIV text note. With the downfall of Jehu's dynasty, the northern kingdom entered a period of political instability (see Hos 1:4). The remaining five kings of the northern kingdom were all assassinated with the exception of Menahem, who reigned ten years, and Hoshea, who was imprisoned by the Assyrians. From the strength and wealth of the reign of Jeroboam II, the decline and fall of the northern kingdom was swift.
15:13 *thirty-ninth year of Uzziah.* 752 B.C. (see note on v. 2). Uzziah is another name for Azariah (see NIV text note on 14:21).
15:14 *Menahem . . . went from Tirzah up to Samaria.* It is likely that Menahem was the commander of a military garrison at Tirzah, the former capital of the northern kingdom (see 1Ki 14:17; 15:21,33). *succeeded him.* For the reign of Menahem see vv. 17–22.
15:15 *annals of the kings of Israel.* See note on 1Ki 14:19.
15:16 *Tiphsah.* There was a Tiphsah located far to the north of Hamath (see 14:25) on the Euphrates River (see 1Ki 4:24). It is unlikely that this was the city intended. Some interpreters prefer the reading "Tappuah" of the Septuagint. Tappuah was a city on the border between Ephraim and Manasseh (Jos 16:8; 17:7–8). Perhaps there was a Tiphsah in Israel not otherwise mentioned. *ripped open all the pregnant women.* See 8:12 and note.

Assyrian Campaigns against Israel and Judah

The Assyrian invasions of the eighth century B.C. were the most traumatic political events in the entire history of Israel.

The brutal Assyrian style of warfare relied on massive armies, superbly equipped with the world's first great siege machines manipulated by an efficient corps of engineers.

Psychological terror, however, was Assyria's most effective weapon. It was ruthlessly applied, with corpses impaled on stakes, severed heads stacked in heaps, and captives skinned alive.

The shock of bloody military sieges on both Israel and Judah was profound. The prophets did not fail to scream out against their horror, while at the same time pleading with the people to see God's hand in history, to recognize spiritual causes in the present punishment.

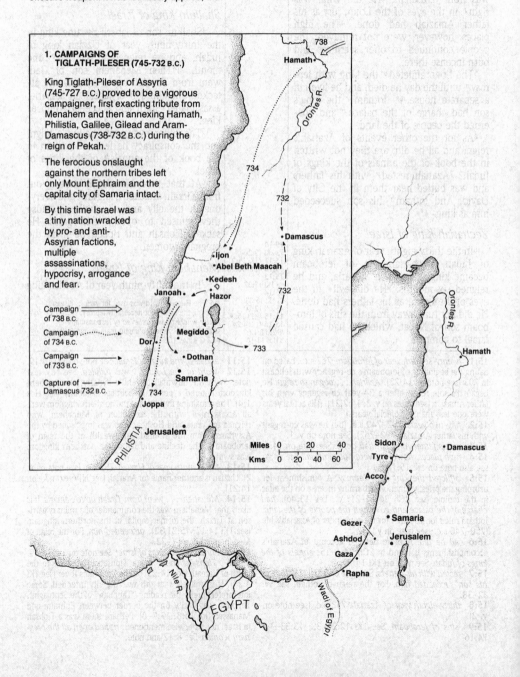

1. CAMPAIGNS OF TIGLATH-PILESER (745-732 B.C.)

King Tiglath-Pileser of Assyria (745-727 B.C.) proved to be a vigorous campaigner, first exacting tribute from Menahem and then annexing Hamath, Philistia, Galilee, Gilead and Aram-Damascus (738-732 B.C.) during the reign of Pekah.

The ferocious onslaught against the northern tribes left only Mount Ephraim and the capital city of Samaria intact.

By this time Israel was a tiny nation wracked by pro- and anti-Assyrian factions, multiple assassinations, hypocrisy, arrogance and fear.

Campaign of 738 B.C.
Campaign of 734 B.C.
Campaign of 733 B.C.
Capture of Damascus 732 B.C.

738
Hamath
Orontes R.
734
732
Damascus
Ijon
Abel Beth Maacah
Kedesh
Janoah
Hazor
732
Megiddo
Dor
733
Dothan
Samaria
734
Joppa
Jerusalem
PHILISTIA

Miles 0 20 40
Kms 0 20 40 60

Orontes R.
Hamath
Sidon
Tyre
Damascus
Acco
Gezer
Samaria
Ashdod
Jerusalem
Gaza
Rapha

Nile R.
EGYPT
Wadi of Egypt

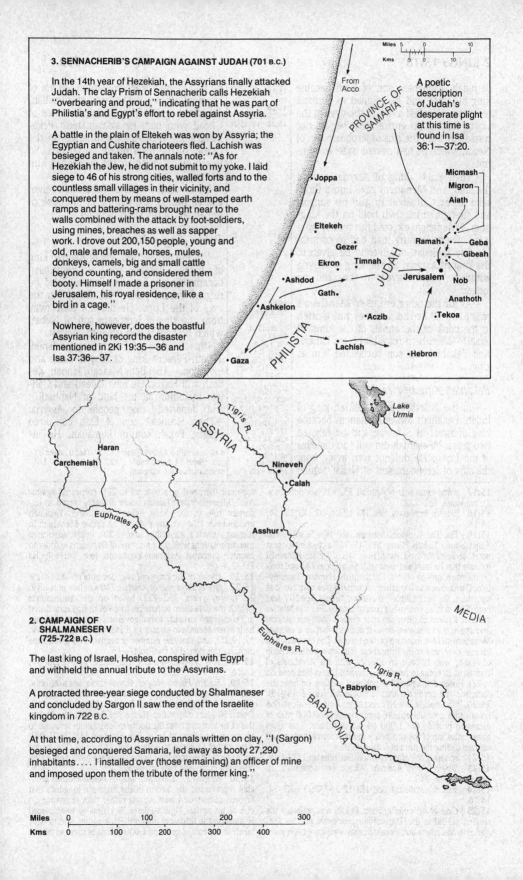

3. SENNACHERIB'S CAMPAIGN AGAINST JUDAH (701 B.C.)

In the 14th year of Hezekiah, the Assyrians finally attacked Judah. The clay Prism of Sennacherib calls Hezekiah "overbearing and proud," indicating that he was part of Philistia's and Egypt's effort to rebel against Assyria.

A battle in the plain of Eltekeh was won by Assyria; the Egyptian and Cushite charioteers fled. Lachish was besieged and taken. The annals note: "As for Hezekiah the Jew, he did not submit to my yoke. I laid siege to 46 of his strong cities, walled forts and to the countless small villages in their vicinity, and conquered them by means of well-stamped earth ramps and battering-rams brought near to the walls combined with the attack by foot-soldiers, using mines, breaches as well as sapper work. I drove out 200,150 people, young and old, male and female, horses, mules, donkeys, camels, big and small cattle beyond counting, and considered them booty. Himself I made a prisoner in Jerusalem, his royal residence, like a bird in a cage."

Nowhere, however, does the boastful Assyrian king record the disaster mentioned in 2Ki 19:35—36 and Isa 37:36—37.

A poetic description of Judah's desperate plight at this time is found in Isa 36:1—37:20.

2. CAMPAIGN OF SHALMANESER V (725-722 B.C.)

The last king of Israel, Hoshea, conspired with Egypt and withheld the annual tribute to the Assyrians.

A protracted three-year siege conducted by Shalmaneser and concluded by Sargon II saw the end of the Israelite kingdom in 722 B.C.

At that time, according to Assyrian annals written on clay, "I (Sargon) besieged and conquered Samaria, led away as booty 27,290 inhabitants.... I installed over (those remaining) an officer of mine and imposed upon them the tribute of the former king."

of Judah, Menahem son of Gadi became king of Israel, and he reigned in Samaria ten years. [18]He did evil[k] in the eyes of the LORD. During his entire reign he did not turn away from the sins of Jeroboam son of Nebat, which he had caused Israel to commit.

[19]Then Pul[q][l] king of Assyria invaded the land, and Menahem gave him a thousand talents[r] of silver to gain his support and strengthen his own hold on the kingdom. [20]Menahem exacted this money from Israel. Every wealthy man had to contribute fifty shekels[s] of silver to be given to the king of Assyria. So the king of Assyria withdrew[m] and stayed in the land no longer.

[21]As for the other events of Menahem's reign, and all he did, are they not written in the book of the annals of the kings of Israel? [22]Menahem rested with his fathers. And Pekahiah his son succeeded him as king.

Pekahiah King of Israel

[23]In the fiftieth year of Azariah king of Judah, Pekahiah son of Menahem became king of Israel in Samaria, and he reigned two years. [24]Pekahiah did evil[n] in the eyes of the LORD. He did not turn away from the sins of Jeroboam son of Nebat, which

he had caused Israel to commit. [25]One of his chief officers, Pekah[o] son of Remaliah, conspired against him. Taking fifty men of Gilead with him, he assassinated[p] Pekahiah, along with Argob and Arieh, in the citadel of the royal palace at Samaria. So Pekah killed Pekahiah and succeeded him as king.

[26]The other events of Pekahiah's reign, and all he did, are written in the book of the annals of the kings of Israel.

Pekah King of Israel

[27]In the fifty-second year of Azariah king of Judah, Pekah[q] son of Remaliah[r] became king of Israel in Samaria, and he reigned twenty years. [28]He did evil in the eyes of the LORD. He did not turn away from the sins of Jeroboam son of Nebat, which he had caused Israel to commit.

[29]In the time of Pekah king of Israel, Tiglath-Pileser[s] king of Assyria came and took Ijon,[t] Abel Beth Maacah, Janoah, Kedesh and Hazor. He took Gilead and Galilee, including all the land of Naphtali,[u] and deported[v] the people to Assyria. [30]Then Hoshea[w] son of Elah conspired against Pekah son of Remaliah. He at-

Cross references (center column):
15:18 *k*1Ki 15:26
15:19 *l*1Ch 5:6, 26
15:20 *m*S 2Ki 12:18
15:24 *n*1Ki 15:26
15:25 *o*2Ch 28:6; Isa 7:1
*p*S 2Ki 12:20
15:27 *q*2Ch 28:6; Isa 7:1 *r*Isa 7:4
15:29 *s*2Ki 16:7; 17:6; 1Ch 5:26; 2Ch 28:20; Jer 50:17
*t*1Ki 15:20
*u*2Ki 16:9; 17:24; 2Ch 16:4; Isa 7:9; 9:1; 10:9,10; 28:1; 36:19; 37:18
*v*2Ki 24:14-16; 1Ch 5:22; Isa 14:6,17; 36:17; 45:13
15:30 *w*2Ki 17:1

q*19* Also called *Tiglath-Pileser*   r*19* That is, about 37 tons (about 34 metric tons)   s*20* That is, about 1 1/4 pounds (about 0.6 kilogram)

15:17 *thirty-ninth year of Azariah.* 752 B.C. (see note on v. 2). *ten years.* 752–742.
15:18 *sins of Jeroboam.* See 1Ki 12:26–32; 13:33–34; 14:16.
15:19 *Pul.* The Babylonian name (see 1Ch 5:26) of the Assyrian ruler Tiglath-Pileser III (745–727 B.C.; see NIV text note). *invaded the land.* Assyrian annals of Tiglath-Pileser III indicate that he marched west with his army in 743 and took tribute from, among others, Carchemish, Hamath, Tyre, Byblos, Damascus, and Menahem of Samaria (see map No. 6 at the end of the Study Bible). *thousand talents.* See NIV text note. This was an enormous sum of money. For the relative value of a talent of silver see note on 5:5. *gain his support and strengthen his own hold.* It appears that as a usurper Menahem still felt insecure on the throne. The opposition to his rule may have come from those following the leadership of Pekah, who favored an alliance with the Arameans of Damascus in order to resist the Assyrian threat (see note on v. 27). Hosea denounced the policy of seeking aid from the Assyrians and predicted that it would fail (Hos 5:13–15).
15:20 *fifty shekels.* See NIV text note. A simple calculation reveals that it would require approximately 60,000 men of means to provide the 1,000 talents of tribute. This gives some indication of the prosperity the northern kingdom had enjoyed during the time of Jeroboam II.
15:21 *annals of the kings of Israel.* See note on 1Ki 14:19.
15:23 *fiftieth year of Azariah.* 742 B.C. (see note on v. 2). *two years.* 742–740.
15:24 *sins of Jeroboam.* See 1Ki 12:26–32; 13:33–34; 14:16.
15:25 *One of his chief officers.* Pekah was probably the ranking official in the Transjordan provinces, but his allegiance to Menahem and Pekahiah may well have been more

apparent than real (see note on v. 27). *conspired against him.* Differences over foreign policy probably played an important role in fomenting Pekah's revolution. Pekahiah undoubtedly followed the policy of his father Menahem in seeking Assyria's friendship (see v. 20). Pekah advocated friendly relations with the Arameans of Damascus in order to counter potential Assyrian aggression (see 16:1–9; Isa 7:1–2,4–6).
15:26 *annals of the kings of Israel.* See note on 1Ki 14:19.
15:27 *fifty-second year of Azariah.* 740 B.C. (see note on v. 2). *twenty years.* 752–732, based on the assumptions (which the data seem to require) that Pekah had established in Transjordan virtually a rival government to that of Menahem when Menahem assassinated Shallum (see notes on vv. 17,19,25), and that the number of regnal years given here includes this period of rival rule.
15:28 *sins of Jeroboam.* See 1Ki 12:26–32; 13:33–34; 14:16.
15:29 *Tiglath-Pileser king of Assyria came.* See note on v. 19. The historical background for this attack is found in 16:5–9; 2Ch 28:16–21; Isa 7:1–17. *Ijon . . . Naphtali.* Over 150 years earlier Ben-Hadad I of Damascus had taken this same territory from the northern kingdom in response to an appeal by a king of Judah (see notes on 1Ki 15:19–20). *deported the people to Assyria.* See 1Ch 5:26. The forced exile of Israelites from their homeland was a fulfillment of the covenant curse (see note on 10:32).
15:30 *Hoshea . . . conspired against Pekah.* Hoshea probably represented the faction in the northern kingdom that favored cooperation with Assyria rather than resistance. In one of his annals Tiglath-Pileser III claims to have placed Hoshea on the throne of the northern kingdom and to have taken ten talents of gold and 1,000 talents of silver as tribute

tacked and assassinated[x] him, and then succeeded him as king in the twentieth year of Jotham son of Uzziah.

[31]As for the other events of Pekah's reign, and all he did, are they not written in the book of the annals[y] of the kings of Israel?

Jotham King of Judah

15:33–38pp — 2Ch 27:1–4,7–9

[32]In the second year of Pekah son of Remaliah king of Israel, Jotham[z] son of Uzziah king of Judah began to reign. [33]He was twenty-five years old when he became king, and he reigned in Jerusalem sixteen years. His mother's name was Jerusha daughter of Zadok. [34]He did what was right[a] in the eyes of the LORD, just as his father Uzziah had done. [35]The high places,[b] however, were not removed; the people continued to offer sacrifices and burn incense there. Jotham rebuilt the Upper Gate[c] of the temple of the LORD.

[36]As for the other events of Jotham's reign, and what he did, are they not written in the book of the annals of the kings of Judah? [37](In those days the LORD began to

send Rezin[d] king of Aram and Pekah son of Remaliah against Judah.) [38]Jotham rested with his fathers and was buried with them in the City of David, the city of his father. And Ahaz his son succeeded him as king.

Ahaz King of Judah

16:1–20pp — 2Ch 28:1–27

16 In the seventeenth year of Pekah son of Remaliah, Ahaz[e] son of Jotham king of Judah began to reign. [2]Ahaz was twenty years old when he became king, and he reigned in Jerusalem sixteen years. Unlike David his father, he did not do what was right[f] in the eyes of the LORD his God. [3]He walked in the ways of the kings of Israel[g] and even sacrificed his son[h] in[t] the fire, following the detestable[i] ways of the nations the LORD had driven out before the Israelites. [4]He offered sacrifices and burned incense[j] at the high places, on the hilltops and under every spreading tree.[k]

[5]Then Rezin[l] king of Aram and Pekah

15:30 *x*S 2Ki 12:20
15:31 *y*1Ki 15:31
15:32 *z*ver 1,5 5;
1Ch 5:17; Isa 1:1;
Hos 1:1
15:34 *a*S 1Ki 14:8
15:35 *b*2Ki 12:3
*c*S Ge 23:10;
2Ch 23:20

15:37 *d*2Ki 16:5;
Isa 7:1; 8:6; 9:11
16:1 *e*Isa 1:1;
7:1; 14:28;
Hos 1:1; Mic 1:1
16:2 *f*S 1Ki 14:8
16:3 *g*2Ki 17:19
*h*S Lev 18:21;
S 2Ki 3:27
*i*S Lev 18:3;
S Dt 9:4
16:4 *j*2Ki 22:17;
23:5 *k*Dt 12:2;
Eze 6:13
16:5 *l*S 2Ki 15:37

t 3 Or even made his son pass through

---

from him. *twentieth year of Jotham.* 732 B.C. (see notes on vv. 32–33). Reference is to his 20th official year, which was his 19th actual year.

15:31 *annals of the kings of Israel.* See note on 1Ki 14:19.

15:32 *second year of Pekah.* 750 B.C. (see note on v. 27).

15:33 *sixteen years.* 750–735 B.C. Jotham was co-regent with his father 750–740 (see note on v. 5). Jotham's reign was in some sense terminated in 735, and his son Ahaz took over. However, Jotham continued to live until at least 732 (see notes on vv. 30,37).

15:34 *as his father Uzziah had done.* See note on v. 3; see also 2Ch 27:2.

15:35 *high places, however, were not removed.* See v. 4; see also note on 1Ki 15:14. *Upper Gate of the temple.* See 2Ch 23:20; Jer 20:2; Eze 8:3; 9:2. Additional information on Jotham's building activities is given in 2Ch 27:3–4.

15:36 *other events of Jotham's reign.* See 2Ch 27:1–6. *annals of the kings of Judah.* See note on 1Ki 14:29.

15:37 This parenthetical statement concerning Jotham's reign supports the idea of an overlap between the reigns of Jotham and Ahaz (see note on v. 33), since 16:5–12; 2Ch 28:5–21; Isa 7:1–17 all place the major effort of Rezin and Pekah in the time of Ahaz.

15:38 *rested with his fathers.* See note on 1Ki 1:21.

16:1 *seventeenth year of Pekah.* 735 B.C. (see note on 15:27). The reign of Ahaz apparently overlapped that of Jotham, with Ahaz serving as a senior partner beginning in 735 (see notes on 15:33,37; see also notes on v. 2; 17:1).

16:2 *twenty years old when he became king.* Perhaps the age at which Ahaz became a senior co-regent with his father Jotham in 735 B.C. (see note on v. 1). Otherwise, according to the ages and dates provided, Ahaz would have been 11 or 12 instead of 14 or 15 years old when his son Hezekiah was born (cf. 18:1–2). *sixteen years.* The synchronizations of the reigns of Ahaz and Hezekiah of Judah with those of Pekah and Hoshea of the northern kingdom present some apparent chronological difficulties (see notes on v. 1; 17:1; 18:1, 9–10). It seems best to take the 16 years specified here as the

number of years Ahaz reigned after the death of Jotham, thus 732–715 (see notes on 15:30,33). The beginning of his reign appears to be dated in a variety of ways in the Biblical text: (1) in 744/743, which presupposes a co-regency with his grandfather Azariah at the tender age of 11 or 12 (see 17:1); (2) in 735, when he became senior co-regent with Jotham (see v. 1); and (3) in 732, when he began his sole reign after the death of Jotham. *Unlike David his father.* Ahaz does not even receive the qualified approval given to Amaziah (14:3), Azariah (15:3) and Jotham (15:34).

16:3 *ways of the kings of Israel.* It is unlikely that Ahaz adhered to the calf worship introduced by Jeroboam I at Bethel and Dan (see 1Ki 12:26–32; 13:33–34; 14:16). The reference here is probably to Baal worship in the spirit of Ahab (see notes on 1Ki 16:31–33; see also 2Ch 28:2). *sacrificed his son.* Israel had been warned by Moses not to engage in this pagan rite (see Lev 18:21; Dt 18:10). In Israel the firstborn son in each household was to be consecrated to the Lord and redeemed by a payment of five shekels to the priests (see Ex 13:1,11–13; Nu 18:16). See also 3:27; 17:17; 21:6; 23:10; 2Ch 28:3; Jer 7:31; 32:35.

16:4 *high places.* See 15:4,35; see also note on 1Ki 15:14. These high places appear to be those assimilated from pagan Baal worship and used for the worship of the Lord in a syncretistic fashion. *under every spreading tree.* Large trees were viewed as symbols of fertility by the pre-Israelite inhabitants of Canaan. Immoral pagan rites were performed at shrines located under such trees. Contrary to the explicit prohibition of the Mosaic covenant, the Israelites adopted this pagan custom (see 17:10; 1Ki 14:23; Dt 12:2; Jer 2:20; 3:6; 17:2; Eze 6:13; 20:28; Hos 4:13–14).

16:5 *Rezin . . . and Pekah . . . marched up to fight against Jerusalem.* See notes on 15:25,37. *could not overpower.* See Isa 7:1–17; 2Ch 28:5–21. Rezin and Pekah desired to replace Ahaz on the throne of the southern kingdom with the son of Tabeel in order to gain another ally in their anti-Assyrian political policy (see notes on 15:19,25). The Lord delivered Judah and Ahaz from this threat in spite of their

son of Remaliah king of Israel marched up to fight against Jerusalem and besieged Ahaz, but they could not overpower him. ⁶At that time, Rezin^m king of Aram recovered Elathⁿ for Aram by driving out the men of Judah. Edomites then moved into Elath and have lived there to this day.

⁷Ahaz sent messengers to say to Tiglath-Pileser^o king of Assyria, "I am your servant and vassal. Come up and save^p me out of the hand of the king of Aram and of the king of Israel, who are attacking me." ⁸And Ahaz took the silver and gold found in the temple of the LORD and in the treasuries of the royal palace and sent it as a gift^q to the king of Assyria. ⁹The king of Assyria complied by attacking Damascus^r and capturing it. He deported its inhabitants to Kir^s and put Rezin to death.

¹⁰Then King Ahaz went to Damascus to meet Tiglath-Pileser king of Assyria. He saw an altar in Damascus and sent to Uriah^t the priest a sketch of the altar, with detailed plans for its construction. ¹¹So Uriah the priest built an altar in accordance with all the plans that King Ahaz had sent from Damascus and finished it before King Ahaz returned. ¹²When the king came back from Damascus and saw the altar, he approached it and presented offerings^u ^u on it. ¹³He offered up his burnt offering^v and grain offering, ^w poured out his drink

offering,^x and sprinkled the blood of his fellowship offerings^{v y} on the altar. ¹⁴The bronze altar^z that stood before the LORD he brought from the front of the temple—from between the new altar and the temple of the LORD—and put it on the north side of the new altar.

¹⁵King Ahaz then gave these orders to Uriah the priest: "On the large new altar, offer the morning^a burnt offering and the evening grain offering, the king's burnt offering and his grain offering, and the burnt offering of all the people of the land, and their grain offering and their drink offering. Sprinkle on the altar all the blood of the burnt offerings and sacrifices. But I will use the bronze altar for seeking guidance."^b ¹⁶And Uriah the priest did just as King Ahaz had ordered.

¹⁷King Ahaz took away the side panels and removed the basins from the movable stands. He removed the Sea from the bronze bulls that supported it and set it on a stone base.^c ¹⁸He took away the Sabbath canopy^w that had been built at the temple and removed the royal entryway outside the temple of the LORD, in deference to the king of Assyria. ^d

¹⁹As for the other events of the reign of

16:6 ^mIsa 9:12
ⁿS 1Ki 9:26
16:7
^oS 2Ki 15:29
^pIsa 2:6; 10:20;
Jer 2:18; 3:1;
Eze 16:28; 23:5;
Hos 10:6
16:8
^qS 1Ki 15:18;
2Ki 12:18
16:9
^rS Ge 14:15;
S 2Ki 15:29
^sIsa 22:6;
Am 1:5; 9:7
16:10 ^tver 11,15,
16; Isa 8:2
16:12
^u2Ch 26:16
16:13
^vLev 6:8-13
^wLev 6:14-23

16:13 ^xS Ex 29:40
^yLev 7:11-21
16:14
^zS Ex 20:24;
S 40:6; S 1Ki 8:64
16:15
^aEx 29:38-41
^b1Sa 9:9
16:17 ^c1Ki 7:27
16:18 ^dEze 16:28

^u12 Or and went up   ^v13 Traditionally peace offerings   ^w18 Or the dais of his throne (see Septuagint)

---

wickedness because of the promises of the Davidic covenant (see 1Ki 11:36; 2Sa 7:13; Isa 7:3–7,14).
16:6 Rezin king of Aram recovered Elath. See note on 14:22. Edomites then moved into Elath. See 2Ch 28:17. The Philistines also took this opportunity to avenge previous defeats (compare 2Ch 26:5–7 with 2Ch 28:18). to this day. See note on 1Ki 8:8.
16:7 Tiglath-Pileser. See notes on 15:19, 29. your servant and vassal. Ahaz preferred to seek security for Judah by means of a treaty with Assyria rather than by obedience to the Lord and trust in his promises (see Ex 23:22; Isa 7:10–16).
16:8 silver and gold found in the temple. The temple treasure must have been restored to some degree by Jotham (see 12:18; 14:14). The name "Jehoahaz of Judah" (Ahaz) appears on a list of rulers (including those of the Philistines, Ammonites, Moabites and Edomites) who brought tribute to Tiglath-Pileser in 734 B.C.
16:9 attacking Damascus and capturing it. In 732 B.C. Tiglath-Pileser III moved against Damascus and destroyed it (see the prophecies of Isa 7:16; Am 1:3–5). deported its inhabitants to Kir. The Arameans were sent back to the place from which they had come (Am 9:7) in fulfillment of the prophecy of Amos (Am 1:5). The location of Kir is unknown, though it is mentioned in connection with Elam in Isa 22:6.
16:10 Ahaz went to Damascus to meet Tiglath-Pileser. As a vassal king to express his gratitude and loyalty to the victorious Assyrian ruler. altar in Damascus. Perhaps that of the god Rimmon (see 5:18; 2Ch 28:23), but more likely a royal altar of Tiglath-Pileser. Ahaz's reproduction of such an altar would have been a further sign of submission to the Assyrians.

16:13 burnt offering . . . grain offering . . . drink offering . . . fellowship offerings. With the exception of the drink offering, these same sacrifices were offered at the dedication of the temple (1Ki 8:64).
16:14 north side of the new altar. Ahaz removed the bronze altar from its prominent place in front of the temple and gave it a place alongside the new stone altar.
16:15 large new altar. Even though fire from heaven had inaugurated and sanctioned the use of the bronze altar for the worship of the Lord (see 2Ch 7:1), Ahaz now replaced it with an altar built on the pattern of the pagan altar from Damascus. Although the bronze altar was quite large (see 2Ch 4:1), the new altar was larger. morning burnt offering. See 3:20; Ex 29:38–39; Nu 28:3–4. evening grain offering. See note on 1Ki 18:29. king's burnt offering and his grain offering. There is no other reference to these special offerings of the king in the OT, with the possible exception of Ezekiel's depiction of the offerings of a future prince (Eze 46:12). I will use the bronze altar for seeking guidance. Seeking omens by the examination of the entrails of sacrificed animals is well attested in ancient Near Eastern texts. Here Ahaz states his intention to follow an Assyrian divination technique in an attempt to secure the Lord's guidance.
16:17 side panels and . . . basins from the movable stands. See 1Ki 7:27–39. removed the Sea from the bronze bulls. See 1Ki 7:23–26. Perhaps the bronze was needed for tribute required by Tiglath-Pileser III.
16:18 in deference to the king of Assyria. As a vassal of Tiglath-Pileser, Ahaz was forced to relinquish some of the symbols of his own royal power.
16:19 other events of the reign of Ahaz. See 2Ch 28, where, among other things, it is said that Ahaz went so far as

all his prophets and seers:[z] "Turn from your evil ways.[a] Observe my commands and decrees, in accordance with the entire Law that I commanded your fathers to obey and that I delivered to you through my servants the prophets."[b]

[14]But they would not listen and were as stiff-necked[c] as their fathers, who did not trust in the LORD their God. [15]They rejected his decrees and the covenant[d] he had made with their fathers and the warnings he had given them. They followed worthless idols[e] and themselves became worthless.[f] They imitated the nations[g] around them although the LORD had ordered them, "Do not do as they do," and they did the things the LORD had forbidden them to do.

[16]They forsook all the commands of the LORD their God and made for themselves two idols cast in the shape of calves,[h] and an Asherah[i] pole. They bowed down to all the starry hosts,[j] and they worshiped Baal.[k] [17]They sacrificed[l] their sons and daughters in[z] the fire. They practiced divination and sorcery[m] and sold[n] themselves to do evil in the eyes of the LORD, provoking him to anger.

[18]So the LORD was very angry with Israel and removed them from his presence.[o] Only the tribe of Judah was left, [19]and even Judah did not keep the commands of the LORD their God. They followed the practices Israel had introduced.[p] [20]Therefore the LORD rejected all the people of Israel; he afflicted them and gave them into the hands of plunderers,[q] until he thrust them from his presence.[r]

[21]When he tore[s] Israel away from the house of David, they made Jeroboam son of Nebat their king.[t] Jeroboam enticed Israel away from following the LORD and caused them to commit a great sin.[u] [22]The Israelites persisted in all the sins of Jeroboam and did not turn away from them [23]until the LORD removed them from his presence,[v] as he had warned[w] through all his servants the prophets. So the people of Israel were taken from their homeland[x] into exile in Assyria, and they are still there.

Samaria Resettled

[24]The king of Assyria[y] brought people from Babylon, Cuthah, Avva, Hamath and Sepharvaim[z] and settled them in the towns of Samaria to replace the Israelites. They took over Samaria and lived in its towns. [25]When they first lived there, they

17:13 [z]S 1Sa 9:9
[a]Jer 4:1; 18:11;
23:22; 25:5;
35:15; 36:3;
Zec 1:4
[b]Mt 23:34
17:14
[c]S Ex 32:9;
Ac 7:51
17:15
[d]S Lev 26:11;
Dt 29:25;
Jdg 2:20;
1Ki 11:11;
2Ki 18:12;
Ps 78:10;
Eze 5:6; Mal 2:10
[e]S Dt 32:21;
Hos 11:2;
Ro 1:21-23
[f]Jer 2:5
[g]S Dt 12:4
17:16 [h]S Ex 32:4
[i]S Dt 16:21
[j]S Ge 2:1;
Isa 40:26;
Jer 19:13
[k]S Jdg 2:11
17:17
[l]S Dt 12:31;
18:10-12;
2Ki 16:3;
Eze 16:21
[m]S Lev 19:26
[n]S 1Ki 21:20;
Ro 7:14
17:18
[o]S Ge 4:14;
S Ex 33:15;
S 2Ki 13:23;
2Th 1:9

17:19 [p]2Ki 16:3;
Jer 3:6-10;
Eze 23:13
17:20 [q]S ver 6
[r]Jer 7:15; 15:1
17:21
[s]S 1Sa 15:27;
S 1Ki 11:11
[t]1Ki 12:20

[u]S 1Ki 12:30 **17:23** [v]Eze 39:23-24 [w]S Jdg 6:8 [x]S 1Ki 9:7
17:24 [y]2Ki 19:37; Ezr 4:2,10; Isa 37:38 [z]ver 31;
S 2Ki 15:29; 18:34; Isa 36:19; 37:13; Am 6:2

[z]17 Or *They made their sons and daughters pass through*

---

enant, but she also spurned the words of prophets the Lord had graciously sent to call his people back to the covenant (see, e.g., 1Ki 13:1–3; 14:6–10; Jdg 6:8–10; 1Sa 3:19–21 as well as the ministries of Elijah, Elisha, Amos and Hosea). *seers.* See note on 1Sa 9:9.
17:14 *stiff-necked.* A figure derived from the obstinate resistance of an ox to being placed under a yoke (see Dt 10:16; Jer 2:20; 7:26; 17:23; 19:15; Hos 4:16).
17:15 *followed worthless idols.* See Dt 32:21; Jer 2:5; 8:19; 10:8; 14:22; 51:18.
17:16 *two idols cast in the shape of calves.* The golden calves of Bethel and Dan (see 1Ki 12:28–30). *Asherah pole.* See note on 1Ki 14:15. *all the starry hosts.* Israel had been commanded not to follow the astral cults of her pagan neighbors (see Dt 4:19; 17:3). Although this form of idolatry is not mentioned previously in 1,2 Kings, the prophet Amos apparently alludes to its practice in the northern kingdom during the reign of Jeroboam II (see note on Am 5:26). It was later introduced in the southern kingdom during the reign of Manasseh (see 21:3,5) and abolished during the reformation of Josiah (see 23:4–5,12; see also Eze 8:16).
17:17 *sacrificed their sons and daughters.* See note on 16:3. *divination and sorcery.* Such practices were forbidden in the Mosaic covenant (see note on 16:15; see also Lev 19:26; Dt 18:10).
17:18 *removed them from his presence.* The exile of the northern kingdom (see v. 6; 23:27). *Only the tribe of Judah was left.* The southern kingdom included elements of the tribes of Simeon and Benjamin, but Judah was the only tribe in the south to retain its complete integrity (see notes on 1Ki 11:31–32; see also note on 2Ki 19:4).
17:20 *afflicted them and gave them into the hands of*

plunderers. See 10:32–33; 13:3,20; 24:2; 2Ch 21:16; 28:18; Am 1:13.
17:21 *tore Israel away from the house of David.* See 1Ki 11:11,31; 12:24. The division of the kingdom was of the Lord, but it came to the nation as a punishment for their sins. *Jeroboam . . . caused them to commit a great sin.* See 1Ki 12:26–32; 13:33–34.
17:23 *warned through all his servants the prophets.* See 1Ki 14:15–16; Hos 10:1–7; 11:5; Am 5:27.
17:24 *king of Assyria.* Primarily Sargon II (722–705 B.C.), though later Assyrian rulers, including Esarhaddon (681–669) and Ashurbanipal (669–627), settled additional non-Israelites in Samaria (see Ezr 4:2,9–10). *Babylon, Cuthah.* Babylon and Cuthah (located about eight miles northeast of Babylon) were forced to submit to Assyrian rule by Sargon II in 709. *Avva.* Probably the same as Ivvah (see 18:34; 19:13). Its association with Hamath, Arpad and Sepharvaim suggests a location somewhere in Aram (Syria). *Hamath.* Located on the Orontes River (see 14:25; 18:34; see also note on Eze 47:15). In 720 Sargon II made the kingdom of Hamath into an Assyrian province. *Sepharvaim.* Perhaps located in Aramean territory, possibly between Damascus and Hamath. *Samaria.* Here a designation for the entire northern kingdom (see note on 1Ki 13:32).
17:25 *did not worship the LORD.* They worshiped their own national deities. *sent lions among them.* Lions had always been present in Canaan (see 1Ki 13:24; 20:36; Jdg 14:5; 1Sa 17:34; Am 3:12). In the aftermath of the disruption and depopulation caused by the conflict with the Assyrians, the lions greatly increased in number (see Ex 23:29). This was viewed by the inhabitants of the land and the writer of Kings as a punishment from the Lord (see Lev 26:21–22).

did not worship the LORD; so he sent lions[a] among them and they killed some of the people. 26It was reported to the king of Assyria: "The people you deported and resettled in the towns of Samaria do not know what the god of that country requires. He has sent lions among them, which are killing them off, because the people do not know what he requires."

27Then the king of Assyria gave this order: "Have one of the priests you took captive from Samaria go back to live there and teach the people what the god of the land requires." 28So one of the priests who had been exiled from Samaria came to live in Bethel and taught them how to worship the LORD.

29Nevertheless, each national group made its own gods in the several towns[b] where they settled, and set them up in the shrines[c] the people of Samaria had made at the high places.[d] 30The men from Babylon made Succoth Benoth, the men from Cuthah made Nergal, and the men from Hamath made Ashima; 31the Avvites made Nibhaz and Tartak, and the Sepharvites burned their children in the fire as sacrifices to Adrammelech[e] and Anammelech, the gods of Sepharvaim.[f] 32They worshiped the LORD, but they also appointed all sorts[g] of their own people to officiate for them as priests in the shrines at the high places. 33They worshiped the LORD, but they also served their own gods in accordance with the customs of the nations from which they had been brought.

34To this day they persist in their former practices. They neither worship the LORD nor adhere to the decrees and ordinances, the laws and commands that the LORD gave the descendants of Jacob, whom he named Israel.[h] 35When the LORD made a covenant with the Israelites, he commanded them: "Do not worship[i] any other gods or bow down to them, serve them or sacrifice to them.[j] 36But the LORD, who brought you up out of Egypt with mighty power and outstretched arm,[k] is the one you must worship. To him you shall bow down and to him offer sacrifices. 37You must always be careful[l] to keep the decrees[m] and ordinances, the laws and commands he wrote for you. Do not worship other gods. 38Do not forget[n] the covenant I have made with you, and do not worship other gods. 39Rather, worship the LORD your God; it is he who will deliver you from the hand of all your enemies."

40They would not listen, however, but persisted in their former practices. 41Even while these people were worshiping the LORD,[o] they were serving their idols. To this day their children and grandchildren continue to do as their fathers did.

Hezekiah King of Judah

18:2–4pp — 2Ch 29:1–2; 31:1
18:5–7pp — 2Ch 31:20–21
18:9–12pp — 2Ki 17:3–7

18 In the third year of Hoshea son of Elah king of Israel, Hezekiah[p] son of Ahaz king of Judah began to reign. 2He was twenty-five years old when he became king, and he reigned in Jerusalem twenty-nine years.[q] His mother's name was Abi-

Cross-references

17:25
[a]S Ge 37:20;
Isa 5:29; 15:9;
Jer 50:17
17:29 [b]Jer 2:28;
11:13
[c]S Lev 26:30;
S 1Ki 12:31
[d]Mic 4:5
17:31 [e]2Ki 19:37
[f]S ver 24
17:32
[g]S 1Ki 12:31

17:34
[h]S Ge 17:5;
S 1Ki 18:31
17:35 [i]S Ex 20:5
[j]S Ex 20:3
17:36
[k]S Ex 3:20;
Ps 136:12
17:37 [l]Dt 5:32
[m]S Lev 19:37
17:38 [n]S Dt 6:12
17:41
[o]S 1Ki 18:21;
Ezr 4:2; Mt 6:24
18:1 [p]Isa 1:1;
Hos 1:1; Mic 1:1
18:2 [q]ver 13;
Isa 38:5

Study notes

17:26 *king of Assyria.* Sargon II. *what the god of that country requires.* According to the religious ideas of that time, each regional deity required special ritual observances, which, if ignored or violated, would bring disaster on the land.

17:27 *one of the priests.* Of the golden calf cult established in the northern kingdom by Jeroboam I (see 1Ki 12:31 and note).

17:28 *came to live in Bethel.* Bethel continued to be the center for the apostate form of Yahweh worship that had been promoted in the northern kingdom since the time of Jeroboam I (see notes on 1Ki 12:28–30).

17:29 *people of Samaria.* The mixed population of the former territory of the northern kingdom. These people of mixed ancestry eventually came to be known as Samaritans. In later times the Samaritans rejected the idolatry of their polytheistic origins and followed the teachings of Moses, including monotheism. In NT times Jesus testified to a Samaritan woman (Jn 4:4–26), and many Samaritans were converted under the ministry of Philip (Ac 8:4–25).

17:32 *officiate for them as priests.* See note on 1Ki 12:31.

17:33 *They worshiped the LORD, but they also served their own gods.* A classic statement of syncretistic religion.

17:34 *To this day.* Until the time of the writing of 1,2 Kings. *worship the LORD.* Here used in the sense of faithful worship. In vv. 32–33 "worship the LORD" refers to a paganized worship.

17:35 *Do not worship any other gods.* The Mosaic covenant demanded exclusive worship of the Lord (Ex 20:5; Dt 5:9). This was the first and great commandment, and it was to distinguish Israel from all other peoples.

17:36 *The LORD, who brought you up out of Egypt . . . you must worship.* Here, as in v. 7, the deliverance from Egypt is cited as the gracious act of the Lord par excellence that entitled him to exclusive claim on Israel's loyalty.

17:39 *will deliver you from . . . all your enemies.* See Ex 23:22; Dt 20:1–4; 23:14.

17:41 *To this day.* See note on v. 34.

18:1 *third year of Hoshea . . . Hezekiah . . . began to reign.* 729 B.C. (see 17:1). Hezekiah was co-regent with his father Ahaz from 729 to 715 (see note on 16:2).

18:2 *became king.* Became sole king of Judah. *twenty-nine years.* 715–686 B.C. See also 2Ch 29–32 and Isa 36–39 for a description of the events of his reign, including a more detailed account of the reformation he led (2Ch 29–31). One of his first acts was to reopen the temple, which had been closed by his father Ahaz (see note on 16:19; see also 2Ch 29:3).

jah[a] daughter of Zechariah. [3]He did what was right[r] in the eyes of the LORD, just as his father David[s] had done. [4]He removed[t] the high places,[u] smashed the sacred stones[v] and cut down the Asherah poles. He broke into pieces the bronze snake[w] Moses had made, for up to that time the Israelites had been burning incense to it. (It was called[b] Nehushtan.[c])

[5]Hezekiah trusted[x] in the LORD, the God of Israel. There was no one like him among all the kings of Judah, either before him or after him. [6]He held fast[y] to the LORD and did not cease to follow him; he kept the commands the LORD had given Moses. [7]And the LORD was with him; he was successful[z] in whatever he undertook. He rebelled[a] against the king of Assyria and did not serve him. [8]From watchtower to fortified city,[b] he defeated the Philistines, as far as Gaza and its territory.

[9]In King Hezekiah's fourth year,[c] which was the seventh year of Hoshea son of Elah king of Israel, Shalmaneser king of Assyria marched against Samaria and laid siege to it. [10]At the end of three years the Assyrians took it. So Samaria was captured in Hezekiah's sixth year, which was the ninth year

of Hoshea king of Israel. [11]The king[d] of Assyria deported Israel to Assyria and settled them in Halah, in Gozan on the Habor River and in towns of the Medes.[e] [12]This happened because they had not obeyed the LORD their God, but had violated his covenant[f]—all that Moses the servant of the LORD commanded.[g] They neither listened to the commands[h] nor carried them out.

[13]In the fourteenth year[i] of King Hezekiah's reign, Sennacherib king of Assyria attacked all the fortified cities of Judah[j] and captured them. [14]So Hezekiah king of Judah sent this message to the king of Assyria at Lachish:[k] "I have done wrong.[l] Withdraw from me, and I will pay whatever you demand of me." The king of Assyria exacted from Hezekiah king of Judah three hundred talents[d] of silver and thirty talents[e] of gold. [15]So Hezekiah gave[m] him all the silver that was found in the temple of the LORD and in the treasuries of the royal palace.

Cross references (center column):

18:3 [r]S 1Ki 14:8; [s]Isa 38:5
18:4 [t]2Ch 31:1; Isa 36:7; [u]2Ki 12:3; 21:3; [v]S Ex 23:24; [w]Nu 21:9
18:5 [x]ver 19; S 1Sa 7:3; 2Ki 19:10; Ps 21:7; 125:1; Pr 3:26
18:6 [y]S Dt 6:18; S 10:20
18:7 [z]S Ge 39:3; S Job 22:25; [a]2Ki 24:1; Ezr 4:19; Isa 36:5
18:8 [b]2Ki 17:9
18:9 [c]Isa 1:1; 36:1
18:11 [d]Isa 37:12; [e]Eze 16:39; 23:9
18:12 [f]S 2Ki 17:15; [g]2Ki 21:8; Da 9:6,10; [h]S 1Ki 9:6
18:13 [i]S ver 2
18:14 [j]Isa 1:7; Mic 1:9; [k]2Ki 19:8; [l]Isa 24:5; 33:8
18:15 [m]S 1Ki 15:18; Isa 39:2

Text notes (center column):

[a]2 Hebrew Abi, a variant of Abijah   [b]4 Or He called it   [c]4 Nehushtan sounds like the Hebrew for bronze and snake and unclean thing.   [d]14 That is, about 11 tons (about 10 metric tons)   [e]14 That is, about 1 ton (about 1 metric ton)

18:3 right . . . as his father David. Hezekiah is one of the few kings who is compared favorably with David. The others are Asa (1Ki 15:11), Jehoshaphat (1Ki 22:43) and Josiah (2Ki 22:2). A qualification is introduced, however, with both Asa and Jehoshaphat: They did not remove the high places (see 1Ki 15:14; 22:43).

18:4 removed the high places. Hezekiah was not the first king to destroy high places (see notes on 1Ki 3:2; 15:14), but he was the first to destroy high places dedicated to the worship of the Lord (see 12:3; 14:4; 15:4,35; 17:9; 1Ki 22:43). This became known even to the Assyrian king, Sennacherib (see v. 22). sacred stones. See 3:2; 10:26–27; 17:10; see also note on 1Ki 14:23. Asherah poles. See 13:6; 17:10,16; 1Ki 16:23; see also note on 1Ki 14:15. Israelites had been burning incense to it. It is unlikely that the bronze snake had been an object of worship all through the centuries of Israel's existence as a nation. Just when an idolatrous significance was attached to it is not known, but perhaps it occurred during the reign of Hezekiah's father Ahaz (see ch. 16). Snake worship of various types was common among ancient Near Eastern peoples.

18:5 no one like him . . . either before him or after him. A difference of emphasis is to be seen in this statement when compared to that of 23:25. Hezekiah's uniqueness is to be found in his trust in the Lord, while Josiah's uniqueness is to be found in his scrupulous observance of the Mosaic law.

18:7 rebelled against the king of Assyria. Judah had become a vassal to Assyria under Ahaz (see 16:7)—which required at least formal recognition of Assyrian deities. Hezekiah reversed the policy of his father Ahaz and sought independence from Assyrian dominance. It is likely that sometime shortly after 705 B.C., when Sennacherib replaced Sargon II on the Assyrian throne, Hezekiah refused to pay the annual tribute due the Assyrians.

18:8 defeated the Philistines. In a reversal of the conditions existing during the time of Ahaz, in which the Philis-

tines captured Judahite cities in the hill country and Negev (see 2Ch 28:18), Hezekiah was able once again to subdue the Philistines. Probably Hezekiah tried to coerce the Philistines into joining his anti-Assyrian policy. In one of his annals Sennacherib tells of forcing Hezekiah to release Padi, king of the Philistine city of Ekron, whom Hezekiah held prisoner in Jerusalem. This occurred in connection with Sennacherib's military campaign in 701 B.C.

18:9 Hezekiah's fourth year. 725 B.C., the fourth year of Hezekiah's co-regency with Ahaz (see notes on v. 1; 17:1).

18:10 three years. See note on 17:5. ninth year of Hoshea. See note on 17:6.

18:11 king of Assyria deported Israel. See note on 17:6.

18:12 violated his covenant. See 17:7–23.

18:13 fourteenth year. Of Hezekiah's sole reign: 701 B.C. (see note on v. 2). Sennacherib . . . attacked. Verses 13–16 correspond very closely with Sennacherib's own account of his 701 campaign against Phoenicia, Judah and Egypt. captured them. In his annals, Sennacherib claims to have captured 46 of Hezekiah's fortified cities, as well as numerous open villages, and to have taken 200,146 of the people captive. He says he made Hezekiah "a prisoner in Jerusalem his royal residence, like a bird in a cage," but he does not say he took Jerusalem.

18:14 three hundred talents of silver and thirty talents of gold. See NIV text notes. The Assyrian and Biblical reports of the amount of tribute paid by Hezekiah to Sennacherib agree with respect to the 30 talents of gold, but Sennacherib claims to have received 800 talents of silver rather than the 300 specified in the Biblical text. This discrepancy may be the result of differences in the weight of Assyrian and Israelite silver talents, or it may simply be due to the Assyrian propensity for exaggeration. For the relative value of this amount of silver and gold see note on 5:5.

18:15 silver . . . in the temple . . . and in the treasuries of the royal palace. See 12:10,18; 14:14; 16:8; 1Ki 7:51; 14:26; 15:18.

16At this time Hezekiah king of Judah stripped off the gold with which he had covered the doors[n] and doorposts of the temple of the LORD, and gave it to the king of Assyria.

Sennacherib Threatens Jerusalem

18:13, 17–37pp — Isa 36:1–22
18:17–35pp — 2Ch 32:9–19

17The king of Assyria sent his supreme commander,[o] his chief officer and his field commander with a large army, from Lachish to King Hezekiah at Jerusalem. They came up to Jerusalem and stopped at the aqueduct of the Upper Pool,[p] on the road to the Washerman's Field. 18They called for the king; and Eliakim[q] son of Hilkiah the palace administrator, Shebna[r] the secretary, and Joah son of Asaph the recorder went out to them.

19The field commander said to them, "Tell Hezekiah:

" 'This is what the great king, the king of Assyria, says: On what are you basing this confidence[s] of yours? 20You say you have strategy and military strength—but you speak only empty words. On whom are you depending, that you rebel against me? 21Look now, you are depending on Egypt,[t] that splintered reed of a staff,[u] which pierces a man's hand and wounds him if he leans on it! Such is Pharaoh king of Egypt to all who depend on him. 22And if you say to me, "We are depending on the LORD our God"—isn't he the one whose high places and altars Hezekiah removed, saying to Judah and Jerusalem, "You must worship before this altar in Jerusalem"?

23" 'Come now, make a bargain with my master, the king of Assyria: I will give you two thousand horses—if you can put riders on them! 24How can you repulse one officer[v] of the least of my master's officials, even though you are depending on Egypt for chariots and horsemen[f]? 25Furthermore, have I come to attack and destroy this place without word from the LORD?[w] The LORD himself told me to march against this country and destroy it.' "

26Then Eliakim son of Hilkiah, and Shebna and Joah said to the field commander, "Please speak to your servants in Aramaic,[x] since we understand it. Don't speak to us in Hebrew in the hearing of the people on the wall."

27But the commander replied, "Was it only to your master and you that my master sent me to say these things, and not to the men sitting on the wall—who, like you, will have to eat their own filth and drink their own urine?"

28Then the commander stood and called out in Hebrew: "Hear the word of the great king, the king of Assyria! 29This is what the king says: Do not let Hezekiah deceive[y] you. He cannot deliver you from my hand. 30Do not let Hezekiah persuade

18:16 [n]2Ch 29:3 **18:17** [o]Isa 20:1 [p]2Ki 20:20; 2Ch 32:4,30; Ne 2:14; Isa 22:9 **18:18** [q]2Ki 19:2; Isa 22:20; 36:3, 11,22; 37:2 [r]ver 26,37; Isa 22:15 **18:19** [s]S ver 5; S Job 4:6 **18:21** [t]Isa 20:5; 31:1; Eze 29:6 [u]2Ki 24:7; Isa 20:6; 30:5,7; Jer 25:19; 37:7; 46:2 **18:24** [v]Isa 10:8 **18:25** [w]2Ki 19:6, 22; 24:3; 2Ch 35:21 **18:26** [x]Ezr 4:7 **18:29** [y]2Ki 19:10

[f]24 Or *charioteers*

18:17–19:37 See Isa 36–37; cf. 2Ch 32.
18:17 *Lachish.* See note on Isa 36:2. *aqueduct . . . Field.* See note on Isa 7:3. It is ironic that the Assyrian officials demand Judah's surrender on the very spot where Isaiah had warned Ahaz to trust in the Lord rather than in an alliance with Assyria for deliverance from the threat against him from Aram and the northern kingdom of Israel (see 16:5–10; Isa 7:1–17).
18:18 *palace administrator.* See note on 1Ki 4:6. *secretary.* See note on 2Sa 8:17. *recorder.* See note on 2Sa 8:16.
18:19 *great king.* A frequently used title of the Assyrian rulers—and occasionally of the Lord (Ps 47:2; 48:2; 95:3; Mal 1:14; Mt 5:35). *says.* The following address is a masterpiece of calculated intimidation and psychological warfare designed to break the resistance of the inhabitants of Jerusalem (see vv. 26–27).
18:21 *depending on Egypt.* See 19:9; Isa 30:1–5; 31:1–3.
18:22 *isn't he the one whose high places and altars Hezekiah removed . . . ?* The Assyrians cleverly attempted to drive a wedge between Hezekiah and the people. They attempted to exploit any resentment that may have existed among those who opposed Hezekiah's reformation and his destruction of the high places (see note on v. 4).
18:23 *if you can put riders on them!* With this sarcastic taunt, the Assyrians undoubtedly accurately suggest that the Judahites were so weak in military personnel that they could not even take advantage of such a generous offer. In contrast with the Assyrians, the army of Judah at the time consisted largely of foot soldiers. The city under siege would have contained few chariots, and it is not known whether the Israelites ever employed mounted men in combat.
18:25 *The LORD himself told me.* Possibly Assyrian spies had informed Sennacherib of the prophecies of Isaiah and Micah.
18:26 *Aramaic.* Had become the international language of the Near East, known and used by those experienced in diplomacy and commerce. It is surprising that the Assyrian officials were able to speak the Hebrew dialect of the common people of Judah (see 2Ch 32:18).
18:27 *men sitting on the wall.* The Assyrian strategy was to negotiate in the hearing of the people in order to demoralize them and turn them against Hezekiah. *eat their own filth and drink their own urine.* A vivid portrayal of the potential hardship of a prolonged siege.
18:29 *the king says.* The Assyrian officials now address their remarks directly to the populace rather than to the officials of Hezekiah, as in vv. 19–27. *Do not let Hezekiah deceive you.* Here and in vv. 30–31 the people are urged three times to turn against Hezekiah.
18:30 *this city will not be given into the hand of the king of Assyria.* Hezekiah could say this on the basis of God's

you to trust in the LORD when he says, 'The LORD will surely deliver us; this city will not be given into the hand of the king of Assyria.'

³¹"Do not listen to Hezekiah. This is what the king of Assyria says: Make peace with me and come out to me. Then every one of you will eat from his own vine and fig tree *z* and drink water from his own cistern, *a* ³²until I come and take you to a land like your own, a land of grain and new wine, a land of bread and vineyards, a land of olive trees and honey. Choose life *b* and not death!

"Do not listen to Hezekiah, for he is misleading you when he says, 'The LORD will deliver us.' ³³Has the god *c* of any nation ever delivered his land from the hand of the king of Assyria? ³⁴Where are the gods of Hamath *d* and Arpad? *e* Where are the gods of Sepharvaim, Hena and Ivvah? Have they rescued Samaria from my hand? ³⁵Who of all the gods of these countries has been able to save his land from me? How then can the LORD deliver Jerusalem from my hand?" *f*

³⁶But the people remained silent and said nothing in reply, because the king had commanded, "Do not answer him." ³⁷Then Eliakim *g* son of Hilkiah the palace administrator, Shebna the secretary and Joah son of Asaph the recorder went to Hezekiah, with their clothes torn, *h* and

told him what the field commander had said.

Jerusalem's Deliverance Foretold

19:1–13pp — Isa 37:1–13

19 When King Hezekiah heard this, he tore *i* his clothes and put on sackcloth and went into the temple of the LORD. ²He sent Eliakim *j* the palace administrator, Shebna the secretary and the leading priests, *k* all wearing sackcloth, *l* to the prophet Isaiah *m* son of Amoz. ³They told him, "This is what Hezekiah says: This day is a day of distress and rebuke and disgrace, as when children come to the point *n* of birth and there is no strength to deliver them. ⁴It may be that the LORD your God will hear all the words of the field commander, whom his master, the king of Assyria, has sent to ridicule *o* the living God, and that he will rebuke *p* him for the words the LORD your God has heard. Therefore pray for the remnant *q* that still survives."

⁵When King Hezekiah's officials came to Isaiah, ⁶Isaiah said to them, "Tell your master, 'This is what the LORD says: Do not be afraid *r* of what you have heard—those words with which the underlings of the king of Assyria have blasphemed *s* me. ⁷Listen! I am going to put such a spirit in him that when he hears a certain report, *t* he will return to his own

Cross references (center column)

18:31
*z*S Nu 13:23;
S 1Ki 4:25
*a*Jer 14:3; La 4:4
18:32 *b*Dt 30:19
18:33 *c*2Ki 19:12
18:34
*d*S 2Ki 17:24;
S Jer 49:23
*e*Isa 10:9
18:35 *f*Ps 2:1-2
18:37 *g*S ver 18;
Isa 33:7; 36:3,22
*h*S 2Ki 6:30

19:1 *i*S Ge 37:34;
S Nu 14:6
19:2 *j*S 2Ki 18:18
*k*Jer 19:1
*l*S Ge 37:34
*m*Isa 1:1
19:3 *n*Hos 13:13
19:4
*o*S 1Sa 17:26
*p*2Sa 16:12
*q*S Ge 45:7;
S Jer 37:3
19:6 *r*S Dt 3:2;
S Jos 1:9
*s*S 2Ki 18:25
19:7 *t*S Ex 14:24;
Jer 51:46

Footnotes (bottom)

promise to him (see 20:6; see also note on Isa 38:6).

18:31 *eat from his own vine and fig tree and drink water from his own cistern.* Depicting peaceful and prosperous times (see 1Ki 4:25; Mic 4:4; Zec 3:10).

18:32 *until I come and take you to a land like your own.* Ultimately surrender meant deportation, but Sennacherib pictured it as something desirable. *Choose life and not death!* The alternatives depicted for the people are: (1) Trust in the Lord and Hezekiah and die, or (2) trust in the Assyrians and enjoy prosperity and peace. These words directly contradict the alternatives placed before Israel by Moses in Dt 30:15–20.

18:33–35 *Has the god of any nation ever delivered his land from the hand of the king of Assyria? . . . How then can the LORD deliver Jerusalem from my hand?* The flaw in the Assyrian reasoning was to equate the one true and living God with the no-gods (Dt 32:21) of the pagan peoples the Assyrians had defeated (see 19:4,6; 2Ch 32:13–19; Isa 10:9–11).

18:34 *Hamath.* See notes on 14:25; 17:24. *Arpad.* A city located near Hamath and taken by the Assyrians in 740 B.C. (see 19:13; Isa 10:9; Jer 49:23). *Sepharvaim.* See note on 17:24. *Hena.* Probably located in the vicinity of the other cities mentioned. *Ivvah.* See note on 17:24.

18:36 *because the king had commanded, "Do not answer him."* The Assyrian attempt to stir up a popular revolt against the leadership and authority of Hezekiah had failed.

18:37 *clothes torn.* An expression of great emotion (see 6:30; 1Ki 21:27). Perhaps in this instance it was motivated by the Assyrian blasphemy against the true God (see 19:4,6; Mt 26:65; Mk 14:63–64).

19:1 *sackcloth.* See note on 6:30.

19:2 *palace administrator.* See note on 1Ki 4:6. *secretary.* See note on 2Sa 8:17. *leading priests.* Probably the oldest members of various priestly families (see Jer 19:1). The crisis involved not only the city of Jerusalem, but also the temple. *prophet Isaiah.* The first reference to Isaiah in the book of Kings, though he had been active in the reigns of Uzziah, Jotham and Ahaz (see Isa 1:1).

19:3 *as when children come to the point of birth and there is no strength to deliver them.* Depicts the critical nature of the threat facing the city.

19:4 *living God.* In contrast to the no-gods of 18:33–35. See 1Sa 17:26,36,45 for another example of ridiculing the living and true God. *pray.* Intercessory prayer was an important aspect of the ministry of the prophets (see, e.g., the intercession of Moses and Samuel: Ex 32:31–32; 33:12–17; Nu 14:13–19; 1Sa 7:8–9; 12:19,23; Ps 99:6; Jer 15:1). *remnant.* Those left in Judah after Sennacherib's capture of many towns and numerous people (see note on 18:13; cf. Isa 10:28–32). Archaeological evidence reveals that many Israelites fled the northern kingdom during the Assyrian assaults and settled in Judah, so that the nation of Judah became the remnant of all Israel.

19:7 *spirit.* Of insecurity and fear. *report.* Some interpreters link this "report" with the challenge to Sennacherib from Tirhakah of Egypt (v. 9). Others regard it as disturbing information from Sennacherib's homeland. *cut down with the sword.* See v. 37. Here the eventual murder of Sennacherib is connected with his blasphemy against the living God.

country, and there I will have him cut down with the sword.*u* ' "

8When the field commander heard that the king of Assyria had left Lachish,*v* he withdrew and found the king fighting against Libnah.*w*

9Now Sennacherib received a report that Tirhakah, the Cushite*g* king of Egypt, was marching out to fight against him. So he again sent messengers to Hezekiah with this word: 10"Say to Hezekiah king of Judah: Do not let the god you depend*x* on deceive*y* you when he says, 'Jerusalem will not be handed over to the king of Assyria.' 11Surely you have heard what the kings of Assyria have done to all the countries, destroying them completely. And will you be delivered? 12Did the gods of the nations that were destroyed by my forefathers deliver*z* them: the gods of Gozan,*a* Haran,*b* Rezeph and the people of Eden who were in Tel Assar? 13Where is the king of Hamath, the king of Arpad, the king of the city of Sepharvaim, or of Hena or Ivvah?"*c*

Hezekiah's Prayer

19:14-19pp — Isa 37:14-20

14Hezekiah received the letter*d* from the messengers and read it. Then he went up to the temple of the LORD and spread it out before the LORD. 15And Hezekiah prayed to the LORD: "O LORD, God of Israel, enthroned between the cherubim,*e* you alone*f* are God over all the kingdoms of the earth. You have made heaven and earth. 16Give ear,*g* O LORD, and hear;*h* open your eyes,*i* O LORD, and see; listen to the words Sennacherib has sent to insult the living God.

17"It is true, O LORD, that the Assyrian kings have laid waste these nations and their lands. 18They have thrown their gods into the fire and destroyed them, for they

were not gods*j* but only wood and stone, fashioned by men's hands.*k* 19Now, O LORD our God, deliver*l* us from his hand, so that all kingdoms*m* on earth may know*n* that you alone, O LORD, are God."

Isaiah Prophesies Sennacherib's Fall

19:20-37pp — Isa 37:21-38
19:35-37pp — 2Ch 32:20-21

20Then Isaiah son of Amoz sent a message to Hezekiah: "This is what the LORD, the God of Israel, says: I have heard*o* your prayer concerning Sennacherib king of Assyria. 21This is the word that the LORD has spoken against*p* him:

"'The Virgin Daughter*q* of Zion
    despises*r* you and mocks*s* you.
The Daughter of Jerusalem
    tosses her head*t* as you flee.
22Who is it you have insulted and
        blasphemed?*u*
    Against whom have you raised your
        voice
and lifted your eyes in pride?
    Against the Holy One*v* of Israel!
23By your messengers
    you have heaped insults on the Lord.
And you have said,*w*
    "With my many chariots*x*
I have ascended the heights of the
        mountains,
    the utmost heights of Lebanon.
I have cut down*y* its tallest cedars,
    the choicest of its pines.
I have reached its remotest parts,
    the finest of its forests.
24I have dug wells in foreign lands
    and drunk the water there.
With the soles of my feet
    I have dried up all the streams of
        Egypt."
25"'Have you not heard?*z*

Cross references (center column)

19:7 *u* ver 37; 2Ch 32:21; Isa 10:12
19:8 *v* 2Ki 18:14 *w* S Nu 33:20; S 2Ki 8:22
19:10 *x* S 2Ki 18:5 *y* 2Ki 18:29
19:12 *z* 2Ki 18:33; 2Ch 32:17 *a* 2Ki 17:6 *b* S Ge 11:31
19:13 *c* Isa 10:9-11; Jer 49:23
19:14 *d* 2Ki 5:7
19:15 *e* S Ge 3:24; S Ex 25:22 *f* S Ge 1:1; S Jos 2:11
19:16 *g* Ps 31:2; 71:2; 88:2; 102:2 *h* S 1Ki 8:29 *i* S Ex 3:16
19:18 *j* Isa 44:9-11; Jer 10:3-10 *k* Dt 4:28; Ps 115:4; Ac 17:29
19:19 *l* Isa 12:10; Job 6:23; Ps 3:7; 71:4 *m* S 1Ki 8:43; 1Ch 16:8 *n* S Jos 4:24; S 1Sa 17:46
19:20 *o* S 1Ki 9:3
19:21 *p* Isa 10:5; 33:1 *q* Isa 47:1; Jer 14:17; 18:13; 31:4; 46:11; La 2:13; Am 5:2 *r* Ps 53:5 *s* Pr 1:26; 3:34 *t* Job 16:4; Ps 44:14; 64:8; 109:25; Jer 18:16
19:22 *u* S 2Ki 18:25 *v* Lev 19:2; 1Sa 2:2; Job 6:10; Ps 16:10; 22:3; 71:22; 78:41; 89:18; Isa 1:4; 6:3; 57:15; Hos 11:9
19:23 *w* Isa 10:18; Jer 21:14; Eze 20:47 *x* Ps 20:7; Jer 50:37 *y* Isa 10:34; 14:8; 33:9; Eze 31:3
19:25 *z* Isa 40:21, 28

g That is, from the upper Nile region

19:8 *Lachish.* See 18:17 (see also note on Isa 36:2). *Libnah.* See note on 8:22.
19:9 *Tirhakah.* See note on Isa 37:9. *Cushite.* See NIV text note.
19:12 *Gozan.* See note on 17:6. *Haran.* See note on Ge 11:31. It is not known just when Haran was taken by the Assyrians. *Rezeph.* Located south of the Euphrates River and northeast of Hamath. *Eden.* See Eze 27:23; Am 1:5; a district along the Euphrates River south of Haran. It was incorporated into the Assyrian empire by Shalmaneser III in 855 B.C. *Tel Assar.* Location unknown.
19:13 *Hamath . . . Ivvah.* See note on 18:34.
19:14 *letter.* See 2Ch 32:17.
19:15 *enthroned between the cherubim.* See notes on Ex 25:18; 1Sa 4:4. *you alone are God.* See notes on 18:33-35; Dt 6:4.
19:18 *fashioned by men's hands.* For the foolishness and

futility of idolatry see Ps 115:3-8; 135:15-18; Isa 2:20; 40:19-20; 41:7; 44:9-20.
19:20 *heard your prayer.* On this occasion Isaiah's message to Hezekiah was unsolicited by the king (contrast v. 2).
19:21-28 The arrogance of the Assyrians and their ridicule of the Israelites and their God are countered with a derisive pronouncement of judgment (cf. Ps 2) on the misconceived Assyrian pride (see Isa 10:5-34).
19:21 *Virgin Daughter of Zion.* A personification of Jerusalem and its inhabitants.
19:22 *Holy One of Israel.* A designation of the God of Israel characteristic of Isaiah (see note on Isa 1:4).
19:24 *dried up all the streams of Egypt.* A presumptuous boast for one who had not even conquered Egypt.
19:25 *I ordained it . . . now I have brought it to pass.* The God of Israel is the ruler of all nations and history. The Assyrians attributed their victories to their own military su-

Long ago I ordained it.
In days of old I planned[a] it;
  now I have brought it to pass,
that you have turned fortified cities
  into piles of stone.[b]
26Their people, drained of power,[c]
  are dismayed[d] and put to shame.
They are like plants in the field,
  like tender green shoots,[e]
like grass sprouting on the roof,
  scorched[f] before it grows up.

27" 'But I know[g] where you stay
  and when you come and go
  and how you rage against me.
28Because you rage against me
  and your insolence has reached my
    ears,
I will put my hook[h] in your nose
  and my bit[i] in your mouth,
and I will make you return[j]
  by the way you came.'

29"This will be the sign[k] for you,
O Hezekiah:

"This year you will eat what grows by
    itself,[l]
and the second year what springs
    from that.
But in the third year sow and reap,
  plant vineyards[m] and eat their fruit.
30Once more a remnant[n] of the house of
    Judah
will take root[o] below and bear fruit
    above.
31For out of Jerusalem will come a
    remnant,[p]

and out of Mount Zion a band of
  survivors.[q]

The zeal[r] of the LORD Almighty will accomplish this.

32"Therefore this is what the LORD says
concerning the king of Assyria:

"He will not enter this city
  or shoot an arrow here.
He will not come before it with shield
  or build a siege ramp against it.
33By the way that he came he will
    return;[s]
  he will not enter this city,
    declares the LORD.
34I will defend[t] this city and save it,
  for my sake and for the sake of
    David[u] my servant."

35That night the angel of the LORD[v]
went out and put to death a hundred and
eighty-five thousand men in the Assyrian
camp. When the people got up the next
morning—there were all the dead bodies![w] 36So Sennacherib king of Assyria
broke camp and withdrew.[x] He returned
to Nineveh[y] and stayed there.

37One day, while he was worshiping in
the temple of his god Nisroch, his sons
Adrammelech[z] and Sharezer cut him
down with the sword,[a] and they escaped
to the land of Ararat.[b] And Esarhaddon[c]
his son succeeded him as king.

Hezekiah's Illness
20:1–11pp — 2Ch 32:24–26; Isa 38:1–8

20 In those days Hezekiah became ill
and was at the point of death. The

Cross references (center column):

19:25 aIsa 22:11
bMic 1:6
19:26 cIsa 13:7;
Eze 7:17;
Zep 3:16
dPs 6:10; 71:24;
83:17; Isa 41:23;
Jer 8:9 eIsa 4:2;
11:1; 53:2;
Jer 23:5
fJob 8:12;
Ps 37:2; 129:6
19:27 gPs 139:1-4
19:28
h2Ch 33:11;
Eze 19:9; 29:4;
38:4; Am 4:2
iIsa 30:28 jver 33
19:29 kS Ex 7:9;
S Dt 13:2;
Lk 2:12 lLev 25:5
mPs 107:37;
Isa 65:21;
Am 9:14
19:30 nS Ge 45:7
oIsa 5:24; 11:1;
27:6; Eze 17:22;
Am 2:9
19:31 pS Ge 45:7

qIsa 66:19;
Zep 2:9;
Zec 14:16 rIsa 9:7
19:33 sver 28
19:34 t2Ki 20:6
uS 2Sa 7:15
19:35
vS Ge 19:13;
S Ex 12:23
wJob 24:24;
Isa 17:14; 41:12;
Na 3:3
19:36
xS 2Ki 12:18
yS Ge 10:11
19:37 z2Ki 17:31
aS ver 7
bS Ge 8:4
cS 2Ki 17:24

---

periority. However, Isaiah said that God alone ordained
these victories (see Isa 10:5–19; cf. Eze 30:24–26).
19:27 *I know.* See Ps 121:8.
19:28 *hook in your nose.* At the top of an Assyrian obelisk
an Assyrian king (probably Esarhaddon, 681–669 B.C.) is
pictured holding ropes attached to rings in the noses of four
of his enemies. Here Isaiah portrays the same thing happening to Sennacherib (see note on Isa 37:29; cf. Eze 38:4; Am
4:2).
19:29 *This year you will eat what grows by itself.* Sennacherib had apparently either destroyed or confiscated the entire
harvest that had been sown the previous fall. The people
would only have use of the later, second growth that came
from seeds dropped from the previous year's harvest (see Lev
25:5). This suggests that Sennacherib came to Judah in
March or April about the time of harvest. *the second year
what springs from that.* Sennacherib's departure would be
too late in the fall (October) for new crops to be planted for
the coming year. In Palestine crops are normally sown in
September and October. *in the third year sow and reap.* The
routine times for sowing and harvesting could be observed in
the following year. The third year is likely a reference to the
third year of harvests detrimentally affected by the Assyrian
presence.
19:30–31 *remnant.* See note on v. 4. For use of the term

"remnant" as a designation for those who will participate in
the future unfolding of God's redemptive program see Isa
11:11,16; 28:5; Mic 4:7; Ro 11:5.
19:32 *not enter this city.* Sennacherib, who was presently
at Libnah (see v. 8; see also note on 8:22), would not be able
to carry out his threats against Jerusalem (see note on 18:13).
19:34 *for the sake of David my servant.* See note on 1Ki
11:13.
19:35 *angel of the LORD.* See note on Ge 16:7. *a hundred
and eighty-five thousand.* See Isa 37:36.
19:36 *Nineveh.* The capital of the Assyrian empire.
19:37 *Nisroch.* The name of this deity does not appear in
preserved Assyrian records. *his sons Adrammelech and
Sharezer.* Ancient records refer to the murder of Sennacherib
by an unnamed son on the 20th of the month of Tebet in the
23rd year of Sennacherib's reign. *Ararat.* See note on Ge 8:4.
Esarhaddon his son succeeded him. And reigned 681–669
B.C. Assyrian inscriptions speak of a struggle among Sennacherib's sons for the right of succession to the Assyrian throne.
Sennacherib's designation of Esarhaddon as heir apparent,
even though he was younger than several of his brothers,
may have sparked the abortive attempt at a coup by Adrammelech and Sharezer.
20:1 *In those days.* Hezekiah's illness (vv. 1–11) as well as
his reception of envoys from Babylon (vv. 12–19) must have

prophet Isaiah son of Amoz went to him and said, "This is what the LORD says: Put your house in order, because you are going to die; you will not recover."

²Hezekiah turned his face to the wall and prayed to the LORD, ³"Remember, ᵈ O LORD, how I have walkedᵉ before you faithfullyᶠ and with wholehearted devotion and have done what is good in your eyes." And Hezekiah wept bitterly.

⁴Before Isaiah had left the middle court, the word of the LORD came to him: ⁵"Go back and tell Hezekiah, the leader of my people, 'This is what the LORD, the God of your father David, says: I have heardᵍ your prayer and seen your tears;ʰ I will heal you. On the third day from now you will go up to the temple of the LORD. ⁶I will add fifteen years to your life. And I will deliver you and this city from the hand of the king of Assyria. I will defendⁱ this city for my sake and for the sake of my servant David.' "

⁷Then Isaiah said, "Prepare a poultice of figs." They did so and applied it to the boil,ʲ and he recovered.

⁸Hezekiah had asked Isaiah, "What will be the sign that the LORD will heal me and that I will go up to the temple of the LORD on the third day from now?"

⁹Isaiah answered, "This is the LORD's signᵏ to you that the LORD will do what he has promised: Shall the shadow go forward ten steps, or shall it go back ten steps?"

¹⁰"It is a simpleˡ matter for the shadow to go forward ten steps," said Hezekiah. "Rather, have it go back ten steps."

¹¹Then the prophet Isaiah called upon the LORD, and the LORD made the shadow go backᵐ the ten steps it had gone down on the stairway of Ahaz.

Envoys From Babylon

20:12–19pp — Isa 39:1–8
20:20–21pp — 2Ch 32:32–33

¹²At that time Merodach-Baladan son of Baladan king of Babylon sent Hezekiah letters and a gift, because he had heard of Hezekiah's illness. ¹³Hezekiah received the messengers and showed them all that was in his storehouses—the silver, the gold, the spices and the fine oil—his armory and everything found among his treasures. There was nothing in his palace or in all his kingdom that Hezekiah did not show them.

¹⁴Then Isaiah the prophet went to King Hezekiah and asked, "What did those men say, and where did they come from?"

"From a distant land," Hezekiah replied. "They came from Babylon."

¹⁵The prophet asked, "What did they see in your palace?"

"They saw everything in my palace," Hezekiah said. "There is nothing among my treasures that I did not show them."

¹⁶Then Isaiah said to Hezekiah, "Hear the word of the LORD: ¹⁷The time will

Cross references

20:3 ᵈS Ge 8:1; Ne 1:8; 5:19; 13:14 ᵉS Ge 5:22 ᶠS 1Ki 2:4; 2Ch 31:20
20:5 ᵍS 1Ki 9:3 ʰPs 6:6,8; 39:12; 56:8
20:6 ⁱS 2Ki 19:34; S 1Ch 17:19
20:7 ʲS Ex 9:9
20:9 ᵏS Dt 13:2; Jer 44:29

20:10 ˡS 2Ki 3:18
20:11 ᵐJos 10:13; 2Ch 32:31

---

preceded the Assyrian campaign in 701 B.C. (see v. 6; see also notes on vv. 12–13). Babylonian records indicate that Merodach-Baladan (v. 12) died in Elam after being expelled from Babylon in 703. *Put your house in order.* Arrangements of a testamentary nature needed to be made, especially with respect to throne succession. *you are going to die.* Assuming that Hezekiah was 25 years old in 715 when he began his sole reign (see 18:2) and that his illness occurred a little more than 15 years prior to his death (see note on v. 6), he would have been about 37 or 38 years old at this time.
20:3 *walked before you faithfully . . . and have done what is good.* Hezekiah's prayer is not an appeal for divine favor that is based on good works, but it expresses the realization that the Lord graciously favors those who earnestly serve him (see note on 2Sa 22:21).
20:5 *I will heal you.* God is the one who sovereignly ordains all that comes to pass (Ps 139:16; Eph 1:11). Hezekiah's petition and God's response demonstrate that (1) divine sovereignty does not make prayer inappropriate but, on the contrary, it establishes it, and (2) both prayer and the divine response to prayer are to be included in one's conception of God's sovereign plan (see 1Ki 21:29; Eze 33:13–16).
20:6 *add fifteen years to your life.* Hezekiah died in 686 B.C. The beginning of the extension of his life is thus to be placed no later than 702. *for my sake and for the sake of my servant David.* See 19:34; see also note on 1Ki 11:13.
20:7 *poultice.* The Lord healed Hezekiah (see v. 5), but divine healing does not necessarily exclude the use of known remedies.

20:9 *steps.* See v. 11 (see also note on Isa 38:8).
20:12 *Merodach-Baladan.* Means "(The god) Marduk has given me a son." He ruled in Babylon 721–710 B.C. before being forced to submit to Assyrian domination by Sargon II of Assyria. Sometime after Sargon's death in 705, Merodach-Baladan briefly reestablished Babylonian independence and ruled in Babylon until Sennacherib forced him to flee in 703 (see note on v. 1). *sent Hezekiah letters and a gift.* See 2Ch 32:31; Isa 39. It is likely that Merodach-Baladan was attempting to draw Hezekiah into an alliance against Assyria. Although Hezekiah rejected the pro-Assyrian policies of his father Ahaz (see 16:7) and rebelled against Assyria (see 18:7), he erred in seeking to strengthen Israel's security by friendship with Babylon and Egypt (see 2Ch 32:31; Isa 30–31; see also notes on 1Sa 17:11; 1Ki 15:19).
20:13 *received the messengers and showed them all.* Hezekiah's reception of the delegation from Babylon was overly hospitable. Perhaps it was an attempt to bolster Judah's security by impressing the Babylonians with the wealth and power of his kingdom as a basis for mutual cooperation against the Assyrians. In principle this was a denial of the covenantal nature of the royal office in Israel (see note on 2Sa 24:2). *silver . . . oil.* The presence of these treasures in Jerusalem is evidence that this incident occurred before the payment of tribute to Sennacherib in 701 B.C. (see 18:15–16).
20:14 *What did those men say . . . ?* Hezekiah gave no response to Isaiah's question concerning the diplomatic purpose of the Babylonian envoys.

surely come when everything in your palace, and all that your fathers have stored up until this day, will be carried off to Babylon.[n] Nothing will be left, says the LORD. [18]And some of your descendants,[o] your own flesh and blood, that will be born to you, will be taken away, and they will become eunuchs in the palace of the king of Babylon."[p]

[19]"The word of the LORD you have spoken is good," Hezekiah replied. For he thought, "Will there not be peace and security in my lifetime?"

[20]As for the other events of Hezekiah's reign, all his achievements and how he made the pool[q] and the tunnel[r] by which he brought water into the city, are they not written in the book of the annals of the kings of Judah? [21]Hezekiah rested with his fathers. And Manasseh his son succeeded him as king.

Manasseh King of Judah

21:1–10pp — 2Ch 33:1–10
21:17–18pp — 2Ch 33:18–20

21 Manasseh was twelve years old when he became king, and he reigned in Jerusalem fifty-five years. His mother's name was Hephzibah.[s] [2]He did evil[t] in the eyes of the LORD, following the detestable practices[u] of the nations the LORD had driven out before the Israelites. [3]He rebuilt the high places[v] his father Hezekiah had destroyed; he also erected

altars to Baal[w] and made an Asherah pole,[x] as Ahab king of Israel had done. He bowed down to all the starry hosts[y] and worshiped them. [4]He built altars[z] in the temple of the LORD, of which the LORD had said, "In Jerusalem I will put my Name."[a] [5]In both courts[b] of the temple of the LORD, he built altars to all the starry hosts. [6]He sacrificed his own son[c] in[h] the fire, practiced sorcery and divination,[d] and consulted mediums and spiritists.[e] He did much evil in the eyes of the LORD, provoking[f] him to anger.

[7]He took the carved Asherah pole[g] he had made and put it in the temple,[h] of which the LORD had said to David and to his son Solomon, "In this temple and in Jerusalem, which I have chosen out of all the tribes of Israel, I will put my Name[i] forever. [8]I will not again[j] make the feet of the Israelites wander from the land I gave their forefathers, if only they will be careful to do everything I commanded them and will keep the whole Law that my servant Moses[k] gave them." [9]But the people did not listen. Manasseh led them astray, so that they did more evil[l] than the nations[m] the LORD had destroyed before the Israelites.

[10]The LORD said through his servants the prophets: [11]"Manasseh king of Judah has committed these detestable sins. He has done more evil[n] than the Amorites[o]

Cross references
20:17 [n]2Ki 24:13; 2Ch 36:10; Jer 20:5; 27:22; 52:17-23
20:18 [o]2Ki 24:15; Da 1:3 [p]Mic 4:10
20:20 [q]S 2Ki 18:17 [r]S 2Sa 5:8
21:1 [s]Isa 62:4
21:2 [t]ver 16; S Dt 4:25; Jer 15:4 [u]Dt 9:4; S 18:9; S 1Ki 14:24; 2Ki 16:3
21:3 [v]S 1Ki 3:3; S 2Ki 18:4
[w]S Jdg 6:28
[x]S Dt 16:21
[y]S Ge 2:1; Dt 17:3; Jer 19:13
21:4 [z]Isa 66:4; Jer 4:1; 7:30; 23:11; 32:34; Eze 23:39
[a]S Ex 20:24; S 2Sa 7:13
21:5 [b]1Ki 7:12; 2Ki 23:12
21:6 [c]S Lev 18:21; S Dt 18:10; S 2Ki 3:27
[d]Dt 18:14
[e]S Lev 19:31
[f]2Ki 23:26
21:7 [g]Dt 16:21; 2Ki 23:4
[h]S Lev 15:31
[i]S Ex 20:24; S 2Sa 7:13
21:8 [j]S 2Sa 7:10
[k]S 2Ki 18:12
21:9 [l]S 1Ki 14:9; Eze 5:7 [m]Dt 9:4
21:11 [n]S 1Ki 14:9
[o]S Ge 15:16

[h]6 Or *He made his own son pass through*

20:17 *carried off to Babylon.* Hezekiah's reception of the Babylonians would bring the exact opposite of what he desired and expected. Isaiah's prediction of Babylonian exile at least 115 years before it happened is all the more remarkable because, when he spoke, it appeared that Assyria rather than Babylon was the world power from whom Judah had the most to fear.

20:18 *some of your descendants . . . will be taken away.* Hezekiah's own son Manasseh was taken by the Assyrians and held prisoner for a while in Babylon (see 2Ch 33:11); later, many more from the house of David were to follow (see 24:15; 25:7; Da 1:3).

20:19 *word . . . is good.* Although it is possible to understand Hezekiah's statement as a selfish expression of relief that he himself would not experience the announced adversity, it seems better to take it as a humble acceptance of the Lord's judgment (see 2Ch 32:26) and as gratefulness for the intervening time of peace that the Lord in his mercy was granting to his people.

20:20 *the pool and the tunnel.* Hezekiah built a tunnel from the Gihon spring (see 1Ki 1:33,38) to a cistern (2Ch 32:30) within the city's walls (see diagram No. 9 at the end of the Study Bible). This greatly reduced Jerusalem's vulnerability to siege by guaranteeing a continuing water supply. In 1880 an inscription (the Siloam inscription; see chart on "Ancient Texts Relating to the OT," p. 5) was found in the rock wall at the entrance to this tunnel, describing the method of its construction. The tunnel, cut through solid rock, is over 1,700 feet long; its height varies from 3 2/3 feet

to 11 1/2 feet and it averages 2 feet in width. *annals of the kings of Judah.* See note on 1Ki 14:29.

20:21 *rested with his fathers.* See note on 1Ki 1:21.

21:1 *twelve years old.* Manasseh was born after Hezekiah's serious illness (see 20:6). *fifty-five years.* 697–642 B.C., including a ten-year co-regency (697–686) with his father Hezekiah. This was the longest reign of any king in either Israel or Judah.

21:2 *detestable practices.* Manasseh reversed the religious policies of his father Hezekiah (see 18:3–5) and reverted to those of Ahaz (see 16:3).

21:3 *high places . . . Hezekiah had destroyed.* See note on 18:4; see also 2Ch 31:1. *Asherah pole.* See 1Ki 14:15,23; 15:13; 16:33. *as Ahab.* Manasseh was the Ahab of Judah (see 1Ki 16:30–33). *bowed down to all the starry hosts.* See note on 17:16.

21:4 *In Jerusalem I will put my Name.* See 1Ki 8:20,29; 9:3.

21:6 *sacrificed his own son.* See note on 16:3; see also 17:17. *practiced sorcery and divination.* See notes on 16:15; 17:17. *consulted mediums and spiritists.* See Lev 19:31; Dt 18:11; 1Sa 28:3,7–9 and notes.

21:7 *carved Asherah pole.* See note on 1Ki 14:15. *David.* See 2Sa 7:13. *Solomon.* See 1Ki 9:3. *chosen out of all the tribes.* See 1Ki 11:13,32,36.

21:9 *nations the LORD had destroyed.* See 1Ki 14:24; Dt 12:29–31; 31:3.

21:10 *his servants the prophets.* See 2Ch 33:10,18.

21:11 *more evil than the Amorites.* See note on 1Ki 21:26.

who preceded him and has led Judah into sin with his idols. p 12Therefore this is what the LORD, the God of Israel, says: I am going to bring such disaster q on Jerusalem and Judah that the ears of everyone who hears of it will tingle. r 13I will stretch out over Jerusalem the measuring line used against Samaria and the plumb line s used against the house of Ahab. I will wipe t out Jerusalem as one wipes a dish, wiping it and turning it upside down. 14I will forsake u the remnant v of my inheritance and hand them over to their enemies. They will be looted and plundered by all their foes, 15because they have done evil w in my eyes and have provoked x me to anger from the day their forefathers came out of Egypt until this day."

16Moreover, Manasseh also shed so much innocent blood y that he filled Jerusalem from end to end—besides the sin that he had caused Judah z to commit, so that they did evil in the eyes of the LORD.

17As for the other events of Manasseh's reign, and all he did, including the sin he committed, are they not written in the book of the annals of the kings of Judah? 18Manasseh rested with his fathers, a was buried in his palace garden, a the garden of Uzza. And Amon his son succeeded him as king.

Amon King of Judah

21:19–24pp — 2Ch 33:21–25

19Amon was twenty-two years old when

he became king, and he reigned in Jerusalem two years. His mother's name was Meshullemeth daughter of Haruz; she was from Jotbah. 20He did evil b in the eyes of the LORD, as his father Manasseh had done. 21He walked in all the ways of his father; he worshiped the idols his father had worshiped, and bowed down to them. 22He forsook c the LORD, the God of his fathers, and did not walk d in the way of the LORD.

23Amon's officials conspired against him and assassinated e the king in his palace. 24Then the people of the land killed f all who had plotted against King Amon, and they made Josiah g his son king in his place.

25As for the other events of Amon's reign, and what he did, are they not written in the book of the annals of the kings of Judah? 26He was buried in his grave in the garden h of Uzza. And Josiah his son succeeded him as king.

The Book of the Law Found

22:1–20pp — 2Ch 34:1–2,8–28

22 Josiah i was eight years old when he became king, and he reigned in Jerusalem thirty-one years. His mother's name was Jedidah daughter of Adaiah; she was from Bozkath. j 2He did what was right k in the eyes of the LORD and walked in all the ways of his father David, not turning aside to the right l or to the left.

3In the eighteenth year of his reign, King Josiah sent the secretary, Shaphan m son of

Cross references (center column)

21:11 pEze 18:12
21:12 q2Ki 23:26; 24:3; Jer 15:4; Eze 7:5
r S 1Sa 3:11
21:13 sIsa 28:17; 34:11; La 2:8; Am 7:7-9
t2Ki 23:27
21:14 uPs 78:60; Jer 12:7; 23:33
v2Ki 19:4; Ezr 9:8; Ne 1:2; Isa 1:9; 10:21; Jer 6:9; 40:15; 42:2; 44:7,28; 50:20; Mic 2:12
21:15 wS Ex 32:22
xJer 25:7
21:16 y2Ki 24:4; Job 22:14; Ps 10:11; 94:7; 106:38; Isa 29:15; 47:10; 59:3,7; Jer 2:34; 7:6; 19:4; 22:17; La 4:13; Eze 7:23; 8:12; 9:9; 22:3,4; Hos 4:2; Zep 1:12
zS ver 2,11
21:18 aver 26; Est 1:5; 7:7
21:20 b1Ki 15:26
21:22 cS 1Sa 8:8
d1Ki 11:33
21:23 eS 2Ki 12:20
21:24 f2Ki 14:5
g2Ch 33:21; Zep 1:1
21:26 hS ver 18
22:1 iJer 1:2; 25:3 jJos 15:39
22:2 kS Dt 17:19; S 1Ki 14:8
lS Dt 5:32
22:3 m2Ch 34:20; Jer 39:14

Study notes (bottom, two columns)

21:12 *ears of everyone who hears of it will tingle.* See Jer 19:3.

21:13 *measuring line . . . plumb line.* Instruments normally associated with construction are used here as symbols of destruction (see Isa 34:11; Am 7:7–9,17).

21:14 *I will forsake.* In the sense of giving over to judgment (see Jer 12:7), not in the sense of abrogation of the covenant (see 1Sa 12:22; Isa 43:1–7). *remnant of my inheritance.* Upon the destruction of the northern kingdom, Judah had become the remnant of the Lord's inheritance (see 1Ki 8:51; Dt 4:20; 1Sa 10:1; Ps 28:9; see also note on 2Ki 19:4).

21:15 The history of Israel was a history of covenant breaking. With the reign of Manasseh the cup of God's wrath overflowed, and the judgment of exile from the land of promise (see note on 17:7) became inevitable (see 24:1–4).

21:16 *innocent blood.* A reference to godly people and perhaps even prophets who were martyred for opposition to Manasseh's evil practices (see vv. 10–11). According to a Jewish tradition (not otherwise substantiated) Isaiah was sawed in two during Manasseh's reign (cf. Heb 11:37).

21:17 *other events of Manasseh's reign.* See 2Ch 33:12–19. *annals of the kings of Judah.* See note on 1Ki 14:29.

21:18 *rested with his fathers.* See note on 1Ki 1:21. *Uzza.* Probably a shortened form of Uzziah (see 14:21–22 and 15:1–7, Azariah; 2Ch 26, Uzziah).

21:19 *two years.* 642–640 B.C. *Jotbah.* Some identify it

with the Jotbathah of Nu 33:33–34 and Dt 10:7, near Ezion Geber. Others, including the church father Jerome, have located it in Judah.

21:20 *did evil.* Amon did not share in the change of heart that characterized his father Manasseh in the last days of his life (see 2Ch 33:12–19). He must have restored the idolatrous practices that Manasseh abolished because these were again in existence in the time of Josiah (see 23:5–7,12).

21:23 *conspired against him.* Whether this palace revolt was motivated by religious or political considerations is not known.

21:24 *people of the land.* The citizenry in general (see 11:14,18; 14:21; 23:30). *killed all who had plotted against King Amon.* It is not clear whether this counterinsurgency was motivated simply by loyalty to the house of David or by other factors.

21:25 *annals of the kings of Judah.* See note on 1Ki 14:29.

21:26 *Uzza.* See note on v. 18.

22:1 *thirty-one years.* 640–609 B.C. (see note on 21:19). *Bozkath.* Located in Judah in the vicinity of Lachish (see Jos 15:39).

22:2 *ways of his father David.* See note on 18:3. Josiah was the last godly king of the Davidic line prior to the exile. Jeremiah, who prophesied during the time of Josiah (see Jer 1:2), spoke highly of him (Jer 22:15–16). Zephaniah also prophesied in the early days of his reign (Zep 1:1).

22:3 *eighteenth year.* 622 B.C. Josiah was then 26 years old

Azaliah, the son of Meshullam, to the temple of the LORD. He said: 4"Go up to Hilkiah[n] the high priest and have him get ready the money that has been brought into the temple of the LORD, which the doorkeepers have collected[o] from the people. 5Have them entrust it to the men appointed to supervise the work on the temple. And have these men pay the workers who repair[p] the temple of the LORD— 6the carpenters, the builders and the masons. Also have them purchase timber and dressed stone to repair the temple. [q] 7But they need not account for the money entrusted to them, because they are acting faithfully."[r]

8Hilkiah the high priest said to Shaphan the secretary, "I have found the Book of the Law[s] in the temple of the LORD." He gave it to Shaphan, who read it. 9Then Shaphan the secretary went to the king and reported to him: "Your officials have paid out the money that was in the temple of the LORD and have entrusted it to the workers and supervisors at the temple." 10Then Shaphan the secretary informed the king, "Hilkiah the priest has given me a book." And Shaphan read from it in the presence of the king. [t]

11When the king heard the words of the Book of the Law,[u] he tore his robes. 12He gave these orders to Hilkiah the priest, Ahikam[v] son of Shaphan, Acbor son of Micaiah, Shaphan the secretary and Asaiah the king's attendant:[w] 13"Go and inquire[x] of the LORD for me and for the people and for all Judah about what is written in this book that has been found. Great is the

LORD's anger[y] that burns against us because our fathers have not obeyed the words of this book; they have not acted in accordance with all that is written there concerning us."

14Hilkiah the priest, Ahikam, Acbor, Shaphan and Asaiah went to speak to the prophetess[z] Huldah, who was the wife of Shallum son of Tikvah, the son of Harhas, keeper of the wardrobe. She lived in Jerusalem, in the Second District.

15She said to them, "This is what the LORD, the God of Israel, says: Tell the man who sent you to me, 16'This is what the LORD says: I am going to bring disaster[a] on this place and its people, according to everything written in the book[b] the king of Judah has read. 17Because they have forsaken[c] me and burned incense to other gods and provoked me to anger by all the idols their hands have made,[i] my anger will burn against this place and will not be quenched.' 18Tell the king of Judah, who sent you to inquire[d] of the LORD, 'This is what the LORD, the God of Israel, says concerning the words you heard: 19Because your heart was responsive and you humbled[e] yourself before the LORD when you heard what I have spoken against this place and its people, that they would become accursed[f] and laid waste,[g] and because you tore your robes and wept in my presence, I have heard you, declares the LORD. 20Therefore I will gather you to your fathers, and you will be buried in peace.[h] Your eyes[i] will not see all the

Cross references (center column)

22:4 [n]Ezr 7:1
[o]2Ki 12:4-5
22:5 [p]2Ki 12:5
22:6
[q]2Ki 12:11-12
22:7 [r]S 2Ki 12:15
22:8 [s]S Dt 28:61; S 31:24; Gal 3:10
22:10 [t]Jer 36:21
22:11 [u]ver 8
22:12
[v]2Ki 25:22; Jer 26:24; 39:14
[w]1Sa 8:14
22:13
[x]S Ge 25:22; S 1Sa 9:9

[y]Dt 29:24-28; S 31:17; Isa 5:25; 42:25; Am 2:4
22:14
[z]S Ex 15:20
22:16
[a]S Dt 31:29; S Jos 23:15; Jer 6:19; 11:11; 18:11; 35:17
[b]Da 9:11
22:17 [c]S 1Ki 9:9
22:18 [d]Jer 21:2; 37:3,7
22:19
[e]S Ex 10:3; Isa 57:15; 61:1; Mic 6:8 [f]Jer 24:9; 25:18; 26:6
[g]Lev 26:31
22:20 [h]Isa 47:11; 57:1; Jer 18:11
[i]S 1Ki 21:29

[i]17 Or by everything they have done

Study notes (bottom)

(see v. 1). He had begun to serve the Lord faithfully at the age of 16 (the 8th year of his reign, 2Ch 34:3). When he was 20 years old (the 12th year of his reign, 2Ch 34:3), he had already begun to purge the land of its idolatrous practices. *secretary, Shaphan.* See note on 2Sa 8:17. Two additional individuals are mentioned as accompanying Shaphan in 2Ch 34:8.
22:4 *Hilkiah.* Father of Azariah and grandfather of Seraiah, the high priest executed at the time of the destruction of Jerusalem by the Babylonians (see 25:18–20). It is unlikely that this Hilkiah was also the father of Jeremiah (see Jer 1:1). *money . . . the doorkeepers have collected.* Josiah used the method devised by Joash for collecting funds for the restoration of the temple (see 12:1–16; 2Ch 34:9).
22:5 *men appointed to supervise.* See 2Ch 34:12–13.
22:8 *Book of the Law.* Some interpreters hold that this refers to a copy of the entire Pentateuch, while others understand it as a reference to a copy of part or all of Deuteronomy alone (see Dt 31:24,26; 2Ch 34:14).
22:11 *tore his robes.* See note on 18:37; contrast Josiah's reaction with that of Jehoiakim to the words of the scroll written by Jeremiah (see Jer 36:24). Perhaps the covenant curses of Lev 26 and/or Dt 28, climaxing with the threat of exile, were the statements that especially disturbed Josiah.
22:12 *Ahikam.* Father of Gedaliah, who was later to be

appointed governor of Judah by Nebuchadnezzar (see 25:22; Jer 39:14). He was also the protector of Jeremiah when his life was threatened during the reign of Jehoiakim (see Jer 26:24). *Acbor.* His son Elnathan is mentioned in 24:8; Jer 26:22; 36:12. *Shaphan the secretary.* See note on v. 3.
22:14 *prophetess Huldah.* Why the delegation sought out Huldah rather than Jeremiah or Zephaniah is not known. Perhaps it was merely a matter of her accessibility in Jerusalem. *Shallum . . . keeper of the wardrobe.* Perhaps the same Shallum who was the uncle of Jeremiah (see Jer 32:7). *Second District.* A section of the city (the Hebrew for this phrase is translated "New Quarter" in Zep 1:10) probably located in a newly developed area between the first and second walls in the northwest part of Jerusalem (see 2Ch 33:14).
22:16 *this place.* Jerusalem.
22:19 *your heart was responsive.* See v. 11.
22:20 *gather you to your fathers.* See note on 1Ki 1:21. *you will be buried in peace.* This prediction refers to Josiah's death before God's judgment on Jerusalem through Nebuchadnezzar and so is not contradicted by his death in battle with Pharaoh Neco of Egypt (see 23:29–30). Josiah was assured that the final judgment on Judah and Jerusalem would not come in his own days.

disaster I am going to bring on this
place.' "
So they took her answer back to the
king.

Josiah Renews the Covenant

23:1–3pp — 2Ch 34:29–32
23:4–20Ref — 2Ch 34:3–7,33
23:21–23pp — 2Ch 35:1,18–19
23:28–30pp — 2Ch 35:20–36:1

23 Then the king called together all
the elders of Judah and Jerusalem.
2 He went up to the temple of the LORD
with the men of Judah, the people of
Jerusalem, the priests and the prophets—all the people from the least to the
greatest. He read[j] in their hearing all the
words of the Book of the Covenant,[k]
which had been found in the temple of the
LORD. 3 The king stood by the pillar[l] and
renewed the covenant[m] in the presence of
the LORD—to follow[n] the LORD and keep
his commands, regulations and decrees
with all his heart and all his soul, thus confirming the words of the covenant written
in this book. Then all the people pledged
themselves to the covenant.
4 The king ordered Hilkiah the high
priest, the priests next in rank and the
doorkeepers[o] to remove[p] from the temple
of the LORD all the articles made for Baal
and Asherah and all the starry hosts. He
burned them outside Jerusalem in the
fields of the Kidron Valley and took the
ashes to Bethel. 5 He did away with the
pagan priests appointed by the kings of
Judah to burn incense on the high places of
the towns of Judah and on those around
Jerusalem—those who burned incense[q] to
Baal, to the sun and moon, to the constel-
lations and to all the starry hosts.[r s] 6 He
took the Asherah pole from the temple of
the LORD to the Kidron Valley[t] outside
Jerusalem and burned it there. He ground
it to powder[u] and scattered the dust over
the graves[v] of the common people.[w] 7 He
also tore down the quarters of the male
shrine prostitutes,[x] which were in the
temple of the LORD and where women did
weaving for Asherah.
8 Josiah brought all the priests from the
towns of Judah and desecrated the high
places, from Geba[y] to Beersheba, where
the priests had burned incense. He broke
down the shrines[j] at the gates—at the entrance to the Gate of Joshua, the city governor, which is on the left of the city gate.
9 Although the priests of the high places did
not serve[z] at the altar of the LORD in
Jerusalem, they ate unleavened bread with
their fellow priests.
10 He desecrated Topheth,[a] which was
in the Valley of Ben Hinnom,[b] so no one
could use it to sacrifice his son[c] or daughter in[k] the fire to Molech. 11 He removed

23:2 [j]S Dt 31:11 [k]S Ex 24:7 **23:3** [l]S 1Ki 7:15 [m]S 2Ki 11:12 [n]S Dt 13:4 **23:4** [o]2Ki 25:18; Jer 35:4 [p]S 2Ki 21:7 **23:5** [q]S 2Ki 16:4 [r]Jer 8:2 [s]Jer 43:13 **23:6** [t]Jer 31:40 [u]S Ex 32:20 [v]S Nu 19:16 [w]Jer 26:23 **23:7** [x]S Ge 38:21; 1Ki 14:24; Eze 16:16 **23:8** [y]S Jos 18:24; S 1Ki 15:22 **23:9** [z]Eze 44:10-14 **23:10** [a]Isa 30:33; Jer 7:31,32; 19:6 [b]S Jos 15:8 [c]S Lev 18:21; S Dt 18:10

[j]8 Or *high places* [k]10 Or *to make his son or daughter pass through*

23:1 *elders.* See note on 10:1.
23:2 *Book of the Covenant.* Although this designation is used in Ex 24:7 with reference to the contents of Ex 20–23, it is here applied to either all or part of the book of Deuteronomy or the entire Mosaic law. Whatever else the scroll contained, it clearly included the covenant curses of Lev 26 and/or Dt 28 (see notes on v. 21; 22:8,11).
23:3 *pillar.* See note on 11:14. *renewed the covenant.* Josiah carries out the function of covenant mediator; cf. Moses (Ex 24:3–8; Dt 1:34), Joshua (Jos 24), Samuel (1Sa 11:14–12:25) and Jehoiada (2Ki 11:17). *follow the LORD.* See notes on 1Sa 12:14,20. *pledged themselves to the covenant.* It is likely that some sort of ratification rite was performed, in which the people participated and pledged by oath to be loyal to their covenant obligations. Whether this was done symbolically (see Jer 34:18) or verbally (see Dt 27:11–26) is not clear.
23:4 *doorkeepers.* See 12:9. *Baal and Asherah.* See note on 1Ki 14:15. *starry hosts.* See note on 17:16. *took the ashes to Bethel.* See vv. 15–16. Bethel was located just over the border between Judah and the former northern kingdom in territory nominally under Assyrian control. With a decline in Assyrian power, Josiah was able to exert his own influence in the north. He apparently deposited the ashes at Bethel in order to desecrate (see note on v. 14) the very place where golden calf worship had originally polluted the land (see notes on 1Ki 12:28,30).
23:5 *pagan priests.* See Hos 10:5; Zep 1:4. *kings of Judah.* A reference to Manasseh and Amon, and perhaps to Ahaz before them. *high places.* See note on 18:4.
23:6 *Asherah pole.* See note on 1Ki 14:15. The Asherah poles destroyed by Hezekiah (18:4) were reintroduced by Manasseh (21:7). When Manasseh turned to the Lord, it is likely that he too got rid of the Asherah poles (see 2Ch 33:15) and that they were then again reintroduced by Amon (2Ki 21:21; 2Ch 33:22). *scattered the dust over the graves of the common people.* Intended as a defilement of the goddess, not as a desecration of the graves of the poor (see Jer 26:23).
23:7 *male shrine prostitutes.* See note on 1Ki 14:24.
23:8 *desecrated the high places.* See note on 18:4. *Geba to Beersheba.* Geba was on the northern border of the southern kingdom (see 1Ki 15:22), and Beersheba was on its southern border (see note on 1Sa 3:20).
23:9 *ate unleavened bread with their fellow priests.* Although not permitted to serve at the temple altar, these priests were to be sustained by a share of the priestly provisions (see Lev 2:10; 6:16–18). They occupied a status similar to that of priests with physical defects (see Lev 21:16–23).
23:10 *Topheth.* The name of an area in the Valley of Hinnom where altars used for child sacrifice were located (see Isa 30:33; Jer 7:31; 19:5–6). *sacrifice his son or daughter.* See 17:17; 21:6; see also note on 16:3. *Molech.* See note on 1Ki 11:5.
23:11 *horses . . . dedicated to the sun.* If live, the horses may have been used to pull chariots bearing images of a sun-god in religious processions. Small images of horses have recently been found in a cult place just outside one of the ancient walls of Jerusalem. *Nathan-Melech.* Perhaps the

from the entrance to the temple of the LORD the horses that the kings of Judah ^{d} had dedicated to the sun. They were in the court near the room of an official named Nathan-Melech. Josiah then burned the chariots dedicated to the sun. ^{e}

12He pulled down ^{f} the altars the kings of Judah had erected on the roof ^{g} near the upper room of Ahaz, and the altars Manasseh had built in the two courts ^{h} of the temple of the LORD. He removed them from there, smashed them to pieces and threw the rubble into the Kidron Valley. ^{i} 13The king also desecrated the high places that were east of Jerusalem on the south of the Hill of Corruption—the ones Solomon ^{j} king of Israel had built for Ashtoreth the vile goddess of the Sidonians, for Chemosh the vile god of Moab, and for Molech ^{l} the detestable ^{k} god of the people of Ammon. ^{l} 14Josiah smashed ^{m} the sacred stones and cut down the Asherah poles and covered the sites with human bones. ^{n}

15Even the altar ^{o} at Bethel, the high place made by Jeroboam ^{p} son of Nebat, who had caused Israel to sin—even that altar and high place he demolished. He burned the high place and ground it to powder, and burned the Asherah pole also. 16Then Josiah ^{q} looked around, and when he saw the tombs that were there on the hillside, he had the bones removed from them and burned on the altar to defile it, in accordance ^{r} with the word of the LORD proclaimed by the man of God who foretold these things.

17The king asked, "What is that tombstone I see?"

The men of the city said, "It marks the tomb of the man of God who came from Judah and pronounced against the altar of Bethel the very things you have done to it."

18"Leave it alone," he said. "Don't let anyone disturb his bones ^{s}." So they spared his bones and those of the prophet ^{t} who had come from Samaria.

19Just as he had done at Bethel, Josiah removed and defiled all the shrines at the high places that the kings of Israel had built in the towns of Samaria that had provoked the LORD to anger. 20Josiah slaughtered ^{u} all the priests of those high places on the altars and burned human bones ^{v} on them. Then he went back to Jerusalem.

21The king gave this order to all the people: "Celebrate the Passover ^{w} to the LORD your God, as it is written in this Book of the Covenant." ^{x} 22Not since the days of the judges who led Israel, nor throughout the days of the kings of Israel and the kings of Judah, had any such Passover been observed. 23But in the eighteenth year of King Josiah, this Passover was celebrated to the LORD in Jerusalem. ^{y}

24Furthermore, Josiah got rid of the mediums and spiritists, ^{z} the household gods, ^{a} the idols and all the other detestable ^{b} things seen in Judah and Jerusalem. This he did to fulfill the requirements of the law written in the book that Hilkiah the priest had discovered in the temple of the LORD. 25Neither before nor after Josiah was there a king like him who turned ^{c} to

---

23:11 ^{d}ver 5,19; Ne 9:34; Jer 44:9 ^{e}S Dt 4:19
23:12 ^{f}2Ch 33:15 ^{g}Jer 19:13; Zep 1:5 ^{h}S 2Ki 21:5 ^{i}S 2Sa 15:23
23:13 ^{j}1Ki 11:7 ^{k}S Dt 27:15 ^{l}Jer 11:13
23:14 ^{m}S Ex 23:24 ^{n}S Nu 19:16; S Ps 53:5
23:15 ^{o}S Jos 7:2; 1Ki 13:1-3 ^{p}S 1Ki 12:33
23:16 ^{q}S 1Ki 13:2 ^{r}1Ki 13:32

23:18 ^{s}1Ki 13:31 ^{t}1Ki 13:29
23:20 ^{u}S Ex 22:20; S 2Ki 11:18 ^{v}S 1Ki 13:2
23:21 ^{w}S Ex 12:11; Dt 16:1-8 ^{x}S Ex 24:7
23:23 ^{y}S Ex 12:11; S Nu 28:16
23:24 ^{z}S Lev 19:31; S Dt 18:11 ^{a}S Ge 31:19 ^{b}Dt 7:26; 2Ki 16:3
23:25 ^{c}S 1Sa 7:3

^{l}13 Hebrew Milcom

---

official in charge of the chariots.
23:12 *altars . . . on the roof.* Altars dedicated to the worship of all the starry hosts (see Jer 19:13; Zep 1:5)—erected by Ahaz (2Ki 16:3–4,10–16), Manasseh (21:3) and Amon (21:21–22).
23:13 *high places . . . Solomon . . . had built.* See note on 1Ki 11:5.
23:14 *covered the sites with human bones.* The bones would defile these sites and make them unsuitable for cultic use in the future (see Nu 19:16).
23:15 *altar at Bethel.* See 1Ki 12:32–33. Nothing is said of the golden calf, which undoubtedly had been sent to Assyria as tribute at the time of the captivity of the northern kingdom (see Hos 10:5–6).
23:16 *tombs.* Of the priests of the Bethel sanctuary (see 1Ki 13:2). *burned on the altar to defile it.* See notes on vv. 6,14. *the man of God who foretold these things.* See 1Ki 13:1–2, 32.
23:18 *prophet who had come from Samaria.* See 1Ki 13:31–32. Samaria is here not to be understood as the city by that name since the prophet came from Bethel (see 1Ki 13:11), and the city Samaria did not yet exist (see 1Ki 16:24). Rather, it is to be taken as a designation for the entire area of the former northern kingdom (see notes on 17:24, 29; 1Ki 13:32).

23:20 *slaughtered all the priests of those high places.* These were non-Levitical priests of the apostate worship practiced in the area of the former northern kingdom (see notes on 17:27–28,33–34). They were treated like the pagan priests of Judah (see v. 5) in contrast to Josiah's treatment of the priests at the high places in Judah (see vv. 8–9). Josiah's actions in this matter conformed to the requirements of Dt 13; 17:2–7.
23:21 *Celebrate the Passover.* A more complete description of this observance is found in 2Ch 35:1–19. *as it is written in this Book of the Covenant.* See note on v. 2. This appears to refer to Dt 16:1–8, where the Passover is described in a communal setting at a sanctuary (see Ex 23:15–17; 34:23–24; Lev 23:4–14) rather than in the family setting of Ex 12:1–14,43–49.
23:22 The uniqueness of Josiah's Passover celebration seems to be in the fact that all the Passover lambs were slaughtered exclusively by the Levites (see 2Ch 35:1–19; cf. 2Ch 30:2–3,17–20 for the Passover observed in the time of Hezekiah).
23:23 *eighteenth year.* See note on 22:3.
23:24 *household gods.* See note on Ge 31:19. *requirements of the law.* See notes on v. 2; 22:8.
23:25 *was there a king like him.* See note on 18:5. *with all his heart . . . soul and . . . strength.* See Dt 6:5.

the LORD as he did—with all his heart and with all his soul and with all his strength, in accordance with all the Law of Moses. *d* ²⁶Nevertheless, the LORD did not turn away from the heat of his fierce anger, *e* which burned against Judah because of all that Manasseh*f* had done to provoke him to anger. ²⁷So the LORD said, "I will remove*g* Judah also from my presence*h* as I removed Israel, and I will reject*i* Jerusalem, the city I chose, and this temple, about which I said, 'There shall my Name be.'*m*"

²⁸As for the other events of Josiah's reign, and all he did, are they not written in the book of the annals of the kings of Judah?

²⁹While Josiah was king, Pharaoh Neco*j* king of Egypt went up to the Euphrates River to help the king of Assyria. King Josiah marched out to meet him in battle, but Neco faced him and killed him at Megiddo. *k* ³⁰Josiah's servants brought his body in a chariot*l* from Megiddo to Jerusalem and buried him in his own tomb. And the people of the land took Jehoahaz son of Josiah and anointed him and made him king in place of his father.

Jehoahaz King of Judah

23:31–34pp — 2Ch 36:2–4

³¹Jehoahaz *m* was twenty-three years old

when he became king, and he reigned in Jerusalem three months. His mother's name was Hamutal*n* daughter of Jeremiah; she was from Libnah. ³²He did evil*o* in the eyes of the LORD, just as his fathers had done. ³³Pharaoh Neco put him in chains at Riblah*p* in the land of Hamath*n q* so that he might not reign in Jerusalem, and he imposed on Judah a levy of a hundred talents*o* of silver and a talent*p* of gold. ³⁴Pharaoh Neco made Eliakim*r* son of Josiah king in place of his father Josiah and changed Eliakim's name to Jehoiakim. But he took Jehoahaz and carried him off to Egypt, and there he died. *s* ³⁵Jehoiakim paid Pharaoh Neco the silver and gold he demanded. In order to do so, he taxed the land and exacted the silver and gold from the people of the land according to their assessments. *t*

Jehoiakim King of Judah

23:36–24:6pp — 2Ch 36:5–8

³⁶Jehoiakim *u* was twenty-five years old when he became king, and he reigned in Jerusalem eleven years. His mother's name was Zebidah daughter of Pedaiah; she was from Rumah. ³⁷And he did evil*v* in the

Cross references (center column)

23:25 *d*Jer 22:15
23:26 *e*2Ki 21:6; Jer 23:20; 30:24
*f*S 2Ki 21:12
23:27 *g*2Ki 21:13; 2Ki 24:3
*h*S Ex 33:15; 2Ki 24:3
*i*Jer 27:10; 32:31
Jer 46:2 *k*2Ki 9:27
23:30 *l*S 2Ki 9:28
23:31 *m*1Ch 3:15; Jer 22:11

*n*2Ki 24:18
23:32 *o*1Ki 15:26
23:33 *p*S Nu 34:11
*q*1Ki 8:65
23:34 *r*2Ki 24:6; 1Ch 3:15; 2Ch 36:5–8; Jer 1:3 *s*Jer 22:12
23:35 *t*Jer 2:16
23:36 *u*Jer 26:1
23:37 *v*1Ki 15:26

*m*27 1 Kings 8:29   *n*33 Hebrew; Septuagint (see also 2 Chron. 36:3) *Neco at Riblah in Hamath removed him*   *o*33 That is, about 3 3/4 tons (about 3.4 metric tons)   *p*33 That is, about 75 pounds (about 34 kilograms)

23:26 *Nevertheless, the LORD did not turn away from the heat of his fierce anger.* The judgment against Judah and Jerusalem was postponed but not rescinded because of Josiah's reformation (see notes on 21:15; 22:20).
23:27 *as I removed Israel.* See 17:18–23. *Jerusalem, the city I chose.* See 21:4,7,13. *this temple, about which I said, 'There shall my Name be.'* See note on 1Ki 8:16.
23:28 *annals of the kings of Judah.* See note on 1Ki 14:29.
23:29 *Pharaoh Neco king of Egypt.* Ruled 610–595 B.C. *help the king of Assyria.* Pharaoh Neco intended to help Ashur-Uballit II, the last Assyrian king, in his struggle against the rising power of Babylon under Nabopolassar. The Assyrian capital, Nineveh, had already fallen to the Babylonians and Medes in 612 (see the book of Nahum). The remaining Assyrian forces had regrouped at Haran, but in 609 they were forced west of the Euphrates. It appears to be at this time that the Egyptians under Neco were coming to the Assyrians' aid. *King Josiah marched out to meet him in battle.* Perhaps Josiah opposed the passage of Neco's army through the pass at Megiddo (see 2Ch 35:20–24) because he feared that the growth of either Egyptian or Assyrian power would have adverse results for the continued independence of Judah.
23:30 *buried him in his own tomb.* See 2Ch 35:24–25. *people of the land.* See note on 21:24. *Jehoahaz son of Josiah.* Jehoahaz was the fourth and youngest son of Josiah. His name was originally Shallum (see 1Ch 3:15; Jer 22:11), which was probably changed to Jehoahaz at the time of his accession to the throne. Perhaps Jehoahaz was chosen by the people over Jehoiakim because it was known that Jehoiakim favored a pro-Egyptian policy instead of the anti-Egyptian policy of Josiah and Jehoahaz. *anointed him.* See note on 1Sa

9:16.
23:31 *three months.* In 609 B.C. *Jeremiah.* Not the prophet (see Jer 1:1). *Libnah.* See note on 8:22.
23:32 *evil . . . as his fathers.* See 16:3; 21:2,21; Eze 19:3.
23:33 *in chains at Riblah.* By either deception or overt force the Egyptians were able to take Jehoahaz captive and impose tribute on Judah (see 2Ch 36:3). Jehoahaz was imprisoned at Neco's military headquarters established at Riblah on the Orontes River. Nebuchadnezzar was later to make his headquarters at the same place (see 25:6,20).
23:34 *Eliakim son of Josiah.* Eliakim was an older brother of Jehoahaz (see 1Ch 3:15). Perhaps he had been bypassed earlier as a successor to Josiah because of a pro-Egyptian political stance. *changed Eliakim's name to Jehoiakim.* The meaning of these two names is similar (Eliakim, "God has established"; Jehoiakim, "Yahweh has established"). Perhaps Neco wanted to use the name change to imply that his actions were sanctioned by Yahweh, the God of Judah (see 18:25; 23:5;21). In any case, the change in name indicated that Jehoiakim was subject to Neco's authority. *took Jehoahaz . . . to Egypt, and there he died.* See 2Ch 36:4; Jer 22:10–12.
23:35 *from the people of the land.* The tribute for Neco was raised by a graduated tax placed on the very people who had supported the kingship of Jehoahaz (see v. 30). Menahem of the northern kingdom had used a similar method of raising funds for tribute (see 15:20).
23:36 *eleven years.* 609–598 B.C.
23:37 *did evil in the eyes of the LORD.* Jehoiakim was responsible for the murder of the prophet Uriah from Kiriath Jearim (Jer 26:20–24), and his rule was characterized by dishonesty, oppression and injustice (see Jer 22:13–19). He

eyes of the LORD, just as his fathers had done.

24 During Jehoiakim's reign, Nebuchadnezzar[w] king of Babylon invaded[x] the land, and Jehoiakim became his vassal for three years. But then he changed his mind and rebelled[y] against Nebuchadnezzar. [2]The LORD sent Babylonian,[q][z] Aramean,[a] Moabite and Ammonite raiders[b] against him. He sent them to destroy[c] Judah, in accordance with the word of the LORD proclaimed by his servants the prophets.[d] [3]Surely these things happened to Judah according to the LORD's command,[e] in order to remove them from his presence[f] because of the sins of Manasseh[g] and all he had done, [4]including the shedding of innocent blood.[h] For he had filled Jerusalem with innocent blood, and the LORD was not willing to forgive.[i]

[5]As for the other events of Jehoiakim's reign,[j] and all he did, are they not written in the book of the annals of the kings of Judah? [6]Jehoiakim rested[k] with his fathers. And Jehoiachin[l] his son succeeded him as king.

[7]The king of Egypt[m] did not march out from his own country again, because the king of Babylon[n] had taken all his territory, from the Wadi of Egypt to the Euphrates River.

Jehoiachin King of Judah

24:8–17pp — 2Ch 36:9–10

[8]Jehoiachin[o] was eighteen years old when he became king, and he reigned in Jerusalem three months. His mother's name was Nehushta[p] daughter of Elnathan; she was from Jerusalem. [9]He did evil[q] in the eyes of the LORD, just as his father had done.

[10]At that time the officers of Nebuchadnezzar[r] king of Babylon advanced on Jerusalem and laid siege to it, [11]and Nebuchadnezzar himself came up to the city while his officers were besieging it. [12]Jehoiachin king of Judah, his mother, his attendants, his nobles and his officials all surrendered[s] to him.

In the eighth year of the reign of the king of Babylon, he took Jehoiachin prisoner. [13]As the LORD had declared,[t] Nebuchadnezzar removed all the treasures[u] from the temple of the LORD and from the royal palace, and took away all the gold articles[v] that Solomon[w] king of Israel had made for the temple of the LORD. [14]He car-

Cross references

24:1 *w*ver 10; 2Ki 25:11; Ezr 5:12; Jer 4:7; 25:1,9; 39:1; 40:1; 50:17; 52:15; Eze 32:2; Da 1:1; 7:4 *x*Jer 35:11 *y*S 2Ki 18:7 **24:2** *z*Jer 5:15; Hab 1:6 *a*Jer 35:11 *b*S 2Ki 5:2 *c*Isa 28:18-19 *d*Jer 12:7-9; 25:1; 26:1; 36:1; Eze 23:23; Da 1:2 **24:3** *e*S 2Ki 18:25 *f*S 2Ki 13:23 *g*S 1Ki 14:9; S 2Ki 21:12; Jer 15:4 **24:4** *h*S 2Ki 21:16; Jer 22:3 *i*S Ex 23:21; La 3:42 **24:5** *j*Jer 22:18-19 **24:6** *k*Jer 22:19; 36:30 *l*1Ch 3:16; Jer 22:24,28; Eze 19:1 **24:7** *m*S Ge 15:18; S 2Ki 18:21; S Jer 46:25 *n*Jer 1:14; 25:9; 46:24 **24:8** *o*1Ch 3:16; Jer 22:24; 37:1 *p*ver 15; Jer 13:18; 22:26; 29:2 **24:9** *q*1Ki 15:26 **24:10** *r*S ver 1 **24:12** *s*2Ki 25:27; Jer 13:18; 22:24-30; 24:1; 29:2 **24:13** *t*2Ki 20:17 *u*2Ki 25:15; Isa 39:6; 42:22 *v*2Ki 25:14; Ezr 1:7; Isa 39:6; Jer 15:13; 17:3; 20:5; 27:16; 28:3; Eze 7:21; Da 1:2; 5:2,23; Zep 1:13 *w*S 1Ki 7:51

*q*2 Or *Chaldean*

Footnotes / Study notes

reintroduced idolatrous worship in the temple (see Eze 8:5–17) and refused to accept the word of the Lord through Jeremiah (see Jer 36). *his fathers.* Manasseh (21:1–18) and Amon (21:19–26).

24:1 *Nebuchadnezzar.* Means "O (god) Nabu, protect my son!" He was the son of Nabopolassar (see note on 23:29) and the most powerful king of the Neo-Babylonian empire (612–539 B.C.), reigning 605–562 (see Da 1–4). *invaded the land.* In 605 Nebuchadnezzar, the crown prince and commander of the Babylonian army, defeated Pharaoh Neco and the Egyptians at the battle of Carchemish and again at Hamath (see 23:29; Jer 46:2). These victories had far-reaching implications in the geopolitical power structure of the eastern Mediterranean world. Nebuchadnezzar went on to conquer all of the "Hatti-country," which, according to Babylonian records, included the "city of Judah." Daniel was among the Judahite hostages taken at this time (see Da 1:1). Perhaps as early as Sept. 6, 605, Nebuchadnezzar acceded to the Babylonian throne upon the death of his father. *three years.* Probably 604–602. In 604 Nebuchadnezzar returned to the west and took tribute from "all the kings of Hatti-land." It is likely that Jehoiakim was included among these kings. *changed his mind and rebelled.* In 601 Nebuchadnezzar again marched west against Egypt and was repulsed by strong Egyptian resistance. This may have encouraged Jehoiakim's rebellion, even though Jeremiah had warned against it (see Jer 27:9–11).
24:2 *Babylonian, Aramean, Moabite and Ammonite raiders against him.* Reaction to Jehoiakim's rebellion was swift. Babylonian troops, perhaps garrisoned in Aram, along with troops of other loyal vassals, were sent to put down the Judahite rebellion.
24:3 *sins of Manasseh.* See 21:11–12; 23:26–27; Jer

15:3–4.
24:4 *innocent blood.* See note on 21:16. *not willing to forgive.* See 22:17.
24:5 *annals of the kings of Judah.* See note on 1Ki 14:29. *rested with his fathers.* See note on 1Ki 1:21. Jehoiakim died shortly before Jerusalem fell to the Babylonian siege (see vv. 8–12). Whether his death was due to natural causes or political intrigue is not indicated.
24:7 *The king of Egypt did not march out from his own country again.* This was due to the Egyptian defeat at Carchemish (see Jer 46:2) in 605 B.C., and it explains why Jehoiakim received no help from Egypt in his rebellion against the Babylonians. *Wadi of Egypt.* See note on 1Ki 8:65.
24:8 *three months.* In 598–597 B.C. Babylonian records place the fall of Jerusalem to Nebuchadnezzar on Mar. 16, 597. This means that the three-month and ten-day reign (see 2Ch 36:9–10) of Jehoiachin began in December, 598.
24:9 *as his father.* See 23:37; Jer 22:20–30.
24:11 *Nebuchadnezzar himself came up to the city.* Babylonian records say that Nebuchadnezzar "encamped against the city of Judah, and on the second day of the month of Addaru [i.e., Mar. 16, 597 B.C.] he seized the city and captured the king."
24:12 *eighth year.* April, 597 B.C. (see 2Ch 36:10; see also note on Jer 52:28, where a different system of dating is reflected).
24:13 *As the LORD had declared.* See 20:13,17.
24:14 *ten thousand.* This figure may include the 7,000 fighting men and 1,000 craftsmen mentioned in v. 16 (see note on Jer 52:28, where a different number of captives is mentioned).

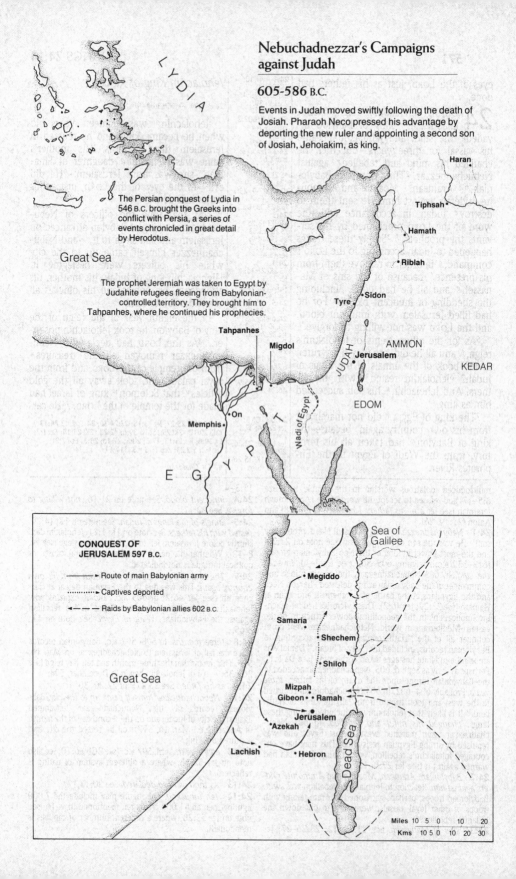

Nebuchadnezzar's Campaigns against Judah

605-586 B.C.

Events in Judah moved swiftly following the death of Josiah. Pharaoh Neco pressed his advantage by deporting the new ruler and appointing a second son of Josiah, Jehoiakim, as king.

The Persian conquest of Lydia in 546 B.C. brought the Greeks into conflict with Persia, a series of events chronicled in great detail by Herodotus.

Great Sea

The prophet Jeremiah was taken to Egypt by Judahite refugees fleeing from Babylonian-controlled territory. They brought him to Tahpanhes, where he continued his prophecies.

LYDIA

Haran

Tiphsah

Hamath

Riblah

Sidon

Tyre

Tahpanhes

Migdol

On

Memphis

Wadi of Egypt

E G Y P T

JUDAH

Jerusalem

AMMON

KEDAR

EDOM

CONQUEST OF JERUSALEM 597 B.C.

→ Route of main Babylonian army

⋯⋯► Captives deported

– – –► Raids by Babylonian allies 602 B.C.

Sea of Galilee

Megiddo

Samaria

Shechem

Shiloh

Mizpah

Gibeon • Ramah

Jerusalem

Azekah

Lachish • Hebron

Great Sea

Dead Sea

Miles 10 5 0 10 20

Kms 10 5 0 10 20 30

Soon a stronger power appeared in the north in the person of Nebuchadnezzar, king of the Chaldeans (Neo-Babylonians), who determined to follow the fierce policies of his Assyrian predecessors.

The tribute of Jehoiakim was paid at a distance when he heard of Nebuchadnezzar's approach. After three years as a Babylonian vassal, he rebelled, bringing a rapid response in the form of small-scale raids from Babylonians, Arameans, Moabites and Ammonites

(c. 602 B.C.). Finally, Nebuchadnezzar's forces controlled all of the coastal territory north of the Wadi of Egypt.

When 18-year-old Jehoiachin had ruled just three months (597 B.C.), the main Babylonian army struck, capturing Jerusalem and exiling the king as a captive in Babylon. Ten thousand persons were deported.

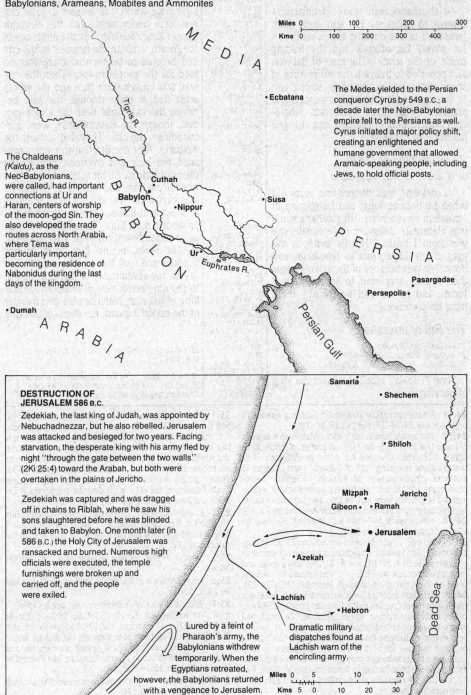

The Medes yielded to the Persian conqueror Cyrus by 549 B.C.; a decade later the Neo-Babylonian empire fell to the Persians as well. Cyrus initiated a major policy shift, creating an enlightened and humane government that allowed Aramaic-speaking people, including Jews, to hold official posts.

The Chaldeans (Kaldu), as the Neo-Babylonians, were called, had important connections at Ur and Haran, centers of worship of the moon-god Sin. They also developed the trade routes across North Arabia, where Tema was particularly important, becoming the residence of Nabonidus during the last days of the kingdom.

DESTRUCTION OF JERUSALEM 586 B.C.

Zedekiah, the last king of Judah, was appointed by Nebuchadnezzar, but he also rebelled. Jerusalem was attacked and besieged for two years. Facing starvation, the desperate king with his army fled by night "through the gate between the two walls" (2Ki 25:4) toward the Arabah, but both were overtaken in the plains of Jericho.

Zedekiah was captured and was dragged off in chains to Riblah, where he saw his sons slaughtered before he was blinded and taken to Babylon. One month later (in 586 B.C.) the Holy City of Jerusalem was ransacked and burned. Numerous high officials were executed, the temple furnishings were broken up and carried off, and the people were exiled.

Lured by a feint of Pharaoh's army, the Babylonians withdrew temporarily. When the Egyptians retreated, however, the Babylonians returned with a vengeance to Jerusalem.

Dramatic military dispatches found at Lachish warn of the encircling army.

ried into exile[x] all Jerusalem: all the officers and fighting men,[y] and all the craftsmen and artisans—a total of ten thousand. Only the poorest[z] people of the land were left.

[15] Nebuchadnezzar took Jehoiachin[a] captive to Babylon. He also took from Jerusalem to Babylon the king's mother,[b] his wives, his officials and the leading men[c] of the land. [16] The king of Babylon also deported to Babylon the entire force of seven thousand fighting men, strong and fit for war, and a thousand craftsmen and artisans.[d] [17] He made Mattaniah, Jehoiachin's uncle, king in his place and changed his name to Zedekiah.[e]

Zedekiah King of Judah

24:18–20pp — 2Ch 36:11–16; Jer 52:1–3

[18] Zedekiah[f] was twenty-one years old when he became king, and he reigned in Jerusalem eleven years. His mother's name was Hamutal[g] daughter of Jeremiah; she was from Libnah. [19] He did evil[h] in the eyes of the LORD, just as Jehoiakim had done. [20] It was because of the LORD's anger that all this happened to Jerusalem and Judah, and in the end he thrust[i] them from his presence.[j]

The Fall of Jerusalem

25:1–12pp — Jer 39:1–10
25:1–21pp — 2Ch 36:17–20; Jer 52:4–27
25:22–26pp — Jer 40:7–9; 41:1–3, 16–18

Now Zedekiah rebelled against the king of Babylon.

25 So in the ninth[k] year of Zedekiah's reign, on the tenth day of the tenth month, Nebuchadnezzar[l] king of Babylon marched against Jerusalem with his whole army. He encamped outside the city and built siege works[m] all around it. [2] The city was kept under siege until the eleventh year of King Zedekiah. [3] By the ninth day of the fourth[r] month the famine[n] in the city had become so severe that there was no food for the people to eat. [4] Then the city wall was broken through,[o] and the whole army fled at night through the gate between the two walls near the king's garden, though the Babylonians[s] were surrounding[p] the city. They fled toward the Arabah,[t] [5] but the Babylonian[u] army pursued the king and overtook him in the plains of Jericho. All his soldiers were separated from him and scattered,[q] [6] and he was captured.[r] He was taken to the king of Babylon at Riblah,[s] where sentence was pronounced on him. [7] They killed the sons of Zedekiah before his eyes. Then they put out his eyes, bound him with bronze shackles and took him to Babylon.[t]

[8] On the seventh day of the fifth month, in the nineteenth year of Nebuchadnezzar king of Babylon, Nebuzaradan commander of the imperial guard, an official of the king

24:14
[x] S Dt 28:36;
S 2Ch 36:20;
S Mt 1:11
[y] Isa 3:1-3
[z] Dt 15:11;
2Ki 25:12;
Job 5:16; Ps 9:18;
Jer 40:7; 52:16
24:15
[a] S 2Ki 20:18;
Eze 19:9 [b] S ver 8;
S 1Ki 2:19
[c] Est 2:6; Isa 39:7;
La 2:9; Eze 1:2;
17:12-14; Da 1:3
24:16 [d] Ezr 2:1;
Jer 24:1
24:17
[e] 1Ch 3:15;
2Ch 36:11;
Jer 1:3; 37:1;
52:1; Eze 17:13
24:18 [f] 1Ch 3:16;
Jer 39:1
[g] 2Ki 23:31
24:19
[h] 1Ki 15:26;
Jer 37:2
24:20 [i] Dt 4:26;
29:27
[j] S Ex 33:15;
S 2Ki 13:23

25:1 [k] Jer 32:1
[l] Jer 21:2; 34:1-7
[m] Isa 23:13; 29:3;
Jer 4:16-17; 32:2;
33:4; Eze 21:22;
24:2
25:3
[n] S Lev 26:26;
Isa 22:2;
Jer 14:18; 37:21;
La 2:20; 4:9
25:4 [o] Job 30:14;
Ps 144:14;
Jer 50:15; 51:44,
58; Eze 33:21
[p] Jer 4:17; 6:3
25:5
[q] S Lev 26:36;
Eze 12:14; 17:21
25:6 [r] Isa 22:3;
Jer 38:23
[s] S Nu 34:11

25:7 [t] S Dt 28:36; Jer 21:7; 32:4-5; 34:3,21; Eze 12:11;
19:9; 40:1

[r] 3 See Jer. 52:6.   [s] 4 Or *Chaldeans*; also in verses 13,
25 and 26   [t] 4 Or *the Jordan Valley*   [u] 5 Or
Chaldean; also in verses 10 and 24

24:15 *Jehoiachin captive to Babylon.* Fulfilling Jeremiah's prophecy (Jer 22:24–27; see 2Ki 25:27–30).
24:17 *Mattaniah, Jehoiachin's uncle.* Mattaniah was a son of Josiah (see 2Ch 3:15; Jer 1:3) and brother of Jehoiachin's father, Jehoiakim. *changed his name to Zedekiah.* Mattaniah's name (meaning "gift of Yahweh") was changed to Zedekiah ("righteousness of Yahweh"). Perhaps Nebuchadnezzar wanted to imply that his actions against Jerusalem and Jehoiachin were just. In any case, the name change signified subjection to Nebuchadnezzar (see note on 23:34).
24:18 *eleven years.* 597–586 B.C. *Jeremiah.* See note on 23:31. *Libnah.* See note on 8:22.
24:19 *did evil . . . as Jehoiakim.* See note on 23:37. During Zedekiah's reign idolatrous practices continued to increase in Jerusalem (see 2Ch 36:14; Eze 8–11). He was a weak and indecisive ruler (see Jer 38:5,19), who refused to heed the word of the Lord given through Jeremiah (2Ch 36:12).
24:20 *Zedekiah rebelled.* Most interpreters link Zedekiah's revolt with the succession to the Egyptian throne in 589 B.C. of the ambitious pharaoh Apries (Hophra). Zedekiah had sworn allegiance to Nebuchadnezzar (Eze 17:13), he had sent envoys to Babylon (see Jer 29:3), and he had made a personal visit (see Jer 51:59). However, he seems to have capitulated to the seductive propaganda of the anti-Babylonian and pro-Egyptian faction in Jerusalem (see Jer 37:5; Eze 17:15–16) in a tragically miscalculated effort to gain independence from Babylon.

25:1 *ninth year . . . tenth day . . . tenth month.* Jan. 15, 588 B.C. (see Jer 39:1; 52:4; Eze 24:1–2). *Nebuchadnezzar . . . marched against Jerusalem.* Earlier, Nebuchadnezzar had subdued all the fortified cities in Judah except Lachish and Azekah (see Jer 34:7). A number of Hebrew inscriptions on potsherds were found at Lachish in 1935 and 1938. These Lachish ostraca (or letters; see chart on "Ancient Texts Relating to the OT," p. 5) describe conditions at Lachish and Azekah during the Babylonian siege.
25:2–3 *eleventh year . . . ninth day . . . fourth month.* July 18, 586 B.C. (see Jer 39:2; 52:5–7). Some scholars follow a different dating system and place the fall of Jerusalem in the summer of 587.
25:3 *famine in the city had become so severe.* See Jer 38:2–9.
25:6 *king of Babylon at Riblah.* See note on 23:33; see also Jer 39:5; 52:9.
25:7 *killed the sons of Zedekiah . . . put out his eyes . . . took him to Babylon.* See Jer 32:4–5; 34:2–3; 38:18; 39:6–7; 52:10–11. Ezekiel (12:13) had predicted that Zedekiah would be brought to Babylon, but that he would not see it. Zedekiah could have spared his own life and prevented the destruction of Jerusalem if he had listened to Jeremiah (see Jer 38:14–28).
25:8 *seventh day . . . fifth month . . . nineteenth year.* Aug. 14, 586 B.C. (see Jer 52:12).

of Babylon, came to Jerusalem. 9He set fire u to the temple of the LORD, the royal palace and all the houses of Jerusalem. Every important building he burned down. v 10The whole Babylonian army, under the commander of the imperial guard, broke down the walls w around Jerusalem. 11Nebuzaradan the commander of the guard carried into exile x the people who remained in the city, along with the rest of the populace and those who had gone over to the king of Babylon. y 12But the commander left behind some of the poorest people z of the land to work the vineyards and fields.

13The Babylonians broke a up the bronze pillars, the movable stands and the bronze Sea that were at the temple of the LORD and they carried the bronze to Babylon. 14They also took away the pots, shovels, wick trimmers, dishes b and all the bronze articles c used in the temple service. 15The commander of the imperial guard took away the censers and sprinkling bowls—all that were made of pure gold or silver. d

16The bronze from the two pillars, the Sea and the movable stands, which Solomon had made for the temple of the LORD, was more than could be weighed. 17Each pillar e was twenty-seven feet v high. The bronze capital on top of one pillar was four and a half feet w high and was decorated with a network and pomegranates of bronze all around. The other pillar, with its network, was similar.

18The commander of the guard took as

prisoners Seraiah f the chief priest, Zephaniah g the priest next in rank and the three doorkeepers. h 19Of those still in the city, he took the officer in charge of the fighting men and five royal advisers. He also took the secretary who was chief officer in charge of conscripting the people of the land and sixty of his men who were found in the city. 20Nebuzaradan the commander took them all and brought them to the king of Babylon at Riblah. 21There at Riblah, i in the land of Hamath, the king had them executed. j

So Judah went into captivity, k away from her land. l

22Nebuchadnezzar king of Babylon appointed Gedaliah m son of Ahikam, n the son of Shaphan, to be over the people he had left behind in Judah. 23When all the army officers and their men heard that the king of Babylon had appointed Gedaliah as governor, they came to Gedaliah at Mizpah—Ishmael son of Nethaniah, Johanan son of Kareah, Seraiah son of Tanhumeth the Netophathite, Jaazaniah the son of the Maacathite, and their men. 24Gedaliah took an oath to reassure them and their men. "Do not be afraid of the Babylonian officials," he said. "Settle down in the land and serve the king of Babylon, and it will go well with you."

25In the seventh month, however, Ishmael son of Nethaniah, the son of Elishama, who was of royal blood, came with ten men and assassinated o Gedaliah and also

25:9 uIsa 60:7; 63:15,18; 64:11
vS Dt 13:16; Ne 1:3; Ps 74:3-8; 79:1; Jer 2:15; 17:27; 21:10; 26:6,18; La 4:11; Am 2:5; Mic 3:12
25:10 wNe 1:3; Jer 50:15
25:11 xS Lev 26:44; 2Ki 24:14
yS Dt 28:36; S 2Ki 24:1
25:12 zS 2Ki 24:14
25:13 aS 1Ki 7:50
25:14 bS Nu 7:14 cS 2Ki 24:13; Ezr 1:7
25:15 dS 2Ki 24:13; Jer 15:13; 20:5; 27:16-22
25:17 e1Ki 7:15-22

25:18 fver 18-21; 1Ch 6:14; Ezr 7:1; Ne 11:11 gJer 21:1; 29:25; 37:3
hS 2Ki 12:9; S 23:4
25:21 iS Nu 34:11 jJer 34:21 kS 1Ki 8:46 lS Ge 12:7; S Jos 23:13
25:22 mJer 39:14; 40:5, 7; 41:18
nS 2Ki 22:12
25:25 oS 2Ki 12:20

v 17 Hebrew eighteen cubits (about 8.1 meters)
w 17 Hebrew three cubits (about 1.3 meters)

25:9 set fire to the temple. See 2Ch 36:19; Jer 39:8; 52:13.
25:13 bronze pillars. See 1Ki 7:15–22. movable stands. See 1Ki 7:27–39. bronze Sea. See 1Ki 7:23–26.
25:14 all the bronze articles used in the temple service. See 1Ki 7:40,45.
25:17 bronze capital . . . was four and a half feet high. See NIV text note. In 1Ki 7:16 and Jer 52:22 the height of the capital is given as seven and a half feet (five cubits). The three-cubit difference may be due to a copyist's error.
25:18 Seraiah the chief priest. Seraiah was the grandson of Hilkiah (see note on 22:4; see also 22:8; 1Ch 6:13–14). His son Jehozadak was taken captive to Babylon. Ezra was one of Jehozadak's descendants (see Ezr 7:1).
25:20 brought them to the king of Babylon at Riblah. See v. 6 and note.
25:21 Judah went into captivity, away from her land. Judah's exile from Canaan fulfilled the prediction of judgment given during the reign of Manasseh (see 23:27). Exile was the most dire of the covenant curses (see Lev 26:33; Dt 28:36; see also Jer 25:8–11).
25:22 Gedaliah. See note on 22:12. Gedaliah shared Jeremiah's nonresistance approach to the Babylonians (see v. 24) and won their confidence as a trustworthy governor of Judah

(see Jer 41:10).
25:23 Mizpah. Had been a town of important political significance in the time just before the establishment of the monarchy (see note on 1Sa 7:5). Jeremiah found Gedaliah there (see Jer 40:1–6). Ishmael son of Nethaniah. Verse 25 gives a fuller genealogy. Elishama, Ishmael's grandfather, was the royal secretary under Jehoiakim (Jer 36:12). Jaazaniah the son of the Maacathite. In 1932 an agate seal was found at Tell en-Nasbeh (Mizpah) bearing the name of Jaazaniah (perhaps the man mentioned here) with the inscription: "Belonging to Jaazaniah the servant of the king."
25:24 Gedaliah urged submission to the Babylonians as the judgment of God. He advocated the restoration of the normal pursuits of a peacetime society (see Jer 27). A similar message had been given by Jeremiah to the captives taken to Babylon in 597 B.C. (see Jer 29:4–7).
25:25 seventh month. October, 586 B.C. assassinated Gedaliah. A more complete account of the assassination of Gedaliah is given in Jer 40:13–41:15. Ishmael appears to have had personal designs on the throne, to have resented Gedaliah's ready submission to the Babylonians, and to have been manipulated by the Ammonites, who also chafed under Babylonian domination (see Jer 40:14; 41:10,15).

the men of Judah and the Babylonians who were with him at Mizpah.[p] [26]At this, all the people from the least to the greatest, together with the army officers, fled to Egypt[q] for fear of the Babylonians.

Jehoiachin Released

25:27–30pp — Jer 52:31–34

[27]In the thirty-seventh year of the exile

25:25	[p]Zec 7:5
25:26	[q]Isa 30:2; Jer 43:7
25:27	[r]S 2Ki 24:12
25:28	[s]S 1Ki 8:50; [t]Ezr 5:5; 7:6,28; 9:9; Ne 2:1; Da 2:48

of Jehoiachin king of Judah, in the year Evil-Merodach[x] became king of Babylon, he released Jehoiachin[r] from prison on the twenty-seventh day of the twelfth month. [28]He spoke kindly[s] to him and gave him a seat of honor[t] higher than those of the

[x]27 Also called Amel-Marduk

25:26 *fled to Egypt.* Pharaoh Apries (Hophra) was then ruler in Egypt (see note on 24:20).
25:27 *thirty-seventh year . . . twenty-seventh day . . . twelfth month.* Mar. 22, 561 B.C. *in the year Evil-Merodach became king of Babylon.* 561 (some scholars place Evil-Merodach's succession to the throne in October, 562; see note on 24:1). His name means "man of (the god) Marduk."

released Jehoiachin from prison. Babylonian administrative tablets (see chart on "Ancient Texts Relating to the OT," p. 5), recording the payment of rations in oil and barley to prisoners held in Babylon, mention Yaukin (Jehoiachin) king of Iahudu (Judah) and five of his sons (cf. 24:15). No reason is given for Jehoiachin's release. Perhaps it was part of a general amnesty proclaimed at the beginning of Evil-

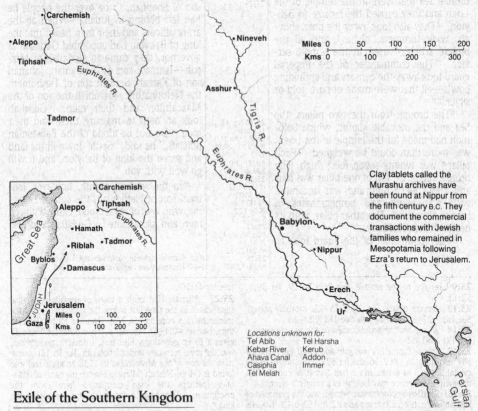

Clay tablets called the Murashu archives have been found at Nippur from the fifth century B.C. They document the commercial transactions with Jewish families who remained in Mesopotamia following Ezra's return to Jerusalem.

Locations unknown for:
Tel Abib   Tel Harsha
Kebar River   Kerub
Ahava Canal   Addon
Casiphia   Immer
Tel Melah

Exile of the Southern Kingdom

Knowledge about the destiny of the captives from Israel and Judah is sparse in the period following the capture of Samaria and the later destruction of Jerusalem.

Assyrians and Babylonians treated their subject peoples essentially the same: overwhelming military force used in a manner inspiring psychological terror, along with mass deportations and heavy tribute.

Three deportations are mentioned in Jer 52:28-30, the largest one consisting of 3,023 Jews who were taken to Babylon along with King Jehoiachin in 597 B.C.

After the destruction of Jerusalem by Nebuzaradan, the commander of the Babylonian army, hundreds of exiles were taken to Riblah "in the land of Hamath," where, in addition to Zedekiah's sons, at least 61 were executed.

Jehoiachin and his family were kept in Babylon, where clay ration receipts bearing his name have been found in a dramatic archaeological confirmation of Biblical history.

Eze 1:1-3 and 3:15 indicate that other captives were placed at Tel Abib and at the Kebar River, both probably in the locale of Nippur, as were other villages mentioned in Ezr 2:59; 8:15, 17; Ne 7:61.

other kings who were with him in Babylon. ²⁹So Jehoiachin put aside his prison clothes and for the rest of his life ate regu-

25:29 *u* S 2Sa 9:7
25:30 *v* Ge 43:34;
Est 2:9; 9:22;
Jer 28:4

larly at the king's table. *u* ³⁰Day by day the king gave Jehoiachin a regular allowance as long as he lived. *v*

Merodach's reign.

25:28 *spoke kindly to him and gave him a seat of honor.* The book of Kings ends on a hopeful note. The judgment of

exile will not destroy the people of Israel or the line of David. God's promise concerning David's house remains (see 2Sa 7:14–16).

1 CHRONICLES

Title

The Hebrew title (*dibre hayyamim*) can be translated "the events (or annals) of the days (or years)." The same phrase occurs in references to sources used by the author or compiler of Kings (translated "annals" in, e.g., 1Ki 14:19,29; 15:7,23,31; 16:5,14,20,27; 22:46). The Septuagint translators (translators of the OT into Greek) called the book "the things omitted," indicating that they regarded it as a supplement to Samuel and Kings. Jerome (A.D. 347-420), translator of the Latin Vulgate, suggested that a more appropriate title would be "chronicle of the whole sacred history." Luther took over this suggestion in his German version, and others have followed him. Chronicles was first divided into two books by the Septuagint translators.

Author, Date and Sources

According to ancient Jewish tradition, Ezra wrote Chronicles, Ezra and Nehemiah (see Introduction to Ezra: Literary Form and Authorship), but this cannot be established with certainty. A growing consensus dates Chronicles in the latter half of the fifth century B.C., thus possibly within Ezra's lifetime. And it must be acknowledged that the author, if not Ezra himself, at least shared many basic concerns with that reforming priest—though Chronicles is not so narrowly "priestly" in its perspective as was long affirmed.

Some believe the text contains evidence here and there of later expansions after the basic work had been composed. While editorial revisions are not unlikely, all specific proposals regarding them remain tentative.

In his recounting of history long past the Chronicler relied on many written sources. About half his work was taken from Samuel and Kings; he also drew on the Pentateuch, Judges, Ruth, Psalms, Isaiah, Jeremiah, Lamentations and Zechariah (though he used texts of these books that varied somewhat from those that have been preserved in the later standardized Hebrew texts). And there are frequent references to still other sources: "the book of the kings of Israel" (9:1; 2Ch 20:34; cf. 2Ch 33:18), "the book of the annals of King David" (27:24), "the book of the kings of Judah and Israel" or ". . . of Israel and Judah" (2Ch 16:11; 25:26; 27:7; 28:26; 32:32; 35:27; 36:8), "the annotations on the book of the kings" (2Ch 24:27). It is unclear whether these all refer to the same source or to different sources, and what their relationship is to Samuel and Kings or to the royal annals referred to in Kings. In addition, the author cites a number of prophetic writings: those of "Samuel the seer" (29:29), "Nathan the prophet" (29:29; 2Ch 9:29), "Gad the seer" (29:29), "Ahijah the Shilonite" (2Ch 9:29), "Iddo the seer" (2Ch 9:29; 12:15; 13:22), "Shemaiah the prophet" (2Ch 12:15), "the prophet Isaiah" (2Ch 26:22), "the seers" (2Ch 33:19). All these he used, often with only minor changes, to tell his own story of the past. He did not invent, but he did select, arrange and integrate his sources to compose a narrative "sermon" for postexilic Israel as she struggled to reorient herself as the people of God in a new situation.

Purpose and Themes

Just as the author of Kings had organized and interpreted the data of Israel's history to address the needs of the exiled community, so the Chronicler wrote for the restored community. The burning issue was the question of continuity with the past: Is God still interested in us? Are his covenants still in force? Now that we have no Davidic king and are subject to Persia, do God's promises to David still have meaning for us? After the great judgment (the dethroning of the house of David, the destruction of the nation, of Jerusalem and of the temple, and the exile to Babylon), what is our relationship to Israel of old? Several elements go into the Chronicler's answer:

1. Continuity with the past is signified by the temple in Jerusalem, rebuilt by the Lord's sovereign

influence over a Persian imperial edict (2Ch 36:22-23). For a generation that had no independent political status and no Davidic king the author takes great pains to show that the temple of the Lord and its service (including its book of prayer and praise, an early edition of the Psalms) are supreme gifts of God given to Israel through the Davidic dynasty. For that reason his account of the reigns of David and Solomon is largely devoted to David's preparation for and Solomon's building of the temple, and David's instructions for the temple service (with the counsel of Gad the seer and Nathan the prophet, 2Ch 29:25, and also of the Levites Asaph, Heman and Jeduthun, 2Ch 35:15). See also the Chronicler's accounts of the reigns of Asa, Jehoshaphat, Joash, Hezekiah and Josiah. The temple of the Lord in the ancient holy city and its service (including the Psalms) were the chief legacy left to the restored community by the house of David.

2. The value of this legacy is highlighted by the author's emphasis on God's furtherance of his gracious purposes toward Israel through his sovereign acts of election: (1) of the tribe of Levi to serve before the ark of the covenant (15:2; see 23:24-32), (2) of David to be king over Israel (28:4; 2Ch 6:6), (3) of Solomon his son to be king and to build the temple (28:5-6,10; 29:1), (4) of Jerusalem (2Ch 6:6,34,38; 12:13; 33:7) and (5) of the temple (2Ch 7:12,16; 33:7) to be the place where God's Name would be present among his people. These divine acts give assurance to postexilic Israel that her rebuilt temple in Jerusalem and its continuing service mark her as God's people whose election has not been annulled.

3. In addition to the temple, Israel has the law and the prophets as a major focus of her covenant life under the leadership of the house of David. Neither the Davidic kings nor the temple had in themselves assured Israel's security and blessing. All had been conditional on Israel's and the king's faithfulness to the law (28:7; 2Ch 6:16; 7:17; 12:1; 33:8). In the Chronicler's account, a primary feature of the reign of every faithful Davidic king was his attempt to bring about compliance with the law: David (6:49; 15:13,15; 16:40; 22:12-13; 29:19), Asa (2Ch 14:4; 15:12-14), Jehoshaphat (2Ch 17:3-9; 19:8-10), Joash (2Ch 24:6,9), Hezekiah (2Ch 29:10,31; 30:15-16; 31:3-4,21), Josiah (2Ch 34:19-21,29-33; 35:6,12,26). And to heed God's prophetic word was no less crucial. The faithful kings, such as David, Asa, Jehoshaphat, Hezekiah and Josiah—and even Rehoboam (2Ch 11:4; 12:6) and Amaziah (2Ch 25:7-10)—honored it; the unfaithful kings disregarded it to their destruction (Jehoram, 2Ch 21:12-19; Joash, 2Ch 24:19-25; Amaziah, 2Ch 25:15-16,20; Manasseh, 2Ch 33:10-11; see 36:15-16). Chronicles, in fact, notes the ministries of more prophets than do Samuel and Kings. Jehoshaphat's word to Israel expresses the Chronicler's view succinctly: "Have faith in the LORD your God and you will be upheld; have faith in his prophets and you will be successful" (2Ch 20:20). In the Chronicler's account of Israel's years under the kings, her response to the law and the prophets was more decisive for her destiny than the reigns of kings.

Thus the law and the prophets, like the temple, are more crucial to Israel's continuing relationship with the Lord than the presence or absence of a king, the reigns of the Davidic kings themselves being testimony.

4. The Chronicler further underscores the importance of obedience to the law and the prophets by emphasizing the theme of immediate retribution. See the express statements of David (28:9), of the Lord (2Ch 7:14) and of the prophets (2Ch 12:5; 15:2,7; 16:7,9; 19:2-3; 21:14-15; 24:20; 25:15-16; 28:9; 34:24-28). In writing his accounts of individual reigns, he never tires of demonstrating how sin always brings judgment in the form of disaster (usually either illness or defeat in war), whereas repentance, obedience and trust yield peace, victory and prosperity.

5. Clearly the author of Chronicles wished to sustain Israel's hope for the promised Messiah, son of David, in accordance with the Davidic covenant (2Sa 7) and the assurances of the prophets, including those near to him (Haggai, Zechariah and Malachi). He was careful to recall the Lord's pledge to David (1Ch 17) and to follow this with many references back to it (see especially his account of Solomon's reign and also 2Ch 13:5; 21:7; 23:3). But perhaps even more indicative are his idealized depictions of David, Solomon, Asa, Jehoshaphat, Hezekiah and Josiah. While not portrayed as flawless, these kings are presented as prime examples of the Messianic ideal, i.e., as royal servants of the Lord whose reigns promoted godliness and covenant faithfulness in Israel. They were crowned with God's favor toward his people in the concrete forms of victories, deliverances and prosperity. They sat, moreover, on the "throne of the LORD" (29:23; see 28:5; 2Ch 9:8) and ruled over the Lord's kingdom (17:14; 2Ch 13:8). Thus they served as types, foreshadowing the David to come of whom the prophets had spoken, and their remembrance nurtured hope in the face of much discouragement (see the book of Malachi). See further the next section on "Portrait of David and Solomon."

6. Yet another major theme of the Chronicler's history is his concern with "all Israel" (see, e.g., 9:1; 11:1-4; 12:38-40; 16:1-3; 18:14; 21:1-5; 28:1-8; 29:21-26; 2Ch 1:1-3; 7:8-10; 9:30; 10:1-3,16; 12:1; 18:16; 28:23; 29:24; 30:1-13,23-27; 34:6-9,33). As a matter of fact, he viewed the restored community as the remnant of all Israel, both north and south (9:2-3). This was more than a theological conceit. His narrative makes frequent note of movements of godly people from Israel to Judah for specifically religious reasons. The first were Levites in the time of Rehoboam (2Ch 11:14). In the reign of Asa others followed from Ephraim and Manasseh (2Ch 15:9). Shortly after the Assyrian destruction of the northern kingdom, many from that devastated land resettled in Judah at Hezekiah's invitation (2Ch 30). Presumably not all who came for Hezekiah's great Passover remained, but archaeology has shown a sudden large increase in population in the region around Jerusalem at this time, and the Chronicler specifically mentions "men of Israel . . . who lived in the towns of Judah" (2Ch 31:6). He also speaks of "the people of Manasseh, Ephraim and the entire remnant of Israel" who joined with "the people of Judah and Benjamin and the inhabitants of Jerusalem" in restoring the temple in the days of Josiah (2Ch 34:9). These were also present at Josiah's Passover (2Ch 35:17-18). So the kingdom of "Judah" had absorbed many from the northern kingdom through the years, and the Chronicler viewed it as the remnant of all Israel from the time of Samaria's fall.

7. The genealogies also demonstrate continuity with the past. To the question "Is God still interested in us?" the Chronicler answers, "He has always been." God's grace and love for the restored community did not begin with David or the conquest or the exodus—but with creation (1:1). For the genealogies see below.

8. The Chronicler often introduces speeches not found in Samuel and Kings, using them to convey some of his main emphases. Of the 165 speeches in Chronicles of varying lengths, only 95 are found in the parallel texts of Samuel and Kings. Cf., e.g., the speeches of Abijah (2Ch 13:4-12), Asa (2Ch 14:11) and Jehoshaphat (2Ch 20:5-12).

Portrait of David and Solomon

The bulk of the Chronicler's history is devoted to the reigns of David (chs. 11-29) and Solomon (2Ch 1-9). His portraits of these two kings are quite distinctive and provide a key to his concerns:

1. The Chronicler has idealized David and Solomon. Anything in his source material (mainly Samuel and Kings) that might tarnish his picture of them is omitted. He makes no reference to the seven-year reign in Hebron before the uniting of the kingdom, the wars between Saul's house and David, the negotiations with Abner, the difficulties over David's wife Michal, or the murders of Abner and Ish-Bosheth (2Sa 1-4). The Chronicler presents David as being immediately anointed king over all Israel after the death of Saul (ch. 11) and enjoying the total support of the people (11:10-12:40; see note on 3:1-9). Subsequent difficulties for David are also not recounted. No mention is made of David's sin with Bathsheba, the crime and death of Amnon, the fratricide by Absalom and his plot against his father, the flight of David from Jerusalem, the rebellions of Sheba and Shimei, and other incidents that might diminish the glory of David's reign (2Sa 11-20). David is presented without blemish, apart from the incident of the census (the Chronicler had a special purpose for including it; see ch. 21 and notes).

The Chronicler handles Solomon similarly. Solomon is specifically named in a divine oracle as David's successor (22:7-10; 28:6). His accession to the throne is announced publicly by David and is greeted with the unanimous support of all Israel (chs. 28-29). No mention is made of the bedridden David, who must overturn the attempted coup by Adonijah at the last moment to secure the throne for Solomon. Nor is there mention that the military commander Joab and the high priest Abiathar supported Adonijah's attempt (1Ki 1). Solomon's execution of those who had wronged David (1Ki 2) is also omitted. The accession of Solomon is without competition or detracting incident. The account of his reign is devoted almost wholly to the building of the temple (2Ch 2-8), and no reference to his failures is included. No mention is made of his idolatry, his foreign wives or of the rebellions against his rule (1Ki 11). Even the blame for the schism is removed from Solomon (1Ki 11:26-40; 12:1-4) and placed on the scheming of Jeroboam. Solomon's image in Chronicles is such that he can be paired with David in the most favorable light (2Ch 11:17).

The David and Solomon of the Chronicler, then, must be seen not only as the David and Solomon of history, but also as typifying the Messianic king of the Chronicler's expectation.

2. Not only is there idealization of David and Solomon, but the author also appears to consciously adopt the account of the succession of Moses and Joshua as a model for the succession of David and Solomon:

a. Both David and Moses fail to attain their goals—one to build the temple and the other to enter

the promised land. In both cases the divine prohibition is related to the appointment of a successor (22:5-13; 28:2-8; Dt 1:37-38; 31:2-8).

b. Both Solomon and Joshua bring the people of God into rest (22:8-9; Jos 11:23; 21:44).

c. There are a number of verbal parallels in the appointments of Solomon and Joshua (compare 22:11-13,16; 28:7-10,20; 2Ch 1:1 with Dt 31:5-8,23; Jos 1:5,7-9).

d. There are both private and public announcements of the appointment of the successors: private (22:6; Dt 31:23); public (28:8; Dt 31:7—both "in the presence/sight of all Israel").

e. Both enjoy the immediate and wholehearted support of the people (29:23-24; Dt 34:9; Jos 1:16-18).

f. It is twice reported that God "exalted" or "made great" Solomon and Joshua (29:25; 2Ch 1:1; Jos 3:7; 4:14).

The Chronicler also uses other models from Pentateuchal history in his portrayal of David and Solomon. Like Moses, David received the plans for the temple from God (28:11-19; Ex 25:9) and called on the people to bring voluntary offerings for its construction (29:1-9; Ex 25:1-7). Solomon's relationship to Huram-Abi, the craftsman from Tyre (2Ch 2:13-14), echoes the role of Bezalel and Oholiab in the building of the tabernacle (Ex 35:30-36:7). See note on 2Ch 1:5.

Genealogies

Analysis of genealogies, both inside and outside the Bible, has disclosed that they serve a variety of functions (with different principles governing the lists), that they vary in form (some being segmented, others linear) and depth (number of generations listed), and that they are often fluid (subject to change).

There are three general areas in which genealogies function: the familial or domestic, the legal-political, and the religious. In the domestic area an individual's social status, privileges and obligations may be reflected in his placement in the lineage (see 7:14-19); the rights of the firstborn son and the secondary status of the children of concubines are examples from the Bible. In the political sphere genealogies substantiate claims to hereditary office or settle competing claims when the office is contested. Land organization and territorial groupings of social units may also be determined by genealogical reckoning—e.g., the division of the land among the 12 tribes. In Israel military levies also proceeded along genealogical lines; several of the genealogies in Chronicles reflect military conscription (5:1-26; 7:1-12,30-40; 8:1-40). Genealogies function in the religious sphere primarily by establishing membership among the priests and Levites (6:1-30; 9:10-34; Ne 7:61-65).

As to form, some genealogical lists trace several lines of descent (segmented genealogies) while others are devoted to a single line (linear genealogies).

Comparison of genealogical lists of the same tribal or family line often brings to light surprising differences. This fluidity of the lists may reflect variation in function. But sometimes changes in the status or relations of social structures are reflected in genealogies by changes in the relationships of names in the genealogy (see 1:35-42; 6:22,27) or by the addition of names or segments to a lineage (see 5:11-22; 6:27; 7:6-12). The most common type of fluidity in Biblical materials is telescoping, the omission of names from the list. Unimportant names are left out in order to relate an individual to a prominent ancestor, or possibly to achieve the desired number of names in the genealogy. Some Biblical genealogies, for example, omit names to achieve multiples of 7: For the period from David to the exile Matthew gives 14 generations (2 times 7), while Luke gives 21 (3 times 7), and the same authors give similar multiples of 7 for the period from the exile to Jesus (Mt 1:1-17; Lk 3:23-38).

The genealogies of Chronicles show variation in all these properties; the arrangements often reflect the purpose for which the genealogies were composed prior to their being adopted by the Chronicler as part of his record.

Outline

I. Genealogies: Creation to Restoration (1Ch 1-9)
   A. The Patriarchs (ch. 1)
   B. The 12 Sons of Jacob/Israel (2:1-2)
   C. The Family of Judah (2:3-4:23)
   D. The Sons of Simeon (4:24-43)
   E. Reuben, Gad and the Half-Tribe of Manasseh (ch. 5)
   F. Levi and Families (ch. 6)
   G. Issachar, Benjamin, Naphtali, Manasseh, Ephraim and Asher (chs. 7-9)
II. The Reign of David (1Ch 10-29)

A. Death of Saul (ch. 10)
B. Capture of Jerusalem; David's Power Base (chs. 11-12)
C. Return of the Ark; Establishment of David's Kingdom (chs. 13-16)
D. Dynastic Promise (ch. 17)
E. David's Conquests (chs. 18-20)
F. The Census (ch. 21)
G. Preparations for the Temple (ch. 22)
H. Organization of the Temple Service (chs. 23-26)
I. Administrative Structures of the Kingdom (ch. 27)
J. David's Final Preparations for Succession and the Temple (28:1-29:20)
K. Succession of Solomon; Death of David (29:21-30)

III. The Reign of Solomon (2Ch 1-9)
A. The Gift of Wisdom (ch. 1)
B. Building the Temple (2:1-5:1)
C. Dedication of the Temple (5:2-7:22)
D. Solomon's Other Activities (ch. 8)
E. Solomon's Wisdom, Splendor and Death (ch. 9)

IV. The Schism, and the History of the Kings of Judah (2Ch 10-36)
A. Rehoboam (chs. 10-12)
B. Abijah (13:1-14:1)
C. Asa (14:2-16:14)
D. Jehoshaphat (17:1-21:3)
E. Jehoram and Ahaziah (21:4-22:9)
F. Joash (22:10-24:27)
G. Amaziah (ch. 25)
H. Uzziah (ch. 26)
I. Jotham (ch. 27)
J. Ahaz (ch. 28)
K. Hezekiah (chs. 29-32)
L. Manasseh (33:1-20)
M. Amon (33:21-25)
N. Josiah (34:1-36:1)
O. Josiah's Successors (36:2-14)
P. Exile and Restoration (36:15-23)

Historical Records From Adam to Abraham

To Noah's Sons

1 Adam,[a] Seth, Enosh, [2]Kenan,[b] Mahalalel,[c] Jared,[d] [3]Enoch,[e] Methuselah,[f] Lamech,[g] Noah.[h]

[4]The sons of Noah:[a] [i]
Shem, Ham and Japheth.[j]

The Japhethites

1:5–7pp — Ge 10:2–5

[5]The sons[b] of Japheth:
Gomer, Magog, Madai, Javan, Tubal, Meshech and Tiras.
[6]The sons of Gomer:
Ashkenaz, Riphath[c] and Togarmah.
[7]The sons of Javan:
Elishah, Tarshish, the Kittim and the Rodanim.

The Hamites

1:8–16pp — Ge 10:6–20

[8]The sons of Ham:
Cush, Mizraim,[d] Put and Canaan.
[9]The sons of Cush:
Seba, Havilah, Sabta, Raamah and Sabteca.
The sons of Raamah:
Sheba and Dedan.
[10]Cush was the father[e] of
Nimrod, who grew to be a mighty warrior on earth.

[11]Mizraim was the father of
the Ludites, Anamites, Lehabites, Naphtuhites, [12]Pathrusites, Casluhites (from whom the Philistines came) and Caphtorites.
[13]Canaan was the father of
Sidon his firstborn,[f] and of the Hittites, [14]Jebusites, Amorites, Girgashites, [15]Hivites, Arkites, Sinites, [16]Arvadites, Zemarites and Hamathites.

The Semites

1:17–23pp — Ge 10:21–31; 11:10–27

[17]The sons of Shem:
Elam, Asshur, Arphaxad, Lud and Aram.
The sons of Aram[g]:
Uz, Hul, Gether and Meshech.
[18]Arphaxad was the father of Shelah, and Shelah the father of Eber.
[19]Two sons were born to Eber:
One was named Peleg,[h] because in his time the earth was divided; his brother was named Joktan.
[20]Joktan was the father of

1:1 [a]Ge 5:1-32; Lk 3:36-38
1:2 [b]S Ge 5:9 [c]S Ge 5:12 [d]S Ge 5:15
1:3 [e]S Ge 5:18; Jude 1:14 [f]S Ge 5:21 [g]S Ge 5:25 [h]S Ge 5:29
1:4 [i]Ge 6:10; 10:1 [j]S Ge 5:32

[a]4 Septuagint; Hebrew does not have *The sons of Noah:* [b]5 *Sons* may mean *descendants* or *successors* or *nations*; also in verses 6-10, 17 and 20. [c]6 Many Hebrew manuscripts and Vulgate (see also Septuagint and Gen. 10:3); most Hebrew manuscripts *Diphath* [d]8 That is, Egypt; also in verse 11 [e]10 *Father* may mean *ancestor* or *predecessor* or *founder*; also in verses 11, 13, 18 and 20. [f]13 Or *of the Sidonians, the foremost* [g]17 One Hebrew manuscript and some Septuagint manuscripts (see also Gen. 10:23); most Hebrew manuscripts do not have this line. [h]19 *Peleg* means *division*.

1:1–9:44 The genealogies succinctly show the restored community's continuity with the past. The great deeds of God on Israel's behalf prior to the rise of David are passed over in silence, but the genealogies serve as a skeleton of history to show that the Israel of the restoration stands at the center of the divine purpose from the beginning (from Adam, v. 1). And the genealogies also serve the very practical purpose of legitimizing the present. They provide the framework by which the ethnic and religious purity of the people can be maintained. They also establish the continuing line of royal succession and the legitimacy of the priests for the postexilic temple service. (See Introduction: Genealogies.)
1:1–2:1 The Chronicler here covers the period from Adam to Jacob, and the materials are drawn almost entirely from Genesis. The subsidiary lines of descent are presented first: Japheth and Ham (vv. 5–16) are given before Shem (vv. 17–27), the sons of Shem other than those in Abraham's ancestry (vv. 17–23) before that line (vv. 24–27), the sons of Abraham's concubines (vv. 28–33) before Isaac's line (v. 34), the descendants of Esau and the Edomite ruling houses (vv. 35–54) before the sons of Israel (2:1). In each case the elect lineage is given last.
Several features of this genealogy are striking when compared with non-Biblical materials. The genealogy begins without an introduction. Two sections of the genealogy have no kinship terms and are only lists of names: the first 13 names (vv. 1–4; see note on v. 4) and vv. 24–27. In vv. 5–16 (and following v. 27) kinship terms are used. Both

segmented (those tracing several lines of descent) and linear (those tracing a single line) genealogies are included. This identical structure is found in a copy of the Assyrian King List: There is no introduction, and the scribe has drawn lines across the tablet dividing it into four sections, two of which are lists of names without kinship terms, alternating with two lists in which relations are specified; both segmented and linear genealogies are used. This suggests that the Chronicler was following a known literary pattern for his composition.
1:1–4 From creation to the flood. This list is taken from Ge 5:1–32 (see notes there). The omission of Cain and Abel demonstrates the Chronicler's interest in the chosen line (see Ge 4:17–25).
1:4 *The sons of Noah.* The phrase is not found in the Hebrew text (see NIV text note); this omission parallels the Assyrian King List (see note on 1:1–2:1). The Chronicler's readers would have known that these were the sons of Noah and would not have needed the kinship notice; the Septuagint (the Greek translation of the OT) and most modern translations insert the phrase to clarify the relationship.
1:5–23 This genealogy is drawn from the table of nations in Ge 10:2–29 (see notes there). The arrangement is primarily geographical and cultural rather than biological. Omitting the Philistines (v. 11) as a parenthesis, a total of 70 nations is achieved: Japheth, 14; Ham, 30; Shem, 26 (see note on Ge 10:2)—an example of a genealogy telescoped to attain multiples of 7 (see Introduction: Genealogies).

Almodad, Sheleph, Hazarmaveth, Jerah, 21Hadoram, Uzal, Diklah, 22Obal,i Abimael, Sheba, 23Ophir, Havilah and Jobab. All these were sons of Joktan.

24Shem,k Arphaxad,j Shelah, 25Eber, Peleg, Reu, 26Serug, Nahor, Terah 27and Abram (that is, Abraham).

The Family of Abraham

28The sons of Abraham:
Isaac and Ishmael.

Descendants of Hagar

1:29-31pp — Ge 25:12-16

29These were their descendants:
Nebaioth the firstborn of Ishmael, Kedar, Adbeel, Mibsam, 30Mishma, Dumah, Massa, Hadad, Tema, 31Jetur, Naphish and Kedemah. These were the sons of Ishmael.

Descendants of Keturah

1:32-33pp — Ge 25:1-4

32The sons born to Keturah, Abraham's concubine:i
Zimran, Jokshan, Medan, Midian, Ishbak and Shuah.
The sons of Jokshan:
Sheba and Dedan.m
33The sons of Midian:
Ephah, Epher, Hanoch, Abida and Eldaah.
All these were descendants of Keturah.

Descendants of Sarah

1:35-37pp — Ge 36:10-14

34Abrahamn was the father of Isaac.o
The sons of Isaac:
Esau and Israel.p

Esau's Sons

35The sons of Esau:q
Eliphaz, Reuel,r Jeush, Jalam and Korah.

36The sons of Eliphaz:
Teman, Omar, Zepho,k Gatam and Kenaz;
by Timna: Amalek.l s
37The sons of Reuel:t
Nahath, Zerah, Shammah and Mizzah.

The People of Seir in Edom

1:38-42pp — Ge 36:20-28

38The sons of Seir:
Lotan, Shobal, Zibeon, Anah, Dishon, Ezer and Dishan.
39The sons of Lotan:
Hori and Homam. Timna was Lotan's sister.
40The sons of Shobal:
Alvan,m Manahath, Ebal, Shepho and Onam.
The sons of Zibeon:
Aiah and Anah.u
41The son of Anah:
Dishon.
The sons of Dishon:
Hemdan,n Eshban, Ithran and Keran.
42The sons of Ezer:
Bilhan, Zaavan and Akan.o
The sons of Dishanp:
Uz and Aran.

The Rulers of Edom

1:43-54pp — Ge 36:31-43

43These were the kings who reigned in

i22 Some Hebrew manuscripts and Syriac (see also Gen. 10:28); most Hebrew manuscripts Ebal   j24 Hebrew; some Septuagint manuscripts Arphaxad, Cainan (see also note at Gen. 11:10)   k36 Many Hebrew manuscripts, some Septuagint manuscripts and Syriac (see also Gen. 36:11); most Hebrew manuscripts Zephi   l36 Some Septuagint manuscripts (see also Gen. 36:12); Hebrew Gatam, Kenaz, Timna and Amalek   m40 Many Hebrew manuscripts and some Septuagint manuscripts (see also Gen. 36:23); most Hebrew manuscripts Alian   n41 Many Hebrew manuscripts and some Septuagint manuscripts (see also Gen. 36:26); most Hebrew manuscripts Hamran   o42 Many Hebrew and Septuagint manuscripts (see also Gen. 36:27); most Hebrew manuscripts Zaavan, Jaakan   p42 Hebrew Dishon, a variant of Dishan

1:24 kS Ge 10:21-25; Lk 3:34-36
1:32 lS Ge 22:24 mS Ge 10:7
1:34 nLk 3:34 oMt 1:2; Ac 7:8 pS Ge 17:5
1:35 qGe 36:19 rS Ge 36:4
1:36 sS Ex 17:14
1:37 tGe 36:17
1:40 uS Ge 36:2

1:24-27 See notes on 1:1-2:1; Ge 11:10-26.
1:28-34 See notes on Ge 25:1-18.
1:35-42 See Ge 36:10-28 and notes.
1:36 sons of Eliphaz. These correspond to Ge 36:11-12, but with one difficulty: The Hebrew text of Chronicles (see second NIV text note on this verse) lists Timna as a son of Eliphaz, while Ge 36:12 designates Timna as the concubine of Eliphaz and mother of Amalek. The NIV follows the Septuagint, which regarded Timna as the mother of Amalek, not as the son of Eliphaz. This solution says that the Hebrew text is here in error, or perhaps that the Chronicler has once again omitted kinship terminology (see notes on 1:1-2:1;

v. 4). Alternatively, some regard this as an example of genealogical fluidity (see Introduction: Genealogies): Since the name Timna also became the name of a chiefdom in Edom (v. 51; Ge 36:40), during the course of time Timna was "promoted" in the Edomite genealogies to the position of a son of Eliphaz and brother of Amalek.
1:43-54 See Ge 36:31-43. The Chronicler continues with extensive coverage of Edom. This is striking in contrast to his omission of the line of Cain and the brief treatment of the line of Ishmael. It probably reflects the fact that the Edomites were important in the Chronicler's own day (see 18:11-13; 2Ch 8:17; 21:8; 25:20; 28:17).

Edom before any Israelite king reigned[q]:

Bela son of Beor, whose city was named Dinhabah.

[44]When Bela died, Jobab son of Zerah from Bozrah succeeded him as king.

[45]When Jobab died, Husham from the land of the Temanites[v] succeeded him as king.

[46]When Husham died, Hadad son of Bedad, who defeated Midian in the country of Moab, succeeded him as king. His city was named Avith.

[47]When Hadad died, Samlah from Masrekah succeeded him as king.

[48]When Samlah died, Shaul from Rehoboth on the river[r] succeeded him as king.

[49]When Shaul died, Baal-Hanan son of Acbor succeeded him as king.

[50]When Baal-Hanan died, Hadad succeeded him as king. His city was named Pau,[s] and his wife's name was Mehetabel daughter of Matred, the daughter of Me-Zahab.
[51]Hadad also died.

The chiefs of Edom were:

Timna, Alvah, Jetheth, [52]Oholibamah, Elah, Pinon, [53]Kenaz, Teman, Mibzar, [54]Magdiel and Iram. These were the chiefs of Edom.

Israel's Sons

2:1–2pp — Ge 35:23–26

2   These were the sons of Israel: Reuben, Simeon, Levi, Judah, Issachar, Zebulun, [2]Dan, Joseph, Benjamin, Naphtali, Gad and Asher.

1:45 [v]S Ge 36:11

Judah

2:5–15pp — Ru 4:18–22; Mt 1:3–6

To Hezron's Sons

[3]The sons of Judah:[w]

Er, Onan and Shelah.[x] These three were born to him by a Canaanite woman, the daughter of Shua.[y] Er, Judah's firstborn, was wicked in the Lord's sight; so the Lord put him to death.[z] [4]Tamar,[a] Judah's daughter-in-law,[b] bore him Perez[c] and Zerah. Judah had five sons in all.

[5]The sons of Perez:[d]

Hezron[e] and Hamul.
[6]The sons of Zerah:

Zimri, Ethan, Heman, Calcol and Darda[t]—five in all.
[7]The son of Carmi:

Achar,[u][f] who brought trouble on Israel by violating the ban on taking devoted things.[v][g]
[8]The son of Ethan:

Azariah.
[9]The sons born to Hezron[h] were:

Jerahmeel, Ram and Caleb.[w]

From Ram Son of Hezron

[10]Ram[i] was the father of

Amminadab,[j] and Amminadab

2:3 [w]S Ge 29:35; 38:2-10
[x]S Ge 38:5
[y]S Ge 38:2
[z]S Nu 26:19
2:4 [a]Ge 38:11-30
[b]S Ge 11:31
[c]S Ge 38:29
2:5 [d]S Ge 46:12
[e]Nu 26:21
2:7 [f]S Jos 7:1
[g]S Jos 6:18
2:9 [h]S Nu 26:21
2:10 [i]Lk 3:32-33
[j]S Ex 6:23

[q]43 Or *before an Israelite king reigned over them*   [r]48 Possibly the Euphrates   [s]50 Many Hebrew manuscripts, some Septuagint manuscripts, Vulgate and Syriac (see also Gen. 36:39); most Hebrew manuscripts *Pai*   [t]6 Many Hebrew manuscripts, some Septuagint manuscripts and Syriac (see also 1 Kings 4:31); most Hebrew manuscripts *Dara*   [u]7 *Achar* means *trouble*; *Achar* is called *Achan* in Joshua.   [v]7 The Hebrew term refers to the irrevocable giving over of things or persons to the Lord, often by totally destroying them.   [w]9 Hebrew *Kelubai,* a variant of *Caleb*

2:1–2 Although there are numerous lists of the 12 tribes in the OT, only four are given in genealogical form: (1) Ge 29:31–30:24; 35:16–20; (2) Ge 35:22–26; (3) Ge 46:8–27; (4) here. Other lists of the tribes are found in 12:24–37; 27:16–22; Ex 1:2–5; Dt 27:12–13; 33; Eze 48:31–34. In other lists the tribe of Levi is omitted, and the number 12 is achieved by dividing Joseph into the tribes of Ephraim and Manasseh (Nu 1:5–15; 1:20–43; 2:3–31; 7:12–83; 10:14–28; 13:4–15; 26:5–51). In this passage the Chronicler appears to follow Ge 35:22–26 except for the position of the tribe of Dan, which is found in seventh instead of ninth place. The list here does not set the order in which the Chronicler will take up the tribes; rather, he moves immediately to his major concern with the house of David and the tribe of Judah (2:3–4:23), even though Judah is fourth in the genealogy. In the lists of these chapters the Chronicler maintains the number 12, but with the following names: Judah, Simeon, Reuben, Gad, half of Manasseh, Levi, Issachar, Benjamin, Naphtali, Ephraim, Manasseh and Asher. Zebulun and Dan are omitted.
2:3–9 The lineage of Judah is traced to Hezron's sons (v. 9), whose descendants are given in 2:10–3:24. Of Judah's five sons, the first two (Er and Onan) died as the result of sin recorded in Ge 38. The lineage of the third son, Shelah, is taken up in 4:21; this section focuses on the remaining two (see Ge 46:12; Nu 26:19–22).
2:6 *Ethan, Heman, Calcol and Darda.* Not immediate descendants of Zerah; rather, they are from the later period of the reign of Solomon (1 Ki 4:31). A Heman and an Ethan were David's musicians (see 15:19; Ps 88–89 titles), but whether these are the same individuals is uncertain. If they are the same, the fact that in 6:33–42 and 15:19 Heman and Ethan are assigned to the tribe of Levi may be another example of genealogical fluidity, where these men's musical skills brought them into the Levitical lineage. Or the reverse may have occurred: As Levites associated with Judah, they were brought into that lineage.
2:7 *Achar.* The change from Achan to Achar (meaning "trouble"; see NIV text note) is probably a play on words reflecting the trouble he brought to Israel (Jos 7).
2:10–3:24 That the Chronicler's primary concern in the genealogy of Judah is with the line of David is seen in his arrangement of this section's material as an inversion:

Descendants of Ram (David's ancestry), 2:10–17

the father of Nahshon,[k] the leader of the people of Judah. [11]Nahshon was the father of Salmon,[x] Salmon the father of Boaz, [12]Boaz[l] the father of Obed and Obed the father of Jesse.[m]

[13]Jesse[n] was the father of
Eliab[o] his firstborn; the second son was Abinadab, the third Shimea, [14]the fourth Nethanel, the fifth Raddai, [15]the sixth Ozem and the seventh David. [16]Their sisters were Zeruiah[p] and Abigail. Zeruiah's[q] three sons were Abishai, Joab[r] and Asahel. [17]Abigail was the mother of Amasa,[s] whose father was Jether the Ishmaelite.

Caleb Son of Hezron

[18]Caleb son of Hezron had children by his wife Azubah (and by Jerioth). These were her sons: Jesher, Shobab and Ardon. [19]When Azubah died, Caleb[t] married Ephrath, who bore him Hur. [20]Hur was the father of Uri, and Uri the father of Bezalel.[u]

[21]Later, Hezron lay with the daughter of Makir the father of Gilead[v] (he had married her when he was sixty years old), and she bore him Segub. [22]Segub was the father of Jair, who controlled twenty-three towns in Gilead. [23](But Geshur and Aram captured Havvoth Jair,[v][w] as well as Kenath[x] with its surrounding settlements—sixty towns.) All these were descendants of Makir the father of Gilead.

[24]After Hezron died in Caleb Ephrathah, Abijah the wife of Hezron

bore him Ashhur[y] the father[z] of Tekoa.

Jerahmeel Son of Hezron

[25]The sons of Jerahmeel the firstborn of Hezron:
Ram his firstborn, Bunah, Oren, Ozem and[a] Ahijah. [26]Jerahmeel had another wife, whose name was Atarah; she was the mother of Onam.

[27]The sons of Ram the firstborn of Jerahmeel:
Maaz, Jamin and Eker.

[28]The sons of Onam:
Shammai and Jada.
The sons of Shammai:
Nadab and Abishur.

[29]Abishur's wife was named Abihail, who bore him Ahban and Molid.

[30]The sons of Nadab:
Seled and Appaim. Seled died without children.

[31]The son of Appaim:
Ishi, who was the father of Sheshan.
Sheshan was the father of Ahlai.

[32]The sons of Jada, Shammai's brother:
Jether and Jonathan. Jether died without children.

[33]The sons of Jonathan:
Peleth and Zaza.
These were the descendants of Jerahmeel.

[34]Sheshan had no sons—only daughters.
He had an Egyptian servant named

x11 Septuagint (see also Ruth 4:21); Hebrew *Salma*
y23 Or *captured the settlements of Jair*   **z**24 *Father* may mean *civic leader* or *military leader*; also in verses 42, 45, 49-52 and possibly elsewhere.   **a**25 Or *Oren and Ozem, by*

Cross references column:
2:10 *k*S Nu 1:7
2:12 *l*S Ru 2:1
*m*S Ru 4:17
2:13 *n*S Ru 4:17
*o*S 1Sa 16:6
2:16 *p*1Sa 26:6
*q*2Sa 2:18
*r*S 2Sa 2:13
2:17 *s*2Sa 17:25
2:19 *t*ver 42,50
2:20 *u*S Ex 31:2
2:21 *v*S Nu 27:1
2:23
*w*S Nu 32:41;
Dt 3:14
*x*Nu 32:42

2:24 *y*1Ch 4:5

Descendants of Caleb, 2:18–24
Descendants of Jerahmeel, 2:25–33
Supplementary material on Jerahmeel, 2:34–41
Supplementary material on Caleb, 2:42–55
Supplementary material on Ram (David's descendants), ch. 3

The Chronicler has structured this central portion of the Judah genealogy to highlight the Davidic ancestry and descent, which frame this section and emphasize the position of David—in line with the Chronicler's interests in the historical portions that follow (see note on 4:1–23).
2:10–17 Verses 10–12 are a linear genealogy from Ram to Jesse; then Jesse's lineage is segmented, reminiscent of 1Sa 16:1–13. The source for most of the material is Ru 4:19–22. In 1Sa 16:10–13 David was the eighth of Jesse's sons to appear before Samuel; in this passage only seven are named, enabling David to occupy the favored place of the seventh son (v. 15; see Introduction: Genealogies). David was the half-uncle of his famous warriors Abishai, Joab, Asahel and Amasa (11:6,20,26; 2Sa 2:13,18; 17:25; 19:13).
2:18–24 For the Chronicler the important name in this

genealogy of the Calebites is Bezalel (v. 20), the wise master craftsman who supervised the building of the tabernacle (Ex 31:1–5). He is mentioned in the Bible only in Exodus and Chronicles. The Chronicler uses Bezalel and Oholiab (Ex 31:6) as a model for his portrait of Solomon and Huram-Abi in the building of the temple (see note on 2Ch 1:5). By inserting a reference to the builder of the tabernacle next to the genealogy of David in vv. 10–17, the Chronicler characteristically juxtaposes the themes of king and temple—so important to his historical narrative.
2:25–33 This section is identified as a separate entity from the supplementary material by its opening and closing formulas: "The sons of Jerahmeel" (v. 25) and "These were the descendants of Jerahmeel" (v. 33). Verses 25–41 are the only genealogical materials on the Jerahmeelites in the Bible. 1Sa 27:10 and 30:27–29 place their settlements in the Negev.
2:34–41 Supplementary material on the line of Sheshan (v. 31); it is a linear genealogy to a depth of 13 generations. The generation of Elishama (v. 41) would be the 23rd since Judah, if there has been no telescoping in this lineage. If no

Jarha. ³⁵Sheshan gave his daughter in marriage to his servant Jarha, and she bore him Attai.

³⁶Attai was the father of Nathan,
Nathan the father of Zabad, ᶻ
³⁷Zabad the father of Ephlal,
Ephlal the father of Obed,
³⁸Obed the father of Jehu,
Jehu the father of Azariah,
³⁹Azariah the father of Helez,
Helez the father of Eleasah,
⁴⁰Eleasah the father of Sismai,
Sismai the father of Shallum,
⁴¹Shallum the father of Jekamiah,
and Jekamiah the father of Elishama.

The Clans of Caleb

⁴²The sons of Caleb ᵃ the brother of Jerahmeel:
Mesha his firstborn, who was the father of Ziph, and his son Mareshah, ᵇ who was the father of Hebron.
⁴³The sons of Hebron:
Korah, Tappuah, Rekem and Shema. ⁴⁴Shema was the father of Raham, and Raham the father of Jorkeam. Rekem was the father of Shammai. ⁴⁵The son of Shammai was Maon ᵇ, and Maon was the father of Beth Zur. ᶜ
⁴⁶Caleb's concubine Ephah was the mother of Haran, Moza and Gazez. Haran was the father of Gazez.
⁴⁷The sons of Jahdai:
Regem, Jotham, Geshan, Pelet, Ephah and Shaaph.
⁴⁸Caleb's concubine Maacah was the mother of Sheber and Tirhanah.
⁴⁹She also gave birth to Shaaph the father of Madmannah ᵈ and to

Sheva the father of Macbenah and Gibea. Caleb's daughter was Acsah. ᵉ ⁵⁰These were the descendants of Caleb.

The sons of Hur ᶠ the firstborn of Ephrathah:
Shobal the father of Kiriath Jearim, ᵍ ⁵¹Salma the father of Bethlehem, and Hareph the father of Beth Gader.
⁵²The descendants of Shobal the father of Kiriath Jearim were:
Haroeh, half the Manahathites, ⁵³and the clans of Kiriath Jearim:
the Ithrites, ʰ Puthites, Shumathites and Mishraites. From these descended the Zorathites and Eshtaolites.
⁵⁴The descendants of Salma:
Bethlehem, the Netophathites, ⁱ Atroth Beth Joab, half the Manahathites, the Zorites, ⁵⁵and the clans of scribes ᶜ who lived at Jabez: the Tirathites, Shimeathites and Sucathites. These are the Kenites ʲ who came from Hammath, ᵏ the father of the house of Recab. ᵈ ˡ

The Sons of David

3:1–4pp — 2Sa 3:2-5
3:5–8pp — 2Sa 5:14-16; 1Ch 14:4-7

3 These were the sons of David ᵐ born to him in Hebron:
The firstborn was Amnon the son of Ahinoam ⁿ of Jezreel; ᵒ
the second, Daniel the son of Abigail ᵖ of Carmel;
²the third, Absalom the son of Maacah daughter of Talmai king of Geshur;

Cross references (center column):

2:36 ᶻ1Ch 11:41
2:42 ᵃS ver 19
2:45 ᵇS Jos 15:55
ᶜS Jos 15:58
2:49 ᵈJos 15:31

ᵉJos 15:16
2:50 ᶠ1Ch 4:4
ᵍS ver 19
2:53 ʰ2Sa 23:38
2:54 ⁱEzr 2:22;
Ne 7:26; 12:28
2:55 ʲS Ge 15:19;
S Jdg 4:11
ᵏJos 19:35
ˡ2Ki 10:15,23;
Jer 35:2-19
3:1 ᵐ1Ch 14:3;
28:5
ⁿS 1Sa 25:43
ᵒS Jos 15:56
ᵖS 1Sa 25:42

ᵇ42 The meaning of the Hebrew for this phrase is uncertain.   ᶜ55 Or of the Sopherites   ᵈ55 Or father of Beth Recab

---

names are omitted, Elishama would likely be contemporary with David, though we know nothing of him.
2:42–55 The same opening and closing formulas noted in vv. 25,33 occur in vv. 42,50a: "The sons of Caleb . . . These were the descendants of Caleb." The list in this section is a mixture of personal and place-names; the phrase "father of" must often be understood as "founder of" or "leader of" a city (see NIV text notes on 1:10; 4:4).
2:50b–55 Resumes the genealogy of Hur (v. 20). The same formulas for identifying the genealogical sections in vv. 25, 33 and in vv. 42,50a are used in v. 50b and 4:4: "The sons of Hur . . . These were the descendants of Hur." The presence of these formulas suggests that this section and 4:1–4 were once a unit; the Chronicler has inserted his record of the Davidic descent (ch. 3) into the middle of this other genealogy, apparently to balance the sections of his material (see notes on 2:10–3:24; 4:1–23). Otherwise the disruption of the genealogy of Hur may have already occurred in the Chronicler's sources.

2:55 Tirathites, Shimeathites and Sucathites. May refer to three families, as translated here, or possibly to three different classes of scribes, perhaps those who (1) read, (2) copied and (3) checked the work. Kenites. Originally a foreign people, many of the Kenites were incorporated into Judah (see Nu 10:29–32; Jdg 1:16; 4:11).
3:1–24 See note on 2:10–3:24.
3:1–9 This list of David's children is largely drawn from 2Sa 3:2–5; 5:13–16; 13:1 (see notes there). The sons born in Jerusalem are repeated in 1Ch 14:3–7. The name Eliphelet occurs twice (vv. 6,8); in 14:5,7 two spellings of the name are given (only one son having this name is mentioned in 2Sa 5:14–16). The reference to David's seven-year rule in Hebron (v. 4) is repeated in 29:27, though the Chronicler does not deal with this period in his narrative. The references to Absalom, Tamar, Adonijah, Amnon and Bathsheba all recall unhappy incidents in the life of David, incidents the Chronicler has omitted from his later narrative (see 2Sa 11–15; 17–18; 1Ki 1).

the fourth, Adonijah[q] the son of Haggith;

[3]the fifth, Shephatiah the son of Abital;

and the sixth, Ithream, by his wife Eglah.

[4]These six were born to David in Hebron,[r] where he reigned seven years and six months.[s] David reigned in Jerusalem thirty-three years, [5]and these were the children born to him there:

Shammua,[e] Shobab, Nathan and Solomon. These four were by Bathsheba[f][t] daughter of Ammiel. [6]There were also Ibhar, Elishua,[g] Eliphelet, [7]Nogah, Nepheg, Japhia, [8]Elishama, Eliada and Eliphelet—nine in all. [9]All these were the sons of David, besides his sons by his concubines. And Tamar[u] was their sister.[v]

The Kings of Judah

[10]Solomon's son was Rehoboam,[w]

Abijah[x] his son,

Asa[y] his son,

Jehoshaphat[z] his son,

[11]Jehoram[h][a] his son,

Ahaziah[b] his son,

Joash[c] his son,

[12]Amaziah[d] his son,

Azariah[e] his son,

Jotham[f] his son,

[13]Ahaz[g] his son,

Hezekiah[h] his son,

Manasseh[i] his son,

[14]Amon[j] his son,

Josiah[k] his son.

[15]The sons of Josiah:

Johanan the firstborn,

Jehoiakim[l] the second son,

Zedekiah[m] the third,

Shallum[n] the fourth.

[16]The successors of Jehoiakim:

Jehoiachin[i][o] his son,

and Zedekiah.[p]

The Royal Line After the Exile

[17]The descendants of Jehoiachin the captive:

Shealtiel[q] his son, [18]Malkiram, Pedaiah, Shenazzar,[r] Jekamiah, Hoshama and Nedabiah.[s]

[19]The sons of Pedaiah:

Zerubbabel[t] and Shimei.

The sons of Zerubbabel:

Meshullam and Hananiah.

Shelomith was their sister.

[20]There were also five others:

Hashubah, Ohel, Berekiah, Hasadiah and Jushab-Hesed.

[21]The descendants of Hananiah:

Cross-reference column

3:2 qIKi 2:22
3:4 rS 2Sa 5:4;
1Ch 29:27
sS 2Sa 5:5
3:5 t2Sa 11:3
3:9 uS 2Sa 13:1
vICh 14:4
3:10
wIKi 14:21-31;
2Ch 12:16
xIKi 15:1-8;
2Ch 13:1
yIKi 15:9-24
z2Ch 17:1-21:3
3:11
a2Ki 8:16-24;
2Ch 21:1
b2Ki 8:25-10:14;
2Ch 22:1-10
c2Ki 11:1-12:21;
2Ch 22:11-24:27
3:12
d2Ki 14:1-22;
2Ch 25:1-28
e2Ki 15:1-7;
2Ch 26:1-23
f2Ki 15:32-38;
2Ch 27:1; Isa 1:1;
Hos 1:1; Mic 1:1
3:13
g2Ki 16:1-20;
2Ch 28:1; Isa 7:1
h2Ki 18:1-20:21;
2Ch 29:1; Isa 1:1;
Jer 26:19;
Hos 1:1; Mic 1:1
i2Ki 21:1-18;
2Ch 33:1
3:14
j2Ki 21:19-26;
2Ch 33:21;
Zep 1:1
k2Ki 22:1;
2Ch 34:1; Jer 1:2;
3:6; 25:3
3:15 lS 2Ki 23:34
mJer 37:1
nS 2Ki 23:31
3:16 oS 2Ki 24:6,
8 pS 2Ki 24:18
3:17 rEzr 3:2
3:18 rEzr 1:8;
5:14 sJer 22:30
3:19 rEzr 2:2;
3:2; 5:2; Ne 7:7;
12:1; Hag 1:1; 2:2; Zec 4:6

e5 Hebrew Shimea, a variant of Shammua   f5 One Hebrew manuscript and Vulgate (see also Septuagint and 2 Samuel 11:3); most Hebrew manuscripts Bathshua   g6 Two Hebrew manuscripts (see also 2 Samuel 5:15 and 1 Chron. 14:5); most Hebrew manuscripts Elishama   h11 Hebrew Joram, a variant of Jehoram   i16 Hebrew Jeconiah, a variant of Jehoiachin; also in verse 17

3:10 Rehoboam. See 2Ch 10–12. Abijah. See 2Ch 13:1–14:1. Asa. See 2Ch 14–16. Jehoshaphat. See 1Ki 22.
3:11 Jehoram. See 2Ch 21.
3:13 Ahaz. See 2Ch 28. Hezekiah. See 2Ch 29–32. Manasseh. See 2Ch 33:1–20.
3:14 Amon. See 2Ch 33:21–25. Josiah. See 2Ki 22:1–23:30; 2Ch 34:1–36:1.
3:15–16 "Johanan the firstborn" is not mentioned elsewhere and may have died before Josiah. The genealogy is segmented at this point, instead of linear as in vv. 10–14. Since Josiah's other three sons would all occupy the throne, the succession was not uniformly father to son. Shallum/Jehoahaz (2Ch 36:2–4; 2Ki 23:30–35) was replaced by Jehoiakim (2Ch 36:5–8; 2Ki 23:34–24:6); Jehoiakim was succeeded by his son Jehoiachin (2Ch 36:9–10; 2Ki 24:8–16). After Jehoiachin was taken captive to Babylon by Nebuchadnezzar, Josiah's third son Zedekiah (2Ki 24:18–20; 2Ch 36:11–14) became the last king of Judah.
3:17–20 Seven sons are attributed to Jehoiachin, but not one succeeded him (see notes on vv. 15–16; Jer 22:30). Tablets found in Babylon dating from the 10th to the 35th year of Nebuchadnezzar (595–570 B.C.) and listing deliveries of rations mention Jehoiachin and five sons as well as other Judahites held in Babylon. Jehoiachin received similar largess from Nebuchadnezzar's successor Evil-Merodach (562–560 B.C.; see 2Ki 25:27–30).
3:18 Shenazzar. May be another spelling of the name Sheshbazzar. If so, the treasures of the temple were con-

signed to his care for return to Judah (Ezr 1:11). He also served for a short time as the first governor of the returnees and made an initial attempt at rebuilding the temple (Ezr 5:14–16). Little is known of him; he soon disappeared from the scene and was overshadowed by his nephew Zerubbabel, who assumes such importance in Ezra, Haggai and Zechariah. But see note on Ezr 1:8.
3:19 Pedaiah. Other texts name Shealtiel (v. 17) as Zerubbabel's father (Ezr 3:2,8; Ne 12:1; Hag 1:12,14; 2:2,23). Suggestions offered to resolve this difficulty are: 1. Shealtiel may have died early, and Pedaiah became the head of the family. 2. Pedaiah may have married the childless widow of Shealtiel; Zerubbabel would then be regarded as the son of Shealtiel according to the law of levirate marriage (Dt 25:5–6). In Lk 3:27 Neri instead of Jehoiachin (v. 17) is identified as the father of Shealtiel. Similar suggestions to those above could be made in this instance as well. It is also interesting to note that the genealogies of Jesus in Mt 1 and Lk 3 both trace his descent to Zerubbabel, but that none of the names subsequent to Zerubbabel (vv. 19–24) is found in the NT genealogies.
3:20 five others. May have been sons of Zerubbabel, but no kinship terms are provided. Since the sons of Hananiah (v. 19) are specified in v. 21, they could also be the sons of Meshullam (v. 19).
3:21 sons of Rephaiah . . . Shecaniah. Probably other Davidic families at the time of Zerubbabel (v. 19) or Pelatiah and Jeshaiah. If they are understood as contemporary with

Pelatiah and Jeshaiah, and the sons of Rephaiah, of Arnan, of Obadiah and of Shecaniah.

22The descendants of Shecaniah:
    Shemaiah and his sons:
    Hattush,*u* Igal, Bariah, Neariah and Shaphat—six in all.
23The sons of Neariah:
    Elioenai, Hizkiah and Azrikam—three in all.
24The sons of Elioenai:
    Hodaviah, Eliashib, Pelaiah, Akkub, Johanan, Delaiah and Anani—seven in all.

Other Clans of Judah

4 The descendants of Judah:*v* Perez, Hezron,*w* Carmi, Hur and Shobal.
2Reaiah son of Shobal was the father of Jahath, and Jahath the father of Ahumai and Lahad. These were the clans of the Zorathites.
3These were the sons*j* of Etam:
    Jezreel, Ishma and Idbash. Their sister was named Hazzelelponi.
4Penuel was the father of Gedor, and Ezer the father of Hushah.
These were the descendants of Hur,*x* the firstborn of Ephrathah and father*k* of Bethlehem.*y*
5Ashhur*z* the father of Tekoa had two wives, Helah and Naarah.
6Naarah bore him Ahuzzam, Hepher, Temeni and Haahashtari. These were the descendants of Naarah.
7The sons of Helah:
    Zereth, Zohar, Ethnan, 8and Koz, who was the father of Anub and

3:22 *u*Ezr 8:2-3
4:1 *v*S Ge 29:35; S 1Ch 2:3
*w*Nu 26:21
4:4 *x*1Ch 2:50
*y*Ru 1:19
4:5 *z*1Ch 2:24

Hazzobebah and of the clans of Aharhel son of Harum.

9Jabez was more honorable than his brothers. His mother had named him Jabez,*l* saying, "I gave birth to him in pain." 10Jabez cried out to the God of Israel, "Oh, that you would bless me and enlarge my territory! Let your hand be with me, and keep me from harm so that I will be free from pain." And God granted his request.

11Kelub, Shuhah's brother, was the father of Mehir, who was the father of Eshton. 12Eshton was the father of Beth Rapha, Paseah and Tehinnah the father of Ir Nahash.*m* These were the men of Recah.

13The sons of Kenaz:
    Othniel*a* and Seraiah.
The sons of Othniel:
    Hathath and Meonothai.*n*
14Meonothai was the father of Ophrah.
Seraiah was the father of Joab, the father of Ge Harashim.*o* It was called this because its people were craftsmen.
15The sons of Caleb son of Jephunneh:
    Iru, Elah and Naam.
The son of Elah:
    Kenaz.
16The sons of Jehallelel:

i3 Some Septuagint manuscripts (see also Vulgate); Hebrew father *k4 Father may mean civic leader or military leader; also in verses 12, 14, 17, 18 and possibly elsewhere.* *l9 Jabez sounds like the Hebrew for pain.* *m12 Or of the city of Nahash* *n13 Some Septuagint manuscripts and Vulgate; Hebrew does not have and Meonothai.* *o14 Ge Harashim means valley of craftsmen.*

4:13 *a*S Jos 15:17

Zerubbabel, his genealogy was carried only two generations (his sons and grandsons) and a date for Chronicles as early as 450 B.C. is possible (see Introduction: Author, Date and Sources).

3:22 *six.* Shemaiah appears to have five sons, but the total is given as six. Either one of the six names is missing, or Shemaiah is to be understood as the brother of the five persons named (in which case there should be a semicolon after "sons" instead of a colon)—all six then being sons of Shecaniah.

4:1–23 None of the genealogies of Judah in this section appears elsewhere in Scripture. Although the section may have the appearance of miscellaneous notes, the careful shaping of the Chronicler is evident in light of the overall inverted structure of the genealogies of Judah:

2:3	Shelah
2:4-8	Perez
2:9-3:24	Hezron
4:1-20	Perez
4:21-23	Shelah

This balancing of the material in inverse order shows the centrality of the section of the lineage of Hezron and the house of David; the same balancing in inverse order is

observed within the Hezron section (see note on 2:10–3:24). The record of Judah's oldest surviving son, Shelah, frames the entire genealogy of Judah. There are 15 fragmentary genealogies in this section, with two to six generations in each.

4:1–2 The descendants of Judah here are not brothers; rather, the genealogy is linear.

4:1 *Carmi.* Either a scribal confusion or an alternative name for Caleb (2:9); the confusion may have been induced by 2:7.

4:2 *Reaiah.* A variant of Haroeh (2:52).

4:5–8 Supplementary to 2:24.

4:9–10 The practice of inserting short historical notes into genealogical records is amply attested in non-Biblical genealogical texts from the ancient Near East as well as in other Biblical genealogies (Ge 4:19–24; 10:8–12).

4:13 *Othniel.* The first of Israel's judges (Jos 15:17; Jdg 1:13; 3:9–11).

4:16–20 This portion of the genealogy is from preexilic times; several of the places named were not included in the province of Judah in the restoration period (e.g., Ziph and Eshtemoa).

Ziph, Ziphah, Tiria and Asarel.
[17]The sons of Ezrah:
Jether, Mered, Epher and Jalon.
One of Mered's wives gave birth to
Miriam,[b] Shammai and Ishbah the
father of Eshtemoa. [18](His Judean
wife gave birth to Jered the father
of Gedor, Heber the father of Soco,
and Jekuthiel the father of Zanoah.[c]) These were the children
of Pharaoh's daughter Bithiah,
whom Mered had married.
[19]The sons of Hodiah's wife, the sister
of Naham:
the father of Keilah[d] the Garmite,
and Eshtemoa the Maacathite.[e]
[20]The sons of Shimon:
Amnon, Rinnah, Ben-Hanan and
Tilon.
The descendants of Ishi:
Zoheth and Ben-Zoheth.
[21]The sons of Shelah[f] son of Judah:
Er the father of Lecah, Laadah the
father of Mareshah and the clans of
the linen workers at Beth Ashbea,
[22]Jokim, the men of Cozeba, and
Joash and Saraph, who ruled in
Moab and Jashubi Lehem. (These
records are from ancient times.)
[23]They were the potters who lived
at Netaim and Gederah; they
stayed there and worked for the
king.

Simeon

4:28-33pp — Jos 19:2-10

[24]The descendants of Simeon:[g]
Nemuel, Jamin, Jarib,[h] Zerah and
Shaul;
[25]Shallum was Shaul's son, Mibsam
his son and Mishma his son.
[26]The descendants of Mishma:
Hammuel his son, Zaccur his son
and Shimei his son.
[27]Shimei had sixteen sons and six
daughters, but his brothers did not have
many children; so their entire clan did not

become as numerous as the people of
Judah. [28]They lived in Beersheba,[i] Moladah,[j] Hazar Shual, [29]Bilhah, Ezem,[k]
Tolad, [30]Bethuel, Hormah,[l] Ziklag,[m]
[31]Beth Marcaboth, Hazar Susim, Beth Biri
and Shaaraim.[n] These were their towns
until the reign of David. [32]Their surrounding villages were Etam, Ain,[o] Rimmon,
Token and Ashan[p]—five towns— [33]and
all the villages around these towns as far as
Baalath.[p] These were their settlements.
And they kept a genealogical record.

[34]Meshobab, Jamlech, Joshah son of
Amaziah, [35]Joel, Jehu son of Joshibiah,
the son of Seraiah, the son of Asiel,
[36]also Elioenai, Jaakobah, Jeshohaiah,
Asaiah, Adiel, Jesimiel, Benaiah, [37]and
Ziza son of Shiphi, the son of Allon,
the son of Jedaiah, the son of Shimri,
the son of Shemaiah.

[38]The men listed above by name were
leaders of their clans. Their families increased greatly, [39]and they went to the
outskirts of Gedor[q] to the east of the valley
in search of pasture for their flocks. [40]They
found rich, good pasture, and the land was
spacious, peaceful and quiet.[r] Some Hamites had lived there formerly.

[41]The men whose names were listed
came in the days of Hezekiah king of
Judah. They attacked the Hamites in their
dwellings and also the Meunites[s] who
were there and completely destroyed[q]
them, as is evident to this day. Then they
settled in their place, because there was
pasture for their flocks. [42]And five hundred
of these Simeonites, led by Pelatiah, Neariah, Rephaiah and Uzziel, the sons of Ishi,
invaded the hill country of Seir.[t] [43]They
killed the remaining Amalekites[u] who had
escaped, and they have lived there to this
day.

4:17 [b]S Ex 15:20
4:18 [c]S Jos 15:34
4:19 [d]S Jos 15:44
[e]S Dt 3:14
4:21 [f]S Ge 38:5
4:24 [g]S Ge 29:33
[h]Nu 26:12

4:28 [i]S Ge 21:14
[j]S Jos 15:26
4:29 [k]S Jos 15:29
4:30 [l]S Nu 14:45
[m]S Jos 15:31
4:31 [n]S Jos 15:36
4:32 [o]S Nu 34:11
[p]S Jos 15:42
4:39 [q]S Jos 15:58
4:40 [r]Jdg 18:7-10
4:41 [s]2Ch 20:1;
26:7
4:42 [t]S Ge 14:6
4:43 [u]S Ge 14:7;
Est 3:1; 9:16

[p]33 Some Septuagint manuscripts (see also Joshua 19:8);
Hebrew *Baal*   [q]41 The Hebrew term refers to the
irrevocable giving over of things or persons to the Lord,
often by totally destroying them.

4:17 *One of Mered's wives.* Pharaoh's daughter (v. 18).
Mered is otherwise unknown; the fact that he married a
daughter of Pharaoh suggests his prominence. The event
may be associated with the fortunes of Israel in Egypt under
Joseph.
4:21,23 This section accurately reflects a feature of ancient
Near Eastern society. Clans were often associated not only
with particular localities but also with special trades or
guilds, such as linen workers (v. 21), potters (v. 23), royal
patronage (v. 23) and scribes (2:55).
4:24-43 The genealogy of Simeon is also found in Ge
46:10; Ex 6:15; Nu 26:12-13. Simeon settled in part of the
territory of Judah; the list of occupied towns should be
compared with Jos 15:26-32,42; 19:2-7. Since Simeon

occupied areas allotted to Judah, this tribe was politically
incorporated into Judah and appears to have lost much of its
own identity in history (see Ge 34:24-31; 49:5-7; see also
notes on Ge 34:25; 49:7). Geographical and historical notes
are inserted in the genealogy (see note on vv. 9-10). Apparently two genealogies are included here: vv. 24-33—ending with the formula, "they kept a genealogical
record"—and vv. 34-43. Overpopulation (v. 38) caused
them to expand toward Gedor and east toward Edom at the
time of Hezekiah (vv. 39-43). The long hostility between
Israel and Amalek surfaced once again (v. 43; cf. Ex
17:8-16; Dt 25:17-19; 1Sa 15; see Introduction to Esther:
Purpose and Theme).

Reuben

5 The sons of Reuben[v] the firstborn of
Israel (he was the firstborn, but when
he defiled his father's marriage bed,[w] his
rights as firstborn were given to the sons of
Joseph[x] son of Israel;[y] so he could not be
listed in the genealogical record in accordance with his birthright,[z] 2and though
Judah[a] was the strongest of his brothers
and a ruler[b] came from him, the rights of
the firstborn[c] belonged to Joseph)— 3the
sons of Reuben[d] the firstborn of Israel:

Hanoch, Pallu,[e] Hezron[f] and Carmi.

4The descendants of Joel:

Shemaiah his son, Gog his son,
Shimei his son, 5Micah his son,
Reaiah his son, Baal his son,
6and Beerah his son, whom Tiglath-
Pileser[r][g] king of Assyria took into
exile. Beerah was a leader of the
Reubenites.

7Their relatives by clans,[h] listed according to their genealogical records:

Jeiel the chief, Zechariah, 8and
Bela son of Azaz, the son of
Shema, the son of Joel. They settled in the area from Aroer[i] to
Nebo[j] and Baal Meon.[k] 9To the
east they occupied the land up to
the edge of the desert that extends
to the Euphrates[l] River, because
their livestock had increased in
Gilead.[m]

10During Saul's reign they waged
war against the Hagrites[n], who
were defeated at their hands; they
occupied the dwellings of the Hagrites throughout the entire region
east of Gilead.

Gad

11The Gadites[o] lived next to them in
Bashan, as far as Salecah:[p]

12Joel was the chief, Shapham the
second, then Janai and Shaphat, in
Bashan.

13Their relatives, by families, were:

Michael, Meshullam, Sheba, Jorai,
Jacan, Zia and Eber—seven in all.

14These were the sons of Abihail son
of Huri, the son of Jaroah, the son
of Gilead, the son of Michael, the
son of Jeshishai, the son of Jahdo,
the son of Buz.

15Ahi son of Abdiel, the son of Guni,
was head of their family.

16The Gadites lived in Gilead, in Bashan and its outlying villages, and
on all the pasturelands of Sharon as
far as they extended.

17All these were entered in the genealogical records during the reigns of Jotham[q] king of Judah and Jeroboam[r] king
of Israel.

18The Reubenites, the Gadites and the
half-tribe of Manasseh had 44,760 men
ready for military service[s]—able-bodied
men who could handle shield and sword,
who could use a bow, and who were
trained for battle. 19They waged war
against the Hagrites, Jetur,[t] Naphish and
Nodab. 20They were helped[u] in fighting
them, and God handed the Hagrites and all
their allies over to them, because they
cried[v] out to him during the battle. He
answered their prayers, because they
trusted[w] in him. 21They seized the live-

5:1 [v]S Ge 29:32 [w]Ge 35:22; 49:4 [x]S Ge 48:16; S 49:26 [y]Ge 48:5 [z]1Ch 26:10 **5:2** [a]S Ge 49:10, 12 [b]S 1Sa 9:16; S 12:12; S 2Sa 6:21; 1Ch 11:2; S 2Ch 7:18; Mt 2:6 [c]S Ge 25:31 **5:3** [d]S Ge 29:32; 46:9; Ex 6:14; Nu 26:5-11 [e]S Nu 26:5 [f]S Nu 26:6 **5:6** [g]ver 26; S 2Ki 15:19; 16:10; 2Ch 28:20 **5:7** [h]Jos 13:15-23 **5:8** [i]S Nu 32:34; Jdg 11:26 [j]S Nu 32:3 [k]S Jos 13:17 **5:9** [l]S Ge 2:14 [m]S Nu 32:26 **5:10** [n]ver 22; 1Ch 27:31

5:11 [o]S Ge 30:11; S Nu 1:25; S Jos 13:24-28 [p]S Dt 3:10 **5:17** [q]S 2Ki 15:32 [r]S 2Ki 14:23 **5:18** [s]S Nu 1:3 **5:19** [t]Ge 25:15 **5:20** [u]Ps 37:40; 46:5; 54:4 [v]1Ki 8:44; 2Ch 6:34; 13:14; 14:11; Ps 20:7-9; 22:5; 107:6 [w]Ps 26:1; Isa 26:3; Da 6:23

[r]6 Hebrew *Tilgath-Pilneser,* a variant of *Tiglath-Pileser,* also in verse 26

5:1–26 The genealogical records of the Transjordan tribes: Reuben, Gad and half of Manasseh (see Nu 32:33–42). The Chronicler's concern with "all Israel" includes incorporating the genealogical records of these tribes that were no longer significant entities in Israel's life in the restoration period, having been swept away in the Assyrian conquests.

5:1–10 The necessity to explain why the birthright of the firstborn did not remain with Reuben (see Ge 35:22; 49:4 for Reuben's sin) interrupts the initial statement (v. 1), which is then repeated after the explanation (v. 3). The parenthetical material (vv. 1–2) shows the writer's partiality for Judah, even though Joseph received the double portion (Ephraim and Manasseh) of the firstborn. The Hebrew term translated "ruler" (v. 2) is used of David in 11:2; 17:7; 2Sa 5:2; 6:21; 7:8; cf. 1Ch 28:4. The use of military titles (vv. 6–7) and a battle account (v. 10) suggest that this genealogy may have functioned in military organization (see Introduction: Genealogies). The source for some of this material on Reuben is Nu 26:5–11. The Chronicler has omitted reference to Eliab and his three sons who perished in the rebellion of Korah (see Nu 26:8–10) and so were not relevant to his purpose.

5:6 *Tiglath-Pileser.* This Assyrian king (745–727 B.C.) attacked Israel (v. 26; 2Ki 15:29) and also imposed tribute on Ahaz of Judah (2Ch 28:19–20; 2Ki 16:7–10).

5:10 *Hagrites.* See vv. 19–22. Named among the enemies of Israel (Ps 83:6), this tribe is apparently associated with Hagar, the mother of Ishmael (Ge 16), but see note on Ps 83:6.

5:11–22 The materials in this list for the tribe of Gad have no parallels in the Bible. The other genealogies of Gad are organized around his seven sons (Ge 46:16; Nu 26:15–18); here four names are given, none found in the other lists. The Chronicler states (v. 17) that these records came from the period of Jotham of Judah (750–732 B.C.) and Jeroboam of Israel (793–753). The presence of military titles and narratives (vv. 12,18–22) suggests that this genealogy originated as part of a military census. The territory of Gad is delineated in Dt 3:12.

5:18–22 The first example of the Chronicler's theme of immediate retribution (see Introduction: Purpose and Themes). Success in warfare is attributed to their crying out to God (v. 20; cf. 2Ch 6:24–25,34–39; 12:7–12; 13:13–16; 14:9–15; 18:31; 20:1–30; 32:1–23).

stock of the Hagrites—fifty thousand camels, two hundred fifty thousand sheep and two thousand donkeys. They also took one hundred thousand people captive, 22and many others fell slain, because the battle[x] was God's. And they occupied the land until the exile.[y]

The Half-Tribe of Manasseh

23The people of the half-tribe of Manasseh[z] were numerous; they settled in the land from Bashan to Baal Hermon, that is, to Senir (Mount Hermon).[a]

24These were the heads of their families: Epher, Ishi, Eliel, Azriel, Jeremiah, Hodaviah and Jahdiel. They were brave warriors, famous men, and heads of their families. 25But they were unfaithful[b] to the God of their fathers and prostituted[c] themselves to the gods of the peoples of the land, whom God had destroyed before them. 26So the God of Israel stirred up the spirit[d] of Pul[e] king of Assyria (that is, Tiglath-Pileser[f] king of Assyria), who took the Reubenites, the Gadites and the half-tribe of Manasseh into exile. He took them to Halah,[g] Habor, Hara and the river of Gozan, where they are to this day.

Levi

6 The sons of Levi:[h]
Gershon, Kohath and Merari.
2The sons of Kohath:

Amram, Izhar, Hebron and Uzziel.[i]

3The children of Amram:
Aaron, Moses and Miriam.[j]
The sons of Aaron:
Nadab, Abihu,[k] Eleazar[l] and Ithamar.[m]

4Eleazar was the father of Phinehas,[n]
Phinehas the father of Abishua,
5Abishua the father of Bukki,
Bukki the father of Uzzi,
6Uzzi the father of Zerahiah,
Zerahiah the father of Meraioth,
7Meraioth the father of Amariah,
Amariah the father of Ahitub,
8Ahitub the father of Zadok,[o]
Zadok the father of Ahimaaz,
9Ahimaaz the father of Azariah,
Azariah the father of Johanan,
10Johanan the father of Azariah[p] (it was he who served as priest in the temple Solomon built in Jerusalem),
11Azariah the father of Amariah,
Amariah the father of Ahitub,
12Ahitub the father of Zadok,
Zadok the father of Shallum,
13Shallum the father of Hilkiah,[q]
Hilkiah the father of Azariah,
14Azariah the father of Seraiah,[r]
and Seraiah the father of Jehozadak.

Cross-reference column

5:22 xS Dt 20:4; 2Ch 32:8 yS ver 10; S 2Ki 15:29
5:23 z1Ch 7:14 aS Dt 3:8,9;
5:25 SS 4:8
bDt 32:15-18; 1Ch 9:1; 10:13; 2Ch 12:2; 26:16; 28:19; 29:6; 30:7; 36:14 cS Ex 34:15; S Lev 18:3
5:26 d1sa 37:7 eS 2Ki 15:19 fS ver 6; S 2Ki 15:29 g2Ki 17:6
6:1 hS Ge 29:34; S Nu 3:17
6:2 iS Ex 6:18
6:3 jS Ex 15:20 kS Lev 10:1; S 10:1-20:2 lLev 10:6 mS Ex 6:23
6:4 nEzr 7:5
6:8 oS 2Sa 8:17; S 1Ch 12:28; S Ezr 7:2
6:10 pS 1Ki 4:2
6:13 q2Ki 22:1-20; 2Ch 34:9; 35:8
6:14 rS 2Ki 25:18; S Ezr 2:2

5:23–26 Manasseh is treated further in 7:14–19; the half-tribe that settled in Transjordan is dealt with here since it shared the same fate as Reuben and Gad, and possibly also so that the Chronicler could keep the total of 12 for his tribal genealogies (see note on 2:1–2). Again immediate retribution is apparent: Just as trust in God can bring victory (vv. 18–22), so also defeat comes to the unfaithful (vv. 25–26). The use of the retributive theme in these two accounts argues for the unity of the genealogies with the historical portions of Chronicles. The list of names given here is not properly a genealogy but a list of clans. Since they are described as brave warriors in connection with a battle report (vv. 24–26), this section too is likely derived from records of military conscription (see note on vv. 1–10; see also 2Ki 15:19,29; 17:6; 18:11).
5:26 *Pul.* Probably Tiglath-Pileser's throne name in Babylon (the Babylonians called him Pulu).
6:1–81 This chapter is devoted to a series of lists, all pertaining to the tribe of Levi. The first section (vv. 1–15) records the line of the high priests down to the exile; the clans of Levi follow (vv. 16–30). David's appointees as temple musicians came from the three clans of Levi: Gershon, Kohath and Merari (vv. 31–47). The generations between Aaron and Ahimaaz are given a separate listing (vv. 49–53), reinforcing the separate duties of priests and Levites (see note on Ex 32:26). The listing of the Levitical possessions among the tribes concludes the chapter (vv. 54–81).
6:1–3 A short segmented genealogy narrows the descendants of Levi to the lineage of Eleazar, in whose line the high priests are presented in linear form (vv. 4–15). The sons of Levi (v. 1) always appear in this order, based on age (v. 16;

Ge 46:11; Ex 6:16; Nu 3:17; 26:57). Of Aaron's four sons (v. 3), the first two died as a result of sacrilege (Lev 10:2; Nu 26:61); succeeding generations of priests would trace their lineage to either Eleazar or Ithamar.
6:4–15 This list of high priests from the time of Eleazar to the exile has been sharply telescoped. The following high priests known from the OT are not mentioned: Jehoiada (2Ki 12:2), Uriah (2Ki 16:10–16), possibly two other Azariahs (2Ch 26:17,20; 31:10–13), Eli (1Sa 1:9; 14:3) and Abiathar (2Sa 8:17). The list is repeated with some variation in Ezr 7:1–5 (see notes there).
6:8 *Ahitub the father of Zadok.* This Zadok was one of David's two priests (18:16; 2Sa 8:17). When David's other priest, Abiathar (see note on vv. 4–15), supported the rebellion of Adonijah, Zadok supported Solomon (1Ki 1). After the expulsion of Abiathar (1Ki 2:26–27), Zadok alone held the office (1Ch 29:22), which continued in his line (1Ki 4:2). The Ahitub mentioned here should not be confused with the priest who was the grandson of Eli (1Sa 14:3) and grandfather of Abiathar (1Sa 22:20); the line of Zadok replaced the line of Eli (1Sa 2:27–36; 1Ki 2:26–27). For the importance of the line of Zadok see Eze 40:46; 43:19; 44:15; 48:11. Ezra was concerned to trace his own priestly lineage to this house (Ezr 7:1–5).
6:13 *Hilkiah.* Discovered the Book of the Law in the temple at the time of Josiah (2Ki 22; 2Ch 34).
6:14 *Seraiah.* Executed by the Babylonians after the conquest of Jerusalem in 586 B.C. (2Ki 25:18–21). *Jehozadak.* Father of Jeshua, the high priest in the first generation of the restoration (Ezr 3:2; 5:2; 10:18; Hag 1:1; 2:2; Zec 3:1; 6:11); his name is also spelled "Jozadak."

[15]Jehozadak[s] was deported when the LORD sent Judah and Jerusalem into exile by the hand of Nebuchadnezzar.

[16]The sons of Levi:[t]
Gershon,[s] Kohath and Merari.[u]
[17]These are the names of the sons of Gershon:
Libni and Shimei.[v]
[18]The sons of Kohath:
Amram, Izhar, Hebron and Uzziel.[w]
[19]The sons of Merari:[x]
Mahli and Mushi.[y]
These are the clans of the Levites listed according to their fathers:
[20]Of Gershon:
Libni his son, Jehath his son, Zimmah his son, [21]Joah his son, Iddo his son, Zerah his son and Jeatherai his son.
[22]The descendants of Kohath:
Amminadab his son, Korah[z] his son,
Assir his son, [23]Elkanah his son, Ebiasaph his son, Assir his son,
[24]Tahath his son, Uriel[a] his son, Uzziah his son and Shaul his son.
[25]The descendants of Elkanah:
Amasai, Ahimoth,
[26]Elkanah his son,[t] Zophai his son, Nahath his son, [27]Eliab his son, Jeroham his son, Elkanah[b] his son and Samuel[c] his son.[u]
[28]The sons of Samuel:
Joel[v][d] the firstborn
and Abijah the second son.
[29]The descendants of Merari:
Mahli, Libni his son,
Shimei his son, Uzzah his son,
[30]Shimea his son, Haggiah his son

and Asaiah his son.

The Temple Musicians

6:54–80pp — Jos 21:4–39

[31]These are the men[e] David put in charge of the music[f] in the house of the LORD after the ark came to rest there. [32]They ministered with music before the tabernacle, the Tent of Meeting, until Solomon built the temple of the LORD in Jerusalem. They performed their duties according to the regulations laid down for them.
[33]Here are the men who served, together with their sons:
From the Kohathites:
Heman,[g] the musician,
the son of Joel,[h] the son of Samuel,
[34]the son of Elkanah,[i] the son of Jeroham,
the son of Eliel, the son of Toah,
[35]the son of Zuph, the son of Elkanah,
the son of Mahath, the son of Amasai,
[36]the son of Elkanah, the son of Joel, the son of Azariah, the son of Zephaniah,
[37]the son of Tahath, the son of Assir, the son of Ebiasaph, the son of Korah,[j]

6:15 [s]Ne 12:1; Hag 1:1,14; 2:2, 4; Zec 6:11
6:16 [t]S Ge 29:34; S Nu 3:17-20 [u]S Nu 26:57
6:17 [v]S Ex 6:17
6:18 [w]S Ex 6:18
6:19 [x]S Ge 46:11; 1Ch 23:21; 24:26 [y]S Ex 6:19
6:22 [z]S Ex 6:24
6:24 [a]1Ch 15:5
6:27 [b]S 1Sa 1:1 [c]S 1Sa 1:20
6:28 [d]ver 33; 1Sa 8:2

6:31 [e]1Ch 25:1; 2Ch 29:25-26; Ne 12:45 [f]1Ch 9:33; 15:19; Ezr 3:10; Ps 68:25
6:33 [g]1Ki 4:31; 1Ch 15:17; 25:1 [h]S ver 28
6:34 [i]S 1Sa 1:1
6:37 [j]S Ex 6:24

[s]*16* Hebrew *Gershom*, a variant of *Gershon*; also in verses 17, 20, 43, 62 and 71   [t]*26* Some Hebrew manuscripts, Septuagint and Syriac; most Hebrew manuscripts *Ahimoth* 26*and Elkanah. The sons of Elkanah*:   [u]*27* Some Septuagint manuscripts (see also 1 Samuel 1:19,20 and 1 Chron. 6:33,34); Hebrew does not have *and Samuel his son.*   [v]*28* Some Septuagint manuscripts and Syriac (see also 1 Samuel 8:2 and 1 Chron. 6:33); Hebrew does not have *Joel.*

6:16–19a Repeated from Ex 6:16–19; Nu 3:17–20; 26:57–61.
6:22–23 *Assir . . . Elkanah . . . Ebiasaph.* Ex 6:24 names these men as sons of Korah, but here they are presented in the form ordinarily used for a linear genealogy of successive generations (see vv. 20–21,25–26,29–30). Either this is another example of genealogical fluidity, or one must understand "his son" as referring to Kohath and not to the immediately preceding name.
6:22 *Amminadab.* The almost parallel genealogy later in this chapter lists Izhar in the place of Amminadab—who is nowhere else listed as a son of Kohath, while every other list includes Izhar (vv. 2,37–38; Ex 6:18,21). Either Amminadab is an otherwise unattested alternative name of Izhar, or he is an otherwise unknown son. Or this may be another example of genealogical fluidity in which the Levites are linked with the tribe of Judah and the lineage of David (see Ru 4:18–22; see also Mt 1:4; Lk 3:33) in view of Aaron's marriage to the daughter of Amminadab of Judah (Ex 6:23; see 1Ch 2:10).
6:24 *Uriel.* Possibly the one who led the Kohathites in David's day (15:5).

6:26–27 *Zophai . . . Nahath . . . Eliab.* Apparently variant names for Zuph, Toah and Eliel (vv. 34–35).
6:27 *Samuel.* His lineage is also given in 1Sa 1:1, where his family is identified as Ephraimite (see note there). Either this is an example of genealogical fluidity, in which Samuel's involvement in the tabernacle (1Sa 3) and performance of priestly duties (9:22; 1Sa 2:18; 3:1) resulted in his incorporation into the Levites, or the term "Ephraimite" is to be understood as a place of residence, not as a statement of lineage.
6:31–48 Each of the three Levitical clans contributed musicians for the temple: Heman from the family of Kohath, Asaph from Gershon, and Ethan from Merari. The Chronicler makes frequent reference to the appointment of the musical guilds by David (15:16,27; 25:1-31; 2Ch 29:25–26; see Ne 12:45–47). The frequent mention of the role of the Levites has led many to assume that the author was a member of the musicians. Non-Biblical literature also attests to guilds of singers and musicians in Canaanite temples. This genealogy appears to function as a means of legitimizing the Levites of the restoration period (Ezr 2:40–41; Ne 7:43–44; 10:9–13, 28–29; 11:15–18; 12:24–47).

38the son of Izhar,k the son of Kohath,

the son of Levi, the son of Israel;
39and Heman's associate Asaph,l who served at his right hand:

Asaph son of Berekiah, the son of Shimea,m
40the son of Michael, the son of Baaseiah,w

the son of Malkijah, 41the son of Ethni,

the son of Zerah, the son of Adaiah,
42the son of Ethan, the son of Zimmah,

the son of Shimei, 43the son of Jahath,

the son of Gershon, the son of Levi;
44and from their associates, the Merarites,n at his left hand:

Ethan son of Kishi, the son of Abdi, the son of Malluch, 45the son of Hashabiah,

the son of Amaziah, the son of Hilkiah,
46the son of Amzi, the son of Bani,

the son of Shemer, 47the son of Mahli,

the son of Mushi, the son of Merari,

the son of Levi.

48Their fellow Leviteso were assigned to all the other duties of the tabernacle, the house of God. 49But Aaron and his descendants were the ones who presented offerings on the altarp of burnt offering and on the altar of incenseq in connection with all that was done in the Most Holy Place, making atonement for Israel, in accordance with all that Moses the servant of God had commanded.

50These were the descendants of Aaron:

Eleazar his son, Phinehas his son, Abishua his son, 51Bukki his son, Uzzi his son, Zerahiah his son,

52Meraioth his son, Amariah his son, Ahitub his son, 53Zadokr his son and Ahimaaz his son.

54These were the locations of their settlementss allotted as their territory (they were assigned to the descendants of Aaron

who were from the Kohathite clan, because the first lot was for them):

55They were given Hebron in Judah with its surrounding pasturelands. 56But the fields and villages around the city were given to Caleb son of Jephunneh.t

57So the descendants of Aaron were given Hebron (a city of refuge), and Libnah,x u Jattir,v Eshtemoa, 58Hilen, Debir,w 59Ashan,x Juttahy and Beth Shemesh, together with their pasturelands. 60And from the tribe of Benjamin they were given Gibeon,z Geba, Alemeth and Anathoth,y together with their pasturelands.

These towns, which were distributed among the Kohathite clans, were thirteen in all.

61The rest of Kohath's descendants were allotted ten towns from the clans of half the tribe of Manasseh.

62The descendants of Gershon, clan by clan, were allotted thirteen towns from the tribes of Issachar, Asher and Naphtali, and from the part of the tribe of Manasseh that is in Bashan.

63The descendants of Merari, clan by clan, were allotted twelve towns from the tribes of Reuben, Gad and Zebulun.

64So the Israelites gave the Levites these townsz and their pasturelands. 65From the tribes of Judah, Simeon and Benjamin they allotted the previously named towns.

66Some of the Kohathite clans were given as their territory towns from the tribe of Ephraim.

67In the hill country of Ephraim they were given Shechem (a city of refuge), and Gezer,a a 68Jokmeam,b Beth Horon,c 69Aijalond and Gath Rimmon,e together with their pasturelands.

70And from half the tribe of Manasseh the Israelites gave Aner and Bileam, together with their pasturelands, to the rest of the Kohathite clans.

6:38 kEx 6:21
6:39 l1Ch 25:1, 9; 2Ch 29:13; Ne 11:17
m1Ch 15:17
6:44 n1Ch 15:17
6:48 o1Ch 23:32
6:49 pEx 27:1-8
qS Ex 30:7; 2Ch 26:18
6:53 rS 2Sa 8:17
6:54 sS Nu 31:10

6:56 tS Jos 14:13; S 15:13
6:57 uS Nu 33:20
vS Jos 15:48
6:58 wS Jos 10:3
6:59 xS Jos 15:42
6:60 yJer 1:1
6:64 zNu 35:1-8
6:67 aS Jos 10:33
6:68 b1Ki 4:12
cS Jos 10:10
6:69 dS Jos 10:12
eS Jos 19:45

w40 Most Hebrew manuscripts; some Hebrew manuscripts, one Septuagint manuscript and Syriac Maaseiah   x57 See Joshua 21:13; Hebrew given the cities of refuge: Hebron, Libnah.   y59 Syriac (see also Septuagint and Joshua 21:16); Hebrew does not have Juttah.   z60 See Joshua 21:17; Hebrew does not have Gibeon.   a67 See Joshua 21:21; Hebrew given the cities of refuge: Shechem, Gezer.

6:49–53 Repeats vv. 4–8 but presumably serves a different function: to legitimize the line of Zadok, which is traced down to Solomon's time, as the only Levitical division authorized to offer sacrifices.

6:54–81 This list of Levitical possessions is taken from Jos 21 with only minor differences (see notes there). The Levites, who were given no block of territory of their own, were distributed throughout Israel.

⁷¹The Gershonites*f* received the following:

From the clan of the half-tribe of Manasseh

they received Golan in Bashan*g* and also Ashtaroth, together with their pasturelands;

⁷²from the tribe of Issachar

they received Kedesh, Daberath,*h*

⁷³Ramoth and Anem, together with their pasturelands;

⁷⁴from the tribe of Asher

they received Mashal, Abdon,*i*

⁷⁵Hukok*j* and Rehob,*k* together with their pasturelands;

⁷⁶and from the tribe of Naphtali

they received Kedesh in Galilee, Hammon*l* and Kiriathaim,*m* together with their pasturelands.

⁷⁷The Merarites (the rest of the Levites) received the following:

From the tribe of Zebulun

they received Jokneam, Kartah,*b* Rimmono and Tabor, together with their pasturelands;

⁷⁸from the tribe of Reuben across the Jordan east of Jericho

they received Bezer*n* in the desert, Jahzah, ⁷⁹Kedemoth*o* and Mephaath, together with their pasturelands;

⁸⁰and from the tribe of Gad

they received Ramoth in Gilead,*p* Mahanaim,*q* ⁸¹Heshbon and Jazer,*r* together with their pasturelands.*s*

Issachar

7 The sons of Issachar:*t*
Tola, Puah,*u* Jashub and Shimron—four in all.

²The sons of Tola:

Uzzi, Rephaiah, Jeriel, Jahmai, Ibsam and Samuel—heads of their families. During the reign of David, the descendants of Tola listed as fighting men in their genealogy numbered 22,600.

³The son of Uzzi:

Izrahiah.

The sons of Izrahiah:

Michael, Obadiah, Joel and Isshiah. All five of them were chiefs.

⁴According to their family genealogy, they had 36,000 men ready for battle, for they had many wives and children.

⁵The relatives who were fighting men belonging to all the clans of Issachar, as listed in their genealogy, were 87,000 in all.

Benjamin

⁶Three sons of Benjamin:*v*

Bela, Beker and Jediael.

⁷The sons of Bela:

Ezbon, Uzzi, Uzziel, Jerimoth and Iri, heads of families—five in all. Their genealogical record listed 22,034 fighting men.

⁸The sons of Beker:

Zemirah, Joash, Eliezer, Elioenai, Omri, Jeremoth, Abijah, Anathoth and Alemeth. All these were the sons of Beker. ⁹Their genealogical record listed the heads of families and 20,200 fighting men.

¹⁰The son of Jediael:

Bilhan.

The sons of Bilhan:

Jeush, Benjamin, Ehud, Kenaanah, Zethan, Tarshish and Ahishahar. ¹¹All these sons of Jediael were heads of families. There were 17,200 fighting men ready to go out to war.

¹²The Shuppites and Huppites were the descendants of Ir, and the Hushites the descendants of Aher.

Naphtali

¹³The sons of Naphtali:*w*

Jahziel, Guni, Jezer and Shillem*c*—the descendants of Bilhah.

Manasseh

¹⁴The descendants of Manasseh:*x*

6:71 *f* 1Ch 23:7
g S Jos 20:8
6:72 *h* S Jos 19:12
6:74 *i* S Jos 19:28
6:75 *j* Jos 19:34
k S Nu 13:21
6:76 *l* Jos 19:28
m S Nu 32:37
6:78 *n* S Jos 20:8
6:79 *o* S Dt 2:26
6:80 *p* Jos 20:8
q S Ge 32:2
6:81 *r* S Nu 21:32
s 2Ch 11:14
7:1 *t* S Ge 30:18
u S Ge 46:13

7:6 *v* S Nu 26:38
7:13 *w* S Ge 30:8
7:14
x S Ge 41:51;
S Jos 17:1;
1Ch 5:23

b 77 See Septuagint and Joshua 21:34; Hebrew does not have *Jokneam, Kartah.*   *c 13* Some Hebrew and Septuagint manuscripts (see also Gen. 46:24 and Num. 26:49); most Hebrew manuscripts *Shallum*

7:1–5 Parts of the genealogy of Issachar are taken from Ge 46:13; Nu 1:28; 26:23–25, though many of the names are otherwise unattested. This list of the clans appears to come from a military muster (vv. 2,4–5) from the time of David (v. 2), perhaps reflecting the census of ch. 21 and 2Sa 24. **7:6–12** There is considerable fluidity among the Biblical sources listing the sons of Benjamin. This list gives three sons; Ge 46:21 records ten; Nu 26:38–39 and 1Ch 8:1–2 both list five (the only name appearing in all these sources is Bela, the firstborn). The variations reflect different origins

and functions for these genealogies. The list here appears to function in the military sphere (vv. 7,9,11). **7:13** Repeats Ge 46:24; Nu 26:48–50. *descendants of Bilhah.* Dan and Naphtali were the actual "sons" of Jacob's concubine Bilhah (Ge 30:3–8), so Naphtali's sons are Bilhah's "descendants." **7:14–19** See note on 5:23–26. The sources for this genealogy are Nu 26:29–34; Jos 17:1–18. The daughters of Zelophehad (v. 15) prompted the rulings on the inheritance rights of women (Nu 26:29–34; 27:1–11; 36:1–12; Jos

Asriel was his descendant through his Aramean concubine. She gave birth to Makir the father of Gilead.[y] [15]Makir took a wife from among the Huppites and Shuppites. His sister's name was Maacah.

Another descendant was named Zelophehad,[z] who had only daughters.

[16]Makir's wife Maacah gave birth to a son and named him Peresh. His brother was named Sheresh, and his sons were Ulam and Rakem.

[17]The son of Ulam:

Bedan.

These were the sons of Gilead[a] son of Makir, the son of Manasseh. [18]His sister Hammoleketh gave birth to Ishhod, Abiezer[b] and Mahlah.

[19]The sons of Shemida[c] were:

Ahian, Shechem, Likhi and Aniam.

Ephraim

[20]The descendants of Ephraim:[d]

Shuthelah, Bered his son,

Tahath his son, Eleadah his son, Tahath his son, [21]Zabad his son and Shuthelah his son.

Ezer and Elead were killed by the native-born men of Gath, when they went down to seize their livestock. [22]Their father Ephraim mourned for them many days, and his relatives came to comfort him. [23]Then he lay with his wife again, and she became pregnant and gave birth to a son. He named him Beriah,[d] because there had been misfortune in his family. [24]His daughter was Sheerah, who built Lower and Upper Beth Horon[e] as well as Uzzen Sheerah.

[25]Rephah was his son, Resheph his son,[e]

Telah his son, Tahan his son,

[26]Ladan his son, Ammihud his son, Elishama his son, [27]Nun his son and Joshua his son.

[28]Their lands and settlements included

Bethel and its surrounding villages, Naaran to the east, Gezer[f] and its villages to the west, and Shechem and its villages all the way to Ayyah and its villages. [29]Along the borders of Manasseh were Beth Shan,[g] Taanach, Megiddo and Dor,[h] together with their villages. The descendants of Joseph son of Israel lived in these towns.

Asher

[30]The sons of Asher:[i]

Imnah, Ishvah, Ishvi and Beriah. Their sister was Serah.

[31]The sons of Beriah:

Heber and Malkiel, who was the father of Birzaith.

[32]Heber was the father of Japhlet, Shomer and Hotham and of their sister Shua.

[33]The sons of Japhlet:

Pasach, Bimhal and Ashvath. These were Japhlet's sons.

[34]The sons of Shomer:

Ahi, Rohgah,[f] Hubbah and Aram.

[35]The sons of his brother Helem:

Zophah, Imna, Shelesh and Amal.

[36]The sons of Zophah:

Suah, Harnepher, Shual, Beri, Imrah, [37]Bezer, Hod, Shamma, Shilshah, Ithran[g] and Beera.

[38]The sons of Jether:

Jephunneh, Pispah and Ara.

[39]The sons of Ulla:

Arah, Hanniel and Rizia.

[40]All these were descendants of Asher—heads of families, choice men, brave warriors and outstanding leaders. The number of men ready for battle, as listed in their genealogy, was 26,000.

The Genealogy of Saul the Benjamite

8:28–38pp — 1Ch 9:34–44

8 Benjamin[j] was the father of Bela his firstborn,

Cross references

7:14 [y]S Nu 26:30
7:15 [z]S Nu 26:33; 36:1-12
7:17 [a]S Nu 26:30
7:18 [b]S Jos 17:2
7:19 [c]Jos 17:2
7:20 [d]S Ge 41:52; S Nu 1:33
7:24 [e]S Jos 10:10
7:28 [f]Jos 10:33
7:29 [g]S Jos 17:11 [h]S Jos 11:2
7:30 [i]S Nu 1:40
8:1 [j]S Ge 46:21

Footnotes

[d] 23 Beriah sounds like the Hebrew for misfortune.
[e] 25 Some Septuagint manuscripts; Hebrew does not have his son.   [f] 34 Or of his brother Shomer: Rohgah
[g] 37 Possibly a variant of Jether

17:3–4). Of the 13 different clans of the tribe of Manasseh known from these genealogies, seven are mentioned in the Samaria ostraca (about 65 inscribed potsherds containing records of deliveries of wine, oil, barley and other commodities in the eighth century B.C.). The prominence of women in this genealogy is unusual; this suggests that it may have functioned in the domestic sphere, perhaps as a statement of the social status of the various clans of Manasseh (see Introduction: Genealogies).

7:20–29 The source for part of the genealogy of Ephraim is Nu 26:35. If Rephah (v. 25) is the grandson of Ephraim, ten generations are recorded from Ephraim to Joshua, a number

that fits very well the 400-year interval when Israel was in Egypt. Joshua's Ephraimite ancestry is also mentioned in Nu 13:8 (where he is called "Hoshea"; see Nu 13:16). The raid against Gath (vv. 21–22) must have taken place well before the conquest of Canaan and must have originated in Egypt. The list of settlements (vv. 28–29) summarizes Jos 16–17.

7:30–40 The genealogy of Asher follows Ge 46:17 for the first three generations; it is also parallel to Nu 26:44–46, except that the name Ishvah (v. 30) is missing there. This genealogy too reflects a military function (v. 40).

8:1–40 The inclusion of a second and even more extensive genealogy of Benjamin (see note on 7:6–12) reflects both the

Ashbel the second son, Aharah the third,
2Nohah the fourth and Rapha the fifth.
3The sons of Bela were:

Addar,k Gera, Abihud,h 4Abishua, Naaman, Ahoah,l 5Gera, Shephuphan and Huram.

6These were the descendants of Ehud,m who were heads of families of those living in Geba and were deported to Manahath:

7Naaman, Ahijah, and Gera, who deported them and who was the father of Uzza and Ahihud.

8Sons were born to Shaharaim in Moab after he had divorced his wives Hushim and Baara. 9By his wife Hodesh he had Jobab, Zibia, Mesha, Malcam, 10Jeuz, Sakia and Mirmah. These were his sons, heads of families. 11By Hushim he had Abitub and Elpaal.

12The sons of Elpaal:

Eber, Misham, Shemed (who built Onon and Lod with its surrounding villages), 13and Beriah and Shema, who were heads of families of those living in Aijalono and who drove out the inhabitants of Gath.p

14Ahio, Shashak, Jeremoth, 15Zebadiah, Arad, Eder, 16Michael, Ishpah and Joha were the sons of Beriah.

17Zebadiah, Meshullam, Hizki, Heber, 18Ishmerai, Izliah and Jobab were the sons of Elpaal.

19Jakim, Zicri, Zabdi, 20Elienai, Zillethai, Eliel, 21Adaiah, Beraiah and Shimrath were the sons of Shimei.

22Ishpan, Eber, Eliel, 23Abdon, Zicri, Hanan, 24Hananiah, Elam, Anthothijah, 25Iphdeiah and Penuel were the sons of Shashak.

26Shamsherai, Shehariah, Athaliah, 27Jaareshiah, Elijah and Zicri were the sons of Jeroham.

28All these were heads of families, chiefs as listed in their genealogy, and they lived in Jerusalem.

29Jeieli the fatherj of Gibeon lived in Gibeon.q

His wife's name was Maacah, 30and his firstborn son was Abdon, followed by Zur, Kish, Baal, Ner,k Nadab, 31Gedor, Ahio, Zeker 32and Mikloth, who was the father of Shimeah. They too lived near their relatives in Jerusalem.

33Nerr was the father of Kish,s Kish the father of Saul,t and Saul the father of Jonathan, Malki-Shua, Abinadab and Esh-Baal.l u

34The son of Jonathan:v

Merib-Baal,m w who was the father of Micah.

35The sons of Micah:

Pithon, Melech, Tarea and Ahaz.

36Ahaz was the father of Jehoaddah, Jehoaddah was the father of Alemeth, Azmaveth and Zimri, and Zimri was the father of Moza. 37Moza was the father of Binea; Raphah was his son, Eleasah his son and Azel his son.

38Azel had six sons, and these were their names:

Azrikam, Bokeru, Ishmael, Sheariah, Obadiah and Hanan. All these were the sons of Azel.

39The sons of his brother Eshek:

Ulam his firstborn, Jeush the second son and Eliphelet the third. 40The sons of Ulam were brave warriors who could handle the bow. They had many sons and grandsons—150 in all.

All these were the descendants of Benjamin.x

8:3 kS Ge 46:21
8:4 lS 2Sa 23:9
8:6 mJdg 3:12-30
8:12 nEzr 2:33; Ne 6:2; 7:37; 11:35
8:13 oS Jos 10:12 pS Jos 11:22

8:29 qS Jos 9:3
8:33 rS 1Sa 28:19 sS 1Sa 9:1 tS 1Sa 14:49 uS 2Sa 2:8
8:34 vS 2Sa 9:12 wS 2Sa 4:4; S 21:7-14
8:40 xS Nu 26:38

h3 Or *Gera the father of Ehud*   i29 Some Septuagint manuscripts (see also 1 Chron. 9:35); Hebrew does not have *Jeiel*.   j29 *Father* may mean *civic leader* or *military leader*.   k30 Some Septuagint manuscripts (see also 1 Chron. 9:36); Hebrew does not have *Ner*.   l33 Also known as *Ish-Bosheth*   m34 Also known as *Mephibosheth*

importance of this tribe and the Chronicler's interest in Saul. Judah, Simeon and part of Benjamin had composed the southern kingdom (1Ki 12:1–21), and their territory largely comprised the restoration province of Judah in the Chronicler's own time. The genealogy of Benjamin is more extensive than that of all the other tribes except Judah and Levi. The Chronicler is also concerned with the genealogy of Saul (vv. 29–38) in order to set the stage for the historical narrative that begins with the end of his reign (ch. 10); Saul's genealogy is repeated in 9:35–44. Several references suggest that this genealogy also originated in the military sphere (vv. 6,10,13,28,40).

8:1–5 Cf. the lists in 7:6–12; Ge 46:21–22; Nu 26:38–41.

8:6–27 Unique to Chronicles.

8:29–38 Essentially the same as the list in 9:35–44.

8:33 For the sons of Saul see 1Sa 14:49; 31:2. *Jonathan.* The firstborn and the best known of the sons of Saul, both for his military prowess and for his friendship with David (1Sa 13–14; 18:1–4; 19:1–7; 20:1–42; 23:16–18; 2Sa 21:13–14). *Esh-Baal.* See NIV text note; see also note on 2Sa 2:8.

8:34 *Merib-Baal.* See NIV text note; see also note on 2Sa 4:4.

9 All Israel[y] was listed in the genealogies recorded in the book of the kings of Israel.

The People in Jerusalem

9:1–17pp — Ne 11:3–19

The people of Judah were taken captive to Babylon[z] because of their unfaithfulness.[a] 2Now the first to resettle on their own property in their own towns[b] were some Israelites, priests, Levites and temple servants.[c]

3Those from Judah, from Benjamin, and from Ephraim and Manasseh who lived in Jerusalem were:

4Uthai son of Ammihud, the son of Omri, the son of Imri, the son of Bani, a descendant of Perez son of Judah.[d]

5Of the Shilonites:
Asaiah the firstborn and his sons.

6Of the Zerahites:
Jeuel.
The people from Judah numbered 690.

7Of the Benjamites:
Sallu son of Meshullam, the son of Hodaviah, the son of Hassenuah;
8Ibneiah son of Jeroham; Elah son of Uzzi, the son of Micri; and Meshullam son of Shephatiah, the son of Reuel, the son of Ibnijah.

9The people from Benjamin, as listed in their genealogy, numbered 956. All these men were heads of their families.

10Of the priests:
Jedaiah; Jehoiarib; Jakin;
11Azariah son of Hilkiah, the son of Meshullam, the son of Zadok, the son of Meraioth, the son of Ahitub, the official in charge of the house of God;

12Adaiah son of Jeroham, the son of Pashhur,[e] the son of Malkijah; and Maasai son of Adiel, the son of Jahzerah, the son of Meshullam, the son of Meshillemith, the son of Immer.

13The priests, who were heads of families, numbered 1,760. They were able men, responsible for ministering in the house of God.

14Of the Levites:
Shemaiah son of Hasshub, the son of Azrikam, the son of Hashabiah, a Merarite; 15Bakbakkar, Heresh, Galal and Mattaniah[f] son of Mica, the son of Zicri, the son of Asaph; 16Obadiah son of Shemaiah, the son of Galal, the son of Jeduthun; and Berekiah son of Asa, the son of Elkanah, who lived in the villages of the Netophathites.[g]

17The gatekeepers:[h]
Shallum, Akkub, Talmon, Ahiman and their brothers, Shallum their chief 18being stationed at the King's Gate[i] on the east, up to the present time. These were the gatekeepers belonging to the camp of the Levites. 19Shallum[j] son of Kore, the son of Ebiasaph, the son of Korah, and his fellow gatekeepers from his family (the Korahites) were responsible for guarding the thresholds of the Tent[n] just as their fathers had been responsible for guarding the entrance to the dwelling of the LORD. 20In earlier times Phinehas[k] son of Eleazar was in charge of the gatekeepers, and the LORD was with him. 21Zechariah[l] son of Meshelemiah

Cross references (center column)

9:1 [y]1Ch 11:1, 10; 12:38; 14:8; 15:3,28; 18:14; 19:17; 21:5; 28:4,8; 29:21,23; 2Ch 1:2; 5:3; 7:8; 10:3,16; 12:1; 13:4,15; 18:16; 24:5; 28:23; 29:24; 30:1 [z]S Dt 21:10 [a]S 1Ch 5:25
9:2 [b]Jos 9:27; Ezr 2:70 [c]Ezr 2:43,58; 8:20; Ne 7:60
9:4 [d]S Ge 38:29; 46:12
9:12 [e]Ezr 2:38; 10:22; Ne 10:3; Jer 21:1; 38:1
9:15 [f]2Ch 20:14; Ne 11:22
9:16 [g]Ne 12:28
9:17 [h]ver 22; 1Ch 26:1; 2Ch 8:14; 31:14; Ezr 2:42; Ne 7:45
9:18 [i]1Ch 26:14; Eze 43:1; 46:1
9:19 [j]Jer 35:4
9:20 [k]Nu 25:11
9:21 [l]1Ch 26:2, 14

[n]19 That is, the temple; also in verses 21 and 23

9:1 *All Israel.* The Chronicler's concern with "all Israel" is one key to why he included the genealogies (see Introduction: Purpose and Themes).
9:2–34 This list of the members of the restored community reflects the Chronicler's concern with the institutions of his own day, especially the legitimacy of officeholders. He lists laity ("Israelites," v. 2) in vv. 3–9, priests in vv. 10–13 and Levites in vv. 14–34. He mentions a fourth class of returnees—the temple servants (v. 2)—but does not give them separate listing in the material that follows. They may have been originally foreigners who were incorporated into the Levites (Jos 9:23; Ezr 8:20) and so are not listed apart from that tribe. A similar office is known in the temple at ancient Ugarit. The list here is related to the one in Ne 11, but less than half the names are the same in the two lists.
9:3 *Ephraim and Manasseh.* Again reflecting his concern with "all Israel," the Chronicler shows that the returnees were not only from Judah and Benjamin but also from the northern tribes.

9:4–6 See 2:3–6; 4:21. The returnees of Judah are traced to Judah's sons Perez, Zerah and Shelah—if the word "Shilonites" (v. 5) is read as "Shelanites" (Nu 26:20). If the reading "Shilonites" is retained, the reference is to Shiloh, the important sanctuary city (Jdg 18:31; Jer 7:12–14; 26:9).
9:10–13 The list of priests is essentially the same as that in Ne 11:10–14. Since it is tied to the list of priests earlier in the genealogies (6:1–15,50–53), contemporary Israel's continuity with her past is shown.
9:15–16 *Asaph . . . Jeduthun.* Leaders of musical groups (6:39; 16:41). Later the Chronicler also lists the musicians (ch. 25) before the gatekeepers (ch. 26).
9:16 *Netophathites.* See note on Ne 12:28.
9:17–21 The Chronicler gives the names of four gatekeepers, while Ne 11:19 mentions only two. The chief of the gatekeepers had the honor of responsibility for the gate used by the king (Eze 46:1–2). The gatekeepers are also listed in ch. 26; Ezr 2:42. These officers traced their origin to Phinehas (v. 20; 6:4; Nu 3:32; 25:6–13).

was the gatekeeper at the entrance to the Tent of Meeting.

22Altogether, those chosen to be gatekeepers[m] at the thresholds numbered 212. They were registered by genealogy in their villages. The gatekeepers had been assigned to their positions of trust by David and Samuel the seer.[n] 23They and their descendants were in charge of guarding the gates of the house of the LORD—the house called the Tent. 24The gatekeepers were on the four sides: east, west, north and south. 25Their brothers in their villages had to come from time to time and share their duties for seven-day[o] periods. 26But the four principal gatekeepers, who were Levites, were entrusted with the responsibility for the rooms and treasuries[p] in the house of God. 27They would spend the night stationed around the house of God,[q] because they had to guard it; and they had charge of the key[r] for opening it each morning.

28Some of them were in charge of the articles used in the temple service; they counted them when they were brought in and when they were taken out. 29Others were assigned to take care of the furnishings and all the other articles of the sanctuary,[s] as well as the flour and wine, and the oil, incense and spices. 30But some[t] of the priests took care of mixing the spices. 31A Levite named Mattithiah, the firstborn son of Shallum the Korahite, was entrusted with the responsibility for baking the offering bread. 32Some of their Kohathite brothers were in charge of preparing for every Sabbath the bread set out on the table.[u]

33Those who were musicians,[v] heads of Levite families, stayed in the rooms of the temple and were exempt from other duties because they were responsible for the work day and night.[w]

34All these were heads of Levite families, chiefs as listed in their genealogy, and they lived in Jerusalem.

Cross references (center column):
9:22 mS ver 17
nS 1Sa 9:9
9:25 o2Ki 11:5
9:26 p1Ch 26:22
9:27 qS Nu 3:38
rIsa 22:22
9:29 sS Nu 3:28;
1Ch 23:29
9:30 tS Ex 30:25
9:32
uLev 24:5-8;
1Ch 23:29;
2Ch 13:11
9:33
vS 1Ch 6:31;
25:1-31;
S 2Ch 5:12
wPs 134:1

9:35 x1Ch 8:29
9:39 yS 1Ch 8:33
zS 1Sa 9:1
a1Sa 13:22
b5 2Sa 2:8
9:40 cS 2Sa 4:4

The Genealogy of Saul

9:34–44pp — 1Ch 8:28–38

35Jeiel[x] the father[o] of Gibeon lived in Gibeon.

His wife's name was Maacah, 36and his firstborn son was Abdon, followed by Zur, Kish, Baal, Ner, Nadab, 37Gedor, Ahio, Zechariah and Mikloth. 38Mikloth was the father of Shimeam. They too lived near their relatives in Jerusalem.

39Ner[y] was the father of Kish,[z] Kish the father of Saul, and Saul the father of Jonathan,[a] Malki-Shua, Abinadab and Esh-Baal.[p][b]

40The son of Jonathan:
Merib-Baal,[q][c] who was the father of Micah.

41The sons of Micah:
Pithon, Melech, Tahrea and Ahaz.[r]

42Ahaz was the father of Jadah, Jadah[s] was the father of Alemeth, Azmaveth and Zimri, and Zimri was the father of Moza. 43Moza was the father of Binea; Rephaiah was his son, Eleasah his son and Azel his son.

44Azel had six sons, and these were their names:
Azrikam, Bokeru, Ishmael, Sheariah, Obadiah and Hanan. These were the sons of Azel.

Saul Takes His Life

10:1–12pp — 1Sa 31:1–13; 2Sa 1:4–12

10 Now the Philistines fought against Israel; the Israelites fled before them, and many fell slain on Mount Gilboa. 2The Philistines pressed hard after Saul and his sons, and they killed his sons Jonathan, Abinadab and Malki-Shua. 3The fighting grew fierce around Saul, and when the archers overtook him, they wounded him.

o35 *Father* may mean *civic leader* or *military leader.*
p39 Also known as *Ish-Bosheth*   q40 Also known as *Mephibosheth*   r41 Vulgate and Syriac (see also Septuagint and 1 Chron. 8:35); Hebrew does not have *and Ahaz.*   s42 Some Hebrew manuscripts and Septuagint (see also 1 Chron. 8:36); most Hebrew manuscripts *Jarah, Jarah*

9:22–27 Twenty-four guard stations were manned in three shifts around the clock; 72 men would be needed for each week. With a total of 212 men, each would have a tour of duty approximately every three weeks (26:12–18).
9:28–34 The Levites not only were responsible for the temple precincts and for opening the gates in the morning, but they also had charge of the chambers and supply rooms (23:28; 26:20–29) as well as the implements, supplies and furnishings (28:13–18; Ezr 1:9–11). In addition they were

responsible for the preparation of baked goods (Ex 25:30; Lev 2:5–7; 7:9). The priests alone prepared the perfumed anointing oil and spices (Ex 30:23–33).
9:35–44 The genealogy of Saul is duplicated here (see 8:29–38) as a transition to the short account of his reign that begins the Chronicler's narration (ch. 10).
10:2 For the strategy of pursuing the king in battle see note on 1Ki 22:31.

⁴Saul said to his armor-bearer, "Draw your sword and run me through, or these uncircumcised fellows will come and abuse me."

But his armor-bearer was terrified and would not do it; so Saul took his own sword and fell on it. ⁵When the armor-bearer saw that Saul was dead, he too fell on his sword and died. ⁶So Saul and his three sons died, and all his house died together.

⁷When all the Israelites in the valley saw that the army had fled and that Saul and his sons had died, they abandoned their towns and fled. And the Philistines came and occupied them.

⁸The next day, when the Philistines came to strip the dead, they found Saul and his sons fallen on Mount Gilboa. ⁹They stripped him and took his head and his armor, and sent messengers throughout the land of the Philistines to proclaim the news among their idols and their people. ¹⁰They put his armor in the temple of their gods and hung up his head in the temple of Dagon.ᵈ

¹¹When all the inhabitants of Jabesh Gileadᵉ heard of everything the Philistines had done to Saul, ¹²all their valiant men went and took the bodies of Saul and his sons and brought them to Jabesh. Then they buried their bones under the great tree in Jabesh, and they fasted seven days.

¹³Saul diedᶠ because he was unfaithfulᵍ to the LORD; he did not keepʰ the word of the LORD and even consulted a mediumⁱ for guidance, ¹⁴and did not inquire of the LORD. So the LORD put him to death and turnedʲ the kingdomᵏ over to David son of Jesse.

Cross references (center column):

10:10 ᵈS Jdg 16:23
10:11 ᵉS Jdg 21:8
10:13 ᶠS 2Sa 1:1
ᵍS 1Ch 5:25
ʰS 1Sa 13:13
ⁱS Lev 19:31;
S 20:6;
Dt 18:9-14
10:14 ʲ1Ch 12:23
ᵏS 1Sa 13:14

11:1 ˡS 1Ch 9:1
ᵐS Ge 13:18;
S 23:19
11:2 ⁿS 1Sa 18:5,
16 ᵒPs 78:71;
Mt 2:6
ᵖS 1Ch 5:2
11:3 ᵠ1Sa 16:1-13
11:4 ʳS Ge 10:16;
S 15:18-21;
S Jos 3:10; S 15:8
11:6 ˢS 2Sa 2:13
11:8 ᵗS 2Sa 5:9;
2Ch 32:5
11:9 ᵘEst 9:4

David Becomes King Over Israel

11:1–3pp — 2Sa 5:1–3

11 All Israelˡ came together to David at Hebronᵐ and said, "We are your own flesh and blood. ²In the past, even while Saul was king, you were the one who led Israel on their military campaigns.ⁿ And the LORD your God said to you, 'You will shepherdᵒ my people Israel, and you will become their ruler.ᵖ' "

³When all the elders of Israel had come to King David at Hebron, he made a compact with them at Hebron before the LORD, and they anointedᵠ David king over Israel, as the LORD had promised through Samuel.

David Conquers Jerusalem

11:4–9pp — 2Sa 5:6–10

⁴David and all the Israelites marched to Jerusalem (that is, Jebus). The Jebusitesʳ who lived there ⁵said to David, "You will not get in here." Nevertheless, David captured the fortress of Zion, the City of David.

⁶David had said, "Whoever leads the attack on the Jebusites will become commander-in-chief." Joabˢ son of Zeruiah went up first, and so he received the command.

⁷David then took up residence in the fortress, and so it was called the City of David. ⁸He built up the city around it, from the supporting terracesᵗ ᵗ to the surrounding wall, while Joab restored the rest of the city. ⁹And David became more and more powerful,ᵘ because the LORD Almighty was with him.

David's Mighty Men

11:10–41pp — 2Sa 23:8–39

¹⁰These were the chiefs of David's

ᵗ8 Or *the Millo*

10:6 *his three sons.* See v. 2 (Ish-Bosheth survived; see note on 1Sa 31:2). *all his house.* His three sons and his chief officials (his official "house"), not all his descendants (see 8:33–34 and notes; 1Sa 31:6).
10:13–14 These verses are not paralleled in the Samuel account; they were put here by the Chronicler in line with his concern with immediate retribution (see Introduction: Purpose and Themes). Seeking mediums was forbidden (Dt 18:9–14) and brought death to Saul. The Chronicler is obviously writing to an audience already familiar with Samuel and Kings, and he frequently assumes that knowledge. Here the consultation with the medium at Endor is alluded to (see 1Sa 28), but the Chronicler does not recount the incident.
11:1–2Ch 9:31 See Introduction: Portrait of David and Solomon.
11:1–3 The material here parallels that in 2Sa 5:1–3, but is recast by the Chronicler in accordance with his emphasis on the popular support given David by "all Israel" (v. 1).

While the Chronicler twice mentions the seven-year reign at Hebron before the death of Ish-Bosheth and the covenant with the northern tribes (3:4; 29:27), these incidents are bypassed in the narrative portion of the book. Most striking is the elimination at this point of the information in 2Sa 5:4–5. Rather, the Chronicler paints a picture of immediate accession over "all Israel," followed by the immediate conquest of Jerusalem (see Introduction: Portrait of David and Solomon). The author once again assumes the reader's knowledge of the parallel account.
11:4–9 See 2Sa 5:6–10 and notes. The "all Israel" theme appears in v. 4 as a substitute for "the king and his men" (2Sa 5:6).
11:10–41a See 2Sa 23:8–39 and notes. In the Samuel account this list of David's mighty men is given near the end of his reign. The Chronicler has moved the list to the beginning of his reign and has greatly expanded it (11:41b–12:40), again as part of his emphasis on the broad support of "all Israel" for the kingship of David (v. 10).

mighty men—they, together with all Israel,[v] gave his kingship strong support to extend it over the whole land, as the LORD had promised[w]— [11]this is the list of David's mighty men:[x]

Jashobeam,[u] a Hacmonite, was chief of the officers[v]; he raised his spear against three hundred men, whom he killed in one encounter.

[12]Next to him was Eleazar son of Dodai the Ahohite, one of the three mighty men. [13]He was with David at Pas Dammim when the Philistines gathered there for battle. At a place where there was a field full of barley, the troops fled from the Philistines. [14]But they took their stand in the middle of the field. They defended it and struck the Philistines down, and the LORD brought about a great victory.[y]

[15]Three of the thirty chiefs came down to David to the rock at the cave of Adullam, while a band of Philistines was encamped in the Valley[z] of Rephaim. [16]At that time David was in the stronghold,[a] and the Philistine garrison was at Bethlehem. [17]David longed for water and said, "Oh, that someone would get me a drink of water from the well near the gate of Bethlehem!" [18]So the Three broke through the Philistine lines, drew water from the well near the gate of Bethlehem and carried it back to David. But he refused to drink it; instead, he poured[b] it out before the LORD. [19]"God forbid that I should do this!" he said. "Should I drink the blood of these men who went at the risk of their lives?" Because they risked their lives to bring it back, David would not drink it.

Such were the exploits of the three mighty men.

[20]Abishai[c] the brother of Joab was chief of the Three. He raised his spear against three hundred men, whom he killed, and so he became as famous as the Three. [21]He was doubly honored above the Three and became their commander, even though he was not included among them.

[22]Benaiah son of Jehoiada was a valiant fighter from Kabzeel,[d] who performed great exploits. He struck down two of Moab's best men. He also went down into a pit on a snowy day and killed a lion.[e] [23]And he struck down an Egyptian who was seven and a half feet[w] tall. Although

the Egyptian had a spear like a weaver's rod[f] in his hand, Benaiah went against him with a club. He snatched the spear from the Egyptian's hand and killed him with his own spear. [24]Such were the exploits of Benaiah son of Jehoiada; he too was as famous as the three mighty men. [25]He was held in greater honor than any of the Thirty, but he was not included among the Three. And David put him in charge of his bodyguard.

[26]The mighty men were:
Asahel[g] the brother of Joab,
Elhanan son of Dodo from Bethlehem,
[27]Shammoth[h] the Harorite,
Helez the Pelonite,
[28]Ira son of Ikkesh from Tekoa,
Abiezer[i] from Anathoth,
[29]Sibbecai[j] the Hushathite,
Ilai the Ahohite,
[30]Maharai the Netophathite,
Heled son of Baanah the Netophathite,
[31]Ithai son of Ribai from Gibeah in Benjamin,
Benaiah[k] the Pirathonite,[l]
[32]Hurai from the ravines of Gaash,
Abiel the Arbathite,
[33]Azmaveth the Baharumite,
Eliahba the Shaalbonite,
[34]the sons of Hashem the Gizonite,
Jonathan son of Shagee the Hararite,
[35]Ahiam son of Sacar the Hararite,
Eliphal son of Ur,
[36]Hepher the Mekerathite,
Ahijah the Pelonite,
[37]Hezro the Carmelite,
Naarai son of Ezbai,
[38]Joel the brother of Nathan,
Mibhar son of Hagri,
[39]Zelek the Ammonite,
Naharai the Berothite, the armorbearer of Joab son of Zeruiah,
[40]Ira the Ithrite,
Gareb the Ithrite,
[41]Uriah[m] the Hittite,
Zabad[n] son of Ahlai,
[42]Adina son of Shiza the Reubenite,

11:10 [v]ver 1
[w]1Ch 12:23
11:11 [x]S 2Sa 17:10
11:14 [y]S Ex 14:30; S 1Sa 11:13
11:15 [z]1Ch 14:9; Isa 17:5
11:16 [a]S 2Sa 5:17
11:18 [b]S Dt 12:16
11:20 [c]S 1Sa 26:6
11:22 [d]S Jos 15:21
[e]1Sa 17:36
11:23 [f]S 1Sa 17:7
11:26 [g]S 2Sa 2:18
11:27 [h]1Ch 27:8
11:28 [i]1Ch 27:12
11:29 [j]S 2Sa 21:18
11:31 [k]1Ch 27:14
[l]S Jdg 12:13
11:41 [m]2Sa 11:6
[n]1Ch 2:36

[u]11 Possibly a variant of *Jashob-Baal*   [v]11 Or *Thirty*; some Septuagint manuscripts *Three* (see also 2 Samuel 23:8)   [w]23 Hebrew *five cubits* (about 2.3 meters)

11:12–14 See 2Sa 23:9b–11a.
11:15–19 David recognizes that he is not worthy of such devotion and makes the water a drink offering to the Lord (see Ge 35:14; 2Ki 16:13; Jer 7:18; Hos 9:4).
11:41b–12:40 See note on vv. 10–41a. The list in 2Sa 23 ends with Uriah the Hittite (2Sa 11); the source for the additional names is not known. The emphasis continues to be on the support of "all Israel"—even Saul's own kinsmen recognized the legitimacy of David's kingship before Saul's death (12:1–7,16–18,23,29).

who was chief of the Reubenites,
and the thirty with him,
43 Hanan son of Maacah,
Joshaphat the Mithnite,
44 Uzzia the Ashterathite,[o]
Shama and Jeiel the sons of Hotham the Aroerite,
45 Jediael son of Shimri,
his brother Joha the Tizite,
46 Eliel the Mahavite,
Jeribai and Joshaviah the sons of
Elnaam,
Ithmah the Moabite,
47 Eliel, Obed and Jaasiel the Mezo-
baite.

Warriors Join David

12 These were the men who came to
David at Ziklag,[p] while he was
banished from the presence of Saul son of
Kish (they were among the warriors who
helped him in battle; 2 they were armed
with bows and were able to shoot arrows
or to sling stones right-handed or left-
handed;[q] they were kinsmen of Saul[r]
from the tribe of Benjamin):

3 Ahiezer their chief and Joash the sons
of Shemaah the Gibeathite; Jeziel and
Pelet the sons of Azmaveth; Beracah,
Jehu the Anathothite, 4 and Ishmaiah
the Gibeonite, a mighty man among
the Thirty, who was a leader of the
Thirty; Jeremiah, Jahaziel, Johanan,
Jozabad the Gederathite,[s] 5 Eluzai,
Jerimoth, Bealiah, Shemariah and
Shephatiah the Haruphite; 6 Elkanah,
Isshiah, Azarel, Joezer and Jashobeam
the Korahites; 7 and Joelah and Zeba-
diah the sons of Jeroham from Ge-
dor.[t]

8 Some Gadites[u] defected to David at his
stronghold in the desert. They were brave
warriors, ready for battle and able to handle the shield and spear. Their faces were
the faces of lions,[v] and they were as swift
as gazelles[w] in the mountains.

9 Ezer was the chief,
Obadiah the second in command,
Eliab the third,
10 Mishmannah the fourth, Jeremiah the
fifth,
11 Attai the sixth, Eliel the seventh,
12 Johanan the eighth, Elzabad the
ninth,
13 Jeremiah the tenth and Macbannai
the eleventh.

14 These Gadites were army commanders; the least was a match for a hundred,[x]
and the greatest for a thousand.[y] 15 It was
they who crossed the Jordan in the first
month when it was overflowing all its
banks,[z] and they put to flight everyone
living in the valleys, to the east and to the
west.

16 Other Benjamites[a] and some men
from Judah also came to David in his
stronghold. 17 David went out to meet
them and said to them, "If you have come
to me in peace, to help me, I am ready to
have you unite with me. But if you have
come to betray me to my enemies when
my hands are free from violence, may the
God of our fathers see it and judge you."

18 Then the Spirit[b] came upon Amasai,[c]
chief of the Thirty, and he said:

"We are yours, O David!
We are with you, O son of Jesse!
Success,[d] success to you,
and success to those who help you,
for your God will help you."

So David received them and made them
leaders of his raiding bands.

19 Some of the men of Manasseh defected to David when he went with the Philistines to fight against Saul. (He and his men
did not help the Philistines because, after
consultation, their rulers sent him away.
They said, "It will cost us our heads if he
deserts to his master Saul.")[e] 20 When David went to Ziklag,[f] these were the men of
Manasseh who defected to him: Adnah,
Jozabad, Jediael, Michael, Jozabad, Elihu
and Zillethai, leaders of units of a thousand
in Manasseh. 21 They helped David against
raiding bands, for all of them were brave
warriors, and they were commanders in
his army. 22 Day after day men came to
help David, until he had a great army, like
the army of God.[x]

Others Join David at Hebron

23 These are the numbers of the men

11:44 [o]S Dt 1:4
12:1 [p]S Jos 15:31
12:2 [q]S Jdg 3:15 [r]S 2Sa 3:19
12:4 [s]Jos 15:36
12:7 [t]S Jos 15:58
12:8 [u]S Ge 30:11 [v]2Sa 17:10 [w]S 2Sa 2:18
12:14 [x]S Lev 26:8 [y]S Dt 32:30
12:15 [z]S Jos 3:15
12:16 [a]S 2Sa 3:19
12:18 [b]S Jdg 3:10; 1Ch 28:12; 2Ch 15:1; 20:14; 24:20 [c]S 2Sa 17:25 [d]1Sa 25:5-6
12:19 [e]1Sa 29:2-11
12:20 [f]S 1Sa 27:6

[x]22 Or *a great and mighty army*

12:1 The Chronicler assumes the reader's knowledge of the events at Ziklag (1Sa 27); see vv. 19–20.
12:8–15 The men of Gad were from Transjordan. Melting snows to the north would have brought the Jordan to flood stage in the first month (March-April) at the time of their crossing (v. 15). The most appropriate time for this incident would have been in the period of David's wandering in the region of the Dead Sea (1Sa 23:14; 24:1; 25:1; 26:1).
12:23–37 The emphasis remains on "all Israel" (v. 38). Though 13 tribes are named, they are grouped in order to maintain the traditional number of 12 (see note on 2:1–2). The northernmost and the Transjordan tribes send the largest number of men (vv. 33–37), reinforcing the degree of support that David enjoyed not only in Judah and Benjamin

armed for battle who came to David at Hebron[g] to turn[h] Saul's kingdom over to him, as the LORD had said:[i]

24men of Judah, carrying shield and spear—6,800 armed for battle;
25men of Simeon, warriors ready for battle—7,100;
26men of Levi—4,600, 27including Jehoiada, leader of the family of Aaron, with 3,700 men, 28and Zadok,[j] a brave young warrior, with 22 officers from his family;
29men of Benjamin,[k] Saul's kinsmen—3,000, most[l] of whom had remained loyal to Saul's house until then;
30men of Ephraim, brave warriors, famous in their own clans—20,800;
31men of half the tribe of Manasseh, designated by name to come and make David king—18,000;
32men of Issachar, who understood the times and knew what Israel should do[m]—200 chiefs, with all their relatives under their command;
33men of Zebulun, experienced soldiers prepared for battle with every type of weapon, to help David with undivided loyalty—50,000;
34men of Naphtali—1,000 officers, together with 37,000 men carrying shields and spears;
35men of Dan, ready for battle—28,600;
36men of Asher, experienced soldiers prepared for battle—40,000;
37and from east of the Jordan, men of Reuben, Gad and the half-tribe of Manasseh, armed with every type of weapon—120,000.

38All these were fighting men who volunteered to serve in the ranks. They came to Hebron fully determined to make David king over all Israel.[n] All the rest of the Israelites were also of one mind to make David king. 39The men spent three days there with David, eating and drinking,[o] for their families had supplied provisions for them. 40Also, their neighbors from as far away as Issachar, Zebulun and Naphtali came bringing food on donkeys, camels, mules and oxen. There were plentiful supplies[p] of flour, fig cakes, raisin[q] cakes, wine, oil, cattle and sheep, for there was joy[r] in Israel.

Bringing Back the Ark

13:1–14pp — 2Sa 6:1–11

13 David conferred with each of his officers, the commanders of thousands and commanders of hundreds. 2He then said to the whole assembly of Israel, "If it seems good to you and if it is the will of the LORD our God, let us send word far and wide to the rest of our brothers throughout the territories of Israel, and also to the priests and Levites who are with them in their towns and pasturelands, to come and join us. 3Let us bring the ark of our God back to us,[s] for we did not inquire[t] of[y] it[z] during the reign of Saul."

Cross references (center column):
12:23 [g]2Sa 2:3-4
[h]1Ch 10:14
[i]S 1Sa 16:1;
1Ch 11:10
12:28 [j]1Ch 6:8;
15:11; 16:39;
27:17
12:29
[k]S 2Sa 3:19
[l]2Sa 2:8-9
12:32 [m]Est 1:13
12:38 [n]S 1Ch 9:1
12:39 [o]2Sa 3:20;
Isa 25:6-8
12:40
[p]S 2Sa 16:1;
17:29 [q]1Sa 25:18
[r]1Ch 29:22
13:3 [s]1Sa 7:1-2
[t]2Ch 1:5

[y]3 Or *we neglected*   [z]3 Or *him*

---

but throughout the other tribes as well. The numbers in this section seem quite high. Essentially two approaches are followed on this question: 1. It is possible to explain the numbers so that a lower figure is actually attained. The Hebrew word for "thousand" may represent a unit of a tribe, each having its own commander (13:1; see Nu 31:14,48,52,54). In this case the numbers would be read not as a total figure, but as representative commanders. For example, the 6,800 from Judah (v. 24) would be read either as six commanders of 1,000 and eight commanders of 100 (see 13:1), or possibly as six commanders of thousands and 800 men. Reducing the numbers in this fashion fits well with 13:1 and with the list of commanders alone found for Zadok's family (v. 28) and the tribe of Issachar (v. 32). Taking the numbers as straight totals would require the presence of 340,800 persons in Hebron for a feast at the same time. 2. Another approach is to allow the numbers to stand and to view them as hyperbole on the part of the Chronicler to achieve a number "like the army of God" (v. 22). This approach would fit well with the Chronicler's glorification of David and with the banquet scene that follows.
12:38–40 The Chronicler's portrait of David is influenced by his Messianic expectations (see Introduction: Purpose and Themes). In the presence of a third of a million people (see note on vv. 23–37) David's coronation banquet typifies the future Messianic feast (Isa 25:6–8). The imagery of the

Messianic banquet became prominent in the intertestamental literature (*Apocalypse of Baruch* 29:4–8; *Enoch* 62:14) and in the NT (see Mt 8:11–12 and Lk 13:28–30; Mt 22:1–10 and Lk 14:16–24; see also Mt 25:1–13; Lk 22:28–30; Rev 19:7–9). The Lord's Supper anticipates that coming banquet (Mt 26:29; Mk 14:25; Lk 22:15–18; 1Cor 11:23–26).
13:1–14 See 2Sa 6:1–11 and notes. The author abandons the chronological order as given in 2Sa 5–6 and puts the transfer of the ark first, delaying his account of the palace building and the Philistine campaign until later (ch. 14). This is in accordance with his portrayal of David; David's concern with the ark was expressed immediately upon his accession—his consultation with the leaders appears to be set in the context of the coronation banquet (12:38–40).
13:1–4 These verses are not found in Samuel and reflect the Chronicler's own concerns with "all Israel." The semimilitary expedition to retrieve the ark in 2Sa 6:1 is here broadened by consultation with and support from the whole assembly of Israel, "throughout the territories" (v. 2), including the priests and Levites—an important point for the Chronicler since only they are allowed to move the ark (15:2,13; 23:25–27; Dt 10:8).
13:3 *we did not inquire of it during the reign of Saul.* 1Sa 14:18 may be an exception (but see NIV text note there).

4The whole assembly agreed to do this, because it seemed right to all the people.

5So David assembled all the Israelites, u from the Shihor River v in Egypt to Leboa Hamath, w to bring the ark of God from Kiriath Jearim. x 6David and all the Israelites with him went to Baalahy of Judah (Kiriath Jearim) to bring up from there the ark of God the LORD, who is enthroned between the cherubim z—the ark that is called by the Name.

7They moved the ark of God from Abinadab's a house on a new cart, with Uzzah and Ahio guiding it. 8David and all the Israelites were celebrating with all their might before God, with songs and with harps, lyres, tambourines, cymbals and trumpets. b

9When they came to the threshing floor of Kidon, Uzzah reached out his hand to steady the ark, because the oxen stumbled. 10The LORD's anger c burned against Uzzah, and he struck him down d because he had put his hand on the ark. So he died there before God.

11Then David was angry because the LORD's wrath had broken out against Uzzah, and to this day that place is called Perez Uzzah. b e

12David was afraid of God that day and asked, "How can I ever bring the ark of God to me?" 13He did not take the ark to be with him in the City of David. Instead, he took it aside to the house of Obed-Edom f the Gittite. 14The ark of God remained with the family of Obed-Edom in his house for three months, and the LORD

blessed his household g and everything he had.

David's House and Family

14:1–7pp — 2Sa 5:11–16; 1Ch 3:5–8

14 Now Hiram king of Tyre sent messengers to David, along with cedar logs, h stonemasons and carpenters to build a palace for him. 2And David knew that the LORD had established him as king over Israel and that his kingdom had been highly exalted i for the sake of his people Israel.

3In Jerusalem David took more wives and became the father of more sons j and daughters. 4These are the names of the children born to him there: k Shammua, Shobab, Nathan, Solomon, 5Ibhar, Elishua, Elpelet, 6Nogah, Nepheg, Japhia, 7Elishama, Beeliada c and Eliphelet.

David Defeats the Philistines

14:8–17pp — 2Sa 5:17–25

8When the Philistines heard that David had been anointed king over all Israel, l they went up in full force to search for him, but David heard about it and went out to meet them. 9Now the Philistines had come and raided the Valley m of Rephaim; 10so David inquired of God: "Shall I go and attack the Philistines? Will you hand them over to me?"

The LORD answered him, "Go, I will hand them over to you."

11So David and his men went up to Baal Perazim, n and there he defeated them. He

Cross references (center column)

13:5 u1Ch 11:1;
15:3 vS Jos 13:3
wS Nu 13:21
xS 1Sa 7:2
13:6 yS Jos 15:9
zS Ex 25:22;
2Ki 19:15
13:7 aS 1Sa 7:1
13:8 b1Ch 15:16,
19,24; 2Ch 5:12;
Ps 92:3
13:10
c1Ch 15:13
dS Lev 10:2
13:11
e1Ch 15:13;
Ps 7:11
13:13
f1Ch 15:18,24;
16:38; 26:4-5,15

13:14
gS 2Sa 6:11
14:1 hS 1Ki 5:6;
1Ch 17:6; 22:4;
2Ch 2:3; Ezr 3:7;
Hag 1:8
14:2 iS Nu 24:7;
S Dt 26:19
14:3 jS 1Ch 3:1
14:4 kS 1Ch 3:9
14:8 l1Ch 11:1
14:9 mver 13;
S Jos 15:8;
S 1Ch 11:15
14:11 nPs 94:16;
Isa 28:21

a5 Or to the entrance to   b11 Perez Uzzah means
outbreak against Uzzah.   c7 A variant of Eliada

13:5–6 The emphasis remains on the united action of "all Israel." Israelites came to participate in this venture all the way from Lebo Hamath in the north and from the Shihor River in the south.
13:5 Shihor. An Egyptian term meaning "the pool of Horus." It appears to be a part of the Nile or one of the major canals of the Nile (see Jos 13:3; Isa 23:3; Jer 2:18 and notes).
13:6 Baalah. The Canaanite name for Kiriath Jearim, also known as Kiriath Baal (Jos 18:14). The Chronicler assumes that his readers are familiar with the account of how the ark came to be at Kiriath Jearim (1Sa 6:1–7:1).
13:7 Uzzah and Ahio. Sons or descendants of Abinadab (2Sa 6:3).
13:10 because he had put his hand on the ark. The ark was to be moved only by Levites, who carried it with poles inserted through the rings in the sides of the ark (Ex 25:12–15). None of the holy things was to be touched, on penalty of death (Nu 4:15). These strictures were observed in the second and successful attempt to move the ark to Jerusalem (15:1–15). It cannot be known whether Uzzah and Ahio were Levites—the Samuel account does not mention the presence of Levites, but the Chronicler's careful inclusion of Levites in this expedition suggests that they were (see note on vv. 1–4). In any case, the ark should not have been moved on a cart (as done by the Philistines, 1Sa 6) or

touched.
13:13 Obed-Edom. Perhaps the same man mentioned in 15:18,21,24. In 26:4 God's blessing on Obed-Edom included numerous sons. This reference also establishes that Obed-Edom was a Levite and that the ark was properly left in his care.
14:1–17 The Chronicler backtracks to pick up material from 2Sa 5 deferred to this point (see note on 13:1–14). The three-month period that the ark remained with Obed-Edom (13:14) was filled with incidents showing God's blessing on David: the building of his royal house (vv. 1–2), his large family (vv. 3–7) and his success in warfare (vv. 8–16)—all because of the Lord's blessing (vv. 2,17).
14:1–2 See 2Sa 5:11–12 and notes.
14:1 Hiram. Later provided materials and labor for building the temple (2Ch 2). His mention here implies international recognition of David as king over Israel and a treaty between David and Hiram.
14:3–7 See 3:5–9; 2Sa 5:13–16. David's children born in Hebron are omitted (3:1–4; 2Sa 3:2–5; see note on 11:1–3).
14:7 Beeliada. Eliada (see NIV text note) in 3:8; 2Sa 5:16.
14:8–12 See 2Sa 5:17–21 and notes.
14:11 break out . . . Perazim. The Hebrew underlying the name of this place where the Lord broke out against the Philistines is the same as that underlying the word used in

said, "As waters break out, God has broken out against my enemies by my hand." So that place was called Baal Perazim. d 12The Philistines had abandoned their gods there, and David gave orders to burn o them in the fire. p

13Once more the Philistines raided the valley; q 14so David inquired of God again, and God answered him, "Do not go straight up, but circle around them and attack them in front of the balsam trees. 15As soon as you hear the sound of marching in the tops of the balsam trees, move out to battle, because that will mean God has gone out in front of you to strike the Philistine army." 16So David did as God commanded him, and they struck down the Philistine army, all the way from Gibeon r to Gezer. s

17So David's fame t spread throughout every land, and the LORD made all the nations fear u him.

The Ark Brought to Jerusalem

15:25–16:3pp — 2Sa 6:12–19

15 After David had constructed buildings for himself in the City of David, he prepared v a place for the ark of God and pitched w a tent for it. 2Then David said, "No one but the Levites x may carry y the ark of God, because the LORD chose them to carry the ark of the LORD and to minister z before him forever."

3David assembled all Israel a in Jerusalem to bring up the ark of the LORD to the place he had prepared for it. 4He called together the descendants of Aaron and the Levites: b

5From the descendants of Kohath,
Uriel c the leader and 120 relatives;

6from the descendants of Merari,
Asaiah the leader and 220 relatives;
7from the descendants of Gershon, e
Joel the leader and 130 relatives;
8from the descendants of Elizaphan, d
Shemaiah the leader and 200 relatives;
9from the descendants of Hebron, e
Eliel the leader and 80 relatives;
10from the descendants of Uzziel,
Amminadab the leader and 112 relatives.

11Then David summoned Zadok f and Abiathar g the priests, and Uriel, Asaiah, Joel, Shemaiah, Eliel and Amminadab the Levites. 12He said to them, "You are the heads of the Levitical families; you and your fellow Levites are to consecrate h yourselves and bring up the ark of the LORD, the God of Israel, to the place I have prepared for it. 13It was because you, the Levites, i did not bring it up the first time that the LORD our God broke out in anger against us. j We did not inquire of him about how to do it in the prescribed way. k" 14So the priests and Levites consecrated themselves in order to bring up the ark of the LORD, the God of Israel. 15And the Levites carried the ark of God with the poles on their shoulders, as Moses had commanded l in accordance with the word of the LORD. m

16David n told the leaders of the Levites o to appoint their brothers as singers p to sing joyful songs, accompanied by musical instruments: lyres, harps and cymbals. q

17So the Levites appointed Heman r son

Cross references (center column)

14:12 oS Ex 32:20
pS Jos 7:15
14:13 qS ver 9
14:16 rS Jos 9:3
sJos 10:33
14:17 tS Jos 6:27
uEx 15:14-16;
S Dt 2:25;
Ps 2:1-12
15:1 vPs 132:1-18
wS 2Sa 6:17;
1Ch 16:1; 17:1
15:2 xS Nu 3:6;
4:15; Dt 10:8;
31:25; 2Ch 5:5
yS Dt 31:9
z1Ch 16:4;
23:13;
2Ch 29:11; 31:2;
Ps 134:1; 135:2
15:3 aS 1Ch 13:5
15:4 bS Nu 3:17-20
15:5 c1Ch 6:24

15:8 dS Ex 6:22
15:9 eEx 6:18
15:11 fS 1Ch 12:28
gS 1Sa 22:20
15:12 hS Ex 29:1;
30:19-21,30;
40:31-32;
S Lev 11:44
15:13 i1Ki 8:4
jS 1Ch 13:11
kS Lev 5:10
15:15 lS Ex 25:14
m2Sa 6:7
15:16 n1Ch 6:31
o2Ch 7:6
pEzr 2:41;
Ne 11:23;
Ps 68:25
qS 1Ch 13:8;
23:5; 2Ch 29:26;
Ne 12:27,36;
Job 21:12;
Ps 150:5; Am 6:5
15:17 rS 1Ch 6:33

d11 Baal Perazim means the lord who breaks out.
e7 Hebrew Gershom, a variant of Gershon

13:11 when the Lord broke out against Uzzah (see NIV text notes).
14:12 gave orders to burn them. 2Sa 5:21 does not mention burning but says that David and his men carried the idols away. Many have seen here an intentional change on the part of the Chronicler in order to bring David's actions into strict conformity with the law, which required that pagan idols be burned (Dt 7:5,25). However, some Septuagint (the Greek translation of the OT) manuscripts of Samuel agree with Chronicles that David burned the idols. This would indicate that the Chronicler was not innovating for theological reasons but was carefully reproducing the text he had before him, which differed from the Masoretic (traditional Hebrew) text of Samuel.
14:13–16 See 2Sa 5:22–25 and notes.
14:17 the LORD made all the nations fear him. Here and elsewhere the Chronicler uses an expression that refers to an incapacitating terror brought on by the sense that the awful power of God is present in behalf of his people (see Ex 15:16). Thus David is seen by the nations as the very representative of God (similarly Asa, 2Ch 14:14; Jehoshaphat,

2Ch 17:10; 20:29).
15:1–16:3 This account of the successful attempt to move the ark to Jerusalem is greatly expanded over the material in 2 Samuel. Only 15:25–16:3 has a parallel (2Sa 6:12–19); the rest of the material is unique to the Chronicler and reflects his own interests, especially in the Levites and cultic musicians (vv. 3–24; see Introduction: Purpose and Themes). Ps 132 should also be read in connection with this account.
15:1 constructed buildings for himself. See 14:1–2 and note on 13:1–14.
15:2–3 See note on 13:10.
15:4–10 The three clans of Levi are represented (Kohath, Merari and Gershon), as well as three distinct subgroups within Kohath (Elizaphan, Hebron and Uzziel)—862 in all.
15:12 consecrate yourselves. Through ritual washings and avoidance of ceremonial defilement (Ex 29:1–37; 30:19–21; 40:31–32; Lev 8:5–35).
15:13–15 The Chronicler provides the explanation for the failure in the first attempt to move the ark, an explanation not found in the Samuel account (see note on 13:10).

of Joel; from his brothers, Asaph[s] son of Berekiah; and from their brothers the Merarites,[t] Ethan son of Kushaiah; [18]and with them their brothers next in rank: Zechariah,[f] Jaaziel, Shemiramoth, Jehiel, Unni, Eliab, Benaiah, Maaseiah, Mattithiah, Eliphelehu, Mikneiah, Obed-Edom[u] and Jeiel,[g] the gatekeepers.

[19]The musicians Heman,[v] Asaph and Ethan were to sound the bronze cymbals; [20]Zechariah, Aziel, Shemiramoth, Jehiel, Unni, Eliab, Maaseiah and Benaiah were to play the lyres according to *alamoth,*[h] [21]and Mattithiah, Eliphelehu, Mikneiah, Obed-Edom, Jeiel and Azaziah were to play the harps, directing according to *sheminith.*[h] [22]Kenaniah the head Levite was in charge of the singing; that was his responsibility because he was skillful at it.

[23]Berekiah and Elkanah were to be doorkeepers for the ark. [24]Shebaniah, Joshaphat, Nethanel, Amasai, Zechariah, Benaiah and Eliezer the priests were to blow trumpets[w] before the ark of God. Obed-Edom and Jehiah were also to be doorkeepers for the ark.

[25]So David and the elders of Israel and the commanders of units of a thousand went to bring up the ark[x] of the covenant of the LORD from the house of Obed-Edom, with rejoicing. [26]Because God had helped the Levites who were carrying the ark of the covenant of the LORD, seven bulls and seven rams[y] were sacrificed. [27]Now David was clothed in a robe of fine linen, as were all the Levites who were carrying the ark, and as were the singers, and Kenaniah, who was in charge of the singing of the choirs. David also wore a linen ephod.[z] [28]So all Israel[a] brought up the ark of the covenant of the LORD with shouts,[b] with the sounding of rams' horns[c] and trumpets, and of cymbals, and the playing of lyres and harps.

[29]As the ark of the covenant of the LORD was entering the City of David, Michal daughter of Saul watched from a window. And when she saw King David dancing and celebrating, she despised him in her heart.

16 They brought the ark of God and set it inside the tent that David had pitched[d] for it, and they presented burnt offerings and fellowship offerings[i] before God. [2]After David had finished sacrificing the burnt offerings and fellowship offerings, he blessed[e] the people in the name of the LORD. [3]Then he gave a loaf of bread, a cake of dates and a cake of raisins[f] to each Israelite man and woman.

[4]He appointed some of the Levites to minister[g] before the ark of the LORD, to make petition, to give thanks, and to praise the LORD, the God of Israel: [5]Asaph was the chief, Zechariah second, then Jeiel, Shemiramoth, Jehiel, Mattithiah, Eliab, Benaiah, Obed-Edom and Jeiel. They were to play the lyres and harps, Asaph was to sound the cymbals, [6]and Benaiah and Jahaziel the priests were to blow the trumpets regularly before the ark of the covenant of God.

David's Psalm of Thanks

16:8–22pp — Ps 105:1–15
16:23–33pp — Ps 96:1–13
16:34–36pp — Ps 106:1,47–48

[7]That day David first committed to Asaph and his associates this psalm[h] of thanks to the LORD:

[8]Give thanks[i] to the LORD, call on his
name;

Cross references

15:17 s1Ch 6:39
t1Ch 6:44
15:18 uS 2Sa 6:10; 1Ch 26:4-5
15:19 v1Ch 16:41; 25:6
15:24 w2Ch 5:12; 7:6; 29:26
15:25 x2Ch 1:4; 5:2; Jer 3:16
15:26 yNu 23:1-4,29
15:27 zS 1Sa 2:18
15:28 aS 1Ch 9:1
bS 1Ki 1:39; Zec 4:7
cS Ex 19:13
16:1 dS 1Ch 15:1
16:2 eS Ex 39:43; Nu 6:23-27
16:3 fIsa 16:7
16:4 gS 1Ch 15:2
16:7 hPs 47:7
16:8 iver 34; Ps 107:1; 118:1; 136:1

Footnotes

f18 Three Hebrew manuscripts and most Septuagint manuscripts (see also verse 20 and 1 Chron. 16:5); most Hebrew manuscripts *Zechariah son and* or *Zechariah, Ben and*   g18 Hebrew; Septuagint (see also verse 21) *Jeiel and Azaziah*   h20,21 Probably a musical term   i1 Traditionally *peace offerings*; also in verse 2

15:18,21,24 *Obed-Edom.* See note on 13:13.
15:24 *priests were to blow trumpets.* See 16:6; Nu 10:1–10.
15:27 Both 2Sa 6:14 and the Chronicler mention David's wearing a linen ephod, a garment worn by priests (1Sa 2:18; 22:18). The Chronicler adds, however, that David (as well as the rest of the Levites in the procession) was wearing a robe of fine linen, further associating him with the dress of the cultic functionaries. Apparently the Chronicler viewed David as a priest-king, a kind of Messianic figure (see Ps 110; Zec 6:9–15).
15:29 Parallel to 2Sa 6:16, but the Chronicler omits the remainder of this incident recorded there (2Sa 6:20–23). Some interpreters regard this omission as part of the Chronicler's positive view of David, so that a possibly unseemly account is omitted. On the other hand, it is equally plausible that the Chronicler here simply assumes the reader's knowledge of the other account (see notes on 10:13–14; 11:1–3;

12:1; 13:6).
16:1–3 David is further associated with the priests in his supervision of the sacrifices and his exercising the priestly prerogative of blessing the people (Nu 6:22–27; see note on 15:27). The baked goods provided by David were for the sacrificial meal following the fellowship offerings (Lev 3:1–17; 7:11–21,28–36).
16:8–36 Similar to various parts of the book of Psalms (for vv. 8–22 see Ps 105:1–15; for vv. 23–33, Ps 96; for vv. 34–36, Ps 106:1,47–48). This psalm is not found in the Samuel account. The use of the lengthy historical portion from Ps 105 emphasizing the promises to Abraham would be particularly relevant to the Chronicler's postexilic audience, for whom the faithfulness of God was a fresh reality in their return to the land. The citation from Ps 106 would also be of immediate relevance to the Chronicler's audience as those who had been gathered and delivered from the nations (v. 35).

make known among the nations[j]
what he has done.
[9]Sing to him, sing praise[k] to him;
tell of all his wonderful acts.
[10]Glory in his holy name;[l]
let the hearts of those who seek the
LORD rejoice.
[11]Look to the LORD and his strength;
seek[m] his face always.
[12]Remember[n] the wonders[o] he has done,
his miracles,[p] and the judgments he
pronounced,
[13]O descendants of Israel his servant,
O sons of Jacob, his chosen ones.

[14]He is the LORD our God;
his judgments[q] are in all the earth.
[15]He remembers[i][r] his covenant forever,
the word he commanded, for a
thousand generations,
[16]the covenant[s] he made with Abraham,
the oath he swore to Isaac.
[17]He confirmed it to Jacob[t] as a decree,
to Israel as an everlasting covenant:
[18]"To you I will give the land of Canaan[u]
as the portion you will inherit."

[19]When they were but few in number,[v]
few indeed, and strangers in it,
[20]they[k] wandered[w] from nation to
nation,
from one kingdom to another.
[21]He allowed no man to oppress them;
for their sake he rebuked kings:[x]
[22]"Do not touch my anointed ones;
do not my prophets[y] no harm."

[23]Sing to the LORD, all the earth;
proclaim his salvation day after day.
[24]Declare his glory[z] among the nations,
his marvelous deeds among all
peoples.
[25]For great is the LORD and most worthy
of praise;[a]
he is to be feared[b] above all gods.[c]
[26]For all the gods of the nations are idols,
but the LORD made the heavens.[d]
[27]Splendor and majesty are before him;
strength and joy in his dwelling place.
[28]Ascribe to the LORD, O families of
nations,
ascribe to the LORD glory and
strength,[e]
[29]   ascribe to the LORD the glory due his
name.[f]
Bring an offering and come before him;

worship the LORD in the splendor of
his[l] holiness.[g]
[30]Tremble[h] before him, all the earth!
The world is firmly established; it
cannot be moved.[i]
[31]Let the heavens rejoice, let the earth be
glad;[j]
let them say among the nations, "The
LORD reigns!"[k]
[32]Let the sea resound, and all that is in
it;[l]
let the fields be jubilant, and
everything in them!
[33]Then the trees[m] of the forest will sing,
they will sing for joy before the LORD,
for he comes to judge[n] the earth.

[34]Give thanks[o] to the LORD, for he is
good;[p]
his love endures forever.[q]
[35]Cry out, "Save us, O God our Savior;[r]
gather us and deliver us from the
nations,
that we may give thanks to your holy
name,
that we may glory in your praise."
[36]Praise be to the LORD, the God of
Israel,[s]
from everlasting to everlasting.

Then all the people said "Amen" and
"Praise the LORD."

[37]David left Asaph and his associates before the ark of the covenant of the LORD to
minister there regularly, according to each
day's requirements.[t] [38]He also left Obed-
Edom[u] and his sixty-eight associates to
minister with them. Obed-Edom son of
Jeduthun, and also Hosah,[v] were gatekeepers.

[39]David left Zadok[w] the priest and his
fellow priests before the tabernacle of the
LORD at the high place in Gibeon[x] [40]to
present burnt offerings to the LORD on the
altar of burnt offering regularly, morning
and evening, in accordance with everything written in the Law[y] of the LORD,
which he had given Israel. [41]With them

16:8 /S 2Ki 19:19
16:9 kS Ex 15:1;
Ps 7:17
16:10 /Ps 8:1;
29:2; 66:2
16:11 mver 10;
1Ch 28:9;
2Ch 7:14; 14:4;
15:2,12; 16:12;
18:4; 20:4; 34:3;
Ps 24:6; 27:8;
105:4; 119:2,58;
Pr 8:17
16:12 nPs 77:11
oS Dt 4:34
pPs 78:43
16:14 qIsa 4:4;
26:9
16:15 rS Ge 8:1;
Ps 98:3; 111:5;
115:12; 136:23
16:16
sS Ge 12:7;
S 15:18;
22:16-18
16:17
tGe 35:9-12
16:18
uGe 13:14-17
16:19 vDt 7:7
16:20
wS Ge 20:13
16:21 xGe 12:17;
S 20:3;
Ex 7:15-18;
Ps 9:5
16:22 yS Ge 20:7
16:24 zIsa 42:12;
66:19
16:25 aPs 18:3;
48:1 bPs 76:7;
89:7 cEx 18:11;
Dt 32:39;
2Ch 2:5;
Ps 135:5;
Isa 40:25
16:26 dPs 8:3;
102:25
16:28 ePs 29:1-2
16:29 fPs 8:1

gS 2Ch 20:21;
Ps 29:1-2
16:30 hPs 2:11;
33:8; 76:8; 99:1;
114:7 iPs 93:1
16:31 jIsa 44:23;
49:13 kPs 9:7;
47:8; 93:1; 97:1;
99:1; 146:10;
Isa 52:7; La 5:19
16:32 lEx 20:11;
Isa 42:10
16:33 mIsa 14:8;
55:12 nIsa 2:10;
Ps 7:8; 96:10;
98:9; 110:6;
Isa 2:4
16:34 oS ver 8;
Ps 105:1; Isa 12:4
pPs 25:7; 34:8;
100:5; 135:3;
145:9; Na 1:7
16:35 qS 2Ch 5:13; 7:3;
Ezr 3:11;
Ps 136:1-26;
Jer 33:11
16:35 rDt 32:15;
Ps 18:46; 38:22;
Mic 7:7
16:36
sS 1Ki 8:15;
Ps 72:18-19
16:37 tS 2Ch 8:14
16:38
uS 1Ch 13:13;
26:4-5

v1Ch 26:10 16:39 wS 1Sa 2:35; S 2Sa 8:17; S 1Ch 12:28
xS Jos 9:3; 2Ch 1:3 16:40 yS Ex 29:38; Nu 28:1-8

i15 Some Septuagint manuscripts (see also Psalm 105:8);
Hebrew Remember   k18-20 One Hebrew manuscript,
Septuagint and Vulgate (see also Psalm 105:12); most
Hebrew manuscripts inherit, / 19though you are but few
in number, / few indeed, and strangers in it." / 20They
l29 Or LORD with the splendor of

16:29 splendor of his holiness. See note on Ps 29:2.
16:39 tabernacle . . . in Gibeon. The tabernacle remained
at Gibeon until Solomon's construction of the temple in
Jerusalem (2Ch 1:13; 5:5), when it was stored within the
temple. The existence of these two shrines—the tabernacle
and the temporary structure for the ark in Jerusalem (v.
1)—accounts for the two high priests: Zadok serving in
Gibeon and Abiathar in Jerusalem (18:16; 27:34; see note
on 6:8).

were Heman[z] and Jeduthun and the rest of those chosen and designated by name to give thanks to the LORD, "for his love endures forever." [42]Heman and Jeduthun were responsible for the sounding of the trumpets and cymbals and for the playing of the other instruments for sacred song.[a] The sons of Jeduthun[b] were stationed at the gate.

[43]Then all the people left, each for his own home, and David returned home to bless his family.

God's Promise to David

17:1–15pp — 2Sa 7:1–17

17 After David was settled in his palace, he said to Nathan the prophet, "Here I am, living in a palace of cedar, while the ark of the covenant of the LORD is under a tent.[c]"

[2]Nathan replied to David, "Whatever you have in mind,[d] do it, for God is with you."

[3]That night the word of God came to Nathan, saying:

[4]"Go and tell my servant David, 'This is what the LORD says: You[e] are not the one to build me a house to dwell in. [5]I have not dwelt in a house from the day I brought Israel up out of Egypt to this day. I have moved from one tent site to another, from one dwelling place to another. [6]Wherever I have moved with all the Israelites, did I ever say to any of their leaders[m] whom I commanded to shepherd my people, "Why have you not built me a house of cedar?[f]" '

[7]"Now then, tell my servant David, 'This is what the LORD Almighty says: I took you from the pasture and from following the flock, to be ruler[g] over my people Israel. [8]I have been with

you wherever you have gone, and I have cut off all your enemies from before you. Now I will make your name like the names of the greatest men of the earth. [9]And I will provide a place for my people Israel and will plant them so that they can have a home of their own and no longer be disturbed. Wicked people will not oppress them anymore, as they did at the beginning [10]and have done ever since the time I appointed leaders[h] over my people Israel. I will also subdue all your enemies.

" 'I declare to you that the LORD will build a house for you: [11]When your days are over and you go to be with your fathers, I will raise up your offspring to succeed you, one of your own sons, and I will establish his kingdom. [12]He is the one who will build[i] a house for me, and I will establish his throne forever.[j] [13]I will be his father,[k] and he will be my son.[l] I will never take my love away from him, as I took it away from your predecessor. [14]I will set him over my house and my kingdom forever; his throne[m] will be established forever.[n]' "

[15]Nathan reported to David all the words of this entire revelation.

David's Prayer

17:16–27pp — 2Sa 7:18–29

[16]Then King David went in and sat before the LORD, and he said:

"Who am I, O LORD God, and what is my family, that you have brought me this far? [17]And as if this were not enough in your sight, O God, you have spoken about the future of the

16:41
zS 1Ch 15:19
16:42 a2Ch 7:6
b1Ch 25:3
17:1 cS 1Ch 15:1
17:2 d1Ch 22:7;
28:2; 2Ch 6:7
17:4 e1Ch 22:10;
28:3
17:6 fS 1Ch 14:1
17:7 gS 2Sa 6:21

17:10 hS Jdg 2:16
17:12 iS 1Ki 5:5
j1Ch 22:10;
2Ch 7:18; 13:5
17:13 k2Co 6:18
l1Ch 28:6;
Lk 1:32; Heb 1:5
17:14
mS 1Ki 2:12;
1Ch 28:5; 29:23;
2Ch 9:8
nPs 132:11;
Jer 33:17

m6 Traditionally *judges*; also in verse 10

16:42 *sounding the trumpets.* See Nu 10:1–10.
17:1–27 See 2Sa 7 and notes.
17:1,10 In these verses the Chronicler omits the statement that David had rest from his enemies (2Sa 7:1,11). Several factors may be at work in this omission: 1. The account of David's major wars is yet to come (chs. 18–20). Chronologically, this passage should follow the account of the wars (v. 8), but the author has placed it here to continue his concern with the ark and the building of the temple (vv. 4–6,12). 2. The Chronicler also views David as a man of war through most of his life (22:6–8), in contrast to Solomon, who is the man of "peace and rest" (22:9) and who will build the temple (22:10). For the Chronicler, David has rest from enemies only late in his life (22:18). 3. As part of his concern to parallel David and Solomon to Moses and Joshua, Solomon (like Joshua) brings the people to rest from enemies (see Introduction: Portrait of David and Solomon).
17:12–14 Though in this context these words refer to

Solomon, the NT applies them to Jesus (Mk 1:11; Lk 1:32–33; Heb 1:5).
17:13 The Chronicler omits from his source (2Sa 7:14) any reference to "punishment with the rod" or "flogging" as discipline for Solomon. This omission reflects his idealization of Solomon as a Messianic figure, for whom such punishment would not be appropriate (see Introduction: Portrait of David and Solomon).
17:14 The Chronicler introduces his own concerns by the changes in the pronouns found in his source (2Sa 7:16); instead of "Your house and your kingdom," the Chronicler reads "my house and my kingdom." This same emphasis on theocracy (God's rule) is found in several other passages unique to Chronicles (28:5–6; 29:23; 2Ch 1:11; 9:8; 13:4–8).
17:16 *sat.* Aside from its parallel in 2Sa 7:18, this is the only reference in the OT to sitting as a posture for prayer.

house of your servant. You have
looked on me as though I were the
most exalted of men, O LORD God.
18“What more can David say to you
for honoring your servant? For you
know your servant, 19O LORD. For the
sake[o] of your servant and according
to your will, you have done this great
thing and made known all these great
promises.[p]
20“There is no one like you, O
LORD, and there is no God but you,[q]
as we have heard with our own ears.
21And who is like your people Israel—the one nation on earth whose
God went out to redeem[r] a people for
himself, and to make a name for yourself, and to perform great and awesome wonders by driving out nations
from before your people, whom you
redeemed from Egypt? 22You made
your people Israel your very own forever,[s] and you, O LORD, have become
their God.
23“And now, LORD, let the promise[t] you have made concerning your
servant and his house be established
forever. Do as you promised, 24so that
it will be established and that your
name will be great forever. Then men
will say, ‘The LORD Almighty, the God
over Israel, is Israel’s God!’ And the
house of your servant David will be
established before you.
25“You, my God, have revealed to
your servant that you will build a
house for him. So your servant has
found courage to pray to you. 26O
LORD, you are God! You have promised these good things to your servant.
27Now you have been pleased to bless
the house of your servant, that it may
continue forever in your sight;[u] for
you, O LORD, have blessed it, and it
will be blessed forever.”

17:19 [o]2Sa 7:16-17; 2Ki 20:6; Isa 9:7; 37:35; 55:3 [p]S 2Sa 7:25 **17:20** [q]S Ex 8:10; S 9:14; S 15:11; Isa 44:6; 46:9 **17:21** [r]S Ex 6:6 **17:22** [s]Ex 19:5-6 **17:23** [t]S 1Ki 8:25 **17:27** [u]Ps 16:11; 21:6

David’s Victories

18:1-13pp — 2Sa 8:1-14

18 In the course of time, David defeated the Philistines and subdued
them, and he took Gath and its surrounding villages from the control of the Philistines.
2David also defeated the Moabites,[v] and
they became subject to him and brought
tribute.
3Moreover, David fought Hadadezer
king of Zobah,[w] as far as Hamath, when he
went to establish his control along the Euphrates River.[x] 4David captured a thousand of his chariots, seven thousand charioteers and twenty thousand foot soldiers.
He hamstrung[y] all but a hundred of the
chariot horses.
5When the Arameans of Damascus[z]
came to help Hadadezer king of Zobah,
David struck down twenty-two thousand
of them. 6He put garrisons in the Aramean
kingdom of Damascus, and the Arameans
became subject to him and brought tribute.
The LORD gave David victory everywhere
he went.
7David took the gold shields carried by
the officers of Hadadezer and brought
them to Jerusalem. 8From Tebah[n] and
Cun, towns that belonged to Hadadezer,
David took a great quantity of bronze,
which Solomon used to make the bronze
Sea,[a] the pillars and various bronze articles.
9When Tou king of Hamath heard that
David had defeated the entire army of
Hadadezer king of Zobah, 10he sent his son
Hadoram to King David to greet him and
congratulate him on his victory in battle

18:2 [v]S Nu 21:29 **18:3** [w]1Ch 19:6 [x]S Ge 2:14 **18:4** [y]S Ge 49:6 **18:5** [z]2Ki 16:9 **18:8** [a]S 1Ki 7:23; 2Ch 4:2-5

[n]*8* Hebrew *Tibhath,* a variant of *Tebah*

17:21–22 The references to the exodus from Egypt would remind the Chronicler’s audience of the second great exodus, the release of the restoration community from the period of Babylonian captivity.

18:1–20:8 The accounts of David’s wars serve to show the blessing of God on his reign; God keeps his promise to subdue David’s enemies (17:10). These accounts are also particularly relevant to a theme developed in the postexilic prophets: that the silver and gold of the nations would flow to Jerusalem; the tribute of enemy peoples builds the temple of God (18:7–8,11; 22:2–5,14–15; cf. Hag 2:1–9,20–23; Zec 2:7–13; 6:9–15; 14:12–14). While this passage of Chronicles portrays God’s blessing on David, it simultaneously explains the Chronicler’s report later (22:6–8; 28:3) that David could not build the temple because he was a man of war. The material in these chapters essentially follows the Chronicler’s source in 2 Samuel. The major differences are not changes the Chronicler introduces into the text, but items he chooses not to deal with—in particular 2Sa 9; 11:2–12:25, where accounts not compatible with his portrait of David occur.

18:1–13 See 2Sa 8:1–14 and notes.

18:2 The Chronicler omits the harsh treatment of the Moabites recorded in 2Sa 8:2, perhaps so that no unnecessary cruelty or brutality would tarnish his portrait of David.

18:5 *Arameans.* Mentioned also among the enemies of Saul (1Sa 14:47, “Zobah”). By the time of David they were united north (Zobah) and south (Beth Rehob, 2Sa 10:6) under Hadadezer. They persisted as a foe of Israel for two centuries until they fell to Assyria shortly before the northern kingdom likewise fell (2Ki 16:7–9).

18:8 *Tebah and Cun.* Located in the valley between the Lebanon and Anti-Lebanon mountain ranges. *which Solomon used to make . . . various bronze articles.* See 2Ch 4:2–5,18.

over Hadadezer, who had been at war with Tou. Hadoram brought all kinds of articles of gold and silver and bronze.

[11]King David dedicated these articles to the LORD, as he had done with the silver and gold he had taken from all these nations: Edom[b] and Moab, the Ammonites and the Philistines, and Amalek.[c]

[12]Abishai son of Zeruiah struck down eighteen thousand Edomites[d] in the Valley of Salt. [13]He put garrisons in Edom, and all the Edomites became subject to David. The LORD gave David victory everywhere he went.

David's Officials

18:14-17pp — 2Sa 8:15-18

[14]David reigned[e] over all Israel,[f] doing what was just and right for all his people. [15]Joab[g] son of Zeruiah was over the army; Jehoshaphat son of Ahilud was recorder; [16]Zadok[h] son of Ahitub and Ahimelech[o][i] son of Abiathar were priests; Shavsha was secretary; [17]Benaiah son of Jehoiada was over the Kerethites and Pelethites;[j] and David's sons were chief officials at the king's side.

The Battle Against the Ammonites

19:1-19pp — 2Sa 10:1-19

19 In the course of time, Nahash king of the Ammonites[k] died, and his son succeeded him as king. [2]David thought, "I will show kindness to Hanun son of Nahash, because his father showed kindness to me." So David sent a delegation to express his sympathy to Hanun concerning his father.

When David's men came to Hanun in the land of the Ammonites to express sympathy to him, [3]the Ammonite nobles said to Hanun, "Do you think David is honoring your father by sending men to you to express sympathy? Haven't his men come to you to explore and spy out[l] the country and overthrow it?" [4]So Hanun seized David's men, shaved them, cut off their garments in the middle at the buttocks, and sent them away.

[5]When someone came and told David about the men, he sent messengers to meet them, for they were greatly humiliated. The king said, "Stay at Jericho till your beards have grown, and then come back."

[6]When the Ammonites realized that they had become a stench[m] in David's nostrils, Hanun and the Ammonites sent a thousand talents[p] of silver to hire chariots and charioteers from Aram Naharaim,[q] Aram Maacah and Zobah.[n] [7]They hired thirty-two thousand chariots and charioteers, as well as the king of Maacah with his troops, who came and camped near Medeba,[o] while the Ammonites were mustered from their towns and moved out for battle.

[8]On hearing this, David sent Joab out with the entire army of fighting men. [9]The Ammonites came out and drew up in battle formation at the entrance to their city,

Cross references

18:11 [b]S Nu 24:18; [c]Nu 24:20
18:12 [d]1Ki 11:15
18:14 [e]1Ch 29:26; [f]1Ch 11:1
18:15 [g]2Sa 5:6-8
18:16 [h]1Ch 6:8; [i]1Ch 24:6
18:17 [j]S 1Sa 30:14; S 2Sa 15:18
19:1 [k]S Ge 19:38; Jdg 10:17-11:33; 2Ch 20:1-2; Zep 2:8-11
19:3 [l]S Nu 21:32
19:6 [m]S Ge 34:30; [n]S 1Ch 18:3
19:7 [o]S Nu 21:30

[o]*16* Some Hebrew manuscripts, Vulgate and Syriac (see also 2 Samuel 8:17); most Hebrew manuscripts *Abimelech*   [p]*6* That is, about 37 tons (about 34 metric tons)   [q]*6* That is, Northwest Mesopotamia

---

18:12 *Abishai.* 2Sa 8:13 speaks only of David (see 1Ki 11:15–16; Ps 60 title).

18:15–17 The titles and duties of these officers at David's court appear to be modeled on the organization of Egyptian functionaries serving Pharaoh.

18:15 For the account of how Joab attained his position over the army see 11:4–6; 2Sa 5:6–8.

18:16 *Zadok... Ahimelech son of Abiathar.* See notes on 6:8; 16:39; 2Sa 8:17.

18:17 *Kerethites and Pelethites.* Apparently a group of foreign mercenaries who constituted part of the royal bodyguard (2Sa 8:18; 20:23; see note on 1Sa 30:14). They remained loyal to David at the time of the rebellions of Absalom (2Sa 15:18) and Sheba (2Sa 20:7) and supported the succession of Solomon against his rival Adonijah (1Ki 1:38,44). *chief officials.* The earlier narrative at this point uses the Hebrew term ordinarily translated "priests" (see note on 2Sa 8:18). The Chronicler has used a term for civil service instead of sacral service. Two approaches to this passage are ordinarily followed: 1. Some scholars see here an attempt by the Chronicler to keep the priesthood restricted to the Levitical line as part of his larger concern with legitimacy of cultic institutions in his own day. 2. Others argue that the Hebrew term used in 2Sa 8:18 could earlier have had a broader meaning than "priest" and could be used

of some other types of officials (cf. 2Sa 20:26; 1Ki 4:5). The Chronicler used an equivalent term, since by his day the Hebrew term for "priest" was restricted to cultic functionaries. The Septuagint, Targum, Old Latin and Josephus all translate the term in Samuel by some word other than "priest."

19:1–20:3 The Chronicler follows 2Sa 10–12 closely (see notes there), apart from his omission of the account of David's sin with Bathsheba (11:2–12:25). The Ammonites were a traditional enemy of Israel (2Ch 20:1–2,23; 27:5; Jdg 3:13; 10:7–9; 10:17–11:33; 1Sa 11:1–13; 14:47; 2Ki 10:32–33; Jer 49:1–6; Zep 2:8–11). Even during the postexilic period Tobiah the Ammonite troubled Jerusalem (Ne 2:19; 4:3,7; 6:1,12,14; 13:4–9).

19:1 *Nahash.* Possibly the same as Saul's foe (1Sa 11:1), or perhaps his descendant.

19:6 *Aram Naharaim, Aram Maacah and Zobah.* 2Sa 10:6 also mentions Beth Rehob and Tob. All these states were north and northeast of Israel and formed a solid block from the region of Lake Huleh through the Anti-Lebanons to beyond the Euphrates.

19:7 *Medeba.* A town in Moab apparently in the hands of Ammon.

19:9 *their city.* The capital city, Rabbah, to which Joab would lay siege the following year (20:1–3).

while the kings who had come were by themselves in the open country.

¹⁰Joab saw that there were battle lines in front of him and behind him; so he selected some of the best troops in Israel and deployed them against the Arameans. ¹¹He put the rest of the men under the command of Abishai^p his brother, and they were deployed against the Ammonites. ¹²Joab said, "If the Arameans are too strong for me, then you are to rescue me; but if the Ammonites are too strong for you, then I will rescue you. ¹³Be strong and let us fight bravely for our people and the cities of our God. The LORD will do what is good in his sight."

¹⁴Then Joab and the troops with him advanced to fight the Arameans, and they fled before him. ¹⁵When the Ammonites saw that the Arameans were fleeing, they too fled before his brother Abishai and went inside the city. So Joab went back to Jerusalem.

¹⁶After the Arameans saw that they had been routed by Israel, they sent messengers and had Arameans brought from beyond the River,^r with Shophach the commander of Hadadezer's army leading them.

¹⁷When David was told of this, he gathered all Israel^q and crossed the Jordan; he advanced against them and formed his battle lines opposite them. David formed his lines to meet the Arameans in battle, and they fought against him. ¹⁸But they fled before Israel, and David killed seven thousand of their charioteers and forty thousand of their foot soldiers. He also killed Shophach the commander of their army.

¹⁹When the vassals of Hadadezer saw that they had been defeated by Israel, they made peace with David and became subject to him.

So the Arameans were not willing to help the Ammonites anymore.

The Capture of Rabbah

20:1–3pp — 2Sa 11:1; 12:29–31

20 In the spring, at the time when kings go off to war, Joab led out the armed forces. He laid waste the land of the Ammonites and went to Rabbah^r and besieged it, but David remained in Jerusalem. Joab attacked Rabbah and left it in ruins.^s ²David took the crown from the head of their king^s—its weight was found to be a talent^t of gold, and it was set with precious stones—and it was placed on David's head. He took a great quantity of plunder from the city ³and brought out the people who were there, consigning them to labor with saws and with iron picks and axes.^t David did this to all the Ammonite towns. Then David and his entire army returned to Jerusalem.

War With the Philistines

2:4–8pp — 2Sa 21:15–22

⁴In the course of time, war broke out with the Philistines, at Gezer.^u At that time Sibbecai the Hushathite killed Sippai, one of the descendants of the Rephaites,^v and the Philistines were subjugated.

⁵In another battle with the Philistines, Elhanan son of Jair killed Lahmi the brother of Goliath the Gittite, who had a spear with a shaft like a weaver's rod.^w

⁶In still another battle, which took place at Gath, there was a huge man with six fingers on each hand and six toes on each foot—twenty-four in all. He also was descended from Rapha. ⁷When he taunted Israel, Jonathan son of Shimea, David's brother, killed him.

⁸These were descendants of Rapha in Gath, and they fell at the hands of David and his men.

David Numbers the Fighting Men

21:1–26pp — 2Sa 24:1–25

21 Satan^x rose up against Israel and incited David to take a census^y of

19:11
pS 1Sa 26:6
19:17 qS 1Ch 9:1

20:1 rS Dt 3:11
sAm 1:13-15
20:3 tS Dt 29:11
20:4 uJos 10:33
vS Ge 14:5
20:5 wS 1Sa 17:7
21:1
xS 2Ch 18:21;
S Ps 109:6
y2Ch 14:8; 25:5

r16 That is, the Euphrates   s2 Or of Milcom, that is, Molech   t2 That is, about 75 pounds (about 34 kilograms)

19:18 *seven thousand.* 2Sa 10:18 has 700, which is evidently a copyist's mistake.
20:1 *when kings go off to war.* Immediately following the spring harvest when there was some relaxation of agricultural labors and armies on the move could live off the land. *Rabbah.* See note on 19:9. Rabbah is the site of modern Amman, Jordan.
20:2–3 The Chronicler assumes that the reader is familiar with 2Sa 12:26–29; he does not offer an explanation of how David, who had remained in Jerusalem (v. 1), came to be at Rabbah.

20:4 *Sibbecai.* See 11:29; 27:11. *Rephaites.* Ancient people known for their large size (see Ge 14:5; Dt 2:11; see also note on 2Sa 21:16).
20:5 See note on 2Sa 21:19. *weaver's rod.* See 11:23; 1Sa 17:7.
20:6 *Rapha.* See note on 2Sa 21:16.
21:1—22:1 See 2Sa 24 and notes. Although the story of David's census is quite similar in both narratives, the two accounts function differently. In Samuel the account belongs to the appendix (2Sa 21–24), which begins and ends with accounts of the Lord's anger against Israel during the reign of

Israel. 2So David said to Joab and the commanders of the troops, "Go and count[z]
the Israelites from Beersheba to Dan. Then
report back to me so that I may know how
many there are."

3But Joab replied, "May the LORD multiply his troops a hundred times over.[a] My
lord the king, are they not all my lord's
subjects? Why does my lord want to do
this? Why should he bring guilt on Israel?"

4The king's word, however, overruled
Joab; so Joab left and went throughout Israel and then came back to Jerusalem.
5Joab reported the number of the fighting
men to David: In all Israel[b] there were
one million one hundred thousand men
who could handle a sword, including four
hundred and seventy thousand in Judah.

6But Joab did not include Levi and Benjamin in the numbering, because the king's
command was repulsive to him. 7This
command was also evil in the sight of God;
so he punished Israel.

8Then David said to God, "I have sinned
greatly by doing this. Now, I beg you, take
away the guilt of your servant. I have done
a very foolish thing."

9The LORD said to Gad,[c] David's seer,[d]
10"Go and tell David, 'This is what the
LORD says: I am giving you three options.
Choose one of them for me to carry out
against you.' "

11So Gad went to David and said to him,
"This is what the LORD says: 'Take your
choice: 12three years of famine,[e] three
months of being swept away[u] before your
enemies, with their swords overtaking
you, or three days of the sword[f] of the
LORD[g]—days of plague in the land, with
the angel of the LORD ravaging every part
of Israel.' Now then, decide how I should
answer the one who sent me."

13David said to Gad, "I am in deep distress. Let me fall into the hands of the
LORD, for his mercy[h] is very great; but do
not let me fall into the hands of men."

14So the LORD sent a plague on Israel,
and seventy thousand men of Israel fell
dead.[i] 15And God sent an angel[j] to destroy Jerusalem.[k] But as the angel was doing so, the LORD saw it and was grieved[l]
because of the calamity and said to the angel who was destroying[m] the people,
"Enough! Withdraw your hand." The angel of the LORD was then standing at the
threshing floor of Araunah[v] the Jebusite.

16David looked up and saw the angel of
the LORD standing between heaven and
earth, with a drawn sword in his hand extended over Jerusalem. Then David and
the elders, clothed in sackcloth, fell facedown.[n]

17David said to God, "Was it not I who
ordered the fighting men to be counted? I
am the one who has sinned and done
wrong. These are but sheep.[o] What have
they done? O LORD my God, let your hand
fall upon me and my family,[p] but do not
let this plague remain on your people."

18Then the angel of the LORD ordered
Gad to tell David to go up and build an
altar to the LORD on the threshing floor[q] of
Araunah the Jebusite. 19So David went up

21:2 [z]1Ch 27:23-24
21:3 [a]S Dt 1:11
21:5 [b]S 1Ch 9:1
21:9 [c]S 1Sa 22:5 [d]S 1Sa 9:9
21:12 [e]S Dt 32:24 [f]Eze 30:25 [g]S Ge 19:13
21:13 [h]Ps 6:4; 86:15; 130:4,7
21:14 [i]1Ch 27:24
21:15 [j]S Ge 32:1 [k]Ps 125:2 [l]S Ge 6:6; S Ex 32:14 [m]S Ge 19:13
21:16 [n]S Nu 14:5; S Jos 7:6
21:17 [o]S 2Sa 7:8 [p]Jnh 1:12
21:18 [q]2Ch 3:1

[u]*12* Hebrew; Septuagint and Vulgate (see also 2 Samuel 24:13) *of fleeing* [v]*15* Hebrew *Ornan,* a variant of *Araunah;* also in verses 18-28

David because of actions by her kings (in ch. 21, an act of Saul; in ch. 24, an act of David). See note on 2Sa 21:1–24:25. The Chronicler appears to include it in order to account for the purchase of the ground on which the temple would be built. The additional material in Chronicles that is not found in Samuel (21:28–22:1) makes this interest clear. The census is the preface to David's preparations for the temple (chs. 22–29).

21:1 See note on 2Sa 24:1. *Satan.* See NIV text notes on Job 1:6; Zec 3:1.

21:4 The Chronicler abridges the more extensive account of Joab's itinerary found in 2Sa 24:4–8; he does not mention that the census required nine months and 20 days (2Sa 24:8).

21:5 *In all Israel . . . one million one hundred thousand men . . . including four hundred and seventy thousand in Judah.* 2Sa 24:9 has 800,000 in Israel and 500,000 (which could be a round number for 470,000) in Judah. The reason for the difference is unclear. Perhaps it is to be related to the unofficial and incomplete nature of the census (see 27:23–24), with the differing figures representing the inclusion or exclusion of certain unspecified groupings among the people (see v. 6). Or perhaps it is simply due to a copyist's mistake. The NIV relieves the problem somewhat by translating the conjunction here as "including" instead of "and."

21:6 The Chronicler adds the note that Joab exempted Levi and Benjamin from the counting. This additional note reflects the Chronicler's concern with the Levites and with the worship of Israel. The tabernacle in Gibeon and the ark in Jerusalem both fell within the borders of Benjamin.

21:9 *Gad.* A longtime friend of David, having been with him when he was a fugitive from Saul (1Sa 22:3–5; cf. 1Ch 29:29; 2Ch 29:25).

21:12 *three years of famine.* See NIV text note on 2Sa 24:13.

21:16 The verse has no parallel in the traditional Hebrew text of 2Sa 24, so some scholars regard it as an addition by the Chronicler reflecting the more developed doctrine of angels in the postexilic period. However, a fragmentary Hebrew text of Samuel from the third century B.C., discovered at Qumran, contains the verse. It now appears that the Chronicler was carefully copying the Samuel text at his disposal, which differed in some respects from the Masoretic (traditional Hebrew) text. Josephus, who appears to be following the text of Samuel, also reported this information. Presumably, he too used a text of Samuel similar to that followed by the Chronicler.

in obedience to the word that Gad had spoken in the name of the LORD.

20While Araunah was threshing wheat,ʳ he turned and saw the angel; his four sons who were with him hid themselves. 21Then David approached, and when Araunah looked and saw him, he left the threshing floor and bowed down before David with his face to the ground.

22David said to him, "Let me have the site of your threshing floor so I can build an altar to the LORD, that the plague on the people may be stopped. Sell it to me at the full price."

23Araunah said to David, "Take it! Let my lord the king do whatever pleases him. Look, I will give the oxen for the burnt offerings, the threshing sledges for the wood, and the wheat for the grain offering. I will give all this."

24But King David replied to Araunah, "No, I insist on paying the full price. I will not take for the LORD what is yours, or sacrifice a burnt offering that costs me nothing."

25So David paid Araunah six hundred shekelsʷ of gold for the site. 26David built an altar to the LORD there and sacrificed burnt offerings and fellowship offerings.ˣ He called on the LORD, and the LORD answered him with fireˢ from heaven on the altar of burnt offering.

27Then the LORD spoke to the angel, and he put his sword back into its sheath. 28At that time, when David saw that the LORD had answered him on the threshing floor of Araunah the Jebusite, he offered sacrifices there. 29The tabernacle of the LORD, which

Moses had made in the desert, and the altar of burnt offering were at that time on the high place at Gibeon.ᵗ 30But David could not go before it to inquire of God, because he was afraid of the sword of the angel of the LORD.

22 Then David said, "The house of the LORD Godᵘ is to be here, and also the altar of burnt offering for Israel."

Preparations for the Temple

2So David gave orders to assemble the aliensᵛ living in Israel, and from among them he appointed stonecuttersʷ to prepare dressed stone for building the house of God. 3He provided a large amount of iron to make nails for the doors of the gateways and for the fittings, and more bronze than could be weighed.ˣ 4He also provided more cedar logsʸ than could be counted, for the Sidonians and Tyrians had brought large numbers of them to David.

5David said, "My son Solomon is youngᶻ and inexperienced, and the house to be built for the LORD should be of great magnificence and fame and splendorᵃ in the sight of all the nations. Therefore I will make preparations for it." So David made extensive preparations before his death.

6Then he called for his son Solomon and charged him to buildᵇ a house for the LORD, the God of Israel. 7David said to Solomon: "My son, I had it in my heartᶜ to buildᵈ a house for the Nameᵉ of the LORD my God. 8But this word of the LORD came to me: 'You have shed much blood

Cross references (center column):

21:20 ʳS Jdg 6:11
21:26 ˢS Ex 19:18; S Jdg 6:21
21:29 ʳS Jos 9:3
22:1 ᵘS Ge 28:17
22:2 ᵛS Ex 1:11; S Dt 20:11; 2Ch 8:10; S Isa 56:6
ʷ1Ki 5:17-18; Ezr 3:7
22:3 ˣS 1Ki 7:47; 1Ch 29:2-5
22:4 ʸS 1Ki 5:6
22:5 ᶻS 1Ch 3:7; 1Ch 29:1
ᵃ2Ch 2:5
22:6 ᵇAc 7:47
22:7 ᶜS 1Ch 17:2
ᵈS 1Ki 8:17
ᵉDt 12:5,11

ʷ25 That is, about 15 pounds (about 7 kilograms)
ˣ26 Traditionally *peace offerings*

21:20–21 The Chronicler reports that Araunah was threshing wheat as the king approached—information not found in 2Sa 24:20. However, Josephus and the fragmentary text of Samuel from Qumran both mention this information (see note on v. 16).
21:25 *six hundred shekels of gold.* 2Sa 24:24 says 50 shekels of silver were paid for the threshing floor and oxen. The difference has been explained by some as the Chronicler's attempt to glorify David and the temple by inflating the price. However, the difference is more likely explained by the Chronicler's statement that this was the price for the "site," i.e., for a much larger area than the threshing floor alone.
21:26 *fire from heaven.* Underscores the divine approval and the sanctity of the site (see 2Ch 7:1; Lev 9:24; 1Ki 18:37–38).
21:28–22:1 This material is not found in 2Sa 24. It reflects the Chronicler's main concern in reporting this narrative (see note on 21:1–22:1).
21:30 *it.* The tabernacle.
22:1–29:30 This material is unique to Chronicles and displays some of the Chronicler's most characteristic interests: the preparations for the building of the temple, the legitimacy of the priests and Levites, and the royal succession. The chapters portray a theocratic "Messianic" kingdom

as it existed under David and Solomon.
22:1 David dedicates this property (21:18–30) as the site for the temple (see vv. 2–6).
22:2–19 Solomon's appointment to succeed David was twofold: (1) a private audience, with David and some leaders in attendance (vv. 17–19), and (2) a public announcement to the people (ch. 28), similar to when Joshua succeeded Moses (see Introduction: Portrait of David and Solomon).
22:2 *aliens . . . stonecutters.* 2Sa 20:24 confirms the use of forced labor by David, but does not specify that these laborers were aliens, not Israelites. Solomon used Israelites in conscripted labor (1Ki 5:13–18; 9:15–23; 11:28), but the Chronicler mentions only his use of aliens (2Ch 8:7–10). Though they were personally free, aliens were without political rights and could be easily exploited. The OT frequently warns that they were not to be oppressed (Ex 22:21; 23:9; Lev 19:33; Dt 24:14; Jer 7:6; Zec 7:10). Isaiah prophesies the participation of foreigners in the building of Jerusalem's walls in the future (Isa 60:10–12).
22:3 *bronze.* See note on 18:8.
22:5 *young.* Solomon's age at the time of his accession is not known with certainty. He came to the throne in 970 B.C. and was likely born c. 991.
22:8–9 See note on 17:1. In 1Ki 5:3 Solomon explains that David could not build the temple because he was too busy

and have fought many wars.[f] You are not to build a house for my Name,[g] because you have shed much blood on the earth in my sight. [9]But you will have a son who will be a man of peace[h] and rest,[i] and I will give him rest from all his enemies on every side. His name will be Solomon,[y][j] and I will grant Israel peace and quiet[k] during his reign. [10]He is the one who will build a house for my Name.[l] He will be my son,[m] and I will be his father. And I will establish[n] the throne of his kingdom over Israel forever.'[o]

[11]"Now, my son, the LORD be with[p] you, and may you have success and build the house of the LORD your God, as he said you would. [12]May the LORD give you discretion and understanding[q] when he puts you in command over Israel, so that you may keep the law of the LORD your God. [13]Then you will have success[r] if you are careful to observe the decrees and laws[s] that the LORD gave Moses for Israel. Be strong and courageous.[t] Do not be afraid or discouraged.

[14]"I have taken great pains to provide for the temple of the LORD a hundred thousand talents[z] of gold, a million talents[a] of silver, quantities of bronze and iron too great to be weighed, and wood and stone. And you may add to them.[u] [15]You have many workmen: stonecutters, masons and carpenters,[v] as well as men skilled in every kind of work [16]in gold and silver, bronze and iron—craftsmen[w] beyond number. Now begin the work, and the LORD be with you."

[17]Then David ordered[x] all the leaders of Israel to help his son Solomon. [18]He said to them, "Is not the LORD your God with you? And has he not granted you rest[y] on every side?[z] For he has handed the inhabitants of the land over to me, and the land

is subject to the LORD and to his people. [19]Now devote your heart and soul to seeking the LORD your God.[a] Begin to build the sanctuary of the LORD God, so that you may bring the ark of the covenant of the LORD and the sacred articles belonging to God into the temple that will be built for the Name of the LORD."

The Levites

23 When David was old and full of years, he made his son Solomon[b] king over Israel.[c]

[2]He also gathered together all the leaders of Israel, as well as the priests and Levites. [3]The Levites thirty years old or more[d] were counted,[e] and the total number of men was thirty-eight thousand.[f] [4]David said, "Of these, twenty-four thousand are to supervise[g] the work[h] of the temple of the LORD and six thousand are to be officials and judges.[i] [5]Four thousand are to be gatekeepers and four thousand are to praise the LORD with the musical instruments[j] I have provided for that purpose."[k]

[6]David divided[l] the Levites into groups corresponding to the sons of Levi:[m] Gershon, Kohath and Merari.

Gershonites

[7]Belonging to the Gershonites:[n] Ladan and Shimei.

[8]The sons of Ladan:
Jehiel the first, Zetham and Joel—three in all.

[9]The sons of Shimei:
Shelomoth, Haziel and Haran—three in all.

Cross references (center column)

22:8 /S 1Ki 5:3
g1Ch 28:3
22:9
hS Jos 14:15;
S 1Ki 5:4 /ver 18;
1Ch 23:25;
2Ch 14:6,7;
15:15; 20:30;
36:21
/S 2Sa 12:24;
S 1Ch 23:1
k1Ki 4:20
22:10
/S 1Ch 17:12
mS 2Sa 7:13
n1Ki 9:5
oS 2Sa 7:14;
S 1Ch 17:4;
2Ch 6:15
22:11
pS 1Sa 16:18;
S 18:12
22:12 q1Ki 3:11
22:13 r1Ki 2:3
s1Ch 28:7
tS Dt 31:6
22:14
u1Ch 29:2-5,19
22:15 vEzr 3:7
22:16 w2Ch 2:7
22:17 x1Ch 28:1
22:18 yS ver 9
z2Sa 7:1

22:19 a2Ch 7:14
23:1 b1Ch 22:9;
28:5; 2Ch 1:8
cS 1Ki 1:30;
1Ch 29:28
23:3 dNu 8:24
e1Ch 21:7
/Nu 4:3-49
23:4 gEzr 3:8
h2Ch 34:13;
Ne 4:10
i1Ch 26:29;
2Ch 19:8;
Eze 44:24
23:5
/S 1Ch 15:16;
Ps 92:3
kNe 12:45
23:6 l2Ch 8:14;
23:18; 29:25
mS Nu 3:17;
1Ch 24:20
23:7 n1Ch 6:71

y9 *Solomon* sounds like and may be derived from the Hebrew for *peace.* z14 That is, about 3,750 tons (about 3,450 metric tons) a14 That is, about 37,500 tons (about 34,500 metric tons)

---

with wars. The Chronicler's nuance is slightly different—not just that wars took so much of his time, but that David was in some sense defiled by them because of the bloodshed. A pun on Solomon's name is woven into the divine oracle (see NIV text note on v. 9).

22:10 See note on 17:12–14.

22:12–13 See Introduction: Portrait of David and Solomon.

22:19 See 2Ch 5:7.

23:1–27:34 David's preparations for the temple were not restricted to amassing materials for the building; he also arranged for its administration and worship. Unique to Chronicles (see note on 22:1–29:30), these details of the organization of the theocracy (God's kingdom) were of vital concern in the Chronicler's own day. Characteristically for the Chronicler, details about religious and cultic matters (chs. 23–26) take precedence over those that are civil and secular (ch. 27). David's arrangements provided the basis and authority for the practices of the restored community.

23:1 *made his son Solomon king.* The account of Solomon's succession is resumed in chs. 28–29. The Chronicler omits the accounts of disputed succession and bloody consolidation recorded in 1Ki 1–2 (see note on 28:1–29:30) since these would not be in accord with his overall portrait of David and Solomon (see Introduction: Portrait of David and Solomon).

23:2–5 The Levites were not counted in the census that had provoked the wrath of God (21:6–7).

23:3 *Levites thirty years old or more.* The census of Levites was made first in accordance with the Mosaic prescription (Nu 4:1–3). Apparently soon after this count, David instructed that the age be lowered to 20 years (vv. 24,27); a similar adjustment to age 25 had been made under Moses (Nu 8:23–24, but see note on Nu 8:24).

23:6 *Gershon, Kohath and Merari.* The Levites were organized by their three clans (ch. 6; Ex 6:16–19; Nu 3). This list parallels those in 6:16–30; 24:20–30.

These were the heads of the families of Ladan.

10 And the sons of Shimei:
Jahath, Ziza,[b] Jeush and Beriah.
These were the sons of Shimei—four in all.

11 Jahath was the first and Ziza the second, but Jeush and Beriah did not have many sons; so they were counted as one family with one assignment.

Kohathites

12 The sons of Kohath:[o]
Amram, Izhar, Hebron and Uzziel—four in all.

13 The sons of Amram:[p]
Aaron and Moses.
Aaron was set apart,[q] he and his descendants forever, to consecrate the most holy things, to offer sacrifices before the LORD, to minister[r] before him and to pronounce blessings[s] in his name forever. 14 The sons of Moses the man[t] of God were counted as part of the tribe of Levi.

15 The sons of Moses:
Gershom and Eliezer.[u]

16 The descendants of Gershom:[v]
Shubael was the first.

17 The descendants of Eliezer:
Rehabiah[w] was the first.
Eliezer had no other sons, but the sons of Rehabiah were very numerous.

18 The sons of Izhar:
Shelomith[x] was the first.

19 The sons of Hebron:[y]
Jeriah the first, Amariah the second, Jahaziel the third and Jekameam the fourth.

20 The sons of Uzziel:
Micah the first and Isshiah the second.

Merarites

21 The sons of Merari:[z]
Mahli and Mushi.[a]
The sons of Mahli:
Eleazar and Kish.

22 Eleazar died without having sons: he had only daughters. Their cousins, the sons of Kish, married them.[b]

23 The sons of Mushi:
Mahli, Eder and Jerimoth—three in all.

24 These were the descendants of Levi by their families—the heads of families as they were registered under their names and counted individually, that is, the workers twenty years old or more[c] who served in the temple of the LORD. 25 For David had said, "Since the LORD, the God of Israel, has granted rest[d] to his people and has come to dwell in Jerusalem forever, 26 the Levites no longer need to carry the tabernacle or any of the articles used in its service."[e] 27 According to the last instructions of David, the Levites were counted from those twenty years old or more.

28 The duty of the Levites was to help Aaron's descendants in the service of the temple of the LORD: to be in charge of the courtyards, the side rooms, the purification[f] of all sacred things and the performance of other duties at the house of God. 29 They were in charge of the bread set out on the table,[g] the flour for the grain offerings,[h] the unleavened wafers, the baking and the mixing, and all measurements of quantity and size.[i] 30 They were also to stand every morning to thank and praise the LORD. They were to do the same in the evening[j] 31 and whenever burnt offerings were presented to the LORD on Sabbaths and at New Moon[k] festivals and at appointed feasts.[l] They were to serve before the LORD regularly in the proper number and in the way prescribed for them.

32 And so the Levites[m] carried out their responsibilities for the Tent of Meeting,[n] for the Holy Place and, under their brothers the descendants of Aaron, for the service of the temple of the LORD.[o]

The Divisions of Priests

24 These were the divisions[p] of the sons of Aaron:[q]

The sons of Aaron were Nadab, Abihu, Eleazar and Ithamar.[r] 2 But Nadab and

23:12 [o]S Ge 46:11; S Ex 6:18 **23:13** [p]Ex 6:20 [q]Ex 30:7-10 [r]S 1Ch 15:2 [s]S Nu 6:23 **23:14** [t]Dt 33:1 **23:15** [u]Ex 18:4 **23:16** [v]1Ch 26:24-28 **23:17** [w]1Ch 24:21 **23:18** [x]1Ch 26:25 **23:19** [y]1Ch 24:23; 26:31 **23:21** [z]S 1Ch 6:19 [a]S Ex 6:19 **23:22** [b]Nu 36:8 **23:24** [c]S Nu 4:3 **23:25** [d]S 1Ch 22:9 **23:26** [e]Nu 4:5, 15; 7:9; Dt 10:8 **23:28** [f]2Ch 29:15; Ne 13:9; Mal 3:3 **23:29** [g]S Ex 25:30 [h]Lev 2:4-7; 6:20-23 [i]Lev 19:35-36; S 1Ch 9:29,32 **23:30** [j]S 1Ch 9:33; Ps 134:1 **23:31** [k]S 2Ki 4:23 [l]Nu 28:9-29:39; Isa 1:13-14; Col 2:16 **23:32** [m]1Ch 6:48 [n]Nu 3:6-8,38 [o]2Ch 23:18; 31:2; Eze 44:14 **24:1** [p]1Ch 23:6; 28:13; 2Ch 5:11; 8:14; 23:8; 31:2; 35:4,5; Ezr 6:18 [q]Nu 3:2-4 [r]S Ex 6:23

[b] *10* One Hebrew manuscript, Septuagint and Vulgate (see also verse 11); most Hebrew manuscripts *Zina*

23:24,27 *twenty years old or more.* See note on v. 3.
23:28–32 See note on 9:28–34. The function of the Levites was to assist the priests. In addition to the care of the precincts and implements, baked goods and music (mentioned as Levitical duties in 9:22–34), the Chronicler adds details on the role of the Levites assisting in sacrifices.
23:30 *morning ... evening.* See Ex 29:38–41; Nu 28:3–8.
24:1–19 There are several lists of priests from the postexilic period (see 6:3–15; 9:10–13; Ezr 2:36–39; Ne 10:1–8; 11:10–12; 12:1–7,12–21).
24:2 *Nadab and Abihu died.* The Chronicler alludes to the events recorded in Lev 10:1–3 (see note on 6:1–3).

Abihu died before their father did,[s] and they had no sons; so Eleazar and Ithamar served as the priests. [3]With the help of Zadok[t] a descendant of Eleazar and Ahimelech a descendant of Ithamar, David separated them into divisions for their appointed order of ministering. [4]A larger number of leaders were found among Eleazar's descendants than among Ithamar's, and they were divided accordingly: sixteen heads of families from Eleazar's descendants and eight heads of families from Ithamar's descendants. [5]They divided them impartially by drawing lots,[u] for there were officials of the sanctuary and officials of God among the descendants of both Eleazar and Ithamar.

[6]The scribe Shemaiah son of Nethanel, a Levite, recorded their names in the presence of the king and of the officials: Zadok the priest, Ahimelech[v] son of Abiathar and the heads of families of the priests and of the Levites—one family being taken from Eleazar and then one from Ithamar.

[7]The first lot fell to Jehoiarib,
  the second to Jedaiah,[w]
[8]the third to Harim,[x]
  the fourth to Seorim,
[9]the fifth to Malkijah,
  the sixth to Mijamin,
[10]the seventh to Hakkoz,
  the eighth to Abijah,[y]
[11]the ninth to Jeshua,
  the tenth to Shecaniah,
[12]the eleventh to Eliashib,
  the twelfth to Jakim,
[13]the thirteenth to Huppah,
  the fourteenth to Jeshebeab,
[14]the fifteenth to Bilgah,
  the sixteenth to Immer,[z]
[15]the seventeenth to Hezir,[a]
  the eighteenth to Happizzez,
[16]the nineteenth to Pethahiah,
  the twentieth to Jehezkel,
[17]the twenty-first to Jakin,
  the twenty-second to Gamul,
[18]the twenty-third to Delaiah
  and the twenty-fourth to Maaziah.

[19]This was their appointed order of min-

istering when they entered the temple of the LORD, according to the regulations prescribed for them by their forefather Aaron, as the LORD, the God of Israel, had commanded him.

The Rest of the Levites

[20]As for the rest of the descendants of Levi:[b]

  from the sons of Amram: Shubael;
    from the sons of Shubael: Jehdeiah.
  [21]As for Rehabiah,[c] from his sons:
    Isshiah was the first.
[22]From the Izharites: Shelomoth;
    from the sons of Shelomoth:
    Jahath.
[23]The sons of Hebron:[d] Jeriah the
    first,[c] Amariah the second, Jahaziel the third and Jekameam the
    fourth.
[24]The son of Uzziel: Micah;
    from the sons of Micah: Shamir.
  [25]The brother of Micah: Isshiah;
    from the sons of Isshiah: Zechariah.
[26]The sons of Merari:[e] Mahli and Mushi.
    The son of Jaaziah: Beno.
[27]The sons of Merari:
    from Jaaziah: Beno, Shoham, Zaccur and Ibri.
[28]From Mahli: Eleazar, who had no
    sons.
[29]From Kish: the son of Kish:
    Jerahmeel.
[30]And the sons of Mushi: Mahli, Eder
    and Jerimoth.

  These were the Levites, according to their families. [31]They also cast lots,[f] just as their brothers the descendants of Aaron did, in the presence of King David and of Zadok, Ahimelech, and the heads of families of the priests and of the Levites. The families of the oldest brother were treated the same as those of the youngest.

Cross references (center column)

24:2 [s]Lev 10:1-2
24:3 [t]S 2Sa 8:17
24:5 [u]ver 31;
  1Ch 25:8; 26:13
24:6 [v]1Ch 18:16
24:7 [w]Ezr 2:36;
  Ne 12:6
24:8 [x]Ezr 2:39;
  10:21; Ne 10:5
24:10 [y]Ne 12:4,
  17; Lk 1:5
24:14 [z]Ezr 2:37;
  10:20; Jer 20:1
24:15 [a]Ne 10:20

24:20 [b]S 1Ch 23:6
24:21 [c]1Ch 23:17
24:23 [d]S 1Ch 23:19
24:26 [e]S 1Ch 6:19
24:31 [f]S ver 5

[c]23 Two Hebrew manuscripts and some Septuagint manuscripts (see also 1 Chron. 23:19); most Hebrew manuscripts *The sons of Jeriah:*

24:3 *Zadok... Ahimelech.* Zadok and Abiathar had served as David's high priests. Here, late in David's life, Abiathar's son Ahimelech appears to have taken over some of his father's duties (see note on 6:8), but see note on 2Sa 8:17.
24:4 *sixteen... eight.* A total of 24 divisions was selected by lot. This would allow for service either in monthly shifts, as was done by priests in Egyptian mortuary temples, or for two-week shifts once each year as found in NT times. The names of the first, second, fourth, ninth and 24th divisions have been found in a Dead Sea scroll from the fourth cave at Qumran (see "The Time between the Testaments," p.

1431).
24:7 *Jehoiarib.* Mattathias, father of the Maccabees, was a member of the Jehoiarib division (in the Apocrypha see 1 Maccabees 2:1).
24:10 *Abijah.* The father of John the Baptist "belonged to the priestly division of Abijah" (Lk 1:5).
24:15 *Hezir.* The division from the family of Hezir was prominent in intertestamental times; the name appears on one of the large tombs in the Kidron Valley, east of Jerusalem.
24:20–31 This list supplements 23:7–23 by extending some of the lines mentioned there.

The Singers

25 David, together with the commanders of the army, set apart some of the sons of Asaph,[g] Heman[h] and Jeduthun[i] for the ministry of prophesying,[j] accompanied by harps, lyres and cymbals.[k] Here is the list of the men[l] who performed this service:[m]

[2]From the sons of Asaph:
Zaccur, Joseph, Nethaniah and Asarelah. The sons of Asaph were under the supervision of Asaph, who prophesied under the king's supervision.

[3]As for Jeduthun, from his sons:[n]
Gedaliah, Zeri, Jeshaiah, Shimei,[d] Hashabiah and Mattithiah, six in all, under the supervision of their father Jeduthun, who prophesied, using the harp[o] in thanking and praising the LORD.

[4]As for Heman, from his sons:
Bukkiah, Mattaniah, Uzziel, Shubael and Jerimoth; Hananiah, Hanani, Eliathah, Giddalti and Romamti-Ezer; Joshbekashah, Mallothi, Hothir and Mahazioth. [5]All these were sons of Heman the king's seer. They were given him through the promises of God to exalt him.[e] God gave Heman fourteen sons and three daughters.

[6]All these men were under the supervision of their fathers[p] for the music of the temple of the LORD, with cymbals, lyres and harps, for the ministry at the house of God. Asaph, Jeduthun and Heman[q] were under the supervision of the king.[r] [7]Along with their relatives—all of them trained and skilled in music for the LORD—they numbered 288. [8]Young and old alike, teacher as well as student, cast lots[s] for their duties.

[9]The first lot, which was for Asaph,[t]
fell to Joseph,
his sons and relatives,[f]   12[g]
the second to Gedaliah,
he and his relatives and sons,   12
[10]the third to Zaccur,
his sons and relatives,   12
[11]the fourth to Izri,[h]

his sons and relatives,   12
[12]the fifth to Nethaniah,
his sons and relatives,   12
[13]the sixth to Bukkiah,
his sons and relatives,   12
[14]the seventh to Jesarelah,[i]
his sons and relatives,   12
[15]the eighth to Jeshaiah,
his sons and relatives,   12
[16]the ninth to Mattaniah,
his sons and relatives,   12
[17]the tenth to Shimei,
his sons and relatives,   12
[18]the eleventh to Azarel,[j]
his sons and relatives,   12
[19]the twelfth to Hashabiah,
his sons and relatives,   12
[20]the thirteenth to Shubael,
his sons and relatives,   12
[21]the fourteenth to Mattithiah,
his sons and relatives,   12
[22]the fifteenth to Jerimoth,
his sons and relatives,   12
[23]the sixteenth to Hananiah,
his sons and relatives,   12
[24]the seventeenth to Joshbekashah,
his sons and relatives,   12
[25]the eighteenth to Hanani,
his sons and relatives,   12
[26]the nineteenth to Mallothi,
his sons and relatives,   12
[27]the twentieth to Eliathah,
his sons and relatives,   12
[28]the twenty-first to Hothir,
his sons and relatives,   12
[29]the twenty-second to Giddalti,
his sons and relatives,   12
[30]the twenty-third to Mahazioth,
his sons and relatives,   12
[31]the twenty-fourth to Romamti-Ezer,
his sons and relatives,   12[u]

[d]3 One Hebrew manuscript and some Septuagint manuscripts (see also verse 17); most Hebrew manuscripts do not have *Shimei*.   [e]5 Hebrew *exalt the horn*   [f]9 See Septuagint; Hebrew does not have *his sons and relatives*.   [g]9 See the total in verse 7; Hebrew does not have *twelve*.   [h]11 A variant of *Zeri*   [i]14 A variant of *Asarelah*   [j]18 A variant of *Uzziel*

25:1 [g]S 1Ch 6:39
[h]S 1Ch 6:33
[i]1Ch 16:41,42; Ne 11:17
[j]S 1Sa 10:5; 2Ki 3:15
[k]S 1Ch 15:16
[l]S 1Ch 6:31
[m]2Ch 5:12; 8:14; 34:12; 35:15; Ezr 3:10
25:3
[n]1Ch 16:41-42
[o]S Ge 4:21; Ps 33:2
25:6
[p]S 1Ch 15:16
[q]S 1Ch 15:19
[r]2Ch 23:18; 29:25
25:8 [s]1Ch 26:13
25:9 [t]S 1Ch 6:39

25:31
[u]S 1Ch 9:33

25:1 *commanders of the army.* David often sought the counsel of military leaders (11:10; 12:32; 28:1), even in cultic affairs (13:1; 15:25). *Asaph, Heman and Jeduthun.* See note on 6:31–48. *ministry of prophesying.* There are several passages in Chronicles, largely in portions unique to these books, where cultic personnel are designated prophets (here; 2Ch 20:14–17; 29:30; 35:15; cf. 2Ki 23:2; 2Ch 34:30). Zechariah the priest also appears to function as a prophet, though he is not so named (2Ch 24:19–22). This may reflect postexilic interest in the prophet-priest-king fig-

ure of Messianic expectation: In Chronicles not only do priests prophesy, but kings also function as priests (see notes on 15:27; 16:1–3). David's organizing of the temple musicians may reflect his overall interest in music (1Sa 16:23; 18:10; 19:9; 2Sa 1:17–27; 6:5,14).

25:5 *fourteen sons and three daughters.* Numerous progeny are a sign of divine blessing (see Job 1:2; 42:13). This is specifically stated for Heman as the result of the promises of God to exalt him. See 3:1–9; 14:2–7; 26:4–5; 2Ch 11:18–21; 13:21; 21:2; 24:3.

The Gatekeepers

26 The divisions of the gatekeepers:[v] From the Korahites: Meshelemiah son of Kore, one of the sons of Asaph.

[2] Meshelemiah had sons:
Zechariah[w] the firstborn,
Jediael the second,
Zebadiah the third,
Jathniel the fourth,
[3] Elam the fifth,
Jehohanan the sixth
and Eliehoenai the seventh.

[4] Obed-Edom also had sons:
Shemaiah the firstborn,
Jehozabad the second,
Joah the third,
Sacar the fourth,
Nethanel the fifth,
[5] Ammiel the sixth,
Issachar the seventh
and Peullethai the eighth.
(For God had blessed Obed-Edom.[x])

[6] His son Shemaiah also had sons, who were leaders in their father's family because they were very capable men. [7] The sons of Shemaiah: Othni, Rephael, Obed and Elzabad; his relatives Elihu and Semakiah were also able men. [8] All these were descendants of Obed-Edom; they and their sons and their relatives were capable men with the strength to do the work—descendants of Obed-Edom, 62 in all.

[9] Meshelemiah had sons and relatives, who were able men—18 in all.

[10] Hosah the Merarite had sons: Shimri the first (although he was not the firstborn, his father had appointed him the first),[y] [11] Hilkiah the second, Tabaliah the third and Zechariah the fourth. The sons and relatives of Hosah were 13 in all.

[12] These divisions of the gatekeepers, through their chief men, had duties for ministering[z] in the temple of the LORD, just as their relatives had. [13] Lots[a] were cast for each gate, according to their families, young and old alike.

[14] The lot for the East Gate[b] fell to Shelemiah.[k] Then lots were cast for his son Zechariah,[c] a wise counselor, and the lot for the North Gate fell to him. [15] The lot for the South Gate fell to Obed-Edom,[d] and the lot for the storehouse fell to his sons. [16] The lots for the West Gate and the Shalleketh Gate on the upper road fell to Shuppim and Hosah.

Guard was alongside of guard: [17] There were six Levites a day on the east, four a day on the north, four a day on the south and two at a time at the storehouse. [18] As for the court to the west, there were four at the road and two at the court itself.

[19] These were the divisions of the gatekeepers who were descendants of Korah and Merari.[e]

The Treasurers and Other Officials

[20] Their fellow Levites[f] were[l] in charge of the treasuries of the house of God and the treasuries for the dedicated things.[g]

[21] The descendants of Ladan, who were Gershonites through Ladan and who were heads of families belonging to Ladan the Gershonite,[h] were Jehieli, [22] the sons of Jehieli, Zetham and his brother Joel. They were in charge of the treasuries[i] of the temple of the LORD.

[23] From the Amramites, the Izharites, the Hebronites and the Uzzielites:[j]

26:1 [v]S 1Ch 9:17
26:2 [w]S 1Ch 9:21
26:5 [x]S 2Sa 6:10; S 1Ch 13:13; S 16:38
26:10 [y]Dt 21:16; 1Ch 5:1
26:12 [z]1Ch 9:22
26:13 [a]S 1Ch 24:5
26:14 [b]S 1Ch 9:18 [c]S 1Ch 9:21
26:15 [d]S 1Ch 13:13; 2Ch 25:24
26:19 [e]2Ch 35:15; Ne 7:1; Eze 44:11
26:20 [f]2Ch 24:5 [g]1Ch 28:12
26:21 [h]1Ch 23:7; 29:8
26:22 [i]1Ch 9:26
26:23 [j]S Nu 3:27

[k]14 A variant of Meshelemiah [l]20 Septuagint; Hebrew As for the Levites, Ahijah was

---

26:1-19 The most extensive of the Chronicler's lists of gatekeepers (see 9:17–27; 16:37–38). A list of gatekeepers in the postexilic period is found in Ezr 2:42 (Ne 7:45).
26:1 *Asaph*. This name appears to be an abbreviation of Ebiasaph (6:23; 9:19); he should not be confused with the temple musician (25:1–2,6).
26:4-5 Numerous sons are again a sign of divine blessing (see note on 25:5).
26:4 *Obed-Edom*. Had cared for the ark when it was left at his house (see note on 13:13).
26:12 *duties*. Elaborated in 9:22–29.
26:14 *East Gate*. The main entrance; it had six guard posts, as opposed to four at the other gates (v. 17).
26:15 *South Gate*. The palaces of David and Solomon were south of the temple mount. The southern gate would be the main one used by the king, and this assignment probably reflects a particular honor for Obed-Edom (see notes on 26:4–5; see also Eze 46:1–10).

26:16 *Shalleketh Gate*. The only reference to a gate by this name; presumably it was on the western side. The Chronicler writes to an audience familiar with these topographical details.
26:20 *treasuries of the house of God*. The Levites in charge of these treasuries received the offerings of the people and cared for the valuable temple equipment (9:28–29). *treasuries for the dedicated things*. Received the plunder from warfare (vv. 27–28). Texts from Mesopotamian temples confirm the presence of temple officers who served as assayers to handle and refine the precious metals received as revenue and offerings. The procedure with reference to the offerings of the people may be seen in the reign of Joash (2Ch 24:4–14; 2Ki 12:4–16). Numerous passages reflect on the wealth collected in the temple (see, e.g., 29:1–9; 2Ch 4:1–22; 34:9–11; 36:7,10,18–19; 1Ki 14:25–28; 15:15, 18; 2Ki 12:4–18; 14:14; 16:8; 25:13–17).

²⁴Shubael,^k a descendant of Gershom son of Moses, was the officer in charge of the treasuries. ²⁵His relatives through Eliezer: Rehabiah his son, Jeshaiah his son, Joram his son, Zicri his son and Shelomith^l his son. ²⁶Shelomith and his relatives were in charge of all the treasuries for the things dedicated^m by King David, by the heads of families who were the commanders of thousands and commanders of hundreds, and by the other army commanders. ²⁷Some of the plunder taken in battle they dedicated for the repair of the temple of the LORD. ²⁸And everything dedicated by Samuel the seerⁿ and by Saul son of Kish, Abner son of Ner and Joab son of Zeruiah, and all the other dedicated things were in the care of Shelomith and his relatives.

²⁹From the Izharites: Kenaniah and his sons were assigned duties away from the temple, as officials and judges^o over Israel.

³⁰From the Hebronites: Hashabiah^p and his relatives—seventeen hundred able men—were responsible in Israel west of the Jordan for all the work of the LORD and for the king's service. ³¹As for the Hebronites,^q Jeriah was their chief according to the genealogical records of their families. In the fortieth^r year of David's reign a search was made in the records, and capable men among the Hebronites were found at Jazer in Gilead. ³²Jeriah had twenty-seven hundred relatives, who were able men and heads of families, and King David put them in charge of the Reubenites, the Gadites and the half-tribe

of Manasseh for every matter pertaining to God and for the affairs of the king.

Army Divisions

27 This is the list of the Israelites—heads of families, commanders of thousands and commanders of hundreds, and their officers, who served the king in all that concerned the army divisions that were on duty month by month throughout the year. Each division consisted of 24,000 men.

²In charge of the first division, for the first month, was Jashobeam^s son of Zabdiel. There were 24,000 men in his division. ³He was a descendant of Perez and chief of all the army officers for the first month.

⁴In charge of the division for the second month was Dodai^t the Ahohite; Mikloth was the leader of his division. There were 24,000 men in his division.

⁵The third army commander, for the third month, was Benaiah^u son of Jehoiada the priest. He was chief and there were 24,000 men in his division. ⁶This was the Benaiah who was a mighty man among the Thirty and was over the Thirty. His son Ammizabad was in charge of his division.

⁷The fourth, for the fourth month, was Asahel^v the brother of Joab; his son Zebadiah was his successor. There were 24,000 men in his division.

⁸The fifth, for the fifth month, was the commander Shamhuth^w the Izrahite. There were 24,000 men in his division.

⁹The sixth, for the sixth month, was Ira^x

26:24
^k1Ch 23:16
26:25
^l1Ch 23:18
26:26
^mS 2Sa 8:11
26:28 ⁿS 1Sa 9:9
26:29
^oDt 17:8-13;
S 1Ch 23:4
26:30
^p1Ch 27:17
26:31
^qS 1Ch 23:19
^rS 2Sa 5:4

27:2 ^s2Sa 23:8
27:4 ^tS 2Sa 23:9
27:5
^u2Sa 23:20
27:7 ^vS 2Sa 2:18
27:8 ^w1Ch 11:27
27:9 ^x2Sa 23:26

26:26 *things dedicated by King David.* See note on 18:1–20:8; see also 2Ch 5:1.

26:27 *plunder taken in battle they dedicated.* Cf. Ge 14:17–20.

26:29–32 These verses designate the 6,000 officials and judges (23:4) who would work outside Jerusalem; they are drawn from two sub-clans of Kohath (6:18). Dt 17:8–13 envisages a judicial function for the priests and Levites (see 2Ch 19:4–11).

26:30,32 *for all the work of the LORD and for the king's service . . . for every matter pertaining to God and for the affairs of the king.* In the theocracy (kingdom of God) there is no division between secular and sacred, no tension in serving God and the king (cf. Mt 22:15–22; Lk 16:10–13; Ro 13:1–7; 1Ti 2:1–4; 1Pe 2:13–17).

26:31 *fortieth year.* The last year of David's reign.

27:1–15 The names of the commanders of David's army are the same as those found in the list of his mighty men (see

11:11–47; see also 2Sa 23:8–39 and notes). Those who had served David while he fled from Saul became commanders in the regular army.

27:1 *24,000.* See note on 12:23–37. Although a national militia consisting of 12 units of 24,000 each (a total of 288,000) is not unreasonable, the stress in this passage on unit commanders and divisions suggests that here too the Hebrew word for "1,000" should perhaps be taken as the designation of a military unit. To designate a division as "1,000" would be to give the upper limit of the number of men in such a unit, though such units would ordinarily not have a full complement of men. If this approach is followed, the figures in the following verses would be read as "24 units" instead of 24,000.

27:2 *Jashobeam.* See 11:11.

27:4 *Dodai.* See 11:12.

27:5 *Benaiah.* See 11:22–25; 18:17.

27:7 *Asahel.* See 11:26; 2Sa 2:18–23.

the son of Ikkesh the Tekoite. There were 24,000 men in his division.

¹⁰The seventh, for the seventh month, was Helez[y] the Pelonite, an Ephraimite. There were 24,000 men in his division.

¹¹The eighth, for the eighth month, was Sibbecai[z] the Hushathite, a Zerahite. There were 24,000 men in his division.

¹²The ninth, for the ninth month, was Abiezer[a] the Anathothite, a Benjamite. There were 24,000 men in his division.

¹³The tenth, for the tenth month, was Maharai[b] the Netophathite, a Zerahite. There were 24,000 men in his division.

¹⁴The eleventh, for the eleventh month, was Benaiah[c] the Pirathonite, an Ephraimite. There were 24,000 men in his division.

¹⁵The twelfth, for the twelfth month, was Heldai[d] the Netophathite, from the family of Othniel.[e] There were 24,000 men in his division.

Officers of the Tribes

¹⁶The officers over the tribes of Israel:

over the Reubenites: Eliezer son of Zicri;

over the Simeonites: Shephatiah son of Maacah;

¹⁷over Levi: Hashabiah[f] son of Kemuel;

over Aaron: Zadok;[g]

¹⁸over Judah: Elihu, a brother of David;

over Issachar: Omri son of Michael;

¹⁹over Zebulun: Ishmaiah son of Obadiah;

over Naphtali: Jerimoth son of Azriel;

²⁰over the Ephraimites: Hoshea son of Azaziah;

over half the tribe of Manasseh: Joel son of Pedaiah;

²¹over the half-tribe of Manasseh in Gilead: Iddo son of Zechariah;

over Benjamin: Jaasiel son of Abner;

²²over Dan: Azarel son of Jeroham.

These were the officers over the tribes of Israel.

²³David did not take the number of the men twenty years old or less,[h] because the LORD had promised to make Israel as numerous as the stars[i] in the sky. ²⁴Joab son of Zeruiah began to count the men but did not finish. Wrath came on Israel on account of this numbering,[j] and the number was not entered in the book[m] of the annals of King David.

The King's Overseers

²⁵Azmaveth son of Adiel was in charge of the royal storehouses.

Jonathan son of Uzziah was in charge of the storehouses in the outlying districts, in the towns, the villages and the watchtowers.

²⁶Ezri son of Kelub was in charge of the field workers who farmed the land.

²⁷Shimei the Ramathite was in charge of the vineyards.

Zabdi the Shiphmite was in charge of the produce of the vineyards for the wine vats.

²⁸Baal-Hanan the Gederite was in charge of the olive and sycamore-fig[k] trees in the western foothills.

Joash was in charge of the supplies of olive oil.

²⁹Shitrai the Sharonite was in charge of the herds grazing in Sharon.[l]

Shaphat son of Adlai was in charge of the herds in the valleys.

³⁰Obil the Ishmaelite was in charge of the camels.

Cross references (center column):

27:10 [y]2Sa 23:26
27:11 [z]S 2Sa 21:18
27:12 [a]2Sa 23:27
27:13 [b]2Sa 23:28
27:14 [c]S 1Ch 11:31
27:15 [d]2Sa 23:29 [e]S Jos 15:17
27:17 [f]1Ch 26:30 [g]S 2Sa 8:17; S 1Ch 12:28
27:23 [h]S 2Sa 24:1; 1Ch 21:2-5 [i]S Ge 12:2
27:24 [j]S 2Sa 24:15; 1Ch 21:14
27:28 [k]S 1Ki 10:27
27:29 [l]SS 2:1; Isa 33:9; 35:2; 65:10

[m]24 Septuagint; Hebrew *number*

27:9–15 The remainder of the commanders were selected from among the Thirty (see the names listed in 11:27–31).
27:16–22 The Chronicler's interest in "all Israel" appears in this list of officers who were over the 12 tribes (see Introduction: Purpose and Themes). The number is kept at 12 by omitting Gad and Asher (see note on 2:1–2).
27:17 *Zadok.* See note on 6:8; see also 12:28; 16:39.
27:18 *Elihu.* Not named elsewhere among the brothers of David. Perhaps he is the unnamed son from the list in 2:10–17 (see note there). Elihu could also be a variant of the name of Jesse's oldest son, Eliab, or the term "brother" could be taken in the sense of "relative," in which case Elihu would be a more distant kinsman.
27:21 *Abner.* A relative of King Saul (see 26:28; 1Sa 14:50–51; 17:55–58; 26:5–16; 2Sa 2:8–4:1).
27:23–24 *number.* Refers to the census narrative in ch. 21 (2Sa 24).

27:23 *twenty years old or less.* The figures reported in ch. 21 and 2Sa 24 were the numbers of those older than 20 years. *promised to make Israel as numerous as the stars.* The patriarchal promises of numerous descendants (Ge 12:2; 13:16; 15:5; 22:17) appear to have been the basis for the objections of Joab (v. 24) to the taking of a census (21:3; 2Sa 24:3).
27:24 *did not finish.* Joab did not count those under age 20, nor did he include the tribes of Levi and Benjamin (21:6).
27:25–31 A list of the administrators of David's property (v. 31). The large cities of the ancient Near East had three basic economic sectors: (1) royal, (2) temple and (3) private. There is no evidence of direct taxation during the reign of David; his court appears to have been financed by extensive landholdings, commerce, plunder from his many wars, and tribute from subjugated kingdoms.

Jehdeiah the Meronothite was in charge of the donkeys.

31Jaziz the Hagrite *m* was in charge of the flocks.

All these were the officials in charge of King David's property.

32Jonathan, David's uncle, was a counselor, a man of insight and a scribe. Jehiel son of Hacmoni took care of the king's sons.

33Ahithophel *n* was the king's counselor. Hushai *o* the Arkite was the king's friend. 34Ahithophel was succeeded by Jehoiada son of Benaiah and by Abiathar. *p*

Joab *q* was the commander of the royal army.

David's Plans for the Temple

28 David summoned *r* all the officials *s* of Israel to assemble at Jerusalem: the officers over the tribes, the commanders of the divisions in the service of the king, the commanders of thousands and commanders of hundreds, and the officials in charge of all the property and livestock belonging to the king and his sons, together with the palace officials, the mighty men and all the brave warriors.

2King David rose to his feet and said: "Listen to me, my brothers and my people. I had it in my heart *t* to build a house as a place of rest *u* for the ark of the covenant of the LORD, for the footstool *v* of our God, and I made plans to build it. *w* 3But God said to me, *x* 'You are not to build a house for my Name, *y* because you are a warrior and have shed blood.' *z*

4"Yet the LORD, the God of Israel, chose me *a* from my whole family *b* to be king over Israel forever. He chose Judah *c* as leader, and from the house of Judah he

chose my family, and from my father's sons he was pleased to make me king over all Israel. *d* 5Of all my sons—and the LORD has given me many *e*—he has chosen my son Solomon *f* to sit on the throne *g* of the kingdom of the LORD over Israel. 6He said to me: 'Solomon your son is the one who will build *h* my house and my courts, for I have chosen him to be my son, *i* and I will be his father. 7I will establish his kingdom forever if he is unswerving in carrying out my commands and laws, *j* as is being done at this time.'

8"So now I charge you in the sight of all Israel *k* and of the assembly of the LORD, and in the hearing of our God: Be careful to follow all the commands *l* of the LORD your God, that you may possess this good land and pass it on as an inheritance to your descendants forever. *m*

9"And you, my son Solomon, acknowledge the God of your father, and serve him with wholehearted devotion *n* and with a willing mind, for the LORD searches every heart *o* and understands every motive behind the thoughts. If you seek him, *p* he will be found by you; but if you forsake *q* him, he will reject *r* you forever. 10Consider now, for the LORD has chosen you to build a temple as a sanctuary. Be strong and do the work."

11Then David gave his son Solomon the plans *s* for the portico of the temple, its buildings, its storerooms, its upper parts, its inner rooms and the place of atonement. 12He gave him the plans of all that the Spirit *t* had put in his mind for the courts of the temple of the LORD and all the surrounding rooms, for the treasuries of the temple of God and for the treasuries for the dedicated things. *u* 13He gave him instructions for the divisions *v* of the priests

Cross references (center column)

27:31
*m*S 1Ch 5:10
27:33
*n*S 2Sa 15:12
*o*S 2Sa 15:37
27:34
*p*S 1Sa 22:20
*q*S 2Sa 2:13
28:1 *r*1Ch 22:17
*s*1Ch 27:1-31;
29:6
28:2 *t*S 1Sa 10:7;
S 1Ch 17:2
*u*2Ch 6:41
*v*Ps 99:5; 132:7;
Isa 60:13
*w*Ps 132:1-5
28:3 *x*S 2Sa 7:5
*y*1Ch 22:8
*z*S 1Ki 5:3;
S 1Ch 17:4
28:4 *a*2Ch 6:6
*b*1Sa 16:1-13
*c*S Ge 49:10;
Nu 24:17-19

*d*1Ch 11:1
28:5 *e*S 1Ch 3:1
*f*S 2Sa 12:24;
S 1Ch 23:1
*g*S 1Ch 17:14
28:6 *h*1Ki 8:20
*i*S 2Sa 7:13;
S 1Ch 17:13
28:7 *j*1Ch 22:13
28:8 *k*S 1Ch 9:1
*l*Dt 6:1 *m*Dt 4:1;
S 17:14-20
28:9
*n*S 1Ch 29:19
*o*S 1Sa 2:3;
2Ch 6:30; Ps 7:9
*p*S 1Ch 16:11;
S Ps 40:16
*q*S Dt 4:31;
S Jos 24:20;
S 2Ch 7:19; 15:2
*r*1Ki 9:7;
Ps 44:23; 74:1;
77:7
28:11
*s*S Ex 25:9;
Ac 7:44; Heb 8:5
28:12
*t*S 1Ch 12:18
*u*1Ch 26:20
28:13
*v*S 1Ch 24:1

27:32–34 A list of David's cabinet members, supplementary to that in 18:14–17.
27:33 *Ahithophel*. Was replaced after he committed suicide, withdrawing his support of Absalom's rebellion (2Sa 15:12,31–37; 16:20–17:23).
27:34 *Benaiah*. See v. 5.
28:1–29:30 The account of the transition from the reign of David to that of Solomon is one of the clearest demonstrations of the Chronicler's idealization of their reigns when it is compared with the succession account in 1Ki 1–2. The Chronicler makes no mention of the infirmities of the aged David (1Ki 1:1–4), the rebellion of Adonijah and the king's sons (1Ki 1:5–10), the court intrigue to secure Solomon's succession (1Ki 1:11–31) or David's charge to Solomon to punish his enemies after his death (1Ki 2:1–9). His selection of material presents a transition of power that is smooth and peaceful and receives the support of "all Israel" (29:25), the officials and the people (28:1–2; 29:6–9,21–25). Instead of the bedridden David who sends others to anoint Solomon (1Ki 1:32–35), David himself is present and in charge of the

ceremonies (see 23:1 and note).
28:1 The assembly is composed largely of the groups named in ch. 27. This public announcement (v. 5) follows the private announcement of Solomon's succession in ch. 22 (see note on 22:2–19).
28:3 *you are a warrior and have shed blood*. See note on 22:8–9.
28:5 *chosen my son Solomon*. See vv. 6,10; 29:1. These are the only uses in the OT of the Hebrew verb for "chosen" with reference to any king after David (see Introduction: Purpose and Themes). The Chronicler's application of this term to Solomon is consistent with his depiction of that king. *kingdom of the LORD*. See note on 17:14.
28:6 *my son*. See 17:12–14 and note; see also 22:10.
28:8–9 See Introduction: Portrait of David and Solomon.
28:12 David provides Solomon with the plans for the temple. This reflects the Chronicler's modeling David after Moses: Just as Moses received the plans for the tabernacle from God (Ex 25–30), so also David received the plans for the temple.

and Levites, and for all the work of serving in the temple of the LORD, as well as for all the articles to be used in its service. [14]He designated the weight of gold for all the gold articles to be used in various kinds of service, and the weight of silver for all the silver articles to be used in various kinds of service: [15]the weight of gold for the gold lampstands[w] and their lamps, with the weight for each lampstand and its lamps; and the weight of silver for each silver lampstand and its lamps, according to the use of each lampstand; [16]the weight of gold for each table[x] for consecrated bread; the weight of silver for the silver tables; [17]the weight of pure gold for the forks, sprinkling bowls[y] and pitchers; the weight of gold for each gold dish; the weight of silver for each silver dish; [18]and the weight of the refined gold for the altar of incense.[z] He also gave him the plan for the chariot,[a] that is, the cherubim of gold that spread their wings and shelter[b] the ark of the covenant of the LORD.

[19]"All this," David said, "I have in writing from the hand of the LORD upon me, and he gave me understanding in all the details[c] of the plan. [d]"

[20]David also said to Solomon his son, "Be strong and courageous,[e] and do the work. Do not be afraid or discouraged, for the LORD God, my God, is with you. He will not fail you or forsake[f] you until all the work for the service of the temple of the LORD is finished.[g] [21]The divisions of the priests and Levites are ready for all the work on the temple of God, and every willing man skilled[h] in any craft will help you in all the work. The officials and all the people will obey your every command."

Gifts for Building the Temple

29 Then King David said to the whole assembly: "My son Solomon, the one whom God has chosen, is young and inexperienced.[i] The task is great, because this palatial structure is not for man but for the LORD God. [2]With all my resources I have provided for the temple of my God—gold[j] for the gold work, silver for

the silver, bronze for the bronze, iron for the iron and wood for the wood, as well as onyx for the settings, turquoise,[n][k] stones of various colors, and all kinds of fine stone and marble—all of these in large quantities.[l] [3]Besides, in my devotion to the temple of my God I now give my personal treasures of gold and silver for the temple of my God, over and above everything I have provided[m] for this holy temple: [4]three thousand talents[o] of gold (gold of Ophir)[n] and seven thousand talents[p] of refined silver,[o] for the overlaying of the walls of the buildings, [5]for the gold work and the silver work, and for all the work to be done by the craftsmen. Now, who is willing to consecrate himself today to the LORD?"

[6]Then the leaders of families, the officers of the tribes of Israel, the commanders of thousands and commanders of hundreds, and the officials[p] in charge of the king's work gave willingly. [q] [7]They[r] gave toward the work on the temple of God five thousand talents[q] and ten thousand darics[r] of gold, ten thousand talents[s] of silver, eighteen thousand talents[t] of bronze and a hundred thousand talents[u] of iron. [8]Any who had precious stones[s] gave them to the treasury of the temple of the LORD in the custody of Jehiel the Gershonite. [t] [9]The people rejoiced at the willing response of their leaders, for they had given freely and wholeheartedly[u] to the LORD. David the king also rejoiced greatly.

David's Prayer

[10]David praised the LORD in the presence of the whole assembly, saying,

"Praise be to you, O LORD,
  God of our father Israel,
  from everlasting to everlasting.

Cross references

28:15 [w]Ex 25:31
28:16 [x]S Ex 25:23
28:17 [y]S Ex 27:3
28:18 [z]Ex 30:1-10; [a]S Ex 25:22; [b]S Ex 25:20
28:19 [c]1Ki 6:38; [d]S Ex 25:9
28:20 [e]S Dt 31:6; 1Ch 22:13; 2Ch 19:11; Hag 2:4; [f]S Dt 4:31; S Jos 24:20; [g]S 1Ki 6:14; 2Ch 7:11
28:21 [h]Ex 35:25-36:5
29:1 [i]1Ki 3:7; 1Ch 22:5; 2Ch 13:7
29:2 [j]ver 7,14, 16; Ezr 1:4; 6:5; Hag 2:8
[k]Isa 54:11
[l]1Ch 22:2-5
29:3 [m]2Ch 24:10; 31:3; 35:8
29:4 [n]S Ge 10:29; [o]1Ch 22:14
29:6 [p]1Ch 27:1; S 28:1; [q]ver 9; Ex 25:1-8; 35:20-29; 36:2; 2Ch 24:10; Ezr 7:15
29:7 [r]S Ge 25:2; Ne 7:70-71
29:8 [s]Ex 35:27; [t]S 1Ch 26:21
29:9 [u]1Ki 8:61

Footnotes

[n]2 The meaning of the Hebrew for this word is uncertain.
[o]4 That is, about 110 tons (about 100 metric tons)
[p]4 That is, about 260 tons (about 240 metric tons)
[q]7 That is, about 190 tons (about 170 metric tons)
[r]7 That is, about 185 pounds (about 84 kilograms)
[s]7 That is, about 375 tons (about 345 metric tons)
[t]7 That is, about 675 tons (about 610 metric tons)
[u]7 That is, about 3,750 tons (about 3,450 metric tons)

28:19 *I have in writing from the hand of the LORD upon me.* The Chronicler may intend no more than the ordinary process of inspiration whereby David wrote under divine influence. On the other hand, he may imply a parallel with Moses, who also received documents from the hand of the Lord (Ex 25:40; 27:8; 31:18; 32:16).

28:20 See Introduction: Portrait of David and Solomon.

29:1 *chosen.* See note on 28:5. *young.* See note on 22:5.

29:2–9 After donating his personal fortune to the construc-

tion of the temple, David appeals to the people for their voluntary gifts. The Chronicler again appears to be modeling his account of David on events from the life of Moses (Ex 25:1–8; 35:4–9,20–29). The willing response of the people aided the building of both tabernacle and temple.

29:7 *darics.* The daric was a Persian coin, apparently named for Darius I (522–486 B.C.) in whose reign it first appears (see Ezr 8:27). Since the Chronicler's readers were familiar with it, he could use it as an up-to-date standard of value for an earlier treasure of gold.

Solomon Asks for Wisdom

1:2–13pp — 1Ki 3:4–15
1:14–17pp — 1Ki 10:26–29; 2Ch 9:25–28

1 Solomon son of David established[a] himself firmly over his kingdom, for the LORD his God was with[b] him and made him exceedingly great. [c]

²Then Solomon spoke to all Israel[d]—to the commanders of thousands and commanders of hundreds, to the judges and to all the leaders in Israel, the heads of families— ³and Solomon and the whole assembly went to the high place at Gibeon, [e] for God's Tent of Meeting[f] was there, which Moses[g] the LORD's servant had made in the desert. ⁴Now David had brought up the ark[h] of God from Kiriath Jearim to the place he had prepared for it, because he had pitched a tent[i] for it in Jerusalem. ⁵But the bronze altar[j] that Bezalel[k] son of Uri, the son of Hur, had made was in Gibeon in front of the tabernacle of the LORD; so Solomon and the assembly inquired[l] of him there. ⁶Solomon went up to the bronze altar before the LORD in the Tent of Meeting and offered a thousand burnt offerings on it.

⁷That night God appeared[m] to Solomon and said to him, "Ask for whatever you want me to give you."

⁸Solomon answered God, "You have shown great kindness to David my father and have made me[n] king in his place. ⁹Now, LORD God, let your promise[o] to my father David be confirmed, for you have made me king over a people who are as numerous as the dust of the earth.[p] ¹⁰Give me wisdom and knowledge, that I may lead[q] this people, for who is able to govern this great people of yours?"

¹¹God said to Solomon, "Since this is your heart's desire and you have not asked for wealth,[r] riches or honor, nor for the death of your enemies, and since you have not asked for a long life but for wisdom and knowledge to govern my people over whom I have made you king, ¹²therefore wisdom and knowledge will be given you. And I will also give you wealth, riches and honor,[s] such as no king who was before you ever had and none after you will have.[t] "

¹³Then Solomon went to Jerusalem from the high place at Gibeon, from before the Tent of Meeting. And he reigned over Israel.

¹⁴Solomon accumulated chariots[u] and horses; he had fourteen hundred chariots and twelve thousand horses,[a] which he kept in the chariot cities and also with him in Jerusalem. ¹⁵The king made silver and gold[v] as common in Jerusalem as stones, and cedar as plentiful as sycamore-fig trees in the foothills. ¹⁶Solomon's horses were imported from Egypt[b] and from Kue[c]—the royal merchants purchased them from Kue. ¹⁷They imported a chariot[w] from Egypt for six hundred shekels[d] of silver, and a horse for a hundred and fifty.[e] They also exported them to all the kings of the Hittites and of the Arameans.

Preparations for Building the Temple

2:1–18pp — 1Ki 5:1–16

2 Solomon gave orders to build a temple[x] for the Name of the LORD and a royal palace for himself.[y] ²He conscripted

Cross references

1:1 [a]S 1Ki 2:12; [b]S 2Ch 12:1
[b]S Ge 21:22; S 39:2; S Nu 14:43
[c]S 1Ch 29:25
1:2 [d]S 1Ch 9:1
1:3 [e]S Jos 9:3
[f]S Lev 17:4
[g]Ex 40:18
1:4 [h]S 1Ch 15:25
[i]2Sa 6:17
1:5 [j]Ex 38:2
[k]S Ex 31:2
[l]1Ch 13:3
1:7 [m]2Ch 7:12
1:8 [n]S 1Ch 23:1
1:9 [o]S 2Sa 7:25; S 1Ki 8:25
[p]S Ge 12:2
1:10 [q]Nu 27:17; 2Sa 5:2; Pr 8:15-16

1:11 [r]S Dt 17:17
1:12
[s]S 1Ch 29:12
[t]S 1Ch 29:25; 2Ch 9:22; Ne 13:26
1:14 [u]S 1Sa 8:11; S 1Ki 9:19
1:15 [v]S 1Ki 9:28; Isa 60:5
1:17 [w]S S 1:9
2:1 [x]S Dt 12:5
[y]Ecc 2:4

Translation notes

[a]14 Or *charioteers*   [b]16 Or possibly *Muzur*, a region in Cilicia; also in verse 17   [c]16 Probably Cilicia
[d]17 That is, about 15 pounds (about 7 kilograms)
[e]17 That is, about 3 3/4 pounds (about 1.7 kilograms)

1:1–9:31 The account of the reign of Solomon is primarily devoted to his building of the temple (chs. 2–7); his endowment with wisdom is mainly to facilitate the building work. Much of the material in Kings that does not bear on building the temple is omitted by the Chronicler; e.g., he does not mention the judgment between the prostitutes (1Ki 3:16–28) or the building of the royal palace (1Ki 7:1–12).
1:1 *established himself.* This expression, or a variation of it, is common in Chronicles (12:13; 13:7–8,21; 15:8; 16:9; 17:1; 21:4; 23:1; 25:11; 27:6; 32:5; 1Ch 11:10; 19:13). Here and in 21:4 it includes the elimination of enemies and rivals to the throne (see 1Ki 2, especially v. 46).
1:2–13 See 1Ki 3:4–15 and notes. Verses 2–6 are largely unique to Chronicles and show some of the writer's concerns: 1. The support of "all Israel" (v. 2) is emphasized (see Introduction to 1 Chronicles: Purpose and Themes). 2. While the writer of Kings is somewhat apologetic about Solomon's visit to a high place (1Ki 3:3), the Chronicler adds the note that this was the location of the tabernacle made by Moses in the desert (v. 3), bringing Solomon's action into line with the provisions of the law (Lev 17:8–9).
1:5 *Bezalel.* See Introduction: The Building of the Temple

in Chronicles. It is specifically in connection with his offering on the altar built by Bezalel (Ex 31:1–11; 38:1–2) that Solomon receives the wisdom from God to reign. In the account that follows, Solomon devotes his gift of wisdom primarily to building the temple, just as Bezalel had been gifted by God to serve as the master craftsman of the tabernacle.
1:7 *God ... said to him.* Both David and Solomon function as prophets (7:1; 29:25; 1Ch 22:8; 28:6,19).
1:9 *numerous as the dust.* In provisional fulfillment of the promise to Abraham (Ge 13:16; 22:17; see note on 1Ch 27:23; cf. Ge 28:14).
1:14–17 The Chronicler does not include the material in 1Ki 3:16–4:34. He moves rather to the account of Solomon's wealth in 1Ki 10:26–29; part of this material is repeated in 2Ch 9:25–28. Recounting Solomon's wealth at this point shows the fulfillment of God's promise (v. 12).
1:16 *Egypt.* See NIV text note; see also note on 1Ki 10:29.
2:1 *palace.* Although the Chronicler frequently mentions the palace Solomon built (7:11; 8:1; 9:11), he gives no details of its construction (see 1Ki 7:1–12).
2:2 See vv. 17–18.

aliens[w] who were in Israel, after the census[x] his father David had taken; and they were found to be 153,600. [18]He assigned[y] 70,000 of them to be carriers and 80,000 to be stonecutters in the hills, with 3,600 foremen over them to keep the people working.

Solomon Builds the Temple

3:1–14pp — 1Ki 6:1–29

3 Then Solomon began to build[z] the temple of the LORD[a] in Jerusalem on Mount Moriah, where the LORD had appeared to his father David. It was on the threshing floor of Araunah[i b] the Jebusite, the place provided by David. [2]He began building on the second day of the second month in the fourth year of his reign.[c]

[3]The foundation Solomon laid for building the temple of God was sixty cubits long and twenty cubits wide[k d] (using the cubit of the old standard). [4]The portico at the front of the temple was twenty cubits[l] long across the width of the building and twenty cubits[m] high.

He overlaid the inside with pure gold. [5]He paneled the main hall with pine and covered it with fine gold and decorated it with palm tree[e] and chain designs. [6]He adorned the temple with precious stones. And the gold he used was gold of Parvaim. [7]He overlaid the ceiling beams, doorframes, walls and doors of the temple with gold, and he carved cherubim[f] on the walls.

[8]He built the Most Holy Place,[g] its length corresponding to the width of the temple—twenty cubits long and twenty cubits wide. He overlaid the inside with six hundred talents[n] of fine gold. [9]The gold nails[h] weighed fifty shekels.[o] He also overlaid the upper parts with gold.

[10]In the Most Holy Place he made a pair[i] of sculptured cherubim and overlaid them with gold. [11]The total wingspan of the cherubim was twenty cubits. One wing of the first cherub was five cubits[p] long and touched the temple wall, while its other wing, also five cubits long, touched the wing of the other cherub. [12]Similarly one wing of the second cherub was five cubits long and touched the other temple wall, and its other wing, also five cubits long, touched the wing of the first cherub. [13]The wings of these cherubim[i] extended twenty cubits. They stood on their feet, facing the main hall.[q]

[14]He made the curtain[k] of blue, purple and crimson yarn and fine linen, with cherubim[l] worked into it.

[15]In the front of the temple he made two pillars,[m] which together were thirty-five cubits[r] long, each with a capital[n] on top measuring five cubits. [16]He made inter-

Cross references (center column)

2:17 wICh 22:2 xS 2Sa 24:2
2:18 yICh 22:2; 2Ch 8:8
3:1 zAc 7:47 aS Ge 28:17 bS 2Sa 24:18
3:2 cEzr 5:11
3:3 dEze 41:2
3:5 eEze 40:16
3:7 fGe 3:24; Eze 41:18
3:8 gS Ex 26:33
3:9 hEx 26:32
3:10 iEx 25:18
3:13 jS Ex 25:18
3:14 kS Ex 26:31, 33 lGe 3:24
3:15 mS 1Ki 7:15; Rev 3:12
n1Ki 7:22

Text notes (center column)

i 1 Hebrew *Ornan*, a variant of *Araunah*   k 3 That is, about 90 feet (about 27 meters) long and 30 feet (about 9 meters) wide   l 4 That is, about 30 feet (about 9 meters); also in verses 8, 11 and 13   m 4 Some Septuagint and Syriac manuscripts; Hebrew *and a hundred and twenty*   n 8 That is, about 23 tons (about 21 metric tons)   o 9 That is, about 1 1/4 pounds (about 0.6 kilogram)   p 11 That is, about 7 1/2 feet (about 2.3 meters); also in verse 15   q 13 Or *facing inward*   r 15 That is, about 52 feet (about 16 meters)

Study notes (bottom)

that alien labor was used (see 8:8).

2:18 *3,600 foremen.* See v. 2. The number given in 1Ki 5:16 is 3,300; however, some manuscripts of the Septuagint (the Greek translation of the OT) also have 3,600. The Chronicler may have been following a different text of Kings from the present Masoretic (traditional Hebrew) text at this point (but see note on 1Ki 5:16).

3:1–17 The Chronicler has considerably curtailed the description of the temple's construction found in Kings, omitting completely 1Ki 6:4–20. This abridgment probably indicates that the Chronicler's audience was familiar with the details of the earlier history and that the temple of the restoration period was less elaborate than the original Solomonic structure (Hag 2:3). On the other hand, the Chronicler goes into more detail on the furnishings and implements (3:6–9; 4:1,6–9).

3:1 *Mount Moriah.* The only passage in the OT where Mount Zion is identified with Mount Moriah, the place where Abraham was commanded to offer Isaac (Ge 22:2, 14). *place provided by David.* See 1Ch 21:18–22:1.

3:2 *second month in the fourth year.* In the spring of 966 B.C. (see note on 1Ki 6:1).

3:4 *overlaid.* Or "inlaid," which perhaps gives a more correct picture: not that the entire interior was covered with gold leaf, but that designs (palm trees, chains) were inlaid with gold leaf (v. 5).

3:6 *Parvaim.* Designates either the source of the gold (perhaps southeast Arabia) or a particular quality of fine gold.

3:7 *cherubim.* See vv. 10–14; see also notes on Ge 3:24; Eze 1:5.

3:8 *twenty cubits long and twenty cubits wide.* It was also 20 cubits high (1Ki 6:20), making the dimensions of the Most Holy Place a perfect cube, as probably also in the tabernacle. In the New Jerusalem there is no temple (Rev 21:22); rather, the whole city is in the shape of a cube (Rev 21:16), for the whole city becomes "the Most Holy Place."

3:9 *gold nails.* The fact that gold is such a soft metal would make it unlikely that nails were made of this substance. It is probable that this small amount (only 1 1/4 pounds; see NIV text note) represents gold leaf or sheeting used to gild the nail heads.

3:10–13 See 1Ki 6:23–27 and notes.

3:14 *curtain.* Also separated the two rooms of the tabernacle (Ex 26:31). Wooden doors could also be closed across the opening (4:22; 1Ki 6:31–32; cf. Mt 27:51; Heb 9:8).

3:15 *together were thirty-five cubits long.* Supplying the word "together" represents an attempt to harmonize this measurement with the 18 cubits (each) in 1Ki 7:15 (also confirmed by 2Ki 25:17—see NIV text note there; Jer 52:21, though the Septuagint at Jer 52:21 has 35). Alternatively, 35 may be the result of a copyist's mistake.

woven chains[s][o] and put them on top of the pillars. He also made a hundred pomegranates[p] and attached them to the chains. [17]He erected the pillars in the front of the temple, one to the south and one to the north. The one to the south he named Jakin[t] and the one to the north Boaz.[u]

The Temple's Furnishings

4:2–6,10–5:1pp — 1Ki 7:23–26,38–51

4 He made a bronze altar[q] twenty cubits long, twenty cubits wide and ten cubits high.[v] [2]He made the Sea[r] of cast metal, circular in shape, measuring ten cubits from rim to rim and five cubits[w] high. It took a line of thirty cubits[x] to measure around it. [3]Below the rim, figures of bulls encircled it—ten to a cubit.[y] The bulls were cast in two rows in one piece with the Sea.

[4]The Sea stood on twelve bulls, three facing north, three facing west, three facing south and three facing east.[s] The Sea rested on top of them, and their hindquarters were toward the center. [5]It was a handbreadth[z] in thickness, and its rim was like the rim of a cup, like a lily blossom. It held three thousand baths.[a]

[6]He then made ten basins[t] for washing and placed five on the south side and five on the north. In them the things to be used for the burnt offerings[u] were rinsed, but the Sea was to be used by the priests for washing.

[7]He made ten gold lampstands[v] according to the specifications[w] for them and placed them in the temple, five on the south side and five on the north.

[8]He made ten tables[x] and placed them in the temple, five on the south side and five on the north. He also made a hundred gold sprinkling bowls.[y]

[9]He made the courtyard[z] of the priests, and the large court and the doors for the court, and overlaid the doors with bronze. [10]He placed the Sea on the south side, at the southeast corner.

[11]He also made the pots and shovels and sprinkling bowls.

So Huram finished[a] the work he had undertaken for King Solomon in the temple of God:

[12]the two pillars;
the two bowl-shaped capitals on top of the pillars;
the two sets of network decorating the two bowl-shaped capitals on top of the pillars;
[13]the four hundred pomegranates for the two sets of network (two rows of pomegranates for each network, decorating the bowl-shaped capitals on top of the pillars);
[14]the stands[b] with their basins;
[15]the Sea and the twelve bulls under it;
[16]the pots, shovels, meat forks and all related articles.

All the objects that Huram-Abi[c] made for King Solomon for the temple of the LORD were of polished bronze. [17]The king had them cast in clay molds in the plain of the Jordan between Succoth[d] and Zarethan.[b] [18]All these things that Solomon made amounted to so much that the

---

Cross references (center column)

3:16 [o]1Ki 7:17
[p]S 1Ki 7:20
4:1 [q]S Ex 20:24; S 40:6; S 1Ki 8:64
4:2 [r]Rev 4:6; 15:2
4:4 [s]Nu 2:3-25; Eze 48:30-34; Rev 21:13
4:6 [t]S Ex 30:18 [u]Ne 13:5,9; Eze 40:38
4:7 [v]S Ex 25:31 [w]Ex 25:40
4:8 [x]S Ex 25:23 [y]S Nu 4:14

4:9 [z]1Ki 6:36; 2Ch 33:5
4:11 [a]1Ki 7:14
4:14 [b]1Ki 7:27-30
4:16 [c]S 1Ki 7:13
4:17 [d]S Ge 33:17

Footnotes

[s]16 Or possibly *made chains in the inner sanctuary;* the meaning of the Hebrew for this phrase is uncertain. [t]17 *Jakin* probably means *he establishes.* [u]17 *Boaz* probably means *in him is strength.* [v]1 That is, about 30 feet (about 9 meters) long and wide, and about 15 feet (about 4.5 meters) high [w]2 That is, about 7 1/2 feet (about 2.3 meters) [x]2 That is, about 45 feet (about 13.5 meters) [y]3 That is, about 1 1/2 feet (about 0.5 meter) [z]5 That is, about 3 inches (about 8 centimeters) [a]5 That is, about 17,500 gallons (about 66 kiloliters) [b]17 Hebrew *Zeredatha,* a variant of *Zarethan*

3:17 *pillars.* Remains of such pillars have been found in the excavations of numerous temples in Palestine. Cf. Rev 3:12. *Jakin . . . Boaz.* See NIV text notes.

4:1 *bronze altar.* The parallel text in Kings does not mention the main altar of the temple described here (1Ki 7:22–23), though several other passages in Kings do refer to it (1Ki 8:64; 9:25; 2Ki 16:14). The main altar of Solomon's temple was similar to the altar with steps that is described in Eze 43:13–17.

4:2 *Sea of cast metal.* Replaced the bronze basin of the tabernacle (Ex 30:18); it was used by the priests for their ceremonial washing (v. 6; Ex 30:21). The NT views these rituals as foreshadowing the cleansing provided by Christ (Tit 3:5; Heb 9:11–14). In the temple of Ezekiel, the Sea, which was on the south side in front of the temple (v. 10), has been replaced by a life-giving river that flows from the south side of the temple (Eze 47:1–12; cf. Joel 3:18; Zec 14:8; Jn 4:9–15; Rev 22:1–2).

4:3 *bulls.* 1Ki 7:24 has "gourds." The Hebrew for the two words is very similar, so the difference may well be due to a

copyist's mistake.

4:4 *twelve bulls.* Possibly symbolic of the 12 tribes, which also encamped three on each side of the tabernacle during the desert journeys (Nu 2; cf. Eze 48:30–35).

4:5 *three thousand baths.* 1Ki 7:26 has 2,000 baths. These figures could easily have been misread by the ancient scribes.

4:6 *ten basins.* See 1Ki 7:38–39.

4:7 *ten gold lampstands.* Instead of one, as in the tabernacle (Ex 25:31–40). *specifications.* See 1Ch 28:15. These lamps were not necessarily of the same shape as described in Ex 25:31–40, but could have resembled the style of lamp depicted in Zec 4:2–6.

4:8 *ten tables.* Instead of one, as in the tabernacle (Ex 25:23–30; 40:4; Lev 24:5–9; 1Sa 21:1–6; Eze 41:22; Heb 9:2; cf. 2Ch 13:11; 29:18).

4:11–16 See 1Ki 7:40–45.

4:17–22 See 1Ki 7:46–50.

4:17 *clay molds.* The clay beds of the Jordan plain made it possible to dig molds for these bronze castings.

weight of the bronze[e] was not determined.

[19]Solomon also made all the furnishings that were in God's temple:

the golden altar;
the tables[f] on which was the bread of the Presence;
[20]the lampstands[g] of pure gold with their lamps, to burn in front of the inner sanctuary as prescribed;
[21]the gold floral work and lamps and tongs (they were solid gold);
[22]the pure gold wick trimmers, sprinkling bowls, dishes[h] and censers;[i] and the gold doors of the temple: the inner doors to the Most Holy Place and the doors of the main hall.

5 When all the work Solomon had done for the temple of the LORD was finished,[j] he brought in the things his father David had dedicated[k]—the silver and gold and all the furnishings—and he placed them in the treasuries of God's temple.

The Ark Brought to the Temple

5:2–6:11pp — 1Ki 8:1–21

[2]Then Solomon summoned to Jerusalem the elders of Israel, all the heads of the tribes and the chiefs of the Israelite families, to bring up the ark[l] of the LORD's covenant from Zion, the City of David. [3]And all the men of Israel[m] came together to the king at the time of the festival in the seventh month.

[4]When all the elders of Israel had arrived, the Levites took up the ark, [5]and they brought up the ark and the Tent of Meeting and all the sacred furnishings in it. The priests, who were Levites,[n] carried them up; [6]and King Solomon and the entire assembly of Israel that had gathered about him were before the ark, sacrificing so many sheep and cattle that they could not be recorded or counted.

[7]The priests then brought the ark[o] of the LORD's covenant to its place in the inner sanctuary of the temple, the Most Holy Place, and put it beneath the wings of the cherubim. [8]The cherubim[p] spread their wings over the place of the ark and covered the ark and its carrying poles. [9]These poles were so long that their ends, extending from the ark, could be seen from in front of the inner sanctuary, but not from outside the Holy Place; and they are still there today. [10]There was nothing in the ark except[q] the two tablets[r] that Moses had placed in it at Horeb, where the LORD made a covenant with the Israelites after they came out of Egypt.

[11]The priests then withdrew from the Holy Place. All the priests who were there had consecrated themselves, regardless of their divisions.[s] [12]All the Levites who were musicians[t]—Asaph, Heman, Jeduthun and their sons and relatives—stood on the east side of the altar, dressed in fine linen and playing cymbals, harps and lyres. They were accompanied by 120 priests sounding trumpets.[u] [13]The trumpeters and singers joined in unison, as with one voice, to give praise and thanks to the LORD. Accompanied by trumpets, cymbals and other instruments, they raised their voices in praise to the LORD and sang:

"He is good;
his love endures forever."[v]

Then the temple of the LORD was filled with a cloud,[w] [14]and the priests could not perform[x] their service because of the cloud,[y] for the glory[z] of the LORD filled the temple of God.

6 Then Solomon said, "The LORD has said that he would dwell in a dark cloud;[a] [2]I have built a magnificent temple for you, a place for you to dwell forever.[b]"

[3]While the whole assembly of Israel was standing there, the king turned around and blessed them. [4]Then he said:

4:18 *e*S 1Ki 7:23
4:19 *f*S Ex 25:23
4:20 *g*Ex 25:31
4:22 *h*S Nu 7:14
5:1 *i*S Lev 10:1
*j*S 1Ki 6:14
*k*S 2Sa 8:11
5:2 *l*S Nu 3:31; S 1Ch 15:25
5:3 *m*S 1Ch 9:1
5:5 *n*S Nu 3:31; S 1Ch 15:2

5:7 *o*Rev 11:19
5:8 *p*S Ge 3:24
5:10 *q*Heb 9:4
*r*S Ex 16:34; S Dt 10:2
5:11 *s*S 1Ch 24:1
5:12 *t*1Ch 10:12; 1Ch 9:33; S 25:1; Ps 68:25
*u*S 1Ch 13:8
5:13 *v*S 1Ch 16:34; 2Ch 7:3; 20:21; Ezr 3:11; Ps 100:5; 106:1; 107:1; 118:1; 136:1; Jer 33:11
*w*S Ex 40:34
5:14 *x*Ex 40:35; Rev 15:8
*y*Ex 19:16
*z*S Ex 29:43; S 40:35
6:1 *a*S Ex 19:9
6:2 *b*Ezr 6:12; 7:15; Ps 135:21

5:1 *things his father David had dedicated.* See notes on 1Ch 18:1–20:8; 22:2–16; 29:2–5; see also 1Ch 26:26.
5:2–14 See 1Ki 8:1–11 and notes.
5:2 *ark.* Had been in a tent provided for it 40 years earlier when David brought it to Jerusalem (1Ch 15:1–16:6).
5:3 *festival in the seventh month.* The Feast of Tabernacles. The month is designated by its Canaanite name Ethanim in 1Ki 8:2; the Hebrew name is Tishri. According to 1Ki 6:38 the temple was completed in the eighth month of Solomon's 11th year, i.e., September-October, 959 B.C. This celebration of dedication took place either a month before the completion of the work or 11 months after, probably the latter (see note on 1Ki 8:2).
5:6 Cf. David's bringing of the ark to Jerusalem (1Ch 15:26; 16:1–3).

5:9 *still there today.* See note on 1Ki 8:8; see also 8:8; 10:19; 20:26; 21:10; 35:25; 1Ch 4:41,43; 5:26; 13:11; 17:5.
5:10 *two tablets.* See Ex 31:18 and note; see also Ex 32:15–16. The ark had earlier contained also the gold jar of manna (Ex 16:32–34) and Aaron's staff (Nu 17:10–11; Heb 9:4). These items were presumably lost, perhaps while the ark was in Philistine hands.
5:12 *fine linen.* See 1Ch 15:27 and note.
5:14 *cloud . . . glory of the LORD.* Cf. 7:1–3. The glory cloud represented the presence of God. It had guided Israel out of Egypt and through the desert, and was present above the tabernacle (Ex 13:21–22; 40:34–38; cf. Eze 43:1–5; Hag 2:9; Zec 1:16; 2:10; 8:3).
6:1–11 See notes on 1Ki 8:12–21.

"Praise be to the LORD, the God of Israel, who with his hands has fulfilled what he promised with his mouth to my father David. For he said, [5]'Since the day I brought my people out of Egypt, I have not chosen a city in any tribe of Israel to have a temple built for my Name to be there, nor have I chosen anyone to be the leader over my people Israel. [6]But now I have chosen Jerusalem[c] for my Name[d] to be there, and I have chosen David[e] to rule my people Israel.'

[7]"My father David had it in his heart[f] to build a temple for the Name of the LORD, the God of Israel. [8]But the LORD said to my father David, 'Because it was in your heart to build a temple for my Name, you did well to have this in your heart. [9]Nevertheless, you are not the one to build the temple, but your son, who is your own flesh and blood—he is the one who will build the temple for my Name.'

[10]"The LORD has kept the promise he made. I have succeeded David my father and now I sit on the throne of Israel, just as the LORD promised, and I have built the temple for the Name of the LORD, the God of Israel. [11]There I have placed the ark, in which is the covenant[g] of the LORD that he made with the people of Israel."

Solomon's Prayer of Dedication

6:12–40pp — 1Ki 8:22–53
6:41–42pp — Ps 132:8–10

[12]Then Solomon stood before the altar of the LORD in front of the whole assembly of Israel and spread out his hands. [13]Now he had made a bronze platform,[h] five cubits[c] long, five cubits wide and three cubits[d] high, and had placed it in the center of the outer court. He stood on the platform and then knelt down[i] before the whole assembly of Israel and spread out his hands toward heaven. [14]He said:

"O LORD, God of Israel, there is no God like you[j] in heaven or on earth—you who keep your covenant of love[k] with your servants who con-

tinue wholeheartedly in your way. [15]You have kept your promise to your servant David my father; with your mouth you have promised[l] and with your hand you have fulfilled it—as it is today.

[16]"Now LORD, God of Israel, keep for your servant David my father the promises you made to him when you said, 'You shall never fail[m] to have a man to sit before me on the throne of Israel, if only your sons are careful in all they do to walk before me according to my law,[n] as you have done.' [17]And now, O LORD, God of Israel, let your word that you promised your servant David come true.

[18]"But will God really dwell[o] on earth with men? The heavens,[p] even the highest heavens, cannot contain you. How much less this temple I have built! [19]Yet give attention to your servant's prayer and his plea for mercy, O LORD my God. Hear the cry and the prayer that your servant is praying in your presence. [20]May your eyes[q] be open toward this temple day and night, this place of which you said you would put your Name[r] there. May you hear[s] the prayer your servant prays toward this place. [21]Hear the supplications of your servant and of your people Israel when they pray toward this place. Hear from heaven, your dwelling place; and when you hear, forgive.[t]

[22]"When a man wrongs his neighbor and is required to take an oath[u] and he comes and swears the oath before your altar in this temple, [23]then hear from heaven and act. Judge between your servants, repaying[v] the guilty by bringing down on his own head what he has done. Declare the innocent not guilty and so establish his innocence.

[24]"When your people Israel have been defeated[w] by an enemy because they have sinned against you and

---

6:6 [c]S Dt 12:5;
S Isa 14:1
[d]S Ex 20:24
[e]S 1Ch 28:4
6:7 [f]S 1Sa 10:7;
S 1Ch 17:2;
Ac 7:46
6:11 [g]S Dt 10:2;
Ps 25:10; 50:5
6:13 [h]Ne 8:4
[i]Ps 95:6
6:14 [j]S Ex 8:10;
15:11 [k]S Dt 7:9

6:15
[l]S 1Ch 22:10
6:16
[m]S 2Sa 7:13,15;
2Ch 23:3
[n]Ps 132:12
6:18 [o]S Rev 21:3
[p]Ps 11:4;
Isa 40:22; 66:1
6:20 [q]S Ex 3:16;
Ps 34:15
6:21 [r]Ps 51:1;
Isa 33:24; 40:2;
43:25; 44:22;
55:7; Mic 7:18
6:22 [u]S Ex 22:11
6:23 [v]Isa 3:11;
65:6; S Mt 16:27
6:24
[w]S Lev 26:17

[c]13 That is, about 7 1/2 feet (about 2.3 meters)
[d]13 That is, about 4 1/2 feet (about 1.3 meters)

6:8–9 Cf. David's speech in 1Ch 28:2–3.
6:12–21 See notes on 1Ki 8:22–30.
6:13 Not in 1Ki 8. Some think that the Chronicler may have wished to clarify the fact that Solomon was not "before the altar" (v. 12) exercising priestly duties. On the other hand, the verse may have been dropped from Kings by a copying error: The phrase "spread out his hands" occurs in vv. 12–13; it is possible that the scribe copying Kings looked back to the second occurrence of the phrase, thus omitting

the verse. The verse would then be present in Chronicles because it was in the particular text of Kings used by the Chronicler.
6:18 Cf. 2:6.
6:22–39 See notes on 1Ki 8:31–46.
6:22–23 See Ex 22:10–11; Lev 6:3–5.
6:24–25 See Lev 26:17,23; Dt 28:25,36–37,48–57,64; Jos 7:11–12.

when they turn back and confess your name, praying and making supplication before you in this temple, ²⁵then hear from heaven and forgive the sin of your people Israel and bring them back to the land you gave to them and their fathers.

²⁶"When the heavens are shut up and there is no rain^x because your people have sinned against you, and when they pray toward this place and confess your name and turn from their sin because you have afflicted them, ²⁷then hear from heaven and forgive^y the sin of your servants, your people Israel. Teach them the right way to live, and send rain on the land you gave your people for an inheritance.

²⁸"When famine^z or plague comes to the land, or blight or mildew, locusts or grasshoppers, or when enemies besiege them in any of their cities, whatever disaster or disease may come, ²⁹and when a prayer or plea is made by any of your people Israel—each one aware of his afflictions and pains, and spreading out his hands toward this temple— ³⁰then hear from heaven, your dwelling place. Forgive,^a and deal with each man according to all he does, since you know his heart (for you alone know the hearts of men),^b ³¹so that they will fear you^c and walk in your ways all the time they live in the land you gave our fathers.

³²"As for the foreigner who does not belong to your people Israel but has come^d from a distant land because of your great name and your mighty hand^e and your outstretched arm—when he comes and prays toward this temple, ³³then hear from heaven, your dwelling place, and do whatever the foreigner^f asks of you, so that all the peoples of the earth may know your name and fear you, as do your own people Israel, and may

know that this house I have built bears your Name.

³⁴"When your people go to war against their enemies,^g wherever you send them, and when they pray^h to you toward this city you have chosen and the temple I have built for your Name, ³⁵then hear from heaven their prayer and their plea, and uphold their cause.

³⁶"When they sin against you—for there is no one who does not sinⁱ—and you become angry with them and give them over to the enemy, who takes them captive^j to a land far away or near; ³⁷and if they have a change of heart^k in the land where they are held captive, and repent and plead with you in the land of their captivity and say, 'We have sinned, we have done wrong and acted wickedly'; ³⁸and if they turn back to you with all their heart and soul in the land of their captivity where they were taken, and pray toward the land you gave their fathers, toward the city you have chosen and toward the temple I have built for your Name; ³⁹then from heaven, your dwelling place, hear their prayer and their pleas, and uphold their cause. And forgive^l your people, who have sinned against you.

⁴⁰"Now, my God, may your eyes be open and your ears attentive^m to the prayers offered in this place.

⁴¹"Now arise,ⁿ O LORD God, and
   come to your resting
    place,^o
   you and the ark of your might.
May your priests,^p O LORD God, be
   clothed with salvation,
   may your saints rejoice in your
    goodness.^q
⁴²O LORD God, do not reject your
   anointed one.^r
Remember the great love^s
   promised to David your
   servant."

6:26 ×Lev 26:19; S Dt 11:17; 28:24; S 2Sa 1:21
6:27 yver 30,39; 2Ch 7:14
6:28 z2Ch 20:9
6:30 aS ver 27
bS 1Sa 2:3; Ps 7:9; 44:21; Pr 16:2; 17:3
6:31 cS Dt 6:13; Ps 34:7,9; 103:11,13; Pr 8:13
6:32 d2Ch 9:6
eS Ex 3:19,20
6:33 fS Ex 12:43

6:34 gDt 28:7
hS 1Ch 5:20
6:36 iS 1Ki 8:46; Job 11:12; 15:14; Ps 143:2; Ecc 7:20; Jer 9:5; 13:23; 17:9; S Ro 3:9; Eph 2:3
jS Lev 26:44
6:37 k1Ki 8:48; 2Ch 7:14; 12:6, 12; 30:11; 33:12, 19,23; 34:27; 36:12; Isa 58:3; Jer 24:7; 29:13
6:39 lS ver 27; 2Ch 30:9
6:40 mS 1Ki 8:29,52; 2Ch 7:15; Ne 1:6, 11; Ps 17:6; 116:1; 130:2; Isa 37:17
6:41 nPs 3:7; 7:6; 59:4; Isa 33:10
o1Ch 28:2
pPs 132:16
qPs 13:6; 27:13; 116:12; 142:7
6:42 rPs 2:2
sPs 89:24,28

6:26–27 See Lev 26:19; Dt 11:10–15; 28:18,22–24.
6:28–31 See Lev 26:16,20,25–26; Dt 28:20–22,27–28, 35,42.
6:32–33 The prophets also envisaged the Gentiles as coming to Jerusalem to worship the Lord (Isa 56:6–8; Zec 8:20–23; 14:16–21; cf. Ps 87).
6:34–35 See Lev 26:7–8; Dt 28:6–7. The Chronicler repeatedly demonstrates God's answer to prayer in time of battle (ch. 13; 14:9–15; 18:31; 20:1–29; 25:5–13; 32:20–22).

6:36 *no one who does not sin.* See Jer 13:23; Ro 3:23. *captive to a land far away.* See 36:15–20; Lev 26:33, 44–45; Dt 28:49–52; 2Ki 17:7–20; 25:1–21.
6:40–42 The Chronicler replaces the ending of Solomon's prayer in Kings (1Ki 8:50–53) with a repetition of Ps 132:8–10, a psalm that deals with bringing the ark to the temple, the theme of this section in Chronicles (5:2–14). The prayer in Kings ends with an appeal to the exodus deliverance under Moses, while in Chronicles the appeal is on the basis of the eternal promises to David.

The Dedication of the Temple

7:1–10pp — 1Ki 8:62–66

7 When Solomon finished praying, fire[t] came down from heaven and consumed the burnt offering and the sacrifices, and the glory of the Lord filled[u] the temple.[v] [2]The priests could not enter[w] the temple of the Lord because the glory[x] of the Lord filled it. [3]When all the Israelites saw the fire coming down and the glory of the Lord above the temple, they knelt on the pavement with their faces to the ground, and they worshiped and gave thanks to the Lord, saying,

"He is good;
his love endures forever."[y]

[4]Then the king and all the people offered sacrifices before the Lord. [5]And King Solomon offered a sacrifice of twenty-two thousand head of cattle and a hundred and twenty thousand sheep and goats. So the king and all the people dedicated the temple of God. [6]The priests took their positions, as did the Levites[z] with the Lord's musical instruments,[a] which King David had made for praising the Lord and which were used when he gave thanks, saying, "His love endures forever." Opposite the Levites, the priests blew their trumpets, and all the Israelites were standing.

[7]Solomon consecrated the middle part of the courtyard in front of the temple of the Lord, and there he offered burnt offerings and the fat[b] of the fellowship offerings,[e] because the bronze altar he had made could not hold the burnt offerings, the grain offerings and the fat portions.

[8]So Solomon observed the festival[c] at that time for seven days, and all Israel[d] with him—a vast assembly, people from Lebo[f] Hamath[e] to the Wadi of Egypt.[f] [9]On the eighth day they held an assembly, for they had celebrated[g] the dedication of the altar for seven days and the festival[h] for seven days more. [10]On the twenty-third day of the seventh month he sent the people to their homes, joyful and glad in heart for the good things the Lord had done for David and Solomon and for his people Israel.

The Lord Appears to Solomon

7:11–22pp — 1Ki 9:1–9

[11]When Solomon had finished[i] the temple of the Lord and the royal palace, and had succeeded in carrying out all he had in mind to do in the temple of the Lord and in his own palace, [12]the Lord appeared[j] to him at night and said:

"I have heard your prayer and have chosen[k] this place for myself[l] as a temple for sacrifices.

[13]"When I shut up the heavens so that there is no rain,[m] or command locusts to devour the land or send a plague among my people, [14]if my people, who are called by my name,[n] will humble[o] themselves and pray and seek my face[p] and turn[q] from their wicked ways, then will I hear[r] from heaven and will forgive[s] their sin and will heal[t] their land. [15]Now my eyes will be open and my ears attentive to the prayers offered in this place.[u] [16]I have chosen[v] and consecrated this temple so that my Name may be there forever. My eyes and my heart will always be there.

[17]"As for you, if you walk before me[w] as David your father did, and do all I command, and observe my decrees[x] and laws, [18]I will establish your royal throne, as I covenanted[y] with

Cross references

7:1 [t]S Ex 19:18; S Lev 9:24; S 1Ki 18:38 [u]S Ex 16:10 [v]Ps 26:8
7:2 [w]S 1Ki 8:11 [x]S Ex 29:43; S 40:35
7:3 [y]S 1Ch 16:34; 2Ch 5:13; Ezr 3:11
7:6 [z]1Ch 15:16 [a]S 1Ch 15:24
7:7 [b]S Ex 29:13
7:8 [c]2Ch 30:26; Ne 8:17 [d]S 1Ch 9:1 [e]S Nu 13:21 [f]S Ge 15:18
7:9 [g]2Ch 30:23 [h]S Lev 23:36
7:11 [i]S 1Ch 28:20
7:12 [j]2Ch 1:7 [k]Dt 12:11 [l]S Dt 12:5
7:13 [m]S Dt 11:17; Am 4:7
7:14 [n]S Nu 6:27 [o]S Ex 10:3; S Lev 26:41; S 2Ch 6:37 [p]S 1Ch 16:11 [q]S 2Ki 17:13; Isa 55:7; Eze 18:32; Zec 1:4 [r]S 2Ch 6:20 [s]S 2Ch 6:27 [t]S Ex 15:26; 2Ch 30:20; Ps 60:2; Isa 30:26; 53:5; 57:18; Jer 33:6; Mal 4:2
7:15 [u]S 1Ki 8:29; S 2Ch 6:40; Ne 1:6
7:16 [v]S Dt 12:5; 2Ch 33:7
7:17 [w]S 1Ki 9:4 [x]S Lev 19:37
7:18 [y]Isa 9:7; Jer 33:17,21

[e]7 Traditionally *peace offerings*   [t]8 Or *from the entrance to*

7:1–22 See 1Ki 8:54–9:9 and notes.
7:1–3 Not found in 1Ki 8. The addition of the fire descending from heaven to consume the sacrifices provides the same sign of divine acceptance as was given at the dedication of the tabernacle (Lev 9:23–24) and David's offering at the threshing floor of Araunah the Jebusite (1Ch 21:26; cf. 1Ki 18:38). While vv. 1–3 are unique to Chronicles, the Chronicler has omitted Solomon's blessing of the congregation (1Ki 8:55–61).
7:1 *glory of the Lord.* See 5:14 and note.
7:3 *He is good . . . forever.* See v. 6; 5:13.
7:6 The verse is unique to Chronicles and reflects the author's overall interest in the Levites, especially the musicians (cf. 29:26–27; see note on 1Ch 6:31–48). *all the Israelites.* See Introduction to 1 Chronicles: Purpose and Themes.
7:8 *from Lebo Hamath to the Wadi of Egypt.* Not only were the patriarchal promises of descendants provisionally fulfilled

under David and Solomon (see 1:9; 1Ch 27:23–24 and notes), but also the promises of land (Ge 15:18–21).
7:9 *eighth day.* The final day of the Feast of Tabernacles (see 5:3 and note; Lev 23:36; Nu 29:35). *seven days . . . seven days.* The dedication had run from the 8th to the 14th day of the month, and the Feast of Tabernacles from the 15th to the 22nd day. The Day of Atonement was on the 10th day of the 7th month (Lev 16; cf. 1Ki 8:65–66).
7:12 *appeared to him.* The second time God appeared to Solomon; the first was at Gibeon (1:3–13; 1Ki 9:2).
7:13–15 Unique to Chronicles. These verses illustrate the writer's emphasis on immediate retribution (see Introduction to 1 Chronicles: Purpose and Themes). The Chronicler subsequently portrays the kings in a way that demonstrates this principle (see v. 22).
7:14 See, e.g., 12:6–7,12.
7:17–18 See 1Ki 9:4–5. Such words as these reinforced ancient Israel's Messianic hopes.

dom. ²⁰All King Solomon's goblets were gold, and all the household articles in the Palace of the Forest of Lebanon were pure gold. Nothing was made of silver, because silver was considered of little value in Solomon's day. ²¹The king had a fleet of trading ships^q manned by Hiram's^r men. Once every three years it returned, carrying gold, silver and ivory, and apes and baboons.

²²King Solomon was greater in riches and wisdom than all the other kings of the earth.^p ²³All the kings^q of the earth sought audience with Solomon to hear the wisdom God had put in his heart. ²⁴Year after year, everyone who came brought a gift^r—articles of silver and gold, and robes, weapons and spices, and horses and mules.

²⁵Solomon had four thousand stalls for horses and chariots,^s and twelve thousand horses,^s which he kept in the chariot cities and also with him in Jerusalem. ²⁶He ruled^t over all the kings from the River^{t u} to the land of the Philistines, as far as the border of Egypt.^v ²⁷The king made silver as common in Jerusalem as stones, and cedar as plentiful as sycamore-fig trees in the foothills. ²⁸Solomon's horses were imported from Egypt^u and from all other countries.

Solomon's Death

9:29–31pp — 1Ki 11:41–43

²⁹As for the other events of Solomon's reign, from beginning to end, are they not written in the records of Nathan^w the prophet, in the prophecy of Ahijah^x the Shilonite and in the visions of Iddo the seer concerning Jeroboam^y son of Nebat? ³⁰Solomon reigned in Jerusalem over all Israel forty years. ³¹Then he rested with his fathers and was buried in the city of David^z his father. And Rehoboam his son succeeded him as king.

9:22 ^pS 1Ki 3:13; S 2Ch 1:12
9:23 ^q1Ki 4:34
9:24 ^r2Ch 32:23; Ps 45:12; 68:29; 72:10; Isa 18:7
9:25 ^sS 1Sa 8:11
9:26 ^tS 1Ki 4:21 ^uPs 72:8-9 ^vGe 15:18-21
9:29 ^wS 2Sa 7:2 ^xS 1Ki 11:29 ^y2Ch 10:2
9:31 ^z1Ki 2:10

Israel Rebels Against Rehoboam

10:1–11:4pp — 1Ki 12:1–24

10 Rehoboam went to Shechem, for all the Israelites had gone there to make him king. ²When Jeroboam^a son of Nebat heard this (he was in Egypt, where he had fled^b from King Solomon), he returned from Egypt. ³So they sent for Jeroboam, and he and all Israel^c went to Rehoboam and said to him: ⁴"Your father put a heavy yoke on us,^d but now lighten the harsh labor and the heavy yoke he put on us, and we will serve you."

⁵Rehoboam answered, "Come back to me in three days." So the people went away.

⁶Then King Rehoboam consulted the elders^e who had served his father Solomon during his lifetime. "How would you advise me to answer these people?" he asked.

⁷They replied, "If you will be kind to these people and please them and give them a favorable answer,^f they will always be your servants."

⁸But Rehoboam rejected^g the advice the elders^h gave him and consulted the young men who had grown up with him and were serving him. ⁹He asked them, "What is your advice? How should we answer these people who say to me, 'Lighten the yoke your father put on us'?"

¹⁰The young men who had grown up with him replied, "Tell the people who have said to you, 'Your father put a heavy yoke on us, but make our yoke lighter'—tell them, 'My little finger is thicker than my father's waist. ¹¹My father laid on you a heavy yoke; I will make it even heavier. My father scourged you with

10:2 ^aS 2Ch 9:29 ^bS 1Ki 11:40
10:3 ^cS 1Ch 9:1
10:4 ^d2Ch 2:2
10:6 ^eJob 8:8-9; 12:12; 15:10; 32:7
10:7 ^fPr 15:1
10:8 ^gS 2Sa 17:14 ^hPr 13:20

^q*21* Hebrew *of ships that could go to Tarshish* ^r*21* Hebrew *Huram,* a variant of *Hiram* ^s*25* Or *charioteers* ^t*26* That is, the Euphrates ^u*28* Or possibly *Muzur,* a region in Cilicia

---

9:26 See 7:8 and note.
9:27 See 1:15.
9:28 The Chronicler omits the accounts of Solomon's wives and the rebellions at the end of his reign (1Ki 11:1–40), both of which would detract from his uniformly positive portrayal of Solomon. *horses . . . Egypt.* See note on 1:16.
9:29–31 See 1Ki 11:41–43.
10:1–36:23 The material covering the divided monarchy in Chronicles is considerably shorter than that in Kings: 27 chapters compared to 36 (1Ki 12–2Ki 25). Moreover, about half of this material is unique to Chronicles and shows no dependence on Kings. The most obvious reason for this is that the Chronicler has written a history of the Davidic dynasty in Judah; the history of the northern kingdom is passed over in silence except where it impinges on that of

Judah. At least two considerations prompt this treatment of the divided kingdom: 1. The Chronicler is concerned to trace God's faithfulness to his promise to give David an unbroken line of descent on the throne of Israel. 2. At the time of the Chronicler the restored community was confined to the returnees of the kingdom of Judah, who were actually the remnant of all Israel (see Introduction to 1 Chronicles: Purpose and Themes).
10:1–19 See 1Ki 12:1–20 and notes. Somewhat in line with his idealization of Solomon, the Chronicler places most of the blame for the schism on the rebellious Jeroboam (cf. 13:6–7).
10:1 *Rehoboam.* Reigned 930–913 B.C.
10:2 *Jeroboam.* His second mention in Chronicles (see 9:29). The Chronicler assumes the reader's familiarity with 1Ki 11:26–40.

whips; I will scourge you with scorpions.'"

[12]Three days later Jeroboam and all the people returned to Rehoboam, as the king had said, "Come back to me in three days." [13]The king answered them harshly. Rejecting the advice of the elders, [14]he followed the advice of the young men and said, "My father made your yoke heavy; I will make it even heavier. My father scourged you with whips; I will scourge you with scorpions." [15]So the king did not listen to the people, for this turn of events was from God,[i] to fulfill the word the LORD had spoken to Jeroboam son of Nebat through Ahijah the Shilonite.[j]

[16]When all Israel[k] saw that the king refused to listen to them, they answered the king:

"What share do we have in David,[l]
    what part in Jesse's son?
To your tents, O Israel!
Look after your own house,
        O David!"

So all the Israelites went home. [17]But as for the Israelites who were living in the towns of Judah, Rehoboam still ruled over them.

[18]King Rehoboam sent out Adoniram,[v][m] who was in charge of forced labor, but the Israelites stoned him to death. King Rehoboam, however, managed to get into his chariot and escape to Jerusalem. [19]So Israel has been in rebellion against the house of David to this day.

11 When Rehoboam arrived in Jerusalem,[n] he mustered the house of Judah and Benjamin—a hundred and eighty thousand fighting men—to make war against Israel and to regain the kingdom for Rehoboam.

[2]But this word of the LORD came to Shemaiah[o] the man of God: [3]"Say to Rehoboam son of Solomon king of Judah and to all the Israelites in Judah and Benjamin, [4]'This is what the LORD says: Do not go up to fight against your brothers.[p] Go home, every one of you, for this is my doing.'" So they obeyed the words of the LORD and turned back from marching against Jeroboam.

Rehoboam Fortifies Judah

[5]Rehoboam lived in Jerusalem and built up towns for defense in Judah: [6]Bethlehem, Etam, Tekoa, [7]Beth Zur, Soco, Adullam, [8]Gath, Mareshah, Ziph, [9]Adoraim, Lachish, Azekah, [10]Zorah, Aijalon and Hebron. These were fortified cities[q] in Judah and Benjamin. [11]He strengthened their defenses and put commanders in them, with supplies of food, olive oil and wine. [12]He put shields and spears in all the cities, and made them very strong. So Judah and Benjamin were his.

[13]The priests and Levites from all their districts throughout Israel sided with him. [14]The Levites[r] even abandoned their pasturelands and property,[s] and came to Judah and Jerusalem because Jeroboam and his sons had rejected them as priests of the LORD. [15]And he appointed[t] his own priests[u] for the high places and for the goat[v] and calf[w] idols he had made. [16]Those from every tribe of Israel[x] who set their hearts on seeking the LORD, the God of Israel, followed the Levites to Jerusalem to offer sacrifices to the LORD, the God of their fathers. [17]They strengthened[y] the kingdom of Judah and supported Rehoboam son of Solomon three years, walking

Cross references (center column):

10:15 [i]2Ch 11:4; 25:16-20
[j]S 1Ki 11:29
10:16 [k]S 1Ch 9:1
[l]S 2Sa 20:1
10:18 [m]S 2Sa 20:24; S 1Ki 5:14
11:1 [n]S 1Ki 12:21
11:2 [o]S 1Ki 12:22; 2Ch 12:5-7,15
11:4 [p]2Ch 28:8-11
11:10 [q]S Jos 10:20; 2Ch 12:4; 17:2, 19; 21:3
11:14 [r]S Nu 35:2-5 [s]1Ch 6:81
11:15 [t]S 1Ki 13:33 [u]S 1Ki 12:31 [v]Lev 17:7 [w]1Ki 12:28; 2Ch 13:8
11:16 [x]2Ch 15:9
11:17 [y]2Ch 12:1

[v]18 Hebrew Hadoram, a variant of Adoniram

10:15 *Ahijah.* The Chronicler assumes the reader's familiarity with 1Ki 11:29–33.

10:18 *Adoniram . . . in charge of forced labor.* Had held the same office under Solomon (1Ki 4:6; 5:14).

10:19 *to this day.* See note on 5:9.

11:1–23 Verses 1–4 are parallel to 1Ki 12:21–24; vv. 5–23 are largely unique to Chronicles. The Chronicler's account of Rehoboam is a good example of his emphasis on immediate retribution (see Introduction to 1 Chronicles: Purpose and Themes). Ch. 11 traces the rewards for obedience to the command of God (vv. 1–4): Rehoboam enjoys prosperity and power (vv. 5–12), popular support (vv. 13–17) and progeny (vv. 18–23). Ch. 12 demonstrates the reverse: Disobedience brings judgment.

11:2 *Shemaiah.* The function of the prophets as guardians of the theocracy (God's kingdom) is prominent in Chronicles; most of Judah's kings are portrayed as receiving advice from prophets (see Introduction to 1 Chronicles: Purpose and Themes).

11:3 *the Israelites in Judah and Benjamin.* A variation from the wording found in 1Ki 12:23, in accordance with the

Chronicler's interest in "all Israel."

11:4 *my doing.* See 10:15.

11:5–10 This list of cities is not found in Kings. Rehoboam fortified his eastern, western and southern borders, but not the north, perhaps demonstrating his hope of reunification of the kingdoms, as well as the threat of invasion from Egypt.

11:13–17 The Chronicler assumes the reader's familiarity with 1Ki 12:26–33. This material is unique to Chronicles and reflects the author's concern both with the temple and its personnel and with showing that the kingdom of Judah was the remnant of all Israel.

11:14 *pasturelands and property.* See 1Ch 6:54–80; Lev 25:32–34; Nu 35:1–5; see also Introduction to 1 Chronicles: Purpose and Themes.

11:15 *goat and calf idols.* The account in Kings mentions only the golden calves (for the worship of goat idols or satyrs see Lev 17:7).

11:17 *three years.* See note on 12:2. *ways of David and Solomon.* Characteristic of the Chronicler's idealization of Solomon; contrast the portrait of Solomon in 1Ki 11:1–13.

Judah raised the battle cry. At the sound of their battle cry, God routed Jeroboam and all Israel[d] before Abijah and Judah. 16The Israelites fled before Judah, and God delivered[e] them into their hands. 17Abijah and his men inflicted heavy losses on them, so that there were five hundred thousand casualties among Israel's able men. 18The men of Israel were subdued on that occasion, and the men of Judah were victorious because they relied[f] on the LORD, the God of their fathers.

19Abijah pursued Jeroboam and took from him the towns of Bethel, Jeshanah and Ephron, with their surrounding villages. 20Jeroboam did not regain power during the time of Abijah. And the LORD struck him down and he died.

21But Abijah grew in strength. He married fourteen wives and had twenty-two sons and sixteen daughters.

22The other events of Abijah's reign, what he did and what he said, are written in the annotations of the prophet Iddo.

14 And Abijah rested with his fathers and was buried in the City of David. Asa his son succeeded him as king, and in his days the country was at peace for ten years.

Asa King of Judah

14:2-3pp — 1Ki 15:11-12

2Asa did what was good and right in the eyes of the LORD his God.[g] 3He removed the foreign altars[h] and the high places,

smashed the sacred stones[i] and cut down the Asherah poles.[a][j] 4He commanded Judah to seek the LORD,[k] the God of their fathers, and to obey his laws and commands. 5He removed the high places[l] and incense altars[m] in every town in Judah, and the kingdom was at peace under him. 6He built up the fortified cities of Judah, since the land was at peace. No one was at war with him during those years, for the LORD gave him rest.[n]

7"Let us build up these towns," he said to Judah, "and put walls around them, with towers, gates and bars. The land is still ours, because we have sought the LORD our God; we sought him and he has given us rest[o] on every side." So they built and prospered.

8Asa had an army of three hundred thousand[p] men from Judah, equipped with large shields and with spears, and two hundred and eighty thousand from Benjamin, armed with small shields and with bows. All these were brave fighting men.

9Zerah the Cushite[q] marched out against them with a vast army[b] and three hundred chariots, and came as far as Mareshah.[r] 10Asa went out to meet him, and they took up battle positions in the Valley of Zephathah near Mareshah.

11Then Asa called[s] to the LORD his God and said, "LORD, there is no one like you

Cross references (center column)

13:15 dS 1Ch 9:1
13:16 eS 2Ch 16:8
13:18 /2Ch 14:11; 16:7; Ps 22:5
14:2 gS 2Ch 21:12
14:3 hS Jdg 2:2

/S Ex 23:24
/S Ex 34:13
kS 1Ch 16:11
14:5 /S 1Ki 15:14
mIsa 27:9; Eze 6:4
14:6 nS 1Ch 22:9
14:7 oS 1Ch 22:9
14:8 pS 1Ch 21:1
14:9 qS 2Ch 12:3
rS Ge 10:8-9; 2Ch 11:8; 24:24
14:11 sS 1Ki 8:44; S 2Ch 13:14; 25:8

a3 That is, symbols of the goddess Asherah; here and elsewhere in 2 Chronicles   b9 Hebrew *with an army of a thousand thousands* or *with an army of thousands upon thousands*

13:21 See note on 11:18–22.
14:1 *peace for ten years.* For the Chronicler peace and prosperity go hand in hand with righteous rule. This first decade of Asa's reign (910–900 B.C.) preceded the invasion by Zerah (14:9–15) and was followed by 20 more years of peace, from the 15th (15:10) to the 35th years (15:19). Contrast this account with the statement that there was war between Asa and Baasha throughout their reigns (see 1Ki 15:16 and note). The tensions between the two kingdoms may have accounted for Asa's fortifications (14:7–8), though actual combat was likely confined to raids until the major campaign was launched in Asa's 36th year (16:1). See 15:8 and note.
14:2–16:14 The account of Asa's reign (910–869 B.C.) here is greatly expanded over the one in 1Ki 15:9–24. The expansions characteristically express the Chronicler's view concerning the relationship between obedience and blessing, disobedience and punishment. The author introduces chronological notes into his account to divide Asa's reign into these periods (see note on 12:2): For ten years Asa did what was right and prospered (14:1–7), and an invasion by a powerful Cushite force was repulsed because he called on the Lord (14:8–15). There followed further reforms (15:1–9) and a covenant renewal in Asa's 15th year (15:10–18), and so he enjoyed peace until his 35th year (15:19). But then came a change: When confronted by an invasion from the northern kingdom in his 36th year (16:1), he hired Aramean reinforcements rather than trusting in the

Lord (16:2–6), and imprisoned the prophet who rebuked him (16:7–10). In his 39th year he was afflicted with a disease (16:12), but still steadfastly refused to seek the Lord. In his 41st year he died (16:13).

14:3 *sacred stones.* See note on 1Ki 14:23.

14:5 *removed the high places.* 1Ki 15:14 states that Asa did not remove the high places. This difficulty is best resolved by the Chronicler's own statement in 15:17, which is properly parallel to 1Ki 15:14: Early in his reign Asa did attempt to remove the high places, but pagan worship was extremely resilient, and ultimately his efforts were unsuccessful (15:17). Statements that the high places both were and were not removed are also found in the reign of Jehoshaphat (17:6; 20:33). Cf. Dt 12:2–3.

14:7 *rest on every side.* See note on 20:30.

14:9 *Zerah the Cushite.* Many identify him with Pharaoh Osorkon I, second pharaoh of the 22nd Egyptian dynasty. However, since he is not called "king" or "pharaoh," and is known as the "Cushite" or "Nubian," some prefer to identify him as an otherwise unknown general serving the pharaoh. The invasion appears to have been an attempt to duplicate the attack of Shishak 30 years earlier (12:1–12), but the results against Asa were quite different.

14:10 *Valley of Zephathah.* Marked the entrance to a road leading to the hills of Judah and Jerusalem. *Mareshah.* Earlier fortified by Rehoboam (11:8) to protect the route mentioned here.

to help the powerless against the mighty. Help us,[t] O LORD our God, for we rely[u] on you, and in your name[v] we have come against this vast army. O LORD, you are our God; do not let man prevail[w] against you."

[12]The LORD struck down[x] the Cushites before Asa and Judah. The Cushites fled, [13]and Asa and his army pursued them as far as Gerar.[y] Such a great number of Cushites fell that they could not recover; they were crushed[z] before the LORD and his forces. The men of Judah carried off a large amount of plunder.[a] [14]They destroyed all the villages around Gerar, for the terror[b] of the LORD had fallen upon them. They plundered all these villages, since there was much booty there. [15]They also attacked the camps of the herdsmen and carried off droves of sheep and goats and camels. Then they returned to Jerusalem.

Asa's Reform

15:16–19pp — 1Ki 15:13–16

15 The Spirit of God came upon[c] Azariah son of Oded. [2]He went out to meet Asa and said to him, "Listen to me, Asa and all Judah and Benjamin. The LORD is with you[d] when you are with him.[e] If you seek[f] him, he will be found by you, but if you forsake him, he will forsake you.[g] [3]For a long time Israel was without the true God, without a priest to teach[h] and without the law.[i] [4]But in their distress they turned to the LORD, the God of Israel, and sought him,[j] and he was found by them. [5]In those days it was not safe to travel about,[k] for all the inhabitants of the lands were in great turmoil. [6]One nation was being crushed by another and one city by another,[l] because God was troubling them with every kind of distress. [7]But as for you, be strong[m] and do not give up, for your work will be rewarded."[n]

14:11
[t]Ps 60:11-12; 79:9
[u]S 2Ch 13:18
[v]S 1Sa 17:45
[w]Ps 9:19
14:12 [x]1Ki 8:45
14:13 [y]Ge 10:19
[z]2Sa 22:38; Ne 9:24; Ps 44:2, 19; 135:10
[a]2Ch 15:11,18
14:14
[b]S Ge 35:5; S Dt 2:25; 11:25
15:1
[c]S Nu 11:25,26
15:2 [d]2Ch 20:17
[e]Jas 4:8
[f]2Ch 7:14; Ps 78:34; Isa 45:19; 55:6; Jer 29:13; Hos 3:5
[g]S Dt 31:17; S 1Ch 28:9
15:3
[h]S Lev 10:11
[i]La 2:9; Am 8:11
15:4 [j]S Dt 4:29
15:5 [k]S Jdg 5:6; 19:20; Zec 8:10
15:6 [l]Isa 19:2; Mt 24:7; Mk 13:8; Lk 21:10
15:7 [m]Jos 1:7,9
[n]1Sa 24:19; Ps 18:20; 58:11; Pr 14:14; Jer 31:16

15:8 [o]1Ki 15:12
[p]2Ch 17:2
[q]S 1Ki 8:64; S 2Ch 8:12
15:9
[r]2Ch 11:16-17
15:10
[s]S Lev 23:15-21
15:11
[t]S 2Ch 14:13
15:12
[u]S 2Ki 11:17
[v]S 1Ch 16:11
15:13
[w]S Ex 22:20; Dt 13:9-16
15:15 [x]Dt 4:29
[y]S 1Ch 22:9
15:16 [z]2Ch 13:2
[a]S 1Ki 2:19
[b]S Ex 34:13
[c]S 2Sa 15:23

[8]When Asa heard these words and the prophecy of Azariah son of[c] Oded the prophet, he took courage. He removed the detestable idols[o] from the whole land of Judah and Benjamin and from the towns he had captured[p] in the hills of Ephraim. He repaired the altar[q] of the LORD that was in front of the portico of the LORD's temple.

[9]Then he assembled all Judah and Benjamin and the people from Ephraim, Manasseh and Simeon who had settled among them, for large numbers[r] had come over to him from Israel when they saw that the LORD his God was with him.

[10]They assembled at Jerusalem in the third month[s] of the fifteenth year of Asa's reign. [11]At that time they sacrificed to the LORD seven hundred head of cattle and seven thousand sheep and goats from the plunder[t] they had brought back. [12]They entered into a covenant[u] to seek the LORD,[v] the God of their fathers, with all their heart and soul. [13]All who would not seek the LORD, the God of Israel, were to be put to death,[w] whether small or great, man or woman. [14]They took an oath to the LORD with loud acclamation, with shouting and with trumpets and horns. [15]All Judah rejoiced about the oath because they had sworn it wholeheartedly. They sought God[x] eagerly, and he was found by them. So the LORD gave them rest[y] on every side.

[16]King Asa also deposed his grandmother Maacah[z] from her position as queen mother,[a] because she had made a repulsive Asherah pole.[b] Asa cut the pole down, broke it up and burned it in the Kidron Valley.[c] [17]Although he did not remove the high places from Israel, Asa's heart was fully committed ‚to the LORD‚ all

[c]8 Vulgate and Syriac (see also Septuagint and verse 1); Hebrew does not have *Azariah son of.*

14:13 *Gerar.* See note on Ge 20:1. *plunder.* Much of this booty (v. 14) made its way to the storehouses of the temple (15:18; see note on 1Ch 18:1–20:8).
14:14 *terror of the LORD.* See note on 1Ch 14:17.
15:1–19 This chapter appears to recount a second stage in the reforms introduced by Asa, beginning with the victory over Zerah and encouraged by the preaching of Azariah (v. 1).
15:3 *priest to teach.* The duties of the priests were not only to officiate at the altar, but also to teach the law (see 17:7–9; Lev 10:11).
15:8 *towns he had captured in . . . Ephraim.* A tacit admission that there had been some fighting between Baasha and Asa prior to Asa's 36th year (16:1); see 17:1.
15:9 *large numbers had come over to him.* Cf. the defection from the northern kingdom that also occurred under Rehoboam (11:13–17).

15:10 *third month of the fifteenth year.* Spring, 895 B.C., the year after Zerah's invasion (v. 19). The Feast of Weeks (or Pentecost) was held in the third month (Lev 23:15–21) and may have been the occasion for this assembly.
15:12 *covenant.* A renewal of the covenant made at Sinai, similar to the covenant renewals on the plain of Moab (Dt 29:1), at Mount Ebal (Jos 8:30–35), at Shechem (Jos 24:25) and at Gilgal (1Sa 11:14; see note there). Later the priest Jehoiada (23:16), as well as Hezekiah (29:10) and Josiah (34:31), would also lead in renewals of the covenant—events of primary significance in the view of the Chronicler.
15:13 *would not seek the LORD.* Would turn to other gods. *were to be put to death.* In accordance with basic covenant law (Ex 22:20; Dt 13:6–9).
15:15 *rest.* See note on 20:30.
15:16 *Asherah pole.* See NIV text note on 14:3.

his life. [18]He brought into the temple of God the silver and gold and the articles that he and his father had dedicated. [d]

[19]There was no more war until the thirty-fifth year of Asa's reign.

Asa's Last Years

16:1–6pp — 1Ki 15:17–22
16:11–17:1pp — 1Ki 15:23–24

16 In the thirty-sixth year of Asa's reign Baasha[e] king of Israel went up against Judah and fortified Ramah to prevent anyone from leaving or entering the territory of Asa king of Judah.

[2]Asa then took the silver and gold out of the treasuries of the LORD's temple and of his own palace and sent it to Ben-Hadad king of Aram, who was ruling in Damascus.[f] [3]"Let there be a treaty[g] between me and you," he said, "as there was between my father and your father. See, I am sending you silver and gold. Now break your treaty with Baasha king of Israel so he will withdraw from me."

[4]Ben-Hadad agreed with King Asa and sent the commanders of his forces against the towns of Israel. They conquered Ijon, Dan, Abel Maim[d] and all the store cities of Naphtali.[h] [5]When Baasha heard this, he stopped building Ramah and abandoned his work. [6]Then King Asa brought all the men of Judah, and they carried away from Ramah the stones and timber Baasha had been using. With them he built up Geba and Mizpah.[i]

[7]At that time Hanani[j] the seer came to Asa king of Judah and said to him: "Because you relied[k] on the king of Aram and not on the LORD your God, the army of the king of Aram has escaped from your hand.

[8]Were not the Cushites[el] and Libyans a mighty army with great numbers[m] of chariots and horsemen[f]? Yet when you relied on the LORD, he delivered[n] them into your hand. [9]For the eyes[o] of the LORD range throughout the earth to strengthen those whose hearts are fully committed to him. You have done a foolish[p] thing, and from now on you will be at war.[q]"

[10]Asa was angry with the seer because of this; he was so enraged that he put him in prison.[r] At the same time Asa brutally oppressed some of the people.

[11]The events of Asa's reign, from beginning to end, are written in the book of the kings of Judah and Israel. [12]In the thirty-ninth year of his reign Asa was afflicted[s] with a disease in his feet. Though his disease was severe, even in his illness he did not seek[t] help from the LORD,[u] but only from the physicians. [13]Then in the forty-first year of his reign Asa died and rested with his fathers. [14]They buried him in the tomb that he had cut out for himself[v] in the City of David. They laid him on a bier covered with spices and various blended perfumes,[w] and they made a huge fire[x] in his honor.

Jehoshaphat King of Judah

17 Jehoshaphat his son succeeded him as king and strengthened[y] himself against Israel. [2]He stationed troops in all the fortified cities[z] of Judah and put garrisons in Judah and in the towns of Ephraim that his father Asa had captured.[a]

[3]The LORD was with Jehoshaphat be-

Cross references (center column)

15:18 dS 2Ch 14:13
16:1 e2Ki 9:9; Jer 41:9
16:2 f2Ch 19:1-20:37; 22:1-9
16:3 g2Ch 20:35; 25:7
16:4 hS 2Ki 15:29
16:6 iJer 41:9
16:7 j1Ki 16:1
kS 2Ch 13:18
16:8 lS Ge 10:6, 8-9; S 2Ch 12:3
m2Ch 24:24
n2Ch 13:16
16:9 oJob 24:23; Ps 33:13-15; Pr 15:3; Jer 16:17; Zec 3:9; 4:10
p1Sa 13:13
q5 1Ki 15:6; 2Ch 19:2; 25:7; 28:16-21
16:10 rS 1Ki 22:27
16:12 s2Ch 21:18; 26:19; Ps 103:3
t2Ch 7:14
uJer 17:5-6
16:14 vS Ge 50:5
wS Ge 50:2
x2Ch 21:19; Jer 34:5
17:1 yS 1Ki 2:12
17:2 zS 2Ch 11:10
a2Ch 15:8

d4 Also known as *Abel Beth Maacah*   e8 That is, people from the upper Nile region   f8 Or *charioteers*

15:17 *did not remove the high places.* See 14:5 and note.
16:1 *thirty-sixth year of Asa's reign Baasha.* According to Kings, Baasha ruled for 24 years and was succeeded by Elah in the 26th year of Asa (1Ki 15:33; 16:8). Obviously Baasha could not have been alive in the 36th year of Asa, where this passage places him—he had been dead for a decade. In order to solve this difficulty, some suggest that the Chronicler here and in 15:19 is dating from the schism in Israel rather than from the year number of Asa's reign: Since Rehoboam had reigned 17 years and Abijah 3, 20 years are deducted with the result that the 35th and 36th years of Asa are in fact the 15th and 16th years of his reign. This would make Baasha's attack come as a possible response to the defections from the northern kingdom (15:9). While this solution may be possible, it has not met with general acceptance. The action described here is not dated in 1Ki 15:17. Perhaps the dates here and in 15:19 are the result of a copyist's error (possibly for an original 25th and 26th).
16:2–9 *Hiring foreign troops brought Asa into a foreign alliance, which showed lack of trust in the Lord. Other examples of condemned foreign alliances are found in the reigns of Jehoshaphat (20:35–37), Ahaziah (22:1–9) and Ahaz (28:16–21). By hiring Ben-Hadad to the north, Asa*

opened a two-front war for Baasha and forced his withdrawal.

16:12 *disease in his feet.* For other examples of disease as punishment for sin see 21:16–20; 26:16–23; Ac 12:23. Cf. 2Ki 15:5.

17:1–21:3 The Chronicler's account of Jehoshaphat's reign is more than twice as long as that in Kings, where the interest in Ahab and Elijah overshadows the space allotted to Jehoshaphat (1Ki 22:1–46). The Chronicler has also used Jehoshaphat's reign to emphasize immediate retribution. This theme is specifically announced in 19:10 and is illustrated in the blessing of Jehoshaphat's obedient faith and in the reproof for his wrongdoing (19:2–3; 20:35–37). Jehoshaphat reigned 872–848 B.C., from 872 to 869 likely as co-regent with his father Asa (see 20:31 and note). The details of his reign may not be in chronological order; the teaching mission of 17:7–9 may have been part of the reforms noted in 19:4–11.

17:2 *cities of Judah . . . towns of Ephraim.* See note on 15:8. Abijah (13:19), Asa (15:8) and now Jehoshaphat had managed to hold these cities; they would be lost under Amaziah (25:17–24).

cause in his early years he walked in the ways his father David[b] had followed. He did not consult the Baals [4]but sought[c] the God of his father and followed his commands rather than the practices of Israel. [5]The LORD established the kingdom under his control; and all Judah brought gifts[d] to Jehoshaphat, so that he had great wealth and honor.[e] [6]His heart was devoted[f] to the ways of the LORD; furthermore, he removed the high places[g] and the Asherah poles[h] from Judah.[i]

[7]In the third year of his reign he sent his officials Ben-Hail, Obadiah, Zechariah, Nethanel and Micaiah to teach[j] in the towns of Judah. [8]With them were certain Levites[k]—Shemaiah, Nethaniah, Zebadiah, Asahel, Shemiramoth, Jehonathan, Adonijah, Tobijah and Tob-Adonijah—and the priests Elishama and Jehoram. [9]They taught throughout Judah, taking with them the Book of the Law[l] of the LORD; they went around to all the towns of Judah and taught the people.

[10]The fear[m] of the LORD fell on all the kingdoms of the lands surrounding Judah, so that they did not make war with Jehoshaphat. [11]Some Philistines brought Jehoshaphat gifts and silver as tribute, and the Arabs[n] brought him flocks:[o] seven thousand seven hundred rams and seven thousand seven hundred goats.

[12]Jehoshaphat became more and more powerful; he built forts and store cities in Judah [13]and had large supplies in the towns of Judah. He also kept experienced fighting men in Jerusalem. [14]Their enrollment[p] by families was as follows:

From Judah, commanders of units of 1,000:

Adnah the commander, with 300,-000 fighting men;

[15]next, Jehohanan the commander, with 280,000;

[16]next, Amasiah son of Zicri, who volunteered[q] himself for the service of the LORD, with 200,000.

[17]From Benjamin:[r]

Eliada, a valiant soldier, with 200,-000 men armed with bows and shields;

[18]next, Jehozabad, with 180,000 men armed for battle.

[19]These were the men who served the king, besides those he stationed in the fortified cities[s] throughout Judah.[t]

Micaiah Prophesies Against Ahab

18:1–27pp — 1Ki 22:1–28

18 Now Jehoshaphat had great wealth and honor,[u] and he allied[v] himself with Ahab[w] by marriage. [2]Some years later he went down to visit Ahab in Samaria. Ahab slaughtered many sheep and cattle for him and the people with him and urged him to attack Ramoth Gilead. [3]Ahab king of Israel asked Jehoshaphat king of Judah, "Will you go with me against Ramoth Gilead?"

Jehoshaphat replied, "I am as you are, and my people as your people; we will join you in the war." [4]But Jehoshaphat also said to the king of Israel, "First seek the counsel of the LORD."

[5]So the king of Israel brought together the prophets—four hundred men—and asked them, "Shall we go to war against Ramoth Gilead, or shall I refrain?"

"Go," they answered, "for God will give it into the king's hand."

[6]But Jehoshaphat asked, "Is there not a

17:3
[b]S 1Ki 22:43
17:4 [c]2Ch 22:9
17:5
[d]S 1Sa 10:27
[e]2Ch 18:1
17:6 /S 1Ki 8:61
[g]S 1Ki 15:14;
2Ch 19:3; 20:33
[h]S Ex 34:13
[i]2Ch 21:12
17:7
/S Lev 10:11;
Dt 6:4-9;
2Ch 19:4-11;
35:3; Ne 8:7;
Mal 2:7
17:8 [k]2Ch 19:8;
Ne 8:7-8; Hos 4:6
17:9 /S Dt 28:61
17:10
[m]S Ge 35:5;
S Dt 2:25
17:11
[n]S 2Ch 9:14
[o]2Ch 21:16
17:14
[p]S 2Sa 24:2

17:16 [q]S Jdg 5:9
17:17 [r]S Nu 1:36
17:19
[s]S 2Ch 11:10
[t]2Ch 25:5
18:1 [u]2Ch 17:5
[v]2Ch 19:1-3;
22:3 [w]2Ch 21:6

17:6 *removed the high places.* Just as his father Asa had attempted to remove the high places, only to have them be restored (14:5; 15:17), so also Jehoshaphat removed them initially, only to have them revive and persist (20:33; cf. 1Ki 22:43). But see notes on 1Ki 3:2; 15:14. *Asherah poles.* See NIV text note on 14:3.
17:7–9 This incident may be part of the reform more fully detailed in 19:4–11. In the theocracy, the law of the Lord was supposed to be an integral part of the law of the land; the king and his officials, as well as the priests and prophets, were representatives of the Lord's kingship over his people.
17:7 *third year.* Perhaps the first year of his sole reign after a co-regency of three years with his father Asa (see 20:31 and note).
17:10–11 See note on 1Ch 18:1–20:8.
17:10 *fear of the Lord.* See note on 1Ch 14:17.
17:14–18 *300,000…280,000…200,000…200,000 …180,000.* Or "300 units … 280 units … 200 units … 200 units … 180 units" (see notes on 1Ch 12:23–37; 27:1).
18:1–19:3 See 1Ki 22:1–40 and notes. To conform with

his interest in the southern kingdom and Jehoshaphat, the Chronicler omits elaboration on the death of Ahab and his succession (1Ki 22:36–40) and adds the material on the prophetic condemnation of Jehoshaphat's involvement (19:1–3).
18:1 Not found in 1Ki 22. The verse enhances the status of Jehoshaphat by mentioning the blessing of wealth for his fidelity, and also sets the stage for an entangling foreign alliance condemned by the prophet in 19:2–3. *allied himself with Ahab by marriage.* This marriage alliance to Athaliah, daughter of Ahab, resulted later in an attempt to exterminate the Davidic line (22:10–23:21).
18:2 The Chronicler further enhances the status of Jehoshaphat by noting the large number of animals Ahab slaughtered in his honor, a note not found in 1Ki 22. *urged him.* Also not found in the parallel text. The Hebrew for this verb is often used in the sense of "inciting to evil" (e.g., 1Ch 21:1) and may express the Chronicler's attitude toward Jehoshaphat's involvement.
18:4 *seek the counsel of the Lord.* This request fits the Chronicler's overall positive portrait of Jehoshaphat.

prophet of the LORD here whom we can inquire of?"

7The king of Israel answered Jehoshaphat, "There is still one man through whom we can inquire of the LORD, but I hate him because he never prophesies anything good about me, but always bad. He is Micaiah son of Imlah."

"The king should not say that," Jehoshaphat replied.

8So the king of Israel called one of his officials and said, "Bring Micaiah son of Imlah at once."

9Dressed in their royal robes, the king of Israel and Jehoshaphat king of Judah were sitting on their thrones at the threshing floor by the entrance to the gate of Samaria, with all the prophets prophesying before them. 10Now Zedekiah son of Kenaanah had made iron horns, and he declared, "This is what the LORD says: 'With these you will gore the Arameans until they are destroyed.' "

11All the other prophets were prophesying the same thing. "Attack Ramoth Gileadˣ and be victorious," they said, "for the LORD will give it into the king's hand."

12The messenger who had gone to summon Micaiah said to him, "Look, as one man the other prophets are predicting success for the king. Let your word agree with theirs, and speak favorably."

13But Micaiah said, "As surely as the LORD lives, I can tell him only what my God says."ʸ

14When he arrived, the king asked him, "Micaiah, shall we go to war against Ramoth Gilead, or shall I refrain?"

"Attack and be victorious," he answered, "for they will be given into your hand."

15The king said to him, "How many times must I make you swear to tell me nothing but the truth in the name of the LORD?"

16Then Micaiah answered, "I saw all Israelᶻ scattered on the hills like sheep without a shepherd,ᵃ and the LORD said, 'These people have no master. Let each one go home in peace.' "

17The king of Israel said to Jehoshaphat, "Didn't I tell you that he never prophesies anything good about me, but only bad?"

18Micaiah continued, "Therefore hear

the word of the LORD: I saw the LORD sitting on his throneᵇ with all the host of heaven standing on his right and on his left. 19And the LORD said, 'Who will entice Ahab king of Israel into attacking Ramoth Gilead and going to his death there?'

"One suggested this, and another that. 20Finally, a spirit came forward, stood before the LORD and said, 'I will entice him.'

" 'By what means?' the LORD asked.

21" 'I will go and be a lying spiritᶜ in the mouths of all his prophets,' he said.

" 'You will succeed in enticing him,' said the LORD. 'Go and do it.'

22"So now the LORD has put a lying spirit in the mouths of these prophets of yours.ᵈ The LORD has decreed disaster for you."

23Then Zedekiah son of Kenaanah went up and slappedᵉ Micaiah in the face. "Which way did the spirit fromᵍ the LORD go when he went from me to speak to you?" he asked.

24Micaiah replied, "You will find out on the day you go to hide in an inner room."

25The king of Israel then ordered, "Take Micaiah and send him back to Amon the ruler of the city and to Joash the king's son, 26and say, 'This is what the king says: Put this fellow in prisonᶠ and give him nothing but bread and water until I return safely.' "

27Micaiah declared, "If you ever return safely, the LORD has not spoken through me." Then he added, "Mark my words, all you people!"

Ahab Killed at Ramoth Gilead

18:28–34pp — 1Ki 22:29–36

28So the king of Israel and Jehoshaphat king of Judah went up to Ramoth Gilead. 29The king of Israel said to Jehoshaphat, "I will enter the battle in disguise, but you wear your royal robes." So the king of Israel disguisedᵍ himself and went into battle.

30Now the king of Aram had ordered his chariot commanders, "Do not fight with anyone, small or great, except the king of Israel." 31When the chariot commanders saw Jehoshaphat, they thought, "This is the king of Israel." So they turned to attack him, but Jehoshaphat cried out,ʰ and the

18:11 ˣ2Ch 22:5
18:13 ʸNu 22:18, 20,35
18:16 ᶻS 1Ch 9:1; ᵃS Nu 27:17

18:18 ᵇDa 7:9
18:21 ᶜ1Ch 21:1; Job 1:6; Zec 3:1; Jn 8:44
18:22 ᵈJob 12:16; Eze 14:9
18:23 ᵉAc 23:2
18:26 ᶠHeb 11:36
18:29 ᵍS 1Sa 28:8
18:31 ʰS 2Ch 13:14

ᵍ23 Or *Spirit of*

18:29 The fact that Ahab disguises himself while directing Jehoshaphat into battle in royal regalia, thus making Jehoshaphat the logical target for attack, is consistent with Israel's dominant position at this time.
18:31 *the LORD helped him. God drew them away from*

him. Not found in 1Ki 22:32. However, some Septuagint (the Greek translation of the OT) manuscripts of Kings do contain the statement that "the LORD helped him," suggesting that the Chronicler was following a Hebrew text of Kings that had these words.

LORD helped him. God drew them away from him, 32for when the chariot commanders saw that he was not the king of Israel, they stopped pursuing him.

33But someone drew his bow at random and hit the king of Israel between the sections of his armor. The king told the chariot driver, "Wheel around and get me out of the fighting. I've been wounded." 34All day long the battle raged, and the king of Israel propped himself up in his chariot facing the Arameans until evening. Then at sunset he died.*i*

19 When Jehoshaphat king of Judah returned safely to his palace in Jerusalem, 2Jehu*j* the seer, the son of Hanani, went out to meet him and said to the king, "Should you help the wicked*k* and love*h* those who hate the LORD?*l* Because of this, the wrath*m* of the LORD is upon you. 3There is, however, some good*n* in you, for you have rid the land of the Asherah poles*o* and have set your heart on seeking God.*p*"

Jehoshaphat Appoints Judges

4Jehoshaphat lived in Jerusalem, and he went out again among the people from Beersheba to the hill country of Ephraim and turned them back to the LORD, the God of their fathers. 5He appointed judges*q* in the land, in each of the fortified cities of Judah. 6He told them, "Consider carefully what you do,*r* because you are not judging for man*s* but for the LORD, who is with you whenever you give a verdict. 7Now let the fear of the LORD be upon

you. Judge carefully, for with the LORD our God there is no injustice*t* or partiality*u* or bribery."

8In Jerusalem also, Jehoshaphat appointed some of the Levites,*v* priests*w* and heads of Israelite families to administer*x* the law of the LORD and to settle disputes. And they lived in Jerusalem. 9He gave them these orders: "You must serve faithfully and wholeheartedly in the fear of the LORD. 10In every case that comes before you from your fellow countrymen who live in the cities—whether bloodshed or other concerns of the law, commands, decrees or ordinances—you are to warn them not to sin against the LORD;*y* otherwise his wrath will come on you and your brothers. Do this, and you will not sin.

11"Amariah the chief priest will be over you in any matter concerning the LORD, and Zebadiah son of Ishmael, the leader of the tribe of Judah, will be over you in any matter concerning the king, and the Levites will serve as officials before you. Act with courage,*z* and may the LORD be with those who do well."

Jehoshaphat Defeats Moab and Ammon

20 After this, the Moabites*a* and Ammonites with some of the Meunites*i b* came to make war on Jehoshaphat.

2Some men came and told Jehoshaphat, "A vast army*c* is coming against you from

h 2 Or *and make alliances with* *i 1* Some Septuagint manuscripts; Hebrew *Ammonites*

Cross-references (center column)

18:34 *i*2Ch 22:5
19:2 /S 1Ki 16:1
*k*S 2Ch 16:2-9
/Ps 139:21-22
*m*2Ch 24:18;
32:25; Ps 7:11
19:3
*n*S 1Ki 14:13
*o*S 2Ch 17:6
*p*S 2Ch 18:1;
20:35; 25:7
19:5 *q*S Ge 47:6;
S Ex 18:26
19:6 *r*S Lev 19:15
*s*Dt 16:18-20;
17:8-13
19:7 *t*S Ge 18:25;
S Job 8:3
*u*S Ex 18:16;
Dt 10:17;
Job 13:10; 32:21;
34:19
19:8 *v*S 1Ch 23:4
*w*Eze 44:24
*x*2Ch 17:8-9
19:10
*y*Dt 17:8-13
19:11
*z*S 1Ch 28:20
20:1 *a*Ps 83:6
*b*S 1Ch 4:41
20:2 *c*2Ch 24:24

19:1–3 Not found in 1Ki 22.

19:2 *Should you help the wicked . . . ?* Jehu's father Hanani had earlier given Jehoshaphat's father Asa the same warning (see 16:7–9). Jehoshaphat later committed the same sin again and suffered for it (20:35–37).

19:3 *Asherah poles.* See NIV text note on 14:3.

19:4 *Jehoshaphat . . . went . . . among the people.* The king traveled throughout the realm personally to promote religious reformation.

19:5 *appointed judges.* The name Jehoshaphat (meaning "The LORD judges") is appropriate for the king who instituted this judicial reform. The arrangement of the courts under Jehoshaphat (vv. 5–11) would be of particular interest to the Chronicler's audience in the postexilic period, when the courts of the restored community would have their own existence and structure legitimized by this precedent.

19:6 Cf. Dt 16:18–20; 17:8–13.

19:7 *let the fear of the LORD be upon you.* Let a terrifying sense of God's presence restrain you from any injustice (see note on 1Ch 14:17).

19:8 *Levites, priests . . . to administer the law.* See note on 1Ch 26:29–32. One effect of this judicial reform appears to be the bringing of the traditional system of justice administered by the elders of the city under closer royal and priestly supervision.

19:11 *any matter concerning the LORD . . . any matter*

concerning the king. This division into the affairs of religion and the affairs of the king reflects the postexilic structure of the Chronicler's day. Cf. the anointing of Solomon and Zadok (1Ch 29:22) and the administration of the postexilic community by Zerubbabel, a Davidic descendant, and Joshua, the high priest (Zec 4:14; 6:9–15).

20:1–30 This episode held special interest for the Chronicler since the restored community was being harassed by the descendants of these same peoples (see Ne 2:19; 4:1–3, 7–9; 6:1–4; 13). He uses it to encourage his contemporaries to trust in the Lord and his prophets, as Jehoshaphat son of David had exhorted (v. 20). The account is significantly structured. Apart from the outer frame, which highlights the reversal of circumstances (vv. 1–4,28–30), it falls into three divisions: (1) Jehoshaphat's prayer (vv. 5–13), (2) the Lord's response (vv. 14–19), (3) the great victory (vv. 20–27). At the center of each is its crucial statement, and these are all linked by a key word: v. 9, "we will stand in your presence before this temple"; v. 17, "stand firm and see the deliverance the LORD will give you"; v. 23, "The men of Ammon and Moab rose up (lit. 'stood up') against the men from Mount Seir to destroy . . . them."

20:1 *Meunites.* A people from the region of Mount Seir in Edom (26:7; 1Ch 4:41; cf. 2Ch 20:10,22–23).

20:2 *Edom.* See NIV text note. Since the Arameans are well to the north and not mentioned among the attackers

a hundred: Azariah son of Jeroham, Ishmael son of Jehohanan, Azariah son of Obed, Maaseiah son of Adaiah, and Elishaphat son of Zicri. [2]They went throughout Judah and gathered the Levites[w] and the heads of Israelite families from all the towns. When they came to Jerusalem, [3]the whole assembly made a covenant[x] with the king at the temple of God.

Jehoiada said to them, "The king's son shall reign, as the LORD promised concerning the descendants of David.[y] [4]Now this is what you are to do: A third of you priests and Levites who are going on duty on the Sabbath are to keep watch at the doors, [5]a third of you at the royal palace and a third at the Foundation Gate, and all the other men are to be in the courtyards of the temple of the LORD. [6]No one is to enter the temple of the LORD except the priests and Levites on duty; they may enter because they are consecrated, but all the other men are to guard[z] what the LORD has assigned to them.[x] [7]The Levites are to station themselves around the king, each man with his weapons in his hand. Anyone who enters the temple must be put to death. Stay close to the king wherever he goes."

[8]The Levites and all the men of Judah did just as Jehoiada the priest ordered.[a] Each one took his men—those who were going on duty on the Sabbath and those who were going off duty—for Jehoiada the priest had not released any of the divisions.[b] [9]Then he gave the commanders of units of a hundred the spears and the large and small shields that had belonged to King David and that were in the temple of God. [10]He stationed all the men, each with his weapon in his hand, around the

king—near the altar and the temple, from the south side to the north side of the temple.

[11]Jehoiada and his sons brought out the king's son and put the crown on him; they presented him with a copy[c] of the covenant and proclaimed him king. They anointed him and shouted, "Long live the king!"

[12]When Athaliah heard the noise of the people running and cheering the king, she went to them at the temple of the LORD. [13]She looked, and there was the king,[d] standing by his pillar[e] at the entrance. The officers and the trumpeters were beside the king, and all the people of the land were rejoicing and blowing trumpets, and singers with musical instruments were leading the praises. Then Athaliah tore her robes and shouted, "Treason! Treason!"

[14]Jehoiada the priest sent out the commanders of units of a hundred, who were in charge of the troops, and said to them: "Bring her out between the ranks[y] and put to the sword anyone who follows her." For the priest had said, "Do not put her to death at the temple of the LORD." [15]So they seized her as she reached the entrance of the Horse Gate[f] on the palace grounds, and there they put her to death.

[16]Jehoiada then made a covenant[g] that he and the people and the king[z] would be the LORD's people. [17]All the people went to the temple of Baal and tore it down. They smashed the altars and idols and killed[h] Mattan the priest of Baal in front of the altars.

23:2 w S Nu 35:2-5
23:3 x S 2Ki 11:17
y S 2Sa 7:12; S 1Ki 2:4;
S 2Ch 6:16; S 7:18; S 21:7
23:6 z Zec 3:7
23:8 a 2Ki 11:9
b S 1Ch 24:1

23:11 c Dt 17:18
23:13 d 1Ki 1:41
e S 1Ki 7:15
23:15 f Jer 31:40
23:16 g 2Ch 29:10; 34:31; Ne 9:38
23:17 h Dt 13:6-9

x 6 Or to observe the LORD's command not to enter
y 14 Or out from the precincts   z 16 Or covenant
between the LORD, and the people and the king that they
(see 2 Kings 11:17)

---

cler divides the reign of Joash (835–796 B.C.) into three parts: (1) the recovery of the throne for the house of David (ch. 23); (2) Joash and Jehoiada—the good years (24:1–16); (3) Joash alone—the bad years (24:17–27). The last section is largely unique to Chronicles and further develops the theme of immediate retribution: Once again chronological notes provide the framework for cycles of obedience and disobedience (24:15–17,23); see notes on 12:2; 14:2–16:14.
23:1–21 See 2Ki 11:4–20. The Chronicler has followed his source rather closely but has introduced material reflecting his own concerns in three areas: 1. The account in Kings has more to say about the participation of the military in the coup; the Chronicler adds material emphasizing the presence of temple officials and their role (vv. 2,6,8,13,18–19). 2. The Chronicler stresses the widespread popular support for the coup by mentioning the presence of large groups of people, such as "all the people" or "the whole assembly" (vv. 3,5–6,8,10,16–17). 3. The Chronicler shows additional concern for the sanctity of the temple area by inserting notes showing the steps taken to ensure that only qualified person-

nel enter the temple precincts (vv. 5–6,19).
23:1 Azariah . . . Elishaphat. The Chronicler names the commanders, which was not done in Kings, but he does not mention the Carites, mercenaries who served as a royal guard (see note on 2Ki 11:4). Verse 20 exhibits the same omission (cf. 2Ki 11:19), the motive for which may have been the Chronicler's concern that only authorized persons enter the temple precincts.
23:2 the Levites and the heads of Israelite families. Reflects both the Chronicler's concerns with the temple personnel and the widespread support for the coup against Athaliah.
23:3 as the LORD promised. See 2Sa 7:11–16.
23:11 copy of the covenant. May refer to the covenant sworn by the assembly (vv. 1,3; cf. v. 16) or to the law of God, by which the king was to rule (see Dt 17:18–20). See note on 2Ki 11:12.
23:13 singers with musical instruments. The Chronicler adds a note (not found in 2Ki 11:14) about the presence of Levitical musicians, who were leading the praises (see note on 1Ch 6:31–48).

18Then Jehoiada placed the oversight of the temple of the LORD in the hands of the priests, who were Levites, *i* to whom David had made assignments in the temple, *j* to present the burnt offerings of the LORD as written in the Law of Moses, with rejoicing and singing, as David had ordered. 19He also stationed doorkeepers *k* at the gates of the LORD's temple so that no one who was in any way unclean might enter. 20He took with him the commanders of hundreds, the nobles, the rulers of the people and all the people of the land and brought the king down from the temple of the LORD. They went into the palace through the Upper Gate *l* and seated the king on the royal throne, 21and all the people of the land rejoiced. And the city was quiet, because Athaliah had been slain with the sword. *m*

Joash Repairs the Temple

24:1–14pp — 2Ki 12:1–16
24:23–27pp — 2Ki 12:17–21

24 Joash was seven years old when he became king, and he reigned in Jerusalem forty years. His mother's name was Zibiah; she was from Beersheba. 2Joash did what was right in the eyes of the LORD *n* all the years of Jehoiada the priest. 3Jehoiada chose two wives for him, and he had sons and daughters.

4Some time later Joash decided to restore the temple of the LORD. 5He called together the priests and Levites and said to them, "Go to the towns of Judah and collect the money *o* due annually from all Israel, *p* to repair the temple of your God. Do it now." But the Levites *q* did not act at once.

6Therefore the king summoned Jehoiada the chief priest and said to him, "Why haven't you required the Levites to bring in from Judah and Jerusalem the tax imposed by Moses the servant of the LORD and by the assembly of Israel for the Tent of the Testimony?" *r*

7Now the sons of that wicked woman Athaliah had broken into the temple of God and had used even its sacred objects for the Baals.

8At the king's command, a chest was made and placed outside, at the gate of the temple of the LORD. 9A proclamation was then issued in Judah and Jerusalem that they should bring to the LORD the tax that Moses the servant of God had required of Israel in the desert. 10All the officials and all the people brought their contributions gladly, *s* dropping them into the chest until it was full. 11Whenever the chest was brought in by the Levites to the king's officials and they saw that there was a large amount of money, the royal secretary and the officer of the chief priest would come and empty the chest and carry it back to its place. They did this regularly and collected a great amount of money. 12The king and Jehoiada gave it to the men who carried out the work required for the temple of the LORD. They hired *t* masons and carpenters to restore the LORD's temple, and also workers in iron and bronze to repair the temple.

13The men in charge of the work were diligent, and the repairs progressed under them. They rebuilt the temple of God according to its original design and reinforced it. 14When they had finished, they brought the rest of the money to the king and Jehoiada, and with it were made articles for the LORD's temple: articles for the service and for the burnt offerings, and also dishes and other objects of gold and silver. As long as Jehoiada lived, burnt offerings were presented continually in the temple of the LORD.

15Now Jehoiada was old and full of

23:18
i S 1Ch 23:28-32
j S 1Ch 23:6;
S 25:6
23:19 *k* 1Ch 9:22
23:20
l S 2Ki 15:35
23:21
m S 2Ch 22:1
24:2 *n* 2Ch 25:2;
26:5
24:5
o S Ex 30:16;
Ne 10:32-33;
Mt 17:24
p 1Ch 11:1
q S 1Ch 26:20

24:6 *r* S Ex 38:21
24:10
s S Ex 25:2;
S 1Ch 29:3,6,9
24:12
t 2Ch 34:11

23:18–19 The Chronicler adds information on the cultic ritual and the guards at the gates (see note on vv. 1–21).
23:20 See note on v. 1.
24:1–14 See 2Ki 12:1–17.
24:1 *forty years.* 835–796 B.C.
24:2 Provides the outline for the Chronicler's treatment of Joash—the good years while Jehoiada was alive (vv. 1–16), and the turn to evil after his death (vv. 17–27). See note on 25:2.
24:3 Another expression of the Chronicler's conviction that large families represent the blessing of God (see v. 27; see also note on 1Ch 25:5).
24:4 *restore the temple.* The vandalism and atrocities of Athaliah (v. 7) required the refurbishing of the temple.
24:5 The writer of 2 Kings speaks of three different sources of revenue (2Ki 12:4–5), whereas the Chronicler mentions only the census tax (see Ex 30:14; 38:26; Mt 17:24). The reason for the tardiness of the priests is not stated (see 2Ki

12:6–8). The writer of Kings notes that the audience with the priests takes place in the 23rd year of Joash's reign, when he is presumably no longer the ward of Jehoiada. Resistance on the part of the priests to the reassignment of the temple revenues for repair work may be the underlying cause.
24:8 *chest.* Mesopotamian texts speak of a similar offering box placed in temples. Representatives of both the king and the temple officials administered temple revenues (see note on 1Ch 26:20).
24:14 See 2Ki 12:13–14. *As long as Jehoiada lived.* An additional note on the part of the Chronicler to introduce the turn to the worse in the reign of Joash upon Jehoiada's death (vv. 15–16).
24:15–22 This section is unique to the Chronicler and shows his emphasis on immediate retribution (see note on 23:1–24:27). After a period of righteous rule until the death of Jehoiada, Joash turns to idolatry and murders Jehoiada's son. In the following year he is invaded and defeated by

brought him to Jerusalem and broke down the wall of Jerusalem from the Ephraim Gate b to the Corner Gate c—a section about six hundred feet i long. 24He took all the gold and silver and all the articles found in the temple of God that had been in the care of Obed-Edom, d together with the palace treasures and the hostages, and returned to Samaria.

25Amaziah son of Joash king of Judah lived for fifteen years after the death of Jehoash son of Jehoahaz king of Israel. 26As for the other events of Amaziah's reign, from beginning to end, are they not written in the book of the kings of Judah and Israel? 27From the time that Amaziah turned away from following the LORD, they conspired against him in Jerusalem and he fled to Lachish e, but they sent men after him to Lachish and killed him there. 28He was brought back by horse and was buried with his fathers in the City of Judah.

Uzziah King of Judah

26:1–4pp — 2Ki 14:21–22; 15:1–3
26:21–23pp — 2Ki 15:5–7

26 Then all the people of Judah f took Uzziah, j who was sixteen years old, and made him king in place of his father Amaziah. 2He was the one who rebuilt Elath and restored it to Judah after Amaziah rested with his fathers.

3Uzziah was sixteen years old when he became king, and he reigned in Jerusalem fifty-two years. His mother's name was Jecoliah; she was from Jerusalem. 4He did what was right in the eyes of the LORD, just as his father Amaziah had done. 5He sought God during the days of Zechariah, who instructed him in the fear k of God. g As long as he sought the LORD, God gave him success. h

6He went to war against the Philistines i and broke down the walls of Gath, Jabneh and Ashdod. j He then rebuilt towns near Ashdod and elsewhere among the Philistines. 7God helped him against the Philistines and against the Arabs k who lived in Gur Baal and against the Meunites. l 8The Ammonites m brought tribute to Uzziah, and his fame spread as far as the border of Egypt, because he had become very powerful.

9Uzziah built towers in Jerusalem at the Corner Gate, n at the Valley Gate o and at the angle of the wall, and he fortified them. 10He also built towers in the desert and dug many cisterns, because he had much livestock in the foothills and in the plain. He had people working his fields and vineyards in the hills and in the fertile lands, for he loved the soil.

11Uzziah had a well-trained army, ready to go out by divisions according to their numbers as mustered by Jeiel the secretary and Maaseiah the officer under the direction of Hananiah, one of the royal officials. 12The total number of family leaders over the fighting men was 2,600. 13Under their

Cross references (center column)

25:23 b2Ki 14:13; Ne 8:16; 12:39
c2Ch 26:9; Jer 31:38
25:24 d5 1Ch 26:15
25:27 e5 Jos 10:3
26:1 f5 2Ch 22:1

26:5 g5 2Ch 24:2
h2Ch 27:6
26:6 i Isa 2:6; 11:14; 14:29; Jer 25:20
jAm 1:8; 3:9
26:7 k5 2Ch 21:16
l2Ch 20:1
26:8 m5 Ge 19:38
26:9 n5 2Ki 14:13; S 2Ch 25:23
o Ne 2:13; 3:13

i 23 Hebrew *four hundred cubits* (about 180 meters)   j 1 Also called *Azariah*   k 5 Many Hebrew manuscripts, Septuagint and Syriac; other Hebrew manuscripts *vision*

25:24 The family of Obed-Edom was the Levitical family into whose care the temple storehouse had been entrusted (1Ch 26:15).

25:27 See note on vv. 14–25.

26:1–23 See 2Ki 15:1–7 and notes. The Chronicler has characteristically divided his account of Uzziah's reign into two parts: the good years, then the bad; cf. his treatment of Uzziah's father Amaziah and his grandfather Joash (see notes on 24:2; 25:1–28). The Chronicler elaborates on the blessings and divine help that flowed from Uzziah's obedience and fidelity (vv. 4–15), whereas the author of Kings only alludes to his fidelity (2Ki 15:3). Where Kings only mentions Uzziah's leprosy (2Ki 15:5), the Chronicler gives additional details to show that the disease was a result of unfaithfulness (vv. 16–21). Under Uzziah and his contemporary in the north, Jeroboam II, the borders of Israel and Judah briefly reached the extent they had attained under David and Solomon (vv. 6–8; 2Ki 14:25). In part, this flourishing of the two kingdoms was facilitated by the removal of the Aramean threat by Assyria under Adadnirari III (802 B.C.), following which Assyria herself went into a period of weakness.

26:1 *Uzziah.* See NIV text note (see also, e.g., 2Ki 15:6–7; 1Ch 3:12). It is likely that Uzziah was a throne name, while Azariah was his personal name.

26:3 *fifty-two years.* 792–740 B.C., including a co-regency with Amaziah from 792 to 767.

26:4 The Chronicler has constructed his account of Uzziah's reign to give it the same outline as that for Amaziah and Joash (see note on vv. 1–23). He has also once again bypassed the statement in the parallel account that the king did not remove the high places (2Ki 15:4), just as he did in the accounts of the other two kings (see note on 25:2).

26:5 *days of Zechariah.* The author again uses chronological notes to portray the cycles of blessing and judgment associated with the individual king's response to God's commands (see note on 12:2).

26:6–8 Uzziah's conquests were toward the southeast and the southwest; Israel's powerful Jeroboam II was in control to the north of Judah.

26:7 *Meunites.* See note on 20:1.

26:9 *Corner Gate . . . Valley Gate.* Found at the northeast and southwest portions of the walls. *fortified.* This construction along the wall of Jerusalem may reflect, in part, repair of the damage done by Jehoash during the reign of Amaziah (25:23).

26:10 *towers . . . cisterns.* Towers and cisterns have been found in several excavations (Qumran, Gibeah, Beersheba). A seal bearing Uzziah's name has been found in a cistern at Tell Beit Mirsim.

26:11 *Uzziah had a well-trained army.* Tiglath-Pileser III of Assyria states that he was opposed in his advance toward the west (743 B.C.) by a coalition headed by "Azriau of Yaudi," perhaps Azariah (Uzziah) of Judah.

command was an army of 307,500 men trained for war, a powerful force to support the king against his enemies. [14]Uzziah provided shields, spears, helmets, coats of armor, bows and slingstones for the entire army.[p] [15]In Jerusalem he made machines designed by skillful men for use on the towers and on the corner defenses to shoot arrows and hurl large stones. His fame spread far and wide, for he was greatly helped until he became powerful.

[16]But after Uzziah became powerful, his pride[q] led to his downfall.[r] He was unfaithful[s] to the LORD his God, and entered the temple of the LORD to burn incense[t] on the altar of incense. [17]Azariah[u] the priest with eighty other courageous priests of the LORD followed him in. [18]They confronted him and said, "It is not right for you, Uzziah, to burn incense to the LORD. That is for the priests,[v] the descendants[w] of Aaron,[x] who have been consecrated to burn incense.[y] Leave the sanctuary, for you have been unfaithful; and you will not be honored by the LORD God."

[19]Uzziah, who had a censer in his hand ready to burn incense, became angry. While he was raging at the priests in their presence before the incense altar in the LORD's temple, leprosy[1][z] broke out on his forehead. [20]When Azariah the chief priest and all the other priests looked at him, they saw that he had leprosy on his forehead, so they hurried him out. Indeed, he himself was eager to leave, because the LORD had afflicted him.

[21]King Uzziah had leprosy until the day he died. He lived in a separate house[m][a] —leprous, and excluded from the temple of the LORD. Jotham his son had charge of the palace and governed the people of the land.

[22]The other events of Uzziah's reign, from beginning to end, are recorded by the prophet Isaiah[b] son of Amoz. [23]Uzziah[c] rested with his fathers and was buried near them in a field for burial that belonged to the kings, for people said, "He had leprosy." And Jotham his son succeeded him as king.[d]

Jotham King of Judah

27:1–4,7–9pp — 2Ki 15:33–38

27 Jotham[e] was twenty-five years old when he became king, and he reigned in Jerusalem sixteen years. His mother's name was Jerusha daughter of Zadok. [2]He did what was right in the eyes of the LORD, just as his father Uzziah had done, but unlike him he did not enter the temple of the LORD. The people, however, continued their corrupt practices. [3]Jotham rebuilt the Upper Gate of the temple of the LORD and did extensive work on the wall at the hill of Ophel.[f] [4]He built towns in the Judean hills and forts and towers in the wooded areas.

[5]Jotham made war on the king of the Ammonites[g] and conquered them. That year the Ammonites paid him a hundred talents[n] of silver, ten thousand cors[o] of wheat and ten thousand cors of barley. The Ammonites brought him the same amount also in the second and third years.

[6]Jotham grew powerful[h] because he walked steadfastly before the LORD his God.

[7]The other events in Jotham's reign, including all his wars and the other things he did, are written in the book of the kings of Israel and Judah. [8]He was twenty-five years old when he became king, and he

Cross references

26:14 *p*Jer 46:4
26:16 *q*S 2Ki 14:10; *r*Dt 32:15; *s*S 1Ch 5:25; *t*2Ki 16:12
26:17 *u*S 1Ki 4:2
26:18 *v*Nu 16:39; *w*Nu 18:1-7; *x*S Ex 30:7; *y*S 1Ch 6:49
26:19 *z*S Nu 12:10
26:21 *a*S Ex 4:6; Lev 13:46; S 14:8; Nu 5:2; S 19:12
26:22 *b*2Ki 15:1; Isa 1:1; 6:1
26:23 *c*Isa 1:1; 6:1 *d*S 2Ki 14:21; Am 1:1
27:1 *e*S 2Ki 15:5, 32; S 1Ch 3:12
27:3 *f*2Ch 33:14; Ne 3:26
27:5 *g*S Ge 19:38
27:6 *h*2Ch 26:5

Footnotes

*1*19 The Hebrew word was used for various diseases affecting the skin—not necessarily leprosy; also in verses 20, 21 and 23.   *m*21 Or *in a house where he was relieved of responsibilities*   *n*5 That is, about 3 3/4 tons (about 3.4 metric tons)   *o*5 That is, probably about 62,000 bushels (about 2,200 kiloliters)

26:15 *machines... to shoot arrows and hurl large stones.* Since the catapult was not known in the military technology of the period, and since torsion-operated devices for shooting arrows did not appear for approximately another three centuries, the devices mentioned here may refer to defensive constructions to protect those shooting arrows and hurling stones from the tops of the walls.
26:16 *after Uzziah became powerful.* See note on v. 5.
26:19 *leprosy.* For disease as a punishment for sin see notes on 16:12; 21:12-15.
26:21 *Uzziah ... died.* See Isa 6:1 and note. *separate house.* See NIV text note; the same phrase in the Canaanite texts from Ugarit suggests a kind of quarantine or separation.
26:22 *recorded by ... Isaiah.* Not a reference to the canonical book but to some other work no longer in existence.
26:23 *buried... in a field... that belonged to the kings.* Cf. 2Ki 15:7. Apparently due to his leprosy, Uzziah was buried in a cemetery belonging to the kings, though not in the tombs of the kings.

27:1–9 See 2Ki 15:32–38 and notes.
27:1 *sixteen years.* 750–735 B.C., including a co-regency with Uzziah (750–740). His reign also overlapped that of his successor Ahaz from 735 to 732.
27:2 *did not enter the temple.* The Chronicler commends Jotham for not making the same error Uzziah did (26:16). *corrupt practices.* Appears to refer to the flourishing high places (2Ki 15:35).
27:3–6 Unique to the Chronicler and an elaboration of his thesis that fidelity to God's commands brings blessing: in construction, military victory and prosperity—all "because he walked steadfastly before the LORD" (v. 6). Judah's relationship with the Ammonites held particular interest for the Chronicler (see notes on 20:1–30; 24:26).
27:7 *all his wars.* See, e.g., 2Ki 15:37.

reigned in Jerusalem sixteen years. [9]Jotham rested with his fathers and was buried in the City of David. And Ahaz his son succeeded him as king.

Ahaz King of Judah

28:1–27pp — 2Ki 16:1–20

28 Ahaz[i] was twenty years old when he became king, and he reigned in Jerusalem sixteen years. Unlike David his father, he did not do what was right in the eyes of the LORD. [2]He walked in the ways of the kings of Israel and also made cast idols[j] for worshiping the Baals. [3]He burned sacrifices in the Valley of Ben Hinnom[k] and sacrificed his sons[l] in the fire, following the detestable[m] ways of the nations the LORD had driven out before the Israelites. [4]He offered sacrifices and burned incense at the high places, on the hilltops and under every spreading tree.

[5]Therefore the LORD his God handed him over to the king of Aram.[n] The Arameans defeated him and took many of his people as prisoners and brought them to Damascus.

He was also given into the hands of the king of Israel, who inflicted heavy casualties on him. [6]In one day Pekah[o] son of Remaliah killed a hundred and twenty thousand soldiers in Judah[p]—because Judah had forsaken the LORD, the God of their fathers. [7]Zicri, an Ephraimite warrior, killed Maaseiah the king's son, Azrikam the officer in charge of the palace, and Elkanah, second to the king. [8]The Israelites took captive from their kinsmen[q] two hundred thousand wives, sons and daughters. They also took a great deal of plunder, which they carried back to Samaria.[r]

[9]But a prophet of the LORD named Oded

was there, and he went out to meet the army when it returned to Samaria. He said to them, "Because the LORD, the God of your fathers, was angry[s] with Judah, he gave them into your hand. But you have slaughtered them in a rage that reaches to heaven.[t] [10]And now you intend to make the men and women of Judah and Jerusalem your slaves.[u] But aren't you also guilty of sins against the LORD your God? [11]Now listen to me! Send back your fellow countrymen you have taken as prisoners, for the LORD's fierce anger rests on you.[v]"

[12]Then some of the leaders in Ephraim—Azariah son of Jehohanan, Berekiah son of Meshillemoth, Jehizkiah son of Shallum, and Amasa son of Hadlai—confronted those who were arriving from the war. [13]"You must not bring those prisoners here," they said, "or we will be guilty before the LORD. Do you intend to add to our sin and guilt? For our guilt is already great, and his fierce anger rests on Israel."

[14]So the soldiers gave up the prisoners and plunder in the presence of the officials and all the assembly. [15]The men designated by name took the prisoners, and from the plunder they clothed all who were naked. They provided them with clothes and sandals, food and drink,[w] and healing balm. All those who were weak they put on donkeys. So they took them back to their fellow countrymen at Jericho, the City of Palms,[x] and returned to Samaria.[y]

[16]At that time King Ahaz sent to the king[p] of Assyria[z] for help. [17]The Edomites[a] had again come and attacked Judah

Cross references

28:1 [i]S 1Ch 3:13; Isa 1:1
28:2 [j]Ex 34:17
28:3 [k]Jos 15:8 [l]S Lev 18:21; S 2Ki 3:27; Eze 20:26 [m]S Dt 18:9; 2Ch 33:2
28:5 [n]Isa 7:1
28:6 [o]S 2Ki 15:25,27 [p]ver 8; Isa 9:21; 11:13
28:8 [q]Dt 28:25-41 [r]2Ch 29:9
28:9 [s]Isa 10:6; 47:6; Zec 1:15 [t]Ezr 9:6; Rev 18:5
28:10 [u]Lev 25:39-46
28:11 [v]2Ch 11:4
28:15 [w]2Ki 6:22; Pr 25:21-22 [x]S Dt 34:3; S Jdg 1:16 [y]Lk 10:25-37
28:16 [z]S 2Ki 16:7; Eze 23:12
28:17 [a]Ps 137:7; Isa 34:5; 63:1; Jer 25:21; Eze 16:57; 25:12; Am 1:11

[p]16 One Hebrew manuscript, Septuagint and Vulgate (see also 2 Kings 16:7); most Hebrew manuscripts *kings*

28:1–27 See 2Ki 16:1–20 and notes, though only the introduction and conclusion in the two accounts are strictly parallel. The reign of Ahaz is the only one for which the Chronicler does not mention a single redeeming feature. In his account the Chronicler appears to adopt explicit parallels from the speech of Abijah condemning the northern kingdom (ch. 13) in order to show that under Ahaz the southern kingdom had sunk to the same depths of apostasy. Judah's religious fidelity, of which Abijah had boasted, was completely overthrown under Ahaz.
28:1 *sixteen years.* 732–715 B.C., not including the co-regency with Jotham (735–732).
28:2 *made cast idols.* Cf. 13:8.
28:3 *Valley of Ben Hinnom.* Cf. 33:6. Josiah put an end to the pagan practices observed there (2Ki 23:10). *sacrificed his sons.* See Lev 20:1–5; Jer 7:31–32. 2Ki 16:3 has the singular "son." Some have regarded the plural as a deliberate inflation on the part of the Chronicler to heighten the wickedness of Ahaz. However, some manuscripts of the Septuagint (the Greek translation of the OT) also have a plural in 2Ki 16:3, suggesting that the Chronicler may have

faithfully copied the text before him.
28:5 Cf. 13:16–17. *God handed him over.* According to the Chronicler's view on immediate retribution, defeat in war is one of the results of disobedience (see note on 20:30). *also given into the hands of the king of Israel.* 2Ki 16:5–6 and Isa 7 make it clear that Rezin (king of Aram) and Pekah acted together against Judah. The Chronicler has chosen either to treat them separately or to report on two different episodes of the Aram-Israel coalition.
28:6 *Pekah.* Reigned over the northern kingdom 752–732 B.C. (see 2Ki 15:27–31). *had forsaken the LORD.* The same charge Abijah made against the northern kingdom (13:11).
28:9–15 The kindness of the northern captors to their captives from Judah, especially as recorded in vv. 14–15, may be the background for Jesus' parable of the Good Samaritan (Lk 10:25–37). Oded's attitude to the north is shown by his willingness to call them "fellow countrymen" (v. 11). In this case, too, the record of ch. 13 has been reversed: The northern tribes are more righteous than the south.
28:17–18 *Edomites . . . attacked Judah . . . Philistines had*

and carried away prisoners,[b] 18while the Philistines[c] had raided towns in the foothills and in the Negev of Judah. They captured and occupied Beth Shemesh, Aijalon[d] and Gederoth,[e] as well as Soco,[f] Timnah[g] and Gimzo, with their surrounding villages. 19The LORD had humbled Judah because of Ahaz king of Israel,[q] for he had promoted wickedness in Judah and had been most unfaithful[h] to the LORD. 20Tiglath-Pileser[r][i] king of Assyria[j] came to him, but he gave him trouble[k] instead of help.[l] 21Ahaz[m] took some of the things from the temple of the LORD and from the royal palace and from the princes and presented them to the king of Assyria, but that did not help him.[n]

22In his time of trouble King Ahaz became even more unfaithful[o] to the LORD. 23He offered sacrifices to the gods[p] of Damascus, who had defeated him; for he thought, "Since the gods of the kings of Aram have helped them, I will sacrifice to them so they will help me." But they were his downfall and the downfall of all Israel.[r]

24Ahaz gathered together the furnishings[s] from the temple of God[t] and took them away.[s] He shut the doors[u] of the LORD's temple and set up altars[v] at every street corner in Jerusalem. 25In every town in Judah he built high places to burn sacrifices to other gods and provoked the LORD, the God of his fathers, to anger.

26The other events of his reign and all his ways, from beginning to end, are written in the book of the kings of Judah and Israel. 27Ahaz rested[w] with his fathers and was buried[x] in the city of Jerusalem, but he was not placed in the tombs of the kings of Israel. And Hezekiah his son succeeded him as king.

Hezekiah Purifies the Temple

29:1–2pp — 2Ki 18:2–3

29 Hezekiah[y] was twenty-five years old when he became king, and he reigned in Jerusalem twenty-nine years. His mother's name was Abijah daughter of Zechariah. 2He did what was right in the eyes of the LORD, just as his father David[z] had done.

3In the first month of the first year of his reign, he opened the doors of the temple of the LORD and repaired[a] them. 4He brought in the priests and the Levites, assembled them in the square on the east side 5and

Cross references (center column)

28:17 [b]2Ch 29:9
28:18 [c]Isa 9:12; 11:14; Jer 25:20; Eze 16:27,57; 25:15
[d]S Jos 10:12
[e]Jos 15:41
[f]S 1Sa 17:1
[g]S Ge 38:12
28:19 [h]S 1Ch 5:25
28:20 [i]S 2Ki 15:29; S 1Ch 5:6
[j]Isa 7:17; 8:7; 10:5-6; 36:1
[k]Isa 10:20
[l]S 2Ki 16:7
28:21 [m]S 2Ch 16:2-9
[n]Jer 2:36
28:22 [o]Jer 5:3; 15:7; 17:23
28:23 [p]S 2Ch 25:14
[q]Isa 10:20; Jer 44:17-18
[r]1Ch 11:1; Jer 18:15
28:24 [s]2Ch 29:19
[t]S 2Ki 16:18
[u]Mal 1:10
[v]2Ch 30:14
28:27 [w]Isa 14:28-32
[x]S 2Ch 21:20
29:1 [y]S 1Ch 3:13
29:2 [z]2Ch 34:2
29:3 [a]2Ki 18:16

q 19 That is, Judah, as frequently in 2 Chronicles
r 20 Hebrew *Tilgath-Pilneser*, a variant of *Tiglath-Pileser*
s 24 Or *and cut them up*

---

raided. Foreign alliances (v. 16) led to further defeats for Ahaz (see note on 16:2–9).
28:19 *The LORD had humbled Judah because of Ahaz.* The same formula used to describe the defeat of the northern tribes in 13:18, though under Ahaz it is Judah that is subdued.
28:20 *Tiglath-Pileser.* King of Assyria 745–727 B.C. (see 1Ch 5:26 and note). *trouble instead of help.* Appears on the surface to contradict the statement in 2Ki 16:9 that Tiglath-Pileser III responded to Ahaz's request by attacking and capturing Damascus, exiling its population and killing Rezin. The Chronicler assumes the reader's familiarity with the other account and knows of the temporary respite for Judah gained by Assyrian intervention against Damascus and the northern kingdom of Israel. But he focuses on the long-range results, in which Judah herself was reduced to vassalage to Assyria.
28:22–23 The Chronicler presumes the reader's familiarity with Ahaz's trip to Damascus and his copying of the altar and practices there (2Ki 16:10–16).
28:24–25 Additional details on Ahaz's alterations are found in 2Ki 16:17–18. The Chronicler also adds details in his description of Hezekiah's reforming activities to correct some of the abuses under Ahaz: Not only had the doors been shut, but also the lamps were put out and offerings were not made at the sanctuary (29:7); the altar and utensils were desecrated, and the table for the consecrated bread was neglected (29:18–19). It is precisely these accoutrements of proper temple service about which Abijah had boasted when he proclaimed the faithfulness of Judah in contrast to that of the northern kingdom (13:11). Now these orthodox furnishings are lacking under Ahaz and make the southern kingdom just like the north (see note on vv. 1–27).
28:27 *not placed in the tombs of the kings.* The third king

whose wickedness resulted in the loss of this honor at death. The others were Jehoram (21:20) and Joash (24:25). Uzziah's sin and leprosy brought the same result, though it is not reported in exactly the same terms (26:23). Cf. also Manasseh (33:20).
29:1–32:33 The Chronicler devotes more attention to Hezekiah than to any other post-Solomonic king. Although the parallel text (2Ki 18–20) has about the same amount of material, only about a fourth of the total relates the same or similar material; only a few verses are strict literary parallels (29:1–2; 32:32–33). In Kings preeminence among the post-Solomonic kings is given to Josiah (2Ki 22–23; cf. 1Ki 13:2), and the record of Hezekiah is primarily devoted to his confrontation with Sennacherib of Assyria. By contrast, the Chronicler highlights almost exclusively Hezekiah's religious reform and his devotion to matters of ceremony and ritual. The parallel passage (2Ki 18:1–6) touches the religious reform only briefly. The numerous parallels in these chapters with the account of Solomon's reign suggest that the Chronicler viewed Hezekiah as a "second Solomon" in his celebration of the Passover (30:2,5,23,25–26), his cultic arrangements (29:7,18,35; 31:2–3), his wealth (32:27–29), the honor accorded him by the Gentiles (32:23) and the extent of his dominion (30:25).
29:1 *twenty-nine years.* 715–686 B.C. (but see note on Isa 36:1), including a 15-year extension of life granted by God (2Ki 20:6) but not mentioned by the Chronicler.
29:3–30:27 Not found in Kings.
29:3 *first year.* 715 B.C., another example of the Chronicler's practice of introducing chronological materials into his narrative (see note on 12:2). *opened the doors of the temple.* Necessary after the actions of Ahaz (28:24). *repaired them.* The repairs to the doors included new gold overlay (2Ki 18:16).

said: "Listen to me, Levites! Consecrate[b] yourselves now and consecrate the temple of the LORD, the God of your fathers. Remove all defilement from the sanctuary. [6]Our fathers[c] were unfaithful;[d] they did evil in the eyes of the LORD our God and forsook him. They turned their faces away from the LORD's dwelling place and turned their backs on him. [7]They also shut the doors of the portico and put out the lamps. They did not burn incense[e] or present any burnt offerings at the sanctuary to the God of Israel. [8]Therefore, the anger of the LORD has fallen on Judah and Jerusalem; he has made them an object of dread and horror[f] and scorn,[g] as you can see with your own eyes. [9]This is why our fathers have fallen by the sword and why our sons and daughters and our wives are in captivity.[h] [10]Now I intend to make a covenant[i] with the LORD, the God of Israel, so that his fierce anger[j] will turn away from us. [11]My sons, do not be negligent now, for the LORD has chosen you to stand before him and serve him,[k] to minister[l] before him and to burn incense."

[12]Then these Levites[m] set to work:
from the Kohathites,
   Mahath son of Amasai and Joel son of Azariah;
from the Merarites,
   Kish son of Abdi and Azariah son of Jehallelel;
from the Gershonites,
   Joah son of Zimmah and Eden[n] son of Joah;
[13]from the descendants of Elizaphan,[o]
   Shimri and Jeiel;
from the descendants of Asaph,[p]
   Zechariah and Mattaniah;
[14]from the descendants of Heman,
   Jehiel and Shimei;
from the descendants of Jeduthun,
   Shemaiah and Uzziel.

[15]When they had assembled their brothers and consecrated themselves, they went in to purify[q] the temple of the LORD, as the king had ordered, following the word of the LORD. [16]The priests went into the sanctuary of the LORD to purify it. They brought out to the courtyard of the LORD's temple everything unclean that they found in the temple of the LORD. The Levites took it and carried it out to the Kidron Valley.[r] [17]They began the consecration on the first day of the first month, and by the eighth day of the month they reached the portico of the LORD. For eight more days they consecrated the temple of the LORD itself, finishing on the sixteenth day of the first month.

[18]Then they went in to King Hezekiah and reported: "We have purified the entire temple of the LORD, the altar of burnt offering with all its utensils, and the table for setting out the consecrated bread, with all its articles. [19]We have prepared and consecrated all the articles[s] that King Ahaz removed in his unfaithfulness while he was king. They are now in front of the LORD's altar."

[20]Early the next morning King Hezekiah gathered the city officials together and went up to the temple of the LORD. [21]They brought seven bulls, seven rams, seven male lambs and seven male goats[t] as a sin offering[u] for the kingdom, for the sanctuary and for Judah. The king commanded the priests, the descendants of Aaron, to offer these on the altar of the LORD. [22]So they slaughtered the bulls, and the priests took the blood and sprinkled it on the altar; next they slaughtered the rams and sprinkled their blood on the altar; then they slaughtered the lambs and sprinkled their blood[v] on the altar. [23]The goats[w] for the sin offering were brought before the king and the assembly, and they laid their hands[x] on them. [24]The priests then slaughtered the goats and presented their blood on the altar for a sin offering to atone[y] for all Israel, because the king had ordered the burnt offering and the sin offering for all Israel.[z]

[25]He stationed the Levites in the temple of the LORD with cymbals, harps and lyres

Cross references (center column)

29:5
[b]S Lev 11:44;
Ne 13:9
29:6 [c]Ezr 9:7;
Ps 106:6-47;
Jer 2:27; 18:17;
Eze 23:35;
Da 9:5-6
[d]S 1Ch 5:25
29:7 [e]S Ex 30:7
29:8 [f]S Dt 28:25
[g]S Lev 26:32;
Jer 18:16; 19:8;
25:9,18
29:9
[h]2Ch 28:5-8,17
29:10
[i]S 2Ki 11:17;
S 2Ch 23:16
[j]S Nu 25:4;
2Ch 30:8;
Ezr 10:14
29:11 [k]S Nu 3:6;
8:6,14
[l]S 1Ch 15:2
29:12
[m]S Nu 3:17-20
[n]2Ch 31:15
29:13 [o]S Ex 6:22
[p]S 1Ch 6:39
29:15
[q]S 1Ch 23:28;
S Isa 1:25

29:16
[r]S 2Sa 15:23
29:19
[s]2Ch 28:24
29:21 [t]Ezr 6:17;
8:35
[u]S Lev 4:13-14
29:22
[v]S Lev 4:18;
Nu 18:17
29:23
[w]S Lev 16:5
[x]Lev 4:15
29:24
[y]S Ex 29:36;
Lev 4:26
[z]1Ch 11:1;
Ezr 8:35

29:5-11 Hezekiah's speech demonstrates again the Chronicler's convictions about the coherence of action and effect: The sins of the past brought difficulty and judgment, but renewed fidelity brings relief.
29:7 Hezekiah reinstitutes these temple arrangements—following the pattern of Solomon (2:4; 4:7).
29:8 *object of dread and horror and scorn.* Echoes the language of the prophets, especially Jeremiah (see Jer 19:8; 25:9,18; 29:18; 51:37). Reference is to the Assyrian devastation of the northern kingdom and much of Judah.
29:12 *Kohathites ... Merarites ... Gershonites.* The three clans of Levi (1Ch 6:1).
29:13-14 *Asaph ... Heman ... Jeduthun.* Founders of

the three families of Levitical musicians (1Ch 6:31-48; 25:1-31).
29:13 *Elizaphan.* A leader of the Kohathites (Nu 3:30), whose family had achieved status almost as a sub-clan (see 1Ch 15:8 and note on 1Ch 15:4-10).
29:16 *carried it out to the Kidron Valley.* Asa also burned pagan cult objects there (15:16; cf. 30:14).
29:18 These actions under Hezekiah mirror those of Solomon (2:4).
29:21 *sin offering.* See Lev 4:1-5:13.
29:22 *sprinkled their blood.* See Lev 17:6; Nu 18:17.
29:23 *laid their hands on them.* See Lev 4:13-15; 8:14-15; Nu 8:12.

in the way prescribed by David[a] and Gad[b] the king's seer and Nathan the prophet; this was commanded by the LORD through his prophets. [26]So the Levites stood ready with David's instruments,[c] and the priests with their trumpets.[d]

[27]Hezekiah gave the order to sacrifice the burnt offering on the altar. As the offering began, singing to the LORD began also, accompanied by trumpets and the instruments[e] of David king of Israel. [28]The whole assembly bowed in worship, while the singers sang and the trumpeters played. All this continued until the sacrifice of the burnt offering[f] was completed.

[29]When the offerings were finished, the king and everyone present with him knelt down and worshiped.[g] [30]King Hezekiah and his officials ordered the Levites to praise the LORD with the words of David and of Asaph the seer. So they sang praises with gladness and bowed their heads and worshiped.

[31]Then Hezekiah said, "You have now dedicated yourselves to the LORD. Come and bring sacrifices[h] and thank offerings to the temple of the LORD." So the assembly brought sacrifices and thank offerings, and all whose hearts were willing[i] brought burnt offerings.

[32]The number of burnt offerings[j] the assembly brought was seventy bulls, a hundred rams and two hundred male lambs—all of them for burnt offerings to the LORD. [33]The animals consecrated as sacrifices amounted to six hundred bulls and three thousand sheep and goats. [34]The priests, however, were too few to skin all the burnt offerings;[k] so their kinsmen the

Levites helped them until the task was finished and until other priests had been consecrated,[l] for the Levites had been more conscientious in consecrating themselves than the priests had been. [35]There were burnt offerings in abundance, together with the fat[m] of the fellowship offerings[t] [n] and the drink offerings[o] that accompanied the burnt offerings.

So the service of the temple of the LORD was reestablished. [36]Hezekiah and all the people rejoiced at what God had brought about for his people, because it was done so quickly.[p]

Hezekiah Celebrates the Passover

30 Hezekiah sent word to all Israel[q] and Judah and also wrote letters to Ephraim and Manasseh,[r] inviting them to come to the temple of the LORD in Jerusalem and celebrate the Passover[s] to the LORD, the God of Israel. [2]The king and his officials and the whole assembly in Jerusalem decided to celebrate[t] the Passover in the second month. [3]They had not been able to celebrate it at the regular time because not enough priests had consecrated[u] themselves and the people had not assembled in Jerusalem. [4]The plan seemed right both to the king and to the whole assembly. [5]They decided to send a proclamation throughout Israel, from Beersheba to Dan,[v] calling the people to come to Jerusalem and celebrate the Passover to the LORD, the God of Israel. It had not been celebrated in large numbers according to what was written.

[6]At the king's command, couriers went

Cross references

29:25 [a]S 1Ch 25:6; 28:19 [b]S 1Sa 22:5
29:26 [c]S 1Ch 15:16 [d]S 1Ch 15:24
29:27 [e]S 1Sa 16:16
29:28 [f]S 2Ch 2:4
29:29 [g]S 2Ch 20:18
29:31 [h]Heb 13:15-16
29:32 [i]S Ex 25:2; 35:22
29:32 [j]Lev 1:1-17
29:34 [k]Eze 44:11

29:35 [l]2Ch 30:3,15 [m]S Ge 4:4; S Ex 29:13 [n]Lev 7:11-21 [o]S Ge 35:14
29:36 [p]2Ch 35:8
30:1 [q]S 1Ch 9:1 [r]S Ge 41:52 [s]S Ex 12:11; S Nu 28:16
30:2 [t]Nu 9:10
30:3 [u]Nu 9:6-13; S 2Ch 29:34
30:5 [v]S Jdg 20:1

[t]35 Traditionally peace offerings

Study notes

29:25 David and Gad . . . and Nathan . . . prophets. The Chronicler considers David among the prophets (see notes on 1:7; 1Ch 28:19).

29:26 David's instruments. See 1Ch 23:5.

29:35 burnt offerings in abundance . . . fellowship offerings . . . drink offerings. Reminiscent of the dedication of the temple under Solomon (7:4–6). For the laws regarding the fellowship offerings see Lev 3; 7:11–21; for the drink offerings see Nu 15:1–12. service of the temple of the LORD was reestablished. Similar to the formula used in 8:16 with reference to Solomon's work.

30:1–27 Unique to the Chronicler; cf. the famous Passover under Josiah (35:1–19; 2Ki 23:21–23). Hezekiah allowed two deviations from the law (Ex 12; Dt 16:1–8) in this observance: (1) the date in the second month (v. 2) and (2) exemption from some ritual requirements (vv. 18–19).

30:1 all Israel and Judah. See Introduction to 1 Chronicles: Purpose and Themes. With the northern kingdom now ended as the result of the Assyrian invasion and deportation (which surprisingly is not mentioned), the Chronicler shows "all Israel" once again united around the Davidic king and the temple (see vv. 5,18–19,25).

30:2 second month. After the division of the kingdom, Jeroboam deferred the sacral calendar of the northern kingdom by one month (1Ki 12:32), possibly to further wean the subjects in the north away from devotion to Jerusalem. By delaying the celebration of Passover one month, Hezekiah not only allows time for the priests to consecrate themselves (v. 3) and for the people to gather (vv. 3,13), but also achieves unity between the kingdoms on the date of the Passover for the first time since the schism more than two centuries earlier. Delaying the date reflects Hezekiah's concern to involve "all Israel." For the first time since Solomon the entire nation observes Passover together, reflecting the Chronicler's view that Hezekiah is a "second Solomon." Passover was prescribed for the 14th day of the first month (Ex 12:2,6; Dt 16:1–8), but could not be celebrated at that time due to the defilement of the temple and the purification rites under way (29:3,17). For celebration of Passover by the restored community shortly after the dedication of the rebuilt temple see Ezr 6:16–22.

30:5 large numbers. Another comparison with the time of Solomon (see v. 26). At the time of its inception, Passover was primarily a family observance (Ex 12). It later became a national celebration at the temple (v. 8; see Dt 16:1–8).

throughout Israel and Judah with letters from the king and from his officials, which read:

"People of Israel, return to the LORD, the God of Abraham, Isaac and Israel, that he may return to you who are left, who have escaped from the hand of the kings of Assyria. [7]Do not be like your fathers[w] and brothers, who were unfaithful[x] to the LORD, the God of their fathers, so that he made them an object of horror,[y] as you see. [8]Do not be stiff-necked,[z] as your fathers were; submit to the LORD. Come to the sanctuary, which he has consecrated forever. Serve the LORD your God, so that his fierce anger[a] will turn away from you. [9]If you return[b] to the LORD, then your brothers and your children will be shown compassion[c] by their captors and will come back to this land, for the LORD your God is gracious and compassionate.[d] He will not turn his face from you if you return to him."

[10]The couriers went from town to town in Ephraim and Manasseh, as far as Zebulun, but the people scorned and ridiculed[e] them. [11]Nevertheless, some men of Asher, Manasseh and Zebulun humbled[f] themselves and went to Jerusalem.[g] [12]Also in Judah the hand of God was on the people to give them unity[h] of mind to carry out what the king and his officials had ordered, following the word of the LORD.

[13]A very large crowd of people assembled in Jerusalem to celebrate the Feast of Unleavened Bread[i] in the second month. [14]They removed the altars[j] in Jerusalem and cleared away the incense altars and threw them into the Kidron Valley.[k]

[15]They slaughtered the Passover lamb on the fourteenth day of the second month. The priests and the Levites were ashamed and consecrated[l] themselves and

brought burnt offerings to the temple of the LORD. [16]Then they took up their regular positions[m] as prescribed in the Law of Moses the man of God. The priests sprinkled the blood handed to them by the Levites. [17]Since many in the crowd had not consecrated themselves, the Levites had to kill[n] the Passover lambs for all those who were not ceremonially clean and could not consecrate their lambs to the LORD. [18]Although most of the many people who came from Ephraim, Manasseh, Issachar and Zebulun had not purified themselves,[o] yet they ate the Passover, contrary to what was written. But Hezekiah prayed for them, saying, "May the LORD, who is good, pardon everyone [19]who sets his heart on seeking God—the LORD, the God of his fathers—even if he is not clean according to the rules of the sanctuary." [20]And the LORD heard[p] Hezekiah and healed[q] the people.[r]

[21]The Israelites who were present in Jerusalem celebrated the Feast of Unleavened Bread[s] for seven days with great rejoicing, while the Levites and priests sang to the LORD every day, accompanied by the LORD's instruments of praise.[u]

[22]Hezekiah spoke encouragingly to all the Levites, who showed good understanding of the service of the LORD. For the seven days they ate their assigned portion and offered fellowship offerings[v] and praised the LORD, the God of their fathers.

[23]The whole assembly then agreed to celebrate[t] the festival seven more days; so for another seven days they celebrated joyfully. [24]Hezekiah king of Judah provided[u] a thousand bulls and seven thousand sheep and goats for the assembly, and the officials provided them with a thousand bulls and ten thousand sheep and goats. A great number of priests consecrated themselves.

Cross references (center column):

30:7 [w]Ps 78:8, 57; 106:6; Jer 11:10; Eze 20:18
[x]S 1Ch 5:25
[y]S Dt 28:25
30:8 [z]S Ex 32:9
[a]S Nu 25:4; S 2Ch 29:10
30:9 [b]Dt 30:2-5; Isa 1:16; 55:7; Jer 25:5; Eze 33:11
[c]S Ex 3:21; S 1Ki 8:50
[d]S Ex 22:27; S Dt 4:31; S 2Ch 6:39; Mic 7:18
30:10 [e]2Ch 36:16
30:11 [f]S 2Ch 6:37 [g]ver 25
30:12 [h]Jer 32:39; Eze 11:19
30:13 [i]S Nu 28:16
30:14 [j]2Ch 28:24 [k]S 2Sa 15:23
30:15 [l]S 2Ch 29:34
30:16 [m]2Ch 35:10
30:17 [n]2Ch 35:11; Ezr 6:20
30:18 [o]Ex 12:43-49; Nu 9:6-10
30:20 [p]S 2Ch 6:20 [q]S 2Ch 7:14; Mal 4:2 [r]Jas 5:16
30:21 [s]Ex 12:15, 17; 13:6
30:23 [t]2Ch 7:9
30:24 [u]1Ki 8:5; 2Ch 35:7; Ezr 6:17; 8:35

[u]21 Or priests praised the LORD every day with resounding instruments belonging to the LORD
[v]22 Traditionally peace offerings

30:8 Come to the sanctuary. Passover was one of three annual pilgrim feasts requiring attendance at the temple (see Nu 28:9–29:39).
30:9 shown compassion by their captors. In Solomon's prayer in 6:39 the Chronicler omitted the phrase found in the parallel account (1Ki 8:50) that their conquerors would "show them mercy." Here the phrase is found in the speech of Hezekiah, again portraying him as a kind of "second Solomon" (see Lev 26:40–42). will come back to this land. Those who repent will have hope of return, even those from the Assyrian captivity.
30:14 threw them into the Kidron Valley. See 29:16 and note.
30:15 The priests and the Levites . . . consecrated themselves. The reproach previously directed against the priests

(v. 3; 29:34) is here broadened to include also the Levites—an exhortation to the priests and Levites of the restored community to be faithful.
30:17 Levites had to kill the Passover lambs. See Ex 12:6; Dt 16:6. According to the law the heads of families were to slay the Passover sacrifice. The Levites perhaps acted for the recent arrivals from the northern kingdom who were not ceremonially clean. Cf. Jn 11:55.
30:18–19 Faith and obedience take precedence over ritual (see Mk 7:1–23; Jn 7:22–23; 9:14–16).
30:20 The response to Hezekiah's prayer recalls the prayer of Solomon (7:14).
30:23 another seven days. The festival was observed for two weeks, just as the observance of the dedication of Solomon's temple had been (7:8–9).

25The entire assembly of Judah rejoiced, along with the priests and Levites and all who had assembled from Israel[v], including the aliens who had come from Israel and those who lived in Judah. 26There was great joy in Jerusalem, for since the days of Solomon[w] son of David king of Israel there had been nothing like this in Jerusalem. 27The priests and the Levites stood to bless[x] the people, and God heard them, for their prayer reached heaven, his holy dwelling place.

31 When all this had ended, the Israelites who were there went out to the towns of Judah, smashed the sacred stones and cut down[y] the Asherah poles. They destroyed the high places and the altars throughout Judah and Benjamin and in Ephraim and Manasseh. After they had destroyed all of them, the Israelites returned to their own towns and to their own property.

Contributions for Worship

31:20–21pp — 2Ki 18:5–7

2Hezekiah[z] assigned the priests and Levites to divisions[a]—each of them according to their duties as priests or Levites—to offer burnt offerings and fellowship offerings,[w] to minister,[b] to give thanks and to sing praises[c] at the gates of the LORD's dwelling.[d] 3The king contributed[e] from his own possessions for the morning and evening burnt offerings and for the burnt offerings on the Sabbaths, New Moons and appointed feasts as written in the Law of the LORD.[f] 4He ordered the people living in Jerusalem to give the portion[g] due the priests and Levites so they could devote themselves to the Law of the LORD. 5As soon as the order went out, the Israelites generously gave the firstfruits[h] of their grain, new wine,[i] oil and honey and all

that the fields produced. They brought a great amount, a tithe of everything. 6The men of Israel and Judah who lived in the towns of Judah also brought a tithe[j] of their herds and flocks and a tithe of the holy things dedicated to the LORD their God, and they piled them in heaps.[k] 7They began doing this in the third month and finished in the seventh month.[l] 8When Hezekiah and his officials came and saw the heaps, they praised the LORD and blessed[m] his people Israel.

9Hezekiah asked the priests and Levites about the heaps; 10and Azariah the chief priest, from the family of Zadok,[n] answered, "Since the people began to bring their contributions to the temple of the LORD, we have had enough to eat and plenty to spare, because the LORD has blessed his people, and this great amount is left over."[o]

11Hezekiah gave orders to prepare storerooms in the temple of the LORD, and this was done. 12Then they faithfully brought in the contributions, tithes and dedicated gifts. Conaniah,[p] a Levite, was in charge of these things, and his brother Shimei was next in rank. 13Jehiel, Azaziah, Nahath, Asahel, Jerimoth, Jozabad,[q] Eliel, Ismakiah, Mahath and Benaiah were supervisors under Conaniah and Shimei his brother, by appointment of King Hezekiah and Azariah the official in charge of the temple of God.

14Kore son of Imnah the Levite, keeper of the East Gate, was in charge of the freewill offerings given to God, distributing the contributions made to the LORD and also the consecrated gifts. 15Eden,[r] Miniamin, Jeshua, Shemaiah, Amariah and Shecaniah assisted him faithfully in the towns[s] of the priests, distributing to their fellow priests

Cross references

30:25 [v]ver 11
30:26
30:27 [w]S 2Ch 7:8
[x]S Ex 39:43
31:1 [y]S 2Ki 18:4; 2Ch 32:12; Isa 36:7
31:2 [z]S 2Ch 29:9 [a]S 1Ch 24:1 [b]S 1Ch 15:2 [c]Ps 7:17; 9:2; 47:6; 71:22 [d]S 1Ch 23:28-32
31:3 [e]S 1Ch 29:3; 2Ch 35:7; Eze 45:17 [f]Nu 28:1-29:40
31:4 [g]S Nu 18:8; S Dt 18:8; Ne 13:10
31:5 [h]S Nu 18:12,24; Ne 13:12; Eze 44:30 [i]Dt 12:17
31:6 [j]S Lev 27:30; Ne 13:10-12 [k]S Ru 3:7
31:7 [l]Ex 23:16
31:8
31:10 [m]Ps 144:13-15
31:12 [n]S 2Sa 8:17 [o]S Ex 36:5; Eze 44:30; Mal 3:10-12 [p]2Ch 35:9
31:13 [q]2Ch 35:9
31:15 [r]2Ch 29:12 [s]Jos 21:9-19

w2 Traditionally *peace offerings*

30:26 *since the days of Solomon.* An explicit indication of the Chronicler's modeling of the reign of Hezekiah after that of Solomon (see note on 29:1–32:33).

30:27 *prayer reached heaven, his holy dwelling place.* Another echo of Solomon's dedication prayer (6:21,30,33, 39).

31:1–21 Apart from the first verse, which parallels 2Ki 18:4, the material of this chapter is unique to the Chronicler, whose interest in the Levites and the temple predominates. Hezekiah's efforts to ensure the material support of the Levites (v. 4) probably had relevance to the postexilic audience for whom the Chronicler wrote.

31:1 *the Israelites . . . the Israelites.* Lit. "all Israel . . . all the Israelites." The Chronicler's interest in "all Israel" as united under Hezekiah is again apparent. *sacred stones.* See note on 1Ki 14:23. *Asherah poles.* See NIV text note on 14:3.

31:2 Echoes 8:14. The Chronicler continues to model Hezekiah as a "second Solomon" (see notes on 29:7,18).
31:3 *king contributed.* The king's giving from his own wealth prompted a generous response from the people, as it had also under David (1Ch 29:3–9).
31:5–6 See Dt 12:5–19; 14:22–27. The grain, new wine and oil had to be brought to the temple (Dt 12:17). Those coming from a distance, however, could bring the value of their offerings and purchase them on arrival (Dt 14:24). Only those who actually lived in Judah brought the tithe of their herds and flocks, a difficult procedure for those who lived farther away. For the restored community's commitment to bring their firstfruits, tithes and offerings see Ne 10:35–39. For their failure to do so see Ne 13:10–13; Mal 3:8–10.
31:7 *third month.* May-June, the time of the Feast of Pentecost and the grain harvest. *seventh month.* September-October, the time of the Feast of Tabernacles and the fruit and vine harvest (see Ex 23:16).

according to their divisions, old and young alike.

16In addition, they distributed to the males three years old or more whose names were in the genealogical records[t]—all who would enter the temple of the LORD to perform the daily duties of their various tasks, according to their responsibilities and their divisions. 17And they distributed to the priests enrolled by their families in the genealogical records and likewise to the Levites twenty years old or more, according to their responsibilities and their divisions. 18They included all the little ones, the wives, and the sons and daughters of the whole community listed in these genealogical records. For they were faithful in consecrating themselves.

19As for the priests, the descendants of Aaron, who lived on the farm lands around their towns or in any other towns,[u] men were designated by name to distribute portions to every male among them and to all who were recorded in the genealogies of the Levites.

20This is what Hezekiah did throughout Judah, doing what was good and right and faithful[v] before the LORD his God. 21In everything that he undertook in the service of God's temple and in obedience to the law and the commands, he sought his God and worked wholeheartedly. And so he prospered.[w]

Sennacherib Threatens Jerusalem

32:9–19pp — 2Ki 18:17–35; Isa 36:2–20
32:20–21pp — 2Ki 19:35–37; Isa 37:36–38

32 After all that Hezekiah had so faithfully done, Sennacherib[x] king of Assyria came and invaded Judah. He laid siege to the fortified cities, thinking to conquer them for himself. 2When Hezekiah saw that Sennacherib had come and that he intended to make war on Jerusalem,[y]

3he consulted with his officials and military staff about blocking off the water from the springs outside the city, and they helped him. 4A large force of men assembled, and they blocked all the springs[z] and the stream that flowed through the land. "Why should the kings[x] of Assyria come and find plenty of water?" they said. 5Then he worked hard repairing all the broken sections of the wall[a] and building towers on it. He built another wall outside that one and reinforced the supporting terraces[y][b] of the City of David. He also made large numbers of weapons[c] and shields.

6He appointed military officers over the people and assembled them before him in the square at the city gate and encouraged them with these words: 7"Be strong and courageous.[d] Do not be afraid or discouraged[e] because of the king of Assyria and the vast army with him, for there is a greater power with us than with him.[f] 8With him is only the arm of flesh,[g] but with us[h] is the LORD our God to help us and to fight our battles."[i] And the people gained confidence from what Hezekiah the king of Judah said.

9Later, when Sennacherib king of Assyria and all his forces were laying siege to Lachish,[j] he sent his officers to Jerusalem with this message for Hezekiah king of Judah and for all the people of Judah who were there:

10"This is what Sennacherib king of Assyria says: On what are you basing your confidence,[k] that you remain in Jerusalem under siege? 11When Hezekiah says, 'The LORD our God will save us from the hand of the king of Assyria,' he is misleading[l] you, to let you die of hunger and thirst. 12Did not Hezekiah himself remove this god's high places and altars, saying to Judah

Cross references (center column):
31:16 [t]1Ch 23:3
31:19
[u]S Nu 35:2-5
31:20
[v]S 2Ki 20:3
31:21 [w]S Dt 29:9
32:1 [x]Isa 36:1; 37:9,17,37
32:2 [y]Isa 22:7; Jer 1:15

32:4 [z]S 2Ki 18:17; Isa 22:9,11; Na 3:14
32:5 [a]Isa 22:10; [b]1Ch 11:8; [c]Isa 22:8
32:7 [d]S Dt 31:6; [e]2Ch 20:15; [f]S Nu 14:9; 2Ki 6:16
32:8 [g]Job 40:9; Isa 52:10; Jer 17:5; 32:21; [h]S Dt 3:22; S 1Sa 17:45; [i]S 1Ch 5:22; Ps 20:7; Isa 28:6
32:9 [j]S Jos 10:3, 31
32:10 [k]Eze 29:16
32:11 [l]Isa 37:10

[x]4 Hebrew; Septuagint and Syriac *king*   [y]5 Or *the Millo*

31:16 *three years.* Although no ancient versions or manuscripts disagree with this figure, it may represent a copyist's mistake for "30 years," the age at which duties were assigned in the temple (1Ch 23:3).
31:20–21 Another brief indication of the Chronicler's emphasis on immediate retribution: Not only does disobedience bring immediate chastening, but obedience and seeking God bring prosperity.
32:1–23 The record of Sennacherib's invasion is much more detailed in 2 Kings and Isaiah (see note on 29:1–32:33).
32:1 The Chronicler omits the date of the invasion (701 B.C., Hezekiah's 14th year; see 2Ki 18:13; Isa 36:1).
32:2–8 Unique to the Chronicler, but normal preparations for invasion.
32:3–4 See v. 30.

32:9 The Chronicler bypasses 2Ki 18:14–16, which records Hezekiah's suit for peace with its accompanying bribe stripped from the temple treasures. These acts were apparently out of accord with the Chronicler's portrait of Hezekiah. He also omits 2Ki 18:17b–18.
32:10 The Chronicler omits 2Ki 18:20–21 (and Isa 36:5–6), containing a portion of the Assyrian commander's speech ridiculing Hezekiah and the citizens of Jerusalem for trusting in Egypt and Pharaoh. This, too, may be theologically motivated, in light of the Chronicler's attitude toward foreign alliances (see note on 16:2–9). The same concern with foreign alliances is also likely the reason for the omission of the material in 2Ki 18:23–27 (and Isa 36:8–12), where mention is again made of the hope of Egyptian intervention (see 2Ki 19:9 for the incursion of Tirhakah).

and Jerusalem, 'You must worship before one altar *m* and burn sacrifices on it'?

13"Do you not know what I and my fathers have done to all the peoples of the other lands? Were the gods of those nations ever able to deliver their land from my hand? *n* 14Who of all the gods of these nations that my fathers destroyed has been able to save his people from me? How then can your god deliver you from my hand? 15Now do not let Hezekiah deceive *o* you and mislead you like this. Do not believe him, for no god of any nation or kingdom has been able to deliver *p* his people from my hand or the hand of my fathers. *q* How much less will your god deliver you from my hand!"

16Sennacherib's officers spoke further against the LORD God and against his servant Hezekiah. 17The king also wrote letters *r* insulting *s* the LORD, the God of Israel, and saying this against him: "Just as the gods *t* of the peoples of the other lands did not rescue their people from my hand, so the god of Hezekiah will not rescue his people from my hand." 18Then they called out in Hebrew to the people of Jerusalem who were on the wall, to terrify them and make them afraid in order to capture the city. 19They spoke about the God of Jerusalem as they did about the gods of the other peoples of the world—the work of men's hands. *u*

20King Hezekiah and the prophet Isaiah son of Amoz cried out in prayer *v* to heaven about this. 21And the LORD sent an angel, *w* who annihilated all the fighting men and the leaders and officers in the camp of the Assyrian king. So he withdrew to his own land in disgrace. And when he went into the temple of his god, some of his sons cut him down with the sword. *x* 22So the LORD saved Hezekiah and the

people of Jerusalem from the hand of Sennacherib king of Assyria and from the hand of all others. He took care of them *z* on every side. 23Many brought offerings to Jerusalem for the LORD and valuable gifts *y* for Hezekiah king of Judah. From then on he was highly regarded by all the nations.

Hezekiah's Pride, Success and Death
32:24-33pp — 2Ki 20:1-21; Isa 37:21-38; 38:1-8

24In those days Hezekiah became ill and was at the point of death. He prayed to the LORD, who answered him and gave him a miraculous sign. *z* 25But Hezekiah's heart was proud *a* and he did not respond to the kindness shown him; therefore the LORD's wrath *b* was on him and on Judah and Jerusalem. 26Then Hezekiah repented *c* of the pride of his heart, as did the people of Jerusalem; therefore the LORD's wrath did not come upon them during the days of Hezekiah. *d*

27Hezekiah had very great riches and honor, *e* and he made treasuries for his silver and gold and for his precious stones, spices, shields and all kinds of valuables. 28He also made buildings to store the harvest of grain, new wine and oil; and he made stalls for various kinds of cattle, and pens for the flocks. 29He built villages and acquired great numbers of flocks and herds, for God had given him very great riches. *f*

30It was Hezekiah who blocked *g* the upper outlet of the Gihon *h* spring and channeled *i* the water down to the west side of the City of David. He succeeded in everything he undertook. 31But when envoys were sent by the rulers of Babylon *j* to ask him about the miraculous sign *k* that had occurred in the land, God left him to test *l* him and to know everything that was in his heart.

32The other events of Hezekiah's reign

32:12
m 2Ch 31:1
32:13 *n* ver 15
32:15 *o* Isa 37:10
p Da 3:15 *q* Ex 5:2
32:17 *r* Isa 37:14
s Ps 74:22;
Isa 37:4,17
t S 2Ki 19:12
32:19 *u* Ps 115:4,
4-8; Isa 2:8;
17:8; 37:19;
Jer 1:16
32:20 *v* Isa 1:15;
37:15
32:21
w S Ge 19:13
x S 2Ki 19:7;
Isa 37:7,38;
Jer 41:2

32:23
y S 1Sa 10:27;
S 2Ch 9:24;
Ps 68:18,29;
76:11; Isa 16:1;
18:7; 45:14;
Zep 3:10;
Zec 14:16-17
32:24 *z* ver 31
32:25
a S 2Ki 14:10
b S 2Ch 19:2
32:26
c Jer 26:18-19
d 2Ch 34:27,28;
Isa 39:8
32:27
e S 1Ch 29:12;
S 2Ch 9:24
32:29 *f* Isa 39:2
32:30
g S 2Ki 18:17
h S 1Ki 1:33
i S 2Sa 5:8
32:31 *j* Isa 13:1;
39:1 *k* S ver 24;
Isa 38:7
l S Ge 22:1;
Dt 8:16

*z*22 Hebrew; Septuagint and Vulgate *He gave them rest*

32:16 *spoke further.* The Chronicler appears to assume his reader's familiarity with the longer account of the Assyrian taunts found in Kings and Isaiah.
32:18 *called out in Hebrew.* Assumes knowledge of the fuller story (2Ki 18:26-28; Isa 36:11-13).
32:20 This brief reference to the prayers of Hezekiah and Isaiah abridges the much longer narrative in 2Ki 19:1-34 (and Isa 37:1-35).
32:21 See 2Ki 19:35-37; Isa 37:36-38. The Chronicler and the parallel accounts telescope events somewhat: Sennacherib's invasion of Judah was in 701 B.C., while his death at the hand of his sons was in 681.
32:23 *highly regarded by all the nations.* Another effort to compare Hezekiah with Solomon (see 9:23-24).
32:24 The Chronicler again abridges the narrative in 2Ki 20:1-11 (and Isa 38:1-8), assuming the reader's familiarity

with the role of Isaiah and the miraculous sign of the shadow reversing ten steps.
32:25-30 Not found in the parallel texts.
32:25-26 *proud . . . pride.* The Chronicler does not specify the nature of Hezekiah's pride (however, see v. 31; 2Ki 20:12-13; Isa 39:1-2). Even for a "second Solomon" like Hezekiah, disobedience brings anger from the Lord.
32:27-29 The Chronicler likens Hezekiah to Solomon also by recounting his wealth (9:13-14).
32:30 See vv. 2-4; 2Ki 20:20.
32:31 See v. 25. The Chronicler assumes the reader's knowledge of the fuller account in 2Ki 20:12-19 (and Isa 39:1-8). The envoys from Babylon were apparently interested in joint efforts against the Assyrians, hoping to open two fronts against them simultaneously.

and his acts of devotion are written in the vision of the prophet Isaiah son of Amoz in the book of the kings of Judah and Israel. [33]Hezekiah rested with his fathers and was buried on the hill where the tombs of David's descendants are. All Judah and the people of Jerusalem honored him when he died. And Manasseh his son succeeded him as king.

Manasseh King of Judah

33:1–10pp — 2Ki 21:1–10
33:18–20pp — 2Ki 21:17–18

33 Manasseh[m] was twelve years old when he became king, and he reigned in Jerusalem fifty-five years. [2]He did evil in the eyes of the LORD,[n] following the detestable[o] practices of the nations the LORD had driven out before the Israelites. [3]He rebuilt the high places his father Hezekiah had demolished; he also erected altars to the Baals and made Asherah poles.[p] He bowed down[q] to all the starry hosts and worshiped them. [4]He built altars in the temple of the LORD, of which the LORD had said, "My Name[r] will remain in Jerusalem forever." [5]In both courts of the temple of the LORD,[s] he built altars to all the starry hosts. [6]He sacrificed his sons[t] in[a] the fire in the Valley of Ben Hinnom, practiced sorcery, divination and witchcraft, and consulted mediums[u] and spiritists.[v] He did much evil in the eyes of the LORD, provoking him to anger.

[7]He took the carved image he had made and put it in God's temple,[w] of which God had said to David and to his son Solomon,

33:1
[m]S 1Ch 3:13
33:2 [n]Jer 15:4
33:3 [o]S Dt 18:9
33:3
[p]Dt 16:21-22;
S 2Ch 24:18
[q]Dt 17:3
33:4 [r]2Ch 7:16
33:5 [s]S 2Ch 4:9
33:6
[t]S Lev 18:21;
S Dt 18:10
[u]S Ex 22:18;
S Lev 19:31
[v]1Sa 28:13
33:7
[w]S 2Ch 7:16

33:8 [x]S 2Sa 7:10
33:9 [y]Jer 15:4;
Eze 5:7
33:11
[z]S Dt 28:36
[a]S 2Ki 19:28;
Isa 37:29;
Eze 29:4; 38:4;
Am 4:2 [b]Ps 149:8
33:12
[c]S 2Ch 6:37
33:14
[d]S 1Ki 1:33
[e]Ne 3:3; 12:39;
Zep 1:10
[f]2Ch 27:3;
Ne 3:26

"In this temple and in Jerusalem, which I have chosen out of all the tribes of Israel, I will put my Name forever. [8]I will not again make the feet of the Israelites leave the land[x] I assigned to your forefathers, if only they will be careful to do everything I commanded them concerning all the laws, decrees and ordinances given through Moses." [9]But Manasseh led Judah and the people of Jerusalem astray, so that they did more evil than the nations the LORD had destroyed before the Israelites.[y]

[10]The LORD spoke to Manasseh and his people, but they paid no attention. [11]So the LORD brought against them the army commanders of the king of Assyria, who took Manasseh prisoner,[z] put a hook[a] in his nose, bound him with bronze shackles[b] and took him to Babylon. [12]In his distress he sought the favor of the LORD his God and humbled[c] himself greatly before the God of his fathers. [13]And when he prayed to him, the LORD was moved by his entreaty and listened to his plea; so he brought him back to Jerusalem and to his kingdom. Then Manasseh knew that the LORD is God.

[14]Afterward he rebuilt the outer wall of the City of David, west of the Gihon[d] spring in the valley, as far as the entrance of the Fish Gate[e] and encircling the hill of Ophel;[f] he also made it much higher. He stationed military commanders in all the fortified cities in Judah.

[15]He got rid of the foreign gods and re-

[a]6 Or He made his sons pass through

33:1–20 See 2Ki 21:1–18 and notes. Manasseh had the longest reign of any of the kings of Judah, a total of 55 years (v. 1). The emphasis in the two accounts differs: While both histories report at length the evil done in Manasseh's reign, only the Chronicler mentions his journey to Babylon and his repentance and restoration to rule. For the writer of Kings, the picture is only a bad one in which Manasseh could be considered almost single-handedly the cause of the exile (2Ki 21:10–15; 23:26). Some scholars regard the record of Manasseh's repentance in Chronicles as motivated by the author's emphasis on immediate retribution: Length of reign is viewed as a blessing for obedience, so that the Chronicler deliberately records some good in Manasseh as a ground for his long reign. However, it must be noted that length of reign is not elsewhere used by the Chronicler as an indication of divine blessing. The usual indicators for such blessing in his account are peace and prosperity, building projects, success in warfare and large families.
33:1 fifty-five years. 697–642 B.C.
33:3 Asherah poles. See NIV text note on 14:3.
33:6 sacrificed his sons. See 28:3–4.
33:10 See note on vv. 1–20. The Chronicler abridges what the Lord said to Manasseh and the people through the prophets; the fuller record is found in 2Ki 21:10–15.
33:11–17 Unique to the Chronicler, showing his stress on immediate retribution: Manasseh's evil brings invasion and

defeat, while his repentance brings restoration to rule.
33:11 took him to Babylon. In extant non-Biblical records there is no reference as yet to Manasseh being taken to Babylon by an Assyrian king. Esarhaddon (681–669 B.C.) lists him among 22 kings required to forward materials for his building projects, and Ashurbanipal (669–627) names him as one of a number of vassals supporting his campaign against Egypt. The fact that an Assyrian king would have him taken to Babylon suggests that this incident may have taken place during the rebellion of Shamash-Shum-Ukin against his brother and overlord Ashurbanipal. This rebellion lasted from 652 to 648, and Manasseh may have joined or at least have been suspected of assisting in the Babylonian defection from Assyria. Manasseh may have been found innocent, or he may have been pardoned on the basis of a renewed pledge of loyalty. Egypt had also bolted from the Assyrian yoke under the new 26th dynasty, and the return of Manasseh to rule may reflect the Assyrian need of a vassal near the border of Egypt.
33:12 The language is reminiscent of Solomon's prayer (7:14).
33:14 rebuilt the outer wall. For the Chronicler such building programs are a sign of divine blessing (8:1–6; 11:5–12; 14:6–7; 26:9–10,14–15; 32:1–5,27–30; 1Ch 11:7–9; 15:1).
33:15–16 Whatever the precise nature of Manasseh's re-

moved[g] the image from the temple of the LORD, as well as all the altars he had built on the temple hill and in Jerusalem; and he threw them out of the city. [16]Then he restored the altar of the LORD and sacrificed fellowship offerings[b] and thank offerings[h] on it, and told Judah to serve the LORD, the God of Israel. [17]The people, however, continued to sacrifice at the high places, but only to the LORD their God.

[18]The other events of Manasseh's reign, including his prayer to his God and the words the seers spoke to him in the name of the LORD, the God of Israel, are written in the annals of the kings of Israel.[c] [19]His prayer and how God was moved by his entreaty, as well as all his sins and unfaithfulness, and the sites where he built high places and set up Asherah poles and idols before he humbled[i] himself—all are written in the records of the seers.[d][j] [20]Manasseh rested with his fathers and was buried[k] in his palace. And Amon his son succeeded him as king.

Amon King of Judah

33:21–25pp — 2Ki 21:19–24

[21]Amon[l] was twenty-two years old when he became king, and he reigned in Jerusalem two years. [22]He did evil in the eyes of the LORD, as his father Manasseh had done. Amon worshiped and offered sacrifices to all the idols Manasseh had made. [23]But unlike his father Manasseh, he

did not humble[m] himself before the LORD; Amon increased his guilt.

[24]Amon's officials conspired against him and assassinated him in his palace. [25]Then the people[n] of the land killed all who had plotted against King Amon, and they made Josiah his son king in his place.

Josiah's Reforms

34:1–2pp — 2Ki 22:1–2
34:3–7Ref — 2Ki 23:4–20
34:8–13pp — 2Ki 22:3–7

34 Josiah[o] was eight years old when he became king,[p] and he reigned in Jerusalem thirty-one years. [2]He did what was right in the eyes of the LORD and walked in the ways of his father David,[q] not turning aside to the right or to the left.

[3]In the eighth year of his reign, while he was still young, he began to seek the God[r] of his father David. In his twelfth year he began to purge Judah and Jerusalem of high places, Asherah poles, carved idols and cast images. [4]Under his direction the altars of the Baals were torn down; he cut to pieces the incense altars that were above them, and smashed the Asherah poles,[s] the idols and the images. These he broke to pieces and scattered over the graves of those who had sacrificed to them.[t] [5]He burned[u] the bones of the

Cross references (center column)

33:15 [g]2Ki 23:12
33:16 [h]Lev 7:11-18
33:19 [i]S 2Ch 6:37 [j]2Ki 21:17
33:20 [k]2Ki 21:18; S 2Ch 21:20
33:21 [l]S 1Ch 3:14
33:23 [m]S Ex 10:3; 2Ch 7:14; Ps 18:27; 147:6; Pr 3:34
33:25 [n]S 2Ch 22:1
34:1 [o]S 1Ch 3:14 [p]Zep 1:1
34:2 [q]2Ch 29:2
34:3
34:4 [r]S 1Ch 16:11 [s]S Ex 34:13 [t]Ex 32:20; S Lev 26:30; 2Ki 23:11; Mic 1:5
34:5 [u]S 1Ki 13:2

b*16* Traditionally *peace offerings*   **c***18* That is, Judah, as frequently in 2 Chron.   **d***19* One Hebrew manuscript and Septuagint; most Hebrew manuscripts *of Hozai*

---

forms, Josiah would later still need to remove "the altars Manasseh had built in the two courts of the temple" (2Ki 23:12).

33:19 *Asherah poles.* See NIV text note on 14:3.

33:20 *buried in his palace.* Cf. 2Ki 21:18. His burial in the palace garden makes Manasseh the fifth king the Chronicler names who was not buried in the tombs of the kings (see note on 28:27).

33:21–25 See 2Ki 21:19–26. The Chronicler's account of the reign of Amon (642–640 B.C.) is quite similar to that in Kings, apart from (1) the additional note that Amon was not repentant like his father Manasseh, a note based on a passage unique to the Chronicler (vv. 12–13), and (2) the absence of the death formula.

34:1–36:1 See 2Ki 22:1–23:30 and notes. Both accounts of Josiah's reign are about the same length and treat the same subjects, but with considerable variation in emphasis. Both deal with three different aspects of Josiah's reform: (1) the removal of foreign cults, (2) the finding of the Book of the Law and the covenant renewal that followed and (3) the celebration of Passover. On the second item the two histories are quite similar. On the first item the writer of Kings goes to great lengths (2Ki 23:4–20), while the Chronicler summarizes it only briefly (34:3–7,33). The account of the Passover is greatly expanded in Chronicles (35:1–19), while only alluded to in 2 Kings (23:21–23). Not only are these items treated at different lengths, but the order is also changed. In Kings the finding of the Book of the Law in the temple in Josiah's 18th year is the first incident mentioned. The writer

appears to have organized his material geographically, i.e., beginning with the temple and spreading through the city, then into the rest of the nation. The Chronicler, on the other hand, has arranged the incidents in order of their occurrence and has characteristically introduced a number of chronological notes into the text: 34:3 (two notes without parallel in Kings); 34:8 (see 2Ki 22:3); 35:19 (see 2Ki 23:23; see also note on 2Ch 12:2). Chronicles makes it clear that the reform began in Josiah's 12th year (34:3), six years before the discovery of the Book of the Law.

34:1–2 See 2Ki 22:1–2.

34:1 *thirty-one years.* 640–609 B.C.

34:3–7 The writer of Kings covers this aspect of Josiah's reform in much greater detail (2Ki 23:4–20). He also delays his account of the removal of pagan cults until after the discovery of the Book of the Law, while the Chronicler places it before.

34:3 Some scholars have sought to tie the events of Josiah's 8th (v. 3), 12th (v. 3) and 18th (v. 8) years to stages in the progressive decline and fall of the Assyrian empire, which had dominated the area for about two centuries. The demise of Assyrian control in Aram and Palestine undoubtedly facilitated and encouraged Josiah's reassertion of Davidic authority over former Assyrian provinces (vv. 6–7). However, one must not undercut religious motives in Josiah's reforms. Otherwise, the reform is reduced to merely a religious expression of an essentially political rebellion. *Asherah poles.* See NIV text note on 14:3.

priests on their altars, and so he purged Judah and Jerusalem. [6]In the towns of Manasseh, Ephraim and Simeon, as far as Naphtali, and in the ruins around them, [7]he tore down the altars and the Asherah poles and crushed the idols to powder[v] and cut to pieces all the incense altars throughout Israel. Then he went back to Jerusalem.

[8]In the eighteenth year of Josiah's reign, to purify the land and the temple, he sent Shaphan son of Azaliah and Maaseiah the ruler of the city, with Joah son of Joahaz, the recorder, to repair the temple of the LORD his God.

[9]They went to Hilkiah[w] the high priest and gave him the money that had been brought into the temple of God, which the Levites who were the doorkeepers had collected from the people of Manasseh, Ephraim and the entire remnant of Israel and from all the people of Judah and Benjamin and the inhabitants of Jerusalem. [10]Then they entrusted it to the men appointed to supervise the work on the LORD's temple. These men paid the workers who repaired and restored the temple. [11]They also gave money[x] to the carpenters and builders to purchase dressed stone, and timber for joists and beams for the buildings that the kings of Judah had allowed to fall into ruin.[y]

[12]The men did the work faithfully.[z] Over them to direct them were Jahath and Obadiah, Levites descended from Merari, and Zechariah and Meshullam, descended from Kohath. The Levites—all who were skilled in playing musical instruments—[a] [13]had charge of the laborers[b] and supervised all the workers from job to job. Some of the Levites were secretaries, scribes and doorkeepers.

The Book of the Law Found

34:14–28pp — 2Ki 22:8–20
34:29–32pp — 2Ki 23:1–3

[14]While they were bringing out the money that had been taken into the temple of the LORD, Hilkiah the priest found the Book of the Law of the LORD that had been given through Moses. [15]Hilkiah said to Shaphan the secretary, "I have found the Book of the Law[c] in the temple of the LORD." He gave it to Shaphan.

[16]Then Shaphan took the book to the king and reported to him: "Your officials are doing everything that has been committed to them. [17]They have paid out the money that was in the temple of the LORD and have entrusted it to the supervisors and workers." [18]Then Shaphan the secretary informed the king, "Hilkiah the priest has given me a book." And Shaphan read from it in the presence of the king.

[19]When the king heard the words of the Law,[d] he tore[e] his robes. [20]He gave these orders to Hilkiah, Ahikam son of Shaphan[f], Abdon son of Micah,[e] Shaphan the secretary and Asaiah the king's attendant: [21]"Go and inquire of the LORD for me and for the remnant in Israel and Judah about what is written in this book that has been found. Great is the LORD's anger that is poured out[g] on us because our fathers have not kept the word of the LORD; they have not acted in accordance with all that is written in this book."

[22]Hilkiah and those the king had sent with him[f] went to speak to the prophetess[h] Huldah, who was the wife of Shallum son of Tokhath,[g] the son of Hasrah,[h] keeper of the wardrobe. She lived in Jerusalem, in the Second District.

[23]She said to them, "This is what the LORD, the God of Israel, says: Tell the man who sent you to me, [24]'This is what the LORD says: I am going to bring disaster[i] on this place and its people[j]—all the curses[k] written in the book that has been read in the presence of the king of Judah. [25]Because they have forsaken me[l] and burned incense to other gods and provoked me to anger by all that their hands have made,[i] my anger will be poured out on this place and will not be quenched.' [26]Tell the king of Judah, who sent you to inquire of the LORD, 'This is what the LORD, the God of Israel, says concerning the words you heard: [27]Because your heart was responsive[m] and you humbled[n] yourself before

34:7 [v]S Ex 32:20
34:9 [w]S 1Ch 6:13
34:11 [x]2Ch 24:12 [y]2Ch 33:4-7
34:12 [z]2Ki 12:15 [a]S 1Ch 25:1
34:13 [b]S 1Ch 23:4

34:15 [c]S 2Ki 22:8; Ezr 7:6; Ne 8:1
34:19 [d]Dt 28:3-68 [e]Isa 36:22; 37:1
34:20 [f]S 2Ki 22:3
34:21 [g]La 2:4; 4:11; Eze 36:18
34:22 [h]S Ex 15:20; Ne 6:14
34:24 [i]Pr 16:4; Isa 3:9; Jer 40:2; 42:10; 44:2,11 [j]2Ch 36:14-20 [k]Dt 28:15-68
34:25 [l]2Ch 33:3-6; Jer 22:9
34:27 [m]S 2Ch 32:26 [n]S Ex 10:3; S 2Ch 6:37

[e]*20* Also called *Acbor son of Micaiah*   [f]*22* One Hebrew manuscript, Vulgate and Syriac; most Hebrew manuscripts do not have *had sent with him.*   [g]*22* Also called *Tikvah*   [h]*22* Also called *Harhas*   [i]*25* Or *by everything they have done*

34:6 *Manasseh, Ephraim and Simeon, as far as Naphtali.* The Chronicler's concern for "all Israel" (see Introduction to 1 Chronicles: Purpose and Themes) is apparent in his recording the involvement of the northern tribes in Josiah's reform (see also vv. 9,21,33). The Chronicler again shows all Israel united under a Davidic king, just as he did under Hezekiah (see note on 30:1). *Simeon.* Perhaps some Simeonites had migrated from Judah to the north.

34:7 *throughout Israel.* Defined by the list of tribes in v. 6.
34:8–21 See 2Ki 22:3–13 and notes.
34:9 *Manasseh, Ephraim and the entire remnant of Israel.* Again as part of his concern with "all Israel," the Chronicler notes that worshipers from the north also brought gifts to the temple (not explicitly indicated in 2Ki 22:4).
34:10–13 Cf. 24:8–12.
34:22–28 See 2Ki 22:14–20 and notes.

God when you heard what he spoke against this place and its people, and because you humbled yourself before me and tore your robes and wept in my presence, I have heard you, declares the LORD. 28Now I will gather you to your fathers, o and you will be buried in peace. Your eyes will not see all the disaster I am going to bring on this place and on those who live here.' " p

So they took her answer back to the king.

29Then the king called together all the elders of Judah and Jerusalem. 30He went up to the temple of the LORD q with the men of Judah, the people of Jerusalem, the priests and the Levites—all the people from the least to the greatest. He read in their hearing all the words of the Book of the Covenant, which had been found in the temple of the LORD. 31The king stood by his pillar r and renewed the covenant s in the presence of the LORD—to follow t the LORD and keep his commands, regulations and decrees with all his heart and all his soul, and to obey the words of the covenant written in this book.

32Then he had everyone in Jerusalem and Benjamin pledge themselves to it; the people of Jerusalem did this in accordance with the covenant of God, the God of their fathers.

33Josiah removed all the detestable u idols from all the territory belonging to the Israelites, and he had all who were present in Israel serve the LORD their God. As long as he lived, they did not fail to follow the LORD, the God of their fathers.

Josiah Celebrates the Passover

35:1,18–19pp — 2Ki 23:21–23

35 Josiah celebrated the Passover v to the LORD in Jerusalem, and the Passover lamb was slaughtered on the fourteenth day of the first month. 2He appointed the priests to their duties and encouraged them in the service of the LORD's temple. 3He said to the Levites, who instructed w all Israel and who had been con-

Cross references (center column)

34:28
o 2Ch 35:20-25
p S 2Ch 32:26
34:30
q S 2Ki 23:2
34:31 r S 1Ki 7:15
s S 2Ki 11:17;
S 2Ch 23:16
t S Dt 13:4
34:33 u S Dt 18:9
35:1
v Ex 12:1-30;
S Nu 28:16
35:3
w S 2Ch 17:7

35:4 x ver 10;
S 1Ch 24:1;
Ezr 6:18
35:6
y S Lev 11:44
35:7
z S 2Ch 30:24
a S 2Ch 31:3
35:8
b S 1Ch 29:3;
2Ch 29:31-36
c S 1Ch 6:13
35:9 d 2Ch 31:12
e 2Ch 31:13
35:10 f S ver 4
g 2Ch 30:16
35:11
h S 2Ch 30:17
35:13
i Ex 12:2-11

secrated to the LORD: "Put the sacred ark in the temple that Solomon son of David king of Israel built. It is not to be carried about on your shoulders. Now serve the LORD your God and his people Israel. 4Prepare yourselves by families in your divisions, x according to the directions written by David king of Israel and by his son Solomon.

5"Stand in the holy place with a group of Levites for each subdivision of the families of your fellow countrymen, the lay people. 6Slaughter the Passover lambs, consecrate yourselves y and prepare the lambs, for your fellow countrymen, doing what the LORD commanded through Moses."

7Josiah provided for all the lay people who were there a total of thirty thousand sheep and goats for the Passover offerings, z and also three thousand cattle—all from the king's own possessions. a

8His officials also contributed b voluntarily to the people and the priests and Levites. Hilkiah, c Zechariah and Jehiel, the administrators of God's temple, gave the priests twenty-six hundred Passover offerings and three hundred cattle. 9Also Conaniah d along with Shemaiah and Nethanel, his brothers, and Hashabiah, Jeiel and Jozabad, e the leaders of the Levites, provided five thousand Passover offerings and five hundred head of cattle for the Levites.

10The service was arranged and the priests stood in their places with the Levites in their divisions f as the king had ordered. g 11The Passover lambs were slaughtered, h and the priests sprinkled the blood handed to them, while the Levites skinned the animals. 12They set aside the burnt offerings to give them to the subdivisions of the families of the people to offer to the LORD, as is written in the Book of Moses. They did the same with the cattle. 13They roasted the Passover animals over the fire as prescribed, i and boiled the holy offerings in pots, caldrons and pans and served them quickly to all the people. 14Af-

---

34:28 *will be buried in peace.* See the death and burial account (35:20–25).

34:29–31 See 2Ki 23:1–3.

34:30 *the priests and the Levites.* Cf. 2Ki 23:2, which has "the priests and the prophets."

34:33 *all the territory belonging to the Israelites . . . all who were present in Israel.* See note on v. 6.

35:1–19 The Chronicler gives much more extensive coverage to Josiah's Passover celebration than is found in the brief allusion in Kings (2Ki 23:21–23).

35:1 *first month.* The traditional month; contrast the Passover of Hezekiah (see note on 30:2).

35:3 *Put the sacred ark in the temple.* Implies that it had been removed, perhaps for protection during the evil reigns of Manasseh and Amon, who preceded Josiah.

35:4 *David . . . Solomon.* The Chronicler specifically parallels David and Solomon in three cases: 7:10 (contrast 1Ki 8:66, where only David is mentioned); 11:17; and here. This tendency reflects his glorification and idealization of both (see Introduction to 1 Chronicles: Portrait of David and Solomon).

35:7–9 The emphasis in Chronicles on voluntary and joyful giving (24:8–14; 29:31–36; 31:3–21; 1Ch 29:3–9) presumably had direct relevance to the postexilic readers for whom the Chronicler wrote.

ter this, they made preparations for themselves and for the priests, because the priests, the descendants of Aaron, were sacrificing the burnt offerings and the fat portions *j* until nightfall. So the Levites made preparations for themselves and for the Aaronic priests.

¹⁵The musicians, *k* the descendants of Asaph, were in the places prescribed by David, Asaph, Heman and Jeduthun the king's seer. The gatekeepers at each gate did not need to leave their posts, because their fellow Levites made the preparations for them.

¹⁶So at that time the entire service of the LORD was carried out for the celebration of the Passover and the offering of burnt offerings on the altar of the LORD, as King Josiah had ordered. ¹⁷The Israelites who were present celebrated the Passover at that time and observed the Feast of Unleavened Bread for seven days. ¹⁸The Passover had not been observed like this in Israel since the days of the prophet Samuel; and none of the kings of Israel had ever celebrated such a Passover as did Josiah, with the priests, the Levites and all Judah and Israel who were there with the people of Jerusalem. ¹⁹This Passover was celebrated in the eighteenth year of Josiah's reign.

The Death of Josiah

35:20–36:1pp — 2Ki 23:28-30

²⁰After all this, when Josiah had set the temple in order, Neco king of Egypt went up to fight at Carchemish *l* on the Euphrates, *m* and Josiah marched out to meet him in battle. ²¹But Neco sent messengers to him, saying, "What quarrel is there between you and me, O king of Judah? It is not you I am attacking at this time, but the

house with which I am at war. God has told *n* me to hurry; so stop opposing God, who is with me, or he will destroy you."

²²Josiah, however, would not turn away from him, but disguised *o* himself to engage him in battle. He would not listen to what Neco had said at God's command but went to fight him on the plain of Megiddo.

²³Archers *p* shot King Josiah, and he told his officers, "Take me away; I am badly wounded." ²⁴So they took him out of his chariot, put him in the other chariot he had and brought him to Jerusalem, where he died. He was buried in the tombs of his fathers, and all Judah and Jerusalem mourned for him.

²⁵Jeremiah composed laments for Josiah, and to this day all the men and women singers commemorate Josiah in the laments. *q* These became a tradition in Israel and are written in the Laments. *r*

²⁶The other events of Josiah's reign and his acts of devotion, according to what is written in the Law of the LORD— ²⁷all the events, from beginning to end, are written in the book of the kings of Israel and

36 Judah. ¹And the people *s* of the land took Jehoahaz son of Josiah and made him king in Jerusalem in place of his father.

Jehoahaz King of Judah

36:2–4pp — 2Ki 23:31-34

²Jehoahaz *i* was twenty-three years old when he became king, and he reigned in Jerusalem three months. ³The king of Egypt dethroned him in Jerusalem and imposed on Judah a levy of a hundred talents *k* of silver and a talent *l* of gold. ⁴The

Cross references (center column):

35:14 /S Ex 29:13
35:15 *k*S 1Ch 25:1; S 26:12-19; 2Ch 29:30; Ne 12:46; Ps 68:25
35:20 /Isa 10:9; Jer 46:2 *m*S Ge 2:14

35:21 *n*S 1Ki 13:18; S 2Ki 18:25
35:22 *o*S 1Sa 28:8
35:23 *p*S 1Ki 22:34
35:25 *q*S Ge 50:10; Jer 22:10,15-16 *r*2Ch 34:28
36:1 *s*S 2Ch 22:1

*i*2 Hebrew *Joahaz*, a variant of *Jehoahaz*; also in verse 4
*k*3 That is, about 3 3/4 tons (about 3.4 metric tons)
*l*3 That is, about 75 pounds (about 34 kilograms)

35:18 *since the days of the prophet Samuel.* Instead of "since the days of the judges" (2Ki 23:22).
35:19 *eighteenth year.* The same year as the discovery of the Book of the Law (34:8,14).
35:20–27 See 2Ki 23:28-30. In 609 B.C. Pharaoh Neco "went up to the Euphrates River to help the king of Assyria" (2Ki 23:29) against the Babylonians.
35:20 *at Carchemish.* Not found in Kings.
35:21–22 Unique to the Chronicler, showing his view on retribution once again: Josiah's death in battle comes as a result of his disobedience to the word of God as heard even in the mouth of the pagan pharaoh.
35:21 *house with which I am at war.* A reference to the Babylonians; Nabopolassar was on the throne of Babylon, while his son Nebuchadnezzar was commanding the armies in the field. Nebuchadnezzar would succeed his father after another battle at Carchemish against Egypt in 605 B.C. Josiah may have been an ally of Babylon (see 32:31; 33:11 and notes).
35:22 *disguised himself.* Cf. Ahab and Jehoshaphat (see

18:29 and note). *plain of Megiddo.* See note on Jdg 5:19.
35:24b–25 Unique to Chronicles.
35:25 *Jeremiah composed laments for Josiah.* Jeremiah held Josiah in high esteem (Jer 22:15–16). The laments he composed are no longer extant. The statement that he composed laments is one of the reasons the book of Lamentations has been traditionally associated with him. *to this day.* See note on 5:9.
36:2–14 Josiah is the only king of Judah to be succeeded by three of his sons (Jehoahaz, Jehoiakim and Zedekiah). The Chronicler's account of the reigns of the remaining kings of Judah is quite brief.
36:2 See 2Ki 23:31–35. With the death of Josiah at the hands of Pharaoh Neco, Judah slipped into a period of Egyptian domination (vv. 3–4). *three months.* In 609 B.C. Neco's assertion of authority over Judah ended the brief 20 years of Judahite independence under Josiah. The Chronicler makes no moral judgment on this brief reign, though the author of Kings does (2Ki 23:32).
36:4 Just as Neco took Jehoahaz into captivity and replaced

king of Egypt made Eliakim, a brother of Jehoahaz, king over Judah and Jerusalem and changed Eliakim's name to Jehoiakim. But Neco[t] took Eliakim's brother Jehoahaz and carried him off to Egypt.[u]

Jehoiakim King of Judah

36:5–8pp — 2Ki 23:36–24:6

[5]Jehoiakim[v] was twenty-five years old when he became king, and he reigned in Jerusalem eleven years. He did evil in the eyes of the LORD his God. [6]Nebuchadnezzar[w] king of Babylon attacked him and bound him with bronze shackles to take him to Babylon.[x] [7]Nebuchadnezzar also took to Babylon articles from the temple of the LORD and put them in his temple[m] there.[y]

[8]The other events of Jehoiakim's reign, the detestable things he did and all that was found against him, are written in the book of the kings of Israel and Judah. And Jehoiachin his son succeeded him as king.

Jehoiachin King of Judah

36:9–10pp — 2Ki 24:8–17

[9]Jehoiachin[z] was eighteen[n] years old when he became king, and he reigned in Jerusalem three months and ten days. He did evil in the eyes of the LORD. [10]In the spring, King Nebuchadnezzar sent for him and brought him to Babylon,[a] together with articles of value from the temple of the LORD, and he made Jehoiachin's uncle,[o] Zedekiah, king over Judah and Jerusalem.

Zedekiah King of Judah

36:11–16pp — 2Ki 24:18–20; Jer 52:1–3

[11]Zedekiah[b] was twenty-one years old when he became king, and he reigned in Jerusalem eleven years. [12]He did evil in the eyes of the LORD[c] his God and did not humble[d] himself before Jeremiah the

prophet, who spoke the word of the LORD. [13]He also rebelled against King Nebuchadnezzar, who had made him take an oath[e] in God's name. He became stiff-necked[f] and hardened his heart and would not turn to the LORD, the God of Israel. [14]Furthermore, all the leaders of the priests and the people became more and more unfaithful,[g] following all the detestable practices of the nations and defiling the temple of the LORD, which he had consecrated in Jerusalem.

The Fall of Jerusalem

36:17–20pp — 2Ki 25:1–21; Jer 52:4–27
36:22–23pp — Ezr 1:1–3

[15]The LORD, the God of their fathers, sent word to them through his messengers[h] again and again,[i] because he had pity on his people and on his dwelling place. [16]But they mocked God's messengers, despised his words and scoffed[j] at his prophets until the wrath[k] of the LORD was aroused against his people and there was no remedy.[l] [17]He brought up against them the king of the Babylonians,[p][m] who killed their young men with the sword in the sanctuary, and spared neither young man[n] nor young woman, old man or aged.[o] God handed all of them over to Nebuchadnezzar.[p] [18]He carried to Babylon all the articles[q] from the temple of God, both large and small, and the treasures of the LORD's temple and the treasures of the king and his officials. [19]They set fire[r] to God's temple[s] and broke down the wall[t] of Jerusalem; they burned

Cross-references (center column)

36:4 [t]Jer 22:10-12 [u]Eze 19:4
36:5 [v]Jer 22:18; 25:1; 26:1; 35:1; 36:1; 45:1; 46:2
36:6 [w]Jer 25:9; 27:6; Eze 29:18 [x]Eze 19:9; Da 1:1
36:7 [y]ver 18; Ezr 1:7; Jer 27:16; Da 1:2
36:9 [z]Jer 22:24-28; 24:1; 27:20; 29:21; 52:31
36:10 [a]ver 18; S 2Ki 20:17; Ezr 1:7; Isa 52:11; Jer 14:18; 21:7; 22:25; 24:1; 27:16,20,22; 29:1; 34:21; 40:1; Eze 17:12; Da 5:2
36:11 [b]S 2Ki 24:17; Jer 27:1; 28:1; 34:2; 37:1; 39:1
36:12 [c]Jer 37:1-39:18 [d]S Dt 8:3; 2Ch 7:14; Jer 44:10
36:13 [e]Eze 17:13 [f]S Ex 32:9; S Dt 9:27
36:14 [g]S 1Ch 5:25
36:15 [h]Isa 5:4; 44:26; Jer 7:25; Hag 1:13; Zec 1:4; Mal 2:7; 3:1; S Mt 5:12 [i]Jer 7:13,25; 11:7; 25:3-4; 35:14,15; 44:4-6
36:16 [j]S 2Ki 2:23; Job 8:2; Isa 28:14; 22; 29:20; 57:4; Jer 5:13; 43:2; Mic 2:11 [k]Ezr 5:12; Pr 1:30-31; Jer 44:3 [l]Ne 9:30; Pr 29:1; Jer 7:26; 20:8; 25:4; 30:12; Da 9:6; Zec 1:2
36:17 [m]S Ge 10:10 [n]Jer 6:11; 9:21; 18:21; 44:7 [o]S Dt 32:25; Jer 51:22 [p]Ezr 5:12; Jer 32:28; La 2:21; Eze 9:6;
23:47 36:18 [q]S ver 7,S 10; Jer 27:20 36:19 [r]Jer 11:16; 17:27; 21:10,14; 22:7; 32:29; 39:8; La 4:11; Eze 20:47; Am 2:5; Zec 11:1 [s]1Ki 9:8-9 [t]S 2Ki 14:13

[m]7 Or *palace* [n]9 One Hebrew manuscript, some Septuagint manuscripts and Syriac (see also 2 Kings 24:8); most Hebrew manuscripts *eight* [o]10 Hebrew *brother*, that is, relative (see 2 Kings 24:17) [p]17 Or *Chaldeans*

Footnotes (bottom)

him with Eliakim, whose name he changed to Jehoiakim, so also Nebuchadnezzar would later take Jehoiachin to Babylon, replacing him with Mattaniah, whose name he changed to Zedekiah (2Ki 24:15–17). Each conqueror wanted to place his own man on the throne; the change of name implied authority over him.

36:5–8 See 2Ki 23:36–24:7. Jehoiakim persecuted the prophets and is the object of scathing denunciation by Jeremiah (Jer 25–26; 36). After the Egyptian defeat at Carchemish (Jer 46:2) in 605 B.C., Jehoiakim transferred allegiance to Nebuchadnezzar of Babylon. When he later rebelled and again allied himself with Egypt, Nebuchadnezzar sent a punitive army against him. But Jehoiakim died before the army arrived, and Nebuchadnezzar took his son Jehoiachin into captivity.

36:5 *eleven years.* 609–598 B.C.
36:9–10 See 2Ki 24:8–17; see also Jer 22:24–28; 24:1;

29:2; 52:31. Although Jehoiachin was taken into captivity (597 B.C.) with a large retinue, including the queen mother and high officials, and was succeeded by Zedekiah, the exiles continued to date in terms of his reign (Jer 52:31; Eze 1:2; cf. Est 2:5–6).

36:9 *three months and ten days.* 598–597 B.C.

36:11–14 See 2Ki 24:18–20; Jer 52:1–3. Verses 13b–14 are unique to the Chronicler (cf. Jer 1:3; 21:1–7; 24:8; 27:1–15; 32:1–5; 34:1–7,21; 37:1–39:7). Zedekiah succumbed to the temptation to look to Egypt for help and rebelled against Nebuchadnezzar. Babylonian reaction was swift. Jerusalem was besieged (Jer 21:3–7) in 588 B.C. and held out for almost two years before being destroyed in the summer of 586.

36:11 *eleven years.* 597–586 B.C.
36:15–16 See 24:19 and note.

all the palaces and destroyed[u] everything of value there.[v]

[20]He carried into exile[w] to Babylon the remnant, who escaped from the sword, and they became servants[x] to him and his sons until the kingdom of Persia came to power. [21]The land enjoyed its sabbath rests;[y] all the time of its desolation it rested,[z] until the seventy years[a] were completed in fulfillment of the word of the LORD spoken by Jeremiah.

[22]In the first year of Cyrus[b] king of Persia, in order to fulfill the word of the LORD spoken by Jeremiah, the LORD

moved the heart of Cyrus king of Persia to make a proclamation throughout his realm and to put it in writing:

[23]"This is what Cyrus king of Persia says:

"'The LORD, the God of heaven, has given me all the kingdoms of the earth and he has appointed[c] me to build a temple for him at Jerusalem in Judah. Anyone of his people among you—may the LORD his God be with him, and let him go up.'"

36:19 [u]La 2:6
[v]Ps 79:1-3
36:20
[w]S Lev 26:44;
S 2Ki 24:14;
Ezr 2:1; Ne 7:6
[x]Jer 27:7
36:21
[y]S Lev 25:4
[z]S 1Ch 22:9
[a]Jer 1:1; 25:11;
27:22; 29:10;
40:1; Da 9:2;
Zec 1:12; 7:5
36:22 [b]Isa 44:28;
45:1,13; Da 1:21;
6:28; 10:1

36:23 [c]S Jdg 4:10

36:20–21 The conclusion of the two Biblical histories is interestingly different: The writer(s) of Samuel and Kings had sought to show why the exile occurred and had traced the sad history of Israel's disobedience to the exile, the time in which the writer(s) of those books lived. With the state at an end, he could still show God's faithfulness to his promises to David (2Ki 25:27–30) by reporting the favor bestowed on his descendants. The Chronicler, whose vantage point was after the exile, was able to look back to the exile not only as judgment, but also as containing hope for the future. For him the purified remnant had returned to a purified land (vv. 22–23), and a new age was beginning. The exile was not judgment alone, but also blessing, for it allowed the land to catch up on its sabbath rests (Lev 26:40–45). And God had

remembered his covenant (Lev 26:45) and restored his people to the land (see next note).
36:22–23 The writer of Kings concluded his history before the restoration, so this text is not paralleled in his account. It is repeated, however, at the beginning of Ezra (1:1–4), which resumes the history at the point where Chronicles ends—indicating that Chronicles and Ezra may have been written by the same author. See the prophecy of Jeremiah (Jer 25:1–14; cf. Da 9). Cyrus also issued decrees for other captive peoples, allowing them to return to their lands. Under God's sovereignty, this effort by a Persian king to win the favor of peoples treated harshly by the Babylonians also inaugurated the restoration period. See notes on Ezr 1: 1–4.

EZRA

Ezra and Nehemiah

Although the caption to Ne 1:1, "The words of Nehemiah son of Hacaliah," indicates that Ezra and Nehemiah were originally two separate compositions, they were combined as one in the earliest Hebrew manuscripts. Josephus (c. A.D. 37-100) and the Jewish Talmud refer to the book of Ezra but not to a separate book of Nehemiah. The oldest manuscripts of the Septuagint (the Greek translation of the OT) also treat Ezra and Nehemiah as one book.

Origen (A.D. 185-253) is the first writer known to distinguish between two books, which he called I Ezra and II Ezra. In translating the Latin Vulgate (A.D. 390-405), Jerome called Nehemiah the second book of Esdrae (Ezra). The English translations by Wycliffe (1382) and Coverdale (1535) also called Ezra "I Esdras" and Nehemiah "II Esdras." The same separation first appeared in a Hebrew manuscript in 1448.

Literary Form and Authorship

As in the closely related books of 1 and 2 Chronicles, one notes the prominence of various lists in Ezra and Nehemiah, which have evidently been obtained from official sources. Included are lists of (1) the temple articles (Ezr 1:9-11), (2) the returned exiles (Ezr 2, which is virtually the same as Ne 7:6-73), (3) the genealogy of Ezra (Ezr 7:1-5), (4) the heads of the clans (Ezr 8:1-14), (5) those involved in mixed marriages (Ezr 10:18-43), (6) those who helped rebuild the wall (Ne 3), (7) those who sealed the covenant (Ne 10:1-27), (8) residents of Jerusalem and other towns (Ne 11:3-36) and (9) priests and Levites (Ne 12:1-26).

Also included in Ezra are seven official documents or letters (all in Aramaic except the first, which is in Hebrew): (1) the decree of Cyrus (1:2-4), (2) the accusation of Rehum and others against the Jews (4:11-16), (3) the reply of Artaxerxes I (4:17-22), (4) the report from Tattenai (5:7-17), (5) the memorandum of Cyrus's decree (6:2b-5), (6) Darius's reply to Tattenai (6:6-12) and (7) the authorization given by Artaxerxes I to Ezra (7:12-26). The documents compare favorably with contemporary non-Biblical documents of the Persian period.

Certain materials in Ezra are first-person extracts from his memoirs: 7:27-28; 8:1-34; 9. Other sections are written in the third person: 7:1-26; 10; see also Ne 8. Linguistic analysis has shown that the first-person and third-person extracts resemble each other, making it likely that the same author wrote both.

Most scholars conclude that the author/compiler of Ezra and Nehemiah was also the author of 1,2 Chronicles. This viewpoint is based on certain characteristics common to both Chronicles and Ezra-Nehemiah. The verses at the end of Chronicles and at the beginning of Ezra are virtually identical. Both Chronicles and Ezra-Nehemiah exhibit a fondness for lists, for the description of religious festivals and for such phrases as "heads of families" and "the house of God." Especially striking in these books is the prominence of Levites and temple personnel. The words for "singer," "gatekeeper" and "temple servants" are used almost exclusively in Ezra-Nehemiah and Chronicles. See Introduction to 1 Chronicles: Author, Date and Sources.

Date

We may date the composition of Ezra c. 440 B.C. and the Nehemiah memoirs c. 430.

The Order of Ezra and Nehemiah

According to the traditional view, Ezra arrived in Jerusalem in the seventh year (Ezr 7:8) of Artaxerxes I (458 B.C.), followed by Nehemiah, who arrived in the king's 20th year (445; Ne 2:1).

Some have proposed a reverse order in which Nehemiah arrived in 445 B.C., while Ezra arrived in the seventh year of Artaxerxes II (398). By amending "seventh" (Ezr 7:8) to either "27th" or "37th," others place Ezra after Nehemiah but maintain that they were contemporaries.

These alternative views, however, present more problems than the traditional position. As the text stands, Ezra arrived before Nehemiah and they are found together in Ne 8:9 (at the reading of the Law) and Ne 12:26,36 (at the dedication of the wall). See chart on "Chronology: Ezra-Nehemiah," p. 674.

Languages

Ezra and Nehemiah were written in a form of late Hebrew with the exception of Ezr 4:8-6:18; 7:12-26, which were written in Aramaic, the international language during the Persian period. Of these 67 Aramaic verses, 52 are in records or letters. Ezra evidently found these documents in Aramaic and copied them, inserting connecting verses in Aramaic.

Return from Exile

1. **RESTORATION** of the exiles began under Cyrus (559-530 B.C.), who allowed them to return to Judah with the captured temple treasures.

2. **THE TEMPLE** was consecrated by official permission of Darius I (522-486 B.C.).

3. **EZRA** won the approval of Artaxerxes I (465-424 B.C.) to return with additional exiles; Nehemiah, to rebuild the walls of Jerusalem.

4. **CLAY TABLETS** from the Murashu archives at Nippur reveal the presence of Jews remaining a half century after Ezra.

Exact location of exiles' villages unknown: Tel Melah, Tel Harsha, Kerub, Addon, Immer

Outline

I. First Return from Exile and Rebuilding of the Temple (chs. 1-6)
   A. First Return of the Exiles (ch. 1)
      1. The edict of Cyrus (1:1-4)
      2. The return under Sheshbazzar (1:5-11)
   B. List of Returning Exiles (ch. 2)
   C. Revival of Temple Worship (ch. 3)
      1. The rebuilding of the altar (3:1-3)
      2. The Feast of Tabernacles (3:4-6)
      3. The beginning of temple reconstruction (3:7-13)
   D. Opposition to Rebuilding (4:1-23)
      1. Opposition during the reign of Cyrus (4:1-5)
      2. Opposition during the reign of Xerxes (4:6)
      3. Opposition during the reign of Artaxerxes (4:7-23)
   E. Completion of the Temple (4:24-6:22)
      1. Resumption of work under Darius (4:24)
      2. A new beginning inspired by Haggai and Zechariah (5:1-2)
      3. Intervention of the governor, Tattenai (5:3-5)
      4. Report to Darius (5:6-17)
      5. Search for the decree of Cyrus (6:1-5)

      6. Darius's order for the rebuilding of the temple (6:6-12)
      7. Completion of the temple (6:13-15)
      8. Dedication of the temple (6:16-18)
      9. Celebration of Passover (6:19-22)
II. Ezra's Return and Reforms (chs. 7-10)
  A. Ezra's Return to Jerusalem (chs. 7-8)
      1. Introduction (7:1-10)
      2. The authorization by Artaxerxes (7:11-26)
      3. Ezra's doxology (7:27-28)
      4. List of those returning with Ezra (8:1-14)
      5. The search for Levites (8:15-20)
      6. Prayer and fasting (8:21-23)
      7. The assignment of the sacred articles (8:24-30)
      8. The journey and arrival in Jerusalem (8:31-36)
  B. Ezra's Reforms (chs. 9-10)
      1. The offense of mixed marriages (9:1-5)
      2. Ezra's confession and prayer (9:6-15)
      3. The people's response (10:1-4)
      4. The calling of a public assembly (10:5-15)
      5. Investigation of the offenders (10:16-17)
      6. The list of offenders (10:18-43)
      7. The dissolution of mixed marriages (10:44)

Cyrus Helps the Exiles to Return

1:1–3pp — 2Ch 36:22–23

1 In the first year of Cyrus king of Persia, in order to fulfill the word of the LORD spoken by Jeremiah,[a] the LORD moved the heart[b] of Cyrus king of Persia to make a proclamation throughout his realm and to put it in writing:

2"This is what Cyrus king of Persia says:

"'The LORD, the God of heaven, has given me all the kingdoms of the earth and he has appointed[c] me to build[d] a temple for him at Jerusalem in Judah. 3Anyone of his people among you—may his God be with him, and let him go up to Jerusalem in Judah and build the temple of the LORD, the God of Israel, the God who is in Jerusalem. 4And the people of any place where survivors[e] may now be living are to provide him with silver and gold,[f] with goods and livestock, and with freewill offerings[g] for the temple of God[h] in Jerusalem.'"[i]

5Then the family heads of Judah and Benjamin,[j] and the priests and Levites—everyone whose heart God had moved[k]—prepared to go up and build the house[l] of the LORD in Jerusalem. 6All their neighbors assisted them with articles of silver and gold,[m] with goods and livestock, and with valuable gifts, in addition to all the freewill offerings. 7Moreover, King Cyrus brought out the articles belonging to the temple of the LORD, which Nebuchadnezzar had carried away from Jerusalem and had placed in the temple of his god.[a][n] 8Cyrus king of Persia had them brought by Mithredath the treasurer, who counted them out to Sheshbazzar[o] the prince of Judah.

9This was the inventory:

gold dishes	30
silver dishes	1,000

Cross references

1:1 *a*Jer 25:11-12; 29:10-14; Zec 1:12-16 *b*Ezr 6:22; 7:27
1:2 *c*S Jdg 4:10; Ps 72:11; Isa 41:2,25; 44:28; 45:13; 46:11; 49:7,23; 60:3,10 *d*Hag 1:2
1:4 *e*Isa 10:20-22 *f*S Ex 3:22
*g*Nu 15:3; Ps 50:14; 54:6; 116:17 *h*Ps 72:8-11; Rev 21:24 *i*Ezr 3:7; 4:3; 5:13; 6:3,14
1:5 *j*2Ch 11:1,3, 10,12,23; 15:2, 8-9; 25:5; 31:1; 34:9; Ezr 4:1; 10:9; Ne 11:4; 12:34 *k*ver 1; Ex 35:20-22; 2Ch 36:22; Hag 1:14; S Php 2:13 *l*Ps 127:1
1:6 *m*S Ex 3:22
1:7 *n*S 2Ki 24:13; S 2Ch 36:7,10; Ezr 5:14; 6:5; Jer 52:17-19
1:8 *o*S 1Ch 3:18
a 7 Or *gods*

1:1–3a Virtually identical with the last two verses of 2 Chronicles. This fact has been used to argue that Chronicles and Ezra-Nehemiah were written and/or edited by the same person, the so-called Chronicler. However, the repetition may have been a device of the author of Chronicles (or less probably of Ezra) to dovetail the narratives chronologically.
1:1 *first year.* Of the reign of Cyrus over Babylon, beginning in March, 538 B.C., after he captured Babylon in October, 539. Cyrus, the founder of the Persian empire, reigned over the Persians from 559 until 530. Isa 44:28; 45:1 speak of him as the Lord's "shepherd" and his "anointed." *to fulfill the word of the LORD spoken by Jeremiah.* Jeremiah prophesied a 70-year Babylonian captivity (Jer 25:11–12; 29:10). The first deportation began in 605, the third year of Jehoiakim (Da 1:1); in 538, approximately 70 years later, the people began to return.
1:2–4 This oral proclamation of Cyrus's decree was written in Hebrew, the language of the Israelite captives, in contrast to the copy of the decree in 6:3–5, which was an Aramaic memorandum for the archives.
1:2 *God of heaven.* Of the 22 OT occurrences of the phrase, 17 occur in Ezra, Nehemiah and Daniel. *temple . . . at Jerusalem.* Jerusalem and the house of God are prominent subjects in Ezra and Nehemiah.
1:3 Cyrus instituted the policy of placating the gods of his subject peoples instead of carrying off their cult images as the Assyrians and the Babylonians had done earlier. His generosity to the Jews was paralleled by his benevolence to the Babylonians.
1:4 *people of any place.* Probably designates the many Jews who did not wish to leave Mesopotamia. *freewill offerings.* A key to the restoration of God's temple and its services (see 2:68; 3:5; 8:28).
1:5 *family heads.* In ancient times families were extended families—more like clans than modern nuclear families. The authority figure was the patriarch, who was the "family head." See 10:16; see also 2:59; Ne 7:61; 10:34. *Judah and Benjamin.* The two main tribes of the kingdom of Judah, which the Babylonians had exiled. *Levites.* See Introduction to Leviticus: Title.

1:7 It was the custom for conquerors to carry off the images of the gods of conquered cities. Since the Jews did not have an image of the Lord (see note on Ex 20:4), Nebuchadnezzar carried away only the temple articles.
1:8 *Mithredath.* A Persian name meaning "given by/to Mithra," a Persian god who became popular among Roman soldiers in the second century A.D. *Sheshbazzar.* A Babylonian name meaning either "Sin, protect the father" or "Shamash/Shashu, protect the father." Sin was the moon-god, and Shamash (Shashu is a variant) was the sun-god. In spite of his Babylonian name, Sheshbazzar was probably a Jewish official who served as a deputy governor of Judah under the satrap in Samaria (see 5:14). Some believe that Sheshbazzar and Zerubbabel were the same person and give the following reasons: 1. Both were governors (5:14; Hag 1:1; 2:2). 2. Both are said to have laid the foundation of the temple (3:2–8; 5:16; Hag 1:14–15; Zec 4:6–10). 3. Jews in Babylon were often given "official" Babylonian names (cf. Da 1:7). 4. Josephus (*Antiquities,* 11.1.3) seems to identify Sheshbazzar with Zerubbabel.
Others point out, however, that the Apocrypha distinguishes between the two men (1 Esdras 6:18). Furthermore, it is likely that Sheshbazzar was an elderly man at the time of the return, while Zerubbabel was probably a younger contemporary. Sheshbazzar also may have been viewed as the official governor, while Zerubbabel served as the popular leader (3:8–11). Whereas the high priest Jeshua is associated with Zerubbabel, no priest is associated with Sheshbazzar. Although Sheshbazzar presided over the foundation of the temple in 536 B.C., so little was accomplished that Zerubbabel had to preside over a second foundation some 16 years later (see Hag 1:14–15; Zec 4:6–10).
Still others hold that Sheshbazzar is to be identified with Shenazzar (1Ch 3:18), the fourth son of King Jehoiachin. Zerubbabel would then have been Sheshbazzar's nephew (compare 3:2 with 1Ch 3:18).
1:9–11 When Assyrian and Babylonian conquerors carried off plunder, their scribes made a careful inventory of all the goods seized. The total of the figures in vv. 9–10 adds up to 2,499 rather than the 5,400 of v. 11. It may be that only the larger and more valuable vessels were specified.

silver pans[b]	29
[10]gold bowls	30
matching silver bowls	410
other articles	1,000

[11]In all, there were 5,400 articles of gold and of silver. Sheshbazzar brought all these along when the exiles came up from Babylon to Jerusalem.

The List of the Exiles Who Returned

2:1–70pp — Ne 7:6–73

2 Now these are the people of the province who came up from the captivity of the exiles,[p] whom Nebuchadnezzar king of Babylon[q] had taken captive to Babylon (they returned to Jerusalem and Judah, each to his own town,[r] [2]in company with Zerubbabel,[s] Jeshua,[t] Nehemiah, Seraiah,[u] Reelaiah, Mordecai, Bilshan, Mispar, Bigvai, Rehum and Baanah):

The list of the men of the people of Israel:

[3]the descendants of Parosh[v]	2,172
[4]of Shephatiah	372
[5]of Arah	775
[6]of Pahath-Moab (through the line of Jeshua and Joab)	2,812
[7]of Elam	1,254
[8]of Zattu	945
[9]of Zaccai	760
[10]of Bani	642
[11]of Bebai	623
[12]of Azgad	1,222
[13]of Adonikam[w]	666
[14]of Bigvai	2,056
[15]of Adin	454
[16]of Ater (through Hezekiah)	98
[17]of Bezai	323
[18]of Jorah	112

Cross references:
2:1 pS 2Ch 36:20
qS 2Ki 24:16; 25:12 rver 70; 1Ch 9:2; Ne 7:73; 11:3
2:2 sS 1Ch 3:19; Mt 1:12; Lk 3:27
tEzr 3:2; 5:2; 10:18; Ne 12:1,8; Hag 1:1,12; 2:4; Zec 3:1-10; 6:9-15
uICh 6:14; Ne 10:2; 11:11; 12:1
2:3 vEzr 8:3; 10:25; Ne 3:25
2:13 wEzr 8:13

b9 The meaning of the Hebrew for this word is uncertain.

1:11 We are not told anything about the details of Sheshbazzar's journey, which probably took place in 537 B.C. Judging from Ezra's later journey (7:8–9), the trip took about four months. See inset to map No. 7 at the end of the Study Bible.
2:1–70 The list of returning exiles in ch. 2 almost exactly parallels the list in Ne 7:6–73 (see also 1 Esdras 5:4–46 in the Apocrypha). The list of localities indicates that people retained the memories of their homes and that exiles from a wide background of tribes, villages and towns returned. In comparing the list here with that in Ne 7, one notes many differences in the names and numbers listed. About 20 percent of the numbers, e.g., are not the same in Ezra and Nehemiah. Many of these differences may be explained, however, by assuming that a cipher notation was used with vertical strokes for units and horizontal strokes for tens, which led to copying errors.
2:1 province. Probably Judah (cf. 5:8, where the Aramaic

word for "province" is translated "district"; see also Ne 1:3).
2:2 Zerubbabel. See notes on 3:2; 5:2. Jeshua. Means "The LORD saves" and is an Aramaic variant of Hebrew "Joshua." The Greek form is "Jesus" (see NIV text note on Mt 1:21). Jeshua is the same as the Joshua of Hag 1:1, the son of the high priest Jehozadak (Jozadak, Ezr 3:2), who was taken into exile (1Ch 6:15). Nehemiah. Not the Nehemiah of the book by that name. Mordecai. A Babylonian name based on that of Marduk the god of Babylon (cf. Jer 50:2). Esther's cousin had the same name (Est 2:7).
2:3 Parosh. Means "flea" (Israelites were often named after insects and animals). Members of this family, as well as of several other families named in vv. 6–14, also returned with Ezra (8:3–14).
2:5 Arah. Probably means "wild ox." Since the name is rare in the OT and has been found in documents from Mesopotamia, it may have been adopted during the exile.

Chronology: Ezra-Nehemiah

Dates below are given according to a Nisan-to-Nisan Jewish calendar (see chart on "Hebrew Calendar," p. 102).
Roman numerals represent months; Arabic numerals represent days.

YEAR	MONTH	DAY	EVENT	REFERENCE
539 B.C.	Oct.	12	Capture of Babylon	Da 5:30
538 to 537	Mar. to Mar.	24 11	Cyrus's first year	Ezr 1:1-4
537(?)			Return under Sheshbazzar	Ezr 1:11
537	VII		Building of altar	Ezr 3:1
536	II		Work on temple begun	Ezr 3:8
536-530			Opposition during Cyrus's reign	Ezr 4:1-5
530-520			Work on temple ceased	Ezr 4:24
520	VI =Sept.	24 21	Work on temple renewed under Darius	Ezr 5:2; Hag 1:14
516	XII =Mar.	3 12	Temple completed	Ezr 6:15

540 B.C.
530
520
510
500
490

[19]of Hashum	223		
[20]of Gibbar	95		
[21]the men of Bethlehem[x]	123		
[22]of Netophah	56		
[23]of Anathoth	128		
[24]of Azmaveth	42		
[25]of Kiriath Jearim,[c] Kephirah and Beeroth	743		
[26]of Ramah[y] and Geba	621		
[27]of Micmash	122		
[28]of Bethel and Ai[z]	223		
[29]of Nebo	52		
[30]of Magbish	156		
[31]of the other Elam	1,254		
[32]of Harim	320		
[33]of Lod, Hadid and Ono	725		
[34]of Jericho[a]	345		
[35]of Senaah	3,630		
[36]The priests:			

2:21 [x]Mic 5:2
2:26 [y]S Jos 18:25
2:28 [z]S Ge 12:8
2:34 [a]1Ki 16:34; 2Ch 28:15

the descendants of Jedaiah[b] (through the family of Jeshua) 973
[37]of Immer[c] 1,052
[38]of Pashhur[d] 1,247
[39]of Harim[e] 1,017

[40]The Levites:[f]

the descendants of Jeshua[g] and Kadmiel (through the line of Hodaviah) 74

[41]The singers:[h]

the descendants of Asaph 128

[42]The gatekeepers[i] of the temple:

the descendants of Shallum, Ater, Talmon, Akkub, Hatita and Shobai 139

2:36 [b]S 1Ch 24:7
2:37 [c]S 1Ch 24:14
2:38 [d]S 1Ch 9:12
2:39 [e]S 1Ch 24:8
2:40 [f]Ge 29:34; Nu 3:9; Dt 18:6-7; 1Ch 16:4; Ezr 7:7; 8:15; Ne 12:24 [g]Ezr 3:9
2:41 [h]S 1Ch 15:16
2:42 [i]1Sa 3:15; S 1Ch 9:17

[c]25 See Septuagint (see also Neh. 7:29); Hebrew *Kiriath Arim.*

2:6 *Pahath-Moab.* Means "governor of Moab" and may have once designated an official title.

2:12 *Azgad.* Cf. 8:12; means "Gad is strong." It is a reference either to Gad (the god of fortune, referred to in Isa 65:11) or to the Transjordanian tribe of Gad.

2:16 *Ater.* Means "left-handed," as in Jdg 3:15; 20:16.

2:21–35 Whereas the names in vv. 3–20 are of families, vv. 21–35 present a series of villages and towns, many of which were in Benjamite territory north of Jerusalem. It is significant that there are no references to towns in the Negev, south of Judah. When Nebuchadnezzar overran Judah in 597 B.C. (Jer 13:19), the Edomites (see the book of Obadiah) took advantage of the situation and occupied that area.

2:21 *men of Bethlehem.* The ancestors of Jesus may have been among the returnees.

2:23 *Anathoth.* See note on Jer 1:1.

2:28 *Bethel.* See note on Ge 12:8. Towns such as Bethel,

Mizpah, Gibeon and Gibeah seem to have escaped the Babylonian assault. Bethel, however, was destroyed in the transition between the Babylonian and Persian periods. Archaeological excavations reveal that there was a small town on the site in Ezra's day.

2:31 See v. 7.

2:33 *Lod.* Modern Lydda.

2:35 *Senaah.* The largest number of returnees—3,630 (3,930 in Ne 7:38)—is associated with Senaah. It has therefore been suggested that they did not come from a specific locality or family, but represented low-caste people, as inferred from the meaning of the name.

2:36–39 Four clans of priests numbering 4,289, about a tenth of the total.

2:40 *Levites.* See Introduction to Leviticus: Title. *74.* The number of Levites who returned was relatively small (cf. 8:15). Since the Levites had been entrusted with the menial tasks of temple service, many of them may have found a

---

YEAR		MONTH	DAY	EVENT	REFERENCE
	458	I =Apr.	1 8	Ezra departs from Babylon	Ezr 7:6-9
480		V =Aug.	1 4	Ezra arrives in Jerusalem	Ezr 7:8-9
		IX =Dec.	20 19	People assemble	Ezr 10:9
470		X =Dec.	1 29	Committee begins investigation	Ezr 10:16
	457	I =Mar.	1 27	Committee ends investigation	Ezr 10:17
460	445 444	Apr. to Apr.	13 2	20th year of Artaxerxes I	Ne 1:1
	445	I =Mar.-Apr.		Nehemiah approaches king	Ne 2:1
		Aug.(?)		Nehemiah arrives in Jerusalem	Ne 2:11
450		VI =Oct.	25 2	Completion of wall	Ne 6:15
		VII =Oct. to Nov.	8 5	Public assembly	Ne 7:73-8:1
440		VII =Oct.	15-22 22-28	Feast of Tabernacles	Ne 8:14
		VII =Oct.	24 30	Fast	Ne 9:1
430 B.C.	433 432	Apr. to Apr.	1 19	32nd year of Artaxerxes; Nehemiah's recall and return	Ne 5:14; 13:6

43The temple servants: /

the descendants of
Ziha, Hasupha, Tabbaoth,
44Keros, Siaha, Padon,
45Lebanah, Hagabah, Akkub,
46Hagab, Shalmai, Hanan,
47Giddel, Gahar, Reaiah,
48Rezin, Nekoda, Gazzam,
49Uzza, Paseah, Besai,
50Asnah, Meunim, Nephussim,
51Bakbuk, Hakupha, Harhur,
52Bazluth, Mehida, Harsha,
53Barkos, Sisera, Temah,
54Neziah and Hatipha

55The descendants of the servants of
Solomon:

the descendants of
Sotai, Hassophereth, Peruda,
56Jaala, Darkon, Giddel,
57Shephatiah, Hattil,
Pokereth-Hazzebaim and Ami

58The temple servants k and the
descendants of the servants of
Solomon   392

59The following came up from the

column reference notes:
2:43 /S 1Ch 9:2; Ne 11:21
2:58 kS 1Ch 9:2
2:59 /S Nu 1:18
2:61 mS 2Sa 17:27
2:62 nNu 3:10; 16:39-40
2:63 oLev 2:3,10
pS Ex 28:30
2:65 qS 2Sa 19:35
2:66 rIsa 66:20

towns of Tel Melah, Tel Harsha,
Kerub, Addon and Immer, but they
could not show that their families
were descended / from Israel:

60The descendants of
Delaiah, Tobiah and Nekoda 652

61And from among the priests:

The descendants of
Hobaiah, Hakkoz and Barzillai (a
man who had married a daughter
of Barzillai the Gileadite m and
was called by that name).

62These searched for their family
records, but they could not find them
and so were excluded from the priesthood n as unclean. 63The governor ordered them not to eat any of the most
sacred food o until there was a priest
ministering with the Urim and Thummim. p

64The whole company numbered
42,360, 65besides their 7,337 menservants and maidservants; and they
also had 200 men and women singers. q 66They had 736 horses, r 245

---

more comfortable way of life in exile.

2:41 *Asaph.* One of the three Levites appointed by David over the temple singers (1Ch 25:1; 2Ch 5:12; 35:15), whose duties are detailed in 1Ch 15:16-24.

2:42 *gatekeepers.* Usually Levites (1Ch 9:26; 2Ch 23:4; 35:15; Ne 12:25; 13:22). They are mentioned 16 times in Ezra-Nehemiah and 19 times in Chronicles. Their primary function was to tend the doors and gates of the temple (1Ch 9:17-27) and to perform other menial tasks (1Ch 9:28-32; 2Ch 31:14).

2:43-57 The temple servants and the descendants of Solomon's servants together numbered 392 (v. 58), which was more than the total of the Levites, singers and gatekeepers together (vv. 40-42).

2:46 *Hanan.* Means "(God) is gracious." The verb "to be gracious" and its derivatives are the components of numerous personal names in the OT—e.g., Johanan ("The LORD is gracious"; see 8:12), which has given us the English name John.

2:51 *Bakbuk.* Means "jar." It may have originally been a nickname for a fat man with a protruding belly. Cf. Jer 19:1,10, where the same Hebrew word is translated "jar"; see NIV text note on Jer 19:7.

2:53 *Barkos.* Means "son of Kos" (or Qos, an Edomite god).

2:55,58 *descendants of the servants of Solomon.* The phrase occurs only here and in Ne 7:57,60; 11:3. These may be the descendants of the Canaanites whom Solomon enslaved (1Ki 9:20-21).

2:55 *Hassophereth.* Probably means "the scribal office/function" and may have once been an official title.

2:59-63 Individuals who lacked evidence of their ancestry.

2:59 *towns.* Places in Mesopotamia where the Jews were settled by their Babylonian captors. *Tel Melah.* Means "mound of salt," possibly a mound on which salt had been scattered (see Jdg 9:45 and note). The Hebrew word *tel* designates a hill-like mound (see note on Jos 11:13) formed

by the remains of a ruined city. The Jewish exiles had been settled along the Kebar River (Eze 1:1), perhaps near Nippur, a city in southern Mesopotamia that was the stronghold of rebels. The Jews had probably been settled on the mounds of ruined cities that had been depopulated by the Babylonians.

2:61 *Barzillai.* Means "man of iron." For another Barzillai see 2Sa 17:27-29; 19:31-39; 1Ki 2:7.

2:63 *governor.* Probably either Sheshbazzar or Zerubbabel (see note on 1:8). *Urim and Thummim.* See note on Ex 28:30.

2:64 *42,360.* Considerably more than the sum of the other figures given:

Categories	Ezra	Nehemiah	1 Esdras
Men of Israel	24,144	25,406	25,947
Priests	4,289	4,289	5,288
Levites, singers, gatekeepers	341	360	341
Temple servants, descendants of Solomon's servants	392	392	372
Men of unproven origin	652	642	652
Totals	29,818	31,089	32,600

It is difficult to account for the difference of about 10,-000-12,000. The figure may refer to an unspecified 10,-000-12,000 women and/or children, and it doubtless includes the priests of unproven origin referred to in vv. 61-63. Some suggest that the groups explicitly counted were returnees from Judah and Benjamin, while the remainder were from other tribes.

2:65 *menservants and maidservants.* The ratio of servants to others (one to six) is relatively high. The fact that so many returned with their masters speaks highly of the benevolent treatment of servants by the Jews. *singers.* The men and women singers listed here may be secular singers who sang at social events such as weddings and funerals (2Ch 35:25), as distinct from the temple singers of v. 41, who were all male.

2:66 *horses.* Perhaps a donation from Cyrus for the nobility. *mules.* Often used by royalty and the wealthy (1Ki 1:33;

mules, 67435 camels and 6,720 donkeys.

68When they arrived at the house of the LORD in Jerusalem, some of the heads of the families s gave freewill offerings toward the rebuilding of the house of God on its site. 69According to their ability they gave to the treasury for this work 61,000 drachmas d of gold, 5,000 minas e of silver and 100 priestly garments.

70The priests, the Levites, the singers, the gatekeepers and the temple servants settled in their own towns, along with some of the other people, and the rest of the Israelites settled in their towns. t

Rebuilding the Altar

3 When the seventh month came and the Israelites had settled in their towns, u the people assembled v as one man in Jerusalem. 2Then Jeshua w son of Jozadak x and his fellow priests and Zerubbabel son of Shealtiel y and his associates began to build the altar of the God of Israel to sacrifice burnt offerings on it, in accordance with what is written in the Law of Moses z the man of God. 3Despite their fear a of the peoples around them, they built the altar on its foundation and sacrificed burnt offerings on it to the LORD, both the morning and evening sacrifices. b 4Then in accordance with what is written, they celebrated the Feast of Tabernacles c with the required number of burnt offerings prescribed for each day. 5After that, they presented the regular burnt offerings,

the New Moon d sacrifices and the sacrifices for all the appointed sacred feasts of the LORD, e as well as those brought as freewill offerings to the LORD. 6On the first day of the seventh month they began to offer burnt offerings to the LORD, though the foundation of the LORD's temple had not yet been laid.

Rebuilding the Temple

7Then they gave money to the masons and carpenters, f and gave food and drink and oil to the people of Sidon and Tyre, so that they would bring cedar logs g by sea from Lebanon h to Joppa, as authorized by Cyrus i king of Persia.

8In the second month j of the second year after their arrival at the house of God in Jerusalem, Zerubbabel k son of Shealtiel, Jeshua son of Jozadak and the rest of their brothers (the priests and the Levites and all who had returned from the captivity to Jerusalem) began the work, appointing Levites twenty l years of age and older to supervise the building of the house of the LORD. 9Jeshua m and his sons and brothers and Kadmiel and his sons (descendants of Hodaviah f) and the sons of Henadad and their sons and brothers—all Levites—joined together in supervising those working on the house of God.

10When the builders laid n the founda-

Cross references

2:68 sS Ex 25:2
2:70 tS ver 1;
S 1Ch 9:2;
Ne 11:3-4
3:1 uNe 7:73
vS Lev 23:24
3:2 wS Ezr 2:2
xHag 1:1;
Zec 6:11
y1Ch 3:17
zS Ex 20:24;
Dt 12:5-6
3:3 aEzr 4:4;
Da 9:25
bS Ex 29:39;
Nu 28:1-8
3:4 cS Ex 23:16;
Nu 29:12-38;
Ne 8:14-18;
Zec 14:16-19

3:5 dS Nu 28:14;
Col 2:16
eLev 23:1-44;
S Nu 29:39
3:7 f1Ch 22:15
gS 1Ch 14:1
hIsa 35:2; 60:13
iS Ezr 1:2-4
3:8 j1Ki 6:1
kZec 4:9
lS Nu 4:3
3:9 mEzr 2:40
3:10 nEzr 5:16;
6:3; Hag 2:15

d69 That is, about 1,100 pounds (about 500 kilograms)
e69 That is, about 3 tons (about 2.9 metric tons)
f9 Hebrew Yehudah, probably a variant of Hodaviah

Isa 66:20).

2:67 donkeys. Were used to carry loads, women or children. Sheep, goats and cattle are not mentioned. They would have slowed the caravan.
2:68 arrive . . . Jerusalem. For the route of the return from exile see inset to map No. 7 at the end of the Study Bible.
2:69 The parallel passage (Ne 7:70–72) gives a fuller description than the account in Ezra. In Ezra the gifts come from the heads of the families (v. 68), while in Nehemiah the gifts are credited to three sources: the governor, the heads of the families, and the rest of the people. drachmas. The drachma was a Greek silver coin. Some believe that the coin intended here was the Persian daric, a gold coin. minas. In the sexagesimal system (based on the number 60) that originated in Mesopotamia, there were 60 shekels in a mina and 60 minas in a talent. A shekel, which was about two-fifths of an ounce of silver, was the average wage for a month's work. Thus a mina would be the equivalent of five years' wages, and a talent would be 300 years' wages.
2:70 Later, Nehemiah (11:1–2) would be compelled to move people by lot to reinforce the population of Jerusalem.
3:1 seventh month. Tishri (September-October), about three months after the arrival of the exiles in Judah (in 537 B.C.). Tishri was one of the most sacred months of the Jewish year (see Lev 23:23–43 and notes).
3:2 Jeshua . . . Zerubbabel. The priest takes precedence over the civil leader in view of the nature of the occasion

(contrast 3:8; 4:3; 5:2; Hag 1:1).
3:4 Feast of Tabernacles. See Lev 23:33–43 and notes.
3:5 New Moon. See note on 1Sa 20:5. appointed sacred feasts. See note on Lev 23:2. freewill offerings. See note on 1:4. It is noteworthy that the restoration of the sacrifices preceded the erection of the temple itself.
3:7 cedar logs. As in the case of the first temple, the Phoenicians cooperated by sending timbers and workmen (1Ki 5:6–12).
3:8 second month. The same month (April-May) in which Solomon had begun his temple (1Ki 6:1). second year. Since the Jews probably returned to Judah in the spring of 537 B.C., the second year would be the spring of 536. twenty years. In earlier times the lower age limit for Levites was 30 (Nu 4:3) or 25 years (Nu 8:24). It was later reduced to 20 (1Ch 23:24,27; 2Ch 31:17), probably because there were so few Levites.
3:10 trumpets. Made of hammered silver (see Nu 10:2 and note). According to Josephus (Antiquities, 3.12.6—written c. A.D. 93), the trumpet was "in length a little short of a cubit; it is a narrow tube, slightly thicker than a flute." With the possible exception of their use at the coronation of Joash (2Ki 11:14; 2Ch 23:13), the trumpets were always blown by priests. They were most often used on joyous occasions, such as here and at the dedication of the rebuilt walls of Jerusalem (Ne 12:35; cf. 2Ch 5:13; Ps 98:6). cymbals. The Hebrew for this word occurs 13 times in the OT, all in Chronicles except

tion of the temple of the LORD, the priests in their vestments and with trumpets,[o] and the Levites (the sons of Asaph) with cymbals, took their places to praise[p] the LORD, as prescribed by David[q] king of Israel.[r] ¹¹With praise and thanksgiving they sang to the LORD:

"He is good;
his love to Israel endures forever."[s]

And all the people gave a great shout[t] of praise to the LORD, because the foundation[u] of the house of the LORD was laid. ¹²But many of the older priests and Levites and family heads, who had seen the former temple,[v] wept[w] aloud when they saw the foundation of this temple being laid, while many others shouted for joy. ¹³No one could distinguish the sound of the shouts of joy[x] from the sound of weeping, be-

cause the people made so much noise. And the sound was heard far away.

Opposition to the Rebuilding

4 When the enemies of Judah and Benjamin heard that the exiles were building[y] a temple for the LORD, the God of Israel, ²they came to Zerubbabel and to the heads of the families and said, "Let us help you build because, like you, we seek your God and have been sacrificing to him since the time of Esarhaddon[z] king of Assyria, who brought us here."[a]

³But Zerubbabel, Jeshua and the rest of the heads of the families of Israel answered, "You have no part with us in building a temple to our God. We alone will build it for the LORD, the God of Israel, as King Cyrus, the king of Persia, commanded us."[b]

Cross references (center column)

3:10 [o]S Nu 10:2; S 2Sa 6:5; 1Ch 16:6; 2Ch 5:13; Ne 12:35
[p]S 1Ch 25:1
[q]S 1Ch 6:31
[r]Zec 6:12
3:11 [s]1Ch 16:34, 41; S 2Ch 7:3; Ps 30:5; 107:1; 118:1; 138:8
[t]S Jos 6:5,10
[u]Hag 2:18; Zec 4:9; 8:9
3:12 [v]Hag 2:3,9
[w]Jer 31:9; 50:4
3:13 [x]Job 8:21; 33:26; Ps 27:6; 42:4; Isa 16:9; Jer 48:33
4:1 [y]Ne 2:20
4:2 [z]S 2Ki 17:24
[a]S 2Ki 17:41
4:3 [b]Ezr 1:1-4

Notes

here and Ne 12:27.
3:11 *sang.* May mean "sang responsively," referring to antiphonal singing by a choir divided into two groups. *He is good . . . endures forever.* See, e.g., 1Ch 16:34; 2Ch 5:13; Ps 100:5. *great shout.* See Jos 6:5,20; 1Sa 4:5; Ps 95:1.
3:13 *shouts of joy . . . sound of weeping.* The people of

Israel were accustomed to showing their emotions in visible and audible ways (10:1; Ne 1:4; 8:9). The same God who had permitted judgment had now brought them back and would enable them to complete the project. A Babylonian cornerstone reads: "I started the work weeping, I finished it rejoicing." Cf. Ps 126:5–6.

Zerubbabel's Temple

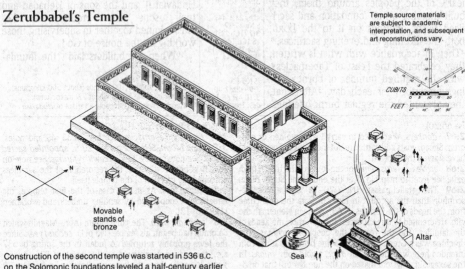

Temple source materials are subject to academic interpretation, and subsequent art reconstructions vary.

CUBITS
FEET

W N
S E

Movable stands of bronze

Altar

Sea

Construction of the second temple was started in 536 B.C. on the Solomonic foundations leveled a half-century earlier by the Babylonians. People who remembered the earlier temple wept at the comparison (Ezr 3:12). Not until 516 B.C., the 6th year of the Persian emperor Darius I (522-486), was the temple finally completed at the urging of Haggai and Zechariah (Ezr 6:13-15).

Archaeological evidence confirms that the Persian period in Palestine was a comparatively impoverished one in terms of material culture. Later Aramaic documents from Elephantine in Upper Egypt illustrate the official process of gaining permission to construct a Jewish place of worship, and the opposition engendered by the presence of various foes during this period.

Of the temple and its construction, little is known. Among the few contemporary buildings, the Persian palace at Lachish and the Tobiad monument at Iraq el-Amir may be compared in terms of technique.

Unlike the more famous structures razed in 586 B.C. and A.D. 70, the temple begun by Zerubbabel suffered no major hostile destruction, but was gradually repaired and reconstructed over a long period. Eventually it was replaced entirely by Herod's magnificent edifice.

© Hugh Claycombe 1986

4Then the peoples around them set out to discourage the people of Judah and make them afraid to go on building.g c 5They hired counselors to work against them and frustrate their plans during the entire reign of Cyrus king of Persia and down to the reign of Darius king of Persia.

Later Opposition Under Xerxes and Artaxerxes

6At the beginning of the reign of Xerxes,h d they lodged an accusation against the people of Judah and Jerusalem. e

7And in the days of Artaxerxesf king of Persia, Bishlam, Mithredath, Tabeel and the rest of his associates wrote a letter to Artaxerxes. The letter was written in Aramaic script and in the Aramaicg language.i,j

8Rehum the commanding officer and Shimshai the secretary wrote a letter against Jerusalem to Artaxerxes the king as follows:

9Rehum the commanding officer and Shimshai the secretary, together with the rest of their associatesh—the judges and officials over the men from Tripolis, Persia,k Erechi and Babylon, the Elamites of Susa,j 10and the other people whom the great and honorable Ashurbanipal¹k deported and settled in the city of Samaria and elsewhere in Trans-Euphrates. l

11(This is a copy of the letter they sent him.)

To King Artaxerxes,

From your servants, the men of Trans-Euphrates:

12The king should know that the Jews who came up to us from you

---

Cross references (center column):

4:4 cS Ezr 3:3
4:6 dEst 1:1; Da 9:1 eEst 3:13; 9:5
4:7 fEzr 7:1; Ne 2:1 g2Ki 18:26; Isa 36:11; Da 1:4; 2:4

4:9 hver 23; Ezr 5:6; 6:6,13 iGe 10:10 jNe 1:1; Est 1:2; Da 8:2 4:10 kS 2Ki 17:24 lver 17; Ne 4:2

g4 Or and troubled them as they built   h6 Hebrew Ahasuerus, a variant of Xerxes' Persian name   i7 Or written in Aramaic and translated   j7 The text of Ezra 4:8—6:18 is in Aramaic.   k9 Or officials, magistrates and governors over the men from   l10 Aramaic Osnappar, a variant of Ashurbanipal

---

4:1–23 A summary of various attempts to thwart the efforts of the Jews. In vv. 1–5 the author describes events in the reign of Cyrus (559–530 B.C.), in v. 6 the reign of Xerxes (486–465) and in vv. 7–23 the reign of Artaxerxes I (465–424). He then reverts in v. 24 to the time of Darius I (522–486), during whose reign the temple was completed (see 5:1–2; 6:13–15; Haggai; Zec 1:1–17; 4:9).
4:1 enemies. The people who offered their "help" (v. 2) were from Samaria. Judah and Benjamin. See notes on 1:5; 1Ki 12:21.
4:2 After the fall of Samaria in 722–721 B.C., the Assyrian kings brought in people from Mesopotamia and Aram. These people served their own gods but also took up the worship of the Lord as the god of the land (2Ki 17:24–41). Esarhaddon. See note on 2Ki 19:37.
4:4 peoples around them. Josephus (Antiquities, 11.2.1) singles out especially the Cutheans (see 2Ki 17:24,30). make them afraid. The Hebrew for this verb often describes the fear aroused in a battle situation (Jdg 20:41; 2Sa 4:1; 2Ch 32:18).
4:5 hired. Cf. the hiring of Balaam (Dt 23:4–5; Ne 13:2) and the hiring of a prophet to intimidate Nehemiah (Ne 6:12–13).
4:6 Xerxes. See the book of Esther. When Darius died in 486 B.C., Egypt rebelled, and Xerxes, the son of Darius, had to march west to suppress the revolt.
4:7 Artaxerxes. Three Persian kings bore this name: Artaxerxes I (465–424 B.C.), II (404–358) and III (358–338). The king here is Artaxerxes I. Mithredath. See 1:8 and note. Tabeel. An Aramaic name (see Isa 7:6 and note). wrote a letter. Near Eastern kings employed an elaborate system of informers and spies. Egyptian sources speak of the "ears and eyes" of Pharaoh. Sargon II of Assyria had agents in Urartu whom he ordered: "Write me whatever you see and hear." The King's Eye and the King's Ear were two officials who reported to the Persian monarch.
4:8—6:18 For this passage the author draws upon Aramaic documents; a further Aramaic section is 7:12–26.
4:8 commanding officer. An official who had the role of a chancellor or commissioner. Perhaps Rehum dictated, and Shimshai wrote the letter in Aramaic. (Alternatively, Shim-

shai may have been a high official rather than a scribe.) The letter would then be read in a Persian translation before the king (v. 18). According to Herodotus (3.128), royal scribes were attached to each governor to report directly to the Persian king.
4:9 associates. See vv. 17,23; 5:3,6; 6:6 ("fellow officials"); 6:13. One of the striking characteristics of Persian bureaucracy was that each responsibility was shared among colleagues. Erech. See note on Ge 10:10. Babylon. During the reign of the Assyrian king Ashurbanipal (669–627 B.C.), a major revolt had taken place (652–648), involving Shamash-Shum-Ukin, the brother of the king and the ruler over Babylonia. After a long siege Shamash-Shum-Ukin hurled himself into the flames. Doubtless these men of Babylon and the other cities mentioned were the descendants of the rebels, whom the Assyrians deported to the west. Susa. The major city of Elam (in southwest Iran). Because of Susa's part in the revolt, Ashurbanipal brutally destroyed it in 640 (two centuries before Rehum's letter).
4:10 Ashurbanipal. The last great Assyrian king, famed for his library at Nineveh. He is not named elsewhere in the Bible, but he is probably the king who freed Manasseh from exile (2Ch 33:11–13). deported. Ashurbanipal may be the unnamed Assyrian king who brought people to Samaria according to 2Ki 17:24. It is characteristic of such deportations that the descendants of populations that had been removed from their homelands nearly two centuries earlier should still stress their origins. Samaria. The murder of Amon king of Judah (642–640 B.C.; see 2Ki 21:23; 2Ch 33:24) was probably the result of an anti-Assyrian movement inspired by the revolt in Elam and Babylonia. The Assyrians may then have deported the rebellious Samaritans and replaced them with the rebellious Elamites and Babylonians. Trans-Euphrates. Lit. "beyond the River," i.e., the Euphrates River. From the Palestinian point of view the land "beyond the River" was Mesopotamia (Jos 24:2–3,14–15; 2Sa 10:16). From the Mesopotamian point of view the land "beyond the River" included the areas of Aram, Phoenicia and Palestine (1Ki 4:24). The Persians also called this area Athura.
4:12 restoring the walls and repairing the foundations. As Isaiah had foretold (Isa 58:13–14).

have gone to Jerusalem and are rebuilding that rebellious and wicked city. They are restoring the walls and repairing the foundations. *m*

¹³Furthermore, the king should know that if this city is built and its walls are restored, no more taxes, tribute or duty *n* will be paid, and the royal revenues will suffer. ¹⁴Now since we are under obligation to the palace and it is not proper for us to see the king dishonored, we are sending this message to inform the king, ¹⁵so that a search may be made in the archives *o* of your predecessors. In these records you will find that this city is a rebellious city, troublesome to kings and provinces, a place of rebellion from ancient times. That is why this city was destroyed. *p* ¹⁶We inform the king that if this city is built and its walls are restored, you will be left with nothing in Trans-Euphrates.

¹⁷The king sent this reply:

To Rehum the commanding officer, Shimshai the secretary and the rest of their associates living in Samaria and elsewhere in Trans-Euphrates: *q*

Greetings.

¹⁸The letter you sent us has been read and translated in my presence. ¹⁹I issued an order and a search was made, and it was found that this city

has a long history of revolt *r* against kings and has been a place of rebellion and sedition. ²⁰Jerusalem has had powerful kings ruling over the whole of Trans-Euphrates, *s* and taxes, tribute and duty were paid to them. ²¹Now issue an order to these men to stop work, so that this city will not be rebuilt until I so order. ²²Be careful not to neglect this matter. Why let this threat grow, to the detriment of the royal interests? *t*

²³As soon as the copy of the letter of King Artaxerxes was read to Rehum and Shimshai the secretary and their associates, *u* they went immediately to the Jews in Jerusalem and compelled them by force to stop.

²⁴Thus the work on the house of God in Jerusalem came to a standstill until the second year of the reign of Darius *v* king of Persia.

Tattenai's Letter to Darius

5 Now Haggai *w* the prophet and Zechariah *x* the prophet, a descendant of Iddo, prophesied *y* to the Jews in Judah and Jerusalem in the name of the God of Israel, who was over them. ²Then Zerubbabel *z* son of Shealtiel and Jeshua *a* son of Jozadak set to work *b* to rebuild the house of God in Jerusalem. And the prophets of God were with them, helping them.

³At that time Tattenai, *c* governor of

Cross-references (center column)

4:12 *m* Ezr 5:3,9
4:13 *n* Ezr 7:24; Ne 5:4
4:15 *o* Ezr 5:17; 6:1 *p* Est 3:8
4:17 *q* S ver 10

4:19 *r* S 2Ki 18:7
4:20 *s* Ge 15:18-21; S Ex 23:31; S Jos 1:4; S 1Ki 4:21; 1Ch 18:3; Ps 72:8-11
4:22 *t* Da 6:2
4:23 *u* S ver 9
4:24 *v* Ne 2:1-8; Da 9:25; Hag 1:1, 15; Zec 1:1
5:1 *w* Ezr 6:14; Hag 1:1,3,12; 2:1, 10,20 *x* Zec 1:1; 7:1
y Hag 1:14-2:9; Zec 4:9-10; 8:9
5:2 *z* S 1Ch 3:19; Hag 1:14; 2:21; Zec 4:6-10
a S Ezr 2:2 *b* ver 8; Hag 2:2-5
5:3 *c* Ezr 6:6

Study notes

4:13 Most of the gold and silver coins that came into Persia's treasury were melted down to be stored as bullion. Very little of the taxes returned to benefit the provinces.
4:14 *we are under obligation to the palace.* Lit. "we eat the salt of the palace." Salt was made a royal monopoly by the Ptolemies in Egypt, and perhaps by the Persians as well.
4:15 *archives.* See 5:17; 6:1; Est 2:23; 6:1-2. There were several repositories of such documents at the major capitals. These royal archives preserved documents for centuries. In the third century B.C. the Babylonian priest Berossus made use of the Babylonian Chronicles in his history of Babylon, which covered events from the Assyrian to the Hellenistic (beginning with Alexander's conquest of Babylon in 330 B.C.) eras.
4:18 *read.* Since the king probably could not read Aramaic, he would have had the document read to him. *translated.* From Aramaic into Persian (see NIV text notes on v. 7; Ne 8:8).
4:19 *rebellion.* There is some truth in the accusation. Jerusalem had rebelled against the Assyrians in 701 B.C. (2Ki 18:7) and against the Babylonians in 600 and 589 (2Ki 24:1,20).
4:21-23 As a result of the intervention of the provincial authorities, Artaxerxes I (see v. 11 and note on v. 7) ordered that the Jews stop rebuilding the walls of Jerusalem (see note on Ne 1:3). The events of vv. 7-23 probably occurred prior to 445 B.C. The forcible destruction of these recently rebuilt

walls rather than the destruction by Nebuchadnezzar would then be the basis of the report made to Nehemiah (Ne 1:3).
4:24 After this long digression describing the opposition to Jewish efforts, the writer returns to his original subject of the rebuilding of the temple (vv. 1-5). *second year of the reign of Darius.* According to Persian reckoning, the second regnal year of Darius I began on Nisan 1 (Apr. 3), 520 B.C., and lasted until Feb. 21, 519. In that year the prophet Haggai (Hag 1:1-5) exhorted Zerubbabel to begin rebuilding the temple on the first day of the sixth month (Aug. 29). Work began on the temple on the 24th day of the month, Sept. 21 (Hag 1:15). During his first two years, Darius had to establish his right to the throne by fighting numerous rebels, as recounted in his famous Behistun (Bisitun) inscription. It was only after the stabilization of the Persian empire that efforts to rebuild the temple could be permitted.
5:1 *Haggai . . . Zechariah.* Beginning on Aug. 29, 520 B.C. (Hag 1:1), and continuing until Dec. 18 (Hag 2:1,10,20), the prophet Haggai delivered a series of messages to stir up the people to resume work on the temple. Two months after Haggai's first speech, Zechariah joined him (Zec 1:1).
5:2 *Zerubbabel.* A Babylonian name meaning "offspring of Babylon," referring to his birth in exile. He was the son of Shealtiel and the grandson of Jehoiachin (1Ch 3:17), the next-to-last king of Judah. Zerubbabel was the last of the Davidic line to be entrusted with political authority by the occupying powers. He was also an ancestor of Jesus (Mt 1:12-13; Lk 3:27). *Jeshua.* See note on 2:2.

Trans-Euphrates, and Shethar-Bozenai[d] and their associates went to them and asked, "Who authorized you to rebuild this temple and restore this structure?"[e] [4]They also asked, "What are the names of the men constructing this building?"[m] [5]But the eye of their God[f] was watching over the elders of the Jews, and they were not stopped until a report could go to Darius and his written reply be received.

[6]This is a copy of the letter that Tattenai, governor of Trans-Euphrates, and Shethar-Bozenai and their associates, the officials of Trans-Euphrates, sent to King Darius. [7]The report they sent him read as follows:

To King Darius:

Cordial greetings.

[8]The king should know that we went to the district of Judah, to the temple of the great God. The people are building it with large stones and placing the timbers in the walls. The work[g] is being carried on with diligence and is making rapid progress under their direction.

[9]We questioned the elders and asked them, "Who authorized you to rebuild this temple and restore this structure?"[h] [10]We also asked them their names, so that we could write down the names of their leaders for your information.

[11]This is the answer they gave us:

"We are the servants of the God of heaven and earth, and we are rebuilding the temple[i] that was built many years ago, one that a great king of Israel built and finished. [12]But because our fathers angered[j] the God of heaven, he handed them over to Nebuchadnezzar the Chaldean, king

of Babylon, who destroyed this temple and deported the people to Babylon.[k]

[13]"However, in the first year of Cyrus king of Babylon, King Cyrus issued a decree[l] to rebuild this house of God. [14]He even removed from the temple[n] of Babylon the gold and silver articles of the house of God, which Nebuchadnezzar had taken from the temple in Jerusalem and brought to the temple[n] in Babylon.[m]

"Then King Cyrus gave them to a man named Sheshbazzar,[n] whom he had appointed governor, [15]and he told him, 'Take these articles and go and deposit them in the temple in Jerusalem. And rebuild the house of God on its site.' [16]So this Sheshbazzar came and laid the foundations of the house of God[o] in Jerusalem. From that day to the present it has been under construction but is not yet finished."

[17]Now if it pleases the king, let a search be made in the royal archives[p] of Babylon to see if King Cyrus did in fact issue a decree to rebuild this house of God in Jerusalem. Then let the king send us his decision in this matter.

The Decree of Darius

6 King Darius then issued an order, and they searched in the archives[q] stored in the treasury at Babylon. [2]A scroll was found in the citadel of Ecbatana in the province of Media, and this was written on it:

Memorandum:

[3]In the first year of King Cyrus, the

Cross references (center column):

5:3 *d*Ezr 6:6
*e*S Ezr 4:12
5:5 *f*S 2Ki 25:28; Ezr 7:6,9,28; 8:18,22,31; Ne 2:8,18; Ps 33:18; Isa 66:14
5:8 *g*S ver 2
5:9 *h*S Ezr 4:12
5:11 *i*1Ki 6:1; 2Ch 3:1-2
5:12 *j*S 2Ch 36:16
*k*S Dt 21:10; S 28:36; S 2Ki 24:1; S Jer 1:3
5:13 *l*S Ezr 1:2-4
5:14 *m*Ezr 1:7
*n*S 1Ch 3:18
5:16 *o*S Ezr 3:10
5:17 *p*S Ezr 4:15
6:1 *q*S Ezr 4:15

---

m4 See Septuagint; Aramaic 4We told them the names of the men constructing this building.   *n14 Or palace*

5:3   *Tattenai.* Probably a Babylonian name. *Shethar-Bozenai.* Perhaps a Persian official.

5:5   *not stopped.* The Persian governor gave the Jews the benefit of the doubt by not stopping the work while the inquiry was proceeding.

5:6–7   *sent to King Darius . . . sent him.* Texts found in the royal city of Persepolis vividly confirm that such inquiries were sent directly to the king himself, revealing the close attention he paid to minute details.

5:8   *timbers.* May refer to interior paneling (1Ki 6:15–18) or to logs alternating with the brick or stone layers in the walls (see note on 6:4).

5:11   *great king of Israel.* According to 1Ki 6:1 Solomon began building the temple in the fourth year of his reign (966 B.C.). The project lasted seven years (1Ki 6:38).

5:12   *Chaldean.* The Chaldeans were the inhabitants of the southern regions of Mesopotamia who established the Neo-Babylonian empire (612–539 B.C.). Their origins are obscure. In the late seventh century B.C. the Chaldeans, led by

Nebuchadnezzar's father Nabopolassar, overthrew the Assyrians.

5:14   *Sheshbazzar . . . governor.* See note on 1:8.

6:1   *archives . . . in the treasury at Babylon.* Many documents have also been found in the so-called "treasury" area of Persepolis (see map on p. 573).

6:2   *Ecbatana.* One of the four capitals (along with Babylon, Persepolis and Susa) of the Persian empire. Located in what is today the Iranian city of Hamadan, its remains have not yet been excavated. This is the only reference to the site in the OT, though there are numerous references in the Apocryphal books (Judith 1:1–4; Tobit 3:7; 7–1; 14:12–14; 2 Maccabees 9:3). *Media.* The homeland of the Medes in northwestern Iran. The Medes were an Indo-European tribe related to the Persians. After the rise of Cyrus in 550 B.C., they became subordinate to the Persians. The name of the area was retained as late as the NT era (Ac 2:9).

6:3–5   Compare this Aramaic memorandum of the decree of Cyrus with the Hebrew version in 1:2–4. The Aramaic is

king issued a decree concerning the temple of God in Jerusalem:

Let the temple be rebuilt as a place to present sacrifices, and let its foundations be laid.[r] It is to be ninety feet[o] high and ninety feet wide, [4]with three courses[s] of large stones and one of timbers. The costs are to be paid by the royal treasury.[t] [5]Also, the gold[u] and silver articles of the house of God, which Nebuchadnezzar took from the temple in Jerusalem and brought to Babylon, are to be returned to their places in the temple in Jerusalem; they are to be deposited in the house of God.[v]

[6]Now then, Tattenai,[w] governor of Trans-Euphrates, and Shethar-Bozenai[x] and you, their fellow officials of that province, stay away from there. [7]Do not interfere with the work on this temple of God. Let the governor of the Jews and the Jewish elders rebuild this house of God on its site.

[8]Moreover, I hereby decree what you are to do for these elders of the Jews in the construction of this house of God:

The expenses of these men are to be fully paid out of the royal treasury,[y] from the revenues[z] of Trans-Euphrates, so that the work will not stop. [9]Whatever is needed—young bulls, rams, male lambs for burnt offerings[a] to the God of heaven, and wheat, salt, wine and oil, as requested by the priests in Jerusalem—must be given them daily without fail, [10]so that they may offer sacrifices pleasing to the God of heaven and pray for the well-being of the king and his sons.[b]

[11]Furthermore, I decree that if anyone changes this edict, a beam is to be pulled from his house and he is to be lifted up and impaled[c] on it. And for this crime his house is to be made a pile of rubble.[d] [12]May God, who has caused his Name to dwell there,[e] overthrow any king or people who lifts a hand to change this decree or to destroy this temple in Jerusalem.

I Darius[f] have decreed it. Let it be carried out with diligence.

Completion and Dedication of the Temple

[13]Then, because of the decree King Darius had sent, Tattenai, governor of Trans-Euphrates, and Shethar-Bozenai and their associates[g] carried it out with dili-

---

6:3 [r]S Ezr 3:10; Hag 2:3
6:4 [s]S 1Ki 6:36 [t]ver 8; Ezr 7:20
6:5 [u]S 1Ch 29:2 [v]S Ezr 1:7
6:6 [w]Ezr 5:3 [x]Ezr 5:3
6:8 [y]S ver 4 [z]S 1Sa 9:20
6:9 [a]Lev 1:3,10
6:10 [b]Ezr 7:23; 1Ti 2:1-2
6:11 [c]S Dt 21:22-23; Est 2:23; 5:14; 9:14 [d]Ezr 7:26; Da 2:5; 3:29
6:12 [e]S Ex 20:24; S Dt 12:5; S 2Ch 6:2 [f]ver 14
6:13 [g]S Ezr 4:9

[o]3 Aramaic *sixty cubits* (about 27 meters)

---

written in a more sober administrative style without any reference to the Lord (Yahweh). A similar memorandum dealing with permission to rebuild the Jewish temple at Elephantine in Upper Egypt was found among fifth-century B.C. Aramaic papyri recovered at that site.

6:3 *ninety feet high and ninety feet wide.* These dimensions, which contrast with those of Solomon's temple (see NIV text note on 1Ki 6:2), are probably not specifications of the temple as built but of the outer limits of a building the Persians were willing to subsidize. The second temple was not as grandiose as the first (3:12; Hag 2:3).

6:4 *large stones . . . timbers.* See 5:8. The same kind of construction is mentioned in 1Ki 6:36; 7:12. Such a design was possibly intended to cushion the building against earthquake shocks. *costs are to be paid by the royal treasury.* In 1973 archaeologists discovered at Xanthos in southwest Turkey a cult foundation charter from the late Persian period that provides some striking parallels with this decree of Cyrus. As in Ezra, amounts of sacrifices, names of priests and the responsibility for the upkeep of the cult are specified. The Persian king seems to have known details of the cult.

6:8 *paid out of the royal treasury.* It was a consistent policy of Persian kings to help restore sanctuaries in their empire. For example, a memorandum concerning the rebuilding of the Jewish temple at Elephantine was written by the Persian governors of Judah and Samaria. Also from non-Biblical sources we learn that Cyrus repaired temples at Uruk (Erech) and Ur. Cambyses, successor to Cyrus, gave funds for the temple at Sais in Egypt. The temple of Amun in the Khargah Oasis was rebuilt by order of Darius.

6:9 That the Persian monarchs were interested in the details of foreign cults is shown clearly by the ordinances of Cambyses and Darius I, regulating the temples and priests in Egypt. On the authority of Darius II (423–404 B.C.) a letter was written to the Jews at Elephantine concerning the keeping of the Feast of Unleavened Bread.

6:10 *pray for the well-being of the king and his sons.* In the inscription on the Cyrus Cylinder (made of baked clay), the king asks: "May all the gods whom I have resettled in their sacred cities ask Bel and Nebo daily for a long life for me." The Jews of Elephantine offered to pray for the Persian governor of Judah. The daily synagogue services included a prayer for the royal family (cf. 1Ti 2:1–2).

6:11 *if anyone changes this edict.* It was customary at the end of decrees and treaties to append a long list of curses against anyone who might disregard them. *impaled.* According to Herodotus (3.159), Darius I impaled 3,000 Babylonians when he took the city of Babylon. See NIV text note on Est 2:23.

6:12 *May God . . . overthrow any king or people.* At the end of his famous Behistun (Bisitun) inscription Darius I warned: "If you see this inscription or these sculptures, and destroy them and do not protect them as long as you have strength, may Ahuramazda strike you, and may you not have a family, and what you do . . . may Ahuramazda utterly destroy." *caused his Name to dwell.* See note on Dt 12:5.

6:13–14 Work on the temple had made little progress not only because of opposition but also because of the preoccupation of the returnees with their own homes (Hag 1:2–9). Because they had placed their own interests first, God sent them famine as a judgment (Hag 1:5–6,10–11). Spurred by the preaching of Haggai and Zechariah, and under the leadership of Zerubbabel and Jeshua, a new effort was begun (Hag 1:12–15).

offerings of the people and priests for the temple of their God in Jerusalem. *p* [17]With this money be sure to buy bulls, rams and male lambs, *q* together with their grain offerings and drink offerings, *r* and sacrifice *s* them on the altar of the temple of your God in Jerusalem.

[18]You and your brother Jews may then do whatever seems best with the rest of the silver and gold, in accordance with the will of your God. [19]Deliver *t* to the God of Jerusalem all the articles entrusted to you for worship in the temple of your God. [20]And anything else needed for the temple of your God that you may have occasion to supply, you may provide from the royal treasury. *u*

[21]Now I, King Artaxerxes, order all the treasurers of Trans-Euphrates to provide with diligence whatever Ezra the priest, a teacher of the Law of the God of heaven, may ask of you— [22]up to a hundred talents *q* of silver, a hundred cors *r* of wheat, a hundred baths *s* of wine, a hundred baths *s* of olive oil, and salt without limit. [23]Whatever the God of heaven has prescribed, let it be done with diligence for the temple of the God of heaven. Why should there be wrath against the realm of the king and of his sons? *v* [24]You are also to know that you have no authority to impose taxes, tribute or duty *w* on any of the

priests, Levites, singers, gatekeepers, temple servants or other workers at this house of God. *x*

[25]And you, Ezra, in accordance with the wisdom of your God, which you possess, appoint *y* magistrates and judges to administer justice to all the people of Trans-Euphrates—all who know the laws of your God. And you are to teach *z* any who do not know them. [26]Whoever does not obey the law of your God and the law of the king must surely be punished by death, banishment, confiscation of property, or imprisonment. *a*

[27]Praise be to the LORD, the God of our fathers, who has put it into the king's heart *b* to bring honor *c* to the house of the LORD in Jerusalem in this way [28]and who has extended his good favor *d* to me before the king and his advisers and all the king's powerful officials. Because the hand of the LORD my God was on me, *e* I took courage and gathered leading men from Israel to go up with me.

List of the Family Heads Returning With Ezra

8 These are the family heads and those registered with them who came up with me from Babylon during the reign of King Artaxerxes: *f*

Cross references (center column)

7:16 *p* Zec 6:10
7:17 *q* S 2Ki 3:4
r Nu 15:5-12
s Dt 12:5-11
7:19 *t* Ezr 5:14; Jer 27:22
7:20 *u* S Ezr 6:4
7:23 *v* S Ezr 6:10
7:24 *w* S Ezr 4:13

x Ezr 8:36
7:25 *y* S Ex 18:21, 26 *z* S Lev 10:11
7:26 *a* S Ezr 6:11
7:27 *b* S Ezr 1:1
c S 1Ch 29:12
7:28
d S 2Ki 25:28
e S Ezr 5:5
8:1 *f* Ezr 7:7

*q*22 That is, about 3 3/4 tons (about 3.4 metric tons)
*r*22 That is, probably about 600 bushels (about 22 kiloliters)   *s*22 That is, probably about 600 gallons (about 2.2 kiloliters)

7:20 *provide from the royal treasury.* Texts from the treasury at Persepolis also record the disbursement of supplies and funds from the royal purse.

7:22 *hundred talents.* An enormous amount (see NIV text note). *hundred cors.* The total was relatively small (see NIV text note). The wheat would be used in grain offerings. *salt without limit.* See note on 4:14. A close parallel is the benefaction of Antiochus III as recorded by Josephus (*Antiquities*, 12.3.3): "In the first place we have decided, on account of their piety, to furnish for their sacrifices an allowance of sacrificial animals, wine, oil and frankincense to the value of 20,000 pieces of silver, and sacred artabae of fine flour in accordance with their native law, and 1,460 medimni of wheat and 375 medimni of salt."

7:23 *wrath against the realm of the king.* Egypt had revolted against the Persians in 460 B.C. and had expelled the Persians with the help of the Athenians in 459. In 458, when Ezra traveled to Jerusalem, the Persians were involved in suppressing this revolt. *his sons.* We do not know how many sons the king had at this time, but he ultimately had 18, according to Ctesias (a Greek physician who wrote an extensive history of Persia).

7:24 *no . . . taxes . . . or duty on any of the priests . . . temple servants.* Priests and other temple personnel were often given exemptions from enforced labor or taxes. A close parallel is found in the Gadates Inscription of Darius I to a governor in western Turkey, granting exemptions to the

priests of Apollo. Antiochus III granted similar exemptions to the Jews: "The priests, the scribes of the temple and the temple singers shall be relieved from the poll tax, the crown tax and the salt tax that they pay" (Josephus, *Antiquities*, 12.3.3).

7:26 *Whoever does not obey . . . must surely be punished.* The extensive powers given to Ezra are striking and extend to secular fields. Perhaps the implementation of these provisions involved Ezra in a great deal of traveling, which would explain the silence about his activities between his arrival and the arrival of Nehemiah 13 years later. A close parallel to the king's commission of Ezra may be found in an earlier commission by Darius I, who sent Udjahorresenet, a priest and scholar, back to Egypt. He ordered the codification of the Egyptian laws by the chief men of Egypt—a task that took from 518 to 503 B.C.

7:28 *me.* The first occurrence of the first person for Ezra—a trait that characterizes the "Ezra Memoirs," which begin in v. 27 and continue to the end of ch. 9.

8:1–21 In vv. 1–14 Ezra lists those who accompanied him in his return from Mesopotamia, including the descendants of 15 individuals. The figures of the men given total 1,496 in addition to the individuals named. There were also women and children (see note on v. 21). About 40 Levites (vv. 18–19) are also included, as are 220 "temple servants" (v. 20).

²of the descendants of Phinehas, Gershom;

of the descendants of Ithamar, Daniel;

of the descendants of David, Hattush ³of the descendants of Shecaniah; *g*

of the descendants of Parosh, *h* Zechariah, and with him were registered 150 men;

⁴of the descendants of Pahath-Moab, *i* Eliehoenai son of Zerahiah, and with him 200 men;

⁵of the descendants of Zattu, *t* Shecaniah son of Jahaziel, and with him 300 men;

⁶of the descendants of Adin, *j* Ebed son of Jonathan, and with him 50 men;

⁷of the descendants of Elam, Jeshaiah son of Athaliah, and with him 70 men;

⁸of the descendants of Shephatiah, Zebadiah son of Michael, and with him 80 men;

⁹of the descendants of Joab, Obadiah son of Jehiel, and with him 218 men;

¹⁰of the descendants of Bani, *u* Shelomith son of Josiphiah, and with him 160 men;

¹¹of the descendants of Bebai, Zechariah son of Bebai, and with him 28 men;

¹²of the descendants of Azgad, Johanan son of Hakkatan, and with him 110 men;

¹³of the descendants of Adonikam, *k* the last ones, whose names were Eliphelet, Jeuel and Shemaiah, and with them 60 men;

¹⁴of the descendants of Bigvai, Uthai and Zaccur, and with them 70 men.

The Return to Jerusalem

¹⁵I assembled them at the canal that flows toward Ahava, *l* and we camped there three days. When I checked among the people and the priests, I found no Levites *m* there. ¹⁶So I summoned Eliezer, Ariel, Shemaiah, Elnathan, Jarib, Elnathan, Nathan, Zechariah and Meshullam, who were leaders, and Joiarib and Elnathan, who were men of learning, ¹⁷and I sent them to Iddo, the leader in Casiphia. I told them what to say to Iddo and his kinsmen, the temple servants *n* in Casiphia, so that they might bring attendants to us for the house of our God. ¹⁸Because the gracious hand of our God was on us, *o* they brought us Sherebiah, *p* a capable man, from the descendants of Mahli son of Levi, the son of Israel, and Sherebiah's sons and brothers, 18 men; ¹⁹and Hashabiah, together with Jeshaiah from the descendants of Merari, and his brothers and nephews, 20 men. ²⁰They also brought 220 of the temple servants *q*—a body that David and the

---

Cross references:
8:3 *g* 1Ch 3:22
h S Ezr 2:3
8:4 *i* Ezr 2:6
8:6 *j* Ezr 2:15;
Ne 7:20; 10:16
8:13 *k* Ezr 2:13
8:15 *l* ver 21,31
m S Ezr 2:40
8:17 *n* Ezr 2:43
8:18 *o* S Ezr 5:5
p ver 24
8:20 *q* S 1Ch 9:2

t 5 Some Septuagint manuscripts (also 1 Esdras 8:32); Hebrew does not have *Zattu.* *u 10* Some Septuagint manuscripts (also 1 Esdras 8:36); Hebrew does not have *Bani.*

8:2 *Gershom.* For the meaning of the name see NIV text note on Ex 2:22, where we learn that Gershom was also the name of the firstborn son of Moses and Zipporah. *Ithamar.* Also the name of the fourth son of Aaron (Ex 6:23).

8:3 *Zechariah.* Cf. v. 11. The name means "The Lord remembers"; it was the name of about 30 individuals mentioned in the Bible, including both the OT prophet and the father of John the Baptist (Lk 1:5–67).

8:4 *Eliehoenai.* Means "On the Lord are my eyes"; the name occurs only here and in 1Ch 26:3. Cf. Ps 25:15.

8:6 *Ebed.* May be a shortened form of Obadiah (cf. v. 9), meaning "servant of the Lord." *Jonathan.* Means "The Lord gives"; it was the name of 15 OT individuals.

8:7 *Athaliah.* Also the name of a famous queen, daughter of Ahab (2Ki 11).

8:8 *Michael.* Means "Who is like God?" It was the name of ten other Biblical personages, including the archangel (Da 10:13; Jude 9; Rev 12:7).

8:10 *Shelomith.* Although it is a feminine form (see also note on SS 6:13), it is often a man's name, as here. The Greek equivalent is Salome.

8:12 *Azgad.* See note on 2:12. *Johanan.* See note on 2:46. *Hakkatan.* Means "the little one"; the name occurs only here.

8:15 *canal that flows toward Ahava.* Probably flows into either the Euphrates or the Tigris (the Kebar "River" in Eze 1:1 was also a canal). *three days.* Perhaps from the 9th to the

12th day of Nisan; the journey began on the 12th (see v. 31). *no Levites.* Since they were entrusted with many menial tasks, they may have found a more comfortable way of life in exile. A rabbinic midrash (comment) on Ps 137 relates the legend that Levites were in the caravan but that they were not qualified to officiate because when Nebuchadnezzar had ordered them to sing for him the songs of Zion, "they refused and bit off the ends of their fingers, so that they could not play on the harps." In the Hellenistic era (following Alexander's conquest of Palestine in 333 b.c.) the role of the Levites declined sharply, though the "Temple Scroll" among the Dead Sea Scrolls from Qumran (see "The Time between the Testaments," p. 1431) assigns important roles to them.

8:16 *Ariel.* Means "lion of God" or "altar hearth" (see note on Isa 29:1,2,7). It occurs only here as a personal name. *Meshullam.* Perhaps means "rewarded." Some assume that he is the same as the Meshullam who opposed the marriage reforms (10:15). *men of learning.* Lit. "those who cause to understand." The Hebrew for this phrase is translated "teacher" in 1Ch 25:8 and "instructed" or "instructing" in 2Ch 35:3; Ne 8:7,9.

8:17 *Casiphia.* Some have located it at the site that was later to become the Parthian capital of Ctesiphon on the Tigris River, north of Babylon.

8:18–19 *18 men . . . 20 men.* Only about 40 Levites from two families were found who were willing to join Ezra's caravan.

officials had established to assist the Levites. All were registered by name.

21There, by the Ahava Canal,r I proclaimed a fast, so that we might humble ourselves before our God and ask him for a safe journeys for us and our children, with all our possessions. 22I was ashamed to ask the king for soldierst and horsemen to protect us from enemies on the road, because we had told the king, "The gracious hand of our God is on everyoneu who looks to him, but his great anger is against all who forsake him.v" 23So we fastedw and petitioned our God about this, and he answered our prayer.

24Then I set apart twelve of the leading priests, together with Sherebiah,x Hashabiah and ten of their brothers, 25and I weighed outy to them the offering of silver and gold and the articles that the king, his advisers, his officials and all Israel present there had donated for the house of our God. 26I weighed out to them 650 talentsv of silver, silver articles weighing 100 talents,w 100 talentsw of gold, 2720 bowls of gold valued at 1,000 darics,x and two fine articles of polished bronze, as precious as gold.

28I said to them, "You as well as these articles are consecrated to the LORD.z The silver and gold are a freewill offering to the LORD, the God of your fathers. 29Guard them carefully until you weigh them out in the chambers of the house of the LORD in Jerusalem before the leading priests and the Levites and the family heads of Israel." 30Then the priests and Levites received the silver and gold and sacred articles that had

been weighed out to be taken to the house of our God in Jerusalem.

31On the twelfth day of the first month we set out from the Ahava Canala to go to Jerusalem. The hand of our God was on us,b and he protected us from enemies and bandits along the way. 32So we arrived in Jerusalem, where we rested three days.c

33On the fourth day, in the house of our God, we weighed outd the silver and gold and the sacred articles into the hands of Meremothe son of Uriah, the priest. Eleazar son of Phinehas was with him, and so were the Levites Jozabadf son of Jeshua and Noadiah son of Binnui.g 34Everything was accounted for by number and weight, and the entire weight was recorded at that time.

35Then the exiles who had returned from captivity sacrificed burnt offerings to the God of Israel: twelve bullsh for all Israel,i ninety-six rams, seventy-seven male lambs and, as a sin offering, twelve male goats.j All this was a burnt offering to the LORD. 36They also delivered the king's ordersk to the royal satraps and to the governors of Trans-Euphrates,l who then gave assistance to the people and to the house of God.m

Ezra's Prayer About Intermarriage

9 After these things had been done, the leaders came to me and said, "The people of Israel, including the priests and

Cross references (center column)

8:21 rS ver 15 sPs 5:8; 27:11; 107:7
8:22 tNe 2:9; Jer 41:16 uS Ezr 5:5 vS Dt 31:17
8:23 wS 2Ch 20:3; Ac 14:23
8:24 xver 18
8:25 yver 33
8:28 zS Lev 21:6; 22:2-3
8:31 aS ver 15 bS Ezr 5:5
8:32 cS Ge 40:13
8:33 dver 25 eNe 3:4,21 fNe 11:16 gNe 3:24
8:35 hS Lev 1:3 iS 2Ch 29:24 jS 2Ch 29:21; S 30:24
8:36 kEzr 7:21-24 lNe 2:7 mEst 9:3

v26 That is, about 25 tons (about 22 metric tons)
w26 That is, about 3 3/4 tons (about 3.4 metric tons)
x27 That is, about 19 pounds (about 8.5 kilograms)

8:20 *temple servants.* See note on 2:43–57.
8:21 *safe journey.* Lit. "straight way"—unimpeded by obstacles and dangers (see v. 31; cf. Pr 3:6). *children.* Elsewhere (e.g., Ge 43:8) the term also includes the elderly and the women. *possessions.* The vast treasures they were carrying with them offered a tempting bait for robbers.
8:22 *I was ashamed.* Scripture speaks often of unholy shame (Jer 48:13; 49:23; Mic 3:7) and on occasion, as here, of holy shame. Ezra was quick to blush with such shame (see also 9:6). Having proclaimed his faith in God's ability to protect the caravan, he was embarrassed to ask for human protection. Grave dangers faced travelers going the great distance between Mesopotamia and Palestine. Some 13 years later Nehemiah was accompanied by an armed escort. The difference, however, does not mean that Nehemiah was a man of lesser faith (see note on Ne 2:9).
8:23 *fasted and petitioned.* For the association of fasting and prayer see Ne 1:4; Da 9:3; Mt 17:21 (NIV text note); Ac 14:23.
8:25 *offering.* Lit. "what is lifted," i.e., dedicated (cf. Ex 25:2; 35:5; Lev 7:14). In Dt 12:6 the Hebrew for this word is translated "special gifts."
8:26 *650 talents . . . 100 talents.* Enormous sums, worth millions of dollars today. See also note on 7:22.
8:27 *darics.* See NIV text note. The word occurs only here

and in 1Ch 29:7 (but see note on 2:69). *polished.* This kind of bronze may have been orichalc, a bright yellow (the Hebrew for "yellow" in Lev 13:30,32,36 is related to the Hebrew for "polished" here) alloy of copper, which resembles gold and was highly prized in ancient times.
8:31 *twelfth day.* See notes on v. 15; 7:7–9.
8:32 *rested three days.* Nehemiah also took a similar rest period after his arrival in Jerusalem (Ne 2:11).
8:33 *Meremoth son of Uriah.* Probably the same as the man who repaired two sections of the wall (Ne 3:4,21).
8:34 *recorded.* According to Babylonian practice (e.g., in the law code of Hammurapi) almost every transaction, including sales and marriages, had to be recorded in writing. Ezra may have had to send back to Artaxerxes a signed certification of the delivery of the treasures.
8:35 *sacrificed.* Except for the identical number of male goats, the offerings here were far fewer than those presented by the returnees under Zerubbabel (6:17), who brought with him a far greater number of families.
9:1 *After these things had been done . . . have not kept themselves separate.* Ezra had reached Jerusalem in the fifth month (7:9). The measures dealing with the problem of intermarriage were announced in the ninth month (10:9), or four months after his arrival. Those who brought Ezra's attention to the problem were probably the ordinary mem-

the Levites, have not kept themselves separate[n] from the neighboring peoples with their detestable practices, like those of the Canaanites, Hittites, Perizzites, Jebusites,[o] Ammonites,[p] Moabites,[q] Egyptians and Amorites.[r] [2]They have taken some of their daughters[s] as wives for themselves and their sons, and have mingled[t] the holy race[u] with the peoples around them. And the leaders and officials have led the way in this unfaithfulness."[v]

[3]When I heard this, I tore[w] my tunic and cloak, pulled hair from my head and beard and sat down appalled.[x] [4]Then everyone who trembled[y] at the words of the God of Israel gathered around me because of this unfaithfulness of the exiles. And I sat there appalled[z] until the evening sacrifice.

[5]Then, at the evening sacrifice,[a] I rose from my self-abasement, with my tunic and cloak torn, and fell on my knees with my hands[b] spread out to the LORD my God [6]and prayed:

"O my God, I am too ashamed[c] and disgraced to lift up my face to you, my God, because our sins are higher than our heads and our guilt has reached to the heavens.[d] [7]From the days of our forefathers[e] until now, our guilt has been great. Because of our sins, we and our kings and our priests have been subjected to the sword[f] and captivity,[g] to pillage and humiliation[h] at the hand of foreign kings, as it is today.

[8]"But now, for a brief moment, the LORD our God has been gracious[i] in leaving us a remnant[j] and giving us a firm place[k] in his sanctuary, and so our God gives light to our eyes[l] and a little relief in our bondage. [9]Though we are slaves,[m] our God has not deserted us in our bondage. He has shown us kindness[n] in the sight of the

---

9:1 [n]S Ezr 6:21
[o]S Ge 10:16;
S Jos 15:8
[p]Ge 19:38
[q]S Ge 19:37
[r]Ex 13:5; 23:28;
Dt 20:17;
S Jos 3:10;
S Jdg 3:5;
1Ki 9:20;
S 2Ch 8:7; Ne 9:8
9:2 [s]S Ex 34:16;
S Ru 1:4
[t]Ps 106:35
[u]S Ex 22:31;
S Lev 27:30;
S Dt 14:2
[v]Ezr 10:2
9:3 [w]S Nu 14:6
[x]S Ex 32:19;
S 33:4
9:4 [y]Ezr 10:3;
Ps 119:120;
Isa 66:2,5
[z]Ne 1:4;
Ps 119:136;
Da 10:2
9:5 [a]S Ex 29:41
[b]Ne 8:6; Ps 28:2;
134:2

9:6 [c]Jer 31:19
[d]S 2Ch 28:9;
Job 42:6; Ps 38:4;
Isa 59:12;
Jer 3:25; 14:20;
Rev 18:5
9:7 [e]S 2Ch 29:6
[f]Eze 21:1-32

[g]S Dt 28:64 [h]S Dt 28:37 **9:8** [i]Ps 25:16; 67:1; 119:58;
Isa 33:2 [j]S Ge 45:7 [k]Ecc 12:11; Isa 22:23 [l]Ps 13:3; 19:8 **9:9**
[m]S Ex 1:14; Ne 9:36 [n]S 2Ki 25:28; Ps 106:46

---

bers of the community rather than the leaders, who were themselves guilty (v. 2). Malachi, who prophesied about the same time as Ezra's mission, indicates that some Jews had broken their marriages to marry daughters of a foreign god (Mal 2:10–16), perhaps the daughters of influential landholders. One of the reasons for such intermarriages may have been the shortage of returning Jewish women who were available. What happened to a Jewish community that was lax concerning intermarriage can be seen in the example of the Elephantine settlement in Egypt, which was contemporary with Ezra and Nehemiah. There the Jews who married pagan spouses expressed their devotion to pagan gods in addition to the Lord. The Elephantine community was gradually assimilated and disappeared. *neighboring peoples.* The eight groups mentioned are representative of the original inhabitants of Canaan before the Israelite conquest (see note on Ex 3:8). Only the Ammonites, Moabites and Egyptians were still living there in the postexilic period (cf. 2Ch 8:7–8). *Canaanites.* See note on Ge 10:6. *Hittites.* See note on Ge 10:15. *Perizzites.* See note on Ge 13:7. *Jebusites.* See note on Ge 10:16. *Ammonites, Moabites.* See note on Ge 19:36–38. *Amorites.* See note on Ge 10:16.
9:2 *holy race.* The Hebrew for this phrase is translated "holy seed" in Isa 6:13. *led the way.* In the wrong direction (see 10:18). *unfaithfulness.* See 10:6; Jos 22:16; Da 9:7. Marrying those who did not belong to the Lord was an act of infidelity for the people of Israel.
9:3 *tore my tunic and cloak.* A common way to express grief or distress (see v. 5; Ge 37:29,34; Jos 7:6; Jdg 11:35; 2Sa 13:19; 2Ch 34:27; Est 4:1; Job 1:20; Isa 36:22; Jer 41:5; Mt 26:65). *pulled hair from my head and beard.* Unique in the Bible. Elsewhere we read about the shaving of one's head and/or beard (Job 1:20; Jer 41:5; 47:5; Eze 7:18; Am 8:10). When Nehemiah was confronted with the same problem of intermarriage, instead of pulling out his own hair he pulled out the hair of the offending parties (Ne 13:25).
9:4 *everyone who trembled.* Cf. Ex 19:16; Isa 66:2; Heb 12:21. *appalled.* See v. 3; cf. Da 4:19; 8:27. *evening sacrifice.* See Ex 12:6. The informants had probably visited Ezra in the morning, so that he must have sat appalled for many

hours. The time of the evening sacrifice, usually about 3:00 P.M., was also the appointed time for prayer and confession (Ac 3:1).
9:5 *self-abasement.* The Hebrew for this word later meant "fasting." See note on Lev 16:29,31. *fell on my knees.* Cf. 1Ki 8:54; Ps 95:6; Da 6:10. *with my hands spread out.* See note on Ex 9:29. Ezra's prayer (vv. 6–15) may be compared with those of Nehemiah (Ne 9:5–37) and Daniel (Da 9:4–19).
9:6 *ashamed and disgraced.* See 8:22 and note; Lk 18:13. Ezra felt both an inner shame before God and an outward humiliation before people for his own sins and the sins of his people. The two Hebrew verbs often occur together; see Ps 35:4; Isa 45:16; Jer 31:19 ("ashamed and humiliated"). *our sins . . . our guilt.* Cf. also vv. 7,13,15; 10:10,19; 1Ch 21:3; 2Ch 24:18; Ps 38:4. *has reached to the heavens.* But God's love is more than a match for our guilt (Ps 103:11–12).
9:7 *From the days of our forefathers.* Israelites were conscious of their corporate solidarity with their ancestors. *sword.* Cf. Ne 4:13. In Eze 21 "the sword of the king of Babylon" (21:19) is described as an instrument of divine judgment. *humiliation.* Cf. Da 9:7–8; 2Ch 32:21.
9:8 *remnant.* See Ge 45:7; Isa 1:9; 10:20–22 and notes. *firm place.* Lit. "nail" or "peg," like a nail driven into a wall (see Isa 22:23 and note) or a tent peg driven into the ground (Isa 33:20; 54:2). *light to our eyes.* An increase in light means vitality and joy (Ps 13:3; 19:8; Ecc 8:1).
9:9 *kings of Persia.* The Achaemenid Persian kings were favorably disposed to the Jews: Cyrus (539–530 B.C.) gave them permission to return (ch. 1); his son Cambyses (530–522), though not named in the Bible, also favored the Jews, as we learn from Elephantine papyri; Darius I (522–486) renewed the decree of Cyrus (ch. 6); his son Xerxes (486–465) granted privileges and protection to Jews (Est 8–10); his son Artaxerxes I (465–424) gave authorizations to Ezra (ch. 7) and to Nehemiah (Ne 2). *repair its ruins.* Isaiah had prophesied that the Lord would restore Jerusalem's ruins (Isa 44:26), which would burst into singing (Isa 52:9; cf. 58:12; 61:4). *wall of protection.* Used of a city wall only in Mic 7:11. The use here is metaphorical (cf. Zec 2:4–5).

kings of Persia: He has granted us new life to rebuild the house of our God and repair its ruins,^{o} and he has given us a wall of protection in Judah and Jerusalem.

¹⁰"But now, O our God, what can we say after this? For we have disregarded the commands^p ¹¹you gave through your servants the prophets when you said: 'The land you are entering^q to possess is a land polluted^r by the corruption of its peoples. By their detestable practices^s they have filled it with their impurity from one end to the other. ¹²Therefore, do not give your daughters in marriage to their sons or take their daughters for your sons. Do not seek a treaty of friendship with them^t at any time, that you may be strong^u and eat the good things^v of the land and leave it to your children as an everlasting inheritance.'^{w}

¹³"What has happened to us is a result of our evil^x deeds and our great guilt, and yet, our God, you have punished us less than our sins have deserved^y and have given us a remnant like this. ¹⁴Shall we again break your commands and intermarry^z with the peoples who commit such detestable practices? Would you not be angry enough with us to destroy us,^{a} leaving us no remnant^b or survivor? ¹⁵O LORD, God of Israel, you are righteous!^{c} We are left this day as a rem-

nant. Here we are before you in our guilt, though because of it not one of us can stand^d in your presence.^{e}"

The People's Confession of Sin

10 While Ezra was praying and confessing,^{f} weeping^g and throwing himself down before the house of God, a large crowd of Israelites—men, women and children—gathered around him. They too wept bitterly. ²Then Shecaniah son of Jehiel, one of the descendants of Elam,^{h} said to Ezra, "We have been unfaithful^i to our God by marrying foreign women from the peoples around us. But in spite of this, there is still hope for Israel.^{j} ³Now let us make a covenant^k before our God to send away^l all these women and their children, in accordance with the counsel of my lord and of those who fear the commands of our God. Let it be done according to the Law. ⁴Rise up; this matter is in your hands. We will support you, so take courage and do it."

⁵So Ezra rose up and put the leading priests and Levites and all Israel under oath^m to do what had been suggested. And they took the oath. ⁶Then Ezra withdrew from before the house of God and went to the room of Jehohanan son of Eliashib. While he was there, he ate no food and drank no water,^{n} because he continued to mourn over the unfaithfulness of the exiles.

⁷A proclamation was then issued throughout Judah and Jerusalem for all the

9:9 oPs 69:35; Isa 43:1; 44:26; 48:20; 52:9; 63:9; Jer 32:44; Zec 1:16-17
9:10 pDt 11:8; Isa 1:19-20
9:11 qDt 4:5
rS Lev 18:25-28
sS Dt 9:4; S 18:9; S 1Ki 14:24
9:12 tS Ex 34:15
uDt 11:8
vS Ge 45:18
wPs 103:17; Eze 37:25; Joel 3:20
9:13 xS Ex 32:22
yJob 11:6; 15:5; 22:5; 33:27; Ps 103:10
9:14 zNe 13:27
aS Dt 9:8
bDt 9:14
9:15
cS Ge 18:25; S 2Ch 12:6; Ne 9:8; Ps 51:4; 129:4; 145:17; Isa 24:16; Jer 12:1; 23:6; 33:16; La 1:18; Da 9:7; Zep 3:5

dPs 76:7; 130:3; Mal 3:2
eS 1Ki 8:47
10:1 f2Ch 20:9; Da 9:20
gS Nu 25:6
10:2 hver 26
iS Ezr 9:2
jDt 30:8-10
10:3 kS 2Ki 11:17
lS Ex 34:16
10:5 mNe 5:12; 13:25
10:6
nS Ex 34:28; Dt 9:18; Ps 102:4; Jnh 3:7

9:11–12 The references are not to a single OT passage but to several passages, such as Dt 11:8–9; Isa 1:19; Eze 37:25. **9:11** *your servants the prophets.* See notes on Jer 7:25; Zec 1:6. *corruption.* Of Canaanite idolatry and the immoral practices associated with it (Lev 18:3; 2Ch 29:5; La 1:17; Eze 7:20; 36:17). The degrading practices and beliefs of the Canaanites are described in texts from ancient Ugarit (see chart on "Ancient Texts Relating to the OT," p. 5). **9:14** *be angry.* God's anger came upon the Israelites because they had violated his covenant with them (Dt 7:4; 11:16–17; 29:26–28; Jos 23:16; Jdg 2:20). **9:15** *you are righteous.* See note on Ps 4:1. *our guilt.* A proper sense of God's holiness makes us aware of our unworthiness. See Isa 6:1–5; Lk 5:8. For comparable passages of national lament see Ps 44; 60; 74; 79–80; 83; 85; 90; 108; 126; 129; 137. **10:1** *weeping.* Not silently but out loud (see 3:13 and note; Ne 1:4; Joel 2:12). *throwing himself down.* The prophets and other leaders used object lessons, even bizarre actions, to attract people's attention (Isa 7:3; 8:1–4,18; Jer 13:1–11; 19; 27:2–12; Eze 4:1–5:4). **10:2** Ezra, as a wise teacher, waited for his audience to draw their own conclusions about what should be done. *Shecaniah.* Perhaps his father Jehiel is the Jehiel mentioned in v. 26 since he was also of the family of Elam. If so, Shecaniah was doubtless grieved that his father had married a non-Jewish woman. Six members of the clan of Elam were

involved in intermarriage (v. 26). **10:3** *make a covenant.* Lit. "cut a covenant" (see note on Ge 15:18). *women and their children.* Mothers were given custody of their children when marriages were dissolved. When Hagar was dismissed, Ishmael was sent with her (Ge 21:14). In Babylonia divorced women were granted their children and had to wait for them to grow up before remarrying, according to the law code of Hammurapi (see chart on "Ancient Texts Relating to the OT," p. 5). In Greece, however, children from broken homes remained with their fathers. **10:4** *Rise up.* Cf. David's exhortation (1Ch 22:16). **10:5** *oath.* The implied curse attendant upon nonfulfillment of a Biblical oath is often expressed in the vague statement, "May God deal with you, be it ever so severely, if . . . ." (see note on 1Sa 3:17). On rare occasions the full implications of the curse are spelled out (Nu 5:19–22; Job 31; Ps 7:4–5; 137:5–6). **10:6** *room.* Such temple chambers were used as storerooms (8:29; Ne 13:4–5). *ate no food and drank no water.* Complete fasting from both food and drink was rare. Moses did it twice (Ex 34:28; Dt 9:18), and the Ninevites also did it (Jnh 3:7). Ordinarily, fasting involved abstaining only from eating (1Sa 1:7; 2Sa 3:35). *mourn.* The Hebrew for this word often describes the reaction of those aware of the threat of deserved judgment (Ex 33:4; Nu 14:39). **10:7–8** While Ezra continued to fast and pray, the officials

exiles to assemble in Jerusalem. 8 Anyone
who failed to appear within three days
would forfeit all his property, in accordance with the decision of the officials and
elders, and would himself be expelled from
the assembly of the exiles.

9 Within the three days, all the men of
Judah and Benjamin[o] had gathered in
Jerusalem. And on the twentieth day of the
ninth month, all the people were sitting in
the square before the house of God, greatly
distressed by the occasion and because of
the rain. 10 Then Ezra[p] the priest stood up
and said to them, "You have been unfaithful; you have married foreign women, adding to Israel's guilt.[q] 11 Now make confession to the LORD, the God of your fathers,
and do his will. Separate yourselves from
the peoples around you and from your foreign wives."[r]

12 The whole assembly responded with a
loud voice:[s] "You are right! We must do
as you say. 13 But there are many people
here and it is the rainy season; so we cannot stand outside. Besides, this matter cannot be taken care of in a day or two, because we have sinned greatly in this thing.
14 Let our officials act for the whole assembly. Then let everyone in our towns who
has married a foreign woman come at a set
time, along with the elders and judges[t] of
each town, until the fierce anger[u] of our
God in this matter is turned away from
us." 15 Only Jonathan son of Asahel and
Jahzeiah son of Tikvah, supported by Meshullam and Shabbethai[v] the Levite, opposed this.

16 So the exiles did as was proposed.
Ezra the priest selected men who were
family heads, one from each family division, and all of them designated by name.
On the first day of the tenth month they
sat down to investigate the cases, 17 and by
the first day of the first month they finished
dealing with all the men who had married
foreign women.

Those Guilty of Intermarriage

18 Among the descendants of the priests,
the following had married foreign
women:[w]

From the descendants of Jeshua[x] son
of Jozadak, and his brothers: Maaseiah, Eliezer, Jarib and Gedaliah.
19 (They all gave their hands[y] in
pledge to put away their wives,
and for their guilt they each
presented a ram from the flock as a
guilt offering.)[z]

20 From the descendants of Immer:[a]
Hanani and Zebadiah.

21 From the descendants of Harim:[b]
Maaseiah, Elijah, Shemaiah, Jehiel
and Uzziah.

22 From the descendants of Pashhur:[c]
Elioenai, Maaseiah, Ishmael, Nethanel, Jozabad and Elasah.

23 Among the Levites:[d]

Jozabad, Shimei, Kelaiah (that is,

10:9 [o]S Ezr 1:5
10:10 [p]Ezr 7:21 [q]2Ch 28:13
10:11 [r]S Dt 24:1; Ne 9:2; Mal 2:10-16
10:12 [s]S Jos 6:5
10:14 [t]Dt 16:18 [u]S Nu 25:4; S 2Ch 29:10
10:15 [v]Ne 11:16
10:18 [w]S Jdg 3:6 [x]S Ezr 2:2
10:19 [y]S 2Ki 10:15 [z]S Lev 5:15; 6:6
10:20 [a]S 1Ch 24:14
10:21 [b]S 1Ch 24:8
10:22 [c]S 1Ch 9:12
10:23 [d]Ne 8:7; 9:4

and elders ordered all the exiles to assemble in Jerusalem. Although Ezra had been invested with great authority (7:25–26), he used it sparingly and influenced the people by his example.

10:8 *within three days.* Since the territory of Judah had been much reduced, the most distant people would not be more than 50 miles from Jerusalem. The borders were Bethel in the north, Beersheba in the south, Jericho in the east and Ono in the west (cf. Ne 7:26–38; 11:25–35). *forfeit.* The Hebrew for this word means "to ban from profane use and to devote to the Lord," either by destruction (see Ex 22:20; Dt 13:12–18 and NIV text notes) or by giving it to the Lord's treasury (cf. Lev 27:28; Jos 6:19; 7:1–15).

10:9,16–17 See chart on "Chronology: Ezra-Nehemiah," p. 674.

10:9 *Judah and Benjamin.* See note on 1:5. *square.* Either the outer court of the temple or the open space before the Water Gate (Ne 8:1). *rain.* The Hebrew for this word is a plural of intensity, indicating heavy torrential rains. The ninth month, Kislev (November-December), is in the middle of the "rainy season" (v. 13), which begins with light showers in October and lasts to mid-April. December and January are also cold months, with temperatures in the 50s and even 40s in Jerusalem. The people shivered not only because they were drenched, but perhaps also because they sensed divine displeasure in the heavy rains (see 1Sa 12:17–18; Eze 13:11,13).

10:10 *adding to Israel's guilt.* See Ex 9:34; Jdg 3:12; 4:1; 2Ch 28:13. The sins and failures of the exiles were great enough, but they added insult to injury by marrying pagan women.

10:11 *Separate yourselves.* See Nu 16:21; 2Co 6:14.

10:12 *with a loud voice.* See Ne 9:4.

10:14 *elders and judges of each town.* See Dt 16:18; 19:12; 21:3,19; Ru 4:2.

10:15 Perhaps these four men opposed the measure because they wanted to protect themselves or their relatives, or they may have viewed it as being too harsh. *Jahzeiah.* Means "May the LORD see" (the name is found only here). *Tikvah.* Means "hope" (found elsewhere only in 2Ki 22:14). *Meshullam.* See note on 8:16. If he is the Meshullam of v. 29, he himself had married a pagan wife. *Shabbethai.* Occurs only here and in Ne 8:7; 11:16; perhaps means "one born on the Sabbath."

10:16–17 The committee completed its work in three months, discovering that about 110 men were guilty of marrying pagan wives.

10:18–22 See 2:36–39.

10:19 *gave their hands.* For the symbolic use of the handshake see 2Ki 10:15; Eze 17:18. *ram.* Guilt offerings were to be made for sins committed unintentionally (Lev 5:14–19) as well as intentionally (Lev 6:1–7), and a ram was the appropriate offering in either case (Lev 5:15; 6:6).

Kelita), Pethahiah, Judah and Elie-
zer.
24From the singers:
Eliashib. *e*
From the gatekeepers:
Shallum, Telem and Uri.

25And among the other Israelites:

From the descendants of Parosh: *f*
Ramiah, Izziah, Malkijah, Mija-
min, Eleazar, Malkijah and Be-
naiah.
26From the descendants of Elam: *g*
Mattaniah, Zechariah, Jehiel, Abdi,
Jeremoth and Elijah.
27From the descendants of Zattu:
Elioenai, Eliashib, Mattaniah, Jere-
moth, Zabad and Aziza.
28From the descendants of Bebai:
Jehohanan, Hananiah, Zabbai and
Athlai.
29From the descendants of Bani:
Meshullam, Malluch, Adaiah, Ja-
shub, Sheal and Jeremoth.
30From the descendants of Pahath-
Moab:
Adna, Kelal, Benaiah, Maaseiah,
Mattaniah, Bezalel, Binnui and
Manasseh.

10:24 *e*Ne 3:1;
12:10; 13:7,28
10:25 /S Ezr 2:3
10:26 *g*S ver 2

31From the descendants of Harim:
Eliezer, Ishijah, Malkijah, Shema-
iah, Shimeon, 32Benjamin, Malluch
and Shemariah.
33From the descendants of Hashum:
Mattenai, Mattattah, Zabad,
Eliphelet, Jeremai, Manasseh and
Shimei.
34From the descendants of Bani:
Maadai, Amram, Uel, 35Benaiah,
Bedeiah, Keluhi, 36Vaniah, Mere-
moth, Eliashib, 37Mattaniah, Mat-
tenai and Jaasu.
38From the descendants of Binnui: *y*
Shimei, 39Shelemiah, Nathan,
Adaiah, 40Macnadebai, Shashai,
Sharai, 41Azarel, Shelemiah,
Shemariah, 42Shallum, Amariah
and Joseph.
43From the descendants of Nebo:
Jeiel, Mattithiah, Zabad, Zebina,
Jaddai, Joel and Benaiah.

44All these had married foreign women,
and some of them had children by these
wives. *z*

y37,38 See Septuagint (also 1 Esdras 9:34); Hebrew *Jaasu
38and Bani and Binnui,*   *z44* Or *and they sent them
away with their children*

10:24 It is striking that only one singer and three gatekeepers were involved. No temple servants (2:43–54) or
descendants of Solomon's servants (2:55–57) sinned
through intermarriage.

10:25–43 See 2:3–20.

10:30 *Bezalel.* Cf. Ex 31:2.

10:31 *Shimeon.* The Hebrew for this name is the same as

that for Simeon, Jacob's second son (see NIV text note on Ge
29:33). In Greek the name became Simon.
10:43 *Nebo.* The Hebrew equivalent of the name of the
Babylonian god Nabu (see Isa 46:1); found only here as a
personal name.
10:44 Some of the marriages had produced children, but
this was not accepted as a reason for halting the divorce
proceedings. See NIV text note.

NEHEMIAH

See Introduction to Ezra.

Outline

I. Nehemiah's First Administration (chs. 1-12)
  A. Nehemiah's Response to the Situation in Jerusalem (ch. 1)
    1. News of the plight of Jerusalem (1:1-4)
    2. Nehemiah's prayer (1:5-11)
  B. Nehemiah's Journey to Jerusalem (ch. 2)
    1. The king's response (2:1-8)
    2. The journey itself (2:9-10)
    3. Nehemiah's nocturnal inspection of the walls (2:11-16)
    4. His exhortation to rebuild (2:17-18)
    5. The opposition of Sanballat, Tobiah and Geshem (2:19-20)
  C. List of the Builders of the Wall (ch. 3)
    1. The northern section (3:1-7)
    2. The western section (3:8-13)
    3. The southern section (3:14)
    4. The eastern section (3:15-32)
  D. Opposition to Rebuilding the Wall (ch. 4)
    1. The derision of Sanballat and Tobiah (4:1-5)
    2. The threat of attack (4:6-15)
    3. Rebuilding the wall (4:16-23)
  E. Social and Economic Problems (ch. 5)
    1. The complaints of the poor (5:1-5)
    2. The cancellation of debts (5:6-13)
    3. Nehemiah's unselfish example (5:14-19)
  F. The Wall Rebuilt Despite Opposition (ch. 6)
    1. Attempts to snare Nehemiah (6:1-9)
    2. The hiring of false prophets (6:10-14)
    3. The completion of the wall (6:15-19)
  G. List of Exiles (7:1-73a)
    1. Provisions for the protection of Jerusalem (7:1-3)
    2. Nehemiah's discovery of the list of returnees (7:4-5)
    3. The returnees delineated (7:6-72)
    4. Settlement of the exiles (7:73a)
  H. Ezra's Preaching and the Outbreak of Revival (7:73b-10:39)
    1. The public exposition of the Scriptures (7:73b-8:12)
    2. The Feast of Tabernacles (8:13-18)
    3. A day of fasting, confession and prayer (9:1-5a)
    4. A recital of God's dealings with Israel (9:5b-31)
    5. Confession of sins (9:32-37)
    6. A binding agreement (9:38)
    7. A list of those who sealed it (10:1-29)
    8. Provisions of the agreement (10:30-39)
  I. New Residents of Judah and Jerusalem (ch. 11)
    1. New residents for Jerusalem (11:1-24)
      a. Introductory remarks (11:1-4a)

      b. Residents from Judah (11:4b-6)
      c. From Benjamin (11:7-9)
      d. From the priests (11:10-14)
      e. From the Levites (11:15-18)
      f. From the temple staff (11:19-24)
    2. New residents for Judah (11:25-36)
      a. Places settled by those from Judah (11:25-30)
      b. Places settled by those from Benjamin (11:31-35)
      c. Transfer of Levites from Judah to Benjamin (11:36)
  J. Lists of Priests and the Dedication of the Wall (ch. 12)
    1. Priests and Levites from the first return (12:1-9)
    2. High priests and Levites since Joiakim (12:10-26)
    3. Dedication of the wall of Jerusalem (12:27-43)
    4. Regulation of the temple offerings and services (12:44-47)
II. Nehemiah's Second Administration (ch. 13)
  A. Abuses during His Absence (13:1-5)
    1. Mixed marriages (13:1-3)
    2. Tobiah's occupation of the temple quarters (13:4-5)
  B. Nehemiah's Return (13:6-9)
    1. His arrival (13:6-7)
    2. His expulsion of Tobiah (13:8-9)
  C. Reorganization and Reforms (13:10-31)
    1. Offerings for the temple staff (13:10-14)
    2. The abuse of the Sabbath (13:15-22)
    3. Mixed marriages (13:23-29)
    4. Provisions of wood and firstfruits (13:30-31)

Nenemiah's Prayer

1 The words of Nehemiah son of Hacaliah:

In the month of Kislev[a] in the twentieth year, while I was in the citadel of Susa,[b] [2]Hanani,[c] one of my brothers, came from Judah with some other men, and I questioned them about the Jewish remnant[d] that survived the exile, and also about Jerusalem.

[3]They said to me, "Those who survived the exile and are back in the province are in great trouble and disgrace. The wall of Jerusalem is broken down, and its gates have been burned with fire.[e] "

[4]When I heard these things, I sat down and wept.[f] For some days I mourned and fasted[g] and prayed before the God of heaven. [5]Then I said:

"O LORD, God of heaven, the great and awesome God,[h] who keeps his covenant of love[i] with those who love him and obey his commands, [6]let your ear be attentive and your eyes open to hear[j] the prayer[k] your ser-

vant is praying before you day and night for your servants, the people of Israel. I confess[l] the sins we Israelites, including myself and my father's house, have committed against you. [7]We have acted very wickedly[m] toward you. We have not obeyed the commands, decrees and laws you gave your servant Moses.

[8]"Remember[n] the instruction you gave your servant Moses, saying, 'If you are unfaithful, I will scatter[o] you among the nations, [9]but if you return to me and obey my commands, then even if your exiled people are at the farthest horizon, I will gather[p] them from there and bring them to the place I have chosen as a dwelling for my Name.'[q]

[10]"They are your servants and your people, whom you redeemed by your great strength and your mighty hand.[r] [11]O Lord, let your ear be attentive[s] to the prayer of this your servant and to the prayer of your servants

---

1:1 *aZec 7:1
bS Ezr 4:9;
S Est 2:8*
1:2 *cNe 7:2
dS 2Ki 21:14;
Ne 7:6; Jer 52:28*
1:3 *eS Lev 26:31;
2Ki 25:10;
Ne 2:3,13,17;
Isa 22:9; Jer 39:8;
52:14; La 2:9*
1:4 *fPs 137:1
gS 2Ch 20:3;
S Ezr 9:4; Da 9:3*
1:5 *hS Dt 7:21;
Ne 4:14;
iS Dt 7:9;
S 1Ki 8:23;
Da 9:4*
1:6 *jS 1Ki 8:29;
S 2Ch 7:15
kS 1Ki 8:30*

lS 1Ki 8:47
1:7 *mPs 106:6*
1:8 *nS Ge 8:1;
S 2Ki 20:3;
Ne 4:14; 5:19;
6:14; 13:22,29,
31 oS Lev 26:33*
1:9 *pS Dt 30:4;
Ps 106:47; 107:3;
Isa 11:12; 56:8;
Jer 42:12;
Eze 11:17
qS 1Ki 8:48;
Jer 29:14;
Eze 11:17;
20:34-38;
36:24-38;
Mic 2:12*
1:10 *rS Ex 32:11;
Isa 51:9-11*
1:11 *sS 2Ch 6:40*

1:1 *The words of.* Originally an introduction to the title of a separate composition (see Jer 1:1; Am 1:1), though the books of Ezra and Nehemiah appear as a single work from earliest times (see Introduction to Ezra: Ezra and Nehemiah). *Nehemiah.* Means "The LORD comforts." *Hacaliah.* Perhaps means "Wait for the LORD," though an imperative in a Hebrew name is quite unusual. The name occurs only here and in 10:1. *Kislev . . . twentieth year.* November-December, 446 B.C. See chart on "Chronology: Ezra-Nehemiah," p. 674. *Susa.* See note on Ezr 4:9.
1:2 *Hanani.* Probably a shortened form of Hananiah, which means "The LORD is gracious." *one of my brothers.* See 7:2. The Elephantine papyri mention a Hananiah who was the head of Jewish affairs in Jerusalem. Many believe that he is to be identified with Nehemiah's brother, and that he may have governed between Nehemiah's first and second terms (see NIV text note on 7:2). *remnant.* See note on Ezr 9:8.
1:3 *province.* See note on Ezr 2:1. *wall of Jerusalem is broken down.* The lack of a city wall meant that the people were defenseless against their enemies. Thucydides (1.89) describes the comparable condition of Athens after its devastation by the Persians in 480–479 B.C. Excavations at Jerusalem during 1961–67 revealed that the lack of a wall on the eastern slopes also meant the disintegration of the terraces there. When Nebuchadnezzar assaulted Jerusalem, he battered and broke down the walls around it (2Ki 25:10). Most, however, do not believe that Nehemiah's distress was caused by Nebuchadnezzar's destruction in 586 but by the episode of Ezr 4:7–23. The Jews had attempted to rebuild the walls earlier in the reign of Artaxerxes I; but after the protest of Rehum and Shimshai, the king ordered the Jews to desist. See note on Ezr 4:21–23.
1:4 *sat down.* Cf. Job 2:13. *wept.* See 8:9; Ezr 3:13 and note; 10:1; Est 8:3. *mourned.* See Ezr 10:6; Da 10:2. *fasted and prayed.* See note on Ezr 8:23. During the exile, fasting became a common practice, including solemn fasts to commemorate the fall of Jerusalem and the murder of Gedaliah (see note on Zec 8:19; see also Est 4:16; Da 9:3;

10:3; Zec 7:3–7). *God of heaven.* See note on Ezr 1:2.
1:5 *love.* Or "faithful love," the quality that honors a covenant through thick and thin.
1:6 *praying before you day and night.* Cf. Ps 42:3; 88:1; Jer 9:1; 14:17; La 2:18; Lk 2:37; 1Th 3:10; 1Ti 5:5; 2Ti 1:3. *sins . . . myself and my father's house.* Nehemiah does not exclude himself or members of his own family in his confession of sins. A true sense of the awesomeness of God reveals the depths of our own sinfulness (Isa 6:1–5; Lk 5:8).
1:7 *commands, decrees and laws.* See note on Ge 26:5. *Moses.* For the prominence of the law of Moses in Ezra and Nehemiah see Ezr 3:2; 6:18; 7:6; Ne 1:8; 8:1,14; 9:14; 10:29; 13:1.
1:8 *Remember.* See note on 13:31; a key word in the book (4:14; 5:19; 6:14; 13:14,22,29,31). *unfaithful . . . scatter.* Dispersion was the inescapable consequence of the people's unfaithfulness. By the NT period there were still more Jews in the Diaspora (dispersion) than in Palestine.
1:9 *I will gather them.* See Dt 30:1–5; a frequent promise, especially in the prophets (e.g., Isa 11:12; Jer 23:3; 31:8–10; Eze 20:34,41; 36:24; Mic 2:12). *chosen as a dwelling for my Name.* See Dt 12:5 and note; Ps 132:13.
1:10 *your people . . . you redeemed.* Although they had sinned and failed, they were still God's people by virtue of his redeeming them (see Dt 4:34; 9:29).
1:11 *Give your servant success today.* Cf. Ge 24:12. *cupbearer.* Lit. "one who gives (someone) something to drink." The Hebrew for this word occurs 11 other times in the OT in the sense of "cupbearer" (Ge 40:1–2,5,9,13,20–21,23; 41:9; 1Ki 10:5; 2Ch 9:4). According to the Greek historian Xenophon (*Cyropaedia*, 1.3.9), one of the cupbearer's duties was to choose and taste the king's wine to make certain that it was not poisoned (see 2:1). Thus Nehemiah had to be a man who enjoyed the unreserved confidence of the king. The need for trustworthy court attendants is underscored by the intrigues that characterized the Achaemenid court of Persia. Xerxes, the father of Artaxerxes I, was killed in his own bedchamber by a courtier.

who delight in revering your name. Give your servant success today by granting him favor ^{t} in the presence of this man."

I was cupbearer ^{u} to the king.

Artaxerxes Sends Nehemiah to Jerusalem

2 In the month of Nisan in the twentieth year of King Artaxerxes, ^{v} when wine was brought for him, I took the wine and gave it to the king. I had not been sad in his presence before; ^{2}so the king asked me, "Why does your face look so sad when you are not ill? This can be nothing but sadness of heart."

I was very much afraid, ^{3}but I said to the king, "May the king live forever! ^{w} Why should my face not look sad when the city^x where my fathers are buried lies in ruins, and its gates have been destroyed by fire?^{y} "

^{4}The king said to me, "What is it you want?"

Then I prayed to the God of heaven,

^{5}and I answered the king, "If it pleases the king and if your servant has found favor in his sight, let him send me to the city in Judah where my fathers are buried so that I can rebuild it."

^{6}Then the king^z, with the queen sitting beside him, asked me, "How long will your journey take, and when will you get back?" It pleased the king to send me; so I set a time.

^{7}I also said to him, "If it pleases the king, may I have letters to the governors of Trans-Euphrates, ^{a} so that they will provide me safe-conduct until I arrive in Judah? ^{8}And may I have a letter to Asaph, keeper of the king's forest, so he will give me timber to make beams for the gates of the citadel ^{b} by the temple and for the city wall and for the residence I will occupy?" And because the gracious hand of my God was upon me, ^{c} the king granted my requests. ^{d} ^{9}So I went to the governors of Trans-Euphrates and gave them the king's letters. The king had also sent army officers and cavalry ^{e} with me.

^{10}When Sanballat^f the Horonite and

Cross references

1:11 ^{t}S Ex 3:21;
^{u}S Ge 40:1
2:1 ^{v}S Ezr 4:7;
S 6:14
2:3 ^{w}1Ki 1:31;
Da 2:4; 3:9;
5:10; 6:6,21
^{x}Ps 137:6
^{y}S Ne 1:3

2:6 ^{z}Ne 5:14;
13:6
2:7 ^{a}S Ezr 8:36
2:8 ^{b}Ne 7:2
^{c}S Ezr 5:5
^{d}S Ezr 4:24
2:9 ^{e}S Ezr 8:22
2:10 ^{f}ver 19;
Ne 4:1,7; 6:1-2,5,
12,14; 13:28

2:1 *Nisan . . . twentieth year.* March-April, 445 B.C. (see chart on "Chronology: Ezra-Nehemiah," p. 674).There was a delay of four months from Kislev, when Nehemiah first heard the news (1:1), to Nisan, when he approached the king. Various reasons have been suggested: 1. The king may have been in his other winter palace at Babylon. 2. Perhaps the king was not in the right mood. 3. Even though Nehemiah was a favorite of the king, he would not have rashly blurted out his request. *sad in his presence.* No matter what one's personal problems were, the king's servants were expected to keep their feelings to themselves and to display a cheerful disposition before him.

2:3 *May the king live forever!* A common form of address to kings. *city.* Nehemiah does not mention Jerusalem by name (see v. 5); he may have wished to arouse the king's sympathy by stressing first the desecration of ancestral tombs.

2:4 *I prayed to the God of heaven.* Before turning to answer the king, Nehemiah utters a brief, spontaneous prayer to God. One of Nehemiah's striking characteristics is his frequent recourse to prayer (1:4; 4:4,9; 5:19; 6:9,14; 13:14,22,29,31).

2:6 *queen.* The Hebrew for this word is used only here and in Ps 45:9 ("royal bride"). It is a loanword from Akkadian and means lit. "(woman) of the palace." The Aramaic equivalent is found only in Da 5:2-3,23, where it is translated "wives." Ctesias, a Greek who lived at the Achaemenid court, informs us that the name of Artaxerxes's queen was Damaspia and that he had at least three concubines. Like Esther, Damaspia may have used her influence with the king (Est 5). The Achaemenid court was notorious for the great influence exercised by the royal women. Especially domineering was Amestris, the cruel wife of Xerxes and mother of Artaxerxes I. *How long will your journey take . . . ?* Nehemiah probably asked for a brief leave of absence, which he then had extended. We can infer from 5:14 that he spent 12 years on his first term as governor of Judah. In the 32nd year of Artaxerxes, Nehemiah returned to report to the king and then came back to Judah for a second term (13:6-7).

2:7 *letters.* A contemporary document from Arsames, the

satrap of Egypt who was at the Persian court, to one of his officers who was returning to Egypt orders Persian officials to provide him with food and drink on the stages of his journey. *Trans-Euphrates.* See note on Ezr 4:10.

2:8 *forest.* The Hebrew for this word is *pardes*, a loanword from Old Persian meaning "enclosure," a pleasant retreat or park. The word occurs elsewhere in the OT only in Ecc 2:5 ("parks") and SS 4:13 ("orchard"). In the Septuagint (the Greek translation of the OT) the Greek transliteration *paradeisos* is used here. In the period between the OT and the NT, the word acquired the sense of the abode of the blessed dead, i.e., "paradise." It appears three times in the NT (Lk 23:43; 2Co 12:4; Rev 2:7). As to the location of the "king's forest," some believe that it was in Lebanon, which was famed for its forests of cedars and other coniferous trees (see notes on Jdg 9:15; Ezr 3:7). But a more plausible suggestion is that it should be identified with Solomon's gardens at Etham, about six miles south of Jerusalem (see Josephus, *Antiquities,* 8.7.3). For city gates, costly imported cedars from Lebanon would not be used but rather indigenous oak, poplar or terebinth (Hos 4:13). *citadel.* Probably refers to the fortress north of the temple, the forerunner of the Antonia fortress built by Herod the Great (Josephus, *Antiquities,* 15.11.4; see Ac 21:34,37; 22:24).

2:9 *army officers and cavalry.* In striking contrast to Ezra (see note on Ezr 8:22), Nehemiah was accompanied by an armed escort since he was officially Judah's governor.

2:10 *Sanballat.* A Babylonian name, meaning "Sin (the moon-god) has given life." *Horonite.* Identifies him as coming from (1) Hauran (Eze 47:16,18), east of the Sea of Galilee, (2) Horonaim, in Moab (Jer 48:34), or, most probably, (3) either Upper or Lower Beth Horon, two key cities 12 miles northwest of Jerusalem, which guarded the main road to Jerusalem (Jos 10:10; 16:3,5; 1 Maccabees 3:16; 7:39). Sanballat was the chief political opponent of Nehemiah (v. 19; 4:1,7; 6:1-2,5,12,14; 13:28). He held the position of governor over Samaria (cf. 4:1-2). An Elephantine papyrus letter of the late fifth century B.C. to Bagohi (Bigvai), governor of Judah, refers to "Delaiah and Shele-

Tobiah[g] the Ammonite official heard about this, they were very much disturbed that someone had come to promote the welfare of the Israelites.[h]

Nehemiah Inspects Jerusalem's Walls

[11]I went to Jerusalem, and after staying there three days[i] [12]I set out during the night with a few men. I had not told anyone what my God had put in my heart to do for Jerusalem. There were no mounts with me except the one I was riding on.

[13]By night I went out through the Valley Gate[j] toward the Jackal[a] Well and the Dung Gate,[k] examining the walls[l] of Jerusalem, which had been broken down, and its gates, which had been destroyed by fire. [14]Then I moved on toward the Fountain Gate[m] and the King's Pool,[n] but there was not enough room for my mount to get through; [15]so I went up the valley by

night, examining the wall. Finally, I turned back and reentered through the Valley Gate. [16]The officials did not know where I had gone or what I was doing, because as yet I had said nothing to the Jews or the priests or nobles or officials or any others who would be doing the work.

[17]Then I said to them, "You see the trouble we are in: Jerusalem lies in ruins, and its gates have been burned with fire.[o] Come, let us rebuild the wall[p] of Jerusalem, and we will no longer be in disgrace.[q]" [18]I also told them about the gracious hand of my God upon me[r] and what the king had said to me.

They replied, "Let us start rebuilding." So they began this good work.

[19]But when Sanballat[s] the Horonite, Tobiah the Ammonite official and Ge-

2:10 [g]Ne 4:3; 13:4-7 [h]Est 10:3
2:11 [i]S Ge 40:13
2:13 [j]S 2Ch 26:9 [k]Ne 3:13; 12:31 [l]S Ne 1:3
2:14 [m]Ne 3:15; 12:37 [n]S 2Ki 18:17
2:17 [o]S Ne 1:3 [p]Ps 102:16; Isa 30:13; 58:12 [q]Eze 5:14
2:18 [r]S Ezr 5:5
2:19 [s]S ver 10

[a]13 Or Serpent or Fig

miah, the sons of Sanballat, governor of Samaria." In 1962 a fourth-century B.C. papyrus was found in a cave north of Jericho, listing the name Sanballat, probably a descendant of Nehemiah's contemporary. *Tobiah.* Means "The LORD is good." He was probably a worshiper of the Lord (Yahweh), as indicated not only by his name but also by that of his son Jehohanan (6:17–18), meaning "The LORD is gracious." Jehohanan was married to the daughter of Meshullam son of Berekiah, the leader of one of the groups repairing the wall (3:4,30; 6:18). Tobiah also had a close relationship with Eliashib the priest (13:4–7). *Ammonite.* See Ezr 9:1; see also note on Ge 19:33. Tobiah was probably governor of Transjordan under the Persians. In later generations a prominent family bearing the name of Tobiah was sometimes associated with the region of Ammon in non-Biblical texts. *very much disturbed.* The reasons for the opposition of Sanballat and Tobiah were not basically religious but political. The authority of the Samaritan governor in particular was

threatened by Nehemiah's arrival.
2:11 *three days.* See note on Ezr 8:32.
2:12 Nehemiah was cautious and discreet as he inspected the city's fortifications. *one I was riding on.* Probably a mule or donkey.
2:13 Nehemiah did not make a complete circuit of the walls, but only of the southern area. Jerusalem was always attacked from the north because it was most vulnerable there, so the walls had probably been completely destroyed in that part of the city. *Valley Gate.* See 3:13. According to 2Ch 26:9 Uzziah fortified towers in the west wall, which overlooked the Tyropoeon Valley, i.e., the central valley between the Hinnom and Kidron valleys. Excavations in 1927–28 uncovered the remains of a gate from the Persian period, which has been identified as the Valley Gate. *Jackal Well.* Many scholars suggest that this was En Rogel (Jos 15:7–8; 18:16; 2Sa 17:17; 1Ki 1:9), a well situated at the junction of the Hinnom and Kidron valleys, 250 yards south

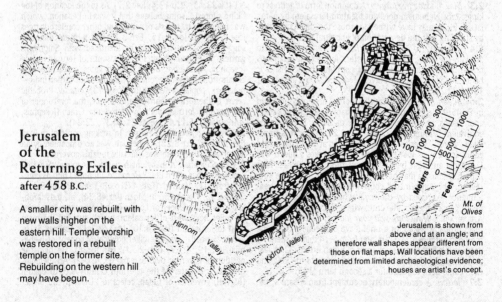

Jerusalem of the Returning Exiles

after 458 B.C.

A smaller city was rebuilt, with new walls higher on the eastern hill. Temple worship was restored in a rebuilt temple on the former site. Rebuilding on the western hill may have begun.

Jerusalem is shown from above and at an angle; and therefore wall shapes appear different from those on flat maps. Wall locations have been determined from limited archaeological evidence; houses are artist's concept.

22The repairs next to him were made by the priests from the surrounding region. 23Beyond them, Benjamin and Hasshub made repairs in front of their house; and next to them, Azariah son of Maaseiah, the son of Ananiah, made repairs beside his house. 24Next to him, Binnui*s* son of Henadad repaired another section, from Azariah's house to the angle and the corner, 25and Palal son of Uzai worked opposite the angle and the tower projecting from the upper palace near the court of the guard. *t* Next to him, Pedaiah son of Parosh*u* 26and the temple servants*v* living on the hill of Ophel*w* made repairs up to a point opposite the Water Gate*x* toward the east and the projecting tower. 27Next to them, the men of Tekoa*y* repaired another section, from the great projecting tower*z* to the wall of Ophel.

28Above the Horse Gate,*a* the priests made repairs, each in front of his own house. 29Next to them, Zadok son of Immer made repairs opposite his house. Next to him, Shemaiah son of Shecaniah, the guard at the East Gate, made repairs. 30Next to him, Hananiah son of Shelemiah, and Hanun, the sixth son of Zalaph, repaired another section. Next to them, Meshullam son of Berekiah made repairs opposite his living quarters. 31Next to him, Malkijah, one of the goldsmiths, made repairs as far as the house of the temple servants and the merchants, opposite the Inspection Gate, and as far as the room above the corner; 32and between the room above the corner and the Sheep Gate*b* the goldsmiths and merchants made repairs.

Opposition to the Rebuilding

4 When Sanballat*c* heard that we were rebuilding the wall, he became angry and was greatly incensed. He ridiculed the Jews, 2and in the presence of his associates*d* and the army of Samaria, he said, "What are those feeble Jews doing? Will they restore their wall? Will they offer sacrifices? Will they finish in a day? Can they bring the stones back to life from those heaps of rubble*e*—burned as they are?"

3Tobiah*f* the Ammonite, who was at his side, said, "What they are building—if even a fox climbed up on it, he would break down their wall of stones!"*g*

4Hear us, O our God, for we are despised.*h* Turn their insults back on their own heads. Give them over as plunder in a land of captivity. 5Do not cover up their guilt*i* or blot out their sins from your sight,*j* for they have thrown insults in the face of*i* the builders.

6So we rebuilt the wall till all of it reached half its height, for the people worked with all their heart.

7But when Sanballat, Tobiah,*k* the Arabs, the Ammonites and the men of Ashdod heard that the repairs to Jerusalem's walls had gone ahead and that the gaps were being closed, they were very angry. 8They all plotted together*l* to come and fight against Jerusalem and stir up trouble against it. 9But we prayed to our God and posted a guard day and night to meet this threat.

10Meanwhile, the people in Judah said,

*i*5 Or *have provoked you to anger before*

Cross references (center column)

3:24 *s*S Ezr 8:33
3:25 *t*Jer 32:2; 37:21; 39:14
*u*S Ezr 2:3
3:26 *v*Ne 7:46; 11:21
*w*S 2Ch 33:14
*x*Ne 8:1,3,16; 12:37
3:27 *y*S ver 5
*z*Ps 48:12
3:28 *a*S 2Ki 11:16
3:32 *b*S ver 1; Jn 5:2

4:1 *c*S Ne 2:10
4:2 *d*S Ezr 4:9-10
*e*Ps 79:1; Jer 26:18
4:3 *f*S Ne 2:10
*g*Job 13:12; 15:3
4:4 *h*Ps 44:13; 123:3-4; Jer 33:24
4:5 *i*Isa 2:9; La 1:22
*j*2Ki 14:27; Ps 51:1; 69:27-28; 109:14; Jer 18:23
4:7 *k*S Ne 2:10
4:8 *l*Ps 2:2; 83:1-18

3:25 *upper palace.* Perhaps the old palace of David (see 12:37). Like Solomon's palace, it would have had a guardhouse (Jer 32:2).
3:26 *Ophel.* See v. 27. The word means "swelling" or "bulge," hence a (fortified) "hill" (as in Mic 4:8; see NIV text note there), specifically the northern part of the southeastern hill of Jerusalem, which formed the original City of David, just south of the temple area (2Ch 27:3). *Water Gate.* So called because it led to the main source of Jerusalem's water, the Gihon spring. It must have opened onto a large area, for the reading of the Law took place there (8:1,3,16; 12:37). *projecting tower.* Perhaps the large tower whose ruins were discovered by archaeologists on the crest of the Ophel hill in 1923–25. Excavations at the base of the tower in 1978 revealed a level dating to the Persian era.
3:27 *men of Tekoa.* The common people of Tekoa did double duty, whereas the nobles of Tekoa shirked their responsibility (see note on v. 5).
3:28 *Horse Gate.* Where Athaliah was slain (2Ch 23:15). It may have been the easternmost point in the city wall—a gate through which one could reach the Kidron Valley (Jer 31:40).
3:29 *East Gate.* May have been the predecessor of the present Golden Gate.

3:31 *goldsmiths.* See v. 8. *Inspection Gate.* In the northern part of the eastern wall.
3:32 *Sheep Gate.* Back to the point of departure (see v. 1).
4:2 *he said.* Disputes between rival Persian governors were frequent. Sanballat asked several derisive questions to taunt the Jews and to discourage them in their efforts. *burned.* Fire had damaged the stones, which were probably limestone, and had caused many of them to crack and crumble.
4:3 *fox.* See Jdg 15:4; SS 2:15. The Hebrew for this word may also mean "jackal" (Ps 63:10; La 5:18; Eze 13:4). The jackal normally hunts in packs, whereas the fox is usually a nocturnal and solitary animal.
4:4–5 As in the so-called imprecatory psalms (Ps 79:12; 83; 94:1–3; 109:14; 137:7–9), Nehemiah does not himself take action against his opponents but calls down on them redress from God. In v. 5 Nehemiah's prayer echoes the language of Jer 18:23.
4:7 *Ashdod.* See note on Isa 20:1. It became a district capital under Persian rule.
4:9 *prayed . . . posted a guard.* Prayer and watchfulness blend faith and action, and also emphasize both the divine side and the human side.
4:10 *giving out.* The picture is of a worker staggering under the weight of his load and ready to fall at any step.

"The strength of the laborers^m is giving out, and there is so much rubble that we cannot rebuild the wall."

^{11}Also our enemies said, "Before they know it or see us, we will be right there among them and will kill them and put an end to the work."

^{12}Then the Jews who lived near them came and told us ten times over, "Wherever you turn, they will attack us."

^{13}Therefore I stationed some of the people behind the lowest points of the wall at the exposed places, posting them by families, with their swords, spears and bows. ^{14}After I looked things over, I stood up and said to the nobles, the officials and the rest of the people, "Don't be afraid^n of them. Remember^o the Lord, who is great and awesome,^{p} and fight^q for your brothers, your sons and your daughters, your wives and your homes."

^{15}When our enemies heard that we were aware of their plot and that God had frustrated it,^{r} we all returned to the wall, each to his own work.

^{16}From that day on, half of my men did the work, while the other half were equipped with spears, shields, bows and armor. The officers posted themselves behind all the people of Judah ^{17}who were building the wall. Those who carried materials did their work with one hand and held a weapon^s in the other, ^{18}and each of

the builders wore his sword at his side as he worked. But the man who sounded the trumpet^t stayed with me.

^{19}Then I said to the nobles, the officials and the rest of the people, "The work is extensive and spread out, and we are widely separated from each other along the wall. ^{20}Wherever you hear the sound of the trumpet,^{u} join us there. Our God will fight^v for us!"

^{21}So we continued the work with half the men holding spears, from the first light of dawn till the stars came out. ^{22}At that time I also said to the people, "Have every man and his helper stay inside Jerusalem at night, so they can serve us as guards by night and workmen by day." ^{23}Neither I nor my brothers nor my men nor the guards with me took off our clothes; each had his weapon, even when he went for water.^{j}

Nehemiah Helps the Poor

5 Now the men and their wives raised a great outcry against their Jewish brothers. ^{2}Some were saying, "We and our sons and daughters are numerous; in order for us to eat and stay alive, we must get grain."

^{3}Others were saying, "We are mortgag-

4:10	^{m}S 1Ch 23:4
4:14	^{n}S Ge 28:15; S Dt 1:29
	^{o}S Ne 1:8
	^{p}S Ne 1:5
	^{q}S 2Sa 10:12
4:15	
	^{r}S 2Sa 17:14; Job 5:12
4:17	^{s}Ps 149:6
4:18	^{t}S Nu 10:2
4:20	^{u}Eze 33:3
	^{v}S Ex 14:14; S Dt 20:4; Jos 10:14

j23 The meaning of the Hebrew for this clause is uncertain.

4:11 *our enemies said.* Either Nehemiah had friendly informants, or the enemy was spreading unsettling rumors.

4:12 *ten times over.* Many times.

4:13 *lowest points . . . exposed places.* Nehemiah posted men conspicuously in the areas that were the most vulnerable along the wall. *spears.* Used as thrusting weapons (Nu 25:7–8; 1Ki 18:28).

4:14 *Don't be afraid of them. Remember the Lord.* See note on 1:8. The best way to dispel fear is to remember the Lord, who alone is to be feared (see Dt 3:22; 20:3; 31:6).

4:16 *shields.* Made primarily of wood or wickerwork and therefore combustible (Eze 39:9). *armor.* The Hebrew for this word designated primarily a breastplate of metal or a coat of mail (see 2Ch 18:33).

4:17 *work with one hand . . . weapon in the other.* Means either that the workers carrried their materials with one hand and their weapons with the other, or simply that the weapons were kept close at hand.

4:18 *trumpet.* See note on Isa 18:3; see also Jos 6:4,6,8, 13.

4:20 *Our God will fight for us!* For the concept of holy war, in which God fights for his people, see Jos 10:14,42; Jdg 4:14; 20:35; 2Sa 5:24; see also Introduction to Joshua: The Conquest and the Ethical Question of War.

4:21 *till the stars came out.* Indicates the earnestness of their efforts, since the usual time to stop working was at sunset (Dt 24:15; Mt 20:8).

4:22 *guards by night.* Even men from outside Jerusalem stayed in the city at night so that some of them could serve as sentries.

4:23 See NIV text note. Although the precise meaning of

the end of the verse is not clear, the implication is that constant preparedness was the rule. According to Josephus (*Antiquities,* 11.5.8), Nehemiah "himself made the rounds of the city by night, never tiring either through work or lack of food and sleep, neither of which he took for pleasure but as a necessity."

5:1–19 During his major effort to rebuild the walls of Jerusalem, Nehemiah faced an economic crisis. Since the building of the wall took only 52 days (6:15), it is surprising that Nehemiah called a "large meeting" (v. 7) in the midst of such a project. Perhaps the economic pressures created by the rebuilding program brought to light problems that had long been simmering and that had to be dealt with before work could proceed. Among the classes affected by the economic crisis were (1) the landless, who were short of food (v. 2); (2) the landowners, who were compelled to mortgage their properties (v. 3); (3) those forced to borrow money at exorbitant rates and sell their children into slavery (vv. 4–5).

5:1 *wives.* The situation was so serious that the wives joined in the protest as they ran short of funds and supplies to feed their families. They complained not against the foreign authorities but against their own countrymen who were taking advantage of their poorer brothers at a time when all were needed for the defense of the country.

5:2 *grain.* About six to seven bushels would be needed for a man to feed his family for a month.

5:3 *mortgaging.* Even those who had considerable property were forced to mortgage it, benefiting the wealthy few (cf. Isa 5:8). In times of economic stress the rich got richer, and the poor got poorer. *famine.* The economic situation was aggravated by the natural conditions that had produced a

pointed prophets to make this proclamation about you in Jerusalem: 'There is a king in Judah!' Now this report will get back to the king; so come, let us confer together."

8I sent him this reply: "Nothing like what you are saying is happening; you are just making it up out of your head."

9They were all trying to frighten us, thinking, "Their hands will get too weak for the work, and it will not be completed."

But I prayed, "Now strengthen my hands."

10One day I went to the house of Shemaiah son of Delaiah, the son of Mehetabel, who was shut in at his home. He said, "Let us meet in the house of God, inside the temple w, and let us close the temple doors, because men are coming to kill you—by night they are coming to kill you."

11But I said, "Should a man like me run away? Or should one like me go into the temple to save his life? I will not go!" 12I realized that God had not sent him, but that he had prophesied against me x because Tobiah and Sanballat y had hired him. 13He had been hired to intimidate me so that I would commit a sin by doing this, and then they would give me a bad name to discredit me. z

14Remember a Tobiah and Sanballat, b O my God, because of what they have done; remember also the prophetess c Noadiah

and the rest of the prophets d who have been trying to intimidate me.

The Completion of the Wall

15So the wall was completed on the twenty-fifth of Elul, in fifty-two days. 16When all our enemies heard about this, all the surrounding nations were afraid and lost their self-confidence, because they realized that this work had been done with the help of our God.

17Also, in those days the nobles of Judah were sending many letters to Tobiah, and replies from Tobiah kept coming to them. 18For many in Judah were under oath to him, since he was son-in-law to Shecaniah son of Arah, and his son Jehohanan had married the daughter of Meshullam son of Berekiah. 19Moreover, they kept reporting to me his good deeds and then telling him what I said. And Tobiah sent letters to intimidate me.

7 After the wall had been rebuilt and I had set the doors in place, the gatekeepers e and the singers f and the Levites g were appointed. 2I put in charge of Jerusalem my brother Hanani, h along with o Hananiah i the commander of the citadel, j because he was a man of integrity and feared k God more than most men do. 3I said to them, "The gates of Jerusalem are not to be opened until the sun is hot. While the gatekeepers are still on duty, have them shut the doors and bar them. Also appoint residents of Jerusalem as

6:10 wNu 18:7
6:12
xEze 13:22-23
yS Ne 2:10
6:13 zJer 20:10
6:14 aS Ne 1:8
bS Ne 2:10
cS Ex 15:20;
Eze 13:17-23;
S Ac 21:9;
Rev 2:20

dJer 23:9-40;
Zec 13:2-3
7:1 e1Ch 9:27;
S 26:12-19
fPs 68:25 gNe 8:9
7:2 hNe 1:2
iNe 10:23
jNe 2:8 k1Ki 18:3

o2 Or Hanani, that is,

6:8 Nothing. Nehemiah does not mince words. He calls the report a lie. He may have sent his own messenger to the Persian king to assure him of his loyalty.
6:9 hands will get . . . weak. Figurative language to express the idea of discouragement. The Hebrew for this phrase is used also in Ezr 4:4; Jer 38:4, as well as on an ostracon from Lachish dated c. 588 B.C.
6:10 Shemaiah . . . was shut in. Perhaps as a symbolic action to indicate that his own life was in danger and to suggest that both Nehemiah and he must flee to the temple (for other symbolic actions see 1Ki 22:11; Isa 20:2–4; Jer 27:2–7; 28:10–11; Eze 4:1–17; 12:3–11; Ac 21:11). Since Shemaiah had access to the temple, he may have been a priest. He was clearly a friend of Tobiah (cf. v. 12), and therefore Nehemiah's enemy. It was at least credible for Shemaiah to propose that Nehemiah take refuge in the temple area at the altar of asylum (see Ex 21:13–14 and notes), but not in the "house of God," the temple building itself.
6:11 Even if the threat against his life was real, Nehemiah was not a coward who would run into hiding. Nor would he transgress the law to save his life. As a layman, he was not permitted to enter the sanctuary (Nu 18:7). When King Uzziah entered the temple to burn incense, he was punished by being afflicted with leprosy (2Ch 26:16–21).
6:12 The fact that Shemaiah proposed a course of action contrary to God's word revealed him as a false prophet (cf. Dt 18:20; Isa 8:19–20).

6:13 If Nehemiah had wavered in the face of the threat against him, his leadership would have been discredited and morale among the people would have plummeted.
6:14 Remember. See note on 1:8. prophetess. See note on Ex 15:20.
6:15 twenty-fifth of Elul. Oct. 2, 445 B.C. fifty-two days. The walls that lay in ruins for nearly a century and a half were rebuilt in less than two months once the people were galvanized into action by Nehemiah's leadership. Archaeological investigations have shown that the circumference of the wall in Nehemiah's day was much reduced. Josephus states (Antiquities, 11.5.8) that the rebuilding of the wall took two years and four months, but he is doubtless including such additional tasks as further strengthening of various sections, embellishing and beautifying, and the like. The dedication of the wall is described in 12:27–47.
6:17–18 Tobiah was related to an influential family in Judah, since his son Jehohanan was married to the daughter of Meshullam, who had helped repair the wall of Jerusalem (3:4,30).
7:2 in charge of Jerusalem. Over Rephaiah and Shallum, who were over sections of the city (3:9,12). Hanani. See note on 1:2. citadel. See notes on 2:8; 3:1.
7:3 until the sun is hot. Normally the gates would be opened at dawn, but their opening would be delayed until the sun was high in the heavens to prevent the enemy from making a surprise attack before most of the people were up.

guards, some at their posts and some near their own houses."

The List of the Exiles Who Returned

7:6–73pp — Ezr 2:1–70

[4]Now the city was large and spacious, but there were few people in it,[l] and the houses had not yet been rebuilt. [5]So my God put it into my heart to assemble the nobles, the officials and the common people for registration by families. I found the genealogical record of those who had been the first to return. This is what I found written there:

[6]These are the people of the province who came up from the captivity of the exiles[m] whom Nebuchadnezzar king of Babylon had taken captive (they returned to Jerusalem and Judah, each to his own town, [7]in company with Zerubbabel,[n] Jeshua, Nehemiah, Azariah, Raamiah, Nahamani, Mordecai, Bilshan, Mispereth, Bigvai, Nehum and Baanah):

The list of the men of Israel:

[8]the descendants of Parosh	2,172
[9]of Shephatiah	372
[10]of Arah	652
[11]of Pahath-Moab (through the line of Jeshua and Joab)	2,818
[12]of Elam	1,254
[13]of Zattu	845
[14]of Zaccai	760
[15]of Binnui	648
[16]of Bebai	628
[17]of Azgad	2,322
[18]of Adonikam	667
[19]of Bigvai	2,067
[20]of Adin[o]	655
[21]of Ater (through Hezekiah)	98
[22]of Hashum	328
[23]of Bezai	324
[24]of Hariph	112
[25]of Gibeon	95
[26]the men of Bethlehem and Netophah[p]	188
[27]of Anathoth[q]	128
[28]of Beth Azmaveth	42
[29]of Kiriath Jearim, Kephirah[r] and Beeroth[s]	743
[30]of Ramah and Geba	621
[31]of Micmash	122
[32]of Bethel and Ai[t]	123
[33]of the other Nebo	52

[34]of the other Elam	1,254
[35]of Harim	320
[36]of Jericho[u]	345
[37]of Lod, Hadid and Ono[v]	721
[38]of Senaah	3,930

[39]The priests:

the descendants of Jedaiah (through the family of Jeshua)	973
[40]of Immer	1,052
[41]of Pashhur	1,247
[42]of Harim	1,017

[43]The Levites:

the descendants of Jeshua (through Kadmiel through the line of Hodaviah)	74

[44]The singers:[w]

the descendants of Asaph	148

[45]The gatekeepers:[x]

the descendants of Shallum, Ater, Talmon, Akkub, Hatita and Shobai	138

[46]The temple servants:[y]

the descendants of
Ziha, Hasupha, Tabbaoth, [47]Keros, Sia, Padon, [48]Lebana, Hagaba, Shalmai, [49]Hanan, Giddel, Gahar, [50]Reaiah, Rezin, Nekoda, [51]Gazzam, Uzza, Paseah, [52]Besai, Meunim, Nephussim, [53]Bakbuk, Hakupha, Harhur, [54]Bazluth, Mehida, Harsha, [55]Barkos, Sisera, Temah, [56]Neziah and Hatipha

[57]The descendants of the servants of Solomon:

the descendants of
Sotai, Sophereth, Perida, [58]Jaala, Darkon, Giddel, [59]Shephatiah, Hattil, Pokereth-Hazzebaim and Amon

[60]The temple servants and the descendants of the servants of Solomon[z]	392

[61]The following came up from the towns of Tel Melah, Tel Harsha, Kerub, Addon and Immer, but they could not show that their families were descended from Israel:

[62]the descendants of

Cross references

7:4 [l]Ne 11:1
7:6
[m]S 2Ch 36:20; S Ne 1:2
7:7 [n]S 1Ch 3:19
7:20 [o]S Ezr 8:6
7:26
[p]S 2Sa 23:28; S 1Ch 2:54
7:27 [q]S Jos 21:18
7:29 [r]S Jos 18:26
[s]S Jos 18:25
7:32 [t]S Ge 12:8

7:36 [u]Ne 3:2
7:37 [v]S 1Ch 8:12
7:44 [w]Ne 11:23
7:45 [x]S 1Ch 9:17
7:46 [y]S Ne 3:26
7:60 [z]S 1Ch 9:2

7:6–73 Essentially the same as Ezr 2. See notes there for the nature of the list and the reasons for the numerous variations in names and numbers between the two lists.

7:7 *Nahamani.* Does not occur in Ezr 2:2.
7:43 *74.* See note on Ezr 2:40.

Delaiah, Tobiah and Nekoda 642

63And from among the priests:

the descendants of
Hobaiah, Hakkoz and Barzillai (a
man who had married a daughter
of Barzillai the Gileadite and was
called by that name).

64These searched for their family
records, but they could not find them
and so were excluded from the priesthood as unclean. 65The governor,
therefore, ordered them not to eat any
of the most sacred food until there
should be a priest ministering with the
Urim and Thummim.ª

66The whole company numbered
42,360, 67besides their 7,337 menservants and maidservants; and they
also had 245 men and women singers.
68There were 736 horses, 245
mules,p 69435 camels and 6,720 donkeys.

70Some of the heads of the families
contributed to the work. The governor
gave to the treasury 1,000 drachmasq
of gold, 50 bowls and 530 garments
for priests. 71Some of the heads of the
familiesb gave to the treasury for the
work 20,000 drachmasr of gold and
2,200 minass of silver. 72The total
given by the rest of the people was
20,000 drachmas of gold, 2,000
minast of silver and 67 garments for
priests.c

73The priests, the Levites, the gatekeepers, the singers and the temple

servants,d along with certain of the
people and the rest of the Israelites,
settled in their own towns.e

Ezra Reads the Law

When the seventh month came and the
Israelites had settled in their towns,f
8 1all the people assembled as one man
in the square before the Water Gate.g
They told Ezra the scribe to bring out the
Book of the Law of Moses,h which the
LORD had commanded for Israel.

2So on the first day of the seventh
monthi Ezra the priest brought the Lawj
before the assembly, which was made up
of men and women and all who were able
to understand. 3He read it aloud from daybreak till noon as he faced the square before the Water Gatek in the presence of
the men, women and others who could
understand. And all the people listened attentively to the Book of the Law.

4Ezra the scribe stood on a high wooden
platforml built for the occasion. Beside
him on his right stood Mattithiah, Shema,
Anaiah, Uriah, Hilkiah and Maaseiah; and
on his left were Pedaiah, Mishael, Malkijah, Hashum, Hashbaddanah, Zechariah
and Meshullam.

5Ezra opened the book. All the people
could see him because he was standingm
above them; and as he opened it, the
people all stood up. 6Ezra praised the

7:65 aS Ex 28:30;
7:71 bS 1Ch 29:7
7:72 cS Ex 25:2

7:73 dNe 1:10;
Ps 34:22; 103:21;
113:1; 135:1
eS Ezr 3:1;
Ne 11:1 fEzr 3:1
8:1 gS Ne 3:26
hS Dt 28:61;
S 2Ch 34:15
8:2
iLev 23:23-25;
Nu 29:1-6
jS Dt 31:11
8:3 kS Ne 3:26
8:4 l2Ch 6:13
8:5 mJdg 3:20

p68 Some Hebrew manuscripts (see also Ezra 2:66); most
Hebrew manuscripts do not have this verse.   q70 That
is, about 19 pounds (about 8.5 kilograms)   r71 That is,
about 375 pounds (about 170 kilograms); also in verse 72
s71 That is, about 1 1/3 tons (about 1.2 metric tons)
t72 That is, about 1 1/4 tons (about 1.1 metric tons)

7:70 drachmas. See note on Ezr 2:69.
7:73 settled in their own towns. See note on Ezr 2:70.
seventh month. October-November, 445 B.C.
8:1–18 According to the traditional view, the reading of
the Law by Ezra would be the first reference to him in almost
13 years since his arrival in 458 B.C. Since he was commissioned to teach the Law (Ezr 7:6,10,14,25–26), it is surprising that there was such a long delay in its public proclamation.
8:1 all the people assembled. See Ezr 3:1, which also
refers to an assembly called in the seventh month (Tishri),
the beginning of the civil year (see chart on "Hebrew Calendar," p. 102). square before the Water Gate. See vv. 3,16;
see also notes on 3:26; Ezr 10:9. Squares were normally
located near a city gate (2Ch 32:6). scribe. See note on Ezr
7:6. Book of the Law of Moses. Cf. vv. 2–3,5,8–9,13–15,
18. Four views have been proposed concerning the extent of
this Book: (1) a collection of legal materials, (2) the priestly
laws of Exodus and Leviticus, (3) the laws of Deuteronomy,
(4) the Pentateuch. Surely Ezra could have brought back
with him the Torah, i.e., the entire Pentateuch.
8:2 first day of the seventh month. Oct. 8, 445 B.C.; the
New Year's Day of the civil calendar (see note on Lev 23:24),
celebrated as the Feast of Trumpets (Nu 29:1–6), with cessation of labor and a sacred assembly. women. See 10:28.

Women did not usually participate in assemblies (see note on
Ex 10:11), but were brought, together with children, on
such solemn occasions (Dt 31:12; Jos 8:35; 2Ki 23:2).
8:3 read it aloud. See Ex 24:7; Ac 8:30. from daybreak till
noon. The people evidently stood (vv. 5,7) for five or six
hours, listening attentively to the reading and exposition
(vv. 7–8,12) of the Scriptures.
8:5 book. Scroll (see note on Ex 17:14). people all stood
up. The rabbis deduced from this verse that the congregation
should stand for the reading of the Torah. It is customary in
Eastern Orthodox churches for the congregation to stand
throughout the service.
8:6 lifted their hands. See Ex 9:29 and note; Ps 28:2;
134:2; 1Ti 2:8. Amen! Amen! See notes on Dt 27:15; Ro
1:25. The repetition conveys the intensity of feeling behind
the affirmation (for other repetitions see Ge 22:11 and note;
cf. 2Ki 11:14; Lk 23:21). worshiped. In its original sense the
Hebrew for this verb meant "to prostrate oneself on the
ground," as the frequently accompanying phrase "to the
ground" indicates. Private acts of worship often involved
prostration "to the ground," as in the case of Abraham's
servant (Ge 24:52), Moses (Ex 34:8), Joshua (Jos 5:14) and
Job (Job 1:20). There are three cases of spontaneous communal worship in Exodus (4:31; 12:27; 33:10). In 2Ch 20:18
Jehoshaphat and the people "fell down in worship before the

LORD, the great God; and all the people lifted their hands[n] and responded, "Amen! Amen!" Then they bowed down and worshiped the LORD with their faces to the ground.

[7]The Levites[o]—Jeshua, Bani, Sherebiah, Jamin, Akkub, Shabbethai, Hodiah, Maaseiah, Kelita, Azariah, Jozabad, Hanan and Pelaiah—instructed[p] the people in the Law while the people were standing there. [8]They read from the Book of the Law of God, making it clear[u] and giving the meaning so that the people could understand what was being read.

[9]Then Nehemiah the governor, Ezra the priest and scribe, and the Levites[q] who were instructing the people said to them all, "This day is sacred to the LORD your God. Do not mourn or weep."[r] For all the people had been weeping as they listened to the words of the Law.

[10]Nehemiah said, "Go and enjoy choice food and sweet drinks, and send some to those who have nothing[s] prepared. This day is sacred to our Lord. Do not grieve, for the joy[t] of the LORD is your strength."

[11]The Levites calmed all the people, saying, "Be still, for this is a sacred day. Do not grieve."

[12]Then all the people went away to eat

and drink, to send portions of food and to celebrate with great joy,[u] because they now understood the words that had been made known to them.

[13]On the second day of the month, the heads of all the families, along with the priests and the Levites, gathered around Ezra the scribe to give attention to the words of the Law. [14]They found written in the Law, which the LORD had commanded through Moses, that the Israelites were to live in booths[v] during the feast of the seventh month [15]and that they should proclaim this word and spread it throughout their towns and in Jerusalem: "Go out into the hill country and bring back branches from olive and wild olive trees, and from myrtles, palms and shade trees, to make booths"—as it is written.[v]

[16]So the people went out and brought back branches and built themselves booths on their own roofs, in their courtyards, in the courts of the house of God and in the square by the Water Gate[w] and the one by the Gate of Ephraim.[x] [17]The whole company that had returned from exile built booths and lived in them.[y] From the days of Joshua son of Nun until that day, the

8:6 [n]S Ezr 9:5; 1Ti 2:8
8:7 [o]S Ezr 10:23 [p]S Lev 10:11; S 2Ch 17:7
8:9 [q]Ne 7:1 [r]Dt 12:7,12; 16:14-15
8:10 [s]1Sa 25:8; S 2Sa 6:19; Est 9:22; Lk 14:12-14 [t]S Lev 23:40; S Dt 12:18; 16:11,14-15

8:12 [u]Est 9:22
8:14 [v]S Ex 23:16
8:16 [w]S Ne 3:26 [x]S 2Ch 25:23
8:17 [y]Hos 12:9

[u]8 Or *God, translating it*   [v]15 See Lev. 23:37-40.

LORD" when they heard his promise of victory.

8:7 *instructed.* See v. 8; Ezr 8:16 and note; Ps 119:34,73, 130; Isa 40:14.

8:8 *read.* See note on v. 3. *making it clear.* Rabbinic tradition understands the Hebrew for this expression as referring to translation from Hebrew into an Aramaic Targum (see NIV text note). But there is no evidence of Targums (free Aramaic translations of OT books or passages) from such an early date. The earliest extensive Targum is one on Job from Qumran, dated c. 150–100 B.C. Targums exist for every book of the OT except Daniel and Ezra-Nehemiah. *understand.* See v. 12.

8:9 *Nehemiah . . . Ezra.* An explicit reference showing that they were contemporaries (see 12:26,36). *Do not mourn.* See Ezr 10:6 and note; Est 9:22; Isa 57:18–19; Jer 31:13. *weep.* See 1:4; Ezr 3:13 and note; 10:1.

8:10 *choice food.* Delicious festive food prepared with much fat. The fat of sacrificial animals was offered to God as the tastiest element of the burnt offering (Lev 1:8,12), the fellowship offering (Lev 3:9–10), the sin offering (Lev 4:8–10) and the guilt offering (Lev 7:3–4). The fat was not to be eaten in these cases. *send some to those who have nothing.* It was customary for God's people to remember the less fortunate on joyous occasions (2Sa 6:19; Est 9:22; contrast 1Co 11:20–22; Jas 2:14–16).

8:14 *booths.* See notes on Ex 23:16; Lev 23:34,42; Jn 7:37–39.

8:15 *olive.* Widespread in Mediterranean countries. It was growing in Canaan before the conquest (Dt 8:8). Because it takes an olive tree 30 years to mature, its cultivation requires peaceful conditions. *wild olive trees.* Lit. "tree of oil," commonly regarded as the wild olive tree. But this is questionable since the "tree of oil" was used as timber (1Ki 6:23,31–33),

whereas the wood of the wild olive tree would have been of little value for use in the temple's furniture. Also, the wild olive tree contains very little oil. The phrase may refer to a resinous tree like the fir. *myrtles.* Evergreen bushes with a pleasing odor (Isa 41:19; 55:13; Zec 1:8,10–11). *palms.* The date palm was common around Jericho (Dt 34:3; 2Ch 28:15). *shade trees.* Cf. Eze 6:13; 20:28. Later Jewish celebrations of the Feast of Tabernacles include waving the *lulav* (made of branches of palms, myrtles and willows) with the right hand and holding branches of the *ethrog* (a citrus native to Palestine) in the left.

8:16 *courts of the house of God.* See note on 13:7. The temple that Ezekiel saw in his visions had an outer and an inner court (see p. 1284). Ezekiel's temple was to some extent patterned after Solomon's, which had an inner court of priests and an outer court (1Ki 6:36; 7:12; 2Ki 21:5; 23:12; 2Ch 4:9; 33:5). The temple of the NT era had a court of the Gentiles and an inner court, which was subdivided into courts of the women, of Israel and of the priests. The Temple Scroll from Qumran has God setting forth in detail an ideal temple. Columns 40–46 describe the outer court as follows: "On the roof of the third story are columns for the constructing of booths for the Feast of Tabernacles, to be occupied by the elders, tribal chieftains and commanders of thousands and hundreds." *Gate of Ephraim.* A gate of the oldest rampart of Jerusalem (see note on 3:6; see also 2Ki 14:13). It was restored by Nehemiah (12:39).

8:17 *From the days of Joshua . . . until that day.* The phrase does not mean that the Feast of Tabernacles had not been celebrated since Joshua's time, because such celebrations took place after the dedication of Solomon's temple (2Ch 7:8–10) and after the return of the exiles (Ezr 3:4). What apparently is meant is that the feast had not been celebrated before with such great joy (cf. 2Ch 30:26; 35:18).

Israelites had not celebrated[z] it like this. And their joy was very great.

[18]Day after day, from the first day to the last, Ezra read[a] from the Book of the Law[b] of God. They celebrated the feast for seven days, and on the eighth day, in accordance with the regulation,[c] there was an assembly.[d]

The Israelites Confess Their Sins

9 On the twenty-fourth day of the same month, the Israelites gathered together, fasting and wearing sackcloth and having dust on their heads.[e] [2]Those of Israelite descent had separated themselves from all foreigners.[f] They stood in their places and confessed their sins and the wickedness of their fathers.[g] [3]They stood where they were and read from the Book of the Law of the LORD their God for a quarter of the day, and spent another quarter in confession and in worshiping the LORD their God. [4]Standing on the stairs were the Levites[h]—Jeshua, Bani, Kadmiel, Shebaniah, Bunni, Sherebiah, Bani and Kenani—who called with loud voices to the LORD their God. [5]And the Levites—Jeshua, Kadmiel, Bani, Hashabneiah, Sherebiah, Hodiah, Shebaniah and Pethahiah—said: "Stand up and praise the LORD your God,[i] who is from everlasting to everlasting.[w]"

"Blessed be your glorious name,[j] and may it be exalted above all blessing and praise. [6]You alone are the LORD.[k] You made the heavens,[l] even the highest heavens, and all their starry host,[m] the earth[n] and all that is on it, the seas[o] and all that is in them.[p] You give life to everything, and the multitudes of heaven[q] worship you.

[7]"You are the LORD God, who chose Abram[r] and brought him out of Ur of the Chaldeans[s] and named him Abraham.[t] [8]You found his heart faithful to you, and you made a covenant with him to give to his descendants the land of the Canaanites, Hittites, Amorites, Perizzites, Jebusites and Girgashites.[u] You have kept your promise[v] because you are righteous.[w]

[9]"You saw the suffering of our forefathers in Egypt;[x] you heard their cry at the Red Sea.[x][y] [10]You sent miraculous signs[z] and wonders[a] against Pharaoh, against all his officials and all the people of his land, for you knew how arrogantly the Egyptians treated them. You made a name[b] for yourself,[c] which remains to this day. [11]You divided the sea before them,[d] so that they passed through it on dry ground, but you hurled their pursuers into the depths,[e] like a stone into mighty waters.[f] [12]By day[g] you led[h] them with a pillar of cloud,[i] and by night with a pillar of fire to give them light on the way they were to take.

[13]"You came down on Mount Sinai;[j] you spoke[k] to them from heaven.[l] You gave them regulations and laws that are just[m] and right, and decrees and commands that are good.[n] [14]You made known to them your holy Sabbath[o] and gave them commands, decrees and laws through your servant Moses. [15]In their hunger you gave them bread from heaven[p] and in their thirst you brought them

Cross references (center column)

8:17 [z]S 1Ki 8:2; S 2Ch 7:8; S 8:13
8:18 [a]Dt 31:11; S 33:10
[b]S Dt 28:61
[c]S Lev 23:40; S Ezr 3:4
[d]S Lev 23:36
9:1 [e]Lev 26:40-45; S Jos 7:6; 2Ch 7:14-16
9:2 [f]S Ezr 6:21; Ne 10:28; 13:3, 30 [g]S Lev 26:40; S Ezr 10:11; Ps 106:6
9:4 [h]S Ezr 10:23
9:5 [i]Ps 78:4 [i]S 2Sa 7:26
9:6 [k]S Dt 6:4 [l]S Ex 8:19 [m]Isa 40:26; 45:12 [n]S Ge 1:1; Isa 37:16 [o]Ps 95:5; 146:6; Jnh 1:9 [p]Dt 10:14; Ac 4:24; Rev 10:6 [q]Ps 103:20; 148:2
9:7 [r]S Ge 16:11 [s]S Ge 11:28 [t]S Ge 17:5
9:8 [u]S Ge 15:18-21; S Ezr 9:1 [v]S Jos 21:45 [w]Ge 15:6; S Ezr 9:15
9:9 [x]Ex 2:23-25; 3:7 [y]Ex 14:10-30
9:10 [z]S Ex 10:1; Ps 74:9 [a]S Ex 3:20; S 6:6 [b]Jer 32:20; Da 9:15 [c]S Nu 6:27
9:11 [d]Ps 78:13 [e]S Ex 14:28 [f]Ex 15:4-5,10; Heb 11:29
9:12 [g]S Dt 1:33 [h]S Ex 15:13 [i]S Ex 13:21
9:13 [j]S Ex 19:11 [k]S Ex 19:19 [l]S Ex 20:22 [m]Ps 119:137 [n]S Ex 20:1; Dt 4:7-8
9:14 [o]S Ge 2:3; Ex 20:8-11
9:15 [p]S Ex 16:4; Ps 78:24-25; Jn 6:31

[w]5 Or God for ever and ever   [x]9 Hebrew Yam Suph; that is, Sea of Reeds

---

8:18 *assembly.* See Nu 29:35.
9:1–37 The ninth chapters of Ezra, Nehemiah and Daniel are devoted to confessions of national sin and to prayers for God's grace.
9:1 *twenty-fourth day.* Oct. 30, 445 B.C.; a day of penance in the spirit of the Day of Atonement, which was held on the tenth day (Lev 16:29–30). *fasting . . . sackcloth . . . dust.* See notes on Ge 37:34; Ezr 8:23; 10:6; Joel 1:13–14.
9:3 *quarter of the day.* About three hours.
9:5–37 One of the most beautiful prayers outside the Psalms, it reviews God's grace and power (1) in creation (v. 6), (2) in the Abrahamic covenant (vv. 7–8), (3) in Egypt and at the Red Sea (vv. 9–11), (4) in the desert and at Sinai (vv. 12–21), (5) during the conquest of Canaan (vv. 22–25), (6) through the judges (vv. 26–28), (7) through the prophets (vv. 29–31) and (8) in the present situation (vv. 32–37). Cf. Ps 78; 105–106.
9:6 *You alone are the LORD.* Though not in the words of Dt 6:4, which expresses the central monotheistic conviction of Israel's faith, the prayer begins with a similar affirmation (cf.

2Ki 19:15; Ps 86:10). *highest heavens.* See Dt 10:14; 1Ki 8:27; 2Ch 2:6; Ps 148:4. *multitudes of heaven worship you.* See Ps 89:5–7.
9:7 *Ur of the Chaldeans.* See note on Ge 11:28. *named him Abraham.* See note on Ge 17:5.
9:8 *faithful.* Compare Ro 4:16–22 with Jas 2:21–23. *made a covenant with him.* See note on Ge 15:18. *Canaanites . . . Girgashites.* See notes on Ge 10:6,15–18; 13:7; Ex 3:8; Ezr 9:1.
9:9 *Red Sea.* See notes on Ex 13:18; 14:2.
9:11 *divided the sea.* See Ex 14:21–22; 1Co 10:1.
9:13 *laws.* The singular form of the Hebrew for this word is *Torah,* which means "instruction," "law," and later the Pentateuch, the five books of Moses.
9:14 *holy Sabbath.* According to the rabbis, "the Sabbath outweighs all the commandments of the Torah." See 10:31–33; 13:15–22.
9:15 *bread from heaven.* See note on Ex 16:4. *water from the rock.* See note on Ex 17:6. *sworn with uplifted hand.* See Ge 14:22 and note; 22:15–17; Ex 6:8; Eze 20:6; 47:14.

water from the rock;*q* you told them to go in and take possession of the land you had sworn with uplifted hand*r* to give them.*s*

16"But they, our forefathers, became arrogant and stiff-necked,*t* and did not obey your commands.*u* 17They refused to listen and failed to remember*v* the miracles*w* you performed among them. They became stiff-necked*x* and in their rebellion appointed a leader in order to return to their slavery.*y* But you are a forgiving God,*z* gracious and compassionate,*a* slow to anger*b* and abounding in love.*c* Therefore you did not desert them,*d* 18even when they cast for themselves an image of a calf*e* and said, 'This is your god, who brought you up out of Egypt,' or when they committed awful blasphemies.*f*

19"Because of your great compassion you did not abandon*g* them in the desert. By day the pillar of cloud*h* did not cease to guide them on their path, nor the pillar of fire by night to shine on the way they were to take. 20You gave your good Spirit*i* to instruct*j* them. You did not withhold your manna*k* from their mouths, and you gave them water*l* for their thirst. 21For forty years*m* you sustained them in the desert; they lacked nothing,*n* their clothes did not wear out nor did their feet become swollen.*o*

22"You gave them kingdoms and nations, allotting to them even the remotest frontiers. They took over the country of Sihon*y p* king of Heshbon and the country of Og king of Bashan.*q* 23You made their sons as numerous as the stars in the sky,*r* and you brought them into the land that you told their fathers to enter and pos-

sess. 24Their sons went in and took possession of the land.*s* You subdued*t* before them the Canaanites, who lived in the land; you handed the Canaanites over to them, along with their kings and the peoples of the land, to deal with them as they pleased. 25They captured fortified cities and fertile land;*u* they took possession of houses filled with all kinds of good things,*v* wells already dug, vineyards, olive groves and fruit trees in abundance. They ate to the full and were well-nourished;*w* they reveled in your great goodness.*x*

26"But they were disobedient and rebelled against you; they put your law behind their backs.*y* They killed*z* your prophets,*a* who had admonished them in order to turn them back to you; they committed awful blasphemies.*b* 27So you handed them over to their enemies,*c* who oppressed them. But when they were oppressed they cried out to you. From heaven you heard them, and in your great compassion*d* you gave them deliverers,*e* who rescued them from the hand of their enemies.

28"But as soon as they were at rest, they again did what was evil in your sight.*f* Then you abandoned them to the hand of their enemies so that they ruled over them. And when they cried out to you again, you heard from heaven, and in your compassion*g* you delivered them*h* time after time.

29"You warned*i* them to return to your law, but they became arrogant*j*

9:15 *q*Ex 17:6; Nu 20:7-13
*r*S Ge 14:22
*s*Dt 1:8,21
9:16 *t*S Ex 32:9; Jer 7:26; 17:23; 19:15
*u*Dt 1:26-33; 31:29
9:17 *v*Jdg 8:34; Ps 78:42
*w*Ps 77:11; 78:12; 105:5; 106:7 *x*Jer 7:26; 19:15 *y*Nu 14:1-4
*z*Ps 130:4; Da 9:9
*a*S Dt 4:31
*b*S Ex 34:6; Ps 103:8; Na 1:3
*c*S Ex 22:27; Nu 14:17-19; Ps 86:15
*d*Ps 78:11; Eze 5:6
9:18 *e*S Ex 32:4
*f*S Ex 20:23
9:19 *g*Ex 13:22
*h*S Ex 13:21
9:20 *i*Nu 9:17; 11:17; Isa 63:11, 14; Hag 2:5; Zec 4:6 /Ps 23:3; 143:10
*k*S Ex 16:15
*l*Ex 17:6
9:21 *m*S Ex 16:35
*n*S Dt 2:7
*o*S Dt 8:4
9:22 *p*S Nu 21:21
*q*S Nu 21:33; Dt 2:26-3:11
9:23 *r*S Ge 12:2; S Lev 26:9; S Nu 10:36

9:24 *s*S Jos 11:23
*t*S Jdg 4:23; S 2Ch 14:13
9:25 *u*S Dt 11:11
*v*S Ex 18:9
*w*Dt 6:10-12
*x*Dt 8:8-11; 32:12-15; Ps 23:6; 25:7; 69:16
9:26 *y*S 1Ki 14:9; Jer 44:10
*z*S Jos 7:25
*a*Jer 2:30; 26:8; Mt 21:35-36; 23:29-36; Ac 7:52
*b*S Jdg 2:12-13
9:27
*c*S Nu 25:17; S Jdg 2:14
*d*Ps 51:1; 103:8; 106:45; 119:156
*e*S Jdg 3:9

9:28 *f*S Ex 32:22; S Jdg 2:17 *g*S 2Sa 24:14 *h*Ps 22:4; 106:43; 136:24 **9:29** *i*S Jdg 6:8 /ver 16-17; Ps 5:5; Isa 2:11; Jer 43:2

*y*22 One Hebrew manuscript and Septuagint; most Hebrew manuscripts *Sihon, that is, the country of the*

9:16 *stiff-necked.* See vv. 17,29; see also notes on 3:5; Ex 32:9.

9:17 *appointed a leader.* Their intention to do so is recorded in Nu 14:4. *gracious . . . abounding in love.* See note on Ex 34:6-7.

9:18 *blasphemies.* See v. 26; Eze 35:12.

9:19 *compassion.* See vv. 27-28; a tender, maternal kind of love (see note on Zec 1:16).

9:20 *Spirit to instruct.* See Ex 31:3.

9:21 *clothes did not wear out.* Evidence of the special providence of God (see Dt 8:4; 29:5; contrast Jos 9:13). *swollen.* Or "blistered"; the Hebrew for this word occurs only here and in Dt 8:4.

9:22 *Sihon . . . Og.* See Nu 21:21-35.

9:23 *numerous as the stars.* See notes on Ge 13:16; 15:5; 22:17.

9:25 See Dt 6:10-12 and note; Jos 24:13. *fertile.* See v.

35; cf. Nu 14:7; Dt 8:7; Jos 23:13. *wells already dug.* Because of the lack of rainfall during much of the year, almost every house had its own well or cistern in which to store water from the rainy seasons (2Ki 18:31; Pr 5:15). By 1200 B.C. the technique of waterproofing cisterns was developed, permitting greater occupation of the central hills of Judah. *vineyards, olive groves and fruit trees.* Cf. Dt 8:8. The Egyptian story of Sinuhe (c. 2000 B.C.) describes Canaan as follows: "Figs were in it, and grapes. It had more wine than water. Plentiful was its honey, abundant its olives. Every (kind of) fruit was on its trees." *well-nourished.* Elsewhere the Hebrew for this word always implies physical fullness and spiritual insensitivity.

9:26–28 See note on Jdg 2:6–3:6.

9:27 *deliverers.* See Introduction to Judges: Title.

9:29 *will live if he obeys.* See note on Lev 18:5. *Stubbornly they turned their backs.* See Zec 7:11; cf. the similar expressions in v. 16; 3:5; Hos 4:16.

and disobeyed your commands. They sinned against your ordinances, by which a man will live if he obeys them.[k] Stubbornly they turned their backs[l] on you, became stiff-necked[m] and refused to listen.[n] ³⁰For many years you were patient with them. By your Spirit you admonished them through your prophets.[o] Yet they paid no attention, so you handed them over to the neighboring peoples.[p] ³¹But in your great mercy you did not put an end[q] to them or abandon them, for you are a gracious and merciful[r] God.

³²"Now therefore, O our God, the great, mighty[s] and awesome God,[t] who keeps his covenant of love,[u] do not let all this hardship seem trifling in your eyes—the hardship[v] that has come upon us, upon our kings and leaders, upon our priests and prophets, upon our fathers and all your people, from the days of the kings of Assyria until today. ³³In all that has happened to us, you have been just;[w] you have acted faithfully, while we did wrong.[x] ³⁴Our kings,[y] our leaders, our priests and our fathers[z] did not follow your law; they did not pay attention to your commands or the warnings you gave them. ³⁵Even while they were in their kingdom, enjoying your great goodness[a] to them in the spacious and fertile land you gave them, they did not serve you[b] or turn from their evil ways.

³⁶"But see, we are slaves[c] today, slaves in the land you gave our forefathers so they could eat its fruit and the other good things it produces. ³⁷Because of our sins, its abundant harvest goes to the kings you have placed over us. They rule over our bodies and our cattle as they please. We are in great distress.[d]

The Agreement of the People

³⁸"In view of all this, we are making a binding agreement,[e] putting it in writ-

ing,[f] and our leaders, our Levites and our priests are affixing their seals to it."

10 Those who sealed it were:

Nehemiah the governor, the son of Hacaliah.

Zedekiah, ²Seraiah,[g] Azariah, Jeremiah,
³Pashhur,[h] Amariah, Malkijah,
⁴Hattush, Shebaniah, Malluch,
⁵Harim,[i] Meremoth, Obadiah,
⁶Daniel, Ginnethon, Baruch,
⁷Meshullam, Abijah, Mijamin,
⁸Maaziah, Bilgai and Shemaiah.
These were the priests.[j]

⁹The Levites:[k]

Jeshua son of Azaniah, Binnui of the sons of Henadad, Kadmiel,
¹⁰and their associates: Shebaniah, Hodiah, Kelita, Pelaiah, Hanan,
¹¹Mica, Rehob, Hashabiah,
¹²Zaccur, Sherebiah, Shebaniah,
¹³Hodiah, Bani and Beninu.

¹⁴The leaders of the people:

Parosh, Pahath-Moab, Elam, Zattu, Bani,
¹⁵Bunni, Azgad, Bebai,
¹⁶Adonijah, Bigvai, Adin,[l]
¹⁷Ater, Hezekiah, Azzur,
¹⁸Hodiah, Hashum, Bezai,
¹⁹Hariph, Anathoth, Nebai,
²⁰Magpiash, Meshullam, Hezir,[m]
²¹Meshezabel, Zadok, Jaddua,
²²Pelatiah, Hanan, Anaiah,
²³Hoshea, Hananiah,[n] Hasshub,
²⁴Hallohesh, Pilha, Shobek,
²⁵Rehum, Hashabnah, Maaseiah,
²⁶Ahiah, Hanan, Anan,
²⁷Malluch, Harim and Baanah.

²⁸"The rest of the people—priests, Levites, gatekeepers, singers, temple servants[o] and all who separated themselves from the neighboring peoples[p] for the sake of the Law of God, together with their wives and all their sons and daughters who are able to understand— ²⁹all these now join their brothers the nobles, and bind

9:29 [k]S Dt 30:16
[l]S 1Sa 8:3
[m]Jer 19:15
[n]Zec 7:11-12
9:30
[o]2Ki 17:13-18; S 2Ch 36:16
[p]Jer 16:11; Zec 7:12
9:31 [q]Isa 48:9; 65:9 [r]S Dt 4:31
9:32 [s]Job 9:19; Ps 24:8; 89:8; 93:4 [t]S Dt 7:21
[u]S Dt 7:9; S 1Ki 8:23; Da 9:4 [v]S Ex 18:8
9:33 [w]S Ge 18:25
[x]Jer 44:3; Da 9:7-8,14
9:34 [y]S 2Ki 23:11
[z]Jer 44:17
9:35 [a]Isa 63:7
[b]Dt 28:45-48
9:36 [c]S Ezr 9:9
9:37 [d]Dt 28:33; La 5:5
9:38
[e]S 2Ch 23:16

[f]Isa 44:5
10:2 [g]S Ezr 2:2
10:3 [h]S 1Ch 9:12
10:5 [i]S 1Ch 24:8
10:8 [j]Ne 12:1
10:9 [k]Ne 12:1
10:16 [l]S Ezr 8:6
10:20
[m]1Ch 24:15
10:23 [n]S Ne 7:2
10:28 [o]Ps 135:1
[p]2Ch 6:26;
S Ne 9:2

9:32 *kings of Assyria.* Including Tiglath-Pileser III, also known as Pul (1Ch 5:26); Shalmaneser V (2Ki 18:9); Sargon II (Isa 20:1); Sennacherib (2Ki 18:13); Esarhaddon (Ezr 4:2); and Ashurbanipal (Ezr 4:10).
9:37 *rule over our bodies.* See 1Sa 8:11-13. The Persian rulers drafted their subjects into military service. Some Jews may have accompanied Xerxes on his invasion of Greece in 480 B.C.
10:1-27 A legal list, bearing the official seal and containing

a roster of 84 names.
10:2-8 About half of these names occur again in 12:1-7.
10:9-13 Most of these names appear also in the lists of Levites in 8:7; 9:4-5.
10:14-27 Almost half of the names in this category are also found in the lists of 7:6-63; Ezr 2:1-61.
10:28 *Levites.* See Introduction to Leviticus: Title. *gatekeepers.* See note on Ezr 2:42. *wives . . . sons and daughters.* See note on 8:2.

themselves with a curse and an oath[q] to follow the Law of God given through Moses the servant of God and to obey carefully all the commands, regulations and decrees of the LORD our Lord.

30"We promise not to give our daughters in marriage to the peoples around us or take their daughters for our sons.[r]

31"When the neighboring peoples bring merchandise or grain to sell on the Sabbath,[s] we will not buy from them on the Sabbath or on any holy day. Every seventh year we will forgo working the land[t] and will cancel all debts.[u]

32"We assume the responsibility for carrying out the commands to give a third of a shekel[z] each year for the service of the house of our God: 33for the bread set out on the table;[v] for the regular grain offerings and burnt offerings; for the offerings on the Sabbaths, New Moon[w] festivals and appointed feasts; for the holy offerings; for sin offerings to make atonement for Israel; and for all the duties of the house of our God.[x]

34"We—the priests, the Levites and the people—have cast lots[y] to determine when each of our families is to bring to the house of our God at set times each year a contribution of wood[z] to burn on the altar of the LORD our God, as it is written in the Law.

35"We also assume responsibility

for bringing to the house of the LORD each year the firstfruits[a] of our crops and of every fruit tree.[b]

36"As it is also written in the Law, we will bring the firstborn[c] of our sons and of our cattle, of our herds and of our flocks to the house of our God, to the priests ministering there.[d]

37"Moreover, we will bring to the storerooms of the house of our God, to the priests, the first of our ground meal, of our grain offerings, of the fruit of all our trees and of our new wine and oil.[e] And we will bring a tithe[f] of our crops to the Levites,[g] for it is the Levites who collect the tithes in all the towns where we work.[h] 38A priest descended from Aaron is to accompany the Levites when they receive the tithes, and the Levites are to bring a tenth of the tithes[i] up to the house of our God, to the storerooms of the treasury. 39The people of Israel, including the Levites, are to bring their contributions of grain, new wine and oil to the storerooms where the articles for the sanctuary are kept and where the ministering priests, the gatekeepers and the singers stay.

"We will not neglect the house of our God."[j]

The New Residents of Jerusalem

11:3–19pp — 1Ch 9:1–17

11 Now the leaders of the people settled in Jerusalem, and the rest of

10:29
qS Nu 5:21;
Ps 119:106
10:30
rS Ex 34:16;
Ne 13:23
10:31 sNe 13:16,
18; Jer 17:27;
Eze 23:38;
Am 8:5
tS Ex 23:11;
Lev 25:1-7
uS Dt 15:1
10:33 vLev 24:6
wNu 10:10;
Ps 81:3; Isa 1:14
xS 2Ch 24:5
10:34
yS Lev 16:8
zNe 13:31

10:35
aS Ex 22:29;
S Nu 18:12
bDt 26:1-11
10:36
cS Ex 13:2;
S Nu 18:14-16
dNe 13:31
10:37
eS Nu 18:12
fS Lev 27:30;
S Nu 18:21
gDt 14:22-29
hEze 44:30
10:38 iNu 18:26
10:39 jNe 13:11,
12

z32 That is, about 1/8 ounce (about 4 grams)

10:31–33 Perhaps a code drawn up by Nehemiah to correct the abuses listed in 13:15–22.
10:31 *sell on the Sabbath.* Though Ex 20:8–11; Dt 5:12–15 do not explicitly prohibit trading on the Sabbath, see Jer 17:19–27; Am 8:5 and note. *seventh year . . . forgo working the land . . . cancel all debts.* See note on Lev 25:4. The Romans misrepresented the Sabbath and the sabbath year as caused by laziness. According to Tacitus, the Jews "were led by the charms of indolence to give over the seventh year as well to inactivity."
10:32 *third of a shekel.* Ex 30:13–14 speaks of a "half shekel" as "an offering to the LORD" from each man who was 20 years old or more as a symbolic ransom. Later Joash used the annual contributions for the repair of the temple (2Ch 24:4–14). In the NT period Jewish men from everywhere sent an offering of a half shekel (actually two drachmas, its equivalent; see Josephus, *Antiquities,* 3.8.2) for the temple in Jerusalem (Mt 17:24). The pledge of a third of a shekel in Nehemiah's time may have been due to economic circumstances.
10:33 *bread.* See note on Lev 24:8.
10:34 *cast lots.* See notes on 11:1; Jnh 1:7. *contribution of wood.* Though there is no specific reference to a wood offering in the Pentateuch, the perpetual burning of fire on the sanctuary altar (Lev 6:12–13) would have required a

continual supply of wood. Josephus mentions "the festival of wood offering" on the 14th day of the fifth month (Ab). The Jewish Mishnah (rabbinic interpretations and applications of Pentateuchal laws) lists nine times when certain families brought wood, and stipulates that all kinds of wood were suitable except the vine and the olive. The Temple Scroll from Qumran describes the celebration of a wood offering festival for six days following a new oil festival.
10:35 *firstfruits.* Brought to the sanctuary to support the priests and Levites (Ex 23:19; Nu 18:13; Dt 26:1–11; Eze 44:30).
10:36 *firstborn.* See note on Ex 13:13.
10:37 *storerooms.* Chambers in the courts of the temple were used as storage rooms for silver, gold and sacred articles (cf. vv. 38–39; 12:44; 13:4–5,9; Ezr 8:28–30). *new wine.* See note on Dt 7:13. Though the Hebrew for this term can refer to freshly pressed grape juice (Isa 65:8; Mic 6:15), it can also be used of intoxicating wine (Hos 4:11). *tithe.* See notes on Ge 14:20; 28:22; Lev 27:30; Am 4:4. *Levites.* Tithes were meant for their support (13:12–13; Nu 18:21–32).
10:39 See 13:11. *We will not neglect.* Haggai (Hag 1:4–9) had accused the people of neglecting the temple.
11:1 *cast lots.* See 10:34. Lots were usually made out of small stones or pieces of wood. Sometimes arrows were used

the people cast lots to bring one out of every ten to live in Jerusalem,[k] the holy city,[l] while the remaining nine were to stay in their own towns.[m] [2]The people commended all the men who volunteered to live in Jerusalem.

[3]These are the provincial leaders who settled in Jerusalem (now some Israelites, priests, Levites, temple servants and descendants of Solomon's servants lived in the towns of Judah, each on his own property in the various towns,[n] [4]while other people from both Judah and Benjamin[o] lived in Jerusalem):[p]

From the descendants of Judah:

Athaiah son of Uzziah, the son of Zechariah, the son of Amariah, the son of Shephatiah, the son of Mahalalel, a descendant of Perez; [5]and Maaseiah son of Baruch, the son of Col-Hozeh, the son of Hazaiah, the son of Adaiah, the son of Joiarib, the son of Zechariah, a descendant of Shelah. [6]The descendants of Perez who lived in Jerusalem totaled 468 able men.

[7]From the descendants of Benjamin:

Sallu son of Meshullam, the son of Joed, the son of Pedaiah, the son of Kolaiah, the son of Maaseiah, the son of Ithiel, the son of Jeshaiah, [8]and his followers, Gabbai and Sallai—928 men. [9]Joel son of Zicri was their chief officer, and Judah son of Hassenuah was over the Second District of the city.

[10]From the priests:

Jedaiah; the son of Joiarib; Jakin; [11]Seraiah[q] son of Hilkiah, the son of Me-

shullam, the son of Zadok, the son of Meraioth, the son of Ahitub,[r] supervisor in the house of God, [12]and their associates, who carried on work for the temple—822 men; Adaiah son of Jeroham, the son of Pelaliah, the son of Amzi, the son of Zechariah, the son of Pashhur, the son of Malkijah, [13]and his associates, who were heads of families—242 men; Amashsai son of Azarel, the son of Ahzai, the son of Meshillemoth, the son of Immer, [14]and his[a] associates, who were able men—128. Their chief officer was Zabdiel son of Haggedolim.

[15]From the Levites:

Shemaiah son of Hasshub, the son of Azrikam, the son of Hashabiah, the son of Bunni; [16]Shabbethai[s] and Jozabad,[t] two of the heads of the Levites, who had charge of the outside work of the house of God; [17]Mattaniah[u] son of Mica, the son of Zabdi, the son of Asaph,[v] the director who led in thanksgiving and prayer; Bakbukiah, second among his associates; and Abda son of Shammua, the son of Galal, the son of Jeduthun.[w] [18]The Levites in the holy city[x] totaled 284.

[19]The gatekeepers:

Akkub, Talmon and their associates, who kept watch at the gates—172 men.

[20]The rest of the Israelites, with the priests and Levites, were in all the towns of Judah, each on his ancestral property. [21]The temple servants[y] lived on the hill

11:1 [k]Ne 7:4
[l]Isa 48:2; 52:1;
64:10;
Zec 14:20-21
[m]S Ne 7:73
11:3 [n]S Ezr 2:1
11:4 [o]S Ezr 1:5
[p]S Ezr 2:70
11:11
[q]S 2Ki 25:18;
S Ezr 2:2

[r]S Ezr 7:2
11:16 [s]Ezr 10:15
[t]S Ezr 8:33
11:17
[u]S 1Ch 9:15;
Ne 12:8
[v]2Ch 5:12
[w]S 1Ch 25:1
11:18
[x]S Rev 21:2
11:21
[y]S Ezr 2:43;
S Ne 3:26

[a]*14* Most Septuagint manuscripts; Hebrew *their*

(Eze 21:21). *one out of every ten to live in Jerusalem.* Josephus (*Antiquities,* 11.5.8) asserts: "But Nehemiah, seeing that the city had a small population, urged the priests and Levites to leave the countryside and move to the city and remain there, for he had prepared houses for them at his own expense." The practice of redistributing populations was also used to establish Greek and Hellenistic cities. It involved the forcible transfer from rural settlements to urban centers. Tiberias on the Sea of Galilee was populated with Gentiles by such a process by Herod Antipas in A.D. 18. *holy city.* See Isa 48:2 and note; Da 9:24; Mt 4:5; 27:53; Rev 11:2; cf. Joel 3:17.

11:2 In addition to those chosen by lot (v. 1), some volunteered out of a sense of duty. But evidently most preferred to stay in their hometowns.

11:3–19 A census roster that parallels 1Ch 9:2–21, a list of the first residents in Jerusalem after the return from Babylonia. About half the names in the two lists are the same.

11:8 *928.* The men of Benjamin provided twice as many men as Judah (v. 6) to live in and protect the city of Jerusalem.

11:9 *Second District.* See 2Ch 34:22 (in Zep 1:10 the Hebrew for this phrase is translated "New Quarter"). Like the "market district" (Zep 1:11), which was probably the Tyropoeon Valley area, the Second District was a new suburb west of the temple area. Excavations indicate that the city had spread outside the walls in this direction by the late eighth century B.C. before the so-called Broad Wall was built c. 700 by Hezekiah (see note on 3:8).

11:16 *outside work.* Duties outside the temple (cf. 1Ch 26:29) but connected with it.

11:17 *Asaph.* See note on Ezr 2:41; see also titles of Ps 50; 73–83. *Jeduthun.* See 1Ch 16:42; 25:1,3; 2Ch 5:12; titles of Ps 39; 62; 77.

11:18 *284.* The relatively small number of Levites, compared with 1,192 priests (the total of 822, 242 and 128 in vv. 12–13), is striking (see note on Ezr 2:40).

11:20 *ancestral property.* Inalienable hereditary possessions—including land, buildings and movable goods—acquired by either conquest or inheritance (Ge 31:14; Nu 18:21; 27:7; 34:2; 36:3; 1Ki 21:1–4).

11:21 *Ophel.* See note on 3:26.

of Ophel, and Ziha and Gishpa were in charge of them.

22The chief officer of the Levites in Jerusalem was Uzzi son of Bani, the son of Hashabiah, the son of Mattaniah, *z* the son of Mica. Uzzi was one of Asaph's descendants, who were the singers responsible for the service of the house of God. 23The singers *a* were under the king's orders, which regulated their daily activity.

24Pethahiah son of Meshezabel, one of the descendants of Zerah *b* son of Judah, was the king's agent in all affairs relating to the people.

25As for the villages with their fields, some of the people of Judah lived in Kiriath Arba *c* and its surrounding settlements, in Dibon *d* and its settlements, in Jekabzeel and its villages, 26in Jeshua, in Moladah, *e* in Beth Pelet, *f* 27in Hazar Shual, *g* in Beersheba *h* and its settlements, 28in Ziklag, *i* in Meconah and its settlements, 29in En Rimmon, in Zorah, *j* in Jarmuth, *k* 30Zanoah, *l* Adullam *m* and their villages, in Lachish *n* and its fields, and in Azekah *o* and its settlements. So they were living all the way from Beersheba *p* to the Valley of Hinnom.

31The descendants of the Benjamites from Geba *q* lived in Micmash, *r* Aija, Bethel *s* and its settlements, 32in Anathoth, *t* Nob *u* and Ananiah, 33in Hazor, *v* Ramah *w* and Gittaim, *x* 34in Hadid, Zeboim *y* and Neballat, 35in Lod and Ono, *z* and in the Valley of the Craftsmen.

36Some of the divisions of the Levites of Judah settled in Benjamin.

Priests and Levites

12 These were the priests *a* and Levites *b* who returned with Zerubbabel *c* son of Shealtiel *d* and with Jeshua: *e* Seraiah, *f* Jeremiah, Ezra, 2Amariah, Malluch, Hattush, 3Shecaniah, Rehum, Meremoth, 4Iddo, *g* Ginnethon, *b* Abijah, *h* 5Mijamin, *c* Moadiah, Bilgah, 6Shemaiah, Joiarib, Jedaiah, *i* 7Sallu, Amok, Hilkiah and Jedaiah. These were the leaders of the priests and their associates in the days of Jeshua.

Cross references (margin)

11:22 *z* 1Ch 9:15
11:23 *a* S 1Ch 15:16; Ne 7:44
11:24 *b* S Ge 38:30
11:25 *c* S Ge 35:27; *d* S Nu 21:30
11:26 *e* Jos 15:26; *f* Jos 15:27
11:27 *g* Jos 15:28; *h* S Ge 21:14
11:28 *i* S 1Sa 27:6
11:29 *j* Jos 15:33; *k* S Jos 10:3; S 15:35
11:30 *l* Jos 15:34; *m* Jos 15:35; *n* S Jos 10:3; 15:39; *o* S Jos 10:10; *p* Jos 15:28
11:31 *q* Jos 21:17; *r* S 1Sa 13:2; *s* S Jos 12:9
11:32 *t* Jos 21:18; Isa 10:30; Jer 1:1; *u* S 1Sa 21:1
11:33 *v* S Jos 11:1; *w* S Jos 18:25; *x* 2Sa 4:3
11:34 *y* 1Sa 13:18
11:35 *z* S 1Ch 8:12
12:1 *a* Ne 10:1-8; *b* Ne 10:9; *c* S 1Ch 3:19; Ezr 3:2; Zec 4:6-10; *d* Ezr 3:2
12:4 *g* ver 16; Zec 1:1 *h* S 1Ch 24:10; Lk 1:5 12:6 *i* S 1Ch 24:7

e S Ezr 2:2 *f* S Ezr 2:2

b 4 Many Hebrew manuscripts and Vulgate (see also Neh. 12:16); most Hebrew manuscripts *Ginnethoi*   *c* 5 A variant of *Miniamin*

11:23 *king's orders . . . regulated.* David had regulated the services of the Levites, including the singers (1Ch 25). The Persian king, Darius I, gave a royal stipend so that the Jewish elders might "pray for the well-being of the king and his sons" (Ezr 6:10). Artaxerxes I may have done much the same for the Levite choir.

11:25–30 An important list, corresponding to earlier lists of towns in Judah. All these names also appear in Jos 15 with the exception of Dibon, Jekabzeel (but see Kabzeel in Jos 15:21), Jeshua, Meconah and En Rimmon (but see Ain and Rimmon in Jos 15:32). The list, however, is not comprehensive, since a number of towns listed in ch. 3; Ezr 2:21–22 are lacking. No Judean coins have been found outside the area designated by vv. 25–30.

11:25 *Kiriath Arba.* See note on Ge 23:2. In the Hellenistic era it fell to the Idumeans, together with other Judean towns.

11:26 *Moladah.* Near Beersheba; later occupied by the Idumeans. *Beth Pelet.* Means "house of refuge," a site near Beersheba.

11:27 *Hazar Shual.* Means "enclosure of a fox" (see 1Ch 4:28). *Beersheba.* See note and NIV text note on Ge 21:31. Archaeological excavations reveal that the city was destroyed by Sennacherib in 701 B.C. and only resettled in the Persian period.

11:28 *Ziklag.* Given to David by Achish, king of Gath (1Sa 27:6), and taken by the Amalekites (1Sa 30:1); see Jos 15:31.

11:29 *En Rimmon.* Means "spring of the pomegranate," probably Khirbet Umm er-Ramamin, nine miles north-northeast of Beersheba (see Jos 15:32). *Zorah.* See note on Jdg 13:2. *Jarmuth.* Eight miles north-northeast of Eleutheropolis (Beit Jibrin), it was one of five Canaanite cities in the south that attempted to halt Joshua's invasion (Jos 10:3–5).

11:30 *Zanoah.* A village in the Shephelah district of low hills between Judah and Philistia. The men of Zanoah re-

paired the Valley Gate (3:13). The site has been identified with Khirbet Zanu, three miles south-southeast of Beth Shemesh. *Adullam.* See note on Ge 38:1. *Lachish.* See Jos 10:3; see also notes on Isa 36:2; Mic 1:13. *Azekah.* See note on Jer 34:7. *Hinnom.* The valley west and south of Jerusalem; Gehenna in the NT.

11:31–35 Most of the Benjamite towns listed here appear also in 7:26–38; Ezr 2:23–35.

11:31 *Geba.* See 12:29; see also note on 1Sa 13:3. *Micmash.* See note on 1Sa 13:2. *Aija.* An alternate name for Ai (see note on Jos 7:2). *Bethel.* See notes on Ge 12:8; Jos 7:2; Ezr 2:28; Am 4:4.

11:32 *Anathoth.* See note on Jer 1:1. *Nob.* See note on 1Sa 21:1. *Ananiah.* Probably Bethany, meaning "house of Ananiah" (see note on Mt 21:17).

11:33 *Gittaim.* Its location is not known.

11:34 *Hadid.* Three to four miles northeast of Lod (see 7:37; Ezr 2:33).

11:35 *Lod.* See note on Ezr 2:33. *Ono.* See note on 6:2. *Valley of the Craftsmen.* See 1Ch 4:14 and NIV text note. It may be the broad valley between Lod and Ono. The name may preserve the memory of the Philistine iron monopoly (1Sa 13:19–20).

12:1 *Zerubbabel son of Shealtiel.* See Ezr 3:2,8; 5:2; see also note on Hag 1:1. *Jeshua.* Returned from Babylonian exile in 538 B.C. (see vv. 10,26; 7:7; Ezr 2:2 and note; Hag 1:1; Zec 3:1 and note). *Ezra.* Not the Ezra of the book, who was the leader of the exiles who returned 80 years later.

12:7 *leaders of the priests.* The rotation of 24 priestly houses was established at the time of David (1Ch 24:3, 7–19). Twenty-two heads of priestly houses are mentioned in vv. 1–7. Inscriptions listing the 24 divisions of the priests probably hung in many synagogues in Palestine. So far, only fragments of two such inscriptions have been recovered—from Ashkelon in the 1920s and from Caesarea in the 1960s (dated to the third and fourth centuries A.D.).

[8]The Levites were Jeshua,[j] Binnui, Kadmiel, Sherebiah, Judah, and also Mattaniah,[k] who, together with his associates, was in charge of the songs of thanksgiving. [9]Bakbukiah and Unni, their associates, stood opposite them in the services.

[10]Jeshua was the father of Joiakim, Joiakim the father of Eliashib,[l] Eliashib the father of Joiada, [11]Joiada the father of Jonathan, and Jonathan the father of Jaddua.

[12]In the days of Joiakim, these were the heads of the priestly families:

of Seraiah's family, Meraiah;

of Jeremiah's, Hananiah;

[13]of Ezra's, Meshullam;

of Amariah's, Jehohanan;

[14]of Malluch's, Jonathan;

of Shecaniah's,[d] Joseph;

[15]of Harim's, Adna;

of Meremoth's,[e] Helkai;

[16]of Iddo's,[m] Zechariah;

of Ginnethon's, Meshullam;

[17]of Abijah's,[n] Zicri;

of Miniamin's and of Moadiah's, Piltai;

[18]of Bilgah's, Shammua;

of Shemaiah's, Jehonathan;

[19]of Joiarib's, Mattenai;

of Jedaiah's, Uzzi;

[20]of Sallu's, Kallai;

of Amok's, Eber;

[21]of Hilkiah's, Hashabiah;

of Jedaiah's, Nethanel.

[22]The family heads of the Levites in the days of Eliashib, Joiada, Johanan and Jaddua, as well as those of the priests, were recorded in the reign of Darius the Persian. [23]The family heads among the descendants of Levi up to the time of Johanan son of Eliashib were recorded in the book of the annals. [24]And the leaders of the Levites[o] were Hashabiah, Sherebiah, Jeshua son of Kadmiel, and their associates, who stood opposite them to give praise and thanksgiving, one section responding to the other, as prescribed by David the man of God.[p]

[25]Mattaniah, Bakbukiah, Obadiah, Meshullam, Talmon and Akkub were gatekeepers who guarded the storerooms at the gates. [26]They served in the days of Joiakim son of Jeshua, the son of Jozadak, and in the days of Nehemiah the governor and of Ezra the priest and scribe.

Dedication of the Wall of Jerusalem

[27]At the dedication[q] of the wall of Jerusalem, the Levites were sought out from where they lived and were brought to Jerusalem to celebrate joyfully the dedication with songs of thanksgiving and with the music of cymbals,[r] harps and lyres.[s] [28]The singers also were brought together from the region around Jerusalem—from

Cross references (center column)

12:8 /S Ezr 2:2
*k*S Ne 11:17
12:10 /S Ezr 10:24; Ne 3:20
12:16 *m*S ver 4
12:17 *n*S 1Ch 24:10
12:24 *o*S Ezr 2:40 *p*S 2Ch 8:14
12:27 *q*Dt 20:5 *r*S 2Sa 6:5 *s*S 1Ch 15:16,28; 25:6; Ps 92:3

Textual footnotes

*d*14 Very many Hebrew manuscripts, some Septuagint manuscripts and Syriac (see also Neh. 12:3); most Hebrew manuscripts *Shebaniah's*   *e*15 Some Septuagint manuscripts (see also Neh. 12:3); Hebrew *Meraioth's*

12:9 *opposite them.* See v. 24; Ezr 3:11 and note; cf. 2Ch 7:6. The singing was antiphonal, with two sections of the choir standing opposite each other. *services.* The Hebrew for this word (*Mishmarot*) is the title of a work from Qumran, which discusses in detail the rotation of the priestly families' service in the temple according to the sect's solar calendar and synchronized with the conventional lunar calendar.

12:10 *Jeshua.* See note on v. 1. *Joiakim.* See vv. 12,26. *Eliashib.* See vv. 22–23; the high priest who assisted in rebuilding the wall (3:1,20–21; 13:28). A priest named Eliashib was guilty of defiling the temple by assigning rooms to Tobiah the Ammonite (13:4,7). It is not known whether this Eliashib was the same as the high priest.

12:11 *Jonathan.* Since v. 22 mentions a Johanan after Joiada and before Jaddua, and v. 23 identifies Johanan as "son" of Eliashib, some believe that "Jonathan" is an error for "Johanan." Further complicating the identification are attempts to identify this high priest with a "Johanan" mentioned in the Elephantine papyri and in Josephus (*Antiquities,* 11.7.1). Such an identification, however, is disputable.

12:12–21 All but one (Hattush, v. 2) of the 22 priestly families listed in vv. 1–7 are repeated (Rehum, v. 3, is a variant of Harim, v. 15; Mijamin, v. 5, is a variant of Miniamin, v. 17) in this later list, which dates to the time of Joiakim (v. 12), high priest in the late sixth and/or early fifth

centuries B.C.

12:22 *Darius the Persian.* Either Darius II Nothus (423–404 B.C.) or Darius III Codamannus (336–331).

12:23 *book of the annals.* Cf. 7:5. This may have been the official temple chronicle, containing various lists and records. Cf. the annals of the Persian kings (Ezr 4:15; Est 2:23; 6:1; 10:2); cf. also the "book of the annals of the kings," mentioned frequently in 1,2 Kings.

12:26 *Nehemiah . . . Ezra.* See note on 8:9.

12:27 *dedication.* See note on Ezr 6:16. *cymbals.* See note on Ezr 3:10. Cymbals were used in religious ceremonies (1Ch 16:42; 25:1; 2Ch 5:12; 29:25). Ancient examples have been found at Beth Shemesh and Tell Abu Hawam. *harps.* See note on Ge 31:27; used mainly in religious ceremonies (1Sa 10:5; 2Sa 6:5; Ps 150:3). Ancient harps have been reconstructed from information derived from the remains of harps at Ur, pictures of harps, and cuneiform texts describing in detail the tuning of harps. *lyres.* Had strings of the same length but of different diameters and tensions (see 1Ch 15:16; Da 3:5).

12:28 *Netophathites.* From Netophah, a town near Bethlehem (7:26).

12:29 *Beth Gilgal.* Perhaps the Gilgal near Jericho (see note on Jos 4:19), or the Gilgal of Elijah (2Ki 2:1), about seven miles north of Bethel.

the villages of the Netophathites, [t] [29]from Beth Gilgal, and from the area of Geba and Azmaveth, for the singers had built villages for themselves around Jerusalem. [30]When the priests and Levites had purified themselves ceremonially, they purified the people, [u] the gates and the wall.

[31]I had the leaders of Judah go up on top[f] of the wall. I also assigned two large choirs to give thanks. One was to proceed on top[g] of the wall to the right, toward the Dung Gate. [v] [32]Hoshaiah and half the leaders of Judah followed them, [33]along with Azariah, Ezra, Meshullam, [34]Judah, Benjamin, [w] Shemaiah, Jeremiah, [35]as well as some priests with trumpets, [x] and also Zechariah son of Jonathan, the son of Shemaiah, the son of Mattaniah, the son of Micaiah, the son of Zaccur, the son of Asaph, [36]and his associates—Shemaiah, Azarel, Milalai, Gilalai, Maai, Nethanel, Judah and Hanani—with musical instruments[y] prescribed by David the man of God. [z] Ezra[a] the scribe led the procession. [37]At the Fountain Gate[b] they continued directly up the steps of the City of David on the ascent to the wall and passed above the house of David to the Water Gate[c] on the east.

[38]The second choir proceeded in the opposite direction. I followed them on top[h] of the wall, together with half the people—past the Tower of the Ovens[d] to the Broad Wall, [e] [39]over the Gate of Ephraim, [f] the Jeshanah[i] Gate, [g] the Fish Gate, [h] the Tower of Hananel[i] and the Tower of the Hundred, [j] as far as the Sheep Gate. [k] At the Gate of the Guard they stopped.

[40]The two choirs that gave thanks then took their places in the house of God; so

did I, together with half the officials, [41]as well as the priests—Eliakim, Maaseiah, Miniamin, Micaiah, Elioenai, Zechariah and Hananiah with their trumpets— [42]and also Maaseiah, Shemaiah, Eleazar, Uzzi, Jehohanan, Malkijah, Elam and Ezer. The choirs sang under the direction of Jezrahiah. [43]And on that day they offered great sacrifices, rejoicing because God had given them great joy. The women and children also rejoiced. The sound of rejoicing in Jerusalem could be heard far away.

[44]At that time men were appointed to be in charge of the storerooms[l] for the contributions, firstfruits and tithes. [m] From the fields around the towns they were to bring into the storerooms the portions required by the Law for the priests and the Levites, for Judah was pleased with the ministering priests and Levites. [n] [45]They performed the service of their God and the service of purification, as did also the singers and gatekeepers, according to the commands of David[o] and his son Solomon. [p] [46]For long ago, in the days of David and Asaph, [q] there had been directors for the singers and for the songs of praise[r] and thanksgiving to God. [47]So in the days of Zerubbabel and of Nehemiah, all Israel contributed the daily portions for the singers and gatekeepers. They also set aside the portion for the other Levites, and the Levites set aside the portion for the descendants of Aaron.[s]

Nehemiah's Final Reforms

13 On that day the Book of Moses was read aloud in the hearing of the people and there it was found written that

[f]31 Or go alongside   [g]31 Or proceed alongside
[h]38 Or them alongside   [i]39 Or Old

Cross references (center column)

12:28
[t]S 1Ch 2:54; 9:16
12:30 [u]Ex 19:10;
Job 1:5
12:31 [v]Ne 2:13
12:34 [w]S Ezr 1:5
12:35 [x]S Ezr 3:10
12:36
[y]S 1Ch 15:16
[z]S 2Ch 8:14
[a]Ezr 7:6
12:37 [b]S Ne 2:14
[c]S Ne 3:26
12:38 [d]Ne 3:11
[e]Ne 3:8
12:39
[f]S 2Ki 14:13
[g]Ne 3:6
[h]S 2Ch 33:14
[i]S Ne 3:1 /[j]Ne 3:1
[k]S Ne 3:1

12:44 [l]Ne 13:4,
13 [m]S Lev 27:30
[n]S Dt 18:8
12:45
[o]S 2Ch 8:14
[p]S 1Ch 6:31;
23:5
12:46
[q]S 2Ch 35:15
[r]2Ch 29:27;
Ps 137:4
12:47 [s]S Dt 18:8

12:30 *purified.* See note on Lev 4:12. The Levites are said to have purified all that was sacred in the temple (1Ch 23:28) and the temple itself (2Ch 29:15) during times of revival. Ritual purity was intended to teach God's holiness and moral purity (Lev 16:30).
12:31 *two large choirs.* See note on v. 38. The two great processions probably started from the area of the Valley Gate (2:13,15; 3:13) near the center of the western section of the wall. The first procession, led by Ezra (v. 36), moved in a counterclockwise direction upon the wall; the second, with Nehemiah (v. 38), moved in a clockwise direction. Both met between the Water Gate (v. 37) and the Gate of the Guard (v. 39), then entered the temple area. Cf. Ps 48:12–13. *to the right.* Or "to the south." The Semite oriented himself facing east, so the right hand represented the south (see Jos 17:7; 1Sa 23:24; Job 23:9). *Dung Gate.* See note on 2:13.
12:35 *trumpets.* See note on Ezr 3:10. Each choir had priests blowing trumpets, as well as Levites playing other musical instruments. *Asaph.* See note on 11:17.
12:36 *Ezra the scribe.* See notes on Ezr 7:1,6.

12:37 *Fountain Gate.* See note on 2:14. *City of David.* See 3:15; see also note on 2Sa 5:7. *Water Gate.* See note on 3:26.
12:38 *choir.* Lit. "thanks," i.e., "thanksgiving choir" (see v. 40). *Tower of the Ovens.* See note on 3:11. *Broad Wall.* See note on 3:8.
12:39 *Gate of Ephraim.* See notes on 3:6; 8:16. *Jeshanah Gate.* See note on 3:6. *Fish Gate.* See note on 3:3. *Tower of Hananel . . . Tower of the Hundred . . . Sheep Gate.* See note on 3:1. *Gate of the Guard.* Cf. Jer 32:2.
12:43 *God had given them great joy.* See 1Ch 29:9; Jnh 4:6. *women.* See 8:2; Ex 15:20 and notes. *heard far away.* See note on Ezr 3:13; cf. 1Ki 1:40; 2Ki 11:13.
12:44 *Judah was pleased.* The people cheerfully contributed their offerings to support the priests and Levites (cf. 2Co 9:7). *ministering.* See Dt 10:8.
12:46 *Asaph.* See note on 11:17.
12:47 *contributed.* The Hebrew for this verb implies continued giving.
13:1–2 See Dt 23:3–6.

no Ammonite or Moabite should ever be admitted into the assembly of God,^{t} ^{2}because they had not met the Israelites with food and water but had hired Balaam^u to call a curse down on them.^{v} (Our God, however, turned the curse into a blessing.)^w ^{3}When the people heard this law, they excluded from Israel all who were of foreign descent.^{x}

^{4}Before this, Eliashib the priest had been put in charge of the storerooms^y of the house of our God. He was closely associated with Tobiah,^{z} ^{5}and he had provided him with a large room formerly used to store the grain offerings and incense and temple articles, and also the tithes^a of grain, new wine and oil prescribed for the Levites, singers and gatekeepers, as well as the contributions for the priests.

^{6}But while all this was going on, I was not in Jerusalem, for in the thirty-second year of Artaxerxes^b king of Babylon I had returned to the king. Some time later I asked his permission ^{7}and came back to Jerusalem. Here I learned about the evil thing Eliashib^c had done in providing Tobiah^d a room in the courts of the house of God. ^{8}I was greatly displeased and threw all Tobiah's household goods out of the room.^{e} ^{9}I gave orders to purify the rooms,^{f} and then I put back into them the

equipment of the house of God, with the grain offerings and the incense.^{g}

^{10}I also learned that the portions assigned to the Levites had not been given to them,^{h} and that all the Levites and singers responsible for the service had gone back to their own fields.^{i} ^{11}So I rebuked the officials and asked them, "Why is the house of God neglected?"^{j} Then I called them together and stationed them at their posts.

^{12}All Judah brought the tithes^k of grain, new wine and oil into the storerooms.^{l} ^{13}I put Shelemiah the priest, Zadok the scribe, and a Levite named Pedaiah in charge of the storerooms and made Hanan son of Zaccur, the son of Mattaniah, their assistant, because these men were considered trustworthy. They were made responsible for distributing the supplies to their brothers.^{m}

^{14}Remember^n me for this, O my God, and do not blot out what I have so faithfully done for the house of my God and its services.

^{15}In those days I saw men in Judah treading winepresses on the Sabbath and bringing in grain and loading it on donkeys, together with wine, grapes, figs and all other kinds of loads. And they were

---

Cross-references (center column):

13:1 ^{t}ver 23; Dt 23:3
13:2 ^{u}Nu 22:3-11 ^{v}S Nu 23:7; S Dt 23:3 ^{w}S Nu 23:11; Dt 23:4-5
13:3 ^{x}ver 23; S Ne 9:2
13:4 ^{y}S Ne 12:44 ^{z}Ne 2:10
13:5 ^{a}S Lev 27:30; S Nu 18:21
13:6 ^{b}S Ne 2:6
13:7 ^{c}S Ezr 10:24 ^{d}S Ne 2:10
13:8 ^{e}Mt 21:12-13; Mk 11:15-17; Lk 19:45-46; Jn 2:13-16
13:9 ^{f}S 1Ch 23:28; S 2Ch 29:5
13:10 ^{g}S Lev 2:1 ^{h}S Dt 12:19 ^{i}S 2Ch 31:4
13:11 ^{j}S Ne 10:37-39; Hag 1:1-9; Mal 3:8-9
13:12 ^{k}S 2Ch 31:6 ^{l}S Dt 18:8; 1Ki 7:51; S 2Ch 31:5; S Ne 10:37-39; Mal 3:10
13:13 ^{m}S Ne 12:44; Ac 6:1-5
13:14 ^{n}S Ge 8:1; S 2Ki 20:3

13:2 *Balaam.* See note on Nu 22:5. An Aramaic inscription of the sixth century B.C. found at Deir 'Alla in Transjordan refers to Balaam.

13:4 *Eliashib.* See note on 12:10. *Tobiah.* See note on 2:10.

13:5 *provided him with a large room.* During Nehemiah's absence from the city to return to the Persian king's court, Tobiah, one of his archenemies, had used his influence with Eliashib to gain entrance into a chamber ordinarily set aside for the storage of tithes and other offerings (see 10:37 and note; cf. Nu 18:21-32; Dt 14:28-29; 26:12-15). Elsewhere we read of the chamber of Meshullam (3:30) and of Jehohanan (Ezr 10:6).

13:6 *thirty-second year of Artaxerxes.* See note on 5:14. *king of Babylon.* The title was assumed by Cyrus after his conquest of Babylon (see Ezr 5:13) and was adopted by subsequent Achaemenid (Persian) kings.

13:7 *came back to Jerusalem.* Nehemiah's second term must have ended before 407 B.C., when Bagohi (Bigvai) was governor of Judah according to the Elephantine papyri. Some have suggested that after Nehemiah's first term he was succeeded by his brother Hanani (see note on 1:2). *courts.* See note on 8:16. Zerubbabel's temple had two courtyards (Zec 3:7; cf. Isa 62:9).

13:8 *displeased . . . threw.* Nehemiah expressed his indignation by taking action (cf. vv. 24-25; 5:6-7). Contrast the reaction of Ezra, who "sat down appalled" (Ezr 9:3). Nehemiah's action reminds us of Christ's expulsion of the money changers from the temple area (Mt 21:12-13).

13:9 *rooms.* Though only a single chamber was mentioned in vv. 5-8, additional rooms were involved. A parallel to the occupation and desecration of the temple by Tobiah comes

from a century earlier in Egypt, where Greek mercenaries had occupied the temple of Neith at Sais. Upon the appeal of the Egyptian priest, Udjahorresnet, the Persian king had the squatters driven out and the temple's ceremonies, processions and revenues restored: "And His Majesty commanded that all the foreigners who had settled in the temple of Neith should be driven out and that all their houses and all their superfluities that were in this temple should be thrown down, and that all their own baggage should be carried for them outside the wall of this temple."

13:10 Nehemiah was apparently correcting an abuse of long standing. Strictly speaking, the Levites had no holdings (Nu 18:20,23-24; Dt 14:29; 18:1), but some may have had private income (Dt 18:8). Therefore the Levites were dependent on the faithful support of the people. This may explain the reluctance of great numbers of Levites to return from exile (see Ezr 8:15-20). For the complaints of those who found little material advantage in serving the Lord see Mal 2:17; 3:13-15.

13:11 *neglected.* See note on 10:39.

13:12 *tithes.* See 12:44. Temples in Mesopotamia also levied tithes for the support of their personnel.

13:13 Of the four treasurers, one was a priest, one a Levite, one a scribe and one a layman of rank. *trustworthy.* Nehemiah appointed honest men to make sure that supplies were distributed equitably, just as the church appointed deacons for this purpose (Ac 6:1-5).

13:15 *treading winepresses.* See notes on Isa 5:2; 16:10. *Sabbath.* The temptation to violate the Sabbath rest was especially characteristic of non-Jewish merchants (see 10:31; Isa 56:1-8). On the other hand, the high regard that many had for the Sabbath was expressed by parents who called their children Shabbethai (see 8:7; 11:16; Ezr 10:15).

bringing all this into Jerusalem on the Sabbath.[o] Therefore I warned them against selling food on that day. [16]Men from Tyre who lived in Jerusalem were bringing in fish and all kinds of merchandise and selling them in Jerusalem on the Sabbath[p] to the people of Judah. [17]I rebuked the nobles of Judah and said to them, "What is this wicked thing you are doing—desecrating the Sabbath day? [18]Didn't your forefathers do the same things, so that our God brought all this calamity upon us and upon this city?[q] Now you are stirring up more wrath against Israel by desecrating the Sabbath."[r]

[19]When evening shadows fell on the gates of Jerusalem before the Sabbath,[s] I ordered the doors to be shut and not opened until the Sabbath was over. I stationed some of my own men at the gates so that no load could be brought in on the Sabbath day. [20]Once or twice the merchants and sellers of all kinds of goods spent the night outside Jerusalem. [21]But I warned them and said, "Why do you spend the night by the wall? If you do this again, I will lay hands on you." From that time on they no longer came on the Sabbath. [22]Then I commanded the Levites to purify themselves and go and guard the gates in order to keep the Sabbath day holy.

Remember[t] me for this also, O my God,

and show mercy to me according to your great love.

[23]Moreover, in those days I saw men of Judah who had married[u] women from Ashdod, Ammon and Moab.[v] [24]Half of their children spoke the language of Ashdod or the language of one of the other peoples, and did not know how to speak the language[w] of Judah. [25]I rebuked them and called curses down on them. I beat some of the men and pulled out their hair. I made them take an oath[x] in God's name and said: "You are not to give your daughters in marriage to their sons, nor are you to take their daughters in marriage for your sons or for yourselves.[y] [26]Was it not because of marriages like these that Solomon king of Israel sinned? Among the many nations there was no king like him.[z] He was loved by his God,[a] and God made him king over all Israel, but even he was led into sin by foreign women.[b] [27]Must we hear now that you too are doing all this terrible wickedness and are being unfaithful to our God by marrying[c] foreign women?"

[28]One of the sons of Joiada son of Eliashib[d] the high priest was son-in-law to Sanballat[e] the Horonite. And I drove him away from me.

[29]Remember[f] them, O my God, because they defiled the priestly office and the covenant of the priesthood and of the Levites.[g]

13:15
[o]Ex 20:8-11;
[s]34:21;
Dt 5:12-15
13:16
[p]S Ne 10:31
13:18 [q]Jer 44:23
[r]S Ne 10:31
13:19 [s]Lev 23:32
13:22 [t]S Ge 8:1;
S Ne 1:8
13:23
[u]Ezr 9:1-2;
Mal 2:11 [v]S ver 1,
S 3; Ex 34:16;
S Ru 1:4;
S Ne 10:30

13:24 [w]Est 1:22;
3:12; 8:9
13:25 [x]S Ezr 10:5
[y]S Ex 34:16
13:26
[z]S 1Ki 3:13;
S 2Ch 1:12
[a]2Sa 12:25
[b]S Ex 34:16;
S 1Ki 11:3
13:27 [c]Ezr 9:14
13:28
[d]S Ezr 10:24
[e]S Ne 2:10
13:29 [f]S Ne 1:8
[g]S Nu 3:12

13:16 *Tyre.* See note on Isa 23:1. *fish.* Most of the fish exported by the Tyrians (Eze 26:4–5,14) was dried, smoked or salted. Fish, much of it from the Sea of Galilee, was an important part of the Israelites' diet (Lev 11:9; Nu 11:5; Mt 15:34; Lk 24:42; Jn 21:5–13). It was sold at the market near the Fish Gate (see note on 3:3).

13:17 *rebuked the nobles.* Because they were the leaders. *desecrating.* Turning what is sacred into common use and so profaning it (see Mal 2:10–11).

13:19 *When evening shadows fell on the gates.* Before sunset, when the Sabbath began. The Israelites, like the Babylonians, counted their days from sunset to sunset (the Egyptians reckoned theirs from dawn to dawn). The precise moment when the Sabbath began was heralded by the blowing of a trumpet by a priest. According to the Jewish Mishnah, "On the eve of Sabbath they used to blow six more blasts, three to cause the people to cease from work and three to mark the break between the sacred and the profane." Josephus (*Jewish War*, 4.9.12) speaks of the location on the parapet of the temple where the priests "gave a signal beforehand, with a trumpet, at the beginning of every seventh day, in the evening twilight, and also at the evening when that day was finished, announcing to the people the respective hours for ceasing work and for resuming their labors." Excavators at the temple mount recovered a stone from the southwest corner of the parapet, which had fallen to the ground in Titus's siege, with the inscription "for the place of the blowing (of the trumpet)."

13:22 *Remember me.* See note on 1:8.

13:23 Ezra had dealt with the same problem of intermarriage some 25 years before (see note on Ezr 9:1). *Ashdod.* See 4:7; Isa 20:1 and notes. *Ammon and Moab.* See note on Ge 19:36–38.

13:24 The Israelites recognized other people as foreigners by their languages (see Dt 3:9; Jdg 12:6; Ps 114:1; Isa 33:19; Eze 3:5–6).

13:25 *pulled out their hair.* See Ezr 9:3; Isa 50:6 and notes. *You are not to give.* Nehemiah's action was designed to prevent future intermarriages, whereas Ezra dissolved the existing unions.

13:26 *Solomon.* Israel's outstanding king in terms of wealth and political achievements (1Ki 3:13; 2Ch 1:12). Solomon began his reign by humbly asking for wisdom from the Lord (1Ki 3:5–9). *he was led into sin.* In later years his foreign wives led him to worship other gods, so that he built a high place for Chemosh, the god of the Moabites (1Ki 11:7).

13:28 *son-in-law to Sanballat.* According to Lev 21:14 the high priest was not to marry a foreigner. The expulsion of Joiada's son followed either this special ban or the general prohibition against intermarriage. The union described in this verse was especially rankling to Nehemiah in the light of Sanballat's enmity (see 2:10). Josephus (*Antiquities,* 11.7.2) records that an almost identical episode, involving a marriage between the daughter of a Sanballat of Samaria and the brother of the Jewish high priest, took place a little over a century later in the time of Alexander the Great.

Median women of the nobility who have heard about the queen's conduct will respond to all the king's nobles in the same way. There will be no end of disrespect and discord.ˢ

¹⁹"Therefore, if it pleases the king,ᵗ let him issue a royal decree and let it be written in the laws of Persia and Media, which cannot be repealed,ᵘ that Vashti is never again to enter the presence of King Xerxes. Also let the king give her royal position to someone else who is better than she. ²⁰Then when the king's edict is proclaimed throughout all his vast realm, all the women will respect their husbands, from the least to the greatest."

²¹The king and his nobles were pleased with this advice, so the king did as Memucan proposed. ²²He sent dispatches to all parts of the kingdom, to each province in its own script and to each people in its own language,ᵛ proclaiming in each people's tongue that every man should be ruler over his own household.

Esther Made Queen

2 Later when the anger of King Xerxes had subsided,ʷ he remembered Vashti and what she had done and what he had

^{1:18} ˢPr 19:13; 27:15
^{1:19} ᵗEcc 8:4
 ᵘEst 8:8; Da 6:8, 12
^{1:22} ᵛS Ne 13:24
^{2:1} ʷEst 7:10

^{2:5} ˣS 1Sa 9:1
^{2:6} ʸS 2Ki 24:15
 ᶻDa 1:1-5; 5:13
^{2:7} ᵃGe 41:45
 ᵇS Ge 39:6

decreed about her. ²Then the king's personal attendants proposed, "Let a search be made for beautiful young virgins for the king. ³Let the king appoint commissioners in every province of his realm to bring all these beautiful girls into the harem at the citadel of Susa. Let them be placed under the care of Hegai, the king's eunuch, who is in charge of the women; and let beauty treatments be given to them. ⁴Then let the girl who pleases the king be queen instead of Vashti." This advice appealed to the king, and he followed it.

⁵Now there was in the citadel of Susa a Jew of the tribe of Benjamin, named Mordecai son of Jair, the son of Shimei, the son of Kish,ˣ ⁶who had been carried into exile from Jerusalem by Nebuchadnezzar king of Babylon, among those taken captive with Jehoiachinᶜʸ king of Judah.ᶻ ⁷Mordecai had a cousin named Hadassah, whom he had brought up because she had neither father nor mother. This girl, who was also known as Esther,ᵃ was lovelyᵇ in form and features, and Mordecai had taken her as his own daughter when her father and mother died.

⁸When the king's order and edict had

ᶜ6 Hebrew *Jeconiah,* a variant of *Jehoiachin*

1:19 *cannot be repealed.* The irrevocability of the Persian laws is mentioned in 8:8 and Da 6:8. *never again to enter.* The punishment corresponds to the crime: Since Vashti refused to appear before the king, it is decreed that she never appear before him again. Furthermore, from this point on she is no longer given the title "Queen" in the book of Esther.
1:22 *proclaiming ... household.* Or "that every man should be ruler over his own household and that his native language should be used in the home," thus referring to the use of the husband's native language in ethnically mixed marriages as a sign of his rule in the home (see Ne 13:23–24).
2:1 *Later.* Esther was taken to Xerxes "in the seventh year of his reign" (v. 16), i.e., in December, 479 B.C., or January, 478. The Greek wars intervened before a new queen was sought (see note on 1:3–4).
2:2 *virgins for the king.* To add to his harem.
2:3–4 The phraseology here is similar to that in Ge 41:34–37. This and numerous other parallels suggest that the author of Esther modeled his work after the Joseph story. Both accounts are set in the courts of foreign monarchs and portray Israelite heroes who rise to prominence and provide the means by which their people are saved (see notes on vv. 9,21–23; 3:4; 4:14; 6:1,8,14; 8:6).
2:5 *in the citadel of Susa a Jew.* As far back as the fall of the northern kingdom in 722–721 B.C. Israelites had been exiled among the cities of the Medes (2Ki 17:6). After the conquest of Babylon by King Cyrus of Persia in 539, some of the Jewish population taken there by the Babylonians (605–586) probably moved eastward into the cities of Medo-Persia. Only 50,000 returned to Israel in the restoration of 538 (Ezr 2:64–67). The presence of a large Jewish population in Medo-Persia is confirmed by the discovery of an archive of texts in Nippur (southern Mesopotamia) from the period of

Artaxerxes I (465–424) and Darius II (424–405). This archive contains the names of about 100 Jews who lived in that city. Some had attained positions of importance and wealth. Similar Jewish populations are probable in many other Medo-Persian cities. *Mordecai.* The name is derived from that of the Babylonian deity Marduk. There are numerous examples in the Bible of Jews having double names—a Hebrew name and a "Gentile" name. Mordecai likely had a Hebrew name, as did Esther (v. 7), Daniel and his friends (Da 1:6–7), Joseph (Ge 41:45) and others, but the text does not mention Mordecai's Hebrew name. A cuneiform tablet from Borsippa near Babylon mentions a scribe by the name of Mardukaya; he was an accountant or minister at the court of Susa in the early years of Xerxes. Many scholars identify him with Mordecai. *son of Jair, the son of Shimei, the son of Kish.* The persons named could be immediate ancestors, in which case Mordecai would be the great-grandson of Kish, who was among the exiles with Jehoiachin in 597 B.C. It is more likely, however, that the names refer to remote ancestors in the tribe of Benjamin (see 2Sa 16:5–14 for Shimei, 1Sa 9:1 for Kish). This association with the tribe and family of King Saul sets the stage for the ongoing conflict between Israel and the Amalekites (see notes on 3:1–6). If the names are those of remote ancestors, the clause "who had been carried into exile" (v. 6) would not apply to Mordecai, who would have been over 100 years old in that case; rather, it would have to be taken as an elliptical construction in the sense "whose family had been carried into exile."
2:6 *Jehoiachin king of Judah.* See 2Ki 24:8–17; 2Ch 36:9–10.
2:7 *Hadassah.* Esther's Hebrew name, meaning "myrtle." The name Esther is likely derived from the Persian word for "star," though some derive it from the name of the Babylonian goddess Ishtar (see note on Jer 7:18).
2:8 *Esther also was taken.* Neither she nor Mordecai

been proclaimed, many girls were brought to the citadel of Susa c and put under the care of Hegai. Esther also was taken to the king's palace and entrusted to Hegai, who had charge of the harem. ⁹The girl pleased him and won his favor. d Immediately he provided her with her beauty treatments and special food. e He assigned to her seven maids selected from the king's palace and moved her and her maids into the best place in the harem.

¹⁰Esther had not revealed her nationality and family background, because Mordecai had forbidden her to do so. f ¹¹Every day he walked back and forth near the courtyard of the harem to find out how Esther was and what was happening to her.

¹²Before a girl's turn came to go in to King Xerxes, she had to complete twelve months of beauty treatments prescribed for the women, six months with oil of myrrh and six with perfumes g and cosmetics. ¹³And this is how she would go to the king: Anything she wanted was given her to take with her from the harem to the king's palace. ¹⁴In the evening she would go there and in the morning return to another part of the harem to the care of Shaashgaz, the king's eunuch who was in charge of the concubines. h She would not return to the king unless he was pleased with her and summoned her by name. i

¹⁵When the turn came for Esther (the girl Mordecai had adopted, the daughter of his uncle Abihail j) to go to the king, k she asked for nothing other than what Hegai,

the king's eunuch who was in charge of the harem, suggested. And Esther won the favor l of everyone who saw her. ¹⁶She was taken to King Xerxes in the royal residence in the tenth month, the month of Tebeth, in the seventh year of his reign.

¹⁷Now the king was attracted to Esther more than to any of the other women, and she won his favor and approval more than any of the other virgins. So he set a royal crown on her head and made her queen m instead of Vashti. ¹⁸And the king gave a great banquet, n Esther's banquet, for all his nobles and officials. o He proclaimed a holiday throughout the provinces and distributed gifts with royal liberality. p

Mordecai Uncovers a Conspiracy

¹⁹When the virgins were assembled a second time, Mordecai was sitting at the king's gate. q ²⁰But Esther had kept secret her family background and nationality just as Mordecai had told her to do, for she continued to follow Mordecai's instructions as she had done when he was bringing her up. r

²¹During the time Mordecai was sitting at the king's gate, Bigthana d and Teresh, two of the king's officers s who guarded the doorway, became angry t and conspired to assassinate King Xerxes. ²²But Mordecai found out about the plot and told Queen Esther, who in turn reported it to the king, giving credit to Mordecai. ²³And when the report was investigated

d21 Hebrew *Bigthan,* a variant of *Bigthana*

Cross references (center column):

2:8 cNe 1:1; Est 1:2; Da 8:2
2:9 dS Ge 39:21
eS Ge 37:3; 1Sa 9:22-24; S 2Ki 25:30; Est 9:19; Eze 16:9-13; Da 1:5
2:10 fver 20
2:12 gPr 27:9; SS 1:3; Isa 3:24
2:14 h1Ki 11:3; SS 6:8; Da 5:2
iEst 4:11
2:15 jEst 9:29
kPs 45:14
2:16 lGe 18:3; S 30:27; Est 5:8; 7:3; 8:5
2:17 mEze 16:9-13
2:18 nS 1Ki 3:15
oS Ge 40:20
pS Est 1:7
2:19 qEst 4:2; 5:13
2:20 rver 10
2:21 sS Ge 40:2
tS Est 1:12; 3:5; 5:9; 7:7

---

would have had any choice in the matter (cf. 2Sa 11:4).
2:9 *special food.* Lit. "her portions." Unlike Daniel and his friends (Da 1:5–10), Esther does not observe the dietary laws, perhaps in part to conceal her Jewish identity (vv. 10,20). Giving such portions is a sign of special favor (1Sa 9:22–24; 2Ki 25:29–30; Da 1:1–10; negatively, Jer 13:25); in the Joseph narrative cf. Ge 43:34. The motif of giving portions appears later as a practice in observing Purim (9:19,22).
2:10 The fact that Esther concealed her identity is reported twice—here and in v. 20 (for the author's use of duplications see Introduction: Purpose, Themes and Literary Features).
2:14 *to another part of the harem.* To the chambers of the concubines.
2:16 *tenth month . . . seventh year.* December, 479 B.C., or January, 478 (see notes on 1:3–4; 2:1). Esther's tenure as queen continued through the events of the book, i.e., through 473 (see 3:7 and note; see also 8:9–13; 9:1). She may have died or fallen from favor shortly thereafter (see note on 1:11).
2:18 *holiday.* The Hebrew for this word, unique to this verse, may imply a remission of taxes, an emancipation of slaves, a cancellation of debts or a remission of obligatory military service.
2:19 See Introduction: Purpose, Themes and Literary Features. The enlargement of the harem apparently continued

unabated. Perhaps there is a causal connection between the second gathering of women and the assassination plot (vv. 21–23); some have suggested that it reflects palace intrigue in support of the deposed Vashti. *king's gate.* The gate of an ancient city was its major commercial and legal center. Markets were held in the gate; the court sat there to transact its business (see Dt 21:18–20; Jos 20:4; Ru 4:1–11; Ps 69:12). A king might hold an audience in the gate (see 2Sa 19:8; 1Ki 22:10). Daniel was at the king's gate as ruler over all Babylon (Da 2:48–49). Mordecai's sitting in the king's gate confirms his holding a high position in the civil service of the empire (see note on v. 5). From this vantage point he might overhear plans for the murder of the king.
2:21–23 Another point of comparison with the Joseph narrative is the involvement of two chamberlains (Ge 40:1–3; see note on vv. 3–4).
2:23 *hanged.* See NIV text note. Among the Persians this form of execution was impalement, as is confirmed in pictures and statues from the ancient Near East and in the comments of the Greek historian Herodotus (3.125,129; 4.43). According to Herodotus (3.159) Darius I impaled 3,000 Babylonians when he took Babylon, an act that Darius himself recorded in his Behistun (Bisitun) inscription. In Israelite and Canaanite practice, hanging was an exhibition of the corpse and not the means of execution itself (Dt 21:22–23; Jos 8:29; 10:26; 1Sa 31:8–10; 2Sa 4:12; 21:9–10). The execution of a chamberlain in the Joseph

and found to be true, the two officials were hanged[u] on a gallows.[e] All this was recorded in the book of the annals[v] in the presence of the king.[w]

Haman's Plot to Destroy the Jews

3 After these events, King Xerxes honored Haman son of Hammedatha, the Agagite,[x] elevating him and giving him a seat of honor higher than that of all the other nobles. [2]All the royal officials at the king's gate knelt down and paid honor to Haman, for the king had commanded this concerning him. But Mordecai would not kneel down or pay him honor.

[3]Then the royal officials at the king's gate asked Mordecai, "Why do you disobey the king's command?"[y] [4]Day after day they spoke to him but he refused to comply.[z] Therefore they told Haman about it to see whether Mordecai's behavior would be tolerated, for he had told them he was a Jew.

[5]When Haman saw that Mordecai would not kneel down or pay him honor, he was enraged.[a] [6]Yet having learned who

Mordecai's people were, he scorned the idea of killing only Mordecai. Instead Haman looked for a way[b] to destroy[c] all Mordecai's people, the Jews,[d] throughout the whole kingdom of Xerxes.

[7]In the twelfth year of King Xerxes, in the first month, the month of Nisan, they cast the pur[e] (that is, the lot[f]) in the presence of Haman to select a day and month. And the lot fell on[f] the twelfth month, the month of Adar.[g]

[8]Then Haman said to King Xerxes, "There is a certain people dispersed and scattered among the peoples in all the provinces of your kingdom whose customs[h] are different from those of all other people and who do not obey[i] the king's laws; it is not in the king's best interest to tolerate them.[j] [9]If it pleases the king, let a decree be issued to destroy them, and I will put ten thousand talents[g] of silver into

2:23
[u]S Ge 40:19;
S Dt 21:22-23;
Ps 7:14-16;
Pr 26:27;
Ecc 10:8 [v]Est 6:1;
10:2 [w]Est 6:2
3:1
[x]S Ex 17:8-16;
S Nu 24:7;
Dt 25:17-19;
1Sa 14:48
3:3 [y]Est 5:9;
Da 3:12
3:4 [z]Ge 39:10
3:5 [a]S Est 2:21

3:6 [b]Pr 16:25
[c]Ps 74:8; 83:4
[d]Est 9:24
3:7 [e]Est 9:24,26
[f]S Lev 16:8;
S 1Sa 10:21 [g]ver
13; Est 9:19
3:8 [h]Ac 16:20-21
[i]Jer 29:7; Da 6:13
[j]Ezr 4:15

[e]23 Or were hung (or impaled) on poles; similarly
elsewhere in Esther   [f]7 Septuagint; Hebrew does not
have And the lot fell on.   [g]9 That is, about 375 tons
(about 345 metric tons)

---

narrative also appears to have been by impalement (Ge 40:19). The sons of Haman were killed by the sword, and then their corpses were displayed in this way (9:5–14). *annals.* The concern of the author of Esther with rhetorical symmetry is seen in the fact that the annals are mentioned in the beginning (here), middle (6:1) and end (10:2) of the narrative. The episode dealing with the plot of Bigthana and Teresh is a good example of the many "coincidences" in the book that later take on crucial significance for the story.
3:1 *After these events.* Four years have elapsed since Esther's selection as queen (v. 7; 2:16–17). The fact that no reason is given for the promotion of Haman provides an ironic contrast between the unrewarded merit of Mordecai (2:21–23; see 6:3) and the unmerited reward of Haman. *son of Hammedatha, the Agagite.* There is some debate about the ancestry of Haman. The name Hammedatha appears to be Persian and probably refers to an immediate ancestor. The title "Agagite" could refer to some other immediate ancestor or to an unknown place; however, it is far more likely that it refers to Agag, king of Amalek (1Sa 15:20). The Amalekites had attacked Israel after she fled from Egypt (Ex 17:8–16; 1Sa 14:47–48); for this reason the Lord would "be at war against the Amalekites from generation to generation" (Ex 17:16). Israel was not to forget, but must "blot out the memory of Amalek from under heaven" (Dt 25:17–19). Saul's attack on Amalek (1Sa 15) resulted in the death of King Agag and most, though not all (1Ch 4:42–43), of the city's population. In Esther, about 500 years after the battle led by the Benjamite Saul, the Benjamite Mordecai (see note on 2:5) continues the war with the Amalekites.
3:2–6 Obedience to the second commandment (Ex 20:4) is not the issue in Mordecai's refusal to bow down to Haman, for the Jews were willing to bow down to kings (see 1Sa 24:8; 2Sa 14:4; 1Ki 1:16) and to other persons (see Ge 23:7; 33:3; 44:14). Only the long-standing enmity between the Jews and the Amalekites accounts both for Mordecai's refusal and for Haman's intent to destroy all the Jews (vv. 5–6). The threat against the Jews "throughout the whole kingdom" (v. 6) is a threat against the ultimate issue of

redemptive history (see Introduction: Purpose, Themes and Literary Features).
3:4 Compare the phraseology with that in the Joseph story (Ge 39:10).
3:7 *twelfth year . . . first month.* April or May, 474 B.C., the fifth year of Esther's reign. *they.* Either indefinite or the astrologers who assisted Haman (5:10,14; 6:12–13). *pur.* See 9:24,26. This word is found in Akkadian texts with the meaning "lot" (as here). The celebration known as Purim takes its name from the plural of this noun (see 9:23–32). There is irony in the fact that the month of the Jews' celebration of the Passover deliverance from Egypt is also the month that Haman begins plotting their destruction (Ex 12:1–11). *twelfth month.* An 11-month delay is contemplated between the securing of the decree and the execution of it in the month Adar (February-March).
3:8–9 The name of the people Haman wishes to destroy is slyly omitted in this blend of the true and the false: The Jews did have their own customs and laws, but they were not disobedient to the king (Jer 29:7).
3:8 *dispersed and scattered.* See 8:11,17; 9:2, 12,16, 19–20,28.
3:9 *ten thousand talents.* Herodotus (3.95) records that the annual income of the Persian empire was 15,000 talents. If this figure is correct, Haman offers two-thirds of that amount—a huge sum. Presumably the money would have come from the plundered wealth of the victims of the decree. Verse 13 implies that those who would take part in the massacre were to be allowed to keep the plunder, perhaps adding financial incentive to the execution of the decree since Xerxes disavows taking the money (v. 11). On the other hand, 4:7 and 7:4 may imply that the king had planned on collecting some of the money. *men who carry out this business.* This clause may represent the title of revenue officers who would bring the money to the treasury, or it could refer to those who carry out the decree. The Amalekites had once before plundered Israel (see note on v. 1); Haman plans a recurrence.

the royal treasury for the men who carry out this business." [k]

[10]So the king took his signet ring[l] from his finger and gave it to Haman son of Hammedatha, the Agagite, the enemy of the Jews. [11]"Keep the money," the king said to Haman, "and do with the people as you please."

[12]Then on the thirteenth day of the first month the royal secretaries were summoned. They wrote out in the script of each province and in the language[m] of each people all Haman's orders to the king's satraps, the governors of the various provinces and the nobles of the various peoples. These were written in the name of King Xerxes himself and sealed[n] with his own ring. [13]Dispatches were sent by couriers to all the king's provinces with the order to destroy, kill and annihilate all the Jews[o]—young and old, women and little children—on a single day, the thirteenth day of the twelfth month, the month of Adar,[p] and to plunder[q] their goods. [14]A copy of the text of the edict was to be issued as law in every province and made known to the people of every nationality so they would be ready for that day.[r]

[15]Spurred on by the king's command, the couriers went out, and the edict was issued in the citadel of Susa.[s] The king and Haman sat down to drink,[t] but the city of Susa was bewildered.[u]

Mordecai Persuades Esther to Help

4 When Mordecai learned of all that had been done, he tore his clothes,[v] put on sackcloth and ashes,[w] and went out into the city, wailing[x] loudly and bitterly. [2]But he went only as far as the king's gate,[y] because no one clothed in sackcloth was allowed to enter it. [3]In every province to which the edict and order of the king

came, there was great mourning among the Jews, with fasting, weeping and wailing. Many lay in sackcloth and ashes.

[4]When Esther's maids and eunuchs came and told her about Mordecai, she was in great distress. She sent clothes for him to put on instead of his sackcloth, but he would not accept them. [5]Then Esther summoned Hathach, one of the king's eunuchs assigned to attend her, and ordered him to find out what was troubling Mordecai and why.

[6]So Hathach went out to Mordecai in the open square of the city in front of the king's gate. [7]Mordecai told him everything that had happened to him, including the exact amount of money Haman had promised to pay into the royal treasury for the destruction of the Jews.[z] [8]He also gave him a copy of the text of the edict for their annihilation, which had been published in Susa, to show to Esther and explain it to her, and he told him to urge her to go into the king's presence to beg for mercy and plead with him for her people.

[9]Hathach went back and reported to Esther what Mordecai had said. [10]Then she instructed him to say to Mordecai, [11]"All the king's officials and the people of the royal provinces know that for any man or woman who approaches the king in the inner court without being summoned[a] the king has but one law:[b] that he be put to death. The only exception to this is for the king to extend the gold scepter[c] to him and spare his life. But thirty days have passed since I was called to go to the king."

[12]When Esther's words were reported to Mordecai, [13]he sent back this answer: "Do not think that because you are in the king's house you alone of all the Jews will escape. [14]For if you remain silent[d] at this time,

Cross references

3:9 [k]Est 7:4
3:10 [l]S Ge 41:42
3:12 [m]S Ne 13:24
[n]S Ge 38:18
3:13 [o]S 1Sa 15:3;
S Ezr 4:6 [p]S ver 7
[q]Est 8:11; 9:10
3:14 [r]Est 8:8; 9:1
3:15 [s]Est 8:14
[t]S Est 1:10
[u]Est 8:15
4:1 [v]S Nu 14:6
[w]S 2Sa 13:19;
Eze 27:30-31
[x]S Ex 11:6;
Ps 30:11
4:2 [y]S Est 2:19

4:7 [z]Est 7:4
4:11 [a]Est 2:14
[b]Da 2:9 [c]Est 5:2;
8:4; Ps 125:3
4:14 [d]Job 34:29;
Ps 28:1; 35:22;
Ecc 3:7;
Isa 42:14; 57:11;
62:1; 64:12;
Am 5:13

3:12 *thirteenth day ... first month.* In the 12th year of Xerxes's reign (v. 7), i.e., Apr. 17, 474 B.C.
3:13 Haman's decree against Israel is the same destruction that had earlier been decreed against Amalek (1Sa 15:3). *thirteenth day ... twelfth month.* Mar. 7, 473 B.C. (see 8:12).
3:15 Haman and the king will drink together again in the story when the fate of the Jews is once again being decided (7:1–2), but then it will be at the dissolution of their relationship and the reversal of the decree here celebrated. The celebration here is in sharp contrast to the fasting and mourning of the Jews (4:1–3,15–16).
4:2 *king's gate.* See note on 2:19.
4:3 See note on 3:15. The prominence of feasting throughout the book of Esther sets the fasts of vv. 3,16 in sharp relief; a pair of fasts matches the prominent pairs of banquets (see Introduction: Purpose, Themes and Literary Features; see also note on 9:31).
4:4–12 The fact that the dialogue of Esther and Mordecai

is mediated by Hathach reflects the prohibition against Mordecai's entering the royal citadel dressed in mourning (v. 2) and the isolation of Esther in the harem quarters.
4:7 See note on 3:9. That Mordecai is aware of the amount Haman promised to the king is a reminder of his high position in the bureaucracy at Susa (2:21–23).
4:11 Herodotus (3.118,140) also notes that anyone approaching the Persian king unsummoned would be killed unless the king gave immediate pardon.
4:12–16 The themes of the book of Esther are most clearly expressed in this passage. Mordecai's confidence in the Jews' deliverance is based on God's sovereignty in working out his purposes and fulfilling his promises. Their deliverance will come, even if through some means other than Esther. Yet that sovereignty is not fatalistic: Unless Esther exercises her individual responsibility, she and her family will perish. Cf. Mt 26:24; Ac 2:23 for similar treatments of the relationship between divine sovereignty and human responsibility.
4:14 *such a time as this.* Cf. Ge 45:5–7 in the Joseph

relief[e] and deliverance[f] for the Jews will arise from another place, but you and your father's family will perish. And who knows but that you have come to royal position for such a time as this?"[g]

[15]Then Esther sent this reply to Mordecai: [16]"Go, gather together all the Jews who are in Susa, and fast[h] for me. Do not eat or drink for three days, night or day. I and my maids will fast as you do. When this is done, I will go to the king, even though it is against the law. And if I perish, I perish."[i]

[17]So Mordecai went away and carried out all of Esther's instructions.

Esther's Request to the King

5 On the third day Esther put on her royal robes[j] and stood in the inner court of the palace, in front of the king's[k] hall. The king was sitting on his royal throne in the hall, facing the entrance. [2]When he saw Queen Esther standing in the court, he was pleased with her and held out to her the gold scepter that was in his hand. So Esther approached and touched the tip of the scepter.[l]

[3]Then the king asked, "What is it, Queen Esther? What is your request? Even up to half the kingdom,[m] it will be given you."

[4]"If it pleases the king," replied Esther, "let the king, together with Haman, come today to a banquet I have prepared for him."

[5]"Bring Haman at once," the king said, "so that we may do what Esther asks."

So the king and Haman went to the banquet Esther had prepared. [6]As they were drinking wine,[n] the king again asked Esther, "Now what is your petition? It will be given you. And what is your request? Even up to half the kingdom,[o] it will be granted."[p]

[7]Esther replied, "My petition and my request is this: [8]If the king regards me with favor[q] and if it pleases the king to grant my petition and fulfill my request, let the king and Haman come tomorrow to the banquet[r] I will prepare for them. Then I will answer the king's question."

Haman's Rage Against Mordecai

[9]Haman went out that day happy and in high spirits. But when he saw Mordecai at the king's gate and observed that he neither rose nor showed fear in his presence, he was filled with rage[s] against Mordecai.[t] [10]Nevertheless, Haman restrained himself and went home.

Calling together his friends and Zeresh,[u] his wife, [11]Haman boasted[v] to them about his vast wealth, his many sons,[w] and all the ways the king had honored him and how he had elevated him above the other nobles and officials. [12]"And that's not all," Haman added. "I'm the only person[x] Queen Esther invited to accompany the king to the banquet she gave. And she has invited me along with the king tomorrow. [13]But all this gives me no satisfaction as long as I see that Jew Mordecai sitting at the king's gate.[y]"

[14]His wife Zeresh and all his friends said to him, "Have a gallows built, seventy-five feet[h] high,[z] and ask the king in the morning to have Mordecai hanged[a] on it. Then go with the king to the dinner and be happy." This suggestion delighted Haman, and he had the gallows built.

Mordecai Honored

6 That night the king could not sleep;[b] so he ordered the book of the chronicles,[c] the record of his reign, to be brought in and read to him. [2]It was found

---

4:14 eEst 9:16,22
/S Ge 45:7;
S Dt 28:29
gS Ge 50:20
4:16
hS 2Ch 20:3;
Est 9:31
iS Ge 43:14
5:1 /Eze 16:13
kPr 21:1
5:2 /S Est 4:11
5:3 mEst 7:2;
Da 5:16; Mk 6:23
5:6 nS Est 1:10
oDa 5:16;
Mk 6:23
pEst 9:12

5:8 qS Est 2:15
rS 1Ki 3:15
5:9 sS Est 2:21;
Pr 14:17
tS Est 3:3
5:10 uEst 6:13
5:11 vPr 13:16
wEst 9:10,13
5:12 xJob 22:29;
Pr 16:18; 29:23
5:13 yS Est 2:19
5:14 zEst 7:9
aEzr 6:11
6:1 bDa 2:1;
6:18 cS Est 2:23

h14 Hebrew *fifty cubits* (about 23 meters)

---

narrative.

4:16 *fast.* See note on v. 3. Prayer, which usually accompanied such fasting, was presumably a part of this fast as well (see Jdg 20:26; 1Sa 7:6; 2Sa 12:16; Ezr 8:21–23; Ne 9:1–3; Isa 58:3; Jer 14:12; Joel 1:14; 2:12–17; Jnh 3:6–9). The omission of any reference to prayer or to God is consistent with the author's intention; absence of any distinctively religious concepts or vocabulary is a rhetorical device used to heighten the fact that it is indeed God who has been active in the whole narrative (see Introduction: Purpose, Themes and Literary Features). *I and my maids will fast.* Note the rhetorical symmetry: Where once Esther and her maids had received special foods (2:9), now they share a fast. *if I perish.* Cf. the similar formulation in the Joseph narrative (Ge 43:14).
5:2 See Pr 21:1.
5:6–7 One can only speculate regarding Esther's reasons for delaying her answer to the king's question until he had

asked it a third time (vv. 3,6; 7:2). The author uses these delays as plot retardation devices that sustain the tension and permit the introduction of new material on Haman's self-aggrandizement (vv. 11–12) and Mordecai's reward (6:6–11).
5:9 Haman's rage is kindled when Mordecai does not rise in his presence—an ironic contrast to his earlier refusal to bow (3:2–6).
5:11 *many sons.* Haman had ten sons (9:7–10). Herodotus (1.136) reports that the Persians prized a large number of sons second only to valor in battle; the Persian king sent gifts to the subject with the most sons (cf. Ps 127:3–5).
5:12–13 See Pr 16:18; 29:23.
5:14 *seventy-five feet high.* There may be a note of hyperbole in the height of the gallows. Others have suggested that the gallows was erected atop some other structure to achieve this height, e.g., the city wall (see 1Sa 31:10). *hanged.* See note on 2:23.

recorded there that Mordecai had exposed Bigthana and Teresh, two of the king's officers who guarded the doorway, who had conspired to assassinate King Xerxes. *d*

3"What honor and recognition has Mordecai received for this?" the king asked.

"Nothing has been done for him,"*e* his attendants answered.

4The king said, "Who is in the court?" Now Haman had just entered the outer court of the palace to speak to the king about hanging Mordecai on the gallows he had erected for him.

5His attendants answered, "Haman is standing in the court."

"Bring him in," the king ordered.

6When Haman entered, the king asked him, "What should be done for the man the king delights to honor?"

Now Haman thought to himself, "Who is there that the king would rather honor than me?" 7So he answered the king, "For the man the king delights to honor, 8have them bring a royal robe*f* the king has worn and a horse*g* the king has ridden, one with a royal crest placed on its head. 9Then let the robe and horse be entrusted to one of the king's most noble princes. Let them robe the man the king delights to honor, and lead him on the horse through the city streets, proclaiming before him, 'This is what is done for the man the king delights to honor!'*h'*"

10"Go at once," the king commanded Haman. "Get the robe and the horse and do just as you have suggested for Mordecai the Jew, who sits at the king's gate. Do not neglect anything you have recommended."

11So Haman got*i* the robe and the

horse. He robed Mordecai, and led him on horseback through the city streets, proclaiming before him, "This is what is done for the man the king delights to honor!"

12Afterward Mordecai returned to the king's gate. But Haman rushed home, with his head covered*j* in grief, 13and told Zeresh*k* his wife and all his friends everything that had happened to him.

His advisers and his wife Zeresh said to him, "Since Mordecai, before whom your downfall*l* has started, is of Jewish origin, you cannot stand against him—you will surely come to ruin!"*m* 14While they were still talking with him, the king's eunuchs arrived and hurried Haman away to the banquet*n* Esther had prepared.

Haman Hanged

7 So the king and Haman went to dine*o* with Queen Esther, 2and as they were drinking wine*p* on that second day, the king again asked, "Queen Esther, what is your petition? It will be given you. What is your request? Even up to half the kingdom,*q* it will be granted.*r*"

3Then Queen Esther answered, "If I have found favor*s* with you, O king, and if it pleases your majesty, grant me my life—this is my petition. And spare my people—this is my request. 4For I and my people have been sold for destruction and slaughter and annihilation.*t* If we had merely been sold as male and female slaves, I would have kept quiet, because no such distress would justify disturbing the king.*i*"

5King Xerxes asked Queen Esther,

i 4 Or *quiet, but the compensation our adversary offers cannot be compared with the loss the king would suffer*

6:2 *d*Est 2:21-23
6:3 *e*Ecc 9:13-16
6:8 *f*S Ge 41:42; S Isa 52:1
g1Ki 1:33
6:9 *h*Ge 41:43
6:11 *i*S Ge 41:42

6:12 *j*2Sa 15:30; Est 7:8; Jer 14:3, 4; Mic 3:7
6:13 *k*Est 5:10
lPs 57:6; Pr 26:27; 28:18
mEst 7:7
6:14 *n*S 1Ki 3:15
7:1
oGe 40:20-22; Mt 22:1-14
7:2 *p*S Est 1:10
qS Est 5:3
rEst 9:12
7:3 *s*S Est 2:15
7:4 *t*Est 3:9;
S 4:7

6:1 This verse marks the literary center of the narrative. When things could not look worse, a series of seemingly trivial coincidences marks a critical turn that brings resolution to the story. The king's inability to sleep, his requesting the reading of the annals, the reading of the passage reporting Mordecai's past kindness, Haman's noisy carpentry in the early hours of the morning (5:14), his sudden entry into the outer court and his assumption that he was the man the king wished to honor—all are events testifying to the sovereignty of God over the events of the narrative. Circumstances that seemed incidental earlier in the narrative take on crucial significance. Just as in the Joseph story (Ge 41:1-45), the hero's personal fortunes are reversed because of the monarch's disturbed sleep (cf. Da 2:1; 6:18).
6:2 The scribe was reading at the time from the annals that recorded events five years earlier (compare 3:7 with 2:16).
6:4-6 Again, the irony is evident: Just as Haman had withheld from the king the identity of the "certain people" (3:8), so now the king unintentionally keeps from Haman the identity of the "man the king delights to honor" (v. 6).
6:8 *royal robe the king has worn.* See 8:15; see also Introduction: Purpose, Themes and Literary Features. Cf. in

the Joseph story Ge 41:41-43. Great significance was attached to the king's garment in ancient times; wearing his garments was a sign of unique favor (1Sa 18:4). To wear another's garments was to partake of his power, stature, honor or sanctity (2Ki 2:13-14; Isa 61:3,10; Zec 3; Mk 5:27). Haman's suggestion is not only a great honor to the recipient, but it is also considerably flattering to the king: Wearing his garment was chosen instead of wealth.
6:13 See Introduction: Purpose, Themes and Literary Features.
6:14 Guests were usually escorted to feasts (see in the Joseph narrative Ge 43:15-26; cf. Mt 22:1-14).
7:2 See 5:3,6.
7:3 See 2:15,17.
7:4 *sold.* Esther refers to the bribe Haman offered to the king (3:9; 4:7); she also paraphrases Haman's edict (3:13). *because no such distress . . . king.* See NIV text note. The statement probably means either (1) that the affliction of the Jews would be less injurious to the king if slavery was all that was involved, or (2) that Esther would not trouble the king if slavery was the only issue.

"Who is he? Where is the man who has dared to do such a thing?"

[6]Esther said, "The adversary and enemy is this vile Haman."

Then Haman was terrified before the king and queen. [7]The king got up in a rage,[u] left his wine and went out into the palace garden.[v] But Haman, realizing that the king had already decided his fate,[w] stayed behind to beg Queen Esther for his life.

[8]Just as the king returned from the palace garden to the banquet hall, Haman was falling on the couch[x] where Esther was reclining.[y]

The king exclaimed, "Will he even molest the queen while she is with me in the house?"[z]

As soon as the word left the king's mouth, they covered Haman's face.[a] [9]Then Harbona,[b] one of the eunuchs attending the king, said, "A gallows seventy-five feet[j] high[c] stands by Haman's house. He had it made for Mordecai, who spoke up to help the king."

The king said, "Hang him on it!"[d] [10]So they hanged[e] Haman[f] on the gallows[g] he had prepared for Mordecai.[h] Then the king's fury subsided.[i]

The King's Edict in Behalf of the Jews

8 That same day King Xerxes gave Queen Esther the estate of Haman,[j] the enemy of the Jews. And Mordecai came into the presence of the king, for Esther had told how he was related to her. [2]The king took off his signet ring,[k] which he had reclaimed from Haman, and

presented it to Mordecai. And Esther appointed him over Haman's estate.[l]

[3]Esther again pleaded with the king, falling at his feet and weeping. She begged him to put an end to the evil plan of Haman the Agagite,[m] which he had devised against the Jews. [4]Then the king extended the gold scepter[n] to Esther and she arose and stood before him.

[5]"If it pleases the king," she said, "and if he regards me with favor[o] and thinks it the right thing to do, and if he is pleased with me, let an order be written overruling the dispatches that Haman son of Hammedatha, the Agagite, devised and wrote to destroy the Jews in all the king's provinces. [6]For how can I bear to see disaster fall on my people? How can I bear to see the destruction of my family?"[p]

[7]King Xerxes replied to Queen Esther and to Mordecai the Jew, "Because Haman attacked the Jews, I have given his estate to Esther, and they have hanged[q] him on the gallows. [8]Now write another decree[r] in the king's name in behalf of the Jews as seems best to you, and seal[s] it with the king's signet ring[t]—for no document written in the king's name and sealed with his ring can be revoked."[u]

[9]At once the royal secretaries were summoned—on the twenty-third day of the third month, the month of Sivan. They wrote out all Mordecai's orders to the Jews, and to the satraps, governors and nobles of the 127 provinces stretching from India to Cush.[k][v] These orders were writ-

---

7:7 [u]S Ge 34:7;
S Est 1:12;
Pr 19:12; 20:1-2
[v]S 2Ki 21:18
[w]Est 6:13
7:8 [x]S Est 1:6;
[y]Ge 39:14;
Jn 13:23
[z]S Ge 34:7
[a]S Est 6:12
7:9 [b]Est 1:10
[c]Est 5:14
[d]S Dt 21:22-23;
Ps 7:14-16; 9:16;
Pr 11:5-6;
S 26:27; S Mt 7:2
7:10 [e]Ge 40:22
[f]Pr 10:28
[g]Est 9:25
[h]Da 6:24 /Est 2:1
8:1 [i]Pr 22:22-23
8:2 [k]S Ge 24:22;
S 41:42

[l]S Ge 41:41;
Pr 13:22; 14:35;
Da 2:48
8:3
[m]S Ex 17:8-16
8:4 [n]S Est 4:11
8:5 [o]S Est 2:15
8:6 [p]Ge 44:34
8:7
[q]S Dt 21:22-23
8:8
[r]S Est 3:12-14
[s]S Ge 38:18
[t]S Ge 41:42
[u]S Est 1:19;
Da 6:15
8:9 [v]Est 1:1

j 9 Hebrew *fifty cubits* (about 23 meters)   **k 9** That is, the upper Nile region

---

7:8 *falling on the couch where Esther was reclining.* Meals were customarily taken reclining on a couch (Am 6:4–7; Jn 13:23). It is ironic that Haman, who became angry when the Jew Mordecai would not bow down (which set the whole story in motion), now falls before the Jewess Esther (see 6:13). The king's leaving the room sets the stage for the final twist that would seal Haman's fate. *covered Haman's face.* See 6:12; see also Introduction: Purpose, Themes and Literary Features.

7:9 Before this moment there is no evidence that Esther had known of Mordecai's triumph earlier in the day (ch. 6); she has pleaded for the life of her people. Harbona's reference to the gallows in effect introduces a second charge against Haman—his attempt to kill the king's benefactor. *Harbona.* See Introduction: Purpose, Themes and Literary Features. He had been sent earlier to bring Vashti and thus set in motion the events that would lead to her fall and the choice of Esther (1:10); now he is instrumental in the fall of Haman and the rise of Mordecai.

7:10 *subsided.* See 2:1; see also Introduction: Purpose, Themes and Literary Features.

8:1–17 The author achieves considerable literary symmetry by recapitulating much of 3:1–4:3 in almost identical terms.

8:1 *gave Queen Esther the estate of Haman.* Herodotus (3.128–129) and Josephus (*Antiquities,* 11.17) confirm that the property of a traitor reverted to the crown; Xerxes presents Haman's wealth (5:11) to Esther.

8:2 Cf. 3:10, where the king's offer of his ring includes Haman's keeping the money; here Mordecai receives the office and the estate of Haman.

8:3–6 Esther and Mordecai are secure (7:4–5), but the irrevocable decree is still a threat to the rest of the Jews.

8:3 *Agagite.* See note on 3:1.

8:5 *favor.* See 4:11; 5:2.

8:6 Cf. the Joseph story (Ge 44:34).

8:8 See 1:19; see also Introduction: Purpose, Themes and Literary Features. The dilemma is the same as the one that confronted Darius the Mede in Daniel (Da 6:8,12,15). The solution is to issue another decree that in effect counters the original decree of Haman without formally revoking it (see note on 9:2–3).

8:9–13 The phraseology is taken from the parallel in 3:12–14. The extent of the destruction is the same as that earlier decreed against Amalek (see note on 3:13).

8:9 *twenty-third day . . . third month.* In Xerxes's 12th year, i.e., June 25, 474 B.C., two months and ten days after the proclamation of Haman's edict (see note on 3:13).

ten in the script of each province and the language of each people and also to the Jews in their own script and language. [w] [10]Mordecai wrote in the name of King Xerxes, sealed the dispatches with the king's signet ring, and sent them by mounted couriers, who rode fast horses especially bred for the king.

[11]The king's edict granted the Jews in every city the right to assemble and protect themselves; to destroy, kill and annihilate any armed force of any nationality or province that might attack them and their women and children; and to plunder[x] the property of their enemies. [12]The day appointed for the Jews to do this in all the provinces of King Xerxes was the thirteenth day of the twelfth month, the month of Adar.[y] [13]A copy of the text of the edict was to be issued as law in every province and made known to the people of every nationality so that the Jews would be ready on that day[z] to avenge themselves on their enemies.

[14]The couriers, riding the royal horses, raced out, spurred on by the king's command. And the edict was also issued in the citadel of Susa.[a]

[15]Mordecai[b] left the king's presence wearing royal garments of blue and white, a large crown of gold[c] and a purple robe of fine linen.[d] And the city of Susa held a joyous celebration.[e] [16]For the Jews it was a time of happiness and joy,[f] gladness and honor.[g] [17]In every province and in every city, wherever the edict of the king went, there was joy[h] and gladness among the Jews, with feasting and celebrating. And many people of other nationalities became Jews because fear[i] of the Jews had seized them.[j]

8:9 [w]S Ne 13:24
8:11 [x]S Ge 14:23;
S Est 3:13; 9:15,
16
8:12 [y]Est 3:13;
9:1
8:13 [z]Est 3:14
8:14 [a]Est 3:15
8:15 [b]Est 9:4;
10:2 [c]S 2Sa 12:30
[d]S Ge 41:42
[e]Est 3:15
8:16 [f]Ps 97:10-12
[g]Est 4:1-3;
Ps 112:4;
Jer 29:4-7
8:17 [h]Ps 35:27;
45:15; 51:8;
Pr 11:10
[i]S Ex 15:14,16;
Dt 11:25; Da 6:26
[j]Est 9:3

9:1 [k]S Est 8:12
[l]Jer 29:4-7
[m]S Est 3:12-14;
Pr 22:22-23
9:2 [n]S Ge 22:17
[o]Ps 35:26; 40:14;
70:2; 71:13,24
9:3 [p]S Ezr 8:36
9Est 8:17
9:4 [r]S Est 8:15
[s]S Ex 11:3
[t]S 2Sa 3:1;
1Ch 11:9
9:5
[u]Dt 25:17-19;
S 1Sa 15:3;
S Ezr 4:6
9:10 [v]S Est 5:11;
Ps 127:3-5
[w]S 1Sa 15:33
[x]S Ge 14:23;
S 1Sa 14:32;
S Est 3:13
9:12 [y]Est 5:6;
7:2

Triumph of the Jews

9 On the thirteenth day of the twelfth month, the month of Adar,[k] the edict commanded by the king was to be carried out. On this day the enemies of the Jews had hoped to overpower them, but now the tables were turned and the Jews got the upper hand[l] over those who hated them.[m] [2]The Jews assembled in their cities[n] in all the provinces of King Xerxes to attack those seeking their destruction. No one could stand against them,[o] because the people of all the other nationalities were afraid of them. [3]And all the nobles of the provinces, the satraps, the governors and the king's administrators helped the Jews,[p] because fear of Mordecai had seized them.[q] [4]Mordecai[r] was prominent[s] in the palace; his reputation spread throughout the provinces, and he became more and more powerful.[t]

[5]The Jews struck down all their enemies with the sword, killing and destroying them,[u] and they did what they pleased to those who hated them. [6]In the citadel of Susa, the Jews killed and destroyed five hundred men. [7]They also killed Parshandatha, Dalphon, Aspatha, [8]Poratha, Adalia, Aridatha, [9]Parmashta, Arisai, Aridai and Vaizatha, [10]the ten sons[v] of Haman son of Hammedatha, the enemy of the Jews.[w] But they did not lay their hands on the plunder.[x]

[11]The number of those slain in the citadel of Susa was reported to the king that same day. [12]The king said to Queen Esther, "The Jews have killed and destroyed five hundred men and the ten sons of Haman in the citadel of Susa. What have they done in the rest of the king's provinces? Now what is your petition? It will be given you. What is your request? It will also be granted."[y]

[13]"If it pleases the king," Esther an-

8:12 *thirteenth day . . . twelfth month.* Mar. 7, 473 B.C. (see 3:13). Some 15 years after this first Purim, Ezra would lead his expedition to Jerusalem (Ezr 7:9).
8:14–17 The phraseology is taken from 3:15–4:3.
8:15 *royal garments.* Mordecai's second investiture (see Introduction: Purpose, Themes and Literary Features; see also note on 6:10).
9:1 See notes on 8:9–13. The Jews carry out the edict of Mordecai eight months and 20 days later. *tables were turned.* The statement that the opposite happened points to the author's concern with literary symmetry: He balances most of the details from the first half of the story with their explicit reversal in the second half.
9:2–3 An illustration of Ge 12:3. Confronted with two conflicting edicts issued in the king's name—the edict of Haman and the edict of Mordecai—the governors follow the edict of the current regime.

9:5–10 The Jews attend to the unfinished business of "blotting out the name of the Amalekites" (Ex 17:16; Dt 25:17–19; see notes on 3:1–6). This incident is presented as the antithesis of 1Sa 15: The narrator is emphatic that the Jews did not take plunder, in spite of the king's permission to do so (8:11). Seizing the plunder 500 years earlier in the battle against Amalek had cost Saul his kingship (1Sa 15:17–19); here, not taking the plunder brings royal power to Mordecai (vv. 20–23). See vv. 15–16; cf. Ge 14:22–24.

9:10 *sons of Haman.* The second reference to Haman's sons (see 5:11; see also Introduction: Purpose, Themes and Literary Features).

9:12 See 5:3,6; 7:2.

9:13 The reference to hanging in this case is to the display of the corpses, not to the means of the execution (see vv. 7–10 and note on 2:23).

swered, "give the Jews in Susa permission to carry out this day's edict tomorrow also, and let Haman's ten sons[z] be hanged[a] on gallows."

[14]So the king commanded that this be done. An edict was issued in Susa, and they hanged[b] the ten sons of Haman. [15]The Jews in Susa came together on the fourteenth day of the month of Adar, and they put to death in Susa three hundred men, but they did not lay their hands on the plunder.[c]

[16]Meanwhile, the remainder of the Jews who were in the king's provinces also assembled to protect themselves and get relief[d] from their enemies.[e] They killed seventy-five thousand of them[f] but did not lay their hands on the plunder.[g] [17]This happened on the thirteenth day of the month of Adar, and on the fourteenth they rested and made it a day of feasting[h] and joy.

Purim Celebrated

[18]The Jews in Susa, however, had assembled on the thirteenth and fourteenth, and then on the fifteenth they rested and made it a day of feasting and joy.

[19]That is why rural Jews—those living in villages—observe the fourteenth of the month of Adar[i] as a day of joy and feasting, a day for giving presents to each other.[j]

[20]Mordecai recorded these events, and he sent letters to all the Jews throughout the provinces of King Xerxes, near and far, [21]to have them celebrate annually the fourteenth and fifteenth days of the month of Adar [22]as the time when the Jews got relief[k] from their enemies, and as the month when their sorrow was turned into joy and their mourning into a day of celebration.[l] He wrote them to observe the days as days of feasting and joy and giving presents of food[m] to one another and gifts to the poor.[n]

[23]So the Jews agreed to continue the celebration they had begun, doing what Mordecai had written to them. [24]For Haman son of Hammedatha, the Agagite,[o] the enemy of all the Jews, had plotted against the Jews to destroy them and had cast the pur[p] (that is, the lot[q]) for their ruin and destruction.[r] [25]But when the plot came to the king's attention,[1] he issued written orders that the evil scheme Haman had devised against the Jews should come back onto his own head,[s] and that he and his sons should be hanged[t] on the gallows.[u] [26](Therefore these days were called Purim, from the word pur.[v]) Because of everything written in this letter and because of what they had seen and what had happened to them, [27]the Jews took it upon themselves to establish the custom that they and their descendants and all who join them should without fail observe these two days every year, in the way prescribed and at the time appointed. [28]These days should be remembered and observed in every generation by every family, and in every province and in every city. And these days of Purim should never cease to be celebrated by the Jews, nor should the memory of them die out among their descendants.

[29]So Queen Esther, daughter of Abihail,[w] along with Mordecai the Jew, wrote with full authority to confirm this second letter concerning Purim. [30]And Mordecai sent letters to all the Jews in the 127 provinces[x] of the kingdom of Xerxes—words of goodwill and assurance— [31]to establish these days of Purim at their designated times, as Mordecai the Jew and Queen Esther had decreed for them, and as they had established for themselves and their descendants in regard to their times of fasting[y] and lamentation.[z] [32]Esther's decree confirmed these regulations about Purim, and it was written down in the records.

9:13 [z]S Est 5:11
[a]S Dt 21:22-23
9:14 [b]S Ezr 6:11
9:15
[c]S Ge 14:23; S Est 8:11
9:16 [d]S Est 4:14
[e]Dt 25:19
[f]S 1Ch 4:43
[g]S Est 8:11
9:17 [h]S 1Ki 3:15
9:19 [i]S Est 3:7
[j]S Est 2:9;
Rev 11:10
9:22 [k]S Est 4:14
[l]Ne 8:12;
Ps 30:11-12
[m]S 2Ki 25:30
[n]S Ne 8:10

9:24
[o]S Ex 17:8-16
[p]S Est 3:7
[q]S Lev 16:8
[r]Est 3:6
9:25 [s]Ps 7:16
[t]S Dt 21:22-23
[u]Est 7:10
9:26 [v]S Est 3:7
9:29 [w]Est 2:15
9:30 [x]S Est 1:1
9:31 [y]S Est 4:16
[z]Est 4:1-3

[1]25 Or when Esther came before the king

9:15–16 See note on vv. 5–10.
9:16,22 *relief from their enemies.* Closely associated with the vengeance on their enemies is the rest promised to Israel (Dt 25:19). The defeat of Haman brings rest to the Jews. Cf. 1Ch 22:6–10; Ps 95:8–11; Isa 32:18; Heb 3:11–4:11.
9:18–19 The author accounts for the tradition of observing Purim on two different days: It is observed on the 14th in most towns, but the Jews of Susa observed it on the 15th. Today it is observed on the 14th except in Jerusalem, where it is observed on the 15th.
9:20 *Mordecai recorded these events.* Some take this as indicating that Mordecai wrote the book of Esther; however, the more natural understanding is that he recorded the events in the letters he sent.

9:22 *presents of food.* See note on 2:9; cf. Ne 8:10,12.
9:24,26 *pur.* See note on 3:7.
9:27 *all who join them.* Some refer this phrase to a period of Jewish proselytism and regard it as important to dating the book. It is more likely that it refers to those mentioned in 8:17.
9:31 *fasting.* See notes on 4:3,16. No date is assigned for this fast. Jews traditionally observe the 13th of Adar, Haman's propitious day (see 3:7,13), as a fast ("the fast of Esther") before the celebration of Purim. These three days of victory celebration on the 13th–15th days of Adar rhetorically balance the three days of Esther's fasting prior to interceding with the king (4:16).

The Greatness of Mordecai

10 King Xerxes imposed tribute throughout the empire, to its distant shores.ᵃ ²And all his acts of power and might, together with a full account of the greatness of Mordecaiᵇ to which the king had raised him,ᶜ are they not written in the book of the annalsᵈ of the kings of Media and Persia? ³Mordecai the Jew was secondᵉ in rankᶠ to King Xerxes,ᵍ preeminent among the Jews, and held in high esteem by his many fellow Jews, because he worked for the good of his people and spoke up for the welfare of all the Jews.ʰ

10:1 ᵃPs 72:10; 97:1
10:2 ᵇS Est 8:15 ᶜS Ge 41:44 ᵈS Est 2:23
10:3 ᵉDa 5:7 ᶠGe 41:43 ᵍGe 41:40 ʰNe 2:10; Jer 29:4-7; Da 6:3

10:1–2 The reference to this taxation may represent material in the author's source, to which he directs the reader for additional information and confirmation (see note on 2:23).

JOB

Author

Although most of the book consists of the words of Job and his counselors, Job himself was not the author. We may be sure that the author was an Israelite, since he (not Job or his friends) frequently uses the Israelite covenant name for God (*Yahweh;* NIV "the LORD"). In the prologue (chs. 1-2), divine discourses (38:1-42:6) and epilogue (42:7-17) "LORD" occurs a total of 25 times (31 times in the Hebrew text), while in the rest of the book (chs. 3-37) it appears only once (12:9).

The unknown author probably had access to oral and/or written sources from which, under divine inspiration, he composed the book that we now have. Of course the subject matter of the prologue had to be divinely revealed to him, since it contains information only God could know. While the author preserves much of the archaic and non-Israelite flavor in the language of Job and his friends, he also reveals his own style as a writer of wisdom literature. The literary structures and the quality of the rhetoric used display the author's literary genius.

Date

Two dates are involved: (1) the date of the man Job and his historical setting, and (2) the date of the inspired writer who composed the book. The latter could be dated anytime from the reign of Solomon to the exile. Although the writer was an Israelite, he mentions nothing of Israelite history. He had a written and/or oral account about the non-Israelite sage Job (1:1), whose setting appears to be during the second millennium B.C. (2000-1000), and probably late in that millennium (see note on 19:24). Like the Hebrew patriarchs, Job lived more than 100 years (42:16). His wealth was measured in cattle (1:3), and he acted as priest for his family (1:5). The raiding of Sabean (1:15) and Chaldean (1:17) tribes fits the second millennium, as does the mention of the *kesitah,* "a piece of silver," in 42:11 (see Ge 33:19; Jos 24:32). The discovery of a Targum (Aramaic paraphrase) on Job from the first or second century B.C. (the earliest written Targum) makes a very late date for authorship highly unlikely.

Language and Text

In many places Job is difficult to translate because of its many unusual words and its style. For that reason, modern translations frequently differ widely. Even the early translator(s) of Job into Greek (the Septuagint) seem(s) often to have been perplexed. The Septuagint of Job is about 400 lines shorter than the accepted Hebrew text, and it may be that the translator(s) simply omitted lines he (they) did not understand. The early Syriac (Peshitta), Aramaic (Targum) and Latin (Vulgate) translators had similar difficulties.

Theme and Message

The book provides a profound statement on the subject of theodicy (the justice of God in light of human suffering). But the manner in which the problem of theodicy is conceived and the solution offered (if it may be called that) is uniquely Israelite. The theodicy question in Greek and later Western thought has been: How can the justice of an almighty God be defended in the face of evil, especially human suffering—and, even more particularly, the suffering of the innocent? In this form of the question, three possible assumptions are left open: (1) that God is not almighty, (2) that God is not just (that there is a "demonic" element in his being) and (3) that man may be innocent. In ancient Israel, however, it was indisputable that God is almighty, that he is perfectly just and that no human is wholly innocent in his sight. These three assumptions were also fundamental to the theology of Job and his friends. Simple logic then dictated the conclusion: Every person's suffering is indicative of the measure of his guilt in the eyes of God. In the abstract, this conclusion appeared inescapable, logically

imperative and theologically satisfying. Hence, in the context of such a theology, theodicy was not a problem because its solution was self-evident.

But what was thus theologically self-evident and unassailable in the abstract was often, as in the case of Job, in radical tension with actual human experience. There were those whose godliness was genuine, whose moral character was upright and who, though not sinless, had kept themselves from great transgression, but who nonetheless were made to suffer bitterly. For these the self-evident theology brought no consolation and offered no guidance. It only gave rise to a great enigma. And the God to whom the sufferer was accustomed to turn in moments of need and distress became himself the overwhelming enigma. In the speeches of chs. 3-37, we hear on the one hand the flawless logic but wounding thrusts of those who insisted on the "orthodox" theology, and on the other hand the writhing of soul of the righteous sufferer who struggles with the great enigma. In addition he suffers from the wounds inflicted by his well-intended friends (see note on 5:27). Here, then, we have a graphic portrayal of the unique form of the problem of theodicy as experienced by righteous sufferers within orthodox Israel.

The "solution" offered is also uniquely Israelite—or, better said, Biblical. The relationship between God and man is not exclusive and closed. A third party intrudes, the great adversary (see chs. 1-2). Incapable of contending with God hand to hand, power pitted against power, he is bent on frustrating God's enterprise embodied in the creation and centered on the God-man relationship. As tempter he seeks to alienate man from God (see Ge 3; Mt 4:1); as accuser (one of the names by which he is called, śaṭan, means "accuser") he seeks to alienate God from man (see Zec 3:1; Rev 12:9-10). His all-consuming purpose is to drive an irremovable wedge between God and man, to effect an alienation that cannot be reconciled.

In the story of Job, the author portrays the adversary in his boldest and most radical assault on God and the godly man in the special and intimate relationship that is dearest to them both. When God calls up the name of Job before the accuser and testifies to the righteousness of this one on the earth—this man in whom God delights—Satan attempts with one crafty thrust both to assail God's beloved and to show up God as a fool. True to one of his modes of operation, he accuses Job before God. He charges that Job's godliness is evil. The very godliness in which God takes delight is void of all integrity; it is the worst of all sins. Job's godliness is self-serving; he is righteous only because it pays. If God will only let Satan tempt Job by breaking the link between righteousness and blessing, he will expose the righteous man for the sinner he is.

It is the adversary's ultimate challenge. For if the godliness of the righteous man in whom God delights can be shown to be the worst of all sins, then a chasm of alienation stands between them that cannot be bridged. Then even redemption is unthinkable, for the godliest of men will be shown to be the most ungodly. God's whole enterprise in creation and redemption will be shown to be radically flawed, and God can only sweep it all away in awful judgment.

The accusation, once raised, cannot be removed, not even by destroying the accuser. So God lets the adversary have his way with Job (within specified limits) so that God and the righteous Job may be vindicated and the great accuser silenced. Thus comes the anguish of Job, robbed of every sign of God's favor so that God becomes for him the great enigma. Also his righteousness is assailed on earth through the logic of the "orthodox" theology of his friends. Alone he agonizes. But he knows in his heart that his godliness has been authentic and that someday he will be vindicated (see 13:18; 14:13-17; 16:19; 19:25-27). And in spite of all, though he may curse the day of his birth (ch. 3) and chide God for treating him unjustly (9:28-35)—the uncalculated outcry of a distraught spirit—he will not curse God (as his wife, the human nearest his heart, proposes; see 2:9). In fact, what pains him most is God's apparent alienation from him.

In the end the adversary is silenced. And the astute theologians, Job's friends, are silenced. And Job is silenced. But God is not. And when he speaks, it is to Job that he speaks, bringing the silence of regret for hasty speech in days of suffering and the silence of repose in the ways of the Almighty (see 38:1-42:6). Furthermore, as his heavenly friend, God hears Job's intercessions for his associates (42:8-10), and he restores Job's beatitude (42:10-17).

In summary, the author's pastoral word to the godly sufferer is that his righteousness has such supreme value that God treasures it more than all. And the great adversary knows that if he is to thwart the purposes of God he must assail the righteousness of man. At stake in the suffering of the truly godly is the outcome of the struggle in heaven between the great adversary and God, with the all-encompassing divine purpose in the balance. Thus the suffering of the righteous has a meaning and value commensurate with the titanic spiritual struggle of the ages.

Literary Form and Structure

Like some other ancient compositions, the book of Job has a sandwich literary structure: prologue (prose), main body (poetry), and epilogue (prose), revealing a creative composition, not an arbitrary compilation. Some of Job's words are lament (cf. ch. 3 and many shorter poems in his speeches), but the form of lament is unique to Job and often unlike the regular format of most lament psalms (except Ps 88). Much of the book takes the form of legal disputation. Although the friends come to console him, they end up arguing over the reason for Job's suffering. The argument breaks down in ch. 27, and Job then proceeds to make his final appeal to God for vindication (chs. 29-31). The wisdom poem in ch. 28 appears to be the words of the author, who sees the failure of the dispute as evidence of a lack of wisdom. So in praise of true wisdom he centers his structural apex between the three cycles of dialogue-dispute (chs. 3-27) and the three monologues: Job's (chs. 29-31), Elihu's (chs. 32-37) and God's (38:1-42:6). Job's monologue turns directly to God for a legal decision: that he is innocent of the charges his counselors have leveled against him. Elihu's monologue—another human perspective on why people suffer—rebukes Job but moves beyond the punishment theme to the value of divine chastening and God's redemptive purpose in it. God's monologue gives the divine perspective: Job is not condemned, but neither is a logical or legal answer given to why Job has suffered. That remains a mystery to Job, though the reader is ready for Job's restoration in the epilogue because he has had the heavenly vantage point of the prologue all along. So the literary structure and the theological significance of the book are beautifully tied together.

Outline

  I. Prologue (chs. 1-2)
     A. Job's Happiness (1:1-5)
     B. Job's Testing (1:6-2:13)
        1. Satan's first accusation (1:6-12)
        2. Job's faith despite loss of family and property (1:13-22)
        3. Satan's second accusation (2:1-6)
        4. Job's faith during personal suffering (2:7-10)
        5. The coming of the three friends (2:11-13)
 II. Dialogue-Dispute (chs. 3-27)
     A. Job's Opening Lament (ch. 3)
     B. First Cycle of Speeches (chs. 4-14)
        1. Eliphaz (chs. 4-5)
        2. Job's reply (chs. 6-7)
        3. Bildad (ch. 8)
        4. Job's reply (chs. 9-10)
        5. Zophar (ch. 11)
        6. Job's reply (chs. 12-14)
     C. Second Cycle of Speeches (chs. 15-21)
        1. Eliphaz (ch. 15)
        2. Job's reply (chs. 16-17)
        3. Bildad (ch. 18)
        4. Job's reply (ch. 19)
        5. Zophar (ch. 20)
        6. Job's reply (ch. 21)
     D. Third Cycle of Speeches (chs. 22-26)
        1. Eliphaz (ch. 22)
        2. Job's reply (chs. 23-24)
        3. Bildad (ch. 25)
        4. Job's reply (ch. 26)
     E. Job's Closing Discourse (ch. 27)
III. Interlude on Wisdom (ch. 28)
 IV. Monologues (29:1-42:6)
     A. Job's Call for Vindication (chs. 29-31)
        1. His past honor and blessing (ch. 29)
        2. His present dishonor and suffering (ch. 30)
        3. His protestations of innocence and final oath (ch. 31)

  B. Elihu's Speeches (chs. 32-37)
    1. Introduction (32:1-5)
    2. The speeches themselves (32:6-37:24)
      a. First speech (32:6-33:33)
      b. Second speech (ch. 34)
      c. Third speech (ch. 35)
      d. Fourth speech (chs. 36-37)
  C. Divine Discourses (38:1-42:6)
    1. God's first discourse (38:1-40:2)
    2. Job's response (40:3-5)
    3. God's second discourse (40:6-41:34)
    4. Job's repentance (42:1-6)
V. Epilogue (42:7-17)
  A. God's Verdict (42:7-9)
  B. Job's Restoration (42:10-17)

Prologue

1 In the land of Uz[a] there lived a man whose name was Job.[b] This man was blameless[c] and upright;[d] he feared God[e] and shunned evil.[f] ²He had seven sons[g] and three daughters,[h] ³and he owned seven thousand sheep, three thousand camels, five hundred yoke of oxen and five hundred donkeys,[i] and had a large number of servants.[j] He was the greatest man[k] among all the people of the East.[l]

⁴His sons used to take turns holding feasts[m] in their homes, and they would invite their three sisters to eat and drink with them. ⁵When a period of feasting had run its course, Job would send and have them purified.[n] Early in the morning he would sacrifice a burnt offering[o] for each of them, thinking, "Perhaps my children have sinned[p] and cursed God[q] in their hearts." This was Job's regular custom.

Job's First Test

⁶One day the angels[a][r] came to present themselves before the LORD, and Satan[b][s] also came with them.[t] ⁷The LORD said to Satan, "Where have you come from?"

Satan answered the LORD, "From roaming through the earth and going back and forth in it."[u]

⁸Then the LORD said to Satan, "Have you considered my servant Job?[v] There is no one on earth like him; he is blameless and upright, a man who fears God[w] and shuns evil."[x]

⁹"Does Job fear God for nothing?"[y] Satan replied. ¹⁰"Have you not put a hedge[z] around him and his household and everything he has?[a] You have blessed the work of his hands, so that his flocks and herds are spread throughout the land.[b] ¹¹But stretch out your hand and strike everything he has,[c] and he will surely curse you to your face."[d]

¹²The LORD said to Satan, "Very well, then, everything he has[e] is in your hands, but on the man himself do not lay a finger."[f]

Then Satan went out from the presence of the LORD.

¹³One day when Job's sons and daughters[g] were feasting[h] and drinking wine at the oldest brother's house, ¹⁴a messenger came to Job and said, "The oxen were plowing and the donkeys were grazing[i] nearby, ¹⁵and the Sabeans[j] attacked and carried them off. They put the servants to the sword, and I am the only one who has escaped to tell you!"

¹⁶While he was still speaking, another messenger came and said, "The fire of God

1:1 ªS Ge 10:23
ᵇEze 14:14,20;
Jas 5:11
ᶜS Ge 6:9;
S Job 23:10
ᵈJob 23:7;
Ps 11:7; 107:42;
Pr 21:29; Mic 7:2
ᵉS Ge 22:12
ᶠver 8; S Dt 4:6;
Job 2:3; 1Th 5:22
1:2 ᵍS Ru 4:15
ʰver 13,18;
Job 42:13;
Ps 127:3; 144:12
1:3 ⁱS Ge 13:2
ʲS Ge 12:16
ᵏver 8; Job 29:25
ˡS Ge 25:6;
Job 42:10;
Ps 103:10
1:4 ᵐver 13,18
1:5 ⁿS Ne 12:30
ᵒS Ge 8:20
ᵖJob 8:4
۹1Ki 21:10,13;
Ps 10:3; 74:10
1:6 ʳS 1Ki 22:19;
ˢⁿ Ge 6:2
ˢS 2Sa 24:1;
S 2Ch 18:21;
S Ps 109:6;
Lk 22:31 ᵗJob 2:1
1:7 ᵘS Ge 3:1;
1Pe 5:8
1:8 ᵛS Jos 1:7

ʷPs 25:12;
112:1; 128:4
ˣS ver 1;
S Ex 20:20
1:9 ʸ1Ti 6:5
1:10
ᶻS 1Sa 25:16 ᵃver
12; Job 2:4;
Ps 34:7 ᵇver 3;
Job 8:7; 29:6;
42:12,17
1:11 ᶜJob 19:21;
Lk 22:31
ᵈLev 24:11;
Job 2:5; Isa 3:8;

65:3; Rev 12:9-10 1:12 ᵉS ver 10 ᶠJob 2:6; 1Co 10:13 1:13
ᵍS ver 2 ʰS ver 4 1:14 ⁱGe 36:24 1:15 ʲS Ge 10:7; S Job 9:24

ª6 Hebrew *the sons of God*   ᵇ6 *Satan* means *accuser.*

1:1 *land of Uz.* A large territory east of the Jordan (see v. 3), which included Edom in the south (see Ge 36:28; La 4:21) and the Aramean lands in the north (see Ge 10:23; 22:21). *blameless and upright.* Spiritually and morally upright. This does not mean that Job was sinless. He later defends his moral integrity but also admits he is a sinner (see 6:24; 7:21). *feared God.* See 28:28; Pr 3:7; see also note on Ge 20:11.
1:2 *seven sons.* An ideal number, signifying completeness (see note on Ru 4:15).
1:3 *seven thousand sheep.* See note on 42:12. Job's enormous wealth was in livestock, not land (see Ge 12:16; 13:2; 26:14). *donkeys.* The Hebrew for this word is feminine in form. Donkeys that produced offspring were very valuable. *people of the East.* The Hebrew for this phrase is translated "eastern peoples" in Ge 29:1; Jdg 6:3 (see note there).
1:5 *period of feasting.* On special occasions, feasts might last a week (see Ge 29:27; Jdg 14:12). *he would sacrifice.* Before the ceremonial laws of Moses were introduced, the father of the household acted as priest (see Ge 15:9–10). *purified.* Made ceremonially clean in preparation for the sacrifices he offered for them (see Ex 19:10,14, where the Hebrew for this verb is translated "consecrate").
1:6 *angels came to present themselves.* See NIV text note here and on 2:1; 38:7. They came as members of the heavenly council who stand in the presence of God (see 1Ki 22:19; Ps 89:5–7; Jer 23:18,22). *Satan.* Lit. "the accuser" (see NIV text note; see also Rev 12:10). In Job the Hebrew for this word is always preceded by the definite article. In the Hebrew of 1Ch 21:1 the article is not used, because by then "Satan" had become a proper name.

1:7 *The LORD.* The Israelite covenant name for God (see Introduction: Author).
1:8 *Have you considered . . . Job?* The Lord, not Satan, initiates the dialogue that leads to the testing of Job. He holds up Job as one against whom "the accuser" can lodge no accusation. *my servant.* See 42:7–8 and note; a designation for one who stands in a special relationship with God and is loyal in service (e.g., Moses, Nu 12:7; David, 2Sa 7:5; see Isa 42:1; 52:13; 53:11).
1:9 "The accuser" boldly accuses the man God commends: He says Job's righteousness, in which God delights, is self-serving—the heart of Satan's attack on God and his faithful servant in the book of Job.
1:10 *hedge.* Symbolizes protection (see Isa 5:5; contrast Job 3:23).
1:11 *stretch out your hand and strike.* See 4:5.
1:12 Satan, the accuser, is given power to afflict (v. 12a) but is kept on a leash (v. 12b). In all his evil among men (vv. 15,17) or in nature (vv. 16,19), Satan is under God's power (compare 1Ch 21:1 with 2Sa 24:1; see 1Sa 16:14; 2Sa 24:16; 1Co 5:5; 2Co 12:7; Heb 2:14). The contest, however, is not a sham. Will Job curse God to his face? If Job does not, the accuser will be proven false and God's delight in Job vindicated.
1:15 *Sabeans.* Probably south Arabians from Sheba, whose descendants became wealthy traders in spices, gold and precious stones (see the account of the queen of Sheba in 1Ki 10:1–13; see also Ps 72:10,15; Isa 60:6; Jer 6:20; Eze 27:22; Joel 3:8). Job 6:19 calls the Sabeans "traveling merchants" and associates them with Tema (about 350 miles southeast of Jerusalem).

fell from the sky[k] and burned up the sheep and the servants,[l] and I am the only one who has escaped to tell you!"

[17]While he was still speaking, another messenger came and said, "The Chaldeans[m] formed three raiding parties and swept down on your camels and carried them off. They put the servants to the sword, and I am the only one who has escaped to tell you!"

[18]While he was still speaking, yet another messenger came and said, "Your sons and daughters[n] were feasting[o] and drinking wine at the oldest brother's house, [19]when suddenly a mighty wind[p] swept in from the desert and struck the four corners of the house. It collapsed on them and they are dead,[q] and I am the only one who has escaped to tell you!"[r]"

[20]At this, Job got up and tore his robe[s] and shaved his head.[t] Then he fell to the ground in worship[u] [21]and said:

"Naked I came from my mother's
 womb,
 and naked I will depart.[c][v]
The LORD gave and the LORD has taken
 away;[w]
 may the name of the LORD be
 praised."[x]

[22]In all this, Job did not sin by charging God with wrongdoing.[y]

Job's Second Test

2 On another day the angels[d][z] came to present themselves before the LORD, and Satan also came with them[a] to present himself before him. [2]And the LORD said to Satan, "Where have you come from?"

Satan answered the LORD, "From roaming through the earth and going back and forth in it."[b]

[3]Then the LORD said to Satan, "Have you considered my servant Job? There is no one on earth like him; he is blameless and upright, a man who fears God and shuns evil.[c] And he still maintains his integrity,[d] though you incited me against him to ruin him without any reason."[e]

[4]"Skin for skin!" Satan replied. "A man will give all he has[f] for his own life. [5]But stretch out your hand and strike his flesh and bones,[g] and he will surely curse you to your face."[h]

[6]The LORD said to Satan, "Very well, then, he is in your hands;[i] but you must spare his life."[j]

[7]So Satan went out from the presence of the LORD and afflicted Job with painful sores from the soles of his feet to the top of his head.[k] [8]Then Job took a piece of broken pottery and scraped himself with it as he sat among the ashes.[l]

[9]His wife said to him, "Are you still holding on to your integrity?[m] Curse God and die!"[n]

[10]He replied, "You are talking like a

1:16
[k]S 1Ki 18:38;
2Ki 1:12;
Job 20:26
[l]S Ge 18:17;
S Lev 10:2;
S Nu 11:1-3
1:17
[m]S Ge 11:28;
S Job 9:24
1:18 [n]S ver 2
[o]S ver 4
1:19 [p]Ps 11:6;
Isa 5:28; 21:1;
Jer 4:11; 13:24;
18:17; Eze 17:10;
Hos 13:15;
Mt 7:25
[q]Job 16:7;
19:13-15
[r]Eze 24:26
1:20
[s]S Ge 37:29;
S Mk 14:63
[t]Isa 3:24; 15:2;
22:12; Jer 7:29;
16:6; Eze 27:31;
29:18; Mic 1:16
[u]1Pe 5:6
1:21 [v]Ecc 5:15;
1Ti 6:7 [w]Ru 1:21;
1Sa 2:7
[x]S Jdg 10:15;
Job 2:10;
Ecc 7:14;
Jer 40:2;
S Eph 5:20;
1Th 5:18;
Jas 5:11
1:22 [y]Job 2:10;
Ps 39:1; Pr 10:19;
13:3; Isa 53:7;
Ro 9:20
2:1 [z]fn Ge 6:2
[a]S Job 1:6

2:2 [b]S Ge 3:1
2:3 [c]S Ex 20:20;
S Job 1:1
[d]Job 6:29; 13:18;
27:6; 31:6; 32:1;
40:8 [e]Job 9:17;
Ps 44:17
2:4 [f]S Job 1:10
2:5 [g]Job 16:8;
19:20; 33:21;
Ps 102:5; La 4:8
[h]S Ex 20:7;
S Job 1:11

2:6 [i]2Co 12:7 [j]S Job 1:12 **2:7** [k]S Dt 28:35; S Job 16:16 **2:8**
[l]Ge 18:27; Est 4:3; Job 16:15; 19:9; 30:19; 42:6; Ps 7:5;
Isa 58:5; 61:3; Jer 6:26; La 3:29; Eze 26:16; Jnh 3:5-8,6;
Mt 11:21 **2:9** [m]Job 6:29; 13:15; 27:5; 33:9; 35:2; 1Th 5:8
[n]S Ex 20:7; S 2Ki 6:33

[c]21 Or will return there   [d]1 Hebrew the sons of God

1:16 *fire of God.* Lightning (see Nu 11:1; 1Ki 18:38; 2Ki 1:12).

1:17 *Chaldeans.* A people who were Bedouin until c. 1000 B.C., when they settled in southern Mesopotamia and later became the nucleus of Nebuchadnezzar's empire.

1:19 *mighty wind.* Tornado.

1:20 *At this, Job got up.* He is silent until his children are killed. *tore his robe and shaved his head.* In mourning (see notes on Ge 37:34; Isa 15:2).

1:21 *depart.* See NIV text note; see also Ge 2:7; 3:19 and note. *The LORD gave and the LORD has taken away.* Job's faith leads him to see the sovereign God's hand at work, and that gives him repose even in the face of calamity.

2:1–3 Except for the final sentence, this passage is almost identical to 1:6–8. He who accused Job of having a deceitful motive is now shown to have a deceitful motive himself: to discredit the Lord through Job.

2:3 *you incited me.* God cannot be stirred up to do things against his will. Though it is not always clear how, everything that happens is part of his divine purpose (see 38:2).

2:4 *Skin for skin!* No doubt a proverb—perhaps originally an expression of willingness to barter one animal skin for another of equal value.

2:5 *strike his flesh and bones.* See 1:11–12; cf. Ge 2:23; Lk 24:39.

2:6 *spare his life.* Satan is still limited by God. Should Job die, neither God nor Job could be vindicated.

2:7 The precise nature of Job's sickness is uncertain, but its symptoms were painful festering sores over the whole body (7:5), nightmares (7:14), scabs that peeled and became black (30:28,30), disfigurement and revolting appearance (2:12; 19:19), bad breath (19:17), excessive thinness (17:7; 19:20), fever (30:30) and pain day and night (30:17). *sores.* The Hebrew for this word is translated "boils" in Ex 9:9; Lev 13:18; 2Ki 20:7.

2:8 *ashes.* Symbolic of mourning (see 42:6; Est 4:3; cf. Jnh 3:6, which speaks of sitting in dust).

2:9 *Curse God.* The Hebrew for this expression here and in 1:5 employs a euphemism (lit. "Bless God"). Satan is using Job's wife to tempt Job as he used Eve to tempt Adam. *and die.* Since nothing but death is left for Job, his wife wants him to provoke God to administer the final stroke due to all who curse him (Lev 24:10–16).

2:10 *Shall we accept good from God, and not trouble?* A key theme of the book: Trouble and suffering are not merely punishment for sin; for God's people they may serve as a trial (as here) or as a discipline that culminates in spiritual gain (see 5:17; Dt 8:5; 2Sa 7:14; Ps 94:12; Pr 3:11–12; 1Co 11:32; Heb 12:5–11).

foolish^e woman. Shall we accept good from God, and not trouble?"^o

In all this, Job did not sin in what he said. ^p

Job's Three Friends

¹¹When Job's three friends, Eliphaz the Temanite,^q Bildad the Shuhite^r and Zophar the Naamathite,^s heard about all the troubles that had come upon him, they set out from their homes and met together by agreement to go and sympathize with him and comfort him. ^t ¹²When they saw him from a distance, they could hardly recognize him; ^u they began to weep aloud,^v and they tore their robes^w and sprinkled dust on their heads. ^x ¹³Then they sat on the ground^y with him for seven days and seven nights. ^z No one said a word to him, ^a because they saw how great his suffering was.

Job Speaks

3 After this, Job opened his mouth and cursed the day of his birth. ^b ²He said:

³"May the day of my birth perish,
  and the night it was said, 'A boy is
    born!' ^c
⁴That day—may it turn to darkness;
  may God above not care about it;
  may no light shine upon it.
⁵May darkness and deep shadow^f ^d
    claim it once more;
  may a cloud settle over it;
  may blackness overwhelm its light.
⁶That night—may thick darkness^e seize
    it;
  may it not be included among the
    days of the year
  nor be entered in any of the months.
⁷May that night be barren;
  may no shout of joy^f be heard in it.

⁸May those who curse days^g curse that
    day, ^g
  those who are ready to rouse
    Leviathan. ^h
⁹May its morning stars become dark;
  may it wait for daylight in vain
  and not see the first rays of dawn, ⁱ
¹⁰for it did not shut the doors of the
    womb on me
  to hide trouble from my eyes.

¹¹"Why did I not perish at birth,
  and die as I came from the womb? ^j
¹²Why were there knees to receive me ^k
  and breasts that I might be nursed?
¹³For now I would be lying down^l in
    peace;
  I would be asleep and at rest ^m
¹⁴with kings and counselors of the earth, ⁿ
  who built for themselves places now
    lying in ruins, ^o
¹⁵with rulers^p who had gold,
  who filled their houses with silver. ^q
¹⁶Or why was I not hidden in the ground
    like a stillborn child, ^r
  like an infant who never saw the
    light of day? ^s
¹⁷There the wicked cease from turmoil, ^t
  and there the weary are at rest. ^u
¹⁸Captives^v also enjoy their ease;
  they no longer hear the slave
    driver's^w shout. ^x
¹⁹The small and the great are there,^y
  and the slave is freed from his
    master.

2:10 ^oS Job 1:21;
S Ecc 2:24;
La 3:38
^pS Job 1:22;
S 6:24; Jas 1:12;
5:11
2:11 ^qS Ge 36:11
^rS Ge 25:2
^sJob 11:1; 20:1
^tS Ge 37:35;
S Job 6:10;
Jn 11:19
2:12 ^uJob 17:7;
Isa 52:14
^vS 2Sa 15:23
^wS Ge 37:29;
S Mk 14:63
^xS Jos 7:6;
S 2Sa 1:2
2:13 ^yIsa 3:26;
47:1; Jer 48:18;
La 2:10;
Eze 26:16;
Jnh 3:6; Hag 2:22
^zS Ge 50:10
^aPr 17:28;
Isa 23:2; 47:5
3:1 ^bJer 15:10;
20:14
3:3 ^cver 11,16;
Job 10:18-19;
Ecc 4:2; 6:3;
Jer 20:14-18;
Mt 26:24
3:5 ^dJob 10:21,
22; 34:22; 38:17;
Ps 23:4; 44:19;
88:12; Jer 2:6;
13:16
3:6 ^eJob 23:17;
30:26
3:7 ^fPs 20:5;
33:3; 65:13;
Isa 26:19;
Jer 51:48

3:8 ^gJob 10:18;
Jer 20:14
^hS Ge 1:21;
Job 41:1,8,10,25;
Ps 74:14; 104:26
3:9 ⁱJob 41:18;
Hab 3:4
3:11 ⁱS ver 3
3:12
^kS Ge 48:12;
Isa 66:12
3:13 ^lJob 17:13;
30:23 ^mver 17;
Job 7:8-10,21;
10:22; 13:19;
14:10-12; 19:27;
21:13,23; 27:19;
Ps 139:11;
Isa 8:22
3:14 ⁿJob 9:24;
12:17; Isa 14:9;
Eze 32:28-32

^oJob 15:28; Jer 51:37; Na 3:7 **3:15** ^pJob 12:21; Isa 45:1
^qJob 15:29; 20:10; 27:17; Ps 49:16-17; Pr 13:22; 28:8;
Ecc 2:26; Isa 2:7; Zep 1:11 **3:16** ^rPs 58:8; Ecc 4:3; 6:3
^sS ver 3; Ps 71:6 **3:17** ^tver 26; Job 30:26; Ecc 4:2; Isa 14:3
^uS ver 13 **3:18** ^vIsa 51:14 ^wS Ge 15:13 ^xJob 39:7 **3:19**
^yJob 9:22; 17:16; 21:33; 24:24; 30:23; Ecc 12:5

^e10 The Hebrew word rendered *foolish* denotes moral deficiency.   ^f5 Or *and the shadow of death*   ^g8 Or *the sea*

2:11 *three friends.* Older than Job (see 15:10). *Eliphaz.* An Edomite name (see Ge 36:11). *Temanite.* Teman was a village in Edom, south of the Dead Sea (see Ge 36:11; Jer 49:7; Eze 25:13; Am 1:12; Ob 9). *Shuhite.* Bildad may have been a descendant of Shuah, the youngest son of Abraham and Keturah (Ge 25:2). *Naamathite.* Apart from 11:1; 20:1; 42:9, this word does not occur elsewhere in the Bible. **2:12** *could hardly recognize him.* Cf. Isa 52:14; 53:3. *tore their robes and sprinkled dust on their heads.* Visible signs of mourning (see note on 1:20). **2:13** *sat on the ground with him.* See Eze 3:15; a commendable expression of sympathy. *seven.* See Ge 50:10; 1Sa 31:13; the number of completeness (see 1:2; see also note on Ru 4:15). *No one said a word to him.* Their mere presence was of more comfort to him than their words of advice would prove to be (see 16:2-3). **3:3** *May the day of my birth perish.* Job's very existence, which has been a joy to him because of God's favor, is now his intolerable burden. He is as close as he will ever come to

cursing God, but he does not do it. **3:4** *may it turn to darkness.* God had said in Ge 1:3, "Let there be light." Job, using similar language, would negate God's creative act. **3:8** *those who curse days.* Eastern soothsayers, like Balaam (see Nu 22-24), who pronounced curses on people, objects and days. *Leviathan.* Using vivid, figurative language, Job wishes that "those who curse days" would arouse the sea monster Leviathan (see note on Isa 27:1) to swallow the day-night of his birth.

3:11-12,16,20-23 A series of rhetorical questions. **3:16** Since in fact his birth had taken place, the next possibility would have been a stillbirth. He would then have lived only in the grave (or Sheol), which he envisions as a place of peace and rest (vv. 13-19; see note on Ge 37:35). Such a situation would be much better than his present intolerable condition, in which he can find neither peace nor rest (v. 26). **3:18** *slave driver's shout.* As in Egypt (see Ex 5:13-14).

20"Why is light given to those in misery,
and life to the bitter of soul, *z*
21to those who long for death that does
not come, *a*
who search for it more than for
hidden treasure, *b*
22who are filled with gladness
and rejoice when they reach the
grave? *c*
23Why is life given to a man
whose way is hidden, *d*
whom God has hedged in? *e*
24For sighing *f* comes to me instead of
food; *g*
my groans *h* pour out like water. *i*
25What I feared has come upon me;
what I dreaded *j* has happened to
me. *k*
26I have no peace, *l* no quietness;
I have no rest, *m* but only turmoil." *n*

Eliphaz

4 Then Eliphaz the Temanite *o* replied:

2"If someone ventures a word with
you, will you be impatient?
But who can keep from speaking? *p*
3Think how you have instructed many, *q*
how you have strengthened feeble
hands. *r*
4Your words have supported those who
stumbled; *s*
you have strengthened faltering
knees. *t*
5But now trouble comes to you, and you
are discouraged; *u*
it strikes *v* you, and you are
dismayed. *w*
6Should not your piety be your
confidence *x*

and your blameless *y* ways your
hope?

7"Consider now: Who, being innocent,
has ever perished? *z*
Where were the upright ever
destroyed? *a*
8As I have observed, *b* those who plow
evil *c*
and those who sow trouble reap it. *d*
9At the breath of God *e* they are
destroyed;
at the blast of his anger they perish. *f*
10The lions may roar *g* and growl,
yet the teeth of the great lions *h* are
broken. *i*
11The lion perishes for lack of prey, *j*
and the cubs of the lioness are
scattered. *k*

12"A word *l* was secretly brought to me,
my ears caught a whisper *m* of it. *n*
13Amid disquieting dreams in the night,
when deep sleep falls on men, *o*
14fear and trembling *p* seized me
and made all my bones shake. *q*
15A spirit glided past my face,
and the hair on my body stood on
end. *r*
16It stopped,
but I could not tell what it was.
A form stood before my eyes,
and I heard a hushed voice: *s*
17"Can a mortal be more righteous than
God? *t*

3:20 *z*S 1Sa 1:10; Eze 27:30-31 **3:21** *a*Rev 9:6 *b*Ps 119:127; Pr 2:4 **3:22** *c*Job 7:16; Ecc 4:3; Jer 8:3 **3:23** *d*Pr 4:19; Isa 59:10; Jer 13:16; 23:12 *e*Job 6:4; 16:13; 19:12; Ps 88:8; La 2:4; 3:7; Hos 2:6 **3:24** *f*Ps 5:1; 38:9; Isa 35:10 *g*Job 6:7; 33:20; Ps 107:18 *h*Ps 22:1; 32:3; 38:8 *i*1Sa 1:15; Job 30:16; Ps 6:6; 22:14; 42:3,4; 80:5; Isa 53:12; La 2:12 **3:25** *j*Job 7:9; 9:28; 30:15; Hos 13:3 *k*S Ge 42:36 **3:26** *l*Isa 48:22; Jn 14:27 *m*Job 7:4,14; Ps 6:6; Da 4:5; Mt 11:28 *n*S ver 17; S Job 10:18; S 19:8 **4:1** *o*S Ge 36:11; Job 15:1; 22:1 **4:2** *p*Job 32:20; Jer 4:19; 20:9 **4:3** *q*Dt 32:2; Job 29:23; Hos 6:3 *r*Job 26:2; Ps 71:9; Isa 13:7; 35:3; Zep 3:16; Heb 12:12 **4:4** *s*Job 16:5; 29:16,25; Isa 1:17 *t*Job 29:11,15; Isa 35:3; Jer 31:8; Heb 12:12 **4:5** *u*S Jos 1:9 *v*Ru 1:13; Job 1:11; 19:21; 30:21; Ps 38:2; Isa 53:4 *w*Job 6:14; Pr 24:10; Ps 27:3; 71:5; Pr 3:26 *y*S Ge 6:9 **4:7** *z*Job 5:11; 36:7; Ps 41:12; 2Pe 2:9 *a*Job 8:20; Ps 37:25;

91:9-10; Pr 12:21; 19:23 **4:8** *b*Job 5:3; 15:17 *c*Jdg 14:18; Job 5:6; 15:35; Ps 7:14; Isa 59:4 *d*Ps 7:15; 9:15; Pr 11:18; 22:8; Isa 17:11; Hos 8:7; 10:13; Gal 6:7-8 **4:9** *e*S Ex 15:10; S Job 41:21; 2Th 2:8 *f*S Lev 26:38; Job 40:13; Isa 25:7 **4:10** *g*Ps 22:13 *h*Ps 17:12; 22:21; Pr 28:15 *i*Job 5:15; 29:17; 36:6; 38:15; Ps 35:10; 58:6 **4:11** *j*Dt 28:41; Job 27:14; Ps 34:10; 58:6; Pr 30:14 *k*Job 5:4 **4:12** *l*ver 17-21; Job 32:13; Jer 9:23 *m*Job 26:14 *n*Job 33:14 **4:13** *o*Job 33:15 **4:14** *p*Job 21:6; Ps 48:6; 55:5; 119:120,161; Jer 5:22; Hab 3:16; S 2Co 7:15 *q*Jer 23:9; Da 10:8; Hab 3:16 **4:15** *r*Da 5:6; 7:15,28; 10:8; Mt 14:26 **4:16** *s*S 1Ki 19:12 **4:17** *t*Job 9:2; 13:18; Ps 143:2

3:21–22 Death has become desirable for Job.
3:23 *whom God has hedged in.* God, who had put a hedge of protection around him (see 1:10 and note), has now, he feels, hemmed him in with turmoil (see v. 26).
4:1 *Eliphaz the Temanite.* See note on 2:11. Teman was an Edomite town noted for wisdom (see Jer 49:7). The speeches of Job's three friends contain elements of truth, but they must be carefully interpreted in context. The problem is not so much with what the friends knew but with what they did not know: God's high purpose in allowing Satan to buffet Job.
4:2 *ventures a word.* Eliphaz seems to be genuinely concerned with Job's well-being and offers a complimentary word (vv. 3–4). *impatient.* See note on 9:2–3.
4:5 *strikes you.* See 1:11; 2:5; 19:21.
4:6–7 Eliphaz counsels Job to be confident that his piety will count with God, that though God is now chastening him for some sin, it is to a good end (see v. 17; 5:17), and he can be assured that God will not destroy him along with the

wicked.
4:6 *piety.* Lit. "fear (of God)" (see note on 1:1). The word is used only by Eliphaz (see 15:4; 22:4).
4:7–9 If Job is truly innocent, he will not be destroyed.
4:8–11 Just as the strongest lions eventually die (vv. 10–11), so the wicked are eventually destroyed (vv. 8–9).
4:9 *blast of his anger.* See Ex 15:7–8. God's judgment is fearfully severe.
4:12–21 Eliphaz tells of a hair-raising (see v. 15), mystical experience mediated through a dream (see v. 13), through which he claims to have received divine revelation and on which he bases his advice to Job.
4:13 *Amid . . . dreams . . . when deep sleep falls on men.* Eliphaz's words are echoed by Elihu in 33:15.
4:14 *all my bones shake.* A sign of great distress (see Jer 23:9; Hab 3:16).
4:17–21 All mortals are sinful; therefore God has a right to punish them. Job should be thankful for the correction God is giving him (see 5:17).

Can a man be more pure than his
  Maker?[u]
[18]If God places no trust in his servants, [v]
  if he charges his angels with error, [w]
[19]how much more those who live in
    houses of clay, [x]
  whose foundations[y] are in the dust, [z]
  who are crushed[a] more readily than
    a moth![b]
[20]Between dawn and dusk they are
    broken to pieces;
  unnoticed, they perish forever. [c]
[21]Are not the cords of their tent pulled
    up, [d]
  so that they die[e] without
    wisdom?'[h][f]

5 "Call if you will, but who will answer
    you?[g]
  To which of the holy ones[h] will you
    turn?
[2]Resentment[i] kills a fool,
  and envy slays the simple.[j]
[3]I myself have seen[k] a fool taking root, [l]
  but suddenly[m] his house was
    cursed. [n]
[4]His children[o] are far from safety, [p]
  crushed in court[q] without a
    defender. [r]
[5]The hungry consume his harvest, [s]
  taking it even from among thorns,
  and the thirsty pant after his wealth.
[6]For hardship does not spring from the
    soil,
  nor does trouble sprout from the
    ground. [t]
[7]Yet man is born to trouble[u]
  as surely as sparks fly upward.

[8]"But if it were I, I would appeal to
    God;
  I would lay my cause before him. [v]

[9]He performs wonders[w] that cannot be
    fathomed, [x]
  miracles that cannot be counted. [y]
[10]He bestows rain on the earth; [z]
  he sends water upon the
    countryside. [a]
[11]The lowly he sets on high, [b]
  and those who mourn[c] are lifted[d] to
    safety.
[12]He thwarts the plans[e] of the crafty,
  so that their hands achieve no
    success.[f]
[13]He catches the wise[g] in their
    craftiness, [h]
  and the schemes of the wily are
    swept away. [i]
[14]Darkness[j] comes upon them in the
    daytime;
  at noon they grope as in the night. [k]
[15]He saves the needy[l] from the sword in
    their mouth;
  he saves them from the clutches of
    the powerful. [m]
[16]So the poor[n] have hope,
  and injustice shuts its mouth. [o]

[17]"Blessed is the man whom God
    corrects;[p]

4:17 [u]Job 8:3; 10:3; 14:4; 15:14; 21:14; 25:4; 31:15; 32:22; 35:10; 36:3,13; 37:23; 40:19; Ps 18:26; 51:5; 119:73; Pr 20:9; Ecc 7:20; Isa 51:13; Mal 2:10; Ac 17:24
4:18 [v]Heb 1:14 [w]Job 15:15; 21:22; 25:5
4:19 [x]Job 10:9; 33:6; Isa 64:8; Ro 9:21; 2Co 4:7; **5:1** [y]Job 22:16 [z]S Ge 2:7 [a]Job 5:4 [b]Job 7:17; 15:16; 17:14; 25:6; Ps 22:6; Isa 41:14
4:20 [c]Job 14:2, 20; 15:33; 20:7; 24:24; Ps 89:47; 90:5-6; Jas 4:14
4:21 [d]Job 8:22; Isa 38:12 [e]Jn 8:24 [f]Job 18:21; 36:12; Pr 5:23; Jer 9:3
5:1 [g]Hab 1:2 [h]Job 15:15; Ps 89:5,7
5:2 [i]Job 21:15; 36:13 [j]Pr 12:16; Gal 5:26
5:3 [k]S Job 4:8 [l]Ps 37:35; Isa 40:24; Jer 12:2; Eze 17:6 [m]Pr 6:15 [n]Job 24:18; Ps 37:22,35-36; 109:9-10; Pr 3:33
5:4 [o]Job 20:10; 27:14 [p]S Job 4:11 [q]Job 4:19; Am 5:12 [r]Ps 109:12; Isa 9:17; 1Jn 2:1
5:5 [s]Lev 26:16; S Jdg 2:15; Job 20:18; 31:8; Mic 6:15
5:6 [t]S Job 4:8
5:7 [u]S Ge 3:17; Job 10:17; 15:35; Ps 51:5; 58:3; 90:10; Ps 22:8
5:8 [v]Job 8:5; 11:13; 13:3,15; 23:4; 40:1;

Ps 35:23; 50:15; Jer 12:1; 1Co 4:4 **5:9** [w]Ps 78:4; 111:2 [x]Dt 29:29; Job 9:4,10; 11:7; 25:2; 26:14; 33:12; 36:5,22, 26; 37:5,14,16,23; 42:3; Ps 40:5; 71:17; 72:18; 86:10; 131:1; 139:6,17; 145:3; Isa 40:28; Ro 11:33 [y]Ps 71:15 **5:10** [z]Mt 5:45 [a]S Lev 26:4; Job 36:28; 37:6,13; 38:28,34; Ps 135:7; Jer 14:22 **5:11** [b]S 1Sa 2:7-8; S Job 4:7; Ps 75:7; 113:7-8 [c]Isa 61:2; Mt 5:4; Ro 12:15 [d]S Mt 23:12; Jas 4:10 **5:12** [e]Ne 4:15; Ps 33:10; Isa 8:10; 19:3; Jer 19:7 [f]Job 12:23; Ps 78:59; 140:8 **5:13** [g]Job 37:24; Isa 29:14; 44:25; Jer 8:8; 18:18; 51:57 [h]Job 15:5; Ps 36:3; Lk 20:23; 1Co 3:19*; 2Co 11:3; Eph 4:14 [i]Job 9:4; 18:7; Pr 21:30; 29:6; Jer 8:9 **5:14** [j]Job 15:22,30; 18:6,18; 20:26; 22:11; 27:20; Isa 8:22; Jn 12:35 [k]S Dt 28:29; S Job 18:5; Am 8:9 **5:15** [l]S Ex 22:23; Job 8:6; 22:27; 33:26; 36:15 [m]S Job 4:10; S 31:22 **5:16** [n]Job 20:19; 31:16; Pr 17:5; 22:22; Isa 11:4; 41:17; 61:1 [o]Ps 63:11; 107:42; Ro 3:19 **5:17** [p]Dt 8:5; Job 33:19; 36:10; Zep 3:7; Jas 1:12

[h]21 Some interpreters end the quotation after verse 17.

4:18–19 If the angels, who are not made of dust, can be guilty in God's sight, how much more man (see 15:15–16)!
4:18 servants. Angels.
4:19 houses of clay. Bodies made of dust (see 10:9; 33:6; see also note on Ge 2:7). moth. A symbol of fragility (cf. 27:18).
4:20 Between dawn and dusk. A vivid picture of the shortness of life.
4:21 tent. A temporary home, like the human body (see 2Co 5:1,4; 2Pe 1:13). without wisdom. Needlessly and senselessly (see v. 20).
5:1 To which . . . will you turn? To plead your case with God. The idea of a mediator, someone to arbitrate between God and Job, is an important motif in the book (see 9:33; 16:19–20; see also NIV text note on 19:25). holy ones. Holy angels, the "sons of God" in the prologue (see NIV text notes on 1:6; 2:1).
5:2 Without mentioning him, Eliphaz implies that Job is resentful against God and that harm will follow. fool. One who pays no attention to God (see NIV text notes on 2:10; Pr 1:7).

5:3 A fool taking root. A wicked man prospering like a tree taking root (see Ps 1:3).
5:6 Unlike a weed, trouble must be sown and cultivated.
5:7 man is born to trouble. See 14:1; proof that no one is righteous in the eyes of God (see 4:17–19). Job should stop behaving like a fool (see vv. 1–7) and should humble himself. Then God would bless, and injustice would shut its mouth (see v. 16). sparks. Lit. "sons of Resheph." In Canaanite mythology, Resheph was a god of plague and destruction. "(Sons of) Resheph" is used as a poetic image in the OT for fire (SS 8:6), bolts of lightning (Ps 78:48) and pestilence (Dt 32:24; Hab 3:5).
5:9 Repeated in 9:10.
5:13 Quoted in part in 1Co 3:19 (the only clear quotation of Job in the NT).
5:17–26 While the preceding hymn (vv. 8–16) spoke of God's goodness and justice, this poem celebrates the blessedness of the man whom God disciplines (see Pr 1:2,7; 3:12; 23:13,23). Eliphaz believed that discipline is temporary and is followed by healing (v. 18), and that the good man will always be rescued. But with Job's wealth gone and his

so do not despise the discipline^q of
the Almighty.^{i r}

¹⁸For he wounds, but he also binds up;^s
he injures, but his hands also heal.^t

¹⁹From six calamities he will rescue^u
you;
in seven no harm will befall you.^v

²⁰In famine^w he will ransom you from
death,
and in battle from the stroke of the
sword.^x

²¹You will be protected from the lash of
the tongue,^y
and need not fear^z when destruction
comes.^a

²²You will laugh^b at destruction and
famine,^c
and need not fear the beasts of the
earth.^d

²³For you will have a covenant^e with the
stones^f of the field,
and the wild animals will be at peace
with you.^g

²⁴You will know that your tent is
secure;^h
you will take stock of your property
and find nothing missing.ⁱ

²⁵You will know that your children will
be many,^j
and your descendants like the grass of
the earth.^k

²⁶You will come to the grave in full
vigor,^l
like sheaves gathered in season.^m

²⁷"We have examined this, and it is true.
So hear itⁿ and apply it to
yourself."^o

Job

6 Then Job replied:

²"If only my anguish could be
weighed

and all my misery be placed on the
scales!^p

³It would surely outweigh the sand^q of
the seas—
no wonder my words have been
impetuous.^r

⁴The arrows^s of the Almighty^t are in
me,^u
my spirit drinks^v in their poison;^w
God's terrors^x are marshaled against
me.^y

⁵Does a wild donkey^z bray^a when it has
grass,
or an ox bellow when it has fodder?^b

⁶Is tasteless food eaten without salt,
or is there flavor in the white of an
egg^j?^c

⁷I refuse to touch it;
such food makes me ill.^d

⁸"Oh, that I might have my request,
that God would grant what I hope
for,^e

⁹that God would be willing to crush^f
me,
to let loose his hand and cut me off!^g

¹⁰Then I would still have this
consolation^h—
my joy in unrelenting painⁱ—
that I had not denied the words^j of
the Holy One.^k

¹¹"What strength do I have, that I should
still hope?
What prospects, that I should be
patient?^l

5:17 ^qPs 94:12;
Pr 3:11; Jer 31:18
^rS Ge 17:1;
S Job 15:11;
Heb 12:5-11
5:18 ^sPs 147:3;
Isa 57:15; 61:1;
Hos 6:1
^tS Dt 32:39
5:19 ^uDa 3:17;
6:16 ^vPs 34:19;
91:10;
Pr 3:25-26;
24:15-16
5:20 ^wver 22;
Ps 33:19; 37:19
^xPs 22:20; 91:7;
140:7; 144:10;
Jer 39:18
5:21 ^yPs 12:2-4;
31:20 ^zPs 23:4;
27:1; 91:5 ^aver
15
5:22 ^bJob 8:21;
39:7,18,22;
41:29 ^cS ver 20
^dS Lev 25:18;
Ps 91:13;
Hos 2:18;
Mk 1:13
5:23 ^eIsa 28:15;
Hos 2:18
^f2Ki 3:19,25;
Ps 91:12; Mt 13:8
^gJob 40:20;
Isa 11:6-9; 65:25;
Eze 34:25
5:24 ^hJob 12:6;
21:9 ⁱJob 8:6;
22:23
5:25 ^jDt 28:4;
Ps 112:2
^kPs 72:16;
Isa 44:3-4; 48:19
5:26 ^lS Ge 15:15;
S Dt 11:21;
S Ecc 8:13
^mPr 3:21-26
5:27 ⁿJob 32:10,
17 ^oJob 8:5;
11:13; 22:27

6:2 ^pJob 31:6;
Pr 11:1; Da 5:27
6:3 ^q1Ki 4:29;
Pr 27:3 ^rver 11,
26; Job 7:11;
16:6; 21:4; 23:2
6:4 ^sS Dt 32:23;
Ps 38:2
^tS Ge 17:1
^uJob 7:20; 16:12,
13; 19:12;
La 3:12
^vJob 21:20
^wS Dt 32:32;
Job 30:21; 34:6;
Jer 15:18; 30:12

^xJob 9:34; 13:21; 18:11; 23:6; 27:20; 30:15; 33:16
^yS Job 3:23; Ps 88:15-18 **6:5** ^zS Ge 16:12 ^aJob 30:7
^bJob 24:6; Isa 30:24 **6:6** ^cJob 33:20; Ps 107:18 **6:7**
^dS Job 3:24 **6:8** ^eJob 14:13 **6:9** ^fJob 19:2 ^gS Nu 11:15;
S Ps 31:22 **6:10** ^hS Job 2:11; 15:11; Ps 94:19 ⁱPs 38:17;
Jer 4:19; 45:3 ^jJob 22:22; 23:12; Ps 119:102; Mk 8:38
^kS Lev 11:44; S 2Ki 19:22; S Isa 31:1 **6:11** ^lS ver 3

ⁱ17 Hebrew *Shaddai*; here and throughout Job   ^j6 The
meaning of the Hebrew for this phrase is uncertain.

children dead, these words about security (v. 24) and children (v. 25) must have seemed cruel indeed to him.
5:17 *Almighty*. The first of 31 times that the Hebrew word
Shaddai is used in Job (see note on Ge 17:1).
5:18–19 See Hos 6:1–2.
5:19 *six . . . seven*. See 33:29; 40:5; Pr 6:16; 30:15,18,
21,29; Ecc 11:2; Am 1:3,6,9,11,13; 2:1,4,6; Mic 5:5. Normally, such number patterns are not to be taken literally but
are a poetic way of saying "many."
5:23 *covenant with the stones*. A figurative way of saying
that stones will "be at peace with you" and will not ruin the
crops (see 2Ki 3:19; Isa 5:2; Mt 13:5).
5:25 *like the grass*. As numerous as blades of grass (see
note on Ge 13:16).
5:26 Eliphaz's prediction was more accurate than he realized (see 42:16–17).
5:27 *apply it to yourself*. Eliphaz's conclusion: Job must
turn from unrighteousness (4:7) and resentment against God
(v. 2) to humility (v. 11) and the acceptance of God's right-

eous discipline (v. 17). Eliphaz's purpose is to offer theological comfort and counsel to Job (2:11), but instead he wounds
him with false accusation.
6:2–3 Job appeals for a sympathetic understanding of the
harsh words he spoke in ch. 3.
6:4 *arrows of the Almighty*. Job shares Eliphaz's "orthodox" theology and believes that God is aiming his arrows of
judgment at him—though he does not know why (see 7:20;
16:12–13; see also La 3:12; cf. Dt 32:23; Ps 7:13; 38:2).
6:5–6 Job claims the right to bray and bellow, since he has
been wounded by God and offered tasteless food (words) by
his friends.
6:8–9 Job repeats the thoughts of ch. 3.
6:10 *Then*. In the afterlife, Job would have the joy of
knowing that he had remained true to God.
6:11–13 With no human resources left, Job considers his
condition hopeless.
6:11 *patient*. See note on 9:2–3.

¹²Do I have the strength of stone?
Is my flesh bronze?[m]
¹³Do I have any power to help myself,[n]
now that success has been driven
from me?

¹⁴"A despairing man[o] should have the
devotion[p] of his friends,[q]
even though he forsakes the fear of
the Almighty.[r]
¹⁵But my brothers are as undependable as
intermittent streams,[s]
as the streams that overflow
¹⁶when darkened by thawing ice
and swollen with melting snow,[t]
¹⁷but that cease to flow in the dry season,
and in the heat[u] vanish from their
channels.
¹⁸Caravans turn aside from their routes;
they go up into the wasteland and
perish.
¹⁹The caravans of Tema[v] look for water,
the traveling merchants of Sheba[w]
look in hope.
²⁰They are distressed, because they had
been confident;
they arrive there, only to be
disappointed.[x]
²¹Now you too have proved to be of no
help;
you see something dreadful and are
afraid.[y]
²²Have I ever said, 'Give something on
my behalf,
pay a ransom[z] for me from your
wealth,[a]
²³deliver me from the hand of the enemy,
ransom me from the clutches of the
ruthless'?[b]

²⁴"Teach me, and I will be quiet;[c]
show me where I have been wrong.[d]
²⁵How painful are honest words![e]
But what do your arguments prove?
²⁶Do you mean to correct what I say,
and treat the words of a despairing
man as wind?[f]
²⁷You would even cast lots[g] for the
fatherless[h]

and barter away your friend.

²⁸"But now be so kind as to look at me.
Would I lie to your face?[i]
²⁹Relent, do not be unjust;[j]
reconsider, for my integrity[k] is at
stake.[k][l]
³⁰Is there any wickedness on my lips?[m]
Can my mouth not discern[n] malice?

7 "Does not man have hard service[o]
on earth?[p]
Are not his days like those of a hired
man?[q]
²Like a slave longing for the evening
shadows,[r]
or a hired man waiting eagerly for his
wages,[s]
³so I have been allotted months of
futility,
and nights of misery have been
assigned to me.[t]
⁴When I lie down I think, 'How long
before I get up?'[u]
The night drags on, and I toss till
dawn.[v]
⁵My body is clothed with worms[w] and
scabs,
my skin is broken and festering.[x]

⁶"My days are swifter than a weaver's
shuttle,[y]
and they come to an end without
hope.[z]
⁷Remember, O God, that my life is but a
breath;[a]
my eyes will never see happiness
again.[b]
⁸The eye that now sees me will see me
no longer;
you will look for me, but I will be no
more.[c]
⁹As a cloud vanishes[d] and is gone,

6:12 ᵐJob 26:2
6:13 ⁿJob 26:2
6:14 ᵒS Job 4:5
ᵖl Sa 20:42;
Job 15:4
ᑫJob 12:4; 17:2,
6; 19:19,21;
21:3; 30:1,10;
Ps 38:11; 69:20;
1Jn 3:17
ʳS Ge 17:1
6:15 ˢJob 13:4;
16:2; 21:34;
Ps 22:1; 38:11;
Jer 15:18
6:16 ᵗPs 147:18
6:17 ᵘJob 24:19
6:19 ᵛS Ge 25:15
ʷS Ge 10:7,28
6:20 ˣJer 14:3;
Joel 1:11
6:21 ʸPs 38:11
6:22
ᶻS Nu 35:31;
Job 33:24;
Ps 49:7
ᵃJer 15:10
6:23
ᵇS 2Ki 19:19
6:24 ᶜS Job 2:10;
33:33; Ps 39:1;
141:3; Pr 10:19;
11:12; 17:27;
Ecc 5:2 ᵈJob 19:4
6:25 ᵉEcc 12:11;
Isa 22:23
6:26 ᶠS ver 3;
S Ge 41:6;
Job 8:2; 15:3;
16:3; Jer 5:13
6:27 ᵍEze 24:6;
Joel 3:3; Ob 1:11;
Na 3:10
ʰS Ex 22:22,24;
Job 31:17,21;
Isa 10:2

6:28 ᶦJob 9:15;
24:25; 27:4;
32:10; 33:1,3;
34:6; 36:3,4
6:29 ʲJob 19:6;
27:2; 40:8;
Isa 40:27
ᵏS Job 2:3
ᶦJob 9:21; 10:7;
11:2; 12:4; 23:7,
10; 33:9,32;
34:5,36; 35:2;
42:6; Ps 66:10;
Zec 13:9
6:30 ᵐJob 27:4
ⁿJob 12:11
7:1 ᵒJob 14:14;
Isa 40:2
ᵖS Job 5:7
ᑫS Lev 25:50
7:2 ʳJob 14:1;
Ecc 2:23
ˢS Lev 19:13;
S Job 14:6
7:3 ᵗJob 16:7;
Ps 6:6; 42:3;
56:8; Ecc 4:1;
Isa 16:9; Jer 9:1;
La 1:2,16

7:4 ᵘDt 28:67 ᵛver 13-14 **7:5** ʷJob 17:14; 21:26; 24:20;
25:6; Isa 14:11 ˣS Dt 28:35 **7:6** ʸJob 9:25; Ps 39:5; Isa 38:12
ᶻJob 13:15; 14:19; 17:11,15; 19:10; Ps 37:4; 52:9 **7:7** ᵃver
16; Ge 27:46; Ps 39:4,5,11; 62:9; 78:39; 89:47; 144:4;
Ecc 7:15; S Jas 4:14 ᵇJob 10:20 **7:8** ᶜS Job 3:13; 8:18; 15:29;
20:7,9,21; 27:17; Ps 37:36; 103:16; Isa 41:12; Jn 16:16;
Ac 20:25 **7:9** ᵈS Job 3:25

ᵏ29 Or *my righteousness still stands*

6:14–15 See Gal 6:1. Job needs spiritual help, but his
friends are proving to be undependable.
6:15 *brothers.* By calling his friends his "brothers," Job
makes their callousness stand out more sharply.
6:19 *Tema.* See note on Isa 21:14. *Sheba.* See note on
1:15.
6:22–23 Job has not asked them for anything except what
will cost them nothing: their friendship and counsel.
6:25 *honest words.* Job is referring to his own words.
6:26 *wind.* See 8:2.
6:27 In addition to dishonesty, Job accuses his friends of
heartless cruelty.
6:29 Job softens his tone, pleading that his friends take

back their false accusations.
7:1–21 Having replied to Eliphaz, Job now addresses his
complaint toward God.
7:1 *hard service.* See 14:14. The Hebrew for this expression sometimes implies military service. It is also used in
reference to the Babylonian exile in Isa 40:2 (see note there).
7:2 *evening shadows.* End of the workday.
7:5 See note on 2:7.
7:7 *my life is but a breath.* As a chronic sufferer he has lost
all sense of purpose in life (see v. 3; see also Ps 144:3–4). He
does not anticipate healing and sees death as his only escape.
7:8 *you will look . . . no more.* See v. 21.
7:9 *he who goes down to the grave does not return.* Such

so he who goes down to the grave[l] [e]
   does not return.[f]
[10]He will never come to his house again;
   his place[g] will know him no more.[h]

[11]"Therefore I will not keep silent;[i]
   I will speak out in the anguish[j] of
    my spirit,
   I will complain[k] in the bitterness of
    my soul.[l]
[12]Am I the sea,[m] or the monster of the
   deep,[n]
   that you put me under guard?[o]
[13]When I think my bed will comfort me
   and my couch will ease my
    complaint,[p]
[14]even then you frighten me with dreams
   and terrify[q] me with visions,[r]
[15]so that I prefer strangling and death,[s]
   rather than this body of mine.[t]
[16]I despise my life;[u] I would not live
   forever.[v]
   Let me alone;[w] my days have no
    meaning.[x]

[17]"What is man that you make so much
   of him,
   that you give him so much
    attention,[y]
[18]that you examine him every morning[z]
   and test him[a] every moment?[b]
[19]Will you never look away from me,[c]
   or let me alone even for an instant?[d]
[20]If I have sinned, what have I done to
   you,[e]
   O watcher of men?
   Why have you made me your target?[f]
   Have I become a burden to you?[m][g]
[21]Why do you not pardon my offenses

and forgive my sins?[h]
For I will soon lie down in the dust;[i]
   you will search for me, but I will be
    no more."[j]

Bildad

8 Then Bildad the Shuhite[k] replied:

[2]"How long will you say such
   things?[l]
   Your words are a blustering wind.[m]
[3]Does God pervert justice?[n]
   Does the Almighty pervert what is
    right?[o]
[4]When your children sinned against him,
   he gave them over to the penalty of
    their sin.[p]
[5]But if you will look to God
   and plead[q] with the Almighty,[r]
[6]if you are pure and upright,
   even now he will rouse himself on
    your behalf[s]
   and restore you to your rightful
    place.[t]
[7]Your beginnings will seem humble,
   so prosperous[u] will your future be.[v]

[8]"Ask the former generations[w]

Cross references

7:9 [e]S Job 3:13; 11:8; 14:13; 17:16; 26:6; 38:17; Am 9:2 [f]2Sa 12:23
7:10 [g]Job 18:21; 21:18; 27:21,23; Ps 58:9; Jer 18:17; 19:8 [h]S ver 8;
Ps 37:10; 104:35
7:11 [i]Job 9:35; 13:13; Ps 22:2; 40:9 [j]Job 10:1; Ps 6:3; Isa 38:15,
17 [k]ver 13; Job 9:27; 21:4; 23:2 [l]S 1Sa 1:10; S Job 6:3
7:12 [m]Job 38:8-11 [n]S Ge 1:21 [o]ver 20; Isa 1:14
7:13 [p]S ver 11
7:14 [q]Job 9:34 [r]S Ge 41:8; S Job 3:26
7:15 [s]1Ki 19:4; Jnh 4:3 [t]Job 6:9; Rev 9:6
7:16 [u]S 1Ki 19:4; Job 9:21 [v]S Job 3:22 [w]ver 19; Job 10:20; Ps 39:13 [x]S ver 7
7:17 [y]S Job 4:19; 22:2; Ps 8:4; 144:3; Heb 2:6
7:18 [z]Ps 73:14 [a]Job 23:10; Ps 139:23 [b]Job 14:3; Ps 17:3; 26:2; 66:10; 139:1-6; 143:2
7:19 [c]S ver 16 [d]Job 9:18; 13:26; 14:6; 27:2; Ps 139:7
7:20 [e]Job 35:6; Jer 17:9; S Job 6:4 [g]S ver 12
7:21 [h]Job 9:28; 10:14; 16:6; Ps 119:120; Isa 43:25; Jer 31:34; Heb 1:3 [i]S Ge 3:19;

Job 10:9; 34:15; Ps 7:5; 22:15; 90:3; 104:29 /S ver 8; S Job 3:13 8:1 [k]S Ge 25:2; Job 18:1; 25:1 8:2 [l]Job 11:2; 18:2 [m]S 2Ch 36:16; S Job 6:26 8:3 [n]S Job 4:17; 34:12; Isa 29:15; Ro 3:5 [o]S Ge 18:25; S Jer 12:1 8:4 [p]Job 1:19 8:5 [q]Job 9:15 [r]S Job 5:8,27 8:6 [s]S Job 5:15; 22:27; 33:26; 34:28; Isa 58:9; 65:24 [t]S Job 5:24 8:7 [u]Job 21:13; 22:21; 36:11; Ps 25:13 [v]S Job 1:10; Jer 29:11; 31:17 8:8 [w]S Dt 32:7; S Ps 71:18

[19] Hebrew *Sheol*   [m]20 A few manuscripts of the Masoretic Text, an ancient Hebrew scribal tradition and Septuagint; most manuscripts of the Masoretic Text *I have become a burden to myself.*

---

statements are based on common observation and are not meant to dogmatize about what happens after death. Mesopotamian descriptions of the netherworld refer to it similarly as the "land of no return" (see note on v. 21).
7:11 *not keep silent.* Job is determined to cry out against the apparent injustice of God who, it seems, will not leave him alone (vv. 17–20). *speak out in ... anguish.* See Jer 4:19. *bitterness of ... soul.* See 10:1; 21:25; 27:2.
7:12 *the sea, or the monster of the deep.* See 3:8 and NIV text note. The boisterous sea monster was a symbol of chaos (see Ps 74:13–14 and note; Isa 27:1; 51:9), and Job objects to being treated like him.
7:13–14 He thinks that even the nightmares that disturb his much-needed sleep are from God.
7:16 *I despise my life.* See note on 9:21.
7:17 *What is man that you make so much of him ...?* See Ps 144:3; cf. Ps 8:4–8, where the answer is given that man is created in God's image to have dominion over the world (see Ge 1:27–28). Job's words (vv. 18–21) are a parody on this theme—as if God's only interest in man is to scrutinize him unmercifully and take quick offense at his slightest fault.
7:19 *even for an instant.* Lit. "long enough for me to swallow my saliva."
7:20 *If I have sinned, what have I done to you ...?* I have not been perfect, but what terrible sin have I committed that

deserves this kind of suffering? *watcher.* The Hebrew for this word is used in a favorable sense in Isa 27:3, but here Job complains that God is too critical. *made me your target.* See note on 6:4. *burden to you.* See NIV text note. Ancient Hebrew scribes report that a change in the text had been made from "you" to "myself" because the reading "you" involved too presumptuous a questioning of God's justice.
7:21 *offenses ... sins.* Job confesses that he is a sinner, but he cannot understand why God refuses to forgive him. *lie down in the dust.* Of the netherworld, as in Mesopotamian descriptions of it (see note on v. 9).
8:2 *How long ...?* See 18:1. In contrast to the older Eliphaz, Bildad is impatient.
8:3 *Does God pervert justice?* But Job has not yet blatantly accused God of injustice.
8:5–6 Bildad reasons as follows: God cannot be unjust, so Job and his family must be suffering as a result of sinfulness. Job should plead for mercy, and if he has been upright, God will restore him.
8:6 *if you are pure and upright.* We know God's verdict about Job (see 1:8; 2:3), but Bildad is confident that Job is a hypocrite (see v. 13).
8:7 See v. 21. Bildad spoke more accurately than he realized (see 42:10–17).
8:8 *Ask the former generations.* Eliphaz appealed to reve-